Daniel's
GEORGIA
CRIMINAL TRIAL
PRACTICE

2018-2019 Edition

Issued in December 2018

By
JACK GOGER

THOMSON REUTERS®

For Customer Assistance Call 1-800-328-4880

Mat #42063822

ISBN: 978-1-539-22603-1

INTRODUCTION TO 2018-2019 EDITION

This 2018-2019 Edition of *Daniel's Georgia Criminal Trial Practice* is a complete guide to the practice of criminal law for the Georgia attorney and incorporates all 2018 legislation. Since last year's edition, new material has been added and/or existing material updated on the following subjects, among others:

- "Knock and announce"
- *Miranda* warnings
- Good faith exception to search warrant requirement
- Cell phone information – retrieval and use
- Consent to search
- Wiretaps, eavesdropping, and surveillance
- Ineffective assistance of counsel
- Grand jury
- Hindering apprehension of a criminal
- Competency evaluation
- Gag orders
- Electronic or photographic coverage of court proceedings
- Nolo contendere pleas – recidivist sentencing
- Review of death-penalty-eligible cases
- Habeas corpus

DEDICATION

For Lee Parks, a great lawyer, a better friend.

Jack Goger
September 2018

PREFACE

I first met Judge Daniel in the late seventies. His law office was on the same floor as mine in the First National Bank Tower in Atlanta. When he left the practice for the bench, our paths parted only to be reunited when I became a judge in 1995. In the winter of 1998, he asked if I would be willing to take over the authorship and editorial duties of his Practice, Evidence and Forms manuals on criminal law. I was honored by his request, but a bit daunted by the responsibility. I was, of course, familiar with the books since they were mandatory tools in the law library and briefcase of every lawyer whose practice involved criminal law. Judge Daniel's work was widely respected and the expectations of those who used the books would by very high.

The Judge dismissed my concerns. He pointed out that the wages were lousy and were usually late in coming. But the work, he promised, would always be interesting and even energizing. He was right. The work has an attraction which is almost addictive. Routinely, I find in the cases inventive and practical approaches to issues crafted by defense lawyers and prosecutors which serve the law well.

I want to thank my current law clerk, Lynette Jimenez, for her critical assistance in putting this volume together. Carla Broyles was a terrific resource in the organization of the materials. I particularly want to acknowledge the work of Noreen White whose effort has been involved in the editorial process since the publication of the first edition.

From the beginning, Judge Daniel relied on the help of law students and practicing lawyers to craft and supplement the materials contained in this volume. Their effort was and continues to be a vital influence on this work. Those persons are: Larry Kupferman, Roxanne Axelrod, Annette Grigsby, Walt Smiley, Anne Lemke, Jim Fisher, Tony Hight, Stan Herndon, Joe Drolet, Millard Farmer, Ed Lipton, Alan Pressman, Brian Limmer, Steve Speer, Gary Wolovick, Beth Taylor, Judge Richard Unis of Portland Oregon, Joyce Bennett, Lorraine Fox, Tom Jones, Barbara Killam, Bob Miller, Joy Raynor, Neal Scott, Dennis White, John Withers, Laurie Mintz, David Bills, D'Andre Berry, Diana Drinkwater Hall, Lani Ray, Monica McFarlin, Genet McIntosh, Allen Meyer, Tracy Aronovitz, Ray Rawls, Frank

DeBorde, Chip Grizzle, Ken Lerman, Tom Powell, Pam Morgan, Stefan Ritter, Ms. Jerry Gerald, Anne Collidge-Kaplan, Mary Pappas, Patty Sellers, Pam Henderson, Emilie Koers, Mary Diversi, Marla Dean Thomas, John "Gee" Aldridge, Greg Miller, Julie Pomerantz, Janice Ward, Robin McLean, Jackie Herring, Chris Goetzinger, Cheryl Harris, Sean McIlhinney, Jennifer Jacobson, Michelle Gopman, Bob Upshaw, Scott Poole, Sheri Beasley, Frank Ilardi, Robert White, Joe Farrell, Megan Mathews, Kate Hakken-Flippen, David Belle Isle, Shirley Plotkin, Nikki Nickerson, Paul Coxe, Teresa Adams, Bonnie Lassiter, Cynthia Chapman, Charles Boring, Nance Tomlinson, Leslie Vaughan, Timothy Tanner, Sarah Moorhead, Todd Boyce, Suzanne Garstin and Boris Ramsey.

I have had the same experience. This book has been blessed by the inspired effort of my former law clerks Nick Sears, Shannon McNulty, Catherine Lawler Jackson, Liegia DiFazio, Jennifer Rodman, Katherine Hughes, and Willis L. Miller, IV, and interns: Ann Caroll, Tyler Watkins, Stephen Rothring, Hector Rojas, Christian Blayne May, Andrew Palmer, Meghan Gordon, Rachel Reed, Rachelle Carmel, Tersugh Tivzenda, Lisa Churvis, Lindsey Allison, Eleanor Patrick, Alex Karam, Jenna Rubin, Sara Phillips, Jason Stephenson, William Newsome, Benjamin Rosichan, Seth Butler, Christopher George, Elizabeth Willett Sullivan, Caroline Welden, Caitlin Dorne, Chelsey McDade, Matthew Rochlin, Ivy White, Paul Schumacher, Marc Robinson, Brandon Palmer, Alicia Harrell, Thomas Flugum, Katherine Cochrane, Peter Gerakitis, Sarah Kinsman, Paul Petersen, Jordan Alford, Scott DeLay, Jeffrey Connelly, Kevin Mason, Chase Ruffin, Autumn Turner, Katrina Carmichael, Kevin Frey, Jacqueline Glass, Timothy Holdsworth, Catharine Luo, Joel Reeves, Jared Hodges, John Phillips, Brian Klein, Michael Oldham, Gloria Won, Raymond Wooten, Sarah Morse, Adam Keating, Jr., Thomas Clarkson, Ashley McMahan, Andreea Neculae, Joshua Vanderhooft, Bradford Gregory Valentine, Adam Reinke, Robert J. Kornhaas, Hannah Ward, Christina Rupp, Janet Hardman, Jeffrey Filipovits, William Gill, Andrew Loeb, Sean Branson Cox; Rosaleen Chou; Priya Palvia; David Willingham; Sean Ryan; Sissy Tran; Noelle Abastillas; Rena Seidler; Ping Yeung; Naiyareh Karimimanesh; Brandy James; Linda Collins; Seth Friedman; Crystal Blackshear; Cara Cook; Jacques Massey; and Ted Woodward.

I am particularly indebted to the criminal defense lawyers and the prosecutors who have allowed me to use materials prepared by them and who regularly provide the constructive criticism which makes this handbook a very valuable resource.

The 2018 Edition is intended to cover legislation passed in 2018 and case law available on Westlaw through September 1, 2018.

Jack Goger
September 2018

THOMSON REUTERS PROVIEW™

This title is one of many now available on your tablet as an eBook.

Take your research mobile. Powered by the Thomson Reuters ProView™ app, our eBooks deliver the same trusted content as your print resources, but in a compact, on-the-go format.

ProView eBooks are designed for the way you work. You can add your own notes and highlights to the text, and all of your annotations will transfer electronically to every new edition of your eBook.

You can also instantly verify primary authority with built-in links to WestlawNext® and KeyCite®, so you can be confident that you're accessing the most current and accurate information.

To find out more about ProView eBooks and available discounts, call 1-800-344-5009.

RELATED PRODUCTS

Many of the following products are part of the highly respected Harrison product line, now published by Thomson Reuters

ALTERNATIVE DISPUTE RESOLUTION

Georgia Alternative Dispute Resolution
Douglas H. Yarn

BUSINESS/CORPORATIONS

Georgia Contracts—Law and Litigation
John K. Larkins, Jr.

Kaplan's Nadler Georgia Corporations, Limited Partnerships and Limited Liability Companies, with Forms
James S. Rankin, Jr., and Elizabeth G. Rankin

CRIMINAL LAW

Molnar's Georgia Criminal Law, Crimes and Punishments
Robert E. Cleary, Jr.

Kurtz Criminal Offenses and Defenses in Georgia
Robert E. Cleary, Jr.

Daniel's Georgia Criminal Trial Practice
John J. Goger

Daniel's Georgia Criminal Trial Practice Forms
Ben W. Studdard

The Georgia DUI Trial Practice Manual
William C. Head and Frank T. Gomez

DAMAGES, REMEDIES AND COLLECTIONS

Georgia Legal Collections
Lewis N. Jones and Elizabeth G. Rankin

Georgia Construction Mechanics' and Materialmen's Liens, with Forms
Daniel F. Hinkel

Georgia Law of Damages, with Forms
Mark D. Link and Eric James Hertz

Punitive Damages in Georgia
Eric James Hertz and Mark D. Link

Georgia Post-Judgment Collection, with Forms
Stuart Finestone

Georgia Enforcement of Security Interests in Personal Property with Forms
James S. Rankin, Jr.

ELDER LAW

Georgia Elder Care, Long-Term Health Care and Nursing Home Litigation
Michael S. Reeves and Stephanie F. Brown

EVIDENCE

Georgia Rules of Evidence
Paul S. Milich

Courtroom Handbook on Georgia Evidence
Paul S. Milich

***Daniel's* Georgia Handbook on Criminal Evidence**
Ben W. Studdard

***Herman and McLaughlin* Admissibility of Evidence in Civil Cases/Manual for Georgia Trial Lawyers**
Michael E. McLaughlin

***Green's* Georgia Law of Evidence**
John D. Hadden

***Agnor's* Georgia Evidence**
Ana Marcela Rountree

Georgia Handbook on Foundations and Objections
Neal W. Dickert

Georgia Admissibility of Expert Testimony
Mary Donne Peters

FORMS

***Ruskell's* Civil Pleading and Practice Forms for Use with West's Official Code of Georgia Annotated**
Richard C. Ruskell

Forms for Pleading Under the Georgia Civil Practice Act

***Brown's* Georgia Pleading, Practice and Legal Forms, Annotated**
Charles R. Adams III and Cynthia Trimboli Adams

Georgia Forms: Legal and Business

GENERAL

Georgia Automobile Insurance Law, Including Tort Law, with Forms
Frank E. Jenkins III and Wallace Miller III

Georgia Property and Liability Insurance Law
J. Stephen Berry

***McConaughey's* Georgia Divorce, Alimony and Child Custody**

David A. Webster and Deborah A. Johnson

Georgia Employment Law
James W. Wimberly, Jr.

Handbook on Georgia Practice with Forms
Charles R. Sheppard, Megan U. Manly,
and John B. Manly

Georgia Juvenile Practice and Procedure, with Forms
Mark H. Murphy

Georgia Law Enforcement Handbook

***Purdom's* Georgia Magistrate Court Handbook with Forms**
John D. Hadden and Lillian N. Caudle

LANDLORD AND TENANT

**Georgia Landlord and Tenant—Breach and Remedies,
with Forms**
William J. Dawkins

Georgia Landlord and Tenant—Lease Forms and Clauses
William J. Dawkins

LITIGATION

***McFadden, Brewer & Sheppard's* Georgia Appellate
Practice, with Forms**
Christopher J. McFadden, Charles R. Sheppard,
Charles M. Cork III, David A. Webster,
and Kelly A. Jenkins

Georgia Civil Discovery, with Forms
Wayne M. Purdom

***Davis and Shulman's* Georgia Practice and Procedure**
Richard C. Ruskell

Georgia Process and Service, with Forms
Phillip Weltner II

Trial Handbook for Georgia Lawyers
Ronald L. Carlson, Julian A. Cook III,
and Michael Scott Carlson

PERSONAL INJURY AND TORTS

**Medical Torts in Georgia: A Handbook on State and
Federal Law**
Preyesh K. Maniklal

Premises Liability in Georgia, with Forms
Michael J. Gorby

Georgia Products Liability
J. Kennard Neal and Catherine Payne

Soft Tissue Injuries in Georgia, Including Whiplash,

with Forms
Houston D. Smith III

Georgia Law of Torts
Charles R. Adams III

Georgia Law of Torts—Trial Preparation and Practice
Kenneth L. Shigley and John D. Hadden

Eldridge's **Georgia Wrongful Death Actions, with Forms**
Robert E. Cleary, Jr.

PROBATE LAW AND TRUSTS

Georgia Guardianship and Conservatorship
Mary F. Radford

Georgia Probate and Administration
Daniel F. Hinkel

Redfearn's **Wills and Administration in Georgia**
Mary F. Radford

Georgia Trusts and Trustees
Mary F. Radford

REAL PROPERTY

Georgia Eminent Domain
Daniel F. Hinkel

**Georgia Real Estate Finance and Foreclosure Law,
with Forms**
Frank S. Alexander, Sarah J. Toering,
and Sarah Bolling Mancini

Pindar's **Georgia Real Estate Law and Procedure,
with Forms**
Daniel F. Hinkel

Georgia Real Estate Sales Contracts
Daniel F. Hinkel

**Georgia Real Estate Title Examinations and Closings, with
Forms**
Daniel F. Hinkel

WORKERS' COMPENSATION

Georgia Workers' Compensation—Law and Practice
James B. Hiers, Jr., Robert R. Potter, and Todd A. Brooks

Georgia Workers' Compensation Claims, with Forms
Jack B. Hood, Benjamin A. Hardy, Jr., and Bobby Lee Cook

Georgia Jurisprudence
West's Code of Georgia Annotated

RELATED PRODUCTS

Georgia Cases
Georgia Court Rules and Procedure—State and Federal
Georgia Digest 2d

———

Thomson Reuters Westlaw™
WESTCheck.com®
KeyCite®

———

Thomson Reuters thanks you for subscribing to this product. Should you have any questions regarding this product please contact Customer Service at 1-800-328-4880 or by fax at 1-800-340-9378. If you would like to inquire about related publications or place an order, please contact us at 1-800-344-5009.

 THOMSON REUTERS®

Thomson Reuters
610 Opperman Drive
Eagan, MN 55123

https://legal.thomsonreuters.com/

Summary of Contents

Table of Contents
INTRODUCTION

CHAPTER 1. INTRODUCTION

PART I. ARREST AND CRIMINAL INVESTIGATIVE PROCEDURES

CHAPTER 2. ARRESTS

CHAPTER 3. STOP-AND-FRISK

CHAPTER 4. SEARCH AND SEIZURE

CHAPTER 5. CONFESSIONS AND SELF-INCRIMINATION

CHAPTER 6. PRE-TRIAL IDENTIFICATION

PART II.   CLIENT-COUNSEL RELATIONSHIP AND PROCEEDINGS PRIOR TO COMMITMENT HEARING

CHAPTER 7.   COUNSEL FOR DEFENDANT

CHAPTER 8.   BONDS

CHAPTER 13. INDICTMENTS AND ACCUSATIONS

CHAPTER 14. PRE-TRIAL PLEAS, DEMURRERS, NOTICES, DEMANDS, AND MOTIONS

CHAPTER 15. PLEA BARGAINING

CHAPTER 18. THE JURY

CHAPTER 19. OPENING STATEMENTS

CHAPTER 20. PRESENTING THE STATE'S CASE AND ATTACKS THEREON

CHAPTER 21. PRESENTING THE DEFENDANT'S CASE AND ATTACKS THEREON

CHAPTER 22. FROM REBUTTAL TO REQUEST TO CHARGE

CHAPTER 27. CONTEMPT

PART V. POST-TRIAL REMEDIES AND PROBATION REVOCATION

CHAPTER 28. JUDICIAL REVIEW

CHAPTER 29. ADMINISTRATIVE REVIEW

CHAPTER 30. PROBATION REVOCATION

INTRODUCTION

Chapter 1

Introduction

§ 1:1   General considerations
§ 1:2   Scope and purpose

KeyCite®: Cases and other legal materials listed in KeyCite Scope can be researched through the KeyCite service on Westlaw®. Use KeyCite to check citations for form, parallel references, prior and later history, and comprehensive citator information, including citations to other decisions and secondary materials.

---

§ 1:1   General considerations

The importance of procedure in the area of substantive criminal law has, in recent years, received the attention it so rightly deserves by commentators and textbook writers alike. From a practical standpoint, the practitioner is well aware that cases can be won or lost on procedural grounds. Thus, this book is designed to aid Georgia practitioners in the handling of a criminal case. It is hoped that through the sequential examination of the various stages of the criminal process from arrest to final judgment, the reader will easily be able to find the point of law with which he is concerned.

While this book focuses on Georgia law, attention is given to federal constitutional law. It should be obvious to anyone who has even a passing knowledge of criminal law that in the past few years the Supreme Court's concern with the constitutional aspects of procedure has taken on great, if not a paramount, importance.

Criminal procedure has also been guided and influenced greatly by the federal courts and to a lesser extent by other sources, such as the American Bar Association Standards for Criminal Justice.[1] In view of the importance of procedure in criminal cases, espe-

---

[Section 1:1]

[1]The A. B. A. Standards which are quoted throughout this book are used with the express permission of the American Bar Association, the holder of the copyright, and Little, Brown and Company, the publisher of the four volume work entitled A. B. A.

1

cially in light of the new sources of criminal procedure, many of which are not readily available to the average practitioner, it was felt that there was a need for this book.

§ 1:2 Scope and purpose

This book was conceived as a handbook of Georgia criminal procedure as practiced in our superior courts. Because of the interrelationship between pre-trial and trial practice, it soon became apparent that criminal procedure prior to trial would have to be included. Basically, however, this book remains a guide to those matters relating to trial practice in our courts of general criminal jurisdiction. Efforts have been made to refer to some of the rules and practices in state courts, city courts, or other special courts as those rules affect the trial of criminal cases.

This book is not intended to be, and is not, a book on substantive criminal law.[1] The prosecution and defense of criminal cases are dealt with only in a general manner without any attempt to discuss the particularities of various kinds of prosecutions and their defenses.

Hopefully, this book will be helpful to those who will be involved in the trial of criminal cases.

Standards for Criminal Justice. Former Chief Justice Burger has said that the A. B. A. Standards are the "single most comprehensive and probably the most monumental undertaking in the field of criminal justice ever attempted by the American legal profession in our national history." Burger, Introduction: The ABA Standards for Criminal Justice, 12 Am. Crim. L. Rev. 251 (1974).

[Section 1:2]

[1] For such works, see Molnar's, Georgia Criminal Law—Crimes and Punishments. Also, particular attention should be given to the admirable Kurtz Criminal Offenses and Defenses in Georgia.

Part I

ARREST AND CRIMINAL INVESTIGATIVE PROCEDURES

Chapter 2

Arrests

KeyCite®: Cases and other legal materials listed in KeyCite Scope can be researched through the KeyCite service on Westlaw®. Use KeyCite to check citations for form, parallel references, prior and later history, and comprehensive citator information, including citations to other decisions and secondary materials.

---

§ 2:1 Scope

This chapter involves the law relating to taking a person into custody in connection with a charge of violating a criminal law. The validity of an arrest has taken on new meaning with the federal constitutional application of the exclusionary rule. In addition to the material on arrests contained in this chapter, stop and frisk is discussed in Chapter 3, and search and seizure is discussed in Chapter 4, which contains sections on searches incident to a valid arrest and material on the question of probable cause. Custodial interrogation is discussed in Chapter 5, and Chapter 6 contains some material on arrest and identification procedures.

§ 2:2 Definitions of arrest

At the threshold, it must be understood that the word "arrest" has two distinct meanings. First, there is a common law, or in some states, a statutory meaning. Second, there is the federal constitutional meaning which has been recognized by the United States Supreme Court.

For the common law definition of the word "arrest,"[1] the Georgia Court of Appeals has stated:

"An arrest is the taking, seizing, or detaining of the person of another, either by touching or putting hands on him, or by any act indicating an intention to take such person into custody, and which subjects such person to the actual control and will of the person making the arrest. It is sufficient if the arrested person

---

[Section 2:2]

[1]Blackstone defined an arrest as "the apprehending or restraining of one's person, in order to be forthcoming to answer an alleged or suspected crime." Blackstone, "Commentaries on the Laws of England" (1769 rpt. Boston Beacon Press 1962) IV, 289.

understands that he is in the power of the one arresting and submits in consequence thereof. The taking of another into custody for the purpose of investigating an alleged crime constitutes an arrest."[2] See § 3:2, infra, on what constitutes a seizure.

The Georgia Supreme Court has more concisely said that "a person is under arrest whenever his liberty to come and go as he pleases is restrained, no matter how slight such restraint may be."[3]

In Georgia, as provided by statute, it is not necessary that a person actually be touched in order to be considered arrested. If the person voluntarily submits or gives in on the condition that he will only be allowed his freedom of movement under the direction of the officer, the arrest is complete.[4]

In addition, it has been held that the seizure of one's property from his immediate presence is the functional equivalent of the seizure of his person. This includes the seizure and retention of personal property or money when the authorities do not make it absolutely clear how they plan to reunite the suspect and his possessions at some time and place.[5]

These statements represent the general common-law concept of arrest.[6] However, this is not the present federal constitutional concept of the term "arrest" or the term "custodial arrest."

Under the federal constitutional concept of arrest, a greater degree of intrusion or restraint is required in order to have an arrest than that which was required at common law. For example, a "stop and frisk" in terms of federal constitutional law amounts to a seizure, not to an arrest; and it does not require probable cause.[7] However, in common-law terms a "stop and frisk" at least generally appears to be an arrest. The person frisked is certainly at least slightly restrained. On the other hand, the United States Supreme Court in the *Terry*[8] case made it clear that the Fourth Amendment applies to "seizures" as well as to arrests.

Thus, from a federal constitutional standpoint, the terms

---

[2]Conoly v. Imperial Tobacco Co., 63 Ga. App. 880, 885, 12 S.E.2d 398 (1940). The rule in Conoly is much like that of Henry v. U.S., 361 U.S. 98, 103, 80 S. Ct. 168, 4 L. Ed. 2d 134 (1959). However, the Supreme Court altered the Conoly rule in Terry v. Ohio, 392 U.S. 1, 88 S. Ct. 1868, 20 L. Ed. 2d 889 (1968). See § 3:1, infra, on *Terry*. A trial court's discretion in resolving the issue of whether and when a defendant is under arrest is very broad. See e.g., Marshall v. State, 286 Ga. App. 86, 648 S.E.2d 674 (2007).

[3]Collier v. State, 244 Ga. 553, 561, 261 S.E.2d 364 (1979) (overruled by, Thompson v. State, 263 Ga. 23, 426 S.E.2d 895 (1993)).

[4]O.C.G.A. § 17-4-1.

[5]Brown v. State, 191 Ga. App. 779, 780, 383 S.E.2d 170 (1989).

[6]6A C.J.S. Arrest § 2.

[7]Terry v. Ohio, 392 U.S. 1, 88 S. Ct. 1868, 20 L. Ed. 2d 889 (1968).

[8]Terry v. Ohio, 392 U.S. 1, 88 S. Ct. 1868, 20 L. Ed. 2d 889 (1968).

"seizure" and "arrest" or "custodial arrest" together seem to approximate the common-law concept of arrest. That is, the common-law term "arrest" applies, of course, to what the United States Supreme Court has called an "arrest" or "custodial arrest" from a federal constitutional standpoint, but the common-law term "arrest" also encompasses a "stop and frisk" or "seizure" as defined by the Supreme Court.

The nomenclature used by the United States Supreme Court is important because a "seizure" or "stop and frisk" is valid if based on reasonable suspicion, which is grounded upon specific and articulable facts, judged against an objective standard. However, when such a "search" is permissible the "search" accompanying such a seizure is much more restricted than in the case of a search incident to a lawful "arrest," as that term is used by the Supreme Court. There may not be a federal constitutional "arrest" in the absence of probable cause, but if there is probable cause (and the arrest is otherwise valid) the search conducted incident to such an arrest may be much broader than in the "stop and frisk" or "seizure" situation. However, where a person thought to be only an eyewitness to a shooting was asked to wait in the back of a police car until he could be questioned about the shooting, and the "witness" made an incriminating statement when a detective approached 17 minutes later, the court concluded that from a federal constitutional standpoint the seizure was reasonable and a less severe intrusion than a traditional arrest and thus declined to suppress the statement.[9]

In *State v. Corbett*,[10] the court held that whether or not a person has been constitutionally arrested depends upon "whether a reasonable person in the suspect's position would have thought the detention would not be temporary." In *State v. Davis*,[11] Judge Johnson pointed out that "[a] person has been 'seized' within the meaning of the Fourth Amendment only if, in view of all of the circumstances surrounding the incident, a reasonable person would have believed that he was not free to leave. Examples of circumstances that might indicate a seizure, even where the person did not attempt to leave, would be the threatening presence of several officers, the display of a weapon by an officer, some physical touching of the person . . ., or the use of language or tone of voice indicating that compliance with the officer's request might be compelled."

It should be noted, however, that notwithstanding the foregoing, not every custodial restraint of an individual by a police of-

[9]U. S. v. Allen, 436 A.2d 1303 (D.C. 1981).

[10]State v. Corbett, 205 Ga. App. 554, 556, 423 S.E.2d 38 (1992).

[11]State v. Davis, 206 Ga. App. 238, 424 S.E.2d 878 (1992).

ficer will constitute an "arrest." A person taken into custody pursuant to an order of *civil* protective custody is not "arrested." In *Lindsey v. State*,[12] for example, an individual who was detained, placed in handcuffs and into a police cruiser and secured while being served with a civil order authorizing the individual's detention for purposes of a mental evaluation was not deemed under "arrest" for purposes of a Fourth Amendment challenge to contraband found during the search.

In *Miranda v. State*,[13] in an opinion by Judge, now Chief Justice, Benham, the Court of Appeals said there are at least three kinds of police-citizen encounters: (1) verbal encounters involving no coercion or detention, (2) brief "stops" or "seizures" which must be accompanied by reasonable suspicion, and (3) "arrests" which must be supported by probable cause.

In *Quinn v. State*,[14] the court pointed out that "[n]ot all encounters between police officers and citizens involve seizures which implicate Fourth Amendment protections. . . . '[E]ven when officers have no basis for suspecting a particular individual, they may generally ask questions . . .; [and] ask to examine the individual's identification . . .;—as long as the police do not convey a message that compliance with their requests is required.' "

See §§ 3:2 et seq., infra, on facts justifying a stop and frisk and what constitutes a seizure.

§ 2:3 Immunity from arrest

Certain persons while performing or preparing to perform official duties may only be arrested for certain offenses. For example, such limited immunity from arrest applies to members of the General Assembly,[1] and militiamen.[2] The federal Constitution provides for this type of immunity from arrest for members of Congress[3] and diplomats of a foreign nation; their families and

---

[12]Lindsey v. State, 282 Ga. App. 644, 639 S.E.2d 584 (2006).

[13]Miranda v. State, 189 Ga. App. 218, 219, 375 S.E.2d 295 (1988).

[14]Quinn v. State, 268 Ga. 70, 72, 485 S.E.2d 483 (1997), relying on and quoting from Florida v. Bostick, 501 U.S. 429, 111 S. Ct. 2382, 115 L. Ed. 2d 389 (1991). See also Muehler v. Mena, 544 U.S. 93, 125 S. Ct. 1465, 161 L. Ed. 2d 299 (2005), where the U.S. Supreme Court found that the questioning of a household occupant about her immigration status during a lawful search of the house did not extend the time of detention and was therefore not an additional seizure within the meaning of the Fourth Amendment.

[Section 2:3]

[1]Ga. Const., Art. III, § IV, ¶ IX. However, the exemption does not apply to arrests for treason, felony or a breach of the peace.

[2]O.C.G.A. § 17-4-2.

[3]U.S. Const. Art. I, § 6 [1].

staffs enjoy a broader immunity under a federal statute.[4]

See § 2:20, infra, on arrest of peace officers.

§ 2:4   Delay in making an arrest

While it is often said that an officer is under a duty to arrest a defendant immediately without a warrant where a crime is committed in his presence,[1] it is established in Georgia, and under the federal Constitution, that a defendant has no general right to an immediate arrest.[2] The United States Supreme Court has held that the Sixth Amendment right to a speedy trial does not apply until the defendant has been indicted or arrested.[3] However, in *United States v. Lovasco*,[4] the Court has acknowledged that the due process clause "has a limited role to play in protecting against oppressive delay." If such a due process violation is asserted and there is "proof of actual prejudice" then it is said that the due process claim is ripe for adjudication, but this does not make the claim automatically valid.[5] A delay for purposes of further investigation normally "does not deprive . . . [a defendant] of due process, even if his defense might have been somewhat prejudiced by the lapse of time."[6] A defendant is entitled to a dismissal of his indictment where the delay is taken by the prosecution as "an intentional device to gain tactical advantage over the accused."[7] The Court in *Lovasco* concluded that a good faith investigative delay of one and one half years did not amount to a due process violation.[8] However, in determining whether or not a delay in obtaining an indictment after an arrest violates the

---

[4]22 U.S.C.A. § 254b.

[Section 2:4]

[1]Yancey v. Fidelity & Cas. Co. of N. Y., 96 Ga. App. 476, 478, 100 S.E.2d 653 (1957).

[2]Koran v. U.S., 469 F.2d 1071 (5th Cir. 1972); Blackwell v. State, 139 Ga. App. 477, 478, 228 S.E.2d 612 (1976).

[3]U.S. v. Marion, 404 U.S. 307, 92 S. Ct. 455, 30 L. Ed. 2d 468 (1971).

[4]U. S. v. Lovasco, 431 U.S. 783, 97 S. Ct. 2044, 52 L. Ed. 2d 752 (1977).

[5]U. S. v. Lovasco, 431 U.S. 783, 789, 97 S. Ct. 2044, 52 L. Ed. 2d 752 (1977).

[6]U. S. v. Lovasco, 431 U.S. 783, 796, 97 S. Ct. 2044, 52 L. Ed. 2d 752 (1977). In Lovasco, the defendant moved to dismiss the indictment and

testified that two material witnesses had died during the delay. However, he did not state how they would have aided the defense had they been willing to testify. The court concluded that in determining the existence of a due process violation, the reason for the delay could be considered and that compelling the defendant to stand trial would not be fundamentally unfair. Accord, Glenn v. State, 144 Ga. App. 557, 241 S.E.2d 447 (1978).

[7]U.S. v. Marion, 404 U.S. 307, 324, 92 S. Ct. 455, 30 L. Ed. 2d 468 (1971). See U.S. v. Butler, 792 F.2d 1528 (11th Cir. 1986); Hilton v. State, 288 Ga. 201, 206 (5), 702 S.E.2d 188 (2010). See Jones v. State, 284 Ga. 320(1), 667 S.E.2d 49 (2008).

[8]U. S. v. Lovasco, 431 U.S. 783, 796, 97 S. Ct. 2044, 52 L. Ed. 2d 752 (1977).

Sixth Amendment right to a speedy trial, the Georgia Supreme Court has applied a less rigorous standard. The Georgia court has evaluated such a delay by the *Barker v. Wingo*[9] standard which the United States Supreme Court has applied to a delay in trial after indictment.[10] This standard is discussed in § 14:70, infra, on right to speedy trial. Nevertheless, from a federal constitutional standpoint the general rule is that "[t]here is no constitutional right to be arrested."[11]

While some states have considered a delay in arrest as a due process violation,[12] it has been said that a dismissal of an indictment is required for pre-arrest or pre-indictment delay only if it is shown that (1) the delay caused substantial prejudice to the defendant's right to a fair trial and that (2) the delay was an intentional device to gain a tactical advantage over the defendant.[13] Thus, it has been held that where a delay only results in a defendant's loss of ability to recall his whereabouts at the time of the alleged offense, the indictment will not be dismissed if there is no indication that the arrest was delayed in order to gain a tactical advantage over the defendant.[14]

Additionally, even prior to *Chimel v. California*,[15] it was held that an officer has no right to use such a delay as an excuse to wait until a defendant is at a particular place which the officer wishes to search incident to an arrest.[16] However, if the officer waits to arrest for the purpose of giving the offender an op-

---

[9]Barker v. Wingo, 407 U.S. 514, 92 S. Ct. 2182, 33 L. Ed. 2d 101 (1972). The factors examined include length of delay, reason for delay, defendant's assertion of his right, and prejudice to the defendant.

[10]Haisman v. State, 242 Ga. 896, 897, 252 S.E.2d 397 (1979).

[11]Hoffa v. U.S., 385 U.S. 293, 310, 87 S. Ct. 408, 17 L. Ed. 2d 374 (1966). See 6A C.J.S. Arrest § 51.

[12]In State v. Griffin, 347 So. 2d 692, 696 (Fla. Dist. Ct. App. 1st Dist. 1977), the court concluded that there had been such a due process violation where there had been an 11-month delay and the defendant had no recollection of where he was or what he was doing and he could not locate any witnesses to his actions or whereabouts on the date in question. The court said that a number of factors should be considered in determining whether there had been a due process violation such as the reason for the delay and the prejudice to the defendant.

[13]Jones v. State, 284 Ga. 320 (1), 667 S.E.2d 49 (2008); Armour v. State, 140 Ga. App. 196, 230 S.E.2d 346 (1976) (citing U.S. v. Marion, 404 U.S. 307, 92 S. Ct. 455, 30 L. Ed. 2d 468 (1971)). In Marion, there was a delay of over three years between the event and the indictment. The court held that the Sixth Amendment did not apply to the defendant until he was indicted. The possible harm to the defendant was insufficient to demonstrate that he could not receive a fair trial as mandated by the due process clause.

[14]Armour v. State, 140 Ga. App. 196, 230 S.E.2d 346 (1976). Accord, Clayton v. State, 145 Ga. App. 541, 244 S.E.2d 67 (1978).

[15]Chimel v. California, 395 U.S. 752, 89 S. Ct. 2034, 23 L. Ed. 2d 685 (1969).

[16]See McKnight v. U.S., 183 F.2d 977 (D.C. Cir. 1950). This case holds that under the circumstances outlined

portunity to repeat the offense, such conduct alone is not objectionable.[17]

§ 2:5 Place of arrest

Georgia provides by statute that, where necessary, an officer with a valid arrest warrant may break into a home to arrest a concealed offender.[1] However, generally an officer has no right in the execution of a search warrant or a warrantless arrest to "break" the door in to arrest a defendant, without first stating his authority and purpose for demanding admission.[2] "[F]or Fourth Amendment purposes, an arrest warrant founded on probable cause implicitly carries with it the limited authority to enter a dwelling in which the suspect lives when there is reason to believe the suspect is within."[3]

In *United States v. Watson,*[4] the Supreme Court held that there may be a warrantless arrest of a suspect in a public place if the officer has probable cause to believe that the suspect has committed a felony. In *Payton v. New York,*[5] the Court further held that an officer has no right to arrest a suspect in the suspect's home without an arrest warrant in the absence of exigent circumstances. However, *Payton* does not prevent a warrantless

---

in the text, the search is illegal regardless of the legality of the arrest.

[17]Geter v. State, 129 Ga. App. 108, 199 S.E.2d 272 (1973). Cf. Hoffa v. U.S., 385 U.S. 293, 310, 87 S. Ct. 408, 17 L. Ed. 2d 374 (1966).

[Section 2:5]

[1]O.C.G.A. § 17-4-3.

[2]See, e.g., Green v. State, 159 Ga. App. 28, 29, 283 S.E.2d 19 (1981); Barclay v. State, 142 Ga. App. 657, 236 S.E.2d 901 (1977). Accord, Miller v. U.S., 357 U.S. 301, 308, 78 S. Ct. 1190, 2 L. Ed. 2d 1332 (1958).

[3]Payton v. New York, 445 U.S. 573, 603, 100 S. Ct. 1371, 63 L. Ed. 2d 639 (1980). See U.S. v. Bervaldi, 226 F.3d 1256 (11th Cir. 2000); Carter v. State, 308 Ga. App. 686, 708 S.E.2d 595 (2011).

[4]U.S. v. Watson, 423 U.S. 411, 422, 96 S. Ct. 820, 46 L. Ed. 2d 598 (1976).

[5]Payton v. New York, 445 U.S. 573, 100 S. Ct. 1371, 63 L. Ed. 2d 639

(1980). In Payton, officers assembled sufficient evidence to establish probable cause that the defendant committed murder. Without obtaining an arrest warrant, the officers went to the defendant's apartment to arrest him. The lights were on and they could hear music coming from the apartment but they received no response to their knock. They broke the door down and found that no one was present. However, they saw in plain view a shell casing and seized it. The United States Supreme Court concluded that it was error to deny the motion to suppress the evidence seized. Accord, Carranza v. State, 266 Ga. 263, 264, 467 S.E.2d 315 (1996). See Minor v. State, 298 Ga. App. 391, 680 S.E.2d 459 (2009) (officer may enter home without a warrant if exigent circumstances require immediate action such as when officer is in hot pursuit of a suspect, or reasonably fears for the imminent destruction of evidence, or reasonably believes suspect is a danger to himself or others).

arrest in a common hallway of an apartment house,[6] or where a defendant "is sitting on his porch,"[7] nor does it prevent an arrest in a defendant's home where the officer attempted to stop the defendant outside his home only to have the defendant retreat into his home.[8] Likewise, in *Kendrick v. State,*[9] the Georgia Court of Appeals held that a warrantless arrest effected after a valid consent to enter the home is not a Payton violation. Nevertheless, in *United States v. Winchenbach,*[10] the court held that when officers have a search warrant for the defendant's residence and have probable cause to arrest him, they may arrest the defendant in his home without an arrest warrant.

In *Welsh v. Wisconsin,*[11] the United States Supreme Court held that officers had no right to a warrantless entry of a defendant's home to arrest him for a non-jailable traffic offense in order to preserve evidence of his intoxication in the absence of other exigency. The Wisconsin Supreme Court had concluded that there were exigent circumstances based on the need to obtain a test of the blood alcohol level of the defendant and hot pursuit. The United States Supreme Court found that "there was no immediate or continuous pursuit of the . . . [defendant] from the scene of a crime," and thus no hot pursuit. The Court also held "that an important factor to be considered when determining whether any exigency exists is the gravity of the underlying offense for which the arrest is being made. Moreover, although no exigency is created simply because there is probable cause to believe that a serious crime has been committed, . . . application of the exigent-circumstances exception in the context of a home entry should rarely be sanctioned when there is probable cause to believe that only a minor offense . . . has been committed."

In *State v. Nichols,*[12] an officer arrested the defendant in his father's home. The defendant backed into a car in the yard and when ordered to stop, he fled into the house. The court affirmed the validity of the arrest pointing out that "hot pursuit" need not involve a high speed chase.

In *McCauley v. State,*[13] deputies responded to a domestic dispute where they found the wife of the defendant outside the residence crying and upset. She indicated that the defendant had

---

[6]U.S. v. Holland, 755 F.2d 253 (2d Cir. 1985).

[7]Collins v. State, 191 Ga. App. 289, 292, 381 S.E.2d 430 (1989).

[8]Brock v. State, 196 Ga. App. 605, 607, 396 S.E.2d 785 (1990).

[9]Kendrick v. State, 211 Ga. App. 599, 601, 440 S.E.2d 53 (1993).

[10]U.S. v. Winchenbach, 197 F.3d 548 (1st Cir. 1999).

[11]Welsh v. Wisconsin, 466 U.S. 740, 753, 104 S. Ct. 2091, 80 L. Ed. 2d 732 (1984).

[12]State v. Nichols, 225 Ga. App. 609, 610, 484 S.E.2d 507 (1997).

[13]McCauley v. State, 222 Ga. App. 600, 475 S.E.2d 669 (1996).

been drinking and had struck and threatened her and their four-month-old infant. With the consent of the wife, the deputies entered the house and determined that the defendant was so impaired as to endanger the child. The appellate court affirmed the conviction, finding that the exigent circumstances justified the warrantless arrest of defendant in his home.

In *Steagald v. United States*,[14] the United States Supreme Court held that an officer with an arrest warrant has no right to enter the home of a third party to search for the defendant unless the officer also has a search warrant to search the premises of the third party without his consent, or unless there are exigent circumstances.

The Eleventh Circuit in *United States v. Bulman*,[15] while recognizing that there may be a lesser expectation of privacy in a motel room than a home, concluded that the Payton[16] rule applied to the arrest of a defendant in his motel room. However, the Steagald rule is intended to protect the third party, whose home has been searched, and not the defendant who is arrested.[17] Hence, it has been held where a defendant is arrested pursuant to an arrest warrant in a third party's home, without a search warrant, the defendant has no standing to move to suppress firearms and ammunition observed in plain view at the time of his arrest.[18]

In *United States v. Reed*,[19] the court said that the following factors may be considered in determining whether or not exigent circumstances exist to arrest a defendant in his home without an arrest warrant: (1) the gravity or violent nature of the offense; (2) whether the suspect is reasonably believed to be armed; (3) "a

---

[14]Steagald v. U.S., 451 U.S. 204, 101 S. Ct. 1642, 68 L. Ed. 2d 38 (1981). See Arp v. State, 327 Ga. App. 340, 759 S.E.2d 57 (2014).

However, in U.S. v. Buckner, 717 F.2d 297 (6th Cir. 1983), the court held that a defendant had no standing to suppress evidence obtained incident to his arrest in his mother's apartment, where he was named in an arrest warrant. Buckner is based on the theory that the search warrant requirement is for the protection of the third person whose home is searched. However, in U.S. v. Morgan, 743 F.2d 1158 (6th Cir. 1984), the court concluded that a defendant had a right to rely on the arrest warrant requirement.

[15]U.S. v. Bulman, 667 F.2d 1374 (11th Cir. 1982); Mowrer v. State, 447 N.E.2d 1129 (Ind. Ct. App. 1983); People v. Oliver, 417 Mich. 366, 338 N.W.2d 167 (1983). Accord, Graham v. State, 406 So. 2d 503 (Fla. Dist. Ct. App. 3d Dist. 1981).

[16]See Payton v. New York, 445 U.S. 573, 100 S. Ct. 1371, 63 L. Ed. 2d 639 (1980).

[17]See, e.g., Patterson v. Com., 630 S.W.2d 73 (Ky. Ct. App. 1981).

[18]U.S. v. Underwood, 717 F.2d 482 (9th Cir. 1983). In Underwood, the court pointed out that a defendant "has no greater right of privacy in another's home than in his own."

[19]U.S. v. Reed, 572 F.2d 412 (2d Cir. 1978).

clear showing of probable cause . . . that the suspect committed the crime"; (4) a "strong reason to believe that the suspect is in the premises being entered"; (5) "a likelihood that the suspect will escape if not swiftly apprehended"; and (6) the peaceful circumstances of the entry by the officer.

In *United States v. Segura*,[20] the Second Circuit found invalid the warrantless security check of the defendant's seventeenth floor apartment after his arrest in the lobby of the building.

§ 2:6 Procedure for arrest

In situations where a lawful arrest cannot be made without a warrant, the officer should have the warrant in his possession at the time of the arrest or so near at hand that it can be exhibited on demand.[1] It has been said that an officer derives no authority or power from a warrant unless he has it with him and can display it.[2] O.C.G.A. § 17-4-20 provides that an officer has a right to arrest with or without a warrant (1) if the offense was committed within his presence or within his immediate knowledge, or (2) if the offender is endeavoring to escape,[3] or (3) if the officer has probable cause to believe an act of family violence has been committed, or (4) if the officer has probable cause to believe that the offender has violated a family violence order, or (5) for other cause if there is likely to be a failure of justice from the want of a duly authorized officer to issue a warrant, or (6) if the officer has probable cause to believe that an offense involving physical abuse has been committed against a vulnerable adult who is defined as being a person 18 years old or older who is unable to protect himself or herself from physical or mental abuse.

In the absence of one of the five instances above, an officer generally has no right to arrest for a violation of a municipal ordinance[4] or a misdemeanor[5] unless the officer has a warrant in

---

[20]U.S. v. Segura, 663 F.2d 411 (2d Cir. 1981). In Segura, the court held that evidence obtained in the "protective sweep" was inadmissible. Officers had remained on the premises illegally for some 19 hours. Finally, a search had been conducted pursuant to a search warrant. The court held that the evidence obtained pursuant to the search warrant was admissible, but evidence obtained during the unlawful stay was not admissible.

[Section 2:6]

[1]Croker v. State, 114 Ga. App. 492, 494, 151 S.E.2d 846 (1966). See Adams v. State, 121 Ga. 163, 48 S.E. 910 (1904). See also 6A C.J.S. Arrest §§ 46, 47.

[2]Giddens v. State, 154 Ga. 54, 61, 113 S.E. 386 (1922).

[3]Porter v. State, 124 Ga. 297, 306, 52 S.E. 283 (1905).

[4]Porter v. State, 124 Ga. 297, 306, 52 S.E. 283 (1905); State v. Koon, 133 Ga. App. 685, 211 S.E.2d 924 (1975).

[5]Porter v. State, 124 Ga. 297, 52 S.E. 283 (1905).

his possession at the time of the attempted arrest.[6] This is said to be true because the officer is bound to have the warrant ready to be produced if asked for.[7] For example, in *Croker v. State,*[8] the court said that where the offense involved was a misdemeanor not committed in the presence of the officer and flight was not involved, the officer had no authority to arrest the defendant even though a warrant had been issued because the warrant was not accessible to the officer at the time. In the case of a felony, it is not necessary for the officer to have the warrant in his possession in order to make a valid arrest.[9] Also, an officer may arrest without a warrant pursuant to O.C.G.A. § 17-4-20(a) or with probable cause.[10] See § 2:13, infra, on warrantless arrests. However, under Georgia law it has been held that if the officer wishes to arrest the defendant without a warrant, he should do so promptly.[11] Without a warrant and in the absence of exigent circumstances, there is no right to make an arrest in a person's home.[12] Moreover, even when an officer has an arrest warrant, the general rule requires that the officer knock and announce his presence before entering.[13] See § 2:19, infra, on arrest warrants.

While it is provided by Georgia statute that where an officer has a warrant he may "break open the door of any house where the offender is concealed,"[14] and it is recognized that an officer may use such force as is reasonably necessary to arrest, nevertheless, he is not authorized to use any more force than is reasonably necessary.[15] But see § 2:5, supra, on place of arrest. It has also been recognized that an officer may use more force to ac-

---

[6]Adorno v. State, 314 Ga. App. 509, 724 S.E.2d 816 (2012). See Shafer v. State, 193 Ga. 748, 755, 20 S.E.2d 34 (1942); Porter v. State, 124 Ga. 297, 52 S.E. 283 (1905). In Croker v. State, 114 Ga. App. 492, 494, 151 S.E.2d 846 (1966), the court pointed out that "a warrant is not in the possession of the officer when it is in his house some distance from the scene of the arrest."

[7]Adams v. State, 121 Ga. 163, 165, 48 S.E. 910 (1904).

[8]Croker v. State, 114 Ga. App. 492, 494, 151 S.E.2d 846 (1966).

[9]Watts v. Cannon, 224 Ga. 797, 164 S.E.2d 780 (1968). See also Croker v. State, 114 Ga. App. 492, 494, 151 S.E.2d 846 (1966).

[10]Durden v. State, 250 Ga. 325, 327, 297 S.E.2d 237 (1982).

[11]Reed v. State, 195 Ga. 842, 849, 25 S.E.2d 692 (1943).

[12]Payton v. New York, 445 U.S. 573, 100 S. Ct. 1371, 63 L. Ed. 2d 639 (1980). See § 2:5, supra, on place of arrest.

[13]See 5 Am. Jur. 2d, Arrest § 93; 6A C.J.S. Arrest § 56. See, e.g., Miller v. U.S., 357 U.S. 301, 78 S. Ct. 1190, 2 L. Ed. 2d 1332 (1958); Barclay v. State, 142 Ga. App. 657, 236 S.E.2d 901 (1977).

[14]O.C.G.A. § 17-4-3. See, e.g., Butler v. State, 159 Ga. App. 895, 897, 285 S.E.2d 610 (1981).

[15]Mullis v. State, 196 Ga. 569, 577, 27 S.E.2d 91 (1943); Byrd v. Cavenaugh, 269 Ga. App. 612, 604 S.E.2d 655 (2004). See 6A C.J.S. Arrest § 49(a).

complish an arrest for a felony than for a misdemeanor.[16]

In *Tennessee v. Garner*,[17] the United States Supreme Court held a statute violative of the Fourth Amendment which permitted officers to use deadly force to prevent the escape of a suspected felon. The Court said that deadly force may not be used unless necessary to prevent escape and the officer has probable cause to believe that the suspect poses a significant threat of death or grave injury to the officer or others. In the case of a misdemeanor, an officer has no right to shoot merely to prevent his escape.[18] This rule applies equally to an arrest for a violation of a municipal ordinance.[19] However, even in the case of a misdemeanor, "in order to overcome declared, open and armed resistance to [the] execution of . . . [a warrant, an officer may] use such force as may be reasonably necessary to effect the arrest."[20]

In 1986, Georgia added to O.C.G.A. § 17-4-20 a provision stating that an officer "may use deadly force to apprehend a suspected felon only when the officer reasonably believes that the suspect possesses a deadly weapon or any object, device, or instrument which, when used offensively against a person, is likely to or actually does result in serious bodily injury; when the officer reasonably believes that the suspect poses an immediate threat of physical violence to the officer or others; or when there is probable cause to believe that the suspect has committed a crime involving the infliction or threatened infliction of serious physical harm. Nothing in this Code section shall be construed so as to restrict such sheriffs or peace officers from the use of such reasonable nondeadly force as may be necessary to apprehend and arrest a suspected felon or misdemeanant."

Unless the person to be arrested knows that the person attempting to arrest him is an officer, the officer should notify him of his authority.[21] Likewise, the person to be taken into custody should be notified of the offense with which he is being charged.[22] If the officer has an arrest warrant, he should tell the suspect by

[16]Mullis v. State, 196 Ga. 569, 578, 27 S.E.2d 91 (1943). In Mullis the court actually says that if the offense is a felony the officer may, if necessary, even slay the suspect to prevent his escape.

[17]Tennessee v. Garner, 471 U.S. 1, 105 S. Ct. 1694, 85 L. Ed. 2d 1 (1985). See 6A C.J.S. Arrest § 49(b).

[18]Savannah News-Press, Inc. v. Harley, 100 Ga. App. 387, 389, 111 S.E.2d 259 (1959); Eaton v. State, 83 Ga. App. 82, 85, 62 S.E.2d 677 (1950).

[19]Holmes v. State, 5 Ga. App. 166, 62 S.E. 716 (1908).

[20]Bennett v. State, 169 Ga. App. 85, 86, 311 S.E.2d 513 (1983).

[21]Jones v. State, 114 Ga. 73, 39 S.E. 861 (1901); 6A C.J.S. Arrest § 48.

[22]Robinson v. State, 93 Ga. 77, 88, 18 S.E. 1018 (1893).

what authority he is being arrested[23] or should display the warrant to the accused.[24] However, if a suspect knows he is being lawfully arrested by an officer, it is the duty of the suspect to submit quietly.[25]

In the case of any offense involving a violation of any law or ordinance involving the operation, licensing, registration, maintenance or inspection of a motor vehicle, the officer may arrest by issuance of a citation if the offense was committed in the presence of the officer. If the offense results in an accident, an investigating officer may issue a citation regardless of whether the offense occurred in his presence. Also, a citation may be issued if the offense occurred before another officer. Any citation issued "shall enumerate the specific charges against the person and the date upon which the person is to appear and answer the charges." If the offense occurred before another officer, "the citation shall list the name of each officer and each must be present when the charges against the accused person are heard."[26]

In *Atwater v. City of Lago Vista,*[27] the United States Supreme Court held that an officer in Texas may, under the federal constitution, arrest the driver of an automobile for not wearing a seat belt even though the failure to utilize a seat belt is a non-jailable misdemeanor punishable only by a fine of not less than $25.00 or more than $50.00. Although the law permits officers to issue citations in lieu of arrest, the court pointed out that "the standard of probable cause 'applie[s]' to all arrests, without the need to 'balance' the interests and circumstances involved in particular situations.' "

See *Criminal Arrest in Georgia,* Institute of Government, University of Georgia (1979), p. 34.

§ 2:7   Right to resist illegal arrest

Certain limitations exist on the power of an officer to arrest an individual. If the arrest is illegal and proceeds so far as to constitute an assault, the alleged offender may resist with such force as is reasonably necessary to prevent his arrest.[1] However, an assault against an arresting officer is not justified unless the officer

---

[23]Douglass v. State, 152 Ga. 379, 392, 110 S.E. 168 (1921). Cf. Davis v. State, 79 Ga. 767, 4 S.E. 318 (1887).

[24]Graham v. State, 143 Ga. 440, 445, 85 S.E. 328 (1915); Jones v. State, 114 Ga. 73, 74, 39 S.E. 861 (1901).

[25]Smith v. State, 144 Ga. App. 785, 787, 242 S.E.2d 376 (1978).

[26]O.C.G.A. § 17-4-23.

[27]Atwater v. City of Lago Vista, 532 U.S. 318, 121 S. Ct. 1536, 149 L. Ed. 2d 549 (2001).

[Section 2:7]

[1]Brooks v. State, 144 Ga. App. 97, 240 S.E.2d 593 (1977).See U.S. v. Timmann, 741 F.3d 1170 (11th Cir. 2013) (the usual inquiry involves an examination of the extent to which the

assaulted the person first.[2] It is generally held that the killing of an individual who is illegally arresting another is manslaughter rather than murder.[3] However, if the arresting officer intended to kill that individual prior to the attempted illegal arrest in order to effect the arrest, such a killing may amount to murder.[4] The "law provides no right to resist a legal arrest."[5] Where an arrest is unlawful, the person making the arrest may be subject to an action for damages[6] and a possible action under the Civil Rights Act.[7]

However, in *Green v. State*,[8] a majority of the Court of Appeals held that where a person is charged with obstruction of a police officer, and his sole defense is that the arrest was illegal, it is not error for the trial judge to refuse to give a charge that "[e]very person has the right to resist an illegal arrest . . .," if the trial judge charges the essential elements of the obstruction offense requiring the state "to prove the lawfulness of the arrest in order to prove an essential element of the offense."

See § 2:11, infra, on probable cause to arrest.

§ 2:8 What persons have an officer's power to arrest?

Ordinarily the word "officer," for purposes of making an arrest, denotes a peace officer who is authorized by statute to make an arrest.[1] An arrest by a security guard or a private citizen, or a citizen's arrest, is discussed in § 2:21, infra.

It should be noted that Georgia has provided by statute[2] that no peace officer shall exercise the power to arrest if the officer has not complied with the Georgia Peace Officer Standards and

---

unlawful police conduct caused the defendant's reaction); Whitener v. State, 272 Ga. App. 28, 611 S.E.2d 707 (2005).

[2]Sosebee v. State, 169 Ga. App. 370, 312 S.E.2d 853 (1983).

[3]Thomas v. State, 91 Ga. 204, 18 S.E. 305 (1892).

In John Bad Elk v. U.S., 177 U.S. 529, 20 S. Ct. 729, 44 L. Ed. 874 (1900), the Supreme Court indicated that a defendant using unreasonable force to resist an unlawful arrest and killing the arresting officer is guilty of manslaughter and not murder. However, in U.S. v. Danehy, 680 F.2d 1311, 1316 (11th Cir. 1982), the Court of Appeals affirmed the refusal of the district court to give such a charge, say-

ing declaring that this rule "has no significant role" in our society today.

[4]Coleman v. State, 121 Ga. 594, 595, 49 S.E. 716 (1905).

[5]Cordis v. State, 236 Ga. App. 629, 631, 513 S.E.2d 45 (1999).

[6]Gordon v. Hogan, 114 Ga. 354, 40 S.E. 229 (1901).

[7]42 U.S.C.A. § 1983. See, e.g., Pierson v. Ray, 386 U.S. 547, 87 S. Ct. 1213, 18 L. Ed. 2d 288 (1967).

[8]Green v. State, 240 Ga. App. 774, 525 S.E.2d 154 (1999).

[Section 2:8]

[1]6A C.J.S. Arrest § 17.

[2]O.C.G.A. § 35-8-17.

Training Act.[3] Also, in *Holstein v. State*[4] the court held that an officer who has not completed the requirements of the Training Act may not obtain a search warrant. However, in *Davis v. State*[5] the court held that an officer who has completed the training requirements of the statute may arrest even though he has not yet received his certification.

In *Williams v. State,*[6] the court held that a federal DEA agent had no authority as an officer to make an arrest for a misdemeanor; however, the agent had the same right as any other citizen to arrest an offender who is committing a misdemeanor in his presence.

O.C.G.A. § 17-4-25 provides in part as follows:

"(a) Under a warrant issued by a judicial officer, an arresting officer may, in any county without regard to the residence of the arresting officer, arrest any person charged with a crime. It is the duty of the arresting officer to take the accused, with the warrant under which he was arrested, to the county in which the offense is alleged to have been committed, for examination before any judicial officer of that county."[7]

This section does not apply to city police officers,[8] but does apply to state officers and county police.[9]

In *Watkins v. State,*[10] the court held that under exigent circumstances a deputy sheriff has authority to make a warrantless arrest beyond the limits of his county.

See generally 6A C.J.S. Arrest § 17. See § 2:21, infra, on the authority of a private citizen to arrest, and § 2:20, infra, on arrest of peace officer. Generally, see § 2:13 et seq., infra, on arrest by an officer.

§ 2:9   Overview of prerequisites for warrantless arrests

In order to have a valid "stop and frisk" or "seizure" of a person in a federal constitutional sense, it is not necessary for an officer to have probable cause. An articulable suspicion is sufficient. See Chapter 3, infra, on stop-and-frisk. However, in order to have a

---

[3]O.C.G.A. §§ 35-8-1 et seq. See, e.g., Williams v. State, 171 Ga. App. 807, 808, 321 S.E.2d 386 (1984).

[4]Holstein v. State, 183 Ga. App. 610, 359 S.E.2d 360 (1987).

[5]Davis v. State, 164 Ga. App. 312, 316, 295 S.E.2d 131 (1982). Cf. Dennis v. State, 220 Ga. App. 420, 469 S.E.2d 494 (1996).

[6]Williams v. State, 171 Ga. App. 807, 808, 321 S.E.2d 386 (1984). Accord, Fajardo v. State, 191 Ga. App. 295, 296, 381 S.E.2d 560 (1989).

[7]See, e.g., Lamb v. Dillard, 94 Ga. 206, 21 S.E. 463 (1894).

[8]1958-59 Op. Att'y Gen., p. 73.

[9]O.C.G.A. § 36-8-5.

[10]Watkins v. State, 207 Ga. App. 766, 772, 430 S.E.2d 105 (1993), overruled on other grounds by West v. Waters, 272 Ga. 591, 533 S.E.2d 88 (2000).

valid arrest, the Fourth Amendment requires that there must be probable cause to believe that the suspect has violated the law,[1] or is violating the law in the officer's presence.[2] See § 2:2, supra, on the definition of an arrest.

By statute, Georgia has stated that an officer may arrest in six situations.[3] However, the absolute prerequisite, which is sometimes lost sight of, is that from a federal constitutional standpoint an arrest is not valid unless there is probable cause, regardless of whether the situation falls within one of the provisions of the Georgia statute authorizing an officer to make a warrantless arrest.[4]

On the other hand, to have a valid arrest in the common law or Georgia tradition, one of the six statutory requirements must exist.[5] §§ 2:13 et seq., infra, discuss the question of whether or not one or more of the statutory requirements for an arrest can exist when there is no probable cause.

In summary, to have a valid arrest from both the federal constitutional and common law standpoint, there must first be probable cause. However, if one of the six situations of the Georgia statute exists there may be a valid "seizure" or "stop and frisk" in the federal constitutional sense, even in the absence of probable cause, if there is an articulable suspicion justifying the action.

[Section 2:9]

[1]Dunaway v. New York, 442 U.S. 200, 99 S. Ct. 2248, 60 L. Ed. 2d 824 (1979). The Dunaway case also held that where such a suspect is taken into custody without probable cause, statements obtained from him and sketches made by him while detained are inadmissible even if he was given *Miranda* warnings and waived the presence of counsel. The Court pointed out that the officers exploited the detention to obtain evidence and that no intervening factors broke the causal link between detention and confession. In U.S. v. Tucker, 610 F.2d 1007, 1010 (2d Cir. 1979), Dunaway was held to be retroactive.

[2]U.S. v. Rabinowitz, 339 U.S. 56, 60, 70 S. Ct. 430, 94 L. Ed. 653 (1950) (overruled in part on other grounds by Chimel v. California, 395 U.S. 752, 89 S. Ct. 2034, 23 L. Ed. 2d 685 (1969).

[3]O.C.G.A. § 17-4-20. Officers also have authority to arrest in extradition situations. See § 2:23, infra, on the Uniform Criminal Extradition Act.

[4]6A C.J.S. Arrest § 16. Michigan v. DeFillippo, 443 U.S. 31, 38, 99 S. Ct. 2627, 61 L. Ed. 2d 343 (1979).

[5]See Thomas v. State, 91 Ga. 204, 206, 18 S.E. 305 (1892). The Thomas case holds that there may be a valid arrest in Georgia when one of the three conditions of O.C.G.A. § 17-4-20 have been met. In 1981 the section was changed to add a fourth situation, i.e., family violence. See § 2:16, infra, discussing the family violence situation authority to arrest. In 1997, a fifth situation was added to the statute, i.e., physical abuse of vulnerable adults and a sixth provision was added in 2013 and it addressed the violation of family violence orders. See § 2:17, infra, discussing an officer's authority to arrest in a situation of physical abuse of a vulnerable adult. Also see Raif v. State, 109 Ga. App. 354, 357, 136 S.E.2d 169 (1964); Graham v. State, 143 Ga. 440, 85 S.E. 328 (1915).

§ 2:10 Probable cause—General

The Fourth Amendment provides as follows:

"The right of the people to be secure in their persons, houses, papers, and effects, against unreasonable searches and seizures, shall not be violated, and no Warrants shall issue, but upon probable cause, supported by Oath or affirmation, and particularly describing the place to be searched, and the persons or things to be seized."[1]

In *Wong Sun v. United States*,[2] the Supreme Court stated that regardless of whether an arrest is made with a warrant or without a warrant, such an arrest "must stand upon firmer ground than mere suspicion . . . though the arresting officer need not have in hand evidence which would suffice to convict. The quantum of information which constitutes probable cause— evidence which would 'warrant a man of reasonable caution in the belief' that a felony has been committed . . . must be measured by the facts of the particular case." In arrests and searches the test, or requirement, of probable cause is objective; it is not a matter to be established by expert opinion nor a question of what the officer thought.[3] However, "the judgment of seasoned officers should be treated with deference." Because of their expertise, these officers are 'able to perceive and articulate meaning in given conduct which would be wholly innocent to the untrained observer.' "[4]

The same quantum of evidence is required to establish probable cause to arrest and probable cause to search.[5] However, there are some different factual aspects of the two. In the case of

---

[Section 2:10]

[1]U.S. Const. Amend. IV.

[2]Wong Sun v. U.S., 371 U.S. 471, 479, 83 S. Ct. 407, 9 L. Ed. 2d 441 (1963). See Madiwale v. Savaiko, 117 F.3d 1321, 1324 (11th Cir. 1997); Brown v. State, 151 Ga. App. 830, 831, 261 S.E.2d 717 (1979) (physical precedent) (probable cause requires "merely a probability less than a certainty but more than a mere suspicion or possibility").

[3]Cuevas v. State, 151 Ga. App. 605, 608, 260 S.E.2d 737 (1979) (citing and relying on Coolidge v. New Hampshire, 403 U.S. 443, 91 S. Ct. 2022, 29 L. Ed. 2d 564 (1971) (search) and Beck v. State of Ohio, 379 U.S. 89, 91, 85 S. Ct. 223, 13 L. Ed. 2d 142 (1964) (arrest)). In Walker v. Bishop, 169 Ga.

App. 236, 240, 312 S.E.2d 349 (1983), a malicious arrest case, the Court of Appeals held that the question of probable cause "was not beyond the ken of the average layman," and, therefore, expert opinion testimony was not required.

[4]Alex v. State, 220 Ga. App. 754, 757, 470 S.E.2d 305 (1996) (citing Brown v. Texas, 443 U.S. 47, 52, 99 S. Ct. 2637, 61 L. Ed. 2d 357 (1979)).

[5]In Spinelli v. U.S., 393 U.S. 410, 416, 89 S. Ct. 584, 21 L. Ed. 2d 637 (1969), in considering probable cause for a search, the Court cited and relied upon the analysis of probable cause to arrest in Draper v. U.S., 358 U.S. 307, 79 S. Ct. 329, 3 L. Ed. 2d 327 (1959). See 2 LaFave, Search and Seizure, § 3.1 (3d ed. 1996).

an arrest without an arrest warrant, probable cause generally must exist before the arrest to believe that the particular person committed or is committing a particular offense,[6] and there is little concern about whether or not the information is stale or current.

However, in the case of a search it is not necessary to name any person. A search and seizure is directed at a place. There is no constitutional requirement that a search warrant name the person who owns or has possession of the premises.[7] In the case of a search there must be probable cause to believe that whatever is sought will be found at the place to be searched. Hence, the information may not be stale.[8]

Lastly, it should be pointed out that even where there is probable cause to arrest a man, this does not mean that there is automatically probable cause to search his home, or place of business.[9] Likewise, if there is probable cause to search a building, this does not mean that there is automatically probable cause to arrest the owner.[10]

§ 2:11 Probable cause to arrest

As previously pointed out, in § 2:9, supra, there can be no valid arrest in the federal constitutional sense unless there is probable cause. And, shown in the last section, probable cause deals with probabilities, not certainties.

How is probable cause obtained? First of all:

"In order to have probable cause to make a warrantless arrest on the basis of personal observation, the presence of the peace officer at the place of observation, and the manner of observing, must be lawful, and this rule applies even where observations are made without entry into a private enclosure."[1] In other words, the information used to establish probable cause must have been legally obtained.[2]

Probable cause to arrest without a warrant has been said to be "a practical, non-technical conception affording the best compromise . . . for accommodating . . . often opposing interests. Requiring more would unduly hamper law enforcement. To allow

---

[6]6A C.J.S. Arrest § 25.

[7]See, e.g., U.S. v. Besase, 521 F.2d 1306 (6th Cir. 1975).

[8]See, e.g., Jackson v. State, 130 Ga. App. 6, 7, 202 S.E.2d 206 (1973).

[9]See Lentile v. State, 136 Ga. App. 611, 613, 222 S.E.2d 86 (1975).

[10]Cf. State v. Doe, 115 N.H. 682, 371 A.2d 167 (1975).

[Section 2:11]

[1]6A C.J.S. Arrest § 34(a).

[2]Wong Sun v. U.S., 371 U.S. 471, 83 S. Ct. 407, 9 L. Ed. 2d 441 (1963) (by implication). Cf. Sacchinelli v. State, 161 Ga. App. 763, 764, 288 S.E.2d 894 (1982).

less would be to leave law-abiding citizens at the mercy of the officers' whim or caprice."[3]

In *Lewis v. State*,[4] the Georgia Supreme Court said "[t]he test of probable cause is whether it would justify a person of reasonable caution in believing that an offense has been or is being committed, and this requires probability which is less than a certainty but more than mere suspicion or possibility."

Nevertheless, the factual basis supporting an officer's assessment of probable cause is at least as stringent as that which is applied when a magistrate weighs the facts in determining whether or not to issue an arrest warrant.[5]

Probable cause must exist at the time of the arrest.[6] In *Vaughn v. State*,[7] the Georgia Supreme Court said:

"Whether that arrest was constitutionally valid depends in turn upon whether, at the moment the arrest was made, the officers had probable cause to make it—whether at that moment the facts and circumstances within their knowledge and of which they had reasonably trustworthy information were sufficient to warrant a prudent man in believing that the . . . [defendant] had committed or was committing an offense."

The fact that reasonable police officers, when considering the totality of known circumstances at the time of arrest, might differ as to whether the suspect has probably committed a crime does not rule out the existence of probable cause. It is for the officer, not the courts, to decide which of the several reasonable inferences to draw.[8]

In determining whether or not probable cause to arrest exists, an officer may also consider what he knows, what he has seen,

---

[3]Beck v. State of Ohio, 379 U.S. 89, 91, 85 S. Ct. 223, 13 L. Ed. 2d 142 (1964) (citing Brinegar v. U.S., 338 U.S. 160, 176, 69 S. Ct. 1302, 93 L. Ed. 1879 (1949)). In U.S. v. Gonzalez-Perez, 426 F.2d 1283 (5th Cir. 1970), the court said that the general test for probable cause is designed to strike a balance between an individual's right to be free from invasion of privacy by the police and the ability of law enforcement to do its job effectively.

[4]Lewis v. State, 255 Ga. 101, 104, 335 S.E.2d 560 (1985).

[5]Whiteley v. Warden, Wyo. State Penitentiary, 401 U.S. 560, 566, 91 S. Ct. 1031, 28 L. Ed. 2d 306 (1971).

[6]Beck v. State of Ohio, 379 U.S. 89, 91, 85 S. Ct. 223, 13 L. Ed. 2d 142 (1964). See, e.g., State v. Koon, 133 Ga. App. 685, 689, 211 S.E.2d 924 (1975).

[7]Vaughn v. State, 247 Ga. 136, 137, 274 S.E.2d 479 (1981) (citing Beck v. State of Ohio, 379 U.S. 89, 91, 85 S. Ct. 223, 13 L. Ed. 2d 142 (1964)).

[8]Hughes v. State, 296 Ga. 744, 770 S.E.2d 636 (2015). See U.S. v. Arvizu, 534 U.S. 266, 274, 122 S. Ct. 744, 151 L. Ed. 2d 740 (2002) (rejects notion that probable cause cannot be found where there is any observation by an officer that is "by itself readily susceptible to an innocent explanation").

and what he has smelled. Thus, in *Berry v. State*,[9] the court held that an officer, who had a degree in chemistry, who had received special training in drug identification, who knew the odor of hydrochloric acid, and who knew that hydrochloric acid is used to process cocaine and heroin, had probable cause to arrest a person fitting the drug courier profile when he detected the odor of hydrochloric acid. See § 3:4, infra, on drug courier profile.

In *State v. Batty*,[10] a trial court's order finding that a police officer lacked probable cause to arrest the defendant for driving while intoxicated was affirmed where it appeared that the only objective evidence of impairment was the odor of alcohol. Although the stop of the defendant's motor vehicle was authorized because of a traffic violation, the trial court ruled that her arrest was not proper after she satisfactorily completed several field sobriety tests.

In *Banks v. State*,[11] the court stated that "[f]light in connection with other circumstances may be sufficient probable cause to uphold" a warrantless arrest. In *State v. Willis*,[12] the court held that where a defendant initially consented to a search and he then fled, these facts, "coupled with . . . [the defendant's] evasive answers regarding his presence in [a] high-crime area, would authorize a finding of probable cause to believe that the bulge in . . . [the defendant's] jacket pocket was contraband. . . ."

The standard for determining reliability of victims and informers in establishing probable cause for a warrantless arrest seem to be the same as in the case of evaluating an affidavit to determine probable cause for a search warrant.[13] See §§ 4:7 et seq., infra, and see also 6A C.J.S. Arrest §§ 28 et seq.

In appraising the trustworthiness of information, and when an officer has to determine whether or not he has probable cause, the standard is an objective one, and subjective good faith alone is not sufficient.[14] However, the known facts and reasonable inferences drawn therefrom may be evaluated from the standpoint of the expertise of the trained and experienced officer.[15]

It must be remembered that it has been held that probable

---

[9]Berry v. State, 163 Ga. App. 705, 708, 294 S.E.2d 562 (1982).

[10]State v. Batty, 259 Ga. App. 431, 577 S.E.2d 98 (2003).

[11]Banks v. State, 187 Ga. App. 280, 282, 370 S.E.2d 38 (1988). Accord, Jones v. State, 195 Ga. App. 868, 869, 395 S.E.2d 69 (1990).

[12]State v. Willis, 207 Ga. App. 76, 77, 427 S.E.2d 306 (1993).

[13]Generally, see 6A C.J.S. Arrest § 29.

[14]Beck v. State of Ohio, 379 U.S. 89, 97, 85 S. Ct. 223, 13 L. Ed. 2d 142 (1964).

[15]U.S. v. Ortiz, 422 U.S. 891, 95 S. Ct. 2585, 45 L. Ed. 2d 623 (1975). In U.S. v. McClard, 333 F. Supp. 158, 164 (E.D. Ark. 1971), the court said, "Actions and things observed by an experienced law enforcement officer may have more significance to him in determining whether the law is being

cause may rest upon the collective knowledge of the police when there is some degree of communication between them, rather than solely on the information possessed by the officer who actually makes the arrest.[16] In *Paxton v. State,*[17] the court pointed out that an NCIC printout is enough to establish probable cause to arrest. Under the rule of *Whiteley v. Warden,*[18] if the officers initiating the NCIC report relating to the defendant did not themselves have probable cause, the arrest pursuant to the NCIC report would not be valid. But in *United States v. Hensley,*[19] a stop-and-frisk situation, the United States Supreme Court held that the collective knowledge concept applies to police departments in two different states where the two departments are not engaging in a joint investigation. In *Hensley,* a "wanted flyer" was issued in Ohio and the stop was made in Kentucky. The Court did not discuss the lack of communication between the two different police departments involved but concluded that the "flyer" itself constituted articulable suspicion justifying a stop. See Chapter 3, infra, on stop and frisk. See § 2:26, infra, on the applicability of the exclusionary rule where there is a mistake in the indexing of a warrant.

The following section contains a discussion of some cases which have considered the problems of determining when probable cause exists.

See Chapter 3, infra, on an articulable suspicion justifying a stop or stop and frisk. See § 3:12, infra, for stop or arrest for the violation of a statute later determined to be unconstitutional. See § 2:19, infra, on arrest warrants.

§ 2:12   Probable cause to arrest—Illustrative cases

The case of *Brinegar v. United States*[1] has been widely cited and relied on in discussing what facts are needed to constitute probable cause to arrest. In *Brinegar,* a government agent had parked beside a highway about five miles from a state line. The defendant drove by. The agent recognized the defendant and the car. The vehicle was proceeding in a direction away from a state in which liquor could be purchased and in the direction of an

---

violated at a given time and place than they would have to a layman."

[16]Goodman v. State, 255 Ga. 226, 229, 336 S.E.2d 757 (1985).

[17]Paxton v. State, 160 Ga. App. 19, 285 S.E.2d 741 (1981).

[18]Whiteley v. Warden, Wyo. State Penitentiary, 401 U.S. 560, 91 S. Ct. 1031, 28 L. Ed. 2d 306 (1971).

[19]U.S. v. Hensley, 469 U.S. 221, 105 S. Ct. 675, 83 L. Ed. 2d 604 (1985). Cf. Westfelt v. State, 192 Ga. App. 791, 792, 386 S.E.2d 542 (1989).

[Section 2:12]

[1]Brinegar v. U.S., 338 U.S. 160, 69 S. Ct. 1302, 93 L. Ed. 1879 (1949). See also Carroll v. U.S., 267 U.S. 132, 45 S. Ct. 280, 69 L. Ed. 543 (1925), discussed in § 4:47, infra.

area where there was a demand for liquor even though the state was dry. The agent had arrested the defendant five months earlier for transporting liquor, had seen him loading liquor in a vehicle in the adjoining state at least twice in the last six months and knew he had a reputation for hauling liquor. The car seemed to be heavily loaded. The defendant tried unsuccessfully to outrun the agent. When the agent approached the car, he called the defendant by name and asked him how much liquor he had this time. The defendant told him not much. There was a case on the front seat which was visible or was covered with a lap robe. The Court concluded that there was probable cause to arrest the defendant.

In *Beck v. Ohio*,[2] police officers who had received unspecified "information" and "heard" about the defendant and who "knew what he looked like" and knew that he had a gambling record, stopped the defendant as he was driving an automobile. Without an arrest or search warrant, the officers placed him under arrest and searched his car, finding nothing of interest. They took him to a police station, where they found some clearinghouse slips on his person, for the possession of which he was subsequently tried. The Court held that no probable cause for petitioner's arrest had been shown, and therefore the arrest, searches, and seizure of the slips were invalid.

In *Maryland v. Pringle*,[3] the Supreme Court found that officers had probable cause to arrest the front-seat passenger of a vehicle where $763 was found in the car's glove compartment and cocaine was found in the backseat of the auto. The Court determined that the officer's discovery of the money and cocaine in their respective locations gave rise to the reasonable inference that the passenger "had knowledge of, and exercised reasonable control over, the cocaine."[4] In addition, the Court distinguished *Ybarra v. Illinois*[5] on the grounds that passengers in a private automobile will often be involved in a common enterprise, unlike a patron in a public tavern.

In *Draper v. United States*,[6] a "special employee" of the Bureau of Narcotics, proven to be reliable in the past, informed a federal agent that the defendant, who was engaged in selling narcotics, was returning to Denver on a certain train and would be wearing

---

[2]Beck v. State of Ohio, 379 U.S. 89, 85 S. Ct. 223, 13 L. Ed. 2d 142 (1964).

[3]Maryland v. Pringle, 540 U.S. 366, 124 S. Ct. 795, 157 L. Ed. 2d 769 (2003).

[4]Maryland v. Pringle, 540 U.S. 366, 124 S. Ct. 795, 157 L. Ed. 2d 769 (2003).

[5]Ybarra v. Illinois, 444 U.S. 85, 100 S. Ct. 338, 62 L. Ed. 2d 238 (1979).

[6]Draper v. U.S., 358 U.S. 307, 79 S. Ct. 329, 3 L. Ed. 2d 327 (1959). See also Crowley v. State, 140 Ga. App. 208, 230 S.E.2d 358 (1976).

certain articles of clothing. The Supreme Court upheld the conviction of Draper, stating that probable cause for arrest exists where an officer receives and corroborates very detailed information from a regular and reliable informer.

In *Wells v. State,*[7] the court held that a tip from a reliable informant when corroborated by the personal observation of an investigating officer is sufficient to establish probable cause.

In *Taylor v. Alabama,*[8] all of the members of the United States Supreme Court agreed there was no probable cause to arrest Taylor. The facts are summarized as follows: "In 1978, a grocery store in Montgomery, Ala., was robbed. There had been a number of robberies in this area, and the police had initiated an intensive manhunt in an effort to apprehend the robbers. An individual who was at that time incarcerated on unrelated charges told a police officer that 'he had heard that . . . Omar Taylor was involved in the robbery. . . .' This individual had never before given similar information to this officer, did not tell the officer where he had heard this information, and did not provide any details of the crime. This tip was insufficient to give the police probable cause to obtain a warrant or to arrest. . . ." Two officers arrested Taylor without a warrant. He was given *Miranda* warnings and fingerprinted. It was determined that his fingerprints matched prints found in the grocery. Based on this information, a warrant was obtained while Taylor was being interrogated. Taylor confessed.

The Court pointed out that the fingerprint information was obtained as a result of Taylor's illegal arrest and the arrest warrant was not valid. Since the confession was obtained through custodial interrogation after an illegal arrest, it was held to be inadmissible.

In *Hill v. California,*[9] officers had sufficient evidence to constitute probable cause to arrest Hill. They went to his apartment without a warrant of any kind. When the officers knocked on a door, a man named Miller went to the door and was arrested. He fit the description of Hill but denied that he was Hill. He pre-

---

[7]Wells v. State, 212 Ga. App. 60, 63, 441 S.E.2d 460 (1994).

[8]Taylor v. Alabama, 457 U.S. 687, 102 S. Ct. 2664, 73 L. Ed. 2d 314 (1982). While Taylor is actually a 5 to 4 decision, the dissenting justices agreed that there was no probable cause to arrest. See § 2:31, n. 6, infra, discussing *Taylor*.

[9]Hill v. California, 401 U.S. 797, 91 S. Ct. 1106, 28 L. Ed. 2d 484 (1971).

In Baker v. McCollan, 443 U.S. 137, 99 S. Ct. 2689, 61 L. Ed. 2d 433 (1979), in a civil rights action under 42 U.S.C.A. § 1983, the Court held that the plaintiff's Fourth Amendment rights were not violated when he was arrested on a valid warrant issued in his name but which was intended for his brother, despite his repeated claims of innocence during the eight-day period he was confined.

sented identification showing that he was Miller and said he was waiting for Hill. He said he knew nothing about any stolen property or guns, but there was a pistol in plain view on a coffee table. The officers were unimpressed with his explanation (which later proved to be true) and the search which they conducted produced evidence which the prosecution later sought to use in Hill's prosecution. The Court held that the officers reasonably mistook Miller for Hill, so Miller's arrest and the resulting search were valid. However, in *Commonwealth v. Collini*,[10] the Pennsylvania Superior Court pointed out that while a reasonable mistaken belief may give probable cause to arrest, an *unreasonable* mistaken belief will not provide probable cause for an arrest.

In *Morris v. State*,[11] the court held "that the defendant's failure to accurately repeat . . . [his] birthday and . . . social security number was sufficient evidence of a false identity as to provide probable cause" to arrest the defendant for giving a false name to a law enforcement officer. See § 3:12, infra, on when a "stop" becomes an "arrest."

In *Ledesma v. State*,[12] the Georgia Supreme Court held probable cause to arrest was justified where Georgia officers received a teletype message from Missouri police that a named person was wanted for a felony in that state and the Georgia officers reasonably believed an arrest warrant had been issued in Missouri.

In *Alex v. State*,[13] the court held that where a defendant refused to voluntarily submit to a search, when validly stopped, officers were authorized to detain him for a reasonable time in which to obtain a search warrant. Also, where under these circumstances the defendant pushed past the agents and shoved an officer with his forearm, the officers had probable cause to arrest him for battery and obstruction of an officer and to search him pursuant to the valid arrest. See § 4:26, infra, on searches incident to lawful arrest.

In *Little v. State*,[14] the defendant became a suspect in connection with the crimes of kidnapping and auto theft. There was no probable cause to arrest the defendant in connection with these crimes. The investigative officer found an old arrest warrant for the defendant on an unpaid traffic fine and arrested the defendant on that warrant so that he could be questioned about the kidnapping and the theft. He was given *Miranda* warnings, questioned

---

[10]Com. v. Collini, 264 Pa. Super. 36, 398 A.2d 1044 (1979).

[11]Morris v. State, 220 Ga. App. 818, 820, 470 S.E.2d 458 (1996).

[12]Ledesma v. State, 251 Ga. 487, 488, 306 S.E.2d 629 (1983).

[13]Alex v. State, 220 Ga. App. 754, 757, 470 S.E.2d 305 (1996).

[14]Little v. State, 153 Ga. App. 574, 266 S.E.2d 265 (1980).

and placed in a lineup where he was identified. The Georgia Court of Appeals held the arrest was valid and the evidence obtained as a result of the arrest was admissible.

In *Hamilton v. State*,[15] the Georgia Court of Appeals, in considering probable cause to arrest, said "the officers were aware that a robbery had taken place less than an hour earlier. The manager-victim was able to identify a black sedan containing three passengers as transporting the probable robbers. A driver's license found at the scene established that Hamilton was probably one of the robbers or at least was present, and that Hamilton probably was driving a black 1967 or 1968 Plymouth Fury. At about 2:00 a.m., the officer saw a 1967 or 1968 black Plymouth Fury with three passengers less than an hour after the robbery about a mile from the scene of the robbery and the car gave indications of attempted evasion. Under such facts we have no hesitancy in concluding the officers had reasonable cause to stop the car and arrest its occupants."

However, in *United States v. Roper*,[16] the Eleventh Circuit concluded that there was not probable cause to arrest the defendant for federal bail jumping at the time the defendant was stopped in an automobile. In this case, an Atlanta police officer saw a bail bondsman's flyer containing "a picture of Roper, his description, his driver's license number, a description of his automobile, and his auto tag number." The same day the officer saw a vehicle matching the description and the tag number described in the flyer. He confirmed through a radio check that the tag number was registered to Roper. However, the court concluded that the facts demonstrated an articulable suspicion justifying a stop. See § 3:7, infra, on articulable suspicion justifying a stop.

In *Chambers v. Maroney*,[17] the United States Supreme Court summarized the facts of the case as follows:

"During the night . . . a . . . service station . . . was robbed by two men, each of whom carried and displayed a gun. The robbers took the currency from the cash register. . . . Two teenagers, who had earlier noticed a blue compact station wagon circling the block in the vicinity of the . . . station, then saw the station wagon speed away from a parking lot close to the . . . station. At the same time, they learned that the . . . station had been robbed. They reported to police, who arrived immediately, that four men were in the station wagon and one was wearing a green

---

[15]Hamilton v. State, 162 Ga. App. 116, 117, 290 S.E.2d 478 (1982).

[16]U.S. v. Roper, 702 F.2d 984 (11th Cir. 1983). See § 3:12, n. 1, infra, discussing *Roper*.

[17]Chambers v. Maroney, 399 U.S. 42, 90 S. Ct. 1975, 26 L. Ed. 2d 419 (1970).

sweater. Kovacich told the police that one of the men who robbed him was wearing a green sweater. A trench coat and incriminating evidence was found in a search of the car. A description of the car and the two robbers was broadcast over the police radio. Within an hour, a light blue compact station wagon answering the description and carrying four men was stopped by the police about two miles from the . . . station. [The defendant] . . . was one of the men in the station wagon. He was wearing a green sweater and there was a trench coat in the car. The occupants were arrested [and incriminating evidence was found in a search of the car]." The Court concluded there was probable cause to arrest.

In *State v. Williams*,[18] the court affirmed the trial court in finding there was no probable cause to arrest where the officer at the suppression hearing "testified that based on the following factors, he believed he had probable cause to transport Williams to the DEA office and procure a warrant to search him: (1) travel characteristics consistent with drug trafficking; (2) incorrect phone number given to Miami ticket agent; (3) manifestations of nervousness; (4) inconsistent answers regarding whom he was visiting in Miami; and (5) the roll of plastic wrap in his backpack." However, the appellate court concluded that "[w]hile these factors may give rise to a reasonable suspicion of illicit drug activity, they are insufficient even when combined to constitute probable cause to believe a suspect is transporting drugs."

Generally, an officer has no right to arrest a person merely because that person was present at the scene of the crime.[19] However, in *United States v. Ashcroft*,[20] the Fifth Circuit held that the agents had probable cause to arrest a man for conspiracy where he was present at two separate major cocaine transactions which were conducted in private.

In *Corbitt v. State*,[21] the Georgia Court of Appeals found there was probable cause to arrest where an officer received information about drug transactions in a certain park, went to the park, and from a concealed position saw the defendant "lighting a half-used portion of [a] cigarette . . . holding it pinched between two fingers and drawing on it . . . in a different manner than you would a regular cigarette." The officer believed the defendant was smoking marijuana. He approached the defendant who moved his hand behind him and when he brought his hand in front of him, there was nothing in it. "A search of the area immediately behind

---

[18]State v. Williams, 242 Ga. App. 34, 36, 528 S.E.2d 554 (2000).

[19]U.S. v. Di Re, 332 U.S. 581, 68 S. Ct. 222, 92 L. Ed. 210 (1948).

[20]U.S. v. Ashcroft, 607 F.2d 1167 (5th Cir. 1979).

[21]Corbitt v. State, 166 Ga. App. 311, 304 S.E.2d 123 (1983).

the bench on which . . . [the defendant had been] sitting revealed a portion of what . . . [the officer] believed to be a marijuana cigarette." The defendant was then arrested.

In *Scott v. State,*[22] at about 10:00 p.m. an officer received a telephone tip that three people were standing in front of a house known for drug sales on a designated street known as an area of drug activity. Officers immediately drove to the area in an unmarked patrol car. The three men separated on seeing the patrol car. The defendant started walking across the street. He was stopped by an officer who conducted a pat-down search. The court concluded that there was probable cause to believe the defendant had possession of contraband or was a party to possession. *Scott* could have been decided on the basis of articulable suspicion and stop and frisk since there was a frisk and a hard object justifying a search.

In *Copeland v. State,*[23] the court pointed out that "[f]light in connection with other circumstances may be sufficient probable cause to uphold a warrantless arrest. . . . " Copeland was in an area known for "a high level of illegal drug use, had been walking in a suspicious manner with a suspected drug dealer, had walked away . . . when the officer attempted to question him, had admitted he was on parole, had voiced despair and run when asked if he had a weapon, and had pulled objects from his pockets and discarded them." The foregoing established probable cause to believe the defendant was committing a crime. In *Bigby v. State,*[24] the court affirmed the trial court in finding that a "trained officer's detection of the odor of marijuana, together with . . . [the defendant's] flight . . . provided probable cause for his arrest."

In *Gober v. State,*[25] the court held that when a gun of the same type as the murder weapon was found in the defendant's bedroom and the officers knew the defendant had used the victim's cellular telephone after the victim's death, there was probable cause to arrest the defendant.

In *Johnson v. State,*[26] the defendant's arrest for driving on a suspended license was supported by probable cause despite the fact that the officer was advised that the defendant had not been served with notice of the suspension of his license. The court

---

[22]Scott v. State, 193 Ga. App. 74, 387 S.E.2d 31 (1989).

[23]Copeland v. State, 213 Ga. App. 39, 41, 443 S.E.2d 869 (1994). Compare Thomas v. State, 322 Ga. App. 734, 746 S.E.2d 216 (2013) (officer's request that defendant "come here, sir" was not sufficient command to amount to probable cause to charge defendant

with obstruction where defendant walked, then ran from officer).

[24]Bigby v. State, 250 Ga. App. 529, 552 S.E.2d 129 (2001).

[25]Gober v. State, 264 Ga. 226, 227, 443 S.E.2d 616 (1994).

[26]Johnson v. State, 297 Ga. App. 254, 676 S.E.2d 884 (2009).

reasoned that once the officer observed the defendant driving, pulled him over for a headlight violation and then learned of the defendant's suspension, he then had sufficient probable cause to arrest the defendant. The court rejected Johnson's contention that the suspension was not effective since he did not receive written notice and concluded that actual or constructive notice would be sufficient. Furthermore, the court held that the officer should not be rendered powerless simply because he lacked information as to whether the defendant had actual or constructive knowledge and therefore, that he had probable cause to proceed with the arrest.

See Sheldon J. Shapiro, Annotation, "What Constitutes Probable Cause for Arrest—Supreme Court Cases," 28 L.Ed.2d 978 (1972). See § 2:14, infra, on other cases illustrating probable cause. See §§ 3:2 et seq., infra, on facts justifying a stop.

§ 2:13   Arrest by officer—General

In considering the question of warrantless arrests there are two possible considerations. Historically, the *first* concern was the provisions of a Georgia statute authorizing warrantless arrests under certain circumstances. The *second* concern addresses the question of whether or not the circumstances establish probable cause which authorized an arrest under the federal Constitution.

Except in the case of extradition matters,[1] Georgia, by statute, authorizes warrantless arrests, as defined by the common law and Georgia authorities. Warrantless arrests may only be made in six situations[2] which are set out in O.C.G.A. § 17-4-20(a). This section provides as follows:

(a) An arrest for a crime may be made by a law enforcement officer:

(1) Under a warrant; or

(2) Without a warrant if:

(A) The offense is committed in such officer's presence or within such officer's immediate knowledge;

[Section 2:13]

[1]O.C.G.A. §§ 17-13-20 to 17-13-49.

[2]There are cases indicating that in the case of a felony, if an officer has probable cause, he may arrest without reference to the statutory requirements of the statute. Richardson v. State, 113 Ga. App. 163, 147 S.E.2d 653 (1966); Morgan v. State, 241 Ga.

485, 487, 246 S.E.2d 198 (1978); Elders v. State, 149 Ga. App. 139, 140, 253 S.E.2d 817 (1979).

Also, there is Georgia authority authorizing an arrest to prevent the imminent commission of a felony. See Savannah News-Press, Inc. v. Harley, 100 Ga. App. 387, 389, 111 S.E.2d 259 (1959). See Criminal Arrest in Georgia, Institute of Government, University of Georgia (1979), p. 20.

(B) The offender is endeavoring to escape;

(C) The officer has probable cause to believe that an act of family violence, as defined in Code Section 19-13-1, has been committed;

(D) The officer has probable cause to believe that the offender has violated a criminal family violence order, as defined in Code Section 16-5-95; provided, however, that such officer shall not have any prior or current familial relationship with the alleged victim or the offender;

(E) The officer has probable cause to believe that an offense involving physical abuse has been committed against a vulnerable adult, who shall be for the purposes of this subsection a person 18 years or older who is unable to protect himself or herself from physical or mental abuse because of a physical or mental impairment; or

(F) For other cause there is likely to be failure of justice for want of a judicial officer to issue a warrant.

This statute has been construed to be a codification of the common law with perhaps a slight enlargement of the power of arrest.[3] It has been applied to all officers authorized to arrest[4] and applied to violations of municipal ordinances, to misdemeanors, and to felonies.[5]

Both the Georgia courts[6] and the federal courts[7] have expressed a preference for arrests pursuant to a warrant. However, the United States Supreme Court has been reluctant to make such a preference a general constitutional mandate when the arrest is in public and is based on probable cause.[8] But see § 2:5, supra, on the place of arrest.

In 1981, in *Vaughn v. State*,[9] the Georgia Supreme Court pointed out that the federal constitutional standard for a war-

---

[3]Porter v. State, 124 Ga. 297, 301, 52 S.E. 283 (1905); Yates v. State, 127 Ga. 813, 818, 56 S.E. 1017 (1907).

[4]Thomas v. State, 91 Ga. 204, 206, 18 S.E. 305 (1892); Porter v. State, 124 Ga. 297, 52 S.E. 283 (1905).

[5]See Thomas v. State, 91 Ga. 204, 205, 18 S.E. 305 (1892); Porter v. State, 124 Ga. 297, 52 S.E. 283 (1905).

[6]Tyson v. State, 241 Ga. App. 288, 290, 526 S.E.2d 603 (1999), vacated, 249 Ga. App. 594, 548 S.E.2d 498 (2001). In Thomas v. State, 91 Ga. 204, 206, 18 S.E. 305 (1892), the court said that "as a general rule the law requires a warrant in order to render an arrest legal." See Gordon v. Hogan, 114 Ga. 354, 40 S.E. 229 (1901); Waters

v. National Woolen Mills, 142 Ga. 133, 82 S.E. 535 (1914).

[7]See Beck v. State of Ohio, 379 U.S. 89, 85 S. Ct. 223, 13 L. Ed. 2d 142 (1964). In Gerstein v. Pugh, 420 U.S. 103, 113, 95 S. Ct. 854, 43 L. Ed. 2d 54 (1975), the Supreme Court said that "while the Court has expressed a preference for the use of arrest warrants when feasible, . . . it has never invalidated an arrest supported by probable cause solely because the officers failed to secure a warrant."

[8]See U.S. v. Watson, 423 U.S. 411, 423, 96 S. Ct. 820, 46 L. Ed. 2d 598 (1976).

[9]Vaughn v. State, 247 Ga. 136, 137, 274 S.E.2d 479 (1981).

rantless arrest is less "stringent" than the requirements of O.C.G.A. § 17-4-20. However, in the 1982 landmark case of *Durden v. State*,[10] the Georgia Supreme Court concluded that *"dual inquiries, one under federal law and one under state law, serve no useful purpose* and result in complicating the law. . . . [W]e find the state rule to be the same as the federal rule. *An arrest and search, legal under federal law, are legal under state law."* (Emphasis added.) In short, the court held that if an officer has probable cause, he may arrest. In 1984, in *Bodiford v. State*,[11] the Court of Appeals said that an arrest which is valid under the federal Constitution is valid in Georgia regardless of whether the statutory requirements have been met.

Georgia has a statute found in O.C.G.A. § 40-8-91 which requires the "marking" of motor vehicles used to make arrests for traffic violations. However, the statute has been held not to invalidate traffic arrests made in unmarked vehicles.[12]

As discussed in § 2:11, supra, an officer has probable cause to arrest in the federal constitutional sense if at the time of the arrest the facts and circumstances, within the knowledge of the officer, and of which he had reasonably trustworthy information, were sufficient to warrant a prudent person in believing that the defendant had committed or was committing an offense, he has probable cause to arrest.

Lastly, it should be remembered that a violator of the law has no right to be promptly arrested. See § 2:4, supra, on delay in arrest.

See § 2:5, supra, on place of arrest, and § 2:6, supra, on procedure for arrest.

§ 2:14 Arrest by officer—Offense committed in presence of officer

First, it should be kept in mind that an officer has no right to arrest, under both Georgia and federal law, unless there is probable cause. However, in federal constitutional terms, there may be a valid stop and frisk or "seizure" based on reasonable suspicion, grounded upon specific and articulable facts, judged against an objective standard.[1] The federal "stop and frisk" is not an arrest.

---

[10]Durden v. State, 250 Ga. 325, 327, 297 S.E.2d 237 (1982). Accord, Battle v. State, 254 Ga. 666, 670, 333 S.E.2d 599 (1985); Mincey v. State, 251 Ga. 255, 304 S.E.2d 882 (1983); State v. Wilson, 179 Ga. App. 334, 336, 346 S.E.2d 111 (1986).

[11]Bodiford v. State, 169 Ga. App. 760, 315 S.E.2d 274 (1984).

[12]State v. Carter, 215 Ga. App. 647, 451 S.E.2d 541 (1994).

[Section 2:14]

[1]See § 2:9, supra, on warrantless

Next we come to the question of what justifies a warrantless "arrest" in common law or traditional Georgia terms where the offense is committed in the presence of the officer. The Georgia statute[2] authorizes a warrantless arrest if the offense is committed in the presence of the officer. However, the Georgia courts are no longer restricted by this statute.[3] Generally, if there is probable cause for the arrest, an officer may arrest. If there is no probable cause, an officer may not arrest. See § 2:13, supra, on arrests by officers. However, in *Carranza v. State*,[4] the Georgia Supreme Court held that where an offense is committed in a defendant's home in the presence of or in the immediate knowledge of an officer, there can be no arrest in that home unless there has been consent for the officer to enter or there are exigent circumstances. See § 2:5, supra, on place of arrest.

For example, in *Rockholt v. State*,[5] probable cause to arrest was found where officers, while searching the premises of a drug supplier pursuant to a valid warrant, observed the defendant drive up and hurriedly attempt to leave when he saw the search in progress. The facts were sufficient to cause the officers to believe that the crime of possession of drugs was being committed in their presence. On the other hand, in *Stanley v. State*,[6] the court concluded that there was not probable cause to arrest where police investigators had arranged to purchase four ounces of MDA and during the transaction undercover officers heard a horn sound continuously and saw the driver of the car motioning them over. Such actions were not sufficient for the officer to reasonably conclude that the defendant was in possession of MDA and thus committing a crime in the officer's presence.

See §§ 2:11 et seq., supra, on probable cause to arrest.

§ 2:15   Arrest by officer—Offender is trying to escape

As noted in the previous section, an arrest may not be conducted in the absence of probable cause. However, a stop and frisk or "seizure," which does not rise to the level of an "arrest," may properly be conducted under the Constitution if it is based on reasonable suspicion, grounded upon specific and articulable

---

arrests.

[2]O.C.G.A. § 17-4-20. See Zilke v. State, 299 Ga. 232, 787 S.E.2d 745 (2016).

[3]Durden v. State, 250 Ga. 325, 297 S.E.2d 237 (1982).

[4]Carranza v. State, 266 Ga. 263, 268, 467 S.E.2d 315 (1996).

[5]Rockholt v. State, 129 Ga. App. 99, 198 S.E.2d 885 (1973).

[6]Stanley v. State, 129 Ga. App. 759, 201 S.E.2d 182 (1973).

facts, and judged against an objective standard.[1]

With these important tenets in mind, we will explore what has justified a warrantless "arrest" in common law or traditional Georgia terms where the offender is attempting to escape.

The Georgia statute[2] provides that an officer may arrest without a warrant if the offender is trying to escape or endeavoring to avoid arrest. It has been previously held that this exception does not apply where an offender simply fails to surrender to authorities.[3] Based on this reasoning it was felt that the evidence must clearly show that the offender was attempting to escape immediately.[4] Thus, it has been held that a policeman had no right to arrest a defendant simply because he walked away and refused to answer questions.[5]

Probable cause has been recognized as playing an important part under the statute in *Watson* v. State.[6] In this case, the court said that where the suspect was attempting to drive away in a car and officers had "sufficient facts and circumstances within their knowledge, based on reasonably trustworthy information, sufficient to warrant a prudent man in believing that the defendant had committed an offense [bank robbery]," an officer could validly stop the car.

Under the literal wording of *Vaughn v. State*[7] and *Bodiford v. State*,[8] the Georgia courts have brushed aside the statute on arrest and are now relying solely on the federal constitutional rule giving an officer the right to arrest whenever there is probable cause and not limiting this right by our statute. See § 2:13, supra, on arrests by officers.

§ 2:16 Arrest by officer—Act of family violence

In 1981, Georgia adopted a family violence act[1] and in the process amended O.C.G.A. § 17-4-20. The amendment provides that an officer may arrest with or without a warrant if he has probable cause to believe that an act of family violence, as defined in O.C.G.A. § 19-13-1, has been committed. Presumably the words "probable cause" in the statute mean the same thing these words

---

[Section 2:15]

[1]See § 2:9, supra, on warrantless arrests.

[2]O.C.G.A. § 17-4-20.

[3]See, e.g., Gordon v. Hogan, 114 Ga. 354, 40 S.E. 229 (1901).

[4]See, e.g., Eaker v. State, 4 Ga. App. 649, 62 S.E. 99 (1908).

[5]Norwell v. City of Cincinnati, Ohio, 414 U.S. 14, 94 S. Ct. 187, 38 L. Ed. 2d 170 (1973).

[6]Watson v. State, 153 Ga. App. 545, 548, 265 S.E.2d 871 (1980). See 6A C.J.S. Arrest § 19.

[7]Vaughn v. State, 247 Ga. 136, 137, 274 S.E.2d 479 (1981).

[8]Bodiford v. State, 169 Ga. App. 760, 315 S.E.2d 274 (1984).

[Section 2:16]

[1]O.C.G.A. §§ 19-13-1 et seq.

mean in the Fourth Amendment.

§ 2:17   Warrantless arrest by officer—Physical abuse against vulnerable adult

Effective January 1, 1998, O.C.G.A. § 17-4-20 authorizes an officer to arrest if the officer "has probable cause to believe that an offense involving physical abuse has been committed against a vulnerable adult," who is defined as a person 18 years of age or older and who is unable, either mentally or physically, to protect himself from physical or mental abuse.

§ 2:18   Warrantless arrest by officer—Failure of justice

It bears repeating that the right of arrest, in the federal constitutional sense, requires probable cause. However, the right to stop and frisk or "seize" requires something less: reasonable suspicion, grounded upon specific and articulable facts, judged against an objective standard.[1]

Against this background, we will consider the question of what justifies a warrantless "arrest" in common law or traditional Georgia terms where, under the requirements of O.C.G.A. § 17-4-20, "for other cause there is likely to be failure of justice for want of a judicial officer to issue a warrant."

In 1966, in *Croker v. State*,[2] the court referred to this "failure of justice" clause as being obscure. In the 1982 landmark case of *Durden v. State*,[3] the court abandoned the Georgia arrest statute and held that any arrest valid under federal law is valid under Georgia law. In other words, if an officer has probable cause, he may arrest. If he does not have probable cause, he may not arrest. See § 2:13, supra, on arrests by officers. In *Fortson v. State*,[4] the court pointed out "that if an officer acquires probable cause to arrest an accused outside his home, a failure of justice is likely to occur as a matter of law if the officer delays the arrest until a warrant is obtained."

§ 2:19   Arrest warrants

An arrest warrant has been said to consist of both an affidavit and a direction to an officer to arrest an offender and present

---

[Section 2:18]

[1]See § 2:9, supra, on warrantless arrests.

[2]Croker v. State, 114 Ga. App. 492, 494, 151 S.E.2d 846 (1966).

[3]Durden v. State, 250 Ga. 325, 327, 297 S.E.2d 237 (1982).

[4]Fortson v. State, 247 Ga. App. 533, 535, 544 S.E.2d 719 (2001).

him before a judicial officer.[1] An affidavit and/or information must be presented to a magistrate[2] before a valid warrant may be issued.

The verified facts presented to the magistrate need not all be set out in the affidavit, but such additional facts may be given in verified oral testimony or in another affidavit.[3] However, the purpose of the verified facts submitted to a judicial officer is to present sufficient facts to enable the magistrate to make a judicial determination of whether or not there is probable cause to believe that a suspect is guilty of the offense charged.[4]

O.C.G.A. § 17-4-41 requires that the affidavit contain the county in which the offense was committed, the time and date it was committed, the place of the offense, the party against whom the offense was committed, and a statement describing the offense. If the offense is theft, the affidavit must also describe the property alleged to have been stolen, the name of the owner, the value of such property, and the name of the person from whose possession the property was taken.[5]

According to the statute, it "is the intent of these requirements that the accused person shall be informed of the specific charge against him and of all basic pertinent particulars pertaining thereto."[6] While older cases have held that a general charge of "misdemeanor" is sufficient where a defendant is accused of committing a misdemeanor,[7] it appears that such a "description" is no longer adequate under the statute.

The Fourth Amendment requires that a warrant "particularly describ[e] . . . the persons . . . to be seized." A warrant not naming the person to be arrested must describe him with some degree of certainty. A "John Doe" warrant without the name of the

---

[Section 2:19]

[1]Cox v. Perkins, 151 Ga. 632, 107 S.E. 863 (1921). In Shadwick v. City of Tampa, 407 U.S. 345, 92 S. Ct. 2119, 32 L. Ed. 2d 783 (1972), the court held that court clerks under the supervision of municipal court judges qualified as neutral and detached magistrates in the issuance of arrest warrants for the violation of city ordinances. See 5 Am. Jur. 2d Arrest § 15.

[2]Thorpe v. Wray, 68 Ga. 359, 1882 WL 3117 (1882). O.C.G.A. § 17-4-40 provides that an arrest warrant may be issued by any judge of a superior, city, state, or magistrate court, or any municipal officer clothed by law with the powers of a magistrate.

See Thornton v. State, 157 Ga. App. 75, 76, 276 S.E.2d 125 (1981) (juvenile judge or small claims court judge may issue arrest warrant).

[3]Ayers v. State, 181 Ga. App. 244, 249, 351 S.E.2d 692 (1986).

[4]Cf. Cox v. Perkins, 151 Ga. 632, 107 S.E. 863 (1921). 5 Am. Jur. 2d Arrest § 16.

[5]O.C.G.A. § 17-4-41.

[6]O.C.G.A. § 17-4-41.

[7]See, e.g., Williams v. State, 107 Ga. 693, 33 S.E. 641 (1899).

person to be arrested or such a description is not valid.[8]

It has been held that an otherwise sufficient arrest warrant is not void because the affidavit fails to specify the time of day that the occurrence took place.[9] However, a warrant which does not state the time other than the date, the place other than the county, or the party against whom the offense was committed, and does not describe the offense more specifically than as "passing a worthless check" is void.[10] An affidavit which merely states the conclusion of a prosecutor, for example, that a defendant has exhibited a certain film which is obscene, is also insufficient.[11] In *Devier v. State*,[12] the Georgia Supreme Court held that the (verified) information supplied to the magistrate must be sufficient to establish probable cause, but the basis of the probable cause does not have to be established in the affidavit alone. It is sufficient if the affidavit and other verified information are sufficient to establish probable cause.

However, there is some relaxation of these requirements in extradition warrants. Thus, in 1975, the Georgia Supreme Court held that an affidavit for an arrest warrant need not contain evidentiary facts.[13] In *Smith v. Stynchcombe*,[14] the Georgia Supreme Court stated that "the probable cause requirements of an affidavit on which a search warrant is issued" do not apply to arrest warrants. The court concluded that it should "require no more of a South Carolina arrest warrant affidavit *than we do in Georgia*." (Emphasis added.) The court, in support of its position, cited an

---

[8]See, e.g., West v. Cabell, 153 U.S. 78, 14 S. Ct. 752, 38 L. Ed. 643 (1894). See also Powe v. City of Chicago, 664 F.2d 639 (7th Cir. 1981).

In U.S. v. Doe, 703 F.2d 745 (3d Cir. 1983), the court said a warrant naming the suspect simply as "John Doe a/k/a Ed" was void and the defect could not be cured by independent personal knowledge of the arresting officer that the person arrested was the person for whom the warrant was intended.

[9]Courtenay v. Randolph, 125 Ga. App. 581, 582, 188 S.E.2d 396 (1972).

[10]Lowe v. Turner, 115 Ga. App. 503, 505, 154 S.E.2d 792 (1967).

[11]See Good v. State, 127 Ga. App. 775, 776, 195 S.E.2d 264 (1972).

[12]Devier v. State, 253 Ga. 604, 610, 323 S.E.2d 150 (1984).

[13]Smith v. Stynchcombe, 234 Ga. 780, 218 S.E.2d 63 (1975). In this case,

the prisoner had argued that the affidavit stated only conclusions, contained no showing of how the information was obtained, did not show that the affiant had personal knowledge, and did not show that the affiant was credible.

In Michigan v. Doran, 439 U.S. 282, 99 S. Ct. 530, 58 L. Ed. 2d 521 (1978), the United States Supreme Court stated that "[o]nce the governor has granted extradition, a court considering release on habeas corpus can do no more than decide (a) whether the extradition documents on their face are in order; (b) whether the petitioner has been charged with a crime in the demanding state; (c) whether the petitioner is the person named in the request for extradition; and (d) whether the petitioner is a fugitive."

[14]Smith v. Stynchcombe, 234 Ga. 780, 781, 218 S.E.2d 63 (1975).

earlier extradition case[15] which held that an affidavit for arrest in an extradition situation need only comply with the provisions of the Uniform Criminal Extradition Act, a statute which requires less detailed information than the present Georgia law for arrest warrants. Generally, see § 2:23, infra, on extradition of fugitives, and also 31A Am. Jur. 2d, Extradition § 59 and 35 C.J.S. Extradition § 16.

In addition to relaxed warrant requirements, it should be pointed out that in an extradition matter, no warrant is necessary in order to have a valid arrest. See § 2:23, infra, on extradition of fugitives.

In the federal area, the United States Supreme Court has held that the Fourth Amendment requirement of probable cause applies to both arrest warrants and search warrants.[16] The Supreme Court, in *Whiteley v. Warden,*[17] stated that before a warrant for either an *arrest* or search can issue, there must be sufficient information presented to the judicial officer to enable him to make "an independent judgment that probable cause exists for the warrant." The Court noted that when an arrest warrant is issued, it must meet the same probable cause requirements as a search warrant.[18] Generally, see 5 Am. Jur. 2d Arrest §§ 12 et seq.

There are important distinctions between an arrest warrant and a search warrant.

An arrest warrant rests on probable cause to believe that the suspect committed an offense; it thus primarily serves to protect an individual's liberty interest against an unreasonable seizure of his

[15]Wollweber v. Martin, 226 Ga. 20, 22, 172 S.E.2d 605 (1970).

[16]Giordenello v. U.S., 357 U.S. 480, 485-486, 78 S. Ct. 1245, 2 L. Ed. 2d 1503 (1958).

[17]Whiteley v. Warden, Wyo. State Penitentiary, 401 U.S. 560, 564, 91 S. Ct. 1031, 28 L. Ed. 2d 306 (1971). In this case, the complaint submitted to the justice of the peace simply stated that the defendant broke into a specified building on a specified date. No other evidence was submitted. The court held that the affidavit's conclusion that the defendant committed the offense was insufficient to justify the issuance of a warrant.

[18]Whiteley v. Warden, Wyo. State Penitentiary, 401 U.S. 560, 566, 91 S. Ct. 1031, 28 L. Ed. 2d 306 (1971). Accord, Green v. State, 615 S.W.2d 700 (Tex. Crim. App. 1980). But see Roberts v. State, 252 Ga. 227, 228, 314 S.E.2d 83 (1984). In Johns v. State, 166 Ga. App. 656, 305 S.E.2d 405 (1983), the court held that a showing of probable cause is not required for the issuance of an arrest warrant.

In Anderson v. State, 249 Ga. 132, 134, 287 S.E.2d 195 (1982), the defendant filed a motion to dismiss an indictment for lack of probable cause. The court stated that "once the grand jury returns an indictment the state is not required to make a further showing of probable cause." If this rule is applied to bench warrants, issued after the return of indictments, then there is no requirement of a showing of probable cause in the issuance of such warrants.

person. A search warrant, by contrast, is grounded in probable cause to believe that the legitimate object of a search is located in a particular place. Rather than protect an individual's person, a search warrant safeguards an individual's interest in the privacy of his home and possessions against the unjustified intrusion of the police.[19]

Thus, probable cause to arrest a person will not necessarily justify a search of his property.

A mere conclusory statement that an accused is engaged in criminal activity is not valid. According to the United States Supreme Court, an affidavit is insufficient where it does not affirmatively state "that the affiant spoke with personal knowledge of the matters contained therein; it does not indicate any sources for . . . [affiant's] belief; and it does not set forth any other sufficient basis upon which a finding of probable cause could be made."[20]

As previously pointed out in this section, an affidavit or verified information is presented before a magistrate so that he may determine whether or not probable cause exists. Georgia provides by statute that in making this decision the magistrate may also consider the facts which he knows. If there is probable cause, the magistrate may ordinarily issue an arrest warrant.

However, Georgia does not require a demonstration of the probable cause necessary for a search warrant before a judicial officer issues an arrest warrant.[21] If the arrest warrant is for the arrest of a peace officer for any offense alleged to have been committed while in the performance of his duties, such a warrant "may be issued only by a judge of a superior court, a judge of a state court, or a judge of a probate court."[22]

A form for an arrest warrant is set out in the Code[23]

In *Watts v. Cannon*,[24] the court held that an arresting officer, who was acting on reliable information that there was an outstanding felony warrant against the defendant, could arrest the defendant even though the officer did not have the warrant. The court cited and relied on a number of United States Supreme Court cases in justifying its conclusion. However, it should be kept in mind that the United States Supreme Court held, in

---

[19]United States v. Griffith, 867 F.3d 1265 (D.C. Cir. 2017) (citations and internal quotations deleted). See Steagald v. U.S., 451 U.S. 204, 212-213, 101 S. Ct. 1642, 68 L. Ed. 2d 38 (1981).

[20]Giordenello v. U.S., 357 U.S. 480, 486, 78 S. Ct. 1245, 2 L. Ed. 2d 1503 (1958). Cf. Cofield v. State, 247

Ga. 98, 109, 274 S.E.2d 530 (1981).

[21]Roberts v. State, 252 Ga. 227, 228(1), 314 S.E.2d 83 (1984).

[22]O.C.G.A. § 17-4-40.

[23]O.C.G.A. § 17-4-46.

[24]Watts v. Cannon, 224 Ga. 797, 164 S.E.2d 780 (1968).

Whiteley v. Warden,[25] that where an arrest is made on a warrant which the officer learned about in a radio bulletin, the arrest is illegal unless the warrant was supported by probable cause. See § 2:26, infra, on arrest where warrant is quash or invalid.

In *State v. Stringer,*[26] the court said "[t]he primary purpose of the bench warrant is to secure the presence of the defendant in court. Once the defendant appears in court, the bench warrant . . . has no force and effect."

O.C.G.A. § 17-4-47 was enacted in 1998. It provides that a judge may conduct applications for the issuance of arrest warrants by video conference. The video conference arrest warrant applications shall be conducted in such a manner that the judge conducting the hearing has visual and audible contact with all affiants and witnesses giving testimony.

For affidavit for arrest and an arrest warrant, see Studdard, *Daniel's Georgia Criminal Trial Practice Forms* (2018–2019 ed.), Chapter 2. See § 2:6, supra, on procedure for arrests and § 2:5, supra, on place of arrest.

§ 2:20 Magistrates who may issue arrest warrants

While there does not seem to be a Georgia case on the precise point, apparently a valid arrest warrant may only be issued by a neutral, detached magistrate.[1] A unanimous United States Supreme Court held that where justices of the peace received five dollars for each search warrant issued, but nothing if they denied the application, the justices of the peace were neither neutral nor detached.[2] This matter is discussed further in § 4:6, infra, on judicial officers who may issue search warrants.

O.C.G.A. § 17-4-40 provides in part as follows: "Any judge of a superior, city, state, or magistrate court, or any municipal officer clothed by law with the powers of a magistrate may issue a warrant for the arrest of any offender against the penal laws, based on probable cause either on the judge's or officer's own knowledge or on the information of others given to the judge or officer under oath. Any retired judge or judge emeritus of a state court may likewise issue arrest warrants if authorized in writing to do so by

---

[25]Whiteley v. Warden, Wyo. State Penitentiary, 401 U.S. 560, 91 S. Ct. 1031, 28 L. Ed. 2d 306 (1971).

[26]State v. Stringer, 258 Ga. 605, 372 S.E.2d 426 (1988).

[Section 2:20]

[1]See Shadwick v. City of Tampa, 407 U.S. 345, 350, 92 S. Ct. 2119, 32 L. Ed. 2d 783 (1972); Giordenello v.

U.S., 357 U.S. 480, 486, 78 S. Ct. 1245, 2 L. Ed. 2d 1503 (1958); Annot., "Requirement, Under Federal Constitution, That Person Issuing Warrant for Arrest or Search Be Neutral and Detached Magistrate—Supreme Court Cases," 32 L.Ed.2d 970 (1973).

[2]Connally v. Georgia, 429 U.S. 245, 97 S. Ct. 546, 50 L. Ed. 2d 444 (1977).

an active judge of the state court of the county wherein the warrants are to be issued. . . . Any warrant for the arrest of a peace officer, law enforcement officer, teacher, or school administrator for any offense alleged to have been committed while in the performance of his or her duties may be issued only by a judge of a superior court, a judge of a state court, or a judge of a probate court."[3] See § 4:2, infra, on search and seizure of documentary evidence in an attorney's possession.

§ 2:21 Arrests by a private citizen

O.C.G.A. § 17-4-60 provides as follows:

"A private person may arrest an offender if the offense is committed in his presence or within his immediate knowledge. If the offense is a felony and the offender is escaping or attempting to escape, a private person may arrest him upon reasonable and probable grounds of suspicion."

The foregoing Code section has been said to be a codification of the preexisting law.[1] The words of the statute, "in his presence" and "within his immediate knowledge" have been held to be synonymous.[2] It has been held that where a suspect admits his guilt of shoplifting to the manager of the store, this places the commission of the crime within the immediate knowledge of the manager.[3]

A citizen's arrest cannot be made for a mere violation of a city ordinance committed in the citizen's presence.[4] If a misdemeanor is committed in the presence of a private citizen, he has a right of arrest if he arrests the offender at that time. However, if he does not immediately arrest, "his power to do so at all is gone."[5] The statute apparently authorizes a citizen's arrest for a felony committed in the citizen's presence.[6] Moreover, as Professor Kurtz points out, a private citizen may arrest upon probable cause if the offense involved was a felony and the offender is escaping or attempting to escape. However, he concludes by saying, "It would

---

[3]O.C.G.A. § 17-4-40(b)(1) also provides that a judge shall schedule a warrant hearing if the warrant application is made by a person other than a peace officer or law enforcement official. Amended effective July 1, 2010, the warrant may be denied without notice to the person whose arrest is sought where the application does not demonstrate probable cause for issuing a warrant.

[Section 2:21]

[1]Graham v. State, 143 Ga. 440,

441, 85 S.E. 328 (1915).

[2]Piedmont Hotel Co. v. Henderson, 9 Ga. App. 672, 72 S.E. 51 (1911).

[3]Young v. State, 238 Ga. 548, 233 S.E.2d 750 (1977).

[4]Graham v. State, 143 Ga. 440, 444, 85 S.E. 328 (1915).

[5]Delegal v. State, 109 Ga. 518, 522, 35 S.E. 105 (1900).

[6]Long v. State, 12 Ga. 293, 1852 WL 1422 (1852).

appear that no other citizens' arrest where the offense was committed outside the citizen's presence is authorized by Georgia law."[7] The arrest powers of a private citizen are not increased because he has an arrest warrant.[8] Despite the authority of a private citizen to arrest, there is no "legal duty on a private citizen to restrain or constrain someone who is drunk or otherwise impaired."[9]

The authority of a citizen's arrest is extended by Georgia statutes to different types of security guards. Under the Georgia Private Detective and Security Agencies Act enacted in 1981, licensees or registrants under the Act have the same authority to arrest as private citizens, which is the authority to arrest for any violation of a misdemeanor or felony which occurs in their presence or within their immediate knowledge. Moreover, if the offense is a felony and the offender is escaping or attempting to escape a licensee or registrant may arrest upon probable cause.[10]

A police officer generally has no greater authority to arrest outside of the city which employs him than a private citizen.[11] However, if a city officer is in pursuit of an offender and unable to arrest him until he has left the city limits, the arrest is valid.[12] In *Glazner v. State*,[13] a majority of the Court of Appeals held that a municipal officer may arrest for traffic violations outside the city, even when not in hot pursuit for an offense committed in the city. The Supreme Court disapproved *Glazner* in *Zilke v. State*,[14] holding that a campus police officer's statutory authority to make

---

[7]Kurtz, Criminal Offenses and Defenses in Georgia Law Enforcement Defense II. C. (2014 ed.).

[8]Coleman v. State, 121 Ga. 594, 49 S.E. 716 (1905).

[9]Armstrong v. State, 244 Ga. App. 871, 872, 537 S.E.2d 147 (2000).

[10]O.C.G.A. § 43-38-13.

[11]O.C.G.A. § 40-13-30. See Russell G. Donaldson, Annot., "Validity, in State Criminal Trial, of Arrest Without Warrant by Identified Peace Officer Outside of Jurisdiction, When Not in Fresh Pursuit," 34 A.L.R.4th 328 (1984).

[12]Wooten v. State, 135 Ga. App. 97, 98, 217 S.E.2d 350 (1975); Delong v. State, 185 Ga. App. 314, 363 S.E.2d 811 (1987).

See State v. Durr, 274 Ga. App. 438, 618 S.E.2d 117 (2005) (arrest by campus police officers in hot pursuit of suspect leaving campus was valid

when suspect was apprehended off campus premises); State v. Picot, 255 Ga. App. 513, 565 S.E.2d 865 (2002) (arrest by county police who observed and pursued a speeding motorist through their jurisdiction was valid when suspect was arrested within a municipality); Poss v. State, 167 Ga. App. 86, 87, 305 S.E.2d 884 (1983) ("the critical elements characterizing 'hot pursuit' are the continuity and immediacy of the pursuit, rather than merely the rate of speed at which pursuit is made").

[13]Glazner v. State, 170 Ga. App. 810, 318 S.E.2d 233 (1984).

[14]Zilke v. State, 299 Ga. 232, 787 S.E.2d 745 (2016) (officer could make an arrest as a private person pursuant to O.C.G.A. § 17-4-60 but "the most he could do would be to deliver [such person] to a judicial officer" or the local police; court expressed "no opinion as to the validity of an extraterritorial

arrests on campus and within 500 yards of campus did not permit the officer to make an arrest after a traffic stop that did not occur on or near campus property. Also a county police officer may arrest for a felony in another county if he has probable cause.[15]

If a private person arrests a person, he must "without any unnecessary delay, take the person arrested before a judicial officer . . . or deliver the person and all effects removed from him to a peace officer of this state."[16] If such a suspect is turned over to a law enforcement officer, the officer may take custody of the person arrested even if the officer has no such personal knowledge of the offense as would enable him to arrest the person without a warrant.[17]

Generally, see § 2:8, supra, on persons who may exercise an officer's power to arrest. Also, generally, see 5 Am. Jur. 2d Arrest §§ 34-36, 6A C.J.S. Arrest §§ 12-15, and *Criminal Arrest in Georgia,* Institute of Government, University of Georgia (1979), page 28 et seq.

§ 2:22   Custody and disposition after arrest

There are special statutory limitations relating to custody where an arrest is made by some officers with limited authority to arrest,[1] and these statutory provisions do not follow a consistent pattern.

Where there is such a limitation, usually it is the duty of the arresting person to turn the suspect over to an officer having a general power of arrest. The preceding section discussed the disposition of a suspect who is arrested by a private citizen.

When a person is taken into custody, he is to be "booked" at the detention facility. It is the responsibility of the person having supervision over the facility to see that the name, age, and address of all persons arrested is recorded on appropriate records which are generally open to public inspection.[2] However, generally, booking is not regarded as a part of the arrest process and a

---

arrest made in 'hot pursuit' of a suspect who flees across the jurisdictions of multiple law enforcement agencies"). See Suggs v. State, 343 Ga. App. 71, 806 S.E.2d 224 (2017) (O.C.G.A. § 17-4-23(a) applies only to municipal officers; O.C.G.A. § 40-13-30 authorizes deputy sheriffs to make arrests outside of their "appointed territories").

[15]State v. Giangregorio, 181 Ga. App. 324, 352 S.E.2d 193 (1986).

[16]O.C.G.A. § 17-4-61. See § 11:4, infra, on statutory procedure of probable cause hearing.

[17]Walker v. State, 144 Ga. App. 838, 839, 242 S.E.2d 753 (1978).

[Section 2:22]

[1]Chief drug inspector or any assistant (deliver to sheriff), O.C.G.A. § 26-4-29; fire marshal (deliver to sheriff), O.C.G.A. § 25-2-9.

[2]O.C.G.A. § 17-4-27.

delay in booking or its absence will not affect a prior valid arrest.[3] In *Franks v. State*,[4] the Georgia Supreme Court limited the "booking exceptions" to *Miranda* and the Fifth Amendment "to requests for basic biographical data, such as the suspect's name, age, address, educational background, marital status, and other information required to complete an arrest form." See § 5:13, infra, on booking questions.

As a part of an officer's duty of keeping a suspect safe after arrest, officers may adopt reasonable measures to provide for the identification and recapture of a person in custody. Thus, officers generally are regarded as having the right to photograph the suspect as well as to take his measurements, weigh him and fingerprint him.[5] In *Rivers v. State*,[6] the court held that it is not necessary to obtain a defendant's consent before his photograph is taken. General questions asked incident to arrest and booking are not regarded as the functional equivalent of questioning,[7] as that term is used in *Miranda*.[8] However, in *Morris v. State*,[9] the Georgia Court of Appeals stated that booking procedures are not per se exempt from the custodial interrogation requirements of *Miranda*. Thus, in *Franks v. State*,[10] the court reversed the trial judge's admission of a statement made by defendant at booking in response to a question about how the defendant's arm was injured.

Also, there seems to be a general right to search a suspect at the detention facility,[11] and, at least in serious cases, it seems that an officer has a right to have the prisoner remove his

---

[3]See 6A C.J.S. Arrest § 61.

[4]Franks v. State, 268 Ga. 238, 239, 486 S.E.2d 594 (1997). Accord, Brooks v. State, 237 Ga. App. 546, 548, 515 S.E.2d 851 (1999). See also, State v. Nash, 279 Ga. 646, 619 S.E.2d 684 (2005), where the Georgia Supreme Court found that an FBI agent's inquiry as to how the suspect came to be in police custody did not fall within the booking exception to *Miranda*.

[5]See 6A C.J.S. Arrest § 62. See, e.g., Bradford v. State, 149 Ga. App. 839, 841, 256 S.E.2d 84 (1979).

[6]Rivers v. State, 265 Ga. 694, 696, 461 S.E.2d 205 (1995).

[7]Price v. State, 160 Ga. App. 245, 248, 286 S.E.2d 744 (1981)).

[8]Miranda v. Arizona, 384 U.S. 436, 86 S. Ct. 1602, 16 L. Ed. 2d 694 (1966).

[9]Morris v. State, 161 Ga. App. 141, 142, 288 S.E.2d 102 (1982). In Morris, one of the crucial points was whether the defendant lived where he had been arrested. At the booking process, the defendant in answer to a question stated that he lived where he had been arrested. The court stated, "In light of the booking officer's motive in asking appellant his address, that portion of the routine booking procedure became custodial interrogation which, if the information gleaned therefrom was to be used against appellant, had to be preceded by informing appellant of his rights. Miranda v. Arizona, 384 U.S. 436, 86 S. Ct. 1602, 16 L. Ed. 2d 694 (1966)."

[10]Franks v. State, 268 Ga. 238, 239, 486 S.E.2d 594 (1997).

[11]Cf. Rusher v. State, 94 Ga. 363, 367, 21 S.E. 593 (1894).

clothing.[12] In the 1999 case of *Taylor v. State,*[13] the court held that it was reasonable that a female defendant could be ordered to remove her clothes by a female employee of a jail as part of the booking process if directed to do so by a police officer who had reason to believe the defendant had contraband hidden beneath her clothes. See § 5:13, infra, on interrogation.

In *Illinois v. Lafayette,*[14] the United States Supreme Court held that officers may search the personal effects of a person under lawful arrest as part of the routine administrative procedure at a police stationhouse incident to booking and jailing the suspect. The court pointed out the "[p]olice conduct that would be impractical or unreasonable—or embarrassingly intrusive—on the street can more readily—and privately—be performed at the station . . . . [I]t is entirely proper for police to remove and list or inventory property found on the person or in the possession of an arrested person who is to be jailed . . . . A standardized procedure for making a list or inventory as soon as reasonable after reaching the stationhouse not only deters false claims but also inhibits theft or careless handling of articles taken from the arrested person. Arrested persons have also been known to injure themselves—or others—with belts, knives, drugs or other items on their person while being detained . . . . It is immaterial whether the police actually fear any particular package or container; the need to protect against such risk arises independently of a particular officer's subjective concerns." In this case, a shoulder bag was searched, and the Court concluded that, while the bag could have been sealed as a unit in a bag or box, the Constitution did not require such a less intrusive inventory. The same rule seems to apply to the search of a wallet at the police

---

In State v. Brown, 291 Or. 642, 634 P.2d 212 (1981), the court held that a defendant, in the booking process, could be searched and that small containers like cigarette boxes and wallets may be searched.

Generally, it is held that purses and shoulder bags may be searched. See, e.g., U.S. v. Moreno, 569 F.2d 1049 (9th Cir. 1978); Sumlin v. State, 266 Ark. 709, 587 S.W.2d 571 (1979); State v. Horton, 44 N.C. App. 343, 260 S.E.2d 780 (1979). But see People v. Redmond, 73 Ill. App. 3d 160, 28 Ill. Dec. 774, 390 N.E.2d 1364 (1st Dist. 1979).

In Carl v. State, 160 Ga. App. 464, 465-66, 287 S.E.2d 379 (1981), the defendant was arrested at the scene of an automobile accident. At the police station, her purse was inventoried and contraband was found. The court stated that the same rules applied in this case which applied to an inventory of an impounded automobile. (See §§ 4:56 and 4:58, infra, on vehicle searches and second search of same area).

[12]Woolfolk v. State, 81 Ga. 551, 562, 8 S.E. 724 (1889). See § 4:57, infra, on strip searches.

[13]Taylor v. State, 239 Ga. App. 858, 860, 522 S.E.2d 266 (1999).

[14]Illinois v. Lafayette, 462 U.S. 640, 103 S. Ct. 2605, 77 L. Ed. 2d 65 (1983).

station.[15] See § 4:26, infra, on the right to search a person incident to a lawful arrest.

In *Carter v. State*,[16] the court held that where a defendant is arrested and in jail, the clothing worn by him at the time of arrest can be seized for evidence and searched without a warrant even if the clothing is no longer worn by the defendant and has been placed in the evidence room.

Georgia provides by statute that in all cases of arrest without a warrant, "the person arresting shall, without delay, convey the offender before the most convenient judicial officer authorized to receive an affidavit and issue a warrant . . . . No such imprisonment shall be legal beyond a reasonable time allowed for this purpose; and any person who is not brought before such judicial officer within 48 hours of arrest shall be released"[17] "from imprisonment or custody until a warrant is obtained . . . ."[18] However, the failure to have a commitment hearing within 48 hours does not render a conviction invalid nor does it automatically render a confession obtained during such unlawful detention inadmissible.[19]

In the case of persons arrested pursuant to an arrest warrant, the officer "shall exercise reasonable diligence in bringing the person arrested before the judicial officer authorized to examine, commit, or receive bail and in any event to present the person arrested before a committing judicial officer within 72 hours after arrest. The accused shall be notified as to when and where the commitment hearing is to be held. An arrested person who is not notified before the hearing of the time and place of the commitment hearing shall be released."[20] However, it should be noted that the statute does not actually require the holding of the commitment hearing within 72 hours but only requires that the suspect be brought before a magistrate during that time.[21] Moreover, and perhaps in a more practical vein, the failure to have a timely commitment hearing is not generally a basis for dismissal

---

[15]In People v. Bean, 107 Ill. App. 3d 662, 63 Ill. Dec. 373, 437 N.E.2d 1295 (3d Dist. 1982), the court held that such a wallet search was not valid. However, the Supreme Court by per curiam order vacated the judgment. Illinois v. Bean, 463 U.S. 1202, 103 S. Ct. 3530, 77 L. Ed. 2d 1383 (1983).

[16]Carter v. State, 224 Ga. App. 367, 480 S.E.2d 376 (1997).

[17]O.C.G.A. § 17-4-62. See § 5:4, infra, on admissibility of confession.

[18]State v. Cade, 184 Ga. App. 347, 348, 361 S.E.2d 494 (1987).

[19]Dollar v. State, 161 Ga. App. 428, 430, 288 S.E.2d 689 (1982). See § 5:4, infra, on admissibility of confession.

[20]O.C.G.A. § 17-4-26.

[21]Dodson v. Grimes, 220 Ga. 269, 270, 138 S.E.2d 311 (1964).

of an indictment,[22] and if an accused is indicted by a grand jury, without ever having had a preliminary hearing, this alone will not prevent a valid conviction at trial.[23]

O.C.G.A. § 42-4-14 provides that Georgia jailers must make a reasonable effort to determine the nationality of the prisoners in their custody and the legality of their status. If the jailer finds that the prisoner is not in the country legally, he is to notify the United States Department of Homeland Security.

See sections 4:26 and 4:28, infra, on search of person and area incident to an arrest. See § 4:57, infra, on scope and intensity of searches. See § 2:25, infra, for cases holding that illegal arrest is no bar to prosecution.

§ 2:23 Extradition of fugitives—The Uniform Criminal Extradition Act

The basic provision for the interstate extradition of fugitives from justice[1] is found in the Constitution of the United States, Article IV, Section 2, Paragraph 2:[2] "A Person charged in any State with Treason, Felony, or other Crime,[3] who shall flee from Justice, and be found in another State, shall on Demand of the executive Authority of the State from which he fled, be delivered up, to be removed to the State having Jurisdiction of the Crime." To implement this constitutional requirement, Georgia and most other states have enacted the Uniform Criminal Extradition Act,[4] while the federal government has enacted a similar statute.[5]

The Uniform Act places an affirmative constitutional duty on the governor of any state in which a fugitive is found to have him arrested and delivered up to the authorities of the state from

---

[22]Mathis v. State, 242 Ga. 761, 763, 251 S.E.2d 305 (1978).

[23]State v. Houston, 234 Ga. 721, 724, 218 S.E.2d 13 (1975).

[Section 2:23]

[1]The term "fugitive from justice" does not require that the accused fled the jurisdiction for the purpose of avoiding arrest and prosecution; it is enough that he is accused of committing a crime in one jurisdiction and can be found within the borders of another. See Hogan v. O'Neill, 255 U.S. 52, 41 S. Ct. 222, 65 L. Ed. 497 (1921); Roberts v. Reilly, 116 U.S. 80, 6 S. Ct. 291, 29 L. Ed. 544 (1885); Jones v. Conway, 269 Ga. 436, 498 S.E.2d 61 (1998). This is true even where the fu-

gitive left the state involuntarily. Brown v. Lowry, 185 Ga. 539, 195 S.E. 759 (1937); Kelly v. Mangum, 145 Ga. 57, 88 S.E. 556 (1916).

[2]GCA § 1-403.

[3]The phrase "treason, felony, or other crime" embraces every criminal offense known to the law of the state from which the accused has fled, including misdemeanors. See Ex parte Reggel, 114 U.S. 642, 5 S. Ct. 1148, 29 L. Ed. 250 (1885); Cf. Graham v. State, 231 Ga. 820, 821, 204 S.E.2d 630 (1974).

[4]O.C.G.A. §§ 17-13-20 et seq.

[5]18 U.S.C.A. § 3182. See § 14:83 et seq., infra, on standing.

which he fled.[6] By law, a demand for extradition must be in writing and must allege (except in cases arising under O.C.G.A. § 17-13-25, discussed infra) that the accused was present in the demanding state at the time the alleged crime was committed,[7] and that he subsequently fled the jurisdiction.[8] The demand must be accompanied by a copy of an indictment against the accused, or by information supported by an affidavit in the state which has jurisdiction of the offense, or by a copy of an affidavit made before a magistrate of the demanding state, together with a copy of any warrant issued or by a copy of a judgment of conviction or of a sentence imposed in execution thereof, together with a statement by the governor of the demanding state that the accused has escaped from confinement or has broken the terms of his bail, probation, or parole. The indictment, affidavit or information must substantially charge the accused with having committed a crime under the law of the demanding state, and be authenticated by the governor of that state.[9]

O.C.G.A. § 17-13-26 provides that when a demand for extradition is made upon the governor, he may call upon any state prosecuting officer, including the Attorney General, to investigate the demand and report whether or not the accused ought to be delivered to the demanding state.[10]

O.C.G.A. § 17-13-24 provides that when a state wishes to have returned to that state a person charged with a crime in that state, but the accused is incarcerated in another state, the governor of the latter state may agree to extradite the prisoner, upon condition that, after he is tried in the demanding state, he be returned to the surrendering state to complete his sentence or to face pending criminal proceedings.[11]

O.C.G.A. § 17-13-25 provides that this state may extradite, pursuant to the requirements of O.C.G.A. § 17-13-23, supra, any

---

[6]O.C.G.A. § 17-13-22; Hart v. Mount, 196 Ga. 452, 453, 26 S.E.2d 453 (1943).

[7]O.C.G.A. § 17-13-23. A person who was not present in the demanding state at the time the alleged crime was committed cannot be extradited under this section. See Dawson v. Smith, 150 Ga. 350, 351, 103 S.E. 846 (1920). However, he may be extradited pursuant to O.C.G.A. § 17-13-25, discussed in this section at n. 12, infra.

[8]O.C.G.A. § 17-13-23.

[9]Where the demanding state relies on an affidavit rather than an indictment, the affidavit must describe the crime allegedly committed with the same particularity required of an indictment. O.C.G.A. § 17-13-1(4). Closer scrutiny is required in affidavit situations than in situations where an indictment has been forwarded. See Ellis v. Grimes, 198 Ga. 51, 30 S.E.2d 921 (1944).

[10]The governor may lawfully delegate his authority to conduct the investigation and need not preside over an extradition hearing. Lively v. Fulcher, 244 Ga. 771, 262 S.E.2d 93 (1979).

[11]See also O.C.G.A. §§ 42-6-20 et seq. (the Interstate Agreement on Detainers), discussed in § 14:71, infra.

person who, although not present in the demanding state at the time the alleged crime was committed, nonetheless committed an act from outside the demanding state which intentionally resulted in a crime being committed within the demanding state.[12]

In *Jenkins v. Garrison*,[13] an Alabama application for extradition noted that Alabama did not contend that the petitioner was present within the state when the crimes were committed. However, the Georgia rendition warrant granting the extradition request stated that the petitioner committed the crimes in Alabama and was a "fugitive from justice." Although the warrant did not give the basis for its issuance, the warrant appeared to be issued pursuant to the mandatory terms of O.C.G.A. § 17-13-23 limiting extradition to a fugitive from justice found in another state, rather than pursuant to O.C.G.A. § 17-13-25 which does not hinge on whether the accused was present in the requesting state when the crimes were committed. Because of this discrepancy and because there was no evidence that gubernatorial discretion was exercised pursuant to O.C.G.A. § 17-13-25 when granting the rendition warrant, the court concluded that habeas corpus relief should have been granted.

When the governor of a state decides to extradite a fugitive to a demanding state, he must issue an arrest warrant, which must recite the facts necessary to the validity of its issuance.[14] The warrant must authorize the peace officers to whom it is directed to arrest the fugitive and, subject to the provisions of O.C.G.A. §§ 17-13-20 et seq., discussed in this section, to deliver him up to the "duly authorized agent of the demanding state."[15] The arresting officer is deemed to have the same authority to command assistance in arresting the fugitive as he has in any criminal process situation.[16]

O.C.G.A. § 17-13-30 provides that before a fugitive is delivered up to the demanding state, he must first be brought before a judge of a court of record of the surrendering state. The judge must inform the accused of (1) "the demand made for his surrender," (2) the crime upon which the demand is based, and (3) his right to counsel.

---

[12]This situation often arises where the defendant, a resident of one state, fails to pay child support to a resident of another state, thereby committing a crime in the latter state without being present there. See Aikens v. Turner, 241 Ga. 401, 402, 245 S.E.2d 660 (1978); Johnstone v. Deyton, 233 Ga. 146, 210 S.E.2d 692 (1974). This provision, as well as the remainder of the Uniform Criminal Extradition Act, was held to be constitutional by the United States Supreme Court in Michigan v. Doran, 439 U.S. 282, 99 S. Ct. 530, 58 L. Ed. 2d 521 (1978).

[13]Jenkins v. Garrison, 265 Ga. 42, 453 S.E.2d 698 (1995).

[14]O.C.G.A. § 17-13-27.

[15]O.C.G.A. § 17-13-28.

[16]O.C.G.A. § 17-13-29.

Should the accused wish to contest the legality of the arrest, a reasonable time is allotted (by the judge of the surrendering state) to allow the accused to petition for habeas corpus relief. If a writ of habeas corpus is applied for, notice thereof shall be given to the prosecuting officer of the county where the arrest was made. The district attorney must answer and defend the habeas corpus unless the governor appoints the attorney general.[17]

In *Michigan v. Doran*,[18] the United States Supreme Court held that once the governor of a state has granted extradition, a court of that state, considering release on habeas corpus, can do no more than decide (1) whether the extradition documents on their face are in order, (2) whether the petitioner has been charged with a crime in the demanding state,[19] (3) whether the petitioner is the person named in the demand for extradition,[20] and (4) it may be necessary to determine whether the petitioner is a fugitive.[21] In the 1998 case of *St. Lawrence v. Bartley*,[22] the Georgia Supreme Court affirmed the granting of a petition for habeas corpus where the demand for extradition alleged that the petitioner was in the demanding state at the time of the alleged crime (see O.C.G.A. § 17-13-23). In this case, Bartley testified that she had not been in South Carolina since she was a toddler and was not a fugitive. Bartley also testified that her checks had been stolen from her and that the theft was reported to the police in Georgia. The court pointed out that although the warrant was prima facie evidence that Bartley had been in South Carolina, the state presented no other evidence that she was in South Car-

---

[17]O.C.G.A. § 17-13-31.

[18]Michigan v. Doran, 439 U.S. 282, 99 S. Ct. 530, 58 L. Ed. 2d 521 (1978). See, e.g., Scott v. Walker, 253 Ga. 695, 324 S.E.2d 187 (1985).

[19]This requires the habeas corpus court to look at the laws of the demanding state but to decide only whether a crime has been substantially charged as a matter of pleading. Ellis v. Grimes, 198 Ga. 51, 30 S.E.2d 921 (1944). See Pearce v. State of Texas, 155 U.S. 311, 15 S. Ct. 116, 39 L. Ed. 164 (1894).

[20]See Annot., "Necessity and Sufficiency of Identification of Accused as the Person Charged, to Warrant Extradition," 93 A.L.R.2d 912 (1964).

[21]In Graham v. State, 231 Ga. 820, 204 S.E.2d 630 (1974), the fugitive had been living in Georgia for almost two years before Tennessee

decided to demand his extradition for a misdemeanor charge. Since moving to Georgia, the fugitive had found a steady job, had gotten married, and had children. The Supreme Court of Georgia held that the habeas corpus court was in error for granting petitioner relief based upon these factors, and granted Tennessee's extradition demand, discussing those factors which the United States Supreme Court in Michigan v. Doran found to be controlling.

However, in Whaley v. State, 254 Ga. 275, 328 S.E.2d 720 (1985), the court said that it is not "necessary . . . that the . . . [defendant] be shown to have been in the demanding state at the time of the commission of the crime, nor that he had fled therefrom."

[22]St. Lawrence v. Bartley, 269 Ga. 94, 495 S.E.2d 18 (1998).

olina when the alleged crime was committed.

Once these requirements are met, any other defenses are to be decided in the demanding state.[23] The guilt or innocence of the accused has no relevance in a habeas corpus proceeding to contest extradition, unless it involves identification of the petitioner as the one charged with the offense[24] or one of the other three matters set out in *Doran.*

In *Oliver v. Barrett,*[25] the Georgia Supreme Court held that "the mental competency of a fugitive is only relevant insofar as it concerns his ability to assist counsel in ascertaining and preparing for the limited issues to be decided in an extradition hearing."

Once the surrendering state makes an initial, prima facie showing that the extradition documents are in order,[26] the burden of proof is on the defendant to show how his arrest and detention is unlawful.[27] Thus, if the defendant contends he is not the person named in the governor's warrant, the burden is on him to show that he is not the person named.[28] It has been said that the purpose of an extradition proceeding is merely to determine whether there is probable cause to transfer a criminal suspect from one jurisdiction to another to stand trial.[29] However, it "is not appropriate for the habeas court to look behind the probable cause finding of the demanding state."[30]

O.C.G.A. § 17-13-32 provides that the officers of both the surrendering state and the demanding state may use the jails of the surrendering state, when necessary, to confine the fugitive while en route, provided that the officers show proof to the keepers of the jails that the prisoner is in fact a fugitive subject to pending extradition proceedings.

O.C.G.A. § 17-13-33 provides that "any credible person" may initiate the extradition process by swearing out a warrant that a crime has been committed in another state and that the accused has been charged with that crime. The accused may then be ar-

---

[23]Fagan v. Massey, 253 Ga. 483, 322 S.E.2d 59 (1984).

[24]See, e.g., O.C.G.A. § 17-13-40; Smithwick v. Olson, 229 Ga. 494, 192 S.E.2d 337 (1972). In re Pace, 250 Ga. 276, 297 S.E.2d 255 (1982), holds that when an extradition proceeding is instituted for non-support, the compliance of a defendant with URESA may be a defense to extradition.

[25]Oliver v. Barrett, 269 Ga. 512, 514, 500 S.E.2d 908 (1998).

[26]In Grubbs v. Stynchcombe, 251 Ga. 39, 302 S.E.2d 552 (1983), the court held that an indictment from another state substantially charging the person with having committed a crime under the laws of the foreign state sufficiently describes the circumstances of its commission.

[27]Smith v. Bell, 246 Ga. 577, 272 S.E.2d 309 (1980).

[28]Covert v. Lee, 256 Ga. 357, 349 S.E.2d 450 (1986).

[29]Campbell v. Smith, 308 F. Supp. 796 (S.D. Ga. 1970).

[30]Rhodes v. State of N.C., 255 Ga. 391, 338 S.E.2d 676 (1986).

rested and brought before a magistrate to answer the complaint.[31]

O.C.G.A. § 17-13-34 provides that a peace officer or a private citizen may arrest a person without a warrant upon reasonable information that the accused is charged in another state with a crime punishable by death or imprisonment for a term greater than one year. The accused must be brought before a magistrate with all practicable speed, where the arresting party must make a complaint under oath setting out the grounds of the arrest; and the accused must be given an opportunity to answer.[32]

Where the magistrate finds that the person being held is the same person as the one who is charged with the alleged offense, and that he has fled from justice (except where O.C.G.A. § 17-13-25 is applicable), it is provided that the magistrate must, by warrant reciting the accusation, commit the accused to the county jail for up to 30 days, to permit an arrest of the accused under a warrant of the governor "on a requisition of the executive authority of the state" which has jurisdiction of the crime.[33] The magistrate may also extend the incarceration for 60 additional days if the accused was not arrested under such a governor's warrant after the initial 30-day period expires, or the magistrate may discharge the accused.[34]

O.C.G.A. § 17-13-36 provides that an accused fugitive may be admitted to bail unless the crime with which he is charged is punishable by death or life imprisonment in the demanding state.[35]

O.C.G.A. § 17-13-39 provides that the governor, in his discretion, may surrender upon demand of the governor of another state any person found in this state, even though that person is incarcerated, on probation or parole, or is facing pending criminal charges in this state. The governor may condition the delivery of the prisoner upon such terms as he may stipulate, including the condition that the prisoner be returned to this state immediately after trial and before commencing the service of his sentence in the demanding state. No surrender of such a prisoner under this section is to be construed as a complete relinquishment of jurisdiction by the surrendering state over the prisoner. However, where the prisoner receives a sentence of death in the demanding state, that sentence may be carried out.

The governor may recall his warrant for the arrest of a fugitive

---

[31]The accused must be released when there is no probable cause that a crime was committed in another state and that the accused was responsible. Batton v. Griffin, 240 Ga. 450, 241 S.E.2d 201 (1978).

[32]See Peterkin v. State, 147 Ga. App. 437, 439, 249 S.E.2d 152 (1978).

[33]O.C.G.A. § 17-13-35.

[34]O.C.G.A. § 17-13-37.

[35]Bond may also be forfeited. O.C.G.A. § 17-13-38.

or issue another warrant at any time.[36]

A person brought into Georgia pursuant to the Uniform Criminal Extradition Act is immune from service of process in civil actions arising out of the same facts as the criminal proceedings for which he was extradited, until he has been convicted, or, if acquitted, until he has had a reasonable opportunity to return to the state from which he was extradited.[37]

In *Palmer v. Dugger,*[38] the Eleventh Circuit held that an indigent who remains in custody while awaiting extradition must get credit when he is sentenced for the time when he was in custody.

O.C.G.A. § 17-13-46 provides that a person arrested pursuant to the Uniform Criminal Extradition Act may waive procedural requirements of the extradition proceedings and may consent in writing to return to the demanding state. The accused must execute such a waiver in the presence of a judge of any court of record within the surrendering state. Before the execution of the waiver becomes valid, the judge must inform the accused of his right to be issued a warrant of extradition and to petition for habeas corpus relief as provided in O.C.G.A. § 17-13-30, discussed supra. Where a waiver has been duly executed, it is filed with the governor, and the accused is delivered to the agent of the demanding state. However, these provisions do not limit the rights of the accused to return to the demanding state voluntarily and without formality and therefore they are not exclusive.

O.C.G.A. § 17-13-47 provides that nothing in the Uniform Criminal Extradition Act is to be construed as limiting the powers of the surrendering state to try a fugitive (for crimes committed in the surrendering state) who has been demanded by another state. Thus, it seems that the surrendering state may retain the fugitive and delay extradition until the proceedings in the surrendering state have been terminated or regain custody of the accused in order to have a trial, sentencing or punishment for any offense committed in the surrendering state.

O.C.G.A. § 17-13-48 provides that after a fugitive has been extradited, he may be tried in the demanding state for other crimes which he allegedly committed in that state as well as those crimes specified in the warrant of extradition.[39]

It has been held that there is no double jeopardy or collateral

---

[36]O.C.G.A. § 17-13-41.

[37]O.C.G.A. § 17-13-45.

[38]Palmer v. Dugger, 833 F.2d 253 (11th Cir. 1987).

[39]The United States Supreme Court has held that a fugitive can be tried in the demanding state for crimes other than the crime for which he was delivered over. Ker v. People of State of Illinois, 119 U.S. 436, 7 S. Ct. 225, 30 L. Ed. 421 (1886). However, the Ker decision was later distinguished in Lascelles v. State, 148 U.S. 537, 543,

estoppel problem where a demand for extradition is rejected by the surrendering state, and a later demand based on the same criminal charge is accepted.[40] It has also been held that the right to challenge the legality of extradition is deemed to have been waived by the fugitive by a failure to petition for habeas corpus relief; the matter cannot be raised after extradition at the trial in the demanding state upon the substantive crime charged.[41]

Although an illegal arrest and extradition result in a civil rights violation actionable under 42 U.S.C.A. § 1983, it cannot be raised as a defense at the trial in the demanding state for the substantive crime charged.[42]

Finally, it must be remembered that a person can only be extradited for a criminal offense and never for the purpose of enforcing the collection of a debt or any private purpose whatsoever,[43] unless the failure to repay the debt also constitutes a crime in the demanding state.[44] See § 14:71, infra, on Interstate Agreement on Detainers.

In *Oliver v. Barrett*,[45] the court pointed out that while Georgia, by statute, "requires that extradition . . . be solely for the purpose of a criminal prosecution, it is not appropriate for the habeas court to look behind the probable cause finding of the demanding state."

Generally, see 35 C.J.S. Extradition §§ 2 et seq.; 31A Am. Jur. 2d Extradition §§ 22 et seq. See § 2:25, infra, on results of illegal arrests and kidnapping of a defendant and on the right of a court to try a defendant where he was illegally brought into the jurisdiction of the court. See Annotation, "Necessity That Demanding State Show Probable Cause to Arrest Fugitive in Extradition Proceedings," 90 A.L.R.3rd 1085 (1979).

§ 2:24 The exclusionary rule—Background

The exclusionary rule, as that term is used in criminal proce-

---

13 S. Ct. 687, 37 L. Ed. 549 (1893).

[40]See Broughton v. Griffin, 244 Ga. 365, 260 S.E.2d 75 (1979). Cf. Harris v. Massey, 241 Ga. 580, 581, 247 S.E.2d 55 (1978); Ward v. Jarvis, 240 Ga. 668, 242 S.E.2d 134 (1978). See Annot., "Discharge on Habeas Corpus of One Held in Extradition Proceedings as Precluding Subsequent Extradition Proceedings," 33 A.L.R.3d 1443 (1970).

[41]See Greene v. United States, 154 Fed. 401 (5th Cir. 1907).

[42]See Lascelles v. State, 148 U.S. 537, 13 S. Ct. 687, 37 L. Ed. 549 (1893). See Annot., "Arrest and Transportation of Fugitive Without Extradition Proceedings as Violation of Civil Rights Actionable Under 42 USCS § 1983," 45 A.L.R.Fed. 871 (1979).

[43]O.C.G.A. § 17-13-1(1), (2).

[44]For example, where the accused is charged with failing to pay child support. See, e.g., Aikens v. Turner, 241 Ga. 401, 245 S.E.2d 660 (1978); Johnstone v. Deyton, 233 Ga. 146, 210 S.E.2d 692 (1974).

[45]Oliver v. Barrett, 269 Ga. 512, 513, 500 S.E.2d 908 (1998).

dure, refers in its broader aspects to the exclusion of some kind of evidence in a judicial proceeding. The term may be used in connection with the sustaining of a hearsay objection at trial, a ruling excluding evidence because of its irrelevancy, or any other valid reason for the non-admission of evidence.

In addition to the broader scope of the meaning of the "exclusionary rule," this term may be applied to a specific statute which provides that certain evidence is not to be admissible in one or more phases of a judicial proceeding. For example, certain confidential communications are excluded on the grounds of public policy.[1] Also, a witness is not obligated to incriminate himself,[2] and a defendant in a criminal case cannot be forced to give evidence for or against himself.[3] By Georgia statute, a confession is not admissible unless it was "made voluntarily, without being induced by another by the slightest hope of benefit or remotest fear of injury."[4] Also, by Georgia statute, any aggrieved defendant may move to suppress any evidence illegally seized in violation of O.C.G.A. §§ 17-5-1 et seq.[5]

However, the term "exclusionary rule" is used most frequently in reference to the exclusion of evidence in some phase of a criminal proceeding as a result of a holding, independent of state law, of the United States Supreme Court. That decision held that evidence obtained by law enforcement officers in violation of the due process clause of the Fourteenth Amendment, or that clause and some provision of the Bill of Rights of the federal Constitution, is not admissible in state trials.[6] In *State v. Chulpayev*,[7] the Georgia Supreme Court noted:

> the exclusionary rule cannot be imposed "as a judicially-created remedy . . . absent a violation of a constitutional right". . . . The legislature may also provide for the exclusion of evidence or its fruits as a matter of statutory law, but suppression is not required merely because evidence was obtained in violation of a statute. . . . Instead, "the exclusionary rule is an appropriate sanction for a statutory violation only where the statute specifically provides for suppression as a remedy or the statutory violation implicates underlying constitutional rights such as the right to be free from unreasonable search and seizure."

[Section 2:24]

[1]O.C.G.A. §§ 24-5-501, 24-5-502, 24-5-501(a)(2), 24-12-1.

[2]Ga. Const. 1983, Art. I, § I, ¶ XVI.

[3]O.C.G.A. § 24-5-506.

[4]O.C.G.A. § 24-8-824.

[5]O.C.G.A. § 17-5-30.

[6]Weeks v. U.S., 232 U.S. 383, 34 S. Ct. 341, 58 L. Ed. 652 (1914).

[7]State v. Chulpayev, 296 Ga. 764, 777, 770 S.E.2d 808 (2015) (citations omitted). See State v. Lampl, 296 Ga. 892, 770 S.E.2d 629 (2015).

In the 1914 decision of *Weeks v. United States,*[8] certain documents were taken from Weeks' room by a United States Marshal who had no authority to enter. The court held that private documents obtained as a result of an illegal search were not admissible as evidence against Weeks at his trial in federal court where he had demanded their return before trial. The court concluded that to admit into evidence such illegally seized evidence "would be to affirm by judicial decision a manifest neglect, if not an open defiance, of the prohibitions of the Constitution, intended for the protection of the people against such unauthorized action."[9] In the 1920 decision of *Silverthorne Lumber Co. v. United States,*[10] Justice Holmes stated that the Fourth Amendment would be reduced "to a form of words" without the use of the exclusionary rule to suppress evidence obtained by an unconstitutional search and seizure.

Nevertheless, the exclusionary rule in Fourth Amendment situations was not applied by the United States Supreme Court in state court proceedings until 1961.[11] The landmark decision of *Mapp v. Ohio*[12] was handed down during that year. *Mapp* involved the admission of evidence obtained in an illegal search and seizure. The majority held that the due process clause of the Fourteenth Amendment made the provisions of the Fourth Amendment applicable to the states; and, consequently, evidence obtained in violation of the Fourth Amendment could not be admitted in a state criminal proceeding. Thereafter, the exclusionary rule has been applied to the states.

In 1936, in *Brown v. Mississippi,*[13] the United States Supreme Court, relying on the due process clause of the Fifth and Fourteenth Amendments, held that an involuntary confession was not admissible in a state criminal trial. In *Escobedo v. Illi-*

---

[8]Weeks v. U.S., 232 U.S. 383, 34 S. Ct. 341, 58 L. Ed. 652 (1914).

[9]Weeks v. U.S., 232 U.S. 383, 394, 34 S. Ct. 341, 58 L. Ed. 652 (1914).

[10]Silverthorne Lumber Co. v. U.S., 251 U.S. 385, 40 S. Ct. 182, 64 L. Ed. 319 (1920).

In Elkins v. United States, 364 U.S. 206, 80 S.Ct. 1437, 4 L.Ed.2d 1669 (1960), the Court clearly and definitely disapproved of the "silver platter" doctrine. Under this doctrine, after the Weeks case, federal courts had continued to admit in federal criminal trials evidence seized by local police officers acting on their own account even though the evidence had been seized in violation of the Fourth Amendment.

[11]See Wolf v. People of the State of Colo., 338 U.S. 25, 69 S. Ct. 1359, 93 L. Ed. 1782 (1949).

[12]Mapp v. Ohio, 367 U.S. 643, 81 S. Ct. 1684, 6 L. Ed. 2d 1081 (1961). Mapp reversed Wolf and applied the exclusionary rule to the states.

[13]Brown v. State of Mississippi, 297 U.S. 278, 56 S. Ct. 461, 80 L. Ed. 682 (1936).

nois,[14] the confession which had been obtained was held inadmissible in a state criminal trial because the confession had been obtained in violation of the Sixth Amendment right to counsel, which was made applicable to the states by the Fourteenth Amendment. Two years later, in *Miranda v. Arizona,*[15] the United States Supreme Court held that the Fifth Amendment was applicable to the states and that admissions and confessions not obtained in compliance with that opinion were not admissible in state or federal courts.

In the field of visual identification of a defendant, the United States Supreme Court in 1967 handed down a decision in *Gilbert v. California.*[16] In that case, the Court held that a defendant in a state criminal trial had been denied his Sixth Amendment right to counsel, made applicable to the states through the Fourteenth Amendment, where he was identified at a lineup after indictment in the absence of his counsel. As a result, evidence of the pre-trial identification of the defendant was held to be inadmissible at his trial.

Lastly, it must be remembered that the federal constitutional exclusionary rule, as pronounced by the United States Supreme Court, represents the minimum constitutional protection due to a defendant in a criminal case.[17] However, a state court may not interpret the federal Constitution to give a defendant any greater right or rights than that given by the interpretation of the federal Constitution by the United States Supreme Court.[18] Nevertheless, a state court may interpret the constitution of the state to give a defendant broader protection than that provided by the federal Constitution as interpreted by the United States Supreme Court.[19] This rule applies even when the wording of the state constitution is exactly like the wording of the federal Constitution on the particular matter.[20] Also, Congress and the state legislatures may extend the exclusionary rule by legislation so as to give a defendant in a criminal case greater protection than he is entitled

---

[14]Escobedo v. State of Ill., 378 U.S. 478, 84 S. Ct. 1758, 12 L. Ed. 2d 977 (1964).

[15]Miranda v. Arizona, 384 U.S. 436, 86 S. Ct. 1602, 16 L. Ed. 2d 694 (1966).

[16]Gilbert v. California, 388 U.S. 263, 271, 87 S. Ct. 1951, 18 L. Ed. 2d 1178 (1967).

[17]Oregon v. Hass, 420 U.S. 714, 719, 95 S. Ct. 1215, 43 L. Ed. 2d 570 (1975).

[18]North Carolina v. Butler, 441 U.S. 369, 376, 99 S. Ct. 1755, 60 L. Ed. 2d 286 (1979); Coley v. State, 231 Ga. 829, 204 S.E.2d 612 (1974); Oregon v. Hass, 420 U.S. 714, 719, 95 S. Ct. 1215, 43 L. Ed. 2d 570 (1975).

[19]Oregon v. Hass, 420 U.S. 714, 95 S. Ct. 1215, 43 L. Ed. 2d 570 (1975); Roberts v. State, 458 P.2d 340 (Alaska 1969).

[20]Pope v. City of Atlanta, 240 Ga. 177, 178, 240 S.E.2d 241 (1977); Bulova Watch Co., Inc. v. Brand Distributors of North Wilkesboro, Inc., 285 N.C. 467, 206 S.E.2d 141 (1974).

to under the federal Constitution.[21]

See Wilkes, "A Most Deplorable Paradox: Admitting Illegally Obtained Evidence in Georgia—Past, Present and Future," 11 Ga. L. R. 105 (1976).

§ 2:25 The exclusionary rule—Present application at trial

The mere fact that an arrest[1] or search is illegal does not prevent a criminal prosecution nor provide a defense to such a prosecution. In *Thompson v. State,*[2] the court pointed out that "the illegality of an arrest neither bars prosecution or affects a conviction." In *Frisbie v. Collins,*[3] the United States Supreme Court held that a court may try a defendant even where the defendant is forcibly abducted and brought within the jurisdiction of the court. In *Lujan v. Gengler,*[4] the court held that where a defendant was kidnapped in a foreign country, not treated in a cruel or inhuman manner, and brought to this country, he was not entitled to be released because of the unconventional way in which he was brought to this county.

In *United States v. Alvarez-Machain,*[5] the United States Supreme Court held that the kidnapping of a Mexican citizen in his home in that country and transporting him to Texas did not amount to a treaty violation nor prevent his trial.

However, primary evidence or evidence directly obtained from a defendant as a result of an arrest[6] or a search and seizure[7] invalid under the Fourth Amendment is not admissible against the

---

[21]Alderman v. U.S., 394 U.S. 165, 175, 89 S. Ct. 961, 22 L. Ed. 2d 176 (1969).

[Section 2:25]

[1]Frisbie v. Collins, 342 U.S. 519, 522, 72 S. Ct. 509, 96 L. Ed. 541 (1952); Lackey v. State, 246 Ga. 331, 333, 271 S.E.2d 478 (1980); Ricks v. State, 204 Ga. App. 441, 442, 419 S.E.2d 517 (1992). See U.S. v. Winter, 509 F.2d 975, 985 (5th Cir. 1975). Cf. U. S. ex rel. Lujan v. Gengler, 510 F.2d 62 (2d Cir. 1975) (unless the abuse is shocking, the illegality of the arrest is no defense).

[2]Thompson v. State, 175 Ga. App. 645, 648, 334 S.E.2d 312 (1985); Shaw v. State, 247 Ga. App. 867, 869, 545 S.E.2d 399 (2001); Mortimer v. State, 177 Ga. App. 679, 680, 340 S.E.2d 649 (1986).

[3]Frisbie v. Collins, 342 U.S. 519,

72 S. Ct. 509, 96 L. Ed. 541 (1952).

[4]U. S. ex rel. Lujan v. Gengler, 510 F.2d 62 (2d Cir. 1975). Accord, U.S. v. Reed, 639 F.2d 896 (2d Cir. 1981). However, in U.S. v. Toscanino, 500 F.2d 267 (2d Cir. 1974), where the defendant was kidnapped in Uruguay, tortured in Brazil, and finally flown to this country to be tried, the Court held the due process required the trial court to divest itself of jurisdiction.

[5]U.S. v. Alvarez-Machain, 504 U.S. 655, 112 S. Ct. 2188, 119 L. Ed. 2d 441 (1992).

[6]Davis v. Mississippi, 394 U.S. 721, 89 S. Ct. 1394, 22 L. Ed. 2d 676 (1969) (fingerprints). See § 3:12, n. 8, infra, on custody to obtain fingerprints. Morales v. State of N. Y., 396 U.S. 102, 90 S. Ct. 291, 24 L. Ed. 2d 299 (1969) (a confession); Brown v. Illinois, 422 U.S. 590, 95 S. Ct. 2254, 45 L. Ed. 2d 416 (1975) (confession);

defendant at his trial[8] if he properly moves to suppress such evidence, except perhaps for purposes of impeachment.[9] See § 3:12, infra, on fingerprinting when there is no probable cause to arrest.

It must be emphasized that the exclusionary rule which is applied to the United States Constitution applies only to *governmental action.* See § 4:60, infra, on applicability of exclusionary rule.

The more difficult question is, what evidence derived from a violation of the Fourth Amendment must be suppressed where the evidence was not obtained directly or immediately from the defendant when the arrest or the search and seizure occurred?

In *Wong Sun v. United States,*[10] the Court said:

"The exclusionary rule has traditionally barred from trial physical, tangible materials obtained either during or as a direct result of an unlawful invasion. It follows . . . that the Fourth Amendment may protect against the overhearing of verbal statements as well as against the more traditional seizure of 'papers and effects.' Similarly, testimony as to matters observed during an unlawful invasion has been excluded in order to enforce the basic constitutional policies . . . . Thus, verbal evidence which derives so immediately from an unlawful entry and an unauthorized arrest as the officers' action in the present case is no less the 'fruit' of official illegality than the more common tangible fruits of the unwarranted intrusion."

Whiteley v. Warden, Wyo. State Penitentiary, 401 U.S. 560, 91 S. Ct. 1031, 28 L. Ed. 2d 306 (1971) (articles found while officers searched the car occupied by defendant at the time of the alleged arrest); Brooks v. State, 129 Ga. App. 109, 198 S.E.2d 892 (1973) (marijuana found on defendant); MacDougald v. State, 124 Ga. App. 619, 620, 184 S.E.2d 687 (1971) (marijuana).

[7]Mapp v. Ohio, 367 U.S. 643, 81 S. Ct. 1684, 6 L. Ed. 2d 1081 (1961).

[8]See Hill v. State, 140 Ga. App. 121, 230 S.E.2d 336 (1976) (defendant's conviction reversed where he was unlawfully arrested, searched and interviewed after which he confessed to stealing a camera found in his backpack).

In Dupree v. State, 247 Ga. 470, 472, 277 S.E.2d 18 (1981), the court pointed out that even though *Miranda* warnings have been given prior to an incriminating statement, the statement may have been voluntary for Fifth Amendment purposes but the statement is nevertheless inadmissible for Fourth Amendment purposes if the statement resulted from the defendant's illegal seizure.

In Moore v. State, 155 Ga. App. 299, 270 S.E.2d 713 (1980), the court held that when the defendant was arrested without probable cause, on motion, evidence of marijuana which was found in an inventory search of the defendant's car after arrest must be suppressed.

[9]Harris v. New York, 401 U.S. 222, 91 S. Ct. 643, 28 L. Ed. 2d 1 (1971); Walder v. U.S., 347 U.S. 62, 74 S. Ct. 354, 98 L. Ed. 503 (1954).

[10]Wong Sun v. U.S., 371 U.S. 471, 485, 83 S. Ct. 407, 9 L. Ed. 2d 441 (1963). In Hoffa v. U.S., 385 U.S. 293, 87 S. Ct. 408, 17 L. Ed. 2d 374 (1966), the Court said "the protections of the Fourth Amendment are surely not limited to tangibles, but can extend as well to oral statements."

In *Brown v. Illinois*,[11] police broke into the defendant's apartment and arrested him, with neither a warrant nor probable cause. Thereafter, the defendant received his *Miranda* warnings and made incriminating statements. The Court rejected the notice that despite the illegality of the arrest, the state could use the statements on the basis that the defendant had been "Mirandized" prior to making them.

In *Silverthorne Lumber Co. v. United States*,[12] Silverthorne had been held in contempt for refusal to obey a subpoena directing the production of certain documents. The government knew of the existence of the documents by reason of a prior illegal search and seizure. In reversing the conviction, the Court, in an opinion by Justice Holmes, said:

"The essence of a provision forbidding the acquisition of evidence in a certain way is that not merely evidence so acquired shall not be used before the court, but that it shall not be used at all. Of course this does not mean that the facts thus obtained become sacred and inaccessible. If knowledge of them is *gained from an independent source* they may be proved like any others, but the knowledge gained by the government's own wrong cannot be used by it . . . . (Emphasis added.)[13]

Tainted evidence not obtained directly from the original invalid search and seizure or arrest has come to be known as derivative evidence or "fruit of the poisonous tree."[14] This term was coined by Justice Frankfurter in *Nardone v. United States*.[15] In that case, the Court noted a second exception to the rule that all derivative evidence must be excluded, by stating that such evidence could "become so attenuated as to dissipate the [original] taint."

The third exception to the rule that all evidence derived from unconstitutional action by officers was mentioned in a footnote of the case *Brewer v. Williams*.[16]

The United States Supreme Court has never held that all de-

---

[11]Brown v. Illinois, 422 U.S. 590, 95 S. Ct. 2254, 45 L. Ed. 2d 416 (1975).

[12]Silverthorne Lumber Co. v. U.S., 251 U.S. 385, 40 S. Ct. 182, 64 L. Ed. 319 (1920).

[13]Silverthorne Lumber Co. v. U.S., 251 U.S. 385, 392, 40 S. Ct. 182, 64 L. Ed. 319 (1920). Accord, Murray v. U.S., 487 U.S. 533, 108 S. Ct. 2529, 101 L. Ed. 2d 472 (1988), where the Court held that evidence discovered during the initial illegal entry is admissible if it is also discovered during a later search pursuant to a warrant that is based on information obtained wholly independent of the initial entry.

[14]Nardone v. U.S., 308 U.S. 338, 341, 60 S. Ct. 266, 84 L. Ed. 307 (1939). Nardone was not actually decided on constitutional grounds but was based on wiretapping—a violation of § 604 of the Federal Communications Act of 1934.

[15]Nardone v. U.S., 308 U.S. 338, 341, 60 S. Ct. 266, 84 L. Ed. 307 (1939).

[16]Brewer v. Williams, 430 U.S. 387, 406, 97 S. Ct. 1232, 51 L. Ed. 2d 424 (1977). Actually, the Williams case involved the right of counsel provided

rivative evidence is to be considered the "fruit of the poisonous tree" "simply because it would not have come to light *but* for the illegal actions of the police.[17] Rather, the more apt question in such a case is 'whether granting establishment of the primary illegality, the evidence to which instant objection is made has been come at by exploitation of that illegality or instead by means sufficiently distinguishable to be purged of the primary taint.' " (Emphasis added.)[18] However, there is no per se exclusion of in-court identification because of suggestive pre-trial identification procedures.[19] See § 6:8, infra, on due process standard of identification.

As previously pointed out, the Supreme Court has at least given passing recognition to three exceptions to the broad language of *Silverthorne* indicating that evidence illegally obtained shall not be used to develop or find other evidence.[20] These exceptions are stated in *United States v. Brookins*[21] as follows: "[First] One form of insufficient connection between the fruit and the tree occurs if physical evidence, a witness' testimony, or the accused's statement has an attenuated link to the illegally secured evidence. . . . [Second] Another type of inadequate connection arises if the derivative evidence has an independent source from the illegally taken objects or statements. . . . A third category of insufficient connection obtains if the derivative evidence . . . would inevitably have been discovered during a police investigation without the aid of the illegally obtained evidence."[22]

Initially the burden has been said to be on the defendant to show that the derivative evidence was obtained by the government as a result of the illegal search. Once this has been done, the government has the burden of establishing that the evidence is admissible under one of the three exceptions set out above.[23]

The following three sections discuss when secondary or derivative evidence is admissible because of the good faith of the officer conducting a search pursuant to a warrant, an independent

---

for in the Sixth Amendment.

[17]Wong Sun v. U.S., 371 U.S. 471, 488, 83 S. Ct. 407, 9 L. Ed. 2d 441 (1963). See Utah v. Strieff, 136 S. Ct. 2056, 195 L. Ed. 2d 400 (2016); Hudson v. Michigan, 126 S. Ct. 2159, 165 L. Ed. 2d 56 (U.S. 2006).

[18]Wong Sun v. U.S., 371 U.S. 471, 488, 83 S. Ct. 407, 9 L. Ed. 2d 441 (1963) (citing Maguire, Evidence of Guilt, 221 (1959)). See Stidham v. State, 299 Ga. App. 858, 683 S.E.2d 906 (2009).

[19]Lindsey v. State, 182 Ga. App.

10, 14, 354 S.E.2d 650 (1987).

[20]However, none of the three cases cited actually turned on the exception which was mentioned in the opinion.

[21]U.S. v. Brookins, 614 F.2d 1037 (5th Cir. 1980).

[22]U.S. v. Brookins, 614 F.2d 1037, 1041 (5th Cir. 1980).

[23]Alderman v. U.S., 394 U.S. 165, 183, 89 S. Ct. 961, 22 L. Ed. 2d 176 (1969); Brown v. Illinois, 422 U.S. 590, 604, 95 S. Ct. 2254, 45 L. Ed. 2d 416 (1975).

source, inevitable discovery, or attenuation.

See § 4:60, infra, on result of school searches.

§ 2:26 The exclusionary rule—Present application at trial—Good faith of officer conducting search pursuant to warrant

In *United States v. Leon*,[1] the Supreme Court held that the Fourth Amendment exclusionary rule does not bar the use in the prosecutor's case-in-chief of evidence obtained by officers acting in reasonable reliance on a search warrant issued by a detached and neutral magistrate but ultimately found to be unsupported by probable cause. In the 1992 case of *Gary v. State*,[2] the Georgia Supreme Court declined to follow the "good faith" exception found by the United States Supreme Court in *Leon*. The Court noted, a "[s]tate is free . . . to impose greater restrictions on police activity than those [the Supreme] Court holds to be necessary under constitutional standards." The Court then held that under the wording of O.C.G.A. § 17-5-30, unless a warrant is supported by probable cause, any evidence obtained as a result thereof must be suppressed. In *State v. New*,[3] the Georgia Court of Appeals stated that because of the express probable cause requirement in O.C.G.A. § 17-5-30, a court-ordered good faith exception would amount to "judicial legislation." However, the court also acknowledged that "[w]ithout a good faith exception in this context, we essentially demand perfection from the police, yet do not require it of prosecutors, defense counsel, or even judges."

In *Arizona v. Evans*,[4] the United States Supreme Court extended the good faith exception to the exclusionary rule to cover errors by employees of the court. In this case, the defendant was arrested and contraband was recovered in a search incident to arrest. The arrest warrant for the defendant had been quashed, but, due to a clerical error by court employees, the computer did not indicate this. The court pointed out that the exclusionary rule was historically used to deter police misconduct and that because there was no police misconduct here, suppression was not necessary. In coming to this conclusion, the Court seemed impressed with the fact that this *type of mistake* occurred very infrequently and that the defendant made no showing that court employees are "inclined to ignore or subvert the Fourth

[Section 2:26]

[1]U.S. v. Leon, 468 U.S. 897, 104 S.Ct. 3405, 82 L.Ed.2d 677 (1984).

[2]Gary v. State, 262 Ga. 573, 574-577, 422 S.E.2d 426 (1992).

[3]State v. New, 331 Ga. App. 139, 142, 770 S.E.2d 239 (2015). See Harper v. State, 293 Ga. 102, 106-107(2), 657 S.E.2d 213 (2008).

[4]Arizona v. Evans, 514 U.S. 1, 115 S. Ct. 1185, 131 L. Ed. 2d 34 (1995).

Amendment." See § 4:20, infra, on execution of invalid warrant.

In *Herring v. United States*,[5] the United States Supreme Court applied the reasoning of *Leon* and *Evans* to find that the exclusionary rule could not be used to suppress drugs and firearms found by officers in a search incident to arrest based on an arrest warrant later found to be defective. The Court held that the deterrent effect to police misconduct provided by the exclusionary rule was not served when the police mistakes were attenuated from the search and were no more than isolated negligence rather than "systemic error or reckless disregard of constitutional requirements."

In *Davis v. United States*,[6] the court made it clear that the exclusionary rule would be applied only as a last resort, reserved for those cases in which the police misconduct exhibits a deliberate, reckless or grossly negligent disregard of the Fourth Amendment. *Davis* involved a case where police conducted a search in reliance on current judicial precedent which was subsequently overturned by *Arizona v. Gant*.[7] Because Davis' conviction had not yet become final at the time *Gant* was announced, the holding in *Gant* was applied to his case retroactively. However, the court declined to exclude the evidence seized in the search finding that any error by the police was the product of good faith reliance on legal precedent only later found to be faulty.

In *Cunningham v. State*,[8] the court affirmed a traffic stop where a patrolman checked with a dispatcher to determine whether a tag on a car belonged on another vehicle. The dispatcher gave erroneous information to the patrolman, who stopped the driver and then arrested him for driving under the influence. The court pointed out that there had been no bad faith and that it was just an "honest human mistake."

However, in *State v. White*,[9] the Florida Supreme Court held that negligence of the sheriff's department in maintaining computer records "falls squarely within the class of governmental ac-

---

[5]Herring v. U.S., 555 U.S. 135, 129 S. Ct. 695, 172 L. Ed. 2d 496 (2009). In Davis v. U.S., 131 S. Ct. 2419, 180 L. Ed. 2d 285 (2011), the U.S. Supreme Court held that warrantless search conducted in compliance with existing precedent is not subject to suppression should the precedent relied upon be subsequently overruled. One commentator suggests that the exclusionary rule provided by Georgia law may be more expansive than that provided by the Fourth Amendment following Herring. 23 *What's the Decision* (Jan. 2009).

[6]Davis v. U.S., 131 S. Ct. 2419, 180 L. Ed. 2d 285 (2011).

[7]Arizona v. Gant, 556 U.S. 332, 129 S. Ct. 1710, 173 L. Ed. 2d 485, 47 A.L.R. Fed. 2d 657 (2009).

[8]Cunningham v. State, 231 Ga. App. 420, 498 S.E.2d 590 (1998).

[9]State v. White, 660 So. 2d 664 (Fla. 1995).

tion that the exclusionary rule was designed to deter." During the stop of the defendant for a minor traffic violation, the deputy sheriff was informed of the existence of an outstanding warrant for the defendant. The defendant was arrested and contraband was discovered during a search of his car. Later it was discovered that the warrant was not outstanding but in fact had been served four days earlier by another deputy and the sheriff's office neglected to supply the computer with that information. The court also pointed out that the collective knowledge rule was also applicable here because other members of the sheriff's department knew that the warrant was no longer outstanding. See § 2:11, supra, and § 4:50, infra, on collective knowledge.

In *Harvey v. State*,[10] the arresting officer ran the defendant's name through NCIC and it showed that there was a bench warrant for his arrest. Harvey was then placed under arrest and, in a search incident to that arrest, cocaine was discovered. At trial the defendant moved to suppress the cocaine because the bench warrant had been quashed a few days before the arrest. This information was not revealed in NCIC records when they were checked by the officer in the field. Nevertheless, the Georgia Supreme Court held that "in hindsight, [this Court] will not declare an arrest to be invalid when the arresting officer reasonably relied upon information which he had no reason to think was incorrect." Because the NCIC report was reliable enough to underlie the reasonable belief which is needed to establish probable cause, the court upheld the admission of the cocaine into evidence. Although the Leon "good faith" exception is not applicable in Georgia, the court in *Harvey* pointed out that it was not implicated here because "[t]he radio transmissions which confirmed the outstanding warrants established the necessary probable cause to arrest."

Also see § 4:22, infra, on good faith exclusionary exception as applied to a warrant not sufficiently particularizing items to be seized. See sections 3:2 and 4:46, infra, on invalidity of law authorizing a stop or search. See § 4:20, infra, on good faith mistaken belief of officer that area being searched was within scope of warrant.

---

[10]Harvey v. State, 266 Ga. 671, 672, 469 S.E.2d 176 (1996). See State v. Edwards, 307 Ga. App. 267, 272–73, 704 S.E.2d 816 (2010) (Court of Appeals very critical of *Harvey* as ignoring clear precedent of *State v. Stringer*, that "receipt of a bulletin or 'computer hit' does not provide probable cause justifying arrest if the information in the computer system is inaccurate." (quoting State v. Stringer, 258 Ga. 605, 607, 372 S.E.2d 426 (1988)). Compare State v. New, 331 Ga. App. 139, 770 S.E.2d 239 (2015) (search based on Fourth Amendment waiver condition of probation was invalid where defendant's probation had terminated eight months earlier despite officer's good faith belief defendant was on probation at time of search).

§ 2:27 The exclusionary rule—Present application at trial—The independent source exception

"The essential aspect of the independent source rule is the existence of evidence which was not illegally seized and which in fact provided an independent basis for the discovery of the challenged evidence."[1] Some courts have interpreted the independent source exception to require the government to show that the challenged evidence was acquired wholly apart from the original illegality.[2] In *Wilder v. State*,[3] the Georgia Supreme Court explained "[t]he independent source doctrine 'allows the prosecution to use evidence only if it was, in fact, obtained by fully lawful means . . . ." This doctrine typically operates when evidence discovered as the result of an initial unlawful search is later discovered in a second search conducted by lawful means using information gained independently of the initial search." However, some other jurisdictions have interpreted this exception more broadly.[4]

Two identification cases serve to illustrate the application of the independent source exception. In *Bynum v. United States*,[5] the defendant had been illegally arrested and fingerprinted. However, the government sought to show that fingerprints which had previously been obtained by the FBI matched the fingerprints left at the scene of the crime. The court held that the older fingerprints were admissible in evidence along with the latent fingerprints taken from the scene.

In *United States v. Crews*,[6] a victim was assaulted in a restroom on the grounds of the Washington Monument. She notified officers and gave a description of her assailant. Several days later, Crews was illegally arrested in the same area because he fit the description given. He was photographed and his picture identified by the victim in a photographic display. Crews was again taken into custody and identified at a lineup. The trial judge

---

[Section 2:27]

[1]1 Ringel, Searches and Seizures, Arrests and Confessions, § 3.3(a) (Clark Boardman 1979); Milner v. State, 180 Ga. App. 97, 98, 348 S.E.2d 509 (1986) (citing Segura v. U.S., 468 U.S. 796, 104 S. Ct. 3380, 82 L. Ed. 2d 599 (1984)). Segura is referred to in a footnote in § 4:28, infra. See Teal v. State, 282 Ga. 319, 647 S.E.2d 15 (2007) for a discussion and comparison of independent source doctrine and inevitable discovery exception.

[2]See U.S. v. Castellana, 488 F.2d 65 (5th Cir. 1974); Waters v. State, 360 So. 2d 347 (Ala. Crim. App. 1978).

[3]Wilder v. State, 290 Ga. 13, 16, 717 S.E.2d 457 (2011) (citing Teal v. State, 282 Ga. 319, 324(2), 647 S.E.2d 15 (2007).

[4]U.S. v. DeMarce, 513 F.2d 755 (8th Cir. 1975); Sheff v. State, 329 So. 2d 270 (Fla. 1976).

[5]Bynum v. U.S., 274 F.2d 767 (D.C. Cir. 1960).

[6]U. S. v. Crews, 445 U.S. 463, 100 S. Ct. 1244, 63 L. Ed. 2d 537 (1980). See the discussion of Crews in § 6:10, infra.

found that the victim's ability to identify Crews was based on her independent and untainted recollection of having seen him at the time of the crime and she was permitted to identify him at the trial. The Supreme Court concluded that the victim's presence in the courtroom at trial was not a result of police misconduct and Crews cannot claim immunity simply because his presence in court was precipitated by an unlawful arrest. Crews was not himself a suppressible fruit of an unlawful arrest. The "Fourth Amendment violation . . . yielded nothing of evidentiary value that the police did not already have in their grasp."[7]

In *Murray v. United States*,[8] the United States Supreme Court held that the exclusionary rule did not apply where officers illegally entered a warehouse and while there "observed in plain view numerous burlap-wrapped bales that were later found to contain marijuana . . ., [l]eft without disturbing the bales, kept the warehouse under surveillance, and did not reenter it until they had a search warrant" issued on the basis of information unrelated to the initial entry.

Generally, see 1 Ringel, *Searches and Seizures, Arrests and Confessions*, § 3 (2014 Thomson Reuters).

§ 2:28 The exclusionary rule—Present application at trial—The inevitable discovery exception

The inevitable discovery exception permits the prosecution to justify the admission of evidence obtained as a result of an unlawful search by showing that the evidence would have been discovered later through legal means.[1]

The Eleventh Circuit Court of Appeals refined the doctrine to also require that "the prosecution . . . demonstrate that the lawful means which made discovery inevitable were possessed by the police and were being actively pursued prior to the occurrence of the illegal conduct."[2] The burden is that of a "reasonable probability" that the evidence would have been recovered lawfully.[3] In *Nix v. Whitman*,[4] the United States Supreme Court noted "inevitable discovery involves no speculative elements but focuses on demonstrated historical facts capable of ready verification or impeachment and does not require a departure from the usual

---

[7]U. S. v. Crews, 445 U.S. 463, 475, 100 S. Ct. 1244, 63 L. Ed. 2d 537 (1980).

[8]Murray v. U.S., 487 U.S. 533, 108 S. Ct. 2529, 101 L. Ed. 2d 472 (1988).

[Section 2:28]

[1]Nix v. Williams, 467 U.S. 431, 104 S. Ct. 2501, 81 L. Ed. 2d 377 (1984).

[2]U.S. v. Terzado-Madruga, 897 F.2d 1099, 1114 (11th Cir. 1990).

[3]U.S. v. Johnson, 777 F.3d 1270, 1274(III)(A) (11th Cir. 2015).

[4]Nix v. Williams, 467 U.S. 431, 460, n.5, 104 S. Ct. 2501, 81 L. Ed. 2d 377 (1984).

burden of proof at suppression hearings." In *Taylor v. State*,[5] the Georgia Supreme Court concluded that as defined by the Eleventh Circuit, the inevitable discovery doctrine was consistent with prior application of the rule in Georgia and decided to expressly adopt it as the rule in this State.

A leading case on inevitable discovery is *Wayne v. United States*,[6] in an opinion written by future Chief Justice Burger. In this case, the court, on the basis of *Wong Sun v. United States*,[7] held a coroner's report concerning the cause of death to be admissible even though the body had been found as the result of an illegal search and seizure. The court pointed out that the body would have been found sooner or later and that the police would have been notified then. This case also demonstrates the close relationship which may exist between the inevitable discovery and independent source exceptions.[8]

In *Nix v. Williams*,[9] the United States Supreme Court considered Williams' second conviction. In the second *Williams* opinion,[10] the Court approved the admissibility of evidence relating to the discovery and condition of the body of the victim since the prosecution had established by a preponderance of the evidence that the body would have been inevitably discovered in the same condition even if there had been no Sixth Amendment violation. The court noted that the prosecution is not required to prove the absence of bad faith on the part of the officers violating the defendant's constitutional rights.

In the 1987 Eleventh Circuit opinion in *United States v. Hernandez-Cano*,[11] the court held that the inevitable discovery doctrine applied where an airline employee would have discovered cocaine even if an officer had not intervened and actually discovered the contraband.

Generally, see 1 Ringel, *Searches and Seizures, Arrests and*

---

[5]Taylor v. State, 274 Ga. 269, 553 S.E.2d 598 (2001) (cases cited by the Court in n. 26 at 275), disapproved on other grounds, State v. Chulpayev, 296 Ga. 764, 770 S.E.2d 808 (2015). See Teal v. State, 282 Ga. 319, 647 S.E.2d 15 (2007) for a discussion and comparison of independent source doctrine and inevitable discovery exception.

[6]Wayne v. U.S., 318 F.2d 205 (D.C. Cir. 1963).

[7]Wong Sun v. U.S., 371 U.S. 471, 83 S. Ct. 407, 9 L. Ed. 2d 441 (1963).

[8]3 LaFave, Search and Seizure 620, § 11.4 (West 1978).

[9]Nix v. Williams, 467 U.S. 431, 104 S. Ct. 2501, 81 L. Ed. 2d 377 (1984). In Williams, the Court compared the inevitable discovery doctrine with the independent source doctrine; both doctrines allow the inclusion of evidence, which if excluded would have put the prosecution in a worse position than it would have been in if no illegality had occurred.

[10]Brewer v. Williams, 430 U.S. 387, 97 S. Ct. 1232, 51 L. Ed. 2d 424 (1977). See § 5:10, infra, on the right to counsel.

[11]U.S. v. Hernandez-Cano, 808 F.2d 779 (11th Cir. 1987).

Confessions, § 3 (2014 Thomson Reuters).

§ 2:29 The exclusionary rule—Present application at trial—Attenuation

The attenuation or purged taint exception to the rule that evidence derived from, or as a result of, an illegal arrest or search is inadmissible finds support in the fact that the United States Supreme Court has pointed out that it has never adopted a "but for" causation test.[1]

In *Hudson v. Michigan,*[2] officers armed with a valid search warrant failed to observe the "knock and announce" rule in violation of the Fourth Amendment. The issue presented was whether the evidence seized by the police should have been suppressed. As the Court explained:

> [E]xclusion may not be premised on the mere fact that a constitutional violation was a "but for" cause of obtaining evidence. Our cases show that but-for causality is only a necessary, not a sufficient, condition for suppression. In this case, . . . the constitutional violation of an illegal manner of entry was not a but-for cause of obtaining the evidence. Whether that preliminary misstep had occurred or not, the police would have executed the warrant they had obtained, and would have discovered the gun and drugs inside the house. But even if the illegal entry here could be characterized as a but-for cause of discovering what was inside, we have "never held that evidence is 'fruit of the poisonous tree' simply because 'it would not have come to light but for the illegal actions of the police.' "

> Attenuation can occur, of course, when the causal connection is remote. Attenuation also occurs when, even given a direct causal connection, the interest protected by the constitutional guarantee that has been violated would not be served by suppression of the evidence obtained. "the penalties visited upon the Government, and in turn upon the public, because its officers have violated the law must bear some relation to the purposes which the law is to serve."

In *Wong Sun v. United States,*[3] federal narcotics agents entered without probable cause and chased Toy to his bedroom, where he was arrested. Toy made a statement implicating Yee. Narcotics were seized from Yee, who implicated Wong Sun. All defendants were arraigned and released. Within a few days, all three made statements to the Narcotics Bureau. The court agreed with Toy's

---

[Section 2:29]

[1]U. S. v. Ceccolini, 435 U.S. 268, 276, 98 S. Ct. 1054, 55 L. Ed. 2d 268 (1978); U.S. v. Leon, 468 U.S. 897, 906, 104 S. Ct. 3405, 82 L. Ed. 2d 677 (1984).

[2]Hudson v. Michigan, 547 U.S. 586, 592–593, 126 S. Ct. 2159, 165 L. Ed. 2d 56, 23 A.L.R. Fed. 2d 823 (2006) (citations and internal punctuation deleted).

[3]Wong Sun v. U.S., 371 U.S. 471, 83 S. Ct. 407, 9 L. Ed. 2d 441 (1963).

contention that his statement and the drugs later seized from Yee were fruits of Toy's illegal arrest. However, the Court concluded that Wong Sun's statement which had been made to agents several days after arraignment was sufficiently attenuated to have dissipated the taint of his illegal arrest. The court pointed out that the taint of the illegal arrest was sufficiently purged by the independent act of the defendant in going to the office and making a statement after his arraignment. The fact that Wong Sun would not have gone to the office of the narcotics agents and made a statement had it not been for his illegal arrest did not prevent the admission of the statement.

In *Burnham v. State*,[4] the Georgia Supreme Court held that "[t]he shorter the lapse in time between the illegal police activity and the defendant's statement, the more likely it is that the defendant's statement was the product of the illegal activity."

In *Brown v. Illinois*,[5] the defendant was illegally arrested, given *Miranda* warnings, and within two hours of the time of his arrest he gave an inculpatory statement concerning a murder and later gave a second statement. The court concluded that the giving of *Miranda* warnings did not automatically break the causal chain so that the statement would be admissible, even if the statement had been made voluntarily under the Fifth Amendment. The court also reasoned that the second statement was the fruit of the first one and that it was not admissible. In the decision, the Court pointed out that each case must turn on its own facts. Of course, if a statement was not voluntarily made, it is not admissible for any purpose. In *Brown*, the Court enumerated some factors which may be considered in determining whether or not the illegal taint has been purged. Those factors are the following:

(1) *Miranda* warnings;

(2) Temporal proximity of the arrest and the confession;

(3) Presence of intervening circumstances;

(4) Purpose of the official misconduct; and

(5) Flagrancy of the official misconduct.[6]

The burden of establishing the sufficiency of the attenuation

---

[4]Burnham v. State, 265 Ga. 129, 133, 453 S.E.2d 449 (1995). *Burham* has since been "disapproved" by the Georgia Supreme Court, Stinski v. State, 281 Ga. 783, 785, 642 S.E.2d 1 (2007).

[5]Brown v. Illinois, 422 U.S. 590, 95 S. Ct. 2254, 45 L. Ed. 2d 416 (1975); Lanier v. South Carolina, 474 U.S. 25, 106 S. Ct. 297, 88 L. Ed. 2d 23 (1985). Cf. Rawlings v. Kentucky, 448 U.S. 98,

107, 100 S. Ct. 2556, 65 L. Ed. 2d 633 (1980), and Devier v. State, 253 Ga. 604, 616, 323 S.E.2d 150 (1984).

[6]Brown v. Illinois, 422 U.S. 590, 603, 604, 95 S. Ct. 2254, 45 L. Ed. 2d 416 (1975). See Utah v. Strieff, 136 S. Ct. 2056, 195 L. Ed. 2d 400 (2016). Compare Vergara v. State, 283 Ga. 175 (2), 657 S.E.2d 863 (2008), where the court concluded that recovery of cocaine was not so attenuated from ille-

from the illegality "rests squarely with the prosecution."[7]

Wong Sun and *Brown* are based on Fourth Amendment violations. However, a different rule applies where there is a violation of the rules of *Miranda.* In *Oregon v. Elstad,*[8] the United States Supreme Court considered a case in which the defendant was arrested, pursuant to a warrant, at his home in connection with a burglary. He was not given *Miranda* warnings, but he voluntarily made an incriminating statement in answer to some questions asked by the officer while sitting in the defendant's living room. One hour later, at police headquarters, he was administered *Miranda* warnings for the first time and he made a full confession, which was typed and signed. The defendant objected to the admissibility of the confession alleging that it was a result of the earlier incriminating statement. The defendant contended that a confession cannot be voluntary "once the cat is out of the bag." Writing for the majority, Justice O'Connor distinguished between "actual" coerced statements resulting from police misconduct and mere "technical" *Miranda* violations. Although the defendant was technically in custody while he was in his living room with the officer, there was no coercion. Because there was no coercion in the first interrogation, and the second confession came after the *Miranda* warnings were given, the second confession was admissible against the defendant. "The Fifth Amendment prohibits the prosecution in its case in chief only of *compelled* testimony. Failure to administer *Miranda* warnings creates a presumption of compulsion." However, "[a] subsequent administration of *Miranda* warnings to a suspect who has given a voluntary but unwarned statement ordinarily should suffice to remove the conditions that precluded admission of the earlier statement."

Elstad, however, does not afford police the opportunity to interrogate suspects without providing *Miranda* warnings with the intention of giving warnings after obtaining incriminating statements and then having the suspect repeat those statements. The United States Supreme Court rejected just such a practice in *Missouri v. Seibert,*[9] where police attempted to circumvent *Miranda* by providing warnings mid-interrogation and post-confession. The opinion states that in determining whether "midstream *Miranda* warnings" could be effective, courts should consider: "the completeness and detail of the questions and

---

gal interrogation as to dissipate the taint.

[7]Jefferson v. State, 217 Ga. App. 747, 752, 459 S.E.2d 173 (1995).

[8]Oregon v. Elstad, 470 U.S. 298, 105 S. Ct. 1285, 84 L. Ed. 2d 222 (1985). See Moore v. State, 263 Ga. 11, 427 S.E.2d 766 (1993).

[9]Missouri v. Seibert, 542 U.S. 600, 124 S. Ct. 2601, 159 L. Ed. 2d 643 (2004).

answers to the first round of interrogation, overlapping contents of the two statements, the timing and setting of the first and second rounds, the continuity of police personnel, and the degree to which the interrogator's questions treated the second round as continuous with the first."[10] This technique is sometimes referred to as "question first."[11]

In *United States v. Street*,[12] the Eleventh Circuit explained:

In determining whether a properly warned confession is admissible where the defendant has first given an unwarned or improperly warned confession we turn to the Supreme Court's decisions in *Oregon v. Elstad*, 470 U.S. 298, 105 S.Ct. 1285, 84 L.Ed.2d 222 (1985), and *Missouri v. Seibert*, 542 U.S. 600, 124 S.Ct. 2601, 159 L.Ed.2d 643 (2004). *Elstad* sets out the general rule that the existence of a pre-warning statement does not require suppression of a post-warning statement that was knowingly and voluntarily made, 470 U.S. at 309, 105 S.Ct. at 1293, while *Seibert* sets out an exception for situations where police employ a deliberate "question first" strategy. 542 U.S. at 617, 124 S.Ct. 2613.

In order to determine whether the second statement was voluntary, "courts are not to presume that the existence of the earlier unwarned statement compelled the defendant to give another one, but instead should assume that ordinarily giving proper *Miranda* warnings removes the effect of any conditions requiring suppression of the unwarned statement."

See § 2:31, note 7, infra, for an application of the Brown rule. Generally, see 1 Ringel, *Searches and Seizures, Arrests and Confessions*, § 3 (2014 Thomas Reuters).

§ 2:30   The exclusionary rule—Present application at trial—Discovery of prosecution witness

In *United States v. Ceccolini*,[1] the Court concluded that "the exclusionary rule should be invoked with much greater reluctance where the claim is based on a causal relationship between a constitutional violation and the discovery of a live witness than when a similar claim is advanced to support suppression of an inanimate object."[2]

In arriving at this conclusion, the Court (1) rejected the conten-

---

[10]Missouri v. Seibert, 542 U.S. 600, 124 S. Ct. 2601, 159 L. Ed. 2d 643 (2004).

[11]See State v. Abbott, 303 Ga. 297, 812 S.E.2d 225 (2018) (court must determine if officers deliberately employed "question first, warning later" interrogation technique to undermine *Miranda* safeguards).

[12]U.S. v. Street, 472 F.3d 1298,

1312 (11th Cir. 2006).

[Section 2:30]

[1]U. S. v. Ceccolini, 435 U.S. 268, 280, 98 S. Ct. 1054, 55 L. Ed. 2d 268 (1978) (witness discovered as the result of an illegal search could properly testify).

[2]Cf. Michigan v. Tucker, 417 U.S. 433, 94 S. Ct. 2357, 41 L. Ed. 2d 182 (1974).

tion of the government that the testimony of a live witness should never be excluded, and (2) reaffirmed the rule that verbal evidence may be the fruit of an unlawful arrest. However, the Court also said that the willingness of the witness to testify is material, since the witness might come forward and offer to testify on his own volition. The time, place and manner of the first questioning is of significance.

§ 2:31 The exclusionary rule—Present application at trial—Confessions obtained

See sections 5:13 and 5:26, infra, on admissibility under Georgia law of a confession made to a private person. As previously pointed out in § 2:29, supra, an incriminating statement obtained from Toy in *Wong Sun v. United States*[1] at the time of his illegal arrest was held to be a direct fruit of the unlawful arrest and therefore inadmissible. However, the statement of Wong Sun after his arraignment was admissible. Also as previously pointed out in § 2:29, supra, in *Brown v. Illinois*,[2] the Court laid down some significant factors to be considered in determining the degree of attenuation which exists.

In *Dunaway v. New York*,[3] the Court held that where a suspect is "picked up," taken to a police station, placed in an interrogation room, given *Miranda* warnings and makes incriminating statements, such statements are not admissible when the officers lacked probable cause to arrest. This is true even if *Miranda* warnings are given and the confession is "voluntary" for purposes of the Fifth Amendment.[4] See § 11:1, infra, on a statement obtained after 48 hours following a warrantless arrest where there has been no probable cause hearing. The Supreme Court of Georgia cited and relied upon *Dunaway* in the 1986 case of *State v. Harris*.[5]

In *Taylor v. Alabama*,[6] the entire Court recognized that "a confession obtained through custodial interrogation after an ille-

---

[Section 2:31]

[1]Wong Sun v. U.S., 371 U.S. 471, 83 S. Ct. 407, 9 L. Ed. 2d 441 (1963).

[2]Brown v. Illinois, 422 U.S. 590, 95 S. Ct. 2254, 45 L. Ed. 2d 416 (1975).

[3]Dunaway v. New York, 442 U.S. 200, 99 S. Ct. 2248, 60 L. Ed. 2d 824 (1979); accord, State v. Guillory, 236 Ga. App. 230, 232, 511 S.E.2d 591 (1999); Ryals v. State, 186 Ga. App. 457, 458, 367 S.E.2d 309 (1988); Jefferson v. State, 217 Ga. App. 747, 750, 459 S.E.2d 173 (1995).

[4]Dunaway v. New York, 442 U.S. 200, 217, 99 S. Ct. 2248, 60 L. Ed. 2d 824 (1979) (cited and relied on in Griffith v. State, 172 Ga. App. 255, 257, 322 S.E.2d 921 (1984)).

[5]State v. Harris, 256 Ga. 24, 25, 343 S.E.2d 483 (1986).

[6]Taylor v. Alabama, 457 U.S. 687, 102 S. Ct. 2664, 73 L. Ed. 2d 314 (1982); Paradise v. State, 212 Ga. App. 166, 167, 441 S.E.2d 497 (1994); Robinson v. State, 166 Ga. App. 741, 305 S.E.2d 381 (1983). See a footnote in § 2:12, supra, discussing *Taylor*. But

gal arrest should be excluded unless intervening events break the causal connection between the illegal arrest and the confession so that the confession is 'sufficiently an act of free will to purge the primary taint.' " In this case, the arrest had been without probable cause. In determining whether the primary taint has been purged, consideration should be given to the factors enumerated in *Brown v. Illinois,*[7] which were discussed in § 2:29, supra. The *Taylor* majority concluded that the primary taint had not been purged. The dissenting justices disagreed. The following facts were discussed on the question of whether the taint had been purged:

(1)   The conduct of the arresting officers had not been blatant.

(2)   Taylor was told at the time of the arrest that he was being arrested for a robbery at a grocery.

(3)   There was no police misconduct other than the arrest.

(4)   Taylor was fingerprinted, placed in a lineup, and told that his fingerprints matched prints found in the store where the robbery had taken place.

(5)   Taylor was given *Miranda* warnings on three occasions.

(6)   Taylor was not represented by counsel.

(7)   Taylor was in custody about six hours before he confessed.

(8)   Taylor's girlfriend talked with him before he confessed. She was, however, emotionally upset at the time.

(9)   Taylor was permitted to talk to a neighbor for a few minutes. Shortly after this conversation, he confessed.

However, in the 1980 case of *Rawlings v. Kentucky,*[8] where Rawlings and some others were detained in a friend's home for about 45 minutes in a "congenial atmosphere" while a search warrant was obtained and *Miranda* warnings were given shortly before an incriminating statement was apparently volunteered, the statement was found to be admissible. The court emphasized the short duration of the detention and that there had been no flagrant misconduct by the officers.

Generally, if two confessions are made and the first is closely connected with the unlawful arrest, or search and seizure, the second confession is also regarded as not being admissible even if some time or intervening circumstances have occurred.[9] In a sense, the second confession is regarded as being the fruit of the

---

cf. Olson v. State, 166 Ga. App. 104, 303 S.E.2d 309 (1983).

[7]Brown v. Illinois, 422 U.S. 590, 95 S. Ct. 2254, 45 L. Ed. 2d 416 (1975).

[8]Rawlings v. Kentucky, 448 U.S. 98, 100 S. Ct. 2556, 65 L. Ed. 2d 633 (1980).

[9]Harrison v. U.S., 392 U.S. 219, 88 S. Ct. 2008, 20 L. Ed. 2d 1047 (1968).

first. However, as in *Oregon v. Elstad,*[10] this is not as likely to be true where the first confession was voluntary but is not admissible simply because of a technical *Miranda* violation.

Where a suspect is confronted with illegally seized items and he confesses to the crime involved, it seems that normally the confession would not be admissible.[11]

In *Green v. State,*[12] the arrest warrant contained no facts justifying that the defendant committed a murder. Since a statement was obtained from the defendant pursuant to the defective warrant, and was admitted at trial, the conviction was reversed. The dissenting opinion emphasized the good faith of the officers and cited *United States v. Williams.*[13] The United States Supreme Court denied certiorari.[14]

However, in *Thompson v. State,*[15] in which Justice Smith dissented and Justice Weltner did not participate, the court held that a confession was admissible despite the fact that it was obtained as a result of an illegal arrest. Here the warrantless arrest was a violation of the Fourth Amendment since the defendant was in his home at the time of the arrest, there were no exigent circumstances; and the defendant did not consent to the arrest. The court emphasized the fact that the officers had probable cause to arrest, honestly thought they did not need an arrest warrant, and did not engage in any purposeful or flagrant misconduct.

Nevertheless, in *United States v. Johnson,*[16] the United States Supreme Court held that the Payton rule,[17] requiring an arrest warrant before a defendant may be arrested in his home in the absence of exigent circumstances, is to be applied retroactively to all cases in which the conviction was not final on the date of the *Payton* decision. *Payton* was decided in 1980. In *Johnson,* the Court held that it was error not to grant the motion to suppress the oral statement which Johnson made shortly after his warrantless arrest at home. The Ninth Circuit concluded in *Johnson*

---

[10]Oregon v. Elstad, 470 U.S. 298, 105 S. Ct. 1285, 84 L. Ed. 2d 222 (1985). See § 2:29, supra, on attenuation. Cf. U.S. v. Trabucco, 424 F.2d 1311 (5th Cir. 1970).

[11]Cf. People v. Robbins, 54 Ill. App. 3d 298, 12 Ill. Dec. 80, 369 N.E.2d 577 (5th Dist. 1977).

[12]Green v. State, 615 S.W.2d 700 (Tex. Crim. App. 1980).

[13]U.S. v. Williams, 622 F.2d 830 (5th Cir. 1980). See § 4:60, infra, on when results of an illegal search may be admissible.

[14]Texas v. Green, 454 U.S. 952, 102 S. Ct. 490, 70 L. Ed. 2d 258 (1981).

[15]Thompson v. State, 248 Ga. 343, 285 S.E.2d 685 (1981). Accord, Okross v. State, 210 Ga. App. 132, 133, 435 S.E.2d 454 (1993).

[16]U.S. v. Johnson, 457 U.S. 537, 102 S. Ct. 2579, 73 L. Ed. 2d 202 (1982).

[17]Payton v. New York, 445 U.S. 573, 100 S. Ct. 1371, 63 L. Ed. 2d 639 (1980).

that the agents had probable cause to arrest. In fact, warrants had been obtained for the arrest of Johnson and another person known to have participated in the offense with him. At one point in *Johnson,* the Court stated, "The Government does not seriously suggest that the retroactivity of a given Fourth Amendment ruling should turn solely on the subjective state of a particular arresting officer's mind. Instead, it offers an 'objective' test: that law enforcement officers 'may properly be charged with knowledge' of all 'settled' Fourth Amendment law." This "objective test" was rejected, however, by the Court. It was reasoned that "if, as the Government argues, all rulings resolving unsettled Fourth Amendment questions should be nonretroactive, then, in close cases, law enforcement officials would have little incentive to err on the side of constitutional behavior."

In the 1990 case of *New York v. Harris,*[18] the United States Supreme Court held that if a warrantless, non-consensual, routine felony arrest in a suspect's home is supported by probable cause, it does not require the suppression of a statement made by the suspect after he was removed from his home. Similarly, in *Carranza v. State,*[19] the Georgia Supreme Court, in a six to one decision, reached the same conclusion.

§ 2:32   The exclusionary rule—Present application at trial—Impeachment

In *Walder v. United States,*[1] the defendant had been tried and convicted of purchasing and possessing heroin. On direct examination Walder testified that he never handled any narcotics. Over objection, on cross-examination the government asked Walder about the heroin unlawfully seized from his home earlier. He denied that narcotics had been taken from his home. The government then put on the stand one of the officers who participated in the unlawful search and seizure as well as the chemist who analyzed the seized heroin. The testimony was allowed and the conviction was affirmed because the defendant "opened the door" for cross-examination regarding his possession of the drugs.

In *Harris v. New York,*[2] the defendant made statements to officers which were not admissible in the government's case in chief under *Miranda.* After Harris testified at trial, prior inconsistent statements he made were held to have been properly

---

[18]New York v. Harris, 495 U.S. 14, 110 S. Ct. 1640, 109 L. Ed. 2d 13 (1990).

[19]Carranza v. State, 266 Ga. 263, 268, 467 S.E.2d 315 (1996). See Pittman v. State, 277 Ga. 475, 479, 592 S.E.2d 72 (2004).

[Section 2:32]

[1]Walder v. U.S., 347 U.S. 62, 74 S. Ct. 354, 98 L. Ed. 503 (1954).

[2]Harris v. New York, 401 U.S. 222, 91 S. Ct. 643, 28 L. Ed. 2d 1 (1971).

See Oregon v. Hass, 420 U.S.

admitted for purposes of impeachment. Likewise, in *Michigan v. Harvey*,[3] the Court held that "the prosecution may use a statement taken in violation of the [*Michigan v.*] *Jackson* prophylactic rule to impeach a defendant's false or inconsistent testimony." (*Jackson* is discussed in § 5:20, infra.)

However, the foregoing situation is to be distinguished from that which exists when a statement or confession was not voluntarily given. Thus, in *Mincey v. Arizona*,[4] a statement obtained by officers from Mincey, while he was in the intensive care unit of a hospital in critical condition, as a result of questioning for four hours while he was in severe pain, was held not to have been voluntarily given. The court then concluded that a confession obtained in this manner could not be used for purposes of impeachment.

Also, the situations in *Walder* and *Harris* are to be distinguished from a case in which a prosecutor seeks to impeach the credibility of a defense *witness* by the use of illegally obtained evidence. *James v. Illinois*[5] is such a case. In *James,* the Court concluded that to permit the impeachment of a defense witness with illegally obtained evidence would lead a defendant not to call the witness and "would not further . . . truthseeking . . . but would appreciably undermine the deterrent effect of the exclusionary rule. . . ." Hence, it is error to admit illegally obtained evidence for the purpose of impeaching a defense witness.

In *United States v. Havens,*[6] the Court considered the admission into evidence of an illegally seized undershirt. On direct examination, Havens testified that he had had no activity with his co-defendant on his visit to Peru. On cross-examination, Havens testified that he had not participated in making a closed pocket on a tee-shirt which the customs officer found the co-defendant wearing. In rebuttal, an agent was permitted to testify to finding

---

714, 95 S. Ct. 1215, 43 L. Ed. 2d 570 (1975). See also Kansas v. Ventris, 556 U.S. 586, 129 S.Ct. 1841, 173 L.Ed.2d 801 (2009) (statements made to government informant while defendant is in custody may be used for impeachment).

[3]Michigan v. Harvey, 494 U.S. 344, 110 S. Ct. 1176, 108 L. Ed. 2d 293 (1990).

[4]Mincey v. Arizona, 437 U.S. 385, 98 S. Ct. 2408, 57 L. Ed. 2d 290 (1978). Cf. Sanders v. State, 281 Ga. 36, 635 S.E.2d 772 (2006) (statement was held voluntary where the defendant was able to engage in meaningful conversations at a time when he was in hospital, in pain and medicated).

[5]James v. Illinois, 493 U.S. 307, 110 S. Ct. 648, 107 L. Ed. 2d 676 (1990).

[6]U.S. v. Havens, 446 U.S. 620, 100 S. Ct. 1912, 64 L. Ed. 2d 559 (1980). But see "Bradley, Havens, Jenkins, and Salvucci, and the Defendant's 'Right' to Testify," 18 Am. Crim. L. R. 419 (1981); Le Bel, "Standing After Havens Reality: A Critique and an Alternative Framework for Analysis," 1982 Duke L. J. 1013 (1982).

a tee-shirt in Havens' bag from which pieces had been cut which matched the pieces sewn to McLeroth's tee-shirt to form pockets which contained the cocaine. Also, the undershirt was admitted into evidence. The Court, in effect, affirmed the trial court and declined to restrict *Walder* to impeachment of direct testimony. The court concluded rather that the cross-examination grew reasonably out of Havens' direct testimony and was not a violation of his constitutional rights.[7]

See Annotation, "Propriety of Using Otherwise Inadmissible Statement, Taken in Violation of *Miranda* Rule, to Impeach Criminal Defendant's Credibility—State Cases," 14 A.L.R.4th 676 (1982).

§ 2:33   Real evidence discovered as a result of *Miranda* violation

Physical evidence discovered as a result of a *Miranda* violation need not be suppressed unless the interrogation involved actual coercion.[1] The fruits from the unwarned statements of criminal suspects may thus be used as evidence against them in subsequent proceedings provided the statements made to the police were given voluntarily.[2] Accordingly, in *Taylor v. State*,[3] a murder weapon discovered through the *Miranda* tainted statement of the defendant was properly admitted at trial because the defendant's statement was voluntary albeit made without counsel, after a proper request for an attorney had been made by the defendant. However, in *Vergara v. State*,[4] the court found that the fruits doctrine applied where there was a direct nexus between the interrogation and the discovery of the cocaine evidence after the defendant had requested counsel and ruled that the evidence should have been suppressed.

§ 2:34   The exclusionary rule—Present application—Non-trial proceedings

"When an attempt is made to apply the [exclusionary] rule in

---

[7]But cf. Agnello v. U.S., 269 U.S. 20, 46 S. Ct. 4, 70 L. Ed. 145 (1925).

[Section 2:33]

[1]State v. Walton, 41 S.W.3d 75, 90 (Tenn. 2001).

[2]Oregon v. Elstad, 470 U.S. 298, 318, 105 S. Ct. 1285, 84 L. Ed. 2d 222 (1985); State v. Woods, 280 Ga. 758, 632 S.E.2d 654 (2006); Wilson v. Zant, 249 Ga. 373, 290 S.E.2d 442 (1982).

[3]Taylor v. State, 274 Ga. 269, 553 S.E.2d 598 (2001), disapproved by State

v. Chulpayev, 296 Ga. 764, 770 S.E.2d 808 (2015) (other evidence or "fruits" obtained as a result of a statement induced by hope of benefit in violation of O.C.G.A. § 24-8-824 is subject to exclusion only if it appears that the statement was not voluntary under the constitutional standard for voluntariness). See Stidham v. State, 299 Ga. App. 858, 683 S.E.2d 906 (2009).

[4]Vergara v. State, 283 Ga. 175 (2), 657 S.E.2d 863 (2008).

contexts other than the initial stages of a criminal prosecution, courts will balance the deterrent effect of the rule's use in the situation at hand against the cost to the government and society of losing the use of probative evidence."[1]

It has been held in Georgia that evidence obtained from a search in violation of the Fourth Amendment may not be used to obtain a search warrant.[2]

In the context of the Fifth Amendment, at least three decisions have concluded that evidence obtained in violation of *Miranda* may not be used to establish probable cause for a search and seizure.[3] However, these cases are open to serious question after *Commonwealth v. White*,[4] a 1977 United States Supreme Court decision where an equally divided court (Justice Powell did not participate) affirmed per curiam the Massachusetts Supreme Judicial Court's exclusion of evidence obtained in violation of *Miranda*.[5]

In the area of grand jury investigations, the United States Supreme Court has held that a witness summoned to appear and testify before the grand jury may not refuse to answer questions on the ground that the questions were based on evidence obtained in an unlawful search and seizure.[6] Also, it seems that it is not necessary to give *Miranda* warnings to a grand jury witness "who is called to testify about criminal activities in which he may have been personally involved."[7]

In the case of parole or probation revocations, some courts have held that the exclusionary rule does not apply.[8] Although Georgia at one time applied the exclusionary rule in probation revocation hearings, in *Thackston v. State*,[9] the Georgia Supreme Court held that it would no longer follow that practice and overruled all

---

[Section 2:34]

[1]Whitebread, Constitutional Criminal Procedure, American Academy of Judicial Education (1978), p. 3.

[2]Kelleher v. State, 185 Ga. App. 774, 778, 365 S.E.2d 889 (1988); Clare v. State, 135 Ga. App. 281, 285, 217 S.E.2d 638 (1975). Accord, State v. Stone, 165 W. Va. 266, 268 S.E.2d 50 (1980) (overruled by, State v. Julius, 185 W. Va. 422, 408 S.E.2d 1 (1991)).

[3]State v. Preston, 411 A.2d 402 (Me. 1980); Com. v. Meehan, 377 Mass. 552, 387 N.E.2d 527 (1979); Com. v. White, 374 Mass. 132, 371 N.E.2d 777 (1977).

[4]Massachusetts v. White, 439 U.S. 280, 99 S. Ct. 712, 58 L. Ed. 2d 519 (1978). See Com. v. White, 374 Mass. 132, 371 N.E.2d 777 (1977).

[5]Generally, see Annot., "Propriety of Considering Hearsay or Other Incompetent Evidence in Establishing Probable Cause for Issuance of Search Warrant," 10 A.L.R.3d 359 (1966).

[6]U.S. v. Calandra, 414 U.S. 338, 94 S. Ct. 613, 38 L. Ed. 2d 561 (1974).

[7]See U.S. v. Mandujano, 425 U.S. 564, 96 S. Ct. 1768, 48 L. Ed. 2d 212 (1976), discussed in § 5:12, n. 3, infra.

[8]U. S. ex rel. Sperling v. Fitzpatrick, 426 F.2d 1161 (2d Cir. 1970); Grimsley v. Dodson, 696 F.2d 303 (4th Cir. 1982).

[9]Thackston v. State, 289 Ga. 412, 716 S.E.2d 517 (2011).

authority to the contrary.

Likewise, some courts have held that the exclusionary rule does not apply to sentencing proceedings,[10] while other courts have applied the exclusionary rule.[11]

See § 4:7, infra, on illegally obtained evidence being considered to establish probable cause, and § 2:25, supra, on applicability of exclusionary rule at trial. See § 5:26, infra, on admissibility of the fruits of an illegally obtained confession.

See sections 3:2 and 4:46, infra, on the application of the exclusionary rule where an officer relied on an invalid law. See § 30:7, infra, on admissibility of evidence obtained in violation of Fourth Amendment in a parole hearing.

§ 2:35   The exclusionary rule—Present application—Civil proceedings

In the case of a forfeiture or condemnation of an automobile, the United States Supreme Court referred to the proceedings as being quasi-criminal and held that the exclusionary rule applied.[1]

However, in *United States v. Janis,*[2] police officers, pursuant to an invalid warrant, conducted a search for evidence of bookmaking. Agents of the Internal Revenue Service were informed of Janis' arrest, resulting in an assessment against Janis for wagering taxes. The court held that the exclusionary rule should not be extended to forbid the use, in a civil proceeding by the federal government, of evidence illegally seized by a criminal law enforcement agent of a state because the likelihood of deterring law enforcement's conduct is not sufficient to outweigh societal costs imposed by the exclusion. Likewise, in *Immigration and Naturalization Service v. Lopez-Mendoza,*[3] the Court held that the Fourth Amendment rule did not apply to a civil deportation proceeding.

---

[10]U.S. v. Schipani, 435 F.2d 26 (2d Cir. 1970). In U.S. v. Pineda, 692 F.2d 284 (2d Cir. 1982), the court held that a taped conversation of the defendant and an informer after the defendant had entered a guilty plea was admissible at sentencing. The court pointed out that ordinarily the government's deliberate use of an informer to elicit incriminating statements violates Massiah v. U.S., 377 U.S. 201, 84 S. Ct. 1199, 12 L. Ed. 2d 246 (1964), but refused to apply that rule to evidence presented at sentencing. (See § 5:9, infra, on Massiah.)

[11]In Gilbert v. California, 388 U.S.

263, 272, 87 S. Ct. 1951, 18 L. Ed. 2d 1178 (1967), the Court held that unconstitutional lineup testimony was not admissible at the sentencing phase of a case. Cf. U.S. v. Weston, 448 F.2d 626 (9th Cir. 1971).

[Section 2:35]

[1]One 1958 Plymouth Sedan v. Com. of Pa., 380 U.S. 693, 85 S. Ct. 1246, 14 L. Ed. 2d 170 (1965).

[2]U.S. v. Janis, 428 U.S. 433, 96 S. Ct. 3021, 49 L. Ed. 2d 1046 (1976).

[3]I.N.S. v. Lopez-Mendoza, 468 U.S. 1032, 104 S. Ct. 3479, 82 L. Ed. 2d 778 (1984).

Georgia courts will also exclude evidence if it was obtained through a violation of privacy.[4] In the case of *Ransom v. Ransom*,[5] the Georgia Supreme Court refused to recognize an exception to this rule for domestic situations. The Georgia Code also specifically defines invasion of privacy with regard to computers.[6]

---

[4]O.C.G.A. §§ 16-11-62, 16-11-67.
[5]Ransom v. Ransom, 253 Ga. 656, 658, 324 S.E.2d 437 (1985); see also

Middleton v. Middleton, 259 Ga. 41, 376 S.E.2d 368 (1989).
[6]O.C.G.A. § 16-9-93(c).

Chapter 3

Stop-and-Frisk

KeyCite®: Cases and other legal materials listed in KeyCite Scope can be researched through the KeyCite service on Westlaw®. Use KeyCite to check citations for form, parallel references, prior and later history, and comprehensive citator information, including citations to other decisions and secondary materials.

---

§ 3:1   General considerations

The police have long felt the need to stop and question and search or frisk suspicious persons. Prior to *Mapp v. Ohio*[1] and the exclusionary rule, the legality of such encounters was not considered to be of great importance and there were few reported cases which addressed the constitutionality of such stops and searches or frisks.[2] However, after the *Mapp* decision in 1961 held that evidence obtained in violation of the Fourth Amendment was inadmissible in a state criminal prosecution, the valid-

---

[Section 3:1]

[1]Mapp v. Ohio, 367 U.S. 643, 81 S.Ct. 1684, 6 L.Ed.2d 1081 (1961).

[2]Generally, see Bogomoly, "State Patrol: The Decision to Stop a Citizen," 12 Crim. L. Bull. 509 (1976). The author concludes that these early cases generally held that mere suspicion was not sufficient to authorize a search or frisk and that the officer had to have probable cause to believe that an offense had been or was being committed.

ity of these searches or frisks began to receive much more attention.[3] Also, the trend toward invalidating vagrancy, loitering, and disorderly conduct statutes[4] further limited the right of officers to search or frisk suspicious persons.

In law enforcement parlance, a "stop" means "a temporary investigative detention of an individual short of an arrest." A "frisk" means the pat-down of an individual's outer clothing to determine whether he is carrying a weapon; a procedure not amounting to a full search.[5] Thus, a stop and frisk represents two distinct occurrences. Even though the facts justify a stop, this does not mean that they justify a frisk. A frisk is more limited than a search incident to a valid arrest. Because both a stop and a frisk are less intrusive than a search incident to a valid arrest, they may be based on something less than probable cause. However, where the police stop a car and ask passengers to exit the vehicle, a frisk conducted pursuant to a policy or standard practice of frisking persons to ensure the officer's safety is unlawful in the absence of a "reasonable suspicion" that the person is armed.[6]

The United States Supreme Court, in *Terry v. Ohio*,[7] first considered the stop-and-frisk situation. The court concluded as follows: (1) In order to justify a stop and follow it with a frisk, the officer had to be able to point to specific and articulable facts which, taken together with reasonable inferences, judged against an objective standard, would justify a reasonable person in believing that the frisk was appropriate.[8] This action may not be justified solely by a hunch, guess, or suspicion.[9] (2) When an officer reasonably concludes that a suspicious person he is investigating at close range is armed and potentially dangerous to the officer or others, it would be unreasonable to prevent the officer from

---

[3]E.g., People v. Mickelson, 59 Cal.2d 448, 30 Cal.Rptr. 18, 380 P.2d 658 (1963); State v. Dilley, 49 N.J. 460, 231 A.2d 353 (1967).

[4]E.g., Soles v. City of Vidalia, 92 Ga. App. 839, 90 S.E.2d 249 (1955); Edelman v. California, 344 U.S. 357, 73 S.Ct. 293, 97 L.Ed. 387 (1953); Hunter v. Allen, 422 F.2d 1158 (5th Cir. 1970), judgment rev'd on other grounds, 401 U.S. 989, 91 S.Ct. 1237, 28 L.Ed.2d 528 (1971); Colten v. Kentucky, 407 U.S. 104, 92 S.Ct. 1953, 32 L.Ed.2d 584, 590 (1972).

[5]State v. Hasenbank, 425 A.2d 1330, 1332 (Me. 1981).

[6]Rogue v. State, 311 Ga. App. 421, 715 S.E.2d 814 (2011) (while pat down without reasonable suspicion that person frisked was armed subsequent consensual search of person is not prohibited).

[7]Terry v. Ohio, 392 U.S. 1, 88 S.Ct. 1868, 20 L.Ed.2d 889 (1968).

[8]Terry v. Ohio, 392 U.S. 1, 21, 88 S.Ct. 1868, 20 L.Ed.2d 889 (1968); Holder v. State, 141 Ga. App. 426, 233 S.E.2d 501 (1977).

[9]Terry v. Ohio, 392 U.S. 1, 22, 27, 88 S.Ct. 1868, 20 L.Ed.2d 889 (1968); Smith v. State, 140 Ga. App. 94, 95, 230 S.E.2d 101 (1976); Brooks v. State, 129 Ga. App. 109, 198 S.E.2d 892 (1973).

determining if he is armed and if so, to prevent him from disarming the person.[10] (3) The sole justification for a frisk is to discover weapons so as to protect the officer and others.[11] The court also pointed out that (4) a frisk is not justified by a need to seize evidence;[12] (5) the frisk, like other searches, must be strictly tied to and justified by the circumstances which initially rendered it permissible;[13] (6) the frisk must be limited to that which is necessary for the discovery of weapons which might be used to harm the officer or others nearby;[14] (7) a stop-and-frisk is not outside the protection of the Fourth Amendment;[15] (8) when a person is restrained so he cannot walk away, he has been seized;[16] (9) a frisk is a serious intrusion on the person frisked;[17] and (10) it is not necessary to have probable cause for an arrest in order to justify a stop-and-frisk.[18]

The scope of the stop-and-frisk area was further delineated in *Sibron v. New York*.[19] In this case, the officer did not have probable cause to arrest. The court concluded that he was looking for narcotics and had no reason to think Sibron was armed. However, the Court pointed out that even if there was probable cause for a limited search or pat-down of his outer clothing for weapons, there was no right to go into his pocket unless a weapon was found in the pat-down.[20]

In *Terry,* the Court emphasized that the stop was solely to obtain weapons, but in *United States v. Hensley*,[21] the United States Supreme Court pointed out that the stop could be based on an articulable suspicion that the person stopped was wanted for a completed felony. See § 3:7, infra, on a report of a crime justifying a stop.

---

[10]Terry v. Ohio, 392 U.S. 1, 24, 88 S.Ct. 1868, 20 L.Ed.2d 889 (1968); Smith v. State, 139 Ga. App. 129, 131, 227 S.E.2d 911 (1976).

[11]Terry v. Ohio, 392 U.S. 1, 29, 88 S.Ct. 1868, 20 L.Ed.2d 889 (1968); Sowers v. State, 146 Ga. App. 701, 702, 247 S.E.2d 225 (1978).

[12]Terry v. Ohio, 392 U.S. 1, 29, 88 S.Ct. 1868, 20 L.Ed.2d 889 (1968).

[13]Terry v. Ohio, 392 U.S. 1, 19, 88 S.Ct. 1868, 20 L.Ed.2d 889 (1968).

[14]Terry v. Ohio, 392 U.S. 1, 26, 88 S.Ct. 1868, 20 L.Ed.2d 889 (1968). *Terry* also points out that the frisk "may realistically be characterized as something less than a 'full' search."

[15]Terry v. Ohio, 392 U.S. 1, 16, 88 S.Ct. 1868, 20 L.Ed.2d 889 (1968).

[16]Terry v. Ohio, 392 U.S. 1, 16, 88 S.Ct. 1868, 20 L.Ed.2d 889 (1968) (quoted with approval in Kelly v. State, 129 Ga. App. 131, 133, 198 S.E.2d 910 (1973)).

[17]Terry v. Ohio, 392 U.S. 1, 17, 88 S.Ct. 1868, 20 L.Ed.2d 889 (1968).

[18]Terry v. Ohio, 392 U.S. 1, 26, 88 S.Ct. 1868, 20 L.Ed.2d 889 (1968).

[19]Sibron v. New York, 392 U.S. 40, 88 S.Ct. 1889, 20 L.Ed.2d 917 (1968).

[20]The remainder of the material in this chapter is taken largely from Daniel, "Stop and Frisk," 17 Ga. St. B. J. 6 (August 1980).

[21]United States v. Hensley, 469 U.S. 221, 105 S.Ct. 675, 83 L.Ed.2d 604 (1985).

In *Michigan v. Chesternut,*[22] the United States Supreme Court held that an "investigatory pursuit" does not violate the Fourth Amendment unless a person has been "seized." Officers "can be said to have seized an individual 'only if, in view of all of the circumstances surrounding the incident, a reasonable person would have believed that he was not free to leave.' "

In *Pennsylvania v. Mimms,*[23] two officers saw the defendant driving an automobile with an expired license plate. The defendant was stopped for the purpose of being issued a traffic summons. He was ordered to get out of the car. When he did, the officer noticed a large bulge under his jacket. The defendant was then frisked and a .38 revolver was found in his waistband. Later he was indicted for carrying a concealed weapon. The court first found that the order to get out of the car after the driver had been detained, was reasonable and therefore permissible under the Fourth Amendment. The court then ruled that the frisk was proper because the officer reasonably concluded that the person whom he legitimately stopped might be armed and presently dangerous. *Mimms* holds that when an officer observes a traffic violation and subsequently issues a citation, the officer may have the driver step out of the car. A number of cases have considered whether the right to have the driver exit the car automatically extends the right of an officer to have passengers in the stopped vehicle step out of the vehicle. This question was answered affirmatively in the 1997 opinion of *Maryland v. Wilson,*[24] which held that "an officer making a traffic stop may order passengers to get out of the car pending completion of the stop." In addition, where the officer has reason to suspect in the context of a traffic stop that a passenger is armed and dangerous, the passenger may be frisked.[25]

In 1979, the Court decided *Ybarra v. Illinois.*[26] In this case, the defendant, Ybarra, was a bar patron at the time of the execution of a search warrant authorizing the search of the bar and one named employee for narcotics and related items. Ybarra was also searched and heroin was found. The court held that it was error to overrule the defendant's motion to suppress. The court found that the officer had no articulable suspicion justifying a weapon

---

[22]Michigan v. Chesternut, 486 U.S. 567, 108 S.Ct. 1975, 100 L.Ed.2d 565 (1988).

[23]Pennsylvania v. Mimms, 434 U.S. 106, 98 S.Ct. 330, 54 L.Ed.2d 331 (1977).

[24]Maryland v. Wilson, 519 U.S. 408, 117 S.Ct. 882, 137 L.Ed.2d 41 (1997).

[25]Arizona v. Johnson, 555 U.S. 323, 129 S.Ct. 781, 172 L.Ed.2d 694 (2009). See Molina v. State, 304 Ga. App. 93, 695 S.E.2d 656 (2010) (in the absence of a reasonable suspicion that the person stopped is armed and dangerous, the police may not proceed to a frisk).

[26]Ybarra v. Illinois, 444 U.S. 85, 100 S.Ct. 338, 62 L.Ed.2d 238 (1979).

frisk, that the Fourth Amendment does not permit a pat down of a person for weapons unless the officer has a reasonable belief that the person is armed and dangerous, and that *Terry* does not permit a search for anything other than weapons. The court later pointed out that the search "was invalid because the police had no reason to believe . . . [Ybarra] had any special connection with the premises, and the police had no other basis for suspecting that he was armed or in possession of contraband."[27] The 1998 Georgia Court of Appeals case of *Clark v. State*[28] is very much like *Ybarra* in its facts and results.

However, in *Michigan v. Summers,*[29] the Court considered an incident involving the execution of a warrant to search a house for narcotics. As the officers approached the house they met the defendant, who was leaving. They requested his assistance in gaining entrance to the house and detained him until they had searched the premises. After learning that the defendant owned the house and after discovering narcotics in the house, the defendant was arrested and searched. Heroin was discovered in his coat pocket. The court said that if there is probable cause to search a citizen's residence for contraband, "it is constitutionally reasonable to require that citizen to remain while officers of the law execute a valid warrant to search his home."

"An investigating officer need not have [an] 'articulable suspicion' before he can approach a stopped vehicle and talk with the driver."[30] But see § 3:9, infra, on roadblocks.

In *Dunaway v. New York,*[31] the defendant was implicated in a murder. The officers did not have "enough information to get a warrant" for the defendant's arrest, but he was "picked up" and brought in. Although the defendant was told he was not under arrest, he would have been physically restrained if he attempted to leave. He was placed in an interrogation room where he waived counsel, made statements and drew sketches that incriminated him. The court held that the defendant's statements and sketches should have been suppressed since the officers did not have probable cause to arrest the defendant and since the acts of taking the defendant into custody and transporting him to the police station could not be regarded as a mere stop approved in *Terry*.

---

[27]Michigan v. Summers, 452 U.S. 692, 696, 101 S.Ct. 2587, 69 L.Ed.2d 340 (1981), n. 4.

[28]Clark v. State, 235 Ga. App. 569, 571 (2), 510 S.E.2d 319 (1998).

[29]Michigan v. Summers, 452 U.S. 692, 101 S.Ct. 2587, 2595, 69 L.Ed.2d 340, 351 (1981) (quoting Payton v. New York, 445 U.S. 573, 602-603, 100 S.Ct. 1371, 63 L.Ed.2d 639 (1980)); Garmon v. State, 271 Ga. 673, 524 S.E.2d 211 (1999).

[30]Molaro v. State, 236 Ga. App. 35, 37 (1), 510 S.E.2d 886 (1999).

[31]Dunaway v. New York, 442 U.S. 200, 99 S.Ct. 2248, 60 L.Ed.2d 824 (1979); State v. Freeman, 59 N.C.App. 84, 295 S.E.2d 619 (1982).

In a plurality opinion, the Court in *United States v. Mendenhall*[32] expanded the scope of frisks under *Terry*. In *Mendenhall*, Drug Enforcement Agency officers approached the defendant as she exited the plane. The officers identified themselves and asked to see her identification and plane ticket. They returned both the identification and ticket to the defendant and only then did they ask her to come with them to a nearby airport office. She consented to go to the office and once there, she further consented to a search of her person. The search revealed heroin. The court established that a person is "seized" only if, in view of all the circumstances, "a reasonable person would have believed that he was not free to leave."[33] On these facts, the Court held that there was no objective reason for the defendant to believe that she was not free to walk away.[34]

The Eleventh Circuit in *United States v. Rodriguez-Franco*[35] held that a stop to obtain identification was not a seizure involving the Fourth Amendment.

In *Immigration and Naturalization Service v. Delgado,*[36] the Court considered "factory surveys" conducted pursuant to a warrant in search of illegal aliens. Each "survey" lasted one to two hours. Agents were posted at factory exits while others asked employees one to three questions relating to citizenship. Four employees were questioned and their union filed an action challenging the constitutionality of the surveys and seeking injunctive relief. The court concluded that the "survey" did not result in the seizure of the entire work force, and the individuals were not seized when they were questioned while at work. In *Florida v. Bostick,*[37] the United States Supreme Court considered a case which it found to be indistinguishable from *Delgado*. In *Bostick,* the question was whether officers without an articulable

---

[32]United States v. Mendenhall, 446 U.S. 544, 100 S.Ct. 1870, 64 L.Ed.2d 497 (1980). The *Terry* "stop-and-frisk" doctrine was established in the limited context where a police officer has a reasonable, articulable suspicion that a person is armed and dangerous; thus, the pat down of exterior clothing was limited to check for weapons. However, in Mendenhall, the Court expanded the scope of a frisk to allow officers to search for narcotics. See also United States v. Cortez, 449 U.S. 411, 101 S.Ct. 690, 66 L.Ed.2d 621 (1981), discussed in § 3:2, infra.

[33]United States v. Mendenhall, 446 U.S. 544, 100 S.Ct. 1870, 64 L.Ed.2d 497 (1980).

[34]Terry v. Ohio, 392 U.S. 1, 34, 88 S.Ct. 1868, 20 L.Ed.2d 889 (1968). Concurring in *Terry*, Justice White noted that if a person chooses to walk away during a *Terry* "stop" this alone does not provide a police officer with probable cause to arrest that person, "although it may alert the officer to the need for continued observation."

[35]United States v. Rodriguez-Franco, 749 F.2d 1555 (11th Cir. 1985).

[36]Immigration and Naturalization Service v. Delgado, 466 U.S. 210, 104 S.Ct. 1758, 80 L.Ed.2d 247 (1984).

[37]Florida v. Bostick, 501 U.S. 429, 111 S.Ct. 2382, 115 L.Ed.2d 389 (1991) (emphasis added).

suspicion could board a bus at a scheduled stop and ask passengers for permission to search their baggage. The court held that the officers' practice of "working busses" is not per se unconstitutional. To determine if such an encounter constitutes a seizure, the Court modified *Mendenhall* in holding that "a court must consider all the circumstances . . . to determine whether the police conduct would have communicated to a reasonable person that the person *was not free to decline* the officers' requests or otherwise terminate the encounter. That rule applies to encounters that take place on a city street or in an airport lobby, and it applies equally to encounters on a bus."

The Supreme Court reversed the 11th Circuit Court of Appeals in *United States v. Drayton*,[38] holding that the Fourth Amendment did not require police officers to advise bus passengers that they did not have to answer questions put to them as part of a routine drug interdiction effort. In the absence of any coercive police conduct, the court found that the cooperation of passengers was voluntary and consensual.

This reasoning was directly applied to traffic stops in *Brendlin v. California*.[39] There, the United States Supreme Court addressed the question of whether a vehicle's passengers are seized for Fourth Amendment purposes and, thus, may challenge the stop's constitutionality. The Court held that, though a passenger, Brendlin was seized from the moment the car came to a halt because a reasonable person in his position would not feel "free to 'terminate the encounter' between the police and himself."[40] However, the court expressly noted that "the relationship between driver and passenger is not the same in a common carrier as it is in a private vehicle, and the expectations of police officers and passengers differ accordingly."[41] In *Solano-Rodriquez v. State*,[42] the Georgia Court of Appeals applying the standard set out in *Florida v. Bostick*[43] held that the proper test for determining when a seizure occurs on a bus is whether the passenger feels free to decline to answer an officer's questions rather than whether the passenger feels free to leave the bus since the passenger most likely has no desire to leave the bus.

---

[38]United States v. Drayton, 536 U.S. 194, 122 S.Ct. 2105, 153 L.Ed.2d 242 (2002).

[39]Brendlin v. California, 551 U.S. 249, 127 S. Ct. 2400, 168 L. Ed. 2d 132 (2007).

[40]Brendlin v. California, 551 U.S. 249, 127 S. Ct. 2400, 168 L. Ed. 2d 132 (2007). This is the so-called "modified *Mendenhall* test." See Florida v. Bostick, 501 U.S. 429, 435-36, 111 S.

Ct. 2382, 115 L. Ed. 2d 389 (1991); Cf. U.S. v. Mendenhall, 446 U.S. 544, 100 S. Ct. 1870, 64 L. Ed. 2d 497 (1980).

[41]Brendlin v. California, 551 U.S. 249, 127 S.Ct. 2400, 2410, 168 L.Ed.2d 132 (2007).

[42]Solano-Rodriquez v. State, 295 Ga. App. 896 (1), 673 S.E.2d 351 (2009).

[43]Florida v. Bostick, 501 U.S. 429, 111 S.Ct. 2382, 115 L.Ed.2d 389 (1991).

See 6A C.J.S. Arrest §§ 38 et seq. See also Annotation, "Law Enforcement Officer's Authority Under Federal Constitution's Fourth Amendment, to Stop and Briefly Detain, and to Conduct Limited Protective Search Of or 'Frisk,' for Investigative Purposes, Person Suspected of Criminal Activity—Supreme Court Cases," 104 L.Ed.2d 1046 (1991).

§ 3:2   Facts justifying the stop—General

In *Terry v. Ohio,*[1] the Court observed that "whenever a police officer accosts an individual and restrains his freedom to walk away he has 'seized' that person," but the Court did not discuss the exact point at which Terry was seized. The court said, however, in footnote number 16 on page 19 of the opinion, that all communications between an officer and a citizen do not involve a "seizure." "Only when the officer, by means of physical force or show of authority, has in some way restrained the liberty of a citizen may we conclude that a 'seizure' has occurred." Thus, in *Edwards v. State,*[2] the Georgia Supreme Court held that there is "no seizure . . . when an individual voluntarily accompanies police in a spirit of cooperation."

It appears, therefore, that under some circumstances an officer may approach a person and ask him some questions even if the officer has no articulable suspicion.[3] As Justice Harlan observed in his concurring opinion in *Terry,* a police officer has "the liberty (again, possessed by every citizen) to address questions to other

---

[Section 3:2]

[1]Terry v. Ohio, 392 U.S. 1, 16, 88 S.Ct. 1868, 20 L.Ed.2d 889 (1968). See § 4:49, infra, on search of vehicle incident to a valid arrest.

    In McShan v. State, 155 Ga. App. 518, 519, 271 S.E.2d 659 (1980), the court quoted from Justice Stewart's opinion in United States v. Mendenhall, 446 U.S. 544, 100 S.Ct. 1870, 64 L.Ed.2d 497, 500 (1980), reh. denied, 448 U.S. 908, 100 S.Ct. 3051, 65 L.Ed.2d 1138 (1980), as follows: "We conclude that a person has been 'seized' within the meaning of the Fourth Amendment only if, in view of all of the circumstances surrounding the incident, a reasonable person would have believed that he was not free to leave. Examples of circumstances that might indicate a seizure, even where the person did not attempt to leave, would be the threatening presence of several officers, the display of a weapon by an officer, some physical touching of the person of the citizen, or the use of language or tone of voice indicating that compliance with the officer's request might be compelled. [Cits.] In the absence of some such evidence, otherwise inoffensive contact between a member of the public and the police cannot, as a matter of law, amount to a seizure of that person." See § 3:3, infra, on when a stop constitutes a seizure.

    See Preiser, "Confrontations Initiated by the Police on Less Than Probable Cause," 45 Albany L. R. 57 (1980).

[2]Edwards v. State, 264 Ga. 615, 616 (2), 449 S.E.2d 516 (1994). Cf. Britton v. State, 220 Ga. App. 120, 469 S.E.2d 272 (1996).

[3]King v. State, 161 Ga. App. 382 (1), 288 S.E.2d 644 (1982).

persons, for ordinarily the person addressed has an equal right to ignore his interrogator and walk away." Justice White, also concurring in *Terry,* said there "is nothing in the Constitution which prevents a policeman from addressing questions to anyone on the streets."[4] It has been held that an officer does not seize a passenger deplaning when the officer displays his credentials and asks permission of the passenger to talk with him.[5]

In *Clark v. State,*[6] the court pointed out that "merely refusing to identify oneself to a police officer is not a crime"; however, "one may commit obstruction when knowingly and willfully hindering an officer in investigating an offense committed by another." Thus, refusal to provide identification can be an obstruction.

In *State v. Dukes,*[7] the court found that, although the defendant's sudden flight arguably gave officers articulable suspicion to detain him, such circumstances only gave the right to conduct a brief investigative stop, not to arrest for obstruction.

In Georgia it has been recognized that there are, "at least theoretically, three tiers of police-citizen encounters: (1) communication between police and citizens involving no coercion or detention and therefore without the compass of the Fourth Amendment, (2) brief 'seizures' that must be supported by reasonable suspicion, and (3) full-scale arrests that must be supported by probable cause."[8] See § 2:2, supra, and § 4:26, infra, on arrests. See § 3:12, infra, on when a stop becomes an arrest.

In *Stokes v. State,*[9] the court pointed out that it has "recognized a distinction between an officer's 'appropriately deferential' request for cooperation and a demand rising to the level of a stop. . . . [A]n officer's approach to a stopped vehicle and inquiry into the situation is not a 'stop' or 'seizure' but rather 'clearly falls within the realm of the first type of police-citizen encounter.' " Thus, police officers may "approach a citizen, ask for identification, ask him to roll down a window or step out of a car, and freely question him without any articulable suspicion, as long as the officers do not detain the citizen or create the impression that

---

[4]The concurring opinions referred to in the text were quoted with approval in United States v. Elmore, 595 F.2d 1036, 1041 (5th Cir. 1979), and in the opinion of Justice Stewart in the decision of United States v. Mendenhall, 446 U.S. 544, 100 S.Ct. 1870, 64 L.Ed.2d 497 (1980), in which then Justice Rehnquist joined.

[5]United States v. Collis, 699 F.2d 832 (6th Cir. 1983).

[6]Clark v. State, 243 Ga. App. 362, 365 (1), 532 S.E.2d 481 (2000).

[7]State v. Dukes, 279 Ga. App. 247, 630 S.E.2d 847 (2006).

[8]Alexander v. State, 166 Ga. App. 233, 303 S.E.2d 773 (1983).

[9]Stokes v. State, 238 Ga. App. 230, 232, 518 S.E.2d 447 (1999); State v. Folk, 238 Ga. App. 206, 207, 521 S.E.2d 194 (1999). But cf. In the Interest of M. J. H., 239 Ga. App. 894, 522 S.E.2d 491 (1999).

the citizen may not leave."[10] Other examples of a first tier police-citizen encounter would include good faith intervention by police in what they believe to constitute emergency medical situations. In this context, police observation or inquiries which lead to the discovery of evidence of criminal activity may not be subject to suppression.[11]

In *In the Interest of S. B.,*[12] the court quoted with approval from the United States Supreme Court in *Florida v. Bostick*[13] that "[m]erely approaching an individual and requesting that he give his consent for a search does *not* constitute a seizure and need *not* be supported by an articulable suspicion. [E]ven when officers have no basis for suspecting a particular individual, they may generally ask questions of that individual . . . and request consent to search . . . as long as the police do not convey a message that compliance with their requests is required." In *State v. Willis,*[14] the court pointed out that "[e]ven when officers have no basis for suspecting a . . . [person], they may generally ask questions . . . to examine the individual's identification . . . and request consent to search. . . ." See § 3:9, infra, on consent during a roadblock and general considerations.

In the 1991 case of *California v. Hodari D.,*[15] the United States Supreme Court considered a case in which officers drove up to a group of four or five persons in a high crime area and the group panicked and fled. One of the officers followed the defendant. When the officer had almost reached the defendant, "he tossed away what appeared to be a small rock. A moment later" the officer tackled the defendant. The rock turned out to be cocaine, and a motion to suppress was filed. The court said the only issue presented was whether the defendant had been "seized" within the meaning of the Fourth Amendment at the time the defendant dropped the drugs. Writing for the majority, Justice Scalia concluded that there was no seizure until the defendant was

---

[10]Akins v. State, 266 Ga. App. 214, 216 (1), 596 S.E.2d 719 (2004) (citations omitted).

[11]See, e.g. Davidson v. State, 257 Ga. App. 260, 263(1), 570 S.E.2d 698 (2002); Childress v. State, 251 Ga. App. 873, 874 (1), 554 S.E.2d 818 (2001).

[12]In the Interest of S. B., 207 Ga. App. 60, 62, 427 S.E.2d 52 (1993).

[13]Florida v. Bostick, 501 U.S. 429, 111 S.Ct. 2382, 115 L.Ed.2d 389, 398 (1991).

[14]State v. Willis, 207 Ga. App. 76, 77, 427 S.E.2d 306 (1993).

[15]California v. Hodari D., 499 U.S. 621, 111 S.Ct. 1547, 113 L.Ed.2d 690 (1991). See Brendlin v. California, 551 U.S. 249, 254, 127 S. Ct. 2400, 168 L. Ed. 2d 132 (2007) ("A police officer may make a seizure by a show of authority and without the use of physical force, but *there is no seizure without actual submission* . . . " (emphasis added). See also, Menuel v. City of Atlanta, 25 F.3d 990 (11th Cir. 1994). Cf. Watson v. State, 247 Ga. App. 498, 499, 544 S.E.2d 469 (2001); Hunt v. State, 205 Ga. App. 490, 423 S.E.2d 24 (1992). Accord, Smith v. State, 217 Ga. App. 680 (2), 458 S.E.2d 704 (1995).

tackled; until he was physically stopped by the officer, the defendant had not yielded to the officer's show of authority. Therefore, the cocaine was not abandoned as a result of a seizure, and the motion to suppress was properly denied. See § 2:2, supra, on what constitutes an arrest.

A citizen who is walking away from an officer, however, may not be "detained" by the officer, and such a citizen is not obligated to answer questions,[16] unless the officer has a specific reasonable articulable suspicion that the citizen is involved in criminal conduct.[17] The standard that is used must be an objective standard, but an officer may evaluate suspicious circumstances in the light of his own experience.[18]

Not only may an officer approach a suspicious person and attempt to talk with him, but in the absence of coercion the officer may ask the person to accompany him to a nearby location to be searched. If the person agrees to do so and freely and voluntarily accompanies the officer, this generally amounts to a waiver or a consent and none of the person's Fourth Amendment rights have been violated. After reaching such place, and after being fully informed that he has a right to refuse to permit a search, if the suspected person intelligently and voluntarily consents to a search of his person and bag (if he has one) and contraband is discovered in the search, it is admissible against him if he is tried for a possessory offense.[19] However, in *United States v. Place*,[20] the United States Supreme Court said that an officer has authority "to make a *forcible stop* of a person when the officer has reasonable, articulable suspicion that the person has been, is, or is about to be engaged in criminal activity."

In *United States v. Cortez*,[21] the United States Supreme Court expressly recognized the right to make an investigatory stop where there are sufficient objective manifestations "that the person stopped is, or is about to be, engaged in criminal activity." The court said:

"Based upon [the] whole picture the detaining officers must have a particularized and objective basis for suspecting the par-

[16]Brown v. Texas, 443 U.S. 47, 99 S.Ct. 2637, 61 L.Ed.2d 357 (1979).

[17]Painter v. State, 227 Ga. App. 875, 877, 490 S.E.2d 544 (1997).

[18]Terry v. Ohio, 392 U.S. 1, 88 S.Ct. 1868, 20 L.Ed.2d 889 (1968); cf. Brown v. Texas, 443 U.S. 47, 99 S.Ct. 2637, 61 L.Ed.2d 357 (1979); United States v. Cortez, 449 U.S. 411, 101 S.Ct. 690, 66 L.Ed.2d 621 (1981); Foster v. State, 208 Ga. App. 699 (1), 431

S.E.2d 400 (1993).

[19]McShan v. State, 155 Ga. App. 518, 519-20, 271 S.E.2d 659 (1980).

[20]United States v. Place, 462 U.S. 696, 103 S.Ct. 2637, 77 L.Ed.2d 110 (1983).

[21]United States v. Cortez, 449 U.S. 411, 101 S.Ct. 690, 695, 66 L.Ed.2d 621 (1981). See Herrington v. State, 221 Ga. App. 354, 471 S.E.2d 289 (1996).

ticular person stopped of criminal activity. . . . The idea that an assessment of the whole picture must yield a particularized suspicion contains two elements, each of which must be present before a stop is permissible. First, the assessment must be based upon all of the circumstances. The analysis proceeds with various objective observations, information from police reports, if such are available, and consideration of the modes or patterns of operation of certain kinds of lawbreakers. From these data, a trained officer draws inferences and makes deductions—inferences and deductions that might well elude an untrained person. . . ."

"The second element contained in the idea that an assessment of the whole picture must yield a particularized suspicion is the concept that the process just described must raise a suspicion that the particular individual being stopped is engaged in wrongdoing."

In *Cortez,* the Court also said: "An investigatory stop must be justified by some objective manifestation that the person stopped is, or is about to be, engaged in criminal activity."[22] The emphasis here is on the right of an officer to stop if he has an objective basis for suspecting the person stopped of criminal activity. In *Terry,* the emphasis seems to be that when an officer has an articulable suspicion "that criminal activity may be afoot and that the person with whom he is dealing may be armed and presently dangerous" there may be a valid "stop."[23] *Cortez* indicates that the "armed and dangerous" element is not now essential.

While *Cortez* emphasizes the right of officers to stop where there is articulable suspicion that the suspect "is engaged in wrongdoing," in *United States v. Hensley*[24] the Court pointed out that officers may stop if they have articulable suspicion that the suspect is wanted for a completed felony. See § 3:7, infra, on crime reports justifying stop.

In *Beck v. State,*[25] the Georgia Court of Appeals pointed out that in the case where one officer is acting on information provided by another, "[t]here is no requirement that the officer making the stop have all the information the original officer had about a suspect and the informant." In *State v. Pennyman*[26] the court pointed out that "[t]he 'collective knowledge' rule provides

---

[22]United States v. Cortez, 449 U.S. 411, 417, 101 S.Ct. 690, 66 L.Ed.2d 621 (1981).

[23]Terry v. Ohio, 392 U.S. 1, 30, 88 S.Ct. 1868, 20 L.Ed.2d 889 (1968).

[24]United States v. Hensley, 469 U.S. 221, 105 S.Ct. 675, 83 L.Ed.2d 604 (1985).

[25]Beck v. State, 216 Ga. App. 532, 534 (1), 455 S.E.2d 110 (1995).

[26]State v. Pennyman, 248 Ga. App. 446, 447, 545 S.E.2d 365 (2001). See Fisher v. State, 267 Ga. App. 426, 599 S.E.2d 361 (2004); Morrow v. State, 257 Ga. App. 707 (2), 572 S.E.2d 58 (2002); State v. Harris, 236 Ga. App. 525 (1), 513 S.E.2d 1 (1999).

that reasonable suspicion may exist based on the collective knowledge of the police when there is reliable communication between the officer supplying the information and the officer acting on that information instead of the arresting officer's knowledge alone. . . . [I]nformation provided by other officers as communicated in a 'be-on-the-lookout' dispatch provides the basis for reasonable and articulable suspicion to justify a stop." See § 3:7, infra, on crime reports justifying a stop.

"[I]t is well settled that police may conduct a brief investigatory stop of a vehicle if they have specific articulable facts that give rise to a reasonable suspicion of criminal conduct."[27] Until the United States Supreme Court decided *Helen v. North Carolina*,[28] a court could find that the reasonable articulable suspicion to justify an investigative stop of a vehicle could be present even in those instances where the officer "may have been mistaken either as to fact or law" on whether a criminal offense may have been committed provided the officer was acting in good faith and not arbitrarily or in a spirit of harassment.[29] In *Helen*, the Supreme Court ruled that only *objectionably reasonable* mistakes of law can give rise to the reasonable suspicion necessary to uphold a search under the Fourth Amendment. In *Harris v. State*,[30] the court noted that in those cases where there is no ambiguity about the law involved, an officer's misunderstanding of its proper application cannot be objectively reasonable. The court also noted that Georgia does not recognize a good faith exception to the exclusionary rule. The method of establishing an articulable suspicion seems to be the same as that used in determining probable cause. See sections 4:7 and 4:50, infra, on probable cause to search.

In order to justify further detention and questioning of a motorist once a routine traffic stop has ended, the officer must have a reasonable suspicion of criminal conduct. In the absence of reasonable suspicion, an officer's continued questioning and detention of the motorist becomes unlawful.[31] As the Eleventh Circuit Court of Appeals observed in *United States v. Purcell*,[32] "only unrelated questions which unreasonably prolong the detention are unlawful; detention, not questioning, is the evil at which *Terry's* prohibition is aimed. Questions which do not extend the duration

---

[27]Lancaster v. State, 261 Ga. App. 348, 350(1), 582 S.E.2d 513 (2003).

[28]Heien v. North Carolina, 135 S. Ct. 530, 190 L. Ed. 2d 475 (2014).

[29]See State v. Cartwright, 329 Ga. App. 154, 764 S.E.2d 175 (2014).

[30]Harris v. State, 344 Ga. App. 572, 810 S.E.2d 660 (2018). See

Abercrombie v. State, 343 Ga. App. 774, 808, 808 S.E.2d 245 (2017).

[31]Salmeron v. State, 280 Ga. 735, 632 S.E.2d 645 (2006).

[32]United States v. Purcell, 236 F.3d 1274, 1280 (11th Cir. 2001). See United States v. Perkins, 348 F.3d 965 (11th Cir. 2003); United States v. Boyce, 351 F.3d 1102 (11th Cir. 2003).

of the initial seizure do not exceed the scope of an otherwise constitutional traffic stop."

In *Michigan v. Summers*,[33] the United States Supreme Court said: "Although no special danger to the police is suggested by the evidence in this record, the execution of a warrant to search for narcotics is the kind of transaction that may give rise to sudden violence or frantic efforts to conceal or destroy evidence. The risk of harm to both the police and the occupants is minimized if the officers routinely exercise unquestioned command of the situation." Thus, in *Summers* the Court seems to be saying that there is a right to "stop" if the "transaction . . . may give rise to sudden violence or frantic efforts to conceal or destroy evidence." If this is true, an officer may "stop" to prevent destruction of evidence—this is an idea which is completely contrary to *Terry*.

In *Brown v. State*,[34] the court said, "Investigative stops of vehicles are analogous to *Terry*-stops . . . and are invalid if based upon only unparticularized suspicion or hunch." Any stop of a moving vehicle has been treated as a detention, and, as pointed out in *Delaware v. Prouse*,[35] an officer generally has no authority to make a stop of a vehicle unless he at least has a reasonable articulable suspicion that a traffic violation has occurred or that an occupant is otherwise subject to seizure,[36] and such a stop constitutes a seizure of its occupants.[37] See text discussing *Delaware v. Prouse* et seq., § 3:9, infra, on roadblocks. See § 3:7, infra, on stop based on a telephone tip. In the case of a parked automobile it has been held that officers have no authority to approach the

---

[33]Michigan v. Summers, 452 U.S. 692, 702, 101 S.Ct. 2587, 69 L.Ed.2d 340 (1981). See § 3:1, n. 29, supra, for a discussion of Summers.

[34]Brown v. State, 188 Ga. App. 184, 187, 372 S.E.2d 514 (1988); Jorgensen v. State, 207 Ga. App. 545, 428 S.E.2d 440 (1993).

[35]Delaware v. Prouse, 440 U.S. 648, 99 S.Ct. 1391, 59 L.Ed.2d 660 (1979). See § 4:49, infra, on warrantless searches of vehicles incident to a valid arrest and § 2:11, supra, on arrests.

[36]United States v. Brignoni-Ponce, 422 U.S. 873, 878-887, 95 S.Ct. 2574, 45 L.Ed.2d 607 (1975).

However, in United States v. Cortez, 449 U.S. 411, 101 S.Ct. 690, 66 L.Ed.2d 621, 628-629 (1981), the Court said "Terms like 'articulable reasons' and 'founded suspicion' are not self-defining; they fall short of providing clear guidance . . . . But the essence of all that has been written is that the totality of the circumstances—the whole picture—must be taken into account. Based upon that whole picture the detaining officers must have a particularized and objective basis for suspecting the particular person stopped of criminal activity." Cf. United States v. Martinez-Fuerte, 428 U.S. 543, 96 S.Ct. 3074, 49 L.Ed.2d 1116 (1976). The court held that no suspicion is required to justify stops at fixed checkpoints at the border. See also § 4:45, infra, on border searches.

[37]United States v. Morrison, 546 F.2d 319 (9th Cir. 1976); State v. Hocker, 113 Ariz. 450, 556 P.2d 784 (1976); Delaware v. Prouse, 440 U.S. 648, 661, 99 S.Ct. 1391, 59 L.Ed.2d 660 (1979) (implication).

car to order occupants to remain in the vehicle in the absence of a reasonable suspicion.[38] In *Hill v. State*[39] police stopped a vehicle driven by the defendant based upon a license plate reader (LPR) alert which indicated that the person driving the vehicle may be the subject of a warrant. An LPR can scan a license plate and quickly report whether it is registered to someone wanted by the authorities. The court held that the information provided to the police by the LPR provided reasonable articulable suspicion for the stop.

In *Montoya v. State*,[40] the court held that "[e]ven the existence of an improper motivation on the part of an officer does not render a stop unreasonable. The validity of the stop depends not on the officer's actual state of mind but on an objective assessment of his actions in light of all the facts and circumstances confronting him at the time."

In *Stanford v. State*,[41] the Court of Appeals set out the standard of review for an order on a motion to suppress as follows:

> First, when a motion to suppress is heard by the trial judge, that judge sits as the trier of facts. The trial judge hears the evidence, and his findings based upon conflicting evidence are analogous to the verdict of a jury and should not be disturbed by a reviewing court if there is any evidence to support it. Second, the trial court's decision with regard to the questions of fact and credibility must be accepted unless clearly erroneous. Third, the reviewing court must construe the evidence most favorably to the upholding of the trial court's finding and judgment. (Cites omitted.)

Applying this standard in *State v. Jones*,[42] the court affirmed the trial court's order granting a motion to suppress where the defendant was stopped by a police officer investigating the defendant's 30 day drive-out tag. After reviewing documents supplied by defendant, which demonstrated that the tag was in or-

---

[38]People v. Harrison, 57 N.Y.2d 470, 457 N.Y.S.2d 199, 443 N.E.2d 447 (1982).

[39]Hill v. State, 321 Ga. App. 817, 743 S.E.2d 489 (2013). See Hernandez-Lopez v. State, 319 Ga. App. 662, 738 S.E.2d 116 (2013). But see Rodriguez v. State, 295 Ga. 362, 761 S.E.2d 19 (2014) (Supreme Court declined to review issue of whether an LPR can provide articulable suspicion for a stop).

[40]Montoya v. State, 232 Ga. App. 24, 25 (1), 499 S.E.2d 680 (1998).

[41]Stanford v. State, 251 Ga. App. 87, 88-89(1), 553 S.E.2d 622 (2001).

See State v. Palmer, 285 Ga. 75, 78, 673 S.E.2d 237 (2009), citing Petty v. State, 283 Ga. 268, 269(2), 658 S.E.2d 599 (2008) ("where . . . the facts are not in dispute and no findings were made by the trial court, the appellate courts owe no deference to the trial court's ruling and the standard of review is de novo").

[42]State v. Jones, 252 Ga. App. 404, 407(1), 556 S.E.2d 495 (2001). See Ward v. State, 277 Ga. App. 790, 793, 627 S.E.2d 862 (2006), where court observed "consent cannot validate a search if the consent is the product of a wrongful detention."

der, the officer detained the defendant with further questions while retaining the defendant's license. The officer requested permission to search the defendant's vehicle, which was given. Suppressing the cocaine found during the search, the trial court determined that the officer's continued detention and questioning of the defendant after having been provided adequate proof regarding the defendant's tag was unreasonable.

In *Brooks v. State*,[43] the court said, "Brooks and a woman companion, driving along a U.S. highway in a pickup truck at about 2:30 a.m. were observed by a sheriff and his deputy to turn onto a side road leading into a woods. They followed the car for some distance, then flashed their top light and brought it to a stop. The sheriff and the defendant got out of their respective vehicles and in the illumination of the headlights the defendant was observed to have a plastic bag sticking out of his shirt pocket. . . ." The court held that there was no articulable suspicion justifying the stop and reversed the denial of the motion to suppress.

The stop must be a "brief stop." It has been said, if not sustained, that "indeed, it is the transitory nature of the stop that justifies the elimination of the probable cause requirement."[44] In applying this standard, the Georgia Court of Appeals has said "it tortures the English language to say" a 40-minute stop is a brief stop or momentary detention.[45] In *Schmidt v. State*,[46] the court held that a 30-minute detention constituted an arrest. On the other hand, in *Sprauve v. State*,[47] the same court held that a 30-minute stop until officers could get a drug dog was not excessive. In *United States v. Sharpe*,[48] the United States Supreme Court said that in "assessing whether a detention is too long in duration to be justified as an investigative stop, we consider it appropriate to examine whether the police diligently

---

[43]Brooks v. State, 129 Ga. App. 109, 198 S.E.2d 892 (1973).

[44]Sharpe v. United States, 660 F.2d 967, 970 (4th Cir. 1981), judgment vacated U.S. v. Sharpe, 457 U.S. 1127, 102 S.Ct. 2951, 73 L.Ed.2d 1345 (1982). In Sharpe, the Court held that a stop of from 30 to 40 minutes could not be considered an investigatory stop.

[45]Radowick v. State, 145 Ga. App. 231, 238-239, 244 S.E.2d 346, 353 (1978). In United States v. Chamberlin, 644 F.2d 1262 (9th Cir. 1980), the court held that the detention of a defendant for 20 minutes was an arrest and not a *Terry* stop.

[46]Schmidt v. State, 188 Ga. App. 85, 87, 372 S.E.2d 440 (1988).

[47]Sprauve v. State, 229 Ga. App. 478, 494 S.E.2d 294 (1997). Cf. Montero v. State, 245 Ga. App. 181, 182, 537 S.E.2d 429 (2000). In Hickman v. State, 279 Ga. App. 558, 631 S.E.2d 778 (2006), the Court of Appeals held that a fifteen minute stop was not unreasonable.

[48]United States v. Sharpe, 470 U.S. 675, 105 S.Ct. 1568, 84 L.Ed.2d 605 (1985). Accord, Buck v. State, 239 Ga. App. 828, 830, 522 S.E.2d 252 (1999). In Buck, the court affirmed the trial court, finding that under the circumstances of the case, a stop of one hour was not unreasonable.

pursued a means of investigation that was likely to confirm or dispel their suspicions quickly, during which time it was necessary to detain the defendant . . . . A court making this assessment should take care to consider whether the police are acting in a swiftly developing situation, and in such cases the court should not indulge in unrealistic second-guessing . . . . The question is not simply whether some other alternative was available, but whether the police acted unreasonably in failing to recognize or pursue it." In *United States v. Roper*,[49] the Eleventh Circuit said, "The distinction between an arrest and an investigatory stop depends upon the nature and degree of the intrusion under all the facts of the particular encounter." See § 3:12, infra, on distinction between stop and arrest.

In *Terry,* the officer thought Terry and his companions were preparing for an armed robbery and the Court discussed a balancing of the interest of a suspected person and the public. However, in *Dunaway v. New York*,[50] the Supreme Court rejected the concept of such a sliding scale where a person was held without probable cause for purposes of investigating an armed robbery and murder.

What situations justify an officer in stopping an individual? As it would be expected, this question may arise in an infinite variety of situations.[51] Also, it must be kept in mind that the existence of one or two suspicious circumstances may not justify a stop, but the existence of several suspicious circumstances may justify a stop. Some of the more common circumstances that have been considered by the courts in determining the validity of a stop are discussed in the following sections of this chapter.

In *Navicky v. State*,[52] the court held that when an officer sees a traffic offense occur, a resulting traffic stop does not violate the Fourth Amendment even if the officer has an ulterior motive in making the stop.

In *Brantley v. State*,[53] the Georgia Court of Appeals followed

---

[49]United States v. Roper, 702 F.2d 984 (11th Cir. 1983). The Eleventh Circuit stated in dicta: "Where at its inception a traffic stop is a valid one for a violation of the law, we doubt that a resultant seizure of no more than seventeen minutes can ever be unconstitutional on account of its durations; the detention is too short." U.S. v. Hernandez, 418 F.3d 1206, 1212 n.7 (11th Cir. 2005).

[50]Dunaway v. New York, 442 U.S. 200, 208-214, 99 S.Ct. 2248, 60 L.Ed.2d 824 (1979).

[51]In Terry v. Ohio, 392 U.S. 1, 30, 88 S.Ct. 1868, 20 L.Ed.2d 889 (1968), the Court said, "Each case of this sort will, of course, have to be decided on its own facts."

[52]Navicky v. State, 245 Ga. App. 284, 537 S.E.2d 740 (2000). See Thompson v. State, 289 Ga. App. 661, 658 S.E.2d 122 (2007).

[53]Brantley v. State, 226 Ga. App. 872 (1), 487 S.E.2d 412 (1997). Accord, Willis v. State, 234 Ga. App. 135 (1),

the United States Supreme Court in *Whren v. United States,*[54] in holding that from a federal constitutional standpoint, "when an officer sees a traffic offense occur, a resulting traffic stop does not violate the Fourth Amendment even if the officer has ulterior motives in initiating the stop, and even if a reasonable officer would not have made the stop under the same circumstances." In *Hines v. State,*[55] the court pointed out that it is inconsequential whether or not a driver is ultimately cited for a traffic violation. See §§ 3:3 and 4:26, infra, on traffic offense justifying stop.

In *Forsman v. State,*[56] the court pointed out that the stop of a vehicle is authorized if the officer observes a traffic offense. The "failure to issue a citation or even an acquittal on an underlying traffic offense is of no consequence in determining the officer's [articulable suspicion necessary] to stop the vehicle. . . ."

In *Michigan v. DeFillippo,*[57] the United States Supreme Court upheld a stop where an officer stopped a person, in good faith, pursuant to a city ordinance authorizing such a stop if the officer had reasonable cause to believe the suspect's behavior warrants further investigation. After the stop, but before a ruling on a motion to suppress, the ordinance had been held unconstitutional. See *Illinois v. Krull,* discussed in § 4:46, infra.

§ 3:3   Facts justifying the stop—Appearance

It has been held that an officer seeing a man with a bulge under his shirt near the scene of a homicide may stop him.[1] The observance of a defendant, apparently with a weapon in his hand, standing behind a car in a parking lot (apparently at night) was found to justify a stop.[2] In another case, however, where police obtained information about 1:30 a.m. that two persons in a restaurant were talking loud and might cause a disturbance and

---

505 S.E.2d 570 (1998).

[54]Whren v. United States, 517 U.S. 806, 116 S.Ct. 1769, 135 L.Ed.2d 89 (1996). Accord, Smith v. State, 240 Ga. App. 150, 151(1), 522 S.E.2d 744 (1999). See also Devenpeck v. Alford, 543 U.S. 146, 125 S. Ct. 588, 160 L. Ed. 2d 537 (2004), where the U.S. Supreme Court declined to adopt the "closely related offense" rule, which would have required an arrest supported by probable cause to be "closely related" to the officer's expressed subjective reason for making the arrest.

[55]Hines v. State, 214 Ga. App. 476, 478, 448 S.E.2d 226 (1994); Accord, State v. Long, 239 Ga. App. 463,

465, 521 S.E.2d 401 (1999); Allenbrand v. State, 217 Ga. App. 609, 610(1), 458 S.E.2d 382 (1995).

[56]Forsman v. State, 239 Ga. App. 612, 613(5), 521 S.E.2d 410 (1999).

[57]Michigan v. DeFillippo, 443 U.S. 31, 99 S.Ct. 2627, 61 L.Ed.2d 343 (1979); see also Ciak v. State, 278 Ga. 27, 597 S.E.2d 392 (2004).

[Section 3:3]

[1]Alexander v. State, 225 Ga. 358, 360 (4), 168 S.E.2d 315 (1969). Cf. Edwards v. State, 165 Ga. App. 527, 301 S.E.2d 693 (1983).

[2]Keating v. State, 141 Ga. App. 377, 378, 233 S.E.2d 456 (1977).

that one of them might be intoxicated, officers were held to have
no right to stop two young, "hippy-looking" men who were simply
walking down a sidewalk some five blocks from the restaurant.[3]

In *State v. Williams,*[4] the appellate court affirmed the granting
of a motion to suppress where a patrolling officer observed four
men during the morning standing on a curb near a housing
project. No illegal or suspicious activity was seen. The officer
testified his attention was drawn to them "as curb areas are
popular locations for drug sales and the area around the housing
project was known for drug activity." However, in *State v. Banks,*[5]
the court held that a stop was not justified by the "fact that a
black man is standing [alone] next to an apartment building with
his hand in his pocket at a reasonable hour. . . ."

In *State v. Kwiatkowski,*[6] the appellate court affirmed the trial
court in granting a motion to suppress evidence of marijuana
found in a car. The case turned on the question of the validity of
the "stop." Officers saw a car in a Department of Transportation
parking lot in a "high drug area" with an out-of-state tag. The
driver had a driver's license from still another state, one of the
occupants seemed nervous, and they denied a request to search.

In *Brooks v. State,*[7] however, the court held that an officer had
no right to stop the driver of a pickup and his companion, where
the pickup was being properly driven along a highway and the
driver turned into a side road leading into the woods.

In *State v. Dubose,*[8] officers were at a bus stop looking for a
suspect in a murder which had occurred 24 hours earlier at the
same bus stop. The men appeared to be gambling and drinking
beer and wine. The court held that the officers had a right to approach the group, ask for identification and frisk the men for
weapons. The men appeared to be engaged in criminal behavior
and the officers conducted the pat-down search for their own
protection.

An officer was held to be entitled to stop a van that was being
driven slowly at 1:30 a.m. through the parking lot of a school
when he knew that a nearby school had been burglarized numerous times.[9] A lookout for a described car with a specified tag

---

[3]Holtzendorf v. State, 125 Ga.
App. 747, 188 S.E.2d 879 (1972).

[4]State v. Williams, 226 Ga. App.
346, 486 S.E.2d 637 (1997).

[5]State v. Banks, 223 Ga. App.
838, 479 S.E.2d 168 (1996).

[6]State v. Kwiatkowski, 238 Ga.
App. 390, 519 S.E.2d 43 (1999).

[7]Brooks v. State, 129 Ga. App.
109, 198 S.E.2d 892 (1973).

[8]State v. Dubose, 161 Ga. App.
144, 291 S.E.2d 39 (1982).

[9]State v. Carter, 240 Ga. 518, 242
S.E.2d 28 (1978). Cf. McQueen v. State,
184 Ga. App. 630, 362 S.E.2d 436
(1987).

number justifies a stop of such car, even a number of miles away.[10] See § 3:7, infra, on identification of auto used in the commission of a crime.

Although later overruled, the court in *Watson v. State*,[11] the court held that an investigative stop was justified where the defendant was in a car having a "drive-out tag rather than a metal license tag" in view of the officer's "knowledge that many cars with drive-out tags turned out to have been stolen."

"[M]erely observing a can of beer in the hand of one who is otherwise driving a car or operating a boat in a safe manner does, in and of itself, constitute an articulable suspicion that a violation of . . . [the law] may be occurring so as to authorize a brief investigatory stop."[12] Moreover, in *Darby v. State*,[13] the trial court was affirmed in ruling that an officer's stop was not pretextual when he pulled the vehicle over to determine whether the crack in the "windshield . . . [had] a starburst or webbing effect" (made unlawful pursuant to O.C.G.A. § 40-8-73(e)).

In *State v. Burns*,[14] the court affirmed the trial court in granting a motion to suppress. The officer had a "be on the lookout" alert for an older, yellow Monte Carlo occupied by two men, one believed to be a white man that had been involved in a purse snatching at a Lowe's store three days earlier. The officer testified that he saw an older yellow or tan Monte Carlo about two miles from the store. There appeared to be two occupants, although the windows were tinted. The court concluded the officer did not have a reasonable suspicion for the stop.

In *Whren v. United States*,[15] the United States Supreme Court held that when an officer has probable cause to believe a driver has committed a traffic offense, the officer may stop the driver even if a reasonable officer would not have stopped the motorist absent some additional law enforcement objective. In *Maxwell v. State*,[16] the court affirmed the denial of a motion to suppress where an officer followed a vehicle with the intention of finding

---

[10]Carney v. State, 145 Ga. App. 660, 244 S.E.2d 603 (1978).

[11]Watson v. State, 190 Ga. App. 696, 379 S.E.2d 817 (1989), overruled by Berry v. State, 248 Ga. App. 874, 547 S.E.2d 664 (2001).

[12]Martin v. State, 204 Ga. App. 782, 783(1), 420 S.E.2d 645 (1992).

[13]Darby v. State, 239 Ga. App. 492 (1), 521 S.E.2d 438 (1999).

[14]State v. Burns, 238 Ga. App. 683, 520 S.E.2d 39 (1999). *But see* State v. Harden, 267 Ga. App. 381, 599 S.E.2d 329 (2004) where stop was upheld after an informant notified police of an inebriated driver about to leave a bank parking lot and police immediately observed a driver leaving that lot.

[15]Whren v. United States, 517 U.S. 806, 116 S.Ct. 1769, 135 L.Ed.2d 89 (1996). Accord, State v. Owens, 239 Ga. App. 722, 723, 521 S.E.2d 860 (1999).

[16]Maxwell v. State, 249 Ga. App. 747, 748, 549 S.E.2d 534 (2001).

"a violation and stop[ping] the vehicle." See § 4:26, infra, on pretextual arrests.

In *State v. Hammang*,[17] an officer stopped a driver for driving without having her headlights on. The officer testified it was almost dark and all other cars he could see had their lights on. The driver was arrested for DUI and filed a motion to suppress based on the fact that the stop was at approximately 9:00 p.m., that sunset that day was at 8:34 p.m. and that she was not required to have her lights on until 9:04 pm. The grant of the motion to suppress was reversed by the appellate court. The court pointed out that "[i]f the officer acting in good faith believes an unlawful act has been committed, his actions are not rendered improper by a later legal determination that the defendant's actions were not a crime according to a technical legal definition or distinction determined to exist in the penal statute." See § 2:26, supra, on good faith exception to exclusionary rule.

§ 3:4 Facts justifying the stop—Airport drug courier profile

The concept of the drug courier profile does not fit precisely into this general material on stop and frisk, but it seems to be more appropriate to discuss it here than elsewhere. General airport searches are discussed in § 4:35, infra. Searches of spectators to recreational events to find contraband are discussed in § 4:37, infra. Inasmuch as the airport drug courier profile stops are somewhat different from other stops discussed in this chapter, this section attempts to discuss not only when such a stop may be made or attempted, but it also discusses what action may be taken by officers after such a stop or attempted stop.

As background information, it should be pointed out that there are "three tiers of police-citizen encounters: [1] communication between police and citizen involving no coercion or detention and therefore without the compass of the Fourth Amendment, [2] brief 'seizures' that must be supported by reasonable suspicion, and [3] full-scale arrests that must be supported by probable cause."[1]

The use of a drug profile as the basis for initiating an investigatory stop has provided considerable context for the issue of when

---

[17]State v. Hammang, 249 Ga. App. 811, 549 S.E.2d 440 (2001). See State v. Cartwright, 329 Ga. App. 154, 764 S.E.2d 175 (2014) (mistaken belief that driving car with non-functioning brake light was a violation of Georgia law does not render traffic stop unlawful unless stop was undertaken arbitrarily or as harassment).

[Section 3:4]

[1]United States v. Berry, 670 F.2d 583, 591 (5th Cir. 1982) (citing United States v. Setzer, 654 F.2d 354 (5th Cir. 1981)).

and how a seizure for purposes of the Fourth Amendment occurs.[2] In *United States v. Ballard,*[3] the United States Court of Appeals for the Fifth Circuit defined the airport drug courier profile as "a compilation of factors considered . . . to be indicative of drug activity. Included among those characteristics listed are: (a) unusual nervousness; (b) no luggage or very limited luggage; (c) possession of an unusually large amount of cash, especially when in bills of small denominations; (d) unusual itinerary, taking circuitous routes from cities known to be source cities for narcotics, such as flying to New Orleans from Los Angeles by way of St. Louis; (e) arriving from a known narcotics source city; (f) paying for an airline ticket in currency of small denominations; (g) purchasing a one-way ticket; (h) use of an alias; (i) use of a false telephone number on an airline reservation; (j) placing a telephone call immediately upon arrival at the airport; and (k) travel by a known narcotics trafficker." The same case pointed out that the elements of the profile that were said to exist in that case did not "in any significant way operate to distinguish Ballard from the general public."[4]

In *United States v. Mendenhall,*[5] the United States Supreme Court was presented with the opportunity to clarify the legality of reliance on the drug courier profile. The question remains unsettled, however, due to lack of agreement on the basis of the decision among the justices forming the majority. While the of-

---

[2]See e.g., Bothwell v. State, 250 Ga. 573, 300 S.E.2d 126 (1983).

[3]United States v. Ballard, 573 F.2d 913 (5th Cir. 1978).

In People v. Kiser, 113 Ill.App.3d 501, 69 Ill.Dec. 423, 447 N.E.2d 858 (1983), the court held that the stop was not valid where "(1) Kiser arrived on a flight from a 'source' city; (2) Kiser was the fifth or sixth passenger to deplane; (3) Kiser was casually dressed; (4) Kiser looked around cautiously as he deplaned; (5) Kiser initially walked down the terminal concourse at a 'slow pace'; (6) Kiser later 'walked at a somewhat faster pace'; (7) Kiser stopped at two water fountains, and (8) Kiser looked over his shoulder '3 or 4 times'. . . . "

[4]In United States v. Hernandez-Cuartas, 717 F.2d 552, 555 (11th Cir. 1983), the court said "Every defendant has a right to be tried based on the evidence against him or her, not on the techniques utilized by law enforcement officers in investigating criminal activity. Drug courier profile evidence is nothing more than the opinion of those officers conducting an investigation. Although this information is valuable in helping drug agents to identify potential drug couriers, we denounce the use of this type of evidence as substantive evidence of a defendant's innocence or guilt." See United States v. Espinoza-Valdez, 889 F.3d 654 (9th Cir. 2018).

For an excellent discussion of the drug courier profiles, see the dissenting opinion of Justice Smith in Bothwell v. State, 250 Ga. 573, 586-588, 300 S.E.2d 126 (1983).

[5]United States v. Mendenhall, 446 U.S. 544, 100 S.Ct. 1870, 64 L.Ed.2d 497 (1980). Cf. United States v. Smith, 649 F.2d 305 (5th Cir. 1981). See Greenberg, "Drug Courier Profiles, Mendenhall and Reid: Analyzing Police Intrusions on Less Than Probable Cause," 19 Am. C. L. Rev. 49 (1981). See § 4:35, infra, on airport searches.

ficers' conduct in stopping and questioning the defendant was found to be lawful, two justices reached this conclusion on the basis that the stop did not constitute a seizure, and three concurring justices assumed that a seizure had occurred but found it justified by a reasonable and articulable suspicion, arising in part from factors included in the profile. The concurring justices noted that reliance on the profile would not necessarily establish a reasonable suspicion, noting that each case must be decided on its own facts. The four dissenting justices found that no reasonable and articulable suspicion of criminal activity had been shown and characterized the stop in question as one based on a mere hunch.

A later decision of the United States Supreme Court, in *Reid v. Georgia*,[6] vacated a decision of the Georgia Court of Appeals[7] holding that there was a reasonable articulable suspicion justifying a stop since the suspect fell within the drug courier profile. The Supreme Court, in a brief per curiam decision with three dissents, did not discuss the "drug courier profile" generally, but the Court concluded that as a matter of law the stop was not justified where "(1) the petitioner had arrived from Fort Lauderdale, which the agent testified is a principal place of origin of cocaine sold elsewhere in the country, (2) the petitioner arrived in the early morning, when law enforcement activity is diminished, (3) he and his companion appeared to the agent to be trying to conceal the fact that they were traveling together, and (4) they apparently had no luggage other than their shoulder bags." The court pointed out that these circumstances "describe a very large category of presumably innocent travelers."

On remand, the Georgia Court of Appeals vacated its earlier decision and affirmed the trial judge's granting of the defendant's motion to suppress.[8] The Georgia Supreme Court then granted certiorari and concluded that the United States Supreme Court found "that the evidence did not as a matter of law show a basis for an articulable or reasonable suspicion sufficient to justify any seizure of Reid, even a '*Terry* stop.'"[9] The Georgia Supreme Court concluded that it must be first determined whether Reid was seized when he was first stopped. If he was seized at this point, the suppression of the trial judge must be sustained. However, the Georgia Supreme Court determined that there was no seizure in the initial encounter between the agent and Reid when it was

---

[6]Reid v. Georgia, 448 U.S. 438, 100 S.Ct. 2752, 65 L.Ed.2d 890 (1980).

[7]State v. Reid, 149 Ga. App. 685, 255 S.E.2d 71 (1979). Actually, the holding in the Georgia Court of Appeals was based on both (1) a justified stop and (2) consent or waiver.

In United States v. Robinson, 625 F.2d 1211 (5th Cir. 1980); U.S. v. Hill, 626 F.2d 429 (5th Cir. 1980).

[8]State v. Reid, 156 Ga. App. 78, 274 S.E.2d 164 (1980).

[9]State v. Reid, 247 Ga. 445, 276 S.E.2d 617 (1981).

suggested that Reid return to the terminal and he was requested to consent to a search.[10] There was nothing to suggest that a reasonable person would have felt he was not free to go. Therefore, the initial approach was not a seizure. Hence, it was error for the trial judge to find that Reid was under arrest when the agent suggested that he go back to the terminal.[11] The case was then remanded for further proceedings consistent with the opinion. Reid again applied to the United States Supreme Court for writ of certiorari, but the petition was denied.[12]

In the Eleventh Circuit's en banc decision of *United States v. Berry*,[13] the Court found no definitive guidance in the opinions of the United States Supreme Court to determine when an airport stop constitutes a seizure under the Fourth Amendment. The court stated that it would turn, therefore, to its own (Fifth Circuit's) opinions, which "though establishing a clearer line of precedent . . . form a confusing thicket. . . ."[14] The *Berry* court concluded "that airport stops of individuals by police, if of extremely restricted scope and conducted in a completely non-coercive manner, do not invoke the Fourth Amendment."[15] Of course, a seizure has occurred if " 'in view of all the circumstances surrounding the incident, a reasonable person would have believed that he was not free to leave.' "[16]Whether or not a stop amounts to a seizure may turn on the tone of voice of the officer, the blocking of a person's path or "otherwise intercepting him to prevent his progress . . . , retaining an individual's ticket for more than a minimal amount of time or by taking a ticket over to a ticket counter,"[17] whether the officers made statements that an investigation had focused on the individual, informing an individ-

---

[10]Cf. Allen v. State, 172 Ga. App. 663, 324 S.E.2d 521 (1984), in which the defendant was stopped and asked a question by an officer in plain clothes. The court held that this non-coercive stop did not amount to a seizure under the Fourth Amendment.

[11]The decision of the Georgia Supreme Court seems to be generally in accord with United States v. Moeller, 644 F.2d 518 (5th Cir. 1981). However, in Moeller the trial judge had found that the defendant consented to the search. But cf. State v. McGee, 173 Ga. App. 287, 325 S.E.2d 899 (1985), in which the suspects were regarded as having been arrested even though the treatment was similar.

[12]Reid v. Georgia, 454 U.S. 883, 102 S.Ct. 369, 70 L.Ed.2d 195 (1981).

[13]United States v. Berry, 670 F.2d 583 (5th Cir. 1982).

[14]United States v. Berry, 670 F.2d 583, 593 (5th Cir. 1982).

[15]United States v. Berry, 670 F.2d 583, 594 (5th Cir. 1982).

[16]United States v. Berry, 670 F.2d 583, 595 (5th Cir. 1982) (quoting with approval from United States v. Mendenhall, 446 U.S. 544, 100 S.Ct. 1870, 64 L.Ed.2d 497 (1980)); McAdoo v. State, 164 Ga. App. 23, 27, 295 S.E.2d 114 (1982).

[17]United States v. Berry, 670 F.2d 583, 597 (5th Cir. 1982) (citing United States v. Bowles, 625 F.2d 526 (5th Cir. 1980), and United States v. Elmore, 595 F.2d 1036 (5th Cir. 1979)). However, in United States v. Wallraff, 705 F.2d 980 (8th Cir. 1983), the court held

ual that an innocent person would cooperate with officers, and whether the passenger is informed that he is free not to consent to a search and is free to call a lawyer.

The *Berry* court pointed out that a match between the defendant and the drug courier profile characteristics does not, of itself, necessarily provide reasonable suspicion: "The profile is nothing more than an administrative tool of the police. The presence or absence of a particular characteristic on any particular profile is of *no* legal significance in the determination of reasonable suspicion."[18] In *United States v. Robinson,*[19] the court held that the Fourth Amendment aspects of *Berry* apply retroactively, at least to all convictions not final at the time the decision was rendered.

The Georgia Court of Appeals, in 1982, in *Berry v. State,*[20] a case completely distinct from *United States v. Berry,* concluded that the "drug courier profile provides sufficient articulable and reasonable suspicion to authorize a '*Terry*-type' stop." Despite the fact that the Eleventh Circuit *Berry* case stated that "[t]he presence or absence of a particular characteristic on any particular profile is of *no* legal significance in the determination of reasonable suspicion," in the four to three decision of *Bothwell v. State,*[21] the Georgia Supreme Court said that the profile characteristics are important in determining "whether there is a basis for a specific and articulable suspicion." In *Pullano v. State,*[22] the Georgia Court of Appeals said that the drug courier profile plus information that the defendant "would be returning to Florida in a few hours, his apparent nervousness, the fact that he deplaned at least three or four minutes after the last passenger left" was sufficient to justify an investigatory stop. In *Murphy v. State,*[23] the court pointed out that although the factors satisfying the drug courier profile are sufficient to justify a stop and frisk, they are still insufficient to establish probable cause for an arrest or search.

---

that retention of a passenger's ticket alone did not coerce a defendant to follow an officer.

[18]United States v. Berry, 670 F.2d 583, 600 (5th Cir. 1982).

[19]United States v. Robinson, 690 F.2d 869 (11th Cir. 1982).

[20]Berry v. State, 163 Ga. App. 705, 709(3), 294 S.E.2d 562 (1982).

[21]Bothwell v. State, 250 Ga. 573, 578, 300 S.E.2d 126 (1983). Bothwell

is discussed in § 3:13, infra.

[22]Pullano v. State, 169 Ga. App. 377, 380, 312 S.E.2d 857 (1983). Cf. Aguero v. State, 169 Ga. App. 462, 313 S.E.2d 735 (1984); Scott v. State, 170 Ga. App. 409, 410, 317 S.E.2d 282 (1984) (not based on drug courier profile but discusses facts which were found to justify a stop).

[23]Murphy v. State, 230 Ga. App. 365, 367(1), 496 S.E.2d 512 (1998).

In *Rebeiro v. State*,[24] the court said the drug courier profile plus the giving of a false name or obviously incorrect information may constitute probable cause for arrest. But in *Rebeiro* the court also said that where information given is not obviously false, probable cause does not exist.

In the 1989 case of *United States v. Sokolow*,[25] the United States Supreme Court stated that in determining the validity of a stop, "[W]e must consider 'the totality of the circumstances—the whole picture.' "In approval of the denial of the motion to suppress, the Court pointed out that while no one of the factors testified to by officers was sufficient to justify the stop, "we think taken together they amount to reasonable suspicion. . . . A court sitting to determine the existence of reasonable suspicion must require the agent to articulate the factors leading to that conclusion, but the fact that these factors may be set forth in a *'profile'* does not somehow detract from their evidentiary significance as seen by a trained agent." (Emphasis added.) However, in *Gordon v. State*,[26] the court pointed out that when a tipster provides "detailed information including [the defendant's] name, his physical description, a description of his clothing . . . , and information regarding his flight itinerary . . . [which were] independently verified . . . [it is sufficient] to justify an investigative stop."

The Fifth Circuit has held that where an individual consents to a pat-down of his outer garments and the officer pats him down in search of weapons or contraband and the officer feels a soft object in an inner pocket which he believes to be contraband, the officer may reach inside the jacket and remove the substance. The court concluded that this amounts only to a reasonable narcotics pat-down.[27]

In *Florida v. Rodriguez*,[28] the United States Supreme Court held that where plainclothes police officers approached citizens in an airport, identified themselves as police officers and asked if the citizens would step aside and talk, it was merely a "consensual encounter" and raised none of the citizens' Fourth Amendment rights. The court expressly did not decide whether continuing a

---

[24]Rebeiro v. State, 186 Ga. App. 518, 519, 367 S.E.2d 857 (1988).

[25]United States v. Sokolow, 490 U.S. 1, 109 S.Ct. 1581, 104 L.Ed.2d 1 (1989). See U.S. v. Arvizu, 534 U.S. 266, 122 S. Ct. 744, 151 L. Ed. 2d 740 (2002) where the Court expressly rejected the Ninth Circuit's analysis of each factor in isolation of the others as being contrary to a totality of the circumstances analysis.

[26]Gordon v. State, 242 Ga. App. 50, 52 (1), 528 S.E.2d 838 (2000).

[27]United States v. Smith, 649 F.2d 305, 308 (5th Cir. 1981).

[28]Florida v. Rodriguez, 469 U.S. 1, 105 S.Ct. 308, 83 L.Ed.2d 165 (1984) (per curiam). See also Voight v. State, 169 Ga. App. 653, 314 S.E.2d 487 (1984); State v. Grimmett, 54 N.C.App. 494, 284 S.E.2d 144 (1981).

discussion, which leads to a search, amounts to a "stop" requiring an articulable suspicion. However, the First Circuit has held that prolonged questioning may amount to a seizure.[29]

In *United States v. Waksal*,[30] the Eleventh Circuit held that where a suspect matching the "drug courier profile" is stopped at an airport, the stop amounts to a seizure where his ticket is obtained and retained, he is not told that he is free to leave and he is asked to accompany the officers to an office. On these facts, the defendant "could not reasonably have felt that he was free to leave."

See § 4:32, infra, on waiver and consent to a search. See § 3:13, infra, on retention of inanimate objects without probable cause. Also see § 4:35, infra, on airport searches connected with aircraft hijackings; § 4:36, infra, on searches on entering courthouses; and § 4:37, infra, on searches of persons entering places of entertainment and recreation. See Annotation, "Propriety of stop and search by law enforcement officers based solely on drug courier profile," 37 A.L.R.5th 1 (1996) and Annotation, "Admissibility of drug courier profile testimony in criminal prosecution," 69 A.L.R.5th 425 (1999).

§ 3:5 Facts justifying the stop—Ships and boats

In the 1983 United States Supreme Court case of *United States v. Villamonte-Marquez*,[1] the Court reasoned that ships are not like automobiles in terms of the Fourth Amendment. The first Congress authorized the boarding of vessels even in the absence of suspicion. "[P]ermanent checkpoints [are not] practical on waters such as these where vessels can move in any direction at any time and need not follow established 'avenues' as automobiles must do. . . . [Also the] documentation requirements with respect to vessels are significantly different than the system of vehicle

---

[29]United States v. Berryman, 717 F.2d 651 (1st Cir. 1983), on rehearing, 717 F.2d 650 (1983).

[30]United States v. Waksal, 709 F.2d 653, 654 (11th Cir. 1983). See UU.S. v. Rangel-Portillo, 586 F.3d 376 (5th Cir. 2009); U.S. v. Tapia, 912 F.2d 1367 (11th Cir. 1990).

In United States v. Thompson, 712 F.2d 1356 (11th Cir. 1983), the court held that when an officer does not suspect criminal activity and he approaches a person in a parked car in a parking lot, asks for his driver's license, retains the license and then asks the person in the vehicle to hand him an object contained therein, he

has been seized and is not free to leave. Hence, the contents of the object handed to the officer should be suppressed since he was being illegally detained when the object was handed to the officer. Compare United States v. Aponte, 662 Fed. Appx. 780 (11th Cir. 2016) (whether an encounter is consensual or coercive requires an examination of all relevant circumstances).

[Section 3:5]

[1]In United States v. Villamonte-Marquez, 462 U.S. 579, 103 S.Ct. 2573, 77 L.Ed.2d 22 (1983).

licensing. . . ." The government relied on 19 U.S.C.A. § 1581(a), which provided in part as follows: "Any officer of the customs may at any time go on board of any vessel . . . at any place in the United States . . . and examine the manifest and other documents and papers . . . and to this end may hail and stop such vessel . . . and use all necessary force to compel compliance." The court defined the issue as follows: "We are asked to decide whether the Fourth Amendment is offended when Customs officials, acting pursuant to this statute and without *any suspicion* of wrongdoing, board for inspection of documents a vessel that is located in waters providing ready access to the open sea." (Emphasis added.) The court concluded that there had not been any Fourth Amendment violation.

In *United States v. Gollwitzer*,[2] the Eleventh Circuit held that a vessel capable of ocean travel could be stopped without reasonable suspicion where the ship was traveling in the Intracoastal Waterway. A few questions may be asked by customs officials and a visual inspection from the customs ship may be made. If what the officers see and the answers they receive provide a reasonable suspicion, the vessel may be boarded. The court suggested that this rule would not apply to smaller crafts which are incapable of ocean travel. In *United States v. Kubiak*,[3] the Eleventh Circuit held that a Coast Guard has authority to stop a 31-foot Chris Craft vessel five or six miles from the coastline "in complete absence of suspicion of criminal activity." The court pointed out that the vessel was in "custom waters" and was subject to 14 U.S.C.A. § 89(a). In *United States v. Hidalgo-Gato*,[4] the same circuit, while pointing out that the territorial waters of the United States extend out three miles from the coast, concluded that there is a contiguous 12-mile zone outside the territorial waters in which a vessel may be stopped, boarded, and searched by customs officials without probable cause or suspicion so long as the search is reasonable. This zone is regarded as the functional equivalent to the border.[5]

In *United States v. One (1) 1982 28%2C International Vessel*,[6] the Eleventh Circuit upheld the search of the lower deck of a ship stopped at a blockade for a routine check. Activity on the ship had been carried on to deceive observers into believing the ship was shrimping. Then the officer discovered that he had

---

[2]United States v. Gollwitzer, 697 F.2d 1357 (11th Cir. 1983).

[3]United States v. Kubiak, 704 F.2d 1545 (11th Cir. 1983).

[4]United States v. Hidalgo-Gato, 703 F.2d 1267 (11th Cir. 1983); United States v. Herrera, 711 F.2d 1546 (11th Cir. 1983).

[5]See § 4:45, infra, on border searches.

[6]United States v. One (1) 1982 28%27 International Vessel, 741 F.2d 1319 (11th Cir. 1984).

stopped the vessel under similar circumstances the previous month. The investigation had revealed "a deck sealed by screws . . . and a space beneath the deck that could not be accounted for."

However, in *Palmer v. State*,[7] the Georgia Court of Appeals held that customs officials may make an investigative stop of a vessel on inland waters "if they are aware of articulable facts which justify a *reasonable suspicion* of illegal activity." Actually, the shrimp boat involved in *Palmer* was apparently in the ocean headed toward the open sea when it was stopped.

In *Jackson v. State*,[8] the Georgia Court of Appeals held that O.C.G.A. § 52-7-25(b)(4) clearly authorized an enforcement officer of the Georgia Department of Natural Resources to stop a boat on Lake Lanier. The court declined to consider the stop under *Terry* standards and pointed out that the officer need not suspect wrongdoing. Such an officer is authorized "to make investigatory stops of watercraft for the sole purpose of *verifying* that the operator has the proper documentation and safety equipment. . . . [T]he boating public does not *necessarily* have the same expectation of privacy on regulated waterways as does the motoring public." In *Peruzzi v. State*,[9] the Supreme Court turned back a constitutional challenge to the statute noting that Georgia now "joins a growing list of states that recognize the legitimacy of suspicionless boat safety inspections and their minimal impact on the privacy of boaters."

See § 3:7, infra, on report of a crime and § 3:8, infra, on a protective sweep.

§ 3:6 Facts justifying the stop—Conduct

An officer on routine patrol in a rural area where several burglaries had occurred was held entitled to stop a car from another county that was being driven slowly on a dirt road, where the passenger looked back and thereafter both the passenger and the driver started doing something in the back seat that caused the officer to think they were hiding something.[1] An officer, however, does not have a reasonable and articulable suspicion to stop a man who went to his car, got in and drove off, after the officer saw him looking in the window of another car parked in a

---

[7]Palmer v. State, 167 Ga. App. 705, 307 S.E.2d 275 (1983).

[8]Jackson v. State, 214 Ga. App. 726, 727, 448 S.E.2d 761 (1994). See Elzey v. State, 239 Ga. App. 47, 519 S.E.2d 751 (1999), on Department of Natural Resources officers checking for hunting licenses.

[9]Peruzzi v. State, 275 Ga. 333, 567 S.E.2d 15 (2002).

[Section 3:6]

[1]State v. Purdy, 147 Ga. App. 340, 248 S.E.2d 683 (1978). Cf. § 3:8, n. 2; § 4:52 (text); and § 4:52, n. 1, infra.

shopping center as though he were going to try to get in the car, when the officer knew that no damage had been done to the parked car.[2] However, in *Darracott v. State*,[3] the court upheld a stop where an officer saw several young people standing in a shopping center parking lot about midnight and there were beer cans and other litter scattered about and the defendant jumped in a vehicle and drove off as the officer approached. Also, the same result was reached in *Stanley v. State*,[4] where the defendant saw a roadblock and backed up his vehicle in an "evasive action."

In *State v. Canidate*,[5] an officer was responding to a call when he noticed a brown Nissan Maxima in the driveway of a house which he knew had previously been raided for drugs. When the officer was returning, he saw a brown Maxima coming toward him. Thinking the driver may have been buying drugs at the house, he pulled around behind the car. The officer said the car appeared to accelerate as he turned around behind it. The officer further testified that he was behind the car for 10 to 15 seconds when the car quickly pulled over into the parking lot of a real estate business. When asked why he was attempting to avoid the police, the driver explained he was trying to get to the real estate agent to see about buying a house. The trial judge found that the initial stop had been based on a hunch, not a particularized articulable suspicion. The appellate court affirmed the verdict and pointed out that the officer admitted that he did not have any basis for stopping the driver when he pulled in behind him. The court further noted that the act of pulling into the parking lot did not create an articulable suspicion.

In *Edgell v. State*,[6] the Court of Appeals reversed the denial of a motion to suppress filed by the defendant passenger in a vehicle which was properly stopped by the arresting officer because of an expired tag. After ticketing the driver and impounding the vehicle, the officer instructed the defendant to exit the vehicle. Because the defendant acted nervously and pursuant to the officer's "routine" of patting down everyone whom he directs to exit a vehicle, he patted down the defendant over his protests. The officer arrested both the defendant and the driver when he felt a hard object in the defendant's pocket. Following the arrest, he placed his hand into the defendant's pockets and discovered a

---

[2]Brooks v. State, 144 Ga. App. 97, 240 S.E.2d 593 (1977). In Commonwealth v. Bacon, 381 Mass. 642, 411 N.E.2d 772 (1980), there was no reasonable suspicion justifying the stop of a four-year-old Cadillac at 4:10 a.m. on a Saturday because its occupants looked too young to be driving such an expensive car.

[3]Darracott v. State, 191 Ga. App. 675 (1), 382 S.E.2d 664 (1989).

[4]Stanley v. State, 191 Ga. App. 603, 604(2), 382 S.E.2d 686 (1989).

[5]State v. Canidate, 220 Ga. App. 276, 469 S.E.2d 710 (1996).

[6]Edgell v. State, 253 Ga. App. 775, 560 S.E.2d 532 (2002).

crack pipe and a small amount of marijuana. Concluding that the officer lacked any articulable suspicion that the defendant was engaged in any criminal activity, the court found that both the detention and the pat down were improper. The Court's observation is worth noting: "An individual's rights under the Fourth Amendment are not automatically waived . . . simply because he or she is asked to step out of a vehicle. The safety of officers is of extreme importance to this court. Nonetheless, our Constitution requires an officer to provide evidence to show that an act alleged to be performed for his safety was actually performed for that purpose in conformance with the requisite standards of *Terry*."[7]

In *McDaniel v. State*,[8] the Court of Appeals upheld an officer's investigative stop of a vehicle where the occupants had been seen peering into a parked car and upon seeing the police car, the driver "slammed on his brakes, turned off his headlights, and immediately put his vehicle in reverse. [The] [d]efendant raced away, unsuccessfully trying to enter a secure complex before abruptly speeding off again." In affirming, the court concluded that "[t]hese odd and evasive circumstances created a reasonable suspicion of criminal activity to permit a limited investigative stop. . . ."

In *State v. Billoups*,[9] the court reversed the granting of a motion to suppress. Here two men broke and ran when they saw an officer about 2:30 a.m. in a high drug area. The court concluded there was probable cause to arrest but the incident seems to fit in better with stop and frisk cases. It is important to note that the court based its reversal on the totality of the circumstances surrounding the transaction. Flight in connection with other circumstances may be sufficient probable cause to uphold a warrantless arrest or search, the surrounding circumstances in this case being the time of night and the area and "certainly these circumstances [give] rise to an articulable suspicion . . . as to authorize a brief investigatory stop."[10]

In *In the Interest of J. L. G.*,[11] an anonymous call to police reported the presence of a person (whose clothing was described) with a hand gun. The officers arrived within minutes. The defendant was dressed as described and when he "saw the police

---

[7]Edgell v. State, 253 Ga. App. 775, 778, 560 S.E.2d 532 (2002).

[8]McDaniel v. State, 227 Ga. App. 364 (1), 489 S.E.2d 112 (1997) (quoting State v. Banks, 223 Ga. App. 838, 841, 479 S.E.2d 168 (1996)). Cf. Merriweather v. State, 228 Ga. App. 246, 247(1), 491 S.E.2d 467 (1997).

[9]State v. Billoups, 191 Ga. App. 834, 383 S.E.2d 198 (1989). Cf. Harris v. State, 205 Ga. App. 813, 814 (1), 423 S.E.2d 723 (1992).

[10]Ransom v. State, 239 Ga. App. 501, 504(2), 521 S.E.2d 430 (1999).

[11]In the Interest of J. L. G., 209 Ga. App. 565, 566, 434 S.E.2d 126 (1993).

car, he stuck his hand in his pocket, [and] turned away from the
officers." When the officers started exiting their car, the defendant
ran and refused to stop on command. The court affirmed the
denial of a motion to suppress pointing out that there was an
articulable suspicion justifying a stop and probable cause to
arrest. In *Davis v. State*,[12] the court pointed out that "[f]light may
be evidence of a consciousness of guilt and may give rise to an
articulable suspicion that a person is engaged in criminal
activity. . . ."

In *Williams v. State*,[13] the Court of Appeals affirmed the denial
of a motion to suppress evidence of contraband and a weapon
seized during a vehicle search based upon police surveillance of
an apartment which revealed considerable foot and vehicle traffic
to and from the premises. The court found that police suspicion
based only upon their observations did not provide a "particularized, and objective basis" to justify the stop. The police had no
reason to stop the defendant other than he appeared to fit a pattern of behavior common to individuals who were going into and
out of a location where police knew drugs were being sold.

"[A]s a general matter, the decision to stop an automobile is
reasonable where the police have probable cause to believe that a
traffic violation has occurred."[14] An officer may stop a driver who
is speeding[15] or who has committed any other violation of the
law.[16] However, driving 49 miles per hour in a location where the
speed limit is 70 miles per hour does not per se create a reasonable suspicion for stopping a car. See § 3:7, infra, on reasonable
suspicion justifying stop.

In *State v. Armstrong*,[17] the court held that an officer is not
required to know with certainty each element of a particular
crime that could be established in order to make a valid stop. "If

---

[12]Davis v. State, 237 Ga. App.
890, 892, 517 S.E.2d 115 (1999).

[13]Williams v. State, 327 Ga. App.
239, 758 S.E.2d 141 (2014). See Hughes
v. State, 269 Ga. 258, 497 S.E.2d 790
(1998); State v. Hopper, 293 Ga. App.
220, 666 S.E.2d 735 (2008).

[14]McBride v. State, 246 Ga. App.
151, 152, 539 S.E.2d 201 (2000).

[15]State v. High, 145 Ga. App. 772,
774, 244 S.E.2d 888 (1978).

However, in People v.
McGaughran, 25 Cal. 3d 577, 159 Cal.
Rptr. 191, 601 P.2d 207 (1979), the
court held that a police officer who
stops a motorist for a minor traffic
violation may only detain the motorist
for the period of time necessary to issue the citation and if a warrant check
cannot be completed in that time, the
motorist should be free to leave.

[16]In State v. Sanders, 154 Ga.
App. 305, 267 S.E.2d 906 (1980), an
officer saw the defendant weaving,
driving in an erratic manner, and
speeding. The detective thought the
driver might have been driving under
the influence. The court held that the
arrest which followed was proper even
though the officer wanted the defendant stopped for another reason.

[17]State v. Armstrong, 223 Ga.
App. 350, 351(2), 477 S.E.2d 635
(1996). See Toole v. State, 340 Ga. App.
633, 798 S.E.2d 288 (2017).

the officer acting in good faith believes that an unlawful act has been committed, his actions are not rendered improper by a later legal determination that the defendant's actions were not a crime according to a technical legal definition. . . ."

In *State v. Blair*,[18] the court affirmed the trial court's granting of a motion to suppress. An officer stopped the car in which the defendant was riding in the back seat because the car was being driven with a dealer's drive-out tag. The officer said he was suspicious because no one produced any proof of ownership of the car. The occupants provided conflicting explanations of the purpose of their journey. All occupants appeared very nervous and the defendant was clutching a bag. The officer thought "something was going on," asked for permission to search and received a negative answer. As another officer drove up, the defendant fled with his bag, which was found to contain marijuana when he was arrested. Here, the officer stopped the car because of the tag. The stop was valid, but the evidence supports the trial judge's finding that the officer abandoned that investigation and held the occupants to conduct a search for drugs.

In *Berry v. State*,[19] the Court of Appeals held that "the critical issue to the validity of a traffic stop is whether the officer had 'a particularized and objective basis for suspecting the particular person stopped of criminal activity.'" Applying this standard to a stop based upon the officer's suspicion that an auto *might* be stolen solely on the basis that it was being operated with a drive-out tag, the court concluded the stop was not authorized. Likewise, the court found in *Bius v. State*,[20] that a stop was not warranted based upon an officer's suspicion that a vehicle *might* not be in compliance with motor vehicle registration laws solely because it was being driven with a drive-out tag.

Brisbane v. State[21] is illustrative of a number of cases involving robberies at service stations in the very early morning hours. An armed robbery by three men occurred at one service station. Later, at about 3:45 a.m., while on routine patrol, an officer stopped at another station that had been the scene of a number

---

[18]State v. Blair, 239 Ga. App. 340, 521 S.E.2d 380 (1999). But cf. Pitts v. State, 221 Ga. App. 309, 311(2), 471 S.E.2d 270 (1996).

[19]Berry v. State, 248 Ga. App. 874, 880(3), 547 S.E.2d 664 (2001), citing Postell v. State, 264 Ga. 249, 250, 443 S.E.2d 628 (1994).

[20]Bius v. State, 254 Ga. App. 634, 563 S.E.2d 527 (2002). See State v. Thompson, 256 Ga. App. 188, 569 S.E.2d 254 (2002) (fact that the defendant acted worried and nervous did not constitute grounds for a reasonable suspicion of criminal activity). See also Lewis v. State, 323 Ga. App. 709, 747 S.E.2d 867 (2013) (discussion of several cases where police lacked reasonable and articulable suspicion to justify stop).

[21]Brisbane v. State, 233 Ga. 339, 211 S.E.2d 294 (1974).

of robberies. The officer noticed an automobile containing three occupants driving slowly by the station. Then the same vehicle approached the station again and slowed down again. The court held that the officer, who stopped the car, had a specific, articulable suspicion justifying the stop.

In *Oboh v. State,*[22] the court reversed the denial of a motion to suppress. The case turned on the validity of the defendant's stop. "The deputy simply saw a stranger drive a van (with bumper stickers with the insignia of a rental car agency) into a bank parking lot, observed bank tellers scrutinize the stranger as he was preparing to leave the bank's parking lot and was informed by one of the tellers that this stranger 'was acting very suspicious.'"

In addition to the right to stop because of an articulable suspicion of a crime, the case of *Dickson v. State*[23] holds that officers have a right to stop a person in an automobile who creates "a safety and traffic hazard."

In *Streicher v. State,*[24] the court reversed the trial judge's denial of a motion to suppress where the officer saw the driver and passenger exchange places in an automobile, at about 8:30 a.m., when the car stopped at a stop sign. The officer did not suspect at the time that the occupants were engaged in criminal conduct, but in his experience every time something like this happened, he had found that there was intoxication or that someone did not have a driver's license. However, in *State v. Templeman,*[25] the court affirmed the trial judge in finding that there was no articulable suspicion where the defendant stopped in the roadway 25 to 50 feet from an intersection for 45 to 60 seconds while facing a green traffic light in order to pick up a friend.

Two decisions worth comparing are *Crowley v. State*[26] and *State v. Newton.*[27] In *Crowley,* an officer stopped the defendant without "a particularized and objective basis for suspecting him of criminal activity," and then subsequently stopped him again after the individual fled.[28] The Court of Appeals held that the defendant's flight provided sufficient reasonable suspicion to uphold the second detention. In contrast, the Court of Appeals in *Newton* concluded that an initial stop where officers exceeded the scope of *Terry* tainted the discovery of evidence found during a subsequent

---

[22]Oboh v. State, 217 Ga. App. 553, 555, 458 S.E.2d 177 (1995).

[23]Dickson v. State, 167 Ga. App. 685, 686(1), 307 S.E.2d 267 (1983).

[24]Streicher v. State, 213 Ga. App. 670, 445 S.E.2d 815 (1994).

[25]State v. Templeman, 229 Ga. App. 6, 492 S.E.2d 902 (1997).

[26]Crowley v. State, 267 Ga. App. 718, 601 S.E.2d 154 (2004).

[27]State v. Newton, 227 Ga. App. 394, 489 S.E.2d 147 (1997).

[28]Crowley v. State, 267 Ga. App. 718, 601 S.E.2d 154 (2004).

stop after the defendant fled. However, these two cases may be harmonized by the fact that the *Newton* Court did not directly address whether or not flight may provide an articulable suspicion to justify a consecutive stop of a suspect.

In *Ewumi v. State*,[29] the court noted that an officer's "feeling" that an individual is committing a crime does not amount to a reasonable particularized suspicion and hence will not provide a basis for an investigatory detention. Thus, while an officer may lawfully initiate a first tier encounter with a person, that person has every right to refuse to participate in a second tier encounter, a brief investigatory detention, even if accomplished by running away from the officer, if there is no reasonable suspicion for the officer to detain the person. Thus, if the attempted detention is not lawful, any subsequent flight by the person is not relevant to the determination of whether the officer had reasonable suspicion to escalate a first tier encounter. Finally, an effort by a person to dispose of contraband or other evidence of a crime while fleeing from or being the subject of an attempted unlawful detention by police authorities does not remove the taint of the wrongful police conduct and all evidence stemming from the wrongful conduct is subject to suppression.[30] One exception to this rule exists where a suspect's response to an illegal stop is to commit another crime. In that case, the "fruit of the poisonous tree" has no application.[31]

See § 4:21, infra, on frisk connected with execution of a search warrant, and § 4:38, infra, on abandoned property.

§ 3:7 Facts justifying the stop—Report of a crime

In *Adams v. Williams*,[1] the United States Supreme Court held that an officer was justified in approaching a man in a car in a

---

[29]Ewumi v. State, 315 Ga. App. 656, 727 S.E.2d 257 (2012). See Hernandez-Espino v. State, 324 Ga. App. 849, 752 S.E.2d 10 (2013) (example of issues which arise when question is whether detention was improperly elevated).

[30]U.S. v. Beck, 602 F.2d 726 (5th Cir. 1979). See U.S. v. Burke, 605 F. Supp. 2d 688 (D. Md. 2009). Compare State v. Walker, 295 Ga. 888, 764 S.E.2d 804 (2014) (person who disregards a police officer's command to "take his hands out of his pockets" and runs away is not "seized" for purposes of the Fourth Amendment).

[31]U.S. v. Bailey, 691 F.2d 1009, 1016(II) (11th Cir. 1982). See U.S. v. Sprinkle, 106 F.3d 613 (4th Cir. 1997).

[Section 3:7]

[1]Adams v. Williams, 407 U.S. 143, 92 S.Ct. 1921, 32 L.Ed.2d 612 (1972). Cf. State v. Noble, 179 Ga. App. 785, 347 S.E.2d 722 (1986); Ates v. State, 155 Ga. App. 97, 270 S.E.2d 455 (1980). In Williams, the informer was known to the officer. However, in United States v. Pearce, 356 F.Supp. 756, 759 (E.D.Pa.1973), the court held that an anonymous tip alone was insufficient to justify a stop.

In United States v. Kent, 691 F.2d 1376 (11th Cir. 1982), the court held that a tip containing considerable detail which was verified by officers justified a stop even though the in-

high crime area during the early morning hours and in questioning him, where the officer had been told by a known informant that the suspect would be found there and that he was armed and carrying narcotics.

In *United States v. White*,[2] an anonymous telephone tipster's information given to an officer plus the verification of some of the innocent details were said to add up to an articulable suspicion justifying a stop of the occupants of a car.

Conversely, "an *unverified* tip from an informant may not supply probable cause for a search or a warrant, [however,] if the information carries enough indicia of reliability, it will authorize a forcible stop of a suspect to maintain the status quo momentarily while obtaining more information."[3]

In *Alabama v. White*,[4] an officer received an anonymous phone call stating that "Vanessa White would be leaving 235-C Lynwood Terrace Apartments at a particular time in a brown Plymouth station wagon with the right taillight lens broken, that she would be going to Dobey's Motel, and that she would be in possession of about an ounce of cocaine inside a brown attache case." The officer drove to the Lynwood Terrace Apartments and saw a brown Plymouth station wagon with a broken right taillight in the parking lot in front of the 235 building. The officer saw the defendant leave the 235 building with nothing in her hands and enter the station wagon. The officer followed the Plymouth as it was driven in the most direct route to Dobey's Motel. The officer stopped the vehicle just before it reached Dobey's Motel. The officer informed the defendant she was stopped because she was suspected of carrying cocaine in the vehicle. He asked for and received permission to search the car. In the search he found an attache case which contained marijuana and in the defendant's pocket book he found cocaine. In upholding the stop, the court declined to say that an "anonymous caller could never provide the reasonable suspicion necessary for a *Terry* stop" but it concluded that "when the officers stopped . . . [the defendant], the anonymous tip had been sufficiently corroborated to furnish reasonable suspicion that . . . [the defendant] was engaged in criminal activity and

former was unproven. The tip included the description of a vessel and its location at a particular time. The court concluded that it could be inferred that the informant obtained his information in a reliable manner.

[2]United States v. White, 648 F.2d 29, 40-45 (D.C.Cir. 1981).

[3]State v. Bassford, 183 Ga. App. 694, 698(1), 359 S.E.2d 752 (1987). See

Sutton v. State, 319 Ga. App. 597, 737 S.E.2d 706 (2013) (anonymous tip based on what tipster had been told by another with only barely relevant corroboration not enough to supply probable cause for warrant).

[4]Alabama v. White, 496 U.S. 325, 110 S.Ct. 2412, 110 L.Ed.2d 301 (1990). Cf. Mack v. State, 212 Ga. App. 187, 188(1), 441 S.E.2d 503 (1994).

that the investigative stop therefore did not violate the Fourth Amendment." In *State v. Williams*,[5] the court quoted from *White* "that 'articulable suspicion' may not be grounded in an anonymous tip alone." See the excellent opinion of Judge Beasley in *State v. Ball*,[6] which follows *White*.

In *Navarette v. California*,[7] the Supreme Court reiterated that an anonymous tip alone will typically fail to demonstrate a sufficient factual basis for providing police with the grounds for an investigative stop. However, it also noted that in the exceptional case an anonymous but well corroborated tip can demonstrate sufficient reliability to justify reasonable suspicion to make an investigative stop. In *Navarette*, the Court held that the investigative stop of the defendant's truck was justified where the tipster was able to provide the license plate and the make and model of a truck which the tipster claimed had run her off the road, as well as the approximate location of where the event occurred and the direction in which the truck was traveling. The Court also found the tip was further verified by the fact that it was reported through the 911 emergency system, which allows for the identification and tracing of callers.

In *Florida v. J. L.*,[8] the United States Supreme Court pointed out that reasonable suspicion existed in *White*, but that case was "borderline." *Florida v. J. L.* then held that "[a]n anonymous tip that a person is carrying a gun is not, without more, sufficient to justify a police officer's stop and frisk. . . ." However, the court also pointed out that in *Florida v. J. L.*, "[a]ll the police had to go on . . . was the bare report of an unknown, unaccountable informant who neither explained how he knew about the gun nor supplied any basis for believing he had inside information about J. L." Furthermore, the court refused to grant an exception for cases involving firearms.

In *McKinley v. State*,[9] the court reversed the trial judge's denial of a motion to suppress where police "received an anonymous

---

[5]State v. Williams, 225 Ga. App. 736, 737(2), 484 S.E.2d 775 (1997). See Register v. State, 315 Ga. App. 776, 728 S.E.2d 292 (2012) (report from anonymous tipster that he observed a "white male" exchange a pill for cash along with a description of vehicle and tag as well as direction it was travelling on a particular highway insufficient to warrant stop because it provided nothing police could corroborate and tipster was unknown to police with no prior history of credibility).

[6]State v. Ball, 207 Ga. App. 729, 429 S.E.2d 258 (1993). Cf. Stanley v. State, 213 Ga. App. 95, 96, 443 S.E.2d 633 (1994).

[7]Navarette v. California, 134 S. Ct. 1683, 188 L. Ed. 2d 680 (2014).

[8]Florida v. J. L., 529 U.S. 266, 120 S.Ct. 1375, 146 L.Ed.2d 254 (2000). See Daniels v. State, 278 Ga. App. 263, 628 S.E.2d 684 (2006), for a thorough discussion of the issues involved in the "anonymous" tip.

[9]McKinley v. State, 213 Ga. App. 738, 445 S.E.2d 828 (1994).

telephone tip that four black males in a white Chevrolet Lumina van with Hillsborough County, Florida, license plates were attempting to sell cocaine on Butler Street in Camilla, Georgia." An officer in an unmarked car followed a white van occupied by two men to a parking lot in front of a convenience store and activated his blue light on his dash. As both the driver and the passenger were getting out of the van, the officer approached the driver and asked to see his driver's license and proof of insurance. The officer told the passenger to get back in the van and close the door. The driver produced his license and rental agreement for the van which did not list him as the renter or as an additional driver. Another officer arrived and told the passenger to get out of the van. Consent to search the van was given, but the appellate court held that the occupants of the van had been seized before the consent was given and that the consent was not freely given.

In the Georgia case of *State v. Holton*,[10] the court cited and relied on *Alabama v. White*.[11] It emphasized that in that case and in the *Holton* case, the anonymous tipster predicted future behavior which was corroborated by observations of the police. The Georgia Court of Appeals said that such a prediction of future conduct and corroboration was necessary to authorize an investigative stop from an anonymous caller. However, in the Eleventh Circuit case of *United States v. Gibson*,[12] the court held that an anonymous tip that a potentially armed person is in a public establishment justifies an investigative stop, without including information as to future conduct, in view of an overriding concern for the safety of the police and the public.

In *United States v. Kent*,[13] the Eleventh Circuit acknowledged that a tip from an informant of unknown reliability will not ordinarily create a reasonable suspicion of criminality, but information from a known informant of unknown reliability has more indicia of reliability than an anonymous telephone tip. Also, cor-

---

[10]State v. Holton, 205 Ga. App. 434, 436, 422 S.E.2d 295 (1992). Accord, Archer v. State, 217 Ga. App. 257, 258(1), 456 S.E.2d 754 (1995); State v. Moon, 217 Ga. App. 790, 459 S.E.2d 441 (1995); Brown v. State, 223 Ga. App. 364, 366, 477 S.E.2d 623 (1996). Compare State v. Williams, 336 Ga. App. 97, 100, 783 S.E.2d 700 (2016), decision vacated and remanded for further clarification of trial court findings, 301 Ga. 60, 799 S.E.2d 779 (2017), and opinion vacated, 344 Ga. App. 311, 809 S.E.2d 844 (2018); Rucker v. State, 276 Ga. App. 683, 624 S.E.2d 259 (2005).

[11]Alabama v. White, 496 U.S. 325, 110 S.Ct. 2412, 110 L.Ed.2d 301 (1990).

[12]United States v. Gibson, 64 F.3d 617 (11th Cir. 1995). Accord, United States v. Clipper, 973 F.2d 944, 949 (D.C.Cir. 1992); United States v. Bold, 19 F.3d 99 (2d Cir. 1994).

[13]United States v. Kent, 691 F.2d 1376 (11th Cir. 1982). Accord, State v. Jarrells, 207 Ga. App. 192 (2), 427 S.E.2d 568 (1993). See also Burse v. State, 209 Ga. App. 276, 278, 433 S.E.2d 386 (1993) (dealing with a known informant of known reliability).

roboration of innocent details may change an otherwise insubstantial tip into a reasonable suspicion of criminal activity. Thus, where a known but unproved informant notified a Customs Patrol Officer that a white yacht-type, 50-foot vessel with three persons on board would be coming into the area of the Coral Gables Waterway within an hour carrying a load of marijuana, and a Customs vessel observed such a vessel about 45 minutes later and it was the only vessel observed in the area at that time, a stop and boarding was justified. See § 3:5, supra, on ships and boats.

In *Archer v. State,*[14] the court held that the stop of the defendant was justified when "the details of that tip, including the predicted timing and route of a particular vehicle driven by a particular individual, were confirmed by the personal observations of the investigating officers."

In *Graves v. State,*[15] an officer was executing a search warrant. Graves was present and the officer had been informed by a reliable informant that Graves always carried a weapon. The Georgia Court of Appeals held that a stop, and a later frisk, were justified.

In *Vansant v. State,*[16] an officer stopped a white van. The officer had followed the vehicle for a half mile observing no traffic violation other than that the vehicle did not stop promptly when the flashing blue light was turned on. The only reason the van was stopped was because a white van had been involved in a hit and run accident about a mile away. The court concluded the facts did not justify an articulable suspicion. "[H]owever, . . . when an officer sees a traffic offense occur, a resulting traffic stop does not violate the Fourth Amendment even if the officer had ulterior motives in initiating the stop . . . "[17] and even if the officer did not charge the defendant with the traffic offense observed.[18] In *State v. Hall,*[19] the court held there may be a *Terry* stop of an automobile if there is an initial minor traffic violation which an officer witnessed. However, the officer must have some other basis (i.e., the officer must have a reasonable suspicion of criminal conduct) for conducting additional questioning and

---

[14]Archer v. State, 217 Ga. App. 395, 396, 457 S.E.2d 679 (1995). Cf. Ledford v. State, 220 Ga. App. 272, 274(1), 469 S.E.2d 401 (1996). Followed, Carter v. State, 248 Ga. App. 821, 823(3), 547 S.E.2d 613 (2001).

[15]Graves v. State, 138 Ga. App. 327, 226 S.E.2d 131 (1976).

[16]Vansant v. State, 264 Ga. 319, 321(2), 443 S.E.2d 474 (1994).

[17]Welborn v. State, 232 Ga. App. 837, 839(2), 503 S.E.2d 85 (1998).

[18]Howard v. State, 233 Ga. App. 861, 505 S.E.2d 270 (1998). In State v. Bute, 250 Ga. App. 479, 481, 552 S.E.2d 465 (2001), also pointed out that "[w]here the officer observes the violation of a traffic law, the resulting stop is not pretextual."

[19]State v. Hall, 235 Ga. App. 412, 414, 509 S.E.2d 701 (1998).

searching a vehicle once a normal traffic stop has ended and the officer has told the motorist he is free to go. "Although this suspicion need not meet the standard of probable cause, it must be more than mere caprice or a hunch or an inclination." See § 4:26, infra, on traffic offense justifying stop.

In contrast to *Vansant*, the court in *State v. Harden*[20] upheld a stop where police received a tip that an inebriated driver was about to leave a bank parking lot, and an officer shortly thereafter observed a vehicle leaving that location. The Court distinguished *Vansant* on the basis that in that case, the defendant's van was stopped a mile away from where the tipster observed the vehicle. Hence, it appears that police may stop a vehicle based on a tip that the driver is inebriated without corroboration of that tip as long as the officer can be reasonably certain that they are stopping the car described by the tipster.

In *Shorter v. State*,[21] the court, citing *Vansant*, held that a general tip to be on the lookout for a white van may not create sufficient articulable suspicion. The court pointed out that "a more particularized description of a suspect vehicle" was needed to justify a *Terry* stop.

However, in *McSwain v. State*,[22] the court held that "an officer's decision to broadcast a lookout" for a described car alone does not "create reasonable suspicion for another officer to stop the vehicle." Here there was no evidence of *collective* knowledge of officers which would give rise to reasonable suspicion that would justify a *Terry* stop.

In *Overand v. State*,[23] the court concluded that "[a] dispatcher who reports a crime at a specified location gives police an articulable suspicion to investigate and detain individuals at the scene, particularly where police observations on arriving at the scene corroborate the dispatcher's report," and the officer is "not required to question dispatchers about the source of the information."

In *McGhee v. State*,[24] the court stated "that when the police received a call to be on the lookout for a car . . . and the car in

---

[20]State v. Harden, 267 Ga. App. 381, 599 S.E.2d 329 (2004). But see Slocum v. State, 267 Ga. App. 337, 599 S.E.2d 299 (2004) where a stop was suppressed on the grounds that a tipster did not provide sufficient information to support the officer's suspicion that defendant's SUV was the vehicle described by the caller.

[21]Shorter v. State, 239 Ga. App. 625, 626(1), 521 S.E.2d 684 (1999).

[22]McSwain v. State, 240 Ga. App. 60, 62, 522 S.E.2d 553 (1999). See Allen v. State, 325 Ga. App. 156, 751 S.E.2d 915 (2013) (BOLO justification too generalized to support stop based on only make, model and nonspecific color of automobile).

[23]Overand v. State, 240 Ga. App. 682, 683(1), 523 S.E.2d 610 (1999).

[24]McGhee v. State, 253 Ga. 278, 279(1), 319 S.E.2d 836 (1984); In the

question roughly fit the description given for the lookout, this provided the basis for an articulable suspicion justifying the stop." See § 3:3, supra, on identification by tag number.

In *Smith v. State*,[25] there had been an armed robbery about 2:30 a.m. The radio bulletin described "the perpetrators . . . [as] two black males armed with sawed-off shotguns and dressed in dark clothing, one of whom was wearing a gray colored toboggan hat." No vehicle description was given. About 3:05 a.m., a few miles away, an officer saw an automobile with a passenger wearing a gray toboggan hat; however, there were three men in the car. The court concluded that a stop of the vehicle was proper.

The Georgia Court of Appeals again found sufficient circumstances to justify a stop in *Butts v. State*,[26] where, at about 3:00 a.m., an officer heard a broadcast stating that a black male had just committed an armed robbery in the immediate area in which he was patrolling. Ten or fifteen minutes after the robbery, he saw a black man running and stopped him. The court found that the officer had a reasonable articulable suspicion that justified the stop. The court did not discuss the very general description of the robber that had been given over the radio.

In *United States v. Hensley*,[27] the United States Supreme Court held that officers in Kentucky were justified in stopping a person in an automobile pursuant to a police "flyer or bulletin [if it had] been issued on . . . articulable facts supporting a reasonable suspicion that the wanted person" had committed a felony in Ohio, and an objective reading of the flyer shows that the stopping officer had information which would warrant a man of reasonable caution to believe that the stop was proper.

In *State v. Mallory*,[28] while an officer was arresting a person for a felony pursuant to a warrant, he saw the defendant approach-

---

Interest of B.K.M., 247 Ga. App. 588, 544 S.E.2d 504 (2001). Cf. Givens v. State, 218 Ga. App. 415, 416-17(1), 461 S.E.2d 579 (1995).

[25]Smith v. State, 165 Ga. App. 333, 299 S.E.2d 891 (1983).

[26]Butts v. State, 149 Ga. App. 492 (2), 254 S.E.2d 719 (1979). But see Anderson v. State, 282 Md. 701, 387 A.2d 281 (1978) (robbery committed six days earlier).

In Burns v. State, 239 Ga. App. 532, 534(1), 521 S.E.2d 217 (1999), rev'd as to Division 2, 241 Ga. App. 886, 528 S.E.2d 547 (2000), the court affirmed the trial court where "the totality of the circumstances, includ-

ing the late hour report of a nearly contemporaneous armed robbery and the place where the defendants were first seen (i.e., the place where the perpetrators were last seen), created a justifiable suspicion concerning defendant's identity and warranted a limited investigative detention to determine if he roughly fit the description of the perpetrators."

[27]United States v. Hensley, 469 U.S. 221, 105 S.Ct. 675, 83 L.Ed.2d 604 (1985).

[28]State v. Mallory, 152 Ga. App. 822, 264 S.E.2d 293 (1979). Cf. Clark v. State, 131 Ga. App. 583 (2), 206 S.E.2d 717 (1974).

ing with his hands in his pockets. "When the officer took his badge out and started to approach the defendant, the defendant turned and walked away, whereupon the officer ordered the defendant to stop." The Georgia Court of Appeals held that the stop was justified in view of the circumstances and the fact that the officer had seen the arrestee with the defendant shortly before executing the warrant; the stop occurred at night in a poorly lighted area, and the officer wanted to be sure the defendant was not armed.

In *Williams v. State*,[29] a druggist in an all-night drug store received a threat stating that a bomb was planted in the store and would be detonated remotely by the caller if the druggist did not deliver certain drugs to a designated point. There were a total of four calls between 2:00 and 4:00 a.m., and a police captain listened to the last call, which was at about 3:30 a.m. At about 4:00 a.m., while waiting for another call, "the druggist and captain were standing at the door of the pharmacy looking out upon a deserted shopping center parking lot." A car drove "from the area of an adjoining highway slowly across the parking lot. At the front door of the drug store, the car more or less stopped and the driver looked through the door and seemingly saw the druggist and presumably the police officer. The car then proceeded on out of the parking lot away from the area." The court concluded that the circumstances were sufficient to present an articulable suspicion justifying a stop of the car.

In *Tarwid v. State*,[30] the court held illegal the stop of a vehicle on an interstate highway for traveling slightly under the maximum speed allowed. The court concluded that this conduct was not indicative that the driver was intoxicated and a radio transmission from a state trooper stating that he had given the driver a warning ticket in another county for speeding and that the vehicle "had shown signs of trafficking" in drugs did not justify the stop. However, in *Taylor v. State*,[31] the appellate court affirmed the trial judge in finding that the officer was justified in stopping the defendant for driving 45 miles per hour in the center lane of I-20 because the driver was creating a traffic hazard. The court pointed out that driving "at such a slow speed as to impede the normal and reasonable movement of traffic" was a violation of O.C.G.A. § 40-6-184(a)(1).

See § 2:12, supra, on probable cause to arrest. See § 4:21, infra, on the right to stop and frisk incident to execution of a search

---

[29]Williams v. State, 163 Ga. App. 866, 868(2), 295 S.E.2d 361 (1982).

[30]Tarwid v. State, 184 Ga. App. 853, 363 S.E.2d 63 (1987). Accord, State v. Aguirre, 229 Ga. App. 736, 494 S.E.2d 576 (1997).

[31]Taylor v. State, 230 Ga. App. 749, 750(1), 498 S.E.2d 113 (1998).

warrant. See § 3:6, supra, on traffic violations.

§ 3:8   Facts justifying the stop—Environment

As previously indicated, the time and place of a stop often supply an important part in determining whether or not an officer has an articulable suspicion to justify a stop. A number of cases have emphasized the fact that the stop was made in a "high crime area."[1] In *Bobo v. State*,[2] the defendant was stopped because he was driving his truck at 2:00 a.m. in a residential area in which vandalism had been reported. However, the court concluded that the facts did not justify the stop. In *Attaway v. State*,[3] the appellate court reversed the trial court's denial of a motion to suppress the evidence obtained from the investigative stop of a car. The officer, aware of past incidents of vandalism in the area, received information from the police dispatcher to be on the lookout for a small red vehicle that had reportedly circled around a named subdivision several times. The court held that the police might have been justified in closely observing the defendant's actions, but that the officer was not justified in making an investigative stop. In *Howden v. State*,[4] the court reversed the trial court's denial of a motion to suppress where the officer "stopped defendant because it was late at night and defendant's warehouse is located in an area known for criminal activity." The defendant's van was backed up to the door of a closed warehouse. The defendant's van pulled out of the area a couple of minutes after the patrol car arrived. The appellate court held the stop which followed was not based on any particular fact that the defendant was engaged in or was about to engage in criminal activity. In *State v. Winnie*,[5] the defendant, after entering a parking lot at 4:00 a.m., pulled away from an approaching officer. Although there was no indication that the officer's decision to stop the defendant was influenced by the defendant's decision to pull away, the court held that "there was no articulable suspicion for

---

[Section 3:8]

[1]E.g., Adams v. Williams, 407 U.S. 143, 92 S.Ct. 1921, 32 L.Ed.2d 612 (1972); Commonwealth v. Almeida, 373 Mass. 266, 366 N.E.2d 756 (1977); State v. Beaty, 57 Wis.2d 531, 205 N.W.2d 11 (1973).

[2]Bobo v. State, 153 Ga. App. 679, 266 S.E.2d 247 (1980). The court also held that it was error to refuse to strike the officer's testimony, since a motion to suppress need not be filed where the state does not attempt to introduce physical evidence. Compare Akins v. State, 266 Ga. App. 214, 596 S.E.2d 719 (2004) (police request to a couple sitting in a motor vehicle to roll down window followed by officer's inquiry regarding woman's well being was first tier encounter which did not require reasonable articulable suspicion of criminal activity).

[3]Attaway v. State, 236 Ga. App. 307, 511 S.E.2d 635 (1999).

[4]Howden v. State, 240 Ga. App. 139, 140, 522 S.E.2d 279 (1999).

[5]State v. Winnie, 242 Ga. App. 228, 529 S.E.2d 215 (2000).

the stop."

In *Raulerson v. State*,[6] the appellate court reversed the finding of the trial judge that there was an articulable suspicion justifying the stopping of an automobile where the defendant was driving at 1:20 a.m. between 25 and 30 m.p.h. in a 55 m.p.h. zone, turned onto a dirt road, and returned to the highway. However, in *Jones v. State*,[7] the court affirmed the trial court's denial of a suppression motion where a car was stopped at 9:30 p.m. as it was leaving a new unoccupied subdivision in which some vandalism had occurred. The only unusual conduct referred to was that the vehicle did not have its lights turned on until the driver saw the officer's car. Likewise, in *Watson v. State*,[8] the court affirmed a finding that the stop of an automobile was justified where an officer had seen the defendant and his two companions in a "high drug area" several times during the day and each time the occupants looked in the opposite direction.

In *Evans v. State*,[9] the court affirmed the denial of a motion to suppress. The officer was patrolling in a high crime area at 12:45 a.m. when he noticed a motion detector had been set off at a convenience store. The officer had checked the store about 10 minutes earlier and found everything in order. Upon receipt of the alarm, the officer pulled out of a gasoline station and saw two persons in a 1969 Plymouth coming up the hill toward the officer about 1,000 yards from the convenience store. No other car or person was in sight. The officer went to the convenience store and noticed the glass in front had been knocked out and cartons of cigarettes were in the parking lot. The officer immediately left the store and followed the 1969 Plymouth. He stopped the car and observed a cigarette carton protruding from a garbage bag under the defendant's leg. The defendant was arrested. The yellow Plymouth was nearly identical to a "lookout" the officer had received earlier regarding other break-ins.

In *State v. Turntime*,[10] the court reversed the granting of a motion to suppress where a defendant was stopped as he was walking in an apartment complex in which he did not live, looking in parked cars, at about 10:30 p.m. There had been a number of automobile break-ins in the area.

---

[6]Raulerson v. State, 223 Ga. App. 556, 557(2), 479 S.E.2d 386 (1996).

[7]Jones v. State, 156 Ga. App. 730, 275 S.E.2d 778 (1980). In Jones, a 5 to 4 decision, there was also testimony that the officer apparently would stop any car he saw entering or leaving the area.

[8]Watson v. State, 181 Ga. App. 512, 513(3), 352 S.E.2d 828 (1987).

[9]Evans v. State, 183 Ga. App. 436, 437(2), 359 S.E.2d 174 (1987).

[10]State v. Turntime, 170 Ga. App. 740, 318 S.E.2d 157 (1984).

In *United States v. Magda,*[11] the Fifth Circuit Court of Appeals found the officers had a sufficient, reasonable and articulable suspicion to stop a man they had seen exchange an object with another man. The exchange took place in an area in which there was a high incidence of narcotic transactions. In *Shaw v. State,*[12] the court affirmed the conclusion of the trial judge holding that a stop was justified where the defendant was seen walking late at night in the vicinity of a burglarized apartment, carrying a dark object over his arm. In *Bozeman v. State,*[13] the opinion affirmed the denial of a motion to suppress and held that a stop was justified where the defendant was in a high crime area and an officer saw him and a companion sitting for no apparent reason in a parked car in a remote part of a motel parking lot at 4:45 a.m. Furthermore, in *Illinois v. Wardlow,*[14] the United States Supreme Court held that when, in an area known for drug trafficking, an officer sees a defendant look toward a police car and flee, those circumstances may give rise to a reasonable suspicion that the defendant is involved in criminal conduct. The court refused to hold that unprovoked flight from officers is always sufficient to justify a stop and reiterated that reasonable suspicion is to be determined by a totality of the circumstances. In *Brown v. Texas,*[15] however, the Supreme Court found that there was no right to stop a suspicious-looking person seen in an alley during the day in a high crime area. Likewise, where officers staked out a ranch while awaiting a search warrant, it was held that they had no Fourth Amendment right to stop a car entering the ranch and frisk the occupants because they feared that the occupants might have had something to do with marijuana activities at that location.[16]

In *Hughes v. State,*[17] the Georgia Supreme Court concluded that "there is no objective manifestation that a person is, or is about to be, engaged in criminal activity merely because the person is a white man in a black neighborhood late at night, who picks up a black man at a location police consider a high-crime area, and who then drives slowly in a circular fashion through the neighborhood."

---

[11]United States v. Magda, 547 F.2d 756 (2d Cir. 1976). But see Jones v. United States, 391 A.2d 1188 (D.C. 1978).

[12]Shaw v. State, 179 Ga. App. 807, 808(1), 348 S.E.2d 132 (1986).

[13]Bozeman v. State, 196 Ga. App. 743 (1), 397 S.E.2d 30 (1990).

[14]Illinois v. Wardlow, 528 U.S. 119, 120 S.Ct. 673, 145 L.Ed.2d 570 (2000).

[15]Brown v. Texas, 443 U.S. 47, 99 S.Ct. 2637, 61 L.Ed.2d 357 (1979).

[16]Hull v. State, 613 S.W.2d 735, 737-740 (Tex.Crim.App.1981).

[17]Hughes v. State, 269 Ga. 258, 261, 497 S.E.2d 790 (1998). Accord, Chinnis v. State, 240 Ga. App. 518, 519(1), 523 S.E.2d 924 (1999).

§ 3:9 Roadblocks

In *Delaware v. Prouse*,[1] the defendant had been stopped at random by a patrolman. The patrolman had not observed any traffic violation or suspicious activity on the part of the defendant, and made the stop only to check the driver's license and the registration. The officer was not acting pursuant to any procedure pertaining to spot checks. During the stop, the patrolman saw marijuana in plain view on the floor of the car. In holding that the marijuana had been properly suppressed, the Court ruled that there must be at least an articulable and reasonable suspicion that a motorist is unlicensed, or that a car is not registered, or that an occupant is otherwise subject to seizure for violation of the law before a driver may be stopped.

In *Brower v. Inyo County*,[2] the Court held that stopping a single motorist with a roadblock amounts to a "seizure" in Fourth Amendment terms. However, this rule does not apply to a roadblock where all vehicles are stopped for a license check.[3]

Based upon its review of the United States Supreme Court's decision in *City of Indianapolis v. Edmond*,[4] and the Georgia Supreme Court's decision in *LaFontaine v. State*,[5] the Georgia Court of Appeals in *Baker v. State*,[6] declared that the constitutional validity of a roadblock is dependent upon the presence of the following features: "(1) the record reflects that the decision to implement the checkpoint in question was made by supervisory officers and not officers in the field *and* that the supervision had a legitimate primary purpose. The phrase 'decision to implement' includes deciding to have this roadblock and where and when to have it . . . (2) all vehicles were stopped as opposed to random stops . . . (3) the delay to motorists was minimal . . . (4) the roadblock operation was well identified as a police checkpoint . . . (5) the screening officer's training and experience were sufficient to qualify him to make an initial determination as to which motorists would be given field tests for intoxication." The court expressly rejected the implication in prior decisions that these

---

[Section 3:9]

[1]Delaware v. Prouse, 440 U.S. 648, 99 S.Ct. 1391, 59 L.Ed.2d 660 (1979). See § 4:2, Protected areas and interests, infra, for discussion of inspections of commercial motor vehicles.

[2]Brower v. Inyo County, 489 U.S. 593, 109 S.Ct. 1378, 103 L.Ed.2d 628 (1989).

[3]Sapp v. State, 188 Ga. App. 700, 374 S.E.2d 114 (1988); State v. Golden, 171 Ga. App. 27, 29(2), 318 S.E.2d 693 (1984); Kan v. State, 199 Ga. App. 170 (1), 404 S.E.2d 281 (1991).

[4]City of Indianapolis v. Edmond, 531 U.S. 32, 121 S.Ct. 447, 148 L.Ed.2d 333 (2000).

[5]LaFontaine v. State, 269 Ga. 251, 497 S.E.2d 367 (1998).

[6]Baker v. State, 252 Ga. App. 695, 556 S.E.2d 892 (2001), disapproved, Brown v. State, 293 Ga. 883, 750 S.E.2d 355 (2013).

criteria were simply guidelines to be applied in weighing the "totality of the circumstances."[7]

In *Baker*, evidence obtained at the roadblock was ruled inadmissible because the state was unable to demonstrate at trial that the decision to implement the checkpoint had in fact been made by supervisory police personnel and not the field officers and there there was a legitimate primary purpose for the roadblock.[8] Since *Baker*, the issue of whether a roadblock was duly authorized by supervising personnel often dictates the outcome of a contest to the admissibility of evidence seized at a roadblock.[9] The state can expect to lose such contests if it fails to produce the responsible supervisory personnel at the hearing and has no other admissible evidence to establish the basis for the roadblock.[10]

In *Brown v. State*,[11] the Supreme Court criticized *Baker* for "merging" the different requirements of *LaFontaine* and *Edmond*, noting that a proper review of the decision to institute a roadblock does not entail a judicial probing of the minds of the of-

---

[7]Baker v. State, 252 Ga. App. 695, 697, 556 S.E.2d 892 (2001), disapproved, Brown v. State, 293 Ga. 883, 750 S.E.2d 355 (2013).

[8]The court overruled a number of decisions on this basis including State v. Sherrill, 247 Ga. App. 708, 710(2), 545 S.E.2d 110 (2001); Boyce v. State, 240 Ga. App. 388, 523 S.E.2d 607 (1999); Albert v. State, 236 Ga. App. 146, 511 S.E.2d 244 (1999); Payne v. State, 232 Ga. App. 591, 502 S.E.2d 526 (1998); Heimlich v. State, 231 Ga. App. 662, 500 S.E.2d 388 (1998); Mims v. State, 201 Ga. App. 277, 410 S.E.2d 824 (1991); and Evans v. State, 190 Ga. App. 856, 380 S.E.2d 332 (1989). See Baker v. State, 252 Ga. App. 695, 702, 556 S.E.2d 892 (2001), disapproved, Brown v. State, 293 Ga. 883, 750 S.E.2d 355 (2013).

[9]See e.g., Harwood v. State, 262 Ga. App. 818, 586 S.E.2d 722 (2003); Blackburn v. State, 256 Ga. App. 800, 570 S.E.2d 36 (2002); Perdue v. State, 256 Ga. App. 765 (1)(a), 578 S.E.2d 456 (2002). In Perdue and Harwood, the courts deemed the roadblocks legitimate despite the fact that in both cases the supervisory officers were also field officers and, in the case of Harwood, the officer was present at the roadblock. In contrast, the court in

Blackburn found insufficient evidence of the roadblock's legitimacy where "the only evidence presented by the state regarding the roadblock came from the testimony of the state trooper who stopped Blackburn at the roadblock." The court reached this finding despite the officer's testimony that a supervising corporal had authorized the roadblock.

[10]Morris v. State, 265 Ga. App. 186, 593 S.E.2d 360 (2004); Blackburn v. State, 256 Ga. App. 800, 570 S.E.2d 36 (2002), a trooper's testimony that a roadblock was conducted at a supervisor's request and for a legitimate purpose was hearsay and therefore inadequate to establish the roadblock's legitimacy; see also Baker v. State, 252 Ga. App. 695, 556 S.E.2d 892 (2001), disapproved, Brown v. State, 293 Ga. 883, 750 S.E.2d 355 (2013).

[11]Brown v. State, 293 Ga. 787, 750 S.E.2d 148 (2013) (Court notes that understaffing of checkpoint is relevant to *LaFontaine* analysis since the presence of only a small number of officers and police vehicles may make the operation less identifiable as a police checkpoint). See Williams v. State, 293 Ga. 883, 750 S.E.2d 355 (2013) (cits omitted).

ficers who conducted the roadblock. The inquiry should be whether the roadblock decision was made in advance of its institution by a supervisor "above and away from 'field officers' on roving patrol, whose unfettered exercise of discretion is feared." The supervisor who orders the roadblock may be at the scene and participate in it, provided the supervisor made the decision in advance and in the capacity of supervisor and not as a field officer. "To summarize, where a defendant challenges his initial stop at a police checkpoint by way of a motion to suppress, the State bears the burden of proving that the seizure was constitutional. This requires the State to prove that the stop was reasonable under the totality of the circumstances. At a minimum, the State must show that the law enforcement agency's checkpoint program had an appropriate primary purpose other than ordinary crime control—a purpose examined at that programmatic level, rather than by trying to determine the motives of the supervisor who implemented and the officers who conducted the particular checkpoint at issue. The State must also prove that the particular checkpoint at which the defendant was stopped was properly implemented and operated—that the five requirements enumerated in *LaFontaine* were met." (Citations omitted).

In *McCoy v. State*,[12] the Court noted that *LaFontaine* is concerned only with the constitutionality of a roadblock. The Court determined that the first four factors address that issue while the fifth is only concerned with *Terry* issues, whether the officer had a "reasonable articulable suspicion" that a crime may have been committed.

Roadblocks which have as a primary purpose the detection of general criminal wrongdoing will not survive scrutiny under the Fourth Amendment. In *Illinois v. Lidster*,[13] the United States Supreme Court considered whether due process was offended by a police roadblock which was designed to question motorists about a crime which had been committed a week earlier at the road-

---

[12]McCoy v. State, 303 Ga. 551, 814 S.E.2d 319 (2018).

[13]Illinois v. Lidster, 540 U.S. 419, 124 S.Ct. 885, 157 L.Ed.2d 843 (2004). The Georgia Court of Appeals had found that a similar checkpoint violated the Fourth Amendment by concluding that its purpose was more in the nature of general crime control. Strickland v. State, 265 Ga. App. 533, 594 S.E.2d 711 (2004). On cert., the Supreme Court of Georgia remanded the case in light of Lidster and the Court of Appeals reversed its earlier opinion accordingly. Strickland v. State, 270 Ga. App. 187, 605 S.E.2d 890 (2004).

In Kellogg v. State, 288 Ga. App. 265 (1), 653 S.E.2d 841 (2007), the court ruled that a roadblock set up to enhance roadway safety by checking for impaired drivers, driver's licenses, seatbelts and insurance was not too much like general crime control and thus the roadblock had a "legitimate primary purpose."

block location and at the approximate time the roadblock was being conducted. The court concluded that the roadblock was proper since its purpose was not a generalized criminal investigation of motorists and the passengers in their cars, but rather a request for help in connection with a criminal investigation. Approved legitimate purposes for roadblock checkpoints include: the interception of illegal aliens; sobriety; verification of driver licenses and vehicle registration; and emergency checkpoints to prevent an imminent terrorist attack or to catch a dangerous criminal thought to be in a particular area.[14]

As noted by the Court in *Loney v. State,*[15] features of a valid roadblock are not "absolute criteria which must be satisfied before a roadblock is legitimate. Rather, this Court looks to the totality of the circumstances surrounding the roadblock to determine whether the factors were satisfied."

In *O'Kelley v. State,*[16] the Georgia Court of Appeals held that there is no "advanced publicity requirement in Georgia" for a roadblock. "Georgia law requires only that the roadblock be identified as a police checkpoint." In *Burns v. State,*[17] the court held that the requirement that supervisory personnel designate the place for the roadblock was sufficiently met where the nightshift supervisor on that night authorized the roadblock even though another officer was the supervisor of the entire shift. In *Hardin v. State,*[18] the court concluded that an auxiliary roadblock assigned to stop drivers attempting to avoid the central roadblock was within the requirements for a proper roadblock, even though its location was not explicitly authorized by supervisory personnel. The court's holding was premised on its finding that the general decision to implement the roadblock had been made by supervisory personnel. Thus, in *Thomas v. State,*[19] the court held that a roadblock was not properly conducted when the decision to implement it was made by officers in the field during the middle of a shift.

---

[14]City of Indianapolis v. Edmond, 531 U.S. 32, 121 S.Ct. 447, 148 L.Ed.2d 333, 340 (2000); Baker v. State, 252 Ga. App. 695, 700, 556 S.E.2d 892 (2001), disapproved, Brown v. State, 293 Ga. 883, 750 S.E.2d 355 (2013); State v. Ayers, 257 Ga. App. 117, 570 S.E.2d 603 (2002).

[15]Loney v. State, 245 Ga. App. 376, 537 S.E.2d 780 (2000) (cits. omitted).

[16]O'Kelley v. State, 210 Ga. App. 686, 687(4), 436 S.E.2d 760 (1993). Cf. Brent v. State, 270 Ga. 160, 161(2), 510 S.E.2d 14 (1998).

[17]Burns v. State, 236 Ga. App. 3, 5(1), 510 S.E.2d 865 (1999).

[18]Hardin v. State, 277 Ga. 242, 587 S.E.2d 634 (2003).

[19]Thomas v. State, 277 Ga. App. 88, 625 S.E.2d 455 (2005).

In *Michigan Department of State Police v. Sitz,*[20] the United States Supreme Court held that the Fourth Amendment was not violated where all motorists were stopped to check for signs of intoxication which were to be determined according to guidelines. In *LaFontaine v. State,*[21] the court required that a "screening" officer at a roadblock checking for persons driving under the influence must have "training and experience . . . sufficient to qualify him to make an initial determination as to which motorists should be given field tests for intoxication."

In *United States v. Prichard,*[22] the court held that a roadblock was constitutional on an interstate highway where officers started by stopping all cars but as soon as 10 cars were backed up, the officers would waive all stopped cars on through. The stops were held valid even though officers admitted that if they saw any evidence of crime while checking licenses and registrations, they planned to enforce the law.

In *Ledford v. State,*[23] the trial judge was affirmed in finding a roadblock valid where "[e]very noncommercial vehicle was stopped at the roadblock, with the exception of noncommercial vehicles which had been checked at the roadblock in one direction and soon came through again in the other direction." But in *State v. Stearns,*[24] the court found a roadblock arbitrary when the "trial court found that there were more than enough officers to stop vehicles traveling in both directions" but police had set up a roadblock north of a cluster of bars and only stopped vehicles being driven north.

In *Gamble v. State,*[25] the court held valid a roadblock which officers set up primarily to check for licenses, insurance and registration; authorized by supervisory personnel; manned by qualified personnel; and identified as a police checkpoint. Motorists were delayed only briefly unless they were unable to produce requisite information. Officers only allowed cars to pass through unchecked when conditions on the road backed up traffic and cre-

---

[20]Michigan Department of State Police v. Sitz, 496 U.S. 444, 110 S.Ct. 2481, 110 L.Ed.2d 412 (1990). Accord, White v. State, 233 Ga. App. 276, 277(2), 503 S.E.2d 891 (1998).

[21]LaFontaine v. State, 269 Ga. 251, 252(2), 497 S.E.2d 367 (1998). Accord, Heimlich v. State, 231 Ga. App. 662, 664, 500 S.E.2d 388 (1998).

[22]United States v. Prichard, 645 F.2d 854, 856-57 (10th Cir. 1981). Cf.

State v. Swift, 232 Ga. 535, 207 S.E.2d 459 (1974); Sowers v. State, 146 Ga. App. 701, 247 S.E.2d 225 (1978); Little v. State, 300 Md. 485, 479 A.2d 903 (1984).

[23]Ledford v. State, 221 Ga. App. 238, 239(2), 470 S.E.2d 796 (1996).

[24]State v. Stearns, 240 Ga. App. 806, 524 S.E.2d 554 (1999).

[25]Gamble v. State, 223 Ga. App. 653, 655(2), 478 S.E.2d 455 (1996).

ated a potential safety hazard. However, in *State v. Manos*[26] the appellate court affirmed the trial court in granting a motion to suppress material seized as a result of a roadblock. The court concluded that the problem with the roadblock was that all cars were stopped unless the officers got too backed up. In that event, officers let every car go until there were no more vehicles in sight before they started stopping cars again. The roadblock "was impermissibly based on an unfettered discretion granted to the field officer."

In *Gamble v. State*,[27] the court held that when a car is validly stopped at a roadblock and the driver could not find proof of insurance, an officer was authorized to make a brief inquiry regarding the driver's and passenger's destination and to request consent to search the vehicle. Where an initial detention or seizure at a roadblock is valid, a secondary detention or seizure does not require additional proof of reasonable and articulable suspicion.[28] In *McCray v. State*,[29] the Court of Appeals upheld the detention of the defendant at a "secondary position" while an officer sought verification of the defendant's driver's license. At the initial roadblock stop the defendant produced a "tattered" license and was unable to furnish a vehicle registration. The court also upheld a subsequent search of the defendant's vehicle after a drug dog alerted officers to the presence of drugs in the defendant's car at that secondary stop. This court was satisfied that the roadblock was set up for a proper purpose, the defendant's detention was appropriate and allowing the dog to walk around the car did not unduly prolong the detention. Independent of the bona fides of a roadblock, evasive measures to avoid a roadblock may give rise to a reasonable suspicion of criminal activity on the part of police authorities. Thus, in *Taylor v. State*,[30] the Court of Appeals affirmed the denial of the defendant's motion to suppress blood alcohol evidence obtained after the evasive and erratic effort of the defendant to avoid a roadblock.

See Annotation, "Validity of Police Roadblocks or Checkpoints for Purpose of Discovery of Alcoholic Intoxication—Post Sitz

---

[26]State v. Manos, 237 Ga. App. 699, 516 S.E.2d 548 (1999). See also Ponce v. State, 271 Ga. App. 408, 609 S.E.2d 736 (2005), judgment vacated on other grounds, 279 Ga. 651, 619 S.E.2d 682 (2005).

[27]Gamble v. State, 223 Ga. App. 653, 656(3), 478 S.E.2d 455 (1996).

[28]Workman v. State, 235 Ga. App. 800, 801, 510 S.E.2d 109 (1998).

[29]McCray v. State, 268 Ga. App. 84, 601 S.E.2d 452 (2004). Note that

the validity of police use of a drug-sniffing dog during a lawful traffic stop where there was no suspicion of drugs was affirmed in Illinois v. Caballes, 543 U.S. 405, 125 S. Ct. 834, 160 L. Ed. 2d 842 (2005). See Rodriguez v. U.S., 135 S. Ct. 1609, 191 L. Ed. 2d 492 (2015).

[30]Taylor v. State, 249 Ga. App. 733, 549 S.E.2d 536 (2001); see also, Richards v. State, 257 Ga. App. 358, 571 S.E.2d 172 (2002).

Cases," 74 A.L.R. 5th 319 (1999).

§ 3:10   The *Terry* frisk

In *Peters v. State,*[1] the court pointed to United States Supreme Court holdings stating that there are

> at least theoretically, three tiers of police-citizen encounters: (1) communication between police and citizens involving no coercion or detention and therefore without the compass of the Fourth Amendment, (2) brief seizures that must be supported by reasonable suspicion, and (3) full-scale arrests that must be supported by probable cause. . . . In the first [tier] police officers may approach citizens, ask for identification, and freely question the citizen without any basis or belief that the citizen is involved in criminal activity, as long as the officers do not detain the citizen or create the impression that the citizen may not leave. The second tier occurs when the officer actually conducts a brief investigative *Terry* stop of the citizen. In this level, a police officer, even in the absence of probable cause, may stop persons and detain them briefly, when the officer has a particularized and objective basis for suspecting the persons are involved in criminal activity.

If there is a sufficient, articulable suspicion to stop a suspect, or if a suspect permits an officer to talk with him, the encounter must not go further than brief questioning of the suspect by the officer unless, after questioning, the officer has *probable cause* to believe the suspect has contraband or if the officer has a justified belief that the person stopped may be armed and dangerous.[2] Likewise, an officer may check "for outstanding warrants or criminal histories on the occupants of a vehicle at a valid traffic stop," provided the officer has a justifiable safety concern during the stop.[3]

If the officer at the end of the "stop phase" has probable cause to believe the suspect has contraband, he may arrest the suspect and then conduct a full-fledged search incident to the arrest.[4] If the officer reasonably believes the suspect is armed and danger-

---

[Section 3:10]

[1]Peters v. State, 242 Ga. App. 816, 531 S.E.2d 386 (2000).

[2]L.B.B. III v. State, 129 Ga. App. 163, 198 S.E.2d 895 (1973); State v. Hunter, 375 So.2d 99 (La.1979).

However, articulable suspicion plus refusal to answer questions may amount to probable cause to arrest. Commonwealth v. Ellis, 233 Pa.Super. 169, 335 A.2d 512, 514-15 (1975). But cf. People v. Howard, 50 N.Y.2d 583, 430 N.Y.S.2d 578, 408 N.E.2d 908

(1980). A number of courts have held that flight together with suspicious behavior can amount to probable cause to arrest. United States v. Vasquez, 534 F.2d 1142, 1145-1146 (5th Cir. 1976); People v. Kreichman, 37 N.Y.2d 693, 376 N.Y.S.2d 497, 339 N.E.2d 182, 187-188 (1975). See § 2:11, supra, on probable cause to arrest.

[3]State v. Williams, 264 Ga. App. 199, 202, 590 S.E.2d 151 (2003) (citations omitted).

[4]Cf. State v. Long, 239 Ga. App. 463, 465, 521 S.E.2d 401 (1999).

ous, he may frisk the suspect for weapons. The frisk, however, may not be justified by the desire to discover or prevent the destruction of evidence in the absence of probable cause[5] and a valid stop alone does not justify a frisk.

Under the rule adopted in *Terry v. Ohio,*[6] a "frisk" is a search within the meaning of the Fourth Amendment. The court in *Terry* also said, however, that unlike a search conducted incident to a lawful arrest, the scope of the frisk must be limited to an intrusion reasonably necessary to discover weapons on or about the person detained.[7]

If a frisk is justified, an officer must ordinarily follow a two-step process. "The officer must pat down first, and then intrude beneath the surface only if he comes upon something which feels like a weapon."[8] A number of courts have emphasized that an officer is not justified in concluding that a search may be conducted if the object felt is soft,[9] but if the object is hard and of substantial size then the officer may remove the item.[10] If an object is felt which the officer believes to be a weapon, the officer may only take such action as is necessary to examine the weapon,[11] or, as McFadden did in *Terry,* remove the object. If the object obtained by the officer turns out to be an illegally concealed weapon or contraband, the officer may at that point arrest the suspect and then conduct a full-blown search.

---

[5]Jones v. State, 126 Ga. App. 841, 844, 192 S.E.2d 171, 174 (1972). See Walker v. State, 299 Ga. App. 788, 683 S.E.2d 867 (2009), where the court found that there was no particularized and objective basis for suspecting criminal activity to support a second-tier *Terry* stop where suspect exhibited nervousness and was standing in a known drug area. The court noted that consent to search obtained as result of illegal detention is not valid.

[6]Terry v. Ohio, 392 U.S. 1, 88 S.Ct. 1868, 20 L.Ed.2d 889 (1968).

[7]Jones v. State, 126 Ga. App. 841, 844, 192 S.E.2d 171, 174 (1972); State v. King, 227 Ga. App. 466, 468, 489 S.E.2d 361 (1997).

[8]Brown v. State, 181 Ga. App. 768, 771(1)(a), 353 S.E.2d 572 (1987); Barrett v. State, 212 Ga. App. 745, 443 S.E.2d 285 (1994); State v. Anonymous, 6 Conn.Cir.Ct. 583, 280 A.2d 816 (1971); State v. Hobart, 94 Wash.2d 437, 617 P.2d 429 (1980); Terry v. Ohio, 392 U.S. 1, 29, 30, 88 S.Ct. 1868, 20

L.Ed.2d 889 (1968); Jones v. State, 126 Ga. App. 841, 192 S.E.2d 171 (1972).

[9]U.S. v. Del Toro, 464 F.2d 520 (2d Cir. 1972); People v. McCarty, 11 Ill. App. 3d 421, 296 N.E.2d 862 (5th Dist. 1973) (abrogated by Minnesota v. Dickerson, 508 U.S. 366, 113 S. Ct. 2130, 124 L. Ed. 2d 334 (1993)). But in the airport drug courier profile situation of United States v. Smith, 649 F.2d 305, 309 (5th Cir. 1981), the court referred to a "reasonable narcotics pat-down," and stated that if a defendant consented to a pat-down of his outer garments and the officer felt what seemed to be contraband in an inside pocket, he could reach his hand inside and remove the substance.

[10]Brown v. State, 181 Ga. App. 768, 771(1)(a), 353 S.E.2d 572 (1987); Ginn v. State, 236 Ga. App. 448, 512 S.E.2d 338 (1999); State v. Bitterman, 304 Minn. 481, 232 N.W.2d 91 (1975).

[11]State v. Cotterman, 544 S.W.2d 322 (Mo.App.1976).

In the 1993 case of *Minnesota v. Dickerson*,[12] the United States Supreme Court held that "[i]f, while conducting a legitimate *Terry* search . . . the officer should . . . discover contraband other than weapons, he clearly cannot be required to ignore the contraband, and the Fourth Amendment does not require its suppression. . . ." If, however, the police lack a reasonable belief that an object felt is contraband or a weapon, the officer has no authority to squeeze, slide, or otherwise manipulate the contents of the defendant's pocket, after the officer knows the pocket does not contain a weapon, in order to determine if the object is contraband. In *Commonwealth v. Johnson*,[13] the court concluded that there was probable cause to arrest where an officer during a *Terry* frisk felt a "crunchy, granular substance" in the defendant's crotch, since it was "immediately apparent" that the defendant possessed contraband. In *Seaman v. State*,[14] Georgia recognized the "plain feel" doctrine and affirmed the denial of a motion to suppress where an experienced narcotics officer in the course of a *Terry* patdown felt what he believed to be a clear plastic baggie containing contraband.[15] There was no evidence the officer "manipulated the object in [the defendant's] pocket in any way before identifying it." Further, in the Georgia case of *Buffington v. State*,[16] the court also applied the "plain feel" test as to a crack pipe in the defendant's pocket because the police officer immediately recognized the pipe as a drug-related object. However, in *State v. Williams*,[17] the court affirmed the suppression where the officer testified he searched the defendant's "pocket because he was concerned that the unidentified object which felt like a bag could be a weapon and because it could 'possibly' be

---

[12]Minnesota v. Dickerson, 508 U.S. 366, 113 S.Ct. 2130, 124 L.Ed.2d 334 (1993). Accord, Boatright v. State, 225 Ga. App. 181, 182(1), 483 S.E.2d 659 (1997); Harris v. State, 239 Ga. App. 537, 539(1), 521 S.E.2d 462 (1999).

[13]Commonwealth v. Johnson, 429 Pa.Super. 158, 631 A.2d 1335, 1337 (1993); State v. Wilson, 112 N.C.App. 777, 437 S.E.2d 387 (1993).

[14]Seaman v. State, 214 Ga. App. 878, 879(2), 449 S.E.2d 526 (1994). Accord, Howard v. State, 220 Ga. App. 579, 582(1), 469 S.E.2d 746 (1996); Andrews v. State, 221 Ga. App. 492, 471 S.E.2d 567 (1996); Stewart v. State, 227 Ga. App. 659, 660(2), 490 S.E.2d 194 (1997).

[15]"Under the plain feel doctrine, if, during a lawful pat-down search, an officer feels an object whose contours or mass makes it *immediately identifiable* as contraband, that officer can seize the item. Thus, for evidence to be admissible under the plain feel doctrine, the searching officer must express a degree of certainty in identifying the item. This is so because a pat-down search is "conducted solely for the purpose of insuring the safety of the officer and of others nearby, not to procure evidence for use at a subsequent trial." Patman v. State, 244 Ga. App. 833, 834-35, 537 S.E.2d 118 (2000). See May v. State, 334 Ga. App. 807, 780 S.E.2d 455 (2015).

[16]Buffington v. State, 229 Ga. App. 450, 494 S.E.2d 272 (1997).

[17]State v. Williams, 220 Ga. App. 100, 101(1), 469 S.E.2d 261 (1996).

contraband." In *Corley v. State*,[18] after a stop, the officer frisked the defendant and felt and saw a bulge in the defendant's watch pocket. There was no evidence that led the officer to believe that the defendant had a weapon in his watch pocket. The defendant emptied his watch pocket when the officer told him to do so and an object which looked like marijuana was removed. The appellate court reversed the denial of the defendant's motion to suppress. See Annotation, "Application of 'Plain-Feel' Exception to Warrant Requirements—State Cases," 50 A.L.R. 5th 581 (1997).

Generally, in the absence of a pretextual stop, if the frisk does not produce a weapon or contraband, the encounter must be terminated at that point unless the officer has obtained probable cause for an arrest.[19] See § 4:26, infra, on pretextual stops. However, in *McGugan v. State*,[20] the officer felt a rather large hard object inside the defendant's inside jacket pocket. The officer asked the defendant to identify the object and the defendant did not respond. The deputy reached inside the defendant's pocket and removed a plastic bag containing a substance later identified as cocaine. The deputy testified he removed the object because the defendant failed to respond to the deputy's request to identify the object. The court concluded that the defendant's refusal to identify the object, coupled with his earlier reluctance to cooperate with the deputy, "created a reasonable suspicion that the defendant was armed" and justified the deputy in placing his hand in the defendant's pocket and removing the object. In *Redd v. State*,[21] the court noted that "an individual's conduct in response to questioning or attempted questioning may rise to the level of probable cause to conduct an arrest or search." The court then held that when an officer has articulable suspicion authorizing a stop and frisk and the defendant "did not respond to the officer's questions, never allowed the officer to get close enough to question him or complete a limited patdown for weapons, ignored several requests to stop, and then fled into the woods," a nonconsensual investigation pursuant to *Terry* was authorized.

In cases where there is an illegal stop and search, which leads to the discovery of evidence of criminal conduct, the evidence may

---

[18]Corley v. State, 236 Ga. App. 302, 304(1), 512 S.E.2d 41 (1999). See Johnson v. State, 297 Ga. App. 847, 678 S.E.2d 539 (2009) (officer is permitted to intrude under suspect's outer clothing only where (1) he comes into contact with something that feels like a weapon or (2) he feels an object whose contour or mass immediately suggests it is contraband).

[19]Arkansas v. Sullivan, 532 U.S. 769, 121 S.Ct. 1876, 149 L.Ed.2d 994 (2001).

[20]McGugan v. State, 215 Ga. App. 535, 536, 451 S.E.2d 460 (1994). See § 4:21, infra, on other aspects of this case.

[21]Redd v. State, 229 Ga. App. 364, 366, 494 S.E.2d 31 (1997).

be admissible if the defendant was the subject of a valid outstanding warrant, despite the manner in which it was obtained if the defendant is arrested under the warrant. In *State v. Cooper*,[22] the defendant was the passenger in a vehicle which was stopped and searched. The defendant sought to suppress the marijuana found in the car. At the time the vehicle was stopped the officer determined that the defendant was the subject of outstanding warrants and arrested him on the basis of these charges. The court concluded that once the warrants were discovered any taint to the evidence found during the search was "cleansed" and the search became justified as one incident to the arrest.

When the suspect is in a car and the articulable suspicion relates to any serious offense, the officer probably may have him get out of the car.[23] Once the suspect is out of the car and on foot, it seems that he is like a pedestrian who has been stopped. In *Maryland v. Wilson*,[24] the United States Supreme Court held that where the driver of a car is stopped for speeding, the "officer making a traffic stop may [also] order passengers to get out of the car pending completion of the stop." In *Rogers v. State*,[25] the court held that "[a]n officer conducting a routine traffic stop may request and examine a driver's license and vehicle registration[,] and run a computer check on the documents." See § 4:26, infra, on search incident to a traffic arrest. In *State v. Blair*,[26] the court pointed out that an investigatory traffic stop is "a brief stop, limited in time to that minimally necessary to investigate the allegation invoking suspicion, and limited in scope to identification and limited questioning reasonably related to the circumstances that justified the initiation of the momentary stop."

Evidence obtained from a pat down of a passenger in a motor

---

[22]State v. Cooper, 260 Ga. App. 333 (2), 579 S.E.2d 754 (2003). See Ruffin v. State, 201 Ga. App. 792(2)(a), 412 S.E.2d 850 (1991); Oliver v. State, 232 Ga. App. 816, 821(3)(a), 503 S.E.2d 28 (1998).

[23]In United States v. White, 648 F.2d 29, 38-39 (D.C.Cir. 1981), the court said that it would be strange to permit an officer to have a driver get out of a car for a minor traffic violation (as in Pennsylvania v. Mimms, 434 U.S. 106, 98 S.Ct. 330, 54 L.Ed.2d 331 [1977]), but not permit an officer to have a suspected narcotics trafficker get out of his car when he is stopped on reasonable suspicion.

[24]Maryland v. Wilson, 519 U.S. 408, 117 S.Ct. 882, 137 L.Ed.2d 41 (1997), cited and followed in Carter v. State, 229 Ga. App. 417, 419, 494 S.E.2d 108 (1997).

[25]Rogers v. State, 206 Ga. App. 654, 657, 426 S.E.2d 209 (1992). See Annots., "Search and Seizure: Lawfulness of Demand for Driver's License, Vehicle Registration, or Proof of Insurance Pursuant to Police Stop to Assist Motorist," 19 A.L.R.5th 884 (1994), and "Permissibility Under Fourth Amendment of Detention of Motorist by Police, Following Lawful Stop for Traffic Offense, to Investigate Matters Not Related To Offense," 118 A.L.R.Fed. 567 (1994).

[26]State v. Blair, 239 Ga. App. 340, 341, 521 S.E.2d 380 (1999).

vehicle conducted by an officer, who admitted that he was not concerned for his safety and administered the search as part of a routine followed in all cases where he directs someone to exit a vehicle, is subject to suppression.[27]

§ 3:11 Extensions of the *Terry* frisk

The material in the foregoing section represents the traditional stereotyped approach to a *Terry* frisk. However, there seems to be an indication in United States Supreme Court opinions and decisions of a number of other courts indicating a departure from the traditional approach. For example, in *Michigan v. Summers*,[1] the Court said that the right to "stop" is not limited to "momentary, on-the-street detention." In footnote 12 the Court said, "[T]he key principle of the Fourth Amendment is reasonableness—the balancing of competing interests. . . . If the purpose underlying a *Terry* stop—investigating possible criminal activity—is to be served, the police must under certain circumstances be able to detain the individual for longer than the brief time period involved in *Terry* and *Adams*." In a like approach the Georgia Court of Appeals said that "[o]nce a '*Terry* stop' has been made, the legality of its scope 'is determined in each case by balancing the extent of the intrusion against the immediacy and importance of the interest in crime prevention or law enforcement which is sought to be advanced.' "[2]

In *Hodges v. State*,[3] the court affirmed the frisk where in addition to the standard *Terry* pat-down, the officer put his fingers under the defendant's "beltline [in the back], on the exterior of the shirt, to feel if there was a weapon secured under the clothing by the belt." This was deemed to be a reasonable search for weapons under the facts of the case which included the fact that the officer himself carried "his weapon in his back when he was off duty." The court also noted, among other things, that the event took place in the early morning hours while it was dark, that the officer went to that area following an emergency 911 call, and that the area was well known for the presence of guns and drugs.

In *Thomas v. State*,[4] the court affirmed the conviction where a defendant exited an automobile and officers informed him that

---

[27]Edgell v. State, 253 Ga. App. 775, 777, 560 S.E.2d 532 (2002).

[Section 3:11]

[1]Michigan v. Summers, 452 U.S. 692, 700, 101 S.Ct. 2587, 69 L.Ed.2d 340 (1981), n. 12.

[2]Van Loo v. State, 187 Ga. App.

290, 291, 370 S.E.2d 44 (1988). Accord, State v. Blair, 239 Ga. App. 340, 341, 521 S.E.2d 380 (1999).

[3]Hodges v. State, 217 Ga. App. 806, 808(2), 460 S.E.2d 89 (1995).

[4]Thomas v. State, 231 Ga. App. 173, 498 S.E.2d 760 (1998).

they had received information that he was carrying drugs. He kept placing his hand in his jacket pocket. After the defendant refused to obey an order to remove his hand from his pocket, the officer, fearing for his own safety, forcibly removed the defendant's hand from the pocket and reached in and found a bag containing the suspected heroin. At that point, the officer arrested the defendant and searched him and the automobile.

In *United States v. Sokolow,*[5] the United States Supreme Court stated that officers are not obligated to use the "least intrusive means available to verify or dispel their suspicions."

As one commentator observed, "It is clear that there are several investigative techniques which may be utilized effectively in the course of a *Terry*-type stop. The most common is interrogation, which may include both a request for identification and inquiry concerning the suspicious conduct of the person detained. Sometimes the officer will communicate with others, either police or private citizens, in an effort to verify the explanation tendered or to confirm the identification or determine whether a person of that identity is otherwise wanted. Or, the suspect may be detained while it is determined if in fact an offense has occurred in the area, a process which might involve checking certain premises, locating and examining objects abandoned by the suspect, or talking with other people. If it is known that an offense has occurred in the area, the suspect may be viewed by witnesses to the crime. There is no reason to conclude that any investigative methods of the type just listed are inherently objectionable; they might cast doubt upon the reasonableness of the detention, however, if their use makes the period of detention unduly long or involves moving the suspect to another locale." 3 LaFave, *Search and Seizure,* § 9.2, pp. 36-37 (West 1978). See § 3:7, supra, on facts justifying a stop where there has been a crime reported.

However, in the 1995 opinion *Smith v. State,*[6] the Georgia Court of Appeals does not speak in terms of exclusion of evidence discovered as a result of unjustified questioning during a stop. The court held that the "scope of the detention must be carefully tailored to its underlying justification." Thus, when a person is stopped for a possible DUI violation, the officer is justified to ask a driver "for his license to establish his identity, and to ask questions reasonably related to whether or not [the driver] was driving under the influence." Once an explanation has been given,

---

[5]United States v. Sokolow, 490 U.S. 1, 109 S.Ct. 1581, 104 L.Ed.2d 1 (1989).

[6]Smith v. State, 216 Ga. App.

453, 454(2), 454 S.E.2d 635 (1995). Cf. Almond v. State, 242 Ga. App. 650, 652(1), 530 S.E.2d 750 (2000).

the officer may "administer a statutorily authorized field sobriety test, or take any other reasonable steps to determine whether [the driver] was, as he originally suspected, driving under the influence." Questions pertaining to the possession of contraband are "beyond the permissible scope of the investigation." The court in *Migliore v. State*[7] relied on *Smith* in holding that "[a]t the point the officer initiated the probe for drugs, he went beyond the permissible scope of the investigation and his further detention of the defendant went beyond that permitted by *Terry* and its progeny."

In *United States v. Purcell*,[8] the 11th Circuit Court of Appeals held that a stop "may not last 'any longer than necessary to process the traffic violation' unless there is articulable suspicion of other illegal activity." In *United States v. Boyce*,[9] the 11th Circuit gave the holding in *Purcell* some added definition by observing that there are only three situations in which a traffic stop may be prolonged: to investigate the driver's license and vehicle registration; to wait for the results of a criminal history check that is part of a routine traffic investigation; and, if there exists an "articulable suspicion of other illegal activity." Thus, when an officer's questioning and detention of the driver and the occupants of a motor vehicle exceeds the scope of reasonable permissible investigation, any evidence obtained as a result may be tainted and subject to suppression at trial.[10]

In *Daniel v. State*,[11] the Supreme Court of Georgia held that evidence obtained as a result of continued questioning and detention after the underlying basis for the initial traffic stop has concluded is not automatically subject to a constitutional

---

[7]Migliore v. State, 240 Ga. App. 783, 785, 525 S.E.2d 166 (1999) (citing Smith v. State, 216 Ga. App. 453, 454 S.E.2d 635 (1995)); State v. Hanson, 243 Ga. App. 532, 539, 532 S.E.2d 715 (2000) (physical precedent).

[8]United States v. Purcell, 236 F.3d 1274, 1277 (11th Cir. 2001).

[9]United States v. Boyce, 351 F.3d 1102, 1106 (11th Cir. 2003).

[10]Cases involving prolonged detention and questioning of the driver and passengers of a motor vehicle are fact intensive. See, e.g., State v. Felton, 297 Ga. App. 35, 676 S.E.2d 434 (2009) (finding that the trial court properly granted a motion to suppress, reasoning that when the officer asked a driver of a car whom he pulled over for a seat belt violation to exit the vehicle, the officer had impermissibly extended the detention and expanded the scope of the traffic stop); see also Evans v. State, 262 Ga. App. 712, 586 S.E.2d 400 (2003); Tiller v. State, 261 Ga. App. 363, 582 S.E.2d 536 (2003); State v. Habib, 260 Ga. App. 229, 581 S.E.2d 576 (2003); Henderson v. State, 250 Ga. App. 278, 551 S.E.2d 400 (2001); Flores v. State, 818 S.E.2d 90 (Ga. Ct. App. 2018) (30-minute vehicle stop was not unduly prolonged by 19-minute wait for a Spanish speaking officer to speak with driver who did not appear to understand officer's questions).

[11]Daniel v. State, 277 Ga. 840 (1), 597 S.E.2d 116 (2004), overruled, Salmeron v. State, 280 Ga. 735 (1), 632 S.E.2d 645 (2006).

challenge. "[W]e hold that a law enforcement officer's continued questioning of a vehicle's driver and passengers outside the scope of a valid traffic stop passes muster under the Fourth Amendment either when the officer has a reasonable articulable suspicion of other illegal activity or when the valid traffic stop has de-escalated into a consensual encounter."[12] In *Daniel*, the police had no reason to suspect criminal activity which would warrant detaining the defendant beyond the scope of the initial stop. Nonetheless, the court concluded that under the totality of the circumstances surrounding the post traffic stop detention, the questioning was consensual in nature and hence the evidence obtained as a result thereof was the product of a lawful investigation and properly admitted at trial.

Following *Daniel*, however, the United States Supreme Court, in *Muehler v. Mena*,[13] held that unless police questioning prolongs detention, the questioning does not amount to an additional seizure, "and, therefore, no additional Fourth Amendment justification" is required. Accordingly, in *Salmeron v. State*,[14] the Supreme Court of Georgia abrogated the totality of the circumstances standard of *Daniel* and substituted the standard announced by the United States Supreme Court in *Muehler*.

As the Georgia Court of Appeals observed in *State v. Davis*[15] following *Salmeron*, "even if police have no basis for suspecting that a person detained at a traffic stop is engaged in criminal activity unrelated to the stop, police may lawfully ask questions during the course of the stop about such unrelated activity, so long as the questioning does not prolong the stop beyond the time reasonably required to complete the purpose of the traffic stop."

---

[12]Daniel v. State, 277 Ga. 840 (1), 597 S.E.2d 116 (2004), overruled, Salmeron v. State, 280 Ga. 735 (1), 632 S.E.2d 645 (2006).

[13]Muehler v. Mena, 544 U.S. 93, 94, 125 S. Ct. 1465, 161 L. Ed. 2d 299 (2005).

[14]Salmeron v. State, 280 Ga. 735, 632 S.E.2d 645 (2006) (seizure justified solely by the issuance of a warning to a motorist can become unlawful if it extends beyond the time reasonably required to complete that mission). Justice Sears sharply dissented in *Salmeron*, noting that a state court is never prohibited from interpreting its state constitution in a way that is not contrary to federal law but none-

theless provides its citizens with greater rights than those allowed by the U.S. Constitution. It should also be noted that *Daniel* and *Muehler* are factually very different cases. *Daniel* involved questioning a motorist about matters unrelated to the initial reason for the stop. *Muehler* was a case brought pursuant to 42 U.S.C.A. § 1983 and arose in the context of the execution of a fairly intrusive search of a residence pursuant to a search warrant.

[15]State v. Davis, 283 Ga. App. 200, 202 (2), 641 S.E.2d 205 (2007). See Duncan v. State, 331 Ga. App. 254, 770 S.E.2d 329 (2015) (good summary of cases treating prolonged detention).

The court also noted in *Hayes v. State*[16] that asking "the driver to step out of the vehicle does not unduly prolong the detention. Further, as a matter of Georgia law, it does not matter whether the request to search comes during the traffic stop or immediately thereafter." However, once the purpose of the traffic stop has been fulfilled, the continued detention of the car and its occupants amounts to a second detention.[17]

The standard for whether or not an officer has reasonable suspicion to stop a vehicle centers on the totality of the circumstances surrounding a particular stop and whether the police questioning unduly prolongs an otherwise proper detention. The United States Supreme Court has expressly recognized that this standard includes analyzing both "innocent factors" and apparently "suspicious factors"[18]

In *Simmons v. State*,[19] the defendant was validly stopped for a traffic violation. The court pointed out that the appropriate legal standard for determining whether further questioning and a walk around the car with a narcotics dog were justified "is whether the officers had a *reasonable suspicion* [rather than probable cause] that [the defendant] was transporting illegal drugs." The appellate court held that the following did not establish such a reasonable suspicion: (1) the defendant and his passenger appeared nervous; (2) the defendant told officers that the vehicle rental agreement was in his wife's name, and his wife was not present; and (3) the defendant told officers he was nervous because the passenger was his girlfriend. After warning him for the traffic violation, the officer should not have detained the defendant further to ask him whether he was transporting narcotics and to

[16]Hayes v. State, 292 Ga. App. 724, 665 S.E.2d 422 (2008) (citations omitted).

[17]See Nunnally v. State, 310 Ga. App. 183, 713 S.E.2d 408 (2011).

[18]United States v. Arvizu, 534 U.S. 266, 122 S.Ct. 744, 151 L.Ed.2d 740 (2002). For example, in Richbow v. State, 293 Ga. App. 556, 559, 667 S.E.2d 418 (2008), the court observed: "Many cases evaluate whether the presence of certain elements constitutes enough evidence to create a reasonable suspicion of criminal activity that permits further inquiry. Regarding the elements of nervousness, cell phones, and air freshener, nervousness alone is not enough, nor are nervousness and meaningless inconsistencies. Traveling a known drug route, nervousness, heavy air freshener and conflicting itinerary accounts may be sufficient. Increasing nervousness and meaningful inconsistencies also may be enough to justify continued detention, but nervousness and a heavy masking scent may not be. Multiple cell phones along with other elements may be sufficient. All three elements of nervousness, multiple cell phones, and a masking scent may or may not be enough to detain someone." (Citations deleted.).

[19]Simmons v. State, 223 Ga. App. 781, 782(2), 479 S.E.2d 123 (1996) (emphasis added). Accord, Berry v. State, 248 Ga. App. 874, 879(3), 547 S.E.2d 664 (2001); Migliore v. State, 240 Ga. App. 783, 785, 525 S.E.2d 166 (1999).

walk a drug dog around his car. In *Dominguez v. State*,[20] the court noted that the "State bears the burden of proving that the search of the car was lawful, and to carry this burden, the State must show that it was lawful to detain [the suspect] until the time the drug dog indicated the presence of drugs." See § 3:12, infra, on when a stop becomes an arrest.

In *State v. Allen*,[21] the Georgia Supreme Court reversed the Court of Appeals which had held that officers may run a computer check of the driver and passengers in an auto provided "an investigatory stop is not unreasonably prolonged" as a result. Detaining the occupants of a vehicle in order to run a record check after the purpose for the stop had been achieved, the Court of Appeals said, would not be proper in the absence of a reasonable articulable suspicion of criminal activity other than the traffic violation. The Supreme Court held that because traffic stops are potentially dangerous situations, it is not unreasonable for officers to run a computer records check even though the period of detention might be extended several minutes as a result. In addition, the Court held that it is permissible for the officers to conduct an open air dog sniff while awaiting the results of the record check.

Once a valid traffic stop has ended, it may de-escalate into a consensual [first tier] encounter. In determining whether a stop has de-escalated into a first tier encounter, one in which a reasonable person would have felt free to leave, "three important factors have been given particular scrutiny: (a) whether the driver's documents have been returned to him; (b) whether the officer informed the driver that he was free to leave; and (c) whether the driver appreciated that the traffic stop had reached an endpoint."[22]

Adams v. Williams[23] represents the exception to the general rule that an officer, at the time of the stop, is to talk with the suspect before determining whether or not to conduct a frisk. In this case, the officer approached Williams, reached to the spot where a gun was thought to be hidden and removed the gun. The court concluded that this conduct was reasonable. After obtaining the pistol, Williams was then arrested for the illegal possession of the weapon and searched as an incident to the arrest. In the

---

[20]Dominguez v. State, 310 Ga. App. 370, 372, 714 S.E.2d 25, 28 (2011) (citations omitted). See also Bodiford v. State, 328 Ga. App. 258, 761 S.E.2d 818 (2014).

[21]State v. Allen, 298 Ga. 1, 779 S.E.2d 248 (2015). The dissent is sharply critical of the opinion. The case is analyzed in 31 *What's the Deci-*sion, November, 2015.

[22]State v. Felton, 297 Ga. App. 35, 37, 676 S.E.2d 434 (2009) (citing State v. Connor, 288 Ga. App. 517, 519, 654 S.E.2d 461 (2007)).

[23]Adams v. Williams, 407 U.S. 143, 92 S.Ct. 1921, 32 L.Ed.2d 612 (1972).

Georgia case *Pace v. State*,[24] officers in a high crime area saw the defendant standing in a parking lot. He stood there about eight minutes before the officers approached in a marked police car. The officers were suspicious that the defendant was there to sell drugs. When the defendant saw the police car, he turned and started walking away. The officers called him and he began acting very nervous and continued to walk away. When the officers approached him "he reached toward his right pocket and attempted several times to reach into it. They stopped him from going into the pocket because they were concerned for their safety . . . . They asked [the defendant] to put his hands on the police car, and the officer reached into the pocket and found [a] razor blade and drugs." There was no earlier pat-down. In affirming the admission of the evidence obtained from the pocket, the court pointed out that "[t]he law permits . . . officers to protect themselves from harm even when conducting a non-coercive lawful stop . . . . The usual police response will be to conduct a frisk, patting the individual's clothing in search of a weapon . . . . [However, a] pat down is not a prerequisite."

In *United States v. Baker*,[25] the Fourth Circuit held that "the reasonableness of a protective search depends on the factual circumstances of each case. . . . Thus, a pat down frisk is but one example of how a reasonable protective search may be conducted. . . . Balancing the officer's interest in self-protection against the resulting intrusion upon Baker's personal security, we hold that [the officer's] direction was reasonable under the circumstances." The officer instructed Baker to lift his shirt far enough to uncover a bulge near his waist so as to reveal the bulge. Baker had been stopped for a traffic violation. The bulge was caused by a gun.

Based on *Terry*, in 1983, the United States Supreme Court in *Michigan v. Long*[26] approved a frisk or search of the passenger compartment of an automobile limited to areas in which a weapon might have been placed. The court said, "[t]he police searched the passenger compartment because they had reason to believe that the vehicle contained weapons. We hold that the protective search

---

[24]Pace v. State, 219 Ga. App. 583, 584-85, 466 S.E.2d 254 (1995) (citations omitted); State v. Ballard, 617 N.W.2d 837 (S.D.2000).

[25]United States v. Baker, 78 F.3d 135 (4th Cir. 1996).

[26]Michigan v. Long, 463 U.S. 1032, 103 S.Ct. 3469, 77 L.Ed.2d 1201 (1983).

See State v. Jones, 289 Ga. App. 176, 657 S.E.2d 253 (2008), where the Court of Appeals expressly disapproved the notion that an officer could justifiably enter an auto and seize a weapon in conjunction with a routine traffic stop in the absence of some evidence of threat to the officer. The court rejected any suggestion to the contrary as expressed in the physical precedent only of Megesi v. State, 277 Ga. App. 855, 627 S.E.2d 814 (2006).

See State v. Jarrells, 207 Ga. App. 192, 193(3), 427 S.E.2d 568 (1993).

of the passenger compartment was reasonable under the principles articulated in *Terry* and other decisions of this Court." In another portion of the opinion the Court said "that the search of the passenger compartment of an automobile, limited to those areas in which a weapon may be placed or hidden, is permissible if the police officer possesses a reasonable belief based on 'specific and articulable facts which, taken together with the rational inferences from those facts, reasonably warrant' the officers in believing that the suspect is dangerous and the suspect may gain immediate control of weapons. . . . '[T]he issue is whether a reasonably prudent man in the circumstances would be warranted in the belief that his safety or that of others was in danger.' "

In *Holsey v. State*,[27] the court held that "a law enforcement officer who detains a person for purposes of investigation should 'not be denied the opportunity to protect himself from attack by a hostile suspect' and may lawfully detain the person in a manner 'reasonably necessary to protect [his] personal safety and to maintain the status quo.' Other courts have held that, in sufficiently dangerous circumstances, law enforcement officers may effect and maintain investigatory detentions by drawing weapons and forcing defendants to lie face down with arms and legs spread. Such methods must be reserved for cases where plausible danger exists to the detaining officer's personal safety, but '[t]o require an officer to risk his life in order to make an investigatory stop would run contrary to the intent of *Terry v. Ohio* . . . .' [Footnotes omitted.]" In *United States v. Holt*,[28] the court held that an officer making a traffic stop may ask the driver if there was a loaded gun in the car.

In *Jackson v. State*,[29] the court held that, in the frisk stage, the officer was justified in handcuffing the defendant where he was regarded as being extremely violent.

In *United States v. Kent*,[30] the Eleventh Circuit held that where Customs officials validly stop a vessel, they have a right to conduct a protective sweep after boarding the vessel.

In *Pitts v. State*,[31] the court affirmed the action of an officer in conducting a "free air search" of the outside of a van by a German Shepherd dog after the officer obtained conflicting versions from the two occupants of the vehicle about their travel itinerary.

---

[27]Holsey v. State, 271 Ga. 856, 861(6), 524 S.E.2d 473 (1999).

[28]United States v. Holt, 264 F.3d 1215 (10th Cir. en banc. 2001).

[29]Jackson v. State, 236 Ga. App. 492 (1), 512 S.E.2d 24 (1999).

[30]United States v. Kent, 691 F.2d 1376 (11th Cir. 1982).

[31]Pitts v. State, 221 Ga. App. 309, 310, 471 S.E.2d 270 (1996). Cf. Edwards v. State, 239 Ga. App. 44, 46(1), 518 S.E.2d 426 (1999).

In *Williams v. State*,[32] the court affirmed the trial court's sanctioning of the opening of an automobile's unlocked trunk without probable cause when the officer thought someone was in the trunk who might pose a threat to his safety.

Some note should be taken of O.C.G.A. § 40-8-76.1(f) which prohibits an officer who stops a motorist because of a seat belt violation from bootstrapping that incident as probable cause for other criminal activity. However, as the court observed in *Blitch v. State*,[33] O.C.G.A. § 40-8-76.1(f) does not preclude an officer from conducting a vehicle search with the drivers consent obtained during a lawful traffic stop for failure to wear a seatbelt.

§ 3:12   When does a "stop" become an "arrest"?

In *United States v. Roper*,[1] the Eleventh Circuit acknowledged that "[t]he distinction between an arrest and an investigatory stop depends upon the nature and degree of the intrusion under all the facts of the particular encounter." However, the court concluded that the stop of an automobile was not converted into an arrest simply because the officer approached the stopped vehicle with a drawn gun.[2] In *Hughes v. State*,[3] a driver of an automobile was informed that he was not free to leave. The Georgia Supreme Court concluded that the evidence supported the conclusion of the trial judge that the defendant was under arrest. However, the "subjective intention of . . . [an] officer to detain the defendant had he attempted to leave is irrelevant except insofar as that intention may have been conveyed to the defendant."[4]

In *Sultenfuss v. State*,[5] the court found that (1) a stop "was not transformed into an arrest merely because one of the officers, who had physically struggled with appellant during a prior incident, drew his weapon on this occasion"; (2) requiring a defendant to step from an automobile did not transform a stop into an arrest; and (3) the detention of the defendant by blocking

---

[32]Williams v. State, 236 Ga. App. 102, 105(2), 511 S.E.2d 216 (1999).

[33]Blitch v. State, 281 Ga. 125(2), 636 S.E.2d 545 (2006). See Temples v. State, 228 Ga. App. 228, 491 S.E.2d 444 (1997).

[Section 3:12]

[1]United States v. Roper, 702 F.2d 984 (11th Cir. 1983). See § 2:12, n. 16, supra, for discussion on *Roper*.

[2]Cf. State v. Burks, 240 Ga. App. 425, 426(1), 523 S.E.2d 648 (1999); Smith v. State, 165 Ga. App. 333, 299 S.E.2d 891 (1983); Edwards v. State, 165 Ga. App. 527, 528, 301 S.E.2d 693 (1983).

[3]Hughes v. State, 259 Ga. 227, 228(1), 378 S.E.2d 853 (1989).

[4]Fowler v. State, 195 Ga. App. 744, 745, 395 S.E.2d 254 (1990) (quoting Sabel v. State, 248 Ga. 10, 282 S.E.2d 61 (1981), disapp. on other grounds in Rower v. State, 264 Ga. 323, 443 S.E.2d 839 (1994)).

[5]Sultenfuss v. State, 185 Ga. App. 47, 48(1), 363 S.E.2d 337 (1987).

his car did not convert the confrontation into an arrest. In *Walton v. State*,[6] the court concluded that a stop was not transformed into an "arrest merely because of the number of police cars used to effect the stop and the manner in which the police blocked his automobile." However, in *State v. Burks*,[7] the court pointed out that after an "initial attempt to stop, '[f]light in connection with other circumstances may be sufficient probable cause to uphold a warrantless arrest or search.'"

However, in *Hayes v. Florida*,[8] the United States Supreme Court held that where "there was no probable cause to arrest," officers have no right to take a suspect to the police station for the purpose of being fingerprinted. However, the Court pointed out that it was saying nothing which implied "that a brief detention in the field for the purpose of fingerprinting, where there is only reasonable suspicion . . . is necessarily impermissible under the Fourth Amendment."[9] In *United States v. Guevara-Martinez*,[10] the court held that when a defendant is illegally detained, his fingerprints, which were not taken as a part of the ordinary booking procedures, were not admissible.

In *People v. Hicks*,[11] the New York Court of Appeals held that where there is a valid *Terry* stop the stop did not become an arrest and was valid even though the defendant was held about 10 minutes and transported to the crime scene for identification.

In the interesting Seventh Circuit case of *United States v. Chaidez*,[12] the Court recognized that there were degrees of intrusion between what is required for a stop and what is required for an arrest. It said that a sliding scale should be applied. The probability requirement should be increased as the intuitiveness increases. There is no reason to "abandon the search for reasonableness when the intrusion falls between arrest and stop."

In *Kolender v. Lawson*,[13] the United States Supreme Court

---

[6]Walton v. State, 194 Ga. App. 490, 492(2), 390 S.E.2d 896 (1990).

[7]State v. Burks, 240 Ga. App. 425, 427(1), 523 S.E.2d 648 (1999).

[8]Hayes v. Florida, 470 U.S. 811, 105 S.Ct. 1643, 84 L.Ed.2d 705 (1985). In Hayes the Court held that seizure was "sufficiently like" an arrest "to invoke the traditional rule that arrest may constitutionally be made only on probable cause." See § 2:25, n. 6, supra, on evidence obtained from arrest.

[9]Hayes v. Florida, 470 U.S. 811, 105 S.Ct. 1643, 84 L.Ed.2d 705, 710 (1985).

[10]United States v. Guevara-Martinez, 262 F.3d 751 (8th Cir. 2001).

[11]People v. Hicks, 68 N.Y.2d 234, 508 N.Y.S.2d 163, 500 N.E.2d 861 (1986). In Hicks, the court pointed out that Hicks was told he would be released if not identified. He was not handcuffed, no gun was drawn and he accompanied the officer without objection.

[12]United States v. Chaidez, 919 F.2d 1193 (7th Cir. 1990).

[13]Kolender v. Lawson, 461 U.S. 352, 103 S.Ct. 1855, 75 L.Ed.2d 903 (1983).

considered the validity of a California statute which required "that an individual provide 'credible and reliable' identification when requested by a police officer who has reasonable suspicion of criminal activity to justify a *Terry* detention." The court held that the statute was unconstitutionally vague on its face and that it vests virtually complete discretion in the police to determine whether the suspect has satisfied the requirements of the statute. However, a stop based upon the violation of a statute later found to be unconstitutional can nonetheless still be considered reasonable.[14] The Georgia Court of Appeals has observed: "[t]he United States Supreme Court has adopted a dual inquiry for evaluating the reasonableness of a lengthy investigative stop. First, we consider whether the officer's action was justified at its inception and second, whether it was reasonably related in scope to the circumstances which justified the interference in the first place. In assessing whether a detention is too long in duration to be justified as an investigative stop, we consider it appropriate to examine whether the police diligently pursued a means of investigation that was likely to confirm or dispel their suspicions quickly, during which time it was necessary to detain the defendant."[15] (citations and punctuation omitted.) Reversing the suppression of evidence obtained following a consensual search initiated seventeen minutes after the initial traffic stop, the Eleventh Circuit stated in dicta: "Where at its inception a traffic stop is a valid one for a violation of the law, we doubt that a resultant seizure of no more than seventeen minutes can ever be unconstitutional on account of its duration: the detention is too short."[16]

See § 2:12, supra, on probable cause which justifies an arrest. See § 2:2, supra, on seizures and arrests. See sections 4:26 and 4:28, infra, on searches incident to lawful arrest. See §§ 4:49 et seq., infra, on automobile searches. See § 3:11, supra, on duty of officer to release a suspect after completion of purpose of frisk.

§ 3:13 Brief retention of inanimate objects without probable cause

In *United States v. Van Leeuwen*,[1] two 12-pound packages were deposited at a post office in Washington near the Canadian

---

[14]Michigan v. DeFillippo, 443 U.S. 31, 99 S. Ct. 2627, 61 L. Ed. 2d 343 (1979). See Ciak v. State, 278 Ga. 27, 597 S.E.2d 392 (2004).

[15]Randolph v. State, 246 Ga. App. 141, 146(3)(b), 538 S.E.2d 139 (2000).

[16]U.S. v. Hernandez, 418 F.3d 1206, 1212 n.7 (11th Cir. 2005). Ac-

cord, Hickman v. State, 279 Ga. App. 558, 631 S.E.2d 778 (2006).

[Section 3:13]

[1]United States v. Van Leeuwen, 397 U.S. 249, 90 S.Ct. 1029, 25 L.Ed.2d 282 (1970).

In People v. Adler, 50 N.Y.2d 730, 431 N.Y.S.2d 412, 415-416, 409

border. Both were mailed "air mail/registered." The mailer represented the packages as containing coins. One package was to be sent to California, the other to Tennessee. The postal clerk was suspicious and it was noticed that the return address given was that of a vacant housing area. The license plates on the mailer's car were from British Columbia. A policeman called on the California address and learned that the addressee was under investigation for dealing in illegal coins. The packages were held overnight until information could be obtained about the addressee in Tennessee. It was learned that the addressee there was under investigation for the same offense. A search warrant for the packages was issued and about 29 hours after the packages had been left with the post office, the warrant was executed. The packages were resealed and sent on their way. The mailer was convicted of illegally importing gold coins. The Supreme Court recognized that the Fourth Amendment applied to first class mail and that it could only be opened pursuant to a warrant. However, the Court concluded that the delaying of the packages until information could be obtained justifying the issuance of a warrant was not unreasonable under the Fourth Amendment. The court also drew an analogy between the facts of this case and those of *Terry*. See Annotation, "Warrantless Detention of Mail for Investigative Purposes as Violative of Fourth Amendment," 115 A.L.R.Fed. 439 (1993).

In *United States v. Klein,*[2] the court found that the officers' observations and information received justified the detention of bags at an airport while the other investigation was being conducted. The court said that this was true even though there was no probable cause for an arrest of the owner. Additionally, although there was no probable cause for an arrest, the court found that there were grounds for a *Terry* stop. In *Yocham v.*

N.E.2d 888 (1980), the court upheld a warrantless search in New York of a package which had been opened in Los Angeles by airline agent who suspected it might contain a hazardous substance. The parcel was then turned over to the police who tested the contents and determined that it contained illicit drugs. The parcel was marked by Los Angeles police, returned to the carrier and shipped to New York. The New York officers were informed of the shipment. When it arrived they obtained the package, tested the contents, returned it to the carrier and arrested defendant when she claimed the package. The court concluded that the original search in Los Angeles was not government action controlled by the Fourth Amendment and nothing prevented them from turning the opened package over to the officers. The search by the New York officers was treated as a continuation of the search which began in California and not as an independent intrusion requiring a warrant.

[2]United States v. Klein, 626 F.2d 22 (7th Cir. 1980).

State,[3] the court said that while "one has a right under the Fourth Amendment to expect privacy of the contents of one's luggage, this right does not extend to the bags' exterior or to control of who actually handles them" once they have been checked. "Having the bags removed from the baggage cart pending further investigation was not an unreasonable seizure."

In *United States v. Place,*[4] the United States Supreme Court said "when an officer's observations lead him reasonably to believe that a traveler is carrying luggage that contains narcotics, the principles of *Terry* and its progeny would permit the officer to detain the luggage briefly to investigate the circumstances that aroused his suspicion, provided that the investigative detention is properly limited in scope. . . . There is no doubt that the agents made a 'seizure' of Place's luggage for the purposes of the Fourth Amendment when, following his refusal to consent to a search, the agent told Place that he was going to take the luggage to a federal judge to secure issuance of a warrant. . . . At the outset, we must reject the Government's suggestion that the point at which probable cause for seizure of luggage from the person's presence becomes necessary is more distant than in the case of a *Terry* stop of the person himself. . . . The precise type of detention we confront here is seizure of personal luggage from the immediate possession of suspect for the purpose of arranging exposure to a narcotics detection dog. . . . [W]hen the police seize luggage from the suspect's custody, we think the limitations applicable to investigative detentions of the person should define the permissible scope of an investigative detention of the person's luggage on less than probable cause. Under this standard, it is clear that the police conduct here exceeded the permissible limits of a *Terry*-type investigative stop. The length of the detention of respondent's luggage alone precludes the conclusion that the seizure was reasonable in the absence of probable cause. . . . [T]he brevity of the invasion of the individual's Fourth Amendment interests is an important factor in determining whether the seizure is so minimally intrusive as to be justifiable on reasonable suspicion. . . . [I]n assessing the effect of the length of the detention, we take into account whether the police diligently purse their investigation. [5] . . . [A]lthough we decline to adopt any outside time limitation for a permissible *Terry* stop, . . . we

---

[3]Yocham v. State, 165 Ga. App. 650, 651(2), 302 S.E.2d 390 (1983).

[4]United States v. Place, 462 U.S. 696, 103 S.Ct. 2637, 77 L.Ed.2d 110 (1983).

[5]The court said, "We note that here the New York agents knew the time of Place's scheduled arrival at LaGuardia, had ample time to arrange for their additional investigation at that location, and thereby could have minimized the intrusion on respondent's Fourth Amendment interests." Cf. United States v. Sharpe, 470 U.S. 675, 105 S.Ct. 1568, 84 L.Ed.2d 605

have never approved a seizure of the person for the prolonged 90-minute period involved here and cannot do so on the facts presented by this case. . . . [Also] the violation was exacerbated by the failure of the agents to accurately inform respondent of the place to which they were transporting his luggage, of the length of time he might be dispossessed, and of what arrangements would be made for return of the luggage if the investigation dispelled their suspicion."

In *Bothwell v. State*,[6] the defendant "traveled alone, from an identified source city, flying under a false name, carried little or no luggage, purchased his expensive airline ticket in cash, acted very nervous, and had given false information to the airline."[7] The stop was based solely on the drug courier profile. See § 3:4, supra. At the time of the stop, one of the officers took the defendant's ticket, retained it and took the defendant to a private office while retaining his boarding pass. He consented to a pat-down search of his person. At first he said he would consent to a search of his bag but after officers retrieved it, he withdrew his consent to the search of his bag. The agents retained the defendant's bag, but the defendant continued his flight to Phoenix. The agents obtained a drug dog. The dog indicated that there were narcotics in the bag. A search warrant was obtained, and a search produced cocaine. The defendant was arrested when he deplaned in Phoenix. In a four to three decision of the Georgia Supreme Court, the court affirmed the denial of the motion to suppress. See *Florida v. Royer,* discussed in § 3:4, supra, on the drug courier profile.

In *State v. Foster*,[8] the defendant fit the "drug courier profile." He was frisked but refused to consent to a search of a shaving bag he was carrying. The court held that the officers could briefly detain the bag under *Terry*. "[W]hen an officer's observations lead him reasonably to believe that a traveler is carrying luggage that contains narcotics, . . . the officer . . . [may] detain the luggage briefly to investigate the circumstances that aroused his suspicion, provided that the investigative detention is properly limited in scope." In this case, a dog sniffed the bag, detected narcotics in the bag, and the defendant was then arrested. The bag was then searched and cocaine was found in it.

(1985). In Sharpe, although the police held the defendant for 20 minutes while waiting for the drug detection dog, the Court held that the seizure was constitutional because the officers exercised "due diligence."

[6]Bothwell v. State, 250 Ga. 573, 300 S.E.2d 126 (1983). But see Pullano

v. State, 169 Ga. App. 377, 380, 312 S.E.2d 857 (1983).

[7]Bothwell v. State, 163 Ga. App. 261, 293 S.E.2d 720 (1982), aff'd, 250 Ga. 573, 300 S.E.2d 126 (1983).

[8]State v. Foster, 209 Ga. App. 143, 145, 433 S.E.2d 109 (1993).

In *Dawson v. State,*[9] the Georgia Court of Appeals concluded that "[w]here a drug dog's alert is the *only* basis for suspecting the presence of contraband . . . , evidence that the dog has been extremely unreliable in the past may lead the trial court to conclude that the dog's alert, by itself, does not indicate a 'fair probability' of the presence of contraband. However, where there are additional indications of the presence of contraband . . . , the totality of the circumstances may support a finding of probable cause notwithstanding evidence of the dog's unreliability."

In *Florida v. Harris,*[10] the Supreme Court held that Florida's interpretation of the Fourth Amendment protocol necessary for a police dog's alert to provide probable cause for a search of a suspect's vehicle runs afoul of the totality of circumstances standard established in *Illinois v. Gates,*[11] and similar precedent. The Florida Supreme Court would require the state to show "the dog's training, certification, field performance records (including any unverified alerts), and evidence concerning the experience and training of the officer handling the dog, as well as any other objective evidence known to the officer about the dog's reliability." The Court rejected the procedure saying that it went far beyond the "more flexible, all things considered approach" approved in *Gates*.

On the other hand, in *State v. Smith,*[12] the defendant arrived at the Atlanta Airport from Fort Lauderdale, a source city. He looked around, staring at people. He appeared nervous. An agent followed the defendant to determine the name on his ticket. The agent learned from the ticket agent the defendant's name, destination, and the fact that the ticket had been paid for with a credit card. The agent called the call-back number in Fort Lauderdale and found it was a hotel there; he estimated that the defendant had remained there about 19 hours. When the defendant was approached, he produced "his ticket, driver's license, and his [real] name." The defendant said he had gone there to look at an airplane. As the defendant was questioned he seemed to become more nervous. He said he was not carrying

---

[9]Dawson v. State, 238 Ga. App. 263, 267(1), 518 S.E.2d 477 (1999) (emphasis by the court).

[10]Florida v. Harris, 133 S. Ct. 1050, 185 L. Ed. 2d 61 (2013) (proof that the drug-sniffing dog has performed satisfactorily in a training or certification is sufficient to establish reliability unless challenged; in that event, the court should consider any competing evidence). See McKinney v. State, 326 Ga. App. 753, 755 S.E.2d 315 (2014). See also Harris v. State,

341 Ga. App. 831, 802 S.E.2d 708 (2017) (to challenge the reliability of a drug-sniffing dog's alert, the defense should be given access to all records relevant to the dog's training, alert history and certification).

[11]Illinois v. Gates, 462 U.S. 213, 103 S. Ct. 2317, 76 L. Ed. 2d 527 (1983).

[12]State v. Smith, 164 Ga. App. 142, 296 S.E.2d 141 (1982).

contraband on his person or in his luggage. He consented to a search of his boots and had a considerable amount of money there. He was given *Miranda* warnings, was accused of carrying drugs in his luggage, and was warned that if he did not consent to a luggage search, he would, if possible, be met in Tulsa by officers and drug dogs. The defendant declined to consent. The agent then retrieved the defendant's checked suitcase, and the defendant was informed of his rights regarding the search of his suitcase. He was told that he was free to leave but that his suitcase would be retained. The defendant left for Tulsa while a search warrant was being obtained for the suitcase. When the suitcase was opened it was found to contain cocaine. The court affirmed the granting of the motion to suppress finding (1) that the stop was not justified by an articulable suspicion, and (2) that the scope of a *Terry* stop had been exceeded and the stop amounted to an illegal detention.

In *State v. Grant*,[13] the court, while disapproving of the conclusion of the trial judge, concluded that a retention of luggage for about an hour was justified where officers acted diligently, the retention was not prolonged needlessly, the agents tried to make arrangements to return the luggage, and the intrusion was minimal and was justifiable.

See § 4:45, infra, on border searches and § 4:46, infra, on search of incoming international mail. See § 3:4, supra, on stops related to the airport drug courier profile. See § 4:35, infra, on searches at airports.

---

[13]State v. Grant, 195 Ga. App.   859, 864(3), 394 S.E.2d 916 (1990).

Chapter 4

Search and Seizure

KeyCite®: Cases and other legal materials listed in KeyCite Scope can be researched through the KeyCite service on Westlaw®. Use KeyCite to check citations for form, parallel references, prior and later history, and comprehensive citator information, including citations to other decisions and secondary materials.

---

§ 4:1 Definitions of search and seizure

A search is a quest for information.[1] The "term implies some exploratory investigation, or an invasion and quest, a looking for or seeking out . . . a prying into hidden places for that which is concealed."[2] In *Maryland v. Macon*,[3] the United States Supreme

---

[Section 4:1]

[1]Lewis v. State, 126 Ga. App. 123, 126, 190 S.E.2d 123 (1972).

[2]79 C.J.S. Searches and Seizures

§ 1.

[3]Maryland v. Macon, 472 U.S. 463, 105 S.Ct. 2778, 86 L.Ed.2d 370 (1985) (citing U.S. v. Jacobsen, 466

Court said, "A search occurs when 'an expectation of privacy that society is prepared to consider reasonable is infringed.' " In that case, the Court held that there was no search where an officer entered a bookstore and examined magazines "that were intentionally exposed to all" who entered the bookstore. In *Florida v. Jardines*,[4] the United States Supreme Court held that the use of a police dog to conduct an open air "sniff" at the front door of the defendant's home and around the outside of the house was a "search" for purposes of the Fourth Amendment.

There is no search when an officer sees from a public road what is in plain view to the unaided eye[5] or, apparently, when the officer sees something from business property generally used by and open to the public.[6]

Based on the theory that "a search ordinarily implies a quest by an officer," the United States Supreme Court in *Wyman v. James*[7] concluded that there was not a search by a social worker in making a home visit to a family receiving Aid to Families with Dependent Children money, even though the visit was to some extent investigative. In *United States v. DeBardeleben*,[8] the court held that the insertion of the keys in the locks of a car was a minimum intrusion which did not amount to a search. See Annotation, "Attachment or Use of Transponder (Beeper) to Monitor Location of Airplane or Automobile as Constituting 'Search' Within Fourth Amendment," 57 A.L.R.Fed. 646 (1982). Also see § 4:2, infra, on protected areas and interests, and sections 14:79 to 14:83, infra, on expectation of privacy. See § 4:40, infra, on field tests of suspected drugs.

The act of taking and removing tangible personal property is a

---

U.S. 109, 104 S. Ct. 1652, 80 L. Ed. 2d 85 (1984)). See also Katz v. United States, 389 U.S. 347, 88 S.Ct. 507, 19 L.Ed.2d 576 (1967).

[4]Florida v. Jardines, 133 S. Ct. 1409, 185 L. Ed. 2d 495 (2013).

[5]Lewis v. State, 126 Ga. App. 123, 126, 190 S.E.2d 123 (1972). However, in State v. Ward, 62 Haw. 509, 617 P.2d 568 (Haw. 1980), the court held that looking into a 17th floor apartment with binoculars from the 14th floor of another building constituted a search. See § 4:2, infra, on Fourth Amendment protection of the home.

[6]Cuevas v. State, 151 Ga. App. 605, 610, 260 S.E.2d 737 (1979).

[7]Wyman v. James, 400 U.S. 309, 91 S.Ct. 381, 27 L.Ed.2d 408 (1971).

[8]In United States v. DeBardeleben, 740 F.2d 440 (6th Cir. 1984), the defendant was arrested in a shopping center for using counterfeit money. In the search incident to his arrest, auto keys were found including keys to a Chrysler. That night an officer returned to the mall when there were only three cars remaining and one was a Chrysler. He tried the keys in the Chrysler and found that the keys to the door and the trunk fit the locks. He relocked the car, obtained a search warrant based on this and other information and searched the car.

seizure.[9] In *Maryland v. Macon*,[10] the Supreme Court said, "A seizure occurs when 'there is some meaningful interference with an individual's possessory interests' in the property seized." No seizure was found in *Maryland* where an officer bought magazines he suspected were obscene that were on display in a store.

It has been held that where officers attempt to maintain a status quo until a warrant can be obtained, there is a seizure where the officers lock the premises or wait inside or outside for the arrival of a warrant.[11] A seizure also occurs when intangible items are obtained, as in the case of overhearing or recording a telephone call improperly.[12]

There is, however, no expectation of privacy in conversations which occur between a prisoner and a visitor in a prison or jail visiting area.[13] Nor is there such an expectation in the case of a telephone call made from a police station reception area.[14] Likewise, conversations between arrestees in the rear seat of a police patrol car which are secretly recorded have no reasonable expectation of privacy.[15]

Finally, it must be noted that seizure of a person occurs not only in the case of an arrest, but also where a person is restrained so that he cannot walk away.[16] See Chapter 2, supra, on arrest, and Chapter 3, supra, on stop-and-frisk.

§ 4:2   Protected areas and interests

Whatever areas and interests are protected by the Fourth Amendment are protected only against governmental action; individuals acting on their own initiative are not within the amendment's scope. See § 4:60, infra, on results of illegal searches.

The Fourth Amendment states that people shall "be secure in their persons, houses, papers and effects, against unreasonable searches and seizures." An admirable opinion written by Judge

---

[9]68 Am. Jur. 2d Searches and Seizures § 8. The "ransacking of a house, apartment or vehicle is generally a 'search.' " 68 Am. Jur. 2d Searches and Seizures § 8.

[10]Maryland v. Macon, 472 U.S. 463, 105 S.Ct. 2778, 86 L.Ed.2d 370 (1985).

[11]United States v. Lomas, 706 F.2d 886 (9th Cir. 1983); United States v. Allard, 634 F.2d 1182 (9th Cir. 1980). See § 4:56, infra, on impoundment.

[12]Katz v. United States, 389 U.S. 347, 88 S.Ct. 507, 19 L.Ed.2d 576 (1967).

[13]Dickerson v. State, 292 Ga. App. 775, 666 S.E.2d 43 (2008). See Karz v. U.S., 389 US 347, 88 S. Ct. 507, 19 L. Ed. 2d 576 (1967); U.S. v. Hearst, 563 F.2d 1331 (9th Cir. 1977).

[14]Meyer v. State, 150 Ga. App. 613, 258 S.E.2d 217 (1979).

[15]Burgeson v. State, 267 Ga. 102, 457 S.E.2d 580 (1996).

[16]Terry v. Ohio, 392 U.S. 1, 13, 88 S.Ct. 1868, 20 L.Ed.2d 889 (1968).

Clark of the Georgia Court of Appeals contains the following: " 'A man's home is his castle. The storm and wind may enter, but the King cannot enter, and all the forces of the Crown cannot cross the threshold of his ruined tenement.' These words by Lord Eldon served as the basis for that portion of the Fourth Amendment in the Bill of Rights declaring that the people shall be secure in their houses against unreasonable searches and seizures. Our state Constitution contains almost identical language as used in the federal document."[1] The Fourth Amendment protection has been extended beyond the home[2] to people,[3] automobiles,[4] boats,[5] the area within the curtilage of a house,[6] apartments,[7] hotel rooms,[8] public telephone booths,[9] offices,[10] desks,[11] a coin-operated locker in a bus station,[12] a tent,[13] and a refrigerator in a locked storage unit.[14]

For example, a warrant authorizing the search of a house was held to give officers authority to search a U-Haul truck within the curtilage of the house.[15] Marijuana found in a cooler about 100 yards from the defendant's house trailer at the end of a path

---

[Section 4:2]

[1]Hogan v. State, 140 Ga. App. 716, 231 S.E.2d 802 (1976).

[2]Chapman v. United States, 365 U.S. 610, 613, 81 S.Ct. 776, 5 L.Ed.2d 828 (1961).

[3]Terry v. Ohio, 392 U.S. 1, 88 S.Ct. 1868, 20 L.Ed.2d 889 (1968). However, in State v. Young, 234 Ga. 488, 216 S.E.2d 586 (1975), the Georgia Supreme Court concluded that the exclusionary rule did not apply to a search of a student by a school principal. See § 4:60, infra, on results of illegal searches.

[4]Gambino v. United States, 275 U.S. 310, 48 S.Ct. 137, 72 L.Ed. 293 (1927).

[5]United States v. Coppolo, 2 F.Supp. 115 (D.N.J.1932).

[6]Norman v. State, 134 Ga. App. 767, 216 S.E.2d 644 (1975).

[7]People v. Stokes, 334 Ill. 200, 165 N.E. 611 (1929); Maxwell v. State, 127 Ga. App. 168, 193 S.E.2d 14 (1972).

[8]United States v. Jeffers, 342 U.S. 48, 72 S.Ct. 93, 96 L.Ed. 59 (1951).

[9]Katz v. United States, 389 U.S. 347, 88 S.Ct. 507, 19 L.Ed.2d 576 (1967).

[10]Go-Bart Importing Co. v. United States, 282 U.S. 344, 51 S.Ct. 153, 75 L.Ed. 374 (1931).

[11]Mancusi v. DeForte, 392 U.S. 364, 88 S.Ct. 2120, 20 L.Ed.2d 1154 (1968). See United States v. Lefkowitz, 285 U.S. 452, 52 S.Ct. 420, 76 L.Ed. 877 (1932). But see § 4:60, infra, on results of illegal searches.

[12]United States v. Durkin, 335 F.Supp. 922, 924 (S.D.N.Y.1971). In United States v. Speights, 557 F.2d 362 (3d Cir. 1977), the same rule was applied to a search of a police officer locker at the police station.

[13]Kelley v. State, 146 Ga. App. 179, 183, 245 S.E.2d 872 (1978). See Annot., "Search and Seizure: reasonable expectation of privacy in a tent or campsight," 66 A.L.R.5th 373 (1999).

[14]State v. Gallup, 236 Ga. App. 321, 323 (1)(b), 512 S.E.2d 66 (1999).

[15]Bellamy v. State, 134 Ga. App. 340, 214 S.E.2d 383 (1975). However, in People v. Sciacca, 45 N.Y.2d 122, 408 N.Y.S.2d 22, 379 N.E.2d 1153 (1978), the court said that a search warrant for a building does not authorize the search of a vehicle on the

from the trailer was also found to be in the curtilage of defendant's home.[16] However, the curtilage concept does not prevent an officer without a warrant from approaching the front door of a house by the same route as would be used by any guest, delivery man, or postal employee. Likewise, the common areas of an apartment building, such as the lobby and the corridors, do not provide a tenant who resides there with a reasonable expectation of privacy where such areas are open and accessible to tenants, visitors, the landlord and its employees as well as the public.[17] See § 4:43, infra, on open fields. Generally, on curtilage, see § 4:19, infra.

The United States Supreme Court, in *Katz v. United States*,[18] pointed out that the common law concept of trespass will no longer determine whether a violation of the Fourth Amendment has occurred, because the Fourth Amendment is intended to protect people, not simply places. However, a place is entitled to Fourth Amendment protection where an individual connected with the place has a reasonable expectation of privacy in that area.[19] Moreover, in *United States v. Jones*,[20] Justice Scalia wrote that *Katz* was not intended to withdraw any of the protection which the Fourth Amendment extends to the home and went on to conclude

---

premises.

In Fixel v. Wainwright, 492 F.2d 480 (5th Cir. 1974), the court found that a fenced area behind an apartment was within the curtilage of the apartment.

In People v. Chavez, 169 Cal.Rptr. 871 (Cal.App.1980), the court held that marijuana lawfully observed growing in a back yard could not be seized without a warrant in the absence of exigent circumstances.

[16]Walker v. State, 140 Ga. App. 418, 231 S.E.2d 386 (1976). See Mason v. State, 146 Ga. App. 557, 559 (5), 247 S.E.2d 118 (1978).

[17]United States v. Miravalles, 280 F.3d 1328 (11th Cir. 2002). This case may have been decided differently if the door to the complex was properly secured and access to the property either more restricted or monitored more carefully.

[18]Katz v. United States, 389 U.S. 347, 351, 88 S.Ct. 507, 19 L.Ed.2d 576 (1967). In this case, the Court said that what a person knowingly exposes to the public is not protected by the Fourth Amendment, but what he seeks to preserve as private may be constitutionally protected. Hence, when a person enters a public telephone booth, shuts the door and pays for his call, he is entitled to assume that what he says will not be broadcast.

[19]United States v. Santana, 427 U.S. 38, 96 S.Ct. 2406, 49 L.Ed.2d 300 (1976) (defendant standing in doorway of her home has no reasonable expectation of privacy); South Dakota v. Opperman, 428 U.S. 364, 96 S.Ct. 3092, 49 L.Ed.2d 1000 (1976) (expectation of privacy in an automobile is much less than in one's home). See United States v. Miller, 425 U.S. 435, 96 S.Ct. 1619, 48 L.Ed.2d 71 (1976) (motion to suppress subpoenaed bank records of defendant denied).

[20]U.S. v. Jones, 132 S. Ct. 945, 181 L. Ed. 2d 911 (2012). See Hamlett v. State, 753 S.E.2d 118, 13 FCDR 4019 (Ga. Ct. App. 2013) (applies *Jones* to hold that installation and monitoring of GPS device constituted search that had to be authorized by probable cause and search warrant).

that the government violated the defendant's Fourth Amendment rights when it "trespassed" on the defendant's private property, his automobile, and installed a GPS tracking device. Generally, on expectation of privacy, see sections 14:79 to 14:83, infra. See § 4:28, infra, on seizure of premises while a search warrant is being obtained.

Generally, articles which can be seen with the naked eye from a place an officer is entitled to be not protected,[21] and this rule seems to apply to the other senses.[22] Thus, in *Cox v. State*,[23] the court stated that officers do not have to obtain prior judicial approval to listen to conversations from a hall outside an apartment or to place the naked ear next to the door to the apartment. In *Maryland v. Macon*,[24] the United States Supreme Court held that there was no reasonable expectation of privacy in an obscene book on display in the public area of an adult bookstore, and the purchase of such a book was not a seizure.

In *United States v. King*,[25] the Eleventh Circuit Court of Appeals held that a private contractor who accessed a military computer network on his personal computer while on a military base located in Saudi Arabia had no reasonable expectation of privacy as to the contents of files that were on a "shared" network, which enabled anyone on that network to access the files.

In *New York v. Burger*,[26] the United States Supreme Court stated, "An expectation of privacy in commercial premises . . . is

---

[21]Harris v. United States, 390 U.S. 234, 88 S.Ct. 992, 19 L.Ed.2d 1067 (1968). See § 4:1, n. 5, supra. See Note, "Telescopes, Binoculars, and the Fourth Amendment," 67 Cornell L. Rev. 379 (1982).

[22]United States v. Pagan, 395 F.Supp. 1052 (D.P.R.1975); State v. Day, 50 Ohio App.2d 315, 362 N.E.2d 1253 (1976).

"[B]oth the eye and the ear as well as the hand, can 'search.'" Smayda v. United States, 352 F.2d 251 (9th Cir. 1965).

[23]Cox v. State, 160 Ga. App. 199, 200, 286 S.E.2d 482 (1981). In United States v. Mankani, 738 F.2d 538 (2d Cir. 1984), the court held that there was no violation of an expectation of privacy when an officer placed his ear to a pre-existing hole between hotel rooms.

[24]Maryland v. Macon, 472 U.S. 463, 105 S.Ct. 2778, 86 L.Ed.2d 370 (1985).

[25]U.S. v. King, 509 F.3d 1338 (11th Cir. 2007).

[26]New York v. Burger, 482 U.S. 691, 107 S.Ct. 2636, 96 L.Ed.2d 601, 612 (1987). The Court's holding was premised upon a determination that: (1) there is a "substantial government interest that informs the regulatory scheme pursuant to which the inspection is made"; (2) the warrantless inspection is "necessary to further the regulatory scheme"; (3) "the statute's inspection program in terms of certainty and regularity of its application [provides] a constitutionally adequate substitute for a warrant." As the Court observed, "[T]he regulatory statute must perform the two basic functions of a warrant: it must advise the owner of the commercial premises that the search is being made pursuant to the law and has a properly defined scope, and it must limit the discretion of the inspecting officers. To perform this

different from, and indeed less than, a similar expectation in an individual's home. . . . This expectation is particularly attenuated in commercial property employed in 'closely regulated' industries." The court then concluded that a state statute was constitutional which was enacted to combat auto theft which authorized a warrantless inspection of junkyards when certain criteria were followed.

In *United States v. Place*,[27] the United States Supreme Court, in considering the sniffing by a dog of luggage of an airline passenger, said "the present course of investigation that the agents intended to pursue here—exposure of respondent's luggage, which was located in a public place, to a trained canine—did not constitute a 'search' within the meaning of the Fourth Amendment." However, in *Bond v. United States*,[28] the Court held that an INS agent conducted an illegal search when he felt of the luggage in the overhead compartment of a bus. The agent detected a "brick-like object" in one of the bags and after receiving consent from the owner, searched and found methamphetamine. The court explained that while "a bus passenger . . . expects that his bag may be handled . . . [he] does not expect that other[s] . . . [will feel the bag] . . . in an exploratory manner."

------

first function, the statute must be sufficiently comprehensive and defined that the owner of commercial property cannot help but be aware that his property will be subject to periodic inspections undertaken for specific purposes. In addition, in defining how a statute limits the discretion of the inspectors, we have observed that it must be carefully limited in time, place, and scope."

[27]United States v. Place, 462 U.S. 696, 103 S.Ct. 2637, 77 L.Ed.2d 110 (1983). In *Place* the Court said, "We have affirmed that a person possesses a privacy interest in the contents of personal luggage that is protected by the Fourth Amendment. Id., at 13. A 'canine sniff' by a well-trained narcotics detection dog, however, does not require opening the luggage. It does not expose noncontraband items that otherwise would remain hidden from public view, as does, for example, an officer's rummaging through the contents of the luggage. Thus, the manner in which information is obtained through this investigative technique is much less intrusive than a typical search. Moreover, the sniff discloses only the presence or absence of narcotics, a contraband item. Thus, despite the fact that the sniff tells the authorities something about the contents of the luggage, the information obtained is limited. This limited disclosure also ensures that the owner of the property is not subjected to the embarrassment and inconvenience entailed in less discriminate and more intrusive investigative methods." See Dawson v. State, 238 Ga. App. 263, 518 S.E.2d 477 (1999) (evidence that dog is well trained and certified in drug detection is prima facie evidence of the dog's reliability). See also, Casey v. State, 246 Ga. App. 786(3)(a), 542 S.E.2d 531 (2000) ("free air" search of auto is limited to space around exterior of car and does not authorize dog's intrusion into the car's interior); O'Keefe v. State, 189 Ga. App. 519, 526, 376 S.E.2d 406 (1988) (citing United States v. Place, 462 U.S. 696, 103 S.Ct. 2637, 77 L.Ed.2d 110 (1983)).

[28]Bond v. United States, 529 U.S. 334, 120 S.Ct. 1462, 146 L.Ed.2d 365 (2000).

In *Carter v. State*,[29] the court held that the use of a dog to smell a package at a UPS station did not interfere with the defendant's possessory interest nor was it a search within the meaning of the Fourth Amendment.

As pointed out in § 4:28, infra, even though a container may be seized, this alone does not mean that the officer has the right to search the container. Abandoned premises and articles lose their protection;[30] open fields[31] and the public portions of business and commercial establishments are not protected.[32]

Surveillance of a stall in public restrooms has sometimes been held to be protected[33] and sometimes held not to be protected.[34] In *Wylie v. State*,[35] the Georgia Court of Appeals affirmed the denial of a motion to suppress where an officer entered a restroom, saw two pairs of feet facing each other under the partition around the commode stall. The officer then looked through the crack between the door and the adjacent wall "and saw two men ingesting a white powder which he took to be and which examination proved was in fact cocaine."

The exterior of a vehicle[36] and articles which can be observed by the public from the outside are not protected.[37] Similarly, in *New York v. Class*,[38] the United States Supreme Court held that a motorist has no reasonable expectation of privacy in a motor vehicle identification number on the dashboard of the car, even if an object on the dash prevented an officer from reading the number from outside the vehicle which the officer had stopped for a traffic violation. The court also held that a gun, discovered by

---

[29]Carter v. State, 222 Ga. App. 345, 347, 474 S.E.2d 240 (1996). See also Illinois v. Caballes, 543 U.S. 405, 125 S. Ct. 834, 160 L. Ed. 2d 842 (2005); Byers v. State, 272 Ga. App. 664, 613 S.E.2d 193 (2005).

[30]Abel v. United States, 362 U.S. 217, 80 S.Ct. 683, 4 L.Ed.2d 668 (1960).

[31]Hester v. United States, 265 U.S. 57, 44 S.Ct. 445, 68 L.Ed. 898 (1924).

[32]Cuevas v. State, 151 Ga. App. 605, 610, 260 S.E.2d 737 (1979).

[33]In People v. Milom, 75 A.D.2d 68, 428 N.Y.S.2d 678 (1980), the court, while acknowledging that an occupant of a toilet stall in a public restroom has a reasonable expectation of privacy, concluded that there is no justified expectation of privacy in the public area of a restroom. Compare State

v. Holt, 48 Or. App. 825, 617 P.2d 962 (1980).

See Annot., "Search and Seizure: Reasonable Expectation of Privacy in Public Restroom," 74 A.L.R.4th 508 (1989).

[34]Smayda v. United States, 352 F.2d 251 (9th Cir. 1965); Mitchell v. State, 120 Ga. App. 447, 170 S.E.2d 765 (1969).

[35]Wylie v. State, 164 Ga. App. 174, 296 S.E.2d 743 (1982). Cf. Mitchell v. State, 120 Ga. App. 447, 170 S.E.2d 765 (1969).

[36]Cardwell v. Lewis, 417 U.S. 583, 94 S.Ct. 2464, 41 L.Ed.2d 325 (1974) (plurality opinion).

[37]Cook v. Commonwealth, 216 Va. 71, 216 S.E.2d 48 (1975).

[38]New York v. Class, 475 U.S. 106, 106 S.Ct. 960, 89 L.Ed.2d 81 (1986).

the officer when he leaned into the vehicle to uncover the identification number, was admissible against the defendant. See section 3-10, supra, on the "plain feel" doctrine.

In *Skinner v. Railway Labor Executives' Association*,[39] the United States Supreme Court held that a blood, urine, and breath test of employees involved in accidents for drugs is a "search" within the ambit of the Fourth Amendment. Even in the absence of a particularized suspicion of drug or alcohol use, the compelling governmental interest in railroad safety outweighs the limited intrusion upon the privacy interest of the employees, and such tests are admissible. The same Court handed down a decision in *National Treasury Employees Union v. Von Raab*[40] on the same day as the *Skinner* case. In the *Von Raab* case, the Court held that the Customs Service may constitutionally require employees seeking promotions to positions requiring the carrying of firearms to undergo blood screening.

In *Chandler v. Miller*,[41] the United States Supreme Court held invalid a Georgia statute requiring certain elective officials to certify that they have tested negative for drugs before qualifying for office. The court held that when public safety is not genuinely in jeopardy, the suspicionless search, no matter how unintrusive or conveniently arranged, is still a violation of the Fourth Amendment. The court pointed out that there was "no evidence of a drug problem among the State's elected officials . . . [that they] do not perform high risk, safety sensitive tasks, and the required certification immediately aids no interdiction effort."

In *Jackson v. State*,[42] the Georgia Court of Appeals concluded that " 'there is no *constitutionally* protected right in a decedent's body. Rather, the courts have evolved the concept of quasi property in recognition of the interests of surviving relatives in the possession and control of decedents' bodies. We do not find this common law concept to be of constitutional dimension.' . . . [Hence, a defendant's] quasi-property interest in [a] stillborn fetus will not support a privacy claim sufficient to implicate the search and seizure provisions of the United States Constitution." (Emphasis in original.)

---

[39]Skinner v. Railway Labor Executives Association, 489 U.S. 602, 109 S.Ct. 1402, 103 L.Ed.2d 639 (1989). See Mitchell v. State, 301 Ga. 563, 802 S.E.2d 217 (2017) (field sobriety test is not a search for purposes of Fourth Amendment and a warrant is not a prerequisite to the admission of defendant's refusal to submit to test).

[40]National Treasury Employees Union v. Von Raab, 489 U.S. 656, 109 S.Ct. 1384, 103 L.Ed.2d 685 (1989).

[41]Chandler v. Miller, 520 U.S. 305, 117 S.Ct. 1295, 137 L.Ed.2d 513 (1997).

[42]Jackson v. State, 208 Ga. App. 391, 392-93 (2), 430 S.E.2d 781 (1993) (quoting Georgia Lions Eye Bank v. Lavant, 255 Ga. 60, 335 S.E.2d 127 (1985)).

In *Ferguson v. Charleston, S.C.,*[43] the United States Supreme Court, in a five to four decision, held a hospital's policy of conducting non-consensual drug tests on pregnant women and turning positive results over to police violates the Fourth Amendment. The court reasoned that the purpose behind the policy takes it outside prior rulings of the court upholding searches conducted under policies that dispense with usual Fourth Amendment requirements in order to serve "special needs" of law enforcement.

The Fourth Amendment does not protect against a misplaced confidence. Thus, where a person invites a guest into his home or room, the guest may later testify as to what he saw or heard while he was in the area into which he was invited, even though the guest is an undercover officer or is working with officers.[44] Likewise, if such a guest is carrying a transmitter to which officers are listening,[45] or if he is carrying a concealed recording device,[46] there is no Fourth Amendment violation. See § 4:59, infra, on electronic surveillance.

In *Zurcher v. Stanford Daily,*[47] the United States Supreme Court held that a search warrant, rather than a subpoena duces tecum, may be used to search the premises of a third party who was not suspected of involvement in the underlying crime. See § 17:11, infra, on subpoenas for production of documents. However, by Georgia statute a search and seizure shall not be conducted without a warrant from a superior court judge, and no search warrant shall be issued for any evidence in the possession of an attorney who is not a criminal suspect unless the application specifies the place to be searched and shows that there is probable cause to believe that such evidence will be secreted or destroyed if a warrant is not issued.[48]

---

[43]Ferguson v. City of Charleston, 532 U.S. 67, 121 S.Ct. 1281, 149 L.Ed.2d 205 (2001).

[44]Hoffa v. U.S., 385 U.S. 293, 87 S. Ct. 408, 17 L. Ed. 2d 374 (1966).

[45]On Lee v. U.S., 343 U.S. 747, 72 S. Ct. 967, 96 L. Ed. 1270 (1952).

[46]Lopez v. U.S., 373 U.S. 427, 83 S. Ct. 1381, 10 L. Ed. 2d 462 (1963).

[47]Zurcher v. Stanford Daily, 436 U.S. 547, 98 S. Ct. 1970, 56 L. Ed. 2d 525 (1978). In this case, a newspaper office was searched for pictures relating to a clash between demonstrators and the police. The court reasoned that the evidence might have "disappeared" if a subpoena duces tecum had been used. Justices Stewart and Marshall dissented and pointed out that (1) the search warrant procedure permits officers to ransack a place and is not as limited as a subpoena, and (2) a subpoena would allow a motion to quash and an adversary hearing. Justice Stevens also dissented. However, the impact of *Zurcher* has been severely limited where the news media are involved by the enactment of 42 U.S.C.A. § 2000aa.

[48]O.C.G.A. § 17-5-32 (if court finds probable cause to believe documentary evidence may be destroyed, it must appoint a special master to accompany person serving warrant).

In *Ledesma v. State*,[49] the Georgia Supreme Court held that when officers recover property reported to be stolen, a good faith inventory of the property may be conducted.

In addition to the protection of the Fourth Amendment, as it is being applied by the United States Supreme Court, there is also a growing number of states which have extended greater protection to their citizens, through their own statutes and state constitutions, than that provided by the federal Constitution.[50]

The United States Supreme Court in *United States v. Verdugo-Urquidez*[51] held that the Fourth Amendment does not apply to the search and seizure by United States agents of property that is owned by a nonresident alien and located in a foreign country. See Annotation, "Expectation of Privacy in Internet Communications," 92 A.L.R.5th 15 (2001).

There seems to be a division of authority on whether or not the use of "bugs" or electronic tracking devices violates the Fourth Amendment.[52] However, in 1983, in *United States v. Knotts*,[53] the United States Supreme Court held that there was no invasion of

---

[49]Ledesma v. State, 251 Ga. 885, 887, 311 S.E.2d 427 (1984).

[50]See Brennan, "State Constitutions and the Protection of Individual Rights," 90 Harv. L. Rev. 489 (1977).

In Mills v. Rogers, 457 U.S. 291, 102 S. Ct. 2442, 73 L. Ed. 2d 16, 23 (1982), the Court said, "Within our federal system the substantive rights provided by the Federal Constitution define only a minimum. State law may recognize liberty interests more extensive than those independently protected by the Federal Constitution."

[51]U.S. v. Verdugo-Urquidez, 494 U.S. 259, 110 S. Ct. 1056, 108 L. Ed. 2d 222 (1990).

[52]In United States v. Perez, 526 F.2d 859 (5th Cir. 1976), the court held that a beeper attached to a television set which had been exchanged for heroin was not illegal. The court said that the defendant had no reasonable expectation that there was no monitoring device on the set. See Case Note, "Electronic Tracking Devices and the Fourth Amendment—United States v. Michael," 16 Ga. L. R. 197 (1981).

In Dunivant v. State, 155 Ga. App. 884, 886-889, 273 S.E.2d 621 (1980), electronic tracking devices were placed (at the direction of the DEA) in boxes containing chemicals which were vital to the manufacture of methamphetamine, before the chemicals were delivered. The court concluded that there was no Fourth Amendment violation since there was no trespass involved and there was probable cause to believe a crime was intended.

Generally, see Dowling, " 'Bumper Beepers' and the Fourth Amendment," 13 Crim. L. Bull. 266 (1977), and Note, "Tracking Katz: Beepers, Privacy and the Fourth Amendment," 86 Yale L. J. 1461-1508 (1977).

[53]United States v. Knotts, 460 U.S. 276, 103 S.Ct. 1081, 75 L.Ed.2d 55 (1983). Cf. United States v. Butts, 729 F.2d 1514 (5th Cir. 1984), rev'g 710 F.2d 1139 (5th Cir. 1983). See Annot., "Use of Electronic Sensing Device to Detect Shoplifting as Unconstitutional Search and Seizure," 10 A.L.R.4th 376 (1981). See also Annot., "Use of Electronic Tracking Device (Beeper) to Monitor Location of Object or Substance Other Than Vehicle or Aircraft as Constituting Search Violating Fourth Amendment," 70 A.L.R.Fed. 747 (1984).

any legitimate expectation of privacy and no "search" or "seizure" within the contemplation of the Fourth Amendment in the use of a beeper to follow an object carried in an automobile on public roads and to a private residence. In *Knotts*, one Armstrong was purchasing chloroform to be used in the manufacture of drugs. Officers arranged to place a beeper inside a chloroform container which was sold to Armstrong. When Armstrong obtained the container, officers followed the car and maintained contact visually and with a monitor. Armstrong transferred the container to one Petschen. Petschen was then followed. Officers lost visual and "beeper" contact at one time but later located the container by the use of a helicopter. The container was then stationary at a cabin of Knotts. The officers then obtained a search warrant and discovered a drug laboratory at Knotts' cabin. The five gallon container was outside the cabin. The court pointed out that the surveillance amounted principally to following automobiles on public streets, that persons driving on public streets have no reasonable expectation of privacy, and that there was no indication that the beeper was used in any way to reveal the movement of the container in the cabin or in any way which would not have been visible to the naked eye outside the cabin. The Georgia Supreme Court applied similar reasoning to hold in *Devega v. State*[54] that the "pinging" of a cell phone in the possession of a defendant while traveling on a "public roadway" in no way violated any Fourth Amendment right of the defendant.

In *State v. Hill*,[55] the court held that "a person lacks a legitimate expectation of privacy in identifying information such as name, address, or the telephone that is used to facilitate the routing of communications by methods such as physical mail, landline telephone or cellular telephone." As a result, the court concluded that the Fourth Amendment did not prevent an officer in lawful possession of the defendant's phone from calling 911 to determine the telephone number assigned to the phone, and name and birthdate of the person associated with the phone.

In *United States v. Karo*,[56] the United States Supreme Court held that, while the installation of a beeper in a drum of ether, with the consent of a dealer, was not a violation of the Fourth Amendment, there is such a violation where the beeper continued to be monitored after the drum had been placed in a private residence. Although the case was later overruled on other grounds

[54]Devega v. State, 286 Ga. 448, 689 S.E.2d 293 (2010). See U.S. v. Skinner, 690 F.3d 772 (6th Cir. 2012).

[55]State v. Hill, 338 Ga. App. 57, 60, 789 S.E.2d 317 (2016) (physical precedent).

[56]United States v. Karo, 468 U.S. 705, 104 S.Ct. 3296, 82 L.Ed.2d 530 (1984). See also United States v. Cassity, 720 F.2d 451 (6th Cir. 1983), judgment vacated, 468 U.S. 1212, 104 S.Ct. 3581, 82 L.Ed.2d 879 (1984).

in *Banks v. State*,[57] the Georgia Court of Appeals summarized its holding as follows: "[O]fficers who find an apparently closed business unlocked during a normal security sweep may conduct a limited intrusion on the business premises for the sole purpose of securing the area and ensuring no intruders are present."

In the case of a GPS device which government investigators secretly attached to the defendant's motor vehicle after having first obtained a search warrant, the Supreme Court in *United States v. Jones*,[58] concluded that such action constituted an unlawful search and that suppression of any evidence obtained as a result was a proper remedy. The search warrant had expired by the time the device was installed. Nonetheless, the government argued that the defendant had no expectation of privacy in the undercarriage of the vehicle where the device was installed. The Court found that the government's action constituted an unlawful trespass on the defendant's property and thus the defendant's expectations of privacy were irrelevant. The Court distinguished earlier electronic monitoring cases such as *Knotts* and *Karo* because there the device had been installed before the object being tracked came into the defendant's possession and with the prior owner's consent.

Jones has no application to passengers in a vehicle which is the subject of a GPS monitor. Although "a passenger has standing to challenge the constitutionality of a traffic stop generally, a passenger cannot challenge his detainment based upon an independent violation of another person's Fourth Amendment rights."[59] These cases rest on the notion that customers do, in fact, have a reasonable expectation of privacy in their travels or comings and goings and thus in their long term cell site location records. By simply using their phones they do not voluntarily turn over that information to a third party. In addition, the intrusion is more personal than in the case of bank records or even in the typical GPS device which is attached to a motor vehicle as in *Jones* since

---

[57]Banks v. State, 229 Ga. App. 414, 416, 493 S.E.2d 923 (1997), overruled on other grounds by Calbreath v. State, 235 Ga. App. 638, 510 S.E.2d 145 (1998).

[58]U.S. v. Jones, 132 S. Ct. 945, 181 L. Ed. 2d 911 (2012). See Hamlett v. State, 753 S.E.2d 118 (Ga. Ct. App. 2013) (applies *Jones* to hold that installation and monitoring of GPS device constituted search that had to be authorized by probable cause and search warrant). See also, Grady v. North Carolina, 135 S. Ct. 1368, 191 L. Ed. 2d 459 (2015) (court remands to trial court to determine whether requiring a recidivist sex offender to wear a tracking device at all times as a condition of probation constitutes an "unreasonable search"); Packingham v. North Carolina, 137 S. Ct. 1730, 198 L. Ed. 2d 273 (2017) (statute prohibiting sex offenders from accessing social networking sites violated First Amendment).

[59]Green v. State, 331 Ga. App. 801, 806-07, 771 S.E.2d 518 (2015). See U.S. v. Davis, 750 F.3d 1186, 1191(A) (10th Cir. 2014).

the customers carry their phones on their person.

As a general proposition, there is no privacy interest in business records kept in the ordinary course. Accordingly, courts have determined that an individual has no standing to contest the state's seizure of a variety of categories of documents held by third parties, including employment records;[60] credit card statements;[61] kilowatt consumption from electric utility records;[62] and motel registration records.[63]

In *U.S. v. Miller*,[64] the United States Supreme Court held that a depositor had no Fourth Amendment interest in bank records consisting of microfilms of checks, deposit slips and other records relating to his bank account and that the subpoenaed records were the records of the bank and not the depositor's private papers. In *Smith v. Maryland*,[65] the United States Supreme Court held that there is no Fourth Amendment violation when a pen register is installed at the central telephone office to record the numbers dialed from a person's telephone. The basis for the holdings in *Miller* and *Smith* is that a person's expectation of privacy in certain information for purposes of the Fourth Amendment vanishes once that information is shared with a third party such as a bank or telephone company. This is sometimes referred to as "The Third Party Rule."

In *Smarr v. State*,[66] the court held that the Fourth Amendment had no application where the state obtained authorization from a

---

[60]U.S. v. Hamilton, 434 F. Supp. 2d 974 (D. Or. 2006).

[61]U.S. v. Phibbs, 999 F.2d 1053, 38 Fed. R. Evid. Serv. 881 (6th Cir. 1993).

[62]U.S. v. Porco, 842 F. Supp. 1393 (D. Wyo. 1994), decision aff'd, 67 F.3d 1497 (10th Cir. 1995), vacated and superseded on reh'g en banc, 83 F.3d 1247 (10th Cir. 1996), and aff'd on other grounds, 83 F.3d 1247 (10th Cir. 1996).

[63]U.S. v. Willis, 759 F.2d 1486, 17 Fed. R. Evid. Serv. 1127 (11th Cir. 1985).

[64]U. S. v. Miller, 425 U.S. 435, 96 S. Ct. 1619, 48 L. Ed. 2d 71 (1976). In Smith v. Maryland, 442 U.S. 735, 99 S. Ct. 2577, 61 L. Ed. 2d 220 (1979), the Court held that neither the Fourth Amendment nor the federal eavesdropping statute applies to a pen register which is installed on telephone company property for the purpose of

recording the numbers dialed from a certain telephone. The court said that a telephone subscriber does not have an expectation of privacy in such a situation.

In U.S. v. Ghidoni, 732 F.2d 814, 15 Fed. R. Evid. Serv. 1186 (11th Cir. 1984), the Court held that there was no Fifth Amendment violation when a judge ordered a defendant to sign a consent or directive that would enable the government to obtain records from a foreign bank. The court emphasized that the form was not a "testimonial communication."

[65]Smith v. Maryland, 442 U.S. 735, 99 S. Ct. 2577, 61 L. Ed. 2d 220 (1979). However, in People v. Sporleder, 666 P.2d 135 (Colo. 1983), the Court held that a pen register violates the Colorado Constitution.

[66]Smarr v. State, 317 Ga. App. 584, 732 S.E.2d 110 (2012). See U.S. v. Skinner, 690 F.3d 772 (6th Cir. 2012).

judge pursuant to 18 U.S.C.A. § 2703 to obtain cell site location detail regarding the defendant's whereabouts at the time a burglary occurred. Several courts that have considered the propriety of government efforts to obtain cell site information regarding the movements of an individual over an extended period of time have required probable cause and a warrant.[67] In *Carpenter v. United States*,[68] the United States Supreme Court held that the Third Party Rule cannot be applied when the sought after information is the defendant's cell site records. The holding was premised upon a recognition by the Court that "individuals have an expectation of privacy in the whole of their movements." The Court also noted that such records are different from the telephone numbers and bank records which were at issue in *Smith* and *Miller*. Cell site records can be used to track a person's location; in this case, the defendant's movements were charted over a period of 127 days with an average of 101 data points recorded daily. The Court also stated that orders entered pursuant to 18 U.S.C.A. § 2703(d) would not be sufficient to compel a carrier to turn over a subscriber's cell site records and that to obtain such information, the government would need probable cause and a warrant.

In *Braswell v. U.S.*,[69] the United States Supreme Court held that there was no violation of the Fifth Amendment privilege of a sole stockholder of a corporation to require him, as custodian of the corporate records, to produce those records pursuant to a subpoena. However, in the Eleventh Circuit opinion of *In re Grand Jury Subpoena,* dated April 9, 1996,[70] the court, relying on *Curcio v. United States*,[71] held that the sole officer and director of a corporation could not be required to testify before a grand jury to the location of the corporate records after she asserted her Fifth Amendment privilege and stated that she did not possess the records. The Georgia Supreme Court, in *Kesler v. State*,[72] cited and followed *Miller* in holding that neither the user of a telephone nor the subscriber to the telephone service has any

---

[67]See, e.g., In re U.S. for an Order Authorizing the Release of Historical Cell-Site Information, 809 F. Supp. 2d 113 (E.D. N.Y. 2011); In re U.S. for Historical Cell Site Data, 747 F. Supp. 2d 827 (S.D. Tex. 2010), subsequently vacated, 724 F.3d 600 (5th Cir. 2013).

[68]Carpenter v. U.S., 138 S. Ct. 2206, 201 L. Ed. 2d 507 (2018) (decision was expressly noted as "limited" to its facts and had four dissenting opinions).

[69]Braswell v. U.S., 487 U.S. 99,

108 S. Ct. 2284, 101 L. Ed. 2d 98, 25 Fed. R. Evid. Serv. 609, 25 Fed. R. Evid. Serv. 632 (1988). See Thompson v. State, 294 Ga. App. 363, 670 S.E.2d 152 (2008).

[70]Grand Jury Subpoena Dated April 9, 1996 v. Smith, 87 F.3d 1198 (11th Cir. 1996).

[71]Curcio v. United States, 354 U.S. 118, 77 S. Ct. 1145, 1 L. Ed. 2d 1225 (1957).

[72]Kesler v. State, 249 Ga. 462, 470(5), 291 S.E.2d 497 (1982).

expectation of privacy in telephone toll and billing records of the telephone company. However, in *Ellis v. State*,[73] the Georgia Supreme Court, while recognizing that from a Fourth Amendment standpoint a pen register does not require a warrant, a warrant *is* required for a pen register under Georgia statutory law.

In *Registe v. State*,[74] the court held that the voluntary release of cell phone records by a provider is governed by 18 U.S.C.A. § 2702(c) of the Stored Wire and Electronic Communications and Transactional Records Access Act (SCA), which authorizes the voluntary release of non-content records, including subscriber information, "to a governmental entity, if the provider, in good faith, believes that an emergency involving danger of death or serious physical injury to any person requires disclosure without delay of information relating to the emergency." In the event the provider is unwilling to voluntarily release the records, 18 U.S.C.A. § 2703 requires police to obtain a warrant, court order or other evidence of the subscriber's consent. However, should the government obtain evidence based upon a search warrant application which does not comply with 18 U.S.C.A. § 2703(d), suppression is not an available remedy.[75]

Whether a court may compel a provider to produce electronic communications at the request of a criminal defendant presents difficult questions as it is not expressly contemplated under the SCA yet it may implicate a defendant's constitutional right to compulsory process. In an unpublished decision, a Georgia superior court held that it may order the release of cell phone records believed to contain material, exculpatory evidence.

In *State v. Williams*,[76] a defendant indicted for murder received information that a witness sent text messages indicating that he had made false statements to police and revealing himself as the

---

[73]Ellis v. State, 256 Ga. 751, 754, 353 S.E.2d 19 (1987). In *Ellis,* the court concluded that a pen register was a "device" under O.C.G.A. § 16-11-60 and O.C.G.A. § 16-11-62. But the case points out that the party seeking suppression must have standing or a legitimate expectation of privacy in order to prevail. See also Duncan v. State, 259 Ga. 278, 282, 379 S.E.2d 507 (1989).

[74]Registe v. State, 292 Ga. 154, 734 S.E.2d 19 (2012). See Hampton v. State, 295 Ga. 665, 763 S.E.2d 467 (2014) (Nahmias, J., concurring, emphasizing that neither state, O.C.G.A. § 16-11-16.1, nor federal, 18 U.S.C.A.

§ 2703(a), law authorize the state government to require providers to disclose the contents of recently stored electronic communications without a properly issued warrant).

[75]See U.S. v. Kennedy, 81 F. Supp. 2d 1103 (D. Kan. 2000) (only available remedy for violation of SCA is civil action and damages). See also U.S. v. Takai, 943 F. Supp. 2d 1315 (D. Utah 2013).

[76]*State v. Williams,* Docket No. 13SC122778, Order on Ex Parte Motion to Compel Production (Ga. Fulton Cnty. Super. Ct. June 16, 2014).

actual shooter in the murder for which the defendant was indicted. Upon finding such evidence necessary to the defense and that the parties to the messages were unavailable, the court granted the defendant's motion to compel the wireless service provider to produce the text messages. Construing the SCA as not precluding a criminal defendant from obtaining such records through common law means of a court order, the court held the defendant's constitutional right to compulsory process includes the right to obtain exculpatory information and that denying a defendant the opportunity to compel its production would violate his right to due process of law and to a fair trial. Other courts have reached different results.[77] Failure to comply with the requirements governing mandatory disclosure of telephone/cell phone records may warrant the suppression of any records obtained pursuant to O.C.G.A. § 16-11-67. There is no statutory remedy in the event of a *voluntary* release of records under state law which does not comply with 18 U.S.C.A. § 2702(c).[78]

In *Hampton v. State,*[79] the Georgia Supreme Court held that a defendant has no standing under either federal or state law to seek the suppression of text messages from a cell phone which is shown to not be his. The Court noted that there is no statutory remedy for suppression under SCA and that state law regulating eavesdropping, surveillance and the interception of telephonic communications only allow for persons who are "aggrieved" by an unlawful seizure to seek suppression, e.g., the owner of the phone or someone with a legal nexus to the account under which the phone is carried, such as being an authorized user of the phone on the account or the de facto user of the account.

The government may compel the production of transactional records such as telephone numbers from the providers of electronic or remote computer services for their subscribers through a properly issued warrant pursuant to 18 U.S.C.A. § 2703(c). In order to gain access to the contents of recently stored communications from such providers, the government must obtain a court order pursuant to 18 U.S.C.A. § 2703(d) based upon a showing of facts "that there are reasonable grounds to

---

[77]See, e.g., *Commonwealth v. Shaun McCarthy,* Docket No. 1059CR2265, Order on Motion to Quash Subpoena (Mass. Plymouth Cnty. Dist. Ct. Sept. 13, 2011) (holding neither a criminal defendant nor the court is a "government agency" under the SCA and, thus, could not compel a provider to produce the electronic records sought); *People v. Pour,* Case No. 08 CF 2781 (Ill. Third Judicial Cir.

July 1, 2010) (holding that defendant's motion to compel product of electronic records from provider pursuant to a subpoena was "barred under federal law").

[78]Registe v. State, 292 Ga. 154, 734 S.E.2d 19 (2012) (Hunstein, C.J., concurring).

[79]Hampton v. State, 295 Ga. 665, 763 S.E.2d 467 (2014).

believe that the contents of a wire or electronic communication . . . are relevant and material to an ongoing criminal investigation."[80]

In *U.S. v. Warshak*,[81] the Sixth Circuit distinguished the bank records in *Miller* which the Supreme Court held were not subject to the Fourth Amendment, from emails "that are stored with or sent or received through a commercial ISP." The Sixth Circuit characterized the bank records as mere business records which the customer conveys to the bank for use in the ordinary course of business. By contrast, the court noted that the commercial ISP is simply facilitating its customer's communications. It is not the intended recipient of the email but more like a warehouse or transporter for the customer's information. The court analogized the email to the written letter or a phone conversation and concluded that a customer does have a reasonable expectation of privacy in his or her emails. The court went on to hold that in order to compel an ISP to produce the email of one of its customers, it must have a warrant based upon probable cause.[82] In addition, the court held "to the extent that the SCA purports to permit the government to obtain such emails warrantlessly, the SCA is unconstitutional."[83]

Unlike email, subscriber information such as individual's name, email address, telephone number and physical address provided to an internet service provider is not subject to the Fourth Amendment. In *Hatcher v. State*,[84] the Georgia Court of Appeals noted:

> The United States Supreme Court consistently has held that a person has no legitimate expectation of privacy in information he voluntarily turns over to third parties. . . . Consistent with this principle, numerous federal courts have concluded that an Internet service customer has no reasonable expectation of privacy in the

---

[80]See U.S. v. Davis, 785 F.3d 498 (11th Cir. 2015); United States v. Graham, 824 F.3d 421 (4th Cir. 2016). See also Ross v. State, 296 Ga. 636, 639, 769 S.E.2d 43 (2015) (cell phone customer has no standing to seek suppression of cell phone "tower dump" records which only show contact between customer and a particular person).

[81]U.S. v. Warshak, 631 F.3d 266 (6th Cir. 2010).

[82]The court was not willing to say that a subscriber agreement would never be broad enough to "snuff out" a reasonable expectation of privacy.

[83]U.S. v. Warshak, 631 F.3d 266, 287 (6th Cir. 2010). The court also noted that after its decision law enforcement could no longer assert good faith reliance pursuant to Illinois v. Krull, 480 U.S. 340, 107 S. Ct. 1160, 94 L. Ed. 2d 364 (1987), on the statute's exception for a warrant or the storage provider's voluntary cooperation with the government based on the subscriber agreement which allows the provider to access the subscriber's email.

[84]Hatcher v. State, 314 Ga. App. 836, 838-839, 726 S.E.2d 117 (2012) (citations omitted).

subscriber information that he gives voluntarily to his Internet service provider. . . . Every federal court to address this issue has held that subscriber information provided to an internet provider is not protected by the Fourth Amendment's privacy expectation. . . . [C]omputer users do not have a legitimate expectation of privacy in their subscriber information because they have conveyed it to another person—the system operator. In light of these decisions, we doubt that an internet service subscriber can have a reasonable expectation of privacy in the subscriber information that he voluntarily conveys to an Internet service provider in order to obtain Internet service.

Computers pose a unique challenge to the case law which has developed around such Fourth Amendment issues as expectation of privacy, probable cause, consent and the extent to which a computer's files may be searched. Although there is law developing in some recent cases, defense counsel, prosecutors and courts should proceed with caution where the subject of a police search resides within a suspect's computer.[85]

It must be kept in mind that the failure to file a timely motion to suppress constitutes a waiver of any violation of the Fourth Amendment with respect to search and seizure.[86]

Indeed, Justice Sotomayor, in her concurring opinion in *Jones v. United States*,[87] warned that "it may be necessary to reconsider the premise that an individual has no reasonable expectation of privacy in information voluntarily disclosed to third parties." Justice Sotomayor noted that in this "digital age" where individuals as a matter of course are required by banks, phone companies and other businesses and institutions to make various sorts of disclosures about themselves, our expectations of privacy must be adjusted by carving out some protection for such disclosures under the Fourth Amendment or simply recognizing that the convenience which they offer is a necessary tradeoff in the diminution of our respective spheres of "private" information.

---

[85]See e.g. U.S. v. Zimmerman, 277 F.3d 426 (3d Cir. 2002); U.S. v. Walser, 275 F.3d 981 (10th Cir. 2001); U.S. v. Carey, 172 F.3d 1268 (10th Cir. 1999); Barton v. State, 286 Ga. App. 49, 648 S.E.2d 660 (2007); Daniels v. State, 278 Ga. App. 332, 629 S.E.2d 36 (2006); Blevins v. State, 270 Ga. App. 388, 606 S.E.2d 624 (2004); Schwindler v. State, 254 Ga. App. 579, 563 S.E.2d 154 (2002). For an excellent discussion regarding the issues surrounding government searches of computers, see Edward T.M. Garland and Donald F. Samuel, *The Fourth Amend-*ment and Computers, Ga.Bar J., Feb. 2009, at page 15.

[86]Tucker v. State, 222 Ga. App. 517, 518 (2), 474 S.E.2d 696 (1996).

[87]U.S. v. Jones, 132 S. Ct. 945, 181 L. Ed. 2d 911 (2012). See Rehberg v. Paulk, 611 F.3d 828 (11th Cir. 2010), aff'd, 132 S. Ct. 1497, 182 L. Ed. 2d 593 (2012) (no protected privacy interest in email sent to another party, even if never received because contents of email were disclosed to internet service).

In *United States v. Walser*,[88] the U.S. Court of Appeals for the Tenth Circuit noted:

> The advent of the electronic age . . . and the development of desktop computers that are able to hold the equivalent of a library's worth of information, go beyond the established categories of constitutional doctrine. Analogies to other physical objects, such as dressers or file cabinets, do not often inform the situations we now face as judges when applying search and seizure law. . . . This does not, of course, mean that the Fourth Amendment does not apply to computers and cyberspace. Rather, we must acknowledge the key differences and proceed accordingly . . . [O]fficers conducting searches (and the magistrates issuing warrants for those searches) cannot simply conduct a sweeping, comprehensive search of a computer's hard drive. Because computers can hold so much information touching on many different areas of a person's life, there is a greater potential for the "intermingling" of documents and a consequent invasion of privacy when police execute a search for evidence on a computer. . . . Thus, when officers come across relevant computer files intermingled with irrelevant computer files, they "may seal or hold" the computer pending "approval by a magistrate of the conditions and limitations on a further search" of the computer. . . . Officers must be clear as to what it is they are seeking on the computer and conduct the search in a way that avoids searching files of types not identified in the warrant. . . .

In *Hawkins v. State*,[89] the Georgia Supreme Court found that "a cell phone is 'roughly analogous' to a container that can be opened and searched for electronic data, similar to a traditional container that can be opened to search for tangible objects of evidence." However, the court cautioned that searches of cell phones, like computers, must be limited in scope "by the object of the search."

In *Riley v. California*,[90] the United States Supreme Court held that the police may not conduct warrantless searches of cell phones in the absence of the case of specific exigent circumstances. As a general rule, the Court noted that neither concerns of officer

---

[88]U.S. v. Walser, 275 F.3d 981,986 (10th Cir. 2001) (citations omitted). See Henson v. State, 314 Ga. App. 152, 723 S.E.2d 456 (2012).

[89]Hawkins v. State, 290 Ga. 785, 723 S.E.2d 924 (2012) (search of cell phone is restricted to object of search).

[90]Riley v. California, 134 S. Ct. 2473, 189 L. Ed. 2d 430 (2014). See Brown v. State, 330 Ga. App. 488, 767 S.E.2d 299 (2014) (child porn discovered on defendant's phone after his arrest for DUI suppressed based upon *Riley* with emphasis by court that

exception for officer's good faith reliance on state of law at time of search is not recognized in Georgia). See also State v. Hill, 338 Ga. App. 57, 789 S.E.2d 317 (2016) (physical precedent). Compare Mobley v. State, 346 Ga. App. 641, 816 S.E.2d 769 (2018) (*Riley* does not apply to information stored on an airbag control monitor [ACM] such as speed just prior to impact because that sort of information is available to anyone who observes the car's movements).

safety nor destruction of evidence are apparent when police seize a suspect's cell phone and hence there is no justification to search the information contained therein without having probable cause and a warrant. The Court did recognize that exigencies may nonetheless occur which would justify a warrantless search of a cell phone where there existed a real possibility that evidence was subject to "imminent destruction, . . . to pursue a fleeing suspect, and to assist persons who are seriously injured or are threatened with immintent injury."

Generally, see 1 LaFave, *Search and Seizure,* 220 et seq. (West 1978). See § 4:59, infra, on electronic surveillance. See §§ 5:22 et seq., infra, on non-testimonial evidence. See § 4:1, supra, on the definition of a "search" and a "seizure." See §§ 14:79 to 14:83, infra, on expectation of privacy. See § 4:60, infra, on school searches. See Annotation, "Validity, Under Fourth Amendment, of 'Mail Cover,' " 57 A.L.R.Fed. 742 (1982). See § 4:43, infra, on material observed from a helicopter or plane.

§ 4:3   Property which may be seized

O.C.G.A. § 17-5-21 provides that a search warrant may issue for the seizure of the following:

(1) Any instruments, articles, or things, including the private papers of any person, which are designed, intended for use, or which have been used in the commission of the offense in connection with which the warrant is issued;

(2) Any person who has been kidnapped in violation of the laws of this state, who has been kidnapped in another jurisdiction and is now concealed within this state, or any human fetus or human corpse;

(3) Stolen or embezzled property;

(4) Any item, substance, object, thing, or matter, the possession of which is unlawful; or

(5) Any instruments, articles or things, any information or data and anything that is tangible or intangible, corporeal or incorporeal, visible or invisible evidence of the commission of the crime for which probable cause is shown, other than the private papers of any person.

When the peace officer is in the process of effecting a lawful search, nothing in this Code section shall be construed to preclude him from discovering or seizing any stolen or embezzled property, any item, substance, object, thing, or matter, the possession of which is unlawful, or any item, substance, object, thing, or matter, other than the private papers of any person, which is tangible evidence of the commission of a crime against the laws of this state.

In *Smith v. State*,[1] the court described the concept of "private papers" as including "diaries, personal letters, and similar documents wherein the author's personal thoughts are recorded." Medical records maintained by a hospital would not constitute "private papers."[2] In *Tuzman v. State*,[3] the court noted that the private papers which are merely "tangible evidence" of a crime are not subject to seizure by a warrant. "Private papers" which are the instrumentalities of a crime, however, are subject to seizure. In *Tuzmon*, a Medicaid fraud case, the papers involved patient records which the court agreed were properly characterized as "private papers." However, because they were also the instruments by which the defendant was able to make the alleged false Medicaid claims, they were subject to seizure.[4]

While it is true that the above statute is couched in terms of a search pursuant to a warrant, it seems that the same persons or things might be seized pursuant to a lawful warrantless search if it is immediately apparent that the person or object falls within this Code section. See §§ 4:39 et seq., infra, on plain view.

In more general terms, in a lawful warrantless search, an officer may seize any contraband,[5] stolen property,[6] or mere evidence of a crime[7] which he sees in plain view and which he immediately recognizes as such, provided that the scope of the search was strictly tied to and justified by the circumstances which rendered it permissible when initiated.[8] Thus, in *United*

[Section 4:3]

[1]Smith v. State, 192 Ga. App. 298, 384 S.E.2d 459 (1989).

[2]Brogdon v. State, 287 Ga. 528, 697 S.E.2d 211 (2010) (disavowing Sears v. State, 262 Ga. 805, 426 S.E.2d 553 (1993), which generally defined "private papers" as those which were the subject of an evidentiary privilege such as attorney-client).

[3]Tuzman v. State, 145 Ga. App. 761, 244 S.E.2d 882 (1978), abrogated on other grounds by State v. Outen, 289 Ga. 579, 714 S.E.2d 581 (2011).

[4]See Flemister v. State, 317 Ga. App. 749, 732 S.E.2d 810 (2012) (a business letter and divorce papers were not "private papers"); Smith v. State, 192 Ga. App. 298, 384 S.E.2d 459 (1989) (checks, deposit slips and business letters were not "private papers").

[5]Fisher v. United States, 425 U.S. 391, 96 S.Ct. 1569, 48 L.Ed.2d 39 (1976).

[6]Harris v. United States, 331 U.S. 145, 67 S.Ct. 1098, 91 L.Ed. 1399 (1947).

[7]Warden v. Hayden, 387 U.S. 294, 87 S.Ct. 1642, 18 L.Ed.2d 782 (1967). In Warden, officers had followed Hayden into a house after a robbery at a cab company. The Fourth Circuit had concluded that clothing seized in the search of the house had been improperly admitted in evidence because the items had "evidential value only." The Supreme Court reversed and held that for search and seizure purposes there is no distinction between "instrumentalities, fruits or contraband" and mere evidence.

[8]Terry v. Ohio, 392 U.S. 1, 88 S.Ct. 1868, 20 L.Ed.2d 889 (1968).

States v. Jones,[9] the court affirmed the trial court in approving a seizure of a handgun in plain view. The officer had been talking to the defendant through a closed screen door and there was another occupant of the room within arm's reach of the weapon.

Generally, see 68 Am. Jur. 2d Searches and Seizures § 85.

§ 4:4 Who may apply for a search warrant?

In Georgia, by statute any officer of this state or its political subdivisions, or a university, college or school charged with the duty of enforcing the criminal laws may file a written complaint for the issuance of a search warrant.[1] An application for the issuance of a search warrant may be conducted by video conference and will be considered a written application if it satisfies statutory requirements.[2] However, an officer is not entitled to obtain a search warrant unless he is certified pursuant to the provisions of O.C.G.A. §§ 35-8-1 et seq.[3] See § 2:8, supra, on persons authorized to arrest.

In *State v. Harber,*[4] the court held that where an officer was "not authorized to obtain and execute an extra-territorial search warrant, this lack of authority would constitute no more than a mere 'technical' defect" not affecting any substantial rights of the defendant.

§ 4:5 Judicial officers who may issue search warrants

Georgia statutes contain several references to the issuance of a search warrant by a "judicial officer."[1] A judicial officer in the strict legal sense is one "who determines causes" between parties or who "renders decisions in a judicial capacity."[2]

O.C.G.A. § 17-5-21 specifically provides that "any judicial officer authorized to hold a court of inquiry . . . may issue a search warrant." It has been expressly held that a magistrate may issue a search warrant for any area of the county in which his district lies.[3] Judges of recorders' court or municipal court may issue

---

[9]United States v. Jones, 239 F.3d 716 (5th Cir. 2001).

[Section 4:4]

[1]O.C.G.A. §§ 17-5-20, 17-5-21.

[2]O.C.G.A. § 17-5-21.1.

[3]Rottenberg v. State, 184 Ga. App. 331 (1), 361 S.E.2d 533 (1987).

[4]State v. Harber, 198 Ga. App. 170, 401 S.E.2d 57 (1990).

[Section 4:5]

[1]O.C.G.A. §§ 17-5-21, 17-5-25, 17-5-29. See Joyner v. State, 817 S.E.2d 822 (Ga. Ct. App. 2018) (probate judges authorized to issue search warrant).

[2]Alexander v. Holmes, 180 Ga. 397, 400, 179 S.E. 77 (1935).

[3]Dye v. State, 114 Ga. App. 299 (1)(a), 151 S.E.2d 164 (1966). Appar-

search warrants[4] apparently for any area within the municipality. In *Campbell v. State*,[5] the court held that a judge of the Municipal Court of the City of College Park could sign a warrant in her home in Fulton County to be executed in Clayton County. The court reasoned that because the municipality of College Park crossed the Fulton County line into Clayton County, the judge's authority extended across the county line to the limits of the municipality. A judge pro hac vice of a municipal court may also issue a search warrant.[6] In *State v. Kirkland*,[7] the court held a judge of the Atlanta City Court lacked authority to authorize a search in Coweta County since no part of the City of Atlanta is in Coweta County. In *McLendon v. State*,[8] the court upheld a warrant issued by a person sitting as a de facto magistrate. A juvenile court judge may issue a search warrant even in matters which are not concerned with juveniles.[9] Of course, a superior court judge may issue a search warrant for execution in any county of his circuit and the warrant may be signed in any county of the circuit, regardless of the county in which the search is to be executed.[10]

Prior to the enactment of the present Georgia statutes on search and seizure, it had been held that a deputy clerk could issue a search warrant if there existed express authorization by

---

ently, a coroner who is also a magistrate may issue a search warrant. Sanders v. State, 151 Ga. App. 590, 260 S.E.2d 504 (1979).

In State v. Varner, 248 Ga. 347, 283 S.E.2d 268 (1981), the court reversed 158 Ga. App. 448, 280 S.E.2d 869 (1981), and held that a Cobb County justice of the peace, while in the City of Marietta, could execute a search warrant to be executed in Cobb County but outside the City of Marietta even though the act creating the State Court of Cobb County abolished the office of justice of the peace within the City of Marietta and "forbade the exercise of the powers of any justice of the peace within the city."

[4]Hall v. State, 113 Ga. App. 587, 588 (2), 149 S.E.2d 175 (1966). In Jackson v. State, 150 Ga. App. 67, 256 S.E.2d 670 (1979), the court, without discussing the question of whether or not a mayor was a judicial officer, said that it is doubtful that he could ever serve as a neutral and detached magistrate in regard to the issuance of a search warrant to city police where he is the chief executive officer of the city and exercises supervisory control over the police department.

In Branch v. State, 248 Ga. 300, 282 S.E.2d 894 (1981), the court held that a judge of a municipality's recorder's court can issue a search warrant for a violation of a state law.

[5]Campbell v. State, 207 Ga. App. 366, 367 (2), 428 S.E.2d 111 (1993).

[6]Pass v. State, 227 Ga. 730, 733, 182 S.E.2d 779 (1971).

[7]State v. Kirkland, 212 Ga. App. 672, 442 S.E.2d 491 (1994).

[8]McLendon v. State, 259 Ga. 778, 779 (2), 387 S.E.2d 133 (1990).

[9]State v. Belcher, 157 Ga. App. 137, 276 S.E.2d 649 (1981).

[10]Allison v. State, 129 Ga. App. 364, 366 (3), 199 S.E.2d 587 (1973).

the legislature.[11] However, such procedure has been recognized as not being valid in that "only a judicial officer can issue a [search] warrant."[12]

Where a motion to suppress is filed and no issue is raised as to the authority of the magistrate to issue the search warrant, this amounts to a waiver of the right of the defendant to object.[13]

In 2001, O.C.G.A. § 17-5-21.1 became effective and provides that a search warrant application may be heard by video conference under the conditions of the statute. In 2013, O.C.G.A. § 17-5-21.1 was amended to provide that search warrants issued by video conference were valid irrespective of the location of the judge at the time of the video conference, provided the judge is authorized to issue such warrants and is physically located within the state.

§ 4:6 Judicial officers who may issue search warrants— Neutral and detached magistrates

It is well recognized that the determination of whether probable cause exists to issue a search warrant must be made by a "neutral and detached magistrate."[1] Thus, it has been held that a magistrate who serves as a weekend dispatcher for the police is disqualified from issuing a search warrant.[2] Likewise, a magistrate who issues search warrants and then takes part in the searches is not regarded as neutral or detached.[3] In *Connally v.*

---

[11]Johnson v. State, 111 Ga. App. 298 (1), 141 S.E.2d 574 (1965).

[12]Hawkins v. State, 130 Ga. App. 426, 427 (2), 203 S.E.2d 622 (1973).

[13]Sampson v. State, 165 Ga. App. 833 (2), 303 S.E.2d 77 (1983).

[Section 4:6]

[1]Coolidge v. New Hampshire, 403 U.S. 443, 449, 91 S.Ct. 2022, 29 L.Ed.2d 564 (1971); Baggett v. State, 132 Ga. App. 266, 208 S.E.2d 23 (1974).

[2]Baggett v. State, 132 Ga. App. 266, 208 S.E.2d 23 (1974). Obviously a police officer who is also a justice of the peace may not issue a valid search warrant. See Hawkins v. State, 130 Ga. App. 426, 203 S.E.2d 622 (1973). In Sanders v. State, 151 Ga. App. 590, 591 (2), 260 S.E.2d 504 (1979), the court indicated that the trial judge holding a motion to suppress will

receive a per se disqualification under the Fourth Amendment rule if the magistrate is personally or otherwise so close to the law enforcement officers as not to be neutral and detached.

[3]Thomason v. State, 148 Ga. App. 513, 251 S.E.2d 598 (1978). In the Thomason case, the magistrate furnished one of the automobiles which were used by officers for the search. He remained present during a 1-½-hour search conversing with officers and the defendant, and his activities were said to be a part of an ongoing practice. However, in Pressel v. State, 163 Ga. App. 188, 190 (1)(c), 292 S.E.2d 553 (1982), the court concluded that a magistrate did not lose his neutrality where in an isolated incident he was picked up by officers at his home, carried to his office to sign a search warrant and thereafter went with officers to the scene of the search but did not participate in the search. See § 4:15,

Georgia,[4] it was held that a magistrate who is paid $5 for issuing a search warrant and receives no fee if he declines to do so is not a neutral and detached magistrate. However, this rule has not been applied retroactively.[5] The Georgia Court of Appeals has concluded that each of these cases must be decided on its own facts and the "test . . . is whether . . . [the magistrate's] welfare is enhanced by positive action and not enhanced by negative action."[6] The Georgia legislature in 1977 attempted to circumvent this problem by amending the statute providing compensation to a justice of the peace (now magistrate) by providing that he will be paid $5 regardless of whether he decides to issue a search warrant.[7] However, the amended statute provides that the fee "shall not exceed $20.00, but this fee may be waived by the issuing magistrate." If the magistrate holds commitment hearings and obtains a fee for this service, the magistrate might be inclined to issue the search warrant so he could obtain fees incident to the preliminary hearing.[8] In *Felker v. State,*[9] the court held that a magistrate was not disqualified where he had a practice of not billing the county if he denied a search warrant but billing the county if he did. However, in *Rains v. State,*[10] the court concluded that a magistrate issuing an arrest warrant is not disqualified by receiving warrant application forms from the county at no cost. Also it has been held that a magistrate is not to be regarded as disqualified to issue a search warrant where in the past in an unrelated incident he signed blank warrants to accommodate officers.[11]

A magistrate is not disqualified merely because of personal association with police officers or regular visits to the sheriff's office

---

infra, on issuance of a search warrant.

[4]Connally v. Georgia, 429 U.S. 245, 97 S.Ct. 546, 50 L.Ed.2d 444 (1977), rev'g Connally v. State, 237 Ga. 203, 227 S.E.2d 352 (1976). See Connally v. State, 238 Ga. 403, 233 S.E.2d 381 (1977). See also Coolidge v. New Hampshire, 403 U.S. 443, 91 S.Ct. 2022, 29 L.Ed.2d 564 (1971), wherein the Court held that the state attorney general, who had personally taken charge of the murder investigation, and was later to serve as chief prosecutor at trial, was not neutral and detached when he issued a search warrant for the defendant's home.

[5]State v. Patterson, 143 Ga. App. 225, 237 S.E.2d 707 (1977); Lawson v. State, 143 Ga. App. 776, 240 S.E.2d 188 (1977); State v. Livingston, 145

Ga. App. 792, 245 S.E.2d 11 (1978); Contreras v. State, 242 Ga. 369, 372 (2), 249 S.E.2d 56 (1978).

[6]State v. Robinson, 142 Ga. App. 705, 237 S.E.2d 1 (1977).

[7]O.C.G.A. § 15-10-82.

[8]See State v. Robinson, 142 Ga. App. 705, 237 S.E.2d 1 (1977). But see Allen v. State, 240 Ga. 567, 242 S.E.2d 61 (1978); Anderson v. State, 166 Ga. App. 459 (1), 304 S.E.2d 550 (1983).

[9]Felker v. State, 252 Ga. 351, 314 S.E.2d 621 (1984), overruled on other grounds by Fleming v. State, 265 Ga. 541, 458 S.E.2d 638 (1995).

[10]Rains v. State, 161 Ga. App. 361 (2), 288 S.E.2d 626 (1982).

[11]Lang v. State, 165 Ga. App. 576, 577 (1), 302 S.E.2d 683 (1983).

and jail or because he was formerly a deputy sheriff. Likewise, an ex officio magistrate is not disqualified because he is also a coroner.[12] In *Clark v. State*,[13] the court held that a magistrate's neutrality was not impaired by the fact that the magistrate's son was a police officer for the same police department which obtained the search warrant where the son was not involved in the case in any way. In Judicial Qualification Opinion No. 101, the Commission concluded that any employee of a law enforcement body is disqualified by conflict of interest from serving as a magistrate.

Where a superior court judge personally impaneled a special investigative grand jury which indicted the defendant, and made suggestions to the district attorney concerning witnesses to be called, he was held not to be a neutral and detached magistrate.[14] However, in *Beal v. State*,[15] the court held that when a judge "notarized" an affidavit submitted in support of a warrant application, it did not keep him from being neutral and detached in examining or issuing the search warrant.

When a warrant is issued for the search and seizure of documentary evidence in the possession of an attorney, the court shall appoint a special master who is a member of the bar to accompany the person serving the warrant. The special master shall specify the items sought, and if the party fails to provide such items, he shall conduct a search.[16] See § 4:2, supra, on warrants for the search and seizure of documentary evidence in an attorney's possession.

§ 4:7 Probable cause required for issuance of search warrant—General

A proceeding to obtain a search warrant can be initiated by any officer of this state or its political subdivisions charged with the duty of enforcing the criminal laws.[1] See § 2:8, supra, on officers who may obtain a search warrant. The Fourth Amendment provides that "no Warrants shall issue, but upon probable cause, supported by Oath or affirmation . . . ." The Georgia Constitu-

---

[12]Tabb v. State, 250 Ga. 317, 297 S.E.2d 227 (1982).

[13]Clark v. State, 217 Ga. App. 113, 117 (2), 456 S.E.2d 672 (1995).

[14]State v. Guhl, 140 Ga. App. 23, 24 (1), 230 S.E.2d 22 (1976), rev'd on other grounds sub nom. Mitchell v. State, 239 Ga. 3, 235 S.E.2d 509 (1977).

[15]Beal v. State, 175 Ga. App. 234 (1)(a), 333 S.E.2d 103 (1985).

[16]O.C.G.A. § 17-5-32.

[Section 4:7]

[1]O.C.G.A. § 17-5-21. In Huff v. Walker, 125 Ga. App. 251, 187 S.E.2d 343 (1972), the court held that a juvenile court probation officer has no authority to apply for a search warrant.

tion[2] and O.C.G.A. § 17-5-21 contain the same threshold requirement.[3]

As previously pointed out, probable cause is based on probabilities—there must be more than mere suspicion, but there is no requirement of proof beyond a reasonable doubt.[4] However, in *State v. Stephens,*[5] the Georgia Supreme Court pointed out that "[b]y no means is probable cause to be equated with proof by even so much as a preponderance of evidence . . . . 'Probable cause does not demand the certainty we associate with formal trials.' The issuing magistrate *now* need only conclude that there is a 'fair probability that contraband or evidence of a crime will be found in a particular place.' " (Emphasis by the court.)

The evidence utilized in the determination of probable cause may be presented in an affidavit,[6] sworn oral testimony,[7] verified complaint,[8] or any combination of the foregoing.[9] In *Williams v. State,*[10] the court held that a magistrate could consider a taped "affidavit" which was sworn to before the magistrate. However, it is necessary to have a written, signed complaint or affidavit before a search warrant may issue, although it is possible to supplement these with oral testimony under oath.[11] Nevertheless, since it is usually impossible for either an officer or a magistrate

---

[2]Ga. Const. 1983, Art. I, § I, ¶ XIII.

[3]See Rule 41 of the Federal Rules of Criminal Procedure.

[4]Wong Sun v. United States, 371 U.S. 471, 479, 83 S.Ct. 407, 9 L.Ed.2d 441 (1963); Brown v. State, 151 Ga. App. 830, 831, 261 S.E.2d 717 (1979).

[5]State v. Stephens, 252 Ga. 181, 184, 311 S.E.2d 823 (1984) (citing and relying on Illinois v. Gates, 462 U.S. 213, 103 S.Ct. 2317, 76 L.Ed.2d 527 (1983)). Accord, Sullivan v. State, 284 Ga. 358, 667 S.E.2d 32 (2008); Galvan v. State, 240 Ga. App. 608, 524 S.E.2d 297 (1999).

[6]E.g., State v. Barnett, 136 Ga. App. 122, 220 S.E.2d 730 (1975); Bell v. State, 128 Ga. App. 426, 196 S.E.2d 894 (1973).

[7]Simmons v. State, 233 Ga. 429, 211 S.E.2d 725 (1975); Reynolds v. State, 142 Ga. App. 549 (2), 236 S.E.2d 525 (1977). However, there is authority holding that while an affidavit may be supplemented by oral testimony, the oral testimony must be recorded and that probable cause requirements

would be significantly weakened if a magistrate could rely on his recollection as to such testimony. United States v. Hittle, 575 F.2d 799 (10th Cir. 1978).

[8]O.C.G.A. § 17-5-21. In State v. Barnett, 136 Ga. App. 122, 220 S.E.2d 730 (1975), the court said that the words "affidavit" and "complaint" are often used interchangeably.

[9]Dailey v. State, 136 Ga. App. 866, 222 S.E.2d 682 (1975); Dawson v. State, 11 Md.App. 694, 276 A.2d 680, 681 (1971); State v. Barber, 148 Ga. App. 743, 744, 252 S.E.2d 911 (1979). See Moore v. State, 130 Ga. App. 184, 202 S.E.2d 555 (1973); Johnston v. State, 227 Ga. 387, 181 S.E.2d 42 (1971); United States v. Hill, 500 F.2d 315, 317 (5th Cir. 1974); Bishop v. State, 155 Ga. App. 611, 612, 271 S.E.2d 743 (1980).

[10]Williams v. State, 188 Ga. App. 334 (1), 373 S.E.2d 42 (1988).

[11]State v. Barnett, 136 Ga. App. 122, 220 S.E.2d 730 (1975). See Roberson v. State, 246 Ga. App. 534, 537(1), 540 S.E.2d 688 (2000) ("oral testimony may be considered in support of the is-

to remember precisely what the officer said in the presence of the magistrate (even if he gives sworn testimony) every reasonable effort should be exercised to see that all the information given the magistrate is in writing or recorded and preserved,[12] but the failure to do so is not error.[13] It has also been held that a magistrate may take into consideration an "on the scene" viewing to which he is taken by an officer.[14] A search warrant may properly issue based on a signed,[15] but unverified affidavit if testimony establishes that the signing party was, in fact, sworn at the time he gave the information to the magistrate.[16] In *Latimer v. State*,[17] the court held that where an officer sought two search warrants at the same time, one for the residence of a suspect and one for his business, it was possible for one affidavit to incorporate allegations of the other by reference.

The *facts* on which the officer relies in seeking the search warrant must be set forth so that a determination of probable cause can be made.[18] An affidavit which merely states a conclusion that narcotics are located in a certain area is not sufficient.[19] Likewise, "observation of activity that fits a 'drug traffic pattern' . . . does not amount to probable cause to search . . . [a] home."[20] However, the reputation of the suspect, whose place is to be searched, is a fact which may be considered in determining whether or not prob-

---

suance of a warrant, in addition to information presented by affidavit"); Galloway v. State, 332 Ga. App. 389, 772 S.E.2d 832 (2015).

[12]Cf. Pines v. State, 166 Ga. App. 724, 305 S.E.2d 459 (1983).

[13]King v. State, 263 Ga. 741, 744 (2)(a), 438 S.E.2d 620 (1994).

[14]Arnsdorff v. State, 152 Ga. App. 515, 516 (4), 263 S.E.2d 176 (1979).

[15]In State v. Barnett, 136 Ga. App. 122, 220 S.E.2d 730 (1975), the court said the "signature of the affiant is necessary to the validity of an affidavit."

[16]State v. Penansky, 140 Ga. App. 405, 231 S.E.2d 152 (1976); Adams v. State, 201 Ga. App. 12, 14 (4), 410 S.E.2d 139 (1991).

[17]Latimer v. State, 134 Ga. App. 372 (1)(a), 214 S.E.2d 390 (1975).

[18]O.C.G.A. § 17-5-21. See Marshall v. State, 113 Ga. App. 143 (1)(a), 147 S.E.2d 666 (1966); Moore v. State, 130 Ga. App. 184, 202 S.E.2d 555 (1973); Wood v. State, 126 Ga. App. 423, 424,

190 S.E.2d 828 (1972). In Hart v. United States, 162 F.2d 74 (10th Cir. 1947), the court said that a search based on a warrant issued without probable cause is unreasonable within the meaning of the Fourth Amendment. In United States v. Bailey, 458 F.2d 408, 412 (9th Cir. 1972), citing United States v. Anderson, 453 F.2d 174, 175 (9th Cir. 1971), the court said that all "data necessary to show probable cause . . . must be contained within the four corners of a written affidavit."

[19]Aguilar v. Texas, 378 U.S. 108, 110, 115, 84 S.Ct. 1509, 12 L.Ed.2d 723 (1964). The information presented to the magistrate must contain the underlying circumstances necessary to enable the magistrate to make an independent judgment as to the validity of the conclusion that contraband is where it is said to be. Spinelli v. United States, 393 U.S. 410, 89 S.Ct. 584, 21 L.Ed.2d 637 (1969).

[20]State v. Brown, 186 Ga. App. 155, 158, 366 S.E.2d 816 (1988).

able cause for a search exists.[21]

Verified facts are presented to a magistrate for the purpose of permitting him to make an independent and detached judgment as to whether probable cause exists for the issuance of a search warrant.[22] Hence, the magistrate must read the affidavit and make such a judicial determination. If the magistrate fails to make a determination as to probable cause, any search warrant which he issues is void.[23]

In determining the existence of probable cause, the evidence presented to the magistrate must be considered as a whole.[24] The courts have indicated that exculpatory material does not have to be inserted in an affidavit for a search warrant "if no misconduct on the affiant's part has occurred."[25] See § 4:10, infra, on reliability of confidential informer. In *Hayes v. State*,[26] the court indicated that failure of an affidavit "to present 'exculpatory' information does not render an affidavit invalid."

The affidavit must be interpreted by the magistrate and reviewing court in a common sense and realistic manner.[27] An officer's affidavit "should not be judged as an entry in an essay contest."[28] In *White v. State*,[29] the court held "[e]laborate specificity is not required in affidavits supporting search warrants and, where the affidavit leaves doubt as to the existence of probable cause, such questions should largely be resolved by a preference accorded warrants." Probable cause in a warrant proceeding is not the equivalent of guilt beyond a reasonable doubt. There need only be probable cause to believe that evidence of a crime has been secreted on specific premises. Probable cause exists where the facts and circumstances would warrant a man of reasonable caution in believing that the evidence sought is in the place described.[30] However, courts should treat the judgment of experienced officers with considerable deference because of their

---

[21]Caffo v. State, 247 Ga. 751, 755, 279 S.E.2d 678 (1981).

[22]Dawson v. State, 11 Md.App. 694, 276 A.2d 680 (1971). In Carson v. State, 221 Ga. 299, 304, 144 S.E.2d 384 (1965), the court said that the affidavit itself must show facts sufficient to authorize the magistrate to conclude that probable cause exists.

[23]Reid v. State, 129 Ga. App. 660, 200 S.E.2d 456 (1973).

[24]Driscoll v. State, 129 Ga. App. 702, 201 S.E.2d 11 (1973).

[25]Redding v. State, 192 Ga. App. 87, 88, 383 S.E.2d 640 (1989); Bowe v. State, 201 Ga. App. 127, 130 (3), 410 S.E.2d 765 (1991).

[26]Hayes v. State, 182 Ga. App. 319, 320 (1), 355 S.E.2d 700 (1987) (implication).

[27]State v. Babb, 134 Ga. App. 302, 214 S.E.2d 397 (1975).

[28]United States v. Harris, 403 U.S. 573, 579, 91 S.Ct. 2075, 29 L.Ed.2d 723 (1971) (citing Spinelli v. United States, 393 U.S. 410, 438, 89 S.Ct. 584, 21 L.Ed.2d 637 (1969)).

[29]White v. State, 225 Ga. App. 74, 75 (1), 483 S.E.2d 329 (1997).

[30]Cf. State v. Alonso, 159 Ga. App. 242, 243, 283 S.E.2d 57 (1981).

expertise which enables them to "articulate meaning in given conduct which would be wholly innocent to the untrained observer."[31] Thus, in *Daniels v. State*,[32] the court upheld the finding of probable cause to search the computer of the defendant, a convicted child molester, where the investigating detective attested that, based on his experience and training, persons involved in the acts of child molestation often use their computers to perpetrate their illegal acts and to maintain files and data related to their illegal acts. There is an indication that less evidence is needed in order to establish probable cause for the issuance of a search warrant than is required for a warrantless search of the premises.[33]

The omission of information from a search warrant application and affidavit will not necessarily justify the suppression of evidence.[34] Indeed, the intentional misrepresentation of the facts presented to the magistrate will not automatically require suppression.[35] The test in each case is whether there exists other corroborative evidence which was presented to the magistrate and which under the totality of circumstances "supplies an alternative basis for finding probable cause, where there are deficiencies in the showing of the informant's veracity, reliability or basis of knowledge."[36]

Probable cause may be established at least in part by smell[37] as well as sight or hearing.[38]

"[T]he time within which proof of probable cause [must exist] . . . . must be of facts closely related to the time of the issuance of the warrant so as to justify such finding at that time."[39] Thus, later conflicting statements of an affiant will not "undo" a finding

---

[31]State v. Grant, 195 Ga. App. 859, 862 (2), 394 S.E.2d 916 (1990).

[32]Daniels v. State, 278 Ga. App. 332, 629 S.E.2d 36 (2006). See also Schwindler v. State, 254 Ga. App. 579, 563 S.E.2d 154 (2002); Blevins v. State, 270 Ga. App. 388, 606 S.E.2d 624 (2004). Cf. Hawkins v. State, 290 Ga. 785, 723 S.E.2d 924 (2012) (search of cell phone is restricted to object of search).

[33]United States v. Ventresca, 380 U.S. 102, 106, 85 S.Ct. 741, 13 L.Ed.2d 684 (1965); Turk v. United States, 429 F.2d 1327, 1330 (8th Cir. 1970); Aguilar v. Texas, 378 U.S. 108, 110, 84 S.Ct. 1509, 12 L.Ed.2d 723 (1964).

[34]Brown v. State, 244 Ga. App. 440, 442 (1), 535 S.E.2d 785 (2000).

[35]Clemons v. State, 257 Ga. App. 96, 574 S.E.2d 535 (2002).

[36]Sanders v. State, 252 Ga. App. 609, 612 (1), 556 S.E.2d 505 (2001).

[37]Brooker v. State, 164 Ga. App. 775 (1), 298 S.E.2d 48 (1982); Johnson v. United States, 333 U.S. 10, 68 S.Ct. 367, 92 L.Ed. 436 (1948). See State v. Kazmierczak, 331 Ga. App. 817, 771 S.E.2d 473 (2015) (odor of marijuana can be sole basis for issuance of warrant provided magistrate also considers all circumstances in warrant affidavit such as officer's training and experience).

[38]See § 4:2, supra, and § 4:40, infra, on plain view discovery.

[39]Callahan v. State, 179 Ga. App. 556, 560, 347 S.E.2d 269 (1986).

of probable cause at the time of issuing a warrant. However, a trial court passing on a motion to suppress must give "great deference" to a magistrate's determination that probable cause exists. " 'A grudging or negative attitude by reviewing courts toward warrants' . . . is inconsistent with the Fourth Amendment. . . . [S]o long as the magistrate had a 'substantial basis for . . . conclud[ing]' that a search would uncover evidence of wrongdoing, the Fourth Amendment requires no more."[40] "A search warrant, regular and proper on its face, is presumptively valid. . . ."[41] However, the issuance of the warrant may not be justified by what is discovered in the later search.[42]

"Minor factual inaccuracies which are only peripherally relevant to the showing will not void the warrant where their presence in the affidavit is not such as to reflect on the credibility of the affiant."[43] In *Houston v. State*,[44] the court pointed out that the defendant has "the burden of showing not only that the false and omitted information was material to the determination of probable cause but that any false information given or material information omitted was done so for the purpose of misleading the magistrate." However, the defendant need not carry the burden of showing that a warrant was obtained through the use of false or misleading information until the State first meets its burden of producing evidence showing the validity of the warrant. At a minimum, this will require the warrant and the supporting affidavit.[45]

Generally, it has been said that if the information set forth in the affidavit is obtained by an illegal wiretap,[46] or in some other illegal manner,[47] a search warrant based thereon is not valid. However, probable cause may be based on evidence obtained

---

[40]Illinois v. Gates, 462 U.S. 213, 103 S.Ct. 2317, 76 L.Ed.2d 527, 547 (1983). Gates is discussed in more detail in § 4:10, infra. Cf. State v. Fultz, 171 Ga. App. 886, 887, 321 S.E.2d 381 (1984); State v. Morrow, 175 Ga. App. 743, 748 (4), 334 S.E.2d 344 (1985).

[41]Hunter v. State, 198 Ga. App. 41, 400 S.E.2d 641 (1990).

[42]Maxwell v. State, 127 Ga. App. 168, 193 S.E.2d 14 (1972).

[43]Dresch v. State, 125 Ga. App. 110 (4), 186 S.E.2d 496 (1971); Summerville v. State, 226 Ga. 854 (1), 178 S.E.2d 162 (1970); Rugendorf v. United States, 376 U.S. 528, 532, 84 S.Ct. 825, 11 L.Ed.2d 887 (1964). See § 14:86, infra, on the identity of an informer.

[44]Houston v. State, 242 Ga. App. 114, 115 (1), 527 S.E.2d 619 (2000).

[45]Davis v. State, 266 Ga. 212, 213, 465 S.E.2d 438 (1996), recon. den. (2/5/1996); Watts v. State, 274 Ga. 373, 376, 552 S.E.2d 823 (2001), recon. den. (10/22/2001), on remand, Watts v. State, 253 Ga. App. 227, 558 S.E.2d 791 (2002).

[46]State v. Toomey, 134 Ga. App. 343, 214 S.E.2d 421 (1975).

[47]See §§ 2:25 and 2:34, supra, on the applicability of the exclusionary rule. In State v. Stone, 165 W.Va. 266, 268 S.E.2d 50, 54-55 (W.Va.1980), overruled by State v. Juluis, 185 W.Va. 422, 408 S.E.2d 1 (1991), the court held that information obtained during

when a warrantless search is conducted by private persons who are not officers.[48] Also, even where an affidavit contains information, which has, in part, been unlawfully obtained, the warrant is not necessarily defective. The question is whether the untainted information is alone sufficient to establish probable cause. If the lawfully obtained information alone is sufficient to constitute probable cause, the evidence seized pursuant to the warrant is admissible.[49] Thus, while it is not appropriate for the police to inform the magistrate that the suspect refused authorities permission to conduct a search of his premises (or for the magistrate to consider the same), if there was enough untainted information in the warrant application to support the issuance of the warrant, any evidence seized as a result will not be suppressed.[50]

In *Evans v. State,*[51] the court held that there is no obligation on the state to produce at trial the officer whose affidavit was the basis of a search warrant.

Generally, see §§ 2:10 et seq., supra, on probable cause, and § 4:26, infra, on warrantless searches. See 68 Am. Jur. 2d Searches and Seizures § 68.

§ 4:8 Probable cause required for issuance of search warrant—Observation of affiant who is officer, victim, or private citizen

The truthfulness or reliability of facts observed and stated in an affidavit or sworn testimony, unless obviously false,[1] may be relied on by the magistrate if the affiant is a police officer,[2] the victim of the crime,[3] or a private citizen.[4] (See § 2:11, supra, on information received by an officer from an informant.) However,

---

an illegal search may not be used to establish probable cause for a later search. As noted, the case was eventually overruled.

[48]United States v. Keuylian, 602 F.2d 1033 (2d Cir. 1979).

[49]Rothfuss v. State, 160 Ga. App. 863, 864, 288 S.E.2d 579 (1982); United States v. Williams, 633 F.2d 742, 744 (2) (8th Cir. 1980); James v. United States, 418 F.2d 1150, 1151 (D.C.Cir. 1969). Cf. Sacchinelli v. State, 161 Ga. App. 763, 764 (1), 288 S.E.2d 894 (1982).

[50]Gardner v. State, 255 Ga. App. 489, 493, 494 (3), 566 S.E.2d 329 (2002), ". . . the trial court's determination that refusal to consent to a search may be taken into account

when determining probable cause is error as a matter of law."

[51]Evans v. State, 161 Ga. App. 468, 470, 288 S.E.2d 726 (1982).

[Section 4:8]

[1]A magistrate is not to believe an incredible affidavit. Theodor v. Superior Court, 8 Cal.3d 77, 89, 104 Cal.Rptr. 226, 501 P.2d 234 (1972).

[2]State v. Causey, 132 Ga. App. 17, 20 (1), 207 S.E.2d 225 (1974).

[3]Simmons v. State, 233 Ga. 429, 211 S.E.2d 725 (1975); Toole v. State, 146 Ga. App. 305, 306 (4), 246 S.E.2d 338 (1978).

[4]Simmons v. State, 233 Ga. 429, 211 S.E.2d 725 (1975); United States v. Hunley, 567 F.2d 822 (8th Cir. 1977);

SEARCH AND SEIZURE   § 4:9

the magistrate is not obligated to believe the facts stated orally
under oath or by affidavit.[5]

An affidavit or testimony for a search warrant must not be
conclusory. Thus, it has been held that an assertion of an affiant
that he had seen "contraband (marijuana residue) in . . .
[defendant's] house" was held to be a mere conclusion and not to
justify the issuance of a search warrant where "the affidavit
contains no information concerning the affiant's ability to
distinguish marijuana residue from tobacco residue."[6]

In *Eaton v. State*,[7] the court held that an anonymous informant
may not be established as a concerned private citizen based on
what the informant told the officer. "If the informant is an 'anonymous tipster,' the information provided to the police must be
detailed enough to provide some basis for predicting the future
behavior of the suspect."[8]

§ 4:9   **Probable cause required for issuance of search
        warrant—Observation of officer, victim, or private
        citizen not appearing before magistrate**

Hearsay may be relied on in order to establish the accuracy of
the facts related by the affiant to the magistrate.[1] Here again, the
magistrate may rely on information related to an officer affiant
by another police officer,[2] the victim of the crime,[3] or by a disinterested private citizen of good reputation.[4] If the source of the
information is a "law abiding concerned citizen," the informant is

---

United States v. Gagnon, 635 F.2d 766 (10th Cir. 1980). But cf. State v. Leistiko, 176 Mont. 434, 578 P.2d 1161 (1978); Devier v. State, 247 Ga. 635, 638 (5), 277 S.E.2d 729 (1981).

[5]See Reid v. State, 129 Ga. App. 660, 200 S.E.2d 456 (1973); Keith v. State, 238 Ga. 157, 158, 231 S.E.2d 727 (1977); Campbell v. State, 226 Ga. 883, 885, 178 S.E.2d 257 (1970).

[6]State v. Casey, 185 Ga. App. 726, 365 S.E.2d 878 (1988).

[7]Eaton v. State, 210 Ga. App. 273, 275, 435 S.E.2d 756 (1993).

[8]Durden v. State, 320 Ga. App. 218, 739 S.E.2d 676 (2013), citing Register v. State, 315 Ga. App. 776, 778, 728 S.E.2d 292 (2012).

[Section 4:9]

[1]In the federal context, Rule 41(c) of the Federal Rules of Criminal Procedure allows the issuance of a search warrant upon oral testimony (by telephone or "other appropriate means") and notes that the finding of probable cause may be based upon hearsay evidence, in whole or in part.

[2]State v. Causey, 132 Ga. App. 17, 207 S.E.2d 225 (1974); Caudell v. State, 129 Ga. App. 229, 230, 199 S.E.2d 550 (1973); Mitchell v. State, 239 Ga. 456, 458, 238 S.E.2d 100 (1977). In Williams v. State, 239 Ga. App. 671, 672, 522 S.E.2d 43 (1999), the court pointed out that "[w]hen a police officer is the informant the reliability of the informant is presumed as a matter of law."

[3]Simmons v. State, 233 Ga. 429, 432, 211 S.E.2d 725 (1975); Williams v. State, 143 Ga. App. 210, 237 S.E.2d 693 (1977).

[4]Davis v. State, 129 Ga. App. 158, 160, 198 S.E.2d 913 (1973).

See Hudson v. State, 253 Ga.

deemed to be reliable.[5] Also, "when a *named* informant makes a declaration against . . . penal interest and based on personal observation, that in itself provides a substantial basis for the magistrate to credit that statement." (Emphasis in original.)[6] However, the fact that the caller was "a well-spoken black lady" without more does not make the caller a "concerned citizen."[7] It is not necessary for the person making the firsthand observation to be named in the affidavit,[8] provided he is sufficiently described so as to make it clear that he falls within one of the above categories and provided the person actually exists.[9]

In *Johnson v. State*,[10] the court pointed out that "information obtained by police officers engaged in an investigation may be used by another officer common to that investigation as a reliable basis for the establishment of probable cause. . . . [However,] where an informant supplies the information to one officer who then relays it to a fellow officer, the reliability . . . of the informant" determines the reliability of the information the second officer received.

In *State v. White*,[11] the court held that an anonymous tipster is not to be regarded as a "concerned citizen" unless facts are presented to the magistrate from which it can be concluded that the tipster is in fact a "concerned citizen." In *Wood v. State*,[12] the court held that the "uncorroborated statement of an unnamed third-party source, as filtered through a reliable informant to a police affiant, did not give rise to probable cause sufficient to support the issuance of a search warrant," and this is true even if

---

App. 210, 211, 558 S.E.2d 420 (2001); Penny v. State, 248 Ga. App. 772, 775, 547 S.E.2d 367 (2001) ("a law-abiding concerned citizen has a built-in credibility and is deemed to be reliable.").

[5]Penny v. State, 248 Ga. App. 772, 775 (2)(b), 547 S.E.2d 367 (2001). See Sutton v. State, 319 Ga. App. 597, 737 S.E.2d 706 (2013).

[6]Tomlinson v. State, 242 Ga. App. 117, 119, 527 S.E.2d 626 (2000). Tomlinson also points out that "[o]ne who knows the police are *already* in a position to charge him with a serious crime will not likely undertake to divert the police down blind alleys." (Emphasis in original.)

[7]Stewart v. State, 217 Ga. App. 45, 47, 456 S.E.2d 693 (1995).

[8]Burns v. State, 119 Ga. App. 678

(2), 168 S.E.2d 786 (1969). See also Baxter v. State, 134 Ga. App. 286, 289-290, 214 S.E.2d 578 (1975).

[9]See § 14:86, infra, on identity of informer. But in Hardy v. State, 162 Ga. App. 797, 799, 292 S.E.2d 902 (1982), the court said that where there is nothing in the affidavit to suggest otherwise, the magistrate may assume "the unnamed individual was a law abiding and trustworthy citizen."

[10]Johnson v. State, 230 Ga. App. 535, 537, 496 S.E.2d 785 (1998).

[11]State v. White, 196 Ga. App. 685, 686, 396 S.E.2d 601 (1990).

[12]Wood v. State, 214 Ga. App. 848 (1), 449 S.E.2d 308 (1994). See Sutton v. State, 319 Ga. App. 597, 737 S.E.2d 706 (2013).

the original statement was against the interest of the declarant.[13] See § 2:11, supra, on probable cause to arrest.

In *Shirley v. State*,[14] the Georgia Court of Appeals addressed the issue of whether a magistrate must view photos of alleged child pornography before issuing a warrant to search the computer files of the accused and if not, what information must be presented to satisfy the probable cause required. The court concluded that the term "child pornography" was a sufficient description of the materials involved and that neither photographic evidence nor expert assistance was necessary. The court was also satisfied that the hearsay information provided by federal and foreign law enforcement authorities contained in the affidavit of the state's investigator was reliable and sufficient. In addition, the court concluded that the information contained in the warrant was not stale because the images were alleged to have been accessed 19 months prior to the application. The warrant requested was directed at the stored data and back-up tapes to the accused's computer. According to the affidavit offered in support of the application, the preference of child pornographers is to store and maintain their pornography in electronic format. Finally, the court held that it is not necessary to establish probable cause that the accused "knowingly" possessed the pornography, only that it was likely to be found in the residence of the accused. On appeal the Georgia Supreme Court reversed, finding that the FBI merely acted as a conduit for the German authorities. The court suggested that the search warrant application might have been sufficient had an agent looked at the website or otherwise offered a reliable source who could confirm that the web site did contain "child pornography."[15]

§ 4:10 Probable cause required for issuance of search warrant—Observation of "informer" not appearing before magistrate

In general terms, anyone who gives an officer information is an informer. However, in the context of probable cause to search, the word often implies a person who is himself, to some extent, involved in unlawful activity. He may be a user of drugs, frequently he has been arrested, perhaps not infrequently he hopes for some special treatment because of his "helping" the

---

[13]State v. Wesson, 237 Ga. App. 789, 791, 516 S.E.2d 826 (1999).

[14]Shirley v. State, 330 Ga. App. 424, 765 S.E.2d 491 (2014).

[15]Shirley v. State, 297 Ga. 722, 777 S.E.2d 444 (2015).

police.[1] On some occasions, the information is given because of jealousy, anger or "to get even" with the person "informed on." This is the kind of person whose credibility is discussed in this section.

A troublesome area in the law of search and seizure involves the credibility of information given to the affiant by an unnamed informer. For instance, although Georgia recognizes the validity of the "statement against interest" rule, it does not apply where the informant is unnamed.[2] It is frequently said that the affidavit or sworn testimony before the magistrate must specifically state sufficient facts to show that the unnamed informer is reliable.[3] In *Mitchell v. State*,[4] the court pointed out that "when the information supplied by the informant is not corroborated, the magistrate must look to see whether the informant himself . . . [is] reliable." In *Pitts v. State*,[5] the court pointed out that a magistrate, in determining reliability of an informer, may consider (1) the type of information previously supplied, (2) the use to which the information was put, and (3) the lapse of time since the information was furnished.

In *Aguilar v. Texas*,[6] the United States Supreme Court held that where an affiant relies on information obtained from an informer, the affidavit must (1) state the underlying circum-

---

[Section 4:10]

[1]See 1 LaFave, Search and Seizure 499, § 3.3 (West 1978). See Wiggins v. State, 331 Ga. App. 447, 771 S.E.2d 135 (2015) (excellent collection of cases on requirements to show informant reliability).

[2]Bellamy v. State, 243 Ga. App. 575, 578 (1), 530 S.E.2d 243 (2000). The "statement against interest rule" by a known informant was explained in Graddy v. State, 277 Ga. 765 (1), 596 S.E.2d 109 (2004): "[a] known informant who makes an inculpatory admission regarding his connection with an offense that has yet to be indicted not only provides probable cause for issuance of a search warrant, but also subjects himself to potential arrest and prosecution for the admitted criminal activity." This rule, however, may not be used to introduce hearsay statements that are against the criminal interest of a third party declarant and exculpatory of the accused at the trial of a criminal case. Stanford v. State, 272 Ga. 267 (4), 528 S.E.2d 246 (2000).

[3]Courson v. State, 125 Ga. App. 373, 187 S.E.2d 554 (1972); Spinelli v. United States, 393 U.S. 410, 89 S.Ct. 584, 21 L.Ed.2d 637 (1969). See § 14:86, infra, on identity of informer.

In Roberson v. State, 246 Ga. App. 534, 537, 540 S.E.2d 688 (2000), the court held that the fact than an affiant states that the informant was reliable is not sufficient.

[4]Mitchell v. State, 239 Ga. App. 735, 736, 521 S.E.2d 873 (1999).

[5]Pitts v. State, 212 Ga. App. 556, 557 (1), 442 S.E.2d 797 (1994); Claire v. State, 247 Ga. App. 648, 649, 544 S.E.2d 537 (2001).

[6]Aguilar v. Texas, 378 U.S. 108, 84 S.Ct. 1509, 12 L.Ed.2d 723 (1964). In Spinelli v. United States, 393 U.S. 410, 89 S.Ct. 584, 21 L.Ed.2d 637 (1969), the Court purported to "explicate" *Aguilar*.

See the excellent opinion of Justice Smith in Tabb v. State, 250 Ga. 317, 322, 297 S.E.2d 227 (1982), in which he discusses and applies the two-prong test.

stances showing the informer's credibility, or the reliability of his information, *and* (2) state the underlying circumstances to support the conclusion that the informer had observed criminal activity.[7] In other words, two essentials must be met: (1) There must be a showing of veracity of the informer and his information—the veracity prong of the two-prong test;[8] and (2) there must be a showing of how or why the informer knew "the narcotics were where he claimed they were" —the basis of knowledge prong of the two-prong test.[9]

The *first* prong of the Aguilar test, reliability of the informer, has often been established by including a statement in the affidavit that the informer has in the past given information which has led to arrests and convictions.[10] Where an informer, alleged to be reliable because of information given on two prior occasions which led to arrests, gave information received from an acquaintance, the Georgia Court of Appeals held the affidavit adequate despite the double hearsay objection.[11] However, the bare assertion that the informer has given reliable information in the past is not sufficient.[12]

The *second* prong of the Aguilar test has been said to require proof to support the informer's conclusion that criminal activity exists. Georgia courts have construed the second prong of the Aguilar test as requiring the affidavit to state how the information was obtained *or* to describe the criminal activity in such detail so that the magistrate can conclude that the informer's information is more than "a casual rumor circulating in the underworld," or a charge based on an individual's general

---

[7]In Hornsby v. State, 124 Ga. App. 724, 725, 185 S.E.2d 623 (1971), the court found an affidavit deficient because it did not state how the informer obtained the information.

[8]Hardy v. State, 162 Ga. App. 797, 292 S.E.2d 902 (1982).

[9]Moylan, "Hearsay and Probable Cause: An 'Aguilar and Spinelli' Primer," 25 Mercer L. Rev. 741, 747 (1974).

[10]Bryan v. State, 137 Ga. App. 169, 223 S.E.2d 219 (1976). See Fair v. State, 284 Ga. 165, 172(b), 664 S.E.2d 227 (2008).

[11]Smith v. State, 136 Ga. App. 17, 220 S.E.2d 11 (1975) (affiant must provide details supporting the cred-

ibility of informant A and the reliability of the information provided by informant A as well as the basis for affiant's belief that information provided to informant A by informant B was reliable in order to support a probable cause determination involving "hearsay on hearsay").

[12]Galgano v. State, 147 Ga. App. 284, 286, 248 S.E.2d 548 (1978) (statement that informant has provided information in the past is insufficient unless affidavit also includes detail as to: type of information provided; how it was used; and, length of time since the information was provided); Burke v. State, 265 Ga. App. 38, 592 S.E.2d 862 (2004).

reputation.[13]

However, all of the foregoing material in this section must be examined in the light of the 1983 United States Supreme Court case of *Illinois v. Gates*.[14] In *Gates* an anonymous letter received by police set out rather detailed information about the drug activities of Mr. and Mrs. Gates. Much of the information was corroborated, but there remained important gaps in the tip. The letter and an affidavit setting out what had been corroborated was used in obtaining a search warrant. A search pursuant to the warrant resulted in a discovery of a large amount of contraband. The Supreme Court said "an informant's 'veracity,' 'reliability' and 'basis of knowledge' are all highly relevant in determining the value of his report. . . . [H]owever . . . these elements should [not] be understood as entirely separate and independent requirements to be rigidly exacted in every case. . . . Rather . . . they should be understood simply as closely intertwined issues that may usefully illuminate the common sense, practical question whether there is 'probable cause' to believe that contraband or evidence is located in a particular place. . . . *[The] totality of the circumstances approach* is far more consistent with our prior treatment of probable cause . . . than is any rigid demand that specific 'tests' be satisfied by every informant's tip. Perhaps the central teaching of our decisions bearing on the probable cause standard is that it is a 'practical, non-technical conception.' . . . [P]robable cause is a fluid concept—turning on the assessment of probabilities in particular factual contexts— not readily, or even usefully, reduced to a neat set of legal rules . . . [T]he 'two-pronged test' directs analysis into two largely independent channels—the informant's 'veracity' or 'reliability' and his 'basis of knowledge.' There are persuasive arguments against according these two elements such independent status. Instead, they are better understood as relevant considerations in the totality of circumstances analysis that traditionally has guided probable cause determinations; a deficiency in one may be compensated for, in determining the overall reliability of a tip, by a strong showing as to the other, or by some other indicia of reliability. . . . [I]t is wiser to abandon the 'two-pronged test' established by our decisions in *Aguilar* and *Spinelli*. . . . In its place we reaffirm the totality of the circumstances analysis. . . ."[15] It is important to recognize that the Court did not completely

---

[13]Buck v. State, 127 Ga. App. 72, 74, 192 S.E.2d 432 (1972); Dailey v. State, 136 Ga. App. 866, 222 S.E.2d 682 (1975).

[14]Illinois v. Gates, 462 U.S. 213, 103 S.Ct. 2317, 76 L.Ed.2d 527 (1983).

Cf. Lewis v. State, 234 Ga. App. 873, 874 (1), 508 S.E.2d 218 (1998). See Coleman v. State, 337 Ga. App. 304, 787 S.E.2d 274 (2016).

[15]Illinois v. Gates, 462 U.S. 213, 103 S.Ct. 2317, 76 L.Ed.2d 527 (1983).

abandon the Aguilar-Spinelli test in *Gates;* the two prongs became part of a balancing test that includes the totality of the circumstances.

In *State v. Stephens,*[16] the Georgia Supreme Court expressly adopted the rule of *Illinois v. Gates*, supra, stating (1) that "it is, at heart, a rule of subjectivity. One judge's 'probable cause' can be another judge's 'inarticulable suspicion' . . . [and (2)] that *Gates be considered as the* outer limit of probable cause. Accordingly we urge that arresting officers and magistrates make every effort to see that supporting affidavits reflect the maximum indication of reliability along the lines of *Aguilar-Spinelli*, whenever and wherever that shall be feasible."

In *Clark v. State,*[17] the court held that *Gates* is to be applied retroactively.

In *Peacock v. State,*[18] the court held that the " 'totality of the circumstances' is a less rigorous test than that of *Aguilar* and *Spinelli* . . . [and] an affidavit that would pass the former test must necessarily meet the 'totality of the circumstances' criterion." However, in *Langford v. State,*[19] the court emphasized that veracity and basis of knowledge are still major concerns and that an affidavit for a search warrant must set forth sufficient facts from which the magistrate can independently determine the reliability of both the information and the informant. In *State v. Palmer,*[20] the court observed that "[t]he magistrate's task in determining if probable cause exists to issue a search warrant is simply to make a practical, common sense decision whether, given all the circumstances set forth in the affidavit before him, including the "veracity" and "basis of knowledge" of persons supplying hearsay information, there is a fair probability that contraband or evidence of a crime will be found in a particular place."

In *Caswell v. State,*[21] the affidavit, which was the sole basis of the warrant, established the reliability of the informant and adequately stated that "[d]uring the past five (5) days affiant has received information from a reliable confidential informant that Bert Caswell had a quantity of methamphetamines in his residence." However, concerning the informant's basis of knowledge, the appellate court pointed out that "[t]here was no indica-

[16]State v. Stephens, 252 Ga. 181, 311 S.E.2d 823 (1984), rev'g 167 Ga. App. 417, 418, 307 S.E.2d 9 (1983) (need a summary of facts set out in affidavit); Mincey v. State, 180 Ga. App. 898, 350 S.E.2d 852 (1986).

[17]Clark v. State, 173 Ga. App. 579, 580 (3), 327 S.E.2d 549 (1985).

[18]Peacock v. State, 170 Ga. App. 309, 310 (1), 316 S.E.2d 864 (1984).

[19]Langford v. State, 213 Ga. App. 232, 233 (1), 444 S.E.2d 153 (1994). Accord, Stewart v. State, 217 Ga. App. 45, 47, 456 S.E.2d 693 (1995).

[20]State v. Palmer, 285 Ga. 75, 77, 673 S.E.2d 237 (2009).

[21]Caswell v. State, 219 Ga. App. 787, 788, 466 S.E.2d 907 (1996).

tion in the affidavit as to whether this information came from the informant's personal knowledge so the informant's tip must be relegated to the status of a casual rumor." At the motion to suppress hearing there was additional information concerning the basis of the informant's knowledge other than that set out in the affidavit. However, the appellate court pointed out that this was irrelevant since it was not given to the magistrate at the time of the issuance of the warrant and reversed the trial court's denial of a motion to suppress.

In *VonLinsowe v. State*,[22] the court pointed out that "[i]n order for the corroboration [by an officer] to be meaningful enough to show reliability, . . . the information corroborated must include 'a range of details relating not just to easily obtained facts and conditions existing at the time of the tip, but to future actions of third parties ordinarily not easily predicted.' . . . In short, the information corroborated will generally need to be a prediction of future behavior, as in [*Gates*] or something similar—that is, inside information not available to the general public." However, in *Wilson v. State*,[23] the court held that this rule relating to a prediction of future behavior "applies to an anonymous telephone tip but not to a tip from a known reliable informant." For instance, in *Fiallo v. State*,[24] the court held that "[m]erely confirming that the accused lives where the informant said he did is not sufficient corroboration of the information regarding illegal activity."

In *Kessler v. State*,[25] the court held that it was not necessary for an affidavit to include the fact that the informant was a felon. See § 14:87, infra, on falsity of affidavits for search warrants. However, in *Perkins v. State*,[26] the court pointed out that "officers seeking warrants should provide the magistrate with any infor-

---

[22]VonLinsowe v. State, 213 Ga. App. 619, 621 (1), 445 S.E.2d 371 (1994) (quoting State v. Bryant, 210 Ga. App. 319, 436 S.E.2d 57 (1993)).

[23]Wilson v. State, 249 Ga. App. 560, 562, 549 S.E.2d 418 (2001).

[24]Fiallo v. State, 240 Ga. App. 278, 279, 523 S.E.2d 355 (1999).

[25]Kessler v. State, 221 Ga. App. 368, 471 S.E.2d 313 (1996).

In Elom v. State, 248 Ga. App. 273, 275 (1), 546 S.E.2d 50 (2001), the appellate court reversed the denial of the trial court to grant a motion to suppress where "(1) the affidavit failed to mention that it was based on hearsay evidence from two confidential informants; (2) the affidavit failed to

disclose that the one informant had a criminal background and was being paid for the information; (3) the affidavit had no information regarding the reliability of the second informant; and (4) the attesting officer had no personal knowledge of the reliability of either informant, the lone statement in the affidavit about one informant's credibility did not constitute sufficient facts from which the magistrate could independently determine the reliability of both the information and the informants."

[26]Perkins v. State, 220 Ga. App. 524, 525 (2), 469 S.E.2d 796 (1996). Accord, Hockman v. State, 226 Ga. App. 521, 522 (1), 487 S.E.2d 102 (1997).

mation they have relevant to a CI's reliability or motivation, including criminal records and any payments made." In *Robertson v. State,*[27] the court reversed the denial of a motion to suppress pointing out that the "officer's failure to inform the magistrate about the informant's criminal background, pending criminal charges and the possible revocation of his probation or parole, and his personal animosity toward . . . [the person whose home was searched] resulted in the magistrate being deprived of the opportunity to independently determine the reliability of the informant." If material information is knowingly or recklessly omitted, "the reviewing court should include it with other information provided the magistrate to determine whether probable cause to issue the warrant existed."[28] "[H]owever, [if] the information directly known by the officers . . . was sufficient to establish probable cause,"[29] a reversal is not required.

In *Pettus v. State,*[30] the court pointed out that "our courts have, on occasion, recognized the affiant's desire to protect the identity of a confidential informant by omitting certain details from the affidavit," such as the exact date drugs were seen on premises.

§ 4:11 Probable cause required for issuance of search warrant—Time

The time of the occurrence of the facts relied upon by the affiant is a prime element in establishing probable cause for the issuance of a search warrant.[1] The magistrate must determine whether the facts presented create a reasonable belief that the same conditions described in the affidavit exist at the time of the presentation of the warrant.[2] However, there has been some relaxation of the requirement of showing that the search warrant is not "stale." Thus, if from all the circumstances set out in the affidavit "there is a fair probability that contraband or evidence of a crime will be found in a particular place," a search warrant may be issued.[3] In *Ayers v. State,*[4] the court said that "the determination of staleness has been modified so that now that issue is

---

[27]Robertson v. State, 236 Ga. App. 68, 70, 510 S.E.2d 914 (1999).

[28]Redding v. State, 192 Ga. App. 87, 383 S.E.2d 640 (1989).

[29]Perkins v. State, 220 Ga. App. 524, 525 (2), 469 S.E.2d 796 (1996).

[30]Pettus v. State, 237 Ga. App. 143, 144 (2), 514 S.E.2d 901 (1999).

[Section 4:11]

[1]Fowler v. State, 121 Ga. App. 22, 23, 172 S.E.2d 447 (1970); Bache-lor v. State, 143 Ga. App. 442, 238 S.E.2d 579 (1977); Dean v. State, 46 Ala.App. 365, 242 So.2d 411 (1970).

[2]Jackson v. State, 130 Ga. App. 6, 202 S.E.2d 206 (1973).

[3]State v. Luck, 252 Ga. 347, 312 S.E.2d 791 (1984).

[4]Ayers v. State, 181 Ga. App. 244, 248 (2), 351 S.E.2d 692 (1986), disapp. on other grounds, Anderson v. State, 267 Ga. 116, 475 S.E.2d 629 (1996). Accord, Carruthers v. State, 272 Ga.

included in the broad overview of 'totality of circumstances.' " As the Court of Appeals observed in *State v. Graddy*,[5] "[t]he mere passage of time does not equate with staleness."

Where an affidavit contains no information relating to the time of the occurrence, a search warrant may not issue.[6] However, in *Scott v. State*,[7] the court held that "the absence of the precise time" the informant observed drug transactions is not necessarily fatal. When an affidavit uses the present tense in stating that a person is selling drugs at a specified location, this may sufficiently show that the information is current and not stale.[8] An affidavit signed on a particular day stating that the informer had within five days prior thereto overheard a specified person state she was using cocaine and planned to use it over the upcoming weekend was held to be sufficient as to timeliness.[9]

When an ongoing activity is described, the passage of time as to some of these events is less significant than in the case of a single, isolated transaction.[10]

Generally, officers are permitted to obtain search warrants in advance when there is a probable cause to believe that the thing to be searched for *will be* at the location described when the search is executed even though the thing to be searched for is not at the location to be searched at the time of the issuance of a warrant.[11] In *United States v. Grubbs*,[12] the Supreme Court held that such "anticipatory" warrants are not categorically unconstitutional and that a "triggering condition" is not required on the face of the warrant to satisfy the Fourth Amendment.

306, 313 (5), 528 S.E.2d 217 (2000).

[5]State v. Graddy, 262 Ga. App. 98, 103 (3), 585 S.E.2d 147 (2003), judgment aff'd, 277 Ga. 765, 596 S.E.2d 109 (2004). See Buckley v. State, 254 Ga. App. 61, 62, 561 S.E.2d 188 (2002) (because the passage of time will not affect materials stored in a computer, the issue of "staleness" may not arise in the context of a search of a computer for pornography). See also U.S. v. Lovvorn, 524 Fed. Appx. 485, 487 (11th Cir. 2013) (files stored in a computer are less likely to disappear over time than other types of contraband).

[6]Fowler v. State, 121 Ga. App. 22, 172 S.E.2d 447 (1970); McMiken v. State, 127 Ga. App. 66, 192 S.E.2d 716 (1972). In Reddish v. State, 161 Ga. App. 170, 171, 288 S.E.2d 266 (1982), the court stated that a mere statement

that two "buys" had been made from the defendant was not sufficient to establish probable cause, since there was no indication of when the "buys" had been made.

[7]Scott v. State, 213 Ga. App. 84, 85 (1), 444 S.E.2d 96 (1994).

[8]Covington v. State, 129 Ga. App. 150, 199 S.E.2d 348 (1973).

[9]Davis v. State, 129 Ga. App. 158, 198 S.E.2d 913 (1973).

[10]Ayers v. State, 181 Ga. App. 244, 248 (2), 351 S.E.2d 692 (1986), disapp. on other grounds, Anderson v. State, 267 Ga. 116, 475 S.E.2d 629 (1996).

[11]2 LaFave, Search and Seizure § 3 (2014); United States v. Outland, 476 F.2d 581 (6th Cir. 1973).

[12]United States v. U.S. v. Grubbs, 126 S. Ct. 1494, 164 L. Ed. 2d 195 (U.S. 2006).

In *McLarty v. State*,[13] a detective obtained a search warrant for drugs at the residence of the defendant but did not execute the warrant until an informant gave the detective confirming information that a person had just left the premises and that drugs were present. The appellate court affirmed the denial of defendant's motion to suppress.

While not directly related to the subject matter of this section, it should be kept in mind that a search warrant is void if not executed within 10 days from the date of issuance.[14]

Generally, see 68 Am. Jur. 2d Searches and Seizures § 70. See also § 4:13, infra, on reason for issuance of a search warrant.

§ 4:12 Probable cause required for issuance of search warrant—Description of place and person to be searched

In order to allege probable cause, an affidavit must meet two essentials concerning the place and person to be searched: (1) an adequate description of the place or person and (2) facts to establish probable cause that the object sought is located at the described place.

The Fourth Amendment, the Georgia Constitution, and the Code all provide that the place to be searched be particularly described.[1] In addition, according to the Georgia statute, if a warrant is to issue for the search of an individual, the person must be specifically described.[2] The Constitution prohibits the issuance of a general warrant.[3] A search warrant which does not particularly describe the place or person to be searched is considered a general warrant.[4] However, the contents of the affidavit may be considered in determining the description of the place to be searched.[5]

The description of the place to be searched must be sufficient to enable a prudent officer executing the warrant to locate the premises "definitely and with reasonable certainty."[6] It has been pointed out that "[s]earch warrants are not directed at persons; they authorize the search of 'places' and the seizure of 'things,'

---

[13]McLarty v. State, 238 Ga. App. 27 (1), 516 S.E.2d 818 (1999).

[14]Fowler v. State, 121 Ga. App. 22, 24, 172 S.E.2d 447 (1970).

[Section 4:12]

[1]U. S. Const. Amend. IV; Ga. Const. 1983, Art. I, § I, ¶ XIII; O.C.G.A. § 17-5-21.

[2]O.C.G.A. § 17-5-21.

[3]State v. Cochran, 135 Ga. App. 47, 48, 217 S.E.2d 181 (1975) (citing Stanford v. Texas, 379 U.S. 476, 481, 85 S.Ct. 506, 13 L.Ed.2d 431 (1965)).

[4]Jackson v. State, 129 Ga. App. 901, 904, 201 S.E.2d 816 (1973).

[5]E.g., Cuevas v. State, 151 Ga. App. 605, 612, 260 S.E.2d 737 (1979).

[6]State v. Hardin, 174 Ga. App. 83, 329 S.E.2d 172 (1985).

and as a constitutional matter they need not even name the person from whom the things will be seized."[7] The slight misspelling of the last name of the person occupying the premises will not necessarily render the affidavit and search warrant invalid,[8] and if the property to be searched is clearly described, a search warrant using a completely incorrect first name does not void a search warrant for the premises.[9]

In *Maryland v. Garrison,*[10] the United States Supreme Court held that whether a mistake as to the place to be searched renders the warrant invalid depends upon the extent to which it was possible for an officer, acting reasonably, to discover a mistake either at the time the warrant was sought or at the time it was executed. Hence, the Georgia Court of Appeals held that a warrant to search a named theater located at "No. 13 West 11th Street" (in a named city) may be used to search a theater of the same name located at "No. 15 West 11th Street" where there is no such theater at the address set out.[11] A search warrant to search lot 14K rather than 15K in a mobile home park was found sufficient where it was difficult to determine what the correct number was. A map was attached and the defendant's car was described and found at the site of the search.[12] However, a warrant to search "283 Rock Springs" cannot be used to search "293 South Rock Springs."[13]

An affidavit describing a room at one of two designated motels

---

[7]Bing v. State, 178 Ga. App. 288, 289 (1), 342 S.E.2d 762 (1986) (quoting Zurcher v. Stanford Daily, 436 U.S. 547, 555, 98 S.Ct. 1970, 56 L.Ed.2d 525 (1978)).

[8]Grant v. State, 130 Ga. App. 237 (2), 202 S.E.2d 675 (1973).

[9]Giles v. State, 149 Ga. App. 263, 264 (c), 254 S.E.2d 154 (1979), rev'd on other grounds, State v. Thackston, 289 Ga. 412, 716 S.E.2d 517 (2011).

[10]Maryland v. Garrison, 480 U.S. 79, 107 S.Ct. 1013, 94 L.Ed.2d 72 (1987). In Garrison, police officers had a warrant to search "the premises known as 2036 Park Avenue third floor apartment." When they arrived to execute the warrant and had already begun the search, the officers realized there were actually two apartments on the third floor. The Court, in a 6-3 opinion, found that neither the warrant nor the search violated the particularity requirement because the officers had been sufficiently diligent in their attempts to ascertain who lived on the third floor prior to seeking the warrant. Neither the informant nor the utility company indicated to the police that there was more than one apartment on the third floor.

[11]State v. Blews, 148 Ga. App. 73, 251 S.E.2d 10 (1978). Cf. Gumina v. State, 166 Ga. App. 592 (2), 305 S.E.2d 37 (1983).

[12]Chambless v. State, 165 Ga. App. 194 (1), 300 S.E.2d 201 (1983). In Martin v. State, 165 Ga. App. 802, 302 S.E.2d 717 (1983), the court relied on a map attached to the search warrant. See U. S. v. Ortiz, 311 F. Supp. 880, 883 (D. Colo. 1970), order aff'd, 445 F.2d 1100 (10th Cir. 1971).

[13]Bell v. State, 124 Ga. App. 139, 182 S.E.2d 901 (1971).

without giving a room number is insufficient.[14] In the case of a warrant to search an apartment house, a dormitory, a motel, a duplex or a partitioned house, the warrant, on its face, must indicate more than a street address for the building.[15] Where a two-story dwelling contained several front and back doors and separate mailboxes in front of each door, a warrant to search the entire first floor was held not to be sufficiently particular.[16] However, where a single-family dwelling is rented by one person but occupied by several who pay rent to the lessee and there are no external signs of occupation by several families, a warrant to search the entire house is valid.[17] In *Andrews v. State*,[18] the court pointed out that where "several persons occupy the premises in common, sharing common living quarters but having separate bedrooms, the courts have held that a single warrant describing the entire premises is valid and justifies the search of the entire premises." Likewise, in *Newby v. State*,[19] a warrant to search "for the person of defendant and the premises known as 2059 East Drive, Decatur, DeKalb County, Georgia" was held sufficiently definite where the warrant also provided that it was "requested for the above residence where [the defendant] rents a room."

In cases where law enforcement authorities seek a warrant to search an apartment house, hotel or some other sub-divided structure suitable for multiple occupancy, the warrant application must describe the particular unit to be searched with sufficient definiteness to preclude a search of one or more units indiscriminately. "There are, however, exceptions to this general rule: '[t]he warrant of a multi-unit structure will be valid where (1) there is probable cause to search each unit; (2) the targets of the investigation have access to the entire structure; or (3) the officers reasonably believe that the premises had only a single unit.' "[20]

In a town or small city, it may be sufficient to describe a build-

---

[14]Garner v. State, 124 Ga. App. 33, 182 S.E.2d 902 (1971). In Garner the court said that where "the name of the owner or occupant is not given, the description of the premises must be exact."

[15]Jackson v. State, 129 Ga. App. 901, 904, 201 S.E.2d 816 (1973). See Annot., 11 A.L.R.3d 1330 (1967).

[16]Jones v. State, 126 Ga. App. 841, 192 S.E.2d 171 (1972).

[17]Jackson v. State, 129 Ga. App. 901, 904, 201 S.E.2d 816 (1973); State v. Capps, 256 Ga. 14, 15, 342 S.E.2d 676 (1986); Bing v. State, 178 Ga. App.

288, 289 (1), 342 S.E.2d 762 (1986). Cf. Maryland v. Garrison, 480 U.S. 79, 107 S.Ct. 1013, 94 L.Ed.2d 72 (1987).

[18]Andrews v. State, 219 Ga. App. 808, 810 (2), 466 S.E.2d 909 (1996) (quoting Bing v. State, 178 Ga. App. 288, 290 (1), 342 S.E.2d 762 (1986)).

[19]Newby v. State, 161 Ga. App. 805, 806 (1), 288 S.E.2d 889 (1982).

[20]Fletcher v. State, 284 Ga. 653, 655(3), 670 S.E.2d 411 (2008), quoting U.S. v. Perez, 484 F.3d 735, 741(4) (5th Cir. 2007) (noting that where the police want a warrant to search more than one residential unit within an

ing or home as the residence of a named person on a particular street in a specified county.[21] However, it has been said that if "the name of the owner or occupant is not given, the description of the premises must be exact."[22] Where a house was incorrectly described as being two-storied when it actually was one-storied but otherwise properly designated, the description was held to be sufficient since the officer could locate the building with "reasonable certainty."[23] However, the description of the place to be searched as a named person's house trailer of a certain color located approximately one and one-half miles east of the intersection of two named roads "to a drive turning north to trailer park, said trailer being last on left in pines with a white station wagon sitting in yard" was found to be insufficient where no city or county was alleged.[24] But in *Mosier v. State*,[25] an affidavit and search warrant were headed "GEORGIA, GWINNETT COUNTY" and described the place to be searched as "6529 Norcross-Tucker Road." The defendant contended that the description was inadequate since the description did not name a county. The court took judicial notice that "Tucker, Georgia" is not an incorporated city, as contended by the defendant, but is merely a community encompassing portions of DeKalb and Gwinnett counties and concluded that the heading was sufficient to enable the officer "to ascertain with reasonable certainty" the place to be searched. See § 4:16 et seq., infra, on execution of search warrants.

A search warrant authorizing the seizure of records may or may not also authorize the seizure of a personal computer which may contain such records. In *Grant v. State*,[26] the court held that if the warrant did not specify a computer or computer disks as items to be seized, those items could not be seized regardless of whether other permitted items could be found on the computer or computer disks. The court found no legal support for the trial court's decision that practical considerations and time constraints justified the overly extensive search. However, cases in other jurisdictions have held that computers may be seized where a warrant authorizes the seizure of records of certain types of crimes, such as drug-dealing, even though the police have no idea

---

apartment building, a separate probable cause determination must be made as to each).

[21]Steele v. State, 118 Ga. App. 433, 434 (3), 164 S.E.2d 255 (1968).

[22]State v. Hatch, 160 Ga. App. 384, 385, 287 S.E.2d 98 (1981).

[23]State v. Megdal, 139 Ga. App. 397, 398 (1), 228 S.E.2d 333 (1976).

[24]Vaughn v. State, 141 Ga. App. 453, 454 (1), 233 S.E.2d 848 (1977); but cf. Miller v. State, 155 Ga. App. 399, 400, 270 S.E.2d 822 (1980).

[25]Mosier v. State, 160 Ga. App. 415, 287 S.E.2d 357 (1981).

[26]Grant v. State, 220 Ga. App. 604, 469 S.E.2d 826 (1996).

what is actually contained on the computers.[27]

A search warrant for a car need not state the location of the vehicle if the description is sufficiently detailed.[28] A warrant describing the person and place as "John Doe #Blue" and "on or about his person or auto (or truck) in the vicinity of Magnolia and Sunset, vehicle being either a green pickup truck or a blue and white Ford" was held sufficient since the affidavit contained a physical description of the individual.[29]

The person or persons to be searched must also be described with particularity.[30] This may be done by using the person's name[31] or by describing him in some other manner.[32] A warrant which states an alias as the name of a person is not invalid if in fact the individual is using the alias.[33] However, a "John Doe" warrant which contains no description of the person to enable an officer to locate the person with reasonable certainty is void.[34] A search warrant for a specified location and "all persons on the premises" is a general warrant as to a commercial customer in the place at the time of the search.[35]

There is some older authority which holds that if a warrant provides for the search of "any other person on said premises who reasonably might be involved in the commission of the aforesaid violation of the laws of Georgia," this is regarded as sufficient particularity to justify the search of those persons present when the warrant is executed.[36] But the addition of such words in a search warrant does not broaden the authority of an officer to search persons coming to the premises during the search or afterwards beyond the limited terms of O.C.G.A. § 17-5-28,[37] which provides that an officer executing a warrant "may reason-

[27]See e.g., People v. Gall, 30 P.3d 145 (Colo. 2001); U.S. v. Musson, 650 F. Supp. 525 (D. Colo. 1986); U.S. v. Sissler, 1991 WL 239000 (W.D. Mich. 1991), aff'd, 966 F.2d 1455 (6th Cir. 1992).

[28]Reed v. State, 126 Ga. App. 323, 190 S.E.2d 587 (1972).

[29]Fomby v. State, 120 Ga. App. 387, 170 S.E.2d 585 (1969). See United States v. Ferrone, 438 F.2d 381, 389 (3d Cir. 1971).

[30]O.C.G.A. § 17-5-21.

[31]Willis v. State, 122 Ga. App. 455, 177 S.E.2d 487 (1970).

[32]See Holloway v. State, 134 Ga. App. 498, 215 S.E.2d 262 (1975).

[33]Thrall v. State, 122 Ga. App. 427, 177 S.E.2d 192 (1970).

[34]See Fowler v. State, 128 Ga. App. 501, 502, 197 S.E.2d 502 (1973).

[35]Wilson v. State, 136 Ga. App. 70, 221 S.E.2d 62 (1975). Generally, see § 4:21, infra, on execution of search warrant.

[36]Willis v. State, 122 Ga. App. 455, 177 S.E.2d 487 (1970); Castillo v. State, 166 Ga. App. 817 (6), 305 S.E.2d 629 (1983). See also Wood v. State, 224 Ga. 121, 125, 160 S.E.2d 368 (1968), approving the search of a vehicle under a warrant authorizing the search of a named person and any other person there who might reasonably be involved in violating the laws of Georgia.

[37]Smith v. State, 139 Ga. App. 129, 132, 227 S.E.2d 911 (1976); Wilson v. State, 136 Ga. App. 70, 221 S.E.2d

ably detain or search any person in the place at the time: (a) To protect himself from attack, or (b) To prevent the disposal or concealment of any instruments, articles or things particularly described in the warrant."

Generally, see 2 LaFave, *Search and Seizure* 72, § 4.5 (West 1978). See § 4:21, infra, on execution of a search warrant. See Annotation, "Search warrant: sufficiency of description of apartment or room to be searched in multiple-occupancy structure," 11 A.L.R.3d 1330 (1967).

§ 4:13 Probable cause required for issuance of search warrant—Reason for searching place and person

Not only must the place or person be particularly described, but the affidavit must contain sufficient facts to show the magistrate that there is probable cause for believing the object sought is located at the place described.[1] However it has been held that "[a]n officer's inference that items sought will be at the place to be searched requires no more than 'a fair presumption' to be reasonable."[2] It has been held that if a reliable informer has recently observed narcotics in the described premises, a finding of probable cause is justified without alleging facts to demonstrate that the informer knew the substance was a narcotic.[3] However, in *State v. Law*,[4] the court held that an affidavit for a search warrant "is not insufficient merely because it fails to show how the informant knew that the substance he saw was a narcotic." Nevertheless, it has been held that if stolen goods are seen on the premises, the informer must state sufficient facts to show how he knew the objects were stolen.[5] An affidavit setting out general suspicious circumstances is insufficient. For example, observation of premises for several weeks, seeing known drug users and pushers there, seeing as many as 15 cars at the home at one time and general information that users and pushers hang around the

---

62 (1975); State v. Cochran, 135 Ga. App. 47, 217 S.E.2d 181 (1975). Cf. Wallace v. State, 131 Ga. App. 204, 205 S.E.2d 523 (1974).

[Section 4:13]

[1]Tuten v. State, 156 Ga. App. 758, 275 S.E.2d 796 (1980).

[2]State v. Staley, 249 Ga. App. 207, 209, 548 S.E.2d 26 (2001).

[3]State v. Hill, 135 Ga. App. 214, 217 S.E.2d 190 (1975) (citing United States v. Ventresca, 380 U.S. 102, 85 S.Ct. 741, 13 L.Ed.2d 684 (1965)). In State v. Kaukani, 59 Haw. 120, 577

P.2d 335 (1978), the affidavit was held adequate which stated that informant saw what "appeared to be" marijuana; however, it failed to mention the extent of the knowledge of the informant in recognizing marijuana.

[4]State v. Law, 208 Ga. App. 744, 745, 432 S.E.2d 110 (1993).

[5]Mahar v. State, 137 Ga. App. 116, 118, 223 S.E.2d 204 (1975). See Hammond v. State, 124 Ga. App. 523, 184 S.E.2d 512 (1971) (mere conclusion that gun seen by officer in a house was "kept . . . for illegal purposes" was insufficient).

house, do not add up to probable cause.[6]

Similar issues arise when the object of a search is a personal computer. Due to the ease with which files and data may be deleted over time, establishing probable cause to search these devices may be problematic. However, law enforcement officials now have various forensic tools which enable them to extrapolate data even long after deletion. In *Buckley v. State*,[7] the court held that because the hard drive on the defendants computer was not perishable, previously obtained information that there were pornographic images on the computer was not stale. Thus, there was probable cause to search the computer.

In *McClain v. State*,[8] the court pointed out that "[a]n officer's inference that items sought will be at the place to be searched requires no more than 'a fair presumption' to be reasonable."

It has been held that a well-defined path from the defendant's premises to a neighbor's property where marijuana was grown justifies issuing a search warrant for the defendant's home.[9]

See § 4:11, supra, on timeliness of information.

§ 4:14 Probable cause required for issuance of search warrant—Person or thing to be seized

The warrant clause of the Fourth Amendment provides in pertinent part that "no Warrants shall issue, but upon probable cause, . . . particularly describing the place to be searched, and the persons or things to be seized." Further defining "persons or things," the Georgia Legislature established that a search warrant may be issued for the following: (1) any things or papers which are designed or intended for use, or have been used, in connection with a crime; (2) any person who has been kidnapped or any human fetus or corpse; (3) stolen or embezzled property; (4) anything which it is unlawful to possess; and (5) anything which is tangible evidence of the commission of a crime except private papers.[1] However, "private papers" which are the instrumentalities of a crime may be seized even though not listed

---

[6]Thornton v. State, 125 Ga. App. 374, 187 S.E.2d 583 (1972); accord, Maxwell v. State, 127 Ga. App. 168, 193 S.E.2d 14 (1972). Cf. State v. Porter, 167 Ga. App. 293, 306 S.E.2d 377 (1983).

[7]Buckley v. State, 254 Ga. App. 61, 561 S.E.2d 188 (2002).

[8]McClain v. State, 267 Ga. 378, 388 (11), 477 S.E.2d 814 (1996). Accord, DeYoung v. State, 268 Ga. 780, 788 (7), 493 S.E.2d 157 (1997).

[9]Brooks v. State, 140 Ga. App. 371, 231 S.E.2d 138 (1976); Steele v. United States, 267 U.S. 498, 503, 45 S.Ct. 414, 69 L.Ed. 757 (1925).

[Section 4:14]

[1]O.C.G.A. § 17-5-21. By statute, Georgia law permits the seizure of "mere evidence" apparently to the full extent permitted by the Fourth Amendment. See Warden v. Hayden, 387 U.S. 294, 87 S.Ct. 1642, 18 L.Ed.2d 782 (1967), which discarded the older

in a search warrant.[2] Deposit slips and checks have been held not to be private papers.[3]

In *Sanford v. Texas*,[4] Justice Stewart expressed the unanimous view of the Supreme Court in holding that under the federal Constitution, the need to particularly describe the "things to be seized" is "accorded the most scrupulous exactitude when the 'things' are books and the basis for their seizure is the ideas they contain." However, in *Hunt v. State*,[5] the Georgia Court of Appeals concluded that under the Georgia Constitution the requirements of *Sanford* for "scrupulous exactitude" applied to *all* search warrants.

The affidavit in support of a search warrant must describe with particularity the person or thing to be seized.[6] In *United States v. Cook*,[7] it was explained that "[a] general order to explore and rummage through a person's belongings is not permitted. The warrant must enable the searcher to reasonably ascertain and identify the things which are authorized to be seized. . . . Circumstances often make an exact description of the property impossible and in those cases the judicial officer issuing the warrant must weigh the practical necessities of law enforcement against the likelihood of a violation of the personal rights of the one whose premises and possessions are to be searched."

"The use of a generic term or a general description in a warrant, however, is acceptable to the judicial officer issuing the warrant only when a more specific description of the things to be seized is unavailable. Thus, in *United States v. Cortellesso*,[8] the First Circuit upheld a warrant issued to search for and seize stolen clothing when the 'labels had been removed from the Pierre Cardin suits so that a more precise description would not have

---

rule of Gouled v. United States, 255 U.S. 298, 41 S.Ct. 261, 65 L.Ed. 647 (1921), preventing the seizure of "mere evidence." See § 5:23, infra, on nontestimonal evidence.

[2]Ledesma v. State, 251 Ga. 885, 890, 311 S.E.2d 427 (1984).

[3]Smith v. State, 192 Ga. App. 298, 384 S.E.2d 459 (1989).

[4]Sanford v. Texas, 379 U.S. 476, 485, 85 S.Ct. 506, 13 L.Ed.2d 431 (1965). See § 4:22, infra, on description of items to be seized.

[5]Hunt v. State, 180 Ga. App. 103, 104, 348 S.E.2d 467 (1986).

[6]O.C.G.A. § 17-5-21; U. S. Const. Amend. IV, and Ga. Const. 1983, Art. I, § I, ¶ XIII.

[7]United States v. Cook, 657 F.2d 730, 733 (5th Cir. 1981). See U.S. v. Aguirre, 664 F.3d 606, 614 (5th Cir. 2011).

[8]United States v. Cortellesso, 601 F.2d 28, 32 (1st Cir. 1979). In Cortellesso a warrant specifying "stolen goods, wares and merchandise valued in excess of $5,000 which have travelled in interstate commerce, in particular men's suits, sports jackets, women's boots, leather coats" was held to be sufficiently particular. See also United States v. Johnson, 541 F.2d 1311, 1313 (8th Cir. 1976) (marijuana, paraphernalia and U. S. currency); United States v. Wilson, 451 F.2d 209, 214 (5th Cir. 1971) ("paraphernalia for making coins").

assisted the [searcher] and, that with respect to other stolen items, only a generic description was known.' Failure to employ the specificity available will invalidate a general description in a warrant." In *United States v. Bright*,[9] the Fifth Circuit held that if the police had possessed a complete list of serial numbers of currency being sought, it would have been necessary to give them in the warrant description because "generic classifications in a warrant are acceptable only when a more precise description is not possible."

A description of "one statue of a Cobra Snake and other items that are fruits of the crime of burglary" is too general except as to the cobra statue.[10] However, an affidavit which describes the things to be seized as "[f]ruits of the crime of the theft of a shipment of assorted shipment of clothing; traveral [sic] sport coats, suits, dresses, swimware [sic], handbags, taken 21 July, 1972, Tucker, Ga." has been held sufficient.[11] In describing a pistol, it is not necessary to set out the exact caliber.[12]

In *Lo-Ji Sales, Inc. v. New York*,[13] the Court held that an open-ended search warrant which authorized the seizure of two films judicially determined to be obscene and the seizure of other items deemed to be obscene was a general warrant and invalid even when the magistrate went along to determine what articles were deemed to be obscene. See § 4:23, infra, on seizure of obscene material. Likewise, in *Dobbins v. State*,[14] the Georgia Supreme Court concluded that the warrant which described the articles sought as "certain property and/or materials of a pornographic nature, to-wit, movies, pictures, and magazines which are contrary to the laws of Georgia" was a general warrant in violation of the Fourth Amendment. The *Dobbins* case concluded that the "warrant left the determination of what items were likely to be

---

[9]United States v. Bright, 630 F.2d 804 (5th Cir. 1980). See Montilla Records of Puerto Rico, Inc. v. Morales, 575 F.2d 324 (1st Cir. 1978); United States v. Klein, 565 F.2d 183 (1st Cir. 1977).

[10]Dugan v. State, 130 Ga. App. 527, 203 S.E.2d 722 (1974). In United States v. Abrams, 615 F.2d 541 (1st Cir. 1980), the court held the following inadequate: "Certain business and billing and medical records of patients of Doctors Abrams, London, Braum, and Abrams, London and Associates, Inc., which show actual medical services performed and fraudulent services claimed to have been performed in a scheme to defraud the United States and to submit false medicare and

medicaid claims for payments to the United States. . . ."

[11]State v. Causey, 132 Ga. App. 17, 207 S.E.2d 225 (1974).

[12]Young v. Caldwell, 229 Ga. 653, 193 S.E.2d 854 (1972).

[13]Lo-Ji Sales, Inc. v. New York, 442 U.S. 319, 99 S.Ct. 2319, 60 L.Ed.2d 920 (1979). But in People v. Superior Court, 25 Cal.3d 67, 157 Cal.Rptr. 716, 598 P.2d 877 (1979), the court held that it was proper for officers to use a burglary victim during the execution of a valid search warrant to identify stolen goods.

[14]Dobbins v. State, 262 Ga. 161, 163 (3), 415 S.E.2d 168 (1992).

'of a pornographic nature' entirely to the discretion of the officers executing the warrant."

However, in the child molestation case of *Cooper v. State*,[15] the court concluded that a search warrant was valid which directed the seizure of "[a]ny video tape showing males/females involved in sexual intercourse or any sexual act" and "[a]ny magazine that shows nude males/females posing/involved in any sexual act . . ." used in the furtherance of the criminal act charged.

If a search warrant is general in nature, but also particularly describes certain articles to be seized, a motion to suppress based on the general nature of the warrant is valid only as to articles seized which were not particularly described.[16] In other words, the valid portion of the search warrant should be severed from the invalid portion and the seizure pursuant to the valid portion should be sustained by the court at a suppression hearing.[17]

A typographical error will not necessarily invalidate a warrant. In *Norton v. State*,[18] the warrant application identified the object of the search as "methamphetamine" but the warrant specified the substance as marijuana. The court was satisfied that the error was made in good faith.

See Annotation, "Sufficiency of Description of Business Records Under Fourth Amendment Requirement of Particularity in Federal Warrant Authorizing Search and Seizure," 53 A.L.R.Fed. 679 (1981). See also § 4:21, infra, on detention and search of person, and § 4:6, supra, on the necessity of having a neutral and detached magistrate.

§ 4:15 Issuance of search warrant

After the magistrate has considered affidavits, written complaints and/or sworn testimony, he must then make an independent determination of whether or not probable cause exists for the issuance of a search warrant. If the magistrate concludes probable cause exists then he should issue a search warrant. The magistrate has no right to issue a warrant to search a place not mentioned in the affidavit. When facts essential to a proper de-

---

[15]Cooper v. State, 212 Ga. App. 34, 36 (2), 441 S.E.2d 448 (1994).

[16]United States v. Cook, 657 F.2d 730, 735 (5th Cir. 1981). Cf. Sovereign News Co. v. United States, 690 F.2d 569, 576 (6th Cir. 1982). In Sovereign, the court held that where some items are specifically described and only items so described are seized, the warrant is not invalidated by the presence of some overly broad language.

[17]Aday v. Superior Court, 55 Cal.2d 789, 797, 362 P.2d 47, 13 Cal.Rptr. 415 (1961); 2 LaFave, Search and Seizure, § 4.6(b) (West 1978).

[18]Norton v. State, 320 Ga. App. 327, 739 S.E.2d 782 (2013). See Lester v. State, 278 Ga. App. 247, 628 S.E.2d 674 (2006) (typographical error regarding address but other descriptive elements of premises were sufficient).

scription of the place to be searched are omitted, this deficiency may not be supplied by the knowledge of the officers attempting to execute the warrant.[1] The Georgia Code, surprisingly, does not contain a form for a search warrant, although certain requirements are set out.[2]

The warrant should state the time and date of issuance.[3] However, if the time of the issuance is not mentioned but it is shown that the warrant was issued prior to the search and seizure, the omission will be regarded only as an irregularity and will not void the warrant.[4] The warrant should also command the search of the place described and the seizure of items enumerated.[5]

A search warrant is not invalid where it is captioned "Superior Court of Hall County, Georgia," but is signed by a magistrate.[6] "[T]he change in name of any court previously known as a police court, recorders court, mayors court, etc. 'shall not affect the validity of any action or prosecution.'"[7]

The magistrate is charged with the duty of keeping a docket record of all warrants issued by him. The warrants shall be executed in duplicate and be directed to all peace officers in the state.[8]

It now appears that a search warrant may be amended after it is issued. If, in such a situation, it were possible to amend the warrant, it would seem that it could only be done by the magistrate issuing it, and then only in conformity with the verified evidence on which the warrant was based.[9] However, in *Green v.*

[Section 4:15]

[1]Durrett v. State, 136 Ga. App. 114, 220 S.E.2d 92 (1975).

[2]O.C.G.A. § 17-5-22.

[3]In Merritt v. State, 121 Ga. App. 832, 833 (2), 175 S.E.2d 890 (1970), the court said that the failure to insert the hour was merely a "technical irregularity" where the evidence is clear that the warrant was issued before the search. See Bostwick v. State, 124 Ga. App. 113, 115 (2), 182 S.E.2d 925 (1971).

[4]Houser v. State, 234 Ga. 209, 214 S.E.2d 893 (1975); Irby v. State, 156 Ga. App. 761, 275 S.E.2d 391 (1980).

[5]O.C.G.A. § 17-5-23. In Commonwealth v. Taylor, 10 Mass.App. Ct. 452, 409 N.E.2d 212, 214-15 (1980),

the court held a search warrant invalid where the warrant was not attached to the affidavit supporting the warrant and the warrant was not specific enough to describe what was to be seized. The affidavit contained a six-page list of items thought to have been stolen but the list was not attached to the warrant. The court implies that the warrant would have been sufficient if the affidavit and its list had been attached.

[6]Robinson v. State, 180 Ga. App. 43, 49 (2)(D), 348 S.E.2d 662 (1986), rev'd on other grounds, 256 Ga. 564, 350 S.E.2d 464 (1986).

[7]Felix v. State, 241 Ga. App. 323, 325 (3), 526 S.E.2d 637 (1999).

[8]O.C.G.A. § 17-5-24.

[9]Delaney v. State, 135 Ga. App. 612, 614, 218 S.E.2d 318 (1975).

State,[10] the Georgia Supreme Court held that "an amendment to a search warrant may be authorized by a second judicial officer upon a proper showing of probable cause." In *State v. Sanders,*[11] the court held that where an officer was about to execute a search warrant, but found the defendant to be registered in a different hotel room from the one mentioned in the search warrant, he could call the magistrate on the telephone and get the magistrate's consent to change the room number, make the change in the search warrant and search the room in which the defendant was registered. In *Oliver v. State,*[12] a search warrant was issued to search "the residence . . . located at 506 Lamar St." The executing officer discovered that the house number was not correct. The next day he returned to the magistrate and orally requested that the number be changed from 506 to 206 on the warrant. Apparently, the number was changed before the search was conducted. The court concluded that the warrant was valid.

§ 4:16   Execution of search warrant—General

"Search warrants are not directed at persons; they authorize the search of 'places' and the seizure of 'things,' and as a constitutional matter they need not even name the person from whom the things will be seized."[1] Thus, a warrant which allows the search of a person and his home does not permit the search of his person at his place of employment.

By statute, a search warrant must be executed within 10 days from the time of its issuance, and any warrant not executed within 10 days will be void.[2] The warrant may be executed at any reasonable time within the 10-day period.[3] When it is executed, the duplicate copy shall be left with the person from whom any

---

[10]Green v. State, 275 Ga. 569, 570 S.E.2d 207 (2002). See Marshall v. State, 273 Ga. App. 17 (1), 614 S.E.2d 169 (2005), second magistrate need not take evidence to correct clerical error.

[11]State v. Sanders, 155 Ga. App. 274, 270 S.E.2d 850 (1980). Accord, Cunrod v. State, 241 Ga. App. 743, 744 (1), 526 S.E.2d 900 (1999). Generally, see Rule 41(c) of the Federal Rules of Criminal Procedure for a method of obtaining search warrants by telephone under federal law.

[12]Oliver v. State, 161 Ga. App. 567, 568, 287 S.E.2d 698 (1982) (alternative holding). Cf. Cunrod v. State,

241 Ga. App. 743, 744 (1), 526 S.E.2d 900 (1999).

[Section 4:16]

[1]State v. Dills, 237 Ga. App. 165, 167, 514 S.E.2d 917 (1999).

[2]Fowler v. State, 121 Ga. App. 22, 24, 172 S.E.2d 447 (1970); O.C.G.A. § 17-5-25.

[3]O.C.G.A. § 17-5-26; Rivers v. State, 250 Ga. 288, 296, 298 S.E.2d 10 (1982). Cf. Williams v. State, 142 Ga. App. 764, 767 (5), 236 S.E.2d 893 (1977). See Annot., "Propriety of Execution of Search Warrant at Nighttime," 41 A.L.R.5th 171 (1996).

articles are seized.[4] It has been held that an officer may make a valid search after exhibiting to the defendant a photocopy of a search warrant rather than the original.[5] Indeed, provided the officer executing the warrant properly informs the resident of the premises sought to be searched of the warrant's existence and if the search does not exceed the scope of the search authorized, the warrant need not be in the physical possession of the officer conducting the search provided it was issued based upon probable cause prior to the commencement of the search.[6]

When necessary, reasonable force may be used to obtain entrance in order to execute a search warrant. The Georgia Code requires that a good-faith attempt be made to give verbal notice of the authority and purpose of the officers before force is used,[7] and in the absence of such notice there is generally no right to enter a place to be searched.[8] However, it has been held that the failure to give advance notice may be excused if such procedure would increase the officers' peril or lead to the destruction of evidence.[9] See Annotation, "Sufficiency of showing of reasonable belief of danger to officers or others excusing compliance with

---

[4]O.C.G.A. § 17-5-25. An unsigned copy of the warrant will satisfy this requirement. State v. Stafford, 277 Ga. App. 852, 627 S.E.2d 802 (2006).

[5]DeFreeze v. State, 136 Ga. App. 10, 220 S.E.2d 17 (1975). Cf. People v. Mahoney, 58 N.Y.2d 475, 462 N.Y.S.2d 410, 448 N.E.2d 1321 (1983) in which officers entered before they obtained a search warrant which had been issued. The court found no Fourth Amendment violation.

[6]State v. Rocco, 255 Ga. App. 565, 566 S.E.2d 365 (2002).

[7]O.C.G.A. § 17-5-27. In Barclay v. State, 142 Ga. App. 657, 658, 236 S.E.2d 901 (1977), the court held that O.C.G.A. § 17-5-27 "represents the enactment of a common law rule dated from Semayne's case in 1603 (77 Eng. Rep. 194, 196 (1603))."

In Dalia v. United States, 441 U.S. 238, 99 S.Ct. 1682, 60 L.Ed.2d 177 (1979), the Court held that neither the Fourth Amendment nor the Omnibus Crime Control and Safe Streets Act prevent per se a covert entry for purposes of installing an electronic eavesdropping device where the eavesdropping order failed to explicitly authorize such an entry.

[8]State v. Smith, 219 Ga. App. 905, 906, 467 S.E.2d 221 (1996); Barclay v. State, 142 Ga. App. 657, 236 S.E.2d 901 (1977).

The following reasons have been given for the announcement requirement:

(1) the "reverence of the law for the individual's right of privacy in his house." Miller v. United States, 357 U.S. 301, 313, 78 S.Ct. 1190, 2 L.Ed.2d 1332 (1958); Commonwealth v. Riccardi, 220 Pa.Super. 72, 283 A.2d 719, 721 (1971);

(2) the prevention of violence which might take place if officers are thought to be intruders. Miller v. United States, 357 U.S. 301, 313, 78 S.Ct. 1190, 2 L.Ed.2d 1332 (1958); People v. Rosales, 68 Cal.2d 299, 66 Cal.Rptr. 1, 437 P.2d 489, 492 (1968); and

(3) notice may result in peaceful admission and elimination of property damage. Cf. United States v. Phillips, 497 F.2d 1131, 1133 (9th Cir. 1974).

[9]Scull v. State, 122 Ga. App. 696 (1), 178 S.E.2d 720 (1970); Jones v. State, 127 Ga. App. 137 (1), 193 S.E.2d 38 (1972); State v. Stevens, 181 Wis.2d 410, 511 N.W.2d 591 (1994). In this connection, it should be pointed out

'knock and announce' requirement—state criminal cases," 17 A.L.R.4th 301 (1982).

The same code section provides that after proper notice, or an attempt in good faith to give such notice, "necessary and reasonable force may be used to effect an entry."[10]

§ 4:17 Who may search?

An officer has a right to apply for a search warrant.[1] An officer having knowledge of exigent circumstances or a search warrant may conduct a search.[2] Officers arriving after the original entry may take part in the search; however, "the later officials must confine their intrusion to the scope of the original invasion unless a warrant or one of the exceptions to the warrant requirement justifies a more thorough or wide ranging search."[3]

§ 4:18 Execution of search warrant—Knock and announce

In the 1995 United States Supreme Court case of *Wilson v. Arkansas,*[1] the Court unanimously held the "common-law 'knock-and-announce' principle forms a part of the reasonableness inquiry under the Fourth Amendment" in a search of a home. However, the Court stated that this was not a "rigid rule" and gave examples when the rule would be excused: (1) cases involving the safety of the officer, (2) cases where a felon has escaped and "retreats to his dwelling," and (3) cases where there is a risk of the destruction of evidence if advance notice is given. Then the Court pointed out that it "need not attempt a comprehensive catalog of the relevant countervailing factors here. For now, we leave to the lower courts the task of determining the circum-

---

that the "no-knock" federal search warrant provision in drug cases of 21 U.S.C.A. § 879 was repealed in 1974. Congress expressed doubt about the constitutionality of the provision and concern for the danger to police and citizens, as was borne out by the fact that police in the District of Columbia had not used this provision from 1971 to 1974 and that federal agents had "requested only three no-knock warrants in the past year." 15 Cr. L. 2460 (1974). See Annot., "What Constitutes Compliance with Knock-and-Announce Rule in Search of Private Premises—State Cases," 70 A.L.R.3d 217 (1976).

[10]See Hourin v. State, 301 Ga. 835, 804 S.E.2d 388 (2017) ("knock and announce" requires that an-

nouncement by police must precede entry; i.e., announcement and entry cannot occur simultaneously).

[Section 4:17]

[1]See § 4:4, supra, on who may apply for a search warrant.

[2]Cf. State v. Peterson, 273 Ga. 657, 659 (1), 543 S.E.2d 692 (2001).

[3]State v. Peterson, 273 Ga. 657, 543 S.E.2d 692 (2001), quoting United States v. Brand, 556 F.2d 1312, 1317 (5th Cir. 1977).

[Section 4:18]

[1]Wilson v. Arkansas, 514 U.S. 927, 115 S.Ct. 1914, 131 L.Ed.2d 976 (1995).

stances under which an unannounced entry is reasonable under the Fourth Amendment."

In *Richards v. Wisconsin*,[2] the United States Supreme Court rejected the blanket exception to the knock-and-announce requirement for felony drug investigations. The court recognized that even though threats of violence and the possibility of destruction of evidence are frequently present in felony drug investigations, these facts do not dispense with the need for a case-by-case evaluation of the manner in which the search is executed. A "no-knock" entry will be justified if the police have a reasonable suspicion that under the circumstances it would be dangerous, futile or it would inhibit a criminal investigation, such as allowing the destruction of evidence, to knock and announce their presence. "This standard . . . strikes the appropriate balance between the legitimate law enforcement concerns . . . and the individual privacy interests affected by no-knock entries."

In *United States v. Jones*,[3] the court affirmed the trial judge in denying a motion to suppress where there had been a "wait" of 15 to 20 seconds between the "knock and announcement" and the time the officers entered an apartment of a suspected drug trafficker, over an objection of the defendant that he was not given time to respond. Similarly, in *United States v. Banks*,[4] the United States Supreme Court held that it was reasonable for the officers to suspect imminent loss of evidence in a drug trafficking case after 15 to 20 seconds without a response based on the facts known to the officers at that time. In *United States v. Ramirez*,[5] the Supreme Court held that the Fourth Amendment does not require "officers to [have] a higher standard . . . when a 'no-knock' entry results in the destruction of property" than when no property is damaged.

One Georgia case has specifically approved the issuance of a search warrant containing a "no-knock" provision where the facts set out in the affidavit demonstrated the potential of danger to the officer and destruction of evidence.[6] However, a "no-knock" request in a search warrant application based solely on the gen-

[2]Richards v. Wisconsin, 520 U.S. 385, 117 S.Ct. 1416, 137 L.Ed.2d 615 (1997). See State v. Williams, 275 Ga. App. 612, 621 S.E.2d 581 (2005); Poole v. State, 266 Ga. App. 113, 596 S.E.2d 420 (2004).

[3]United States v. Jones, 133 F.3d 358 (5th Cir. 1998).

[4]United States v. Banks, 540 U.S. 31, 124 S.Ct. 521, 157 L.Ed.2d 343 (2003).

[5]United States v. Ramirez, 523 U.S. 65, 118 S.Ct. 992, 140 L.Ed.2d 191 (1998).

[6]Jones v. State, 127 Ga. App. 137 (1), 193 S.E.2d 38 (1972); Brannon v. State, 220 Ga. App. 572, 574 (3), 469 S.E.2d 716 (1996) (peril to officers). But in Reynolds v. State, 46 Ala.App. 77, 238 So.2d 557, 559 (1970), the

eral experience of the law enforcement officer making the application that drug traffickers will destroy contraband if they know the police are at the door or that such persons generally have access to firearms is insufficient. A "no knock" warrant is only justified upon a particularized showing of danger to the police or the likelihood that evidence will be destroyed if the police announce their presence.[7] Even without a "no-knock" provision in a search warrant, where officers knock, identify themselves, and receive no response, after a reasonable time they may use reasonable force to gain entrance.[8] In *Swan v. State*,[9] the Court of Appeals approved as reasonable a three to five second interval between the knock/announcement and the entry into the home. The Court found that the interval was sufficient in light of explicit judicial recognition that firearms are common to the drug trade. In Georgia it seems that even if there is no "no-knock" provision and even if the officers did not "knock and announce," the execution of a search warrant is still not illegal if exigent circumstances are found to exist, such as danger to the officers or destruction of evidence.[10] In *Adams v. State*,[11] the court held that even where a "no-knock" provision was erroneously included by the magistrate, this did not invalidate a search where the officers entered in a good faith belief that they were so authorized because of the peril created by the presence of a dangerous dog.

Violation of the knock-and-announce requirement does not necessitate application of the exclusionary rule. In *Hudson v. Michigan*[12] the Supreme Court declined to suppress evidence obtained following a failure to knock-and-announce where the police had the ability to execute a previously obtained search

---

court said that the general propensity of narcotics violators to destroy evidence as soon as they are aware of the presence of officers does not justify an unannounced forcible entry into a house with a search warrant.

[7]See State v. Cash, 316 Ga. App. 324, 728 S.E.2d 918 (2012).

[8]Jackson v. State, 129 Ga. App. 901, 905, 201 S.E.2d 816 (1973); 68 Am. Jur. 2d § 91 (1973). See Annot., "What Constitutes Compliance with Knock-and-Announce Rule in Search of Private Premises—State Cases," 70 A.L.R.3d 217 (1976). Also see Annot., "What Constitutes Violation of 18 U.S.C.A. § 3109 Requiring Federal Officer to Give Notice of His Authority and Purpose Prior to Breaking Open Door or Window or Other Part of House to Execute Search Warrant," 21

A.L.R.Fed. 820 (1974).

[9]Swan v. State, 257 Ga. App. 704 (3), 572 S.E.2d 64 (2002).

[10]Scull v. State, 122 Ga. App. 696, 178 S.E.2d 720 (1970); Martin v. State, 165 Ga. App. 760, 302 S.E.2d 614 (1983); Neal v. State, 173 Ga. App. 71, 325 S.E.2d 457 (1984); Hunter v. State, 198 Ga. App. 41, 44 (2), 400 S.E.2d 641 (1990).

See Annot., "Sufficiency of Showing of Reasonable Belief of Danger to Officers or Others Excusing Compliance with 'Knock and Announce' Requirement—State Criminal Cases," 17 A.L.R.4th 301 (1982).

[11]Adams v. State, 201 Ga. App. 12, 14 (3), 410 S.E.2d 139 (1991).

[12]Hudson v. Michigan, 126 S. Ct. 2159, 165 L. Ed. 2d 56 (U.S. 2006).

warrant. The court went on to explain in dicta that, even if the failure to knock-and-announce is the "but-for" cause of discovery of the evidence sought to be excluded, such evidence may still be admitted where the causation is attenuated or where the deterrence benefits of suppression are outweighed by "substantial social costs."[13] Attenuation occurs when the causal connection is remote, or when, "given a direct causal connection, the interest protected by the constitutional guarantee that has been violated would not be served by suppression of the evidence obtained." Because the knock-and-announce rule does not protect "one's interest in preventing the government from seeing or taking evidence described in a warrant," the *Hudson* court found that the presence of "but-for" causation would not have affected its ruling.[14] See Annotation, "What constitutes compliance with knock-and-announce rule in search of private premises—state cases," 85 A.L.R.5th 1 (2001) and 70 A.L.R.3d 217 (1976).

§ 4:19   Execution of search warrant—Area to be searched—Curtilage

Officers may search the premises which are located at the place described in the search warrant.[1] The right to search also includes the curtilage around a home.[2] The right to search the curtilage of a dwelling includes the right to search "the yards and grounds of a particular address, its gardens, barns [and] buildings,"[3] as well as vehicles within the curtilage,[4] but it does not include the right to search beyond the property lines of the dwelling specified in the warrant.[5] In *Albert v. State*,[6] the court referred to a service station as having a curtilage and approved of a search of a car at

---

[13]Hudson v. Michigan, 126 S. Ct. 2159, 2164-2165, 165 L. Ed. 2d 56 (U.S. 2006).

[14]Hudson v. Michigan, 126 S. Ct. 2159, 2165, 165 L. Ed. 2d 56 (U.S. 2006). See Jackson v. State, 280 Ga. App. 716(1), 634 S.E.2d 846 (2006).

[Section 4:19]

[1]In State v. Manzella, 392 So.2d 403 (La.1980), officers obtained a search warrant to search 6176 Pontchartrain Blvd. The officers went to that address and were told by the defendant's sister that he lived next door at 6178. The officers went to 6178 and searched it. The court held that the motion to suppress should have been sustained.

[2]Rosencranz v. United States,

356 F.2d 310 (1st Cir. 1966). See 68 Am. Jur. 2d Searches and Seizures § 20; Gumina v. State, 166 Ga. App. 592 (2), 305 S.E.2d 37 (1983). See § 4:2, supra, and § 4:43, infra, on curtilage. Cf. Dunbar v. State, 163 Ga. App. 243 (1), 292 S.E.2d 897 (1982).

[3]Landers v. State, 250 Ga. 808, 301 S.E.2d 633 (1983), rev'g 164 Ga. App. 657, 297 S.E.2d 748 (1982).

[4]Bellamy v. State, 134 Ga. App. 340, 214 S.E.2d 383 (1975), approved, Landers v. State, 250 Ga. 808, 301 S.E.2d 633 (1983).

[5]Landers v. State, 250 Ga. 808, 301 S.E.2d 633 (1983), rev'g 164 Ga. App. 657, 297 S.E.2d 748 (1982).

[6]Albert v. State, 155 Ga. App. 99, 270 S.E.2d 220 (1980). In Goggins v. State, 161 Ga. App. 571, 572, 289

the station which was owned by a third person since the vehicle was deemed to be connected with the premises. But in *State v. Crank*,[7] the court held that a search warrant for the defendant's home and vehicles located there did not authorize the following of the defendant's car for miles, then stopping and searching it. See § 4:2, supra, on areas protected by the Fourteenth Amendment, and § 4:43, infra, on open field warrantless searches.

In *Barton v. State*,[8] the Georgia Court of Appeals stated that the word "premises" in a search warrant authorized the search of the home and a shed about 20 feet behind the house. The court stated that "premises" refers to the "entire living area used by its occupant. Living area may be otherwise expressed as the 'curtilage.' The word 'curtilage' includes yards and grounds of a particular address together with the gardens, barn and buildings thereon. . . . The principle of curtilage comes to us from the common law and traditionally has included out-buildings, which may be searched as part of the 'premises' though not specifically described so long as permission has been obtained to search the 'premises.' "

In *Payton v. State*,[9] the court stated, "Whether the place searched is within the curtilage is to be determined from the facts, including its proximity or annexation to the dwelling, its inclusion within the general enclosure surrounding the dwelling, and its use and enjoyment as an adjunct to the domestic economy of the family."

See § 4:2, supra, and § 4:43, infra, on curtilage.

In *Espinoza v. State*,[10] a search warrant was issued for "251-B Dickson Road." Officers searched both 251-B and 251-A, as well as the "stethoscope shaped" driveway, a part of which served both units. 251-A is on the left side of the duplex. Drugs were found in bushes several feet to the left of the 251-A driveway, outside the stethoscope. The resident of 251-A was indicted. The Georgia Court of Appeals found that the drugs were "not found within the curtilage shared by both apartments." Subsequently, the Georgia Supreme Court "granted the writ of certiorari to consider whether the Court of Appeals properly applied the concept of curtilage." The court explicitly stated, "We disapprove of the term 'common area curtilage,' on which the Court of Ap-

S.E.2d 771 (1982), the court recognized a curtilage around a country club.

[7]State v. Crank, 212 Ga. App. 246, 249, 441 S.E.2d 531 (1994).

[8]Barton v. State, 161 Ga. App. 591, 592 (1), 288 S.E.2d 914 (1982). Cf. Woods v. State, 258 Ga. 540, 541 (2), 371 S.E.2d 865 (1988).

[9]Payton v. State, 177 Ga. App. 104, 105, 338 S.E.2d 462 (1985) (citing Care v. United States, 231 F.2d 22, 25 (10th Cir. 1956)).

[10]Espinoza v. State, 265 Ga. 171, 172 (2), 174 (4), 454 S.E.2d 765 (1995), rev'g 212 Ga. App. 814, 818, 442 S.E.2d 911 (1994).

peals relied." The court reversed on the ground that "police officers discovered the evidence within the curtilage of the defendant's apartment for which they did not have a search warrant." The court reasoned that "[t]he resident of 251-B would have no reasonable expectation of privacy in a portion of the yard that was not directly connected to that unit, its driveway, or its side of the duplex." The court affirmed the trial court's grant of a motion to suppress because the resident of 251-A "was the only resident who had a reasonable expectation of privacy in the yard outside the driveway leading to his unit." See Annotation, "Search and Seizure: Reasonable Expectation of Privacy in Driveways," 60 A.L.R.5th 1 (1998).

Nevertheless, in *Maryland v. Garrison*,[11] a description in a search warrant turned out to be ambiguous when the officers, acting in good faith, learned at the time of the execution of the warrant that there was a distinction between McWebb's apartment for which they had a search warrant, and the third floor of the building in that there were two apartments on that floor. Before the officers realized they were in the defendant's apartment rather than McWebb's apartment, they discovered contraband. The United States Supreme Court held that "a good-faith mistaken belief on the part of officers that the area being searched is within the scope of the warrant that is being executed docs not mandate suppression."[12] See § 4:12, supra, on description of place to be searched.

However, it must be remembered that while a search, justified by a search warrant, may not be extended beyond the dwelling described and its curtilage, no warrant is required to search an area beyond the curtilage of a house since no constitutional protection extends "to open fields, orchards, or other lands not an immediate part of the dwelling site."[13] See § 4:43, infra, on open fields.

§ 4:20 Execution of search warrant—Purpose of search

In 1999, the United States Supreme Court held in *Wilson v. Layne*[1] that it is a Fourth Amendment violation to permit news media to enter a suspect's home to witness a search or arrest when their presence "was not in aid of the execution of the warrant."

---

[11]Maryland v. Garrison, 480 U.S. 79, 107 S.Ct. 1013, 94 L.Ed.2d 72 (1987). See § 4:12, supra, on further discussion of *Maryland v. Garrison*.

[12]Hamil v. State, 198 Ga. App. 869, 870 (2), 403 S.E.2d 828 (1991).

[13]Ray v. State, 181 Ga. App. 42 (1), 351 S.E.2d 490 (1986).

[Section 4:20]

[1]Wilson v. Layne, 526 U.S. 603, 119 S.Ct. 1692, 143 L.Ed.2d 818 (1999).

In *Massachusetts v. Sheppard*,[2] the United States Supreme Court considered a case in which a magistrate used an improper form when he intended to issue a search warrant. The warrant was issued by a magistrate at his home on Sunday. The officer had taken a form search warrant to the magistrate which was used in drug cases. The officer told the magistrate about this and the judge assured the officer he had made the necessary changes so that a search could be conducted for evidence related to a homicide. Actually, the warrant, as issued, provided only for a search for controlled substances. Without knowledge of the actual contents of the warrant, the officer searched and found evidence of the homicide. The court held that the exclusionary rule did not apply where the "officers reasonably believed that the search they conducted was authorized by a valid warrant." The court noted that the purpose of the exclusionary rule is to deter police misconduct. Because the defect of this warrant was caused by the judge's error, excluding the results of the search would not serve the goal of the exception. But see § 2:26, supra, on good faith exception to exclusionary rule.

In general terms, an officer may search anywhere within the permissible area in which the object or objects of the search may be located, but not in an area in which the object of the search could not be located.[3] Thus, an officer has no right to search desk drawers in search of a stolen television.[4]

While officers may search in every place in which the object of the search warrant may be located, such officers must be careful to avoid unnecessary damage to the premises and personal property located therein.[5]

In *Bradley v. State*,[6] the court held that officers were entitled to search a camera bag of a resident of a house being searched even though the defendant was not named in the search warrant.

After a search of the designated area, an officer may apply for and obtain a second search warrant if probable cause is shown.[7]

Generally, see § 4:14, supra, on person or thing to be seized and § 4:58, infra, on second search. See § 2:26, supra, on the application of the exclusionary rule where the officer acts in good faith pursuant to a warrant.

----

[2]Massachusetts v. Sheppard, 468 U.S. 981, 104 S.Ct. 3424, 82 L.Ed.2d 737 (1984).

[3]See § 4:57, infra, on scope and intensity of search.

[4]U.S. v. Highfill, 334 F.Supp. 700 (D.Ark.1971).

[5]2 LaFave, Search and Seizure 161, § 4.10 (West 1978).

[6]Bradley v. State, 213 Ga. App. 468, 469 (1), 444 S.E.2d 842 (1994).

[7]Harris v. State, 260 Ga. 860, 862 (2), 401 S.E.2d 263 (1991).

§ 4:21 Execution of search warrant—Detention and search of person present

O.C.G.A. § 17-5-28 provides that an officer in the execution of a search warrant may reasonably detain or search any person in the place at the time (1) to protect himself from attack or (2) to prevent the disposal or concealment of any instruments, articles, or things particularly described in the warrant.[1] Officers may not broaden their power to search persons beyond the provisions of this Code section.[2]

This Code section has been said to describe the maximum extent, consistent with the Constitution, to which officers may go in seizing persons not described in the search warrant.[3] In *State v. Holmes,*[4] the court pointed out that, in connection with the first statutory requirement, "the officer must be able to articulate specific facts that would support a reasonable belief or suspicion that the person to be searched was armed and dangerous."

In *Collins v. State,*[5] the court held that the inclusion "in a search warrant of 'other persons' on the premises being searched" does not automatically convert an otherwise valid warrant into a general warrant. However, a warrant authorizing the search of places and persons for drugs in all automobiles located on a certain premises was found to be a general warrant and unconstitutional.[6]

In *State v. Hawkins,*[7] the court pointed out that in order to search a person under subsection (2) of the statute, "there must be a nexus between what the officers are authorized to search for[,] . . . the nature of the evidence sought, the environment in which the search is authorized, and the person searched." Where there was *probable cause* to believe those coming to a certain residence were carrying lottery tickets, the search of such individu-

---

[Section 4:21]

[1]See Louis v. State, 188 Ga. App. 435, 436 (1), 373 S.E.2d 231 (1988).

[2]State v. Cochran, 135 Ga. App. 47, 49, 217 S.E.2d 181 (1975).

[3]Wallace v. State, 131 Ga. App. 204, 205, 205 S.E.2d 523 (1974).

[4]State v. Holmes, 240 Ga. App. 332, 333, 525 S.E.2d 698 (1999).

[5]Collins v. State, 187 Ga. App. 430, 432, 370 S.E.2d 648 (1988).

[6]State v. Cochran, 135 Ga. App. 47, 217 S.E.2d 181 (1975); Wilson v. State, 136 Ga. App. 70, 221 S.E.2d 62 (1975). State v. Sims, 382 A.2d 638, 75 N.J. 337 (N.J.1978), contains an excellent discussion of this material. Cf. Wyatt v. State, 151 Ga. App. 207, 208, 259 S.E.2d 199 (1979).

[7]State v. Hawkins, 187 Ga. App. 826, 828, 371 S.E.2d 668 (1988). For example, an officer would be justified in searching a person who was in a position to assist in the disposal or concealment of the drugs sought by the warrant, or if [she] had attempted flight from inside the house subject to the warrant. (citations and footnotes omitted). State v. Holmes, 240 Ga. App. 332, 333, 525 S.E.2d 698 (1999). See Norton v. State, 283 Ga. App. 790, 643 S.E.2d 278 (2007).

als was held lawful despite the lack of express authorization by the warrant.[8] In the absence of such probable cause, a third party entering premises which are being searched may not himself be searched where he has no opportunity to conceal any of the items described in the search warrant.[9] In *State v. Anderson,*[10] the court held that in the absence of "independent probable cause," a person present at the time of the search but not named in the warrant may be searched only (1) to protect the officer from attack or (2) to prevent disposal or concealment of contraband described in the warrant.

Searches of persons not named in a search warrant but found on the premises to be searched are illegal without an independent justification for a private search.[11] If an officer has an articulable reasonable suspicion to think that a person on the premises is armed, he has a right to "pat-down" the person for weapons.[12] In *McGugan v. State,*[13] officers had obtained a search warrant to search a named individual and his residence for evidence relating to the sale of cocaine. A deputy remained outside to "secure the scene." The deputy saw the defendant drive by and then back into the driveway. The deputy approached the defendant's vehicle, identified himself, informed the defendant that a search was in progress and asked the defendant to step out of his vehicle. The defendant became nervous, looked around and did not get out. The deputy opened the door of the defendant's car and instructed the defendant for the third time to step

---

[8]Logan et al. v. State, 135 Ga. App. 879, 885 (3), 219 S.E.2d 615 (1975). Cf. Wood v. State, 224 Ga. 121, 124 (2), 160 S.E.2d 368 (1968). See § 4:12, supra.

[9]Wallace v. State, 131 Ga. App. 204, 205 S.E.2d 523 (1974); Smith v. State, 292 Ala. 120, 289 So.2d 816 (1974).

[10]State v. Anderson, 195 Ga. App. 793, 395 S.E.2d 50 (1990).

[11]Hayes v. State, 141 Ga. App. 706, 707, 234 S.E.2d 360 (1977). Accord, State v. Varner, 239 Ga. App. 347, 348, 521 S.E.2d 247 (1999). See § 4:12, supra. In Ybarra v. Illinois, 444 U.S. 85, 100 S.Ct. 338, 62 L.Ed.2d 238 (1979), the state tried to justify a search under an Illinois statute exactly like O.C.G.A. § 17-5-28. The United States Supreme Court concluded the police had no articulable suspicion justifying weapons frisk, and even if there had been a reasonable basis for

believing that the defendant was armed, this does not permit a frisk for narcotics.

[12]Jones v. State, 126 Ga. App. 841, 844, 192 S.E.2d 171 (1972).

In Wyatt v. State, 151 Ga. App. 207, 210, 259 S.E.2d 199 (1979), the court said that the sole justification for such a frisk was to discover weapons and an officer cannot go any further unless he finds something which feels like a weapon. However, O.C.G.A. § 17-5-28(2) has been held to permit a personal search where the warrant stated that known drug abusers had been observed entering and leaving the premises and persons not specified in the warrant were found in the same room with named suspects where contraband could be easily passed around or concealed.

[13]McGugan v. State, 215 Ga. App. 535, 451 S.E.2d 460 (1994). See § 3:10, supra, on other aspects of this case.

outside. The defendant complied, but tried to pull away. The deputy frisked the defendant for weapons. The appellate court affirmed the trial court's finding that the frisk was justified by the officer's reasonable belief that the frisk was necessary to protect himself.

If an officer has probable cause to think that a person who is present is attempting to conceal the substance described in the warrant, he may arrest the person and have him empty his pockets.[14] In *Travis v. State*,[15] the court held that the defendant's presence at the time the search warrant for drugs was executed, coupled with his flight, provided probable cause to believe he had possession of contraband. Hence, his arrest was valid and a search conducted incident to the arrest was valid. On searches of persons present who are in some way described in the search warrant, see § 4:12, supra.

In *Ybarra v. Illinois*,[16] the United States Supreme Court held that, where an officer is executing a warrant for the search of a bar and a certain named individual for narcotics and related items, a weapon frisk or a pat-down of Ybarra was not justified where the officer had no reasonable belief that he was armed and dangerous. The court also pointed out that a *Terry* frisk does not permit a search for anything other than weapons. In retrospect the Court said the search "was invalid because the police had no reason to believe . . . [Ybarra] had any special connection with the premises, and the police had no other basis for suspecting that he was armed or in possession of contraband."[17]

However, in *Michigan v. Summers*,[18] the United States Supreme Court considered an incident involving the execution of a warrant to search a house for narcotics. As the officers approached the house they met the defendant, who was leaving. They requested his assistance in gaining entrance to the house and then detained him until they had searched the premises. After learning that the defendant owned the house and after having discovered narcotics in the house, the defendant was arrested and searched. In his coat pocket heroin was found. The court said

---

[14]Patton v. State, 148 Ga. App. 793, 794, 252 S.E.2d 678 (1979).

[15]Travis v. State, 192 Ga. App. 695, 385 S.E.2d 779 (1989).

[16]Ybarra v. Illinois, 444 U.S. 85, 100 S.Ct. 338, 62 L.Ed.2d 238 (1979). Accord, Bundy v. State, 168 Ga. App. 90, 308 S.E.2d 213 (1983).

[17]Michigan v. Summers, 452 U.S. 692, 696, 101 S.Ct. 2587, 69 L.Ed.2d 340 (1981), n. 4.

[18]Michigan v. Summers, 452 U.S. 692, 101 S.Ct. 2587, 2595, 69 L.Ed.2d 340 (1981). See Bailey v. U.S., 133 S. Ct. 1031, 185 L. Ed. 2d 19 (2013) (*Summers* authorizes detention of occupants and persons within immediate vicinity of premises and prohibits the arrest of persons allowed to leave once they have traveled as much as one mile away.). Accord, Martin v. State, 211 Ga. App. 849, 850 (1), 440 S.E.2d 736 (1994).

that if there is probable cause to search a citizen's residence for contraband "it is constitutionally reasonable to require that citizen to remain while officers of the law execute a valid warrant to search his home." In the 2001 case of *Illinois v. McArthur,*[19] the United States Supreme Court held that where officers had probable cause to believe that the defendant had hidden contraband in his home, they could prevent the defendant from entering his home unaccompanied by an officer for about two hours while officers obtained a search warrant. However, in *State v. Mallard,*[20] the Georgia Court of Appeals affirmed the trial court in granting a motion to suppress where the defendant was found to have possession of marijuana when he was stopped by an officer shortly after leaving a residence on which a warrant to search the house for marijuana was about to be executed. The officer stopped the defendant in order to determine if the owner of the house was in the car, and, after quickly determining that the owner of the house was not present and checking the defendant's driver's license, the officer asked the defendant if he had any marijuana. The defendant produced a baggy of marijuana. The officer had no information implicating the defendant of wrongdoing.

A person's suitcase or purse which he carries has been held to be included in his personal immunity from search so long as it is evident that it belongs to the owner.[21] In *Hayes v. State,*[22] police officers obtained a warrant to search "the person of . . . and the premises known as: the residence of Mark, being [a particularly described apartment]" for marijuana. The officers entered the apartment and found the defendant sleeping on the couch. The defendant's suitcase was next to the couch. His name, "Daniel Hayes," was on the outside of the suitcase and the officer testified that immediately upon opening it he found an airline ticket issued in the defendant's name. The officer continued to search the suitcase and found a quantity of illegal drugs. The Georgia Court of Appeals held that because the officer had notice that the

---

[19]Illinois v. McArthur, 531 U.S. 326, 121 S.Ct. 946, 148 L.Ed.2d 838 (2001). See U.S. v. Laist, 702 F.3d 608 (11th Cir. 2012) (25-day delay in seeking search warrant following seizure of defendant's computers in possession of child pornography case deemed reasonable based on totality of circumstances). Compare U.S. v. Mitchell, 565 F.3d 1347 (11th Cir. 2009) (error to deny motion to suppress where government agents' failure to obtain warrant to search defendant's hard drive in child pornography case for 21 days was deemed unreasonable under

totality of circumstances).

[20]State v. Mallard, 246 Ga. App. 357, 358, 541 S.E.2d 46 (2000). See Pritchard v. State, 300 Ga. App. 14, 684 S.E.2d 88 (2009).

[21]Hayes v. State, 141 Ga. App. 706, 708, 234 S.E.2d 360 (1977); United States v. Graham, 638 F.2d 1111 (7th Cir. 1981) (shoulder purse).

[22]Hayes v. State, 141 Ga. App. 706, 234 S.E.2d 360 (1977). Cf. Brown v. State, 181 Ga. App. 768, 772 (2), 353 S.E.2d 572 (1987).

defendant was not the person specified in the warrant, and there was no independent justification for his arrest and subsequent search of his suitcase, the trial judge should have granted the defendant's motion to suppress. The same rule applies to a purse of a visitor which is near the visitor and evidently is owned by her.[23] However, if a woman is in a house which is searched pursuant to a search warrant, and her pocketbook is on a bed in another room, it has been held that her purse may be searched even when there is no right to search her person.[24] However, an officer's "investigation based on other similar and related incidents which, when studied as parts of a scheme or design, would lead the reasonable mind to light upon the particular suspect, comprises good probable cause."[25]

In *Wright v. State*,[26] the court pointed out that when there is no notice of ownership of personal property, "the police are entitled to assume that all objects within the premises [are] lawfully subject to [a] search" as a part of the premises to be searched under a warrant. "Whether the police . . . [knew or should have known] that an object belonged to a visitor must be determined by the trial court on the facts of each case; and the trial court's determination will be upheld if there is any evidence to support it . . . ."

See Annotation, "Sufficiency of description in warrant of person to be searched," 43 A.L.R.5th 1 (1996). See § 3:6, supra, on conduct justifying stop. See §§ 4:7 et seq., supra, on probable cause to issue a search warrant for a person or thing to be seized. See sections 4:26 and 4:28, infra, on searches incident to a lawful arrest. Also see sections 4:22 and 4:28, infra, on protective sweeps. In addition, see § 4:22, infra, on search of personal items in premises searched. See § 4:38, infra, on abandoned property. See Annotation, "Propriety of Search of Nonoccupant Visitor's Belongings Pursuant to Warrant Issued for Another's Premises," 51 A.L.R.5th 375 (1997).

§ 4:22 Execution of search warrant—Property which may be seized—General

Generally, the Fourth Amendment permits law enforcement officers executing a search warrant to seize only those persons or

---

[23]Childers v. State, 158 Ga. App. 613, 281 S.E.2d 349 (1981); Hawkins v. State, 165 Ga. App. 278, 300 S.E.2d 224 (1983).

[24]United States v. Teller, 397 F.2d 494 (7th Cir. 1968), cited with approval in Hayes v. State, 141 Ga. App. 706, 708, 234 S.E.2d 360 (1977). Cf. Daugherty v. State, 171 Ga. App. 95, 96 (4), 318 S.E.2d 803 (1984).

[25]State v. Tedford, 195 Ga. App. 372, 374, 393 S.E.2d 502 (1990) (quoting Wilkes v. State, 166 Ga. App. 771, 305 S.E.2d 388 (1983)).

[26]Wright v. State, 221 Ga. App. 559, 472 S.E.2d 128 (1996).

items *"particularly"* described in the warrant.[1] The fact that the officers make the decision as to what objects are listed in the warrant, and therefore subject to seizure, does not alone invalidate the warrant.[2] In *Reaves v. State*,[3] the court observed that while "a warrant cannot leave the determination of what articles fall within its description and are to be seized entirely to the judgment and opinion of the officer executing the warrant, the degree of specificity in the description is flexible and will vary with the circumstances involved." Thus, where the warrant identifies specified items of potential evidence, "residual clauses" such as "other items related to the crime of murder" or "evidence of child molestation and sexual exploitation of children" have been deemed sufficient to pass muster under the Fourth Amendment. However, in *Groh v. Ramirez*,[4] the Supreme Court held that a warrant was facially invalid for "provid[ing] no description of the type of evidence sought," even though the application for the warrant adequately described the things to be seized. The court declined to allow the description contained in the application to be incorporated by reference into the actual warrant because the officer failed to leave a copy of the application at the premises to be searched. The court concluded that the search was unreasonable because the person whose premises were the subject of the search would have no way of ascertaining the proper subject and scope of the warrant. In *Battle v. State*,[5] the Georgia Court of Appeals adopted *Groh*. The court noted that the

---

[Section 4:22]

[1]Marron v. United States, 275 U.S. 192, 196, 48 S.Ct. 74, 72 L.Ed. 231 (1927); O.C.G.A. § 17-5-23.

[2]Strauss v. Stynchcombe, 224 Ga. 859, 860 (2)(c), 864, 165 S.E.2d 302 (1968). Here the records of certain named corporations were subpoenaed and the court held that the officers could go through the papers found to determine if they were records of the named corporations. However, in Marron v. United States, 275 U.S. 192, 196, 48 S.Ct. 74, 72 L.Ed. 231 (1927), the Court said that nothing is to be "left to the discretion of the officer executing the warrant."

In United States v. Humphrey, 104 F.3d 65 (5th Cir. 1997), the court upheld the search for all financial records in a residence which was also used as the primary place of business. Nevertheless, the Court pointed out "that the Fourth Amendment requires much closer scrutiny of an all records search of a residence; however, we conclude that, in the present case, the search warrant was valid in the light of the pervasive nature of the fraud, the considerable overlap of the [defendants'] business and personal lives, and the limitation of the warrant to records pertaining to financial transactions."

[3]Reaves v. State, 284 Ga. 181, 185 (2)(d), 664 S.E.2d 211 (2009).

[4]Groh v. Ramirez, 540 U.S. 551, 124 S.Ct. 1284, 157 L.Ed.2d 1068 (2004).

[5]Battle v. State, 275 Ga. App. 301, 304, 620 S.E.2d 506 (2005). In U.S. v. Pratt, 438 F.3d 1264, 1270 (11th Cir. 2006), the Eleventh Circuit found that, "when a warrant is not in evidence at a suppression hearing, a prosecutor must prove, by a preponderance of the evidence, the missing search warrant's *exact* language describing the place to

"apparently widespread custom of preparing warrants which describe the place to be searched only by reference to the probable cause affidavit is not the better practice and should not be encouraged by judges who approve search warrants." The court concluded that a warrant which refers to another documents, e.g., the application, for a description of the premises to be searched and the things to be seized is invalid unless the other document is delivered and left at the subject premises.

Although the Fourth Amendment prevents officers from entering people's homes to conduct exploratory searches for evidence, both the search incident to a lawful arrest[6] and plain view[7] doctrines are used to justify seizure of property not listed in the search warrant if the discovery "resulted from a bona fide search for the items named in the warrant."[8] Thus, an officer conducting a lawful search is not prevented "from seizing tangible evidence of the commission of a crime" if he has probable cause to believe it is such, despite the fact that it was not listed on the warrant.[9]

If in the course of the execution of a search warrant, an officer obtains probable cause to arrest an individual found in the premises searched, the officer as an incident to the lawful arrest may search the individual and the area within his reach, lunge, or grab, and articles found are admissible not pursuant to the search warrant but pursuant to a search incident to a lawful arrest.[10] Once a valid search warrant gets an officer into premises which he has a right to search, he does not have to close his eyes to obvious contraband which he sees in plain view while validly executing a search warrant for other articles.[11]

From a federal constitutional standpoint,[12] subject to some limitations hereinafter set out, and regardless of what objects are named in the search warrant, the following articles are also subject to seizure: (1) contraband,[13] (2) stolen property,[14] and (3) evidence of the commission of a crime.[15]

An officer executing a valid warrant has a right to search any

---

be searched and the persons or items to be seized" (emphasis in original).

[6]United States v. Crouch, 648 F.2d 932 (4th Cir. 1981).

[7]Texas v. Brown, 460 U.S. 730, 103 S.Ct. 1535, 75 L.Ed.2d 502 (1983).

[8]Smith v. State, 194 Ga. App. 870, 871, 392 S.E.2d 56 (1990).

[9]Nichols v. State, 210 Ga. App. 134, 136 (3)(b), 435 S.E.2d 502 (1993).

[10]Marron v. United States, 275 U.S. 192, 198, 48 S.Ct. 74, 72 L.Ed. 231 (1927).

[11]Coolidge v. New Hampshire, 403 U.S. 443, 91 S.Ct. 2022, 29 L.Ed.2d 564 (1971).

[12]Cf. O.C.G.A. § 17-5-21.

[13]See §§ 4:39 et seq., infra, for a discussion of plain view seizures. See Reynolds v. State, 142 Ga. App. 549 (1), 236 S.E.2d 525 (1977); Gurleski v. United States, 405 F.2d 253, 258 (5th Cir. 1968).

[14]State v. Scigliano, 120 Ariz. 6, 583 P.2d 893 (1978).

[15]Warden v. Hayden, 387 U.S.

area in which the object sought might be located. However, he has no right to look where the object could not be located.[16] Nevertheless, once the officer knows he has found what the search warrant directs him to seize, the search must stop.[17]

The "plain view" doctrine "may not be used to extend a general exploratory search from one object to another until something incriminating at last emerges."[18] However, when an officer is executing a warrant he may also seize not only what is described in the warrant, but also contraband, stolen property, or evidence of a crime in "plain view." See section § 4:42, infra, on the plain view doctrine.

Even when officers have received a consent to search for narcotics, they have no right to rummage through the premises and read through the defendant's papers in search of anything indicating that the defendant was engaged in illegal activity.[19]

However, it has been held that a warrant sufficiently identifies items of a specific crime where a more precise description was not possible under the circumstances.[20] In *United States v. Ladd*,[21] the court upheld a warrant to seize all property relating to "smuggling, packing, distribution, and use of controlled substances."

In a case where a search warrant is issued to search a specified automobile for "tools and instrumentalities of the crime of burglary," the officers were found to be authorized in seizing and searching a small black leather bag found strapped under the hood of the car.[22] In *Furfano v. State*,[23] a search warrant was issued authorizing the search of a car for a "handgun, projectiles,

---

294, 87 S.Ct. 1642, 18 L.Ed.2d 782 (1967); Harp v. State, 136 Ga. App. 897, 898 (1), 222 S.E.2d 623 (1975). In Cady v. Dombrowski, 413 U.S. 433, 448, 93 S.Ct. 2523, 37 L.Ed.2d 706 (1973), the Court held that where a valid search warrant was executed for the search of a car, a bloody seat and a briefcase, contained in the car, it was proper for the officer to seize a sock and floor mat which were in plain view when the search was conducted.

[16]United States v. Chadwell, 427 F.Supp. 692 (D.Del.1977).

[17]United States v. Feldman, 366 F.Supp. 356 (D.Haw.1973). Cf. Purcell v. State, 325 So.2d 83 (Fla.App.1976); State v. Starke, 81 Wis.2d 399, 260 N.W.2d 739 (1978).

[18]Coolidge v. New Hampshire, 403 U.S. 443, 91 S.Ct. 2022, 29 L.Ed.2d 564 (1971).

[19]United States v. Dichiarinte, 445 F.2d 126, 129 (7th Cir. 1971).

[20]United States v. George, 975 F.2d 72, 76 (2d Cir. 1992).

[21]United States v. Ladd, 704 F.2d 134 (4th Cir. 1983). In Fair v. State, 284 Ga. 165, 664 S.E.2d 227 (2008), the court held that a warrant authorizing executing officers to search a residence for "evidence of the crime of Violation of Georgia Controlled Substance[s] Act" provided enough description to survive a motion to suppress.

[22]Dressler v. State, 158 Ga. App. 11, 12 (3), 279 S.E.2d 454 (1981). In Dressler, the court emphasized that the case was not a suitcase or piece of luggage but its appearance, size and location suggested that it was a repository for burglary tools.

blood, fingerprints, [and] other evidence pertaining to the crime of aggravated assault." A 35-millimeter film canister was among the items seized. The officer said it could have contained bullets or film which could have contained fingerprints. The court affirmed the denial of the motion to suppress.

Generally, the illegal seizure of items not authorized by the warrant or the plain view doctrine does not require the suppression of all articles, but only the suppression of those illegally seized.[24] Nevertheless, if the officers' unlawful seizure of other materials led to the discovery of other evidence, this derivative evidence is not admissible.[25] See section § 2:25, supra, on "fruits of the poisonous tree."

In *United States v. Fitzgerald,*[26] the court held a seizure of a pistol valid under the plain view doctrine even though some portions of the warrant did not sufficiently describe some of the items to be seized. The court said that it recognized that "police might be tempted to frame warrants in general terms, adding a few specific clauses in the hope that under the protection of those clauses they could engage in a general rummaging . . . and then contend that any incriminating evidence they recovered was found in plain view. . . . We believe, however, that careful administration of the rule will afford full protection to individual rights. First, magistrates must exercise vigilance to detect pretext and bad faith on the part of law enforcement officials. Second, courts should rigorously apply the exclusionary rule to evidence seized pursuant to the invalid portions of the warrant. Third, items not described in the sufficiently particular portions of the warrant will not be admissible unless it appears that (a) the police found the item in a place where one would reasonably have expected them to look in the process of searching for the objects described in the sufficiently particular portions of the warrant, (b) the police found the item before they found all the objects described in the sufficiently particular portions of the warrant (that is, before their lawful authority to search expired), and (c) the other requirements of the plain view rule—inadvertent discovery and probable cause to associate the item with criminal activity—are met."

In *Teems v. State,*[27] while officers were executing a search warrant for drugs, the phone rang. It was answered by an officer.

---

[23]Furfano v. State, 212 Ga. App. 472 (1), 442 S.E.2d 305 (1994).

[24]Hunt v. State, 180 Ga. App. 103, 106, 348 S.E.2d 467 (1986); United States v. Mendoza, 473 F.2d 697 (5th Cir. 1973).

[25]Waller v. State, 251 Ga. 124 (2), 303 S.E.2d 437 (1983), rev'd on other grounds, 467 U.S. 39, 104 S.Ct. 2210, 81 L.Ed.2d 31 (1984).

[26]United States v. Fitzgerald, 724 F.2d 633 (8th Cir. 1983) (en banc).

[27]Teems v. State, 161 Ga. App. 339, 287 S.E.2d 774 (1982); United

The caller asked for Ronald. The defendant was named Ronald, but the defendant was not present at the time. The officer replied that he was "Ronald." The caller said he "needed 300 Rubies and a quarter-of-a-pound of pot." The court held that the conversation was admissible.

Both the Eleventh Circuit[28] and California[29] have concluded that under the good faith exception of searches conducted pursuant to warrants, the particularity requirement for items to be seized has been relaxed to some extent insofar as the exclusionary rule is concerned. See § 2:26, supra, for the general application of the exclusionary rule where an officer conducts a search in good faith pursuant to a warrant.

See § 4:28, infra, on protective sweeps. See § 4:22, supra, on what property may be seized and searched pursuant to a search warrant. See Annotation, "Seizure of Books, Documents or Other Papers Under Search Warrant Not Describing Such Items," 54 A.L.R.4th 391 (1987). See Annotation, "Validity of Search or Seizure of Computer, Computer Disk or Computer Peripheral Equipment," 84 A.L.R.5th 1 (2000).

§ 4:23   Execution of search warrant—Property which may be seized—Obscene material

Because of First Amendment protection, it has been held that an officer has no authority to indiscriminately seize what he considers to be obscene publications without a prior judicial determination as to whether the material is, in fact, obscene.[1] However, where an officer knows that a magistrate has deter-

---

States v. Passarella, 788 F.2d 377 (6th Cir. 1986). See § 4:59, infra, on electronic surveillance.

[28]United States v. Accardo, 749 F.2d 1477 (11th Cir. 1985).

[29]People v. MacAvoy, 162 Cal.App.3d 746, 209 Cal.Rptr. 34 (1984).

[Section 4:23]

[1]State v. Smalley, 138 Ga. App. 747, 227 S.E.2d 488 (1976). But see Maryland v. Macon, 472 U.S. 463, 105 S.Ct. 2778, 86 L.Ed.2d 370 (1985); Ball v. State, 149 Ga. App. 270, 271 (2), 253 S.E.2d 886 (1979). Cf. M. G. T. Corp. v. State, 149 Ga. App. 588, 254 S.E.2d 909 (1979). In Walter v. United States, 447 U.S. 649, 100 S.Ct. 2395, 65 L.Ed.2d 410 (1980), a majority of the Justices agreed that an FBI agent had

no right to view film without a warrant which had been improperly delivered by a carrier. In Walter, sealed packages containing obscene movie film were shipped by private carrier to Atlanta, Georgia. The film was mistakenly delivered to the wrong business. An employee opened the film and "attempted without success to view portions of the film by holding it up to a light." Shortly thereafter the FBI was called and an agent picked up the packages. Without obtaining a warrant or attempting to communicate with the consignor or consignee of the shipment, the agent viewed the film. The court pointed out that the authority to possess was distinct from the authority to examine its contents.

Walter also summarizes the rule of Stanley v. Georgia, 394 U.S. 557, 569, 89 S.Ct. 1243, 22 L.Ed.2d 542

mined that a certain issue of a certain magazine is probably obscene, he may seize a copy of the same issue of the same magazine from a store.[2] Also, in *Simpson v. State*,[3] the court held that sexual paraphernalia prohibited by O.C.G.A. § 16-12-80(b), which without doubt are designed primarily for the stimulation of genital organs and which are in plain view, may be confiscated.

In *New York v. P. J. Video, Inc.*,[4] the United States Supreme Court pointed out that there is a distinction between seizing films to destroy them and the seizing of a single copy of a film for the bona fide purpose of preserving it as evidence in a criminal case. The court then held that no greater probable cause showing is necessary in the case of seizure of materials presumptively protected by the First Amendment than in other contexts. In order to establish probable cause to seize a copy of a film it is not necessary for the magistrate to actually view the film. It is sufficient if an officer has seen the film and he adequately describes the obscene nature of the film.

In *N & N, Inc. v. Veline*,[5] the Georgia Supreme Court considered the seizure, pursuant to a warrant, of 42 eight-millimeter projectors. The Georgia case cited *Heller v. New York*[6] and summarized its holding as follows: "[T]he Constitution does not require an adversary hearing on the issue of probable obscenity prior to the issuance of a warrant for the seizure of a film to be used as evidence where the issuing judge has viewed the film and found it to be obscene . . . . 'If such a seizure (for use as evidence) is pursuant to a warrant, issued after a determination of probable cause by a neutral magistrate, and, following the seizure, a prompt judicial determination of the obscenity issue in an adversary proceeding is available at the request of an interested party, the seizure is constitutionally permissible.' "

(1969), by stating "that the warrantless projection of motion picture films was an unconstitutional invasion of the privacy of the owner" where, as Justice Stewart's concurrence in Stanley noted, "the contents of the films could not be determined by mere inspection."

In Zurcher v. Stanford Daily, 436 U.S. 547, 564-65, 98 S.Ct. 1970, 56 L.Ed.2d 525 (1978), the Court said, "Where presumptively protected materials are sought to be seized, the warrant requirement should be administered to leave as little as possible to the discretion or whim of the officer in the field. Similarly, where seizure is sought of allegedly obscene materials, the judgment of the arresting officer alone is insufficient to justify issuance of a search warrant or a seizure without a warrant incident to arrest."

[2]Kervin v. State, 172 Ga. App. 478, 480, 323 S.E.2d 643 (1984).

[3]Simpson v. State, 144 Ga. App. 657, 242 S.E.2d 265 (1978).

[4]New York v. P.J. Video, Inc., 475 U.S. 868, 106 S.Ct. 1610, 89 L.Ed.2d 871 (1986).

[5]N & N, Inc. v. Veline, 253 Ga. 51, 52, 315 S.E.2d 908 (1984).

[6]Heller v. New York, 413 U.S. 483, 93 S.Ct. 2789, 37 L.Ed.2d 745 (1973). See § 4:14, supra.

The *Veline* decision then remanded the case for an adversary hearing since it was obvious that N & N, Inc., wanted such a hearing. "In such a hearing evidence should be presented to allow the trial court to determine: (1) If the seizure was pursuant to a warrant; (2) issued after a determination of probable cause; (3) by a neutral magistrate; (4) that the projectors were used to show obscene films; (5) the seizure was for the bona fide purpose to preserve the projectors as evidence; and (6) not to block distribution or exhibition of the films."

See section §§ 4:39 et seq., infra, on plain view. See § 4:14, supra, on description of obscene materials to be seized. See § 10:2, infra, on forfeitures.

§ 4:24 Return by officer

After the search has been completed, it is the duty of the officer to file a verified list of the items seized with the magistrate named in the warrant, or before a court having jurisdiction.[1] However, failure to swear to the inventory will not invalidate the search[2] and items seized and not listed on an inventory are not rendered inadmissible for this reason.[3] By Georgia statute, on demand, the individual whose person or premises were searched shall be entitled to a copy of the inventory.[4] However, such request should be made to the magistrate issuing the warrant and not to the trial judge or the district attorney.[5]

A search pursuant to a warrant issued by a state court judge of one county for a search in that county is not invalidated by reason of the return being filed in that state court when the defendant is being tried for a felony in another county.[6]

§ 4:25 Warrantless searches—General

There is a constitutional preference for searches pursuant to a warrant rather than without one.[1] Under the Fourth Amendment, "a governmental search and seizure should represent both

---

[Section 4:24]

[1]O.C.G.A. § 17-5-29.

[2]Waters v. State, 122 Ga. App. 808, 809, 178 S.E.2d 770 (1970). In Lewis v. State, 126 Ga. App. 123, 125 (2)(a), 190 S.E.2d 123 (1972), the court said that the failure to make a return on the search warrant is a ministerial act and does not affect the validity of the search. Wallace v. State, 165 Ga. App. 804 (1), 302 S.E.2d 718 (1983), cites *Lewis* with approval.

[3]Hall v. State, 143 Ga. App. 706, 707 (3), 240 S.E.2d 125 (1977).

[4]O.C.G.A. § 17-5-29.

[5]Jones v. State, 155 Ga. App. 926, 274 S.E.2d 1 (1980).

[6]Rivers v. State, 250 Ga. 288, 294 (2), 298 S.E.2d 10 (1982).

[Section 4:25]

[1]United States v. Ventresca, 380 U.S. 102, 106, 85 S.Ct. 741, 13 L.Ed.2d 684 (1965). "The warrant clause of the Fourth Amendment is not dead language. . . . It is not an inconvenience to be somehow 'weighed' against the

the efforts of the officer to gather evidence of wrongful acts and the judgment of the magistrate that the collected evidence is sufficient to justify invasion of a citizen's private premises. . . ."[2]

Searches conducted without prior approval by a judge or magistrate are per se unreasonable subject only to a few "specifically established and well-delineated exceptions."[3] In other words, "a search conducted pursuant to a search warrant, regular and proper on its face, is presumed to be valid and the burden is on the person who moves to suppress the items found to show that the search warrant was invalid."[4] Thus, in cases which are close or marginal on the question of probable cause, if there is a warrant, the court should largely find there was probable cause, but if there is no warrant in such a case the court should find that there is an absence of probable cause.[5] The preference for a warrant is also demonstrated by the fact that the exclusionary rule does not apply where officers demonstrate an objective reasonable reliance on a warrant later found not to be supported by probable cause.[6]

In general terms, it has been said that in order to justify a warrantless search two essentials must exist: (1) It must be established that the circumstances at the time of the search were

---

claims of police efficiency." United States v. United States District Court, 407 U.S. 297, 315, 92 S.Ct. 2125, 32 L.Ed.2d 752 (1972). Generally, as background on the importance of the Fourth Amendment, see Underwood v. State, 13 Ga. App. 206, 78 S.E. 1103 (1913).

[2]United States v. United States District Court, 407 U.S. 297, 316, 92 S.Ct. 2125, 32 L.Ed.2d 752 (1972). In Agnello v. United States, 269 U.S. 20, 33, 46 S.Ct. 4, 70 L.Ed. 145, 149 (1925), the Court in referring to a search and seizure said, "Absence of any judicial approval is persuasive authority that it is unlawful."

[3]Schneckloth v. Bustamonte, 412 U.S. 218, 219, 93 S.Ct. 2041, 36 L.Ed.2d 854 (1973); State v. Guhl, 140 Ga. App. 23, 24 (1), 230 S.E.2d 22 (1976), rev'd on other grounds sub nom. Mitchell v. State, 239 Ga. 3, 235 S.E.2d 509 (1977) (quoting Coolidge v. New Hampshire, 403 U.S. 443, 454, 91 S.Ct. 2022, 29 L.Ed.2d 564 (1971)). Also see G. M. Leasing Corp. v. United States, 429 U.S. 338, 97 S.Ct. 619, 50 L.Ed.2d 530 (1977); State v. Slaughter,

252 Ga. 435, 436, 315 S.E.2d 865 (1984); State v. Estrado, 170 Ga. App. 889, 890 (2), 318 S.E.2d 505 (1984). See Case Note entitled "Search Warrant Requirements in IRC § 6331(b) Jeopardy Income Tax Assessments," 29 Mercer L. Rev. 359 (1977), discussing G. M. Leasing Corp. case.

[4]Ayers v. State, 181 Ga. App. 244, 252 (5)(b), 351 S.E.2d 692 (1986) (quoting with approval from Massachusetts v. Upton, 466 U.S. 727, 104 S.Ct. 2085, 2086, 80 L.Ed.2d 721 (1984)), disapp. on other grounds, Anderson v. State, 267 Ga. 116, 475 S.E.2d 629 (1996).

[5]State v. Slaughter, 252 Ga. 435, 437, 315 S.E.2d 865 (1984); Branton v. State, 240 Ga. App. 106, 108, 522 S.E.2d 694 (1999); McConville v. State, 228 Ga. App. 463, 467 (2), 491 S.E.2d 900 (1997); Munson v. State, 211 Ga. App. 80, 83, 438 S.E.2d 123 (1993).

[6]United States v. Leon, 468 U.S. 897, 104 S.Ct. 3405, 82 L.Ed.2d 677 (1984) (see § 2:26, supra); Rodriguez v. State, 191 Ga. App. 241, 242 (1), 381 S.E.2d 529 (1989).

sufficient to require immediate action which necessitated not complying with the restrictions of the warrant requirement of the Fourth Amendment. (2) Also, and of equal importance, the manner and scope of the search which was conducted must be reasonably related to the justification of the search.[7] In *Mincey v. Arizona*,[8] the United States Supreme Court said that "the mere fact that law enforcement may be made more efficient can never by itself justify disregard of the Fourth Amendment. . . . The investigation of crime would always be simplified if warrants were unnecessary. But the Fourth Amendment reflects the views of those who wrote the Bill of Rights that the privacy of a person's home and property may not be totally sacrificed in the name of maximum simplicity in enforcement of the criminal law. . . . For this reason, warrants are generally required to search a person's home or his person unless 'the exigencies of the situation' make the needs of law enforcement so compelling that the warrantless search is objectively reasonable under the Fourth Amendment." In the 1999 case of *Flippo v. West Virginia*,[9] the United States Supreme Court again "rejected the contention that there is a 'murder scene exception' to the Warrant Clause of the Fourth Amendment." However, if officers "reasonably believe a person is in need of immediate aid," they may make a prompt warrantless search of the murder scene. In addition, a search conducted in compliance with existing precedent is not subject to suppression should the precedent relied upon be subsequently overruled.[10]

In *United States v. Ross*,[11] the Supreme Court held that a warrantless search which is authorized by an exception to the warrant requirement "is no broader and no narrower than a magistrate could legitimately authorize by warrant."

Exceptions to the warrant requirement may arise in the situations which are hereinafter listed. Also, the list includes a reference to the material contained in this book which relates to each of these exceptions.

(1) Search incident to a lawful arrest (§ 4:26 and § 4:28, infra).

(2) Valid stop-and-frisk (§ 4:29, infra, Chapter 3, supra).

(3) Where exigent circumstances exist (§ 4:30, infra).

(4) Where an officer is in hot pursuit (§ 4:31, infra).

(5) Where there is valid consent (§§ 4:32 through 4:34, infra).

---

[7]Cleary, "Recent Developments in the Law of Search and Seizure," 1 Nat'l J. Crim. Def. 21, 40 (1975).

[8]Mincey v. Arizona, 437 U.S. 385, 393-394, 98 S.Ct. 2408, 57 L.Ed.2d 290 (1978). See § 4:30, infra, on exigent circumstances justifying a warrantless search.

[9]Flippo v. West Virginia, 528 U.S. 11, 120 S.Ct. 7, 145 L.Ed.2d 16 (1999).

[10]Davis v. U.S., 131 S. Ct. 2419, 180 L. Ed. 2d 285 (2011).

[11]United States v. Ross, 456 U.S. 798, 102 S.Ct. 2157, 72 L.Ed.2d 572 (1982).

(6) Airport searches (§ 4:35, infra).

(7) Courthouses and public buildings (§ 4:36, infra).

(8) Places of recreation and entertainment (§ 4:37, infra).

(9) Searches of abandoned property (§ 4:38, infra).

(10) Property in plain view (§ 4:40, infra).

(11) Property in open fields (§ 4:43, infra).

(12) Searches of probationers and inmates (§ 4:44, infra).

(13) Border searches (§ 4:45, infra).

(14) Administrative searches (§ 4:46, infra).

(15) Vehicle searches (§§ 4:47 through 4:56, infra).

The Fourth Amendment does not actually apply to "border searches." Also, some of the other situations are not true exceptions since the interest involved is not actually protected by the Fourth Amendment. Moreover, it has been said that some of the other exceptions to the warrant requirement listed above are actually not "true exceptions" in that the Fourth Amendment only prevents "unreasonable" searches and seizures and the so-called "exceptions," when they apply, are regarded as being reasonable.[12]

§ 4:26 Warrantless searches—Incident to lawful arrest— Person

More than 50 years ago, Justice Cardozo wrote, "The peace officer empowered to arrest must be empowered to disarm. If he may disarm, he may search, lest a weapon be concealed."[1] In *Washington v. Chrisman*,[2] the United States Supreme Court said, "The absence of an affirmative indication that an arrested person might have a weapon available or might attempt to escape does not diminish the arresting officer's authority to maintain custody over the arrested person. . . . Every arrest must be presumed to present a risk of danger to the arresting officer." After an arrest, the officer has a right to remain literally at the defendant's elbow; and if the officer sees contraband while he is with or near the defendant, he may seize it.

---

[12]Generally, see Annot., "Construction and Application of National Security Exemption to Fourth Amendment Search Warrant Requirement," 39 A.L.R.Fed. 646 (1978).

[Section 4:26]

[1]People v. Chiagles, 237 N.Y. 193, 142 N.E. 583 (1923). For an illuminating discussion of a search incident to an arrest, see the dissenting opinion of Justice Frankfurter in Davis v.

United States, 328 U.S. 582, 594, 66 S.Ct. 1256, 90 L.Ed. 1453 (1946).

[2]Washington v. Chrisman, 455 U.S. 1, 102 S.Ct. 812, 70 L.Ed.2d 778 (1982).

However, the Washington Supreme Court, relying on its state constitution, declined to follow the United States Supreme Court. State v. Chrisman, 100 Wash.2d 814, 676 P.2d 419 (1984).

In *Preston v. United States,*[3] a unanimous Court held, "Unquestionably, when a person is lawfully arrested, the police have the right, without a search warrant, to make a contemporaneous search of the person of the accused for weapons or for the fruits of or implements used to commit the crime." In *Wade v. State,*[4] the Georgia Court of Appeals stated that the motivation of a search pursuant to an arrest is irrelevant.

A search incident to an arrest will not be valid unless the arrest itself is lawful.[5] However, a stop based upon the violation of a statute later found to be unconstitutional can nonetheless be considered reasonable.[6] Likewise, a stop based upon an officer's *reasonable*, but incorrect understanding of the law can give rise to the reasonable suspicion necessary to uphold a seizure against a Fourth Amendment challenge.[7] In *Brock v. State,*[8] the court held that an officer is not prevented from making an arrest for a traffic violation even though the officer is authorized to simply issue a traffic citation. The arrest may not be made as a pretext for conducting a search,[9] and it will not be validated by what is found in the search.[10] When the validity of an arrest is challenged, the burden is on the state to prove its legality.[11] The arrest must generally precede the search[12] or be substantially contemporaneous with the search.[13] Where a search is incident to an arrest, the search is limited to the defendant and the area within his imme-

---

[3]Preston v. United States, 376 U.S. 364, 367, 84 S.Ct. 881, 11 L.Ed.2d 777 (1964).

[4]Wade v. State, 184 Ga. App. 97, 360 S.E.2d 647 (1987).

[5]Holtzendorf v. State, 125 Ga. App. 747, 188 S.E.2d 879 (1972); Kelly v. State, 129 Ga. App. 131, 198 S.E.2d 910 (1973).

[6]Michigan v. DeFillippo, 443 U.S. 31, 99 S. Ct. 2627, 61 L. Ed. 2d 343 (1979).

[7]Heien v. North Carolina, 135 S. Ct. 530, 190 L. Ed. 2d 475 (2014).

[8]Brock v. State, 196 Ga. App. 605, 606 (1), 396 S.E.2d 785 (1990).

[9]Urquhart v. State, 261 So.2d 535 (Fla.App.1971); State v. Hoven, 269 N.W.2d 849 (Minn.1978).

[10]MacDougald v. State, 124 Ga. App. 619, 620, 184 S.E.2d 687 (1971).

[11]Baez v. State, 206 Ga. App. 522, 529, 425 S.E.2d 885 (1992)

[12]Kelly v. State, 129 Ga. App. 131, 134, 198 S.E.2d 910 (1973); State v. Aguillard, 357 So.2d 535 (La.1978); Willis v. State, 122 Ga. App. 455, 457, 177 S.E.2d 487 (1970). However, there is some authority holding that if there is probable cause for an arrest before the search, the fact that the search slightly preceded the formal arrest will not render the search unlawful when both the search and the arrest take place as part of the same transaction. Holt v. Simpson, 340 F.2d 853, 856 (7th Cir. 1965). See Henderson v. United States, 405 F.2d 874 (5th Cir. 1968). See U.S. v. McCauley, 2010 WL 697286 (W.D. Wis. 2010), aff'd, 659 F.3d 645 (7th Cir. 2011). See also Cupp v. Murphy, 412 U.S. 291, 93 S. Ct. 2000, 36 L. Ed. 2d 900 (1973).

[13]United States v. Burnett, 526 F.2d 911 (5th Cir. 1976).

diate control.[14] Contraband or other fruits or instrumentalities of a crime may be seized in connection with the search.[15] In *Lopez v. State,*[16] a defendant's cell phone was confiscated at the time of his arrest and later examined for stored phone numbers of co-defendants involved in a drug trafficking scheme. The Court of Appeals did not disturb the trial court's order denying the motion to suppress because it was narrowly tailored to the circumstances of the case. However, in *Hawkins v. State,*[17] the Georgia Supreme Court found that "a cell phone is 'roughly analogous' to a container that properly can be opened and searched for electronic data, similar to a traditional container that can be opened to search for tangible objects of evidence." The court cautioned that searches of cell phones, like computers, must be limited in scope "by the object of the search."

In the interesting case of *Sprinkles v. State,*[18] the court pointed out that "[f]light after a lawful command to halt constitutes obstruction of an officer" and justifies an arrest for obstruction and the defendant may be searched as an incident of the arrest. However, the command to stop must be lawful. See sections 2:2 and 3:1, supra, on lawful stops.

The United States Supreme Court has held that the right to search incident to a valid arrest is an exception to the warrant requirement of the Fourth Amendment. "This general exception has historically been formulated into two distinct propositions. The first is that a search may be made of the *person* of the arrestee. . . . The second is that a search may be made of the area within the control of the arrestee."[19] The remainder of this section is devoted to what is considered a search of the person.

If there is a valid custodial arrest, the officer may make a full search of the person.[20] The extent of a search incident to a lawful arrest is not limited to a frisk, which has been discussed in

---

[14]Chimel v. California, 395 U.S. 752, 89 S.Ct. 2034, 23 L.Ed.2d 685 (1969). Cf. Brannon v. State, 231 Ga. App. 847, 500 S.E.2d 597 (1998).

[15]Bagwell v. State, 214 Ga. App. 15, 446 S.E.2d 739 (1994).

[16]Lopez v. State, 267 Ga. App. 532, 601 S.E.2d 116 (2004).

[17]Hawkins v. State, 290 Ga. 785, 723 S.E.2d 924 (2012) (search of cell phone restricted to object of search).

[18]Sprinkles v. State, 227 Ga. App. 112, 113 (1), 488 S.E.2d 492 (1997).

[19]United States v. Robinson, 414 U.S. 218, 224, 94 S.Ct. 467, 38 L.Ed.2d 427 (1973).

[20]O.C.G.A. § 17-5-1. Generally, see Annot. (originally compiled before Chimel but later supplemented), entitled "Modern Status of Rule as to Validity of Non-Consensual Search and Seizure Made Without Warrant After Lawful Arrest as Affected by Lapse of Time Between, or Difference in Places of, Arrest and Search," 19 A.L.R.3d 727 (1968). See 1 Federal Trial Handbook: Criminal § 36:30 (2014); 9 Ga. Proc. Criminal Procedure § 8:145 (2015).

Chapter 3, supra. In *Gustafson v. Florida*,[21] the United States Supreme Court held that an officer "was entitled to make a full search" of Gustafson's person, incident to a lawful arrest for driving without a license. The court pointed out that where a defendant is arrested for driving without a license, it is immaterial (1) that the defendant had had no previous encounter with the arresting officer; (2) that only a minor offense was involved; (3) that no police regulations required the officer to take the defendant into custody; (4) that there was no police department policy requiring a full-scale search; and (5) that the officer had no fear of the defendant.[22]

In the Georgia case of *Baker v. State*,[23] the court held that even though an officer could have only required the driver to surrender her license in lieu of bond or arrest for a minor traffic offense, this does not prevent the officer from taking the driver into custody and conducting an inventory search of her purse. In *Taylor v. State*,[24] the Georgia Court of Appeals held that the search incident to the defendant's arrest was valid even though the officer would not have arrested the defendant for the offense if the defendant had consented to a search. Likewise, in the Texas case of *Williams v. State*,[25] the court held that a search was valid where the defendant was guilty of a parking violation even though the formal arrest did not take place until after the search of the car and the reason for searching the car had little, if anything, to do with the parking violation. In *Williams v. State*,[26] where an officer would not have stopped a vehicle for speeding had the officer not had a suspicion that it was carrying illicit drugs, the stop was, nonetheless, found valid. In *Jones v. State*,[27] the court held "[t]he stop of a vehicle is authorized, and not pretextual, if the officer observed a traffic offense." In *Sanchez v. State*,[28] the court held that when there is actual reason to take a defendant into custody because the officer believed he was violating the Georgia Controlled Substances Act, the arrest is not invalidated even though the initial charge was no proof of insur-

---

[21]Gustafson v. Florida, 414 U.S. 260, 94 S.Ct. 488, 38 L.Ed.2d 456 (1973). See, U.S. v. Robinson, 414 U.S. 218, 94 S.Ct. 467, 38 L.Ed.2d 427 (1973). See also, Maryland v. Wilson, 519 U.S. 408, 117 S. Ct. 882, 137 L.Ed.2d 41 (1997).

[22]Gustafson v. Florida, 414 U.S. 260, 94 S.Ct. 488, 38 L.Ed.2d 456 (1973).

[23]Baker v. State, 202 Ga. App. 73 (1), 413 S.E.2d 251 (1991). But cf. State v. Lamb, 202 Ga. App. 69, 413 S.E.2d 511 (1991).

[24]Taylor v. State, 181 Ga. App. 703, 704, 353 S.E.2d 619 (1987); Hunter v. State, 190 Ga. App. 24, 25, 378 S.E.2d 352 (1989).

[25]Williams v. State, 726 S.W.2d 99 (Tex.Crim.App. 1986).

[26]Williams v. State, 187 Ga. App. 409, 410 (1), 370 S.E.2d 497 (1988).

[27]Jones v. State, 200 Ga. App. 666 (1), 409 S.E.2d 251 (1991).

[28]Sanchez v. State, 197 Ga. App. 470, 472 (1), 398 S.E.2d 740 (1990).

ance and there was probable cause to believe he was guilty of that offense even though as a matter of fact he was not guilty of that offense. In *Whren v. United States*,[29] the United States Supreme Court held that where a driver violated a traffic law, an officer *could stop* the vehicle even if the officer would not have stopped it had it not been for some other reason. In *Brantley v. State*,[30] the Georgia Court of Appeals followed *Whren*. In *Birchfield v. North Dakota*,[31] the Supreme Court held that a breath test is allowed as a search incident to arrest. See sections 3:2 and 3:3, supra, on facts and appearance justifying a stop. See § 3:10, supra, on investigations following traffic stops.

However, under Georgia's seat belt law, absent additional offenses, an officer has no right to search a person or an automobile solely because an occupant of the front seat failed to wear a seat belt.[32]

The defendant may be searched at the place of the arrest, and he may be searched at the jail when officers inventory his property,[33] if this is part of the routine booking procedures.[34] In *United States v. Edwards*,[35] the Court said, "It is also plain that searches and seizures that could be made on the spot at the time of the ar-

---

[29]Whren v. United States, 517 U.S. 806, 116 S.Ct. 1769, 135 L.Ed.2d 89 (1996), cited and followed in Buffington v. State, 228 Ga. App. 810, 812, 492 S.E.2d 762 (1997). See also Devenpeck v. Alford, 543 U.S. 146, 125 S. Ct. 588, 160 L. Ed. 2d 537 (2004), where the U.S. Supreme Court declined to adopt the "closely related offense' rule, which would have required an arrest supported by probable cause to be " closely related" to the officer's expressed subjective reason for making the arrest.

[30]Brantley v. State, 226 Ga. App. 872 (1), 487 S.E.2d 412 (1997).

[31]Birchfield v. North Dakota, 136 S. Ct. 2160, 195 L. Ed. 2d 560 (2016) (breath test amounts to minimal physical intrusion and may be conducted without a warrant where officer has reason to believe driver is impaired; absent exigent circumstances warrant is necessary to conduct a blood test because it is invasive and privacy concern is heightened).

[32]Richardson v. State, 232 Ga. App. 398, 400 (1), 501 S.E.2d 885 (1998).

[33]Abel v. United States, 362 U.S. 217, 239, 80 S.Ct. 683, 4 L.Ed.2d 668 (1960); Charles v. United States, 278 F.2d 386 (9th Cir. 1960). See Annot., 19 A.L.R.3d 727, 738 (1968).

An inventory search at the place of confinement has been sustained (1) to protect the property of the person arrested, United States v. Taggart, 334 F.Supp. 206 (D.Del.1971); (2) to protect officers from false claims, United States v. Gardner, 480 F.2d 929 (10th Cir. 1973); (3) to safeguard the institution and its inmates from objects which might be harmful or used as a means of escape, People v. Glaubman, 175 Colo. 41, 485 P.2d 711 (1971); and (4) to establish the identity of the arrestee, State v. Scroggins, 297 Minn. 144, 210 N.W.2d 55 (1973). See 2 LaFave, Search and Seizure 306, § 5.3(a) (West 1978).

[34]United States v. Frankenberry, 387 F.2d 337 (2d Cir. 1967).

[35]United States v. Edwards, 415 U.S. 800, 803, 94 S.Ct. 1234, 39 L.Ed.2d 771 (1974). Accord, Carter v. State, 224 Ga. App. 367, 480 S.E.2d 376 (1997).

rest may legally be conducted later when the accused arrives at the place of detention."

However, any search of clothing or other property of the defendant at the police station should be done promptly, and it has been held that once property has been inventoried and put in storage, there is no right to a further examination of it without a search warrant.[36]

Fingernail scrapings may be taken from an arrestee.[37] Likewise, in *Jackson v. State*,[38] exigent circumstances justified a warrantless penile swab of a rape suspect where he was discovered near the victim's apartment shortly after the alleged assault. The suspect fit the description of the man fleeing the apartment and investigators feared that any evidence that could be obtained as a result of the swab would be compromised within a very short period of time and long before a warrant could be obtained. There is a right to conduct a careful examination of the defendant's clothing[39] and even to subject his clothing to a laboratory analysis.[40] Although not sustained on appeal, it has also been held that when a suspect is arrested, his hands may be swabbed with cotton for purposes of a neutron activation test to determine the presence of the gunpowder residue.[41]

In *Maryland v. King*,[42] the Supreme Court held that the DNA identification of arrestees constitutes a reasonable search that can be considered part of a routine booking procedure. The Court premised its holding on the fact that arrestees are in custody and that the Maryland DNA Collection Act serves several legitimate government interests.

---

[36]Brett v. United States, 412 F.2d 401 (5th Cir. 1969). Compare U.S. v. Edwards, 415 U.S. 800, 94 S. Ct. 1234, 39 L. Ed. 2d 771 (1974); U.S. v. Andrews, 22 F.3d 1328, 1334 (5th Cir. 1994).

[37]Cupp v. Murphy, 412 U.S. 291, 93 S.Ct. 2000, 36 L.Ed.2d 900 (1973). Actually Murphy was not under arrest at the time the scrapings were obtained, but the Court held that since there was probable cause for his arrest and the evidence was highly destructible, the Fourth Amendment was not violated.

[38]Jackson v. State, 336 Ga. App. 140, 784 S.E.2d 7 (2016).

[39]People v. Pinette, 42 Mich.App. 250, 201 N.W.2d 692 (1972); Gaddis v. State, 497 P.2d 1087 (Okla.Crim.App. 1972). Also, it has been held that a defendant's billfold may be searched since knives and small weapons could be concealed in a billfold. United States v. Simpson, 453 F.2d 1028 (10th Cir. 1972).

[40]United States v. Edwards, 415 U.S. 800, 94 S.Ct. 1234, 39 L.Ed.2d 771 (1974).

[41]State v. Ulrich, 187 Mont. 347, 609 P.2d 1218 (1980). Cf. Strickland v. State, 247 Ga. 219, 224 (18), 275 S.E.2d 29 (1981); Cupp v. Murphy, 412 U.S. 291, 93 S.Ct. 2000, 36 L.Ed.2d 900 (1973).

[42]Maryland v. King, 133 S. Ct. 1958, 186 L. Ed. 2d 1 (2013).

In *United States v. Ross,*[43] the United States Supreme Court abandoned the constitutional distinction between warrantless searches of "worthy" and "unworthy" containers. The court held that "a traveler who carries a toothbrush and a few articles of clothing in a paper bag or knotted scarf claims an equal right to conceal his possessions from official inspection as the sophisticated executive with the locked attache case. . . ." However, "the protection afforded by the [Fourth] Amendment varies in different settings. . . . A container carried at the time of arrest often may be searched without a warrant and even without specific suspicion concerning its contents."

In *United States v. Teller,*[44] the court formulated what is now referred to as the "possession test." This allows officers to search personal items such as purses or clothing that are not in their owners' possession when police find them in executing a premises search warrant. In *Teller*, the officers were involved in the process of executing a warrant when the defendant arrived at her home and left her purse on her bed. The officers searched the purse and found drugs. The court upheld the search reasoning that the purse was no longer "an extension of her person" once she left it on her bed.

The possession test has been adopted in a number of jurisdictions.[45] Others find that it is too broad and choose instead to focus upon the relationship between the person and the place to be searched. Thus, in *United States v. Micheli,*[46] the court concluded it was proper when executing a warrant to search an office to allow the search of the owner's briefcase because of his relationship to the place searched but noted the case would be otherwise had the briefcase belonged to a visitor or a mere passerby.

Although a court may order a peace officer to apprehend a person pursuant to O.C.G.A. § 37-7-41(b) and, under certain conditions, take him or her to a drug treatment facility, the officer may not search the person who is the subject of the order. An apprehension is not the equivalent of an arrest which would warrant a search.[47]

See § 4:28, infra, on seizures and searches around a person arrested, and § 4:56, infra, on inventories of automobiles. See § 3:7,

---

[43]United States v. Ross, 456 U.S. 798, 102 S.Ct. 2157, 72 L.Ed.2d 572 (1982).

[44]U.S. v. Teller, 397 F.2d 494 (7th Cir. 1968). See U.S. v. Young, 909 F.2d 442 (11th Cir. 1990).

[45]See, e.g., U.S. v. Johnson, 475 F.2d 977, 979 (D.C. Cir. 1973).

[46]U.S. v. Micheli, 487 F.2d 429, 431 (1st Cir. 1973). See U.S. v. Young, 909 F.2d 442 (11th Cir. 1990).

[47]Lindsey v. State, 282 Ga. App. 644, 639 S.E.2d 584 (2006).

supra, on automobile searches following a stop for a traffic violation. See § 4:58, infra, on second search of articles taken from an arrested defendant in an automobile. See § 2:22, supra, on search incident to "booking." See § 4:49, infra, on vehicle searches incident to an arrest. See § 3:2, supra, on investigative stops.

§ 4:27   Warrantless searches—Incident to lawful arrest— Cell phones and Personal Computers

The modern standard of a "reasonable expectation of privacy" in the context of digital information operates off of the two-fold requirement developed by Justice Harlan's concurrence in *Katz v. United States*.[1] The standard requires that (1) a person has exhibited an actual, subjective expectation of privacy, and (2) that the expectation is one that society recognizes as reasonable. The subjective prong was further clarified in *Smith v. Maryland*,[2] where the court explained that the "individual [must have] shown that 'he seeks to preserve something as private.' " Additionally, in *Katz* the court created the "third party doctrine" which holds that what a person knowingly exposes to the public, even from a private space such as a home or office, is not subject to Fourth Amendment Protection.[3] Courts have struggled to apply these standards to law enforcement's ability to conduct digital information searches. Currently there is no uniform application; the court's interpretation has varied not only by jurisdiction, but also by context of surveillance.

As a general matter, courts have held that an individual has an objectively reasonable expectation of privacy in data that they have stored on their personal computer. For example, an individual has an absolute privacy interest in a computer that is in their home,[4] password protected,[5] and not connected to any networks. However, an individual's expectation of privacy decreases significantly once the individual accesses the internet. Often information is passively disclosed by an individual who has not un-

---

[Section 4:27]

[1]Katz v. U.S., 389 U.S. 347, 360–61, 88 S. Ct. 507, 19 L. Ed. 2d 576 (1967).

[2]Smith v. Maryland, 442 U.S. 735, 740, 99 S. Ct. 2577, 61 L. Ed. 2d 220 (1979).

[3]Katz v. U.S., 389 U.S. 347, 351, 88 S. Ct. 507, 19 L. Ed. 2d 576 (1967).

[4]See U.S. v. Lifshitz, 369 F.3d 173, 190, 4 A.L.R.6th 697 (2d Cir. 2004) ("Individuals generally possess a rea-sonable expectation of privacy in their home computers."); Guest v. Leis, 255 F.3d 325, 333, 2001 FED App. 0206P (6th Cir. 2001) ("Homeowners would of course have a reasonable expectation of privacy in their homes and in their belongings—including computers—inside the home.").

[5]Trulock v. Freeh, 275 F.3d 391, 403 (4th Cir. 2001) (consent to search a computer did not extend to co-tenant's password protected files).

dertaken any action other than accessing a website. For instance, transmitting information to an internet service provider ("ISP") opens one's information, including one's internet protocol ("IP") address,[6] to government access.[7] Courts have held that when individuals engage in uploading and downloading files, or "file-sharing," they lack a reasonable expectation of privacy in files stored on their computer.[8]

Further, law enforcement officers have been given great latitude to affirmatively gather information on individuals by using online tools like chat rooms, social networking sites and fake website links. For example, in *United States v. Borowy*,[9] the court held that an FBI agent did not violate a defendant's Fourth Amendment rights by logging onto a program as part of a child pornography investigation and using a keyword search to locate files held on the defendant's shared folder. The court found that the shared folder was accessible to anyone with a file-sharing program and, therefore, was entirely exposed to public view. Although an individual has a reasonable expectation of privacy of information held on their personal computer, once an individual has engaged in sharing or receiving files, in any manner, they do not have a reasonable expectation of privacy.

In *Riley v. California*,[10] the Supreme Court held that neither the interest in protecting an officer nor in preventing the destruction of evidence justified dispensing with the warrant requirement for searches of cell phone data. The court held that the officers were limited to ensuring the cell phone itself was not a weapon. Additionally, the Fifth Circuit has held that an individual has a reasonable expectation of privacy regarding the content

---

[6]A unique string of numbers separated by periods that identifies each computer using the Internet Protocol to communicate over a network.

[7]See Courtney v. State, 340 Ga. App. 496, 797 S.E.2d 496 (2017) (defendant lacked reasonable expectation of privacy in subscriber information and, thus, lacked standing to challenge search of internet provider).

[8]See U.S. v. Ganoe, 538 F.3d 1117, 1128 (9th Cir. 2008) (defendant installed and used file-sharing software, thereby opening his computer to anyone else with the same freely available program. Therefore, agent's use of file-sharing software program to access

child pornography files on the defendant's computer was not a violation of the defendant's Fourth Amendment rights). See also U.S. v. Stults, 575 F.3d 834 (8th Cir. 2009).

[9]U.S. v. Borowy, 595 F.3d 1045 (9th Cir. 2010).

[10]Riley v. California, 134 S. Ct. 2473, 189 L. Ed. 2d 430, 42 Media L. Rep. (BNA) 1925 (2014). See Davis v. State, 301 Ga. 397, 801 S.E.2d 897 (2017) (no *Riley* issue where police seized and held defendant's phone during interview conducted prior to arrest after defendant appeared to be manipulating it until they could obtain a search warrant).

of data in their phone. In *United States v. Zavala*,[11] the court held that "cell phones contain a wealth of private information, including emails, text messages, call histories, address books, and subscriber numbers. [The defendant] had a reasonable expectation of privacy regarding this information."[12] However, courts have been more willing to allow warrantless searches of identifier information, such as phone numbers and email addresses. In *Smith v. Maryland*,[13] the Supreme Court held that police may use devices to record phone numbers because individuals share this information with their telephone company by both sending and receiving calls. In general, courts have required the use of a warrant to obtain data that is stored on a cell phone, but have lowered the expectation of privacy when data has been transmitted from the cell phone user to a third party. In *State v. Hill*,[14] the court held that "a person lacks a legitimate expectation of privacy in identifying information such as name, address, or telephone that is used to facilitate the routing of communications by methods such as physical mail, landline telephone or cellular telephone." As a result, the court concluded that the Fourth Amendment did not prevent an officer in lawful possession of the defendant's phone from calling 911 to determine the telephone number assigned to the phone, and name and birthdate of the person associated with the phone.

Related issues involving the search of cell phones and computers are discussed in: § 4-2, supra, on privacy interest in cell phone, emails and computer records; §§ 4-12 and 4-13, supra, on probable cause for warrant to search computer; § 14-79, infra, on motion to suppress cell phone and computer records; Studdard, *Daniel's Georgia Handbook on Criminal Evidence (2018 ed.)* § 8:13, on business record hearsay exception for computer and cell phone records; § 9:18 on general authentication of computer printouts, emails and web pages.

§ 4:28   Warrantless searches—Incident to lawful arrest— Articles and area around person arrested[1]

---

[11]U.S. v. Zavala, 541 F.3d 562, 577 (5th Cir. 2008).

[12]U.S. v. Zavala, 541 F.3d 562, 577 (5th Cir. 2008).

[13]Smith v. Maryland, 442 U.S. 735, 736 n.1, 99 S. Ct. 2577, 61 L. Ed. 2d 220 (1979) ("We therefore conclude that petitioner in all probability entertained no actual expectation of privacy in the phone numbers he dialed, and that, even if he did, his expectation was not 'legitimate.' The installation and use of a pen register, consequently, was not a 'search,' and no warrant was required.").

[14]State v. Hill, 338 Ga. App. 57, 60, 789 S.E.2d 317 (2016) (physical precedent).

[Section 4:28]

[1]The general comments contained in the first two paragraphs of the last section apply equally to the

In *Chimel v. California,*[2] the United States Supreme Court established the validity of and limitations to a search of the area around an arrestee. The court held that officers have the right to search the defendant as well as the area within his "immediate control," or "wingspan," to remove any weapons and prevent the concealment or destruction of evidence. However, *Chimel* does not give arresting officers the authority to walk the defendant through his home so that they can search everywhere within his reach; nor does the case permit police to search "through all the desk drawers or other closed or concealed areas in [the] room itself."[3]

O.C.G.A. § 17-5-1 provides that an officer has a right, incident to a lawful arrest, to search in the "immediate presence" of the person arrested[4] for weapons to prevent the person from escaping, or to discover fruits of the crime or instruments used in commission of the crime for which the arrest is made. No Georgia cases have explicitly compared the meaning of the words "immediate control" in *Chimel* with the "immediate presence" language used in the statute.[5] Presumptively, they mean the same thing.

An arrest cannot be used as a pretext to search a home where the true purpose for entering is to search and not to arrest the defendant who lives there.[6] However, after a lawful arrest, the officer has a right to remain literally at the defendant's elbow; and if the officer sees contraband while he is with or near the

---

searches discussed in this section.

[2]Chimel v. California, 395 U.S. 752, 89 S.Ct. 2034, 23 L.Ed.2d 685 (1969).

[3]Chimel v. California, 395 U.S. 752, 763, 89 S.Ct. 2034, 23 L.Ed.2d 685 (1969). Glover v. State, 139 Ga. App. 162, 227 S.E.2d 921 (1976), holds that at the time of a lawful arrest, officers may make a full search of the defendant, a limited area within his control, and the car in his possession at the scene of the arrest.

[4]Smallwood v. State, 166 Ga. App. 247, 304 S.E.2d 95 (1983). The Smallwood case does refer to the area of the search as being "within the arrestee's 'lunging area.' "

[5]In Glover v. State, 139 Ga. App. 162, 164, 227 S.E.2d 921 (1976), the court seems to have confused the search of the person and the area in which the search took place despite

the fact that United States v. Robinson, 414 U.S. 218, 94 S.Ct. 467, 38 L.Ed.2d 427 (1973), which the Georgia court relied on, clearly distinguishes between the two.

[6]Jones v. United States, 357 U.S. 493, 78 S.Ct. 1253, 2 L.Ed.2d 1514 (1958). In *Jones*, the Court said the search was invalid even though the officers had probable cause to believe the defendant was engaged in operating an illicit distillery in his home. In United States v. Reed, 572 F.2d 412 (2d Cir. 1978), the court held that absent exigent circumstances and an arrest warrant, there is no right to arrest a person in his home even if there is probable cause for the arrest. But cf. People v. Payton, 45 N.Y.2d 300, 408 N.Y.S.2d 395, 380 N.E.2d 224 (1978), rev'd sub nom., Payton v. New York, 445 U.S. 573, 100 S.Ct. 1371, 63 L.Ed.2d 639 (1980). See § 4:30, infra, on warrantless searches.

defendant, he may seize it.[7]

While there is no right to search an entire house incident to a lawful arrest, officers are authorized to make a "limited protective sweep in conjunction with an in-home arrest when the searching officer possesses a reasonable belief based on specific and articulable facts that the area to be swept harbors an individual posing a danger to those on the arrest scene."[8] Such a sweep "may extend only to a cursory inspection of those spaces where a person may be found."[9] In *Maryland v. Buie,*[10] police officers had arrest warrants for two men. When they entered one defendant's home, they conducted a "protective sweep" and seized a red running suit observed in plain view. The United States Supreme Court upheld the "sweep" as well as the seizure because the defendant was wanted for a robbery in which the assailant wore a red running suit. See §§ 4:21 and 4:22, supra, on what property may be seized and searched pursuant to a search warrant. In *Inglett v. State,*[11] the court held "[p]olice officers are authorized to make a protective sweep in conjunction with an in-home arrest when they possess 'articulable facts which, taken together with the rational inferences from those facts, would warrant a reasonably prudent officer in believing that the area to be swept harbors an individual posing a danger to those on the arrest scene.' "

In *Belton v. New York,*[12] the United States Supreme Court dealt with the scope of automobile searches when the occupants are arrested. The court held "when a policeman has made a lawful custodial arrest of the occupant of an automobile, he may, as a contemporaneous incident of that arrest, search the passenger

---

[7]Washington v. Chrisman, 455 U.S. 1, 102 S.Ct. 812, 70 L.Ed.2d 778 (1982). In Hartline v. State, 161 Ga. App. 847, 849 (3), 288 S.E.2d 902 (1982), officers were executing an arrest warrant for the defendant. The officers asked for identification. The defendant stated that he would have to get his driver's license. The officers followed him into his residence. In the house they saw marijuana in plain view as well as scales and plastic bags. The court affirmed the overruling of the motion to suppress.

[8]Maryland v. Buie, 494 U.S. 325, 110 S.Ct. 1093, 108 L.Ed.2d 276 (1990).

See State v. Scott, 176 Ga. App. 887, 890 (3), 339 S.E.2d 276 (1985). Cf. Lush v. State, 168 Ga. App. 740, 741 (1), 310 S.E.2d 287 (1983).

[9]Maryland v. Buie, 494 U.S. 325, 110 S.Ct. 1093, 108 L.Ed.2d 276 (1990).

[10]Maryland v. Buie, 494 U.S. 325, 110 S.Ct. 1093, 108 L.Ed.2d 276 (1990). See Causey v. State, 334 Ga. App. 170, 778 S.E.2d 800 (2015) (mere "hunch" that other dangerous persons may be in home where police serve warrant and arrest a person is not sufficient reason to conduct a warrantless sweep of the premises).

[11]Inglett v. State, 239 Ga. App. 524, 525 (1), 521 S.E.2d 241 (1999).

[12]New York v. Belton, 453 U.S. 454, 101 S.Ct. 2860, 69 L.Ed.2d 768 (1981).

compartment of that automobile." In *Thornton v. United States,*[13] the Supreme Court held that *Belton* still applies "when an officer does not make contact until the person arrested has left the vehicle." However, in *Arizona v. Gant,*[14] the Supreme Court held that *Belton* should not be construed to warrant a search incident to arrest which extends beyond the space within the defendant's immediate control. Even then, a search would only be justified by the arresting officer's reasonable belief that the area might contain a weapon or evidence of the crime for which the defendant was arrested. State and federal cases suggesting otherwise should be reviewed carefully in light of *Gant.*[15] Although the United States Supreme Court has held that *Gant* should not be applied retroactively if the police in good faith believed that they were acting within the bounds of applicable legal precedent, both the Georgia Supreme Court and the Court of Appeals have applied *Gant* retroactively.[16] "However, warrantless searches of luggage or other property seized at the time of an arrest cannot be justified as incident to that arrest either if the search is remote in time or place from the arrest, or no exigency exists. Once law enforcement officers have reduced luggage or other personal property not immediately associated with the person of the arrestee to their exclusive control, and there is no longer any danger that the arrestee might gain access to the property to seize a weapon or destroy evidence, a search of that property is no longer an incident of the arrest."[17] See § 4:49 and § 4:50, infra, on searches of vehicles and containers found therein.

When police search the area within the arrestee's "immediate control" or "immediate presence," they are sometimes allowed to search articles they find therein.

---

[13]Thornton v. United States, 541 U.S. 615, 124 S.Ct. 2127, 158 L.Ed.2d 905 (2004).

[14]Arizona v. Gant, 556 U.S. 332, 129 S.Ct. 1710, 173 L.Ed.2d 485 (2009). See Grimes v. State, 303 Ga. App. 808, 695 S.E.2d 294 (2010).

[15]See Martinez v. State, 303 Ga. App. 166, 692 S.E.2d 766 (2010) (court held that *Gant* does not prohibit search of vehicle where officer has probable cause to believe that the car contains contraband regardless of whether there is some exigency in the attendant circumstances). Cf. Boykins v. State, 290 Ga. 71, 717 S.E.2d 474 (2011) (warrantless search of vehicle not authorized where officer has no probable cause to believe vehicle contains evidence of criminal activity re-lated to stop and suspect has no access to vehicle after being removed therefrom).

[16]See Davis v. U.S., 131 S. Ct. 2419, 180 L. Ed. 2d 285 (2011). Compare Canino v. State, 314 Ga. App. 633, 725 S.E.2d 782 (2012); Boykins v. State, 290 Ga. 71, 717 S.E.2d 474 (2011); Holsey v. State, 306 Ga. App. 75, 701 S.E.2d 538 (2010).

[17]U.S. v. Chadwick, 433 U.S. 1, 14, 97 S. Ct. 2476, 53 L. Ed. 2d 538 (1977) (abrogated on other grounds by, California v. Acevedo, 500 U.S. 565, 111 S. Ct. 1982, 114 L. Ed. 2d 619 (1991)) (citation, interior quotation marks and footnote omitted). See Kennebrew v. State, 299 Ga. 864, 792 S.E.2d 695 (2016).

In *Chester v. State*,[18] the court considered the search of a suitcase located in a house apparently owned by the defendant. Officers had a search warrant for the premises, and the suitcase had the defendant's surname on it. The court upheld the search even though the defendant's name did not appear in the warrant. The court pointed out that there is a distinction between the search of a suitcase of a visitor to the premises and the search of a suitcase of the owner of the premises.

In *State v. Browning*,[19] police responded to a complaint of noise in an apartment. When a man opened the door, the officers observed four other persons in the apartment, one of whom was female. The man assured the officers they would keep the noise down and closed the door. As the door closed, the officers smelled marijuana, knocked on the door again, and heard a back door shut. When the officers entered the apartment there were only two men present, drug paraphernalia was in plain sight, and a woman's purse was "open" on the floor. An officer examined the contents of the purse and found marijuana. At trial the officer admitted he was searching the personal effects of a visitor and the judge granted the motion to suppress that evidence. The appellate court affirmed and concluded that the woman had a substantial interest in the privacy of all her possessions and that there was sufficient evidence to find that the purse had not been abandoned.

In *Rawlings v. Kentucky*,[20] the United States Supreme Court denied a motion to suppress evidence discovered pursuant to a search warrant because the defendant did not have a reasonable expectation of privacy in the contents of a woman's purse, even though it was his belongings (illegal drugs) that were seized therein. In *Rawlings*, the defendant and others were kept in a house for about 45 minutes while police obtained a search warrant. The defendant contended that his admission of ownership of the drugs was a result of an illegal detention and that the search of his person was illegal. The court assumed that the detention was unconstitutional, but found that it was sufficiently attenuated from the admission to make the statement of ownership admissible. The search of the defendant's person was valid because it was incident to his arrest.

In *Segura v. United States*,[21] the Court held that an earlier illegal entry into an apartment did not require suppression of evi-

---

[18]Chester v. State, 162 Ga. App. 10, 290 S.E.2d 117 (1982).

[19]State v. Browning, 209 Ga. App. 197, 198 (1), 433 S.E.2d 119 (1993); Wade v. State, 184 Ga. App. 289, 291, 361 S.E.2d 266 (1987).

[20]Rawlings v. Kentucky, 448 U.S. 98, 100 S.Ct. 2556, 65 L.Ed.2d 633 (1980).

[21]Segura v. United States, 468 U.S. 796, 104 S.Ct. 3380, 82 L.Ed.2d 599 (1984). See § 2-27, supra, on excep-

dence seized later pursuant to a valid warrant which was issued on information obtained by police before the illegal entry into the apartment.

See section § 2:25 et seq., supra, on results of illegal arrest. Also see § 4:49, infra, on search of vehicle incident to an arrest and § 4:50, infra, on probable cause to search a motor vehicle. See § 4:58, infra, on a second search of articles taken from an arrested defendant. See § 4:26, supra, on search of a person incident to a lawful arrest. See § 4:56, infra, on conducting an inventory of contents of a vehicle. See § 2:22, supra, on search at police stations.

§ 4:29   Warrantless searches—Valid stop-and-frisk

Stop-and-frisk situations are discussed in Chapter 3, supra.

§ 4:30   Warrantless searches—Exigent circumstances

A warrantless search may be valid in some emergency situations where there is an immediate necessity to search and no opportunity to obtain a warrant.[1] Although "hot pursuit" is a type of emergency or exigent circumstance, it will be discussed separately in the following section. In *People v. Mitchell*,[2] the court held that in order to establish the existence of an emergency situation, the following basic elements must appear: "(1) The police must have reasonable grounds to believe that there is an emergency at hand and an immediate need for their assistance for the protection of life or property. (2) The search must not be primarily motivated by intent to arrest and seize evidence. (3) There must be some reasonable basis, approximating probable cause, to associate the emergency with the area or place to be searched." In 2006, however, *Mitchell* was abrogated by *Brigham City v. Stuart*,[3] wherein the United States Supreme Court held that a warrantless entry under exigent circumstances does not run afoul of the Fourth Amendment "as long as the circumstances, viewed *objectively*, justify [the] action."[4] (Emphasis in original).

"Circumstances which have seemed relevant to courts include (1) the degree of urgency involved and the amount of time neces-

tion to exclusionary rule.

[Section 4:30]

[1]See Brewer v. State, 129 Ga. App. 118, 199 S.E.2d 109 (1973); Ricks v. State, 140 Ga. App. 298, 231 S.E.2d 113 (1976).

[2]People v. Mitchell, 39 N.Y.2d 173, 383 N.Y.S.2d 246, 347 N.E.2d 607, 609 (1976).

[3]Brigham City, Utah v. Stuart, 547 U.S. 398, 126 S. Ct. 1943, 164 L. Ed. 2d 650 (2006).

[4]Brigham City, Utah v. Stuart, 547 U.S. 398, 126 S. Ct. 1943, 164 L. Ed. 2d 650 (2006), quoting Scott v. U.S., 436 U.S. 128, 138, 98 S. Ct. 1717, 56 L. Ed. 2d 168 (1978). See Michigan v. Fisher, 130 S. Ct. 546, 175 L. Ed. 2d 410, 58 A.L.R.6th 839 (2009).

sary to obtain a warrant, (2) reasonable belief that the contraband is about to be removed, (3) the possibility of danger to police officers guarding the site of the contraband while a search warrant is sought, (4) information indicating the possessors of the contraband are aware that the police are on their trail, and (5) the ready destructibility of the contraband and the knowledge 'that efforts to dispose of narcotics and to escape are characteristic behavior of persons engaged in the narcotics traffic.' " *United States v. Manning,* 448 F.2d 992, 998-999 (2d Cir. 1971); *United States v. Davis,* 461 F.2d at 1031-1032.

In *Welsh v. Wisconsin,*[5] the United States Supreme Court, in considering a warrantless home arrest, pointed out that the seriousness of the crime may be considered in determining whether exigent circumstances exist. The court said, "Our hesitation in finding exigent circumstances . . . is especially appropriate when the underlying offense for which there is probable cause to arrest is relatively minor. Before agents of the government may invade the sanctity of the home, the burden is on the government to demonstrate exigent circumstances that overcome the presumption of unreasonableness that attaches to all warrantless home entries. . . . When the government's interest is only to arrest for a minor offense, that presumption of unreasonableness is difficult to rebut, and the government usually should be allowed to make such arrests only with a warrant issued upon probable cause by a neutral and detached magistrate."

A number of cases have held that if there is probable cause to believe that contraband will be discovered, but would be destroyed unless there is an immediate search, the search may be conducted without a warrant.[6] In *United States v. Rubin,*[7] the Third Circuit held that where government agents have probable cause to believe that contraband is present and, based on surrounding circumstances or the information at hand, the agents have reason to conclude that the evidence will be destroyed or removed before they can secure a search warrant, a warrantless search is justified. The court cautioned that a case by case scrutiny of the circumstances is always necessary. According to *Rubin:*

---

[5]Welsh v. Wisconsin, 466 U.S. 740, 104 S.Ct. 2091, 80 L.Ed.2d 732 (1984).

[6]Cupp v. Murphy, 412 U.S. 291, 93 S.Ct. 2000, 36 L.Ed.2d 900 (1973) (fingernail scrapings where police had probable cause to believe defendant strangled his wife); U.S. v. Johnson, 467 F.2d 630, 638 (2d Cir. 1972) (evi-dence in suitcases near the rear door of apartment building in a high crime area); U.S. v. Brown, 457 F.2d 731 (1st Cir. 1972) (accomplices were at large and could have taken evidence). See Jackson v. State, 336 Ga. App. 140, 784 S.E.2d 7 (2016).

[7]United States v. Rubin, 474 F.2d 262, 268 (3d Cir. 1973).

"The emergency circumstances will vary from case to case, and the inherent necessities of the situation at the time must be scrutinized. Circumstances which have seemed relevant to courts include (1) the degree of urgency involved and the amount of time necessary to obtain a warrant, (2) reasonable belief that the contraband is about to be removed, (3) the possibility of danger to police officers guarding the site of the contraband while a search warrant is sought, (4) information indicating the possessors of the contraband are aware that the police are on their trail, and (5) the ready destructibility of the contraband and the knowledge 'that efforts to dispose of narcotics and to escape are characteristic behavior of persons engaged in the narcotics traffic' " (citations omitted).[8]

In *Herring v. State,*[9] an officer operating on a tip that a certain homeowner had drugs in his possession engaged in a permissible knock-and-talk procedure in order to investigate a report of a crime. Once the door was opened, the offer observed in plain view evidence of drug use. The officer also observed the defendant get up from a sofa and start walking toward the back of the hours. The court found the officer's warrantless entry to be justified by the likelihood that the contraband was in danger of immediate destruction.

Although the Supreme Court, in *Agnello v. United States,*[10] stated that even when probable cause exists that evidence will be found in a certain area, a search for an article in a dwelling is unlawful in the absence of a search warrant, the Court alluded to the legality of a warrantless search where there is an emergency situation necessitating prompt action.[11] If there is probable cause and no exigent circumstances, it may be permissible for officers to seize premises to secure the area while a search warrant is obtained;[12] but generally, "they may not enter a home without a warrant merely because they plan to obtain one subsequently."[13] The United States Supreme Court reversed a conviction resulting from the search of a house for narcotics where the state failed to

---

[8]United States v. Rubin, 474 F.2d 262, 268-269 (3d Cir. 1973).

[9]Herring v. State, 279 Ga. App. 162, 630 S.E.2d 776 (2006).

[10]Agnello v. United States, 269 U.S. 20, 46 S.Ct. 4, 70 L.Ed. 145 (1925) (cited with approval in Black v. State, 119 Ga. App. 855, 856, 168 S.E.2d 916 (1969)); Phillips v. State, 167 Ga. App. 260, 261, 305 S.E.2d 918 (1983).

[11]Johnson v. United States, 333 U.S. 10, 15, 68 S.Ct. 367, 92 L.Ed. 436 (1948); Chapman v. United States, 365 U.S. 610, 81 S.Ct. 776, 5 L.Ed.2d 828 (1961); Bratt v. Genovese, 660 Fed. Appx. 837 (11th Cir. 2016).

[12]See § 4:21, supra.

[13]Griffith v. State, 172 Ga. App. 255, 257, 322 S.E.2d 921 (1984).

show any exigent circumstances.[14]

In *Wayne v. United States,*[15] then Judge, later Chief Justice Burger, in an opinion on exigent circumstances, stated that: "Breaking into a home by force is not illegal if it is reasonable in the circumstances. . . . [A] warrant is not required to break down a door to enter a burning home to rescue occupants or extinguish a fire, to prevent a shooting or to bring emergency aid to an injured person. The need to protect or preserve life or avoid serious injury is justification for what would be otherwise illegal absent an exigency or emergency. Fires or dead bodies are reported to police by cranks where no fires or bodies are to be found. Acting in response to reports of 'dead bodies,' the police may find the 'bodies' to be common drunks, diabetics in shock, or distressed cardiac patients. But the business of policemen and firemen is *to act,* not to speculate or meditate on whether the report is correct. People could well die in emergencies if police tried to act with the calm deliberation associated with the judicial process. Even the apparently dead often are saved by swift police response. A myriad of circumstances could fall within the terms 'exigent circumstances' . . . e.g., smoke coming out a window or under a door, the sound of gunfire in a house, threats from the inside to shoot through the door at police, reasonable grounds to believe an injured or seriously ill person is being held within."

If an officer reasonably believes there are wounded people in a home, he may enter without a warrant.[16] The police have the right to enter without a warrant if they receive a credible call that an individual is dead in a house.[17] Where officers find a man lying unconscious on a public street, they may search him to learn his identity and to obtain information about his medical history. If narcotics are discovered in the search, they are admissible if the defendant is tried for possession.[18]

In a case where an officer found a vehicle parked at 3 a.m. with

---

[14]Vale v. Louisiana, 399 U.S. 30, 90 S.Ct. 1969, 26 L.Ed.2d 409 (1970). In Black v. State, 119 Ga. App. 855, 856, 168 S.E.2d 916 (1969), the court said, citing Jones v. United States, 357 U.S. 493, 497, 78 S.Ct. 1253, 2 L.Ed.2d 1514 (1958), "[P]robable cause for belief that certain articles subject to seizure are in a dwelling cannot of itself justify a search without a warrant." In Kelley v. State, 146 Ga. App. 179, 184, 245 S.E.2d 872 (1978), the court held that the same rule applies to a search of the curtilage of a dwelling. See Gordon v. State, 277 Ga. App. 247, 626 S.E.2d 214 (2006).

[15]Wayne v. United States, 318 F.2d 205, 212 (D.C.Cir. 1963).

[16]Carthern v. State, 238 Ga. App. 670 (1), 519 S.E.2d 490 (1999).

[17]Patrick v. State, 227 A.2d 486, 489 (Del.1967). See State v. Chapman, 250 A.2d 203 (Me.1969). In State v. Epperson, 571 S.W.2d 260 (Mo.1978), the court said that officers who discovered bodies in a bedroom had authority to search the house for "readily accessible evidence of the crime."

[18]Vauss v. United States, 370 F.2d 250 (D.C.Cir. 1966). Cf. Owens v. State, 236 Ga. App. 534, 535, 512 S.E.2d 394

its motor running and a man lying on the front seat, the court concluded that the policeman had the right to try to rouse the man, and contraband found in the process was admissible.[19] Likewise, a limited search of the trunk of an auto without a warrant was valid where officers smelled a strong odor of ether coming from the trunk and officers knew of its highly explosive character.[20]

It must be remembered that probable cause does not permit a warrantless intrusion into one's home in the absence of a showing that the exigencies of the situation make such a search imperative.[21] Thus, it has been held that an officer investigating a complaint about a loudly playing stereo in the early morning has no authority to enter an apartment uninvited when the defendant comes to the door in response to his knock.[22]

In *United States v. Place,*[23] the United States Supreme Court said, "Where law enforcement authorities have probable cause to believe that a container holds contraband or evidence of a crime, but have not secured a warrant, the Court has interpreted the Amendment to permit seizure of the property, pending issuance of a warrant to examine its contents, if the *exigencies* of the circumstances demand it or some other recognized exception to the warrant requirement is present. . . . For example, 'objects such as weapons or contraband found in a public place may be seized by the police without a warrant,' . . . because, under these circumstances, the risk of the item's disappearance or use for its intended purpose before a warrant may be obtained outweighs the interest in possession." (Emphasis added.) However, the mere "presence of contraband without more does not give rise to exigent circumstances."[24]

In *Strozier v. State,*[25] an officer saw marijuana plants in pots being watered by the defendant. The defendant was in a fenced yard standing at the corner of his carport. The trial court's deter-

---

(1999).

[19]Thompson v. State, 140 Ga. App. 293, 231 S.E.2d 110 (1976).

[20]People v. Clements, 661 P.2d 267 (Colo.1983).

[21]United States v. Reed, 572 F.2d 412 (2d Cir. 1978). But cf. People v. Payton, 45 N.Y.2d 300, 408 N.Y.S.2d 395, 380 N.E.2d 224 (1978). See U.S. v. Hackett, 638 F.2d 1179 (9th Cir. 1980); Bogan v. State, 165 Ga. App. 851, 303 S.E.2d 48 (1983).

[22]Clare v. State, 135 Ga. App. 281, 284, 217 S.E.2d 638 (1975). See Felton v. State, 322 Ga. App. 630, 745 S.E.2d

832 (2013) (pat down of defendant during investigatory stop was not justified based solely on officer's suspicion that defendant might be "hiding something" rather than objectively reasonable grounds that defendant was armed).

[23]United States v. Place, 462 U.S. 696, 103 S.Ct. 2637, 77 L.Ed.2d 110 (1983).

[24]Welchel v. State, 255 Ga. App. 556, 559, 565 S.E.2d 870 (2002).

[25]Strozier v. State, 244 Ga. App. 514, 535 S.E.2d 847 (2000).

mination that there were exigent circumstances was affirmed in view of the mobility of the plants. Conversely, in *Gates v. State*,[26] the court held that exigent circumstances did not exist justifying seizure when a police officer observed marijuana growing on the defendant's property. However, if an occupant "sees" the officer, then the facts may amount to exigent circumstances and will justify an immediate seizure.[27]

On the other hand, because of the mobility of the automobile, exigent circumstances justifying a warrantless search were found where officers received reliable information that a person possessed marijuana in a described automobile at a certain location.[28] In *Meadows v. State*,[29] officers received information describing the automobile defendant was driving and that the defendant was transporting cocaine to Cusseta from Columbus. Forty-five minutes later on the designated highway, an officer stopped Meadows, ordered him out of the car and patted him down for weapons and drugs. The officer removed a bag which appeared to contain cocaine residue. The appellate court affirmed the trial court in denying the motion to suppress the bag obtained in the search.

Where an officer, while executing a valid search warrant, answered a telephone call from the defendant, who mistook him for the resident, and made arrangements to meet the defendant to purchase marijuana, the warrantless arrest of the defendant and warrantless search were justified because the officer did not know in advance where the actual transaction was going to take place.[30]

In a case where a defendant was arrested at a hospital for suspicion of murder following the death of his wife, the search of his home to see if there was any injured person was held reasonable under the circumstances.[31] However, in *Mincey v. Arizona*,[32] the United States Supreme Court pointed out that (1) "the

[26]Gates v. State, 229 Ga. App. 766, 767-768, 495 S.E.2d 113 (1997).

[27]Carranza v. State, 266 Ga. 263, 266, 467 S.E.2d 315 (1996) (implication).

[28]Smith v. State, 135 Ga. App. 424, 218 S.E.2d 133 (1975). On auto searches, see §§ 4:48 et seq., infra.

[29]Meadows v. State, 247 Ga. App. 634, 635 (1), 545 S.E.2d 76 (2001).

[30]Lentile v. State, 136 Ga. App. 611, 612 (1), 222 S.E.2d 86 (1975).

[31]Thomas v. State, 118 Ga. App. 359, 163 S.E.2d 850 (1968). This is an

alternative holding because the court placed considerable emphasis on the fact that the door of the house was found open when the officer arrived. Also, there was testimony that the son of the defendant requested the officer to go to the house.

In Gilreath v. State, 247 Ga. 814, 818 (1), 279 S.E.2d 650 (1981), the court pointed out that an officer may enter the curtilage to knock on a door to locate a missing person when he has reason to believe a person within is in need of immediate aid.

[32]Mincey v. Arizona, 437 U.S. 385, 98 S.Ct. 2408, 57 L.Ed.2d 290 (1978).

seriousness of the offense under investigation [does not] itself [create] exigent circumstances," and (2) a warrantless search must be "strictly circumscribed by the exigencies which justify its initiation."

Nevertheless, *Mincey* continued to recognize "that the Fourth Amendment does not bar police officers from making warrantless entries and searches when they reasonably believe that a person within is in need of immediate aid. Similarly, when the police come upon the scene of a homicide, they may make a prompt warrantless search of the area to see if there are other victims or if a killer is still on the premises. . . .'The need to protect or preserve life or avoid serious injury is justification for what would be otherwise illegal absent an exigency or emergency.' "[33] One of the cases cited in *Mincey* with approval was *People v. Mitchell*.[34] Note, however, that in the 2006 decision of *Brigham City v. Stuart*,[35] the U.S. Supreme Court abrogated *Mitchell* to the extent that it allows for consideration of an officer's subjective intent in making a warrantless entry of a home potentially occupied by persons in need of emergency assistance. A warrantless entry under such circumstances does not run afoul of the Fourth Amendment "as long as the circumstances, viewed *objectively*, justify [the] action."[36] (Emphasis in original).

In *State v. Peterson*,[37] the court held that "temporary care of minor children left without adult supervision by police requires police to care for the children until responsibility for their care and custody is undertaken by a responsible adult. . . . The absence of responsible adult supervision of children is an exigent circumstance justifying a warrantless entry."

In the Mincey case there was a warrantless search of a "murder scene" which was in the defendant's home. See § 4:25, supra.

[33]Mincey v. Arizona, 437 U.S. 385, 392, 98 S.Ct. 2408, 57 L.Ed.2d 290 (1978); Delay v. State, 258 Ga. 229, 230 (2)(b), 367 S.E.2d 806 (1988). See Kentucky v. King, 131 S. Ct. 1849, 179 L. Ed. 2d 865 (2011); Wayne v. United States, 318 F.2d 205 (D.C.Cir. 1963), opinion by then Judge Burger. See 2 LaFave, Search and Seizure 455, § 6.5(d) (West 1978).

[34]People v. Mitchell, 39 N.Y.2d 173, 383 N.Y.S.2d 246, 347 N.E.2d 607 (1976), discussed in n. 2, supra.

[35]Brigham City, Utah v. Stuart, 547 U.S. 398, 126 S. Ct. 1943, 164 L. Ed. 2d 650 (2006).

[36]Brigham City, Utah v. Stuart, 547 U.S. 398, 126 S. Ct. 1943, 164 L. Ed. 2d 650 (2006), quoting Scott v. U.S., 436 U.S. 128, 138, 98 S. Ct. 1717, 56 L. Ed. 2d 168 (1978).

[37]State v. Peterson, 273 Ga. 657, 660 (2), 543 S.E.2d 692 (2001). In MacKay v. State, 291 Ga. App. 733, 662 S.E.2d 814 (2008), the Court had no trouble finding exigent circumstances justifying a warrantless entry when officers entered a mobile home, unoccupied at the time, in pursuit of a marauding Rottweiler which had caused havoc in the neighborhood.

In *Burk v. State*,[38] the Georgia Court of Appeals adopted the lead taken by several other jurisdictions and held that "a reasonable belief that minors are consuming alcohol in a residence constitutes an exigent circumstance . . . ." The court cited as the basis for its ruling, public safety concerns as well as the likelihood that any evidence tending to show the crime of serving alcohol to minors would likely be destroyed if officers were forced to seek a warrant.

In *Thompson v. Louisiana*,[39] the United States Supreme Court, in a 1984 per curiam opinion, held that a search was unlawful which had been conducted by two members of a homicide unit 35 minutes after officers arrived and found a corpse and an unconscious person who had attempted suicide. The homicide investigators conducted an exploratory search for about two hours. The first officers had already searched the premises for other victims and suspects. There was time to secure a warrant before the search.

Nevertheless, in *Overman v. State*,[40] the Georgia Supreme Court held that officers who were called to the defendant's apartment where his former girlfriend had been shot and where the defendant consented to their entering had a right to "seize and secure possible evidence in plain view while investigating the scene." This right was said to include the right to seize a telephone tape recorder from the defendant's bedroom.

The 11th Circuit has held that where exigent circumstances demand an immediate response because of the possibility of danger to human life, a limited warrantless intrusion into a home may be justified by officers responding to a 911 call.[41]

In *Hatten v. State*,[42] the court approved a murder scene warrantless search of the defendant's home and yard three to six hours after the police first arrived.

See § 4:57, infra, on scope and intensity of a search. See Annotation, "Belief That Burglary is in Progress or Has Been Recently Committed As Exigent Circumstances Justifying Warrantless Search of Premises," 64 A.L.R.5th 637 (1998).

---

[38]Burk v. State, 284 Ga. App. 843, 844-45, 644 S.E.2d 914 (2007).

[39]Thompson v. Louisiana, 469 U.S. 17, 105 S.Ct. 409, 83 L.Ed.2d 246 (1984).

[40]Overman v. State, 250 Ga. 494, 496 (2), 299 S.E.2d 542 (1983). See 2

LaFave, Search and Seizure, § 6.5(e) (West 1978).

[41]United States v. Holloway, 290 F.3d 1331 (11th Cir. 2002).

[42]Hatten v. State, 253 Ga. 24, 25 (2), 315 S.E.2d 893 (1984).

§ 4:31 Warrantless searches—Officer in hot pursuit

In *Warden v. Hayden,*[1] the United States Supreme Court recognized the hot-pursuit exception to the warrant requirement. This case, which is typical of the hot-pursuit exception, involved a fleeing robber who entered a certain house. The police were informed of the robbery, knocked at the house, were admitted,[2] and searched the entire house. Hayden was found in an upstairs bedroom feigning sleep, and he was arrested. Meanwhile, an officer discovered a shotgun and pistol in the adjoining bathroom, while another policeman found a jacket and trousers of the kind worn by the robber in a washing machine in the basement.

The Supreme Court affirmed the warrantless search, stating that under the exigencies of the situation, the search was imperative.[3] "The Fourth Amendment does not require police officers to delay in the course of an investigation if to do so would gravely endanger their lives or the lives of others." Where speed is essential, a thorough search for persons and weapons is permissible to insure that the police can gain control of all weapons which can be used against them or to effect an escape.

In *Welsh v. Wisconsin,*[4] the United States Supreme Court concluded that there was no "hot pursuit" where "there was no immediate or continuous pursuit of the . . . [defendant] from the scene of a crime."

In Georgia, the hot-pursuit exception was held to be applicable when officers, after a robbery, obtained an automobile license number which was traced to the defendant's wife and immediately proceeded to the defendant's residence where the defendant and the automobile were searched.[5] In *Darby v. State,*[6] the Georgia Court of Appeals recognized that to establish the hot pursuit exception to the warrant requirement, "[t]he critical ele-

---

[Section 4:31]

[1]Warden v. Hayden, 387 U.S. 294, 87 S.Ct. 1642, 18 L.Ed.2d 782 (1967). Cf. Minnesota v. Olson, 495 U.S. 91, 110 S.Ct. 1684, 109 L.Ed.2d 85 (1990) (see § 14:81, infra, on standing to object to illegally obtained tangible evidence).

[2]The court did not pass on the question of whether consent for the search was given.

[3]Warden v. Hayden, 387 U.S. 294, 298, 87 S.Ct. 1642, 18 L.Ed.2d 782 (1967); Commonwealth v. DiSanto, 8 Mass.App.Ct. 694, 397 N.E.2d 672 (1979).

[4]Welsh v. Wisconsin, 466 U.S. 740, 104 S.Ct. 2091, 80 L.Ed.2d 732 (1984) (discussed in § 2:5, supra).

[5]Hall v. State, 135 Ga. App. 690, 691 (3), 218 S.E.2d 687 (1975). Generally, on auto searches, see §§ 4:48 et seq., infra. In United States v. Prescott, 581 F.2d 1343 (9th Cir. 1978), the court held that absent exigent circumstances, officers may not enter a house without an arrest warrant to arrest a person, even where they have probable cause to make the arrest and reasonable grounds to believe the suspect is in the dwelling. See § 2:5, supra, on place of arrest.

[6]Darby v. State, 216 Ga. App. 781, 782 (1), 455 S.E.2d 850 (1995).

ments that need to be satisfied . . . are (1) continuity of pursuit, and (2) immediacy of pursuit."

However, in the thought provoking Georgia case of *Hamrick v. State*,[7] the court held that the doctrine of hot pursuit did not justify an arrest of a defendant in his home for a traffic violation (misdemeanor) where the circumstances did not make an immediate arrest necessary. See discussion of *Welsh v. Wisconsin* in § 4:30, supra.

In the Fifth Circuit case of *United States v. Kreimes*,[8] the court found that the warrantless search of a zippered piece of luggage was justified for the purpose of learning the identity of a person who fled from a truck which was found to be loaded with marijuana.

§ 4:32   Warrantless searches—Valid consent—General

A valid consent to a search eliminates an officer's need to obtain a warrant[1] and the need for probable cause.[2] However, a consent to search is not a consent to seize. Thus, an officer may only seize items which he has probable cause to believe are stolen or embezzled property, contraband, or instrumentalities or fruits of a crime.[3] Likewise, consents have been strictly construed against the state; thus, it has been held that a consent to let an officer determine whether or not a key will fit a car is not a consent to a search of the car.[4] It has been said that a consent to look inside a pick-up truck is not a consent to open a drawstring bag on the front seat.[5] In *United States v. Elliott*,[6] an officer asked the defendant if he could "look through the trunk [of a car] and see

---

[7]Hamrick v. State, 198 Ga. App. 124, 401 S.E.2d 25 (1990).

[8]United States v. Kreimes, 649 F.2d 1185, 1192 (5th Cir. 1981).

[Section 4:32]

[1]Dean v. State, 250 Ga. 77, 80, 295 S.E.2d 306 (1982); Davis v. United States, 328 U.S. 582, 593, 66 S.Ct. 1256, 90 L.Ed. 1453 (1946); Zap v. United States, 328 U.S. 624, 630, 66 S.Ct. 1277, 90 L.Ed. 1477 (1946).

[2]Hall v. State, 239 Ga. 832, 238 S.E.2d 912 (1977); Hunter v. State, 190 Ga. App. 52, 53, 378 S.E.2d 338 (1989); Davis v. State, 192 Ga. App. 214, 384 S.E.2d 275 (1989); Eaves v. State of Georgia, 236 Ga. App. 279, 280 (2), 511 S.E.2d 621 (1999).

[3]See State v. Causey, 132 Ga. App. 17, 207 S.E.2d 225 (1974). A

search conducted pursuant to a valid consent must be reasonably limited to the area to which the consent was given. Hence, it has been held that a consent to search a residence does not ordinarily give officers the right to intercept incoming telephones calls.

[4]Love v. State, 144 Ga. App. 728, 733, 242 S.E.2d 278 (1978) (overruled on other grounds in Parker v. State, 161 Ga. App. 37, 288 S.E.2d 852 (1982). See State v. Austin, 310 Ga. App. 814, 714 S.E.2d 671 (2011); McNeil v. State, 248 Ga. App. 70, 71, 545 S.E.2d 130 (2001) ("intrusiveness of the search is limited by the permission granted").

[5]State v. Corley, 201 Ga. App. 320, 323, 411 S.E.2d 324 (1991).

[6]United States v. Elliott, 107 F.3d 810 (10th Cir. 1997).

what you got in there? I don't want to look through each item." The officer also testified that he told the defendant he just wanted to see how things were packed. The defendant responded by releasing the trunk latch. The court held that this consent did not authorize the officer to conduct a thorough search of the contents of a bag located in the trunk. However, as pointed out in *Caster v. State,*[7] a consent to a thorough search of everything found in a car is not limited "to a 'look inside' or 'in' the car and its contents." Thus, in *Caster* the court affirmed a finding that, because of the consent, an officer noticing a loose back seat was authorized to lift it and observe contraband.

It has been pointed out that "[c]onsent may be as limited as the consenter wishes. . . . The suspect is not required to call a halt when the search has gone beyond the scope of consent given; the burden remains on the [s]tate to show that the scope of the officer's search did not exceed the permission given."[8] Thus, in *State v. Neese,*[9] police were deemed to have exceeded the scope of the defendant's consent to search his backpack for identification and weapons when the police unscrewed a small flashlight and found crystal methamphetamine. However, where a general consent to search is given, its validity should be regarded as continuing until the consent is revoked or otherwise withdrawn.[10] Nonetheless, mere "acquiescence to a claim of lawful authority" will not suffice as consent to extend a *Terry* pat-down into a more intrusive search.[11]

Where two or more officers undertake a warrantless search and one officer discovers contraband without actually knowing that one of the other officers has obtained a valid consent to search, the consent legitimized the search.[12] In *State v. Sutton,*[13] the court held that a valid written consent executed after a prior warrantless entry ratified the prior search.

The burden of proof is on the prosecution to show that the

[7]Caster v. State, 210 Ga. App. 809, 811 (3), 437 S.E.2d 608 (1993).

[8]Springsteen v. State, 206 Ga. App. 150, 152, 424 S.E.2d 832 (1992).

[9]State v. Neese, 302 Ga. App. 829, 691 S.E.2d 883 (2010).

[10]McDaniel v. State, 227 Ga. App. 364, 366 (2), 489 S.E.2d 112 (1997); Bell v. State, 162 Ga. App. 79, 81, 290 S.E.2d 187 (1982); Mixon v. State, 184 Ga. App. 623, 624, 362 S.E.2d 111 (1987).

[11]Johnson v. State, 297 Ga. App. 847, 678 S.E.2d 539 (2009) (consent to *Terry* pat-down not shown to extend to officer's request that passenger in vehicle turn over identification card).

[12]Atkins v. State, 173 Ga. App. 9, 12 (4), 325 S.E.2d 388 (1984) (implication), rev'd on other grounds, 254 Ga. 641, 331 S.E.2d 597 (1985). See Annot., "Effect of Retroactive Consent on Legality of Otherwise Unlawful Search and Seizure," 76 A.L.R.5th 563 (2000).

[13]State v. Sutton, 258 Ga. 382 (2), 369 S.E.2d 249 (1988).

consent was, in fact, freely and voluntarily given.[14] "The proper standard for a trial court's determination of whether there is consent to search is preponderance of the evidence," and it is not necessary for the judge to find beyond a reasonable doubt that consent was given.[15] The same standard applies in determining the voluntariness of a consent to a search as pertains to confessions.[16] Thus, a court looks to the totality of the surrounding circumstances.

In determining the question of voluntariness, the United States Supreme Court has considered such factors as the youth of the accused, his lack of education, failure to be informed of his constitutional rights, length of detention, prolonged nature of questioning, deprivation of food or sleep, and the psychological impact of these things on the accused.[17] In *Schneckloth v. Bustamonte*,[18] the United States Supreme Court held no single factor is controlling. In *Rogers v. State*,[19] the court held that even where a person has been seized, if his "subsequent search was pursuant to a voluntary consent which was not a product of the illegal detention, the taint of that illegal detention would not require suppression of the evidence." In *VonLinsowe v. State*,[20] the court held that where a defendant is being unlawfully detained, if the

---

[14]Bumper v. North Carolina, 391 U.S. 543, 548, 88 S.Ct. 1788, 20 L.Ed.2d 797 (1968); Clare v. State, 135 Ga. App. 281, 284 (3), 217 S.E.2d 638 (1975). See Lewis v. U.S., 385 U.S. 206, 87 S. Ct. 424, 17 L. Ed. 2d 312 (1966) (where defendant's home is converted to a commercial center to which outsiders are invited for purpose of conducting unlawful business, government agent can accept invitation to do business and enter premises without a search warrant).

[15]State v. Barnett, 233 Ga. App. 496, 497 (2), 504 S.E.2d 531 (1998).

[16]Schneckloth v. Bustamonte, 412 U.S. 218, 229, 93 S.Ct. 2041, 36 L.Ed.2d 854 (1973). In United States v. Watson, 423 U.S. 411, 96 S.Ct. 820, 46 L.Ed.2d 598, 609 (1976), in the context of the Fourth Amendment stated there may be a valid consent even though the defendant does not know he has a right to refuse to consent. Generally, see Annot., "Validity, Under Federal Constitution, of Consent to Search—Supreme Court Cases," 36 L.Ed.2d 1143 (1974). See Olevik v. State, 302 Ga. 228, 806

S.E.2d 505 (2017) (compelling a DUI suspect to undergo a breath test violates a person's right not to incriminate himself; Georgia's implied consent warning is not per se coercive).

[17]In Martinez v. State, 239 Ga. App. 662, 663, 522 S.E.2d 53 (1999), the court pointed out that whether or not a consent to search was voluntary "is determined by the totality of the circumstances, 'including such factors as the age of the accused, his education, his intelligence, the length of detention, whether the accused was advised of his constitutional rights, the prolonged nature of questioning, the use of physical punishment, and the psychological impact of all these factors on the accused.' "

[18]Schneckloth v. Bustamonte, 412 U.S. 218, 226, 93 S.Ct. 2041, 36 L.Ed.2d 854, 862 (1973).

[19]Rogers v. State, 206 Ga. App. 654, 660 (4), 426 S.E.2d 209 (1992).

[20]VonLinsowe v. State, 213 Ga. App. 619, 622 (2), 445 S.E.2d 371 (1994).

search was pursuant to a voluntary consent which was not a product of the illegal detention, the illegal detention would not require suppression of the evidence seized. "However, in order to eliminate any taint from an involuntary seizure or arrest, there must be proof both that the consent was voluntary and that it was not the product of the illegal detention. Proof of a voluntary consent alone is not sufficient. The relevant factors include temporal proximity of an illegal seizure and consent, intervening circumstances, and the purpose and flagrancy of the official misconduct."

In *Bowers v. State,*[21] the defendant was stopped for "changing lanes without using a turn signal." There were no other vehicles in the area. After the defendant had been questioned in the cold for about 20 minutes, the defendant "consented" to a search of the car and contraband was found. The trial court denied a motion to suppress which the appellate court reversed. The court pointed out that a turn signal need not be given when the movement can be made with reasonable safety. There was no objective manifestation that the person being stopped was or was "about to be engaged in criminal activity." There was no significant lapse of time or intervening circumstances between the unlawful detention and the consent. "Therefore, . . . the consent was the product of the illegal detention. . . ." Likewise, in *Bolton v. State,*[22] the Court of Appeals determined that the consent to search in that case was tainted by the police. If there is a lack of valid consent or a lack of exigent circumstances, any entry onto the subject premises is unreasonable. Thus any consent to search after an unwarranted entry or any evidence recovered in such a search would be considered tainted and thus subject to suppression.

In order to show a valid consent, it is not always essential for an officer to inform a person of his Fourth Amendment protections or his right to refuse to consent.[23] However, a judge may "consider the absence of any attempt by . . . [an officer] to advise defendant of his constitutional rights . . ." in determining whether the State failed to satisfy its burden.[24] In *State v. Westmoreland,*[25] an officer, without articulable suspicion, asked the defendant and others if they would consent to be searched. The defendant asked if the officer had a search warrant. The officer replied that he did not need a warrant. The court pointed out

[21]Bowers v. State, 221 Ga. App. 886, 473 S.E.2d 201 (1996). See Hernandez-Espino v. State, 324 Ga. App. 849, 752 S.E.2d 10 (2013).

[22]Bolton v. State, 258 Ga. App. 217, 573 S.E.2d 479 (2002).

[23]Schneckloth v. Bustamonte, 412 U.S. 218, 234, 93 S.Ct. 2041, 36 L.Ed.2d 854, 862 (1973).

[24]State v. Norrington, 203 Ga. App. 574, 575, 417 S.E.2d 203 (1992).

[25]State v. Westmoreland, 204 Ga. App. 312, 314 (2), 418 S.E.2d 822 (1992).

that the answer was not true. It was held that when the evidence shows that a defendant must consent, "such evidence weighs heavily against a finding that [a] consent was voluntary."

If a suspect is given *Miranda* warnings and is informed that the results of a search may be used against him, the search is not considered the result of illegal coercion simply because there is no showing that he knew he could withhold his consent.[26]

Where consent is obtained through coercion, it will not be deemed voluntary. In *Bumper v. North Carolina*,[27] the consent to a search of a house by the defendant's grandmother was held to be involuntary where an officer falsely claimed to have a search warrant. Deception on the part of an officer may prevent a consent from being valid.[28]

In *Darby v. State*,[29] the court held that "[w]hen an officer represents to an accused that a warrant to search will be obtained if consent [to search] is refused and [the officer] does not have probable cause to secure the warrant, then the accused's consent is invalid." However, it has been held that deception on the part of an officer does not automatically prevent a consent from being valid,[30] unless the method used offends due process.[31] Thus, a consent to search is not invalid for the reason that the consent was given to an officer working outside his jurisdiction.[32]

In *State v. Sims*,[33] the Court of Appeals explained in the context of a warrantless search of an automobile that it is the unreasonable search and seizure which is prohibited by the Fourth Amendment. "The 'touchstone . . . is reasonableness' . . . [which] . . ., in turn, is measured in objective terms by examining the totality of the circumstances."[34] Thus, "if the officer *continues to detain* the subject after the conclusion of the traffic stop

---

[26]United States v. Watson, 423 U.S. 411, 96 S.Ct. 820, 46 L.Ed.2d 598, 609 (1976).

[27]Bumper v. North Carolina, 391 U.S. 543, 88 S.Ct. 1788, 20 L.Ed.2d 797 (1968); Lo-Ji Sales, Inc. v. New York, 442 U.S. 319, 99 S.Ct. 2319, 60 L.Ed.2d 920 (1979).

[28]Graves v. Beto, 424 F.2d 524 (5th Cir. 1970). But cf. United States v. Hill, 508 F.2d 345 (5th Cir. 1975).

See Warner, Government Deception in Consent Searches, 34 U. Miami L. Rev. 57 (1979).

[29]Darby v. State, 216 Ga. App. 781, 783 (2), 455 S.E.2d 850 (1995). Accord, Palmer v. State, 257 Ga. App. 650 (2), 572 S.E.2d 27 (2002).

[30]Bagley v. State, 161 Ga. App. 688, 691, 288 S.E.2d 332 (1982); Suddeth v. State, 162 Ga. App. 460 (1), 291 S.E.2d 430 (1982); People v. Abrams, 95 A.D.2d 155, 465 N.Y.S.2d 208 (1983).

[31]Cf. Rogers v. Richmond, 365 U.S. 534, 81 S.Ct. 735, 5 L.Ed.2d 760 (1961); Frazier v. Cupp, 394 U.S. 731, 89 S.Ct. 1420, 22 L.Ed.2d 684 (1969) (confessions involved).

[32]State v. Rezvani, 181 Ga. App. 328, 352 S.E.2d 197 (1986).

[33]State v. Sims, 248 Ga. App. 277, 278, 546 S.E.2d 47 (2001).

[34]State v. Sims, 248 Ga. App. 277, 279, 546 S.E.2d 47 (2001), citing Florida v. Jimeno, 500 U.S. 248, 250,

and interrogates him to seek consent to search without reasonable suspicion of criminal activity, the officer has exceeded the scope of a permissible investigation of the initial traffic stop."[35] Accordingly, what may begin as a reasonable setting in which to conduct a search may progress to one which, because of its "intensity and scope," violates the Fourth Amendment.[36] The Court applied *Sims* in *Padron v. State*,[37] to exclude contraband discovered during the search of a motor vehicle belonging to a Spanish-speaking couple whose proficiency in English was suspect. Admitting that he was acting only on a "hunch" when he requested leave to search the vehicle, the officer discovered cocaine in a suitcase in the trunk after the apparent protest of the driver that the search terminate. The officer did not present the couple with departmental consent to search forms printed in Spanish and did not request an interpreter until after the arrest was effected. The Court concluded that the officer never had a reasonable basis for conducting the search and that any "consent" obtained by the officer was the result of the coercive nature of the couple's detention during the search.[38] *Salmeron v. State*,[39] has since displaced *Padron* and the notice that an officer cannot question an individual on matters outside the scope of the reason for the stop. Instead, the court in *Salmeron* said the inquiry should be whether the police questioning unduly *prolonged* the detention initiated by the reason for the stop.

It has been held that the refusal of the defendant to consent to a search is not admissible since a defendant is not to be penalized for exercising a constitutional right.[40]

See § 26:19, note 37, infra, on the validity of consent to warrantless searches as a condition of probation. Generally, see 2 LaFave, *Search and Seizure,* §§ 8.1 et seq. (West 1978). See § 3:11, supra, on extension of the *Terry* frisk. See § 4:2, supra, on admission because of misplaced confidence or deception. See § 5:10, infra, on statement made in presence of an acquaintance on the mistaken belief that the statement would not be revealed. See § 4:53, infra, on the nature of search of automobile permitted. See Studdard, *Daniel's Georgia Handbook on Criminal Evidence* (2018 ed.), § 7:26, on the use which may be made of blood drawn

---

111 S.Ct. 1801, 114 L.Ed.2d 297 (1991); Ohio v. Robinette, 519 U.S. 33, 39, 117 S.Ct. 417, 136 L.Ed.2d 347 (1996).

[35]State v. Sims, 248 Ga. App. 277, 279, 546 S.E.2d 47 (2001) (emphasis in original).

[36]State v. Sims, 248 Ga. App. 277, 279, 546 S.E.2d 47 (2001).

[37]Padron v. State, 254 Ga. App. 265, 562 S.E.2d 244 (2002).

[38]Padron v. State, 254 Ga. App. 265, 269-270, 562 S.E.2d 244 (2002).

[39]Salmeron v. State, 280 Ga. 735, 632 S.E.2d 645 (2006).

[40]People v. Redmond, 111 Cal.App.3d 742, 169 Cal.Rptr. 253 (1980).

from a driver under the implied consent statute.

§ 4:33 Warrantless searches—Valid consent by defendant

If the state seeks to justify a warrantless search on the theory that the defendant consented to the search, it "has the burden of proving that the consent was, *in fact,* freely and voluntarily given."[1] In *State v. Williams,*[2] the Georgia Court of Appeals pointed out that "although silence in the face of a request for permission to search may, when accompanied by other conduct, sometimes be interpreted as acquiescence, such 'acquiescence cannot . . . substitute for free consent.' " It has been held that if a search is "consented to" because the officer says he has a search warrant, the consent is not valid.[3] In *Murphy v. State,*[4] the court held that "[w]hen an officer represents to an accused that a warrant to search will be obtained if consent is refused, and does not have probable cause to secure a warrant, then the accused's consent is invalid." Likewise, a defendant who provides his consent to search after the police represent that they have the authority to enter and search the premises against the will of the defendant, if necessary, can still claim that the consent was not voluntary.[5] "Consent which is the product of coercion or deceit on the part of the police is invalid. Consent is not voluntary when it is the result of duress or coercion, express or implied."[6]

Some cases have treated a consent much like a confession and have concluded that if the consent was given because of an induced hope of reward, it is invalid. But generally, the validity of a defendant's consent to a search is determined by a totality of the circumstances.[7] For example: (1) The fact that the defendant was in custody at the time the consent was given does not alone

---

[Section 4:33]

[1]Clare v. State, 135 Ga. App. 281, 284 (3), 217 S.E.2d 638 (1975) (citing Bumper v. North Carolina, 391 U.S. 543, 548, 88 S.Ct. 1788, 20 L.Ed.2d 797 (1968)).

[2]State v. Williams, 212 Ga. App. 164, 165 (1), 441 S.E.2d 501 (1994).

[3]See Bumper v. North Carolina, 391 U.S. 543, 548, 88 S.Ct. 1788, 20 L.Ed.2d 797 (1968).

[4]Murphy v. State, 230 Ga. App. 365, 496 S.E.2d 512 (1998) (quoting Darby v. State, 216 Ga. App. 781, 455 S.E.2d 850 (1995)).

[5]State v. Jones, 269 Ga. App. 325, 604 S.E.2d 228 (2004).

[6]State v. Jourdan, 264 Ga. App. 118, 120 (1), 589 S.E.2d 682 (2003). Compare United States v. Spivey, 861 F.3d 1207 (11th Cir. 2017) (deceit employed by agent to obtain defendant's consent to search premises did not render consent involuntary).

[7]Schneckloth v. Bustamonte, 412 U.S. 218, 223, 93 S.Ct. 2041, 36 L.Ed.2d 854 (1973); Fazio v. State, 302 Ga. 295, 806 S.E.2d 544 (2017) (compelling a DUI suspect to undergo a breath test violates a person's right not to incriminate himself; consent warning is not per se coercive).

In United States v. McCraney, 705 F.2d 449 (5th Cir. 1983), the defendant was arrested and demanded that he be allowed to consult with his at-

show that it was coerced.[8] (2) The absence of proof that the defendant knew he could withhold his consent does not alone prevent the consent from being valid.[9] (3) A threat to obtain a warrant does not alone invalidate the consent.[10] In *Blitch v. State*,[11] the fact that the defendant was in handcuffs at the time he gave consent to search his automobile did not preclude a determination that the consent was voluntary where the defendant was advised of the reason for the stop and there was no evidence to suggest coercion or deceit on the part of the officer. However, all of these factors may be considered under the totality of the circumstances.[12] In *Setser v. State*,[13] the court held that "[a]lthough [a defendant's] consent may have been the product of his erroneous assumption, based on previous arrests, that the officers would proceed with a search anyway, such an erroneous assumption does not constitute coercion . . . and . . . [t]he consent was valid."

In *Lane v. State*,[14] the court held that "[a] warrantless search may be upheld if the law enforcement officer conducting the

---

torney. The court held that under these circumstances it is necessary for the prosecution to show that the defendant "by his own considered decision elected to permit the search without first consulting an attorney." In this case, the court relied upon Edwards v. Arizona, 451 U.S. 477, 101 S.Ct. 1880, 68 L.Ed.2d 378 (1981), which is discussed in § 5:20, infra. See State v. Brogan, 340 Ga. App. 232, 797 S.E.2d 149 (2017).

[8]Woodruff v. State, 233 Ga. 840, 844 (3), 213 S.E.2d 689 (1975); Crider v. State, 114 Ga. App. 523 (1), 151 S.E.2d 792 (1966). However, it has been held that in a custodial situation there is increased possibility of coercion and the burden on the prosecution increases when the defendant's alleged consent was given while he was in custody. United States v. Wiener, 534 F.2d 15 (2d Cir. 1976); Hayes v. Cady, 500 F.2d 1212 (7th Cir. 1974); Dean v. State, 250 Ga. 77, 80, 295 S.E.2d 306 (1982).

[9]United States v. Watson, 423 U.S. 411, 96 S.Ct. 820, 46 L.Ed.2d 598 (1976). See State v. Durrence, 295 Ga. App. 216, 671 S.E.2d 261 (2008).

[10]Barlow v. State, 280 A.2d 703 (Del.1971); Bailey v. State, 147 Ga.

App. 621, 622, 249 S.E.2d 675 (1978). But see Poe v. Oklahoma City, 483 P.2d 1190 (Okla.Crim.App. 1971); Cuevas v. State, 151 Ga. App. 605, 609, 260 S.E.2d 737 (1979).

In Code v. State, 234 Ga. 90, 95, 214 S.E.2d 873 (1975), the court stated that a threat to get a search warrant did not invalidate a consent to a search if the officer had probable cause to obtain a warrant.

[11]Blitch v. State, 323 Ga. App. 677, 747 S.E.2d 863 (2013). See Maloy v. State, 293 Ga. App. 648, 667 S.E.2d 688 (2008).

[12]U.S. v. Patayan Soriano, 361 F.3d 494, 501-09 (9th Cir. 2004) (government has burden to show "consent was freely and voluntarily given" based upon inter alia (1) whether the defendant was in custody; (2) whether the arresting officers had their guns drawn; (3) whether Miranda warnings were given; (4) whether the defendant was notified that she had a right not to consent; and (5) whether the defendant had been told a search warrant could be obtained).

[13]Setser v. State, 209 Ga. App. 57, 59 (2), 432 S.E.2d 652 (1993).

[14]Lane v. State, 250 Ga. App. 160, 162, 549 S.E.2d 468 (2001).

search *reasonably* (albeit erroneously) believes the consent given was valid." (emphasis in original.)

In *Ohio v. Robinette*,[15] the United States Supreme Court held that where a driver is stopped for a traffic offense, the failure of the officer to tell the driver that he was "free to go" did not alone prevent the driver's consent to search from being voluntary. The court emphasized (1) that the subjective thoughts of the officer are immaterial when he asks a driver to get out of the car if the officer was objectively justified in doing so; and (2) that the voluntariness of a consent "is a question of fact to be determined from all the circumstances."

Often the voluntariness of the defendant's consent turns on the meaning intended by his words,[16] and it must be kept in mind that what may be a consent as to others may not always be regarded as a consent to law enforcement officers.[17]

In *Gonzales v. State*,[18] the Court of Appeals observed that once the investigation associated with a routine traffic stop has terminated, additional questioning or further searching of the vehicle must close in the absence of reasonable suspicion or valid consent. In this case, after stopping the defendants because of a partially obscured license plate, the officers continued questioning one of the defendants about whether there was any contraband in his car and searching the vehicle even after being told that the defendants would not consent to the search. The officer contended that his "reasonable suspicion" for the search was justified by the "nervousness" of the defendants. The Court ruled that "nervousness" without more is not sufficient to establish reasonable suspicion for detention and investigation for illicit drug activity.

Acquiescence to apparent authority where the defendant is under arrest is not necessarily regarded as consent, and this seems to be particularly true if the defendant is under illegal arrest, or if an illegal search of one area has already taken place.[19] The Eleventh Circuit has said "that the standard remains the

---

[15]Ohio v. Robinette, 519 U.S. 33, 117 S.Ct. 417, 136 L.Ed.2d 347 (1996).

[16]Zimmerman v. State, 131 Ga. App. 793, 207 S.E.2d 220 (1974). In this case, officers searched a warehouse with a warrant for weapons. In the process three typewriters were found in the storage area, covered with yellow plastic bags, and carried to the office. No weapons were found. The defendant told the officers they could take the typewriters which later turned out to have been stolen. The

consent was said to have been invalid since it was given after the seizure.

[17]Ivins v. State, 129 Ga. App. 865, 868, 201 S.E.2d 683 (1973).

[18]Gonzales v. State, 255 Ga. App. 149, 564 S.E.2d 552 (2002). See Adkins v. State, 298 Ga. App. 229, 679 S.E.2d 793 (2009). Cf. United States v. Simms, 385 F.3d 1347 (11th Cir. 2004).

[19]See, U.S. v. Jenson, 462 F.3d 399 (5th Cir. 2006); U.S. v. Freymuller, 571 F. Supp. 61 (N.D. Ill. 1983). See also, Johnson v. State, 297 Ga. App.

same whether the defendant is in custody under arrest or merely stopped at the time of consent."[20] A threat to arrest a defendant and all occupants of a house if a consent is not given may render the consent invalid.[21] "Consent which is the product of coercion or deceit on the part of the police is invalid. Consent is not voluntary when it is the result of duress or coercion, express or implied."[22]

A condition of a defendant's probation in a previous case that he submit himself, his premises, or motor vehicle to search by any law enforcement officer, and that any evidence seized is admissible against the defendant, was held in *State v. Bethune*[23] to amount to a consent. In *State v. Hall*,[24] the court affirmed the granting of a motion to suppress where a defendant was told that if he did not consent to a search of a car, the car would be impounded and he "would be arrested until they get a search warrant from the judge." See § 26:19, infra, on consent to search as condition of probation.

In *Pupo v. State*,[25] the court pointed out that to the extent the driver of a car had no authority to consent to a search, he clearly lacked standing to complain that the search violated the Fourth Amendment.

In *Beasley v. State*,[26] the defendant consented to a urine test after he was told that the purpose of the results of the test were to be used in connection with the defendant's request for a bond. After the defendant tested positive for cocaine, he was charged with possession of cocaine. The court concluded that the consent was not voluntary since he had not been informed that he might be supplying evidence against himself in an independent criminal prosecution. However, in *Gadson v. State*,[27] the defendant was arrested for assaulting a victim. He was given his *Miranda* rights and was asked for a sample of blood. He consented and signed a form consenting to give his blood without a search warrant and

---

847, 678 S.E.2d 539 (2009).

[20]United States v. Espinosa-Orlando, 704 F.2d 507 (11th Cir. 1983).

[21]State v. Reid, 167 Ga. App. 81, 306 S.E.2d 61 (1983).

[22]State v. Jourdan, 264 Ga. App. 118, 120 (1), 589 S.E.2d 682 (2003). Compare United States v. Spivey, 861 F.3d 1207 (11th Cir. 2017) (deceit employed by agent to obtain defendant's consent to search premises did not render consent involuntary).

[23]State v. Bethune, 207 Ga. App. 340 (2), 427 S.E.2d 795 (1993).

[24]State v. Hall, 229 Ga. App. 194, 196 (2), 493 S.E.2d 718 (1997).

[25]Pupo v. State, 187 Ga. App. 765, 767 (5), 371 S.E.2d 219 (1988).

[26]Beasley v. State, 204 Ga. App. 214, 216, 419 S.E.2d 92 (1992). See Andrews v. State, 331 Ga. App. 353, 771 S.E.2d 59 (2015) (consent to DNA test given for purposes of determining paternity could be used in criminal prosecution of statutory rape where defendant was told by police that DNA test could be used in criminal case).

[27]Gadson v. State, 223 Ga. App. 342, 345 (4), 477 S.E.2d 598 (1996).

stating that anything found could be used as evidence in any court. The appellate court affirmed the admission of DNA evidence based on the blood in view of the defendant's freely and voluntarily given consent with "no limits on the scope of his consent." See Studdard, *Daniel's Georgia Handbook on Criminal Evidence* (2018 ed.), § 7:26, on DNA examination of blood taken from driver under implied consent.

In *Cole v. State*,[28] the court concluded that the defendant's consent to search his automobile was voluntary following a valid traffic stop made because of an improper lane change. After stopping the vehicle, the officer detected the smell of marijuana and requested permission to search the vehicle. The officer did admit that he might have stated that if the defendant did not consent, he would get a drug dog. The court ruled that the State did not have to affirmatively show that the officer did not make the statement. Rather, it is "up to the trial court to consider the weight to be given the possibility that it was made."[29]

In *Fincher v. State*,[30] the Court of Appeals noted that under appropriate circumstances the State may prove that consent to search given by the defendant or by an authorized third party after a search will serve to validate an otherwise illegal search.

See § 26:19, infra, on validity of consent to search as a condition of probation. See Annotation, "When is Consent Voluntarily Given so as to Justify Search Conducted on Basis of That Consent—Supreme Court Cases," 148 A.L.R.Fed. 271 (1998).

§ 4:34 Warrantless searches—Valid consent by third person

In *Illinois v. Rodriguez*,[1] the United States Supreme Court held that concerning the validity of a consent to search by a third person, the "consent to enter must 'be judged against an objective standard: would the facts available to the officer at the moment . . . warrant a man of reasonable caution in the belief that the consenting party had authority over the premises?' . . . If not, then warrantless entry without further inquiry is unlawful unless authority actually exists." Thus, "a warrantless search based on unauthorized consent could nonetheless be upheld if the law enforcement officer conducting the search *reasonably* (albeit erro-

---

[28]Cole v. State, 254 Ga. App. 424 (2), 562 S.E.2d 720 (2002).

[29]Cole v. State, 254 Ga. App. 424, 425, 562 S.E.2d 720 (2002). See U.S. v. Castillo, 866 F.2d 1071, 1082 (9th Cir. 1988).

[30]Fincher v. State, 276 Ga. 480, 578 S.E.2d 102 (2003).

[Section 4:34]

[1]Illinois v. Rodriguez, 497 U.S. 177, 110 S.Ct. 2793, 111 L.Ed.2d 148 (1990). Rodriguez was cited, quoted, and followed in Taylor v. State, 228 Ga. App. 325, 328 (1)(c), 491 S.E.2d 417 (1997).

neously) believed the consent given was valid."[2]

A person may consent to a search if he possesses "common authority over or other sufficient relationship to the premises or effects sought to be inspected."[3] The test is, do "the facts available to the officer at the moment warrant a man of reasonable caution in the belief that the consenting party had authority over the premises? If not, then warrantless entry without further inquiry is unlawful. . . ."[4]

Common authority means "mutual use of the property by persons generally having joint access or control for most purposes, so that it is reasonable to recognize that any of the co-inhabitants has the right to permit the inspection in his own right and that the others have assumed the risk that one of their number might permit the common area to be searched."[5] Thus, in *Atkins v. State*,[6] the court held that the defendant's 17-year-old brother had sufficient authority to give a valid consent.

In *Park v. State*,[7] officers went to the defendant's apartment and asked her 24-year-old daughter if she would mind looking around to see if she could find certain documents. The daughter consented. She found some of the documents which were given to the officers. The court did not regard this as a search by the officers and held the documents admissible.

In *Davis v. State*,[8] the Georgia Supreme Court considered a case in which the defendant's ten-year-old stepson called 911 to report drugs in his home. The child had a key to the house and called his mother as soon as he got in from school. His mother

---

[2]Ford v. State, 214 Ga. App. 284, 286 (3), 447 S.E.2d 334 (1994) (citation and punctuation omitted).

[3]People v. Adams, 53 N.Y.2d 1, 439 N.Y.S.2d 877, 422 N.E.2d 537, 540 (1981) (citing United States v. Matlock, 415 U.S. 164, 171, 94 S.Ct. 988, 39 L.Ed.2d 242 (1974)); Coolidge v. New Hampshire, 403 U.S. 443, 91 S.Ct. 2022, 29 L.Ed.2d 564 (1971); Frazier v. Cupp, 394 U.S. 731, 89 S.Ct. 1420, 22 L.Ed.2d 684 (1969); State v. Colvard, 296 Ga. 381, 768 S.E.2d 473 (2015); Tidwell v. State, 285 Ga. 103, 104 (2), 674 S.E.2d 272 (2009).

[4]Illinois v. Rodriguez, 497 U.S. 177, 188-89, 110 S. Ct. 2793, 111 L. Ed. 2d 148 (1990); State v. Rucker, 337 Ga. App. 875, 879, 789 S.E.2d 281 (2016).

[5]United States v. Matlock, 415 U.S. 164, 171 n. 7, 94 S.Ct. 988, 39 L.Ed.2d 242 (1974) (quoted with approval in Smith v. State, 264 Ga. 87, 88 (2), 441 S.E.2d 241 (1994)). In Turner v. State, 246 Ga. App. 49, 51 (2), 539 S.E.2d 553 (2000), the Georgia Court of Appeals quoted from Matlock that "[a] warrantless search of a residence may be authorized by the consent of any person who possesses a sufficient relationship to the premises to be inspected. . . ."

[6]Atkins v. State, 173 Ga. App. 9, 10 (2), 325 S.E.2d 388 (1984), rev'd on other grounds, 254 Ga. 641, 331 S.E.2d 597 (1985).

[7]Park v. State, 154 Ga. App. 348, 350 (4), 268 S.E.2d 401 (1980).

[8]Davis v. State, 262 Ga. 578, 422 S.E.2d 546 (1992).

came in from work about 4:30 p.m. He was not permitted to invite anyone into the house or to go outside during this period of about 1-½ hours. On the afternoon in question, he found what he believed to be drugs in his parents' bedroom. In making the call, the child acted on advice he received in a drug abuse class at school. In his call, he stated he would like to get some help for his parents. When the deputy arrived, he followed the child into the house and into the defendant's bedroom where the child obtained a mirror with white powder and a razor blade on it and pulled a bag of marijuana and "rolling papers" from a nightstand. The deputy saw a " 'marijuana joint' in an ashtray." The defendant contended that his stepson lacked authority to consent. The trial judge denied the motion to suppress. The Georgia Supreme Court held that the motion to suppress should have been granted. The court identified the following factors which should be considered in determining the validity of such a search: (1) "whether the minor lived on the premises; [2] whether the minor had a right of access to the premises and the right to invite others thereto; [3] whether the minor was of an age at which he or she could be expected to exercise at least minimal discretion; and [4] whether officers acted reasonably in believing that the minor had sufficient control over the premises to give a valid consent to search."

The court then emphasized the importance of examining "a child's mental maturity and his ability to understand the circumstances . . . and the consequences of his actions. . . . The younger a child the less likely that he or she can be said to have the minimal discretion required. . . ." The court concluded that based on the foregoing criteria, the child involved did not have authority to validly consent, the circumstances did not justify a finding of present danger to the child, nor were there exigent circumstances. Lastly, the court pointed out the facts of this case did not warrant affirmance under the "independent source" or "inevitable discovery exception." See § 2:27, supra, on the independent source exception, and § 2:28, supra, on the inevitable discovery exception. In 1997, Georgia enacted O.C.G.A. § 16-7-21, which provides that a minor may not permit a lawful entry if the "parent or guardian has previously given notice that such entry is forbidden or notice to depart." See Annotation, "Admissibility of Evidence Discovered in Search of Adult Defendant's Property or Residence Authorized by Defendant's Minor Child—State Cases," 51 A.L.R.5th 425 (1997). Also see Annotation, "Admissibility of Evidence Discovered in Search of Adult Defendant's Property or Residence Authorized by Defendant's Minor Relative," 152 A.L.R.Fed. 475 (1999) and Annotation, "Admissibility of Evidence Discovered in Search of a Defendant's Property or Residence Authorized by Defendant's Spouse (resident or nonresident)—State Cases," 65 A.L.R.5th (1999). However, the 1999 case of *Rainwater v. State*,[9] the court, relying on *Davis*, said a 15-year-old gave valid consent to search her home.

It has been held that a father may consent to the search of his son's car which is parked on the father's premises.[10] In *Fears v. State*,[11] the court said that when the defendant left a bag at his sister's house, he assumed the risk that she might consent to a search of the bag and her consent was valid. In *Varriano v. State*,[12] the consent of a vehicle's driver to search the entire car was sufficient to authorize the officer to search a passenger's closed book bag on the rear seat. However, in *State v. Colvard*,[13] the court found police could not have reasonably believed that the defendant's uncle had the authority to provide the police with consent to search the defendant's room in the uncle's house with whom defendant resided where it appeared that the defendant kept the door to his room locked preventing entry except with the use of force.

There have been cases involving all kinds of factual situations relating to third party consents. Some of the more significant situations will be mentioned here; others are referred to in the footnotes. Generally, a spouse or roommate can consent to a search of common premises.[14] In order for the consent of a third party to be valid, that party must possess "common authority

---

[9]Rainwater v. State, 240 Ga. App. 370, 523 S.E.2d 586 (1999).

[10]Tolbert v. State, 224 Ga. 291, 294, 161 S.E.2d 279 (1968). Accord, State v. West, 237 Ga. App. 185, 514 S.E.2d 257 (1999). See Soloman v. State, 143 Ga. App. 449, 238 S.E.2d 573 (1977); Marsh v. State, 223 Ga. 590 (1), 157 S.E.2d 273 (1967).

See Annots., "Admissibility of Evidence Discovered in Search of Defendant's Property or Residence Authorized by Defendant's Relative," 48 A.L.R.Fed. 131 (1980); "Admissibility of Evidence Discovered in Search of Defendant's Property or Residence Authorized by Defendant's Spouse (Resident or Nonresident)—State Cases," 1 A.L.R.4th 673 (1980).

[11]Fears v. State, 152 Ga. App. 817, 264 S.E.2d 284 (1979).

See Annot., "Admissibility of Evidence Discovered in Search of Defendant's Property or Residence Authorized by Defendant's Adult Relative Other Than Spouse—State Cases," 4 A.L.R.4th 196 (1981).

[12]Varriano v. State, 312 Ga. App. 266, 718 S.E.2d 14 (2011).

[13]State v. Colvard, 296 Ga. 381, 768 S.E.2d 473 (2015).

[14]United States v. Thompson, 421 F.2d 373 (5th Cir. 1970), judgment vacated on other grounds, 400 U.S. 17, 91 S.Ct. 122, 27 L.Ed.2d 17 (1970). This seems to be true even if the spouse is a common-law spouse, United States v. Matlock, 415 U.S. 164, 94 S.Ct. 988, 39 L.Ed.2d 242 (1974); and the same thing applies to a paramour if the premises have been jointly occupied for some time, White v. United States, 444 F.2d 724 (10th Cir. 1971).

See Annots., "Admissibility of Evidence Discovered in Search of Defendant's Property or Residence Authorized by Defendant's Spouse," 1 A.L.R.4th 673 (1980); "Admissibility of Evidence Discovered in Search of Defendant's Property or Residence Authorized by One, Other Than Relative, Who Is Co-Tenant or Common Resident With Defendant—State Cases," 4 A.L.R.4th 1050 (1981).

over or other sufficient relationship to the premises or effects sought to be inspected."[15] Hence, the mere fact that a third person was present in a house does not mean that the third person could validly consent to a search of the house.[16] However, in *Dover v. State*,[17] the court held that where a husband had given his mother-in-law a key to his house and said she was welcome at any time, she had authority to enter the house in the absence of the owner and to consent to a search of the house when the circumstances reasonably indicated it might be necessary in the interest of the householders or safeguarding the house. The owner of a car may turn over to officers luggage of an acquaintance which has been placed in the automobile.[18] However, in *United States v. Welch*,[19] the court held that the consent of a male to search a rental car did not authorize the search of a purse found in the trunk which belonged to his female companion. If the owner of a car is present and the driver consents to a search, the driver's consent has been considered sufficient.[20] An employer may give a valid consent to a search of the employer's truck which is driven by an employee.[21] In *United States v. Jenkins*,[22] the Court concluded that a driver of a rig has apparent authority to consent to a search of the trailer. A taxi cab driver's consent to search his cab extended to a passenger's bag which was within "easy reach" of the driver, ownership of the bag was not determined until after the search occurred, and "the bag was not secured in any way."[23] On the other hand, a hotel clerk cannot validly consent to the search of a guest's room until it is vacated;[24] a landlord cannot validly consent to the search of his tenant's

---

[15]United States v. Matlock, 415 U.S. 164, 171, 94 S.Ct. 988, 39 L.Ed.2d 242 (1974).

[16]State v. Floyd, 161 Ga. App. 49, 50, 289 S.E.2d 8 (1982). See State v. Holtzclaw, 341 Ga. App. 639, 802 S.E.2d 254 (2017) (visitor in home of defendant had no authority to consent to police search of premises). See also Kennebrew v. State, 299 Ga. 864, 792 S.E.2d 695 (2016) (consent of defendant's girlfriend to search her dorm room did not authorize police to take items that police knew belonged to someone else).

[17]Dover v. State, 250 Ga. 209, 211 (1), 296 S.E.2d 710 (1982).

[18]Mooney v. State, 243 Ga. 373, 374, 254 S.E.2d 337 (1979), abrogated on other grounds, Horton v. California, 496 U.S. 128, 110 S. Ct. 2301, 110 L.

Ed. 2d 112 (1990). See Wilder v. State, 290 Ga. 13, 717 S.E.2d 457 (2011).

[19]United States v. Welch, 4 F.3d 761 (9th Cir. 1993).

[20]Pupo v. State, 187 Ga. App. 765, 767 (5), 371 S.E.2d 219 (1988).

[21]Braddock v. State, 127 Ga. App. 513, 194 S.E.2d 317 (1972).

[22]United States v. Jenkins, 92 F.3d 430 (6th Cir. 1996).

[23]U.S. v. Barber, 777 F.3d 1303 (11th Cir. 2015) (court found that the passenger had reasonable expectation of privacy and standing to bring motion).

[24]Stoner v. California, 376 U.S. 483, 84 S.Ct. 889, 11 L.Ed.2d 856 (1964). See Bowden v. State, 304 Ga. App. 896, 698 S.E.2d 372 (2010) (director of housing authority not authorized

quarters;[25] and a nurse cannot consent to a search of a patient's clothing.[26] See Annotation, "Admissibility of Evidence Discovered in Warrantless Search of Rental Property Authorized by Lessor of Property—State Cases," 61 A.L.R.5th 149 (1998).

In *Browning v. State,*[27] the court said, "An officer's belief that a third party has authority to consent to the search of another person's property should not only be based on information previously obtained in his investigation, but should also be based on the facts and circumstances existent at the time of the search." In *State v. Gray,*[28] the court noted: "[t]o resolve the issue of third party consent, we must determine whether the objective facts available to the officer at the time would warrant a person of reasonable caution to conclude that the third person had authority over the premises."

In determining whether a consent given by a third party is voluntary, the "totality of circumstances" test is applicable,[29] but it is not always necessary for the prosecution to establish that the

---

to give police consent to search absent tenant's apartment).

[25]Browning v. State, 176 Ga. App. 420, 421 (1), 336 S.E.2d 41 (1985); Chapman v. United States, 365 U.S. 610, 81 S.Ct. 776, 5 L.Ed.2d 828 (1961); State v. Oliver, 183 Ga. App. 92, 94, 357 S.E.2d 889 (1987).

In Warner v. State, 299 Ga. App. 56, 681 S.E.2d 624 (2009), the court found the parents were acting as heads of household as opposed to landlords when they allowed the search of their son's room while he was home from college. Additionally, the court held that "even if the parents in fact did not have the authority to consent to a search of Warner's bedroom, the circumstances led the police to reasonably believe that the parents had that authority, and therefore the search was valid." Cf., Looney v. State, 293 Ga. App. 639, 667 S.E.2d 893 (2008) (where search held unlawful when the landlord was the tenant's parent despite officer's good faith belief that the parent had authority to consent).

See Annots., "Admissibility of Evidence Discovered in Warrantless Search of Rental Property Authorized by Lessor of Such Property—State Cases," 2 A.L.R.4th 1173 (1980); "Admissibility of Evidence Discovered in

Warrantless Search of Rental Property Authorized by Lessor of Such Property—State Cases," 2 A.L.R.4th 1173 (1980).

[26]Commonwealth v. Silo, 480 Pa. 15, 389 A.2d 62 (1978).

[27]Browning v. State, 176 Ga. App. 420, 336 S.E.2d 41 (1985). See, e.g., Hunt v. State, 302 Ga. App. 578, 691 S.E.2d 368 (2010) (suppression motion improperly denied where consent to search house provided by individual who may have informed police prior to search that he did not live there and police had no information about the homeowner or residents before knocking on the door).

[28]State v. Gray, 285 Ga. App. 124, 127, 645 S.E.2d 598 (2007). See Tidwell v. State, 285 Ga. 103, 104(1), 674 S.E.2d 272 (2009) (police needed a warrant to search defendant's private locker used in connection with sleeping quarters at work despite receiving permission to search the facility from a co-worker).

[29]In Traylor v. State, 165 Ga. App. 226, 227, 299 S.E.2d 911 (1983), the court held that "tacit consent" to a sheriff's seizure of shoes may be sufficient.

In Rajappa v. State, 200 Ga.

person who consented knew that he had a right to refuse to consent.[30]

An interesting question posed to the Georgia Court of Appeals was the validity of a consent to search given by one occupant to a premises where another occupant, also present at the time, had already refused such access to the police. In *Randolph v. State*,[31] the court concluded that in a case involving a married couple, one spouse could not waive the other's right to privacy by allowing a police search in their residence after the other spouse had refused to permit the search. The court's decision was upheld by the Supreme Court of Georgia and the U.S. Supreme Court granted certiorari in order to resolve a split of authority among the Federal Courts of Appeal. In *Georgia v. Randolph*,[32] the U.S. Supreme Court affirmed the judgment of the Supreme Court of Georgia, making clear, however, that their decision is strictly limited to those situations involving a physically present co-occupant objector.[33] *Randolph* should not affect the capacity of the police to protect victims of domestic violence. For example, if the consenting occupant inside the dwelling indicates that he or

---

App. 372, 374 (3), 408 S.E.2d 163 (1991), the court said, "In cases where the person consenting to the search has not attained the age of eighteen, the courts have measured the minor's control over the area searched by examining whether the minor lived on the premises, whether the minor had a right of access to the premises and the right to invite others thereto; whether the minor was of an age at which he or she could be expected to exercise at least minimal discretion; and whether officers acted reasonably in believing that the minor had sufficient control over the premises to give a valid consent to search."

[30]Schneckloth v. Bustamonte, 412 U.S. 218, 232, 93 S.Ct. 2041, 36 L.Ed.2d 854 (1973).

[31]Randolph v. State, 264 Ga. App. 396, 590 S.E.2d 834 (2003), affirmed, 278 Ga. 614, 604 S.E.2d 835 (2003), affirmed, Georgia v. Randolph, 547 U.S. 103, 126 S.Ct. 1515, 164 L.Ed.2d 208 (2002). As the concurring opinions and the dissent in this case indicate, the implications of this case could be far reaching. Compare United States v. Bacus, 33 F.3d 62 (10th Cir. 1994).

[32]Georgia v. Randolph, 126 S. Ct. 1515, 164 L. Ed. 2d 208 (U.S. 2006). Compare Spence v. State, 281 Ga. 697, 642 S.E.2d 856 (2007) where subsequent consent by defendant's roommate trumped a defective warrant; Valle v. State, 282 Ga. App. 223, 638 S.E.2d 394 (2006), where consent to search by one occupant made search lawful as to *that* occupant even though other occupant did not consent. In Preston v. State, 296 Ga. App. 655, 675 S.E.2d 553 (2009), the court held that Randolph excludes evidence obtained from a search to which a non-present co-occupant consented but to which the present co-occupant did not expressly consent.

[33]Georgia v. Randolph, 126 S. Ct. 1515, 1527, 164 L. Ed. 2d 208 (U.S. 2006). Justice Souter explicitly distinguished U.S. v. Matlock, 415 U.S. 164, 94 S. Ct. 988, 39 L. Ed. 2d 242 (1974) and Illinois v. Rodriguez, 497 U.S. 177, 110 S. Ct. 2793, 111 L. Ed. 2d 148 (1990), explaining that there is still a valid warrantless entry in the case of a potential objector who is nearby but not privy to the colloquy between his or her co-occupant and the police regarding consent.

she is in need of police protection, then police entry is justified regardless of the other occupant's refusal to consent.[34]

In *Fernandez v. California*,[35] the Supreme Court expanded on the *Randolph* holding. Here, police observed a suspect in a violent robbery run into an apartment building. Upon arrival they heard "sounds of screaming and fighting" coming from one of the apartments. A female answered the door and it was obvious that she had been in a fight, a fact which she confirmed. The defendant then appeared and told the police to leave. He was arrested for assaulting the woman. Later, the police returned and received the woman's consent to search the apartment. In the apartment, officers found gang paraphernalia, weapons and clothing worn by the robbery suspect. The Court held that "[A]n occupant who is absent due to a lawful detention or arrest stands in the same shoes as an occupant who is absent for any other reason." The test for whether the detention of the absent occupant is simply pre-text so police can get consent to search from the other occupant should focus on whether the occupant's removal was "objectively reasonable" rather than the subjective intent of the officers.

However, in *Preston v. State*,[36] the Georgia Court of Appeals held that police could not arrest the defendant at his home and then initiate a search of the home consented to by a live-in girlfriend that was not incident to the arrest without first informing the defendant the basis of the search and giving him an opportunity to object.

In *State v. Kuhnhausen*,[37] the appellate court affirmed the grant of the defendant's motion to suppress evidence seized in a warrantless search of a mobile home shared by the defendant and his brother. Though the defendant's brother had consented to the search, the mobile home had been permanently divided with the construction of a wall and there was no interior access between the units. The court held that "one individual cannot waive the Fourth Amendment rights of another individual on their independent, separate, private property."

---

[34]Georgia v. Randolph, 126 S. Ct. 1515, 1525, 164 L. Ed. 2d 208 (U.S. 2006).

[35]Fernandez v. California, 134 S. Ct. 1126, 188 L. Ed. 2d 25 (2014). See United States v. Jones, 861 F.3d 638 (7th Cir. 2017) (defendant was deemed to have voluntarily exited the premises when he did so at request of officer who then handcuffed him and detained him 20 feet from house after which they obtained consent of other occupant to search premises).

[36]Preston v. State, 296 Ga. App. 655, 675 S.E.2d 553 (2009).

[37]State v. Kuhnhausen, 289 Ga. App. 489, 491 (1), 657 S.E.2d 592 (2008).

In *Sevilla-Carcamo v. State*,[38] the court held that the trial court was correct to deny the defendant's motion to suppress the search of her auto where the consent to search was provided by the person she requested to take safekeeping of the car after she was arrested for DUI. The defendant refused at the time of her arrest to allow the police to search the car. The court declined to extend *Randolph* to a motor vehicle which had been entrusted to another by the owner since it would be reasonable to assume that he might allow someone else to look inside.

In the context of a third party's consent to a warrantless search of another person's computer, the issues of whether the third party's actual or apparent authority over the premises where the computer is located as well as the person's access to the computer must be examined.[39] Courts considering these questions have attempted to analogize computers to other items more commonly seen in Fourth Amendment jurisprudence. Individuals' expectation of privacy in computers have been likened to their expectations of privacy in "a suitcase or briefcase."[40] Password-protected files have been compared to a "locked footlocker" inside the bedroom.[41] The issues arise in frequently when the third party providing the consent is the parent of the person under investigation.

Parental consent to the search of a minor's property, including computers, and living space is almost always valid. Searches authorized by a "parent or guardian have been justified on three grounds: 1) the parent is the head of the household or owner of the property; 2) the parent is exercising his or her parental authority and control over the un-emancipated minor child; and/or 3) the parent is a cotenant or common resident of jointly occupied property."[42] Even in situations where the minor makes extraordinary efforts to exclude their parent from their property, courts have held that the parents' authority over their own home

[38]Sevilla-Carcamo v. State, 335 Ga. App. 788, 783 S.E.2d 150 (2016) (physical precedent). See Pupo v. State, 187 Ga. App. 765, 767, 371 S.E.2d 219 (1988) (driver had authority to give consent to search when registered owner, a passenger, did not object).

[39]See U.S. v. McAlpine, 919 F.2d 1461, 1463 (10th Cir. 1990) ("This notion of 'common authority' over the object of the search does not rest solely on abstract principles of property, but rather stems from a practical understanding of the way in which the par-

ties to a given relationship have access to and share certain property").

[40]U.S. v. Aaron, 33 Fed. Appx. 180, 184 (6th Cir. 2002).

[41]Trulock v. Freeh, 275 F.3d 391, 403 (4th Cir. 2001) (live-in girlfriend lacked actual authority to search boyfriend's computer files where they shared household computer but the files of each were password protected).

[42]In re Tariq A-R-Y, 347 Md. 484, 701 A.2d 691 (1997).

trumps the child's efforts.[43]

When children residing with the parents are adults, the determination of the validity of the parent's consent to the search of their living space and possessions is more difficult. Courts have focused on factors such as the child's age, whether they pay rent, and whether they have made an effort to prevent their parents from accessing their computer.

In *United States v. Andrus*,[44] the officer sought and gained consent to search the defendant's computer from the defendant's father. The defendant, a 51-year-old male, resided with his father and kept his laptop in the common living quarters of the premises. The Tenth Circuit court held that because the laptop was in a commonly accessed area, the defendant's father owned the house, the defendant was not paying rent, and the defendant's father did not indicate that he did not have access to the laptop, the officer's warrantless search of the laptop was valid. The court found that a reasonable person would believe that the defendant's father had apparent authority over the laptop.

That said, when suspects are older, pay rent, and/or deny their parents access to their living space and computers, courts have generally held that the parent's consent to search is not valid.[45] For example, in *United States v. Durham*,[46] the court held that a mother held neither actual nor apparent authority to consent to the search of her son's room because the son paid rent and had changed the locks on his room door. The court must consider the tenancy relationship of an adult child, as well as their efforts to exclude third parties from access.

Courts have often considered whether an employer can validly consent to a warrantless search of an employee's workplace property. In *O'Connor v. Ortega*,[47] the United States Supreme Court held that searches and seizures by government employers or supervisors of private property are subject to the restraints of the Fourth Amendment. However, courts have held than an employer does not have actual authority to provide third party consent to the warrantless search of an employee's computer that

---

[43]See In Interest of Salyer, 44 Ill. App. 3d 854, 3 Ill. Dec. 648, 358 N.E.2d 1333 (3d Dist. 1977) (holding a mother's consent to a police search of her 15-year-old son's room effective despite son keeping a combination lock on the outside of the room and also having an inside lock on the door).

[44]U.S. v. Andrus, 483 F.3d 711 (10th Cir. 2007), decision clarified on

denial of reh'g, 499 F.3d 1162 (10th Cir. 2007).

[45]United States Department of Justice, Department of Justice Manual, Comment 9-7.100 (Vol. 6, 2017).

[46]U.S. v. Durham, 1998 WL 684241, *4 (D. Kan. 1998).

[47]O'Connor v. Ortega, 480 U.S. 709, 717, 107 S. Ct. 1492, 94 L. Ed. 2d 714 (1987).

was provided by the employer. In *United States v. Ziegler*,[48] the Court held that the defendant's employer exercised common authority over the defendant's workspace including his laptop computer. The workplace computer was the "type of property that remained within the control of the employer even if an employee places personal items on that computer."[49] Accordingly, as a general rule, an employee who is provided a computer by his employer should not entertain the notion that he has a constitutionally protected right of privacy with respect to any personal information stored in that computer.

See Annotation, "Admissibility of Evidence Discovered in Search of Defendant's Property or Residence Authorized by Defendant's Adult Relative Other Than Spouse—State Cases," 55 A.L.R.5th 125 (1998) (this annotation is almost 300 pages long); Annotation, "Admissibility of Evidence Discovered in Search of Defendant's Property or Residence Authorized by Defendant's Adult Relative Other Than Spouse," 160 A.L.R.Fed. 165 (2000); and Annotation, "Admissibility of Evidence Discovered in Search of Defendant's Property or Residence Authorized by One, Other Than Relative, Who is Co-Tenant or Common Resident With Defendant—State Cases," 68 A.L.R.5th 343 (1999).

§ 4:35 Warrantless searches—Airport searches

The frequency of aircraft hijackings in the past has led to the adoption of measures to deal with the critical time when passengers board an airplane.[1]

Federal Aviation Administration regulations[2] require the presence of armed officers throughout the screening of departing passengers. Also, searches may be conducted in critical preboarding areas even if the passenger does not meet the FAA "profile" of a potential hijacker or otherwise appear suspicious.[3] "[S]earch in an airport gate area or security checkpoint . . . [does] not require probable cause or even reasonable suspicion, but instead 'mere suspicion of possible illegal activity.' "[4] Once commenced, a consent search may continue until the officers, in their profes-

---

[48]U.S. v. Ziegler, 474 F.3d 1184 (9th Cir. 2007).

[49]U.S. v. Ziegler, 474 F.3d 1184, 1191 (9th Cir. 2007).

[Section 4:35]

[1]See Annot., 14 A.L.R.Fed. 286 (1973), for a discussion of the validity of such measures; Case Note, "Constitutional Law—Fourth Amendment Search and Seizure in the Context of Air Piracy," 25 Mercer L. Rev. 355 (1974).

[2]14 C.F.R. Part 107.

[3]United States v. Skipwith, 482 F.2d 1272, 1276 (5th Cir. 1973). However, it has been held that if there is no reasonable ground to indicate that defendant was armed or constituted a danger to others, there is no right to search him. People v. Erdman, 69 Misc.2d 103, 329 N.Y.S.2d 654 (1972).

[4]United States v. Herzbrun, 723 F.2d 773, 776 (11th Cir. 1984).

sional judgment, conclude that no harm will result from the passenger boarding the plane.[5]

The use of metal-detecting devices called magnetometers has been held to constitute a search under the Fourth Amendment.[6] Georgia courts have approved the use of such devices as reasonable and have upheld the validity of the search or frisk based upon the magnetometer reading.[7]

In some cases there has been an attempt to justify airport searches on the theory that a person traveling by airplane consents to airport security procedures.[8] However, most cases seem to have rejected the implied consent theory,[9] since such a "consent" is not freely and voluntarily given. "To make one choose between flying to one's destination and exercising one's constitutional right . . . in many situations [is] a form of coercion."[10] Nevertheless, in State v. Rosof,[11] the Georgia Court of Appeals held that persons "presenting themselves at a security checkpoint thereby consent automatically to a search" if there is a sign informing persons entering the area that they will be subject to search. Likewise, it has been said that when a "passenger presents himself at an airport security check-point, he has consented to the screening of his luggage by the X-ray machine."[12] Most of the more recent cases have justified such security measures on the theory that although initially there is not enough probable cause to justify a search, if the passenger activates a magnetometer and follow-up procedures do not satisfy the officer, there is

---

[5]McSweeney v. State, 183 Ga. App. 1, 4, 358 S.E.2d 465 (1987); United States v. Cyzewski, 484 F.2d 509, 513 (5th Cir. 1973). In Santiago v. State, 50 Md.App. 20, 435 A.2d 499 (1981), the court held that an airport security search may extend into small containers and packages which could not contain conventional weapons.

[6]United States v. Epperson, 454 F.2d 769, 770 (4th Cir. 1972).

[7]State v. David, 130 Ga. App. 872, 204 S.E.2d 773 (1974).

[8]United States v. Allen, 349 F.Supp. 749 (N.D.Cal.1972). However, the court held that there was no consent under the circumstances.

In Shapiro v. State, 390 So.2d 344, 347-50 (Fla.1980), the court said that a passenger had no reasonable expectation of privacy which prevented

his being searched for weapons or other devices which could be used in hijackings, hence the Fourth Amendment did not apply. Even if it is assumed that the Fourth Amendment applied, passengers consent to be searched. Also, the search is reasonable and therefore does not violate the Fourth Amendment.

[9]United States v. Lopez, 328 F.Supp. 1077, 1093 (E.D.N.Y.1971). But see United States v. Skipwith, 482 F.2d 1272 (5th Cir. 1973), which treated a search of carry-on luggage like a border search.

[10]United States v. Albarado, 495 F.2d 799, 806 (2d Cir. 1974).

[11]State v. Rosof, 180 Ga. App. 637, 640, 350 S.E.2d 36 (1986).

[12]McSweeney v. State, 183 Ga. App. 1, 3, 358 S.E.2d 465 (1987).

at least probable cause for a frisk.[13] The courts have not been impressed with the distinction that a typical frisk situation is designed to protect the officer, whereas in the airport context the purpose of the frisk is to protect the passengers once the plane has departed,[14] and it has been pointed out that an airport search is "not to be condemned as violating the Fourth Amendment simply because it does not precisely fit into one of the previously recognized categories for dispensing with a search warrant."[15]

In *State v. Crisanti*,[16] the court held that once a person who is subject to an investigatory stop admits a weapon is present, officers are privileged to search the area to uncover that weapon, and pointed out that the reasonableness of the action of officers is to be measured by the "foresight of the policeman on the scene. . .

In the 1980 case of *Shapiro v. State*,[17] the Florida Supreme Court concluded that a passenger had no reasonable expectation of privacy which prevented his being searched for weapons or other devices which could be used in hijackings. Therefore, the court concluded, the Fourth Amendment did not apply.

The right to search without a warrant at an airport applies only to searches of passengers and the luggage they carry on board.[18] In Georgia, it has been held that where an airline employee on his own initiative searches checked luggage which accidentally sprang open, the search is a private search not covered by the protection of the Fourth Amendment.[19]

The search by Drug Enforcement Administration officers for drugs on passengers arriving in airports from other points in the United States,[20] or the search of passengers arriving from foreign countries and passing through customs,[21] are situations beyond the scope of this section.

Generally, on scope of a search and seizure, see § 4:57, infra. Also see § 3:4, supra, on drug courier profile and § 4:30, supra, on

---

[13]See Chapter 3, supra, on "Stop-and-Frisk." Also see United States v. Kirsch, 493 F.2d 465 (5th Cir. 1974).

[14]See United States v. Lindsey, 451 F.2d 701, 703 (3d Cir. 1971).

[15]United States v. Edwards, 498 F.2d 496, 498 (2d Cir. 1974).

[16]State v. Crisanti, 220 Ga. App. 705, 709, 470 S.E.2d 314 (1996).

[17]Shapiro v. State, 390 So.2d 344, 347 (Fla.1980).

[18]Corngold v. United States, 367 F.2d 1 (9th Cir. 1966), cited apparently with approval in Andreu v. State, 124

Ga. App. 793, 796, 186 S.E.2d 137 (1971). See State v. Salit, 613 P.2d 245 (Alaska 1980), on the "ground rules" to be used in the search of carry-on luggage.

[19]Andreu v. State, 124 Ga. App. 793, 186 S.E.2d 137 (1971); United States v. Fannon, 590 F.2d 794 (9th Cir. 1979). But see Snyder v. State, 585 P.2d 229 (Alaska 1978).

[20]On this subject, see the very fine opinion in United States v. Van Lewis, 409 F.Supp. 535, 541 (E.D.Mich.1976).

[21]This situation is referred to briefly in § 4:45, infra.

exigent circumstances. Generally, on airport searches, see 68 Am. Jur. 2d Searches and Seizures § 59 (1973), and 3 LaFave, *Search and Seizure* 327, § 10.6 (West 1978).

§ 4:36 Warrantless searches—Courthouses and public buildings

In the South Carolina case of *State v. Shelton*,[1] the trial judge received reliable information that a party in a pending action carried a gun and had threatened one of the attorneys in the case. The trial judge ordered the party searched. The appellate court said:

"A trial judge has the inherent power to preserve order in his court and to see that justice is not obstructed by any person or persons. He has the authority to take such measures as appear reasonably necessary to secure orderly proceedings and to preserve the security of those participating in the trial or lawfully attending the proceedings. The exercise of this authority by the trial judge is not inhibited by the guarantees of the Fourth Amendment. Therefore, the Fourth Amendment protection against unreasonable searches and seizures is inapplicable to a courtroom in the exercise of the trial judge's authority and duty to preserve security and order."

However, generally a court does not know the identity of a person who is armed. Hence, where there are threats or have been acts of violence, magnetometers, or metal detecting devices, may be used to screen persons entering a courthouse.

In *McMorris v. Alioto*,[2] the court in effect approved the requirement that persons entering a courthouse must pass through a metal detector. If the detector indicated the presence of metal, the person could empty his pockets and pass through the detector again. If the detector was activated again, the person was frisked before being permitted to enter. Briefcases and articles capable of concealing weapons were also subject to inspection. The court pointed out that any person could leave the courthouse without a further search or questioning if he activated the metal detector, and concluded that there was sufficient freedom from compulsion to meet the requirements of the Fourth Amendment.

In some cases, even more severe or intensive means of search-

---

[Section 4:36]

[1]State v. Shelton, 270 S.C. 577, 243 S.E.2d 455 (1978).

[2]McMorris v. Alioto, 567 F.2d 897 (9th Cir. 1978). Cf. Downing v. Kunzig, 454 F.2d 1230 (6th Cir. 1972); In re "Trials of Pending and Future Crimi-

nal Cases," 306 F.Supp. 333 (N.D.Ill.1969); Barrett v. Kunzig, 331 F.Supp. 266 (M.D.Tenn.1971).

See Annot., "Validity, Under Federal Constitution of Search Conducted as Condition of Entering Public Building," 53 A.L.R.Fed. 888 (1981).

ing have been used.[3] These security measures are sometimes said to be justified on a consent theory[4] or on a theory of the inherent power of the court to maintain order.[5]

See 3 LaFave, *Search and Seizure,* § 10.7(a) (West 1978); 1 Ringel, *Searches and Seizures,* Arrests and Confessions, § 16.3 (Clark Boardman 1979); Annotation, "Validity, Under Federal Constitution, of Search Conducted as Condition of Entering Public Building," 53 A.L.R.Fed. 888 (1981).

§ 4:37   Warrantless searches—Places of recreation and entertainment

Several cases have arisen involving the search of persons entering a stadium or some other such facility. These cases have arisen where spectators were required to submit to a search for drugs, alcohol, or weapons as a prerequisite to the right to enter. Justification of these checks or searches has generally been sought by drawing an analogy between such checks and airport searches. However, thus far the analysis has been rejected because (1) there is no showing of public necessity; (2) the intensity required of such a search, if it is to be effective, is intolerable; and (3) the searches have been used on a selective basis.

For the foregoing reasons such searches have been held unconstitutional if they are a result of government action.[1]

See 1 Ringel, *Searches and Seizures, Arrests and Confessions,* § 16.4 (Clark Boardman 1979); 1 LaFave, *Search and Seizure,* § 10.7(a) (West 1978); Annotation, "Validity, Under Federal Constitution, of Search Conducted as Condition of Entering Public Building," 53 A.L.R.Fed. 888 (1981).

---

[3]See Jesmore, "The Courthouse Search," 21 U.C.L.A. L. Rev. 797 (1974).

[4]United States v. Sihler, 562 F.2d 349 (5th Cir. 1977).

[5]Cf. United States v. Bell, 457 F.2d 1231 (5th Cir. 1972).

[Section 4:37]

[1]Collier v. Miller, 414 F.Supp. 1357 (D.Tex. 1976); Wheaton v. Hagan, 435 F.Supp. 1134 (M.D.N.C.1977); State v. Williams, 297 So.2d 52 (Fla.

App.1974); Stroeber v. Commission Veteran's Auditorium, 453 F.Supp. 926 (S.D.Iowa 1977); Gaioni v. Folmar, 460 F.Supp. 10 (M.D.Ala.1978); State v. Carter, 267 N.W.2d 385 (Iowa 1978). Contra, Jensen v. City of Pontiac, 113 Mich.App. 341, 317 N.W.2d 619 (1982).

See Annot., "Searches and Seizures: Validity of Searches Conducted as Condition of Entering Public Premises—State Cases," 28 A.L.R.4th 1250 (1984).

§ 4:38 Warrantless searches—Abandoned property

The United States Supreme Court has held that the Fourth Amendment does not apply to abandoned property.[1] Thus, if property has been abandoned it may be seized by officers without a warrant.[2] Momentarily divesting oneself of contraband inside an automobile does not constitute abandonment.[3] "The question of abandonment for Fourth Amendment purposes does not turn on strict property concepts but on whether the accused has relinquished his interest in the property to the extent that he no longer has a reasonable expectation of privacy . . . at the time of the search."[4] "Abandonment is primarily a question of intent, and intent may be inferred from words spoken, acts done, and other objective facts. All relevant circumstances existing at the time of the alleged abandonment should be considered. Police pursuit or the existence of a police investigation does not of itself render abandonment involuntary."[5] If a defendant abandons an automobile after being chased by police, he may not object to the search.[6] In *Williams v. State,*[7] the defendant's car "was found over 100 yards from the nearest home on land not belonging to the defendant: it was down a deserted field road, the tag and battery had been removed, and the vehicle was covered with freshly cut bushes and debris." The court said that the issue of abandonment is one of fact and will not be disturbed by an appellate court if there is any evidence to support it. Here there was adequate evi-

---

[Section 4:38]

[1]Hester v. United States, 265 U.S. 57, 44 S.Ct. 445, 68 L.Ed. 898 (1924); United States v. Wilson, 492 F.2d 1160 (5th Cir. 1974); Jackson v. State, 45 Ala.App. 621, 235 So.2d 382 (1970). However, abandonment has been treated as relating to the standing or expectation of privacy of a defendant rather than to the inapplicability of the Fourth Amendment. Commonwealth v. Richardson, 476 Pa. 571, 383 A.2d 510 (1978).

[2]Hester v. United States, 265 U.S. 57, 44 S.Ct. 445, 68 L.Ed. 898 (1924); Hawkins v. State, 146 Ga. App. 312, 313, 246 S.E.2d 343 (1978). In United States v. Edwards, 644 F.2d 1, 2 (5th Cir. 1981), a ship was caught in a raging storm on a reef. The defendant called the Coast Guard for help, abandoned ship and went with the Coast Guard. The court concluded that the defendant gave up his Fourth Amendment rights.

[3]Rios v. United States, 364 U.S. 253, 262, 80 S.Ct. 1431, 4 L.Ed.2d 1688 (1960), n. 6.

[4]Browning v. State, 176 Ga. App. 420, 336 S.E.2d 41 (1985) (quoting Bloodworth v. State, 233 Ga. 589, 590 (2), 212 S.E.2d 774 (1975)).

[5]Young v. State, 190 Ga. App. 775, 776, 380 S.E.2d 309 (1989).

[6]Powell v. State, 270 Ga. App. 707, 607 S.E.2d 909 (2004); Whitlock v. State, 124 Ga. App. 599 (3)(b), 185 S.E.2d 90 (1971), rev'd in part on other grounds, 230 Ga. 700, 198 S.E.2d 865 (1973). Compare State v. Nesbitt, 305 Ga. App. 28, 699 S.E.2d 368 (2010).

[7]Williams v. State, 171 Ga. App. 546, 547 (2), 320 S.E.2d 389 (1984). Cf. State v. Nesbitt, 305 Ga. App. 28, 699 S.E.2d 368 (2010) (merely fleeing from a vehicle that is parked, even carelessly parked, with the keys in the ignition is not per se evidence of abandonment).

dence to support a finding of abandonment. "In order to determine whether property has been abandoned, we must ask: Did the complaining party retain a legitimate expectation of privacy in the article allegedly abandoned?"

In *Berger v. State*,[8] the court held that when a briefcase was left unlocked in the lobby of a hotel, an officer could open it and look in it to determine who the owner is. In *Ramsey v. State*,[9] the court held that where a defendant denied ownership or any interest in a briefcase, this amounted to an abandonment of the briefcase and its contents and justified a warrantless search.

When a person drops or throws contraband away while he is being followed or approached by an officer, the property is treated as having been abandoned.[10] This abandonment situation, in some parts of the country, has led to what has been commonly referred to as the "dropsy" cases and the "perjury routine" in which officers have been accused of routinely testifying that a defendant dropped the drugs when he saw the officer approaching.[11] However, if the officer is attempting to make an illegal arrest which causes the defendant to dispose of the contraband, the property is not treated as having been abandoned.[12] Likewise, where officers illegally stop a person and as a result of the stop the person abandons contraband, this is not regarded as voluntary abandonment and the contraband has been held not admissible.[13]

However, if "a defendant is in a state of flight when he discards or abandons property . . . his being pursued does not result in the 'seizure' of property he abandoned." Hence, when a defendant is in a state of flight when he discards contraband, and has not submitted to any show of authority by the police, the contraband is "not discovered as a result of an illegal search or seizure, regardless of whether the police had probable cause to stop . . .

---

[8]Berger v. State, 150 Ga. App. 166, 257 S.E.2d 8 (1979).

[9]Ramsey v. State, 183 Ga. App. 48, 49 (1), 357 S.E.2d 869 (1987).

[10]Green v. State, 127 Ga. App. 713, 194 S.E.2d 678 (1972); Golden v. State, 163 Ga. App. 519, 295 S.E.2d 333 (1982); Ransom v. State, 239 Ga. App. 501, 503, 521 S.E.2d 430 (1999).

[11]See People v. McMurty, 64 Misc.2d 63, 314 N.Y.S.2d 194 (1970). E.g., People v. Quinones, 61 A.D.2d 765, 402 N.Y.S.2d 196 (1978). See 1 Ringel, Searches and Seizures, Arrests and Confessions, § 8.5(a)(1) (Clark Boardman 1979).

[12]Fletcher v. Wainwright, 399 F.2d 62, 63 (5th Cir. 1968) (where defendants seek to dispose of contraband as officers attempt illegal entry into their premises, any evidence recovered as a result is tainted by illegal entry and subject to suppression). See U.S. v. Simpson, 944 F. Supp. 1396 (S.D. Ind. 1996).

[13]United States v. Beck, 602 F.2d 726 (5th Cir. 1979) (seeking to dispose of contraband because of police misconduct is not the equivalent of a voluntary abandonment of one's property). See U.S. v. Cooley, 552 F. Supp. 2d 1284 (N.D. Ala. 2008).

[the defendant's] vehicle."[14]

The case of *Abel v. United States*[15] exemplifies an abandonment situation. In *Abel,* the defendant was arrested in his hotel room. After he had been taken away, an officer with the consent of the hotel manager searched the wastepaper basket in the room and discovered incriminating evidence. The court held the items had been abandoned and were thus admissible. However, a tenant who is evicted retains a reasonable expectation of privacy and an officer has no right to sift through his possessions before moving them onto the street.[16]

Several cases involving the search of garbage cans placed on the street have held that the items in question were abandoned.[17] See § 14:83, infra, on expectation of privacy. Likewise, it has been held that substances obtained from the feces of a hospitalized drug suspect are admissible.[18] However, where personal property such as a wallet is merely lost and not abandoned, the owner does maintain an expectation of privacy, albeit a somewhat diluted one. Addressing the issue for the first time, the Court of Appeals in *Wolf v. State*,[19] held that a person's expectations of privacy in their personal effects, does not vanish simply because the item is lost or mislaid. It is, however, diminished to the extent that police may examine the contents thereof in order to find the rightful owner. See Annotation, "Searches and Seizures: Reasonable Expectation of Privacy in Contents of Garbage or Trash Receptacle," 62 A.L.R.5th 1 (1998).

In addition to personal property, the doctrine of abandonment

---

[14]Brown v. State, 239 Ga. App. 674, 676 (1), 522 S.E.2d 41 (1999).

[15]Abel v. United States, 362 U.S. 217, 80 S.Ct. 683, 4 L.Ed.2d 668 (1960). Cf. Buttrum v. State, 249 Ga. 652, 653 (2), 293 S.E.2d 334 (1982). In Witt v. State, 157 Ga. App. 564, 278 S.E.2d 145 (1981), the court pointed out that where a tenant's lease has expired and he has moved out, whatever was left is considered abandoned and the landlord may permit officers to search.

[16]Boone v. State, 39 Md.App. 20, 383 A.2d 412 (1978).

[17]United States v. Shelby, 573 F.2d 971 (7th Cir. 1978); United States v. Crowell, 586 F.2d 1020 (4th Cir. 1978); United States v. Vahalik, 606 F.2d 99 (5th Cir. 1979); United States v. Mustone, 469 F.2d 970, 972 (1st Cir. 1972); United States v. Dzialak, 441 F.2d 212, 215 (2d Cir. 1971); State v. Stevens, 120 Wis.2d 334, 354 N.W.2d 762 (Wis.App.1984).

In United States v. Kramer, 711 F.2d 789 (7th Cir. 1983), the court held that a defendant had no legitimate expectation of privacy in discarded garbage placed in garbage bags in cans located just inside a low fence around defendant's yard even though officers committed trespass to obtain the garbage.

See Annot., "Searches and Seizures: Reasonable Expectation of Privacy in Contents of Garbage or Trash Receptacle," 28 A.L.R.4th 1219 (1984).

[18]Venner v. State, 30 Md.App. 599, 354 A.2d 483 (1976).

[19]Wolf v. State, 291 Ga. App. 876 (1), 663 S.E.2d 292 (2008).

also applies to real estate. In *Bloodworth v. State,*[20] the defendant physically moved out of a house, but he retained possession until the day after the warrantless search. The court said that strict property concepts did not apply and the question was whether or not he had relinquished his interest in the property to such an extent that he no longer had a reasonable expectation of privacy. Therefore, the court concluded that the evidence authorized a finding that the premises had been abandoned.

In *Smith v. State,*[21] a search was upheld on the theory of abandonment where the defendant was temporarily living elsewhere, the rent had not been paid for several months, the owner had initiated proceedings to take possession of the premises, the water had been turned off and the telephone disconnected several months before the search, and the house was said to be uninhabitable. In *Hollingsworth v. State,*[22] the court upheld the warrantless search of an apparently vacant house which had been condemned by the city.

In *United States v. Tolbert,*[23] the court held that the definition of the word "abandonment" has a traditional concept in property law, but the same word may have a different meaning under the Fourth Amendment. The court then concluded that the defendant had no expectation of privacy in a checked suitcase left in an air terminal where the defendant vociferously denied owning the suitcase. See § 3:6, supra, on conduct justifying stop. See § 4:21, supra, on frisk executed in connection with execution of search warrant. See sections 14:79 to 14:83, infra, on standing and expectation of privacy. See Annotation, "Search and Seizure: What Constitutes Abandonment of Personal Property Within Rule That Search and Seizure of Abandoned Property Is Not Unreasonable—Modern Cases," 40 A.L.R.4th 382 (1985).

§ 4:39   Warrantless searches—Plain view—General

In a sense the plain view doctrine or rule is not an exception to the warrant requirement for a search. This is true in that articles discovered as a result of "plain view" are not discovered as a

---

[20]Bloodworth v. State, 233 Ga. 589 (2), 212 S.E.2d 774 (1975).

[21]Smith v. State, 160 Ga. App. 26, 27 (2), 285 S.E.2d 749 (1981).

[22]Hollingsworth v. State, 155 Ga. App. 878, 880, 273 S.E.2d 639 (1980).

[23]United States v. Tolbert, 692 F.2d 1041 (6th Cir. 1982); United States v. Miller, 589 F.2d 1117, 1131 (1st Cir. 1978). Cf. United States v. Kendall, 655 F.2d 199 (9th Cir. 1981); United States v. Berd, 634 F.2d 979 (5th Cir. 1981); United States v. Washington, 677 F.2d 394 (4th Cir. 1982).

result of a search.[1] No warrant is required since no search is conducted. Thus, the plain view doctrine is a seizure doctrine, not a search doctrine. However, absent exigent circumstances, an officer has no right to seize contraband unless he has a legal right to go where the contraband is located.[2]

In *Texas v. Brown*,[3] four Justices of the United States Supreme Court said that " '[p]lain view' is perhaps better understood, . . . not as an independent 'exception' to the warrant clause but simply as an extension of whatever the prior justification for the officer's 'access to an object' may be. The principle is grounded on the recognition that when a police officer has observed an object in 'plain view' the owner's remaining interests in the object are merely those of possession and ownership. . . . Likewise, it reflects the fact that requiring police to obtain a warrant once they have obtained a first-hand perception of contraband, stolen property or incriminating evidence generally would be a 'needless inconvenience,' . . . which might involve danger to the police and public."[4]

The "plain view" exception to the warrant requirement is based on the theory that the discovery of the particular incriminating evidence is not the result of a search.[5] In *Coolidge v. New Hampshire*,[6] the Court said that in order for the plain view exception to apply, three requirements must be met: (1) the object must be inadvertently discovered, (2) the officer discovering the object must have a legal right to be where he is at the time of the discovery,[7] and (3) it must be immediately apparent that the seized item is stolen property, contraband, or other fruits or evi-

[Section 4:39]

[1]Pickens v. State, 225 Ga. App. 792, 795 (1)(b), 484 S.E.2d 731 (1997).

[2]Gates v. State, 229 Ga. App. 766, 768, 495 S.E.2d 113 (1997); Cates v. State, 232 Ga. App. 262, 264, 501 S.E.2d 262 (1998). Contra, Hornblower v. State, 351 So.2d 716 (Fla.1977); 1 Ringel, Searches and Seizures, Arrests and Confessions, § 10.1 (Clark Boardman 1979).

[3]Texas v. Brown, 460 U.S. 730, 103 S.Ct. 1535, 75 L.Ed.2d 502 (1983).

[4]Quoted with approval in Mitchell v. State, 181 Ga. App. 470, 352 S.E.2d 647 (1987).

[5]United States v. Lee, 274 U.S. 559, 47 S.Ct. 746, 71 L.Ed. 1202 (1927). On the general subject, see Lewis and Mannie, "Warrantless Searches and the 'Plain View' Doctrine: Current Perspective," 12 Crim. L. Bull. 5 (1976); Moylan, "The Plain View Doctrine: Unexpected Child of the Great 'Search Incident' Geography Battle," 26 Mercer L. Rev. 1047 (1975).

[6]Coolidge v. New Hampshire, 403 U.S. 443, 91 S.Ct. 2022, 29 L.Ed.2d 564 (1971) (plurality opinion).

[7]Harris v. United States, 390 U.S. 234, 88 S.Ct. 992, 19 L.Ed.2d 1067 (1968); Ker v. California, 374 U.S. 23, 83 S.Ct. 1623, 10 L.Ed.2d 726 (1963). See Lewis v. State, 126 Ga. App. 123, 126, 190 S.E.2d 123 (1972); Kelley v. State, 146 Ga. App. 179, 183, 245 S.E.2d 872 (1978).

In State v. Brooks, 160 Ga. App. 381, 287 S.E.2d 95 (1981), a different situation was found to exist where an officer had a right to be where he was. In Brooks, an officer was investigating an anonymous complaint of gambling and walked up the drive to defendant's

dence of a crime.[8] However, in the 1990 case of *Horton v. California*,[9] the United States Supreme Court held that the "inadvertent discovery requirement" of the plain view rule is no longer required.

In reading the cases on "plain view," it becomes readily apparent that these words in the Fourth Amendment context do not mean what they would seem to mean in lay English. It has been suggested that " '[o]pen view' is a better term to describe the non-intrusional visual observation from a vantage point outside a constitutionally protected area. The 'plain view doctrine' of Coolidge 'refers exclusively to the legal justification—the reasonableness—for the seizure of evidence . . . in the course of a constitutional search already in progress or in the course of an otherwise justifiable intrusion into a Constitutionally protected area. . . .' Because an 'open view' encompasses that which is readily observable or clearly visible from an observation point which is not within a constitutionally protected confine, this sighting of evidence needs no further justification for a seizure."[10]

See § 4:22, supra, on property which may be seized when a warrant is executed. See § 4:41, infra, on enhanced vision of officer by the use of a light or binoculars. See § 4:43, infra, on aerial view of premises. See § 3:10, supra, on identification of a substance by feel.

§ 4:40 Warrantless searches—Plain view—Inadvertent discovery

In the 1990 case of *Horton v. California*,[1] the United States Supreme Court held that "the absence of inadvertence" does not prevent a seizure from being valid under the plain view doctrine. The court pointed out that (1) "evenhanded law enforcement is best achieved by the application of objective standards of conduct, rather than standards that depend upon the subjective state of mind of the officer." (2) The inadvertence requirement is not required to prevent a "specific warrant" from being converted into a general warrant.

---

house. He observed growing marijuana and seized it. The seizure was approved. Cf. State v. Nichols, 160 Ga. App. 386, 287 S.E.2d 53 (1981).

[8]Cook v. State, 134 Ga. App. 712, 715 (4), 215 S.E.2d 728 (1975).

[9]Horton v. California, 496 U.S. 128, 110 S.Ct. 2301, 110 L.Ed.2d 112 (1990).

[10]Merriman v. State, 201 Ga. App. 817, 819, 412 S.E.2d 598 (1991). See Morgan v. State, 285 Ga. App. 254, 645 S.E.2d 745 (2007).

[Section 4:40]

[1]Horton v. California, 496 U.S. 128, 110 S.Ct. 2301, 110 L.Ed.2d 112 (1990).

In *Nichols v. State,*[2] the Georgia Court of Appeals followed *Horton*. However, in the 2006 case of *Mauge v. State,*[3] the Court of Appeals listed inadvertent discovery as one of three requirements under the plain view doctrine.

For Georgia law before *Horton,* see *State v. Scott*[4] and *Whittington v. State.*[5]

§ 4:41 Warrantless searches—Plain view—Right of officer to be where he was at time of discovery

The officer must have a right to be where he is at the time he sees the item. Thus, looking into a motel window from a parking lot was held not objectionable because there existed no reasonable expectation of privacy,[1] but if an officer goes on private property without a warrant and peers in a window and thus obtains probable cause for an arrest, the arrest and search incident to it are illegal.[2] However, in *Pickens v. State,*[3] the court held that the Fourth Amendment is not violated where an officer goes on private property only to the extent of knocking on outer doors, even if the officer does not have an articulable suspicion. In *State v. O'Bryant,*[4] pursuant to an anonymous tip of possible drug dealing, officers went to the defendant's residence without a warrant to speak with the defendant. There was no response to their knock at the front door and the officers walked to the side of the house, knocked at a basement door and received no response. They noticed a Toyota truck parked in the driveway in which one of the officers had seen marijuana roaches in the ashtray on a prior occasion. At this time they saw through a tinted window what appeared to be a plastic bag of marijuana. One of the officers obtained a search warrant for the vehicle and the house. The search of the house yielded 20 pounds of marijuana. The appellate court affirmed the granting of the motion to suppress, pointing out that the officers had no right to be where they were

[2]Nichols v. State, 210 Ga. App. 134, 136 (3)(d), 435 S.E.2d 502 (1993).

[3]Mauge v. State, 279 Ga. App. 36, 38, 630 S.E.2d 174 (2006).

[4]State v. Scott, 159 Ga. App. 869, 285 S.E.2d 599 (1981).

[5]Whittington v. State, 165 Ga. App. 763, 302 S.E.2d 617 (1983).

[Section 4:41]

[1]Gil v. Beto, 440 F.2d 666 (5th Cir. 1971). See Oldfield v. State, 291 Ga. App. 432, 662 S.E.2d 243 (2008).

[2]Texas v. Gonzales, 388 F.2d 145, 146 (5th Cir. 1968).

In United States v. Wheeler, 641 F.2d 1321, 1324-28 (9th Cir. 1981), the court found that evidence which was the later basis of a search warrant was not tainted where an officer stood on two automobile tires in order to look over a six-foot privacy fence.

[3]Pickens v. State, 225 Ga. App. 792, 793 (1)(a), 484 S.E.2d 731 (1997).

[4]State v. O'Bryant, 219 Ga. App. 862, 863, 467 S.E.2d 342 (1996). See State v. Vickers, 339 Ga. App. 272, 793 S.E.2d 167 (2016) (physical precedent).

when they looked into the Toyota.

It has been held in some jurisdictions that the use of a telescope to watch a defendant in his apartment was illegal and information so obtained was inadmissible.[5] In *Patterson v. State*,[6] the Georgia Court of Appeals held that it was proper for officers to use binoculars to watch a defendant harvest marijuana growing in a field. Also, such surveillance is proper under the open fields exception, which is discussed in the next section, and it is not to be compared with looking in a home. In *Kyllo v. United States*,[7] the United States Supreme Court held that the warrantless use of a thermal imaging device to scan the home of the defendant in connection with an investigation involving an indoor marijuana farm was improper.

The plain view doctrine does not apply to objects found while searching furniture or wastebaskets,[8] nor will it justify an exploratory search from one object to another until incriminating evidence is found.[9]

Despite the lesser expectation of privacy in a motor vehicle, it has been held that an officer has no authority to stick his head

---

[5]United States v. Kim, 415 F.Supp. 1252 (D.Haw.1976); United States v. Taborda, 635 F.2d 131 (2d Cir. 1980). See Commonwealth v. Meunley, 263 A. 2d 905 (Pa. 1970). But cf. State v. Louis, 296 Or. 57, 672 P.2d 708 (1983). See § 4:1, supra, on searches, and § 4:2, supra, on Fourth Amendment protection of the home.

[6]Patterson v. State, 133 Ga. App. 742, 212 S.E.2d 858 (1975). See Annot., 48 A.L.R.3d 1185 (1973). Also see Annot., "Observation Through Binoculars as Constituting Unreasonable Search," 48 A.L.R.3d 1178 (1973). See § 4:2, supra, on areas not protected by the Fourteenth Amendment and § 4:43, infra, on open field exception to surveillance.

However, in Wheeler v. State, 659 S.W.2d 381, 390 (Tex.Crim.App. 1982), the court held that prolonged surveillance of an isolated greenhouse from air and ground with telescopes of increasing magnitude violated the Fourth Amendment where a 600-millimeter telescope was ultimately used and the observation was made through a five-inch opening in the louvers of the exhaust fan.

[7]Kyllo v. U.S., 533 U.S. 27, 121 S. Ct. 2038, 150 L. Ed. 2d 94 (2001). See Brundige v. State, 291 Ga. 677, 735 S.E.2d 583 (2012) (heat loss recorded by a thermal scanner does not fit within the scope of "tangible evidence," i.e., "evidence that is essentially an object with a material form," and as such is not a proper subject for a search warrant under O.C.G.A. § 17-5-21(a)(5)). Cf. Florida v. Jardines, 569 U.S. 1, 133 S. Ct. 1409, 185 L. Ed. 2d 495 (2013) (use of police dog to "sniff" home of defendant from front door and around the outside of home is a "search" for purposes of Fourth Amendment); Mitchell v. State, 323 Ga. App. 739, 747 S.E.2d 900 (2013) (warrant based upon information obtained while officer is in the curtilage of defendant's residence without the consent of defendant was improper and evidence garnered as a result was suppressed).

[8]United States v. Lefkowitz, 285 U.S. 452, 52 S.Ct. 420, 76 L.Ed. 877 (1932). See Annot. on the Supreme Court's development of "open fields doctrine," 80 L.Ed.2d 860 (1986).

[9]Lentile v. State, 136 Ga. App. 611, 614, 222 S.E.2d 86 (1975).

inside a windowless cargo van parked in a public place. The officer had found the sliding door open from 15 to 18 inches.[10]

The plain view doctrine does not mean that the human senses may never be assisted in any way. In *United States v. Lee*,[11] the United States Supreme Court held that the plain view doctrine was not violated where a search light was directed on a boat, revealing a number of cans of alcohol. The court also drew an analogy between the use of the search light and the use of field glasses and said that their use was constitutionally proper. Generally, courts have held that the use of a flashlight to see an object did not violate the concept of the plain view doctrine, particularly when related to automobiles.[12] Also, the use of a flashlight in looking in an unlighted garage through an open door has been upheld.[13]

In the unusual Eleventh Circuit case of *United States v. Sentovich*,[14] the court concluded that probable cause to obtain a search warrant could be based, in part, on the assertion of a DEA agent that he could smell marijuana inside of a closed suitcase at an airport.

In *Lo-Ji Sales, Inc. v. New York*,[15] the Court said that "there is no basis for the notion that [where] a retail store invites the public to enter, it consents to wholesale searches and seizures that do not conform to Fourth Amendment guarantees."

In *Merriman v. State*,[16] pursuant to an anonymous call that marijuana was growing in the defendant's backyard, officers went

---

[10]Commonwealth v. Podgurski, 386 Mass. 385, 436 N.E.2d 150 (1982).

[11]United States v. Lee, 274 U.S. 559, 47 S.Ct. 746, 71 L.Ed. 1202 (1927).

[12]Parker v. State, 229 Ga. App. 217, 219 (3), 493 S.E.2d 558 (1997); State v. Hodges, 184 Ga. App. 21, 25, 360 S.E.2d 903 (1987); United States v. Lara, 517 F.2d 209 (5th Cir. 1975); Marshall v. United States, 422 F.2d 185 (5th Cir. 1970); Caito v. State, 130 Ga. App. 831, 204 S.E.2d 765 (1974). However, some courts have held that objects seen in a car when a flashlight is shined through the window are not in plain view. See People v. Smith, 42 N.Y.2d 961, 398 N.Y.S.2d 142, 367 N.E.2d 648 (1977); United States v. Taborda, 491 F.Supp. 50 (E.D.N.Y. 1980); State v. Harriman, 467 A.2d 745 (Me. 1983).

[13]People v. Wheeler, 28 Cal.App.3d 1065, 105 Cal.Rptr. 56 (1972). Cf. United States v. Wright, 449 F.2d 1355 (D.C.Cir. 1971), in which the court approved the use of a flashlight in looking through an eight-inch space in the door.

[14]United States v. Sentovich, 677 F.2d 834 (11th Cir. 1982). Accord, Brooker v. State, 164 Ga. App. 775 (1), 298 S.E.2d 48 (1982). See § 4:28, supra; §§ 4:48 to 4:53, infra; and § 4:56, infra, on warrantless searches.

See Annot., "Odor of Narcotics as Providing Probable Cause for Warrantless Search," 5 A.L.R.4th 681 (1981).

[15]Lo-Ji Sales, Inc. v. New York, 442 U.S. 319, 99 S.Ct. 2319, 60 L.Ed.2d 920 (1979).

[16]Merriman v. State, 201 Ga. App. 817, 412 S.E.2d 598 (1991). This case has an outstanding opinion by Judge Beasley in which she discusses a num-

to the defendant's house and found the yard enclosed partly by a high brick wall and partly by a wooden fence about eight feet tall. They moved through a heavily wooded area behind the wooden fence and, looking through cracks in the fence, they saw growing marijuana. The seizure was affirmed.

See §§ 4:32 and 4:33, supra, on inviting an undercover officer into a house to sell him contraband. See § 4:43, infra, on warrantless searches of open fields and on aircraft surveillance. See § 4:58, infra, on "second search" and a controlled delivery. See § 14:79, infra, on expectations of privacy and standing. See Annotation, "Permissibility and Sufficiency of Warrantless Use of Thermal Imager or Forward Looking Infra-Red Radar (F.L.I.R.)," 78 A.L.R.5th 309 (2000).

§ 4:42   Warrantless searches—Plain view—Illegality of seized items immediately apparent

In *State v. David*,[1] the Georgia Supreme Court pointed out that "[a]n officer's observation of . . . contraband from outside the apartment and his recognition of it as contraband, standing alone . . . [does] not authorize the officer to make a warrantless entry into the apartment to arrest the occupants and seize the material." For the plain view doctrine to authorize seizure, the officer must enter the home by consent or there must be exigent circumstances.

It must be immediately apparent to the officer that the object seized is subject to seizure.[2] However, in *State v. Field*,[3] the court held that where an officer sees suspicious items and he moves nothing but merely takes a closer look, this meets the requirements of immediate apparency of the plain view rule. In *State v. Sharer*,[4] the Georgia Court of Appeals upheld the seizure of a brown bottle, two to three inches in height, with a white cap and no label of any sort. The bottle was opened and found to contain yellow capsules and blue pills. The bottle was found in plain view on the floor of an automobile. A further check of the car pursuant to a warrant led to the discovery of more bottles containing pills and capsules. The court concluded that having "lawfully discovered the pill bottles, the officers had probable cause to conclude from their location and appearance and the circumstances of their discovery that they contained contraband."

---

ber of similar cases.

[Section 4:42]

   [1]State v. David, 269 Ga. 533, 535 (2), 501 S.E.2d 494 (1998).

   [2]Hogan v. State, 140 Ga. App. 716, 718, 231 S.E.2d 802 (1976).

   [3]State v. Field, 188 Ga. App. 639, 641, 373 S.E.2d 815 (1988).

   [4]State v. Sharer, 161 Ga. App. 811, 289 S.E.2d 19 (1982). In *Sharer*, the defendant was arrested for driving under the influence of alcohol. His automobile was impounded.

However, in *Stone v. State,*[5] officers approached a truck and saw a brown paper bag on the floorboard. The bag had "enough torn places in it for the officers to see 'some white tablets, some white looking powder and some brownish material,' in plastic bags inside." One officer, who had been a policeman for six years, "had a suspicion" there were drugs in the bag. The trained officer testified that "to his personal knowledge what he observed, 'was not any controlled substance or was not anything that appeared to be a controlled substance.' " The court affirmed the holding of the trial judge that "the incriminating nature of the evidence" was not immediately apparent and that the seizure and search was not valid.

In *Texas v. Brown,*[6] the United States Supreme Court considered the "immediately apparent" requirement of the plain view rule. Here a police officer stopped Brown at a driver's license checkpoint. The officer asked for his license, shined his flashlight into the car and saw an opaque party balloon, knotted near the tip, fall from Brown's hand to the seat. The officer was aware that drugs were frequently placed in such balloons. The officer then noticed small plastic vials, loose white powder and an open bag of party balloons in the glove compartment. Brown said he did not have a license with him and got out of the car as requested. The officer picked up the balloon which had fallen. The balloon seemed to have a powdery substance in the tied off portion. Brown was informed that he was under arrest, and the car was inventoried on the scene. A motion to suppress was denied by the trial judge. The Texas Court of Criminal Appeals reversed because the officer did not "*know* that 'incriminating evidence was before him when he seized the balloon.' " In a plurality opinion, the Supreme Court reversed. Chief Justice Burger and Justices Rehnquist, White, and O'Connor disregarded *Coolidge v. New Hampshire*[7] as binding precedent and the opinion seems to go out of its way to point this out. The opinion says that "if, while lawfully engaged in an activity in a particular place, police officers perceive a suspicious object they may seize it immediately. . . . This rule merely reflects an application of the Fourth Amendment's central requirement of reasonableness to the law governing seizures of property. . . . [I]t is plain that . . . [the officer] possessed probable cause to believe that the balloon . . . contained an illicit substance." Justices Powell and Black-

---

[5]Stone v. State, 162 Ga. App. 654, 656, 292 S.E.2d 525 (1982).

[6]Texas v. Brown, 460 U.S. 730, 103 S.Ct. 1535, 75 L.Ed.2d 502 (1983).

In State v. Ball, 124 N.H. 226, 471 A.2d 347 (1983), the court relied on the constitution of its state and refused to follow *Brown*.

[7]Coolidge v. New Hampshire, 403 U.S. 443, 91 S.Ct. 2022, 29 L.Ed.2d 564 (1971).

mun concurred in the judgment, saying that if probable cause must be shown to justify a seizure, it existed in this case, but they disagreed with the criticism of *Coolidge*. Justices Stevens, Brennan, and Marshall concurred in the judgment but said that the court failed to deal adequately with the search of the balloon as opposed to its seizure.

However, in *Arizona v. Hicks*,[8] the United States Supreme Court held that "immediately apparent" means the officer must have probable cause to believe that the object is subject to seizure. Thus, while there is nothing to prevent an officer from recording serial numbers which may be easily seen, an officer may not move an article or turn it over to see the serial number unless there is probable cause where such moving of equipment is outside the scope of the exigency that justified the warrantless entry. However, in *Downey v. State*,[9] the trial court was affirmed in denying a motion to suppress where officers conducted a search with the consent of the owner which was granted in connection with the execution of an arrest warrant for her son. During the search, one officer saw the stock of a rifle in a styrofoam gun box in the attic. He noted the serial number and handed the rifle down to be "cleared." The officer then went to his patrol car to check his notes from a previous burglary. The weapon was determined to be stolen.

In *Brown v. State*,[10] the court recognized that "if the police see a person in possession of a highly suspicious object . . . which because of other circumstances is reasonably suspected to be contraband, and then observe that person make an apparent attempt to conceal that object from police view, probable cause is then present."

In *Whittington v. State*,[11] officers were executing a search warrant for marijuana. In the attic they found a pillow case sewn together at both ends. They opened it and found 79 pieces of silverware of differing patterns. One of the officers said he recognized some of it as being of the same pattern as some which had been stolen. However, the owner was unable to describe the patterns which he said had been stolen. The court concluded that all of these facts, including the location, added up to probable cause to believe the silverware was stolen; and the seizure was, therefore, valid. Also, the court pointed out that "[i]t is not necessary under the law that the officer know with certainty that the

[8]Arizona v. Hicks, 480 U.S. 321, 107 S.Ct. 1149, 94 L.Ed.2d 347 (1987).

[9]Downey v. State, 241 Ga. App. 821, 527 S.E.2d 909 (2000).

[10]Brown v. State, 269 Ga. 830, 832 (2), 504 S.E.2d 443 (1998). Taylor v. State, 249 Ga. App. 538, 540 (1), 548 S.E.2d 662 (2001).

[11]Whittington v. State, 165 Ga. App. 763, 302 S.E.2d 617 (1983).

item is stolen [or contraband] at the time of the seizure, only that there be probable cause to believe that this is the case." In *Mozier v. State,*[12] a search warrant was issued to search for items taken from the victim, and where the affidavit stated that she had been beaten, the court upheld the seizure of brass knuckles.

In *United States v. Jacobsen,*[13] the Supreme Court held that the DEA's field test of a white powder, discovered by an employee of a private freight carrier, was not a search within the meaning of the Fourth Amendment because it was sui generis. Thus, the motion to suppress was not valid.

See § 3:10, supra, on objects identified by feel during a frisk. See § 4:30, supra, on exigent circumstances justifying seizure of contraband seen at a home.

§ 4:43　Warrantless searches—Open fields

Writing for the Court, in 1924, Justice Holmes held, in *Hester v. United States,*[1] that the Fourth Amendment protects individuals in their "persons, houses, papers and effects" and its protection does not extend to open fields. Thus, it has been held that no search warrant is necessary for a search of an open field[2] or orchard,[3] or a beach,[4] or some other such area. In *Oliver v. United States,*[5] the Supreme Court seems to say the open fields doctrine applies to all land outside the curtilage regardless of how remote the land is and regardless of the efforts of the property owner to keep others out. The court said "that the term 'open fields' may

---

[12]Mozier v. State, 207 Ga. App. 264, 267, 427 S.E.2d 551 (1993).

[13]United States v. Jacobsen, 466 U.S. 109, 104 S.Ct. 1652, 80 L.Ed.2d 85 (1984).

[Section 4:43]

[1]Hester v. United States, 265 U.S. 57, 44 S.Ct. 445, 68 L.Ed. 898 (1924).

[2]Hester v. United States, 265 U.S. 57, 44 S.Ct. 445, 68 L.Ed. 898 (1924) (citing 4 Bl. Com. 223, 225-226); Anderson v. State, 133 Ga. App. 45, 46 (1), 209 S.E.2d 665 (1974). In Reece v. State, 152 Ga. App. 760, 761 (1-A), 264 S.E.2d 258 (1979), the court held that no warrant was required to fly over open fields in an effort to locate stolen vehicles.

See Annot., "Aerial Observation or Surveillance as Violative of Fourth Amendment Guaranty Against Unrea-

sonable Search and Seizure," 56 A.L.R.Fed. 772 (1982).

See Note, "Aerial Surveillance: Overlooking the Fourth Amendment," 50 Fordham L. Rev. 271 (1981).

[3]Frazier v. State, 138 Ga. App. 640, 646, 227 S.E.2d 284 (1976).

[4]Walter v. United States, 447 U.S. 649, 100 S.Ct. 2395, 65 L.Ed.2d 410 (1980).

[5]Oliver v. United States, 466 U.S. 170, 104 S.Ct. 1735, 80 L.Ed.2d 214 (1984). But see Morse v. State, 288 Ga. App. 725(1), 655 S.E.2d 217(2007), where Georgia Court of Appeals, while acknowledging that it was bound to follow *Oliver*, nonetheless questioned "how the Oliver majority could have concluded that an expectation of privacy" in open fields is unreasonable even where the landowner takes steps to keep intruders out.

include any unoccupied or undeveloped area outside of the curtilage. An open field need be neither 'open' nor a 'field' as those terms are used in common speech. . . . [A] thickly wooded area . . . may be an open field as that term is used in construing the Fourth Amendment."[6]

In *United States v. Dunn,*[7] the Court said that "the extent of the curtilage is determined by factors that bear upon whether an individual reasonably may expect that the area in question should be treated as the home itself. . . . [T]he central component of this inquiry [is] . . . whether the area harbors the 'intimate activity associated with the 'sanctity of a man's home and the privacies of life' . . . [C]urtilage questions should be resolved with particular reference to four factors: [1] the proximity of the area claimed to be curtilage to the home, [2] whether the area is included within an enclosure surrounding the home, [3] the nature of the uses to which the area is put, and [4] the steps taken by the resident to protect the area from observation by people passing by." The court then concluded that a barn was not located within the curtilage where it was located about 50 yards from a fence which surrounded the house.

Even prior to *Oliver,* the term "open field" was not limited to unfenced land.[8] It has been applied to land posted with no trespassing signs[9] and has not been limited to what is in plain view.[10]

However, the area within the curtilage of a farm dwelling, as well as any building in that location, is protected. It has been held that a shed on a farm, located 45 to 60 yards from the house, is protected as being within the curtilage.[11] A field separated by fence and some other objects has been found not to be within the

---

[6]Oliver v. United States, 466 U.S. 170, 104 S.Ct. 1735, 80 L.Ed.2d 214, 225, n. 11 (1984).

[7]United States v. Dunn, 480 U.S. 294, 107 S.Ct. 1134, 94 L.Ed.2d 326 (1987). See Corey v. State, 320 Ga. App. 350, 739 S.E.2d 790 (2013) (homeowner's garage considered curtilage and entitled to Fourth Amendment protection when officer entered to question homeowner regarding possible DUI and examined vehicle which had just been parked in garage). Cf. Gravley v. State, 181 Ga. App. 400, 352 S.E.2d 589 (1986).

[8]Giddens v. State, 156 Ga. App. 258, 259 (1), 274 S.E.2d 595 (1980); LoGiudice v. State, 164 Ga. App. 709, 297 S.E.2d 499 (1982), vacated on other grounds, 251 Ga. 711, 309 S.E.2d 355 (1983).

[9]McDowell v. United States, 383 F.2d 599 (8th Cir. 1967). Accord, Manley v. State of Georgia, 217 Ga. App. 556, 557 (2), 458 S.E.2d 179 (1995); Quintrell v. State, 231 Ga. App. 268, 269 (1), 499 S.E.2d 117 (1998).

[10]Anderson v. State, 133 Ga. App. 45, 209 S.E.2d 665 (1974).

[11]McGee v. State, 133 Ga. App. 184, 210 S.E.2d 355 (1974). See Collins v. Virginia, 138 S. Ct. 1663, 201 L. Ed. 2d 9 (2018) (where officer has reason to believe motorcycle under tarp in suspect's driveway was stolen and used in two incidents, he must obtain search warrant before coming onto property to lift tarp and inspect motor-

curtilage even though it was only 35 feet from the residence.[12] Likewise, the backyard of the house in which the defendant lives in a city is not within the open field doctrine, but is regarded as being within the curtilage of the house.[13] The curtilage concept does not, however, prevent an officer from going to the front door of a house by the same route which would be used by "any guest, deliveryman, postal employee, or other caller."[14] In *State v. Lyons,*[15] the Georgia Court of Appeals held that when, pursuant to a complaint, an officer went to the front door of a house which he reasonably believed to be occupied and he could get no response, he could enter the backyard even though fenced to reach the back door. The court distinguished the case from one where the officer entered the backyard for the purpose of conducting a warrantless search. In *Olson v. State,*[16] the court treated an unoccupied abandoned house and its "curtilage" pursuant to the open fields doctrine. See §§ 4:2 and 4:19, supra, on curtilage.

In *Dow Chemical Co. v. United States,*[17] the United States Supreme Court held that the open areas of an industrial complex are not analogous to the curtilage of a dwelling. The court found that aerial photographing of the complex from a plane in public navigable airspace was not a violation of the Fourth Amendment. Thus, the Court does not extend the coverage of the Fourth Amendment curtilage of an industrial complex to the extent of the protection of the curtilage of the home, but it still enjoys a greater protection than the true open field. See sections § 4:2 and § 4:19, supra, on curtilage.

In *California v. Ciraolo,*[18] decided the same day as *Dow Chemical,* the Court held that aerial naked-eye observation, from an altitude of 1,000 feet, of the fenced curtilage of a home did not violate the Fourth Amendment because there is no reasonable expectation of privacy within the curtilage of what could be seen by the naked eye from the navigable air space. Hence, the information obtained from these observations could be used to obtain

---

cycle); State v. Gravitt, 289 Ga. App. 868, 658 S.E.2d 424 (2008). See also, §§ 4:2 and 4:19, supra, on curtilage.

[12]Karlovich v. State, 165 Ga. App. 761, 762, 302 S.E.2d 396 (1983).

[13]Fixel v. Wainwright, 492 F.2d 480 (5th Cir. 1974). See also § 4:19, supra.

[14]Cf. Galloway v. State, 178 Ga. App. 31, 34, 342 S.E.2d 473 (1986); State v. Nichols, 160 Ga. App. 386, 287 S.E.2d 53 (1981); State v. Zackery, 193 Ga. App. 319, 387 S.E.2d 606 (1989); Dean v. State, 200 Ga. App. 752, 753

(1), 409 S.E.2d 667 (1991); Jenkins v. State, 223 Ga. App. 486, 487 (1), 477 S.E.2d 910 (1996).

[15]State v. Lyons, 167 Ga. App. 747, 748, 307 S.E.2d 285 (1983).

[16]Olson v. State, 166 Ga. App. 104 (1), 303 S.E.2d 309 (1983).

[17]Dow Chemical Co. v. United States, 476 U.S. 227, 106 S.Ct. 1819, 90 L.Ed.2d 226 (1986).

[18]California v. Ciraolo, 476 U.S. 207, 106 S.Ct. 1809, 90 L.Ed.2d 210 (1986).

a search warrant for the search and seizure of marijuana growing in the fenced yard.

In *Florida v. Riley*,[19] the United States Supreme Court
concluded that "surveillance of the interior of a partially covered
greenhouse in a residential backyard from the vantage point of a
helicopter located 400 feet above the greenhouse [does not consti-
tute] a 'search' for which a warrant is required under the Fourth
Amendment. . . ."

In *Katz v. United States*,[20] the United States Supreme Court
emphasized that the Fourth Amendment protected persons and
not places, and held that in determining whether the Fourth
Amendment had been violated, the question was whether or not
the officer's conduct "violated the privacy upon which [the
defendant] justifiably relied." Prior to *Oliver*, some courts applied
Katz to open fields cases.[21] However, Georgia and a number of
other jurisdictions have always followed *Hester*.[22]

Generally, warrantless aerial observations have not been
regarded as violative of the Fourth Amendment because it is said
that no reasonable expectation of privacy is violated.[23]

See section §§ 4:39 et seq., supra, on plain view warrantless
searches. See Annotation, "Admissibility in Evidence of Aerial
Photographs," 85 A.L.R.5th 671 (2001).

§ 4:44　Warrantless searches—Jails, prisons, probationers, and inmates

A person on probation, like all other persons, has a right to be
free from unreasonable searches and seizures.[1] His probationary

---

[19]Florida v. Riley, 488 U.S. 445,
109 S.Ct. 693, 102 L.Ed.2d 835 (1989).
See Thomas v. State, 203 Ga. App. 529,
417 S.E.2d 353 (1992).

[20]Katz v. United States, 389 U.S.
347, 88 S.Ct. 507, 19 L.Ed.2d 576
(1967).

[21]State v. Wert, 550 S.W.2d 1
(Tenn.Crim.App.1977); United States
v. Freie, 545 F.2d 1217 (9th Cir. 1976).

[22]Anderson v. State, 133 Ga. App.
45, 209 S.E.2d 665 (1974); Williams v.
State, 157 Ga. App. 476, 277 S.E.2d
923 (1981); United States v. Brown,
473 F.2d 952 (5th Cir. 1973); Conrad v.
State, 63 Wis.2d 616, 218 N.W.2d 252
(1974); United States v. Oliver, 686
F.2d 356 (6th Cir. 1982) (en banc).

[23]State v. Ryder, 315 N.W.2d 786
(Iowa 1982). See n. 1, supra.

[Section 4:44]

[1]Evans v. State, 318 Ga. App.
706, 734 S.E.2d 527 (2012); Brown v.
Kearney, 355 F.2d 199 (5th Cir. 1966).
See also Annot., 32 A.L.R.Fed. 155
(1977), concerning the validity of a
warrantless search of a parolee or his
property by parole officer. For an annotation regarding Fourth Amendment protection of prisoners against
unreasonable searches or seizures, see
Annot., 32 A.L.R.Fed. 601 (1977). And
see Annot., "Admissibility, in Federal
Probation Revocation Proceeding, of
Evidence Obtained Through Unreasonable Search and Seizure or in Absence of *Miranda* Warnings," 30
A.L.R.Fed. 824 (1976).

status is not an automatic exception to the warrant requirement.[2]

The defendant's status as a probationer, however, is a circumstance to be considered in determining whether a search by a probation officer is reasonable.[3] The Georgia Court of Appeals concluded that a warrantless search of a probationer is reasonable if, under all the circumstances, the probation officer acts reasonably to effectuate the legitimate operation of the probation supervisory process.[4]

In *Griffin v. Wisconsin*,[5] the United States Supreme Court considered a state statute which authorized a warrantless search of a probationer's home by a probation officer where there are "reasonable grounds." The court held the statute to be constitutional and pointed out that although the Fourth Amendment requires that all home searches be reasonable, probationers and parolees "do not enjoy the 'absolute liberty to which every citizen is entitled, but only . . . conditional liberty properly dependent on observance of special 'restrictions.' . . . . These restrictions are meant to assure that probation serves as a period of genuine rehabilitation and that the community is not harmed by probationers being at large.' " As a result, in *Fox v. State*,[6] the Georgia Supreme Court has held that "[a]t a minimum, when a probationer has not consented to a search, a warrantless search of a probationer's home must be based upon reasonable grounds to believe that the probationer has contraband in the home or is engaged in some criminal activity there." Nevertheless, a waiver of Fourth Amendment rights may be valid if it has been negotiated through the plea bargaining process. However, if a defendant did not agree to the condition of probation, a waiver of Fourth Amendments rights is not valid.[7] But in *Johnson v. State*,[8] the court concluded that the defendant "impliedly consented" to a

---

[2]United States v. Bradley, 571 F.2d 787 (4th Cir. 1978). Contra, Latta v. Fitzharris, 521 F.2d 246, 250 (9th Cir. 1975).

[3]Jones v. State, 282 Ga. 784, 653 S.E.2d 456 (2007).

[4]Hunter v. State, 139 Ga. App. 676, 677 (2), 229 S.E.2d 505 (1976); Lillard v. State, 156 Ga. App. 54, 274 S.E.2d 96 (1980); Howard v. State, 168 Ga. App. 143, 308 S.E.2d 424 (1983). See Hess v. State, 296 Ga. App. 300, 674 S.E.2d 362 (2009); Spencer v. State, 293 Ga. App. 450, 667 S.E.2d 223 (2008); Reece v. State, 257 Ga. App. 137 (2)(b), 570 S.E.2d 424 (2002).

[5]Griffin v. Wisconsin, 483 U.S. 868, 107 S.Ct. 3164, 97 L.Ed.2d 709 (1987). Cf. Anderson v. State, 209 Ga. App. 676, 677, 434 S.E.2d 122 (1993).

In United States v. Knights, 534 U.S. 112, 122 S.Ct. 587, 151 L.Ed.2d 497 (2001), the U.S. Supreme Court approved the warrantless search of a probationer's apartment where the condition of probation authorized such a search based upon the reasonable suspicions of law enforcement authorities.

[6]Fox v. State, 272 Ga. 163, 166 (2), 527 S.E.2d 847 (2000).

[7]Fox v. State, 272 Ga. 163, 164 (1), 527 S.E.2d 847 (2000). See Jones v. State, 282 Ga. 784(11), 653 S.E.2d 456 (2007).

waiver of his Fourth Amendment rights where the defendant was specifically informed of the waiver at sentencing in the presence of counsel and his counsel did not object. In *Woody v. State*,[9] the court held that where a defendant agrees to consent as a condition of probation, it is valid. In *Samson v. California*,[10] the United States Supreme Court upheld the validity of a state statute that required all parolees to consent to a search of their premises when requested by law enforcement officers "with or without a search warrant and with or without cause." However, the waiver of Fourth Amendment rights provided as a condition of probation or parole cannot be used after the fact to justify a warrantless search by officers who were not aware of the waiver.[11]

In *Howard v. State*,[12] the Georgia Court of Appeals held that corrections officials have authority to condition a visit to a correctional institution on the willingness of the visitor to submit to a search for contraband or other items prohibited by O.C.G.A. § 42-5-15. The same case also held that where a warning sign has been placed at an entrance way stating that vehicles passing through the "guard line" of the prison are subject to a search, prison officials also have authority to search a vehicle of an employee parked inside the "guard line."

In *Florence v. County of Burlington*,[13] the United States Supreme Court clarified that local jail authorities may conduct strip searches of prisoners as part of the jail's routine intake process without violating the civil and constitutional rights of the prisoners. It is not necessary that jail authorities demonstrate a reasonable suspicion that the prisoner has possession of a weapon or contraband before conducting the search. The Court noted that such searches were justified on the institution's general security concerns, including the detection of contraband.

In the case of border searches, including searches of persons

---

[8]Johnson v. State, 248 Ga. App. 454, 455 (2), 546 S.E.2d 562 (2001).

[9]Woody v. State, 247 Ga. App. 684, 545 S.E.2d 83 (2001). In *Woody* the special condition of probation provided that "[p]robationer shall submit to a search of his/her business, person, houses, papers and/or effects as these terms of the Fourth Amendment to the United States Constitution and Article I, Section I, Paragraph XIII of Georgia Constitution are defined by the Courts, any time of the day or night with or without a search warrant whenever requested to do so by a probation officer, surveillance officer, or any law enforcement officer and specifically consents to the use of anything seized as evidence in any proceeding against him/her."

[10]Samson v. California, 126 S. Ct. 2193, 165 L. Ed. 2d 250 (2006). See State v. Cauley, 282 Ga. App. 191(1), 638 S.E.2d 351 (2006).

[11]Cantrell v. State, 295 Ga. App. 634, 673 S.E.2d 32 (2009).

[12]Howard v. State, 185 Ga. App. 465 (1), 364 S.E.2d 600 (1988).

[13]Florence v. Board of Chosen Freeholders of County of Burlington, 132 S. Ct. 1510, 182 L. Ed. 2d 566 (2012).

before or after boarding airplanes, officers must have a particularized reasonable suspicion before conducting a strip search. See § 4:45, infra, on border searches.

In *Hudson v. Palmer*,[14] the United States Supreme Court held that "society is not prepared to recognize as legitimate any subjective expectation of privacy that a prisoner might have in his prison cell and that, accordingly, the Fourth Amendment proscription against unreasonable searches does not apply within the confines of a prison cell. The recognition of privacy rights for prisoners in their individual cells simply cannot be reconciled with the concept of incarceration and the needs and objectives of penal institutions." However, prisoners must "be accorded those rights not fundamentally inconsistent with imprisonment itself or incompatible with the objectives of incarceration."

In *State v. Henderson*,[15] the court rejected the state's contention that a valid search warrant was not required before searching the defendant's cell, finding that when a search of a cell of a pretrial detainee is "conducted by representatives of the prosecution solely for the purpose of uncovering incriminating evidence which could be used against the detainee at trial, rather than out of concern for any of the legitimate prison objectives . . . , the pre-trial detainee retains a limited but legitimate expectation of privacy that he would be protected in such circumstances from an unreasonable search. . . ."

In *Franklin v. State*,[16] the court recognized the right of officials to censor letters written by a defendant during pre-trial confinement as an aid to maintenance of discipline in the confinement facility. The court also concluded that an incriminating letter written by a defendant while incarcerated was admissible. In *Thomas v. State*,[17] the Georgia Supreme Court held that "[f]or security and maintenance purposes, jail officials must have access

---

[14]Hudson v. Palmer, 468 U.S. 517, 526, 104 S.Ct. 3194, 82 L.Ed.2d 393, 402 (1984) (quoted with approval in State v. Henderson, 271 Ga. 264 (1), 517 S.E.2d 61 (1999)).

In Wolff v. McDonnell, 418 U.S. 539, 555, 94 S.Ct. 2963, 41 L.Ed.2d 935 (1974), the United State Supreme Court said that though a prisoner's "rights may be diminished by the needs and exigencies of the institutional environment, a prisoner is not wholly stripped of constitutional protections when he is imprisoned for crime." In Procunier v. Martinez, 416 U.S. 396, 405, 94 S.Ct. 1800, 40 L.Ed.2d 224 (1974), overruled on other

grounds by Thornburgh v. Abbott, 490 U.S. 401, 109 S.Ct. 1874, 104 L.Ed.2d 459 (1989), the United States Supreme Court said, "When a prison regulation or practice offends a fundamental constitutional guarantee, federal courts will discharge their duty to protect constitutional rights." Cf. State v. Sapp, 214 Ga. App. 428, 432, 448 S.E.2d 3 (1994).

[15]State v. Henderson, 271 Ga. 264, 266 (3), 517 S.E.2d 61 (1999).

[16]Franklin v. State, 166 Ga. App. 375 (2), 304 S.E.2d 501 (1983).

[17]Thomas v. State, 263 Ga. 85, 87, 428 S.E.2d 564 (1993).

to the cells and personal effects of all prisoners. . . . Letters found as a result of these searches . . . [are] not within the scope of the Fourth Amendment and . . . [are] therefore admissible."

In *Block v. Rutherford*,[18] the United States Supreme Court held that an inmate in a jail has no due process right to be present during irregular "shake down" searches of cells.

However, in discussing the search of inmates' body cavities, the Court of Appeals in *McCullough v. State*[19] stated that, while inmates have a decreased expectation of privacy and that body cavity searches may normally be conducted without a warrant, such searches must still be conducted in a reasonable manner. In order to justify such searches, the government "must show that a legitimate penological need necessitated the search, that the need could not have been satisfied by a more narrow means, and that the search and any consequent seizure were conducted in a reasonable manner." See § 4:57, infra, on scope and intensity of search.

See § 4:58, infra, on second search. See § 5:22, infra, on non-testimonial evidence under the United States Constitution. See § 26:19, infra, on the validity of consent to warrantless searches as a condition of probation. See § 14:83, infra, on expectation of privacy, and § 4:57, infra, on scope and intensity of a search. See Annotations, "Validity, Under Fourth Amendment, of Warrantless Search of Parolee or His Property by Parole Officer," 32 A.L.R.Fed. 155 (1977); "Fourth Amendment as Protecting Prisoner Against Unreasonable Searches and Seizures," 32 A.L.R.Fed. 601 (1977); "Censorship and Evidentiary Use of Unconvicted Prisoners' Mail," 52 A.L.R.3d 548 (1973); "Censorship of Convicted Prisoners' 'Nonlegal' Mail," 47 A.L.R.3d 1192 (1973).

§ 4:45 Warrantless searches—Border searches

A search at a border incident to the entrance of a person into the United States is not protected by the Fourth Amendment; hence, there is no warrant requirement for such searches. "Travelers may be . . . stopped in crossing an international boundary, because of national self-protection reasonably requiring one entering the country to identify himself as entitled to

---

[18]Block v. Rutherford, 468 U.S. 576, 104 S.Ct. 3227, 82 L.Ed.2d 438 (1984). *Block* also held that a detainee has no due process rights to contact visits with outsiders where a rule preventing such visits is reasonable and was adopted in response to legitimate security concerns.

See Annot., "Fourth Amendment as Protecting Prison Visitor Against Unreasonable Searches and Seizures," 69 A.L.R.Fed. 856 (1984).

[19]McCullough v. State, 177 Ga. App. 741, 743, 341 S.E.2d 241 (1986); Scott v. State, 216 Ga. App. 692, 696 (5), 455 S.E.2d 609 (1995).

come in, and his belongings as effects which may be lawfully brought in."[1]

Rules applying to border searches are important in Georgia since an airport at which passengers arrive after a non-stop flight from outside the country is "the functional equivalent to a border" of the United States.[2] A search by customs agents of passengers at such an airport is not limited by the Fourth Amendment.[3] Thus, a person and his baggage arriving at a customs area may be searched without the slightest suspicion[4] even after the passenger has cleared the customs area.[5]

There is authority which indicates that the defendant must be kept under constant surveillance from the time he leaves the customs area until he is searched in order to protect the privacy of the person and to ensure that any unlawful items found on him were not obtained in this country.[6] However, the validity of a search removed from the customs area depends upon the totality of the circumstances, including the amount of time which has elapsed, the distance, and the extent of surveillance.[7] See Annotation, "Validity of Warrantless Search Under Extended Border Doctrine," 102 A.L.R.Fed. 269 (1991).

While border searches are not controlled by the Fourth Amendment, the nature and extent of the search by custom officials is

---

[Section 4:45]

[1]Carroll v. United States, 267 U.S. 132, 154, 45 S.Ct. 280, 69 L.Ed. 543 (1925); United States v. Ramsey, 431 U.S. 606, 97 S.Ct. 1972, 52 L.Ed.2d 617 (1977); United States v. Garcia, 672 F.2d 1349 (11th Cir. 1982). Generally, see Annot., 6 A.L.R.Fed. 317 (1966); D.E. v. John Doe, 834 F.3d 723, 95 Fed. R. Serv. 3d 730 (6th Cir. 2016).

[2]See Almeida-Sanchez v. United States, 413 U.S. 266, 273, 93 S.Ct. 2535, 37 L.Ed.2d 596 (1973). See Annot., "What Constitutes Functional Equivalent of Border for Purpose of Border Exception to Requirements of Fourth Amendment," 94 A.L.R.Fed. 372 (1989).

[3]See United States v. Warner, 441 F.2d 821, 832 (5th Cir. 1971).

[4]See Henderson v. United States, 390 F.2d 805, 808 (9th Cir. 1967).

In United States v. Sandler, 644 F.2d 1163, 1169 (5th Cir. 1981) (en banc), the court concluded that customs agents need only a mere suspicion of criminal activities to justify a frisk or a request to remove outer clothing, such as coats or shoes, or a request to empty pockets, a wallet or purse of persons entering the country.

[5]Thomas v. United States, 372 F.2d 252 (5th Cir. 1967). Here the defendant was searched within 1-½ hours after return to the country and within a distance of six blocks from the border.

[6]See 8 San Diego L. Rev. 435 (1970).

[7]E.g., Willis v. United States, 370 F.2d 604 (5th Cir. 1966); United States v. Weil, 432 F.2d 1320, 1323 (9th Cir. 1970).

In United States v. Fogelman, 586 F.2d 337 (5th Cir. 1978), a search of a truck in Atlanta, Georgia, was upheld as an extended border search where officers watched the truck being loaded in Savannah and kept it under constant surveillance. The search was less than a day after the truck was loaded.

limited. Mere suspicion alone will not justify certain types of searches. If a customs official wishes to have a person disrobe, a real suspicion justifying the search must exist. It has been held that if an examination of body cavities is made, there must be a clear indication that contraband will be found.[8] In *United States v. Ek,*[9] the court said, "As a search becomes more intrusive, it must be justified by a corresponding higher level of suspicion of wrongdoing."

On April 16, 1984, the Eleventh Circuit handed down at least seven opinions involving the scope and intensity permitted in border searches in this Circuit.[10] In *United States v. Vega-Barvo,*[11] a border crossing case, the court held that a strip search requires a particularized "reasonable suspicion." This standard is met when "a person behaves in an articulably suspicious manner." "To determine the level of intrusiveness of a search we must focus on the indignity of the search. . . . [P]ersonal indignity suffered by the individual searched controls the level of suspicion required to make the search reasonable. . . . [T]hree factors . . . contribute to personal indignity . . . : (1) physical contact between the searcher and the person searched; (2) exposure of intimate body parts; and (3) use of force." The court then concluded that requiring a person to submit to a warrantless but properly taken x-ray at a hospital is no more intrusive than a strip search.[12] The facts of the case justify a finding of reasonable suspicion that the defendant was a "mule" to carry cocaine in her

---

[8]Henderson v. United States, 390 F.2d 805, 808 (9th Cir. 1967). See Rivas v. United States, 368 F.2d 703, 710 (9th Cir. 1966) (there should be a "clear indication or plain suggestion"); also see United States v. Briones, 423 F.2d 742, 744 (5th Cir. 1970).

[9]United States v. Ek, 676 F.2d 379 (9th Cir. 1982). In *Ek*, the court held that "the stricter standard required for a body search also applies to an X-ray search."

[10]United States v. De Montoya, 729 F.2d 1369 (11th Cir. 1984); United States v. Henao-Castano, 729 F.2d 1364 (11th Cir. 1984); United States v. Castaneda-Castaneda, 729 F.2d 1360 (11th Cir. 1984); United States v. Pino, 729 F.2d 1357 (11th Cir. 1984); United States v. Mosquera-Ramirez, 729 F.2d 1352 (11th Cir. 1984); United States v. Vega-Barvo, 729 F.2d 1341 (11th Cir.

1984); United States v. Padilla, 729 F.2d 1367 (11th Cir. 1984).

[11]United States v. Vega-Barvo, 729 F.2d 1341 (11th Cir. 1984). But cf. United States v. Hernandez, 739 F.2d 484 (9th Cir. 1984). In United States v. Castaneda-Castaneda, 729 F.2d 1360 (11th Cir. 1984), the defendants were attempting to smuggle cocaine in their digestive tracts. When they were questioned by customs officials they confessed and x-rays confirmed their confessions. They had been given *Miranda* warnings. The court concluded that the confessions were voluntary.

[12]Contra, United States v. Ek, 676 F.2d 379, 382 (9th Cir. 1982). See Simpson v. State, 263 Ga. App. 496, 588 S.E.2d 445 (2003); Safford v. State, 240 Ga. App. 80 (1), 522 S.E.2d 565 (1999).

digestive tract. In *United States v. Mosquera-Ramirez*,[13] the court upheld the warrantless detention of 12 hours until the defendant discharged the contents of his stomach where there was reasonable suspicion and the defendant refused to consent to an x-ray examination. Likewise, in *United States v. Montoya de Hernandez*,[14] a similar case, the United States Supreme Court upheld an incommunicado detention of 16 hours to await the defendant's bowel movement. Thereafter, a rectal examination was conducted pursuant to court order. In *United States v. Pino*,[15] the court said that in order to conduct a rectal search "the facts must be sufficient to raise the level of required suspicion in the minds of experts . . . and . . . the review should not be an *ad hoc* determination of whether those facts would arouse the suspicion of the court, or an inexperienced person. . . . What is necessary are facts . . . which would cause these inspectors to reasonably believe that contraband was being carried internally and would be revealed in a rectal search: an articulable, particularized suspicion as to the person, and a particularized suspicion as to the location of the drugs."

The statutory provision for border searches[16] does not provide for warrantless searches of residences, but only of people and vehicles. Hence, the Fifth Circuit has found that a warrantless search of the motel room of a person who had just entered the country was invalid.[17] However, in *United States v. Richards*,[18] the Fifth Circuit held that the border search exception permits the warrantless search of a piece of international mail, even after its delivery to the addressee, if there has been continuous surveillance of the mail and reasonable suspicion exists to believe that it contains contraband.

The Eleventh Circuit in *United States v. Chemaly*[19] declined to decide whether the Fourth Amendment applied to passengers leaving the country. However, the court held that a warrant is required to search a person leaving for alleged currency violations under 31 U.S.C.A. § 5317.

---

[13]United States v. Mosquera-Ramirez, 729 F.2d 1352 (11th Cir. 1984). In United States v. Henao-Castano, 729 F.2d 1364 (11th Cir. 1984), the court affirmed the conviction where the defendant refused to consent to an x-ray and he was detained for four hours until he excreted the contents of his stomach. Cf. United States v. De Montoya, 729 F.2d 1369 (11th Cir. 1984).

[14]United States v. Montoya de Hernandez, 473 U.S. 531, 105 S.Ct. 3304, 87 L.Ed.2d 381 (1985).

[15]United States v. Pino, 729 F.2d 1357 (11th Cir. 1984).

[16]19 U.S.C.A. § 482.

[17]United States v. Steinkoenig, 487 F.2d 225, 229 (5th Cir. 1973). See also Montoya v. United States, 392 F.2d 731 (5th Cir. 1968).

[18]United States v. Richards, 638 F.2d 765 (5th Cir. 1981).

[19]United States v. Chemaly, 741 F.2d 1346 (11th Cir. 1984).

See § 3:13, supra, on retention of inanimate objects without probable cause and § 4:46, infra, on search of incoming international mail. See § 3:5, supra, on stops and searches of vessels.

§ 4:46 Warrantless searches—Administrative searches

Border searches,[1] airport searches,[2] searches of prisoners, and perhaps parolees and probationers,[3] may all be considered as a kind of administrative search. They have been discussed before and will not be considered further in this section.

In *Camara v. Municipal Court,*[4] the United States Supreme Court considered a "safety inspection" of a dwelling by an employee of the Department of Health. Camara refused to permit a warrantless search and was convicted of violating an ordinance requiring occupants to submit to such inspections. The court concluded that in the absence of consent, a search warrant was required before an occupant had to submit to such an inspection. However, the Court also pointed out that a different kind of probable cause or a lesser degree of probable cause was required in the case of such an administrative search than that which is required in the traditional criminal search warrant. The court said that the probable cause required for such an administrative "area warrant" "must exist if reasonable legislative or administrative standards for conducting an area inspection are satisfied with respect to a particular dwelling. Such standards, which will vary with the municipal program being enforced, may be based upon the passage of time, the nature of the building (e.g., a multifamily apartment house), or the condition of the entire area, but they will not necessarily depend upon specific knowledge of the condition of the particular dwelling."[5]

However, in *Wyman v. James,*[6] the United States Supreme Court held that a home visit by a social worker to a family receiving Aid to Families with Dependent Children money was not a search in the traditional criminal law context of the Fourth Amendment; even if the visit had some characteristics of a search, it was reasonable, and no search warrant was required.

[Section 4:46]

[1]See § 4:45, supra, on border searches.

[2]See § 4:35, supra, on airport searches.

[3]See § 4:44, supra, on warrantless searches of prisoners and probationers.

[4]Camara v. Municipal Court, 387 U.S. 523, 87 S.Ct. 1727, 18 L.Ed.2d 930 (1967).

[5]Camara v. Municipal Court, 387 U.S. 523 at 538, 87 S.Ct. 1727, 18 L.Ed.2d 930 (1967).

[6]Wyman v. James, 400 U.S. 309, 91 S.Ct. 381, 27 L.Ed.2d 408 (1971).

In *Illinois v. Krull*,[7] the United States Supreme Court held that the exclusionary rule did not apply where officers, in good faith, relied on a statute authorizing a warrantless administrative search which was later held to violate the Fourth Amendment. See *Michigan v. DeFillippo*, discussed in § 3:2, supra. However, in *Yingsum Au v. State*,[8] the Georgia Supreme Court applied the exclusionary rule where an officer relied on an ordinance of the City of Marietta in conducting a search and the court found the ordinance in violation of the Fourth Amendment.

In connection with the search of business premises the United States Supreme Court held in *United States v. Biswell*[9] that when a federal treasury agent requests entry into a locked storeroom of a federally licensed firearms dealer for the purpose of inspecting firearms and ammunition, he has a right to conduct an inspection without first obtaining a search warrant. The court emphasized the broad authority which has historically been recognized in relation to dealers in alcohol[10] and firearms. "When a dealer chooses to engage in this pervasively regulated business and to accept a federal license, he does so with the knowledge that his business records, firearms, and ammunition will be subject to effective inspection." Similarly, in *Donovan v. Dewey*,[11] the Court held that an inspector acting under the Federal Mine Safety and Health Act could inspect a mine to insure compliance with health and safety standards without first obtaining a search warrant. The court discussed problems of mine safety and pointed out that the Act notifies operators that inspections will be conducted on a regular basis.

However, in *Marshall v. Barlow's, Inc.*,[12] the United States Supreme Court held that an inspector working pursuant to the Occupational Safety and Health Act (OSHA) had no authority to conduct a warrantless inspection of the private areas of an ordinary business against which no complaints had been filed; but the Court again pointed out that probable "cause in the criminal law sense is not required" to obtain an administrative search warrant. Probable cause justifying an administrative search war-

---

[7]Illinois v. Krull, 480 U.S. 340, 107 S.Ct. 1160, 94 L.Ed.2d 364 (1987). In Davis v. U.S., 131 S. Ct. 2419, 180 L. Ed. 2d 285 (2011), the United States Supreme Court held that warrantless search conducted in compliance with existing precedent is not subject to suppression should the precedent relied upon be subsequently overruled.

[8]Yingsum Au v. State, 258 Ga. 419, 369 S.E.2d 905 (1988).

[9]United States v. Biswell, 406 U.S. 311, 92 S.Ct. 1593, 32 L.Ed.2d 87 (1972).

[10]Colonnade Catering Corp. v. United States, 397 U.S. 72, 90 S.Ct. 774, 25 L.Ed.2d 60 (1970).

[11]Donovan v. Dewey, 452 U.S. 594, 101 S.Ct. 2534, 69 L.Ed.2d 262 (1981).

[12]Marshall v. Barlow's, Inc., 436 U.S. 307, 98 S.Ct. 1816, 56 L.Ed.2d 305 (1978).

rant may be based not only on specific evidence of an existing violation but also on a showing that "reasonable legislative or administrative standards for conducting an . . . inspection are satisfied with respect to a particular [establishment]."[13]

In the fire investigations field, in *Michigan v. Tyler*,[14] the Court held "that an entry to fight a fire requires no warrant, and that once in the building, officials may remain there for a reasonable time to investigate the cause of the blaze." However, a fire may be so devastating that no reasonable expectation of privacy interest remains. If the building is "totally consumed by the fire," there is no violation of the Fourth Amendment by a later warrantless search.[15]

Administrative decisions involving tax levies were involved in *G. M. Leasing Corp. v. United States*.[16] After determining that the corporation was the alter ego of a delinquent taxpayer, agents, acting without a warrant, seized several automobiles of the corporation from public streets, parking lots, and other open areas. The agents also went to the corporation's office in a cottage-type building and made a forced entry. No seizure was made. However, two days later they again entered the office without a warrant and seized books, records and other property. The Supreme Court concluded that the seizure of the automobiles did not violate the Constitution. However, the warrantless search and seizure of the articles from the office violated the Fourth Amendment since no exigent circumstances existed.

The search of incoming international mail was involved in *United States v. Ramsey*.[17] In this case, a customs inspector found eight letter-size airmail envelopes in the same mail bag from Thailand. All eight envelopes appeared to have been addressed

---

[13]Marshall v. Barlow's, Inc., 436 U.S. 307, 98 S.Ct. 1816, 56 L.Ed.2d 305 (1978).

[14]Michigan v. Tyler, 436 U.S. 499, 98 S.Ct. 1942, 56 L.Ed.2d 486 (1978). Another aspect of *Tyler* is discussed in § 4:58, infra. Anglin v. Green, 254 Ga. 87, 326 S.E.2d 740 (1985), is in accord with *Tyler*.

In Michigan v. Clifford, 464 U.S. 287, 104 S.Ct. 641, 78 L.Ed.2d 477 (1984), firefighters extinguished a blaze about 7 a.m. About 1:00 p.m., arson investigators arrived to investigate. They found work crews boarding up the house and pumping water out of the basement. They entered about 1:00 p.m. without a warrant. The court concluded that evidence discovered in the house was not admissible.

See Annot., "Admissibility, in Criminal Case, of Evidence Discovered by Warrantless Search in Connection with Fire Investigation—Post Tyler Cases," 31 A.L.R.4th 194 (1984).

[15]Pervis v. State, 181 Ga. App. 613, 614 (1), 353 S.E.2d 200 (1987). See also Riley v. State, 278 Ga. 677, 604 S.E.2d 488 (2004).

[16]G. M. Leasing Corp. v. United States, 429 U.S. 338, 97 S.Ct. 619, 50 L.Ed.2d 530 (1977).

[17]United States v. Ramsey, 431 U.S. 606, 97 S.Ct. 1972, 52 L.Ed.2d 617 (1977). See § 3:13, supra, on search of inanimate objects without probable cause and § 4:45, supra, on border searches.

on the same typewriter. All were bulky and weighed from 3 to 6 times as much as normal international mail. He opened the envelopes without a warrant and found them to contain heroin.

The court concluded that the inspector had "reasonable cause to suspect" that the envelopes contained merchandise or contraband. Thus, the Fourth Amendment did not prohibit the action taken by the inspector because (a) border searches without probable cause and a warrant are reasonable within the meaning of the Fourth Amendment; (b) the inclusion of international mail within the border search exception does not represent any "extension" of that doctrine; (c) the border search exception is not based on exigent circumstances but is a longstanding historically recognized exception to the Fourth Amendment's general requirement that a warrant must be obtained; and (d) the opening of international mail under the guidelines of the statute, when the customs official has reason to believe the mail contains something other than correspondence, does not impermissibly chill free speech under the First Amendment. See § 3:1, supra, on factory surveys to locate illegal aliens.

However, in *New York v. Burger*,[18] the United States Supreme Court pointed out that the expectation of privacy is greater in a home than in commercial premises and that there is no expectation of privacy in "[c]ertain industries [which] have a history of governmental oversight." Therefore, a warrant was not necessary for officers to conduct an inspection of a junkyard. The Supreme Court has applied this rule in the case of liquor dealers,[19] firearms in a pawnshop,[20] and mines.[21]

See 3 LaFave, *Search and Seizure*, §§ 10.1 et seq. (West 1978); 1 Ringel, *Searches and Seizures, Arrests and Confessions*, §§ 14.1 et seq. (Clark Boardman 1979); 68 Am. Jur. 2d Searches and Seizures § 15; Annotation, "Fourth Amendment's Prohibition of Unreasonable Search and Seizure as Applied to Administrative Inspections of Private Property," 69 L.Ed.2d 1078 (1982). See Annotation, "State and local administrative inspection of and administrative warrants to search pharmacies," 29 A.L.R.4th 264 (1984). See O.C.G.A. § 2-2-11 on agricultural inspection warrants.

---

[18]New York v. Burger, 482 U.S. 691, 107 S.Ct. 2636, 96 L.Ed.2d 601 (1987). The Eleventh Circuit noted in Bruce v. Beary, 498 F.3d 1232 (11th Cir. 2007), that the administrative search exception does not authorize law enforcement to ignore the warrant requirement where the primary purpose of the search is to seize evidence of ordinary criminal wrongdoing. However, an administrative search is not rendered invalid simply because it is accompanied by "some suspicion of wrongdoing."

[19]Colonnade Catering Corp. v. United States, 397 U.S. 72, 90 S.Ct. 774, 25 L.Ed.2d 60 (1970).

[20]United States v. Biswell, 406 U.S. 311, 92 S.Ct. 1593, 32 L.Ed.2d 87 (1972).

[21]Donovan v. Dewey, 452 U.S. 594, 101 S.Ct. 2534, 69 L.Ed.2d 262 (1981).

§ 4:47 Warrantless searches—Vehicles—Overview of some United States Supreme Court cases

In *Carroll v. United States,*[1] the defendant was driving a car from Detroit, to Grand Rapids, Michigan. Agents recognized his car, personally knew Carroll dealt in illegal liquor, and had seen the car on that highway before. The agents also knew the car had been used in the illegal liquor business, and because Detroit is located on an international boundary it was one of the most active centers for introducing illegal liquors into the country. These factors combined gave the agents reasonable cause to believe the defendant was carrying illegal liquor. Because of this, the warrantless stop, search, and seizure was valid, since it was not reasonably practical to get a search warrant for a moving vehicle. In *Maryland v. Dyson,*[2] the court reaffirmed *Carroll* and pointed out that the automobile exception provides that an officer may search a car without a warrant if he has probable cause to believe it contains contraband even if there are no exigent circumstances preventing the officer from getting a search warrant.

In *Chambers v. Maroney,*[3] a service station attendant was robbed. The robbers and the vehicle they drove were described in a police broadcast. Within an hour, and within two miles of the station, a car and occupants were sighted and stopped by an officer. The occupants were arrested and the car was driven to the police station where it was searched without a warrant and incriminating evidence discovered. The court, in holding the search valid, pointed out that the validity of the search was not dependent on the right to arrest but was dependent on the reasonable cause the seizing officer has for his belief that the contents of the auto offend the law. Since there was probable cause to search where the car was stopped, it could also be searched after it had been towed to the police station.

In *Coolidge v. New Hampshire,*[4] the court concluded that where Coolidge was arrested in his house there was no right to search his automobile parked in his drive as an incident to the arrest. Also, there was no right to search the vehicle based on probable

---

[Section 4:47]

[1]Carroll v. United States, 267 U.S. 132, 45 S.Ct. 280, 69 L.Ed. 543 (1925); cf. Brinegar v. United States, 338 U.S. 160, 69 S.Ct. 1302, 93 L.Ed. 1879 (1949), discussed in § 2:12, supra.

[2]Maryland v. Dyson, 527 U.S. 465, 119 S.Ct. 2013, 144 L.Ed.2d 442 (1999). Accord, Benton v. State, 240 Ga. App. 243, 245 (2), 522 S.E.2d 726 (1999).

[3]Chambers v. Maroney, 399 U.S. 42, 90 S.Ct. 1975, 26 L.Ed.2d 419 (1970).

[4]Coolidge v. New Hampshire, 403 U.S. 443, 91 S.Ct. 2022, 29 L.Ed.2d 564 (1971). See Williams v. State, 296 Ga. 817, 819, 771 S.E.2d 373 (2015) ("searches conducted outside judicial process are per se unreasonable under the Fourth Amendment, subject only to a few specifically established and well-delineated exceptions").

cause since there were no exigent circumstances. The defendant was in custody. All the members of his immediate family were elsewhere, and guards had been placed at his home. The offense he was thought to have committed had taken place over four weeks before. The court also said, "The word 'automobile' is not a talisman in whose presence the Fourth Amendment fades away and disappears." Likewise, the search may not be justified under the plain view doctrine since its discovery was not inadvertent and there were no exigent circumstances.

§ 4:48   Warrantless searches—Vehicles—General

While the Fourth Amendment limitations apply to vehicles,[1] warrantless examinations of automobiles have been upheld in circumstances in which a search of a home or office would not have been validated.[2] The courts have recognized Fourth Amendment distinctions between homes and automobiles.[3] The following factors have been given as reasons for a somewhat different application of the Fourth Amendment to vehicle searches: (1) The mobility of motor vehicles, as a matter of necessity, prevents rigorous enforcement of the warrant requirement; (2) an individual's expectation of privacy is less in an automobile;[4] (3) automobiles are frequently subject to governmental regulations, such as

---

[Section 4:48]

[1]Gambino v. United States, 275 U.S. 310, 48 S.Ct. 137, 72 L.Ed. 293 (1927); Carroll v. United States, 267 U.S. 132, 45 S.Ct. 280, 69 L.Ed. 543 (1925).

In United States v. Hensler, 625 F.2d 1141 (4th Cir. 1980), the court treated a boat stranded on a sandbar under the "automobile exception."

[2]Cardwell v. Lewis, 417 U.S. 583, 589-590, 94 S.Ct. 2464, 41 L.Ed.2d 325 (1974). In Cardwell, the defendant was arrested and shortly thereafter his car was towed from the public parking lot to a police impoundment lot. Paint scrapings and tire impressions which were obtained without a warrant were held not to have violated the Fourth Amendment. See Chambers v. Maroney, 399 U.S. 42, 90 S.Ct. 1975, 26 L.Ed.2d 419, 426 (1970).

[3]California v. Carney, 471 U.S. 386, 105 S.Ct. 2066, 85 L.Ed.2d 406 (1985). See Collins v. Virginia, 138 S. Ct. 1663, 201 L. Ed. 2d 9 (2018) (where officer has reason to believe motorcycle under tarp in suspect's driveway was stolen and used in two incidents, he must obtain search warrant before coming onto property to lift tarp and inspect motorcycle).

[4]In U.S. v. Chadwick, 433 U.S. 1, 97 S. Ct. 2476, 53 L. Ed. 2d 538 (1977) (abrogated on other grounds by, California v. Acevedo, 500 U.S. 565, 111 S. Ct. 1982, 114 L. Ed. 2d 619 (1991)), the Court said: "Our treatment of automobiles has been based in part on their inherent mobility, which often makes obtaining a judicial warrant impracticable. . . . [W]e, have also sustained 'warrantless searches of vehicles . . . in cases in which the possibilities of the vehicle's being removed or evidence in it destroyed were remote, if not nonexistent.' Cady v. Dombrowski, 413 U.S. 433, 441-442, 93 S.Ct. 2523, 37 L.Ed.2d 706 (1973). . . . The answer lies in the diminished expectation of privacy which surrounds the automobile: 'One has a lesser expectation of privacy in a motor vehicle [1] because its function is transportation and it seldom serves as

those relating to licensing and inspection; and (4) the contents of impounded vehicles are routinely inventoried to protect the property of the owner, protect the officers against claims for lost or stolen property, and protect the police from potential danger.[5]

Despite the foregoing considerations, the requirement of a search warrant for a vehicle has been said to be the general rule,[6] and where there is a search without a warrant, the burden is on the government to show the search falls within one of the exceptions to the Fourth Amendment requirement of a warrant.[7] Generally, the following exceptions or limitations may apply to the rule requiring a warrant:

(1) Search incident to a valid arrest.

(2) Where there is probable cause to search.

(3) Where the car is impounded or placed in storage.

(4) Where there is consent to the search.

(5) Search of a car at or near a border of the United States.

(6) Search of abandoned vehicle.

These exceptions to the warrant requirement will be discussed as listed above. Consent searches have been discussed earlier[8] and border searches have been referred to previously.[9]

It should be pointed out that where a defendant is arrested in a stolen automobile, he is said to have no standing or expectation of privacy which will enable him to object to an illegal search of the vehicle.[10]

Also, the United States Supreme Court in *Cardwell v. Lewis*[11] found that the owner of a car had no expectation of privacy in the

---

one's residence or as the repository of personal effects. . . . [2] It travels public thoroughfares where both its occupants and its contents are in plain view.' Cardwell v. Lewis, 417 U.S. 583, 590, 94 S.Ct. 2464, 41 L.Ed.2d 325 (1974). . . . Other factors reduce automobile privacy. [3] 'All States require vehicles to be registered and operators to be licensed. [4] States and localities have enacted extensive and detailed codes regulating the condition and manner in which motor vehicles may be operated on public streets and highways.' Cady v. Dombrowski, supra, at 441, 413 U.S. 433, 93 S.Ct. 2523, 37 L.Ed.2d 706. [5] Automobiles periodically undergo official inspection, and they are often taken into police custody in the interests of public safety."

[5]South Dakota v. Opperman, 428 U.S. 364, 96 S.Ct. 3092, 49 L.Ed.2d 1000 (1976). Generally, see Annot., 26 L.Ed.2d 893 (1971).

[6]See Coolidge v. New Hampshire, 403 U.S. 443, 461-462, 91 S.Ct. 2022, 29 L.Ed.2d 564 (1971).

[7]O.C.G.A. § 17-5-30(a)(1), (b); Merritt v. State, 133 Ga. App. 956 (1), 213 S.E.2d 84 (1975).

[8]Consent searches, see §§ 4:32 et seq., supra.

[9]See § 4:45, supra.

[10]Brinks v. State, 232 Ga. 13 (3), 205 S.E.2d 247 (1974); Dutton v. State, 228 Ga. 850 (1), 188 S.E.2d 794 (1972).

[11]Cardwell v. Lewis, 417 U.S. 583, 94 S.Ct. 2464, 41 L.Ed.2d 325 (1974). However, the Lewis decision does point out that there was probable cause in the case to conduct a warrantless

exterior of his car. Here the defendant was suspected of having used his automobile to push the victim's vehicle over an embankment. The court said, " 'What a person knowingly exposes to the public, even in his own home or office, is not a subject of Fourth Amendment protection' . . . With the 'search' limited to the examination of the tire on the wheel and the taking of paint scrapings from the exterior of the vehicle left in the public parking lot, we fail to comprehend what expectation of privacy was infringed."[12]

In *Illinois v. Caballes*,[13] the United States Supreme Court held that the warrantless use of a drug-sniffing dog during a lawful traffic stop does not violate the defendant's legitimate privacy interests where the use of the dog does not impermissibly extend the traffic stop. In so holding, the Court distinguished *Kyllo v. United States*,[14] stating, "The legitimate expectation that information about perfectly lawful activity will remain private is categorically distinguishable from respondent's hopes or expectations concerning the nondetection of contraband in the trunk of his car." As such, "[a] dog sniff conducted during a concededly lawful traffic stop that reveals no information other than the location of a substance that no individual has any right to possess, does not violate the Fourth Amendment." However, in the absence of articulable suspicion, a non-consensual drug dog sniff *following* completion of a routine traffic stop violates the Fourth Amendment.[15]

In *State v. Allen*,[16] the Georgia Supreme Court reversed the Court of Appeals which had held that officers may run a computer check of the driver and passengers in an auto provided "an investigatory stop is not unreasonably prolonged" as a result.

---

search of the car.

[12]Cardwell v. Lewis, 417 U.S. 583, 591, 94 S.Ct. 2464, 41 L.Ed.2d 325 (1974) (citing Katz v. United States, 389 U.S. 347, 351, 88 S.Ct. 507, 19 L.Ed.2d 576 (1967)).

[13]Illinois v. Caballes, 543 U.S. 405, 125 S. Ct. 834, 160 L. Ed. 2d 842 (2005). Compare Bennett v. State, 285 Ga. App. 796, 648 S.E.2d 126 (2007), detaining defendant while waiting for another officer to arrive with a "warning" citation was unreasonable under the facts, and drugs found in defendant's car by K-9 unit who arrived with the second officer were suppressed.

[14]Kyllo v. United States, 533 U.S. 27, 121 S.Ct. 2038, 150 L.Ed.2d 94 (2001).

[15]Rodriguez v. U.S., 135 S. Ct. 1609, 191 L. Ed. 2d 492 (2015). See Watts v. State, 334 Ga. App. 770, 780 S.E.2d 431 (2015) (de minimis period of detention after purpose of stop is served, is improper). Compare State v. Allen, 298 Ga. 1, 779 S.E.2d 248 (2015) (computer records check of passengers in vehicle is an ordinary police safety measure which can permissibly extend traffic stop; open air dog sniff conducted while officer waits for return of records check is not improper).

[16]State v. Allen, 298 Ga. 1, 779 S.E.2d 248 (2015). The dissent is sharply critical of the opinion. The case is analyzed in 31 *What's the Decision*, November, 2015.

Detaining the occupants of a vehicle in order to run a record check after the purpose for the stop had been achieved, the Appeals Court said, would not be proper in the absence of a reasonable articulable suspicion of criminal activity other than the traffic violation. The Supreme Court held that because traffic stops are potentially dangerous situations, it is not unreasonable for officers to run a computer records check even though the period of detention might be extended several minutes as a result. In addition, the court held that it is permissible for the officers to conduct an open air dog sniff while awaiting the results of the record check.

See Annotation, "Validity, Under Federal Constitution, of Warrantless Search of Motor Vehicle—Supreme Court Cases," 66 L.Ed.2d 882 (1982). See § 14:83, infra, on examples of expectation of privacy.

§ 4:49 Warrantless searches—Vehicles—Incident to valid arrest

In the vehicle field it is frequently difficult to determine whether a search which was found to be valid by appellate courts was permitted on the theory that the search was incident to a valid arrest or because there was probable cause to conduct the search. Of course, both theories may apply in a given case. The two concepts have been confused and at times improperly lumped together, or used interchangeably.[1] Yet they are different and much of the confusion which exists in the area of automobile searches has resulted from the failure to clearly separate the two concepts.

In *Chambers v. Maroney,*[2] the United States Supreme Court said "that the search of an auto on probable cause proceeds on a theory wholly different from that justifying the search incident to an arrest: 'The right to search and the validity of the seizure are not dependent on the right to arrest. They are dependent on the reasonable cause the seizing officer has for belief that the contents of the automobile offend against the law.' "

In 1925 it was held that a search incident to an arrest is limited to the immediate area where the defendant is at the time of the

---

[Section 4:49]

[1]E.g., Glover v. State, 139 Ga. App. 162, 227 S.E.2d 921 (1976); Adams v. Williams, 407 U.S. 143, 92 S.Ct. 1921, 32 L.Ed.2d 612 (1972); Williams v. State, 150 Ga. App. 852, 853, 857, 258 S.E.2d 659 (1979) (dissent). See

Kurtz, "Criminal Law" Annual Survey of Ga. Law, 29 Mercer L. Rev. 55, 68 (1977).

[2]Chambers v. Maroney, 399 U.S. 42, 49, 90 S.Ct. 1975, 26 L.Ed.2d 419 (1970).

arrest,[3] and is to be made, for the most part, contemporaneously with the arrest.[4] The purpose of a search incident to an arrest is to locate weapons and evidence related to the offense for which the arrest is made.[5] The officer has a right, for his own personal safety and the safety of others, to locate weapons which might be used by the defendant in order to escape or to wound or kill an officer or other person. Likewise, the officer has a right to locate and preserve any evidence of the crime for which the defendant is arrested so as to prevent the defendant from destroying such evidence.[6]

In *New York v. Belton,*[7] the Court emphasized the need for a "straight forward rule" from a federal constitutional standpoint so that "a court will apply a settled principle to a recurring factual situation [so] that a person [can] . . . know the scope of his constitutional protection, . . . [and so] a policeman [can] know the scope of his authority." This was later referred to as a "bright line rule." The court then held "that when a policeman has made a lawful custodial arrest of the occupant of an automobile, he may, as a contemporaneous incident of that arrest, search the passenger compartment of that automobile." This right to search also applies to containers located in the passenger compartment.

The right to search the passenger compartment incident to a valid arrest is not lost at the time the defendant is placed in a police car and when the contents are no longer in the control of the defendant.[8] The vehicle rule has been held applicable to a small

---

[3]Agnello v. United States, 269 U.S. 20, 30-32, 46 S.Ct. 4, 70 L.Ed. 145 (1925); Preston v. United States, 376 U.S. 364, 367, 84 S.Ct. 881, 11 L.Ed.2d 777 (1964).

See also Thompson v. State, 155 Ga. App. 101, 104, 270 S.E.2d 313 (1980), which concerned an inventory search, and Askew v. State, 145 Ga. App. 164 (1), 243 S.E.2d 334 (1978), in which the court found that there was probable cause for the search.

[4]Coolidge v. New Hampshire, 403 U.S. 443, 456, 91 S.Ct. 2022, 29 L.Ed.2d 564 (1971).

See United States v. Chadwick, 433 U.S. 1, 97 S.Ct. 2476, 53 L.Ed.2d 538 (1977) (abrogated on other grounds by, California v. Acevedo, 500 U.S. 565, 111 S. Ct. 1982, 114 L. Ed. 2d 619 (1991)), and Arkansas v. Sanders, 442 U.S. 753, 99 S.Ct. 2586, 61 L.Ed.2d 235 (1979). See § 4:28, supra, on

search of area around arrestee.

In United States v. Dien, 609 F.2d 1038 (2d Cir. 1979), Sanders was applied retroactively.

[5]Chimel v. California, 395 U.S. 752, 763, 89 S.Ct. 2034, 23 L.Ed.2d 685 (1969).

[6]This is apparently the reason the court held the search of an automobile trunk illegal where a defendant was "arrested" for running a stoplight in Rowland v. State, 117 Ga. App. 577, 161 S.E.2d 422 (1968).

[7]New York v. Belton, 453 U.S. 454, 101 S.Ct. 2860, 69 L.Ed.2d 768 (1981). Accord, State v. Weathers, 234 Ga. App. 376, 377, 506 S.E.2d 698 (1998).

[8]New York v. Belton, 453 U.S. 454, 101 S.Ct. 2860, 69 L.Ed.2d 768 (1981); McDowell v. State, 172 Ga. App. 643 (1), 324 S.E.2d 211 (1984); Maddox v. State, 188 Ga. App. 883, 884

airplane,[9] a ship, a motor boat, and a wagon.[10] In *New York v. Belton*,[11] in a footnote, the Court said, " 'Container' here denotes any object capable of holding another object. It thus includes closed or open glove compartments, consoles, or other receptacles located anywhere within the passenger compartment, as well as luggage, boxes, bags, clothing, and the like. Our holding encompasses only the interior of the passenger compartment of an automobile and does not encompass the trunk." In *Boyd v. State*,[12] the Georgia Court of Appeals held that under the Belton rule officers could search an open overnight bag in the open bed of a pickup when the officers arrested the occupants of the truck. However, in *Arizona v. Gant*,[13] the Supreme Court held that *Belton* should not be construed to warrant a search incident to arrest which extends beyond the space within the defendant's immediate control. Even then, a search would only be justified by the arresting officer's reasonable belief that the area might contain a weapon or evidence of the crime for which the defendant was arrested. State and federal cases suggesting otherwise should be reviewed carefully in light of *Gant*.

In *State v. Escobar*,[14] the Georgia Court of Appeals affirmed the granting of a motion to suppress where there had been a valid arrest, a search of the interior of a van, and then the removal of a misaligned piece of molding from the outside of the vehicle. After the removal of the molding, with the aid of a flashlight and through a crack about an inch wide, officers "observed yellow and

---

(1), 374 S.E.2d 810 (1988).

[9]United States v. Thomas, 536 F.Supp. 736, 743 (M.D.Ala.1982).

[10]Chambers v. Maroney, 399 U.S. 42, 48, 90 S.Ct. 1975, 26 L.Ed.2d 419 (1970).

[11]New York v. Belton, 453 U.S. 454, 460, n. 4, 101 S.Ct. 2860, 69 L.Ed.2d 768 (1981).

In State v. Hopkins, 163 Ga. App. 141, 142 (2), 293 S.E.2d 529 (1982), the court discussed and applied Belton where the defendant was handcuffed and placed in the patrol car while officers were waiting for a wrecker service to tow the car to an impoundment lot. The court did not cite or discuss O.C.G.A. § 17-5-1, which authorizes a search incident to a lawful arrest of "the area within . . . [the defendant's] immediate presence." However, it should be kept in mind that this statute does not expressly prohibit a search outside the immedi-

ate presence of the person arrested.

[12]Boyd v. State, 168 Ga. App. 246, 249 (3), 308 S.E.2d 626 (1983).

[13]Arizona v. Gant, 129 S. Ct. 1710, 173 L. Ed. 2d 485, 47 A.L.R. Fed. 2d 657 (2009). See Martinez v. State, 303 Ga. App. 166, 692 S.E.2d 766 (2010) (court held that Gant does not prohibit search of vehicle where officer has probable cause to believe that the car contains contraband regardless of whether there is some exigency in the attendant circumstances). Cf. Boykins v. State, 290 Ga. 71, 717 S.E.2d 474 (2011) (warrantless search of vehicle not authorized where officer has no probable cause to believe vehicle contains evidence of criminal activity related to stop and suspect has no access to vehicle after being removed therefrom).

[14]State v. Escobar, 193 Ga. App. 535, 388 S.E.2d 534 (1989).

brown wrapped material. The compartment was later accessed by drilling into the vehicle, and eighteen individually wrapped kilogram packages of cocaine were recovered." It was the removal of the van's body molding that was outside the parameters of a legal search and thus illegal.

In 1977, the United States Supreme Court held that when a driver is stopped for driving a vehicle with an expired license plate, the officer may order the driver to step out of the automobile before he asks the driver for his driver's license.[15] Apparently this rule will be applied to all cases where a defendant is stopped for a traffic violation. However, as pointed out in the chapter on stop-and-frisk, supra, an officer generally has no authority to make a stop of a vehicle unless he at least has a reasonable articulable suspicion that a traffic violation has occurred or that an occupant is otherwise subject to seizure.[16]

However, where an officer stops a motorist for speeding and it is "the standard procedure when he arrested someone for a traffic violation . . . to issue the driver a standard citation and offer him the choice of leaving his driver's license with the [officer] . . . in lieu of bond or proceeding to the sheriff's office to make [a] . . . bond," the officer may not take the driver into custody and impound the car so as to make an inventory search.[17] But in *Dixon v. State*,[18] the court held that when a driver is arrested for speeding and having no proof of insurance or a driver's license, the passenger compartment may be validly searched even if it is later determined that the defendant had a valid license.

Of course, if there is a valid custodial arrest, the officer has the right to search the defendant.[19] If there is a valid custodial arrest of a defendant in an automobile, as an incident of the arrest, the officer may search the passenger compartment of the car as set out above even after the defendant is removed from the immedi-

---

[15]Pennsylvania v. Mimms, 434 U.S. 106, 110-111, 98 S.Ct. 330, 54 L.Ed.2d 331 (1977).

[16]Delaware v. Prouse, 440 U.S. 648, 99 S.Ct. 1391, 59 L.Ed.2d 660 (1979); United States v. Brignoni-Ponce, 422 U.S. 873, 878, 95 S.Ct. 2574, 45 L.Ed.2d 607 (1975).

[17]Rohrig v. State, 148 Ga. App. 869, 871, 253 S.E.2d 253 (1979). In Rohrig, the highway patrol had received a call telling the patrol office that a car of the description of the defendant's was being driven north on

I-75 transporting drugs. The caller was unknown. The court also held that there was no probable cause to search the car. See § 3:7, supra, on stop-and-frisk.

[18]Dixon v. State, 180 Ga. App. 222, 225 (4), 348 S.E.2d 742 (1986).

[19]Gustafson v. Florida, 414 U.S. 260, 263, 266, 94 S.Ct. 488, 38 L.Ed.2d 456 (1973). See § 4:26, n.21, supra. See also United States v. Robinson, 414 U.S. 218, 236, 94 S.Ct. 467, 38 L.Ed.2d 427 (1973).

ate area of the automobile or even driven away by the police.[20] In *Gooden v. State*,[21] the court pointed out that the Belton rule does not apply in Georgia "where there is some necessity for the police to take custody of the vehicle and conduct an inventory search for the protection of the police department and the defendant."

In order to justify a search of an automobile as incident to an arrest, the initial arrest must be valid.[22] There is no right to search an automobile as an incident of a valid arrest after it has been moved to another location.[23] Unlike a search incident to a valid arrest, if there is *probable* cause to search the car at the scene of the arrest, then the search may be delayed until the defendant and the automobile have been taken to another location.[24] However, where a defendant is arrested in his home and his car is parked on his drive, there is no right as an incident to the arrest to take the car to the police station and search it without a warrant.[25] Likewise, where a defendant is arrested and found in possession of parking-meter keys, a search of his legally parked automobile a half-block away is not incident to the arrest.[26] In *State v. Bell*,[27] the Court of Appeals affirmed the trial court's order granting a motion to suppress evidence seized from the defendant's auto after the defendant had been arrested and charged with the offense of consuming alcohol in the vicinity of a liquor store in violation of a municipal ordinance. The court ruled that the seizure could not properly be characterized as a search incident to arrest because: the defendant had left his vehicle on his own initiative; the arrest was in no way related to the operation of the motor vehicle; and, the arresting officer's safety was

---

[20]State v. Watkins, 182 Ga. App. 431, 433, 356 S.E.2d 82 (1987).

[21]Gooden v. State, 196 Ga. App. 295, 297, 395 S.E.2d 634 (1990).

[22]Henry v. United States, 361 U.S. 98, 80 S.Ct. 168, 4 L.Ed.2d 134 (1959). Generally, on the subject of the search of vehicles following arrest for traffic violations, see Annot., 10 A.L.R.3d 314 (1966).

[23]United States v. Edwards, 554 F.2d 1331 (5th Cir. 1977), rev'd en banc on other grounds, 577 F.2d 883 (5th Cir. 1978); Arrington v. United States, 382 A.2d 14 (D.C.App.1978).

[24]Glover v. State, 139 Ga. App. 162, 165, 227 S.E.2d 921 (1976); Chambers v. Maroney, 399 U.S. 42, 47, 52, 90 S.Ct. 1975, 26 L.Ed.2d 419 (1970); Texas v. White, 423 U.S. 67, 96 S.Ct. 304, 46 L.Ed.2d 209 (1975). Cf. Hunter v. State, 127 Ga. App. 664, 194 S.E.2d 680 (1972).

[25]Coolidge v. New Hampshire, 403 U.S. 443, 455-457, 91 S.Ct. 2022, 29 L.Ed.2d 564 (1971). And see Dunkum v. State, 138 Ga. App. 321, 324, 226 S.E.2d 133 (1976), which holds that where defendant's car is legally parked on defendant's private property and his arrest is not connected with the car, there is no right to conduct an inventory search. See § 4:55, infra, on "abandoned" vehicle search.

[26]State v. Creel, 142 Ga. App. 158 (1), 235 S.E.2d 628 (1977).

[27]State v. Bell, 259 Ga. App. 328, 577 S.E.2d 39 (2003).

never in jeopardy. In *State v. Lejeune*,[28] the Supreme Court in reversing a trial court's order denying a motion to suppress based upon the "automobile exception" to the general requirement of a warrant for a search observed: "the 'automobile exception' cases do not hold that a search warrant is *never* needed to search a car. There is an automobile exception to the search warrant requirement, not an exemption." (emphasis in original). However, in a case where a driver is stopped for a defective taillight and then arrested for driving under the influence, the court held that the officer had the right to search the trunk of the car, not as an incident to the arrest, but because of facts giving the officer probable cause for searching the car for marijuana such as the odor of marijuana, a passenger being seen trying to throw something out of the car, and other facts.[29]

In addition to a search incident to an arrest, the Georgia courts have recognized the limited right of officers to momentarily detain a citizen for a routine license check though there is no probable cause for an arrest. During a license check, probable cause for an arrest may be discovered by the officer. However, such license checks are "not [to] be used as a subterfuge to detain citizens for the purpose of searching their automobiles when they are under no founded suspicion."[30] Roadblocks to check licenses are regarded as preventive therapy to determine if drivers meet the legislative determination of fitness to drive.[31] See § 3:9, supra, on roadblocks. Nevertheless, an officer has no right to a *Terry* frisk of the driver of a vehicle simply because the officer is suspicious or because the defendant acts in a suspicious manner.[32] Moreover, it has been held that even when there is a right to conduct a *Terry* frisk, if the occupants get out of the car and the officers are between the occupants and vehicle, there is no justification for one of the officers sticking his head in the vehicle to check for weapons.[33]

---

[28]State v. Lejeune, 276 Ga. 179, 576 S.E.2d 888 (2003); compare Wright v. State, 276 Ga. 454, 579 S.E.2d 214 (2003).

[29]Rogers v. State, 131 Ga. App. 136, 139 (3), 205 S.E.2d 901 (1974) (quoting Carroll v. United States, 267 U.S. 132, 158, 45 S.Ct. 280, 69 L.Ed. 543 (1925)). See Cook v. State, 136 Ga. App. 908, 222 S.E.2d 656 (1975). Cf. State v. Massa, 273 Ga. App. 596, 615 S.E.2d 652 (2005).

[30]Brisbane v. State, 233 Ga. 339, 343, 211 S.E.2d 294 (1974). See State v. LeJeune, 327 Ga. App. 327, 759 S.E.2d 53 (2014).

[31]State v. Swift, 232 Ga. 535, 207 S.E.2d 459 (1974). See Hardin v. State, 277 Ga. 242, 587 S.E.2d 634 (2003).

[32]In Holder v. State, 141 Ga. App. 426, 233 S.E.2d 501 (1977), the officer testified that he had to "investigate a suspicious person."

[33]Canal Zone v. Bender, 573 F.2d 1329 (5th Cir. 1978). In the *Bender* case, an officer stuck his head in the car after the occupants had gotten out, smelled a faint odor of marijuana and

In *State v. Watts,*[34] in discussing the search of an auto, the court said that to establish probable cause for the issuance of a warrant by a magistrate or to establish exigent circumstances justifying a search without a warrant three elements are essential: "[1] that there is reason to accept the informer's reliability; [2] that the facts are sufficient to show how the informer obtained his information or that the criminal activity is described in such detail as to negate its being a mere rumor; and [3] that the information is current, not stale."

See § 2:11, supra, on probable cause to arrest without a warrant for an offense committed in the presence of an officer; §§ 4:26 and 4:28, supra, on general searches incident to an arrest; and § 4:15, supra. In connection with the search of suitcases in a vehicle driven by a defendant at the time of his arrest, see §§ 4:26 and 4:28, supra. See § 4:50, infra, on search of an automobile based on probable cause and § 3:11, supra, on frisk of a vehicle. See Annotation, "Validity, Under Federal Constitution, of Warrantless Search of Motor Vehicle—Supreme Court Cases," 66 L.Ed.2d 882, 887 (1982).

§ 4:50 Warrantless searches—Vehicles—Probable cause— General

In *Carroll v. United States,*[1] the United States Supreme Court held that officers may search a stopped automobile without a warrant if there is probable cause to believe that contraband or other evidence of crime is within the vehicle and it is not practicable to secure a warrant. Thus, in the case of a motor vehicle, if there is probable cause to believe that it contains evidence which is seizable and there are exigent circumstances, an officer may conduct a warrantless search.[2] In the 1996 case of *Pennsylvania v. Labron,*[3] the United States Supreme Court held that a search of an automobile based on probable cause does not require exigent or unforeseen circumstances. " '[R]eady mobility' [amounts to] an exigency sufficient to excuse failure to obtain a search warrant. . . . If a car is readily mobile and probable cause exists to believe it contains contraband, the Fourth Amendment thus permits police to search the vehicle without more." The

---

then reached under the front seat and found contraband there. The court said that the car was not within the "area of control" of the occupants.

[34]State v. Watts, 154 Ga. App. 789 (3), 270 S.E.2d 52 (1980).

[Section 4:50]

[1]Carroll v. United States, 267 U.S. 132, 156, 45 S.Ct. 280, 69 L.Ed. 543 (1925).

[2]United States v. Ross, 456 U.S. 798, 102 S.Ct. 2157, 72 L.Ed.2d 572 (1982).

[3]Pennsylvania v. Labron, 518 U.S. 938, 116 S.Ct. 2485, 135 L.Ed.2d 1031 (1996).

United States Supreme Court, in *Maryland v. Dyson*[4] in 1999, upheld the stopping of a vehicle and a warrantless search of a vehicle based on probable cause even though there was sufficient time after the informant's tip to obtain a warrant and it would not have been significantly difficult to get a warrant. This has been said to be true because of the mobility of automobiles. A vehicle can quickly be moved out of the jurisdiction in which a warrant is obtained. However, the same rule has been applied to an automobile which has been rendered immobile as a result of a collision.[5] The Carroll rule has been held to be applicable to an airplane.[6]

In *Chambers v. Maroney*,[7] the United States Supreme Court held that if there is probable cause to search the vehicle where it is stopped or located, the search may be delayed until the automobile is moved to another location. In *California v. Carney*,[8] the Court applied the Carroll rule to an operable motor home on a public parking lot, and in *United States v. Hamilton*,[9] the Ninth Circuit applied the Carroll rule to a motor home parked in a private drive.

It would be unreasonable to authorize officers to stop every automobile on the chance of finding contraband. In order to stop and search a car on a public highway, there must be probable cause for believing that the vehicle contains contraband.[10] The "probable cause determination must be based on objective facts that could justify the issuance of a warrant by a magistrate and

---

[4]Maryland v. Dyson, 527 U.S. 465, 119 S.Ct. 2013, 144 L.Ed.2d 442 (1999).

[5]Fluker v. State, 171 Ga. App. 415, 416, 319 S.E.2d 884 (1984).

[6]United States v. Olson, 670 F.2d 185 (11th Cir. 1982); United States v. Nigro, 727 F.2d 100 (6th Cir. 1984).

[7]Chambers v. Maroney, 399 U.S. 42, 90 S.Ct. 1975, 26 L.Ed.2d 419 (1970); Texas v. White, 423 U.S. 67, 96 S.Ct. 304, 46 L.Ed.2d 209 (1975).

In Texas v. White, 423 U.S. 67, 96 S.Ct. 304, 46 L.Ed.2d 209 (1975), the defendant was arrested at 1:30 p.m. in Amarillo while he was attempting to pass fraudulent checks at a drive-in window of a bank. The officers directed the defendant "to park his auto at the curb. While parking the car, respondent was observed by . . . one of the officers attempting to 'stuff'

between the seats." The defendant was arrested and his car was driven to the station house by one of the officers. At the station house the defendant was questioned for 30 to 45 minutes. The defendant declined to consent to a search of the car. However, officers did search the car. The Supreme Court, in upholding the search, said that the "probable cause factor" that developed on the scene "still obtained at the station house."

[8]California v. Carney, 471 U.S. 386, 105 S.Ct. 2066, 85 L.Ed.2d 406 (1985).

[9]United States v. Hamilton, 792 F.2d 837 (9th Cir. 1986).

[10]United States v. Ross, 456 U.S. 798, 102 S.Ct. 2157, 72 L.Ed.2d 572 (1982) (quoting with approval from Carroll v. United States, 267 U.S. 132, 153, 45 S.Ct. 280, 69 L.Ed. 543 (1925)).

not merely on subjective good faith of the police officers."[11] In addition, where the initial action of the police is improper, e.g., stopping a motorist without some objective basis for suspicion of wrongdoing, an intervening legitimate ground for stopping the driver, e.g., resisting arrest, may serve to purge the taint of an otherwise illegal stop and justify the use of any evidence seized in connection therewith.[12]

In *Colorado v. Bannister*,[13] the United States Supreme Court held that where there was probable cause to believe that articles appearing in plain view in an automobile were stolen property, the officer may seize the items without a search warrant. In *Michigan v. Thomas*,[14] the United States Supreme Court held that a second search could be conducted by officers, without a search warrant, even after the vehicle had been immobilized by being in police custody. In *Boggs v. State*,[15] the Georgia Court of Appeals held that where an officer has "probable cause to believe that contraband was contained somewhere in appellant's automobile, he was authorized to conduct a search of its contents, including the locked strongbox." In *California v. Acevedo*,[16] the United States Supreme Court pointed out that "[t]o the extent that the Chadwick-Sanders rule protects privacy, its protection is minimal. . . . Sanders was explicitly undermined in Ross. [See § 4:53, infra.] . . . [I]t is better to adopt one clear-cut rule to govern automobile searches and eliminate the warrant requirement for closed containers set forth in Sanders. . . 'Probable cause to believe that a container placed in the trunk of [an automobile] contains contraband or evidence does not justify a search of the

---

[11]United States v. Ross, 456 U.S. 798, 102 S.Ct. 2157, 72 L.Ed.2d 572 (1982); King v. State, 210 Ga. App. 828, 829, 437 S.E.2d 809 (1993).

[12]See State v. Stilley, 261 Ga. App. 868, 584 S.E.2d 9 (2003); Eichelberger v. State, 252 Ga. App. 801, 557 S.E.2d 439 (2001); see also, U.S. v. Bailey, 691 F.2d 1009 (11th Cir. 1982). But see Hameen v. State, 246 Ga. App. 599, 541 S.E.2d 668 (2000).

[13]Colorado v. Bannister, 449 U.S. 1, 101 S.Ct. 42, 66 L.Ed.2d 42 (1980).

In United States v. Ramapuram, 632 F.2d 1149 (4th Cir. 1980), the court upheld the warrantless search of the trunk of an apparently abandoned auto located in an open field where there was probable cause.

[14]Michigan v. Thomas, 458 U.S. 259, 102 S.Ct. 3079, 73 L.Ed.2d 750

(1982). In *Thomas*, the Court said "that the justification to conduct such a warrantless search does not vanish once the car has been immobilized; nor does it depend upon a reviewing court's assessment of the likelihood in each particular case that the car would be driven away, or that its contents would have been tampered with, during the period required for the police to obtain a warrant." Accord, Florida v. Meyers, 466 U.S. 380, 104 S.Ct. 1852, 80 L.Ed.2d 381 (1984). See § 4:56, infra, on warrantless inventory search of impounded, stored or condemned vehicle.

[15]Boggs v. State, 194 Ga. App. 264, 390 S.E.2d 423 (1990).

[16]California v. Acevedo, 500 U.S. 565, 111 S.Ct. 1982, 114 L.Ed.2d 619 (1991).

entire [vehicle].' . . . In the case before us, the police had probable cause to believe that the paper bag in the automobile's trunk
contained marijuana. That probable cause now allows a warrantless search of the paper bag. . . . The police may search an
automobile and the containers within it where they have probable cause to believe contraband or evidence is contained."

There must be at least as much probable cause for a vehicular
search without a warrant as would be required to obtain a search
warrant from a magistrate.[17] In *Love v. State,*[18] the Georgia Court
of Appeals said, "An automobile search may be conducted without
a warrant provided it is based on facts that would justify the issuance of a warrant." The facts known to the officers involved
must be such as would lead a prudent man in the same circumstances to believe that contraband is illegally possessed in a vehicle or that tools or fruits of a crime are there.[19] In *McKinney v.
State,* the court held that exigent circumstances were not necessary to justify the warrantless search of an automobile.[20]
However, exigent circumstances plus a general inarticulable
suspicion are not sufficient.[21] The presence or absence of probable
cause is to be determined from the totality of circumstances.[22]
The fact that it is the usual practice among officers to search
stopped cars will not render a search valid.[23]

The doctrine of collective knowledge of officers conducting a
common investigation applies to the search of an automobile just
as it applies to an arrest.[24] See § 2:11, supra, on probable cause to
arrest. Thus, the Georgia Court of Appeals, in *Parker v. State,*[25]
stated that especially "when an officer is operating under the
exigent circumstances required for a warrantless search of a car,

---

[17]See State v. Perry, 234 Ga. 842,
218 S.E.2d 559 (1975). Cf. Peters v.
State, 148 Ga. App. 850, 253 S.E.2d
214 (1979), where the informant was
known to be reliable.

[18]Love v. State, 173 Ga. App. 85
(1), 325 S.E.2d 449 (1984).

[19]Cunningham v. State, 133 Ga.
App. 305, 307-308, 211 S.E.2d 150
(1974). See Glenn v. State, 285 Ga.
App. 872, 874, 648 S.E.2d 177 (2007)
(a determination of probable cause
"merely requires that the facts available to the officer would warrant a
man of reasonable caution in the belief
that certain items may be contraband
or stolen property or useful as evidence of a crime; it does not demand
any showing that such a belief be correct or more likely true than false. A

practical, nontechnical probability
that incriminating evidence is involved
is all that is required. Cit").

[20]Parker v. State, 161 Ga. App.
37, 38 (1), 288 S.E.2d 852 (1982);
McKinney v. State, 184 Ga. App. 607,
362 S.E.2d 65 (1987).

[21]State v. Creel, 142 Ga. App. 158,
159 (3), 235 S.E.2d 628 (1977). But see
United States v. Staller, 616 F.2d 1284
(5th Cir. 1980).

[22]Cook v. State, 136 Ga. App. 908,
909 (1), 222 S.E.2d 656 (1975).

[23]Brewer v. State, 129 Ga. App.
118, 121, 199 S.E.2d 109 (1973).

[24]See § 2:11, supra.

[25]Parker v. State, 161 Ga. App.
37, 39 (4), 288 S.E.2d 852 (1982).

we cannot require a police officer to radio to another officer all the information he has about a suspect, the source of his information, and the background of his informant in order that the receiving officer may make an independent determination as to whether he has probable cause to stop and search the automobile in question. . . . [The] searching officer need not personally be aware of all the facts which would support a probable cause determination so long as it can be established by evidence that the searching officer's actions were the end result of a chain of information-sharing; one link of which is an officer in possession of the 'information requisite to support an independent judicial assessment of probable cause.' " However, in *Duke v. State*,[26] the Court of Appeals acknowledged in response to a motion to suppress that the state was entitled to rely on the collective knowledge of law enforcement to satisfy the probable cause element to a warrantless search of an auto and its driver. However, while the arresting officer was acting appropriately by performing a stop and search, after receiving orders from his dispatch to stop a specific vehicle believed to be involved in drug activity, the Court nonetheless suppressed the evidence because the State failed to show the source of the information provided over the police radio or any reason for the order to make the stop. See § 2:11, § 3:2, § 3:7, and § 4:9, supra, on collective knowledge establishing an articulable suspicion.

See § 2:11, supra, on probable cause to arrest and § 4:7, supra, on probable cause to obtain a search warrant. See § 4:53, infra, on nature of search permitted. Also see § 4:30, supra, on exigent circumstances. Generally, see Annotation, "Validity, Under Federal Constitution, of Warrantless Search of Motor Vehicle—Supreme Court Cases," 66 L.Ed.2d 882, 889 (1982).

§ 4:51 Warrantless searches—Vehicles—Circumstances not amounting to probable cause

The following situations illustrate cases in which the Georgia Court of Appeals determined that probable cause to search a vehicle did not exist where (1) the police were notified by campus police from the local college to be on the lookout for a car fitting the description of a defendant's vehicle because of a campus traffic violation;[1] (2) an officer recognized a driver as one he believed

---

[26]Duke v. State, 257 Ga. App. 609, 571 S.E.2d 414 (2002).

[Section 4:51]

[1]Davidson v. State, 125 Ga. App. 502, 188 S.E.2d 124 (1972) (inference).

to possess marijuana and observed a cigarette paper in the car;[2] (3) marijuana could not be seized from a car where an officer's most favorable testimony to the state was that he saw, through the window of the automobile and through the open aperture of the unlit glove compartment, a bag containing a substance he believed was contraband;[3] (4) officers observed a man in a car who matched the description of a person who had reportedly recently retrieved a plastic bag from under some leaves, they had no right to search the man's car, even though they smelled alcohol from within the automobile;[4] (5) an officer observed the passing of a paper bag from one car to another late at night, the car to which the bag is passed pulls away with its lights off, and, on stopping the vehicle, there is a paper sack which the officer partially sees behind the passenger seat; the officer asked, "What's in the paper bag?" and the driver said, "What paper bag?";[5] (6) there is no probable cause to search a car, which was not seen violating any law, but which was seen in a commercial district in the early morning hours approximately 500 yards from a place officers later learned had been burglarized;[6] (7) likewise, the observation of black suspects near a Cadillac in the driveway of a residence in a "white" neighborhood and their shortly driving away did not constitute probable cause for an arrest for burglary;[7] (8) officers had probable cause to search the defendant's car and the defendant was arrested a number of miles away from the car, there were found to be no exigent circumstances justifying a warrantless search where officers could have obtained a search warrant;[8] and, (9) the "mere entry and exit of a house where drugs had been found six months earlier does not rise to the level of reasonable, articulable suspicion of a drug purchase" and hence would not provide the probable cause to stop the motor vehicle which took the defendant to and from the house.[9]

---

[2]L. B. B. v. State, 129 Ga. App. 163, 198 S.E.2d 895 (1973). State v. Thompson, 256 Ga. App. 188, 569 S.E.2d 254 (2002) (nervousness, shaky hands, not making eye contact with officer and a strong smell of laundry detergent or dryer sheets which can be used to mask the odor of illegal substances are not sufficient to justify prolonged investigation of traffic stop).

[3]Humkey v. State, 129 Ga. App. 750, 201 S.E.2d 190 (1973). See State v. Massa, 273 Ga. App. 596, 615 S.E.2d 652 (2005).

[4]Bethea v. State, 127 Ga. App. 97, 192 S.E.2d 554 (1972).

[5]Vincent v. State, 178 Ga. App. 199, 200 (1), 342 S.E.2d 382 (1986).

[6]State v. Avret, 156 Ga. App. 527, 275 S.E.2d 113 (1980).

[7]Davis v. State, 158 Ga. App. 271, 279 S.E.2d 720 (1981).

[8]State v. Padgett, 159 Ga. App. 204, 283 S.E.2d 36 (1981).

[9]State v. Morgan, 260 Ga. App. 263(2), 581 S.E.2d 296 (2003).

§ 4:52 Warrantless searches—Vehicles—Circumstances amounting to probable cause

The observation by police officers of an object passed out of a car in exchange for money has been held to establish probable cause where the officers had reliable information that the car was being used to transport drugs.[1] Where a car sped off when officers approached and officers noted the odor of marijuana when the car was stopped, there was probable cause to search the automobile.[2] In *State v. Folk*,[3] the court held that "a trained police officer's perception of the odor of burning marijuana, provided his ability to identify that odor is placed into evidence, constitutes sufficient probable cause to support the warrantless search of a vehicle," and pointed out that the court has previously found "the 'alert' of a trained narcotics dog, standing alone, sufficient to provide probable cause for the search of a vehicle."

In *Pittman v. State*,[4] the court concluded that there was probable cause and exigent circumstances justifying a search of a car, including its trunk. Exigent circumstances seem clear. However, the report of the case fails to indicate how the known reliable informant obtained the information he furnished to the officer. The informant stated that the defendant was going to meet a black female at the Gulf station on Riverside Drive in the next few minutes and that the defendant would have a quantity of cocaine and be alone in a late model Oldsmobile Toronado. The officer went to the location, and the defendant arrived within five minutes alone in a car as described. The defendant walked behind the station and returned with a black female. The defendant looked around "apparently to see if the area was clear." Both persons got in the defendant's car and drove off. The officer stopped the car and searched it. The court pointed to "the detailed nature of his tip, and the corroboration of his information" as establishing probable cause.

Where a rape occurred in a red and white car in a rural area and such a vehicle was found with blood both on the inside and outside, a search of the car was held valid.[5] After a high-speed chase, the arrest of a murder suspect has been held to constitute

---

[Section 4:52]

[1]Johnson v. State, 126 Ga. App. 93, 189 S.E.2d 900 (1972).

[2]Cook v. State, 136 Ga. App. 908, 222 S.E.2d 656 (1975). Cf. State v. Boykins, 50 N.J. 73, 232 A.2d 141 (N.J.1967).

[3]State v. Folk, 238 Ga. App. 206, 209, 521 S.E.2d 194 (1999). See State v. Kazmierczak, 331 Ga. App. 817, 771 S.E.2d 473 (2015).

[4]Pittman v. State, 162 Ga. App. 51, 289 S.E.2d 531 (1982).

[5]Abrams v. State, 223 Ga. 216, 218, 154 S.E.2d 443 (1967); Barlow v. State, 148 Ga. App. 717, 252 S.E.2d 214 (1979).

probable cause to search the interior of the car.[6]

§ 4:53 Warrantless searches—Vehicles—Nature of search permitted

In *United States v. Ross*,[1] officers received information from a reliable informant that a described person was selling narcotics and kept the contraband in the trunk of a car at a certain location. After locating the automobile, the officers left the area and returned about five minutes later. They observed the vehicle being driven away and stopped it. The interior of the car was searched, and one of the officers looked into the trunk, where he found a closed brown paper bag. He opened the bag and found glassine bags containing a white powder. Ross was charged with possession of heroin with intent to distribute. The officer also found a leather zipped pouch in the trunk. The Supreme Court held that the warrantless search of the bag and the pouch was valid. The court stated:

"A lawful search of fixed premises generally extends to the entire area in which the object of the search may be found and is not limited by the possibility that separate acts of entry or opening may be required to complete the search. Thus, a warrant that authorizes an officer to search a home for illegal weapons also provides authority to open closets, chests, drawers, and containers in which the weapon might be found. A warrant to open a footlocker to search for marijuana would also authorize the opening of packages found inside. A warrant to search a vehicle would support a search of every part of the vehicle that might contain the object of the search. When a legitimate search is under way, and when its purpose and its limits have been precisely defined, nice distinctions between closets, drawers, and containers, in the case of a home, or between glove compartments, upholstered seats, trunks, and wrapped packages, in the case of a vehicle, must give way to the interest in the prompt and efficient completion of the task at hand.

"This rule applies equally to all containers. . . .

---

[6]Whitlock v. State, 124 Ga. App. 599, 602 (3)(c), 185 S.E.2d 90 (1971) (alternative holding). See Raymond v. State, 129 Ga. App. 17, 198 S.E.2d 430 (1973), in which the search seems to have been approved as incident to an arrest with probable cause to search and consent.

(1982). See State v. Kazmierczak, 331 Ga. App. 817, 771 S.E.2d 473 (2015) (the validity of a warrantless search under the automobile exception based upon probable cause is satisfied if the facts would justify the issuance of a warrant).

[Section 4:53]

[1]United States v. Ross, 456 U.S. 798, 102 S.Ct. 2157, 72 L.Ed.2d 572

"The scope of a warrantless search based on probable cause is no narrower—and no broader—than the scope of a search authorized by a warrant supported by probable cause. Only the prior approval of the magistrate is waived; the search otherwise is as the magistrate could authorize.

"The scope of a warrantless search of an automobile thus is not defined by the nature of the container in which the contraband is secreted. Rather, it is defined by the object of the search and the places in which there is probable cause to believe that it may be found. Just as probable cause to believe that a stolen lawnmower may be found in a garage will not support a warrant to search an upstairs bedroom, probable cause to believe that undocumented aliens are being transported in a van will not justify a warrantless search of a suitcase. Probable cause to believe that a container placed in the trunk of a taxi contains contraband or evidence does not justify a search of the entire cab. . . .

"The Fourth Amendment proscribes all unreasonable searches and seizures, and it is a cardinal principle that 'searches conducted outside the judicial process, without prior approval by judge or magistrate, are *per se* unreasonable under the Fourth Amendment—subject only to a few specifically established and well-delineated exceptions.' . . .

"The exception recognized in *Carroll* is unquestionably one that is 'specifically established and well-delineated.' We hold that the scope of the warrantless search authorized by that exception is no broader and no narrower than a magistrate could legitimately authorize by warrant. If probable cause justifies the search of a lawfully stopped vehicle, it justifies the search of every part of the vehicle and its contents that may conceal the object of the search."

In *United States v. Johns*,[2] the United States Supreme Court held that where there is probable cause to search a vehicle and probable cause to search a package taken from the vehicle, it is not necessary to obtain a search warrant in order to search the package removed from the vehicle three days after its seizure.

The United States Supreme Court in *California v. Acevedo*[3] held that where there is probable cause to search a vehicle for contraband and there is probable cause to search a paper bag or container found in the vehicle, officers may search the bag. *Acevedo* is discussed in § 4:50, supra. In *Wyoming v. Houghton*,[4] the United States Supreme Court held that where probable cause

---

[2]United States v. Johns, 469 U.S. 478, 105 S.Ct. 881, 83 L.Ed.2d 890 (1985).

[3]California v. Acevedo, 500 U.S.

565, 111 S.Ct. 1982, 114 L.Ed.2d 619 (1991).

[4]Wyoming v. Houghton, 526 U.S. 295, 119 S.Ct. 1297, 143 L.Ed.2d 408

exists to believe a vehicle contains contraband, the officer has a right to search any container large enough to conceal the object in the vehicle regardless of whether the container belongs to the driver or a passenger.

In *Florida v. Jimeno*,[5] the Court held that a consent to search a vehicle included a consent to search a folded brown bag found on the floorboard. In *United States v. Jaras*,[6] the Fifth Circuit held that the consent of a motorist to a search of the car he was driving did not amount to a consent to search suitcases in the trunk which were identified as belonging to a passenger, and the passenger's silence did not amount to a consent.

See §§ 4:26 and 4:28, supra, on searches of articles around arrestee. Also see § 4:49, supra, on searches incident to the arrest of a driver of a vehicle, and § 4:54, infra, on searches of occupants of vehicles. See § 3:11, supra, on frisk of a motor vehicle. See § 4:30, supra, on exigent circumstances justifying a warrantless search.

§ 4:54   Warrantless searches—Vehicles—Search of occupants

Generally, it has been held that a passenger in an automobile may not be searched simply because the driver is stopped for speeding[1] or for possession of contraband.[2] However, in *Pennsylvania v. Mimms*,[3] the Supreme Court held that where a driver is stopped for driving with an expired license plate, the officer may order him to get out of the car before looking at his driver's license. The dissenting opinion concludes that this case means a passenger in any vehicle stopped for a traffic violation may be ordered to get out of the car, but the majority opinion does not mention this. By mere presence in an automobile, a person does not lose his Fourth Amendment protection from search of his person.[4] However, it has been held that if an officer alone is making an arrest for driving without a license and recognizes the

---

(1999). See also Autry v. State, 277 Ga. App. 305, 626 S.E.2d 528 (2006).

[5]Florida v. Jimeno, 500 U.S. 248, 111 S.Ct. 1801, 114 L.Ed.2d 297 (1991).

[6]United States v. Jaras, 86 F.3d 383 (5th Cir. 1996).

[Section 4:54]

[1]Hunt v. State, 133 Ga. App. 444, 211 S.E.2d 399 (1974). But see United States v. Berryhill, 445 F.2d 1189 (9th Cir. 1971).

[2]United States v. Di Re, 332 U.S. 581, 68 S.Ct. 222, 92 L.Ed. 210 (1948).

[3]Pennsylvania v. Mimms, 434 U.S. 106, 98 S.Ct. 330, 54 L.Ed.2d 331 (1977).

[4]In United States v. Di Re, 332 U.S. 581, 68 S.Ct. 222, 92 L.Ed. 210 (1948), the defendant was seated in an automobile with the owner, from whom counterfeit gasoline coupons had been purchased. Both the owner and the defendant were arrested. On searching the defendant it was found he had counterfeit gasoline coupons. The court

passengers in the automobile as suspects in a recent crime, he may frisk them where there is a substantial risk of possible danger to his safety.[5] It is not necessary that the officer be frightened by the threat of danger if he is aware of sufficient specific facts to suggest that he is in danger.[6] In *Arizona v. Johnson,*[7] the United States Supreme Court clarified the issue of whether police needed an articulable suspicion that the passenger in a vehicle stopped by the police has committed a crime before being subjected to a search. The court concluded that once the police detain the passenger by asking him or her to step out of the car, the passenger may be subject to search provided only that the police have reason to believe the passenger is armed.

Where a driver is arrested and there is probable cause to believe that evidence pertaining to the crime is in the automobile, the police officer may require the passengers to get out so that he may safely and effectively search the vehicle,[8] and to prevent them from destroying the evidence. However, where defendants are stopped driving a stolen car and there is probable cause to arrest them, they may be searched incident to their arrests, like any one else who is arrested.[9]

Pursuant to *Belton,* discussed in § 4:49, supra, a California court has held that where an occupant of an automobile is arrested, officers may search containers in the passenger compartment which belong to occupants who have not been arrested.[10]

See §§ 4:49 and 4:50, supra, on automobile searches. Also see §§ 4:26 and 4:28, supra, on searches incident to an arrest. See § 14:81, infra, on standing of a passenger to challenge use of evidence seized following the search of a motor vehicle.

§ 4:55　Warrantless searches—Vehicles—Abandonment

Abandoned vehicles may generally be searched without a

---

held that there was no probable cause to arrest the defendant.

See Ybarra v. Illinois, 444 U.S. 85, 100 S.Ct. 338, 62 L.Ed.2d 238 (1979).

[5]See United States v. Berryhill, 445 F.2d 1189, 1193 (9th Cir. 1971). However, in State v. Larson, 93 Wash.2d 638, 611 P.2d 771 (1980), the court concluded that where a car is stopped for a traffic offense at 3 a.m. in a high crime area, officers had no right to request identification of a passenger. See § 3:8, supra.

[6]See United States v. Berryhill, 445 F.2d 1189 (9th Cir. 1971), which held that where officers arrested the defendant, who was in a car driven by his wife, they had the right under *Terry* to check the wife's pocketbook for weapons where the pocketbook seemed to be filled beyond its capacity.

[7]Arizona v. Johnson, 555 U.S. 323, 129 S.Ct. 781, 172 L.Ed.2d 694 (2009). See Molina v. State, 304 Ga. App. 93, 695 S.E.2d 656 (2010).

[8]Johnson v. Wright, 509 F.2d 828 (5th Cir. 1975).

[9]Coley v. State, 135 Ga. App. 810, 813 (4), 219 S.E.2d 35 (1975).

[10]People v. Mitchell, 36 Cal.App. 4th 672, 42 Cal.Rptr.2d 537 (Cal.App. 1 Dist.1995).

warrant.[1] Sometimes such a warrantless search is said to be valid because the owner has no standing or expectation of privacy.[2]

Strictly speaking, the question of whether or not a vehicle can be searched should probably turn on whether the owner had a reasonable expectation of privacy in the vehicle under all the circumstances existing.[3] It has also been found that an automobile may be temporarily abandoned.[4] A vehicle may be abandoned if it is given to another person.[5] Also, a vehicle may be abandoned by leaving it at a service station for an unreasonable period of time.[6] More commonly, a vehicle is deemed to have been abandoned when it has been chased by police, and after a wreck the driver flees.[7]

§ 4:56   Warrantless searches—Vehicles—Inventory search after impound, put in storage, or condemned[1]

In *South Dakota v. Opperman*,[2] the United States Supreme Court held that, from a federal constitutional standpoint, a locked automobile impounded for a parking violation may be inventoried even if it has to be unlocked, and evidence discovered in the glove compartment[3] during the process is admissible in evidence against the owner if the police department has a standard procedure of inventorying the contents of such vehicles.

[Section 4:55]

[1]Johnson v. State, 305 Ga. App. 635, 700 S.E.2d 612 (2010). Compare State v. Nesbitt, 305 Ga. App. 28, 699 S.E.2d 368 (2010).

[2]State v. Achter, 512 S.W.2d 894 (Mo.App.1974).

[3]State v. Achter, 512 S.W.2d 894 (Mo.App.1974); cf. Duncan v. State, 281 Md. 247, 378 A.2d 1108 (1977).

[4]State v. Tungland, 281 N.W.2d 646 (Minn.1979).

[5]Commonwealth v. Sero, 478 Pa. 440, 387 A.2d 63 (1978).

[6]U.S. v. Gulledge, 469 F.2d 713 (5th Cir. 1972).

[7]Whitlock v. State, 124 Ga. App. 599 (3)(b), 185 S.E.2d 90 (1971); United States v. Edwards, 441 F.2d 749 (5th Cir. 1971).

[Section 4:56]

[1]Generally, see Annot., "Lawfulness of 'Inventory Search' of Motor Vehicle Impounded by Police," 48 A.L.R.3d 537 (1973). See the excellent Article, Reamey, "Reevaluating the Vehicle Inventory," 19 Crim. L. Bull. 325 (1983).

[2]South Dakota v. Opperman, 428 U.S. 364, 96 S.Ct. 3092, 49 L.Ed.2d 1000 (1976). See § 4:49, supra. When the Opperman case went back to the South Dakota Supreme Court, the court considered whether or not the search violated the state constitution, concluded that the search was unreasonable, and reversed the defendant's conviction. State v. Opperman, 247 N.W.2d 673 (S.D.1976).

In Bennett v. State, 160 Ga. App. 684, 288 S.E.2d 17 (1981), the court pointed out that the inventory may be valid even though officers were already suspicious of the contents of the vehicle.

[3]The court in Opperman emphasized that the glove compartment was unlocked. However, in United States v. Martin, 566 F.2d 1143 (10th Cir. 1977), the court held that officers had a right to look into a locked trunk of an auto in the inventory process.

In *Colorado v. Bertine,*[4] the United States Supreme Court held that the Fourth Amendment does not prevent the "inventory search" of a closed container in the passenger compartment of an automobile which had been impounded, even if some less intrusive method might achieve the purpose of the inventory provided the inventory was carried out in compliance with standard police procedures. The court emphasized the importance of a "single familiar standard . . . to guide police officers."

In *Florida v. Wells,*[5] the United States Supreme Court considered a case in which the defendant was arrested for driving under the influence of alcohol. Pursuant to permission, during an inventory search the officers found two marijuana cigarettes in the vehicle and a locked suitcase in the trunk. The suitcase contained a large amount of marijuana. The highway patrol had no policy on opening closed containers. Based on this, the Florida court suppressed evidence of the contraband found in the locked suitcase. In affirming, the United States Supreme Court pointed out that "[a] police officer may be allowed sufficient latitude to determine whether a particular container should or should not be opened in light of the nature of the search and characteristics of the container itself. Thus, while policies of opening all containers or of opening no containers are unquestionably permissible, it would be equally permissible, for example, to allow the opening of closed containers whose contents officers determine they are unable to ascertain from examining the containers exteriors. The allowance of the exercise of judgment based on concerns related to the purposes of an inventory search does not violate the Fourth Amendment." In *Martin v. State,*[6] the court held that "[w]hether there was a department inventory policy and whether the officer knew it, if there was one, is not determinative of the issue although the existence of a policy would be relevant . . . . Justification of such a search, however, is premised upon the validity of the impoundment."

In *State v. Evans,*[7] the Georgia Court of Appeals held that pursuant to standard procedure, an officer may unlock the trunk of an automobile and inventory an unlocked container found within even in the absence of probable cause. In *Michigan v. Thomas,*[8] the United States Supreme Court upheld the search of an air

---

[4]Colorado v. Bertine, 479 U.S. 367, 107 S.Ct. 738, 93 L.Ed.2d 739 (1987). Cf. Ahmad v. State, 312 Ga. App. 703, 719 S.E.2d 563 (2011); Garner v. State, 154 Ga. App. 839, 269 S.E.2d 912 (1980); Gaston v. State, 155 Ga. App. 337, 270 S.E.2d 877 (1980).

[5]Florida v. Wells, 495 U.S. 1, 110 S.Ct. 1632, 109 L.Ed.2d 1 (1990).

[6]Martin v. State, 201 Ga. App. 716, 717, 411 S.E.2d 910 (1991).

[7]State v. Evans, 181 Ga. App. 422 (2), 352 S.E.2d 599 (1986).

[8]Michigan v. Thomas, 458 U.S. 259, 102 S.Ct. 3079, 73 L.Ed.2d 750 (1982).

vent under the dash after an earlier inventory search had disclosed contraband in the glove compartment. The court emphasized that the right to make a probable cause search is not lost by the impoundment of the vehicle.

Where there is such a standard policy, there is the right to inventory an impounded vehicle for the purpose of (1) protecting the owner's property while he is in custody or elsewhere; (2) protecting the officer against claims of the owner for alleged missing property; (3) protecting the public and the police from illegal weapons which might be contained in the car; and (4) determining whether the vehicle has been stolen. In *Pierce v. State,*[9] the Georgia Court of Appeals said, "[i]nventory searches have two purposes: [1] to protect the vehicle and the property in it, and [2] to safeguard the police or other officers from claims of lost possessions." In conducting such an inventory, an officer may presumably check all areas of the automobile which he has reasonable probable cause to believe might contain any of the items to be inventoried.[10] These areas normally include an inspection of the glove compartment, the trunk, the top of the seats, under the front seat and the floor of the automobile.[11] In *Whatley v. State,*[12] the court upheld an inventory conducted under the hood of a vehicle and said the areas examined need only be related to the purposes set out in *Opperman.* Of course, if in conducting such an inventory the officer finds contraband or stolen property, he may seize it. However, an inventory of the contents may not be used as a pretext for an investigatory police search.[13] In *State v. Lowe,*[14] the court pointed out that an impoundment "is valid only if there is some necessity for the police to take charge of [the car] . . . . In each instance, the ultimate test for the validity of the police's conduct is whether, under the circumstances then confronting the police, their conduct was reasonable within the meaning of the Fourth Amendment . . . . The existence of a

---

[9]Pierce v. State, 194 Ga. App. 481 (1), 391 S.E.2d 3 (1990).

[10]United States v. Edwards, 577 F.2d 883, 894 (5th Cir. 1978). In this case, the court held that there was a right incident to an inventory to look under the overlapping carpeting on the floor of the car.

In United States v. Wilson, 636 F.2d 1161, 1165 (8th Cir. 1980), the court held "that the needs of . . . an inventory search may be ordinarily accomplished without the serious intrusion into the locked trunk of an automobile."

[11]Arnold v. State, 155 Ga. App. 581 (1), 271 S.E.2d 714 (1980) (citing with approval United States v. Edwards, 577 F.2d 883, 894 (5th Cir. 1978)).

[12]Whatley v. State, 196 Ga. App. 73, 77 (4), 395 S.E.2d 582 (1990); United States v. Lumpkin, 159 F.3d 983 (6th Cir. 1998).

[13]People v. Hicks, 197 Colo. 168, 590 P.2d 967 (1979).

[14]State v. Lowe, 224 Ga. App. 228, 229, 480 S.E.2d 611 (1997). Accord, Staley v. State, 224 Ga. App. 806, 807, 482 S.E.2d 459 (1997).

department policy is relevant but not determinative" of the right to impound and inventory.

If the impoundment is not valid, the inventory or search is not valid.[15] Thus, where the owner of an automobile is arrested a half block away from his legally parked automobile and there is nothing to indicate the police intended to impound the car, the police may not search the car for the purpose of discovering fruits of the crime for which the defendant was arrested.[16] Likewise, it has been held that where a defendant is arrested for speeding and driving under the influence while driving a borrowed car and the defendant asks that a passenger be permitted to return the car to the owner at a designated address, it is improper for the officer to have the vehicle impounded without seeking instructions from the owner.[17] Where an owner makes his own arrangements to have his car towed away, an arresting officer has no right to conduct an inventory search of the vehicle.[18]

It has been held that where an officer arrests the driver of an automobile for being drunk in a private parking lot owned by the driver, the officer has no right to call a wrecker and inventory the contents of the car.[19] Likewise, officers have no right to impound a vehicle parked in a shopping mall where the owner is arrested.[20] It has been held that where a defendant meets an undercover agent in a parking lot of a night club and goes into the building and comes back with a large amount of marijuana which is placed in the agent's car and the defendant is arrested, there is no right to impound and inventory the defendant's car.[21] But where a defendant is arrested and separated from his automobile which is parked on a yellow curb and is obstructing traffic, the car can be impounded and inventoried.[22] Likewise, where a driver is arrested driving under the influence and his car is impounded and inventoried, marijuana found in the trunk is admissible.[23]

---

[15]Dunkum v. State, 138 Ga. App. 321, 325, 226 S.E.2d 133 (1976). But see Mooney v. State, 243 Ga. 373, 376, 254 S.E.2d 337 (1979).

[16]State v. Creel, 142 Ga. App. 158 (2), 235 S.E.2d 628 (1977).

[17]State v. Ludvicek, 147 Ga. App. 784, 250 S.E.2d 503 (1978).

[18]Mulling v. State, 156 Ga. App. 404, 274 S.E.2d 770 (1980). See Rowland v. State, 302 Ga. App. 337, 691 S.E.2d 254 (2010).

[19]State v. McCranie, 137 Ga. App. 369, 223 S.E.2d 765 (1976); Grimes v. State, 303 Ga. App. 808, 695 S.E.2d 294 (2010). But see Mooney v. State, 243 Ga. 373, 376, 254 S.E.2d 337 (1979).

[20]State v. Darabaris, 159 Ga. App. 121, 282 S.E.2d 744 (1981).

[21]Dunkum v. State, 138 Ga. App. 321, 226 S.E.2d 133 (1976). But see Mooney v. State, 243 Ga. 373, 376, 254 S.E.2d 337 (1979).

[22]Denson v. State, 128 Ga. App. 456, 197 S.E.2d 156 (1973).

[23]Pierce v. State, 134 Ga. App. 14, 213 S.E.2d 162 (1975).

However, in *Mooney v. State,*[24] the Georgia Supreme Court, in 1979, in a murder case said that the validity of a seizure and an inventory search is not dependent "upon the absolute necessity for the police to take charge of property to preserve it." The court cited with approval the case of *United States v. Gravitt,*[25] in which police arrested men and seized and inventoried their car, which was parked at a motel. Their rent had been paid for two days beyond the time of the seizure of the car. However, officers had reason to expect that the detention would last much longer than two days. The court concluded that the car might have been stolen from the parking lot or some of the contents might have been taken; thus, it was convenient and reasonable for the car to be taken immediately after the arrest.

Nevertheless, in *Strobhert v. State,*[26] the Georgia Court of Appeals reversed the denial of a motion to suppress. Here the defendant was arrested for possession of beer in a park. The defendant was standing by his lawfully parked car when arrested. The vehicle belonged to a member of his family. The defendant had a friend with him when he was arrested. The court held that while an absolute necessity to impound is not required, "a seizure must still be reasonable under the circumstances. . . . [Here] the impoundment was not reasonably necessary. . . . [T]he officer . . . did not even inquire into whether the companion could be trusted with the vehicle. The officer also had not asked about nor given appellant the opportunity to make alternative arrangements for the removal of the vehicle. . . ." There is no right of impoundment "when a driver is arrested and a reliable friend is present who may be authorized and capable of removing the vehicle or where the arrestee expresses some preference for a private towing service."[27] In *Reed v. State,*[28] a passenger was allowed to drive the vehicle from the place of the defendant's arrest to the sheriff's office. A check gave officers no reason to think the van had been stolen. The court reversed the trial judge after making a finding that the impoundment had not been reasonably necessary. But where a passenger in an automobile tells the arresting officer that he does not have any identification, the officer may assume that the passenger does not have a driver's license

[24]Mooney v. State, 243 Ga. 373, 375, 254 S.E.2d 337 (1979).

[25]United States v. Gravitt, 484 F.2d 375 (5th Cir. 1973).

[26]Strobhert v. State, 165 Ga. App. 515, 301 S.E.2d 681 (1983). See Canino v. State, 314 Ga. App. 633, 725 S.E.2d 782 (2012).

[27]Cf. Phillips v. State, 167 Ga. App. 260, 262, 305 S.E.2d 918 (1983); State v. King, 191 Ga. App. 706, 707, 382 S.E.2d 613 (1989).

[28]Reed v. State, 195 Ga. App. 821, 823, 395 S.E.2d 294 (1990).

and impound the vehicle without offering to let him take it.[29]

In Florida, a court held that an automobile slightly damaged in an accident may not be inventoried by officers simply because the owner is arrested, if the defendant has a friend who is willing to take charge of the vehicle.[30] However, if a vehicle does not have a valid inspection sticker or proper lights (if arrest is at night), it would be unlawful for it to be operated by anyone; hence, officers are not obligated to let a friend of the arrested driver take the car.[31] Likewise, if a car does not have a "valid license plate and current revalidation sticker, if required," it is illegal to operate such a vehicle and it may be impounded.[32] An officer has no right to make an inventory search of a badly wrecked automobile if the driver is not under arrest and has a wrecker of his choice come to tow the car away.[33]

It has been held that if a vehicle is lawfully seized for forfeiture or condemnation, it may apparently be "searched" without a warrant and not simply subjected to an "inventory" of its contents.[34] In *Florida v. White,*[35] the United States Supreme Court held that if officers have probable cause to believe a vehicle is subject to civil forfeiture, the officers may seize the vehicle if it is located in a public place.

Also, if there is probable cause to arrest a driver, the passenger compartment of a vehicle may be searched before the vehicle is impounded.[36] See § 4:49, supra, on search of a vehicle incident to a valid arrest.

If a defendant fails to raise the issue of impoundment in a motion to suppress, there is no burden on the state to prove that the impoundment was proper.[37]

---

[29]Howard v. State, 187 Ga. App. 74, 76, 369 S.E.2d 271 (1988).

[30]Altman v. State, 335 So.2d 626 (Fla.App.1976). See Highland v. State, 144 Ga. App. 594, 595, 241 S.E.2d 477 (1978); Martasin v. State, 155 Ga. App. 396, 397 (1), 271 S.E.2d 2 (1980).

[31]Curry v. State, 155 Ga. App. 829, 830 (2), 273 S.E.2d 411 (1980).

[32]State v. Sims, 170 Ga. App. 229, 316 S.E.2d 835 (1984).

[33]State v. Travitz, 140 Ga. App. 351, 231 S.E.2d 127 (1976). Compare Rowland v. State, 302 Ga. App. 337, 691 S.E.2d 254 (2010).

[34]United States v. Johnson, 572 F.2d 227 (9th Cir. 1978). The *Johnson* case upholds a thorough investigatory

search of the automobile some two weeks after the initial seizure for forfeiture purposes and after an initial inventory which did not disclose narcotics. See Cooper v. California, 386 U.S. 58, 87 S.Ct. 788, 17 L.Ed.2d 730 (1967); United States v. La Vecchia, 513 F.2d 1210 (2d Cir. 1975); United States v. Shye, 473 F.2d 1061 (6th Cir. 1973); United States v. Edge, 444 F.2d 1372 (7th Cir. 1971); United States v. Stout, 434 F.2d 1264 (10th Cir. 1970).

[35]Florida v. White, 526 U.S. 559, 119 S.Ct. 1555, 143 L.Ed.2d 748 (1999).

[36]Oswell v. State, 181 Ga. App. 35, 351 S.E.2d 221 (1986).

[37]Wilson v. State, 197 Ga. App. 181, 183, 397 S.E.2d 744 (1990).

In *State v. Haddock*,[38] the court held that the trial judge "erred as a matter of law in granting . . . [a] motion to suppress" because the state failed to produce the impound inventory sheet.

See § 4:50, supra, on probable cause and exigent circumstances justifying a search.

§ 4:57 Scope and intensity of search

The validity of the scope of a search depends, generally, upon the reasonableness of the search in light of its purpose.[1] A search which is initially valid may violate the Fourth Amendment because of "its intolerable intensity and scope."[2] The "scope of [a] search must be 'strictly tied to and justified by' the circumstances which rendered its initiation permissible."[3] Some of the limits of a search as they apply under the various circumstances have been discussed in those sections which deal with the particular situations.

In *United States v. Irizarry*,[4] the First Circuit pointed out that the officers had no authority to search the space adjacent to an open ceiling tile in a motel bathroom after the occupant of the room had been arrested outside the motel room and then taken back inside after a crowd began to gather. The government contended that *Chimel v. California*[5] did not apply because of exigent circumstances and probable cause to believe that the defendant possessed a pistol and contraband in the room. However, the Court concluded that there were no exigent circumstances after the defendant had been arrested. Hence, there was sufficient time to get a search warrant.

Even when officers are executing a valid search warrant, this does not mean that they may conduct an intensive examination of all parts of the premises described in the warrant. They may

---

[38]State v. Haddock, 235 Ga. App. 726, 727, 510 S.E.2d 561 (1998).

[Section 4:57]

[1]Holtzendorf v. State, 125 Ga. App. 747, 188 S.E.2d 879 (1972). See Howard v. State, 253 Ga. App. 158, 558 S.E.2d 745 (2002); United States v. Edwards, 577 F.2d 883 (5th Cir. 1978) (en banc). In Ker v. California, 374 U.S. 23, 33, 83 S.Ct. 1623, 10 L.Ed.2d 726 (1963), the Court said the reasonableness of a search must be determined by federal constitutional standards. Actually this means that protection of the defendant may not be less than that required by the federal constitution. See § 4:49, n.19, supra.

[2]Terry v. Ohio, 392 U.S. 1, 18, 88 S.Ct. 1868, 20 L.Ed.2d 889 (1968).

[3]Terry v. Ohio, 392 U.S. 1, 19, 88 S.Ct. 1868, 20 L.Ed.2d 889 (1968) (cited in Chimel v. California, 395 U.S. 752, 762, 89 S.Ct. 2034, 23 L.Ed.2d 685 (1969)). In Tinetti v. Wittke, 620 F.2d 160 (7th Cir. 1980), the court held that there was no right to a strip search for a traffic violation.

[4]United States v. Irizarry, 673 F.2d 554 (1st Cir. 1982). Cf. State v. Young, 135 Ariz. 437, 661 P.2d 1138 (App.1982).

[5]Chimel v. California, 395 U.S. 752, 89 S.Ct. 2034, 23 L.Ed.2d 685 (1969).

only look where the items described in the warrant might be. Thus, if an officer is executing a search warrant for a stolen television set, he has no right to rummage through desk drawers of other places too small to contain a television set.[6] "The same meticulous investigation which would be appropriate in a search for two small canceled checks could not be considered reasonable where agents are seeking a stolen automobile or an illegal still."[7]

Officers are justified in staying on premises only as long as it is necessary to conduct a reasonable search.[8] A search warrant does not confer on the officer executing it the authority to make an unreasonable search. The officer must not exceed his authority and should be considerate of the comfort, convenience and feelings of the occupants.[9] Officers are obligated to avoid unnecessary damage to the premises[10] and to terminate the search as soon as the object of the search has been discovered.[11]

Where officers, following information received from a reliable source, used a drug detection dog to sniff out marijuana in the defendant's suitcases at an airline terminal in a public area, the search was held to be reasonable.[12] In *State v. Montford*,[13] the court held that where there is a reasonable suspicion that a vehicle contains illegal drugs, an officer is authorized to walk a drug dog around the vehicle to see if the dog alerts for drugs. If "the dog alerted for drugs, that factor, combined with the factors prompting the use of the drug dog . . . established probable cause . . . authorizing the . . . search of [the car's] interior." However, it has also been held that a police officer has no right to take a trained dog into the baggage room, an area not open to the pub-

---

[6]United States v. Highfill, 334 F.Supp. 700 (E.D.Ark.1971).

[7]Harris v. United States, 331 U.S. 145, 152, 67 S.Ct. 1098, 91 L.Ed. 1399 (1947). Actually, *Harris* deals with a search incident to an arrest.

[8]United States v. American Brewing Co., 296 Fed. 772 (E.D.Pa. 1924). But cf. Hess v. State, 309 So.2d 606 (Fla.App.1975).

[9]McMahan's Adm'x. v. Draffen, 242 Ky. 785, 47 S.W.2d 716 (1932).

[10]Buckley v. Beaulieu, 104 Me. 56, 71 A. 70 (1908); Moore v. Kilmer, 185 Okla. 158, 90 P.2d 892 (1939).

[11]United States v. Feldman, 366 F.Supp. 356 (D.Haw.1973).

[12]United States v. Bronstein, 521 F.2d 459 (2d Cir. 1975). In U.S. v. Goldstein, 635 F.2d 356, 360-61 (5th Cir. 1981), the court concluded that air travelers who checked their luggage with an airline had no reasonable expectation that it would not be handled by DEA agents or sniffed by a dog. See United States v. Solis, 536 F.2d 880 (9th Cir. 1976), which did not involve an airport but holds that such a search with a warrant is not unreasonable because a dog was used to locate marijuana. See Peebles, "The Uninvited Canine Nose and the Right to Privacy: Some Thoughts on Katz and Dogs," 11 Ga. L. R. 75 (1976).

[13]State v. Montford, 217 Ga. App. 339, 340 (1), 457 S.E.2d 229 (1995). See Rodriguez v. U.S., 135 S. Ct. 1609, 191 L. Ed. 2d 492 (2015) (in the absence of articulable suspicion, a nonconsensual drug sniff *following* completion of a routine traffic stop violates the Fourth Amendment).

lic, to sniff all the baggage in a general exploratory search or
"fishing expedition."[14]

Where officers make a warrantless entry in a search of a person
believed to require immediate aid and they find a body, they may
make a prompt warrantless search of the area to determine if
there are other victims present or if the killer is still present.[15]
Likewise, officers may make a protective "sweep" of a house in
which a body is discovered.[16] See § 4:28, supra, on protective
sweeps.

The courts seem to apply a rule of reason in determining the
quantity of material which may be validly seized even where the
search is legal. Thus, the seizure of the entire contents of a cabin[17]
or all of the defendant's files[18] has been held unreasonable.

An inventory of an impounded or forfeited automobile is limited
to (1) inventorying the owner's personal articles in the vehicle,
(2) searching for illegal weapons, and (3) looking for evidence of
ownership of the vehicle.[19] In the case of a search of an automobile
based on reasonable probable cause to believe that contraband or
stolen property is in a vehicle, an officer may search any part of
the automobile where it is reasonable to believe such articles
might be concealed.[20]

The forcible extraction of evidence, such as illegal drugs, from

---

[14]People v. Williams, 51
Cal.App.3d 346, 124 Cal.Rptr. 253
(1975). On this whole subject, see Annot., 31 A.L.R.931 (1924), and Annot.,
"Use of Trained Dog to Detect Narcotics or Drugs as Unreasonable Search
in Violation of Fourth Amendment,"
150 A.L.R.Fed. 399 (1998). See Illinois
v. Caballes, 543 U.S. 405, 125 S. Ct.
834, 160 L. Ed. 2d 842 (2005) (use of
narcotics-detection dog to sniff around
exterior of auto does not offend Fourth
Amendment provided stop is not extended beyond that necessary to conduct routine inquiry incident to the
reason for the stop).

[15]Gilreath v. State, 247 Ga. 814,
821 (1), 279 S.E.2d 650 (1981).

[16]Mincey v. Arizona, 437 U.S. 385,
392-93, 98 S.Ct. 2408, 57 L.Ed.2d 290
(1978).

[17]Kremen v. United States, 353
U.S. 346, 77 S.Ct. 828, 1 L.Ed.2d 876
(1957). The inventory of the items
seized takes up pp. 349-359. See also
United States ex rel. Mishkin v.
Thomas, 282 F.Supp. 729 (S.D.N.Y.

1968) (thousands of books were
seized).

[18]United States v. Kleefield, 275
F.Supp. 761 (S.D.N.Y.1967). Here the
search was said to be incident to an
arrest. There was also the added fact
that defendant was refused permission
to copy parts of the records.

[19]See South Dakota v. Opperman,
428 U.S. 364, 96 S.Ct. 3092, 49 L.Ed.2d
1000 (1976).

[20]See United States v. Faulkner,
488 F.2d 328, 330 (5th Cir. 1974) and
United States v. Gorman, 355 F.2d
151, 154-155 (2d Cir. 1965), and generally, Mintz, J. and Dalbey, D.,
"Search of Motor Vehicles," in 56 Federal Bureau of Investigation (1969)
(also available in FBI Law Enforcement Bulletin, March through December, 1967). The right to search a vehicle generally authorizes a
contemporaneous search of containers
which might reasonably be used to
contain contraband or weapons. United
States v. Anderson, 500 F.2d 1311,
1315 (5th Cir. 1974).

a suspect's body has been limited by *Rochin v. California*.[21] In *Rochin*, the United States Supreme Court condemned the use of a stomach pump to forcibly seize swallowed narcotics by saying that such conduct "shocks the conscience." In *Merriweather v. State*,[22] the court affirmed the use of "a Heimlich Maneuver" to expel contraband from defendant's mouth. The court said that "[a]lthough forceful extraction of contraband from a criminal suspect implicates the Fourth Amendment and should be avoided whenever possible, a criminal suspect does not have a right to destroy evidence and 'the police are authorized to use reasonable but not excessive force in preventing the destruction or concealment of evidence.' "

In *Bell v. Wolfish*,[23] the United States Supreme Court found no Fourth Amendment violation in requiring that a prisoner, after conviction, be required to submit to strip searches and to expose body cavities for visual inspection after each contact visit with a person from outside the institution and persons in jails and prisons. In *Florence v. County of Burlington*,[24] the United States Supreme Court clarified that local jail authorities may conduct strip searches of prisoners as part of the jail's routine intake process without violating the civil and constitutional rights of the prisoners. It is not necessary that jail authorities demonstrate a reasonable suspicion that the prisoner has possession of a weapon or contraband before conducting the search. The Court noted that such searches were justified on the institution's general security concerns, including the detection of contraband. See § 4:44, supra, on search of probationers and inmates.

In the case of border searches, including searches of persons before or after boarding airplanes, officers must have a particualrized reasonable suspicion before conducting a strip search. See § 4:45, supra, on border searches.

See § 3:13, supra, on retention of inanimate objects and §§ 4:39 et seq., supra, on plain view. See § 4:26, supra, on search incident to a lawful arrest. See sections 5:22 and 5:23, infra, on the use of surgery on the human body to obtain evidence. See § 4:45, supra, on border searches. See § 4:32, supra, on consent. See Annota-

---

[21]Rochin v. California, 342 U.S. 165, 72 S.Ct. 205, 96 L.Ed. 183 (1952). Cf. People v. Sanders, 268 Cal.App.2d 802, 74 Cal.Rptr. 350 (1969), where the defendant was choked to obtain drugs which he was attempting to swallow; Hill v. Bogans, 735 F.2d 391 (10th Cir. 1984).

[22]Merriweather v. State, 228 Ga. App. 246, 248 (3), 491 S.E.2d 467 (1997) (quoting State v. Young, 15 Wash.App.

581, 550 P.2d 689, 691-92 (1976)). Accord, Sanders v. State, 247 Ga. App. 170, 543 S.E.2d 452 (2000).

[23]Bell v. Wolfish, 441 U.S. 520, 558, 99 S.Ct. 1861, 60 L.Ed.2d 447 (1979).

[24]Florence v. Board of Chosen Freeholders of County of Burlington, 132 S. Ct. 1510, 182 L. Ed. 2d 566 (2012).

tion, "Propriety of Search Involving Removal of Natural Substance or Foreign Object From Body by Actual or Threatened Force," 66 A.L.R.Fed. 119 (1984). See Annotation, "Validity, Under Federal Constitution, of Regulations, Rules, or Statutes Allowing Drug Testing of Students," 87 A.L.R.Fed. 148 (1988). See Annotation, "Federal and State Constitutions as Protecting Against Unreasonable Searches and Seizures," 85 A.L.R.5th 261 (2001).

§4:58 Second search

The validity of an initial search, pursuant to a warrant or under an exception to the warrant requirement, generally will not sustain a later search of the same area unless a new warrant is obtained, or unless there again exists a right to search without a warrant.[1] Generally a search of a person and his effects at the time of arrest does not prevent a search at the time the defendant reaches the station house.[2]

In *People v. Richards*,[3] the court held that a defendant has no reasonable expectation of privacy in items which were inventoried by police at the time of his processing. The item involved was a necklace which the defendant had at the time of his arrest. The Illinois Supreme Court pointed out that the necklace was not in any kind of container and that there was only a "second inspection" of it in order to give the victim of a theft an opportunity to see if she could identify the necklace as the one taken from her. The court concluded that there was no violation of the Fourth Amendment in such a "second inspection." In *Williams v. State*,[4] the Georgia Supreme Court arrived at the same conclusion without considering expectation of privacy.

Likewise, in *Florida v. Meyers*,[5] the United States Supreme Court held that where a vehicle has been impounded by officers at the time the defendant was arrested, a second warrantless search some eight hours later is valid even though the car has been retained in a locked secured area.

[Section 4:58]

[1]Delaney v. State, 135 Ga. App. 612, 218 S.E.2d 318 (1975). See Green v. State, 275 Ga. 569, 570 S.E.2d 207 (2002).

[2]United States v. Burnette, 698 F.2d 1038 (9th Cir. 1983). In *Burnette*, the court approved the search of the defendant's purse at the station house when the defendant reached there even though the purse had remained in the possession of officers and even though it had been searched at the time of arrest. See §2:22, n. 10, supra.

[3]People v. Richards, 94 Ill.2d 92, 67 Ill.Dec. 839, 445 N.E.2d 319 (Ill. 1983).

[4]Williams v. State, 258 Ga. 281, 368 S.E.2d 742 (1988).

[5]Florida v. Meyers, 466 U.S. 380, 104 S.Ct. 1852, 80 L.Ed.2d 381 (1984). Cf. Michigan v. Thomas, 458 U.S. 259, 102 S.Ct. 3079, 73 L.Ed.2d 750 (1982).

In *Michigan v. Tyler*,[6] the United States Supreme Court held that the warrantless entry and inspection of fire marshals of a burning building is proper under the emergency exception to the warrant requirement. Also, their return some four hours later (after daylight) was treated as a continuation of their earlier investigation. However, a still later return and investigation required a search warrant. See § 4:46, supra, on administrative searches.

One exception to the second search doctrine is that which applies in the case of a controlled delivery. In *Illinois v. Andreas*,[7] the United States Supreme Court held that where contraband is lawfully found in a sealed container and it is resealed by officers and delivered to the addressee under police supervision and there is "no substantial likelihood . . . that the contents of the shipping container were changed during . . . [a] gap in surveillance," it is not necessary for officers to obtain a warrant before seizing and again opening and searching the container. This is said to be true because there is no expectation of privacy in the contents of the container after it is first opened and found to contain contraband. "The simple act of resealing the container to make a controlled delivery does not operate to revive or restore the lawfully invaded privacy rights."

In *State v. Fultz*,[8] the Georgia Court of Appeals, in a warrant situation and without citing *Andreas*, arrived at the same conclusion in reversing the grant of a motion to suppress. The trial court had concluded that there had not been a "controlled buy," apparently because the "purchaser" had not been searched before the "buy." The appellate court's reversal was actually based on the failure of the trial court to give sufficient deference to the magistrate's determination of probable cause. See § 4:7, supra, on probable cause.

In *State v. Johnston*,[9] the manager of a mini-warehouse discovered that the locking device on a unit leased to the defendant had been cut. The manager opened the door and discovered several bags of pills. He recognized the pills as Quaalude, took a number of pills, closed the door, and called officers. When the officers arrived, the manager gave the officer the pills and told him what he had found. The officer then searched the unit. The court sustained the warrantless search on

---

[6]Michigan v. Tyler, 436 U.S. 499, 98 S.Ct. 1942, 56 L.Ed.2d 486 (1978).

[7]Illinois v. Andreas, 463 U.S. 765, 103 S.Ct. 3319, 77 L.Ed.2d 1003 (1983). See § 4:30, n.18, supra; Anderson v. State, 193 Ga. App. 6, 387 S.E.2d 148, 150 (1989).

[8]State v. Fultz, 171 Ga. App. 886, 321 S.E.2d 381 (1984).

[9]State v. Johnston, 171 Ga. App. 224, 319 S.E.2d 83 (1984). See Hobbs v. State, 272 Ga. App. 148, 611 S.E.2d 775 (2005).

the theory that the defendant had no expectation of privacy after the manager had seen the pills.[10]

See § 4:44, supra, on searches of prisoners and probationers. See § 4:20, supra, on obtaining a second search warrant. See § 4:26, supra, on search and/or seizure of clothing worn at time of arrest.

§ 4:59 Electronic surveillance—General

In *Osborn v. United States*,[1] *Berger v. New York*,[2] and *Katz v. United States*,[3] the United States Supreme Court has shown that when appropriate procedural safeguards are met, a narrowly written statute providing for a system of electronic surveillance does not constitute an unreasonable search and seizure under the Fourth Amendment.[4] The appropriate procedural safeguards required include (1) that an order permitting the surveillance (or an order renewing a previous order) be obtained from a neutral and detached judicial officer;[5] (2) that the applicant show, with the particularity required of a search warrant, that there is probable cause that a crime has been or is being committed and that the defendant is responsible;[6] (3) that the surveillance which is authorized be limited in time and scope to the investigation at hand, so as not to become a series of intrusions, searches, and seizures pursuant to a single showing of probable cause;[7] (4) that the statute overcome the lack of notice by requiring a showing of exigent circumstances as a precondition to the judicial authorization;[8] and (5) that the order be executed and the warrant returned with a dispatch.[9] Pursuant to 18 U.S.C.A. 2703(a), the contents of electronic communications less than 180 days old can only be obtained pursuant to a warrant issued after a showing of prob-

---

[10]The court cited United States v. Jacobsen, 466 U.S. 109, 104 S.Ct. 1652, 80 L.Ed.2d 85 (1984), cited and discussed in § 4:42, supra.

[Section 4:59]

[1]Osborn v. United States, 385 U.S. 323, 87 S.Ct. 429, 17 L.Ed.2d 394 (1966), reh. denied, 386 U.S. 938, 87 S.Ct. 951, 17 L.Ed.2d 813 (1967).

[2]Berger v. New York, 388 U.S. 41, 87 S.Ct. 1873, 18 L.Ed.2d 1040 (1967).

[3]Katz v. United States, 389 U.S. 347, 88 S.Ct. 507, 19 L.Ed.2d 576 (1967).

[4]United States v. Cox, 462 F.2d 1293, 1302-1303 (8th Cir. 1972).

[5]Berger v. New York, 388 U.S. 41, 87 S.Ct. 1873, 18 L.Ed.2d 1040 (1967); Katz v. United States, 389 U.S. 347, 88 S.Ct. 507, 19 L.Ed.2d 576 (1967).

[6]Berger v. New York, 388 U.S. 41, 87 S.Ct. 1873, 18 L.Ed.2d 1040 (1967); Katz v. United States, 389 U.S. 347, 88 S.Ct. 507, 19 L.Ed.2d 576 (1967).

[7]Berger v. New York, 388 U.S. 41, 87 S.Ct. 1873, 18 L.Ed.2d 1040 (1967); United States v. Cox, 462 F.2d 1293, 1302-1303 (8th Cir. 1972).

[8]Berger v. New York, 388 U.S. 41, 87 S.Ct. 1873, 18 L.Ed.2d 1040 (1967).

[9]United States v. Cox, 462 F.2d 1293 (8th Cir. 1972).

able cause.[10] Of course, no prior judicial authorization is necessary where one party to the communication consents to the monitoring.[11]

O.C.G.A. § 16-11-64.3 was enacted in 2000, providing for application process of an investigation warrant in an emergency situation. Specifically, it must be shown to the Attorney General or a district attorney with jurisdiction that the situation involves "the immediate danger of death or serious physical injury . . . [requiring] the immediate interception . . ." and that "[t]here are grounds upon which [a] . . . warrant pursuant to O.C.G.A. § 16-11-64 could be issued." Additionally, the Code section prevents the subsequent use of evidence obtained if the application is denied or the procurement is terminated prior to a warrant being issued.

In *Whatley v. State*,[12] the court pointed out that "[t]he standard of probable cause for a wiretap authorization is the same as the standard for a regular search warrant."

All forms of electronic surveillance must be conducted pursuant to the Omnibus Crime Control and Safe Streets Act (Title III) of 1968,[13] as well as to the provisions of O.C.G.A. §§ 16-11-60 through 16-11-69, where those provisions are applicable.[14] Wiretap recordings are to be returned to and sealed by the issuing judge immediately upon the expiration of the order. This rule

---

[10]See O.C.G.A. §§ 16-11-66.1, 17-5-21; State v. Harris, 301 Ga. 234, 799 S.E.2d 801 (2017).

[11]18 U.S.C.A. § 2511(2)(c); O.C.G.A. § 16-11-66; U.S. v. White, 1971-1 C.B. 380, 401 U.S. 745, 91 S. Ct. 1122, 28 L. Ed. 2d 453 (1971); McKenzie v. State, 248 Ga. 294, 296 (5), 282 S.E.2d 95 (1981).

[12]Whatley v. State, 218 Ga. App. 608, 610 (1), 462 S.E.2d 779 (1995) (quoting Ayers v. State, 181 Ga. App. 244, 248, 351 S.E.2d 692 (1986), disapp. on other grounds, Anderson v. State, 267 Ga. 116, 475 S.E.2d 629 (1996)).

[13]18 U.S.C.A. §§ 2510 to 2520. Title III was designed to create limited authority for electronic surveillance in the investigation of specified crimes thought to be within the province of organized criminal activity. It was designed to conform to the prevailing constitutional standards, and has been declared constitutional only because of its precise requirements and its provi-

sions for close judicial scrutiny. See United States v. Sklaroff, 506 F.2d 837 (5th Cir. 1975).

[14]Both laws must be complied with. Orkin v. State, 236 Ga. 176, 179 (2)(a), 223 S.E.2d 61 (1976). Thus, in order to authorize electronic surveillance by state officers, the state statute must be read as complementing Title III. Cross v. State, 225 Ga. 760, 171 S.E.2d 507 (1969); Granese v. State, 232 Ga. 193, 206 S.E.2d 26 (1974). Title III permits the existence of state statutes "in conformity with" the federal statute; the state statute need not be a "carbon copy" of Title III, however. Cox v. State, 152 Ga. App. 453, 263 S.E.2d 238 (1979). The constitutionality of Georgia's electronic surveillance provisions was upheld in Granese v. State, 232 Ga. 193, 206 S.E.2d 26 (1974). The Georgia Supreme Court upheld the constitutionality of the federal statute in Dudley v. State, 228 Ga. 551, 556, 186 S.E.2d 875 (1972).

applies in cases where the wiretap is terminated prior to the expiration of the warrant. The recordings need only be returned to the court for sealing upon the expiration of the warrant.[15] See Annotation, "Who May Apply or Authorize Application For Order to Intercept Wire or Oral Communications Under Title III of Omnibus Crime Control and Safe Streets Act of 1968 (18 U.S.C.A. §§ 2510, et seq.)," 169 A.L.R.Fed 169 (2001).

In *Porter v. State*,[16] tapes of wiretapped conversations were made from February 20 to March 7; however, these tapes were not delivered to the superior court for sealing until March 28. The appellate court held that the defendants' motion to suppress the contents of the tapes should have been granted since the tapes were not submitted to the court for sealing *immediately* after the recording occurred as is required by 18 U.S.C.A. § 2518(8)(a).

In *King v. State*,[17] the Georgia Supreme Court held that the harmless error rule did not apply where a trial judge failed to place a judicial seal on tapes which had been made pursuant to a wiretap order. The court pointed out that 18 U.S.C.A. § 2518(8) requires such a seal or a satisfactory explanation for its absence and the absence thereof prevents admissibility of the tapes.

In *Williams v. State*,[18] the Georgia Supreme Court held that failure to comply with former O.C.G.A. § 16-11-64(b)(5) and (b)(6) did not require suppression of evidence unless the violation would result in prejudice to the defendant. However, the court concluded that violations that affect the quality or quantity of the evidence or the gathering or safeguarding of the evidence may require suppression.

The recording or divulging of the conversations of a child under the age of 18 years old without the consent of the child's parent

---

[15]Finney v. State, 298 Ga. 620, 783 S.E.2d 598 (2016) (court acknowledges federal case law authority which requires that wiretap recordings be returned immediately upon the end of surveillance, e.g., U.S. v. Williams, 124 F.3d 411 (3d Cir. 1997)). See North v. State, 250 Ga. App. 622, 552 S.E.2d 554 (2001).

[16]Porter v. State, 209 Ga. App. 27, 31 (1), 432 S.E.2d 629 (1993). See U.S. v. Ojeda Rios, 495 U.S. 257, 110 S. Ct. 1845, 109 L. Ed. 2d 224 (1990) (seal is required to insure integrity of recording and where there is a delay in sealing or an absence of a seal, government is required by statute to provide

a reasonable explanation therefore); U.S. v. Martin, 618 F.3d 705 (7th Cir. 2010).

[17]King v. State, 262 Ga. 147, 414 S.E.2d 206 (1992).

[18]Williams v. State, 265 Ga. 471, 457 S.E.2d 665 (1995). O.C.G.A. § 16-11-64 was amended in 2002 by replacing the procedure for the application and execution of investigative warrants then provided in the Code Section with a requirement that surveillance be conducted in a manner consistent with Chapter 119 of Title 18 of the United States Code Annotated (18 U.S.C.A. §§ 2510 et seq.).

or a court order is prohibited by O.C.G.A. § 16-11-66(b).[19]

The electronic "devices" regulated by O.C.G.A. §§ 16-11-60 et seq. include any instrument or apparatus used for overhearing, recording, intercepting, or transmitting sounds, or for observing, photographing, videotaping, recording, and transmitting visual images.[20] O.C.G.A. § 16-11-64(c) provides that "the district attorney having jurisdiction over prosecution of the crime under investigation or the Attorney General" may seek an "investigative warrant" permitting the use of an eavesdropping device as defined in Code Section 16-11-60 "for the surveillance of a person or place to the extent the same is consistent with and subject to the terms, conditions and procedures provided for by 18 U.S.C. Chapter 119 . . .."[21]

In *Evans v. State*,[22] the court affirmed a superior court judge in Fulton County authorizing wiretaps of telephones in other counties. Under the system used, an inductor coil was placed in each county where each such telephone was located. Here the actual "listening post" was in Fulton County and the court concluded that the inductor coil was not a "device used to overhear, record or intercept . . ." within the meaning of the statute. In *Luangkhat v. State*,[23] the court held that a judge in county "A" may not sign a wiretap order that allows police to wiretap cell phones unless the subject phones would be used in

---

[19]See London v. State, 333 Ga. App. 332, 775 S.E.2d 787 (2015) (trial court erred by failing to suppress recorded telephone conversation of a minor in absence of court order or parental consent).

[20]O.C.G.A. § 16-11-60. This provision specifically declines to regulate hearing aids and magnifying glasses.

[21]18 U.S.C.A. § 2516 details the type of criminal activity which are proper subjects for an investigation warrant and 18 U.S.C.A. § 2518 for the general procedures which the state must follow in obtaining and executing the warrant. See Finney v. State, 298 Ga. 620, 783 S.E.2d 598 (2016) (failure to "immediately" present recordings to be sealed as required by 18 U.S.C.A. § 25-18(8)(a) without satisfactory reason for 16 days after execution of wiretap order requires that recording be excluded at trial); North v. State, 250 Ga. App. 622, 552 S.E.2d 554 (2001) (wiretapping and surveillance are the subjects of federal and

state law and compliance is required where applicable); State v. Harrell, 323 Ga.App. 56, 744 S.E.2d 867 (2013) (O.C.G.A. § 16-11-64(c) provides authority for superior court judges to issue warrants but does not prohibit use of evidence gathered pursuant to federal wiretap application process in connection with a federal investigation.).

[22]Evans v. State, 252 Ga. 312, 318, 314 S.E.2d 421 (1984). See Luangkhot v. State, 292 Ga. 423, 736 S.E.2d 397 (2013) (recognized that the federal definition of intercept was expanded by 18 U.S.C.A. 2510(4) in recognition of current technology such as electronic pagers, email and computer communications to include the "listening post" where the communications are overheard as well as the sites of the tapped phone from which the contents of the communications are being redirected).

[23]Luangkhot v. State, 292 Ga. 423, 736 S.E.2d 397 (2013).

county "A" or that the listening post is located in county "A." In response to *Luangkhat*, the legislature amended O.C.G.A. § 16-11-64 to provide that the state should seek a wiretap or electronic surveillance warrant from the superior court having jurisdiction over the "crime under investigation" and further that "[s]uch warrant shall have statewide application and interception of communications shall be permitted in any location in this state."

However, generally under both state and federal law a party to a telephone conversation may permit a third person to listen to the conversation without the knowledge of the other person, and an informant may conceal a radio transmitter or recorder and carry on a conversation without the knowledge of the other person.[24] See Studdard, *Daniel's Georgia Handbook on Criminal Evidence* (2018 ed.), § 9:16. In *United States v. Yonn*,[25] the Eleventh Circuit applied the same rule to the warrantless planting of an electronic monitoring device in the defendant's motel room by government agents. The informer reserved the room for the defendant at his request. The device was then used to monitor the conversation between the defendant and the informer. In *Smith v. State*,[26] the Court of Appeals ruled that consent to the monitoring of an inmate's phone calls may be implied where the institution in which the inmate is confined has a published policy which states that inmates' phone calls are monitored. Proof of such a policy or practice may consist of: lectures which describe the policy to inmates; written notices near the phones used by the inmates; manuals regarding such procedures which are provided to inmates; or recorded messages played on the prison phones before communication can begin.

In the 1992 case of *Salmon v. State*,[27] the Georgia Court of Appeals held that under Georgia law as it then existed there was no prohibition against the interception of a cellular telephone conversation and that cellular telephone users had no justifiable expectation of privacy. However, in 1993 the Legislature enacted O.C.G.A. § 16-11-66.1, which has the effect of reversing *Salmon*. Under this statute, it is unlawful to intentionally intercept a cellular telephone conversation.

In the Georgia case of *Uhler v. State*,[28] the court held that it is not necessary to make a written application in order to have the

---

[24]Tackett v. State, 211 Ga. App. 664, 666 (1), 440 S.E.2d 74 (1994). See § 4:2, supra.

[25]United States v. Yonn, 702 F.2d 1341 (11th Cir. 1983). Contra, United States v. Padilla, 520 F.2d 526 (1st Cir. 1975).

[26]Smith v. State, 254 Ga. App.

107, 109, 561 S.E.2d 232 (2002).

[27]Salmon v. State, 206 Ga. App. 469, 470 (1), 426 S.E.2d 160 (1992).

[28]Uhler v. State, 180 Ga. App. 767, 769 (2), 350 S.E.2d 281 (1986), disapp. on other grounds, Anderson v. State, 267 Ga. 116, 475 S.E.2d 629 (1996).

telephone company assist the state by tracing the "call-forwarding" process since this did not involve the interception of electric signals from the telephone lines.

In *United States v. Torres*,[29] the Seventh Circuit held that Title III was not violated by a video surveillance or by surveillance of other than oral communications.

To be "aggrieved" under Georgia law and suppress the result of a wiretap, "the violation must have occurred on the movants' premises or the unlawfully heard conversation must have been of the movants themselves."[30]

"Minor factual inaccuracies [in an affidavit] which are only peripherally relevant to the showing" of probable cause will not void a warrant for a wiretap.[31]

The exclusionary rule generally applies to any information obtained in violation of Georgia law.[32] In *Jordan v. State*,[33] the court pointed out the difference between the United States and Georgia statutes regarding use of evidence obtained as a result of an illegal wiretap. 18 U.S.C.A. § 2515 provides that "no part of the contents of such [illegal] communication and *no evidence derived therefrom* may be received in evidence in any trial. . . ." (Emphasis in original.) However, O.C.G.A. § 16-11-67 does not contain any language precluding derivative evidence.

It is not reversible error for the trial judge to refuse to exclude spectators at a motion to suppress and conduct a closed hearing unless "the party seeking to close the hearing . . . advance[s] an over-riding interest that [he] is likely to be prejudiced. . . . [T]he closure must be no broader than necessary to protect that interest."[34] See § 17:2, infra, on fair and open trial.

The exclusionary rule also applies to a violation of 18 U.S.C.A. § 2518(10)(a).[35] This provision of the statute provides in part as follows:

"(10)(a) Any aggrieved person . . . may move to suppress the contents of any wire or oral communication intercepted pursuant to this chapter, or evidence derived therefrom, on the grounds that—

---

[29]United States v. Torres, 751 F.2d 875 (7th Cir. 1984).

[30]Van Nice v. State, 180 Ga. App. 112, 114 (1), 348 S.E.2d 515 (1986).

[31]Van Nice v. State, 180 Ga. App. 112, 115 (2), 348 S.E.2d 515 (1986).

[32]O.C.G.A. § 16-11-67.

[33]Jordan v. State, 211 Ga. App. 86, 89 (1)(a), 438 S.E.2d 371 (1993).

[34]Ayers v. State, 181 Ga. App. 244, 246 (1)(b), 351 S.E.2d 692 (1986), disapp. on other grounds, Anderson v. State, 267 Ga. 116, 475 S.E.2d 629 (1996).

[35]Cf. Ayers v. State, 181 Ga. App. 244, 246 (1)(a), 351 S.E.2d 692 (1986), disapp. on other grounds, Anderson v. State, 267 Ga. 116, 475 S.E.2d 629 (1996); United States v. Giordano, 416 U.S. 505, 94 S.Ct. 1820, 40 L.Ed.2d 341 (1974).

"(i) the communication was unlawfully intercepted;

"(ii) the order of authorization or approval under which it was intercepted is insufficient on its face; or

"(iii) the interception was not made in conformity with the order of authorization or approval.

"Such motion shall be made before the trial, hearing, or proceeding unless there was no opportunity to make such motion or the person was not aware of the grounds of the motion. . . ."

Under Georgia law the interception of a "wire, oral or electronic communication" is permissible by either party to the conversation provided one of the parties gives his or her consent. This is sometimes referred to as the "one party consent rule."[36]

Unlawful eavesdropping or surveillance is addressed in O.C.G.A. § 16-11-62. Section 16-11-62(1) prohibits the intentional act or attempt "to overhear, transmit or record . . . the private conversations of another person which shall originate in any private place." O.C.G.A. § 16-11-62(2) prohibits "[a]ny person . . . without the consent of all persons involved, to observe, photograph, transmit or record the activities of another which occur in any private place and out of public view . . .." A "private place" is defined in § 16-11-60(3) as "a place where there is a reasonable expectation of privacy."[37] Thus, it is improper to admit a video recording of two people privately engaged in sexual acts where only one of the parties consents to the publication.[38]

There are, however, a number of exceptions to § 16-11-62(2). O.C.G.A. § 16-11-62(2)(A) provides that "it shall not be unlawful" for jails and correctional institutions to record and video the activities of persons incarcerated therein other than when discussing their case with counsel.

O.C.G.A. § 16-11-67 provides that "[n]o evidence obtained [in violation of O.C.G.A. § 16-11-62] shall be admissible . . . except to prove" a violation of said statute. O.C.G.A. § 16-11-62(2)(d) provides that "a law enforcement officer or his or her agent . . . in the lawful performance of his or her official duties [may]

---

[36]O.C.G.A. § 16-11-66(a). See Smith v. State, 254 Ga. App. 107, 561 S.E.2d 232 (2002) (inmate in county jail who knew his phone calls were being monitored implicitly consented to recording conversations for purposes of O.C.G.A. § 16-11-66(a)). See Gavin v. State, 292 Ga. App. 402, 664 S.E.2d 797 (2008).

[37]See Gary v. State, 338 Ga. App. 403, 790 S.E.2d 150 (2016) (term "private place" refers to a physical location and not to an area of a person's body; statute did not apply to defendant's actions in filming underneath a woman's skirt in a grocery store which court found not to be a "private place").

[38]State v. Cohen, 302 Ga. 616, 807 S.E.2d 861 (2017) (O.C.G.A. § 16-11-66(a), one party consent rule has no application to "observational devices"). See Gavin v. State, 292 Ga. App. 402, 664 S.E.2d 797 (2008).

observe, photograph, videotape, or record the activities of persons that occur in the presence of such officer or his or her agent." Pursuant to O.C.G.A. § 50-18-72(a)(26.2) audio and video recordings made by police authorities in a place "where there is a reasonable expectation of privacy" may be obtained by an accused in a criminal case provided it is relevant to his or her case and there is no pending investigation.

In *Jordan v. State*,[39] the court implies (1) that an improper wiretap by a private individual "without the preknowledge and acquiescence of law enforcement authorities" will not prevent the use by the state of derivative evidence, and (2) the fruit of the poisonous tree doctrine and the inevitable discovery rule do not apply where there was no illegal conduct by state agents.

In *Barlow v. Barlow*,[40] the court held that Georgia's wiretapping statutes apply to cordless telephone conversations.

See § 4:2, supra, on protected areas and interests. See Studdard, *Daniel's Georgia Criminal Trial Practice Forms* (2018–2019 ed.), §§ 3:35, 3:38, and 3:39, on motion to suppress based on electronic surveillance. See Studdard, *Daniel's Georgia Handbook on Criminal Evidence* (2018 ed.), § 9:16, on sound recordings and § 9:15 on method and location of surveillance. See § 4:2, supra, on pen registers and § 4:7, supra, on probable cause affidavits based on illegal wiretaps.

§ 4:60   Results of illegal search

The material contained in this section is in summary form. The exclusionary rule is treated in far greater depth in §§ 2:24 et seq., supra.

Generally, if a search or seizure is illegal, the articles obtained are not admissible in evidence[1] in the prosecution's case in chief against a person who has standing[2] to object to the search or seizure. However, the aggrieved party must make a timely motion to suppress the evidence.[3] The person who conducts an illegal search or seizure may be liable in damages to the aggrieved person.[4] Pursuant to O.C.G.A. § 17-5-30(a) "[a] defendant aggrieved by an unlawful search and seizure may move the court

---

[39]Jordan v. State, 211 Ga. App. 86, 90-91 (1)(a), (c), (d), 438 S.E.2d 371 (1993).

[40]Barlow v. Barlow, 272 Ga. 102 (1), 526 S.E.2d 857 (2000).

[Section 4:60]

[1]Mapp v. Ohio, 367 U.S. 643, 81 S.Ct. 1684, 6 L.Ed.2d 1081 (1961).

[2]"Standing" is discussed in

§§ 14:79 to 14:83, infra.

[3]Failure to file a timely motion to suppress amounts to a waiver of the Fourth Amendment protections. Gilmore v. State, 117 Ga. App. 67, 68 (2), 159 S.E.2d 474 (1967).

[4]A common-law action may be brought in state court or an action may be brought under 42 U.S.C.A. § 1983, and Georgia has provided in

for the return of property, the possession of which is not otherwise unlawful and to suppress as evidence anything so obtained." Because the code section applies only to a criminal defendant, a party to an administrative investigative proceeding can not rely upon it as authority for the recovery of evidence improperly seized by a state agency or its suppression in any future proceeding.[5]

Evidence obtained in an illegal search and seizure can be used for purposes of impeachment of the aggrieved party if he testifies to facts contrary to those existing in the search or seizure.[6] Likewise, illegally obtained evidence may be used to impeach a defendant's false testimony obtained in response to proper cross-examination which was reasonably suggested by the defendant's direct examination.[7] Also, the exclusionary rule does not generally apply to civil proceedings.[8]

In Georgia, the exclusionary rule is based not only on federal constitutional requirements as interpreted in *Mapp v. Ohio*,[9] but also on statutory law.[10]

Generally, the exclusionary rule, from a federal constitutional standpoint, applies only to governmental employees[11] and does not apply to searches by private citizens.[12] However, a joint operation of a credit card company and law enforcement officers has

O.C.G.A. § 36-33-4 a right to bring an action against city police officers.

[5]National Viatical, Inc. v. State of Georgia, 258 Ga. App. 408, 410(1), 574 S.E.2d 337 (2002).

[6]E.g., Harris v. New York, 401 U.S. 222, 91 S.Ct. 643, 28 L.Ed.2d 1 (1971), held that even though a confession was obtained without the required *Miranda* warnings, the confession nevertheless could be used to impeach the defendant when he testified on direct examination contrary to what he said in his confession. See § 2:32, supra, on exclusionary rule and impeachment.

[7]United States v. Havens, 446 U.S. 620, 100 S.Ct. 1912, 64 L.Ed.2d 559 (1980). See Betancourt v. State, 322 Ga.App. 201, 744 S.E.2d 419 (2013) (exclusionary rule doesn't apply to similar transaction evidence of traffic stop in another state). See also, § 5:21, infra, on duty to speak.

[8]In United States v. Janis, 428 U.S. 433, 96 S.Ct. 3021, 49 L.Ed.2d 1046 (1976), the Court held that where state officers were acting in good faith under a defective warrant, the evidence was admissible in a civil action in federal court involving a levy under an assessment for wagering taxes.

[9]Mapp v. Ohio, 367 U.S. 643, 81 S.Ct. 1684, 6 L.Ed.2d 1081 (1961).

[10]O.C.G.A. § 17-5-30.

[11]Marks v. State, 174 Ga. App. 711, 715, 330 S.E.2d 900 (1985); Watson v. United States, 391 F.2d 927 (5th Cir. 1968); Burdeau v. McDowell, 256 U.S. 465, 41 S.Ct. 574, 65 L.Ed. 1048 (1921). However, it is possible that the rule of Burdeau is limited by Elkins v. United States, 364 U.S. 206, 80 S.Ct. 1437, 4 L.Ed.2d 1669 (1960). In Moore v. State, 562 S.W.2d 484 (Tex.Crim. App. 1978), the court held that the exclusionary rule applied where an off-duty officer searched a vehicle as a favor to a neighbor. See Gasaway v. State, 137 Ga. App. 653, 655 (2), 224 S.E.2d 772 (1976).

[12]Hyatt v. State, 210 Ga. App. 425 (1), 436 S.E.2d 540 (1993).

been held to be limited by the Fourth Amendment,[13] and officers may not evade the requirements of the Fourth Amendment by the use of a private person to do what the officer could not do.[14]

In *United States v. McGreevy*,[15] Petrie was a full-time police officer who worked the midnight shift. He also worked for Federal Express about six hours a week doing security work and acting as liaison between the company and law enforcement agencies. He was called by the Federal Express station manager in regard to a suspicious package. He opened the package and found contraband. The court concluded that he was not acting under color of state law when he opened the package.

In *Goodwin v. State*,[16] an off-duty police officer, while working security on private property, was instructed by his employer to stop all cars entering the premises. In doing so, he smelled alcohol on the breath of a driver and notified the police, who subsequently arrested the defendant. The court held that the defendant's claim that the initial stop lacked articulable suspicion and was not justified was without merit since the officer was "acting in his capacity as a hotel security officer and not attempting to search for incriminating evidence."

In *United States v. Miller*,[17] the Ninth Circuit held that there are two critical factors to be considered in determining whether a private person was acting as an agent of the government in conducting a search: "(1) whether the government knew of or acquiesced in the intrusive conduct, and (2) whether the party performing the search intended to assist law enforcement efforts or to further his own ends." The court then concluded that a theft victim was not acting as an agent or instrumentality of law enforcement even though officers had asked the victim to help them identify the property stolen, agreed to his plan to enter the suspect's property for that purpose, and to some extent provided protection for him.

In *State v. Lovig*,[18] the court said that the test is whether the

---

[13]Stapleton v. Superior Court, 70 Cal.2d 97, 73 Cal.Rptr. 575, 447 P.2d 967 (1968). In Wilson v. State, 237 Ga. 13, 226 S.E.2d 575 (1976), an automobile was repossessed and the evidence discovered by the repossessor was held admissible.

[14]State v. Betsill, 144 Ga. App. 267, 268, 240 S.E.2d 781 (1977). Compare Higdon v. State, 261 Ga. App. 729, 583 S.E.2d 556 (2003).

[15]United States v. McGreevy, 652 F.2d 849 (9th Cir. 1981).

[16]Goodwin v. State, 222 Ga. App. 285, 286 (1), 474 S.E.2d 84 (1996).

[17]United States v. Miller, 688 F.2d 652 (9th Cir. 1982).

[18]State v. Lovig, 189 Ga. App. 436, 437, 376 S.E.2d 229 (1988). See Williams v. State, 302 Ga. 474, 807 S.E.2d 350 (2017) (statements made by defendant to emergency room nurse for purposes of receiving medical attention while under custody were not subject to suppression because she was not acting as an agent of the police

private person, "in light of all circumstances of the case must be regarded as having acted as an 'instrument' or agent" of the government when he produced the evidence. In this regard, two cases worth comparing are *Cook v. State*[19] and *Pruitt v. State*.[20] In *Cook*, a statement made by the defendant to his father, who was also an F.B.I. agent, did not require suppression since, at the time it was made, the defendant's father was not acting in his capacity as a law enforcement officer but rather as a parent offering comfort to a troubled son. In *Pruitt*, the court ruled that evidence seized by a police officer father from his son's motor vehicle should have been suppressed since, under the totality of the circumstances, it never appeared that the police officer subordinated his official status to that of his parental status.

In *State v. Young*,[21] the court considered a motion to suppress marijuana found by the assistant principal of a school on the person of a student. In refusing to uphold the suppression motion, the court concluded that persons conducting searches are to be divided into three groups: (1) searches by private persons, (2) searches by agents of the state, and (3) searches by law enforcement agents.[22] The court said that searches by the second class of persons are not subject to the exclusionary rule, and that a principal or assistant principal of a school fits into this category.[23]

Statements obtained by school officials acting in concert with

---

while conducting the patient interviews); Hitchcock v. State, 291 Ga. App. 455, 662 S.E.2d 155 (2008).

[19]Cook v. State, 270 Ga. 820 (2), 514 S.E.2d 657 (1999).

[20]Pruitt v. State, 263 Ga. App. 814 (2), 589 S.E.2d 591 (2003). See Robbins v. State, 290 Ga. App. 323 (3), 659 S.E.2d 628 (2008), confession to wife who was also a police officer made with assurance of collateral benefit that she would not divorce him was not made to her in her capacity as an agent of the state.

[21]State v. Young, 234 Ga. 488, 493, 216 S.E.2d 586 (1975); State v. J. T., 155 Ga. App. 812, 273 S.E.2d 214 (1980).

In Farmer v. State, 156 Ga. App. 837, 839 (2), 275 S.E.2d 774 (1980), the court concluded that where a school official called a law enforcement officer in connection with a student suspected of having marijuana "the officer was acting as an extension of an arm of school discipline at the time of

the search." Cf. D. R. C. v. Alaska, 646 P.2d 252 (Alaska App.1982).

[22]In State v. Trippe, 146 Ga. App. 210, 246 S.E.2d 122, 246 (1978), the court found that a deputized school security officer who was asked by the dean to assist in some room checks was acting as a law enforcement officer.

[23]The exclusionary rule has no application to searches conducted by school officials provided they are acting in that capacity and law enforcement personnel are not involved. However, a police search of a student on campus, even though conducted at the direction of a school official, requires probable cause. State v. K.L.M., 278 Ga. App. 219, 628 S.E.2d 651 (2006). See Patman v. State, 244 Ga. App. 833, 537 S.E.2d 118 (2000), disapproved on other grounds by State v. Kazmierczak, 331 Ga. App. 817, 771 S.E.2d 473 (2015). But see Wilkes, "A Most Deplorable Paradox: Admitting Illegally Obtained Evidence in Georgia—Past, Present and Future," 11 Ga. L. Rev.

or at the direction of police authorities may also be subject to exclusion. Whether the school officials were acting in such a capacity must be determined on a case by case basis by viewing the totality of the circumstances.[24]

However, in *New Jersey v. T. L. O.*,[25] the United States Supreme Court considered the validity of a search of a pupil by a public school official. The court found that the Fourth Amendment does apply to school officials, and that such officials act as representatives of the state, but that this conclusion does not mean probable cause is required for a search. The court concluded that under the Fourth Amendment a lesser standard of reasonableness is appropriate for school children. Thus, "the legality of a search of a student should depend simply on the reasonableness, under all the circumstances, of the search." There must be "reasonable grounds for *suspecting* that the search will turn up evidence that the student has violated or is violating either the law or the rules of the school." (Emphasis added.) "[T]he measures adopted [must be] reasonably related to the objective of the search and not excessively intrusive in the light of the age and sex of the student and the nature of the infraction."

In the 1987 case of *O'Connor v. Ortega*,[26] the United States Supreme Court cited and relied on *T. L. O.* Ortega was a physician and psychiatrist who was Chief of Professional Education at a state hospital. Five of the Justices agreed that searches and seizures conducted by government supervisors of the private property of their employees are subject to scrutiny under the Fourth Amendment. The case did not involve criminal charges but was related to administrative concerns about possible improprieties involving sexual harassment by Dr. Ortega. "In contrast to law enforcement officials, . . . public employers are not enforcers of the criminal law; instead, public employers have a direct and overriding interest in ensuring that the work of the agency is conducted in a proper and efficient manner. . . . Balanced against the substantial government interests in the efficient and proper operation of the workplace are the privacy

---

105, 136 (1976).

[24]See Cook v. State, 270 Ga. 820 (2), 514 S.E.2d 657 (1999); In re T.A.G., 292 Ga. App. 48, 663 S.E.2d 392 (2008); State v. J.T., 155 Ga. App. 812, 273 S.E.2d 214 (1980).

[25]New Jersey v. T. L. O., 469 U.S. 325, 105 S.Ct. 733, 83 L.Ed.2d 720 (1985). Accord, Patman v. State, 244 Ga. App. 833, 834, 537 S.E.2d 118 (2000), disapproved on other grounds by State v. Kazmierczak, 331 Ga. App.

817, 771 S.E.2d 473 (2015). A strip search of a student in an effort to determine whether she was in possession of prescription strength ibuprofen is not reasonable. Safford Unified School Dist. No. 1 v. Redding, 557 U.S. 364, 129 S.Ct. 2633, 174 L.Ed.2d 354 (2009).

[26]O'Connor v. Ortega, 480 U.S. 709, 107 S.Ct. 1492, 94 L.Ed.2d 714 (1987).

interests of government employees in their place of work which, while not insubstantial, are far less than those found at home or in some other contexts. . . . '[S]pecial needs, beyond the normal need for law enforcement make the . . . probable-cause requirement impracticable. . . .' " Instead, the intrusion of government supervisors on the constitutionally protected privacy interests of government employees for non-investigatory, work-related purposes, as well as for investigations of work-related misconduct, should be judged by the "standard of reasonableness under all the circumstances." Under this standard, both the inception and the scope of the intrusion must be reasonable.

However, in *City of Ontario v. Quon*,[27] the United States Supreme Court concluded that even assuming a city police officer had a reasonable expectation of privacy in personal text messages sent by way of a city issued pager, the city's review of the messages as part of an audit related to their usage minutes was reasonable and based upon a legitimate work related rationale.

In *Twiggs v. State*,[28] the court held that the search of the defendant's computer pursuant to a warrant obtained by the state could properly be performed at the request of the state by an F.B.I. officer trained to conduct such searches.

See § 4:57, supra, on drug tests of students. See §§ 14:79 et seq., infra, on the expectation of privacy. See an exhaustive annotation of over 250 pages entitled "Search Conducted by School Official or Teacher as Violation of Fourth Amendment or Equivalent State Constitutional Provision," 31 A.L.R.5th 229 (1995). See § 2:26, supra, on erroneous information as constituting probable cause to arrest.

---

[27]City of Ontario, Cal. v. Quon, 130 S. Ct. 2619, 177 L. Ed. 2d 216 (2010). See Rehberg v. Paulk, 611 F.3d 828 (11th Cir. 2010), aff'd, 132 S.Ct. 1497, 182 L.Ed. 593 (2012).

[28]Twiggs v. State, 315 Ga. App. 191, 726 S.E.2d 680 (2012).

Chapter 5

Confessions and Self-Incrimination

KeyCite®: Cases and other legal materials listed in KeyCite Scope can be researched through the KeyCite service on Westlaw®. Use KeyCite to check citations for form, parallel references, prior and later history, and comprehensive citator information, including citations to other decisions and secondary materials.

---

§ 5:1 Confessions—Definition

Historically in Georgia, a confession has been regarded as a voluntary[1] admission of guilt[2] of every essential element of the crime involved,[3] without including any legal excuse or justification.[4] In order to be admissible, the confession must be made "without being induced by another by the slightest hope of benefit or remotest fear of injury."[5] A number of older cases have emphasized that a statement which constitutes a confession must be so comprehensive as to include every essential element of the crime.[6]

However, in 1974, in *Robinson v. State,*[7] the Georgia Supreme Court held that an inculpatory statement may amount to a confession even though the defendant does not admit all the essential elements of the crime. In distinguishing between admissions and confessions, the court said that "the true determinant is whether the statement is offered by the accused as exculpatory or inculpatory."[8] In *Robinson,* the defendant was charged with rape. He gave a statement which made no mention of penetration and stated only that everything started getting "fuzzy." However, Robinson did not state that he abandoned his attempt to rape, and unlike the statement in *Bloodworth v. State,*[9] the statement of Robinson was considered a confession. In *Robinson,* the attack in question upon the child was admitted subject to the memory lapse, without justification, and the statement is not one from which the jury could infer innocence. "The statement, taken as a whole, can only be thought to have been given by Robinson for the purpose of assuming responsibility for the crime charged" and constitutes a confession. Since the *Robinson* decision, the courts have reaffirmed the rule laid down in that case several times.[10]

Even when reference is made to a statement of the defendant, it is not necessary for the trial judge to give a charge distinguishing between a confession and an admission when there is no

---

[Section 5:1]

[1]O'Neal v. State, 213 Ga. 232, 234, 98 S.E.2d 376 (1957).

[2]Harvey v. State, 111 Ga. App. 279 (1), 141 S.E.2d 604 (1965).

[3]Bloodworth v. State, 216 Ga. 572 (1), 118 S.E.2d 374 (1961).

[4]Daniel v. State, 187 Ga. 411, 413 (4), 1 S.E.2d 6 (1939).

[5]O.C.G.A. § 24-8-824.

[6]See, e.g., Johnson v. State, 204 Ga. 528, 530, 50 S.E.2d 334 (1948).

[7]Robinson v. State, 232 Ga. 123, 205 S.E.2d 210 (1974).

[8]Robinson v. State, 232 Ga. 123, 126, 205 S.E.2d 210 (1974); Wells v. State, 247 Ga. 792, 797, 279 S.E.2d 213 (1981).

[9]Bloodworth v. State, 216 Ga. 572, 118 S.E.2d 374 (1961). In *Bloodworth*, the defendant's statement that he "tried to have intercourse with her and she started to cry and he stopped" was held to be an admission.

[10]Gaines v. State, 239 Ga. 98, 100, 236 S.E.2d 55 (1977); Kennedy v. State, 156 Ga. App. 792, 275 S.E.2d 339 (1980); Merritt v. State, 292 Ga. 327, 737 S.E.2d 673 (2013).

mention of a confession.[11]

Confessions may be oral, written or recorded.[12] If oral, they need not be reduced to writing.[13] A confession may be partly oral and partly in writing.[14] It has been held that a written confession must be contained in a single document.[15] However, in view of *Robinson v. State,* this rule may not still be applicable.

The admissibility of a confession is not destroyed solely because it includes other transactions.[16] See Studdard, *Daniel's Georgia Handbook on Criminal Evidence* (2018 ed.), § 4:40, on similar transactions, and § 4:56 on res gestae.

Where a hearing impaired person is legally arrested, if a qualified interpreter is not available, the arresting officer may interrogate or take a statement from the person, provided that, if the hearing impaired person cannot hear the spoken word with a hearing aid or similar device, "such interrogation and answers thereto shall be in writing and shall be preserved and turned over to the court" in the event the person is tried for the alleged offense.[17] Additionally, an interpreter shall be provided and present during consultation between the hearing impaired person and the court appointed counsel.[18] See Studdard, *Daniel's Georgia Handbook on Criminal Evidence* (2018 ed.), § 6:6, on interpreters.

The trial court in *Newman v. State*[19] suppressed the results of an interrogation where the police officers failed to comply with the provisions concerning the interrogation of deaf persons.

See § 5:2, infra, on admissions.

§ 5:2 Admissions—Definition

Under present Georgia law, an "admission of the main fact, from which the essential elements of the criminal act may be inferred, amounts to an admission of the crime itself. If the main fact is admitted with a qualifying exclusion of a necessary ingredient of the crime charged, the crime is not confessed." Therefore, "a mere [admission] is made where the accused, though admit-

---

[11]Williams v. State, 157 Ga. App. 157, 158, 276 S.E.2d 649 (1981).

[12]See Herrmann v. State, 235 Ga. 400, 401, 220 S.E.2d 2 (1975); Harris v. State, 237 Ga. 718, 724 (5), 230 S.E.2d 1 (1976).

[13]Hilliard v. State, 128 Ga. App. 157, 158 (3), 195 S.E.2d 772 (1973).

[14]3 Torcia, Wharton's Criminal Evidence, § 665 (13th Ed.).

[15]Johnson v. State, 204 Ga. 528, 530, 50 S.E.2d 334 (1948).

[16]Fairfield v. State, 155 Ga. 660, 662, 118 S.E. 395 (1923). See Postell v. State, 226 Ga. App. 843, 487 S.E.2d 422 (1997); Cade v. State, 180 Ga. App. 314, 348 S.E.2d 769 (1986).

[17]O.C.G.A. §§ 17-4-30, 24-6-653. See § 17:9, n. 17, infra, on availability of a court reporter.

[18]O.C.G.A. § 24-6-654.

[19]Newman v. State, 237 Ga. 376, 228 S.E.2d 790 (1976).

ting to damaging circumstances, nonetheless attempts to deny responsibility for the crime charged by putting forward exculpatory or legally justifying facts. Thus . . . '[a] statement which includes facts or circumstances which show excuse or justification is not a confession of guilt even if it admits the main fact.' "[1] For example, if a person is charged with burglary and he acknowledges that he entered the house, this is not a confession but it is an admission.[2]

While it is sometimes difficult to distinguish between an admission and a confession, it is important for the trial judge to properly distinguish between the two when he instructs the jury. If the statement amounts to an admission and not a confession, it is error for the court to charge on confessions.[3] However, a mere passing use of the word "confession" does not require a reversal even if the statement was an admission.[4] The Georgia Supreme Court has said that "[i]f the trial judges would avoid the use of the word 'confession' in questionable cases and instead use the word 'admission' in each instance where they might otherwise use the word 'confession' or 'statement,' the entire problem would vanish."[5] However, it has been held that the "quantum of evidence necessary to corroborate a confession is entirely for the jury to decide."[6]

In *Griggs v. State*,[7] the court concluded that under the facts of the case it was error to charge on a confession and on an incriminating statement and to let the jury determine which category the statement fell into. However, if a defendant does not admit that a statement is a confession, and if there is no request to charge on the need for corroboration of a confession, it is not error for the court to fail to so charge.[8] An incriminating statement not amounting to a confession is an admission.[9]

[Section 5:2]

[1]Robinson v. State, 232 Ga. 123, 126, 205 S.E.2d 210 (1974) (citing Owens v. State, 120 Ga. 296, 299, 48 S.E. 21 (1904). See Key v. State, 289 Ga. App. 317, 657 S.E.2d 273 (2008); Pendergrass v. State, 245 Ga. 626, 266 S.E.2d 225 (1980) (admission in criminal case is acknowledgment of a fact or circumstance from which guilt may be inferred but is not equivalent to a confession of guilt).

[2]Edwards v. State, 171 Ga. App. 264, 266, 319 S.E.2d 101 (1984).

[3]Edwards v. State, 213 Ga. 552, 556, 100 S.E.2d 172 (1957); Norrell v. State, 116 Ga. App. 479 (2), 486 (2), 157 S.E.2d 784 (1967); Logue v. State, 149 Ga. App. 797, 798 (2), 256 S.E.2d 31 (1979).

[4]Richards v. State, 251 Ga. 447, 449 (1), 306 S.E.2d 302 (1983).

[5]Golden v. State, 250 Ga. 428, 429 (4), 297 S.E.2d 479 (1982).

[6]Jones v. State, 174 Ga. App. 783, 785 (2), 331 S.E.2d 633 (1985).

[7]Griggs v. State, 146 Ga. App. 694, 695 (4), 247 S.E.2d 219 (1978).

[8]Lane v. State, 238 Ga. 407, 408 (3), 233 S.E.2d 375 (1977).

[9]Norrell v. State, 116 Ga. App.

Under *Miranda v. Arizona,*[10] both confessions and admissions are treated alike in determining their admissibility under the federal Constitution.

Where the state relies on a defendant's admission alone to establish an essential element of the case and the accused's inculpatory statement is coupled with exculpatory matter, the jury must consider both statements. However, this rule is inapplicable if there is other evidence contradicting the defendant's exculpatory statement.[11]

See § 5:1, supra, on confessions. See § 10:2, infra, on admissions in pleadings in condemnation cases.

§ 5:3 Admissibility—General

O.C.G.A. § 24-8-824 provides as follows:

"To make a confession admissible, it must have been made voluntarily, without being induced by another by the slightest hope of benefit or remotest fear of injury." Thus, according to this statute, there are three conditions which must exist before a pre-trial confession or admission[1] is admissible in evidence at a criminal trial: (1) It must be made voluntarily. It must not be produced by or result from (2) "the slightest hope of benefit" or (3) the "remotest fear of injury." These essentials will be discussed in the following sections.

From a federal constitutional standpoint, the essential element of voluntariness is not to be regarded as being limited by the words "without being induced by another by the slightest hope of benefit or remotest fear of injury." Voluntariness based on a totality of *all* the surrounding facts and circumstances is an essential element of due process.[2] In *Wan v. United States,*[3] the United States Supreme Court said, "A confession is voluntary in law if, and only if, it was, in fact, voluntarily made."

O.C.G.A. § 24-8-823 provides as follows:

"All admissions shall be scanned with care, and confessions of guilt shall be received with great caution. A confession alone, un-

---

479, 486 (2), 157 S.E.2d 784 (1967). See Griffin v. State, 302 Ga. App. 807, 808-809, 692 S.E.2d 7 (2010).

[10]Miranda v. Arizona, 384 U.S. 436, 476, 86 S.Ct. 1602, 16 L.Ed.2d 694 (1966).

[11]Thomas v. State, 141 Ga. App. 192, 233 S.E.2d 41 (1977).

[Section 5:3]

[1]In Moore v. State, 222 Ga. 748,

751, 152 S.E.2d 570 (1966), the court said that the same rule applies to both admissions and confessions (decided under former O.C.G.A. § 24-3-50). See Flowers v. State, 252 Ga. 476, 314 S.E.2d 206 (1984).

[2]Haynes v. Washington, 373 U.S. 503, 83 S.Ct. 1336, 10 L.Ed.2d 513 (1963).

[3]Wan v. United States, 266 U.S. 1, 45 S.Ct. 1, 69 L.Ed. 131 (1924).

corroborated by any other evidence, shall not justify a conviction." Blackstone wrote in the Eighteenth Century that confessions are regarded as "the weakest and most suspicious of all testimony; ever liable to be obtained by artifice, false hopes, promises of favour or menaces."[4]

Despite the language of the statute, there is a line of Georgia cases stating that a "confession of guilt freely and voluntarily made by the accused, is direct evidence of the highest character and sufficient to authorize a conviction when corroborated by proof of the corpus delicti."[5]

In *McGowan v. State*,[6] the court held that the defendant has no standing to raise a question as to the violation of the witness' right not to be forced to give certain information. Also, a defendant "may not invoke another's privilege, even if the other is his co-defendant."[7]

For motions to suppress statements, see Studdard, *Daniel's Georgia Criminal Trial Practice Forms* (2018–2019 ed.), §§ 5:1 et seq. See Studdard, *Daniel's Georgia Handbook on Criminal Evidence* (2018 ed.), §§ 1:22, 6:16, 6:36, and 8:9.

§ 5:4　Admissibility—Voluntariness—General

Today, as a result of *Miranda v. Arizona*,[1] most litigation about confessions centers on the applicability of the Fifth Amendment. But until 1966, when *Miranda* was decided, the Court relied on other mechanisms for determining the validity of confessions. In the 1936 case *Brown v. Mississippi*,[2] the United States Supreme Court gave the "voluntariness" test constitutional stature under the Due Process Clause of the Fourteenth Amendment[3] in reversing the defendants' convictions that rested solely upon confes-

---

[4]4 Blackstone Commentaries 357. See also 8 Wigmore, Evidence (3rd Ed.), 309 et seq., quoted with approval in Kelly v. State, 182 Ga. App. 7, 354 S.E.2d 647 (1987). In Escobedo v. Illinois, 378 U.S. 478, 488, 84 S.Ct. 1758, 12 L.Ed.2d 977 (1964), the court said: "We have learned the lesson of history, ancient and modern, that a system of criminal law enforcement which comes to depend on the 'confession' will, in the long run, be less reliable and more subject to abuses than a system which depends on extrinsic evidence independently secured through skillful investigation."

[5]Lowe v. State, 225 Ga. 56, 165 S.E.2d 861 (1969); Fields v. State, 232 Ga. 723 (2), 208 S.E.2d 822 (1974).

[6]McGowan v. State, 173 Ga. App. 438 (3), 326 S.E.2d 805 (1985). Accord, Riley v. State, 257 Ga. 91, 93 (2), 355 S.E.2d 66 (1987).

[7]Frazier v. State, 257 Ga. 690, 693 (8), 362 S.E.2d 351 (1987).

[Section 5:4]

[1]Miranda v. Arizona, 384 U.S. 436, 86 S.Ct. 1602, 16 L.Ed.2d 694 (1966).

[2]Brown v. Mississippi, 297 U.S. 278, 56 S.Ct. 461, 80 L.Ed. 682 (1936).

[3]When the Court decided Brown v. Mississippi, 297 U.S. 278, 56 S.Ct. 461, 80 L.Ed. 682 (1936), neither the Fifth nor the Sixth Amendment had

sions extracted after they were severely beaten by police.

When determining voluntariness, the "totality of circumstances" that preceded the confession must be examined.[4] In *Payne v. Arkansas*,[5] the Court held that the defendant's confession was not "voluntary" because it came after he was held incommunicado for three days, was denied food for long periods of time, and was threatened by the chief of police that a lynch mob would get him if he did not confess.

In 1964, with the cases *Massiah v. United States*[6] and *Escobedo v. Illinois*,[7] the Supreme Court's focus shifted from "voluntariness" of confessions under the Due Process Clause to a defendant's right to "assistance of counsel" as provided by the Sixth Amendment. But, two years later, the Court decided *Miranda*, which made Fifth Amendment analysis the driving force behind inquiries into the admissibility of confessions.

However, the due process standard of voluntariness still applies, even where there is a Miranda violation in connection with a confession. If there is a Miranda violation, the statement obtained from the defendant is not admissible in the prosecution's case in chief. But the shield of "*Miranda* cannot be perverted into a license to use perjury" and a statement obtained from a defendant in violation of *Miranda* may be used to impeach an earlier statement made by the defendant during the trial if its "trustworthiness . . . satisfies legal standards."[8] Similarly, *Miranda* does not require suppression of the physical fruits of a

---

been applied to the states. In an earlier case, Bram v. United States, 168 U.S. 532, 18 S.Ct. 183, 42 L.Ed. 568 (1897), the Court excluded a confession, on Fifth Amendment grounds, that was obtained after the defendant was stripped and interrogated in a foreign police station regarding the murder of three persons on the high seas. However, this approach remained dormant until Miranda v. Arizona, 384 U.S. 436, 86 S.Ct. 1602, 16 L.Ed.2d 694 (1966).

[4]Fikes v. Alabama, 352 U.S. 191, 77 S.Ct. 281, 1 L.Ed.2d 246 (1957). Note that the totality of circumstances approach was highly fact-specific, and eventually gave way to Miranda's prophylactic, per se rules designed to prevent coercive police tactics from eliciting involuntary confessions. See Miranda v. Arizona, 384 U.S. 436, 86 S.Ct. 1602, 16 L.Ed.2d 694 (1966).

[5]Payne v. Arkansas, 356 U.S. 560, 78 S.Ct. 844, 2 L.Ed.2d 975 (1958). Accord, Haynes v. Washington, 373 U.S. 503, 513, 83 S.Ct. 1336, 10 L.Ed.2d 513 (1963), where the confession was found to be involuntary when the defendant was held incommunicado until he signed it. The court said "the true test of admissibility is that the confession is made freely, voluntarily and without compulsion or inducement of any sort."

[6]Massiah v. United States, 377 U.S. 201, 84 S.Ct. 1199, 12 L.Ed.2d 246 (1964).

[7]Escobedo v. Illinois, 378 U.S. 478, 84 S.Ct. 1758, 12 L.Ed.2d 977 (1964).

[8]Harris v. New York, 401 U.S. 222, 225, 91 S.Ct. 643, 28 L.Ed.2d 1 (1971) followed in State v. Byrd, 255 Ga. 665, 666-667, 341 S.E.2d 455 (1986) and Richards v. State, 250 Ga. App. 712, 715 (3), 552 S.E.2d 114 (2001).

suspect's voluntary, but unwarned statements.[9] However, in "*any criminal trial the use against a defendant of his involuntary statement is a denial of due process.*"[10] Of course, unless a confession or statement was given voluntarily, it fails to pass the Georgia statutory test.

In *Colorado v. Connelly,*[11] the United States Supreme Court held that a confession cannot be held to be involuntary under the due process clause unless it is linked to coercion by government agents. The court then concluded that a confession was voluntary and hence admissible where the statement was made by the defendant because he thought he was being directed by God to confess.

In *King v. State,*[12] the Georgia Supreme Court said voluntary "is practically synonymous with spontaneously, of his own free will; and not when overmastered by the will of another." But in a civil case it was held that an admission was not inadmissible simply because it was made after a polygraph examination.[13]

Prolonged grilling prevents a confession from being voluntary.[14] However, it has been held that the fact that a defendant is a drug addict and is undergoing withdrawal symptoms at the time of his confession does not alone make it involuntary.[15] In *Ryan v. State,*[16] the court held that "[t]he mere fact that a defendant was emotionally upset did not render [his statement] inadmissible." The giving of cigarettes and soft drinks to a suspect does not alone prevent a confession from being voluntarily given.[17] In a dubious case, it has been held that if a defendant, while in a drunken stupor or asleep, makes an admission, the jury may determine whether or not it should be considered.[18] In *Shelby v.*

---

[9]United States v. Patane, 542 U.S. 630, 124 S.Ct. 2620, 159 L.Ed.2d 667 (2004). See Reaves v. State, 284 Ga. App. 181, 664 S.E.2d 211 (2008).

[10]Mincey v. Arizona, 437 U.S. 385, 98 S.Ct. 2408, 57 L.Ed.2d 290 (1978).

[11]Colorado v. Connelly, 479 U.S. 157, 107 S.Ct. 515, 93 L.Ed.2d 473 (1986), cited with approval in Wilson v. State, 257 Ga. 444, 448 (9), 359 S.E.2d 891 (1987).

[12]King v. State, 155 Ga. 707, 715, 118 S.E. 368 (1923).

[13]Johnson v. Aetna Insurance Co., 124 Ga. App. 112, 113, 183 S.E.2d 85 (1971).

[14]King v. State, 155 Ga. 707, 715, 118 S.E. 368 (1923) (three hours). Cf.

Ashcraft v. Tennessee, 322 U.S. 143, 64 S.Ct. 921, 88 L.Ed. 1192 (1944).

[15]Fields v. State, 232 Ga. 723, 724 (4), 208 S.E.2d 822 (1974).

[16]Ryan v. State, 226 Ga. App. 180, 181 (3), 486 S.E.2d 397 (1997).

[17]Coverson v. State, 162 Ga. App. 497, 292 S.E.2d 196 (1982).

[18]Sutton v. State, 237 Ga. 418, 419 (2), 228 S.E.2d 815 (1976). Likewise, in Forehand v. State, 271 Ga. App. 746, 611 S.E.2d 78 (2005), evidence that an otherwise coherent defendant was intoxicated without more, will not render a statement inadmissible as not being voluntary and made with an informed waiver of rights. In Hamm v. State, 146 Ga. App. 628, 247 S.E.2d 211 (1978), the court said a

State,[19] the Georgia Supreme Court affirmed a finding that a statement was freely and voluntarily given despite the fact that the defendant's blood alcohol level was .24 percent. A statement is not regarded as having been made involuntarily simply because the defendant was using drugs at the time it was given.[20] In one case, however, where a defendant made a confession while in the hospital and under the influence of morphine, the statement was held to be involuntary.[21] In *Brown v. State*,[22] the court pointed out that "[i]lliteracy . . . 'does not dictate a determination that there has been no voluntary knowledgeable waiver.' " In *Vance v. Bordenkircher*,[23] the court concluded that a confession in a murder case was voluntary even though given by a 15-year-old who had an I.Q. of 62 and a mental age of nine. In a similar case, *Willis v. State*,[24] the court pointed out that "[a] mere showing that an accused . . . has a high blood alcohol level or may be suffering from some mental disability is not a sufficient basis to automatically exclude a statement." In *Horton v. State*,[25] the court held that the fact officers did not inform the defendant she would be charged with murder until after she made a statement did not render the statement involuntary. In *Oliver v. State*,[26] the court pointed out that the "mere showing that a person who confessed to a crime may have suffered from some mental disability is not a sufficient basis on which to exclude the statement." See Annotation, "Admissibility of Expert Testimony Regarding Reliability of Accused's Confession Where Accused Allegedly Suffered From Mental Disorder or Defect at Time of Confession," 82 A.L.R.5th 591 (2000). Generally, see § 5:19, infra, on Miranda waivers.

It is not necessary for the trial judge to charge a jury on the

---

statement is not regarded as having been given involuntarily simply because the defendant was using drugs at the time it was given.

[19]Shelby v. State, 265 Ga. 118, 119 (2), 453 S.E.2d 21 (1995).

[20]Hamm v. State, 146 Ga. App. 628, 247 S.E.2d 211 (1978). But intoxication may prevent a valid waiver of Miranda rights. Commonwealth v. White, 374 Mass. 132, 371 N.E.2d 777 (1977).

See Annot., "Sufficiency of Showing That Voluntariness of Confession or Admission Was Affected by Alcohol or Other Drugs," 25 A.L.R.4th 419 (1983).

[21]Beecher v. Alabama, 408 U.S. 234, 92 S.Ct. 2282, 33 L.Ed.2d 317 (1972) (defendant's written and oral

confessions were held invalid in this case).

[22]Brown v. State, 250 Ga. App. 147, 150 (3), 550 S.E.2d 701 (2001).

[23]Vance v. Bordenkircher, 692 F.2d 978 (4th Cir. 1982). See Colton v. State, 296 Ga. 172, 766 S.E.2d 38 (2014) (cognitive impairment is only one of several factors to consider when weighing waiver and voluntariness of defendant's statement to police).

[24]Willis v. State, 263 Ga. 597, 599 (2), 436 S.E.2d 204 (1993).

[25]Horton v. State, 258 Ga. 489, 490 (3), 371 S.E.2d 384 (1988).

[26]Oliver v. State, 232 Ga. App. 816, 821 (3)(b), 503 S.E.2d 28 (1998) (quoting Marlowe v. State, 187 Ga. App. 255, 370 S.E.2d 20 (1988)).

necessity of voluntariness of a confession unless a timely written request has been filed.[27]

Generally, a confession will be deemed admissible if, considering the totality of the circumstances, it was made voluntarily, "without being induced by hope of benefit or coerced by threats."[28] However, in *State v. Gardner,*[29] the Georgia Supreme Court held that a "confession made by one who is insane is not the product of 'a rational intellect and a free will,' and is, thus, not voluntarily made." Nevertheless, a person who is "mentally ill" may make a voluntary confession.[30]

O.C.G.A. § 17-4-62 requires that a person arrested without a warrant must be brought before a magistrate within 48 hours of arrest or be released. However, it has been held that where the defendant is not presented before a magistrate within 48 hours after a warrantless arrest and a statement is obtained after the 48 hours, there is no right to a per se exclusion of the statement because the arrest is not necessarily violative of the federal Constitution and a violation of the Georgia statute does not automatically authorize a defendant to have the statement excluded.[31] But see *County of Riverside v. McLaughlin,*[32] which is discussed in § 11:1, infra. While there is no per se exclusion of such a statement, it must be remembered that where there is a warrantless arrest, the Fourth Amendment requires a probable cause determination "promptly after arrest."[33] If a confession is obtained after a warrantless arrest but before a prompt probable cause hearing, it may be that it is subject to suppression as a violation of the Fourth Amendment. See §§ 2:24 et seq., supra, on the exclusionary rule.

In *Arizona v. Fulminante,*[34] the United States Supreme Court held that the erroneous admission of a coerced confession can be harmless error.

---

[27]Rogers v. State, 155 Ga. App. 685, 687 (3), 272 S.E.2d 549 (1980); Blackmon v. State, 197 Ga. App. 247, 398 S.E.2d 229 (1990). See Poellnitz v. State, 296 Ga. 134, 765 S.E.2d 343 (2014) (jury charge regarding voluntariness of statement not required where the statement involved is that of a *witness*).

[28]Reynolds v. State, 275 Ga. 548, 549-550(3), 569 S.E.2d 847 (2002). In the case of a juvenile there are a range of factors to consider for purposes of whether a confession is admissible. See § 5:8 infra, on confessions of a juvenile.

[29]State v. Gardner, 254 Ga. 264, 265, 328 S.E.2d 546 (1985).

[30]Johnson v. State, 256 Ga. 259, 260 (4), 347 S.E.2d 584 (1986).

[31]Vaughn v. State, 248 Ga. 127, 130, 281 S.E.2d 594 (1981).

[32]County of Riverside v. McLaughlin, 500 U.S. 44, 111 S.Ct. 1661, 114 L.Ed.2d 49 (1991).

[33]Baker v. McCollan, 443 U.S. 137, 142, 143, 99 S.Ct. 2689, 61 L.Ed.2d 433 (1979) (dicta).

[34]Arizona v. Fulminante, 499 U.S. 279, 111 S.Ct. 1246, 113 L.Ed.2d 302 (1991), rehearing denied, 500 U.S. 938, 111 S.Ct. 2067, 114 L.Ed.2d 472 (1991).

See § 5:7, infra, on confessions obtained by trickery. See Annotation, "Admissibility of Confession as Affected by Delay in Arraignment of Prisoner," 19 A.L.R.2d 1331 (1951). See Annotation, "Mental Subnormality of Accused as Affecting Voluntariness or Admissibility of Confession," 8 A.L.R.4th 16 (1981). See also § 5:5, infra, on confessions obtained by a hope of benefit.

§ 5:5 Admissibility—Voluntariness—Hope of benefit

A confession which is obtained by a promise to confer a benefit on the suspect is involuntary and inadmissible.[1] Where a confession is obtained by offering the defendant immunity, it is induced by a hope of reward and is inadmissible.[2] Likewise, a promise to reduce or dismiss charges or recommend a relatively light sentence for the charge renders a confession involuntary.[3] So, too, is a statement induced by the promise that the defendant would not be among those charged.[4] A confession given to obtain the release from custody of the defendant's girlfriend has been held to be involuntary because of the circumstances surrounding the confession.[5] This rule applies not only to full blown confessions, but to any sort of inculpatory admission or statement induced through "the slightest hope of benefit or the remotest fear of injury."[6] In *Starr v. State*,[7] for example, the court found on appeal that an incriminating statement made by the defendant during a taped interview with police investigators which placed him alone with the victim in a child molestation case should have been excluded at trial since it was induced by the hope of special considerations in the disposition of the case and was for that reason not made voluntarily. However, in Georgia it has been held that a confession obtained as a result of a promise of a collateral

[Section 5:5]

[1]O.C.G.A. § 24-8-824.

[2]Bryant v. State, 132 Ga. App. 186, 187, 207 S.E.2d 671 (1974); Porter v. State, 143 Ga. App. 640, 239 S.E.2d 694 (1977). Generally, see Ga. Digest, West Pub. Co., Criminal Law, Key No. 520.

[3]Johnson v. State, 238 Ga. 27, 230 S.E.2d 849 (1976).

[4]Foster v. State, 283 Ga. 484 (2), 660 S.E.2d 521 (2008).

[5]Ferguson v. Boyd, 566 F.2d 873 (4th Cir. 1977). Cf. United States v. Robertson, 582 F.2d 1356 (5th Cir. 1978) (en banc); Stein v. People of State of New York, 346 U.S. 156, 73 S.Ct. 1077, 97 L.Ed. 1522 (1953); Coleman v. State, 245 So.2d 642 (Fla.App. 1971).

In Copeland v. State, 162 Ga. App. 398, 400, 291 S.E.2d 560 (1982), the court concluded that a confession was not rendered involuntary by an officer's statement to the defendant that the defendant's wife could be charged with theft by receiving stolen property. The court said this statement was "a truism" and affirmed the defendant's conviction of burglary.

[6]King v. State, 155 Ga. 707, 712-713, 118 S.E. 368 (1923).

[7]Starr v. State, 269 Ga. App. 466(2), 604 S.E.2d 297 (2004) (overruled on other grounds by, Hatley v. State, 290 Ga. 480, 722 S.E.2d 67 (2012)).

benefit is not excludable for that reason.[8] See § 5:6, infra, on admissibility of confession obtained on fear of injury. Thus, in *Burton v. State*,[9] the court held that an "officer's statement to the accused that substance abuse counseling was available was an offer of a collateral benefit which does not invalidate the [defendant's] statement."

An officer's promise to recommend a lighter punishment[10] or statements to the effect that "everybody asks how cooperative has a suspect been with you"[11] or that it would be better for him to make a confession[12] have been regarded as holding out a hope of benefit. In *Askea v. State*,[13] the court held that an investigator's statement to the defendant that his cooperation "would probably help him in court" impermissibly held out some hope of benefit. However, in *Lyles v. State*,[14] the court pointed out that where a detective told the defendant he would let the district attorney know about his cooperation and this might result in a reduced sentence, no promises were made. Moreover, this defendant signed a form acknowledging that his statement was made without promise or hope of reward. Therefore, the Georgia Court of Appeals upheld the admissibility of the defendant's confession.

But a comment by an officer that it is always better to tell the truth does not invalidate a confession.[15] If a defendant makes a confession implicating himself and others as a result of a plea bargain, but subsequently refuses to plead guilty and is tried, the

---

[8]Johnson v. State, 170 Ga. App. 71, 72 (2), 316 S.E.2d 160 (1984). See Annot., "Voluntariness of Confession as Affected by Police Statements that Suspect's Relatives Will Benefit by the Confession," 51 A.L.R.4th 495 (1987).

[9]Burton v. State, 212 Ga. App. 100, 102 (2), 441 S.E.2d 470 (1994).

[10]Biddy v. State, 127 Ga. App. 212 (2), 193 S.E.2d 31 (1972). In Canty v. State, 286 Ga. 608, 690 S.E.2d 609 (2010), the defendant's confession was held inadmissible when he incriminated himself only after he was told he might get a "shorter term" by doing so. In Hillard v. State, 286 Md. 145, 406 A.2d 415 (1979), a statement was held to have been involuntarily obtained from a defendant even though given in the presence of his attorney after an officer told the suspect that he would "go to bat" for him with the district attorney if he confessed.

[11]Robinson v. State, 229 Ga. 14, 15, 189 S.E.2d 53 (1972).

[12]McLemore v. State, 181 Ga. 462 (4), 466, 182 S.E. 618 (1935). The opinion in this case contains an excellent discussion of what constitutes a promise by an officer.

[13]Askea v. State, 153 Ga. App. 849, 851 (3), 267 S.E.2d 279 (1980). See State v. Robinson, 326 Ga. App. 63, 755 S.E.2d 869 (2014) (statement by investigator that "person that cooperates is the person that gets help" was hope of benefit). Cf. State v. Ray, 272 Ga. 450, 451 (2), 531 S.E.2d 705 (2000).

[14]Lyles v. State, 221 Ga. App. 560, 561 (1), 472 S.E.2d 132 (1996) (the "slightest hope of benefit" has generally referred to promises of lighter sentence, reduced charge or no charge at all). Accord, Martin v. State, 271 Ga. 301, 305 (2), 518 S.E.2d 898 (1999).

[15]Minton v. State, 99 Ga. 254, 25 S.E. 626 (1896); Rogers v. State, 142 Ga. App. 387, 388, 236 S.E.2d 134 (1977); Carroll v. State, 142 Ga. App.

confession is not admissible because it was given with the hope of benefit induced by another.[16] However, in 1997 the Georgia Supreme Court in *Carswell v. State*[17] held that an officer's agreement to tell the judge of the defendant's cooperation is not the kind of "hope of benefit" contemplated by former O.C.G.A. § 24-3-50 (replaced by Code Section 24-8-824 effective January 1, 2013). Likewise, "[o]ffering to make known a suspect's confession to the district attorney and the trial judge is not an offer of benefit."[18] In the same vein, a detective's suggestion made during the interrogation of a murder suspect that the suspect probably did not intend to murder the victim was not the equivalent of a hope of benefit, but mere routine police questioning designed to elicit a response from the suspect.[19] In *Brown v. State*,[20] the court held it was error for the trial court to exclude the defendant's statement to police as being the product of a hope of benefit where the statement was made after the officer promised that regardless of what the defendant told him, "short of murder," he would allow the defendant to return home that evening. The Court ruled that a "promise" made by police authorities, which does not relate to the charges or possible punishment, constitutes only a collateral benefit and as such does not necessitate the exclusion of statements made by the accused in response.

In *Patrick v. State*,[21] the court held that a promise to keep a defendant out of Reidsville if he made a statement was not a

---

428, 236 S.E.2d 159 (1977).

In Stephens v. State, 164 Ga. App. 398, 399 (3), 297 S.E.2d 90 (1982), the court held that no "hope of benefit" was offered the defendant when the interrogating officer stated that the defendant "was helping himself by telling the truth, that judges love to hear that defendants helped the police, and that although telling the truth put appellant 'right in the hot seat', it also showed that he cooperated." The officer also told the defendant that he "could not promise any help." See Miller v. State, 323 Ga. App. 412, 744 S.E.2d 926 (2013).

[16]Williams v. State, 239 Ga. 327 (1), 236 S.E.2d 672 (1977); Johnson v. State, 238 Ga. 27 (1), 230 S.E.2d 849 (1976).

[17]Carswell v. State, 268 Ga. 531, 533 (2), 491 S.E.2d 343 (1997). Accord, Bailey v. State, 248 Ga. App. 120, 121, 545 S.E.2d 659 (2001).

[18]Sims v. State, 260 Ga. 782, 399

S.E.2d 924 (1991) (quoting McKenzie v. State, 187 Ga. App. 840, 371 S.E.2d 869 (1988)). Accord, Evans v. State, 248 Ga. App. 99, 102(2), 545 S.E.2d 641 (2001).

[19]Pittman v. State, 277 Ga. 475, 478 (3), 592 S.E.2d 72 (2004). A mere promise to reduce bond does not constitute a "hope of benefit" under O.C.G.A. § 24-8-824. Only promises which implicate sentence or the pending charges qualify as the sort of benefit which would render a confession inadmissible. Gonzalez v. State, 283 Ga. App. 843 (2)(a), 643 S.E.2d 8 (2007).

[20]Brown v. State, 290 Ga. 865, 725 S.E.2d 320 (2012).

[21]Patrick v. State, 169 Ga. App. 302 (1), 312 S.E.2d 385 (1983), aff'd, 252 Ga. 509, 314 S.E.2d 909 (1984). Cf. Hazen v. Rich's, Inc., 137 Ga. App. 258, 260, 223 S.E.2d 290 (1976). In Hillard v. State, 286 Md. 145, 406 A.2d 415 (1979), the court held that a state-

promise of lighter punishment, was collateral in nature, and did not render a confession inadmissible. This was treated as being similar to a promise to inform the court of the defendant's cooperation. In *Arline v. State*,[22] the court held that "the slightest hope of benefit" means "the hope of a lighter sentence." Where an officer tells a suspect that telling the truth "would probably help in court," this holds out some hope of reward.[23]

However, in *Tyler v. State*,[24] the court held that no hope of benefit was held out to the defendant where she was told that if she had anything to do with the crime, the best thing to do "was to go ahead and get it off her chest; that sometimes people did things for various reasons; . . . and whatever she told me I'd be willing to present it to the court." Also, where an officer tells a suspect that he will feel better if he confesses, this does not prevent the admission of a confession.[25] In the questionable case of *Johnson v. State*,[26] the court held that an agreement to put the defendant in a private cell, to seek psychiatric examination for the defendant, and to tell the judge of his cooperation, was held not to be the kind of hope of benefit which would keep a confession from being voluntary. In *White v. State*,[27] the court held there was no "hope of benefit" where a defendant was to be transferred from a non-smoking jail to one where he could smoke. In *Duke v. State*,[28] the court affirmed the admission of a statement where officers told defendant that if a third person committed the crime, then the defendant should tell the officers or risk being charged himself.

In *Sizemore v. State*,[29] the court concluded that a defendant's statement was admissible when made to an officer who had "promised to let the defendant see his children [the victims] if he

---

ment obtained from a suspect was not admissible, even though defense counsel was present, where an officer told the defendant he would "go to bat" for him with the district attorney if he confessed.

[22]Arline v. State, 264 Ga. 843, 844 (2), 452 S.E.2d 115 (1995).

[23]Askea v. State, 153 Ga. App. 849, 851 (3), 267 S.E.2d 279 (1980).

[24]Tyler v. State, 247 Ga. 119, 122, 274 S.E.2d 549 (1981).

[25]Caffo v. State, 247 Ga. 751, 755 (3), 279 S.E.2d 678 (1981).

[26]Johnson v. State, 238 Ga. 27 (1), 230 S.E.2d 849 (1976); State v. Miller, 76 N.J. 392, 388 A.2d 218 (1978). But see United States v. Maroney, 287

F.Supp. 420 (E.D.Pa.1968) and People v. Rhoads, 73 Ill.App.3d 288, 29 Ill.Dec. 249, 391 N.E.2d 512 (1979).

[27]White v. State, 266 Ga. 134, 135 (3), 465 S.E.2d 277 (1996).

[28]Duke v. State, 268 Ga. 425, 426 (2), 489 S.E.2d 811 (1997).

[29]Sizemore v. State, 201 Ga. App. 431, 432 (1), 411 S.E.2d 505 (1991), rev'd on other grounds, 262 Ga. 214, 416 S.E.2d 500 (1992). See Edison v. State, 327 Ga. App. 366, 759 S.E.2d 247 (2014) (statement by officer that defendant would not be taken to jail if she submitted to drug recognition exam was collateral to charges and not "hope of benefit" under former O.C.G.A. § 24-3-50).

would make a statement."

In *Williams v. State*,[30] the court held that a statement was not the product of a "hope of reward" where defense counsel told the defendant that if the defendant made a statement, the district attorney might negotiate a sentence agreement. In *State v. Todd*,[31] a majority of the appellate court reversed the trial court, which had held that an officer had induced the defendant's statement where the officer told the defendant that "if after we talk with you, we believe that probable cause doesn't exist, we are certainly not going to keep you arrested." The appellate court held that "this sort of mere truism, mere explanations of Todd's arrest and of the law, does not constitute an improper offer of some hope of benefit." Likewise, in *Heard v. State*,[32] the court held that a confession was valid even though the defendant thought he could obtain a reduction in his bond if he confessed.

In *Tyson v. State*,[33] the court indicated that implied promises based on a course of conduct with law enforcement officers over a number of years will not prevent a confession from being admissible.

See 1 Ringel, *Searches and Seizures, Arrests and Confessions*, § 25.2(c) (Clark Boardman 1979).

§ 5:6 Admissibility—Voluntariness—Fear of injury

A confession induced by fear on the part of the accused, as a result of a threat, is involuntary and not admissible. O.C.G.A. § 24-8-824 provides as follows: "To make a confession admissible, it shall have been made voluntarily, without being induced by another by the slightest hope of benefit or remotest fear of injury." Although the Code section uses the term "confession," "[i]t has long been the law in this State that the rule as to the admissibility of an incriminatory statement is the same as that applied to a

---

[30]Williams v. State, 250 Ga. 553, 559, 300 S.E.2d 301 (1983).

[31]State v. Todd, 250 Ga. App. 265, 266, 549 S.E.2d 821 (2001).

[32]Heard v. State, 165 Ga. App. 252, 300 S.E.2d 213 (1983); Pounds v. State, 189 Ga. App. 809, 810, 377 S.E.2d 722 (1989). Cf. State v. Johnson, 273 Ga. App. 324, 615 S.E.2d 163 (2005), where the officer's statement to the defendant that she would be held without bond for a year unless she confessed, followed by the officer's promise to obtain a reduced bond if she confessed, was found to constitute a "hope or benefit" rendering the defendant's confession involuntary. In so holding, the court distinguished Pounds v. State finding the officer's statements to be "more akin to a fear of injury or a sentencing issue than a collateral benefit such as bond reduction, the promise of a solitary cell, or communication with the judge about cooperation."

[33]Tyson v. State, 165 Ga. App. 22, 23 (2), 299 S.E.2d 69 (1983).

[full] confession."[1] The phrase "slightest hope of benefit" has generally been understood to refer to "promises related to reduced criminal punishment—a shorter sentence, lesser charges, or no charges at all."[2]

Thus, a confession made because of fear induced by torture is not admissible,[3] and even advice by an officer to a suspect in custody, to the effect that if he knew anything he had better tell it, prevents a confession from being admissible.[4] "The promise of a benefit that will render a confession involuntary . . . must relate to the charge or sentence facing the suspect. . . . Generally, the 'hope of benefit' to which the statute refers has been construed as a hope of lighter punishment."[5]

In *Anderson v. State,*[6] the appellate court held that the defendant's confession was not a result of a threat of injury or promise of benefit where the officer told the defendant that he was considering charging the defendant's girlfriend as an accessory to the crime. The court concluded that the officer's statement was a mere "truism" or recounting of facts.

In *Lynumn v. Illinois,*[7] the Supreme Court held that an oral confession, which was made after the defendant had been told that "state financial aid for her infant children would be cut off, and her children taken away from her, if she did not 'cooperate,'" was involuntary. The court stated that "the confession cannot be deemed 'the product of a rational intellect and a free will.'" See § 5:5, supra, on admissibility of confession obtained on hope of benefit.

In *Garrity v. New Jersey,*[8] "police officers were investigated for allegedly fixing traffic tickets. The officers were informed that they could exercise their Fifth Amendment privilege against self-incrimination if they wished, but doing so would cost them their jobs. . . . The [United States] Supreme Court held that the state-

---

[Section 5:6]

[1]Vergara v. State, 283 Ga. 175, 177, 657 S.E.2d 863 (2008).

[2]See State v. Chulpayev, 296 Ga. 764, 771, 770 S.E.2d 808, 815 (2015) (statements and evidence obtained by state as a result of a § 24-8-824 violation will not be excluded by poisonous tree doctrine unless the original statement can be characterized as involuntary based upon the totality of the circumstances).

[3]Cf. Burns v. State, 61 Ga. 192 (1878).

[4]Dixon v. State, 113 Ga. 1039, 39 S.E. 846 (1901).

[5]Foster v. State, 283 Ga. 484, 485, 660 S.E.2d 521 (2008) (citations omitted). See Morales v. State, 337 Ga. App. 614, 788 S.E.2d 535 (2016).

[6]Anderson v. State, 224 Ga. App. 608, 610 (1), 481 S.E.2d 595 (1997).

[7]Lynumn v. Illinois, 372 U.S. 528, 534, 83 S.Ct. 917, 9 L.Ed.2d 922 (1963). Cf. United States v. Tingle, 658 F.2d 1332 (9th Cir. 1981).

[8]Garrity v. New Jersey, 385 U.S. 493, 87 S.Ct. 616, 17 L.Ed.2d 562 (1967).

ments obtained under threat of removal from office cannot be used . . . ."[9]

In *State v. Aiken*,[10] the Georgia Supreme Court adopted the totality of circumstances test used in *Garrity* for determining whether a public employees statement was coerced through an implied or express threat of termination. The Court observed:

Factors that a court may consider include those discussed in the foregoing cases, including whether the State actor made an overt threat to the defendant of the loss of his job if he did not speak with investigators or whether a statute, rule, or ordinance of which the defendant was aware provided that the defendant would lose his job for failing to answer questions. If no express threat is present, the court may examine whether the defendant subjectively believed that he could lose his job for failing to cooperate and whether, if so, that belief was reasonable given the State action involved. In determining whether the defendants belief was objectively reasonable, the court may examine whether the defendant was aware of any statutes, ordinances, manuals, or policies that required cooperation and provided generally, without specifying a penalty, that an employee could be subject to discipline for failing to cooperate. The court may also consider whether the investigator implicitly communicated any threat of dismissal either in written or oral form; whether, before the interrogation began, the defendant was told he was free to leave at any time; and whether the defendant was told he had the right to have a lawyer present. A trial court, of course, is free to consider any other factor that it determines is relevant to the determination of voluntariness. We conclude that the totality of the circumstances test is in keeping with the spirit of *Garrity* and with the discretion our courts have historically enjoyed in determining whether a defendants statement is voluntary.

(citations and footnotes omitted).

However, in *State v. Stinson*,[11] the Georgia Court of Appeals held that this rule does not apply where there is neither an overt threat to terminate employment nor a subjective belief by such public employee that he would be terminated if he failed to answer questions.

In *Roberts v. State*,[12] the court held that advising a defendant of the evidence the state has against him does not constitute

---

[9]Quoted from State v. Stinson, 244 Ga. App. 622, 624, 536 S.E.2d 293 (2000).

[10]State v. Aiken, 282 Ga. 132, 132-36(2), 646 S.E.2d 222 (2007). See Lengsfeld v. State, 324 Ga. App. 775, 751 S.E.2d 566 (2013).

[11]State v. Stinson, 244 Ga. App. 622, 625, 536 S.E.2d 293 (2000). Citing People v. Sapp, 934 P.2d 1367, 1373 (Colo. 1997), the court explained that, in order for *Garrity* to apply, the state must play a role "in creating the impression that the refusal to give a statement will be met with termination of employment." See Lengsfeld v. State, 324 Ga. App. 775, 751 S.E.2d 566 (2013).

[12]Roberts v. State, 223 Ga. App. 167, 168 (1), 477 S.E.2d 345 (1996).

coercion.

§ 5:7 Admissibility—Voluntariness—Trickery

The general rule is that the confession of a suspect, if freely and voluntarily made, is not rendered inadmissible although it is induced by some trick, artifice or deception,[1] unless the trickery amounts to a violation of due process.[2] O.C.G.A. § 24-8-825 provides as follows:

"The fact that a confession has been made under a spiritual exhortation, a promise of secrecy, or a promise of collateral benefit shall not exclude it."

While Georgia also has a code section which provides that an admission obtained by fraud is not admissible,[3] this section has not been held to apply in criminal cases.[4]

In *DeYoung v. State,*[5] the court held that "[c]onfessions are admissible though obtained by artifice, trick, or deception, so long as the means employed to procure them are not calculated to elicit an untrue statement. . . . That a confession is obtained by such means does not preclude a finding that the confession was freely and voluntarily given." However, in *State v. Ritter,*[6] the Georgia Supreme Court pointed out "that use of trickery and deceit to obtain a confession does not render it inadmissible, so long as the means employed are not calculated to procure an untrue statement." "Thus, while deceit may not on its own render a statement inadmissible (where not calculated to procure an untrue statement), we hold that in looking to the totality of the circumstances . . . the employment of deceit may result in the inadmissibility of a statement in those situations where the particular deception used, by constituting a 'slightest hope of benefit or remotest fear of injury' . . ., has induced a party to confess, thereby rendering the confession involuntary." Therefore, the

---

[Section 5:7]

[1]Hudson v. State, 153 Ga. 695 (3), 113 S.E. 519 (1922); Blackwell v. State, 113 Ga. App. 536, 148 S.E.2d 912 (1966); Cornwall v. State, 91 Ga. 277, 278 (4), 18 S.E. 154 (1893); Tyson v. State, 165 Ga. App. 22, 23 (2), 299 S.E.2d 69 (1983).

[2]Rogers v. Richmond, 365 U.S. 534, 81 S.Ct. 735, 5 L.Ed.2d 760 (1961).

[3]O.C.G.A. § 24-4-408.

[4]Moore v. State, 230 Ga. 839, 199 S.E.2d 243 (1973).

[5]DeYoung v. State, 268 Ga. 780, 789 (8), 493 S.E.2d 157 (1997). Accord, Berry v. State, 210 Ga. App. 789, 790 (2), 437 S.E.2d 630 (1993). See State v. Woods, 280 Ga. 758, 632 S.E.2d 654 (2006); State v. Ritter, 268 Ga. 108, 110 (1), 485 S.E.2d 492 (1997). Compare Brewer v. Williams, 430 U.S. 387, 97 S. Ct. 1232, 51 L. Ed. 2d 424 (1977), officer who gave "Christian burial" speech despite agreement with defense counsel to refrain from questioning defendant, violated defendant's right to counsel.

[6]State v. Ritter, 268 Ga. 108, 485 S.E.2d 492 (1997).

court concluded that a statement obtained from the defendant was not admissible where the defendant was told that the victim was awake when he was actually dead. This is consistent with the principles expressed in O.C.G.A. § 24-8-824. Likewise, the Georgia Supreme Court held in *Carswell v. State*[7] that the statement obtained from the defendant was not subject to suppression even though the investigator told the defendant they were speaking "off the record" when they were being recorded. However, in *State v. Ritter*[8] the Georgia Supreme Court pointed out that "deceit may result in the inadmissibility of a statement . . . where the particular deception used, by constituting a 'slightest hope of benefit or remotest fear of injury' . . . has induced a party to confess, thereby rendering the confession involuntary."

In *State v. Parks*,[9] the Court of Appeals rejected the notion that the defendant's statement was not voluntary where he agreed to follow police officers to the station for the purpose of being questioned and, while there, was interrogated in a room where the door could not, in fact, be locked. With respect to the officers' employment of trickery during the questioning of the defendant, the court observed that "the use of trickery or deception does not bear on the issue of whether [the defendant] was in custody or reasonably believed himself to be in custody. (Citations omitted). Rather, trickery may compromise the *voluntariness* of a statement if it constitutes 'the slightest hope of benefit or remotest fear of injury.' "[10]

In *Miranda v. Arizona*,[11] the Supreme Court said, "[A]ny evidence that the accused was threatened, tricked, or cajoled into a waiver will, of course, show that the defendant did not voluntarily waive his privilege." Technically this language refers to the waiver of Miranda rights and not to the voluntariness of the confession itself, but it may indicate the attitude of the Court toward trickery. However, the United States Supreme Court never seems to have indicated any particular kind of trickery which would alone render a confession inadmissible.[12] It has been said that a confession is not rendered inadmissible because of trickery or deception "as long as the means employed are not calculated to

---

[7]Carswell v. State, 268 Ga. 531, 533 (2), 491 S.E.2d 343 (1997).

[8]State v. Ritter, 268 Ga. 108, 110, 485 S.E.2d 492 (1997).

[9]State v. Parks, 273 Ga. App. 682, 616 S.E.2d 456 (2005).

[10]State v. Parks, 273 Ga. App. 682, 616 S.E.2d 456 (2005) quoting

Richardson v. State, 265 Ga. App. 711, 715 (1), 595 S.E.2d 565 (2004).

[11]Miranda v. Arizona, 384 U.S. 436, 476, 86 S.Ct. 1602, 16 L.Ed.2d 694 (1966).

[12]White, "Police Trickery in Inducing Confessions," 127 Pa. L. R. 581, 583 (1979).

produce an untrue statement."[13] See § 5:10, infra, on right to counsel.

Generally, see 1 Ringel, *Searches and Seizures, Arrests and Confessions,* § 25.2(d) (Clark Boardman 1979).

§ 5:8 Admissibility—Confession of juvenile

Major amendments to the Juvenile Code went into effect on January 1, 2014. Both O.C.G.A. § 15-11-28 and O.C.G.A. § 15-11-479 address confessions made by juveniles who are charged and treated as such and not as adults. According to O.C.G.A. § 15-11-28, no admission, confession, or incriminating information obtained from a child in the course of any screening or treatment that is undertaken in conjunction with juvenile proceedings, including but not limited to court ordered screenings, court ordered detention or risk assessments and evaluations shall be admitted into evidence, except as rebuttal or impeachment evidence, in any adjudication hearing in which a child is accused under this chapter. Such admission, confession, or incriminating information may be considered by the court at disposition.

"Child" is defined under O.C.G.A. § 15-11-2(10) and includes, but is not limited to, children under the age of 18 and children under the age of 17 alleged to have committed a delinquent act. A "delinquent act" is defined by O.C.G.A. § 15-11-2(19), which in part defines the term as "[a]n act committed by a child designated a crime by the laws of this state, or by the laws of another state if the act occurred in that state, under federal laws, or by local ordinance, and the act is not an offense applicable only to a child or a juvenile traffic offense."

O.C.G.A. § 15-11-479 provides that voluntary statements made by a delinquent child, a child who has committed a delinquent act and is in need of treatment or rehabilitation, in the course of intake screening, treatment, or anything related shall be inadmissible when the child is the accused and shall not be considered by the court except as rebuttal or impeachment evidence.

A confession from a juvenile is "scanned with more care and received with greater caution" than that of an adult.[1] The provisions of O.C.G.A. § 15-11-502 apply to a confession by a juvenile even when the juvenile is tried as an adult.[2] This statute provides in part as follows:

A person taking an alleged delinquent child into custody, with all

---

[13]Matter of D. A. S., 391 A.2d 255 (D.C.App.1978).

[Section 5:8]

[1]Crawford v. State, 240 Ga. 321, 323 (1), 240 S.E.2d 824 (1977); Hance v. State, 245 Ga. 856, 858 (2), 268 S.E.2d 339 (1980).

[2]Williams v. State, 238 Ga. 298, 232 S.E.2d 535 (1977).

reasonable speed and without first taking such child elsewhere, shall:

(1) Immediately release such child, without bond, to his or her parent, guardian, or legal custodian upon such person's promise to bring such child before the court when requested by the court;

(2) Immediately deliver such child to a medical facility if such child is believed to suffer from a serious physical condition or illness which requires prompt treatment and, upon delivery, shall promptly contact a juvenile court intake officer. Immediately upon being notified by the person taking such child into custody, the juvenile court intake officer shall determine if such child can be administered a detention assessment and if so, shall conduct such assessment and determine if such child should be released, remain in protective custody, or be brought before the court; or

(3) Bring such child immediately before the juvenile court or promptly contact a juvenile court intake officer. The court or juvenile court intake officer shall determine if such child should be released or detained. All determinations and court orders regarding detention shall comply with the requirements of this article and shall be based on an individual detention assessment of such child and his or her circumstances.

In *Bussey v. State*,[3] the Court of Appeals observed:

The person taking a child into custody shall promptly give notice thereof, together with a statement of the reason for taking the child into custody, to a parent, guardian, or other custodian and to the court. Any temporary detention or questioning of the child necessary to comply with this Code section shall conform to the procedures and conditions prescribed by this article and rules of court.

These provisions apply to both juvenile court proceedings and criminal cases.[4] However, a confession is not to be automatically excluded if the provisions of the Juvenile Code are not complied with.[5] In *Lattimore v. State*,[6] the Georgia Supreme Court pointed out that "the issue to be considered is whether there is a knowing

---

[3]Bussey v. State, 144 Ga. App. 875, 243 S.E.2d 99 (1978).

[4]Jackson v. State, 146 Ga. App. 375, 376, 246 S.E.2d 407 (1978) (dicta). In R. A. S. v. State, 156 Ga. App. 366, 274 S.E.2d 752 (1980), overruled by In Interest of R.D.F., 266 Ga. 294, 466 S.E.2d 572 (1996), the defendant was not given an informal detention hearing within 72 hours of detention pursuant to former O.C.G.A. § 15-11-49 (repealed and replaced by § 15-11-506 effective January 1, 2014). No confession was obtained, but the appellate court held that the proceeding had

been properly dismissed for failure to comply with the former jurisdictional time limitations. See In Interest of R. D. F., 266 Ga. 294, 466 S.E.2d 572 (1996), holding that the failure to comply with O.C.G.A. § 15-11-49 results in a dismissal without prejudice and overruling R. A. S. to the extent it holds to the contrary.

[5]Massey v. State, 243 Ga. 228 (1), 253 S.E.2d 196 (1979). Here the defendant misrepresented his age and was given Miranda warnings. Accord, Barber v. State, 267 Ga. 521, 522 (2), 481 S.E.2d 813 (1997). However, in

and intelligent waiver by . . . [the defendant] of his constitutional rights in making the incriminating statements. . . . [If a defendant] knowingly and intelligently waived his constitutional rights . . . and voluntarily made the statement in question . . ." it is not error for the trial judge to deny a motion to suppress the statement. Thus, in *Paxton v. State*,[7] the court pointed out that the requirements of the predecessor, but similar, statute to O.C.G.A. § 15-11-502(a)(2) are to be construed as directory and not mandatory. The same case also holds that there is no requirement that "an accused juvenile . . . be advised that he has a right to have a parent, guardian or adult present during questioning."[8]

In *Marshall v. State*,[9] the court affirmed the trial judge's finding that a confession of a 14-year-old juvenile was admissible. The defendant, after being arrested for murder, was taken first to the police station for booking and to obtain hair samples, rather than being handled as provided in the predecessor statute to O.C.G.A. § 15-11-502. The court stated that this did not amount to a per se violation of the Juvenile Code. The juvenile was advised of his rights, and both he and his mother signed a waiver of rights form. After booking, he was taken to the Youth Development Center for detention. The court pointed out that there is no requirement that one or both parents be present during questioning. The admissibility of such a confession from a juvenile is dependent upon the totality of the circumstances.

There are nine criteria to be considered in determining whether the waiver was voluntarily and knowingly given: (1) age of the

---

Manning v. State, 162 Ga. App. 494, 495, 292 S.E.2d 95 (1982) (dicta), the court said that the "[f]ailure to comply with the statutory safeguards . . . renders the confession of a juvenile inadmissible."

[6]Lattimore v. State, 265 Ga. 102, 104, 454 S.E.2d 474 (1995). See Williams v. State, 273 Ga. App. 42, 45(4), 614 S.E.2d 146 (2005). Accord, Skidmore v. State, 226 Ga. App. 130, 131 (2), 485 S.E.2d 540 (1997).

[7]Paxton v. State, 159 Ga. App. 175, 178, 282 S.E.2d 912 (1981); Barnes v. State, 178 Ga. App. 205, 206-207 (2), 342 S.E.2d 388 (1986).

[8]Paxton v. State, 159 Ga. App. 175, 180, 282 S.E.2d 912 (1981). In Green v. State, 282 Ga. 672, 673 (1), 653 S.E.2d 23 (2007), a juvenile was informed of his rights under the predecessor statute to O.C.G.A. § 15-11-502(a) to have a parent present during a police interview, but the juvenile did not invoke that right. The Georgia Supreme Court held that a violation of the statute, such as a failure to contact a parent or guardian, does not require automatic exclusion of a juvenile's statement. Rather, the Riley factors must be applied to determine the question of waiver. The predecessor to O.C.G.A. § 16-11-502 was former O.C.G.A. § 15-11-47 which itself replaced former GCA § 24A-1402.

[9]Marshall v. State, 248 Ga. 227, 282 S.E.2d 301 (1981); J. E. W. v. State, 256 Ga. 464, 467, 349 S.E.2d 713 (1986). Cf. Spradley v. State, 161 Ga. App. 180, 288 S.E.2d 133 (1982); Howe v. State, 250 Ga. 811, 301 S.E.2d 280 (1983).

accused; (2) education of the accused; (3) knowledge of the accused as to both the substance of the charge and the nature of his rights to consult with an attorney and remain silent; (4) whether the accused is held incommunicado or allowed to consult with relatives, friends or an attorney; (5) whether the accused is interrogated before or after formal charges are filed; (6) methods used in interrogation; (7) length of interrogation; (8) whether vel non the accused refuses to voluntarily give statements on prior occasions; and (9) whether the accused repudiates an extrajudicial statement at a later date.[10] Where it appears that a juvenile delegates to a parent or guardian the decision to proceed without counsel, any subsequent statement may be subject to suppression as not being knowing and voluntary.[11] In addition, the court is required to make the juvenile aware of the danger of proceeding without the assistance of counsel.[12]

Statements obtained by school officials acting in concert with or at the direction of police authorities may also be subject to exclusion. Whether the school officials were acting in such a capacity must be determined on a case by case basis by viewing the totality of the circumstances.[13]

§ 5:9 Admissibility—Massiah and Escobedo—Pre-*Miranda* theories based on the Sixth Amendment

The inadmissibility of incriminating statements obtained simply because of the absence of counsel was perhaps first recognized in 1964 by the United States Supreme Court in *Mas-*

---

[10]These criteria were enunciated in West v. United States, 399 F.2d 467, 469 (5th Cir. 1968). See J.D.B. v. North Carolina, 131 S. Ct. 2394, 180 L. Ed. 2d 310 (2011) (*Miranda* custody analysis is an objective inquiry and a juvenile's age is a factor which should be considered). Cf. Attaway v. State, 244 Ga. App. 5, 6, 534 S.E.2d 580 (2000). In Vergara v. State, 283 Ga. 175, 177-178 (1), 657 S.E.2d 863 (2008), the Georgia Supreme Court held that the "nine factor analysis" is not applicable to a confession by an adult.

[11]State v. Rodriguez, 274 Ga. 728, 729, 559 S.E.2d 435 (2002). See Boyd v. State, 315 Ga. App. 256, 726 S.E.2d 746 (2012) (failure to disclose severity of charges juvenile was facing at time officer asked him to "straighten out what the hell happened this evening" while permissible questions in the case of an adult could have implied a promise of leniency to a juvenile suspect). On a somewhat related issue, the Supreme Court noted in Cook v. State, 270 Ga. 820, 823 (2), 514 S.E.2d 657 (1999) that the voluntariness of a statement given by a child to a parent who is employed in a law enforcement capacity is subject to a case by case analysis.

[12]In re S.M., 322 Ga. App. 678, 745 S.E.2d 863 (2013).

[13]See Cook v. State, 270 Ga. 820 (2), 514 S.E.2d 657 (1999); In re: T.A.G., 292 Ga. App. 48, 663 S.E.2d 392 (2008); State v. J.T., 155 Ga. App. 812, 273 S.E.2d 214 (1980).

siah v. United States.[1] In *Massiah* the Court held that the Sixth Amendment guarantee of "the assistance of counsel" in all "criminal prosecutions" is violated where government agents "deliberately elicit" post-indictment statements from a suspect in the absence of counsel.[2] The fact that Massiah was already indicted when his incriminating statements were made is important to the decision of that case, as well as future Sixth Amendment cases, because the Sixth Amendment right to counsel only attaches at the initiation of adversary criminal proceedings. Therefore, before this "critical period of the proceedings,"[3] a suspect in a criminal investigation has no Sixth Amendment right to counsel. However, while the state may not use such statements in its case in chief, it may use the statements to impeach a defendant who elects to testify at trial.[4]

Five weeks after *Massiah,* the United States Supreme Court

[Section 5:9]

[1]Massiah v. United States, 377 U.S. 201, 84 S.Ct. 1199, 12 L.Ed.2d 246 (1964). Massiah had been indicted for heroin trafficking and was released on bail. A "friend" of his allowed government agents to install a radio transmitter in his car and then invited Massiah into his car. Massiah made several incriminating statements pertaining to the crime for which he had already been indicted. Those statements were heard by police via the radio transmitter and were later used at trial to convict him. See also Brown v. State, 198 Ga. App. 590, 402 S.E.2d 341 (1991). But cf. Conner v. State, 160 Ga. App. 202, 286 S.E.2d 441 (1981).

In Rollins v. State, 153 Ga. App. 848, 267 S.E.2d 262 (1980), the court held that there was no Massiah violation where a defendant who was free on bond visited and talked, on his own initiative, with a third party who was in jail and who secretly recorded conversations in which defendant incriminated himself. In Drake v. State, 245 Ga. 798, 800 (1), 267 S.E.2d 237 (1980), rev'd on other grounds by Harwell v. State, 270 Ga. 765, 512 S.E.2d 892 (1999), the court found that there had been no Massiah violation where Drake had been indicted and was represented by counsel in a tire conspiracy case, and where an informer made a concealed tape record-

ing of a conversation involving a completely separate murder.

In Georgia, where a police officer talked with a defendant after a preliminary hearing and after an attorney was employed, incriminating statements were not per se inadmissible; and whether or not such statements are admissible depends on a totality of the circumstances. Pierce v. State, 235 Ga. 237, 238 (2), 219 S.E.2d 158 (1975). Cf. Williams v. State, 566 S.W.2d 919 (Tex.Crim.App. 1978).

The Massiah doctrine was made binding on the states under the Fourteenth Amendment in McLeod v. Ohio, 381 U.S. 356, 85 S.Ct. 1556, 14 L.Ed.2d 682 (1965) (per curium).

[2]See Higuera-Hernandez v. State, 289 Ga. 553, 714 S.E.2d 236 (2011) (reviews the factors to be considered in determination as to whether informant is a government agent citing "one common principle" that the informant must be acting at direction of government official).

[3]Massiah v. United States, 377 U.S. 201, 205, 84 S.Ct. 1199, 12 L.Ed.2d 246 (1964) (quoting Powell v. Alabama, 287 U.S. 45, 53 S.Ct. 55, 77 L.Ed. 158 (1932)).

[4]Kansas v. Ventris, 556 U.S. 586, 129 S.Ct. 1841, 173 L.Ed.2d 801 (2009).

decided *Escobedo v. Illinois*.[5] Escobedo was arrested for murder, questioned, and then released the same day. He had counsel at the time of the initial arrest, and was later re-arrested and questioned again. During the second questioning, which lasted four hours, Escobedo was not permitted to speak with his lawyer, despite repeated requests to do so by both Escobedo and his attorney who was present at the police station while Escobedo was being questioned. Although the interrogation here was conducted before Escobedo was indicted, the Court noted that "in the context of this case, that fact should make no difference." Writing for the Court, Justice Goldberg narrowly held that (1) where an investigation "has begun to focus on a particular suspect, [(2)] the suspect has been taken into policy custody, [(3)] the police carry out a process of interrogations that lends itself to eliciting incriminating statements, [(4)] the suspect has requested and been denied an opportunity to consult with his lawyer, and [(5)] the police have not effectively warned him of his absolute constitutional right to remain silent, the accused has been denied 'the Assistance of Counsel' in violation of the Sixth Amendment . . . ."[6]

In *Miranda v. Arizona*,[7] the Court effectively limited the *Escobedo* holding to its facts.

§ 5:10 Admissibility—Right to counsel—The confusing relationship between the Fifth and Sixth Amendments

The Fifth Amendment provides that "[n]o person . . . shall be compelled in any criminal case to be a witness against himself." In *Miranda v. Arizona*,[1] the United States Supreme Court interpreted the above quoted clause as providing a defendant with a right to have counsel present during custodial interrogation. The Sixth Amendment provides that "[i]n all criminal prosecutions, the accused shall . . . have the Assistance of Counsel for his defense." The Fifth Amendment refers to compulsion; the Sixth Amendment does not. Thus, there is an independent basis for the applicability of these two amendments. A statement or confession admissible under *Miranda* may be inadmissible under the Sixth Amendment. Thus, a voluntary

---

[5]Escobedo v. Illinois, 378 U.S. 478, 84 S.Ct. 1758, 12 L.Ed.2d 977 (1964). See Cervi v. State, 248 Ga. 325, 282 S.E.2d 629 (1981). But Cf. Blanks v. State, 254 Ga. 420, 422, 330 S.E.2d 575 (1985), discussed in § 5:17, infra.

[6]Escobedo v. Illinois, 378 U.S. 478, 490-91, 84 S.Ct. 1758, 12 L.Ed.2d 977 (1964).

[7]Miranda v. Arizona, 384 U.S. 436, 86 S.Ct. 1602, 16 L.Ed.2d 694 (1966).

[Section 5:10]

[1]Miranda v. Arizona, 384 U.S. 436, 467, 86 S.Ct. 1602, 16 L.Ed.2d 694 (1966).

statement made after the initiation of judicial proceedings by a defendant, either in custody or not in custody, in the absence of counsel may be inadmissible under the Sixth Amendment right to counsel.[2] It is most difficult to generalize from the United States Supreme Court cases in this area; hence, the facts of each such case take on added significance.

In *Brewer v. Williams,*[3] the defendant turned himself in in Davenport, Iowa, pursuant to telephone advice from his lawyer in Des Moines. He was booked in Davenport for abducting a 10-year-old girl in Des Moines. He was advised of his *Miranda* rights, conferred with a Davenport attorney, and was arraigned before a magistrate. The following day, officers from Des Moines drove the 160 miles to Davenport to get Williams. There was an express agreement that Williams was not to be questioned. On the way back, one of the officers talked with Williams extensively. The officer told Williams that they would be going back near the area where he thought the body had been disposed of and pointed out that the parents should be entitled to a Christian burial. It was snowing at the time and the officer said that after the snowstorm was over, they might not be able to find the body. Some time later Williams directed them to the body. The United States Supreme Court concluded that Williams' Sixth Amendment right to counsel had been violated and that, constitutionally, the case was indistinguishable from *Massiah*. Because adversary proceedings had begun against the defendant, he had a right to counsel when the officers interrogated him.

Rhode Island v. Innis[4] was decided on the basis of whether or not there had been any custodial interrogation of the defendant. Innis had been arrested for a shotgun robbery. The defendant had been given *Miranda* warnings, and he said he wanted to talk with a lawyer. As he was being driven to the police station by

---

[2]See Fellers v. United States, 540 U.S. 519, 124 S.Ct. 1019, 157 L.Ed.2d 1016 (2004), where the Supreme Court held that defendant's voluntary statement was made in violation of the Sixth Amendment because it was "deliberately elicited" by the police after the defendant had already been indicted.

[3]Brewer v. Williams, 430 U.S. 387, 97 S.Ct. 1232, 51 L.Ed.2d 424 (1977). See § 2:28, supra, for a further discussion of Williams. In State v. Woods, 280 Ga. 758, 632 S.E.2d 654 (2006), the defendant expressly requested counsel at the time of his arrest in connection with the disappear-

ance of his uncle. Nonetheless, a police officer gave the defendant the "Christian burial" speech, after which the defendant admitted his guilt and told the police where the body could be found. The Georgia Supreme Court determined that *Brewer* did not apply since the defendant was not represented at the time he made his statement. Concluding that the officer's comments were in no way coercive, the Court found that the statement was voluntary and could be admitted.

[4]Rhode Island v. Innis, 446 U.S. 291, 100 S.Ct. 1682, 64 L.Ed.2d 297 (1980).

two officers, one of the officers said to the other that there was a school for handicapped children in the area and a lot of children were running around. "God forbid one of them might find a weapon with shells . . . they might hurt themselves." The defendant interrupted the officers, stating that they should turn the car around and he would show them where the gun was located. The court concluded that the defendant volunteered the information and that it did not result from interrogation. In *Rai v. State*,[5] the court explained that before an informant can be considered an agent for the government there must first be an agreement between the informant and the government that the informant will receive something of value such as money or leniency in exchange for incriminating information and secondly some action by the informant designed to deliberately elicit the incriminating information from the defendant.

In *United States v. Henry*,[6] the Court held that incriminating statements made to a cellmate, after the defendant was indicted, were in violation of the Sixth Amendment right to counsel. An FBI agent instructed the cellmate in advance to be alert to any statement made by the defendant, but not to initiate any conversation with the defendant and not to question him. The informer understood that he was to be paid if he furnished information.

In *Henry,* the Court distinguished *Hoffa v. United States.*[7] Hoffa was convicted of endeavoring to bribe members of a jury who had tried him for an alleged earlier violation of the Taft-Hartley Act. A substantial part of the evidence against Hoffa was contributed by a paid informer named Partin, who testified to several incriminating statements made by Hoffa in his presence. The court concluded that (1) none of Hoffa's Fourth Amendment rights were violated because Partin was present by invitation and the conversations were knowingly carried on in his presence. All of Hoffa's statements were voluntary. The Fourth Amendment does not protect against the misplaced belief that Partin would not reveal the conversations; (2) Hoffa's Fifth Amendment rights were not violated because his incriminating statements were voluntary and not the product of coercion; (3) Hoffa's Sixth Amend-

---

[5]Rai v. State, 297 Ga. 472, 775 S.E.2d 129 (2015).

[6]United States v. Henry, 447 U.S. 264, 100 S.Ct. 2183, 65 L.Ed.2d 115 (1980); State v. Rogers, 173 Ga. App. 653, 654, 327 S.E.2d 782 (1985). Cf. Cagle v. Davis, 520 F.Supp. 297 (E.D. Tenn.1980).

[7]Hoffa v. United States, 385 U.S. 293, 87 S.Ct. 408, 17 L.Ed.2d 374 (1966).

In United States v. Lisenby, 716 F.2d 1355 (11th Cir. 1983), the court held that there was no Massiah violation where an informer was used to get admissions from defendant about a crime other than that for which he was being held.

ment rights were not violated because the informer Partin was not present when Hoffa talked with his lawyer, and he could not complain that he was not taken into custody while the earlier trial was in progress even though the government had sufficient grounds for doing so.

In *Henry,* the Court said that in *Hoffa* there was no violation of the right to counsel by " 'deliberately eliciting incriminating statements.' . . . An accused speaking to a known government agent is typically aware that his statements may be used against him. . . . When the accused is in the company of a fellow inmate who is acting by prearrangement as a Government agent, the same cannot be said." The fact that Henry was incarcerated is also a factor because of the psychological inducement to reach for aid when a person is confined.

The *Henry* Court felt that *Hoffa* was different because, in *Hoffa,* the government used "incriminating statements from persons not in custody but suspected of criminal activity prior to the time charges [were] filed." In *Kuhlmann v. Wilson,*[8] the United States Supreme Court held that the intentional placing of an informant in a cell with a defendant did not violate the Sixth Amendment where the informant does not take "some action, beyond merely listening, that was designed deliberately to elicit incriminating remarks." In *Illinois v. Perkins,*[9] the United States Supreme Court held that *Miranda* warnings did not have to be given to an incarcerated suspect before an officer, posing as a fellow inmate, questioned the suspect.

The 1981 case of *Estelle v. Smith*[10] should be considered. Smith was charged with murder. Apparently, defense counsel had been appointed to represent him. The trial judge, without notice to defense counsel, directed a psychiatric examination of Smith by a Dr. Grigson to determine Smith's competence to stand trial. Dr. Grigson was later called as a witness by the state to testify at the

---

[8]Kuhlmann v. Wilson, 477 U.S. 436, 106 S.Ct. 2616, 91 L.Ed.2d 364 (1986).

[9]Illinois v. Perkins, 496 U.S. 292, 110 S.Ct. 2394, 110 L.Ed.2d 243 (1990).

[10]Estelle v. Smith, 451 U.S. 454, 101 S.Ct. 1866, 68 L.Ed.2d 359 (1981).

However, in United States v. Morrison, 449 U.S. 361, 101 S.Ct. 665, 66 L.Ed.2d 564 (1981), the Court unanimously held that an indictment should not have been dismissed with prejudice for government interference where agents who knew the defendant had counsel try to get the defendant to cooperate with them in a related investigation. The agents disparaged the defendant's attorney, told the defendant she should think of the kind of representation she would get, and said she would be better represented by the public defender. The agent indicated that the defendant would obtain certain benefits if she cooperated. The defendant refused to cooperate and failed to incriminate herself in the prosecution. If the agents had obtained incriminating information, the remedy would have been suppression of such information.

penalty stage of the bifurcated trial after Smith had been found guilty of murder. The psychiatrist testified that Smith was a severe sociopath and would continue his previous behavior. Smith was sentenced to death. The United States Supreme Court held that Smith's Sixth Amendment right to counsel was violated when he was sent to Dr. Grigson for evaluation, because defense counsel were not notified in advance that the psychiatric examination would encompass the issue of their client's future dangerousness, and Smith was denied his attorneys' assistance in making the decision of whether to submit to the examination and to what end the psychiatrist's findings could be used.

In *Maine v. Moulton,*[11] the United States Supreme Court said that "the right to counsel granted by the Sixth and Fourteenth Amendments means at least that a person is entitled to the help of a lawyer at or after the time that judicial proceedings have been initiated against him." The court held that a recording of a conversation, made in the absence of counsel after the defendant had been indicted, between the defendant and a co-defendant who was a government informer, violated the Sixth Amendment.

However, in 1986, in *Moran v. Burbine,*[12] the United States Supreme Court held that where a suspect was given *Miranda* warnings, and waived his right to remain silent, the waiver was not voided by (1) the failure of officers to inform suspect that counsel had been employed for him by a third person, or (2) in failing to inform suspect that counsel was attempting to reach him, or (3) by giving counsel misleading information regarding the officer's intention to interrogate the defendant. The court emphasized that the Sixth Amendment right to counsel did not apply until the initiation of adversary judicial proceedings, stating that *Escobedo* is now viewed not as a Sixth Amendment case but as a Fifth Amendment self-incrimination case. The court said that *Miranda* does not forbid such police deception relating to an attorney, and such conduct was not so offensive as to deprive the suspect of fundamental fairness guaranteed in the due process clause of the Fourteenth Amendment.

In *Cahill v. Rushen,*[13] the Ninth Circuit held that a confession of the defendant after his conviction was not admissible when he was re-tried after obtaining a reversal of his earlier conviction. The defendant had told officers that the confession could not adversely affect him at that point, and he then confessed. The court concluded that there had been a denial of the defendant's right to counsel.

---

[11]Maine v. Moulton, 474 U.S. 159, 106 S.Ct. 477, 88 L.Ed.2d 481 (1985).

[12]Moran v. Burbine, 475 U.S. 412, 106 S.Ct. 1135, 89 L.Ed.2d 410 (1986).

[13]Cahill v. Rushen, 678 F.2d 791 (9th Cir. 1982).

In *Spence v. State*,[14] the court said that Georgia has limited the Massiah rule to post-indictment statements made outside the presence of counsel. In *Baxter v. State*,[15] the Georgia Court of Appeals found *Henry* not to apply where the defendant made incriminating statements to two fellow inmates, who had encouraged the statements in the hope of lenient treatment. Since lenient treatment had not been promised by the state, the inmates were not state agents. See Studdard, *Daniel's Georgia Handbook on Criminal Evidence* (2018 ed.), § 6:3.

In *United States v. Karr*,[16] the Ninth Circuit held that the *Miranda* warnings plus being told that formal judicial proceedings had begun against him is sufficient information to enable a defendant to waive his Sixth Amendment right to counsel. In *Patterson v. Illinois*,[17] the United States Supreme Court considered a post indictment statement made to an officer in absence of counsel. The defendant knew what he was charged with, was given *Miranda* warnings and signed a *Miranda* waiver. The court rejected Patterson's argument that the Sixth Amendment right to counsel is superior to "the fifth amendment right." The court then pointed out "that whatever warnings suffice for *Miranda* purposes will also be sufficient in the context of post indictment questioning."

In *Potter v. State*,[18] the defendant, after being properly given his *Miranda* warnings, gave a voluntary statement while in custody. While the defendant was being interrogated, the public defender's office was attempting to gain access to the defendant to determine whether he qualified for and wanted its representation. The court rejected the defendant's argument that his statement should not have been admitted at trial because of the public defender's actions. In addition to noting that defendant had signed written waivers of his rights and had not invoked his right to counsel, the court observed that "[n]o attorney, acting without consulting [the defendant], was empowered to invoke a right to counsel for him."

In *Starks v. State*,[19] the Georgia Supreme Court considered the admissibility of a non-custodial statement made to a probation officer. The court concluded that if the statement was obtained after the defendant had asserted his Sixth Amendment right to

---

[14]Spence v. State, 252 Ga. 338, 342, 313 S.E.2d 475 (1984).

[15]Baxter v. State, 254 Ga. 538, 546 (12), 331 S.E.2d 561 (1985). Accord, Burgan v. State, 258 Ga. 512, 515 (5), 371 S.E.2d 854 (1988).

[16]United States v. Karr, 742 F.2d 493 (9th Cir. 1984).

[17]Patterson v. Illinois, 487 U.S. 285, 108 S.Ct. 2389, 101 L.Ed.2d 261 (1988).

[18]Potter v. State, 283 Ga. 576, 577 (2), 662 S.E.2d 128 (2008).

[19]Starks v. State, 262 Ga. 244, 245 (3), 416 S.E.2d 520 (1992).

counsel, and the conversation had been initiated by the officer, the statement was not admissible.

Generally, see 1 Ringel, *Searches and Seizures, Arrests and Confessions,* §§ 29.1 et seq. (Clark Boardman 1979). See § 5:13, infra, on interrogation.

§ 5:11 Confessions and admissions—*Miranda v. Arizona*— General

Much controversy has centered around *Miranda v. Arizona,*[1] handed down in 1966.[2] However, thus far the United States Supreme Court has declined to reverse *Miranda* although it has had ample opportunity to do so.[3] In a persuasive opinion in 1999, *United States v. Dickerson,*[4] the Fourth Circuit held that the rules set out in *Miranda* are not required by the United States Constitution and that the provisions of 18 U.S.C.A. § 3501 contain the test for admitting confessions in federal courts. However, *Dickerson* was reversed by the United States Supreme Court, which held that *Miranda* was an interpretation of the requirements of the Constitution.[5]

In essence, *Miranda* holds the following:

(1) The warnings established by *Miranda* govern unless other equally effective methods are found.[6]

(2) "Volunteered statements of any kind are not barred" by *Miranda.*[7]

(3) The rules apply when an individual in custody is first subjected to police questioning.[8]

(4) The prescribed warnings must be given regardless of the

[Section 5:11]

[1]Miranda v. Arizona, 384 U.S. 436, 86 S.Ct. 1602, 16 L.Ed.2d 694 (1966).

[2]E.g., see Wren, *"Miranda* Years: Another Decade?" Trial Magazine, July, 1977, at p. 45. This article points out in a footnote that Miranda himself was killed in Phoenix, Arizona, in a tavern on January 31, 1976.

[3]E.g., Michigan v. Tucker, 417 U.S. 433, 94 S.Ct. 2357, 41 L.Ed.2d 182 (1974).

[4]United States v. Dickerson, 166 F.3d 667 (4th Cir. 1999), judgment reversed by Dickerson v. U.S., 530 U.S. 428, 120 S.Ct. 2326, 147 L.Ed.2d 405 (2000).

[5]Dickerson v. United States, 530 U.S. 428, 120 S.Ct. 2326, 147 L.Ed.2d 405 (2000).

[6]Miranda v. Arizona, 384 U.S. 436, 467, 86 S.Ct. 1602, 16 L.Ed.2d 694 (1966).

[7]Miranda v. Arizona, 384 U.S. 436, 478, 86 S.Ct. 1602, 16 L.Ed.2d 694 (1966). See § 5:13, infra, on application of *Miranda* in interrogations.

[8]Miranda v. Arizona, 384 U.S. 436, 477, 86 S.Ct. 1602, 16 L.Ed.2d 694 (1966). In Grogins v. State, 154 Ga. App. 606 (2), 269 S.E.2d 98 (1980), the court said that *Miranda* warnings did not have to be given by a welfare case worker who was checking on overpayments.

In Turner v. State, 246 Ga. App. 49, 539 S.E.2d 553 (2000), the court held that a paramedic is not a lawful

knowledge of the person in custody.[9]

(5) An individual is free to exercise his right to remain silent if he indicates in any manner at any time prior to or during questioning that he wishes to remain silent. If he does, questioning must cease immediately.[10]

(6) If a statement is obtained in the absence of counsel, the prosecution has the burden of demonstrating that the defendant knowingly and intelligently waived his privilege against self-incrimination. A waiver of the privilege cannot be inferred from silence after the *Miranda* warnings have been given nor from the fact that a confession was obtained.[11]

(7) An accused may not be penalized for exercising his privilege against self-incrimination.[12]

(8) Unless and until warnings and waivers are demonstrated by the prosecution, no evidence obtained as a result of a violation of *Miranda* is admissible in evidence.[13] However, it seems that generally statements made by a defendant in the absence of *Miranda* warnings are admissible where the primary purpose of questioning was to save the life of a victim.[14] Thus, in *New York v. Quarles,*[15] the United States Supreme Court held that it was not necessary for an officer to give *Miranda* warnings to a suspect in custody before asking "where is the gun" because there were

---

law enforcement officer.

[9]Miranda v. Arizona, 384 U.S. 436, 469, 86 S.Ct. 1602, 16 L.Ed.2d 694 (1966). See State v. Walden, 336 N.W.2d 629 (N.D. 1983) (defendant can waive right to warnings where he refuses to listen). See also Nguyen v. State, 269 Ga. App. 730, 605 S.E.2d 130 (2004) finding that where the record shows that a defendant's *Miranda* rights were duly explained and understood, an imperfect translation thereof will not foreclose a valid rights waiver.

[10]Miranda v. Arizona, 384 U.S. 436, 473, 474, 86 S.Ct. 1602, 16 L.Ed.2d 694 (1966).

[11]Miranda v. Arizona, 384 U.S. 436, 475, 86 S.Ct. 1602, 16 L.Ed.2d 694 (1966). But see Rachell v. State, 210 Ga. App. 106, 107 (2), 435 S.E.2d 480 (1993), where the Georgia Court of Appeals held that "[o]nce *Miranda* warnings are given and [the] person in custody gives a statement to police without invoking his right to remain silent and without requesting an attorney, he has in effect waived his

rights."

[12]Miranda v. Arizona, 384 U.S. 436, 468, n. 37, 86 S.Ct. 1602, 16 L.Ed.2d 694 (1966).

[13]Miranda v. Arizona, 384 U.S. 436, 479, 86 S.Ct. 1602, 16 L.Ed.2d 694 (1966). Harris v. New York, 401 U.S. 222, 91 S.Ct. 643, 28 L.Ed.2d 1 (1971), which was cited with approval in Alexander v. State, 138 Ga. App. 618, 619 (2), 226 S.E.2d 807 (1976), held that even if *Miranda* warnings were not given, a confession obtained could be used for purposes of impeachment where defendant on direct examination testified contrary to the confession.

[14]People v. Dean, 39 Cal.App.3d 875, 114 Cal.Rptr. 555 (1974). See Annot., "Concern for Possible Victim (Rescue Doctrine) as Justifying Violation of *Miranda* Requirements," 9 A.L.R.4th 595 (1981).

[15]New York v. Quarles, 467 U.S. 649, 104 S.Ct. 2626, 81 L.Ed.2d 550 (1984).

"overriding considerations of public safety" as measured by an objective standard. See Annotation on "public safety" exception to *Miranda,* 81 L.Ed.2d 990 (1986). See § 5:14, infra, on *Miranda* warnings.

(9) The rules set forth in *Miranda* apply to both confessions and admissions.

The *Miranda* decision is not retroactive.[16]

In *United States v. Mesa,*[17] the Third Circuit held that a suspect barricaded in a motel room was not in custody when officers tried to talk him into a peaceful surrender. The fact that the motel was surrounded does not mean that the suspect was in custody.

In summary, it must be remembered that *Miranda* does not apply at all unless there are both (1) *custody* and (2) *interrogation.*[18] If there is interrogation of an in-custody suspect, *Miranda* does apply. If *Miranda* is applicable, no statement obtained from a suspect is admissible unless both of the following requirements have been met: (1) The suspect must have been given *adequate warnings,* and (2) the suspect must have validly *waived* his right of silence.

If *Miranda* is applicable and there is a violation, the only result is the suppression of the in-custody statement and not a dismissal of the charges against the defendant.[19]

§ 5:12 Confessions and admissions—*Miranda v. Arizona*— Custody[1]

The necessity of giving the *Miranda* warnings exists *only* when an individual is questioned while in custody.[2] According to *Miranda,* "custodial interrogation" means "questioning initiated by

---

[16]Miranda v. Arizona, 384 U.S. 436, 476, 86 S.Ct. 1602, 16 L.Ed.2d 694 (1966); Johnson v. New Jersey, 384 U.S. 719, 86 S.Ct. 1772, 16 L.Ed.2d 882 (1966); Green v. State, 115 Ga. App. 685, 687, 155 S.E.2d 655 (1967). The date of the *Miranda* decision was June 13, 1966.

[17]United States v. Mesa, 638 F.2d 582, 587 (3d Cir. 1980). In People v. Riddle, 83 Cal.App.3d 563, 148 Cal.Rptr. 170 (1978), the court held that *Miranda* did not apply where there was a possibility of saving human life, no other course of action was available, and rescue was the primary purpose of the interrogation.

[18]Indeed, as long as a person is not in custody, it is irrelevant to the

Miranda analysis that investigators "(1) might have focused their suspicions upon the person being questioned, or (2) have already decided that they will take the person into custody and charge [him] with an offense." Robinson v. State, 278 Ga. 299, 302(2), 602 S.E.2d 574 (2004).

[19]Hardwick v. State, 210 Ga. App. 468, 469 (2), 436 S.E.2d 676 (1993).

[Section 5:12]

[1]Because cases involving questions of whether a defendant was in "custody" or was "interrogated" are so closely related, the author suggests that both §§ 5:12 and 5:13 be read together to provide a complete picture.

[2]Wilburn v. State, 230 Ga. 675, 679 (2), 198 S.E.2d 857 (1973); Moses

law enforcement officers after a person has been taken into custody or otherwise deprived of his freedom of action in any significant way."[3] As a general rule, a person "who is the subject of a general on-the-scene investigation is not in custody," and neither the fact that the officer "would not have allowed any of the bystanders to leave until he had received some answers to his questions nor his conclusion that all of them were in his legal custody may be considered controlling on the issue of whether there had in fact been an official exercise of control or authority over the defendant amounting to an arrest."[4] A person is not regarded as being in custody simply because he and other potential witnesses went to the jail, pursuant to request, and where they are called into an investigator's office individually for questioning.[5] However, deprivation of freedom of action is an element to be considered in determining whether an individual is in custody.[6] Thus, in *Reinhardt v. State*,[7] the Georgia Supreme Court held that the defendant was in custody for *Miranda* purposes

---

v. State, 264 Ga. 313, 314 (1), 444 S.E.2d 767 (1994). See § 5:13, infra, on interrogations.

[3]Miranda v. Arizona, 384 U.S. 436, 444, 86 S.Ct. 1602, 16 L.Ed.2d 694 (1966). Thus, in Orozco v. Texas, 394 U.S. 324, 89 S.Ct. 1095, 22 L.Ed.2d 311 (1969), the Court held that *Miranda* warnings had to be given to a suspect who was questioned about a murder in his bedroom, at about 4:00 a.m., where officers testified that he was not free to go but was under arrest. Compare Oregon v. Mathiason, 429 U.S. 492, 97 S. Ct. 711, 50 L. Ed. 2d 714 (1977) (suspect questioned in State Patrol office behind closed door and released shortly after he gives confession deemed to be not in custody); California v. Beheler, 463 U.S. 1121, 103 S. Ct. 3517, 77 L. Ed. 2d 1275 (1983) (suspect who voluntarily comes to police station for interview and thereafter is allowed to leave is deemed to be not in custody). Accord, Williams v. State, 162 Ga. App. 363, 291 S.E.2d 89 (1982). Cf. Woods v. State, 242 Ga. 277, 248 S.E.2d 612 (1978); Chester v. State, 157 Ga. App. 191, 276 S.E.2d 684 (1981). See also U. S. v. Mandujano, 425 U.S. 564, 96 S. Ct. 1768, 48 L. Ed. 2d 212 (1976) (failure to give complete Miranda warning to "virtual" defendant called

before grand jury did not require suppression of statements made in connection with perjury prosecution).

[4]Mason v. State, 177 Ga. App. 184, 185 (1), 338 S.E.2d 706 (1985). See Anguiano v. State, 313 Ga. App. 449, 721 S.E.2d 652 (2011) (statement made to reporter during a child molestation "sting" scenario conducted by television network with the knowledge of local law enforcement was not subject to Miranda because the reporter was not an agent of the police and defendant was not in police custody at time he made the statement).

[5]Hardeman v. State, 252 Ga. 286, 287 (1), 313 S.E.2d 95 (1984). In State v. Parks, 273 Ga. App. 682, 616 S.E.2d 456 (2005), the questioning of the defendant was found to be noncustodial where the defendant voluntarily followed the officers to the police station in his own vehicle, was questioned in a room with a door that could not be locked, and was repeatedly told that he was not under arrest and was free to leave.

[6]Shy v. State, 234 Ga. 816, 819, 218 S.E.2d 599 (1975). *Shy* has since been disapproved by the Georgia Supreme Court to the extent it required considering subjective intent of the police and whether there was probable cause to arrest the defendant when

when he was questioned by officers in a hospital room.

In *Stansbury v. California*,[8] the United States Supreme Court pointed out that *Miranda* warnings need only be given "where there has been such a restriction on a person's freedom as to render him 'in custody.' . . . [A] court must examine all of the circumstances surrounding the interrogation but 'the ultimate inquiry is simply whether there [was] a "formal arrest or restraint on freedom of movement." ' . . . [T]he initial determination of custody depends on the *objective* circumstances of the interrogation, not on the *subjective* views harbored by either the interrogating officers or the person being questioned. . . . [T]he only relevant inquiry is how a reasonable man in the suspect's shoes would have understood his situation. . . . [A] police officer's subjective view that the individual under questioning is a suspect, if undisclosed, does not bear upon the question [of] whether the individual is in custody for purposes of *Miranda*. "However, '[a]n officer's knowledge or beliefs may bear upon the custody issue if they are conveyed, by word or deed, to the individual being questioned . . . , [but] [t]hose beliefs are relevant only to the extent they would affect how a reasonable person in the position of the individual being questioned would gauge the breadth of his or her "freedom of action." ' "[9]

In the 1995 United States Supreme Court case of *Thompson v. Keohane*,[10] the Court concluded that two discrete inquiries are essential to a determination of "in custody for *Miranda* purposes: '[F]irst, what were the circumstances surrounding the interrogation; and second, given those circumstances, would a reasonable

---

making an "in custody" evaluation for *Miranda* purposes. State v. Folsom, 285 Ga. 11, 673 S.E.2d 210 (2009). See Sewell v. State, 283 Ga. 558, 662 S.E.2d 537 (2008).

[7]Reinhardt v. State, 263 Ga. 113, 114 (3), 428 S.E.2d 333 (1993), overruled on other grounds, Vergara v. State, 283 Ga. 175(1), 657 S.E.2d 863 (2008). See State v. Carder, 301 Ga. App. 901, 689 S.E.2d 347 (2009), where the defendant was deemed "in custody" where police requested that hospital personnel detain her until they could question her; Mayberry v. State, 267 Ga. App. 620, 600 S.E.2d 703 (2004), where the Court of Appeals held that defendant was in custody for purposes of *Miranda* where police questioned him in a hospital while he was handcuffed to a stretcher and his legs were restrained. The court reached this

conclusion despite the fact that police told defendant that he was not under arrest prior to the questioning.

[8]Stansbury v. California, 511 U.S. 318, 114 S.Ct. 1526, 128 L.Ed.2d 293 (1994) (emphasis added). Accord, Hardin v. State, 269 Ga. 1, 494 S.E.2d 647 (1998); Sutton v. State, 223 Ga. App. 721, 722 (1), 478 S.E.2d 910 (1996). Cf. State v. Wintker, 223 Ga. App. 65, 66, 476 S.E.2d 835 (1996).

[9]Indeed, the fact that an individual is the *prime* suspect in an investigation is not a conclusive determination for purposes of whether *Miranda* warnings are necessary before interrogation. Heckman v. State, 276 Ga. 141(1), 576 S.E.2d 834 (2003).

[10]Thompson v. Keohane, 516 U.S. 99, 116 S.Ct. 457, 133 L.Ed.2d 383 (1995).

person have felt he or she was not at liberty to terminate the interrogation and leave. . . . [T]he court must apply an objective test. . . . The first inquiry . . . is distinctly factual. . . . The second inquiry . . . presents a 'mixed question of law and fact. . . .' " In *State v. Brannan,*[11] the Georgia Court of Appeals said that in determining if a person is in custody, "we apply an objective standard and determine whether a reasonable person in his situation would have believed he was physically deprived of his freedom of action in a significant way." In *Hadley v. State,*[12] the court pointed out that the factors to consider in determining whether or not a defendant was in custody "include: probable cause to arrest, substantive intent of the police, subjective belief of the defendant, and the focus of the investigation." In *Johnson v. State,*[13] the court pointed out that the term "reasonable person" . . . "does not mean a person with a guilty conscience who knows as soon as they see the blue light that they will be arrested for matters known to them, but [which] are not as yet known to the police."

In *Hodges v. State,*[14] the court cited *Stansbury* and held that there is no automatic need to Mirandize a person being questioned simply because the officer has probable cause to arrest.

In *Berkemer v. McCarty,*[15] the United States Supreme Court pointed out that "detention of a motorist pursuant to a traffic stop is presumptively temporary and brief . . . [and] circumstances associated with the typical traffic stop are not such that the motorist feels completely at the mercy of the police. . . . In short, the atmosphere surrounding an ordinary traffic stop is substantially less 'police dominated' than that surrounding the kinds of interrogation at issue in *Miranda*. . . . [T]he usual traffic stop is more analogous to a so called '*Terry* stop. . . .' "

In *Crum v. State,*[16] the Georgia Court of Appeals held that

---

[11]State v. Brannan, 222 Ga. App. 372, 374 (2), 474 S.E.2d 267 (1996). Accord, Hardin v. State, 269 Ga. 1, 3 (2), 494 S.E.2d 647 (1998).

[12]Hadley v. State, 235 Ga. App. 737, 738, 510 S.E.2d 569 (1998).

[13]Johnson v. State, 234 Ga. App. 116, 119 (2), 506 S.E.2d 234 (1998) (quoting Brown v. State, 223 Ga. App. 364, 367, 477 S.E.2d 623 (1996)).

[14]Hodges v. State, 265 Ga. 870, 872 (2), 463 S.E.2d 16 (1995).

[15]Berkemer v. McCarty, 468 U.S. 420, 104 S.Ct. 3138, 82 L.Ed.2d 317 (1984). In Pennsylvania v. Bruder, 488 U.S. 9, 109 S.Ct. 205, 102 L.Ed.2d 172 (1988), the United States Supreme Court quoted from *Berkemer* as follows: The "noncoercive aspects of ordinary traffic stops prompts us to hold that persons temporarily detained pursuant to such stops are not 'in custody' for purposes of *Miranda*." Cf. Lipscomb v. State, 188 Ga. App. 322, 372 S.E.2d 853 (1988).

[16]Crum v. State, 194 Ga. App. 271, 272, 390 S.E.2d 295 (1990). In Lipscomb v. State, 188 Ga. App. 322, 372 S.E.2d 853 (1988), the court said "[t]reatment of this sort cannot fairly be characterized as the functional

roadside questioning during the investigation of a routine traffic incident generally does not constitute a custodial situation. In *State v. Pastorini*,[17] the court held that where an officer obtained the defendant's driver's license and insurance card while investigating an accident, and then administered field sobriety tests after observing signs of drunkenness, the defendant was not in custody as contemplated by *Miranda* until he was formally arrested. In *Sutton v. State*,[18] the court pointed out that "an officer conducting a routine traffic stop may request and examine a driver's license and vehicle registration and run a computer check on the documents."

However, in *State v. O'Donnell*,[19] the defendant was involved in a two-car accident. The defendant left the scene and was almost immediately involved in a second accident, where he was arrested. An officer questioned him and had him perform field sobriety tests. The appellate court held that since the defendant was under arrest, "a *Miranda* warning must be given regardless of whether the questioning occurs in the context of a routine investigation of a traffic offense."

In *Olevik v. State*,[20] the Georgia Supreme Court determined that a citizen's constitutional protections against compelled testimony applies to speech as well as compelled actions such as a breath test for D.U.I. However, the court also found that the implied consent notice is not per se coercive so as to make a driver's "consent" not voluntary. Instead, the trial court must consider the totality of the circumstances when the issue is raised to determine whether the manner in which the implied consent warning was administered, e.g., did the officer appear menacing or threatening, render a suspect's consent coerced and not voluntary.

In *Quinn v. State*,[21] an officer with an arrest warrant for the defendant went to the defendant's house. "Before he placed defendant under arrest, the officer told defendant about the shooting incident, adding that he was 'not quite clear on everything that happened,' but that he did know that a 'shiny nickel weapon' was used. . . . Then he asked defendant if he owned a similar

---

equivalent of formal arrest." Accord, Sutton v. State, 223 Ga. App. 721, 723, 478 S.E.2d 910 (1996).

[17]State v. Pastorini, 222 Ga. App. 316, 474 S.E.2d 122 (1996).

[18]Sutton v. State, 223 Ga. App. 721, 723 (1), 478 S.E.2d 910 (1996).

[19]State v. O'Donnell, 225 Ga. App. 502, 504 (1), 484 S.E.2d 313 (1997). *O'Donnell* has no application to the state-administered breath test since a defendant under arrest is deemed to have given consent when an adequate warning pursuant to O.C.G.A. § 40-5-67.1(b) has been provided. State v. Lord, 236 Ga. App. 868, 513 S.E.2d 25 (1999).

[20]Olevik v. State, 302 Ga. 228, 806 S.E.2d 505 (2017).

[21]Quinn v. State, 209 Ga. App. 480, 481 (2), 433 S.E.2d 592 (1993).

weapon. [The] [d]efendant replied that he did; he 'went inside,' brought the gun out and 'voluntarily' gave it to the officer." Thereupon, he was placed under arrest and then advised of his rights. The court affirmed the finding that there was no *Miranda* violation because he was not in custody until after the gun was handed to the officer.

The fact that a prisoner is questioned about an offense which occurred outside of the prison, and is unrelated to the one for which he is in custody, does not necessarily mean that the prisoner must be provided with a *Miranda* warning. Likewise, the fact that the questioning takes place in isolation from other prisoners is not enough to create a "custodial" interrogation. It must appear from all the attendant circumstances that the prisoner could reasonably believe that his failure to cooperate would have adverse consequences or that he would not be allowed to terminate the questioning whenever he wanted and return to his cell or wherever else he would normally have access to within the institution.[22] In *Minnesota v. Murphy*,[23] the United States Supreme Court held that a defendant was not in custody at the time he made a confession to his probation officer in another case.

If a defendant, after an automobile collision, is found by the side of the road and questioned by the police, *Miranda* warnings are not required until questioning becomes accusatory.[24]

In addition to *Miranda* warnings being required before a person in custody is questioned by police or representatives of the district attorney, the United States Supreme Court held in *Estelle v. Smith*[25] that *Miranda* warnings have to be given before a psychiatric interview ordered by a trial judge on his own initiative where the defendant was being held for murder.

---

[22]Howes v. Fields, 132 S. Ct. 1181, 182 L. Ed. 2d 17 (2012). Cf. Mathis v. U.S., 391 U.S. 1, 88 S. Ct. 1503, 20 L. Ed. 2d 381 (1968).

[23]Minnesota v. Murphy, 465 U.S. 420, 104 S.Ct. 1136, 79 L.Ed.2d 409 (1984).

[24]See Thompson v. State, 313 Ga. App. 844, 723 S.E.2d 85 (2012) (on-the-scene inquires to ascertain the nature of the situation are permissible unless the questioning is pursued to establish a suspect's guilt).

[25]Estelle v. Smith, 451 U.S. 454, 101 S.Ct. 1866, 68 L.Ed.2d 359 (1981). In Battie v. Estelle, 655 F.2d 692 (5th Cir. 1981), the rule of the Smith case was found to be retroactive. See § 14:92, infra, on general insanity issues.

§ 5:13 Confessions and admissions—*Miranda v. Arizona*—Interrogation

Generally, on-the-scene questioning of citizens as to the facts surrounding a crime is not curtailed by *Miranda*.[1] Routine police questioning not related to the investigation of the case does not amount to a custodial interrogation within the meaning of *Miranda*.[2] An officer's question, "What are you doing here?" asked of a suspect who was apprehended at gunpoint is not an interrogation.[3] The statement, volunteered by a defendant, "Well, you all got me," blurted out in a police car is admissible, even though not preceded by *Miranda* warnings.[4] "Furthermore, a police officer's question, prompted by defendant's volunteered remark falls under the same exception."[5]

A public safety exception to *Miranda* warnings is "not [depen-

---

[Section 5:13]

[1]Miranda v. Arizona, 384 U.S. 436, 477, 86 S.Ct. 1602, 16 L.Ed.2d 694 (1966). The Supreme Court notes that the *Miranda* decision "is not intended to hamper the traditional function of police officers in investigating crime." Miranda v. Arizona, 384 U.S. 436, 477, 86 S.Ct. 1602, 16 L.Ed.2d 694 (1966). See Brackins v. State, 139 Ga. App. 94, 227 S.E.2d 891 (1976); Westley v. State, 143 Ga. App. 344, 345 (2), 238 S.E.2d 701 (1977); Barnes v. State, 163 Ga. App. 61, 62, 293 S.E.2d 717 (1982). See Annot., "What Constitutes 'Custodial Interrogation' Within Rule of Miranda v. Arizona Requiring That Suspect Be Informed of His Federal Constitutional Rights Before Custodial Interrogation?" 31 A.L.R.3d 565 (1970).

[2]Shy v. State, 234 Ga. 816, 822, 218 S.E.2d 599 (1975), disapproved on other grounds, State v. Folsom, 285 Ga. 11, 673 S.E.2d 210 (2009). In Tucker v. State, 237 Ga. 777 (2), 229 S.E.2d 617 (1976), when an officer approached defendant's apartment, the defendant opened the door and said, "Officer, I shot my wife. I think she's dead." The officer saw the body through the open door and asked, "Where is the weapon?" The defendant obtained the pistol and gave it to the officer. The court concluded that the question of the officer was a threshold inquiry and the defendant's actions would have

been admissible even if the defendant had been in custody. In Gainer v. State, 144 Ga. App. 703, 704 (1), 242 S.E.2d 286 (1978), the court reviewed a number of Georgia and other cases on the meaning of interrogation.

[3]Shy v. State, 234 Ga. 816, 822, 218 S.E.2d 599 (1975), disapproved on other grounds, State v. Folsom, 285 Ga. 11, 673 S.E.2d 210 (2009). Cf. Bailey v. State, 153 Ga. App. 178 (1), 264 S.E.2d 710 (1980).

[4]Sellers v. Smith, 412 F.2d 1002, 1004-1005 (5th Cir. 1969). Cf. Hobgood v. State, 146 Ga. App. 737, 247 S.E.2d 517 (1978). But see United States v. Blum, 614 F.2d 537 (6th Cir. 1980).

[5]People v. Giuchici, 118 Mich.App. 252, 324 N.W.2d 593 (1982). In Giuchici, the defendant, while in the booking room, stated, "It was like a bad dream." The officer said, "What's like a bad dream?" This was not regarded as interrogation.

In State v. Ladd, 308 N.C. 272, 302 S.E.2d 164 (1983), the court officers went to defendant's home to arrest him. When the defendant went to the door he was told he was under arrest. The defendant asked, "What for?" One of the officers said, "You know why." The defendant replied, "Yeah, just don't wake up my family. I don't want them to know." The officer's reply, "You know why," was held not to constitute interrogation.

dent] upon the motivation for the individuals involved."[6] This is a reversal of the holding in *State v. Overby*,[7] which limited the exception to situations in which the *sole* purpose of questioning was for determining danger to persons at the scene.

Confessions which are volunteered are not affected by *Miranda*.[8] In *Beeks v. State*,[9] the defendant reported to the sheriff that a certain individual stole his car. While the defendant was in a car with two officers en route to report the theft, he made incriminating statements which were held voluntary and admissible.

The four cases making up the *Miranda* decision all involved action of law enforcement officials in attempting to get statements or confessions, and *Miranda* applies only to interrogations by law enforcement officers.[10] The Georgia Supreme Court has held that questions asked by family members fall outside *Miranda* protection.[11] In *Cook v. State*,[12] the Georgia Supreme Court held that case by case analysis should be used when determining if the *Miranda* protections apply to the statements made by a child to a parent who is employed in law enforcement. Furthermore, the Georgia Court of Appeals has held that *Miranda* does not apply to the in-custody statement made to a caseworker of the Department of Family and Children Services in a cruelty to children case because the caseworker was not a law enforcement officer.[13] Additionally, *Miranda* was held to be inapplicable in a situation where a private citizen was protecting his property.[14] However, it has been pointed out that most of the courts consider-

---

[6]Davis v. State, 244 Ga. App. 708, 711, 536 S.E.2d 596 (2000).

[7]State v. Overby, 249 Ga. 341, 290 S.E.2d 464 (1982).

[8]Miranda v. Arizona, 384 U.S. 436, 478, 86 S.Ct. 1602, 16 L.Ed.2d 694 (1966). See Cash v. State, 224 Ga. 798, 799 (1), 164 S.E.2d 558 (1968). In Perkins v. State, 151 Ga. App. 199, 204 (4), 259 S.E.2d 193 (1979), the court held that where two defendants were in custody and the arresting officer was writing out tickets, the officer could testify what the defendants said to each other even though no *Miranda* warnings had been given.

[9]Beeks v. State, 225 Ga. 200, 201 (2), 167 S.E.2d 156 (1969).

[10]State v. Bolan, 27 Ohio St.2d 15, 271 N.E.2d 839, 841 (1971) (and a number of cases cited therein); State v. Kelly, 113 N.J.Super. 169, 273 A.2d 371 (1971) (security guards).

[11]Jackson v. State, 272 Ga. 191, 194 (3), 528 S.E.2d 232 (2000).

[12]Cook v. State, 270 Ga. 820, 514 S.E.2d 657 (1999). In that case the court determined that the defendant's parents' actions were those of a parent and not of a state actor, where the defendant asked to speak to his father, who was a FBI agent, and subsequently confessed to a double murder. Compare Pruitt v. State, 263 Ga. App. 814 (2), 589 S.E.2d 591 (2003), in which the court determined that the parent employed in law enforcement to be a state actor when the parent was actively helping the police search the defendant child's vehicle.

[13]Rucker v. State, 203 Ga. App. 358 (2), 416 S.E.2d 871 (1992).

[14]Carnes v. State, 115 Ga. App. 387, 392, 154 S.E.2d 781 (1967); Glean

ing the question have held that the requirements of *Miranda* apply to a statement obtained by a parole officer from questioning related to the parole function.[15]

Once *Miranda* warnings are given and the suspect indicates his desire to remain silent, the questioning must cease.[16] However, there is no blanket prohibition against subsequent questioning with the voluntariness of any later incriminating statement depending upon the facts of the individual case.[17] However, in *Edwards v. Arizona,*[18] the United States Supreme Court distinguished the right to remain silent from the right to counsel under the Fifth Amendment and held that "when an accused has invoked his right to have counsel present during custodial interrogation, a valid waiver of that right cannot be established by showing only that he responded to further police-initiated custodial interrogation even if he has been advised of his rights." See § 5:20, infra, on *Miranda* right to counsel.

In *Rhode Island v. Innis,*[19] the United States Supreme Court said that interrogation, as conceptualized in *Miranda,* "must

---

v. State, 197 Ga. App. 34, 35 (4), 397 S.E.2d 459 (1990).

[15]Marrs v. State, 53 Md.App. 230, 452 A.2d 992 (1982). See Eldridge v. State, 270 Ga. App. 84, 86(2), 606 S.E.2d 95 (2004).

[16]Miranda v. Arizona, 384 U.S. 436, 473-474, 86 S.Ct. 1602, 16 L.Ed.2d 694 (1966). The accused may indicate "in any manner, at any time prior to or during questioning, that he wishes to remain silent."

[17]Michigan v. Mosley, 423 U.S. 96, 96 S.Ct. 321, 46 L.Ed.2d 313 (1975). In this case, a suspect in a robbery chose to remain silent after *Miranda* warnings were given; questioning immediately stopped. Two hours later, after again being given *Miranda* warnings, the defendant was questioned by another officer about another crime. At the second questioning, the defendant did not ask for counsel, but he did make incriminating statements which were held admissible. On the other hand, in Westover v. United States, 384 U.S. 436, 494, 86 S.Ct. 1602, 16 L.Ed.2d 694 (1966), a confession was obtained during a second interrogation by FBI agents at which *Miranda* warnings were given. However, warnings were not given before

the first interrogation by police, and the confession was held inadmissible. The Supreme Court stated that a "different case would be presented if an accused were taken into custody by the second authority, removed both in time and place from his original surroundings, and then adequately advised of his rights and given an opportunity to exercise them." Westover v. United States, 384 U.S. 436, 496, 86 S.Ct. 1602, 16 L.Ed.2d 694.

In the 2006 case of Griffin v. State, 280 Ga. 683, 631 S.E.2d 671 (2006) citing Fields v. State, 266 Ga. 241(1), 466 S.E.2d 202 (1996), the Georgia Supreme Court held that "a second interrogation regarding the same crime may also be constitutional under *Mosley* . . . where the initial invocation of the right to remain silent was scrupulously honored."

[18]Edwards v. Arizona, 451 U.S. 477, 484, 101 S.Ct. 1880, 68 L.Ed.2d 378 (1981).

[19]Rhode Island v. Innis, 446 U.S. 291, 100 S.Ct. 1682, 64 L.Ed.2d 297 (1980) (emphasis added). In *Innis*, the defendant was given *Miranda* warnings. One officer said to another that there were a lot of handicapped children in a school nearby and said that "one of them might find a weapon with

reflect a measure of compulsion above and beyond that inherent in custody itself . . . *Miranda* safeguards come into play whenever a person in custody is subjected to either express questioning or its *functional equivalent.* . . . [*Miranda* applies] to any words or actions on the part of the police (other than those normally attendant to arrest and custody) that the police should know are reasonably likely to elicit an incriminating response from the suspect. . . . A practice that the police should know is reasonably likely to evoke an incriminating response from a suspect thus amounts to interrogation" even if no direct question is asked. See § 14:29, infra, on discovery of a defendant's statements while in custody. However, in the 1990 case of *Illinois v. Perkins,*[20] the United States Supreme Court held that *Miranda* warnings do not have to be given by an undercover policeman, posing as an inmate, before he questions an inmate about a crime the officer is investigating.

---

shells and they might hurt themselves." When the defendant heard this he directed the officers to take him to the area where he led them to the shotgun because he "wanted to get the gun out of the way because of the kids." The court held that this was not interrogation under the circumstances. See Teele v. State, 319 Ga. App. 448, 738 S.E.2d 277 (2012). Cf. Brewer v. Williams, 430 U.S. 387, 392, 97 S.Ct. 1232, 51 L.Ed.2d 424 (1977). In *Brewer*, a Sixth Amendment case, the Court reasoned that, where one of the detectives who was transporting the defendant knew that Williams "was a former mental patient, and knew also that he was deeply religious," the detective's recitation of a Christian Burial Speech was intended to deliberately elicit incriminating information from Williams and thus was "tantamount to interrogation." See § 5:4, supra, and Kamisap, *"Brewer v. Williams, Massiah* and *Miranda*: What Is Interrogation? When Does It Matter?" 67 Geo. L. J. 1 (1979).

See White, "Interrogation Without Questions: Rhode Island v. Innis and United States v. Henry," 78 Mich. L. R. 1209 (1980). See § 5:10, supra, for a further discussion of *Rhode Island v. Innis.*

In Murray v. State, 155 Ga. App. 816, 273 S.E.2d 219 (1980), an incriminating statement was made by defendant after his arrest, after having been given his *Miranda* rights, and after he had said he did not want to make a statement without having an attorney present. Despite this statement, an officer engaged him in an informal conversation about marijuana. The officer admitted asking some questions but the incriminating statement was apparently not a direct reply to a question. The court cited Innis with approval and said the conversation amounted to interrogation. Accord, Walton v. State, 267 Ga. 713, 717, 482 S.E.2d 330 (1997). Cf. United States v. Henry, 447 U.S. 264, 100 S.Ct. 2183, 65 L.Ed.2d 115 (1980), discussed in § 5:10, supra. Also see § 5:20, infra, on questioning after defendant says he wants counsel.

[20]Illinois v. Perkins, 496 U.S. 292, 110 S.Ct. 2394, 110 L.Ed.2d 243 (1990). The court in *Perkins* reasoned that *Miranda* warnings are designed to dispel the coercive pressure of custodial interrogation by law enforcement. Because *Perkins* did not know the "inmate" was an undercover police officer, there was no coercive pressure for *Miranda* warnings to guard against.

In *Carr v. State*,[21] two defendants were arrested and placed in a patrol car where a hidden recorder recorded the conversation between the defendants. The court found that this was not interrogation and that officers "do not interrogate a suspect simply by hoping that he will incriminate himself."

In *Washington v. State*,[22] where the defendant indicated that he did not wish to talk and stated that the police did not have any evidence against him, the court held that there was no interrogation where an officer informed the defendant of the evidence against him and the defendant then decided to talk. However, in *State v. Darby*,[23] the court ruled that telling a suspect that he could only tell "his side" of things if he first signed a *Miranda* waiver was improper. The court noted that the suspect should have been advised that "he could make a voluntary statement but that he could not be interrogated by the officers without first signing the waiver."

In *Williams v. State*,[24] the Georgia Supreme Court concluded that there was nothing to suggest that a sheriff should have known that his conduct was "reasonably likely to elicit an incriminating response from Williams" in taking him "back to the location where the killing occurred while he was still intoxicated and disoriented."

In *Johnson v. State*,[25] the defendant, who was in custody on unrelated charges, was brought to the interview room for questioning where he was shown a picture of the victim prior to being informed of his *Miranda* rights. He stated, "I guess I know why I'm here now. I didn't shoot that man. I never got out of the car." The appellate court affirmed the action of the trial judge in admitting this statement in evidence as voluntary.

In *Pennsylvania v. Muniz*,[26] the defendant was arrested for driving under the influence. He was taken routinely to a booking center and told that his voice and actions would be taped. Without being given *Miranda* warnings, he was asked questions about his name, address, height, weight, eye color, date of birth and current age. He was also asked and was not able to give the date of his sixth birthday. The United States Supreme Court held that the defendant's response to the date of his sixth birthday was testimonial and not admissible. The other questions were not

[21]Carr v. State, 267 Ga. 547, 552 (3), 480 S.E.2d 583 (1997).

[22]Washington v. State, 192 Ga. App. 678, 680, 385 S.E.2d 767 (1989).

[23]State v. Darby, 284 Ga. 271, 272, 663 S.E.2d 160 (2008).

[24]Williams v. State, 249 Ga. 839, 842, 295 S.E.2d 74 (1982).

[25]Johnson v. State, 266 Ga. 775, 777 (5), 470 S.E.2d 637 (1996).

[26]Pennsylvania v. Muniz, 496 U.S. 582, 110 S.Ct. 2638, 111 L.Ed.2d 528 (1990).

regarded as interrogation. The taping of the sobriety test and incriminating statements of the defendant during the test were held admissible. See § 2:22, supra, on booking.

In Georgia it has been held that routine questions to the defendant at the time of arrest, such as the defendant's name or date of birth, are not generally regarded as interrogation.[27] In *Edwards v. State*,[28] the court found that there was no interrogation when a booking officer obtains information such as name, address, telephone number, social security number, date and place of birth, employer, height, and weight.

Police conduct, however, can negate a valid *Miranda* warning. In *United States v. Beale*,[29] the officer responded to a defendant's inquiry as to the "pros and cons" of having a lawyer rather than signing a waiver, by telling him that a lawyer would only tell him not to answer questions which could "hurt" him. The court concluded that the officer's statement contradicted the *Miranda* warning that anything a suspect says can be used against him in court. Thus, the court held that statements of the defendant made after he executed a written waiver of counsel should have been suppressed and their admission at trial was error.

See § 5:19, infra, on waiver and assertion of *Miranda* rights. See § 5:10, supra, on confessions made to a cellmate.

§ 5:14   Confessions and admissions—*Miranda v. Arizona*—Warnings

As pointed out in § 5:11, supra, if there is in-custody interrogation by law enforcement officers and the prosecution wishes to introduce into evidence a statement by a defendant, it must be shown (1) that the defendant was adequately warned and (2) that he knowingly and intelligently waived his right to remain silent and his right to presence of counsel at the time of the interrogation.

In *Miranda*, the Court summarized the warnings required as follows: Prior to any questioning, the person must be warned (1) that he has a right to remain silent, (2) that any statement he makes *may* be used as evidence against him,[1] (3) that he has a right to the presence of an attorney, and (4) that if he cannot afford an attorney, one will be appointed for him prior to any

---

[27]White v. State, 168 Ga. App. 794, 796, 310 S.E.2d 540 (1983).

[28]Edwards v. State, 220 Ga. App. 74, 76 (2), 467 S.E.2d 379 (1996). Accord, Slaughter v. State, 240 Ga. App. 758, 760 (3), 525 S.E.2d 130 (1999).

[29]U.S. v. Beale, 921 F.2d 1412, 32

Fed. R. Evid. Serv. 783 (11th Cir. 1991). See U.S. v. Lall, 607 F.3d 1277 (11th Cir. 2010).

[Section 5:14]

[1]See § 5:16, infra, on warning not required that statement "can and will" be used against defendant.

questioning if he so desires. If the accused indicates in any manner at any stage of the process that he wishes to consult with an attorney, questioning must cease. Likewise, if the individual is alone and indicates in any manner that he does not wish to be interrogated, the police may not question him. The mere fact that he may have answered some questions or volunteered statements does not deprive him of the right to refrain from answering any further inquiries until he has consulted with an attorney and thereafter consents to further questioning.[2]

However, in *Duckworth v. Eagan*,[3] the United States Supreme Court held that the *Miranda* warnings were satisfactory even though they contained a statement that the officers had "no way of giving you a lawyer, but one will be appointed for you, if you wish, if and when you go to court."

Miranda warnings are commonly given by reading them from a card which has been prepared for this purpose. However, an officer may give the warnings from memory rather than reading them.[4] Many officers in Georgia currently use a *Miranda* warning card which contains the following material:[5]

"1. You have the right to remain silent.

"2. Anything you say *can and will* be used against you in a court of law.

"3. You have the right to talk to a lawyer and have him present with you while you are being questioned.[6]

"4. If you cannot afford to hire a lawyer, one will be appointed to represent you before any questioning, if you wish."

On the card quoted from above, a fifth statement is included:

"5. You can decide at any time to exercise these rights and not answer any questions or make any statements."[7]

The reverse side of the card contains the following:

[2]Miranda v. Arizona, 384 U.S. 436, 479, 86 S.Ct. 1602, 16 L.Ed.2d 694 (1966). See Florida v. Powell, 130 S. Ct. 1195, 1199-1200 (2010), which held *Miranda* satisfied where suspect advised that he has "the right to talk to a lawyer before answering any of [the law enforcement officers'] questions" and that he can invoke this right "at any time . . . during the interview."

[3]Duckworth v. Eagan, 492 U.S. 195, 109 S.Ct. 2875, 106 L.Ed.2d 166 (1989).

[4]Richards v. State, 260 Ga. 775, 400 S.E.2d 320 (1991).

[5]These warning cards have been prepared by the Prosecuting Attorney's Council of Georgia and are printed on a card which easily fits into a billfold.

[6]See § 5:17, infra, defendant's right to have counsel present during interrogation.

[7]Number 5 on the warning card is actually not required by *Miranda* but is helpful in conveying the complete meaning of the *Miranda* rights to a person in custody. Thomas v. State, 158 Ga. App. 668, 669 (2)(a), 281 S.E.2d 646 (1981).

In Watters v. State, 241 Ga. 307, 245 S.E.2d 281 (1978), the court held

"WAIVER

"After the warning and in order to secure a waiver, the following questions should be asked and an affirmative reply secured to each question.[8]

"1. Do you understand each of these rights I have explained to you?

"2. Having these rights in mind, do you wish to talk to us now?"

All of the warnings as prescribed in *Miranda* must be given, not just a part of them.[9] Number 5 as set out above is not required.

The pre-questioning warnings must be given in a clear manner[10] and in language understandable to the suspect.[11] However, a person under arrest may be given a document containing the warnings. If the accused reads the warnings and signs a statement saying he clearly understands them, the warnings are generally considered to have been satisfactorily given even if the defendant later testifies that he did not comprehend all of the words.[12]

In the opinion in *In the Interest of D. T. C.*,[13] the court pointed out that the "facts that D. T. C. has an I.Q. of 64, has an intellectual deficiency and may be mentally retarded do not automatically invalidate his waiver of *Miranda* rights." In *Coppock v. State*,[14] the Georgia Supreme Court held that "the fact that an individual may be moderately retarded is not sufficient to exclude . . . [his] statement."

---

that where the jury is charged on the necessity of a statement being freely and voluntarily given and on his constitutional rights, it is not error for the judge to fail to charge the jury, in the absence of a request, "that one of those rights was the right to stop answering questions at any time." Accord, Montgomery v. State, 241 Ga. 396, 397 (4), 245 S.E.2d 652 (1978).

[8]It is not necessary to ask these questions if the defendant is fully apprised of his constitutional rights and he in fact wants to waive such rights. See Gainer v. State, 144 Ga. App. 703, 706 (3), 242 S.E.2d 286 (1978).

[9]See Miranda v. Arizona, 384 U.S. 436, 479, 86 S.Ct. 1602, 16 L.Ed.2d 694 (1966).

[10]Id. See also De La Fe v. United States, 413 F.2d 543 (5th Cir. 1969). The *Miranda* warnings must convey to the accused that he is entitled to counsel at the present time, not just in the future.

[11]De La Fe v. United States, 413 F.2d 543 (5th Cir. 1969). See U.S. v. Torres, 1986 WL 7267 (S.D.N.Y. 1986) (warnings given to Spanish speaking defendant in English satisfied *Miranda* where officers testified that defendant spoke English as well as Spanish and appeared to understand the dialogue).

[12]Gould v. State, 138 Ga. App. 159, 225 S.E.2d 916 (1976). Cf. State v. Appleton, 459 A.2d 94 (R.I.1983); Daniel v. State, 171 Ga. App. 171, 319 S.E.2d 66 (1984).

[13]In the Interest of D.T.C., 226 Ga. App. 364, 366, 487 S.E.2d 21 (1997).

[14]Coppock v. State, 273 Ga. 324 (2), 540 S.E.2d 187 (2001).

Despite the broad language of *Miranda,* a number of courts have held that the need to give the prescribed warnings does not apply for routine traffic violations.[15] Some of these courts have found an absence of the required custody,[16] while others have regarded questions asked a driver as a limited on-the-scene investigation rather than an interrogation.[17] However, if an officer determines that a driver should be arrested,[18] *Miranda* warnings must be given. In the 1984 case of *Berkemer v. McCarty,*[19] the United States Supreme Court held that *Miranda* safeguards must be complied with whenever there is custodial interrogation, regardless of the severity of the offense. However, the Court also pointed out that a routine traffic stop does not ordinarily amount to custody under *Miranda.* See § 5:12, supra, on traffic violations.

In *Foster v. State,*[20] the Georgia Supreme Court held that statements made by officers to the defendant that his confession "was not going to hurt 'a thing' and that it would be 'as much for your benefit as ours . . .'" is not consistent with warnings required by *Miranda.*

It seems that in emergency situations, at least when there is not time to give *Miranda* warnings, questions asked to protect

---

[15]E.g., United States v. LeQuire, 424 F.2d 341 (5th Cir. 1970), where police officer stopped automobile for speeding. See Annot., 25 A.L.R.3d 1076 (1969). In "Does *Miranda* Apply to Traffic Arrests?" 27 Wayne L. R. 193 (1980), the author argues that it is the arrest itself, not the offense, which *Miranda* addresses.

　　See Berkemer v. McCarty, 468 U.S. 420, 104 S.Ct. 3138, 82 L.Ed.2d 317 (1984); Pennsylvania v. Bruder, 488 U.S. 9, 109 S.Ct. 205, 102 L.Ed.2d 172 (1988). Accord, Shy v. State, 234 Ga. 816, 218 S.E.2d 599 (1975) disapproved on other grounds, State v. Folsom, 285 Ga. 11, 673 S.E.2d 210 (2009), which held that a *Terry* stop-and-frisk does not require *Miranda* warnings.

[16]Gustafson v. State, 243 So.2d 615 (Fla.App. 1971), quashed in part by State v. Gustafson, 258 So.2d 1 (Fla.1972), overruled on other grounds, 414 U.S. 260, 94 S.Ct. 488, 38 L.Ed.2d 456 (1973).

[17]United States v. Chase, 414 F.2d 780 (9th Cir. 1969), where police officer asked driver for identification and vehicle registration slip without giving defendant *Miranda* warnings.

[18]See Campbell v. Superior Court of Maricopa County, 106 Ariz. 542, 479 P.2d 685 (1971). Cf. People v. Lowe, 200 Colo. 470, 616 P.2d 118 (1980).

[19]Berkemer v. McCarty, 468 U.S. 420, 104 S.Ct. 3138, 82 L.Ed.2d 317 (1984).

[20]Foster v. State, 258 Ga. 736, 742 (8)(b), 374 S.E.2d 188 (1988). See Spence v. State, 281 Ga. 697, 642 S.E.2d 856 (2007), officer's promise to keep defendants' statement confidential contradicts *Miranda*'s premise that anything said by suspect could be used in court and hence statement cannot be admitted even though defendant had already executed a *Miranda* waiver prior to making statement. See also State v. Clark, 301 Ga. 7, 799 S.E.2d 192 (2017).

the safety of a person or persons are not prohibited by *Miranda*.[21] See § 5:11, supra, on confessions and admissions.

Generally, it is not necessary to inform a suspect of the nature of the offense with which he is being charged.[22]

Although *Miranda* warnings must be given before questioning begins,[23] it has been held that it is not necessary to repeat the warnings prior to a later session of interrogation[24] if the interrogations are continuing in nature and separated by only a short time span.[25] Where one investigating officer replaces another, a suspect who has been provided his rights and signed a waiver need not be given additional warnings where the lapse between the questioning was brief.[26] In *McSears v. State*,[27] the defendant was given *Miranda* warnings in connection with one case. Later during the interview, without *Miranda* warnings being given again, the defendant made a statement about another case. He was tried for the second case. The appellate court affirmed the admissibility of the admissions made during the interview relating to the second case. It has also been pointed out that if full warnings are given a defendant, at subsequent questionings it is not necessary that they be preceded by the complete warning if the defendant is reminded that he was previously advised of his rights.[28] Where a defendant's attorney informs an officer that his client wishes to make a statement, there is no need to give the *Miranda* warnings.[29] On the other hand, the United States Supreme Court has held inadmissible incriminating statements obtained by officers where there had been an agreement between the officers and the suspect's attorney that the suspect would not be questioned while being transported from one city to another.[30]

---

[21]U.S. v. Freeman, 591 Fed. Appx. 855 (11th Cir. 2014). See U.S. v. Ayala, 2011 WL 1769146 (E.D. Tex. 2011); United States v. Castellana, 500 F.2d 325 (5th Cir. 1974); State v. Hudson, 325 A.2d 56 (Me.1974); State v. Roadenbaugh, 234 Kan. 474, 673 P.2d 1166 (1983); State v. Hein, 138 Ariz. 360, 674 P.2d 1358 (1983).

[22]Gaines v. State, 179 Ga. App. 623, 624 (1), 347 S.E.2d 673 (1986); Gainer v. State, 144 Ga. App. 703, 706 (2), 242 S.E.2d 286 (1978).

[23]Miranda v. Arizona, 384 U.S. 436, 479, 86 S.Ct. 1602, 16 L.Ed.2d 694 (1966). See § 5:11, n. 7, supra, on volunteered statements.

[24]Watson v. State, 227 Ga. 698, 700, 182 S.E.2d 446 (1971); United States v. Kinsey, 352 F.Supp. 1176 (E. D.Pa.1972).

[25]McKenzie v. State, 187 Ga. App. 840, 844, 371 S.E.2d 869 (1988).

[26]Wallace v. State, 253 Ga. App. 220, 222, 558 S.E.2d 773 (2002).

[27]McSears v. State, 226 Ga. App. 90, 92 (2), 485 S.E.2d 589 (1997).

[28]Hubbard v. State, 187 Ga. App. 542, 544, 371 S.E.2d 116 (1988).

[29]Dempsey v. State, 225 Ga. 208 (1), 166 S.E.2d 884 (1969).

[30]Brewer v. Williams, 430 U.S. 387, 97 S.Ct. 1232, 51 L.Ed.2d 424 (1977).

§ 5:15 Confessions and admissions—*Miranda v. Arizona*— Warnings—Right to remain silent

Prior to any questioning, a person in custody must be warned of the right to remain silent.[1] In fact, it appears that the remainder of the warnings are intended in large measure to implement this first warning.[2] As noted in *Miranda,* an accused needs a warning concerning the right to remain silent because of the inherently compelling nature of in-custody interrogations.[3]

The exercise of the right to remain silent must be unequivocal. In *Perez v. State,*[4] the Georgia Supreme Court ruled that the statements made by an accused after ambiguous assertions of the right, such as " . . . I can stop the interrogation. Right? Yes or no?" will not qualify and police may continue questioning. In *Berghuis v. Thompkins,*[5] the United States Supreme Court reached a result similar to that in *Perez,* holding that a suspect who remains silent after being advised of his rights under *Miranda* has not invoked the right to remain silent. A suspect's right to remain silent, like the right to counsel, must be asserted without equivocation and, in the absence of an unconditional statement that the suspect chooses to remain silent, the police may conduct an interrogation. In addition, police are under no obligation to ask clarifying questions of the accused as to whether he or she fully comprehends the extent of the right to remain silent. Although acknowledging that such clarifying questions might be good police practice, the United States Supreme Court, in *Davis v. United States,*[6] refused to apply such a rule where the right to counsel was concerned.

If a defendant chooses to remain silent after receiving *Miranda* warnings,[7] it is a violation of the Due Process Clause of the Fourteenth Amendment for the prosecution to use the accused's

---

[Section 5:15]

[1]Miranda v. Arizona, 384 U.S. 436, 444, 86 S.Ct. 1602, 16 L.Ed.2d 694 (1966).

[2]Miranda v. Arizona, 384 U.S. 436, 468, 86 S.Ct. 1602, 16 L.Ed.2d 694 (1966).

[3]Miranda v. Arizona, 384 U.S. 436, 469, 86 S.Ct. 1602, 16 L.Ed.2d 694 (1966). The "warning may serve to make the individual more acutely aware that he is faced with a phase of the adversary system—that he is not in the presence of persons acting solely in his interest."

[4]Perez v. State, 283 Ga. 196, 657 S.E.2d 846 (2008).

[5]Berghuis v. Thompkins, 130 S. Ct. 2250 (2010). See Barnes v. State, 287 Ga. 423, 696 S.E.2d 629 (2010).

[6]Davis v. U.S., 512 U.S. 452, 114 S. Ct. 2350, 129 L. Ed. 2d 362 (1994).

[7]In Fletcher v. Weir, 455 U.S. 603, 607, 102 S.Ct. 1309, 71 L.Ed.2d 490 (1982), the Court said that there was no federal constitutional limitation on the use of post-arrest silence to impeach a defendant where no *Miranda* warnings have been given.

silence to impeach him.[8] However, in *Jackson v. State,*[9] the Georgia Supreme Court held that when a defendant on direct examination testifies that he made no statement, he may be cross-examined about his post-arrest silence. In *Osborne v. State,*[10] the Georgia Court of Appeals held that "[t]he silence of an arrestee prior to his receipt of the *Miranda* warnings may be used by the State for purposes of impeachment." In *Fallen v. State,*[11] "defense counsel elicited from his client the statement that he was never asked . . . to make a written statement." The court found no error in the district attorney bringing out on cross-examination that he was not asked to make a statement, because on being given his *Miranda* warnings, he elected to remain silent.

The Georgia Supreme Court has held this prohibition to be inapplicable to earlier cases where the issue was not raised in the trial court and to appeals which were completed before June 17, 1976, the date of the decision in *Doyle v. Ohio.*[12] The rule against using a defendant's silence to impeach him does not apply retroactively in habeas corpus or other post-appeal attacks unless the point was properly raised in the trial court.[13]

It is error for the trial judge to allow an officer "to testify that after being read his rights and after answering one question, the defendant refused to answer a second question and then said his lawyer would be available the next day. The defendant has the right to remain silent and to be represented by counsel and the exercise of these rights is not to be used as evidence against him."[14]

However, if a defendant does not elect to remain silent and he makes a statement and if at trial he makes a different statement, the earlier statement is admissible for purposes of impeachment[15] if the statement is freely and voluntarily made.[16] In addition, a defendant's refusal to answer some questions and responding to others during interrogation may be the subject of testimony at trial provided the defendant's silence cannot be construed as an

---

[8]Doyle v. Ohio, 426 U.S. 610, 96 S.Ct. 2240, 49 L.Ed.2d 91 (1976); Howard v. State, 237 Ga. 471, 473, 228 S.E.2d 860 (1976); Hosch v. State, 246 Ga. 417, 419, 271 S.E.2d 817 (1980).

[9]Jackson v. State, 258 Ga. 322, 323 (3), 368 S.E.2d 760 (1988).

[10]Osborne v. State, 193 Ga. App. 276 (1), 387 S.E.2d 383 (1989) (quoting Lanham v. State, 184 Ga. App. 554, 362 S.E.2d 131 (1987)); Mattox v. State, 196 Ga. App. 64 (1), 395 S.E.2d 288 (1990).

[11]Fallen v. State, 191 Ga. App. 233, 381 S.E.2d 410 (1989).

[12]Doyle v. Ohio, 426 U.S. 610, 96 S.Ct. 2240, 49 L.Ed.2d 91 (1976).

[13]Clark v. State, 237 Ga. 901, 902, 230 S.E.2d 277 (1976).

[14]Hosch v. State, 246 Ga. 417, 271 S.E.2d 817 (1980).

[15]Brown v. State, 167 Ga. App. 61, 63 (4), 305 S.E.2d 870 (1983); Milline v. State, 172 Ga. App. 468, 323 S.E.2d 678 (1984).

[16]Mincey v. Arizona, 437 U.S. 385, 98 S.Ct. 2408, 57 L.Ed.2d 290 (1978).

attempt to assert his right to remain silent and cut off all questioning.[17]

See § 5:21, infra, on duty to speak and tacit admissions. Also see § 7:7, subparagraph (5), infra, on suggested advice to defendant in custody not to participate in any tests or try on clothing. Also see § 5:19, infra, on questioning a defendant after he says he wants counsel.

§ 5:16 Confessions and admissions—*Miranda v. Arizona*—Warnings—Use in court of any statements

In summarizing the warning requirements, the United States Supreme Court in *Miranda* noted that any statement an accused makes "*may* be used against him."[1] However, another part of the opinion goes on to state that the warnings should include a statement that "anything said *can and will* be used against the individual in court."[2] It appears that a warning advising a suspect that any statement he makes "can and will" be used against him is not necessary.[3]

§ 5:17 Confessions and admissions—*Miranda v. Arizona*—Warnings—Right to have counsel present

The right to have counsel present at an in-custody interrogation is "indispensable to the protection of the Fifth Amendment privilege."[1] However, *Miranda* does not require an officer to inform a defendant how he can obtain counsel.[2] Also, the Georgia Supreme Court has held that the *Miranda* warnings do not have to contain a statement that if during the course of questioning the suspect wishes an attorney, he may cease answering questions and will not be required to answer further questions until his attorney is present.[3]

While questioning must cease when a suspect in custody says

---

[17]Rogers v. State, 290 Ga. 401, 721 S.E.2d 864 (2012).

[Section 5:16]

[1]Miranda v. Arizona, 384 U.S. 436, 444, 86 S.Ct. 1602, 16 L.Ed.2d 694 (1966).

[2]Miranda v. Arizona, 384 U.S. 436, 469, 86 S.Ct. 1602, 16 L.Ed.2d 694 (1966). See also United States v. Grady, 423 F.2d 1091 (5th Cir. 1970).

[3]In Morris v. State, 228 Ga. 39, 44, 184 S.E.2d 82 (1971), the court held that the difference between "could and may be used" and "can and will be used" was inconsequential. See Staple-

ton v. State, 235 Ga. 513, 515, 220 S.E.2d 269 (1975).

[Section 5:17]

[1]Miranda v. Arizona, 384 U.S. 436, 469, 86 S.Ct. 1602, 16 L.Ed.2d 694 (1966). See Annot., "Necessity That *Miranda* Warnings Include Express Reference to Right to Have Attorney Present During Interrogation," 77 A.L.R.Fed. 123 (1986).

[2]Reynolds v. State, 168 Ga. App. 555, 556 (3), 309 S.E.2d 867 (1983).

[3]Katzensky v. State, 228 Ga. 6, 8, 183 S.E.2d 749 (1971).

that he wants counsel, unless the right to counsel is later waived,[4] a request to talk with some other person, such as a probation officer[5] or a relative,[6] does not require that questioning stop.

Signing a waiver to counsel after being told that counsel was not immediately available is still a valid waiver, even though the suspect was never provided with counsel during the interrogation.[7] Likewise, a custodial statement was deemed properly admitted in *Moore v. State*,[8] where the defendant agreed to an interrogation after signing a waiver and communicating, "I guess I'll get a lawyer too."

While a suspect has a right to invoke his right to counsel, this right is personal and cannot be invoked by another. Thus, where an attorney calls officers who have a defendant in custody and requests that questioning of the defendant cease until counsel arrives, this does not amount to an exercise of the defendant's right to counsel at the time of questioning.[9] Likewise, in *Blanks v. State*,[10] the Georgia Supreme Court held that where a suspect had been given the *Miranda* warnings a number of times, had waived his right to be silent, and was making a loud statement, officers were not obligated to inform him that an attorney had been hired for him and that the attorney wanted to confer with him. Moreover, in *Davis v. United States*,[11] the United States Supreme Court held that for a defendant to invoke his right to counsel under the Fifth Amendment, the request must be unambiguous. The Georgia Supreme Court has since adapted the reasoning in *Davis* and in the absence of an unambiguous request for counsel, police may question an accused who has been properly advised of his rights to counsel.[12]

---

[4]Cf. Rouse v. State, 255 Ind. 670, 266 N.E.2d 209 (1971).

[5]Fare v. Michael C., 442 U.S. 707, 99 S.Ct. 2560, 61 L.Ed.2d 197 (1979).

[6]In United States v. Weston, 519 F.Supp. 565, 572 (W.D.N.Y.1981), the defendant asked for his wife and brother-in-law. The court stated that the "defendant had an absolute right to have his lawyer present, not his wife."

[7]Simon v. State, 279 Ga. App. 844(1), 632 S.E.2d 723 (2006).

[8]Moore v. State, 263 Ga. App. 548, 550-51(2), 588 S.E.2d 327 (2003). See Crawford v. State, 288 Ga. 425, 704 S.E.2d 772 (2011) (custodial ques-

tion to officer by defendant as to whether he needed an attorney was not unequivocal request for attorney).

[9]Edwards v. State, 167 Ga. App. 681, 682, 307 S.E.2d 264 (1983).

[10]Blanks v. State, 254 Ga. 420, 330 S.E.2d 575 (1985).

[11]Davis v. United States, 512 U.S. 452, 114 S.Ct. 2350, 129 L.Ed.2d 362 (1994).

[12]Jordan v. State, 267 Ga. 442(1), 480 S.E.2d 18 (1997). In Perez v. State, 283 Ga. 196, 657 S.E.2d 846 (2008) the Court apparently rejected prior suggestions by members of the Georgia Supreme Court that the Georgia Constitution might require a rule which places a responsibility upon police

§ 5:18 Confessions and admissions—*Miranda v. Arizona*— Warnings—Right to have counsel appointed

The *Miranda* warnings must effectively advise the accused of his right to a court-appointed counsel.[1] However, it is not necessary to furnish counsel to a suspect where he can afford to employ an attorney on his own.[2] Thus, it has been held that a warning is not defective if the provision for the appointment of counsel is omitted unless it appears that the defendant was indigent.[3]

§ 5:19 Confessions and admissions—*Miranda v. Arizona*— Waiver—Right to remain silent

As previously pointed out in § 5:11, supra, if there is in-custody interrogation by the state or its representatives, a statement of the defendant obtained by officers is not admissible unless (1) the defendant was adequately warned (§ 5:14, supra) and (2) the defendant validly waived his right of silence and, if counsel was not present, his right to the presence of counsel at the time of the interrogation.

An in-custody suspect must clearly and affirmatively waive his right to silence and counsel.[1] A waiver cannot be implied from the silence of the suspect nor from the fact that a confession was obtained.[2] There is no presumption that the defendant knowingly and intelligently waived his *Miranda* rights.[3] In fact, the "courts must presume that a defendant did not waive his rights; the prosecution's burden is great." However, the failure of a suspect to expressly waive (in writing or orally) his right to remain silent does not automatically prevent the admission of a statement which he thereafter makes.[4]

---

conducting interviews to obtain an un-equivocal response from a criminal suspect in custody to the question of whether counsel is requested. Luallen v. State, 266 Ga. 174, 179, 465 S.E.2d 672 (1996) (Fletcher, P.J., concurring); Carroll v. State, 275 Ga. 160, 563 S.E.2d 125 (2002) (Sears, P.J., concurring).

[Section 5:18]

[1]See, e.g., Duckworth v. Eagan, 492 U.S. 195, 109 S. Ct. 2875, 106 L. Ed. 2d 166 (1989). Cf. Florida v. Powell, 130 S. Ct. 1195 (2010).

[2]See Miranda v. Arizona, 384 U.S. 436, 473, 86 S.Ct. 1602, 16 L.Ed.2d 694 (1966). See § 2:30, supra,

on the exclusionary rule and discovery of a live witness.

[3]Griffith v. State, 223 Ga. 543, 156 S.E.2d 903 (1967).

[Section 5:19]

[1]Colbert v. State, 124 Ga. App. 283 (1), 183 S.E.2d 476 (1971); State v. Stephens, 300 N.C. 321, 266 S.E.2d 588 (1980).

[2]Miranda v. Arizona, 384 U.S. 436, 475, 86 S.Ct. 1602, 16 L.Ed.2d 694 (1966).

[3]Tague v. Louisiana, 444 U.S. 469, 100 S.Ct. 652, 62 L.Ed.2d 622 (1980).

[4]North Carolina v. Butler, 441

In *Michigan v. Mosley*,[5] the defendant, who had been arrested in connection with certain robberies, exercised his right to remain silent after he was advised of his *Miranda* rights. More than two hours later, a different officer took the defendant to another part of the building, Mirandized the defendant again, and asked him questions about an unrelated holdup murder. At that time defendant made incriminating statements. The United States Supreme Court used a totality of circumstances analysis and held that the defendant's statements were obtained lawfully under the Fifth Amendment and were therefore properly admitted against him at trial. The court considered that (1) the defendant had been advised of his *Miranda* rights at both interrogations, (2) when the defendant exercised his right to remain silent at the first interrogation, the officer immediately ceased the questioning, and (3) the second interrogation occurred after a significant time lapse, was directed solely at the murder holdup, to which the defendant had not invoked his *Miranda* rights, and was conducted at another location in the building by another officer.

In the 2006 case of *Griffin v. State*,[6] the Georgia Supreme Court considered the case of a defendant who sought to suppress incriminating statements where an officer honored the defendant's right to remain silent in the first interview, but then returned four days later to question the defendant about the same crime. The court affirmed the denial of the defendant's motion to suppress, holding that "a second interrogation regarding the same crime may also be constitutional under *Mosley* . . . where the initial invocation of the right to remain silent was scrupulously honored."[7]

It has generally been held that it is not necessary to show that a suspect was informed of the charge against him.[8] In *Vaughan v.*

U.S. 369, 373, 99 S.Ct. 1755, 60 L.Ed.2d 286 (1979). In Butler the court, quoting from Johnson v. Zerbst, 304 U.S. 458, 464, 58 S.Ct. 1019, 82 L.Ed. 1461 (1938), said the question of waiver must be determined by "the particular facts and circumstances surrounding [the] . . . case, including the background, experience, and conduct of the accused." See Williams v. State, 244 Ga. 485, 488, 260 S.E.2d 879 (1979). See Aldridge v. State, 258 Ga. 75, 76 (3), 365 S.E.2d 111 (1988) "refusal to sign a waiver form does not constitute an invocation of the right to remain silent or the right to counsel."

Accord, Hunter v. State, 273 Ga. App. 52 (3), 614 S.E.2d 179 (2005).

[5]Michigan v. Mosley, 423 U.S. 96, 96 S.Ct. 321, 46 L.Ed.2d 313 (1975).

[6]Griffin v. State, 280 Ga. 683, 631 S.E.2d 671 (2006) citing Fields v. State, 266 Ga. 241(1), 466 S.E.2d 202 (1996).

[7]Griffin v. State, 280 Ga. 683, 631 S.E.2d 671 (2006) citing Fields v. State, 266 Ga. 241(1), 466 S.E.2d 202 (1996).

[8]James v. State, 230 Ga. 29, 195 S.E.2d 448 (1973); Peebles v. State, 196 Ga. App. 176, 395 S.E.2d 640

State,[9] the court held that the failure of an officer "to advise a suspect as to the crimes about which he is to be questioned prior to the suspect's waiver of his *Miranda* rights is not relevant to the question of whether the suspect's waiver was knowing and voluntary."

In *Colorado v. Spring,*[10] the United States Supreme Court held that the failure of an officer to inform a suspect that he would be questioned about a murder did not invalidate the interrogation. " '[O]ne who is told he is free to refuse to answer questions . . . [cannot] later complain that his answers were compelled.' . . . Here, the additional information could affect only the wisdom of a *Miranda* waiver, not its essentially voluntary and knowing nature. Accordingly, the failure of the law enforcement officials to inform Spring of the subject matter of the interrogation could not affect Spring's decision to waive his Fifth Amendment privilege in a constitutionally significant manner."

The fact that a person declined to sign a written waiver does not mean that a later statement which is obtained is automatically inadmissible.[11] In *Moore v. State,*[12] the Georgia Court of Appeals held that the defendant's refusal to sign a transcription of his confession, based on his belief that the unsigned statement could not be used against him, did not prevent the admissibility of the confession.

While the burden rests on the government to demonstrate that the defendant voluntarily, knowingly, and intelligently waived his privilege against self-incrimination and his right to retained or appointed counsel, where there is questioning of an in-custody suspect without the presence of an attorney,[13] a defendant is not entitled to counsel to help him determine whether to waive his

---

(1990).

[9]Vaughan v. State, 210 Ga. App. 381, 383 (3)(a), 436 S.E.2d 19 (1993).

[10]Colorado v. Spring, 479 U.S. 564, 107 S.Ct. 851, 93 L.Ed.2d 954 (1987).

[11]Mitchell v. State, 254 Ga. 353, 355 (7), 329 S.E.2d 481 (1985); Spain v. State, 243 Ga. 15, 16, 252 S.E.2d 436 (1979). See Humphreys v. State, 287 Ga. 63, 694 S.E.2d 316 (2010) (although not required, better practice is to have waiver in writing). Cf. North Carolina v. Butler, 441 U.S. 369, 99 S. Ct. 1755, 60 L. Ed. 2d 286 (1979) (written waiver does not automatically establish waiver).

[12]Moore v. State, 207 Ga. App.

802, 430 S.E.2d 115 (1993).

[13]Edwards v. Arizona, 451 U.S. 477, 101 S.Ct. 1880, 68 L.Ed.2d 378 (1981); Miranda v. Arizona, 384 U.S. 436, 475, 86 S.Ct. 1602, 16 L.Ed.2d 694 (1966); Smith v. State, 132 Ga. App. 491, 492, 208 S.E.2d 351 (1974). In Canal Zone v. Gomez, 566 F.2d 1289 (5th Cir. 1978), the court pointed out that a waiver is ineffective unless the defendant understands the language in which the warnings are given. In United States v. Massey, 550 F.2d 300 (5th Cir. 1977), the court said that waiver was invalid where a defendant is misled into believing that the questioning would not relate to the crime under investigation.

Miranda rights.[14]

In *Colorado v. Connelly*,[15] the United States Supreme Court held that the burden placed on the state is to prove waiver by a preponderance of the evidence, and pointed out *Miranda* is concerned with governmental coercion and is not concerned "with moral and psychological pressures to confess emanating from sources other than official coercion."

In *United States v. Hernandez*,[16] the Fifth Circuit pointed out that the "more times police inform a suspect of his rights in the face of his repeated invocation of one of those rights—the right to remain silent—the clearer it becomes that the police must not mean what they say. This is exactly the type of subtle coercive pressure which the *Miranda* opinion condemned."

Intoxication does not automatically prevent a valid waiver.[17] A waiver by the defendant whose blood alcohol percentage was .27 has been upheld.[18] Where a defendant had been shot and he contended that he was under the influence of alcohol and drugs and was suffering a great deal of pain, he was found to have understood and waived his *Miranda* rights when making a statement at a hospital.[19] In *Felts v. State*,[20] the Court of Appeals pointed out that "where a suspect is coherent and his demeanor indicates that he understands his rights and has waived those rights, intoxication will not be a defense."

Furthermore, a suspect need not have a great deal of intelligence to waive his *Miranda* rights.[21] A waiver by a suspect with

---

[14]United States v. Britt, 460 F.2d 1023 (5th Cir. 1972). See § 5:10, supra, on defendant's Sixth Amendment right to counsel.

[15]Colorado v. Connelly, 479 U.S. 157, 107 S.Ct. 515, 93 L.Ed.2d 473 (1986). See § 5:4, n. 11, supra.

[16]United States v. Hernandez, 574 F.2d 1362 (5th Cir. 1978). In *Hernandez,* the defendant was given *Miranda* warnings and he exercised his right to remain silent. He was confined for five hours in a police wagon. Within 45 minutes of his arrival at the police station he was given the warnings again and officers attempted to question him. This occurred at least two more times. Finally, the defendant made an admission.

[17]In Cunningham v. State, 255 Ga. 727, 729 (2), 342 S.E.2d 299 (1986), the court held that a .30 blood-

alcohol level did not prevent a valid waiver. But see United States v. Martin, 434 F.2d 275 (5th Cir. 1970).

[18]Smith v. State, 164 Ga. App. 624, 298 S.E.2d 587 (1982), modified on other grounds, 268 Ga. 196, 486 S.E.2d 819 (1997).

[19]Durden v. State, 250 Ga. 325, 327 (2), 297 S.E.2d 237 (1982).

[20]Felts v. State, 207 Ga. App. 31, 32 (1), 427 S.E.2d 25 (1993).

[21]Colton v. State, 296 Ga. 172, 766 S.E.2d 38 (2014) (cognitive impairment is only one of several factors to consider when weighing waiver and voluntariness of statement). See Fife v. State, 306 Ga. App. 425, 428(2), 702 S.E.2d 454 (2010) (evidence was sufficient to show that mildly retarded defendant "knowingly" waived his Miranda rights". Compare Cooper v. Griffin, 455 F.2d 1142 (5th Cir. 1972)

a mental age of 6 and I. Q. of 60 has been upheld.[22] Likewise, the fact that a defendant is illiterate and was in a special education class when he was in school does not mean he is "incapable of understanding his *Miranda* rights when they are read to him."[23] Also a waiver may be valid even though the "defendant may have been suffering from some mental condition" or is moderately retarded.[24] In *Kerr v. State*,[25] there was evidence that the defendant ranked in the lower 3% of the population in range of intelligence. The defendant contended that "he could not have made an *intelligent* waiver of *Miranda* rights, because he is not 'intelligent.' " In affirming the trial judge's finding that the defendant knowingly and voluntarily waived his *Miranda* rights, the court pointed out that there is no requirement that a suspect have a high or average degree of intelligence "but *requires* a knowing waiver."

Neither does an imperfect translation of a defendant's *Miranda* rights necessarily nullify an otherwise valid rights waiver. In *Nguyen v. State*,[26] the court upheld the trial court's admission of the defendant's confession where the record showed that the defendant's *Miranda* rights were duly explained and that the defendant understood such rights. Under such circumstances, an imperfect translation of the defendant's rights will not foreclose a valid rights waiver.

It has been held that there is a distinction between the weight of the evidence required to show that a statement was made voluntarily and the evidence required to show a *Miranda* waiver. Thus, where an individual is "distraught, upset, weeping and obviously out of control" even if his statements were voluntary for the purpose of the Fifth Amendment, his condition may be such as to prevent a showing of "the higher standard . . . [required] with respect to waiver of the right to counsel that applies when the Sixth Amendment has attached."[27] See § 5:4, supra, on voluntariness of confession.

In *United States v. Reyna*,[28] the defendant underwent custodial interrogation without receiving the *Miranda* warnings and

---

(15- and 16-year-old suspects not capable of making "knowing and intelligent" waiver where they had low IQ and reading comprehension).

[22]United States v. Bush, 466 F.2d 236 (5th Cir. 1972).

[23]Donaldson v. State, 249 Ga. 186, 189 (5), 289 S.E.2d 242 (1982).

[24]Parker v. State, 161 Ga. App. 478 (1), 288 S.E.2d 297 (1982).

[25]Kerr v. State, 194 Ga. App. 604, 605 (2), 391 S.E.2d 449 (1990).

[26]Nguyen v. State, 269 Ga. App. 730, 605 S.E.2d 130 (2004).

[27]United States v. Satterfield, 558 F.2d 655 (2d Cir. 1976) (citing Judge Friendly's dissent in United States v. Massimo, 432 F.2d 324, 327 (2d Cir. 1970)).

[28]United States v. Reyna, 563 F.2d 1169 (5th Cir. 1977). Accord, State v. Baker, 238 Ga. App. 802, 803 (2), 521 S.E.2d 24 (1999).

confessed. Immediately thereafter he was given the warnings, and he repeated the confession. The Fifth Circuit held that the "first" confession was tainted and that neither the "first" nor "second" confession was admissible. The confessions were said to be "so closely related in time and circumstance that they were one and the same." The idea is that the defendant "let the cat out of the bag" when he made the first statement.

However, in *Oregon v. Elstad*,[29] the United States Supreme Court said that a "suspect who has once responded to unwarned . . . [and] uncoercive questioning is not thereby disabled from waiving his rights and confessing after he has been given the requisite *Miranda* warnings," even though he had made an admission of being present at the scene of the crime in response to his earlier questioning. In *Thornton v. State*,[30] while in jail the defendant wrote a note to an investigator asking how he could "turn state's evidence." The investigator conducted a video interview with the defendant in which he proclaimed his innocence. No *Miranda* warnings had been given. The Georgia Supreme Court held that "[u]nwarned statements that are otherwise voluntary within the meaning of the Fifth Amendment must nevertheless be excluded from evidence under *Miranda*."

In *Sliger v. State*,[31] the Georgia Supreme Court held that the Unified Appeal Procedure giving the defendant an opportunity to state any objections he may have to defense counsel is not compelling the defendant to be a witness against himself.

It has been held that the best evidence of waiver by an in-custody suspect is a signed written waiver form.[32] Such a waiver is set out in *Moody v. State*.[33] However, there is no obligation on the state to give the defendant a copy of the signed waiver form, and there is no requirement that a copy of the waiver be furnished to defense counsel pursuant to a request for a copy of

---

[29]Oregon v. Elstad, 470 U.S. 298, 105 S.Ct. 1285, 84 L.Ed.2d 222 (1985). Compare Missouri v. Seibert, 542 U.S. 600, 124 S.Ct. 2601, 159 L.Ed.2d 643 (2004), where the Supreme Court rejected admissibility of statements where police deliberately questioned the defendant without giving her *Miranda* warnings, and then, after she confessed, provided warnings and had defendant repeat her confession.

[30]Thornton v. State, 264 Ga. 563, 570 (8)(c), 449 S.E.2d 98 (1994).

[31]Sliger v. State, 248 Ga. 316, 319 (3), 282 S.E.2d 291 (1981).

[32]United States v. Ellis, 457 F.2d 1204 (8th Cir. 1972). In Brooks v. United States, 416 F.2d 1044, 1050 (5th Cir. 1969), and Grimsley v. State, 251 So.2d 671 (Fla.App.1971), the courts said a signed written waiver is usually sufficient if the defendant can read. However, the Court in North Carolina v. Butler, 441 U.S. 369, 99 S.Ct. 1755, 60 L.Ed.2d 286 (1979), said that a written waiver does not automatically establish a waiver.

[33]Moody v. State, 224 Ga. 301, 161 S.E.2d 856 (1968).

statements made by the defendant while in custody.[34] See § 14:29, infra, for a request for a copy of such statements. Even when there is a valid waiver of counsel and a suspect begins to answer questions, he may at any time change his mind and exercise his right to remain silent. If he exercises this right, questioning must cease immediately.[35]

§ 5:20 Confessions and admissions—*Miranda v. Arizona*—Waiver—Right to counsel

In *Edwards v. Arizona*,[1] the United States Supreme Court established a per se rule, holding that once the *Miranda* right to counsel has been invoked, any further conversation between police and suspect (1) must be *initiated* by the suspect, and (2) "waivers of counsel must not only be voluntary, but constitute a knowing and intelligent relinquishment or abandonment of a known right or privilege." In *Edwards*,[2] the defendant was arrested and Mirandized, after which he told police he wanted to "make a deal." Edwards then told officers he wanted "an attorney before making a deal" and the questioning ceased. The following morning, before the defendant had access to counsel, two different officers Mirandized the defendant again, he waived his rights, and confessed to the same crime about which he was questioned earlier. The court held that Edwards' incriminating statements should not have been admitted against him at trial.[3]

The per se rule in *Edwards* was adopted to preserve the "integ-

---

[34]Brady v. State, 206 Ga. App. 497, 498 (1), 426 S.E.2d 15 (1992).

[35]See § 5:11, n. 10, supra.

[Section 5:20]

[1]Edwards v. Arizona, 451 U.S. 477, 101 S.Ct. 1880, 1883-1887, 68 L.Ed.2d 378 (1981). This is a tougher standard than that which applies to a consent to search and waivers of Fourth Amendment rights. See Chapter 4, supra, on search and seizure. Cf. Hopkins v. State, 263 Ga. 354, 357 (3)(a), 434 S.E.2d 459 (1993).

[2]Edwards v. Arizona, 451 U.S. 477, 101 S.Ct. 1880, 68 L.Ed.2d 378 (1981). It is important to note that the Court, referring to *Miranda*, distinguished between invoking the right to remain silent (i.e., Michigan v. Mosley, 423 U.S. 96, 96 S.Ct. 321, 46 L.Ed.2d 313 (1975)) and the right to counsel under the Fifth Amendment. Invoking the right to counsel essentially means that defendant is saying "I am unable to proceed without a lawyer's advice."

There is an interesting dichotomy between *Moseley* and *Edwards*. In *Moseley*, defendant invoked the right to remain silent which is explicitly provided for in the text of the Fifth Amendment and the Court used a case-by-case approach which allowed the re-interrogation. However, in *Edwards*, where defendant invoked the right to counsel, which is not in the text of the Fifth Amendment, the Court adopted a per se rule. So, it appears that the actual right (to remain silent) provided for in the Constitution receives less protection than a procedural right (to counsel) created by the Court in *Miranda*. See § 5:19, supra, for a discussion of Michigan v. Mosley, 423 U.S. 96, 96 S.Ct. 321, 46 L.Ed.2d 313 (1975), and waiver of the right to remain silent.

[3]Accord, Walton v. State, 267 Ga.

rity of an accused's choice to communicate with police only through counsel."[4] The concern was that an accused in custody might be subject to police badgering to waive a previously asserted right to counsel.[5] In *Maryland v. Shatzer*,[6] the Court distinguished the case of an accused subject to multiple police interrogation efforts while in uninterrupted custody from that of an accused who initially requested counsel but is later re-interrogated after a break in custody. In the latter case, the Court held that the line drawn in *Edwards* is not crossed if the second request for a statement comes at least 14 days after the accused is released from custody. The Court's reasoning was premised upon its finding that 14 days is enough time for the accused to assimilate back into his or her accustomed surroundings, consult with friends and counsel and relieve the coercive atmosphere that comes with a custodial setting.

The Georgia Supreme Court in *Gissendaner v. State*[7] considered a case in which the lawyer, not the suspect, told officers he wanted to be present at any interviews between the suspect and officers. The court, in reversing the conviction, treated the statement of counsel as being the invocation by the suspect of her right to have counsel present before officers talked with the defendant.

In *Oregon v. Bradshaw*,[8] the United States Supreme Court clarified what it means for a suspect to "initiate" a conversation under *Edwards*. In the plurality opinion, then Justice Rehnquist defined "initiation" of a conversation as when the suspect "evince[s] a willingness and desire for a generalized discussion

---

713, 715, 482 S.E.2d 330 (1997).

[4]Patterson v. Illinois, 487 U.S. 285, 291, 108 S. Ct. 2389, 101 L. Ed. 2d 261 (1988).

[5]Michigan v. Harvey, 494 U.S. 344, 350, 110 S. Ct. 1176, 108 L. Ed. 2d 293 (1990).

[6]Maryland v. Shatzer, 130 S. Ct. 1213 (2010).

[7]Gissendaner v. State, 269 Ga. 495, 497, 500 S.E.2d 577 (1998).

[8]Oregon v. Bradshaw, 462 U.S. 1039, 103 S.Ct. 2830, 77 L.Ed.2d 405 (1983). In *Bradshaw*, police were transporting the defendant from the police station to the jail when he asked the officer, "Well, what is going to happen to me now?" Eight Justices agreed that the test in *Edwards* is that further interrogation or re-interrogation is improper unless two steps are established by the prosecution: First, the suspect must himself initiate further communication with officers. However, this alone does not justify further questioning by officers. There are some inquiries of a defendant "such as a request for a drink of water or a request to use a telephone that are so routine that they cannot be fairly said to open up a more generalized discussion relating directly or indirectly to the investigation. Such inquiries or statements, by either an accused or a police officer relating to routine incidents of the custodial relationship will not generally 'initiate' a conversation in the sense in which that word was used in Edwards." Second, the prosecution must also establish that the suspect at that time validly waived his right.

about the investigation." In *Sanders v. State,*[9] the Georgia Court of Appeals cited *Bradshaw* and said that where an in-custody defendant requests a lawyer, an analysis of whether the in-custody defendant who has invoked his right to counsel under *Miranda* "has later waived that right proceeds in two steps. First, a determination as to whether the *defendant* initiated further talks with the police, and second, if so, whether his waiver was shown to be voluntary under the totality of the circumstances."

Applying *Bradshaw,* the Supreme Court in *Connecticut v. Barrett*[10] held that a suspect did not invoke his right to counsel within the meaning of *Edwards* where he received *Miranda* warnings and then stated that "he would not give police any written statements [without having counsel present] but [that] he had no problem in talking about the incident." The court regarded this statement as ambiguous; therefore, the oral statement which followed was admissible.

The Edwards rule applies where the right to counsel is invoked "during custodial interrogation." However, this situation is to be distinguished from that in *Michigan v. Mosley,*[11] where the defendant was arrested and exercised his right to remain silent after receiving *Miranda* warnings. In *Moseley,* some hours after arrest and exercising his right to remain silent, another officer Mirandized the defendant and questioned him about an unrelated crime. The defendant made a statement which was admitted into evidence at trial. The Supreme Court affirmed the admission of the statement. In *Fields v. State,*[12] the court cited *Moseley* and said *Fields* is similar to *Moseley* except in *Fields* officers sought the same information at each encounter. However, in *Fields* there was a 10-month period between the two instances and the defendant wished to make a statement at the later time. The court affirmed the admission of the statement.

In the 2006 case of *Griffin v. State,*[13] the Georgia Supreme Court considered the case of a defendant who sought to suppress incriminating statements where an officer honored the defen-

---

[9]Sanders v. State, 182 Ga. App. 581, 582 (1), 356 S.E.2d 537 (1987) (emphasis supplied). In Vasser v. State, 272 Ga. App. 327, 612 S.E.2d 543 (2005), the Court of Appeals found that the defendant's post-invocation of counsel query about whether he might qualify to become a policeman was not sufficient to "initiate" conversation under Oregon v. Bradshaw, 462 U.S. 1039, 103 S.Ct. 2830, 77 L.Ed.2d 405 (1983).

[10]Connecticut v. Barrett, 479 U.S. 523, 107 S.Ct. 828, 93 L.Ed.2d 920

(1987); Moore v. State, 272 Ga. 359, 360 (2), 528 S.E.2d 793 (2000). Accord, Harris v. State, 197 Ga. App. 695, 696 (2), 399 S.E.2d 284 (1990).

[11]Michigan v. Mosley, 423 U.S. 96, 96 S.Ct. 321, 46 L.Ed.2d 313 (1975).

[12]Fields v. State, 266 Ga. 241, 242 (1), 466 S.E.2d 202 (1996).

[13]Griffin v. State, 280 Ga. 683, 631 S.E.2d 671 (2006) citing Fields v. State, 266 Ga. 241(1), 466 S.E.2d 202 (1996).

dant's right to remain silent in the first interview, but then returned four days later to question the defendant about the same crime. The court affirmed the denial of the defendant's motion to suppress, holding that "a second interrogation regarding the same crime may also be constitutional under *Mosley* . . . where the initial invocation of the right to remain silent was scrupulously honored."[14] However, in *Hill v. State*,[15] the court held that a police officer's testimony that the defendant waived his right to counsel, made an oral statement, but refused to sign a written statement or give a recorded one, did not constitute an impermissible comment on the right of the defendant to remain silent. The police officer's statement was made in response to questions by the defense as to whether the defendant was given an opportunity to make a written statement.

In *Mack v. State*,[16] the Georgia Supreme Court adopted the following rule:

> Accordingly, we now expressly adopt this rule: a suspect will be considered to have "initiated" renewed contact with law enforcement authorities, so as to permit further interrogation, only if the renewed contact by the suspect was not the product of past police interrogation conducted in violation of the suspect's previously-invoked rights. In determining the causal connection between the prior unlawful interrogation and the suspect's renewal of contact, the entire sequence of events leading up to the suspect's renewal of contact must be considered, including but not limited to the lapse of time between the unlawful interrogation and the renewed contact, any change in location or in the identity of the officers involved from one interview to the next, and any break in custody between interviews. The State bears the burden of proving an effective "initiation" under the circumstances.

In the 1986 case of *Michigan v. Jackson*,[17] the United States Supreme Court held that where a defendant at arraignment requests counsel, the police may not thereafter initiate interrogation with the defendant. The court found the reasoning of *Edwards*, which was based on the Fifth Amendment, to apply with even greater force in this situation where the right was based on the Sixth Amendment right to counsel. *Jackson*, however, was

---

[14]Griffin v. State, 280 Ga. 683, 631 S.E.2d 671 (2006) citing Fields v. State, 266 Ga. 241(1), 466 S.E.2d 202 (1996).

[15]Hill v. State, 290 Ga. 493, 722 S.E.2d 708 (2012).

[16]Mack v. State, 296 Ga. 239, 248, 765 S.E.2d 896 (2014) (citations omitted) (court emphasized that on review the appellate court must accept trial court findings of fact on issue of "initiation" unless clearly erroneous but must review de novo "whether the facts so found constitute an effective initiation in the legal sense").

[17]Michigan v. Jackson, 475 U.S. 625, 106 S.Ct. 1404, 89 L.Ed.2d 631 (1986). In *Jackson*, the detective in charge of the investigation was present at the arraignment.

overruled in *Montejo v. Louisiana*.[18] The court found that *Jackson* was simply not tenable, at least with respect to a defendant's right to counsel where, after the appointment of counsel, the defendant voluntarily executes a proper waiver of counsel and speaks with police. The court said that *Jackson* was designed to prohibit police "badgering" and that *Miranda* warnings were sufficient to assure only voluntary waivers of counsel. Accordingly, police may not approach a represented defendant and request an interview without counsel being present provided only that the defendant is first advised of his right to counsel and then voluntarily waives that right.

In *McNeil v. Wisconsin*,[19] the United States Supreme Court considered a case in which McNeil was represented by counsel at a bond hearing and was not released on bond, and then while still in jail and on the same day as the bond hearing, he was approached by officers, was given *Miranda* warnings, and was questioned about an unrelated murder, and he gave a statement. The court found that there had been no *Miranda* violation. The assertion of the Sixth Amendment right of counsel in one case does not bar the statement obtained in the unrelated case. However, in *State v. Jenkins*,[20] the same court held that "[t]he fact that . . . [the defendant] was questioned by a detective other than the one to whom he had made the request for counsel does not excuse the continued questioning after the request."

In *Texas v. Cobb*,[21] the United States Supreme Court considered a case in which the defendant was charged with burglary and counsel was appointed for him in that case. Law enforcement officers approached the defendant and interrogated him about a murder which was factually related to the burglary. The court held that officers may interrogate the defendant about the other offense or offenses as long as the other offense or offenses have not been formally charged and the officers comply with the requirements of *Miranda*.

In *Vaughn v. State*,[22] the Georgia Supreme Court cited and followed the rule of *Edwards*. However, the Georgia Supreme Court has held that "fruits" of a voluntary statement obtained in viola-

---

[18]Montejo v. Louisiana, 556 U.S. 778, 129 S.Ct. 2079, 173 L.Ed.2d 955 (2009) (5-4 decision with a scathing dissent).

[19]McNeil v. Wisconsin, 501 U.S. 171, 111 S.Ct. 2204, 115 L.Ed.2d 158 (1991).

[20]State v. Jenkins, 257 Ga. 741, 742, 363 S.E.2d 551 (1988).

[21]Texas v. Cobb, 532 U.S. 162, 121 S.Ct. 1335, 149 L.Ed.2d 321 (2001). In Chenoweth v. State, 281 Ga. 7(2), 635 S.E.2d 730 (2006), the Georgia Supreme Court declined an invitation to construe the right to counsel under the Georgia constitution in a manner consistent with *Cobb*, finding that under the facts presented, the crimes involved were not "closely related."

[22]Vaughn v. State, 248 Ga. 127, 130, 281 S.E.2d 594 (1981).

tion of *Edwards* are admissible even though the statement itself is not admissible at trial.[23]

In *Roper v. State*,[24] the Georgia Supreme Court held that "once an accused in custody invokes the right to counsel, he should not be subject to further interrogation by the authorities until counsel is *present,* unless the accused himself initiates further communication. . . ." (Emphasis added.) It is the duty of law enforcement authorities "to maintain a procedure to enable an officer who proposes to initiate an interrogation to determine whether a suspect has previously invoked the right to counsel. . . . The fact that the interrogating officers had no actual knowledge that . . . [the defendant] had made a request for counsel is constitutionally insignificant. . . . [The defendant's] negative answer to the question of whether he had a lawyer did not answer the question of whether he had invoked the right to counsel, nor could it constitute a waiver."

In *State v. Hatcher*,[25] after the defendant was arrested "he was provided with and completed at the jail an 'eligibility affidavit form' for appointed counsel." The form stated that he could not afford a lawyer and wanted the court to appoint one for him. Two days later an investigator, who was generally aware of the booking procedures including the request for a lawyer, interviewed the defendant and gave him *Miranda* warnings. The defendant signed a waiver and made a confession. The Georgia Supreme Court held that the confession was admissible since "the form at issue was offered by the police and completed by appellant as a housekeeping measure; not for the questioning which was to take

---

[23]State v. Woods, 280 Ga. 758, 632 S.E.2d 654 (2006); Wilson v. Zant, 249 Ga. 373, 376 (1), 290 S.E.2d 442 (1982), disapp. on other grounds, Morgan v. State, 267 Ga. 203, 476 S.E.2d 747 (1996). Accord, Widdowson v. State, 171 Ga. App. 134, 136 (1), 318 S.E.2d 820 (1984).

[24]Roper v. State, 258 Ga. 847, 849, 375 S.E.2d 600 (1989). Cf. Ashley v. State, 261 Ga. 488, 489 (1), 405 S.E.2d 657 (1991). See McDougal v. State, 277 Ga. 493, 591 S.E.2d 788 (2004), where the court examines the admissibility of several in-custody statements provided by the defendant, suppressing some and allowing others, after determining: the defendant's custodial status; his request for counsel; and his initiation of further communication with the police officers. See also State v. Brown, 287 Ga. 473, 697 S.E.2d 192

(2010) (court defined interrogation as express questioning or words or actions that police should know can produce an incriminating response. Merely being in the presence of defendant and responding to questions posed by defendant does not constitute interrogation).

[25]State v. Hatcher, 264 Ga. 556, 558, 448 S.E.2d 698 (1994), rev'g 212 Ga. App. 46, 48 (1), 441 S.E.2d 673 (1994). Compare Stone v. State, 296 Ga. App. 305, 674 S.E.2d 31 (2009), where defendant requested and received counsel at first appearance hearing and thereafter requested counsel for all future proceedings, statements subsequently made to state investigator without presence of defense counsel should not have been admitted.

place a few days later, but as a prospective request for counsel 'when the government's role [would shift] from investigation to accusation.' . . . [T]he form was promulgated to satisfy an accused's Sixth Amendment right to counsel and cannot reasonably be read to constitute an invocation of right to counsel for purposes of the Fifth Amendment."

In *Cansler v. State*,[26] the court held that "whether or not the detective knew of the request for an attorney is not dispositive. . . . [Also] the . . . [defendant's] later denial of the statement [does not] refute the contention that the detective initiated the interrogation."

In *Minnick v. Mississippi*,[27] the defendant invoked his right to counsel. Counsel was then appointed and spoke with the defendant. Thereafter the police returned and, without an attorney, the defendant made statements later used against him at trial. The United States Supreme Court held that the fact that the defendant consulted with counsel did not suspend his Fifth Amendment rights in a way that would allow police to interrogate the defendant in the absence of his attorney, unless the defendant initiates the conversation and waives his rights.

In *Petty v. State*,[28] the Georgia Supreme Court rejected the notion that *Edwards* had any application to a non-custodial interrogation and overruled *Nobles v. State*,[29] to the extent it suggested that police must cease questioning an accused who is not in custody after he or she requests an attorney. In *Peebles v. State*,[30] the court held that the assertion of the right to counsel does not render inadmissible any statement made by the defendant before he asserted the right of counsel. See Annotation, "What Constitutes Assertion of Right to Counsel Following *Miranda* Warnings—State Cases," 83 A.L.R.4th 443.[31]

However, in *State v. Bymes*,[32] the Georgia Supreme Court held that because of "a 21-month break in custody between the initial interrogation and the final interrogation," *Edwards* did not ap-

---

[26]Cansler v. State, 261 Ga. 693, 694 (3), 409 S.E.2d 504 (1991).

[27]Minnick v. Mississippi, 498 U.S. 146, 111 S.Ct. 486, 112 L.Ed.2d 489 (1990); Cansler v. State, 261 Ga. 693, 694 (3), 409 S.E.2d 504 (1991); Smith v. State, 265 Ga. 495 (1), 458 S.E.2d 347 (1995), rev'd on other grounds by Smith v. State, 268 Ga. 196, 486 S.E.2d 819 (1997).

[28]Petty v. State, 283 Ga. 268 (2), 658 S.E.2d 599 (2008).

[29]Nobles v. State, 191 Ga. App. 594(1)(a), 382 S.E.2d 637 (1989).

[30]Peebles v. State, 196 Ga. App. 176, 178 (1)(b), 395 S.E.2d 640 (1990).

[31]This annotation is over 150 pages in length and contains cases from 43 states, including a number from Georgia.

[32]State v. Bymes, 258 Ga. 813, 814, 375 S.E.2d 41 (1989).

ply; and in the 1994 case of *Wilson v. State,*[33] the court held that *Edwards* did not apply where there was a seven-month break in custody.

It has been pointed out "that a waiver is possible if the request for counsel is equivocal."[34] Thus, in Georgia it has been held that where a defendant was given *Miranda* warnings and an officer asked if he wanted to talk and the defendant said, "Well, it's no use," and the officer said it was up to him and asked again if he wanted to talk, and the defendant said yes and made a statement, there was no Edwards violation.[35] However, in *Wilson v. State,*[36] the United States Supreme Court held that once a defendant expresses a desire for counsel, questioning must cease and response to further interrogation cannot be used to cast doubt on the initial request. In *Lucas v. State,*[37] the Georgia Supreme Court reversed the trial court, concluding that the defendant's statement during questioning that his lawyer told him not to say anything was an invocation of the Fifth Amendment. The concurring opinion by two justices stated that the officers should have sought clarification of his "equivocal request" before asking any other questions other than those related to whether or not the defendant wanted to stop talking.

In *Vasser v. State,*[38] when the investigator mentioned the right to an attorney during the reading of the defendant's *Miranda* warnings, the defendant, in custody at the time, stated, "That's what I want. I want a lawyer." However, when the investigator again asked the defendant if he wanted an attorney at the conclusion of the *Miranda* warnings, the defendant responded, "It doesn't matter. I don't have nothing to hide." The investigator then proceeded to conduct an interrogation of the defendant, during the course of which the defendant asked, "After I beat this case, can I be a policeman, an investigator or something?" Finding that the defendant's question did not constitute an attempt to "initiate" conversation about the charges, the Court of Appeals held that the defendant clearly invoked his right to counsel and

---

[33]Wilson v. State, 264 Ga. 287, 290 (2), 444 S.E.2d 306 (1994).

[34]Souder v. State, 170 Ga. App. 413, 414, 317 S.E.2d 251 (1984).

[35]Tucker v. State, 170 Ga. App. 782 (1), 318 S.E.2d 147 (1984); Hall v. State, 255 Ga. 267, 270, 336 S.E.2d 812 (1985); Turner v. State, 245 Ga. App. 294, 295 (3), 536 S.E.2d 814 (2000).

[36]Smith v. Illinois, 469 U.S. 91, 105 S.Ct. 490, 83 L.Ed.2d 488 (1984).

[37]Lucas v. State, 273 Ga. 88, 538 S.E.2d 44 (2000).

[38]Vasser v. State, 272 Ga. App. 327, 612 S.E.2d 543 (2005). See Smith v. Illinois, 469 U.S. 91, 105 S. Ct. 490, 83 L. Ed. 2d 488 (1984) (once a defendant expressed a desire for counsel, questioning must cease and response to further interrogation cannot be used to undercut request for counsel); Wheeler v. State, 289 Ga. 537, 713 S.E.2d 393 (2011).

suppressed the in-custody statements.

In *Davis v. United States*,[39] the defendant waived his right to remain silent and to have counsel, both orally and in writing. After being questioned for one and one-half hours the defendant said, "Maybe I should talk to a lawyer." The defendant was asked to clarify his comment to which he stated he was not asking for a lawyer. The defendant was then reminded of his rights and the questioning was continued. About one hour later the defendant said, "I think I want a lawyer before I say anything else." Questioning was stopped at this point. The United States Supreme Court held that "the suspect must unambiguously request counsel . . . [H]e must articulate his desire to have counsel present sufficiently clearly that a reasonable police officer in the circumstances would understand the statement to be a request for an attorney. If the statement fails to meet the requisite level of clarity, *Edwards* does not require that the officers stop questioning the suspect." The Georgia Supreme Court has expressly adopted *Davis* and has repudiated prior authority which required police to clarify ambiguous requests for counsel by a criminal suspect before interrogation could continue.[40]

In *Berry v. State*,[41] the Georgia Supreme Court held that if a request for counsel "was unambiguously limited to the taking of a polygraph examination and did not encompass the custodial interrogation," this did not prevent further questioning. In *Baird v. State*,[42] the defendant said that he "might ought to talk to a lawyer" in response to a request to search his vehicle. The *Baird* court held (1) that this was not an assertion of his Fifth Amendment right to counsel, and (2) that where a limited request for counsel is made, officers are "required to honor [it] to no greater extent than the express limits of his reservation." Also, the court declined "to adopt a rule requiring officers to ask clarifying questions."

---

[39]Davis v. United States, 512 U.S. 452, 114 S.Ct. 2350, 129 L.Ed.2d 362 (1994). *Davis* was cited, relied upon, and quoted in Jordan v. State, 267 Ga. 442, 444 (1), 480 S.E.2d 18 (1997). See Roundtree v. State, 270 Ga. 504, 506 (4), 511 S.E.2d 190 (1999); Tucker v. State, 228 Ga. App. 321, 322 (1), 491 S.E.2d 420 (1997). Cf. Anderson v. State, 228 Ga. App. 617, 618 (1)(a), 492 S.E.2d 252 (1997).

[40]Perez v. State, 283 Ga. 196, 657 S.E.2d 846 (2008) overruling Hatcher v. State, 259 Ga. 274, 379 S.E.2d 775

(1989). See Reaves v. State, 292 Ga. 582, 586(2)(b), 740 S.E.2d 141 (2013) (mere reference to "attorney" or "lawyer," without more, does not automatically invoke right to counsel).

[41]Berry v. State, 254 Ga. 101, 104, 326 S.E.2d 748 (1985). Cf. Comley v. State, 218 Ga. App. 520, 521, 462 S.E.2d 432 (1995). Cf. Jackson v. State, 222 Ga. App. 843, 845 (1)(a), 476 S.E.2d 615 (1996).

[42]Baird v. State, 263 Ga. 868, 870 (1), 440 S.E.2d 190 (1994).

In *Hall v. State*,[43] the Georgia Supreme Court pointed out that "where the accused asks a question that contains an ambiguous or equivocal reference to the availability of counsel, an interrogating officer must be given considerable latitude in formulating a reasonable and responsive answer."

In the interesting case of *Underwood v. State*,[44] the defendant, after having been given his *Miranda* rights, handed the agents his lawyer's business card. On the back of "the card" there was a preprinted statement as follows: "I refuse to consent to any search of my premises, the location of my arrest, my car or my effects. I wish to exercise my rights under the fifth and sixth amendments to remain silent and to have my attorney present for any questioning or line up. If you ignore my wish to exercise these rights and attempt to procure a waiver I wish to confer with my attorney prior to any conversation with law enforcement agents on subject of waiver." When presented with the card, the officers "immediately terminated the interview." The court did not pass on the issue of "whether such an ambiguous act place[d] a burden on law enforcement officers to inquire whether any of the rights addressed on the preprinted business card are, in fact, being asserted." However, while the defendant was going back to the jail area, he stated "there were some things we could talk about." He was read the *Miranda* warnings and he signed the *Miranda* form. The appellate court affirmed the trial judge in admitting the defendant's statements which were given.

In *Ottis v. State*,[45] the Georgia Supreme Court affirmed the conviction where the defendant said "she wished to talk to the detectives if her attorney was contacted." The detective was "unable to contact her attorney" and so informed the defendant. Then the defendant "initiated the discussion with the police which led to her spontaneous . . . statement placing her at the scene of the crimes, thereby knowingly and intelligently waiving the right she had invoked."

In the 2000 case of *Lucas v. State*,[46] the defendant told the interrogating officer that his "lawyer told me . . . to say nothing."

---

[43]Hall v. State, 255 Ga. 267, 274 (3), 336 S.E.2d 812 (1985). Cf. Davis v. State, 232 Ga. App. 450, 453 (2)(b), 501 S.E.2d 241 (1998).

[44]Underwood v. State, 218 Ga. App. 530, 533 (2), 462 S.E.2d 434 (1995). The contents of the card do not appear in the opinion, but the card is a part of the record.

[45]Ottis v. State, 269 Ga. 151, 153 (2), 496 S.E.2d 264 (1998). Compare

State v. Philpot, 299 Ga. 206, 787 S.E.2d 181 (2016) (defendant's unambiguous request to detectives that they should call his girlfriend to get his lawyer's number after first asking that they call the lawyer directly was invocation of right to counsel and further interrogation should have been halted).

[46]Lucas v. State, 273 Ga. 88, 90, 538 S.E.2d 44 (2000). Compare State v. Darby, 284 Ga. 271, 663 S.E.2d 160

Later during the interview the defendant said "[my lawyer] told me . . . to answer nothing." The interrogation continued without pause in both instances. The Georgia Supreme Court concluded "that under the circumstances . . . a reasonable police officer would have understood . . . [the defendant's] statements to be a request for counsel to be present during questioning." The court reversed the trial court's admission of the defendant's statement saying that it was "clearly erroneous."

Also, the Edwards rule does not apply unless the defendant is in custody.[47] The Edwards rule also does not apply to a request of officers for routine booking information.[48] In *Allen v. State*,[49] the defendant was given *Miranda* warnings and stated "I'll talk to you after I've talked to my lawyer." The Georgia Supreme Court held that the defendant's initial invocation of his right to counsel could not have been clearer. Statements made while in custody but which are not the product of interrogation may not be subject to *Miranda* unless they are made in response to a statement by a police officer which is likely to illicit an incriminating response.[50]

In *Woodard v. State*,[51] the Court of Appeals reversed the trial court order denying a motion to suppress statements made by the defendant in response to questions of police investigators after being advised of his *Miranda* rights and executing a written waiver of them. At the time he made the statements, he was represented by appointed counsel and because he had not initiated the conversations which led to the incriminating statements there was no waiver of his right to counsel.

In *Beck v. State*,[52] the court pointed out that "the mere completion of an application to obtain appointed counsel, without more, is not sufficient to invoke the Fifth Amendment. . . ."

In *Arizona v. Roberson*,[53] the defendant was arrested for burglary and given his warnings, at which point he stated that he wanted a lawyer "before answering any questions." Three days

(2008), where the court found that statements made by defendant were improperly induced through the pretext of "advice" given by officer regarding preliminary hearing procedure.

[47]Cf. Wright v. State, 169 Ga. App. 693, 694, 314 S.E.2d 709 (1984).

[48]Hibbert v. State, 195 Ga. App. 235, 236, 393 S.E.2d 96 (1990).

[49]Allen v. State, 259 Ga. 63, 66, 377 S.E.2d 150 (1989).

[50]Gonzalez v. State, 277 Ga. App. 362, 626 S.E.2d 569 (2006). See Teele v. State, 319 Ga. App. 448, 738 S.E.2d 277 (2012).

[51]Woodard v. State, 256 Ga. App. 464, 568 S.E.2d 528 (2002).

[52]Beck v. State, 235 Ga. App. 707, 709 (2), 510 S.E.2d 368 (1998).

[53]Arizona v. Roberson, 486 U.S. 675, 108 S.Ct. 2093, 100 L.Ed.2d 704 (1988). This case extended *Edwards* by distinguishing *Moseley* because *Moseley* involved only the right to remain silent. Butler v. McKellar, 494 U.S. 407, 110 S.Ct. 1212, 108 L.Ed.2d 347 (1990), held that this rule does not apply retrospectively to cases on collateral review.

later, and as yet without counsel, a different officer Mirandized the defendant, he waived his rights, and implicated himself in another burglary. The United States Supreme Court held that Roberson's statements were inadmissible because the *Miranda* right to counsel is *not* offense specific.

In *Arizona v. Mauro*,[54] the United States Supreme Court held that the defendant had waived his *Miranda* rights where the defendant stated that he did not want to answer questions without the presence of an attorney, but his wife insisted on talking with the defendant and was permitted to talk with him in the presence of an officer who openly recorded the conversation. The court concluded that the incriminating statements were not the result of interrogation by the officer.

In *Krier v. State*,[55] where the defendant was arrested in New Orleans, the Georgia Supreme Court concluded that a request for counsel "in the asylum state [does not operate] to prevent any further inquiry by authorities in [Georgia] as to whether the accused would like to speak to them, where [Georgia] authorities reasonably understood that no request for counsel had been made."

In the unusual case of *Roberson v. State*,[56] the defendants were advised of their *Miranda* rights after arrest and invoked the right to counsel. The defendants' mother suggested to a television and radio reporter that the reporter interview one of the defendants in jail. Then the other defendant requested an interview. Consequently, the sheriff's office, on request, arranged the interviews. The police escorted the defendants to the interview but did not initiate or participate in the interview. The defendants signed waiver forms stating that they voluntarily agreed to the interviews, realizing they had the right to refuse and reserving the right to terminate the interviews at any time. The court affirmed the convictions finding that there was no violation of their rights to counsel.

The *Miranda* warnings currently in use by some Georgia officers are set out in § 5:14, supra. The opposite side of the card from which officers read the warnings states certain questions to be asked pertaining to waivers. These "waiver" questions have also been set out in § 5:14, supra. See § 5:13, supra, on the meaning of "interrogation." See § 5:15, supra, on the right to remain silent.

---

[54]Arizona v. Mauro, 481 U.S. 520, 107 S.Ct. 1931, 95 L.Ed.2d 458 (1987).
[55]Krier v. State, 249 Ga. 80, 82,

287 S.E.2d 531 (1982).
[56]Roberson v. State, 265 Ga. 658, 659 (1), 461 S.E.2d 212 (1995).

§ 5:21 Confessions and admissions—*Miranda v. Arizona*— Duty to speak

Prior to January 1, 2013, the state was prohibited from commenting on a defendant's silence or failure to come forward under circumstances which could reasonably be viewed as requiring a denial or some other form of conduct similar thereto. In *Mallory v. State*,[1] such tacit admissions on the part of the defendant could not be introduced even in the case of a defendant who testified at trial.[2] Effective January 1, 2013, O.C.G.A. § 24-8-801(d)(2)(B) expressly authorizes the introduction of the tacit admission in those cases where there is not good reason for the defendant's silence other than the defendant's exercise of his right to remain silent in connection with a police interview. However, in order to satisfy the rule, "two criteria must be met. First, the statement must be such that an innocent defendant would normally be induced to respond. Second, there must be sufficient foundational facts from which the jury could infer that the defendant 'heard, understood and acquiesced in the statement.' . . . Generally, before admitting a statement as an adoptive admission, the trial court must determine whether a jury could reasonably find that the defendant comprehended and acquiesced in the statement."[3] Given the Georgia Supreme Court's emphatic endorsement in 2009 of *Mallory* in *Reynolds v. State*,[4] however, at least one commentator[5] has expressed uncertainty as to whether Georgia will construe § 24-8-801(d)(2)(B) any differently than it did under the statute it replaced. See Studdard, *Daniel's Georgia Handbook on Criminal Evidence* §§ 3:14 and 8:3 (2018 ed.) on adoption of tacit admissions.

[Section 5:21]

[1] Mallory v. State, 261 Ga. 625(5), 409 S.E.2d 839 (1991), overruled on other grounds by Chapel v. State, 270 Ga. 151, 510 S.E.2d 802 (1998). See Reynolds v. State, 285 Ga. 70, 673 S.E.2d 854 (2009) (court empathetically endorsed *Mallory* expressly overruling cases which restricted its scope). See also State v. Sims, 296 Ga. 465, 471, 769 S.E.2d 62 (2015) (court explicitly declined to express an opinion on the vitality of *Mallory* in light of 2013 revision to Georgia Evidence Code).

[2] Jarrett v. State, 265 Ga. 28, 453 S.E.2d 461 (1995); Mallory v. State, 261 Ga. 625(5), 409 S.E.2d 839 (1991), overruled on other grounds by Chapel v. State, 270 Ga. 151, 510 S.E.2d 802 (1998). Cf. Sanders v. State, 230 Ga. App. 176(3), 495 S.E.2d 653 (1998) (court concluded that there was no impropriety in an officer testifying that the defendant made a statement and then stated that he wanted to talk to a lawyer before giving any additional information).

[3] See U.S. v. Joshi, 896 F.2d 1303, 29 Fed. R. Evid. Serv. 1114 (11th Cir. 1990).

[4] Reynolds v. State, 285 Ga. 70, 673 S.E.2d 854 (2009).

[5] Milich Georgia's New Evidence Code—An Overview, Ga. St. U. L. Rev. 379, 411–13 (Winter 2012).

In *Doyle v. Ohio*,[6] the United States Supreme Court held that an accused's silence after the giving of the *Miranda* warnings could not be used as evidence of his guilt.[7] However, in *Fletcher v. Weir*,[8] the United States Supreme Court stated that where a defendant had not been informed that he had a right to remain silent, there is no due process violation in permitting the defendant to be "cross examined as to his post-arrest silence when the defendant chooses to take the stand." In addition, it is not improper for a prosecutor to inform a jury of the defendant's termination of a custodial interview and invocation of the right to counsel.[9]

An improper comment on the defendant's silence does not necessarily mandate a new trial.[10] Evidence of a defendant's election to remain silent warrants reversal only if it points directly at the substance of the defense or otherwise prejudices the defendant in the eyes of the jury.[11]

It must be kept in mind, however, that *Miranda* applies only where a defendant is in custody. Hence, in *Jenkins v. Anderson*,[12] the Court held that the silence of a suspect who was not taken into custody for two weeks after a homicide could be constitutionally used for impeachment purposes on cross-examination when the suspect testifies to self-defense at his trial. The court pointed out that its decision does not force a state to allow impeachment by pre-arrest silence, but it shows that impeachment in such a

---

[6]Doyle v. Ohio, 426 U.S. 610, 96 S.Ct. 2240, 49 L.Ed.2d 91 (1976); Howard v. State, 237 Ga. 471, 475, 228 S.E.2d 860 (1976).

[7]In Bridges v. State, 242 Ga. 251, 254 (10), 248 S.E.2d 647 (1978), the defendant, although given *Miranda* warnings, voluntarily discussed his version of the event. At trial, the defendant claimed for the first time that the other man had a gun. The court pointed out that in such a situation the defendant may be asked why he did not tell this to investigators.

For an excellent discussion of Jenkins v. Anderson, 447 U.S. 231, 100 S.Ct. 2124, 65 L.Ed.2d 86 (1980), and United States v. Havens, 446 U.S. 620, 100 S.Ct. 1912, 64 L.Ed.2d 559 (1980), see "The Supreme Court, 1979 Term," 94 Harv. L. Rev. 1, 77 (1980). See § 2:32, supra, on using statements not admissible under *Miranda* for impeachment purposes.

[8]Fletcher v. Weir, 455 U.S. 603, 607, 102 S.Ct. 1309, 71 L.Ed.2d 490 (1982). Accord, Hollis v. State, 174 Ga. App. 627, 330 S.E.2d 817 (1985). Cf. Cromwell v. State, 218 Ga. App. 481, 482 (1), 462 S.E.2d 388 (1995). See Clark, "Impeachment with Post Arrest Silence: The Emergence of a 'New Federalism' Approach," 19 Amer. Cr. L. Rev. 751 (1972).

[9]Rowe v. State, 276 Ga. 800 (4), 582 S.E.2d 119 (2003).

[10]Parks v. State, 281 Ga. App. 679, 681(2), 637 S.E.2d 46 (2006).

[11]Whitaker v. State, 283 Ga. 521, 524(3), 661 S.E.2d 557 (2008); Taylor v. State, 272 Ga. 559, 532 S.E.2d 395 (2000).

[12]Jenkins v. Anderson, 447 U.S. 231, 100 S.Ct. 2124, 65 L.Ed.2d 86 (1980). See Bradley, "Havens, Jenkins and Salvucci, and the Defendant's 'Right' to Testify," 18 Am. Crim. L. Rev. 419 (1981).

situation does not violate the federal Constitution. In *Salinas v. Texas*,[13] the United States Supreme Court held that a defendant's pre-*Miranda* noncustodial silence may be admitted into evidence and be commented upon by the prosecutor during closing. The Court's holding was premised upon the principle that a defendant cannot assert the privilege against self-incrimination by simply remaining mute in response to police questioning. The privilege must be expressly invoked in order to fall within the bounds of its protection.

In *Norris v. State*,[14] the defendant contended he was coerced into escaping. The appellate court said that it could consider the failure of the defendant to tell an investigator about the coercion in determining whether the evidence was sufficient to justify his conviction.

In *DeBerry v. State*,[15] the Georgia Supreme Court said that a defendant's Fifth Amendment rights were violated where an officer testified that the defendant made no statements to the police when arrested, but the failure of defense counsel to object waived the right of the defendant to later complain. The same right of silence was recognized where a defendant was given *Miranda* warnings, answered some questions, and then remained silent when he was asked a particularly incriminating question.[16]

In *Gibbs v. State*,[17] the prosecuting attorney asked an officer if the defendant provided the officer with any statement after he was in custody. The officer replied, "I advised him of his rights and he refused to give a statement." The court held that "the record shows an error of constitutional dimension." It is "fundamentally unfair to simultaneously afford a suspect a constitutional right to silence at arrest and yet allow the implication of that silence to be used against him. . . ."

In the unusual case of *Williams v. State*,[18] the defendant pled

[13]Salinas v. Texas, 133 S. Ct. 2174, 186 L. Ed. 2d 376 (2013).

[14]Norris v. State, 227 Ga. App. 616, 619 (4), 489 S.E.2d 875 (1997).

[15]DeBerry v. State, 241 Ga. 204, 205 (1), 243 S.E.2d 864 (1978); Lattimore v. State, 265 Ga. 154, 454 S.E.2d 496 (1995). See Alderman v. State, 241 Ga. 496, 246 S.E.2d 642 (1978) (majority declines to reverse where there was no contemporaneous objection and testimony was elicited on direct rather than on cross for purposes of impeachment).

[16]Durden v. State, 250 Ga. 325, 327 (3), 297 S.E.2d 237 (1982). Accord, Gibbs v. State, 217 Ga. App. 614, 615, 458 S.E.2d 407 (1995).

[17]Gibbs v. State, 217 Ga. App. 614, 458 S.E.2d 407 (1995). See State v. Moore, 318 Ga. App. 118, 733 S.E.2d 418 (2012) (ineffective assistance in failing to object to prosecutor's remarks during closing about defendant's failure to respond to police officer's inquiries about rape allegations during phone interview).

[18]Williams v. State, 242 Ga. 757, 759 (3), 251 S.E.2d 254 (1978); Baldwin v. State, 253 Ga. 721, 723 (1), 325 S.E.2d 128 (1985).

temporary insanity at the time of the crime. In an effort to show that the defendant was not insane at that time, the state was permitted to show that at the time of defendant's arrest, he was given *Miranda* warnings and he elected to remain silent. However, in *Wainwright v. Greenfield,*[19] the United States Supreme Court held that there was a violation of the Due Process Clause of the Fourteenth Amendment where the prosecutor used the defendant's silence, after he had been given *Miranda* warnings, as evidence of the defendant's sanity.

In *Jones v. Dugger,*[20] the Eleventh Circuit held that there was no error in permitting an officer to testify to his observations of the mental condition of Jones at the time of questioning even if there had not been a valid *Miranda* waiver. The officer was not permitted to testify as to what Jones said, but he could testify that Jones seemed to be rational and well-oriented and his answers seemed to be responsive to the questions asked.

Even when there is an improper reference to the defendant's silence and the point has been preserved by proper objection, this does not automatically require reversal. The error may be considered to be harmless beyond a reasonable doubt.[21] The test is whether the evidence of the election to remain silent pointed "directly at the substance of the defendant's defense or otherwise substantially prejudiced the defendant in the eyes of the jury."[22]

See § 5:15, supra, on the right to remain silent and § 5:13, supra, on interrogation. Also, generally, see § 5:11, supra, on *Miranda.*

§ 5:22 Nontestimonial evidence—Under United States Constitution

In *Schmerber v. California,*[1] the United States Supreme Court held that the compulsory taking of non-testimonial blood-sample evidence from a defendant does not violate the federal Constitution, although noting that the Fifth Amendment prevents the use

---

[19]Wainwright v. Greenfield, 474 U.S. 284, 106 S.Ct. 634, 88 L.Ed.2d 623 (1986).

[20]Jones v. Dugger, 839 F.2d 1441 (11th Cir. 1988).

[21]Hill v. State, 250 Ga. 277, 283, 295 S.E.2d 518 (1982). Cf. Nihart v. State, 227 Ga. App. 272, 276 (1)(e), 488 S.E.2d 740 (1997).

[22]Taylor v. State, 272 Ga. 559, 561(2)(d), 532 S.E.2d 395 (2000); Whitaker v. State, 283 Ga. 521 (3), 661 S.E.2d 557 (2008).

[Section 5:22]

[1]Schmerber v. California, 384 U.S. 757, 86 S.Ct. 1826, 16 L.Ed.2d 908 (1966). In this case, the blood sample was taken from the defendant over his objection while he was in a hospital. See Quarterman v. State, 282 Ga. 383, 651 S.E.2d 32 (2007). See also, Annot., "Admissibility in Criminal Cases of Blood-Alcohol Test Where Blood Was Taken Despite Defendant's Objection or Refusal to Submit to Test," 14 A.L.R.4th 690 (1982).

of testimonial evidence in the situation where an accused is compelled to speak against himself. The court found that while the constitutional privilege against self-incrimination applies to all forms of communications which an accused might make, it has no application to the comparison of blood evidence from the body of the accused because his "testimonial capacities were in no way implicated." And, because of the threat that the blood evidence which the officer wanted to recover might dissipate during the time it would take to get a warrant, the officer's actions in directing the extraction of the defendant's blood was deemed an appropriate incident to his arrest.

In *Missouri v. McNeeley*,[2] the court rejected a per se rule that the natural metabolization of alcohol in a person's bloodstream constitutes an exigency justifying an exception to the Fourth Amendment's search warrant requirement for non-consensual blood testing in all DUI cases. Instead it concluded that:

> While the natural dissipation of alcohol in the blood may support a finding of exigency in a specific case, as it did in *Schmerber*, it does not do so categorically. Whether a warrantless blood test of a drunk-driving suspect is reasonable must be determined case by case based on the totality of the circumstances.

In *Williams v. State*,[3] the Georgia Supreme Court expressly adopted the rule announced in *McNeeley* and overruled Georgia authority to the contrary. Although the Court noted that a search warrant would not be necessary in the case of a driver who *actually* consents to a blood test, it expressed some doubt as to whether the statutory implied consent is the equivalent of the "actual" consent to a blood test for purposes of the Fourth Amendment in the context of a DUI investigation. The court concluded that while a driver's expression of consent after being advised of the required implied consent notice is a factor to consider, a trial court must determine based upon the totality of the circumstances whether the defendant freely and voluntarily consented to the blood test requested by the police officer.

---

[2]Missouri v. McNeely, 133 S. Ct. 1552, 1563(II)(B), 185 L. Ed. 2d 696 (2013) (Court noted that *Schmerber* found that there was an imminent threat that the evidence of the defendant's BAC would dissipate in the time it took to obtain a warrant, a circumstance that may no longer exist with modern technology).

[3]Williams v. State, 296 Ga. 817, 771 S.E.2d 373 (2015). See Kendrick v. State, 335 Ga. App. 766, 782 S.E.2d 842 (2016) (rejected a Williams challenge based upon defendant's sense she was being coerced into giving her consent because she was under arrest at the time it was requested by police). See State v. Bowman, 337 Ga. App. 313, 787 S.E.2d 284 (2016) (evidence supported trial court order granting motion to suppress based upon finding that driver's consent under totality of circumstances was not voluntary where driver appeared disoriented, intoxicated, and physically ill).

In *Birchfield v. North Dakota*,[4] the U.S. Supreme Court held that the Fourth Amendment permits warrantless breath tests as a search incident to a lawful arrest for drunk driving, but not warrantless blood tests. Warrantless blood tests incident to arrests for drunk driving are not permitted under the Fourth Amendment because blood tests implicate significant privacy concerns "and their reasonableness must be judged in light of the availability of the less invasive alternative of a breath test." The court also found that motorists may not be deemed to have consented to a blood test on pain of criminal punishment under implied-consent laws.

The federal Constitution does not, however, entitle a defendant to refuse to submit to fingerprinting, photographing,[5] or measurements. He or she must repeat words for identification, appear in court, assume certain positions, walk, make particular gestures, and furnish handwriting exemplars.[6] Likewise, in *South Dakota v. Neville*,[7] the same Court held that the admission in evidence of a refusal of a defendant to submit to a blood-alcohol test is not a violation of the Fifth Amendment. If a defendant refuses to give handwriting exemplars, it is proper for the court in its charge, and for the prosecution in summation, to refer to the accused's failure to provide this non-testimonial evidence.[8] Generally, a person may be required under the federal Constitution to

---

[4]Birchfield v. North Dakota, 136 S. Ct. 2160, 195 L. Ed. 2d 560 (2016). See Fazio v. State, 302 Ga. 295, 806 S.E.2d 544 (2017) (implied consent statute does not violate Fourth Amendment prohibition against unreasonable searches); Jacobs v. State, 338 Ga. App. 743, 791 S.E.2d 844 (2016) (*Birchfield* does not apply to Georgia's implied consent statute because it does not expose driver to criminal penalty upon driver's refusal).

[5]DeYoung v. State, 268 Ga. 780, 790 (13), 493 S.E.2d 157 (1997).

[6]Schmerber v. California, 384 U.S. 757, 764, 86 S.Ct. 1826, 16 L.Ed.2d 908 (1966). See United States v. Dionisio, 410 U.S. 1, 93 S.Ct. 764, 35 L.Ed.2d 67 (1973) (compelled voice exemplars for identification purposes before grand jury); Bowling v. State, 289 Ga. 881, 717 S.E.2d 190 (2011) (defendant's medical records including lab results for blood and urine not protected by Fifth Amendment); Ferega v. State, 286 Ga. App. 808, 650 S.E.2d

286 (2007) (evidence that defendant refused to submit to field sobriety test is not barred by Fifth Amendment). Accord, U.S. v. Kallstrom, 446 F. Supp. 2d 772 (E.D. Mich. 2006).

In United States v. Campbell, 732 F.2d 1017 (1st Cir. 1984), the court held that a defendant could not be required to furnish handwriting exemplars by writing down what is dictated. This amounts to giving a defendant a spelling test. But see United States v. Pheaster, 544 F.2d 353 (9th Cir. 1976).

[7]South Dakota v. Neville, 459 U.S. 553, 103 S. Ct. 916, 74 L. Ed. 2d 748 (1983).

[8]United States v. Nix, 465 F.2d 90 (5th Cir. 1972). The court also noted that there is no reasonable expectation of privacy in voice or handwriting exemplars, thus no violation of the Fourth Amendment. See Ingram v. State, 253 Ga. 622, 323 S.E.2d 801 (1984) (requiring defendant to strip to waist and be photographed in respect to tattoos on his body identified by

give voice exemplars[9] and handwriting exemplars to a grand jury.[10] Likewise, it has been held that hair samples may be taken involuntarily from a defendant pursuant to a search warrant.[11]

A defendant can be compelled to allow the removal of a bullet from his body by a physician pursuant to a search warrant if there is no risk involved in the procedure.[12] However, a defendant cannot be compelled to undergo a risky operation to remove a bullet from the spinal cavity. In *Winston v. Lee*,[13] the United States Supreme Court said, "The reasonableness of surgical intrusions beneath the skin depends on a case-by-case approach, in which the individual's interest in privacy and security are weighed against society's interest in conducting the procedure. . . . Schmerber . . . provides the appropriate framework of analysis for such cases." The court then concluded that the state had failed to demonstrate that surgical removal of the bullet would be reasonable in view of the evidence which the state had and the disputed evidence about the risks of such an operation.

In *Andresen v. Maryland*,[14] the United States Supreme Court held that a defendant's incriminating business records are non-testimonial and thus admissible. In *Doe v. United States*,[15] the United States Supreme Court held that there was no Fifth Amendment violation in requiring a depositor to sign a "consent directive" which directs foreign banks to disclose records of the depositor.

On incrimination by lineups, see § 6:4, infra. Also see § 4:26, supra, on searches incident to an arrest and § 4:32, supra, on consent to search. See § 21:3, infra, on voice exemplars as testimony. See § 5:13, supra, on video taping of sobriety tests.

---

victim did not compel defendant to incriminate himself); Anglin v. State, 302 Ga. 333, 806 S.E.2d 573 (2017).

[9]United States v. Dionisio, 410 U.S. 1, 93 S.Ct. 764, 35 L.Ed.2d 67 (1973).

[10]United States v. Mara, 410 U.S. 19, 93 S.Ct. 774, 35 L.Ed.2d 99 (1973).

[11]United States v. Ellis, 739 F.2d 1250 (7th Cir. 1984).

[12]Creamer v. State, 229 Ga. 511, 192 S.E.2d 350 (1972).

[13]Winston v. Lee, 470 U.S. 753, 105 S.Ct. 1611, 84 L.Ed.2d 662 (1985).

[14]Andresen v. Maryland, 427 U.S.

463, 96 S.Ct. 2737, 49 L.Ed.2d 627 (1976). See Fisher v. United States, 425 U.S. 391, 96 S.Ct. 1569, 48 L.Ed.2d 39 (1976), where the defendant's attorney was ordered to produce the defendant's private papers which he had obtained from the defendant's accountant. The court held that the attorney could be forced to produce the papers. See Note, "The Rights of Criminal Defendants and the Subpoena Duces Tecum: The Aftermath of Fisher v. United States," 95 Harv. L. Rev. 683 (1982).

[15]Doe v. United States, 487 U.S. 201, 108 S.Ct. 2341, 101 L.Ed.2d 184 (1988).

§ 5:23 Nontestimonial evidence—Under Georgia Constitution and Georgia law

Georgia has long asserted that it grants more protection to its citizens than that afforded by the United States Constitution.[1] The Georgia Constitution provides that "[n]o person shall be compelled to give testimony tending in any manner to criminate himself."[2] In *Creamer v. State*,[3] the Georgia Supreme Court construed the word "testimony" so as to limit the state from forcing the individual to present evidence, oral or real.

Georgia law regarding non-testimonial evidence has been summarized as follows:

"[N]o man is bound to accuse himself of any crime or to furnish any evidence to convict himself of any crime. . . . The constitutional guaranty protects one from being compelled to furnish evidence against himself, either in the form of oral confessions or incriminating admissions of an involuntary character, or of doing an act against his will which is incriminating in its nature."[4]

The Georgia statute on self-incrimination provides as follows:

"No person, who shall be charged in any criminal proceeding with the commission of any indictable offense or any offense punishable on summary conviction shall be compellable to *give evidence* for or against himself." (Emphasis added.)[5]

Thus, a defendant cannot be forced to do an affirmative act which would be incriminating such as placing his foot in a footprint near a burglary[6] or placing his hand in his pocket and surrendering a pistol,[7] based on these provisions. Likewise, it is improper for a district attorney during a trial to ask a defendant to stand and raise his shirt so as to reveal identifying scars on his chest.[8] In *Robinson v. State*,[9] relying on *Creamer,* the Georgia Court of Appeals held that a defendant's state constitutional rights were not violated where, pursuant to a warrant, samples of blood and urine were taken to determine if he had cocaine in his system.

[Section 5:23]

[1]Creamer v. State, 229 Ga. 511, 515, 192 S.E.2d 350 (1972).

[2]Ga. Const. 1983, Art. I, § I, ¶ XVI.

[3]Creamer v. State, 229 Ga. 511, 516, 192 S.E.2d 350 (1972).

[4]Calhoun v. State, 144 Ga. 679, 680, 87 S.E. 893 (1916).

[5]O.C.G.A. § 24-5-506.

[6]Day v. State, 63 Ga. 667 (1879).

[7]Evans v. State, 106 Ga. 519, 32 S.E. 659 (1899).

[8]See Sheets v. State, 143 Ga. App. 510 (1), 239 S.E.2d 196 (1977). See § 5:22, supra, on nontestimonial evidence under the United States Constitution.

[9]Robinson v. State, 180 Ga. App. 43, 50 (3), 348 S.E.2d 662 (1986), rev'd on other grounds, 256 Ga. 564, 350 S.E.2d 464 (1986).

In *Price v. State*,[10] the court relied on *Creamer* in holding valid a search warrant which required a leg hair to be removed from a defendant who was not under arrest at the time. The court again emphasized that there is "a distinction between forcing an accused to *do* an act, and compelling him to *submit* to an act." (Emphasis in original.) The court explained that forcing a defendant to give evidence violates the right of the defendant not to incriminate himself, but forcing an accused to submit to the removal of a hair was not a violation of his rights.

In *Pinson v. State*,[11] the Georgia Court of Appeals pointed out "that requiring a blood test for the purpose of proving or disproving paternity" would not compel a defendant to be a witness against himself within the meaning of the Fifth Amendment nor would the procedure compel him to give testimony tending to incriminate himself within the meaning of the Georgia Constitution.

As pointed out in the foregoing section, nothing in the United States Constitution prevents a defendant from being forced to give voice exemplars[12] and in Georgia it has been held that a defendant may also be required to give such exemplars.[13] However, there is older Georgia authority holding that a defendant may not be forced by court order to produce incriminating evidence.[14] Thus, in *State v. Armstead*,[15] the court held that a defendant cannot be forced to produce a handwriting exemplar to be used against him. However, the Georgia Court of Appeals has held that a defendant can be required to give voice exemplars[16] and to repeat certain words in a lineup.[17] Likewise, in *State v. Thornton*,[18] the Georgia Supreme Court said, "We decline to extend our Constitution so far as would prohibit reasonable police practices, such as the taking of fingerprints [and]

---

[10]Price v. State, 194 Ga. App. 453, 455 (2), 390 S.E.2d 663 (1990).

[11]Pinson v. State, 194 Ga. App. 506, 391 S.E.2d 28 (1990).

[12]United States v. Wade, 388 U.S. 218, 87 S.Ct. 1926, 18 L.Ed.2d 1149 (1967).

[13]Lowe v. State, 185 Ga. App. 606, 607, 365 S.E.2d 479 (1988); Robinson v. State, 184 Ga. App. 398, 401, 361 S.E.2d 542 (1987).

[14]Walter v. State, 131 Ga. App. 667, 206 S.E.2d 662 (1974). But in Tate v. State, 153 Ga. App. 508, 510, 265 S.E.2d 818 (1980), the court seems to erroneously conclude that under Georgia law a defendant can be forced to utter specified words for identification purposes. But see Davis v. State, 158

Ga. App. 549, 552 (5), 281 S.E.2d 305 (1981).

[15]State v. Armstead, 152 Ga. App. 56, 57 (2), 262 S.E.2d 233 (1979).

[16]Tate v. State, 153 Ga. App. 508, 510 (2), 265 S.E.2d 818 (1980).

[17]Davis v. State, 158 Ga. App. 549, 551 (5), 281 S.E.2d 305 (1981); Jenkins v. State, 167 Ga. App. 840, 841, 308 S.E.2d 14 (1983); Robinson v. State, 184 Ga. App. 398, 400, 361 S.E.2d 542 (1987).

[18]State v. Thornton, 253 Ga. 524, 525, 322 S.E.2d 711 (1984) (overruled on other grounds by, Neal v. State, 290 Ga. 563, 722 S.E.2d 765 (2012)). See Bell v. State, 278 Ga. 69, 597 S.E.2d 350 (2004).

. . . taking . . . dental impressions. . . ."

In the interesting case of *Weems v. State*,[19] the Georgia Supreme Court held that the Fourth Amendment right of a victim to be secure against an unreasonable search prevented a defendant from compelling a victim to undergo surgery for the removal of a bullet to be used in his defense. Likewise, in *Park v. State*,[20] the court held that the defendant was not entitled to force the victim to be examined by an expert selected by the defendant.

Unlike the situation under the federal Constitution, in Georgia private papers which are merely tangible evidence of the commission of a crime may not be seized.[21] However, it has been held that if the papers are the instrumentalities of a crime, they may be seized.[22]

See § 6:12, infra, on voice identification. See § 5:22, supra, on compelling non-testimonial evidence under the federal Constitution and § 5:25, infra, on officers requiring an incriminating act. See Studdard, *Daniel's Georgia Handbook on Criminal Evidence* (2018 ed.), § 1:27, on cross-examination and the right of an accused to confront witnesses. See Note, "The Georgia Right Against Self-Incrimination: Historical Anomaly or Vanguard of Justice?" 15 Georgia Law Review 1104 (1981). See Studdard, *Daniel's Georgia Handbook on Criminal Evidence* (2018 ed.), § 7:29, on use of DNA results like fingerprints, and §§ 7-30 and 7-31 on identification by DNA records.

§ 5:24 Statutes requiring incriminating acts

If a statute requires a defendant to incriminate himself, he cannot be convicted for failing to comply with the terms of the statute.[1] Therefore, a federal law requiring gamblers to pay a wagering tax and to register their names violates the privilege against self-incrimination under the Fifth Amendment.[2] In one case, the United States Supreme Court held that a state statute

---

[19]Weems v. State, 268 Ga. 142, 145 (8), 485 S.E.2d 767 (1997).

[20]Park v. State, 230 Ga. App. 274 (1), 495 S.E.2d 886 (1998).

[21]O.C.G.A. § 17-5-21(a)(5).

[22]Tuzman v. State, 145 Ga. App. 761, 244 S.E.2d 882 (1978), abrogated on other grounds by State v. Outen, 289 Ga. 579, 714 S.E.2d 581 (2011). In *Tuzman*, the court said that Medicaid records were seizable where defendant was charged with making false claims for dental work. The case fails to define just what Medicaid records

were seized. If the records were those sent to the state, the reasoning of the case may be valid; if not, the case seems to overlook O.C.G.A. § 17-5-21(a)(5).

[Section 5:24]

[1]Haynes v. United States, 390 U.S. 85, 88 S.Ct. 722, 19 L.Ed.2d 923 (1968).

[2]Marchetti v. United States, 390 U.S. 39, 88 S.Ct. 697, 19 L.Ed.2d 889 (1968), where required registration and payment of wagering tax violated accused's privilege against self-

infringes on the Fifth Amendment privilege against self-incrimination where it provides that if an officer of a political party, subpoenaed by a grand jury to testify concerning the conduct of his office, refuses to testify or to waive immunity against prosecution, he shall lose his office.[3] However, in *California v. Byers*,[4] a defendant charged with violating the "hit-and-run" law requiring a driver involved in a collision to stop at the scene and give his name and address was held not to suffer substantial risk of self-incrimination if he complied with the law, but rather to face the possibility of civil damages.[5] However, in *Chandler v. Miller*[6] the United States Supreme Court held unconstitutional a Georgia statute which required candidates running for certain offices to pass a urinalysis drug test before running for office. The court concluded that there was no "special need" for such tests.

In *Bd. Of Ed. Of Indep. Sch. Dist. No. 92 of Pottawatomie County v. Earls*,[7] the United States Supreme Court approved a school district's policy which required all middle and high school students to consent to drug testing as a condition to participate in extracurricular activities. The Court based its decision on a finding that the policy was a reasonable device for detecting and preventing drug use among students.

Georgia has shown considerable reluctance in finding compelled acts to be so incriminating as to justify a defendant's refusal to

---

incrimination.

[3]Lefkowitz v. Cunningham, 431 U.S. 801, 97 S.Ct. 2132, 53 L.Ed.2d 1 (1977).

[4]California v. Byers, 402 U.S. 424, 91 S.Ct. 1535, 29 L.Ed.2d 9 (1971).

[5]The court also pointed out that even if the statute caused self-incrimination, the information which it sought to have given was non-testimonial insofar as the Fifth Amendment was concerned. California v. Byers, 402 U.S. 424, 433, 91 S.Ct. 1535, 29 L.Ed.2d 9 (1971).

In United States v. Ward, 448 U.S. 242, 100 S.Ct. 2636, 2641-2642, 65 L.Ed.2d 742 (1980), the Court considered a statute which required any person in charge of a vessel, an onshore facility or an offshore facility to report oil spills to the government or be liable for fine and imprisonment.

Such a person who reports the oil spill would be subject to civil penalties for the spill, but not fine or imprisonment, and the information obtained could not be used in a criminal case except in one relating to the falsity of the report. The court concluded that the Act was not violative of the self-incrimination provision of the Fifth Amendment.

[6]Chandler v. Miller, 520 U.S. 305, 117 S.Ct. 1295, 137 L.Ed.2d 513 (1997).

[7]Bd. of Ed. of Indep. Sch. Dist. No. 92 of Pottawatomie County v. Earls, 536 U.S. 822, 122 S.Ct. 2559, 153 L.Ed.2d 735 (2002). See Vernonia School Dist. v. Acton, 515 U.S. 646, 115 S.Ct. 2386, 132 L.Ed.2d 564 (1995) where random drug testing for school students as a prerequisite for athletic participation was upheld. See Annot., "Supreme Court's View on Mandatory Testing for Drugs or Alcohol," 145 A.L.R. Fed 335 (1998).

act. Thus, in *Dennis v. State*,[8] the Georgia Supreme Court held a statute valid which required a driver to drive his truck on a weighing scale, even though the law imposed a penalty on the driver for failure to follow such instructions.

In *Raines v. White*,[9] the appellant Raines was a defendant in an action brought under O.C.G.A. §§ 19-7-40 et seq. to determine paternity. The defendant contended that O.C.G.A. § 19-7-45 was violative of the federal and state Constitutions. The court concluded that the defendant could be required to submit to a blood test as provided for in that section.

In *Keenan v. State*,[10] the Georgia Supreme Court upheld the validity of O.C.G.A. § 40-6-392(d), holding that it was not error for the trial judge to admit the refusal of a defendant to take a state-administered breath test. In *Olevik v. State*,[11] the Georgia Supreme Court held that the implied consent to a blood or breath test by a DUI suspect does not amount to a per se voluntary consent to a warrantless search. The state must show that under the totality of the circumstances, the suspect's consent to be tested was in fact voluntary.

In *Garner v. United States*,[12] the United States Supreme Court held that a federal income tax return in which the defendant stated he was a professional gambler was admissible against the defendant when he was charged with conspiracy to violate gambling laws. The defendant was said to have made the disclosure instead of claiming the privilege on his tax returns; his disclosures were not regarded as compelled incriminations.

See § 5:22, supra, on compelling non-testimonial evidence under the federal Constitution; § 5:23, supra, on non-testimonial evidence under the Georgia Constitution and law; and § 5:25, infra, on officers requiring incriminating acts.

---

[8]Dennis v. State, 226 Ga. 341, 175 S.E.2d 17 (1970). The court expressly refused to follow Sark v. State, 118 Ga. App. 529, 164 S.E.2d 266 (1968), which was factually very much like *Dennis v. State*.

[9]Raines v. White, 248 Ga. 406, 284 S.E.2d 7 (1981).

[10]Keenan v. State, 263 Ga. 569 (1), 436 S.E.2d 475 (1993).

[11]Olevik v. State, 302 Ga. 228, 806 S.E.2d 505 (2017). See State v. Herrera-Bustamante, 818 S.E.2d 552 (Ga. 2018) (*Olevik* did not consider whether O.C.G.A. §§ 40-6-391(a) and 40-5-67.1(b), which allow for admission of a defendant's refusal to take a chemical

analysis of his blood, violate defendant's right under state and federal constitutions not to incriminate one's self). See also Birchfield v. North Dakota, 136 S. Ct. 2160, 195 L. Ed. 2d 560 (2016) (consent to blood or breath test by motorist may not be deemed voluntary where refusal to undergo test may subject motorist to criminal punishment under implied consent statute). See Fazio v. State, 302 Ga. 295, 806 S.E.2d 544 (2017) (implied consent statute does not violate Fourth Amendment prohibition against unreasonable searches).

[12]Garner v. United States, 424 U.S. 648, 96 S.Ct. 1178, 47 L.Ed.2d 370 (1976).

§ 5:25 Officers requiring incriminating acts

"An individual must show three things to fall within the ambit of the Fifth Amendment: (1) complusion, (2) a testimonial communication or act, and (3) incrimination."[1] The United States Supreme Court has noted "two ways in which an act of production is *not testimonial*. First, the Fifth Amendment privilege is not triggered where the Government merely compels some physical act, i.e. where the individual is not called upon to make use of the contents of his or her mind. The most famous example is the key to the lock of a strongbox containing documents, but the Court has also used this rationale in a variety of other contexts. Second, under the 'foregone conclusion' doctrine, an act of production is not testimonial—even if the act conveys a fact regarding the existence or location, possession, or authenticity of the subpoenaed materials—if the Government can show with 'reasonable particularity' that, at the time it sought to compel the act of production, it already knew of the materials, thereby making any testimonial aspect a 'foregone conclusion.' "[2] In *Chafin v. State*,[3] the defendant was required to sign a property receipt card which was kept in the normal course of business by the police department. The card was introduced at trial to allow a comparison of the signature with a signature on a motel registration form. The Georgia Supreme Court concluded that this was not a *Miranda* violation.

In the event an individual subpoenaed by the state refuses to perform "an act of production" on Fifth Amendment grounds, a grant of immunity would extend to information obtained as a result of the production. In *In re: Grand Jury Subpoena Duces Tecum dated March 25, 2011*,[4] the defendant was ordered, after receiving immunity over his assertion of his Fifth Amendment privilege, to decrypt certain computer files. The court found that "even if the decryption and production of the hard drives themselves are not incriminating, they are a 'link in the chain of evidence' that is designed to lead to incriminating evidence; this

[Section 5:25]

[1]U.S. v. Ghidoni, 732 F.2d 814, 816, 15 Fed. R. Evid. Serv. 1186 (11th Cir. 1984) (order requiring defendant to execute consent directive to bank to turn over records was neither testimonial nor incriminating because directive did not confirm existence of accounts or defendant's control of them).

[2]In re Grand Jury Subpoena Duces Tecum Dated March 25, 2011, 670 F.3d 1335, 1344 (11th Cir. 2012), citing U.S. v. Hubbell, 530 U.S. 27, 120 S. Ct. 2037, 147 L. Ed. 2d 24 (2000) (citations omitted) (Government cannot use grand jury to compel an individual to unlock or decrypt files unless it can show that it knows what is in the files.).

[3]Chafin v. State, 246 Ga. 709 (9), 716, 273 S.E.2d 147 (1980).

[4]In re Grand Jury Subpoena Duces Tecum Dated March 25, 2011, 670 F.3d 1335, 84 A.L.R.6th 677 (11th Cir. 2012).

is sufficient to invoke the Fifth Amendment privilege." The court noted that merely delivering the encrypted computer files to the government was not testimonial, and therefore not protected. It was the compelled act of producing unencrypted files which was, in effect, testimonial and thereby qualified for the assertion of the privilege. Because the court found that the immunity which the government provided was limited to the act of production, and was not co-extensive with the Fifth Amendment use and derivative use of immunity, the defendant's refusal to deliver the unencrypted files was justified.

In *State v. Armstead*,[5] the state filed a motion to compel the accused to produce handwriting exemplars. The Court of Appeals affirmed the trial court's decision to deny the motion, citing *Creamer v. State*.[6] "[A]lthough evidence may be compulsorily adduced from an accused, it is constitutionally impermissible to compel an accused to perform an act which results in the production of incriminating evidence. . . . The distinction is between forcing an accused to *do* an act against his will and requiring an accused to *submit* to an act. While the latter 'takes evidence from the defendant' . . . and is constitutionally acceptable, the former compels the defendant, in essence, to *give* evidence which violates an individual's right not to incriminate himself." (Emphasis in original.)

The Court of Appeals recognized that the United States Supreme Court, in *Gilbert v. California*,[7] held "that handwriting exemplars can be compelled," but asserted that the state can grant more (but not less) protection to its citizens than the federal Constitution. The *Armstead* court cited *Creamer*: " 'While the language in the United States Constitution has long been construed to be limited to "testimony," the Georgia Constitution has been construed to limit the State from forcing the individual to present *evidence*, oral or real.' "(Emphasis in original.) However, in a case involving a lineup,[8] the Georgia Supreme Court cited *United States v. Wade*,[9] and stated "one's voluntary consent to a lineup does not violate his Fifth Amendment right against self-incrimination, since the lineup process involves no compulsion of the accused to give evidence of a testimonial nature

---

[5]State v. Armstead, 152 Ga. App. 56, 262 S.E.2d 233 (1979).

[6]In Creamer v. State, 229 Ga. 511, 192 S.E.2d 350 (1972), the court stated: "You cannot force a defendant to act, but you can, under proper circumstances, produce evidence from his person."

[7]Gilbert v. California, 388 U.S.

263, 87 S.Ct. 1951, 18 L.Ed.2d 1178 (1967).

[8]Disby v. State, 238 Ga. 178 (2), 231 S.E.2d 763 (1977); Howard v. State, 160 Ga. App. 487, 287 S.E.2d 392 (1981).

[9]United States v. Wade, 388 U.S. 218, 222, 87 S.Ct. 1926, 18 L.Ed.2d 1149 (1967).

against himself." Similarly, the Georgia Supreme Court has held that a suspect can be forced to take part in a lineup.[10] In *Graham v. State*[11] the Georgia Court of Appeals held that the state has a right to demand the presence of the defendant so that he can be identified.

In *Tate v. State*,[12] the Georgia Court of Appeals asserted that "[o]ur appellate courts have held, or recognized, that requiring a suspect in a criminal case to verbalize specified words for identification purposes, whether or not the words used are the same as those allegedly used during the commission of the offense, does not violate an accused's privilege against self-incrimination accorded the accused by the United States' Constitution and the state's statutes and Constitution." No Georgia cases were cited.

The idea that a suspect may be forced to speak certain words seems to be contrary to historic Georgia law which prevents a suspect from being forced to perform any affirmative act which might incriminate him. See § 5:23, supra, on Georgia constitutional protection against self-incrimination.

In *Montgomery v. State*,[13] the Georgia Court of Appeals held that a DUI suspect is not "compelled" to incriminate himself by taking field sobriety tests when the police neither threaten him with criminal sanctions nor use physical force, and the suspect does not refuse to perform the tests upon request.

Elder v. State[14] involved testimony of witnesses in a murder trial where evidence was given that the defendant's foot fitted tracks leading from a field near the victim's house. The defendant, while under arrest and handcuffed, was brought by the sheriff and several others to the place where the tracks were being examined. The sheriff commanded the defendant to put his foot in the track. The Georgia Supreme Court held that this evidence should have been excluded, and because it was not, the case was remanded for a new trial. The court found that the defendant did

[10]Wilson v. State, 237 Ga. 657, 229 S.E.2d 424 (1976).

[11]Graham v. State, 171 Ga. App. 242, 253 (12), 319 S.E.2d 484 (1984). See § 17:8, infra, on presence of defendant.

[12]Tate v. State, 153 Ga. App. 508, 510, 265 S.E.2d 818 (1980). See Campbell v. State, 228 Ga. App. 258, 491 S.E.2d 477 (1997).

[13]Montgomery v. State, 174 Ga. App. 95, 329 S.E.2d 166 (1985). See Clark v. State, 289 Ga. App. 884, 658 S.E.2d 372 (2008).

[14]Elder v. State, 143 Ga. 363 (1), 85 S.E. 97 (1915). See Butler v. State, 277 Ga. App. 57, 625 S.E.2d 458 (2005), judgment aff'd, 281 Ga. 310, 637 S.E.2d 688 (2006) (there is a difference between compelling one to submit his body for purposes of having evidence removed such as a bullet or having his body displayed for purpose of identification and acts where defendant is forced to provide incriminatory evidence such as in *Elder*).

not voluntarily put his foot in the track and stated: "the evidence as to the foot of the accused fitting the track should have been excluded upon objection being made thereto under the provision of the constitution of this State, which declares that 'No person shall be compelled to give testimony tending in any matter to criminate himself' . . . [W]e think in the present case, under the circumstances, there was such a show of force as amounted to the actual use of force and to coercion."

In Georgia, a defendant may not be compelled to produce a handwriting exemplar. However, the state may use a voluntary writing by the defendant, such as a signature on a check or even an indictment for such purposes.[15] The rule in federal court is otherwise.[16]

In *Mobley v. State*,[17] the court pointed out that compelling a defendant to undergo a psychiatric examination to determine his competency to stand trial and his insanity defense does not violate the defendant's privilege against self-incrimination.

See § 5:23, supra, on non-testimonial evidence under the Georgia Constitution and law. See § 5:4, supra, on coercing an employee to give a statement. See Studdard, *Daniel's Georgia Handbook on Criminal Evidence* (2018 ed.), § 7:16 on performing a sobriety test without being warned against self-incrimination.

§ 5:26   Results of illegally obtained evidence

The material in this section is in summary form. The exclusionary rule is treated in far greater depth in §§ 2:24 et seq., supra.

From the standpoint of the federal exclusionary rule, any admission or confession of the defendant which is obtained in violation of the *Miranda* requirements is not admissible against the defendant[1] if he makes a proper objection to the introduction of such evidence.[2] Also if a confession or an admission is not

---

[15]See Williams v. State, 259 Ga. App. 742, 578 S.E.2d 128 (2003).

[16]See In re Grand Jury Subpoena No.2002r02810 (163), No.2005-01 to John Doe, 176 Fed. Appx. 72 (11th Cir. 2006) (handwriting exemplar is an identifying physical characteristic that falls outside Fifth Amendment right against self-incrimination).

[17]Mobley v. State, 269 Ga. 738, 741 (2), 505 S.E.2d 722 (1998).

[Section 5:26]

[1]Miranda v. Arizona, 384 U.S. 436, 479, 86 S.Ct. 1602, 16 L.Ed.2d 694 (1966). See also Colbert v. State, 124 Ga. App. 283, 183 S.E.2d 476 (1971).

[2]Mallory v. State, 230 Ga. 657, 198 S.E.2d 677 (1973). This case points out that if defendant fails to object to the admissibility of a confession at trial, the admission of a confession may not be complained of later.

freely and voluntarily made, it is not admissible.[3] However, *Harris v. New York,*[4] holds that if an accused makes a voluntary statement, even in the absence of proper *Miranda* warnings, it may be used to impeach him where the defendant testifies at trial. However, if the statement was not voluntarily made it may not be used even for purposes of impeachment.[5] In addition, the admission of such a statement may constitute reversible error unless "the jury is expressly instructed that the evidence is admitted for the purpose of impeachment only, whether or not a request to so charge be made, and whether or not any exceptions are made to the charge as given."[6]

Under Georgia law a confession is not admissible unless it was "made voluntarily, without being induced by another by the slightest hope of benefit or remotest fear of injury."[7]

In *Griffin v. State,*[8] the Georgia Court of Appeals held that under Georgia law, there must be a determination of voluntariness, regardless of whether the confession is obtained by an officer or a private person, before a statement is submitted to the jury for its consideration. Additionally, it is better practice for a hearing to be held outside the presence of the jury with both the state and the defendant given the opportunity to present evidence. Where the confession is obtained by a private actor who is not a state public law enforcement officer, there is no requirement that the suspect be provided with *Miranda* warnings.[9]

In *Wilson v. Zant,*[10] the Georgia Supreme Court concluded that the exclusionary rule did not apply to the fruits of a voluntary statement obtained in violation of *Edwards v. Arizona*[11] even though the statement itself is inadmissible at trial. In the case of

---

[3]See Jackson v. Denno, 378 U.S. 368, 84 S. Ct. 1774, 12 L. Ed. 2d 908, 1 A.L.R.3d 1205 (1964).

[4]Harris v. New York, 401 U.S. 222, 91 S.Ct. 643, 28 L.Ed.2d 1 (1971). See also Alexander v. State, 138 Ga. App. 618, 619, 226 S.E.2d 807 (1976); Colbert v. State, 124 Ga. App. 283, 183 S.E.2d 476 (1971). Cf. United States v. Rada-Solano, 625 F.2d 577 (5th Cir. 1980).

[5]Mincey v. Arizona, 437 U.S. 385, 98 S.Ct. 2408, 57 L.Ed.2d 290 (1978); New Jersey v. Portash, 440 U.S. 450, 99 S.Ct. 1292, 59 L.Ed.2d 501 (1979); Platt v. State, 163 Ga. App. 776, 296 S.E.2d 113 (1982); Green v. State, 154 Ga. App. 295, 296 (1), 267 S.E.2d 898 (1980).

[6]Askea v. State, 153 Ga. App.

849, 853 (5), 267 S.E.2d 279 (1980); Dukes v. State, 264 Ga. App. 820, 592 S.E.2d 473 (2003).

[7]O.C.G.A. § 24-8-824.

[8]See Davenport v. State, 277 Ga. App. 758(1), 627 S.E.2d 133 (2006); Wiley v. State, 245 Ga. App. 580(3), 538 S.E.2d 483 (2000); Griffin v. State, 230 Ga. App. 318, 496 S.E.2d 480 (1998).

[9]Singleton v. State, 231 Ga. App. 694, 500 S.E.2d 411 (1998).

[10]Wilson v. Zant, 249 Ga. 373, 378, 290 S.E.2d 442 (1982), disapp. on other grounds, Morgan v. State, 267 Ga. 203, 476 S.E.2d 747 (1996).

[11]Edwards v. Arizona, 451 U.S. 477, 101 S.Ct. 1880, 68 L.Ed.2d 378 (1981). See State v. Woods, 280 Ga. 758, 632 S.E.2d 654 (2006), statement

United States v. Patane,[12] the District Court granted, and the Appellate court affirmed, the defendant's motion to suppress a firearm where the weapon was discovered as a result of the defendant's voluntary statements made without *Miranda* warnings. However, the United States Supreme Court reversed on the grounds that "[t]he Self-incrimination Clause . . . is not implicated by the admission into evidence of the physical fruit of a voluntary statement."[13] Hence, neither *Miranda* nor the "fruits-of-the-poisonous-tree" doctrine requires suppression of physical evidence seized as a result of voluntary statements made in the absence of *Miranda* warnings.

The issue, however, may be different where the defendant's right to counsel has attached. In *Vergara v. State,*[14] the defendant had requested counsel and sometime thereafter requested to speak with police investigators. The defendant's statements led to the discovery of contraband. The court concluded that based upon the totality of the circumstances, the state failed to show that the defendant had waived his previously invoked right to counsel and the fruits doctrine required the exclusion of the evidence.

Even if there is error on the part of the court in admitting such evidence, a reviewing court may still consider it harmless error and thus refuse to reverse the conviction.[15] Also, a defendant lacks standing to attack a violation of the constitutional rights of a co-defendant who has confessed to a crime and thereby implicated the defendant.[16]

See § 2:27, supra, on the effect of an illegal arrest on identification and § 6:9, infra, on the right to place a suspect in a lineup.

---

obtained after unambiguous request for attorney in response to "Christian Burial" speech was found to be voluntary and fruits of statements, recovery of victims' bodies, were admissible.

[12]United States v. Patane, 542 U.S. 630, 124 S.Ct. 2620, 159 L.Ed.2d 667 (2004).

[13]United States v. Patane, 542 U.S. 630, 124 S.Ct. 2620, 159 L.Ed.2d 667 (2004). See Reaves v. State, 284 Ga. App. 181(2)(b), 664 S.E.2d 211 (2008).

[14]Vergara v. State, 283 Ga. 175 (2), 657 S.E.2d 863 (2008), the court concluded that recovery of cocaine was not so attenuated from illegal interrogation as to dissipate the taint.

[15]See Brown v. State, 122 Ga. App. 570, 572, 177 S.E.2d 801 (1970). In Wilson v. Zant, 249 Ga. 373, 377, 290 S.E.2d 442 (1982), disapp. on other grounds, Morgan v. State, 267 Ga. 203, 476 S.E.2d 747 (1996), the court stated that the admission of a statement obtained in violation of *Miranda* is not a basis for habeas corpus where the statement "was harmless beyond a reasonable doubt. Schneble v. Florida, 405 U.S. 427, 432, 92 S.Ct. 1056, 31 L.Ed.2d 340 (1972). . . ."

[16]Sims v. State, 243 Ga. 83, 84 (2), 252 S.E.2d 501 (1979).

Chapter 6

Pre-Trial Identification

> **KeyCite®:** Cases and other legal materials listed in KeyCite Scope can be researched through the KeyCite service on Westlaw®. Use KeyCite to check citations for form, parallel references, prior and later history, and comprehensive citator information, including citations to other decisions and secondary materials.

§ 6:1 Scope

In this chapter consideration is given to some methods of identifying a person, normally a defendant. A defendant may be identified in a number of ways, including eyewitness identification, photographic identification, voice identification, handwriting identification, fingerprint and palm print identification, footprint identification, and some other perhaps less commonly used methods of identification. This chapter is concerned only with eyewitness identification, photographic identification, and voice identification. Other methods of identification are treated elsewhere in this book.

§ 6:2 Eyewitness identification—Background

There have been cases in which a defendant was convicted of a crime because of the testimony of an eyewitness who incorrectly

443

identified him as the person committing the crime.[1] In some of these incidents, the evidence has been extremely weak.[2] It has been stated that "erroneous identification of the accused constitutes the major cause of known wrongful convictions."[3] Also, it has been said that the hazard of a mistaken eyewitness identification is particularly pronounced in a situation where the witness is a member of one race and the suspect is a member of another race.[4]

It has been held that the fact that a victim cannot accurately describe the assailant to the police because of darkness and because he was attacked from the rear does not prevent an in-court identification.[5] The Georgia Supreme Court has said that where an eyewitness positively identifies an assailant, this is not opinion evidence[6] and consequently it is not error for the trial court to fail to charge on non-expert opinion evidence.[7] However, some have referred to identification testimony as opinion testimony.[8]

Until the case of *United States v. Wade,*[9] decided in 1967 and discussed in the next section, it was generally thought that a jury question existed as to the identity of the defendant in all cases in which there was a dispute as to the identity of the perpetrator of a crime.[10] It always has been true that the identity of a defendant as the guilty party may be shown by circumstantial evidence as

---

[Section 6:2]

[1]E.g., see Wood and Ross, "Nothing but the Truth" (Doubleday & Co. 1960), which is based on a trial in Georgia. The Georgia Supreme Court affirmed the conviction and death sentence in this case. The decision is reported as Foster v. State, 213 Ga. 601, 100 S.E.2d 426 (1957). See The Atlanta Journal and Constitution, p. 14B, Sunday, July 8, 1979. See Loftus, "Reconstructing Memory: The Incredible Eyewitness," Psychology Today, p. 116, Dec. 1974.

[2]E. Borchard, "Convicting the Innocent" (1932); "Unreliability of Eyewitness Identification," 18 Am. Jur. Proof of Facts 2d 361.

[3]Frank & Frank, "Not Guilty," p. 61 (1957).

[4]"The Neglected Dimension in Eyewitness Identification," 4 Crim. Def., No. 3, p. 5, May-June, 1977.

[5]Styles v. State, 139 Ga. App. 128, 228 S.E.2d 28 (1976).

[6]Contra, Wiggins v. Henson, 68 Ga. 819 (1882).

[7]Salisbury v. State, 223 Ga. 414, 416 (4), 156 S.E.2d 48 (1967); Brown v. State, 137 Ga. App. 331 (1), 223 S.E.2d 753 (1976).

[8]For an excellent discussion of some of the Georgia cases and other authority on this point, see the opinion of Judge Quillian in Cowans v. State, 145 Ga. App. 693 (2), 244 S.E.2d 624 (1978).

[9]United States v. Wade, 388 U.S. 218, 87 S.Ct. 1926, 18 L.Ed.2d 1149 (1967).

[10]E.g., Randall v. State, 73 Ga. App. 354, 36 S.E.2d 450 (1945). Here the court holds that a witness may give his opinion as to the identity of the defendant when he states the facts on which the opinion is based. In this case, the perpetrator wore a mask below his eyes and a cap which was pulled down to cover most of his forehead. In Daniel v. State, 150 Ga. App. 798, 258 S.E.2d 604 (1979), the court

well as direct evidence,[11] but if the evidence is entirely circumstantial, it may be insufficient to support a conviction.[12]

In *Wade,* the United States Supreme Court stated that eyewitness identification by the victim or witnesses is peculiarly riddled with dangers which may prevent a fair trial, and a major cause of miscarriages of justice result from mistaken identification.[13] Despite the dangers which exist in eyewitness identifications, such identification is regarded as essential to most criminal cases. Yet, every experienced lawyer who tries criminal cases knows how devastating such eyewitness identification testimony frequently is, even when the witness has had very little opportunity to view the person who committed the crime. Nevertheless, the rule remains that generally, eyewitness testimony is admissible[14] and the jury determines how much weight it should be given.[15] However, there are situations so extreme that some such evidence is not admissible.[16]

Identification testimony in court may conceivably come from three sources: (1) a witness pointing out the defendant in court; (2) asking the eyewitness if he has identified the defendant earlier; and (3) having a third person testify that the witness identified the defendant on an earlier occasion. However, Georgia has placed limitations on the third possibility which are discussed later in this section.

In the first situation there is no per se exclusionary rule. There is no authority for the proposition that an in-court identification is subject to the same safeguards required for a pre-trial identification at a line up or by way of a photographic array.[17] However, if the pre-trial procedures have been such as to undermine the reliability of the eyewitness identification, there may be a due process violation.[18] Thus, if the suggestiveness of the identification amounts to "a very substantial likelihood of irreparable misidentification" based on a totality of the circum-

---

stated, quoting from Manson v. Brathwaite, 432 U.S. 98, 113, 97 S.Ct. 2243, 53 L.Ed.2d 140 (1977), "[R]eliability is the linchpin in determining the admissibility of an identification."

[11]Jester v. State, 193 Ga. 202 (1), 17 S.E.2d 736 (1941).

[12]Rutland v. State, 129 Ga. App. 313, 199 S.E.2d 595 (1973).

[13]United States v. Wade, 388 U.S. 218, 228, 87 S.Ct. 1926, 18 L.Ed.2d 1149 (1967).

[14]See Randall v. State, 73 Ga. App. 354 (2-4), 367, 36 S.E.2d 450 (1945).

[15]Garrett v. State, 141 Ga. App. 584, 586 (3), 234 S.E.2d 161 (1977); Thornton v. State, 161 Ga. App. 296, 297 (1), 287 S.E.2d 749 (1982).

[16]See West's Georgia Digest, Criminal Law Key No. 339.11.

[17]Milner v. State, 258 Ga. App. 425, 574 S.E.2d 457 (2002).

[18]Foster v. California, 394 U.S. 440, 89 S.Ct. 1127, 22 L.Ed.2d 402 (1969).

stances,[19] then such testimony of pre-trial identification is not admissible.[20]

In the second situation and possibly in the third, where a defendant was identified by a witness or the victim at a pre-trial lineup or showup, there is a per se exclusionary rule which applies to the admission of such pre-trial identification testimony if the defendant had no opportunity to be represented by counsel at the lineup or showup and if the adversary criminal judicial proceeding had already been instituted against the defendant.[21]

Also, in the second and third situations, there may be a less precise due process violation which may apply to such pre-trial identification testimony if (1) the identification procedure was so unduly suggestive (2) that it was conducive to irreparable mistaken identification.[22]

Aside from the constitutional limitation which may require the exclusion of extrajudicial pre-trial identifications which are involved in situations two and three, there are other questions. In the second situation, Georgia and most jurisdictions seem to permit a witness to testify in court about his pre-trial identification of the defendant.[23] In *United States v. Owens*,[24] the United States Supreme Court held that there was no violation of the Confrontation Clause where there was testimony of an out-of-court identification statement of a witness who was present for trial as a witness and who had since lost his memory of the event so that he was not able to testify as to the basis for the identification. See Goger, *Daniel's Georgia Handbook on Criminal Evidence* (2017 ed.), § 1:27, on cross-examination. However, a few states will not permit such testimony on hearsay grounds[25] or because it is regarded as unduly bolstering the in-court identification.[26]

---

[19]Manson v. Brathwaite, 432 U.S. 98, 97 S.Ct. 2243, 53 L.Ed.2d 140 (1977) (quoting Simmons v. United States, 390 U.S. 377, 88 S.Ct. 967, 19 L.Ed.2d 1247 (1968)); United States v. Gidley, 527 F.2d 1345 (5th Cir. 1976).

[20]Neil v. Biggers, 409 U.S. 188, 93 S.Ct. 375, 34 L.Ed.2d 401 (1972).

[21]Gilbert v. California, 388 U.S. 263, 87 S.Ct. 1951, 18 L.Ed.2d 1178 (1967).

[22]Cf. Stovall v. Denno, 388 U.S. 293, 302, 87 S.Ct. 1967, 18 L.Ed.2d 1199 (1967).

[23]Cf. Ingram v. State, 233 Ga. App. 356, 357 (1), 504 S.E.2d 254 (1998). See Thomas v. State, 128 Ga. App. 538, 542 (4), 197 S.E.2d 452 (1973); Duffey v. State, 151 Ga. App. 673, 261 S.E.2d 421 (1979). See 29 Am. Jur. 2d Evidence § 372.

Also see Annot., "Admissibility and Weight of Extrajudicial or Pretrial Identification Where Witness Was Unable or Failed to Make In-Court Identification," 29 A.L.R.4th 104 (1984).

[24]United States v. Owens, 484 U.S. 554, 108 S.Ct. 838, 98 L.Ed.2d 951 (1988).

[25]Wilson v. State, 111 Tex.Crim. 134, 11 S.W.2d 803 (App.1928).

[26]State v. Baldwin, 317 Mo. 759, 297 S.W. 10 (1927).

In the 2001 case of *White v. State*,[27] the Georgia Supreme Court held that "[i]n the absence of some other viable hearsay exception, such as 'necessity' or 'res gestae,' a law enforcement officer may not testify to a pre-trial identification of the accused unless the person who actually made the identification testifies at trial and is subject to cross-examination." In *Abrams v. State*,[28] the court affirmed the trial court in permitting an investigator to testify that the victim and an eyewitness identified the defendant, and over objection, the investigator testified that the victim told him the defendant "was the right size and the clothing was right." The court also pointed out that the victim and the eyewitness both testified and were available for cross-examination. See an excellent annotation, "Admissibility of Evidence as to Extrajudicial or Pretrial Identification of Accused," 71 A.L.R.2d 449 (1960).

It is within a trial court's discretion whether or not to admit expert testimony regarding eyewitness identification.[29] However, "[w]here eyewitness identification of the defendant is a key element of the State's case and there is no substantial corroboration of that identification by other evidence, trial courts may not exclude expert testimony without carefully weighing whether the evidence would assist the jury in assessing the reliability of eyewitness testimony and whether eyewitness testimony is the only effective way to reveal any weakness in an eyewitness

---

[27]White v. State, 273 Ga. 787, 788, 546 S.E.2d 514 (2001). The *White* case overruled Haralson v. State, 234 Ga. 406, 408 (4), 216 S.E.2d 304 (1975), Neal v. State, 211 Ga. App. 829, 830 (1)(b), 440 S.E.2d 717 (1994), and a number of earlier Georgia cases. The Supreme Court explained in In re L.J.P., 277 Ga. 135, 136-37, 587 S.E.2d 15 (2003): "Evidence of an extrajudicial identification is admissible, not only to corroborate an identification made at the trial, but as independent evidence of identity. Unlike other testimony that cannot be corroborated by proof of prior consistent statements unless it is first impeached, evidence of an extrajudicial identification is admitted regardless of whether the testimonial identification is impeached, because the earlier identification has greater probative value than an identification made in the courtroom after the suggestions of others and the circum-stances of the trial may have intervened to create a fancied recognition in the witness' mind. The failure of the witness to repeat the extra judicial identification in court does not destroy its probative value, for such failure may be explained by loss of memory or other circumstances. The extrajudicial identification tends to connect the defendant with the crime, and the principal danger of admitting hearsay evidence is not present since the witness is available at the trial for cross-examination. The fact that the victim was excused as a witness before his pre-hearing statements were offered through [a police officer's] testimony does not in any way require their exclusion."

[28]Abrams v. State, 229 Ga. App. 152, 153 (1), 493 S.E.2d 561 (1997).

[29]Johnson v. State, 272 Ga. 254, 257, 526 S.E.2d 549 (2000).

identification."[30] In *Brodes v. State*,[31] the trial judge excluded expert testimony on the accuracy of eyewitness identification. The Appellate Court reversed, finding that the expert's testimony was "highly relevant" to the case, which involved "cross-racial identifications by victims who were at gunpoint . . . ."[32] Following trial and conviction, *Brodes* eventually found its way to the Supreme Court of Georgia and there the Court reversed the trial court, which, relying on the pattern charge, instructed the jury that one of the factors it was to consider in reviewing the testimony of the eyewitnesses was the level of certainty in their identification. The Court was persuaded by the empirical research presented that there exists a distinct "lack of correlation between a witness's certainty in his or her identification of someone as the perpetrator of a crime and the accuracy of that identification . . . "[33] The Court went on to "advise" trial courts to refrain from using the level of certainty factor as part of their eyewitness identification charge. However, *Brodes* in no way is an impediment to a witness testifying about his or her level of certainty of identification. Such testimony would, of course, be subject to challenge by way of "cross examination, expert testimony or the presentation of testimony from other eye witnesses."[34]

Effective July 1, 2016, "any law enforcement agency that conducts live lineups, photo lineups, or show-ups shall adopt written policies for using such procedures for the purpose of determining whether a witness identifies someone as the perpetrator of an alleged crime."[35] See § 6:4, infra, on lineups.

The next section discusses in chronological order some United States Supreme Court decisions which have considered problems of eyewitness identification. Then the general aspects of lineups are treated followed by material on showups and photographic identification. Next, consideration is given to the right to counsel at the time of identification and then due process consideration is discussed. After material on motions for lineups there is a discussion on hearings on motions to suppress identification.

See Annotation, "Propriety of Requiring Suspect or Accused to

---

[30]Johnson v. State, 272 Ga. 254, 257, 526 S.E.2d 549 (2000).

[31]Brodes v. State, 250 Ga. App. 323, 551 S.E.2d 757 (2001).

[32]Brodes v. State, 250 Ga. App. 323, 325, 551 S.E.2d 757 (2001).

[33]Brodes v. State, 279 Ga. 435, 614 S.E.2d 766 (2005). The same pattern charge criticized in *Brodes* includes a reference to the "intelligence" of witnesses as one of the factors jurors should assess in weighing the credibility of witnesses. The Court of Appeals found this part of the instruction confusing and ill defined in McKenzie v. State, 293 Ga. App. 350, 667 S.E.2d 142 (2008), and suggested that trial courts discontinue its use in future cases.

[34]Clark v. State, 285 Ga. App. 182, 185(4), 645 S.E.2d 671 (2007); Best v. State, 279 Ga. App. 309(3), 630 S.E.2d 900 (2006).

[35]O.C.G.A. § 17-20-2(a).

Alter, or Refrain From Altering, Physical or Bodily Appearance," 24 A.L.R.4th 592 (1983).

§ 6:3 Overview of some United States Supreme Court cases on eyewitness identification

On June 12, 1967, the United States Supreme Court handed down decisions in three landmark cases on eyewitness identification. The first case, in terms of where it is reported, is the case of *United States v. Wade.*[1]

In *Wade,* the defendant was indicted for bank robbery some six months after the robbery. He was arrested about a week later. Fifteen days after counsel had been appointed for him, FBI agents, without notice to Wade's attorney, arranged to have two bank employees observe a lineup of Wade and five or six other prisoners. Before the lineup the bank employees observed, through an open door, Wade, who was standing in the hall with an FBI agent. The other five or six prisoners appeared and a lineup was conducted in the courtroom. Each person in the lineup was directed to say something like "put the money in the bag." Both employees identified Wade at the lineup. At trial both employees on direct examination identified Wade. Prior lineup identification was elicited from both employees on cross-examination. At the close of the testimony, defense counsel moved for a judgment of acquittal or alternatively to strike the courtroom identification on the ground that the lineup without notice to, and in the absence of, defense counsel violated the Sixth Amendment right to assistance of counsel and violated the Fifth Amendment. The Court of Appeals for the Fifth Circuit reversed and ordered a new trial at which the in-court identification evidence was to be excluded because of the Sixth Amendment violation and the court concluded that there had been no Fifth Amendment violation. The Supreme Court pointed out that a defendant is entitled to the presence of counsel "at any stage of the prosecution, formal or informal, in court or out, where counsel's absence might derogate from the accused's right to a fair trial."[2] Identification may take the form of a lineup or showup "as in the present case, or presentation of the suspect alone to the witness . . . risks of suggestion attend either form of confrontation. . . ."[3] "The presence of counsel at such critical confrontations . . . operates to assure that the accused's interests

---

[Section 6:3]

[1]United States v. Wade, 388 U.S. 218, 87 S.Ct. 1926, 18 L.Ed.2d 1149 (1967).

[2]United States v. Wade, 388 U.S. 218, 226, 87 S.Ct. 1926, 18 L.Ed.2d 1149 (1967).

[3]United States v. Wade, 388 U.S. 218, 229, 87 S.Ct. 1926, 18 L.Ed.2d 1149 (1967).

will be protected. . . ."[4] The "presence of counsel itself can often avert prejudice and assure a meaningful confrontation at trial, there can be little doubt that for Wade the . . . lineup was a critical stage of the prosecution. . . ."[5] Both Wade and his counsel should have been notified of the lineup and his counsel's presence should have been required unless this right was waived. Counsel's presence is necessary as an observer "to preserve the defendant's basic right to a fair trial as affected by his right meaningfully to cross-examine the witnesses against him and to have effective assistance of counsel at the trial itself."[6] The court expressly left open the question of whether substitute counsel would suffice if the presence of his counsel would have resulted in prejudicial delay.[7] The "accused's inability effectively to reconstruct at trial any unfairness that occurred at the lineup may deprive him of his only opportunity meaningfully to attack the credibility of the witnesses' courtroom identification."[8]

In summary, the United States Supreme Court said that the court of appeals did not apply the proper test. The court directed the conviction vacated "pending a hearing to determine whether the in-court identifications had an independent source, or whether, in any event, the introduction of the evidence was harmless error . . . and . . . [directed] the District Court to reinstate the conviction or order a new trial, as may be proper."[9] However, the Court pointed out that the Government must be given "the opportunity to establish by *clear and convincing* evidence that the in-court identifications were based upon observations of the suspect other than [at] the lineup identification." (Emphasis added.)[10] The question to be determined in the trial court was whether the in-court identification was based on the lineup which was without counsel or whether it had an independent source. "Application of this test in the present context requires consideration of various factors; for example, [1] the prior opportunity to observe the alleged criminal act, [2] the existence of any discrepancy between any pre-lineup description and the defendant's actual description, [3] any identification prior to lineup of another person, [4] the identification by picture of the defendant

---

[4]United States v. Wade, 388 U.S. 218, 227, 87 S.Ct. 1926, 18 L.Ed.2d 1149 (1967).

[5]United States v. Wade, 388 U.S. 218, 236, 87 S.Ct. 1926, 18 L.Ed.2d 1149 (1967).

[6]United States v. Wade, 388 U.S. 218, 227, 240, 87 S.Ct. 1926, 18 L.Ed.2d 1149 (1967).

[7]United States v. Wade, 388 U.S. 218, 237, 87 S.Ct. 1926, 18 L.Ed.2d 1149 (1967).

[8]United States v. Wade, 388 U.S. 218, 231, 87 S.Ct. 1926, 18 L.Ed.2d 1149 (1967).

[9]United States v. Wade, 388 U.S. 218, 242, 87 S.Ct. 1926, 18 L.Ed.2d 1149 (1967).

[10]United States v. Wade, 388 U.S. 218, 240, 87 S.Ct. 1926, 18 L.Ed.2d 1149 (1967).

prior to the lineup, [5] failure to identify the defendant on a prior occasion, and [6] the lapse of time between the alleged act and the lineup identification. [7] It is also relevant to consider those facts which despite the absence of counsel, are disclosed concerning the conduct of the lineup."[11]

The second of the three cases to be reported was *Gilbert v. California*.[12] After counsel had been appointed, a lineup was held in an auditorium after indictment for armed robbery of a savings and loan association. At trial Gilbert moved to strike the testimony of a cashier of the association on the ground that she identified him at the lineup which was conducted in the absence of his counsel. The trial judge denied a hearing at which the defendant sought to show that the witness' trial testimony was based at least in part on the lineup. On cross-examination the witness testified to her identification of the defendant at the lineup. Apparently other prosecution witnesses testified at the sentencing phase of the trial as to other robberies committed by the defendant and their lineup identification of the defendant. The conviction was vacated and the case remanded. The testimony of the witnesses at the sentencing phase of the case was subject to a per se exclusion because the defendant was not represented by counsel at the lineup identification. It was error for the trial judge to permit the in-court identification testimony of the witnesses at the savings and loan association without first determining that their testimony would not be tainted by the lineup. Unless "the California Supreme Court is 'able to declare a belief that it was harmless beyond a reasonable doubt' . . . Gilbert will be entitled on remand to a new trial or, if no prejudicial error is found on the guilt stage but only in the penalty stage, to whatever relief California law affords where the penalty stage must be set aside."

The last of the three cases is *Stovall v. Denno*.[13] Stovall was arrested in 1961 the day after a doctor was stabbed to death in his kitchen and the doctor's wife also had been stabbed a number of times. The wife was placed in a hospital in critical condition and major surgery was performed on her. Stovall was brought to the wife's hospital room on the day after surgery for purposes of identification without being given an opportunity to obtain counsel. He was handcuffed and was the only black person in the room. After Stovall repeated a few words as directed, he was identified as the assailant. The victim testified at trial to her identification of Stovall in her room and also made an in-court

[11]United States v. Wade, 388 U.S. 218, 241, 87 S.Ct. 1926, 18 L.Ed.2d 1149 (1967).

[12]Gilbert v. California, 388 U.S. 263, 87 S.Ct. 1951, 18 L.Ed.2d 1178 (1967).

[13]Stovall v. Denno, 388 U.S. 293, 87 S.Ct. 1967, 18 L.Ed.2d 1199 (1967).

identification of him. The state's conviction was attacked by federal habeas corpus. The Supreme Court concluded that the right to counsel at a lineup as recognized in *Wade* and *Gilbert* was to be applied only to identifications after June 12, 1967, the date of the decisions in those cases. However, even though the right to counsel at the time of an identification was not applied, Stovall still had a right to relief in the "event the confrontation . . . was so unnecessarily suggestive and conducive to irreparable mistaken identification that he was denied due process of law. . . . The practice of showing suspects singly to persons for the purpose of identification, and not as part of a lineup, has been widely condemned." However, whether or not due process has been violated depends on a totality of the circumstances surrounding it. Here the showing of Stovall to the victim was imperative. She was the only one who could have exonerated him. She might have died. The hospital was not far from the jail. She could not go to the jail and a lineup was out of the question. Hence, there was found to be no due process violation in the identification.

In *Simmons v. United States*,[14] a savings and loan association in Chicago was robbed by two men in 1964. Officers located a car matching the one described by an employee of the association. A man named Andrews was a suspect. FBI agents obtained pictures of Andrews and Simmons from Andrews' sister who told agents that Andrews and Simmons were together on the day of the robbery. The agents showed the employees at least six snapshots which consisted mostly of group pictures of Andrews and Simmons. The pictures were exhibited to each employee separately. All of the employees identified Simmons, but none of them identified Andrews. They later reaffirmed their identification from pictures. Simmons claimed that the identification procedure fatally tainted his conviction. The United States Supreme Court pointed out that improper use of pictures may cause witnesses to err in identification and that the danger is increased where several pictures are displayed and the picture of one person recurs. However, despite the hazards, identification by photograph is widely used by officers. The court stated, "[W]e hold that each case must be considered on its own facts, and that convictions based on eyewitness identification at trial following a pretrial identification by photograph will be set aside on that ground only if the photographic identification procedure was so impermissibly suggestive as to give rise to a very substantial likelihood of

---

[14]Simmons v. United States, 390   1247 (1968).
U.S. 377, 88 S.Ct. 967, 19 L.Ed.2d

irreparable misidentification."[15] The court then pointed out that in this case photographic identification had to be resorted to. The perpetrators were still at large. The agents needed to determine if they were on the right tract. There was little likelihood of misidentification of Simmons. All employee witnesses identified Simmons. The bank had been well-lighted. The robbers did not wear masks. Andrews was not identified. Witnesses had no doubt. Hence, the identification procedures did not violate due process.

In *Foster v. California*,[16] Davis, the night manager of a Western Union office, had been robbed by three men. Clay surrendered and implicated Foster and Grice. Only Davis and the robbers were witnesses to the crime. Davis was called to the police station to view a lineup of three men. Foster was about 6' tall, the other two in the lineup were about 5' 6". Foster wore a leather jacket similar to one worn by one of the robbers. Davis could not identify Foster positively but thought he was the man. Davis asked to talk with Foster and did so alone in a room with him. Davis was still uncertain. Ten days later police arranged another lineup. Foster was the only man in the second lineup who had been in the first. This time Davis was convinced that Foster was the man. At trial Davis testified to his identification of Foster in the lineups as set out above. The only other evidence against Foster was the testimony of Clay, an acknowledged accomplice in the robbery. The identification was made before the decision in *Wade*. However, the Court pointed out that judged by a totality of the circumstances, the conduct of an identification may be so unnecessarily suggestive and conducive to irreparable mistaken identity as to amount to a denial of due process. The court concluded that the facts of this case amounted to such a due process violation and reversed the conviction. The court concluded that *all* the identification testimony should have been excluded.[17]

In *Moore v. Illinois*,[18] the defendant was arrested for rape. The victim appeared the next day at a preliminary hearing which was conducted to determine whether or not the defendant was to be bound over to the grand jury. The defendant's name was called and he was lead before the bench. The victim was in the courtroom and also was called by the judge. The prosecuting attorney outlined evidence connecting the defendant with the crime and moved for a continuance of the hearing until fingerprint evi-

---

[15]Simmons v. United States, 390 U.S. 377, 384, 88 S.Ct. 967, 19 L.Ed.2d 1247 (1968).

[16]Foster v. California, 394 U.S. 440, 89 S.Ct. 1127, 22 L.Ed.2d 402 (1969).

[17]Neil v. Biggers, 409 U.S. 188, 197, 93 S.Ct. 375, 34 L.Ed.2d 401 (1972).

[18]Moore v. Illinois, 434 U.S. 220, 98 S.Ct. 458, 54 L.Ed.2d 424 (1977). Moore is discussed at length in Eiland v. State, 246 Ga. 112, 114 (2), 268 S.E.2d 922 (1980).

dence could be presented. The victim identified the defendant and a continuance was granted. Moore was not represented by counsel at the time. Counsel was appointed for Moore after he had been indicted. Defense counsel moved to suppress the identification of Moore by the victim because he was not represented by counsel. The motion was denied and at trial on direct examination the victim testified that she had identified Moore at the preliminary hearing and that she also had made an in-court identification. The defendant's conviction was affirmed by the Illinois courts and Moore sought a writ of habeas corpus in federal court. The Supreme Court pointed out (1) that the *Wade* per se exclusionary rule of pre-trial identification testimony applied to an uncounseled identification at a preliminary hearing. The right attaches "at or after the initiation of adversary judicial criminal proceedings—whether by way of formal charge, preliminary hearing, indictment, information, or arraignment."[19] The court also pointed out that (2) counsel's presence can serve both his client's interests and those of the prosecution "by objecting to suggestive features of a procedure before they influence a witness' identification";[20] (3) the testimony of pre-trial identification elicited by the prosecution in its case-in-chief enhances the witnesses' in-court identification; (4) where testimony is the direct result of an illegal lineup, the prosecution is not entitled to an opportunity to show that the testimony had an independent source;[21] (5) the right to have counsel present at an identification at or after the initiation of adversary criminal proceedings exists whether the identification is at a lineup, a one-on-one identification or a judicial proceeding.[22] The denial of habeas corpus was reversed and the case was remanded for a determination of whether the failure to exclude that evidence was harmless constitutional error.

In *Neil v. Biggers,*[23] the victim had been raped in 1965. She saw her assailant in the lighted house and then saw him in the moonlight for some 10 or 15 minutes. She gave a description of her assailant to officers. During the next seven months she was shown suspects in lineups and showups and some 30 or 40 photos. She did not identify any of them. The defendant, Biggers, was be-

---

[19]Moore v. Illinois, 434 U.S. 220, 226, 98 S.Ct. 458, 54 L.Ed.2d 424 (1977) (citing Kirby v. Illinois, 406 U.S. 682, 92 S.Ct. 1877, 32 L.Ed.2d 411 (1972)). In Lomax v. Alabama, 629 F.2d 413, 414 (5th Cir. 1980), the court said that the adversary criminal proceeding did not begin with an arrest pursuant to a warrant.

[20]Moore v. Illinois, 434 U.S. 220,

225, 98 S.Ct. 458, 54 L.Ed.2d 424 (1977).

[21]Moore v. Illinois, 434 U.S. 220, 226, 98 S.Ct. 458, 54 L.Ed.2d 424 (1977).

[22]Moore v. Illinois, 434 U.S. 220, 229, 98 S.Ct. 458, 54 L.Ed.2d 424 (1977).

[23]Neil v. Biggers, 409 U.S. 188, 93 S.Ct. 375, 34 L.Ed.2d 401 (1972).

ing held in jail on an unrelated charge and the victim was called
to the police station to look at him. Officers said they were unable to get persons looking like Biggers so as to arrange a lineup,
so a showup was conducted. At that showup, at the victim's
request, Biggers said "shut up or I'll kill you." He was positively
identified at that time and later convicted. The Tennessee
Supreme Court affirmed and he filed a petition for habeas corpus
in federal court asserting a due process violation. The United
States Supreme Court concluded that the identification was unnecessarily suggestive but pointed out it "is the likelihood of misidentification which violates a defendant's right to due process
. . . [s]uggestive confrontations are disapproved because they
increase the likelihood of misidentification . . . the admission of
evidence of a showup without more does not violate due process."[24]
The "central question [is] whether under the 'totality of the circumstances' the identification was reliable even though the
confrontation procedure was suggestive. . . ." The "factors to be
considered in evaluating the likelihood of misidentification
include [1] the opportunity of the witness to view the criminal at
the time of the crime, [2] the witness' degree of attention, [3] the
accuracy of the witnesses' prior description of the criminal, [4]
the level of certainty demonstrated by the witness at the
confrontation, and [5] the length of time between the crime and
the confrontation." After reviewing the facts of the case in light of
the factors suggested, the Court concluded that there was no
substantial likelihood of misidentification and held that the habeas corpus should not be granted.

In *Perry v. New Hampshire*,[25] the United States Supreme Court
addressed for the first time, the issue of whether an identification
which is not tainted by suggestive circumstances created by the
police is a proper subject for a pre-trial motion to suppress or
exclude. After car break-ins in an apartment complex, in response
to a police investigator's request for a description of the man she
saw breaking into the cars, the witness responded by simply
pointing out her kitchen window at an African American, the
defendant, who, at the time, was talking to another police officer
in the parking lot. At a subsequent photo lineup, the witness was
unable to identify the defendant. The Court held that in the
absence of "improper law enforcement activity," the reliability of
a witness's identification should be tested through "the rights
and opportunities generally designed for that purpose[:] . . . the
presence of counsel at postindictment lineups, vigorous cross-

---

[24]Neil v. Biggers, 409 U.S. 188, 198, 93 S.Ct. 375, 34 L.Ed.2d 401 (1972).

[25]Perry v. New Hampshire, 132 S. Ct. 716, 181 L. Ed. 2d 694 (2012). See Gandy v. State, 290 Ga. 166, 718 S.E.2d 287 (2011).

examination, protective rules of evidence and jury instructions on both the fallibility of eyewitness identification and the requirement of proof beyond a reasonable doubt." The Court concluded that unless a witness's identification is procured through unnecessarily suggestive procedures arranged by police authorities, due process does not require a pre-trial judicial inquiry into the reliability of a witness's identification of a defendant. The holding was premised on the basis that the exclusion of identification testimony which is tainted by improper police conduct serves as a deterrent to such procedures by law enforcement. When the police are not involved, the right to counsel and cross-examination of eyewitnesses is sufficient to secure a fair trial for the defendant.

§ 6:4 Lineups

A lineup is distinguished from a showup by the fact that a lineup requires the witness to identify the alleged perpetrator of a crime from among a number of persons while a showup is a one-on-one identification whereby the witness is shown only one person and in effect asked if this is the person who committed the crime.

Lineups must be considered from two standpoints: First, in some situations there is a per se exclusion of the pre-trial identification testimony. Second, the due process standard must be considered. Due process considerations are discussed in § 6:8, infra.

Under the authority of *United States v. Wade*[1] and *Moore v. Illinois,*[2] there is a general per se exclusionary rule which applies to a pre-trial identification at or after the initiation of adversary judicial criminal proceedings unless the defendant is represented by counsel who is present at the time of the identification. In *Moore,* " 'adversary judicial criminal proceedings' were [said to be] initiated when a preliminary hearing was held," but this rule has been held not to apply where the pre-trial identification was at the place scheduled for a preliminary hearing but no evidence was introduced and the case was simply referred to juvenile court.[3] In *Victorine v. State,*[4] the Georgia Supreme Court continued to rely on a Georgia case decided before *Moore* and

---

[Section 6:4]

[1]United States v. Wade, 388 U.S. 218, 87 S.Ct. 1926, 18 L.Ed.2d 1149 (1967). *Wade* is discussed in § 6:3, supra.

[2]Moore v. Illinois, 434 U.S. 220, 98 S.Ct. 458, 54 L.Ed.2d 424 (1977).

Moore is discussed in § 6:3, supra. Contra, Jones v. State, 171 Ga. App. 184, 185 (1), 319 S.E.2d 18 (1984).

[3]Wilson v. State, 181 Ga. App. 435, 436 (2), 352 S.E.2d 618 (1987). In Ferguson v. State, 211 Ga. App. 218, 220 (1), 438 S.E.2d 682 (1993), the

concluded that "there is no right to counsel at a pre-indictment photo lineup." In *Phillips v. State*,[5] the Georgia Court of Appeals pointed out that the Sixth Amendment right to counsel at a lineup is *"offense-specific."* Thus, "[t]he right does not apply with respect to one offense where adversary proceedings have been commenced with respect to a different offense, but not that offense." In *Phillips*, the defendant had been indicted for burglary at the time of the lineup, but he had not yet been indicted for the unrelated charge of rape.

Nevertheless, a defendant may waive his right to the presence of counsel at a lineup.[6] In *Jenkins v. State*,[7] the Georgia Court of Appeals held that where defense counsel is notified of a lineup and he simply elects not to attend, this amounts to a waiver of the right to have counsel present. However, an identification in the absence of counsel at such time does not prevent an in-court identification at the time of trial if the in-court identification has an independent origin.[8] Also, it must be remembered that there is no due process right to a pre-trial lineup.[9]

A number of sets of rules or guidelines for lineup identifications have been suggested by and for various groups of law enforcement officers.[10] These suggestions may be helpful to counsel attending a lineup and in connection with the cross-examination of witnesses who have given eyewitness identification testimony.

Some of the most important guidelines or rules which have been suggested are as follows:[11]

(1) All persons in the lineup should be of the same general age

---

court stated that "[n]o constitutional right exists to have counsel present at a pre-indictment lineup."

[4]Victorine v. State, 264 Ga. 580, 582 (5), 449 S.E.2d 91 (1994).

[5]Phillips v. State, 204 Ga. App. 698, 699 (1), 420 S.E.2d 316 (1992); McNeil v. Wisconsin, 501 U.S. 171, 111 S.Ct. 2204, 115 L.Ed.2d 158 (1991).

[6]Martin v. State, 132 Ga. App. 658 (2), 209 S.E.2d 103 (1974).

[7]Jenkins v. State, 167 Ga. App. 840 (1), 308 S.E.2d 14 (1983). In *Jenkins*, the court also held that it was immaterial that defense counsel was not told that officers would also seek a voice identification.

[8]United States v. Wade, 388 U.S. 218, 87 S.Ct. 1926, 18 L.Ed.2d 1149 (1967).

[9]Code v. Montgomery, 725 F.2d 1316 (11th Cir. 1984).

[10]6 Am. Crim. L. Q. 93 (1968); 4 Defender Newsletter 55 (1967), based on Clark County (Las Vegas), Nevada, also reported in 4 Crim. L. Bull. 98 (1968); Sobel, "Assailing Suggestion: Evolving Limitations on Abuse of Pretrial Criminal Identification Methods," 38 Brooklyn L. Rev. 261, 304 (1971). See Annot., 39 A.L.R.3d 487 (1971); "Eye Witness Identification," 20 Am. Jur. Proof of Facts 2d 539; Read, "Lawyers at Lineups: Constitutional Necessity or Avoidable Extravagance," 17 U.C.L.A. L. Rev. 339 (1969); Comment, 29 U. Pitt. L. Rev. 651 (1967).

[11]These proposals have been taken from a model statute proposed by Murray, "The Criminal Lineup at Home and Abroad," 610 Utah L. Rev.

and race and have similar characteristics.[12]

(2) Clothing worn by each person should be similar.[13]

(3) Any movements or statements should be made by each person in the lineup, one at a time. It now seems clear that under Georgia law a person in a lineup may be compelled to speak certain words.[14]

(4) A color photograph of the lineup should be taken and developed as soon as possible.

(5) A witness should be prevented from seeing the defendant in custody prior to lineup.[15]

(6) Witnesses should not be shown a photograph of the defendant before the lineup.[16]

(7) If more than one person is to view a lineup, the witnesses should do so one at a time and out of the presence of the other.[17]

(8) No actions should be taken or statements made to a witness to suggest that a suspect is standing in any particular place.[18]

(9) As few persons as possible should be allowed in the room when the lineup is conducted.

(10) The witness, before entering the room where the lineup is to be conducted, should be given a form on which his identification can be marked and signed.

(11) There should be at least six persons in the lineup.

(12) Statements by persons in a lineup should not be requested

---

627-628 (1966), and have been quoted with approval in United States v. Wade, 388 U.S. 218, 236, 87 S.Ct. 1926, 18 L.Ed.2d 1149 (1967). For pertinent Georgia cases, see West's Georgia Digest, Criminal Law, Key No. 339.8.

[12]Meeks v. Moore, 216 F.3d 951 (11th Cir. 2000); Young v. State, 243 Ga. 546, 255 S.E.2d 20 (1979); Smith v. State, 239 Ga. 744, 238 S.E.2d 884 (1977) (no due process violation in lineup where several members had facial scars and all members were the same race despite small variation in members' heights and ages).

[13]Cf. Heng v. State, 251 Ga. App. 274, 554 S.E.2d 243 (2001) (lineup impermissibly suggestive where only defendant wore an orange, sleeveless jacket that matched victim's description of suspect's clothing); Raheem v. Kelly, 257 F.3d 122, 134(II)(A)(1) (2d Cir. 2001) (citing U.S. v. Williams, 469

F.2d 540 (D.C. Cir. 1972)). But cf. Cooper v. State, 281 Ga. 760, 760(2), 642 S.E.2d 817 (2007).

[14]Tate v. State, 153 Ga. App. 508, 510, 265 S.E.2d 818 (1980). See Campbell v. State, 228 Ga. App. 258, 262(3)(A), 491 S.E.2d 477 (1997).

[15]See Banks v. State, 203 Ga. App. 355, 416 S.E.2d 866 (1992). But see Mobley v. State, 277 Ga. App. 267, 269(1), 626 S.E.2d 248 (2006).

[16]See Thornton v. State, 238 Ga. 160, 231 S.E.2d 729 (1977).

[17]Young v. State, 243 Ga. 546, 255 S.E.2d 20 (1979). See McKenzie v. State, 162 Ga. App. 522, 292 S.E.2d 722 (1982).

[18]In Hodnett v. State, 269 Ga. 115, 118 (4), 498 S.E.2d 737 (1998), the court held that a lineup is not flawed by the fact that a police officer told the defendant where to stand.

unless a witness suggests it. If statements are made, all participants should repeat the same words.

(13) If counsel is present, he should be allowed to make suggestions.[19]

(14) Prior to the lineup, the witness should give a detailed description of the perpetrator. This description should be reduced to writing before the lineup.

(15) If possible, law enforcement officers should not be used in lineups.

(16) Some authorities feel that "blank lineups"—lineups which are held in the absence of the suspect—should be utilized. Blank lineups could prevent a witness from picking out the person in the lineup looking most like the accused even if the person is not the perpetrator of the crime.[20]

(17) The names and addresses of all persons participating in the lineup should be preserved.

Since July 1, 2016, law enforcement agencies which conduct live or photo lineups are now required to adopt written policies for using such procedures for the purpose of determining whether a witness can identify someone as the perpetrator of an alleged crime.[21] These procedures must include such requirements as: who can conduct a live or photo lineup; the manner in which a photo lineup is to be conducted; instructions to be provided to the witness; the minimum number of "fillers," individuals who are not suspects, for live and photo lineups; and that the witness's level of confidence in his or her identification be documented in the words of the witness. These policies must be made available for public inspection. The failure of a law enforcement agency to comply with the statute and/or its policies adopted thereto, may be considered by the court in connection with a motion to suppress the identification but will not mandate that exclusion is

---

[19]Foster v. State, 156 Ga. App. 672, 676, 275 S.E.2d 745 (1980) (Quillian, J. concurring) (citing Moore v. Illinois, 434 U.S. 220, 225, 98 S. Ct. 458, 54 L. Ed. 2d 424 (1977)).

[20]In People v. White, 151 Misc. 2d 171, 174, 572 N.Y.S.2d 840, 842 (Sup 1991) (where an eyewitness views a "blank lineup," one which does not include defendant but all participants closely resemble defendant, and makes no identification, a subsequent identification in another lineup would constitute "extraordinarily strong evidence"). In People v. Guerea, 78

Misc.2d 907, 358 N.Y.S.2d 925, 928 (1974), the court said, "Even where there has been no pre-lineup suggestive conduct, a witness viewing a lineup usually believes that a suspect is within the array. . . . Logically, the police would not have brought him to the lineup if there were no suspect. The use of a 'blank' lineup would serve to minimize this inherent suggestiveness by testing the witness' ability to make no identification in a situation which suggests the presence of a suspect."

[21]O.C.G.A. § 17-20-2.

required.[22]

In Georgia, it has been held that a suspect has no right to refuse to take part in a lineup.[23] Generally, if a person is lawfully incarcerated on an unrelated charge, he may be forced to be a "stand in" in a lineup.[24]

In *Foster v. State*,[25] the Georgia Court of Appeals treated a pretrial identification in the courtroom as a lineup. The court said that two witnesses to a robbery (who had never identified the defendant during a four-month period between the crime and the trial) were asked by a representative of the district attorney to identify the assailant from a group of defendants seated in the jury box of the courtroom, before the trial started. At the trial defense counsel objected to the identification testimony of one of these witnesses. The court concluded that if defense counsel was not present when the witness (who testified over objection as to the identity of the defendant) identified the defendant in the jury box, the admission of such pre-trial identification, and all of the witnesses' identification testimony, was error unless the trial judge determined that the witness' in-court identification had an origin independent "from her lineup identification, based on the standards set forth in . . . *Wade*." The court distinguished *Foster* from *Prater v. State*[26] where witnesses on their own initiative attended a court proceeding where they expected to see the defendant. The court indicated that *Wade* condemned state action in providing for identification in the absence of defense counsel. In *Robinson v. State*,[27] the court found that there was no lineup where a witness on her own initiative attended an arraignment calendar call. The district attorney talked to the witness when she was noticed and asked if she could identify any of the robbers. The witness then pointed out the defendant. The court reasoned that the identification was not orchestrated by the police or the district attorney.

---

[22]O.C.G.A. § 17-20-3.

[23]Wilson v. State, 237 Ga. 657, 229 S.E.2d 424 (1976). In People v. Nelson, 40 Ill.2d 146, 238 N.E.2d 378 (1968), the court approved an identification where the defendant was uncooperative during the procedure and attempted to hide his face from the witness at the time of the identification. In 22A C.J.S. Criminal Law § 616, we find the statement that "the quantum of suspicion required to compel a person to participate in a lineup is the existence of facts sufficient to constitute probable cause to arrest . . . ." See § 6:9, infra, on motions for lineups.

[24]E.g., People v. Whitaker, 64 N.Y.2d 347, 486 N.Y.S.2d 895, 476 N.E.2d 294 (1985).

[25]Foster v. State, 156 Ga. App. 672, 275 S.E.2d 745 (1980).

[26]Prater v. State, 148 Ga. App. 831, 841 (7), 253 S.E.2d 223 (1979). Accord, Daniels v. State, 252 Ga. 30, 31 (1), 310 S.E.2d 904 (1984).

[27]Robinson v. State, 164 Ga. App. 379, 382, 296 S.E.2d 225 (1982). Cf. Brown v. State, 171 Ga. App. 70, 72 (3), 318 S.E.2d 498 (1984).

In *Ely v. State*,[28] the court pointed out that evidence of such a courtroom identification arranged by the district attorney and without the knowledge of the defendant was not admissible under *Wade*. However, this alone does not prevent the witness, during the trial, from identifying the defendant if the trial identification has an independent origin.

In *Wiley v. State*,[29] the court upheld the admissibility at trial of an identification at a "lineup" at which only the hands of participants were visible. The victim had previously given a detailed description of her assailant's hands. However, she had been unable to identify him at an earlier conventional lineup, presumably because her assailant was wearing a mask at the time of the crime. Because counsel was present at the lineup, the court properly applied the general two-step due process standard discussed in § 6:8, infra.

The statement of an officer to a witness before a lineup that a suspect had been arrested has been said to be no more suggestive than the lineup itself.[30] However, such statements should be avoided.[31]

See 29 Am. Jur. 2d, Evidence § 628 (1994) on suggestive lineups. Generally, see "Lineups and Showups: Admissibility and Effect of Pretrial Identification," 19 Am. Jur. Proof of Facts 2d 435; "Unreliability of Eyewitness Identification," 18 Am. Jur. Proof of Facts 2d 361. See also 29 Am. Jur. 2d Evidence § 371.4. See Annotation, "Admissibility of In-Court Identification as Affected by Pretrial Encounter That Was Not Result of Action by Police, Prosecutors and the Like," 86 A.L.R.5th 463 (2001).

§ 6:5 Showups

As previously mentioned, a showup occurs when a witness views a single individual for purposes of identification. This means of identification is inherently suggestive[1] and has been widely condemned[2] when used by law enforcement officers.[3]

---

[28]Ely v. State, 172 Ga. App. 737, 324 S.E.2d 569 (1984).

[29]Wiley v. State, 250 Ga. 343, 346 (1)(a), 296 S.E.2d 714 (1982).

[30]Mitchell v. State, 236 Ga. 251, 254, 223 S.E.2d 650 (1976).

[31]Reid v. State, 210 Ga. App. 783, 786 (2), 437 S.E.2d 646 (1993).

[Section 6:5]

[1]See Butler v. State, 290 Ga. 412, 721 S.E.2d 876 (2012).

[2]Stovall v. Denno, 388 U.S. 293, 302, 87 S.Ct. 1967, 18 L.Ed.2d 1199 (1967).

[3]In Duck v. State, 250 Ga. 592, 597, 300 S.E.2d 121 (1983), the court emphasized that the Due Process Clause of the Fourteenth Amendment relates only to state action. In the *Duck* case a witness attended a preliminary hearing of the defendant at the request of a neighbor. The witness recognized the defendant and identified him at the trial.

Nonetheless, as the court observed in *Horne v. State*,[4] "the identification need not be excluded as long as the identification was reliable notwithstanding any suggestive procedure under all the circumstances. The factors to be considered in evaluating the likelihood of misidentification include the opportunity of the witness to view the criminal at the time of the crime, the witness' degree of attention, the accuracy of the witness' prior description of the criminal, the level of certainty demonstrated by the witness at the confrontation, and the length of time between the crime and the confrontation." (Citations omitted.)

However, courts have generally upheld admission of in-court identification when the prior one-on-one showups were reasonably and fairly conducted at or near the time of the offense.[5] Such early identification is needed (1) to guide officers in determining whether or not to look further for the perpetrator; (2) because the accuracy and reliability of identification is likely to be greater at that time; and (3) to permit the speedy release of an innocent person who is in custody.[6] For these reasons, delays in identification of as much as two or three hours have not been condemned.[7] However, an identification after a delay of as much as four or five hours has been held to be too suggestive.[8]

In *M. A. K. v. State*,[9] a juvenile was arrested and carried to the victim of a burglary to see if he were the burglar. The victim identified the juvenile. The Georgia statute, the material parts of which are set out in § 5:8, supra, provides that a "person taking a child into custody, with all reasonable speed and without first taking the child elsewhere, shall . . . [take] the child immediately before the juvenile court or promptly contact a juvenile court intake officer." The juvenile contended that this statute had been violated by taking him to the victim of the burglary for

---

[4]Horne v. State, 260 Ga. App. 640, 643 (4), 580 S.E.2d 644 (2003).

[5]Rogers v. State, 205 Ga. App. 739, 741 (1), 423 S.E.2d 435 (1992); Kirby v. Illinois, 406 U.S. 682, 92 S.Ct. 1877, 32 L.Ed.2d 411 (1972) (identification at police station shortly after arrest). Kirby is discussed in § 6:3, supra. See Bates v. United States, 405 F.2d 1104 (C.A.D.C. 1968), opinion by later Chief Justice Burger.

See 29 Am. Jur. 2d Evidence §§ 371.2, 371.6.

See Brown v. State, 161 Ga. App. 55, 56 (2), 289 S.E.2d 9 (1982); Horton v. State, 163 Ga. App. 809, 810 (1), 295 S.E.2d 554 (1982); Hoffa v. State, 165 Ga. App. 512, 301 S.E.2d 679 (1983); Wright v. State, 166 Ga.

App. 295 (1), 304 S.E.2d 105 (1983) ("a little over an hour").

[6]Arnold v. State, 155 Ga. App. 782, 272 S.E.2d 751 (1980); Bennefield v. Brown, 228 Ga. 705, 187 S.E.2d 865 (1972); Russell v. United States, 408 F.2d 1280 (D.C.Cir. 1969).

[7]Bennefield v. Brown, 228 Ga. 705, 187 S.E.2d 865 (1972) (two hours); Hoover v. Slayton, 341 F.Supp. 317 (W.D.Va.1972) (three or four hours).

[8]Smith v. Coiner, 473 F.2d 877 (4th Cir. 1973) (five hours); McRae v. United States, 420 F.2d 1283 (D.C.Cir. 1969) (four hours).

[9]M.A.K. v. State, 171 Ga. App. 151, 152, 318 S.E.2d 828 (1984).

identification. The court held that the statute was directory and did not limit the authority of the officer to take the juvenile for identification.

After the exigencies connected with an identification shortly after an arrest have dissipated, there is a right to the presence of counsel at such identification at or after the initiation of the adversary criminal judicial proceeding.[10] See § 6:4, supra, on lineups. If this right to counsel is violated at such an identification there is a per se rule which prevents the admission of such pre-trial identification at the trial. However, this alone does not prevent an in-court identification at the time of trial.[11]

If the showup or lineup takes place before the initiation of the adversary criminal judicial proceeding, but after the dissipation of the exigencies connected with the arrest, it seems that in-court testimony of the pre-trial identification will be excluded only if the pre-trial identification amounts to a due process violation, i.e., if it was so suggestive as to result in misidentification.[12] However, here again, the tainted pre-trial identification does not automatically prevent a later in-court identification of the defendant at the time of trial.[13]

An "accidental" identification of a defendant by a witness even after the initiation of the adversary criminal judicial proceeding will not automatically prevent in-court testimony of the pre-trial identification.[14] Thus, in *Herron v. State*,[15] the victim and her brother had been at the police station to view some pictures. The victim could not positively identify her assailant from the pictures but two of the pictures reminded her of her assailant. The defendant was then released and he left at the same time as the victim. The evidence was that the victim by chance saw the defendant. The victim then stated that the defendant was her assailant. The trial judge was affirmed in refusing to strike the one-on-one showup identification testimony because there was no showing that the confrontation was staged. The court concluded that the confrontation had not been arranged and thus there was

---

[10]Moore v. Illinois, 434 U.S. 220, 98 S.Ct. 458, 54 L.Ed.2d 424 (1977). Moore is discussed in § 6:3, supra.

[11]United States v. Wade, 388 U.S. 218, 87 S.Ct. 1926, 18 L.Ed.2d 1149 (1967); Anthony v. State, 160 Ga. App. 842, 844, 287 S.E.2d 686 (1982).

[12]Neil v. Biggers, 409 U.S. 188, 198, 93 S.Ct. 375, 34 L.Ed.2d 401 (1972).

[13]Neil v. Biggers, 409 U.S. 188, 198, 93 S.Ct. 375, 34 L.Ed.2d 401 (1972).

[14]United States v. Wade, 388 U.S. 218, 87 S.Ct. 1926, 18 L.Ed.2d 1149 (1967). Cf. United States v. Isenberg, 343 F.Supp. 25 (W.D.Pa.1972); Cantrell v. State, 162 Ga. App. 699, 700 (2), 293 S.E.2d 2 (1982).

[15]Herron v. State, 155 Ga. App. 791, 793 (3), 272 S.E.2d 756 (1980). Cf. Duffy v. State, 156 Ga. App. 847, 849 (5), 275 S.E.2d 658 (1980) (chance encounter); State v. Flash, 418 A.2d 158 (Me.1980); United States v. Brown, 461 F.2d 134 (C.A.D.C.1971).

no due process violation. There was said not to be a "very substantial likelihood of irreparable misidentification" and the pre-trial identification was not impermissibly suggestive. Hence, testimony of the pre-trial identification was admissible.

See § 6:8, infra, on due process and identification. See Annotation, "Admissibility of Evidence of Showup Identification as Affected by Allegedly Suggestive Showup Procedures," 39 A.L.R.3d 791 (1971).

See 29 Am. Jur. 2d, Evidence § 629 (1994). Generally, see "Lineups and Showups: Admissibility and Effect of Pretrial Identification," 19 Am. Jur. Proof of Facts 2d 435; "Unreliability of Eyewitness Identification," 18 Am. Jur. Proof of Facts 2d 361.

§ 6:6 Picture identification

Much of what has been said about lineup and showup identification applies to an identification based on pictures, in that reliability is the linchpin of any identification procedure.[1] However, there is one very important difference. Whereas there is generally a per se right to the exclusion of a pre-trial identification at a lineup or showup, at or after the initiation of the adversary judicial criminal proceeding if counsel is not present, no such automatic exclusion applies to testimony regarding a photographic identification.[2]

In *United States v. Ash*,[3] the United States Supreme Court concluded that the dangers of mistaken identification are not sufficient to require a per se exclusionary rule of testimony of a photographic identification. However, the admissibility of such testimony is still limited by the due process clause. In *Branch v. Estelle*,[4] the Fifth Circuit pointed out that the distinction between a review of a corporal lineup and a photographic lineup is the fact that a photographic lineup can be reconstructed for purposes of trial and appellate court review. However, the court said that in a situation where officers fail to preserve the photographic array, there is a presumption that the array is impermissibly suggestive. Nevertheless, in *Daniel v. State*,[5] the Georgia Court of Appeals held that the failure to preserve the photos used in a pre-trial lineup "merely goes to the weight to be afforded the pictorial lineup and not to its admissibility."

[Section 6:6]

[1]Daniel v. State, 150 Ga. App. 798, 258 S.E.2d 604 (1979).

[2]United States v. Ash, 413 U.S. 300, 93 S.Ct. 2568, 37 L.Ed.2d 619 (1973).

[3]United States v. Ash, 413 U.S. 300, 93 S.Ct. 2568, 37 L.Ed.2d 619 (1973).

[4]Branch v. Estelle, 631 F.2d 1229, 1234 (5th Cir. 1980).

[5]Daniel v. State, 185 Ga. App. 228, 230 (2), 363 S.E.2d 634 (1987). Cf. Allison v. State, 213 Ga. App. 195, 197 (2), 444 S.E.2d 347 (1994).

In *Brewer v. State*,[6] the court affirmed the admission of a photograph of the defendant even though the photograph on the back contained the signature of the victim which had been placed there at the time she identified the photograph.

In *Huggins v. State*,[7] the court held that testimony of a picture identification was admissible even though the pictures used had been lost ("the absence of the pictures at the time of trial . . . goes to the weight").

In the 2001 case of *White v. State*,[8] the Georgia Supreme Court held that "[i]n the absence of some other viable hearsay exception, such as 'necessity' or 'res gestae,' a law enforcement officer may not testify to a pre-trial identification of the accused unless the person who actually made the identification testifies at trial and is subject to cross-examination."

The display of a single picture is regarded as being too suggestive.[9] Hence, where there is such an impermissibly suggestive identification, it must be determined whether under a totality of the circumstances the display of a single photograph was conducive to irreparable mistaken identification.[10] Even though the display of a single photograph is impermissibly suggestive, still this does not prevent an in-court identification if the in-court identification has an independent source.[11]

If there are a number of pictures and the picture of one person appears more than once,[12] or if an officer tells a witness that he has other evidence that one of the persons pictured committed the crime, the chance of misidentification increases.[13] It has been

---

[6]Brewer v. State, 219 Ga. App. 16, 18 (2), 463 S.E.2d 906 (1995).

[7]Huggins v. State, 173 Ga. App. 457, 459 (2), 326 S.E.2d 821 (1985). Cf. Jackson v. State, 261 Ga. 734, 735 (4), 410 S.E.2d 115 (1991).

[8]White v. State, 273 Ga. 787, 788, 546 S.E.2d 514 (2001). The *White* case overruled Haralson v. State, 234 Ga. 406, 408 (4), 216 S.E.2d 304 (1975), Neal v. State, 211 Ga. App. 829, 830 (1)(b), 440 S.E.2d 717 (1994), and a number of earlier Georgia cases.

[9]Talley v. State, 137 Ga. App. 548, 551, 224 S.E.2d 455 (1976); Simmons v. United States, 390 U.S. 377, 383, 88 S.Ct. 967, 19 L.Ed.2d 1247 (1968). However, this alone generally is not regarded as violating due process. State v. Hill, 209 Kan. 688, 498 P.2d 92 (1972) (violates due pro-

cess); United States v. Baxter, 492 F.2d 150 (9th Cir. 1973) (does not violate due process).

See Bonner v. State, 278 Ga. App. 855, 630 S.E.2d 127 (2006) (suggestive pre-trial lineup may still be admissible under totality of circumstances).

[10]Bradley v. State, 152 Ga. App. 902, 903, 264 S.E.2d 332 (1980).

[11]United States v. Cannington, 729 F.2d 702 (11th Cir. 1984).

[12]However, it has been held that this alone does not amount to a due process violation. United States v. McQueen, 458 F.2d 1049 (3d Cir. 1972). Accord, Cleveland v. State, 164 Ga. App. 478, 480, 298 S.E.2d 22 (1982).

[13]Simmons v. United States, 390 U.S. 377, 383, 88 S.Ct. 967, 19 L.Ed.2d 1247 (1968).

held that the fact that the picture of the defendant was eight years old does not make the array impermissible.[14]

Ideally the pictures presented should be of the same kind,[15] size[16] and appearance.[17] In *Wright v. State*,[18] the court held the photographic identification was not impermissibly suggestive where six photographs of black males who appeared to be about the same age as the defendant with similar medium complexion, hair, and no facial hair were presented to the victim. However, in *Cheeves v. State*,[19] there was some indication that the backgrounds of some of the photographs were different, two of the photographs were slightly smaller than the others, and some of the persons pictured had on hats while others did not. The Georgia Court of Appeals affirmed the trial judge's action in overruling the defendant's request to exclude the eyewitness identification. In *Heard v. State*,[20] the court affirmed the trial judge's finding that the photo array was not impermissibly suggestive where the defendant's picture had a different colored background and his face may have been larger than the faces in the other photos. Likewise, in *Brewer v. State*,[21] the court held that "[t]he contention that the shading and tone of defendant's photograph made

---

[14]McDaniel v. State, 169 Ga. App. 123, 124 (2), 312 S.E.2d 159 (1983).

[15]But in People v. Hudson, 7 Ill.App.3d 333, 287 N.E.2d 297 (1972), no due process violation was found where defendant's picture was in color and the others were in black and white.

[16]However, in State v. Farrow, 61 N.J. 434, 294 A.2d 873 (1972), it was found that there was no due process violation simply because defendant's picture was an inch wider than the other four.

[17]But in United States ex rel. Clemmer v. Mazurkiewicz, 365 F.Supp. 1158 (E.D.Pa.1973), due process was found not to have been violated where all pictures were mug shots except for that of defendant. However, in Smith v. State, 244 Ga. App. 165, 166, 534 S.E.2d 903 (2000), the court affirmed a photographic lineup even though the defendant was the only person shown without a shirt where the attacker was not wearing a shirt at the time of the attack.

In Harper v. State, 251 Ga. 183 (2), 304 S.E.2d 693 (1983), the court

held that a photographic array was not impermissibly suggestive even though "(1) all but the appellant's photograph and one other in the array were noticeably green in color; [and] (2) . . . [the witness] was told by police prior to being shown the photographic array, that they had a suspect in custody . . . ."

In Jones v. State, 251 Ga. 361, 362 (1), 306 S.E.2d 265 (1983), the court held that there was no substantial likelihood of irreparable mistaken identification where one of the pictures shown to witnesses "had a different tint than the others."

[18]Wright v. State, 228 Ga. App. 779, 781 (2), 492 S.E.2d 680 (1997).

[19]Cheeves v. State, 157 Ga. App. 566, 278 S.E.2d 148 (1981). Accord, Whitaker v. State, 269 Ga. 462, 463 (2), 499 S.E.2d 888 (1998).

[20]Heard v. State, 210 Ga. App. 805, 806 (2), 437 S.E.2d 496 (1993), overruled on other grounds, 274 Ga. 196, 552 S.E.2d 818 (2001).

[21]Brewer v. State, 219 Ga. App. 16, 20 (6), 463 S.E.2d 906 (1995). Accord, Karim v. State, 244 Ga. App. 282, 284 (2), 535 S.E.2d 296 (2000).

. . . [the] identification procedure unduly suggestive is without merit." In *Padilla v. State*,[22] the Georgia Supreme Court affirmed the trial court in the pretrial identification of the defendant "even though he was the only mixed-race male in the photographs." In *Hendry v. State*,[23] the court concluded that the fact that "the individuals in the photographs had on the same clothing as the individuals the witness saw in the show-up is not in and of itself impermissively [sic] suggestive." In *Jackson v. State*,[24] the court held that a photographic lineup was not rendered impermissibly suggestive merely because the defendant's co-indictee was pictured in one of the six pictures displayed.

Nevertheless, in *Passman v. Blackburn*,[25] a photographic identification was found to be impermissibly suggestive where officers used a single, colored photograph of a front view of the defendant and the remaining 11 pictures were black-and-white mug shots with front and side views. Also, the court pointed out that four of the black-and-white pictures were significantly smaller. Nevertheless, in *Graham v. State*,[26] the court held, "The variance in size and texture in the pictures used does not render the procedure impermissibly suggestive." In *Colston v. State*,[27] the court held that a photographic lineup was not impermissibly suggestive "because of the different backgrounds of the pictures, different sizes of the photographs and the fact that defendant's photograph was the second largest."

In the Tenth Circuit case of *United States v. Sanchez*,[28] the court pointed out that "[t]he larger the number of pictures used in an array, the less likely it is that a minor difference, such as background color or texture, will have a prejudicial effect on selection. . . . Conversely, when a relatively low number of photographs are used . . . , minor differences such as background color can make a picture stand out, and can act to repeatedly draw a witness's eyes to that picture."

In asking a witness to view a photographic array, an officer

---

[22]Padilla v. State, 273 Ga. 553, 554 (1), 544 S.E.2d 147 (2001).

[23]Hendry v. State, 177 Ga. App. 439, 440, 339 S.E.2d 650 (1986).

[24]Jackson v. State, 209 Ga. App. 53, 54 (1), 432 S.E.2d 649 (1993).

[25]Passman v. Blackburn, 652 F.2d 559 (5th Cir. 1981). However, the court concluded that the in-court identification of Passman, in the light of the totality of the circumstances, did not result in a very substantial likelihood of irreparable misidentification. Cf. O'Brien v. Wainwright, 738 F.2d 1139 (11th Cir. 1984).

[26]Graham v. State, 171 Ga. App. 242, 253, 319 S.E.2d 484 (1984); Simpson v. State, 193 Ga. App. 439, 440, 388 S.E.2d 39 (1989).

[27]Colston v. State, 205 Ga. App. 782, 783 (1), 423 S.E.2d 714 (1992).

[28]United States v. Sanchez, 24 F.3d 1259 (10th Cir. 1994).

should not tell the witness that the suspect has been arrested.[29] However, a pre-trial photographic identification is not rendered impermissibly suggestive by an officer's telling the victim that there is a suspect in the seven pictures displayed.[30]

It has been said pictures should be displayed to only one eyewitness at a time, and if there are other eyewitnesses they should not be present when the identification is being attempted.[31] However, in a case where two photo spreads are used and only the defendant's picture appeared in both, the court concluded that the identification was not impermissibly defective.[32]

Suggestions made by officers may cause a due process violation at the time of a photographic identification.[33] The witness should not be informed that the defendant's picture is in the array,[34] and no picture should be pointed out to a witness.[35] In *Cridiso v. State*,[36] the court said that "it may not be good practice for a police officer to indicate to a witness that he has chosen the 'right guy.' "However, the test for admissibility at trial following a tainted pre-trial identification (either photographic or physical) is "whether the in-court identification had an independent origin."[37]

Georgia has recognized that a composite drawing of a suspect made up of data supplied by witnesses may be shown to a witness for purposes of identification.[38] However, the inability of a victim to verbally convey the picture of the assailant to an artist

---

[29]Dodd v. State, 236 Ga. 572, 224 S.E.2d 408 (1976); Lowe v. State, 141 Ga. App. 433, 233 S.E.2d 807 (1977).

[30]Harper v. State, 172 Ga. App. 69 (2), 321 S.E.2d 805 (1984).

[31]See United States v. Hopkins, 464 F.2d 816 (D.C.Cir. 1972); People v. Norfleet, 4 Ill.App.3d 758, 281 N.E.2d 761 (1972). See also Thornton v. State, 238 Ga. 160, 231 S.E.2d 729 (1977).

[32]Dudley v. State, 179 Ga. App. 252, 253 (1), 345 S.E.2d 888 (1986).

[33]United States v. Johnson, 452 F.2d 1363 (D.C.Cir. 1971); Dodd v. State, 236 Ga. 572, 224 S.E.2d 408 (1976); Lowe v. State, 141 Ga. App. 433, 233 S.E.2d 807 (1977); Talley v. State, 137 Ga. App. 548, 224 S.E.2d 455 (1976). But see also Eiland v. State, 246 Ga. 112, 268 S.E.2d 922 (1980), where the fact that the officer who was conducting the photographic identification told the witness to "[t]ake all the time you need, we want

to be sure we've got the man in jail for murder, we want to be sure we've got the right one" did not render the witness' identification unnecessarily suggestive.

[34]Dodd v. State, 236 Ga. 572, 224 S.E.2d 408 (1976); Lowe v. State, 141 Ga. App. 433, 233 S.E.2d 807 (1977); Talley v. State, 137 Ga. App. 548, 224 S.E.2d 455 (1976). But see Eiland v. State, 246 Ga. 112, 268 S.E.2d 922 (1980).

[35]Talley v. State, 137 Ga. App. 548, 224 S.E.2d 455 (1976).

[36]Cridiso v. State, 200 Ga. App. 342, 344 (4), 408 S.E.2d 153 (1991).

[37]Cf. State v. Willis, 218 Ga. App. 402, 403 (2), 461 S.E.2d 576 (1995).

[38]Clark v. State, 149 Ga. App. 641, 643, 255 S.E.2d 110 (1979). See Annot., "Admissibility in Evidence of Composite Picture or Sketch Produced by Police to Identify Offender," 23 A.L.R. 5th 672 (1994) (updated weekly).

has been held not to prevent a photo or physical identification.[39] In *Williams v. State*,[40] the court held that a composite drawing was not objectionable as hearsay where the police artist did not testify at trial. See Annotation, "Admissibility in Evidence of Composite Picture or Sketch Produced by Police to Identify Offender," 42 A.L.R.3d 1217 (1972). Also, in Georgia it has been held that a defendant may be identified by permitting a witness to look through "mug" books.[41]

Some psychologists believe that in an array of photographs, if one picture is not in line with the others, that is if it is "crooked" in the array, it is more likely to be picked out. Likewise, some have concluded that a picture of a person with a different expression from the persons in the other pictures or different clothing from the others is more likely to be selected.[42]

In *Lynch v. State*,[43] the defendant contended that the victim's in-court identification was tainted by a photographic lineup of eight photographs and that the array was misleading because the pictures (from chest up) showed the heights of the suspects. However, there was no testimony that the identification was based on any height information. The court concluded that in view of the totality of the circumstances, it was not error to admit the in-court identification testimony.

In *Baier v. State*,[44] an officer displayed three black and white photographs to the witness. Two of the pictures depicted the accused, including one with a mustache added. The witness tentatively identified the accused, pointing out that the mustache was incorrectly drawn. Later the witness saw him in a showup at jail and "recognized him." In reversing the conviction, the court concluded that there had been "an impermissibly suggestive photographic confrontation, followed by a suggestive in person confrontation at a critical stage of the proceedings conducted without counsel . . . making it impossible to determine that the courtroom identification is untainted. . . ." However, in *Futch v.*

---

[39]Robinson v. State, 179 Ga. App. 616, 618, 347 S.E.2d 667 (1986).

[40]Williams v. State, 181 Ga. App. 693, 694 (1), 353 S.E.2d 563 (1987).

[41]Blue v. State, 170 Ga. App. 304 (1), 316 S.E.2d 862 (1984).

[42]Buckhout, "Eyewitness Identification and Psychology in the Courtroom," 4 Crim. Def., No. 5, p. 5, Sept.-Oct. 1977.

[43]Lynch v. State, 158 Ga. App. 643, 281 S.E.2d 640 (1981).

[44]Baier v. State, 124 Ga. App. 334, 183 S.E.2d 622 (1971). Cf. United States v. Bell, 457 F.2d 1231 (5th Cir. 1972). "In-court identification following a pretrial identification by photograph is improper if the photographic procedure was so impermissibly suggestive as to give rise to a very substantial likelihood of irreparable misidentification, but it has been held not to be improper if the photographic procedure is not so impermissibly suggestive." 22A C.J.S. Criminal Law § 616; Mata v. Sumner, 696 F.2d 1244 (9th Cir. 1983).

State[45] the court stated that "[c]onvictions based on eyewitness identification at trial following a pretrial identification by photograph will be set aside only if the photographic identification procedure was so impermissibly suggestive as to give rise to a very substantial likelihood of irreparable misidentification. . . . Moreover, '(e)ven if a pretrial identification is tainted, an in-court identification is not constitutionally inadmissible if it does not depend upon the prior identification but has an independent origin.' "

It has been pointed out that a photographic array is a less reliable means of identification than a corporal lineup and that the use of such a less reliable identification is a factor which may be used in determining whether an identification was reliable.[46] However, even though "a corporal lineup is the most reliable identification procedure and for that reason the most preferable, . . . a defendant has no constitutional right to a lineup."[47]

In *Boscaino v. State*,[48] the victim positively identified the defendant at a photographic lineup conducted three days after the incident. However, he could not positively identify the defendant in court. The court held that the failure to positively identify the defendant in court did not invalidate his earlier positive identification.

On the other hand, it was held in *Banks v. State*[49] that "[t]he victims' failure to identify . . . [the defendant] from the photographic lineup does not require the conclusion that their in-court identification was based solely on the" viewing of the defendant in the courtroom at the time of trial.

Generally, see Annotations, "Admissibility of Evidence of Photographic Identification as Affected by Allegedly Suggestive Identification Procedures," 39 A.L.R.3d 1000 (1971); "Lineups and Showups: Admissibility and Effect of Pretrial Identification," 19 Am. Jur. Proof of Facts 2d 435, 446; "Unreliability of Eyewitness Identification," 18 Am. Jur. Proof of Facts 2d 361. See also 29 Am. Jur. 2d Evidence (1994) § 630. See § 6:9, infra, on an arrest to take a suspect's picture. See Annotation, "Admissibility in Evidence of Composite Picture or Sketch Produced by Police to Identify Offender," 23 A.L.R.5th 672 (1994), and Goger, *Daniel's Georgia Handbook on Criminal Evidence* (2017 ed.), § 7:8.

---

[45]Futch v. State, 192 Ga. App. 345, 346, 385 S.E.2d 18 (1989) (quoting Evans v. State, 188 Ga. App. 379, 373 S.E.2d 70 (1988)).

[46]People v. Holiday, 47 Ill.2d 300, 265 N.E.2d 634 (1970); State v. Thorkelson, 25 Wash.App. 615, 611 P.2d 1278 (1980).

[47]Branch v. Estelle, 631 F.2d 1229, 1234 (5th Cir. 1980).

[48]Boscaino v. State, 186 Ga. App. 133 (1), 366 S.E.2d 789 (1988).

[49]Banks v. State, 203 Ga. App. 355, 356, 416 S.E.2d 866 (1992). Cf. Chergi v. State, 234 Ga. App. 548, 549 (1), 507 S.E.2d 795 (1998).

§ 6:7 Presence of counsel

As previously mentioned, defense counsel has a right to be present when his client is present at any kind of identification at or after the initiation of the adversary criminal proceeding.[1] Conversely, there is no right to counsel at an identification before the initiation of the adversary criminal proceeding.[2] Also, like most other rights, the presence of counsel may be waived.[3] Nevertheless, the giving of the *Miranda* warning alone has been held not to constitute a waiver of the right to have counsel present at a lineup.[4] Also, it may be possible to utilize substitute counsel if the defendant's counsel cannot be present or there would be a prejudicial delay in waiting for the defendant's counsel.[5]

After the time at which the defendant constitutionally is entitled to counsel, when he is present for identification, the failure to have counsel present results in a per se exclusion of testimony of the pre-trial identification[6] at least in the absence of an accidental or unanticipated identification[7] or perhaps when the identification can be justified by exigent circumstances.[8] If the defendant's right to counsel is violated, testimony of the pre-trial identification is inadmissible regardless of whether there was an independent source of the witness' identification at the

---

[Section 6:7]

[1]Moore v. Illinois, 434 U.S. 220, 98 S.Ct. 458, 54 L.Ed.2d 424 (1977); Coleman v. State, 160 Ga. App. 158 (1), 286 S.E.2d 494 (1981).

In Bonner v. State, 160 Ga. App. 902, 903 (1), 288 S.E.2d 612 (1982), the victim of a robbery was subpoenaed to a probation revocation hearing. The Court of Appeals seems to have summarily concluded that a probation revocation hearing is not a showup and there was no right to counsel. No mention was made about whether the adversary criminal robbery proceeding had been initiated. If the adversary proceeding had been initiated, it does not seem that this part of the decision is sound in view of Moore v. Illinois, 434 U.S. 220, 98 S.Ct. 458, 54 L.Ed.2d 424 (1977).

[2]Cf. Brown v. State, 160 Ga. App. 226, 286 S.E.2d 487 (1981).

[3]United States v. Wade, 388 U.S. 218, 237, 87 S.Ct. 1926, 18 L.Ed.2d 1149 (1967); Messer v. State, 247 Ga. 316, 276 S.E.2d 15 (1981).

[4]State v. Williams, 279 N.C. 663, 185 S.E.2d 174 (1971). Cf. United States v. Ayers, 426 F.2d 524 (2d Cir. 1970). See 22A C.J.S. Criminal Law § 616.

[5]United States v. Wade, 388 U.S. 218, 237, 87 S.Ct. 1926, 18 L.Ed.2d 1149 (1967).

[6]Pearson v. United States, 389 F.2d 684 (5th Cir. 1968). In People v. Yopp, 25 Mich.App. 69, 180 N.W.2d 897 (1970), the court said that there are no exceptions to the rule stated in the body of the text.

[7]Cf. United States v. Isenberg, 343 F.Supp. 25 (W.D.Pa.1972); United States v. Brown, 461 F.2d 134 (C.A.D. C.1971) (due process grounds).

[8]Cf. United States v. Moore, 459 F.2d 1360 (D.C.Cir. 1972); Stidham v. Commonwealth, 444 S.W.2d 110 (Ky. 1969).

confrontation.[9]

However, the fact that there has been a pre-trial identification of a defendant in violation of his right to counsel does not necessarily mean that the in-court identification testimony of the witness is to be excluded. If the witness' in-court identification was independent of any tainted pre-trial identification, the in-court identification testimony is admissible.[10]

As previously pointed out, however, the defendant is not entitled to be represented by counsel at a photographic identification regardless of when it takes place.[11]

What is counsel's role at an identification? Clearly it is envisioned that counsel is present as a witness and so that he may better cross-examine the identifying witness or witnesses at trial.[12] The idea of having defense counsel act as a witness at a critical stage of the proceeding may place the attorney in an unusual position. If there is a disagreement about what took place or the arrangement of the lineup, he may have to withdraw from the case in order to testify. However, in *Moore v. Illinois*,[13] a more active role was suggested by the United States Supreme Court. The court said that defense counsel may object to suggestive features before they influence a witness' identification.

There is some older authority indicating that defense counsel can do nothing but observe and that he cannot prevent an unfair lineup[14] nor make suggestions which must be followed.[15] In addition, officers have authority to eject argumentative defense counsel from the lineup room if his efforts impede the efforts of officers to conduct the proceeding effectively.[16] With the possible exception of the situation involving disruption of the proceeding, the validity of these views is at least open to question since *Moore*. However, if counsel does have a right to object or make suggestions, his failure to do so may amount to a waiver.

---

[9]Moore v. Illinois, 434 U.S. 220, 231, 98 S.Ct. 458, 54 L.Ed.2d 424 (1977).

[10]United States v. Wade, 388 U.S. 218, 87 S.Ct. 1926, 18 L.Ed.2d 1149 (1967); Foster v. State, 160 Ga. App. 326, 287 S.E.2d 323 (1981).

[11]United States v. Ash, 413 U.S. 300, 93 S.Ct. 2568, 37 L.Ed.2d 619 (1973).

[12]United States v. Wade, 388 U.S. 218, 230, 231, 236, 87 S.Ct. 1926, 18 L.Ed.2d 1149 (1967); Uviller, "The Role of the Defense Lawyer at a Lineup in the Light of the Wade, Gilbert and Stovall Decisions," 4 Crim. L. Bull. 273, 278, 286 (1968).

[13]Moore v. Illinois, 434 U.S. 220, 225, 98 S.Ct. 458, 54 L.Ed.2d 424 (1977). In People v. Bustamante, 30 Cal.3d 88, 177 Cal.Rptr. 576, 634 P.2d 927 (1981), the majority envisioned counsel's role at a lineup as being a passive one.

[14]Vernon v. State, 12 Md.App. 430, 278 A.2d 609 (1971).

[15]Mason v. United States, 414 F.2d 1176 (D.C.Cir. 1969).

[16]United States v. Cunningham, 423 F.2d 1269 (4th Cir. 1970).

Generally, see "Lineups and Showups: Admissibility and Effect of Pretrial Identification," 19 Am. Jur. Proof of Facts 2d 435 and 22A C.J.S. § 616.

§ 6:8   Due process standard

The due process requirement applies to all testimony involving pre-trial identifications, at least in the absence of a waiver.[1] These requirements apply to all lineups,[2] showups, and photographic displays regardless of whether there was a constitutional right to the presence of counsel at the time.[3] Thus, even if the right to counsel was waived by the defendant at the time of a pre-trial identification, it may still be possible for defense counsel to exclude testimony of the identification if the confrontation violated due process.[4] The due process standard is the only standard which applies to a photographic pre-trial identification[5] and it is the standard which applies to accidental confrontations and confrontations produced by exigent circumstances.[6] Of course, it was the only standard which applied to pre-trial identifications before June 12, 1967.[7]

The due process standard applies to two different kinds of identification testimony. First, it applies to the admissibility at trial of a pre-trial identification. Second, the due process standard applies to the question of whether or not the witness will be permitted to identify the defendant in court at the time of trial.

"It is error to allow testimony concerning a pre-trial identification of the defendant if the identification procedure was impermissibly suggestive and, under the totality of the circumstances, the suggestiveness gave rise to a substantial likelihood of misidentification."[8] "A court need not consider whether there was a substantial likelihood of misidentification if it determines that

---

[Section 6:8]

[1]Simmons v. United States, 390 U.S. 377, 88 S.Ct. 967, 19 L.Ed.2d 1247 (1968); Gilbert v. California, 388 U.S. 263, 87 S.Ct. 1951, 18 L.Ed.2d 1178 (1967).

[2]See Annot., "Admissibility of Evidence of Lineup Identification as Affected by Allegedly Suggestive Lineup Procedures," 39 A.L.R.3d 487 (1971).

[3]Stovall v. Denno, 388 U.S. 293, 87 S.Ct. 1967, 18 L.Ed.2d 1199 (1967); United States v. Gidley, 527 F.2d 1345 (5th Cir. 1976), reh'g denied, 530 F.2d 976 (5th Cir. 1976).

[4]Long v. United States, 424 F.2d 799 (D.C.Cir. 1969).

[5]United States v. Ash, 413 U.S. 300, 93 S.Ct. 2568, 37 L.Ed.2d 619 (1973).

[6]Bush v. State, 149 Ga. App. 448, 254 S.E.2d 453 (1979).

[7]Stovall v. Denno, 388 U.S. 293, 87 S.Ct. 1967, 18 L.Ed.2d 1199 (1967); Coleman v. Alabama, 399 U.S. 1, 90 S.Ct. 1999, 26 L.Ed.2d 387 (1970).

[8]Miller v. State, 270 Ga. 741, 743 (2), 512 S.E.2d 272 (1999) (citing Neil v. Biggers, 409 U.S. 188, 93 S.Ct. 375, 34 L.Ed.2d 401 (1972), and Reid v. State, 210 Ga. App. 783, 437 S.E.2d

the identification procedure was not impermissibly suggestive."[9] "An identification procedure is impermissibly suggestive when it leads the witness to an 'all but inevitable identification' of the defendant as the perpetrator . . . or as was held in *Heyward v. State*,[10] is the equivalent of the authorities telling the witness, 'This is our suspect.' "[11]

In cases where there is a question of a due process violation in a pre-trial identification, testimony of the pre-trial identification is to be excluded if the violation was so suggestive as to result in misidentification.[12] If the pre-trial identification "was so unnecessarily suggestive and conducive to mistaken identification" as judged by a totality of the circumstances surrounding it, the defendant is said to have been denied due process of law and testimony of the pre-trial identification should be excluded.[13]

However, in the 2000 Georgia Supreme Court case of *Jones v. State*,[14] the court held that "[w]hen a trial court concludes that an identification procedure is impermissibly suggestive, the issue becomes whether there was a substantial likelihood of irreparable misidentification. If not, then both the pre-trial and in-court identifications are admissible."

Insofar as admission of in-court identification where there is a question of whether or not due process has been violated, a two-step analysis now is used. First, the threshold inquiry is whether the identification procedure used was impermissibly suggestive, and only if it was, is the second question reached.[15] Second, was

---

646 (1993)).

[9]Miller v. State, 270 Ga. 741, 743 (2), 512 S.E.2d 272 (1999) (citing Whatley v. State, 266 Ga. 568, 468 S.E.2d 751 (1996)).

[10]Heyward v. State, 236 Ga. 526, 224 S.E.2d 383 (1976).

[11]Miller v. State, 270 Ga. 741, 743 (2), 512 S.E.2d 272 (1999); Cowan v. State, 243 Ga. App. 388, 394 (6), 531 S.E.2d 785 (2000). See also Brewer v. State, 219 Ga. App. 16, 463 S.E.2d 906 (1995).

[12]Neil v. Biggers, 409 U.S. 188, 198, 93 S.Ct. 375, 34 L.Ed.2d 401 (1972). See Messer v. State, 247 Ga. 316, 276 S.E.2d 15 (1981).

[13]Stovall v. Denno, 388 U.S. 293, 302, 87 S.Ct. 1967, 18 L.Ed.2d 1199 (1967).

In Manson v. Brathwaite, 432 U.S. 98, 97 S.Ct. 2243, 53 L.Ed.2d 140 (1977), a single photograph was presented to a witness in non-exigent circumstances. It was acknowledged that the procedure was suggestive. The court declined to adopt a per se rule excluding testimony at trial of unnecessarily suggestive pre-trial identifications, and pointed out that testimony of pre-trial identification should not be excluded from the jury, even though the identification was unnecessarily suggestive, if the identification was reliable. In determining whether or not such pre-trial identification is admissible, the factors to be considered are set out in Neil v. Biggers, 409 U.S. 188, 199, 93 S.Ct. 375, 34 L.Ed.2d 401 (1972).

[14]Jones v. State, 273 Ga. 213, 216 (2), 539 S.E.2d 143 (2000).

[15]Odim v. State, 228 Ga. App. 158,

there a substantial likelihood of irreparable misidentification?[16] These questions are to be answered in the light of a totality of the circumstances surrounding the identification.[17] Insofar as the question of likelihood of irreparable misidentification is concerned, it comes down "to the central question whether under the 'totality of the circumstances' the identification was reliable even though the confrontation was suggestive."[18] In *Neil v. Biggers,*[19] the United States Supreme Court said that the "factors to be considered in evaluating the likelihood of misidentification include [1] the opportunity of the witness to view the criminal at the time of the crime, [2] the witness' degree of attention, [3] the accuracy of the witness' prior description of the criminal, [4] the level of certainty demonstrated by the witness at the confrontation, and [5] the length of time between the crime and the confrontation." In *Semple v. State,*[20] the court held that *Biggers* "deals with the suggestiveness of an identification procedure used by police, and applies only to state action."

However, in *Davis v. State,*[21] the Georgia Court of Appeals recognized that even in a situation as "inherently suggestive" as a one-on-one showup, "any psychological effect a one-on-one showup may have on a potential witness is greatly diminished when that witness is a law enforcement officer who, through experience, training or both, has learned certain witness identification techniques and procedures."

A discrepancy between a pre-lineup description and the actual description, the identification of another person before a lineup, the failure to identify the defendant on an earlier occasion,[22] the identification of the defendant by picture, and the lapse of time between the crime and the lineup are all significant factors to

159 (2), 491 S.E.2d 218 (1997); Graham v. State, 171 Ga. App. 242, 253 (11), 319 S.E.2d 484 (1984).

[16]Anderson v. State, 168 Ga. App. 243, 245, 308 S.E.2d 623 (1983); Pack v. State, 182 Ga. App. 618, 619, 356 S.E.2d 557 (1987); Morgan v. State, 197 Ga. App. 823, 824, 399 S.E.2d 578 (1990).

[17]Daniel v. State, 150 Ga. App. 798, 799, 258 S.E.2d 604 (1979); Gravitt v. State, 239 Ga. 709, 710, 239 S.E.2d 149 (1977); Bloodworth v. Hopper, 539 F.2d 1382 (5th Cir. 1976); Woody v. State, 166 Ga. App. 666 (1), 305 S.E.2d 365 (1983); Arnold v. State, 166 Ga. App. 313 (4), 304 S.E.2d 118 (1983).

[18]Neil v. Biggers, 409 U.S. 188,

199, 93 S.Ct. 375, 34 L.Ed.2d 401 (1972). Cf. Payne v. State, 233 Ga. 294, 299, 210 S.E.2d 775 (1974); Moye v. State, 122 Ga. App. 14, 17, 176 S.E.2d 180 (1970).

[19]Neil v. Biggers, 409 U.S. 188, 199, 93 S.Ct. 375, 34 L.Ed.2d 401 (1972); Tate v. State, 153 Ga. App. 508 (1), 265 S.E.2d 818 (1980).

[20]Semple v. State, 271 Ga. 416, 417 (2), 519 S.E.2d 912 (1999).

[21]Davis v. State, 216 Ga. App. 580, 581 (2), 455 S.E.2d 115 (1995).

[22]In State v. Falkins, 356 So.2d 415 (La.1978), the court reversed the conviction because the district attorney failed to disclose prior mistaken identification by witness.

consider.[23] However, in *Price v. State*,[24] the court held that an identification is not "inherently unreliable" because of inconsistencies in the description given by the witness where the witness is available for cross-examination.

Where an identification is made, it is improper for an officer to tell the witness that he has chosen the right person.[25]

In *Swicegood v. Alabama*,[26] the court, on the basis of a due process violation in the identification of the defendant, pointed out that (1) the defendant, who was 35 years of age at the time, was 9 to 15 years older than the other participants in the lineup; (2) the two witnesses had an unsupervised opportunity to discuss the lineup between the first viewing when neither identified the defendant and the second viewing when they both positively identified the defendant; (3) one witness was allowed to view those in the lineup without masks although he had never seen the robber without a mask; (4) one witness had given only a very general description, and neither witness was asked to give a more precise description prior to the lineup; (5) neither witness had a good opportunity during the offense to see or hear the robber (one was locked in a closet the entire time and the other wore a blindfold covering her eyes for all except about two seconds, and her ears were covered for at least part of the time); (6) the lineup was held nearly three weeks after the robbery; (7) the in-court certainty may have been tainted by the remark of a police officer to the effect that the witnesses had identified the "right man"; and (8) even though the defendant generally fit the description of the witnesses, so did the others in the lineup. The court concluded that the lineup raised due process considerations sufficient enough to require an examination of the reliability of the identification. The court then examined each of the five factors set out in *Biggers* in light of the evidence in the present case and concluded by saying, "We cannot say that the likelihood of misidentification was slight or that the suggestiveness of the lineup was an uncorrupting influence. . . . [U]nder all the circumstances of this case, the suggestiveness of the lineup and the unreliability of the identifications coalesce to produce a due process violation."

In *Clark v. State*,[27] the court held that a lineup was not impermissible because the defendant was the only person to ap-

---

[23]Griffin v. State, 229 Ga. 165, 166, 190 S.E.2d 61 (1972).

[24]Price v. State, 194 Ga. App. 453, 454 (1), 390 S.E.2d 663 (1990); Grier v. State, 206 Ga. App. 93, 94 (1), 424 S.E.2d 358 (1992).

[25]Dodd v. State, 236 Ga. 572, 573,

224 S.E.2d 408 (1976).

[26]Swicegood v. Alabama, 577 F.2d 1322 (5th Cir. 1978). In this case, the court in a habeas corpus action in effect reversed Swicegood v. State, 343 So.2d 806 (Ala.Crim.App. 1977).

[27]Clark v. State, 166 Ga. App. 366

pear in both an earlier pictorial identification and the lineup.

In *Hodnett v. State*,[28] the Georgia Supreme Court pointed out that a lineup would not be flawed simply by an officer's telling a defendant to take a certain position in the lineup.

Lastly, the failure to hold any kind of pre-trial identification is not a due process violation of a defendant.[29]

See § 6:5, supra, on showups.

Generally, see "Lineups and Showups: Admissibility and Effect of Pretrial Identification," 19 Am. Jur. Proof of Facts 2d 435 and "Unreliability of Eyewitness Identification," 18 Am. Jur. Proof of Facts 2d 361.

§ 6:9 Motions for lineups

In Georgia it has been said that a defendant has no right to refuse to participate in a lineup,[1] at least if it is properly arranged and conducted. Even if he is on bond, it seems he may be required to appear for a lineup.[2] Georgia courts do not seem to have considered expressly a situation in which law enforcement officers desire to have a suspect placed in a lineup even though they do not have sufficient probable cause to justify an arrest of the suspect. Most courts seem to hold that a suspect may not be forced to appear in a lineup unless there is probable cause to arrest the suspect.[3] However, a person lawfully held in custody for one offense has been held not to have a right to complain when

---

(3), 304 S.E.2d 494 (1983).

[28]Hodnett v. State, 269 Ga. 115, 118 (4), 498 S.E.2d 737 (1998).

[29]Cf. Code v. Montgomery, 725 F.2d 1316 (11th Cir. 1984).

[Section 6:9]

[1]Wilson v. State, 237 Ga. 657, 229 S.E.2d 424 (1976).

[2]Wilson v. State, 237 Ga. 657, 229 S.E.2d 424 (1976). In *Wilson* the defendant apparently was under arrest for another charge. See Allen v. Estelle, 568 F.2d 1108 (5th Cir. 1978); Kirby v. Illinois, 406 U.S. 682, 687, 92 S.Ct. 1877, 32 L.Ed.2d 411 (1972).

[3]In re Armed Robbery, Albertson's on August 31, 1981, 99 Wash.2d 106, 659 P.2d 1092 (1983) (en banc). Contra, Wise v. Murphy, 275 A.2d 205 (D.C.App.1971); see § 6:4, supra, on lineups.

In State v. Hall, 93 N.J. 552, 461 A.2d 1155 (1983), the court held that a court has authority to order a lineup on less than probable cause where [1] the detention is "based upon sufficient evidence to demonstrate that a particular crime has occurred; [2] the crime is unsolved; [3] it is under active investigation"; [4] police "demonstrate a reasonable and well-grounded basis to believe that the individual sought as the subject of the investigative detention may have committed the crime under investigation"; [5] "the results of the detention will significantly advance the criminal investigation and will serve to determine whether or not the suspect probably committed the crime"; and [6] "it must appear that these investigative results cannot be otherwise practically obtained." However, even when a lineup may be ordered "appropriate procedures must be fashioned to assure that the intrusiveness of the detention is properly circumscribed."

he is used as a "filler" in a lineup in connection with an unrelated offense.[4] It has been held that when there is probable cause, pursuant to a warrant, there may be an arrest of a suspect for purposes of fingerprinting and photography.[5] However, it seems that a grand jury at least may do so.[6] Also, it should be remembered that if officers think they have probable cause for a valid arrest and they do not, this does not mean that in-court identification is automatically suppressible even if a picture made as a result of the illegal arrest was used as a means of a pre-trial identification.[7]

Likewise, Georgia does not seem to have expressly passed on the question of whether or not a defendant on his own motion is entitled to a pre-trial lineup. Courts in other jurisdictions have differed on this question, some holding that a defendant under some circumstances is entitled to a pre-trial lineup[8] and some

---

[4]People v. Whitaker, 64 N.Y.2d 347, 486 N.Y.S.2d 895, 476 N.E.2d 294 (1985).

[5]Baker v. State, 449 N.E.2d 1085 (Ind.1983).

[6]In re Maguire, 571 F.2d 675 (1st Cir. 1978). Accord, Wise v. Murphy, 275 A.2d 205, 207 (D.C.App. 1971); cf. Rigney v. Hendrick, 355 F.2d 710, 715 (3d Cir. 1965) and United States v. Jones, 403 F.2d 498 (7th Cir. 1968). See also State v. Gengler, 294 Minn. 503, 200 N.W.2d 187 (Minn. 1972). In the case of In the Matter of Kelley, 433 A.2d 704 (D.C.1981), the court held that where a grand jury directs a suspect to appear in a lineup, he may be forced to do so without "a preliminary showing establishing a nexus between the person and the alleged crime."

[7]Cf. United States v. Crews, 445 U.S. 463, 100 S.Ct. 1244, 63 L.Ed.2d 537 (1980); Baker v. State, 39 Md.App. 133, 383 A.2d 698 (1978).

[8]Commonwealth v. Sexton, 485 Pa. 17, 400 A.2d 1289 (1979); Evans v. Superior Court, 11 Cal.3d 617, 114 Cal.Rptr. 121, 522 P.2d 681 (1974). Cf. United States v. Gilmore, 398 F.2d 679 (7th Cir. 1968).

Moore v. Illinois, 434 U.S. 220, 231, 98 S.Ct. 458, 54 L.Ed.2d 424 (1977), involved an identification at a preliminary hearing. In n. 5, the court stated:

"For example, counsel could have requested that the hearing be postponed until a lineup could be arranged at which the victim would view petitioner in a less suggestive setting. See, e.g., United States v. Ravich, 421 F.2d 1196, 1202-1203 (2nd Cir.,1970); Mason v. United States, 134 U.S. App. D. C. 280, 283 n. 19, 414 F.2d 1176, 1179 n. 19 (1969). Short of that, counsel could have asked that the victim be excused from the courtroom while the charges were read and the evidence against petitioner was recited, and that petitioner be seated with other people in the audience when the victim attempted an identification. See Allen v. Rhay, 431 F.2d 1160, 1165 (9th Cir. 1970). Counsel might have sought to cross-examine the victim to test her identification before it hardened. Cf. Haberstroh v. Montanye, 493 F.2d 483, 485 (2d Cir. 1974); United States ex rel. Riffert v. Rundle, 464 F.2d 1348, 1351 (3d Cir. 1972). Riffert v. Johnson, 415 U.S. 927, 94 S.Ct. 1434, 39 L.Ed.2d 484 (1974). Because it is in the prosecution's interest as well as the accused's that witnesses' identification remain untainted, see United States v. Wade, 388 U.S. 218, 238, 87 S.Ct. 1926, 18 L.Ed.2d 1149 (1967), we cannot assume that such requests would have been in vain. Such requests ordi-

holding that a defendant is not entitled to such a lineup.[9]

§ 6:10 Admissibility of in-court identification testimony at trial

In §§ 6:4 to 6:9, supra, the emphasis was on whether testimony of a pre-trial identification is admissible at trial. The thrust of this section is to determine when the pre-trial taint is so severe or the witness' view of the defendant so fleeting[1] that a witness should be prevented from testifying at trial that "the defendant is the man I saw commit the crime." Some of the cases previously discussed in this chapter have considered this problem.

If a pre-trial identification arranged by officers[2] violates the right to counsel or if there is a due process violation, such as was discussed above, then on motion it is the duty of the trial judge to determine whether the witness has an independent recollection of the appearance of the defendant which is based on having seen him at the time of the crime and which is independent of the tainted pre-trial identification.[3] If the witness can testify independently of the pre-trial identification, the witness' in-court

---

narily are addressed to the sound discretion of the court. See *United States v. Ravich*, supra, at 1203; we express no opinion as to whether the preliminary hearing court would have been required to grant any such requests."

[9]Cf. United States v. Hamilton, 420 F.2d 1292 (D.C.Cir. 1969); United States v. McGhee, 488 F.2d 781, 786 (5th Cir. 1974); State v. Wright, 316 So.2d 380 (La.1975); Clark v. State, 156 Ga. App. 326, 274 S.E.2d 718 (1980); Berryman v. United States, 378 A.2d 1317 (D.C.App.1977). In State v. Boettcher, 338 So.2d 1356 (La.1976), the court held that a trial judge has discretion to grant a defense request for an out-of-court pre-trial lineup. Accord, People v. Lopez, 86 Misc.2d 111, 382 N.Y.S.2d 609 (1976). See Note, "Pretrial Identification Procedures: The Expanded Duty to Disclose Favorable Evidence," 50 Notre Dame Law. 508 (1975); Comment, "Due Process Failure Requires That Accused Be Given a Pretrial Discovery Right to a Lineup," 24 Cath. U. L. Rev. 360 (1975).

[Section 6:10]

[1]In Strickland v. State, 348 So.2d 1105 (Ala.Crim.App. 1977), the court held that where an officer sees a defendant at night and the defendant flees and there is no question of improper pre-trial identification procedures, the defendant is not entitled to a hearing on a motion to suppress his identification testimony. The weight and credibility to be given such testimony is a question which is addressed solely to the jury.

[2]In United States v. Peele, 574 F.2d 489 (9th Cir. 1978), the court held that, where an identification allegedly was influenced improperly by a newspaper picture, the admissibility of the in-court identification was not affected and the weight and credit to be given the in-court identification testimony was solely a question for the jury.

[3]Gilbert v. California, 388 U.S. 263, 272, 87 S.Ct. 1951, 18 L.Ed.2d 1178 (1967).

In McKenzie v. State, 162 Ga. App. 522, 524, 292 S.E.2d 722 (1982), the court concluded "that the lineup was not impermissibly suggestive and

identification testimony is admissible.[4] If the witness cannot testify in-court as to the defendant's identity independently of the tainted pre-trial identification, his in-court identification testimony should be excluded.[5] In *Paxton v. State,*[6] the Georgia Court of Appeals pointed out that an independent origin of an in-court identification may be shown by the fact that "the victim was able to give a precise and accurate description of his assailant before he viewed the photographic lineup."

If there is a tainted pre-trial identification and the state wishes to show that the witness should be permitted to identify the defendant in-court, the burden is on the state "to establish by clear and convincing evidence that the in-court identification . . . [would be] based upon the observations of the suspect" at some time other than at the tainted identification.[7]

In *Tiller v. State,*[8] the court pointed out that "even where a pre-trial identification has been found to be tainted, a subsequent in-court identification is admissible if it does not depend on the prior, tainted identification but has some other independent basis."

In *Smith v. State,*[9] the Georgia Court of Appeals considered whether a pre-trial photographic lineup was so impermissibly suggestive as to give rise to a substantial likelihood of irreparable misidentification. In determining whether the in-court

---

that it did not create a substantial likelihood of misidentification. [Hence] the court did not err in allowing the witnesses' in-court identification testimony."

In Velez v. Schmer, 724 F.2d 249 (1st Cir. 1984), the court held that the due process violations of officers and an analysis of the case in the light of the four criteria of Neil v. Biggers, 409 U.S. 188, 93 S.Ct. 375, 34 L.Ed.2d 401 (1972), there was such a "substantial likelihood of irreparable misidentification" that it was error to permit an in-court identification.

[4]United States v. Crews, 445 U.S. 463, 100 S.Ct. 1244, 63 L.Ed.2d 537 (1980); Jacobs v. State, 207 Ga. App. 714, 715 (1), 429 S.E.2d 256 (1993); Price v. State, 159 Ga. App. 662, 284 S.E.2d 676 (1981); Aiken v. State, 226 Ga. 840, 847, 178 S.E.2d 202 (1970); McCoy v. State, 161 Ga. App. 97, 99, 289 S.E.2d 301 (1982). See 22A C.J.S. Criminal Law § 616.

[5]Foster v. State, 156 Ga. App. 672, 275 S.E.2d 745 (1980); Respess v. State, 145 Ga. App. 570, 244 S.E.2d 251 (1978); Herron v. State, 155 Ga. App. 791, 792 (2), 272 S.E.2d 756 (1980). In Green v. Loggins, 614 F.2d 219 (9th Cir. 1980), the court found that a prolonged accidental confrontation rendered the witness' in-court identification unreliable. See United States v. Weston, 519 F.Supp. 565, 572 (W.D.N.Y.1981).

[6]Paxton v. State, 160 Ga. App. 19, 20 (2), 285 S.E.2d 741 (1981). Cf. Jones v. State, 258 Ga. 25, 27, 365 S.E.2d 263 (1988).

[7]United States v. Wade, 388 U.S. 218, 240, 87 S.Ct. 1926, 18 L.Ed.2d 1149 (1967).

[8]Tiller v. State, 222 Ga. App. 840, 841, 476 S.E.2d 591 (1996); Humphrey v. State, 281 Ga. 596(1), 642 S.E.2d 23 (2007).

[9]Smith v. State, 160 Ga. App. 60, 286 S.E.2d 45 (1981).

identification was tainted, the court considered each of the five criteria set out in *Neil v. Biggers,*[10] viz., (1) the opportunity of the witness to view the perpetrator at the time of the crime; (2) the witness' degree of attention; (3) the accuracy of the witness' prior description of the criminal; (4) the level of certainty demonstrated by the witness; and (5) the length of the time between the crime and the confrontation. The court then concluded that there was no substantial likelihood of misidentification at either the pre-trial or in-court identification.

It has been pointed out that reliability is to be determined from a totality of the circumstances.[11] Thus, it has been held that an "in-court identification based upon the scene of the crime was not impermissibly tainted solely because the appellant sat at the defendant's table and was the only black male in the courtroom."[12] Likewise, an in-court identification is not inadmissible solely because the victim was unable to identify the defendant at a lineup shortly after the crime[13] or failed to identify the defendant at a photo lineup.[14] In *Buckner v. State,*[15] the court held that "uncertainty expressed by the victim regarding his in-court identification of [the defendant] was merely a factor to be considered by the jury in determining the weight of this testimony."

In *Brodes v. State,*[16] the Georgia Supreme Court reversed the trial court, which, relying on the pattern charge, instructed the jury that one of the factors it was to consider in reviewing the testimony of the eyewitnesses was the level of certainty in their identification. The Court was persuaded by the empirical research presented that there exists a distinct "lack of correlation between a witness's certainty in his or her identification of someone as the perpetrator of a crime and the accuracy of that identification . . ." The Court went on to "advise" trial courts to refrain from using the level of certainty factor as part of their eyewitness identification charge. However, *Brodes* in no way is an impedi-

---

[10]Neil v. Biggers, 409 U.S. 188, 93 S.Ct. 375, 34 L.Ed.2d 401 (1972). See § 6:3, supra, on eyewitness identification.

[11]United States v. Richardson, 651 F.2d 1251, 1255 (8th Cir. 1981).

[12]Manning v. State, 162 Ga. App. 494 (1), 292 S.E.2d 95 (1982).

[13]Waddell v. State, 165 Ga. App. 147, 149, 300 S.E.2d 519 (1983).

[14]West v. State, 218 Ga. App. 341 (1), 461 S.E.2d 300 (1995).

[15]Buckner v. State, 209 Ga. App. 107, 108 (1)(c), 433 S.E.2d 94 (1993). The same pattern charge criticized in Brodes includes a reference to the "intelligence" of witnesses as one of the factors jurors should assess in weighing the credibility of witnesses. The Court of Appeals found this part of the instruction confusing and ill defined in McKenzie v. State, 293 Ga. App. 350, 667 S.E.2d 142 (2008) and suggested that trial courts discontinue its use in future cases.

[16]Brodes v. State, 279 Ga. 435, 614 S.E.2d 766 (2005).

ment to a witness testifying about his or her level of certainty of identification. Such testimony would, of course, be subject to challenge by way of "cross examination, expert testimony or the presentation of testimony from other eye witnesses."[17]

In *Clay v. State*,[18] the court held that when the jury has been adequately charged on the presumption of innocence, reasonable doubt, burden of proof, credibility of witnesses and impeachment, there is no error should the court fail, *sua sponte,* to charge the jury on identification even if it constitutes the sole defense.

It should be pointed out that the United States Supreme Court held in *United States v. Crews*[19] that where a defendant was illegally arrested and photographed and identified by the victim of the robbery by the picture and later in a pre-trial lineup, the victim was not prevented from identifying the defendant in court at the time of the trial where the trial judge found that her in-court identification was based on her original encounter with the defendant.[20] However, it was conceded that her testimony as to the photographic identification and the lineup was suppressible as a result of the Fourth Amendment violation.

It must be emphasized that the failure of defense counsel to object to an in-court identification generally prevents a later attack based on an allegedly tainted prior identification.[21] On the other hand, a pre-trial lineup or display of a photograph or photographs to a witness is not a prerequisite to an in-court identification.[22]

It is within a trial court's discretion whether or not to admit expert testimony regarding eyewitness identification.[23] However, "[w]here eyewitness identification of the defendant is a key element of the State's case and there is no substantial corroboration of that identification by other evidence, trial courts may not exclude expert testimony without carefully weighing whether the evidence would assist the jury in assessing the reliability of eye-

---

[17]Clark v. State, 285 Ga. App. 182, 185(4), 645 S.E.2d 671 (2007); Best v. State, 279 Ga. App. 309(3), 630 S.E.2d 900 (2006).

[18]Clay v. State, 232 Ga. App. 656, 658(2), 503 S.E.2d 560 (1998). See Harris v. State, 331 Ga. App. 32, 769 S.E.2d 749 (2015).

[19]United States v. Crews, 445 U.S. 463, 100 S.Ct. 1244, 63 L.Ed.2d 537 (1980).

[20]The U.S. Supreme Court has said that the exclusionary rule should be invoked with much greater reluc-

tance than in other Fourth Amendment situations where identification of the defendant by a live witness is at issue. United States v. Ceccolini, 435 U.S. 268, 280, 98 S.Ct. 1054, 55 L.Ed.2d 268 (1978).

[21]Respess v. State, 145 Ga. App. 570, 571 (2), 244 S.E.2d 251 (1978); May v. State, 159 Ga. App. 565, 566 (2), 284 S.E.2d 70 (1981).

[22]Price v. State, 159 Ga. App. 662, 663, 284 S.E.2d 676 (1981).

[23]Johnson v. State, 272 Ga. 254, 257, 526 S.E.2d 549 (2000).

witness testimony and whether eyewitness testimony is the only effective way to reveal any weakness in an eyewitness identification."[24]

Finally, it should be noted that a defendant who voluntarily absents himself from court during the testimony of the eyewitness cannot thereafter complain about the lack of an in-court identification.[25]

See 21A Am. Jur. 2d Criminal Law § 803. See Goger, *Daniel's Georgia Handbook on Criminal Evidence* (2017 ed.), § 7:8, on expert testimony relating to accuracy of eyewitness identification.

§ 6:11 Hearing on motion to suppress identification testimony

An objection to the admissibility of in-court identification may be raised at trial.[1] Also, where there is a tainted pre-trial identification, most jurisdictions recognize the right of a defendant to file a pre-trial motion to suppress[2] the in-court identification and to have an evidentiary hearing on the question raised.[3]

In *Kemp v. State,*[4] the Georgia Court of Appeals strongly indicated that the point should be raised before the trial starts and that a defendant may waive his right to an evidentiary hearing by not making a timely motion for such a hearing.

Regardless of how the point is raised, any such hearing should be conducted outside the presence of the jury. In *Watkins v. Sowders,*[5] the United States Supreme Court concluded that while the Due Process Clause of the Fourteenth Amendment does not

---

[24]Johnson v. State, 272 Ga. 254, 257, 526 S.E.2d 549 (2000).

[25]See Hill v. State, 290 Ga. 493, 722 S.E.2d 708 (2012).

[Section 6:11]

[1]Foster v. State, 156 Ga. App. 672, 275 S.E.2d 745 (1980); Dodson v. State, 237 Ga. 607, 229 S.E.2d 364 (1976).

[2]Hunter v. State, 202 Ga. App. 195, 196 (2), 413 S.E.2d 526 (1991).

[3]Clemons v. United States, 408 F.2d 1230 (D.C.Cir. 1968); United States v. Driber, 546 F.2d 18 (3d Cir. 1976); United States v. Allison, 414 F.2d 407 (9th Cir. 1969); State v. DeMasi, 118 R.I. 494, 374 A.2d 806 (1977); Bruce v. State, 268 Ind. 180, 375 N.E.2d 1042, 1059 (1978); People

v. Rodriguez, 68 Cal.App.3d 874, 137 Cal.Rptr. 594 (1977).

[4]Kemp v. State, 158 Ga. App. 570, 571 (1), 281 S.E.2d 315 (1981). See also Dodson v. State, 237 Ga. 607, 229 S.E.2d 364 (1976); Sims v. State, 159 Ga. App. 692 (1), 285 S.E.2d 65 (1981).

[5]Watkins v. Sowders, 449 U.S. 341, 101 S.Ct. 654, 66 L.Ed.2d 549 (1981). The facts of Watkins are discussed in n. 3, supra, sub nomine *Summit v. Bordenkircher* and *Watkins v. Bordenkircher*. In Merriweather v. State, 588 S.W.2d 564 (Tenn.Crim. App. 1979), the court held that there was no error in failing to have a hearing outside the presence of the jury where there was no substantial likelihood of misidentification under a totality of the circumstances. See also

always require a hearing outside the presence of the jury, the "prudence of such a hearing has been emphasized by many decisions. . . . A judicial determination outside the presence of the jury of the admissibility of identification evidence may often be advisable. In some circumstances . . . such a determination may be constitutionally necessary. But it does not follow that the constitution requires a per se rule compelling such a procedure in every case."

In a motion to suppress identification testimony, the judge is the trier of fact and he is to determine credibility, weight, and conflicts in the evidence. It has been said that if there is evidence to support the ruling of the trial judge, the ruling will not be disturbed.[6]

In *Moore v. State*,[7] the court held that a trial judge may deny, without a hearing, a pre-trial motion to suppress identification testimony. The Georgia Court of Appeals held in *Davis v. State*[8] that in reviewing the denial of a motion to suppress identification testimony, the appellate court may consider "the evidence adduced both at the suppression hearing and at trial."

See § 14:78, infra, on motions to suppress and motions in limine. For motions to suppress identification, see Studdard, *Daniel's Georgia Criminal Trial Practice Forms* (2017–2018 ed.), Chapter 6.

§ 6:12 Voice identification

Much of what has been said about eyewitness identification applies to voice identification.[1] For example, the California Court of Appeals has ruled that a defendant has a right to have his counsel present at a "voice lineup."[2] Under the United States Constitution[3] and under Georgia law, a defendant may be required to give

---

Duffey v. State, 151 Ga. App. 673, 261 S.E.2d 421 (1979).

[6]Arnold v. State, 155 Ga. App. 569, 570 (1), 271 S.E.2d 702 (1980); Woods v. State, 165 Ga. App. 39, 40 (1), 299 S.E.2d 97 (1983).

[7]Moore v. State, 215 Ga. App. 626 (1), 451 S.E.2d 534 (1994).

[8]Davis v. State, 216 Ga. App. 580, 581 (1), 455 S.E.2d 115 (1995).

[Section 6:12]

[1]In re Crane, 171 Ga. App. 31, 32 (1), 318 S.E.2d 709 (1984), rev'd on other grounds, 253 Ga. 667, 324 S.E.2d 443 (1985). Cf. Morris v. State, 150 Ga.

App. 652, 654, 258 S.E.2d 302 (1979). In Wallace v. State, 156 Ga. App. 525, 275 S.E.2d 110 (1980), the court said, quoting Willingham v. State, 134 Ga. App. 603, 606, 215 S.E.2d 521 (1975), vocal "verification is analogous to visual verification." However, in Brown v. Harris, 666 F.2d 782, 785 (2d Cir. 1981), the court stated that it was doubtful whether an analogy between a voice identification and a photo showup was valid.

[2]People v. Reese, 121 Cal.App.3d 606, 175 Cal.Rptr. 214 (1981).

[3]Fisher v. United States, 425 U.S. 391, 96 S.Ct. 1569, 48 L.Ed.2d 39

voice exemplars[4] and to repeat any words, including those which the witness said the perpetrator used at the time of the offense,[5] and he may be forced to stand in a lineup.[6] If a law enforcement officer requests individuals to speak over the telephone for purposes of identification and none of them refuse, the identification is admissible even though no *Miranda* warnings are given.[7] See § 5:23, supra, on compelling a suspect to give non-testimonial evidence in Georgia.

Another difference between the two types of identification concerns their accuracy, particularly where spectrographic identification is used. Whereas eyewitness identification is frequently open to much dispute, voiceprints or spectrographic voice identifications are said to be quite accurate and are gaining acceptance in the scientific community.[8] In fact, a voiceprint has been said to have the same accuracy as fingerprint identification. Some courts, however, have rejected voiceprints as unreliable.[9]

One other distinction should be pointed out. While the general rule regards voice identification as direct testimony,[10] the Georgia rule is that such testimony is opinion evidence and, consequently, is not admissible unless the witness testifies to the basis for his opinion.[11]

In *Reese v. State,*[12] the Georgia Court of Appeals declined to hold that where voice identification is involved, it is necessary to have persons in the lineup with a similar distinctive voice as that of the assailant.

(1976).

[4]Davis v. State, 158 Ga. App. 549, 552, 281 S.E.2d 305 (1981); Tate v. State, 153 Ga. App. 508, 510, 265 S.E.2d 818 (1980); Jenkins v. State, 167 Ga. App. 840, 841, 308 S.E.2d 14 (1983); Robinson v. State, 184 Ga. App. 398, 401, 361 S.E.2d 542 (1987); Lowe v. State, 185 Ga. App. 606, 607, 365 S.E.2d 479 (1988).

[5]Tate v. State, 153 Ga. App. 508, 510, 265 S.E.2d 818 (1980).

[6]Wilson v. State, 237 Ga. 657, 229 S.E.2d 424 (1976).

[7]Bradford v. State, 118 Ga. App. 457, 164 S.E.2d 264 (1968). See Annot., 24 A.L.R.3d 1261 (1969).

[8]Moenssens, Moses & Inbau, "Scientific Evidence in Criminal Cases," p. 516 (Foundation Press 1973). See Jones v. State, 156 Ga. App.

543, 275 S.E.2d 119 (1980).

[9]People v. King, 266 Cal.App.2d 437, 72 Cal.Rptr. 478 (1968). In State ex rel. Trimble v. Hedman, 291 Minn. 442, 192 N.W.2d 432 (1971), the court concluded that the process was extremely unreliable. See State v. Cary, 56 N.J. 16, 264 A.2d 209 (1970). Generally, see Annot., 49 A.L.R.3d 915 (1973).

[10]Alea v. State, 265 So.2d 96 (Fla. App.1972); Lindsey v. State, 279 So.2d 913 (Miss.1973); McInturf v. State, 544 S.W.2d 417 (Tex.Crim.App.1976).

[11]Willingham v. State, 134 Ga. App. 603, 604, 215 S.E.2d 521 (1975); Brown v. State, 278 Ga. 369 (1), 602 S.E.2d 834 (2004).

[12]Reese v. State, 145 Ga. App. 453, 456, 243 S.E.2d 650 (1978).

In *Jefferson v. State*,[13] the victim was approached from the rear, blindfolded, and raped. The assailant spoke to the victim a number of times, and she described his voice. While the defendant was being questioned at the police department on the day of the arrest, the police had the victim listen to the defendant's voice just outside the room where he was being questioned. The victim positively identified the voice of the defendant. The court concluded that the voice identification was admissible under the test of *Neil v. Biggers*.[14] See § 6:3, supra, on eyewitness identification. The Georgia court held that the factors to be considered in evaluating the likelihood of misidentification include (1) the opportunity to hear the voice at the time of the crime; (2) the degree of attention of the witness; (3) the witness' prior description of the voice; (4) the level of certainty of the witness at the time of confrontation; and (5) the length of time between the crime and the confrontation. The court then concluded that there was no substantial likelihood of irreparable misidentification.

Generally, see Goger, *Daniel's Georgia Handbook on Criminal Evidence* (2017 ed.), § 6:30, on the defendant as a witness, and § 9:6, on voice identification, and sections 5:22 and 5:23, supra, on non-testimonial evidence. See 1 Wharton's Criminal Evidence, § 189. See also 22A C.J.S. Criminal Law § 616(b)(4).

See 29 Am. Jur. 2d Evidence § 368, on identification by voice. See Annotations, "Admissibility of Evidence of Voice Identification of Defendant as Affected by Alleged Suggestive Voice Lineup Procedures," 55 A.L.R.5th 423 (1998), and "Cautionary Instructions to Jury as to Reliability of, or Factors to Be Considered in Evaluating, Voice Identification Testimony," 17 A.L.R.5th 851 (1994).

---

[13]Jefferson v. State, 206 Ga. App. 544, 545 (2), 425 S.E.2d 915 (1992).

[14]Neil v. Biggers, 409 U.S. 188, 93 S.Ct. 375, 34 L.Ed.2d 401 (1972); Zachery v. State, 238 Ga. App. 191, 193 (3), 517 S.E.2d 71 (1999).

Part II

CLIENT-COUNSEL RELATIONSHIP AND PROCEEDINGS PRIOR TO COMMITMENT HEARING

Chapter 7

Counsel for Defendant

> **KeyCite®:** Cases and other legal materials listed in KeyCite Scope can be researched through the KeyCite service on Westlaw®. Use KeyCite to check citations for form, parallel references, prior and later history, and comprehensive citator information, including citations to other decisions and secondary materials.

§ 7:1   General considerations

In *Penson v. Ohio,*[1] the United States Supreme Court said "the right to be represented by counsel is among the most fundamental rights. . . . '[L]awyers in criminal courts are necessities, not luxuries.' " The same court in *Perry v. Leeke*[2] said "that a

---

[Section 7:1]

[1]Penson v. Ohio, 488 U.S. 75, 84, 109 S.Ct. 346, 102 L.Ed.2d 300 (1988).

[2]Perry v. Leeke, 488 U.S. 272, 268, 109 S.Ct. 594, 102 L.Ed.2d 624 (1989).

defendant has the right to the aid of counsel at each critical stage of the adversary process." In *Benjamin v. Fraser*,[3] the court held that requiring counsel to wait hours to see his counsel is a violation of the Sixth Amendment.

A person who has been arrested needs to employ counsel as quickly as possible. Generally, where a defendant can afford to employ his own counsel, he may be defended by an attorney of his own selection[4] who has been admitted to practice in Georgia. However, in *United States v. Koblitz*,[5] the Eleventh Circuit said, "The right to counsel of choice is not absolute. It must be balanced against the government's interest in the fair, orderly, and effective administration of the courts which, in a given case, may require an accused to resort to his second choice of counsel . . . . In giving effect to this governmental interest, however, a trial judge must be mindful that 'acting in the name of calendar control, [he] cannot arbitrarily and unreasonably interfere with a client's right to be represented by the attorney [the client] has selected.' " The Eleventh Circuit then concluded that the trial court erred in requiring retained counsel to obtain substitute counsel while retained counsel is engaged in a protracted case.[6] However, counsel should take notice of the caveat on a defendant's right to retain the counsel of his/her choice expressed by the court in *Davis v. State:*[7] [a] "defendant must use reasonable diligence in obtaining retained counsel. A defendant may not use a request for change of counsel as a dilatory tactic." In addition, where a defendant is represented by counsel, he cannot also seek to represent himself. Accordingly, motions filed by a defendant, who is a lay person and who has representation, are deemed "unauthorized and without effect."[8]

It is within the discretion of the trial court to permit a non-Georgia attorney to represent a defendant in isolated cases.[9] See Rule 4.4 of the Uniform Rules for the Superior Courts for special

---

[3]Benjamin v. Fraser, 264 F.3d 175 (2d Cir. 2001).

[4]Long v. State, 119 Ga. App. 82, 166 S.E.2d 365 (1969). However, in United States v. Brown, 591 F.2d 307 (5th Cir. 1979), it was held that the Sixth Amendment does not require that the defendant be appointed counsel of his choice. In State v. Fleming, 245 Ga. 700, 703 (2), 267 S.E.2d 207 (1980), the court said that while the right to select a particular person as counsel is not an absolute right, the arbitrary dismissal by a judge of a defendant's counsel of choice violates the defendant's right to counsel.

See Turman v. State, 272 Ga. App. 570, 613 S.E.2d 126 (2005).

[5]United States v. Koblitz, 803 F.2d 1523, 1528 (11th Cir. 1986) (quoting Linton v. Perini, 656 F.2d 207 (6th Cir. 1981)).

[6]United States v. Koblitz, 803 F.2d 1523, 1529 (11th Cir. 1986).

[7]Davis v. State, 295 Ga. 168, 169 (2), 758 S.E.2d 296 (2014) (citations and interior quotations omitted).

[8]See Cotton v. State, 279 Ga. 358, 613 S.E.2d 628 (2005).

[9]Stone v. State, 272 Ga. 351, 353 (2), 529 S.E.2d 136 (2000); Pence v.

admission of attorneys from other states. While an accused has the right to be represented by counsel and a limited right to represent himself (see § 7:3, infra), an accused has no right to be represented by a non-lawyer.[10]

Not only is an accused person entitled to have counsel, that attorney must have reasonable access to the defendant even if he remains in custody, and this is particularly true during trial.[11] However, in *Perry v. Leeke,*[12] the United States Supreme Court held that "the Federal Constitution does not compel every trial judge to allow the defendant to consult with his lawyer while his testimony is in progress if the judge decides that there is a good reason to interrupt the trial for a few minutes." Prior to trial, incarcerated suspects and indicted defendants are entitled to meaningful access to counsel. This includes the right to jail or prison facilities which can accommodate confidential conferences with counsel.[13]

"The benefit of counsel guaranteed by the Georgia Constitution is not satisfied merely because the defendant is represented by counsel . . . [at] trial, but his counsel is entitled to a reasonable time after his employment to prepare a defense . . . ."[14]

Counsel has an ethical duty not to present known or suspected perjury. When a client insists on testifying in a fashion which counsel believes will be perjurious, he or she has a duty to either withdraw or allow the defendant to testify over counsel's objection, in a narrative manner without any direction or questions from counsel. Counsel should inform the court of the situation in

---

Seaboard Coast Line, 128 Ga. App. 161, 196 S.E.2d 182 (1973); Williams v. State, 157 Ga. App. 494 (2), 277 S.E.2d 781 (1981).

See Leis v. Flynt, 439 U.S. 438, 99 S.Ct. 698, 58 L.Ed.2d 717 (1979) (absent state statutory authority nonresident attorney does not have a "right" to represent defendant pro hac vice).

[10]Lebrun v. State, 255 Ga. 406, 407 (2), 339 S.E.2d 227 (1986); Robinson v. State, 182 Ga. App. 423, 425 (5), 356 S.E.2d 55 (1987); Mercier v. State, 203 Ga. App. 494 (2), 417 S.E.2d 430 (1992). See Annot., "Criminal Defendant's Representation by Person Not Licensed to Practice Law as Violation of Right to Counsel," 19 A.L.R.5th 351 (1994).

[11]In Geders v. United States, 425 U.S. 80, 96 S.Ct. 1330, 47 L.Ed.2d 592 (1976), the court entered an order preventing defense counsel from consulting with the defendant during an overnight recess between the defendant's direct and cross-examination to prevent counsel from improperly attempting to influence his testimony. All eight justices participating agreed this was a violation of the defendant's Sixth Amendment right to counsel. Cf. Carter v. State, 156 Ga. App. 633, 275 S.E.2d 716 (1980).

[12]Perry v. Leeke, 488 U.S. 272, 109 S.Ct. 594, 102 L.Ed.2d 624 (1989).

[13]Wright v. State, 250 Ga. 570, 300 S.E.2d 147 (1983); Brown v. Incarcerated Public Defender Clients Div. 3, 288 Ga. App. 859, 655 S.E.2d 704 (2007).

[14]Lowrance v. State, 183 Ga. App. 421, 422, 359 S.E.2d 196 (1987).

an ex-parte fashion. The court should then inform the defendant of counsel's concern and advise that, other than asking some preliminary questions, counsel will not participate in the defendant's presentation of testimony.[15] See § 7:7, infra, on the right of counsel to control the defense of the case.

§ 7:2 Appointment of counsel

If for financial reasons a person is unable to hire an attorney, it is the duty of the court having jurisdiction of the case to appoint counsel for him.[1] Since the passage of the Georgia Indigent Defense Act[2] in 2003, the Georgia Public Defender Council (formerly the Georgia Public Defender Standards Council) has provided counsel to defend the indigent throughout the state with the exception of a limited number of counties which opted not to participate. Counties which do not receive funding under the Act are required to provide indigent defense pursuant to Unif. Sup. Ct. R. 29.1 et seq. The funding of indigent defense both before and after the Georgia Indigent Defense Act has been the subject of considerable criticism. However, there is no right to appointment of counsel prior to the initiation of the adversary judicial proceeding against the defendant such as "formal charge, preliminary hearing, indictment, information or arraignment."[34]

The definition of indigency under The Act varies according to the nature of the offense charged. In the case of a misdemeanor offense, a person is deemed indigent if he or she earns less than 100% of the federal guidelines for poverty. In the case of a felony, the number rises to 150% of the guidelines. In the case of a juvenile, the qualifying number is less than 125% of the guidelines.

Although there is some authority for the notion that a trial court's rulings regarding indigence are not subject to review, these cases are probably best cited in the context of applications

---

[15]Miller v. State, 295 Ga. 769, 764 S.E.2d 135 (2014). See Georgia Rules of Professional Conduct, Rules 1.7, 3.3.

[Section 7:2]

[1]See generally Annot., "Indigent Accused's Right to Choose Particular Counsel Appointed to Assist Him," 66 A.L.R.3d 996 (1975).

[2]See generally O.C.G.A. §§ 17-12-1, et seq.

[3]U.S. v. Gouveia, 467 U.S. 180, 188, 104 S. Ct. 2292, 81 L. Ed. 2d 146 (1984). See U.S. v. Moody, 206 F.3d 609, 2000 FED App. 0088P (6th Cir. 2000).

[4]United States v. Gouveia, 467 U.S. 180, 104 S.Ct. 2292, 81 L.Ed.2d 146 (1984). In Gouveia, the defendant was in prison. He and three other inmates were placed in administrative confinement while a murder of an inmate was investigated. He was so held for 19 months. After indictment, and appointment of counsel, the defendant moved to dismiss the indictment. The court recognized that the defendant's confinement might handicap his ability to work on the case, but this possibility is not enough. There has never been a "right to counsel . . . to provide a defendant with a preindictment investigator."

to proceed *in forma pauperis* in connection with civil cases.[5] Their application in the context of a criminal case has been limited and, given the duty imposed on a trial court by Uniform Rule 30.2 and in cases where a defendant elects to proceed to trial without counsel, a record without appropriate findings would not survive an appeal.[6]

In the Maryland case of *Baldwin v. State*,[7] the court pointed out that the financial ability of a defendant must be determined upon the basis of resources he controls or has a right to control. The court then concluded that the defendant was indigent and entitled to representation by a public defender even though he was free on a $100,000 bond posted by his family, was a college graduate, lived rent-free with his parents, and officers had seized about $17,000 in cash where controlled substances had been found. However, in *Thomas v. State*,[8] the court affirmed the trial court's denial of appointed counsel for a 19-year old defendant who had $428 in monthly earnings but lived with his mother and stepfather who earned $4,000 monthly. The court held that a judge should consider "other resources that might reasonably be used to employ a lawyer" besides the defendant's own income when determining the indigence of misdemeanor defendants.

The appointment of counsel for the indigent is guaranteed under the Sixth Amendment of the United States Constitution. It was apparently recognized that an indigent defendant's right to the appointment of counsel exists in the case of felonies,[9] misdemeanors[10] and other situations in which there is a potential risk of imprisonment upon a finding of guilt.[11] However, in *Scott v. Illinois*,[12] the United States Supreme Court held that there is no right under the Sixth and Fourteenth Amendments to have a state-appointed counsel where the defendant is charged with an

---

[5]See, e.g., Harris v. State, 170 Ga. App. 726, 318 S.E.2d 315 (1984); Quarterman v. Weiss, 212 Ga. App. 563, 564 (5), 442 S.E.2d 813 (1994); Rolleston v. Estate of Sims, 253 Ga. App. 182, 558 S.E.2d 411 (2001); Morris v. Department of Transportation, 209 Ga. App. 40, 432 S.E.2d 638 (1993).

[6]Ford v. State, 254 Ga. App. 413, 563 S.E.2d 170 (2002). See § 7:3, infra.

[7]Baldwin v. State, 51 Md.App. 538, 444 A.2d 1058 (1982).

[8]Thomas v. State, 297 Ga. App. 416, 421, 677 S.E.2d 433, 437 (2009).

[9]Gideon v. Wainwright, 372 U.S. 335, 83 S.Ct. 792, 9 L.Ed.2d 799 (1963), dicta.

[10]Gideon v. Wainwright, 372 U.S. 335, 83 S.Ct. 792, 9 L.Ed.2d 799 (1963).

[11]Argersinger v. Hamlin, 407 U.S. 25, 92 S.Ct. 2006, 32 L.Ed.2d 530 (1972). Contra, Hill v. Bartlett, 227 Ga. 385, 181 S.E.2d 57 (1971), holding that there was no right to appointment of counsel where defendant was charged with violating a city ordinance. This case also seems to be contrary to O.C.G.A. § 17-12-4. Accord, Parker v. State, 220 Ga. App. 303, 304 (2), 469 S.E.2d 410 (1996).

[12]Scott v. Illinois, 440 U.S. 367, 99 S.Ct. 1158, 59 L.Ed.2d 383 (1979). See § 26:28, infra.

offense for which imprisonment upon conviction was authorized if the conviction did not actually lead to imprisonment.

In *Alabama v. Shelton*,[13] the United States Supreme Court in a 5-4 decision concluded that the Sixth Amendment requires that counsel be appointed in any case where an uncounseled indigent defendant *may* be incarcerated as a result of a conviction. Thus, a suspended or probated sentence which may be activated or revoked in the event of a violation of a condition of suspension or revocation is now invalid if the defendant was indigent at the time sentence was imposed and was not represented by counsel and did not waive the right to counsel. In *Howard v. United States*,[14] the 11th Circuit held that the right recognized in *Shelton* is retroactively applicable. In *Alford v. State*,[15] the Georgia Supreme Court agreed with *Howard*. Recognizing that *Shelton* represented a "new rule," the court held that the case "relates to the accuracy of a decision and alters our understanding of the bedrock procedural elements essential to the fairness of a proceeding"[16] and for that reason must be applied retroactively.

In the 1995 case of *Flanagan v. State*,[17] the court held that while a judge "does not have the duty to appoint counsel for [a non-indigent defendant] [the judge] does have the discretion to do so. . . . [T]his discretion must be affirmatively exercised, based on the individual circumstances of each case. . . . [If the trial judge] appoints counsel, it may order the non-indigent defendant to reimburse the county over time."

The 1997 case of *Flanagan v. State*,[18] involved the same case decided in 1995. In this case, the defendant, who had an eighth-grade education, wanted a lawyer to represent him at trial and had contacted several attorneys. He was forced to represent himself and was convicted. On appeal, the Court reversed the conviction. The defendant had no assets and had earned $1,169 a

---

[13]Alabama v. Shelton, 535 U.S. 654, 122 S.Ct. 1764, 152 L.Ed.2d 888 (2002). See Barnes v. State, 275 Ga. 499, 501(2), 570 S.E.2d 277 (2002) ("absent a knowing and intelligent waiver, no indigent person may be imprisoned for any offense, or sentenced to a probated or suspended prison term, unless he was represented by counsel"). Cf. Miller v. Deal, 295 Ga. 504, 761 S.E.2d 274 (2014) (no due process right to counsel for defendant subject to civil contempt action because of non-payment of child support).

[14]Howard v. U.S., 374 F.3d 1068 (11th Cir. 2004).

[15]Alford v. State, 287 Ga. 105, 695 S.E.2d 1 (2010).

[16]Alford v. State, 287 Ga. 105, 695 S.E.2d 1 (2010).

[17]Flanagan v. State, 218 Ga. App. 598, 600, 462 S.E.2d 469 (1995). See also Rules 29.4 and 29.5 of the Uniform Rules for the Superior Courts. Accord, McCall v. State, 232 Ga. App. 684, 686 (1), 503 S.E.2d 578 (1998); Pierce v. State, 222 Ga. App. 245, 247 (2), 474 S.E.2d 112 (1996).

[18]Flanagan v. State, 224 Ga. App. 272, 480 S.E.2d 299 (1997).

month. His employer had loaned him $1,200 before trial, and he did not think his employer would lend him any more money. He had not been able to get a lawyer to represent him for less than $5,000. It appeared that no responsible lender would lend him $3,800. Nevertheless, the trial judge refused to appoint counsel. The appellate court concluded that in view of the foregoing and the trial judge's "failure to consider its power to order defendant to reimburse the county for the cost of a court-appointed attorney . . . [this] persuades us that the trial court . . . manifestly abused its discretion in finding that defendant failed to act reasonably in attempting . . . to retain an attorney." See the reference to Rule 29.5, supra.

The right to appointed counsel is fully retroactive and applicable to cases decided before *Gideon v. Wainwright.*[19] However, a defendant may waive his right to counsel and insist on representing himself even at trial.[20] However, in *Williams v. State,*[21] the court held that where a defendant elects to represent himself and then declines to do so, the trial judge may appoint counsel for the defendant and have the trial proceed. See § 14:93, infra, on mental incompetence of a defendant.

A defendant is entitled to the guiding hand of counsel at every stage of his prosecution at which he would be prejudiced by the

---

[19]Gideon v. Wainwright, 372 U.S. 335, 83 S.Ct. 792, 9 L.Ed.2d 799 (1963); Kitchens v. Smith, 401 U.S. 847, 91 S.Ct. 1089, 28 L.Ed.2d 519 (1971), rev'g 226 Ga. 667, 177 S.E.2d 87 (1970), as to misdemeanors. Berry v. Cincinnati, 414 U.S. 29, 94 S.Ct. 193, 38 L.Ed.2d 187 (1973), holds that the rule is retroactive as to any case in which imprisonment may be imposed. See also Rule 44 of the Federal Rules of Criminal Procedure, regarding the right to appointed counsel in federal courts:

"(a) **Right to Appointed Counsel**. A defendant who is unable to obtain counsel is entitled to have counsel appointed to represent the defendant at every stage of the proceeding from initial appearance through appeal, unless the defendant waives the right.

"(b) **Appointment procedure**. Federal law and local court rules govern the procedure for implementing the right to counsel.

"(c) **Inquiry Into Joint Representation**.

(1) **Joint Representation**. Joint representation occurs when:

(A) two or more defendants have been charged jointly under Rule 8(b) or have been joined for trial under Rule 13; and

(B) the defendants are represented by the same counsel, or counsel who are associated in law practice.

(2) **Court's Responsibilities in Cases of Joint Representation**. The court must promptly inquire about the propriety of joint representation and must personally advise each defendant of the right to the effective assistance of counsel, including separate representation. Unless there is good cause to believe that no conflict of interest is likely to arise, the court must take appropriate measures to protect each defendant's right to counsel.

[20]Faretta v. California, 422 U.S. 806, 95 S.Ct. 2525, 45 L.Ed.2d 562 (1975); Taylor v. Ricketts, 239 Ga. 501, 238 S.E.2d 52 (1977). See Wilkerson v. State, 286 Ga. 201, 686 S.E.2d 648 (2009).

[21]Williams v. State, 169 Ga. App. 812, 315 S.E.2d 42 (1984).

absence of an attorney.[22] However, it has been held in Georgia that if a defendant is not indigent at the time of his conviction, his failure to retain counsel amounts to a waiver of his right to an attorney.[23] Such a ruling, however, appears contrary to several Supreme Court decisions which emphasize the necessity of the defendant's understanding of the charges, range of allowable punishment, possible defenses, and mitigating circumstances before he can intelligently waive his right to counsel.[24]

Where a defendant expresses dissatisfaction with appointed counsel and refuses to employ counsel despite having had an adequate opportunity to do so, courts have found this to constitute a waiver to the right to counsel.[25] Likewise, an indigent defendant has no absolute right to discharge a court-appointed attorney and have another appointed to represent him.[26] In *Cotton v. State,*[27] the defendant insisted on discharging appointed counsel in midtrial and refused to let counsel represent him. Defendant then engaged in an effort to delay trial without justification, which amounted to a waiver to be represented by counsel. In *Rivers v. State,*[28] the court held that a defendant "is not entitled to counsel of his own choosing." In *Phipps v. State,*[29] the court pointed out that "[a] defendant is not entitled to an attorney who agrees with the defendant's personal views of the prevailing law or the equities of the prosecutor's case. A defendant is entitled to an attorney who will consider the defendant's views and seek to accommodate all reasonable requests with respect to trial preparation and trial tactics. . . . [He] is entitled to appointment of an attorney with whom he can communicate reasonably, but has no right to an attorney who will docilely do as he is told." In

---

[22]Coleman v. Alabama, 399 U.S. 1, 90 S.Ct. 1999, 26 L.Ed.2d 387 (1970).

[23]Bostick v. Ricketts, 236 Ga. 304, 306 (2), 223 S.E.2d 686 (1976). Cf. Scott v. State, 151 Ga. App. 840, 841, 262 S.E.2d 198 (1979); Braswell v. State, 240 Ga. App. 510 (1), 523 S.E.2d 904 (1999).

[24]See Johnson v. Zerbst, 304 U.S. 458, 58 S.Ct. 1019, 82 L.Ed. 1461 (1938); Faretta v. California, 422 U.S. 806, 95 S.Ct. 2525, 45 L.Ed.2d 562 (1975). See also Campbell v. State, 128 Ga. App. 74, 76, 195 S.E.2d 664 (1973), in which the court says there is a presumption against waiver of counsel.

[25]Hose v. State, 161 Ga. App. 401,

288 S.E.2d 675 (1982). See Partlow v. State, 346 Ga. App. 473, 816 S.E.2d 474 (2018). But see § 7:3, infra.

[26]Newby v. State, 161 Ga. App. 805, 807 (2), 288 S.E.2d 889 (1982); Mock v. State, 163 Ga. App. 320, 293 S.E.2d 525 (1982).

[27]Cotton v. State, 223 Ga. App. 288, 290 (2), 477 S.E.2d 425 (1996). See Sims v. State, 265 Ga. App. 476, 594 S.E.2d 693 (2004).

[28]Oliver v. State, 246 Ga. App. 32, 36, 538 S.E.2d 837 (2000); Rivers v. State, 250 Ga. 303, 308 (6), 298 S.E.2d 1 (1982); United States v. Ely, 719 F.2d 902 (7th Cir. 1983).

[29]Phipps v. State, 200 Ga. App. 18, 19, 406 S.E.2d 493 (1991).

Durham v. State,[30] the court held that a request by an indigent defendant to discharge one appointed counsel and have another substituted addresses itself to the sound discretion of the trial judge. In *Morris v. Slappy,*[31] the United States Supreme Court held that an indigent defendant has no right to counsel with whom he will develop a rapport or a *"meaningful attorney*-client relationship." Likewise, in *Stephens v. State,*[32] the court held that it was not error for the trial judge to deny a motion for a continuance where the defendant hired a new lawyer on the day of trial because he just felt "totally unsafe" with the former lawyer. In *United States v. Moore,*[33] the court held that a defendant's "persistent unreasonable demand for dismissal of counsel and appointment of new counsel . . . is the . . . equivalent of a knowing and voluntary waiver of counsel." In *Jefferson v. State,*[34] the court pointed out that "any act of defendant which effectively terminated his counsel would not have . . . the effect of 'triggering' a duty upon the part of the trial court to appoint another attorney for defendant. . . . If the defendant does not have a good reason for discharging his court-appointed attorney, the trial court does not err in requiring him to choose between representation by that attorney and proceeding pro se."

However, in *Amadeo v. State,*[35] the Georgia Supreme Court said that while "the court's discretion in the appointment of counsel is not to be limited or constrained by a defendant's bare statement of personal preference, we hold that when that statement of preference, timely made, is supported by objective considerations of the consequence here involved, and where there are no countervailing considerations of comparable weight, it is an abuse of sound judicial discretion to deny the defendant's request to appoint the counsel of his preference."

Further, in *Roberts v. State,*[36] the Georgia Supreme Court held that not only does a trial judge have the authority to appoint counsel for an indigent defendant, the judge also has a constitutional duty to do so, even where the defendant is already

---

[30]Durham v. State, 185 Ga. App. 163, 164 (1), 363 S.E.2d 607 (1987).

[31]Morris v. Slappy, 461 U.S. 1, 103 S.Ct. 1610, 75 L.Ed.2d 610 (1983).

[32]Stephens v. State, 208 Ga. App. 620 (1), 431 S.E.2d 422 (1993).

[33]United States v. Moore, 706 F.2d 538 (5th Cir. 1983) (citing Wilks v. Israel, 627 F.2d 32 (7th Cir. 1980); McKee v. Harris, 649 F.2d 927 (2d Cir. 1981)).

[34]Jefferson v. State, 209 Ga. App. 859, 861 (1), 434 S.E.2d 814 (1993).

[35]Amadeo v. State, 259 Ga. 469, 471, 384 S.E.2d 181 (1989) (quoting Harris v. People, 19 Cal.3d 786, 140 Cal.Rptr. 318, 567 P.2d 750 (1977)); Davis v. State, 261 Ga. 221, 222, 403 S.E.2d 800 (1991). See Hulett v. State, 296 Ga. 49, 766 S.E.2d 1 (2014) (the rule is different post-conviction where there is a record and trial counsel's effectiveness may be an issue).

[36]Roberts v. State, 263 Ga. 764, 766 (1), 438 S.E.2d 905 (1994).

represented by pro bono counsel or counsel paid for by a third party. Also, the right to appointed counsel may be raised by the indigent defendant's current legal representative.

On the right of an indigent defendant to counsel on appeal, see § 28:6, infra. See § 7:3, infra, on waiver of right to counsel. See § 7:4, infra, on necessity of counsel being admitted to practice law.

§ 7:3 Waiver of counsel

In *Faretta v. California*,[1] the United States Supreme Court held that a defendant has a federal constitutional right to waive his right of counsel and represent himself at the trial stage. If a defendant makes a pre-trial, unequivocal assertion of the right to self-representation, the request must be followed by a hearing to insure that the defendant knowingly and intelligently waives the traditional benefits associated with the right to counsel and understands the disadvantages of self-representation so that the record will establish that he knows what he is doing and his choice is made with eyes open.[2]

In *Martinez v. Court of Appeals of California*,[3] the United States Supreme Court limited *Faretta* by holding that a non-lawyer has no federal constitutional right to represent himself on a direct appeal from a conviction. Nevertheless, this case points out that its holding does not prevent a state from recognizing such a right under its own constitution. As a result of the wording of the Georgia Constitution of 1976, it has been held that at trial a defendant has a right to represent himself alone and also to represent himself as co-counsel even though he is adequately represented.[4] Additionally, in *Cook v. State*,[5] the Georgia Court of Appeals recognized that the wording of the Georgia Constitution also guarantees a right to self-representation on appeal. However, it has been pointed out that, under the present Georgia Constitution, a lay person does not have "the right to represent himself and also be represented by an attorney,"[6] and that this is not a violation of the Sixth Amendment of the United States

---

[Section 7:3]

[1]Faretta v. California, 422 U.S. 806, 95 S.Ct. 2525, 45 L.Ed.2d 562 (1975).

[2]Thaxton v. State, 260 Ga. 141, 142, 390 S.E.2d 841 (1990) (punctuation and citation omitted). See Wiggins v. State, 298 Ga. 366, 782 S.E.2d 31 (2016).

[3]Martinez v. Court of Appeal of California, 528 U.S. 152, 120 S.Ct.

684, 145 L.Ed.2d 597 (2000).

[4]Jackson v. State, 149 Ga. App. 496, 499 (1), 254 S.E.2d 739 (1979); Burney v. State, 244 Ga. 33, 257 S.E.2d 543 (1979); Moody v. State, 153 Ga. App. 866, 267 S.E.2d 291 (1980); Garvey v. State, 176 Ga. App. 268, 269, 335 S.E.2d 640 (1985).

[5]Cook v. State, 296 Ga. App. 496, 675 S.E.2d 245 (2009).

[6]Jones v. State, 171 Ga. App. 184,

Constitution.[7] In other words, a non-lawyer "defendant has a right to represent himself, [but] he does not have the right to act as co-counsel."[8] In *Seagraves v. State*,[9] the court held that a defendant who also happens to be a lawyer does have the right to represent himself and act as co-counsel to his private or appointed attorney. However, it is error to advise a defendant wishing to proceed pro se that thereafter he cannot reverse his decision once trial begins. The trial court has discretion to appoint counsel for a pro se defendant during trial. The court's discretion in the face of such a request should be tempered by the potential for disruption to the trial. Accordingly, the better practice for trial courts is to appoint standby counsel for the defendant who chooses to proceed to trial without counsel.[10]

Before allowing a defendant to proceed pro se, a trial court must ascertain whether or not the defendant is mentally competent to represent himself, assuming competency is an issue, and must "apprise the defendant of the 'dangers and disadvantages' inherent in representing himself . . . ."[11] After a court has determined competency and informed the defendant of these "dangers and disadvantages," a "defendant who nevertheless chooses voluntarily to proceed pro se has validly waived the right to counsel . . . and is entitled to exercise his or her constitutional right to self representation."[12] In *Lamar v. State*,[13] the Supreme Court of Georgia found reversible error where the trial court denied the defendant the opportunity to represent himself after questioning him about his legal knowledge of death penalty law, rather than informing him of the dangers of self-representation

---

186 (2), 319 S.E.2d 18 (1984).

[7]Cargill v. State, 255 Ga. 616, 622 (3), 340 S.E.2d 891 (1986) (citing McKaskle v. Wiggins, 465 U.S. 168, 104 S.Ct. 944, 79 L.Ed.2d 122, 136 (1984)). See also Daguilar v. State, 275 Ga. App. 756, 621 S.E.2d 846 (2005).

[8]Isaacs v. State, 259 Ga. 717, 731 (24), 386 S.E.2d 316 (1989); Eagle v. State, 264 Ga. 1, 3 (5), 440 S.E.2d 2 (1994).

[9]Seagraves v. State, 259 Ga. 36, 38, 376 S.E.2d 670 (1989). Accord, Miller v. State, 219 Ga. App. 213, 214 (1), 464 S.E.2d 621 (1995).

[10]See Wilkerson v. State, 286 Ga. 201, 686 S.E.2d 648 (2009). See also Cotton v. State, 279 Ga. 358, 613 S.E.2d 628 (2005), where the court noted that a pro se motion filed by a convicted defendant while represented

by counsel is "unauthorized and without effect."

[11]Lamar v. State, 278 Ga. 150, 598 S.E.2d 488 (2004); Faretta v. California, 422 U.S. 806, 835 (V), 95 S.Ct. 2525, 45 L.Ed.2d 562 (1975) (stating that when a defendant chooses to represent himself, the record must reflect that "he knows what he is doing and his choice is made with eyes open.").

[12]Lamar v. State, 278 Ga. 150, 598 S.E.2d 488 (2004).

[13]Lamar v. State, 278 Ga. 150, 598 S.E.2d 488 (2004). See Bettis v. State, 328 Ga. App. 167, 761 S.E.2d 570 (2014) (failure to advise defendant about dangers of self-representation who asserted unequivocal desire to represent himself on eve of trial was error).

pursuant to *Faretta*.

In *Indiana v. Edwards*,[14] the trial court properly denied the defendant's right to waive assigned counsel when a mentally ill defendant was competent enough to stand trial, but not competent enough to defend himself at trial. The U.S. Supreme Court held there is nothing in the U.S. Constitution which prohibits a state from insisting that a mentally ill defendant be represented by counsel.

In *McKaskle v. Wiggins*,[15] the court said, "A defendant's Sixth Amendment rights are not violated when a trial judge appoints standby counsel—even over the defendant's objection." However, "the Faretta right must impose some limits on the extent of standby counsel's unsolicited participation. First, the pro se defendant is entitled to preserve actual control over the case he chooses to present to the jury. . . . Second, participation by standby counsel without defendant's consent should not be allowed to destroy the jury's perception that the defendant is representing himself. . . . [T]he appearance of a pro se defendant's self representation will not be unacceptably undermined by counsel's participation outside the presence of the jury. Thus, Faretta rights are adequately vindicated in proceedings outside the presence of the jury if the pro se defendant is allowed to address the court freely on his own behalf and if disagreements between counsel and the pro se defendant are resolved in the defendant's favor. . . ." A defendant can waive his Faretta rights. Once a pro se defendant invites or agrees to any substantial participation by counsel, subsequent appearances by counsel must be presumed to be with the defendant's acquiescence, at least until the defendant expressly and unambiguously renews his request that standby counsel be silenced.

In *Powers v. State*,[16] the court held that if a defendant asserts his right to represent himself but co-counsel has been appointed and co-counsel is lead counsel, the trial judge may require co-counsel to conduct the examination of witnesses.

---

[14]Indiana v. Edwards, 554 U.S. 164, 128 S. Ct. 2379, 171 L.Ed.2d 345 (2008). See Duckett v. State, 331 Ga. App. 24, 769 S.E.2d 743 (2015) (trial court not required to sua sponte conduct competency hearing during trial after defendant who is proceeding without counsel displays obvious signs of mental and emotional instability but never appeared so impaired as to warrant denying her right to represent herself).

[15]McKaskle v. Wiggins, 465 U.S. 168, 104 S.Ct. 944, 79 L.Ed.2d 122 (1984), rev'g Wiggins v. Estelle, 681 F.2d 266 (5th Cir. 1982). See Barnes v. Secretary, Department of Corrections, 888 F.3d 1148 (11th Cir. 2018) (right to proceed pro se not violated by appointment of special counsel over objection of defendant to investigate and present mitigation evidence in penalty phase of death case).

[16]Powers v. State, 168 Ga. App. 642, 643 (3), 310 S.E.2d 260 (1983).

In the unusual case of *Williams v. State*,[17] shortly after the trial had started, the defendant decided he did not want appointed counsel to represent him and asked for other counsel. Original counsel had been appointed two months earlier, had conferred with the defendant and was prepared. The court refused to appoint new counsel and ordered that the trial continue. The defendant refused to represent himself and said that he would not permit the original counsel to represent him in any way, and voluntarily remained out of the courtroom during nearly all of the remainder of the trial. The court permitted the earlier appointed counsel to remain in the courtroom and directed him "to exercise his best judgment in entering objections to evidence." Counsel did make some objections. The appellate court affirmed the conviction.

A defendant's insistence that appointed counsel pursue "a frivolous and baseless line of defense" may be the functional equivalent of a knowing and voluntary waiver of counsel.[18] However, the record must reflect that the court made the defendant aware of his right to counsel and the dangers of proceeding pro se.[19]

In *Wyman v. State*,[20] the Court of Appeals noted that where "a defendant does not have a good reason for discharging his court-appointed counsel, the trial court does not err in requiring him to choose between representation by that attorney and proceeding pro se." Thus, in *Holsey v. State*,[21] a trial court's decision to require defendant to either proceed with appointed counsel or pro se was affirmed even though defendant had filed a bar complaint against his attorney, claiming that his attorney had not communicated with him for several months. The trial court was satisfied by counsel's representation that he was prepared and ready for trial.

In *Thaxton v. State*,[22] the Georgia Supreme Court pointed out that prior to trial a defendant must make an unequivocal assertion of his right to represent himself, and a defendant "cannot

[17]Williams v. State, 169 Ga. App. 812, 315 S.E.2d 42 (1984).

[18]Calmes v. State, 312 Ga. App. 769, 719 S.E.2d 516 (2011).

[19]Walker v. State, 288 Ga. 174, 702 S.E.2d 415 (2010).

[20]Wyman v. State, 267 Ga. App. 118(1), 598 S.E.2d 855 (2004).

[21]Holsey v. State, 291 Ga. App. 216(2), 661 S.E.2d 621 (2008).

[22]Thaxton v. State, 260 Ga. 141, 142 (2), 390 S.E.2d 841 (1990); Chambers v. State, 213 Ga. App. 414, 417 (4), 444 S.E.2d 820 (1994). The denial of a defendant's request to represent himself first asserted during trial is not reversible error. Stewart v. State, 267 Ga. App. 100 (1), 598 S.E.2d 837 (2004); Mallory v. State, 225 Ga. App. 418 (4), 483 S.E.2d 907 (1997). See Tyner v. State, 334 Ga. App. 890, 780 S.E.2d 494 (2015) (physical precedent only) (trial court erred in refusing defendant's request that his attorney resume as counsel in the case shortly after granting defendant's request that he act as his own counsel).

frivolously change his mind in midstream." Failure to assert the right to self representation prior to the start of trial may amount to a waiver.[23]

In a case in which a defendant says he wants to represent himself, a special burden rests upon the trial judge. He must be sure the record discloses that the defendant voluntarily, knowingly and intelligently waives counsel and in the process he must be advised of his right to counsel and informed that if he cannot afford counsel, the judge will appoint counsel to represent him.[24] There is a presumption that a defendant does not waive his right to counsel and the trial judge must determine whether or not there has been a valid waiver.[25] Indeed, in those cases where a defendant appears pro se at a first appearance or arraignment calendar and attempts without success to resolve the case with the state's representatives, any statements made in conjunction therewith may be subject to suppression at trial unless the defendant first properly waives the right to counsel.[26] A trial judge's affidavit, submitted by the State on appeal, which states

---

[23]Danenberg v. State, 291 Ga. 439, 729 S.E.2d 315 (2012). See Owens v. State, 298 Ga. 813, 783 S.E.2d 611 (2016) (mid-trial election by defendant to represent herself properly denied).

[24]Rogers v. State, 156 Ga. App. 466, 274 S.E.2d 815 (1980); Fernandez v. State, 171 Ga. App. 290, 292, 319 S.E.2d 503 (1984). In Clarke v. Zant, 247 Ga. 194, 197, 275 S.E.2d 49 (1981), the court said that "in future cases, the record should reflect a finding on the part of the trial court that the defendant has validly chosen to proceed pro se. The record should also show that this choice was made after the defendant was made aware of his right to counsel and the dangers of proceeding without counsel." See Watkins v. State, 291 Ga. App. 343 (1), 662 S.E.2d 544 (2008) where the defendant waived his right to counsel at arraignment, but later insisted on appointed counsel just prior to trial. The Court of Appeals held that the trial court erred in failing to appoint counsel because the record was devoid of an informed waiver of counsel other than a waiver form that was executed at the defendant's arraignment.

[25]Johnson v. Zerbst, 304 U.S. 458, 58 S.Ct. 1019, 82 L.Ed. 1461 (1938).

See § 16:3, particularly n. 1, infra, on guilty plea.

In United States v. Weninger, 624 F.2d 163, 164 (10th Cir. 1980), the court, quoting from Von Moltke v. Gillies, 332 U.S. 708, 724, 68 S.Ct. 316, 92 L.Ed. 309 (1948), pointed out that a "judge can make certain that an accused's professed waiver of counsel is understandingly and wisely made only from a penetrating and comprehensive examination of all the circumstances under which such a plea is tendered." The court also said that "[d]uring trial, the judge repeatedly tried to persuade Weninger to secure representation. . . . The record and surrounding circumstances sufficiently demonstrate that Weninger had a reasonable opportunity to retain counsel, [yet] . . . he strategically chose to appear pro se . . . Weninger's stubborn failure to hire an attorney constituted a knowing and intelligent waiver of the right to assistance of counsel. . . . Since we hold that Weninger was properly permitted to appear pro se, his lack of legal expertise cannot be the basis for a reversal."

[26]State v. Pinkerton, 262 Ga. App. 858, 586 S.E.2d 743 (2003).

that the defendant was informed of her right to counsel and a trial by jury will not satisfy the State's burden to show that a guilty plea was voluntary where the affidavit is not part of the trial record.[27]

Pre-trial waiver forms might be helpful if they fully set out the defendant's voluntary and knowledgeable decision to proceed without counsel. The defendant's right to counsel and the dangers of proceeding without one should be fully described. In addition, "the form should be signed by the defendant and by the trial court."[28] In the absence of a satisfactory explanation as to the rights which the defendant is waiving, a waiver form will not be deemed to constitute a knowing and voluntary waiver of counsel.[29]

Where the trial judge determines that the defendant is not indigent and, consequently, not entitled to appointment of counsel, "the record should reflect a finding on the part of the trial court that the defendant . . . was made aware of his right to [employ] counsel *and the dangers* of proceeding without counsel."[30]

In *Barnes v. State*,[31] the Supreme Court of Georgia observed "[i]n addition to an indigent defendant's right to court appointed counsel, Georgia precedent recognizes an independent and broader constitutional right to be defended by counsel of [one's] own selection whenever [one] is willing and able to employ such counsel." The Court proceeded to note that whether the right to counsel of one's choosing has been waived is an "independent and separate inquiry from whether the right to court appointed counsel exists." It has been said that the trial "judge must investigate as long and as thoroughly as the circumstances of the case before him demand. . . . To be valid . . . [a waiver of counsel] must be made with an apprehension of [1] the nature of the charges, [2] the statutory offenses included within them, [3] the range of allowable punishments thereunder, [4] possible defenses to the charges and [5] circumstances in mitigation thereof, and [6] all other facts essential to a broad understanding of the whole

---

[27]Helmer v. State, 256 Ga. App. 717, 569 S.E.2d 606 (2002).

[28]Brooks v. State, 243 Ga. App. 246, 248 (1)(a), note 1, 532 S.E.2d 763 (2000); Tucci v. State, 255 Ga. App. 474, 565 S.E.2d 831 (2002). Both of these cases disapproved of the forms used by the trial courts.

[29]See Williams v. State, 336 Ga. App. 442, 784 S.E.2d 808 (2016).

[30]Horton v. State, 161 Ga. App. 664, 665, 289 S.E.2d 788 (1982) (quoting Clarke v. Zant, 247 Ga. 194, 197, 275 S.E.2d 49 (1981)). Cf. Callaway v. State, 197 Ga. App. 606, 607, 398 S.E.2d 856 (1990).

[31]Barnes v. State, 275 Ga. 499, 501(1), 570 S.E.2d 277 (2002) (citing Deren v. State, 237 Ga. App. 387, 515 S.E.2d 191 (1999)).

matter."[32] In addition, the defendant should also be advised that he or she will be responsible for such strategic decisions as which witnesses to call, conducting voir dire and selecting a jury. The defendant should understand the necessity of creating and preserving a record for purposes of appeal.[33] However, in *Wayne v. State*,[34] the Georgia Supreme Court held that while it might be helpful, "it is not incumbent upon a trial court to ask each of . . . [these] questions. . . . The record need only reflect that the accused was made aware of the dangers of self-representation and nevertheless made a knowing and intelligent waiver." The test of a valid waiver is not whether it appears that the defendant is capable of adequately representing himself, but whether the waiver is made knowingly and intelligently.[35]

In *Reviere v. State*,[36] the court pointed out that "[t]here is no magic language that must be used by a trial judge in determining that a defendant has made a valid waiver of his right to counsel. Rather, such determination must depend upon the particular facts and circumstances of each case." As noted by the court in *Manning v. State*,[37] simply warning a defendant who elects to proceed without counsel that it was "an unwise decision" and "extremely ill advised" was not sufficient to allow for a finding that the defendant's waiver was knowing and voluntary.

In *Mitchell v. State*,[38] the court held that where a non-indigent defendant appears for trial without counsel, "the judge has a duty to delay the proceedings long enough to ascertain whether the defendant has acted with reasonable diligence in obtaining an attorney's service and whether the absence of an attorney is attributable to reasons beyond the defendant's control."

---

[32]Von Moltke v. Gillies, 332 U.S. 708, 723-24, 68 S.Ct. 316, 92 L.Ed. 309 (1948); State v. Watson, 244 Ga. App. 484, 536 S.E.2d 170 (2000); Prater v. State, 220 Ga. App. 506, 508, 469 S.E.2d 780 (1996).

[33]Bush v. State, 268 Ga. App. 200(2), 601 S.E.2d 511 (2004).

[34]Wayne v. State, 269 Ga. 36, 38, 495 S.E.2d 34 (1998); Allen v. State, 273 Ga. App. 227 (1), 614 S.E.2d 857 (2005). See Merritt v. State, 261 Ga. App. 597 (1), 583 S.E.2d 283 (2003). See also, Jones v. Walker, 540 F.3d 1277 (11th Cir. 2008), where the 11th Circuit held that a defendant can voluntarily waive counsel through uncooperative conduct. To be an effective waiver, the defendant must still be ad-

vised by the court of the dangers of proceeding pro se.

[35]Seymour v. State, 312 Ga. App. 462, 718 S.E.2d 354 (2011).

[36]Reviere v. State, 231 Ga. App. 329, 330, 498 S.E.2d 332 (1998); King v. State, 231 Ga. App. 775, 776, 501 S.E.2d 19 (1998).

[37]Manning v. State, 260 Ga. App. 171, 581 S.E.2d 290 (2003).

[38]Mitchell v. State, 225 Ga. App. 520, 521 (2), 484 S.E.2d 271 (1997), rev'd on other grounds, 268 Ga. 592, 492 S.E.2d 204 (1997). See Houston v. State, 205 Ga. App. 703, 423 S.E.2d 431 (1992). Cf. Lang v. State, 226 Ga. App. 729, 733 (7), 487 S.E.2d 485 (1997).

In *Jones v. Wharton*,[39] the Georgia Supreme Court made several significant points on waiver of counsel. (1) "When the record is silent, waiver is never presumed and the burden is on the state to present evidence of a valid waiver." (2) "Waiver of counsel requires more than a showing of a knowledge of right to counsel; there must also be evidence of relinquishment." (3) "Merely finding that a request for counsel was not made is insufficient to establish waiver . . . ; the right to be furnished counsel does not depend on a request." (4) In both felony cases and misdemeanor cases where the defendant faces imprisonment "the record should reflect a finding on the part of the trial court that the defendant has validly chosen to proceed pro se. The record should also show that this choice was made after the defendant was made aware of his right to counsel and the dangers of proceeding without counsel."[40]

In *Carswell v. State*,[41] the court rejected the argument that the burden was on the defendant to complete an application for appointment of counsel and that there is no obligation on the part of the trial court to appoint counsel until this has been done.

In *Godinez v. Moran*,[42] the United States Supreme Court held that the competence of a defendant to waive counsel is the same as the competence required to stand trial or plead guilty.

See § 7:2, supra, on waiver of right to counsel by refusing to accept appointed counsel or employ an attorney. Also see § 5:10, supra, on right of a defendant to counsel.

§ 7:4 Ineffective assistance of counsel—Deficiency and prejudice

The right to counsel means the right of the defendant to be represented by a person who has been admitted to practice law.[1] In *Cornwell v. Dodd*,[2] the Georgia Supreme Court held that "an attorney . . . [who] is suspended for failure to pay dues or complete continuing legal education is still counsel for purposes of the sixth amendment." It has also been held that if counsel is subsequently disbarred for professional misconduct in unrelated

---

[39]Jones v. Wharton, 253 Ga. 82, 83, 316 S.E.2d 749 (1984).

[40]Clarke v. Zant, 247 Ga. 194, 197, 275 S.E.2d 49 (1981). But see Singleton v. State, 176 Ga. App. 733, 337 S.E.2d 350 (1985).

[41]Carswell v. State, 244 Ga. App. 516, 521 (4), 534 S.E.2d 568 (2000).

[42]Godinez v. Moran, 509 U.S. 389, 113 S.Ct. 2680, 125 L.Ed.2d 321 (1993).

[Section 7:4]

[1]Solina v. United States, 709 F.2d 160 (2d Cir. 1983).

[2]Cornwell v. Dodd, 270 Ga. 411 (1), 509 S.E.2d 919 (1999). Cf. Spears v. State, 234 Ga. App. 498, 506 S.E.2d 446 (1998) (involving at least some question of whether the solicitor of a state court had paid his bar dues).

matters, it is not a per se denial of counsel.[3] In *People v. Tin Trung Ngo,*[4] the court held that there was no automatic disqualification of an attorney where he was involuntarily placed on inactive status by the bar for failing to comply with mandatory CLE requirements. In *United States v. Hoffman,*[5] the Ninth Circuit held that there was no per se disqualification of defense counsel where counsel was suspended during trial from the Florida Bar without the knowledge of the trial judge.

In the outstanding Texas case of *Cantu v. State,*[6] the defendant's lawyer was suspended for refusal to respond to a commission on grievances. Counsel did not know of the suspension until he learned of it during trial. The court concluded that action or inaction of defendant's counsel to the commission on grievances did not indicate an inability to represent the defendant competently. The court pointed out that four reasons have been given for finding a per se Sixth Amendment violation when a defendant is represented by a non-lawyer: (1) absence of counsel is a jurisdictional defect; (2) to prevent a conflict of interest; (3) to maintain confidence in the judicial system; and (4) to protect the defendant's right to effective assistance of counsel. However, "[a] different rule obtains for attorneys who were once validly licensed but have subsequently been suspended or disbarred. We believe the Sixth Amendment's concerns are satisfied by a case-by-case approach. A suspended or disbarred attorney is incompetent as a matter of law if the reasons for the discipline imposed reflect so poorly upon the attorney's competence that it may reasonably be inferred that the attorney was incompetent to represent the defendant in the proceeding in question. . . . In either event, relevant factors for determining whether an attorney is incompetent as a matter of law include, but are not necessarily limited to, the following: (1) severity of the sanction (suspension versus disbarment; length of suspension), (2) the reasons for the discipline, (3) whether the discipline was based upon an isolated incident or a pattern of conduct, (4) similarities between the type of proceeding resulting in discipline and the type of proceeding in question, (5) similarities between kinds of conduct resulting in the attorney's discipline and any duties or responsibilities the attorney had in connection with the proceeding in question, (6) temporal proximity between the conduct for which the attorney was disciplined and the proceeding in question, and (7) the nature and extent of

---

[3]Williams v. State, 211 Ga. App. 393, 395 (2)(a), 439 S.E.2d 11 (1993). Cf. Kemp v. State, 163 Ga. App. 680, 681 (1), 296 S.E.2d 71 (1982).

[4]People v. Tin Trung Ngo, 14 Cal.4th 30, 924 P.2d 97, 57 Cal.Rptr.2d 456 (1996).

[5]United States v. Hoffman, 733 F.2d 596 (9th Cir. 1984).

[6]Cantu v. State, 930 S.W.2d 594 (Tex.Cr.App.1996).

the lawyer's professional experience and accomplishments."

In *White v. State,*[7] the Georgia Supreme Court held that the defendant was not denied effective assistance of counsel where his trial counsel was disbarred after the defendant's trial on a matter unrelated to the defendant's case.

Not only is a defendant entitled to the assistance of counsel, he is entitled to the reasonably effective assistance of counsel.[8] In *Hawes v. State,*[9] the Georgia Supreme Court said that effective assistance is said not to mean "errorless counsel . . . [nor] counsel judged ineffective by hindsight, but counsel reasonably likely to render and rendering reasonably effective assistance." Generally, the "burden is on the defendant to establish his claim of ineffective assistance of counsel[,]"[10] which is determined by looking at the totality of the representation and not by evaluating the effectiveness of counsel based upon isolated trial errors.[11]

The United States Supreme Court, in the 1984 case of *Strickland v. Washington,*[12] held that from a Sixth Amendment standpoint, (1) counsel must render "reasonably effective assistance"; however, (2) "a court must indulge a strong presumption that counsel's conduct falls within the wide range of reasonable professional assistance." The court also held that in order for a convicted defendant to obtain a reversal because of defective assistance of counsel, two requirements must be met. "First, the defendant must show that counsel's performance was deficient. This requires showing that counsel made errors so serious that counsel was not functioning as the 'counsel' guaranteed that defendant by the Sixth Amendment. Second, the defendant must show that the deficient performance prejudiced the defense." In order for a defendant to show that he was prejudiced by action or inaction of his counsel, he must show "that there is a reasonable probability that, but for counsel's unprofessional errors, the result of the proceeding would have been different."

---

[7]White v. State, 267 Ga. 523, 524 (7), 481 S.E.2d 804 (1997).

[8]Young v. State, 239 Ga. 53, 60, 236 S.E.2d 1 (1977). See also Herring v. Estelle, 491 F.2d 125, 127 (5th Cir. 1974) (citing MacKenna v. Ellis, 280 F.2d 592 (5th Cir. 1960)).

[9]Hawes v. State, 240 Ga. 327, 329 (1), 240 S.E.2d 833 (1977) (quoting MacKenna v. Ellis, 280 F.2d 592, 599 (5th Cir. 1960)). Accord, McGill v. State, 263 Ga. 81, 82 (2), 428 S.E.2d 341 (1993).

[10]Cauley v. State, 203 Ga. App. 299, 301 (2), 416 S.E.2d 575 (1992).

[11]Dansby v. State, 165 Ga. App. 41, 43 (2)(c), 299 S.E.2d 579 (1983); Hicks v. State, 169 Ga. App. 542, 314 S.E.2d 113 (1984).

[12]Strickland v. Washington, 466 U.S. 668, 104 S.Ct. 2052, 80 L.Ed.2d 674 (1984); Schofield v. Gulley, 279 Ga. 413, 614 S.E.2d 740 (2005) ("reasonable possibility" does not mean "certain" or even "more likely than not"); Davenport v. State, 172 Ga. App. 848, 851, 325 S.E.2d 173 (1984); Smith v. Francis, 253 Ga. 782, 783, 325 S.E.2d 362 (1985); Gabler v. State, 177 Ga. App. 3, 6 (2), 338 S.E.2d 469 (1985).

In *Strickland,* supra, the Supreme Court observed that there are at least three situations where a defendant does not have to prove prejudice: "1) an actual or constructive denial of counsel, 2) government interference with counsel and 3) counsel that labors under an actual conflict of interest that adversely affects his performance."[13] In *Heath v. State,*[14] where the defense counsel did no investigation of potential defenses available to his client, never consulted with his client during the 13 months between arraignment and the entry of the plea, and gave completely incorrect advice regarding the likely sentence to be imposed on a plea of guilty, the Georgia Court of Appeals reversed the trial court's denial of the defendant's motion to withdraw his plea. The Court concluded that "any defendant who receives less than an absolute minimum level of representation in any given case such that in effect, he has received no representation at all should be entitled to a presumption of prejudice."[15] The Supreme Court, however, reversed the Court of Appeals concluding that the defendant's assertions of his counsel's ineffectiveness should have been analyzed under the prejudice prong of *Strickland* and remanded the case accordingly.[16] On remand, the Court of Appeals reversed the trial court's denial of the defendant's motion to withdraw his guilty pleas after applying the prejudice component of *Strickland*. This component was met by showing that there was a "reasonable probability that, but for counsel's errors, the defendant would not have pleaded guilty and would have insisted on going to trial."[17] The United States Supreme Court reached a similar conclusion in *Lee v. United States.*[18] Georgia does not recognize the cumulative error rule.[19] That is, an ineffective claim cannot be sustained only on the basis of any number of harmless errors attributable

---

[13]State v. Heath, 277 Ga. 337, 338, 588 S.E.2d 738 (2003) citing *Strickland v. Washington*, supra. In the case of U.S. v. Gonzalez-Lopez, 126 S. Ct. 2557, 165 L. Ed. 2d 409 (U.S. 2006), the U.S. Supreme Court ruled that prejudice may be presumed where the trial court wrongfully denies the defendant the right to his retained counsel of choice. See Calloway v. State, 313 Ga. App. 708, 722 S.E.2d 422 (2012) (constructive denial of counsel is present only where defense counsel entirely fails to hold state to its burden of proof).

[14]Heath v. State, 258 Ga. App. 612, 574 S.E.2d 852 (2002).

[15]Heath v. State, 258 Ga. App. 612, 617, 574 S.E.2d 852 (2002), judg-ment reversed by State v. Heath, 277 Ga. 337 588 S.E.2d 738 (2003).

[16]Heath v. State, 268 Ga. App. 235, 601 S.E.2d 758 (2004). See also Machuca v. State, 279 Ga. App. 231, 630 S.E.2d 828 (2006), no presumption of prejudice where trial counsel failed to object to prosecution's repeated use of the word "rape," but trial court instructed jury on distinction between rape and consensual sex.

[17]State v. Heath, 277 Ga. 337, 338, 588 S.E.2d 738 (2003).

[18]Lee v. U.S., 137 S. Ct. 1958, 198 L. Ed. 2d 476 (2017).

[19]Bridges v. State, 268 Ga. 700(a), 492 S.E.2d 877 (1997). But see Darst v. State, 323 Ga.App. 614, 746 S.E.2d 865 (2013) (reversing trial court on

to counsel. Unless actual prejudice arising from counsel's errors can be demonstrated, a claim based upon ineffective assistance cannot prevail. Nonetheless, the cumulative effect of counsel's errors may be considered as *part* of such a claim.[20] Under the cumulative error rule in the Eleventh Circuit, a conviction may be reversed if the cumulative effect of errors is prejudicial, even if the prejudice caused by each individual error is harmless.[21]

In *Kirkland v. State*,[22] the Georgia Supreme Court found that prejudice could be "implied" in a case where defense counsel failed to strike for cause jurors who owned stock in a corporate victim in a criminal case. Because such jurors are legally presumed to be biased, the court concluded that counsel's error was harmful per se. In *Edwards v. Lewis*,[23] the Georgia Supreme Court concluded that trial and appellate counsel were presumptively ineffective because of a conflict of interest which kept them from pursuing a challenge to the composition of the jury array. The Court's ruling was premised upon a finding that the DeKalb County Superior Court Judges had implicitly struck a bargain with the county Public Defender's Office to update the jury pool data base with more recent census information provided the Public Defender's Office would not challenge the racial composition of grand and petit jurors in the defendant's case as well as all other previous cases. The Court concluded that their agreement absolutely conflicted defendant's counsel. In cases such as these, the Court found that to require an aggrieved defendant to show that the conflict resulted in actual prejudice that could have altered the outcome of the trial was too high a bar.

The prejudice requirement demands a showing "that counsel's errors were so serious as to deprive the defendant of a fair trial, a trial whose result is reliable." "[A]n analysis focusing solely on mere outcome determination, without attention to whether the result of the proceeding was fundamentally unfair or unreliable, is defective."[24] Thus, "[a]n error by counsel, even if professionally unreasonable, does not warrant setting aside the judgment . . .

---

grounds of ineffective assistance of counsel after looking at the "cumulative effect" of multiple errors by the defendant's counsel during the trial).

[20]Schofield v. Holsey, 281 Ga. 809, 642 S.E.2d 56 (2007). See Ojemuyiwa v. State, 285 Ga. App. 617, 647 S.E.2d 598 (2007); Waits v. State, 282 Ga. 1, 644 S.E.2d 127 (2007).

[21]U.S. v. Capers, 708 F.3d 1286 (11th Cir. 2013).

[22]Kirkland v. State, 274 Ga. 778, 560 S.E.2d 6 (2002).

[23]Edwards v. Lewis, 283 Ga. 345, 658 S.E.2d 116 (2008).

[24]Lockhart v. Fretwell, 506 U.S. 364, 113 S.Ct. 838, 122 L.Ed.2d 180 (1993). The court held that failure to make a federal constitutional claim based on a then existing case, which was subsequently overruled, was not prejudicial and was not a denial of effective assistance of counsel because the result was neither unreliable nor fundamentally unfair. *Lockhart* also provides a good synopsis of the prejudice prong of *Strickland*. Compare

if the error had no effect on the judgment."[25]

"Unless a defendant . . . [shows both deficiency and prejudice], it cannot be said that the conviction or death sentence resulted from a breakdown in the adversary process that renders the result unreliable."[26] In the absence of evidence to the contrary, a court should assume that the fact finder acted according to law and not by virtue of idiosyncracies. "[A] court need not determine whether counsel's performance was deficient before examining the prejudice suffered by the defendant. . . . If it is easier to dispose of [a] claim on the ground of lack of sufficient prejudice, . . . that course should be followed."

In *Miller v. State*,[27] the Georgia Supreme Court held that a petitioner does not need to prove "but for" counsel's error the outcome of the case would have been different in order to prevail on an ineffective assistance claim. The court noted that *Strickland* requires only a "reasonable probability" that the outcome would have been different, and disapproved cases in both the Supreme Court and the Court of Appeals which held otherwise.

In *Spence v. State*,[28] the court held that the same standard applied to both retained and appointed counsel. But only four years later, in *Donaldson v. State*,[29] the same court stated that "[w]henever a defendant selects his own counsel, that counsel truly represents the defendant and no mistake or error of his, made in good faith and with earnest and honest purpose to serve his client, can be made the basis of a claim of reversible error." Similarly, "when a criminal defendant elects to represent himself, either solely or in conjunction with representation or assistance by an attorney, he will not thereafter be heard to assert a claim

---

Miller-Roy v. State, 255 Ga. App. 575, 565 S.E.2d 899 (2002), where the court ruled that a defendant who is charged only with a traffic violation is not entitled to counsel or to any special warnings from the court regarding the dangers of proceeding pro se since a traffic violation does not rise to the level of a misdemeanor and does not expose the defendant to the possibility of incarceration.

[25]Goodwin v. Cruz-Padillo, 265 Ga. 614, 615, 458 S.E.2d 623 (1995).

[26]Strickland v. Washington, 466 U.S. 668, 104 S.Ct. 2052, 80 L.Ed.2d 674 (1984). See also Lajara v. State, 263 Ga. 438, 440 (3), 435 S.E.2d 600 (1993); Scapin v. State, 204 Ga. App. 725, 420 S.E.2d 385 (1992).

[27]Miller v. State, 285 Ga. 285, 676 S.E.2d 173 (2009). See Harrington v. Richter, 131 S. Ct. 770, 178 L. Ed. 2d 624 (2011) (*Strickland* test asks whether it is "reasonably likely" that the result at trial would have been different but for counsel's representation).

[28]Spence v. State, 163 Ga. App. 198 (1), 292 S.E.2d 908 (1982). The *Spence* opinion by Judge Pope is rich in its consideration of a large number of alleged deficiencies of defense counsel. See also Blatch v. State, 389 So.2d 669 (Fla.App.1980), relying on Cuyler v. Sullivan, 446 U.S. 335, 100 S.Ct. 1708, 64 L.Ed.2d 333 (1980).

[29]Donaldson v. State, 180 Ga. App. 879, 880 (3), 350 S.E.2d 849 (1986).

of ineffective assistance of counsel with respect to any stage of the proceedings wherein he was counsel."[30]

In *House v. Balkcom*,[31] the Eleventh Circuit stated that "a court considers that more is required from trial counsel than from counsel whose defendant pleads guilty to the charges. . . . A court must also consider that, although a capital case is judged by the same standards as any other case '[t]he seriousness of the charges against the defendant is a factor that *must be* considered in assessing counsel's performance.' "

Ineffective assistance of counsel applies not only when a defendant is tried and convicted, but also when a defendant enters a guilty plea.[32] In the 1997 Georgia Supreme Court case of *Brantley v. State*,[33] the court held that the two-prong test of *Strickland* applies where the defendant enters a guilty plea "and requires that the defendant establish the reasonable probability that, but for counsel's errors, he would not have pleaded guilty and would have insisted on going to trial."

In determining whether representation was inadequate, a factual inquiry should be conducted to determine (1) whether the defendant had a defense which was not presented; (2) whether counsel consulted sufficiently with the defendant; (3) whether counsel adequately investigated the facts and the law; and (4) whether omissions charged resulted from inadequate preparation rather than unwise choices of strategy.[34]

In *Belton v. State*,[35] the Georgia Supreme Court held that "[t]o show deficient performance, [a defendant] must demonstrate that . . . counsel's performance was not reasonable under the circumstances confronting . . . counsel at the time, without resorting to

---

[30]Mullins v. Lavoie, 249 Ga. 411, 412, 290 S.E.2d 472 (1982); Ellis v. State, 235 Ga. App. 837 (1), 510 S.E.2d 127 (1998); Wallis v. State, 170 Ga. App. 354, 355 (2), 317 S.E.2d 331 (1984); Moss v. State, 196 Ga. App. 81 (1), 395 S.E.2d 363 (1990).

[31]House v. Balkcom, 725 F.2d 608 (11th Cir.). See also Goodpaster, "The Trial For Life: Effective Assistance of Counsel in Death Penalty Cases," 58 N.Y.U. L. Rev. 299 (1983).

[32]In McCroskey v. State, 280 Ga. App. 638(2), 634 S.E.2d 824 (2006), the court observed that advising a client that a non-negotiated plea may be withdrawn as a matter of right after

sentence is imposed is ineffective. See § 15:1, infra, on duty of defense counsel to relay all offers of the prosecution to the defendant.

[33]Brantley v. State, 268 Ga. 151, 152 (1), 486 S.E.2d 169 (1997).

[34]Hawes v. State, 240 Ga. 327, 329, 240 S.E.2d 833 (1977) (citing Brubaker v. Dickson, 310 F.2d 30, 32 (9th Cir. 1962)). See also Johnson v. Zant, 249 Ga. 812, 813, 295 S.E.2d 63 (1982).

[35]Belton v. State, 270 Ga. 671, 673 (3), 512 S.E.2d 614 (1999) (quoting Turpin v. Mobley, 269 Ga. 635, 502 S.E.2d 458 (1998)).

hindsight." In *Potter v. State*,[36] the court held that "lack of experience alone does not constitute grounds for a claim of ineffective assistance of counsel."

An attorney should always see that witnesses of both state and defense are interviewed.[37] However, there are inherent dangers which exist when counsel attempts to personally interview a witness in that if counsel later wishes to impeach the witness' in-court testimony, it may be necessary for him to withdraw from the case.[38] A lawyer cannot be both counsel and witness unless his or testimony is about an uncontested issue; revolves around the services provided in the case; or if not being allowed to testify would cause such lawyer's client substantial hardship.[39]

In *Flanigan v. State*,[40] the Georgia Supreme Court pointed out that there is a presumption of effective assistance of counsel, and, at least by implication, this presumption must be overcome by clear and convincing evidence if the defendant is to prevail. The Georgia Court of Appeals has stated that where "retained counsel is a member in good standing of the State Bar of Georgia, a prima facie case of competence is made out,"[41] and mere shortness of time for preparation does not alone show a denial of the right to effective counsel.[42] However, it has been held that the defendant is deprived of his right to effective counsel when the attorney is not prepared to try his case, regardless of the

---

[36]Potter v. State, 273 Ga. 325, 326, 540 S.E.2d 184 (2001).

[37]See Harrell v. State, 139 Ga. App. 556, 558 (3), 228 S.E.2d 723 (1976); A.B.A. Standards, The Defense Function, Vol. I, Standard 4-4.1. But see Mulligan v. Kemp, 771 F.2d 1436 (11th Cir. 1985), in which the Eleventh Circuit found no ineffective assistance of counsel where the defendant insisted on using an alibi defense which defense counsel came to rely upon. Counsel had failed to see that all the prosecution's witnesses had been interviewed and he was surprised by fingerprint testimony placing the defendant at the scene of the crime.

[38]E.g., Waldrop v. State, 424 So.2d 1345 (Ala.Crim.App.1982).

[39]Rule 3.7 of the Rules of Professional Conduct, effective January 1, 2001, and superseding the Canons of Ethics. See Gonzalez v. State, 175 Ga. App. 217, 218 (1), 333 S.E.2d 132 (1985); Potts v. State, 259 Ga. 812, 815, 388 S.E.2d 678 (1990); Thomas v. State, 192 Ga. App. 744, 745 (2), 386 S.E.2d 402 (1989).

[40]Flanigan v. State, 269 Ga. 160, 162, 496 S.E.2d 255 (1998).

[41]Payne v. State, 161 Ga. App. 233, 291 S.E.2d 236 (1982); Suits v. State, 150 Ga. App. 285, 286, 257 S.E.2d 306 (1979).

[42]Ward v. State, 165 Ga. App. 163, 164 (2), 300 S.E.2d 528 (1983); Tucker v. State, 172 Ga. App. 86 (1), 321 S.E.2d 817 (1984); Tahamtani v. State, 177 Ga. App. 52, 53, 338 S.E.2d 488 (1985). See also Morris v. Slappy, 461 U.S. 1, 103 S.Ct. 1610, 75 L.Ed.2d 610 (1983) (public defender's one week preparation was not deprivation); Washington v. State, 216 Ga. App. 352, 353 (1), 454 S.E.2d 214 (1995).

competency of counsel.[43] "[C]ounsel is entitled to a reasonable length of time to prepare."[44] Furthermore, there is a presumption of ineffective assistance of counsel when an attorney is appointed at the last minute[45] or where an attorney has spoken with the accused for only a few minutes prior to trial.[46] However, in *Williams v.* State,[47] the court pointed out that there is "no specified amount of time which a counsel must spend in preparation for trial; each situation must be judged upon its own circumstances and in light of its own degree of complexity."

In *Ross v. Kemp,*[48] the Georgia Supreme Court said that "[t]he presentation of a fractured defense, and the placement of [the defendant] on the stand with no preparation whatsoever in a trial in which his life hung in the balance is evidence of inef-

---

[43]United States v. Woods, 487 F.2d 1218 (5th Cir. 1973). Where the only attempted communication between the defendant and court-appointed attorney was a letter by the accused to counsel which went unanswered, and no further contact between attorney and client occurred until trial, the court warned that while the accused in this situation was deprived of his right to counsel, "these circumstances should not be construed as sanctioning dilatory tactics by a defendant whose tardy objections to an attorney's representation frustrates the orderly course of litigation."

In Georgia, it has been held that a defendant will not be permitted to use change of counsel as a dilatory tactic to obtain a continuance. Hightower v. State, 166 Ga. App. 744 (2), 305 S.E.2d 372 (1983), rev'd on other grounds, 252 Ga. 220, 312 S.E.2d 610 (1984).

[44]Smith v. State, 215 Ga. 362 (1), 110 S.E.2d 635 (1959). However, in Jones v. Henderson, 549 F.2d 995, 997 (5th Cir. 1977), the court said that the "brevity of the time spent in consultation with counsel [relative to a defendant's constitutional rights before arraignment] is only a factor to be considered in the totality of the circumstances. . . ."

[45]Avery v. Alabama, 308 U.S. 444, 60 S.Ct. 321, 84 L.Ed. 377 (1940).

[46]Grant v. State, 131 Ga. App. 759, 206 S.E.2d 709 (1974). In Chambers v. Maroney, 399 U.S. 42, 54, 90 S.Ct. 1975, 26 L.Ed.2d 419 (1970), the court said that "the courts should make every effort to effect early appointments of counsel in all cases. But we are not disposed to fashion a per se rule requiring reversal of every conviction following tardy appointment of counsel" or to hold that an evidentiary hearing is necessary in every habeas corpus petition alleging belated appointment of counsel.

[47]Williams v. State, 219 Ga. App. 167, 168 (2), 464 S.E.2d 404 (1995) (quoting Datz v. State, 210 Ga. App. 517, 168 (3)(a), 436 S.E.2d 506 (1993)). Accord, Benefield v. State, 231 Ga. App. 80, 81, 497 S.E.2d 650 (1998).

[48]Ross v. Kemp, 260 Ga. 312, 315, 393 S.E.2d 244 (1990) (quoting House v. Balkcom, 725 F.2d 608 (11th Cir. 1984)). Accord, Cochran v. State, 262 Ga. 106, 108, 414 S.E.2d 211 (1992). *Ross* represented an egregious situation and is the exception to the general requirement that an ineffective claim must be demonstrated by both deficient attorney performance and that such performance caused prejudice. The Court did note that, where counsel is available to assist the accused during trial, prejudice may still be presumed if counsel labors under the circumstances that make effective representation unlikely. Turpin v. Curtis, 278 Ga. 698 (1), 606 S.E.2d 244 (2004).

fectiveness 'so pervasive that a particularized inquiry into prejudice would be unguided speculation' . . . [and we] conclude that [the defendant] did not receive . . . effective assistance of counsel."

But in *United States v. Cronic*,[49] the Supreme Court held that an inference of ineffective assistance of counsel was not justified where defense counsel was appointed about a month before trial, the government had spent four and one-half years in working up the case, and defense counsel had never tried a criminal case before. In *Roland v. State*,[50] the Georgia Supreme Court held that a two-week preparation period in a murder case is not inadequate as a matter of law. In *Morris v. Slappy*,[51] the United States Supreme Court held a six-day preparation period was adequate where the defendant was charged with rape, robbery, and burglary of the same female.

In *Tenorio v. State*,[52] the Court of Appeals noted that the defense counsel's failure to interview key witnesses, who might be able to support an alibi, constituted ineffective assistance of counsel. The fact that the failure to identify and interview witnesses was attributable to an investigator rather than defense counsel is of no importance because the defense counsel is "ultimately responsible for ensuring a thorough investigation."[53]

Errors of judgment and tactics do not constitute ineffective assistance of counsel. "Counsel's actions are usually based, quite properly, on informed strategic choices made by the defendant and on information supplied by the defendant. . . . [W]hen a defendant has given counsel reason to believe that pursuing certain investigations would be fruitless or even harmful, counsel's failure to pursue those investigations may not later be challenged as unreasonable."[54] Also, in *Rogers v. Zant*,[55] the court held that " 'strategy' can include a decision not to investigate [a

---

[49]United States v. Cronic, 466 U.S. 648, 104 S.Ct. 2039, 80 L.Ed.2d 657 (1984) (for constructive denial of counsel to be found it must appear that the attorney failed entirely to subject the state's case to "meaningful testing"). See Bell v. Cone, 535 U.S. 685, 122 S. Ct. 1843, 152 L. Ed. 2d 914 (2002); Charleston v. State, 292 Ga. 678, 743 S.E.2d 1 (2013).

[50]Roland v. State, 266 Ga. 545, 546 (3), 468 S.E.2d 378 (1996).

[51]Morris v. Slappy, 461 U.S. 1, 103 S.Ct. 1610, 75 L.Ed.2d 610 (1983).

[52]Tenorio v. State, 261 Ga. App. 609 (3), 583 S.E.2d 269 (2003).

[53]Tenorio v. State, 261 Ga. App. 609 (3), 583 S.E.2d 269 (2003). See Tezeno v. State, 343 Ga. App. 623, 808 S.E.2d 64 (2017) (ineffective assistance claim supported where co-counsel who was to conduct the examination was unavailable at trial due to back injury but counsel failed to alert court to his co-counsel's absence or to seek accommodation from the court but instead let the examination go on with only two "cursory" objections).

[54]Strickland v. Washington, 466 U.S. 668, 104 S.Ct. 2052, 80 L.Ed.2d 674 (1984). But cf. Turpin v. Christenson, 269 Ga. 226, 231 (12), 497 S.E.2d 216 (1998) (a death penalty case in-

defense] . . . . [T]he ineffectiveness question turns on whether the decision not to make a particular investigation was reasonable. . . . This correct approach toward investigation reflects the reality that lawyers do not enjoy the benefit of endless time, energy or financial resources. . . . 'At some point a trial lawyer has done enough,' [even though] 'a lawyer can almost always do something more in every case' . . . as long as [the] decision was reasonable under [the] circumstances, counsel may elect to forego [a] line of defense without first investigating it substantially." In this regard, counsel should note that as a practical matter when trying to show that a trial attorney's actions at trial were *ineffective* rather than *strategic*, it is critical to have the trial attorney testify at the hearing on the motion for new trial. Without the trial attorney's testimony as to the "why and how" of the tactics employed at trial, it is difficult to overcome the presumption that counsel's conduct resulted from reasonable trial strategy.[56]

Ineffective assistance of counsel jurisprudence, however, has no application when the issue involves one of the client's autonomy rather than the competence of defense counsel. A criminal defendant has the basic right under the Sixth Amendment to make fundamental decisions about his/her own defense. Violation of that right constitutes "structural" error. An error is deemed to be structural when it involves a fundamental principle, such as defendant's right to "make his own choices about the proper way to protect his own liberty."[57] This is different than strategic decisions such as which witnesses to call or questions to ask them. Thus, in *McCoy v. Louisiana*,[58] the court held that the trial committed structural error and violated the defendant's Sixth Amendment right to choose the direction of his defense when it allowed defense counsel, over the objection of the defendant, to concede that the defendant "committed [the] three murders" based upon his judgment that this strategy represented the defendant's best chance to avoid the death penalty. The defendant opposed any admission of guilt and insisted that the defense should be based

---

volving ineffective assistance of counsel connected with the penalty phase of the trial).

[55]Rogers v. Zant, 13 F.3d 384 (11th Cir. 1994). See Poole v. State, 291 Ga. 848, 734 S.E.2d 1 (2012) ("counsel has a duty to make reasonable investigations or to make a reasonable decision that makes particular investigation unnecessary"). See also Ferrell v. State, 261 Ga. 115, 119 (3), 401 S.E.2d 741 (1991); Pitts v. State, 209 Ga. App. 47,

49 (2), 432 S.E.2d 643 (1993). Cf. Gates v. Zant, 863 F.2d 1492, 1498 (11th Cir. 1989).

[56]Brown v. State, 288 Ga. 902, 708 S.E.2d 294 (2011). See Russell v. State, 269 Ga. 511, 501 S.E.2d 206 (1998).

[57]Weaver v. Massachusetts, 137 S. Ct. 1899, 1908, 198 L. Ed. 2d 420 (2017).

[58]McCoy v. Louisiana, 138 S. Ct. 1500, 200 L. Ed. 2d 821 (2018).

upon the alibi that he was not in the state at the time of the murders.

Prior to July 1, 2007, counsel could reserve objections to the jury charge pending a motion for new trial or appeal.[59] At that time, it was considered the better practice, at a minimum, to always reserve objections. O.C.G.A. § 17-8-58 now requires that counsel make specific objections to the charge before jury deliberations begin. One commentator has suggested that conscientious counsel should be sure to record charge conferences and take care to articulate objections to the charge. If necessary, counsel may want to request time after the charge to formulate objections.[60] Counsel would do well to request from the court a written copy of the charge to be given just as soon as it can be made available.

There is, however, a strong indication from the United States Supreme Court that the tactical decisions made by counsel may in the future receive less deference and more scrutiny. In *Wiggins v. Smith*,[61] a death penalty case, the Court concluded that the election by counsel not to introduce mitigation evidence, much less conduct an adequate investigation of such evidence, constituted ineffective assistance. The Court ruled that pursuant to *Strickland*, counsel's effectiveness will be measured by an objective review, "measured for reasonableness under prevailing norms including a context dependent consideration of the challenged conduct as seen from counsel's perspective at the time of that conduct."

In *Florida v. Nixon*,[62] the United States Supreme Court held that defense counsel's decision to concede guilt in a capital case was not the functional equivalent of a guilty plea. The Court further held that counsel's failure to obtain the defendant's express consent to a strategy of conceding guilt in a capital trial does not by itself render counsel's performance functionally deficient under *Stickland*.

The failure to raise a defense might also constitute ineffective

---

[59]See e.g., McCoy v. State, 262 Ga. 699, 425 S.E.2d 646 (1993).

[60]*What's the Decision*, Volume 33, Issue 4, April, 2007. See Hughes v. State, 309 Ga. App. 150, 709 S.E.2d 900 (2011) (failure to separately object to jury instruction or join in co-defendant's objection waives any error).

[61]Wiggins v. Smith, 539 U.S. 510, 123 S.Ct. 2527, 156 L.Ed.2d 471 (2003). See Rompilla v. Beard, 545 U.S. 374, 125 S. Ct. 2456, 162 L. Ed. 2d 360 (2005) (failure of counsel to review transcripts of defendant's prior trials where counsel knew that prosecutor intended to read portions of victim testimony impaired ability of defense to respond thereto and was ineffective.); Williams v. Taylor, 529 U.S. 362, 120 S.Ct. 1495, 146 L.Ed.2d 389 (2000).

[62]Florida v. Nixon, 543 U.S. 175, 125 S. Ct. 551, 160 L. Ed. 2d 565 (2004).

assistance of counsel. In *Guzman v. State*,[63] the court found that the appellant's defense attorney was ineffective at trial by failing to raise a defense based upon the defendant's medical condition. This defense was the only defense available to the defendant and defense counsel's failure to adequately investigate its merit was the basis for the court's ruling.

Likewise, a defendant may not refuse to cooperate with his counsel "and then claim that, because of that lack of cooperation, he was not effectively represented."[64] In addition, the United States Supreme Court held that a defendant is not deprived of the effective assistance of counsel where defense counsel refuses to cooperate with the defendant in presenting false testimony at trial.[65]

"The decisions on which witnesses to call, whether and how to conduct cross examinations, what jurors to accept or strike, what trial motions should be made, and all other strategies and tactical decisions are the exclusive province of the lawyer after consultation with his client."[66] Likewise, decisions as to "which charges will be requested fall within the realm of trial tactics and strategy. They provide no grounds for reversal unless such tactical decisions are so patently unreasonable that no competent attorney would have chosen them."[67] In *Jones v. State*,[68] the court held that "[i]neffective assistance of counsel does not result from the refusal of counsel to" call a witness whom counsel reasonably believes would present perjured testimony. In *Adams v. State*,[69] the court pointed out that in "the absence of testimony to the contrary, counsel's actions are presumed strategic." In *Jefferson v. Zant*,[70] the court held that whether a trial attorney's tactics are reasonable is a question of law. The court then said "[t]he test for

---

[63]Guzman v. State, 260 Ga. App. 689, 580 S.E.2d 654 (2003).

[64]Rivers v. State, 250 Ga. 303, 308 (6), 298 S.E.2d 1 (1982); Jefferson v. State, 209 Ga. App. 859, 861 (1), 434 S.E.2d 814 (1993). See also Caldwell v. United States, 651 F.2d 429 (6th Cir. 1981).

[65]Nix v. Whiteside, 475 U.S. 157, 106 S.Ct. 988, 89 L.Ed.2d 123 (1986). See Miller v. State, 295 Ga. 769, 764 S.E.2d 135 (2014). Accord, Stephenson v. State, 206 Ga. App. 273, 424 S.E.2d 816 (1992). See Studdard, *Daniel's Georgia Handbook on Criminal Evidence* (2018 ed.), § 6:31.

[66]Austin v. Carter, 248 Ga. 775, 779, 285 S.E.2d 542 (1982); Scapin v. State, 204 Ga. App. 725, 420 S.E.2d 385 (1992). Cf. Williams v. State, 247 Ga. App. 99, 102, 543 S.E.2d 408 (2000).

[67]Champion v. State, 238 Ga. App. 48, 49 (1) (b), 517 S.E.2d 595 (1999) (citations omitted).

[68]Jones v. State, 239 Ga. App. 832, 836 (2)(b), 521 S.E.2d 614 (1999).

[69]Adams v. State, 217 Ga. App. 532, 533 (2), 458 S.E.2d 171 (1995).

[70]Jefferson v. Zant, 263 Ga. 316, 318 (3)(a), 431 S.E.2d 110 (1993), quoting White v. Singletary, 972 F.2d 1218, 1220 (11th Cir. 1992) (quoted with approval in Mency v. State, 228 Ga. App. 640, 643 (2)(a), 492 S.E.2d 692 (1997)). Accord, Stansell v. State, 270 Ga. 147, 150 (2), 510 S.E.2d 292 (1998).

reasonable attorney performance 'has nothing to do with what the best lawyers would have done. Nor is the test even what most good lawyers would have done. We ask only whether some reasonable lawyer at the trial could have acted, in the circumstances, as defense counsel acted at trial . . . we are not interested in grading lawyers' performances; we are interested in whether the adversarial process at trial, in fact, worked adequately.' " In *Brady v. State,*[71] the court held that "[A] defense attorney may face finite resources of time and money such that a reasonably competent attorney often must rely on his own experience and judgment, without the benefit of a substantial investigation, when deciding whether or not to forego a particular line of defense."

Nevertheless, in *Van Alstine v. State,*[72] the court concluded "that it is critically important for defense lawyers . . . to consult fully with accuseds in . . . [making a] decision whether to pursue an 'all or nothing' defense and whether to request [a charge on] the lesser included offenses. . . ." But the right to effective assistance of counsel does not mean assistance of counsel satisfactory to the defendant.[73] See § 7:2, supra, on appointment of counsel.

In *Muff v. State,*[74] the defendant contended that his counsel was ineffective in that the defendant was not informed that he would be sentenced to a mandatory life sentence if convicted of selling cocaine. The court held: (1) that failure to inform the defendant of the consequences of rejecting a guilty plea was less than reasonable professional assistance and (2) that the facts of each case must be examined, and if there is "an inference from the evidence that the defendant would have accepted the offer as made or something similar[,]" then the defendant has established prejudice.

The Supreme Court has noted that the failure of defense counsel to put before a jury mental health expert testimony of a mitigating character of which counsel is aware in the sentencing phase of a capital case would be "unreasonable conduct" and would support a claim of ineffective assistance of counsel.[75] In

---

[71]Brady v. State, 270 Ga. 574, 576 (4), 513 S.E.2d 199 (1999).

[72]Van Alstine v. State, 263 Ga. 1, 4, 426 S.E.2d 360 (1993).

[73]Bailey v. State, 240 Ga. 112, 114 (1), 239 S.E.2d 521 (1977).

[74]Muff v. State, 210 Ga. App. 309, 311 (2), 436 S.E.2d 47 (1993). See Lloyd v. State, 258 Ga. 645, 647 (2) (a), 373 S.E.2d 1 (1988); Avans v. State, 251 Ga. App. 575, 554 S.E.2d 766 (2001).

Accord, Hall v. State, 210 Ga. App. 792, 437 S.E.2d 634 (1993). See Annot., "Adequacy of Defense Counsel's Representation of Criminal Client Regarding Guilty Pleas," 10 A.L.R.4th 8 (1981).

[75]Head v. Thomason, 276 Ga. 434, 578 S.E.2d 426 (2003). See also Turpin v. Lipham, 270 Ga. 208, 510 S.E.2d 32 (1998) (failure to have defendant's medical history reviewed by mental health expert in connection with

Schoefield v. Gulley,[76] the court found that the failure of defense counsel to investigate and present evidence at the mitigation stage of trial that the defendant had been responsible for saving the lives of two persons was both deficient and prejudicial. In *Emilio v. State*,[77] the Georgia Court of Appeals determined that the failure of defense counsel to redact bad character evidence from a defense exhibit was deficient performance.

In *Crabbe v. State*,[78] the Court determined that the defense attorney rendered ineffective assistance when he "affirmatively misrepresented" the defendant's parole eligibility prior to the entry of his guilty plea. In *Davis v. Murrell*,[79] the Georgia Supreme Court found both deficient performance and prejudice in a case where defense counsel affirmatively misrepresented the time after which the defendant would be eligible for parole by some ten years. In addition, counsel told the defendant, incorrectly, that the sentence was qualified for sentence review.

As a general proposition, a guilty plea which is knowingly and voluntarily entered with the assistance of competent counsel, will operate as a waiver of a constitutional double jeopardy claim.[80] However, the failure of counsel to properly advise the defendant

---

mitigation/sentencing phase of a death penalty case may provide a basis for an ineffective assistance claim); Martin v. Barrett, 279 Ga. 593, 619 S.E.2d 656 (2005) (failure to properly investigate client's mental health when counsel has notice that it may be an issue can be ineffective.)

[76]Schofield v. Gulley, 279 Ga. 413(1), 614 S.E.2d 740 (2005). See Cullen v. Pinholster, 131 S. Ct. 1388, 179 L. Ed. 2d 557 (2011) (*Strickland* does not require that counsel put up mitigation evidence if, e.g., it could open door to damaging evidence). See also, Hulett v. State, 296 Ga. 49, 766 S.E.2d 1 (2014) (no "rigid" requirement for mitigation specialist such as where counsel employed investigator familiar with death cases to do mitigation investigation).

[77]Emilio v. State, 263 Ga. App. 604(1), 588 S.E.2d 797 (2003). See Whitaker v. State, 276 Ga. App. 226(1), 622 S.E.2d 916 (2005). Compare Floyd v. State, 293 Ga. App. 235(2), 666 S.E.2d 611 (2008) (where counsel failed to properly advise defendant about parole eligibility, the court found that ineffective assistance in this regard

was irrelevant since defense strategy was to avoid recidivist sentence); Humphrey v. Williams, 295 Ga. 536, 761 S.E.2d 297 (2014) (trial counsel ineffective where he failed to obtain readily available court documents which would have discredited similar transaction witness's testimony).

[78]Crabbe v. State, 248 Ga. App. 314, 546 S.E.2d 65 (2001). See, Rollins v. State, 277 Ga. 488, 591 S.E.2d 796 (2004); State v. Patel, 280 Ga. 181, 626 S.E.2d 121 (2006); Holmes v. United States, 876 F.2d 1545 (11th Cir. 1989).

[79]Davis v. Murrell, 279 Ga. 584(1), 619 S.E.2d 662 (2005). See Smith v. Williams, 277 Ga. 778(1), 596 S.E.2d 112 (2004). Compare Stinson v. State, 286 Ga. 499, 689 S.E.2d 323 (2010) (fact that defendant did not understand he was ineligible for parole for a period of 30 years was a collateral consequence which did not affect voluntariness of plea).

[80]United States v. Broce, 488 U.S. 563, 109 S.Ct. 757, 102 L.Ed.2d 927 (1989); Clark v. Caldwell, 229 Ga. 612, 193 S.E.2d 816 (1972).

of the implications of double jeopardy prior to the entry of a plea can constitute ineffective assistance.[81] Moreover, part of effective representation in a criminal alien case requires that counsel investigate the immigration consequences of a proposed plea. Merely advising the client of the possibility of adverse consequences is insufficient.[82]

In *United States v. Campbell*,[83] although a guilty plea could subject a defendant to automatic deportation, it was nonetheless regarded only as a collateral consequence of the plea. Therefore, failure of counsel to advise the client of that consequence was not considered ineffective assistance of counsel. The United States Supreme Court has never made a distinction between the direct and collateral consequences of a guilty plea for purposes of reviewing whether a defendant received effective assistance of counsel. However, in *Padilla v. Kentucky*,[84] the Court found that because its consequences are so severe, the failure to advise a client of possible exposure to deportation as a result of a guilty plea is ineffective assistance of counsel, and abrogated all case authority to the contrary. Based in part on *Padilla*, the United States Supreme Court held in *Missouri v. Frye*[85] that defense counsel has a duty to accurately communicate formal offers of a plea made by the prosecution. If such an offer is not communicated in

---

[81]278 Ga. 641(3), 604 S.E.2d 462 (2004).

[82]Encarnacion v. State, 295 Ga. 660, 763 S.E.2d 463 (2014).

[83]U.S. v. Campbell, 778 F.2d 764 (11th Cir. 1985). See § 16:10, infra, on waivers of defendant and collateral consequences doctrine.

[84]Padilla v. Kentucky, 130 S. Ct. 1473, 176 L. Ed. 2d 284 (2010). See Smith v. State, 304 Ga. App. 846, 698 S.E.2d 355 (2010) (Georgia Supreme Court follows *Padilla*, holding that failure to advise non-citizen that guilty plea may result in deportation is ineffective assistance and satisfies first prong of *Strickland*). See also Lee v. United States, 137 S.Ct. 1958, 198 L.Ed.2d 476 (2017) (failure to properly advise defendant regarding deportation in case where it was the critical issue to plea constitutes deficient performance even though evidence of guilt in case was overwhelming and likelihood of longer sentence and deportation was probable); Smith v. State, 287 Ga. 391, 697 S.E.2d 177 (2010) (defen-

dant must also show that he was unaware of risks of deportation because of plea from any other source such as an immigration attorney or an ongoing immigration proceeding); Taylor v. State, 304 Ga. App. 878, 698 S.E.2d 384 (2010) (failure to advise defendant of sex offender registry requirements mandated by plea was deficient representation); State v. Addaquay, 302 Ga. 412, 807 S.E.2d 413 (2017) (*Padilla* does not apply to failure of plea counsel to properly advise defendant about consequences of plea to future application for citizenship). Cf. § 14:64, infra, on retroactive application of new rules of criminal law.

[85]Missouri v. Frye, 132 S. Ct. 1399, 182 L. Ed. 2d 379 (2012) (Recommended that trial courts adopt ABA guidelines for documenting formal offers in writing and that such offers be made a part of the record either when plea is entered or before trial commences). See Harris v. Upton, 292 Ga. 491, 739 S.E.2d 300 (2013); Lloyd v. State, 258 Ga. 645, 373 S.E.2d 1 (1988).

a timely fashion, and as a result, the defendant either goes to trial or accepts a plea which results in terms and conditions more harsh than the prior plea offer, the defendant may be entitled to relief based upon a claim of ineffective assistance of counsel. In order to prevail on such a claim, the defendant would have to demonstrate a reasonable probability that the offer, if properly communicated would have been accepted and that the trial court would have imposed it. In *Lafler v. Cooper*,[86] the Court held that in certain cases an appropriate remedy may be to require the state to "re-offer" the rejected offer.

> If, for example, an offer was for a guilty plea to a count or counts less serious than the ones for which a defendant was convicted after trial, or if a mandatory sentence confines a judge's sentencing discretion after trial, a resentencing based on the conviction at trial may not suffice. In these circumstances, the *proper exercise of discretion* to remedy the constitutional injury *may* be to require the prosecution to reoffer the plea proposal. Once this has occurred, the judge can then exercise discretion in deciding whether to vacate the conviction from trial and accept the plea or leave the conviction undisturbed.

If the case is one involving multiple counts, the court might also vacate some of the convictions and resentence the defendant accordingly. The Eleventh Circuit has held that *Frye* and *Lafler* are not "new rules" of constitutional law and hence may not be applied retroactively.[87]

In *Alexander v. State*,[88] the Georgia Supreme Court adopted the reasoning expressed in *Padilla* and *Lafley*, holding that the failure to properly advise a client that his plea to a recidivist sentence eliminated his eligibility for parole and thereby constituted ineffective assistance of counsel. In doing so, the court rejected the notion that parole eligibility was merely a collateral and not a direct consequence of a plea and criminal sentence. The

---

[86]Lafler v. Cooper, 132 S. Ct. 1376, 1389 (II)(C), 182 L.Ed.2d 398 (2012) (emphasis added; citations omitted). See Maines v. State, 330 Ga. App. 247, 765 S.E.2d 382 (2014) (trial court did not abuse discretion in not ordering re-tender of plea offer where the issue involved a more severe sentence to the same charge for which the defendant was convicted rather than a lesser offense or one which involved a mandatory sentence). See also Ingram v. State, 338 Ga. App. 552, 790 S.E.2d 641 (2016) (defendant who pled guilty to avoid recidivist sentence received ineffective assistance when counsel failed to investigate and discover that one of the convictions which state relied upon for recidivist sentence was entered under First Offender statute).

[87]In re Perez, 682 F.3d 930 (11th Cir. 2012).

[88]Alexander v. State, 297 Ga. 59, 772 S.E.2d 655 (2015). See Kennedy v. Kohnle, 303 Ga. 95, 810 S.E.2d 543 (2018) (*Alexander* created a "new rule" and is not to be applied retroactively).

court overruled *Williams v. Duffy*[89] and its progeny which had held that a lawyer's failure to advise a client (as contrasted with affirmatively misrepresenting) the consequences of a guilty plea did not constitute ineffective assistance.

The Court noted that when evaluating whether the failure to advise a client about the collateral consequences of a plea amounted to constitutionally deficient performance, the trial court should take into consideration the guidelines suggested by the United States Supreme Court in *Padilla v. Kentucky*:[90]

> In addition to professional guidelines, our courts can look to these factors when weighing advice concerning a collateral consequence: (1) whether the collateral consequence is intimately related to the criminal process and is "nearly an automatic result" flowing from the conviction; (2) whether the consequence is a "drastic measure" or a penalty with harsh ramifications for the client; and (3) whether the law imposing the consequence is "succinct, clear and explicit."

In *Johnson v. State*,[91] the Georgia Supreme Court held that the defendant, facing a mandatory minimum sentence of life without parole, received ineffective assistance of counsel when his attorney failed to advise that he could have pled prior to arraignment and received a sentence of twenty years.

In *Carson v. State*,[92] the defendant's claim of ineffective assistance of counsel was rejected where counsel advised only that a mandatory sentence was possible when in fact it was likely. The court concluded that it was sufficient that the defendant understood that the "consequences of refusing the state's plea offer could be harsher than the consequences of accepting it."

---

[89]Williams v. Duffy, 270 Ga. 580, 513 S.E.2d 212 (1999).

[90]Padilla v. Kentucky, 559 U.S. 356, 365-69, 130 S. Ct. 1473, 176 L. Ed. 2d 284 (2010) (where "law is not succinct and straightforward . . . a criminal defense attorney need to do no more than advise a non-citizen client that pending criminal charges may carry a risk of adverse immigration consequences"). See State v. Aduka, 303 Ga. 309, 812 S.E.2d 266 (2018).

[91]Johnson v. State, 289 Ga. 532, 712 S.E.2d 811 (2011) (unaware of plea offer, defendant wanted counsel to investigate alibi defense which counsel failed to do). See Cox v. Howerton, 290 Ga. 693, 723 S.E.2d 891 (2012) (court

denied habeas relief to petitioner who claimed she received erroneous information about parole possibility from counsel in the absence of a showing that petitioner placed particular emphasis on parole eligibility in decision to plead guilty).

[92]Carson v. State, 264 Ga. App. 763, 764, 592 S.E.2d 161 (2003) (citing Sutton v. State, 263 Ga. App. 188, 190 (1), 587 S.E.2d 379 (2003)). See State v. Lexie, 331 Ga. App. 400, 771 S.E.2d 97 (2015) (counsel was ineffective when he convinced defendant to go to trial rather than to plead and receive a probated sentence and avoid a mandatory sentence of life plus twenty-five years).

In *Caudell v. State*,[93] appellant claimed that the circumstances of the fee arrangement between counsel and appellant created a conflict of interest because it violated certain rules of professional conduct. The Court of Appeals found that "[a]n ethics violation does not necessarily establish a claim of ineffectiveness of counsel."[94] The appellant in such a situation must still meet the two-part test established in *Strickland*.

In *Morrison v. State*,[95] the Georgia Supreme Court stated that an attorney is not merely his client's "mouthpiece," but is "an 'independent . . . professional representative.' "However, after a defendant has "been informed, the defendant, and not his attorney, makes the ultimate decision about . . . what line of defense to pursue, . . . whether or not to testify in his own behalf, . . . whether or not to plead guilty, . . . and whether or not to present witnesses in mitigation." The court then held that "where a properly informed, competent defendant insists that he prefers a death sentence to life imprisonment, his attorney does not violate any right of the defendant by attempting to 'comply with his client's wishes . . . and by arguing to the sentencer in favor of the death sentence' " where the defendant is able to "exercise proper judgment." However, in *Francis v. Spraggins*,[96] the Eleventh Circuit held that there was ineffective assistance of counsel where the attorney in a death case at the innocence-guilt phase stated that he believed the defendant committed the crime.

In cases where the defendant claims that appellate counsel was ineffective because of a failure to assert an error on appeal, the reviewing court is required to determine whether the decision was a "reasonable tactical choice which any competent attorney in the same situation would have made" and whether the omitted error outweighed the errors which counsel selected to enumerate on appeal. It must then appear that the failure to raise the error on appeal prejudiced the defense.[97] In *Griffin v. Terry*,[98] the Georgia Supreme Court held that "to show prejudice under *Strickland* where appellate ineffectiveness is alleged due to the failure to assert an error that carries presumed prejudice on direct appeal

---

[93]Caudell v. State, 262 Ga. App. 44, 584 S.E.2d 649 (2003).

[94]Caudell v. State, 262 Ga. App. 44, 584 S.E.2d 649 (2003), citing Blackshear v. State, 274 Ga. 842, 560 S.E.2d 688 (2002).

[95]Morrison v. State, 258 Ga. 683, 686, 373 S.E.2d 506 (1988).

[96]Francis v. Spraggins, 720 F.2d 1190 (11th Cir. 1983).

[97]Shorter v. Waters, 275 Ga. 581, 571 S.E.2d 373 (2002); Shorter v. Waters, 278 Ga. 558, 604 S.E.2d 472, 475 (2004) (reversing and remanding the judgment of the habeas court and finding that appellate counsel's failure to make an ineffective assistance claim based on trial counsel's failure to preserve the issue of a reckless conduct charge was "outside the range of reasonable professional conduct").

[98]Griffin v. Terry, 291 Ga. 326, 729 S.E.2d 334 (2012).

[such as a right to be present claim], the appellant must establish a reasonable probability that the error would have been reversible on appeal, and to do so, must establish a reasonable probability of a different outcome at trial had the error been prevented or corrected."

Review of the factual findings in ineffective counsel claims on appeal is restricted to a "clearly erroneous" standard which is the same as the "any evidence" rule.[99]

"The proper method for raising a claim of ineffective assistance after entry of a guilty plea is for a defendant to file either a timely motion to withdraw the guilty plea, a direct appeal challenging the validity of the plea, or an action seeking relief through habeas corpus."[100] See § 28:11, infra, on notice of appeal.

Defense counsel should note the growing skepticism expressed by the Georgia Court of Appeals of trial counsel who testify about their ineffective representation in support of a former client's application for post trial relief. In *Carrie v. State*,[101] the court noted that there appears to be a "dangerous" trend by defense counsel to admit to "bad lawyering" at trial in support of a former client's claim of ineffective assistance of counsel. While not expressing an opinion on the candor of the lawyer witness in that case, the court viewed such efforts as a threat to the "administration of justice in the absence of consequences for lawyers who irresponsibly assert their ineffectiveness as trial counsel."

See § 16:10, infra, on waivers of defendant and collateral consequences doctrine; Annotation, "Adequacy of Defense Counsel's Representation of Criminal Client—Conduct Occurring at Time of Trial Regarding Issues of Diminished Capacity, Intoxication, and Unconsciousness," 78 A.L.R.5th 197 (2000).

§ 7:5   Ineffective assistance of counsel—Failure to file notice of appeal

In *Haynes v. State*,[1] the Georgia Court of Appeals considered a case in which the defendant contended his trial counsel had been

---

[99]Washington v. State, 276 Ga. 655, 581 S.E.2d 518 (2003); Hanson v. Kent, 263 Ga. 124, 428 S.E.2d 785 (1993); Gravitt v. State, 301 Ga. App. 131, 687 S.E.2d 150 (2009).

[100]Pierce v. State, 294 Ga. 842, 755 S.E.2d 732 (2014).

[101]Carrie v. State, 298 Ga. App. 55, 679 S.E.2d 30 (2009); Nejad v. State, 296 Ga. App. 163, 169, 674 S.E.2d 60 (2009), judgment rev'd on other grounds, 286 Ga. 695, 690 S.E.2d 846

(2010) (concurring opinion of, Adams, J., in Court of Appeals case).

[Section 7:5]

[1]Haynes v. State, 227 Ga. App. 64, 65, 488 S.E.2d 119 (1997). As noted by the Georgia Court of Appeals in Towns v. State, 228 Ga. App. 267, 491 S.E.2d 497 (1997) (disapproved of on other grounds by, Raheem v. State, 339 Ga. App. 859, 794 S.E.2d 418 (2016)), "the right to effective assistance of counsel includes the defendants right

ineffective in refusing his request to appeal his conviction. The court held that a defendant is entitled to an out-of-time appeal if the defendant "was denied his right of appeal through counsel's negligence or ignorance, or if the appellant was not adequately informed of his appeal rights. . . . [T]he right to appeal is violated when the appointed lawyer deliberately [foregoes] the direct appeal without first obtaining his client's consent." In addition, when a defendant claims that his or her right to appeal was frustrated by ineffective assistance of counsel, the trial court must conduct an evidentiary hearing on the claim, and the failure to do so constitutes an abuse of discretion.[2] See § 28:11, infra, on appeals.

However, in the 2000 case of *Roe v. Flores-Ortega*,[3] the United States Supreme Court extended the application of *Strickland*[4] *to include claims that "counsel was constitutionally ineffective for failing to file a notice of appeal." The court split the first prong of* Strickland into two questions. First, the hearing court must determine whether counsel consulted the defendant, i.e., talked to the defendant "about the advantages and disadvantages of taking an appeal and [made] a reasonable effort to discover the defendant's wishes. If counsel has consulted with the defendant, . . . [c]ounsel performs in a professionally unreasonable manner only by failing to follow the defendant's express instructions with respect to an appeal." This Court points out that "counsel has a constitutionally-imposed duty to consult with the defendant about an appeal when there is reason to think either (1) that a rational defendant would want to appeal . . . or (2) that this particular defendant reasonably demonstrated to counsel that he was interested in appealing." A critical factor to be considered in the determination is whether the defendant is appealing a trial verdict or a guilty plea. If the defendant is appealing a guilty plea, this reduces the scope of appealable issues. Moreover, the guilty plea may reflect the defendant's wish to end any judicial proceedings. Further, with a guilty plea, "the court must consider such factors as whether the defendant received the sentence bargained for as part of the plea and whether the plea expressly reserved or waived some or all appeal rights." *Strickland's* second

---

to be informed of . . . the right to counsel on appeal including the right to appointed counsel for indigent defendants." See Hill v. State, 285 Ga. App. 310(1), 645 S.E.2d 758 (2007). See also Stephens v. State, 291 Ga. 837, 733 S.E.2d 266 (2012) (issues that defendant seeks to raise on appeal from a guilty plea must be such that they can be resolved using the exist-ing record).

[2]Simmons v. State, 276 Ga. 525, 579 S.E.2d 735 (2003).

[3]Roe v. Flores-Ortega, 528 U.S. 470, 120 S.Ct. 1029, 145 L.Ed.2d 985 (2000).

[4]Strickland v. Washington, 466 U.S. 668, 104 S.Ct. 2052, 80 L.Ed.2d 674 (1984).

prong, as applied in this context, requires that the defendant show a "reasonable probability that, but for counsel's deficient failure to consult [the defendant] about an appeal, [the defendant] would have timely appealed." Once it appears that the defendant will benefit from the filing of a notice of appeal, a presumption of prejudice arises. The court points to two "highly determinative" factors to be considered: (1) that the defendant presented evidence of "nonfrivolous grounds for appeal," or (2) that the defendant "promptly expressed a desire to appeal." However, the hearing court need not discuss the merit of an appeal. Further, a defendant who shows nonfrivolous grounds for appeal may satisfy both prongs of *Strickland* at once.

> The Georgia Court of Appeals stated that "[a]n out-of-time appeal is appropriate where due to the ineffective assistance of counsel, no appeal has been taken. However, an attorney renders effective assistance of counsel with regard to the decision whether to appeal when he advises his client of his appellate rights, and does not preempt his client's decision to appeal. Neither the sixth amendment nor the fourteenth amendment requires that the record reflect that the defendant made a knowing and intelligent decision not to appeal before he can be precluded from appellate review. The grant or denial of a motion for an out-of-time appeal is within the discretion of the trial court, and its decision will not be reversed absent abuse of such discretion."[5]

In cases where a defendant has an ineffective appellate attorney who prosecutes the defendant's first appeal but fails to identify and raise a meritorious issue, the proper remedy is to order a new trial. This is so because it provides the defendant with the new trial he would have received had his appeal been properly presented. In cases where a pro se defendant has been improperly denied counsel in his first directed appeal, an appellate court would have no way of knowing what issues an attorney would have raised. Thus, the only remedy in such cases is to provide an attorney to the defendant for purpose of presenting a new appeal.[6]

§ 7:6 Ineffective assistance of counsel—When issue must be raised

The testimony of counsel that he provided ineffective assistance to both of his clients because he was hindered by his role as counsel for both at a joint trial has been said to be "inherently

---

[5]Davis v. State, 242 Ga. App. 101, 527 S.E.2d 602 (2000) (quoting Lunsford v. State, 237 Ga. App. 696, 515 S.E.2d 198 (1999)). See also Penrod v. State, 233 Ga. App. 532, 504 S.E.2d 757 (1998).

[6]Trauth v. State, 295 Ga. 874, 763 S.E.2d 854 (2014).

suspicious," because of the attorney's disregard of legal ethics.[1]

In connection with effective representation, it should be pointed out that in *Polk County v. Dodson*,[2] the United States Supreme Court held that a public defender, representing an indigent defendant, "does not act under color of state law when performing a lawyer's traditional functions as counsel. . . ." Hence, when so acting, a public defender is not subject to action under 42 U.S.C.A. § 1983. However, in *Tower v. Glover*,[3] the court held that a public defender does not have immunity where the petitioner alleges that he conspired with various state officials including trial and appellate judges and the Attorney General to deprive him of his constitutional rights.

It has been held that the right to effective assistance of counsel does not attach until the initiation of the adversary judicial proceeding.[4] "[A]ny contention concerning the violation of the constitutional right to counsel should be made at the earliest practicable moment[,]"[5] and "the counsel whose proficiency is under attack should be given an opportunity to be heard."[6]

In the 1996 case of *Glover v. State*,[7] the Georgia Supreme Court reiterated that a claim for ineffective assistance of counsel must be raised " 'at the earliest practicable moment' "and must "be raised *before appeal* if the opportunity to do so is available." (Emphasis in original.) In *Glover*, after conviction a new counsel was appointed for appeal. Appellate counsel filed a notice of appeal rather than a motion for new trial. The court remanded the case for a hearing on ineffectiveness of counsel, saying that it is unfair to hold the defendant to the rule of this case since there has been some inconsistency in the cases. However, the court

---

[Section 7:6]

[1]Keen v. State, 164 Ga. App. 81, 84, 296 S.E.2d 91 (1982). But see Annot., "Ineffective Assistance of Counsel: Right of Attorney to Withdraw, as Appointed Defense Counsel, Due to Self-Avowed Incompetence," 16 A.L.R.5th 118 (1993).

[2]Polk County v. Dodson, 454 U.S. 312, 102 S.Ct. 445, 70 L.Ed.2d 509 (1981). Generally, see Annot., "Court-Appointed Attorney as Subject to Liability Under 42 U. S. C. S. § 1983," 36 A.L.R.Fed. 594 (1978).

[3]Tower v. Glover, 467 U.S. 914, 104 S.Ct. 2820, 81 L.Ed.2d 758 (1984).

In Ferri v. Ackerman, 444 U.S. 193, 100 S.Ct. 402, 62 L.Ed.2d 355 (1979), the court held that a complaint for negligence by a former indigent defendant against counsel appointed under the federal Criminal Justice Act of 1964 was not subject to dismissal because of immunity of counsel.

[4]People v. Claudio, 59 N.Y.2d 556, 466 N.Y.S.2d 271, 453 N.E.2d 500 (1983). In *Claudio*, counsel's conduct in connection with the giving of a confession was said to be "woefully inadequate." However, the court declined to suppress the statement. See § 14:89, n. 1, infra, on failure to file a motion to suppress.

[5]Smith v. State, 255 Ga. 654, 656 (3), 341 S.E.2d 5 (1986).

[6]Lynn v. State, 181 Ga. App. 461, 462 (1), 352 S.E.2d 602 (1986).

[7]Glover v. State, 266 Ga. 183 (2), 465 S.E.2d 659 (1996).

made it clear that "a defendant's failure to raise a claim of ineffectiveness before appeal under the circumstances of this case is a procedural bar to raising the claim at a later date." The court expressly overruled *Sixayaketh v. State*,[8] *Dozier v. State*,[9] and *King v. State*.[10]

In a series of cases culminating with *Wilson v. State*,[11] it is now clear that the claim of ineffective assistance of counsel must be raised in the trial court by way of a motion for new trial. The failure to do so by appellate counsel will result in the waiver of that issue on appeal. If the issue is raised in the trial court but the defendant does not request an evidentiary hearing on the motion, review of trial counsel's effectiveness will be restricted to the trial court record and no remand for an evidentiary hearing will be available. However, since "an attorney cannot reasonably be expected to assert or argue his or her own ineffectiveness, claims of ineffective assistance of counsel are often properly raised for the first time in a habeas corpus petition."[12] Indeed, the Georgia Supreme Court has held that in all cases where an indigent defendant wishes to raise the issue of ineffective assistance on appeal, trial counsel is conflicted from acting as counsel on appeal. This would include other attorneys in the office of the trial counsel or the office of the public defender who tried the case.[13]

A trial court's finding of effective assistance will be affirmed unless clearly erroneous.[14] However, in *Suggs v. State*,[15] the Georgia Supreme Court pointed out that "the clearly erroneous stan-

---

[8]Sixayaketh v. State, 261 Ga. 690, 410 S.E.2d 112 (1991), overruled by Glover v. State, 266 Ga. 183, 465 S.E.2d 659 (1996).

[9]Dozier v. State, 217 Ga. App. 835, 836 (3), 459 S.E.2d 463 (1995), overruled by Glover v. State, 266 Ga. 183, 465 S.E.2d 659 (1996).

[10]King v. State, 208 Ga. App. 77, 78-79 (2), 430 S.E.2d 640 (1993), overruled by Glover v. State, 266 Ga. 183, 465 S.E.2d 659 (1996).

[11]Wilson v. State, 277 Ga. 195, 586 S.E.2d 669 (2003). *Wilson* overruled contrary authority which held that in the absence of an evidentiary hearing on trial counsel's effectiveness, the issue was waived. In so doing, the court clarified that by including the claim in the motion for new trial, appellate review was secured but limited to the record on appeal and that no remand would be available to develop the issue if a hearing thereon by the trial court had not been requested.

See Wilson v. State, 286 Ga. 141, 686 S.E.2d 104 (2009), where the Supreme Court adopted the Court of Appeals' rule that claims of trial counsel's ineffectiveness not raised in a motion for new trial are waived and may not be resuscitated by assertions that appellate counsel was ineffective in failing to assign those claims as error in the initial appeal.

[12]White v. Kelso, 261 Ga. 32, 401 S.E.2d 733 (1991). See Williams v. Moody, 287 Ga. 665, 697 S.E.2d 199 (2010).

[13]Garland v. State, 283 Ga. 201, 657 S.E.2d 842 (2008).

[14]Smith v. State, 256 Ga. 483, 351 S.E.2d 641 (1986); Gibbs v. State, 213

dard applies solely to the trial court's factual findings and . . . [an appellate court owes] no deference to the trial court's legal conclusions."

In *Ponder v. State,*[16] the court held that a challenge to counsel's efficacy could be raised in an out-of-time appeal only if the appellate counsel pursues a motion for new trial subsequent to the grant of appeal and raises the issue. In *Maxwell v. State,*[17] the court elaborated on this holding by concluding that even if a defendant had filed a motion for new trial prior to the grant of his out-of-time appeal, he was not precluded from filing a second motion for new trial following the grant of appeal and was in fact required to do so within 30 days after the grant to preserve the issue of ineffective assistance of counsel. The court expressly recognized the trial court's discretion to refuse to reopen issues already decided in the first motion for new trial.

In *Thompson v. State,*[18] the court held that after November 5, 1987, any claim of ineffective assistance of counsel would be deemed waived if an appellant employs new counsel after conviction and the new attorney files a motion for new trial without raising ineffective assistance of counsel. However, the defendant's right to claim ineffective assistance of counsel is not barred if a member of the same law firm or a different public defender from the same defender's office fails to raise ineffective assistance of counsel.[19]

In *Rucker v. State,*[20] the defendant contended that the "new counsel" representing him at the hearing on motion for a new trial was deficient in failing to secure the testimony of a newly discovered witness. The court, in remanding the case, pointed out that the defendant had not had an earlier opportunity to challenge the performance of "new counsel."

Ga. App. 117, 118 (1), 443 S.E.2d 708 (1994).

[15]Suggs v. State, 272 Ga. 85, 88 (4), 526 S.E.2d 347 (2000).

[16]Ponder v. State, 260 Ga. 840, 841 (1), 400 S.E.2d 922 (1991). Accord, Peavy v. State, 213 Ga. App. 79, 443 S.E.2d 705 (1994).

[17]Maxwell v. State, 262 Ga. 541, 542 (3), 422 S.E.2d 543 (1992).

[18]Thompson v. State, 257 Ga. 386, 359 S.E.2d 664 (1987); Porter v. State, 258 Ga. 94, 365 S.E.2d 438 (1988). Cf. Maxwell v. State, 262 Ga. 541, 542 (3), 422 S.E.2d 543 (1992).

[19]Ryan v. Thomas, 261 Ga. 661, 662, 409 S.E.2d 507 (1991).

In Kennebrew v. State, 267 Ga. 400, 401(2), 480 S.E.2d 1 (1996), the court held that it was error for the trial judge to refuse to appoint counsel for defendant on his appeal to raise the issue of ineffective assistance of counsel where a public defender, in the same office as that of the public defender who represented defendant at trial, also represented defendant in the appeal on all issues other than ineffective assistance.

[20]Rucker v. State, 268 Ga. 406, 408(3), 489 S.E.2d 844 (1997).

In *Baldwin v. State*,[21] new counsel filed a motion for a new trial and alleged ineffective assistance of counsel. However, the motion contained "no factual allegations nor any demand for an *evidentiary* hearing. A rule nisi schedules *some* type of hearing. . . . However, there is no transcript of that hearing. . . ." The appellate court concluded that the defendant's claim of ineffective assistance of trial counsel was "procedurally barred and no remand is required." Thus, in *Upshaw v. State*,[22] the court found that claims of ineffective assistance that are procedurally barred because the defendant failed to assert them in a timely fashion cannot be resuscitated by "bootstrapping" them to claims of ineffective assistance of appellate counsel. "Once a claim is procedurally barred there is nothing for this Court to review. To hold otherwise would eviscerate the rule requiring that ineffectiveness claims be raised at the earliest practicable moment."[23]

See Annotations, "Adequacy of Defense Counsel's Representation of Criminal Client Regarding Post-Plea Remedies," 13 A.L.R.4th 533 (1982), and "Adequacy of Defense Counsel's Representation of Criminal Client Regarding Search and Seizure Issues," 12 A.L.R.4th 318 (1982). See § 7:11, infra, on conflicts of evidence preventing effective assistance of counsel. On effective assistance of appellate counsel, see § 28:6, infra. Generally, see Rule 29.8 of the Uniform Rules for the Superior Courts on the levels of experience and competency for various cases.

§ 7:7   Telephone call from defendant in custody

If counsel receives a telephone call from a defendant in custody wishing to have the attorney represent him, or if counsel wishes to reach a defendant by telephone after he has been approached by a friend or relative concerning the representation of the accused, counsel should consider covering the following in his conversation with the defendant:

1. Do not ask the defendant about any of the facts connected with the incident.
2. Tell the defendant that you will go to the jail to see him in person as soon as possible and give him a tentative date and time.
3. Warn the defendant not to discuss the alleged crime with anyone, in person or over the phone, including but not limited to friends, relatives, prosecutors, detectives, officers, jailors, cell mates or other persons in custody.

---

[21]Baldwin v. State, 217 Ga. App. 866, 867(1), 460 S.E.2d 80 (1995).

[22]Upshaw v. State, 257 Ga. App. 199, 202(4), 570 S.E.2d 640 (2002).

[23]Upshaw v. State, 257 Ga. App. 199, 202, 570 S.E.2d 640 (2002) citing Adams v. State, 239 Ga. App. 42, 43(2), 520 S.E.2d 746 (1999).

4. Tell him not to give voice or handwriting exemplars to anyone.

5. Tell him not to participate in any tests or try on any clothing, hat, cap, gloves or shoes.

§ 7:8 The initial interview

Normally, counsel will want to speak with the defendant prior to accepting his case. Where counsel has been appointed, he will still need to talk to the defendant for the purpose of determining whether there is some reason why he should not undertake to represent the accused. If any such reason exists, it should be made known immediately to the appointing judge so that substitute counsel may be appointed. In either event, counsel should interview the defendant as soon as possible. If for any reason counsel will not be available to interview the defendant, he should consider having an associate or another attorney speak with the accused in his absence as quickly as possible.

Counsel needs to personally interview the defendant as soon as possible.[1] If it appears at the initial interview that the defendant will be promptly released on bond, a brief interview may be adequate. However, if there will be any delay in obtaining the defendant's release, or he is not likely to be released on bond, counsel should conduct an in-depth discussion with him at the time of the initial interview.

Regardless of location, a thorough, detailed interview must be conducted as soon as possible. Defendants, like other witnesses, forget facts which may be crucial in the defense of the case. Counsel needs to explore every aspect related to the offense with which the defendant is charged while the facts are fresh in the accused's mind. At the same time, counsel should investigate the background of the defendant, including his prior record if any, his family and friends, and persons willing to help with the cost of attorney's fees, investigation and bond.

The defendant needs to understand from the beginning that counsel will be the one who makes tactical decisions about the handling of the case if he is employed.[2] The defendant should be fully informed that the trial motions to be made and all other

---

[Section 7:8]

[1]A.B.A. Standards, The Defense Function, Vol. I, Standards 4-3.1 and 4-3.2(a).

[2]Burns v. State, 145 Ga. App. 357, 358 (2), 243 S.E.2d 746 (1978); A.B.A. Standards, The Defense Function, Vol. I, Standards 4-3.1(b) and

4-5.2.

In Fortson v. State, 240 Ga. 5 (1), 239 S.E.2d 335 (1977), the court said that the "decisions on which witnesses to call, whether and how to conduct cross-examinations, what jurors to accept or strike, what trial motions should be made, and all other strategic and tactical decisions are the

trial strategies are within the exclusive province of counsel.[3]

After counsel has talked to the defendant, he should speak with the investigating and arresting officers in order to determine their version of the facts. After completing this task, the attorney will be in a position to talk intelligently about attorney's fees and investigative expenses.

For examples of client interview sheets, see Studdard, *Daniel's Georgia Criminal Trial Practice Forms* (2018–2019 ed.), §§ 6:6 and 6:7.

§ 7:9 Contract of employment

Experienced criminal defense lawyers feel that they should be paid in full in advance. There is much to support this belief, but counsel needs to first make an adequate appraisal of the time and expenses which will be involved in representing the defendant, as well as the ability of the defendant, his family, or friends to pay.

There are probably cases in which counsel should ask for a retainer fee in order to at least cover his loss of time involved in initially interviewing the defendant, particularly if the defendant is in custody. There are other situations in which such practice would be inappropriate. If a defendant is financially responsible, an attorney might consider charging a certain amount for his services through a commitment hearing and an additional specified amount for his services through a motion to suppress if one seems to be in order. A specified fee might be charged for entering a guilty plea. If the defendant is financially responsible, counsel might consider taking the case based on a specified retainer plus or against an hourly rate for his services.[1]

If the defendant is of limited financial means, and perhaps in certain other situations, counsel may think it best to charge a sizable lump sum for representing the defendant through the trial court. If the defendant, his family, and friends are so limited financially that counsel feels they cannot raise sufficient funds to adequately compensate him for the time and expenses he thinks will be involved, he needs to tell the defendant so. Unless the attorney is willing to handle the matter effectively for a lesser amount, he should have the defendant see an attorney who might

---

exclusive province of the lawyer after consultation with his client," quoting from A.B.A. Standards, The Defense Function, Vol. I, Standard 4-5.2(b).

[3]Willis v. State, 249 Ga. 261, 266 (6), 290 S.E.2d 87 (1982). See § 7:4, supra.

[Section 7:9]

[1]Fogarty v. State, 270 Ga. 609, 613, 513 S.E.2d 493 (1999). Generally, on the question of fees, see A.B.A. Standards, The Defense Function, Vol. I, Standard 4-3.3(a).

be able to handle the matter for a smaller amount, or he should attempt to have counsel appointed for the defendant. Attorneys should be careful not to accept a case for too small an amount and then attempt to take shortcuts by doing a less than professional job in representing the defendant.

There may be other situations in which counsel can take a case for a smaller amount where the defendant says that he is guilty and wants to enter a plea of guilty or nolo contendere. However, an attorney should not knowingly coerce a defendant into entering a guilty plea because he has quoted a fee for trying the case which the defendant cannot pay.

Whatever agreement counsel has with the defendant about representing him, it is imperative that said agreement be set out in writing. The agreement should point out that counsel is not promising to obtain any particular disposition of the case and that all the attorney can do is represent the client to the best of his ability.[2] If a family member or a friend is paying for counsel's representation of the defendant, the attorney at the outset must make it clear to everyone that his entire duty and loyalty is to the defendant and not to the person who may be paying for the defendant's representation. If there appears to be any conflict of interest between the person who has offered to pay and the defendant, counsel would be well advised not to accept the payment under these circumstances from the third person or any payment which counsel knows comes from such third person.[3] See § 7:11, infra, on conflicts of interest.

See O.C.G.A. § 17-12-5 on compensation of appointed counsel and payment of expenses necessarily incurred in the defense of an indigent defendant.[4] Generally, on "Fees and Employment Agreements," see Kadish and Brofman, 1 *Criminal Law Advocacy* (Trial Investigation and Preparation, para. 3.01 et seq.) (Mat-

---

[2]An agreement providing for a certain payment contingent on a disposition of the case favorable to defendant is void and against public policy. However, counsel is entitled to recover on a quantum meruit basis even if he had such a contract. Genins v. Geiger, 144 Ga. App. 244, 245 (2)(B), 240 S.E.2d 745 (1977).

[3]A.B.A. Standards, The Defense Function, Vol. I, Standard 4-3.5(c).

Standard 4-3.5. Conflict of interest

"(c) In accepting payment of fees by one person for the defense of another, a lawyer should be careful to determine that he or she will not be confronted with a conflict of loyalty since the lawyer's entire loyalty is due the accused. It is unprofessional conduct for the lawyer to accept such compensation except with the consent of the accused after full disclosure. It is unprofessional conduct for a lawyer to permit a person who recommends, employs, or pays the lawyer to render legal services for another to direct or regulate the lawyer's professional judgment in rendering such legal services."

[4]See § 14:5, infra, on payment of expenses incurred in the defense of an indigent defendant.

thew Bender 1982).

For a sample attorney's contract of employment, see Studdard, *Daniel's Georgia Criminal Trial Practice Forms* (2018–2019 ed.), §§ 6:2, 6:3 and 6:4.

§ 7:10   Appearance and withdrawal of counsel

Rule 4.6 of the Uniform Rules for the Superior Courts provides in part as follows: "[P]romptly upon agreeing to represent any client, the new attorney shall notify the appropriate calendar clerk in writing . . . and . . . the district attorney . . . of such representation. . . ."

Rule 4.2 provides in part as follows: "No attorney shall appear in that capacity before a superior court until the attorney has entered an appearance by filing a signed entry of appearance form or by filing a signed pleading in a pending action. An entry of appearance and all pleadings shall state: (1) the style and number of the case; (2) the identity of the party for whom the appearance is made; and (3) the name, assigned state bar number, and current office address and telephone number of the attorney. The filing of any pleading shall contain the information required by this paragraph and shall constitute an appearance by the person(s) signing such pleading unless otherwise specified by the court. The filing of a signed entry of appearance alone shall not be a substitute for the filing of an answer or any other required pleading. The filing of an indictment or accusation shall constitute an entry of appearance by the district attorney."

Rule 4.2 also provides that an attorney admitted to practice in Georgia may not file an appearance if he has failed "to maintain active membership in good standing in the State Bar of Georgia."

Rule 4.3 sets out a procedure for withdrawal of counsel prior to arraignment. However, Rule 30.2 provides in part as follows: "Upon arraignment, the attorney, if any, who announces for or on behalf of an accused, or who is entered as counsel of record, shall represent the accused in that case throughout the trial, unless other counsel and the defendant notify the judge prior to trial that such other counsel represents the accused and is ready to proceed, or counsel is otherwise relieved by the judge."

§ 7:11   Conflicts of interests

In *Glasser v. United States*,[1] the United States Supreme Court said that "the Sixth Amendment contemplates that such assis-

---

[Section 7:11]

[1]Glasser v. United States, 315 U.S. 60, 70, 62 S.Ct. 457, 86 L.Ed. 680 (1942) (quoted with approval in Mitchell v. State, 261 Ga. 347, 349, 405 S.E.2d 38 (1991)).

tance [of effective counsel] be untrammeled and unimpaired by a court order requiring that one lawyer shall simultaneously represent conflicting interests." The conflict-of-interest problems are particularly prone to arise where counsel attempts to represent two or more defendants jointly charged with an offense. Some experienced lawyers think that counsel should never undertake to represent two jointly indicted defendants.[2] This view would probably be considered extreme by most attorneys in Georgia today. However, while there is much to be said for caution in this area,[3] "[s]ingle representation of multiple defendants raises no per se presumption of conflict of interest or prejudice."[4]

A few of the problems which may be encountered in a situation of dual representation are: (1) What happens if defense counsel thinks that one defendant should testify against the other defendant? (2) Suppose it is in the best interest of one defendant to plead guilty? (3) Suppose one defendant has confessed? (4) What if it is in the best interest of one defendant to testify and this may adversely affect the other defendant?

The real difficulty is that the conflict of interests may not appear until the time of trial or during the course of the trial. If counsel realizes that there is a conflict of interest, he should not continue to represent both defendants, and since presumably he will have received confidential information from both, he probably should not continue to represent either defendant. This is not only a problem for trial counsel, but it is a burden on the trial court, which is now faced with a half-tried case with counsel who feels that he can no longer represent the defendants.

If one defendant's defense is that the other defendant, and not he, committed the crime, or that the culpability of one is less than the other, or that in mitigation of the punishment of one, the bad influence of the other should be considered, then from a constitutional standpoint, each defendant must have separate counsel. If counsel cannot vigorously pursue the defense of one defendant because it will impair the defense of the other, sepa-

---

[2]See "Criminal Co-defendants and the Sixth Amendment: The Case for Separate Counsel," 6 Crim. L. Bull. 432 (1970); Baker v. State, 202 So.2d 563, 566 (Fla.1967).

"A lawyer shall not represent a client if the representation of that client will be directly adverse to another client, unless . . . [the lawyer] reasonable believes the representation will not adversely affect the relationship with the other client; and . . . each client consents after consultation."

Rule 1.7 of the Rules of Professional Conduct, effective January 1, 2001, and superseding the Canons of Ethics.

[3]A.B.A. Standards, The Defense Function, Vol. I, Standard 4-3.5(a), (b).

See Annot., "Circumstances Giving Rise to Prejudicial Conflict of Interests Between Criminal Defendant and Defense Counsel—State Cases," 18 A.L.R.4th 360 (1982).

[4]Hamilton v. State, 255 Ga. 468, 470 (2), 339 S.E.2d 707 (1986).

rate counsel are needed. However, it has been said that the defenses do not have to be "entirely consistent."[5]

In 1978, the United States Supreme Court, in *Holloway v. Arkansas*,[6] held that if a trial counsel has been appointed to defend two or more defendants and a timely motion is made by defense counsel to have separate counsel appointed, the failure to appoint separate counsel or to take adequate steps to determine if the risk of a conflict of interest was too remote to warrant separate counsel, is a violation of the Sixth Amendment regardless of whether or not prejudice is shown. The court also cited, with apparent approval, a number of cases holding that "an attorney's request for the appointment of separate counsel, based on his representations as an officer of the court regarding a conflict of interest, should be granted."[7] In the 1980 case of *Cuyler v. Sullivan*,[8] the same court said that in "order to establish a violation of the Sixth Amendment, a defendant who raised no objection at trial must demonstrate that an actual conflict of interest adversely affected his lawyer's performance. . . ."[9] [T]he possibility of conflict is insufficient to impugn a criminal conviction." "The conflict of interest 'must be palpable and have a substantial basis in fact. A theoretical or speculative conflict will not impugn a conviction [or sentence] which is supported by competent evidence.' "[10]Additionally, the Court in *Cuyler* pointed out that "[a]bsent special circumstances, . . . trial courts may assume either that multiple representation entails no conflict or that the lawyer and his clients knowingly accept such risk of conflict."[11] See § 7:12, infra, on disqualification of counsel.

---

[5]Davis v. State, 129 Ga. App. 796, 799, 201 S.E.2d 345 (1973). In Lemley v. State, 245 Ga. 350 (1), 264 S.E.2d 881 (1980), the defendant was indicted for murder. The defendant's girlfriend was indicted for hindering the apprehension of a criminal because she had taken the defendant to another county to obtain medical attention. Apparently the girlfriend had witnessed the shooting. The same attorney was appointed to represent the defendant and the girlfriend. The girlfriend was later granted immunity and ordered to testify for the state. The court held that counsel did not have a conflict of interest and pointed out that even if she had not been granted immunity, she would not have had any defenses inconsistent with that of the defendant.

[6]Holloway v. Arkansas, 435 U.S.

475, 98 S.Ct. 1173, 55 L.Ed.2d 426 (1978). Cf. Clark v. State, 152 Ga. App. 627, 628, 263 S.E.2d 512 (1979). Cf. Wilson v. State, 257 Ga. 352, 353, 359 S.E.2d 661 (1987).

[7]Quoted with approval in Mitchell v. State, 261 Ga. 347, 349, 405 S.E.2d 38 (1991).

[8]Cuyler v. Sullivan, 446 U.S. 335, 348, 100 S.Ct. 1708, 64 L.Ed.2d 333 (1980). See White v. State, 298 Ga. 416, 782 S.E.2d 280 (2016).

[9]Kennedy v. State, 177 Ga. App. 543, 544 (1), 340 S.E.2d 204 (1986); Stephens v. State, 214 Ga. App. 183, 187 (9)(b), 447 S.E.2d 26 (1994).

[10]Henry v. State, 269 Ga. 851, 854 (3), 507 S.E.2d 419 (1998) (quoting Lamb v. State, 267 Ga. 41, 472 S.E.2d 683 (1996)).

[11]Cuyler v. Sullivan, 446 U.S. 335,

The Georgia Supreme Court, in the 1980 case of *Fleming v. State,*[12] concluded that in the future the same attorney shall not represent co-defendants in cases in which the death penalty is sought because of the difficulty in assessing possible conflicts of interest. In *Fleming,* the court expressly left open the question of multiple representation where the death penalty is not being requested.[13] However, in *Ford v. State,*[14] the court declined to apply the rule of *Fleming* to a capital case in which the district attorney had recommended a life sentence after plea bargaining and a guilty plea had been entered by the defendant. In *Zant v. Hill,*[15] the court concluded that the rule of *Fleming* of automatic disqualification should be "limited to cases in which each of two or more defendants is charged with capital felonies arising out of the same criminal transaction or event."

In *Ruffin v. Kemp,*[16] the Eleventh Circuit held a lawyer who attempts to represent two defendants in a murder case and tries to work out a plea bargain in which one defendant is to testify against the other defendant, renders the defendant who is not the beneficiary of the plea agreement ineffective assistance of counsel. In *Tarwater v. State,*[17] the court held "that when counsel representing multiple defendants negotiates a plea bargain *conditioned upon more than one pleading guilty,* that attorney has suffered a conflict of interest which *per se adversely affects his representation* of each defendant affected." (Emphasis added.)

In *State v. Abernathy,*[18] the Supreme Court of Georgia held that in order to assert an ineffective assistance claim based upon an actual conflict of interest, the defendant "must demonstrate that the conflict of interest existed and that it significantly affected counsel's performance." The court went on to note:

> The critical question is whether the conflict significantly affected the *representation,* not whether it affected the outcome of the

---

346, 100 S.Ct. 1708, 64 L.Ed.2d 333 (1980); Angevine v. State, 171 Ga. App. 658, 660, 320 S.E.2d 578 (1984).

[12]Fleming v. State, 246 Ga. 90, 270 S.E.2d 185 (1980).

[13]Fleming v. State, 246 Ga. 90, 92 n. 5, 270 S.E.2d 185 (1980).

[14]Ford v. State, 248 Ga. 241, 282 S.E.2d 308 (1981).

[15]Zant v. Hill, 262 Ga. 815, 816 (2), 425 S.E.2d 858 (1993).

[16]Ruffin v. Kemp, 767 F.2d 748 (11th Cir. 1985). Accord, Ford v. Ford, 749 F.2d 681 (11th Cir. 1985).

[17]Tarwater v. State, 259 Ga. 516, 519, 383 S.E.2d 883 (1989). See The State v. Mamedov, 288 Ga. 858, 708 S.E.2d 279 (2011) (once an actual conflict is proven, the only issue is whether the conflict adversely affected counsel's representation of the client). See also Fogarty v. State, 270 Ga. 609, 513 S.E.2d 493 (1999) (petitioner need not show that outcome at trial would have been different but only that conflict adversely affected lawyer's performance).

[18]State v. Abernathy, 289 Ga. 603, 604–605, 715 S.E.2d 48 (2011) (citations and punctuation omitted; emphasis in original).

underlying *proceedings*. That is precisely the difference between
ineffective assistance of counsel claims generally where prejudice
must be shown, and ineffective assistance of counsel claims involving actual conflicts of interest, which require only a showing of a
significant effect on the representation. A significant effect on the
representation may be found, for example, where counsel is shown
to have refrained from raising a potentially meritorious issue due
to the conflict; where counsel negotiates a plea bargain for more
than one defendant in a case conditioned on acceptance of the plea
by all such defendants; or where one of the State's witnesses was a
current client of defense counsel in an unrelated criminal matter,
thereby constraining counsel's ability to cross-examine the witness.

If, in a particular case, counsel determines that he can, in good
faith, defend two or more joint defendants, he must be sure to
inform both of the possibility of a conflict of interests and make a
full disclosure of the situation to each defendant.[19] In such a situation, it would be wise for counsel to require a letter or memo
from each defendant stating that (1) he fully understands his
right to have individual counsel, (2) he recognizes the possibility
of a conflict of interest developing at some later point in time, (3)
counsel has explained the situation to him, (4) he sees no possibility of a conflict of interest, (5) he knowingly and voluntarily
waives his right to individual counsel, and (6) he requests counsel
to represent him and the other defendant(s) whom he names.[20]
Indeed, the dissent in *Woods v. State*,[21] suggests that, in the
future a written waiver of conflict of interest may not be sufficient to satisfy the requirement that the waiver be knowing,
intelligent and voluntary. Chief Justice Fletcher wrote that in
the absence of a dialogue on the record, similar to that required
by Fed. R. Crim. p. 44(c) between the court and the defendant, a
pro forma written waiver of conflict is unlikely to adequately
reflect that it was executed with a full appreciation of the dangers
inherent in sharing counsel with a co-defendant.

However, "[w]here a co-defendant does not object to multiple
representation until after trial, a conflict of interest will not be

---

[19]Cf. Rice v. State, 226 Ga. App.
770, 771 (1), 487 S.E.2d 517 (1997).

[20]In Collins v. State, 144 Ga. App.
102, 104 (1), 240 S.E.2d 597 (1977),
the court held that defendants may
knowingly, intelligently and intentionally waive their rights to separate
counsel even where one of the defendants has made a confession implicating the other. Contra, Baker v.
Wainwright, 422 F.2d 145 (5th Cir.
1970).

In Shirley v. State, 166 Ga. App.

456 (2), 304 S.E.2d 468 (1983), the
court said that where each defendant
"confirmed, on the record, that they
had discussed the case thoroughly
with their counsel, and each stated
that there was no conflict of interest
. . . [and] that they were satisfied to
proceed with one counsel . . . if any
error occurred it was induced by these
defendants' statements and induced
error is impermissible."

[21]Woods v. State, 275 Ga. 844,
852, 573 S.E.2d 394 (2002).

presumed; and in order to establish a Sixth Amendment violation, it must be shown that an actual conflict existed which adversely affected the attorney's performance."[22] In *Brumelow v. State*,[23] the court pointed out, "Where [two] defendants state on the record that they have discussed the case with counsel, that there is no conflict of interest and that they are satisfied to proceed with one counsel, any error was induced by defendants' statements, and induced error is impermissible."

In 1982, the Georgia Attorney General made two unofficial rulings relating to conflicts of interest. First he ruled that public officers and public employees are not prevented from representing a defendant in a criminal proceeding.[24] Second, he ruled that it is impermissible for a person holding a continuing appointment as a Special Assistant Attorney General to represent a defendant in a criminal case. However, this latter rule does not apply to a one-time or infrequent appointee.[25] In *Capers v. State*,[26] the court pointed out that "single representation of multiple defendants raises no per se presumption of conflict of interest or prejudice. . . . A mere possibility of conflict is insufficient to impugn a criminal conviction amply supported by competent evidence. . . . '[A]ctive representation of conflicting interests' connotes more than merely cross-examining a former client.' "

In *Hudson v. State*,[27] the court held that an attorney who is a state court solicitor or a probate judge is not automatically disqualified from representing a defendant in a criminal case. In *Thompson v. State*,[28] the Georgia Supreme Court held that where a part time solicitor of a state court has an associate in his firm, there is no per se disqualification preventing the associate from representing a defendant in superior court. In *Reeves v. State*,[29] the defendant contended that he was denied effective assistance of counsel because defense counsel did not inform him before trial that he had accepted a position as assistant district attorney. The defendant contends he would not have waived a jury trial if he had been properly informed of the distinctions between a bench

---

[22]Acierno v. State, 176 Ga. App. 600, 601 (3), 337 S.E.2d 39 (1985); Griggs v. State, 262 Ga. 766, 769 (4)(b), 425 S.E.2d 644 (1993).

[23]Brumelow v. State, 239 Ga. App. 119, 123 (6), 520 S.E.2d 776 (1999).

[24]Ga. Atty. Gen. U82-44.

[25]Ga. Atty. Gen. U82-45.

[26]Capers v. State, 220 Ga. App. 869, 873, 470 S.E.2d 887 (1996).

[27]Hudson v. State, 250 Ga. 479, 482 (1), 299 S.E.2d 531 (1983). Cf.

O'Melia v. State, 255 Ga. 476, 477, 339 S.E.2d 586 (1986).

[28]Thompson v. State, 254 Ga. 393, 395 (2), 330 S.E.2d 348 (1985).

[29]Reeves v. State, 231 Ga. App. 22, 497 S.E.2d 625 (1998). In Howerton v. Danenberg, 279 Ga. 861(1), 621 S.E. 2d. 738 (2005) impermissible conflict of interest in death penalty case where defense counsel was concurrently representing district attorney in federal civil rights action.

trial and a jury trial. The appellate court reversed the conviction. See § 17:6, infra, on district attorneys.

In *Burger v. Kemp*,[30] the United States Supreme Court held that there is no per se conflict of interest where two co-defendants are each represented at separate trials by counsel who are partners. Likewise, there is no per se conflict for one of these counsel to prepare briefs for both defendants on appeal after their convictions.

Also, there are "inherent dangers that arise when a criminal defendant is represented by a lawyer hired and paid by a third party, particularly when the third party is the operator of the alleged criminal enterprise." One risk is that the lawyer will prevent his client from obtaining leniency by preventing the client from offering testimony against the one who is paying his fee. Another risk is that the person paying the lawyer may have an interest in establishing a legal precedent which might sacrifice the interest of the client.[31]

In *Mitchell v. State*,[32] the Georgia Supreme Court held that the rules about conflicts of interest "apply with equal force to alleged conflicts arising from defense counsel's representation of a prosecution witness in unrelated matters." In *Hill v. State*,[33] the same court, in an opinion by Justice Sears, considered the situation in which defense counsel had previously represented a witness who had testified for the state. The court pointed out that there is a "legal presumption . . . that an attorney-client relationship terminates once the case or controversy in which the attorney was originally employed is resolved by the entry of final judgment. . . . [However, courts] must examine the particular circumstances to determine whether counsel's undivided loyalties remain with his or her current client, as they must. . . . [F]actors that arguably may interfere with effective cross-examination . . . include '(1) concern that the lawyer's pecuniary interest in possible future business may cause him [or her] to avoid vigorous cross-examination which might be embarrassing or offensive to the witness; (2) . . . the possibility that privileged information . . . [in the earlier representation] might be relevant to cross-examination' [and (3)] whether 'the subject matter of the first representation is substantially related to that of the second.' "

---

[30]Burger v. Kemp, 483 U.S. 776, 107 S.Ct. 3114, 97 L.Ed.2d 638 (1987).

[31]Wood v. Georgia, 450 U.S. 261, 268, 101 S.Ct. 1097, 67 L.Ed.2d 220 (1981).

[32]Mitchell v. State, 261 Ga. 347, 350, 405 S.E.2d 38 (1991). See Bourassa v. State, 345 Ga. App. 463, 811 S.E.2d 113 (2018).

[33]Hill v. State, 269 Ga. 23 (2), 494 S.E.2d 661 (1998) (quoting United States v. Jeffers, 520 F.2d 1256 (7th Cir. 1975), and United States v. Ross, 33 F.3d 1507 (11th Cir. 1994)).

In *United States v. Reynoso*,[34] the court held that an attorney employed by the Federal Defender need not be disqualified from representing a defendant just because another lawyer in the Federal Defender's office had represented a prospective witness in another case. In *Burns v. State*,[35] the Georgia Supreme Court declined to adopt a "presumed or per se rule of conflict of interest involving attorneys in the same PDO [Public Defender Office] . . . and held that two attorneys from the same PDO can represent criminal co-defendants in those cases where no conflict exists." In 2013 the Court published Formal Advisory Opinion 10-1 in which it held that "if it is determined that a single public defender in the circuit public defender's office of a particular judicial circuit has an impermissible conflict of interest concerning the representation of co-defendants, then that conflict of interest is imputed to all of the public defenders working in the circuit public defender office of that particular judicial circuit."[36]

The Court reiterated that simply because a public defender in a particular office represents one of several defendants in a given case, another attorney in the same office is not *per se* barred from representing a co-defendant in the same case. It is only when a single attorney in the office has an in fact impermissible conflict of interest which would prevent that attorney from representing another defendant in the case that other attorneys in the office are conflicted from representing the other defendant. The Court's reasoning was based upon its conclusion that, in many respects, the public defender's office for a circuit is analogous to a law firm and should treat the representation of clients in the same way as law firms do in the case of a conflict.

In *Odum v. State*,[37] the Georgia Court of Appeals interpreted for the first time O.C.G.A. § 17-12-22, which became effective January 1, 2005 as part of the Indigent Defense Act of 2003. This code section addresses the issue of conflict of interest within a public defender's office. The court ruled that before the public de-

---

[34]United States v. Reynoso, 6 F.Supp.2d 269 (S.D.N.Y. 1998).

[35]Burns v. State, 281 Ga. 338, 340, 638 S.E.2d 299 (2006) (citations omitted). See Lytle v. State, 290 Ga. 177, 718 S.E.2d 296 (2011) (no conflict for public defender representing defendant who worked in same office as other public defenders representing co-defendants and who shared the office's only investigator where no evidence that attorneys or investigators shared confidential information). But see White v. State, 287 Ga. 713, 699 S.E.2d 291 (2010) (public defender's office policy of never pleading to a life sentence was a conflict where trial verdict added thirteen years to sentence).

[36]In re Formal Advisory Opinion 10-1, 293 Ga. 397, 744 S.E.2d 798 (2013) (Georgia Rules of Professional Conduct 1.10(a) applies to the office of a circuit public defender in the same way it does to a private law firm). See Pryor v. State, 333 Ga. App. 408, 776 S.E.2d 474 (2015).

[37]Odum v. State, 283 Ga. App. 291, 641 S.E.2d 279 (2007).

fender's office begins actual representation of a client, it is the sole arbiter of whether a conflict exists. Once the public defender undertakes to represent a client, however, any effort to withdraw representation from a client because of a perceived conflict would have to be submitted to the discretion of the trial court.

In *Wharton v. Thomas*,[38] the court held that "[w]hen conflict of interest is raised in a post-conviction proceeding, the [defendant] must show actual conflict which caused his counsel's performance to be adversely affected." However, in *Sallie v. State*,[39] the Georgia Supreme Court unanimously reversed the defendant's conviction and held that where defense counsel in a death case was a full-time law clerk in the same court and he had never informed the defendant that he was a law clerk in the circuit, this was a conflict of interest.

See Annotation, "Multiple Representation of Defendants in Criminal Cases as Violative of Sixth Amendment Right to Counsel—Federal Cases," 64 L.Ed.2d 907 (1981), and Annotation, "Attorney: Disqualification of Member of Law Firm as Requiring Disqualification of Entire Firm—State Cases," 6 A.L.R.5th 242 (1992). See § 7:9, supra, on fees which may be set.

See § 7:12, infra, on disqualification and removal of counsel. See Annotation, "Circumstances Giving Rise to Prejudicial Conflict of Interest Between Criminal Defendant and Defense Counsel—Federal Cases," 53 A.L.R.Fed. 140 (1981) and 18 A.L.R.4th 360 (1982) on state cases.

§ 7:12 Disqualification and removal of counsel

The general rule is that a defendant is entitled to a reasonable opportunity to employ counsel of his choice and to be represented by such counsel at trial.[1] However, a trial judge has authority to disqualify, even retained counsel, and to prevent such counsel from representing a defendant in some situations. For example, if defense counsel has a conflict of interest he may be disqualified by the court.[2] In like manner it has been held that where defense

---

[38]Wharton v. Thomas, 256 Ga. 76, 77, 343 S.E.2d 694 (1986); Hance v. Kemp, 258 Ga. 649, 659 (5), 373 S.E.2d 184 (1988). Cf. Green v. State, 221 Ga. App. 694, 697 (6), 472 S.E.2d 457 (1996).

[39]Sallie v. State, 269 Ga. 446, 447 (2), 499 S.E.2d 897 (1998).

[Section 7:12]

[1]23 C.J.S. 932, Criminal Law § 979(5) (1961).

[2]Cf. State ex rel. Bradford v. Dinwiddie, 361 Mo. 940, 237 S.W.2d 179 (1951); Matter of Darr, 143 Cal.App.3d 500, 191 Cal.Rptr. 882 (1983). See Lowenthal, "Successive Representation by Criminal Lawyers," 93 Yale L. J. 1 (1983).

counsel is implicated in the crime with which the defendant has been charged he may be disqualified.[3] Moreover, it has been held that in such a situation a defendant may not "waive any ethical problems in order to have the benefit of his attorney's continued representation . . . because the ethical violations involve public perception of the lawyer and the legal system."[4]

In *Wheat v. United States,*[5] the United States Supreme Court said that the trial judge "must be allowed substantial latitude in refusing waivers of conflicts of interest not only in those rare cases where an actual conflict may be demonstrated before trial, but in the more common cases where a potential for conflict exists which may or may not burgeon into an actual conflict as the trial progresses." While a trial judge "must recognize a presumption in favor of . . . [the defendant's] counsel of choice . . . that presumption may be overcome not only by a demonstration of actual conflict but by a showing of a serious potential for conflict."

In *Flores v. State,*[6] the court held that if it becomes apparent to the trial judge during the course of a trial that the representation of two defendants is a violation of the Code of Professional Responsibility, the judge may disqualify the attorney. Thus, in *Davenport v. State,*[7] the Georgia Supreme Court approved a trial court's decision to remove an appointed attorney over the defendant's objection after the trial court determined that counsel was willing to proceed to trial although unprepared and without properly asserting several of his client's rights.

As a general proposition, there are two grounds for disqualification of a prosecuting attorney. The first is conflict of interest. For example, a prosecutor who either represented or provided professional advice to the accused in connection with the case would have such a conflict. A prosecutor would also be subject to disqualification if he or she acquires a personal stake in the defendant's prosecution and conviction. This is also referred to as "forensic misconduct." An example would be public statements by the prosecutor expressing belief in the defendant's guilt which

---

[3]United States v. Hobson, 672 F.2d 825 (11th Cir. 1982) (abrogated by Flanagan v. U.S., 465 U.S. 259, 104 S. Ct. 1051, 79 L. Ed. 2d 288 (1984)); United States v. Garrett, 727 F.2d 1003 (11th Cir. 1984).

[4]United States v. Hobson, 672 F.2d 825, 829 (11th Cir. 1982) (abrogated by Flanagan v. U.S., 465 U.S. 259, 104 S. Ct. 1051, 79 L. Ed. 2d 288 (1984)).

[5]Wheat v. United States, 486 U.S. 153, 108 S.Ct. 1692, 100 L.Ed.2d

140 (1988). See Registe v. State, 287 Ga. 542, 697 S.E.2d 804 (2010). See also Heidt v. State, 292 Ga. 343, 736 S.E.2d 384 (2013) (defense counsel who represented defendant and his co-defendant girlfriend disqualified because of likelihood of conflict in advising girlfriend of possible plea bargain).

[6]Flores v. State, 159 Ga. App. 336, 337 (1), 283 S.E.2d 372 (1981).

[7]Davenport v. State, 283 Ga. 29 (2b), 656 S.E.2d 514 (2008).

are calculated "to prejudice the defendant in the minds of the jurors. . . ."[8]

In *State v. Clausell*,[9] the Florida Supreme Court held that where some of the district attorney's office are disqualified from taking part since they are to testify against the defendant this does not require that all the attorneys in the district attorney's office be disqualified. In *Holiday v. State*,[10] the Georgia Supreme Court held that the disqualification of an assistant district attorney does not disqualify all the staff of the district attorney. Likewise, in *Brown v. State*,[11] the court held that the disqualification of the district attorney himself, simply because he was to be a witness, does not require the disqualification of his entire office.

In *Love v. State*,[12] the court affirmed the action of a trial judge in disqualifying a law firm with which a former assistant district attorney had become associated where the former assistant district attorney had represented the state at a preliminary hearing of the case.

In *Stinson v. State*,[13] the court pointed out that it was "improper to disqualify an attorney based solely on an appearance of impropriety, particularly when the appearance of impropriety resulted not from the attorney's conduct but from his status as the spouse of an attorney affiliated with the opposing party." However, if defense counsel's spouse is called as a witness, this would prevent adequate representation of the client.

The state is not authorized to appeal a trial court's denial of a motion to disqualify an attorney under O.C.G.A. § 5-7-1.[14]

See § 7:11, supra, on conflicts of interest. See § 17:6, infra, on disqualification of a prosecuting attorney. See Annotations, "Grounds for Disqualification of Criminal Defendant's Chosen and Preferred Attorney in Federal Prosecution," 127 A.L.R.Fed. 67 (1995) and "Disqualification of Member of Law Firm as Requiring Disqualification of Entire Firm—State Cases," 6 A.L.R.5th 242 (1992).

[8]Williams v. State, 258 Ga. 305, 314(2)(B), 369 S.E.2d 232 (1988) (citations omitted).

[9]State v. Clausell, 474 So.2d 1189 (Fla.1985), rev'g 455 So.2d 1050 (1984).

[10]Holiday v. State, 258 Ga. 393, 397 (9), 369 S.E.2d 241 (1988).

[11]Brown v. State, 261 Ga. 66, 72 (9), 401 S.E.2d 492 (1991).

[12]Love v. State, 202 Ga. App. 889, 416 S.E.2d 99 (1992).

[13]Stinson v. State, 210 Ga. App. 570, 436 S.E.2d 765 (1993). Likewise, the personal relationship between an investigator in the prosecutor's office and the victim will not provide grounds to disqualify the office provided the investigator is not involved in the victim's case. Head v. State, 253 Ga. App. 757, 758 (2), 560 S.E.2d 536 (2002).

[14]State v. Redd, 248 Ga. App. 312, 313, 546 S.E.2d 68 (2001).

Chapter 8

Bonds

KeyCite®: Cases and other legal materials listed in KeyCite Scope can be researched through the KeyCite service on Westlaw®. Use KeyCite to check citations for form, parallel references, prior and later history, and comprehensive citator information, including citations to other decisions and secondary materials.

---

§ 8:1   General considerations

Defense counsel will normally attempt to have his client released on bond if he is still in custody at the time counsel is employed. Generally, nothing is achieved from a defense standpoint by leaving the defendant in jail pending trial. Of course, the fact that the defendant is in jail may keep him from getting into additional trouble. However, generally an accused can be of little help to himself, his family, or his counsel as long as he remains in custody. If he is released he may work, care for his family and more actively assist defense counsel in the preparation of his case.[1] From the standpoint of the prosecution, it may be desirable to keep the defendant in custody to prevent his escape, commission of other crimes, or intimidation of witnesses.

While the Eighth Amendment of the United States Constitution states that bail shall not be excessive, it does not expressly provide that a defendant has a right to bail. Although the United

---

[Section 8:1]

[1]The court recognized the importance of having a defendant charged with murder released in United States v. Reese, 463 F.2d 830 (D.C.Cir. 1972). In this case, the defendant was re-leased in custody of a marshal so that he could assist defense counsel in finding an exculpatory witness. Cf. Young v. State, 149 Ga. App. 533, 534 (3), 254 S.E.2d 749 (1979); State v. Ruff, 176 Ga. App. 303, 335 S.E.2d 687 (1985).

States Supreme Court has never expressly held that the Eighth Amendment applies to the states, a number of federal courts have so regarded its application.[2] However, in *Schall v. Martin*,[3] the court did consider whether or not criteria for release violated the due process clause of the Fourteenth Amendment.

The Georgia Constitution parallels the provision of the federal Constitution concerning bail.[4] O.C.G.A. § 17-6-1 provides that all "offenses . . . are bailable by a court of inquiry" except the following:

"(1) Treason;

"(2) Murder;

"(3) Rape;

"(4) Aggravated sodomy;

"(5) Armed robbery;

"(6) Aircraft hijacking and hijacking a motor vehicle;

"(7) Aggravated child molestation;

"(8) Aggravated sexual battery;

"(9) Manufacturing, distributing, delivering, dispensing, administering, or selling any controlled substance classified under O.C.G.A. § 16-13-25 as Schedule I or under O.C.G.A. § 16-13-26 as Schedule II;

"(10) Violating O.C.G.A. § 16-13-31 or O.C.G.A. § 16-13-31.1 (drug offenses);

"(11) Kidnapping, arson, aggravated assault, or burglary if the person, at the time of the alleged kidnapping, arson, aggravated assault, or burglary, had previously been convicted of, was on probation or parole with respect to, or was on bail for kidnapping, arson, aggravated assault, burglary, or one or more of the offenses listed in paragraphs (1) through (10) of this subsection; and

"(12) Aggravated stalking."[5]

The offenses named in paragraphs (1) through (12) in this Code

---

[2]See Goodman v. Ault, 358 F.Supp. 743 (N.D.Ga.1973); Goodine v. Griffin, 309 F.Supp. 590 (S.D.Ga.1970); Boyer v. Orlando, 402 F.2d 966 (5th Cir. 1968); Pilkinton v. Circuit Court, 324 F.2d 45, 46 (8th Cir. 1963); Dawkins v. Crevasse, 391 F.2d 921 (5th Cir. 1968); Sheldon v. State of Nebraska, 401 F.2d 342, 346 (8th Cir. 1968); Kinney v. Lenon, 425 F.2d 209 (9th Cir. 1970).

[3]Schall v. Martin, 467 U.S. 253, 104 S.Ct. 2403, 81 L.Ed.2d 207 (1984).

See § 8:3, infra, for a discussion of Martin.

[4]Ga. Const. 1983, Art. I, § I, ¶ XVII.

[5]O.C.G.A. § 17-6-1. In United States v. Abrahams, 575 F.2d 3 (1st Cir. 1978), the court stated that the Eighth Amendment does not require that a defendant be allowed bail in all non-capital cases. In this case, the defendant had already failed to appear once.

subsection are not bailable unless a judge of the superior court fixes a bond.[6] In 1983, the legislature repealed a provision of the law which gave a defendant in capital cases a right to bond where the defendant filed a demand for trial at the term in which his indictment was returned where he was not tried at that term.[7] See § 8:4, infra, on the fixing of a bond in superior court for the offenses named above.

In 1991, O.C.G.A. § 17-6-1(b) was amended to also provide that a person charged with driving under the influence whose blood alcohol concentration, at the time of arrest, was 0.10 grams or more "may be detained for a period . . . up to six hours after booking and prior to being released."

In the case of a defendant charged with an offense only bailable in superior court, if a defendant has had a commitment hearing scheduled and it is continued at the request of either party or of the court, it seems that a superior court judge on motion may after that time fix a bond in the case even though the defendant has not been bound over.[8] However, if a magistrate erroneously rules that an offense is bailable only before the Superior Court and denies a request for bond, this is not a basis for quashing an indictment which is later returned.[9]

O.C.G.A. § 17-6-1(h) provides that except in the cases in which life imprisonment or death may be imposed, a superior court judge may delegate his or her authority to any judge of a court of inquiry within the superior court circuit. However, such delegated authority may not be exercised outside the county in which the judge of the court of inquiry was elected or appointed. Such a delegation is valid for one year unless revoked by the superior court judge before that time.

In determining whether or not to set a bond and in determining the amount of such a bond, the court should consider the same criteria which are relevant in considering a bond on appeal.[10] See § 28:5, infra, on bonds pending appeal and § 8:4, infra, for

---

[6]O.C.G.A. § 17-6-1.

[7]O.C.G.A. § 17-7-171.

[8]Lane v. State, 247 Ga. 387, 388, 276 S.E.2d 644 (1981).

[9]Nixon v. State, 256 Ga. 261, 262 (1), 347 S.E.2d 592 (1986).

[10]Lane v. State, 247 Ga. 387, 388, 276 S.E.2d 644 (1981). In Lane, the case was remanded to the trial court to determine whether or not a bond should be granted in the light of the opinion. The opinion says that "the trial court, in an order denying bond, must set forth the basis of its decision." It is not clear whether this is a general requirement in all cases where a bond is denied or whether this requirement is intended to apply only to that case.

However, in Benford v. State, 161 Ga. App. 87, 88 (3), 289 S.E.2d 253 (1982), the court stated that, in the absence of a transcript of the bond hearing, the appellate court must assume as a matter of law that the evidence presented at the hearing supported the findings of the trial judge.

criteria for bonds in superior court for certain offenses. If the trial judge denies a bond, the court must set out the reason for the denial so that appellate courts can better determine whether there has been an abuse of discretion.[11] In passing on the question of whether or not to fix a bond, the trial judge may consider prior convictions, even if the defendant's sentences have been commuted and his civil and political rights have been restored.[12]

Under Georgia law, if a defendant posts bond before a preliminary or commitment hearing, the bond remains valid after such hearing unless the amount is increased.[13] Officials of a municipality have the authority to accept cash bonds for violations of municipal ordinances[14] and since 1969, there has been general statutory authority to deposit cash in lieu of a bond.[15] Prior to the enactment of the 1969 statute authorizing the acceptance of a cash bond, cash was commonly accepted by sheriffs and their agents although the money accepted was regarded as being held in trust for the depositor.[16]

Also, a statute[17] was passed in 1982 authorizing certain county officers to accept cash bonds. This statute provides that any sheriff, deputy sheriff, county peace officer, or other county officer charged with the duty of enforcing the laws of this state relating to (1) traffic or the operation or licensing of motor vehicles or operators; (2) the width, height, or length of vehicles and loads; (3) motor common carriers and motor contract carriers; (4) road taxes on motor carriers as provided in O.C.G.A. §§ 48-9-30 et seq.; (5) game and fish; (6) boating; or (7) litter control who makes an arrest outside the corporate limits of any municipality of this state for a violation of said laws and who is authorized, as provided therein by a court of record having jurisdiction over such offenses, to accept cash bonds may accept a cash bond from the person arrested in lieu of a statutory bond or recognizance. No such officer may accept a cash bond unless he is authorized to receive cash bonds in such cases by an order of the court having

---

Morton v. State, 166 Ga. App. 170, 303 S.E.2d 509 (1983).

[11]Foster v. State, 165 Ga. App. 137, 299 S.E.2d 420 (1983).

[12]Morton v. State, 166 Ga. App. 170, 303 S.E.2d 509 (1983).

[13]O.C.G.A. § 17-6-14; AAA Bonding Co. v. State, 192 Ga. App. 684, 685 (3), 386 S.E.2d 50 (1989).

[14]O.C.G.A. § 17-6-10. See also O.C.G.A. § 15-16-27, which authorizes sheriffs in certain counties to deposit cash bonds and cash reserves of professional bondspersons in interest-bearing accounts.

[15]O.C.G.A. §§ 9-10-10, 17-6-4. Also see O.C.G.A. § 17-6-5, which contains a special provision for cash bonds where authorized by a judge for violations of traffic, game, fish, boat, and littering offenses.

[16]Washburn v. Foster, 87 Ga. App. 132, 73 S.E.2d 240 (1952). See O'Neal, Criminal Law, 5 Mercer L. Rev. 52, 53 (1953).

[17]O.C.G.A. § 17-6-5.

jurisdiction over such offenses and unless such order has been entered on the minutes of the court. Any such order may be granted, revoked, or modified by the court at any time.

O.C.G.A. § 17-6-2(a)(1) provides: "In all cases wherein a licensed driver of this state has been arrested, incarcerated, and charged with a violation of state law and where said violation is a misdemeanor, the sheriff of the county wherein the violation occurred shall be authorized, unless otherwise ordered by a judicial officer, after the individual has been incarcerated for not less than five days, to accept the individual's driver's license as collateral for any bail which has been set in the case, up to and including the amount of $1,000.00, provided such license is not under suspension or has not expired or been revoked." The provisions of this section of the Code apply except when an individual has been charged with a violation of O.C.G.A. § 40-6-391, relating to driving under the influence of alcohol or drugs, at which time the provisions of O.C.G.A. § 40-5-67 apply. Taking of the driver's license as required by O.C.G.A. § 40-5-67 does not prohibit any law enforcement officer or agency from requiring any cash bond authorized by O.C.G.A. § 17-6-1.

A committing magistrate, or a judge having jurisdiction to try the defendant, may in his discretion release the accused on his own recognizance.[18] A surety bond may also be given.[19] Rule 27 et seq. of the Uniform Rules for the Superior Courts authorizes a county to establish a pre-trial release program.

The officials of a county in which a defendant is arrested on a warrant from another county have no authority to permit the defendant to post bond.[20]

Where bond is forfeited, the defendant may not post another bond unless the court permits him to do so.[21] A bond, once posted, unless revoked or forfeited, remains in force until the defendant is sentenced.[22] The bond is considered void after sentencing or acquittal.[23]

For years, under Georgia statutory law, a married woman could not sign a bond as surety in a criminal case because of the wording of GCA § 53-503. However, this Code section was amended in 1976 in order to expressly allow a married woman to sign as

[18]O.C.G.A. § 17-6-12.

[19]See Andrews v. Hardwick, 29 Ga. App. 251, 114 S.E. 644 (1922); O.C.G.A. § 17-6-1, O.C.G.A. § 17-6-71.

[20]Weatherly v. Beavers, 139 Ga. 122, 76 S.E. 853 (1912).

[21]O.C.G.A. § 17-6-13.

[22]Andrews v. Hardwick, 29 Ga. App. 251 (1), 114 S.E. 644 (1922).

[23]Roberts v. Gordon, 86 Ga. 386, 12 S.E. 648 (1890).

surety on a bond.[24] Then, the entire section as amended was repealed in 1979. Since the original statute was the impediment which prevented a married woman from signing as a surety, and it has been repealed along with the 1976 amendment, there is no present reason why a married woman cannot sign a bond.

O.C.G.A. § 17-6-11 provides that in lieu of posting a bond, a person may display his or her driver's license when apprehended for a traffic offense other than one for which a license may be suspended for a first offense by the Commissioner of Drivers Services and other offenses including those covered by O.C.G.A. § 40-5-54 (mandatory suspension of license for crimes committed while operating a motor vehicle, e.g., vehicular homicide); §§ 40-6-390, et seq. (serious traffic offenses); and other offenses related to common carriers, motor contact carriers and hazardous materials transportation.

O.C.G.A. § 17-6-10 provides that the forfeiture of a cash bond posted with a municipality does not prevent the defendant from later being tried for the offense for which he posted the cash bond. However, in *Wilson v. State*[25] the court held that where a cash bond on a driving under the influence case is forfeited and the court enters an order reciting that the bond was forfeited in open court "and is declared to be a final disposition of" the case, the defendant may not thereafter be tried over a plea in bar.

Where a person is held in custody and is refused bail, he is entitled to have the charge against him heard by a grand jury within 90 days from the commencement of his confinement.[26] Generally, if his case is not heard by the grand jury within 90 days, or within such extended period of confinement as is granted by the court (not to exceed 90 additional days), the accused may have bail set upon application to the court unless the person is arrested for a crime for which the death penalty is being sought.[27] In *Rawls v. Hunter*,[28] the court held that where a defendant is incarcerated for more than 90 days without being indicted by the

---

[24]Ga. Laws 1976, p. 478.

[25]Wilson v. State, 167 Ga. App. 421, 306 S.E.2d 704 (1983).

[26]See Tatis v. State, 289 Ga. 811, 716 S.E.2d 203 (2011) (defendant placed in hospital at time of arrest under police custody is in confinement for purposes of O.C.G.A. § 17-5-50).

[27]O.C.G.A. § 17-7-50. However, in this event, the defendant is only entitled to a bond on the charge or charges for which he/she was arrested. Thus, in Bryant v. Vowell, 282 Ga. 437, 651 S.E.2d 77 (2007) (overruled on

other grounds by, Brown v. Crawford, 289 Ga. 722, 715 S.E.2d 132 (2011)), shortly after the 90-day period following arrest had expired, the grand jury returned an indictment with six separate charges. Since the defendant had only been charged with two charges in the arrest warrant the court agreed with the trial court that the defendant was not entitled to bond pursuant to § 17-7-50 on those charges set out for the first time in the indictment.

[28]Rawls v. Hunter, 267 Ga. 109, 475 S.E.2d 609 (1996). In State v. English, 276 Ga. 343(3), 578 S.E.2d

state, the defendant is entitled to have a reasonable bond set on request even if he is indicted on the ninety-first day and regardless of whether he has been indicted at the time of the consideration of the request for a bond. However, this "90 day" statute was amended in 1996 to provide that if the arrest is "for a crime for which the death penalty is being sought, the superior court may, upon motion of the district attorney for an extension and after a hearing and good cause shown, grant one extension to the 90 day period not to exceed 90 additional days." Where such additional period is granted, the defendant has no automatic right on application to a bond until the expiration of the extension.

See § 28:5, infra, on bonds pending an appeal.

§ 8:2 Posting bond as waiver of commitment hearing

In *Watts v. Pitts,*[1] the Georgia Supreme Court held that a person who is arrested and released on bond within the time provided by law is not entitled to a commitment hearing. See § 11:4, infra, on probable cause hearing.

§ 8:3 Motion to fix bond

Various methods may be used to determine the amount of bond where there is an automatic right to post bond.[1] The bond may be fixed by a magistrate soon after a defendant is arrested, by the officer issuing an arrest warrant at the time the warrant is issued, or according to a fixed schedule providing for bonds in certain amounts for specified offenses.[2] However, only a judicial officer may set bail in a case involving an act of family violence involving serious injury to the victim when the arresting officer has the opinion that additional conditions of bail are necessary. If a bond is not fixed prior to a preliminary or commitment hearing, the presiding magistrate will set a bond if the offense is one for which there exists a right to bond.

There is considerable variation throughout Georgia in the amount set for bonds for the same offense.[3] In *Stack v. Boyle,*[4] the United States Supreme Court held that since the primary purpose

---

413, 418 (2003), the Court ruled that a defendant who is incarcerated for a period of 90 days has been effectively "refused bail" and hence no application for bond must be made *and* denied during that period in order for O.C.G.A. § 17-7-50 to apply.

[Section 8:2]

[1]Watts v. Pitts, 253 Ga. 501, 322 S.E.2d 252 (1984); State v. Gilstrap,

230 Ga. App. 281, 495 S.E.2d 885 (1998).

[Section 8:3]

[1]See O.C.G.A. § 17-6-1.

[2]O.C.G.A. § 17-6-1(f)(1) provides that a "judge of any court of inquiry may by written order establish a schedule of bails."

[3]It should be noted in passing that a number of successful pre-trial

of bail is to ensure the defendant's presence at trial, a bond which is higher than the amount calculated to effect such an end is excessive.[5] However, in *United States v. Salerno*,[6] the same court said that the rule of *Stack* applies only when the government's "only interest is in preventing flight." Reasonableness is determined in terms of the particular defendant.[7] However, the fact that a defendant cannot post a bond in the amount fixed does not, in and of itself, demonstrate that the bond is excessive.[8] In *Howard v. State*,[9] the court pointed out that in addition to considering whether the amount of the bond is sufficient to cause the defendant to be present for trial, it is proper to consider "the accused's ability to pay, the seriousness of the offense and the accused's character and reputation."

The American Bar Association's Standards for Criminal Justice presume that a defendant should be released on his own recognizance.[10] Generally, if release on the accused's own recognizance is unwarranted, the judicial officer should impose the least onerous condition necessary to assure the defendant's appearance in court.[11] If money bail must be set to assure the defendant's presence at trial, the amount should not be greater than the amount necessary to assure his appearance.[12] However, violating a special condition of a bond would not subject the defendant to a contempt of court charge.[13]

Pursuant to O.C.G.A. § 17-6-1(d), a motion for bond must be heard within ten days of filing. However, there is no remedy for a court's failure to act within that time.[14]

---

release programs exist in Georgia in conjunction with the ordinary bond system. One such program is conducted in Cobb County and the other in Hall County. These programs have been developed by outstanding judges with the goal of improving the existing bail system.

[4]Stack v. Boyle, 342 U.S. 1, 72 S.Ct. 1, 96 L.Ed. 3 (1951).

[5]Stack v. Boyle, 342 U.S. 1, 5, 72 S.Ct. 1, 96 L.Ed. 3 (1951).

[6]United States v. Salerno, 481 U.S. 739, 107 S.Ct. 2095, 95 L.Ed.2d 697 (1987).

[7]Bennett v. United States, 36 F.2d 475, 477 (5th Cir. 1929).

[8]Simon v. Woodson, 454 F.2d 161 (5th Cir. 1972).

[9]Howard v. State, 197 Ga. App. 693, 694, 399 S.E.2d 283 (1990) (quot-ing Spence v. State, 252 Ga. 338, 313 S.E.2d 475 (1984)).

[10]See A.B.A. Standards, Pretrial Release, Vol. II, Standard 10-5.1.

[11]See A.B.A. Standards, Pretrial Release, Vol. II, Standard 10-5.2.

[12]See A.B.A. Standards, Pretrial Release, Standard 10-5.3.

[13]Salter v. Greene, 226 Ga. App. 384, 386 (2), 486 S.E.2d 650 (1997).

[14]Capestany v. State, 289 Ga. App. 47(3), 656 S.E.2d 196 (2007). See Taylor v. Chitwood, 266 Ga. 793, 471 S.E.2d 511 (1996) where Justice Sears, in a concurring opinion, suggested that the failure to provide a timely hearing on a bond motion might, in the appropriate case, subject the state to civil liability.

In *Clarke v. State*,[15] the court held that a trial judge has inherent authority to impose reasonable conditions when setting the amount of bail. "[I]n lieu of setting a higher bail . . . a trial court may choose to impose reasonable restrictions on a defendant's behavior. [For example,] [w]hen a defendant is charged with a violent crime against a specific victim, . . . [the trial court may] require that the defendant avoid any contact with the victim . . . ." Indeed, a bond order can include as a condition a waiver of the defendant's Fourth Amendment rights.[16] The trial judge has authority to revoke a bond if, following a hearing, he determines that the defendant has violated a condition of a bond.

When bail or bond is thought of, a cash bond or surety bond usually comes to mind, and the Fifth Circuit has held that the equal protection clause of the Fourteenth Amendment does not require that a bond procedure include a presumption against the requirement of a money bond.[17]

In *Spence v. State*,[18] the court held that it was not error for a trial judge to impose a $90,000 total bond for three theft charges involving not more than $500 where the defendant was suspected of murdering his mother, and his father feared for his safety. In *Rocco v. State*,[19] the Georgia Court of Appeals held that it was reasonable to make the defendant's Fourth Amendment waiver a condition of bond. However, a warrantless entry into the defendant's home on the basis of the waiver must be predicated upon the reasonable suspicion of the police that the defendant was involved in criminal activity.

In the United States Supreme Court case of *Schall v. Martin*,[20] the court held that a New York statute was not violative of the due process clause of the Fourteenth Amendment even though it provided under certain circumstances for preventive pre-trial detention of juveniles for a period not to exceed 17 days. The court emphasized the fact that juveniles and adults do not have to be treated exactly alike. The New York statute required a "notice, a hearing, and a statement of facts and reasons" prior to any pre-trial preventive detention. "A formal probable cause hearing is then held within a short while thereafter, if the fact finding hearing is not itself scheduled within three days. These . . . procedures . . . are adequate under the Fourteenth Amendment."

---

[15]Clarke v. State, 228 Ga. App. 219, 220 (1), (2), 491 S.E.2d 450 (1997).

[16]Roco v. State, 267 Ga. App. 900 (1), 601 S.E.2d 189 (2004).

[17]Pugh v. Rainwater, 572 F.2d 1053 (5th Cir. 1978) (en banc).

[18]Spence v. State, 252 Ga. 338, 340 (2b), 313 S.E.2d 475 (1984).

[19]Rocco v. State, 267 Ga. App. 900, 601 S.E.2d 189 (2004).

[20]Schall v. Martin, 467 U.S. 253, 104 S.Ct. 2403, 81 L.Ed.2d 207 (1984).

In *United States v. Salerno*,[21] the United States Supreme Court found constitutional a provision of the Federal Bail Reform Act which authorized the pre-trial detention of a defendant charged with certain serious felonies on the grounds of a finding of future dangerousness to individuals or the community and where there are no release provisions which can dispel such dangerousness. The court pointed out (1) "that preventing danger to the community is a legitimate regulatory goal," (2) that "the government must convince a neutral decisionmaker by *clear and convincing evidence* that no conditions of release can reasonably assure the safety of the community or any person" (emphasis added) and (3) that "[i]n our society liberty is the norm, and detention prior to trial . . . is the carefully limited exception."

If the trial court denies a defendant a bond, the judge must explain its "reasons for denying bond to assist appellate review. . . . The granting or denial of bail will not be set aside unless there is a manifest and flagrant abuse of discretion." Initially the defendant has the burden of showing "that he . . . poses no significant risk of fleeing, threatening the community, committing another crime, or intimidating a witness. . . . This burden . . . means that a person charged with murder must present evidence . . . on factors that indicate roots in the community. . . . These factors include the defendant's length and character of residence in the community, employment status and history, past history of responding to legal process, and prior criminal record. . . . [T]he state [then] has the burden of persuasion in convincing the superior court that a defendant is not entitled to pretrial release. This . . . means the state has the burden of proving by a preponderance of the evidence that the trial court should deny bail either to secure the defendant's appearance in court or to protect the community. Depending on the quality of the defendant's evidence, the state may not need to present any evidence to carry its burden of persuasion. . . ."[22]

Once the amount of bond has been fixed, it is possible to request, orally or by written motion, that the bond be reduced if the defendant cannot post a bond in the amount set. If a defendant is in custody for an offense for which there is no automatic right to obtain a bond, counsel may make a motion before the superior court having jurisdiction to fix a bond as soon as the defendant has been bound over. In requesting that a bond be reduced, or set, counsel for the defendant should be sure that the judge has the information concerning the defendant which is set out in Standard 10-5.1(b) of the A.B.A. Standards on Pretrial

[21]United States v. Salerno, 481 U.S. 739, 107 S.Ct. 2095, 95 L.Ed.2d 697 (1987).

[22]Ayala v. State, 262 Ga. 704, 705, 425 S.E.2d 282 (1993).

Release.[23] In *Jones v. Grimes,*[24] the court pointed out that excessive bail is equivalent to a refusal to set a bond.

For motions for bond, see Studdard, *Daniel's Georgia Criminal Trial Practice Forms* (2018–2019 ed.), §§ 7:3 et seq. For admissibility of hearsay evidence at bond hearings, see Studdard, *Daniel's Georgia Handbook on Criminal Evidence* (2018 ed.), § 8:34.

§ 8:4 Statutory criteria for the granting of a bond in superior court

§ 8:1, supra, enumerates offenses which are bailable only before a superior court judge.

A person charged with an offense bailable only before a judge of the superior court may petition the superior court requesting that he be released on bail. The superior court is obligated to notify the district attorney and set a date for a hearing within 10 days of the time of the filing of the petition. The superior court is authorized to release the petitioner if the judge determines that the defendant:

"(1) Poses no significant risk of fleeing from the jurisdiction of the court or failing to appear in court when required;

"(2) Poses no significant threat or danger to any person, or to the community, or to any property in the community;

"(3) Poses no significant risk of committing any felony pending trial; and

"(4) Poses no significant risk of intimidating witnesses or otherwise obstructing the administration of justice."[1]

In *Pullin v. Dorsey,*[2] the court pointed out that "the foremost consideration when fixing bail is the probability that the accused, if freed, will appear at trial . . . ."

In *Camphor v. State,*[3] the court held that "[w]hen a defendant is charged with a violent crime . . . it is within the trial court's inherent powers to require that the defendant avoid any contact with the victim as a condition of remaining free pending trial."

---

[23]Generally, see Annot., "Considerations Affecting Grant, Continuance, Reduction, or Revocation of Bail by Individual Justice of Supreme Court," 30 L.Ed.2d 952 (1973).

[24]Jones v. Grimes, 219 Ga. 585, 134 S.E.2d 790 (1964).

[Section 8:4]

[1]O.C.G.A. § 17-6-1(e). See Ayala v. State, 262 Ga. 704 (1), 425 S.E.2d 282 (1993).

[2]Pullin v. Dorsey, 271 Ga. 882, 525 S.E.2d 87 (2000).

[3]Camphor v. State, 272 Ga. 408, 410, 529 S.E.2d 121 (2000).

O.C.G.A. § 17-6-1(b)(3), as a condition of setting a bond amount in cases involving stalking, provides that the judge may "prohibit the defendant from entering or remaining present at the victim's school, place of employment, or other specified places at times when the victim is present."

If a trial judge denies a bond, he should set out in his order the reason for his refusal to set a bond.[4]

Where a defendant is entitled to a bond pending trial he is only entitled, as a matter of right, to be released once on bail.[5] If his bond is forfeited, release on bail is at the discretion of the court.

See § 8:3, supra, on conditions which may be imposed. See § 28:5, infra, on bonds pending an appeal. See § 28:23, infra, on appeal from the denial of a bond. For admissibility of hearsay evidence at bond hearings, see Studdard, *Daniel's Georgia Handbook on Criminal Evidence* (2018 ed.), § 8:34.

§ 8:5 Pre-trial review of denial of bond

In *Howard v. State*,[1] the court pointed out that an appeal from a refusal to set a bond is an interlocutory matter and the defendant consequently must follow the procedure set out in O.C.G.A. § 5-6-34(b). The trial court has authority to consider a habeas corpus review of the defendant's contention that he was illegally denied bail by another judge in the circuit.[2]

§ 8:6 Reduction of bond by habeas corpus in federal court

As pointed out above, the fixing of the amount of a bond is a matter largely resting in the discretion of the trial judge. "Ordinarily, the denial of a motion for pretrial bail is an interlocutory matter requiring a defendant to follow the interlocutory procedure set forth in OCGA § 5-6-34(b)."[1] In determining whether the denial of a bond was proper, the appellate court applies a "flagrant abuse" standard.[2] A defendant may file a petition for federal habeas corpus asking that he be released or, in the alternative, that he be released on a bond of a reasonable

[4]Foster v. State, 165 Ga. App. 137, 299 S.E.2d 420 (1983).

[5]O.C.G.A. § 17-6-13.

[Section 8:5]

[1]Howard v. State, 194 Ga. App. 857, 392 S.E.2d 562 (1990).

[2]Banks v. Waldrop, 272 Ga. 475, 531 S.E.2d 708 (2000).

[Section 8:6]

[1]Howard v. State, 194 Ga. App. 857, 392 S.E.2d 562 (1990); Woods v. State, 238 Ga. App. 54, 517 S.E.2d 592 (1999).

[2]Hardy v. State, 192 Ga. App. 860 (2), 386 S.E.2d 731 (1989).

amount while his case is pending in state court.[3] However, the prisoner must exhaust his state remedies to obtain a bond in a reasonable amount before a federal court will grant such a petition. The filing of a state habeas corpus action is not necessary in the exhaustion of state remedies.[4]

A federal court cannot substitute its judgment for that of the state court and it must be shown that bail is excessive or arbitrary before the federal court will grant a petition. If the trial judge went "beyond the range within which judgments could rationally differ," the result would "amount in effect to legal arbitrariness"[5] and justify action by a federal court.

§ 8:7 Revocation of bond

In *Hood v. Carsten*,[1] the court held invalid an order revoking a defendant's bond "without a hearing structured to insure that the finding of a violation of a condition of bond and the exercise of the court's discretion to revoke bond were based on verified facts. . . ." The *Hood* case also pointed out that "revocation of bail sua sponte, in chambers without providing notice or opportunity to be heard, is an arbitrary denial of due process."

---

[3]Pilkinton v. Circuit Court, 324 F.2d 45 (8th Cir. 1963) (court held that no question of excessiveness of bail was raised where bail had been fixed at $500 on each of two charges against a state prisoner); Goodine v. Griffin, 309 F.Supp. 590 (S.D.Ga.1970).

[4]Goodine v. Griffin, 309 F.Supp. 590 (S.D.Ga.1970).

[5]Goodine v. Griffin, 309 F.Supp. 590, 592 (S.D.Ga.1970), where at the hearing, a law enforcement officer testified as to the reasons for his recommendation that bail be fixed in large amounts varying from $50,000 to $100,000. While the defendants "offered evidence at the hearing in respect to their residence, occupation, marital status, criminal record and other matters deemed relevant to the probability of their appearance on the date of trial," it was within the discretion of the judge to set the amount of bail. See Mastrian v. Hedman, 326 F.2d 708, 711 (8th Cir. 1964).

[Section 8:7]

[1]Hood v. Carsten, 267 Ga. 579, 481 S.E.2d 525 (1997).

Chapter 9

Civil Actions Related to the Defense of Criminal Cases

§ 9:1   General considerations and scope
§ 9:2   Extraordinary remedies in state court
§ 9:3   Extraordinary remedies in federal court

KeyCite®: Cases and other legal materials listed in KeyCite Scope can be researched through the KeyCite service on Westlaw®. Use KeyCite to check citations for form, parallel references, prior and later history, and comprehensive citator information, including citations to other decisions and secondary materials.

---

§ 9:1   General considerations and scope

This chapter will consider certain extraordinary remedies, such as actions for injunctions and mandamus as related to the criminal process. Reference is made to the possibility of instituting a civil action to aid in the defense of a criminal proceeding, such as in the case of discovery in § 14:4, infra. Also, the possibility of bringing a habeas corpus action is discussed in § 11:4, infra.

Some lawyers contend that actions for false arrest, malicious prosecution and civil right violations also help to obtain fair treatment in the disposition of criminal cases. However, these actions will not be discussed herein because of their special nature, and in fact they are not normally considered as a part of the defense of a criminal case.

§ 9:2   Extraordinary remedies in state court

The general rule expressed in O.C.G.A. § 9-5-2, relating to extraordinary remedies in state courts, provides as follows: "Equity will take no part in the administration of the criminal law. It will neither aid criminal courts in the exercise of their jurisdiction, nor will it restrain or obstruct them." Thus, it has been said that a court "exercising equitable jurisdiction will not enjoin prosecutions under municipal ordinances, even where the ordinances are allegedly invalid and there are threats of arrest and multiplicity of prosecutions, unless it is shown that the threatened prosecutions are for the sole purpose of unlawfully taking or destroying property or the business of the plaintiff, or that they will in fact result in irreparable injury thereto, *and* unless the complaining party has no plain and adequate remedy at law which is as practical and efficient to the ends of justice and its prompt administration as the remedy in equity."[1]

Georgia courts have sometimes stated that equity has no jurisdiction to enjoin criminal prosecutions.[2] However, such language or terminology does not seem to be accurate, since in some situations injunctions may properly be issued in connection with a criminal prosecution.[3] While it is generally true that equity cannot be used to enforce the criminal laws,[4] equity may restrain a threatened or existing nuisance which involves the violation of a criminal law.[5]

There are some limited situations in which equity will enjoin a criminal prosecution.[6] For example, if it is clear that a criminal prosecution is being threatened to prevent the exercise of civil rights,[7] or for the purpose of unlawfully taking or destroying property, or for preventing the exercise of a franchise granted by the state,[8] or because of repeated prosecutions in recorder's court which would cause irreparable damage to property rights,[9] equity

---

[Section 9:2]

[1]Arnold v. Mathews, 226 Ga. 809, 810 (1), 177 S.E.2d 691 (1970). See Harris v. Entertainment Sys., Inc., 259 Ga. 701, 704, 386 S.E.2d 140 (1989).

[2]Morrow v. City of Atlanta, 162 Ga. 228 (4), 232 (3), 133 S.E. 345 (1926). See Annot., "Availability of Writ of Prohibition or Similar Remedy Against Acts of Public Prosecutor," 16 A. L. R. 4th 112 (1982).

[3]E.g., Benton Brothers Drayage & Storage Co. v. Mayor of City of Savannah, 219 Ga. 172, 132 S.E.2d 196 (1963).

[4]Bennett v. Kimmel, 163 Ga. 725, 733, 137 S.E. 60 (1927); Forehand v. Moody, 200 Ga. 166, 36 S.E.2d 321 (1945).

[5]Bennett v. Bennett, 161 Ga. 936, 942, 132 S.E. 528 (1926).

[6]It has been said that these situations are not to be regarded as exceptions to the general rule, since equity takes jurisdiction in these cases, not because of the criminal aspects of the case, but in spite of it, for the purpose of preventing irreparable injury. 10A E. G. L. Equity (1999 Rev.), § 42.

[7]Georgia Railroad and Banking Co. v. City of Atlanta, 118 Ga. 486 (8), 45 S.E. 256 (1903).

[8]See Mayor & Council of Shellman v. Saxon, 134 Ga. 29 (2), 67 S.E. 438 (1910).

In Total Vending Service, Inc. v. Gwinnett County, 153 Ga. App. 109, 264 S.E.2d 574 (1980), the court held that an action for declaratory judgment stated a claim where it alleged that law enforcement officers threatened to prosecute the plaintiff if pinball machines were installed pursuant to a 1962 local law. The plaintiff had entered into a contract to supply pinball machines to a bowling establishment. There was a question about whether the 1962 act had been superseded by a 1978 statute.

[9]Cutsinger v. City of Atlanta, 142 Ga. 555, 556 (4), 573 (4), 83 S.E. 263 (1914). But a mere multiplicity of prosecutions alone will not require the issuance of an injunction. City of Douglas v. South Georgia Grocery Co., 178 Ga. 657 (3), 174 S.E. 127 (1934). But cf. Columbus, Georgia v. Granco, Inc., 240 Ga. 850, 852, 242 S.E.2d 607 (1978).

will step in. In the 1986 case of *Majmundar v. Veline,*[10] the Georgia Supreme Court pointed out that "when injury to property is threatened, . . . injunction will lie notwithstanding the fact that in the process a criminal prosecution is involved."

In addition to the Georgia courts' rulings on injunctions in criminal cases, it has also been held that a declaratory judgment action will not lie to determine the validity and application of a criminal statute where there is no justiciable controversy.[11] Likewise, a writ of prohibition or an injunction will not lie to prevent a grand jury or a district attorney from prosecuting or indicting a defendant.[12] Yet, a mandamus action will lie where a void judgment is the cause of the refusal of the Board of Pardons and Paroles to consider a defendant's application for parole.[13]

In *Russell v. Evans,*[14] the court considered a writ of prohibition where the plaintiff had been imprisoned for a number of months on a civil contempt. The court held that in such a situation "where there is no means of reviewing the legality of his restraint; . . . [a person] who otherwise had exhausted available remedies, is entitled to the protection of the writ of prohibition."

In *Henry v. James,*[15] the court pointed out that a writ of prohibition "is available only where there is lack of jurisdiction of the subject-matter, or where the act complained of was in excess of the jurisdiction of the court . . . and is not generally available for the relief of grievances which may be redressed in the ordinary course of judicial proceedings. . . ."

---

[10]Majmundar v. Veline, 256 Ga. 8 (1), 342 S.E.2d 682 (1986) (citing Moultrie Milk Shed v. City of Cairo, 206 Ga. 348, 351, 57 S.E.2d 199 (1950)).

[11]Jenkins v. Thomas, 124 Ga. App. 286, 289, 183 S.E.2d 489 (1971). Also, where petitioners have been arrested and charged with unlawfully "establishing and promoting a lottery" in violation of O.C.G.A. § 16-12-22, a declaratory judgment action does not lie to test the constitutionality of state laws and city ordinances where the criminal prosecution is pending and there is insufficient showing of irreparable injury to justify equity in issuing an injunction. Pendleton v. City of Atlanta, 236 Ga. 479, 224 S.E.2d 357 (1976). Generally, see 10 A. L. R. 3d 727 (1966). But in Galer v. Board of Regents of the University System, 239 Ga. 268, 236 S.E.2d 617 (1977), a declaratory judgment action was brought to invalidate O.C.G.A. § 16-10-9. Here, the plaintiff had been elected a state representative. She taught at Columbus College. The statute prevents an employee of the General Assembly from employment by the executive branch of government. The Court, over one dissent, passed on the merits of the case.

[12]Stynchcombe v. Hardy, 228 Ga. 130, 133, 184 S.E.2d 356 (1971).

[13]Riley v. Garrett, 219 Ga. 345 (2)(b), 351, 133 S.E.2d 367 (1963); and see Solomon v. State, 232 Ga. 306, 206 S.E.2d 436 (1974).

[14]Russell v. Evans, 260 Ga. 754 (1), 400 S.E.2d 11 (1991).

[15]Henry v. James, 264 Ga. 527, 532 (2), 449 S.E.2d 79 (1994).

In *Bartlett v. Caldwell*,[16] the court held that a citizen has no right to a writ of mandamus to force a magistrate to issue an arrest warrant or a district attorney to prosecute a case.

In the 1997 case of *Nalley v. Howell*,[17] the court held that mandamus will not issue to compel a judicial officer to issue an arrest warrant in the absence of a gross abuse of discretion.

§ 9:3 Extraordinary remedies in federal court[1]

In considering possible federal action to aid a defendant in a state criminal prosecution, several federal statutes should be considered.[2] At the outset, the defendant is faced with a problem that the federal courts will not normally intervene in a pending state prosecution.[3] But, if a criminal prosecution has not yet begun, the petitioner is confronted with the general rule that a federal court is reluctant to interfere by way of an injunction in what is no more than a threat of a possible state criminal prosecution.[4] It seems, however, that a defendant's chances of obtaining federal injunctive relief are much better if there is no pending state criminal prosecution.[5] The basis for the reluctance to intervene is that usually a defendant can sufficiently raise any federal statutory or constitutional question in the state proceeding.[6]

In the case of a petition in federal court to enjoin a state criminal proceeding, the plaintiff must show extraordinary circum-

---

[16]Bartlett v. Caldwell, 265 Ga. 52, 452 S.E.2d 744 (1995).

[17]Nalley v. Howell, 268 Ga. 63, 487 S.E.2d 600 (1997).

[Section 9:3]

[1]Generally, see Annot., 44 L.Ed.2d 692 (1976). See also "Supreme Court's Construction of Eleventh Amendment Restricting Federal Judicial Power to Entertain Suits Against a State," 50 L.Ed.2d 928 (1977).

[2]See The Anti-Injunction Act, 28 U.S.C.A. § 2283; The Civil Rights Act, 42 U.S.C.A. § 1983; The Declaratory Judgment Act, 28 U.S.C.A. § 2201.

[3]Outdoor American Corp. v. Philadelphia, 333 F.2d 963 (3d Cir. 1964); Douglas v. City of Jeannette, 319 U.S. 157, 163, 63 S.Ct. 877, 87 L.Ed. 1324 (1943).

[4]E.g., Golden v. Zwickler, 394 U.S. 103, 109, 89 S.Ct. 956, 22 L.Ed.2d 113 (1969). This was a declaratory judgment action in which the court concluded that there was no evidence of a controversy of sufficient immediacy or reality to warrant issuance of a declaratory judgment.

[5]See Doran v. Salem Inn, Inc., 422 U.S. 922, 95 S.Ct. 2561, 45 L.Ed.2d 648 (1975); Younger v. Harris, 401 U.S. 37, 91 S.Ct. 746, 27 L.Ed.2d 669 (1971). In Septum, Inc. v. Keller, 614 F.2d 456 (5th Cir. 1980), the court held that an agreement between prosecutor and film exhibitor to give the exhibitor prior notice if local government decides to prosecute and the exhibitor has made it clear that it will stop showing a film rather than face a prosecution does not prevent an action for an injunction and declaratory relief in federal court challenging the constitutionality of a Georgia statute.

[6]Wallach v. City of Pagedale, 376 F.2d 671 (8th Cir. 1967); Outdoor American Corp. v. Philadelphia, 333 F.2d 963 (3d Cir. 1964).

stances, such as a threat of irreparable injury,[7] bad faith conduct in a prosecution,[8] or a prosecution brought for purposes of harassment.[9] The threat of injury must be both great and immediate.[10] The cost, anxiety, and inconvenience of having to defend against a single criminal prosecution does not alone constitute irreparable injury.[11]

It has been held that a civil rights action under 42 U.S.C.A. § 1983 is an exception to the anti-injunction provisions set out in 28 U.S.C.A. § 2283.[12] Even so, civil rights actions are limited by the "principles of equity, comity, and federalism."[13] Thus, it appears that the present Supreme Court attaches little, if any, weight to the provisions of the Civil Rights Act as set out in 42 U.S.C.A. § 1983.

In some cases, an effort has been made to avoid the anti-injunction statute by bringing a declaratory judgment action. It has been held, however, that injunctive and declaratory relief are ordinarily virtually identical and where injunctive relief is not appropriate, neither is declaratory relief.[14]

In the area of ordinances or laws which allegedly violate First Amendment rights, the courts appear to be more liberal in issuing an injunction than in other areas.[15] This attitude is demonstrated in 1977 in a well-publicized case.[16]

In the case of federal officers, the supremacy clause of the

---

[7]Younger v. Harris, 401 U.S. 37, 91 S.Ct. 746, 27 L.Ed.2d 669 (1971).

[8]Pcrez v. Ledesma, 401 U.S. 82, 91 S.Ct. 674, 27 L.Ed.2d 701 (1971); Floyd v. Anders, 440 F.Supp. 535 (D.S. C.1977).

[9]See Roe v. Wade, 410 U.S. 113, 93 S.Ct. 705, 35 L.Ed.2d 147 (1973).

[10]Mitchum v. Foster, 407 U.S. 225, 92 S.Ct. 2151, 32 L.Ed.2d 705 (1972).

[11]Kugler v. Helfant, 421 U.S. 117, 124, 95 S.Ct. 1524, 44 L.Ed.2d 15 (1975).

[12]Mitchum v. Foster, 407 U.S. 225, 92 S.Ct. 2151, 32 L.Ed.2d 705 (1972).

[13]Rizzo v. Goode, 423 U.S. 362, 96 S.Ct. 598, 46 L.Ed.2d 561 (1976).

[14]Samuels v. Mackell, 401 U.S. 66, 73, 91 S.Ct. 764, 27 L.Ed.2d 688 (1971).

[15]See Doran v. Salem Inn, Inc., 422 U.S. 922, 95 S.Ct. 2561, 45 L.Ed.2d 648 (1975).

[16]Wooley v. Maynard, 430 U.S. 705, 97 S.Ct. 1428, 51 L.Ed.2d 752 (1977). In this case, a Jehovah's Witness was tried and convicted for obscuring the state motto "Live Free or Die" on his automobile license plate without appealing his conviction and after a second case had been begun against him for the same offense, the defendant sought injunctive and declaratory relief in a federal district court against future enforcement of the law for which he had been convicted. The court pointed out that the right of freedom of thought protected by the First Amendment included the right to speak or refrain from speaking and said that the state statute caused the defendant to use his automobile as a mobile billboard for the state's ideological message as a condition to driving an automobile. The court concluded that the state's interest was not sufficient to justify compelling the display of the state motto and affirmed an order enjoining the

federal constitution prevents the state prosecution of such officers for state crimes committed while acting within the scope of their duties.[17]

In *Rowe v. Griffin,*[18] the Eleventh Circuit held that the state prosecution of a defendant who had been promised transactional immunity was "per se bad faith justifying a federal court in enjoining the criminal prosecution."

See § 8:6, supra, on reduction of bond in federal court.

For examples of complaints in this area, see Studdard, *Daniel's Georgia Criminal Trial Practice Forms* (2018–2019 ed.), § 8:4.

---

state from arresting and prosecuting the defendant in the future for covering his license plate.

[17]In re Neagle, 135 U.S. 1, 10 S.Ct. 658, 34 L.Ed. 55 (1890); Clifton v. Cox, 549 F.2d 722 (9th Cir. 1977). See § 14:91, infra, on transfer to federal court.

In Baucom v. Martin, 677 F.2d 1346, 1347 (11th Cir. 1982), "A special agent of the FBI, . . . Baucom, brought this suit seeking declaratory and injunctive relief to prevent his threatened state prosecution by . . . Martin, District Attorney *pro tem,* for the Stone Mountain Judicial Circuit, Georgia. Baucom had participated during the course of an investigation in an alleged bribery attempt of a state prosecutor. The district court granted plaintiff declaratory judgment finding that his acts in the bribery scheme were within his authority as an FBI agent, and that . . . any state conviction of him for those acts would contravene the Supremacy Clause. . . . The

defendant appeal[ed]. . . ." The Circuit Court affirmed, but pointed out that "a federal official does not enjoy absolute state immunity. . . . That a deliberate violation of state law may render law enforcement more convenient is insufficient to shield the agent from state prosecution. More is required lest the issue, at least initially, be left to state court resolution." (677 F.2d at 1350.)

In order for the supremacy clause to apply, there were found to be two requirements: First, is the requirement "that the federal officer be in the performance of an act which he is authorized by federal law to do as a part of his duty." Second, is the requirement that "what the officer did was 'no more than what was necessary and proper for him to do.' "(677 F.2d at 1350.) The court concluded that both requirements were met in this case.

[18]Rowe v. Griffin, 676 F.2d 524 (11th Cir. 1982).

Chapter 10

Condemnations and Forfeitures

> **KeyCite®:** Cases and other legal materials listed in KeyCite Scope can be researched through the KeyCite service on Westlaw®. Use KeyCite to check citations for form, parallel references, prior and later history, and comprehensive citator information, including citations to other decisions and secondary materials.

---

§ 10:1 Background

The early English common law, which adopted Saxon law, provided that a person convicted of a felony, and in certain instances a misdemeanor, forfeited all of his personal property to the crown.[1] Real property became the property of the crown perpetually or for the lifetime of the convicted individual.[2]

In addition to Saxon rules dealing with forfeiture, the common law, subsequent to the Norman Conquest, adopted the doctrine of corruption of blood.[3] According to this doctrine, a convicted felon's blood was said to be corrupted so that he could not transmit his estate at death to his heirs.[4] Rather, the convicted felon's prop-

---

[Section 10:1]

[1]See 13 C.J.S. 192, Convicts, § 3.
See also 18 C.J.S. 102, Convicts, § 2.

[2]2 Blackstone Comm. 251, 252 (1766).

[3]Avery v. Everett, 18 N.E. 148, 110 N.Y. 317 (1888).

[4]Holmes v. King, 113 So. 274, 275, 216 Ala. 412 (1927).

erty escheated to his lord or to the crown.[5] Furthermore, descendants of persons of attainted blood could not inherit from that ancestor.[6]

Under modern law, the United States Constitution limits the right of Congress to provide for attainder, corruption of blood, or forfeiture.[7] Georgia law prevents the corruption of blood and forfeiture of a person's property to the state.[8]

From a federal constitutional standpoint, a delay in instituting forfeiture proceedings is to be considered in light of the criteria set out in *Barker v. Wingo*[9] and the Sixth Amendment right to a speedy trial.[10] See § 14:61, infra, on limitations of prosecution.

§ 10:2   General principles and statutes providing for condemnation, forfeiture, confiscation, and disposition or return of personal property in custody of law enforcement

Georgia has numerous statutes which provide for confiscation or forfeiture.[1] Several of these statutes are of particular signifi-

---

[5]Holmes v. King, 113 So. 274, 275, 216 Ala. 412 (1927).

[6]Sir Salathiel Lovell's Case, 16 Kings' Bench Book 80. 91 Eng. Reprint 80.

[7]U.S. Const., Art. III, § 3, ¶ 2.

[8]Ga. Const. 1983, Art. I, § I, ¶ XX; O.C.G.A. § 44-5-210. However, the last Code section does provide that the state shall have a lien on all of person's property "for the cost of the prosecution against him." In this connection, it should be pointed out that today a defendant is not liable for court costs for his conviction in any felony case. O.C.G.A. § 15-16-21(e). Thus, the lien would apparently be limited to court costs incurred in convicting a defendant of a misdemeanor. Query: Is a fine a part of the court costs for lien purposes?

[9]Barker v. Wingo, 407 U.S. 514, 92 S.Ct. 2182, 33 L.Ed.2d 101 (1972). *Barker* is discussed in § 14:70, infra.

[10]United States v. Eight Thousand Eight Hundred and Fifty Dollars ($8,850) in United States Currency, 461 U.S. 555, 103 S.Ct. 2005, 76 L.Ed.2d 143 (1983). Under the facts of this case, the court held that there was no violation of the Sixth Amendment where the forfeiture proceeding was filed 18 months after the seizure.

[Section 10:2]

[1]See, e.g., O.C.G.A. § 3-10-12 (raw materials, fixtures, apparatus, and implements used in the manufacture of illegal intoxicating liquors); O.C.G.A. § 3-10-11 (apparatus used in manufacturing and conveyances used to carry illegal intoxicating liquors); O.C.G.A. § 10-1-186 (substandard brake fluid); O.C.G.A. § 26-2-232 (unwholesome dairy products); O.C.G.A. § 26-2-38 (adulterated and misbranded foods); O.C.G.A. § 16-12-32 (vehicles used in transporting gambling information and devices); O.C.G.A. § 26-2-85 (meat and meat products); O.C.G.A. § 27-3-48 (articles used in illegal night hunting); O.C.G.A. § 27-3-68 (trapping equipment illegally used); O.C.G.A. § 48-2-82 (public revenue contraband articles); O.C.G.A. § 16-13-49 (controlled substances); O.C.G.A. § 17-5-51 (weapons); O.C.G.A. § 46-9-253 (explosives which are shipped and not properly marked).

cance in the criminal law field since they relate to weapons,[2] controlled substances,[3] and the manufacture and transportation of illegal liquors.[4] In 2015, these statutes and others[5] were amended to expressly provide that property deemed "contraband" under the statutes' provisions is subject to forfeiture pursuant to the procedures set forth in Chapter 16 of Title 9 of the Georgia Code, which now provides a uniform procedure for civil forfeitures in Georgia, effective July 1, 2015. See §10:4, infra, on uniform forfeiture procedure.

Contraband per se is subject to seizure or forfeiture. An article is deemed to be contraband per se if its possession is illegal. Thus, where a vehicle is used to transport illegal liquor or contraband, the vehicle may be seized.[6] However, in a five to four

---

[2]O.C.G.A. §§ 17-5-51 et seq.

[3]O.C.G.A. § 16-13-49 (provides generally for the forfeiture of controlled substances as well as, inter alia, any property used to facilitate a violation of the criminal drug laws of Georgia, all other states and the United States).

[4]O.C.G.A. §§ 3-10-10 et seq.

[5]See, e g., O.C.G.A. § 16-5-44.1 (highjacking a motor vehicle); O.C.G.A. § 16-5-46 (trafficking of persons for labor or sexual servitude); O.C.G.A. § 16-6-13.2 (pimping and pandering); O.C.G.A. § 16-7-95 (bombs, explosives, and chemical and biological weapons); O.C.G.A. 16-8-5.2 (retail property fencing); O.C.G.A. § 16-8-60 (unauthorized reproduction and distribution of recorded materials); O.C.G.A. § 16-8-85 (motor vehicle chop shops and stolen and altered property); O.C.G.A. § 16-8-106 (residential mortgage fraud); O.C.G.A. § 16-9-4 (false identification documents); O.C.G.A. § 16-11-11 (subversive organizations); O.C.G.A. § 16-12-100 (sexual exploitation of children); O.C.G.A. § 16-13-30.1 (transactions involving non-controlled substances); O.C.G.A. § 16-13-30.2 (transactions involving imitation controlled substances); O.C.G.A. § 16-13-30.4 (licensing of distributors of products containing pseudoephedrine); O.C.G.A. §§ 16-13-32 and 16-13-32.1 (transactions involving drug related objects); O.C.G.A. §§ 16-14-1 to 16-4-12 (Georgia RICO violations); O.C.G.A. § 16-15-5 (violations of Georgia Street Gang Terrorism and Prevention Act); O.C.G.A. § 16-16-2 (burglary, armed robbery or home invasion); O.C.G.A. §§ 3-10-10 and 3-10-11 (unlawful sale or possession of distilled spirits); O.C.G.A. § 7-1-916 (unlawful currency transactions); O.C.G.A. § 10-1-454 (forging or counterfeiting trademarks, service marks, or copyrighted or registered designs); O.C.G.A. § 10-13A-8 (sale of unstamped and authorized tobacco products); O.C.G.A. § 12-4-48 (violation of regulations relating to deep drilling for oil, gas and minerals); O.C.G.A. §§ 12-5-133 and 12-5-137 (unlicensed or unauthorized water well drilling); O.C.G.A. § 12-8-2 (unlawful disposal of sanitary sewer, kitchen or toilet wastes); O.C.G.A. §§ 17-5-51, 17-5-52, (former) 17-5-52.1, and 17-5-54 (unlawful possession of weapons and weapons used in commission of crimes); O.C.G.A. § 27-3-12 (unlawful hunting substances and equipment); O.C.G.A. § 27-3-26 (unlawful bear hunting); O.C.G.A. §§ 27-4-133, 27-4-134, 27-4-137 (regulations regarding shrimping); O.C.G.A. § 40-6-391.2 (habitual violators for driving under the influence); and O.C.G.A. § 40-11-20 (unlawful removal, alteration of falsification of motor vehicle's identification number of a component part's identification number).

[6]Blackmon v. Brotherhood Protective Order of Elks, Toccoa Lodge No.

decision in *Seaman v. State*,[7] a majority held that the state had no right to confiscate VCRs used to copy pornographic video tapes. Georgia law exempts from forfeiture the interest in any property of an "innocent" owner or interest holder who did not know and should not reasonably have known of the conduct making the property subject to forfeiture.[8]

In *United States v. Bajakajian*,[9] the United States Supreme Court held that a forfeiture may violate the Eighth Amendment if it is "grossly disproportional" to the seriousness of the underlying crime.[10] See § 14:66, infra, on limitations of prosecution.

In *Howell v. State*,[11] the Georgia Supreme Court set out the standard by which a forfeiture should be tested for excessiveness. The Court adapted the following from *von Hofe v. U.S.*:[12]

> We . . . frame our excessiveness inquiry in terms of the following considerations: (1) the harshness, or gross disproportionality, of the forfeiture in comparison to the gravity of the offense, giving due regard to (a) the offense committed and its relation to other criminal activity, (b) whether the claimant falls within the class of persons for whom the statute was designed, (c) the punishments available, and (d) the harm caused by the claimant's conduct; (2) the nexus between the property and the criminal offenses, including the deliberate nature of the use and the temporal and spatial extent of the use; and (3) the culpability of each claimant.[13]

The trial court should consider the above factors and make findings on the record when ruling on a challenge to a forfeiture judgment under the Excessive Fines Clause of the Eighth Amendment.[14]

Generally, forfeitures are not favored in the law and are to be

---

1820, 232 Ga. 671, 672, 673, 208 S.E.2d 483 (1974).

[7]Seaman v. State, 196 Ga. App. 634, 396 S.E.2d 525 (1990).

[8]O.C.G.A. § 9-16-17(a)(2). See § 10:4, infra, on uniform forfeiture procedure.

[9]U.S. v. Bajakajian, 524 U.S. 321, 118 S. Ct. 2028, 141 L. Ed. 2d 314, 172 A.L.R. Fed. 705 (1998).

[10]Austin v. U.S., 509 U.S. 602, 609-10, 113 S. Ct. 2801, 125 L. Ed. 2d 488 (1993) (federal law which provides for forfeiture of property used to facilitate drug-related crimes is subject to the limitations of the Eighth Amendment's Excessive Fines Clause, which "limits the government's power to extract payments, whether in cash or in kind, as punishment for some of-

fense"). See Deborah F. Buckman, Annotation, "When Does Forfeiture of Motor Vehicle Pursuant to Federal Statute Violate Excessive Fines Clause of the Eighth Amendment," 169 A. L. R. Fed. 615 (2001).

[11]Howell v. State, 283 Ga. 24, 656 S.E.2d 511 (2008).

[12]von Hofe v. U.S., 492 F.3d 175, 186 (2d Cir. 2007).

[13]See Tipton v. State, 321 Ga. App. 870, 743 S.E.2d 532 (2013) (forfeiture of vehicle worth between $1,600 and $2,500 may be an excessive fine in violation of the Eighth Amendment where defendant was accused of selling an amount of cocaine worth only approximately $30).

[14]Buchanan v. State, 319 Ga. App. 525, 527, 737 S.E.2d 321 (2013).

avoided if possible.[15] Statutes providing for forfeiture or penalties are strictly construed by the courts,[16] and the state has the burden of proof to establish that the condemnation is authorized.[17] Pursuant to O.C.G.A. § 9-16-17(a)(1), forfeiture proceedings are reviewed under a preponderance of the evidence standard.[18]

The exclusionary rule of *Mapp v. Ohio*[19] applies to such proceedings and mandates that probable cause for forfeiture cannot rest upon tainted evidence.[20] In *Pitts v. State*,[21] where a forfeiture action preceded a related criminal action, the Court of Appeals of Georgia held that the trial judge erred in disallowing evidence concerning the legality of the search when the validity of the underlying search had not been previously adjudicated in the related criminal proceeding. The court concluded that "in those instances where the issue of the legality of the underlying search has not been resolved in the context of a criminal action" it can be raised as a collateral attack in the context of the forfeiture proceedings.

O.C.G.A. § 16-14-7, a provision in Georgia's Racketeer Influenced and Corrupt Organizations Act, allows for the forfeiture of "[a]ll property of every kind used or intended for use in the course of, derived from, or realized through a pattern of racketeering activity." This Code Section was amended considerably in 2015 in the same legislation that enacted the Uniform Civil Forfeiture Procedure Act such that now RICO related forfeitures are to be

---

[15]Sale v. Leachman, 218 Ga. 834, 837, 131 S.E.2d 185 (1963) (citing Renfroe v. Colquitt, 74 Ga. 618, 1885 WL 215 (1885)); Brooks v. Hicks, 230 Ga. 500, 501, 197 S.E.2d 711 (1973); Kitchens v. Atlantic Steel Co., 123 Ga. App. 812, 815, 182 S.E.2d 530 (1971), judgment aff'd, 228 Ga. 708, 187 S.E.2d 824 (1972).

[16]State v. Jackson, 197 Ga. App. 619, 620, 399 S.E.2d 88 (1990); Polk v. Thomason, 130 Ga. 542, 545, 61 S.E. 123 (1908). In Chappell v. Stapleton, 58 Ga. App. 138, 198 S.E. 109 (1938), two slot machines were confiscated; however, the court held that the owner was entitled to a return of the money in the machines. In Balkcom v. Heptinstall, 152 Ga. App. 539, 263 S.E.2d 275 (1979), a large sum of money was confiscated from a prisoner because prisoners were prohibited from having currency. The court concluded the prisoner was entitled to a return of the money when he was released from

prison, noting the "need for a statute setting forth with particularity the circumstances under which money may or may not be appropriated by the state for its own use." In the absence of "clear authority from the legislature providing for such a forfeiture," the court held the prisoner did not forfeit his right to reclaim it upon his release from prison. However, the result of this case seems to be changed by the enactment of O.C.G.A. § 42-5-62.

[17]Morrow v. State, 186 Ga. App. 615, 616, 367 S.E.2d 854 (1988).

[18]Sanders v. State, 259 Ga. App. 422, 425(2), 577 S.E.2d 94, 97 (2003).

[19]Mapp v. Ohio, 367 U.S. 643, 81 S. Ct. 1684, 6 L. Ed. 2d 1081, 86 Ohio L. Abs. 513, 84 A.L.R.2d 933 (1961).

[20]Vance v. U.S., 676 F.2d 183, 188 (5th Cir. 1982).

[21]Pitts v. State, 207 Ga. App. 606, 607(1), 428 S.E.2d 650 (1993).

conducted in accordance with the uniform procedure set forth in Chapter 16 of Title 9. Like former O.C.G.A. § 16-14-7(c) and (m), the uniform procedure provides for both in rem and in personam actions[22]—both of which are expressly intended to be civil in nature under the uniform law.[23]

However, in *Cisco v. State*[24] the Georgia Supreme Court found that the in personam RICO forfeiture procedure under the old law, unlike in rem forfeitures which authorize the condemnation of property used in or derived from an unlawful purpose, was punitive in effect and premised upon a finding of criminal activity by the defendant. Thus, despite the description of a RICO forfeiture as a "civil procedure,"[25] the court proceeded to find former O.C.G.A. § 16-14-7(m) to impose a criminal penalty and held it unconstitutional to the extent that it allowed for the prejudgment seizure of the defendant's property without the due process accorded a defendant in a criminal proceeding. It is unclear whether the uniform procedure will be found to contain sufficient "procedural safeguards" to address the constitutional concerns raised in *Cisco*.[26]

---

[22]O.C.G.A. §§ 9-16-12 and 9-16-13.

[23]See O.C.G.A. § 9-16-2(2) (defining "civil forfeiture proceeding" as "a quasi-judicial forfeiture initiated pursuant to Code Section 9-16-11 or a complaint for forfeiture initiated pursuant to Code Section 9-16-12 [in rem actions] or 9-16-13 [in personam actions]").

[24]Cisco v. State, 285 Ga. 656, 680 S.E.2d 831, 58 A.L.R.6th 809 (2009).

[25]See former O.C.G.A. § 16-14-7(a).

[26]In Cisco v. State, 285 Ga. 656, 680 S.E.2d 831, 58 A.L.R.6th 809 (2009), the court referenced "procedural flaws" of former O.C.G.A. § 16-14-7(m) that were raised in a dissenting opinion in Pimper v. State ex rel. Simpson, 274 Ga. 624, 627, 555 S.E.2d 459 (2001) (Hunstein, J., dissenting), which included, inter alia, constitutional concerns regarding self-incrimination and the possibility of "sidestepping established constitutional procedures and protections regarding searches and seizures" in the context of pre-indictment and pre-judgment in personam forfeiture proceedings). See also Pittman v. State, 288 Ga. 589, 594, 706 S.E.2d 398 (2011) (Hunstein, J., concurring) (finding former O.C.G.A. § 16-14-7(m) to be "so woefully lacking in mandatory constitutional protections that, until those constitutional deficiencies are corrected by the Legislature, it must be clearly understood that there can be no constitutional 'civil' in personam RICO proceedings in our state courts"). The uniform procedure appears to address some but possibly not all of these constitutional concerns. Compare O.C.G.A. § 9-16-6 (providing for seizure of property upon issuance of warrant showing probable cause exists for forfeiture or, if without process, only if probable causes exists to believe the property is subject to forfeiture or if the seizure is incident to arrest or search pursuant to a search warrant or to an inspection under an inspection warrant) and O.C.G.A. § 9-16-15 (upon a showing of good cause civil forfeiture proceedings may be stayed "during the pendency of criminal proceedings resulting from a related indictment or accusation until such time as the criminal proceedings result in a

In *Ali v. State*,[27] parties who had been the subject of a RICO criminal prosecution objected to a subsequent RICO forfeiture action brought against them and sums of currency which the state claimed were used in connection with the criminal activities for which the individuals had already been prosecuted. The claim of double jeopardy by the defendants was rejected by the court finding that while the state had to prove the predicate racketeering activity, which happened to involve the defendants, the subject of the forfeiture action was the currency and it was the state's burden to prove that it was used in connection with that activity.[28]

Various state courts have ruled that state homestead exemption laws prevent forfeiture of the homestead.[29] However, the Eleventh Circuit has held that federal forfeiture statutes preempt a state's constitutional homestead exemption.[30]

Once a criminal prosecution has been concluded, "personal property seized for use as evidence at trial must be returned to its rightful owner, unless the property constitutes contraband or is subject to forfeiture."[31] Chapter 5 of Title 17 of the Georgia Code addresses searches and seizures by the government, and Article 3 of that chapter addresses the disposition of various categories of property after they have been seized. See O.C.G.A. §§ 17-5-50 to 17-5-56. Among the provisions found in Article 3, O.C.G.A. § 17-7-54 addresses the disposition of personal property in the custody of a "law enforcement agency" to its "rightful owner." Subsection (c) of that statute provides in part:

(1) Except as provided in Chapter 16 of Title 9 [addressing civil for-

---

plea of guilty, a conviction after trial, or an acquittal after trial or are otherwise concluded before the trial court") with O.C.G.A. § 9-16-13(a), (b), and (e) (state's in personam forfeiture complaint must allege the "essential elements of the criminal violation which is claimed to exist" to which a defendant is compelled to file a verified answer or risk default judgment). Cf. Sanders v. State, 259 Ga. App. 422, 426, 577 S.E.2d 94 (2003) (in an in personam civil forfeiture under O.C.G.A. § 16-13-49, finding inferences can be drawn from a defendant's invocation of his privilege against self-incrimination and that such inferences may properly "constitute admissions unfavorable to him" in the civil proceeding).

[27]Ali v. State, 328 Ga. App. 203, 761 S.E.2d 601 (2014).

[28]Cuellar v. State, 230 Ga. App. 203, 496 S.E.2d 282 (1998) (finding a forfeiture proceeding is a civil sanction that does not constitute punishment for purposes of a double jeopardy defense under either the U.S. or Georgia Constitutions).

[29]Cf. State ex rel. Means v. Ten (10) Acres of Land, 1994 OK 71, 877 P.2d 597 (Okla. 1994); People v. One Residence Located at 1403 East Parham Street, 251 Ill. App. 3d 198, 190 Ill. Dec. 573, 621 N.E.2d 1026 (5th Dist. 1993); Butterworth v. Caggiano, 605 So. 2d 56, 16 A.L.R.5th 1118 (Fla. 1992).

[30]U.S. v. Lot 5, Fox Grove, Alachua County, Fla., 23 F.3d 359 (11th Cir. 1994).

[31]Norman v. Yeager, 335 Ga. App. 470, 472, 781 S.E.2d 580 (2016).

feiture proceedings], Code Sections 17-5-55 [addressing the disposition of evidence designated as dangerous or contraband by state or federal law] and 17-5-56 [addressing the maintenance of evidence containing biological material], and subsection (b) of this Code section, when a law enforcement agency assumes custody of any personal property which is the subject of a crime or has been abandoned, a disposition of such property shall be made in accordance with the provisions of this Code section.

(2) When a final verdict and judgment is entered finding a defendant guilty of the commission of a crime, any personal property used as evidence in the trial shall be returned to the rightful owner of the property within 30 days following the final judgment; provided, however, that if the judgment is appealed or if the defendant files a motion for a new trial and if photographs, videotapes, or other identification or analysis of the personal property will not be sufficient evidence for the appeal of the case or new trial of the case, such personal property shall be returned to the rightful owner within 30 days of the conclusion of the appeal or new trial, whichever occurs last.

(3) Any person claiming to be a rightful owner of property shall make an application to the entity holding his or her property and shall furnish satisfactory proof of ownership of such property and present personal identification. The person in charge of such property may return such property to the applicant. The person to whom property is delivered shall sign, under penalty of false swearing, a declaration of ownership, which shall be retained by the person in charge of the property. Such declaration, absent any other proof of ownership, shall be deemed satisfactory proof of ownership for the purposes of this Code section; provided, however, that with respect to motor vehicles, paragraph (3) of subsection (b) and subsection (f) of this Code section shall govern the return of motor vehicles.[32]

§ 10:3   Uniform forfeiture procedure

In 2015, the Georgia General Assembly enacted the Georgia Uniform Civil Forfeiture Procedure Act, §§ 9-16-1 et seq., effective July 1, 2015. The Act establishes a comprehensive procedure applicable to civil forfeiture proceedings in Georgia. The legislation also repealed or amended a number of Code Sections so that they now reference §§ 9-16-1 et seq. in order to provide a uniform process for the forfeiture of contraband related to or used in the commission of certain criminal offenses and other violations that are subject to civil penalties.[1]

The uniform procedure models itself in large part after former

---

[32]O.C.G.A. § 17-5-50 treats the return to the rightful owner of property alleged to have been stolen or "otherwise unlawfully obtained" and brought into the custody of a law enforcement agency; O.C.G.A. §§ 17-5-51 and 17-5-52 treat the disposition of weapons used in the commission of a crime.

[Section 10:3]

[1]See, e.g., O.C.G.A. § 16-5-44.1 (highjacking a motor vehicle); O.C.G.A. § 16-5-46 (trafficking of persons for

O.C.G.A. § 16-13-49 which provides for the forfeiture of contraband used for and arising from drug related crimes and which has now been amended to refer back to the uniform procedure set forth in §§ 9-16-1 et seq. Thus, to the extent the new law adopts the language of former O.C.G.A. § 16-13-49, case law involving drug related forfeitures should continue to be instructive when construing the new law.

O.C.G.A. § 9-16-2 provides a number of definitions now uniformly applicable to civil forfeitures that are subject to Chapter 16 of Title 9, and defines a civil forfeiture proceeding as "a quasi-judicial forfeiture" initiated pursuant to O.C.G.A. § 9-16-11 or a complaint for forfeiture initiated under O.C.G.A. §§ 9-16-12 (in rem actions) or 9-16-13 (in personam actions).[2]

Pursuant to O.C.G.A. § 9-16-3 a "state attorney,"[3] acting on behalf of the state, should file a civil forfeiture action in the

---

labor or sexual servitude); O.C.G.A. § 16-6-13.2 (pimping and pandering); O.C.G.A. § 16-7-95 (bombs, explosives, and chemical and biological weapons); O.C.G.A. § 16-8-5.2 (retail property fencing); O.C.G.A. § 16-8-60 (unauthorized reproduction and distribution of recorded material); O.C.G.A. § 16-8-85 (motor vehicle chop shops and stolen and altered property); O.C.G.A. § 16-8-106 (residential mortgage fraud); O.C.G.A. § 16-9-4 (false identification documents); O.C.G.A. § 16-11-11 (subversive organizations); O.C.G.A. § 16-12-32 (gambling and related offenses); O.C.G.A. § 16-12-100 (sexual exploitation of children); O.C.G.A. § 16-13-30.1 (transactions involving non-controlled substances); O.C.G.A. § 16-13-30.2 (transactions involving imitation controlled substances); O.C.G.A. § 16-13-30.4 (licensing of distributors of products containing pseudoephedrine); O.C.G.A. §§ 16-13-32 and 16-13-32.1 (transactions involving drug related objects); O.C.G.A. §§ 16-13-49 and former 16-13-53 (regulation of controlled substances); O.C.G.A. §§ 16-14-1 to 16-4-12 (Georgia RICO violations); O.C.G.A. § 16-15-5 (violations of Georgia Street Gang Terrorism and Prevention Act); O.C.G.A. § 16-16-2 (burglary, armed robbery or home invasion); O.C.G.A. §§ 3-10-10 and 3-10-11 (unlawful sale or possession of distilled spirits); O.C.G.A. § 7-1-916 (unlawful currency transactions); O.C.G.A. § 10-1-454 (forging or counterfeiting trademarks, service marks, or copyrighted or registered designs); O.C.G.A. § 10-13A-8 (sale of unstamped and authorized tobacco products); O.C.G.A. 12-4-48 (violation of regulations relating to deep drilling for oil, gas and minerals); O.C.G.A. §§ 12-5-133 and 12-5-137 (unlicensed or unauthorized water well drilling); O.C.G.A. § 12-8-2 (unlawful disposal of sanitary sewer, kitchen or toilet wastes); O.C.G.A. §§ 17-5-51, 17-5-52, (former) 17-5-52.1, and 17-5-54 (unlawful possession of weapons and weapons used in commission of crimes); O.C.G.A. § 27-3-12 (unlawful hunting substances and equipment); O.C.G.A. § 27-3-26 (unlawful bear hunting); O.C.G.A. §§ 27-4-133, 27-4-134, 27-4-137 (regulations regarding shrimping); O.C.G.A. § 40-6-391.2 (habitual violators for driving under the influence); and O.C.G.A. § 40-11-20 (unlawful removal, alteration of falsification of motor vehicle's identification number of a component part's identification number); O.C.G.A. § 46-9-253 (unlawful transport of gun powder, dynamite or other dangerous explosive).

[2]O.C.G.A. § 9-16-2(2).

[3]See O.C.G.A. § 9-16-2(12) (defining state attorney as "a district attorney of this state or his or her designee or, when specifically authorized by

superior court. An in rem action may be filed in the judicial circuit where the property is located[4] while an in personam action can be filed in the judicial circuit in which the defendant resides.[5] Alternatively, a state attorney having jurisdiction over any offense that arose out of the conduct making the property subject to forfeiture may file the action in that jurisdiction.[6] However, if more than one state attorney has jurisdiction, the attorney that has "primary jurisdiction" over the conduct giving rise to the forfeiture will have priority.[7]

With respect to venue, a complaint for forfeiture brought in rem against real property must be tried in the county where the property is located,[8] while an in rem proceeding against personal property must be tried in the county where the property is located or where it will be located during the pendency of the forfeiture action.[9] Article VI, Section II of the Georgia Constitution governs forfeiture actions filed in personam.

Property subject to forfeiture can be seized by any Georgia law enforcement officer or any political subdivision having the power to make arrests or execute process or a search warrant issued by any court having jurisdiction over the property.[10] A court may issue a warrant authorizing the seizure of property upon the execution of an affidavit showing that probable causes exists for the forfeiture or that a final judgment of forfeiture concerning the property has previously been entered by a U.S. court.[11] However, property may be seized without process if probable cause exists to believe that it is properly subject to forfeiture or if the seizure is incident to an arrest or a search or inspection pursuant to a search or inspection warrant.[12] A court's jurisdiction will not be affected by a seizure later found to be unconstitutional if made with process or in a good faith belief that probable cause existed.[13]

If property is seized for forfeiture or a forfeiture lien is filed without a judicial determination of probable cause, an order of

---

law, the Attorney General or his or her designee").

[4]O.C.G.A. § 9-16-3(a)(1).

[5]O.C.G.A. § 9-16-3(a)(2).

[6]O.C.G.A. § 9-16-3(a)(3).

[7]O.C.G.A. § 9-16-3(b). The seizing agency or district attorney can transfer the forfeiture proceeding by discontinuing the action in favor of another civil forfeiture proceeding initiated by another agency or district attorney. See O.C.G.A. § 9-16-9(b).

[8]Where a single tract of land is divided by a county line, the case may be tried in the superior court of either

county. O.C.G.A. § 9-16-4(a).

[9]O.C.G.A. § 9-16-4. In accordance with Uniform Superior Court Rules, an in rem or in personam forfeiture action may be assigned to the same judge hearing any other forfeiture complaint or criminal proceeding that involves substantially the same parties or the same property. O.C.G.A. § 9-16-9(d).

[10]O.C.G.A. § 9-16-6(a).

[11]O.C.G.A. § 9-16-6(a).

[12]O.C.G.A. § 9-16-6(b).

[13]O.C.G.A. § 9-16-6(c).

forfeiture, or a hearing as provided in O.C.G.A. § 9-16-14(2), and upon timely application by an owner or interest holder and five days' notice to the state, the court may issue a show cause order for a hearing on the sole issue of whether probable cause exists for the forfeiture.[14] If the court does not find probable cause, the property should be released. In deciding whether probable cause exists, the court must apply the rules of evidence, however, hearsay is admissible.[15]

Pursuant to O.C.G.A. § 9-16-15, "[i]f a seized vehicle is registered to a person or entity that was not present at the scene of the seizure and whose conduct did not give rise to the seizure, the seizing officer or his or her designee shall make a reasonable effort to determine the name of the registered owner of the seized vehicle and, upon learning such registered owner's telephone number or address, inform such registered owner that the vehicle has been seized."

When property that is intended to be forfeited is seized, within 30 days the seizing officer must report the seizure, conduct an inventory and estimate the value of the property.[16] This information must be reported to the district attorney having jurisdiction in the county where the seizure occurred. Within 60 days of the seizure, the state should initiate a forfeiture proceeding.[17]

O.C.G.A. § 9-16-20(e) provides that a civil forfeiture proceeding must be brought "within four years after the last conduct giving rise to forfeiture or to the claim for relief became known or should have become known, excluding any time during which either the property or defendant is out of the state or in confinement or during which criminal proceedings relating to the same conduct are in progress."

The state has three available approaches for forfeiting contraband property.[18] In the first approach, if the property sought to be forfeited is personal property valued at $25,000.00 or less, the state may initiate a "quasi-judicial forfeiture" pursuant to O.C.G.A. § 9-16-11 by serving a notice of seizure; only if an owner or interest holder timely files a claim to the property would the state then have to file a formal forfeiture complaint, otherwise

---

[14]O.C.G.A. § 9-16-14(4).

[15]O.C.G.A. § 9-16-14(4).

[16]O.C.G.A. § 9-16-7(a).

[17]O.C.G.A. § 9-16-7(b).

[18]O.C.G.A. § 9-16-7(b). Upon the commencement of any civil forfeiture or criminal proceeding or when property is seized for forfeiture, the state may file a forfeiture lien which constitutes notice to any person claiming an interest in the property and creates a lien in favor of the state as it relates to the property or to any named persons with respect to the property. The forfeiture lien secures the amount of potential liability for civil judgment and secures the fair market value of the property with respect to any civil forfeiture action initiated to enforce the lien. O.C.G.A. § 9-16-8.

the unclaimed property is forfeited to the state by operation of law. Another approach available to the state is to proceed in rem where a complaint for forfeiture is filed against the property to be forfeited as provided in O.C.G.A. § 9-16-12. The third approach is to proceed in personam pursuant to O.C.G.A. § 9-16-13 where a complaint for forfeiture is filed against the person whose conduct gave rise to the property being forfeitable. If the seizing officer fails to properly report the seizure or if the state fails to initiate one of the foregoing forfeiture proceedings within 60 days of the seizure and unless the property is being held as evidence, it must be released at the request of the owner or interest holder until a forfeiture complaint is filed.[19] A discussion of the procedure for each forfeiture approach follows.

To initiate a "quasi-judicial forfeiture" proceeding involving personal property seized and valued at $25,000.00 or less, the state must post a notice of the seizure in a prominent location in the courthouse of the county where the seizure occurred.[20] The notice must include: (1) a description of the property; (2) the date and location of the seizure; (3) the conduct giving rise to the seizure; (4) the alleged violation of law; and (5) a statement that the owner or interest holder of the property has 30 days to serve a claim to the property on the state attorney.

Also, the state attorney must serve a copy of the notice on the owner, interest holder, and person that was in possession of the property at the time of the seizure.[21] If the name and current address of any of these individuals is known, the district attorney must have them personally served or mail a copy by certified or

---

[19]O.C.G.A. § 9-16-7(c). See Johnson v. State, 266 Ga. App. 171, 172, 596 S.E.2d 693 (2004) (construing a similar provision under former O.C.G.A. § 16-13-49(h), affirming forfeiture of property and finding sole remedy for state's failure to initiate a forfeiture proceeding within 60 days of seizure was the return of the property to the owner pending further forfeiture proceedings). Cf. Smith v. State, 301 Ga. App. 870, 690 S.E.2d 208 (2010); Green v. State, 250 Ga. App. 440, 550 S.E.2d 736 (2001). When a court releases seized property to an owner or interest holder due to a failure to timely report the seizure or to initiate a forfeiture proceeding, the state may seek the imposition of conditions on the release, including, inter alia: a restraining order or injunction; the execution of performance bonds; the appointment of a receiver, conser-

vator, or trustee; or other action to secure, maintain or preserve the availability of the property subject to forfeiture. See O.C.G.A. §§ 9-16-7(c) and 9-16-14(1).

[20]O.C.G.A. § 9-16-11(a).

[21]O.C.G.A. § 9-16-11(b). See O.C.G.A. §§ 9-16-2(8) (defining "owner" as "a person, other than an interest holder, who has an interest in property and is in compliance with any statute requiring its recordation or reflection in public records in order to perfect the interest against a bona fide purchaser for value"); O.C.G.A. §§ 9-16-2(7) (defining "interest holder" as "a secured party within the meaning of Code Section 11-9-102, the claim of a beneficial interest, or a perfected encumbrance pertaining to an interest in property").

overnight mail. If the name and address of any of these individuals is by law required to be recorded in order to perfect an interest in the property, the state attorney may mail a copy of the notice by certified mail or overnight delivery to the address on record. However, if the identity or contact information of the person in possession or the owner or interest holder is not on record and is otherwise unknown, the state may serve by publication by publishing a copy of the notice of seizure once a week for two consecutive weeks in the legal organ of the county where the seizure occurred.

An owner or interest holder seeking to make a claim to the seized property must serve their claim on the state attorney by certified mail or statutory overnight delivery within 30 days after being served or within 30 days after the second publication, whichever occurs later.[22] The claim must include information such as the claimant's name and address, a description of his interest in the property along with any documentation supporting such interest, and the claimant's relationship with the person in possession of the property at the time it was seized.[23]

If a claim is served, the state is required to file a complaint for forfeiture as provided in O.C.G.A. §§ 9-16-12 (in rem action) or 9-16-13 (in personam action) within 30 days of receiving the claim, even if the state attorney believes the information provided in the claim is insufficient.[24] The complaint must specifically address the property claimed and any individual who has served a claim upon the state attorney must be joined as a party to the action.

If no claim to the property is timely made, "all right, title, and interest in the property" is forfeited to the state by operation of law and the state can dispose of the property pursuant to O.C.G.A. § 9-16-19.[25] However, the state must serve a copy of the court order forfeiting the property via first class mail on any

---

[22]O.C.G.A. § 9-16-11(c)(1). In Holmes v. State, 233 Ga. App. 872, 506 S.E.2d 157 (1998), the court pointed out that "to contest a forfeiture, a party must be an 'owner' or 'interest holder.'" A purely equitable interest in the property subject to forfeiture will not suffice. See State v. Centers, 310 Ga. App. 413, 713 S.E.2d 479 (2011); McFarley v. State, 268 Ga. App. 621, 602 S.E.2d 341 (2004). The rule is different, however, where the party contesting the forfeiture is a secured party. The holder of an unperfected security interest in the property subject to forfeiture who has no actual or constructive knowledge that the property involved was somehow used in connection with illegal activity may prevail over the state in a forfeiture proceeding. See Tolliver v. State, 276 Ga. App. 755, 625 S.E.2d 403 (2005); Farmers & Merchants Bank of Trenton v. State, 167 Ga. App. 77, 306 S.E.2d 11, 36 U.C.C. Rep. Serv. 1740 (1983); Hallman v. State, 141 Ga. App. 527, 233 S.E.2d 839 (1977).

[23]O.C.G.A. § 9-16-11(c)(2).

[24]O.C.G.A. § 9-16-11(c)(3).

[25]O.C.G.A. § 9-16-11(c)(4).

person who was served with the notice of seizure.

Under the second approach, in rem forfeiture actions must comply with O.C.G.A. § 9-16-12.[26] Certain contraband can only be forfeited through an in rem action.[27] The subject property should be named a defendant in the verified complaint for forfeiture[28] which must, inter alia, describe the property with "reasonable particularity," state the name of the property's custodian and owner or interest holder, allege the essential elements of the criminal violation(s) leading to the seizure and provide information regarding the seizure itself.[29] The complaint and summons must be served on any person known to be an owner or interest holder or who is in possession of the property, and should be served as provided in O.C.G.A. § 9-11-4(a), (b), (c), and (e).[30] However, if the forfeiture is with respect to real property or the owner or interest holder is unknown, resides out of state or leaves the state and cannot after due diligence be found or if the person conceals himself to avoid service, the state can effectuate service by publishing a copy of the notice of the complaint for forfeiture once a week for two consecutive weeks in the county's legal organ.[31]

An owner or interest holder may file a verified answer asserting a claim to the property within 30 days after service, or if service is made by publication, within 30 days after the final

---

[26]Pursuant to O.C.G.A. § 9-11-12(g), any action in rem can be brought by the state attorney in addition to or in lieu of any other in rem or in personam action filed under Chapter 16 of Title 9.

[27]See, e.g., O.C.G.A. § 12-4-48(e)(2) (illegal minerals seized due to a violation of the Oil and Gas and Deep Drilling Act of 1975); O.C.G.A. § 27-4-137 (boats and equipment seized due to unlawful shrimping).

[28]The complaint should be verified by an authorized state agent as provided in Article 5 of Chapter 10 of Title 9. O.C.G.A. § 9-16-12(a). However, construing a similar provision in former O.C.G.A. § 16-13-49(o), in McMichen v. State, 209 Ga. App. 169, 433 S.E.2d 92 (1993), the Court of Appeals of Georgia affirmed the denial of a motion to dismiss based on the state's failure to have the forfeiture complaint verified by an authorized agent, finding "substantial compli-ance" sufficient and that the complaint could be subsequently amended to include a proper verification.

[29]O.C.G.A. § 9-16-12(a). If the complaint for forfeiture concerns tangible property that has not been seized, the court can order the sheriff or other law enforcement officer to take possession of it, or if taking actual possession is impractical, the sheriff can execute process by conspicuously affixing a copy of the complaint and summons to the property and leaving another copy with the person in possession of it. In cases involving a vessel or aircraft, the sheriff or other law enforcement officer is authorized to make a written request to the appropriate government agency not to allow the vessel or aircraft to depart from its location until notified that the property has been released. O.C.G.A. § 9-16-12(b)(4).

[30]O.C.G.A. § 9-16-12(b)(1) to (2).

[31]O.C.G.A. § 9-16-12(b)(3).

publication.[32] The pleading must comply with the Civil Practice Act's general rules regarding filing an answer as provided under Article 3 of Chapter 11 of Title 9 and, additionally, must include information such as the claimant's identity and contact information, the circumstances surrounding his interest in the property, the nature of the relationship between the claimant and the person in possession of the property at the time of the seizure, and any supporting documentation.[33] The claimant may not file any counterclaim or cross-claim and cannot bring or maintain any civil action regarding the validity of his interest in the property other than as provided under the Uniform Civil Forfeiture Procedure Act.[34]

If an answer is filed, a bench trial[35] should be held within 60 days after the last claimant was served, unless the court finds good cause to continue the trial.[36] The 60-day requirement is mandatory and a request for continuance must be made within that time to "ensure a speedy resolution of contested forfeiture cases in the courts, as well as speedy resolution of property rights."[37] In the event a continuance is granted, the outermost limits of a continuance would be another 60-day period before ei-

---

[32]O.C.G.A. § 9-16-12(c).

[33]O.C.G.A. § 9-16-12(c)(1). If the state finds the answer deficient in some respect, pursuant to subsection (c)(2) of this Code Section the state attorney can move the court to require the claimant to file a more definite statement. If the motion is granted and the claimant does not sufficiently supplement his answer within 15 days after notice of the court's order or such other time as the court fixes, the court may strike the pleading. This is similar to former O.C.G.A. § 16-13-49(o). See Coffey v. State, 339 Ga. App. 367, 793 S.E.2d 557 (2016); Crimley v. State, 330 Ga. App. 639, 768 S.E.2d 813 (2015); Holmes v. State, 270 Ga. App. 882, 608 S.E.2d 325 (2004). Compare Williams v. State, 222 Ga. App. 270, 474 S.E.2d 98 (1996).

[34]O.C.G.A. § 9-16-20(d).

[35]See Swails v. State, 263 Ga. 276, 431 S.E.2d 101 (1993) (finding former O.C.G.A. § 16-13-49(o)(5) and (p)(6) which also required that forfeiture hearings be held by court without a jury did not violate the jury trial provision of Article I, Section I, Paragraph XI(a) of the Constitution of the State of Georgia).

[36]O.C.G.A. § 9-16-12(f). However, when considering a similar forfeiture provision under former O.C.G.A. § 16-13-49(o)(5), it has been held that the court's power to grant such extensions is limited. See Bourassa v. State, 323 Ga. App. 435, 436(1), 746 S.E.2d 815 (2013) (trial court improperly stayed forfeiture proceeding to allow a civil case to proceed in federal court that was filed by the property owner against the prosecutor and case agent involved in the forfeiture action); McDowell v. State, 290 Ga. App. 538, 540, 660 S.E.2d 24 (2008) ("[E]ven if a continuance is granted for good cause thereby causing the State to miss the original 60–day deadline, the outermost limits of a continuance would be another 60–day period before either the matter is heard or another continuance is granted") (citations and punctuation omitted).

[37]See State v. Henderson, 263 Ga. 508, 511, 436 S.E.2d 209 (1993) (decided under former O.C.G.A. § 16-13-49).

ther the matter is heard or another continuance is granted.[38] In the event the matter is not heard within the 60-day period or within such time as it may be continued, an order of dismissal is required.[39]

Discovery is generally not allowed, however, any party can move the court to allow discovery. If allowed, the court should establish the scope and duration of any discovery and may continue the trial to a date not more than 60 days after the end of the ordered discovery period, unless the court finds good cause to continue the trial further. If no answer is timely filed, the district attorney may seek a default judgment under O.C.G.A. § 9-11-55, and if granted the court may order disposition of the property pursuant to O.C.G.A. § 9-16-19.[40]

Finally, under the third approach to forfeiture, in personam forfeiture actions must comply with O.C.G.A. § 9-16-13. The complaint must be verified under oath by an authorized state agent and must describe the property sought to be forfeited with particularity and include information such as the property's current custodian, the owner or interest holder (if known), the essential elements of the criminal violation(s) alleged, and the place of seizure if the property has been seized.[41] The complaint and summons should be served as provided by O.C.G.A. § 9-11-4(a), (b), (c), and (d).[42] If the defendant is unknown, resides out of state, departs the state and cannot after diligent search be found, or if he conceals himself to avoid service, publishing notice of the complaint for forfeiture once a week for two consecutive weeks in the county's legal organ will be deemed sufficient notice to that defendant.[43]

A defendant's answer must be verified and filed within 30 days after service, or if service was by publication, within 30 days of the final publication.[44] If no answer is timely filed, the district attorney can seek a default judgment and, if granted, the court may order the disposition of the property as provided in O.C.G.A. § 9-16-19.[45] If an answer is filed, as with in rem forfeiture actions, a bench trial should be held within 60 days after the last claimant was served unless the court allows additional time for

---

[38]Blanks v. State, 240 Ga. App. 175, 178 (1), 522 S.E.2d 770 (1999). See McDowell v. State, 290 Ga. App. 538, 539 (2), 660 S.E.2d 24 (2008) (decided under former O.C.G.A. § 16-13-49(O)(5)).

[39]Rounsaville v. State, 345 Ga. App. 899, 815 S.E.2d 212 (2018).

[40]O.C.G.A. § 9-16-12(e).

[41]O.C.G.A. § 9-16-13(a).

[42]O.C.G.A. § 9-16-13(b).

[43]O.C.G.A. § 9-16-13(b).

[44]O.C.G.A. § 9-16-13(c).

[45]O.C.G.A. § 9-16-13(e).

discovery and/or for good cause shown.[46] Upon a determination of the liability of a person for conduct giving rise to the forfeiture, the court will enter a judgment of forfeiture against the subject property and authorize the state attorney or an authorized officer to seize any property ordered forfeited and not previously seized.[47] Upon entry of a forfeiture order, the state may also request an "appropriate order" to protect the state's interest in the forfeited property. In *Loveless v. State of Georgia*,[48] defendant's answer was struck when the court determined that the defendant failed to include in his answer information as to the nature and extent of his interest in the cash which was the subject of the forfeiture case. Instead of seeking a stay of the civil proceeding pending the resolution of the criminal case, he filed a general denial to the essential allegations of the complaint. In addition, the defendant contended that the property was seized in violation of his Fourth Amendment rights and stated that he was facing criminal charges in a related criminal matter and for that reason he was asserting his Fifth Amendment rights. The court struck the answer because it failed to state what interest the defendant had in the cash and thus his assertions that the answer raised disputed questions of fact and some constitutional concerns was without merit. Although decided under the former forfeiture procedure, counsel should take note that in order to contest a forfeiture, a party must plead with particularity what interest the party has in the subject property.

In a forfeiture proceeding, the state must prove by a preponderance of the evidence that seized property is forfeitable. There is a rebuttable presumption that a person's property is subject to forfeiture if the state establishes by a preponderance of evidence that: (1) the person engaged in the conduct giving rise to the forfeiture; (2) the property was acquired by the person during the time that he or she was engaged in such conduct or within a reasonable time thereafter; and (3) there is no other likely source of the property other than that conduct.[49]

In conjunction with any civil forfeiture action or criminal proceeding involving forfeiture, the state attorney may apply for other forms of court ordered relief, including seeking: a restraining order or injunction; appointment of a receiver, conservator, appraiser, accountant or trustee; or a warrant for the property's seizure and writ of attachment.[50]

Pursuant to O.C.G.A. § 9-16-18, "[a]ll property declared to be

---

[46]O.C.G.A. § 9-16-13(f).

[47]O.C.G.A. § 9-16-13(g).

[48]Loveless v. State, 337 Ga. App. 250, 786 S.E.2d 899 (2016).

[49]O.C.G.A. § 9-16-17(a)(1) and (b).

[50]O.C.G.A. § 9-16-14(1). See subsections (2) and (3) of this Code Section for requirements regarding notice

forfeited vests in the state at the time of commission of the conduct giving rise to forfeiture together with the proceeds of the property after that time."[51] Thus, if property or proceeds are transferred after the conduct that made the property forfeitable occurs, the property remains subject to forfeiture and can be ordered forfeited unless the transferee establishes that he is a bona fide purchaser for value whose interest is exempt from forfeiture under O.C.G.A. § 9-16-17(a)(2).

O.C.G.A. § 9-16-20 provides that a court must order the forfeiture of any property of a claimant or defendant up to the value of the property found to be subject to forfeiture if any of the forfeited property:

(1) Cannot be located;

(2) Has been transferred or conveyed to, sold to, or deposited with a third party;

(3) Is beyond the jurisdiction of the court;

(4) Has been substantially diminished in value while not in the actual physical custody of the receiver or governmental agency directed to maintain custody of the property; or

(5) Has been commingled with other property that cannot be divided without difficulty.

Further, the state may initiate a civil action in any U.S. court against any person acting with knowledge or any person to whom notice of seizure, a forfeiture lien, or forfeiture proceeding has been provided if property subject to seizure is "conveyed, alienated, disposed of, or otherwise rendered unavailable for forfeiture" after the filing of a forfeiture lien, notice of seizure, or a civil forfeiture action.[52]

Upon a showing of good cause by the state, an owner, or an interest holder, the court may stay civil forfeiture proceedings pending a final resolution of a related criminal proceeding.[53] An acquittal or dismissal in a criminal case will not bar pursuit of a civil forfeiture.[54] However, evidence of the acquittal may be admissible by the acquitted defendant in a related forfeiture proceeding but is generally not admissible by third party claimants.[55]

If a defendant is convicted in a criminal case, he cannot later

---

and hearing.

[51]See U.S. v. Monsanto, 491 U.S. 600, 109 S. Ct. 2657, 105 L. Ed. 2d 512 (1989) (neither the Fifth nor Sixth Amendment requires that a defendant be permitted to use assets which are subject to forfeiture to pay his attorney).

[52]O.C.G.A. § 9-16-20(b).

[53]O.C.G.A. § 9-16-15(a).

[54]O.C.G.A. § 9-16-15(b). See U.S. v. Burch, 294 F.2d 1 (5th Cir. 1961).

[55]Duncan v. State, 149 Ga. 195, 99 S.E. 612 (1919). See also Chester v. State, 162 Ga. App. 10, 13, 290 S.E.2d 117 (1982) (where a criminal defendant charged with possession of drugs admitted in his pleadings in a related

deny the essential allegations of the offense for which he was convicted in a related forfeiture proceeding brought against him.[56] This is so even if an appeal of the conviction is pending, although evidence that an appeal is pending is admissible.

Under O.C.G.A. § 9-16-16, an "injured person"[57] who has provided the state contact information pursuant to the Crime Victims' Bill of Rights[58] should be served with the complaint for forfeiture, whether in rem or in personam, and must be given notice at least 30 days before the entry of a final judgment that he or she may intervene in the action. If such an individual timely intervenes, that person will have a claim to the forfeited property or to its proceeds that is superior to any right of the state or local government, other than for costs and notwithstanding the distribution provisions of O.C.G.A. § 9-16-19.[59] Likewise, any owner, interest holder or person in possession of the property who qualifies as an "injured person" is entitled to intervene in a civil forfeiture action as provided by Chapter 11 of Title 9.[60]

The uniform forfeiture law includes a defense to forfeiture commonly known as the "innocent owner" exception.[61] O.C.G.A. § 9-16-17(a)(2) provides:

> (2) A property interest shall not be subject to forfeiture under this chapter if the owner of the interest or interest holder establishes that the owner or interest holder:
>
> (A) Is not privy to criminal conduct giving rise to its forfeiture;
> (B) Did not consent to the conduct giving rise to the forfeiture;
> (C) Did not know of the conduct giving rise to the forfeiture;
> (D) Did not know the conduct giving rise to the forfeiture was likely to occur;
> (E) Should not have reasonably known the conduct giving rise to

---

forfeiture action that money had been seized from his home, admission of defendant's unverified pleadings in the forfeiture action for the limited purpose of establishing ownership of the premises held proper).

[56]O.C.G.A. § 9-16-15(c).

[57]See O.C.G.A. § 9-16-16(a) (defining "injured person" as "any person who suffers a pecuniary loss or physical injury due to a violation of" Code Section 16-5-46 [trafficking of persons for labor or sexual servitude], Article 4 or 5 of Chapter 8 of Title 16 [involving motor vehicle chop shops, stolen and altered property, and residential mortgage fraud], or Chapter 14 of Title 16 [Georgia RICO violations]).

[58]O.C.G.A. §§ 17-17-1 et seq.

[59]O.C.G.A. § 9-16-16(c).

[60]O.C.G.A. §§ 9-16-12(d), 9-16-13(d).

[61]See Holiday v. State, 332 Ga. App. 747, 774 S.E.2d 793 (2015) ("[O]nce the State has presented a prima facie case for forfeiture, a claimant asserting that he is an innocent owner of the subject property bears the burden of proving such status by a preponderance of the evidence") (citing Little v. State, 279 Ga. App. 329, 330, 630 S.E.2d 903 (2006)). See, e.g., State v. Davis, 292 Ga. App. 387, 665 S.E.2d 350 (2008); State v. Jackson, 197 Ga. App. 619, 399 S.E.2d 88 (1990).

the forfeiture was likely to occur;

(F) Had not acquired and did not stand to acquire substantial proceeds from the conduct giving rise to its forfeiture other than as an interest holder in an arm's length commercial transaction;

(G) With respect to conveyances for transportation only, did not hold the property jointly, in common, or in community with a person whose conduct gave rise to the forfeiture;

(H) Does not hold the property for the benefit of or as nominee for any person whose conduct gave rise to its forfeiture, and, if the owner or interest holder acquired the interest through any such person, the owner or interest holder acquired it as a bona fide purchaser for value without knowingly taking part in an illegal transaction; and

(I) Acquired the interest:

(i) Before the completion of the conduct giving rise to its forfeiture and the person whose conduct gave rise to its forfeiture did not have the authority to convey the interest to a bona fide purchaser for value at the time of the conduct; or

(ii) After the completion of the conduct giving rise to its forfeiture:

(I) As a bona fide purchaser for value without knowingly taking part in an illegal transaction;

(II) Before the filing of a forfeiture lien on it and before the effective date of a notice of pending forfeiture relating to it and without notice of its seizure for forfeiture; and

(III) At the time the interest was acquired, was reasonably without cause to believe that the property was subject to forfeiture or likely to become subject to forfeiture.

Thus, an individual claiming to be an innocent owner must meet all of the above criteria in order for the individual's property interest not to be subject to forfeiture.[62]

With respect to vehicles forfeited as a result of a person being

---

[62]See, e.g., Sanders v. State, 259 Ga. App. 422, 577 S.E.2d 94 (2003) (claimant's invocation against self-incrimination when questioned about the presence of drugs and cash in his vehicle constituted admissions that he either consented to the criminal conduct giving rise to the forfeiture or that he knew or reasonably should have known of the conduct such that forfeiture was authorized); State v. Tucker, 242 Ga. App. 3, 528 S.E.2d 523 (2000) (auto dealership failed to show innocent ownership of vehicle that dealership's president's son used to transport drugs and cash where dealership, through president, could have reasonably known of the son's criminal conduct or that it was likely to oc-

cur); James v. State, 240 Ga. App. 288, 523 S.E.2d 354 (1999) (mother properly denied innocent owner status and forfeiture affirmed where state established son used the vehicle to transport and sell drugs and that the mother was aware of her son's criminal conduct given that officers warned her on several occasions that her son was selling drugs from the car). See also Bennis v. Michigan, 516 U.S. 442, 116 S. Ct. 994, 134 L. Ed. 2d 68 (1996) (neither the Due Process Clause of the Fourteenth Amendment nor the Takings Clause of the Fifth Amendment is violated where an "owner's interest in property [is] forfeited by reason of the use to which the property is put even though the owner did not know that it was to be put to such use").

declared a habitual violator under O.C.G.A. § 40-6-391.2, i.e. three or more offenses for driving under the influence, the 2015 legislation creates an exception where a vehicle subject to forfeiture is the "only family vehicle." O.C.G.A. § 40-6-391.2(b) provides that in such cases "the court may, if it determines that the financial hardship to the family as a result of the forfeiture and sale outweighs the benefit to the state from such forfeiture, order the title to the vehicle transferred to such other family member who is a duly licensed operator and who requires the use of such vehicle for employment or family transportation purposes." However, the transfer is subject to any valid liens and will be "granted only once."

The new law includes detailed provisions addressing how forfeited property is to be distributed and the order in which distributions are to be made.[63] Depending on the order of the court and the applicable law, the forfeited property may be destroyed, title placed in the name of the state, transferred, sold or otherwise disposed of in a "commercially reasonable manner." The state attorney must submit to the court a proposed order of distribution that includes a time for the transfer of forfeited property and the entity responsible for effectuating the transfer.[64]

Additionally, in the Uniform Civil Forfeiture Procedure Act the Georgia Legislature expresses an intent that there be "accountability and transparency" in the distribution of forfeited property and income derived from its sale such that "appropriate accounting and auditing standards shall be applicable to such distribution."[65] Thus, entities receiving forfeited property or proceeds or income resulting from their sale must submit an annual report specifying what was received and how it was used.

§ 10:4   Forfeiture of weapons

O.C.G.A. § 17-5-51 provides that any weapon used in the commission or attempted commission of a crime or the possession of which constitutes a criminal offense is contraband that may be forfeited.[1]

In such cases, upon the entry of a final judgment and when the

---

[63]O.C.G.A. § 9-16-19.

[64]O.C.G.A. § 9-16-19(f)(1).

[65]O.C.G.A. § 9-16-19(g).

[Section 10:4]

[1]See Cannington v. State, 154 Ga. App. 557, 269 S.E.2d 62 (1980) (individual who pled guilty to voluntary manslaughter not entitled to the return of the weapon he used to commit the crime). Compare Holland v. State, 204 Ga. App. 22, 418 S.E.2d 400 (1992) (individual who pled nolo contendere to charge of reckless conduct for pointing a gun at another not entitled to the return of the gun used during the offense but was entitled to the return of five other firearms seized from his home at the time of his arrest). See also O.C.G.A. § 17-5-2 (provides that if a person is arrested and released

weapon is no longer needed for evidentiary purposes, it should be turned over to the law enforcement agency or sheriff that seized it, who within one year must return or sell it pursuant to O.C.G.A. § 17-5-54.[2] However, if the weapon is subject to forfeiture, forfeiture proceedings should commence. Such proceedings are generally conducted pursuant to Georgia's Uniform Civil Forfeiture Procedure Act,[3] with the exception of the "time frames set forth in Code Section 9-16-7."[4] Instead, O.C.G.A. § 17-5-52 requires that a state attorney seeking forfeiture of a weapon under that Code Section must commence civil forfeiture proceedings within 60 days of when the final judgment is entered. Otherwise, the forfeiture of weapons is subject to the provisions of the uniform law. See § 10:3, supra, on uniform forfeiture procedure.

§ 10:5   Forfeitures relating to beverage alcohol

In 1980, the Georgia Alcoholic Beverage Code was enacted as former GCA section 5A-101 et seq. (now O.C.G.A. §§ 3-1-1 et seq.).[1] This Code expressly repeals former GCA Title 58 on Intoxicating Liquors,[2] and all amendments to former GCA Title 58. All provisions relating to forfeiture connected with intoxicants are now found in O.C.G.A. § 3-2-35 and O.C.G.A. §§ 3-10-1 et seq. O.C.G.A. § 3-2-35 and O.C.G.A. §§ 3-10-1 et seq. provide for forfeitures in two different situations. The first situation relates to a forfeiture anywhere in the state initiated by the State Revenue Commissioner or his agents where there is a seizure of contraband found in the possession of any person in violation of O.C.G.A. §§ 3-1-1 et seq. The second situation applies only to seizures in counties or municipalities in which sales of distilled spirits are not lawful. Apparently all these condemnation statutes are to be construed strictly against the state.[3]

First, O.C.G.A. § 3-2-35 provides for a seizure of contraband, other than unlawfully manufactured alcoholic beverages, found

---

without being charged, "all instruments, articles, or things seized" in a search without a search warrant, other than contraband or stolen property, must be returned upon the person's release).

Under the common law of deodand, any personal property which was an immediate cause of a negligent or willful death of a human being was forfeited to the king. See J. W. Goldsmith, Jr., Grant Co. v. U.S., 254 U.S. 505, 510, 41 S. Ct. 189, 65 L. Ed. 376 (1921); Fields v. Metropolitan Life

Ins. Co., 147 Tenn. 464, 249 S.W. 798, 36 A.L.R. 1250 (1923).

[2]O.C.G.A. § 17-5-52.

[3]O.C.G.A. §§ 9-16-1 et seq.

[4]O.C.G.A. § 17-5-52.

[Section 10:5]

[1]Ga. Laws 1980, p. 1573 et seq.

[2]Ga. Laws 1980, pp. 1573, 1652.

[3]See Leath v. Rosser, 52 Ga. App. 587 (1), 183 S.E. 839 (1936); Premium Distributing Co. v. State, 89 Ga. App. 222, 230, 79 S.E.2d 57 (1953).

in the possession of a person in violation of O.C.G.A. §§ 3-1-1 et seq. Upon such a seizure the commissioner or his agent shall give a receipt to the person from whom the contraband is taken, stating the place of seizure, the person from whom the contraband was seized, and a description of the seized property. A copy of the receipt must be filed with the commissioner and shall be open to public inspection. An additional copy of the receipt is to be posted at the courthouse of the county in which the contraband was seized.

Any person wishing to claim the contraband property shall file a claim with the Georgia Revenue Commissioner in Atlanta within 10 days of the seizure. Such a claimant is entitled to a hearing, provided by the commissioner, within 30 days of the receipt of the claim. At the hearing the claimant has the right "to show his entitlement to the seized items."[4] The burden of proof at such a hearing is on the claimant "to establish his claim to the items seized and to show compliance with, or justification for noncompliance" with the provisions of this section.[5] The commissioner must issue a written order granting or denying the claim within 30 days from the hearing. The statute provides for an appeal to the Superior Court of Fulton County by filing a notice of appeal within 15 days from the decision of the commissioner. The appeal is based on the record, and the "court shall review the record for errors of law, violation of constitutional or statutory provisions, violation of the statutory authority of the agency, lawfulness of the procedure, lack of any evidence to support the decision, and arbitrariness and abuse of discretion. However, the court shall not substitute its judgment for that of the hearing officer as to the weight of evidence on questions of fact."[6] Lastly, the statute provides for the method of disposition by the commissioner of alcoholic beverages on which taxes have been paid.

Second, O.C.G.A. §§ 3-10-1 et seq. contain three separate statutes which apply in counties and municipalities in which sales of distilled spirits are unlawful, except as otherwise provided in O.C.G.A. § 3-10-11, discussed below.[7] They are discussed below in the order in which they appear.

(1) O.C.G.A. § 3-10-10 provides that no property rights exist in distilled spirits or vessels kept or used for purposes of violating any provision of this Chapter nor in any such liquors when received, possessed, or stored at any place forbidden or anywhere in a quantity forbidden by law or stored or deposited for the purpose of sale or unlawful disposition, distribution or furnishing. All such distilled spirits and receptacles in which distilled spirits

---

[4]O.C.G.A. § 3-2-35(d).   [6]O.C.G.A. § 3-2-35(e).
[5]O.C.G.A. § 3-2-35(d).   [7]O.C.G.A. § 3-10-1.

are contained and property kept or used for the purpose of violating this Chapter are declared contraband and are subject to seizure and forfeiture pursuant to the Georgia Uniform Civil Forfeiture Procedure Act.[8] See § 10:3, supra, on uniform forfeiture procedure.

(2) O.C.G.A. § 3-10-11 provides all "apparatus or appliances which are used for the unlawful purpose of distilling or manufacturing any distilled spirits are declared to be contraband." No person is deemed to have any property right in such contraband.

"Whenever apparatus or appliances used or about to be used for the unlawful purpose of manufacturing, using, holding, or containing any distilled spirits are found or discovered by any sheriff, deputy sheriff, or other law enforcement officer of this state, the same shall be summarily destroyed and rendered useless by him without any formal order of the court."[9]

Subsection (b) provides that all vehicles and conveyances of every kind, including boats which are used in unlawfully conveying, removing, concealing, or storing any distilled spirits are deemed contraband and are also subject to seizure and forfeiture pursuant to the Georgia Uniform Civil Forfeiture Procedure Act, including in those counties and municipalities in which the sale of distilled spirits is lawful. See § 10:3, supra, on uniform forfeiture procedure.

(3) The last statute relating to condemnation in Title 3 is found in O.C.G.A. § 3-10-12 and provides that, in counties or municipalities in which the sale of distilled spirits is not lawful,[10] "[a]ny raw materials or substances, including, but not limited to, sugar . . . and any fixture, implement, or apparatus used or intended for use in the unlawful distilling or manufacturing of any distilled spirits are declared to be contraband." No person has any property interest in such contraband. Any property used or about to be so used which is discovered by an officer, sheriff, deputy sheriff, or revenue agent in transit or storage or at the site of such unlawful distillation or manufacture is forfeited. If discovered at a site of unlawful manufacture or distillation, it may be summarily destroyed or rendered useless without court order. In the event any raw material or substance is fit for human consumption or if any fixture or apparatus is useful to the educational authorities of the county for use in any of their educational programs, they may be delivered to the public schools of the county. However, the officer delivering such items shall obtain an itemized receipt for them from proper school authorities and must report that information pursuant to O.C.G.A. § 9-

---

[8]O.C.G.A. §§ 9-16-1 et seq.

[9]Cf. the first sentence of former

GCA § 58-207.

[10]O.C.G.A. § 3-10-1.

16-19(g). If such items are destroyed by such officer he shall execute an affidavit itemizing the items destroyed. Such receipts and affidavits shall be maintained by the officer and shall be open to public inspection on request.[11] However, such items discovered in transit or storage by said officers shall be seized and forfeited pursuant to the Georgia Uniform Civil Forfeiture Procedure Act. See § 10:3, supra, on uniform forfeiture procedure.

In 1991, Georgia enacted O.C.G.A. § 40-6-391.2, which provides for the forfeiture of a motor vehicle operated by a person who has been declared an habitual violator, whose license has been revoked, and who is arrested for driving under the influence. Such a proceeding should also be conducted in accordance with Georgia's uniform forfeiture procedures. See § 10:3, supra, on uniform forfeiture procedure. However, O.C.G.A. § 40-6-391.2(b) provides an exception where a vehicle subject to forfeiture is the "only family vehicle." That Code section provides that in such cases "the court may, if it determines that the financial hardship to the family as a result of the forfeiture and sale outweighs the benefit to the state from such forfeiture, order the title to the vehicle transferred to such other family member who is a duly licensed operator and who requires the use of such vehicle for employment or family transportation purposes." However, the transfer is subject to any valid liens and will be "granted only once."[12]

§ 10:6 Forfeitures relating to drugs[1]

O.C.G.A. §§ 16-13-49, 16-13-30.1, and 16-13-30.2 provide for forfeiture of property used in or maintained by illegal drug transactions. These statutes were amended in 2015 upon the enactment of the Georgia Uniform Civil Forfeiture Procedure Act,[2] which establishes a comprehensive and uniform procedure applicable to civil forfeiture proceedings in Georgia. Effective July 1, 2015, property and proceeds used to facilitate such illegal drug transactions or derived therefrom are subject to forfeiture in accordance with the uniform procedure. See § 10:3, supra, on uniform forfeiture procedure.

The uniform procedure models itself in large part after former O.C.G.A. § 16-13-49. Thus, to the extent the new law adopts the language of former O.C.G.A. § 16-13-49, case law involving drug related forfeitures should continue to be instructive when

---

[11]Cf. former GCA § 58-210(1).

[12]Frank v. State, 257 Ga. App. 164, 570 S.E.2d 613 (2002).

[Section 10:6]

[1]The majority of foregoing material was originally prepared by J. David Fowler, Director of Drug Prosecutions, Prosecuting Attorneys' Council of Georgia, Drug Prosecutions Division.

[2]O.C.G.A. §§ 9-16-1, et seq.

construing the new law.

O.C.G.A. § 16-13-49 sets up six categories of property that are subject to forfeiture as contraband under its provisions:

(1) Any controlled substances, raw materials, or controlled substance analogs that have been manufactured, distributed, dispensed, possessed, or acquired in violation of this article;

(2) Any property which is, directly or indirectly, used or intended for use in any manner to facilitate a violation of this article and any proceeds;

(3) Any property located in this state which was, directly or indirectly, used or intended for use in any manner to facilitate a violation of this article or the laws of the United States relating to controlled substances that is punishable by imprisonment for more than one year and any proceeds;

(4) Any interest, security, claim, or property or contractual right of any kind affording a source of influence over any enterprise that a person has established, operated, controlled, conducted, or participated in the conduct of in violation of this article or the laws of the United States relating to controlled substances that is punishable by imprisonment for more than one year and any proceeds;

(5) Any property found in close proximity to any controlled substance or other property subject to forfeiture under this Code section;[3] and

(6) Any weapon available for any use in any manner to facilitate a violation of this article.[4]

However, property is not subject to forfeiture under this Code Section for a violation "involving only one gram or less of a mixture containing cocaine or four ounces or less of marijuana" unless the property was used to facilitate the purchase or sale of a controlled substance.[5]

O.C.G.A. § 16-13-30.1 prohibits transactions involving noncon-

---

[3]See State v. Tucker, 242 Ga. App. 3, 7(2), 528 S.E.2d 523 (2000) (briefcase containing $4,010 located in cab of truck found to be in sufficient proximity to cocaine and pills found in bait box in the bed of the same truck so as to authorize forfeiture of money); Gearin v. State, 218 Ga. App. 390, 391(2), 461 S.E.2d 562 (1995) (methamphetamine found in the pocket of a driver stopped at a police road block and suspected of DUI found to be "in close proximity" to truck such as to render truck subject to forfeiture).

[4]O.C.G.A. § 16-13-49(b).

[5]O.C.G.A. § 16-13-49(d). See Bell v. State, 249 Ga. App. 296, 296, 548 S.E.2d 35 (2001) (construing a similar provision under former OCGA § 16-13-49(e), finding state must demonstrate that seized cocaine consists of more than one of gram of "pure" cocaine, rather than it merely testing positive for an undetermined amount of cocaine, in order to sustain forfeiture). Accord State v. Foote, 225 Ga. App. 222, 483 S.E.2d 628 (1997).

trolled substances represented as controlled substances and provides in part:

It is unlawful for any person knowingly to manufacture, deliver, distribute, dispense, possess with the intent to distribute, or sell a noncontrolled substance upon either: (A) The express or implied representation that the substance is a narcotic or nonnarcotic controlled substance; (B) The express or implied representation that the substance is of such nature or appearance that the recipient of said delivery will be able to distribute said substance as a controlled substance; or (C) The express or implied representation that the substance has essentially the same pharmacological action or effect as a controlled substance.

Any property that is used in any way, whether directly or indirectly, to facilitate a violation of O.C.G.A. § 16-13-30.1 as well as any proceeds from such violation and nonconstrolled substances manufactured or distributed in violation of the statute are deemed contraband subject to forfeiture in accordance with the uniform forfeiture procedures set forth in Chapter 16 of Title 9.[6]

O.C.G.A. 16-13-30.2 prohibits transactions involving any "imitation controlled substance" which is defined as:

(A) A product specifically designed or manufactured to resemble the physical appearance of a controlled substance such that a reasonable person of ordinary knowledge would not be able to distinguish the imitation from the controlled substance by outward appearances; or

(B) A product, not a controlled substance, which, by representations made and by dosage unit appearance, including color, shape, size, or markings, would lead a reasonable person to believe that, if ingested, the product would have a stimulant or depressant effect similar to or the same as that of one or more of the controlled substances included in Schedules I through V of Code Sections 16-13-25 through 16-13-29.[7]

Any materials that are manufactured, distributed or possessed in violation of O.C.G.A. § 16-13-30.2 as well as any proceeds derived therefrom are deemed contraband that is also subject to forfeiture pursuant to the uniform forfeiture procedures.[8]

In *United States v. James Daniel Good Real Property*,[9] the United States Supreme Court held that in a drug forfeiture case "[u]nless exigent circumstances are present, the Due Process Clause requires the Government to afford notice and a meaning-

---

[6]O.C.G.A. § 16-13-30.1(f).

[7]O.C.G.A. § 16-13-21(12.1).

[8]O.C.G.A. § 16-13-30.2(d).

[9]United States v. James Daniel Good Real Property, 510 U.S. 43, 114 S.Ct. 492, 126 L.Ed.2d 490 (1993).

ful opportunity to be heard before seizing real property subject to civil forfeiture. To establish exigent circumstances, the Government must show that less restrictive measures—*i.e.,* a *lis pendens,* restraining order, or bond—would not suffice to protect the Government's interests in preventing the sale, destruction, or continued unlawful use of the real property."

Various state courts have ruled that state homestead exemption laws prevent forfeiture of the homestead.[10] However, the Eleventh Circuit has held that federal forfeiture statutes preempt a state's constitutional homestead exemption.[11] In *Cuellar v. State,*[12] the court held that a forfeiture under former O.C.G.A. § 16-13-49 is a civil sanction and does not constitute punishment insofar as double jeopardy is concerned. See § 10:2, supra, on excessiveness in forfeiture statutes.

§ 10:7　Civil disabilities[1]

A person convicted of a crime may forfeit certain civil rights. The loss of these rights is usually referred to as "civil disabilities." Among these are the right to vote, hold public office, and engage in various kinds of employment requiring licensing. Further, since a criminal record ipso facto precludes any presumption of good character, certain other employment positions open to individuals of "good character" are inaccessible to those who have been convicted of a crime.

The right to vote[2] and to seek public office[3] is forfeited in Georgia upon conviction of a crime involving moral turpitude which is punishable with imprisonment in the penitentiary. This is also sufficient ground for divorce when the convicted spouse is sentenced to the penitentiary for two years or more.[4] A notary public commission is automatically canceled upon conviction of a crime involving turpitude.[5]

A state or county officer automatically loses his position upon

---

[10]Cf. State ex rel. Means v. 10 Acres of Land, 1994 OK 71, 877 P.2d 597 (1994); People v. One Residence Located at 1403 East Parham, 251 Ill.App.3d 198, 190 Ill.Dec. 573, 621 N.E.2d 1026 (1993); Butterworth v. Caggiano, 605 So.2d 56 (Fla. 1992).

[11]United States v. Lot 5, Fox Grove, Alachua County, Fla., 23 F.3d 359 (11th Cir. 1994).

[12]Cuellar v. State, 230 Ga. App. 203, 496 S.E.2d 282 (1998).

[Section 10:7]

[1]Generally, on this subject, see

the excellent special project entitled "The Collateral Consequences of a Criminal Conviction," 23 Vand. L. Rev. 931-1241 (1970).

[2]Ga. Const. 1983, Art. II, § I, ¶ III; O.C.G.A. § 21-2-217, O.C.G.A. § 21-2-231.

[3]Ga. Const. 1983, Art. II, § II, ¶ III; O.C.G.A. § 21-2-8.

[4]O.C.G.A. § 19-5-3.

[5]O.C.G.A. § 45-17-9.

conviction of a felony.[6] A felony conviction also bars a person whose civil rights have not been restored from service as a grand juror[7] and dissolves any partnership of which the convicted person is a party.[8] An insurance agent may have his license revoked upon conviction of a felony involving moral turpitude.[9]

A driver's license may be suspended upon conviction of an offense related to the use of a motor vehicle,[10] and insurance carriers may cancel automobile coverage of the insured upon his conviction of a felony.[11] Limitations are imposed on the right of a person convicted of certain crimes to obtain a license to carry a pistol or revolver.[12]

Practically all of the professions, businesses, and trades which are regulated by State Boards or Commissions in Georgia have provisions in the Annotated Code regarding the qualifications of license applicants and providing for disciplinary action in the event anyone licensed under their authority is convicted of "a felony" or "moral turpitude" or "a crime involving moral turpitude."[13] These provisions usually require a Board hearing before any action is taken, but the person who has been convicted

---

[6]O.C.G.A. § 45-5-2. In Ramsey v. Powell, 244 Ga. 745, 262 S.E.2d 61 (1979), the court held that if the crime is a felony but punishment is reduced to a misdemeanor, the defendant is still disqualified.

[7]O.C.G.A. § 15-12-60 (includes persons sentenced as a first offender; persons charged with a felony who are in a pre-trial release program; persons sentenced as a felon who have not completed the terms of the sentence imposed; persons participating in a drug or similar court sponsored program; and persons who are mentally incompetent).

[8]O.C.G.A. § 14-8-7.

[9]O.C.G.A. § 33-23-21.

[10]O.C.G.A. § 40-5-54.

[11]O.C.G.A. § 33-24-45.

[12]O.C.G.A. § 16-11-129.

[13]See O.C.G.A. § 26-4-60 and O.C.G.A. § 26-4-41 (pharmacists and pharmacies), O.C.G.A. § 43-3-27 (public accountants), O.C.G.A. § 43-6-16 (auctioneers), O.C.G.A. § 43-4-13 (architects), O.C.G.A. § 43-9-12 (chiropractors), O.C.G.A. § 43-11-47 (dentists and dental hygienists), O.C.G.A. § 43-34-8 (medical practitioners), O.C.G.A. § 43-30-9 (optometrists), O.C.G.A. § 43-40-15 (real estate brokers and salespersons), O.C.G.A. § 43-50-41 (veterinarians), O.C.G.A. § 43-15-19 (engineers and land surveyors), O.C.G.A. § 43-18-46 (funeral directors and embalmers), O.C.G.A. § 43-19-16 (geologists), O.C.G.A. § 43-33-18 (physical therapists), O.C.G.A. § 43-39-13 (psychologists), O.C.G.A. § 43-29-12 (opticians), O.C.G.A. § 43-47-10 (used car dealers), O.C.G.A. § 43-45-9 (pest control operators), O.C.G.A. § 43-23-12 (landscape architects), O.C.G.A. § 43-20-16 (hearing aid dealers and distributors), O.C.G.A. § 43-34-107 (physicians' assistants), O.C.G.A. § 43-38-6, O.C.G.A. § 43-38-11 (private detectives and security agents), O.C.G.A. § 43-28-13 (occupational therapists), O.C.G.A. § 43-5-10 (athletic trainers), O.C.G.A. § 43-47-8 (used motor vehicle and motor vehicle parts dealers), O.C.G.A. § 43-10A-17 (marriage and family counselors), and O.C.G.A. § 43-11A-15 (dieticians). Also see Rule 4-201 of the Rules and Regulations for Organization and Government of the State Bar of Georgia, which provides for disciplinary proceedings against attorneys.

may have his license suspended or revoked.

In *Carter v. Caldwell*,[14] the court held that where a person is discharged from his employment for failure to be present for work because he is incarcerated as a result of his conviction, he is not entitled to unemployment compensation.

While at common law one convicted of a felony or treason forfeited his civil rights of citizenship and was deemed to be civilly dead, this is not true in Georgia. A person convicted of a crime continues to have all the rights of an ordinary citizen except those which are expressly or by necessary implication taken from him by law.[15] A person convicted of a felony may still sue and be sued in Georgia.[16] Hence, one convicted of a felony is not thereby disqualified from suing for personal injuries sustained during his imprisonment.[17] Moreover, up until 1984, the statute of limitations did not run against a prisoner during the time he was imprisoned;[18] but in 1984, O.C.G.A. § 9-3-90 was amended so as to provide that the limitation period is no longer tolled by imprisonment.[19]

See § 10:8, infra, on restoration of civil rights.

§ 10:8   Restoration of civil rights

A pardon, as defined in an opinion by Justice Erskine in 1868, is "an act of mercy flowing from the fountain of bounty and grace; its effect, when it is a full pardon, is to obliterate every stain which the law attached to the offender, to place him where he stood before he committed the pardoned offense, and to free him from the penalties and forfeitures to which the law had subjected his person and property."[1] Perhaps more precisely, a grant of pardon by the State Board of Pardons and Paroles relieves a person from the legal consequences of a particular conviction and removes all legal disabilities by restoring that person's civil and political rights.[2]

The authority of the State Board of Pardon and Paroles to grant pardons and remove disabilities is granted in O.C.G.A. § 42-9-45

---

[14]Carter v. Caldwell, 151 Ga. App. 687 (1), 261 S.E.2d 431 (1979).

[15]Westbrook v. State, 133 Ga. 578, 585, 66 S.E. 788 (1909).

[16]Scott v. Scott, 192 Ga. 370 (1), 15 S.E.2d 416 (1941).

[17]Dade Coal Co. v. Haslett, 83 Ga. 549, 10 S.E. 435 (1889).

[18]Maddox v. Hall County, 162 Ga. App. 371 (1), 291 S.E.2d 442 (1982); Turner v. Evans, 251 Ga. 486, 306 S.E.2d 921 (1983).

[19]Hughes v. Montgomery Contracting Co., 189 Ga. App. 814, 377 S.E.2d 723 (1989).

[Section 10:8]

[1]United States v. Athens Armory, 35 Ga. 344, 362 (1868).

[2]Rule 475-3-.10(6) of the State Board of Pardon and Paroles; Morris v. Hartsfield, 186 Ga. 171, 174 (3), 197 S.E. 251 (1938).

and the Georgia Constitution.[3] The Constitution of 1983 states, "Except as otherwise provided in this Paragraph, the State Board of Pardons and Paroles shall be vested with the power of executive clemency, including the powers to grant reprieves, pardons, and paroles; to commute penalties; to remove disabilities imposed by law; and to remit any part of a sentence for any offense against the state after conviction."

The Rules of the State Board of Pardons and Paroles in Rule 475-3-.10 provides in part that a pardon which does not imply innocence may be granted after an applicant "has completed his full sentence obligation, including serving any probated sentence and paying any fine, and who has thereafter completed five years without any criminal involvement."[4] The waiting period "may be waived if [it] is shown to be detrimental to the applicant's livelihood."[5] The Board has forms which are available on request.

Conditional releases are applicable to convictions before July 1, 1964, and "[c]onsideration for conditional release is automatic when the [defendant] has served his minimum sentence."[6]

"The Board automatically restores civil and political rights to a felony parolee or Youthful Offender Conditional Releasee upon discharge from supervision if he has no other sentence to serve or pending criminal charge against him."[7]

Nevertheless, aside from the exception set out in the previous two paragraphs, a convicted felon's civil rights are not restored until he makes an application for such restoration.[8]

O.C.G.A. § 42-9-54 provides in part as follows: "All pardons shall relieve those pardoned from civil and political disabilities imposed because of their convictions."

It has been held that the removal of disabilities after a felony conviction restores a citizen's civil and political rights, including the restoration of the right to vote, to hold public office, and to sit on a jury.[9] In addition, an unconditional pardon of a defendant's aggravated sodomy conviction obviates the duty of a convicted sex offender to register as a sex offender.[10]

An opinion of the Attorney General concluded that the civil disabilities which may be restored are the customary civil rights ordinarily belonging to a citizen of the state which are generally

---

[3]Ga. Const. 1983, Art. IV, § II, ¶ II(a).

[4]Rule 475-3-.10(3)(b), State Board of Pardons and Paroles.

[5]Rule 475-3-.10(3)(b), State Board of Pardons and Paroles.

[6]Rule 475-3-.10(4), State Board of Pardons and Paroles.

[7]Rule 475-3-.10(6)(a), State Board of Pardons and Paroles.

[8]Rule 475-3-.10(6), State Board of Pardons and Paroles.

[9]Morton v. State, 166 Ga. App. 170, 171, 303 S.E.2d 509 (1983).

[10]State v. Davis, 303 Ga. 684, 814 S.E.2d 701 (2018).

recognized to be the right to hold office, to vote, and to serve on a jury.[11] However, a pardon does not restore a person to an office he forfeited as a result of a conviction,[12] although it does restore a convicted person to a general eligibility to hold office;[13] and apparently it does not affect the right to operate a motor vehicle or to practice a profession nor does it affect extraordinary rights granted and regulated by the state under its police power.[14] If an attorney is disbarred because of a criminal conviction, he is not entitled to be reinstated automatically as a lawyer because he received a pardon, but a pardon is one of the factors which may be considered if he seeks readmission to the bar.

If a person has served his sentence and/or his probation for a criminal offense, he does not need a pardon or restoration of rights in order to register and vote.[15]

Under the provisions of O.C.G.A. § 16-11-131(c), a convicted felon who later receives a pardon is not thereafter guilty of violating this statute which makes it a felony for a convicted felon to have possession of a firearm.[16] Generally, the same result is applied under 18 U.S.C.A. § 922(g),[17] if the defendant's civil rights have been restored under federal law. However, in *Beecham v. United States*,[18] the United States Supreme Court held that a defendant could be convicted under 18 U.S.C.A. § 922(g), which prohibits the possession of a firearm by a convicted felon, if his civil rights have not been restored under federal law, even though he has obtained a restoration of his civil rights in a state proceeding.

See § 28:23, infra, on civil suits by prisoners.

§ 10:9   May a person convicted of a felony serve on a trial jury?

O.C.G.A. § 15-12-163 provides that either the state or the defense may object to a juror serving if "the juror has been convicted of a felony . . . and the juror's civil rights have not been restored. . . ."

In *Dodys v. State*,[1] the court held that when a question arises as to whether or not a prospective juror has been convicted of a

---

[11]Op. Atty. Gen., 1954, p. 506.

[12]Hulgan v. Thornton, 205 Ga. 753, 55 S.E.2d 115 (1949).

[13]Morris v. Hartsfield, 186 Ga. 171, 197 S.E. 251 (1938).

[14]Op. Atty. Gen., 1954, p. 506.

[15]Op. Atty. Gen., 84-33, p. 71.

[16]Fain v. State, 259 Ga. 708, 386 S.E.2d 144 (1989).

[17]Cf. United States v. Swanson, 947 F.2d 914 (11th Cir. 1991). But see United States v. Jones, 993 F.2d 1131 (4th Cir. 1993).

[18]Beecham v. United States, 511 U.S. 368, 114 S.Ct. 1669, 128 L.Ed.2d 383 (1994).

[Section 10:9]

[1]Dodys v. State, 73 Ga. App. 483, 486 (1), 37 S.E.2d 173 (1946).

crime involving moral turpitude, it is immaterial how the trial judge determines whether or not there has been such a conviction and a certified copy of the conviction is not required.

It has been held that there are at least three methods by which a person who has been convicted of a felony may serve on a jury: (1) a pardon is granted by the State Board of Pardon and Paroles;[2] (2) a removal of disabilities is granted by the State Board of Pardon and Paroles;[3] and (3) upon the discretion of the court. The distinction between a pardon and the removal of disabilities has been pointed out in *Harrison v. Wigington*,[4] however, both a pardon and a removal of disabilities are sufficient to restore a person's civil and political rights, which includes the right to sit on a trial jury.

It has been held that under certain circumstances a convicted felon may serve on a jury even without a pardon or removal of disabilities. Typically, the defense must have knowledge of the conviction and fail to raise an objection upon the receipt of that knowledge.[5] O.C.G.A. § 15-12-60 states that a person convicted of a felony shall not be eligible to serve on a grand jury. The common law, however, has disqualified jurors on the basis of a felony conviction.[6] In *Williams v. State*,[7] the court noted that in the absence of any provision by the General Assembly, "a jury trial in Georgia, to be valid, must be governed by the same rules as prevailed in England at the time . . . [Georgia] adopted . . . [the] constitution." The common law in England at that time entitled a citizen to a trial before 12 "upright and intelligent" peers. Because the convicted felon was not considered to meet the "upright" standard, a new trial was ordered in that case. However, the court expressly stated that one could be found by a court to be upright and intelligent even if convicted of a crime involving moral turpitude "because it has sometimes happened that men who afterward became model citizens had in their youth committed offenses which were fully expiated or atoned for by a subsequent course of exemplary rectitude."[8] This standard was upheld in *Bennett v. State*.[9]

---

[2]Rule 475-3-.10(3), State Board of Pardon and Paroles.

[3]Rule 475-3-.10(6), State Board of Pardon and Paroles.

[4]Harrison v. Wigington, 269 Ga. 388, 497 S.E.2d 568 (1998).

[5]Bennett v. State, 262 Ga. 149, 150, 414 S.E.2d 218 (1992); Wright v. Davis, 184 Ga. 846, 853, 193 S.E. 757 (1937).

[6]Williams v. State, 12 Ga. App. 337 (3), 77 S.E. 189 (1913).

[7]Williams v. State, 12 Ga. App. 337, 339, 77 S.E. 189 (1913).

[8]Williams v. State, 12 Ga. App. 337, 77 S.E. 189 (1913).

[9]Bennett v. State, 262 Ga. 149, 150, 414 S.E.2d 218 (1992).

In *Bennett v. State*,[10] the juror had only one felony conviction, traffic-offense habitual-violator, from several years before. The court held that the conviction was not severe enough nor recent enough to disqualify the juror where the defense knew of the conviction during the trial and failed to raise a valid objection. In *Wright v. State*,[11] a juror who was twice convicted of car theft obtained a place on the jury by fraudulently impersonating another. The court held that the defendant was denied the right to a jury "composed entirely of upright men." Important distinctions between *Bennett* and *Wright* are the nature of the juror's convictions, the number of convictions, the manner in which jury service was obtained, and the point in time at which the defense knew of the convictions.

Conversely, a conviction by another state or the federal government does not disqualify a citizen from service on a Georgia jury. In considering the issue of whether a convicted felon is competent to serve on a jury, the Georgia Supreme Court has held that the disqualification of a juror in Georgia's courts may not be determined by the law and judgment of another state or the federal government.[12] Also, a juror is not considered incompetent when he is charged with a felony in a pending case.[13]

See § 10:8, supra, on restoration of civil rights. See Annotation, "Disqualification or Exemption of Juror for Conviction of or Prosecution for Criminal Offense," 75 A.L.R. 5th 295 (2000). See § 18:34, infra, on excusal of convicted felon.

---

[10]Bennett v. State, 262 Ga. 149, 151, 414 S.E.2d 218 (1992).

[11]Wright v. Davis, 184 Ga. 846, 853, 193 S.E. 757 (1937).

[12]Brady v. State, 199 Ga. 566, 575, 34 S.E.2d 849 (1945).

[13]Turnipseed v. State, 54 Ga. App. 442, 444, 188 S.E. 260 (1936).

Part III

PRE-TRIAL JUDICIAL PROCEEDINGS

Chapter 11

Pre-Indictment Proceedings

KeyCite®: Cases and other legal materials listed in KeyCite Scope can be researched through the KeyCite service on Westlaw®. Use KeyCite to check citations for form, parallel references, prior and later history, and comprehensive citator information, including citations to other decisions and secondary materials.

---

§ 11:1   First appearance

Rule 26.1 of the Uniform Rules for the Superior Courts provides as follows:

"Immediately following any arrest but not later than 48 hours if the arrest was without a warrant, or 72 hours following an arrest with a warrant, unless the accused has made bond in the meantime, the arresting officer or the law officer having custody of the accused shall present the accused in person before a magistrate or other judicial officer for first appearance.

"At the first appearance, the judicial officer shall:

"(A) Inform the accused of the charges;

"(B) Inform the accused of the right to remain silent, that any statement made may be used against the accused, and of the right to the presence and advice of an attorney, either retained or appointed;

"(C) Determine whether or not the accused desires and is in

need of an appointed attorney and, if appropriate, advise the accused of the necessity for filing a written application;

"(D) Inform the accused of his or her right to a later pre-indictment commitment hearing, unless the first appearance covers the commitment hearing issues, and inform the accused that giving a bond shall be a waiver of the right to a commitment hearing;[1]

"(E) In the case of a warrantless arrest, make a fair and reliable determination of the probable cause for the arrest unless a warrant has been issued before the first appearance;

"(F) Inform the accused that of the right to grand jury indictment in felony cases and the right to trial by jury, and when the next grand jury will convene; [In State Court, see State Court Rule 26.1(F).]

"(G) Inform the accused that if he or she desires to waive these rights and plead guilty, then the accused shall so notify the judge or the law officer having custody, who shall in turn notify the judge.

"(H) Set the amount of bail if the offense is not one bailable only by a superior court judge, or so inform the accused if it is."

In *Ellison v. State*,[2] the court held "that obtaining an arrest warrant from a neutral magistrate within 48 hours of a warrantless arrest, even without an adversarial hearing, satisfies the statute."

In *County of Riverside v. McLaughlin*,[3] the United States Supreme Court held that the Fourth Amendment requires a prompt judicial probable cause hearing for a person arrested without a warrant. The court went further and held that such a hearing within 48 hours of arrest is presumed to be valid but if there is not such a hearing within 48 hours, "the burden shifts to the government to demonstrate the existence of a bona fide emergency or other extraordinary circumstance." Intervening weekends are not such extraordinary circumstances.[4]

[Section 11:1]

[1]The alternative Uniform Magistrate Court Rule 25.1(4) is similar to Uniform Superior Court Rule 26.1(D) but adds that "a magistrate may in his or her discretion hold a commitment hearing pursuant to Rule 25.2(A) ." The author points out the contradiction between the two rules, but it appears it is within the magistrate's discretion whether an accused on bond can have a preliminary hearing.

[2]Ellison v. State, 242 Ga. App. 636, 637 (1), 530 S.E.2d 524 (2000).

[3]County of Riverside v. McLaughlin, 500 U.S. 44, 111 S.Ct. 1661, 114 L.Ed.2d 49 (1991).

[4]Cf. AM v. Jay Martin, Zell Miller and Fulton County, Civil Action File No. 1:96-CV-2316-JEC, U. S. D. C., Northern District of Ga., Atlanta Division (1/23/98).

In *Powell v. Nevada*,[5] the Supreme Court held that *McLaughlin* applies retroactively to all cases on direct review or not yet final. The date of the *McLaughlin* decision was May 13, 1991. Powell had been arrested on November 3, 1989. A magistrate did not find probable cause to hold him for a preliminary hearing until November 7 and he was not personally brought before a magistrate until November 13. On November 7, Powell had made a statement which officers used against him at his trial. The court pointed out that the delay was presumptively unreasonable under "*McLaughlin's* 48-hour rule." The decision of the Nevada Supreme Court was vacated and the case was remanded.

In *Taylor v. Chitwood*,[6] the court held that "the failure to hold a timely first appearance hearing provides no basis for release once the defendant has been indicted and had an opportunity to seek bail." In *State v. Gilstrap*,[7] the court held that "the remedy for failing to hold a probable cause hearing within the statutory period is a release from custody and not a dismissal of the charges."

In *O'Kelley v. State*,[8] the Georgia Supreme Court overruled *Ross v. State*[9] which had held that the Sixth Amendment right to counsel did not attach at a first appearance hearing before a magistrate where the only issues to resolve were scheduling an arraignment on a date when the defendant would actually confront a prosecutor. In *O'Kelley*,[10] the court concluded that while "often not a critical stage of a criminal proceeding in its own right requiring the actual presence of a criminal defense attorney [an initial appearance] is a formal legal proceeding wherein the Sixth Amendment right to counsel attaches." However, the court noted that while the right may attach at such a hearing, that does not mean that counsel must be present and available at the hearing. The defendant can elect to proceed without counsel but should the defendant request counsel, the magistrate would then have to suspend the hearing until such time as counsel is available.

§ 11:2 General considerations of probable cause hearing

At common law, it was customary for an accused and the witnesses to be brought before a justice of the peace soon after ar-

---

[5]Powell v. Nevada, 511 U.S. 79, 114 S.Ct. 1280, 128 L.Ed.2d 1 (1994).

[6]Taylor v. Chitwood, 266 Ga. 793 (1), 471 S.E.2d 511 (1996).

[7]State v. Gilstrap, 230 Ga. App. 281, 282, 495 S.E.2d 885 (1998). Cf. Chiasson v. State, 250 Ga. App. 63, 64 (2), 549 S.E.2d 503 (2001).

[8]O'Kelley v. State, 278 Ga. 564, 604 S.E.2d 509 (2004).

[9]Ross v. State, 254 Ga. 22 (3) (b), 326 S.E.2d 194 (1985).

[10]O'Kelley v. State, 278 Ga. 564, 604 S.E.2d 509 (2004).

rest in order to determine whether there was reason to believe that the person arrested had committed a crime.[1] Today, under Georgia statutory law, the magistrate holding the commitment hearing decides whether there is sufficient reason to suspect the guilt of the accused and to bind him over for trial.[2] It has been held that after a magistrate has conducted such a hearing and an accusation has been filed, a state court may not transfer the case back for another preliminary hearing.[3]

From a practical standpoint, a preliminary hearing provides a defendant with an opportunity for discovery.[4] It is difficult to overemphasize the importance of the discovery aspect of the preliminary hearing. The hearing affords defense counsel the opportunity to subpoena potentially hostile witnesses and to question them under oath. It has been held that since the magistrate *"shall hear all legal evidence submitted* by either party,"[5] the hearing is imperfect where the committing magistrate prevents defense counsel from questioning subpoenaed witnesses who may be potential witnesses for the state. Such action, however, on the part of a committing magistrate is not a basis for habeas corpus before indictment[6] and not a ground for a motion to quash the indictment.[7] However, if the magistrate refuses to permit defense counsel to fully cross-examine a prosecution witness, the

---

[Section 11:2]

[1]Gerstein v. Pugh, 420 U.S. 103, 114-15, 95 S.Ct. 854, 43 L.Ed.2d 54 (1975).

[2]O.C.G.A. § 17-7-23.

[3]State v. Johnson, 195 Ga. App. 855, 395 S.E.2d 67 (1990).

[4]Manor v. State, 221 Ga. 866, 869, 148 S.E.2d 305 (1966), overruled by State v. Middlebrooks, 236 Ga. 52, 54, 222 S.E.2d 343 (1976). See the dissenting opinion of Justice Ingram in Phillips v. Stynchcombe, 231 Ga. 430, 441, 202 S.E.2d 26 (1973).

[5]O.C.G.A. § 17-7-28 (emphasis added). However, in Day v. State, 237 Ga. 538, 539, 228 S.E.2d 913 (1976), the court held that the trial judge was not authorized to grant a motion to quash an indictment or to grant a new trial where defense counsel was not permitted by the magistrate to examine potential witnesses for the state who had been subpoenaed by the defendant.

In Baldwin v. Sapp, 238 Ga. 597, 234 S.E.2d 513 (1977), the defendant in a criminal case filed a pre-indictment habeas corpus complaining about the preliminary hearing which had been conducted. The justice of the peace after hearing one prosecution and one defense witness declined to hear other witnesses subpoenaed by the defendant, found probable cause and bound the defendant over. The appellate court concluded that this was harmless error. However, the court pointed out that if the defendant contends that he was injured, "this may be established only upon the trial of the case."

[6]Baldwin v. Sapp, 238 Ga. 597, 598, 234 S.E.2d 513 (1977).

[7]Day v. State, 237 Ga. 538, 228 S.E.2d 913 (1976). In Kurtz, "Criminal Law, Annual Survey of Georgia Law," 29 Mercer L. Rev. 55, 72 (1977), the author concludes that the effect of the Day and Baldwin cases is to make "misconduct at a commitment hearing . . . nonreviewable, so long as an indictment can be obtained." Hope-

testimony of that witness would not later be available to the state if the witness is inaccessible.[8] Defense counsel should consider subpoenaing and interrogating all witnesses from whom he may later have difficulty getting a statement. A defendant does not forfeit his right to a fair trial by insisting on a preliminary hearing or by subpoenaing the victims of the crime.[9]

Defense counsel needs to prepare the defendant, and perhaps his family, for the preliminary hearing well in advance. The defendant should understand that the prosecution need not prove his guilt beyond a reasonable doubt and that if there is any conflict in the testimony as to the accused's guilt, he will probably be bound over. Under most circumstances, it is to the defendant's advantage not to testify at the preliminary hearing. If he testifies inaccurately at this early stage of the proceedings, his testimony may be used against him at some future time.

From the standpoint of the prosecution, it may be best to introduce just enough evidence at the preliminary hearing to make out a prima facie case. The prosecutor, at this time, is not obligated to inform the defendant of all the evidence which may be available to the state. However, the prosecutor may want to have a witness testify at the hearing if he is not likely to be available for trial.[10]

Generally, counsel should be sure that a court reporter is present.[11] See § 11:4, infra, and also § 17:9, infra, on the necessity of a transcript.

However, Rule 26.2 of the Uniform Rules for the Superior Courts requires the judicial officer to "[c]ause an accurate record to be made of the testimony and proceeding by any reliable method." In the absence of a court reporter, any person who was present at the preliminary hearing may testify at the trial to impeach the testimony of a witness who testified at the commitment hearing.[12] O.C.G.A. § 24-8-804(b)(1) provides generally that the rule against hearsay will not apply to the testimony of a witness previously given at a prior hearing if the witness is legally unavailable to appear and the party against whom the testimony is being offered was present at the time the prior testimony was given and had an opportunity to examine the witness.[13]

---

fully, this is an exaggeration.

[8]See California v. Green, 399 U.S. 149, 90 S.Ct. 1930, 26 L.Ed.2d 489 (1970).

[9]Wright v. State, 164 Ga. App. 587, 588, 298 S.E.2d 294 (1982).

[10]LaCount v. State, 237 Ga. 181, 182 (1), 227 S.E.2d 31 (1976).

[11]But see § 28:7, n. 1, infra, on the right of an indigent to a copy of a transcript of the preliminary hearing.

[12]See Hollis v. State, 77 Ga. 74 (1886).

[13]See Goger, *Georgia Handbook on Criminal Evidence* § 8:36 (2017 ed.) on former testimony.

Under present Georgia law, a defendant is entitled to a copy of the record made at a preliminary hearing upon paying of costs.[14]

Defense counsel may wish to waive a preliminary hearing in extreme cases, such as where a key prosecution witness resides out of state or is unlikely to be available for trial. If a defendant waives his right to a commitment hearing,[15] there is apparently no way in which the prosecutor can successfully insist on a hearing.

See the discussion by the United States Supreme Court in *County of Riverside v. McLaughlin* in § 11:1, supra, on the necessity of a prompt probable cause hearing in case of a warrantless arrest.

For motions for a preliminary hearing, see Studdard, *Daniel's Georgia Criminal Trial Practice Forms* (2018–2019 ed.), §§ 10:1 et seq.

§ 11:3   The rule on commitment hearings by a court of inquiry

Rule 26.2 of the Uniform Rules for the Superior Courts provides as follows:

"(A) At the commitment hearing by the court of inquiry, the judicial officer shall perform the following duties:

"(1) Explain the probable cause purpose of the hearing;

"(2) Repeat to the accused the rights explained at the first appearance;

"(3) Determine whether the accused intends to plead 'guilty,' or 'not guilty,' or waives the commitment hearing;

"(4) If the accused intends to plead guilty or waives the hearing, the court shall immediately bind the entire case over to the court having jurisdiction of the most serious offense charged;

"(5) If the accused pleads 'not guilty' the court shall immediately proceed to conduct the commitment hearing unless, for good cause shown, the hearing is continued to a later scheduled date;

"(6) Cause an accurate record to be made of the testimony and proceeding by any reliable method.

"(7) The judicial officer shall bind the entire case over to the court having jurisdiction of the most serious offense for which probable cause has been shown by sufficient evidence and dismiss any charge for which probable cause has not been shown.

"(8) On each case which is bound over, a memorandum of the

---

[14]Barnes v. State, 184 Ga. App. 513 (2), 361 S.E.2d 876 (1987).

[15]O.C.G.A. § 17-6-16.

commitment shall be entered on the warrant by the judicial officer. The warrant, bail bond, and all other papers pertaining to the case shall be forwarded to the clerk of the appropriate court having jurisdiction over the offense for delivery to the district attorney. Each bail bond shall contain the full name, telephone number, residence, business and mailing address(es) of the accused and any surety.

"(9) A copy of the record of any testimony and the proceedings of the first appearance and the commitment hearing shall be provided to the proper prosecuting officer and to the accused upon payment of the reasonable cost for preparation of the record.

"(10) A judicial officer, conducting a commitment hearing, is without jurisdiction to make final disposition of the case or cases at the hearing by imposing any fine or punishment, except where the only charge arising out of the transaction at issue is the violation of a county ordinance.

"(B) At the commitment hearing, the following procedures shall be utilized:

"(1) The rules of evidence shall apply except that hearsay may be allowed;

"(2) The prosecuting entity shall have the burden of proving probable cause; and may be represented by a law enforcement officer, a district attorney, a solicitor, a private attorney or otherwise as is customary in that court;

"(3) The accused may be represented by an attorney or may appear pro se; and,

"(4) The accused shall be permitted to introduce evidence."

O.C.G.A. §§ 24-1-2(d) and 17-7-28 both provide that hearsay "shall" be admissible at preliminary or commitment hearings.

§ 11:4   Outline of statutory procedure of probable cause hearing

Little has changed in the practice and procedure during a preliminary hearing since the adoption of U.S.C.R. 26-2. Therefore, the following material is presented largely as it was before the adoption of the Rules. The Georgia statutes outline the appropriate procedures for preliminary or commitment hearings. Essentially, any judge of the superior court, or a state court, a magistrate, any officer who has the criminal jurisdiction of a magistrate, and any mayor, recorder, or other proper officer presiding in any court of a municipal corporation may hold a preliminary or commitment hearing.[1] Likewise, a probate judge may hold a preliminary hearing.[2]

After the defendant has been arrested, the officer shall carry the prisoner before the most convenient and accessible judicial officer authorized to hear the case. However, if the defendant objects and there are no grounds for suspicion of improper motive, the arresting officer shall carry the defendant before another judicial officer.[3] Every person arrested under a warrant shall be brought before a committing officer promptly, and in any event within 72 hours after arrest.[4] It is necessary to bring the accused before a magistrate within 72 hours after arrest, but it is not necessary that the commitment or preliminary hearing take place within 72 hours.[5]

Where a defendant is indicted prior to arrest, no commitment hearing need be held.[6] If a defendant is arrested without a warrant, he must be brought before magistrate without delay and within a reasonable time. The statute provides that if the accused is not carried before a magistrate within 48 hours of his warrantless arrest, he shall be released.[7] However, it has been held that such delay will not automatically render a confession inadmissible, even though it is given while the defendant is illegally imprisoned.[8] But see the discussion by the United States Supreme Court in *Riverside County v. McLaughlin* in § 11:1, supra, on the necessity of a prompt probable cause hearing in the case of a warrantless arrest.

If a defendant wishes to assert his right to a commitment hear-

---

[Section 11:4]

[1]O.C.G.A. § 17-7-20, O.C.G.A. § 17-7-22. Apparently, any such judge may associate one or more magistrates to sit with him. O.C.G.A. § 17-7-21.

[2]O.C.G.A. § 17-7-20.

[3]O.C.G.A. § 17-4-21.

[4]O.C.G.A. § 17-4-26. This statute also provides that if the officer fails to give the accused advance notice of the time and place of the hearing, the defendant shall be released.

[5]Dodson v. Grimes, 220 Ga. 269, 270 (1), 138 S.E.2d 311 (1964); Tidwell v. Paxton, 282 Ga. 641, 651 S.E.2d 714 (2007).

[6]See Cannon v. Grimes, 223 Ga. 35, 36 (3), 153 S.E.2d 445 (1967). See Baldivia v. State, 267 Ga. App. 266, 273(5)(a), 599 S.E.2d 188 (2004) (once an indictment is returned, probable cause is established and need for preliminary hearing vanishes).

[7]O.C.G.A. § 17-4-62. Cf. Rule 5(c) of the Federal Rules of Criminal Procedure.

[8]Blake v. State, 109 Ga. App. 636, 137 S.E.2d 49 (1964); Mace v. State, 144 Ga. App. 496, 498 (2), 241 S.E.2d 615 (1978). In *Mace*, the court pointed out that in determining whether or not a statement had been voluntarily given, the court should consider the legality, duration and conditions of the detention. Cf. § 5:4, supra.

However, in State v. Benbo, 174 Mont. 252, 570 P.2d 894 (1977), the court excluded an incriminating statement and in effect adopted the McNabb rule. See § 5:4, supra, and its footnotes.

ing, he must do so promptly and before indictment. He may file a habeas corpus petition based on the denial of a preliminary hearing.[9]

Both defendant and prosecutor shall be given a reasonable time to prepare for the hearing. A defendant, by statute, cannot be forced to a preliminary hearing without an attorney if there is a reasonable probability of his securing counsel without too great a delay.[10] If, however, the defendant appears before a magistrate without benefit of counsel, and he has not waived his right to counsel at the preliminary hearing, error may not be raised until such time as the defendant is found guilty.[11]

The magistrate has the responsibility for setting time and place of the hearing.[12] O.C.G.A. § 17-7-25 provides for the subpoenaing of witnesses who live in the county.[13] However, under the confrontation clause of the Sixth Amendment, it seems that there must be a right to subpoena witnesses from outside the county.

If the defendant testifies at the hearing, he is subject to cross-examination. Failure to testify creates no presumption against him nor may it be the subject of comment.

According to O.C.G.A. § 17-7-28, the court shall hear all legal evidence submitted by either party.[14] However, despite the clear language of the statute, the Georgia Supreme Court has held that the refusal of a magistrate to permit defense counsel's questioning of subpoenaed witnesses is not grounds for a motion to quash the indictment.[15]

Formerly, a Georgia statute required that if a defendant was charged with a felony, the court had to cause an abstract of all the evidence to be made.[16] But the failure of the magistrate to comply with the statute did not render the commitment or later indictment void.[17] Rule 26.2 of the Uniform Rules for the Superior Courts provides that "[a] copy of the record of any testimony and

[9]McClure v. Hopper, 234 Ga. 45, 48, 214 S.E.2d 503 (1975).

[10]O.C.G.A. § 17-7-24.

[11]State v. Houston, 234 Ga. 721, 218 S.E.2d 13 (1975); State v. Hightower, 236 Ga. 58, 222 S.E.2d 333 (1976); Pointer v. Texas, 380 U.S. 400, 85 S.Ct. 1065, 13 L.Ed.2d 923 (1965).

[12]O.C.G.A. § 17-7-20.

[13]O.C.G.A. § 17-7-25.

[14]O.C.G.A. § 17-7-28.

[15]Day v. State, 237 Ga. 538, 228 S.E.2d 913 (1976).

[16]GCA § 27-406. This section was

not carried forward into the O.C.G.A. See § 28:7, infra, on the right of an indigent defendant to a copy of a transcript of his preliminary hearing. In Graham v. State, 147 Ga. App. 202, 248 S.E.2d 332 (1978), the court said that a defendant is not entitled to an abstract or transcript of a committal hearing.

[17]Miller v. State, 224 Ga. 627 (1), 163 S.E.2d 730 (1968); Chenault v. State, 234 Ga. 216, 221, 215 S.E.2d 223 (1975).

In Nettles v. State, 144 Ga. App. 473 (1), 241 S.E.2d 589 (1978), the court held that defendant did not have

the proceedings of the first appearance and the commitment hearing shall be provided to the proper prosecuting officer and to the accused upon payment of the reasonable cost for preparation of the record." However, as a general proposition, the failure to provide the defendant with a copy of the transcript from his preliminary hearing will not constitute grounds for reversal unless it can be shown that such can be attributed to the state and resulted in unfair prejudice to the defense.[18]

The purpose of the preliminary hearing is to determine "whether there is sufficient reason to suspect the guilt of the accused." If there is probable cause, it is the duty of the magistrate to bind the defendant over.[19] If evidence indicates that the defendant is guilty of an offense other than that charged, he may be bound over for the other offense.[20] The form of a commitment is set out in the Code.[21]

It has been held that the jurisdiction of the committing magistrate is to determine whether probable cause exists. Thus, he has no authority to dismiss a warrant on the ground that it was not issued by a neutral and detached magistrate or to rule on a question of res judicata.[22]

Not only does a committing magistrate have authority to bind a defendant over to a higher court, but if the accused is bound over, the judge may require witnesses for either or both parties to post a bond to insure their appearance at trial or to have them confined until trial.[23] If a defendant is bound over to the superior court, the magistrate must endorse, on the warrant, the name of

---

to be furnished an abstract or transcript of the hearing. But in Roberts v. LaVallee, 389 U.S. 40, 88 S.Ct. 194, 19 L.Ed.2d 41 (1967), the court considered a New York law which provided that a transcript of a preliminary hearing be furnished a defendant on payment of costs. As an indigent, the defendant requested a free transcript. The defendant's request was denied. He was convicted and sentenced. In a habeas corpus action the court held that the denial of a free transcript to the indigent defendant violated the equal protection clause provision of the federal constitution.

[18]See Joyner v. State, 278 Ga. App. 60, 628 S.E.2d 186 (2006) (failure to provide manuscript of commitment hearing which defendant needed to impeach police witness at trial was not attributable to state and no prejudice shown where there was "ample" evidence to support conviction).

[19]O.C.G.A. § 17-7-23.

[20]O.C.G.A. § 17-7-29.

[21]O.C.G.A. § 17-7-30.

[22]Bradshaw v. State, 163 Ga. App. 819, 820 (2), 296 S.E.2d 119 (1982).

[23]O.C.G.A. § 17-7-26, O.C.G.A. § 17-7-27. These statutes apparently do not violate the federal constitution. See Hurtado v. United States, 410 U.S. 578, 93 S.Ct. 1157, 35 L.Ed.2d 508 (1973) (reh'g denied). This case also held that a witness in custody for a federal prosecution is not entitled to be paid the $20 per day witness fee until the trial begins.

each witness for the state.[24] If the defendant is bound over and not released on bond, the commitment shall be given to the officer to whom custody of the prisoner is delivered. The officer shall then deliver the commitment, along with the defendant, to the jailer. The warrant and other documents shall be delivered to the clerk of the court having jurisdiction of the case. The clerk shall then forward the papers to the district attorney.[25] If the district attorney decides to dismiss the case without filing an accusation or seeking an indictment, "he or she shall file a notice of such fact with the clerk of court having jurisdiction over the offense." The clerk must transmit the notice to the Georgia Crime Information Center within 30 days.[26]

Lastly, it should be noted that a defendant may waive his right to a preliminary hearing if he so desires.[27] No defendant is entitled to be discharged on a writ of habeas corpus because of an informality in a commitment proceeding if the statutory provisions have essentially been met.[28]

§ 11:5   Failure to have probable cause hearing at which defendant is represented by counsel

In *Coleman v. Alabama*,[1] two defendants charged with assault with intent to murder were not represented by counsel at the preliminary hearing. The Supreme Court concluded that the preliminary hearing was a critical stage in Alabama's criminal procedure and as such required the presence of counsel.

In *Gerstein v. Pugh*,[2] the Supreme Court held, that because of the non-adversary character of the Florida procedure, preliminary hearing was not a critical stage in the prosecution. The court noted that the Fourth Amendment requires a state to provide a fair and reliable determination of probable cause by a judicial officer as a condition of any significant restraint.

In *Coleman v. Alabama*, the court noted the following benefits are available where counsel is present at preliminary hearing: (1) an opportunity to expose a fatal weakness in the case which might lead to a dismissal, (2) a means of gathering evidence to use for impeachment purposes at trial, (3) a means of preserving testimony favorable to the defendant, (4) an opportunity to discover the prosecution's case and thus aid the preparation of a defense, and (5) an opportunity to make arguments for the

---

[24]O.C.G.A. § 17-7-31.

[25]O.C.G.A. § 17-7-32.

[26]O.C.G.A. § 17-7-32.

[27]O.C.G.A. § 17-6-16.

[28]O.C.G.A. § 17-7-34.

[Section 11:5]

[1]Coleman v. Alabama, 399 U.S. 1, 90 S.Ct. 1999, 26 L.Ed.2d 387 (1970).

[2]Gerstein v. Pugh, 420 U.S. 103, 95 S.Ct. 854, 43 L.Ed.2d 54 (1975).

defendant on such matters as the necessity of psychiatric examination and/or bond. However, the court noted that the defendant's convictions would be reversed on remand only if the failure to have counsel at the preliminary hearing was shown to have been harmful to the defendant.

In *Mitchell v. State,*[3] the Georgia Court of Appeals found that several benefits were not lost by a defendant due to the absence of counsel at the preliminary hearing, including the opportunity to (1) gather impeachment evidence, (2) secure and preserve favorable testimony which may be unavailable at trial, (3) discover the state's case, and (4) assert arguments about the need for a psychiatric examination or a bond.

The Georgia Supreme Court has also concluded that a preliminary hearing is a critical stage in a criminal prosecution.[4] However, an illegal arrest or detention does not necessarily void a later conviction. Thus, detention without a valid preliminary hearing will not prevent a grand jury indictment,[5] and the Supreme Court has said that failure to have a commitment hearing is not reversible error nor a required step in a felony prosecution.[6] Once an indictment has been returned, it has been held that a court does not have jurisdiction to hold a commitment hearing.[7]

Furthermore, in *Bright v. State,*[8] a death penalty case, the court held that failure to have a preliminary hearing does not require reversal of a conviction.

In *State v. Hightower,*[9] the defendant had a preliminary hearing at which he was not represented by counsel. The defendant filed a motion to quash the indictment for failure to have counsel. While the court concluded that it was error for the defendant not to have representation at the hearing, the error was said to have been harmless beyond a reasonable doubt, since it did not contribute to the accused's conviction.

---

[3]Mitchell v. State, 173 Ga. App. 560, 561, 327 S.E.2d 537, 539 (1985).

[4]State v. Houston, 234 Ga. 721, 723, 218 S.E.2d 13 (1975). In doing so, the court held that Georgia's preliminary hearing is more like that of Alabama (see Coleman v. Alabama, 399 U.S. 1, 90 S.Ct. 1999, 26 L.Ed.2d 387 (1970)) than that of Florida (see Gerstein v. Pugh, 420 U.S. 103, 95 S.Ct. 854, 43 L.Ed.2d 54 (1975)).

[5]State v. Houston, 234 Ga. 721, 724, 218 S.E.2d 13 (1975).

[6]State v. Middlebrooks, 236 Ga. 52, 222 S.E.2d 343 (1976). In this case, the defendant was not taken before a magistrate and not given a commitment hearing. He was indicted a few weeks later. Bridges v. State, 154 Ga. App. 811, 270 S.E.2d 60 (1980).

[7]First National Bank & Trust Co. v. State, 237 Ga. 112, 227 S.E.2d 20 (1976).

[8]Bright v. State, 265 Ga. 265, 278 (4), 455 S.E.2d 37 (1995).

[9]State v. Hightower, 236 Ga. 58, 222 S.E.2d 333 (1976). See Tarpkin v. State, 236 Ga. 67, 222 S.E.2d 364 (1976).

When a defendant is not represented by counsel at a commitment hearing and a habeas corpus is filed after conviction, the trial court must consider the facts of the case and determine whether the defendant waived his right to counsel.[10] If there was no such waiver, then the trial court must determine whether the error of lack of representation was harmless.

Based on the above cases, it is clear that the failure of a defendant to have a commitment hearing or the failure to have representation at such hearing provides no basis for an automatic quashing of an indictment or a reversal of a conviction.

In order to obtain any relief after conviction, a defendant must show that he was materially prejudiced by the lack of representation. Thus, if it can be shown that the defendant was deprived of an opportunity to impeach a state witness, secure favorable testimony or attain a psychiatric examination, the defendant could presumably obtain relief.[11]

See § 8:2, supra, on waiver of hearing by posting a bond.

§ 11:6 Dismissal or bind over from probable cause hearing

The judgment of the magistrate does not determine the guilt or innocence of the defendant. If the defendant is bound over to a court having jurisdiction to try him, he may raise all available defenses.[1] The Code sets out the form of the commitment which may be used when a defendant is bound over.[2] Under Georgia law, a defendant may be bound over for an offense not charged in the warrant providing the evidence demonstrates the violation.[3]

As a practical matter, a magistrate's decision not to bind a defendant over will probably end the prosecution in most cases. However, a finding of insufficient probable cause will not prevent a grand jury from later indicting the defendant for the same offense.[4]

---

[10]Hannah v. Stone, 236 Ga. 65, 222 S.E.2d 362 (1976).

[11]See Tarpkin v. State, 236 Ga. 67, 68, 222 S.E.2d 364 (1976).

[Section 11:6]

[1]See Hyden v. State, 40 Ga. 476, 478 (1869).

[2]O.C.G.A. § 17-7-30.

[3]O.C.G.A. § 17-7-29.

[4]Johnson v. State, 242 Ga. 822, 251 S.E.2d 563 (1979); Wells v. Stynchcombe, 231 Ga. 199, 200 S.E.2d 745 (1973). In Boyce v. State, 184 Ga. App. 578, 362 S.E.2d 229 (1987), aff'd, 258 Ga. 171, 366 S.E.2d 684 (1988), the Georgia Court of Appeals held that a defendant can still be indicted even if the court of inquiry finds no probable cause to commit. The dismissal of the charges at the preliminary hearing stage is irrelevant and inadmissible evidence as against the indictment. Also see Moore v. Commonwealth, 218 Va. 388, 237 S.E.2d 187 (1977).

§ 11:7   Judicial review of probable cause hearing

The right to a pre-indictment petition for habeas corpus exists where the accused is denied a commitment hearing.[1] No appeal is allowed from a judgment of a magistrate committing a defendant.[2] However, should it appear that the detention of the accused is unlawful, the remedy of a habeas petition is available.[3] A habeas corpus action for insufficient evidence to bind the defendant over is rendered moot if the defendant is indicted before the habeas corpus hearing.[4]

In *Spears v. Johnson*,[5] a petition for writ of habeas corpus was filed for failure to have a preliminary hearing. The trial judge took the matter under advisement after a hearing. After the hearing and before an order had been entered, the defendant was indicted. The trial judge then denied the writ on the ground that the indictment rendered the proceeding moot. The Georgia Supreme Court affirmed, pointing out that the return of the indictment established probable cause and the state did not have to make any additional showing of probable cause.

[Section 11:7]

[1]McClure v. Hopper, 234 Ga. 45, 48, 214 S.E.2d 503 (1975); Lang v. Baker, 248 Ga. 831, 286 S.E.2d 433 (1982).

[2]Harris v. Norris, 188 Ga. 610, 612, 4 S.E.2d 840 (1939).

[3]See Sanders v. Paschal, 186 Ga. 837, 199 S.E. 153 (1938).

[4]Walker v. City of Atlanta, 238 Ga. 723, 235 S.E.2d 28 (1977). Cf. Ross v. Lemacks, 264 Ga. 839, 452 S.E.2d 109 (1995).

[5]Spears v. Johnson, 256 Ga. 518, 350 S.E.2d 468 (1986); Pruitt v. State, 258 Ga. 583, 585 (2), 373 S.E.2d 192 (1988).

Chapter 12

Grand Jury

KeyCite®: Cases and other legal materials listed in KeyCite Scope can be researched through the KeyCite service on Westlaw®. Use KeyCite to check citations for form, parallel references, prior and later history, and comprehensive citator information, including citations to other decisions and secondary materials.

---

§ 12:1   Introduction

A significant number of indictments have been found to be invalid because of the composition of the grand jury, and apparently a still larger number would have been found to be defective if the defendant had attacked the composition prior to indictment. Thus, from the standpoint of the defense, an early challenge or objection to the grand jury cannot be overemphasized. These attacks on indictments have stimulated interest not only in the general composition of grand juries but also on the entire subject of the grand jury procedures.

The following material discusses some of the important aspects of the background of grand juries, the methods of their selection, objections and challenges to grand juries, their deliberation, and general procedures relating to the returning of indictments.

§ 12:2   Historical background

The grand jury is deeply rooted in the English common law. It has been said that the modern criminal grand jury had its origin in the Assize of Clarendon, issued by Henry II in 1166, which provided for a body of 12 men in each county whose duty was to report persons suspected of crimes. However, the grand jury gradually developed an independence from the king, and its proceedings became veiled in secrecy. It began to hear witnesses in secrecy, and representatives of the king were not permitted to be present when the witnesses were being examined or when the grand jury was deliberating. The grand jurors took an oath of secrecy, and judges ceased to examine them on their findings. It is said that the true independence of the grand jury was established in 1681 in the trial of Stephen College and in the trial of the Earl of Shaftsbury. The defendants in both of these cases were accused by the Crown of treason. The prosecution ordered the grand juries to hear witnesses in open court. After having done so, each of these grand juries demanded, and were granted, the right to examine the witnesses and to deliberate their findings in private. Both grand juries refused to indict.

Grand jury secrecy developed to protect jurors and accused persons from the tyranny of the king. The grand jury was brought to this country in much the same form as it existed in England, and the attitude of distrust for the power of government is reflected in the Fifth Amendment of the United States Constitution which requires grand jury sanction before a person can be tried for any serious crime.[1] However, the grand jury provision does not apply directly to a state criminal proceeding, nor does the due process clause of the Fourteenth Amendment make the provision applicable to the states.[2]

From a historical standpoint, the grand jury has been regarded as a shield to protect the innocent defendant accused of crime by law enforcement officers.[3] However, the influence of the prosecuting attorney on the grand jury has increased, and from a practi-

---

[Section 12:2]

[1]See In the Matter of Russo, 53 F.R.D. 564 (C.D.Cal.1971).

[2]Hurtado v. California, 110 U.S. 516, 4 S.Ct. 111, 28 L.Ed. 232 (1884). While the Georgia Constitution provides for grand jurors, it does not require a grand jury indictment before any criminal prosecution. Ga. Const. 1983, Art. I, § I, ¶ XI.

[3]See United States v. Mandujano, 425 U.S. 564, 96 S.Ct. 1768, 48

cal standpoint, much of the independence of the grand jury has been lost in the ordinary case.[4] Perhaps for these reasons, the use of the grand jury has been abolished in 22 states,[5] and grand jury proceedings have been severely criticized by legal writers.[6]

In Georgia, district attorneys have the duty to "attend on the grand juries, advise them in relation to matters of law, and swear and examine witnesses before them"[7] as well as to "draw up all indictments or presentments, when requested by the grand jury."[8] While it is said that the grand jury is but an arm of the superior court,[9] with the duty to make presentments of any violations of the law of which it has knowledge,[10] in most cases the knowledge they have about crimes comes to them largely from the district attorney.

The grand jury has been called an "engine for discovery against organized and far-reaching crime."[11] This attitude toward the grand jury is probably responsible for the legislature's authorization of "special grand juries," "special purpose grand juries," and "investigative grand juries" for certain counties.[12] Also, this attitude may be responsible for much of the opposition which has been voiced against the grand jury.[13]

See 38 C. J. S. Grand Juries § 1.

L.Ed.2d 212 (1976).

[4]See Hawthorne v. Director of Internal Revenue, 406 F.Supp. 1098, 1119 (E.D.Pa.1975). Judge Thornberry, in a concurring opinion in Martin v. Beto, 397 F.2d 741 (5th Cir. 1968), in considering pre-indictment publicity, said that today "the grand jury is an accusatory body which does not have to be impartial."

[5]See People v. Sears, 49 Ill.2d 14, 273 N.E.2d 380, 390 (1971).

[6]See Grand Jury Law & Practice § 9-1 (2d ed.) (2016).

[7]O.C.G.A. § 15-18-6(2). Also the State Attorney General may obtain indictments in any court when so requested by the governor. Ga. Const. 1983, Art. V, § III, ¶ IV; statutory provisions, see O.C.G.A. §§ 45-15-3 et seq.; Meredith v. State, 148 Ga. App. 853, 854 (1), 253 S.E.2d 220 (1979) (overruled on other grounds by, Hamm v. State, 294 Ga. 791, 756 S.E.2d 507 (2014)).

[8]O.C.G.A. § 15-18-6(4); A.B.A.

Standards, The Prosecution Function § 3.5.

[9]Gates v. State, 73 Ga. App. 824, 826, 38 S.E.2d 311 (1946).

[10]O.C.G.A. § 15-12-74; Groves v. State, 73 Ga. 205 (1884).

[11]Howard v. State, 60 Ga. App. 229, 236, 4 S.E.2d 418 (1939) (quoting In re Grand Jury Proceedings, 4 F.Supp. 283 (3) (E.D.Pa. 1933)).

[12]See O.C.G.A. § 15-12-100 (authorizes impaneling of special purpose grand jury to investigate alleged public corruption); State v. Lampl, 296 Ga. 892, 770 S.E.2d 629 (2015) (no statutory authority to dismiss an indictment returned by special grand jury which exceeded the scope of its investigatory charge). Compare, Kenerly v. State, 311 Ga. App. 190, 715 S.E.2d 688 (2011) (special purpose grand jury has no statutory authority to return an indictment).

[13]E.g., 63 A.B.A. J. 775 (June 1977).

§ 12:3   Making up grand jury lists

O.C.G.A. § 15-12-40.1 directs the Council of Superior Court Clerks of Georgia to compile a state-wide jury list. The Georgia Supreme Court is authorized to establish rules and standards for the distribution of the state-wide master jury list and the county jury list. The Jury Composition Rule crafted by the Court directs the council to compile the state-wide master jury list by using a list of drivers' license and personal identification card holders provided by the Department of Driver Services and a list of registered voters provided by the Secretary of State. The lists provided by the Department of Driver Services and the Secretary of State shall be submitted to the council in electronic format. Once each calendar year the council shall provide a county master jury list, in electronic format to the respective clerk.[1] The stated purpose for the Rule "is to set reasonable standards for the preparation, dissemination and technological improvements of inclusive statewide and county master jury lists."[2]

[Section 12:3]

[1]In addition, O.C.G.A. § 15-12-40.1 requires that at the request of the Council: the Department of Driver Services provide whatever racial information it has collected; the Department of Public Health provide "data relating to death certificates for . . . the 15 year period preceding the date of the request"; the Department of Corrections provide the name, race and address of all persons convicted of a felony offense; the Board of Pardons and Paroles provide the name, race and address of all persons who have had their civil rights restored.

[2]The Rule establishes three sources of data for the creation of the statewide and county master jury lists. Identified as the "Primary Records Sources," they are:

Department of Driver Services

Records shall be secured from the Georgia Department of Driver Services ("DDS"). Such records shall include data relating to all persons 18 years of age or older and residents of this state with any of the following:

(a) Valid driver's licenses;

(b) Driver's licenses expired for 730 days or less;

(c) State issued personal identification documents; or

(d) Convictions for driving without a license in Georgia or another state.

The records provided by DDS exclude persons who driver's licenses have been suspended or revoked due to a felony conviction, persons whose driver's licenses have been expired more than 730 days, and persons who have been identified as not being citizens of the United States. See O.C.G.A. § 15-12-40.1(b).

Secretary of State Voter Registration Records

Voter registration records shall be secured from the Georgia Secretary of State. Such records shall include data relating to all persons registered to vote within the state, including persons identified by the Secretary of State as "active" and "inactive."

Previous Year Statewide Master Jury List

The preceding year's statewide master jury list shall be used as a primary record source for the purposes of maintaining continuity of the Statewide Juror Number from year to year.

In *Ricks v. State,*[3] the Georgia Supreme Court held that Fulton County's Jury Order which provided for routine revisions to the master list provided by the Council of Superior Court Clerks violated the Supreme Court's Jury Composition Rule. Pursuant to the Supreme Court's Order, the County employed a vendor which utilized "legacy data" to add names to the master list and programs designed to delete addresses which were identified as "undeliverable." The county also allowed its jury officials to excuse, defer or inactivate jurors known to be ineligible to serve. Because the case was one in which the state was seeking the death penalty, it was before the Supreme Court for interim review. The Court expressly declined to rule on whether the procedure employed by the county was so defective as to amount to "reversible or prejudicial error."

See § 12:8, infra, on the timing of objections to grand jurors and see § 12:9, infra, on challenge to array for failure to have a representative cross section of the county. See § 12:4, infra, on the composition of the grand jury list.

§ 12:4 Composition of grand jury list

By statute, grand jurors must be 18 years of age or older, of sound mind, and residents in the county for at least 6 months preceding the time of serving.[1] It has been held that these requirements do not violate the due process or equal protection clauses of the State or United States Constitution.[2]

The United States Supreme Court has emphasized the importance of having a pool of jurors who are representative of the area.[3] While a defendant does not have the right to have a grand jury of any particular makeup,[4] he is entitled to a grand jury selected from a grand jury list from which the state has not deliberately and systematically eliminated members of any race,[5] class,[6] or any other identifiable group in the community,[7] such as

---

[3]Ricks v. State, 301 Ga. 171, 800 S.E.2d 307 (2017).

[Section 12:4]

[1]O.C.G.A. § 15-12-60.

[2]White v. State, 230 Ga. 327, 196 S.E.2d 849 (1973).

[3]See Taylor v. Louisiana, 419 U.S. 522, 95 S.Ct. 692, 42 L.Ed.2d 690 (1975).

[4]Jugiro v. Brush, 140 U.S. 291, 11 S.Ct. 770, 35 L.Ed. 510 (1891); Swain v. Alabama, 380 U.S. 202, 85 S.Ct. 824, 13 L.Ed.2d 759 (1965).

[5]Alexander v. Louisiana, 405 U.S. 625, 628, 92 S.Ct. 1221, 31 L.Ed.2d 536 (1972), says that the state may not deliberately and systematically eliminate members of the defendant's race. In Peters v. Kiff, 407 U.S. 493, 92 S.Ct. 2163, 33 L.Ed.2d 83 (1972), a Georgia case, the United States Supreme Court held that a white may challenge a grand jury from which black persons have been arbitrarily excluded.

[6]Hoyt v. Florida, 368 U.S. 57, 82 S.Ct. 159, 7 L.Ed.2d 118 (1961).

women.[8]

The Georgia Supreme Court, in reversing a finding that persons 18 through 20 years of age were a distinct group, expressed doubt that any age group is significantly identifiable.[9] However, the Georgia Court of Appeals has held that where 9 out of 10 of the grand jurors on the list were white males averaging 69 years of age, there was obviously not a representative cross section of the county.[10] Further, in *DeYoung v. State*,[11] the court pointed out that young adults, Hispanics, Asians and other minorities "have not been found to be cognizable classes for purposes of a constitutional challenge."

While it is necessary that a grand juror be a resident of the county in which he is serving, a plea in abatement to an indictment based upon the non-residence of a grand juror is not valid unless the defendant did not have an opportunity to challenge the grand jury before indictment.[12] However, where an indictment is returned by a grand jury which contained an alien, a plea in abatement may be filed at arraignment.[13]

Pursuant to O.C.G.A. § 15-12-60, the following persons are not eligible to serve as grand jurors: a person convicted of a felony whose civil rights have not been restored; a person charged with a felony offense who is in a pretrial release and diversion program; a person sentenced as a first offender who has not completed the terms of the sentence imposed; a person participating in a drug court or similar type of court program; and anyone judicially determined to be mentally incompetent. However, the fact that an indictment is returned by a grand jury which included a person who was not eligible to serve as such will not provide a basis to quash the indictment without something more.[14] Law enforcement officers are not automatically excused from grand jury service.[15]

The exclusion of persons convicted of a felony who have not been pardoned or had their civil rights restored does not apply to convictions prior to 1976, the date of the above statute. Likewise,

---

[7]Swain v. Alabama, 380 U.S. 202, 205, 85 S.Ct. 824, 13 L.Ed.2d 759 (1965); Peters v. Kiff, 407 U.S. 493, 92 S.Ct. 2163, 33 L.Ed.2d 83 (1972).

[8]Taylor v. Louisiana, 419 U.S. 522, 95 S.Ct. 692, 42 L.Ed.2d 690 (1975).

[9]State v. Gould, 232 Ga. 844, 209 S.E.2d 312 (1974). But see Zeigler, "Young Adults as a Cognizable Group in Jury Selection," 76 Mich. L. Rev. 1045 (1978); "Age Group Underrepresentation in Grand Jury or Petit Jury Venire," 62 A.L.R.4th 859 (1988).

[10]Julian v. State, 134 Ga. App. 592, 215 S.E.2d 496 (1975).

[11]DeYoung v. State, 268 Ga. 780, 790 (13), 493 S.E.2d 157 (1997).

[12]Edwards v. State, 121 Ga. 590, 591 (2), 49 S.E. 674 (1905).

[13]Reich v. State, 53 Ga. 73 (1874).

[14]O.C.G.A. § 15-12-60(d).

[15]Stinski v. State, 281 Ga. 783, 788(5), 642 S.E.2d 1 (2007).

a conviction of a felony in another state or in federal court does not disqualify a person for grand jury service.[16]

A grand juror is not disqualified to serve simply because he is related within the third degree to a person who contributed to a reward fund for arrest and conviction of an accused.[17] However, he is disqualified if he is related by blood or marriage within the third degree to any party interested in the outcome of the case.[18] Such objection, however, may not be raised for the first time after indictment.[19]

If the objection of a defendant is to the under-representation or non-representation of a cognizable group, the defendant is said to have no standing to object unless he is a member of such group.[20]

See § 12:9, infra, on a challenge to the array based on a failure to have a representative cross section of the county.

§ 12:5 Selecting a grand jury

O.C.G.A. § 15-12-62.1 provides:

The clerk shall choose a sufficient number of persons to serve as grand jurors from the county master jury list in the same manner as trial jurors are chosen. The clerk, not less than 20 days before the commencement of each term of court at which a regular grand jury is impaneled, shall issue summonses by mail to the persons chosen for grand jury service.

O.C.G.A. § 15-12-65.1 provides:

On and after July 1, 2012, the clerk shall be authorized to mail all summonses by first-class mail addressed to the prospective jurors' most notorious places of abode at least 25 days prior to the date of the court the prospective jurors shall attend. Failure to receive the notice personally shall be a defense to a contempt citation.

A grand jury is made up of not more than 23 nor less than 16 persons.[1] The judge will determine which of the summoned grand jurors are present and which ones have some reason to be

---

[16]Clark v. State, 255 Ga. 370, 371 (1), 338 S.E.2d 269 (1986).

[17]Blevins v. State, 220 Ga. 720, 141 S.E.2d 426 (1965).

[18]O.C.G.A. § 15-12-70.

[19]Farrar v. State, 187 Ga. 401, 402 (1), 200 S.E. 803 (1939); Smith v. State, 203 Ga. 569 (1), 47 S.E.2d 579 (1948).

[20]Frazier v. State, 257 Ga. 690, 691 (2), 362 S.E.2d 351 (1987).

[Section 12:5]

[1]O.C.G.A. § 15-12-61. However, it seems that an alternate may not be substituted after the grand jury has started hearing evidence on a present-ment or indictment. See Commonwealth v. Levinson, 480 Pa. 273, 389 A.2d 1062 (1978). This is the same number as prescribed for a fed-eral grand jury. Rule 6(a), Federal Rules of Criminal Procedure. However, if an indictment only names 15 grand

excused.[2] The grand jury will normally be made up of the first 23 on the list who are present[3] and have not been excused. However, if there are less than 23 persons summoned as grand jurors remaining after the judge has excused some, the grand jury will be made up of such smaller number provided that there are not less than 16 names remaining on the list. The law has been changed so as to provide that three alternate grand jurors may also be sworn and an alternate may serve so long as the number serving does not exceed 23 at any sitting.[4]

As previously noted, under Georgia law, a grand jury may not be composed of more than 23 members. An indictment returned by a grand jury of 24 members is void. However, if a defendant knows that a grand jury will investigate his case and he does not object to the number until after indictment, the objection is too late.[5] Apparently, if an objection were made before deliberations commenced, the judge could cure the defect by excusing the last grand juror.[6] The votes of at least 12 grand jurors are necessary to return a bill of indictment or to make a presentment.[7]

If an indictment is returned and the name of a person appears on the indictment as a grand juror when such individual is not on the grand jury list, a plea in abatement is good.[8] It has been said that if there is one disqualified grand juror, the indictment is void.[9] However, it appears that the defect must be raised at the proper time.

See § 12:9, infra, on failure to have a representative cross section of the county.

---

jurors it is not void, but the defect may be taken advantage of by special demurrer. Such a defect is not a valid ground for a motion in arrest of judgment. See Giddens v. State, 152 Ga. 195, 108 S.E. 788 (1921). See § 12:17, infra.

[2]Excusing a grand juror seems to be a matter almost completely within the discretion of the judge. Williams v. State, 69 Ga. 11 (1882).

[3]See Dickens v. State, 137 Ga. 523, 524 (1), 73 S.E. 826 (1912).

[4]O.C.G.A. § 15-12-61.

[5]Evans v. State, 17 Ga. App. 120 (2), 86 S.E. 286 (1915).

[6]Dickens v. State, 137 Ga. 523, 524 (1), 73 S.E. 826 (1912).

[7]O.C.G.A. § 15-12-61(a).

[8]Bazemore v. State, 28 Ga. App. 556, 112 S.E. 160 (1922). In Cross v. State, 64 Ga. 443 (3) (1879), the Court said that the fact a "grand juror's name is on the minutes of the court as properly drawn, is a sufficient reply to an exception to the indictment that his name was not in the jury box." But if all the grand jurors are qualified and one grand juror's name is drawn but his name does not appear on the revised list made before he was impaneled, a plea in abatement after indictment is not good. Williams v. State, 72 Ga. 180 (2) (1883); Williams v. State, 55 Ga. 391 (1) (1875).

[9]Dicta, Crawford v. Crow, 114 Ga. 282, 284, 40 S.E. 286 (1901). See Harper v. State, 283 Ga. 102, 657 S.E.2d 213 (2008), challenge to indictment returned by grand jury which included someone not selected by Grand Jury Commissioners will be sustained if filed timely.

§ 12:6 Organizing the grand jury

The judge either appoints a foreperson of the grand jury or directs the jurors to elect their own foreperson.[1] Each member of the grand jury is given an oath as set out in the Code, which among other things provides for secrecy unless called upon to testify.[2] The oath is apparently regarded as valid even if a judge who administers it is disqualified in a case later considered by the grand jury. Hence, an oath so administered affords no grounds for a plea in abatement.[3] Also, if a grand juror violates his oath of secrecy, this is not a valid basis for a plea in abatement.[4]

If a plea in abatement is filed alleging that the grand jury was not sworn, the issue may be determined from the minutes of the clerk.[5]

A grand juror is disqualified from participating in the consideration of any case or matter if he is related by blood or marriage within the third degree to any party interested in the outcome of the case.[6] Again, however, the point may not ordinarily be raised for the first time after indictment.[7]

§ 12:7 Kinds of objections and challenges to grand jury

There are different methods of classifying challenges or objections to grand juries. One method is by distinguishing between a challenge to the array and a challenge to the poll. A challenge to the array is a challenge to all the grand jurors selected for a term

---

[Section 12:6]

[1]Johnson v. State, 177 Ga. 881, 171 S.E. 699 (1933). See Rose v. Mitchell, 443 U.S. 545, 99 S. Ct. 2993, 61 L. Ed. 2d 739 (1979) (appointment of foreperson must be nondiscriminatory); Hobby v. U.S., 468 U.S. 339, 104 S. Ct. 3093, 82 L. Ed. 2d 260 (1984) (discriminatory selection of foreperson in federal court does not implicate due process concerns because the position involves only clerical and administrative duties); Ingram v. State, 253 Ga. 622, 323 S.E.2d 801 (1984) (discriminatory selection of foreperson has no effect on due process rights of an accused because the duties are ministerial).

[2]O.C.G.A. § 15-12-67. See O.C.G.A. § 15-12-72, O.C.G.A. § 15-12-73.

[3]Cabaniss v. State, 8 Ga. App. 129, 137 (6), 68 S.E. 849 (1910).

[4]Howard v. State, 60 Ga. App. 229, 4 S.E.2d 418 (1939).

[5]Bird v. State, 53 Ga. 602 (2) (1875).

[6]O.C.G.A. § 15-12-70.

[7]Farrar v. State, 187 Ga. 401, 403 (1), 200 S.E. 803 (1939); Smith v. State, 203 Ga. 569 (1), 47 S.E.2d 579 (1948). The unfortunate thing about these cases is that they do not consider the fact that a grand juror should disqualify himself and leave the grand jury room if a case comes to the attention of the grand jury and he is related to a party interested in the outcome of the case. The statute says he is disqualified. How is a person who is later indicted to know that such a grand juror was not going to "disqualify" himself and not participate in the particular case?

of court. A challenge to the array must be based upon some defect in the grand jury as a whole.[1] It must be in writing and apparently must be based on the theory that the grand jury was not fairly or properly selected and/or that the grand jury list was not fairly or properly compiled.[2] On the other hand, a challenge to the poll is a challenge to an individual grand juror or individual jurors because of some disqualification of the particular grand juror or grand jurors.[3]

A challenge to the poll or to a specified individual or individuals on a grand jury may be further subdivided into the following categories. First, defects propter affectum. That is, a defect because of relationship to one of the parties, or because of prejudice or bias, or because of an expression of opinion. This defect may not be raised for the first time after indictment.[4] Thus, even though Georgia law requires the disqualification of members of a grand jury who are related by blood or marriage to interested parties within the third degree (O.C.G.A. § 15-12-70), the disqualification of a juror is not a ground for quashing the indictment.[5] Second, defects propter defectum. This term has been used to apply to a challenge to a grand juror where he is a

---

[Section 12:7]

[1]See Bryan v. State, 124 Ga. 79, 80, 52 S.E. 298 (1905).

[2]See O.C.G.A. § 15-12-162. This section was probably enacted with a view solely to a challenge to the array of traverse or trial jurors, but there seems to be no reason to think that a different standard would apply to grand jury. No Georgia case has been found which clearly defines a challenge to the array of a grand jury or when such a challenge will lie.

[3]E.g., Mize v. State, 135 Ga. 291, 69 S.E. 173 (1910) (the grand juror challenged was a non-resident); Hawkins v. State, 86 Ga. App. 872, 72 S.E.2d 778 (1952) (grand juror challenged served as a grand juror at immediate preceding term).

[4]Hall v. State, 7 Ga. App. 115 (1), 116 (1), 66 S.E. 390 (1909) (relationship to prosecutor); Simpson v. State, 100 Ga. App. 726, 112 S.E.2d 314 (1959) (member of REA from which materials were stolen); Betts v. State, 66 Ga. 508, 514 (4) (1881) (expression of opinion). A grand juror is not disqualified to serve simply because he is related within the third degree to a person who contributed to a reward fund for the arrest and conviction of the person killing the victim. Blevins v. State, 220 Ga. 720, 141 S.E.2d 426 (1965). But in Lascelles v. State, 90 Ga. 347, 372, 16 S.E. 945 (1892), aff'd, 148 U.S. 537, 13 S.Ct. 687, 37 L.Ed. 549 (1893), the court said the objection of relationship between a grand juror and a prosecution witness could not be made by a plea in abatement "at least if the accused has had an opportunity to . . . challenge before the . . . indictment." Cf. Phillips v. State, 167 Ga. App. 260, 264 (3), 305 S.E.2d 918 (1983).

[5]Brown v. State, 295 Ga. 240, 759 S.E.2d 489 (2014) (plea in abatement not available where several grand jurors were possible victims of defendant's alleged crimes; vigorous dissent to majority by Hunstein, J.); Black v. State, 264 Ga. 550, 552 (2), 448 S.E.2d 357 (1994).

non-resident of the county[6] or where he served on the grand jury for the previous term.[7] Challenges of this kind must be filed before indictment.[8] Third, defect propter delictum, that is, a defect because the grand juror is not qualified to serve because of conviction of a crime. This defect may not be raised for the first time after verdict.[9]

In *Isaacs v. State*,[10] the court pointed out that "bias, prejudice, and exposure to pre-trial publicity are not mentioned in" O.C.G.A. § 15-12-82(a) as possible grounds for disqualification of grand jurors. The court also quoted the following authority:

"Generally, in the absence of a controlling statutory provision, a person is not disqualified or incompetent to serve as a grand juror by reason of bias or prejudice on his part, by the fact that he has heard or read about the case under investigation or has even formed or expressed an opinion as to the guilt of the accused, or by his interest in a prosecution other than a direct pecuniary interest. . . . [38 Am. Jur. 2d 951, Grand Jury, § 7]."

In addition to a challenge to the poll as classified above, without attempting to classify the challenge, it has been held that (1) a plea in abatement is not valid, where it attempts to show that J. A. Huger, Jr., served as a grand juror even though the name of J. A. Huger had been drawn, unless the defendant could overcome the presumption that the man who served was in fact the man whose name was drawn;[11] and (2) a plea in abatement filed after indictment is not valid when it attempts to show that a grand juror had been excused at a prior term of court and then served on the later grand jury which indicted the defendant, after having been given a choice of serving on the grand jury at the later

---

[6]Mize v. State, 135 Ga. 291, 295, 69 S.E. 173 (1910). But if a person on a grand jury is an alien, the point may be raised by a plea in abatement after indictment. Reich v. State, 53 Ga. 73 (2) (1874).

[7]Hawkins v. State, 86 Ga. App. 872, 874, 72 S.E.2d 778 (1952); West v. State, 19 Ga. App. 142 (1), 91 S.E. 216 (1917). However, if a person does not know that the grand jury is to consider a case against him, a plea in abatement after indictment is good. McFarlin v. State, 121 Ga. 329, 330, 49 S.E. 267 (1904).

[8]Betts v. State, 66 Ga. 508, 514 (1881), contains a dictum which states that a challenge propter defectum voids an indictment. This case has apparently never been overruled.

[9]Mitchell v. State, 69 Ga. App. 771, 781 (7), 26 S.E.2d 663 (1943). In Gunn v. State, 245 Ga. 359, 361 (1), 264 S.E.2d 862 (1980), the court held that a grand juror is not disqualified by reason of a federal conviction before 1976.

[10]Isaacs v. State, 259 Ga. 717, 719 (2), 386 S.E.2d 316 (1989). See Brown v. State, 322 Ga. App. 446, 745 S.E.2d 699 (2013), judgment aff'd, 295 Ga. 240, 759 S.E.2d 489 (2014).

[11]Turner v. State, 78 Ga. 174, 175 (2) (1886).

term or a traverse jury at the prior term.[12] Likewise, (3) a plea in abatement was held to be properly overruled where the defendant alleged that Claire Ehler's name appeared on the indictment and her name did not appear on the list of grand jurors selected for that term of court. The state alleged that she had been called for the previous term but excused until the following term. Her name appeared on the list for the previous term and was on the master list. Her married name was Mrs. Carroll Ehler. The court concluded that the plea was insufficient since the defendant had failed to show that the grand juror was not qualified to serve.[13]

Generally, see 38 Am. Jur. 2d Grand Jury § 7, on effect of bias, prejudice or interest. For a motion to voir dire grand jury, see Studdard, *Daniel's Georgia Criminal Trial Practice Forms* (2018– 2019 ed.), §§ 11:3 and 11:4.

§ 12:8 Timing of objections to grand jury and challenges to the array

The case law surrounding challenges to grand juries on the theory that the manner in which they are selected fails to include significant identifiable groups within the community has been developing since the 1960's. These attacks have concentrated on the underrepresentation of African Americans, and to a lesser extent, Hispanics, females and the young. Georgia courts have continued to place great emphasis on the timeliness of challenges to grand juries. On the other hand, in an effort to have these challenges adjudicated on the merits in trial courts, the United States Supreme Court has indicated an attitude of some indifference toward the "timing" of the objections.

As a general rule, a challenge to the composition of the grand jury must be made prior to the return of the indictment or the defendant must show that he had no knowledge, either actual or constructive, of such alleged illegal composition of the grand jury prior to the time the indictment was returned; otherwise, the objection is deemed to be waived.[1] However, in *Vasquez v. Hillery*,[2] the United States Supreme Court affirmed a federal writ of habeas corpus which had been granted 16 years after the prisoner's trial. The prisoner had contended after indictment that the indictment had been returned "by a grand jury from which blacks had been systematically excluded." The court held that the

---

[12]Burke v. State, 116 Ga. App. 753, 159 S.E.2d 176 (1967).

[13]Dawson v. State, 166 Ga. App. 515 (2), 304 S.E.2d 570 (1983).

[Section 12:8]

[1]Clark v. State, 255 Ga. 370, 372(2), 338 S.E.2d 269 (1986). See Langlands v. State, 282 Ga. 103, 646 S.E.2d 253 (2007).

[2]Vasquez v. Hillery, 474 U.S. 254, 106 S.Ct. 617, 88 L.Ed.2d 598 (1986).

conviction by a proper jury did not render the earlier defect harmless. The court pointed out that, while a state showing that it has been prejudiced by delay in filing a petition for federal habeas corpus is a basis for dismissal of the petition, the difficulties that a state will face because of a retrial do not justify a dismissal of such a petition.

In Georgia, grand jurors lists are public records and are open to inspection at reasonable times.[3] It may be contended that the public has constructive notice on the names of grand jury lists.[4]

The United States Supreme Court has indicated that where a defendant is represented by counsel in a criminal case, he may not raise an objection to the makeup of the grand jury for the first time in a federal habeas corpus action without showing why the challenge was not filed on time and without showing actual prejudice.[5] It also appears that a defendant who is represented by counsel must challenge the grand jury, if he wishes to do so, no later than the time of the arraignment.[6]

In the 1982 case of *Walraven v. State*,[7] the Georgia Supreme Court held that the timing of a challenge to the array is different in a death penalty case under the Georgia Unified Appeal Procedure than that in other criminal cases. In a death penalty case a challenge to the array may be made after indictment.

Ideally, defense counsel should file an objection or challenge to the array before indictment, and after indictment he should file a challenge to the array in the form of a plea in abatement on the

---

[3]Unofficial opinion of Attorney General, October 16, 1967.

[4]Hayes v. State, 138 Ga. App. 666, 667 (2), 226 S.E.2d 819 (1976), points out that the defendant had access to the names of the grand jury before he was indicted.

[5]Francis v. Henderson, 425 U.S. 536, 96 S.Ct. 1708, 48 L.Ed.2d 149 (1976). The Georgia Supreme Court has said that a defendant waives an attack on the composition of the grand jury if the issue is not raised until a state habeas corpus is filed. Mitchell v. Hopper, 239 Ga. 781, 239 S.E.2d 2 (1977).

[6]In Thomas v. State, 239 Ga. 734, 238 S.E.2d 888 (1977), the court said that where a defendant did not have counsel until after indictment, he is still not excused for failure to challenge the array until the case is appealed. Since *Thomas* was decided, the

time for filing pre-trial motions has been changed from at or before the time of arraignment to within ten days after arraignment pursuant to O.C.G.A. § 17-7-110.

In Sullivan v. State, 246 Ga. 426, 428, 271 S.E.2d 823 (1980), the court acknowledged that Reich v. State, 53 Ga. 73 (1874), and Cobb v. State, 218 Ga. 10 (3), 126 S.E.2d 231 (1962), appear to say that a challenge to the array of grand jurors may be made by a plea in abatement filed at or before arraignment. However, in *Sullivan*, the opinion said the *Reich* and *Cobb* decisions have been construed to apply only where there was no opportunity to raise the question before indictment.

Cf. Cunningham v. State, 248 Ga. 558, 284 S.E.2d 390 (1981).

[7]Walraven v. State, 250 Ga. 401, 404 (1), 297 S.E.2d 278 (1982).

same grounds as his earlier objection. However, if counsel fails to object to the grand jury before indictment, he should still file a challenge to the array after indictment just as though he had filed the objection before indictment.

If a defendant does not know that the grand jury will be considering a case against him, it seems clear that he should be able to challenge the grand jury by a plea in abatement after indictment.[8]

However, it has been held that a defendant may not attack an indictment because of the make-up of the grand jury where his counsel expected the regular grand jury to consider the matter several weeks later rather than the specially summoned grand jury which returned the indictment.[9] In 1980, the Georgia Supreme Court said that "Georgia law requires that objection to the composition of the grand jury be made at the earliest practical opportunity."[10] Thus, a challenge to the composition of the grand jury filed for the first time in a motion for new trial would not be timely.[11]

Apparently, the purpose of requiring a defendant to file an objection to a grand jury or jurors before indictment is to give the court the opportunity to select another grand jury not subject to the same infirmities raised by the defendant's objections and to allow the "new" grand jury to consider the case.[12]

Caution would indicate that an objection to a grand jury should set out fully all of the reasons which the defendant has for objecting to the grand jury. A copy should be filed with the clerk of the court having jurisdiction over the alleged crime, together with a certificate of service showing the date of service and the fact that the district attorney has been served.

§ 12:9 Challenge to the array—Failure to have a representative cross section of county

In making up a jury list and a grand jury list, it has been said that there is a presumption that the jury commissioners have

---

[8]See Langlands v. State, 282 Ga. 103, 646 S.E.2d 253 (2007). In Reece v. Georgia, 350 U.S. 85, 89, 76 S.Ct. 167, 100 L.Ed. 77 (1955), the court said that "the right to object to a grand jury presupposes an opportunity to exercise that right."

[9]Godfrey v. State, 243 Ga. 302, 305 (3), 253 S.E.2d 710 (1979), rev'd on other grounds, 446 U.S. 420, 100 S.Ct. 1759, 64 L.Ed.2d 398 (1980).

[10]Sullivan v. State, 246 Ga. 426, 428, 271 S.E.2d 823 (1980) (quoting Thomas v. State, 239 Ga. 734, 735 (1), 238 S.E.2d 888 (1977)).

[11]Griffin v. State, 245 Ga. 345(2), 265 S.E.2d 20 (1980).

[12]See Parris v. State, 125 Ga. 777 (3), 54 S.E. 751 (1906); Mize v. State, 135 Ga. 291 (1), 69 S.E. 173 (1910).

acted properly,[1] at least in the absence of evidence to the contrary. Although the role of jury commissioners has been abolished, the same presumption should apply to the state and county jury master lists assembled pursuant to O.C.G.A. § 15-12-40.1. If a defendant wishes to make out a prima facie case of invidious discrimination, he has the burden of proof.[2] Purposeful discrimination is not established by introducing evidence that a single grand jury or a single venire of traverse jurors fails to contain a large or identifiable segment of the community or that such an identifiable class is underrepresented.[3] "There is no constitutional guarantee that the grand or petit juries, impaneled in a particular case will constitute a representative cross-section of the entire community."[4]

However, in *Whitus v. Georgia* in 1967,[5] the United States Supreme Court said a prima facie case of discrimination against blacks is shown where jury commissioners use a tainted source for names and there is a marked disparity between the number of blacks on the jury rolls and the percentage of the blacks in the total community, even though jury commissioners testify that no one was rejected because of race or color.[6] The rule of *Whitus* is retroactive.[7]

In *Taylor v. Louisiana*,[8] the United States Supreme Court said that the list of trial jurors must represent a fair cross section and this is a requirement of the Sixth Amendment. Also, under *Taylor*, it is no longer necessary to show an opportunity to discriminate in the selection process. *Taylor* merely requires a showing of a systematic exclusion of any distinct group regardless of how the

---

[Section 12:9]

[1]Jones v. State, 223 Ga. 157, 154 S.E.2d 228 (1967), judgment rev'd on other grounds, 389 U.S. 24, 88 S.Ct. 4, 19 L.Ed.2d 25 (1967).

[2]Swain v. Alabama, 380 U.S. 202, 209, 85 S.Ct. 824, 13 L.Ed.2d 759 (1965).

[3]White v. State, 230 Ga. 327, 331 (2), 196 S.E.2d 849 (1973); Scudiere v. State, 130 Ga. App. 477, 482 (12), 203 S.E.2d 581 (1973) (petit jury).

[4]Singleton v. State, 229 Ga. App. 135, 136 (1), 493 S.E.2d 556 (1997) (quoting Truitt v. State, 212 Ga. App. 286, 441 S.E.2d 800 (1994)).

[5]Whitus v. Georgia, 385 U.S. 545, 551, 87 S.Ct. 643, 17 L.Ed.2d 599 (1967). Cf. Castaneda v. Partida, 430 U.S. 482, 97 S.Ct. 1272, 51 L.Ed.2d 498 (1977). In this case, the "key man"

method of jury selection was used. Even though the grand jury which indicted the defendant was made up of 50% Mexican-Americans, the court held that a prima facie case of discrimination had been established where 79% of the population was Mexican-American but only 39% of those summoned for grand jury over a period of 10 years were Mexican-Americans.

[6]In this case, the jury commissioners used an old jury list which had previously been condemned and names from a segregated tax digest in making up the new list.

[7]Brown v. State, 239 Ga. 435, 437, 238 S.E.2d 21 (1977).

[8]Taylor v. Louisiana, 419 U.S. 522, 95 S.Ct. 692, 42 L.Ed.2d 690 (1975).

exclusion occurred.[9] Likewise, in the 1979 case of *Duren v. Missouri*,[10] the court followed the Taylor rule. Nevertheless, the Georgia Supreme Court in the 1981 case of *Thomas v. State*[11] continued to list as a requirement for a prima facie case of discrimination that "an opportunity for discrimination against . . . [the] group existed from the source of the jury list." As previously pointed out, this is no longer a requirement.

In 1982, in *Walraven v. State*,[12] the Georgia Supreme Court pointed out that when "a defendant makes a Sixth Amendment fair-cross-section attack upon the composition of the traverse jury, 'the fair-cross-section requirement involves a comparison of the makeup of jury venires . . . with the makeup of the *community*, not of the voter registration lists.' " In the 1998 decision of the United States Supreme Court in *Campbell v. Louisiana*,[13] the Court held that under the equal protection and due process clauses of the Fourteenth Amendment, a white defendant may assert a claim of discrimination against blacks in the selection of the grand jury which indicted him.

In *Parks v. State*,[14] the Georgia Supreme Court has recognized that persons from 18 to 30 years of age may constitute a distinct and cognizable group. However, whether or not age is a cognizable class is a question of fact which "depends upon the time and location of the trial."[15] Likewise, in *Willis v. Zant*,[16] the Eleventh Circuit recognized that adults from 18 to 30 could constitute a

---

[9]Whitebread, Constitutional Criminal Procedure (1978), p. 325 (American Academy of Judicial Education).

[10]Duren v. Missouri, 439 U.S. 357, 99 S.Ct. 664, 58 L.Ed.2d 579 (1979).

[11]Thomas v. State, 248 Ga. 247, 249, 282 S.E.2d 316 (1981). Accord, Cunningham v. State, 248 Ga. 558, 559, 284 S.E.2d 390 (1981).

[12]Walraven v. State, 250 Ga. 401, 406 (3), 297 S.E.2d 278 (1982).

[13]Campbell v. Louisiana, 523 U.S. 392, 118 S.Ct. 1419, 140 L.Ed.2d 551 (1998).

[14]Parks v. State, 254 Ga. 403, 410, 330 S.E.2d 686 (1985).

In Hopkins v. State, 19 Md.App. 414, 311 A.2d 483 (1973), the court said: "In order for a group to be 'cognizable' it must be shown that the particular group has a definite composition and that membership does not shift from day to day. . . . The group must have cohesion. 'There must be a common thread which runs through the group, a basic similarity in attitudes or ideas or experience which is present in members of the group and which cannot be adequately represented if the group is excluded from the jury selection process.' United States v. Guzman . . . 337 F.Supp. at 143; Wilkins v. State, 16 Md.App. 587, 300 A.2d 411 (1973). Moreover, the possibility must exist that the exclusion of the group from jury service will result in bias, partiality or prejudice being practiced against members of the group by juries hearing cases in which members of the group are involved. . . . United States v. Greenberg, 200 F.Supp. 382, 391 (S.D.N.Y.1961)."

[15]Hicks v. State, 256 Ga. 715, 718 (7), 352 S.E.2d 762 (1987).

[16]Willis v. Zant, 720 F.2d 1212 (11th Cir. 1983). In *Willis* the case was remanded to the district judge to conduct a hearing to determine whether

cognizable group.

The Georgia Supreme Court has declined to consider an underrepresentation of women prior to 1975, since the case of *Taylor v. Louisiana*[17] in 1975 is not regarded as being retroactive.[18]

In a challenge to the array, it is not necessary to show that the defendant is a member of the underrepresented group,[19] nor that all persons in the underrepresented group would vote alike.[20]

The Georgia Supreme Court has recognized different standards for gauging disparity (1) in "classifications based upon race, nationality, or sex" and (2) in "classifications based on age." In the case of race, nationality, or sex there is a call for close or strict judicial scrutiny. In classifications based on age, they are not subjected to such scrutiny.[21]

In *Bryant v. State*,[22] the defendant challenged the array of traverse jurors based on alleged underrepresentation of residents aged 18 to 29. The court held that "[w]hether a group is suf-

---

or not the age group of 18 to 30 constitutes a cognizable group in terms of the Sixth Amendment in the particular case. The court said, "The distinctiveness and homogeneity of a group under the Sixth Amendment depends upon the time and location of the trial. For example, Latins have been held to be a cognizable group in Miami, Florida. . . . In another community, they might not be. To show that a group is distinct or cognizable under the Sixth Amendment, a defendant must show: (1) that the group is defined and limited by some factor (i.e., that the group has a definite composition such as by race or sex); (2) that a common thread or basic similarity in attitude, ideas, or experience runs through the group; and (3) that there is a community of interest among members of the group such that the group's interests cannot be adequately represented if the group is excluded from the jury selection process." The last sentence quoted from the Willis case was quoted with approval in Potts v. State, 259 Ga. 812, 813 (1), 388 S.E.2d 678 (1990).

[17]Taylor v. Louisiana, 419 U.S. 522, 95 S.Ct. 692, 42 L.Ed.2d 690 (1975). In this case, 53% of the persons eligible for jury service were female, but the females on the jury list represented not more than 10% of the persons on the list and none were selected

for the venire from which the defendant's jury was selected. Louisiana had a statute which provided that no female's name was to be put on the jury list unless she had previously filled out a declaration of her desire to serve. The general Georgia statute exempting certain persons from jury duty is found in O.C.G.A. § 15-12-1.1.

[18]Barrow v. State, 239 Ga. 162, 164 (2), 236 S.E.2d 257 (1977) (citing Daniel v. Louisiana, 420 U.S. 31, 95 S.Ct. 704, 42 L.Ed.2d 790 (1975), which held that *Taylor* was not to be retroactive). Accord, Young v. State, 239 Ga. 53, 55 (1), 236 S.E.2d 1 (1977).

[19]Peters v. Kiff, 407 U.S. 493, 92 S.Ct. 2163, 33 L.Ed.2d 83 (1972) (white defendant and exclusion of blacks); Taylor v. Louisiana, 419 U.S. 522, 526, 95 S.Ct. 692, 42 L.Ed.2d 690 (1975) (male defendant complained of underrepresentation of women).

[20]Peters v. Kiff, 407 U.S. 493, 503, 92 S.Ct. 2163, 33 L.Ed.2d 83 (1972).

[21]Parks v. State, 254 Ga. 403, 410, 330 S.E.2d 686 (1985). In *Parks*, the court concluded that a 15% underrepresentation of young persons on the traverse jury list did not require reversal.

[22]Bryant v. State, 268 Ga. 664 (2), 665, 492 S.E.2d 868 (1997).

ficiently distinct is a question of fact which depends upon the time and location of the trial" and is to be determined by the trial judge. Even if a defendant shows that persons aged 18 to 29 constitute a cognizable class in the county, the defendant must also prove a consistent underrepresentation of that class.

Some of the Georgia cases on challenges to the array have been based on federal constitutional grounds and some on a violation of former O.C.G.A. § 15-12-40 and frequently the basis for the challenge was not clear. Previously, under former O.C.G.A. § 15-12-40, if there was (1) an opportunity for discrimination and (2) a significant disparity in representation, a prima facie case of discrimination was established,[23] which was not overcome even if the jury commissioners were to testify that they did not discriminate in making up the grand jury and traverse jury lists.[24] However, even if there is no showing of an opportunity to discriminate, a marked disparity of representation may be so extreme as to establish, as a matter of law, a case of discrimination.[25] In 1982, in *Walraven v. State*,[26] the Georgia Supreme Court said, " 'The fair cross section analysis employs a prima facie test which is virtually identical to the equal protection prima facie test for establishing a presumption of discrimination. . . . There is a significant distinction, however, in the way that each prima facie case may be rebutted. For an equal protection claim, the presumption can be rebutted by proving an absence of discriminatory intent. . . . In a fair cross section analysis, purposeful discrimination is irrelevant since the emphasis is purely on the structure of the jury venire; a prima facie case can be rebutted only by establishing a significant government interest which justifies the imbalance of classes.' "[27] O.C.G.A. § 15-12-40 has now been replaced by O.C.G.A. § 15-12-40.1 and whether it is sufficiently inclusive has not yet been tested. However, if it is challenged, it will have to satisfy the fair cross section analysis discussed in *Walraven*.

The cases discussed in the remainder of this section will illustrate the application of these rules to specific factual situations.

In *Pass v. Caldwell*,[28] decided in 1973, there was no mention of an opportunity for discrimination. The court held that where

---

[23]Barrow v. State, 239 Ga. 162, 236 S.E.2d 257 (1977); Brown v. State, 239 Ga. 435, 436, 238 S.E.2d 21 (1977).

[24]State v. Gethers, 139 Ga. App. 1, 227 S.E.2d 832 (1976); Brown v. State, 239 Ga. 435, 436, 238 S.E.2d 21 (1977).

[25]Sanders v. State, 237 Ga. 858, 230 S.E.2d 291 (1976).

[26]Walraven v. State, 250 Ga. 401, 406 (3), 297 S.E.2d 278 (1982).

[27]Quoted from United States v. Perez-Hernandez, 672 F.2d 1380, 1384, n. 5 (11th Cir. 1982). Cf. Devier v. State, 250 Ga. 652, 653, 300 S.E.2d 490 (1983).

[28]Pass v. Caldwell, 231 Ga. 192, 200 S.E.2d 720 (1973).

blacks made up 11% of the population of the county and 5.13% of persons on the grand jury list, this did not establish a prima facie case of discrimination.

In 1974, the Georgia Court of Appeals, in *Gould v. State*,[29] considered a situation in which women were 91.2% under-represented on the grand jury list and 69.7% on the petit jury list, and blacks were 49.5% underrepresented on the grand jury list and 61.7% on the petit jury list, and there were as many upright and intelligent women as men and blacks as whites in the county. The court concluded that the jury list violated former O.C.G.A. § 15-12-40 and the defendant was denied a fairly representative cross section of the intelligent citizens of the county.[30] It should be noted that in this case, the court pointed out that O.C.G.A. § 15-12-40 was not under attack, that the court did not have jurisdiction to pass on the constitutionality of the statute, and that its decision was based primarily on Georgia statutes and case law.[31]

In 1976, the Georgia Supreme Court considered the case of *Sanders v. State*.[32] In this case, the petit jury was made up of 53% women as compared to 55% women in the county and 20% blacks on the petit jury list as compared with 22-½% of the population of the county. The court concluded that the difference was too slight to establish a prima facie case of purposeful discrimination.[33] However, the grand jury list was composed of 15% women as compared with 55% of the population in the county and 8% blacks as compared with a county population of 22-½% blacks. The court concluded that such a marked disparity showed as a matter of law that the grand jury list was not fairly representative of the community. Such a disparity may not be considered harmless where the grand jury which indicted a defendant was composed of 19 persons, only 4 of whom were

---

[29]Gould v. State, 131 Ga. App. 811, 822, 207 S.E.2d 519 (1974), rev'd in part and aff'd in part, 232 Ga. 844, 209 S.E.2d 312 (1974).

[30]Effective July 1, 2012, O.C.G.A. § 15-12-40 was replaced by O.C.G.A. § 15-12-40.1.

[31]Gould v. State, 131 Ga. App. 811, 820, 207 S.E.2d 519 (1974).

[32]Sanders v. State, 237 Ga. 858, 230 S.E.2d 291 (1976).

[33]In State v. Gethers, 139 Ga. App. 1, 3, 227 S.E.2d 832 (1976), the evidence showed that blacks comprised 17.8% of the county's population but only 6.7% of the traverse jury list and

are underrepresented by 62.4%; that females comprised 52.1% of the population but only 26.3% of the jury list and are underrepresented by 49.5%; that whites are 82.2% of the population, 93.5% of the jury list and are overrepresented by 13.5%; and that males are 47.9% of the population, comprised 73.7% of the jury list and are overrepresented by 53.9%. The appellate court concluded that there was sufficient evidence to affirm the sustaining of the challenge to the array in the trial court even though the statistical evidence seems to have been the only evidence.

women and only 2 of whom were blacks.[34] It is not clear whether this case turns on statutory or constitutional grounds or a combination of the two. It should be noted that in *Sanders,* there is nothing in the opinion to indicate any tainted source of names such as that referred to in *Whitus.*

However, in *Hudson v. State,*[35] another 1977 case, there was no evidence of a historical pattern of discrimination against blacks or women. The jury commissioners mailed out approximately 10,000 cards to persons on the voters list, and all persons not ineligible or exempt by law were placed on the list. The voters list was supplemented from the city directory and other sources. There were advertisements in the newspaper asking anyone who wanted to be on the list to contact the commissioners. The court concluded that the commissioners carried the burden of showing no purposeful discrimination and had made a bona fide effort to get a cross section of the community even though there was some imprecise testimony indicating that 22.67% of the county was black and only 11.94% of those on the grand jury list were black and 51.92% of the county was female and only 23.51% of those on the grand jury list were female.

In *Fouts v. State,*[36] the court held that where 50% of the population was female and 22.7% of the grand jury list was female, this was a significant underrepresentation but concluded that because of testimony of the diligence of the jury commissioners (half of whom were female) to obtain a representative grand jury list, there was sufficient evidence to support the trial judge's denial of the challenge to the grand jury.

---

[34]Sanders v. State, 237 Ga. 858, 230 S.E.2d 291 (1976). Query: Does the statement relating to the composition of the indicting grand jury indicate that harmless error would have existed if the particular grand jury happened to contain a fair cross-section of the community even though the grand jury list was not representative? The court has previously said that the make-up of a particular grand jury did not establish discrimination. The thing which had to be shown was that the overall list was not representative. See White v. State, 230 Ga. 327, 331, 196 S.E.2d 849 (1973); Hardwick v. State, 231 Ga. 181, 183 (5), 200 S.E.2d 728 (1973).

However, in Sims v. State, 221 Ga. 190, 144 S.E.2d 103 (1965), the court said that jury "lists for prior years would not be relevant in the face of a showing that no discrimination existed in the composition of the present juries." But the Sims case was reversed on other grounds, 385 U.S. 538, 87 S.Ct. 639, 17 L.Ed.2d 593 (1967).

[35]Hudson v. State, 240 Ga. 70, 72, 239 S.E.2d 330 (1977). In this case, the court, on page 72, mentioned the difficulty of obtaining women because of the exemption given mothers with children under 14 years of age. No consideration was given to whether this exemption was constitutional.

[36]Fouts v. State, 240 Ga. 39, 41 (c), 239 S.E.2d 366 (1977) (Justices Undercofler, Hall and Hill dissented).

In *Sears v. State,*[37] the evidence showed that blacks comprised 9.2% of the population but only 5.4% of the voter registration list. The grand jury list was drawn at random from the voter list and 5.4% of those on the grand jury list were black. Thus, there was a disparity of 3.8%. The traverse list had no disparity. The court pointed to the difficulty of supplementing such a large list and overruled the challenge.

In *Cook v. State,*[38] the court stated that "[a]s a general proposition, absolute disparities under 10% usually are sufficient to satisfy constitutional requirements."

In *Davis v. State,*[39] a majority of the court affirmed the overruling of a challenge to the array of trial jurors in view of hearsay evidence relied upon by the defendant and the mechanical method used for selecting jurors from the voters' list.

In *Cochran v. State,*[40] the court held that the trial judge erred in refusing to allow the defendant to call jury commissioners as witnesses to explain the relatively small percentage of blacks on the grand jury list. The court pointed out that there had been an opportunity for discrimination since the jury list (from which the grand jury list was selected) had come from the voters' list which was segregated by race.

In a number of cases involving the alleged underrepresentation of Hispanics on juries in Hall county, the Supreme Court framed a three part test to be used for determining the existence of a prima facie Sixth Amendment fair-cross-section violation which is: ". . . 1) whether the group alleged to be excluded is a 'distinctive' group in the community; 2) whether the representation of this group in jury pools is not fair and reasonable in relation to the number of such persons in the community; and 3) whether their underrepresentation is due to systematic exclusion of the group in the jury selection process."[41] Applying this analysis in

---

[37]Sears v. State, 262 Ga. 805, 806 (2), 426 S.E.2d 553 (1993).

[38]Cook v. State, 255 Ga. 565, 571 (11), 340 S.E.2d 843 (1986).

[39]Davis v. State, 241 Ga. 376, 377, 388, 247 S.E.2d 45 (1978). In this case, census figures showed about 28% of the population was black and about 53% female. The jury list was 13.7% black and 34.5% female. However, Davis was granted federal habeas corpus relief in Davis v. Zant, 721 F.2d 1478 (11th Cir. 1983).

[40]Cochran v. State, 151 Ga. App. 478, 260 S.E.2d 391 (1979). The opinion in the *Cochran* case after the earlier reversal is found in Cochran v. State, 155 Ga. App. 418, 271 S.E.2d 864 (1980). In this decision, the court affirmed the trial judge's conclusion that defendant did not show discrimination where the jury commissioners (one of whom was black) made up the jury list from the voter's list by taking every fourth person on the voters' list.

[41]Smith v. State, 275 Ga. 715, 716 (1), 571 S.E.2d 740 (2002) (citing Morrow v. State, 272 Ga. 691 (1), 532 S.E.2d 78 (2000)).

Smith v. State,[42] the Court concluded that Hispanics were not underrepresented on juries in Hall county because although a "distinctive" group for purposes of a fair-cross-section analysis, the number of Hispanics on the jury list was not significantly less than the number of Hispanics within the community who were eligible to serve jury duty. Thus, the court held that citizenship is properly considered in jury composition claims. However, "[t]o establish a prima facie case of a fair-cross-section Sixth Amendment violation, Smith had to show an actionable disparity between the percentage of Hispanics on the traverse jury list and the percentage of Hispanics in Hall County who are jury-eligible."[43]

In *Torres v. State*,[44] the court pointed out that "[t]here is no constitutional guarantee that grand or petit juries, impaneled in a particular case, will constitute a representative cross-section of the entire community. . . . The proper inquiry concerns the procedures for compiling the jury lists and not the actual composition . . . in a particular case. . . . The Constitution requires only that the State not deliberately and systematically exclude identifiable and distinct groups from jury lists. . . ."

In order "[t]o establish a prima facie case of jury discrimination, a defendant must show the following: '(1) that a distinctive group or recognizable class in the community has been excluded from the jury list; (2) that an opportunity for discrimination against this group existed from the source of the jury list; and (3) that use of the infected source produced a significant disparity between the percentages found present in the source and those actually appearing on the jury panels.' "[45] However, it seems that a disparity which is less than 10 percent, as a general proposition, satisfies constitutional requirements.[46] In *Morrow v. State*,[47] the defendant failed the third prong of establishing a prima facie case because the 4 percent disparity of the number of Hispanics from the census and the percentage on the jury list was well within the general rule of less than 10 percent.

It should be noted, however, that the Uniform Appeal Procedure (UAP) sets the limit for under-representation of a cognizable group at five percent. In *Edwards v. State*,[48] the Georgia Supreme Court concluded that well settled case law which

---

[42]Smith v. State, 275 Ga. 715, 716 (1), 571 S.E.2d 740 (2002).

[43]Smith v. State, 275 Ga. 715, 716, 571 S.E.2d 740 (2002).

[44]Torres v. State, 272 Ga. 389, 391 (4), 529 S.E.2d 883 (2000).

[45]Montijo v. State, 238 Ga. App. 696, 702 (5), 520 S.E.2d 24 (1999)

(quoting Bowen v. State, 244 Ga. 495, 260 S.E.2d 855 (1979)).

[46]Cook v. State, 255 Ga. 565(1), 340 S.E.2d 843 (1986).

[47]Morrow v. State, 272 Ga. 691, 692 (11), 532 S.E.2d 78 (2000).

[48]Edwards v. State, 281 Ga. 108, 636 S.E.2d 508 (2006).

established the disparity benchmark at 10 percent trumped the court promulgated rules set out in the UAP and ruled that an under-representation of white jurors by 6.04 percent was not unconstitutional.

The UAP also mandates the statewide use of the Decennial Census as the comprehensive source of data as an objective, readily implemented test of whether cognizable groups are adequately represented on jury source lists. The Supreme Court has approved this methodology even in the case where there is evidence that at some point during the ten years between census a cognizable group becomes underrepresented on a county's jury source list.[49]

See § 12:3, supra, on making up of grand jury list.

For challenges to the array of grand jurors see Studdard, *Daniel's Georgia Criminal Trial Practice Forms* (2018–2019 ed.), §§ 11:1, et seq. See § 12:4, supra, on the general requirements for grand jurors.

§ 12:10 Grand jury secrecy

Grand jury proceedings are secret proceedings and the grand jurors are sworn to secrecy.[1] The classic justification for grand jury secrecy, to the extent it exists, is said to be based upon the following reasons: (1) Witnesses will be more likely to testify freely and fully;[2] (2) perjury and subornation of perjury may be prevented by withholding knowledge of facts testified to before a grand jury which, if known, could be of use to the defendant and confederates; (3) to conceal the fact that a defendant is under investigation, and thus, prevent his escape;[3] (4) to insure that the grand jurors will be free from fear in stating their opinions and voting; and (5) so that an innocent accused will not be openly accused with a groundless charge.[4]

While Georgia has a statute providing for a grand juror to disclose everything which occurred at a grand jury proceeding if

---

[49]Ramirez v. State, 276 Ga. 158, 575 S.E.2d 462 (2003). See Williams v. State, 287 Ga. 735, 699 S.E.2d 25 (2010).

[Section 12:10]

[1]O.C.G.A. § 15-12-67. See also O.C.G.A. § 15-12-73. See Olsen v. State, 302 Ga. 288, 806 S.E.2d 556 (2017) (oath of secrecy does not apply to district attorney and staff as well as expert witness employed by state; district attorney and staff may be present during presentations of evidence but must leave grand jury during deliberations).

[2]See U. S. v. Procter & Gamble Co., 356 U.S. 677, 682, 78 S. Ct. 983, 2 L. Ed. 2d 1077 (1958).

[3]Howard v. State, 60 Ga. App. 229, 236, 4 S.E.2d 418 (1939).

[4]In the Matter of Russo, 53 F.R.D. 564 (C.D.Cal.1971). Cf. Douglas Oil Co. of California v. Petrol Stops Northwest, 441 U.S. 211, 99 S.Ct. 1667, 60 L.Ed.2d 156 (1979).

necessary,[5] another statute states that admissions and communications among grand jurors are not admissible in evidence as a matter of public policy.[6] A number of cases also hold that grand jurors cannot impeach their own findings.[7]

However, a grand juror is not prevented from testifying in support of the action the grand jury has taken.[8] He may apparently testify as to the nature of an oath administered to a witness, the testimony which the witness delivered before the grand jury,[9] the number of grand jurors present and the manner in which they voted in returning an indictment.[10] It appears that a grand juror can testify to the testimony of a witness before the grand jury for purposes of impeaching the witness at trial[11] and in a trial for perjury.[12]

If the district attorney was present at the grand jury, he may be sworn as a witness and compelled to testify as to the events which occurred in the proceeding.[13] A court reporter or other individual present in the grand jury room would apparently not be disqualified from also testifying at trial.[14] Although no one other than grand jurors can be present in the grand jury room when it

---

[5]O.C.G.A. § 15-12-72. Generally, see Annot., "Accused's Right to Inspection of Minutes of State Grand Jury," 20 A.L.R.3d 7 (1968).

[6]O.C.G.A. § 15-12-73. See also O.C.G.A. § 24-5-501(a)(3) which excludes communications among grand jurors from evidence.

[7]Turner v. State, 57 Ga. 107 (1876); Simms v. State, 60 Ga. 145 (2) (1878) (where a grand jury voting for indictment was not permitted to testify that a witness was not sworn).

[8]Simms v. State, 60 Ga. 145 (1878).

[9]See Switzer v. State, 7 Ga. App. 7, 11 (2), 65 S.E. 1079 (1909). But cf. Simms v. State, 60 Ga. 145, 146 (1) (1878).

In Butterworth v. Smith, 494 U.S. 624, 110 S.Ct. 1376, 108 L.Ed.2d 572 (1990), the court held that a Florida law preventing a grand jury witness from disclosing his testimony after the discharge of the grand jurors is a violation of the First Amendment.

[10]See Tanner v. State, 163 Ga. 121 (1), 134, 135 S.E. 917 (1926). But see Eubanks v. State, 5 Okla.Crim. 325, 114 P. 748 (1911); State v. Hartfield,

290 Or. 583, 624 P.2d 588 (1981).

[11]State v. Wood, 53 N.H. 484 (1873). But see State v. Terrebonne, 256 La. 385, 236 So.2d 773 (1970), holding that a transcript of testimony before a grand jury may not be used for impeachment; Brown v. Dewell, 123 Fla. 785, 167 So. 687 (1936).

[12]Izer v. State, 77 Md. 110, 26 A. 282 (1893), where the court states that the grand juror's oath of secrecy "cannot be made the means to defeat the punishment of crime." Grand jury testimony has been held admissible at trial when a witness refuses to testify because of threats made by the defendant. United States v. Carlson, 547 F.2d 1346 (8th Cir. 1976).

[13]Switzer v. State, 7 Ga. App. 7 (2), 65 S.E. 1079 (1909).

[14]The Federal Rules of Criminal Procedure, in Rule 6(e), expressly recognize the propriety of the presence of a court reporter. However, in United States v. Head, 586 F.2d 508 (5th Cir. 1978), the court held that it is not necessarily reversible error for a prosecutor to fail to have the testimony of some witnesses recorded while recording that of others even when the nonrecording resulted from the prosecu-

votes on whether to indict an accused, there are no rules restricting the number of qualifications of persons who may be present when the state presents evidence.[15] However, an indictment may be invalidated where the presence of a person in the grand jury room is prejudicial to the defendant.[16]

§ 12:11 Discovery of grand jury testimony

The material in § 12:10, supra, sets out the Georgia statutory and case law as it relates to grand jury secrecy. To summarize, Georgia statutes provide (1) that a grand juror may, in court, whenever it becomes necessary, disclose everything[1] and (2) that communications between grand jurors are not discoverable.[2]

The area presenting the greatest difficulty is that related to communications between grand jurors. There is a recognized and sound public policy which is intended to prevent the disclosure of grand jury deliberations. Yet it has been held that grand jurors may testify how they voted on an indictment.[3] Also, if anyone is in the grand jury room other than the grand jurors when the grand jury is deliberating, it seems that the presence of this person keeps the communications from being privileged and the third person can testify to what took place.[4] The Georgia courts have apparently treated the presence of an outsider, even the district attorney, as being analogous to a third person overhearing a conversation between a husband and wife[5] and thus have permitted or required the testimony of such an outsider if such evidence is relevant. Since this rule has been applied to the district attorney, it would certainly seem to also apply to a court reporter or anyone else in the room.

The need for protection or secrecy related to grand jury proceedings would seem to be less in a situation involving the testimony of a witness before a grand jury than in the case of the actual deliberations among the grand jurors as discussed above. It has

---

tor's desire to limit the number of Jencks statements. Reversible error will exist only where the defendant can show that the selective recording prejudiced him in making his defense.

[15]Olsen v. State, 302 Ga. 288, 806 S.E.2d 556 (2017).

[16]See U.S. v. Bowdach, 324 F. Supp. 123 (S.D. Fla. 1971) (presence of FBI agent); U.S. v. Borys, 169 F. Supp. 366 (Terr. Alaska 1959) (mother of child victim). Compare U.S. v. Braniff Airways, Inc., 428 F. Supp. 579 (W.D. Tex. 1977) (presence of unauthorized persons in grand jury room is per se ground for abating indictment without proof of actual prejudice).

[Section 12:11]

[1]O.C.G.A. § 15-12-72.

[2]O.C.G.A. §§ 24-5-501(a)(3), 15-12-73.

[3]See Tanner v. State, 163 Ga. 121, 123 (1), 135 S.E. 917 (1926).

[4]Switzer v. State, 7 Ga. App. 7 (2), 65 S.E. 1079 (1909).

[5]Hudson v. State, 153 Ga. 695, 113 S.E. 519 (1922).

been pointed out that the need for grand jury secrecy is ended after an indictment has been returned and if the ends of justice require it, statements of grand jury witnesses may be made available to defense counsel.[6] However, there is no general rule which permits defense counsel to obtain such statements automatically.[7] The rule in the federal courts is that defense counsel has to show a "particularized need" for such a statement or statements.[8] This same rule is growing in acceptance in state courts.[9] Whether or not a particularized need exists is ordinarily a question which necessarily addresses itself to the sound discretion of the trial judge.[10]

It must be kept in mind, however, that all of the foregoing must be considered in the light of *Brady v. Maryland*.[11]

See 38 Am. Jur. 2d Grand Jury § 41 on limitations or exceptions to the rule of secrecy.

§ 12:12   Swearing the grand jury witnesses

O.C.G.A. § 15-12-68 provides that the following oath shall be

---

[6]See United States v. Socony-Vacuum Oil Co., 310 U.S. 150, 234, 60 S.Ct. 811, 84 L.Ed. 1129 (1940).

[7]In fact, the general rule has historically been that the defense is not entitled to inspection of grand jury minutes or statements. Gaines v. State, 146 Ala. 16, 41 So. 865, 867 (1906); Jackman v. State, 140 So.2d 627, 630 (Fla.App. 1962); Commonwealth v. Jordan, 207 Mass. 259, 93 N.E. 809, 811 (1911).

[8]Pittsburgh Plate Glass Co. v. United States, 360 U.S. 395, 79 S.Ct. 1237, 3 L.Ed.2d 1323 (1959). Also see Dennis v. United States, 384 U.S. 855, 872, 86 S.Ct. 1840, 16 L.Ed.2d 973 (1966), which seems to indicate a loosening of the requirements needed to show a particularized need.

[9]West v. State, 3 Tenn.Crim.App. 671, 466 S.W.2d 524, 525 (1971); Dinning v. State, 256 Ind. 399, 269 N.E.2d 371, 373 (Ind. 1971); Commonwealth v. Carita, 356 Mass. 132, 249 N.E.2d 5, 10 (1969).

[10]E.g., State v. Gillespie, 227 So.2d 550, 559 (Fla.App.1969); State v. James, 327 S.W.2d 278 (Mo.1959); State v. Faux, 9 Utah 2d 350, 345 P.2d 186 (1959); Shelby v. District Court, 82 Nev. 204, 414 P.2d 942 (1966); Burkholder v. State, 491 P.2d 754 (Alaska 1971) (sufficiency of evidence for indictment); People v. Bellanca, 386 Mich. 708, 194 N.W.2d 863 (1972). Generally, see Comment, "Grand Jury Minutes; The Unreasonable Rule of Secrecy," 48 Va. L. Rev. 668 (1962); Comment, "Pre-Trial Discovery of Grand Jury Testimony in Criminal Cases," 66 Dick. L. Rev. 379 (1962); Comment, "The Impact of Jencks v. United States and Subsequent Legislation on the Secrecy of Grand Jury Minutes," 27 Fordham L. Rev. 244 (1958); "Pre-Trial Disclosure in Federal Grand Jury Testimony," 48 Walsh L. Rev. 423 (1973); Calkin and Wiley, "Grand Jury Secrecy Under Illinois Criminal Code—Unconstitutional," 59 Nw. U. L. Rev. 581 (1964); Calkin, "Grand Jury Secrecy," 63 Mich. L. Rev. 455 (1965).

[11]Brady v. Maryland, 373 U.S. 83, 83 S.Ct. 1194, 10 L.Ed.2d 215 (1963), discussed in §§ 14:33 et seq., infra. Also, generally, see Annot., "Withholding or Suppression of Evidence by Prosecution in Criminal Case as Vitiating Conviction," 34 A.L.R.3d 16 (1970).

administered to witnesses who are to testify before the grand jury:

"Do you solemnly swear or affirm that the evidence you shall give the grand jury on this bill of indictment or presentment shall be the truth, the whole truth, and nothing but the truth? So help you God."

In *State v. Williams*,[1] the court held, " 'Unless the oath prescribed by the statute is taken by the witness, his testimony before the grand jury does not amount to evidence, and, if false, would not be a basis upon which perjury . . . could be assigned. . . . [T]he witness must be sworn [on a particular case]. . . . The right to question the witness is limited to the special case upon which he was sworn. . ..' " However, in *State v. Bartel*,[2] the court held that the above oath is not to be used for witnesses appearing before a grand jury in a civil investigation.

§ 12:13 Witnesses and evidence before grand jury

At the outset it must be pointed out that the district attorney in his sole discretion may dismiss a case prior to indictment. This power to dismiss is regarded as a part of the power of his office.[1] In *Lee v. State*,[2] the court stated, "Whether to prosecute and what charge to bring before a grand jury are decisions that generally rest in the prosecutor's discretion."

" '[A]s a prerequisite to valid testimony before a grand jury, there must before the grand jury some pleading, either in the form of a bill of indictment or a special presentment, charging a named person with a specified offense.' "[3] As set out in § 12:12, supra, the witness must be sworn upon that particular case.

By statute, the district attorney[4] and the foreperson of the grand jury[5] have the authority to swear and examine witnesses. However, any member of the grand jury apparently can interrogate witnesses.[6] If there is a substantial difference between the

---

[Section 12:12]

[1]State v. Williams, 181 Ga. App. 204, 205, 351 S.E.2d 727 (1986); Inman v. State, 187 Ga. App. 652, 371 S.E.2d 230 (1988).

[2]State v. Bartel, 223 Ga. App. 696, 699, 479 S.E.2d 4 (1996).

[Section 12:13]

[1]State v. Hanson, 249 Ga. 739, 744, 295 S.E.2d 297 (1982).

[2]Lee v. State, 177 Ga. App. 698, 700 (1), 340 S.E.2d 658 (1986) (quoted with approval in Slater v. State, 185 Ga. App. 889 (1), 366 S.E.2d 240 (1988)).

[3]State v. Williams, 181 Ga. App. 204, 205, 351 S.E.2d 727 (1986).

[4]O.C.G.A. § 15-18-6(2).

[5]O.C.G.A. § 15-12-67; Bird v. State, 50 Ga. 585 (1874).

[6]See Davis v. State, 72 Ga. App. 347, 349, 33 S.E.2d 728 (1945).

oath required by statute[7] and that actually administered, a motion to quash the indictment will lie[8] if the only evidence before the grand jury on the indictment was the testimony of the witness to whom the defective oath was administered.[9]

The oath of the witness is not sufficient if he is merely sworn in reference to "a case against a party for a specified offense, without in fact having the case stated in the form of an indictment."[10] An indictment may not be returned without the grand jury having heard such testimony. The right to question the witness is limited to the special case upon which he is sworn.[11] In addition to subpoenaing witnesses to appear before a grand jury, the clerk of the court may issue a subpoena duces tecum to have documents produced before a grand jury,[12] but such a subpoena may not be so broad as to violate the Fourth Amendment.[13]

In Georgia, there is no requirement that a grand jury keep minutes of its proceedings. If the clerk or secretary of the grand jury does keep minutes, this does not prevent a witness from testifying as to events or statements made in the grand jury room in considering an indictment if the testimony is otherwise admissible.[14]

A grand jury has no right to subpoena an accused and force him to testify to matters related to a pending charge against him. If it does, a plea in abatement is good even if the grand jury also hears the testimony of other witnesses.[15]

It should be kept in mind that "the grand jury sits not to

---

[7]O.C.G.A. § 15-12-68.

[8]Ashburn v. State, 15 Ga. 246 (1854); Switzer v. State, 7 Ga. App. 7 (1), 65 S.E. 1079 (1909). Also, if a witness is not properly sworn before he testifies before a grand jury, he may not be prosecuted for perjury even if his testimony before the grand jury is not true. Aldridge v. State, 39 Ga. App. 484, 487, 147 S.E. 414 (1929).

See Annot., "Failure to Swear or Irregularity in Swearing Witness Appearing Before Grand Jury as Ground for Dismissal of Indictment," 23 A.L.R.4th 154 (1983).

[9]Lennard v. State, 104 Ga. 546, 30 S.E. 780 (1898).

[10]Switzer v. State, 7 Ga. App. 7, 11-12, 65 S.E. 1079 (1909).

[11]Switzer v. State, 7 Ga. App. 7 (1), 11, 65 S.E. 1079 (1909); In re Lester, 77 Ga. 143, 144 (1886).

[12]Blitch v. State, 145 Ga. 882, 90 S.E. 42 (1916).

[13]United States v. Calandra, 414 U.S. 338, 346, 94 S.Ct. 613, 38 L.Ed.2d 561 (1974).

[14]Thompson v. State, 18 Ga. App. 488, 89 S.E. 607 (1916).

[15]Jenkins v. State, 65 Ga. App. 16, 14 S.E.2d 594 (1941). However, there is no federal constitutional reason which prevents a suspect from being subpoenaed to testify before a grand jury and then being indicted by the grand jury. Also, from a federal constitutional standpoint, the case of United States v. Wong, 431 U.S. 174, 97 S.Ct. 1823, 52 L.Ed.2d 231 (1977), holds that it is not necessary to warn a person testifying before a grand jury that he is a potential defendant where he is given the *Miranda* warnings before he testifies, and a witness who testifies before a grand jury may be

determine innocence or guilt, but to assess whether there is adequate basis for bringing a criminal charge."[16] Except in the case of a public official or peace officer, an accused has no right to submit evidence on his behalf before a grand jury even if the district attorney consents,[17] nor may he be present when the grand jury hears testimony against him.[18] A grand jury will usually hear only the accusative evidence.[19] The failure of the state to call witnesses who would have weakened the state's case is generally not a violation of the defendant's due process right.[20] The United States Supreme Court in *United States v. Williams*[21] held that a prosecutor has no duty to present exculpatory evidence before a grand jury. However, several courts have suggested that prosecutors, while not obliged to present every form of exculpatory evidence of an accused to the grand jury, may have a duty to present evidence that clearly negates guilt. These courts find this standard promotes judicial economy. "If a fully informed grand jury cannot find probable cause to indict, there is little chance the prosecution could have proved guilt beyond a reasonable doubt."[22]

Subject only to the Fifth Amendment right against self-incrimination, a witness appearing before a grand jury has no right to refuse to answer questions. Likewise, a grand jury witness is not entitled to Miranda warnings.[23] A grand jury witness may not on federal constitutional grounds refuse to answer questions because they are the product of an unlawful search and seizure.[24] Furthermore, there is no constitutional requirement

---

prosecuted for perjury even if he does not understand the *Miranda* warnings given him because of his limited knowledge of the English language.

[16]United States v. Williams, 504 U.S. 36, 112 S.Ct. 1735, 118 L.Ed.2d 352 (1992).

[17]United States v. Blodgett, (1867). Cf. United States v. Salsedo, 607 F.2d 318 (9th Cir. 1979).

[18]Harper v. State, 131 Ga. 771 (1), 63 S.E. 339 (1909).

[19]Rafe v. State, 20 Ga. 60, 65 (1) (1856).

[20]United States v. Ruyle, 524 F.2d 1133, 1135 (6th Cir. 1975).

[21]United States v. Williams, 504 U.S. 36, 112 S.Ct. 1735, 118 L.Ed.2d 352 (1992).

[22]U.S. v. Page, 808 F.2d 723, 728 (10th Cir. 1987) (court noted that where *substantial* exculpatory evidence is known to government, this should be provided to grand jury); U.S. v. Flomenhoft, 714 F.2d 708, 712 (7th Cir. 1983); U.S. v. Ciambrone, 601 F.2d 616, 622-623 (2d Cir. 1979).

[23]See U. S. v. Mandujano, 425 U.S. 564, 96 S. Ct. 1768, 48 L. Ed. 2d 212 (1976).

[24]In re Grand Jury Proceedings, 522 F.2d 196 (5th Cir. 1975). The ABA has taken the position that "[e]very witness before a grand jury shall be informed of his privilege against self-incrimination and right to counsel and shall be advsied that false answers may result [in perjury charges]. Target witnesses shall be told they are possible indictees." *House of Delegates Adopts Advertising D.R. and Endorses a Package of Grand Jury Reforms*, 63

that the exclusionary rule be applied.[25] However, in *Gelbard v. United States*,[26] the United States Supreme Court held that a grand jury witness could refuse to answer questions based on information obtained from illegal wiretapping.

There is Georgia authority stating that a grand jury may not force a witness to disclose general knowledge of violations of the criminal laws.[27] It is the responsibility of the grand jury to determine infractions of the criminal law, but it has no authority to make a man spy upon the conduct of his neighbors and to compel him to divulge information he has received in confidence.[28]

Valid testimony[29] must be heard on each presentment. An affidavit alone apparently is not sufficient to authorize the grand jury to return a true bill.[30] However, generally a court will not consider "admissibility, confidentiality, relevance or prejudice of evidence" presented to a grand jury.[31]

In *Morris v. State*,[32] the Georgia Supreme Court considered the question of relevancy and materiality of documents subpoenaed by a grand jury. On a motion to quash such a subpoena, the grand jury initially "has the burden of going forward, and . . . the duty to make a prima facie showing that the subpoenaed documents are relevant to a legitimate grand jury investigation." After that has been done the party "moving to quash . . . has the general burden of persuasion. . . . The reason for this allocation of the burden of going forward is that the secrecy of grand jury deliberations insures that the party moving to quash a subpoena duces tecum has no precompliance knowledge of the subject matter of the investigation. 'Relevance and materiality necessarily are terms of broader content in their use as to a grand jury investigation than in their use as to the evidence of a trial.' . . . Thus, we hold that the required prima facie showing of relevancy entails proof of the following: (1) the existence of a grand jury investigation; (2) a general characterization of the subject matter and purpose of said investigation; and (3) the fact that each general

---

A.B.A. J. 1234, 1237 (Sept. 1977).

[25]United States v. Calandra, 414 U.S. 338, 351, 94 S.Ct. 613, 38 L.Ed.2d 561 (1974).

[26]Gelbard v. United States, 408 U.S. 41, 92 S.Ct. 2357, 33 L.Ed.2d 179 (1972). In re: iPhone Application Litigation, 844 F.Supp. 2d. 1040, 1061 (N.D. Cal. 2012) (notes that *Gelbard* was based on an outdated version of the Wiretap Act which was broader than the current version of 18 U.S.C. 2510(8)).

[27]See Vaughn v. State, 259 Ga.

325, 381 S.E.2d 30 (1989).

[28]In re Lester, 77 Ga. 143, 147 (1886). See § 12:18, infra. See State v. Williams, 181 Ga. App. 204, 351 S.E.2d 727 (1986).

[29]See Switzer v. State, 7 Ga. App. 7, 11, 65 S.E. 1079 (1909).

[30]See Williams v. State, 107 Ga. App. 794, 131 S.E.2d 567 (1963).

[31]Mitchell v. State, 239 Ga. 456, 459, 238 S.E.2d 100 (1977).

[32]Morris v. State, 246 Ga. 510, 272 S.E.2d 254 (1980).

category of the subpoenaed documents bears *some* relevance to the investigation being pursued." On motions to quash subpoenas, see § 17:12, infra.

A court will not generally inquire into the sufficiency of the evidence upon which an indictment was returned.[33] However, if it was returned without any evidence[34] or wholly upon illegal evidence,[35] a plea in abatement will lie. In *Felker v. State,*[36] the court held that when "it appears that a competent witness or witnesses were sworn and examined before the grand jury . . . a plea in abatement on the ground that it was found on insufficient evidence or illegal evidence, or no evidence, *will not be sustained,* because it comes under the rule that no inquiry into sufficiency or legality of the evidence is indulged." The Fifth Circuit has held that the Fifth Amendment prevents the returning of an indict-

---

[33]Buchanan v. State, 215 Ga. 791 (2), 113 S.E.2d 609 (1960); Powers v. State, 172 Ga. 1 (3), 157 S.E. 195 (1931); Mitchell v. State, 239 Ga. 456, 459 (3), 238 S.E.2d 100 (1977); Mullen v. State, 203 Ga. App. 170, 172 (1), 416 S.E.2d 784 (1992). But see United States v. Provenzano, 423 F.Supp. 662 (S.D.N.Y.1976).

In United States v. Calandra, 414 U.S. 338, 94 S.Ct. 613, 38 L.Ed.2d 561 (1974), the court said, "The grand jury's sources of information are widely drawn, and the validity of an indictment is not affected by the character of the evidence considered."

[34]See Johnson v. State, 148 Ga. 546 (1), 97 S.E. 515 (1918); Chapman v. State, 148 Ga. 531 (1), 97 S.E. 546 (1918).

[35]See Meriwether v. State, 63 Ga. App. 667, 668, 11 S.E.2d 816 (1940); State v. Lawler, 221 Wis. 423, 267 N.W. 65, 68 (1936); People v. Aday, 226 Cal.App.2d 520, 38 Cal.Rptr. 199, 203 (1964).

In Costello v. United States, 350 U.S. 359, 76 S.Ct. 406, 100 L.Ed. 397 (1956), cited with approval in Reaves v. State, 242 Ga. 542, 545, 250 S.E.2d 376 (1978), the United States Supreme Court in its supervisory authority over federal courts, refused to establish a rule permitting defendants in criminal cases to challenge indictments on the ground that they were based solely on hearsay evidence. See Annot., "Compe-tency or Sufficiency of Evidence Before Grand Jury as Affecting Validity of Indictment or Conviction in Federal Court," 100 L. Ed. 404, 407 (1955). In United States v. Estepa, 471 F.2d 1132 (2d Cir. 1972), the court held valid a motion to dismiss an indictment where apparently the only grand jury witness testified from hearsay to detailed facts about which he had no personal knowledge and he failed to make it clear to the grand jury that his testimony was based on hearsay; accord, Burkholder v. State, 491 P.2d 754 (Alaska 1971).

A.B.A. Standards, The Prosecution Function, Standard 3-4.6 sets out a number of responsibilities which a prosecutor should meet, including advising a grand jury when the evidence presented does not warrant an indictment; ensuring that grand jurors are properly instructed as to their ability to ask questions and seek evidence; advising the grand jurors of the request by a target of an investigation to appear and present non-frivolous evidence; and, advising a target of an investigation who wishes to testify of his or her right against self-incrimination.

[36]Jackson v. State, 270 Ga. 494, 496 (2), 512 S.E.2d 241 (1999); Felker v. State, 252 Ga. 351, 314 S.E.2d 621 (1984), overruled on other grounds by Fleming v. State, 265 Ga. 541, 458 S.E.2d 638 (1995); State v. Bragg, 213 Ga. App. 795, 446 S.E.2d 226 (1994).

ment solely on informal unsworn hearsay testimony.[37] It should be noted, however, that an indictment is presumed to be returned on competent evidence. The burden is on the defendant to show the contrary.[38]

There must be separate hearing of testimony on each indictment.[39]

See § 12:10, supra, on persons who may be in the grand jury room.

§ 12:14 Witness immunity—Background—General

There are at least three general kinds of immunity: (1) complete immunity, which is a promise to the witness that he will not be prosecuted for anything, including perjury, in connection with his testimony; (2) transactional immunity, or a promise not to prosecute the witness for anything related to the transaction about which he testifies but not including immunity for perjury; and (3) use and derivative use immunity, which means that none of the testimony of the witness and nothing derived directly or indirectly from it can be used against him.[1]

---

[37]United States v. Hodge, 496 F.2d 87 (5th Cir. 1974). In this case, the defendant was indicted in February 1973 for conspiracy to make and transport forged money orders after the original grand jury had been discharged. A mistake was made in the wording on the indictment. In August of 1973 the prosecuting attorney appeared before another grand jury, explained that the scrivener made a mistake in the first indictment and it failed to describe the money orders as counterfeit. No witnesses appeared and a new indictment was returned. The court said: "An indictment may rest upon hearsay, Costello v. United States, 350 U.S. 359, 76 S.Ct. 406, 100 L.Ed. 397 (1956), and we see no problem if government agents did in fact give sworn testimony before the second grand jury as to what they and other witnesses had stated to the first grand jury. But informal unsworn hearsay from the mouth of the prosecutor only is something else altogether. This, we think, is interdicted by the Fifth Amendment. . . . [A]n indictment must be based on competent evidence."

[38]See Meriwether v. State, 63 Ga. App. 667, 668, 11 S.E.2d 816 (1940).

[39]Evans v. State, 17 Ga. App. 120 (3), 86 S.E. 286 (1915).

[Section 12:14]

[1]In United States v. Frumento, 552 F.2d 534 (3d Cir. 1977) (en banc), the court pointed out that a witness could be prosecuted for perjury committed in the trial even though his testimony was immunized. However, the Constitution requires that a valid grant of immunity be as broad as the Fifth Amendment privilege. If a witness does not testify, obviously his testimony may not be used to impeach him. Hence, immunized testimony may not be used to impeach the witness if he later testifies in another case.

In U.S. v. Balsys, 524 U.S. 666, 118 S. Ct. 2218, 141 L. Ed. 2d 575, 49 Fed. R. Evid. Serv. 371 (1998), the Supreme Court held that the risk that a resident alien's testimony might subject him to deportation was not a sufficient ground for asserting the Fifth Amendment protection from self-

In *Counselman v. Hitchcock,*[2] the United States Supreme Court said that any valid immunity statute "must afford absolute immunity against future prosecution for the offense to which . . . [questioning] relates." Thus, transactional immunity came to be regarded as the minimum constitutional protection which could be given a witness.

In 1970, Congress enacted 18 U. S. C. §§ 6001 to 6003, which provide for use and derivative use immunity in federal courts. In 1972, the United States Supreme Court considered these statutes in *Kastigar v. United States,*[3] in which the defendant was subpoenaed to testify before a federal grand jury and was granted use and derivative use immunity under this statute. A district court order was issued directing the defendant to answer questions and produce evidence before the grand jury. The defendant objected to this order contending that the immunity provided by the statute was not coextensive with the Fifth Amendment privilege against self-incrimination.[4] The trial court rejected his contention and directed that he testify before the grand jury.[5] The defendant refused and was found to be in contempt. The Supreme Court held that the use and derivative use immunity provided by the statute was as broad as the Fifth Amendment privilege against self-incrimination. The court pointed out that once a defendant shows that he has testified to related matters, the prosecution has the burden of showing that their evidence is not tainted and "the affirmative duty to prove that the evidence it proposes to use is derived from a legitimate source wholly independent of the compelled testimony."[6] This is generally referred to as a *Kastigar* hearing.

In 1975, Georgia enacted an immunity statute which applies to

---

incrimination. The Court noted that concern with prosecution by a foreign government was beyond the scope of the Fifth Amendment.

[2]Counselman v. Hitchcock, 142 U.S. 547, 12 S.Ct. 195, 35 L.Ed. 1110 (1892).

[3]Kastigar v. United States, 406 U.S. 441, 92 S.Ct. 1653, 32 L.Ed.2d 212 (1972). See In re Grand Jury Subpoena Duces Tecum Dated March 25, 2011, 670 F.3d 1335, 84 A.L.R.6th 677 (11th Cir. 2012). Cf. Garrity v. New Jersey, 385 U.S. 493, 87 S.Ct. 616, 17 L.Ed.2d 562 (1967).

[4]Generally, see Annot., "Adequacy, Under Federal Constitution of Immunity Granted in Lieu of Privilege Against Self-Incriminations—Supreme Court Cases," 32 L.Ed.2d 869 (1973).

[5]However, before a witness is cited for contempt for refusal to answer questions after a grant of immunity, the trial judge must specifically explain the grant of immunity to the witness. State v. Paquette, 117 R.I. 638, 369 A.2d 1096 (1977).

[6]Kastigar v. United States, 406 U.S. 441, 460, 92 S.Ct. 1653, 32 L.Ed.2d 212 (1972). In 1977, the American Bar Association recommended that the federal law be changed and that grand jury witnesses be granted transactional rather than use immunity. 5 Criminal Justice No. 2, Sept. 1977, p. 1. See Gerstein and Robinson, "Remedy for the Grand Jury: Retain but Reform," 64 A.B.A. J. 337, 338 (March 1978).

testimony given before grand juries as well as in the trial of criminal cases.[7] This statute provides that while a person shall not be excused from testifying on the basis of his privilege against self-incrimination, testimony required under court order concerning proceedings or prosecution for a crime or offense shall not be used against him.

The Georgia courts have recognized the husband-wife relationship as an exception to the immunity statute. Hence, if immunity is given to a wife, she still cannot be forced to testify against her husband to matters which would incriminate him.[8]

The Georgia Supreme Court has said that there is no common law transactional immunity in Georgia and former O.C.G.A. § 24-9-28 (repealed and replaced by O.C.G.A. § 24-5-507 effective July 1, 2013), which provides use immunity for a witness compelled to testify, provides adequate constitutional protection.[9]

With court approval, the district attorney may validly promise to forego prosecution of specific crimes or crimes arising out of a specified transaction.[10] In *Lee v. King*,[11] the court pointed out that such an agreement must be in writing. However, such an agreement is binding only in the circuit of the district attorney who

---

[7]O.C.G.A. § 24-5-507. Cf. O.C.G.A. § 10-5-11 on a grant of immunity by the Georgia Commissioner of Securities in conducting an investigation involving securities; O.C.G.A. § 34-8-253 relating to records pertaining to industrial relations.

In Corson v. Hames, 239 Ga. 534 (1), 238 S.E.2d 75 (1977), the court said that the title of former § 24-9-28 (now § 24-5-507) "Immunity from prosecution" is inaccurate since the section only authorizes "a grant of use and derivative use immunity." The same case says that absent statutory authority, the validity of a grant of transactional immunity is an open question, citing Ingram v. Prescott, 111 Fla. 320, 321, 149 So. 369 (1933).

[8]State v. Smith, 237 Ga. 647, 229 S.E.2d 433 (1976), aff'g 138 Ga. App. 683, 227 S.E.2d 84 (1976). See Studdard, *Daniel's Georgia Handbook on Criminal Evidence* § 5:2 (2018 ed.), on spousal privilege.

[9]State v. Hanson, 249 Ga. 739, 742, 295 S.E.2d 297 (1982), aff'g result in 161 Ga. App. 536, 287 S.E.2d 764 (1982).

In Rowe v. Griffin, 676 F.2d 524, 527-28 (11th Cir. 1982), the state of Alabama, without statutory authority, granted transactional immunity to *Rowe*. Years later he was indicted for murder. The court stated, "We believe that, as a matter of fair conduct, the government ought to be required to honor such an agreement when it appears from the record that: (1) an agreement was made; (2) the defendant has performed on his side; and (3) the subsequent prosecution is directly related to offenses in which the defendant, pursuant to the agreement, either assisted with the investigation or testified for the government." The court then affirmed the district court's grant of a permanent injunction preventing the state prosecution.

[10]State v. Hanson, 249 Ga. 739, 747, 295 S.E.2d 297 (1982).

See Annot., "Enforceability of Agreement by Law Enforcement Officials Not to Prosecute if Accused Would Help in Criminal Investigation or Would Become Witness Against Others," 32 A.L.R.4th 990 (1984).

[11]Lee v. King, 263 Ga. 116, 117 (1), 428 S.E.2d 326 (1993).

makes the agreement.[12]

In *State v. Dean*,[13] the court recognized the concept of equitable immunity as being applicable to the circumstances of that case.

For a petition for immunity, see Studdard, *Daniel's Georgia Criminal Trial Practice Forms* (2018–2019 ed.), §§ 11:5 et seq. on petition, order for witness immunity; Studdard, *Daniel's Georgia Handbook on Criminal Evidence*, (2018 ed.) § 5:23 on grant of immunity.

§ 12:15   Witness immunity—Procedure

If a witness declines to testify or to produce evidence when subpoenaed to appear before a grand jury or at the trial of a criminal case because of a fear of self-incrimination, immunity is sometimes granted in order to obtain the testimony or evidence.

O.C.G.A. § 24-5-507 provides that if the Attorney General or any district attorney requests the court in writing to order a person to testify or produce evidence and the judge signs the order, that person shall not be excused from testifying on the basis of self-incrimination, but the testimony or evidence so given and any information derived directly or indirectly therefrom may not be used against the person in any prosecution or proceeding unless he is charged with perjury or false swearing in connection with his testimony.[1] In *State v. Mosher*,[2] the trial judge expressed doubts as to the co-defendant's credibility and hence refused to enter an order granting immunity. On appeal, the court pointed out that the statute does not mandate that the judge automatically enter an immunity order, but while the Attorney General or any district attorney has the initial statutory discretion, the judge has the ultimate discretion to order that the witness testify. However, the judge abused his discretion in refusing to sign an order based on his own determination of credibility because issues of witness credibility are reserved for the jury. The Georgia

---

[12]Bryant v. State, 164 Ga. App. 555, 556, 296 S.E.2d 792 (1982).

[13]State v. Dean, 212 Ga. App. 724, 728 (2), 442 S.E.2d 830 (1994).

[Section 12:15]

[1]In United States v. Apfelbaum, 445 U.S. 115, 100 S.Ct. 948, 63 L.Ed.2d 250 (1980), the court in considering federal immunity provided for in 18 U.S.C.A. § 6002 said that neither the statute nor the Fifth Amendment prevents prosecution for perjury after a grant of use and derivative use immunity.

The court also concluded that the prosecution could not only introduce the defendant's false statements but could also introduce his truthful testimony, which was intended to put the false statements in context and to show that the defendant knew the false statements were not true. See Hoffman, "The Privilege Against Self-Incrimination and Immunity Statutes: Permissible Uses of Immunized Testimony," 16 Crim. L. Bull. 421 (1980).

[2]State v. Mosher, 265 Ga. 666, 461 S.E.2d 219 (1995).

Supreme Court has said that even if a witness' testimony or evidence involves a violation of a federal law or a criminal offense in another jurisdiction, he can be forced to testify.[3]

The statute also says that no compelled evidence nor any evidence derived directly or indirectly therefrom can be used against the witness in any court, including federal courts. Thus, a grant of immunity prevents the use of such evidence against the witness in any county in the state.[4] The grant of immunity must be as broad in scope as the privilege it replaces and it must demonstrate the applicability of the immunity to the witness before he is ordered to testify.[5] The grant of immunity may not be conditional. Hence, the state may not condition a grant of immunity on the testimony of the witness being "full," "complete" and "truthful."[6] Likewise, immunized grand jury testimony may not be used to impeach a defendant if he later testifies at his trial.[7]

It has been held that when a defendant has been granted immunity under a state immunity grant and the federal government seeks to prosecute him, the defendant may show that he testified pursuant to a state immunity grant on a matter related to the federal prosecution. The defendant is then entitled to a hearing to determine if any of the evidence the government obtained was connected with his immunized testimony. The government must affirmatively prove that its evidence comes from sources independent of the immunized testimony. It is not sufficient for the government to simply deny that it has seen or heard the immunized testimony. If the evidence before the grand jury which indicted the witness is not found to be from an independent source, the indictment against the witness should be dismissed. At the trial of the case, if the immunized evidence was used, a new trial must be granted.[8]

---

[3]Brooks v. State, 238 Ga. 435, 436, 233 S.E.2d 208 (1977), disapproving Powell v. Allen, 140 Ga. App. 186, 230 S.E.2d 343 (1976). The Ninth Circuit has held that the possibility of a criminal prosecution in a foreign country is not regarded as justifying a witness in refusing to testify if he has been granted use and derivative use immunity. See In re Federal Grand Jury Witness, 597 F.2d 1166 (9th Cir. 1979).

[4]Brooks v. State, 238 Ga. 435, 233 S.E.2d 208 (1977).

[5]See U.S. v. Balsys, 524 U.S. 666, 681, 118 S. Ct. 2218, 141 L. Ed. 2d 575, 49 Fed. R. Evid. Serv. 371 (1998).

[6]Corson v. Hames, 239 Ga. 534, 535, 238 S.E.2d 75 (1977).

[7]New Jersey v. Portash, 440 U.S. 450, 99 S.Ct. 1292, 59 L.Ed.2d 501 (1979). In *Portash*, the court held that since the defendant's grand jury testimony had been compelled by the grant of immunity, it was not admissible for impeachment.

[8]United States v. Nemes, 555 F.2d 51 (2d Cir. 1977). Cf. United States v. Tantalo, 680 F.2d 903 (2d Cir. 1982).

In *In re Long*,[9] the court concluded that the failure of the trial judge to make a specific finding that the witness's testimony was necessary to the public interest rendered the immunity order invalid.

In *Greenwood v. State*,[10] the court held if immunity is granted to a witness and the witness nevertheless makes it clear that he will refuse to answer any questions, it is error to permit the district attorney to call the witness and ask leading questions based on the witness' prior testimony. The court pointed out that this kind of procedure in effect permitted the district attorney to testify and circumvent meaningful cross-examination.

There is authority holding that if the prosecuting attorney does not object, immunity may be granted to a witness in a civil case.[11]

The United States Supreme Court said, in *United States v. Calandra*,[12] that if a grand jury witness is granted immunity, he has no right to refuse to answer questions which were predicated on information obtained as a result of an unlawful search and seizure. However, the court was careful to point out that this decision was limited to grand jury testimony, which is not regarded as an adversary proceeding, and is not limited by technical evidentiary rules.[13] The general rule is that immunity statutes are for the benefit of the state and not for the benefit of the defendant.[14]

In *U.S. v. Quinn*,[15] the court was emphatic in its holding that the judiciary is not authorized to order witness immunity. However, the court did recognize that the selective use of witness immunity, witness intimidation, and other forms of prosecutorial

---

[9]In re Long, 276 Ga. App. 306(1), 623 S.E.2d 181 (2005).

[10]Greenwood v. State, 203 Ga. App. 901, 902, 418 S.E.2d 160 (1992). Cf. Lawrence v. State, 257 Ga. 423, 424 (3), 360 S.E.2d 716 (1987).

[11]Daly v. Superior Court of San Francisco, 19 Cal.3d 132, 137 Cal.Rptr. 14, 560 P.2d 1193 (1977).

[12]United States v. Calandra, 414 U.S. 338, 94 S.Ct. 613, 38 L.Ed.2d 561 (1974).

In Pillsbury Co. v. Conboy, 459 U.S. 248, 103 S.Ct. 608, 74 L.Ed.2d 430 (1983), the court held that a witness who has been granted immunity under 18 U.S.C.A. § 6002 cannot be forced by a trial court in a civil case to answer questions based on immunized answers he gave to a grand jury over

a valid assertion of the Fifth Amendment privilege unless he is given a new grant of immunity as to his answers.

[13]United States v. Calandra, 414 U.S. 338, 94 S.Ct. 613, 38 L.Ed.2d 561 (1974). However, on non-constitutional grounds, the court held that an immunized witness before a federal grand jury could refuse to answer questions based on illegal wiretapping and electronic surveillance. Gelbard v. United States, 408 U.S. 41, 92 S.Ct. 2357, 33 L.Ed.2d 179, 180 (1972).

[14]Brown v. State, 295 Ga. 804, 764 S.E.2d 376 (2014). See Dampier v. State, 249 Ga. 299, 290 S.E.2d 431 (1982).

[15]U.S. v Quinn, 728 F.3d 243 (3rd Cir. 2013).

misconduct may operate to deprive an accused of a fair trial. If the harm caused by the government can be ameliorated by compelling the testimony of a witness for the defense through a grant of immunity, the remedy may well be to afford the government the option of providing the witness with use immunity or dismissing the case.

> Courts sometimes refer to this remedy as "compelling the Government to immunize the witness," . . . but that is imprecise. Dismissing the charges unless the witness is immunized leaves prosecutorial decisions in the hands of the Government. It may grant immunity to the witness and attempt to convict the defendant in a fair trial, or it may decide that denying the witness immunity is more important to its goals than seeking that conviction. But the remedy does not compel the Government to do anything. It simply prevents prosecutors from obtaining a conviction through a process that lacks the fairness afforded by due process.

In *King v. State*,[16] the court ruled that a defendant has no standing to object to the grant of use immunity to a codefendant.

On contempt procedure, see §§ 27:4 et seq., infra. See Studdard, *Daniel's Georgia Handbook on Criminal Evidence* (2018 ed.), § 6:33, on immunity for a defense witness. Generally, see 21 Am. Jur. Criminal Law §§ 210 et seq. See § 15:2, infra, on enforceability of agreement not to prosecute.

§ 12:16　Proceedings against officials and peace officers

Prior to 2016, O.C.G.A. § 45-11-4 set forth special procedures for grand jury hearings on allegations of criminal acts by public officials. Peace officers charged with crimes committed while in the performance of their duties could avail themselves of similar procedures pursuant to O.C.G.A. § 17-7-52. The special procedures under both Code sections allowed the accused to be present throughout the grand jury proceedings, and at the end of the state's case in chief, to make a statement to the grand jury. Neither the district attorney nor the grand jury could question the officer about his or her statement.

Ga. Laws 2016, Act 350 (H.B. 941), enacted in 2016 amid a nationwide negative reaction to officer-involved shootings, reformed grand jury proceedings for peace officers and other public officials. H.B. 941's two major objectives were the elimination of many of the protections afforded to public officials and law enforcement officers in grand jury proceedings under O.C.G.A. §§ 45-11-4 and 17-7-52, and granting grand juries the ability to independently review cases involving a police officer's use of

---

[16]King v. State, 273 Ga. 258(15), 539 S.E.2d 783 (2000). See Gilbert v. State, 306 Ga. App. 776, 703 S.E.2d 374 (2010).

deadly force that resulted in serious bodily injury or death.

Law enforcement officers may no longer make uncontested, unquestioned statements to the grand jury. An officer may not be compelled to appear before a grand jury but he or she has the right to do so. If the officer chooses to testify, "the case shall proceed as in any other criminal case heard by a grand jury." The officer may not be present for the testimony of other witnesses. Like all other witnesses, the officer "may be questioned by the prosecuting attorney or members of the grand jury" Prior to questioning, however, the officer may still give a sworn statement without interruption.[1]

At the request of the district attorney, or when deemed necessary by eight or more members of the grand jury, a grand jury "shall conduct a review of any incident in which a peace officer's use of deadly force resulted in death or serious bodily injury to another." If the grand jury deems an investigation necessary, it may only conduct its review upon completion and submission of the investigative report from the incident. The grand jury cannot conduct a review if the district attorney decides to bring the case to the grand jury for an indictment. Grand jury reviews must be recorded by a court reporter.[2]

If, after conducting a review, the grand jury does not request that the district attorney create a bill of indictment or special presentment, it must prepare a report that includes a summary of the evidence and the grand jury's findings of fact, and publish it in open court. The district attorney must make the evidence from the review available, subject to redactions for privilege. If the grand jury requests that the district attorney create a bill of indictment or special presentment, none of the records from the grand jury review may be disclosed.[3]

Although no longer afforded all of the protections provided by former O.C.G.A. § 17-7-52, peace officers still have some degree of procedural protection before the grand jury. If the officer is represented by counsel, the attorney may be present in the grand jury room while the officer testifies. Counsel may consult with the officer outside the grand jury room as well. However, counsel may not propound questions to the officer nor interpose evidentiary objections to questions put to the officer.

Prior to 2016, the appellate courts addressed under what circumstances peace officers should be afforded such protection. In *Morrill v. State*,[4] the court pointed out "that a police officer charged with participating in a burglary while in uniform and on

---

[Section 12:16]

[1]O.C.G.A. § 17-7-52.

[2]O.C.G.A. § 15-12-71(b)(5)(B) to

(D).

[3]O.C.G.A. § 15-12-71(e).

[4]Morrill v. State, 216 Ga. App.

duty [is not entitled to the foregoing] protections, inasmuch as the performance of such official duties does not include the commission of burglaries." As the Court of Appeals explained in *State v. Galloway*:[5]

> These rights have been found to apply where prison officers were charged with involuntary manslaughter for confining a prisoner under conditions which caused his death by heat prostration, and where a police officer on duty was charged with speeding and failing to reduce his speed when approaching an intersection. However, these rights have been found not to apply to situations where officers have stepped aside from the performance of their official duties in order to commit crimes. For instance, we have held that officers charged with committing burglary, armed robbery, and aggravated assault while on duty are not entitled to these rights inasmuch as the performance of their official duties does not include the commission of such crimes. Likewise, this court has held that the performance of official duties does not include rape.

O.C.G.A. § 45-11-4 as amended applies to certain public officials including probate judges, county commissioners, and the mayor or member of any municipal governing authority who are charged with "malpractice, misfeasance or malfeasance in office." The Code section has no application to any other crime alleged to have been committed by a public official while in the performance of an official duty. Previously, these categories of public officials were afforded the right to appear with counsel before the grand jury and make an unsworn statement at the conclusion of the state's presentation. However, that right was taken away by the 2016 amendment to O.C.G.A. § 45-11-4.

See O.C.G.A. § 15-18-27 on the procedure to be taken to present or indict the district attorney.

For a plea in abatement for failure to permit a peace officer to appear before a grand jury, see Studdard, *Daniel's Georgia Criminal Trial Practice Forms* (2018–2019 ed.), §§ 11:11 and 11:12.

§ 12:17 Handling of the indictment

A judge has no authority to give any direction whatsoever to a

---

468, 470(2), 454 S.E.2d 796 (1995).

[5]State v. Galloway, 270 Ga. App. 184, 185, 606 S.E.2d 273 (2004). See State v. Dorsey, 342 Ga. App. 188, 802 S.E.2d 61 (2017) (deputy charged with restraining and sexually assaulting woman during working hours was acting outside official duties and not entitled to rights provided in O.C.G.A. §§ 17-5-52 and 45-11-4). Compare Wiggins v. State, 280 Ga. 268(1), 626 S.E.2d 118 (2006) (officer charged with falsifying a police report to cover up his criminal action was entitled to the protection afforded by O.C.G.A. §§ 17-7-52 and 45-11-4); State v. Peabody, 343 Ga. App. 362, 807 S.E.2d 107 (2017) (officer responsible for care of a K-9 unit deemed to be acting in performance of duties when charged with aggravated cruelty to animals involving death of dog resulting from being left in officer's unventilated vehicle while he was attending to personal matter).

grand jury concerning the return of an indictment against a particular person.[1]

As previously noted, a grand jury cannot return an indictment against an accused without hearing sworn evidence on the specific charge.[2] If the grand jury, however, determines that the evidence shows the commission of another offense, the accused may be indicted for the other offense.[3] On the trial of the case, the defendant is not entitled to show that the offense for which he was indicted was not the crime for which he was initially being investigated by the grand jury.[4] Generally, for a discussion of the terms "indictment" and "special presentments," see § 13:2, infra.

Grand jurors must vote individually on each charge and may not vote on indictments in block.[5] At common law, a concurrence of at least 12 of the panel was necessary in order to return an indictment.[6] Since this has not been changed by statute, it is apparently still true.[7] The same rule also applies in federal court.[8]

It has been said that a grand jury is the judge of the law and the facts.[9] The Fifth Amendment requirements are met if a grand jury declines to indict a defendant unless it has probable cause to

---

[Section 12:17]

[1]Thompson v. State, 109 Ga. 272, 276, 34 S.E. 579 (1899) (dictum).

[2]In re Lester, 77 Ga. 143 (1886); Switzer v. State, 7 Ga. App. 7 (1), 11, 65 S.E. 1079 (1909).

[3]Oglesby v. State, 121 Ga. 602 (4), 49 S.E. 706 (1905).

[4]Davis v. State, 105 Ga. 783, 32 S.E. 130 (1898). In this case, the defendant actually was prevented from using the foreman of the grand jury to testify that initially the grand jury was investigating a separate transaction.

[5]Evans v. State, 17 Ga. App. 120 (3), 86 S.E. 286 (1915).

[6]See Cannon v. State, 62 Fla. 20, 57 So. 240 (1911); Barney v. State, 20 Miss. 68, 12 Smedes & Marshall 68 (1849); State v. Perry, 122 N.C. 1018, 29 S.E. 384 (1898); McCampbell v. State, 116 Tenn. 98, 93 S.W. 100 (1905); Clyncard's Case, 78 Eng. Reprint 893.

In United States v. Lang, 644 F.2d 1232 (7th Cir. 1981), the court said that the Fifth Amendment does not limit the number of substitutions which can be made in grand jury membership and refused to void an indictment where only 11 members heard all the evidence on a particular case.

See § 12:5, supra, on selecting grand jury.

See Annot., "Validity of Indictment As Affected by Substitution or Addition of Grand Jurors After Commencement of Investigation," 2 A.L.R.4th 980 (1980).

[7]See Thurman v. State, 25 Ga. 220, 221 (1858); Tanner v. State, 163 Ga. 121, 124, 135 S.E. 917 (1926).

[8]Rule 6(b)(2), Federal Rules of Criminal Procedure. Rule 6(c) imposes on the foreperson of a federal grand jury the responsibility of keeping a record of the number of jurors concurring in the returning of each indictment. On motion, counsel for defendant is entitled to this record. If there was no such record kept, the defendant is entitled to a hearing to determine if 12 or more grand jurors did concur. United States v. Bullock, 448 F.2d 728 (5th Cir. 1971).

[9]State v. Lawler, 221 Wis. 423, 267 N.W. 65, 69 (1936).

believe him guilty.[10] The probable cause rule has been said to be the common law rule and the modern rule unless a higher degree of proof is required by statute.[11] It has been held that when a grand jury has evidence before it "which is competent and credible which excites in its mind after careful consideration an honest reasonable belief that the accused committed the offense charged, it is warranted in returning an indictment."[12] Some states permit the returning of an indictment if "the evidence . . . presented, taken together, if unexplained or uncontradicted, would in the grand jury's judgment warrant a conviction by a trial jury."[13]

After the grand jury has voted on an indictment, an entry is made on the back of the charges showing that either a "true bill" or a "no bill" has been returned. This is normally done by simply inserting the word "true" or "no" before or above the word "bill" on the back of the presentment.[14] In *State v. Auerswald,*[15] the court pointed out that "the tabling of an indictment . . . [is not] the legal equivalent of a no bill" an a grand jury may defer action in a particular case.

If a grand jury returns a "no bill," the case is probably terminated. However, it is legally possible for the same grand jury to reconsider the case and return a "true bill," or an indictment, against the accused at that term.[16] Also, after an earlier "no bill," it is possible for a grand jury at a later term of court to indict the defendant.[17]

O.C.G.A. § 17-7-53.1 was enacted in 1987. It provides that when two "true bills" of indictments for the same offense are returned and the indictment is quashed for the second time "whether by ruling on a motion, demurrer, special plea or exception, or other pleading of the defendant or by the court's own motion, such actions shall be a bar to any future prosecution of such defendant

---

[10]Beavers v. Henkel, 194 U.S. 73, 84, 24 S.Ct. 605, 48 L.Ed. 882 (1904). This case quotes from 4 Blackstone Commentaries 303, which provides in part as follows: "[T]he grand jury are only to inquire . . . whether there be sufficient cause to call upon the party to answer it. A grand jury, however, ought to be thoroughly persuaded of the truth of an indictment, so far as their evidence goes; and not to rest satisfied merely with remote probabilities."

[11]41 Am. Jur. 2d Indictments and Informations § 21; cf. 38 C. J. S. Grand Juries § 42(c).

[12]State v. Lawler, 221 Wis. 423, 267 N.W. 65, 71 (1936).

[13]People v. Fernandez, 172 Cal.App.2d 747, 342 P.2d 309, 312 (1959).

[14]See Barlow v. State, 127 Ga. 58, 63, 56 S.E. 131 (1906).

[15]State v. Auerswald, 198 Ga. App. 183, 185 (4), 401 S.E.2d 27 (1990).

[16]Fuss v. State, 31 Ga. App. 147, 120 S.E. 37 (1923).

[17]McNeely v. State, 25 Ga. App. 328 (1), 103 S.E. 189 (1920).

for the offense." In *State v. Griffin*,[18] the Georgia Supreme Court held that "OCGA § 17-7-53.1 applies only when two quashed indictments originate in the grand jury of a single county." However, this statute does not apply to an indictment returned before the effective date of the statute.[19] In *Smith v. State*,[20] the court held that even where two indictments have been returned against a defendant, neither has been quashed, and he is "brought to trial on the second reindictment," the statute does not prevent his being tried. The court pointed out that the statute "contemplates the trial court's actual quashing of two prior indictments, not the trial court's mere denial of two prior special demurrers." In *Gourley v. State*,[21] the court held that the consent of the trial judge to an entry of nolle prosequi to two indictments does not equate to the quashing of an indictment within the meaning of O.C.G.A. § 17-7-53.1 and did not amount to a statutory bar to defendant's trial on a third indictment which contained the same language found in the two previous indictments. However, in *Evans v. State*,[22] the court applied O.C.G.A. § 17-7-53.1 even though the trial judge refused to reduce to writing the ruling on the second motion to quash.

On the other hand, if a grand jury indicts a defendant and subsequently in their general presentments recommends that the indictment be nol prossed, it is within the discretion of the court whether to follow this recommendation or not.[23] After the return of an indictment has been placed on the minutes of the court, a grand jury loses its jurisdiction and cannot recall the "true bill," erase the "true bill" entry, and make an entry of "no bill" on the indictment.[24] Where a defendant is indicted for murder and the words "True Bill—Voluntary Manslaughter" are written on the back and a line is drawn through the word "murder" on the back and a line with an arrow from the stricken word murder is drawn to the "voluntary manslaughter" notation, the indictment has been held to be a valid voluntary manslaughter indictment.[25]

Where a grand jury has returned a "no bill" and a second grand jury returns another "no bill" on the same charges, the prosecution is terminated unless the returns have been procured by fraud

---

[18]State v. Griffin, 268 Ga. 540, 543, 491 S.E.2d 340 (1997).

[19]State v. Smith, 187 Ga. App. 249, 370 S.E.2d 15 (1988).

[20]Smith v. State, 260 Ga. 746, 399 S.E.2d 66 (1991).

[21]Gourley v. State, 268 Ga. 235, 486 S.E.2d 342 (1997).

[22]Evans v. State, 217 Ga. App. 548, 550, 458 S.E.2d 357 (1995).

[23]Edwards v. State, 121 Ga. 590 (1), 49 S.E. 674 (1905).

[24]Gibson v. State, 162 Ga. 504, 134 S.E. 326 (1926); Fields v. State, 121 Ala. 16, 25 So. 726 (1899); Banks v. State, 185 Ark. 539, 48 S.W.2d 847 (1932).

[25]Carter v. State, 155 Ga. App. 49, 270 S.E.2d 233 (1980).

or unless there exists newly discovered evidence. In the case of fraud or newly discovered evidence, the judge may allow a third presentation of the case.[26] However, the rule set out in this paragraph does not apply where accusations are involved.[27]

If a defendant is in jail, he is entitled to be released as soon as a "no bill" is returned.[28] Likewise, if the accused is on bond, he and his surety are released subject to his being re-arrested if he is later indicted.[29]

One member of the grand jury signs the "true bill" or "no bill."[30] Normally, this is done by the foreperson,[31] but this apparently was not a requirement at common law and is not required by Georgia law.[32] If it is not signed by him, it will be presumed that the person signing acted as foreperson with the authority of the grand jury.[33] The "true bill," or indictment, does not have to be signed by the district attorney,[34] although his name will usually be typed or printed on it.

Once the charges have been marked either "true bill" or "no bill" and signed, the document is normally delivered to the bailiff,[35] who delivers it to the judge in open court, or it may be

---

[26]O.C.G.A. § 17-7-53. However, in Chafin v. State, 246 Ga. 709, 712 (1), 273 S.E.2d 147 (1980), the court pointed out that the mere failure of two successive grand juries to indict the defendant did not prevent a later grand jury from indicting him. In Nelson v. State, 247 Ga. 172, 174 (3), 274 S.E.2d 317 (1981), the court pointed out that "a mere failure of the grand jury to indict does not constitute the return of a no bill."

[27]State v. Roca, 203 Ga. App. 267, 268, 416 S.E.2d 836 (1992).

[28]See Lowry v. Thompson, 53 Ga. App. 71, 72, 184 S.E. 891 (1936).

[29]Curcio v. Sanders, 109 Ga. App. 548, 136 S.E.2d 406 (1964), says that an accused, after return of a "no bill," is released "subject to being re-arrested and new recognizance required upon the initiation of a new bill of indictment." It seems, though, that there would be no need for a bond until indictment.

[30]In Harrell v. State, 11 Ga. App. 407 (1), 75 S.E. 507 (1912), the court held that if the "true bill" contained the names of the 18 persons making up the grand jury who acted on it and the minutes of the court showed that these persons made up the regularly impaneled grand jury, it was a clerical error for the foreman to fail to sign his full name on the back, but the error was said to be immaterial. In Barlow v. State, 127 Ga. 58, 62-63, 56 S.E. 131 (1906), the court said that if the indictment is properly returned and so appears on the minutes of the court, this is probably sufficient.

[31]See White v. State, 27 Ga. App. 769, 109 S.E. 917 (1921).

[32]See Barlow v. State, 127 Ga. 58, 62, 56 S.E. 131 (1906).

[33]McGuffie v. State, 17 Ga. 497 (1855) (this may be rebutted by the minutes of the court, but the court does not indicate what the result would be if the person signing was established not to be the foreman).

[34]Ellison v. State, 82 Ga. App. 760, 62 S.E.2d 407 (1950).

[35]See Davis v. State, 74 Ga. 869, 870 (8) (1885), limited by Bowen v. State, 81 Ga. 482, 8 S.E. 736 (1889).

delivered by the grand jury as a body to the judge in open court.[36] The bailiff cannot simply deliver it to the clerk of the court after court for that day has adjourned.[37] A bailiff may retain indictments overnight, however, and return them in open court the next day if the grand jury has not been discharged.[38] After the grand jury has been discharged by the court, the bailiff may not make a return of an indictment.[39] In *State v. Brown*,[40] the Georgia Supreme Court held that "open court" means that the indictment must be returned in a place where court is being held open to the public with the judge and clerk in attendance. The Court also held that the failure to return the indictment causes "per se" injury to the defendant.

The district attorney has no legal authority to return an indictment into court for the grand jury,[41] but if the grand jury is present in a body in open court and an indictment is handed to the district attorney in the presence of the judge and he hands it to the clerk, the return is valid.[42] If the minutes of the court show that the "true bill" was returned at that term of court, there is a presumption that it was regularly returned, although this presumption may be rebutted.

"Open court," as the term is used in connection with an indictment, means the place where court is held which is open to the public with the judge and clerk of the court present.[43] The rationale underlying the requirement is the deterrence of indictments returned in secret and the appearance of a grand jury acting as a "Star Chamber."[44] Since indictments are to be returned in open court, a plea in abatement will lie where the bailiff delivers an indictment to the judge in the hallway of the courthouse and is directed by the judge to deliver the indictment to the clerk.[45] Also, where the bailiff delivers an indictment to the judge's office

---

[36]Zugar v. State, 194 Ga. 285, 21 S.E.2d 647 (1942).

[37]Sampson v. State, 124 Ga. 776, 53 S.E. 332 (1906). But see Danforth v. State, 75 Ga. 614 (1) (1886).

[38]Dalton v. State, 100 Ga. App. 732, 733, 112 S.E.2d 446 (1959).

[39]Dalton v. State, 100 Ga. App. 732 (2), 112 S.E.2d 446 (1959).

[40]State v. Brown, 293 Ga. 493, 748 S.E.2d 376 (2013). See Thomas v. State, 331 Ga. App. 641, 771 S.E.2d 255 (2015) (objection that indictment was not returned in open court is waived if not raised prior to trial).

[41]Bowen v. State, 81 Ga. 482, 8 S.E. 736 (1889).

[42]Bowen v. State, 81 Ga. 482, 8 S.E. 736 (1889).

[43]Zugar v. State, 194 Ga. 285, 289, 21 S.E.2d 647 (1942); State v. Brown, 293 Ga. 493, 748 S.E.2d 376 (2013) (the court held that the requirement to return an indictment in open court must be complied with in every case and that the failure to do so is not subject to a harmless error inquiry).

[44]State v. Brown, 293 Ga. 493, 748 S.E.2d 376 (2013).

[45]Zugar v. State, 194 Ga. 285, 21 S.E.2d 647 (1942).

while the clerk is present, a plea in abatement is good.[46] Where there is a visiting judge trying a case because the regular judge is disqualified, an indictment returned to the visiting judge in open court is valid.[47]

If as a matter of fact an indictment is improperly returned and the minutes of the court indicate that it was regularly returned, the defendant should file a motion to correct the minutes.[48]

The fact that the judge before whom an indictment was returned would be disqualified to try the case does not constitute an improper return, and a plea in abatement based on this is not valid.[49]

In *In re Floyd County,*[50] the court held that in the absence of specific statutory authority, "[a] grand jury has no right to file a report charging or casting reflections of misconduct in office upon a public officer or impugning his character, except by present-ment or true bill of indictment charging such individual with a specific offense . . . and it is the . . . right of the one who is the subject of such . . . report to have it expunged from the official records."

For a motion to amend and correct grand jury minutes, see Studdard, *Daniel's Georgia Criminal Trial Practice Forms* (2018–2019 ed.), § 11:13.

§ 12:18 Witnesses subpoenaed to testify before grand jury[1]

Reference has been made previously to the provisions in some counties for investigative or special grand juries.[2] Such investiga-tive grand juries have long been used by the federal courts al-though there has been a cry for reform.[3] The theory of the investigative grand jury is that witnesses who would be unwill-ing to talk to law enforcement officials can be subpoenaed before a grand jury and forced to testify under the threat of contempt.

O.C.G.A. § 15-12-68 provides an oath which is to be adminis-tered to witnesses who are to testify before a grand jury in crimi-

[46]Cadle v. State, 101 Ga. App. 175, 180, 113 S.E.2d 180 (1960).

[47]Wilson v. State, 215 Ga. 446, 111 S.E.2d 32 (1959).

[48]See Cadle v. State, 101 Ga. App. 175, 178, 113 S.E.2d 180 (1960).

[49]Clinkscales v. State, 102 Ga. App. 670, 117 S.E.2d 229 (1960).

[50]In re Floyd County, 225 Ga. App. 705, 707 (1), 484 S.E.2d 769 (1997).

[Section 12:18]

[1]See Fahringer, "Representing a Witness Before a Grand Jury," 15 Crim. L. Bull. 571 (1979).

[2]See § 12:2, supra, on historical background of grand jury.

[3]See 122 Congressional Record No. 127. See the splendid article, Rodis, "A Lawyer's Guide to Grand Jury Abuse," 14 Crim. L. Bull. 123 (1978).

nal cases. However, in *Robinson v. State*,[4] the court held that the failure to administer the requisite oath does not entitle a defendant to a new trial.

If counsel represents a witness summoned to testify before a grand jury,[5] he will want to be sure that none of the answers sought from the witness could incriminate him. If a possibility of incrimination exists, the witness should be instructed to consider invoking the Fifth Amendment privilege against self-incrimination. In this connection, it should be remembered that the United States Supreme Court has held that it is not necessary for a grand jury witness to be given Miranda warnings.[6]

It is generally conceded that counsel for the witness has no right to enter the witness room.[7] Yet, a witness has a right to consult with counsel outside the grand jury room as long as he is acting in good faith.[8]

There is authority holding that a grand jury witness has a right to consult with his counsel after each question asked him.[9] Some counsel are careful to tell the witness to write down each question which he may wish to discuss with counsel. In many cases, it is probably wise for counsel to write out certain "stock" answers which may be appropriate. These answers might cover such matters as (1) the witness's refusing to answer on the ground that it may incriminate him, and (2) the witness's declining to answer the question until he has had an opportunity to consult with his counsel as provided for by the Sixth Amendment.

If the witness is granted immunity as discussed previously,[10] then he is faced with the dilemma of answering the questions put to him or facing the possibility of punishment for contempt in refusing to answer. If it is determined that the immunity is suf-

---

[4]Robinson v. State, 221 Ga. App. 865, 867 (4), 473 S.E.2d 519 (1996).

[5]Generally, on this subject, see Grand Jury Defense Office of the National Lawyers Guild, Representation of Witnesses Before Federal Grand Juries 566 (2d ed. 1976, Clark Boardman Co.).

[6]United States v. Mandujano, 425 U.S. 564, 96 S.Ct. 1768, 48 L.Ed.2d 212 (1976).

[7]In re Groban, 352 U.S. 330, 77 S.Ct. 510, 1 L.Ed.2d 376 (1957). However, in 1977 the American Bar Association recommended that the federal law be changed so that grand jury witnesses will have the right to take lawyers into the grand jury room. 5 Crim. Just. No. 2, p. 1, Sept. 1977. See

Gerstein and Robinson, "Remedy for the Grand Jury: Retain but Reform," 64 A.B.A. J. 337, 338 (March 1978). In Losavio v. J.L., 195 Colo. 494, 580 P.2d 23 (1978), the court upheld a Colorado statute which permitted a witness to have his counsel with him in the grand jury room.

[8]In re Tierney, 465 F.2d 806 (5th Cir. 1972), but a witness may not, as a matter of constitutional right, insist on being represented by counsel. See United States v. Mandujano, 425 U.S. 564, 96 S.Ct. 1768, 48 L.Ed.2d 212, 225 (1976).

[9]United States v. George, 444 F.2d 310 (6th Cir. 1971).

[10]See §§ 12:14 and 12:15, supra.

ficiently broad to protect the witness, it may be well for counsel
to remind him that under Georgia's use and derivative use immunity, the more information he reveals, the broader his immunity will be.

It should be noted that under Georgia law, a grand jury has no
right to force a witness to testify to any general information he
has about violation of the law. Furthermore, a grand jury has no
authority to compel a witness to divulge information he has
received in confidence.[11]

§ 12:19 Action of grand jury after being discharged

In the 1993 case of *State v. Grace*,[1] the Georgia Supreme Court
held "that a grand jury properly summoned, sworn, and charged
to serve during a particular term of the court, may recess and
reconvene as it sees fit to conduct its business in the course of
that term, and need not be resworn or recharged by the court
during that term."

---

[11]In re Lester, 77 Ga. 143, 147
(1886), and see § 12:13, supra.

[Section 12:19]

[1]State v. Grace, 263 Ga. 220, 221,
430 S.E.2d 583 (1993), overruling Ward
v. State, 205 Ga. App. 485, 423 S.E.2d

22 (1992), and State v. Byrd, 197 Ga.
App. 661, 399 S.E.2d 267 (1990). Garcia
v. State, 207 Ga. App. 794, 429 S.E.2d
164 (1993), had followed and relied
upon *Byrd*. *Garcia* is not cited or
referred to in *Grace*, but it will not be
followed.

Chapter 13

Indictments and Accusations

> **KeyCite®:** Cases and other legal materials listed in KeyCite Scope can be researched through the KeyCite service on Westlaw®. Use KeyCite to check citations for form, parallel references, prior and later history, and comprehensive citator information, including citations to other decisions and secondary materials.

§ 13:1 Scope

This chapter will discuss indictments, presentments, and accusations, along with the essentials of each. Matters such as joinder of parties,[1] joinder of offenses,[2] surplusage,[3] and idem sonans[4] (two names spelled differently but which are pronounced the same) are covered in the material on pre-trial motions. Demurrers, motions for a directed verdict of acquittal, and matters such as variance are discussed in the material on trials. See § 13:4, infra, on variance. See Studdard, *Daniel's Georgia Handbook on Criminal Evidence* (2018 ed.), §§ 1:40 et seq. on indictments.

§ 13:2 Background

At common law and formerly in Georgia, the grand jury would return a special presentment from which the prosecuting attorney would file an indictment. The distinction between indictments and special presentments has been abolished. Special presentments of the grand jury are returned into court and treated as indictments. Thus, defendants may still be arraigned and tried on special presentments,[1] and the term "indictment" commonly refers to a special presentment.[2] The term "special presentment" is seldom used.

The term "accusation" is a generic term which includes an indictment, but the term "indictment" or "special presentment" does not include an accusation. In Georgia, the term "accusation" has a specialized meaning. It is said that an accusation is the

---

[Section 13:1]

[1]See § 14:72, infra, on motion to sever parties.

[2]See § 14:73, infra, on motion to sever offenses.

[3]See § 14:41, infra, on special demurrers. Also see § 13:4, infra, on contents of indictments.

[4]See § 14:45, infra, on plea of misnomer.

[Section 13:2]

[1]Switzer v. State, 7 Ga. App. 7, 10, 65 S.E. 1079 (1909); Barlow v. State, 127 Ga. 58, 60, 56 S.E. 131 (1906); O.C.G.A. § 17-7-51.

In Carmichael v. State, 228 Ga. 834, 837, 188 S.E.2d 495 (1972), the court said that the technical distinction between an indictment and a special presentment is "that in an indictment the accusation is presented by a prosecutor, and in a special presentment it is preferred by the grand jury without a prosecutor."

[2]O.C.G.A. § 17-7-51.

equivalent of an information at common law.[3]

There is no state constitutional provision granting a defendant the right to be tried only by indictment,[4] and the requirement under the federal constitution of a grand jury indictment does not apply to a state criminal prosecution.[5] The Georgia Supreme Court has expressly held that a defendant may be tried in a city court for a misdemeanor on an accusation.[6] However, an indictment must be used if a defendant is charged with a felony, unless he waives it.[7] Thus, accusations are commonly used in misdemeanor cases tried in city and state courts, while indictments or special presentments are utilized in cases tried in superior court.[8]

In *Bass v. State*,[9] an accusation was returned charging the defendant with entering an auto with intent to commit theft. He was tried, convicted, and given a misdemeanor sentence in the State Court of Thomas County. The defendant appealed, and the Court of Appeals reversed his conviction, holding that the offense for which he had been tried was a felony, even though misdemeanor punishment was authorized. The court said that the trial court "did not have jurisdiction . . . and all proceedings held in the state court pursuant . . . [to the accusation] are a nullity."

§ 13:3   Formal parts

An indictment which uses the form set out in the Code or one which plainly states the nature of the offense charged is adequate.[1] The statutory form is as follows:

"Georgia, _____ County.

"The grand jurors selected, chosen, and sworn for the County of _____, to wit: _____, in the name and behalf of the citizens of Georgia, charge and accuse (name of the accused) of the county and state aforesaid, with the offense of _____; for that the said (name of the accused) (state with sufficient certainty the offense and the time and place of committing the same), contrary to the laws of said state, the good order, peace, and dignity thereof."

The same Code section also provides that where there is more than one count to the charge, each additional count shall begin

---

[3]Wright v. Davis, 120 Ga. 670, 676, 48 S.E. 170 (1904).

[4]Hopkins v. State, 5 Ga. App. 699, 700, 63 S.E. 718 (1909).

[5]Hurtado v. California, 110 U.S. 516, 4 S.Ct. 111, 28 L.Ed. 232 (1884).

[6]Green v. State, 119 Ga. 120, 45 S.E. 990 (1903).

[7]Cunningham v. State, 80 Ga. 4, 8, 5 S.E. 251 (1888).

[8]The rule at common law was that a person charged with a felony had to be indicted by a grand jury. See Gordon v. State, 102 Ga. 673, 675, 29 S.E. 444 (1897).

[9]Bass v. State, 169 Ga. App. 520, 313 S.E.2d 776 (1984).

[Section 13:3]

[1]O.C.G.A. § 17-7-54.

as follows:

"And the jurors aforesaid, in the name and behalf of the citizens of Georgia, further charge and accuse (name of the accused) with having committed the offense of _____; for that the said (name of the accused) (state with sufficient certainty the offense and the time and place of committing the same) contrary to the laws of said state, the good order, peace, and dignity thereof."[2]

If the indictment fails to contain the words "contrary to the laws of said state, the good order, peace, and dignity thereof" or words of similar import, the indictment is subject to demurrer;[3] but it is not necessary for these words to appear at the conclusion of each count.[4] If an indictment for burglary charges that the defendant did "unlawfully and with force and arms" enter, etc., it is subject to demurrer.[5]

The district attorney need not sign an indictment or special presentment.[6] The typed[7] or printed[8] name of the district attorney on the indictment is treated as his signature.

§ 13:4   Contents—General

An indictment has been said not to be subject to a general demurrer when it is written in the form set out in O.C.G.A. § 17-7-54, and couched in the language of the statute alleged to have been violated.[1] However, an indictment need not quote the exact

---

[2]In Holtzendorf v. State, 146 Ga. App. 823, 247 S.E.2d 599 (1978), the court said that it is not necessary for each count to be numbered.

[3]Tarver v. State, 123 Ga. 494, 496, 51 S.E. 501 (1905). This case also points out that there was a similar requirement at common law. See Jackson v. State, 301 Ga. 137, 800 S.E.2d 356 (2017) (indictment must (1) recite the language of the statute that sets out all the elements of the offense charged or (2) allege the facts necessary to establish violation of a criminal statute).

[4]Morris v. State, 82 Ga. App. 420, 61 S.E.2d 297 (1950).

[5]In Smith v. State, 130 Ga. App. 390, 391, 203 S.E.2d 375 (1973), the court said that the quoted words are not part of the burglary statute and they are not contained in the statutory form prescribed for indictments and are surplusage.

[6]See Newman v. State, 101 Ga. 534 (4), 28 S.E. 1005 (1897); Ellison v. State, 82 Ga. App. 760, 62 S.E.2d 407 (1950). In federal court, it has been said that a true bill does not become an indictment until it is signed by the United States Attorney and that the court has no authority to order him to sign it. In re Grand Jury Jan. 1969, 315 F.Supp. 662 (D.Md.1970). Generally, see Annot., "Necessity and Sufficiency of Government Attorney's Signature on Indictment or Information," 5 A.L.R.Fed. 922 (1970). But cf. Thompson v. State, 109 Ga. 272, 276, 34 S.E. 579 (1899).

[7]See Byrd v. State, 72 Ga. App. 840, 841 (1), 35 S.E.2d 385 (1945).

[8]Hillman v. State, 67 Ga. App. 292 (1), 20 S.E.2d 91 (1942).

[Section 13:4]

[1]Smith v. State, 130 Ga. App. 390, 203 S.E.2d 375 (1973). Cf. Tidwell v. State, 216 Ga. App. 8, 9 (1), 453

language of the statute.[2] If an indictment does not recite language from the Code, it must allege every essential element of the crime charged.[3] An indictment should set out the alleged offense with sufficient specificity so as to give the defendant ample opportunity to prepare his defense, but it need not specify the crime by a specific name[4] or Code section number.[5] In *Smith v. Hardrick*,[6] the court pointed out that an "indictment which does not recite language from the Code must allege every essential element of the crime charged." "Due process requires that the indictment inform the accused of the charges so that he may defend them at trial."[7] The name given a crime in an indictment is not what determines the crime for which the defendant is to be tried; the descriptive language determines the crime for which the defendant is to be tried.[8] See § 13:15, infra, on crimes which could be committed in more than one way. In *Bentley v. State*,[9] the court held that "[a]n alleged variance between the offense as named or the Code section cited and the allegations specified in the indictment [describing the charge] goes only to the form of the indictment." See § 14:41, infra, on special demurrers.

It has been said that the true test of the adequacy and "sufficiency of the indictment is not whether it could have been made more definite and certain, but whether it contains the elements of the offense intended to be charged, and sufficiently apprises the defendant of what he must be prepared to meet, and, in case any other proceedings are taken against him for a similar offense, whether the record shows with accuracy to what extent he may plead a former acquittal or conviction."[10] It has been said that "if all the facts which the indictment charges can be admit-

---

S.E.2d 64 (1994). But cf. Russell v. United States, 369 U.S. 749, 82 S.Ct. 1038, 8 L.Ed.2d 240 (1962) on indictments in federal courts.

In Wagner v. State, 282 Ga. 149(1), 646 S.E.2d 676 (2007), the Georgia Supreme Court noted that "where a special demurrer points out an immaterial defect, the trial court should strike out or otherwise correct the immaterial defect. Where a special demurrer points out a *material* defect, the trial court must quash the defective count of the indictment." (Emphasis in original).

[2]Farrar v. State, 187 Ga. 401 (2), 200 S.E. 803 (1939).

[3]Davis v. State, 272 Ga. 818, 819 (1), 537 S.E.2d 327 (2000); State v. Bolman, 222 Ga. App. 534, 474 S.E.2d

721 (1996).

[4]Allen v. State, 120 Ga. App. 533, 171 S.E.2d 380 (1969).

[5]Curtis v. State, 80 Ga. App. 244, 246, 55 S.E.2d 758 (1949).

[6]Smith v. Hardrick, 266 Ga. 54, 55 (1), 464 S.E.2d 198 (1995).

[7]Bilbrey v. State, 254 Ga. 629, 632 (2), 331 S.E.2d 551 (1985).

[8]State v. Eubanks, 239 Ga. 483, 484, 238 S.E.2d 38 (1977).

[9]Bentley v. State, 210 Ga. App. 862 (1), 438 S.E.2d 110 (1993).

[10]Fletcher v. State, 157 Ga. App. 707 (2), 278 S.E.2d 444 (1981) (citing State v. Black, 149 Ga. App. 389, 390, 254 S.E.2d 506 (1979)). As the Court of Appeals observed in Gentry v. State, 281 Ga. App. 315(1), 635 S.E.2d 782

ted, and still the accused be innocent, the indictment is bad; but if, taking the facts alleged as premises, the guilt of the accused follows as a legal conclusion, the indictment is good."[11]

In *Smarr v. State,*[12] the court observed:

> It is well established that under Georgia law, we no longer adhere to an overly technical application of the fatal-variance rule, "focusing instead on materiality." Thus, the threshold inquiry is not whether there "has been a variance in proof, but whether there has been such a variance as to affect the substantial rights of the accused." We make this determination by exploring whether the underlying reasons for the fatal-variance rule have been served, namely (1) whether the allegations definitely inform the accused as to the charges against him so that he may present his defense and not to be taken by surprise, and (2) whether the allegations adequately protect the accused against another prosecution for the same offense. Only if the allegations fail to satisfy either of these two tests is the variance considered "fatal." (cits omitted).

An indictment sufficiently describes an offense when the nature of the charge may be readily understood by the jury.[13] However, where a body is so decomposed that the cause of death cannot be determined, the cause of death does not have to be alleged.[14] It is often said that the test of sufficiency of the indictment to withstand a general demurrer is whether the defendant can admit the charges alleged and still be innocent. If he can, the indictment is fatally defective.[15] Since the Georgia statutes are not intended to dispense with the substance of good pleadings, nothing should be left to inference or implication.[16] There are offenses which cannot be described in the language of the Code alone,[17] and in such a case it is necessary to plead the evidence which establishes the ultimate facts which the prosecution

---

(2006), "the test for validity of an indictment is twofold: first, the indictment must not mislead the defendant, so that he is unable to prepare a defense; and second, the indictment must protect the defendant from double jeopardy." Accord, State v. Greene, 171 Ga. App. 329, 330, 320 S.E.2d 183 (1984).

[11]Newman v. State, 63 Ga. 533, 534 (1879).

[12]Smarr v. State, 317 Ga. App. 584, 732 S.E.2d 110 (2012).

[13]Knowles v. State, 166 Ga. 182 (1), 142 S.E. 676 (1928); Locke v. State, 3 Ga. 534 (1847); O'Brien v. State, 109 Ga. 51, 52 (1), 35 S.E. 112 (1900). Rule

7(c)(1) of the Federal Rules of Criminal Procedure provides in part as follows: "The indictment or the information shall be a plain, concise and definite written statement of the essential facts constituting the offense charged."

[14]Phillips v. State, 258 Ga. 228 (1), 367 S.E.2d 805 (1988).

[15]Dukes v. State, 9 Ga. App. 537 (2), 71 S.E. 921 (1911).

[16]Locke v. State, 3 Ga. 534, 541 (1847); O'Brien v. State, 109 Ga. 51, 52 (1), 35 S.E. 112 (1900).

[17]Moore v. State, 54 Ga. App. 218, 219, 187 S.E. 595 (1936).

expects to prove.[18]

If the jurors cannot easily understand the nature of the charge in the indictment, the indictment may be defective even where stated "in the precise language of the statute." If the definition of the offense includes generic terms, it is not sufficient to merely use the statutory language.[19] In such cases, "the indictment must state the species of acts charged; 'it must descend to particulars.' "[20] Where a crime can be committed in more than one way, the particular manner in which the crime was committed must be set forth.[21]

Generally, an indictment should contain a complete description of the offense charged, including every essential element of the crime.[22] However, a robbery case that is charged in the language of the Code is adequate, even though it does not allege that the taking was with an intent to steal,[23] and in a capital case it is not necessary to set out aggravating circumstances which the state intends to use to support the death penalty.[24] An indictment is not amended by evidence which shows the commission of a crime not charged in the indictment.[25] See Studdard, *Daniel's Georgia Handbook on Criminal Evidence* (2018 ed.), § 1:40.

In Georgia it is said that a "prosecution is commenced 'with the return of the indictment or the filing of the accusation.' "[26]

An indictment should be captioned with the name of the state and county involved.[27]

It is not necessary for an indictment to show upon its face the

---

[18]Abel v. State, 64 Ga. App. 448 (6), 13 S.E.2d 507 (1941); Wellborn v. State, 78 Ga. App. 520 (1)(a), 51 S.E.2d 588 (1949).

[19]Russell v. United States, 369 U.S. 749, 765, 82 S.Ct. 1038, 8 L.Ed.2d 240 (1962).

[20]Lee v. State, 117 Ga. App. 765, 162 S.E.2d 229 (1968), quoting Harris v. State, 37 Ga. App. 113, 138 S.E. 922 (1927). See State v. Delaby, 298 Ga. App. 723, 725, 681 S.E.2d 645 (2009).

[21]Roughlin v. State, 17 Ga. App. 205, 207, 86 S.E. 452 (1915).

[22]Martin v. State, 96 Ga. App. 557, 558, 100 S.E.2d 645 (1957); Phillips v. State, 240 Ga. 453, 241 S.E.2d 203 (1978). In United States v. Simmons, 96 U.S. (6 Otto) 360, 362, 24 L.Ed. 819 (1877), the Court said, "[T]he accused must be apprised by the indictment, with reasonable certainty, of the nature of the accusation

against him, to the end that he may prepare his defense, and plead the judgment as a bar to any subsequent prosecution for the same offense."

In Steele v. State, 154 Ga. App. 59, 267 S.E.2d 500 (1980), the conviction was set aside because the indictment failed to allege that the owner or the lessor were damaged by the theft by conversion.

[23]Rutherford v. State, 183 Ga. 301 (1), 188 S.E. 442 (1936).

[24]Smith v. State, 236 Ga. 12, 20 (6), 222 S.E.2d 308 (1976); Jarrell v. Hopper, 242 Ga. 617, 250 S.E.2d 446 (1978).

[25]Tuggle v. State, 145 Ga. App. 603, 605 (2), 244 S.E.2d 131 (1978).

[26]Smith v. State, 190 Ga. App. 246, 247, 378 S.E.2d 493 (1989).

[27]See Reed v. State, 148 Ga. 18 (1), 95 S.E. 692 (1918).

665

term of court at which it was returned; it is sufficient if this information appears on the back of the indictment where the return of the grand jurors is entered.[28]

In *Bostic v. State*,[29] the court held that where an indictment alleges an illegal drug sale, "it is not necessary that it allege to whom the sale was made, the amount sold or the price received." In *Latimer v. State*,[30] the court held that "[i]t is not necessary to plead the amount of marijuana in an indictment or accusation where trial is had in a superior court. . . ." If the evidence showed the amount was in excess of one ounce, the defendant may be sentenced for a felony.

An indictment is not objectionable because it contains on its back a list of witnesses who testified before the grand jury, and it is not objectionable if it has printed on the back a statement that the defendant waives a "copy of a bill of indictment and list of witnesses before the grand jury and arraignment."[31]

There are cases holding that upon timely demand by demurrer, a defendant has a right to be tried on an indictment which is perfect in *form* and *substance*.[32] This rule applies where the indictment contains surplusage[33] or does not contain allegations which should be stated.[34] However, since *State v. Eubanks*[35] applied the harmless error rule to the overruling of a special demurrer, the importance of the foregoing is questionable. See § 14:41, infra, on special demurrers.

An indictment is to be strictly construed against the state when a demurrer has been filed against it.[36] However, where a defendant does not demur to the indictment, after verdict, it is to be construed so as to uphold the verdict.[37]

O.C.G.A. § 16-8-41(c)(1) provides that in any case in which the defendant commits criminal robbery and in the course thereof unlawfully takes a controlled substance from a pharmacy, such

---

[28]Nixon v. State, 121 Ga. 144 (1), 48 S.E. 966 (1904).

[29]Bostic v. State, 173 Ga. App. 494 (1), 326 S.E.2d 849 (1985).

[30]Latimer v. State, 134 Ga. App. 372, 374 (4), 214 S.E.2d 390 (1975).

[31]Estep v. State, 129 Ga. App. 909, 914 (7), 201 S.E.2d 809 (1973); White v. State, 230 Ga. 327, 339 (8), 196 S.E.2d 849 (1973).

[32]Harris v. State, 37 Ga. App. 113, 138 S.E. 922 (1927). See Annot., "Use of Abbreviation in Indictment or Information," 92 A.L.R.3d 494 (1979).

[33]See Smith v. State, 130 Ga. App. 390, 203 S.E.2d 375 (1973).

[34]Harris v. State, 37 Ga. App. 113, 114, 138 S.E. 922 (1927).

[35]State v. Eubanks, 239 Ga. 483, 238 S.E.2d 38 (1977).

[36]Scott v. State, 53 Ga. App. 61, 65-66, 185 S.E. 131 (1936), aff'd, 184 Ga. 164, 190 S.E. 582 (1937); Gilbert v. State, 175 Ga. 276, 165 S.E. 120 (1932). But see Bond v. State, 104 Ga. App. 627 (1), 122 S.E.2d 310 (1961).

[37]Cordovano v. State, 61 Ga. App. 590, 594 (2), 7 S.E.2d 45 (1940); Gazaway v. State, 9 Ga. App. 194, 70 S.E. 978 (1911); King v. State, 103 Ga. App. 272, 119 S.E.2d 77 (1961).

facts shall be charged in the indictment or accusation, and upon a conviction, the defendant shall be punished by imprisonment for not less than 15 years.

Generally, see 1 Torcia, *Wharton's Criminal Procedure,* §§ 256 et seq. (12th Ed. 1976); see §§ 14:39 et seq., infra, on demurrers.

§ 13:5   Contents—Classification of offense

An indictment need not specify whether an offense charged is a felony or a misdemeanor if the offense is adequately set out.[1] It has been held that an indictment is not subject to a demurrer if it refers to an offense as a felony when in fact it is a misdemeanor.[2] However, in *State v. Phillips,*[3] the court held that the words "High and Aggravated Misdemeanor" were not a material allegation which must be set out in reference to a charge of driving under the influence where the defendant had two prior convictions for DUI; and, thus, the words must be amended and omitted if submitted to the jury. Rather, the court determined that "High and Aggravated Misdemeanor" falls within the category of other legislative directions as to punishment.

Failure to name the crime charged does not render the indictment invalid.[4] In *Phillips v. State,*[5] the court said that a "variance between the offense as named or the Code section cited and the allegations specified in the indictment goes only to the form of the indictment," and the indictment is not defective if it properly describes the elements of the crime.[6] Likewise, it is immaterial that the name given a crime is incorrect if the description of the crime is proper.[7] However, in a burglary indictment where a defendant is charged with entering "with intent to commit a felony," the indictment is fatally defective if the felony is not specified.[8]

In an indictment charging felony murder, the omission of an essential element of the predicate felony murder may be cured if the felony offense is completely set out in a separate count. For example, if the felony murder count was premised upon the felony offense of reckless driving, but omitted the critical allegation that

---

[Section 13:5]

[1]See Gray v. State, 6 Ga. App. 428 (2-a), 65 S.E. 191 (1909).

[2]Hixon v. State, 35 Ga. App. 392, 133 S.E. 285 (1926); Lummus v. State, 17 Ga. App. 414, 87 S.E. 147 (1915).

[3]State v. Phillips, 206 Ga. App. 421, 422, 425 S.E.2d 412 (1992).

[4]Sisson v. State, 141 Ga. App. 559, 561 (6), 234 S.E.2d 146 (1977).

[5]Phillips v. State, 215 Ga. App. 526 (2), 451 S.E.2d 517 (1994).

[6]Corsini v. State, 238 Ga. App. 383, 387 (4), 519 S.E.2d 39 (1999).

[7]Rank v. State, 179 Ga. App. 28 (1), 345 S.E.2d 75 (1986).

[8]Ealey v. State, 136 Ga. App. 292, 221 S.E.2d 50 (1975). See Polk v. State, 275 Ga. App. 467(1), 620 S.E.2d 857 (2005).

the defendant drove the vehicle with reckless disregard for the safety of persons or property, the count will nonetheless survive if the offense is fully set out with all the necessary allegations in a separate count in the indictment.[9]

"Multiplicity is the charging of the same crime in several counts of the charging document."[10] In *State v. Williams*,[11] the defendant filed a motion to dismiss because of "multiplicity" where 47 counts in an indictment charged the defendant with possession of a separate and distinct image of child pornography. The court noted that it is the legislature's responsibility to determine whether a course of conduct can result in separate violations of the same statute, each of which may be subject to an independent sentence and not be subject to merger. The court held that O.C.G.A. § 16-12-100(b)(8) reflects such an intention and that the trial court was correct in denying the motion.

§ 13:6   Contents—Time

Generally, it has been held that an indictment must state the date of the commission of the alleged offense.[1] The year, month, and day of the month should be alleged.[2] However, in *Hutton v. State*,[3] a child molestation case, the court held that an indictment may charge that the offenses occurred between two specified dates, "the exact dates being unknown to the Grand Jurors." The rule is otherwise, however, where the state can identify the dates of the offenses alleged.[4]

It has never been necessary for the indictment to state the

---

[9]State v. Grant, 274 Ga. 826, 561 S.E.2d 94 (2002); Howard v. State, 252 Ga. App. 487 (2), 555 S.E.2d 884 (2001).

[10]Chancey v. State, 256 Ga. 415, 349 S.E.2d 717 (1986). See § 26:33, infra, on merger limitations.

[11]State v. Williams, 818 S.E.2d 256 (Ga. Ct. App. 2018).

[Section 13:6]

[1]Goldberg v. State, 22 Ga. App. 122 (1), 95 S.E. 541 (1918); Braddy v. State, 102 Ga. 568, 27 S.E. 670 (1897); Lyles v. State, 215 Ga. 229, 231, 109 S.E.2d 785 (1959).

[2]Tipton v. State, 119 Ga. 304, 46 S.E. 436 (1904). But in Callahan v. State, 148 Ga. App. 555, 251 S.E.2d 790 (1978), the court said that it was not error to overrule a demurrer to an indictment which alleged a theft of a car "between June 30, 1977 and July 7, 1977."

In Chesser v. State, 159 Ga. App. 261, 283 S.E.2d 24 (1981), the court held that a motion to quash an indictment was properly overruled where the defendant was indicted about 18 months after the thefts took place and the indictment charged the theft as taking place in January or February 1979. The court said that the indictment did not have to be dismissed because the precise date could not be determined.

[3]Hutton v. State, 192 Ga. App. 239, 241 (4), 384 S.E.2d 446 (1989). Cf. Johns v. State, 181 Ga. App. 510 (1), 352 S.E.2d 826 (1987).

[4]See Cole v. State, 334 Ga. App. 752, 780 S.E.2d 406 (2015).

exact time of day of the offense.[5] The date alleged in the indictment must be within the statute of limitations for the offense charged.[6]

An indictment must show on its face that the offense was committed before the indictment was returned. Thus, the date alleged must be a date before the return of the indictment; otherwise, the conviction is illegal and will be set aside.[7]

If the time of death is material to the defense of the case, the defendant is entitled to be informed of the date and time of death.[8]

Even though it has been held that a definite date of an offense should be alleged in an indictment, the state is not restricted to proof of the date stated.[9] It is sufficient if the evidence demonstrates that the offense was committed at any time within the statute of limitations.[10] However, if it appears that the state can reasonably narrow the range of dates during which the crime or crimes are alleged to have been committed, the indictment is subject to a special demurrer.[11] If the indictment alleges that the date of the offense is material, the proof must correspond to the date alleged.[12] In addition, where the defense is alibi, the defendant is entitled to know the date that the state claims the offense occurred.[13]

If there are several similar offenses covering a period within the statute of limitations, the indictment may charge a particular offense on a specific date, in which event the state can then prove any one or more of the offenses. However, if the indictment is drawn in counts which state in each that the date alleged is an essential averment of the transaction, the defendant may receive a separate sentence for each count on which he is convicted, but in this situation the defendant may not be convicted on any count unless it is proved that he committed the offense charged on the

---

[5]Miller v. State, 224 Ga. 627, 630 (3), 163 S.E.2d 730 (1968); Bostic v. State, 173 Ga. App. 494, 326 S.E.2d 849 (1985).

[6]Dixon v. State, 111 Ga. App. 556, 142 S.E.2d 304 (1965).

[7]Minhinnett v. State, 106 Ga. 141, 32 S.E. 19 (1898).

[8]State v. Williams, 247 Ga. 200, 202 (1), 275 S.E.2d 62 (1981).

[9]Grayson v. State, 39 Ga. App. 673 (1), 148 S.E. 309 (1929).

[10]Jefferson v. State, 136 Ga. App. 63, 66 (5), 220 S.E.2d 71 (1975).

[11]State v. Meeks, 309 Ga. App. 855, 711 S.E.2d 403 (2011). See Cole v. State, 334 Ga. App. 752, 780 S.E.2d 406 (2015) (where state apparently had ability to identify specific dates of numerous allegedly fraudulent medical claims, indictment which indicated only a range of dates without an averment that the state could not be more specific is subject to special demurrer). See also Herring v. State, 334 Ga. App. 50, 778 S.E.2d 57 (2015).

[12]Crawford v. State, 233 Ga. App. 323 (1)(a), 504 S.E.2d 19 (1998).

[13]Bradford v. State, 285 Ga. 1, 673 S.E.2d 201 (2009).

exact date set out.[14] Likewise, where a defendant is charged in an indictment, in two or more counts, with the commission of an identical crime, except for the date, only one sentence may be imposed unless each count alleges that the date is an essential element of the offense.[15]

However, in *Hamilton v. State*,[16] the indictment charged the defendant in four counts with the offense of meter tampering. The dates alleged were in Count 1 "between April 21, 1982, and May 20, 1982; Count 2 between May 20, 1982, and June 18, 1982; Count 3 being between June 18, 1982, and July 18, 1982; . . ." etc. The defendant was acquitted on three of the counts but convicted on the fourth. On appeal, the conviction was affirmed. The court concluded that each count referred to a different period of time and that the time was "an essential averment of the transaction."

Nevertheless, in *State v. Stamey*,[17] the court sustained a motion to quash an indictment charging embezzlement between January 2, 1991 and January 10, 1992. The court pointed out that the indictment did not allege "and the State does not argue, that the exact date or dates were unknown to the grand jurors." In *South v. State*,[18] a trial court's order denying defendant's special demurrer to an indictment which charged him with the offense of aggravated stalking was reversed where the state simply alleged that the incidents of stalking occurred between two dates and failed to set out that the state was unable to identify the exact dates of the alleged conduct. In *State v. Layman*,[19] the Georgia Supreme Court concluded: ". . . if an indictment alleges that a crime occurred between two particular dates, and if evidence presented to the trial court shows that the State can reasonably narrow the range of dates during which the crime is alleged to have occurred, the indictment is subject to a special demurrer."

The repeal, repeal and reenactment, or amendment of any law

---

[14]Martin v. State, 73 Ga. App. 573, 574 (4-8), 37 S.E.2d 411 (1946); Bloodworth v. State, 128 Ga. App. 657, 197 S.E.2d 423 (1973).

[15]LaPan v. State, 167 Ga. App. 250, 253 (4), 305 S.E.2d 858 (1983).

[16]Hamilton v. State, 167 Ga. App. 370, 306 S.E.2d 673 (1983).

[17]State v. Stamey, 211 Ga. App. 837, 838 (1), 440 S.E.2d 725 (1994). (The author is indebted to Stanley Lawson of Cleveland, Georgia for calling this case to his attention.)

[18]South v. State, 268 Ga. App. 110, 601 S.E.2d 378 (2004). Citing Dennard v. State, 243 Ga. App. 868 (2), 534 S.E.2d 182 (2000), the court noted that had the defendant challenged the form of the indictment after trial rather than by way of a pre-trial special demurrer, no relief would have been available in the absence of prejudice.

[19]State v. Layman, 279 Ga. 340, 341, 613 S.E.2d 639 (2005). See Blackmon v. State, 272 Ga. App. 854, 614 S.E.2d 118 (2005).

of this state which prohibits any act or omission to act and which provides for any criminal penalty therefor, whether misdemeanor, misdemeanor of a high and aggravated nature, or felony, shall not affect or abate the status as a crime of any such act or omission which occurred prior to the effective date of the act repealing, repealing and reenacting, or amending such law, nor shall the prosecution of such crime be abated as a result of such repeal, repeal and reenactment, or amendment unless the legislature expressly declares otherwise in the act repealing, repealing and reenacting, or amending such law.[20]

The text of O.C.G.A. § 16-1-11 seems on its face to be in direct opposition to the following language of the Georgia Supreme Court in *Daker v. Williams:*[21]

"In general, '[w]hen a statute making described conduct a crime is repealed prior to final judgment on a conviction, the repeal ends the prosecution if the legislature has not provided otherwise in [sic] saving clause.' (cites omitted). In other words, if, due to a statutory amendment prior to the entry of a final judgment on a conviction, the actions for which a defendant was indicted no longer constitute a crime, the prior conviction is abated in the absence of a savings clause providing otherwise. On the other hand, a prosecution may continue towards a final disposition where the actions for which the defendant was indicted were not decriminalized by the subsequent statutory amendment. A conviction may stand if it was authorized under both the original definition of the crime and the revised definition contained in the statutory amendment. (citation omitted)."

In order to reconcile the two authorities, § 16-1-11 must be read as speaking only to the circumstances described in the latter portion of the above quotation, i.e., the refusal of the legislature following the repeal of the statute to "decriminalize" the actions for which the defendant was indicted.

In *Bassett v. Lemacks,*[22] the Georgia Supreme Court said, "Understanding the rule of abatement of prosecution by repeal of a criminal statute becomes easier by examining a series of illustrations. Question 1: The legislature repeals a criminal law on Day 1 and enacts a slightly modified version of that law one year later on Day 2. If after Day 1, but prior to Day 2, a person commits acts which would have made out the criminal offense under the repealed statute, may he be convicted? No. No crime has been committed because the conduct is not proscribed by the legislature. Question 2: The person commits the proscribed

---

[20]O.C.G.A. § 16-1-11.

[21]Daker v. Williams, 279 Ga. 782, 621 S.E.2d 449 (2005).

[22]Bassett v. Lemacks, 258 Ga. 367, 369, 370 S.E.2d 146 (1988).

conduct before Day 1. He is indicted after Day 1, but prior to Day 2. Is he entitled to have his indictment quashed? Yes. See Gunn v. State, 227 Ga. 786, 183 S.E.2d 389 (1971) and Gunn v. Balkcom, 228 Ga. 802, 188 S.E.2d 500 (1972). Question 3: The person commits the proscribed acts prior to Day 1, is indicted and convicted before Day 1 and the conviction is on appeal on Day 1. Will his conviction stand? No, he is entitled to raise this issue on direct appeal and have the conviction set aside. See Mason v. Carter, 223 Ga. 2 (153 S.E.2d 162) (1967). Question 4: The person commits the formerly proscribed acts after Day 1, but prior to Day 2. The new version of the statute outlawing the proscribed acts goes into effect on Day 2. May he be prosecuted under the new version? No. See 1983 Georgia Constitution, Art. I, Sec. I, Par. X."

See § 14:66, infra, on alleging an exception to the statute of limitations. See § 14:41, infra, on sustaining and overruling a special demurrer.

§ 13:7 Contents—Place

An indictment must allege the county in which the offense charged was committed.[1] Generally, no other allegation as to location need be set out.[2] However, if the location is determinative of whether an act is criminal, the indictment must allege the location within the county.[3]

In an indictment charging burglary, it is not sufficient to simply allege that the defendant burglarized a building of a certain person located in a named county. Since the person named may own another building in the county, the defendant is not specifically informed of the burglary he is called upon to defend.[4] However, in *Askea v. State*,[5] the court held that an indictment was not subject to special demurrer where it alleged that the defendant unlawfully entered and remained "within the residence and dwelling house of" a named victim. The court concluded that a residence of a person in a named county sufficiently described the location of the house involved.

See § 14:41, infra, on sustaining and overruling a special

[Section 13:7]

[1]Conley v. State, 83 Ga. 496, 10 S.E. 123 (1889); State v. Ramos, 145 Ga. App. 301, 243 S.E.2d 693 (1978).

[2]Hall v. State, 120 Ga. 142, 47 S.E. 519 (1904); Reddish v. State, 101 Ga. App. 759 (2), 115 S.E.2d 736 (1960); Gentry v. State, 235 Ga. App. 328, 330 (3), 508 S.E.2d 671 (1998).

[3]Burkes v. State, 7 Ga. App. 39, 65 S.E. 1091 (1909). Generally, see Flanders v. State, 97 Ga. App. 779, 104 S.E.2d 538 (1958).

[4]State v. Green, 135 Ga. App. 622, 218 S.E.2d 456 (1975). But see Mobley v. State, 164 Ga. App. 154 (1), 296 S.E.2d 617 (1982).

[5]Askea v. State, 153 Ga. App. 849, 850 (1), 267 S.E.2d 279 (1980).

demurrer.

§ 13:8 Contents—Names of grand jurors

The names of the grand jurors returning the indictment must be listed in its body.[1] However, this defect may not be successfully raised for the first time after conviction.[2] In *Hawkins v. State*,[3] the court held that the trial judge did not err in refusing to delete from the indictment the names of the grand jurors even though the defendant argued that "the publishing of names of prominent and influential members of the small community lent undue credibility to the charges against him."

If an indictment contains more than one count, the names of the grand jurors need not be repeated in each count. The second and subsequent counts may commence by simply saying the "grand jurors aforesaid."[4]

It is not essential that the full names of the grand jurors be set out. The jurors may be named by initials.[5] A grand juror listed as "Mrs. Ed Brown" is sufficient.[6]

A slight mistake in the indictment as to the spelling of the names of the grand jurors is immaterial where the evidence introduced at trial on a plea in abatement shows that there was no doubt as to the identity of the grand jurors.[7]

Where an indictment lists 23 grand jurors and 5 names have a line drawn through them, the indictment is not invalid unless the defendant can show that he was prejudiced.[8] The striking out of names indicates that particular person did not participate in the returning of the indictment.

It is not essential that one of the grand jurors be designated as foreman in the indictment.[9]

[Section 13:8]

[1]Willerson v. State, 14 Ga. App. 451, 81 S.E. 391 (1914).

[2]Williams v. State, 107 Ga. 721, 33 S.E. 648 (1899); Hopper v. Kemp, 236 Ga. 615, 225 S.E.2d 15 (1976).

[3]Hawkins v. State, 260 Ga. 138, 139 (4)(a), 390 S.E.2d 836 (1990).

[4]O.C.G.A. § 17-7-54.

[5]Minor v. State, 63 Ga. 318 (1879).

[6]Mitchell v. State, 157 Ga. App. 683, 684, 278 S.E.2d 192 (1981).

[7]Cole v. State, 68 Ga. App. 179 (1), 180 (1), 22 S.E.2d 529 (1942).

[8]Woodring v. State, 130 Ga. App. 247, 202 S.E.2d 696 (1973).

[9]Taylor v. State, 121 Ga. 362, 364, 49 S.E. 317 (1904).

§ 13:9   Contents—Name of defendant

It has been held that the surname of the defendant, if it is known, must be alleged in the charging part of the indictment.[1] In *Noeske v. State,*[2] the court stated that it could "think of nothing more basic which should be properly charged in an accusation or indictment than the name of the alleged perpetrator." In *Noeske,* a two count accusation was involved with one charge of driving with a revoked license and one charge of speeding. In the first count, the defendant was named as the one charged, and, in the second count, the prosecuting law enforcement officer was named as the perpetrator. The court held that the latter count was fatally defective.

It is preferable to set out the full name of the accused, but if the full name or true name is not known, the indictment may use the name by which the accused is commonly known.[3] In *Frazier v. State,*[4] the court held that a defendant could be validly indicted "under a name by which he is generally known and called, whether this be his true name or not." If only an initial in addition to a surname is known, it may be preferable for the indictment to allege that the full name is unknown.[5] If the name of the accused is unknown, the indictment should state that his name is not known and set out a description of him.[6]

An indictment is not subject to demurrer because it does not set out the accused's middle initial,[7] nor will a plea in abatement lie if the initials are transposed.[8]

If an accused is known by more than one name and the grand jury is uncertain as to which name is correct, one name may be set out followed by the word "alias" and then another name by which he is known.[9] The Georgia courts do not regard such procedure as putting the defendant's character into evidence;[10] however, there is authority in other jurisdictions indicating that

---

[Section 13:9]

[1]Culpepper v. State, 173 Ga. 799, 161 S.E. 623 (1931). Here the name of the prosecutor was apparently inserted instead of that of the defendant. The court held that the error was fatal.

[2]Noeske v. State, 181 Ga. App. 778, 779 (2), 353 S.E.2d 635 (1987).

[3]Eaves v. State, 113 Ga. 749, 755 (4), 39 S.E. 318 (1901).

[4]Frazier v. State, 257 Ga. 690, 692 (7), 362 S.E.2d 351 (1987) (quoting Roland v. State, 127 Ga. 401, 56 S.E. 412 (1907)).

[5]Wiggins v. State, 80 Ga. 468, 469 (1), 5 S.E. 503 (1888).

[6]See Wiggins v. State, 80 Ga. 468, 470, 5 S.E. 503 (1888).

[7]Veal v. State, 116 Ga. 589, 42 S.E. 705 (1902). Generally, see Annot., "Sufficiency of Indictment, Information, or Other Form of Criminal Complaint, Omitting or Misstating Middle Name or Initial of Person Named Therein," 15 A.L.R.3d 968 (1967).

[8]Timberlake v. State, 100 Ga. 66, 27 S.E. 158 (1896).

[9]Radford v. State, 140 Ga. App. 195, 230 S.E.2d 345 (1976).

[10]Andrews v. State, 196 Ga. 84, 26

this practice may needlessly prejudice an accused unless the aliases are relevant to the facts of the case.[11]

In *Hawes v. State,*[12] the court held that there is "nothing presumptively improper about the State indicting [a defendant] under both his legal and alias names." However, the court indicated that the use of an alias may be improper if the defendant presents evidence that its use will "prejudice him in the eyes of the jury by conjuring images of" his guilt of the crime charged.

In *Thompson v. State,*[13] the defendant was indicted as "Floyd Thompson." The sentence identified him as "Willie Floyd Thompson." The court concluded that no corrective action was necessary since the defendant alleged no harm and this was an obvious clerical error.

In *Palmer v. State,*[14] the court held that the proper time for filing a plea of misnomer is before arraignment.

See § 14:45, infra, on plea of misnomer. See § 13:10, infra, on name of injured party.

§ 13:10 Contents—Name of injured party

In order to protect the accused, it is necessary that an indictment set out the name of the injured party, if it is known, or the name by which he is commonly known.[1] Likewise, "[a] variance between the victim's name as alleged in the indictment and as proven at trial is not fatal if the two names in fact refer to the same individual, such as where a mere misnomer is involved."[2] If only a portion of the injured person's name is known, the known part should be set out together with a statement that the remainder is unknown.[3] This rule applies to cases involving minor victims. Thus, because a defendant is entitled to an indictment which is perfect in form and substance, an indictment which

S.E.2d 263 (1943), overruled in part on other grounds, Frady v. State, 212 Ga. 84, 90 S.E.2d 664 (1955). See Brown v. State, 295 Ga. 804, 806(2), 764 S.E.2d 376 (2014).

[11]United States v. Beedle, 463 F.2d 721 (3d Cir. 1972); but see State v. Swift, 290 N.C. 383, 226 S.E.2d 652 (1976).

[12]Hawes v. State, 266 Ga. 731, 732 (2), 470 S.E.2d 664 (1996).

[13]Thompson v. State, 163 Ga. App. 828, 829 (4), 296 S.E.2d 123 (1982).

[14]Palmer v. State, 271 Ga. 234, 241 (3), 517 S.E.2d 502 (1999).

[Section 13:10]

[1]Irwin v. State, 117 Ga. 722, 45 S.E. 59 (1903); Dennard v. State, 243 Ga. App. 868, 876 (2), 534 S.E.2d 182 (2000). Compare, Presley v. State, 251 Ga. App. 823, 555 S.E.2d 156 (2001) which held that the name of an individual is not necessary where defendant is charged with conspiracy to commit aggravated assault in connection with a plan to escape from jail.

[2]Strozier v. State, 277 Ga. 78, 80, 586 S.E.2d 309 (2003).

[3]See Eaves v. State, 113 Ga. 749, 755, 39 S.E. 318 (1901).

identifies a minor victim by initials rather than by name is subject to a special demurrer.[4]

A claim that an indictment improperly identifies the victim is a challenge to the form of the instrument and must be raised by way of demurrer. After conviction, the challenge must be raised by way of a motion in arrest of judgment. A motion for directed verdict on this basis is not proper and is not subject to review because the issue will be deemed to have been waived.[5]

In *Murphy v. State,*[6] the court held that a defendant could be punished for aggravated assault on a peace officer even though the named victim was not referred to as a peace officer in the indictment, provided that the evidence shows that he was a peace officer.

If a name purports on its face to be one of a corporation, it is not necessary to allege that it is incorporated.[7] However, if a name purports to be that of a partnership, an indictment is fatally defective if it does not set out the names of the partners.[8]

In an indictment for robbery, ownership of property taken may be laid in the person having actual lawful possession, even though it is merely being held for another who is the true owner.[9]

However, where the injured party is the public at large, no particular victim need be identified. Examples of such cases are solicitation of a prostitute[10] and the distribution of child pornography.[11]

See § 13:9, supra, on name of defendant.

§ 13:11 Contents—Description of stolen property

Where a defendant is charged with theft[1] and with theft by receiving stolen property,[2] the property stolen must be described in the indictment in sufficient detail so as to reasonably inform the defendant of the event referred to and put him in a position

---

[4]Sellers v. State, 263 Ga. App. 144, 587 S.E.2d 276 (2003). See Cole v. State, 334 Ga. App. 752, 780 S.E.2d 406 (2015) (initials used to identify victims who were minors were sufficient when accompanied by other details of identification).

[5]Strozier v. State, 277 Ga. 78(3), 586 S.E.2d 309 (2003).

[6]Murphy v. State, 146 Ga. App. 721, 726 (5), 247 S.E.2d 186 (1978).

[7]Gray v. State, 6 Ga. App. 428, 432 (2)(b), 65 S.E. 191 (1909); Hill v. State, 117 Ga. App. 721, 161 S.E.2d 917 (1968).

[8]Buffington v. State, 124 Ga. 24, 52 S.E. 19 (2, 3) (1905).

[9]Cline v. State, 153 Ga. App. 576, 577 (2), 266 S.E.2d 266 (1980).

[10]Day v. State, 70 Ga. App. 819, 820, 29 S.E.2d 659 (1944).

[11]Coalson v. State, 251 Ga. App. 761, 764, 555 S.E.2d 128 (2001).

[Section 13:11]

[1]Ayers v. State, 3 Ga. App. 305, 59 S.E. 924 (1907).

[2]Brown v. State, 116 Ga. 559 (2), 42 S.E. 795 (1902).

to prepare to defend the case. The description is required in order to "individualize the transaction, and enable the court to see that . . . [the items taken] are, in law, the subjects of larceny. . . . There must be such certainty as will enable the jury to say whether the chattel proved to be stolen is the same . . . [as that set out in the indictment]. Still another reason given why the description should be definite is, that a judgment may be pleaded in bar of a subsequent prosecution. . . ."[3] Thus, it has been said or held that an indictment is not sufficient for theft or receipt of stolen property which simply describes the property as "a lot of cord wood of the personal goods of certain named persons, of the value of ten dollars";[4] "a certain lot of brass, to wit: five thousand pounds";[5] "various items of men's clothing, same being the property of [a named person] . . .";[6] "one black leather sample case, one black fibre sample case, one tan fibre sample case of the value of $15, eighty pounds of assorted candies of the value of $25, one book of photographs of candy of the value of $25, all the property of [a named person]";[7] "one shovel of the value of one dollar";[8] "a chair, a shovel, a table, a watermelon, or a pocket-knife";[9] "two and one-half gallons of syrup."[10] On the other hand, it has been held that the following descriptions were sufficient: "one Oldsmobile Starfire Coupe automobile of the value of $3,000.00 and the property of [a named company]";[11] "one five-passenger Ford automobile of the value of four hundred ($400.00) dollars and the property of [a named person]";[12] "two 1965 Chevrolet Impala Supersport chrome hubcaps";[13] "one bicycle painted red and bearing trade-mark 'Climax' and of the value of $15.00, and the personal goods of [a named partnership]."[14]

It has been held that it is not necessary for an indictment to

[3]Walthour v. State, 114 Ga. 75, 76, 39 S.E. 872 (1901). Cf. Wages v. State, 165 Ga. App. 587, 589 (4), 302 S.E.2d 112 (1983).

[4]Walthour v. State, 114 Ga. 75, 39 S.E. 872 (1901).

[5]Brown v. State, 116 Ga. 559 (2), 42 S.E. 795 (1902). The indictment charged the accused with receiving stolen property: "[C]ertain lot of brass fittings . . . four hundred pounds of the value of three hundred dollars, knowing the same to have been stolen by the person from whom received. . . ."

[6]Pippin v. State, 128 Ga. App. 355, 196 S.E.2d 664 (1973).

[7]Pharr v. State, 44 Ga. App. 363, 161 S.E. 643 (1931).

[8]Melvin v. State, 120 Ga. 490, 48 S.E. 198 (1904).

[9]Bright v. State, 10 Ga. App. 17, 72 S.E. 519 (1911).

[10]Tucker v. State, 112 Ga. App. 622, 624, 145 S.E.2d 751 (1965) (citing Mathis v. State, 27 Ga. App. 229, 107 S.E. 629 (1921)).

[11]Gee v. State, 110 Ga. App. 439 (1), 138 S.E.2d 700 (1964). The Gee case pointed out that it is not necessary to set out the year, model, the serial number or the motor number.

[12]Carson v. State, 22 Ga. App. 551, 96 S.E. 500 (1918).

[13]Tucker v. State, 112 Ga. App. 622, 145 S.E.2d 751 (1965).

[14]Adams v. State, 21 Ga. App. 152, 94 S.E. 82 (1917).

set out the year, license number or serial number of four motor vehicles allegedly stolen when the charge specified the make and model of the trucks as well as the date of the alleged theft.[15] Where there is an alleged theft of money, it is not necessary "for the indictment to specifically identify the form of the currency taken."[16]

An indictment charging the theft of "the personal goods of [a named person] . . . 100 pounds of seed cotton of the value of $10.00" is insufficient.[17] However, a theft from the house of "125 pounds of upland or short cotton in the seed, of the value of $5.00 the personal property of [a named person]" was held to be sufficient.[18] Likewise, an indictment for theft of "six 125 pound bag[s] of peanuts, of a value exceeding $200 and the property of J. M. Henson Company, 673 Wells Street" was held not to be subject to special demurrer.[19] Also, in *Bailey v. State*,[20] the court held that an indictment was not subject to special demurrer in a theft by taking case where the defendant was charged with unlawfully appropriating "merchantable pine timber."

A "compound larceny" is considered to be a theft from a house[21] or from the person.[22] In the case of compound larceny a more general description is said to be permissible, since the aggravating fact is regarded as "individualizing the transaction."[23] Thus, in such a case, the following descriptions have been regarded as sufficient: "one watch and chain of the value of seventy-five dollars, and the property of [a named person]";[24] "one double-case silver watch, of the personal goods of [a named person] . . . and of the value of thirty dollars";[25] "one iron anvil, two buggy-axles and the front springs and back springs from a buggy, and two forge grates of the personal goods of [a named person]";[26] "a Ford touring model automobile of the value of $580.00 and the property of [a named person], from which the motor number—the same being a mark of identification—had been removed and

[15]Martin v. State, 179 Ga. App. 551, 552 (2), 347 S.E.2d 247 (1986).

[16]State v. Stamey, 211 Ga. App. 837, 839 (3), 440 S.E.2d 725 (1994), rev'd as to Division (2), State v. Forthe, 237 Ga. App. 134, 514 S.E.2d 890 (1999).

[17]Bright v. State, 10 Ga. App. 17, 72 S.E. 519 (1911).

[18]Lindsey v. State, 9 Ga. App. 299, 70 S.E. 1114 (1911).

[19]State v. Traylor, 158 Ga. App. 786, 282 S.E.2d 376 (1981).

[20]Bailey v. State, 169 Ga. App. 802, 803 (3), 315 S.E.2d 297 (1984).

[21]Blackmon v. State, 24 Ga. App. 384, 100 S.E. 730 (1919); Cannon v. State, 125 Ga. 785, 54 S.E. 692 (1906).

[22]Anderson v. Winfree, 85 Ky. 597, 4 S.W. 351, 352 (1887).

[23]Pharr v. State, 44 Ga. App. 363, 365, 161 S.E. 643 (1931).

[24]Powell v. State, 88 Ga. 32, 13 S.E. 829 (1891).

[25]Patterson v. State, 122 Ga. 587, 50 S.E. 489 (1905).

[26]Fuller v. State, 57 Ga. App. 809, 197 S.E. 58 (1938).

altered for the purpose of concealment and misrepresenting the identity of said automobile."[27] However, it should be remembered that if an indictment is for burglary, no description of goods taken is necessary.[28]

In *Ayers v. State*,[29] the defendant was charged with larceny. The property alleged to have been taken was described as "one Eclipse Frick engine, 25 horse power, 1 Frick Box Boiler, 3 log carts, 1 set lumber-trucks and track-irons, all of the value of $500 and of the personal goods of [a named person] a constable." The court held that the description was sufficient since the indictment also stated that said property had been seized under a specified levy. The court concluded that the items taken were individualized by reference to the levy.

Under the former law charging theft of a hog, it was only necessary to describe the hog so the owner could identify it.[30] Thus, the old hog-stealing cases are probably not authoritative now. In a case involving larceny after trust, the court held sufficient a description of "15 head of beef cattle worth $20.00 per head, which had been entrusted to him by [a named person]."[31] However, the court said that this would not have been sufficient if simple larceny had been charged.

Where the value of an item or items determines whether an offense is a misdemeanor or a felony, the indictment need only allege whether the value is over or under $500 and is not subject to either a special or general demurrer. Further, where an indictment does not specify the amount taken, it will not be "subject to a general demurrer, because such amount is not an essential element of the offense."[32]

§ 13:12 Contents—Value

In *State v. Forthe*,[1] the Georgia Court of Appeals, in an eight to two opinion, held that in a theft case the indictment as to value does not have to allege anything other than of "a value of more than $500" or "a value of less than $500."

See Studdard, *Daniel's Georgia Handbook on Criminal Evidence* (2018 ed.), §§ 1:41 and 7:5, on establishing value.

---

[27]Glass v. State, 26 Ga. App. 157, 106 S.E. 13 (1921).

[28]Boyd v. State, 4 Ga. App. 273, 61 S.E. 134 (1908); Lanier v. State, 76 Ga. 304 (1)(a) (1886).

[29]Ayers v. State, 3 Ga. App. 305, 59 S.E. 924 (1907).

[30]Former GCA § 26-2610 (Code of 1933).

[31]Sanders v. State, 86 Ga. 717, 723, 12 S.E. 1058 (1891).

[32]State v. Forthe, 237 Ga. App. 134, 514 S.E.2d 890 (1999).

[Section 13:12]

[1]State v. Forthe, 237 Ga. App. 134, 514 S.E.2d 890 (1999).

§ 13:13   Contents—Exceptions

Generally, an exception is regarded as a part of the description of the offense if it is embodied in the language of the enacting clause of a statute. If the exception is a part of the definition of the offense, the indictment must allege that the exception does not exist.[1] But, where a statute makes a certain act criminal and the legislature enacts certain exemptions, it is not necessary for an indictment to negate the exceptions.[2] Furthermore, an exception or proviso in a statute which exempts certain persons from an offense need not be negatived in an indictment.[3]

For example, where a statute makes it unlawful to discharge firearms near a public highway except in defense of person or property, the indictment must allege that the shooting was not done in defense of person or property.[4] Similarly, an indictment charging a violation of the sale of malted beverages without compliance with the provisions of the governing statute must allege that the accused violated the statutory provisions.[5] Where a statute makes it a crime to produce a miscarriage and abortion except under the advice of two physicians, an indictment charging the offense must allege that the defendant acted without the advice of the physicians.[6] However, where a statute makes it a crime to sell intoxicating liquors and in a subsequent section provides that the prohibition shall not prevent practicing physicians from furnishing such intoxicants to their patients, it is not necessary for an indictment to allege that the accused is not a licensed physician.[7] An indictment for assault with intent to murder need not negative the exception in the statute by stating that the act was not done in self-defense or under other circumstances of justification.[8] In *Greenhill v. State*,[9] the court held that an indictment charging a violation of the Securities Act does not have to allege that the activity charged was not an exempt transaction.

§ 13:14   Contents—Exceptions—Statute of limitations

See § 14:66, *infra*, on the requirement that an indictment al-

---

[Section 13:13]

[1]Holloway v. State, 90 Ga. App. 86, 82 S.E.2d 235 (1954); Plemmons v. State, 58 Ga. App. 131, 133, 198 S.E. 104 (1938).

[2]Tigner v. State, 119 Ga. 114 (1), 45 S.E. 1001 (1903).

[3]Blocker v. State, 12 Ga. App. 81, 76 S.E. 784 (1912); Kitchens v. State, 116 Ga. 847 (1), 43 S.E. 256 (1903).

[4]Rumph v. State, 119 Ga. 121, 45 S.E. 1002 (1903).

[5]Plemmons v. State, 58 Ga. App. 131, 198 S.E. 104 (1938).

[6]Holloway v. State, 90 Ga. App. 86 (1), 82 S.E.2d 235 (1954).

[7]Oglesby v. State, 121 Ga. 602 (2), 49 S.E. 706 (1905).

[8]Isom v. State, 83 Ga. 378, 9 S.E. 1051 (1889).

[9]Greenhill v. State, 199 Ga. App. 218, 219 (2), 404 S.E.2d 577 (1991).

lege why the statute of limitations has been tolled if it appears from the face of the indictment that the statute of limitations for the offense charged has already run. See § 14:46, infra, on pleading the statute of limitations as a plea in bar, and § 14:66, infra, on limitations of prosecution.

§ 13:15 Contents—Charging in the alternative and conjunctive

Where an offense may be committed in more than one way, an indictment may not allege that it was committed in one way "or" in the other. Thus, where an indictment charges that an accused did "bet for money or other things of value," the indictment is subject to a special demurrer.[1]

A Georgia statute prevents an act of "omission or neglect causing unjustifiable physical pain, suffering or death of any living animal." In *Military Circle Pet Center v. State*,[2] the defendants were "charged only with causing unjustifiable physical pain, suffering, or death by 'neglect' without specifying the manner in which they were negligent." The court concluded that since the "negligence could have taken many forms, such as failure to provide adequate food and water, physical abuse, failure to treat a disease, etc., the failure to charge the manner in which the crime was committed subjected the accusations to a special demurrer."

An indictment charging a defendant with stabbing a named person with a knife "or some other like instrument" is subject to a demurrer.[3] However, if the disjunctive matter is merely descriptive of the material it precedes, the indictment is not defective.[4] If the disjunctive and subsequent material can be treated as surplusage, then the alternative allegation is not a ground for quashing the indictment. If the alternative allegation can be construed as being synonymous to the allegation, the indictment is not defective. Thus, an indictment charging the theft of a horse of a

---

[Section 13:15]

[1]Haley v. State, 124 Ga. 216, 52 S.E. 159 (1905). See Isom v. State, 71 Ga. App. 803, 32 S.E.2d 437 (1944); Statham v. State, 50 Ga. App. 165, 177 S.E. 522 (1934).

[2]Military Circle Pet Center v. State, 181 Ga. App. 657, 658 (1)(a), 353 S.E.2d 555 (1987), rev'd on other grounds, 257 Ga. 388, 360 S.E.2d 248 (1987).

[3]Henderson v. State, 113 Ga. 1148, 39 S.E. 446 (1901).

[4]E.g., Whitaker v. State, 11 Ga. App. 208, 75 S.E. 258 (1912). Here the accused was charged with selling stock in an incorporated bank. The indictment alleged that he sold "two shares of said stock or what purported to be two shares of stock" of said bank. The court concluded that the alternative provision merely amplified the previous allegation.

"bay or brown" color is valid.[5]

If an indictment in one count charges the commission of a crime in two ways and uses the conjunctive "and" where the statute contains the word "or," the indictment is not defective. The accused may be convicted by proof that he violated the statute in either way.[6]

If an offense is properly charged in general terms and this is followed by descriptive matter and the descriptive matter negates the general allegations, the indictment is defective.[7]

If an indictment charges a crime which may be committed in more than one way, a failure to charge the manner in which the crime was committed subjects the indictment to special demurrer.[8] "[W]here one felony is set out in various ways in . . . different counts to meet diversities in the proofs, no election of counts will ordinarily be required."[9] Likewise, "the state . . . [does not have] to elect between malice and felony murder before presenting the case to the jury."[10]

§ 13:16   Contents—Residence of defendant

While the form of an indictment set out in the statute[1] contains an allegation of the defendant's residence, it is not necessary that an indictment contain this information in order to be valid.[2]

§ 13:17   Contents—Intent

In *Bowman v. State,*[1] the court held that "[w]here the indictment alleges an offense, . . . and alleges that the act was unlawfully committed, and that it was contrary to the laws of the State, and employs language from which it must necessarily be inferred that criminal intent existed, it is not void because it fails to *expressly* allege the criminal intent."

---

[5]See Henderson v. State, 113 Ga. 1148, 39 S.E. 446 (1901).

[6]Southern Express Co. v. State, 1 Ga. App. 700, 58 S.E. 67 (1907); Jones v. State, 75 Ga. App. 610 (4), 44 S.E.2d 174 (1947).

[7]Woodson v. State, 114 Ga. 844, 847 (2), 40 S.E. 1013 (1902).

[8]State v. Black, 149 Ga. App. 389, 391 (4), 254 S.E.2d 506 (1979); Gilmore v. State, 242 Ga. App. 470, 530 S.E.2d 221 (2000).

[9]Hogan v. State, 178 Ga. App. 534, 537, 343 S.E.2d 770 (1986) (quoting Sutton v. State, 124 Ga. 815, 816-17, 53 S.E. 381 (1906)); Conyers v.

State, 260 Ga. 506, 507 (2), 397 S.E.2d 423 (1990).

[10]Usher v. State, 259 Ga. 835, 836 (1), 388 S.E.2d 686 (1990).

[Section 13:16]

[1]O.C.G.A. § 17-7-54.

[2]Wooten v. State, 160 Ga. App. 747, 288 S.E.2d 94, 95 (1981).

[Section 13:17]

[1]Bowman v. State, 227 Ga. App. 598, 600 (1), 490 S.E.2d 163 (1997) (quoting Hammock v. State, 201 Ga. App. 614, 411 S.E.2d 743 (1991)) (emphasis in original).

§ 13:18 Contents—Former convictions

An accused cannot receive a sentence greater than that prescribed by law for the offense of which he was convicted.[1] While it is necessary for the defendant to have notice of the prior convictions to be used against him, it has been held that it is not necessary for the former conviction to be set out in the indictment.[2] Also, while "a written notification . . . [to the defendant] is preferable, it is not required as long as the notification is clear."[3] However, the jury may not be informed of a prior conviction simply because it is to serve as the basis of the recidivist punishment,[4] and "it is error for the jury to be made aware of the prior convictions during the guilt/innocence phase of the trial."[5] In fact, a defendant no longer has a right to a jury determination of the recidivism issue, since this is now a matter to be considered by the judge at the time of sentencing.[6] However, "where the nature of the offense is changed from misdemeanor to felony by its repetition, such as felony shoplifting under O.C.G.A. § 16-8-14(b)(1)(C), recidivism must be alleged . . . 'so that the indictment reflects the maximum punishment to which the defendant can be sentenced.' "[7]

It has been held that only convictions or pleas which are valid[8] and which were obtained against the defendant prior to the returning of the new indictment[9] and which are not on appeal[10] may be set out in an indictment as a basis of a recidivist

---

[Section 13:18]

[1]Black v. Caldwell, 231 Ga. 589, 592, 203 S.E.2d 208 (1974).

[2]Anderson v. State, 176 Ga. App. 255, 256, 335 S.E.2d 487 (1985); Anderson v. State, 199 Ga. App. 559, 561 (3), 405 S.E.2d 558 (1991).

[3]Moss v. State, 206 Ga. App. 310, 312, 425 S.E.2d 386 (1992).

[4]Riggins v. Stynchcombe, 231 Ga. 589, 592, 203 S.E.2d 208 (1974).

[5]Favors v. State, 182 Ga. App. 179 (1), 355 S.E.2d 109 (1987).

[6]State v. Freeman, 198 Ga. App. 553, 556 (3), 402 S.E.2d 529 (1991).

[7]Wainwright v. State, 208 Ga. App. 777, 778 (2), 432 S.E.2d 555 (1993).

[8]Burgett v. Texas, 389 U.S. 109, 88 S.Ct. 258, 19 L.Ed.2d 319, 324 (1967). In *Burgett*, the court held that the guilty plea was invalid because there was no showing of a valid waiver of counsel and hence the plea could not be used as a basis of recidivist punishment.

[9]Williams v. State, 130 Ga. App. 418, 419, 203 S.E.2d 627 (1973).

[10]Croker v. Smith, 225 Ga. 529, 532, 169 S.E.2d 787 (1969). When a former conviction is the basis of a recidivist indictment, and even though the case is not on appeal at the time, if it is later determined that the prior conviction is invalid (because no valid waiver of counsel appears), the recidivist punishment entered on the later indictment must be set aside as a constitutional matter. United States v. Tucker, 404 U.S. 443, 92 S.Ct. 589, 597, 30 L.Ed.2d 592 (1972).

indictment.[11]

In *Chappell v. State*,[12] the defendant was charged with armed robbery and the remainder of the indictment charged the defendant with having previously pled guilty to an armed robbery and two burglaries. The indictment did not allege that the defendant was being charged as an habitual offender under O.C.G.A. § 17-10-7. No challenge was made to the indictment prior to the return of a guilty verdict. The defendant "knew he had been indicted as a habitual offender." The defendant was sentenced as a habitual offender and then claimed that he had been illegally convicted and sentenced as a recidivist. The court affirmed the conviction, pointing out that the defendant had not been misled. See §§ 14:39 et seq., infra, on demurrers and § 28:13, infra, on motion in arrest of judgment.

See § 24:18, infra, on sending the indictment to the jury room where the defendant has been indicted as a recidivist, and § 26:28, infra, on recidivism punishment.

Also see § 24:10, infra, on charge of court.

§ 13:19 Contents—Counts

While distinct offenses cannot ordinarily be joined in the same count of an indictment,[1] different grades of the same offense[2] and various methods of committing the crime[3] may be included in one count. Offenses not of the same nature, if they constitute but one transaction, may be joined in one count in the same indictment.[4] See sections 14:72 and 14:73, infra, on severance.

Due process requires that a defendant be put on notice in an indictment of all crimes with which he is charged. In *Lewis v. State*,[5] the court ruled that "[a] defendant is held to have notice of all crimes charged in the indictment, as well as lesser crimes shown by the facts alleged therein." While it has been said that

---

[11]However, in Wooten v. State, 160 Ga. App. 747, 288 S.E.2d 94 (1981), the court found that there was no error in the refusal of the trial judge to quash, where one of the prior convictions had been reversed and on retrial the defendant was found not guilty of the offense, and the reversed conviction was not called to the attention of the jury nor considered by the judge in imposing sentence.

[12]Chappell v. State, 164 Ga. App. 77 (1), 296 S.E.2d 629 (1982).

[Section 13:19]

[1]Gilbert v. State, 65 Ga. 449 (1) (1880); Evans v. State, 252 Ga. 312, 320, 314 S.E.2d 421 (1984) (citing Goldin v. State, 104 Ga. 549, 30 S.E. 749 (1898)); State v. Williams, 247 Ga. 200 (2), 275 S.E.2d 62 (1981).

[2]Warren v. State, 32 Ga. App. 359, 123 S.E. 182 (1924).

[3]Hall v. State, 8 Ga. App. 747 (1), 70 S.E. 211 (1911).

[4]Chester v. State, 262 Ga. 85, 87, 414 S.E.2d 477 (1992).

[5]Lewis v. State, 283 Ga. 191, 196(6), 657 S.E.2d 854 (2008). See Hill v. Williams, 296 Ga. 753, 770 S.E.2d 800 (2015).

each count of an indictment must be complete within itself,[6] still one count can incorporate by reference from another count.[7] A single count of an indictment may not allege more than one separate and distinct offense. However, there are two exceptions to this rule: (1) where a lesser included offense is involved, and (2) where the other offense is a part of the same transaction. The second exception has been recognized where the count charged aggravated assault and reckless conduct involving one victim.[8]

In *Lumpkins v. State,*[9] the court pointed out that "an indictment for a single crime which may have been committed in more than one way can take one of two recognized forms. One . . . is . . . a *single count* which contains alternative allegations as to the various ways in which the crime may have been committed. . . ." The other is that of an *"alternative counts* form from which the State [chooses] to employ in the [particular] case." In *State v. Corbitt,*[10] the court pointed out that "the *same offense,* that is the same species of offense, may be charged in different ways in *several* counts to meet the evidence [which may come out]. Accordingly . . . an indictment which contains such alternative counts is *not* subject to a motion to dismiss."

§ 13:20 Amendments

In Georgia and other jurisdictions, it is well-established that an indictment may not be materially amended by striking from or adding to its allegations except by the grand jury before the indictment is returned into court, and it has been said, "It is bad practice for the court to do either; and if such additions or subtractions materially affect the indictment, it becomes void."[1]

---

[6]Smith v. Hardrick, 266 Ga. 54, 56 (3), 464 S.E.2d 198 (1995); Perry v. State, 62 Ga. App. 115, 117, 8 S.E.2d 425 (1940). Accord, Gamble v. State, 235 Ga. App. 777, 779 (3), 510 S.E.2d 69 (1998).

[7]Durden v. State, 152 Ga. 441, 110 S.E. 283 (1921).

[8]State v. Williams, 247 Ga. 200, 203, 275 S.E.2d 62 (1981). In Jones v. State, 206 Ga. App. 604 (2), 426 S.E.2d 179 (1992), count one of the accusation charged the defendant with driving a motor vehicle under the influence. Count two charged the defendant with concentration of 0.12 grams but failed to specify driving a motor vehicle. The appellate court affirmed the conviction on each count and pointed

out that one count may incorporate another; however, an examination of the accusation shows that it contained no express provision in one count incorporating allegations of the other count.

[9]Lumpkins v. State, 264 Ga. 255, 256 (3), 443 S.E.2d 619 (1994).

[10]State v. Corbitt, 221 Ga. App. 304, 471 S.E.2d 261 (1996) (emphasis in original).

[Section 13:20]

[1]Gentry v. State, 63 Ga. App. 275, 276, 11 S.E.2d 39 (1940); Ingram v. State, 211 Ga. App. 252, 253 (1), 438 S.E.2d 708 (1993). However, Robinson v. State, 93 Ga. App. 203, 91 S.E.2d 52 (1956), clearly states that an indictment is not amendable. See Ex parte Bain, 121 U.S. 1, 7 S.Ct. 781, 30 L.Ed.

However, in Georgia it has been held that slight surplusage may be stricken on special demurrer without rendering the remainder void if the nature of the charge remains the same,[2] but no material defect may be corrected by an amendment.[3] However, if an indictment misnames the crime charged but sets out the essential allegations of the crime, the trial judge has authority to strike the erroneous name and permit the defendant to be tried on the indictment as changed.[4] An indictment may not be amended to conform to the evidence.[5]

Where a criminal trial ends in a mistrial because of the inability of the jury to agree on a verdict, the defendant may be reindicted for the original charge, including an addition of a recidivist count.[6]

If an alteration appears on the face of an indictment, it is presumed that the charge was made before the grand jury returned the indictment.[7] If a defendant wishes to establish that an alteration was made after the indictment was returned, he must proceed by a plea in abatement[8] and not by demurrer.[9]

Where defendant and his counsel agree to permit the district attorney to amend an indictment, the district attorney may do so and in such a case the defendant may not later object to the amendment.[10] In *Sewell v. State*,[11] there is a passing reference to an oral amendment in open court. *Sewell* cites *Reed v. State*[12] as authority for such an action. However, in *Reed* the amendment was not to an indictment, but to an accusation.

The prosecuting attorney has some flexibility in amending an

---

849 (1887). In Russell v. United States, 369 U.S. 749, 770, 82 S.Ct. 1038, 8 L.Ed.2d 240 (1962), the court said, "[A]n indictment may not be amended except by resubmission to the grand jury, unless the change is merely a matter of form."

[2]Brooks v. State, 47 Ga. App. 226, 170 S.E. 406 (1933), aff'd, 178 Ga. 784, 175 S.E. 6 (1934). The Georgia Supreme Court in this case, in headnote 3, said: "The words stricken added nothing to the indictment and their elimination took nothing from it."

[3]See Gentry v. State, 63 Ga. App. 275, 11 S.E.2d 39 (1940); Robinson v. State, 93 Ga. App. 203, 91 S.E.2d 52 (1956). Sutton v. State, 54 Ga. App. 349, 351, 188 S.E. 60 (1936), says that it is a violation of due process to permit even an accusation to be amended in substance.

[4]State v. Eubanks, 239 Ga. 483, 490, 238 S.E.2d 38 (1977).

[5]Pruitt v. State, 135 Ga. App. 677, 680 (4), 218 S.E.2d 679 (1975).

[6]Lassiter v. State, 175 Ga. App. 338, 339 (2), 333 S.E.2d 412 (1985).

[7]Owens v. State, 54 Ga. App. 417 (3), 187 S.E. 890 (1936); Cook v. State, 119 Ga. 108, 110, 46 S.E. 64 (1903).

[8]Allen v. State, 123 Ga. 499 (1), 51 S.E. 506 (1905).

[9]Gunn v. State, 10 Ga. App. 819 (2), 74 S.E. 312 (1912).

[10]Green v. Russell, 176 Ga. 354, 168 S.E. 65 (1933).

[11]Sewell v. State, 229 Ga. App. 685, 690 (2)(b), 494 S.E.2d 512 (1997).

[12]Reed v. State, 205 Ga. App. 209, 211 (2), 422 S.E.2d 15 (1992).

accusation.[13] However, at least prior to 1980,[14] an accusation could not be amended in substance, but it has been held that an amendment could be made to conform the accusation to the affidavit on which it was based, or to amplify the charge contained in the affidavit.[15] An unsigned accusation has been said not to be wholly void, and it may be signed by the prosecuting attorney at any time before arraignment[16] unless an amendment is prohibited by the legislative act creating the court, in which the case is pending.[17]

In *Freeman v. State*[18] the court concluded that the accusation "stated the offense of simple assault so plainly that the nature of the offense could be easily understood . . . [and was] 'sufficiently technical and correct.' "The court then held that "prior to trial, the prosecuting attorney may amend an accusation to allege or to change the allegations regarding any offense arising out of the same conduct of the defendant which gave rise to any offense alleged or attempted to be alleged in the original accusation."

§ 13:21 Reindictments

In *Larochelle v. State,*[1] the court held that " '[A]n indictment obtained without the dismissal of a prior indictment is a superseding indictment. A grand jury is not prevented from returning another indictment against an accused, even though an indictment is pending, where there has been no jeopardy. . . .' "However, " '[a] reindictment increasing the severity of the charges following the exercise of certain procedural rights may create an appearance of vindictiveness, and where it does so, the burden is shifted to the government to prove that the decision to reindict . . . did not result from any vindictive motive.' "

However, in *United States v. Goodwin,*[2] the United States Supreme Court pointed out that "[a]n initial indictment—from which the prosecutor embarks on a course of plea negotiation—

---

[13]Sutton v. State, 54 Ga. App. 349, 351, 188 S.E. 60 (1936). In this case, the act creating the court expressly provided that accusations could be amended in form and substance, but the court concluded that an amendment in substance was still not effective.

[14]See § 13:23, infra, on accusations.

[15]Goldsmith v. State, 2 Ga. App. 283, 284, 58 S.E. 486 (1907).

[16]Cook v. Walker, 161 Ga. 551, 555, 131 S.E. 288 (1926).

[17]See Jackson v. State, 4 Ga. App. 461 (1), 61 S.E. 862 (1908).

[18]Freeman v. State, 194 Ga. App. 905, 908, 392 S.E.2d 330 (1990).

[Section 13:21]

[1]Larochelle v. State, 219 Ga. App. 792, 794, 466 S.E.2d 672 (1996) (quoting 41 Am. Jur. 2d Indictments and Informations § 54 (1995) and 42 C.J.S. Indictments and Informations § 27 (1991)).

[2]United States v. Goodwin, 457 U.S. 368, 379, 102 S.Ct. 2485, 73 L.Ed.2d 74 (1982).

does not necessarily define the extent of the legitimate interest in prosecution. . . . In the course of preparing a case for trial, the prosecutor may uncover additional information that suggests a basis for further prosecution or he simply may come to realize that information possessed by the State has a broader significance. . . . The possibility that a prosecutor would respond to a defendant's pretrial demand for a jury trial by bringing charges not in the public interest that could be explained only as a penalty imposed on the defendant is so *unlikely* that a presumption of vindictiveness certainly is not warranted." (Emphasis in original.)

A superseding indictment may be brought after the statute of limitations on the charged offenses has expired, provided: "(i) the original indictment is still pending; (ii) the original indictment was timely; and (iii) the *superseding indictment does not broaden or substantially amend the original charged.*"[3] The determination of whether the indictment broadens or substantially amends the original charges is an issue of law for the court.[4]

§ 13:22   Waiver

As previously noted, a defendant has no right to insist on an indictment if he is charged with a misdemeanor.[1] In all misdemeanor cases which may be prosecuted in superior court, the district attorney can, with or without the consent of the defendant, prefer an accusation against the defendant rather than present the matter to the grand jury for an indictment.[2]

In all felony cases except capital felonies[3] where a defendant is bound over to superior court, or is in jail awaiting a commitment, or has waived a preliminary hearing, the district attorney shall have a right to prefer an accusation against him if the defendant waives, in writing, indictment by a grand jury. In the event such a waiver is executed, the defendant may be tried on the accusation.

Where the defendant wishes to enter a guilty plea, a judge of the superior court may, at any time, accept such plea without the presence of a grand jury or traverse jury if the defendant and

---

[3]Martinez v. State, 306 Ga. App. 512, 523 (2), 702 S.E.2d 747 (2010) (citations and punctuation omitted; emphasis in original).

[4]Lee v. State, 289 Ga. 95, 96, 709 S.E.2d 762 (2011).

[Section 13:22]

[1]See § 13:2, supra, on background of indictments and accusa-

tions; O.C.G.A. § 17-7-71.

[2]O.C.G.A. § 17-7-70. In Garmon v. Johnson, 243 Ga. 855, 257 S.E.2d 276 (1979), the court said that for purposes of this section, armed robbery, rape and kidnapping are not regarded as capital offenses.

[3]See Keener v. MacDougall, 232 Ga. 273, 278, 206 S.E.2d 519 (1974); O.C.G.A. § 17-7-70.

judge consent thereto. The judge may try the defendant upon the accusation without a jury if the defendant waives indictment, consents to a trial, and is represented by counsel.[4]

The waiver should expressly state that the defendant waives "indictment by a grand jury." The signing of a statement on the accusation to the effect that the defendant waives "formal arraignment, copy of bill of indictment, list of witnesses sworn before the grand jury . . ." does not amount to a waiver of indictment.[5] However, if a defendant signs a waiver embodying the above-quoted language and subsequently enters a guilty plea, he has waived his defense to the deficiency of the waiver.[6]

For a waiver of indictment and agreement to prosecution on accusation, see Studdard, *Daniel's Georgia Criminal Trial Practice Forms* (2018–2019 ed.), §§ 12:2 et seq.

§ 13:23 Accusations

The word "accusation" is a broad term which may include in its general use an indictment or any form in which a charge can be made against a person. In misdemeanor cases, and in certain non-capital felony cases where the defendant has waived indictment, it may have a more specific and technical meaning, referring to the form of the charge utilized in courts. In this technical capacity, an accusation is the equivalent of a common law information.[1] When used in this sense, an accusation takes the place of an indictment.[2] Ordinarily, an accusation is used only in some court inferior to a superior court.[3] For purposes of this section, the word "accusation" is used in its restricted, technical sense. Because of an amendment to existing law by the legislature in 2002, O.C.G.A. § 17-7-71 now provides that a criminal proceeding in all misdemeanor cases may be commenced by accusation in all courts and that this would include municipal courts which have jurisdiction over misdemeanor offenses. In addition, O.C.G.A. § 36-32-10.2 now provides ". . . in municipal courts

---

[4]O.C.G.A. § 17-7-70.

[5]Nelms v. State, 132 Ga. App. 689, 209 S.E.2d 110 (1974).

[6]Balkcom v. McDaniel, 234 Ga. 470, 471 (2), 216 S.E.2d 328 (1975).

[Section 13:23]

[1]Gordon v. State, 102 Ga. 673, 679, 29 S.E. 444 (1897).

[2]Flint v. State, 12 Ga. App. 169, 76 S.E. 1032 (1913). However, for bond purposes an accusation is not the same thing as an indictment, and where a bond is given conditioned on the ap-

pearance of defendant to answer an indictment, the bondsman is not obligated to produce defendant until an indictment is returned, even if there is an accusation for the same offense where defendant has waived indictment. Felton v. State, 91 Ga. 553, 18 S.E. 432 (1893).

[3]But under O.C.G.A. § 17-7-70, a district attorney can prosecute a defendant in superior court by an accusation if a defendant waives indictment (in all felony cases, except capital felony cases).

which have jurisdiction over misdemeanor offenses or ordinance violations, such offenses or violations may be tried upon a uniform traffic citation, summons, citation, or an accusation."[4]

In *Lamberson v. State,*[5] the Georgia Supreme Court held that "the substitution of an accusation for indictment for the specific felonies enumerated in O.C.G.A. § 17-7-70.1 does not violate the Due Process Clause of the Fourteenth Amendment."

O.C.G.A. § 17-7-71 provides a form to be used for an accusation. This section was amended in 1980 so as to provide that an accusation need not be supported by an affidavit where the defendant has already been arrested for the offense.[6]

In addition, O.C.G.A. § 17-7-71(b)(1) provides generally for the trial of misdemeanors arising out of traffic laws by a trial on a uniform traffic citation. In *Pryor v. State,*[7] the court held that such a citation was sufficient even though the attesting signature appearing below the officer's signature did not have a notary seal affixed. In a like vein, in *Miller v. State,*[8] the court pointed out that a citation was sufficient even if there is "a misstatement of the code section making DUI a crime . . . and under 'remarks' on the citation for speeding the entry 'S. on Ga. 21' when the defendant was in fact driving north on Georgia Highway 21." Likewise, in *Brown v. State,*[9] the court affirmed the refusal to quash where the traffic citation was not a uniform traffic citation but there was no indication that the defendant had been misled. Similarly, in *Lockett v. State,*[10] the trial court's refusal to quash a citation was affirmed where the court found that while by statute a uniform traffic citation should charge no more than one offense, the state could proceed on a citation charging two offenses in the absence of any evidence that the defendant was confused or misled. The later issuance of an accusation supersedes "any uniform traffic citation as the charging instrument."[11] However, while the traffic citation was created to provide a uniform device for charging motorists with traffic violations, its application is

---

[4]See also Beaman v. City of Peachtree City, 256 Ga. App. 62, 65, 567 S.E.2d 715 (2002).

[5]Lamberson v. State, 265 Ga. 764, 766, 462 S.E.2d 706 (1995).

[6]Daniel v. State, 169 Ga. App. 722 (1), 314 S.E.2d 737 (1984); Blankenship v. State, 208 Ga. App. 710, 711, 431 S.E.2d 481 (1993); Military Circle Pet Center v. State, 181 Ga. App. 657, 659 (1)(c), 353 S.E.2d 555 (1987), rev'd on other grounds, 257 Ga. 388, 360 S.E.2d 248 (1987).

[7]Pryor v. State, 182 Ga. App. 79, 80 (1), 354 S.E.2d 690 (1987).

[8]Miller v. State, 182 Ga. App. 700, 701, 356 S.E.2d 900 (1987).

[9]Brown v. State, 202 Ga. App. 371, 372 (2), 414 S.E.2d 505 (1991).

[10]Lockett v. State, 257 Ga. App. 412(1), 571 S.E.2d 192 (2002).

[11]Ellerbee v. State, 215 Ga. App. 102, 104 (3), 449 S.E.2d 874 (1994), overruled on other grounds, Felix v. State, 271 Ga. 534, 523 S.E.2d 1 (1999).

not restricted to such offenses. For example, it was approved as the charging instrument in a case involving underage possession of alcohol brought in a municipal court in *City of Peachtree City v. Shaver*.[12]

Except where an affidavit is not necessary as set out above, in order to issue an accusation, an affidavit supporting the accusation must exist.[13] Where the accusation does not refer to an affidavit and no affidavit is attached, the whole trial is a nullity.[14] If an accusation refers to an affidavit but it is not attached, and on demand it is not produced, there can be no conviction.[15] However, if the accusation alleges that it is based on an affidavit and no demand is made for the affidavit, it has been held that this is not reversible error where this point is not raised until after conviction.[16]

In *State v. Litz*,[17] the court held that an arrest warrant is not required for a valid misdemeanor accusation.

Frequently, blank printed forms which have an affidavit at the top and accusation at the bottom of the same page are utilized.[18] It is error for an affidavit for an arrest and an arrest warrant to be included in or attached to an accusation, since a jury is not permitted to have an arrest warrant.[19] If the accusation shows on its face that it is based on an affidavit, the failure to state this fact is not ground for demurrer.[20] If the affidavit is not attested by a person having authority to swear the affiant[21] or is void for other reasons, the error may be raised even after sentencing, if

---

[12]City of Peachtree City v. Shaver, 276 Ga. 298, 578 S.E.2d 409 (2003). Compare Bush v. State, 273 Ga. 861, 548 S.E.2d 302 (2001), where the use of a traffic citation charging a non-traffic related offense resulted in a void judgment since the court in which the case was brought, the Atlanta Traffic Court, was one in which jurisdiction is limited to traffic offenses and related charges not above the grade of misdemeanor.

[13]In Bickley v. State, 243 Ga. 488, 489, 255 S.E.2d 31 (1979), the court said that an affidavit is necessary for an accusation in superior court and in state courts.

[14]Martin v. State, 139 Ga. App. 8, 228 S.E.2d 15 (1976); Scroggins v. State, 55 Ga. 380 (3) (1875).

[15]Chauncey v. State, 129 Ga. App. 207, 208, 199 S.E.2d 391 (1973).

[16]Gilreath v. State, 140 Ga. App. 213, 230 S.E.2d 362 (1976).

[17]State v. Litz, 210 Ga. App. 200, 435 S.E.2d 724 (1993).

[18]E.g., Faulkner v. State, 146 Ga. App. 604, 605 (2), 247 S.E.2d 147 (1978).

[19]Cain v. State, 113 Ga. App. 477, 481 (5), 148 S.E.2d 508 (1966). However, in Morris v. State, 149 Ga. App. 793, 257 S.E.2d 549 (1979), the court implied that a valid arrest warrant issued by a justice of the peace might be sufficient support for an accusation if it is filed with the court or is attached to the accusation.

[20]Mitchell v. State, 126 Ga. 84 (6), 54 S.E. 931 (1906).

[21]Unless the statute creating the court prescribes the person before whom the affidavit is to be made, it may be signed before a notary public. Shuler v. State, 125 Ga. 778, 54 S.E. 689 (1906).

the affidavit is necessary to support the accusation.[22]

The accusation must be specific enough to "meet the requirements of criminal pleading by putting the defendant on notice of the identical charge he is expected to meet, and enable him to prepare to defend against the charge."[23] In *Jackson v. State,*[24] the court held that an indictment or accusation at a minimum must (1) recite the language of the statute that sets out all the elements of the offense charged or (2) allege the facts necessary to establish violation of a criminal statute; if either of these requisites is met, then the accused cannot admit the allegations of the indictment and yet be not guilty of the crime charged and overruled all authority to the contrary.

Thus, a defendant may be tried for a traffic offense on a properly completed and signed traffic citation alone,[25] except in superior court,[26] and in *Wood v. State,*[27] the court affirmed the defendant's conviction even though there was no attestation of the ticket in view of the fact the defendant did not demonstrate any prejudice. Likewise, a prosecution may proceed even if the ticket is not on a "uniform traffic citation" form which omitted some information called for in a uniform citation if the defendant was not misled or prejudiced.[28] However, in *Burks v. State,*[29] the court pointed out it is not necessary that the "prosecution must proceed upon the uniform traffic citation form" which has been initially issued; the prosecuting attorney has authority to file a later formal accusation on the charge. Additionally, the subsequent issuance of a formal accusation does not amend the uniform traffic citation, but such accusation supersedes any uniform traffic citation as the charging instrument.[30] The statute of limitations runs between the date of the offense and the date the accusation is charged. The statute of limitations does not begin to run after the traffic citation is issued because the citation is an accusation and its validity remains unaffected.[31]

The statute also prescribes a form which may be used as an accusation. However, older forms may continue to be used. The law does not affect the validity of any prosecution commenced

---

[22]Scroggins v. State, 55 Ga. 380 (3) (1875).

[23]Lepinsky v. State, 7 Ga. App. 285, 66 S.E. 965 (1910).

[24]Jackson v. State, 301 Ga. 137, 800 S.E.2d 356 (2017).

[25]Weaver v. State, 179 Ga. App. 641, 347 S.E.2d 295 (1986).

[26]Prindle v. State, 240 Ga. App. 461 (1), 523 S.E.2d 44 (1999).

[27]Wood v. State, 190 Ga. App. 733, 380 S.E.2d 289 (1989).

[28]Harris v. State, 199 Ga. App. 457 (2), 405 S.E.2d 501 (1991).

[29]Burks v. State, 195 Ga. App. 516 (1), 394 S.E.2d 136 (1990).

[30]Smith v. State, 239 Ga. App. 515, 517 (2), 521 S.E.2d 450 (1999).

[31]See Prindle v. State, 240 Ga. App. 461, 462 (1), 523 S.E.2d 44 (1999).

before the effective date of the Act.[32]

This same statute as amended in 2002 in O.C.G.A. § 17-7-71(f) now provides that a summons or citation as well as an accusation may be amended prior to trial so as "to allege, or to change the allegations regarding any offense arising out of the same conduct of the defendant." A copy of such an amendment must be served on the defendant or his counsel and the original must be filed with the clerk. The court is specifically authorized to "grant the defendant a continuance which is reasonably necessitated by an amendment." Indeed, the statute specifically provides that if "any additional charges against the defendant are made, the judge shall advise the defendant that he or she has an automatic right to a continuance." See § 13:20, supra, on amendments of accusations.

O.C.G.A. § 15-18-66(b)(10) now provides that "[n]o accusation, citation, or summons shall be considered filed unless such filing has been done with the consent, direction or approval of the solicitor-general. . . ."[33]

O.C.G.A. § 17-7-70.1 provides that when a defendant has been bound over to superior court or has waived a commitment hearing, the district attorney may proceed with the trial by accusation of cases involving theft by taking, shoplifting, entering an automobile, forgery in first or second degree, deposit account fraud, financial transaction card theft, financial transaction card fraud, unauthorized use of financial transaction card, escape, purchase, possession or distribution of a controlled substance or marijuana, or habitual violators.

In *Lamberson v. State,*[34] the court held that O.C.G.A. § 17-7-70.1 was not violative of the Fifth and Fourteenth Amendments.

It has been held that a criminal prosecution against a corporation must be by indictment and not by accusation.[35]

§ 13:24 Guilty pleas on accusations

O.C.G.A. § 17-7-70(b) provides that a trial judge may receive and act on a guilty plea entered on an accusation for any felony except a capital felony if the defendant waives his right to indictment by a grand jury. The term "capital felony" applies to "those felonies to which the death penalty is affixed as a punishment" regardless of whether or not the district attorney has elected to

---

[32]Ga. Laws 1980, pp. 452, 455.

[33]State v. Rish, 222 Ga. App. 729, 732, 476 S.E.2d 50 (1996).

[34]Lamberson v. State, 265 Ga. 764, 462 S.E.2d 706 (1995) (quoted in Hood v. State, 223 Ga. App. 573, 479 S.E.2d 400 (1996)).

[35]Progress Club v. State, 12 Ga. App. 174 (2), 76 S.E. 1029 (1913). But see State v. Military Circle Pet Center, 257 Ga. 388, 360 S.E.2d 248 (1987).

seek the death penalty. Hence, the trial judge cannot accept a guilty plea to an accusation charging murder and the defendant cannot by consent confer jurisdiction on the court to accept such a guilty plea to an accusation.[1]

O.C.G.A. § 17-7-70.1 provides for trial upon accusations in certain non-capital felony cases in which the "defendants have either been bound over to the superior court based on a finding of probable cause pursuant to a commitment hearing under Article 2 [17-7-20, et seq.] or have expressly or by operation of law waived a commitment hearing, the district attorney shall have authority to prefer accusations, and the defendant shall be tried on such accusations according to the same rules of substantive and procedural laws relating to the defendants who have been indicted by a grand jury."

This provision applies to the following offenses:

I. Felony cases involving O.C.G.A. § 16-8-2 (theft by taking), § 16-8-14 (theft by shoplifting), § 16-8-18 (entering automobile or other motor vehicle with intent to commit theft or felony), § 16-9-1 (forgery in the first degree), § 16-9-2 (forgery in the second degree), § 16-9-20 (deposit account fraud), § 16-9-31 (financial transaction card theft), § 16-9-33 (financial transaction card fraud), § 16-9-37 (unlawful use of financial transaction card), § 16-10-52 (escape), § 40-5-58 (habitual offenders), or § 16-11-131 (possession of firearm by convicted felon or first offender probationer)

II. Article 1 of Chapter 8 of Title 16 relating to theft.

III. Chapter 9 of Title 16 relating to forgery and fraudulent practices.

IV. Article 3 of Chapter 10 of Title 16 relating to escape and other offenses related to confinement.

However, in *Brackins v. State*,[2] the court held that a felony obstruction charge may not be tried on an accusation.

§ 13:25   Transfer of indictment to inferior court

When a defendant is indicted by a grand jury for a misdemeanor, the superior court may transfer the case to the state court of the county for trial.[1]

In criminal cases where the accused runs the risk of having his or her parental rights terminated if convicted, "a superior court may transfer a criminal case to a family treatment court division of a juvenile court for treatment and a report back to the superior

---

[Section 13:24]

[1]Weatherbed v. State, 271 Ga. 736, 738, 524 S.E.2d 452 (1999).

[2]Brackins v. State, 249 Ga. App. 788, 789 (2), 549 S.E.2d 775 (2001).

[Section 13:25]

[1]Turner v. State, 152 Ga. App. 354, 355 (1), 262 S.E.2d 618 (1979).

court," provided the prosecutor and the accused agree to the transfer.[2] The court may transfer an eligible case prior to sentencing with consent of the prosecutor as part of the sentence, or upon consideration of a petition to revoke probation.[3] The juvenile court may transfer the case back to the superior court at any time.[4] See § 13:27, infra, on the transfer of offenses committed by juveniles.

§ 13:26   Transfer of accusation from municipal or recorders court to state or superior court

O.C.G.A.'s § 40-6-376(a) provides that a traffic offense which violates state law as well as a local ordinance may, at the discretion of the prosecution, be charged as a violation of the state statute or the local ordinance. O.C.G.A.'s § 40-6-376(b) permits a defendant to request a traffic offense charged as a violation of a local ordinance to be transferred to the appropriate state tribunal where the conduct also violates state law. In *State v. Johnson*,[1] the Court of Appeals ruled that even though the statute does not expressly state that the prosecution may request the transfer of a case from Recorders Court to State Court, there is no prohibition to such a motion and reversed a trial court's order finding that the solicitor lacked the authority to request the transfer.

§ 13:27   Offenses committed by juveniles

O.C.G.A. § 15-11-561 provides in part as follows:

(a) After a petition alleging delinquency has been filed but before the adjudication hearing, on its own motion or on a motion by a prosecuting attorney, the court may convene a hearing to determine whether to transfer the offense to the appropriate superior court for criminal trial if the court determines that:

(1) There is probable cause to believe that a child committed the alleged offense;

(2) Such child is not committable to an institution for the developmentally disabled or mentally ill; and

(3) The petition alleges that such child:

(A) Was at least 15 years of age at the time of the commission of the offense and committed an act which would be a felony if committed by an adult; or

(B) Was 13 or 14 years of age and either committed an act for which

---

[2]O.C.G.A. § 15-11-15(d). This subsection was added by the General Assembly in 2016 along with the statute creating juvenile court family treatment divisions, O.C.G.A. § 15-11-70.

[3]O.C.G.A. § 15-11-70(a)(3).

[4]O.C.G.A. § 15-11-15(d).

[Section 13:26]

[1]State v. Johnson, 257 Ga. App. 162, 570 S.E.2d 627 (2002); see State v. Serio, 257 Ga. App. 369(2), 571 S.E.2d 168 (2002).

the punishment is loss of life or confinement for life in a penal institution or committed aggravated battery resulting in serious bodily injury to a victim.

(b) At least three days prior to the scheduled transfer hearing, written notice shall be given to a child and his or her parent, guardian, or legal custodian. The notice shall contain a statement that the purpose of the hearing is to determine whether such child is to be tried in the juvenile court or transferred for trial as an adult in superior court. A child may request and the court shall grant a continuance to prepare for the transfer hearing.[1]

O.C.G.A. § 15-11-560(b) provides that the superior court has exclusive jurisdiction of a child 13 to 18 years of age who is charged with murder, murder in the second degree, voluntary manslaughter, rape, aggravated sodomy, aggravated child molestation, aggravated sexual battery, armed robbery if committed with a firearm, or aggravated battery upon a public safety officer.[2] O.C.G.A. § 15-11-560(d) also provides that the district attorney may decline to prosecute a juvenile charged with such an offense in superior court and can instead transfer the case to juvenile court for disposition. Code Section 15-11-560(e) authorizes a superior court to transfer to juvenile court issues in which a child 13 to 18 years of age is charged with voluntary manslaughter, aggravated sodomy, aggravated child molestation, or aggravated sexual battery. The court is required to consider the criteria set forth in Code Section 15-11-562 before entering a transfer order. That criteria includes such factors as: the age of the child; whether violence was involved; the culpability of the child; the child's history of bad conduct; the programs and facilities available in juvenile court; and, the best interests of the community. A superior court's transfer order under this Code Section is subject to appeal by the state. O.C.G.A. § 15-11-602 provides that when a child has committed a designated felony act, the order of disposition shall be made within 20 days of the conclusion of the disposition hearing.[3] If the order provides for placement in restrictive custody, then it shall include specific written findings of fact as to why this placement is necessary based on each of the factors set forth in O.C.G.A. § 15-11-602(b) which include the child's: age and maturity; needs and best interests; record of bad conduct; culpability; and mitigating conduct. The court will also consider

---

[Section 13:27]

[1]A party may seek review of a transfer to superior court under this Code section by way of direct appeal, pursuant to O.C.G.A. § 15-11-564. See In Interest of K.S., 303 Ga. 542, 814 S.E.2d 324 (2018).

[2]The concurrent jurisdiction of the superior court over capital felonies extends to related lesser crimes which are part of the same criminal transaction. Reynolds v. State, 266 Ga. 235(2), 466 S.E.2d 218 (1996).

[3]See O.C.G.A. § 15-11-2 for definitions of "Class A designated felony acts" and "Class B designated felony acts."

whether the child injured anyone in connection with the incident. The disposition of the case will be entered by the court in accordance with O.C.G.A. § 15-11-601.[4]

In *In the Interest of T. C. S.,*[5] the defendant was charged with child molestation and the court held "that the juvenile court lacked jurisdiction . . . until the entire process was completed, including the filing of the petition for delinquency . . . ."

In *In the Interest of J. D.,*[6] the court pointed out that "[w]hether the child is amenable to treatment in the juvenile system is a factor to consider in balancing the interests of the child and community . . . . The state is not required to show, nor is the transfer order required to explain, why the child is not amenable to treatment when that factor is not relied on as the basis for the transfer."

In *In the Interest of J. T. D.,*[7] the court pointed out that the age at the time of the offense, not the age at the time of the adjudicatory hearing, determines the jurisdiction of the juvenile court. In *In the Interest of D. L.,*[8] when D. L. was 16, he allegedly shot a man in the stomach and would have been guilty of aggravated assault if he had been an adult. After he turned 17, the juvenile court entered an order closing the case without an adjudicatory hearing. After he became 18, the case was reopened, a transfer hearing was conducted, and the case was transferred to superior court. The appellate court affirmed the juvenile court in transferring the case to superior court and held that the juvenile court did not lose jurisdiction over D. L. when he turned 17.

Pursuant to O.C.G.A. § 15-11-560, prior to indictment the superior court and the juvenile court have concurrent jurisdiction

---

[4]See In Interest of C.T., 197 Ga. App. 300, 303(3), 398 S.E.2d 286 (1990) (requiring trial court to make findings will assist appellate court in determining whether trial court abused its discretion). See also, In re K.F., 316 Ga. App. 437, 439(2), 729 S.E.2d 575 (2012).

[5]In the Interest of T. C. S., 220 Ga. App. 545, 547 (2), 469 S.E.2d 802 (1996).

[6]In the Interest of J. D., 264 Ga. 836, 452 S.E.2d 105 (1995). However, in Pascarella v. State, 294 Ga. App. 414, 669 S.E.2d 216 (2008) (citing Chapman v. State, 259 Ga. 592, 385 S.E.2d 661 (1989)), the court held that a defendant does not have a constitutional right to be treated as a juvenile.

Rather, "[A]ny right a defendant may have to be treated as a juvenile is not an inherent right specifically protected by the constitution, but one created by statute." Although there may be conflicting determinations regarding the juvenile's amenability to treatment in the juvenile system, the court may still transfer the case if "it finds that the amenability factor is outweighed by the interest of the community in treating the child as an adult." (Citation omitted.) In the Interest of W.N.J., 268 Ga. App. 637, 640 (2), 602 S.E.2d 173 (2004).

[7]In the Interest of J. T. D., 242 Ga. App. 243, 529 S.E.2d 377 (2000).

[8]In the Interest of D. L., 228 Ga. App. 503 (1), 492 S.E.2d 273 (1997).

over those cases involving children under the age of 13 and which would be considered a crime if tried in superior court and for which the child may be punished by loss of life or life in prison with or without the possibility of parole. For children between the ages of 13 and 18, the superior court has exclusive jurisdiction over cases involving murder, voluntary manslaughter, rape, aggravated sodomy, aggravated child molestation, aggravated sexual battery, and armed robbery if committed with a firearm.[9] After indictment, the court may transfer any such case to juvenile court for extraordinary cause unless the offense involved is punishable by loss of life or life in prison with or without the possibility of parole.[10] Although "extraordinary" is not defined in the statute, the Court of Appeals in *State v. Ware*,[11] affirmed the superior court's finding that the "youth of the child" was a sufficient basis for the order of transfer in a case involving allegations of child molestation. In addition, prior to indictment, the superior court acting on its own volition does not have the authority to transfer such a case to juvenile court after the district attorney has already invoked the jurisdiction of the superior court.[12]

Indictments charging juveniles with crimes which fall within the jurisdiction of the superior court pursuant to O.C.G.A. § 15-11-560 or O.C.G.A. § 15-11-561 must be presented within 180 days of the date of detention. The state can seek one extension for good cause not to exceed 90 days. If the case is not timely indicted, it must be returned to juvenile court.[13]

In the case of *In the Interest of J.C.*,[14] the Court of Appeals was highly critical of a Juvenile Court which entered an adjudication

---

[9]O.C.G.A. § 15-11-560(b).

[10]O.C.G.A. § 15-11-560(e). In State v. Harper, 271 Ga. App. 761 (2), 610 S.E.2d 699 (2005), a trial court's order transferring an indicted armed robbery case to juvenile court was reversed since the offense is punishable by life in prison.

[11]State v. Ware, 258 Ga. App. 564, 574 S.E.2d 632 (2002).

[12]State v. Henderson, 281 Ga. 623, 641 S.E.2d 515 (2007).

[13]O.C.G.A. § 17-7-50.1. See Hill v. State, 309 Ga. App. 531, 710 S.E.2d 667 (2011). See also In re C.B., 313 Ga. App. 778, 723 S.E.2d 21 (2012) (once the case is transferred back to juvenile court because indictment was not timely, state may not thereafter seek to have case returned to superior court); Nunnally v. State, 311 Ga. App.

558, 716 S.E.2d 608 (2011) (the request for a 90-day extension to obtain indictment must be made within 180 days of juvenile's detention). See also Edwards v. State, 323 Ga. App. 864, 748 S.E.2d 501 (2013) (granting defendant bond does not toll the 180-day mandate); State v. Baxter, 300 Ga. 268, 794 S.E.2d 49 (2016) (juvenile can waive 180-day limit provided waiver is made knowingly and voluntarily). See In Interest of M.D.H., 300 Ga. 46, 793 S.E.2d 49 (2016) (trial court is required to dismiss *without prejudice* only, if state fails to file delinquency petition within 30 days from filing a complaint against juvenile who is not detained unless within that time it obtains an extension of time).

[14]In the Interest of J.C., 242 Ga. 737, 251 S.E.2d 299 (2002).

for reckless driving without regard for the most basic notions of due process. The concurring opinion reflected what might be a concern of the entire Court, that the rights of juveniles are not being routinely observed in juvenile courts generally. The concurring judges suggested that the Acknowledgement of Rights form should be substantially revised so as to provide a more substantive and explicit description of a juvenile's rights in those courts.

Pursuant to O.C.G.A. § 15-11-160(a), the juvenile court must issue a summons to the parents of an allegedly delinquent child as necessary and proper parties to the delinquency actions. As the Court of Appeals observed in *In the interest of J.L.B.*,[15] "the parents' status as necessary parties to a delinquency action implicitly recognizes that the parents are the natural custodians of their child and that, upon an adjudication of delinquency and the court's issuance of a dispositional order, the consequences of complying with the order will fall on both the parents and their child." Accordingly, in a case of first impression, the *J.L.B.* court recognized that parents have the right to appeal the judgment of a juvenile court and to participate in the appellate process.

See § 21:9, infra, on the age of criminal responsibility. See § 5:8, supra, on admissibility of confessions by a juvenile.

§ 13:28 Parties to a crime—General

The Criminal Code of Georgia treats as parties to a crime persons who were formerly regarded as principals in the first degree, principals in the second degree and accessories before the fact.[1] "Accessories after the fact" are not parties to the crime, and their punishment is addressed in O.C.G.A. § 16-10-24, O.C.G.A. § 16-10-50, and O.C.G.A. § 16-10-94.[2]

The Georgia Criminal Code designates parties to a crime as follows:

" O.C.G.A. § 16-2-20 Parties to crime; punishment

"(a) Every person concerned in the commission of a crime is a party thereto and may be charged with and convicted of commission of the crime.

"(b) A person is concerned in the commission of a crime only if

---

[15]In re J.L.B., 280 Ga. App. 556(1), 634 S.E.2d 514 (2006).

[Section 13:28]

[1]Jones v. State, 250 Ga. 11, 13, 295 S.E.2d 71 (1982). See Judge Dean's excellent opinion in Hannah v. State, 125 Ga. App. 596, 598 (2), 188 S.E.2d 401 (1972).

[2]Huckabee v. State, 287 Ga. 728, 699 S.E.2d 531 (2010); see Higuera-Guiterrez v. State, 298 Ga. 41, 779 S.E.2d 288 (2015) (defendant's conviction as a party to the crime of felony murder reversed where court found that he was "at best" an accessory after the fact); Vergara v. State, 287 Ga. 194, 695 S.E.2d 215 (2010). Cf. Jones v. State, 250 Ga. 11, 13, 295 S.E.2d 71 (1982).

he:

"(1) Directly commits the crime;

"(2) Intentionally causes some other person to commit the crime under such circumstances that the other person is not guilty of any crime either in fact or because of legal incapacity;

"(3) Intentionally aids or abets in the commission of the crime; or

"(4) Intentionally advises, encourages, hires, counsels, or procures another to commit the crime."

Professor Kurtz summarizes the four categories of O.C.G.A. § 16-2-20(b) as follows: (1) those who actually commit the crime directly; (2) those who use an innocent or non-responsible agent to commit the crime directly; (3) those who intentionally aid or abet in the direct commission of the crime; and (4) those who intentionally advise, encourage, hire, counsel or procure others to commit the crime directly.[3]

In *Jordan v. State*,[4] the Court of Appeals explained "party to a crime" this way: "A participant to a crime may be convicted although he is not the person who directly commits the crime. A person who intentionally aids or abets in the commission of a crime or intentionally advises, encourages, hires, counsels or procures another to commit the crime may be convicted of the crime. Mere presence at the scene is not sufficient to convict one of being a party to a crime, but criminal intent may be inferred from conduct before, during and *after* the commission of a crime." In addition, there must be some evidence of a common criminal intent to establish that one is a party to a crime.[5]

In *Nalls v. State*,[6] the Georgia Supreme Court overruled prior precedent which held that convictions for the offenses of murder and hindering in the apprehension of a criminal are mutually exclusive. The court found its reasoning in the prior cases to be seriously flawed, observing that a party who participates in the commission of the primary crime can also be involved in the subsequent crime of hindering the apprehension of another who also is a party to that crime.

---

[3]Kurtz Criminal Offenses and Defenses in Georgia PARTIES TO CRIME II. (2018 ed.); State v. Freeman, 272 Ga. 813, 815 (2), 537 S.E.2d 92 (2000) (overruled on other grounds by, Nalls v. State, 815 S.E.2d 38 (Ga. 2018)).

[4]Jordan v. State, 281 Ga. App. 419, 636 S.E.2d 151 (2006).

[5]Higuera-Guiterrez v. State, 298 Ga. 41, 779 S.E.2d 288 (2015).

[6]Nalls v. State, 304 Ga. 168, 815 S.E.2d 38 (2018) (overruling Jordan v. State, 272 Ga. 395, 530 S.E.2d 192 (2000), and all other case law to the extent they suggest that one can *never* be convicted of both hindering and murder).

In *Guzman v. State*,[7] the defendant was convicted of vehicular homicide although he was neither driving nor riding in the vehicle involved in the fatal accident. His conviction was premised upon his role as a party to the crime because he gave car keys and beer to the 14-year-old driver who was operating the car at the time of the offense. The case turns on the issue of intent. Only a general intent is required for the offense of DUI. The minor's actions satisfy that element of the case but only as to his criminal exposure. The adult defendant's intent, the court concluded, could be inferred from the fact that he gave an alcoholic beverage and permission and the means to operate a motor vehicle to an individual who lacked the legal capacity to handle either.

In *Butts v. State*,[8] that court noted that a co-conspirator to a robbery may be convicted of armed robbery even if he did not have actual prior knowledge that his fellow conspirator intended to use a gun, provided that the state can show that the use of the weapon was naturally or necessarily done in furtherance of the robbery.

In *Osborn v. State*,[9] the Georgia Court of Appeals, in referring to O.C.G.A. § 16-2-20(b)(3), (4), stated that while the "Code section does not use the word 'conspiracy,' it is plain that it embodies the theory of conspiracy insofar as it renders one not directly involved in the commission of a crime responsible as a party thereto." As in the case of conspiracy, "the indictment need not charge the defendant with being a party to a crime in order for the State to prove his culpability in that manner."[10]

It is not error for a trial judge to charge the jury that a defendant may be found guilty, even though he did not directly commit the crime if he is a "party to the crime," even though the indictment does not refer to the defendant as being a party to the crime.[11]

It is no longer necessary for the actual perpetrator to be tried at the same time or before the accessory before the fact, and the conviction of the principal is not a prerequisite to the conviction of an accomplice.[12] This rule is made clear in O.C.G.A. § 16-2-21,

[7]Guzman v. State, 260 Ga. App. 689 (1), 580 S.E.2d 654 (2003).

[8]Butts v. State, 297 Ga. 766, 778 S.E.2d 205 (2015).

[9]Osborn v. State, 161 Ga. App. 132, 133 (1), 291 S.E.2d 22 (1982); Hernandez v. State, 182 Ga. App. 797, 800, 357 S.E.2d 131 (1987).

[10]Wakily v. State, 225 Ga. App. 56, 60 (7), 483 S.E.2d 313 (1997); Monteagudo v. State, 247 Ga. App. 801, 803 (2), 545 S.E.2d 351 (2001).

[11]Jenkins v. State, 172 Ga. App. 715, 717, 324 S.E.2d 491 (1984). Cf. Smith v. State, 234 Ga. App. 586, 590 (3), 506 S.E.2d 406 (1998).

[12]White v. State, 181 Ga. App. 354, 352 S.E.2d 205 (1986), rev'd, 257 Ga. 236, 356 S.E.2d 875 (1987).

which provides as follows:

"Any party to a crime who did not directly commit the crime may be indicted, tried, convicted, and punished for commission of the crime upon proof that the crime was committed and that he was a party thereto, although the person claimed to have directly committed the crime has not been prosecuted or convicted, or has been convicted of a different crime or degree of crime, or is not amenable to justice or has been acquitted."

In *Harden v. State*,[13] the court held that the general statute quoted above does not apply to a person who knowingly aids another in an escape, since there is a specific statute covering this situation and the special statute is regarded as preempting the general statute.

In *Martinez v. State*,[14] the court pointed out that under O.C.G.A. § 16-2-21 an accessory after the fact is not a party to the crime but such acts constitute the separate offense of obstruction of justice under O.C.G.A. § 16-10-24.

The mere agreement of one person to buy contraband which another agrees to sell does not establish that the two acted in concert so as to support a finding of conspiracy.[15] However, when the supplier "fronts" contraband to another who is expected to sell it and pay the supplier from the proceeds, the supplier retains a sufficient interest in the later sale to establish that he acted in concert with the other person to distribute the contraband.[16] See Studdard, *Daniel's Georgia Handbook on Criminal Evidence* (2018 ed.), § 6:35, on testimony of accomplices, and § 8:9, on conspiracy.

In *Porter v. State*,[17] the court pointed out that evidence of the guilt of the person who directly committed the crime is admissible, and in *White v. State*,[18] the court held that the acquittal of the principal is relevant and admissible. However, the viability of *White* has since been questioned in *Davis v. State*[19] as being out of step with the majority view on the admissibility of an accomplice's acquittal. In *Davis*, the court restricted *White* to its facts, a case in which the defendant was "distinctly" charged as an "aider, abettor, encourager or counselor in the commission of the

---

[13]Harden v. State, 184 Ga. App. 371, 372, 361 S.E.2d 696 (1987).

[14]Martinez v. State, 222 Ga. App. 497, 499 (2), 474 S.E.2d 708 (1996). Accord, Bullard v. State, 242 Ga. App. 843 (6), 530 S.E.2d 265 (2000).

[15]United States v. Mancillas, 580 F.2d 1301, 1307 (7th Cir. 1978).

[16]Osborn v. State, 161 Ga. App. 132, 134 (1), 291 S.E.2d 22 (1982).

[17]Porter v. State, 200 Ga. 246, 255, 36 S.E.2d 794 (1946).

[18]White v. State, 257 Ga. 236, 356 S.E.2d 875 (1987), rev'g 181 Ga. App. 354, 352 S.E.2d 205 (1986). See Davis v. State, 296 Ga. 126, 765 S.E.2d 336 (2014).

[19]Davis v. State, 296 Ga. 126, 765 S.E.2d 336 (2014).

crime."

§ 13:29   Parties to a crime—Corporations

The Criminal Code of Georgia provides as follows:

"16-2-22 Criminal responsibility of corporations

"(a) A corporation may be prosecuted for the act or omission constituting a crime only if:

"(1) The crime is defined by a statute which clearly indicates a legislative purpose to impose liability on a corporation, and an agent of the corporation performs the conduct which is an element of the crime while acting within the scope of his office or employment and in behalf of the corporation; or

"(2) The commission of the crime is authorized, requested, commanded, performed, or recklessly tolerated by the board of directors or by a managerial official who is acting within the scope of his employment in behalf of the corporation.

"(b) For the purposes of this Code section, the term:

"(1) 'Agent' means any director, officer, servant, employee, or other person who is authorized to act in behalf of the corporation.

"(2) 'Managerial official' means an officer of the corporation or any other agent who has a position of comparable authority for the formulation of corporate policy or the supervision of subordinate employees."

The intent seems to have been "to limit corporate liability for crimes, except those indicating a clear legislative intent to impose liability on corporations to violations of the law as a result of 'corporate policy' or 'corporate action' formulated, carried out or recklessly tolerated by directors or other top management officials."[1]

The United States Justice Department has now published a document giving guidance to United States attorneys on the prosecution of corporations.[2]

§ 13:30   Conspiracy—General

Except as related to the admission of hearsay evidence, the doctrine of conspiracy is largely a matter of substantive criminal law and not criminal procedure, with which this book attempts to deal. In order to obtain an insight into the law of conspiracy from

---

[Section 13:29]

[1]Committee Notes to former GCA §§ 26-801 et seq. (now O.C.G.A. §§ 16-2-20 et seq.) reported in GCA Vol. 10, Pt. 1, p. 236 (1998 revision).

[2]Federal Prosecution of Corporations, U.S. Attorneys' Manual, Title 9, Criminal Resource Manual 163 (Feb. 2000).

this book, the reader needs to consider the sections on parties to a crime, § 13:28, supra; motions to sever parties, § 14:72, infra; motions to sever offenses, § 14:73, infra; the substantive law of conspiracy which is referred to in § 13:31, infra; attempts, see § 21:4, infra; and double jeopardy considerations, see §§ 14:47 et seq., infra.

§ 13:31 Conspiracy—Substantive aspects

O.C.G.A. § 16-4-8 provides as follows:

"A person commits the offense of conspiracy to commit a crime when he together with one or more persons conspires to commit any crime and any one or more of such persons does any overt act to effect the object of the conspiracy. A person convicted of the offense of criminal conspiracy to commit a felony shall be punished by imprisonment for not less than one year nor more than one-half the maximum period of time for which he could have been sentenced if he had been convicted of the crime conspired to have been committed, by one-half the maximum fine to which he could have been subjected if he had been convicted of such crime, or both. A person convicted of the offense of criminal conspiracy to commit a misdemeanor shall be punished as for a misdemeanor. A person convicted of the offense of criminal conspiracy to commit a crime punishable by death or by life imprisonment shall be punished by imprisonment for not less than one year nor more than ten years."

In every conspiracy there must be (1) an agreement and (2) a basic or object offense or offenses, toward which the conspiracy is directed.

It must be remembered that such agreements are rarely established by direct testimony. The mutual understanding can be, and usually is, established by circumstantial evidence.[1] Under the Georgia statute, the state must prove an overt act to effect the object of the conspiracy.[2] "A defendant may be said to 'conspire' even if he did not intend the underlying act himself; the government must only prove that the defendant reached an agreement with the intent that the crime be committed by some member of the conspiracy."[3]

Intent of two kinds is required to establish a conspiracy. First,

---

[Section 13:31]

[1]Harris v. State, 236 Ga. 242, 245 (2), 223 S.E.2d 643 (1976); Blackstone v. Andre, 232 Ga. 715, 208 S.E.2d 815 (1974); Chesser v. State, 141 Ga. App. 657, 234 S.E.2d 121 (1977).

[2]Kurtz Criminal Offenses and Defenses in Georgia CONSPIRACY II. (2014 ed.).

[3]Hourin v. State, 301 Ga. 835, 839-840, 804 S.E.2d 388 (2017) (defendant non-physician could be prosecuted for conspiracy to distribute a controlled substance in violation of

there must be an intent to agree,[4] and lack of capacity to agree may negate this requirement.[5] Second, a defendant must have intended to realize a criminal objective, but not necessarily the one which resulted. Thus, in *Berryhill v. State*,[6] the court concluded that where two persons conspire to rob a third person, one agrees to watch while the other enters a building to rob, and in the furtherance of the design to rob, the person entering the building kills the intended victim, the one who remained outside to watch was guilty of murder. However, a conspiracy charge would not be appropriate in the case of a buyer and seller of drugs. The "mere agreement of one person to buy contraband which another agrees to sell does not establish that the two acted in concert."[7]

Pursuant to O.C.G.A. § 24-8-801(d)(2)(E), the statement of a co-conspirator of a party is admissible if it was made "during the course of and in furtherance of the conspiracy, including a statement made during the concealment phase of a conspiracy." Such statements are admissions and are not considered hearsay. They may be used against every party to the conspiracy.[8] A party to a conspiracy is not only responsible for any actions taken in furtherance of the conspiracy, but also for collateral acts "incident to and growing out of the original purpose."[9] To be held criminally responsible for the collateral acts, however, they must be a "natural and probable consequence of the conspiracy."[10] For example,

---

O.C.G.A. § 16-13-42 which applies to "practitioners" without being subject to conviction for underlying offense).

[4]Underwood v. State, 29 Ga. App. 479, 115 S.E. 919 (1923).

[5]See Underwood v. State, 29 Ga. App. 479, 115 S.E. 919 (1923).

[6]Berryhill v. State, 151 Ga. 416, 107 S.E. 158 (1921). In Jenkins v. State, 159 Ga. App. 183, 283 S.E.2d 49 (1981), the victim was abducted from the bus station by Jenkins and another man. She was taken to a house, robbed, and sexually molested by Jenkins. All three left the house. Jenkins left the victim and the other man. The other man forced the victim to return to the house and he raped her. Jenkins was convicted of robbery and kidnapping with bodily harm. The bodily harm consisted of the rape. The conviction was affirmed, even though Jen-

kins was not present when the rape occurred.

[7]Pruitt v. State, 264 Ga. App. 44, 47 (2), 589 S.E.2d 864 (2003).

[8]See State v. Wilkins, 302 Ga. 156, 805 S.E.2d 868 (2017) (O.C.G.A. § 24-8-801(a)(2)(E) only applies to statements made in furtherance of a conspiracy and "retrospective" statements regarding a past event not designed to enlist others to conspiracy or advance an objective of the conspiracy do not qualify).

[9]Everritt v. State, 277 Ga. 457, 459, 588 S.E.2d 691 (2003) (quoting Burke v. State, 234 Ga. 512, 514, 216 S.E.2d 812 (1975)).

[10]Everritt v. State, 277 Ga. 457, 459, 588 S.E.2d 691 (2003) (citing Huffman v. State, 257 Ga. 390, 392 (3), 359 S.E.2d 910 (1987)).

in *Everritt v. State*,[11] the defendant had entered into a conspiracy
to commit arson. One of the defendant's co-conspirators murdered
another co-conspirator without the knowledge of the defendant.
Under the theory of conspiracy, the defendant was convicted of
malice murder. The Georgia Supreme Court reversed the
defendant's conviction because it found that a conspiracy to commit arson does not "naturally, necessarily and probably result in
the murder of one co-conspirator by another."

It should be remembered that O.C.G.A. § 16-4-9 provides that a
"coconspirator may be relieved [of his responsibility for a conspir-
acy] if he can show that before the overt act occurred he withdrew
his agreement to commit a crime."

In *Scott v. State*,[12] the Georgia Supreme Court held that a
defendant may not be convicted of violating the conspiracy statute if the conspired crime has in fact been committed. However,
in *English v. State*,[13] the court held the crime of conspiracy to
defraud the state (under the peculiar wording of that statute)
does not merge into the underlying criminal offense.

In *Rowe v. State*,[14] the Court of Appeals held that a defendant
could not be convicted of the conspiracy statute if the indictment
does not charge that offense. Nonetheless, the state may seek to
prove at trial that the defendant was engaged in a conspiracy as
a party to a crime pursuant to O.C.G.A. § 16-2-20 and obtain a
jury charge thereon although the defendant was not indicted
under the theory of conspiracy as set out in O.C.G.A. § 16-4-8.[15]

See the excellent material in Kurtz, *Criminal Offenses and Defenses in Georgia* (4th ed.), p. 114 et seq., and Marcus, *Prosecution and Defense of Criminal Conspiracy Cases* (Matthew Bender
1978).

§ 13:32 Conspiracy—Procedural aspects

Until 1969, conspiracy was not itself an indictable offense, but
its importance was as a theory of connecting a person to a particular substantive crime.[1] This conspiracy rule is common in the

---

[11]Everritt v. State, 277 Ga. 457,
459, 588 S.E.2d 691 (2003).

[12]Scott v. State, 229 Ga. 541, 544,
192 S.E.2d 367 (1972); McCormick v.
State, 163 Ga. App. 267 (1), 293 S.E.2d
35 (1982). See, Grant v. State, 227 Ga.
App. 243, 488 S.E.2d 763 (1997).

[13]English v. State, 202 Ga. App.
751, 752 (1), 415 S.E.2d 659 (1992).

[14]Rowe v. State, 166 Ga. App. 836,
305 S.E.2d 624 (1983).

[15]Wiley v. State, 238 Ga. App. 334,
335 (4), 519 S.E.2d 10 (1999).

[Section 13:32]

[1]Kurtz Criminal Offenses and
Defenses in Georgia CONSPIRACY I.
(2014 ed.).

United States[2] and is preserved in O.C.G.A. § 16-2-20(b)(4), which defines a party to a crime as a person who "[i]ntentionally advises, encourages, hires, counsels, or procures another to commit the crime."[3]

A conspiracy may be proven, even though it is not alleged in the indictment.[4] However, in *Rowe v. State*,[5] the court held that a defendant could not be convicted of the Georgia Conspiracy Statute (O.C.G.A. § 16-4-8) unless he is charged in the indictment with that offense. If the evidence tends to show a conspiracy, it is not error for the trial judge to charge the jury on the substantive statute on conspiracy set out in O.C.G.A. § 16-4-8, even if a crime under this statute is not set out in the indictment;[6] it seems that a party may be convicted under this section if he is not convicted of the charge actually contained in the indictment.[7] However, a defendant is not as a matter of right entitled to a jury instruction on O.C.G.A. § 16-4-8, where the evidence shows without dispute that the basic offense was committed.[8]

At least a large part of the material set out above results from the minority view[9] of the Georgia courts that a defendant may not be convicted of a conspiracy if he is found guilty of the basic, underlying, or object crime.[10]

In a conspiracy case, venue is properly laid in the county in which the substantive offense was committed even though the defendant may have never entered that county.[11] However, where a case is based on the activities of a co-conspirator and those activities took place in a county other than the one in which the prosecution is brought, a special instruction on venue is necessary to clarify the nature of the criminal activities for which he is on trial.[12]

See § 13:28, supra, on parties to a crime.

---

[2]See 16 Am. Jur. 2d Conspiracy § 1 (1979).

[3]Dutton v. State, 228 Ga. 850, 853, 188 S.E.2d 794 (1972).

[4]Knowles v. State, 159 Ga. App. 239, 240 (4), 283 S.E.2d 51 (1981); Osborn v. State, 161 Ga. App. 132, 133 (1), 291 S.E.2d 22 (1982); Wright v. State, 165 Ga. App. 790 (1), 302 S.E.2d 706 (1983).

[5]Rowe v. State, 166 Ga. App. 836, 305 S.E.2d 624 (1983).

[6]Cordova v. State, 191 Ga. App. 297, 298 (1), 381 S.E.2d 436 (1989).

[7]Cf. Jones v. State, 243 Ga. 820, 829 (11), 256 S.E.2d 907 (1979).

[8]Cf. Dutton v. State, 228 Ga. 850, 852 (3), 188 S.E.2d 794 (1972).

[9]LaFave & Scott, Criminal Law, § 62 at p. 494 (West 1972). E.g., Iannelli v. United States, 420 U.S. 770, 95 S.Ct. 1284, 43 L.Ed.2d 616 (1975).

[10]Dutton v. State, 228 Ga. 850, 853, 188 S.E.2d 794 (1972); Crosby v. State, 232 Ga. 599, 602, 207 S.E.2d 515 (1974); Bennett v. State, 135 Ga. App. 615, 218 S.E.2d 455 (1975); Scott v. State, 229 Ga. 541, 543, 192 S.E.2d 367 (1972).

[11]Osborn v. State, 161 Ga. App. 132, 133 (1), 291 S.E.2d 22 (1982).

[12]Osborn v. State, 161 Ga. App. 132, 136 (3), 291 S.E.2d 22 (1982).

Chapter 14

Pre-Trial Pleas, Demurrers, Notices, Demands, and Motions

KeyCite®: Cases and other legal materials listed in KeyCite Scope can be
researched through the KeyCite service on Westlaw®. Use KeyCite to check
citations for form, parallel references, prior and later history, and comprehensive citator information, including citations to other decisions and secondary
materials.

---

§ 14:1 General considerations

After an indictment has been returned, defense counsel has an
opportunity to utilize a great number of pleas, demurrers,
demands, notices, and motions. For the sake of brevity, such
pleas, demurrers, notices, demands, and motions are sometimes
loosely referred to as "pleadings." The facts of the particular case
will determine which of these pleadings are to be utilized.

It has been said that defense counsel is generally limited only by the extent of his imagination and insight into the law as to the pleadings he should use. Some unusual pleadings have on occasion established new and better law.[1]

It should be pointed out that a defendant has no right to file a written answer to an indictment admitting certain allegations and denying or explaining others as is done in a civil case.[2] The general issue of guilt or innocence is made by a plea of not guilty, which entitles the defendant to any defense within the scope of the general issue.[3]

There may be a number of reasons for filing pleadings. For example, a demurrer or a plea may result in the dismissal of an indictment or of one or more counts in an indictment. A demand for a list of witnesses, a notice to produce, or a discovery motion may assist defense counsel in the preparation of his case for trial. A motion to suppress may result in the exclusion of evidence which is vital to the state's prosecution of a case.

There may be pleadings which defense counsel considers must be granted to insure his client a fair trial. There may be others which are not vital to the defense of the case, and the defendant may be better off if they are denied or overruled, particularly since such ruling may constitute a basis for a reversal in the event of a conviction.

Where an order in favor of the defendant is not vital to a fair trial, some defense counsel will file a pleading which is a "form" or reproduction of an older pleading. Such a form or copy may not receive as a careful judicial scrutiny as one which appears to be "brand-new," carefully drawn, and freshly typed.[4] The legal effect of a photostated pleading properly signed is the same as that of a typed original. In the average case which ends in a conviction, there is generally nothing more unfortunate for the defendant or defense counsel than having to appeal only on the general ground that the evidence does not support the verdict. However, in *Black*

[Section 14:1]

[1]E.g., in Ferguson v. Georgia, 365 U.S. 570, 81 S.Ct. 756, 5 L.Ed.2d 783 (1961), counsel attacked the rule that defense counsel had no right to ask a defendant questions when he made a statement. The court concluded that this deprived the defendant of his right of counsel and was a violation of the due process clause of the Fourteenth Amendment.

[2]McBride v. State, 119 Ga. App. 418, 167 S.E.2d 374 (1969).

[3]McBride v. State, 119 Ga. App. 418 (1), 167 S.E.2d 374 (1969).

[4]In the landmark case of Gould v. State, 131 Ga. App. 811, 207 S.E.2d 519 (1974), while it does not appear in the opinion, Millard Farmer, the visionary counsel for the defendant in the trial court, filed a photostated plea in abatement which was promptly, if not summarily, overruled.

v. State,[5] the court emphasized that the trial court make a ruling on each point which is a basis of appeal. A defendant must fairly raise each issue and not a laundry list of objections and must present argument on only one or two. As noted by Judge Randall Evans while sitting on the Georgia Court of Appeals: "[A] part of the trial lawyer's job during the trial is to see that points are made which will allow defendant's counsel to do something more than to merely accept the verdict of guilty. . . . A lawyer should never be proud of saying he made no points during the trial on which to base an appeal."[6]

It should be remembered that the role of defense counsel is to represent his client to the best of his ability by any legal, ethical means. It is improper for defense counsel not to vigorously assert any defense available if it will permanently terminate the prosecution of his client. Furthermore, counsel has no right to weakly assert a position in the trial court which will dispose of the case with the idea that he will appeal an adverse ruling and make "new law" in an appellate court. However, counsel has the obligation "not to clog the courts with frivolous motions or appeals."[7] Thus, an attorney is not to be considered "incompetent for his failure to file any pretrial motions, especially where no necessity of or benefit from such is indicated."[8]

In determining what motions may be appropriate in a particular case, it should be kept in mind that the arbitrary denial of a state-created right has been held to be a violation of due process.[9]

It has been pointed out that lawyers are encouraged to embrace civility and "avoid incivility's evil consequences of discord, disrespect, irresponsibility and blind advocacy. . . . [R]espect, courtesy, politeness, graciousness and basic good manners . . . [are] an essential part of effective advocacy."[10]

Substance or contents, not the name or title given by the pleader, determine what a pleading is.[11] In *Prater v. State*,[12] the court pointed out that under O.C.G.A. § 17-1-1(a) every written

---

[5]Black v. State, 248 Ga. App. 626 (1), 548 S.E.2d 9 (2001).

[6]Barnes v. State, 135 Ga. App. 190, 191, 217 S.E.2d 443 (1975).

[7]Polk County v. Dodson, 454 U.S. 312, 102 S.Ct. 445, 70 L.Ed.2d 509 (1981). Cf. Hammond v. State, 264 Ga. 879, 887 (10), 452 S.E.2d 745 (1995). Cf. Sewell v. State, 229 Ga. App. 685, 687 (1)(a), 494 S.E.2d 512 (1997).

[8]Johnson v. State, 171 Ga. App. 851, 853, 321 S.E.2d 402 (1984).

[9]Hicks v. Oklahoma, 447 U.S. 343, 100 S.Ct. 2227, 65 L.Ed.2d 175 (1980). Cf. Greenholtz v. Inmates of the Nebraska Penal and Correctional Complex, 442 U.S. 1, 99 S.Ct. 2100, 60 L.Ed.2d 668 (1979).

[10]Concurring opinion of Chief Justice Benham, Butts v. State, 273 Ga. 760, 772, 546 S.E.2d 472 (2001).

[11]Garcia v. State, 207 Ga. App. 794, 795, 429 S.E.2d 164 (1993). Accord, Welborn v. State, 232 Ga. App. 837, 838 (1), 503 S.E.2d 85 (1998); Boney v. State, 236 Ga. App. 179, 180, 510 S.E.2d 892 (1999).

motion must be served on the opposite party "absent authority for an ex parte hearing." This statute also provides "service shall be made upon a party's attorney . . . by delivering a copy to him or by mailing it to him at his last known address. . . . Service by mail shall be deemed complete upon mailing."[13]

§ 14:2   Time of filing

Rule 31.1 of the Uniform Rules for the Superior Courts provides in part as follows:

"All motions, demurrers, and special pleas shall be made and filed at or before the time set by law (10 days after arraignment, O.C.G.A. § 17-10-110), unless time therefor is extended by the judge in writing prior to trial. Unless otherwise provided by law, notice of the state's intention to introduce child victim hearsay statements, notice of the defense's intention to raise the issue of insanity or mental illness, or the defense's intention to introduce evidence of specific acts of violence by the victim against third persons, shall be given and filed at least ten (10) days before trial unless the time is shortened or lengthened by the judge."

An "authorized judicial official" may declare a "judicial emergency" and suspend deadlines, time schedules or filing requirements in the event that a "natural disaster, civil disturbance, or other emergency situation" interferes with a litigant's or a state official's ability to comply with these deadlines.[1]

Under O.C.G.A. § 9-10-150 all judges are to continue any hearing, on or without a motion, when any party or his attorney is absent because of his membership in the General Assembly.

If a defendant elects into the reciprocal discovery statutes by giving written notice "at or prior to arraignment, or at such time as the court permits," certain specific requests or demands are no longer necessary. See § 14:9, infra, on the reciprocal discovery for felony cases.

In *Hardeman v. State,*[2] the court held that "an accused cannot launch an initial constitutional challenge in the context of a mo-

---

[12]Prater v. State, 222 Ga. App. 486, 488, 474 S.E.2d 684 (1996).

[13]Cabell v. State, 250 Ga. App. 530, 531, 551 S.E.2d 386 (2001); O.C.G.A. § 17-1-1(b)(1)(3).

[Section 14:2]

[1]O.C.G.A. §§ 38-3-60 to 38-3-64. A plea in bar or a general demurrer challenging the validity of the indictment may be filed at any time and may assert a defense of the statute of limitations at trial. See State v. Barker, 277 Ga. App. 84, 625 S.E.2d 500 (2005). See also §§ 14:39, 14:61, infra, on demurrers.

[2]Hardeman v. State, 272 Ga. 361, 529 S.E.2d 368 (2000). This includes challenges to an indictment based upon contentions that the statute involved is unconstitutionally vague both on its face and as applied to the defendant. Robles v. State, 277 Ga. 415, 421 (9), 589 S.E.2d 566 (2003).

tion for a new trial." However, a constitutional challenge to the sentence to be imposed following conviction is timely if made after verdict but prior to sentencing.[3]

In *State v. Grandison*,[4] the court emphasized that the authorization of a trial judge to file motions after arraignment must be authorized in *writing*.

In Watson v. State,[5] the court held that the failure to timely file a motion or a demurrer amounts to a waiver of the contents of the motion or demurrer.

In *State v. Mendoza*,[6] a demurrer was not filed until after the waiver of arraignment. Defense counsel withdrew. The defendant obtained new counsel who filed a special demurrer within 10 days of his employment. A few weeks later the trial judge signed an order extending the time for filing pre-trial motions. The state contended that the demurrer was improper since it was filed after the time of arraignment and before the signing of the order extending time. The appellate court affirmed the trial court judge's action in considering the demurrer and sustaining it.

In *Roberts v. State*,[7] the Georgia Supreme Court ruled that the doctrine of judicial estoppel could not be employed in the context of a motion for speedy trial filed in a criminal case. A motion for speedy trial filed pursuant to O.C.G.A. § 17-7-170 may not be filed until an indictment has been returned or an accusation proffered. At the defendant's scheduled preliminary hearing, the state announced that the hearing would be unnecessary because an indictment had been returned. The defendant filed his motion for speedy trial accordingly. However, in fact the indictment was not returned until the following day. As a result, the defendant's motion was premature and as such was a "nullity".[8] The defendant invoked the doctrine of judicial estoppel contending that because the prosecutor had stated in open court that the defendant had been indicted, he had, thereby, been deprived of his preliminary hearing. The defense contended that the state should not be allowed to rely on the actual date of the indictment to further deprive the defendant of another of his rights under Georgia criminal procedure, the right to a speedy trial. The court concluded that to apply the doctrine of judicial estoppel in the context of a criminal case would in the final analysis only serve to undermine the public's interest in the prosecution of criminal

---

[3]Woods v. State, 279 Ga. 28(1), 608 S.E.2d 631 (2005).

[4]State v. Grandison, 192 Ga. App. 473, 385 S.E.2d 139 (1989).

[5]Watson v. State, 190 Ga. App. 671, 673 (3), 379 S.E.2d 811 (1989).

[6]State v. Mendoza, 190 Ga. App. 831 (2), 380 S.E.2d 357 (1989).

[7]Roberts v. State, 278 Ga. 610, 604 S.E.2d 781 (2004).

[8]Day v. State, 187 Ga. App. 175(2), 369 S.E.2d 796 (1988).

conduct.

§ 14:3 Time of hearing

Rule 31.2 of the Uniform Rules for the Superior Courts provides as follows:

"All such motions, demurrers, special pleas and notices shall be heard and considered at such time, date, and place as set by the judge. Generally, such will be heard at or after the time of arraignment and prior to the time at which such case is scheduled for trial."

§ 14:4 Discovery—General

Regardless of the competency of counsel, his effectiveness in a particular case is determined in large measure by his preparation.[1] In order to perform a creditable job, counsel must learn the witnesses' views of the facts.

It has been said that at common law there was no right of the defendant to examine the evidence in the case against him prior to trial.[2] During the latter part of the 20th century there was a trend toward discovery based at least partially on notions of due process and the right of the effective benefit of counsel.[3] However, in *Weatherford v. Bursey*,[4] the United States Supreme Court pointed out that "[t]here is no general constitutional right to discovery in a criminal case and Brady did not create one." Some states, such as Florida and Illinois, have enacted comprehensive discovery statutes much like those provided for civil cases.[5]

Georgia followed suit in 1994 by enacting O.C.G.A. §§ 17-16-1 et seq. The radical changes in the discovery act apply only to felony defendants who elect in writing to have the rules govern their case.

Once a defendant elects in, no further demands are required with respect to discovery covered by the Act. As a general rule, discovery covered by the Act must be disclosed as provided in O.C.G.A. § 17-6-4. The discovery rules are now reciprocal and the defendant's duty to disclose certain information arises once the state has fulfilled its disclosure duty. A defendant who does not elect to opt into reciprocal discovery is under no obligation to

---

[Section 14:4]

[1]See United States v. Woods, 487 F.2d 1218 (5th Cir. 1973).

[2]Rex v. Holland, 100 Eng. Rep. 1248 (1792).

[3]See A.B.A. Standards, Discovery and Procedure Before Trial § 11-5.1.

[4]Weatherford v. Bursey, 429 U.S. 545, 559, 97 S.Ct. 837, 51 L.Ed.2d 30 (1977). Accord, Shearer v. State, 259 Ga. 51 (1), 376 S.E.2d 194 (1989).

[5]See A.B.A. Standards, Discovery and Procedure Before Trial § 11-2.1; Ellis v. State, 248 Ga. 414, 416, 283 S.E.2d 870 (1981).

provide the state with witness information, alibi detail, expert information or other materials to which the state would otherwise be entitled to receive under reciprocal discovery. However, the defendant who does not elect to participate in reciprocal discovery is restricted to statutory discovery devices such as the notice to produce provided for in O.C.G.A. § 24-13-27.

Discovery in misdemeanor cases is covered by O.C.G.A. §§ 17-16-20 et seq., which simply reenacted the old discovery statutes, former O.C.G.A. §§ 17-7-110, 17-7-210 and 17-7-211, without substantial change. The case law discussed in the following sections which has interpreted these reenacted statutes continues to be applicable.

Once defense counsel learns the names of the witnesses, he needs to obtain statements from them if possible. However, if a minor witness has a guardian, it is completely within the discretion of the guardian to allow or not to allow a representative of the defendant to interview the ward in advance of trial.[6] Normally, it is preferable to use an investigator for this purpose.[7] If counsel obtains statements from a witness who later changes his earlier statement, the attorney is left in the dubious role of being both an advocate and a witness in the same case, and he may have to take the witness stand and testify to the witness' statement to him.[8]

In *Wright v. State,*[9] the Georgia Supreme Court found that defense counsel improperly acted as witness and advocate where he called a witness he had interviewed and later testified as to what the witness told him earlier. The court then pointed out that DR 5-102 provides in part that "except when essential to the ends of justice a lawyer should avoid testifying in court in behalf of his client" and "the ABA Standards for Criminal Justice propose one way of handling this problem by stating that, '[u]nless the lawyer for the accused is prepared to forgo impeachment of a witness by the lawyer's own testimony as to what the witness stated in an interview or to seek leave to withdraw from the case in order to prevent such impeaching testimony, the lawyer should avoid interviewing a prospective witness except in the presence of a third party.' "

---

[6]Willett v. State, 223 Ga. App. 866, 871 (2), 479 S.E.2d 132 (1996).

[7]Generally, on the right of an indigent defendant to an investigator, see § 14:5, infra. See § 7:4, supra.

[8]See Annot., "Defense Attorney as Witness for His Client in State Criminal Case," 52 A.L.R.3d 887 (1973). In Commonwealth v. Rondeau, 378 Mass. 408, 392 N.E.2d 1001 (1979), the court held that when trial counsel potentially becomes a very important witness, he must withdraw from the case.

[9]Wright v. State, 267 Ga. 496, 497 (2)(b), 480 S.E.2d 13 (1997).

In *Reedman v. State,*[10] the court pointed out that the effective assistance of counsel does not "entitle a defendant to bail 'in order to personally assist counsel' . . . [and] a defendant's entitlement to bail does not increase because he . . . represent[s] himself."

Witnesses do not belong to either the prosecution or the defense, as they are not parties to the case.[11] Thus, the state may not instruct witnesses to refuse to talk to the defense counsel or his investigator. Likewise, defense counsel has no right to instruct witnesses not to talk to a representative of the district attorney.[12] However, a witness may not be compelled to submit to an interview with a representative of either the state or the defense.[13] "[W]hen the witness is a child, the child's guardian may make this decision."[14] If either party wishes to obtain the testimony of a witness, it is not improper for the investigator or attorney to acquaint the witness with other facts surrounding the case if this is necessary in order to obtain the cooperation of the witness.[15] See Studdard, *Daniel's Georgia Handbook on Criminal Evidence* (2018 ed.), § 6:3. See § 14:22, infra, on the prosecution's obligation to furnish the defense with certain witness information under the new reciprocal discovery statutes for felony cases.

It is misconduct for the prosecution[16] or the defense[17] to conceal a witness or to transport or have a witness transported out of the

---

[10]Reedman v. State, 193 Ga. App. 688, 689 (1), 388 S.E.2d 763 (1989).

[11]Jaynes v. Blake, 119 Ga. App. 748, 168 S.E.2d 832 (1969). In Woods v. State, 240 Ga. 265, 239 S.E.2d 786 (1977), the trial judge ordered the district attorney to inform witnesses who were to testify for the state that they should feel free to discuss the case with defense counsel.

[12]See Wilson v. State, 93 Ga. App. 229, 91 S.E.2d 201 (1956); Gregory v. United States, 369 F.2d 185 (C.A.D.C. 1966). In United States v. Barnes, 486 F.2d 776 (8th Cir. 1973), an informer was an active participant in the alleged crime of possession of narcotics. The government did not plan to call him and did not reveal his name and address to defendant. The court held that the prosecution had a duty to locate the informer so defendant could interview him and use him as a witness if he wished. In Clingan v. United States, 400 F.2d 849 (5th Cir. 1968), the court said that where a paid government informer or one acting in concert with officers refused to be interviewed by the defense attorney, there is enough prejudice to permit defendant to call the informer as an adverse witness.

[13]Cf. Mullins v. State, 147 Ga. App. 330, 331 (1), 248 S.E.2d 708 (1978); Rutledge v. State, 245 Ga. 768, 770 (2), 267 S.E.2d 199 (1980); Foster v. State, 170 Ga. App. 222, 223 (2), 316 S.E.2d 828 (1984); Baxter v. State, 254 Ga. 538, 541 (4), 331 S.E.2d 561 (1985); Kelly v. State, 197 Ga. App. 811, 813 (1), 399 S.E.2d 568 (1990).

[14]Dover v. State, 250 Ga. 209, 212 (2), 296 S.E.2d 710 (1982); Sosebee v. State, 190 Ga. App. 746, 748 (3), 380 S.E.2d 464 (1989).

[15]Mincey v. State, 251 Ga. 255 (16), 304 S.E.2d 882 (1983).

[16]See United States v. Calzada, 579 F.2d 1358 (7th Cir. 1978); People v. Wilson, 24 Ill.2d 425, 182 N.E.2d 203 (1962); Freeman v. Georgia, 599 F.2d 65 (5th Cir. 1979).

jurisdiction of the court.

O.C.G.A. § 35-3-34 provides that criminal history records of the defendant and witnesses in a criminal case contained in the Georgia Crime Information Center are available to counsel for the defendant in a criminal action at cost upon receipt of a request from counsel. If a defendant has been found to be indigent, the costs are waived. The request must "contain the style of the case and the name and identifying information for each person whose records." Subsection (a)(2)(C) states that "[d]isclosure of criminal history information to the defendant's counsel as provided in this paragraph shall be solely in such counsel's capacity as an officer of the court. Any use of such information in a manner not authorized by law or the court in which such action is pending where the records were disclosed shall constitute a violation of O.C.G.A. § 35-3-38. . . ." See § 14:13, infra, on the prosecutor's duty to furnish to the defendant a copy of the defendant's Georgia Crime Information Center criminal history under the new reciprocal discovery statutes for felony cases.

However, the district attorney is not obligated to determine the criminal records of the state's witnesses and disclose them to the defense.[18] However, these records are available to defense counsel as set out earlier in this section.

In *Thomason v. State*,[19] the court held that the trial judge did not "abuse its discretion in denying Thomason's motion for notice by the State of its intention to use any evidence 'arguably subject to a motion to suppress,' as the law does [not] require the State to make such a disclosure."

The opportunity for discovery arises at any type of evidentiary hearing, such as a motion to set or reduce bond, motion to suppress evidence, or change of venue. In some cases, consideration may be given to the possibility of filing a civil action related to the subject matter of the criminal charge in order that the broad rules of discovery for civil cases can govern.[20] For example, in an arson case, an action might be brought against the fire insurance

---

[17]Henderson v. Commonwealth, 185 Ky. 232, 215 S.W. 53 (1919).

[18]Hall v. State, 261 Ga. 778, 783 (10), 415 S.E.2d 158 (1991).

[19]Thomason v. State, 268 Ga. 298, 312 (13), 486 S.E.2d 861 (1997).

[20]In United States v. Kordel, 397 U.S. 1, 90 S.Ct. 763, 25 L.Ed.2d 1 (1970), the court held that information obtained by the government by interrogatories in a civil condemnation action, instituted by the government against a corporation, could be used in a later criminal proceeding brought against the president and vice-president of the corporation.

In Campbell v. Eastland, 307 F.2d 478, 487 (5th Cir. 1962), the court held that the use of civil discovery rules to obtain tax fraud files would give the defendant an unfair advantage in a criminal case. The court said a "trial judge in the civil proceeding should not ignore the effect discovery would have on a criminal proceeding

company. In a case of aggravated assault or murder, an action might be brought for a civil assault and battery. However, a decision to file a civil action should not be lightly made since civil discovery is reciprocal. A defense counsel may find that probing interrogatories will be sent to his client. The opposing counsel may want to take the defendant's deposition. While presumably a defendant could decline to answer interrogatories[21] or questions asked him during a deposition[22] on the grounds of self-incrimination, the refusal to answer may be embarrassing to explain in certain situations, such as where the defendant claims self-defense. Also, it has been indicated that a defendant may not be able to refuse to answer self-incriminating questions when the defendant files a civil action arising out of a criminal matter.[23] In *Christopher v. State*,[24] the court held that even in a condemnation case a trial judge has no right to postpone discovery indefinitely. This is particularly true where the district attorney fails to demonstrate present *facts* showing that a criminal prosecution would be prejudiced by such a stay.

In federal practice, a motion for a bill of particulars is sometimes loosely referred to as a discovery device.[25] Georgia has no provision in its law for anything comparable to a bill of particulars.[26]

See § 5:10, supra, on the right of officers to obtain information from a defendant after the prosecution has begun.

Even if a defendant has not elected reciprocal discovery, there is some limited discovery which a defendant is entitled to without the filing of any discovery device. For example, if a witness commits perjury on the stand relating to a promise of leniency, it is the duty of the prosecuting attorney to correct the false evidence.[27]

In federal courts defense counsel is entitled to a copy of statements of a government witness after he has given his direct

---

that is pending or just about to be brought." The court pointed out that it lacked authority to amend the criminal rules to conform to the civil rules and the trial judge is under an affirmative duty "to prevent the rules and policies applicable to one suit from doing violence to those pertaining to the other."

[21]Townsend v. Northcutt, 121 Ga. App. 230, 173 S.E.2d 470 (1970).

[22]O.C.G.A. § 24-5-505.

[23]Savannah Surety Associates, Inc. v. Master, 240 Ga. 438, 241 S.E.2d 192 (1978).

[24]Christopher v. State, 185 Ga. App. 532, 364 S.E.2d 905 (1988). See Chumley v. State, 282 Ga. App. 117, 637 S.E.2d 828 (2006).

[25]See Rule 7(b) of the Federal Rules of Criminal Procedure.

[26]Brooks v. State, 141 Ga. App. 725, 730 (3), 234 S.E.2d 541 (1977); Megar v. State, 144 Ga. App. 564 (3), 241 S.E.2d 447 (1978).

[27]Giglio v. United States, 405 U.S. 150, 92 S.Ct. 763, 31 L.Ed.2d 104 (1972); Allen v. State, 128 Ga. App. 361, 196 S.E.2d 660 (1973).

testimony.[28] These statements are referred to as Jencks statements and may be used in the cross-examination of the witness. In *Jencks v. United States*,[29] the United States Supreme Court recognized this right on non-constitutional grounds. The Jencks Act was then enacted by Congress to limit the rights of the defendant under the *Jencks* decision. Georgia and most other states have not recognized the practice followed in the federal courts.[30] But see § 14:21, infra, on the obligation of both the prosecution and the defense to furnish witness statements under the new reciprocal discovery statutes for felony cases.

For a motion to cause witnesses to confer with counsel, see Studdard, *Daniel's Georgia Criminal Trial Practice Forms* (2018–2019 ed.), §§ 14:49, 14:50.

§ 14:5 Discovery—Pre-trial examination and analysis of physical objects

Expert examination of critical evidence in criminal cases has been recognized in more recent Georgia cases. In the past, most decisions have held that the granting of a motion to examine physical objects was a matter completely within the discretion of the trial judge.[1] See § 14:14, infra, on the defense and prosecution's duty to allow the other party to inspect and copy or photograph tangible evidence, including books, papers, documents, photographs, tangible objects, audio and visual tapes, films and recordings, under Georgia's reciprocal discovery statutes.

In *Barnard v. Henderson*,[2] the defendant moved to permit a ballistics expert of his own choosing to inspect and analyze the murder weapon and projectile. The court held that the refusal to allow the defendant such an examination violated his right of fundamental fairness. However, if it is clear that no meaningful test could be performed on shotgun pellets which would have been material to the defense, it is not error to deny such a

---

[28]See 18 U.S.C.A. § 3500.

[29]Jencks v. United States, 353 U.S. 657, 77 S.Ct. 1007, 1 L.Ed.2d 1103 (1957).

[30]Odom v. State, 156 Ga. App. 119, 120 (1), 274 S.E.2d 117 (1980).

[Section 14:5]

[1]E.g., Herrin v. State, 138 Ga. App. 729, 732 (10), 227 S.E.2d 498 (1976); Butler v. State, 134 Ga. App.

131, 134 (3), 213 S.E.2d 490 (1975).

[2]Barnard v. Henderson, 514 F.2d 744 (5th Cir. 1975). The court states that "fundamental fairness is violated when a criminal defendant on trial for his liberty is denied the opportunity to have an expert of his own choosing, bound by appropriate safeguards imposed by the court, examine a piece of critical evidence whose nature is subject to varying expert opinion."

request.[3]

In *Patterson v. State,*[4] the Georgia Supreme Court held that where a timely[5] motion for an independent analysis of alleged marijuana is made, a defendant may have an expert of his own choosing independently analyze the substance. Any such motion must be filed with 10 days after the arraignment.[6] However, the trial court may impose safeguards to insure that the evidence is unchanged and will be preserved for the trial.[7] Generally, the experts should be allowed to examine the substance at the state laboratory under the control and supervision of the state. The trial court, in its discretion, may refuse to permit an analysis where a valid reason exists, such as where the quantity remaining is too small.[8]

Until the 1981 case of *Sabel v. State,*[9] the Georgia Supreme Court limited the right to pre-trial examination and analysis to

---

[3]Roberts v. State, 243 Ga. 604, 606 (4)(b), 255 S.E.2d 689 (1979).

[4]Patterson v. State, 238 Ga. 204, 206, 232 S.E.2d 233 (1977). Actually, in this case the court refused to reverse the action of the trial court in view of the fact that the defendant was arrested in 1971 and did not file his request to examine the substance until 1975, which was after the State Crime Laboratory had destroyed the sample. In Gilliland v. State, 142 Ga. App. 374, 235 S.E.2d 780 (1977), the Court of Appeals reversed the defendant's conviction where the defendant's request for examination of an alleged controlled substance was timely.

[5]The importance of promptly filing and obtaining a ruling on a motion for a scientific examination is emphasized in Pressel v. State, 163 Ga. App. 188, 192 (4), 292 S.E.2d 553 (1982). In *Pressel*, the motion was filed on May 14. A motion to suppress was denied on September 28. The defendant then sought a hearing for a scientific examination. The district attorney said he considered the motion to have been abandoned. The defendant contended that the motion was valid and that he had not wanted to go to the expense of obtaining an independent examination until he learned that his motion to suppress was being overruled. The trial judge concluded that the motion for an examination had been aban-

doned, and the Court of Appeals affirmed.

[6]O.C.G.A. § 17-7-110. Pursuant to Uniform Superior Court Rule 31.1, this time may be extended by the judge in writing prior to trial.

[7]Haynie v. State, 141 Ga. App. 688, 234 S.E.2d 406 (1977), judgment rev'd on other grounds, 240 Ga. 866, 242 S.E.2d 713 (1978). In Griffin v. State, 148 Ga. App. 311, 251 S.E.2d 161 (1978), the court held that the trial judge did not abuse his discretion in limiting an examination by a defense expert of hair samples to an examination conducted "at State Crime Lab under their supervision" even though defense desired a "Neutron Activation Analysis" and equipment for such an examination was not available at the State Crime Laboratory.

The crime laboratory may also promulgate reasonable rules regarding tests to be conducted there. Tant v. State, 148 Ga. App. 419, 420, 251 S.E.2d 349 (1978).

[8]E.g., Baker v. State, 250 Ga. 187, 194 (2), 297 S.E.2d 9 (1982). But cf. Smith v. State, 270 Ga. 68, 70 (6), 508 S.E.2d 145 (1998).

[9]Sabel v. State, 248 Ga. 10, 17 (6), 282 S.E.2d 61 (1981), disapp. on other grounds in Rower v. State, 264 Ga. 323, 443 S.E.2d 839 (1994).

prohibited substances which would be determinative of guilt or innocence.[10] However, in *Sabel* the court held on due process grounds that a defendant in a criminal case "is entitled on motion timely made to have an expert of his choosing, bound by appropriate safeguards imposed by the court, examine critical evidence [here paint samples] whose nature is subject to varying expert opinion." The court continued to adhere to the safeguards announced in *Patterson,* but indicated that if more sophisticated equipment is available outside of the crime laboratory, the examination may be made somewhere else; however, the state must remain in control of the evidence. In *Blanos v. State,*[11] the court held that there was no right to have an expert examine evidence gathering equipment which was used by the state in a criminal investigation. The defendant in *Blanos* was convicted of driving under the influence of alcohol. The court denied his request for an independent expert to examine the Intoximeter 3000 that was used to test his breath.

In *Morris v. State,*[12] the court noted that there are limitations on the "safeguards" a trial court can require in granting a defendant's expert access to evidence in the possession of the government. There, the defense wanted to inspect the hard drive to the defendant's computer for any child pornography it might contain. The trial court ordered that before the hard drive could be delivered and inspected, the parties were required to obtain written assurance from the U.S. Attorney that possession and inspection of the hard drive by the defense would not result in federal prosecution of the expert for possession of child pornography. The Court of Appeals ruled that the trial court had no authority to order such a requirement.

"Critical evidence," as used above, has been defined "for purposes of the due process clause . . . [as] evidence that, when developed by skilled counsel and experts, could induce a reasonable doubt in the minds of enough jurors to avoid a conviction."[13] In *Rogers v. State,*[14] the court emphasized that for the Sabel rule to apply, (1) the evidence must be critical, and (2) the request for examination must be specific rather than general for potentially

---

[10]In Duckworth v. State, 246 Ga. 631, 636 (8), 272 S.E.2d 332 (1980), the court declined to extend *Patterson* to bullet fragments involved in that case.

[11]Blanos v. State, 192 Ga. App. 835 (1), 386 S.E.2d 714 (1989).

[12]Morris v. State, 324 Ga. App. 756, 751 S.E.2d 551 (2013). See Reaves v. State, 284 Ga. 181, 664 S.E.2d 211 (2008) (trial court does not have au-

thority to order government lab to conduct tests for benefit of defense).

[13]Ellis v. State, 164 Ga. App. 366, 372, 296 S.E.2d 726 (1982) (quoting White v. Maggio, 556 F.2d 1352, 1357 (5th Cir. 1977)); Carpenter v. State, 252 Ga. 79, 80 (1), 310 S.E.2d 912 (1984).

[14]Rogers v. State, 224 Ga. App. 359, 480 S.E.2d 368 (1997).

exculpatory evidence.

In *Tatum v. State*,[15] the court stated "that a request for funds by an indigent must create a reasonable probability that expert assistance is necessary to the defense and that without such assistance the defendant's trial would be rendered fundamentally unfair." In *Brooks v. State*,[16] the court stated that when an indigent defendant moves for funds to employ a scientific expert, he must disclose "with a reasonable degree of precision, [1] why certain evidence is critical, [2] what type of scientific testimony is needed, [3] what that expert proposes to do regarding the evidence, and [4] the anticipated costs for services." *Brooks* also points out that any hearing on a motion for funds shall be ex parte but shall be reported and transcribed as a part of the record and sealed. However, the "state may always be represented when a defendant is examined as to his indigency."

In *Kendrix v. State*,[17] the court held that a defendant has "no right to seek, and the trial court . . . [has] no authority to order, that the State Crime Lab conduct tests *for. . . [the defendant's]* benefit."

In *McAdoo v. State*,[18] the court held that the trial judge may conduct a hearing to determine if the expert designated by the defendant is qualified to conduct the contemplated examination. If such an expert cannot legally possess the substance, this is a basis for refusing to let him have possession of the substance outside the State Crime Laboratory.

Before 2003, indigent defense was the responsibility of the various counties and municipalities. Trial courts appointed counsel for indigent defendants and when appropriate, ordered the county to provide funds necessary for a proper defense to include expert assistance and investigative assistance. In 2003, the legislature enacted the Georgia Indigent Defense Act[19] and the Standards Defender Council (renamed Georgia Public De-

---

[15]Tatum v. State, 259 Ga. 284, 286 (2), 380 S.E.2d 253 (1989). See Dingler v. State, 281 Ga. App. 721(1), 637 S.E.2d 120 (2006); Coalson v. State, 251 Ga. App. 761(3), 555 S.E.2d 128 (2001).

[16]Brooks v. State, 259 Ga. 562, 565, 385 S.E.2d 81 (1989) (quoting Roseboro v. State, 258 Ga. 39, 365 S.E.2d 115 (1988)). Accord, Crawford v. State, 267 Ga. 881, 883 (2), 485 S.E.2d 461 (1997); Thomason v. State, 268 Ga. 298, 310 (7), 486 S.E.2d 861 (1997). See Putnal v. State, 303 Ga. 569, 814 S.E.2d 307 (2018) (court violated defendant's due process right to communicate ex parte with court when it entered an order on the public record rather than under seal as requested by the defense denying motion to allow mental health experts to have access to defendant while in custody).

[17]Kendrix v. State, 206 Ga. App. 627, 628 (2), 426 S.E.2d 251 (1992). See also Brown v. State, 242 Ga. App. 106, 108, 528 S.E.2d 868 (2000).

[18]McAdoo v. State, 164 Ga. App. 23, 28 (2), 295 S.E.2d 114 (1982).

[19]O.C.G.A. §§ 17-12-1, et seq.

fender Council effective July 1, 2015) was created to supervise indigent defense throughout the state. Counties had the option to opt out of the program and a small number chose to do so. The Council also provides counsel to indigents when a county public defender is conflicted from representing the person. In addition, the Council provides the funds to employ expert assistance where needed. The Council has a capital defender division which provides defense to indigents charged with capital offenses. The funding and the administration of the program has been the subject of criticism.

See § 14:30, infra, on the right of a defendant to obtain copies of scientific reports. See § 14:15, infra, if reciprocal discovery has been elected by the defendant.

For motions for scientific examinations, see Studdard, *Daniel's Georgia Criminal Trial Practice Forms* (2018–2019 ed.), §§ 14:56, et seq. See Annotation, "Right of Indigent Defendant in State Criminal Prosecution to Ex Parte In-Camera Hearing on Request for State-Funded Expert Witness," 83 A.L.R.5th 541 (2000).

§ 14:6 Discovery—Duty of state to preserve

In *California v. Trombetta,*[1] the United States Supreme Court held that the due process clause of the Fourteenth Amendment does not require officers to preserve breath samples of drivers suspected of driving under the influence. The court concluded that the officers acted in good faith in accordance with their normal practices. "Whatever duty the Constitution imposes on the States to preserve evidence, that duty must be limited to evidence that might be expected to play a significant role in the suspect's defense. . . . [T]he chances are extremely low that preserved samples would have been exculpatory." In *Hopper v. State,*[2] the Georgia Court of Appeals followed *Trombetta* and also found that this rule was not violative of the Georgia Constitution.

[Section 14:6]

[1]California v. Trombetta, 467 U.S. 479, 104 S.Ct. 2528, 81 L.Ed.2d 413 (1984). Accord, Kuptz v. State, 179 Ga. App. 150, 152 (9), 345 S.E.2d 670 (1986). See State v. Brooks, 301 Ga. App. 355, 687 S.E.2d 631 (2009), where the court held that it is improper to dismiss a case when the record did not reflect whether the evidence had an exculpatory value or the police acted in bad faith.

In Penny v. State, 248 Ga. App. 772, 774 (1), 547 S.E.2d 367 (2001),

the court emphasized that under Trombetta before a duty to preserve evidence attaches, " 'an exculpatory value . . . [must have been] apparent before the evidence was destroyed' and it is 'of such a nature that the defendant would be unable to obtain comparable evidence by other reasonably available means.' "

[2]Hopper v. State, 175 Ga. App. 358 (1), 333 S.E.2d 201 (1985). Cf. Bartell v. State, 181 Ga. App. 148, 150 (3), 351 S.E.2d 495 (1986).

In *Sanders v. State*,[3] the Georgia Court of Appeals held that "the fact that . . . evidence was destroyed between the time of . . . testing and the offer of the test results in evidence did not render those results inadmissible." In *United States v. Agurs*,[4] the court determined that exculpatory value must be known prior to the destruction of the evidence to meet constitutional materiality; the testing officer would not have this knowledge. Also, the defendants had "alternative means of demonstrating their innocence." In *Arizona v. Youngblood*,[5] the United States Supreme Court considered a case in which the state failed to preserve semen samples taken from the victim's body and clothing. The principal defense was mistaken identification. The court said "that unless a criminal defendant can show bad faith on the part of the police, failure to preserve potentially useful evidence does not constitute a denial of due process of law."

In *Walker v. State*,[6] the Georgia Supreme Court discussed the interplay between *Trombetta* and *Youngblood*:

> In dealing with the failure of the state to preserve evidence which might have exonerated the defendant, a court must determine both whether the evidence was material and whether the police acted in bad faith in failing to preserve the evidence. To meet the standard of constitutional materiality, the evidence must possess an exculpatory value that was apparent before it was destroyed, and be of such a nature that the defendant would be unable to obtain comparable evidence by other reasonably available means.

In *United States v. Nabors*,[7] the Eleventh Circuit, while pointing out that "[t]he government has a concomitant responsibility to try in good faith to preserve important material and locate it once the defendant moves for discovery," still "where the material has been destroyed in spite of the government's good faith attempt to preserve it, testimony as to the nature of the material need not be suppressed absent some showing that the testing of the material by another expert would have been reasonably likely to produce evidence favorable to the defendant." In such a case it

---

[3]Sanders v. State, 226 Ga. App. 650, 652 (3), 487 S.E.2d 442 (1997).

[4]United States v. Agurs, 427 U.S. 97, 109, 96 S.Ct. 2392, 49 L.Ed.2d 342 (1976).

[5]Arizona v. Youngblood, 488 U.S. 51, 109 S.Ct. 333, 102 L.Ed.2d 281 (1988); accord, Walker v. State, 264 Ga. 676, 680, 449 S.E.2d 845 (1994); Swanson v. State, 248 Ga. App. 551 (1), 545 S.E.2d 713 (2001); Milton v. State, 232 Ga. App. 672, 679 (6), 503 S.E.2d 566 (1998); Spaulding v. State, 195 Ga. App. 420, 421 (1), 394 S.E.2d 111 (1990).

[6]Walker v. State, 264 Ga. 676, 680, 449 S.E.2d 845 (1994). See State v. Miller, 287 Ga. 748, 699 S.E.2d 316 (2010).

[7]United States v. Nabors, 707 F.2d 1294 (11th Cir. 1983). Cf. Black v. State, 167 Ga. App. 204, 205, 305 S.E.2d 837 (1983); West v. State, 251 Ga. 458, 459 (3), 306 S.E.2d 909 (1983); Hilliard v. Spalding, 719 F.2d 1443 (9th Cir. 1983).

is proper to look at "the government's culpability and prejudice to the defendant." It is not, however, appropriate to give the jury a spoliation charge based upon O.C.G.A. § 24-14-22 in a criminal case.[8]

In *Blackwood v. State*,[9] the court noted:

> The State has a constitutional obligation to preserve evidence that might be expected to play a significant role in the suspect's defense. But *the failure to preserve evidence does not constitute a constitutional violation, unless it is shown that the missing evidence was potentially useful to the defense and was destroyed in bad faith on the part of the police.* Accordingly, the prosecution may be penalized if it loses or destroys evidence that could potentially have been helpful to the defense only if the defense shows that the evidence was material and that the State acted in bad faith in failing to preserve it. *To be material, the evidence must have had an apparent exculpatory value before it was lost, and be of such as nature that the defendant cannot obtain comparable evidence by other reasonable means.*

O.C.G.A. § 17-5-56(a) requires the state to maintain "physical evidence collected at the time of the crime that contains biological material, including, but not limited to, stains, fluids or hair samples that relate to the identity of the perpetrator of the crime." O.C.G.A. § 17-5-56(b) sets out the length of time the state must maintain the evidence depending on the severity level of the offense involved. The Code section does not specify the consequences of the state's failure to maintain such evidence.[10]

See Annotation, "Failure of Police to Preserve Potentially Exculpatory Evidence as Violating Criminal Defendant's Rights Under the United States Constitution," 40 A.L.R.5th 113 (1996). See Annotation, "Right of Accused in State Courts to Have Expert Inspect, Examine, or Test Physical Evidence in Possession of

---

[8]Doyal v. State, 287 Ga. App. 667, 653 S.E.2d 52 (2007).

[9]Blackwood v. State, 277 Ga. App. 870, 873–874 (2), 627 S.E.2d 907, 24 A.L.R.6th 819 (2006) (citations and punctuation omitted; emphasis supplied). See Clayton County v. Austin-Powell, 321 Ga. App. 12, 740 S.E.2d 831 (2013) (in order for there to have been spoliation, the evidence in question must have: existed; been in the possession of a party; and, relate to the destruction or failure to preserve evidence that is necessary to contemplated or pending litigation). See Sachtjen v. State, 340 Ga. App. 612, 798 S.E.2d 114 (2017) (spoliation presumption does not apply in criminal

proceedings).

[10]See State v. Mussman, 289 Ga. 586, 713 S.E.2d 822 (2011) (suppression not warranted where officers disposed of evidence in accordance with standard policy and there was no basis to find that either policy or officer's actions demonstrated some intent to wrongfully withhold evidence from defendant). See Clay v. State, 290 Ga. 822, 725 S.E.2d 260 (2012) (Code section applies only to preservation of biological materials that "relate to the identity of the perpretator" and not to such materials as may relate to any other issue, such as an individual's leval of intoxication.).

Prosecution," 27 A.L.R.4th 1188 (1984).

§ 14:7 Discovery—Depositions in criminal cases

O.C.G.A. § 24-13-130 provides for the taking of depositions in certain limited situations in criminal cases.[1] A summary of that statute follows.

Any time after a defendant has been charged with an offense, upon motion of a party and after notice to the parties, the court can order the taking of a material witness' testimony. In order to be entitled to take a witness' deposition, it must be shown to the satisfaction of the court that the witness is material to the case and one of the following: (1) the witness is in imminent danger of death; (2) the witness has been threatened with death or great bodily harm because of his or her status as a witness; (3) the witness is preparing to leave the state and there are reasonable grounds to believe the witness will be unable to attend trial; (4) the witness is so sick or infirm that there are reasonable grounds to believe the witness will be unable to attend trial; (5) the witness is being detained as a material witness and there are reasonable grounds to believe that the witness will flee if released; or (6) the witness is a non-resident alien.[2] The moving party is also entitled to have produced at the taking of such a deposition designated books, records, documents, recordings, papers and material which is not privileged.

The statute also provides for the taking of a deposition upon motion of the state or the defendant of a physician whose testimony is relevant to a criminal case where the defendant has been charged with child molestation, aggravated child molestation or physical or sexual abuse of a child.

In *Maryland v. Craig*,[3] the Supreme Court set forth what has since become known as the *Craig* test holding that a defendant's right to confront "any accusatory witness may be satisfied absent a physical face-to-face confrontation at trial only where the denial of such confrontation is necessary to further an important policy and only where the reliability of the testimony is otherwise

---

[Section 14:7]

[1]O.C.G.A. § 24-13-130. The Georgia statute follows closely, but is not identical to, Fed. R. Crim. P. 15 and 18 U.S.C.A. § 3503.

[2]An explicit finding of the reason for allowing the use of the deposition should be made on the record by the trial court. Austin v. State, 275 Ga. App. 560, 621 S.E.2d 546 (2005). In addition, the proponent of the deposi-

tion should be careful to satisfy the requirements of O.C.G.A. § 24-13-130 or risk its exclusion at trial. Evans v. State, 275 Ga. App. 621, 621 S.E.2d 584 (2005).

[3]Maryland v. Craig, 497 U.S. 836, 844 (11), 110 S. Ct. 3157, 111 L. Ed. 2d 666, 30 Fed. R. Evid. Serv. 1 (1990). See In Interest of E. T., 342 Ga. App. 710, 804 S.E.2d 725 (2017); U.S. v. Yates, 438 F.3d 1307 (11th Cir. 2006).

assured." Under *Craig*, it is the state's burden to make a satisfactory demonstration of necessity during an evidentiary hearing. The Court held that the defendant's right of confrontation did not categorically prohibit a child sexual victim from testifying by one way closed circuit television. See § 19:3, infra, on taping a child's testimony.

In *United States v. Jacobs*,[4] a case involving a witness with medical issues, the Court held that:

> The [trial] court must determine the necessities of the specific case by weighing the importance of the absent witness for the case; the nature and extent of the cross-examination; the nature of the illness; the expected time of recovery; the reliability of the evidence of the probable duration of the illness; and any special circumstances counseling against delay.

The Court concluded that requiring the defendant to complete cross-examination by video conferencing was prohibited by the defendant's Sixth Amendment right of confrontation where the state failed to show, and the trial court did not require evidence of, the particular medical circumstances of the witness which would justify allowing the witness to testify by video.

In *Brumley v. Wingard*,[5] the Sixth Circuit held that a defendant's constitutional right of confrontation was violated when the trial court admitted the videotaped deposition of an out-of-state and incarcerated witness without first making a finding of constitutional unavailability, i.e., whether the state has made a good faith effort to secure the presence of the witness.

The motion to take a deposition of a material witness or physician must include the nature of the charge, the status of the criminal proceeding, the name and address of the witness in Georgia, an assertion that the testimony is material and why the taking of the deposition is proper or that the testimony is that of a physician and that the physician's testimony is relevant to a charge of sexual or physical abuse of a child.

The party moving for an order allowing the taking of a deposition shall give at least one day's notice of the hearing to the opposing party.[6] If the court believes that a deposition is necessary and authorized by law, the court shall enter an order setting a time period of not more than 30 days during which the deposition can be taken.

---

[4]U.S. v. Jacobs, 97 F.3d 275, 282, 45 Fed. R. Evid. Serv. 1013 (8th Cir. 1996).

[5]Brumley v. Wingard, 269 F.3d 629, 57 Fed. R. Evid. Serv. 599, 2001 FED App. 0365P (6th Cir. 2001).

[6]However in the extreme case of Davis v. State, 238 Ga. App. 84, 86 (2), 517 S.E.2d 808 (1999), the court found that the defendant waived the requirement of notice by intentionally delaying the trial.

It is necessary that the moving party give reasonable written notice of the time and place of taking the deposition to every party to the case. The notice must state the name and address of the person(s) to be examined. Upon proper motion of a party upon whom the notice is served, the court may reschedule the time and place for taking the deposition. Under Rule 31.1 of the Uniform Rules for the Superior Courts, any such motion must be filed at or before the time set by law (10 days after arraignment, O.C.G.A. § 17-7-110) unless time therefor is extended by the judge in writing prior to trial.

If the defendant is in custody, the officer in charge of a defendant must produce him at the examination and keep him in the presence of the witness during the examination. However, the statute states that a motion to take a deposition may be filed "[a]t any time after a defendant has been charged." A defendant not in custody has a right to be present at the taking of the deposition; however, in the absence of good cause, the failure of a defendant not in custody to appear after notice and tender of expenses will constitute a waiver of his right to be present, and also to any objection to the taking and use of the deposition based on that right.

If a defendant does not have counsel, the court must advise him of his rights and assign counsel to represent him unless the defendant elects to proceed without counsel or is able to obtain counsel of his own choice.

If the deposition is taken on the motion of the state, the cost of the deposition shall be borne by the state. If a deposition is taken at the instance of the defendant, the costs shall be paid for by the defendant. However, if the defendant is unable to pay the cost of such a deposition, the court shall direct that the reasonable expenses of travel and subsistence of the defendant and his attorney for attendance at the examination be paid out of the fine and forfeiture fund of the county where venue is laid.

A deposition of a defendant himself may not be taken without his consent.

The scope of examination and cross-examination shall be such as would be allowed by the trial itself. On request of the defendant, or with the defendant's waiver, the court may direct that a deposition be taken on written interrogatories as provided for in civil actions. Depositions may be taken, recorded, and preserved by the use of audio-visual equipment. Objections to receiving in evidence a deposition or any part of it are to be made as in civil cases.

The statute says that the state is obligated to make available to the defendant, at the taking of the deposition, any statement of the witness who is being deposed which is in the possession of the state, and which the state would be required to make available to the defendant if the witness were testifying at the trial.

If at the time of trial or any hearing a witness is unavailable, all or part of a deposition may be used if otherwise admissible under the rules of evidence. A witness is not unavailable if such unavailability is due to the wrongdoing of the party offering the deposition at the hearing or trial. Any deposition may be used by any party to contradict or impeach the testimony of the deponent as a witness. If only part of a deposition is offered in evidence by a party, an adverse party may require the party to offer all of it which is relevant to the part already offered and any party may offer other parts.

If the court finds that any party or counsel for a party is using the deposition procedures for the purpose of harassment or delay, the court may punish such conduct as contempt of court.[7]

In *McGuire v. State*,[8] the Arkansas Supreme Court upheld the constitutionality of a statute providing for the video deposition of a victim's testimony in a child abuse case rather than having the child give such testimony in open court. The statute required that "good cause" be shown before a deposition could be taken, and provided for the presence of the judge, district attorney, defendant and defense counsel, allowing defense counsel to cross-examine. See § 19:3, infra, on taping a child's testimony.

§ 14:8 Discovery—Notice to produce

O.C.G.A. § 24-13-27 provides that by notice to produce, a party may compel production of books, writings, and other documents or tangible things in the possession, custody, or control of the opposite party. In *Deal v. State*,[1] the court held that a defendant could not compel the production of a video tape by a notice to produce. In *Sims v. State*,[2] the court pointed out that a notice to produce lies only where the state has "books, etc., [which] would be admissible and are needed for use as evidence on behalf of the defendant." Thus, the court concluded that the state did not have to produce diaries so that defense counsel could use them in cross-examination. The notice must be in writing, signed by the party seeking production, or by his attorney, and directed to the opposite party or his attorney.

---

[7]O.C.G.A. § 24-13-139.

[8]McGuire v. State, 288 Ark. 388, 706 S.W.2d 360 (1986). But see Long v. State, 742 S.W.2d 302 (Tex.Crim.App. 1987).

[Section 14:8]

[1]Deal v. State, 199 Ga. App. 184, 187 (3), 404 S.E.2d 343 (1991).

[2]Sims v. State, 251 Ga. 877, 879, 311 S.E.2d 161 (1984).

In *Phillips v. State*,[3] the court emphasized in obiter dictum that a notice to produce may be used by the state to obtain information from the defendant. However, as pointed out above, the right of the state to use a notice to produce is limited to matters which would not violate the constitutional rights of the defendant. Thus, in *Johnson v. State*,[4] the court held that in Georgia a defendant may not be required, pursuant to a notice "to produce evidence, oral or real, regardless of whether or not it is 'testimonial.'"

In *Brown v. State*,[5] the Georgia Supreme Court for the first time recognized that the notice-to-produce provisions of former O.C.G.A. § 24-10-26 (now § 24-13-27) applied to criminal cases. The court noted that the words "insofar as consistent with the Constitution" constituted a limitation on the state's use of the notice to produce, and not on its use by the accused.[6]

In *Stevens v. State*,[7] the court said defense counsel is not entitled to pre-trial statements of key witnesses for the state pursuant to a notice to produce. In *Natson v. State*,[8] the court said that a notice to produce may not be used to obtain "(a) the work product of the district attorney, (b) the addresses and telephone numbers of the state's witnesses, (c) . . . reports, memoranda, and documents in the files of . . . officers . . . [or] (d) the names and addresses of any other persons with knowledge of the facts."

---

[3]Phillips v. State, 146 Ga. App. 423, 425 (5), 246 S.E.2d 438 (1978). This case was actually remanded to the trial court "to determine the issue of failure to produce items requested" by the defendant. The defendant had filed a motion to produce, but the state had not responded. The court denied the motion without a hearing or argument by either side, emphasizing the difference between a *Brady* motion and notice to produce. The court then referred to Rule 16 of the Federal Rules of Criminal Procedure and some of the A.B.A. Standards and commended Rule 16 and §§ 11-2.1(a)(i) and 11-4.4 of the Standards to trial judges for their guidance.

[4]Johnson v. State, 156 Ga. App. 496, 498, 274 S.E.2d 837 (1980) (citing State v. Armstead, 152 Ga. App. 56, 57, 262 S.E.2d 233 (1979)).

[5]Brown v. State, 238 Ga. 98, 231 S.E.2d 65 (1976). Generally, see Comment, "Criminal Discovery: The Use of Notice to Produce," 30 Mercer L. R. 331 (1978).

[6]Brown v. State, 238 Ga. 98, 100, 231 S.E.2d 65 (1976).

[7]Stevens v. State, 242 Ga. 34, 247 S.E.2d 838 (1978). This disappointing opinion cites Barker v. State, 144 Ga. App. 339, 241 S.E.2d 11 (1977), as being in accord, but *Barker* seems to be more directed to the duty of the district attorney to make a copy of statements for defense counsel. But see James v. State, 143 Ga. App. 696, 698, 240 S.E.2d 149 (1977). Contra, Chambliss v. State, 149 Ga. App. 654, 656 (2), 255 S.E.2d 120 (1979). Hill v. State, 161 Ga. App. 346, 347 (3), 287 S.E.2d 779 (1982), is substantially in accord with *Stevens*.

[8]Natson v. State, 242 Ga. 618, 623 (5), 250 S.E.2d 420 (1978); Carter v. State, 150 Ga. App. 119 (1), 257 S.E.2d 11 (1979); Wilson v. State, 246 Ga. 62, 65, 268 S.E.2d 895 (1980).

In *Wilson v. State*,[9] the court indicated that the district attorney does not have to produce investigative reports pursuant to a notice to produce, but in *Goldsmith v. State*,[10] the court said that an affidavit of a physician whose name had been forged and whose photograph had been used in a photographic identification should be produced pursuant to a notice to produce. Likewise, in *Kesler v. State*,[11] it was held that telephone records in possession of the district attorney should be produced pursuant to a proper notice to produce. In *Holbrook v. State*,[12] the court held that statements of witnesses are not subject to a notice to produce.

If a notice to produce is "unreasonably oppressive, broad, indefinite and inclusive," the trial court on motion may modify it so as to delete the objectionable features.[13] Also, a notice to produce does not lie to require the district attorney to obtain evidence from the prosecuting witness or some third party.[14] A notice to produce reaches only material which is in the possession of the state[15] and cannot be used to require production of "reports, memoranda and documents in the files of law enforcement officers."[16] Thus, when the prosecution moves to quash because items are said not to be in existence and the defendant does not make a showing to the contrary, it is not error for the trial judge to grant the motion to quash.[17] See § 14:4, supra, on discovery of criminal records of witnesses.

The notice to produce statute does not normally provide for discovery in advance of trial,[18] as is possible in civil cases.[19] However, defense counsel may have documents produced by the

[9]Watson v. State, 147 Ga. App. 847, 848 (2), 250 S.E.2d 540 (1978).

[10]Goldsmith v. State, 148 Ga. App. 786, 787 (2), 252 S.E.2d 657 (1979).

[11]Kesler v. State, 249 Ga. 462, 470 (5), 291 S.E.2d 497 (1982).

[12]Holbrook v. State, 162 Ga. App. 400, 401, 291 S.E.2d 729 (1982); Welch v. State, 251 Ga. 197 (8), 304 S.E.2d 391 (1983).

[13]Haynie v. State, 141 Ga. App. 688, 694, 234 S.E.2d 406 (1977), rev'd on other grounds, 240 Ga. 866, 242 S.E.2d 713 (1978); State v. Bradshaw, 145 Ga. App. 278, 243 S.E.2d 547 (1978).

[14]Young v. State, 146 Ga. App. 167, 245 S.E.2d 866 (1978); Fletcher v. State, 157 Ga. App. 707, 708 (3), 278 S.E.2d 444 (1981).

[15]Wheat v. State, 171 Ga. App. 583 (1), 320 S.E.2d 808 (1984).

[16]Lockwood v. State, 184 Ga. App. 262, 264, 361 S.E.2d 195 (1987), rev'd on other grounds, 257 Ga. 796, 364 S.E.2d 574 (1988).

[17]Patterson v. State, 154 Ga. App. 877, 270 S.E.2d 86 (1980).

[18]Brooks v. State, 141 Ga. App. 725, 731 (4), 234 S.E.2d 541 (1977); Sims v. State, 251 Ga. 877, 879 (4), 311 S.E.2d 161 (1984).

[19]Gilstrap v. State, 256 Ga. 20, 21 (2), 342 S.E.2d 667 (1986). See O.C.G.A. § 9-11-34. However, where the document or article to be produced is needed for purposes of a scientific examination, it has been strongly indicated that the defendant is entitled to have the notice complied with sufficiently in advance of trial to permit such an examination. Haynie v. State, 141 Ga. App. 688, 234 S.E.2d 406

prosecution at the commencement of the case,[20] and if the documents or tangible evidence must be deliberately examined prior to trial in order for them to be of value to the defendant,[21] he may have them produced sufficiently in advance of trial to give the defendant a reasonable opportunity for such an examination.[22] It is said that if there is inadequate authority under the notice to produce provisions for such an advance examination of evidence, the deficiency is taken care of by a pre-trial examination and analysis of physical objects discussed in § 14:5, supra.

Under Rule 31.1 of the Uniform Rules of Superior Courts, a notice to produce must be filed at or before the time set by law (10 days after arraignment, O.C.G.A. § 17-7-110) unless time therefor is extended by the judge in writing prior to trial.

A notice to produce is not equivalent to a stipulation that the document sought is admissible in evidence, and the same rule applies to a copy of an in-custody statement made by the defendant, and copies of scientific reports.[23]

In *Farmer v. State,*[24] the court pointed out that "[a] notice to produce cannot be used to enable defense counsel to examine, in advance of trial or evidentiary hearing, the contents of the district attorney's file. . . . [A] notice to produce cannot be used . . . to require the district attorney's work product; reports, memoranda and documents in the files of law enforcement officers; addresses and telephone numbers of state's witnesses; or names and addresses of other persons with knowledge of the facts. . . . In short, a notice to produce cannot be used as a discovery tool to circumvent discovery reciprocity under the discovery act."

Likewise, in *Fleming v. State,*[25] the court held that the defendant is not entitled to a pre-trial review of the jury records that the prosecution has.

In *Wansley v. State,*[26] the defendant sought production from the district attorney of records which would disclose which potential

---

(1977), rev'd on other grounds, 240 Ga. 866, 242 S.E.2d 713 (1978).

[20]It should be noted that in federal court the defendant is not, as a matter of right, entitled to a copy of a witness' statement until after he has testified. Then, on demand, defense counsel is entitled to copies of all statements of that witness, and these statements may be used in cross-examination of the witness. 18 U.S.C.A. § 3500.

[21]Haynie v. State, 141 Ga. App. 688, 694, 234 S.E.2d 406 (1977), rev'd on other grounds, 240 Ga. 866, 242

S.E.2d 713 (1978).

[22]But cf. Howard v. State, 144 Ga. App. 208, 211 (4), 240 S.E.2d 908 (1977).

[23]Bragg v. State, 175 Ga. App. 640, 643, 334 S.E.2d 184 (1985).

[24]Farmer v. State, 222 Ga. App. 506, 508 (2), 474 S.E.2d 711 (1996).

[25]Fleming v. State, 269 Ga. 245, 248 (5), 497 S.E.2d 211 (1998). Accord, Wansley v. State, 256 Ga. 624, 625 (2), 352 S.E.2d 368 (1987).

[26]Wansley v. State, 256 Ga. 624, 625 (2), 352 S.E.2d 368 (1987).

jurors "in this case had previously served on a jury, and, if so, whether their verdict was guilty or not guilty." The court pointed out that in Georgia the prosecution is not required to reveal or produce investigatory work routinely performed in criminal cases unless it is subject to discovery under O.C.G.A. § 17-16-22 (statements by defendant in custody) or O.C.G.A. § 17-16-23 (scientific reports), or under *Brady v. Maryland*[27] (exculpatory evidence).

See § 17:11, infra, on subpoenas for production of documents.

For notices to produce, see Studdard, *Daniel's Georgia Criminal Trial Practice Forms* (2018–2019 ed.), §§ 14:70, 14:81, 14:82, 14:86, 14:87 and 14:103.

§ 14:9 Discovery—Reciprocal discovery in felony cases—Bird's eye view

O.C.G.A. § 17-16-2(a) provides that the defendant may elect in writing to have these statutes apply to his case. The failure to formally opt in to reciprocal discovery deprives a defendant of all the discovery devices available thereunder.[1] However, a defendant who chooses not to opt in is entitled to *Brady* information upon demand.[2]

O.C.G.A. § 17-16-4 provides that upon written election of defense counsel to engage in reciprocal discovery, the district attorney must provide the defendant with *any* statement made by him at any time to law enforcement or a district attorney, whether the defendant was in custody at the time of the statement or not. The defendant can also get statements of co-conspirators that are attributable to the defendant and arguably admissible against the defendant. The defendant can get his criminal history, if it is in the possession of the district attorney, upon written request. The defendant gets open files from the state as to: (1) documents and physical evidence; (2) the right to examine and test evidence at GBI; and (3) results of physical and mental exams and scientific tests. The prosecuting attorney is also required to provide the defendant no later than ten days prior to trial with notice of any evidence in aggravation of punishment that the state intends to introduce in sentencing. However, the defendant cannot get information about psychiatric treatment of the victim or a witness. If the defendant requests the open file of the district attorney, then the district attorney gets the open file

---

[27]Brady v. Maryland, 373 U.S. 83, 83 S.Ct. 1194, 10 L.Ed.2d 215 (1963).

[Section 14:9]

[1]See Brown v. State, 274 Ga. 202, 203(2), 552 S.E.2d 812 (2001); Davis v. State, 232 Ga. App. 320, 322(2), 501 S.E.2d 836 (1998) (unless procured in bad faith, defendant who chooses not to opt into reciprocal discovery has no basis to complain of last minute test of suspected marijuana).

[2]Mondy v. State, 229 Ga. App. 311, 494 S.E.2d 176 (1997).

including all of the above listed evidence from the defendant. Any additional evidence discovered by either must be turned over to the other party as soon as discovered. The trial court has discretion to limit any discovery that would cause physical or economic harm to a witness.

In 2005, the Georgia Legislature made substantial additions to the defendant's obligations under reciprocal discovery. O.C.G.A. §§ 17-16-4(b)(3)(A), (B) and (C) now provide as follows:

"(b)(3)(A) The defendant shall, no later than the announcement of the verdict of the jury or if the defendant has waived a jury trial at the time the verdict is published by the court, serve upon the prosecuting attorney all books, papers, documents, photographs, tangible objects, audio and visual tapes, films and recordings, or copies or portions thereof and to inspect and photograph buildings or places which are within the possession, custody, or control of the defendant and which the defendant intends to introduce as evidence in the presentence hearing.

"(b)(3)(B) The defendant shall, no later than the announcement of the verdict of the jury or if the defendant has waived a jury trial at the time the verdict is published by the court, serve upon the prosecuting attorney all reports of any physical or mental examinations and scientific tests or experiments, including a summary of the basis for the expert opinions rendered in the reports, or copies thereof, if the defendant intends to introduce in evidence in the presentence hearing the results of the physical or mental examination or scientific test or experiment. If the report is oral or partially oral, the defendant shall reduce all relevant and material oral portions of such report to writing and shall serve opposing counsel with such portions.

"(b)(3)(C) The defendant shall, no later than five days before the trial commences, serve upon the prosecuting attorney a list of witnesses that the defendant intends to call as a witness in the presentence hearing. No later than the announcement of the verdict of the jury or if the defendant has waived a jury trial at the time the verdict is published by the court, the defendant shall produce for the opposing party any statement of such witnesses that is in the possession, custody, or control of the defendant or the defendant's counsel that relates to the subject matter of the testimony of such witnesses unless such statement is protected from disclosure by the privilege contained in paragraph (5), (6), (7), or (8) of subsection (a) of Code Section 24-5-501."

The applicability of the reciprocal discovery provisions to the sentencing phase presents a special problem for defense counsel. To wit, it should be borne in mind that, although a mitigation witness will obviously be helpful during the presentence hearing, such a witness may also possess information that could be used to incriminate the defendant during the guilt/innocence phase. The decision of whether or not to participate in reciprocal discovery should therefore be carefully considered. In *Muhammad v. State*,[3] the Georgia Supreme Court recognized this issue and concluded that O.C.G.A. § 17-16-6 provides the trial court with discretion "to specify the time, place, and manner of making the discovery" and to enter such orders as seem "just under the circumstances" when such concerns become apparent. The court suggested that defense counsel should request appropriate relief from the trial court in the form of a protective order or a continuance to make discovery on mitigation witnesses until the guilt/innocence phase has concluded.

O.C.G.A. § 17-16-5 provides that if the district attorney requests it, the defendant must provide the district attorney with notice of the alibi defense, including a list of witnesses. The district attorney must in turn disclose alibi rebuttal witnesses of the state. Any additional alibi witnesses found by either side must be immediately disclosed to the other party. The trial court can limit disclosure if the witness will be harmed. If the defendant withdraws notice of intention to rely on alibi, the notice is not admissible. See § 14:19, infra, on alibi witnesses in felony cases.

O.C.G.A. § 17-16-6 provides that the court can order compliance or grant a continuance if either side fails to comply in good faith. Upon a showing of prejudice and bad faith, the evidence may be suppressed.

O.C.G.A. § 17-16-7 provides that prior to trial or at the time of any evidentiary hearing, both sides must produce any statements of any witnesses that the party intends to call. This provision has no application to oral witness statements which are neither recorded nor memorialized in any way.[4] As a general rule, an investigator's notes are not subject to reciprocal discovery.[5]

O.C.G.A. § 17-16-8 provides that at the request of either party,

---

[3]Muhammad v. State, 282 Ga. 247(3)(c), 647 S.E.2d 560 (2007) the courts holding was premised on concerns that disclosure by the defendant of a mitigation witness who could incriminate the defendant during the guilt/innocence phase of the trial could implicate Fifth Amendment considerations. See Stinski v. State, 286 Ga. 839, 691 S.E.2d 854 (2010) (notes and summaries of witness statements made by mitigation specialist at direction of attorney should be regarded as "notes or summaries" of counsel and as such not subject to reciprocal discovery). See also Smith v. Smith, 223 Ga. 551, 156 S.E.2d 916 (1967) (notes and work of investigation done under supervision of counsel not subject to discovery).

[4]Burges v. Smith, 276 Ga. 185, 576 S.E.2d 863 (2003).

[5]See State v. Brown, 333 Ga. App. 643, 777 S.E.2d 27 (2015); Brannon v. State, 298 Ga. 601, 783 S.E.2d 642 (2016).

the other shall furnish in confidence certain identifying information about witnesses to be called.

O.C.G.A. § 17-16-9 provides that a party providing material will be reimbursed. However, if a defendant is indigent, the court may determine the means of reimbursement.

In *State v. Dickerson*,[6] the Georgia Supreme Court pointed out that "[g]enerally a defendant has a duty to request a continuance to cure any prejudice which may have resulted from the State's failure to comply with the provisions of O.C.G.A. §§ 17-16-1 et seq."

There is a striking resemblance between the 1994 Georgia discovery statutes in criminal cases and the American Bar Association Standards for Criminal Justice: Discovery, Third Edition, approved by the House of Delegates in August 1994. However, one major difference between the two procedures is that the Georgia statutes apply only if a defendant elects to have them apply, whereas the ABA procedure applies regardless of the defendant's acquiescence or lack of acquiescence.[7]

§ 14:10 Discovery—Reciprocal discovery in felony cases— Applicability of the statute

O.C.G.A. § 17-16-2 governs the applicability of reciprocal discovery. If an indictment or accusation contains one or more felony charges and if the defendant elects to have the 1994 statutory provisions for reciprocal discovery apply to the case, such an election must be made prior to arraignment "or at such time as the court permits." The election must be made in writing and served on the prosecuting attorney.[1] If there is more than one defendant in a case, an election by one defendant to engage in reciprocal discovery applies to all defendants unless a severance is granted. If a defendant so elects, the provisions of this article shall also apply to sentencing hearings and the sentencing phase of a death penalty trial except as provided in O.C.G.A. § 17-16-4(b)(3).[2] Other statutes in the law apply if the defendant is charged only with one or more misdemeanor offenses or the defendant does not elect to have the reciprocal discovery statutes apply. None of the discovery statutes apply in juvenile court proceedings unless automatically invoked under O.C.G.A. § 17-16-2(c).

---

[6]State v. Dickerson, 273 Ga. 408, 411 (2), 542 S.E.2d 487 (2001).

[7]56 Cr. L. 2001 (Oct. 5, 1994).

[Section 14:10]

[1]Davis v. State, 232 Ga. App. 320, 322 (2), 501 S.E.2d 836 (1998).

[2]O.C.G.A. § 17-16-2(e).

DFACS and other such records are confidential and access thereto prohibited except as provided by O.C.G.A. § 49-5-41(a)(11). That Code section grants access to DFACS and other records in the possession of law enforcement and child advocacy centers and agencies by way of subpoena based upon a court's finding that access to the records may be necessary for proceedings before the court provided that the subpoenaed records first be produced to the court for in-camera review and a determination of materiality and necessity to the case.[3]

In *Miller v. State*,[4] the court emphasized that the defendant must provide *written* notice to the prosecuting attorney that the defendant elects to have reciprocal discovery in the case. In *Bennett v. State*,[5] the court held that the defendant had failed to make the "requisite demand" under O.C.G.A. § 17-16-2(a). Therefore, the provisions for reciprocal discovery did not apply.

However, reciprocal discovery shall be deemed automatically invoked, without written notice required in O.C.G.A. § 17-16-2(a) when a defendant seeks discovery pursuant to Chapter 11 of Title 9, the "Georgia Civil Practice Act," pursuant to O.C.G.A. § 15-11-541, or pursuant to the Uniform Rules for Juvenile Court of Georgia where such discovery material is the same as the discovery material that may be provided with notice.[6] Moreover, except as provided in paragraph (3) of subsection (b) of O.C.G.A. § 17-16-4, "if a defendant has elected to have the provisions of this article apply, the provisions of this article shall also apply to sentencing hearings and the sentencing phase of a death penalty trial."[7] See also, O.C.G.A. § 17-6-4.

Except as provided in O.C.G.A. § 17-16-8, which relates to lists of names and information concerning witnesses, these provisions for discovery do not apply to the "discovery or inspection of attorney work product."

§ 14:11 Discovery—Reciprocal discovery in felony cases—Copy of indictment or accusation and list of witnesses furnished

O.C.G.A. § 17-16-3 provides that prior to arraignment every person charged with a criminal offense shall receive a copy of the indictment and a list of witnesses which shall be supplemented pursuant to the provisions of the reciprocal discovery statutes.

---

[3]See Grier v. State, 339 Ga. App. 778, 792 S.E.2d 737 (2016).

[4]Miller v. State, 235 Ga. App. 724, 725, 510 S.E.2d 560 (1998).

[5]Bennett v. State, 228 Ga. App. 254 (2), 491 S.E.2d 481 (1997).

[6]O.C.G.A. § 17-16-2(c).

[7]O.C.G.A. § 17-16-2(e).

In *State v. Lucious*,[1] the Georgia Supreme Court held that a defendant was not entitled to a witness list with addresses and telephone numbers unless he elects to engage in reciprocal discovery.

§ 14:12   Discovery—Reciprocal discovery in felony cases—Statements attributable to defendant

Readers should review § 14-29, infra, on discovery of defendant's statements in misdemeanor cases and felonies docketed prior to January 1, 1995. Discovery in these cases is conducted pursuant to O.C.G.A. § 17-16-22 which is essentially a restatement of former O.C.G.A. § 17-7-210. Much of the case law thereunder is still good law and is a helpful guide to discovery in criminal cases today.

O.C.G.A. § 17-16-4(a)(1) provides that "[t]he prosecuting attorney shall, no later than ten days prior to trial, or at such time as the court orders, disclose to the defendant and make available . . . any relevant written or recorded statements made by the defendant, or copies thereof, within the possession . . . of the state or prosecution and that portion of any written record containing the substance of any relevant oral statement made by the defendant, whether before or after arrest, in response to interrogation by any person then known to the defendant to be a law enforcement officer or member of the prosecuting attorney's staff. The prosecuting attorney shall also disclose . . . the substance of any other relevant oral statement made by the defendant, before or after arrest, in response to interrogation by . . . law enforcement [or a] member of the prosecuting attorney's staff if the state intends to use that statement at trial." Furthermore, any other statement made by the defendant while in custody must be furnished whether or not in response to interrogation. In addition, "[s]tatements of coconspirators that are attributable to the defendant and arguably admissible against the defendant at trial also shall be disclosed. . . ."

In *Marshall v. State*,[1] the court pointed out that a statement of the defendant made while in custody and provided by a witness to a law enforcement officer is regarded as being in the possession of the prosecutor and is not "newly discovered" despite the prosecutor's actual ignorance of it. However, the recollections of a witness about a statement of the defendant which are in addition to those contained in the written statement of the witness does not constitute a "statement of a witness" for purposes of O.C.G.A.

[Section 14:11]

[1]State v. Lucious, 271 Ga. 361, 518 S.E.2d 677 (1999).

[Section 14:12]

[1]Marshall v. State, 230 Ga. App. 116, 495 S.E.2d 585 (1998).

§ 17-16-1(2) which must be produced prior to trial.[2]

In *Lawson v. State*,[3] the court held that this statute does not require the state to actually *serve* defense counsel with defendant's statement; it is sufficient if the state makes the defendant's statement "available for inspection, copying, or photographing" by the defense.

If the defendant is a corporation, partnership, association, or labor union, the court may grant the defendant upon motion, the discovery of any witness who is so situated as an officer or employee as to be legally capable of binding the defendant to the conduct charged.

In *Bell v. State*,[4] the defendant contended that the trial judge erred in denying a motion for a mistrial where an officer volunteered an incriminating statement which defendant uttered at his arrest. The state had not provided the defendant with a copy. The appellate court found that there was no prejudice to the defendant and pointed out that under the statute the trial judge has the authority to exclude the defendant's statement only where there is a showing of prejudice and bad faith by the state. However, in *Johnson v. State*,[5] the Court of Appeals held that defense counsel was ineffective for failing to object to the admission of a statement attributed to the defendant which had not previously been provided during discovery and after its admission failing to move for a mistrial. The court said that prejudice could be "presumed" since counsel's trial preparation was necessarily incomplete. Having no notice of the statement, the defense was in no position to refute or rebut its implications.

In *Crews v. State*,[6] the state failed to provide defendant with notice of his admission to police that he owned the truck. This admission was given in conjunction with his consent to search. The defendant claimed he was harmed by this failure because his defense at trial was that the cocaine belonged to someone else and his possession of the truck linked him with the crack pipe discovered. The appellate court held that reversal is not required when the state fails to disclose a statement which was not directly incriminating or inculpatory but becomes so only as a result of a defense theory at trial. However, by eliciting testimony from a police officer on direct examination that the defendant admitted at the time he was being booked into jail that "the drugs were

---

[2]Hinds v. State, 296 Ga. App. 80 (4), 673 S.E.2d 598 (2009).

[3]Lawson v. State, 224 Ga. App. 645, 647 (3)(a), 481 S.E.2d 856 (1997). Accord, Guild v. State, 234 Ga. App. 862, 868 (3), 508 S.E.2d 231 (1998).

[4]Bell v. State, 224 Ga. App. 191, 192, 480 S.E.2d 241 (1997).

[5]Johnson v. State, 281 Ga. App. 455, 636 S.E.2d 178 (2006).

[6]Crews v. State, 226 Ga. App. 232, 234 (2), 486 S.E.2d 61 (1997).

his," the court found that the state violated O.C.G.A. § 17-16-4(a)(1) where it appeared that the state knew in advance how the officer would testify and that it had not disclosed the statement to the defense prior to trial.[7]

In *Pattman v. State*,[8] the court held that there had been a sufficient compliance with the discovery statute where the state opened its file to the defendant several weeks before the trial and the file contained a transcript of a condemnation hearing in which the defendant made an admission that he owned the cocaine involved in the trial.

§ 14:13 Discovery—Reciprocal discovery in felony cases—Criminal history of defendant

O.C.G.A. § 17-16-4(a)(2) provides that no later than 10 days prior to trial the prosecuting attorney shall furnish the defendant a copy of his Georgia Crime Information Center criminal history, if any, that is in the possession of the prosecutor or any law enforcement agency involved in the investigation of the case being prosecuted.

§ 14:14 Discovery—Reciprocal discovery in felony cases—Examination of pictures, documents and tangible evidence

Readers should review § 14:30, infra, on discovery of scientific reports in misdemeanor cases and felonies docketed prior to January 1, 1995. Discovery in these cases is conducted pursuant to O.C.G.A. § 17-16-23 which is essentially a restatement of former O.C.G.A. § 17-7-211. Much of the case law thereunder is still good law and is a helpful guide to discovery in criminal cases today. O.C.G.A. § 17-16-4(a)(3) provides that "[t]he prosecuting attorney shall . . . permit the defendant at a time agreed to by the parties or ordered by the court to inspect and copy or photograph books, papers, documents, photographs, tangible objects, audio and visual tapes, films and recordings, or copies or portions thereof and to inspect and photograph buildings or places which are within the possession, custody, or control of the state . . . and are intended for use by the prosecuting attorney as evidence in the prosecution's case-in-chief or rebuttal at the trial or were obtained from or belong to the defendant. Evidence that is within the possession, custody, or control of the Forensic Sciences

---

[7]Johnson v. State, 328 Ga. App. 702, 760 S.E.2d 682 (2014). See Marshall v. State, 230 Ga. App. 116, 495 S.E.2d 585 (1998).

[8]Pattman v. State, 236 Ga. App.

786, 787 (2), 513 S.E.2d 761 (1999). See Hudson v. State, 284 Ga. 595(3), 669 S.E.2d 94 (2008); Acey v. State, 281 Ga. App. 197(2), 635 S.E.2d 814 (2006).

Division of the Georgia Bureau of Investigation or other laboratory for the purpose of testing and analysis may be examined, tested, and analyzed at the facility . . . pursuant to reasonable rules and regulations adopted by the Forensic Sciences Division. . ."

O.C.G.A. § 17-16-4(a)(5), as amended July 1, 2005, provides that "[t]he prosecuting attorney shall, no later than ten days prior to trial, or at such time as the court orders but in no event later than the beginning of the trial, provide the defendant with notice of any evidence in aggravation of punishment that the state intends to introduce in sentencing."

In *McSears v. State*,[1] the court pointed out that the duty of the prosecution is to permit the defendant to copy or photograph the documents referred to in the Code. There is no duty on the prosecution to copy or photograph such documents.

According to O.C.G.A. § 17-16-4(b)(1), the defendant is then under an obligation to produce discovery of the same nature that is in the control of the defendant and which the defendant intends to use at trial within 10 days of timely compliance by the prosecuting attorney, but no later than five days prior to trial.

See Studdard, *Daniel's Georgia Handbook on Criminal Evidence* (2018 ed.), § 5:14, on requiring the prosecution to submit documents on selective prosecution.

In *Tucker v. State*,[2] the court held that the trial judge may prohibit the state from introducing evidence improperly withheld from the defense, but only if there has been "a showing *of prejudice* to the defense *and bad faith* by the state." (Emphasis added.)

§ 14:15 Discovery—Reciprocal discovery in felony cases— Results of examinations and tests

Readers should review § 14:30, infra, on discovery of scientific reports in misdemeanor cases and felonies docketed prior to January 1, 1995. Discovery in these cases is conducted pursuant to O.C.G.A. § 17-16-23 which is essentially a restatement of former O.C.G.A. § 17-7-211. Much of the case law thereunder is still good law and is a helpful guide to discovery in criminal cases today.

O.C.G.A. § 17-16-4(a)(4) requires the prosecuting attorney to "permit the defendant at a time agreed to by the parties or ordered by the court to inspect and copy or photograph any results or reports of physical or mental examinations and of sci-

---

[Section 14:14]

[1]McSears v. State, 226 Ga. App. 90, 91 (1), 485 S.E.2d 589 (1997).

[2]Tucker v. State, 222 Ga. App. 517, 518 (3), 474 S.E.2d 696 (1996).

entific tests or experiments, including a summary of the basis for the expert opinion rendered in the report, or copies thereof, which are within the possession . . . of the state or prosecution which the state intends to introduce in evidence. . . . [However, nothing in this statute] shall require the disclosure of any material, note, or memorandum relating to the psychiatric or psychological treatment or therapy of any victim or witness." O.C.G.A. § 17-16-4 requires that the prosecution shall reduce to writing all relevant material of an oral or partially oral report and serve it upon opposing counsel no later than ten days prior to trial.

Possession, custody or control of the state or prosecution "means an item which is within the possession, custody, or control of the prosecuting attorney or *any law enforcement agency* involved in the investigation of the case being prosecuted." (Emphasis in original.)[1]

Note that, beginning July 1, 2005, the defendant may now be required to produce the material covered in O.C.G.A. § 17-16-4(a)(4) in the context of a presentence hearing. Subsection O.C.G.A. § 17-16-4(b)(3)(B) now provides: "The defendant shall, no later than the announcement of the verdict of the jury or if the defendant has waived a jury trial at the time the verdict is published by the court, serve upon the prosecuting attorney all reports of any physical or mental examinations and scientific tests or experiments, including a summary of the basis for the expert opinions rendered in the reports, or copies thereof, if the defendant intends to introduce in evidence in the presentence hearing the results of the physical or mental examination or scientific test or experiment. If the report is oral or partially oral, the defendant shall reduce all relevant and material oral portions of such report to writing and shall serve opposing counsel with such portions."

In *Aleman v. State*,[2] the court held that a failure to comply with O.C.G.A. § 17-16-4(a)(3) may be grounds for prohibiting the state from introducing evidence. However, this sanction "applies only where there has been a showing of prejudice to the defense and bad faith by the State." In *Felder v. State*,[3] the court held that giving "counsel an opportunity to inspect . . . items before their introduction into evidence . . . is a permissible response to the State's failure to comply with criminal discovery provisions."

[Section 14:15]

[1]Baker v. State, 238 Ga. App. 285, 286 (1), 518 S.E.2d 455 (1999) (quoting O.C.G.A. § 17-16-1(1)).

[2]Aleman v. State, 224 Ga. App. 391, 393 (2), 480 S.E.2d 393 (1997).

[3]Felder v. State, 270 Ga. 641, 645 (6), 514 S.E.2d 416 (1999) (citing O.C.G.A. § 17-16-6). The articles involved included "ski masks, articles of clothing and plaster casts of shoe prints."

In *Lawson v. State*,[4] the court held that compliance with O.C.G.A. § 17-16-4(a)(4) does not require the state to affirmatively serve upon the defendant such a report; making the report available for inspection and copying is sufficient.

In *Garey v. State*,[5] the court pointed out that the above statute "does not require the state to have its expert prepare a report; rather it requires that if such a report exists it be made available to the defendant." In *Beck v. State*,[6] the court pointed out that "[t]he defendant is not required to have the opinions of experts reduced to writing nor" is the defendant required to produce any report he will not offer at trial.

O.C.G.A. § 17-16-4(b)(2) requires that once the prosecutor complies with his disclosure duty, the defendant is required to produce the same within 10 days, but no later than 5 days prior to trial, if the defendant plans to use the reports at trial.

In 2003, subsections (a)(4) and (b)(2) of O.C.G.A. § 17-6-4 were amended. Subsection (a)(4) now provides the following:

If the [expert's] report is oral or partially oral, the prosecuting attorney shall reduce all relevant and material oral portions of such report to writing and shall serve opposing counsel with such portions no later than ten days prior to trial.

The added language of amended subsection (b)(4), dealing with the defendant's duty to provide a reduced report to opposing counsel, is identical to that of subsection (a)(4), with the sole exception being the defendant's duty to serve opposing counsel with the expert's report no later than five days prior to trial. Accordingly, to the extent they conflict with amended subsections (a)(4) and (b)(2) of O.C.G.A. § 17-16-4, *Lawson, Garey* and *Beck* may no longer be good law.

In *Cook v. State*,[7] the court held that a defendant is not entitled to the internal documents and work product of the Crime Lab under O.C.G.A. § 17-16-4.

§ 14:16 Discovery—Reciprocal discovery in felony cases— Crime lab reports

O.C.G.A. § 35-3-154.1 provides:

"(a) A copy of a report of the methods and findings of any examination or analysis conducted by an employee of the state crime laboratory or an employee of the laboratory with which the

---

[4]Lawson v. State, 224 Ga. App. 645, 648 (3)(c), 481 S.E.2d 856 (1997). Accord, Aleman v. State, 224 Ga. App. 391, 393 (2), 480 S.E.2d 393 (1997).

[5]Garey v. State, 273 Ga. 133, 136 (1), 539 S.E.2d 123 (2000).

[6]Beck v. State, 250 Ga. App. 654, 658 (4), 551 S.E.2d 68 (2001).

[7]Cook v. State, 270 Ga. 820, 831 (13), 514 S.E.2d 657 (1999).

state crime laboratory has a contract for the provision of laboratory or scientific examination or analysis, authenticated under oath, is prima-facie evidence in court proceedings in the state of the facts contained therein.

"(b) The report shall have the effect as if the person who performed the analysis or examination had personally testified and shall have an affidavit of the employee stating:

(1) That he or she is certified to perform the requisite analysis or examination;

(2) His or her experience as a chemist or analyst and as an expert witness testifying in court; and

(3) That he or she conducted the tests shown on the report using procedures approved by the Bureau and the report accurately reflects his opinion regarding the results.

"(c) The prosecuting attorney shall serve a copy on defendant's attorney of record or on defendant if pro se, prior to the first proceeding in which the report is to be used against defendant.

"(d) Any report under this Code section shall contain notice of the right to demand the testimony of the person signing the report.

"(e) The defendant may object in writing any time after service of the report, but at least ten days prior to trial, to the introduction of the report. If objection is made, the judge shall require the employee to be present to testify. The state shall diligently investigate the witness' availability and report to the court. If the witness is not available on a timely basis, the court shall grant a continuance."

If defense counsel wishes to examine the analyst responsible for the preparation of any such report, care should be taken to interpose a timely objection to its use without the witness at least ten (10) days before trial.

§ 14:17 Discovery—Reciprocal discovery in felony cases— Additional evidence discovered

O.C.G.A. § 17-16-4(c) requires that a party that discovers additional evidence or material previously requested or ordered which is subject to discovery under the reciprocal discovery statute must notify the other party of the existence of the additional evidence and make the same available.

§ 14:18 Discovery—Reciprocal discovery in felony cases— Threat of physical or economic harm

O.C.G.A. § 17-16-4(d) provides that upon a sufficient showing that a discovery required by this article would create a substantial threat of physical or economic harm to a witness, the court may order that the discovery or inspection be denied, restricted, or deferred or make some other appropriate order. Such showing may be made in whole or in part in the form of a written statement to be examined by the judge alone. If the court grants relief, the "entire text of the party's statement shall be sealed and preserved" for an appeal.

§ 14:19 Discovery—Reciprocal discovery in felony cases— Alibi witnesses

O.C.G.A. § 17-16-5 provides that upon written demand by the prosecuting attorney within 10 days after arraignment, or at such time as the court permits, stating the time, date and place of the alleged offense, the defendant shall serve within 10 days of the demand or 10 days prior to trial, whichever is later, or as ordered by the court, upon the prosecuting attorney a written notice of the defendant's intention to offer a defense of alibi. Such notice of the defendant shall state the specific place or places "the defendant claims to have been at the time of the alleged offense and the names, addresses, dates of birth, and telephone numbers of the witnesses, if known to the defendant, upon whom the defendant intends to rely to establish such alibi . . . ."

"The prosecuting attorney shall serve upon the defendant within five days of the defendant's written notice but no later than five days before trial, whichever is later, a written notice stating the names, addresses, dates of birth, and telephone numbers of the witnesses, if known to the state, upon whom the state intends to rely to rebut the defendant's evidence of alibi . . . ."

If either party learns of an additional witness whose identity, if known, should have been included in the information he previously furnished, the party shall promptly notify the opposite party of the additional witness or witnesses.

"Upon a showing that a disclosure required by [O.C.G.A. § 17-16-5] would create a substantial threat of physical or economic harm to a witness, the court may grant an exception to the requirements" of the section.

"If the defendant withdraws the notice of intention to rely upon an alibi defense, the notice and intention to rely upon an alibi defense is not admissible. However, the prosecuting attorney may offer any other evidence regarding alibi."

In *State v. Charbonneau*,[1] the Georgia Supreme Court held that a defendant was required under O.C.G.A. § 17-16-5(a) to

---

[Section 14:19]

[1]State v. Charbonneau, 281 Ga. 46, 635 S.E.2d 759 (2006), the majority opinion drew a sharp dissent which

give the state notice of an alibi defense where the defendant is the only witness to be offered in support of the defense. The court did note that the defense was not required to disclose the substance of the defendant's testimony, only that the defense of alibi would be presented. In addition, the court observed that the defendant could avoid the alibi notice requirement by not participating in reciprocal discovery.

In *Malaguti v. State*,[2] the court held that if the state fails to comply with O.C.G.A. § 17-16-5, the court is vested with discretion (1) to permit the defense to interview the witness, (2) to grant a continuance, or (3) upon showing prejudice and bad faith to prohibit the state from introducing the evidence not disclosed or presenting the witness not disclosed or to enter such order as it deems just under the circumstances.

In *Tubbs v. State*,[3] a trial court's decision *sua sponte* to order a mistrial after the defense referred to undisclosed alibi witnesses in its opening statement was affirmed on the basis of manifest necessity. In reviewing the action by the trial court, the Supreme Court determined that the mistrial was necessary since a continuance would not have provided the state with a fair opportunity to interview and prepare for the unexpected testimony and excluding the witnesses would have deprived the defendant of evidence essential to the defense.

In *Davis v. State*,[4] the appellate court affirmed the trial court's finding that the defense acted in bad faith by disclosing only the names of three proposed alibi witnesses without their addresses and telephone numbers and affirmed the trial court's grant of a motion in limine preventing the three witnesses from testifying. In *Hayes v. State*,[5] the court held that the state may not rely on its general witness list as a substitute for compliance with O.C.G.A. § 17-16-5(b). Likewise, in *White v. State*,[6] the defense must identify alibi witnesses as such and not merely include

---

was critical of the court's application of Johnson v. State, 272 Ga. 468(1), 532 S.E.2d 377 (2000). In *Johnson*, the court held that a defendant did not have to give notice of alibi testimony which was to be provided by the defendant, finding that for purposes of O.C.G.A. § 17-16-5(a) the defendant was not considered a "witness" as defined by O.C.G.A. § 17-16-1(3).

[2]Malaguti v. State, 273 Ga. 398, 401 (2), 543 S.E.2d 1 (2001).

[3]Tubbs v. State, 276 Ga. 751 (3), 583 S.E.2d 853 (2003). See Huckabee v. State, 287 Ga. 728, 699 S.E.2d 531

(2010) (unjustified failure of defendant to provide timely notice of alibi witnesses warranted sanction of their exclusion). See also Card v. State, 273 Ga. App. 367, 615 S.E.2d 139 (2005).

[4]Davis v. State, 226 Ga. App. 83, 84 (1), 485 S.E.2d 508 (1997). Compare Ware v. State, 298 Ga. App. 232, 679 S.E.2d 797 (2009) (error to exclude untimely disclosure of alibi witnesses in the absence of bad faith).

[5]Hayes v. State, 249 Ga. App. 857, 862 (4), 549 S.E.2d 813 (2001).

[6]White v. State, 271 Ga. 130(1), 518 S.E.2d 113 (1999).

them in its general witness list. In addition, the Supreme Court in *Tubbs v. State*,[7] rejected a defendant's position that the label of "alibi" witness be limited to those who can testify to the defendant's whereabouts at the specific time of the alleged offense. The Court ruled that anyone whom the defense intends to call in support of the alibi defense must be specifically identified as an alibi witness pursuant to O.C.G.A. § 17-16-5(a). The witnesses who will testify regarding the alibi defense for the state must be disclosed to the defense.

§ 14:20 Discovery—Reciprocal discovery in felony cases— Failure to comply

O.C.G.A. § 17-16-6 states that if it comes to the attention of the court that the state or the defendant has failed to comply with the requirements of this article, the court may order such party to "permit the discovery or inspection, interview of the witness, grant a continuance, or, upon a showing of prejudice and bad faith, prohibit the [party] from introducing the evidence not disclosed or presenting the witness not disclosed, or may enter such other order as it deems just under the circumstances. The court may specify the time, place, and manner of making the discovery, inspection, and interview and may prescribe such terms and conditions as are just."

In *Corbin v. State*,[1] the court pointed out the statute gives trial courts wide latitude in remedying discovery violations.

In *Franklin v. State*,[2] the court emphasized that the power of the trial judge to exclude evidence for failure to comply with reciprocal discovery is dependent on a showing of both prejudice *and* bad faith. However, it may be an abuse of discretion by the trial court to exclude a witness or evidence which is only discovered during the course of trial or just prior thereto where it is not apparent that the same information could have been discovered earlier had counsel's investigation been more diligent.[3]

---

[7]Tubbs v. State, 276 Ga. 751 (1), 583 S.E.2d 853 (2003).

[Section 14:20]

[1]Corbin v. State, 240 Ga. App. 788, 790, 525 S.E.2d 365 (1999).

[2]Franklin v. State, 224 Ga. App. 578 (2), 481 S.E.2d 852 (1997). Accord, Ware v. State, 298 Ga. App. 232, 679 S.E.2d 797 (2009); Guild v. State, 236 Ga. App. 444, 446 (3), 512 S.E.2d 343 (1999). Cf. Blankenship v. State, 229 Ga. App. 793, 794, 494 S.E.2d 758 (1997). See Ware v. State, 298 Ga. App. 232, 679 S.E.2d 797 (2009), where the court held the exclusion of testimony from a witness who is not timely disclosed is improper unless both prejudice and bad faith are shown; rather, the trial court should have considered a less severe remedy, such as permitting an interview before the witness testifies or by granting a continuance.

[3]See Mitchell v. State, 326 Ga. App. 899, 755 S.E.2d 308 (2014).

In *Crawley v. State*,[4] the prosecuting attorney and defense counsel together, and at the same time, discovered $143 in cash in the bloody pants of an accomplice. Because the pants had been available to both counsel before but neither had examined them, there was no violation of the discovery statute.

In *Bertholf v. State*,[5] the court held that a showing of prejudice is not established by a claim that earlier disclosure "would have allowed for better trial preparation, or would have caused him to call additional witnesses or testify on his own behalf [since] '[m]ere speculation . . . that he "might" have pursued a different course of action had he received the evidence earlier, is not sufficient.' "

However, in *Baker v. State*,[6] the court concluded that "[w]hen wrongfully withheld evidence is disclosed for the first time at the start of the trial, the defendant may be presumed to have been prejudiced, as his attorney has not had the opportunity to reflect upon such evidence and to determine what other investigation may be required as a result of its use and how it impacts the existing trial strategy and the subpoena and call of witnesses."

In *Clark v. State*,[7] the defendant disclosed a witness five days before trial and filed the disputed witness' statement three days before trial. The statement was made four months prior to its filing. Finding prejudice to the state and bad faith on the part of the defendant, the Court of Appeals upheld the trial court's decision to bar the presentation of the witness.

In *State v. Brown*,[8] the trial court excluded important evidence from the state's case as a sanction because notes taken by an investigator in connection with her surveillance and used by her to prepare a search warrant application and affidavit were not made available to the defense in discovery. The investigator discarded the notes, made on scraps of paper, after completing the search warrant documents. The Court of Appeals reversed holding that there is no duty under the discovery requirements in criminal cases to retain "everything associated with [every] case." Informal notes of an investigation used in connection with the preparation of other documents are generally not subject to discovery.

---

[4]Crawley v. State, 240 Ga. App. 891, 892 (1), 525 S.E.2d 739 (1999).

[5]Bertholf v. State, 224 Ga. App. 831 (1), 482 S.E.2d 469 (1997).

[6]Baker v. State, 238 Ga. App. 285, 287 (1), 518 S.E.2d 455 (1999).

[7]Clark v. State, 271 Ga. App. 534, 610 S.E.2d 165 (2005).

[8]State v. Brown, 333 Ga. App. 643, 777 S.E.2d 27 (2015). See Brannon v. State, 298 Ga. 601, 783 S.E.2d 642 (2016) (notes made by law enforcement officials are not among the materials state is required to turn over to defense as part of reciprocal discovery).

In *Moceri v. State*,[9] the Court of Appeals held that the trial court did not abuse its discretion by excluding from the defendant's case evidence that the vehicle operated by the defendant at the time of the charged vehicular homicide had a possible mechanical malfunction which caused the fatal crash. The evidence consisted of testimony from an expert based on his examination of the automobile. The trial court's action was taken following its determination that the defense had acted in bad faith by failing to preserve the car for inspection by the state as ordered.

§14:21 Discovery—Reciprocal discovery in felony cases—Statements of witnesses

O.C.G.A. § 17-16-1(2) defines a witness statement to include (a) any written or recorded statement, or copies thereof, made by the witness that is signed or otherwise adopted or approved by the witness, (b) a substantially verbatim recital of an oral statement made by the witness that is recorded contemporaneously with the making of the oral statement, or (c) a summary of the substance of a statement made by a witness contained in a memorandum or report other than notes made by counsel.

O.C.G.A. § 17-16-1(3) provides that a witness does not include the defendant.

O.C.G.A. § 17-16-7 states that "[n]o later than ten days prior to trial, or at the time of any post-indictment pre-trial evidentiary hearing other than a bond hearing, [both parties] shall produce for the opposing party any statement of any witness that is in the possession, custody, or control" of the state or of the defendant or defendant's counsel that relates to the testimony of a witness the party intends to call as a witness at a post-indictment pre-trial evidentiary hearing or at trial.

However, in *Lawson v. State*,[1] the court held that it is not necessary that the state furnish or serve any statement referred to in O.C.G.A. § 17-16-7 on the defense; it is sufficient to make the statements available to the defense.

In *Forehand v. State*,[2] the court held that this rule does not apply where "a witness merely makes an oral statement. There can

---

[9]Moceri v. State, 338 Ga. App. 329, 788 S.E.2d 899 (2016).

[Section 14:21]

[1]Lawson v. State, 224 Ga. App. 645, 648 (3)(b), 481 S.E.2d 856 (1997). Accord, Taylor v. State, 272 Ga. 562, 564, 532 S.E.2d 669 (2000).

[2]Forehand v. State, 267 Ga. 254,

255 (3), 477 S.E.2d 560 (1996). Accord, Lewis v. State, 293 Ga. 110, 744 S.E.2d 21 (2013); Baldwin v. State, 232 Ga. App. 335, 501 S.E.2d 548 (1998); Grabowski v. State, 234 Ga. App. 222, 224 (2), 507 S.E.2d 472 (1998); Thompson v. State, 240 Ga. App. 26, 29 (3), 521 S.E.2d 876 (1999). Cf. Kinney v. State, 234 Ga. App. 733, 736

be no 'possession, custody or control' of a witness' statement which has neither been recorded nor committed to writing. . . . Accordingly if, but only if, the eyewitness' statement has been recorded or committed to writing other than 'in notes or summaries made by counsel,' it would be discoverable."

In *Sauls v. State,*[3] the court held that this section does not apply before a defendant has been indicted.

In *Williams v. State,*[4] the court pointed out that notes or summaries prepared by counsel are not statements of witnesses and do not have to be produced. Further, notes of an investigator or specialist working under an attorney's direction in a criminal matter are not discoverable.[5]

§ 14:22　Discovery—Reciprocal discovery in felony cases— Lists of names and information concerning witnesses

O.C.G.A. § 17-16-8 states that upon election by the defendant to engage in reciprocal discovery, "[t]he prosecuting attorney, not later than ten days before trial, and the defendant's attorney, within ten days after compliance by the prosecuting attorney but no later than five days prior to trial, or as otherwise ordered by the court, shall furnish to the opposing counsel as an officer of the court, in confidence, the names, current locations, dates of birth, and telephone numbers of that party's witnesses, unless for good cause the judge allows an exception to this requirement, in which event the counsel shall be afforded an opportunity to interview such witnesses prior to the witness being called to testify." However, the above statute was amended in 1996 to provide that the prosecuting attorney is not required "to furnish the home address, date of birth, or home telephone number of a

---

(6), 506 S.E.2d 441 (1998). Compare Bohannon v. State, 230 Ga. App. 829, 835, 498 S.E.2d 316 (1998) (witness's recorded statement did not qualify for a work product exception as it was a statement of a witness within the meaning of O.C.G.A. § 17-16-1(2)(A) and "did not merely constitute 'notes or summaries made by counsel' within the meaning of O.C.G.A. § 17-16-1(2)(C)").

[3]Sauls v. State, 220 Ga. App. 115, 468 S.E.2d 771 (1996).

[4]Williams v. State, 226 Ga. App. 313, 315, 485 S.E.2d 837 (1997).

[5]See Stinski v. State, 286 Ga. 839, 845, 691 S.E.2d 854 (2010) ("notes and summaries" of a mitigation specialist working at the direction of trial counsel in a death penalty case "should be regarded as 'notes or summaries made by counsel' within the meaning of the criminal discovery procedure"). Cf. McGee v. State, 272 Ga. 363, 529 S.E.2d 366 (2000) (even if notes taken by an investigator during pre-trial interviews with state witnesses were not provided, such is not constitutional error because Brady v. Maryland, 373 U.S. 83, 83 S. Ct. 1194, 10 L. Ed. 2d 215 (1963) "does not require that agents of the state retain rough notes made in the course of their investigation").

witness who is a law enforcement officer." But the prosecuting attorney shall furnish defense counsel the "current work location and work phone number" of such witness. However, in *Boone v. State*,[1] a case in which an investigator whose name was not on the list of witnesses furnished by the state to testify at trial was allowed to testify at the trial, the court held that the defendant was not harmed where the defendant "was given open access to the state's file and the investigator's name and reports were included in the file." Where the trial court determines not to exclude a witness whose name was not on the list, proper remedies include a request for a continuance or a mistrial.

In *State v. Dickerson*,[2] the court held "that a party charged with producing the statutorily required information may not rest *solely* on the fact that it is not within their possession. Instead the statute imposes an affirmative duty on the producing party to attempt to acquire the information. . . . If, after a diligent effort to obtain the information, a party has demonstrated an inability to do so, the trial court is authorized to exercise its discretion in deciding whether good cause has been shown for nondisclosure and in fashioning a remedy under O.C.G.A. § 17-16-6." (Emphasis added.)

In *Sibert v. State*,[3] the court held that while Rule 30.3 of the Uniform Rules for the Superior Courts requires the defendant to be furnished the names and addresses of the witnesses the state intends to call, the district attorney is not required to notify defense counsel of the actual location where the witnesses may be located. Likewise, in *Davis v. State*,[4] the court held that the state was not obligated to provide updated addresses for potential witnesses it chose not to call. In *Massey v. State*,[5] the court held that the address requirement was complied with when the state gave a mailing address and not the address where the witness lived.

It has been held that even where defense counsel makes a proper demand for a list of witnesses, if counsel signs the "form"

[Section 14:22]

[1]Boone v. State, 250 Ga. App. 133, 138(9), 549 S.E.2d 713 (2001). See also Morris v. State, 268 Ga. App. 325, 601 S.E.2d 804 (2004), where the Court of Appeals found no prejudice resulted to the defendant where the state failed to include the names of certain witnesses on its formal witness list, but the defendant was aware, *inter alia*, of the witnesses' identity and the state's intention to call them as witnesses. The court also noted that the defendant was provided an opportunity to interview the witnesses and that the state never attempted to conceal the witnesses' names.

[2]State v. Dickerson, 273 Ga. 408, 410 (1), 542 S.E.2d 487 (2001).

[3]Sibert v. State, 259 Ga. 323, 324(2), 380 S.E.2d 698 (1989).

[4]Davis v. State, 209 Ga. App. 755, 759(4), 434 S.E.2d 752 (1993).

[5]Massey v. State, 263 Ga. 379, 381(3), 434 S.E.2d 467 (1993).

on the back of the indictment which "waives copy of indictment, list of witnesses" the earlier demand for a list of witnesses has been considered waived.[6] However, in *Brown v. State*,[7] the Georgia Supreme Court held that where defense counsel had twice in writing demanded a list of witnesses which had not been complied with, and on the morning of the trial the defendant entered a plea and the words "list of witnesses" were not marked through because his counsel did not think it was necessary, the trial court should have permitted defense counsel "to withdraw what was clearly an unintentional and inadvertent waiver." Likewise, in *Rogers v. State*,[8] the court reversed a conviction where such a waiver was signed but prosecution sent defense counsel a list of witnesses and updates, but failed to explain why a witness was not on the amended list. Also, the trial judge denied the defense an opportunity to interview the witness.

Although the statute authorizes the exclusion of certain testimony, it has been said that the exclusion of a witness is not mandatory where the judge, in his discretion, determines that the defendant can be protected in some other way.[9] In *Berry v. State*,[10] the Georgia Supreme Court pointed out that "the prosecution's failure to list a witness may be remedied by allowing the defense to interview the witness before the testimony is given." In *Butler v. State*,[11] the defendant had made a timely demand for a list of witnesses, and the prosecuting attorney had failed to comply. Nevertheless, the defendant announced "ready" when the case was called. Subsequently, the defense objected to the state calling a witness whose name had not been on the accusation on the ground that the names listed thereon constituted a list of witnesses. The state argued that the defense counsel waived his right to insist on a list of witnesses when he announced ready. The trial court resolved the issue by allowing the defense the opportunity to interview the "unlisted" witness. The appellate court concluded that the defendant did not show substantial prejudice.

---

[6]Parr v. State, 117 Ga. App. 484, 160 S.E.2d 865 (1968); Lashley v. State, 132 Ga. App. 427, 429(6), 208 S.E.2d 200 (1974).

[7]Brown v. State, 242 Ga. 536, 250 S.E.2d 438 (1978).

[8]Rogers v. State, 261 Ga. 649(1), 409 S.E.2d 655 (1991).

[9]Davis v. State, 135 Ga. App. 203, 207, 217 S.E.2d 343 (1975); Powell v. State, 171 Ga. App. 876, 879, 321 S.E.2d 745 (1984).

In Smith v. Estelle, 602 F.2d 694 (5th Cir. 1979), judgment aff'd, 451 U.S. 454, 101 S. Ct. 1866, 68 L. Ed. 2d 359 (1981), the court held that there was a due process violation, where the prosecution over objection used a "devastating" witness whose name was not on a list of witnesses given by the district attorney to defense counsel pursuant to court order.

[10]Berry v. State, 268 Ga. 437, 440(3), 490 S.E.2d 389 (1997).

[11]Butler v. State, 139 Ga. App. 92, 227 S.E.2d 889 (1976).

In *Price v. State*,[12] the court pointed out that "[a]llowing defense counsel an opportunity to interview . . . [a] newly discovered witness is a procedure which is permitted as an alternative to [granting a motion for] a continuance."

If the district attorney does not know the name of an employee from the crime laboratory who is to testify, such witness may not be excluded if his name is given to the defendant as soon as the district attorney learns of it.[13] The same rule has been applied to a custodian of the Department of Public Safety records.[14] However, it has been held that where a list of names is given to the defense and no reference is made to the person who gave an intoxication test, the individual may not testify over objection.[15]

An investigating officer's knowledge of a witness is not imputed to the district attorney in the absence of reciprocal discovery.[16] The district attorney can allow a witness to testify whose name has not been given to the defense if the district attorney did not know about the witness until the night before trial.[17]

Where an indictment names a person as the victim of the assault charged[18] or as a co-defendant,[19] or as the person to whom contraband was sold,[20] it is proper to permit such person to testify even though his name does not appear on the list of witnesses, since the defendant has already been put on notice as to the existence of the person. The same rule applies to a co-defendant who pleads guilty and then testifies for the state[21] or is convicted and then called as a witness for the state.[22] Likewise, the same rule applies to other witnesses whose names appear on the copy of the

---

[12]Price v. State, 223 Ga. App. 185, 186, 477 S.E.2d 353 (1996). See also Morris v. State, 268 Ga. App. 325, 601 S.E.2d 804 (2004), where the Court of Appeals found no prejudice resulted to the defendant where the state failed to include the names of certain witnesses on its formal witness list, but the defendant was aware, *inter alia,* of the witnesses' identity and the state's intention to call them as witnesses. The court also noted that the defendant was provided an opportunity to interview the witnesses and that the state never attempted to conceal the witnesses' names.

[13]Yeomans v. State, 229 Ga. 488(1), 192 S.E.2d 362 (1972).

[14]Parks v. State, 180 Ga. App. 31(1), 348 S.E.2d 481 (1986).

[15]Hyatt v. State, 134 Ga. App. 703, 707(3), 215 S.E.2d 698 (1975).

[16]Abner v. State, 139 Ga. App. 600, 603(4), 229 S.E.2d 83 (1976); Harris v. State, 142 Ga. App. 37(6), 234 S.E.2d 798 (1977).

[17]Moye v. State, 129 Ga. App. 52, 54(1), 198 S.E.2d 514 (1973).

[18]Huff v. State, 141 Ga. App. 66, 232 S.E.2d 403 (1977).

[19]Byrd v. State, 216 Ga. App. 510, 512(4), 455 S.E.2d 318 (1995).

[20]Hibbs v. State, 133 Ga. App. 407, 211 S.E.2d 24 (1974).

[21]Anderson v. State, 141 Ga. App. 249, 233 S.E.2d 240 (1977).

[22]Redmond v. State, 252 Ga. 142, 312 S.E.2d 315 (1984).

indictment.[23]

The district attorney may supplement an earlier list even though the new names are not "newly discovered" if the complete list is available to defense counsel early enough so as to give him an opportunity to interview the witnesses before trial.[24] In fact, it has been held that the state may supplement its list a number of times, even by telephone.[25] However, the defendant must receive the information at a reasonable time before trial.[26] Thus, where the defendant received a supplemental list four days before trial to which he promptly objected and the district attorney made no showing that the additional witnesses were newly discovered, it was error to permit the witnesses on the supplemental list to testify.[27]

The district attorney's non-compliance with the demand for a list of witnesses does not entitle the defendant to a directed verdict of acquittal. The defendant must move for a mistrial or continuance.[28] Likewise, where the compliance is completed the day before trial,[29] or where the district attorney does not comply until the jury has been struck,[30] the defendant should request a continuance and not merely object to the testimony of the witnesses when they are called.[31] It has been held that if, after demanding a list of witnesses, defense counsel announces ready, he waives his demand.[32]

The delivery of a "padded list," intended to provide extra work for defense counsel, does not comply with the statute.[33]

In some cases, the error of the district attorney in failing to

---

[23]Lewis v. State, 159 Ga. App. 135, 282 S.E.2d 750 (1981).

[24]Hicks v. State, 232 Ga. 393, 399, 207 S.E.2d 30 (1974) (holding modified on other grounds by, Tribble v. State, 248 Ga. 274, 280 S.E.2d 352 (1981)). In Williams v. State, 242 Ga. 757(1), 251 S.E.2d 254 (1978), a list of witnesses was supplemented three times. None of the supplemental lists contained the name of a particular witness who was named on the original list. The court held that such witness could testify even though he was named only on the first list.

[25]Cf. Logan v. State, 170 Ga. App. 809, 318 S.E.2d 516 (1984).

[26]Newman v. State, 237 Ga. 376, 381, 228 S.E.2d 790 (1976).

[27]Smith v. State, 130 Ga. App. 390, 392(4), 203 S.E.2d 375 (1973).

[28]Hunnicutt v. State, 135 Ga. App. 774, 219 S.E.2d 22 (1975). In Posey v. State, 222 Ga. App. 405, 406(2), 474 S.E.2d 206 (1996), the court said that "the proper remedy when a witness is called whose name was not on the list is to request a continuance, not the exclusion of the witness' testimony."

[29]Alexander v. State, 134 Ga. App. 201, 213 S.E.2d 560 (1975); Parham v. State, 135 Ga. App. 315, 217 S.E.2d 493 (1975).

[30]Davis v. State, 135 Ga. App. 203, 206(3), 217 S.E.2d 343 (1975).

[31]See Burrell v. State, 140 Ga. App. 900, 901(2), 232 S.E.2d 172 (1977).

[32]Hardin v. State, 142 Ga. App. 795, 796(1), 237 S.E.2d 202 (1977).

[33]See Griffin v. State, 133 Ga. App. 508, 211 S.E.2d 382 (1974); Irby

comply with a demand for a list of witnesses may prove to be harmless.[34] Where the district attorney puts defense counsel on notice that he plans to introduce certain records, it is not harmful to the defendant for the court to allow the custodian, whose name is not on the list, to identify the records.[35]

There is no requirement that the state call all persons whose names are set out in the list.[36] If no timely demand is made, the district attorney is not obligated to notify defense counsel of the witnesses the state will call.[37]

Generally, it is not necessary for the state to give the defendant the names of witnesses who will be used in rebuttal[38] unless the district attorney knows the witness will be called.[39] However, when the state offers a witness who is not on the list and the defense counsel's objection is sustained, the state cannot then call the same witness in rebuttal.[40] Where there is a retrial and no new demand for a list of witnesses, it is not error for the court to permit a witness who testified at the former trial to testify again even though his name was not on the list of witnesses.[41]

Where witnesses are to be sequestered at the trial, it has been held that it is within the discretion of the court to require the names of defense witnesses to be revealed to the district attorney if there is a need to keep defense witnesses from entering the

---

v. State, 60 Wis. 2d 311, 210 N.W.2d 755, 759 (1973). But it has been held that it is not necessary that addresses of witnesses be furnished. However, in Chafin v. State, 246 Ga. 709, 713(4), 273 S.E.2d 147 (1980), the court said that absent "a showing of prejudice or of bad faith" the giving of a list of 213 persons and calling of only 27 witnesses was not a denial of the defendant's right to a list. The state later broke the list down into two lists (a list of 142 "possible witnesses" and a list of 71 the state expected to use), and the principal investigator said from 500 to 1,000 people had been interviewed.

[34]Huffaker v. State, 119 Ga. App. 742, 168 S.E.2d 895 (1969). In Ervin v. State, 144 Ga. App. 504, 505(1), 241 S.E.2d 650 (1978), the court concluded that the demand for a list of witnesses was filed merely for purposes of delay, when arraignment was to be immediately before trial and the defense motion for a continuance was overruled.

[35]Clark v. State, 138 Ga. App. 266, 268(3), 226 S.E.2d 89 (1976); Arnold v. State, 163 Ga. App. 94, 95, 292 S.E.2d 891 (1982).

[36]Griffin v. State, 133 Ga. App. 508, 211 S.E.2d 382 (1974); Looney v. State, 240 Ga. 691, 694(3), 242 S.E.2d 86 (1978); Glover v. State, 149 Ga. App. 369, 371(3), 254 S.E.2d 492 (1979); cf. State v. Boushee, 284 N.W.2d 423 (N.D. 1979).

[37]See Green v. State, 223 Ga. 611, 612(1), 157 S.E.2d 257 (1967); Baker v. State, 143 Ga. App. 302, 305(4), 238 S.E.2d 241 (1977).

[38]See Yeomans v. State, 229 Ga. 488, 490(2), 192 S.E.2d 362 (1972).

[39]Vinson v. State, 127 Ga. App. 607, 608(2), 194 S.E.2d 583 (1972).

[40]Cunningham v. State, 137 Ga. App. 758, 225 S.E.2d 98 (1976).

[41]Upton v. State, 128 Ga. App. 547, 548(3), 197 S.E.2d 478 (1973).

757

courtroom.[42] However, in *Evans v. State*,[43] the court held that it is error for the trial judge to order the defendant to disclose a list of witnesses to be called and then restrict the defendant to the use of the listed witnesses. The court did not address the question of whether or not a defendant can be required under any circumstances to submit a list of defense witnesses to be called or what sanction could be imposed if the defendant refused to comply with such an order. However, the court concluded that the order of the trial court judge was harmless error since the defendant did not tender the testimony of any witness who was disallowed under the order.

A defendant has no right to demand a list of witnesses whom the prosecution expects to call at a commitment hearing.[44] For various demands for a list of witnesses, see Studdard, *Daniel's Georgia Criminal Trial Practice Forms* (2018-2019 ed.), §§ 14:32, et seq.

§ 14:23　Discovery—Reciprocal discovery in felony cases— Reimbursement of costs

O.C.G.A. § 17-16-9 states that "[a]ny party providing documents or statements to another party under [O.C.G.A. §§ 17-16-1 et seq.] shall be reimbursed for the actual cost incurred in providing such documents. If the court has determined the defendant to be indigent, the court shall determine the means of reimbursement."

§ 14:24　Discovery—Reciprocal discovery in felony cases— Material or information already furnished; who may be called as witness?

O.C.G.A. § 17-16-10 provides that "[t]he defendant need not include in materials and information furnished to the prosecuting attorney . . . any material . . . which the prosecuting attorney has already furnished to the defendant. . . ." and vice versa. Either party may call as a witness any person listed on either the prosecuting attorney's or defendant's witness list.

In *Davis v. State*,[1] the court held that, where a defendant was being tried on the re-indictment of the same original charges,

---

[42]Nance v. State, 123 Ga. App. 410, 411(5), 181 S.E.2d 295 (1971); Butler v. State, 172 Ga. App. 405, 406(1), 323 S.E.2d 628 (1984); Baxter v. State, 254 Ga. 538, 544(9), 331 S.E.2d 561 (1985); Fugitt v. State, 254 Ga. 521, 522(4), 330 S.E.2d 714 (1985).

[43]Evans v. State, 161 Ga. App.

504, 505(4), 288 S.E.2d 629 (1982).

[44]Sutton v. State, 237 Ga. 423, 424, 228 S.E.2d 820 (1976).

[Section 14:24]

[1]Davis v. State, 240 Ga. App. 301, 302 (2), 522 S.E.2d 729 (1999).

and the state complied with its discovery obligation under the original indictment, it is not necessary for the state "to submit the same evidence a second time. . . ."

§ 14:25 Discovery—Reciprocal discovery in felony cases— Pre-sentence evidence

In 2005, the Georgia legislature amended O.C.G.A. § 17-16-4 to provide for pre-sentence reciprocal discovery and disclosure. Generally, the state must disclose evidence it intends to use in aggravation of punishment ten days prior to trial or at such time as the court may direct, not later than the start of the trial.[1] The intention of the state to use the defendant's past history of criminal convictions must be "unmistakable."[2] The purpose of the notice is to provide the defendant with ample opportunity to examine his record in order to determine whether the convictions are in fact his or whether there was some defect in the prior cases, such as the absence of defense counsel, which might render them inadmissible during the pre-sentence hearing.[3] The defense must disclose no later than verdict all evidence which it intends to offer in mitigation including mental and physical health reports. The defense is required to disclose at least five days prior to trial the names of any witnesses it intends to call at the pre-sentence hearing if one is necessary and no later than verdict, any statement which the witness may have provided to the defense.[4]

§ 14:26 Other statutory discovery, misdemeanor cases

Discovery in misdemeanor cases as well as those felony cases accused prior to January 1, 1995, is governed by O.C.G.A. §§ 17-16-20 et seq., which replaced without substantial change the discovery statutes in effect prior to the adoption of reciprocal discovery.[1]

In *Brooks v. State*,[2] the Court of Appeals noted the discovery provisions applicable to misdemeanor prosecutions are not the same as those in felony prosecutions. Thus, the misdemeanor defendant there was not entitled to discovery of recordings, crime scene photos, the victim's criminal history, witness statements and the like. The state was required only to provide the defense

---

[Section 14:25]

[1]O.C.G.A. § 17-16-4(a)(5).

[2]Evans v. State, 290 Ga. App. 746, 748, 660 S.E.2d 841 (2008).

[3]Hightower v. State, 210 Ga. App. 216, 436 S.E.2d 31 (1993).

[4]O.C.G.A. § 17-16-4(b)(3).

[Section 14:26]

[1]The parties to felony cases indicted prior to January 1, 1995, can agree to reciprocal discovery.

[2]Brooks v. State, 267 Ga. App. 663, 664, 600 S.E.2d 737 (2004) (quoting Brown v. State, 246 Ga. App. 517, 520, 541 S.E.2d 112 (2000)).

with a copy of the accusation, a list of the state's witnesses and the defendant's criminal history.

§ 14:27 Other statutory discovery, misdemeanor cases— Copy of indictment or accusation

The 1983 Constitution[1] and O.C.G.A. § 17-16-21, as enacted in 1994, provide that "every person charged with a criminal offense shall be furnished with a copy of the indictment or accusation," and the statute provides that it shall be furnished to the defendant prior to arraignment. Hence, it seems that it is no longer necessary for the defendant to demand a copy of the indictment or accusation in a misdemeanor case. This is true whether or not the defendant elects into the new reciprocal discovery statutes. See § 14:11, supra, on the defendant's right to a copy of the indictment under the reciprocal discovery statutes for felony cases.

For a demand for copy of indictment, see Studdard, *Daniel's Georgia Criminal Trial Practice Forms* (2018-2019 ed.), § 14:2.

§ 14:28 Other statutory discovery, misdemeanor cases— Witness lists

Discovery in misdemeanor cases as well as those felony cases accused prior to January 1, 1995, is governed by O.C.G.A. §§ 17-16-20 et seq., which replaced without substantial change the discovery statutes in effect prior to the adoption of reciprocal discovery.[1] Several of the cases discussed in this section arose under the predecessor statute, former O.C.G.A. § 17-7-110, but remain as good authority.

Rule 30.3 of the Uniform Rules for the Superior Courts is also a basis for this section, and Rule 30.3 has been neither repealed nor amended. Rule 30.3 provides as follows: "Upon request of defense counsel, the district attorney shall furnish to defense counsel as an officer of the court, in confidence, the addresses and telephone numbers of the state's witnesses to the extent such are within the knowledge of the district attorney, unless for good cause the judge allows an exception to this requirement, in which event defense counsel shall be afforded an opportunity to interview such witnesses prior to the witness being called to

---

[Section 14:27]

[1]In Byrd v. State, 182 Ga. App. 284, 285 (1), 355 S.E.2d 666 (1987), the court held that there was no reversible error in that case where the copy of the indictment did not contain a list of the grand jurors, and a copy of one count was omitted. See Ga. Const. 1983, Art. I, § I, ¶ XIV.

[Section 14:28]

[1]The parties to felony cases indicted prior to January 1, 1995, can agree to reciprocal discovery.

testify."

See § 14:22, supra, on the new statutory provisions on the obligation of the defendant and the state to provide a list of witnesses under the new reciprocal discovery statutes for felony cases.

O.C.G.A. § 17-16-21 states that upon "demand, [the defendant shall be furnished] with a list of the witnesses on whose testimony the charge against such person is founded. Without the consent of the defendant, no witness shall be permitted to testify for the state whose name does not appear on the list . . . unless the prosecuting attorney shall state that the evidence . . . is newly discovered. . . ."

Prior to arraignment, a defendant has a right to make a written demand for a list of those witnesses whom the district attorney plans to have testify at trial.[2] Such a demand must be in writing.[3]

The purpose of O.C.G.A. § 17-16-21, formerly § 17-7-110, is to give defense counsel, or his investigator, the opportunity to interview witnesses before trial so as to avoid surprise by testimony at trial.[4] To effectuate the purpose of the statute, the list of witnesses should be served on the defendant.[5] While it has been said that delivery on the following day is adequate, delivery of a list of witnesses a few moments before the commencement of the trial is not a sufficient compliance even if the delivery is made on the first working day following the demand.[6] However, it appears that if the trial is not to be held promptly after arraignment, the list may be delivered much later if the defendant will still have a reasonable opportunity to interview the witnesses.

The demand should be made in accordance with Rule 30.3 of the Uniform Rules for Superior Courts. One copy must be served on the district attorney,[7] while another copy should be filed with the clerk of the court. The demand should be accompanied by a certificate of service. Where counsel strikes through the word "waives" preceding the words "list of witnesses" on the back of an indictment and inserts the word "demands," this is not sufficient to comply with the statute.[8]

Unlisted witnesses may testify in misdemeanor cases over

---

[2]O.C.G.A. § 17-16-21. Cf. Tenn. Code Ann., § 40-17-106.

[3]Ronskowsky v. State, 190 Ga. App. 147, 148 (1), 378 S.E.2d 185 (1989).

[4]See Mowery v. State, 234 Ga. App. 801, 507 S.E.2d 821 (1998).

[5]Driver v. State, 188 Ga. App. 301, 302 (2), 372 S.E.2d 841 (1988).

[6]Fishman v. State, 128 Ga. App. 505 (4), 511, 197 S.E.2d 467 (1973); State v. Haag, 176 Mont. 395, 578 P.2d 740 (1978).

[7]Beeks v. State, 225 Ga. 200 (1), 167 S.E.2d 156 (1969).

[8]Yeomans v. State, 229 Ga. 488,

objection where the defense fails to make a demand for a list of the state's witnesses prior to trial.[9] In addition, witnesses who come to the attention of the state shortly before or at the trial of the case may testify over the objection that their names were not provided in response to the defendant's demand as "newly discovered."[10]

A trial court may exercise its discretion and allow the defense a continuance of the trial in order to prepare for any unlisted witnesses which the state wants to call at trial.[11]

See § 14:22, supra, on reciprocal discovery of witness names and information in felony cases.

§ 14:29   Other statutory discovery, misdemeanor cases— Defendant's statements

Former O.C.G.A. § 17-7-210 (former GCA § 27-1302), which formed the basis for the material in this section, was repealed and reenacted without substantial change at O.C.G.A. § 17-16-22 as of January 1, 1995. The provisions of former O.C.G.A. § 17-7-210 (former GCA § 27-1302) now apply to misdemeanor cases and felony cases docketed before January 1, 1995.[1] The most important provisions of the former law and the cases decided thereunder are discussed in this section. That case law is still applicable under O.C.G.A. § 17-16-22. See § 14:12, supra, on the prosecution's duty to furnish the defendant with a copy of his statements and/or the statements of his co-conspirators under the new reciprocal discovery rules for felony cases.

A defendant may request in writing, within any reasonable period of time before trial, a copy of any statement[2] of the defendant made by him while in police custody.[3] In *Brinson v. State,*[4] the defendant "filed a 'motion for production of statement of defendant' in which he asks for 'any oral or written statement made by the defendant pursuant to the investigation giving rise to the

---

489-490, 192 S.E.2d 362 (1972).

[9]See, e.g., Brown v. State, 246 Ga. App. 517, 541 S.E.2d 112 (2000).

[10]Brice v. State, 242 Ga. App. 163, 529 S.E.2d 178 (2000).

[11]Major v. State, 306 Ga. App. 342, 702 S.E.2d 684 (2010).

[Section 14:29]

[1]Park v. State, 230 Ga. App. 274, 276 (2)(b), 495 S.E.2d 886 (1998).

[2]In Franklin v. State, 166 Ga. App. 375 (2), 304 S.E.2d 501 (1983), the court held that a letter written by

a defendant while in custody before trial was not a "statement" under the statute.

[3]Hudgins v. State, 186 Ga. App. 883, 884 (2), 369 S.E.2d 54 (1988).

In Williams v. State, 165 Ga. App. 69, 70 (3), 299 S.E.2d 402 (1983), the court held that the statute did not apply to statements made by the defendant at the time of the crime since the defendant was not in custody at that time. Merritt v. State, 165 Ga. App. 597 (1), 302 S.E.2d 136 (1983).

[4]Brinson v. State, 261 Ga. 884, 885 (2), 413 S.E.2d 443 (1992).

indictment.' "The court held the request was insufficient to require discovery pursuant to former O.C.G.A. § 17-7-210. In *Byars v. State*,[5] the court emphasized that on request the defendant is entitled to "any" statement of the defendant made while in police custody. Thus, it is error for the state to fail to produce an in-custody statement the defendant made during the investigation of a prior rape. However, statements or utterances made by a defendant "during the commission of, or in connection with, the crime charged do not constitute statements given 'while in custody.' "[6] In *Deal v. State*,[7] the court held that a defendant was not entitled to the production of a video tape of a surveillance of a motel under a request for the defendant's statements. Also, a defendant has no right to a copy of a co-conspirator's statement under the statute.[8] But see §§ 14:12 and 14:22, supra, on the defendant's right to co-conspirators' statements under the new reciprocal discovery rules in felony cases.

A consent to search form which was signed by the defendant is not regarded as a "statement,"[9] and a waiver of Miranda rights is not regarded as a statement. (See § 5:19, supra.) However, statements of the defendant which are not incriminating or inculpatory need not be furnished.[10] In *Byrd v. State*,[11] the court held that the defendant need only be furnished with a summary of his statement and that de minimis discrepancies are "of no legal consequence." The court noted, "[t]he law has historically declined to take notice of very small or trifling matters." In *Williams v. State*,[12] the court held that a letter written by a defendant while in jail to the victim's mother was not a "statement" covered by former O.C.G.A. § 17-7-210.

In order for such a request to be timely, it must be made prior to 10 days before the trial of the case.[13] The request for a statement or statements is not regarded as a "motion" as that word is

---

[5]Byars v. State, 198 Ga. App. 793, 795 (4), 403 S.E.2d 82 (1991).

[6]Adams v. State, 197 Ga. App. 81, 82, 397 S.E.2d 497 (1990) (quoting Holbrook v. State, 162 Ga. App. 400, 291 S.E.2d 729 (1982)).

[7]Deal v. State, 199 Ga. App. 184, 187 (3), 404 S.E.2d 343 (1991).

[8]Chase v. State, 179 Ga. App. 71, 74, 345 S.E.2d 149 (1986).

[9]Reeves v. State, 169 Ga. App. 665, 666 (2), 314 S.E.2d 682 (1984).

[10]Jackson v. State, 207 Ga. App. 190 (1), 427 S.E.2d 566 (1993); Williamson v. State, 188 Ga. App. 307, 308 (1), 372 S.E.2d 685 (1988).

[11]Byrd v. State, 216 Ga. App. 510 (2), 455 S.E.2d 318 (1995).

[12]Williams v. State, 202 Ga. App. 728, 729 (2), 415 S.E.2d 327 (1992).

[13]Blanchard v. State, 247 Ga. 415, 419, 276 S.E.2d 593 (1981). Cf. State v. Meminger, 249 Ga. 561, 564, 292 S.E.2d 681 (1982). For a discussion of the interpretation of the requirements for a timely request, see § 14:30, infra.

used in Rule 31.1 of the Uniform Rules for the Superior Courts.[14] However, in *Pealor v. State*,[15] the Georgia Court of Appeals held that where counsel was appointed for the defendant less than 10 days before trial and counsel filed a request for the defendant's statements on the day after appointment, the filing was timely. If the state wished to use the defendant's statements, it should have requested a continuance. In order for a request under this statute to be valid it "must either make specific reference to § 27-1302 [former O.C.G.A. § 17-7-210], or make it clear that written copies of the defendant's own statements are to be furnished to the defense at least ten days prior to trial."[16] Thus, the Georgia Supreme Court found the following to be an inadequate request under the statute: "[A] Brady motion requesting, among other things '[a]ll written and recorded statements and all summaries or memoranda of any oral or written statements made by the named defendant . . . [requested to be produced] at the trial . . . and at any and all non-jury hearings.' "[17]

As pointed out earlier, the statute only applies to statements of the defendant while in custody. In *Magher v. State*,[18] the court held that the test for determining whether a person was in custody within the meaning of the statute "is if a reasonable person in the suspect's position would have thought the detention would not be temporary." In *Hudgins v. State*,[19] the Court of Appeals treated the statutory words "in police custody" as meaning the same thing as "taken into custody" in connection with interrogation under *Miranda*. The court then concluded that the defendant had not been "taken into custody" when he was stopped by an officer while driving and he made a statement "before he was placed under arrest." Likewise, in *Daugherty v. State*,[20] statements made during the roadside questioning of a person in connection with an accident investigation after a routine traffic stop were not considered as having been made while in custody. See § 5:12, supra, on custodial interrogation.

Pursuant to such a proper request, the defendant is entitled to have a copy of any such statement given by him, whether written

---

[14]Livingston v. State, 222 Ga. App. 298, 299, 474 S.E.2d 1 (1996).

[15]Pealor v. State, 165 Ga. App. 387, 299 S.E.2d 904 (1983).

[16]McCarty v. State, 249 Ga. 618, 620, 292 S.E.2d 700 (1982); Williams v. State, 164 Ga. App. 148, 149 (2), 296 S.E.2d 739 (1982).

[17]McCarty v. State, 249 Ga. 618, 619, 292 S.E.2d 700 (1982); Tabb v. State, 250 Ga. 317, 323 (3), 297 S.E.2d 227 (1982).

[18]Magher v. State, 199 Ga. App. 508, 509 (4), 405 S.E.2d 327 (1991) (quoting Hughes v. State, 259 Ga. 227, 378 S.E.2d 853 (1989)).

[19]Hudgins v. State, 176 Ga. App. 719, 720 (1), 337 S.E.2d 378 (1985). Cf. Mitchell v. State, 174 Ga. App. 594, 597 (2), 330 S.E.2d 798 (1985).

[20]Daugherty v. State, 248 Ga. App. 181, 546 S.E.2d 310 (2001).

or oral, at least 10 days prior to the trial of the case.[21] If the state is unable to provide the defense with the statements in a timely fashion, at least ten days prior to trial, its remedy is to seek a continuance or risk having the statements excluded in its case in chief.[22] Where a request has been timely made and the statement delivered one day before trial, it has been held error to admit the statement over objection.[23] The prosecution must furnish in writing all relevant and material portions of the defendant's oral or partially oral statement.[24] The state is not excused from its duty to produce such a statement by virtue of the fact that the statement or conversation was initiated by the defendant after the commission of the crime.[25] In *Looney v. State*,[26] the defense moved for a copy of in-custody statements of the defendant. The state failed to respond. At trial, over objection, the prosecution was permitted to play a video tape recording (without sound) of the defendant while he was being given a breath test. The appellate court affirmed after concluding that the visual portion of the tape was not a statement covered by former O.C.G.A. § 17-7-210.

Likewise, where there is a proper request under this statute for copies of statements of the defendant, a copy of a statement made by the defendant to another inmate must be given to the defendant if the state seeks to use the testimony of the inmate.[27] However, it has been held that the statute does not apply to statements that are not incriminating or inculpatory.[28] In *O'Kelley*

---

[21]See Pealor v. State, 165 Ga. App. 387, 299 S.E.2d 904 (1983) (where defendant first obtained counsel less than ten days prior to trial, a request for statements made by defendant was considered timely and the trial court's ruling to the contrary was error).

[22]Garner v. State, 159 Ga. App. 244, 282 S.E.2d 909 (1981).

[23]Smith v. State, 181 Ga. App. 595, 596 (1), 353 S.E.2d 35 (1987); Bright v. State, 265 Ga. 265, 281 (6), 455 S.E.2d 37 (1995).

[24]Reed v. State, 163 Ga. App. 364, 365, 295 S.E.2d 108 (1982). However, in McCarty v. State, 161 Ga. App. 444, 288 S.E.2d 249 (1982), the court held that the trial judge did not err in permitting evidence as to the contents of an oral statement made by the defendant pursuant to this Code section where an officer had testified at a

hearing on motion to suppress three months before trial as to the defendant's oral statement. The Court of Appeals reasoned that the statute was to inform the defendant of the allegations which were to be used against the defendant and that, under the facts of the case, this object had already been satisfied.

[25]Henderson v. State, 162 Ga. App. 320, 323 (3), 292 S.E.2d 77 (1982).

[26]Looney v. State, 180 Ga. App. 693 (1), 350 S.E.2d 29 (1986); Orr v. State, 209 Ga. App. 832, 834, 434 S.E.2d 723 (1993).

[27]Walraven v. State, 250 Ga. 401, 405 (2), 297 S.E.2d 278 (1982); Bell v. State, 179 Ga. App. 491 (2), 347 S.E.2d 321 (1986).

[28]Holland v. State, 190 Ga. App. 169, 378 S.E.2d 513 (1989); Furlow v. State, 172 Ga. App. 185, 186 (2), 322 S.E.2d 317 (1984).

v. State,[29] the court held that the statute did not require the state to present shorthand notes of a statement of the defendant where a transcript of an in-custody statement of the defendant had been given to defense counsel.

If the prosecution fails to comply with the defendant's request, the oral or written statement shall be excluded and suppressed from the prosecution's use in its case-in-chief and in rebuttal.[30] However, in *Keller v. State,*[31] the court held that a recorded in-custody statement of a defendant which had not been furnished to the defendant in accordance with former O.C.G.A. § 17-7-210(a) was admissible for impeachment purposes since the defendant testified on direct examination to an issue which the state could not introduce in its case-in-chief or rebuttal. If the defendant's statement was oral, no relevant and material portion of such statement may be used against the defendant if the defendant has properly requested such statement and has not been properly supplied with a copy of such statement.[32] In *Simpson v. State,*[33] the court held that an officer could not interpret the meaning of a word used by a defendant in a statement unless the defendant was appraised of the interpretation pursuant to the statute. In *Ludy v. State,*[34] the court pointed out that, where a defendant had made a proper request for statements he made while in custody and the state had supplied some statements, it is error to permit an officer to testify to custodial statements not given to the defendant. However, in *Moon v. State,*[35] the court held that when the state provided the defendant with an incomplete in-custody statement, it was proper to apply the "highly probable that it did not contribute to the verdict" test and to affirm the conviction where the error was harmless. In *Walls v. State,*[36] the court emphasized that "the state is required to furnish *in* writing" a copy of the in-custody statement upon request and the fact that the district attorney has "opened his file" to defense counsel does not meet the requirement of the statute. However, if a defendant has made general statements about his education, his family, and his description, and pursuant to a defense request

---

[29]O'Kelley v. State, 175 Ga. App. 503, 506 (2), 333 S.E.2d 838 (1985).

[30]Garner v. State, 159 Ga. App. 244, 282 S.E.2d 909 (1981); Garard v. State, 159 Ga. App. 248, 283 S.E.2d 27 (1981).

[31]Keller v. State, 208 Ga. App. 589, 590 (2), 431 S.E.2d 411 (1993).

[32]In Lee v. State, 166 Ga. App. 644 (2), 305 S.E.2d 175 (1983), the court, in referring to an oral statement allegedly made by the defendant, held

that there is no absolute right to a mistrial if there is some reference made to a statement of the defendant.

[33]Simpson v. State, 181 Ga. App. 558, 353 S.E.2d 55 (1987).

[34]Ludy v. State, 177 Ga. App. 767, 768, 341 S.E.2d 224 (1986).

[35]Moon v. State, 208 Ga. App. 540, 542 (1)(b), 431 S.E.2d 128 (1993).

[36]Walls v. State, 169 Ga. App. 80, 82, 311 S.E.2d 243 (1983).

this information is not summarized and the state does not present such evidence and defense counsel brings it out on cross-examination of the state's witnesses, this does not require the granting of a motion for a continuance to investigate what the defendant had said.[37]

Nothing in the statute requires the State to inform a defendant of the name of the persons to whom he made statements while in custody. A summary of an oral statement or verbatim transcript is not to be regarded as an insufficient compliance of the statute simply because the defendant was not informed that material supplied related to two different statements.[38] However, "the written summary provided by the State [must] accurately and completely reflect those portions of a defendant's interrogation that the State intends to use against the defendant."[39]

In *Causey v. State*,[40] a "verbatim account of defendant's statement [is] not required, where counsel [is] given a written summary of the statement prior to trial which include[s] all relevant and material portions of the . . . statements," even in cases where the state plans to introduce a video taped confession into evidence.

It has been held that where an oral statement is involved, the failure of the district attorney to notify defense counsel that the defendant requested a lawyer is not "relevant and material" to any issue in the case.[41] The failure of the state to prepare and produce summaries of unrecorded statements made by the defendant to police, including one in which he denied his guilt, did not require the exclusion of an inculpatory tape recorded statement of the defendant in *Brown v. State*.[42] The court stated: "Because the defendant's prior denials of guilt were separate and

---

[37]Hilburn v. State, 166 Ga. App. 357 (3), 304 S.E.2d 480 (1983). Cf. Ledesma v. State, 251 Ga. 487, 489 (5), 306 S.E.2d 629 (1983).

[38]Roman v. State, 185 Ga. App. 32, 34 (2), 363 S.E.2d 329 (1987); Orr v. State, 209 Ga. App. 832, 834, 434 S.E.2d 723 (1993).

[39]Holland v. State, 221 Ga. App. 821, 824 (1), 472 S.E.2d 711 (1996).

[40]Causey v. State, 215 Ga. App. 723, 726 (7), 452 S.E.2d 564 (1994). Accord, Holland v. State, 221 Ga. App. 821, 824 (1), 472 S.E.2d 711 (1996).

[41]Carter v. State, 160 Ga. App. 588, 287 S.E.2d 627 (1981).

[42]Brown v. State, 161 Ga. App. 544, 545 (3), 288 S.E.2d 882 (1982).

Video recorded police interrogations of criminal defendants may be a source of improper opinion which should be excluded from a jury's consideration where the interrogator offers opinions during the questioning about the credibility of the person being questioned. In such cases, if the video is offered as evidence the trial court should consider redacting any improper expression concerning the credibility of the person being interrogated. Compare Axelburg v. State, 294 Ga. App. 612, 669 S.E.2d 439 (2008) (redaction necessary), and Hames v. State, 278 Ga. 182(3), 598 S.E.2d 459 (2004) ("aggressive" interrogation technique used to test truthfulness of defendant's statements different than sworn testimony and designed only to elicit statements

disassociated from his [inculpatory] tape-recorded statement, and because the state made no attempt to use them as evidence, we hold that the failure to reduce them to writing and furnish them to the defense did not require the exclusion of the tape recording."

However, when the state offers evidence of a statement of the defendant without complying with this statute, after a proper request and when the defendant does not object, he waives his right under the statute.[43] Thus, after the state's witnesses have testified to such statements on direct and cross-examination, a motion to strike their testimony is not valid.[44] While non-compliance by the state with the statute does not result in reversal if the error is harmless,[45] the Georgia Court of Appeals has said that the burden is on the state to show that in fact the error was harmless to the defendant.[46]

Former GCA § 27-1302(e) stated the following: "The provisions of this section shall not apply to newly discovered evidence. Such evidence shall be produced as soon as possible after it has been discovered." Former O.C.G.A. § 17-7-210(e) and current § 17-16-22(e) read as follows: "This Code section shall not apply to evidence discovered after a request has been filed.[47] If a request has been filed, such evidence shall be produced as soon as possible after it has been discovered."[48] However, the newly discovered evidence exception has been held not to apply to in-custody statements made to an investigating officer where there has been a timely request for statements.[49]

Lastly, it must be kept in mind that the failure of the district attorney to respond to a timely demand does not prevent the defendant from being tried again and the same evidence used

---

from defendant).

[43]Henderson v. State, 162 Ga. App. 320, 323 (3), 292 S.E.2d 77 (1982).

[44]Henderson v. State, 162 Ga. App. 320, 328, 292 S.E.2d 77 (1982). See Osborne v. State, 166 Ga. App. 439, 304 S.E.2d 416 (1983).

[45]Van Kleeck v. State, 250 Ga. 551, 299 S.E.2d 735 (1983).

In Tyson v. State, 165 Ga. App. 22 (1), 299 S.E.2d 69 (1983), prior to retrial defendant made a demand for copies of statements defendant had made while in custody. While the district attorney did not respond, the defense counsel had a transcript of the prior trial.

[46]Reed v. State, 163 Ga. App. 364, 365, 295 S.E.2d 108 (1982).

[47]Hampton v. State, 162 Ga. App. 672, 674 (3), 292 S.E.2d 544 (1982). In *Hampton*, the district attorney first learned of an oral statement late Wednesday afternoon. On Friday, the morning of the trial, the district attorney gave defense counsel a synopsis of the statement. The court held that it was not error for the trial judge to admit testimony of the statement. Cf. Jenkins v. State, 167 Ga. App. 840, 843 (2), 308 S.E.2d 14 (1983).

[48]See Ellison v. State, 158 Ga. App. 419, 420 (3), 280 S.E.2d 371 (1981), overruled on other grounds by Talley v. State, 251 Ga. 42, 302 S.E.2d 355 (1983).

[49]Talley v. State, 251 Ga. 42, 302 S.E.2d 355 (1983).

against the defendant if the district attorney has complied with the statute.[50]

§ 14:30 Other statutory discovery, misdemeanor cases— Scientific reports

Former O.C.G.A. § 17-7-211 (former GCA § 27-1303), which forms the basis for this section of this book, was repealed and re-enacted without substantial change as O.C.G.A. § 17-16-23 as of January 1, 1995. This statute now applies to misdemeanor cases and felony cases docketed before January 11, 1995. Case law decided under O.C.G.A. § 17-7-110 remains generally applicable to cases decided since its repeal. See § 14:15, supra, on the right of the prosecution and defense to inspect and copy reports of any physical or mental examinations and of scientific tests or experiments under the new reciprocal discovery statutes applicable to felony cases.

The Code provides that a defendant may request in writing a copy of any written scientific reports available to the prosecution.[1] Such a request "should give the state reasonable notice that the defense desires the disclosure of all available scientific reports no later than ten days before trial; this notice would be adequate if the defense specifically refers to § 27-1303 [O.C.G.A. § 17-16-23], or if it makes clear that scientific reports, whether inculpatory or exculpatory, should be furnished prior to the ten-day limit."[2] Thus, it has been held that there was no sufficient demand under this statute where there was a Brady motion or a notice to produce, requesting "[r]esults of any scientific tests, experiments or studies made in connection with the . . . case and copies of all such reports . . . [s]ufficiently in advance of trial to give the defendant a reasonable opportunity to prepare a proper defense."[3]

The statute provides that this request should be made at ar-

---

[50]Tyson v. State, 165 Ga. App. 22 (1), 299 S.E.2d 69 (1983) (dicta).

[Section 14:30]

[1]In Billings v. State, 161 Ga. App. 500, 501 (3), 288 S.E.2d 622 (1982), overruled on other grounds by Bangs v. State, 198 Ga. App. 404, 401 S.E.2d 599 (1991), the state in rebuttal used a forensic scientist to establish that the deceased was shot in the back at a distance of more than two feet. The defendant had testified that the pistol was against the victim at the time the shot was fired. The district attorney stated that he had not intended to use the expert when the trial began. The district attorney had no scientific report at the time the trial began, and there was nothing to suggest bad faith on his part. The court affirmed the action of the trial judge in permitting the expert to testify despite the district attorney's not having given defense counsel a copy of a scientific report of the expert's findings pursuant to the defendant's demand.

[2]State v. Meminger, 249 Ga. 561, 563 (1), 292 S.E.2d 681 (1982); Dunn v. State, 251 Ga. 731, 732 (2), 309 S.E.2d 370 (1983).

[3]State v. Madigan, 249 Ga. 571, 573 (2), 292 S.E.2d 406 (1982). Cf. Massey v. State, 251 Ga. 515, 516 (2),

raignment or within any reasonable time prior to trial. "What is reasonable is in the sound discretion of the trial judge . . . . Nothing in the statute indicates the report becomes non-discoverable solely because a request is untimely. Obviously, the ten day time period may be reduced if ten days are not available either because the defendant delays the request, or because indictment or arraignment occurs within ten days of trial. The defendant is nonetheless entitled to production within such time as is reasonable. If the prosecuting attorney furnishes a copy but not in the time frame specified, there is nothing in the statute to require exclusion of the document from evidence. Perhaps late furnishing of a copy will mean the defendant is entitled to a continuance or recess. . . ."[4] O.C.G.A. § 17-7-110 provides that all pretrial motions, demurrers and special pleas shall be filed within 10 days after arraignment.

O.C.G.A. § 17-7-211 (now O.C.G.A. § 17-16-23) provides that " 'written scientific reports' includes, but is not limited to, reports from the Division of Forensic Sciences of the Georgia Bureau of Investigation; an autopsy report by the coroner of a county or by a private pathologist; blood alcohol test results done by a law enforcement agency or a private physician; and similar types of reports that would be used as scientific evidence by the prosecution. . . ." However, in *State v. Mulkey,*[5] the court indicates, if it does not hold, that the statute was limited to "tests which generally are carried out during the course of the investigation of a crime." Thus, in an arson case the court concluded that the statute did not apply to "ignition tests . . . . [which] did not originate in the state's investigation and preparation for trial, and merely constituted a portion of the body of scientific experience, training, and knowledge. . . ."[6] In *Conklin v. State,*[7] the court held that the statute did not apply to a death certificate or "the failure to provide public information to which the defendant already had access." In *Wester v. State,*[8] the defendant filed a motion to obtain a copy of the report of an expert fingerprint witness. This report was provided to the defense. However, the state did not provide the defendant with a written report of the officer who actually lifted the fingerprints. The report of the expert referred

---

307 S.E.2d 489 (1983) (Brady motion).

[4]Law v. State, 251 Ga. 525, 527, 307 S.E.2d 904 (1983), disapproving State v. Meminger, 249 Ga. 561, 292 S.E.2d 681 (1982), and State v. Madigan, 249 Ga. 571, 292 S.E.2d 406 (1982).

[5]State v. Mulkey, 252 Ga. 201, 203, 312 S.E.2d 601 (1984), rev'g 167 Ga. App. 627, 629 (4), 307 S.E.2d 117

(1983); Kosal v. State, 204 Ga. App. 708, 712 (4), 420 S.E.2d 621 (1992).

[6]State v. Mulkey, 252 Ga. 201, 203, 312 S.E.2d 601 (1984), rev'g 167 Ga. App. 627, 629 (4), 307 S.E.2d 117 (1983).

[7]Conklin v. State, 254 Ga. 558, 566 (3)(a), 331 S.E.2d 532 (1985).

[8]Wester v. State, 205 Ga. App. 336, 422 S.E.2d 433 (1992).

to the officer's report. The defendant contends that the officer and the expert should not have been allowed to testify. The court concluded that the officer's report was not a scientific report and the state was not obligated to present it to the defendant. In *Hullander v. State*,[9] the court also held a "police report was not an official scientific report, but merely a recordation of what the officer recollected" to which the defendant had no early disclosure rights. In the 1997 case of *Harmon v. State*,[10] involving the "new" O.C.G.A. § 17-16-23(a), the court held that a certificate of inspection required by O.C.G.A. § 40-6-392(f) is not a written scientific report; however, the results of a defendant's blood test should have been provided to the defendant. The printed results of a gas chromatograph analysis of a defendant's blood is discoverable under O.C.G.A. § 40-6-392(a)(4).[11]

In *Ramsey v. State*,[12] the court held that a letter of transmittal is not a scientific report and in *Walker v. State*,[13] the court held that a computer print-out which was an internal document of the Crime Lab was not a "scientific report," even though it was attached to the report used by the employee from the lab. Likewise, in *Williams v. State*[14] the court held that graphs were not scientific reports where they did not contain conclusions of a scientist, but which "had to be interpreted" by him in order to attain significance. In *Causey v. State*,[15] the court held that "x-rays [are] not discoverable as written scientific reports" when they do not contain a doctor's conclusions and findings but must be interpreted by a doctor to attain significance. However, in *Taylor v.*

---

[9]Hullander v. State, 271 Ga. 580, 581 (2), 522 S.E.2d 658 (1999).

[10]Harmon v. State, 224 Ga. App. 890, 893 (3)(a), (b), 482 S.E.2d 730 (1997); Fantasia v. State, 268 Ga. 512, 515 (4), 491 S.E.2d 318 (1997) (overruled on other grounds by, Olevik v. State, 302 Ga. 228, 806 S.E.2d 505 (2017)).

[11]Price v. State, 269 Ga. 222, 498 S.E.2d 262 (1998). However, allowing an expert to testify about the results of such an analysis where the state has failed to provide the printout despite a proper request therefor will not constitute reversible error in the absence of prejudice to the defendant or bad faith on the part of the prosecutor. Birdsall v. State, 254 Ga. App. 555, 562 S.E.2d 841 (2002).

In Massey v. State, 331 Ga. App. 430, 771 S.E.2d 122 (2015), the court affirmed a decision denying a defendant's discovery request pursuant to O.C.G.A. § 40-6-392(a)(4) where the defendant refused to submit to a blood test and sought discovery of test results and other data generated from a compelled blood test obtained through a search warrant. The defendant failed to preserve for appeal and the court declined to consider whether the denial of such discovery amounts to a denial of due process.

[12]Ramsey v. State, 165 Ga. App. 854, 856, 303 S.E.2d 32 (1983).

[13]Walker v. State, 168 Ga. App. 130, 131 (3), 308 S.E.2d 404 (1983).

[14]Williams v. State, 251 Ga. 749, 754, 312 S.E.2d 40 (1983); Cothran v. State, 177 Ga. App. 58, 60 (3), 338 S.E.2d 513 (1985).

[15]Causey v. State, 215 Ga. App. 723, 726 (8), 452 S.E.2d 564 (1994).

State,[16] the court held that the report of a polygraph examiner should have been produced even though the defendant had stipulated the admissibility of the results of the examination. In *Griffin v. State,*[17] the court held that a latent fingerprint card was not a scientific report. Likewise, dental impressions and x-rays[18] as well as photographs[19] have been held not to be discoverable as scientific reports; but, in *Worth v. State,*[20] the court held that "the emergency room record of the exam" is included in the statute. In *Paggett v. State,*[21] the court held that an emergency room record is a scientific report, but where the record originated with a neutral third person and the defendant knows of the report and has an equal opportunity to obtain the report, it is not a violation of the statute for the state to fail to produce the report. In *Mercer v. State,*[22] the court made the questionable passing remark that a chart enlargement of a fingerprint was not discoverable since it was regarded as "work product." In *Thompson v. State,*[23] the court pointed out that generally interim papers generated in the course of scientific examination "are not discoverable, for they are merely internal documents of the examining agency and products of the examiner's work as it is being undertaken." In *Pierce v. State,*[24] the court held that the state is not required "to furnish defendant with its expert's notes, work product, recordation of data, internal documents, or graphs."

In *Renschen v. State,*[25] the court held that a certificate of inspection showing that an Intoxilyzer 5000 had been examined by the Division of Forensic Sciences of the GBI was not generated in the course of the state's investigation of the crime with which the defendant was accused and was not a "scientific report" as used in O.C.G.A. § 17-16-23. In *Ratliff v. State,*[26] the court held that the statute relating to scientific reports applied to a printout of an intoximeter breath test to prove the defendant's intoxication,

---

[16]Taylor v. State, 172 Ga. App. 408, 409 (2), 323 S.E.2d 212 (1984).

[17]Griffin v. State, 183 Ga. App. 386, 387 (1), 358 S.E.2d 917 (1987).

[18]Harris v. State, 260 Ga. 860, 864 (4), 401 S.E.2d 263 (1991).

[19]Taylor v. State, 261 Ga. 287, 292 (6)(a), 404 S.E.2d 255 (1991).

[20]Worth v. State, 183 Ga. App. 68, 71 (2)(a), 358 S.E.2d 251 (1987).

[21]Paggett v. State, 188 Ga. App. 174, 175, 372 S.E.2d 504 (1988).

[22]Mercer v. State, 169 Ga. App. 723, 728 (4), 314 S.E.2d 729 (1984).

[23]Thompson v. State, 175 Ga. App. 645, 649 (4), 334 S.E.2d 312 (1985).

[24]Pierce v. State, 209 Ga. App. 366, 367 (2), 433 S.E.2d 641 (1993).

[25]Renschen v. State, 225 Ga. App. 678, 679 (3), 484 S.E.2d 753 (1997). Cf. Self v. State, 232 Ga. App. 735, 736 (3), 503 S.E.2d 625 (1998).

[26]Ratliff v. State, 207 Ga. App. 112, 113, 427 S.E.2d 85 (1993). Cf. Lewis v. State, 215 Ga. App. 486, 489 (4), 451 S.E.2d 116 (1994). See State v. Fen Yue Tan, 305 Ga. App. 55, 699 S.E.2d 74 (2010) (intoxilyzer test slip which shows no result because of an insufficient breath sample is not a scientific report subject to discovery under O.C.G.A. § 17-16-23).

but a notation of the test results on the traffic ticket given to the defendant is sufficient. In *Vincent v. State*,[27] there was a question of whether the prosecutor served defense counsel with intoxilyzer test results. The court pointed out that since the defendant had been provided with a copy of test results at the time of the test, the defendant was not harmed by any failure to serve defense counsel with the results. Furthermore, in *Prindle v. State*,[28] the court recognized that "horizontal gaze nystagmus" (HGN) test results are discoverable as scientific reports while "certificates of inspections" of breath test machines are not.

The obligation of the prosecution, upon request, is to supply defense counsel with copies of such reports. However, in *Brown v. State*,[29] the court held that the district attorney complies with this obligation when he delivers copies of the reports which he has or are available to him. In *Alexander v. State*,[30] the court held that a scientific report in the possession of the crime laboratory is available to the district attorney. In *Alexander*, the trial judge was reversed for admitting scientific testimony on the subject matter of the report where a copy of the report was delivered to defense counsel the morning of the trial even though the district attorney had earlier served defense counsel with "a handwritten statement that the crime lab report indicated a trace of cocaine." Hence, under certain circumstances the statute has been said to be complied with, even if the report is in part illegible.[31] Likewise, defense counsel may not validly object to an expert witness testifying to various tests which he made where this information is not included in the scientific report.[32]

The statute provides that failure to furnish the defendant with a copy of the report after a proper and timely written demand shall result in the report being excluded and suppressed from evidence in the prosecution's case-in-chief and in rebuttal. In addition, both the Georgia Supreme Court[33] and Court of Appeals[34] have held that the failure to supply defense counsel with a copy

---

[27]Vincent v. State, 228 Ga. App. 691 (1), 492 S.E.2d 604 (1997).

[28]Prindle v. State, 240 Ga. App. 461, 463 (3), 523 S.E.2d 44 (1999).

[29]Brown v. State, 161 Ga. App. 544 (1), 288 S.E.2d 882 (1982).

[30]Alexander v. State, 203 Ga. App. 375, 376, 416 S.E.2d 762 (1992).

[31]Brown v. State, 161 Ga. App. 544 (1), 288 S.E.2d 882 (1982).

[32]Hartline v. State, 161 Ga. App. 847, 848 (2), 288 S.E.2d 902 (1982); Ramsey v. State, 165 Ga. App. 854,

856, 303 S.E.2d 32 (1983). See Metts v. State, 162 Ga. App. 641, 291 S.E.2d 405 (1982).

[33]Wester v. State, 260 Ga. 228, 391 S.E.2d 765 (1990); State v. Madigan, 249 Ga. 571, 573, 292 S.E.2d 406 (1982). Cf. Crowe v. State, 265 Ga. 582, 587 (7), 458 S.E.2d 799 (1995) (no error where prosecutor gave defendant open access to its files and permitted him to photocopy anything contained therein).

[34]Tanner v. State, 160 Ga. App. 266, 268, 287 S.E.2d 268 (1981).

of such a report, pursuant to a timely demand, also prevents the scientist who prepared the report from testifying over timely objection. In *Tanner v. State*,[35] the court compared any other interpretation of the statute as making it "a toothless tiger" or "a fish that cannot swim." The state argued unsuccessfully that the failure to produce an autopsy report only prevented the report from being introduced in evidence. Thus, in *Metts v. State*,[36] the court held that it was error for the trial judge to admit the testimony of the experts who performed the tests involved where the defendant had properly requested copies of scientific reports under this statute and was not supplied with the report, even though the report was not offered in evidence. Furthermore, in *Carson v. State*,[37] the court said the state "should limit its examination of its forensic witness to the material contained in the scientific report given to the defendant. . . ."

Presumably, the failure of the district attorney in response to a timely demand to furnish defense counsel with a copy of such a report does not *in the absence of an objection* prevent an expert from testifying about his examination.[38] However, in *Asbell v. State*,[39] the court held that when a proper request has been made and the report is not given to defense counsel until the morning of the trial, it is error to overrule a motion for continuance and to permit the expert to testify where the expert's testimony is vital to the state's case. In *Horne v. State*,[40] the court held that even though there is a timely demand, "there is nothing in the statute to require exclusion of the document from evidence" because of a tardy compliance with the demand.

---

[35]Tanner v. State, 160 Ga. App. 266, 267, 287 S.E.2d 268 (1981) (quoting Garner v. State, 159 Ga. App. 244, 282 S.E.2d 909 (1981)). Accord, Metts v. State, 162 Ga. App. 641, 291 S.E.2d 405 (1982).

In State v. Madigan, 249 Ga. 571, 572, 292 S.E.2d 406 (1982), the Georgia Supreme Court expressly approved *Tanner v. State*.

In Odom v. State, 248 Ga. 434, 283 S.E.2d 885 (1981), the Georgia Supreme Court found it unnecessary to pass on the issue decided in *Tanner*, but did discuss some of the pros and cons of the *Tanner* rule. Meminger v. State, 160 Ga. App. 509, 511 (6), 287 S.E.2d 296 (1981), was reversed in State v. Meminger, 249 Ga. 561, 564, 292 S.E.2d 681 (1982), because the request was not timely filed. Madigan

v. State, 160 Ga. App. 656, 288 S.E.2d 34 (1981), was reversed in State v. Madigan, 249 Ga. 571, 573 (2), 292 S.E.2d 406 (1982), because there was no proper request filed pursuant to the statute.

[36]Metts v. State, 162 Ga. App. 641, 643 (5), 291 S.E.2d 405 (1982).

[37]Carson v. State, 192 Ga. App. 52, 53 (1), 383 S.E.2d 619 (1989).

[38]Cf. Henderson v. State, 162 Ga. App. 320, 323, 292 S.E.2d 77 (1982); McDaniel v. State, 169 Ga. App. 254, 255 (3), 312 S.E.2d 363 (1983).

[39]Asbell v. State, 163 Ga. App. 514 (1), 295 S.E.2d 182 (1982).

[40]Horne v. State, 192 Ga. App. 528, 532 (4), 385 S.E.2d 704 (1989).

In *Wellborn v. State*,[41] the court held that the "statute does not prohibit the prosecution from introducing evidence of scientific tests performed immediately prior to or during the trial absent a showing that the prosecution attempted to circumvent the discovery process."

In *Luck v. State*,[42] the court emphasized that the district attorney must comply with the statute if the report is *available* to him. If the report is in the possession of the crime lab, it is regarded as being available to the district attorney even if he does not actually have the report. Thus, where a request was timely made and the district attorney received an oral report from the crime lab which was relayed to defense counsel and the district attorney did not actually get the report until the day before the trial and a copy was given to defense counsel on the morning of trial, it was held to be error to permit testimony connected with the report. Likewise, in *Walls v. State*,[43] the court pointed out that the oral communication of the contents of a scientific report to defense counsel is not a substantial compliance with the statute.

However, in *Durden v. State*,[44] decided in 1988, the court held that it was error for the trial judge, over objection, to permit a forensic witness to testify at length as to test results which were not stated in the crime lab report. The opinion pointed out that "when the State or its witness chooses to leave out of its 'written report' the quantifying substance of the forensic case against the defendant, the prejudice to the defendant in being denied his discovery rights under O.C.G.A. § 17-7-211 is the same whether done in bad faith or not. . . . The failure to produce this evidence in the 'written scientific report' left the defense counsel at a huge disadvantage in trying to cross-examine the State's witness as to the implications of these test results and the formation of her opinion based upon them." The *Durden* case was affirmed by the Georgia Supreme Court.

In *Law v. State*,[45] the court held that if there is "no writing, there is nothing to which the statute attaches." The statute is not "intended to deal with oral reports." Thus, the statute has been

---

[41]Wellborn v. State, 258 Ga. 570, 572 (1), 372 S.E.2d 220 (1988); Hand v. State, 206 Ga. App. 501, 503 (4), 426 S.E.2d 18 (1992).

[42]Luck v. State, 163 Ga. App. 657, 658 (2), 295 S.E.2d 584 (1982); Heard v. State, 170 Ga. App. 130, 134 (10), 316 S.E.2d 504 (1984).

[43]Walls v. State, 169 Ga. App. 80, 82 (1), 311 S.E.2d 243 (1983).

[44]Durden v. State, 187 Ga. App. 154, 157, 369 S.E.2d 764 (1988), aff'd, 258 Ga. 720, 375 S.E.2d 610 (1988).

[45]Law v. State, 251 Ga. 525, 528 (2), 307 S.E.2d 904 (1983); Hair v. State, 262 Ga. 284, 417 S.E.2d 657 (1992); Gay v. State, 228 Ga. App. 248, 249, 491 S.E.2d 469 (1997); Brown v. State, 268 Ga. 354, 359 (5), 490 S.E.2d 75 (1997).

held not to apply to a fingerprint taken from a defendant at the jail at an overnight recess during a trial where the prints were not shown to the expert until the following day and there was no opportunity for the expert to prepare a report.[46] Likewise, in 1994, in *Harley v. State*,[47] the Georgia Supreme Court unanimously affirmed the trial court holding that a luminal test need not be produced under O.C.G.A. § 17-7-211 since it was never reduced to writing. However, the Georgia Supreme Court has apparently not ruled on the question of whether the statute is "violated if a district attorney knows of the results of a scientific experiment and specifically instructs the examiner or expert not to reduce his writings to the form of a written report."[48]

Some cases have indicated that the harmless error rule applies to the failure of the district attorney to supply a copy of a scientific report pursuant to a timely request,[49] and other cases have indicated that the harmless error rule does not apply.[50] In *Carey v. State*,[51] the Georgia Supreme Court refused to apply a harmless error rule and said that where the trial judge offered the defense a continuance of one week, which was declined, it was not error to admit evidence of a report at a trial which began on September 29 when the district attorney did not get the report until September 26 and it was delivered to the defense on the same day.

In *Osborne v. State*,[52] the court held that when a conviction is reversed because a laboratory technician was permitted to testify, even though a copy of his report had not been furnished to defense counsel, this does not prevent the defendant from being re-tried and does not prevent the admission of such testimony on retrial if defense counsel is properly furnished a copy of such report.

The Georgia statute is limited to requiring the district attorney, pursuant to request, to supply a copy of a report.[53] Thus, the statute does not require the district attorney to supply defense

---

[46]Lemons v. State, 167 Ga. App. 863, 864 (5), 307 S.E.2d 747 (1983).

[47]Harley v. State, 263 Ga. 875, 878 (4), 440 S.E.2d 178 (1994).

[48]Williams v. State, 251 Ga. 749, 753 n. 1, 312 S.E.2d 40 (1983).

In McDaniel v. State, 169 Ga. App. 254, 255 (3), 312 S.E.2d 363 (1983), the court pointed out that there was nothing to indicate bad faith on the part of the prosecution.

[49]Mackler v. State, 164 Ga. App. 874, 876 (3), 298 S.E.2d 589 (1982). In *Mackler*, the physician had testified at the previous trial of the case and the

defendant knew the testimony would be given; the court pointed out that the defendant could not have been harmed. Cf. Prater v. State, 171 Ga. App. 122 (1), 318 S.E.2d 816 (1984).

[50]Metts v. State, 162 Ga. App. 641, 643 (5), 291 S.E.2d 405 (1982).

[51]Carey v. State, 257 Ga. 134, 135 (3), 356 S.E.2d 507 (1987).

[52]Osborne v. State, 166 Ga. App. 439, 304 S.E.2d 416 (1983). See Henderson v. State, 162 Ga. App. 320, 292 S.E.2d 77 (1982).

[53]Law v. State, 251 Ga. 525, 528 (2), 307 S.E.2d 904 (1983); Perry v.

counsel with information concerning the method utilized in conducting an examination or the names of the persons handling or conducting an examination.[54] However, in *Box v. State*,[55] involving a driving under the influence case, the court held that the results of a chemical test were inadmissible where the crime laboratory report presented to the defendant did not show the actual test results.

In *Owens v. State*,[56] the court pointed out that the improper non-production of a scientific report only results in "the exclusion of the evidence" and does not require the grant of a motion for a mistrial.

In *Sabel v. State*,[57] the Georgia Supreme Court seems to hold that where a trial judge pursuant to court order allows an expert employed on behalf of the defendant to examine physical objects which the state has, the judge may, or perhaps should, direct that the expert supply the district attorney as well as the defendant with a copy of his report. However, in *Rower v. State*,[58] the court limited *Sabel* to hold that "the state is entitled only to those discovery rights specifically granted to the defendant by O.C.G.A. § 17-7-211." Thus, "[t]he state may discover any written reports of [the defendant's] experts which [the defendant] intends to introduce at trial . . . . With regard to the state's right to call [the defendant's] expert witnesses as its own, or to argue the inference arising from [the defendant's] failure to call his own experts," the "state is put to an election" to *either* argue the inference arising from the failure to call the witness *or to call the expert as a witness for the state*.[59] See Studdard, *Daniel's Georgia Handbook on Criminal Evidence* (2018 ed.), § 7:9.

State, 255 Ga. 490, 492 (3), 339 S.E.2d 922 (1986).

[54]Sears v. State, 161 Ga. App. 515, 288 S.E.2d 757 (1982). See Brown v. State, 161 Ga. App. 544, 288 S.E.2d 882 (1982).

[55]Box v. State, 187 Ga. App. 260, 370 S.E.2d 28 (1988); Camarata v. State, 188 Ga. App. 41, 42 (1), 371 S.E.2d 885 (1988).

[56]Owens v. State, 204 Ga. App. 5, 6 (1), 418 S.E.2d 631 (1992).

[57]Sabel v. State, 248 Ga. 10, 17 (6), 282 S.E.2d 61 (1981). In *Sabel*, the court said, "[W]e find that requiring the report of the defendant's expert to be reduced to writing and made available to the state will further the search for the truth. If the defendant does not call the expert as a witness, the state may call the defendant's expert without adding his or her name to the list of witnesses, or may argue to the jury that the defendant would have called the expert had the result of the testing been favorable to the defendant."

[58]Rower v. State, 264 Ga. 323, 325 (5), 443 S.E.2d 839 (1994); Thornton v. State, 264 Ga. 563, 574 (16), 449 S.E.2d 98 (1994); Childress v. State, 266 Ga. 425, 432 (3), 467 S.E.2d 865 (1996); Freeman v. State, 268 Ga. 185, 187 (3), 486 S.E.2d 348 (1997).

[59]Blige v. State, 264 Ga. 166, 168, 441 S.E.2d 752 (1994).

In *Johnson v. State*,[60] the trial judge issued an order requiring the defendant "to disclose the names and addresses of all experts whom he intends to call at trial and to have the opinions of all testifying experts reduced to writing and supplied to the state . . . ." The Supreme Court held that under *Rower* "the state is entitled *only* to those *existing,* written scientific reports which the defense intends to introduce." (Emphasis added.) "[T]he court's order is erroneous to the extent that it requires the defense to reduce unwritten opinions to writing and to produce written reports which it does not intend to introduce at trial."

See § 14:14, supra, on the defendant's right to have an expert examine and analyze physical objects.

§ 14:31 Discovery in juvenile court

O.C.G.A. §§ 15-11-541, et seq., allows for limited discovery in an action against a juvenile. The juvenile, upon written request to the prosecution or party having actual custody, control, or possession of the material to be produced, shall have full access to the complaint, the petition, the names and last known addresses of each witness, any written or oral statements of the child or any witness, except the work product of counsel, any scientific or other reports intended to be introduced at the hearing or that pertains to physical evidence to be introduced, and photographs and physical evidence that is intended to be introduced at the hearing. If the child makes such a request, the State is entitled to names, addresses, and telephone numbers of witnesses for the defense, any written statements made by such witnesses, any scientific or other report, photographs, and any physical evidence to be introduced at the hearing. A request for discovery or reciprocal discovery shall be complied with no later than 48 hours before the adjudicatory hearing. If a request is made less than 48 hours before such a hearing, the discovery response should be made in a timely manner.

O.C.G.A. § 15-11-543 provides that upon written request by the prosecution the juvenile shall produce "a written notice of the child's intention to offer a defense of alibi." The child will also furnish the prosecution with "the place or places at which the child claims to have been at the time of the delinquent act" and any witness upon whom the child intends to rely in order to establish such an alibi. A request must be complied with promptly and not later than 48 hours before the hearing. If the request is made fewer than 48 hours before trial the alibi evidence shall be produced in a timely fashion. In response the prosecution must

---

[60]Johnson v. State, 265 Ga. 833, 834, 463 S.E.2d 123 (1995); Fielding v. State, 266 Ga. 26, 463 S.E.2d 489 (1995).

furnish the child with all the witnesses upon whom the state intends to rely on to rebut the child's evidence of alibi. If the child "withdraws the notice of intention to rely upon an alibi defense, the notice and intention to rely on an alibi defense are inadmissible," however, the prosecution may offer any other evidence regarding the alibi.

O.C.G.A. § 15-11-542 provides that if a request for discovery is refused, an application for a court order compelling discovery can be made. The court may deny, otherwise limit or set conditions concerning the discovery if the party against whom discovery is sought can sufficiently show that discovery would: "(1) [j]eopardize the safety of a party, witness, or confidential informant (2) [c]reate a substantial threat of physical or economic harm to a witness or other person (3) [e]ndanger physical evidence (4) disclose privileged information [or] (5) [i]mpede the criminal prosecution of a minor who is being prosecuted as an adult or an adult who is being prosecuted for an offense arising out of the same transaction or occurrence." However, nothing "shall prohibit the court from ordering the disclosure of any information that the court deems necessary and appropriate for proper adjudication."

O.C.G.A. § 15-11-545 provides that if either side fails to comply with a court order under this section, the court may grant a continuance, may prohibit the violating party from introducing into evidence any information not disclosed, or enter such an order as the court deems just under the circumstances. All information given to the child shall remain in that child's exclusive custody.

§ 14:32 Discovery—By prosecution

It must be kept in mind that the Georgia Constitution provides that no person "shall be compelled to give testimony tending in any manner to incriminate himself."[1] Also, no party is required to discover matters tending to incriminate himself.[2] However, in *Williams v. Florida*,[3] the United States Supreme Court found the reciprocal discovery provisions of the Florida statute to be valid under the federal Constitution.

Generally see an annotation entitled, "Right of Prosecution to Pretrial Discovery, Inspection, and Disclosure," 96 A.L.R.2d 1224 (1964).

[Section 14:32]

[1]Ga. Const. 1983, Art. I, § I, ¶ XVI. See also O.C.G.A. § 24-5-505.

[2]O.C.G.A. § 24-5-505.

[3]Williams v. Florida, 399 U.S. 78, 90 S.Ct. 1893, 26 L.Ed.2d 446 (1970).

§ 14:33   Discovery—Brady motion—Background

In *Brady v. Maryland*,[1] the United States Supreme Court established that the prosecution has a constitutional duty to disclose certain information to the defense. Brady requested that the district attorney give him copies of statements made by a co-defendant. Although several statements made by the co-defendant were given to Brady, one statement, in which the co-defendant admitted to being the "trigger-man," was not provided. Brady, who was tried first, admitted participation, but denied actually doing the shooting. After Brady's conviction, the defense learned of the statement they had not received. The court held that failure by the prosecution to disclose this statement to the defense was a violation of the Due Process Clause of the Fourteenth Amendment of the United States Constitution because the defense specifically requested the evidence and was, therefore, entitled to it as long as it "would tend to exculpate him or reduce the penalty."

The Brady rule grew out of the prosecution's constitutional duty to reveal any use of perjured testimony. In *Mooney v. Holohan*,[2] and its progeny, the United States Supreme Court ruled that the knowing use of perjured testimony must be disclosed to the defense. When the prosecution knowingly allows a witness to create a false impression, a violation of the Due Process Clause of the Fourteenth Amendment results unless the prosecution informs the defense. For example, in *Napue v. Illinois*,[3] the United States Supreme Court held that a conviction was invalid where a prosecutor failed to inform the defense a witness testified falsely regarding whether he had received promises of consideration in exchange for his testimony.

In *Giglio v. United States*,[4] the United States Supreme Court held that even when one prosecutor was not aware that another prosecutor had made a deal with a witness, disclosure of the witness' false testimony concerning the deal is still required. See § 14:34, infra, on scope of revelation. The court suggested that procedures should be developed by the prosecution to prevent further Giglio-type problems.

[Section 14:33]

[1]Brady v. Maryland, 373 U.S. 83, 83 S.Ct. 1194, 10 L.Ed.2d 215 (1963). See also A.B.A. Standards, Discovery and Procedure Before Trial, §§ 11-2.1 and 11-2.6. Cf. Chavis v. North Carolina, 637 F.2d 213 (4th Cir. 1980).

[2]Mooney v. Holohan, 294 U.S. 103, 55 S.Ct. 340, 79 L.Ed. 791 (1935). See also Pyle v. Kansas, 317 U.S. 213,

63 S.Ct. 177, 87 L.Ed. 214 (1942); Alcorta v. Texas, 355 U.S. 28, 78 S.Ct. 103, 2 L.Ed.2d 9 (1957); Napue v. Illinois, 360 U.S. 264, 79 S.Ct. 1173, 3 L.Ed.2d 1217 (1959).

[3]Napue v. Illinois, 360 U.S. 264, 79 S.Ct. 1173, 3 L.Ed.2d 1217 (1959).

[4]Giglio v. United States, 405 U.S. 150, 92 S.Ct. 763, 31 L.Ed.2d 104 (1972).

In the 2000 case of *Byrd v. Owen*,[5] the Georgia Supreme Court in effect granted a petition for habeas corpus where the state had failed to respond to a Brady motion by failing to reveal where (1) "the State's immunity agreement with its primary trial witness had [not] been disclosed as required . . . there is a substantial likelihood that the outcome of the trial could have been different; and . . . [2] concealment of the agreement interfered with counsel's ability to render effective assistance at trial and on appeal."

The Supreme Court of the United States clarified the Brady rule in *United States v. Agurs*.[6] In *Agurs*, the Court divided Brady material into three categories. First, as in *Mooney*, the prosecution is required to disclose any perjured testimony used by the prosecution. Second, in the case of a specific request for information which is material to the issue of guilt, the prosecution has a duty to provide the requested evidence. Third, in the case of a general request for exculpatory evidence, or no request at all, the prosecutor maintains a duty to disclose any "evidence [which] is obviously of such substantial value to the defense that elementary fairness requires it to be disclosed even without a specific request." Quoting *Berger v. United States*,[7] the Court held that a prosecutor has a two-fold aim, which is "that guilt shall not escape or innocence suffer."

In *United States v. Bagley*,[8] the United States Supreme Court explained the standard for materiality in Brady challenges. The court held:

> The evidence is material only if there is a reasonable probability that, had the evidence been disclosed to the defense, the result of the proceeding would have been different. A "reasonable probability" is a probability sufficient to undermine confidence in the outcome.[9]

This standard applies to the disclosure of evidence in both the guilt and the sentencing phases of trial. It also applies equally to exculpatory and impeachment evidence. In addition, *Brady* material need not be "admissible" evidence. "[I]nadmissible evidence may be material [under *Brady*] if it could have led to the discovery

---

[5]Byrd v. Owen, 272 Ga. 807, 536 S.E.2d 736 (2000).

[6]United States v. Agurs, 427 U.S. 97, 96 S.Ct. 2392, 49 L.Ed.2d 342 (1976). Accord, Williams v. State, 250 Ga. 463, 465, 298 S.E.2d 492 (1983).

[7]Berger v. United States, 295 U.S. 78, 88, 55 S.Ct. 629, 79 L.Ed. 1314 (1935).

[8]United States v. Bagley, 473 U.S. 667, 105 S.Ct. 3375, 87 L.Ed.2d 481 (1985).

[9]United States v. Bagley, 473 U.S. 667, 682, 105 S.Ct. 3375, 87 L.Ed.2d 481 (1985).

of [material] admissible evidence."[10]

In *Kyles v. Whitley*,[11] the Supreme Court of the United States explained that there are four "aspects of materiality" under *Brady*. First is an assessment of whether a reasonable probability exists that, but for the failure of the prosecution to disclose the exculpatory evidence, a different result would have occurred. Second, that this assessment is not a test of the sufficiency of the evidence to support a conviction. Third, that if a violation is material, it cannot be harmless error. And fourth, that all the evidence must be viewed collectively in determining the existence of the reasonable probability. The court in *Kyles* also held that evidence known only to the police may be covered by *Brady*. (Cf. § 14:37, infra.) In order to comply with *Brady*, the prosecution "remains responsible for gauging [the cumulative effect of all undisclosed evidence] regardless of any failure by the police to bring favorable evidence to the prosecutor's attention."

In *Wood v. Bartholomew*,[12] the United States Supreme Court, in a five to four decision, held that no Brady violation occurs when the prosecution withholds the results of a polygraph examination indicating deception by a state's witness. In making this determination, the Court held that the assumption that the information would lead to admissible evidence was "mere speculation," and the information itself was not admissible and, therefore, "not 'evidence' at all." The court also mentioned the "overwhelming evidence" against Bartholomew.

In contrast, the Supreme Court remanded the case of *Banks v. Dretke*,[13] where the state's key witness, who had been "intensively coached" by prosecutors, testified in court that he had not spoken to anyone about his testimony, and had not talked to the prosecutor until a few days before the trial. The prosecutor not only failed to correct the witness's misrepresentation, but also proceeded to argue that the witness had been truthful.[14]

In the 1999 United States Supreme Court case of *Strickler v. Greene*,[15] the Court further explained the standard for materiality in Brady challenges. The court emphasized that the inquiry is

---

[10]Johnson v. Folino, 705 F.3d 117, 130 (3d Cir. 2013).

[11]Kyles v. Whitley, 514 U.S. 419, 115 S.Ct. 1555, 131 L.Ed.2d 490 (1995). Accord, Chaney v. State, 224 Ga. App. 663, 664, 482 S.E.2d 398 (1997).

[12]Wood v. Bartholomew, 516 U.S. 1, 116 S.Ct. 7, 133 L.Ed.2d 1 (1995).

[13]Banks v. Dretke, 540 U.S. 668, 124 S.Ct. 1256, 157 L.Ed.2d 1166 (2004).

[14]See also United States v. Scheer, 168 F.3d 445 (11th Cir. 1999), where prosecutor's failure to reveal to the defense a "threat" he made to a witness prior to that witness's testimony constituted a *Brady* violation.

[15]Strickler v. Greene, 527 U.S. 263, 119 S.Ct. 1936, 144 L.Ed.2d 286 (1999).

not based on a sufficiency of the evidence to support the verdict in light of the undisclosed evidence, nor is the standard that the defendant would *more likely than not* have received a different verdict with the suppressed evidence. To support a Brady violation, the court must find that there is a *reasonable probability* that the defendant's conviction would have been different, rendering the verdict unworthy of confidence. The court in *Strickler* held that a violation of *Brady* occurs where the suppressed, "favorable evidence could reasonably be taken to put the whole case in such a different light as to undermine confidence in the verdict."[16] The court stated that, "[t]hus the term 'Brady violation' is sometimes used to refer to any breach of the broad obligation to disclose exculpatory evidence—that is, to any suppression of so-called 'Brady material'—although, strictly speaking, there is never a real 'Brady violation' unless the nondisclosure was so serious that there is a reasonable probability that the suppressed evidence would have produced a different verdict."[17]

For Brady discovery motions, see Studdard, *Daniel's Georgia Criminal Trial Practice Forms* (2018–2019 ed.), §§ 14:17, 14:18, and 14:67.

§ 14:34 Discovery—Brady motion—Discoverable material

The United States Supreme Court in *Moore v. Illinois*[1] said, "We know of no constitutional requirement that the prosecution make a complete and detailed accounting to the defense of all police investigatory work on a case." In *Broom v. State*,[2] the court pointed out that no Georgia statute or rule of practice entitles a defendant, "as a matter of right to receive copies of police reports and investigation reports made in the course of preparing the case against a defendant. . . . " But see § 14:9, supra, on reciprocal discovery. However, the material discoverable under the Brady rule has been held to include statements favorable to the defendant.[3] More specifically, it has been held that the defendant is entitled to information on the existence of witnesses favorable

---

[16]Strickler v. Greene, 527 U.S. 263, 119 S.Ct. 1936, 144 L.Ed.2d 286, 307 (1999) (citing Kyles v. Whitley, 514 U.S. 419, 115 S.Ct. 1555, 131 L.Ed.2d 490 (1995)).

[17]Strickler v. Greene, 527 U.S. 263, 119 S.Ct. 1936, 144 L.Ed.2d 286, 302 (1999). Accord, Bolick v. State, 244 Ga. App. 567, 573 (2), 536 S.E.2d 242 (2000).

[Section 14:34]

[1]Moore v. Illinois, 408 U.S. 786,

795, 92 S.Ct. 2562, 33 L.Ed.2d 706 (1972). Cf. Morrill v. State, 216 Ga. App. 468, 472, 454 S.E.2d 796 (1995).

[2]Broom v. State, 209 Ga. App. 42, 43, 432 S.E.2d 823 (1993).

[3]Jackson v. Wainwright, 390 F.2d 288 (5th Cir. 1968). In Monroe v. Blackburn, 607 F.2d 148 (5th Cir. 1979), a witness' in-court testimony referred to hearing a noise shortly before he was robbed. In an earlier statement given police, no reference was made to a noise. The court found a *Brady* viola-

to the defendant.[4] In *Giglio v. United States*,[5] the United States Supreme Court held that a defendant is entitled to discover promises of leniency or promises of non-prosecution of a key government witness if a proper motion is filed requesting such information. In *Klinect v. State*,[6] the Georgia Supreme Court held that the state "was under an obligation to reveal any agreement it had with [a witness who had allegedly had a role in the crime] concerning future prosecution, and failure to reveal such an agreement would constitute a due process violation."

The mere fact that some information might have helped the defense or might have affected the outcome of the trial does not make it discoverable under *Brady*.[7] The defendant has the burden of showing that the evidence withheld "so impaired his defense that he was denied a fair trial within the meaning of the Brady rule."[8] Thus, it has been held that where there was a general *Brady* demand in a murder case and the defendant did not claim self-defense, it was not a violation of *Brady* for the district attorney to fail to inform the defense counsel that a knife had been found near the location of the crime.[9] As the court observed in *Gresham v. State*,[10] the general rule is that mere "speculation by [the defendant] that he 'might' have pursued a different course of action had he received the evidence earlier is not sufficient" to

---

tion requiring reversal, since the use of the statement by defense counsel may have affected the outcome of the case.

    In Hughes v. Hopper, 629 F.2d 1036 (5th Cir. 1980), the court concluded that the *Brady* rule was not violated where defense counsel failed to receive a report, but was aware of its contents.

[4]United States ex rel. Meers v. Wilkins, 326 F.2d 135 (2d Cir. 1964).

[5]Giglio v. United States, 405 U.S. 150, 92 S.Ct. 763, 31 L.Ed.2d 104 (1972); United States v. Bagley, 473 U.S. 667, 105 S.Ct. 3375, 87 L.Ed.2d 481 (1985). See Wearry v. Cain, 136 S. Ct. 1002, 1003-04, 194 L. Ed. 2d 78 (2016) (*Brady* violation where state failed to disclose identity of two witnesses who cast doubt on credibility of state's central witness and fact that state's second main witness had twice sought a "deal" in exchange for agreement to testify against defendant).

[6]Klinect v. State, 269 Ga. 570, 572 (2), 501 S.E.2d 810 (1998). In this case, there is no mention of a motion to reveal such an agreement, but the witness at a pretrial hearing testified that he had received no promise of leniency.

[7]Castell v. State, 250 Ga. 776, 781, 301 S.E.2d 234 (1983); Powell v. State, 171 Ga. App. 876, 880, 321 S.E.2d 745 (1984).

[8]Wallin v. State, 248 Ga. 29, 33, 279 S.E.2d 687 (1981); Donaldson v. State, 249 Ga. 186, 189, 289 S.E.2d 242 (1982); Rose v. State, 249 Ga. 628, 629 (1), 292 S.E.2d 678 (1982); Duncan v. State, 163 Ga. App. 148, 150, 294 S.E.2d 365 (1982); Brooks v. State, 182 Ga. App. 144, 145 (1), 355 S.E.2d 435 (1987).

[9]Smith v. State, 248 Ga. 507, 508, 284 S.E.2d 406 (1981).

[10]Gresham v. State, 265 Ga. 730, 732, 462 S.E.2d 370 (1995).

support a *Brady* violation. However, in *Nelson v. Zant*,[11] the court granted a petition for habeas corpus where a defendant had been convicted on circumstantial evidence and there had apparently been a general request for discovery and, "[u]nknown to the defense at the original trial, the hair sample had been examined not just by the expert who testified for the state at trial, but also by the FBI crime laboratory . . . [which] concluded . . . that the state's hair sample [was] 'not suitable for significant comparison purposes.' "

In *Holbrook v. State*,[12] the court held that pursuant to a Brady motion, the defense is entitled to those statements of witnesses in the custody of the district attorney which are exculpatory. However, in *Singleton v. State*,[13] the court held that "[t]he State does not suppress allegedly exculpatory evidence if that evidence is not in the State's possession." It has also been held there is no Brady violation where the prosecuting attorney fails to inform defense that a key witness has started vacillating about his testimony.[14] In *Riley v. State*,[15] the court held that if a witness was originally arrested as a suspect in the crime for which the defendant is charged, a suggestion of bias arises. Impeachment evidence showing this bias falls within the Brady rule. In *Speed v. State*,[16] the court held there was no Brady violation where the trial court permitted the state to withhold evidence that the officers who had worked with the victim were arrested over a year after the victim had been shot for committing crimes such as burglary and armed robbery. In *Gray v. State*,[17] the court pointed out that when the district attorney is aware before trial of potential contradictions, a prior contradictory statement is not discoverable as impeachment evidence until the witness testifies. Also, in *Houston v. State*,[18] the court held that there was no Brady violation where the district attorney failed to reveal to the defense that the victim was unable to identify the defendant. In *Mitchell v. State*,[19] the court held that there was no Brady violation where the three crime victims were unable to visually identify the defendant, particularly when the victims could identify the perpetrator by "another means such as by his clothing, manner,

---

[11]Nelson v. Zant, 261 Ga. 358, 360 (3), 405 S.E.2d 250 (1991).

[12]Holbrook v. State, 162 Ga. App. 400, 401, 291 S.E.2d 729 (1982).

[13]Singleton v. State, 240 Ga. App. 240, 522 S.E.2d 734 (1999), judgment vacated on other grounds, 243 Ga. App. 429, 533 S.E.2d 457 (2000).

[14]United States v. Brown, 582 F.2d 197 (2d Cir. 1978).

[15]Riley v. State, 242 Ga. App. 720, 722, 531 S.E.2d 138 (2000).

[16]Speed v. State, 270 Ga. 688, 699 (53), 512 S.E.2d 896 (1999).

[17]Gray v. State, 213 Ga. App. 507, 510 (2), 445 S.E.2d 328 (1994).

[18]Houston v. State, 187 Ga. App. 335, 338 (3), 370 S.E.2d 178 (1988).

[19]Mitchell v. State, 250 Ga. App. 292, 294 (1), 551 S.E.2d 404 (2001).

or voice." However, in *People v. Cowart*,[20] the court found that there was a Brady violation where the prosecution failed to disclose a tape-recorded interview with a key state witness which contradicted material parts of the witness' trial testimony. Likewise, in *Harridge v. State*,[21] the court held there was a Brady violation where the state failed to inform the defendant that a preliminary laboratory test from the state crime lab showed the presence of cocaine and marijuana in the victim's urine. In *Head v. Stripling*,[22] the defendant obtained habeas corpus relief when he was able to show the state had suppressed parole records which would have supported his claim of mental retardation. In *Wansley v. State*,[23] the court held that defense counsel is not entitled to obtain jury records which would disclose whether or not a potential juror had served on a jury and whether or not a jury, on which a juror served, had returned a guilty or not guilty verdict.

In *Gilreath v. State*,[24] the Georgia Supreme Court held that the state does not have to inform the defendant that evidence against the defendant was seized without a warrant. The court in *Gilreath* also held that the state has no duty under the Brady rule to produce a statement made by the defendant since the defendant is presumed to know the contents of any statement he has made.[25] But see § 14:12, supra, on obtaining the statement of a defendant. In *Henderson v. State*,[26] the court held that it is not error for a trial judge to refuse defense's motion asking that the state be required to produce rough notes made in the course of a criminal investigation. However, there is authority holding that a defendant is entitled to information concerning the existence of witnesses favorable to the defendants[27] and to records of convic-

---

[20]People v. Cowart, 114 Misc.2d 881, 452 N.Y.S.2d 774 (N.Y.Sup. 1982). See § 17:6, infra.

[21]Harridge v. State, 243 Ga. App. 658, 659 (1), 534 S.E.2d 113 (2000).

[22]Head v. Stripling, 277 Ga. 403 (1), 590 S.E.2d 122 (2003).

[23]Wansley v. State, 256 Ga. 624, 625 (2), 352 S.E.2d 368 (1987); King v. State, 273 Ga. 258, 263 (12), 539 S.E.2d 783 (2000).

[24]Gilreath v. State, 247 Ga. 814, 822 (2), 279 S.E.2d 650 (1981); Glaser v. State, 272 Ga. 757, 759 (3), 535 S.E.2d 231 (2000). Cf. Bromley v. State, 259 Ga. 377, 378 (2), 380 S.E.2d 694 (1989).

[25]Gilreath v. State, 247 Ga. 814, 826 (6), 279 S.E.2d 650 (1981); McCarty v. State, 249 Ga. 618, 620, 292 S.E.2d 700 (1982); Driver v. State, 240 Ga. App. 513, 515 (2), 523 S.E.2d 919 (1999); Williams v. State, 164 Ga. App. 148, 149 (2), 296 S.E.2d 739 (1982).

[26]Henderson v. State, 182 Ga. App. 513, 356 S.E.2d 241 (1987), judgment aff'd in part, rev'd in part on other grounds, 257 Ga. 618, 362 S.E.2d 346 (1987). Accord, McGee v. State, 272 Ga. 363 (2), 529 S.E.2d 366 (2000).

[27]United States ex rel. Meers v. Wilkins, 326 F.2d 135 (2d Cir. 1964).

tions of state witnesses to be used for purposes of impeachment.[28]

In *Ex parte Lewis*,[29] the Texas Court of Criminal Appeals held that a prosecutor had a duty to disclose evidence he had on the defendant's competency. There is also authority holding that pursuant to a proper Brady motion, the prosecution must produce a record of the convictions of its witnesses which can be used for purposes of impeachment.[30] However, in Georgia the prosecution is not required, in responding to a Brady motion, to furnish the defense with criminal records of state witnesses which are not known to the prosecution and are not within the prosecutor's file.[31] But if the district attorney has such information and there is a proper *Brady* demand, the defense is entitled to the information.[32] The general rule in Georgia is that the prosecution is not under a burden to uncover exculpatory evidence, even if the defendant is indigent.[33] See § 14:4, supra, on obtaining criminal history records from the Georgia Crime Information Center.

In Georgia, a distinction has been made between what a defense counsel is entitled to see and obtaining a copy of material which is discoverable. Thus, the Georgia Supreme Court has held that a district attorney is not obligated to make a copy of discoverable material for defense counsel if defense counsel is given an adequate opportunity to examine such material.[34] In *Rini v. State*,[35] the court held that where the district attorney has a statement which exculpates the defendant, it is error for the court to overrule the defendant's motion for production of the

---

[28]Lewis v. United States, 408 A.2d 303 (D.C. 1979).

[29]Ex parte Lewis, 587 S.W.2d 697 (1979).

[30]Lewis v. United States, 408 A.2d 303 (D.C. 1979). See Annot., "Accused Right to Discovery or Inspection of 'Rap Sheets' or Similar Police Records About Prosecution Witnesses," 95 A.L.R.3d 832 (1979). See "Exploring the Limits of Brady v. Maryland: Criminal Discovery as a Due Process Right in Access to Police Investigation and State Crime Laboratories," 15 U. Richmond L. R. 189 (1980).

[31]Hines v. State, 249 Ga. 257, 258, 290 S.E.2d 911 (1982).

[32]Hayes v. State, 168 Ga. App. 94, 95 (3), 308 S.E.2d 227 (1983).

[33]Pulliam v. Balkcom, 245 Ga. 99, 104, 263 S.E.2d 123 (1980); Plemons v. State, 155 Ga. App. 447, 450, 270 S.E.2d 836 (1980).

In Rini v. State, 236 Ga. 715, 718, 225 S.E.2d 234 (1976) (quoting from Hicks v. State, 232 Ga. 393, 395, 207 S.E.2d 30 (1974)), the court said, "The prosecution does not 'suppress' evidence by refusing to search for it, even though the evidence may be more accessible to the state than to the defense." Cf. State v. Pemental, 434 A.2d 932 (R.I.1981).

Cf. Watts v. State, 141 Ga. App. 127, 128 (2), 232 S.E.2d 590 (1977), overruled on other grounds, Graham v. State, 153 Ga. App. 658, 660, 266 S.E.2d 316 (1980). The State v. Graham was in turn reversed at 246 Ga. 341, 271 S.E.2d 627 (1980).

[34]Burnett v. State, 240 Ga. 681, 685 (2), 242 S.E.2d 79 (1978); Hill v. State, 248 Ga. 304, 305 (2), 283 S.E.2d 252 (1981); Crowe v. State, 265 Ga. 582, 587 (7), 458 S.E.2d 799 (1995).

[35]Rini v. State, 235 Ga. 60, 64, 218 S.E.2d 811 (1975).

statement. Nevertheless, it has been held that if the district attorney makes such statements available for examination by defense counsel, it is not required that the state make a copy for the defense. However, in *Fields v. State*,[36] the court directed that a defendant be furnished with "a copy of a videotape the police made of the crime scene."

The extent of required *Brady* disclosures appears more limited in the context of a plea bargain. In *United States v. Ruiz*,[37] the United States Supreme Court concluded that provided the government turns over all information which establishes a defendant's innocence, there is no obligation to disclose evidence having a material impeachment character before concluding a plea agreement with a criminal defendant.

See 2 Torcia, *Wharton's Criminal Procedure*, § 381 (12th Ed. 1976). See also Annotation, "Accused's Right to Discovery or Inspection of 'Rap Sheets' or Similar Police Records About Prosecution Witness," 95 A.L.R.3d 832 (1979).

§ 14:35   Discovery—Brady motion—Application of the rule

In the 1994 case of *Zant v. Moon*,[1] the Georgia Supreme Court held that to establish a Brady violation the defendant must show "(1) that the State possessed evidence favorable to the defense; (2) that the defendant did not possess the evidence nor could he obtain it himself with any reasonable diligence; [2] (3) that the prosecution suppressed the favorable evidence; and (4) that had the evidence been disclosed to the defense, a reasonable probability exists that the outcome of the proceedings would have been different."

According to *Wells v. State*,[3] the defendant must prove, along with the above four criteria, (5) that access to such evidence was denied to the defendant, and (6) that the disclosure would have benefited the defense by providing evidence for the defense or impeaching prior inconsistent statements.

---

[36]Fields v. State, 260 Ga. 331, 335 (8), 393 S.E.2d 252 (1990).

[37]United States v. Ruiz, 536 U.S. 622, 122 S.Ct. 2450, 153 L.Ed.2d 586 (2002).

[Section 14:35]

[1]Zant v. Moon, 264 Ga. 93, 100 (3), 440 S.E.2d 657 (1994); Tessmer v. State, 273 Ga. 220, 225 (6), 539 S.E.2d 816 (2000); Ramsay v. State, 220 Ga. App. 618, 624 (6), 469 S.E.2d 814 (1996). Cf. Ferguson v. State, 226 Ga. App. 681, 682 (2), 487 S.E.2d 467 (1997).

[2]However, "Brady 'does not impose an affirmative obligation on the prosecution to seek out information for the defense, even if such information is more accessible to the prosecution than to the defense.' "Adams v. State, 271 Ga. 485, 487 (3), 521 S.E.2d 575 (1999).

[3]Wells v. State, 237 Ga. App. 109, 514 S.E.2d 245 (1999).

In *Garrison v. Maggio,*[4] the Fifth Circuit Court held that where there is no request by the defense for beneficial material, a distinction is to be drawn between cases where the non-disclosed evidence goes to a substantive issue in the trial and where it is useful only for impeachment. Where the evidence is useful only for impeachment, a new trial must be granted, but only if the new evidence would have probably resulted in an acquittal. The Fifth Circuit Court also pointed out that in *United States v. Agurs,*[5] the evidence which was not disclosed went to a substantive issue in the trial—the defendant's self-defense.

In these Fifth Circuit cases the court equates a general request to no request. However, in either of these situations, if the prosecution has failed to give defense counsel evidence which, in addition to the other evidence introduced in the case, would have been of sufficient importance to create a reasonable doubt, this is a basis for a reversal.[6] In other words, the defendant "has the burden of establishing [that] his defense was so impaired as to deprive him of a fair trial."[7] In *Potts v. State,*[8] the court held that where a general request for exculpatory information has been made, the prosecution is only obligated to "disclose evidence which creates a reasonable doubt of guilt which did not otherwise exist."

At the threshold, an appellant must show that the exculpatory evidence which was not produced is material.[9] In *Smith v. State,*[10] the court emphasized that "[t]he suppression by the prosecution of evidence favorable to an accused upon request violates due process where the evidence is material either to guilt or to punishment, irrespective of the good or bad faith of the prosecution."

In *Walker v. State,*[11] the Court of Appeals pointed out that "the trial court should consider and make appropriate findings of fact and conclusions of law on whether there have been violations of due process requirements of *Brady.* . . . If the trial court determines that such violations have occurred, the trial court

---

[4]Garrison v. Maggio, 540 F.2d 1271 (5th Cir. 1976).

[5]United States v. Agurs, 427 U.S. 97, 96 S.Ct. 2392, 49 L.Ed.2d 342 (1976).

[6]United States v. Agurs, 427 U.S. 97, 96 S.Ct. 2392, 49 L.Ed.2d 342, 355 (1976). The rather confusing case of Moore v. Illinois, 408 U.S. 786, 92 S.Ct. 2562, 33 L.Ed.2d 706 (1972), involved a general request for all statements taken by the police.

[7]Lee v. State, 177 Ga. App. 698, 701 (3), 340 S.E.2d 658 (1986).

[8]Potts v. State, 207 Ga. App. 863, 868 (7), 429 S.E.2d 526 (1993).

[9]Gross v. State, 161 Ga. App. 489, 490 (2), 288 S.E.2d 733 (1982); Mason v. State, 162 Ga. App. 167, 290 S.E.2d 499 (1982).

[10]Smith v. State, 221 Ga. App. 306, 308, 471 S.E.2d 227 (1996) (quoting Brady v. Maryland, 373 U.S. 83, 87, 83 S.Ct. 1194, 10 L.Ed.2d 215 (1963)).

[11]Walker v. State, 214 Ga. App. 691, 696 (2), 448 S.E.2d 924 (1994).

should also consider and make appropriate findings and conclusions of law on whether 'the [undisclosed] evidence is material in the sense that its suppression undermined confidence in the outcome of the trial,' i.e., 'only if there is a reasonable probability that, had the evidence been disclosed to the defense, the result of the proceeding would have been different.' "[12] In *Gulley v. State*,[13] the Georgia Supreme Court held that "*Brady* does not require that the defendant be given copies of material exculpatory evidence, but only that such evidence be made available to him."

In the Maryland case of *Wilson v. State*,[14] the court held that a prosecutor must disclose the precise terms of any plea agreement made with a key witness so that defense counsel has an opportunity to effectively challenge the witnesses on the contents of the agreements and to impeach the witnesses' credibility.

The United States Supreme Court does not seem to have ever passed on the question of just when a defendant is entitled to Brady material. In *Castell v. State*,[15] the Georgia Supreme Court at least indicated that *Brady* does not require pre-trial compliance. In *Fuqua v. State*,[16] the court held that *Brady* does not require pre-trial disclosure. Evidence which the state introduces at trial but has not disclosed to the defendant before trial, even though the defendant has moved for disclosure of exculpatory material, is not a violation of *Brady* under Georgia's interpretation of the case, but the failure to disclose may still deprive the defendant of a fair trial.[17] In *Knight v. State*,[18] the Georgia Supreme Court held that "[a] Brady violation does not exist where the information sought by the defendant becomes available at

---

[12]This is not to say that the defendant must show that, but for the nondisclosure, the jury's verdict would have been one of acquittal, but rather that the verdict returned was not the product of a fair trial and worthy of confidence. The Georgia Court of Appeals has explained that "[a] 'reasonable probability' of a different result is accordingly shown when the government's evidentiary suppression 'undermines confidence in the outcome of a trial.' " Nikitin v. State, 257 Ga. App. 852, 856 (1), 572 S.E.2d 377 (2002). Accord, Brownlow v. Schofield, 277 Ga. 237, 238 (2), 587 S.E.2d 647 (2003).

[13]Gulley v. State, 271 Ga. 337, 342 (5), 519 S.E.2d 655 (1999).

[14]Wilson v. State, 363 Md. 333, 768 A.2d 675 (2001).

[15]Castell v. State, 250 Ga. 776, 781, 301 S.E.2d 234 (1983). In *Castell* the court did point out that "[e]arlier disclosure would not have benefited the defense, and the delayed disclosure did not deprive him of a fair trial."

[16]Fuqua v. State, 183 Ga. App. 414, 417, 359 S.E.2d 165 (1987). Accord, Brantley v. State, 199 Ga. App. 623, 624 (2), 405 S.E.2d 533 (1991); Davis v. State, 266 Ga. 801, 802 (2), 471 S.E.2d 191 (1996).

[17]Bentley v. State, 178 Ga. App. 90, 91, 342 S.E.2d 25 (1986) (citing Parks v. State, 254 Ga. 403 (3), 330 S.E.2d 686 (1985)).

[18]Knight v. State, 271 Ga. 557, 560 (3), 521 S.E.2d 819 (1999).

trial." In *Carroll v. State*,[19] the Georgia Court of Appeals held that "Brady material must be disclosed in time to benefit the defense." However, cases from other jurisdictions have held that *Brady* does not ordinarily require pre-trial compliance.[20]

If a request for discovery is made and there is no compliance by the state, defense counsel must be sure the record shows that there was no compliance. If the issue is not raised in the trial court, it may not later be raised on appeal.[21] In *Williams v. State*,[22] the court held that an oral request for a specific document could validly be made during the trial.

If Brady material is suppressed prior to trial but is made available during trial, the defendant "must show that earlier disclosure would have benefitted the defense and that the delayed disclosure deprived him of a fair trial."[23] In *Masters v. State*,[24] the court held there is no reversible error where exculpatory evidence is made available to the defense during trial but before the witness testified.

See Annotation, "Constitutional Duty of Federal Prosecutor to Disclose Brady Evidence Favorable to Accused," 158 A.L.R.Fed. 401 (1999).

§ 14:36   Discovery—Brady motion—In camera inspection

In *Tribble v. State*,[1] the Georgia Supreme Court, in response to certified questions, held that where a general or a specific Brady motion is filed, the trial judge is not required to conduct an in camera inspection. However, after the state has made its response to the motion, the defendant may request an in camera inspection and the trial judge must comply with this request.[2] But, if the defendant does not ask the court to conduct an in

---

[19]Carroll v. State, 222 Ga. App. 560, 562, 474 S.E.2d 737 (1996). Cf. Schwartzmiller v. Winters, 99 Idaho 18, 576 P.2d 1052 (1978); Grant v. Alldredge, 498 F.2d 376 (2d Cir. 1974); United States v. Donatelli, 484 F.2d 505, 507 (4) (1st Cir. 1973); United States v. Thevis, 84 F.R.D. 47, 52 (N. D.Ga.1979).

[20]Cf. United States v. Shelton, 588 F.2d 1242, 1247 (9th Cir. 1978); United States v. Baxter, 492 F.2d 150, 174 (21) (9th Cir. 1973).

[21]Carter v. State, 142 Ga. App. 351, 352 (3), 235 S.E.2d 750 (1977).

[22]Williams v. State, 250 Ga. 463, 466, 298 S.E.2d 492 (1983). In *Williams* the request was made after clos-

ing arguments but before the jury was charged.

[23]West v. State, 213 Ga. App. 362, 364 (1)(a), 444 S.E.2d 398 (1994); Jordan v. State, 217 Ga. App. 420, 421 (1), 457 S.E.2d 692 (1995). Cf. Johnson v. State, 244 Ga. App. 128, 133 (2), 534 S.E.2d 480 (2000).

[24]Masters v. State, 186 Ga. App. 795, 799 (5), 368 S.E.2d 557 (1988).

[Section 14:36]

[1]Tribble v. State, 248 Ga. 274, 280 S.E.2d 352 (1981); McCullough v. State, 162 Ga. App. 866, 867 (1), 293 S.E.2d 455 (1982).

[2]Osborn v. State, 161 Ga. App. 132, 137 (5), 291 S.E.2d 22 (1982).

camera inspection *after* the state's response, the court is not required to examine the file.[3] The *Tribble* decision seems to indicate, however, that if the trial judge fails to comply with the request after the district attorney's response, the defendant still bears the burden of showing prejudice.[4] In *McNeal v. State*,[5] the court pointed out that the failure of the trial judge to conduct an in camera examination of the state's file after a timely request from the defendant is still "not reversible error as the error may be cured by post-trial examination of the State's file." In *Carpenter v. State*,[6] the trial judge failed to conduct an in camera inspection pursuant to a proper request. The Georgia Supreme Court directed the trial judge to conduct a post-conviction examination of the district attorney's file.

In a case originating in Georgia, a Brady motion was considered in the Fifth Circuit case of *Williams v. Dutton*,[7] where defense counsel had moved in the trial court for the production of nine categories of information. The defendant's motion was denied. After conviction, the defendant sought review on the ground that his Fourteenth Amendment rights had been denied. The state contended there had been no showing that the evidence demanded was favorable to Williams. However, the Fifth Circuit said that due process may not be sidestepped, and, in effect, remanded the case to the trial judge to make an in camera inspection to determine if any of the material requested was favorable to the defendant as to the issues of guilt or punishment. If the trial judge found any such favorable information, Williams was to be given a new trial. However, in *Mobley v. State*,[8] the court held that it is not error for a trial judge to refuse "to inspect the files of the Georgia Bureau of Investigation and other state law enforcement agencies or police files."

In *Williams v. State*,[9] the court said, "If the trial court performs an in camera inspection and denies the defendant access to certain information, on appeal the appellant has the burden of showing both the materiality and the favorable nature of the evidence sought. . . . Mere speculation that the items the appellant wishes to review possibly contain exculpatory information does

---

[3]Watts v. State, 170 Ga. App. 614, 615 (2), 317 S.E.2d 654 (1984); Holmes v. State, 187 Ga. App. 214 (1), 369 S.E.2d 533 (1988); Swann v. State, 256 Ga. 254 (2), 347 S.E.2d 555 (1986).

[4]Cf. Tribble v. State, 160 Ga. App. 358, 287 S.E.2d 83 (1981).

[5]McNeal v. State, 263 Ga. 397, 399, 435 S.E.2d 47 (1993).

[6]Carpenter v. State, 252 Ga. 79, 81, 310 S.E.2d 912 (1984). Accord,

McNeal v. State, 263 Ga. 397, 399, 435 S.E.2d 47 (1993).

[7]Williams v. Dutton, 400 F.2d 797 (5th Cir. 1968).

[8]Mobley v. State, 219 Ga. App. 789, 791 (6), 466 S.E.2d 669 (1996).

[9]Williams v. State, 251 Ga. 749, 789, 312 S.E.2d 40 (1983). See Stephens v. State, 305 Ga. App. 339, 699 S.E.2d 558 (2010).

not satisfy this burden. . . . 'If the appellant desires to have this inspection reviewed by . . . [an appellate] court, . . . [he] must point out what material . . . [he] believes to have been suppressed and show how . . . [he] has been prejudiced.' " In *Byrd v. State*,[10] the court held that an appellate court will not assume the burden of going through materials sealed by the trial judge to see whether there is anything favorable to the defendant which was withheld. It is the responsibility of the defendant to designate what is favorable to him. Further, if a defendant desires to have the inspected material sealed for the record, he should so request.[11]

In *Plemons v. State*,[12] the Georgia Court of Appeals set out the following "procedure for appellate review of in camera inspections of the state's files where defendant's counsel is not granted an opportunity to review the files: A photocopy of the files shall be prepared whereupon the original and the photocopy, together with a certificate by the prosecuting attorney that the entire case file is included, shall be transmitted to the trial judge, who shall make a determination that the photocopy is . . . a true, exact and complete copy of the original files as examined by such trial judge. The files shall then be made part of the record for review and shall be transmitted to this court. After review by the appellate court, the files shall be resealed and returned to the clerk of the trial court for transmission to the district attorney with the notation thereon that they shall not be opened without court order by anyone other than the district attorney or his designee." However, the Court of Appeals in *Barnes v. State*,[13] while upholding the procedural requirements to protect the prosecutor's file, overruled the Plemons requirement that the entire file be forwarded to the appellate court unless the defendant can show that particular evidence was suppressed. Nevertheless, it should be remembered that the Georgia Supreme Court in *Wilson v. State*[14] said:

> Where a Brady motion is made and the prosecutor does not make the specified material available to defense counsel, the trial judge should make an in camera inspection of the material sought. . . . On motion by the defendant, the material examined in camera should either be sealed and filed . . . or an inventory or record of the examined material made, so as to permit appellate review. . . .

---

[10]Byrd v. State, 171 Ga. App. 344, 345 (3), 319 S.E.2d 460 (1984).

[11]Taylor v. State, 230 Ga. App. 749, 498 S.E.2d 113 (1998).

[12]Plemons v. State, 155 Ga. App. 447, 270 S.E.2d 836 (1980).

[13]Barnes v. State, 157 Ga. App. 582, 585, 277 S.E.2d 916 (1981).

[14]Wilson v. State, 246 Ga. 62, 65, 268 S.E.2d 895 (1980). Cf. Wills v. Composite State Board of Medical Examiners, 259 Ga. 549, 553 (3), 384 S.E.2d 636 (1989).

However, in *Jenkins v. State*,[15] the court held where the trial court determined the district attorney's file did not contain evidence favorable to the defendant and the court denied the defense motion to seal a copy of the prosecutor's file for appellate review, any error is harmless unless the defendant makes a "specific claim that any particular exculpatory evidence was in fact suppressed."

In 1999, the Georgia Supreme Court in *Johnson v. State*[16] declined to reverse the trial court where the trial court reviewed the state's file and found nothing exculpatory had been withheld and failed to include a sealed copy of the file, as defendant had requested, for the appellate record. The court pointed out that the defendant "cannot now be heard to complain that the [State's file] was not in fact sealed in spite of the trial judge's apparent agreement to do so and the prosecution's lack of objection. . . . If this was not thereafter done, defense counsel should have persevered and insisted that it be done. His failure to do so amount[s] to a waiver."

§ 14:37 Discovery—Brady motion—Information known only to police

In the Fifth and Eleventh Circuits,[1] there is federal constitutional authority supporting the applicability of a Brady motion to information in the hands of the police as well as the prosecuting attorney.[2] However, in 1996 the Georgia Court of Appeals held in *Mobley v. State*[3] that the defense is "entitled only to exculpatory material contained in the state prosecutor's file or about which the prosecutor had knowledge." Likewise, in the 1989 case *Massengale v. State*,[4] the court concluded that "a prosecutor has no obligation to contact local law enforcement and judicial agencies on behalf of the defense to uncover any information which might be remotely relevant. . . . [Also, in] the absence of a clear showing that this information was wilfully and intentionally concealed from the defense, we are included *not to impute* to the prosecutor

---

[15]Jenkins v. State, 229 Ga. App. 556, 494 S.E.2d 311 (1997).

[16]Johnson v. State, 271 Ga. 375, 379 (7), 519 S.E.2d 221 (1999).

[Section 14:37]

[1]In Bonner v. City of Prichard, Alabama, 661 F.2d 1206, 1207 (11th Cir. 1981), the court held "that the decisions of the . . . Fifth Circuit . . . as that court existed on September 30, 1981, handed down by that court prior to the close of business on that date, shall be binding as precedent in the Eleventh Circuit."

[2]Freeman v. Georgia, 599 F.2d 65, 69 (5th Cir. 1979); Emmett v. Ricketts, 397 F.Supp. 1025, 1041 (N.D. Ga.1975).

[3]Mobley v. State, 219 Ga. App. 789, 791 (6), 466 S.E.2d 669 (1996). Cf. Frazier v. State, 249 Ga. App. 463 (1), 549 S.E.2d 133 (2001).

[4]Massengale v. State, 189 Ga. App. 877, 881 (4), 377 S.E.2d 882 (1989).

knowledge possessed by the local police and probation authorities." (Emphasis in original.)

However, in 1995 the Supreme Court of the United States held in *Kyles v. Whitley*[5] that Brady material includes evidence known only to police and not to the prosecution. The court held "that the individual prosecutor has a duty to learn of any favorable evidence known to others acting on the government's behalf in the case, including the police." The prosecutor remains responsible "regardless of any failure by the police to bring favorable evidence to the prosecutor's attention."

The Georgia Court of Appeals limited this duty though, in the unusual case of *Ferguson v. State*,[6] where a federal informant testified against a defendant on trial in superior court for drug trafficking. In exchange for his testimony, federal authorities promised the informant leniency on his own federal criminal charges. This deal was not disclosed to the defendant. The Georgia Court of Appeals found that there was no Brady violation and upheld the defendant's conviction. In doing so, the court reasoned that while a prosecutor has a duty under *Brady* to learn of any favorable evidence known to others acting on "the government's behalf," that duty extends only to those persons "over whom the prosecutor has authority. Whether a person is on the prosecution team and subject to the authority of the prosecutor depends in each case on the extent of interaction, cooperation, and dependence of the agents working on the case."

In *Head v. Stripling*,[7] the Georgia Supreme Court made the following observation on the scope of those whose knowledge regarding Brady material must be disclosed to the defense: "Our definition of the prosecution team responsible for Brady disclosures cannot be a monolithic view of government that would impute to the prosecutor the knowledge of persons in state agencies not involved in the prosecution. Such a wide definition would be unworkable."

In *Zant v. Moon*,[8] the court held that a *Brady* demand did not require the district attorney to reveal evidence in the possession

---

[5]Kyles v. Whitley, 514 U.S. 419, 115 S.Ct. 1555, 131 L.Ed.2d 490 (1995).

[6]Ferguson v. State, 226 Ga. App. 681, 684, 487 S.E.2d 467 (1997) (citing Zant v. Moon, 264 Ga. 93, 100, 440 S.E.2d 657 (1994)).

[7]Head v. Stripling, 277 Ga. 403, 408 (1), 590 S.E.2d 122 (2003) (citations omitted) where Attorney General's office was deemed part of prosecution team for purposes of *Brady* because it represented the state with respect to defense request for defendant's parole records which in post trial habeas proceedings revealed information helpful to defendant's mental retardation claim.

[8]Zant v. Moon, 264 Ga. 93, 100 (3), 440 S.E.2d 657 (1994) (quoting United States v. Meros, 866 F.2d 1304 (11th Cir. 1989)). See Guzman v. Secretary, Dept. of Corrections, 663 F.3d

of a Tennessee officer who testified for the prosecution. The court pointed out that "*Brady* requires information to be revealed only when it is 'possessed by the prosecutor or anyone over whom the prosecutor has authority.' "

§ 14:38   Discovery—Brady motion—Discovery of informer

In *Glover v. State*,[1] the court held that a "general Brady motion does not normally encompass the disclosure of the identity of a confidential informant."

In *Thornton v. State*,[2] the Georgia Supreme Court held that where a Brady motion was filed seeking the identity of an informer, it was error[3] for the trial judge to fail to conduct a hearing to determine (1) if the informer was "a pure tipster who neither participated in nor witnessed the offense," or (2) whether the informer was a witness to the transaction, or (3) whether the informer was a participant in the transaction. The court recognized the need to protect informers, emphasized in *Roviaro v. United States*,[4] and said that this need must be weighed by the trial judge against the right of the defendant to a full and fair opportunity to defend himself.[5] In considering *Roviaro*, Professor Kurtz concluded that *Roviaro* "permits the state's interest in maintaining confidential informants to be weighed against the defendant's right to defend himself in deciding whether to reveal the name of any anonymous informant to the defendant. The

---

1336(11th Cir. 2011) (new trial ordered where, unknown to prosecutor, police officer testified falsely that no benefit had been provided to witness when in fact crack-addicted witness had been paid $500).

[Section 14:38]

[1]Glover v. State, 203 Ga. App. 853 (1), 418 S.E.2d 127 (1992).

[2]Thornton v. State, 238 Ga. 160, 165, 231 S.E.2d 729 (1977); Stiggers v. State, 151 Ga. App. 546, 549 (2), 260 S.E.2d 413 (1979); Merritt v. State, 165 Ga. App. 597, 598 (2), 302 S.E.2d 136 (1983).

[3]However, in Thornton the court did not reverse the trial judge, but remanded the case for a post-trial hearing. "If on the basis of evidence introduced at such hearing the trial judge concludes that identity disclosure should be compelled . . . (the trial judge) must order a new trial." Stiggers v. State, 151 Ga. App. 546,

550, 260 S.E.2d 413 (1979).

[4]Roviaro v. United States, 353 U.S. 53, 77 S.Ct. 623, 1 L.Ed.2d 639, 645 (1957).

Also see Thornton v. State, 239 Ga. 693, 695, 238 S.E.2d 376 (1977), in which the court said that the earlier Thornton case held that "the identity of a mere tipster is absolutely privileged."

In United States v. Barnes, 486 F.2d 776, 779 (8th Cir. 1973), the court said that as a rule, if an informer is a participant in the crime on demand, his name and address should be disclosed to the defense prior to trial. Apparently, if the informer cannot be located and is a material witness whom the prosecution does not plan to use, "it owes a duty to make every reasonable effort to have the informant made available to defendant to interview or use as a witness, if desired."

[5]Moore v. State, 187 Ga. App. 387, 391, 370 S.E.2d 511 (1988).

court resolved this balancing question by announcing a two-step
process for trial courts to follow. . . . First, a hearing must be
held on the Brady motion to determine its merits. Then, if the
identity of the informant is found to be evidence favorable to the
defendant and material to his guilt, the trial court must
determine whether the state's privilege under *Roviaro* outweighs
the defendant's right to have the identity disclosed." Professor
Kurtz had described the "two-step analysis . . . [as] indefensible,"
and said that if the defendant convinces the trial judge of the
materiality of the informer's identity, it is a violation of due process for the state to refuse to reveal the identity of the informer.[6]

In 1998, in *Ivory v. State*,[7] the Georgia Court of Appeals summarized the procedure to be followed in determining if the
confidential informant's identity should be revealed by the state
as follows:

> [T]he trial court must conduct a two-step hearing. Initially, the
> trial court should hear evidence to determine: (a) that the
> confidential informant is an alleged informer-witness or informer
> participant whose testimony appears to be material to the defense
> on the issue of guilt or punishment; (b) that the testimony for the
> prosecution and the defense is or will be in conflict; and (c) that the
> CI was the only available witness who could amplify or contradict
> the testimony of these witnesses. Once this threshold has been met,
> the trial court must conduct an in camera hearing of the CI's
> testimony [and apply the balancing test] set forth in *Thornton v.
> State,* 238 Ga. 160, 231 S.E.2d 729 (1977), and *Moore v. State*, 187
> Ga. App. 387, 388 (2), 389, 370 S.E.2d 511 (1988) supra. [Emphasis
> omitted.]

In *State v. Martin*,[8] the court concluded that in the case of a
mere tipster, the public policy of the state toward non-disclosure

---

[6]Kurtz, "Criminal Law," Annual
Survey of Georgia Law, 29 Mercer L.
Rev. 55, 64 (1977).

In Thornton v. State, 238 Ga.
160, 231 S.E.2d 729 (1977), Justice
Ingram, concurring specially, stated:

"[D]oes the majority really mean
to say that if a trial judge decides that
evidence in the hands of the state is so
material to the defense that suppression of the evidence will result in an
unfair trial that it may, nevertheless,
be withheld by the state under its
privilege? If this is the intended holding of the majority, I believe the due
process clause has been dealt a body
blow. It is difficult for me to accept the
proposition that the state has an overriding public policy that would convict

an innocent person of a crime. Theoretically, this could be the result if the
majority reasoning is extended to a
logical conclusion."

See § 14:86, infra. Also see Annot., "Accused's Right to and Prosecution's Privilege Against Disclosure of
Identity of Informer," 76 A.L.R.2d 262
(1961).

[7]Ivory v. State, 234 Ga. App. 858,
859 (2), 508 S.E.2d 421 (1998) (quoting Grant v. State, 230 Ga. App. 330,
496 S.E.2d 325 (1998)). See Little v.
State, 280 Ga. App. 60, 633 S.E.2d 403
(2006).

[8]In State v. Martin, 156 Ga. App.
554, 555, 275 S.E.2d 129 (1980), an affidavit for a search warrant stated
that an officer had driven a confiden-

of an informer would not be overcome; a mere tipster would not be material the defendant's innocence or guilt nor helpful to the defendant, because his testimony would be inadmissible.

Likewise, it has been held that where "a person merely takes an undercover police officer to a location and . . . introduces the officer to the defendant, and the officer arranges for and buys contraband from the defendant, and the person witnesses such sale, . . . a disclosure of his name . . . to the defendant is not required as a matter of law. . . ."[9] However, it has been argued that if the informer was a witness or participant in the transaction, then it would seem that his identity would be material to the defendant and the trial judge would have to weigh the right of the defendant to fairly defend himself against the normal right of the state not to disclose the identity of an informer.[10] Nevertheless, in *Leonard v. State*,[11] the court pointed out that "[t]he movant must establish the relevance, materiality, and necessity of the identity of the informant as a predicate for disclosure. . . . [Even when an] informant . . . takes the police to a drug buy, introduces the officer, and witnesses the sale . . . [as] an eyewit-

---

tial informer to the defendant's residence. He had searched the informer before he went in. When he returned he had marijuana which he stated he purchased in the house. The informer also reported he saw another sale while he was in the house and the officer had seen this person leave the house. The court concluded as a matter of law that the informer was a mere tipster whose identity was privileged. The court also pointed out that there had been no showing that this information would be beneficial to the defendant. Also, the prosecution need not disclose the name of an informer who merely provided probable cause for a search. Cf. McCray v. Illinois, 386 U.S. 300, 87 S.Ct. 1056, 18 L.Ed.2d 62 (1967), and Rugendorf v. United States, 376 U.S. 528, 84 S.Ct. 825, 11 L.Ed.2d 887 (1964); Branch v. State, 248 Ga. 300, 301 (2), 282 S.E.2d 894 (1981).

[9]Statiras v. State, 170 Ga. App. 739, 740, 318 S.E.2d 156 (1984). Cf. Carver v. State, 175 Ga. App. 599, 600 (1), 333 S.E.2d 697 (1985); Brinson v. State, 188 Ga. App. 214, 215, 372 S.E.2d 487 (1988); Wilson v. State, 191 Ga. App. 833, 383 S.E.2d 197 (1989).

[10]In Usher v. State, 148 Ga. App. 719, 720 (3), 252 S.E.2d 677 (1979), the court in an alternative holding said that disclosure is not required "if it is clear that disclosure of the informant's identity could have been of no benefit to appellant except possibly to allow him to impeach the agent's testimony." See Chandler v. State, 317 Ga. App. 406, 731 S.E.2d 88 (2012) (identity of informant who was a participant in charged drug sale need not be disclosed if only value of testimony is impeachment of informer or investigating officer). Accord, Paras v. State, 247 Ga. 75, 77 (3), 274 S.E.2d 451 (1981).

In State v. Royal, 247 Ga. 309, 312 (2), 275 S.E.2d 646 (1981), the court said, "Where a defendant charges that a confidential informant has entrapped him outside the presence of any other witnesses, Roviaro would ordinarily require disclosure of the informant's identity, since the defense of entrapment would rest upon allegations which only the informant could confirm or deny." But see Little v. State, 165 Ga. App. 389, 392 (4), 300 S.E.2d 540 (1983).

[11]Leonard v. State, 228 Ga. App. 792, 795 (2), 492 S.E.2d 747 (1997).

ness . . . the trial court, in balancing the respective rights of the defendant and the . . . State, can in the exercise of sound discretion, deny disclosure."

In *Davidson v. State,*[12] the court said where a Brady motion has been filed to determine the identity of the informer, the defendant is entitled to a hearing to determine if the evidence is material to the defendant. If the evidence is material under *Brady,* the trial judge must weigh this benefit to the defendant against the state's privilege under *Roviaro.* However, if the defendant is a "mere tipster," the defendant is not entitled to a hearing.[13] Also, the "[p]ublic policy in Georgia favors nondisclosure of the identity of an informant in the interest of the free flow of information about criminal activity."[14] "The mere possibility of [obtaining] impeachment [material] . . . is not a sufficient basis to require the disclosure of a confidential informant."[15] But in applying the balancing test, all relevant evidence in all hearings and the trial may be considered by the judge.[16]

Although the case was later overruled, in *State v. Mason,*[17] the court pointed out "that the privilege [of the state] is not simply one against disclosing identity of a confidential informant; but the public and the informant have a clear interest which can, and

---

[12]Davidson v. State, 156 Ga. App. 457, 274 S.E.2d 807 (1980); Dyer v. State, 162 Ga. App. 773, 774 (2), 293 S.E.2d 42 (1982). In Henderson v. State, 162 Ga. App. 320, 322 (2), 292 S.E.2d 77 (1982), the court emphasized that before a trial judge must direct the revealing of the identity of an informer, the defendant must make a showing that the testimony of the informer would be favorable and material to the defendant.

In Little v. State, 165 Ga. App. 389, 392 (4), 300 S.E.2d 540 (1983), the court said that "where it appears that disclosure of the informant's identity would at most serve to provide possible testimony to impeach the agent's testimony . . . nondisclosure [is not] an abuse of discretion. . . ."

In Gilmore v. State, 168 Ga. App. 76, 77, 308 S.E.2d 232 (1983), the court said, "Where a person merely takes an undercover agent to a location and identifies or introduces the agent to a seller of drugs, with all arrangements for the sale being wholly made by the agent, even if the sale is witnessed by the introducer, such introducer is nothing more than an informer and acts as a tipster only and not as a decoy so as to require a disclosure of name, address or similar information. . . . Under the facts . . . there were no discovery rights in the tipster mandated by Brady . . . and thus the disclosure rested within the sound discretion of the trial court."

[13]Brown v. State, 229 Ga. App. 87, 89 (1), 493 S.E.2d 230 (1997).

[14]Wells v. State, 212 Ga. App. 60, 63 (3), 441 S.E.2d 460 (1994); Roden v. State, 181 Ga. App. 287, 290 (1), 351 S.E.2d 713 (1986); Skipworth v. State, 185 Ga. App. 636, 637 (3), 365 S.E.2d 284 (1988); Grimes v. State, 168 Ga. App. 372, 376 (5), 308 S.E.2d 863 (1983).

[15]Tuff v. State, 202 Ga. App. 772, 772, 415 S.E.2d 702 (1992).

[16]Bannister v. State, 202 Ga. App. 762, 763, 415 S.E.2d 912 (1992).

[17]State v. Mason, 181 Ga. App. 806, 809 (3), 353 S.E.2d 915 (1987), overruled by Watts v. State, 274 Ga. 373, 552 S.E.2d 823 (2001).

in the particular case should, be protected even when the informant's identity has been disclosed or discovered. In *Roviaro v. United States,* . . . the court said: 'What is usually referred to as the informer's privilege is in reality the Government's privilege.' . . . '[I]t is . . . [the informant's right and duty] to communicate to . . . officers any information which he has of the commission of an offense against those laws. . . . [I]t is the duty of that government to see that he may exercise this right freely, and *to protect him from violence while so doing, or on account of so doing.* . . .' Re Quarles, 158 U.S. 532, 15 S.Ct. 959, 39 L.Ed. 1080 (1895). . . . A confidential informant, though his identity might become known *or guessed,* has a real interest in not being subjected to enforced testimony. . . ." In *State v. Morris,*[18] the court held that the trial judge erred in holding that where an informant had waived the privilege, the privilege no longer existed, since the state can still invoke the privilege.

In *Smith v. State,*[19] the court said, "[T]here are particular requirements placed upon the defendant to justify identifying or summonsing the informer. The defendant must ask the trial court for an in-camera examination of the matter, by first showing not only the *materiality* but the *necessity* of the witness' testimony . . . ." The defendant should ask the trial court to make the state present the information; then the defendant must show its materiality and the necessity of disclosure and show how the evidence would exonerate him. At such an in camera hearing, neither the defendant nor his counsel are entitled to be present when the informant is examined by the judge.[20] However, in *Moore v. State,*[21] the court directed that at such a hearing the state is required to disclose the identity of the informant to the trial judge. The informant is to be sworn, and his testimony shall be reported and transcribed. But the informant should not reveal his name, address, or place of business nor cause such information to be recorded. The transcript of the informant's testimony shall be sealed. If the state cannot produce the informant for such a hearing, the judge shall determine the circumstances of the informant's absence, but the state should not be required to reveal the identity at the hearing. Both the defendant and the state shall be entitled to present any relevant evidence or to argue on the sole issue of whether the defendant would be prejudiced by the trial judge's not disclosing the informant's

---

[18]State v. Morris, 202 Ga. App. 344, 345 (2), 414 S.E.2d 656 (1991), rev'd on other grounds, 262 Ga. 446, 421 S.E.2d 524 (1992).

[19]Smith v. State, 192 Ga. App. 144 (1), 384 S.E.2d 677 (1989) (emphasis by the court).

[20]Gray v. State, 204 Ga. App. 33 (2), 418 S.E.2d 412 (1992).

[21]Moore v. State, 187 Ga. App. 387, 392, 370 S.E.2d 511 (1988).

identity. In *State v. Sears*,[22] the court held that it was not error for the trial judge to fail to conduct a hearing to determine the identity of an informant where the defendant did not ask the trial judge for an in camera examination into the matter.

Likewise, in *Ezzard v. State*,[23] the court held that the trial judge is not necessarily required to conduct an in camera hearing. In *Ezzard* the court affirmed the trial court in concluding after argument that because the inmate was a "mere tipster," no further inquiry by the trial court was required.

However, in *Jones v. State*[24] the Georgia Court of Appeals considered a case in which an officer purchased a quantity of cocaine but did not make an immediate arrest of the seller. The defendant was later arrested and charged with the sale. Although "[t]he officer positively identified . . . [defendant] as the perpetrator," the defendant "denied any participation in the transaction and claimed misidentification by the officer. Under these circumstances, the disclosure of the identity of the confidential informant was material to the issue of . . . [defendant's] guilt."

Likewise, in *Hampton v. State*,[25] the court held if there was no known witness to an alleged sale other than the defendant and the officer and the informant was the only witness in a position to amplify or contradict the testimony of the officer, the identity of the informant should be required.

In *Little v. State*,[26] the Georgia Court of Appeals, in conducting the two-step Brady and Roviaro analysis, noted that (1) "the confidential informant was an informer-witness or informer-participant;" (2) there was conflicting testimony as to whether the defendant was home at the time of the alleged transaction, as well as a "conflict between the testimony of the police officer and . . . [another witness] as to the defendant's guilt; and [(3)] that the confidential informant was the only available witness who could amplify or contradict their testimony." The court held that the trial court "should . . . [require] the State to disclose the identity of the confidential informant to the trial judge *only* and an in-camera hearing should . . . [be] held to determine if, in fact, the confidential informer was an eyewitness and, if so, whether his testimony would be inculpatory, impeaching or

[22]State v. Sears, 202 Ga. App. 352, 353 (4), 414 S.E.2d 494 (1991).

[23]Ezzard v. State, 230 Ga. App. 147, 495 S.E.2d 620 (1998).

[24]Jones v. State, 192 Ga. App. 186, 187, 384 S.E.2d 273 (1989).

[25]Hampton v. State, 215 Ga. App. 57, 449 S.E.2d 654 (1994). Cf. Jones v. State, 192 Ga. App. 186, 384 S.E.2d 273 (1989).

[26]Little v. State, 230 Ga. App. 803, 808 (3), 498 S.E.2d 284 (1998) (emphasis by the court), quoting Thornton v. State, 238 Ga. 160, 231 S.E.2d 729 (1977); Rapier v. State, 245 Ga. App. 211, 214 (2), 535 S.E.2d 860 (2000).

exculpatory to the defendant's guilt or punishment. . . . [A]fter making a determination that the testimony of the confidential information . . . [is] exculpatory to the defendant's guilt or punishment, . . . [the trial judge should] go further and 'weigh the materiality of the informer's identity to the defense against the [S]tate's privilege not to disclose his name under *Roviaro*.' "

In *Wilson v. State*,[27] the court held that where "the accused makes a credible initial showing that the informant may not have been merely mistaken as to the name of the person selling drugs to undercover police . . . on the occasion in question, the police privilege against revealing the name of its informant must yield to a defendant's right to a fair trial. A possible exception is where the State responds to defendant's assertion by showing beyond all doubt that the informant must have been mistaken in his or her original identification."

In *Taylor v. State*,[28] the court held that disclosure of the informant's identity for impeachment purposes only cannot be compelled.

In *Boatright v. State*,[29] the court stated that "if the confidential informer acts as the entrapper, and if the defendant can show that he has an arguably persuasive defense of entrapment—the state might have a duty to produce such a witness."

In *Glenn v. State*,[30] the Georgia Supreme Court held that the state is not entitled to appeal an order of a trial judge directing the disclosure of a confidential informant.

See § 14:86, infra, on informers and a motion to suppress. See Studdard, *Daniel's Georgia Handbook on Criminal Evidence* (2018 ed.), § 1:27, on scope of cross-examination, and § 5:13, on government privilege.

§ 14:39 Demurrers

A demurrer is a document which is used in order to have the trial judge pass on the sufficiency and appropriateness of some pleading.[1] It is sometimes referred to as a pleading or as a "motion to quash."[2] However, the term "motion to quash" is a general term used to refer to demurrers and pleas which do not raise a question as to a defect appearing on the face of the document

---

[27]Wilson v. State, 209 Ga. App. 436, 438, 433 S.E.2d 703 (1993).

[28]Taylor v. State, 216 Ga. App. 572, 455 S.E.2d 340 (1995).

[29]Boatright v. State, 260 Ga. 534, 536 (1), 397 S.E.2d 689 (1990).

[30]Glenn v. State, 271 Ga. 604, 523 S.E.2d 13 (1999).

[Section 14:39]

[1]See Seaboard Air Line Ry. Co. v. Jolly, 160 Ga. 315, 318, 127 S.E. 765 (1925).

[2]See Baskin v. State, 137 Ga. App. 840, 841 (2), 225 S.E.2d 77 (1976).

which is being attacked.[3] However, in *Traylor v. State*,[4] the court said that a motion to quash is classified as a general demurrer in determining when it may be filed.

A demurrer calls attention to a defect in the pleading. Normally, a demurrer to an indictment must be in writing unless the indictment is so deficient that a motion in arrest of judgment would be valid.[5]

> O.C.G.A. § 17-7-110 and Uniform Superior Court Rule 31.1 combine to require a demurrer or plea in bar to be filed within ten days after the date of arraignment, unless the time for filing is extended by the court. But this court long ago held in *Hollingsworth v. State* that even though courts on the civil side require a defendant to plead the statute of limitation by way of defense, that rule should not be applied in criminal cases. Thus unlike the situation which usually exists where pleas and demurrers are not filed, even if the plea or demurrer is not filed before trial, the defendant may still assert the defense of the statute of limitations in the trial of the case.[6]

In the case of an indictment, a demurrer can only be directed at a defect which appears in the indictment[7] or at the constitutionality of the statute which is the basis of the indictment.[8] If the introduction of any evidence is necessary in order to raise a particular point, the document is not a demurrer, but some other kind of plea. See § 14:41, infra, on a speaking demurrer.

A demurrer raises a question of law which is to be passed on by the trial judge.[9] The sustaining of a general or special demurrer to an indictment usually results in a dismissal of the indictment.[10] Furthermore, it has been held that at least in the case of a general demurrer, if the demurrer is overruled by the trial judge and his ruling is later reversed, the entire procedure following the overruling of the demurrer is a nullity.[11] The sustaining of a demurrer does not prevent the reindictment and

---

[3]E.g., Allen v. State, 110 Ga. App. 56, 137 S.E.2d 711 (1964).

[4]Traylor v. State, 165 Ga. App. 226, 228, 299 S.E.2d 911 (1983).

[5]O.C.G.A. § 17-7-111. However, if the defect raised is one which would be good in a motion in arrest of judgment, it may be orally made. Gilmore v. State, 118 Ga. 299 (1), 45 S.E. 226 (1903).

[6]State v. Barker, 277 Ga. App. 84, 87, 625 S.E.2d 500 (2005); citing Hollingsworth v. State, 7 Ga. App. 16, 65 S.E. 1077 (1909) (interior quotes deleted). See Lynch v. State, 815 S.E.2d 340 (Ga. Ct. App. 2018).

[7]Jackson v. State, 64 Ga. 344, 346 (1879); State v. Holmes, 142 Ga. App. 847, 848, 237 S.E.2d 406 (1977).

[8]See Cohen v. State, 7 Ga. App. 5 (3), 65 S.E. 1096 (1909).

[9]See Geele v. State, 203 Ga. 369, 376, 47 S.E.2d 283 (1948).

[10]See Goddard v. State, 27 Ga. App. 226, 107 S.E. 888 (1921).

[11]See McMichen v. State, 59 Ga. App. 896, 2 S.E.2d 507 (1939), and McLendon v. State, 16 Ga. App. 262, 264 (6), 85 S.E. 200 (1915). On the effect of erroneously overruling a special demurrer, see State v. Eubanks, 239 Ga. 483, 238 S.E.2d 38 (1977). But see

trial of the defendant unless the demurrer was directed at the alleged unconstitutionality of the statute on which the indictment was based[12] or at the dismissal of the indictment for the second time. See § 12:17, supra, on grand jury handling of the indictment.

In *State v. Mendoza,*[13] the court held that where the sustaining of a special demurrer results in striking from or adding "to the material allegations of an indictment, [this] is equivalent to sustaining a general demurrer and quashing the indictment."

If an indictment is drawn in more than one count and a demurrer is sustained as to one count, the court may strike the defective count and permit the trial to proceed on the remaining valid count.[14] Where a count has been dismissed from an indictment, defense counsel should insist that the defendant be tried on an indictment which has no reference to the stricken count or counts.[15] The appearance of stricken counts may have the effect of (1) placing the defendant's character in evidence without his consent, (2) providing the jury with information about a separate crime, (3) depriving the defendant of the presumption of innocence, (4) lessening the state's burden of proving the defendant's guilt beyond a reasonable doubt, and (5) depriving the defendant of due process of law.

Defense counsel should obtain a signed order from the court sustaining or overruling all demurrers which have been filed. It is error for the trial judge to refuse to rule on a demurrer.[16] However, the fact that the judge refused to rule on a demurrer must appear on the record if the defense wishes to be able to take advantage of this error.

The overruling of a demurrer is not a valid ground for a motion for new trial.[17] The point, nevertheless, may be raised on appeal.

If a demurrer to an indictment is filed without expressly reserving the defendant's right to an arraignment, a waiver of arraign-

---

§ 14:41, infra, on the harmless error rule.

[12]See Brown v. State, 109 Ga. 570, 34 S.E. 1031 (1900); United States v. Oppenheimer, 242 U.S. 85, 87, 37 S.Ct. 68, 61 L.Ed. 161 (1916). See §§ 14:51 and 14:58, infra.

However, in United States v. Ball, 163 U.S. 662, 16 S.Ct. 1192, 41 L.Ed. 300 (1896), the court held that an acquittal on a defective indictment would bar a later prosecution for the same offense charged in a new indictment.

[13]State v. Mendoza, 190 Ga. App. 831 (1), 380 S.E.2d 357 (1989).

[14]Martin v. State, 10 Ga. App. 795, 74 S.E. 304 (1912); Williams v. State, 165 Ga. App. 72 (1), 299 S.E.2d 405 (1983).

[15]See Wingfield v. State, 231 Ga. 92, 104, 105, 200 S.E.2d 708 (1973).

[16]Birt v. State, 127 Ga. App. 532, 194 S.E.2d 335 (1972); and see Waldrop v. Wolff, 114 Ga. 610, 613 (3), 40 S.E. 830 (1902).

[17]Cleveland v. State, 109 Ga. 265, 34 S.E. 572 (1899).

ment results.[18] Preserving the right to an arraignment may be important, not only for the arraignment itself, but also because of the other pleadings which must be filed before arraignment, such as a demand for a list of witnesses, another demurrer, a plea in abatement, or a plea in bar.

§ 14:40 Demurrers—General demurrers

Demurrers are divided in two categories: (1) general and (2) special. A general demurrer attacks the sufficiency of the indictment. The validity of a general demurrer depends on whether the defendant can admit the charge as made and still be innocent.[1] If he can, the indictment is fatally defective. When a demurrer is filed to an indictment, the indictment is to be strictly construed against the pleader.[2]

As a general proposition, "an indictment couched in the language of the statute alleged to have been violated is not subject to a general demurrer."[3] Normally, it is proper to file a general demurrer where the indictment fails to set out an essential element of the crime or there exists some general defect in the indictment. Thus, a general demurrer is adequate if it simply states that the indictment fails to set out a specific violation of Georgia law.[4] However, if a general demurrer is filed because of the alleged unconstitutionality of the statute on which the indictment is based, extreme care must be used. In *Wallin v. State*,[5] the court said that in order to raise the question of the constitutionality of a law "at least three things must be shown: (1) The statute or the particular part or parts of the statute which the party would challenge must be stated or pointed out with fair

---

[18]Baskin v. State, 137 Ga. App. 840, 841, 225 S.E.2d 77 (1976); Kincade v. State, 14 Ga. App. 544, 81 S.E. 910 (1914).

[Section 14:40]

[1]Dukes v. State, 9 Ga. App. 537 (2), 71 S.E. 921 (1911); Jenkins v. State, 121 Ga. App. 103, 104, 172 S.E.2d 845 (1970); Marshall v. State, 229 Ga. 841, 842, 195 S.E.2d 12 (1972).

[2]Green v. State, 109 Ga. 536 (1), 35 S.E. 97 (1900); Johnson v. State, 233 Ga. App. 450, 504 S.E.2d 290 (1998).

[3]State v. Wyatt, 295 Ga. 257, 260(2), 759 S.E.2d 500 (2014) (citation and punctuation omitted).

[4]Jenkins v. State, 121 Ga. App. 103, 172 S.E.2d 845 (1970). See also Douglas, Augusta and Gulf Railway Co. v. Swindle, 2 Ga. App. 550, 59 S.E. 600 (1907). See Kimbrough v. State, 300 Ga. 878, 799 S.E.2d 229 (2017) (motion to dismiss for failure to state a claim under O.C.G.A. § 9-11-12(b)(6) in a civil case serves the same function as a general demurrer).

[5]Wallin v. State, 248 Ga. 29, 30, 279 S.E.2d 687 (1981) (citing Richmond Concrete Products Co. v. Ward, 212 Ga. 773, 774, 95 S.E.2d 677 (1956)). See, Chester v. State, 262 Ga. 85, 88(3), 414 S.E.2d 477 (1992); Lindsey v. State, 259 Ga. App. 389, 577 S.E.2d 78 (2003).

precision;[6] (2) the provision of the Constitution which it is claimed has been violated must be clearly designated; and (3) it must be shown wherein the statute, or some designated part of it, violates such constitutional provision." The Georgia Supreme Court "will not rule on a challenge to the constitutionality of a statute unless the issue has been raised and ruled on in a trial court."[7] However, the former requirement preventing designation of a statute only by numbers unless the statute were in the 1933 Code[8] has been eliminated.[9]

A general demurrer should be filed before arraignment. If the defect attacked is one which would support a motion to arrest judgment, it may be filed any time during trial.[10] It has been held that a general demurrer may be filed even after a trial and before a second trial where a new trial is obtained.[11] However, Rule 31.1 of the Uniform Rules for the Superior Courts provides that all demurrers are to be filed "at or before the time set by law (ten days after arraignment, O.C.G.A. § 17-7-110) unless time therefor is extended by the judge in writing prior to trial." If a demurrer is not filed prior to the entry of judgment on the verdict, a motion in arrest of judgment or habeas corpus are the only available remedies to attack a conviction based upon a defective indictment.[12]

In *LaFontaine v. State*,[13] the court held that where a defendant failed to obtain a ruling on a timely filed general demurrer until after the trial had begun, such conduct amounted to a waiver to have the demurrer considered by the court.

If an indictment is so defective that a motion in arrest of judgment would lie, the defect may be attacked by an oral motion to dismiss or quash[14] "at any time during the trial."[15]

Some careful and diligent practitioners believe that a general demurrer should be filed to every indictment where any likeli-

---

[6]In Wiggins v. State, 249 Ga. 302, 303, 290 S.E.2d 427 (1982), the court said, "We now hold that the statutory provision attacked is identified 'with fair precision' where its substantive provisions are set forth with sufficient particularity to enable it to be found among and distinguished from other statutory provisions although neither its official nor its unofficial citation is set forth in the pleading raising the constitutional challenge."

[7]In Re L.C., 273 Ga. 886, 889 (2), 548 S.E.2d 335 (2001).

[8]Mack v. State, 219 Ga. 829 (2), 136 S.E.2d 320 (1964).

[9]Grantham v. State, 244 Ga. 775, 262 S.E.2d 777 (1979).

[10]Gilmore v. State, 118 Ga. 299 (1), 45 S.E. 226 (1903). See § 28:13, infra.

[11]Bramblett v. State, 239 Ga. 336, 338, 236 S.E.2d 580 (1977).

[12]Harris v. State, 258 Ga. App. 669(1), 574 S.E.2d 871 (2002); Jackson v. State, 284 Ga. App. 619(2), 644 S.E.2d 491 (2007).

[13]LaFontaine v. State, 269 Ga. 251, 497 S.E.2d 367 (1998).

[14]Stone v. State, 151 Ga. App. 531, 260 S.E.2d 405 (1979).

hood of trial exists. Sometimes omissions in indictments are not readily noticeable. These defects, if they relate to the sufficiency of the indictment, may be raised in support of a general demurrer which was filed earlier.

For examples of a general demurrer, see Studdard, *Daniel's Georgia Criminal Trial Practice Forms* (2018-2019 ed.), §§ 12:9 et seq.

§ 14:41 Demurrers—Special demurrers

A special demurrer raises an objection to the form of the indictment. A defendant has been said to have a right to be tried on an indictment which is perfect in form and substance. In *State v. Shepherd Construction Co.,*[1] the court first said that a defendant "is entitled to an indictment perfect in form as well as substance if he raises the question on special demurrer." The court then pointed out that the indictment should have set out the names of the "other" conspirators or stated that they were unknown or unindicted. However, the court then concluded that, since defendant had been supplied the names of the other conspirators in response to a Brady motion, it was error for the trial judge to sustain a special demurrer attacking the indictment for failure to set out the names of the "other" conspirators. It has been held that even where a special demurrer has been filed, pointing out a defect, and the demurrer is erroneously overruled, "a defendant's entitlement to a perfect indictment . . . [has] no literal application to a post-conviction review" unless the defendant was misled to his prejudice.[2] In a case in which no demurrer had been filed and the defendant was convicted, the court said a defendant would not be heard after conviction to urge defects in an indictment unless the indictment was absolutely void.[3]

As a general matter, an indictment which fails to state with specificity the date on which the crime occurred will be subject to a special demurrer. In some cases, however, the state may not be able to do more than state a range of dates between which the criminal conduct occurred. In such a case, the indictment may still be subject to a special demurrer if it appears that the state

---

[15]Pullen v. State, 199 Ga. App. 881, 406 S.E.2d 283 (1991).

[Section 14:41]

[1]State v. Shepherd Construction Co., 248 Ga. 1, 3, 281 S.E.2d 151 (1981). See Cole v. State, 334 Ga. App. 752, 780 S.E.2d 406 (2015) (a trial court's ruling on a special demurrer is reviewed de novo).

[2]State v. Eubanks, 239 Ga. 483, 484, 238 S.E.2d 38 (1977). See Andemical v. State, 336 Ga. App. 661, 786 S.E.2d 238 (2016).

[3]Lanier v. State, 5 Ga. App. 472, 63 S.E. 536 (1909); Foy v. State, 40 Ga. App. 617, 150 S.E. 917 (1929).

can in fact narrow the range of dates during which the alleged crime occurred.[4]

In *State v. Thomas*,[5] an indictment alleging a single count of theft by taking through the use of the defendant's employer's credit card was subject to special demurrer because it failed to allege with any particularity the manner in which the crime occurred or the date or dates on which it occurred other than to state a date range of several weeks.

In *State v. Wyatt*,[6] the indictment alleged that defendant committed aggravated assault with "an object the exact nature of which is unknown to the . . . Grand Jury." This was deemed sufficient to withstand a special demurrer. The court did note, however, that should the state at trial seek to prove its case by identifying a specific object, the defendant might then be able to claim a "fatal variance" between the indictment and the proof at trial.

A special demurrer must be in writing.[7] It must be free from imperfection and "put its finger on the exact point of weakness."[8] A special demurrer to an indictment is construed strictly against the defendant.[9]

A demurrer which states that an indictment is duplicitous because two separate and distinct offenses have been improperly joined is fatally defective unless it alleges what the offenses are.[10] If an indictment is good in substance, it will not be stricken on a demurrer which in general terms characterizes the indictment as "vague, uncertain and indefinite."[11] However, where an indictment charges a defendant with taking "one set of twelve golf clubs . . . and various items of men's clothing," the latter allegation will be stricken on a special demurrer, since it is an insufficient description of the clothing.[12] If an indictment names a crime but alleges the essential elements of another crime, and not the elements of the named crime, it is subject to a special demurrer. However, the trial court has authority to strike the erroneous name and to permit the case to be tried on the indict-

---

[4]State v. Layman, 279 Ga. 340, 613 S.E.2d 639 (2005); Blackmon v. State, 272 Ga. App. 854, 614 S.E.2d 118 (2005).

[5]State v. Thomas, 331 Ga. App. 220, 770 S.E.2d 301 (2015).

[6]State v. Wyatt, 295 Ga. 257, 759 S.E.2d 500 (2014).

[7]See King v. State, 117 Ga. 39(1), 43 S.E. 426 (1903).

[8]Boatwright v. State, 26 Ga. App. 67, 68, 105 S.E. 381 (1920).

[9]McElmurray v. State, 76 Ga. App. 604, 606, 47 S.E.2d 139 (1948).

[10]Gatlin v. State, 18 Ga. App. 9 (6), 89 S.E. 345 (1916).

[11]Jones v. State, 115 Ga. 814, 42 S.E. 271 (1902).

[12]Pippin v. State, 128 Ga. App. 355, 196 S.E.2d 664 (1973).

ment as charged.[13]

In *State v. Jones*,[14] the court held that "[w]here a crime may be committed in more than one way, the failure to charge the manner in which the crime was committed subjects the indictment or accusation to a proper special demurrer."

A demurrer which alleges that an affidavit on which an accusation is based is insufficient, is itself invalid if it fails to set out reasons for the affidavit's insufficiency.[15]

A demurrer alleging facts which do not appear in the indictment and which are not judicially known or legally presumed is called a "speaking demurrer" and is void.[16] If a demurrer is predicated on facts that are judicially known, they must be set out. The failure to allege judicially known facts renders the demurrer invalid.[17]

The sustaining of a special demurrer, the result of which is either to strike from or add to the material allegations of the indictment, is the equivalent to sustaining a general demurrer and dismissing the indictment, but this is not true of an immaterial allegation.[18]

In former Georgia civil practice it was frequently possible to obtain more detailed information by means of a special demurrer.[19] Under that system of pleading in civil cases, if a special demurrer was sustained, the opposite party normally amended to meet the requirement of the court order sustaining the demurrer. Today, a motion for a more definite statement under the Civil Practice Act serves many of the same purposes that the special demurrer did under the former Civil Practice Procedure in Georgia.[20] Even though a special demurrer may still be filed in a criminal case, it may not generally be used for purposes of discovery, since an indictment cannot be amended to

---

[13]State v. Eubanks, 239 Ga. 483, 238 S.E.2d 38 (1977). However, this decision reversed Eubanks v. State, 141 Ga. App. 569, 234 S.E.2d 95 (1977), and the Georgia Supreme Court held that it was error to reverse the trial court, since it was not shown that the defendant was prejudiced by the overruling of the demurrer.

[14]State v. Jones, 246 Ga. App. 482, 483, 540 S.E.2d 622 (2000).

[15]Lucas v. State, 38 Ga. App. 449 (2), 451, 144 S.E. 138 (1928).

[16]Walters v. State, 90 Ga. App. 360, 365, 83 S.E.2d 48 (1954); State v. Givens, 211 Ga. App. 71, 72, 438 S.E.2d 387 (1993). However, in some cases

such a motion has been treated as a plea and passed on as such. State v. Holmes, 142 Ga. App. 847, 849, 237 S.E.2d 406 (1977). See State v. Grube, 293 Ga. 257, 744 S.E.2d 1 (2013).

[17]See Cole v. State, 68 Ga. App. 179, 182, 22 S.E.2d 529 (1942).

[18]Gentry v. State, 63 Ga. App. 275, 276, 11 S.E.2d 39 (1940). But cf. State v. Eubanks, 239 Ga. 483, 490, 238 S.E.2d 38 (1977).

[19]Driskal v. Mutual Benefit Life Insurance Co., 144 Ga. 534, 87 S.E. 668 (1916).

[20]Kimbrough v. State, 300 Ga. 878, 799 S.E.2d 229 (2017).

add additional facts.[21] However, since an accusation can be amended, it seems at least in theory that a special demurrer to an accusation may be sometimes used for the purpose of discovery. Also, of course, the sustaining of a special or general demurrer may force the district attorney to obtain a new indictment which contains information which was lacking in the earlier indictment.

In the 1977 case of *State v. Eubanks,*[22] the Georgia Supreme Court considered a case in which the indictment set out the essentials of one crime but incorrectly named the crime. A special demurrer was erroneously overruled. On appeal, the court said that the name of the crime was immaterial and the trial court had the power and duty to strike the erroneous name. This conclusion does no great violence to Georgia criminal procedure and finds support in earlier cases. However, the court concluded that unless the defendant was harmed by the overruling of the special demurrer, this is not a basis for reversing the conviction. Prior to this case, there was at least respectable Georgia authority which seemed to hold that if a special demurrer was erroneously overruled, all proceedings thereafter were rendered nugatory.[23] The *Eubanks* decision applies the harmless error doctrine to the overruling of a special demurrer and says that unless a defendant can show that he was prejudiced by being tried on the defective indictment, the erroneous overruling of a special demurrer is not a basis for reversal.[24] Thus, the court found no error in overruling a special demurrer to an indictment because it did not state the exact date of the crime where there was no showing that the absence of the date materially affected the ability of the defendant to present his defense.[25] The overruling of a special demurrer to a burglary indictment for failure to give an exact address of the building was held not to be error where the defendant failed to show that he was unable to prepare his defense or was subjected to a possible later prosecution for the same offense.[26]

In *State v. Grube,*[27] the defendant was charged with the offense of attempting to entice, over the internet, a person identified in

---

[21]Gentry v. State, 63 Ga. App. 275, 11 S.E.2d 39 (1940).

[22]State v. Eubanks, 239 Ga. 483, 238 S.E.2d 38 (1977).

[23]E.g., Haley v. State, 124 Ga. 216, 52 S.E. 159 (1905); Gilbert v. State, 175 Ga. 276, 277, 165 S.E. 120 (1932); Isom v. State, 71 Ga. App. 803, 805, 32 S.E.2d 437 (1944).

[24]McKinney v. State, 155 Ga. App.

930, 935 (6), 273 S.E.2d 888 (1980), overruled on other grounds by McKinney v. State, 184 Ga. App. 607, 609, 362 S.E.2d 65 (1987).

[25]Massengale v. State, 164 Ga. App. 57, 58 (1), 296 S.E.2d 371 (1982).

[26]Mobley v. State, 164 Ga. App. 154 (1), 296 S.E.2d 617 (1982).

[27]State v. Grube, 293 Ga. 257, 744 S.E.2d 1 (2013) (the ruling is consis-

the indictment only as "Tiffany." In reversing the Court of Appeals, the Supreme Court held that the indictment satisfied the principal requirements of due process for a formal criminal accusation, to wit: "(1) it must contain the essential elements of the crimes and apprise a defendant of what he must be prepared to meet at trial; and (2) it must show with accuracy to what extent the defendant may plead a former acquittal or conviction." The Court concluded that typically the manner in which a victim is identified in an indictment is by his or her full and correct name. However, it concluded that the same purpose is served by identifying the "victim" by his or her assumed name where the alleged criminal activity is directed at an undercover officer who is using an assumed name since that is the only identity of the "victim" the defendant has experienced.

For examples of some special demurrers, see Studdard, *Daniel's Georgia Criminal Trial Practice Forms* (2018–2019 ed.), §§ 12:13 et seq.

§ 14:42 Pleas

A plea may be utilized to attack a defect which does not appear on the face of an indictment. A plea attacking the indictment waives arraignment unless the defendant expressly reserves his right to arraignment.[1] The plea must be in writing and filed "at or before the time set by law unless time therefor is extended by the judge in writing prior to trial."[2]

Where a plea is filed, the district attorney may file a traverse if he contends that the facts set out in the plea are not truthful,[3] or a demurrer[4] or an oral motion to dismiss[5] if he believes that the plea is insufficient as a matter of law. If the plea is not stricken on demurrer, the defendant may introduce evidence in support of the plea. It is error for the trial court to prohibit the defendant from introducing the evidence in support of the plea.[6] If no evidence is introduced by the defendant, the plea must be overruled.[7] Furthermore, if a plea is filed and the defendant goes to trial without invoking any action of the court, the plea is treated as

---

tent with indictments which identify victims using the name by which he or she is known).

[Section 14:42]

[1]Baskin v. State, 137 Ga. App. 840, 841, 225 S.E.2d 77 (1976).

[2]Ga. Unif. Super. Ct. R. 31.1.

[3]Wells v. State, 118 Ga. 556, 557 (9), 45 S.E. 443 (1903).

[4]E.g., Fisher v. State, 93 Ga. 309 (1), 20 S.E. 329 (1894).

[5]See Meriwether v. State, 63 Ga. App. 667, 669, 11 S.E.2d 816 (1940).

[6]See Allen v. State, 110 Ga. App. 56, 137 S.E.2d 711 (1964).

[7]Wells v. State, 118 Ga. 556, 557 (8), 45 S.E. 443 (1903).

having been abandoned.[8] Likewise, a defendant's motions will not be treated as overruled where no order appears in the record on the motions.[9]

Pleas are usually passed upon by the trial judge without the intervention of a jury, except in the case of a special plea of insanity. This is true despite the fact that the Georgia Constitution states that the right to trial by jury shall remain inviolate except where otherwise provided,[10] unless a defendant waives his right to a jury trial.[11] While a long line of cases recognizes the right to a jury trial where there is no consent to the trial judge's passing or to the questions of fact raised in support of a plea,[12] in practice, the judge will normally pass on the plea himself, since a trial by jury requires more time. Several cases have stated directly that a plea in abatement should be submitted to a jury.[13] Other cases deal with directing a verdict against a plea.[14] Likewise, it has been held that a jury issue is formed where the defendant files a plea in abatement and the district attorney files a general denial.[15]

While most of the cases recognizing the right to a jury trial have involved a plea in abatement, the same rule applies to a plea in bar.[16] Granting a defendant a jury trial can be imperative in a plea in bar since such a plea can permanently dispose of a prosecution.[17]

If a plea is filed, the district attorney may demur to it or file a traverse denying the allegations. The burden of proof is on the defendant to establish the truth of the allegations set out in the

---

[8]Norwood v. State, 3 Ga. App. 325, 59 S.E. 828 (1907).

[9]Dowdy v. State, 152 Ga. App. 145, 146, 262 S.E.2d 511 (1979).

[10]Ga. Const. 1983, Art. I, § I, ¶ XI.

[11]Logan v. State, 86 Ga. 266, 270, 12 S.E. 406 (1890).

[12]E.g., Futch v. State, 37 Ga. App. 151, 139 S.E. 110 (1927); Burns v. State, 191 Ga. 60, 64, 11 S.E.2d 350 (1940); Wilson v. State, 69 Ga. 224, 236 (1882); Chancey v. State, 141 Ga. 54, 80 S.E. 287 (1913).

[13]Moore v. State, 64 Ga. App. 171, 173, 12 S.E.2d 410 (1940); Washington v. State, 113 Ga. 698, 39 S.E. 294 (1901). However, Williams v. State, 60 Ga. App. 636, 637, 4 S.E.2d 719 (1939), said that pleas "in abatement, pleas to the jurisdiction, a special plea of a deed relied on in an ejectment case, and pleas of former jeopardy are pleas which *may* be tried as separate issues." (Emphasis added.)

[14]Harris v. State, 193 Ga. 109, 112, 17 S.E.2d 573 (1941); Heaton v. State, 167 Ga. 147, 148 (4), 144 S.E. 782 (1928).

[15]Switzer v. State, 7 Ga. App. 7, 9, 65 S.E. 1079 (1909).

[16]See Ruffin v. State, 28 Ga. App. 40, 46 (3), 110 S.E. 311 (1921); Dennard v. State, 154 Ga. App. 283, 284, 267 S.E.2d 886 (1980).

[17]Ruffin v. State, 28 Ga. App. 40, 46, 110 S.E. 311 (1921), holds that in case of a plea in bar, the issue should be determined by a jury. Accord, Harris v. State, 43 Ga. App. 485, 487, 159 S.E. 603 (1931), a jury trial was used to pass on the question of fact presented in a plea in bar, viz., autrefois convict.

plea, and if the defendant fails to introduce evidence in support of the plea, the judge may direct a verdict against the defendant.[18] If the defendant submits evidence on the essential elements of the plea in abatement, it is error for the court to direct a verdict against the defendant on the plea.[19]

The sustaining of a plea terminates the prosecution; however, the defendant may be re-indicted and re-tried unless the plea sustained was a plea in bar. If a plea has been denied and the defendant convicted, he can appeal, and if the denial of the plea is reversed, all proceedings after the denial of the plea are considered void.[20]

§ 14:43   Plea in abatement

A plea in abatement is a dilatory plea. It must leave nothing to implication, and every inference is construed against the pleader.[1] Pleas in abatement are not favored and must be verified.[2]

In keeping with this policy of strictly construing a plea in abatement, a plea attacking an indictment on the ground that the proper oath was not administered to a named witness who testified before the grand jury is subject to demurrer where it is not alleged that the indictment against the defendant was returned based solely on the testimony of that witness.[3] A plea in abatement alleging that no precept has ever been issued or ordered as the law directed for the summoning of grand jurors is subject to demurrer, since it does not allege that no precept at all was issued.[4]

A plea in abatement may not be used to attack the validity of a law which is the basis of the indictment; the proper method of attacking such a statute is by demurrer.[5] However, the question of venue may be raised in a plea in abatement.[6] A plea in abatement may attack an indictment because there was no evidence before the grand jury to support it.[7]

---

[18]Harris v. State, 193 Ga. 109, 112, 17 S.E.2d 573 (1941).

[19]Heaton v. State, 167 Ga. 147, 148 (4), 144 S.E. 782 (1928), rev'g 37 Ga. App. 195, 139 S.E. 103 (1927).

[20]Nichols v. State, 17 Ga. App. 593, 610, 87 S.E. 817 (1916).

[Section 14:43]

[1]Jones v. State, 219 Ga. 848, 849 (2), 136 S.E.2d 358 (1964).

[2]Meriwether v. State, 63 Ga. App. 667, 669, 11 S.E.2d 816 (1940).

[3]Lennard v. State, 104 Ga. 546 (1), 30 S.E. 780 (1898).

[4]Williams v. State, 69 Ga. 11, 26, 27 (1882).

[5]Davis v. City of Fitzgerald, 6 Ga. App. 532, 65 S.E. 319 (1909).

[6]Knight v. State, 15 Ga. App. 474 (2), 83 S.E. 797 (1914).

[7]Whitehead v. State, 126 Ga. App. 570, 574, 191 S.E.2d 336 (1972).

In *Garcia v. State*,[8] the court pointed out that "Georgia courts have long recognized authority for treating motions to quash as pleas in abatement."

§ 14:44 Plea in abatement—Defective grand jury

An objection to the grand jury prior to indictment is most frequently called a challenge to the array or the poll. If an objection is raised after indictment, it is a plea in abatement. The objections and requirements of challenges before indictment apply equally to a plea in abatement filed after indictment. This material is discussed in more detail in the chapter on the Grand Jury and particularly in sections 12:3 through 12:9, supra.

§ 14:45 Plea in abatement—Misnomer

O.C.G.A. § 17-7-112 provides for the filing of a plea of misnomer. The plea must state the defendant's true name and allege that he has never been known by any other name and he is not called by the name under which he was indicted.[1] The plea must be verified[2] and filed "at or before the time set by law unless time therefor is extended by the judge in writing prior to trial."[3]

Most cases involving such pleas have dealt with the doctrine of *idem sonans*. Under this doctrine, if two names, although spelled differently, sound alike or are pronounced alike, they are regarded as the same.[4] By way of illustration, a plea of misnomer is invalid in the following situations: "Bickers" instead of "Biggers,"[5] "Fielder" instead of "Fielding,"[6] "Gittings" instead of "Giddans,"[7] "Hudson" instead of "Hutson,"[8] "Ila" instead of "Ira,"[9] "King" instead of "Keen,"[10] "L" instead of "Ell,"[11] "Maria S." instead of "Marie S."[12] and "Welsh" instead of "Welch."[13] However,

---

[8]Garcia v. State, 207 Ga. App. 794, 795, 429 S.E.2d 164 (1993).

[Section 14:45]

[1]O.C.G.A. § 17-7-112; Wiggins v. State, 80 Ga. 468, 5 S.E. 503 (1888).

[2]It has been referred to as a plea in abatement (see Johnson v. State, 7 Ga. App. 551, 552, 67 S.E. 224 (1910)), and pleas in abatement must be verified. Former GCA § 81-403 (not carried forward into O.C.G.A.); 7B E. G. L. Criminal Procedure (2000 Rev.), § 55; 22 C. J. S. Criminal Law § 430(b).

[3]Ga. Unif. Super. Ct. R. 31.1.

[4]Webb v. State, 149 Ga. 211, 99 S.E. 630 (1919).

[5]Biggers v. State, 109 Ga. 105, 34 S.E. 210 (1899).

[6]Fielding v. State, 30 Ga. App. 664, 118 S.E. 601 (1923).

[7]Woody v. State, 113 Ga. 927 (1), 39 S.E. 297 (1901).

[8]Chapman v. State, 18 Ga. 736 (1) (1855).

[9]Roberts v. State, 40 Ga. App. 732 (1), 151 S.E. 240 (1930).

[10]King v. State, 28 Ga. App. 228 (2), 111 S.E. 84 (1922).

[11]Rountree v. State, 34 Ga. App. 668, 670, 130 S.E. 919 (1925).

[12]Watkins v. State, 18 Ga. App. 500, 89 S.E. 624 (1916).

"Lizzie" is not idem sonans for "Eliza."[14]

If the district attorney files a demurrer to the plea of misnomer because the names sound alike, the trial judge may rule on the question of idem sonans as a matter of law.[15] However, where there is a question as to the exact name contained in the indictment, the defendant may have a jury determine the factual issue.[16]

The use of initials, instead of a full name, followed by a surname is immaterial.[17]

The overruling of a plea of misnomer is not grounds for a motion for a new trial,[18] although it may be assigned as error on appeal.

In *Hughes v. State*,[19] the Georgia Court of Appeals indicated that where an indictment contains an alias, a plea of misnomer is valid if the defendant has never been known by the alias.

See § 13:9, supra, on the name of the defendant in an indictment.

§ 14:46 Plea in bar

In a civil context, it has been said that a plea in bar attacks the merits of the case.[1] No Georgia criminal case appears to have defined such a plea. It would seem that if a plea asserts a defense which would demonstrate that no later prosecution may be successfully brought for the same crime, the plea would be a plea in bar. But if a plea will not prevent a later prosecution for the same offense, but only cause the district attorney to start the proceeding again, the plea is one in abatement. However, it has been said that a plea of res judicata is a plea in abatement,[2] and a plea of autrefois acquit is a plea in bar.[3]

A plea based on the statute of limitations is a plea in bar, and

---

[13]Webb v. State, 149 Ga. 211 (1), 99 S.E. 630 (1919).

[14]Jordan v. State, 60 Ga. 656 (1878).

[15]See King v. State, 28 Ga. App. 228 (1), 111 S.E. 84 (1922).

[16]See Washington v. State, 113 Ga. 698 (1), 39 S.E. 294 (1901).

[17]Eaves v. State, 113 Ga. 749, 750 (4), 39 S.E. 318 (1901).

[18]Lively v. State, 30 Ga. App. 633 (1), 118 S.E. 476 (1923).

[19]Hughes v. State, 161 Ga. App. 824 (1), 288 S.E.2d 916 (1982). Accord, Jenkins v. State, 229 Ga. App. 556, 494 S.E.2d 311 (1997).

[Section 14:46]

[1]Leverett, Hall, Christopher, Davis and Shulman, *Georgia Procedure and Practice*, § 10-4 (1957).

[2]Futch v. State, 37 Ga. App. 151, 139 S.E. 110 (1927). Contra, Loveless v. Carten, 64 Ga. App. 54 (1), 12 S.E.2d 175 (1940).

[3]Ruffin v. State, 28 Ga. App. 40, 46 (3), 110 S.E. 311 (1921). This case says that the plea goes to the merits of the charge as laid and it should be determined by a jury. State v. Rowe, 138 Ga. App. 904, 905 (1), 228 S.E.2d 3 (1976), overruled on other grounds

the burden is on the state to prove that the prosecution is not barred by the statute.[4] A motion alleging a denial of the constitutional right to a speedy trial is a plea in bar,[5] and an acquittal as a result of a demand for trial under O.C.G.A. § 17-7-170 is a plea in bar.[6]

Where a plea in bar is filed, the defendant is entitled to a jury trial on the plea if there is any question of fact.[7] If there is no question of fact involved, the trial judge may rule on the plea in bar as a matter of law.[8]

In *State v. Tuzman*,[9] the Georgia Court of Appeals pointed out that a defendant is not entitled to a pre-trial hearing on a plea in bar and it would be proper for the trial judge to dismiss the plea as a pre-trial matter reserving the merits for the trial of the defendant. However, it is not error for the trial judge to determine the merits of a plea in bar at a pre-trial evidentiary hearing, and such a pre-trial hearing "may be a very effective, fair and expedient method to deal with" a statute of limitations question. "Merely because the issue [is] to be determined pre-trial, the state is not relieved of its burden to prove that the case falls with in the exception . . ." to the statute of limitations.

In *Jenkins v. State*,[10] the Georgia Supreme Court disapproved *Tuzman* to the extent it said that a trial court could refuse a pre-trial hearing on a plea in bar based upon the statute of limitations. The court noted, "we believe that the proper procedure for litigating a plea in bar based upon the statute of limitations should be analogous to a pretrial *Jackson v. Denno* hearing, wherein if the defendant prevails on the issue of the voluntariness of a statement, the jury never hears the statement; if the State prevails on a pretrial *Jackson v. Denno* hearing the statement is admissible, but the defendant is still entitled to present

---

by Cleary v. State, 258 Ga. 203, 205, 366 S.E.2d 677 (1988).

[4]State v. Tuzman, 145 Ga. App. 481, 483 (3), 243 S.E.2d 675 (1978) (abrogated on other grounds by, State v. Outen, 289 Ga. 579, 714 S.E.2d 581 (2011)).

[5]State v. King, 137 Ga. App. 26, 222 S.E.2d 859 (1975); State v. Fields, 137 Ga. App. 726, 224 S.E.2d 829 (1976).

[6]State v. Benton, 246 Ga. 132, 269 S.E.2d 470 (1980).

[7]Daniels v. State, 78 Ga. 98 (1886); Harrell v. State, 196 Ga. App. 101, 102 (1), 395 S.E.2d 598 (1990).

[8]Bell v. State, 249 Ga. 644, 292 S.E.2d 402 (1982).

[9]State v. Tuzman, 145 Ga. App. 481, 483 (2), 243 S.E.2d 675 (1978) (abrogated on other grounds by, State v. Outen, 289 Ga. 579, 714 S.E.2d 581 (2011)).

[10]Jenkins v. State, 278 Ga. 598 (1), 604 S.E.2d 789 (2004). See Lynch v. State, 815 S.E.2d 340 (Ga. Ct. App. 2018) (plea in bar based upon the statute of limitations may be raised at any time including during the trial of the case); Lee v. State, 289 Ga. 95, 709 S.E.2d 762 (2011) (failure of state to prove date that prosecution was commenced left jury with no basis to find that accusation was timely filed).

evidence and argument that it was not voluntary, and the State must prove otherwise. If a defendant prevails on a pretrial plea in bar on the statute of limitations, the charge should be dismissed; if the State prevails on this issue before trial, the defendant may still require the State to prove at trial that the charge is not barred by the statute of limitations." (citations omitted).

§ 14:47 Double jeopardy

The Fifth Amendment of the United States Constitution states that no person shall "be twice put in jeopardy of life or limb" for the same offense.[1] The Fifth Amendment applies to the states through the due process clause of the Fourteenth Amendment.[2] The Georgia Constitution similarly provides that "[n]o person shall be put in jeopardy of life or liberty more than once for the same offense except when a new trial has been granted after conviction or in case of mistrial."[3] However, the statutory protections afforded by the state against double jeopardy do not apply to civil proceedings.[4]

In *Monge v. California*,[5] the United States Supreme Court pointed out that the Fifth Amendment "protects against successive prosecutions for the same offense . . . and against multiple criminal punishments for the same offense. . . . [However, historically the] double jeopardy protections [have been] inapplicable to sentencing proceedings . . . because the determinations at issue do not place a defendant in jeopardy for an 'offense'. . . ." See Annotation, "Double Jeopardy Considerations in Federal Criminal Cases—Supreme Court Cases," 162 A.L.R.Fed. 415 (2000).

The prohibition against double jeopardy is a fundamental principle deeply embedded in the common law and is older than

---

[Section 14:47]

[1]U.S. Const. Amend. V. See Annot., "Supreme Court's Views of Fifth Amendment's Double Jeopardy Clause Pertinent to or Applied in Federal Criminal Cases," 50 L.Ed.2d 830 (1977).

[2]Benton v. Maryland, 395 U.S. 784, 89 S.Ct. 2056, 23 L.Ed.2d 707 (1969). See Annot., "Limitations Under Double Jeopardy Clause of Fifth Amendment Upon State Criminal Prosecutions—Supreme Court Cases," 25 L.Ed.2d 968 (1970).

See Annot., "Limitations Under Double Jeopardy Clause of Fifth Amendment Upon State Criminal Prosecutions—Supreme Court Cases," 67 L.Ed.2d 831 (1982).

[3]Ga. Const. 1983, Art. I, § I, ¶ XVIII. In Jackson v. State, 154 Ga. App. 367 (1), 268 S.E.2d 418 (1980), the court makes it clear that it does not matter "how a defendant obtains a new trial—by direct appeal from . . . [a] conviction or after the denial of his motion for new trial." In either case, the defendant waives his right to assert double jeopardy.

[4]Durfee v. State, 221 Ga. App. 211, 212 (1), 471 S.E.2d 32 (1996).

[5]Monge v. California, 524 U.S. 721, 118 S.Ct. 2246, 141 L.Ed.2d 615, 623 (1998).

the Constitution.[6] It was known in a primitive form in the Greek and Roman civilizations.[7] As applied, it prevents successive prosecutions for the same offense.[8] This is referred to as the procedural aspect of the double jeopardy rule, the purpose of which is to prevent harassment of the accused. It has yet another aspect, which is to prevent multiple convictions.[9] This is said to be the substantive aspect. The theory behind the bar to multiple convictions is to prevent multiple and excessive punishments.[10]

The prohibition against double jeopardy only applies to criminal proceedings.[11] In *Waye v. State*,[12] officers executed a search warrant at the defendant's residence and seized $78,254 and discovered cocaine. The officers transferred the money to federal officials who initiated federal forfeiture proceedings. After the defendant was indicted, he filed a motion to dismiss which was denied. The court pointed out that the double jeopardy clause of the Georgia Constitution is construed no more broadly than the federal Constitution. Although Georgia statutes "extend the proscription beyond those constitutional limits," they do not apply to civil proceedings. The forfeiture proceeding was civil. Similarly, in *Murphy v. State*,[13] the court held that a civil forfeiture in a drug case does not prevent a later criminal prosecution based on the same acts.

For purposes of due process and equal protection, corporations are treated as "persons."[14] Accordingly, "[i]t follows that a corporation is entitled to the double jeopardy protection afforded by the Georgia Constitution."[15]

See § 20:4, infra, on venue where there is a series of crimes in different counties.

§ 14:48 Double jeopardy—Some situations not constituting double jeopardy

Although many situations may appear to be of criminally procedural nature, they nonetheless do not amount to double

---

[6]Black v. State, 36 Ga. 447, 449 (1867).

[7]Keener v. State, 238 Ga. 7, 230 S.E.2d 846 (1976).

[8]See O.C.G.A. § 16-1-8.

[9]See O.C.G.A. § 16-1-7.

[10]Keener v. State, 238 Ga. 7, 8, 230 S.E.2d 846 (1976); State v. Estevez, 232 Ga. 316, 317 (1), 206 S.E.2d 475 (1974), overruled by, Drinkard v. Walker, 281 Ga. 211, 636 S.E.2d 530 (2006)).

[11]Alexander v. State, 129 Ga. App. 395, 397 (2), 199 S.E.2d 918 (1973).

[12]Waye v. State, 219 Ga. App. 22, 464 S.E.2d 19 (1995) (quoting State v. Martin, 173 Ga. App. 370, 371, 326 S.E.2d 558 (1985)).

[13]Murphy v. State, 219 Ga. App. 474, 475, 465 S.E.2d 497 (1995), aff'd, 267 Ga. 120, 475 S.E.2d 907 (1996).

[14]Eckles v. Atlanta Technology Group, Inc., 267 Ga. 801, 485 S.E.2d 22 (1997).

[15]Wilbros, LLC v. State, 294 Ga. 514, 755 S.E.2d 145 (2014).

jeopardy. A person placed in a lineup on three different occasions is not deemed to have been put in jeopardy,[1] and a person is not placed in jeopardy by having a preliminary or commitment hearing, even if the charges against him were dismissed at that time.[2] Where a police officer is terminated for choking a victim, he may be tried criminally.[3] Where an inmate receives administrative punishment for an escape, this does not prevent a criminal prosecution for the same offense.[4] Likewise, where a driver is declared an habitual violator by the Department of Public Safety (now Department of Motor Vehicle Safety), his driver's license is revoked, and he is indicted as an habitual violator after a DUI arrest, the prior action of the Department does not prevent his trial under the habitual violator indictment.[5] In *Martinez v. State*,[6] the court affirmed the denial of a plea in bar where defendant was charged with driving under the influence and an earlier administrative license suspension hearing was "resolved in defendant's favor . . . when the arresting officer failed to appear. . . ." In *Thompson v. State*,[7] the court affirmed the denial of a plea in bar where defendant's driver's license was suspended for a year after he was arrested for driving under the influence. He complied with O.C.G.A. § 40-5-67.2(a)(1) by submitting evidence of completion of a DUI alcohol risk reduction program and paid a $200 fee to get his driver's license back. The court held that the defendant's payment of the $200 was voluntary. Where a defendant is tried for driving under the influence in a county recorder's court (which has no authority to try him for this offense), this does not prevent his later trial in a court which has jurisdiction.[8] In *Boone v. State*,[9] the Court of Appeals observed that for purpose of double jeopardy, an administrative suspen-

---

[Section 14:48]

[1]Atkins v. Martin, 229 Ga. 815, 816 (4), 194 S.E.2d 463 (1972). See § 14:51, infra, on administrative punishment.

[2]Wells v. Stynchcombe, 231 Ga. 199, 200 S.E.2d 745 (1973); Moore v. Commonwealth, 218 Va. 388, 237 S.E.2d 187 (1977).

[3]Pennyman v. State, 222 Ga. App. 779, 476 S.E.2d 71 (1996).

[4]Anderson v. State, 250 Ga. 500, 300 S.E.2d 163 (1983); Flowers v. State, 166 Ga. App. 740, 306 S.E.2d 16 (1983). But see Annot., "Doctrine of Res Judicata or Collateral Estoppel as Barring Relitigation in State Criminal Proceedings of Issues Previously Decided in Administrative Proceedings,"

30 A.L.R.4th 856 (1984).

[5]Webster v. State, 170 Ga. App. 102, 316 S.E.2d 503 (1984). Accord, Kirkpatrick v. State, 219 Ga. App. 307, 464 S.E.2d 882 (1995); Jackson v. State, 218 Ga. App. 677, 678, 462 S.E.2d 802 (1995). Cf. Nolen v. Georgia, 218 Ga. App. 819, 820, 463 S.E.2d 504 (1995); Ford v. State, 221 Ga. App. 155, 470 S.E.2d 537 (1996).

[6]Martinez v. State, 221 Ga. App. 483, 471 S.E.2d 551 (1996).

[7]Thompson v. State, 229 Ga. App. 526, 494 S.E.2d 306 (1997). Accord, Morgan v. State, 229 Ga. App. 861, 495 S.E.2d 138 (1997).

[8]Cf. Duncan v. State, 185 Ga. App. 854, 366 S.E.2d 154 (1988), overruled on other grounds by Kolker

sion of a driver's license will not be considered a punishment so as to bar a prosecution for the related criminal offense, e.g., D.U.I. "[b]ecause a driver's license is a privilege and not an absolute right, that privilege may be revoked or suspended for cause."

In *Prock v. State*,[10] the defendant was indicted in Count 1 for furnishing alcohol to an underage person on August 18, 1998, in Count 2 with the sale of marijuana on August 27, 1998, and in Count 3 with unlawful possession of marijuana. The defendant filed a plea in bar to the charge of selling alcohol in the Henry County Probate Court. Later the defendant filed a plea in bar to the indictment charges contending that the defendant's guilty plea to the charge of selling alcohol to a minor constituted double jeopardy. While the trial court accepted the plea regarding the alcohol charge, the plea for double jeopardy was properly denied since the probate court did not have jurisdiction over the felony charges.

A defendant is not placed in jeopardy by an administrative change of the Georgia Crime Information Center to show a conviction in lieu of first offender treatment.[11] In *Jackett v. State*,[12] the court held that a defendant was not put in jeopardy when he was tried by a magistrate sitting as a state court judge and the magistrate did not meet the statutory requirements to sit as a state court judge. If a defendant is tried by a court not having venue of the crime, he may be tried in a court which does have venue.[13] In *Jennings v. State*,[14] the court held that a defendant is not placed in jeopardy by the admission of evidence at a former trial that he committed the crime for which he is now on trial.

Neither is the defendant placed in jeopardy by being indicted. Hence, the pendency of a former indictment for the same offense is no basis for a plea,[15] even if the defendant was arraigned and filed a plea to the earlier indictment.[16] Where an indictment is dismissed on demurrer, the defendant has not been put in

---

v. State, 193 Ga. App. 306 (1), 387 S.E.2d 597 (1989).

[9]Boone v. State, 256 Ga. App. 220, 223, 568 S.E.2d 91 (2002).

[10]Prock v. State, 246 Ga. App. 703, 704, 541 S.E.2d 685 (2000).

[11]McKinney v. State, 240 Ga. App. 812, 813 (1), 525 S.E.2d 395 (1999).

[12]Jackett v. State, 209 Ga. App. 112, 432 S.E.2d 586 (1993).

[13]Kimmel v. State, 261 Ga. 332, 334 (1), 404 S.E.2d 436 (1991).

[14]Jennings v. State, 230 Ga. App. 661, 663 (1), 497 S.E.2d 13 (1998).

[15]Irwin v. State, 117 Ga. 706, 45 S.E. 48 (1903). In Cox v. State, 203 Ga. App. 869, 870, 418 S.E.2d 133 (1992), the court held that O.C.G.A. § 9-2-5, which prohibits the state from two proceedings for the same offense at the same time, does not apply to criminal proceedings.

[16]Geckles v. State, 177 Ga. App. 70, 71, 338 S.E.2d 473 (1985); Leatherwood v. State, 212 Ga. App. 342, 344 (4), 441 S.E.2d 813 (1994).

jeopardy.[17] (But see § 12:17, supra, on the second dismissal of an indictment.) An arraignment does not place the defendant in jeopardy or prevent the return of a later indictment for the same offense.[18]

The admission of guilt of a separate crime during a sentencing does not amount to jeopardy as to the separate crime.[19] In *Witte v. United States,*[20] the Court held that the double jeopardy clause does not prevent the prosecution of a defendant for a crime which was used in a prior sentencing hearing to enhance the defendant's sentence under the Federal Sentencing Guidelines. A guilty plea, pursuant to plea negotiations, to a lesser included offense does not prevent a trial for the greater offense, where the guilty plea is withdrawn.[21]

Likewise, if a defendant's probation is revoked for the commission of a later crime, this does not prevent his trial for the later crime[22] or other violation of the conditions of his probation.[23] Also, jeopardy does not attach in a probation revocation hearing.[24] In *State v. Jones,*[25] the defendant had been sentenced to probation in an earlier case; later he was indicted for robbery; the defendant's parole officer petitioned for a revocation of probation, based on the later offense of robbery; the trial judge's order stated that he did "not find a violation." This probation hearing and order did not serve as collateral estoppel of the defendant's guilt or innocence of robbery. Where a trial judge dismisses, without prejudice, a rule nisi order on a probation revocation petition because the state does not have its witnesses present, this does not prevent the trial judge from issuing a new rule nisi order and conducting the probation revocation hearing.[26] Where a hearing is conducted on revocation of probation for commission of robbery and the trial judge declines to revoke his probation, this does not

[17]Brown v. State, 109 Ga. 570, 34 S.E. 1031 (1900). See § 14:58, infra.

[18]Gray v. State, 6 Ga. App. 428, 65 S.E. 191 (1909). In Illinois v. Somerville, 410 U.S. 458, 93 S.Ct. 1066, 35 L.Ed.2d 425 (1973), the court held that where an indictment is fatally defective, and this comes to the attention of the district attorney after the introduction of some evidence, and his motion for a mistrial is granted over the objection of the defense, the defendant's double jeopardy rights are not violated by a later trial for the same offense.

[19]In re M.E.J., 260 Ga. 805, 806, 401 S.E.2d 254 (1991).

[20]Witte v. United States, 515 U.S. 389, 115 S.Ct. 2199, 132 L.Ed.2d 351 (1995). Witte was cited with approval and followed in Nance v. State, 266 Ga. 816, 471 S.E.2d 216 (1996).

[21]Klobuchir v. Commonwealth, 639 F.2d 966 (3d Cir. 1981).

[22]Morris v. State, 166 Ga. App. 137 (2), 303 S.E.2d 492 (1983).

[23]In the Interest of B. N. D., 185 Ga. App. 906, 907, 366 S.E.2d 187 (1988).

[24]Smith v. State, 171 Ga. App. 279, 282, 319 S.E.2d 113 (1984).

[25]State v. Jones, 196 Ga. App. 896, 397 S.E.2d 209 (1990).

[26]Brooks v. State, 162 Ga. App. 485, 292 S.E.2d 89 (1982).

prevent the defendant's later indictment and trial for robbery.[27] In addition, the modification of the conditions of a defendant's probation after the imposition of sentence does not amount to double jeopardy.[28]

Likewise, a dismissal for "want of prosecution" without prejudice does not prevent a later trial of a defendant for the same charge.[29] Additionally, no jeopardy attaches where a trial is dismissed because of lack of venue.[30] Where a nolle prosequi of an indictment is properly entered in superior court so that the case may be transferred to the state court of that county, double jeopardy does not prevent the trial in state court.[31]

A gun owner's acquittal of a criminal firearms charge does not prevent a later forfeiture proceeding against the firearms.[32] In *United States v. Ursery*,[33] the United States Supreme Court held that a civil forfeiture proceeding against a house for alleged drug activity did not violate the double jeopardy clause because (1) Congress intended the forfeiture to be a remedial civil sanction instead of a criminal penalty, and (2) the forfeiture proceeding was not so punitive in effect that it may not legitimately be viewed as civil in nature, since the legislative intent was to establish a civil remedial mechanism.

Likewise, a hearing on a motion to suppress does not place a defendant in jeopardy.[34] The defendant's civil commitment for mental illness does not prevent a later prosecution even though the evidence of the same incident was considered in the civil commitment.[35] Likewise, a person is not placed in jeopardy by the trial of a case in which he is named as an unindicted co-

---

[27]Teague v. State, 169 Ga. App. 285 (1), 312 S.E.2d 818 (1983).

[28]Stephens v. State, 289 Ga. 758, 716 S.E.2d 154 (2011). Cf. Gould v. Patterson, 253 Ga. App. 603, 560 S.E.2d 37 (2002) (the revocation of a defendant's probation based upon the violation of a condition of probation which the defendant never had notice may violate defendant's right to due process).

[29]State v. Roca, 203 Ga. App. 267, 268, 416 S.E.2d 836 (1992).

[30]Sewell v. State, 229 Ga. App. 685, 686, 494 S.E.2d 512 (1997). The same is true where the trial court directs a verdict of acquittal because the state failed to prove venue. Hudson v. State, 296 Ga. App. 758 (1), 675 S.E.2d 603 (2009).

[31]Newman v. State, 166 Ga. App. 609, 305 S.E.2d 123 (1983).

[32]United States v. One Assortment of 89 Firearms, 465 U.S. 354, 104 S.Ct. 1099, 79 L.Ed.2d 361 (1984).

[33]United States v. Ursery, 518 U.S. 267, 116 S.Ct. 2135, 135 L.Ed.2d 549 (1996). Followed, Battista v. State, 223 Ga. App. 369, 370, 477 S.E.2d 665 (1996). Accord, Murphy v. State, 267 Ga. 120, 475 S.E.2d 907 (1996).

[34]Waters v. State, 177 Ga. App. 374, 375 (1), 339 S.E.2d 608 (1985).

[35]Wiggins v. State, 171 Ga. App. 358, 360 (2), 319 S.E.2d 528 (1984).

conspirator.[36] Generally, when a mistrial is granted, at the request of the defendant, the defendant may be tried again.[37] The double jeopardy clause does not generally prevent the retrial of a defendant where he was successful in getting his conviction set aside "because of some error in the proceedings leading to the conviction."[38] But see § 14:58, infra, on retrial where a conviction is set aside for lack of evidence.

In *Moser v. Richmond County Board of Commissioners*,[39] the court held that a revocation of a license to operate a health spa, after the owner pled nolo contendere to a sexual offense, did not amount to double jeopardy.

Generally, a defendant is not considered as having been placed in jeopardy when a cash or property bond is revoked.[40] However, if a defendant posts a cash bond, fails to appear, "and the judge enters an order forfeiting the bond and declaring such forfeiture to be a final disposition of the case," this bars a later prosecution.[41] But there is said to be no prosecution and thus no jeopardy where a defendant simply pays a fine on a speeding charge to a clerk.[42] Georgia has a special statute (O.C.G.A. § 17-6-8) which applies to certain misdemeanors and provides that a cash bond may be forfeited without a compliance with statutory procedure provided for the forfeiture of statutory bail bonds. "A judgment ordering the case disposed of and settled may be entered by the court and the proceeds shall be applied in the same manner as fines. If the court does not enter a judgment ordering the case disposed of and settled, the forfeiture of a cash bond shall not be a bar to subsequent prosecution. . . ." This statutory procedure applies only to any person arrested for a misdemeanor arising out of a violation of the laws of this state relating to (1) traffic or the operation or licensing of motor vehicles or operators; (2) the width, height, or length of vehicles and loads; (3) motor common carriers and motor contract carriers; (4) road taxes on motor carriers as provided in O.C.G.A. §§ 48-9-30 et seq.; (5) game and fish; (6) boating; or (7) litter control. Also, O.C.G.A. § 17-6-10 provides that a forfeited bond given for the violation of a municipal ordinance prevents a later prosecution for that offense in cities which do not have a provision in their charters relating "to

---

[36]Caldwell v. State, 171 Ga. App. 680, 320 S.E.2d 888 (1984).

[37]Sanders v. State, 197 Ga. App. 867 (1), 399 S.E.2d 734 (1990). See § 14:58, infra.

[38]Allen v. State, 262 Ga. 240, 241, 416 S.E.2d 290 (1992).

[39]Moser v. Richmond County Board of Commissioners, 263 Ga. 63,

428 S.E.2d 71 (1993).

[40]O.C.G.A. § 17-6-8.

[41]Collins v. State, 177 Ga. App. 758, 341 S.E.2d 288 (1986) (citing Wilson v. State, 167 Ga. App. 421, 306 S.E.2d 704 (1983)).

[42]Collins v. State, 177 Ga. App. 758, 341 S.E.2d 288 (1986).

the subject matter of this Code section."

In the interesting case of *Clark v. State*,[43] the court held that there was no double jeopardy violation where the defendant was suspended from high school because of an armed robbery and he was then charged with armed robbery. The court pointed out that determining whether the suspension is punishment requires " 'a particularized assessment of the penalty imposed and the purposes that the penalty may fairly be said to serve.' . . . Whether a sanction constitutes punishment is not to be determined from the defendant's perspective, but rather, 'it is the purpose *actually served* by the sanction in question, not the underlying nature of the proceeding giving rise to the sanction, that must be evaluated.' "[44]

In *Shepherd v. State*,[45] the Georgia Supreme Court held that the mandatory psychiatric treatment of an insanity acquitee does not implicate the Double Jeopardy Clause's prohibition against multiple punishments where the acquitee also faces jail time for charges arising out of the same offense. Relying on *United States v. Halper*,[46] the *Shepherd* court found that the defendant's civil commitment "advanced remedial goals with respect to the treatment of an insanity acquitee," and accordingly held that "[Georgia's] statutory scheme 'permitting psychiatric treatment rather than merely imprisonment alone,' [citation omitted], is not punitive, and double jeopardy's multiple punishment concerns are not implicated."[47]

In *Jackson v. State*,[48] the court held that the defendant's double jeopardy challenge was foreclosed by his later guilty plea and a judgment of conviction.

---

[43]Clark v. State, 220 Ga. App. 251, 469 S.E.2d 250 (1996) (quoting United States v. Halper, 490 U.S. 435, 109 S.Ct. 1892, 104 L.Ed.2d 487 (1989)) (emphasis in original). See Simile v. State, 259 Ga. App. 106, 576 S.E.2d 83 (2003) where a plea of former jeopardy by a Georgia Tech student to a DUI prosecution was rejected where it was premised upon University administrative sanctions imposed because of the same conduct.

[44]Department of Revenue of Montana v. Kurth Ranch, 511 U.S. 767, 114 S.Ct. 1937, 128 L.Ed.2d 767 (1994).

[45]Shepherd v. State, 280 Ga. 245, 626 S.E.2d 96 (2006).

[46]U.S. v. Halper, 490 U.S. 435, 109 S. Ct. 1892, 104 L. Ed. 2d 487 (1989). *Halper* has since been abrogated by U.S. v. Hudson, 522 U.S. 93, 118 S.Ct. 488, 139 L.Ed.2d 450 (1997), wherein the Court held that for double jeopardy to apply in a criminal case which follows a civil case involving the same conduct, the sanctions in the civil case must clearly have been punitive.

[47]Shepherd v. State, 280 Ga. 245, 252, 626 S.E.2d 96 (2006), citing U.S. v. Halper, 490 U.S. 435, 109 S. Ct. 1892, 104 L. Ed. 2d 487 (1989).

[48]Jackson v. State, 246 Ga. App. 673, 674 (1), 541 S.E.2d 672 (2000).

In *Brown v. State*,[49] the court ruled that double jeopardy had no application on the resentencing of a defendant who reneged on a negotiated plea bargain which required his participation as a state's witness in the trial of his co-defendant.

Pursuant to O.C.G.A. § 16-5-44.1, the offense of motor vehicle hijacking is to be considered as a separate offense, punished as such and not to be merged with any other offense. In *Mathis v. State*,[50] the Georgia Supreme Court held that this code section does not violate the prohibition against double jeopardy since the Georgia constitutional provision which protects against multiple punishment for the same offense does not forbid additional punishment "for a separate offense which the General Assembly has deemed to warrant separate sanctions." The court concluded that motor vehicle hijacking is such an offense and that the code section is a clear expression of the Legislature's intent to impose a punishment for that offense, separate from and additional to, any punishment for conduct which violates other criminal statutes.

§ 14:49 Double jeopardy—Necessity of plea

A plea relating to the successive prosecutions of a defendant for the same offense must be filed promptly by the defendant. If such a plea is not timely filed, the right of the defendant to assert the defense is generally lost.[1]

However, it has been held that if the state has failed to respond to a Brady motion for discovery of information favorable to defendant, and to inform defense counsel of a former conviction, the right to file a plea of double jeopardy is not waived. The knowledge of the defendant himself makes no difference in a collateral estoppel situation.[2]

Generally, a plea in bar of former jeopardy based on successive prosecutions for the same offense must be made within 10 days after arraignment unless that time is extended in writing by the court prior to trial.[3]

However, there is a distinction between successive prosecutions for the same offense as prohibited in O.C.G.A. § 16-1-7 and

---

[49]Brown v. State, 261 Ga. App. 115, 582 S.E.2d 13 (2003). Compare Evans v. State, 293 Ga. App. 371, 667 S.E.2d 183 (2008), where defendant's efforts to plead double jeopardy after he was rejected by drug court because of his physical and mental condition was denied.

[50]Mathis v. State, 273 Ga. 508, 509(1), 543 S.E.2d 712 (2001).

[Section 14:49]

[1]See Phelps v. State, 130 Ga. App. 344, 203 S.E.2d 320 (1973); United States v. Hoyland, 264 F.2d 346 (7th Cir. 1959); United States v. Hill, 473 F.2d 759 (9th Cir. 1972).

[2]Clark v. State, 144 Ga. App. 69, 70, 240 S.E.2d 270 (1977).

[3]Ga. Unif. Super. Ct. R. 31.1; O.C.G.A. § 17-7-110.

a prohibition against successive punishments for the same offense as prohibited in O.C.G.A. § 16-1-7. See §§ 14:54, 14:55 and 14:56, infra. Thus, in *McClure v. State*,[4] the Georgia Court of Appeals held that "the failure to file a written plea of former jeopardy prior to trial will not defeat an accused's right to be free of multiple convictions for the criminal act."

See §§ 14:53 to 14:57, infra, on double jeopardy for the same offense and collateral estoppel.

§ 14:50   Double jeopardy—Requirements of plea

As previously noted, a plea of former jeopardy for successive prosecutions for the same offense must be made in writing. The common law plea of "autrefois attaint," formerly convicted, is now obsolete. Instead, the plea of "autrefois convict" is now utilized where a former conviction is pled to prevent a later prosecution.[1]

A plea of former jeopardy for successive prosecutions must allege that the offenses are identical or that there exists some other provision of law which would serve to bar a second trial. The result of the former trial must be set out.[2] Furthermore, a plea is fatally defective if it fails to set out a copy of the former indictment[3] or accusation.[4]

A defendant is entitled to a separate jury trial of the plea where he files a plea of former jeopardy and the state files a traverse.[5]

Since courts do not take judicial notice of municipal ordinances, where the plea of former jeopardy states that the defendant has been convicted in a municipal court of violating a city ordinance, a copy of the ordinance should be included.[6]

For pleas of double jeopardy, see Studdard, *Daniel's Georgia*

---

[4]McClure v. State, 179 Ga. App. 245, 246 (1), 345 S.E.2d 922 (1986); Dotson v. State, 213 Ga. App. 7, 11 (2), 443 S.E.2d 650 (1994).

[Section 14:50]

[1]Jenkins v. State, 14 Ga. App. 276 (3), 279, 80 S.E. 688 (1914). This case points out that at common law there was some doubt whether, under a plea of former conviction, it was necessary to set out the judgment of conviction or whether or not it was sufficient to allege simply that a verdict of guilty had been rendered on an indictment which on its face appeared to be valid. The court concluded that whatever the rule was at common law, in Georgia it is sufficient to show that a verdict of guilty had been returned

on a valid indictment.

[2]See Lock v. State, 122 Ga. 730 (2), 50 S.E. 932 (1905).

[3]Thomas v. State, 24 Ga. App. 350 (1), 100 S.E. 760 (1919); State v. Fowler, 182 Ga. App. 897, 357 S.E.2d 329 (1987).

[4]Honiker v. State, 230 Ga. App. 597, 598, 497 S.E.2d 70 (1998); State v. Fowler, 182 Ga. App. 897, 357 S.E.2d 329 (1987); Welch v. State, 53 Ga. App. 255, 257, 185 S.E. 390 (1936); Jackson v. State, 246 Ga. App. 673, 674 (2), 541 S.E.2d 672 (2000).

[5]McWilliams v. State, 110 Ga. 290, 34 S.E. 1016 (1900).

[6]Howell v. State, 13 Ga. App. 74, 78 S.E. 859 (1913); State v. Fowler, 182 Ga. App. 897, 357 S.E.2d 329 (1987).

Criminal Trial Practice Forms (2018–2019 ed.), §§ 27:9 et seq.

§ 14:51 Double jeopardy—When jeopardy attaches

Generally, in Georgia, jeopardy attaches when the jury is impaneled and sworn,[1] or in a non-jury case, after the first witness has been sworn and the court begins to hear testimony.[2] However, the swearing of a witness does not conclusively establish that the trial had commenced because sworn testimony is often given during pre-trial proceedings.[3] In *Nguyen v. State*,[4] the court held that a defendant is not placed in jeopardy where another individual was erroneously put on trial earlier with the mistaken belief that the person put on trial was the defendant.

In *Weaver v. State*,[5] the court held that the entering of a nolo contendere plea constitutes jeopardy even though entered before a jury was impaneled and sworn.

Where a defendant files a demurrer to the indictment which is overruled, and the judge later during trial sustains the demurrer, the defendant's plea of double jeopardy is invalid. The plea is not good, regardless of whether the indictment was defective or not, since the defendant has asked that the earlier indictment be dismissed.[6] However, when a *nolle prosequi* is entered over the objection of the defendant after a jury has been empaneled, a retrial on those charges would be barred.[7]

In *Wilson v. State*,[8] the court held that jeopardy attached where a defendant forfeited a cash bond and the court entered an order stating that the forfeiture of cash bonds is a final disposition of these cases. Jeopardy cannot attach until after the return of an

---

[Section 14:51]

[1]Newsom v. State, 2 Ga. 60, 62 (1847); Franklin v. State, 85 Ga. 570, 11 S.E. 876 (1890); Ferguson v. State, 219 Ga. 33, 35, 131 S.E.2d 538 (1963); Shaw v. State, 239 Ga. 690, 692, 238 S.E.2d 434 (1977); Von Burleson v. Estelle, 666 F.2d 231 (5th Cir. 1982).

However, in Crist v. Bretz, 437 U.S. 28, 98 S.Ct. 2156, 57 L.Ed.2d 24 (1978), the court held jeopardy attaches when the jury is impaneled and sworn; this rule is an integral part of the Fifth Amendment and is made applicable to the states through the Fourteenth Amendment.

[2]White v. State, 143 Ga. App. 315, 317, 238 S.E.2d 247 (1977).

[3]Henderson v. State, 236 Ga. App. 72, 73, 510 S.E.2d 879 (1999).

[4]Nguyen v. State, 257 Ga. 281, 284, 358 S.E.2d 247 (1987).

[5]Weaver v. State, 224 Ga. App. 243, 480 S.E.2d 286 (1997).

[6]See Brown v. State, 109 Ga. 570(1), 34 S.E. 1031 (1900); Hill v. Nelms, 122 Ga. 572, 50 S.E. 344 (1905).

[7]Marshall v. State, 275 Ga. 218(2), 563 S.E.2d 868 (2002). Compare Smith v. State, 279 Ga. 396, 614 S.E.2d 79 (2005) and Hubbard v. State, 225 Ga. App. 154, 483 S.E.2d 115 (1997).

[8]Wilson v. State, 167 Ga. App. 421, 306 S.E.2d 704 (1983).

indictment or the filing of an accusation.[9]

In *Smith v. Massachusetts,*[10] the trial judge, at the conclusion of the prosecution's case, granted the defendant's motion for a finding of not guilty on one count of the indictment. During the defendant's case, however, the trial judge announced orally that she was reversing her previous ruling on the motion, thus allowing the previously dismissed count to go to the jury. Following conviction on all counts of the indictment, the defendant filed an appeal, contending that double jeopardy prohibited a "second" prosecution after the trial judge's initial ruling of acquittal. On appeal, the United States Supreme Court concluded that "[i]f, after a facially unqualified midtrial dismissal of one count, the trial has proceeded to the defendant's introduction of evidence, the acquittal must be treated as final . . ." in the absence of some recognized procedure which would expressly allow for the reconsideration of midtrial orders of dismissal.

If an indictment is fatally defective, no jeopardy attaches.[11] In the unusual case of *Williams v. State,*[12] the defendant was being tried for arson in the first degree. At the close of the evidence the defendant moved for a directed verdict on the ground that the indictment was "fatally defective." The trial judge agreed that the indictment did not allege the crime of arson in the first degree, but allowed the case to go to the jury on the lesser included offense of arson in the second degree. The Court of Appeals affirmed the conviction of arson in the second degree.

Similarly, if a defendant is tried or pleads guilty in a court not having jurisdiction to try the case, jeopardy does not attach.[13] If a defendant is tried in one county in a court having jurisdiction of

---

[9]Cf. Roberts v. State, 171 Ga. App. 131, 132 (1), 319 S.E.2d 42 (1984).

[10]Smith v. Massachusetts, 543 U.S. 462, 125 S. Ct. 1129, 160 L. Ed. 2d 914 (2005).

[11]Conley v. State, 85 Ga. 348 (1), 11 S.E. 659 (1890); Lee v. United States, 432 U.S. 23, 97 S.Ct. 2141, 53 L.Ed.2d 80 (1977); see comment on *Illinois v. Somerville* in n. 18 of § 14:48, supra.

In Benton v. Maryland, 395 U.S. 784, 89 S.Ct. 2056, 23 L.Ed.2d 707 (1969), a defendant was tried for larceny and burglary and was found not guilty of larceny, but guilty of burglary. He appealed and the conviction was set aside because the indictment was void due to the oath administered to the grand jurors. The defendant, given

the option of demanding reindictment and retrial, chose to have his conviction set aside, and a new indictment was returned, charging the defendant with burglary and larceny. The court held that his retrial on the larceny charge (even though originally tried on a void indictment) violated the double jeopardy clause.

See United States v. Jenkins, 490 F.2d 868 (2d Cir. 1973), for a discussion of the rule at common law.

[12]Williams v. State, 162 Ga. App. 350, 351, 291 S.E.2d 425 (1982).

[13]Perkins v. State, 279 Ga. 506, 614 S.E.2d 92 (2005); Mayo v. State, 277 Ga. 645, 594 S.E.2d 333 (2004); Weatherbed v. State, 271 Ga. 736, 524 S.E.2d 452 (1999).

the offense, but the crime occurred in another county, no jeopardy attaches.[14]

In *Jones v. State*,[15] a jury was selected and sworn, the court recessed for lunch. Before proceeding further with the trial, the district attorney informed the court that a specified juror was a man with whom the prosecuting witness had had unfriendly contacts concerning the defendant's prosecution. He asked defense counsel to agree to try the case with 11 jurors. The defense counsel refused, and the court granted the district attorney's motion for a mistrial on the ground that the juror had made false answers in denying knowledge of the prosecution witness. The court overruled the defendant's plea of double jeopardy, and the defendant was convicted. The Georgia Supreme Court, in affirming the conviction, said that a trial judge in very limited situations has authority to declare a mistrial if in his opinion there is a "manifest necessity" to do so or if the ends of justice would otherwise be defeated.[16]

In *Jones v. State*,[17] in a two-count indictment, the defendant was indicted for rape and burglary arising out of the same transaction. The defendant pled guilty to burglary. The state then attempted to try him for rape. The court affirmed the denial of his autrefois convict defense.

See § 14:48, supra, for a discussion of a number of criminal or quasi criminal procedural situations held not to be jeopardy. See §§ 14:58 and 14:61, infra, on new trials and re-trials.

§ 14:52 Double jeopardy—Lesser included offense

O.C.G.A. § 16-1-6 provides as follows: "An accused may be convicted of a crime included in a crime charged in the indictment or accusation. A crime is so included when: (1) It is established by proof of the same or less than all the facts or a less culpable mental state than is required to establish the commission of the crime charged; or (2) It differs from the crime charged only in the respect that a less serious injury or risk of injury to the same person, property, or public interest or a lesser kind of culpability suffices to establish its commission."

In *State v. Sallie*,[1] the court held that the provisions of O.C.G.A. § 16-1-6(1) "pertaining to a proof of the same facts test is but a

---

[14]Barrs v. State, 22 Ga. App. 642, 97 S.E. 86 (1918).

[15]Jones v. State, 232 Ga. 324, 206 S.E.2d 481 (1974).

[16]This opinion quoted from United States v. Perez, 22 U.S. (9 Wheat.) 579, 6 L.Ed. 165 (1824), and also relied on

Illinois v. Somerville, 410 U.S. 458, 93 S.Ct. 1066, 35 L.Ed.2d 425 (1973).

[17]Jones v. State, 169 Ga. App. 4, 5, 311 S.E.2d 485 (1983).

[Section 14:52]

[1]State v. Sallie, 206 Ga. App. 732, 734, 427 S.E.2d 11 (1992).

variant application of the 'uses up all the evidence' test. . . ." In connection with this statute, the "actual evidence" test is to be applied. *Sallie* also pointed out that when multiple crimes occur within more than one county and one crime which is included within one of the multiple crimes was committed in only one of the counties, defendant cannot be tried in more than one county for that same included offense. The opinion ends with the following: "Thus it behooves prosecutors in such cases to coordinate local prosecutorial efforts with prosecutors of other counties to best protect the interests of the citizens of Georgia and to insure that an accused's right to fundamental fairness within the judicial system is not abused."

In *State v. Burgess*,[2] the court pointed out that in determining if a lesser crime is included in a crime charged under O.C.G.A. § 16-1-6(1), the "actual evidence test" is to be applied. "Under the actual evidence test, a lesser crime is included in the crime charged if the evidence actually presented at trial to establish the elements of the crime charged also establishes all the elements of lesser crime." In *Drinkard v. Walker*,[3] the Georgia Supreme Court disapproved the actual evidence test and adopted the "required evidence" test in order to determine when one offense is included in another for purposes of O.C.G.A. § 16-1-6(1). Accordingly, a single act may constitute an offense which violates more than one statute, and "if each statute requires proof of an additional fact which the other does not, an acquittal or conviction under either statute does not exempt the defendant from prosecution and punishment under the other."[4]

§ 14:53   Double jeopardy—Same offense—General

In Georgia, the guarantee against double jeopardy for the same offense has several aspects. First, there is the protection against multiple or successive prosecutions for crimes arising from the same conduct.[1] This is a procedural protection which prevents the defendant from being unduly harassed by successive

[2]State v. Burgess, 263 Ga. 143, 144 (1), 429 S.E.2d 252 (1993).

[3]Drinkard v. Walker, 281 Ga. 211, 215, 636 S.E.2d 530 (2006). The "required evidence" test comes from the United States Supreme Court decision in Blockburger v. U.S., 284 U.S. 299, 52 S. Ct. 180, 76 L. Ed. 306 (1932). In Stepp v. State, 286 Ga. 556, 690 S.E.2d 161 (2010), the Georgia Supreme Court held under separate statutes that different culpable mental states are not distinguishing facts for

purposes of the "required evidence" test and thus a conviction or acquittal under one would not bar prosecution under the other.

[4]Pryor v. State, 238 Ga. 698, 700, 234 S.E.2d 918 (1977) (overruled on other grounds by Montes v. State, 262 Ga. 473, 421 S.E.2d 710 (1992)), quoting Gavieres v. U.S., 220 U.S. 338, 342, 31 S. Ct. 421, 55 L. Ed. 489 (1911).

[Section 14:53]

[1]State v. Estevez, 232 Ga. 316, 317-19, 206 S.E.2d 475 (1974),

prosecutions. Two protections are given here: (1) O.C.G.A. § 16-1-7(b) mandates that different crimes arising from the same conduct and known to the prosecution must be tried in a single prosecution; (2) O.C.G.A. § 16-1-8(a), (b) sets out when a second prosecution is barred. Basically, this section states that a defendant should not twice be put in danger of being convicted of the "same offense" for which he has initially been tried.

In *United States v. Halper*,[2] the court held that a civil sanction could rise to the level of punishment for purposes of double jeopardy if the sanction involved was so severe as to be punitive in effect. The Supreme Court has since disavowed *Halper*, holding that punishment for purposes of double jeopardy must take the form of criminal sanctions and a civil penalty, regardless of its severity, may not constitute criminal punishment if its purpose is clearly civil in nature.[3]

Second, O.C.G.A. § 16-1-7(a), in conjunction with O.C.G.A. § 16-1-6, limits the convictions and punishments that may be imposed for crimes arising from the same criminal conduct. This is known as the substantive aspect of the guarantee against double jeopardy.[4]

In *Sanders v. State*,[5] the court held that the application of O.C.G.A. § 16-1-7 was a matter for the trial judge and not for a jury.

In *Blockburger v. United States*,[6] the United States Supreme Court held that "each of the offenses created requires proof of a different element. Where the same act or transaction constitutes a violation of two distinct statutory provisions, the test to be applied to determine whether there are two offenses or only one is whether each provision requires proof of an additional fact which the other does not." However, in *Grady v. Corbin*,[7] the same court held that "if two successive prosecutions are not barred by the Blockburger test, the second prosecution would [still] be barred if

---

overruled by, Drinkard v. Walker, 281 Ga. 211, 636 S.E.2d 530 (2006)); O.C.G.A. § 16-1-7(b), O.C.G.A. §§ 16-1-8(a), (b), (c).

[2]U.S. v. Halper, 490 U.S. 435, 109 S. Ct. 1892, 104 L. Ed. 2d 487 (1989).

[3]U.S. v. Hudson, 522 U.S. 93, 118 S.Ct. 488, 139 L.Ed.2d 450 (1997). But see Shepherd v. State, 280 Ga. 245 (2), 626 S.E.2d 96 (2006) (detention in a mental institution following civil commitment based on insanity verdict is not punishment for purposes of double jeopardy).

[4]Chitwood v. State, 170 Ga. App. 599, 601, 317 S.E.2d 589 (1984).

[5]Sanders v. State, 212 Ga. App. 832 (2), 442 S.E.2d 923 (1994).

[6]Blockburger v. United States, 284 U.S. 299, 304, 52 S.Ct. 180, 76 L.Ed. 306 (1932). See Baker v. State, 263 Ga. App. 462, 588 S.E.2d 288 (2003).

[7]Grady v. Corbin, 495 U.S. 508, 110 S.Ct. 2084, 109 L.Ed.2d 548 (1990), rev'd, United States v. Dixon, 509 U.S. 688, 113 S.Ct. 2849, 125 L.Ed.2d 556 (1993).

the prosecution sought to establish an essential element of the second crime by proving the conduct for which the defendant was convicted in the first prosecution." However, in 1993, *Grady v. Corbin* was reversed in *United States v. Dixon*.[8] In *Dixon*, the United States Supreme Court held that a prosecution based on an indictment charging a defendant with simple assault was barred by a prior contempt proceeding predicated on the same act arising out of a violation of a protective order prohibiting abusive action of any kind against the victim.[9] On purely federal constitutional grounds in *Henderson v. State*,[10] the court concluded that there was a double jeopardy violation where the defendant was convicted of violating a county ordinance on disorderly conduct prohibiting the engaging "in conduct or behavior likely to provoke or incite an immediate breach of the peace" and simple battery and criminal damage to property in the second degree. The court pointed out that to prove simple battery and criminal damage to property the state would have to prove the ordinance violation. "[T]he Double Jeopardy Clause bars any subsequent prosecution in which the government, to establish an essential element of an offense charged in that prosecution, will prove *conduct* that constitutes an offense for which the defendant has already been prosecuted." Moreover, "[i]f all the elements of one of the two crimes are included in the other, the two crimes are the same as a matter of law and successive prosecutions are barred, no matter whether the greater or lesser offense is tried first."[11]

In *Tanks v. State*,[12] a defendant, who was before a DeKalb County court facing a nonsummary criminal contempt proceeding arising out of a violation of a protective order, claimed that an indictment charging him with aggravated stalking issued by the Fulton County Grand Jury for the same conduct constituted double jeopardy. The DeKalb County proceedings had been stayed pending the outcome of the Fulton County case. The Court of Appeals agreed that if jeopardy had attached in the DeKalb County case the Fulton County indictment would be barred.

In *Sallie v. State*,[13] the defendant was indicted in Liberty County for two counts of false imprisonment arising out of an

[8]United States v. Dixon, 509 U.S. 688, 113 S.Ct. 2849, 125 L.Ed.2d 556 (1993).

[9]See Tanks v. State, 292 Ga. App. 177, 663 S.E.2d 812 (2008).

[10]Henderson v. State, 206 Ga. App. 642, 426 S.E.2d 264 (1992).

[11]Potts v. State, 261 Ga. 716, 718 (1)(a), 410 S.E.2d 89 (1991) (citations

omitted). See Gerisch v. Meadows, 278 Ga. 641, 644 (2), 604 S.E.2d 462 (2004).

[12]Tanks v. State, 292 Ga. App. 177, 663 S.E.2d 812 (2008) (the case was remanded to determine if jeopardy had attached in the contempt case by the swearing of a witness).

[13]Sallie v. State, 216 Ga. App. 502, 455 S.E.2d 315 (1995).

event originating in Bacon County. The defendant had been convicted in Bacon County for murder, burglary, aggravated assault, and two counts of kidnapping with bodily injury. The appellate court reversed the denial of the defendant's plea of former jeopardy since as a matter of law the false imprisonment charge in this case is a lesser included offense of kidnapping with bodily injury. The court pointed out that when he entered Liberty County it was a continuation of the kidnapping and not a separate offense of false imprisonment.

Nevertheless, in *Potts v. State*,[14] the court held that where "a criminal defendant goes on a multi-county crime spree, the Double Jeopardy Clause does not preclude successive prosecutions in separate counties for separate crimes arising out of a single criminal episode—even if they have factual elements in common—where they are not the 'same offense' as a matter of fact or of law." Likewise, in *Johns v. State*,[15] the defendant's guilty plea to criminal trespass (Family Violence Act) did not bar the prosecution for DUI which arose "out of the same incident" but not out of the "same transaction." Following an argument with his live-in girlfriend during which the defendant damaged some of her clothes, the defendant left the premises and was stopped by police who had been alerted that the defendant was driving and drinking. The defendant was arrested and charged with criminal trespass and DUI. The court reasoned that each offense could have been separately presented to a trier of fact without any reference to the other.

For a discussion of the two procedural aspects of jeopardy, see §§ 14:54 and 14:55, infra. For a discussion of the substantive aspects of double jeopardy, see §§ 14:56 and 26:30, infra.

§ 14:54   Double jeopardy—Procedural aspects—Multiple prosecutions for same conduct

The Criminal Code of Georgia divides the procedural aspect of the double jeopardy principle into two categories: (1) Multiple prosecutions for the same conduct—O.C.G.A. § 16-1-7 (discussed herein); and (2) When prosecution is barred by former prosecution—O.C.G.A. § 16-1-8 (see discussion in § 14:55, infra.)

The Criminal Code of Georgia in O.C.G.A. § 16-1-7(b) provides the following:

"If the several crimes arising from the same conduct are known to the proper prosecuting officer at the time of commencing the

---

[14]Potts v. State, 261 Ga. 716, 720 (1), 410 S.E.2d 89 (1991); Norwood v. State, 249 Ga. App. 507, 508, 548 S.E.2d 478 (2001).

[15]Johns v. State, 319 Ga. App. 718, 738 S.E.2d 304 (2013). See State v. Stewart, 317 Ga. App. 82, 729 S.E.2d 478 (2012).

prosecution and are within the jurisdiction of a single court, they must be prosecuted in a single prosecution. . . ."[1] See § 20:4, infra, on criminal cases which may be prosecuted in more than one county.

O.C.G.A. § 16-1-7, despite the title which it carries, relates to successive prosecutions in state and municipal courts for the same conduct.[2]

The bar to successive prosecutions is sometimes referred to as the procedural aspect of double jeopardy, and is intended to prevent the harassment of a defendant.[3] However, it must also be remembered that O.C.G.A. § 16-1-7(b) prevents a later prosecution for crimes (1) arising from the same transaction, (2) known to the prosecuting officer, and (3) which are within the jurisdiction of a *single court*.

In *Armfield v. State*,[4] the defendant contended that his malice murder charge should have been prosecuted with his three previous drug charges. In rejecting this contention, the court pointed out that the plan to murder the victim did not arise until the defendant learned of the victim's involvement in his "arrest for selling marijuana—the murder itself not occurring until a month and a half after the last drug sale. . . . Thus, the offenses . . . did not arise from the same conduct."

The words "known to the prosecuting officer" mean that the crimes were "*actually* known to the prosecuting officer *actually* handling the proceedings"[5] and also mean that such prosecuting officer must have actually known that the other crime or crimes arose from the same transaction.[6] Obviously, knowledge by the arresting officer of all crimes arising out of the transaction does

---

[Section 14:54]

[1]O.C.G.A. § 16-1-7(b) also provides for an exception not set out in the body. This exception is set out in the next paragraph of the section and provides as follows:

"(c) When two or more crimes are charged as required by subsection (b) . . . the court in the interest of justice may order that one or more of such charges be tried separately."

[2]Brock v. State, 146 Ga. App. 78, 80, 245 S.E.2d 442 (1978); State v. Burroughs, 149 Ga. App. 183, 185, 254 S.E.2d 144 (1979), aff'd, 246 Ga. 393, 271 S.E.2d 629 (1980).

[3]Coleman v. State, 163 Ga. App. 173, 175, 293 S.E.2d 395 (1982); Keener v. State, 238 Ga. 7, 8, 230 S.E.2d 846

(1976).

[4]Armfield v. State, 259 Ga. 43, 44 (1), 376 S.E.2d 369 (1989).

[5]Baker v. State, 257 Ga. 567, 569, 361 S.E.2d 808 (1987) (quoting McCannon v. State, 252 Ga. 515, 315 S.E.2d 413 (1984)) (emphasis in original); Hill v. State, 234 Ga. App. 173, 175 (1), 507 S.E.2d 3 (1998). Accord, Turner v. State, 238 Ga. App. 438, 518 S.E.2d 923 (1999); Anderson v. State, 200 Ga. App. 530, 532, 408 S.E.2d 829 (1991).

[6]Powe v. State, 257 Ga. 563, 361 S.E.2d 811 (1987); Bonner v. State, 249 Ga. App. 358, 360 (1), 548 S.E.2d 84 (2001). Compare Collins v. State, 177 Ga. App. 758, 341 S.E.2d 288 (1986) and Brown v. State, 251 Ga. App. 569, 554 S.E.2d 760 (2001), where the de-

not bring the situation within the prohibition of O.C.G.A. § 16-1-7(b).[7] In *Zater v. State*,[8] the court held that the words of the statute "proper prosecuting officer" mean "the prosecuting attorney for the state." The burden is on the defendant to show "that the proper prosecuting attorney had actual knowledge of all the charges."[9] However, in *Smith v. State*,[10] a case involving an accusation for a traffic offense and an indictment for drug violations which arose out of the same conduct, both bearing the name of the district attorney, the court held that "[t]hese documents constitute conclusive circumstantial evidence that the district attorney had actual knowledge of all the offenses. . . ." The appellate court held that it was error for the trial judge to deny the plea in bar even though an assistant district attorney who disposed of the traffic offense had begun his job only the month before.

In *Billups v. State*,[11] the defendant appealed the denial of his plea of former jeopardy for aggravated assault. The appellate court reversed. Here, "the assistant solicitor testified she read the arrest report before taking appellant's plea to reckless conduct but she did not 'see all the elements of [aggravated assault].' She admitted she contacted the District Attorney's office to determine whether . . . [defendant] had been convicted of any felonies. . . . [The District Attorney's employee mentioned] 'that there were other charges pending.' " The court pointed out that "it is both reasonable and necessary to expect prosecutors to know what *crimes* arise from certain conduct, so long as they know all the *facts* of that conduct." (Emphasis in original.)

There is no requirement that the court which tried the first case must have also had jurisdiction over the offenses charged in the second case provided the crime charged in the first case is a

---

fendants unsuccessfully asserted a plea in bar after paying fines to the clerk of court for minor traffic offenses associated with substantive criminal charges. In each case the court found that the clerk of court is not the equivalent of a "prosecuting officer" for purposes of O.C.G.A. § 16-1-7(b).

[7]Webb v. State, 176 Ga. App. 576, 577, 336 S.E.2d 838 (1985). Accord, Dodd v. State, 240 Ga. App. 48, 49, 522 S.E.2d 538 (1999).

[8]Zater v. State, 197 Ga. App. 648 (1), 399 S.E.2d 222 (1990). Accord, Rowe v. State, 218 Ga. App. 746, 747, 463 S.E.2d 21 (1995).

[9]Blackwell v. State, 232 Ga. App. 884, 885, 502 S.E.2d 774 (1998); Hayles

v. State, 188 Ga. App. 281 (2), 372 S.E.2d 668 (1988); State v. Cornette, 229 Ga. App. 487, 488, 494 S.E.2d 289 (1997).

[10]Smith v. State, 190 Ga. App. 6, 378 S.E.2d 349 (1989), aff'd, 259 Ga. 352, 381 S.E.2d 37 (1989); Mack v. State, 249 Ga. App. 424, 426, 547 S.E.2d 697 (2001).

[11]Billups v. State, 228 Ga. App. 804, 806 (1), 493 S.E.2d 8 (1997). See Dean v. State, 309 Ga. App. 459, 711 S.E.2d 42 (2011) (guilty plea to DUI in probate court barred prosecution on related traffic offenses in superior court where prosecutor in DUI case was aware of pending related charges).

necessary element of the charge to be tried in the second case. For example, in *Brock v. State*,[12] the defendant was driving and had a collision in which a man was killed; was charged in state court with speeding, driving on the left, and driving under the influence; he pled nolo contendere to speeding and driving under the influence; and was sentenced and fined. The court held that he could not later be tried in superior court for vehicular homicide arising out of the same incident. In *State v. Kennedy*,[13] the defendant was charged with driving an automobile on the wrong side of the road. As a result, there was a fatal accident. The citation charging the defendant with driving on the wrong side of the road was filed in the state court of the county. The defendant later "paid the ticket at the sheriff's office. The bond was forfeited in open court . . . and on that date the order from the State Court judge approving the forfeiture and disposing of the case was filed." About two weeks later the state filed an accusation in the state court charging the defendant with vehicular homicide. The defendant filed a plea of prior jeopardy. The state claimed the prosecuting officer did not know of the charge of driving on the wrong side of the road, but the trial judge concluded that "since the accusation and indictment bore the name of the district attorney, they constituted 'conclusive circumstantial evidence that the district attorney had actual knowledge of all the offenses arising from the same conduct and the pendency of both prosecutions, but chose to proceed separately as to each.' "The appellate court affirmed the sustaining of the plea of former jeopardy find-

---

[12]Brock v. State, 146 Ga. App. 78, 245 S.E.2d 442 (1978). In State v. Burroughs, 149 Ga. App. 183, 254 S.E.2d 144 (1979), aff'd, 246 Ga. 393, 271 S.E.2d 629 (1980), the defendant was in violation of a city ordinance entitled "disorderly conduct—violent interference with another's pursuit of a lawful occupation" and a statute on simple battery on a police officer arising out of the same incident. The conviction of the ordinance violation in municipal court prevented a trial in state court of the battery charge.

In Mann v. State, 160 Ga. App. 527, 287 S.E.2d 325 (1981), the defendant was arrested and found to have marijuana and several pills of amobarbital and secobarbital in a bag. The defendant entered a guilty plea in state court to possession of less than an ounce of marijuana. He was then indicted in superior court for possession of the pills. The defendant entered a plea of former jeopardy based on O.C.G.A. § 16-1-7(b). The Court of Appeals reversed the denial of the plea.

In State v. Stowe, 167 Ga. App. 65, 306 S.E.2d 663 (1983), the defendant was indicted for murder, vehicular homicide in the first degree and second degree, reckless driving, driving under the influence, leaving the scene of an accident, and driving to the left of the center line. At trial only the murder count was submitted to the jury because of statute of limitations problems. The jury was unable to agree on a verdict, and the trial judge declared a mistrial. The defendant was re-indicted on all counts in such a way as to attempt to avoid the statute of limitations. The court held that a trial for any offense other than murder was barred by O.C.G.A. § 16-1-7(b).

[13]State v. Kennedy, 216 Ga. App. 405, 454 S.E.2d 600 (1995).

ing a violation of O.C.G.A. § 16-1-7.

In *Keener v. State*,[14] the court noted that "[w]here crimes are tried separately it is generally held that if multiple convictions arising out of a single prosecution are barred they will likewise be barred from successive prosecution. Therefore when crimes are to be prosecuted separately the more serious known crimes should be prosecuted first to avoid the conviction of a lesser crime barring a subsequent prosecution for a more serious crime."

In *Asberry v. State*,[15] the defendant was indicted for possession of a firearm during the commission of a crime and for possession of a firearm by a convicted felon. In a separate indictment returned the same day and arising from the same incident, the defendant was indicted for violating the Georgia Controlled Substances Act, the facts of which form the basis for the underlying crime necessary to support the firearm charge. At the time of trial one of the defendant's co-defendants announced he was not ready to proceed on the drug charge. Over objection the defendant was tried on the firearms charge. The defendant was found guilty on that charge. The defendant "filed a motion in autrefois convict to have the drug charge dismissed on double jeopardy grounds," which the trial court denied. In reversing the trial court's decision, the appellate court pointed out that the burden is "on the State to establish that severance under O.C.G.A. § 16-1-7(c) was required in the interest of justice and the trial court so held at the time of the severance, or that defendant had waived his right to procedural due process." Here, no written motion to sever the charges under O.C.G.A. § 16-1-7(c) was filed, nor did the prosecution seek permission of the court to do so. The trial judge exercised no discretion on the issue of severance. The defendant did not waive his procedural double jeopardy protection.

In *State v. Willis*,[16] the court held that where a defendant drove from one county to another while intoxicated, *a plea* of nolo contendere in one county prevented a prosecution for driving under the influence in the other; however, the court also held that he could be tried and convicted in both counties for speeding.

Also, where a driver pleads guilty in state court to driving with a revoked license and driving under the influence, he may not be tried in superior court as an habitual violator whose license has been revoked (O.C.G.A. § 40-5-58(c)), where the habitual violator case arose from "the same conduct" and in the same transaction;

---

[14]Keener v. State, 238 Ga. 7, 8, 230 S.E.2d 846 (1976).

[15]Asberry v. State, 221 Ga. App. 809, 472 S.E.2d 562 (1996).

[16]State v. Willis, 149 Ga. App. 509, 511, 254 S.E.2d 743 (1979).

O.C.G.A. § 16-1-7 bars such successive prosecutions.[17]

In *In the Interest of J. B. W.*,[18] the court held that O.C.G.A. § 16-1-7(b) applies to a trial in juvenile court.

However, in *Puckett v. State*,[19] the defendant was charged with the state offenses of DUI-less safe driver and failure to maintain a lane. He was also charged with a municipal ordinance violation of "resisting/interfering with arrest." The defendant requested having all three charges bound over to the state court. The municipal court bound over the two state charges, but found the defendant guilty of the municipal offense. The defendant filed a plea in bar in state court, which was denied. The appellate court affirmed, pointing out that the municipal court initially had jurisdiction of all three charges but, when the defendant requested a jury trial, the municipal court was divested of jurisdiction over the two state charges. However, the municipal court could dispose of the ordinance violation, because "O.C.G.A. § 16-1-7(b) does not preclude successive state and municipal prosecutions, only successive prosecutions for state crimes."

§ 14:55 Double jeopardy—Procedural aspects— Prosecution barred by former prosecution

Another aspect of the procedural protection afforded by Georgia's double jeopardy provisions is found in O.C.G.A. § 16-1-8, which provides as follows:

"(a) A prosecution is barred if the accused was formerly prosecuted for the same crime based upon the same material facts, if such former prosecution:

"(1) Resulted in either a conviction or an acquittal; or

"(2) Was terminated improperly after the jury was impaneled and sworn or, in a trial before a court without a jury, after the first witness was sworn. . . ."

In *McCannon v. State*,[1] the Georgia Supreme Court summarized O.C.G.A. § 16-1-8(b) as follows: "A prosecution is barred if the accused was formerly prosecuted for a different crime . . . if such former prosecution:

---

[17]State v. Gilder, 242 Ga. 285, 248 S.E.2d 659 (1978).

[18]In the Interest of J. B. W., 230 Ga. App. 673, 497 S.E.2d 1 (1998). O.C.G.A. § 15-11-523(c) (after jeopardy attaches new charges may not be added to petition). See In re J.H., 335 Ga. App. 848, 783 S.E.2d 367 (2016) (error to allow state to make material change to delinquency petition after hearing had commenced without first providing juvenile with proper service, notice and time to prepare).

[19]Puckett v. State, 239 Ga. App. 582, 583 (1), 521 S.E.2d 634 (1999).

[Section 14:55]

[1]McCannon v. State, 252 Ga. 515, 315 S.E.2d 413 (1984). Accord, McCrary v. State, 171 Ga. App. 585, 320 S.E.2d 567 (1984), aff'd, 253 Ga. 747, 325 S.E.2d 151 (1985).

"(1) resulted in either a conviction or acquittal and:

"(i) the subsequent prosecution is for a crime of which the accused could have been convicted on the former prosecution; or [note the disjunctive[2]]

"(ii) is for a crime with which the accused should have been charged on the former prosecution (unless the court ordered a separate trial of such charge); or [note the disjunctive[3]]

"(iii) is for a crime which involves the same conduct, unless[4]

"(A) each prosecution requires proof of a fact not required on the other prosecution or

"(B) the crime was not consummated when the former trial began."

"The phrase 'the same conduct' in this statute has been used interchangeably with the phrase 'the same transaction.' "[5]

In *McCannon,* the conviction was reversed because the crime resulting in the latter conviction should have been tried with the former prosecution. Here the defendant had been stopped by an officer and drove away injuring the officer. The defendant entered a plea of nolo contendere to an accusation in superior court for possession of less than an ounce of marijuana.[6] About three months later the superior court judge overruled the defendant's contention that he should have been prosecuted in a single prosecution. The Supreme Court pointed out that the district attorney knew of both offenses. "They were within the jurisdiction of a single court. They arose out of the same conduct or transaction," thus coming within O.C.G.A. § 16-1-7(b). The second prosecution was also barred under item (ii) above in that the prosecutions could have been brought together.

The statutes prevent the re-prosecution of a defendant for the same crime based upon the same material facts.[7] This provision provides a statutory implementation of the constitutional guarantee.[8]

The statute (O.C.G.A. § 16-1-8(b)) further prohibits the prose-

---

[2]McCannon v. State, 252 Ga. 515, 517, n. 3, 315 S.E.2d 413 (1984).

[3]McCannon v. State, 252 Ga. 515, 517, n. 4, 315 S.E.2d 413 (1984).

[4]In McCannon v. State, 252 Ga. 515, 519, 315 S.E.2d 413 (1984), the court pointed out that item (iii) "is traditional double jeopardy."

[5]State v. Steien, 214 Ga. App. 345, 346, 447 S.E.2d 701 (1994).

[6]See State v. Pruiett, 324 Ga. App. 789, 751 S.E.2d 579 (2013) (plea

of guilty on record and acceptance by court constitutes jeopardy for purposes of O.C.G.A. §§ 16-1-7(b) and 16-1-8(b)). See also State v. Smith, 185 Ga. App. 694, 365 S.E.2d 846 (1988).

[7]O.C.G.A. § 16-1-8(a). Generally, see Note, "Double Jeopardy: Multiple Prosecutions Arising From Same Transaction," 15 Am. Crim. L. Rev. 259 (1978).

[8]Committee Notes, Criminal Code of Georgia, Ch. 26-5, 1988 rev. at p. 78.

cution of a defendant where he was formerly prosecuted for a different crime, or for the same crime based upon different facts, if (1) the defendant could have been convicted of the "new" offense on the former prosecution, or (2) the defendant should have been charged on the former prosecution with the "new" offense,[9] or (3) the "new" crime involves the same conduct of the former prosecution ("unless each prosecution requires proof of a fact not required on the other"), or (4) unless the "new" crime was not consummated when the former trial began.[10] These provisions are said to embrace the concept of res judicata and to prevent further prosecutions which could have been prosecuted under the former law.[11] "A prerequisite to this type of procedural double jeopardy claim is knowledge of the crimes arising from the same conduct by the prosecuting [attorney] who handled the first prosecution."[12]

The remainder of this material on procedural double jeopardy relates to the procedural protections afforded by the federal constitutional double jeopardy guarantees.[13] As indicated above, the minimum standards in some cases are not as broad as those provided for by Georgia law. A defendant tried on one offense but convicted of a lesser included offense, upon obtaining a new trial, may only be re-tried on the offense for which he was convicted. Where a defendant is tried for murder and convicted of voluntary manslaughter, and then after a successful appeal he is re-tried over his objection for murder, this violates the double jeopardy provision of the Fifth Amendment.[14] The court reasoned that with the verdict of voluntary manslaughter, the defendant's jeopardy on the greater charge of murder had ended.[15] The court noted that the state could have re-tried the defendant for voluntary

---

[9]O.C.G.A. § 16-1-8(b)(1): ". . . (unless the court ordered a separate trial of such charge). . . ."

[10]O.C.G.A. § 16-1-8(b). See Ellis v. State, 285 Ga. 756, 684 S.E.2d 263 (2009) (child cruelty conviction does not bar subsequent murder charge arising from the same conduct where crime of murder not complete at time of child cruelty conviction as child had not yet died).

[11]Committee Notes, Criminal Code of Georgia, GCA Ch. 26-5, 1988 rev., at p. 78.

[12]White v. State, 284 Ga. App. 805, 644 S.E.2d 903 (2007); Baker v. State, 257 Ga. 567, 361 S.E.2d 808 (1987). See Goodwin v. State, 341 Ga. App. 530, 802 S.E.2d 3 (2017).

[13]In United States v. Inmon, 568 F.2d 326 (3d Cir. 1977), the court held that where a defendant makes a non-frivolous showing that a later charge was the same as that for which he was formerly placed in jeopardy, the burden of establishing separate crimes is on the prosecution. The court pointed out that the government has access to the evidence which it will use and controls the way indictments are drawn.

See Mead, "Double Jeopardy Protection—Illusion or Reality?" 13 Ind. L. Rev. 863 (1980).

[14]Price v. Georgia, 398 U.S. 323, 90 S.Ct. 1757, 26 L.Ed.2d 300 (1970).

[15]Price v. Georgia, 398 U.S. 323, 327-30, 90 S.Ct. 1757, 26 L.Ed.2d 300 (1970).

manslaughter under the theory of "continuing jeopardy."[16]

Where a defendant is convicted of a crime, he may not later be indicted and tried for a lesser included offense which had to be proved in order for him to be convicted of the greater offense.[17] Also, an acquittal or conviction on an indictment phrased in general terms prevents a later trial for the same crime which was committed before the indictment.[18] In addition, where "all the elements of one of the two crimes are included in the other, the two crimes are the same, as a matter of law, and successive prosecutions are barred, no matter whether the greater or lesser offense is tried first."[19]

In a state having a statute which makes theft of an automobile a crime, with a separate statute making joyriding a crime, a guilty plea to joyriding prevents a prosecution for theft of the automobile.[20] The United States Supreme Court has said that for "purposes of the double jeopardy clause of the Fifth Amendment, a lesser included offense requires no proof beyond that which is required for conviction of the greater offense, and the greater offense is therefore by definition the 'same' for purposes of double jeopardy as any lesser offense included in it."[21]

When crimes are tried separately, from the standpoint of the

---

[16]Price v. Georgia, 398 U.S. 323, 327-30, 90 S.Ct. 1757, 26 L.Ed.2d 300 (1970).

[17]Harris v. Oklahoma, 433 U.S. 682, 97 S.Ct. 2912, 53 L.Ed.2d 1054 (1977). In this case, a clerk in a grocery was shot and killed by a companion of the defendant. The defendant was convicted of murder. In order to justify his conviction, the underlying felony of robbery with a firearm had to be proved in order to establish the necessary intent. Later he was tried for robbery with a firearm, and over his double jeopardy objection, he was convicted. The second conviction was reversed by the United States Supreme Court.

[18]McCoy v. State, 121 Ga. 359, 49 S.E. 294 (1904).

[19]Potts v. State, 261 Ga. 716, 718 (1)(a), 410 S.E.2d 89 (1991) (citations omitted).

[20]Brown v. Ohio, 432 U.S. 161, 97 S.Ct. 2221, 53 L.Ed.2d 187 (1977).

In Illinois v. Vitale, 447 U.S. 410, 100 S.Ct. 2260, 65 L.Ed.2d 228 (1980), the defendant was convicted of failing to reduce speed to avoid an accident. Later he was charged with manslaughter by automobile under a different statute. The court vacated the decision of the Illinois Supreme Court, holding that the second case violated double jeopardy, and remanded the case. Whether double jeopardy was violated depends on whether each statute requires proof of a fact which the other does not. If manslaughter by automobile does not always entail proof of a failure to reduce speed, then the two are not the same. The mere possibility that the state will seek to rely on all the elements of the first offense would not be sufficient to bar the later prosecution. However, if, as a matter of Illinois law, the careless failure to reduce speed is always a necessary element of manslaughter by automobile, then the two offenses are the same.

[21]Brock v. State, 146 Ga. App. 78, 82, 245 S.E.2d 442 (1978) (quoting with approval from Brown v. Ohio, 432 U.S. 161, 97 S.Ct. 2221, 53 L.Ed.2d 187 (1977)).

prosecution, the more serious offense should be tried first so that the conviction of a lesser crime will not bar the later prosecution of a more serious crime.[22] However, a conviction of one crime which is included in the other during a single prosecution does not prevent a retrial on the major crime where the defendant obtains a reversal of the more serious offense.[23]

In *Evans v. Michigan*,[24] the defendant's retrial was barred by the Double Jeopardy Clause even though the defendant's acquittal at the original trial was due to the trial court's misunderstanding of the law applicable to the case.

Also see § 14:60, infra, on trial in inferior court. See §§ 14:62 and 26:30 et seq., infra, on multiple counts or multiple indictments for the same conduct.

§ 14:56   Double jeopardy—Same offense—Substantive aspects

The substantive aspect of double jeopardy, set forth in O.C.G.A. § 16-1-7(a) places limits on the number of convictions and punishments which may be imposed for crimes arising from the same criminal conduct. O.C.G.A. § 16-1-7 reads as follows:

"(a) When the same conduct of an accused may establish the commission of more than one crime, the accused may be prosecuted for each crime. He may not, however, be convicted of more than one crime if:

"(1) One crime is included in the other;[1] or

"(2) The crimes differ only in that one is defined to prohibit a designated kind of conduct generally and the other to prohibit a specific instance of such conduct."

The material which discusses the above statute and its applications is in § 26:30, infra, on sentencing. See also related topics at sections 14:51, 14:52, and 14:54, supra, and at §§ 25:3, 25:5, and 26:29, infra.

---

[22]Keener v. State, 238 Ga. 7, 8, 230 S.E.2d 846 (1976).

[23]Keener v. State, 238 Ga. 7, 9, 230 S.E.2d 846 (1976).

[24]Evans v. Michigan, 133 S. Ct. 1069, 185 L. Ed. 2d 124 (2013).

[Section 14:56]

[1]Rules for determining whether one crime is included in the other are set out at O.C.G.A. § 16-1-6. See also § 14:52, supra.

§ 14:57 Double jeopardy—Collateral estoppel

Under the doctrine of collateral estoppel, an issue of ultimate fact, once resolved against the state[1] by a final judgment, may not again be litigated between the parties. It is incumbent upon the party asserting collateral estoppel to introduce those portions of the record of the prior proceedings that "affirmatively demonstrate that the fact at issue was already litigated and determined in the party's favor in the earlier case."[2] In *Ashe v. Swenson,*[3] the United States Supreme Court held that the doctrine of collateral estoppel was embodied in the Fifth Amendment's double jeopardy provision and applicable to the states through the due process clause of the Fourteenth Amendment.[4] "[C]ollateral estoppel . . . means simply that when an issue of ultimate fact has once been determined by a valid and final judgment, that issue cannot again be litigated between the same parties in any future lawsuit."[5] The doctrine of collateral estoppel in criminal cases was recognized in Georgia[6] long before the *Ashe* case.[7]

In *Ashe,* six men playing poker were robbed by three or four masked men. Ashe was first tried for robbing one of the players and was found not guilty. Six weeks later, Ashe was brought to trial again for the robbery of another of the poker players. His motion to dismiss the second prosecution because of his earlier acquittal was overruled, and he was convicted. The United States Supreme Court reversed the case, holding that the issue of whether Ashe was one of the robbers had already been determined at his first trial.

[Section 14:57]

[1]State v. Ingenito, 87 N.J. 204, 432 A.2d 912 (1981).

[2]Johnson v. State, 292 Ga. 22, 26, 733 S.E.2d 736 (2012).

[3]Ashe v. Swenson, 397 U.S. 436, 90 S.Ct. 1189, 25 L.Ed.2d 469 (1970); Harris v. State, 193 Ga. 109, 17 S.E.2d 573 (1941) ("The plea of former acquittal may be sustained by showing that the defendant could not have been guilty of the crime with which he is now charged without also being guilty of that of which he has been acquitted."). See Bravo-Fernandez v. United States, 137 S.Ct. 352, 196 L.Ed.2d 242 (2016) (Double Jeopardy Clause does not bar retrial of defendants where jury returns inconsistent verdicts which are later vacated because of inconsistency). See also Giddens v. State, 299 Ga. 109, 121, 786 S.E.2d 659 (2016); Yeager v. U.S., 557 U.S. 110, 129 S. Ct. 2360, 174 L. Ed. 2d 78 (2009).

[4]Harris v. Washington, 404 U.S. 55, 92 S.Ct. 183, 30 L.Ed.2d 212 (1971). This case held that where a defendant is tried for murder resulting from the explosion of a bomb and is acquitted, he cannot later be tried for murder of another person who was killed in the same explosion.

[5]Sanchez v. State, 242 Ga. App. 686, 688 (3), 530 S.E.2d 775 (2000).

[6]Lindsey v. State, 227 Ga. 48, 52 (2), 178 S.E.2d 848 (1970).

[7]Harris v. State, 193 Ga. 109, 17 S.E.2d 573 (1941); see also O.C.G.A. § 16-1-8(b).

In *Yeager v. United States*,[8] the defendant was charged with several counts of federal securities violations. The defendant was acquitted on the fraud counts but the jury was unable to reach a verdict as to the "insider trader" counts. When the government sought to retry the defendant as to those counts, the defendant argued and the Court agreed that if the possession of insider information was an element as to all the charges in the indictment, it was estopped or precluded from relitigating that issue in a second trial because it had already been resolved adversely to the government in the first trial. Likewise, in *Roesser v. State*,[9] the defendant was acquitted of murder and felony murder charges, but the jury was unable to reach a verdict on the lesser included offense of voluntary manslaughter which was before the jury only because of the request by the defendant. The Georgia Supreme Court held that double jeopardy and the doctrine of collateral estoppel precluded the defendant's retrial on the charge of voluntary manslaughter where it was obvious from the record that because the entire case rested on whether the defendant had acted in self-defense, the jury must have determined that the defendant had acted in self-defense.

In *Giddins v. State*,[10] the Georgia Supreme Court held "that a defendant's retrial for convictions that have been reversed or vacated due to trial error is not barred by an inconsistent acquittal." The Court noted "[t]he bedrock of collateral estoppel in criminal cases is that the court must determine, honor, and apply the facts that the jury actually and necessarily decided in the defendant's favor."[11] As the Eleventh Circuit explained in *United States v. Ohayon*:[12]

> Where a previous judgement of acquittal was based upon a general verdict, as is usually the case, a court must ask whether a rational jury could have grounded its verdict upon an issue other than that which the defendant seeks to foreclose from consideration. When

---

[8]Yeager v. U.S., 557 U.S. 110, 119, 129 S. Ct. 2360, 174 L. Ed. 2d 78 (2009).

[9]Roesser v. State, 294 Ga. 295, 751 S.E.2d 297 (2013).

[10]Giddens v. State, 299 Ga. 109, 786 S.E.2d 659 (2016).

[11]Giddens v. State, 299 Ga. 109, 786 S.E.2d 659 (2016).

[12]U.S. v. Ohayon, 483 F.3d 1281, 1286 (11th Cir. 2007) (citations and punctuation omitted). See Robinson v. State, 334 Ga. App. 646, 780 S.E.2d 86 (2015).

In U.S. v. Hernandez, 572 F.2d 218, 220 (9th Cir. 1978), the court used a three-step analysis in determining whether a former trial collaterally estopped a later trial. The steps included: (1) identification of the issues in the two cases to determine whether the issues are sufficiently similar and material in both actions to justify invoking the doctrine; (2) examination of the record in the earlier case to determine whether the issue was litigated there; and (3) examination of the record of the prior proceeding to determine whether the issue was necessarily decided in the first case.

making this determination, a court must examine the record of a prior proceeding, taking into account the pleadings, evidence, charge, and other relevant matter. This inquiry must be set in a practical frame, and a court is not to conduct its analysis with the hypertechnical and archaic approach of a 19th century pleading book, but with realism and rationality.

If a defendant is charged with two or more crimes and is found not guilty of one which necessarily includes a finding against a fact which is essential to the conviction of the other(s), the conviction of the other(s) must be reversed. Thus, where a defendant is charged with battery and obstructing an officer by biting and kicking him and both charges arose out of the same incident, if he is acquitted of battery, he must be acquitted of obstruction of an officer.[13]

In another state it has been held that collateral estoppel applies to the state on a motion to suppress. Hence, if a co-defendant's motion to suppress evidence obtained from a car occupied by both defendants is granted, the remaining defendant is entitled to the benefit of the earlier ruling.[14]

In *Johnson v. Estelle*,[15] the defendant was found not guilty of burglary of a residence with intent to rape. Later he was convicted of assault with intent to rape in connection with the same incident. The court concluded that the doctrine of collateral estoppel prevented the second trial. However, in *Martin v. State*,[16] where the defendant was charged with aggravated assault and rape, he contended that he could not be convicted of both, but the court concluded that the assault occurred with a tire jack before the rape and affirmed the two convictions of both offenses.

An administrative finding of fact made in connection with a license suspension hearing that the State has failed to show that

[13]Evans v. State, 138 Ga. App. 620, 621 (1), 227 S.E.2d 448 (1976). In *Evans* the court reasoned that if the defendant "committed no battery upon the officers by biting or kicking them [this] precludes a finding that the defendant obstructed the officers by committing these same disapproved acts."

In Taylor v. Redman, 500 F.Supp. 453 (D.C.Del.1980), the court held that the defendant's acquittal by reason of insanity in one county prevented his later trial in another county on charges arising out of the same criminal episode. The ultimate fact in the second trial was the defendant's insanity and this had been determined in the first trial.

[14]State v. Gonzalez, 75 N.J. 181, 380 A.2d 1128 (1977). Cf. Cook v. State, 141 Ga. App. 241, 233 S.E.2d 60 (1977), holding that where a defendant's motion to suppress is sustained in a case charging him with possession of marijuana this prevented the introduction of the marijuana in a later case charging him with selling marijuana after his second motion to suppress was overruled.

[15]Johnson v. Estelle, 506 F.2d 347 (5th Cir. 1975). Cf. McDonald v. Wainwright, 493 F.2d 204 (5th Cir. 1974).

[16]Martin v. State, 151 Ga. App. 9 (1), 258 S.E.2d 711 (1979).

the defendant was properly advised of her implied consent rights will not bar the state from litigating that issue in a subsequent criminal trial.[17] Administrative decisions are not afforded the dignity of collateral estoppel in a subsequent judicial proceeding under Georgia law unless: (1) both proceedings involve the same parties or their privies; (2) the issue must have actually been litigated and determined in the first proceeding; (3) that determination must have been essential to the judgment in the first proceeding; and (4) the party against whom the doctrine is asserted must have had a full opportunity to litigate the issue in question.[18] Because the State may not appeal an administrative summary determination regarding a license suspension, it does not have a "full opportunity" to litigate the issue and hence the findings made in such hearings will not be afforded preclusive effect against the State in subsequent judicial proceedings.[19]

See §§ 26:33 et seq., infra, on merger. See § 26:33, infra, on the trial of an acquitted defendant for perjury at his earlier trial.

§ 14:58 Double jeopardy—Mistrial—New trial

The Georgia Constitution provides that no person shall be put in jeopardy "more than once for the same offense except when a new trial has been granted after conviction or in case of mistrial."[1] Thus, generally a defendant may not complain of former jeopardy if he moves for a new trial,[2] or appeals his conviction.[3] The same result is reached under the federal Constitution.[4]

If a defendant moves for a mistrial and the motion is granted,

---

[17]Swain v. State, 251 Ga. App. 110, 114 (1), 552 S.E.2d 880 (2001).

[18]Swain v. State, 251 Ga. App. 110, 113, 552 S.E.2d 880 (2001).

[19]Swain v. State, 251 Ga. App. 110, 113, 552 S.E.2d 880 (2001). See O.C.G.A. § 40-5-67.1(h).

[Section 14:58]

[1]The Georgia Constitution expressly excepts the grant of mistrials from constituting double jeopardy. Ga. Const. 1983, Art. I, § I, ¶ XVIII. Generally, see Note, "Mistrials and Double Jeopardy," 15 Am. Crim. L. Rev. 169 (1977).

[2]Staggers v. State, 225 Ga. 581 (1), 170 S.E.2d 430 (1969).

[3]Daniels v. State, 165 Ga. App. 397, 398 (3), 299 S.E.2d 746 (1983). See Patterson v. Haskins, 470 F.3d 645 (6th Cir. 2006). See also Levin v. Morales, 295 Ga. 781, 764 S.E.2d 145 (2014) (concurring opinion notes that unlike some other jurisdictions, Georgia has never addressed the issue of whether double jeopardy applies to the re-trial of a case which is reversed on appeal due to a determination that the evidence was insufficient but only because of a post-trial change in the law).

[4]U.S. Const. Amend. V. The double jeopardy provision of the Fifth Amendment is made applicable to the states through the due process clause of the Fourteenth Amendment. Benton v. Maryland, 395 U.S. 784, 89 S.Ct. 2056, 23 L.Ed.2d 707 (1969).

normally he may be tried again.[5] If a motion for mistrial is denied, and curative instructions are given by the court, it must be renewed or it will be deemed waived for purposes of appeal.[6]

It has been held in Georgia that a defendant's retrial is barred where a mistrial is granted on the grounds of prosecutorial over-reaching and such was motivated by bad faith on the part of the prosecuting attorney or with the intention to harass or prejudice the defendant.[7] However, in *State v. Beck*,[8] the court held that "intentional prosecutorial misconduct, standing alone, is *not* sufficient to bar retrial. Double jeopardy does not attach unless the prosecutorial misconduct was intended to subvert the protections afforded by the double jeopardy clause." But from a federal constitutional standpoint, the United States Supreme Court, in the 1982 case of *Oregon v. Kennedy*,[9] held that where a defendant moves for a mistrial because of prosecutorial misconduct, he may be tried again unless the conduct of the district attorney "was intended to provoke the defendant into moving for a mistrial." In *Potts v. State*,[10] the court referred to the intentional misconduct of the district attorney which would prevent a retrial after a mistrial as being the "prosecutorial misconduct justifying mistrial

---

[5]Lovett v. State, 80 Ga. 255, 4 S.E. 912 (1888). In Lyde v. State, 241 Ga. 111, 243 S.E.2d 64 (1978), the court said that if defense counsel has no objection to the granting of a mistrial, this bars a plea of double jeopardy. But it has been held that if a mistrial should have been granted because of the bad faith conduct of the prosecuting attorney, United States v. Dinitz, 424 U.S. 600, 611, 96 S.Ct. 1075, 47 L.Ed.2d 267 (1976), or because of his gross negligence, United States v. Martin, 561 F.2d 135 (8th Cir. 1977), a second trial is prevented. Intentional government misconduct seriously prejudicing defendant's right to a fair trial and causing defendant to move for a mistrial prevents defendant's retrial. United States v. Kessler, 530 F.2d 1246, 1256 (5th Cir. 1976).

See United States v. Scott, 437 U.S. 82, 98 S.Ct. 2187, 57 L.Ed.2d 65 (1978).

[6]Wells v. State, 243 Ga. App. 629, 631 (3), 534 S.E.2d 106 (2000).

[7]Studyvent v. State, 153 Ga. App. 161, 162, 264 S.E.2d 695 (1980); State v. Maddox, 185 Ga. App. 674, 675, 365 S.E.2d 516 (1988). Cf. Cobb v. State,

246 Ga. 619, 620, 272 S.E.2d 296 (1980).

State v. Traylor, 281 Ga. 730, 642 S.E.2d 700 (2007). Egregious case of prosecutorial misconduct which provoked defense motion for mistrial did not amount to double jeopardy bar to re-trial. Compare, Anderson v. State, 285 Ga. App. 466, 645 S.E.2d 647 (2007).

[8]State v. Beck, 200 Ga. App. 557, 558, 409 S.E.2d 57 (1991), rev'd on other grounds, 261 Ga. 826, 412 S.E.2d 530 (1992). Accord, Nance v. State, 274 Ga. 311, 553 S.E.2d 794 (2001); State v. D'Auria, 229 Ga. App. 34, 35, 492 S.E.2d 918 (1997).

[9]Oregon v. Kennedy, 456 U.S. 667, 102 S.Ct. 2083, 72 L.Ed.2d 416 (1982).

In Wright v. State, 284 Ga. App. 169, 643 S.E.2d 538 (2007), the Court of Appeals held that a prosecutor may be called as a witness at the hearing on a plea in bar in order to show motive where the state's conduct prompted a mistrial.

[10]Potts v. State, 257 Ga. 402, 403, 359 S.E.2d 916 (1987).

which resulted from the fear of the prosecutor that a jury might otherwise acquit." In *State v. Whitehead*,[11] the court said, "Only where the governmental conduct in question is intended to 'goad' the defendant into moving for a mistrial may a defendant raise the bar of double jeopardy to a second trial after having succeeded in aborting the first trial on his own motion. . . . Thus the standard is the intent of the prosecutor in connection with the misconduct. In the words of the holding, 'conduct . . . intended to provoke the defendant into moving for a mistrial' is what will bar retrial on the federal constitutional double jeopardy ground." This is a question of fact for the trial court and its finding on that issue will be upheld on appeal if there is any evidence to support it.[12] In *State v. Maddox*,[13] the court pointed out that an officer and the district attorney "have different scopes of employment and authority; . . . [I]n the absence of a showing that the prosecutor in . . . [a] case actively aided, counselled, or became a willing party to the error generated by the officer, we see no reason to bar . . . defendant's retrial."

Where the basis for the motion for mistrial is evidentiary in nature, the failure to make an objection at the time the evidence is offered is not timely and will be considered waived.[14]

In the case of a hung jury, double jeopardy will not normally prevent a subsequent trial.[15] If a defendant has been tried twice and both trials end in a hung jury, he may still be tried again.[16] However, if a mistrial is declared on defendant's motion after a testifying officer improperly places defendant's character in issue, the state may not, on retrial, add additional counts arising out of the same conduct which formed the basis for the original indictment.[17] See § 24:27, infra, on mistrials.

In *Benford v. State*,[18] the defendant had obtained a new trial because of the refusal of the trial judge to charge on involuntary manslaughter. The evidence was substantially the same at the second trial, and the trial judge again refused to give the requested charge. The Court of Appeals reversed. However, it

---

[11]State v. Whitehead, 184 Ga. App. 162, 163, 361 S.E.2d 41 (1987) (quoting Oregon v. Kennedy, 456 U.S. 667, 102 S.Ct. 2083, 72 L.Ed.2d 416 (1982)); Beck v. State, 261 Ga. 826, 412 S.E.2d 530 (1992). See also Reed v. State, 222 Ga. App. 376, 474 S.E.2d 264 (1996).

[12]Roscoe v. State, 286 Ga. 325, 687 S.E.2d 455 (2009).

[13]State v. Maddox, 185 Ga. App. 674, 676, 365 S.E.2d 516 (1988).

[14]Thaxton v. State, 260 Ga. 141, 143(5), 390 S.E.2d 841 (1990); Nel v. State, 252 Ga. App. 761, 763(3), 557 S.E.2d 44 (2001).

[15]Hobbs v. State, 229 Ga. 556, 192 S.E.2d 903 (1972).

[16]Orvis v. State, 237 Ga. 6, 226 S.E.2d 570 (1976).

[17]Herrington v. State, 315 Ga. App. 101, 726 S.E.2d 625 (2012).

[18]Benford v. State, 164 Ga. App. 733, 298 S.E.2d 39 (1982).

failed to find a double jeopardy violation because it could not "say that this was prompted by a conscious intent to harass the defendant or jeopardize his rights." Nevertheless, the court strongly indicated that a failure of the trial judge to properly instruct the jury at a third trial would prevent the defendant's retrial.

In the event of a mistrial in a felony case, the trial judge may in his discretion, with or without an application from the state and/or the defendant, direct that "a brief or transcript of the testimony be filed by the court reporter."[19] As a matter of equal protection, a defendant is generally entitled to a copy of such a transcript.[20] However, if a defendant wants such a transcript, he must request it promptly; if he fails to do so, the lack of a transcript at the time of a retrial does not automatically entitle a defendant to a continuance.[21]

An exception is found to the foregoing material where a case is appealed and the appellate court finds that there was no evidence to support the verdict. In this situation the defendant may not be tried for the offense again.[22] In *Ricketts v. Williams*,[23] the Georgia Supreme Court seemed to retreat from this position by qualifying its broad reach. The court said that if a new trial is granted because the trial judge finds the verdict "contrary to the evidence and principles of justice and equity" or that the verdict is "decidedly and strongly against the weight of the evidence," a later trial is permissible. However, in *Gentry v. State*,[24] the court pointed out that under O.C.G.A. §§ 16-1-8(a)(1) and (d)(2), a retrial is barred where it has been determined that there was insufficient evidence to support an earlier conviction. In *Burks v.*

---

[19]O.C.G.A. § 17-8-5.

[20]Britt v. North Carolina, 404 U.S. 226, 92 S.Ct. 431, 30 L.Ed.2d 400 (1971).

[21]Walker v. State, 156 Ga. App. 478, 274 S.E.2d 680 (1980).

[22]Marchman v. State, 234 Ga. 40, 215 S.E.2d 467 (1975). In Parham v. State, 137 Ga. App. 498, 224 S.E.2d 485 (1976), the defendant was tried for murder and convicted of voluntary manslaughter. On appeal, the court determined there was no evidence of voluntary manslaughter and reversed the conviction. The defendant was later indicted for voluntary manslaughter for the same homicide. The court held that the overruling of his plea in bar based on the former prose-cution was error.

[23]Ricketts v. Williams, 240 Ga. 148, 240 S.E.2d 41 (1977), judgment vacated, 438 U.S. 902, 98 S.Ct. 3119, 57 L.Ed.2d 1145 (1978). On remand, the Georgia Supreme Court held that a finding by a trial court that the verdict is against the weight of the evidence is not a finding "that the evidence is legally insufficient so as to bar a second trial." Ricketts v. Williams, 242 Ga. 303, 304, 248 S.E.2d 673 (1978). See Nelson v. State, 317 Ga. App. 527, 731 S.E.2d 770 (2012). Accord, Priest v. State, 265 Ga. 399 (1), 456 S.E.2d 503 (1995).

[24]Gentry v. State, 206 Ga. App. 490, 491 (1), 426 S.E.2d 52 (1992).

United States,[25] the United States Supreme Court held that the Fifth Amendment prevents a second trial, once an appellate court has found the evidence insufficient to sustain the jury's verdict of guilty. This rule applies to trials in state court.[26] However, in *Lockhart v. Nelson*,[27] the United States Supreme Court held that "the Double Jeopardy Clause allows retrial when a reviewing court determines that a defendant's conviction must be reversed because evidence was erroneously admitted against [the defendant], . . . and also concludes that without the inadmissible evidence there was insufficient evidence to support [the] conviction. . . ."

The United States Supreme Court vacated Georgia's decision in *Ricketts*, and remanded the case for further consideration in the light of *Greene* and *Burks*, which are cited in the footnotes.[28] Nevertheless, when the Georgia Supreme Court again considered *Ricketts*, it again held that there could be a retrial after a motion for new trial had been granted because "the verdict is decidedly and strongly against the weight of the evidence." The court pointed out that there has always been a distinction between such a new trial which is discretionary and a reversal because of insufficient evidence.[29] Thereafter, the United States Supreme Court denied certiorari.[30]

In *Tibbs v. Florida*,[31] the United States Supreme Court, in a five to four decision, held that a reversal based upon the weight

---

[25]Burks v. United States, 437 U.S. 1, 98 S.Ct. 2141, 57 L.Ed.2d 1 (1978). In Hudson v. Louisiana, 450 U.S. 40, 101 S.Ct. 970, 67 L.Ed.2d 30 (1981), the court said that the rationale of Burks applies when either a reviewing court or the trial judge determines the evidence to be insufficient, not just when there is no evidence to support the conviction.

In Lewis v. State, 248 Ga. 566, 285 S.E.2d 179 (1981), the court pointed out that the rule in *Burks* does not prevent the Court of Appeals from withdrawing an opinion in which it found that the evidence did not support the verdict and substituting a new opinion on rehearing. Accord, Holcomb v. Peachtree City, 187 Ga. App. 258, 370 S.E.2d 23 (1988).

Dinning v. State, 267 Ga. 879, 880, 485 S.E.2d 464 (1997), followed *Burks*, supra. However, in Mosley v. State, 230 Ga. App. 890, 891 (1), 497 S.E.2d 608 (1998), the court mistak-

enly reached the opposite conclusion. Cf. Childress v. State, 268 Ga. 386, 387 (1), 489 S.E.2d 799 (1997).

[26]See Greene v. Massey, 437 U.S. 19, 98 S.Ct. 2151, 57 L.Ed.2d 15 (1978). Also, this rule applies even when an erroneous ruling of the trial court results in the insufficiency of the evidence which causes the trial judge to render an acquittal. See Sanabria v. United States, 437 U.S. 54, 98 S.Ct. 2170, 57 L.Ed.2d 43 (1978).

[27]Lockhart v. Nelson, 488 U.S. 33, 109 S.Ct. 285, 102 L.Ed.2d 265 (1988).

[28]Williams v. Ricketts, 438 U.S. 902, 98 S.Ct. 3119, 57 L.Ed.2d 1145 (1978).

[29]Ricketts v. Williams, 242 Ga. 303, 248 S.E.2d 673 (1978).

[30]Williams v. Ricketts, 439 U.S. 1135, 99 S.Ct. 1059, 59 L.Ed.2d 97 (1979).

[31]Tibbs v. Florida, 457 U.S. 31, 102 S.Ct. 2211, 72 L.Ed.2d 652 (1982).

of the evidence does not prevent a retrial, but that a reversal based on the insufficiency of the evidence does prevent a retrial on double jeopardy grounds. Thus, if a conviction is reversed because the evidence presented fails to comply with the due process requirement of *Jackson v. Virginia,*[32] the reversal is based on insufficient evidence and the defendant may not be tried again.

In *Patterson v. State,*[33] the Georgia Court of Appeals recognized another exception to the Burks rule in a situation where venue was not sufficiently established at the first trial. In *Patterson* the defendant moved for a new trial because the state did not prove venue. Then the defendant moved for an acquittal on double jeopardy grounds. The trial judge found no double jeopardy violation. The appellate court concluded that *Burks* applied only when the deficiency in the evidence related to some fundamental matter in the judicial process. Venue does not "go to the guilt or innocence of the accused and thus is not substantive in the manner indicated by *Burks.*"

In *Stone v. Superior Court,*[34] the California Supreme Court considered a situation in which the jury foreman announced that the jury was unanimous for acquittal of first and second degree murder. However, some of the jurors had voted for a finding of guilt for voluntary manslaughter, some for involuntary manslaughter, some for justifiable homicide and none for acquittal. The trial judge concluded that the jury was hopelessly deadlocked and declared a mistrial. The appellate court concluded that it is a double jeopardy violation for the trial judge to fail to return a partial verdict finding the defendant not guilty of the two greater offenses of which the jury had concluded unanimously that the defendant was not guilty. However, in *Blueford v. Arkansas,*[35] the United States Supreme Court held that double jeopardy did not bar retrial of murder charges after the jury announced that it had unanimously agreed against them but remained deadlocked on lesser included offenses. After an *Allen* charge, the jury deliberated further but reported it was still deadlocked on the lesser charges. The Supreme Court based its holding on the failure of the jury to formally provide a verdict after it had received the *Allen* charge and again reported its deadlock on the lesser counts in the indictment.

[32]Jackson v. Virginia, 443 U.S. 307, 99 S.Ct. 2781, 61 L.Ed.2d 560 (1979). In *Jackson*, the court held that the due process clause forbids a conviction on evidence insufficient to persuade a rational factfinder of guilt beyond a reasonable doubt.

[33]Patterson v. State, 162 Ga. App. 455, 291 S.E.2d 567 (1982).

[34]Stone v. Superior Court, 31 Cal.3d 503, 183 Cal.Rptr. 647, 646 P.2d 809 (1982).

[35]Blueford v. Arkansas, 132 S. Ct. 2044, 182 L. Ed. 2d 937 (2012).

In *Hall v. State,*[36] the court limited still further the application of the double jeopardy clause by holding that if the insufficiency of the evidence results from a "trial error," this does not prevent the retrial of the defendant. In this bad check case, the manager of the bank's bookkeeping department testified from records which he admitted he did not prepare and which were not properly authenticated. The court excluded the records since a proper foundation was not made under former O.C.G.A. § 24-3-14 (now § 24-8-803(6)). On appeal, the court held that it was error for the trial judge not to strike the manager's testimony. The striking of his testimony would have resulted in insufficient evidence to warrant a conviction. However, the court concluded that the "trial error" would not prevent a retrial.

In *Taylor v. State,*[37] the defendant was tried for vehicular homicide, driving under the influence, and one count of reckless driving. The jury convicted him of reckless driving and driving under the influence. The jury was unable to reach a verdict on vehicular homicide. The appellate court, in affirming the denial of the defendant's motion in autrefois convict, pointed out that "where, as here, the State seeks to prosecute a defendant for two offenses in a single prosecution, one of which is included in the other, and the defendant receives a mistrial on the greater offense, the remaining conviction of the lesser offense does not bar retrial of the greater offense."

In *Hunter v. State,*[38] the court held that *Burks* did not apply where the case was reversed for insufficient evidence where the lack of evidence resulted from an erroneous ruling of the trial judge on a motion of the defendant.

In *Richardson v. United States,*[39] the United States Supreme Court held that the legal insufficiency of the evidence to convict is not established where the jury fails to reach a verdict and the trial judge declares a mistrial for this reason. However, in *Smalis v. Pennsylvania,*[40] the court held that where a case in a trial is terminated by the judge, determining that there is insufficient evidence to justify a conviction, this prevents a re-trial of the defendant even if in fact the trial judge erroneously terminated the trial. See § 24:27, infra, on grant of a mistrial because of the jury's inability to reach a verdict.

---

[36]Hall v. State, 244 Ga. 86, 91 (4), 259 S.E.2d 41 (1979).

[37]Taylor v. State, 238 Ga. App. 753 (1), 520 S.E.2d 267 (1999) (quoting Rower v. State, 267 Ga. 46, 472 S.E.2d 297 (1996)). See Smith v. State, 292 Ga. 478, 738 S.E.2d 621 (2013).

[38]Hunter v. State, 257 Ga. 571, 574 (4), 361 S.E.2d 787 (1987).

[39]Richardson v. United States, 468 U.S. 317, 104 S.Ct. 3081, 82 L.Ed.2d 242 (1984).

[40]Smalis v. Pennsylvania, 476 U.S. 140, 106 S.Ct. 1745, 90 L.Ed.2d 116 (1986).

If a trial is improperly terminated after the jury has been impaneled and sworn, a later trial is barred.[41] But it has been said that if the defendant, or his counsel, through his improper conduct is responsible for the mistrial, a plea of double jeopardy may not be successfully raised.[42] However, the Fifth Circuit has held that even if a defense counsel's misconduct causes the court to grant a mistrial, unless there is a showing of manifest necessity to grant the mistrial, a later trial on the same offense will constitute double jeopardy.[43] If a defendant has moved for a directed verdict of acquittal after the close of evidence, and obtains a judgment of acquittal notwithstanding the mistrial,[44] where the jury is unable to reach a verdict, another trial may not be held.[45]

In *State v. Johnson*,[46] Johnson and Weems were tried together. Although Weems' attorney moved for a mistrial, Johnson's attorney neither joined in the motion nor commented or participated in the discussion of the motion. The trial judge granted a mistrial to both. Johnson then moved for dismissal of the charges based on double jeopardy. The trial judge granted Johnson's motion. The Georgia Supreme Court reversed, holding that Johnson's silence impliedly amounted to a consent to the declaration of a mistrial.

In extreme cases a judge may grant a mistrial where there is manifest necessity for a second trial, lest otherwise the end of public justice be defeated.[47] The lack of consent of the defendant to the granting of a mistrial in this situation will not prevent an-

---

[41]O.C.G.A. § 16-1-8(a); Oliveros v. State, 120 Ga. 237, 238 (2), 47 S.E. 627 (1904); State v. Battaglia, 221 Ga. App. 283, 288, 470 S.E.2d 755 (1996).

[42]Pleas v. State, 268 Ga. 889, 495 S.E.2d 4 (1998); Fraser v. State, 21 Ga. App. 154 (1), 94 S.E. 79 (1917). See Bagwell v. State, 129 Ga. 170, 171, 58 S.E. 650 (1907); State v. Abdi, 162 Ga. App. 20, 21, 288 S.E.2d 772 (1982), aff'd, 249 Ga. 827, 294 S.E.2d 506 (1982), rev'd, 744 F.2d 1500 (11th Cir. 1984).

[43]United States v. Dinitz, 492 F.2d 53 (5th Cir. 1974), rev'd on other grounds, 424 U.S. 600, 96 S.Ct. 1075, 47 L.Ed.2d 267 (1976).

[44]E.g., Phillips v. State, 133 Ga. App. 461, 211 S.E.2d 411 (1974). But see § 28:9, infra, on judgment of acquittal notwithstanding a mistrial.

[45]See United States v. Martin

Linen Supply Co., 430 U.S. 564, 97 S.Ct. 1349, 51 L.Ed.2d 642 (1977). See § 14:61, infra, on retrial.

[46]State v. Johnson, 267 Ga. 305, 477 S.E.2d 579 (1996).

[47]In Arizona v. Washington, 434 U.S. 497, 98 S.Ct. 824, 54 L.Ed.2d 717 (1978), the court recognized this rule, emphasizing the need of the trial judge to exercise his sound discretion under the facts of the particular case, and said that it is not necessary for the trial judge to make a formal finding of fact.

In United States v. Aguiar, 610 F.2d 1296 (5th Cir. 1980), the trial judge severed the defendant from an earlier trial after the defendant had testified as a result of the defendant's counsel informing the court he was planning to comment on the failure of the other defendants to testify. The court said the severance was a result

other trial.[48] However, where a defendant moves for a mistrial, the doctrine of manifest necessity is said not to apply.[49]

In *Laster v. State*,[50] the court observed: "Once a jury is impaneled and sworn, jeopardy attaches and an accused is entitled to have the trial proceed to an acquittal or conviction by that jury. The trial court may interrupt the proceedings and declare a mistrial over the defendant's objection only if the prosecutor demonstrates manifest necessity for the mistrial. Manifest necessity exists when the accused's right to have the trial completed by a particular tribunal is subordinate to 'the public interest in affording the prosecutor one full and fair opportunity to present his evidence to an impartial jury.' The classic example of a proper basis for a mistrial is the trial judge's belief that the jury is unable to reach a verdict; at the other extreme are the cases where the prosecutor seeks a mistrial to buttress weaknesses in the state's evidence. When there is no prosecutorial misconduct, the trial court has broad discretion in deciding whether to grant a mistrial." However the failure of the state to timely secure evidence necessary to its case "does not constitute . . . manifest necessity, because the Double Jeopardy Clause forbids a second trial for the purpose of affording the prosecution another opportunity to supply evidence which it failed to muster in the first

---

of manifest necessity and the defendant could be tried later.

In Chatham v. State, 247 Ga. 95, 274 S.E.2d 473 (1981), rev'g 155 Ga. App. 154, 270 S.E.2d 274 (1980), a mistrial was granted because defense counsel was not prepared. The Supreme Court found that there was no manifest necessity, because the conduct of the district attorney and trial judge in calling that case and finding defense counsel in contempt was fundamentally unfair.

In Cobb v. State, 246 Ga. 619, 272 S.E.2d 296 (1980), the court concluded that it was error to grant a mistrial over the defendant's objection. The jury was out only 13 minutes, came back in the courtroom, and told the judge that the jury did not think either side had presented enough evidence, but that the foreman thought the jury could reach a verdict. The court said there was no manifest necessity for declaring a mistrial. See Otis v. State, 298 Ga. 544, 782 S.E.2d 654 (2016) (no manifest necessity where judge declared mistrial because defense failed to provide state with pre-

trial notice of intent to present insanity defense with testimony of lay witnesses; Ga. Unif. Super. Ct. R. 31.1 only requires notice when defense is supported by expert testimony).

[48]Jones v. State, 232 Ga. 324, 327, 206 S.E.2d 481 (1974). In Kelly v. State, 145 Ga. App. 780 (1), 245 S.E.2d 20 (1978), the court cited United States v. Perez, 22 U.S. (9 Wheat.) 579, 6 L.Ed. 165 (1824), and said that a mistrial caused by the failure of the jury to reach a verdict did not constitute double jeopardy, because of the doctrine of manifest necessity. In United States v. McKoy, 591 F.2d 218 (3d Cir. 1979), the court said that the burden is on the government to show that the trial judge had no alternative to granting a mistrial.

[49]Oregon v. Kennedy, 456 U.S. 667, 102 S.Ct. 2083, 72 L.Ed.2d 416 (1982).

[50]Laster v. State, 268 Ga. 172, 173 (1), 486 S.E.2d 153 (1997) (footnotes omitted). See Ogletree v. State, 300 Ga. App. 365, 685 S.E.2d 351 (2009).

proceeding."[51] This rule would not apply where the prosecution had properly subpoenaed a necessary witness who then fails to appear at trial.[52]

The doctrine of manifest necessity means just what the name implies. "The decision to declare a mistrial is not to be undertaken lightly."[53] The "failure of a trial judge to consider adequately less severe alternatives to a mistrial shows 'an inadequate concern for the severe consequences of ordering a mistrial without the accused's consent.' "[54] In *Smith v. State*,[55] the court held that "a trial court should give careful, deliberate, and studious consideration to whether the circumstances demand a mistrial, with a keen eye toward other, less drastic, alternatives, calling for a recess if necessary and feasible to guard against hasty mistakes. . . ." Thus, it was error for a trial judge to declare a mistrial over the objection of the defendant, where a juror's mother died after the trial began without considering how long

---

[51]Jackson v. State, 305 Ga. App. 727, 729, 700 S.E.2d 714 (2010).

[52]Julian v. State, 319 Ga. App. 808, 738 S.E.2d 647 (2013).

[53]United States v. Starling, 571 F.2d 934 (5th Cir. 1978).

In Blount v. State, 169 Ga. App. 215, 216, 312 S.E.2d 197 (1983), the court found that there was manifest necessity where the trial judge granted a mistrial because a juror was found to be distraught due to fear of other jurors. See Meadows v. State, 303 Ga. 507, 813 S.E.2d 350 (2018) (double jeopardy barred retrial where trial court abused its discretion in declaring mistrial over defendant's objection based on concern for jury safety in contentious trial of gang member).

In Davis v. State, 170 Ga. App. 748, 318 S.E.2d 202 (1984), the court held that there was manifest necessity to grant a mistrial where the 15-year-old alleged victim, who had been subpoenaed, failed to appear in court. See Griffin v. State, 264 Ga. 232, 233, 443 S.E.2d 612 (1994).

In Payne v. State, 269 Ga. App. 662, 605 S.E.2d 75 (2004), the Court of Appeals found that there was no manifest necessity warranting a mistrial where the evidence which had been the subject of a motion in limine was heard by the jury.

[54]Cherry v. Director, State Board of Corrections, 613 F.2d 1262, 1266 (5th Cir. 1980); Brady v. Samaha, 667 F.2d 224 (1st Cir. 1981); Bradfield v. State, 211 Ga. App. 318, 439 S.E.2d 100 (1993); Stevens v. State, 215 Ga. App. 718, 719, 452 S.E.2d 176 (1994).

[55]Smith v. State, 263 Ga. 782, 783 (1), 439 S.E.2d 483 (1994). See Honester v. State, 336 Ga. App. 166, 784 S.E.2d 30 (2016). See also Dotson v. State, 213 Ga. App. 7, 8 (1), 443 S.E.2d 650 (1994) (determine manifest necessity by weighing the defendant's right to a particular tribunal against the public's interest in just judgments).

In Jefferson v. State, 224 Ga. App. 8, 479 S.E.2d 406 (1996), the defendant was issued two uniform traffic citations. After the defendant appeared and the jury was impaneled and sworn, the State charged him with yet another accusation. The defendant announced that he was ready to proceed on the original citations but objected to proceeding on the additional count, asserting that he needed more time on the additional count. Over the defendant's objection, the court granted a mistrial. The appellate court held that it was error for the trial judge to deny the defendant's motion for discharge and acquittal based on double jeopardy.

the juror would need to be absent, or whether or not the juror would have been willing to continue with the trial. Also, the trial judge failed to give each side an opportunity to explain its position on a mistrial.[56] In *Johnson v. State*,[57] the sua sponte order of mistrial over the defendant's objection following a series of abusive remarks and behavior directed at the court and the prosecution by defense counsel was reversed where it did not appear from the record that the defendant's case could not have been fairly decided by the jury. In *Julian v. State*,[58] the Court of Appeals held that it was error for the trial court to grant a mistrial on grounds of "manifest necessity" when the state was not allowed to present a witness by way of Skype over the objection of the defendant and should have granted the defendant's motion for discharge and acquittal after the state sought to retry the case. The court noted that the state conceded it did not finally decide to present the witness until after the jury was impaneled. See Annotation, "What Constitutes 'Manifest Necessity' for State Prosecutor's Dismissal of Action, Allowing Subsequent Trial Despite Jeopardy's Having Attached," 14 A.L.R.4th 1014 (1982). See § 18:38, infra, on ordering a mistrial because of an improper communication with a juror. In *Terrell v. State*,[59] the court held that "the failure of the trial [court] to affirmatively state on the record the alternatives . . . [the court] considered and rejected, prior to announcing the mistrial, does not, standing alone, render . . . [the court's] determination so unwarranted as to preclude the defendant's retrial. . . ." However, "[w]here inadmissible evidence has been introduced and curative instructions cannot 'free the jury's mind of prejudice,' a trial court should declare a mistrial."[60]

---

[56]Cherry v. Director, State Board of Corrections, 613 F.2d 1262 (5th Cir. 1980), in effect rev'g Cherry v. State, 220 Ga. 695, 141 S.E.2d 412 (1965).

In Webb v. Hutto, 720 F.2d 375 (4th Cir. 1983), the court held that there was no double jeopardy violation where a trial judge on motion of the prosecution granted a five-day continuance in order for additional witnesses to be obtained.

[57]Johnson v. State, 258 Ga. App. 33(1), 572 S.E.2d 669 (2002). The Court of Appeals in another case involving a defendant with the last name of Johnson ruled there was no manifest necessity which would justify an order of mistrial of a four count accusation where the jury was dead-locked on only one of the charges. Johnson v. State, 256 Ga. App. 730, 569 S.E.2d 625 (2002).

In McGee v. State, 287 Ga. App. 839, 652 S.E.2d 822 (2007), a trial court's sua sponte declaration of mistrial and denial of the defendant's motion to dismiss because of double jeopardy was reversed because the court failed to give the parties advance notice of its intentions and thereby allow for them to suggest alternative remedies.

[58]Julian v. State, 319 Ga. App. 808, 738 S.E.2d 647 (2013).

[59]Terrell v. State, 236 Ga. App. 163, 165, 511 S.E.2d 555 (1999).

[60]Bentley v. State, 262 Ga. App. 541 (3), 586 S.E.2d 32 (2003).

In *Knight v. State,*[61] the court held that the postponement of a trial in progress for 48 hours because of the illness of a juror was not a violation of double jeopardy, since a continuance of a case is not a termination of the trial. In contrast, however, is the case of *Puplampu v. State.*[62] There, after the first witness for the state was sworn, but before providing any evidence, the court terminated and rescheduled the case for the next week before a different judge after the court determined that the State was unprepared. The Court of Appeals ruled that the defendant had been placed in double jeopardy as a result.

In *Julian v. State,*[63] the Court of Appeals held that it was error for the trial court to grant a mistrial on grounds of "manifest necessity" when the state was not allowed to present a witness by way of Skype over the objection of the defendant and should have granted the defendant's motion for discharge and acquittal after the state sought to retry the case. The court noted that the state conceded it did not finally decide to present the witness until after the jury was empanelled.

In the interesting Eleventh Circuit case of *United States v. Chica,*[64] involving four criminal defendants, two of the defendants moved for a mistrial on the ground that they had been prejudiced by certain testimony. The other two defendants, Chica and Ramos, had not been prejudiced. Counsel for Chica and Ramos wanted to continue the trial with these two defendants. The trial judge granted the motion for a mistrial as to all four defendants in the interest of judicial economy. The appeals court held that judicial economy was insufficient to meet the necessary high standard for granting a mistrial over objection and, thus, retrial of Chica and Ramos violated the Double Jeopardy Clause. In dismissing the case, the Eleventh Circuit pointed out that "the Double Jeopardy Clause does not contain a judicial economy exception."

It has been said that jeopardy does not attach if a defendant is tried on an indictment which is fatally defective.[65] If a defendant files a demurrer to an indictment and after the introduction of

---

[61]Knight v. State, 197 Ga. App. 250, 398 S.E.2d 202 (1990).

[62]Puplampu v. State, 257 Ga. App. 5, 6, 570 S.E.2d 83 (2002).

[63]Julian v. State, 319 Ga. App. 808, 738 S.E.2d 647 (2013).

[64]United States v. Chica, 14 F.3d 1527, 1532 (11th Cir. 1994).

[65]Conley v. State, 85 Ga. 348 (1), 11 S.E. 659 (1890).

However, in Benton v. Maryland, 395 U.S. 784, 797, 89 S.Ct. 2056, 23 L.Ed.2d 707 (1969), the court said that the state may not allege its own error to deprive the defendant of the benefit of an acquittal by jury, even if the indictment was voidable because of an improper grand jury. But in the case of United States v. Ewell, 383 U.S. 116, 86 S.Ct. 773, 15 L.Ed.2d 627 (1966), the court said that if a defendant is convicted on a fatally defective indictment, he may be not only tried for the offense again, but the new indictment

evidence the court sustains the demurrer, this does not prevent the defendant from being tried again on a new indictment[66] if the dismissal of the indictment is not the second dismissal of the charge. See § 12:17, supra, on indictments. However, if a defendant is tried on a defective indictment for two or more crimes and he is acquitted of one crime, he may not again be tried for the offense for which he was acquitted.[67]

O.C.G.A. § 5-7-1 provides the state with a limited right of appeal from orders regarding select issues entered prior to trial. In addition, the state has the right to an interlocutory appeal from an order excluding evidence. However, the statute does not have double jeopardy implications since the events upon which it authorizes an appeal by the state occur before jeopardy attaches. See § 14:51, supra, on double jeopardy; § 28:4, infra, on the state's right of appeal; and § 14:99, infra, on interlocutory appeals.

§ 14:59 Double jeopardy—Dual sovereignty

Pursuant to O.C.G.A. § 16-1-8(c), an accused who has been formerly prosecuted in federal court may not be prosecuted in state court "for the same conduct, unless each prosecution requires proof of a fact not required in the other prosecution or unless the crime was not consummated when the former trial began." The statute does not oust the Georgia courts from jurisdiction, but merely bars a second trial for an offense previously tried in federal court. For example, where a defendant is indicted

---

may also include offenses not included in the defective indictment.

In Keener v. State, 238 Ga. 7, 230 S.E.2d 846 (1976), the court said that where the defendant waived an indictment alleging armed robbery, burglary, and possession of a sawed-off shotgun during a robbery, the waiver of an indictment to the armed robbery was invalid since this was a capital felony. However, even though the remaining convictions were valid, this did not prevent the defendant from being tried for the armed robbery again. The court said that "where there is a conviction of two crimes in a single prosecution one of which is included in the other and the defendant obtains a reversal of the major crime for lack of jurisdiction the remaining conviction of the lesser crime does not bar a retrial on the major crime." Simmons v. State, 106 Ga. 355 (2), 32 S.E. 339 (1899).

[66]Culpepper v. State, 44 Ga. App. 351 (1), 161 S.E. 849 (1931). But cf. Benton v. Maryland, 395 U.S. 784, 89 S.Ct. 2056, 23 L.Ed.2d 707 (1969); Lee v. United States, 432 U.S. 23, 97 S.Ct. 2141, 53 L.Ed.2d 80 (1977). See §§ 14:39 and 14:51, supra.

[67]In Arizona v. Washington, 434 U.S. 497, 98 S.Ct. 824, 54 L.Ed.2d 717 (1978), the court said "The Double Jeopardy Clause does protect a defendant against government actions intended to provoke mistrial requests and thereby subject defendants to the substantial burdens imposed by multiple prosecutions. It bars retrials where 'bad faith conduct by judge or prosecutor' threatens the harassment of accused by successive prosecutions or declaration of mistrial so as to afford the prosecution a more favorable opportunity to convict the defendant."

in both federal and state court for crimes arising out of the same transaction, to-wit, bank robbery, and he pleads guilty and is sentenced in federal court, he may not thereafter be tried in state court for a crime arising out of the bank robbery.[1]

In *Sullivan v. State*,[2] however, the Georgia Supreme Court concluded that O.C.G.A. § 16-1-8(c) would not bar the state from trying the defendant for malice and felony murder even though the defendant had been acquitted of "murder for hire" charges involving the same victim and event in federal court. The court ruled that unless the federal prosecution was for a crime over which the state had concurrent jurisdiction, double jeopardy had no application. The court found that the interstate commerce and communication elements of the federal law precluded a finding of such jurisdiction.

There is no comparable federal statute to prevent a prosecution in federal court after a prosecution in state court for substantially the same crime. However, the United States Department of Justice has adopted a policy of not prosecuting an accused for essentially the same crime after he has been prosecuted by a state.[3] This policy is known as the Petite[4] policy and prevents a second prosecution except for compelling reasons; the United States Attorney "is required to obtain authorization from an appropriate Assistant Attorney General."[5]

The federal Constitution does not prevent the state or the federal government from prosecuting a defendant after he has been prosecuted by the other for substantially the same crime.[6]

[Section 14:59]

[1]Dorsey v. State, 237 Ga. 876, 230 S.E.2d 307 (1976). But cf. Brown v. State, 181 Ga. App. 795, 797, 354 S.E.2d 3 (1987), holding that "a criminal agreement to import cocaine is not the same as a criminal agreement to actually and knowingly possess more than 400 grams of cocaine."

[2]Sullivan v. State, 279 Ga. 893, 622 S.E.2d 823 (2005). This is a divided opinion which drew a very sharp dissent. Compare Calloway v. State, 303 Ga. 48, 810 S.E.2d 105 (2018).

[3]See In re Washington, 531 F.2d 1297 (5th Cir. 1976). Here, two defendants were convicted in state court for conspiracy to rob, and were likewise convicted in federal court for federal crimes arising out of the same facts. Affirmed en banc, 544 F.2d 203 (5th Cir. 1976), rev'd sub nom. on other grounds, Rinaldi v. United States, 434 U.S. 22, 98 S.Ct. 81, 54 L.Ed.2d 207 (1977).

[4]Petite v. United States, 361 U.S. 529, 80 S.Ct. 450, 4 L.Ed.2d 490 (1960).

[5]See Rinaldi v. United States, 434 U.S. 22, 98 S.Ct. 81, 54 L.Ed.2d 207 (1977). In Delay v. United States, 602 F.2d 173 (8th Cir. 1979), the court held that the petite policy is an internal rule of the Department of Justice which cannot be enforced by the defendant. See Annot., 51 A.L.R.Fed. 852 (1981).

[6]Bartkus v. Illinois, 359 U.S. 121, 131, 79 S.Ct. 676, 3 L.Ed.2d 684 (1959).

In United States v. Wheeler, 435 U.S. 313, 98 S.Ct. 1079, 55 L.Ed.2d

However, this practice has been severely criticized,[7] and this attitude is perhaps responsible for the Georgia statute and the Department of Justice's policy.

In *Heath v. Alabama*,[8] the United States Supreme Court held that the double jeopardy clause was not violated where a defendant pled guilty to " 'malice' murder" in Georgia and was given a life sentence, and then an Alabama court tried, convicted, and sentenced the defendant to death for "murder during a kidnapping" arising out of the same course of conduct.

See § 14:48, supra, on how the double jeopardy aspects of the defendant's conduct in a present crime was used in an earlier proceeding in aggravation of sentence.

§ 14:60   Double jeopardy—Trial in an inferior court

For purpose of double jeopardy, a state and municipality are considered to be the same sovereign. In *Waller v. Florida*,[1] the defendant and others removed a canvas mural from a wall of the City Hall and carried it through the streets of the city. The defendant was charged with and found guilty of the violation of two city ordinances: destruction of city property and disorderly breach of the peace. Later, over objection, he was charged with

---

303 (1978), the court held that double jeopardy did not prevent a federal prosecution of an Indian who had been convicted of a lesser included offense in an Indian tribal court, since two different sovereigns were involved. However, in State v. Hogg, 118 N.H. 262, 385 A.2d 844 (1978), the court held that the New Hampshire constitution barred a later trial in state court where the defendant had previously been tried in federal court for the same offense.

[7]See Fisher, "Double Jeopardy, Two Sovereignties, and the Intruding Constitution," 28 U. Chi. L. Rev. 591 (1961). Also see "Acquittal or Conviction in State Court as Bar to Federal Prosecution Based on Same Act or Transaction," Annot., 18 A.L.R.Fed. 393 (1974).

See Annot., "Conviction or Acquittal in Federal Court as Bar to Prosecution in State Court for State Offense Based on Same Facts—Modern View," 6 A.L.R.4th 802 (1981).

[8]Heath v. Alabama, 474 U.S. 82, 106 S.Ct. 433, 88 L.Ed.2d 387 (1985).

See also Jackson v. State, 284 Ga. 826, 672 S.E.2d 640 (2009) (where the Georgia Supreme Court held that double jeopardy did not bar the prosecution of a defendant for theft by receiving in Kentucky and theft by taking in Georgia for the same incident).

[Section 14:60]

[1]Waller v. Florida, 397 U.S. 387, 90 S.Ct. 1184, 25 L.Ed.2d 435 (1970). The continued validity of *Waller v. Florida* was recognized in Brown v. Ohio, 432 U.S. 161, 97 S.Ct. 2221, 53 L.Ed.2d 187 (1977).

In Fugate v. New Mexico, 470 U.S. 904, 105 S.Ct. 1858, 84 L.Ed.2d 777 (1985), a defendant was convicted in a municipal court for driving under the influence and careless driving. He was later convicted of vehicular homicide based on the same event in a higher court. The state Supreme Court found no double jeopardy bar. The United States Supreme Court was evenly divided, and, thus, the case was affirmed.

and convicted of grand larceny, a felony. The United States Supreme Court in a unanimous decision concluded that a state may not try a defendant for an offense for which he has already been tried in a municipal court. The court said, "Political subdivisions of States—counties, cities, or whatever—never were and never have been considered as sovereign entities. Rather, they have been traditionally regarded as subordinate governmental instrumentalities created by the State to assist in the carrying out of state governmental functions." The ruling is fully retroactive to all cases decided before *Waller*.[2]

In *State v. Burroughs*,[3] the Georgia Supreme Court on federal constitutional grounds said that a person who has been convicted of a crime having several elements may not later be tried for a lesser included offense consisting solely of one or more of the elements of the crime for which he had already been convicted[4] or tried. Likewise, a conviction or trial of a lesser included offense bars a later trial on the greater offense.[5]

In *State v. Gilder*,[6] the defendant pled guilty to driving under the influence in state court. He was later indicted in superior court as a habitual violator. The court held that the defendant's plea in bar was valid, since the habitual violator charge (a felony) was based in part on the driving under the influence case, and the election by the state to charge the defendant with the misdemeanor prevented the later indictment based in part on the earlier case. However, in *Rogers v. State*,[7] a defendant was arrested for driving under the influence of intoxicants, driving without a valid driver's license, and possession of diazepam (a felony). The defendant entered a nolo contendere plea in state

---

[2]Robinson v. Neil, 409 U.S. 505, 93 S.Ct. 876, 35 L.Ed.2d 29 (1973). However, in Swisher v. Brady, 435 U.S. 913, 98 S.Ct. 1465, 55 L.Ed.2d 504 (1978), the court held that a Maryland statute, providing that the state may file exceptions to a report of a master who makes recommendations to a juvenile judge, does not place the juvenile in jeopardy twice, since the juvenile judge is the ultimate adjudicator of the case.

[3]State v. Burroughs, 246 Ga. 393, 394, 271 S.E.2d 629 (1980).

[4]In re Nielsen, 131 U.S. 176, 9 S.Ct. 672, 33 L.Ed. 118 (1889).

[5]Illinois v. Vitale, 447 U.S. 410, 100 S. Ct. 2260, 65 L. Ed. 2d 228 (1980). But in Singer v. State, 156 Ga. App. 416, 274 S.E.2d 612 (1980), the defendant entered a plea of nolo contendere to trespass and possession of marijuana in a magistrate's court two days after his arrest. As soon as a laboratory's report identified a substance, which defendant also had at the time of his arrest for trespass, as MDA, he was indicted for possession of MDA. The court held that the earlier case did not bar the later charge, and pointed out that the district attorney had no knowledge of the MDA until the report was received and also had no knowledge of the earlier nolo contendere plea.

[6]State v. Gilder, 145 Ga. App. 731, 245 S.E.2d 3 (1978), aff'd, 242 Ga. 285, 248 S.E.2d 659 (1978).

[7]Rogers v. State, 166 Ga. App. 299, 304 S.E.2d 108 (1983).

court to the misdemeanor charges and was sentenced to 12 months on probation and a fine. The defendant was then indicted for possession of diazepam. He filed a motion of autrefois convict. The Georgia Court of Appeals affirmed the denial of the motion. The court said that while the accusation had charged the defendant with driving under the influence of wines, beers, liquors, and drugs, there was no evidence that the plea was entered for the offense of driving under the influence of drugs. "The offenses here did arise out of the same conduct, that is, the act of driving, but his possession of the controlled substances is separate and distinct from the conduct required to establish the offense of driving under the influence."

In *Barber v. State*,[8] the defendant was prosecuted in municipal court for disorderly conduct. After introduction of evidence, the case was dismissed and the defendant was then charged with simple battery in state court. The court held that the evidence of defendant striking prosecutrix and pulling her hair would support a conviction for both charges and that the second trial amounted to double jeopardy. Also, in *State v. Burroughs*,[9] the court held that where a defendant was tried in municipal court for violently interfering with another's pursuit of his lawful occupation, this prevented a later trial in state court for simple battery arising out of the same incident.

However, in *Fuller v. State*,[10] the defendant was convicted of public drunkenness in a municipal court. When he was charged in state court with driving under the influence, he pled double jeopardy. The plea was overruled, and he was convicted of driving under the influence. In affirming the second conviction, the court said that O.C.G.A. § 16-1-7(a) does not prevent successive state and municipal prosecution but only successive prosecutions for state crimes. Since the municipal court had no jurisdiction over misdemeanors, it is presumed the conviction in municipal court was for violating a municipal ordinance. Also the court said that there was nothing in the record to show that both convictions were based on the same facts.

In addition, a person is not subjected to double jeopardy by a criminal prosecution for a violation of a state statute governing

---

[8]Barber v. State, 146 Ga. App. 523, 246 S.E.2d 510 (1978). Cf. State v. Burroughs, 246 Ga. 393, 271 S.E.2d 629 (1980), which overruled *Barber* "insofar as it implies that the *statutory double jeopardy* provision controls the issue of successive state and municipal prosecutions" (emphasis added), aff'g 149 Ga. App. 183, 254

S.E.2d 144 (1979).

[9]State v. Burroughs, 149 Ga. App. 183, 254 S.E.2d 144 (1979), aff'd, 246 Ga. 393, 271 S.E.2d 629 (1980).

[10]Fuller v. State, 169 Ga. App. 468 (3), 313 S.E.2d 745 (1984); Parker v. State, 170 Ga. App. 333 (1), 317 S.E.2d 209 (1984); Dickinson v. State, 191 Ga. App. 467, 468, 382 S.E.2d 187 (1989).

the control of alcoholic beverages, although he was previously subjected to a civil penalty by the Department of Revenue for the same conduct.[11] Likewise, punishment received by a prisoner and administered by officials of the Executive Department of the state government will not bar a later criminal charge for the same offense.[12] However, by statute, if a person is convicted of a violation of most any traffic offense in a municipal court, he may not later be tried for that offense in a higher court.[13]

In *Perkins v. State*,[14] the court was confronted with a case in which the defendant had been arrested for the sale of more than an ounce of marijuana. Three months later he pled guilty in State Court to possession of less than an ounce of marijuana. One month before this guilty plea he had been indicted for sale of more than one ounce. The defendant contended and the appellate court held that the State Court proceeding barred the prosecution in Superior Court.

Double jeopardy does not attach if the inferior court did not have jurisdiction to try the case which was before it. Thus, where a defendant is tried in a municipal court for theft by taking, this does not prevent a later trial in a state court for the same offense.[15]

In *State v. Perkins*,[16] a divided Court of Appeals ruled that the trial court properly dismissed a felony vehicular homicide where the defendant pled guilty to the lesser included offense of reckless driving in Probate Court. O.C.G.A. § 40-6-376(d) prohibits the prosecution of any offense arising out of a felony vehicular homicide case except in a court having jurisdiction to hear the felony case. Although the Probate Court did not have jurisdiction to hear the felony vehicular homicide case, it did have jurisdiction over misdemeanor vehicular homicide cases. Since the guilty plea to the reckless driving charge was entered before the vehicular indictment was returned, a majority of the court found that the felony prosecution was barred on former jeopardy grounds.

The Supreme Court however, reversed, finding that because the defendant had been charged with felony vehicular homicide

---

[11]Alexander v. State, 129 Ga. App. 395, 199 S.E.2d 918 (1973).

[12]Carruth v. Ault, 231 Ga. 547, 203 S.E.2d 158 (1974).

[13]O.C.G.A. § 40-6-376.

[14]Perkins v. State, 143 Ga. App. 124, 237 S.E.2d 658 (1977); Mann v. State, 160 Ga. App. 527, 287 S.E.2d 325 (1981).

[15]State v. Ramsey, 143 Ga. App. 191, 237 S.E.2d 666 (1977). In this case, by statute the City Court of East Point only had jurisdiction over "offenses against the laws and ordinances of said city." Cf. Rangel v. State, 217 Ga. App. 152, 456 S.E.2d 739 (1995) (tried for simple battery in a municipal court).

[16]State v. Perkins, 256 Ga. App. 855, 569 S.E.2d 910 (2002).

on the Uniform Traffic Citation issued at the time of arrest, the Probate Court never had jurisdiction over the offense. The Court concluded that the indictment simply superseded the UTC as the charging document.[17]

See §§ 14:52 to 14:56, supra, on lesser included offenses. See § 13:27, supra, on transfers involving juveniles. See § 14:54, supra, on conviction of a city ordinance in municipal court.

§ 14:61   Double jeopardy—Retrial

Where a defendant is charged with murder and the jury makes no finding as to that count but returns a guilty verdict on the lesser included offense of involuntary manslaughter, the defendant may not be retried on the murder count in the event the defendant obtains a new trial. This is premised upon the implicit verdict of not guilty as to the murder charge when the jury returns a verdict of guilty on the lesser included offense.[1] If a defendant is to be tried again, he may file a plea of double jeopardy to be sure that he is not tried again for the greater offense. There are various other options available to him: (1) he may ask that a new indictment be returned charging him with the lesser offense; (2) the indictment may be written so as to only show the lesser crime; (3) the indictment need not go to the jury room;[2] or (4) by stipulation the parties may waive an indictment and an accusation charging the defendant with the lesser offense.[3]

If a defendant is on retrial to be tried on a lesser included offense, no mention should be made to the jury of the former charge.[4]

If a defendant is convicted of two crimes in a single transaction, and on appeal the conviction of the more serious crime is reversed while that of the lesser crime is affirmed, the defendant

---

[17]State v. Perkins, 276 Ga. 621, 580 S.E.2d 523 (2003).

[Section 14:61]

[1]Price v. Georgia, 398 U.S. 323, 90 S.Ct. 1757, 26 L.Ed.2d 300 (1970). In Blackledge v. Perry, 417 U.S. 21, 94 S.Ct. 2098, 40 L.Ed.2d 628 (1974), the court held that where a defendant successfully appealed from a misdemeanor conviction, it is a violation of due process to indict and try him for a felony arising out of the same transaction, since this was a result of prosecutorial vindictiveness and would discourage an appeal. Cf. Johnson v. State, 396 A.2d 163 (Del.1978). In Miracle v. Estelle, 592 F.2d 1269 (5th Cir. 1979), the court held that a defendant could not be charged with a more serious offense, based on the same activity, on his retrial. This amounted to prosecutorial vindictiveness.

[2]See § 24:18, infra, on sending the indictment and evidence to the jury room.

[3]Harrison v. State, 143 Ga. App. 883, 885, 240 S.E.2d 263 (1977).

[4]Harrison v. State, 143 Ga. App. 883, 886, 240 S.E.2d 263 (1977).

may still be re-tried on the greater crime.[5] Likewise, "where the State sought to prosecute a defendant on two offenses in a single prosecution [felony murder and arson in the first degree], one of which is included in the other, and the defendant receives a mistrial on the greater offense, the remaining conviction of the lesser offense does not bar retrial of the greater offense." In *Hogan v. State*,[6] the defendant was charged with driving under the influence. Count I charged him with being in control while intoxicated. Count II charged him with being in control with at least.12% blood alcohol. The defendant was found guilty of Count I and not guilty of Count II, and a motion for a new trial was granted on Count I. The court held that retrial on Count I was not violative of double jeopardy, even though the defendant was acquitted of Count II which was *"the same crime,"* (emphasis in original) because he could have been convicted on Count I and the retrial was the result of the defendant's efforts.

However, if the state retries the defendant "for felony-murder and receives a conviction, . . . the trial court must set aside the conviction for the underlying felony of arson in the first degree."[7]

The double jeopardy clause also prevents the "adult" trial of a youth who has already been placed in jeopardy by a juvenile court proceeding in which it was determined that he committed criminal acts,[8] and this is true even if it is determined that he was unsuitable for care and treatment within the juvenile system.[9]

In *Curry v. State*,[10] the defendant was indicted for assault on a peace officer and for simple battery. The jury was unable to reach a verdict. The defendant was then re-indicted for the original two offenses and also for two additional offenses: obstruction of an officer and abusive language. All of the offenses arose out of the same incident. The defendant raised a double jeopardy defense. The court concluded that the third and fourth counts of the new indictment should have been stricken.

---

[5]Keener v. State, 238 Ga. 7, 230 S.E.2d 846 (1976).

[6]Hogan v. State, 178 Ga. App. 534, 343 S.E.2d 770 (1986). See Williams v. State, 288 Ga. 7, 700 S.E.2d 564 (2010) (double jeopardy precludes retrial of counts merged by application of Edge v. State, 261 Ga. 865, 414 S.E.2d 463 (1992), into voluntary manslaughter conviction reversed on defendant's appeal).

[7]Bell v. State, 249 Ga. 644, 647, 292 S.E.2d 402 (1982).

[8]Lincoln v. State, 138 Ga. App. 234, 235 (3), 225 S.E.2d 708 (1976).

[9]Breed v. Jones, 421 U.S. 519, 95 S.Ct. 1779, 44 L.Ed.2d 346 (1975). In this case, a 17-year-old was found at an adjudicatory hearing to have violated the robbery law. At the dispositional hearing he was found unsuitable for punishment as a juvenile. He was then tried and convicted as an adult. The court found that the adult trial violated double jeopardy.

[10]Curry v. State, 248 Ga. 183, 281 S.E.2d 604 (1981).

From a federal constitutional standpoint, it is not necessary that a new trial be given for the conviction of a crime that was double jeopardy, if the appellate court can reduce the conviction to a lesser included offense which is not barred by double jeopardy, unless the defendant "demonstrate[s] a reasonable probability that he would not have been convicted of the non-jeopardy-barred offense absent the presence of the jeopardy-barred offense."[11]

See § 14:58, supra, on mistrials and new trials. See § 26:11, infra, on retrial of a capital case where the conviction is reversed for lack of evidence.

§ 14:62   Double jeopardy—Sentencing

In *North Carolina v. Pearce*,[1] the court held that neither the double jeopardy nor equal protection clauses of the federal Constitution prohibit a trial judge from imposing a more severe sentence after a second conviction for the same offense. But the due process clause prevents the imposition of a greater sentence by the trial judge unless the trial judge makes finding of fact based on facts occurring subsequent to the first trial, to justify the greater sentence. However, in *Wasman v. United States*,[2] the Supreme Court held *Pearce* was not intended to confine the trial judge's consideration solely to "conduct" occurring between the two sentences but to "events" during this time. Hence, the trial judge may impose a greater sentence where the defendant has been convicted of another crime during the interval between the

---

[11]Morris v. Mathews, 475 U.S. 237, 106 S.Ct. 1032, 89 L.Ed.2d 187 (1986). See "Morris v. Mathews: A Constitutional Salve for Double Jeopardy Violations," 38 Mercer L. Rev. 715 (1987).

[Section 14:62]

[1]North Carolina v. Pearce, 395 U.S. 711, 89 S.Ct. 2072, 23 L.Ed.2d 656 (1969), overruled by Alabama v. Smith, 490 U.S. 794, 109 S. Ct. 2201, 104 L. Ed. 2d 865 (1989). This rule is not retroactive. Michigan v. Payne, 412 U.S. 47, 93 S.Ct. 1966, 36 L.Ed.2d 736 (1973). Cf. Blackledge v. Perry, 417 U.S. 21, 94 S.Ct. 2098, 40 L.Ed.2d 628 (1974), in which the defendant was charged with a misdemeanor, convicted and sentenced to six months. He filed an appeal to superior court where he was entitled to a de novo trial. The district attorney then ob-

tained a felony indictment against him for the same conduct. He was sentenced to five years when he was tried on the indictment. The United States Supreme Court held that the defendant was deprived of due process, unless the state shows that it would have been impossible to proceed with the more serious charge at the outset. See § 15:2, infra.

In German v. State, 159 Ga. App. 638 (1), 284 S.E.2d 654 (1981), the defendant withdrew his guilty plea to involuntary manslaughter before sentence was pronounced. He was tried and found guilty of voluntary manslaughter. The conviction was affirmed.

[2]Wasman v. United States, 468 U.S. 559, 104 S.Ct. 3217, 82 L.Ed.2d 424 (1984).

two sentences for conduct of the defendant before the first sentence. In *Texas v. McCullough*,[3] the United States Supreme Court concluded that there was no Pearce violation or violation of the due process clause. McCullough was sentenced by the trial judge to 50 years even though he had been previously sentenced to 20 years by a jury. Unlike *Pearce*, the trial judge had granted a new trial after the earlier conviction. The Supreme Court held that there was no basis for a presumption of vindictiveness, and that, even if vindictiveness was presumed, the explanation of the trial judge overcame the presumption, justifying the sentence imposed. The Supreme Court pointed out that an increased sentence could be justified by facts existing at the time of the earlier sentence. *Alabama v. Smith*[4] finally overruled *Pearce*, noting that in subsequent cases, such as *McCullough*, it had made clear that *Pearce's* "presumption of vindictiveness" does not automatically arise in every case on retrial where the defendant receives a harsher sentence.

Where a jury fixes punishment on retrial, the jury is not limited to the sentence imposed by the former jury.[5] However, if a defendant is tried for a capital felony and is sentenced to life imprisonment, if he is re-tried, the jury may not impose the death sentence at his second trial.[6] But if a defendant is sentenced to life imprisonment for one crime and death for another, and his death sentence is set aside and he is re-sentenced, he may be sentenced to consecutive life sentences.[7]

In the interesting case of *Sattazahn v. Pennsylvania*,[8] the jury returned a verdict on a murder charge, but deadlocked during

---

[3]Texas v. McCullough, 475 U.S. 134, 106 S.Ct. 976, 89 L.Ed.2d 104 (1986).

[4]Alabama v. Smith, 490 U.S. 794, 109 S. Ct. 2201, 104 L. Ed. 2d 865 (1989).

[5]Chaffin v. Stynchcombe, 412 U.S. 17, 93 S.Ct. 1977, 36 L.Ed.2d 714 (1973). Contra, State v. Eden, 163 W.Va. 370, 256 S.E.2d 868 (W.Va.1979).

[6]Ward v. State, 239 Ga. 205, 208, 236 S.E.2d 365 (1977). However, this case is not based on double jeopardy, but is based on O.C.G.A. § 17-10-35(c)(3). The court said it is impossible for it to say that the death penalty was not disproportionate, where on the previous trial of the same case the jury imposed life imprisonment.

In Bullington v. Missouri, 451 U.S. 430, 101 S.Ct. 1852, 68 L.Ed.2d 270 (1981), the court held on double jeopardy grounds that where a defendant at a trial is sentenced by jury to life imprisonment and thereafter obtains a new trial and is re-tried, the state may not seek the death sentence at the second trial.

In Arizona v. Rumsey, 467 U.S. 203, 104 S.Ct. 2305, 81 L.Ed.2d 164 (1984), a life sentence was imposed after the trial judge found there were no aggravating circumstances as a result of an erroneous interpretation of the law. The court said that the double jeopardy clause bars the state from later sentencing the defendant to death for the same crime.

[7]Thomas v. State, 150 Ga. App. 341, 342, 258 S.E.2d 28 (1979).

[8]Sattazahn v. Pennsylvania, 537 U.S. 101, 123 S.Ct. 732, 154 L.Ed.2d 588 (2003).

the penalty phase. Pursuant to state law, the defendant was sentenced to life in prison. The Unites States Supreme Court held that double jeopardy did not bar the state from seeking the death penalty on retrial because there was no determination by the jury at the penalty phase of the first trial.

If a defendant who has received a death sentence obtains a new trial, the jury at the second trial may find aggravating circumstances justifying the death sentence which the jury during the first trial did not find to be aggravating circumstances.[9]

In *United States v. DiFrancesco*,[10] the United States Supreme Court held that there was no double jeopardy violation where the government appealed a sentence pursuant to the Organized Control Act to increase a sentence of a "dangerous special offender."

In *Wilford v. State*,[11] the court held that the constitutional prohibition against double jeopardy is not offended where a defendant's sentence as a First Offender is revoked after the trial court discovers that the defendant was not eligible to be sentenced as such and thereafter proceeds to impose a harsher sentence. The Georgia First Offender Act specifically contemplates the prospect of resentencing in the event a person is improperly sentenced as a First Offender and for that reason there is no expectation of finality in the original sentence.

In *United States v. Broce*,[12] the defendant had entered guilty pleas to two indictments. The first indictment charged the defendant with entering into an agreement about April 1978 to rig bids on a particular highway project. The second indictment charged the defendant with entering into a similar agreement about July 1979 to rig bids on a different project. Later, in a collateral attack, the defendant sought to show that there had been only one conspiracy and that the conviction of both indictments constituted double jeopardy. The Supreme Court held that since the guilty plea had been counseled and voluntarily and understandingly entered, this foreclosed the double jeopardy claim. See § 12:17, supra, on the second quashing of an indictment.

See § 14:61, supra, on double jeopardy in retrial. See § 26:11, infra, on retrial of a capital case. Also see §§ 15:2, infra, on plea bargaining; 16:1, infra, on arraignment; and 26:28 and 26:30 et

---

[9]Redd v. State, 242 Ga. 876, 883 (6), 252 S.E.2d 383 (1979).

[10]United States v. DiFrancesco, 449 U.S. 117, 101 S.Ct. 426, 66 L.Ed.2d 328 (1980); Note, "United States v. DiFrancesco: Court Upholds State Initiated Sentence Appeal," 32 Mercer L. Rev. 1261 (1981).

[11]Wilford v. State, 278 Ga. 718, 606 S.E.2d 252 (2004). See United States v. DiFrancesco, 449 U.S. 117, 101 S.Ct. 426, 66 L.Ed.2d 328 (1980).

[12]United States v. Broce, 488 U.S. 563, 109 S.Ct. 757, 102 L.Ed.2d 927 (1989).

seq., infra, on sentencing. See Annotation, "Retrial on Greater Offenses Following Reversal of Plea-Based Conviction of Lesser Offense," 14 A.L.R.4th 970 (1982).

§ 14:63 Retroactive application of penal statutes—Ex post facto

The federal and state constitutions prohibit the retroactive application of a penal statute to criminalize and punish conduct which was not criminal before the enactment of the statute. In *Smith v. Doe*,[1] the United States Supreme Court held that a statutory provision for retroactive registration of sex offenders was not punitive and thus was not an ex post facto law. In *Thompson v. State*,[2] the Georgia Supreme Court explained:

> To determine whether a penal statute is an ex post facto law, we employ a three step analysis: First, we ask whether the law applies retrospectively. If it does not, our inquiry is at an end. If it does, we look to see if the law is punitive or regulatory. If it is punitive, the statute is an ex post facto law. If it is regulatory, we examine the statute's effect. If the effect of the statute is punitive, the statute is deemed ex post facto—even if the statute was intended to be regulatory. But, again, if the statute is not retrospective we need not determine whether it is punitive . . . . A penal statute is retrospective if it alters the consequences for crimes committed prior to its enactment. [Citations omitted.]

The overhaul of the Georgia rules of evidence should not run afoul of the Ex Post Facto Clause. In *Hall v. Vargas*,[3] the court observed that regardless of whether a rule may have some effect on whether a defendant can be convicted, "[o]rdinary rules of evidence do not violate the Clause."

In *Landers v. State*,[4] the court observed "[i]n determining whether a statute is being applied in an ex post facto manner, the definitive time period to be considered is the date on which the criminal offense was committed." In that case, the court was examining the statute which punishes the possession of a firearm by a convicted felon. The critical date was that of the offense of the possession of the firearm and not the underlying conviction. The defendant was being punished for a new offense; that of possession of a firearm, an element of which was the defendant's status as a convicted felon.

[Section 14:63]

[1]Smith v. Doe, 538 U.S. 84, 123 S.Ct. 1140, 155 L.Ed.2d 164 (2003).

[2]Thompson v. State, 278 Ga. 394, 395-396, 603 S.E.2d 233 (2004).

[3]Hall v. Vargas, 278 Ga. 868, 870, 608 S.E.2d 200 (2005).

[4]Landers v. State, 250 Ga. 501, 504 (4), 299 S.E.2d 707 (1983).

In *Thompson v. State*,[5] the Georgia Supreme Court held that the statute which makes it a felony for a person required to register as a sex offender to reside in certain locations "does not alter the consequences for the offense of child molestation; rather it creates a new crime based in part on an offender's status as a child molester." See § 4:64, infra, on retroactive application of new rules of criminal law and § 30:2, infra, on violation of conditions of probation.

In *Peugh v. United States*,[6] the Supreme Court held that sentencing guidelines different than those in effect on the date the defendant is sentenced which are more severe than those in effect on the date the offense was committed may amount to an ex-post facto violation.

§ 14:64   Retroactive application of new rules of criminal law

As a general proposition, "new" rules of criminal law may not be applied retroactively. A rule of criminal law is considered "new" if it "breaks new ground or imposes a new obligation on the States or the Federal Government or if the result was not dictated by precedent existing at the time the defendant's conviction became final."[1]

However, there are two noted exceptions to this proposition. "First, a new rule should be applied retroactively if it places 'certain kinds of primary, private individual conduct beyond the power of the criminal law-making authority to proscribe.' Second, a new rule should be applied retroactively if it requires the observance of 'those procedures that . . . are implicit in the concept of ordered liberty.' "[2] For example, in the case of *Brewer v. State*,[3] the Georgia Supreme Court held that "force is a separate essential element which the State is required to prove to obtain a conviction for aggravated sodomy against a victim under the age of consent." Previously, the state could prove force simply based

---

[5]Thompson v. State, 278 Ga. 394, 395-396, 603 S.E.2d 233 (2004).

[6]Peugh v. U.S., 133 S. Ct. 2072, 186 L. Ed. 2d 84 (2013).

[Section 14:64]

[1]Teague v. Lane, 489 U.S. 288, 109 S. Ct. 1060, 103 L. Ed. 2d 334 (1989).

[2]Teague v. Lane, 489 U.S. 288, 307, 109 S. Ct. 1060, 103 L. Ed. 2d 334 (1989), quoting Williams v. United States, 401 U.S. 667, 692, 91 S. Ct. 1171, 28 L. Ed. 2d 404 (1971). See State

v. Sosa, 291 Ga. 734, 733 S.E.2d 262 (2012). See also, State v. Addaquay, 302 Ga. 412, 807 S.E.2d 413 (2017) (court declined to consider retroactivity of ineffective assistance rule regarding counsel's failure to properly advise client about deportation consequences of guilty plea announced in Padilla v. Kentucky, 559 U.S. 356, 130 S. Ct. 1473, 176 L. Ed. 2d 284 (2010), because case failed to satisfy either of *Teague* exceptions).

[3]Brewer v. State, 271 Ga. 605, 606, 523 S.E.2d 18 (1999).

on the underage status of the victim. Subsequently, the Georgia Supreme Court held that the *Brewer* case created a new criminal rule requiring the state to prove force as a separate element in an aggravated sodomy case and that this new rule was to be applied retroactively to cases on collateral review.[4] Thus, in *Alford v. State*,[5] the Georgia Supreme Court found that because the right to counsel "in all stages of the adjudication process is imperative to the fact-finding process," the requirement that its waiver be voluntary and intelligent as recognized in *Alabama v. Shelton*[6] would apply to cases on both direct and collateral review.

The second exception concerns "watershed" rules regarding procedures that are implicit in the concept of ordered liberty and that implicate the fundamental fairness and accuracy of the criminal proceedings. The Supreme Court ruling of *Gideon v. Wainwright*,[7] giving defendants the right to counsel in certain criminal proceedings, is a model example of a watershed rule. Over the past 15 years, the United States Supreme Court has reviewed at least 11 cases of criminal procedure in which the petitioner claimed the watershed rule exception would apply. In all eleven cases, the Supreme Court held them not to fall under the watershed exception.[8]

---

[4]Luke v. Battle, 275 Ga. 370 (2), 371, 565 S.E.2d 816 (2002). "[O]ur decision in *Brewer* must be considered a new rule of substantive criminal law. In this regard, before *Brewer*, this Court and the Court of Appeals had construed the term 'force' in the aggravated sodomy statute to permit the State to convict a person of aggravated sodomy by showing only that he had engaged in an act of sodomy with an underage victim. In *Brewer*, however, we construed the term 'force' in the aggravated sodomy statute to mean acts of physical force" (citations omitted).

[5]Alford v. State, 287 Ga. 105, 107, 695 S.E.2d 1 (2010). Cf. Green v. State, 303 Ga. App. 210, 692 S.E.2d 784 (2010) (defendant was not entitled to retroactive application of substantive changes to sodomy laws because current offense was failure to register as a sex offender which offense came about because of prior sodomy conviction).

[6]Alabama v. Shelton, 535 U.S. 654, 122 S. Ct. 1764, 152 L. Ed. 2d 888 (2002).

[7]Gideon v. Wainwright, 372 U.S. 335, 83 S. Ct. 792, 9 L. Ed. 2d 799, 93 A.L.R.2d 733 (1963) (indigent defendants have the right to court-appointed counsel in all criminal prosecutions).

[8]U.S. v. Mandanici, 205 F.3d 519, 530 (2d Cir. 2000). See O'Dell v. Netherland, 521 U.S. 151, 117 S. Ct. 1969, 138 L. Ed. 2d 351 (1997) (rule announced in Simmons v. South Carolina, 512 U.S. 154, 114 S. Ct. 2187, 129 L. Ed. 2d 133 (1994), that a capital defendant must be permitted to inform his sentencing jury that he is parole-ineligible if the prosecution argues that he is a future danger); Lambrix v. Singletary, 520 U.S. 518, 539–40, 117 S. Ct. 1517, 137 L. Ed. 2d 771 (1997) (rule announced in Espinosa v. Florida, 505 U.S. 1079, 112 S. Ct. 2926, 120 L. Ed. 2d 854 (1992), that in certain states where a sentencing judge is required to give deference to a jury's advisory sentencing recommendation with respect to the death pen-

In *Fortson v. State*,[9] the Georgia Supreme Court held that a motion to withdraw a guilty plea is a critical stage at which the right to counsel attaches. In *Carter v. Johnson*,[10] the Court held that the rule in *Fortson* was a new rule because it imposed a new obligation on the state to appoint counsel during a motion to withdraw a guilty plea and this result was not dictated by Georgia precedent existing when the defendant's conviction became final. The Court held that this was not a change in substantive law, nor would not fall under the watershed rule exception. Accordingly, the court declined to give its ruling retroactive application.

See § 14:63, supra, on ex post facto.

---

alty, neither the jury nor the judge is permitted to consider invalid aggravating circumstances); Gray v. Netherland, 518 U.S. 152, 116 S. Ct. 2074, 135 L. Ed. 2d 457 (1996) (rule that state's failure to give adequate notice of some of the evidence it intended to use in the petitioner's capital sentence proceeding violates due process); Goeke v. Branch, 514 U.S. 115, 120-21, 115 S. Ct. 1275, 131 L. Ed. 2d 152 (1995) (per curiam) (rule that due process generally prohibits a state appellate court from dismissing the appeal of a recaptured fugitive); Caspari v. Bohlen, 510 U.S. 383, 114 S. Ct. 948, 127 L. Ed. 2d 236 (1994) (rule that twice subjecting a defendant to a noncapital sentence enhancement proceeding violates the Double Jeopardy Clause); Gilmore v. Taylor, 508 U.S. 333, 345–46, 113 S. Ct. 2112, 124 L. Ed. 2d 306 (1993) (rule announced in Falconer v. Lane, 905 F.2d 1129 (7th Cir. 1990), that the failure to instruct jury that it could not return a murder conviction if it found that the defendant possessed a mitigating mental state violates due process); Graham v. Collins, 506 U.S. 461, 113 S. Ct. 892, 122 L. Ed. 2d 260 (1993) (proposed rule that jury instructions preventing a petitioner's sentencing jury from considering mitigating evidence in a capital sentencing proceeding violate the petitioner's Eighth and Fourteenth Amendment rights); Sawyer v. Smith, 497 U.S. 227, 241–45, 110 S. Ct. 2822, 111 L. Ed. 2d 193 (1990)

(rule announced in Caldwell v. Mississippi, 472 U.S. 320, 105 S. Ct. 2633, 86 L. Ed. 2d 231 (1985), that the Eighth Amendment prohibits the imposition of a death sentence by a jury that has been led to the false belief that responsibility for determining the appropriateness of the capital sentence lies elsewhere); Saffle v. Parks, 494 U.S. 484, 110 S. Ct. 1257, 108 L. Ed. 2d 415 (1990) (proposed rule that the trial court's instruction in the petitioner's capital sentence proceeding, telling the jury to "avoid any influence of sympathy" violates the Eighth Amendment); Butler v. McKellar, 494 U.S. 407, 110 S. Ct. 1212, 108 L. Ed. 2d 347 (1990) (rule announced in Arizona v. Roberson, 486 U.S. 675, 108 S. Ct. 2093, 100 L. Ed. 2d 704 (1988), that the Fifth Amendment bars police-initiated interrogation following a suspect's request for counsel in the context of a separate investigation); Teague v. Lane, 489 U.S. 288, 109 S. Ct. 1060, 103 L. Ed. 2d 334 (1989) (plurality opinion) (rule announced in Taylor v. Louisiana, 419 U.S. 522, 95 S. Ct. 692, 42 L. Ed. 2d 690 (1975), that the Sixth Amendment's fair cross-section requirement applies to a petit jury).

[9]Fortson v. State, 272 Ga. 457, 532 S.E.2d 102 (2000).

[10]Carter v. Johnson, 278 Ga. 202, 599 S.E.2d 170 (2004).

§ 14:65 Quashing second indictment as barring further prosecution

O.C.G.A. § 17-7-53.1 provides as follows:

"If, upon the return of two 'true bills' of indictments or presentments by a grand jury on the same offense, charge, or allegation, the indictments or presentments are quashed for the second time, whether by ruling on a motion, demurrer, special plea or exception, or other pleading of the defendant or by the court's own motion, such actions shall be a bar to any further prosecution of such defendant for the offense, charge, or allegation."

In *Redding v. State*,[1] the court held that the entering of a nolle prosequi is not the quashing of an indictment within the meaning of O.C.G.A. § 17-7-53.1. See § 17:19, infra, on entering of nolle prosequi.

§ 14:66 Limitations of prosecution

O.C.G.A. § 17-3-1 provides for the following limitations of prosecution:

"(a) A prosecution for murder may be commenced at any time.[1]

"(b) Except as otherwise provided in Code Section 17-3-2.1, prosecution for other crimes punishable by death or life imprisonment shall be commenced within seven years after the commission of the crime; provided, however, that prosecution for the crime of forcible rape must be commenced within 15 years after the commission of the crime.

"(c) Except as otherwise provided in Code Section 17-3-2.1, prosecution for felonies other than those specified in subsections (a), (b) and (d) of this Code section shall be commenced within four years after the commission of the crime, provided that pros-

---

[Section 14:65]

[1]Redding v. State, 205 Ga. App. 613, 614 (2), 423 S.E.2d 10 (1992).

[Section 14:66]

[1]This applies to the offense of felony murder as well since Georgia does not require the charging and conviction of the underlying felony only that the murder was committed in connection with the felony. Accordingly, the expiration of the statute of limitations for the felony offense underlying a charge of felony murder will not time-bar the felony murder prosecution. State v. Jones, 274 Ga. 287 (1), 553 S.E.2d 612 (2001). Note, however,

"the statute of limitations applicable in a criminal case is that which relates to the offense charged in the indictment, and not to any minor offense included therein of which the accused might be found guilty. The provisions of the statute of limitations applicable to an indictment for voluntary manslaughter will not bar a conviction of that offense under an indictment for murder; there being no statutory limitation as to indictments for murder." (Citations and punctuation omitted.) Glidewell v. State, 279 Ga. App. 114, 630 S.E.2d 621 (2006), overruled by Reynolds v. State, 285 Ga. 70, 673 S.E.2d 854 (2009).

ecution for felonies committed against victims who are at the time of the commission of the offense under the age of 18 years shall be commenced within seven years after the commission of the crime.[2]

"(d) A prosecution for the following offenses may be commenced at any time when deoxyribonucleic acid (DNA) evidence is used to establish the identity of the accused:

(1) Armed robbery, as defined in Code Section 16-8-41;

(2) Kidnapping, as defined in Code Section 16-5-40;

(3) Rape, as defined in Code Section 16-6-1;

(4) Aggravated child molestation, as defined in Code Section 16-6-4;

(5) Aggravated sodomy, as defined in Code Section 16-6-2; or

(6) Aggravated sexual battery, as defined in Code Section 16-6-22.2; provided, however, that a sufficient portion of the physial evidence tested for DNA is preserved and available for testing by the accused and provided, further, that, if the DNA evidence does not establish the identity of the accused, the limitation on prosecution shall be as provided in subsections (b) and (c) of this Code Section.

"(e) Prosecution for misdemeanors shall be commenced within two years after the commission of the crime."[3]

O.C.G.A. § 17-3-1 was amended effective July 1, 2002 to allow without a time limitation the prosecution of serious violent offenses where DNA evidence is used to establish the identity of the accused "provided that a sufficient portion of the physical evidence tested for DNA is preserved and available for testing by the accused and provided, further, that if the DNA evidence does not establish the identity of the accused, the limitation on prosecution . . ." shall be as otherwise provided by law. However, there is a general provision which excludes from the time limits set out above or in any other statute of limitations "any period in which:

"(1) The accused is not usually and publicly a resident within this state;[4]

"(2) The person committing the crime is unknown or the crime is unknown;

"(3) The accused is a government officer or employee and the crime charged is theft by conversion of public property while such

---

[2]In 2002 this section was amended to raise the age of child victims from 14 to 18.

[3]O.C.G.A. § 17-3-1.

[4]See Dennard v. State, 154 Ga. App. 283, 284, 267 S.E.2d 886 (1980). In Danuel v. State, 262 Ga. 349, 352, 418 S.E.2d 45 (1992), the court held that whether the statute is tolled does not depend solely upon the legal residence of the defendant.

an officer or employee; or

"(4) The accused is a guardian or trustee and the crime charged is theft by conversion of property of the ward or beneficiary."[5]

In 1992, O.C.G.A. § 17-3-2.1, dealing with limiting the prosecution of certain offenses involving a victim who is under the age of 16, was enacted, stating as follows:

"(a) If the victim of a violation of:

"(1) O.C.G.A. § 16-5-70, relating to cruelty to children;

"(2) O.C.G.A. § 16-6-1, relating to rape;

"(3) O.C.G.A. § 16-6-2, relating to sodomy and aggravated sodomy;

"(4) O.C.G.A. § 16-6-3, relating to statutory rape;

"(5) O.C.G.A. § 16-6-4, relating to child molestation and aggravated child molestation;[6]

"(6) O.C.G.A. § 16-6-5, relating to enticing a child for indecent purposes; or

"(7) O.C.G.A. § 16-6-22, relating to incest,

"is under 16 years of age on the date of the violation, the applicable period within which a prosecution must be commenced under O.C.G.A. § 17-3-1 or other applicable statute shall not begin to run until the victim has reached the age of 16 or the violation is reported to a law enforcement agency, prosecuting attorney, or other governmental agency, whichever occurs earlier. Such law enforcement agency or other governmental agency shall promptly report such allegation to the appropriate prosecuting attorney.

"(b) This Code section shall apply to any offense designated in paragraphs (1) through (7) of subsection (a) of this Code section occurring on or after July 1, 1992."

Additionally, O.C.G.A. § 17-3-2.2 provides that for victims who are 65 years old or older the statute of limitations will not start running until the violation is "reported to or discovered by a law enforcement agency, prosecuting attorney, or other governmental agency, whichever occurs earlier."[7] Furthermore, prosecution cannot begin more than 15 years after the crime has been committed

---

[5]O.C.G.A. § 17-3-2.

[6]State v. Godfrey, 309 Ga. App. 234, 709 S.E.2d 572 (2011) (statute not tolled pursuant to O.C.G.A. § 17-3-2.1 where indictment fails to allege that victim is under age of 16).

[7]See State v. Mullins, 321 Ga. App. 671, 742 S.E.2d 490 (2013) (prosecution time barred where victims were over age 65, but State failed to show any delay in reporting crime or its discovery). See also Harper v. State, 292 Ga. 557, 738 S.E.2d 584 (2013). See State v. Outen, 296 Ga. 40, 764 S.E.2d 848 (2014) (tolling of limitations period under Section 17-3-3 runs from the date of the trial court's order and is not extended further in the event of an appeal by the state).

unless the statute of limitations for that crime is greater than 15 years.

In addition to these provisions which toll the statute of limitations in certain situations, where an indictment is dismissed pursuant to a plea or demurrer or where a nolle prosequi is entered, O.C.G.A. § 17-3-3 provides that the period is "extended six months from the time the first indictment is quashed or the nolle prosequi entered" if the earlier indictment was not void.[8]

It should be noted that the Ex Post Facto Clause of the United States Constitution prohibits states from enacting statutes that extend limitation periods for crimes where the applicable limitation periods of the crimes have already expired.[9]

In *State v. Barrett*,[10] the court held that where a defendant and his counsel signed a plea agreement which "waived his right to rely upon the statutes of limitation in exchange for first offender treatment. This waiver . . . is enforceable beyond the execution of his sentence."

If it appears on the face of the indictment that the statute of limitations has run, this defense may be raised by demurrer.[11] If the defect does not appear on the face of the indictment, the defense may be raised by a plea,[12] which probably should be considered as a plea in bar.[13] However, unlike the situation which usually exists where pleas and demurrers are not filed, even if

---

[8]Hodges v. State, 214 Ga. 614 (1), 106 S.E.2d 795 (1959). The *Hodges* case points out that the six-month period does not apply if the former indictment contained a fatal defect or was void, but the six-month period is applicable where an indictment is nolle prossed because of an "informality" or some other reason which did not render it void.

[9]Stogner v. California, 539 U.S. 607, 123 S.Ct. 2446, 156 L.Ed.2d 544 (2003).

[10]State v. Barrett, 215 Ga. App. 401, 407, 451 S.E.2d 82 (1994) (abrogated on other grounds by, State v. Outen, 289 Ga. 579, 714 S.E.2d 581 (2011)).

[11]Hansford v. State, 54 Ga. 55, 56 (4) (1875).

[12]See § 14:39, supra, on demurrers. In Moss v. State, 220 Ga. App. 150(3), 469 S.E.2d 325 (1996) (citations and punctuation omitted), the Georgia Court of Appeals explained:

"It has long been the law in Georgia in a criminal case, where an exception is relied upon to prevent the bar of the statute of limitations, it must be alleged and proved. Such proof is inadmissible unless the exception sought to be proved is alleged. Furthermore, the exception must be alleged in the indictment. As no exception was alleged in the indictment, the State [is] incapable of proving an exception to toll the applicable . . . statute of limitation, as such proof was inadmissible." See, State v. Aycock, 283 Ga. App. 876, 643 S.E.2d 249 (2007).

[13]State v. Tuzman, 145 Ga. App. 481, 482 (2), 243 S.E.2d 675 (1978) (abrogated on other grounds by, State v. Outen, 289 Ga. 579, 714 S.E.2d 581 (2011)). In Dennard v. State, 154 Ga. App. 283, 284, 267 S.E.2d 886 (1980), the terms of plea in bar and plea in abatement seem to be used interchangeably in a statute of limitations case. In State v. Brannon, 154 Ga. App. 285, 267 S.E.2d 888 (1980), such a plea

the plea or demurrer is not filed before trial, the defendant may still assert the defense of the statute of limitations in the trial of the case.[14] The issue must be raised at or before trial if it is to be preserved for appeal. Otherwise, the proper remedy is a motion in arrest of judgment or habeas corpus.[15]

From the standpoint of the district attorney, it must be emphasized that if there is any exception to the general statute governing limitation of prosecution, the exception or reason for tolling the statute must be alleged in the indictment.[16] It is probably sufficient if the exception relied on by the state is set out in the language of the Code.[17] Under Georgia law prior to the adoption of the Criminal Code of Georgia, if the offense or offender were unknown, the limitation did not begin to run until they became known.[18] However, former GCA § 27-601 was repealed in 1968 by the adoption of the Criminal Code of Georgia, which contains section 17-3-2,[19] quoted above. This statute provides that it does not begin to run if the person committing the crime is unknown,[20] but if a law enforcement officer knows a person has committed an act, the statute begins to run, even if the officer does not know that the conduct constitutes a crime.[21] In addition, the "tolling exception to the statute of limitations cannot be based upon the subjective opinion of the district attorney as to whether there was enough evidence to file charges against a particular

---

is referred to as a plea in bar.

[14]Hollingsworth v. State, 7 Ga. App. 16, 18, 65 S.E. 1077 (1909). The defendant can raise the issue prior to trial by way of plea in bar and, even if unsuccessful, he or she can still require the state to prove at trial that the charge is not barred by the statute. Jenkins v. State, 278 Ga. 598, 604 S.E.2d 789 (2004). See § 14:46, supra, on plea in bar.

[15]Zabain v. State, 315 Ga. App. 749, 728 S.E.2d 273 (2012).

[16]State v. Shepherd Construction Co., 248 Ga. 1, 4, 281 S.E.2d 151 (1981). The state has the burden of presenting evidence establishing an exception to the statute of limitations. State v. Robins, 296 Ga. App. 437, 674 S.E.2d 615 (2009). See Sallie v. State, 276 Ga. 506, 578 S.E.2d 444 (2003) (this rule has no application where an indictment is timely filed but then nolle prossed; O.C.G.A. § 17-3-3 pro-

vides that the period of limitations for an offense is *extended* by six months from the date the nolle prosequi is entered); Johnson v. State, 335 Ga. App. 886, 782 S.E.2d 50 (2016).

[17]Saunders v. State, 43 Ga. App. 59, 158 S.E. 433 (1931).

[18]Former GCA § 27-601.

[19]State v. Shepherd Construction Co., 248 Ga. 1, 281 S.E.2d 151 (1981); State v. Benton, 168 Ga. App. 665, 666, 310 S.E.2d 243 (1983).

[20]O.C.G.A. § 17-3-2(b). See Kenerly v. State, 325 Ga. App. 412, 750 S.E.2d 822 (2013) (no requirement that state exercise "reasonable diligence" to find wrongdoer only that the person who committed the crime is unknown).

[21]Holloman v. State, 133 Ga. App. 275, 280(6), 211 S.E.2d 312 (1974). See State v. Bragg, 332 Ga. App. 608, 774 S.E.2d 182 (2015).

person."[22] An allegation in an indictment that the offender was unknown until a specified date within the statute of limitations is adequate against the demurrer to show that the indictment was timely. When this tolling provision "is relied upon, the tolling period ends when the state acquires 'actual knowledge' of the defendant's identity."[23] Thus, the "person unknown" tolling exception will not apply unless "there is no identified suspect among the universe of all potential suspects."[24] In this regard, the knowledge of the victim and others interested in the prosecution come "within the class of persons whose knowledge will satisfy the statute," provided that such knowledge is actual, i.e., that the state knew the identity of the person alleged to have committed the crime.[25]

O.C.G.A. § 17-3-2.1 provides that infancy shall toll the statute of limitation for certain offenses involving a victim under 16 years of age or until the violation is reported to law enforcement officers, whichever is earlier. *State v. Sears*[26] established that the statute of limitations was not tolled during the infancy of a child victim where she knew the acts were wrong, but was not aware that the acts were criminal. Thus, under *Sears* the statute of limitations would start running on an 11 year old child who was a victim of molestation if she knew it was a crime. "The knowledge at issue in O.C.G.A. § 17-3-2(2) is the knowledge of the State, including that imputed to the State, through the knowledge of the prosecution, the knowledge of someone interested in the prosecution or the knowledge of someone injured by the offense."[27] When the case involves a crime against the public, which also involves "a wrong upon an individual who is not a party to the crime, the knowledge of the victim is imputed to the State, even though the victim does not represent the State in an official capacity."[28] O.C.G.A. § 17-3-2.1 provides that infancy shall toll the statute of limitations for certain offenses involving a victim under 16 years of age or until the violation is reported to law enforcement authorities, whichever is earlier. In *State v. Mullins*,[29] the court ruled that the prosecution was time-barred and that the provisions of O.C.G.A. § 17-3-2.2 had no application. Al-

[22]Jenkins v. State, 278 Ga. 598(1), 604 S.E.2d 789 (2004).

[23]Scales v. State, 310 Ga. App. 48, 49 (1), 712 S.E.2d 555 (2011).

[24]Jenkins v. State, 278 Ga. 598, 603 (1)(A), 604 S.E.2d 789 (2004).

[25]Beasley v. State, 244 Ga. App. 836, 839 n.5, 536 S.E.2d 825 (2000) (constructive knowledge, such as in the exercise of due diligence the state could have discovered the identity of the alleged perpetrator, is insufficient).

[26]Sears v. State, 182 Ga. App. 480, 356 S.E.2d 72 (1987).

[27]Lowman v. State, 204 Ga. App. 655, 420 S.E.2d 94 (1992).

[28]Lowman v. State, 204 Ga. App. 655, 420 S.E.2d 94 (1992).

[29]State v. Mullins, 321 Ga. App. 671, 742 S.E.2d 490 (2013). See Harper

though the victims were over the age of 65, the state failed to show that there had been any delay in reporting the crime or its discovery and hence the normally applicable four-year statute controlled.

If a law enforcement officer,[30] district attorney,[31] grand juror,[32] or other person having the duty to report a crime and act thereon knows of the commission of an offense, this is sufficient to start the running of the statute. Also, if the victim of a crime or someone interested in the prosecution knows of the commission of an offense, this brings the running of the statute.[33]

As previously mentioned, defense counsel may file a demurrer or plea, whichever is appropriate, or he may reserve the question about the statute of limitations until the time of trial. Generally, the date of an offense set out in an indictment is not material, and the state may show that the offense was committed at any time within the statute of limitations. But the defendant may object to the admission of evidence of an offense, the prosecution of which is barred by the statute of limitations, unless some exception to the statute was alleged in the indictment.[34] In *Moss v. State,*[35] the court held that proof of an exception to the statute of limitations is not admissible unless the exception is alleged in the indictment.

The running of the statute of limitations on the prosecution of criminal cases is not stopped or suspended by the issuance of an arrest warrant. The time continues to run until an indictment is returned or an accusation is completed;[36] but the statute of limitations ceases to run when an indictment is returned, and the actual time of trial does not determine whether or not the statute has run.[37] If there is a change in the statute of limitations, the

---

v. State, 292 Ga. 557, 738 S.E.2d 584 (2013).

[30]Holloman v. State, 133 Ga. App. 275, 278, 211 S.E.2d 312 (1974).

[31]Duncan v. State, 193 Ga. App. 793, 389 S.E.2d 365 (1989).

[32]Taylor v. State, 44 Ga. App. 64, 72, 160 S.E. 667 (1931).

[33]State v. Brannon, 154 Ga. App. 285, 287, 267 S.E.2d 888 (1980). See State v. Bair, 303 Ga. App. 183, 692 S.E.2d 806 (2010).

[34]Hollingsworth v. State, 7 Ga. App. 16, 19, 65 S.E. 1077 (1909). However, if the crime for which a defendant is being tried involves continuous or repeated acts in a series of embezzle-

ments extending over a long period of time, some falling within the statutory period and some before that, even if the indictment does not allege that the statute did not run as to the earlier offenses, they may be admissible to show intent. Mangham v. State, 11 Ga. App. 427, 438 (3), 75 S.E. 512 (1912) (dictum).

[35]Moss v. State, 220 Ga. App. 150, 469 S.E.2d 325 (1996).

[36]Flint v. State, 12 Ga. App. 169, 76 S.E. 1032 (1913). See Annot., "Finding or Return of Indictment, or Filing of Information, as Tolling Limitation Period," 18 A.L.R.4th 1202 (1982).

[37]Hall v. Hopper, 234 Ga. 625, 216 S.E.2d 839 (1975); Freeman v. State,

statute in effect on the date of the offense controls.[38]

In *Wooten v. State*,[39] the court held if an accusation is timely and still pending, a superseding indictment returned after the running of the statute of limitations which "does not broaden or substantially amend the original charges" is not barred. In order to determine "whether the first indictment tolled the limitations period, the crucial inquiry is whether approximately the same facts were used as the basis for both indictments."[40] Some of the considerations in determining whether a subsequent indictment broadens a timely and pending prior indictment include "[w]hether the additional pleadings allege violations of a different statute, contain different elements, rely on different evidence, or expose the defendant to a potentially greater sentence."[41] The central concern is whether the prior indictment gave the defendant adequate notice to enable him to prepare his defense to the superseding indictment. Where the charges and allegations in the prior and subsequent indictments are substantially the same, the assumption is that the defendant was on notice that he would be called to account for certain activities and should prepare his defense accordingly.[42]

The statute of limitations relating to the time in which an indictment may be returned or the time of an accusation has no relation to the actual disposition of a criminal case. There is no

---

194 Ga. App. 905, 907(8), 392 S.E.2d 330 (1990). See Martinez v. State, 306 Ga. App. 512, 702 S.E.2d 747 (2010) (re-issued indictment which included new charges not previously made in original indictment which had been dismissed do not relate back to date of original indictment and were time-barred by applicable period of limitations). But see State v. Thompson, 261 Ga. App. 828, 829 (2), 584 S.E.2d 7 (2003) (finding the statute of limitations tolled by the solicitor's delivery of accusations to the clerk's office, even though the clerk did not file-stamp the accusation, because "a document is considered filed when it is delivered to and received by the proper officials to be kept on file"). In State v. Thompson, 261 Ga. App. 828 (2), 584 S.E.2d 7 (2003), the court ruled that the statute of limitations was tolled by the delivery of accusations to the clerk's office by the solicitor. The date stamp on the documents was that of the solicitor and not the clerk whose practice was to separately indicate the date of

receipt only when it conflicted with the solicitor's date. The court concluded, "a document is considered filed when it is delivered to and received by the proper official to be kept on file."

[38]Cf. State v. Williams, 172 Ga. App. 708, 709, 324 S.E.2d 557 (1984).

[39]Wooten v. State, 240 Ga. App. 725, 726 (2)(a), 524 S.E.2d 776 (1999).

[40]U.S. v. Italiano, 894 F.2d 1280, 1285 (11th Cir. 1990). See State v. Outen, 342 Ga. App. 457, 461, 751 S.E.2d 109 (2013), affirmed 296 Ga. 40, 764 S.E.2d 848 (2014) (superseding indictment which specifies manner in which crime was committed does not materially broaden scope of original indictment).

[41]United States v. Liu, 731 F.3d 982, 996-997 (9th Cir. 2013) (citations omitted).

[42]United States v. Italiano, 894 F.2d 1280, 1283 (11th Cir. 1990). See State v. Outen, 296 Ga. 40, 764 S.E.2d 848 (2014).

provision in Georgia law for the dismissal of an indictment or accusation after the lapse of a specified time from its date, such as the five-year rule which applies in a civil case.[43] Of course, a defendant may file a demand for trial as discussed in § 14:67, supra, and § 14:69, infra, and there are constitutional limitations discussed in section § 14:70, infra, which to some extent limit the right of the state to insist on a trial long after the return of an indictment.

In *Early v. State*,[44] the court pointed out that a defendant may waive the protection provided by the statute of limitations if this is done "knowingly and voluntarily." Here, however, the court held that where the prosecutor, defense counsel and the judge are all mistaken as to the applicable statute of limitations, there is no waiver and a sentence on the offense after the statute had run was clear error.

See § 13:23, supra, on the tolling of the statute by the issuance of a traffic citation.

§ 14:67 Statutory speedy trial demand for trial under O.C.G.A. § 17-7-170

When a defendant has been indicted for a non-capital offense, he may, as a matter of right, file a demand for trial at that term of court or at the next following regular[1] term.[2] Such a demand should be filed with the clerk of the court, served upon the prosecutor of the case and upon the assigned judge, or, if no judge is assigned, upon the chief judge of the court in which the case is pending.[3] In addition, beginning July 1, 2006, a demand for a speedy trial must: (1) be filed as "a separate, distinct, and individual document;" (2) clearly be titled "Demand For Speedy Trial;" (3) reference O.C.G.A. § 17-7-170 within the pleading; and (4) "identify the indictment number or accusation number for which such demand is being made."[4] The above requirements also apply to a demand for speedy trial made in a capital case, beginning

---

[43]O.C.G.A. § 9-11-41(e).

[44]Early v. State, 218 Ga. App. 869, 870, 463 S.E.2d 706 (1995).

[Section 14:67]

[1]In Buxton v. State, 253 Ga. 137, 139 (2), 317 S.E.2d 538 (1984), the court held that special terms of court were not to be considered "regular terms."

[2]In State v. Ramsey, 147 Ga. App. 150, 248 S.E.2d 289 (1978), the court held that the provisions of O.C.G.A. § 17-7-170 do not apply to criminal trials in state courts where a later special act exists, granting more time for a trial after a demand.

But in State v. Majia, 254 Ga. 660, 333 S.E.2d 834 (1985), the court said that the demand for trial provisions of a state court "must give way to an inconsistent rule contained in the general provisions of Georgia's criminal-procedure law." But see n. 47, infra.

[3]O.C.G.A. § 17-7-170.

[4]O.C.G.A. § 17-7-170, as amended July 1, 2006. See Hudson v.

July 1, 2006.[5]

Failure to serve the court will invalidate the demand.[6] After the second term, the demand may only be filed if the court grants permission.[7] If a defendant files a pro se demand for a speedy trial while represented by counsel, the trial court is "authorized to find that the pro se demand [has] . . . no legal effect whatsoever." This is true because in Georgia a defendant no longer has the right to represent himself if he is represented by counsel.[8] The Georgia Supreme Court held that a public defender's office is to be considered a law firm in deciding whether a defendant has representation. "This . . . means a defendant is not unrepresented merely because different attorneys from the same office represent him at different times."[9] In addition to the specific statutory limitations, there is a more general right of a defendant to a speedy trial which is contained in the Constitution. The leading case of the United States Supreme Court is *Barker v. Wingo.*[10]

Where a statutory demand for a speedy trial is filed and there are juries impaneled and qualified[11] to try the defendant at the time, he shall be acquitted of the offense charged[12] if he is not tried at that term or at the next term if there is a jury at the next term qualified to try him.[13] "A 'term or a *remainder* of a term in which no jurors are impaneled and qualified to try the

---

State, 311 Ga. App. 206, 715 S.E.2d 442 (2011) (although motion must be filed separately, its service on state can be reflected on a certificate which shows service of other motions as well).

[5]O.C.G.A. § 17-7-171.

[6]Baker v. State, 270 Ga. App. 762(1), 608 S.E.2d 38 (2004).

[7]O.C.G.A. § 17-7-170. In State v. Benton, 246 Ga. 750, 272 S.E.2d 718 (1980), the court pointed out that if a demand is not made at the term of the accusation or at the next regular term thereafter, the demand is not effective unless it is permitted by the court.

[8]Maddox v. State, 218 Ga. App. 320, 461 S.E.2d 286 (1995). See Ditman v. State, 301 Ga. App. 187, 687 S.E.2d 155 (2009).

[9]Ware v. State, 267 Ga. 510 (1), 480 S.E.2d 599 (1997).

[10]Barker v. Wingo, 407 U.S. 514, 92 S.Ct. 2182, 33 L.Ed.2d 101 (1972), cited and followed in Jackson v. State, 272 Ga. 782, 534 S.E.2d 796 (2000).

[11]The requirement that there must be jurors qualified to try the defendant relates to the general qualifications of the panels, not the disqualification of individual jurors on the panels. It relates to having enough jurors present to permit the striking of a jury in the defendant's case. Campbell v. State, 6 Ga. App. 539, 540, 65 S.E. 307 (1909).

In Wilson v. State, 156 Ga. App. 53, 274 S.E.2d 95 (1980), the court affirmed the denial of an acquittal, where the trial judge found that there were no jurors qualified to try defendant who were impaneled at the term at which demand was made or at the following term. The appellate court said that this finding could only be overcome by clear and uncontradictory testimony to the contrary.

[12]O.C.G.A. § 17-7-170; Adams v. State, 129 Ga. App. 839, 201 S.E.2d 649 (1973); Hurt v. State, 62 Ga. App. 878 (1), 10 S.E.2d 136 (1940).

[13]Roebuck v. State, 57 Ga. 154 (1)

case is not counted for purposes of O.C.G.A. § 17-7-170.' . . . If jurors have been dismissed and are not subject to recall when the demand is filed, the term in which the demand is filed does not count for computation of the two-term requirement. . . ." (Emphasis in original.)[14] The trial must be started before the end of the second term, but need not be completed before the term ends.[15]

If a defendant has not been tried by the expiration of the second term, he may file a motion for his discharge. The motion must allege that qualified jurors were impaneled to try him at both terms.[16] But even in the absence of a motion, the court should enter an order of discharge because a defendant stands automatically discharged at the expiration of the second term. The formal entry of discharge may be made at any time nunc pro tunc.[17] In light of "the extreme nature of the sanction of absolute discharge and acquittal, it is applied only where there has been strict compliance with O.C.G.A. § 17-7-170 or O.C.G.A. § 17-7-171, whichever is the applicable statute prescribing the means by which a criminal defendant may assert a demand for trial."[18] A defendant loses his right to automatic discharge if he withdraws his demand for trial before the end of the second term.[19]

An adjourned or special term after a regular term does not constitute a second term of court.[20] As a general proposition, a trial which ends in a hung jury or mistrial resulting from other than "inevitable accident such as the death or sickness of the judge or one or more of the jurors" does not constitute a trial that satisfies the state's obligation under the demand for trial statutes.[21] However, where a mistrial is declared due to the inability of the

(1876). See also McIver v. State, 212 Ga. App. 670, 671, 442 S.E.2d 855 (1994).

[14]Union v. State, 273 Ga. 666, 543 S.E.2d 683 (2001).

[15]Bailey v. State, 209 Ga. App. 390, 391 (1), 433 S.E.2d 610 (1993).

[16]Woodall v. State, 25 Ga. App. 8, 10, 102 S.E. 913 (1920). In State v. McDonald, 242 Ga. 487, 249 S.E.2d 212 (1978), rev'g 146 Ga. App. 83 (1), 245 S.E.2d 446 (1978), the court said that where a demand is filed, stating that at the time there were "jurors impaneled and qualified to try the case," and the judge entered an order reciting that the demand was true; nevertheless, it may be shown that this statement was not true.

[17]Collins v. Smith, 7 Ga. App. 653,

654, 67 S.E. 847 (1910).

[18]State v. Varner, 277 Ga. 433, 434, 589 S.E.2d 111 (2003) (citations omitted). See Uribe v. State, 346 Ga. App. 264, 816 S.E.2d 113 (2018) (failure to file demand as a separate document clearly titled as a "Demand for Speedy Trial" rendered motion improper and was denied).

[19]Dempsey v. State, 156 Ga. App. 806, 275 S.E.2d 671 (1980).

[20]Stripland v. State, 115 Ga. 578, 41 S.E. 987 (1902); Buxton v. State, 253 Ga. 137, 139 (2), 317 S.E.2d 538 (1984).

[21]Geiger v. State, 25 Ga. 667, 668 (1858); State v. Varner, 277 Ga. 433, 589 S.E.2d 111 (2003) (citations omitted).

jury to come to closure on a unanimous verdict on the last day of the term in a case in which a demand for trial has been filed, the demand will be carried over to the next term if there are no jurors available to retry the case in the term of the mistrial.[22] The benefit of a demand for trial is not lost by a nolle prosequi entered without the defendant's consent.[23] See § 17:19, infra, on entering of nolle prosequi.

Demand may not be made until indictment has been returned[24] or the accusation is filed with the clerk.[25] A Uniform Traffic Citation (UTC) is not considered an accusation in itself. To become an accusation, a UTC must first be filed with the court.[26] In *State v. Gerbert,*[27] the Georgia Supreme Court held "that the right to a speedy trial under O.C.G.A. § 17-7-170 attaches when the state files the Uniform Traffic Citation with the court" regardless of whether or when a formal accusation is filed. In *Millan v. State,*[28] the court emphasized that *the state* must file the citation with the court and held that where a defendant requests a jury trial in recorder's court and the case is bound over to state court and the citation is filed by the clerk of recorder's court with the clerk of the state court, there has not been a filing of the citation *by the state* in state court. Hence, the filing of a demand for trial in state court before a filing of the citation or accusation *by the state* in that court was premature and a nullity.

In *Vedder v. State,*[29] the court held that "[a] demand for speedy trial filed in a municipal court, which is not a court of record having both regular terms and the authority to impanel juries, is

---

[22]State v. Varner, 277 Ga. 433, 434, 589 S.E.2d 111 (2003).

[23]Bond v. State, 212 Ga. App. 608, 609, 442 S.E.2d 482 (1994); Fisher v. State, 143 Ga. App. 493, 238 S.E.2d 584 (1977); Brown v. State, 85 Ga. 713, 11 S.E. 831 (1890).

[24]O.C.G.A. § 17-7-170; Groom v. State, 212 Ga. App. 133, 441 S.E.2d 259 (1994); Day v. State, 187 Ga. App. 175, 176 (2), 369 S.E.2d 796 (1988).

[25]Lagyak v. State, 245 Ga. App. 546, 548, 538 S.E.2d 467 (2000).

[26]State v. Frazier, 201 Ga. App. 6 (1), 410 S.E.2d 134 (1991); Meservey v. State, 230 Ga. App. 382, 383, 496 S.E.2d 518 (1998); State v. Lipsky, 191 Ga. App. 842, 383 S.E.2d 204 (1989). The current version of O.C.G.A. § 17-7-170 requires that the accusation must be "filed with the clerk" while an older version merely required the ac-

cusation to be "preferred." See Majia v. State, 174 Ga. App. 432, 330 S.E.2d 171 (1985); Keller v. State, 183 Ga. App. 717, 719, 359 S.E.2d 714 (1987); Collins v. State, 154 Ga. App. 651 (1), 269 S.E.2d 509 (1980); all decided based on "preferred."

[27]State v. Gerbert, 267 Ga. 169, 475 S.E.2d 621 (1996). Accord, Clark v. State, 271 Ga. 519, 520 S.E.2d 694 (1999); Hayek v. State, 269 Ga. 728, 729 (3), 506 S.E.2d 372 (1998); Tyler v. State, 224 Ga. App. 550, 481 S.E.2d 228 (1997). Cf. Shire v. State, 225 Ga. App. 306, 307 (1)(a), 483 S.E.2d 694 (1997).

[28]Millan v. State, 231 Ga. App. 121, 497 S.E.2d 664 (1998).

[29]Vedder v. State, 241 Ga. App. 578, 579, 527 S.E.2d 249 (1999). See also, Oliver v. State, 262 Ga. App. 637, 586 S.E.2d 333 (2003).

ineffective, and if the case is transferred to State Court even without a request from the defendant, the only valid demand for speedy trial is that which has been filed anew in the transferee State Court."

In *Copeland v. State*,[30] the court pointed out that a speedy trial demand is "binding only in the court in which the demand is filed, except where the case is transferred from one court to another without a request from the defendant." A speedy trial filed in Fulton County has no bearing on charges brought in Clayton County.

In *Willingham v. State*,[31] the defendant filed a demand for trial and a motion to quash the indictment. The motion to quash was granted. Two months later, the defendant was reindicted. The defendant filed a motion for discharge and acquittal contending that the speedy trial demand was viable and he had not been tried on the original indictment. The court held that the defendant's demand for trial did not survive the quashing of the original indictment. However, a defendant's demand for trial will survive a dismissal of the indictment and upon its adoption apply to all of the charges set out in any subsequent indictment which were also contained in the indictment which was dismissed. The demand will not apply to any new charges contained in the second indictment.[32]

A demand for trial filed before indictment or accusation but after an arrest on a warrant has been treated as a nullity[33] and cannot "be resuscitated by a later returned accusation (or indictment). . . ."[34] Formal arraignment is usually waived by filing a demand for trial and a motion to suppress.[35] However, the period for filing a demand for trial may expire before arraignment.[36]

In *Smith v. State*,[37] the court held that a defendant is not entitled to file a valid demand for trial where the defendant had unilaterally filed a waiver of indictment. The court emphasized that "O.C.G.A. § 17-7-170 is available *only* to those 'against whom a true bill of indictment or an accusation is filed with the clerk.' " (Emphasis in original.) In addition, because a defendant who

---

[30]Copeland v. State, 248 Ga. App. 346, 349 (2), 546 S.E.2d 351 (2001).

[31]Willingham v. State, 232 Ga. App. 244, 501 S.E.2d 575 (1998).

[32]Banks v. State, 251 Ga. App. 421, 423 (1), 554 S.E.2d 500 (2001); State v. Daniels, 206 Ga. App. 443, 445 (2), 425 S.E.2d 366 (1992).

[33]E.g., Little v. State, 188 Ga. App. 410 (1), 373 S.E.2d 260 (1988);

State v. Hicks, 183 Ga. App. 715, 716, 359 S.E.2d 712 (1987).

[34]State v. McKenzie, 184 Ga. App. 191, 192, 361 S.E.2d 54 (1987).

[35]Ferrell v. State, 149 Ga. App. 405, 406 (3), 254 S.E.2d 404 (1979).

[36]Smith v. State, 207 Ga. App. 762, 429 S.E.2d 149 (1993).

[37]Smith v. State, 218 Ga. App. 392, 461 S.E.2d 561 (1995).

demands a speedy trial must be available for trial, when the accused is in the custody of a different sovereign and the Interstate Agreement on Detainers Act doesn't apply, the accused is not "available for trial." This is because the courts in Georgia have no "inherent authority" to compel the presence of a defendant in the custody of the federal government or another state or country.[38]

"A demand for trial . . . [is] effective to invoke the statutory sanction of mandatory acquittal only if filed in a court of record having both regular terms and the authority to impanel juries."[39] In *Marks v. State*,[40] the court held that a demand for trial filed in a court which does not have regular terms and cannot impanel jurors, "will not per se invoke the right to acquittal and discharge within the language of the statute," but requires a request in such a lower court which amounts to a request to transfer the case to a court "which can impanel juries and has regular terms . . . . [A] defendant whose demand for trial requires a transfer to another court *must* make a new demand in that second court." (Emphasis added.) *Marks* also points out that a demand may be filed in the second court even if no demand was made in the first court. However, in *State v. Bostwick*,[41] the court held that if a case is transferred to another court, the demand is also deemed to be transferred.

O.C.G.A. § 15-12-130.1(a) provides that if there is any court in a county "having county-wide jurisdiction concurrent with the superior courts . . . to try any, all, or any type of case not within the exclusive jurisdiction of the superior courts," any juror summoned for trial in a civil or criminal case will be competent to serve as a juror in the other court. Thus, in determining whether there were jurors impanelled and qualified to serve at a term of a state court for which no jurors were summoned, it must be determined whether the superior court had such jurors.[42] However, this Code section does not apply unless three criteria are met: First, the jurors must be drawn by the judge of the superior court in accordance with O.C.G.A. § 15-12-120.1, who announces in open court the name or names of the court or courts other than superior court wherein jurors shall be competent to

---

[38]Gosline v. State, 341 Ga. App. 708, 708–09, 802 S.E.2d 275 (2017). See State v. Collins, 201 Ga. App. 500, 501, 411 S.E.2d 546 (1991).

[39]Cliatt v. State, 194 Ga. App. 110, 389 S.E.2d 568 (1989) (quoting Adams v. State, 189 Ga. App. 345, 375 S.E.2d 642 (1988)).

[40]Marks v. State, 192 Ga. App. 106, 107, 384 S.E.2d 186 (1989). Accord, Groom v. State, 212 Ga. App. 133,

441 S.E.2d 259 (1994); Cliatt v. State, 194 Ga. App. 110, 389 S.E.2d 568 (1989). Cf. Fausnaugh v. State, 244 Ga. App. 263, 264 (1), 534 S.E.2d 554 (2000).

[41]State v. Bostwick, 181 Ga. App. 508, 352 S.E.2d 824 (1987).

[42]Dean v. State, 177 Ga. App. 678, 340 S.E.2d 647 (1986); Scott v. State, 206 Ga. App. 17, 424 S.E.2d 325 (1992).

serve. Second, the precept issued in accordance with O.C.G.A. § 15-12-65.1 must show the jurors listed thereon as jurors in courts other than the superior court and show the name of such court or courts. Third, the summons to each juror must be properly served and show the name of all courts wherein the juror is eligible to serve.[43]

In *Kaysen v. State*,[44] the court held that "in computing the time allowed by the two-term requirement, terms or remainders of terms during which no jury is impancled are not counted." When a demand for trial "is filed during a term in which there is no jury impaneled to try the case 'the time allowed by the two-term trial requirement [does] not begin to run until the term following that during which the demand was filed' "[45] if at the following term there were jurors impaneled and qualified to try the defendant.[46] A term, or a remainder of a term, in which no jurors are impaneled and qualified to try the defendant's case is not counted for purposes of the statutory right to a speedy trial. If jurors have been dismissed and are not subject to recall when the speedy trial demand is filed, the term in which the demand is filed does not count for computation of the two-term requirement. In *Williamson v. State*,[47] the Court noted "that the statute does not require that courts examine how many jurors were serving on other trials or had been committed for other trials." The court went on to hold that "juries must merely be qualified and impaneled for that term to count. For purposes of [O.C.G.A. § 17-7-170(b)], we conclude that impaneled means jurors who have been summoned, have appeared for service, and have not yet been discharged." In *Williamson,* there were 37 jurors who were impaneled and qualified to serve. Although 14 of these had been assigned to another courtroom and 18 had been committed to other courtrooms the same day, the Supreme Court held that the requisite number of jurors were qualified and impaneled for that term to count against the two term limit under the statute. O.C.G.A. § 17-7-170 is regarded as a general statute governing state courts even though there is a special law relating to the

---

[43]Cf. George v. State, 229 Ga. App. 632, 633, 494 S.E.2d 526 (1997).

[44]Kaysen v. State, 191 Ga. App. 734, 382 S.E.2d 737 (1989). Cf. Deadwiley v. State, 192 Ga. App. 229, 384 S.E.2d 221 (1989).

[45]Kaysen v. State, 191 Ga. App. 734, 382 S.E.2d 737 (1989).

[46]Smith v. State, 199 Ga. App. 771, 406 S.E.2d 118 (1991).

[47]Williamson v. State, 295 Ga. 185, 758 S.E.2d 790 (2014). See Birts v. State, 192 Ga. App. 476, 385 S.E.2d 120 (1989) (O.C.G.A. § 17-7-170 is not conditional upon there being "enough" juries impaneled and qualified or how many jury trials are scheduled or if there are "enough" judges).

particular court providing a different rule.[48]

In 1985, O.C.G.A. § 17-7-170 was amended, in the case of misdemeanors, so as to provide that in determining the term at which trial shall be had, "there shall be excluded any civil term of court in a county in which civil and criminal terms of court are designated."

In *Cross v. State,*[49] the court held that the statute creating a state court with limited jurisdiction may determine the terms of that court.

In 1987, the statute was amended so as to expressly require that the demand be "served on the prosecutor and shall be binding only in the court in which the demand is filed, except where the case is transferred from one court to another without a request from the defendant."[50] In *Carter v. State,*[51] the court held that "merely sending a demand to the trial court and having it filed in the clerk's office . . . [is] insufficient service *on the State.*" (Emphasis in original.) But where time is lost in the transmission between courts of a case resulting solely from the deceit of the defendant, the defendant may not take advantage of the delay and secure a dismissal under the statute.[52]

"*Any affirmative action* of the defendant which results in a continuance of the case, or a failure to try it within the time fixed by the statute after the filing of a demand, has the effect of tolling the time."[53] This can include a request by counsel for a leave of absence of any duration which the court finds to be inordinate in light of the defendant's demand for a speedy trial.[54] However, the "State has the burden of showing that the defendant or his counsel took such affirmative action resulting in a waiver. . . ."[55] Likewise, it has been held that a defendant waives his right to a

[48]Dean v. State, 177 Ga. App. 678, 340 S.E.2d 647 (1986).

[49]Cross v. State, 272 Ga. 282, 528 S.E.2d 241 (2000).

[50]In Vondolteren v. State, 184 Ga. App. 344, 361 S.E.2d 833 (1987), the court held that under O.C.G.A. § 17-1-1 a demand for trial was not valid where the prosecuting attorney was not served with a copy. See also Turner v. State, 188 Ga. App. 267, 372 S.E.2d 826 (1988).

[51]Carter v. State, 226 Ga. App. 198, 199, 486 S.E.2d 79 (1997).

[52]Ramsey v. State, 189 Ga. App. 91, 94, 375 S.E.2d 63 (1988).

[53]Sykes v. State, 236 Ga. App. 518, 520, 511 S.E.2d 566 (1999); State v. Waters, 170 Ga. App. 505, 508 (3), 317 S.E.2d 614 (1984) (quoting Letbedder v. State, 129 Ga. App. 196, 199 S.E.2d 270 (1973)). See also Jackson v. State, 172 Ga. App. 359, 360, 323 S.E.2d 198 (1984). Cf. Fisher v. State, 273 Ga. 721, 545 S.E.2d 895 (2001), involving a notice of conflict letter given pursuant to USCR 17.1(B).

[54]State v. Dodge, 251 Ga. App. 361, 366 (2), 553 S.E.2d 831 (2001). See Jones v. State, 276 Ga. 171, 575 S.E.2d 456 (2003).

[55]State v. Grant, 217 Ga. App. 358, 359, 457 S.E.2d 263 (1995).

speedy trial by agreeing to a continuance from the second term[56] or by filing a motion to suppress "if the motion is granted and the State elects to have [an] appellate determination made."[57]

In *Ballew v. State,*[58] the court held that "A waiver of the demand would result from a continuance granted on the motion of the accused, or *from any other act on his part showing affirmatively that he consented to passing the case until a subsequent term.*" (Emphasis by the court.) Merely filing a notice of conflict letter pursuant to Superior Court Rule 17.1(B) does not amount to a waiver of an otherwise timely demand.[59] Likewise, the fact that a defendant does not object to a scheduling order which sets a trial date outside the two-term limit imposed by O.C.G.A. § 17-7-170(b), is not considered a waiver of a previously filed motion for speedy trial.[60]

A defendant does not waive his right to a trial if he merely asks for a postponement until a later time because of the unavailability of a witness,[61] or if he consents to a continuance to a later time within the time permitted by law,[62] or if he is granted a continuance which does not postpone the trial to another term,[63] or because he asks for a preliminary hearing,[64] or if he files with his demand a notice to produce and inspect recordings "well in advance of trial" and the motion is never set for a hearing,[65] or if the defendant's motion for mistrial is granted and the state fails to try him again within two terms when time exists to do so.[66] In *Jackson v. State,*[67] the defendant timely filed a demand for trial. He asked for a continuance, and the trial judge told him he could either go to trial immediately or have the case continued and that if the case was continued, the "speedy trial demand would have to be refiled to start the clock ticking again." The defendant

---

[56]State v. Stewart, 191 Ga. App. 35, 381 S.E.2d 50 (1989).

[57]State v. Waters, 170 Ga. App. 505, 508, 317 S.E.2d 614 (1984); Smith v. State, 192 Ga. App. 604, 386 S.E.2d 370 (1989).

[58]Ballew v. State, 211 Ga. App. 672, 673, 440 S.E.2d 76 (1994).

[59]Gifford v. State, 301 Ga. App. 50, 686 S.E.2d 831 (2009).

[60]State v. Marshall, 337 Ga. App. 336, 787 S.E.2d 290 (2016).

[61]Walker v. State, 89 Ga. 482, 15 S.E. 553 (1892); Campbell v. State, 6 Ga. App. 539, 540, 65 S.E. 307 (1909). But cf. State v. Stewart, 191 Ga. App. 35, 36, 381 S.E.2d 50 (1989). See also O.C.G.A. § 17-8-31 for continuances in the case of a material witness who is absent due to military service. In such a case, the court is required to continue the case until the witness is available and the time for the speedy trial is tolled in the interim.

[62]Adams v. State, 129 Ga. App. 839, 842, 201 S.E.2d 649 (1973).

[63]Weidlund v. State, 191 Ga. App. 668, 671, 382 S.E.2d 709 (1989).

[64]Frank v. State, 145 Ga. App. 678, 244 S.E.2d 619 (1978).

[65]State v. Smith, 156 Ga. App. 133, 134, 274 S.E.2d 130 (1980).

[66]State v. Allen, 165 Ga. App. 86, 88, 299 S.E.2d 158 (1983).

[67]Jackson v. State, 231 Ga. App. 187, 188, 498 S.E.2d 780 (1998).

opted for a continuance. The defendant filed another speedy trial demand without asking for permission to do so. The court rejected the defendant's contention that the court had already given him permission.

A valid demand for trial must "identify the charges upon which defendant demanded a speedy trial by 'name, date, term of court or case number.' "[68] But in *Baker v. State,*[69] the court held that a demand was sufficient which contained only the style of the case and the indictment number and stated, "Come now [defendants] by and through their attorney-at-law . . . before arraignment and demand a speedy trial." In *Verscharen v. State,*[70] the court held that a demand was sufficient when the defendant's name appeared in the caption even though the body of the demand had another name.

According to O.C.G.A. § 17-7-170 any demand shall expire upon the entry of a plea of guilty or nolo contendere or upon the conclusion of the trial. If the case "is reversed upon direct appeal, a new demand for trial must be filed within the term of the court in which the remittitur from the appellate court is received by the clerk of the court" or in the next successive term. If a case in which a demand for trial has been filed results in a mistrial, the case will be tried in the next regular term of the court.

In *State v. Wright,*[71] a demand for trial was filed which the state contended was inaccurate in that the number listed for the indictment was that of a nol prossed indictment and not that of the active case. However, the appellate court affirmed the action of the trial judge in finding that the demand was valid and the state was fully aware that the incident was the same in both indictments.

In a non-capital case, a defendant is not required to be present in court when the case is called for trial, but he is required to be available for trial.[72] However, he need not take any further steps to bring the case to trial.[73] It has been held that if the court asks whether there are any other jury trials at the time, the defendant

---

[68]Cummins v. State, 202 Ga. App. 155, 413 S.E.2d 773 (1991). Accord, Aranza v. State, 213 Ga. App. 192, 193 (2), 444 S.E.2d 349 (1994).

[69]Baker v. State, 212 Ga. App. 731, 442 S.E.2d 815 (1994).

[70]Verscharen v. State, 188 Ga. App. 746, 374 S.E.2d 349 (1988).

[71]State v. Wright, 221 Ga. App. 584, 472 S.E.2d 144 (1996).

[72]State v. Collins, 201 Ga. App. 500, 411 S.E.2d 546 (1991); McKnight

v. State, 215 Ga. App. 899, 903 (3), 453 S.E.2d 38 (1994), aff'd, 265 Ga. 701, 462 S.E.2d 142 (1995). See n. 84, infra.

[73]Thornton v. State, 7 Ga. App. 752, 753, 67 S.E. 1055 (1910) ("[N]o such waiver results from mere inactivity on [the defendant's] part, provided he does not absent himself from court, so that he can not be tried. The State is the pursuer; he is the pursued; until the State moves toward him, he may remain still. [I]f the State neglects to try him within the time prescribed by

may remain silent, allow the jury to be discharged, and then insist on his being discharged for the failure to try him.[74] However, in the 1995 case of *State v. McKnight*,[75] the Georgia Supreme Court pointed out that "a speedy trial demand may be waived where defense counsel is absent because of an *unjustified* belief that counsel was excused or 'on call' and nothing can be construed as authority approving the unexcused unjustified 'disappearance' of counsel." (Emphasis in original.) The material set out in this paragraph does not apply to capital cases.[76] See § 14:68, infra, on O.C.G.A. § 17-7-171.

A defendant in custody must be within the subpoena power of the court at the time the demand is filed. Thus, the demand for trial under O.C.G.A. § 17-7-170 is not valid if the defendant was in federal custody[77] or custody of another state at the time the demand was filed. See § 14:71, infra, on obtaining trial of a defendant in federal custody.

When a defendant files a demand for trial, files a pre-trial appeal or an appeal after conviction, and is granted a new trial, he need not file another demand.[78] "[U]pon the filing of the remittitur from the appellate court by the clerk's office of the trial court, the State shall have the remainder of that term and one additional regular term of court in which to try the defendant pursuant to his demand for trial, provided there are juries impaneled and qualified to try the defendant."[79] However, in *Pope v. State*,[80] the court held "that jurors must be present and available to serve after the remittitur is filed for a court term to count as one of the two terms in which the state must try the defendant."

In *State v. Rowe*,[81] a defendant made a demand for trial at the June term of court after two indictments were returned against him, one charging kidnapping and the other armed robbery in one count and robbery by intimidation in the second count. He was not tried at the June or September terms of court. Since two terms of court passed without a trial, the court discharged and

---

law, it operates as a conclusive and final abandonment of the prosecution . . .."). See also Mager v. State, 21 Ga. App. 139, 94 S.E. 82 (1917).

[74]Dublin v. State, 126 Ga. 580, 583, 55 S.E. 487 (1906).

[75]State v. McKnight, 265 Ga. 701, 462 S.E.2d 142 (1995). Cf. Cates v. State, 226 Ga. App. 519, 486 S.E.2d 654 (1997).

[76]Riley v. State, 212 Ga. App. 519, 520, 442 S.E.2d 7 (1994).

[77]Hunt v. State, 147 Ga. App. 787, 250 S.E.2d 517 (1978); McIver v. State,

205 Ga. App. 648, 423 S.E.2d 27 (1992). See Gosline v. State, 341 Ga. App. 708, 802 S.E.2d 275 (2017).

[78]Doehling v. State, 238 Ga. App. 293, 294, 518 S.E.2d 137 (1999).

[79]Henry v. James, 264 Ga. 527, 531, 449 S.E.2d 79 (1994).

[80]Pope v. State, 265 Ga. 473, 458 S.E.2d 115 (1995).

[81]State v. Rowe, 138 Ga. App. 904, 228 S.E.2d 3 (1976), overruled by Cleary v. State, 258 Ga. 203, 366 S.E.2d 677 (1988).

acquitted the defendant of kidnapping and robbery by intimidation and sustained the defendant's plea of autrefois acquit on the armed robbery count. On appeal by the state, the court held that robbery by intimidation is a lesser included offense of armed robbery. The defendant was entitled to an acquittal of the lesser offense because the state failed to try the case within two terms, and this was a bar to his trial for armed robbery, which arose out of the same transaction. However, in *Cleary v. State,*[82] the court disapproved *Rowe* and held "that where a multi-count indictment includes both capital and noncapital offenses, the time for trial upon a proper demand . . . is the time allowed . . . for the more serious offenses."

A demand for trial under O.C.G.A. § 17-7-170 does not apply to unindicted offenses pending in other counties.[83] See § 17:19, infra, on entering a nolle prosequi after a demand for trial is filed. See § 14:99, infra, on interlocutory appeals.

In *Mason v. Banks,*[84] a non-capital case, the defendant entered a guilty plea. After his probation was revoked, he sought to show that he had been denied a speedy trial. The court held that where he voluntarily entered a guilty plea, he could not later raise as a defense "his right to a speedy and public trial." In *Tutt v. State,*[85] there was a demand filed in a capital case, but the case was disposed of by a guilty plea. The court pointed out that "[o]nce a defendant solemnly admits in open court that he is in fact guilty . . . he may not thereafter raise independent claims . . . that occurred prior to the entry of the guilty plea."

In *Cooper v. State,*[86] the defendant was indicted in Georgia in April of 1995 while incarcerated in Florida on an unrelated charge. On June 11, 1995, he made a demand for a speedy trial, even though he was still incarcerated in Florida. He was returned to Georgia on August 28, 1995. The court held that the demand for a speedy trial was premature and could not validly be filed until the defendant was released from custody in Florida and was available for trial in Georgia.

In addition to the general statute providing for a demand for trial, which has been discussed above, and the statute applicable to capital cases, which is discussed in the next section, Georgia has a special statute, discussed in § 14:69, infra, which applies to a demand for trial by a person who is already confined to a Georgia penal or correctional institution under the jurisdiction of the

---

[82]Cleary v. State, 258 Ga. 203, 205, 366 S.E.2d 677 (1988).

[83]Garrett v. Arrington, 245 Ga. 47, 262 S.E.2d 808 (1980).

[84]Mason v. Banks, 242 Ga. 292, 293 (2), 248 S.E.2d 664 (1978).

[85]Tutt v. State, 267 Ga. 49, 50, 472 S.E.2d 306 (1996).

[86]Cooper v. State, 224 Ga. App. 621, 481 S.E.2d 607 (1997).

State Department of Corrections on another offense.[87] In general terms, if the inmate requests final disposition of the matter forming the basis of the detainer, and if the inmate is not tried within two terms of court, the detainer based on such "new" indictment shall be dismissed.[88]

Georgia has a separate statute[89] which relates to interstate agreements on detainers. This legislation provides that a prisoner

---

[87]O.C.G.A. §§ 42-6-1 et seq.; Butler v. State, 126 Ga. App. 22, 189 S.E.2d 870 (1972). On this statute, see Spurlin v. State, 228 Ga. 2, 183 S.E.2d 765 (1971).

[88]O.C.G.A. § 42-6-3, O.C.G.A. § 42-6-4.

[89]O.C.G.A. §§ 42-6-20 et seq. Generally, see United States v. Fusco, 436 U.S. 340, 98 S.Ct. 1834, 56 L.Ed.2d 329 (1978), for an interesting discussion on the Interstate Agreement on Detainers. In Smith v. Hooey, 393 U.S. 374, 89 S.Ct. 575, 21 L.Ed.2d 607 (1969), the court said that where a defendant is serving time in one state and charges are pending against him in a second state, if the defendant demands trial, the second state must make a diligent effort to get him and try him. Failure of the second state to do so is a violation of the Sixth Amendment, made applicable to the states through the Fourteenth Amendment.

The Interstate Detainers Act provides that the defendant's trial shall commence within 120 days of his arrival in the receiving state, but for good cause shown in open court with prisoner or his counsel present, reasonable continuances may be granted. Reaves v. State, 242 Ga. 542, 553, 250 S.E.2d 376 (1978).

In Braden v. Kentucky, 410 U.S. 484, 93 S.Ct. 1123, 35 L.Ed.2d 443 (1973), *Braden* was indicted in Kentucky. He escaped from custody before trial and went to Alabama, where he was convicted of felonies and imprisoned. A Kentucky detainer was lodged against him. He requested a speedy trial in Kentucky. He remained in Alabama, was not tried in Kentucky, and then filed a federal habeas corpus action in Kentucky, contending that he had been denied a speedy trial. The court in effect approved an order of the federal district court ordering Kentucky to try Braden within 60 days or dismiss the indictment.

In United States v. Dobson, 585 F.2d 55 (3d Cir. 1978), the court held that the Interstate Agreement on Detainers Act does not apply, prior to a parole revocation, for an alleged violation of parole.

In Walker v. King, 448 F.Supp. 580 (S.D.N.Y., 1978), the court held that under the Act, a receiving state must sentence a convicted prisoner before returning him to the sending state.

In Duchac v. State, 151 Ga. App. 374, 377, 259 S.E.2d 740 (1979), the court concluded that where defendant properly requested his statutory right to a speedy trial under the Interstate Agreement and when no continuances are obtained (as provided for in the Act) and no circumstances tolling the 180-day period are shown in the record, it is error not to dismiss the indictment with prejudice.

In Cobb v. State, 244 Ga. 344, 346 (1), 260 S.E.2d 60 (1979), the court found that the 120-day time limit was tolled by defendant's numerous pre-trial motions.

Generally, see Annot., "Validity, Construction and Application of Interstate Agreement on Detainers," 98 A.L.R.3d 160 (1980).

In Cuyler v. Adams, 449 U.S. 433, 101 S.Ct. 703, 66 L.Ed.2d 641 (1981), the court held that the interpretation of the Interstate Detainer Act is a federal question, even where the United States is not a party to a controversy involving two states.

serving a sentence in another state (which has enacted a statute substantially like that of Georgia) may obtain a prompt trial in Georgia or have the detainer lifted by following the provisions set out. Of course, the statute, being reciprocal, also applies to requests from other states received in Georgia, for a prisoner serving time in Georgia. See § 14:71, infra, on the Interstate Detainer Act or interstate agreements.

An order denying a pre-trial demand for a speedy trial pursuant to O.C.G.A. § 17-7-170 is subject to direct appeal.[90]

If a defendant is in federal custody or in custody in another state, this Georgia statute does not apply and the defendant must seek relief under the Interstate Agreement on Detainers.[91]

For demands for trial, see Studdard, *Daniel's Georgia Criminal Trial Practice Forms* (2018–2019 ed.), §§ 18:1, et seq.

§ 14:68   O.C.G.A. § 17-7-171

In 1983, the Georgia law was changed to permit a demand for trial in capital cases.[1] "A capital offense within the terms of [O.C.G.A. § 17-7-171] refers to offenses defined by statute as capital offenses, not necessarily offenses for which the state could or actually does seek the death penalty."[2] The time for filing a demand is the same as in non-capital cases. If more than two

---

[90]Williamson v. State, 321 Ga. App. 25, 740 S.E.2d 841 (2013). See Hubbard v. State, 254 Ga. 694, 333 S.E.2d 827 (1985). Compare Sosniak v. State, 292 Ga. 35, 734 S.E.2d 362 (2012) (reversing Callaway v. State, 275 Ga. 332, 567 S.E.2d 13 (2002))) (no right to direct review of denial of constitutional speedy trial demand; subject only to review by interlocutory appeal prior to trial).

[91]Cf. Luke v. State, 180 Ga. App. 378, 379, 349 S.E.2d 391 (1986), overruled on other grounds by State v. Collins, 201 Ga. App. 500, 411 S.E.2d 546 (1991).

[Section 14:68]

[1]O.C.G.A. § 17-7-171.

[2]Cleary v. State, 258 Ga. 203, 204, 366 S.E.2d 677 (1988); White v. State, 202 Ga. App. 370, 371, 414 S.E.2d 296 (1991); Harper v. State, 203 Ga. App. 775, 776, 417 S.E.2d 435 (1992).

The Supreme Court explained in Cook v. State, 242 Ga. 657, 658, 251 S.E.2d 230 (1978), "[A] capital crime is one for which the death penalty may be imposed. Our Code law continues to prescribe that the death penalty . . . cannot be imposed where no death results. This difference between what the Code prescribes and the Constitution allows has created some confusion. We have held as follows: (1) Convictions of rape, armed robbery and kidnapping with bodily injury where no death results are not capital felonies for appellate jurisdictional purposes and appeals in such cases go to the Court of Appeals. (2) A crime, such as kidnapping with bodily injury [or rape], on which the death penalty cannot be imposed, is nevertheless "another capital felony" for purposes of aggravating circumstances under [O.C.G.A. § 17-10-30(b)(2)]. (3) Under [O.C.G.A. § 17-7-95], a plea of nolo contendere to a charge of rape was not authorized because rape was a capital felony for purposes of that Code section, but such plea and sentence thereon were beneficial to the defendant and thus were harmless error."

regular terms are convened and adjourned after the term at which the demand was filed, the defendant shall be acquitted, if at both terms juries were impaneled, qualified to try the case and the defendant was present in court, announcing ready for trial and requesting a trial.[3]

In 1988, Georgia amended this statute to provide that in a case in "which the death penalty is sought, if a demand for trial is entered, the counting of terms under subsection (b) . . . shall not begin until the convening of the first term following the completion of pretrial review proceedings in the Supreme Court. . . ."

In *Franks v. State*,[4] the court held that the counting of terms of court shall not begin in a death penalty case until the convening of the first term after completion of pre-trial review in the Georgia Supreme Court. If the trial judge determines that a review is warranted, and has filed a report to that effect, the pre-trial review proceedings in the Supreme Court, "which include and may be limited to, the determination whether to grant interim review, are not complete, and the counting of terms under subsection (b) has not begun. However, [if] the trial court conclude[s] that no issues warrant . . . certification for pretrial appellate review and enter[s] an order obviating such review," the demand shall begin to run at that time.

In *Rice v. State*,[5] the court held that any request for a continuance, in a capital case, after the filing of a demand for speedy trial operates as a waiver of the demand. This rule does not apply to a demand filed in a non-capital case. See § 14:67, supra, on speedy trial demand.

Beginning July 1, 2006, a defendant in a capital case who wishes to file a speedy trial demand must follow the same procedures as a defendant in a non-capital case. To wit, a demand for speedy trial in a capital case must be filed with the clerk of the court and served upon the prosecutor and upon the judge to whom the case is assigned, or, if the case is not assigned, upon the chief judge of the court in which the case is pending. In addi-

---

(citations omitted).

In Morrow v. State, 147 Ga. App. 395, 249 S.E.2d 110 (1978), the Court of Appeals concluded that rape is a capital offense for purposes of the speedy trial statutes.

[3]O.C.G.A. § 17-7-171. See Walker v. State, 290 Ga. 696, 723 S.E.2d 894 (2012). See also Levester v. State, 270 Ga. 485, 486, 512 S.E.2d 258 (1999).

In order for a defendant to be discharged, the record must show that he was in court announcing ready and requesting trial for two terms after that at which demand was filed. Dennis v. Grimes, 216 Ga. 671, 118 S.E.2d 923 (1961), disapp. on other grounds, Henry v. James, 264 Ga. 527, 530, 449 S.E.2d 79 (1994); Sheats v. State, 237 Ga. 757 (1), 229 S.E.2d 600 (1976).

[4]Franks v. State, 266 Ga. 707, 708, 469 S.E.2d 651 (1996).

[5]Rice v. State, 264 Ga. 846, 452 S.E.2d 492 (1995). Accord, Davis v. State, 221 Ga. App. 168, 170 (1), 471 S.E.2d 14 (1996).

tion, the demand must: (1) be filed as "a separate, distinct, and individual document;" (2) clearly be titled "Demand For Speedy Trial;" (3) reference § 17-7-171 within the pleading; and (4) "identify the indictment number or accusation number for which such demand is being made." Finally, "the demand for speedy trial shall be binding only in the court in which such demand is filed, except where the case is transferred from one court to another without a request from the defendant."[6]

It must be remembered that in a capital case the defendant must be present in court when his case is called for trial. The defendant must not only be present, but he must be "announcing ready for trial and requesting a trial on the indictment."[7] In *Walker v. State,*[8] the court held that this rule applies even when a defendant is in custody. The defendant must at least exercise due diligence to be "present in court announcing ready for trial and requesting a trial on the indictment." However, counsel can announce ready for the defendant.

In *Abiff v. State,*[9] the court held that when a defendant is convicted, appeals, obtains a reversal, and then files a demand for trial, the demand is not valid unless the defendant obtained "special permission of the court." The reversal entitles the defendant to a new trial, not a new indictment. The reversal of a conviction does not start again the running of the statutory period provided.

However, this statute does not apply when the defendant is unable to appear as required because of an involuntary extradition to another state. In the event of such an extradition after a demand for trial, it has been held that the defendant's right to a speedy trial is determined by the Interstate Agreement on Detainers,[10] which is discussed in § 14:71, infra.

§ 14:69 Demand for trial by prison inmate—General

O.C.G.A. §§ 42-6-1 through 42-6-6 provide that when a defendant is serving a sentence under the Department of Corrections and there is pending in a state court an accusation or indictment against the defendant which is the basis of a detainer filed against him, he shall be brought to trial within two terms of the court in which the action is pending, after the inmate has had delivered to the clerk of the court and the prosecutor of the court

---

[6]O.C.G.A.   § 17-7-171,   as amended July 1, 2006.

[7]State v. Collins, 201 Ga. App. 500, 411 S.E.2d 546 (1991).

[8]Walker v. State, 216 Ga. App. 236, 454 S.E.2d 156 (1995). Accord,

Burns v. State, 265 Ga. 763, 462 S.E.2d 622 (1995).

[9]Abiff v. State, 260 Ga. 434 (1), 396 S.E.2d 483 (1990).

[10]Bashlor v. State, 165 Ga. App. 329 (1), 299 S.E.2d 418 (1983).

a request for trial. The request for trial must be accompanied by a certificate of the Department of Corrections "stating the term of commitment under which the inmate is being held, the computed expiration date of the commitment, and the time of parole eligibility of the inmate." The notice and request shall be delivered to the Commissioner of the Department of Corrections, who is to promptly forward it and the attached certificate to the prosecuting officer and court by registered mail. The warden or his representative having custody of the inmate shall inform the inmate of the source of and a copy of any detainer within 15 days and shall also inform him of his right to request a final disposition of the charge upon which the detainer is based.

A request for final disposition of a pending indictment or accusation operates as a request for final disposition of all untried indictments or accusations on the basis of which detainers have been filed against the inmate from the county of the prosecuting attorney who filed the detainer. The Commissioner of the Department of Corrections shall promptly notify all interested prosecuting officers and courts in the jurisdictions within the county to which the request for final disposition is being sent. The trial judge is authorized to grant continuances, and such a continuance extends the period within which an inmate may be tried. After an inmate has filed a request for final disposition, if the inmate escapes, this voids the request.

The statute does not require the filing of a detainer with the Department of Corrections or that a detainer be filed at any particular time.[1] A letter to the Department of Corrections stating that there was an outstanding warrant for the defendant and that the State intended to prosecute substantially complies with O.C.G.A. § 42-6-1(3).[2] However, in *Street v. State*,[3] the court held that a trial court order directing the Department of Offender Rehabilitation to produce a defendant for arraignment on a specified date and for trial on another specified date did not constitute a detainer because the statute requires that the instrument must be *"executed by the prosecuting officer of the court."* (Emphasis by the court.)

§ 14:70 General right to speedy trial

In addition to limitations of prosecution imposed by Georgia statutes which were discussed in the last sections, a defendant

---

[Section 14:69]

[1]Riley v. State, 180 Ga. App. 409, 412 (3), 349 S.E.2d 274 (1986).

[2]Riley v. State, 180 Ga. App. 409, 412 (3), 349 S.E.2d 274 (1986). Cf. 21 Am. Jur. 2d 669, Criminal Law § 404 (1981).

[3]Street v. State, 211 Ga. App. 230, 231, 438 S.E.2d 693 (1993).

has a broader though less precise constitutional right of a speedy trial under both the United States Constitution[1] and the Georgia Constitution.[2] The federal constitutional Sixth Amendment provision for a speedy trial applies to state prosecutions through the due process clause of the Fourteenth Amendment.[3] The right to a speedy trial begins to run "at the time of arrest or when formal charges are brought, whichever is earlier."[4] "The Sixth Amendment's speedy trial guarantee does not apply once a defendant has been found guilty at trial or has pleaded guilty to criminal charges."[5]

In *Barker v. Wingo*,[6] the United States Supreme Court said that the right to a speedy trial is different from other constitutional rights in that (1) society has an interest in the prompt trial of those charged with crime, and long imprisonment prior to trial may have a destructive effect on a defendant; (2) a delay may work to the defendant's benefit; (3) the right to a speedy trial is a more vague concept than other procedural rights.

The court said that in speedy trial cases the following factors are to be considered: (1) the length of the delay;[7] (2) the reason for the delay;[8] (3) assertion by the defendant of his right to a

---

[Section 14:70]

[1]U.S. Const. Amend. VI. See Annot., "Accused's Right to Speedy Trial Under Federal Constitution—Supreme Court Cases," 71 L.Ed.2d 983 (1983).

[2]Ga. Const. 1983, Art. I, § I, ¶ XI.

[3]Klopfer v. North Carolina, 386 U.S. 213, 87 S.Ct. 988, 18 L.Ed.2d 1 (1967).

[4]Boseman v. State, 263 Ga. 730, 731 (1), 438 S.E.2d 626 (1994) (overruled on other grounds by, Sosniak v. State, 292 Ga. 35, 734 S.E.2d 362 (2012)).

[5]Betterman v. Montana, 136 S. Ct. 1609, 194 L. Ed. 2d 723 (2016).

[6]Barker v. Wingo, 407 U.S. 514, 92 S.Ct. 2182, 33 L.Ed.2d 101 (1972).

In Crapse v. State, 180 Ga. App. 321, 349 S.E.2d 190 (1986), the court found there was no speedy trial violation where there was a delay of over five years between indictment and trial.

See Glidewell v. State, 169 Ga. App. 858, 859 (2), 314 S.E.2d 924 (1984).

[7]In Simpson v. State, 150 Ga. App. 814, 815, 258 S.E.2d 634 (1979), there was a delay of 34 months between arrest and arraignment, and the court said that the mere passage of time does not alone constitute a denial of due process. See State v. Giddens, 280 Ga. App. 586, 634 S.E.2d 526 (2006), delay of five years, although excessive, was not a per se denial of right to speedy trial where defendant did not timely and vigilantly assert right and was otherwise unable to show prejudice to defense counsel by delay.

[8]For example, a deliberate attempt to hinder a defendant weighs heavily against the state. Overcrowded courts may be considered. A missing witness should justify an appropriate delay. A looming issue is whether the funding of public defense is so inadequate that delay caused due to the failure of the state to provide counsel and a properly funded defense may amount to a constitutional speedy trial violation requiring the dismissal of the indictment with prejudice. See Phan v.

speedy trial;[9] and (4) prejudice to the defendant.[10] In *Johnson v. State*,[11] the court held that in determining the prejudice to the defendant, the court must consider three interests: (1) preventing oppressive pretrial incarceration; (2) minimizing anxiety and concern of the defendant, and (3) limiting the possibility that the defense will be impaired. However, in *Moore v. Arizona*, the United States Supreme Court held that it is not necessary to

State, 287 Ga. 697, 699 S.E.2d 9 (2010). Cf., Vermont v. Brillon, 129 S. Ct. 1283, 173 L. Ed. 2d 231 (2009).

In Simpson v. State, 150 Ga. App. 814, 816, 258 S.E.2d 634 (1979), the court pointed out that negligence or overcrowded courts may be considered, but these factors weigh less heavily against the state.

In Strunk v. United States, 412 U.S. 434, 436, 93 S.Ct. 2260, 37 L.Ed.2d 56 (1973), the court said that the ultimate responsibility for overcrowded dockets and understaffed prosecutors is on the government.

In Vermont v. Brillon, 129 S. Ct. 1283, 173 L. Ed. 2d 231 (2009), the United States Supreme Court noted that a "systemic 'breakdown in the public defender system' could be charged to the state." It did not do so in *Brillon* because the issue was not raised in that case. In Weis v. State, 287 Ga. 46, 694 S.E.2d 350 (2010), the Georgia Supreme Court agreed with *Brillon* that while the failure of the state's public defender system could be charged against the state for purposes of a speedy trial analysis it declined to do so, finding that the reason for the delay in bringing the defendant's death penalty case to trial was attributable to defense counsel. There were any number of delays in the case due to a lack of funding for defense counsel and experts. Appointed defense counsel were removed from the case when they insisted they could not proceed without proper funding and were never replaced by salaried public defenders. Appointed counsel later sought to get back into the case. The dissent in this split decision is sharply critical of the state's public defender system.

[9]An assertion of the right to trial is entitled to strong evidentiary weight in determining if a defendant is being deprived of his Sixth Amendment right. Failure of the defendant to assert the right will make it difficult to show that he was denied a speedy trial. The court should also consider how forcefully the defendant asserted his right to a trial. Cf. Simpson v. State, 150 Ga. App. 814, 816, 258 S.E.2d 634 (1979).

In State v. Alexander, 295 Ga. 154, 758 S.E.2d 289 (2014), the court noted that the weight to this factor may be subject to mitigation at the discretion of the court in cases where the defendant failed to assert the right because, e.g., he was without counsel; because of the defendant's limited education; or, because of the difficulty of preparing a defense while incarcerated.

[10]Pre-trial incarceration, anxiety, possibility of impairment of his defense are examples cited as showing prejudice to a defendant.

In Lett v. State, 164 Ga. App. 584, 298 S.E.2d 541 (1982), the defendant was indicted in 1975. He had no knowledge of the indictment until 1982. In the meantime the sheriff who arrested and questioned him had died. His co-indictee could not be located. The court held that it was error for the trial judge to deny the plea in bar and dismiss the indictment.

[11]Johnson v. State, 268 Ga. 416, 417 (2), 490 S.E.2d 91 (1997). See State v. Pickett, 288 Ga. 674(4)(c), 706 S.E.2d 561 (2011) (within court's discretion to find that defendant's bond condition which prohibited contact with his children after a five and one-half year delay was sufficiently prejudicial).

show affirmatively that the defendant has been prejudiced in order to show a denial of his constitutional right to a speedy trial.[12] The failure of the defendant to assert his or her demand for a speedy trial "is entitled to strong evidentiary weight against the defendant."[13] However, the defendant's failure to assert the demand in a timely fashion may be mitigated by defendant's lack of representation, incarceration and/or limited education.[14]

The trial court, defense counsel and the state all share responsibility for the expeditious resolution of criminal cases. In *Threatt v. State*,[15] the Georgia Court of Appeals noted that the trial court and the prosecutor could not sit idly when it was or should have been apparent that the defendant's court appointed counsel allowed the case to languish.

In *State v. Yates*,[16] the court affirmed the dismissal of DUI charges where the defendant was arrested on August 14, 1993, and on July 13, 1995, the defendant's only witness died. The case had been continued several times at the request of the state.[17]

A number of Georgia cases have cited *Barker* and applied the criteria set out.[18] The trial court's weighing of each *Barker* speedy trial factor and its balancing of all four factors are reviewed on appeal only for abuse of discretion. However, where the trial court has clearly erred in some of its findings of fact or misapplied the law, the deference owed to the trial court's decision is "diminished."[19]

It has been recognized that a demand for trial is not a prerequisite to a plea in bar for failure to have a speedy trial.[20] Likewise, it has been held that the "[m]ere passage of time, standing alone,

---

[12]Moore v. Arizona, 414 U.S. 25, 94 S.Ct. 188, 38 L.Ed.2d 183 (1973). But see Crapse v. State, 180 Ga. App. 321, 324, 349 S.E.2d 190 (1986).

[13]Brannen v. State, 274 Ga. 454, 456, 553 S.E.2d 813 (2001).

[14]See State v. Alexander, 295 Ga. 154, 758 S.E.2d 289 (2014).

[15]Threatt v. State, 282 Ga. App. 884, 640 S.E.2d 316 (2006).

[16]State v. Yates, 223 Ga. App. 403, 477 S.E.2d 670 (1996).

[17]Compare Brannen v. State, 274 Ga. 454, 553 S.E.2d 813 (2001) (52 month delay) and Nelloms v. State, 274 Ga. 179, 549 S.E.2d 381 (2001) (51 month delay). State allowed to proceed to trial because it could alleviate prejudice from delay by essentially stipulating to facts lost to defense during

delay due to death of witness.

[18]State v. Carr, 278 Ga. 124, 598 S.E.2d 468 (2004); Hester v. State, 268 Ga. App. 94, 601 S.E.2d 456 (2004) (noteworthy because Court of Appeals considered the pre-indictment delay of 63 months in concluding that defendant's right to speedy trial had been violated); Mullinax v. State, 273 Ga. 756, 758 (2), 545 S.E.2d 891 (2001). E.g., Hall v. State, 131 Ga. App. 786, 787, 206 S.E.2d 644 (1974); State v. King, 137 Ga. App. 26, 222 S.E.2d 859 (1975); State v. Weeks, 136 Ga. App. 637, 639, 222 S.E.2d 117 (1975); Perry v. Mitchell, 253 Ga. 593, 594, 322 S.E.2d 273 (1984).

[19]State v. Porter, 288 Ga. 524, 705 S.E.2d 636 (2011).

[20]State v. King, 137 Ga. App. 26, 222 S.E.2d 859 (1975). In this case,

does not compel a finding of denial of due process. . . . Nevertheless, . . . [a] delay of 17 months raises a threshold presumption of prejudice."[21]

In *United States v. Loud Hawk,*[22] the United States Supreme Court held that the period of time after a dismissal by the trial judge during which time the defendant was not subject to indictment or any restraint on his freedom must be excluded from calculations under the speedy trial clause.

While there is generally no right to a speedy arrest,[23] the time between arrest and indictment, as well as between indictment and trial, may be considered in determining whether or not a defendant has been denied a speedy trial.[24] Although there is no constitutional "right" to a speedy indictment, egregious delay between the time of arrest and indictment may deprive a defendant of due process.[25] However, in *Lenear v. State,*[26] the court held a refusal to dismiss the indictment for lack of a speedy trial was not error unless it is shown that the "delay was purposeful, oppressive, or prejudicial."

In *United States v. MacDonald,*[27] the defendant had been charged with the murder of his wife in 1970 while he was in the Army. Later that year, the charges were dismissed. The defendant was honorably discharged based upon hardship. In 1975, he was indicted by a federal grand jury. He was convicted and appealed, contending that his Sixth Amendment right to a speedy trial had been denied. The court concluded that the time between the dis-

---

there was a 27-month delay between indictment and the time of the filing of the plea because of a heavy case load.

[21]Jernigan v. State, 239 Ga. App. 65, 66, 517 S.E.2d 370 (1999).

[22]United States v. Loud Hawk, 474 U.S. 302, 106 S.Ct. 648, 88 L.Ed.2d 640 (1986).

[23]See § 2:4, supra.

[24]Dillingham v. United States, 423 U.S. 64, 96 S.Ct. 303, 46 L.Ed.2d 205 (1975). Here there was a delay of 22 months between arrest and indictment and 12 months delay between indictment and trial.

[25]U.S. v. Lovasco, 431 U.S. 783, 97 S. Ct. 2044, 52 L. Ed. 2d 752 (1977); U.S. v. Marion, 404 U.S. 307, 92 S. Ct. 455, 30 L. Ed. 2d 468 (1971); Griffin v. State, 282 Ga. 215(5), 647 S.E.2d 36 (2007); Moore v. State, 278 Ga. 473, 604 S.E.2d 139 (2004).

[26]Lenear v. State, 239 Ga. 617, 618 (2), 238 S.E.2d 407 (1977). In this case, the delay was said to have resulted from the defendant's use of an alias. In State v. Hight, 156 Ga. App. 246, 248, 274 S.E.2d 638 (1980), the defendant was arrested on February 18, 1978, indicted on January 15, 1980, and scheduled for trial on February 26, 1980, when he filed a motion to dismiss on speedy trial grounds. Despite the 23-month delay between arrest and indictment, the appellate court reversed the dismissal, where the defendant had not been in "confinement, did not demand trial . . . [showed] no actual prejudice and the record . . . [did] not demonstrate the delay was deliberate or [was] taken for purpose of tactical advantage over the defendant."

[27]United States v. MacDonald, 456 U.S. 1, 102 S.Ct. 1497, 71 L.Ed.2d 696 (1982).

missal of the military charges and the later indictment was not to be considered in determining whether the defendant's right to a speedy trial had been violated. A delay prior to arrest or indictment may give rise to a claim of a violation of the due process clause of the Fifth Amendment. However, the speedy trial clause does not apply until a defendant has been indicted, arrested or otherwise officially accused. After the military charges were dismissed, any restraint on liberty, disruption, strain on financial resources, exposure to public obloquy, or stress and anxiety was no different than that experienced by anyone who is openly subject to criminal investigation. The defendant was not under arrest or in custody and was, therefore, legally and constitutionally in the same posture as if he had never been formerly charged.

In *Doggett v. United States*,[28] there was a delay of eight and one-half years between indictment and arrest. The defendant was out of the country for approximately two years from about the time of his indictment. He apparently did not know he had been indicted. The United States Supreme Court held that the defendant's motion to dismiss the indictment for a speedy trial violation (1) should have been granted. The court pointed out that Doggett would prevail if he could show that the government had intentionally held back the prosecution to gain some impermissible advantage at trial, citing *Barker*. However, (2) if the government pursued Doggett with reasonable diligence from indictment to arrest, his speedy trial claim would fail. There is a middle ground between (1) and (2). Negligence is to be weighed more lightly than deliberate intent to harm the accused. Condoning prolonged and unjustified delays in prosecution would both penalize many defendants for the state's fault and simply encourage the government to gamble with the interests of criminal suspects. "To be sure, to warrant granting relief, negligence unaccompanied by particularized trial prejudice must have lasted longer than negligence demonstrably causing such prejudice. But even so, the Government's egregious persistence in failing to prosecute Doggett is clearly sufficient. . . . When the Government's negligence thus causes delay six times as long as that generally sufficient to trigger judicial review, . . . and when the presumption of prejudice, albeit unspecified, is neither extenuated, . . . as by the defendant's acquiescence . . . nor persuasively rebutted, . . . the defendant is entitled to relief."

In *Doggett*,[29] the court held that "post-accusation delay [is] presumptively prejudicial at least as it approaches one year . . . ..

---

[28]Doggett v. United States, 505 U.S. 647, 112 S.Ct. 2686, 120 L.Ed.2d 520 (1992).

[29]Doggett v. U.S., 505 U.S. 647, 652 n.1, 112 S. Ct. 2686, 120 L. Ed. 2d 520 (1992). Cawley v. State, 330 Ga. App. 22, 766 S.E.2d 581 (2014).

We note that, as the term is used in this threshold context, 'presumptive prejudice' does not necessarily indicate a statistical probability of prejudice; it simply marks the point at which courts deem the delay unreasonable enough to trigger the *Barker* enquiry."

In *Wooten v. State,*[30] the Georgia Supreme Court affirmed the defendant's conviction for a 1978 murder at a trial in 1991, where charges were "dropped" at a preliminary hearing, but after new evidence was discovered, he was indicted in 1990. The Georgia court relied on *MacDonald* but did not refer to *Doggett.* The court treated the 1978 warrant as having been orally dismissed, and found that the defendant was not restrained of his liberty after the preliminary hearing. The court concluded that the delay of Wooten's trial should be considered under the due process standard of (1) prejudice and (2) intent to gain tactical advantage. The court pointed out that "any prejudice which results merely from the passage of time cannot create the requisite prejudice." As to the "second prong," the defendant did not allege that the delay was an intentional attempt to gain a tactical advantage. However, if the delay is deemed to be presumptively prejudicial, then the criteria of the Barker analysis are to be considered. The presumption alone cannot establish a Sixth Amendment violation without a Barker analysis.[31] In *Snow v. State,*[32] the court affirmed the trial judge in finding that defendant had not been denied his right to a speedy trial where the defendant was arrested in 1992 and convicted in 1996, but did not file a motion to dismiss until about 10 months before he was convicted. The court found that there was no evidence of pretrial incarceration and minimal evidence that anxiety had been caused, and at best there was some question of prejudice in not being able to find a witness.

At some point, however, excessive delay by the state in getting a case to trial becomes so prejudicial that the defendant need not show "particularized prejudice" in order to prevail on a constitutional speedy trial claim. This is because a lengthy delay impairs the fundamental fairness of a trial due to the potential lost or unreliable memory of the witness and the staleness of the evidence. In such cases it becomes the burden of the state to affirmatively show that the defense has not been impaired by the delay.[33] Georgia courts have generally agreed that a delay in excess of five years entitles a defendant to a strong presumption of prejudice which need not require any particularized showing of

---

[30]Wooten v. State, 262 Ga. 876, 878 (2), 426 S.E.2d 852 (1993).

[31]Boseman v. State, 263 Ga. 730, 732, 438 S.E.2d 626 (1994). See Harris v. State, 284 Ga. 455, 667 S.E.2d 361 (2008).

[32]Snow v. State, 229 Ga. App. 532, 494 S.E.2d 309 (1997).

[33]Grizzard v. State, 301 Ga. App. 613, 688 S.E.2d 402 (2009).

prejudice.[34]

In *Stoner v. State*,[35] the Alabama Court of Criminal Appeals concluded that there was no due process violation in a 19-year delay where the defendant was indicted on September 20, 1977, for unlawfully exploding dynamite dangerously near an inhabited dwelling on June 29, 1958. The court pointed out that (1) the Sixth Amendment right to a speedy trial applies only to prosecutions formally begun; (2) the mere passage of time is not a per se due process violation; (3) the burden is on the defendant to show actual prejudice; (4) diminished recollection of witnesses alone does not constitute substantial prejudice; (5) prosecutions may be delayed for lack of evidence; (6) in the absence of proof, a court will not assume the state intentionally delayed a prosecution to gain a tactical advantage or made a knowingly reckless disregard of the defendant's ability to defend himself. The United States Supreme Court denied certiorari.[36]

If the defendant is denied his constitutional right to a speedy trial, the charges against him must be dismissed. While this has been said to be an unsatisfactory and severe remedy, it is the only possible remedy.[37]

In *Boseman v. State*,[38] the court emphasized that in considering a motion to dismiss on speedy trial grounds, "it is essential for the trial court to enter findings of fact and conclusions of law consistent with the *Barker v. Wingo* factors." In the absence of such findings, the case must be remanded.[39]

In *Sosniak v. State*,[40] the Georgia Supreme Court held that the denial of a pre-trial motion to dismiss based upon speedy trial grounds is not directly appealable and overruled all authority to the contrary. Review of such an order is available only by way of

---

[34]Arbegast v. State, 301 Ga. App. 462, 688 S.E.2d 1 (2009).

[35]Stoner v. State, 418 So.2d 171 (Ala.Cr.App.1982), aff'd, 418 So.2d 184 (Ala.1982).

[36]Stoner v. State, 418 So.2d 171 (Ala.Cr.App.1982), aff'd, 418 So.2d 184 (Ala. 1982). In Stoner v. Graddick, 751 F.2d 1535 (11th Cir. 1985), the court affirmed the denial of a petition for federal habeas corpus.

[37]Strunk v. United States, 412 U.S. 434, 93 S.Ct. 2260, 37 L.Ed.2d 56 (1973).

[38]Boseman v. State, 263 Ga. 730, 731, 438 S.E.2d 626 (1994). See State v. Porter, 288 Ga. 524, 705 S.E.2d 636 (2011); Goddard v. State, 310 Ga. App.

2, 712 S.E.2d 528 (2011); Higgenbottom v. State, 288 Ga. 429, 704 S.E.2d 786 (2011).

[39]Richardson v. State, 311 Ga. App. 369, 715 S.E.2d 774 (2011). See Butler v. State, 309 Ga. App. 86, 709 S.E.2d 293 (2011), opinion vacated, 312 Ga. App. 513, 718 S.E.2d 869 (2011) (review may be had where trial court incorporates by specific references its verbal findings set forth in hearing transcript).

[40]Sosniak v. State, 292 Ga. 35, 734 S.E.2d 362 (2012) (overruling Callaway v. State, 275 Ga. 332, 567 S.E.2d 13 (2002)), and Boseman v. State, 263 Ga. 730, 438 S.E.2d 626 (1994))).

a certificate of immediate review. However, denial of a statutory speedy trial request is directly appealable under O.C.G.A. § 5-6-34(a).[41]

In addition to the constitutional right of a defendant to a speedy trial, Congress has felt that more expedition is needed in the trial of federal criminal cases. Hence, it has enacted the Speedy Trial Act of 1974.[42] This act provides for a progressive reduction in time for the disposition of various steps in a criminal prosecution over a period of several years. Georgia has no comparable statute.

See § 14:67, supra, on demand for trial, and § 2:4, supra, on the right to a speedy arrest.

For a motion to dismiss for failure to have a speedy trial, see Studdard, *Daniel's Georgia Criminal Trial Practice Forms* (2018–2019 ed.), § 18:7, 18:8 and 18:9.

§ 14:71 Interstate agreement on detainers[1]

When a defendant is serving time in federal custody or in one state and criminal charges are pending against him in another state or in a federal court, the jurisdiction in which charges are pending should make a diligent effort to obtain custody over him and to try him, if he demands a trial; failure to do so is a violation of the Sixth Amendment right to a speedy trial, which applies to the states through the Fourteenth Amendment.[2] In order to minimize the uncertainties resulting from outstanding criminal charges against a prisoner by another jurisdiction, Georgia has become a party to the Interstate Agreement on Detainers.[3] Forty-seven other states, the District of Columbia, Puerto Rico, and the Virgin Islands have also become parties to the

---

[41]Williamson v. State, 321 Ga. App. 25, 740 S.E.2d 841 (2013). See Hubbard v. State, 254 Ga. 694, 333 S.E.2d 827 (1985).

[42]18 U.S.C.A. §§ 3161 et seq. Generally, see Russ and Mandelkern, "The Speedy Trial Act of 1974: A Trap for the Unwary Practitioner," 2 Nat'l J. Crim. Def. 1 (1976).

[Section 14:71]

[1]See Annot., "Validity, Construction, and Application of Interstate Agreement on Detainers," 98 A.L.R.3d 160 (1980). Also see United States v. Fusco, 436 U.S. 340, 98 S.Ct. 1834, 56 L.Ed.2d 329 (1978), for an interesting discussion of the agreement. A de-

tainer is defined as "a written instrument executed by the prosecuting officer of a court and filed with the department requesting that the department retain custody of an inmate pending delivery of the inmate to the proper authorities to stand trial upon a pending indictment or accusation contain[ing] a statement that the prosecuting officer desires and intends to bring the inmate to trial upon the pending indictment or accusation. . . ." O.C.G.A. § 42-6-1.

[2]Smith v. Hooey, 393 U.S. 374, 89 S.Ct. 575, 21 L.Ed.2d 607 (1969).

[3]O.C.G.A. §§ 42-6-20 et seq.

agreement.[4] The Agreement provides that a prisoner serving a sentence in another state which has a similar statute in effect may obtain a prompt[5] trial in Georgia or have the detainer lifted. The statute, being reciprocal,[6] provides the procedures by which another state can gain custody over and try a prisoner serving a sentence in Georgia.

The purpose of the Agreement is to encourage the expeditious and orderly disposition of charges that are outstanding against prisoners incarcerated in other states, as well as the expeditious and orderly determination of the proper status of detainers based on untried indictments, informations, or complaints.[7] The Agreement promotes cooperative procedures between the party states to effectuate proceedings relating to charges and detainers originating from another jurisdiction.[8] However, the Agreement or Act does not apply until the defendant has been indicted.[9]

Custody of a prisoner may be temporarily changed from the "Sending State" (where the prisoner is incarcerated at the time change of custody proceedings are initiated)[10] to the "Receiving State" (where the trial is to be held)[11] in order to achieve a final disposition of all untried indictments, informations, and complaints on which detainers have been filed against the prisoner, and any other charges arising out of the same transaction.[12] However, the Agreement has no application to mere arrest warrants. The charging instrument must be one upon which the state can proceed to trial such as an indictment, information or complaint.[13]

Temporary change of custody of a prisoner may be brought about in two ways.[14] When a prisoner is incarcerated in a party state, and in another party state there is pending any untried indictment, information, or complaint for which a detainer has

---

[4]Carchman v. Nash, 473 U.S. 716, 105 S.Ct. 3401, 87 L.Ed.2d 516 (1985). In Duchac v. State, 151 Ga. App. 374, 259 S.E.2d 740 (1979), the court said 45 states have adopted the Act.

[5]The Agreement provides that the defendant's trial shall commence within 120 days of his arrival in the receiving state. O.C.G.A. § 42-6-20 (Art. IV(c)) . However, reasonable continuances may be granted for good cause shown in open court in the presence of the defendant or his counsel. O.C.G.A. § 42-6-20 (Art. IV(c)) ; Reaves v. State, 242 Ga. 542, 553, 250 S.E.2d 376 (1978).

[6]O.C.G.A. § 42-6-20.

[7]O.C.G.A. § 42-6-20 (Art. I) .

[8]O.C.G.A. § 42-6-20 (Art. I) .

[9]Bernyk v. State, 182 Ga. App. 329, 330 (1), 355 S.E.2d 753 (1987).

[10]O.C.G.A. § 42-6-20 (Art. II(b)) .

[11]O.C.G.A. § 42-6-20 (Art. II(c)) .

[12]O.C.G.A. § 42-6-20 (Art. II(b), (c), Art. V(d)) .

[13]State v. Carlton, 276 Ga. 693, 583 S.E.2d 1 (2003).

[14]O.C.G.A. §§ 42-6-20 (Art. III) (prisoner's request for final disposition), 42-6-20 (Art. IV) (receiving state's request for custody or availability).

been lodged against the prisoner, the prisoner may request in writing that a final disposition be made of the indictment, information, or complaint.[15]

The written request for final disposition is delivered to the warden or any other proper authority having custody over the prisoner.[16] Article III(b) of the Interstate Agreement on Detainers provides: "The written notice and request for final disposition referred to in paragraph (a) hereof *shall* be given or sent by the prisoner to the warden, commissioner of corrections or other official having custody of him, who *shall* promptly forward it together with the certificate *to the appropriate prosecuting official and court by registered or certified mail or statutory overnight delivery, return receipt requested.*"[17] The notice requirements of Article III(b) must be strictly complied with. Therefore, in *Clater v. State,*[18] the court held that "[t]he facsimile transmission of the request . . . [does] not satisfy the requirement . . . that the request shall be sent by registered or certified mail [or statutory overnight delivery], return receipt requested."

The material required to be sent, along with a certificate from the proper official exercising custody over the prisoner (stating time served, good-time earned, etc.) is forwarded to the appropriate prosecuting official and court of the receiving state.[19] The prisoner will be entitled to a trial within 180 days[20] after the Certificate of Inmate's Status is submitted to the official having custody of him.[21] However, in *Fex v. Michigan,*[22] the United States Supreme Court held that the 180 day period does not begin to

---

[15]O.C.G.A. § 42-6-20 (Art. III(a)).

[16]O.C.G.A. § 42-6-20 (Art. III(b)).

[17]O.C.G.A. § 42-6-20 (Art. III(b)) (emphasis added).

[18]Clater v. State, 266 Ga. 511, 512 (3), 467 S.E.2d 537 (1996) (emphasis in original).

[19]O.C.G.A. § 42-6-20 (Art. III(a)). In Reed v. Stynchcombe, 249 Ga. 344, 290 S.E.2d 469 (1982), the court pointed out that the absence of the certificate is fatal to the claim.

[20]O.C.G.A. § 42-6-20 (Art. III(a)). For good cause shown in open court, in the presence of the defendant or his counsel, reasonable continuances may be granted. See n. 5, supra.

In Duchac v. State, 151 Ga. App. 374, 377, 259 S.E.2d 740 (1979), the court held that where the defendant properly requested a final disposition

under the Agreement, no continuances were obtained and no circumstances justifying the tolling of the 180-day period appeared in the record, it was error not to dismiss the indictment with prejudice. For cases involving the failure of the prisoner to properly and completely comply with the provisions of O.C.G.A. § 42-6-20 (Art. III) , see Johnson v. State, 154 Ga. App. 512, 268 S.E.2d 782 (1980), and Greathouse v. State, 156 Ga. App. 491, 274 S.E.2d 835 (1980).

Cf. Reed v. Farley, 512 U.S. 339, 114 S.Ct. 2291, 129 L.Ed.2d 277 (1994). In Georgia the time for trial is 180 days, not 120 days as it is in Indiana.

[21]Thompson v. State, 186 Ga. App. 379, 381, 367 S.E.2d 247 (1988).

[22]Fex v. Michigan, 507 U.S. 43, 113 S.Ct. 1085, 122 L.Ed.2d 406 (1993).

run "until the prisoner's request for final disposition . . . has actually been delivered to the court and prosecuting officer of the jurisdiction that lodged the detainer against him." In *Parrott v. State*,[23] the court pointed out that a reasonable continuance can be granted where necessary. The agreement provides that a motion for continuance is to be made "in open court with the prisoner or his counsel being present."[24] In *Carchman v. Nash*,[25] the United States Supreme Court held that this time limitation does not apply to detainers which are based on probation violation charges. The prisoner's request for final disposition constitutes consent to the production of his body in any court where his presence may be required to effectuate the purposes of the Agreement and also constitutes consent to be returned to the original place of incarceration pursuant to the terms of the Agreement.[26]

In *New York v. Hill*,[27] the United States Supreme Court held that a defendant waived his right to be tried within 180 days where he agreed to a trial date beyond the 180 day period.

A request for final disposition by the prisoner is also deemed to constitute a waiver of extradition with respect to any charge or proceeding to which the Agreement is applicable, and also constitutes a waiver of extradition to the receiving state for purposes of serving his sentence there, after he completes his sentence in the sending state.[28]

Should the prisoner escape after the execution of his request for final disposition, the request becomes void.[29]

The second method of temporarily changing the custody of a prisoner is provided in O.C.G.A. § 42-6-20 (Art. IV). The appropriate officer of any party state in which an untried indictment, information, or complaint is pending may have a prisoner, against whom he has lodged a detainer, made available by making a written request for temporary custody or availability to the proper officials in the party state in which the prisoner is incarcerated.[30] The sending state then has 30 days to process the request, during which time the governor of the sending state may disapprove the request, upon either his motion or upon a motion

---

[23]Parrott v. State, 206 Ga. App. 829, 834 (4), 427 S.E.2d 276 (1992).

[24]O.C.G.A. § 42-6-20 (Art. III (a)) . Cf. Judge v. State, 240 Ga. App. 541, 542 (1), 524 S.E.2d 4 (1999).

[25]Carchman v. Nash, 473 U.S. 716, 105 S.Ct. 3401, 87 L.Ed.2d 516 (1985).

[26]O.C.G.A. § 42-6-20 (Art. III(e)) .

[27]New York v. Hill, 528 U.S. 110, 120 S.Ct. 659, 145 L.Ed.2d 560 (2000).

[28]O.C.G.A. § 42-6-20 (Art. III(e)) . This section also provides that the sentence handed down by the receiving state may run concurrently with the sentence the prisoner is serving in the sending state if otherwise permissible by law.

[29]O.C.G.A. § 42-6-20 (Art. III(f)) .

[30]O.C.G.A. § 42-6-20 (Art. IV(a)) .

by the prisoner himself.[31] Although under certain circumstances the prisoner may have the right to contest the legality of the transfer of custody, he may not do so on the grounds that the governor of the sending state did not affirmatively consent to or order such transfer.[32] In fact there are only four issues which may be raised by a defendant. They are the same issues which may be raised at extradition hearings, to-wit: "a) whether the . . . documents on their face are in order; b) where the petitioner has been charged with a crime in the demanding state; c) whether the petitioner is the person named in the request . . .; and d) whether the petitioner is a fugitive."[33]

When the officials of the sending state receive the written request for temporary custody, they then furnish the requesting officer with a certificate stating the length of the prisoner's term, the amount of time left to serve and the length of time served, the amount of good time earned, when the prisoner is eligible for parole, and decisions made by the state parole agency.[34] Simultaneously, the sending state furnishes all other officers and courts in the receiving state who had lodged detainers against the prisoner with similar certificates, informing them of the request for custody or availability and the reasons therefor.[35]

After the prisoner arrives in the receiving state, trial must commence within 120 days.[36] If a trial on any indictment, information, or complaint is not had before the prisoner is returned to the place where he was originally incarcerated, such indictment, information, or complaint becomes null and void and must be dismissed with prejudice.[37]

---

[31]O.C.G.A. § 42-6-20 (Art. IV(a)) .

[32]O.C.G.A. § 42-6-20 (Art. IV(d)) .

[33]Lambert v. Jones, 250 Ga. 603, 604, 299 S.E.2d 716 (1983).

[34]O.C.G.A. § 42-6-20 (Art. IV(b)) .

[35]O.C.G.A. § 42-6-20 (Art. IV(b)).

[36]O.C.G.A. § 42-6-20 (Art. IV(c)) . As noted previously (nn. 5 and 19, supra), reasonable continuances may be granted.

[37]O.C.G.A. § 42-6-20 (Art. IV(e)) ; Morrison v. State, 280 Ga. 222, 626 S.E.2d 500 (2006); State v. Thompson, 284 Ga. App. 744, 644 S.E.2d 889 (2007). Compare Barton v. Atkinson, 228 Ga. 733(1), 187 S.E.2d 835 (1972). In Braden v. Kentucky, 410 U.S. 484, 93 S.Ct. 1123, 35 L.Ed.2d 443 (1973),

Braden was indicted in Kentucky. He escaped from custody before trial and went to Alabama, where he was convicted of felonies and imprisoned. A Kentucky detainer was lodged against him, and he requested a speedy trial in that state. He remained in Alabama and was not tried in Kentucky; he then filed a federal habeas corpus action in Kentucky, contending that he had been denied a speedy trial. The court in effect approved an order of the federal district court that ordered Kentucky to try Braden within 60 days or dismiss the indictment.

In Cobb v. State, 244 Ga. 344, 346 (1), 260 S.E.2d 60 (1979), the court found that the 120-day time limit was tolled by defendant's numerous pre-trial motions.

In *Alabama v. Bozeman,*[38] the United States Supreme Court pointed out that the defendant must be tried within the statutory time. If during that time the defendant is returned to his "original place of imprisonment" prior to the expiration of that time, the charges against him shall be dismissed with prejudice. In *Bozeman,* the court held that even a very brief violation of this rule requires dismissal of the case.

For the procedure by which custody of prisoners is transferred pursuant to the Agreement, see O.C.G.A. § 42-6-20 (Art. V) .

The United States Supreme Court has upheld the constitutionality of the Interstate Agreement on Detainers over claims that the Agreement violates the Sixth, Eighth, and Fourteenth Amendments.[39] The same court has also held that the writ of habeas corpus ad prosequendum is not a detainer within the meaning of the Agreement.[40]

It has been held that where outstanding detainers are based on probation or parole violations, they are not based on "untried" charges as the Agreement requires and hence, a prisoner cannot request final disposition of such charges.[41]

In *State v. Sassoon,*[42] the prisoner has been in federal custody. Georgia initiated change of custody proceedings, gained temporary custody of Sassoon, arraigned him, and returned him to federal custody pending his trial in Georgia. Sassoon contended that since he was returned to his original place of incarceration without being tried on the charge, the charge must be dismissed pursuant to O.C.G.A. § 42-6-20 (Art. V(e)) . The Georgia Supreme Court assumed but did not decide that a technical violation of this provision had taken place; the Court refused to dismiss the charge, finding that a brief removal of a prisoner to the receiving

---

[38]Alabama v. Bozeman, 533 U.S. 146, 121 S.Ct. 2079, 150 L.Ed.2d 188 (2001).

[39]Pollard v. State, 128 Ga. App. 470 (2), 197 S.E.2d 158 (1973); Cuyler v. Adams, 449 U.S. 433, 101 S.Ct. 703, 66 L.Ed.2d 641 (1981). In *Cuyler,* the court also held that because the Agreement is an interstate compact approved by Congress, interpretation of the Agreement presents a federal question, even where the dispute is between two states and the United States is not a party to the action. Finally, the court concluded that as a matter of federal law, prisoners transferred pursuant to the Agreement do not forfeit any pre-existing rights they may have under state or federal law

to challenge the legality of their transfer.

[40]United States v. Mauro, 436 U.S. 340, 98 S.Ct. 1834, 56 L.Ed.2d 329 (1978). The court noted that a detainer puts prison officials on notice that a prisoner is wanted by another jurisdiction upon his release, while the writ, authorized by statute in the federal courts, requires the prisoner's immediate presence. Thus, the writ does not remain lodged against prisoners for lengthy periods of time as do detainers.

[41]Suggs v. Hopper, 234 Ga. 242, 215 S.E.2d 246 (1975).

[42]State v. Sassoon, 240 Ga. 745, 242 S.E.2d 121 (1978).

jurisdiction for an arraignment and his prompt return to the sending state pending trial was consonant with the policy of the Agreement.

See O.C.G.A. §§ 42-6-1 through 42-6-6 for provisions regarding prisoners within Georgia. Generally, on the Interstate Act, see 21 Am. Jur. Criminal Law § 404 (1981). See also Interstate Agreement on Detainers Act, 98 A.L.R.3d 160. See § 14:96, infra, on the Uniform Act to Secure the Attendance of Witnesses from Without the State. See § 14:69, supra, for a request for trial by an inmate serving in custody of the Georgia Department of Corrections. See § 2:23, supra, on extraditions.

§ 14:72 Motion to sever—Parties

Georgia law was radically changed, for purposes of judicial economy in 1971 and 1972, so as to permit the joint trial of two or more defendants.[1] O.C.G.A. § 17-8-4 provides that any defendant who is jointly indicted with another for a capital offense is still entitled to be tried separately, unless he agrees to be tried with the other defendant or co-defendants, or the state agrees to waive the death penalty. When defendants are tried for a case in which "the death penalty is waived, or for a felony less than capital, or for a misdemeanor, such defendants may [generally] be tried jointly or separately in the discretion of the trial court."[2]

Formerly, there was authority in Georgia drawing a distinction between a motion to sever where separate indictments were returned against two defendants and the situation where a single indictment charged two defendants with a crime. It was said that defendants have a right to have separate trials if they were indicted separately.[3] However, more recently the distinction has been disapproved[4] and the present rule is that the same criteria are to be applied in determining whether the trial judge is to grant a severance, regardless of whether or not there is one indictment against two defendants or more, or a separate indictment against each defendant.[5]

[Section 14:72]

[1] Under the former law, if two or more persons were jointly indicted, it was necessary to have separate trials unless the defendants agreed to be tried together.

[2] O.C.G.A. § 17-8-4. See Durham v. State, 240 Ga. 203, 240 S.E.2d 14 (1977).

[3] State v. Connelly, 138 Ga. App. 121, 225 S.E.2d 519 (1976).

[4] Allen v. State, 144 Ga. App. 233, 234 (2), 240 S.E.2d 754 (1977).

[5] Allen v. State, 144 Ga. App. 233, 234 (2), 240 S.E.2d 754 (1977) (citing and relying on Padgett v. State, 239 Ga. 556, 238 S.E.2d 92 (1977)).

In *Wilkerson v. State*,[6] the court pointed out that the Supreme Court of Georgia, in cases involving multiple defendants, has urged trial courts "to give a separate instruction which details the jury's duty to consider each charge in the indictment against each defendant separately and which reminds the jury that the guilt of one defendant does not require the return of a guilty verdict against the other defendant."

In *Padgett v. State*,[7] the Georgia Supreme Court held that there may be a joinder of defendants and related offenses. However, in *Nicholson v. State*,[8] the court, although finding no error, pointed out that it is a better practice for the trial judge, in a trial of joint defendants, to give separate instructions detailing the jury's duty to consider each charge in the indictment against each defendant separately and remind the jury that the finding of the guilt of one defendant does not require a finding of the guilt of the other defendant.

If a defendant wants to be tried separately, he must file a motion to sever. Georgia appellate courts have indicated that, except in the case of a capital felony, it is never error to fail to sever where a motion for severance is not filed.[9] Thus, where the state's motion for severance was denied, a defendant cannot complain of the overruling of the motion where he did not file such a motion himself.[10] "Similarly, a defendant who does not join his co-defendant's motion to sever before or during trial waives that right absent an abuse of discretion by the trial court."[11]

In *Morris v. State*,[12] the court held that a severance should be granted "before or during the trial whenever it appears 'necessary to achieve a fair determination of the guilt or innocence of a defendant.' "

While the trial judge has the power to determine whether a party should be severed on a proper motion, there are definite limitations on his discretion. According to the Georgia Supreme

---

[6]Wilkerson v. State, 244 Ga. App. 307, 535 S.E.2d 505 (2000).

[7]Padgett v. State, 239 Ga. 556, 238 S.E.2d 92 (1977) (two or more defendants charged with different offenses may be tried together where the offenses were part of a common scheme, but on motion, severance should be granted where court finds that such promotes fair determination of the charges against each defendant).

[8]Nicholson v. State, 265 Ga. 711, 714 (3), 462 S.E.2d 144 (1995).

[9]Worley v. State, 237 Ga. 521,

228 S.E.2d 895 (1976); Lenear v. State, 239 Ga. 617, 619 (6), 238 S.E.2d 407 (1977).

[10]Ingram v. State, 137 Ga. App. 412, 224 S.E.2d 527 (1976); Way v. State, 239 Ga. 316 (2), 236 S.E.2d 655 (1977).

[11]Smith v. State, 267 Ga. 372, 373 (2), 477 S.E.2d 827 (1996).

[12]Morris v. State, 204 Ga. App. 437 (1), 419 S.E.2d 733 (1992) (quoting Terry v. State, 190 Ga. App. 570, 379 S.E.2d 604 (1989)).

Court, the trial judge should consider the following questions: "(1) Will the number of defendants create confusion of the evidence and law applicable to each individual defendant? (2) Is there a danger that evidence admissible against one defendant will be considered against another despite the admonitory precaution of the court? (3) Are the defenses of the defendants antagonistic to each other or to each other's rights?"[13]

If the defendant can show that failure to sever will prejudice him under one or more of these considerations, his motion should presumably be granted.[14] Thus, a trial judge should grant a severance whenever it is necessary to achieve a fair determination of the guilt or innocence of a defendant.[15] However, an appellate court will not hold that the denial of a motion to sever is an abuse of discretion unless it appears that the defendant suffered prejudice which amounted to a denial of due process.[16] In *Linares*

---

[13]Adams v. State, 264 Ga. 71 (3), 440 S.E.2d 639 (1994); Cain v. State, 235 Ga. 128, 129, 218 S.E.2d 856 (1975); Chandler v. State, 213 Ga. App. 46 (1), 443 S.E.2d 679 (1994). In Birge v. State, 143 Ga. App. 632, 634 (3), 239 S.E.2d 395 (1977), the court said that antagonism alone is not sufficient to require separate trials. Accord, Whitlock v. State, 148 Ga. App. 203 (2), 251 S.E.2d 59 (1978). See Stephens v. State, 170 Ga. App. 267 (1), 316 S.E.2d 847 (1984); Marlow v. State, 207 Ga. App. 269, 271 (1), 427 S.E.2d 600 (1993). See Brinson v. State, 288 Ga. 435, 704 S.E.2d 756 (2011) (fact that a co-defendant may offer witness testimony antagonistic to defendant is insufficient for severance, because co-defendant could have offered the same testimony at a separate trial.

[14]Cain v. State, 235 Ga. 128, 129, 218 S.E.2d 856 (1975); Oliver v. State, 253 Ga. 284, 285, 319 S.E.2d 856 (1984). Cf. Myrick v. State, 155 Ga. App. 496, 497, 271 S.E.2d 637 (1980). In Murphy v. State, 246 Ga. 626, 629 (2), 273 S.E.2d 2 (1980), the court said that a defendant "must do more than raise the possibility that a separate trial would give him a better chance of acquittal. He must make a clear showing of prejudice and a consequent denial of due process."

[15]See A.B.A. Standards, Joinder and Severance, Vol. II, Standard 13-3.2. See also Baker v. State, 238 Ga. 389, 391 (2), 233 S.E.2d 347 (1977). Accord, Padgett v. State, 142 Ga. App. 139, 235 S.E.2d 545 (1977).

In Crawford v. State, 148 Ga. App. 523, 526, 251 S.E.2d 602 (1978), the court held that it was error not to grant a motion to sever where there was minimal evidence against the defendant and substantial evidence against the co-defendants. The court concluded that the defendant's conviction might well have resulted from a "spillover" of the evidence against the other two defendants.

[16]Owen v. State, 266 Ga. 312, 314 (2), 467 S.E.2d 325 (1996); Mayfield v. State, 220 Ga. App. 19, 20 (2), 467 S.E.2d 352 (1996); Carroll v. State, 147 Ga. App. 332, 333 (1), 248 S.E.2d 702 (1978). In Magouirk v. State, 158 Ga. App. 517, 518, 281 S.E.2d 283 (1981), the court acknowledged the following: (1) there is the possibility of incriminating evidence against one defendant being considered against another; (2) strategy may have to be altered because of co-counsel; and (3) despite the benefit to the court or the district attorney, the accused's rights to a fair trial take precedence. However, the court affirmed the denial of the severance in that case.

But in Price v. State, 155 Ga. App. 844, 846, 273 S.E.2d 225 (1980),

v. State,[17] the court held that on appeal a defendant must show "clear prejudice."

The burden is on the defendant requesting the severance to make a clear showing of prejudice.[18] He must show more than a "possibility that a separate trial would give him a better chance of acquittal."[19] The fact that two defendants are indicted and each blames the other for the crime does not necessarily mean that they were prejudiced by being tried together, even where one of the defendants is a repeat offender whose prior convictions were alleged in the indictment.[20] Severance is warranted because of the antagonistic defenses of co-defendants only where they are "antagonistic to the point of being mutually exclusive or irreconcilable, so that the jury, in order to believe the core of one defense, must necessarily disbelieve the core of the other."[21] Severance on the basis of the antagonistic defenses of co-defendants rarely occurs. Generally, a jury charge to the effect that the evi-

---

rev'd on other grounds, 247 Ga. 58, 273 S.E.2d 854 (1981), the court said that "if the defendant can demonstrate harm resulting from the failure to sever, then such failure to sever becomes error." In *Price*, the testimony was said to be overwhelming against the co-defendant and very slight against Price; the court concluded that Price made "a clear showing of prejudice and a consequent denial of due process."

[17]Linares v. State, 266 Ga. 812, 815 (4), 471 S.E.2d 208 (1996).

[18]See Zafiro v. U.S., 506 U.S. 534, 538–540, 113 S. Ct. 933, 122 L. Ed. 2d 317 (1993); U.S. v. Blankenship, 382 F.3d 1110, 1122-1124 (11th Cir. 2004); Owen v. State, 266 Ga. 312, 467 S.E.2d 325 (1996); Cain v. State, 235 Ga. 128, 129, 218 S.E.2d 856 (1975). Cf. Armour v. State, 151 Ga. App. 254, 259 S.E.2d 662 (1979). See Dawson, "Joint Trials of Defendants in Criminal Cases: An Analysis of Efficiencies and Prejudices," 77 Mich. L. Rev. 1379 (1979), in which the author refers to "the substantial risk of prejudice inherent in joint trials," and suggests that the burden of justifying a joint trial should be on the party desiring a joint trial.

[19]Stovall v. State, 236 Ga. 840, 225 S.E.2d 292 (1976) (quoting with approval from Tillman v. United States, 406 F.2d 930 (5th Cir. 1969)); Cook v. State, 221 Ga. App. 831, 832 (1), 472 S.E.2d 686 (1996); Culpepper v. State, 156 Ga. App. 331 (2), 274 S.E.2d 616 (1980). Generally, see the exhaustive Annot., "Right of Defendants in Prosecution for Criminal Conspiracy to Separate Trials," 82 A.L.R.3d 366 (1978).

[20]Davis v. State, 129 Ga. App. 796, 201 S.E.2d 345 (1973). Cf. Jordan v. State, 210 Ga. App. 30 (1), 435 S.E.2d 256 (1993). But see De Luna v. United States, 308 F.2d 140 (5th Cir. 1962), where one defendant did not testify and the other defendant stated the contraband belonged to the non-testifying defendant. The attorney for the testifying defendant argued guilt of other defendant and the fact that he did not testify. The testifying defendant was acquitted by the jury and the other was convicted. On appeal the conviction was reversed.

See *United States v. Aguiar*, § 14:58, n. 42, supra. See Annot., "Antagonistic Defenses as Ground for Separate Trials of Codefendants in Criminal Cases," 82 A.L.R.3d 245 (1978).

[21]U.S. v. Sandoval, 847 F.2d 179, 183 (5th Cir. 1988) (citations and punctuation omitted). See U.S. v. Daniels, 281 F.3d 168, 177(1) (5th Cir. 2002).

dence is to be weighed and considered as to each defendant separately is considered "to cure any prejudice caused when co-defendants accuse each other of the crime."[22] In *Dennard v. State*,[23] the court held that antagonism between co-defendants is not enough in itself to require severance.

It has been held that a severance is not required merely because there is a great amount of evidence against one defendant and a small amount of evidence against the other defendant.[24] In *Banks v. State*,[25] the court held that "[a]dmission of similar crimes evidence against a co-defendant does not mandate severance where . . . the trial judge gave specific limiting instructions regarding that evidence and the evidence itself did not implicate . . ." the complaining defendant. Moreover, in *Stevens v. State*,[26] the court pointed out that the fact that a defendant will lose the right to open and close during concluding argument does not require severance. However, a conviction was reversed where a motion to sever was denied and it appeared from the transcript that numerous disagreements existed between defense counsels with respect to the admission or exclusion of evidence.[27]

In *Brown v. State*,[28] the Georgia Supreme Court affirmed the denial of a motion to sever "based largely on the state's announced intention to introduce evidence . . . of statements, made by . . . [a co-defendant] shortly after the crime occurred, in which . . . [the co-defendant] implicated himself and . . . [Brown] in . . . [a] murder." At trial the co-defendant's statements were introduced, the co-defendant did not take the stand and was not available for cross-examination. It was held that the statements made while the co-defendant was not in custody to an acquaintance of his, and not an officer, were designated as a declaration of a conspirator not a confession and were admissible where the requirements of former O.C.G.A. § 24-3-5 (now § 24-8-801(d)(2)(E)) were met.

---

[22]U.S. v. Stouffer, 986 F.2d 916, 924(II)(C) (5th Cir. 1993).

[23]Dennard v. State, 263 Ga. 453, 455 (5), 435 S.E.2d 26 (1993), rev'd on other grounds, Sanders v. State, 281 Ga. 36(1), 635 S.E.2d 772 (2006).

[24]Kesler v. State, 249 Ga. 462, 469, 291 S.E.2d 497 (1982). In *Kesler*, the court stated that "where a conspiracy is shown, where the defenses of the co-defendants being tried are not antagonistic, and where . . . the jury is carefully instructed on conspiracy and to consider the state's case against each defendant separately," it is not an abuse of discretion to refuse to grant a motion to sever because of the hazard of the effect of the "spillover evidence" on the defendant against whom there is less evidence.

[25]Banks v. State, 230 Ga. App. 881, 882 (2), 497 S.E.2d 821 (1998).

[26]Stevens v. State, 210 Ga. App. 355, 356 (2), 436 S.E.2d 82 (1993).

[27]See Reeves v. State, 237 Ga. 1, 4, 226 S.E.2d 567 (1976); United States v. Johnson, 478 F.2d 1129, 1131 (5th Cir. 1973).

[28]Brown v. State, 262 Ga. 223, 416 S.E.2d 508 (1992).

In *Harper v. State*,[29] severance was denied where the alleged prejudice arose from contentions asserted in a non-testifying co-defendant's opening statement. While the court noted that opening statements do not constitute evidence, its holding rests on the finding that the evidence against the defendant was overwhelming and hence the refusal to sever, if made in error, was harmless. However the case does not rule out the propriety of severance where the antagonistic nature of co-defendant's defenses become prejudicial through the opening statements of one or both of the defendants.

In *Bruton v. United States*,[30] Evans and Bruton were tried together for robbery. While Evans did not testify, an officer testified to Evans' oral confession that both committed the robbery. The trial court instructed the jury that Evans' confession was inadmissible against Bruton. Both men were convicted. The United States Supreme Court reversed, since Evans did not testify and could not be cross-examined. The Georgia Supreme Court has recognized the Bruton rule and follows it.[31] In *Boone v.*

---

[29]Harper v. State, 300 Ga. App. 757, 686 S.E.2d 375 (2009). See Character v. State, 285 Ga. 112, 674 S.E.2d 280 (2009); Owen v. State, 266 Ga. 312, 467 S.E.2d 325 (1996).

[30]Bruton v. United States, 391 U.S. 123, 88 S.Ct. 1620, 20 L.Ed.2d 476 (1968). Accord, Hardy v. State, 223 Ga. App. 597, 598 (1), 478 S.E.2d 423 (1996). Cf. State v. LaBarge, 275 S.C. 168, 268 S.E.2d 278 (S.C.1980). In Rachel v. State, 247 Ga. 130, 133 (4), 274 S.E.2d 475 (1981), Rachel, Robinson and Wright had been tried for felony murder arising out of an armed robbery. Two women testified that they heard Wright say that Ruff (the victim) had a lot of money and that he could find some one "to do him in." Both women testified that they thought Wright was kidding and he said he was kidding. The only other evidence offered linking Wright to the crime was the confession of Robinson, who did not testify at the trial. Wright had moved for a severance, but did not give the confession of Robinson as a reason for severance. The court reversed Wright's conviction for the Bruton violation.

In Holloway v. State, 168 Ga. App. 294, 296 (4), 308 S.E.2d 641 (1983), the court held that there is no Bruton violation where the confessing defendant testified at trial.

In Davis v. State, 154 Ga. App. 357, 268 S.E.2d 409 (1980), the defendant and a co-defendant were tried for rape. The co-defendant did not testify, but a statement of the co-defendant was admitted in which he admitted having sexual relations with the prosecutrix. The court held that this was not a Bruton violation.

See Marcus, "The Confrontation Clause and Co-Defendant Confessions: The Drift From Bruton to Parker v. Randolph," 1979 U. Ill. L. F. 559 (1979); Hadad, "Post-Bruton Developments: A Reconsideration of the Confrontation Rationale, and a Proposal for a Due Process Evaluation of Limiting Instructions," 18 Am. Crim. L. Rev. 1 (1980).

[31]See Reeves v. State, 237 Ga. 1, 3, 226 S.E.2d 567 (1976); Knowles v. State, 246 Ga. 378, 385 (11), 271 S.E.2d 615 (1980), overruled on other grounds by Hanifa v. State, 269 Ga. 797, 505 S.E.2d 371 (1998); Hall v. State, 161 Ga. App. 521, 522, 289 S.E.2d 313 (1982).

State,[32] the court summarized *Bruton* by stating that "a defendant's Sixth Amendment right of confrontation is violated when: (a) co-defendants are tried jointly, (b) one co-defendant's statement is used to implicate the other co-defendant in the crime, and (c) the co-defendant who made the implicating statement employs the Fifth Amendment right not to testify and thus does not take the stand to face cross-examination about the statement." However, the mere finding of a violation of the Bruton rule does not automatically require a reversal,[33] and there is no violation of the Bruton rule if all defendants testify and can be cross-examined.[34] In order "[f]or the admission of a co-defendant's statements to constitute a *Bruton* violation, the statements *standing alone* must *clearly inculpate* the defendant."[35] It has been held that there is no Bruton violation where two defendants are tried together and one has given a confession which does not incriminate the other defendant and where the confessing defendant does not testify.[36] In *Morton v. State*,[37] the Georgia Court of Appeals "held that there is no Bruton violation when the testimony presented by the co-defendant's confession is supported by the complaining defendant's own confession."

It has been held that *Bruton* does not apply to the non-custodial statements (as opposed to a confession) of a co-defendant which implicate the defendant. The Georgia Supreme Court has observed that in such cases the appropriate analysis is whether

[32]Boone v. State, 250 Ga. App. 133, 135 (2), 549 S.E.2d 713 (2001).

[33]Reddish v. State, 238 Ga. 136, 138, 231 S.E.2d 737 (1977). In this case, the court pointed out that unless there was a reasonable possibility that the improperly admitted evidence contributed to the conviction, a reversal is not necessary.

In Depree v. State, 246 Ga. 240, 241 (1), 271 S.E.2d 155 (1980), the court approved the editing of a confession of one of the defendants on trial, so that it would not identify another defendant who was on trial. However, when the confessing defendant took the stand to denounce a part of the statement, the state was free to cross-examine him about the identity of the other participant.

In Brown v. State, 164 Ga. App. 505 (2), 296 S.E.2d 215 (1982), the court said "when a co-defendant's confession is edited so as to delete all reference to another defendant,

whether by name or by other identifying phrases, the confession is admissible at a joint trial." Cf. Blue v. State, 168 Ga. App. 868 (1), 310 S.E.2d 748 (1983).

[34]Durham v. State, 240 Ga. 203, 204 (2), 240 S.E.2d 14 (1977). In Tifford v. Wainwright, 588 F.2d 954 (5th Cir. 1979), a petition for habeas corpus was granted where plaintiff's motion to sever had been denied, preventing plaintiff's use of exculpatory testimony which would have been available if there had been separate trials.

[35]Thomas v. State, 268 Ga. 135, 137 (a), 485 S.E.2d 783 (1997). See Wallace v. State, 267 Ga. App. 801 (4), 600 S.E.2d 808 (2004) (citations and punctuation omitted; emphasis in original).

[36]Mock v. State, 163 Ga. App. 319, 294 S.E.2d 361 (1982).

[37]Morton v. State, 181 Ga. App. 781 (1), 353 S.E.2d 852 (1987).

the statement is admissible under the co-conspirator exception to the hearsay rule.[38] However, in *Colton v. State*,[39] the Court held that such statements are subject to exclusion under *Crawford v. Washington*[40] where they are of a testimonial character. The distinction in the cases is between statements made by the declarant to the police during the course of an investigation and those made by a non-testifying co-defendant who is not in custody to an acquaintence rather than a police officer. See Studdard, *Daniel's Georgia Handbook on Criminal Evidence* § 8:9 (2018 ed.) on conspiracy hearsay exception.

In *Parker v. Randolph*,[41] in 1979, the United States Supreme Court held that when a defendant's confession agrees with a co-defendant's confession, the confessions are admissible against both defendants when the court gives a limiting instruction. Georgia courts have followed this holding. However, the *Parker* holding was rejected by the United States Supreme Court in 1987 in *Cruz v. New York*,[42] which holds that use of a nontestifying co-defendant's confession incriminating the defendant is a violation of the Confrontation Clause even if the jury is instructed not to consider it against the defendant and even if the defendant's own confession is admitted into evidence. The court went on to say that this violation may be rendered harmless by the introduction of the defendant's interlocking confession. In *Hanifa v. State*,[43] the Georgia Supreme Court followed *Cruz* and, in doing so, overruled many Georgia cases which had relied on *Parker*.[44] In *Hanifa* the Court held:

---

[38]See Burgess v. State, 278 Ga. 314, 602 S.E.2d 566 (2004); Neason v. State, 277 Ga. 789, 596 S.E.2d 120 (2004); Fetty v. State, 268 Ga. 365, 489 S.E.2d 813 (1997).

[39]Colton v. State, 292 Ga. 509, 739 S.E.2d 380 (2013).

[40]Crawford v. Washington, 541 U.S. 36, 124 S. Ct. 1354, 158 L. Ed. 2d 177, 63 Fed. R. Evid. Serv. 1077 (2004).

[41]Parker v. Randolph, 442 U.S. 62, 99 S.Ct. 2132, 60 L.Ed.2d 713 (1979).

[42]Cruz v. New York, 481 U.S. 186, 107 S.Ct. 1714, 95 L.Ed.2d 162 (1987).

[43]Hanifa v. State, 269 Ga. 797, 505 S.E.2d 731 (1998). However, in the Eighth Circuit (en banc) case of United States v. Logan, 210 F.3d 820 (8th Cir. 2000), the court held that a co-defendant's confession could be sanitized by substituting "another individ-

ual" for the name of the non-confessing defendant.

[44]Georgia cases overruled by Hanifa v. State, 269 Ga. 797, 505 S.E.2d 731 (1998), include Freeman v. State, 265 Ga. 709 (1), 462 S.E.2d 139 (1995); Satterfield v. State, 256 Ga. 593, 351 S.E.2d 625 (1987); Allen v. State, 255 Ga. 513, 516, 340 S.E.2d 187 (1986); Tatum v. State, 249 Ga. 422, 291 S.E.2d 701 (1982); Fortner v. State, 248 Ga. 107 (1), 281 S.E.2d 533 (1981); Knowles v. State, 246 Ga. 378 (4), 271 S.E.2d 615 (1980); Casper v. State, 244 Ga. 689 (1), 261 S.E.2d 629 (1979); Hall v. State, 230 Ga. App. 378 (1), 496 S.E.2d 475 (1998); Sawyer v. State, 217 Ga. App. 406 (1), 457 S.E.2d 685 (1995); Kesler v. State, 215 Ga. App. 553 (1), 451 S.E.2d 496 (1994); Yeargin v. State, 164 Ga. App. 835 (4), 298 S.E.2d 606 (1982); Edwards v. State, 162 Ga. App. 216 (1), 290 S.E.2d 553 (1982).

Unless the statement is otherwise directly admissible against the defendant, the Confrontation Clause is violated by the admission of a nontestifying co-defendant's statement which inculpates the defendant by referring to the defendant's name or existence, regardless of the existence of limiting instructions and of whether the incriminated defendant made an interlocking incriminating statement.

A co-defendant's statement meets the Confrontation Clause's standard for admissibility when it does not refer to the existence of the defendant and is accompanied by instructions limiting its use to the case against the confessing co-defendant. The fact that the jury might infer from the contents of the co-defendant's statement in conjunction with other evidence, that the defendant was involved does not make the admission of the co-defendant's statement a violation of the Confrontation Clause.[45]

The court then went on to hold that although a violation had occurred, it was harmless based on the evidence, which included the defendant's statement that she was present at the scene of the crime, that she was aware of the criminal acts of others, and her own admission to limited participation in the assaults.

On the same day of the opinion in *Cruz,* the United States Supreme Court handed down an opinion in *Richardson v. Marsh,*[46] which also involved the Bruton rule. In *Richardson,* the court found no Bruton violation and summarized its holding as follows: "[T]he Confrontation Clause is not violated by the admission of a nontestifying codefendant's confession with a proper limiting instruction when, as here, the confession is redacted to eliminate not only the defendant's name, but any reference to [the] existence [of the defendant]." The court pointed out that the confession in *Richardson* "was not incriminating on its face, and became so only when linked with evidence introduced later at trial (the defendant's own testimony). . . . Where the necessity of such linkage is involved, it is a less valid generalization that the jury will not likely obey the instruction to disregard the evidence."

In *Bryant v. State,*[47] the Georgia Supreme Court affirmed the trial court in denying motions to sever where "each co-defendant's custodial statement was extensively redacted prior to its introduction, in accordance with *Bruton.* . . . When the . . . [defendants'] statements were introduced, the trial court clearly instructed the jury that each statement was admissible only against the declarant, and did not impact upon the adjudication of the other co-defendants' guilt or innocence. After the admission of all the

---

[45]Hanifa v. State, 269 Ga. 797, 803 (2), 505 S.E.2d 731 (1998).

[46]Richardson v. Marsh, 481 U.S. 200, 107 S.Ct. 1702, 95 L.Ed.2d 176 (1987). Cf. Harris v. State, 218 Ga. App. 472, 473-74 (2), 462 S.E.2d 425 (1995).

[47]Bryant v. State, 270 Ga. 266, 269-270 (2), 507 S.E.2d 451 (1998).

custodial statements, the trial court again gave . . . [a] limiting instruction."

In the 1998 case of *Gray v. Maryland,*[48] the United States Supreme Court held that redacting a confession by substituting a blank space or the word "deleted" for the name of one defendant amounted to a Bruton violation. In *McDonald v. State,*[49] the court held that the use of a statement given by a co-defendant who did not testify was a Bruton violation where the state simply replaced the name of the co-defendant with a blank. Also, where a defendant was on trial with two co-defendants who made statements but only one testified, and each statement had blanks left for two persons, the court concluded that since the defendant had two co-defendants, the jury would readily fill in the blanks with the names of the co-defendants. In *United States v. Gonzalez,*[50] the Eleventh Circuit held that it was error for the redacted statement to refer to the number of co-defendants.

In *Owens v. State,*[51] the court stated that "[f]or the admission of a co-defendant's statements to constitute a Bruton violation, however, the statements *standing alone* must *clearly inculpate the defendant.*" (Emphasis by the court.) In *Hicks v. State,*[52] the court held that there was no Bruton violation "where the incriminating statements were made shortly after the crime[,] . . . were made prior to arrest, and were non-custodial statements made to acquaintances . . . rather than to police . . . [and] the requirements of [former] O.C.G.A. § 24-3-5 [now § 24-8-801(d)(2)(E)] have been met."

In *Alexander v. State,*[53] the court pointed out that the factors to be considered in determining whether a violation of *Bruton* is harmful include (1) the importance of the witness' testimony in the prosecution's case, (2) whether the testimony was cumulative, (3) the presence or absence of evidence corroborating or contradicting the testimony of the witness on material points, (4) the extent of cross-examination otherwise permitted, and (5) the overall strength of the prosecution's case. However, in *Collins v.*

---

[48]Gray v. Maryland, 523 U.S. 185, 118 S.Ct. 1151, 140 L.Ed.2d 294 (1998). In *Gray* the court held that "to replace the [defendant's name] with an obvious blank will not likely fool anyone."

[49]McDonald v. State, 210 Ga. App. 689, 690 (2), 436 S.E.2d 811 (1993).

[50]United States v. Gonzalez, 183 F.3d 1315 (1999).

[51]Owens v. State, 193 Ga. App. 661, 662 (3), 388 S.E.2d 712 (1989);

Baugher v. State, 212 Ga. App. 7, 440 S.E.2d 768 (1994). Accord, Owen v. State, 266 Ga. 312, 314 (4), 467 S.E.2d 325 (1996); Moore v. State, 224 Ga. App. 797, 799 (2), 481 S.E.2d 892 (1997).

[52]Hicks v. State, 262 Ga. 756 (1), 425 S.E.2d 877 (1993).

[53]Alexander v. State, 236 Ga. App. 142, 145, 511 S.E.2d 249 (1999).

State,[54] the court held "to be harmless, a Bruton error must be harmless beyond a reasonable doubt."

In the unusual case of *Martin v. State,*[55] the motion to sever had been denied, and two defendants were tried together. One of the defendants had stipulated the admissibility of the result of a polygraph examination. The examiner was permitted to testify against the defendant who had been examined. The court concluded that this did not amount to a Bruton violation.

The use of multiple juries is another method that has been occasionally employed as an alternative to severance as a means of avoiding the Bruton problem. Although the use of multiple juries has been upheld on appeal, it has not been well received by appellate courts.[56]

The Bruton rule does not apply to non-jury trials.[57] However, in a bench trial the trial judge may not consider any testimony which violates the Bruton rule as substantive evidence. That is, in the absence of "indicia of reliability" there is a weighty presumption against the admission of uncross-examined evidence contained in a co-defendant's earlier confession.[58]

In a joint trial of more than one defendant, defense counsel may be prejudiced by not having as many jury strikes available where only one client is being tried. By statute, however, the trial judge, upon request, is required to allow an equal number of additional strikes, not to exceed five, to each defendant. Also, the trial judge "may allow the state additional strikes not to exceed

---

[54]Collins v. State, 242 Ga. App. 450, 452 (1), 529 S.E.2d 412 (2000) (quoting Schneble v. Florida, 405 U.S. 427, 92 S.Ct. 1056, 31 L.Ed.2d 340 (1972)).

[55]Martin v. State, 162 Ga. App. 703, 704 (3), 292 S.E.2d 864 (1982). However, in Martin, Judges Pope and Sognier only concurred in the affirmance.

[56]In Ewish v. State, 110 Nev. 221, 871 P.2d 306 (1994), the court affirmed a conviction where multiple juries were used. However, the court concluded that multiple juries should not be used until courts have guidelines for their use.

The use of two juries was also reluctantly approved in State v. Corsi, 86 N.J. 172, 430 A.2d 210 (1981). In this case, there was some evidence which was admissible against one defendant but not the other. A motion to sever was denied by the trial judge, but he did grant the application for two juries. Separate opening statements and closing arguments were made. Evidence admissible against both defendants was presented to the two juries jointly. When evidence was presented which was admissible against only one defendant, the jury trying the other defendant was removed from the courtroom. Each jury was charged separately and, of course, the juries returned separate verdicts. Cf. People v. Rainge, 112 Ill.App.3d 396, 68 Ill.Dec. 87, 445 N.E.2d 535 (1983); People v. Church, 102 Ill.App.3d 155, 57 Ill.Dec. 679, 429 N.E.2d 577 (1981).

[57]Rogers v. McMackin, 884 F.2d 252 (6th Cir. 1989).

[58]Lee v. Illinois, 476 U.S. 530, 546, 106 S.Ct. 2056, 90 L.Ed.2d 514 (1986).

the number of additional strikes as are allowed to the defendants."[59] See § 18:30, infra, on peremptory strikes.

In *DeLuna v. United States*,[60] the Fifth Circuit held that "[w]hen one of two defendants jointly tried . . . exercises his right not to testify . . . the Fifth Amendment protects him from prejudicial comments on his silence made to the jury by an attorney for the co-defendant." The Georgia Court of Appeals declined to follow *DeLuna* in *Head v. State*.[61]

In *Givens v. State*,[62] the court held that there had been no prejudice requiring reversal where the defendant was tried with a co-defendant who had prior convictions which were made known to the jury. However, in *Morris v. State*,[63] a co-defendant was called as a witness by the state. After the testimony of the co-defendant, Morris sought to impeach the testimony of the co-defendant by introducing his prior convictions. The appellate court held that the trial judge was correct in refusing to permit Morris to present this impeachment evidence but erred in refusing to grant Morris' motion to sever.

There are special problems which arise where there is a motion to sever so that one defendant will be able to call the other defendant as a witness. In *Stevens v. State*,[64] the Georgia Court of Appeals applied the criteria used by the Fifth Circuit in *United States v. Butler*.[65] In *Butler* the court said, "In order to be entitled to a severance . . . , the movant must demonstrate: (1) a bona fide need for the testimony; (2) the substance of the testimony; (3) its exculpatory nature and effect; and (4) that the co-defendant will in fact testify if the cases are severed. . . . Given such a showing, the court should (1) examine the significance of the testimony in relation to the defendant's theory of defense; (2) assess the extent of prejudice caused by the absence of the

---

[59]O.C.G.A. § 17-8-4.

[60]De Luna v. United States, 308 F.2d 140, 1 A.L.R.3d 969 (5th Cir. 1962) (where the attorney for a testifying co-defendant comments on the other defendant's failure to testify, the prejudice caused thereby may warrant retrial and may be basis for severance if parties know prior to trial that one defendant plans to testify). See U.S. v. Blankenship, 382 F.3d 1110 (11th Cir. 2004) (good discussion of *DeLuna* and severance issues where one defendant wants to testify or use an incriminatory statement of a co-defendant to shift blame).

[61]Head v. State, 256 Ga. App. 624, 569 S.E.2d 548 (2002) (the facts in Head were not compelling).

[62]Givens v. State, 184 Ga. App. 498, 499 (1), 361 S.E.2d 830 (1987).

[63]Morris v. State, 204 Ga. App. 437 (1), 419 S.E.2d 733 (1992).

[64]Stevens v. State, 165 Ga. App. 814, 817, 302 S.E.2d 724 (1983). See also Keener v. State, 215 Ga. App. 117, 118 (1), 449 S.E.2d 669 (1994); Marquez v. State, 298 Ga. 448, 782 S.E.2d 648 (2016).

[65]United States v. Butler, 611 F.2d 1066 (5th Cir. 1980). See Westmoreland v. State, 287 Ga. 688, 693 (5), 699 S.E.2d 13 (2010); Green v. State, 274 Ga. 686, 687–88, 558 S.E.2d 707 (2002).

testimony; (3) pay close attention to judicial administration and economy; (4) give weight to the timeliness of the motion."

According to O.C.G.A. § 17-8-4, "[w]hen separate trials are ordered in any case, the defendants shall be tried in the order requested by the state." The court in the 1912 case *Dixon v. State*[66] held that the state maintains the right to choose which defendant will be tried first, "especially when it is not made to appear that the rights of the accused were prejudiced by the State's determination to try one of the defendants before the other." Where one defendant's testimony would have had "little exonerative significance" on the other's trial, there is an absence of prejudice sufficient to require the court to compel the state to try one defendant before the other.[67]

Bruton does not apply to the non-custodial statements (as opposed to a confession) of a co-defendant which implicate the defendant. The Georgia Supreme Court has observed that in such cases the appropriate analysis is whether the statement is admissible under the co-conspirator exception to the hearsay rule.[68]

In *Zafiro v. United States*,[69] the Supreme Court established a two-step test for determining whether a defendant is entitled to a new trial due to a district court's refusal to sever prior to trial or to grant a mistrial once the trial had commenced. First, a defendant must demonstrate that he was somehow prejudiced by a joint trial. However, the Court clarified that "[m]utually antagonistic defenses are not prejudicial *per se*." The Court specifically rejected the notion that defendants who have contradictory defenses are inherently prejudiced simply because "a jury will conclude [either] that both defendants are lying and convict them both on that basis, or that at least one of the two must be guilty without regard to whether the Government has proved its case beyond a reasonable doubt."

"After finding that a defendant has suffered prejudice under step one of the *Zafiro* test, we then turn to the second step— determining whether severance (or a mistrial) is the proper remedy for that prejudice." The Court emphasized, "*Rule 14* does not require severance . . . . [R]ather, it leaves the tailoring of the relief to be granted, if any, to the district court's sound discretion." In *United States v. Blankenship*,[70] the Eleventh Circuit noted:

There are only two circumstances in which severance is the only

---

[66]Dixon v. State, 12 Ga. App. 17, 76 S.E. 794 (1912).

[67]House v. State, 203 Ga. App. 55, 416 S.E.2d 108 (1992).

[68]See Burgess v. State, 278 Ga. 314, 602 S.E.2d 566 (2004); Neason v. State, 277 Ga. 789, 596 S.E.2d 120 (2004); Fetty v. State, 268 Ga. 365, 489 S.E.2d 813 (1997).

[69]Zafiro v. U.S., 506 U.S. 534, 113 S. Ct. 933, 122 L. Ed. 2d 317 (1993).

[70]U.S. v. Blankenship, 382 F.3d

permissible remedy.

[W]hen defendants properly have been joined under *Rule 8(b)*, a district court should grant severance under *Rule 14* only if there is a serious risk that a joint trial would compromise a specific trial right of one of the defendants, or prevent the jury from making a reliable judgement about guilt or innocence.

Aside from the two categories of defendants specified by the Supreme Court, most other defendants prejudiced by a joint trial are entitled only to curative instructions.

The first scenario for mandatory severance (or mistrial) described by the Court exists only where a joint trial leads to the denial of a constitutional right. Regarding the second scenario mentioned by *Zafiro*, the Court did not clearly explain what it meant by a jury being prevented from "making a reliable judgement." Based on the Court's ensuing discussion, however, as well as an examination of subsequent precedent, it seems that courts have applied this exception in primarily three situations. While this list appears to be fairly comprehensive, it is quite possible that other factors could also prevent a jury from "making a reliable judgement."

First, severance is mandated where compelling evidence that is not admissible against one or more of the co-defendants is to be introduced against another co-defendant. This is a concern, for example, "where the . . . gruesome evidence against one defendant overwhelms the *di minimus* evidence against the co-defendant(s)". . . .

In general, the strong presumption is that jurors are able to compartmentalize evidence by respecting limiting instructions specifying the defendants against whom the evidence may be considered.

The mere fact that there may be an "enormous disparity in the evidence admissible against [one defendant] compared to the other defendants" is not a sufficient basis for reversal. A defendant does not suffer compelling prejudice, sufficient to mandate a severance, simply because much of the evidence at trial is applicable to co-defendants. . . .

Severance must be granted where evidence is admissible against only one defendant only where that evidence is so convincing that not even limiting instructions are likely to prevent the jury from considering the evidence against all co-defendants. . . .

The "reliable judgement" exception also applies in an extremely narrow range of cases in which the sheer number of defendants and charges with different standards of proof and culpability, along with the massive volume of evidence, makes it nearly impossible for a jury to juggle everything properly and assess the guilt or innocence of each defendant independently. See *United States v. Cassano*, 132 F.3d 646, 651 (11th Cir. 1998).

Finally, severance is required under *Zafiro* where one defendant is being charged with a crime, that while somehow related to the other defendants or their overall criminal scheme, is significantly

_____

1110 (11th Cir. 2004) (citations omit-   ted).

different from those of the other defendants.

See sections 7:11 and 7:12, supra, on representing multiple defendants. See section 20-6, infra, on *Jackson v. Denno* hearings. Generally, on prejudicial joinder, see Kadish and Brofman, *1 Criminal Law Advocacy, Trial Investigation and Preparation,* ¶ 10.04 (Matthew Bender 1982).

For motions to sever parties, see Studdard, *Daniel's Georgia Criminal Trial Practice Forms* (2018-2019 ed.), §§ 13:16 et seq.

§ 14:73 Motion to sever—Offenses

In *Brown v. State,*[1] the court pointed out that severance of offenses is designed to protect a defendant from, among other things, " 'the great risk of prejudice from a joint disposition of unrelated charges' and confusion of law and evidence by the trier of the fact and the 'smear' effect such confusion can produce."

O.C.G.A. § 16-1-7, regarding joinder of offenses, provides as follows:

"(a) When the same conduct of an accused may establish the commission of more than one crime, the accused may be prosecuted for each crime. He may not, however, be convicted of more than one crime if:

"(1) One crime is included in the other; or

"(2) The crimes differ only in that one is defined to prohibit a designated kind of conduct generally and the other to prohibit a specific instance of such conduct.

"(b) If the several crimes arising from the same conduct are known to the proper prosecuting officer at the time of commencing the prosecution and are within the jurisdiction of a single court, they must be prosecuted in a single prosecution except as provided in subsection (c) of this Code section.

"(c) When two or more crimes are charged as required by subsection (b) of this Code section, the court in the interest of justice may order that one or more of such charges be tried separately."

By statute, Georgia has also defined "included crime" as follows:

"An accused may be convicted of a crime included in a crime charged in the indictment or accusation. A crime is so included when:

"(1) It is established by proof of the same or less than all the facts or a less culpable mental state than is required to establish

[Section 14:73]

[1]Brown v. State, 230 Ga. App. 190, 193, 495 S.E.2d 858 (1998) (quot-ing Dingler v. State, 233 Ga. 462, 211 S.E.2d 752 (1975)).

the commission of the crime charged; or

"(2) It differs from the crime charged only in the respect that a less serious injury or risk of injury to the same person, property, or public interest or a lesser kind of culpability suffices to establish its commission."[2]

If criminal offenses are to be joined, they must arise from the "same conduct" of the accused. However, the fact that several offenses arose out of the same conduct does not necessarily mean that they may be joined.

In *Dingler v. State*,[3] the Georgia Supreme Court held that severance is mandatory where offenses are joined solely on the ground they are of the same or similar character. However, it has been held that offenses may be joined for trial "based (1) 'on the same conduct' or (2) 'a series of acts connected together' or (3) 'on a series of acts constituting parts of a single scheme or plan.' "[4] In *Cobb v. State*,[5] the court pointed out that "[o]ffenses are not joined solely because they are of the same or similar character where the similarity reaches the level of a pattern evincing a common motive, plan, scheme or bent of mind."

In considering the kinds of offenses which constitute the "same kind of crime" the conduct of a defendant in other transactions is generally irrelevant. Thus, where count one of an indictment charged a burglary on May 13 and count two charged an attempt to steal a motor vehicle on May 22, the trial court erred in overruling a special demurrer charging an improper joinder of offenses[6] since the elements of both crimes differed.

The A.B.A. Standards set out below on joinder of offenses and severance of offenses have been recognized to be a definite statement of Georgia law and have been adopted by the Georgia Supreme Court as a part of our law.[7] These standards provide as follows:

---

[2]O.C.G.A. § 16-1-6.

[3]Dingler v. State, 233 Ga. 462, 211 S.E.2d 752 (1975); Mangrum v. State, 244 Ga. App. 559, 536 S.E.2d 217 (2000). Accord, Carter v. State, 261 Ga. 344 (1), 404 S.E.2d 432 (1991).

[4]Barber v. State, 176 Ga. App. 103, 104, 335 S.E.2d 594 (1985); Phillips v. State, 160 Ga. App. 345, 346, 287 S.E.2d 69 (1981); Floyd v. State, 186 Ga. App. 777 (1), 368 S.E.2d 541 (1988). In Stewart v. State, 239 Ga. 588, 589 (3), 238 S.E.2d 540 (1977), the court said a judge may "refuse a motion for severance of the trial

of multiple charges where crimes alleged were a part of a continuous transaction conducted over a short period of time, and . . . it would be almost impossible to present to a jury evidence of one of the crimes without also permitting evidence of the other."

[5]Cobb v. State, 236 Ga. App. 265, 268 (2), 511 S.E.2d 522 (1999) (quoting Whitfield v. State, 217 Ga. App. 402, 457 S.E.2d 682 (1995)).

[6]Fair v. State, 129 Ga. App. 565, 200 S.E.2d 296 (1973).

[7]Dingler v. State, 233 Ga. 462, 464, 211 S.E.2d 752 (1975).

"Standard 13-2.1. Joinder of offenses

"Any two or more offenses committed by the same defendant:

"(a) may be joined in one accusatory instrument, with each offense stated in a separate count; or

"(b) may be joined for trial, upon the application of the prosecuting attorney or the defense."

"Standard 13-3.1. Severance of offenses

"(a) Whenever two or more unrelated offenses have been joined for trial, the prosecuting attorney or the defendant shall have a right to a severance of the offenses.

"(b) The court, on the application of either the prosecuting attorney or the defendant, should grant a severance of related offenses:

"(i) before trial, whenever severance is deemed appropriate to promote a fair determination of the defendant's guilt or innocence of each offense; or

"(ii) during trial, whenever, upon the consent of the defendant or upon a finding of manifest necessity, severance is deemed necessary to achieve a fair determination of the defendant's guilt or innocence of each offense.

"(c) When evaluating whether severance is 'appropriate to promote' or 'necessary to achieve' a fair determination of the defendant's guilt or innocence for each offense, the court should consider among other factors whether, in view of the number of offenses charged and the complexity of the evidence to be offered, the trier of fact will be able to distinguish the evidence and apply the law intelligently as to each offense."

Thus, where offenses are joined solely on the ground that they are of the same or of similar character, the defendant is entitled to severance "because of the great risk of prejudice from a joint disposition of unrelated charges."[8] However, in *Loyless v. State*,[9] the court held that a "[s]everance is not mandated . . . where the similarity of the offenses is coupled with evidence of a pattern which shows a common motive, plan, scheme, or bent of mind." On motion, it is error for the trial judge not to allow separate trials on each count of an indictment charging separate and distinct crimes of the same species,[10] unless the two offenses arose from the same conduct, occurred at the same place, and involved the

---

[8]Dingler v. State, 233 Ga. 462, 211 S.E.2d 752 (1975); Coats v. State, 234 Ga. 659, 662 (4), 217 S.E.2d 260 (1975); Stone v. State, 155 Ga. App. 357, 271 S.E.2d 22 (1980); Haisman v. State, 242 Ga. 896, 899 (3), 252 S.E.2d 397 (1979); Thompson v. State, 181 Ga. App. 163, 165, 351 S.E.2d 483 (1986).

[9]Loyless v. State, 210 Ga. App. 693, 695 (3), 436 S.E.2d 814 (1993).

[10]Dingler v. State, 134 Ga. App. 223, 224, 214 S.E.2d 6 (1975). See the excellent opinion of Chief Judge Quillian in Davis v. State, 159 Ga. App. 356

same persons, or unless "the offenses are so similar that they show a common scheme or plan or have an identical modus operandi."[11] A relevant consideration in this regard is that of whether the evidence of one offense would be admissible in a trial of the other offense if they were to be tried separately.[12] However, in these latter circumstances, it is not error to deny a severance of the trials unless it appears that the joint trial of offenses will make it difficult for the jury to distinguish the evidence and apply the law intelligently.[13] Where separate crimes charged in an indictment did not arise out of the same conduct, did not involve the same victims or witnesses, and the evidence relating to one would not be admissible in the trial of the other, it is an abuse of discretion to deny a motion to sever.[14]

In *Rivers v. State*,[15] the court held that "unless the offenses were joined *solely* because they are of the same or similar character," the trial judge has discretion to join or sever offenses. (Emphasis in original.)

In *Weaver v. State*,[16] the court held that two thefts "were part of the same conduct" where the defendant took a locked Cougar and a week later ran out of gas in the Cougar, and later took the Cadillac after a person who offered to take defendant to get gas stepped out of the car to get directions. In *Jordan v. State*,[17] the court held that five charges of child molestation occurring from January 1982 to March of 1983 could be joined for trial.

In *Brown v. State*,[18] the court noted that the criteria for introducing "similar transaction" evidence is significantly more rigorous than the criteria used for determining "similarity of conduct" for joinder purposes. To determine "similarity of conduct," the state is obligated to show only that the conduct itself is similar. The standard for determining the admissibility of "similar transaction" evidence, however, requires that the state demonstrate not only that the conduct is similar, but also that the offenses are of a "like character."

---

(1), 283 S.E.2d 286 (1981).

[11]Mack v. State, 163 Ga. App. 778 (1), 296 S.E.2d 115 (1982); Gilbert v. State, 163 Ga. App. 688, 689 (3), 295 S.E.2d 173 (1982).

[12]Stewart v. State, 277 Ga. 138, 587 S.E.2d 602 (2003).

[13]Stewart v. State, 277 Ga. 138, 587 S.E.2d 602 (2003). See, Underwood v. State, 144 Ga. App. 684, 685 (2), 242 S.E.2d 339 (1978); Price v. State, 155 Ga. App. 206, 270 S.E.2d 203 (1980), rev'd on other grounds, 247 Ga. 58, 273 S.E.2d 854 (1981).

[14]Booker v. State, 231 Ga. 598, 599 (1), 203 S.E.2d 194 (1974).

[15]Rivers v. State, 225 Ga. App. 558, 560 (1), 484 S.E.2d 519 (1997).

[16]Weaver v. State, 169 Ga. App. 890 (1), 315 S.E.2d 467 (1984).

[17]Jordan v. State, 172 Ga. App. 496 (1), 323 S.E.2d 657 (1984).

[18]Brown v. State, 230 Ga. App. 190, 495 S.E.2d 858 (1998). Accord, Smith v. State, 225 Ga. App. 553, 555 (1), 484 S.E.2d 515 (1997).

Where joinder is based on the same conduct or a series of acts constituting parts of a single plan, severance lies within the discretion of the judge. The court should consider whether, in view of the number of offenses charged and the complexity of the case, the jury will be able to distinguish the evidence and apply the law intelligently to each offense.[19] Thus, courts have considered the likelihood of evidence of one crime also demonstrating the commission of another offense, the length of time from the beginning of the first crime until the completion of the last offense, and whether the crimes were all part of one continuous transaction. It was held not to be error to deny a motion to sever where the defendant was charged with bigamy, incest, and murder over a period of 20 hours or less, all naming the victim.[20]

As noted previously, offenses may be joined in an indictment where two or more counts charge a defendant with the same crime against separate persons and where the offenses arise out of a series of acts constituting a single plan. If more than a single crime against an accused falls into one or both of these categories, they may not be joined if "(1) One crime is included in the other; or (2) The crimes differ only in that one is defined to prohibit a designated kind of conduct generally and the other to prohibit a specific instance of such conduct."[21] For example, possession is a lesser included offense to the charge of the sale of contraband. Thus, both offenses may be charged in separate counts in an indictment. However, the defendant cannot be convicted of both crimes since the possession charge is deemed to merge into the greater offense of selling.[22] Similarly, where a defendant is charged with both felony murder and the predicate felony of armed robbery of the same person, he may not be convicted and sentenced for both.[23] See §§ 26:33 et seq., infra, on merger.

---

[19]Coats v. State, 234 Ga. 659, 662 (4), 217 S.E.2d 260 (1975); Fluellen v. State, 163 Ga. App. 425 (2), 294 S.E.2d 653 (1982).

In Stewart v. State, 277 Ga. 138, 587 S.E.2d 602 (2003), referring to the A.B.A. Standards on Joinder of Offenses, the court observed: "[u]nder these Standards, a trial court must first determine whether the offenses are joined solely because they are of the same or similar character. If they are, severance is *mandatory*. If they are not, the court must then decide whether severance would promote a just determination of guilt or innocence as to each offense." (emphasis supplied and citations omitted).

[20]Owens v. State, 233 Ga. 905, 910, 213 S.E.2d 860 (1975).

[21]O.C.G.A. § 16-1-7(a).

[22]State v. Estevez, 232 Ga. 316, 320, 206 S.E.2d 475 (1974) overruled on other grounds by, Drinkard v. Walker, 281 Ga. 211, 636 S.E.2d 530 (2006) (criteria for determining whether one crime is included in another so as to bar conviction for more than one crime is set forth in O.C.G.A. § 16-1-7(a)). Refer to §§ 26:33 et seq., infra, regarding merger.

[23]Atkins v. Hopper, 234 Ga. 330, 216 S.E.2d 89 (1975).

If the prosecuting officer is aware at the time of the commencement of the prosecution that the accused is guilty of several crimes arising from the same course of conduct all within the jurisdiction of a single court, the offenses must be included in a single indictment.[24] In this situation, failure to include all known offenses in a single indictment appears to bar a later prosecution of those crimes which were not included.[25] However, in a case where a defendant stole two trucks from the same person on the same day, the act constituted one offense and could not be charged in two separate counts of an indictment.[26]

A motion to sever counts may be either oral or written[27] or by demurrer if the defect appears on the face of the indictment,[28] and must be made or filed "at or before the time set by law unless time therefor is extended by the judge in writing prior to trial."[29] However, the filing of a written motion supported by affidavits covering any factual matters involved in the case appears to be the better practice.

Even though it may be permissible, or even mandatory, to join offenses in a single indictment, the trial court may, in the "interest of justice," order one or more charges to be tried separately.[30] But, if counts in an indictment have been joined solely on the ground that the offenses are of the same or similar character, the trial court must grant a motion to sever for purposes of trial.[31] In *Smith v. State*,[32] the appellate court reversed the defendant's conviction where the trial court denied the defendant's motion to sever the offense of child molestation of his grandson from the trial of offenses relating to the rape of his neighbor. The court reasoned that the two incidents arose from unrelated transactions and that the joint trial caused a "smear effect." However, if such a motion is made and no ruling is obtained on the motion, the failure to grant the severance is not generally reversible error.[33]

There has been some indication that where there are two or more separate indictments against the same defendant, the trial

---

[24]O.C.G.A. § 16-1-7(b).

[25]See Henderson v. State, 227 Ga. 68, 75, 76, 179 S.E.2d 76 (1970), judgment vacated in part on other grounds, 408 U.S. 938, 92 S.Ct. 2868, 33 L.Ed.2d 758 (1972).

[26]Breland v. State, 135 Ga. App. 478, 218 S.E.2d 153 (1975).

[27]See Wigley v. State, 140 Ga. App. 145, 230 S.E.2d 108 (1976).

[28]However, it is unusual for an indictment to show on its face that a joinder is improper. See Wingfield v. State, 231 Ga. 92, 105, 200 S.E.2d 708 (1973).

[29]Ga. Unif. Super. Ct. R. 31.1.

[30]O.C.G.A. § 16-1-7(c).

[31]Wigley v. State, 140 Ga. App. 145, 230 S.E.2d 108 (1976).

[32]Smith v. State, 249 Ga. App. 39, 40 (1), 547 S.E.2d 598 (2001).

[33]Hunsucker v. State, 160 Ga. App. 846 (1), 287 S.E.2d 689 (1982).

judge may not consolidate them for trial over the objection of the defendant.[34] However, in *Whisenhunt v. State*,[35] the court treated different accusations as different counts of the same accusation, holding that the trial judge could consolidate separate accusations for trial where "they are based (1) on the same conduct or (2) on a series of acts connected together, or (3) a series of acts constituting parts of a single scheme or plan." In *Stone v. State*,[36] the court pointed out that "[i]n determining whether separate offenses should be considered 'consolidated for trial' for purposes of recidivist sentencing, we look to the totality of the circumstances."

In *Cherry v. State*,[37] the court pointed out that "indictments for continuing sales of the same type of contraband may be . . . [joined for trial] because they 'constitute[d] parts of a single scheme or plan.' "

In *Weaver v. State*,[38] the court held that "[w]here the evidence of one crime would be admissible in the trial of the other crime, it cannot be said that the trial court abused its discretion in denying [the] motion for severance." See Studdard, *Daniel's Georgia Handbook on Criminal Evidence* (2018 ed.), § 4:37.

See § 13:18, supra, on indictments alleging a former conviction. For motions to sever offenses, see Studdard, *Daniel's Georgia Criminal Trial Practice Forms* (2018–2019 ed.), §§ 13:21 et seq. See § 14:54, supra, on merger of offenses. See § 17:24, infra, on bifurcation.

§ 14:74 Motion to change venue—Background and statutory procedure

The Sixth Amendment to the Constitution guarantees a defendant the right to a jury trial. This provision is applicable to the states through the due process clause of the Fourteenth Amendment.[1] Thus, a defendant has the right to a trial by a fair and impartial jury.[2]

O.C.G.A. § 17-7-150 provides a method for obtaining a change

---

[34]Bradford v. State, 126 Ga. App. 688, 191 S.E.2d 545 (1972), disapproved in Smith v. State, 199 Ga. App. 410 (2), 405 S.E.2d 107 (1991).

[35]Whisenhunt v. State, 156 Ga. App. 583, 587 (10), 275 S.E.2d 82 (1980).

[36]Stone v. State, 245 Ga. App. 728, 538 S.E.2d 791 (2000).

[37]Cherry v. State, 230 Ga. App. 443, 445 (3), 496 S.E.2d 764 (1998) (quoting Little v. State, 165 Ga. App. 389, 300 S.E.2d 540 (1983)).

[38]Weaver v. State, 206 Ga. App. 560, 561 (1), 426 S.E.2d 41 (1992). Accord, Morrow v. State, 226 Ga. App. 833, 834 (1), 487 S.E.2d 669 (1997).

[Section 14:74]

[1]Duncan v. Louisiana, 391 U.S. 145, 88 S.Ct. 1444, 20 L.Ed.2d 491 (1968).

[2]Ga. Const. 1983, Art. I, § I, ¶ XI(a) . Rideau v. Louisiana, 373 U.S. 723, 83 S.Ct. 1417, 10 L.Ed.2d 663 (1963), involved a motion for change of venue and the court held that it was a

of venue to insure that a defendant will be tried by a fair and impartial jury and the criteria to be considered.[3] If a defendant in a criminal case[4] does not feel he can obtain a fair trial in the county where the crime was allegedly committed, he may request a change of venue by filing a written petition.[5] Since the Georgia Constitution provides for the trial of criminal cases in the county where the offense took place,[6] a change of venue on motion of the district attorney would violate the defendant's constitutional rights.[7] However, where the defendant makes the request, he waives this right to be tried where the incident occurred. In *Patterson v. Faircloth,*[8] the Georgia Supreme Court concluded on non-constitutional grounds that a trial judge on his own motion does not have the right to change the venue over the objection of the defendant on the ground that a fair and impartial jury cannot be obtained in that county.

When a motion for a change of venue is filed, the trial judge must conduct a hearing and give the defendant an opportunity to present evidence.[9] "In a motion for a change of venue, the petitioner must show (1) that the setting of the trial was inherently prejudicial or (2) that the jury selection process showed actual prejudice to a degree that rendered a fair trial

---

denial of due process for the state to deny such change, where the defendant was charged with armed robbery, kidnapping and murder, and there had been a televised interview of the defendant by the local sheriff during which the defendant made admissions. Cf. People v. Gay, 407 Mich. 681, 289 N.W.2d 651 (1980).

[3]See Annot., "Federal Prosecutor's Pretrial Statements of Affecting Defendant's Right to Fair Trial," 22 A.L.R.Fed. 556 (1975), and "Validity and Construction of Federal Court's Pretrial Order Precluding Publicity or Comment About Pending Case by Counsel, Parties or Witnesses," 5 A.L.R.Fed. 948 (1970).

[4]The case of Slaughter v. State, 61 Ga. App. 619, 7 S.E.2d 215 (1940), holds that only a superior court judge may grant a motion to change venue. If the Georgia statute prevents a state court judge from transferring a misdemeanor case to another county when an impartial jury cannot be obtained

in the first county, the statute seems unconstitutional. Groppi v. Wisconsin, 400 U.S. 505, 91 S.Ct. 490, 27 L.Ed.2d 571 (1971), holds that denial in a misdemeanor case of defendant's right to a change of venue based on community prejudice is violative of the Fourteenth Amendment.

See Annot., "Right of Accused in Misdemeanor Prosecution to Change of Venue on the Grounds of Inability to Secure Fair Trial and the Like," 34 A.L.R.3d 804 (1970).

[5]O.C.G.A. § 17-7-150. See Rule 462(a) of the Uniform Rules of Criminal Procedure.

[6]Ga. Const. 1983, Art. VI, § II, ¶ VI. See O.C.G.A. § 17-2-2.

[7]See Kohl v. Lehlback, 160 U.S. 293, 16 S.Ct. 304, 40 L.Ed. 432, 435 (1895).

[8]Patterson v. Faircloth, 256 Ga. 489, 492, 350 S.E.2d 243 (1986).

[9]Villa v. State, 190 Ga. App. 530, 532 (2), 379 S.E.2d 417 (1989).

impossible."[10]

O.C.G.A. § 17-7-150(a)(1) provides in part that at such a hearing "it shall not be necessary to examine all persons in the county liable to serve on juries, but the judge shall hear evidence by affidavit or oral testimony in support of or against the motion."

In determining the county to which the case shall be transferred, O.C.G.A. § 17-7-150(2), as amended in 1995, contains a long list of considerations and procedures to be used by the trial judge once the determination to transfer the case is made.

Rule 19.2(A) of the Uniform Rules for the Superior Courts provides as follows:

"When a criminal action is to be transferred to the superior court of a county different from that in which initially brought, the superior court judge granting the venue change, unless disqualified, shall continue as presiding judge in the action."

In *Glean v. State*,[11] the court held that today where a motion for change of venue is granted, the jury *selection and trial* shall be conducted in the county to which the case has been transferred. However, as a result of a statutory change, the remainder of the actual trial may be conducted physically in the original county.[12]

In *Coleman v. Kemp*,[13] a capital case involving the murders of the Alday family in rural south Georgia, the Eleventh Circuit found that a showing by the defendant of an enormous amount of pre-trial publicity and public opinion amounted to a presumption of prejudice. While noting that this standard is rarely met, the court found that prejudice is presumed "when pretrial publicity is sufficiently prejudicial and inflammatory and the prejudicial pre-trial publicity saturated the community where the trials were held."

See 21 Am. Jur. Criminal Law §§ 372 et seq. (1981). For motions for a change of venue, see Studdard, *Daniel's Georgia Criminal Trial Practice Forms* (2018–2019 ed.), §§ 13:27 et seq.

§ 14:75 Right of trial judge to change venue because of danger

In addition to the right to grant a change of venue because an impartial jury cannot be obtained, the trial judge on his own motion, with or without petition, may change the venue of the trial

---

[10]Happoldt v. State, 267 Ga. 126, 128 (2), 475 S.E.2d 627 (1996); Powell v. State, 297 Ga. 352, 773 S.E.2d 762 (2015); Culver v. State, 230 Ga. App. 224, 234 (14), 496 S.E.2d 292 (1998).

[11]Glean v. State, 268 Ga. 260, 263

(2)(c), 486 S.E.2d 172 (1997).

[12]Pruitt v. State, 270 Ga. 745, 748 (2), 514 S.E.2d 639 (1999).

[13]Coleman v. Kemp, 778 F.2d 1487 (11th Cir. 1985).

"whenever, in his judgment, there is danger of violence being committed on the defendant."[1] "Such a determination is [to be] based on circumstances as they exist at the time of trial; a decision as to the danger of violence at trials at some future undetermined time is" not proper.[2] A defendant may also request a change of venue by petition because of danger of violence. The word "violence" in this connection is not limited to physical violence to the defendant, but also includes the danger of violence to witnesses whom the defendant wishes to call. Thus, if the threat of danger to a defense witness in a certain county will prevent the defendant from having the witness present, this may entitle the defendant to a change of venue because this constitutes "violence to the defendant's fundamental right to a fair trial."[3]

If the motion for change of venue is denied, there is no automatic right of immediate appeal.[4] If the defendant wishes an immediate appeal, he must obtain a certificate for immediate review[5] and comply with the Appellate Practice Act.[6]

Whenever venue is changed, the clerk of the transferring court must send all papers connected with the case to the clerk of the newly designated court.[7] The receiving judge shall have the same power as the first judge to transfer the case to another county if an impartial jury cannot be obtained.[8]

§ 14:76 Motion to change venue—Practical and legal suggestions

Various practical concerns should underlie the decision of whether to seek a change of venue, and a defendant should carefully consider the pros and cons of the situation. While he might obtain a panel of jurors who are less likely to have heard of his case, this might be more than offset by the inconvenience and additional expense of having to go to another county for trial. The defendant should also consider whether the jury he is likely to

---

[Section 14:75]

[1]O.C.G.A. § 17-7-150. See Ruffin v. State, 28 Ga. App. 40, 41 (4), 110 S.E. 311 (1921).

[2]Freeman v. State, 264 Ga. 27, 30 (3), 440 S.E.2d 181 (1994).

[3]Yancey v. State, 98 Ga. App. 797, 801, 107 S.E.2d 265 (1959).

[4]Under the former statute, there was a provision for an immediate appeal. See Arkwright v. State, 226 Ga. 192, 173 S.E.2d 179 (1970), judgment vacated in part on other grounds, 408 U.S. 936, 92 S.Ct. 2859, 33 L.Ed.2d 752 (1972).

[5]Brooks v. State, 229 Ga. 593, 194 S.E.2d 256 (1972).

[6]O.C.G.A. § 17-7-150, O.C.G.A. § 5-6-34.

[7]O.C.G.A. § 17-7-151. See Ruffin v. State, 28 Ga. App. 40, 45, 110 S.E. 311 (1921).

[8]O.C.G.A. § 17-7-152; Ruffin v. State, 28 Ga. App. 40, 41 (5), 110 S.E. 311 (1921).

obtain in a new location will be more or less conservative than a jury in the county where he is indicted. Other concerns to be weighed include: (1) Will the defendant be able to have his witnesses appear at the place where the case is likely to be transferred? (2) How will the new jury relate to the defendant and his counsel? (3) If the crime has received statewide attention by the news media, are people at the new location likely to have heard of and formed opinions about the incident? (4) Is the change likely to be granted if requested? (5) Will a defendant's motion for change of venue cause even more hostility toward him if the motion is not granted? Of course, it is obvious that there may be a local atmosphere which is so hostile to the defendant that the decision is obvious and another venue must be sought. However, in the average case, all factors should be carefully considered, since the defendant cannot have his case transferred back to the original county once a petition for change of venue has been granted.[1]

Rule 19.2 of the Uniform Rules for the Superior Courts provides as follows:

"(A) When a criminal action is to be transferred to the superior court of a county different from that in which initially brought, the superior court judge granting the venue change, unless disqualified, shall continue as presiding judge in the action.

"(B) When there has been an order granting change of venue to the superior court of a county other than that in which the action theretofore pended, the trial jury shall be selected from qualified jurors of the transferee county although trial of the action may, in the discretion of the presiding judge, take place in the transferor county."

However, in *Hardwick v. State*,[2] the court held that Rule 19.2(B) is unenforceable absent the consent of the parties because it is inconsistent with O.C.G.A. § 17-7-150(a). Nevertheless, in *Pruitt v. State*,[3] the Georgia Supreme Court approved the action of the trial judge in granting a change of venue from Lumpkin County to Cherokee County. The trial judge ordered the jury would be selected from Cherokee but the actual trial would physically take place in Lumpkin. The court pointed out that in 1995, after the date of *Hardwick*, the General Assembly amended O.C.G.A. § 17-7-150(a)(3) so as to provide for the procedure used in *Pruitt*.

A request for change of venue should be made by written peti-

---

[Section 14:76]

[1]Graham v. State, 143 Ga. 440 (1), 85 S.E. 328 (1915).

[2]Hardwick v. State, 264 Ga. 161,

164 (2), 442 S.E.2d 236 (1994).

[3]Pruitt v. State, 270 Ga. 745, 748 (2), 514 S.E.2d 639 (1999).

tion of the defendant.[4] It is not legally necessary for the district attorney to file an answer to such a petition,[5] but filing an answer may have some practical and psychological advantages. Also, it has been held that where the state neither answers the petition nor introduces any evidence, the case resolves itself into a question of law, and the only issue is whether the defendant's evidence brings him within the statutory provisions for a change of venue.[6]

The determination of whether or not to grant a change of venue is a question for the judge and not a jury.[7] At one time it was necessary for the judge to examine all persons who were liable to serve on juries before the venue could be changed,[8] but this is no longer necessary. Evidence may be offered by affidavit or oral testimony.[9] However, a verified petition for a change of venue is not evidence unless it is formally introduced in evidence.[10] Wide news coverage does not necessarily show pervasive prejudice in the community.[11] Also generally courts will "be less likely to closely scrutinize the prejudicial effect of publicity . . . in cases where that publicity is created by the defendant's escape attempt than in cases where the publicity stems from other sources."[12] There are a number of cases holding that if the defendant fails to introduce any evidence, it is not error to overrule the motion.[13]

However, there are also cases holding that where a motion for change of venue has been filed on the basis that an impartial jury cannot be obtained, a positive duty is imposed on the judge to inform himself of the truth of the allegations in the petition.[14] Although the ultimate granting or denial of a motion for a change

---

[4]O.C.G.A. § 17-7-150.

[5]See Robinson v. State, 86 Ga. App. 375 (2), 71 S.E.2d 677 (1952).

[6]Yancey v. State, 98 Ga. App. 797, 801, 107 S.E.2d 265 (1959).

[7]Ruffin v. State, 28 Ga. App. 40, 41 (3), 110 S.E. 311 (1921).

[8]Blackman v. State, 80 Ga. 785, 7 S.E. 626 (1888), overruled in part on other grounds by Corbin v. State, 211 Ga. 400, 86 S.E.2d 221 (1955). See White v. State, 100 Ga. 659, 663 (1), 28 S.E. 423 (1897).

[9]O.C.G.A. § 17-7-150. See Cook v. State, 22 Ga. App. 770, 775, 97 S.E. 264 (1918).

[10]Rawlings v. State, 33 Ga. App. 825, 127 S.E. 881 (1925).

[11]Lingo v. State, 224 Ga. 333 (2), 162 S.E.2d 1 (1968). But generally, see Annot., "Pretrial Publicity in Criminal Case as Ground for Change of Venue," 33 A.L.R.3d 17 (1970).

[12]Goodman v. State, 255 Ga. 226, 230 (14), 336 S.E.2d 757 (1985).

[13]Cook v. State, 22 Ga. App. 770, 775, 97 S.E. 264 (1918); Atkins v. State, 228 Ga. 578 (1), 187 S.E.2d 132 (1972); Wise v. State, 146 Ga. App. 194 (4), 246 S.E.2d 6 (1978).

[14]Grenoble v. State, 41 Ga. App. 663, 154 S.E. 304 (1930); Best v. State, 26 Ga. App. 671, 107 S.E. 266 (1921); Wilson v. State, 28 Ga. App. 574, 575 (2), 112 S.E. 295 (1922); Blevins v. State, 108 Ga. App. 738, 740(2), 134 S.E.2d 496 (1963).

of venue lies within the discretion of the judge,[15] in determining the issue of whether an impartial jury can be obtained, the judge should consider opinions of witnesses on this question based on the facts to which they testify.[16] In determining whether or not there should be a change of venue, the crucial question is not whether a person has an opinion as to the innocence or guilt of the defendant, but whether or not his opinion can be laid aside and the issues determined solely upon the evidence presented to the jury.[17] In *Crawford v. State*,[18] the court said, "The relevant question is not whether the community remembered the case, but whether the jurors at [this] trial had such fixed opinions that they could not judge impartially the guilt of the defendant [or the sentence that might be imposed]." The Georgia Supreme Court has stated that it has "grave reservations about the admissibility" of public opinion polls.[19]

The test of whether or not the defendant can have a fair trial in spite of publicity is said to be determined by whether jurors summoned to try the case have a firm opinion of the guilt or innocence of the defendant.[20] The A.B.A. Standards recommend the granting of a motion for change of venue where "because of the dissemination of potentially prejudicial material, there is a substantial likelihood that in the absence of such relief a fair trial by an impartial jury cannot be had."[21] However, Georgia has declined to adopt an earlier version of this standard.[22]

In order to show that a defendant did not receive a fair trial, he must show "(1) that the setting of the trial was inherently

---

[15]Jarrell v. State, 234 Ga. 410, 415, 216 S.E.2d 258 (1975).

[16]Jones v. State, 101 Ga. App. 851, 852 (3)(a), 115 S.E.2d 576 (1960); Pierce v. State, 125 Ga. App. 490, 188 S.E.2d 181 (1972).

[17]Berryhill v. State, 249 Ga. 442, 291 S.E.2d 685 (1982) (abrogated on other grounds by Jones v. State, 261 Ga. 665, 409 S.E.2d 642 (1991)).

[18]Crawford v. State, 257 Ga. 681, 683, 362 S.E.2d 201 (1987). The statement in the body is substantially a quotation from Patton v. Yount, 467 U.S. 1025, 1035, 104 S.Ct. 2885, 81 L.Ed.2d 847 (1984).

[19]Berryhill v. State, 249 Ga. 442, 291 S.E.2d 685 (1982) (abrogated on other grounds by Jones v. State, 261 Ga. 665, 409 S.E.2d 642 (1991)).

[20]Krist v. Caldwell, 230 Ga. 536, 537 (2), 198 S.E.2d 161 (1973); Shinhol-ster v. State, 150 Ga. App. 221, 257 S.E.2d 342 (1979). In Brooks v. State, 244 Ga. 574, 577, 261 S.E.2d 379 (1979), judgment vacated on other grounds, 446 U.S. 961, 100 S.Ct. 2937, 64 L.Ed.2d 821 (1980), the court pointed out that the jurors do not have to be totally ignorant of the case and its facts. But in Pamplin v. Mason, 364 F.2d 1 (5th Cir. 1966), the court said, "It is immaterial that the voir dire did not demonstrate community prejudice."

[21]A.B.A. Standards, Fair Trial and Free Press, Vol. II, Standard 8-3.3.

[22]Mooney v. State, 243 Ga. 373, 254 S.E.2d 337 (1979) (abrogated on other grounds by Horton v. California, 496 U.S. 128, 110 S. Ct. 2301, 110 L. Ed. 2d 112 (1990)); Beasley v. State, 161 Ga. App. 737 (3), 288 S.E.2d 759 (1982).

prejudicial, or (2) that the jury selection process showed actual prejudice to a degree which rendered a fair trial impossible."[23] "The second test involves review of the voir dire examination of potential jurors." It is particularly difficult to show a violation of the first test if it is demonstrated on voir dire that fair and impartial jurors were selected.[24]

"Traditionally, a defendant seeking a change of venue on the basis that the setting of the trial is *inherently prejudicial* relies heavily if not primarily or exclusively on news media reports. . . . However, widespread or even adverse publicity is not in itself grounds for a change of venue. . . . On appeal, the impact of media publicity is evaluated by various factors, such as [1] the size of the community and the extent of media coverage (number of articles and their circulation); [2] whether it related to the discovery of the crime (e.g., facts regarding the victim) or [3] to the apprehension or interrogation of the defendant (and whether any publicized confession was admitted at trial); [4] the prominence and content of the reports (e.g., facts vs. speculation and emotionalism, and the accuracy and admission into evidence of those facts); and [5] the time interval between the publicity and the trial. . . . Although some of these considerations cannot be resolved until the evidence is closed, on appellate review the impact of the pretrial publicity of evidence and the admission of evidence can be compared." (Emphasis supplied.)[25]

In *Jenkins v. State*,[26] the Georgia Supreme Court held that to determine the percentage of jurors excused for cause resulting from pretrial publicity, the court should contrast "the percentage of jurors influenced by pretrial publicity to the total number of jurors *questioned* . . . [and] not . . . to the total number of jurors *excused*."

In determining whether the jury selection process showed actual prejudice to a degree which rendered a fair trial impossible, the courts have considered the number of jurors who were excused for prejudice for having a fixed opinion as to the guilt or

---

[23]Brooks v. State, 244 Ga. 574, 577, 261 S.E.2d 379 (1979); Taft v. State, 154 Ga. App. 566, 567(3), 269 S.E.2d 69 (1980); Lemley v. State, 258 Ga. 554, 556(4), 372 S.E.2d 421 (1988); Cargill v. State, 255 Ga. 616, 627(9), 340 S.E.2d 891 (1986); Berry v. State, 267 Ga. 605, 481 S.E.2d 203 (1997); Maddox v. State, 272 Ga. App. 440 (1), 612 S.E.2d 484 (2005); Morgan v. State, 276 Ga. 72, 75(4), 575 S.E.2d 468 (2003); Eckman v. State, 274 Ga. 63,

68(4), 548 S.E.2d 310 (2001).

[24]Kesler v. State, 249 Ga. 462, 472, 291 S.E.2d 497 (1982).

[25]Kesler v. State, 249 Ga. 462, 472, 291 S.E.2d 497 (1982).

[26]Jenkins v. State, 268 Ga. 468, 469 (2), 491 S.E.2d 54 (1997) (emphasis by the court), overruled on other grounds by Hamm v. State, 294 Ga. 791, 756 S.E.2d 507 (2014).

innocence of the defendant. In *Berryhill v. State*,[27] the court pointed out that 67 prospective jurors were examined and six were excused for prejudice. The court stated that this represented only about eight percent of those called and "strongly corroborates the expressions of impartiality by the other jurors who were not excused for prejudice." The court then cited the percentage figures in several other cases. The highest figure referred to was a 46 percent dismissal for cause, which was also said to corroborate an absence of prejudicial bias for the remainder.

In *Perkinson v. State*,[28] the trial court denied the defendant's motion to change venue, finding that "relatively few" prospective jurors had read a newspaper article that include inadmissible information. The Georgia Supreme Court upheld the trial court's decision, finding that the pretrial media coverage was " 'neither so extensive and inflammatory nor so reflective of "an atmosphere of hostility" as to require a change of venue.' "[29]

In *Jones v. State*,[30] the Georgia Supreme Court said that a trial judge "will order a change of venue for death penalty trials in those cases in which a defendant can make a substantive showing of the likelihood of prejudice by reason of extensive publicity." The court stated that this is a new standard.

However, it has also been recognized that "if the atmosphere surrounding the trial is sufficiently inflammatory, the trial judge should disregard" the statements of prospective jurors that they can and will disregard what they have heard about a case and render a verdict based on the evidence.[31] If a defendant's motion for a change of venue is overruled because an impartial jury cannot be obtained, and defense counsel wishes to be able to assign error to this ruling in the event the defendant is convicted, he should be careful to exhaust his peremptory strikes when he selects the jury,[32] since the failure to exhaust peremptory strikes generally precludes a successful challenge to the denial of a mo-

[27]Berryhill v. State, 249 Ga. 442, 444, 291 S.E.2d 685 (1982). Cf. Harper v. State, 249 Ga. 519, 530, 292 S.E.2d 389 (1982); Blige v. State, 211 Ga. App. 771, 772 (2), 440 S.E.2d 521 (1994).

[28]Perkinson v. State, 279 Ga. 232, 610 S.E.2d 533 (2005).

[29]Perkinson v. State, 279 Ga. 232, 610 S.E.2d 533 (2005), quoting Gissendaner v. State, 272 Ga. 704, 706, 532 S.E.2d 677 (2000).

[30]Jones v. State, 261 Ga. 665, 666 (2)(b), 409 S.E.2d 642 (1991).

[31]Reaves v. State, 242 Ga. 542,

549, 250 S.E.2d 376 (1978); Brooks v. State, 244 Ga. 574, 578, 261 S.E.2d 379 (1979). In Dick v. State, 246 Ga. 697, 699 (1), 273 S.E.2d 124 (1980), the court in ruling on whether or not the trial judge erroneously refused to grant a change of venue attached great weight to the percentage of jurors who were excused for prejudice (10%) and the fact that defense counsel did not exhaust his peremptory challenges. The court also compared the percentages of jurors excused for prejudice in a number of other cases.

[32]See Coleman v. State, 237 Ga.

tion for a change of venue.[33] A change of venue based on the danger of violence to the defendant may be ordered by the judge on his own motion, without hearing any testimony, if in his own judgment, based on his familiarity with local conditions, he feels that there is danger to the accused if he remains in the county where the crime was alleged to have been committed.[34]

Rule 19.2 of the Uniform Rules for the Superior Courts provides that when a criminal case is transferred to another county, the judge granting the change, unless disqualified, shall continue to preside in the action.

See sections 18:25 to 18:28, infra, on voir dire examination of jurors.

§ 14:77 Motion for a change of judge

The filing of a motion to have a judge disqualify or excuse himself must be undertaken with care. Several results may occur: (1) The judge may resent the suggestion that he will not be impartial in the trial; thus, his hostility may adversely affect the moving party during the trial; (2) he may lean over backward to be fair, once made aware of his difficult position; or (3) he may grant the motion although, statistically, it is unlikely. Also, as in the case of a petition for a change of venue, a motion to have the judge recuse himself may cause hostility or additional hostility against a defendant.

O.C.G.A. § 15-1-8 in summary form provides that a judge is disqualified from presiding in any case in which he has a pecuniary interest or is related within the third degree to any party interested in the outcome of the case or in any case in which he has been of counsel or employed in the case or in which he has presided in an inferior judicature when his ruling or decision is the subject of review.[1] However, in *Gillis v. City of Waycross,*[2] the court held that "Canon 3E (formerly 3C) of the Code of Judicial Conduct provides 'a broader rule of disqualification' than that provided in the statute, and . . . both the statute and the canon

---

84, 92, 226 S.E.2d 911 (1976).

[33]Brady v. State, 270 Ga. 574, 575 (3), 513 S.E.2d 199 (1999); Lloyd v. State, 226 Ga. App. 401, 402 (2), 487 S.E.2d 44 (1997).

[34]Ruffin v. State, 28 Ga. App. 40, 41 (4), 110 S.E. 311 (1921).

[Section 14:77]

[1]In Gray v. Barlow, 241 Ga. 347, 348, 245 S.E.2d 299 (1978), the court pointed out that the word "party" in this code section "is not restricted to

the technical limitation of a party to the case, but includes those who are interested in the result of the case . . . [but the] interest of a person not a party to the record which will disqualify a judge [who is related to such person] is a pecuniary interest in the result of the litigation."

[2]Gillis v. City of Waycross, 247 Ga. App. 119, 543 S.E.2d 423 (2000) (quoting Stephens v. Stephens, 249 Ga. 700, 701 (2), 292 S.E.2d 689 (1982)).

provide grounds for recusal." If a judge is to testify, even in a non-jury matter, he must disqualify himself.[3]

Rules 25.1, 25.2, and 25.3 of the Uniform Rules for the Superior Courts provide as follows:

"25.1 Motions

"All motions to recuse or disqualify a judge presiding in a particular case or proceeding shall be timely filed in writing and all evidence thereon shall be presented by accompanying affidavit(s) which shall fully assert the facts upon which the motion is founded. Filing and presentation to the judge shall be not later than 5 days after the affiant first learned of the alleged grounds for disqualification, and not later than 10 days prior to the hearing or trial which is the subject of recusal or disqualification, unless good cause be shown for failure to meet such time requirements. In no event shall the motion be allowed to delay the trial or proceeding."

"25.2 Affidavit

"The affidavit shall clearly state the facts and reasons for the belief that bias or prejudice exists, being definite and specific as to time, place, persons and circumstances of extra-judicial conduct or statements, which demonstrate either bias in favor of any adverse party, or prejudice toward the moving party in particular, or a systematic pattern of prejudicial conduct toward persons similarly situated to the moving party, which would influence the judge and impede or prevent impartiality in that action. Allegations consisting of bare conclusions and opinions shall not be legally sufficient to support the motion or warrant further proceedings."

"25.3 Duty of the Trial Judge

"When a judge is presented with a motion to recuse, or disqualify, accompanied by an affidavit, the judge shall temporarily cease to act upon the merits of the matter and shall immediately determine the timeliness of the motion and the legal sufficiency of the affidavit, and make a determination, assuming any of the facts alleged in the affidavit to be true, whether recusal would be warranted. If it is found that the motion is timely, the affidavit sufficient and that recusal would be authorized if some or all of the facts set forth in the affidavit are true, another judge shall be assigned to hear the motion to recuse. The allegations of the motion shall stand denied automatically. The trial judge shall not otherwise oppose the motion."

Georgia Uniform Superior Court Rule 25.3 does not require that a trial court conduct an evidentiary hearing to decide the

---

[3]Collins v. State, 141 Ga. App. 121, 122 (2), 232 S.E.2d 635 (1977).

legal question as to whether a motion to recuse meets the threshold requirements of the rule. A hearing is required only in those cases where the court determines that the motion satisfies the conditions of Rule 25.3 At that hearing, the assigned judge may take evidence or decide the case on the basis of the affidavits.[4]

In *Isaacs v. State*,[5] the Georgia Supreme Court held "that after a legally sufficient motion to recuse has been assigned for hearing, the judge against whom the motion is directed may not oppose the motion." This is said to be true since a "judge has no interest in sitting on a particular case. . . . His efforts at defending himself against a motion to recuse will invariably create an appearance of partiality."

Rule 25.4 outlines the procedure to be followed in assigning the matter to a judge for a hearing. Also see Rule 25.7 on voluntary recusal and Rule 25.5 on selection of the judge to hear a recusal motion.

Rule 2.11 of the Georgia Code of Judicial Conduct provides in part:

(A) Judges shall disqualify themselves in any proceeding in which their impartiality might reasonably be questioned, or in which:

(1) The judge has a personal bias or prejudice concerning a party or a party's lawyer, or personal *knowledge* of disputed evidentiary facts concerning an *impending matter* or a *pending proceeding*.

(2) The judge is within the third *degree of relationship* to any of the following listed persons, or the judge's spouse, *domestic partner intimate partner*, or any other *member of a judge's family residing in the judge's household* is within the third *degree of relationship* to any of the following persons:

(a) a party to the proceeding, or any officer, director, or trustee of a party;

(b) a lawyer in the proceeding;

(c) a person *known* by the judge to have a more than *de minimis* interest that could be substantially affected by the outcome of the proceeding; or

(d) a person who to the judge's *knowledge* is likely to be a material witness in the proceeding.

In addition, the rule provides other grounds for recusal, including: cases involving parties or attorneys who have made campaign contributions to the judge to an extent that there is "a

---

[4]See Henderson v. State, 295 Ga. 333, 759 S.E.2d 827 (2014). See Birt v. State, 256 Ga. 483, 484(1), 350 S.E.2d 241 (1986) (original judge cannot make threshold determinations after case has been assigned to a different judge).

[5]Isaacs v. State, 257 Ga. 126, 355 S.E.2d 644 (1987). See Post v. State, 298 Ga. 241, 779 S.E.2d 624 (2015) (court reminds trial judges to consider motion to recuse without a hearing to avoid being drawn into consideration of facts beyond those set out in motion and supporting affidavit).

reasonable question as to the judge's impartiality;" and cases which touch on matters involving issues about which the judge as a judicial candidate made statements of commitment.

The American Bar Association's Standards for Criminal Justice, Standard 6-1.7 of *Special Functions of the Trial Judge* also states: "The trial judge should recuse himself or herself whenever the judge has any doubt as to his or her ability to preside impartially in a criminal case or whenever the judge believes his or her impartiality can reasonably be questioned." The Georgia Court of Appeals has approved this ABA standard.[6] The Georgia Supreme Court in *Stephens v. Stephens*[7] relied on the Code of Judicial Conduct in concluding that a judge should recuse himself from a case where the attorney handling the case is the employer of the judge's son. The court pointed out that the judge's "impartiality might reasonably be questioned." However, in *Baxter v. State*,[8] the court held that bias against counsel, rather than a party, is not per se a ground of recusal. See § 14:85, infra, on judge signing search warrant and passing on a motion to suppress.

In *Liteky v. United States*,[9] the United States Supreme Court, in construing 28 U.S.C.A. § 455(a), held that (1) "judicial rulings alone almost never constitute valid basis for [showing] bias or partiality" of a judge, and (2) "opinions formed by the judge on the basis of facts introduced or events occurring in the course of the current proceedings, or of prior proceedings, do not constitute a basis for a bias or partiality motion unless they display a deep-seated favoritism or antagonism that would make fair judgment impossible."

A judge may not preside over a matter in which the judge has testified on a substantive matter. "Simply stated, if a judge testifies as a material witness with regard to an issue in a case, the remainder of the case must be heard by another judge."[10]

In *Pope v. State*,[11] the court considered a case in which the judge's law clerk had accepted a position with the district at-

---

[6]Johnson v. State, 140 Ga. App. 284, 285, 231 S.E.2d 87 (1976).

In Carter v. State, 246 Ga. 328, 329, 271 S.E.2d 475 (1980), the court stated that any alleged bias must arise "from an extrajudicial source and result in an opinion on the merits on some basis other than what the judge learned from his participation in the case." United States v. Grinnell Corp., 384 U.S. 563, 583, 86 S.Ct. 1698, 16 L.Ed.2d 778 (1966).

[7]Stephens v. Stephens, 249 Ga.

700, 292 S.E.2d 689 (1982).

[8]Baxter v. State, 176 Ga. App. 154, 155 (1), 335 S.E.2d 607 (1985) (emphasis in original).

[9]Liteky v. United States, 510 U.S. 540, 114 S.Ct. 1147, 127 L.Ed.2d 474 (1994).

[10]Lewis v. State, 275 Ga. 194, 565 S.E.2d 437 (2002), citing Code of Judicial Conduct, Canon 3 (E)(1)(b).

[11]Pope v. State, 256 Ga. 195, 345 S.E.2d 831 (1986), overruled on other grounds by Nash v. State, 271 Ga. 281,

torney but had not yet started to work for the district attorney. The court held that the trial judge should have disclosed this fact, and if defense counsel did not know of the situation and raised the point at the first opportunity after learning of it, the conviction would be reversed.

In *Sendula v. State*,[12] the Court of Appeals reversed a trial court's order denying a defendant's motion to recuse based upon an alleged "close relationship" between the judge and the district attorney who had served as the judge's campaign manager and treasurer in a recent election. The motion requested an evidentiary hearing to determine if recusal was warranted, which was denied, as was the request that the judge refer the issue to another judge for resolution. The appeals court noted that the allegations of a "close relationship" between the judge and the district attorney were insufficient to require recusal when unsupported by facts which suggest a prejudice or bias. Nonetheless, it ruled the trial court should have told the parties about the nature and extent of the relationship for their consideration as to whether either or both might want to move for a change of judge, and having failed to do so, reversed the defendant's conviction.

In *King v. State*,[13] the court noted that because the elected district attorney is "of counsel" as to all criminal cases in his or her circuit, a trial judge should recuse from any criminal matter which was addressed "in any case" while the judge was serving as district attorney. In *Gude v. State*,[14] the court ruled that a judge who previously served as a senior district attorney should recuse from presiding over any criminal matter which was managed by personnel over whom the judge had supervision authority during the time the judge served as an assistant senior district attorney. The United States Supreme Court has noted that in cases where the presiding judge in a case also had an integral role at some point in the prosecution of the same case there exists "[a] constitutionally intolerable probability of bias" which

---

519 S.E.2d 893 (1999).

[12]Serdula v. State, 344 Ga. App. 587, 812 S.E.2d 6 (2018).

[13]King v. State, 246 Ga. 386 (7), 271 S.E.2d 630, 16 A.L.R.4th 545 (1980).

[14]Gude v. State, 289 Ga. 46 (2), 709 S.E.2d 206 (2011) (Court also held that a judge should recuse from any case involving an attorney or a party who made an "exceptionally large"

campaign contribution). See Caperton v. A.T. Massey Coal Co., Inc., 556 U.S. 868, 129 S. Ct. 2252, 173 L. Ed. 2d 1208 (2009) (constitutional due process violated when judge refuses to recuse from a case involving a party who gave the judge an exceptionally large campaign contribution). See also Patterson v. Butler, 187 Ga. App. 740, 371 S.E.2d 268 (1988) (fact that a party worked in judge's campaign is not a per se reason for recusal).

requires recusal.[15] "However, the fact that a judge in the judge's previous capacity as district attorney prosecuted the defendant on another charge not currently pending before the judge is not, standing alone, a ground for disqualification."[16] In *Sears v. State*,[17] the court held that recusal generally is not mandated simply because the judge knows one of the parties or their attorneys socially.

In addition, recusal may not be required simply because the judge previously worked in the office of the district attorney during the time the case was pending. If the judge was not involved in the prosecution of the case, recusal would not be required. Also, simply because the district attorney is a friend of the judge or made contributions to his/her election campaign, recusal will not be required. Campaign contributions are also not a basis for recusal unless the contribution is unusually large.[18]

When a judge recuses himself, the case should be impartially assigned by someone other than the recused judge[19] to another judge in the circuit, or the case may be turned over to the administrative judge in the circuit for reassignment, or it may be assigned to a judge of another circuit.[20] "[O]nce a superior court judge, against whom a motion to recuse has been filed, refers the motion to recuse to another judge, he is no longer qualified to hear any phase of the recusal hearing."[21]

In *State v. Fleming*,[22] the Georgia Supreme Court said that when a trial judge, in a case pending before that judge, is presented with a motion to recuse accompanied by an affidavit, the

---

[15]Williams v. Pennsylvania, 136 S. Ct. 1899, 195 L. Ed. 2d 132 (2016).

[16]Leverette v. State, 291 Ga. 834, 835, 732 S.E.2d 255 (2012).

[17]Sears v. State, 262 Ga. 805, 426 S.E.2d 553 (1993). See Barnett v. State, 300 Ga. 551, 796 S.E.2d 653 (2017) (fact that judge had formerly represented a victim is not a per se reason for recusal).

[18]Gude v. State, 289 Ga. 46, 709 S.E.2d 206 (2011). See Cheney v. U.S. Dist. Court for Dist. of Columbia, 541 U.S. 913, 124 S. Ct. 1391, 158 L. Ed. 2d 225 (2004).

[19]Ferry v. State, 245 Ga. 698, 699, 267 S.E.2d 1 (1980).

[20]Ferry v. State, 151 Ga. App. 436, 260 S.E.2d 351 (1979), aff'd, 245 Ga. 698, 267 S.E.2d 1 (1980).

[21]Birt v. State, 255 Ga. 693, 342 S.E.2d 303 (1986). See State v. Nejad, 286 Ga. 695, 690 S.E.2d 846 (2010) (once the trial judge is recused, he or she is generally only authorized to complete the ministerial acts "necessary to have the case transferred to another judge").

[22]State v. Fleming, 245 Ga. 700, 702, 267 S.E.2d 207 (1980).

In Riggins v. State, 159 Ga. App. 791, 285 S.E.2d 579 (1981) (citing Wilson v. State, 145 Ga. App. 33 (1), 243 S.E.2d 304 (1978)), the court pointed out that where a motion to recuse is unsupported by an affidavit or other evidence, it is not error to overrule it. The court also stated that "[i]n the absence of any evidence to the contrary, it is presumed that the trial judge's conduct . . . in performing his official duties was proper." See O.C.G.A. § 24-14-26.

judge whose recusal is sought shall only pass "on the legal sufficiency" of the affidavit, and if, assuming all the facts alleged in
the affidavit to be true, recusal would be warranted, then another judge must be assigned to hear the motion to recuse. The
affidavit must set out *facts* sufficient to warrant the recusal of
the judge.[23]

In *Baptiste v. State*,[24] the court pointed out that "under . . .
[Uniform Superior Court Rule] 25.1, there is no provision for any
discovery to find a basis for recusal, because the movant for
recusal is supposed to have all the evidence of the grounds at the
time the motion is filed."

The fact that a judge receives death threats does not mandate
a judge's recusal. Any other rule would allow a defendant to delay
trial and otherwise subvert the criminal justice system.[25]

Generally, see Annotation, "Review of Federal Judge's Grant or
Denial of Motion to Recuse," 64 A.L.R.Fed. 433 (1983), and An-
notation, "Waiver or Loss of Right to Disqualify Judge by
Participation in Proceedings—Modern State Criminal Cases," 27
A.L.R.4th 597 (1984).

§ 14:78 Motion to suppress—General

The term "motion to suppress" commonly refers to the suppression of illegally obtained tangible evidence.[1] There is no reason
why the term should not refer to intangible evidence as well.[2]
The purpose of the motion to suppress is to determine, in advance
of trial, whether or not particular evidence will be admissible at
the trial. If the evidence is not admissible, the district attorney

---

[23]Brown v. State, 156 Ga. App.
201, 274 S.E.2d 572 (1980). In the
Brown case, the court concluded that
the following affidavit was inadequate:
"(1) That this Court did on October 15,
1979, find Counsel for the Defendant
guilty of contempt of court. (2) That
this Honorable Court did on October
15, 1979, accuse counsel for the defendant of obstructing and delaying the
administration of justice and the procedures of the Court. (3) That this
Court did exhibit evidence of personal
bias and prejudice against Counsel for
the Defendant whereby Defendant
believes that he will be unable to
secure a fair and impartial trial by
this Court." See Hunnicutt v.
Hunnicutt, 248 Ga. 516, 519 (1), 283
S.E.2d 891 (1981).

[24]Baptiste v. State, 229 Ga. App.
691, 698 (2), 494 S.E.2d 530 (1997).

[25]Battle v. State, 298 Ga. 661, 784
S.E.2d 381 (2016).

[Section 14:78]

[1]In Bobo v. State, 153 Ga. App.
679, 266 S.E.2d 247 (1980), the court
held that, on motion, a trial judge
should strike the testimony of an officer who improperly stops a suspect,
even though no motion to suppress is
filed. The court pointed out that a motion to suppress only needs to be filed
when physical evidence is obtained.

[2]In Warden v. Hayden, 387 U.S.
294, 87 S.Ct. 1642, 18 L.Ed.2d 782
(1967), the court said we "have held
. . . that intangible as well as tangible
evidence may be suppressed. . . ."

may realize that he cannot make out a case and thus dead docket or enter a nolle prosequi. On the other hand, a defendant may be more likely to enter a plea of guilty if he knows the trial judge will admit the evidence to which he will object. Thus, a motion to suppress may avoid wasted time.

As a general proposition, "[o]nce a motion to suppress has been filed, the burden of proving the lawfulness of the warrant is on the [S]tate and that burden never shifts. [Cits.] The only burden upon the challenger of a search warrant is that of producing evidence to support his challenge, which burden is shifted to him only after the [S]tate has met its initial burden of producing evidence showing the validity of the warrant." [Cit.][3]

A motion to suppress identification evidence is a specific type of motion to suppress. The Georgia courts have stated that the suppression of identification testimony is beyond the scope of a motion to suppress as contemplated by O.C.G.A. § 17-5-30.[4] Likewise, it has been held that the admissibility of a confession may not be determined by a motion to suppress.[5] While it is true that O.C.G.A. § 17-5-30 relates to the suppression of tangible evidence in a search and seizure context, it also allows the court "to suppress as evidence anything" obtained by an illegal search.[6]

The Georgia Supreme Court has summarily indicated that a pre-trial motion to suppress identification testimony does not lie in any case.[7] In considering a pre-trial motion to suppress a confession, the Supreme Court quoted[8] with approval a Court of Appeals decision which said: "If a motion to suppress were held to apply to testimony because it is for some reason inadmissible, the court would be required to hold a pre-trial full scale trial for determining what portions of the testimony or other evidence may be inadmissible upon grounds directed to the court's attention, and even that would not preclude the objecting to it on yet other grounds when it is tendered on the trial. It is simply impractical to test in advance the admissibility of testimony that may or may not be tendered on the trial and a requirement that

---

[3]Davis v. State, 266 Ga. 212, 213, 465 S.E.2d 438 (1996) (citations omitted). In Graddy v. State, 277 Ga. 765, 767 (3), 596 S.E.2d 109 (2004), the court expressly overruled State v. Towe, 246 Ga. App. 808, 541 S.E.2d 423 (2000) and "any other decision which places the burden of proof on the defendant who challenges a search warrant. . . ."

[4]Baker v. State, 230 Ga. 741, 742 (1), 199 S.E.2d 252 (1973); Foote v. State, 141 Ga. App. 18, 232 S.E.2d 366 (1977). Contra, Kirby v. Superior Court, 8 Cal.App.3d 591, 87 Cal.Rptr. 577 (1970).

[5]State v. High, 145 Ga. App. 772, 773 (1), 244 S.E.2d 888 (1978).

[6]O.C.G.A. § 17-5-30(a).

[7]Day v. State, 237 Ga. 538, 541 (3)(a), 228 S.E.2d 913 (1976). See Pass v. State, 227 Ga. 730 (5), 182 S.E.2d 779 (1971); Williams v. State, 147 Ga. App. 268, 248 S.E.2d 548 (1978).

[8]Jarrell v. State, 234 Ga. 410, 417 (3), 216 S.E.2d 258 (1975).

the court attempt to do so would be intolerable."[9]

Since it is recognized that a motion to suppress an in-court identification should be heard outside the presence of the jury[10] and that pre-trial identification is not admissible at trial if it was unnecessarily suggestive,[11] there is no valid reason why a defendant should not be able to obtain a ruling on a motion to suppress identification testimony prior to trial. See § 6:11, supra, on motion to suppress identification testimony.

A motion in limine is typically used to seek a pre-trial determination of the admissibility of specific evidence at trial. A motion in limine is recognized in an increasing number of states;[12] however, Georgia seems to have been reluctant to accept it.[13] The Georgia Court of Appeals has said that a judge has the inherent authority to grant a motion in limine,[14] and the Georgia Supreme Court has held that if the motion is granted and the opposing counsel asks a question relating to the area protected by the order, it is not necessary for an objection to be made at the time of

---

[9]Reid v. State, 129 Ga. App. 660, 662-63, 200 S.E.2d 456 (1973). Cf. Luce v. United States, 469 U.S. 38, 105 S.Ct. 460, 83 L.Ed.2d 443 (1984) (defendant lost right to claim improper impeachment with a prior conviction because he did not testify at trial). See Warbington v. State, 316 Ga. App. 614, 730 S.E.2d 90 (2012) (Court of Appeals followed *Luce*).

[10]Holcomb v. State, 128 Ga. App. 238 (1), 196 S.E.2d 330 (1973). In the *Holcomb* case the court said that if there is a written motion to suppress eyewitness identification, there should be a hearing on the motion outside the presence of the jury.

[11]Stovall v. Denno, 388 U.S. 293, 302, 87 S.Ct. 1967, 18 L.Ed.2d 1199, 1206 (1967).

[12]See Annot., 63 A.L.R.3d 311 (1975).

[13]In Cauley v. State, 130 Ga. App. 278, 282, 203 S.E.2d 239 (1973), the defendant moved to suppress all testimony that resulted from an illegal interception of telephone conversation to which the defendant was a party. The court held that the motion was directed at anticipated testimony rather than property and, therefore, it would not lie. Dr. Agnor concludes that this was error. He says, "clearly under Katz v. United States [389 U.S. 347, 88 S.Ct. 507, 19 L.Ed.2d 576 (1967)] the interception without authority of a telephone conversation is a search and seizure. The resulting testimony would be 'anything so obtained' under O.C.G.A. § 17-5-30 (Rev. 1972) and should be suppressed." 26 Mercer L. Rev. 93, 104-105 (1974). In Norrell v. State, 116 Ga. App. 479, 488, 157 S.E.2d 784 (1967), the court held that a motion to suppress "oral statements of defendant" secured as the result of an illegal arrest did not lie but that the statements could be objected to at trial. See Hawkins v. State, 117 Ga. App. 70, 159 S.E.2d 440 (1967); Reed v. State, 126 Ga. App. 323, 190 S.E.2d 587 (1972).

[14]Harley-Davidson Motor Co., Inc. v. Daniel, 149 Ga. App. 120, 121 (1), 253 S.E.2d 783 (1979), disapproved of on other grounds, 244 Ga. 284, 260 S.E.2d 20 (1979).

In O.C.G.A. § 24-4-412, the legislature has provided a special rule in the trial of rape, aggravated sodomy, aggravated child molestation, and aggravated sexual battery cases which, even in the absence of a motion in limine, requires the trial judge to rule in advance on the admissibility of evidence of the "past sexual behavior" of the complaining witness.

the question[15] in order to preserve the alleged error for appellate review.[16] However, in *State v. Johnston*,[17] the court held that a trial judge "has an absolute right to refuse to decide the admissibility of evidence, allegedly violative of some ordinary rule of evidence, prior to trial."

A motion in limine may be made either orally or in writing.[18] However, the trial judge may modify a ruling on a motion in limine at the time of trial.[19]

In *Smith v. State*,[20] the court pointed out "that a motion to suppress is not a proper procedural device for raising a challenge to the admissibility of a blood-alcohol test based merely on noncompliance with agency regulations governing the administration of such tests. . . . [However, a] trial court would nevertheless be authorized to reach the merits of a motion to suppress predicated on such grounds by treating it as a motion in limine."

In the 1982 case of *Wiggins v. State*,[21] the Georgia Supreme Court discussed judicial economy[22] and then held that "the admissibility of evidence gained by use of a radar speed detection device properly may be raised by a motion in limine although the motion may be styled as, or in the form of, a motion to suppress, and that the trial court has discretion to hear the motion pretrial or to reserve ruling on the admissibility of the evidence until it is offered as evidence during trial."

As with the motion to suppress identification material, a motion in limine should be heard before trial. "It is commonly understood by trial lawyers that prejudice implanted or stimulated in the minds of jurors can win trials, that objecting to the prejudicial material may only emphasize it, and that traditional 'curative' actions taken by trial judges when prejudicial material is objected to are ineffective and unrealistic and may aggravate the potential harm. In order to avoid this dilemma, counsel has

---

[15]Harley-Davidson Motor Co., Inc. v. Daniel, 244 Ga. 284, 285 (1), 260 S.E.2d 20 (1979).

[16]Reno v. Reno, 249 Ga. 855, 295 S.E.2d 94 (1982).

[17]State v. Johnston, 249 Ga. 413 (1), 415, 291 S.E.2d 543 (1982); Pierce v. State, 173 Ga. App. 551 (2), 327 S.E.2d 531 (1985). Cf. Holt v. State, 181 Ga. App. 798, 799 (1), 354 S.E.2d 167 (1987).

[18]Brown v. State, 192 Ga. App. 864, 865 (1), 386 S.E.2d 734 (1989).

[19]Gregg v. State, 201 Ga. App. 238, 239 (2), 411 S.E.2d 65 (1991); Woityra v. State, 213 Ga. App. 89, 90 (3), 443 S.E.2d 867 (1994).

[20]Smith v. State, 185 Ga. App. 531, 364 S.E.2d 907 (1988).

[21]Wiggins v. State, 249 Ga. 302, 303, 290 S.E.2d 427 (1982).

[22]In State v. Johnston, 160 Ga. App. 71, 73, 286 S.E.2d 47 (1981), aff'd, 249 Ga. 413, 291 S.E.2d 543 (1982), the court held that considerations of judicial economy permit an accused to challenge the admissibility of the results of an intoximeter test either by way of a motion to suppress or by objection at the time the test results are offered as evidence.

often sought to secure in advance the exclusion from trial of prejudicial evidence or other references to prejudicial matters by means of a preliminary motion, sometimes called a motion in limine."[23]

In *Ruffin v. State*,[24] the court held that the failure to file a motion to suppress constitutes a waiver of the constitutional guarantee with respect to a search and seizure.

In *Hatcher v. State*,[25] the court held that when a defendant has been aggrieved by an unlawful search pursuant to a warrant, a motion to suppress must be in writing stating facts showing the unlawfulness and must be made at or before arraignment.

The Georgia Court of Appeals has stated that the purpose of a motion to suppress is to "avoid the interruption of the trial for the purpose of investigating the collateral issue."[26] The same purpose applies to a motion in limine. Furthermore, if ruled on in advance of trial, a motion in limine will prevent the jury from hearing inadmissible evidence, a desirable practice since instructions from the trial court to disregard certain comments are usually ineffective.[27]

The Federal Rules of Evidence provide: "In jury cases, proceedings shall be conducted, to the extent practicable, so as to prevent inadmissible evidence from being suggested to the jury by any means, such as making statements or offers of proof or asking questions in the hearing of the jury."[28] Judge Weinstein and Dr. Berger have stated in connection with Rule 103(c) that "a ruling excluding evidence in a jury case may be pointless if the jury is already aware of the evidence."[29]

Even when a motion in limine is granted, the trial judge may modify his ruling in order to prevent "manifest injustice."[30]

A defendant generally waives his right to formal arraignment by filing a demand for trial and a motion to suppress.[31]

A motion to suppress illegally seized evidence must be filed in

---

[23]63 A.L.R.3d 313 (1975). This quotation is reproduced with the express permission of Lawyers Cooperative Publishing Company, Rochester, New York, copyright owner.

[24]Ruffin v. State, 201 Ga. App. 792 (1), 412 S.E.2d 850 (1991).

[25]Hatcher v. State, 224 Ga. App. 747, 748 (1), 482 S.E.2d 443 (1997). Accord, State v. Roddy, 231 Ga. App. 91, 93 (1), 497 S.E.2d 653 (1998). Cf. Belcher v. State, 230 Ga. App. 235, 236 (1), 496 S.E.2d 306 (1998).

[26]Thomas v. State, 118 Ga. App. 359, 361, 163 S.E.2d 850 (1968).

[27]Nash v. Hess Oil, 123 Ga. App. 132, 179 S.E.2d 778 (1970).

[28]See Rule 103(c) of the Federal Rules of Evidence.

[29]Weinstein's Evidence ¶ 103-41 (05) (Matthew Bender, 1975).

[30]Henley v. State, 169 Ga. App. 682 (1), 314 S.E.2d 697 (1984).

[31]Ferrell v. State, 149 Ga. App. 405, 406 (3), 254 S.E.2d 404 (1979).

"a court with jurisdiction to try the offense."[32]

See § 6:11, supra, on motions to suppress identification. For examples of motions in limine, see Studdard, *Daniel's Georgia Criminal Trial Practice Forms* (2018–2019 ed.), Chapter 15.

§ 14:79 Motion to suppress—Illegally obtained tangible evidence—Expectation of privacy or standing— General

This section and those following will discuss first, the necessity of standing or expectation of privacy and next, the meaning of these terms under Georgia law, with some reference to the federal constitutional requirement. There will then be some reference to who has the burden of establishing the existence or lack of existence of standing or expectation of privacy, and then the federal constitutional meaning of these terms will be discussed in light of current United States Supreme Court authority. Next, some of the criteria of the expectation of privacy will be discussed. Finally, some examples will be given on expectation of privacy.

Even when there has been an unlawful search and/or seizure, a defendant has no right to suppress the fruits of such a search unless he has standing under the Georgia statute,[1] or unless the seizure violated the defendant's legitimate expectation of privacy in the area searched under the federal constitution.[2] The Georgia statute provides that a "defendant aggrieved by an unlawful search and seizure may move . . . to suppress" unlawfully obtained evidence.[3] In the 1986 case of *Sanders v. State,*[4] the court held that a person does not become "aggrieved" within the meaning of the statute unless the alleged illegal search "occurred on [his] premises or [his] Fourth Amendment rights . . . have been infringed in some other manner." The court then stated, "We decline to accept the proposition that defendant achieved the status of one 'aggrieved' under O.C.G.A. § 17-5-30(a), merely because the objective of the search warrant was the interception of the cocaine delivery, since it is the recognized relationship of the person with the property searched that gives rise to the protective device of suppression."

---

[32]Harbin v. State, 193 Ga. App. 248, 250 (3), 387 S.E.2d 367 (1989).

[Section 14:79]

[1]Dutton v. State, 228 Ga. 850 (1), 188 S.E.2d 794 (1972).

[2]United States v. Salvucci, 448 U.S. 83, 100 S.Ct. 2547, 65 L.Ed.2d 619 (1980). In United States v. Bell, 651 F.2d 1255 (8th Cir. 1981), the court pointed out that the defendant had no standing in a motion to suppress cocaine illegally seized from a third person.

[3]O.C.G.A. § 17-5-30(a).

[4]Sanders v. State, 181 Ga. App. 117, 119 (1), 351 S.E.2d 666 (1986). See Hampton v. State, 295 Ga. 665, 668 (1), 763 S.E.2d 467 (2014).

One of the few Georgia cases which really discusses the meaning of the statutory words "aggrieved by an unlawful search and seizure" is the 1967 case of *Norrell v. State*.[5] Most of the cases have discussed the question of standing as though there were no difference between the requirements of the Fourth Amendment and O.C.G.A. § 17-5-30.[6]

In *United States v. Suarez-Blanca*,[7] United States Magistrate Alan Baverman explains:

> The Fourth Amendment protects an individual in those places where he can demonstrate a reasonable expectation of privacy against government intrusion. *See Katz v. United States*, 389 U.S. 347, 353, 88 S.Ct. 507, 19 L.Ed.2d 576 (1967). Fourth Amendment rights, however, are personal, and only individuals who actually enjoy the reasonable expectation of privacy have standing to challenge the validity of a government search. *Rakas v. Illinois*, 439 U.S. 128, 133–34, 143, 99 S.Ct. 421, 58 L.Ed.2d 387 (1978); *United States v. Cooper*, 203 F.3d 1279, 1284 (11th Cir.2000). To have standing to challenge a search, one must manifest a subjective expectation of privacy in the invaded area that "society is prepared to recognize as reasonable." *Rakas*, 439 U.S. at 143 & n. 12; *United States v. Cooper*, 133 F.3d 1394, 1398 (11th Cir.1998). Further, "[l]egitimation of expectations of privacy by law must have a source outside of the Fourth Amendment, either by reference to concepts of real or personal property law or to understandings that are recognized and permitted by society." *Rakas*, 439 U.S. at 143 n. 12.
>
> Thus, an individual asserting Fourth Amendment rights "must demonstrate that he personally has an expectation of privacy in the place searched, and that his expectation is reasonable [.]" *Minnesota v. Carter*, 525 U.S. 83, 88, 119 S.Ct. 469, 142 L.Ed.2d 373 (1998). That is, a defendant must establish both a subjective and an objective expectation of privacy. *United States v. Segura-Baltazar*, 448 F.3d 1281, 1286 (11th Cir.2006); *United States v. Robinson*, 62 F.3d 1325, 1328 (11th Cir.1995). " 'The subjective component requires that a person exhibit an actual expectation of privacy, while the objective component requires that the privacy expectation be one that society is prepared to recognize as reasonable.' " *Carter*, 525 U.S. at 88; *see also Smith v. Maryland*, 442 U.S. 735, 740–41, 99 S.Ct. 2577, 61 L.Ed.2d 220 (1979) (noting that an individual's expectation, viewed objectively, must be justifiable under the circumstances) (quoting *Katz*, 389 U.S. at 383); *Cooper*, 133 F.3d at 1398. The subjective prong is a factual inquiry. *United States v. McKennon*, 814 F.2d 1539, 1543 (11th Cir.1987); *see also United*

---

[5]Norrell v. State, 116 Ga. App. 479, 488, 157 S.E.2d 784 (1967) (citing Jones v. United States, 362 U.S. 257, 261, 80 S.Ct. 725, 4 L.Ed.2d 697 (1960)). See also Brewer v. State, 129 Ga. App. 118, 122, 199 S.E.2d 109 (1973).

[6]E.g., Norrell v. State, 116 Ga.

App. 479 (3), 157 S.E.2d 784 (1967); Nealey v. State, 233 Ga. 326, 327, 211 S.E.2d 286 (1974); Brewer v. State, 129 Ga. App. 118, 122, 199 S.E.2d 109 (1973).

[7]U.S. v. Suarez-Blanca, 2008 WL 4200156 (N.D. Ga. 2008).

States v. Jones, 184 Fed. Appx. 943, 947 (11th Cir.2006). The objective prong is a question of law. *Id.*

The subscriber to a telephone service or a person whose voice is heard on a wiretap has standing to challenge illegal phone surveillance; "[w]hen the voice of an individual is not heard and the tap is not on his premises, he has no standing."[8] See § 4:58, supra, on electronic surveillance. Computers pose a unique challenge to the case law which has developed around such Fourth Amendment issues as expectation of privacy, probable cause, consent and the extent to which a computer's files may be searched. In *Henson v. State,*[9] for example, an officer armed with a warrant which authorized the search of the suspect's premises for evidence related to the sale and distribution of marijuana, including both written and electronic records thereof, discovered pictures of child pornography during the search of the defendant's computer. The search was terminated while the officers obtained another warrant authorizing the search of the computer for further evidence of child pornography. The seizure of the computer and subsequent discovery of hundred of photographs and dozens of videos depicting child pornography was found lawful based upon the court's finding that the initial search of the computer was reasonable and within the scope of the warrant.

It is now well established that an internet service customer has no reasonable expectation of privacy in subscriber information that he voluntarily turns over to an internet provider and for that reason lacks standing to challenge the search of his subscriber information.[10]

Although the law is still developing, defense counsel, prosecutors and courts should proceed with caution where the object of a police search resides within a suspect's computer.[11]

See § 4:26, supra, on warrantless searches, and § 4:59, supra, on school searches.

---

[8]Ellis v. State, 256 Ga. 751, 755, 353 S.E.2d 19 (1987). See Deleon-Alvarez v. State, 324 Ga. App. 694, 751 S.E.2d 497 (2013).

[9]Henson v. State, 314 Ga. App. 152, 723 S.E.2d 456 (2012) (court relied on U.S. v. Walser, 275 F.3d 981 (10th Cir. 2001).

[10]Ensley v. State, 330 Ga. App. 258, 765 S.E.2d 374 (2014).

[11]See, e.g., U.S. v. Zimmerman, 277 F.3d 426 (3d Cir. 2002); U.S. v. Walker, 275 F.3d 981 (10th Cir. 2001); U.S. v. Carey, 172 F.3d 1268 (10th Cir. 1999); Barton v. State, 286 Ga. App. 49, 648 S.E.2d 660 (2007); Daniels v. State, 278 Ga. App. 332, 629 S.E.2d 36 (2006); Blevins v. State, 270 Ga. App. 388, 606 S.E.2d 624 (2004); Schwindler v. State, 254 Ga. App. 579, 563 S.E.2d 154 (2002). See also Hawkins v. State, 290 Ga. 785, 723 S.E.2d 924 (2012) (search of cell phone is restricted to object of search).

§ 14:80 Motion to suppress—Illegally obtained tangible evidence—Burden of proving standing

Who has the burden of proving standing or the lack of it? In the area of federal constitutional law, the burden of establishing a defendant's reasonable expectation of privacy falls on the defendant. "Petitioner, of course, bears the burden of proving not only that the search [. . .] was illegal, but also that he had a legitimate expectation of privacy [. . .]."[1]

While the Georgia statute provides that the burden of proving that a search was lawful is on the state,[2] Georgia courts have consistently referred only to the federal Constitution in assigning the burden of proving standing to the defendant.[3]

In *Keishian v. State*,[4] the Georgia Court of Appeals held that "a defendant charged with possessory offense who moves to suppress the item . . . is . . . obligated to establish at the suppression hearing that the police conduct of which he complained violated his own Fourth Amendment rights. . . . Ownership of the seized contraband alone is not sufficient to entitle a defendant to challenge the search; he bears the burden of proving . . . that he had a legitimate expectation of privacy in the area searched."

Counsel should note that in order for a defendant to carry his burden, he must either stipulate to evidence introduced by the government or present his own. A defendant cannot rely on the government's assertion that he was a party to a recorded phone conversation for purposes of establishing standing to move for the suppression of the recording without also admitting that he was in fact a party to the conversation.[5]

§ 14:81 Motion to suppress—Illegally obtained tangible evidence—Supreme Court rulings on standing

Historically, from a federal constitutional standpoint, standing generally seemed to have followed the common law concept of the

---

[Section 14:80]

[1]Rawlings v. Kentucky, 448 U.S. 98, 104, 100 S.Ct. 2556, 65 L.Ed.2d 633 (1980). See also Rakas v. Illinois, 439 U.S. 128, 131, 99 S.Ct. 421, 58 L.Ed.2d 387 (1978); United States v. Salvucci, 448 U.S. 83, 95, 100 S.Ct. 2547, 65 L.Ed.2d 619 (1980).

[2]O.C.G.A. § 17-5-30(b).

[3]E.g., Gray v. State, 260 Ga. App. 197, 201, 581 S.E.2d 279 (2003); Shelton v. State, 252 Ga. App. 444,

445, 556 S.E.2d 540 (2001); In re M.H., 247 Ga. App. 84, 85, 543 S.E.2d 390 (2000); Atwater v. State, 233 Ga. App. 339, 340 (2), 503 S.E.2d 919 (1998).

[4]Keishian v. State, 202 Ga. App. 718, 719, 415 S.E.2d 324 (1992).

[5]Bourassa v. State, 345 Ga. App. 463, 811 S.E.2d 113 (2018) (state's witness "believed" defendant's voice could be heard on recording; no other evidence offered to establish defendant was a party to conversation).

ownership of property until 1960 in *Jones v. United States*.[1] In *Jones*, the court first defined a "person aggrieved by an unlawful search and seizure" as one who is a "victim of a search or seizure, one against whom the search was directed, as distinguished from one who claims prejudice only through the use of evidence gathered as a consequence of a search or seizure directed at someone else."[2] However, the court concluded that it was not proper to incorporate into the protection of the Fourth Amendment the subtle distinctions of the common law. Hence, "anyone legitimately on premises where a search occurs may challenge its legality . . . when its fruits are proposed to be used against him." *Jones* also established what was known as automatic standing where a defendant was charged with a possessory crime. Automatic standing was adopted for two reasons: (1) a defendant should not have to admit ownership of contraband in order to attempt to suppress it, since this testimony might be used against him at trial if his motion to suppress was unsuccessful; and (2) it is inconsistent for the government to claim at a suppression hearing that the defendant did not own the contraband and then contend at trial that he did.

In 1967, in *Katz v. United States*,[3] the court held that the Fourth Amendment was intended to protect people and not places; thus, when Katz entered a public telephone booth, closed the door, and paid for a long distance call, he was entitled to the protection of the Fourth Amendment.

The next year, in *Simmons v. United States*,[4] the court held that testimony given at a suppression hearing could not be admitted over objection against a defendant at the trial-in-chief.

Also in 1968 the court decided *Mancusi v. DeForte*,[5] in which DeForte was found to have standing to suppress documents seized in his presence from a union office which he shared with other officials, since he had a reasonable expectation of privacy in the area searched.

In the 1969 wiretapping case of *Alderman v. United States*,[6] the court held that where a person's telephone was illegally tapped, he had standing to object to eavesdropping upon

---

[Section 14:81]

[1]Jones v. United States, 362 U.S. 257, 80 S.Ct. 725, 4 L.Ed.2d 697 (1960).

[2]Jones v. United States, 362 U.S. 257, 261, 80 S.Ct. 725, 4 L.Ed.2d 697 (1960).

[3]Katz v. United States, 389 U.S. 347, 88 S.Ct. 507, 19 L.Ed.2d 576 (1967).

[4]Simmons v. United States, 390 U.S. 377, 88 S.Ct. 967, 19 L.Ed.2d 1247 (1968).

[5]Mancusi v. DeForte, 392 U.S. 364, 88 S.Ct. 2120, 20 L.Ed.2d 1154 (1968); Harper v. State, 283 Ga. 102, 657 S.E.2d 213 (2008).

[6]Alderman v. United States, 394 U.S. 165, 89 S.Ct. 961, 22 L.Ed.2d 176 (1969).

conversations occurring upon his premises, even though he was not present at the time of the call and was not a party to the call.

In 1978, the court decided the case of *Rakas v. Illinois*.[7] In this case, officers stopped a car in which Rakas, King, and two females were riding. One of the females owned the automobile. The vehicle was stopped because it fit the description of one which had been used as a getaway car in a robbery. The occupants were ordered out and the car was searched; a box of rifle shells was found in the glove compartment, and a sawed-off rifle was found under the front passenger seat. The males moved to suppress the rifle and shells. The court first rejected the "target" theory of standing, under which a defendant at whom a search was directed would have standing, even though the Fourth Amendment violation was that of a third person. The court also rejected derivative standing by saying "Fourth Amendment rights are personal rights that may not be asserted vicariously."[8]

In Justice Rehnquist's majority opinion, he stated that the court could think of no decided case of the United States Supreme Court which would have been decided differently if the rule of *Rakas* had been applied in those cases. Thus, it could be said that *Rakas* affirmed the results reached in prior search and seizure cases in that court, and that the court expressly affirmed the result of *Jones*. However, the court disapproved the statement in *Jones* that anyone "legitimately on premises" where a search occurs may challenge its legality.[9] The court said this "would permit a casual visitor who has never seen, or been permitted to visit the basement of another's house to object to a search of the basement if the visitor happened to be in the kitchen of the house at the time of the search."[10] The Fourth Amendment protects a person from unreasonable governmental intrusion in a place where he has a legally sufficient interest. Legitimate presence is not irrelevant, but it is not controlling. In this case, the defendants asserted no property interest in the automobile nor in the property seized, and showed no legitimate expectation of

---

[7]Rakas v. Illinois, 439 U.S. 128, 99 S.Ct. 421, 58 L.Ed.2d 387 (1978). Cf. Wood v. State, 159 Ga. App. 221 (1), 283 S.E.2d 79 (1981); Dunbar v. State, 163 Ga. App. 243 (1), 292 S.E.2d 897 (1982).

[8]Rakas v. Illinois, 439 U.S. 128, 133, 99 S.Ct. 421, 58 L.Ed.2d 387 (1978). At 439 U.S. 128, 99 S.Ct. 421, 58 L.Ed.2d 387 the court said that "the issue of standing involves two inquiries: first, whether the proponent of a particular legal right has alleged

'injury in fact,' and, second, whether the proponent is asserting his own legal rights and interests rather than basing his claim for relief upon the rights of third parties."

[9]Jones v. United States, 362 U.S. 257, 264, 80 S.Ct. 725, 4 L.Ed.2d 697 (1960). Cf. Cuevas v. State, 151 Ga. App. 605, 610, 260 S.E.2d 737 (1979).

[10]Rakas v. Illinois, 439 U.S. 128, 142, 99 S.Ct. 421, 58 L.Ed.2d 387 (1978).

privacy in the areas searched.[11] Their presence does not give them the right to suppress. While the expectation of privacy is significantly different in a vehicle than in a home, the outcome would have been the same if the defendants had been in a dwelling. In *Rakas,* the defendant raised no question of the propriety of the stopping of the automobile.[12] In *Byrd v. United States,*[13] the Court held that a driver in lawful possession or control of a rental car has a reasonable expectation of privacy even though he is not listed on the rental agreement as an authorized driver.

The full impact of *Rakas* was not felt until *Salvucci* and *Rawlings* which were decided in 1980. In *United States v. Salvucci,*[14] Salvucci and Zackular were charged with possession of stolen mail. The mail was discovered when police searched, pursuant to a warrant, an apartment rented by the mother of the defendant Zackular. The court treated the warrant as being defective and began its opinion by reversing the automatic standing rule laid down in *Jones* as to possessory offenses. The court concluded that *Simmons* and other events have eliminated the need for automatic standing. However, the court expressly reserved the question of whether testimony at a suppression hearing could be used to impeach a defendant at his trial, since the suppression had been tried on the theory of automatic standing. The case was reversed and remanded so as to give the defendants an opportunity to demonstrate, if they could, that their own Fourth Amendment rights were violated. The court pointed out that while ownership of seized property is a factor in determining whether a defendant's Fourth Amendment rights have been violated, an illegal search only violates the rights of those who have a "legitimate expectation of privacy in the invaded place."[15] Possession "of a seized good . . . [is not] a substitute for a factual finding that the owner of the good had a legitimate expectation of privacy in the area

---

[11]Cf. Marshall v. State, 153 Ga. App. 198, 264 S.E.2d 718 (1980).

[12]Rakas v. Illinois, 439 U.S. 128, 155, n. 4, 99 S.Ct. 421, 58 L.Ed.2d 387, concurring opinion (court noted that its ruling would not prevent a visitor to a residence from contesting the lawfulness of a search if the visitor's property was seized) and 160, n. 5, dissenting opinion (they would have had standing to challenge the legality of the stop), 439 U.S. 128, 99 S.Ct. 421, 58 L.Ed.2d 387 (1978) (apparently, they would have had standing to have contended that the stop was invalid and that the evidence was obtained as a result of an unlawful stop).

[13]Byrd v. U.S., 138 S. Ct. 1518, 200 L. Ed. 2d 805 (2018).

[14]United States v. Salvucci, 448 U.S. 83, 100 S.Ct. 2547, 65 L.Ed.2d 619 (1980). See U.S. v. Bushay, 859 F. Supp. 2d 1335, 1352 (N.D. Ga. 2012) (declined to extend standing to a challenge of the *seizure* of property based upon one's possessory interest therein noting that only one trial court had done so since Salvucci was decided). See also, State v. Scott, 176 Ga. App. 887, 339 S.E.2d 276 (1985).

[15]Gilbert v. State, 159 Ga. App. 326, 327 (1), 283 S.E.2d 361 (1981).

searched."[16]

In *Rawlings v. Kentucky,*[17] officers entered a house to arrest one Marquess. While unsuccessfully searching for him, the officers smelled marijuana smoke and saw marijuana seed. Two of the officers left to get a search warrant. They were gone about 45 minutes. During the time they were gone, the officers refused to let anyone leave without undergoing a body search.

When the officers returned with a search warrant, Miranda warnings were given. Officers told Ms. Cox to empty her purse on a table. She did, and then told Rawlings to take what was his. He immediately claimed the drugs which had been in Ms. Cox's purse. There seems to be some question as to the validity of the search warrant insofar as Cox's purse is concerned.[18] However, the Supreme Court considered the case as though the warrant did not authorize the search of her purse. In concluding that Rawlings did not have a reasonable expectation of privacy in Cox's purse, the court mentioned the following factors: First, Rawlings had the burden of establishing that he has a legitimate expectation of privacy in her purse;[19] second, he dumped thousands of dollars worth of illegal drugs in her purse when he had known her only a few days; third, he "had never sought or received access to her purse prior to that sudden bailment"; fourth, Rawlings had no right to exclude others from the purse, and another person other than Cox did have free access to the purse; fifth, "the precipitous nature of the transaction hardly supports a reasonable inference that petitioner took normal precautions to maintain his privacy"; sixth, Rawlings frankly admitted "that he had no subjective expectation that Cox's purse would remain free from governmental intrusion."

The court acknowledged that Rawlings' ownership of the drugs was "undoubtedly one fact to be considered . . . [however] Rakas emphatically rejected the notion that 'arcane' concepts of property law ought to control the ability to claim the protections of the Fourth Amendment." If he had placed the drugs in plain view, he would still have owned them, but he would not have any legitimate expectation of privacy. The threshold question in determining suppression after *Rakas* is "whether governmental officials violated any legitimate expectation of privacy held by petitioner." The court concluded that it could find no reason to overturn the lower court's conclusion that petitioner had no legit-

---

[16]United States v. Salvucci, 448 U.S. 83, 92, 100 S.Ct. 2547, 65 L.Ed.2d 619 (1980).

[17]Rawlings v. Kentucky, 448 U.S. 98, 100 S.Ct. 2556, 65 L.Ed.2d 633 (1980).

[18]Rawlings v. Kentucky, 448 U.S. 98, 110, 100 S.Ct. 2556, 65 L.Ed.2d 633 (1980).

[19]Rawlings v. Kentucky, 448 U.S. 98, 104, 100 S.Ct. 2556, 65 L.Ed.2d 633 (1980).

imate expectation of privacy in Cox's purse at the time of the search.[20]

In *Minnesota v. Olson*,[21] the United States Supreme Court considered the non-consensual, warrantless entry of a home to arrest a guest in the home. The guest was suspected of driving the getaway car used in a robbery-murder. The guest was found hiding in a closet and arrested. Soon thereafter he made incriminating statements. The court affirmed the suppression of these statements in view of the absence of exigent circumstances. The court held that the guest's "status as an overnight guest is alone enough to show that he had an expectation of privacy in the home . . . ." In *Minnesota v. Carter*,[22] the United States Supreme Court held that while an individual making an overnight stop may have an expectation of privacy, an expectation of privacy in commercial property is less than an expectation of privacy in a home. One who is merely present with the consent of the householder may not have an expectation of privacy. A defendant who was not an overnight guest but was essentially present for a business transaction and was in the house for a matter of hours has no legitimate expectation of privacy.

A passenger in an automobile who makes no claim of a possessory interest in the auto or the items within it has no standing to challenge a search of the vehicle directly. However, as the Court of Appeals observed in *Migliore v. State*[23] "[s]tanding to contest the search and standing to contest the *Terry* seizure and detention are two separate and distinct questions, and different privacy interests are involved." In a case involving the standing of a defendant to move for the exclusion of evidence seized from the motor vehicle in which he had been a passenger, the Court of Appeals in *State v. Cooper*,[24] observed: "[a] passenger does have standing to challenge the stop and detention of the car . . . because the interest in freedom of movement and the interest in being free of fear and surprise are personal to all occupants of the vehicle . . . an individual's interest is not diminished simply because he is a passenger as opposed to the driver when the stop occurred." The Court then concluded that the defendant had

---

[2]Rawlings v. Kentucky, 448 U.S. 98, 16, 100 S.Ct. 2556, 65 L.Ed.2d 633 (1980).

[2]Minnesota v. Olson, 495 U.S. 91, 110 S.Ct. 1684, 109 L.Ed.2d 85 (1990). Cf. Warden v. Hayden, 387 U.S. 294, 87 S.Ct. 1642, 18 L.Ed.2d 782 (1967) (see § 30, supra).

[22]Minnesota v. Carter, 525 U.S. 83, 119 S.Ct. 469, 142 L.Ed.2d 373 (1998).

[23]Migliore v. State, 240 Ga. App. 783, 787, 525 S.E.2d 166 (1999).

[24]State v. Cooper, 260 Ga. App. 333, 334(1), 579 S.E.2d 754 (2003). As authority for its position, the Court cited: United States v. Kimball, 25 F.3d 1 (1st Cir. 1994). United States v. Green, 275 F.3d 694, 699 (8th Cir. 2001). See, Tiller v. State, 261 Ga. App. 363, 582 S.E.2d 536 (2003).

standing to challenge the use of evidence obtained as a result of his unlawful detention.

In *United States v. Padilla*,[25] the court held that the existence of a conspiracy did not give an absent co-conspirator an expectation of privacy in cocaine found in the trunk of a vehicle driven by another conspirator. "[A] Fourth Amendment violation can be successfully urged only by those whose rights were violated by the search itself, not by those who are aggrieved solely by the introduction of damaging evidence."

See § 4:59, supra, on expectation of privacy of a student or a governmental employee in his desk and file cabinet. See § 4:2, supra, on protected areas and interests.

§ 14:82   Motion to suppress—Illegally obtained tangible evidence—Criteria for determining expectation of privacy

What are the criteria today for determining whether or not a defendant has a legitimate expectation of privacy in the premises searched? First, the court has emphasized the right to exclude others from the area.[1] Non-owners may also have a right to exclude others from the premises.[2] Conversely, a denial of ownership or interest in an object may demonstrate a lack of an

---

[25]United States v. Padilla, 508 U.S. 77, 113 S.Ct. 1936, 123 L.Ed.2d 635 (1993).

[Section 14:82]

[1]Rakas v. Illinois, 439 U.S. 128, 143, n. 12, 99 S.Ct. 421, 58 L.Ed.2d 387 (1978).

[2]Rakas v. Illinois, 439 U.S. 128, 149, 99 S.Ct. 421, 58 L.Ed.2d 387 (1978). At 439 U.S. 128, 99 S.Ct. 421, 58 L.Ed.2d 387, the court also pointed out that when Katz entered the telephone booth, he "shut the door behind him to exclude all others and paid the toll, which 'entitled [him] to assume that the words he utter[ed] into the mouthpiece [would] not be broadcast to the world.' "See Katz v. United States, 389 U.S. 347, 88 S.Ct. 507, 19 L.Ed.2d 576 (1967).

It has been suggested that if a person can validly consent to admit others, he has a right to exclude others. Cf. United States v. Matlock, 415 U.S. 164, 94 S.Ct. 988, 39 L.Ed.2d 242 (1974).

A guest of long duration is not to be regarded in the same light as one for an hour. Cf. Morrison v. State, 508 S.W.2d 827 (Tex.Crim.App. 1974).

In United States v. Haydel, 649 F.2d 1152 (5th Cir. 1981), agents searched the home of the defendant's parents and discovered a cardboard box of gambling records under the bed of the defendant's parents. The defendant sought to suppress the contents of the box. The court, in support of its conclusion that the defendant had a legitimate expectation of privacy in the records, pointed out the following: (1) the defendant's parents had given him permission to use their home and had given him a key, thus providing him free access; (2) although he did not reside regularly there, he kept some clothing there and sometimes spent the night; (3) he conducted a significant portion of his gambling activities at his parents' home and owned the records seized; (4) it was reasonable to assume that the defendant had authority to exclude persons other than his parents and their guests; and

expectation of privacy.[3] Second, free access at will over a long period of time may establish a legitimate expectation of privacy in the area.[4] Third, while mere legitimate presence is not enough,[5] this does not mean that legitimate presence plus some other interest in the place searched or the thing seized is not enough. Fourth, has the defendant taken reasonable precautions to exclude others from the thing seized?[6] Fifth, the subjective expectation of privacy, or lack of it, was at least sufficient to cause the court to discuss it in *Rawlings*.[7] Sixth, a possessory interest in the thing seized has some significance in evaluating a person's expectation of privacy.[8] Lastly, there seems to be significance in whether or not conduct of officers rises to a "level of conscious or flagrant misconduct requiring prophylactic exclusion."[9]

Generally, see Slobogin, "Capacity to Contest a Search and Seizure: the Passing of Old Rules, and Some Suggestions for New

---

(5) the defendant demonstrated a subjective expectation that the contents of the box were to remain private.

[3]United States v. Tolbert, 692 F.2d 1041 (6th Cir. 1982). See § 4:37, supra.

[4]United States v. Jeffers, 342 U.S. 48, 72 S.Ct. 93, 96 L.Ed. 59 (1951).

[5]Rakas v. Illinois, 439 U.S. 128, 142, 99 S.Ct. 421, 58 L.Ed.2d 387 (1978).

In Neely v. State, 159 Ga. App. 737, 285 S.E.2d 190 (1981), the court concluded that a mere overnight guest in an apartment had no standing to suppress fruits of a search of the apartment.

[6]Frederick v. State, 226 Ga. App. 540, 541 (1), 487 S.E.2d 107 (1997). In U.S. v. Chadwick, 433 U.S. 1, 97 S. Ct. 2476, 53 L. Ed. 2d 538 (1977) (abrogated on other grounds by California v. Acevedo, 500 U.S. 565, 111 S. Ct. 1982, 114 L. Ed. 2d 619 (1991)), the court emphasized that the defendant, by placing his personal effects in "a double-locked footlocker, . . . manifested an expectation that the contents would remain free from public examination." In Rawlings v. Kentucky, 448 U.S. 98, 105, 100 S.Ct. 2556, 65 L.Ed.2d 633 (1980), the court said "the precipitous nature of the transaction

hardly supports a reasonable inference that petitioner took normal precautions to maintain his privacy."

There would seem to be no expectation of privacy in abandoned property. Anderson v. State, 133 Ga. App. 45, 47, 209 S.E.2d 665 (1974); Abel v. United States, 362 U.S. 217, 241, 80 S.Ct. 683, 4 L.Ed.2d 668 (1960). Generally, see § 4:37, supra. Compare State v. Nesbitt, 305 Ga. App. 28, 699 S.E.2d 368 (2010).

There is no expectation of privacy in what a person knowingly exposes to the public. Rawlings v. Kentucky, 448 U.S. 98, 106, 100 S.Ct. 2556, 65 L.Ed.2d 633 (1980).

In Traylor v. State, 165 Ga. App. 226, 227 (1), 299 S.E.2d 911 (1983), the court pointed out that the defendant could have no reasonable expectation of privacy in the unenclosed carport of his father's house, where he was a frequent visitor rather than a resident.

[7]Rawlings v. Kentucky, 448 U.S. 98, 105, 100 S.Ct. 2556, 65 L.Ed.2d 633 (1980).

[8]Rawlings v. Kentucky, 448 U.S. 98, 105, 100 S.Ct. 2556, 65 L.Ed.2d 633 (1980); United States v. Salvucci, 448 U.S. 83, 91, n. 6, 100 S.Ct. 2547, 65 L.Ed.2d 619 (1980).

[9]Cf. Rawlings v. Kentucky, 448 U.S. 98, 110, 100 S.Ct. 2556, 65 L.Ed.2d 633 (1980).

Ones," 18 Am. Crim. L. Rev. 387 (1981); Gutterman, " 'A Person Aggrieved': Standing to Suppress Illegally Seized Evidence in Transition," 23 Emory L. J. 111 (1974); 3 LaFave, *Search and Seizure,* § 11.3 (West 1978); 1 Ringel, *Searches and Seizures, Arrests and Confessions* § 20.3 (Clark Boardman 1979); 68 Am. Jur. 2d Searches and Seizures, § 37 (1973). See § 4:2, supra, on protected areas and interests.

§ 14:83   Motion to suppress—Illegally obtained tangible evidence—Examples of expectation of privacy

In *United States v. Barry,*[1] the Sixth Circuit concluded that a person dealing in drugs has no expectation of privacy in drugs sent by Federal Express, a private carrier. Pills, contained in four large bottles and from which the prescription numbers had been effaced, were visible after the package was damaged in transit. The court stated that the defendant had assumed "the risk of exposure" of the contraband. The "possibility that Federal Express would for some purpose open the package, be it for reasons of security, or accident, or damage, is a risk that must, or at least should have been considered by" the defendant.

In *Hatcher v. State,*[2] the Georgia Court of Appeals noted:

> The United States Supreme Court consistently has held that a person has no legitimate expectation of privacy in information he voluntarily turns over to third parties. . ... Consistent with this principle, numerous federal courts have concluded that an Internet service customer has no reasonable expectation of privacy in the subscriber information that he gives voluntarily to his Internet service provider. . ... Every federal court to address this issue has held that subscriber information provided to an internet provider is not protected by the Fourth Amendment's privacy expectation. . ... [C]omputer users do not have a legitimate expectation of privacy in their subscriber information because they have conveyed it to another person – the system operator. In light of these decisions, we doubt that an internet service subscriber can have a reasonable expectation of privacy in the subscriber information that he volun-

---

[Section 14:83]

[1]United States v. Barry, 673 F.2d 912, 919 (6th Cir. 1982).

[2]Hatcher v. State, 314 Ga. App. 836, 838-39, 726 S.E.2d 117 (2012) (citations omitted) (physical precedent). See Ensley v. State, 330 Ga. App. 258, 765 S.E.2d 374 (2014) (confirming *Hatcher* finding that defendant lacked reasonable expectation of privacy in information supplied to his internet service provider); Courtney v. State, 340 Ga. App. 496, 797 S.E.2d 496 (2017) (O.C.G.A. § 16-9-109(b) sets forth process by which prosecutor may obtain subscriber information from internet provider). See also U.S. v. Jones, 132 S. Ct. 945, 181 L. Ed. 2d 911 (2012) (concurring opinion of Sotomayor, J., questions whether third party rule should be re-examined in light of current technological advances which require the disclosure of information in performance of "mundane tasks" that might reasonably be considered "private").

tarily conveys to an Internet service provider in order to obtain Internet service.

In *Stone v. State,*[3] the defendant was the driver of a pickup which contained a controlled substance. Gravitt was a first cousin of the defendant and was a passenger in the vehicle. The pickup had been purchased by Gravitt with his mother's money. She apparently had legal title. She could not drive the vehicle. It had been purchased to haul her "garbage and stuff like that." The truck stayed at her house, usually with the key in it. If the key was not in it, either the defendant or Gravitt had to get the key from her. The defendant and Gravitt had equal access to use the pickup without asking permission. The defendant lived next door to the owner. However, Gravitt was living five or six miles away during the month involving the incident. The pickup had been in the possession of the defendant at his house for about 10 days before the incident so that he could do some repair work on it. The trial judge granted Gravitt's motion to suppress, since the officer did not have probable cause to search the vehicle. However, the defendant's motion to suppress was denied on the basis that the defendant had no reasonable expectation of privacy in the pickup. The Court of Appeals reversed, holding that the defendant and Gravitt had equal access to the truck, and the defendant had a legitimate expectation of privacy in the pickup.

The equal access defense is of a limited application. As the court in *Newman v. State,*[4] observed: "[t]he equal access rule, entitling a defendant to acquittal where evidence is presented that others had equal access to a vehicle or that the vehicle had been recently used by others, applies only where the sole evidence of possession of contraband found in the vehicle is the defendant's ownership or possession of the vehicle." The rule does not apply to eliminate the presumption of possession where "all persons allegedly having equal access to the contraband are alleged to have been in joint constructive possession of that contraband."[5] Thus, merely finding contraband on premises occupied by the defendant is not sufficient under the equal access rule to support a conviction if it "affirmatively appears from the evidence that persons other than the defendant had equal op-

---

[3]Stone v. State, 162 Ga. App. 654, 656, 292 S.E.2d 525 (1982).

[4]Newman v. State, 216 Ga. App. 73, 75(3), 453 S.E.2d 117 (1995). See also Stovall v. State, 275 Ga. App. 244, 620 S.E.2d 462 (2005); Davis v. State, 272 Ga. App. 33(1), 611 S.E.2d 710 (2005).

[5]Heller v. State, 275 Ga. App. 637, 638(1), 621 S.E.2d 591 (2005). See also Wilkerson v. State, 269 Ga. App. 190(2), 603 S.E.2d 728 (2004); Thompson v. State, 234 Ga. App. 74(3), 506 S.E.2d 201 (1998). See Reyes v. State, 322 Ga.App. 496, 745 S.E.2d 738 (2013).

portunity to commit the crime."[6] In *Hodges v. State*,[7] the court noted that a finding of "constructive possession must be based upon some connection between the defendant and the contraband other than spatial proximity. Evidence of mere presence at the scene of the crime and nothing more to show participation of a defendant in the illegal act, is insufficient to support a conviction." In *Hodges* the court determined that there was no such connection between the defendant and the contraband where the defendant was merely a passenger in a car and the drugs involved were located in a package hidden behind the seat of the driver. In order for a person to be in constructive possession of an object, he or she must "knowingly [have] both the power and intention at a given time to exercise dominion over the object."[8] In *Sanchez-Villa v. State*,[9] the court noted "a charge on the equal access defense is appropriate only to counter a jury instruction on the presumption of possession, and when no instruction is given on the presumption, an equal access instruction is not required."

A number of cases beginning with *Reid v. State*,[10] held that when more than one occupant in an auto "has equal access to hidden contraband, but only one occupant is prosecuted for possession of the contraband, the State has the burden of proving that the prosecuted occupant 'was in *sole* constructive possession' [cit] of the contraband."[11] In *Maddox v. State*,[12] the Court of Appeals rejected those cases, noting that the State may elect to prosecute one or more of the several occupants in a motor vehicle containing contraband either "jointly or separately, [cit] . . . or may elect to prosecute only one of the occupants for directly committing the crime, but nevertheless prove the sole prosecuted occupant was guilty as a party to the crime. [cit]."

See Studdard, *Daniel's Georgia Handbook on Criminal Evidence* § 3:17 (2018 ed.), on possession of contraband.

Several cases have held that an owner of an automobile has no expectation of privacy in the vehicle while it is loaned to another.[13] A person in a stolen automobile has no legitimate expectation of

---

[6]Brookins v. State, 256 Ga. App. 884, 885, 570 S.E.2d 72 (2002).

[7]Hodges v. State, 277 Ga. App. 174, 626 S.E.2d 133 (2006). See Brown v. State, 285 Ga. App. 330, 332, 646 S.E.2d 273 (2007), "mere spatial proximity combined with flight is insufficient to connect a defendant to nearby contraband." See also Coney v. State, 290 Ga. App. 364(3), 659 S.E.2d 768 (2008).

[8]Wofford v. State, 262 Ga. App. 291, 292, 585 S.E.2d 207 (2003).

[9]Sanchez-Villa v. State, 341 Ga. App. 264, 273 (2), 799 S.E.2d 364, 372(2) (2017).

[10]Reid v. State, 212 Ga. App. 787, 442 S.E.2d 852 (1994), overruled by Maddox v. State, 322 Ga. App. 811, 746 S.E.2d 280 (2013).

[11]Maddox v. State, 322 Ga. App. 811, 814, 746 S.E.2d 280 (2013).

[12]Maddox v. State, 322 Ga. App. 811, 814, 746 S.E.2d 280 (2013).

[13]Espinoza v. State, 244 Ga. App. 96, 98 (4), 534 S.E.2d 824 (2000);

privacy in the vehicle.[14] Likewise, passengers occupying an automobile could not assert the protection of the Fourth Amendment "with respect to a search of the vehicle where they 'asserted neither a property nor a possessory interest in the automobile, nor an interest in the property seized.' "[15] "[A] mere passenger who asserts an interest in neither the car nor the property found in it has no standing to object to the search of the automobile."[16] But where a passenger in a vehicle pays the driver to transport the passenger, his family and belongings, the passenger has standing.[17] In *Hall v. State*,[18] the appellate court affirmed the trial court's finding that "an unlicensed and unauthorized driver of a rental vehicle [did not] . . . have a reasonable expectation of privacy in vehicle after he [had] been placed under arrest and acquiesced in the impoundment of the vehicle." In *State v. Duran*,[19] Guerra was in a vehicle with her common law husband and their two children. The defendant testified that the vehicle was loaned to her common law husband, that he did all the driving, and that he never gave her the keys. The trunk of the car contained clothing belonging to both husband and wife. The trial judge found that she had a legitimate expectation of privacy and standing to object to the search.

Despite the foregoing, a number of jurisdictions have approved motions to exclude evidence found in a motor vehicle in which the movant was merely a passenger, provided that the movant can show that he or she was the subject of unlawful detention and that the search of the vehicle was unlawful. In *State v. Cooper*,[20] the Georgia Court of Appeals citing these other jurisdictions with approval concluded that a defendant passenger in a motor vehicle which was improperly searched would have standing to contest the admissibility of contraband found in the car.

Gresham v. State, 204 Ga. App. 540, 540 (1), 420 S.E.2d 71 (1992); Prothro v. State, 186 Ga. App. 836, 838 (3), 368 S.E.2d 793 (1988); United States v. One 1977 Mercedes Benz, 708 F.2d 444 (9th Cir. 1983); United States v. Dyar, 574 F.2d 1385 (5th Cir. 1978); United States v. Dall, 608 F.2d 910 (1st Cir. 1979).

[14]Sanborn v. State, 251 Ga. 169 (1), 304 S.E.2d 377 (1983); Morrison v. State, 258 Ga. 683, 685 (2), 373 S.E.2d 506 (1988).

[15]Mecale v. State, 186 Ga. App. 276, 278, 367 S.E.2d 52 (1988); Ballard v. State, 216 Ga. App. 315, 316, 454 S.E.2d 200 (1995); State v. Saia, 249 Ga. App. 69, 70, 547 S.E.2d 407 (2001).

Cf. Keishian v. State, 202 Ga. App. 718, 415 S.E.2d 324 (1992); Robinson v. State, 208 Ga. App. 528, 530 (2), 430 S.E.2d 830 (1993).

[16]Gilbert v. State, 245 Ga. App. 809, 810, 539 S.E.2d 506 (2000).

[17]State v. Diaz, 191 Ga. App. 830, 831 (1), 383 S.E.2d 195 (1989).

[18]Hall v. State, 223 Ga. App. 211 (1), 477 S.E.2d 364 (1996).

[19]State v. Duran, 220 Ga. App. 296, 297 (1), 469 S.E.2d 429 (1996).

[20]State v. Cooper, 260 Ga. App. 333, 579 S.E.2d 754 (2003). There are a number of federal and state decisions noted in the decision which are not referenced here.

Although the Court noted that there are distinct questions of standing peculiar to a *Terry* detention and the automobile search, it concluded that in each case the interest in freedom of movement without fear is paramount and should not be diminished in the case of a passenger.

There is no expectation of privacy in the identification numbers of automobiles parked in an outdoor lot of a repair shop where the numbers are visible through the windshield.[21]

In *Sims v. State*,[22] the court said a person "has a reasonable expectation of privacy in the contents of a covered shoebox hidden under a bed in his parents' home," even though he does not reside in their dwelling. Likewise, in *State v. Gay*,[23] the court held that a guest in an apartment retained a reasonable expectation of privacy with respect to the contents of a backpack belonging to him and located under the bed on which he was sleeping. In this case, the lessee of the apartment had given police permission to search the premises and the court concluded that in the absence of a search warrant or the permission of the defendant guest to search the backpack, the motion to suppress was properly granted.

In the interesting case of *United States v. Brown*,[24] the Eleventh Circuit held that when two persons are traveling together and one is searched and contraband is found concealed on him and the two men are charged with "aiding and abetting each other to possess with intent to distribute a controlled substance," the defendant not carrying contraband has standing to challenge the search of the other defendant. However, on reconsideration the same panel concluded that the defendant did not have a reasonable expectation of privacy under the Fourth Amendment.[25]

In *Robinson v. State*,[26] the appellate court affirmed the denial of a motion to suppress. A passenger in the defendant's car was wearing the defendant's jacket when he was patted down and cocaine was found in a jacket pocket. The court pointed out that the defendant gave up any expectation of privacy in the jacket when he let the passenger use the jacket.

---

[21]Shaw v. State, 253 Ga. 382, 320 S.E.2d 371 (1984).

[22]Sims v. State, 251 Ga. 877, 882, 311 S.E.2d 161 (1984) (citing and relying on United States v. Haydel, 649 F.2d 1152 (5th Cir. 1981)).

[23]State v. Gay, 269 Ga. App. 331, 604 S.E.2d 572 (2004).

[24]United States v. Brown, 731 F.2d 1491, modified, 743 F.2d 1505 (11th Cir. 1984).

[25]United States v. Brown, 743 F.2d 1505 (11th Cir. 1984); Ransom v. State, 239 Ga. App. 501, 503 (1)(b), 521 S.E.2d 430 (1999).

[26]Robinson v. State, 226 Ga. App. 406, 408 (2), 486 S.E.2d 667 (1997).

In *Lester v. State*,[27] the court said that a defendant who is not a resident or tenant of the apartment and who has no interest in the apartment has no standing to suppress contraband which was seized from the apartment. A mere visitor has no expectation of privacy in the premises of another.[28] Likewise, in *Smallwood v. State*,[29] the court pointed out that a defendant's own Fourth Amendment rights must be violated before the exclusionary rule is applied. Thus, it was not error to deny a motion to suppress marijuana found on property adjacent to that leased by the defendant.

In *Minnesota v. Olson*,[30] the United States Supreme Court held that overnight guests in a home had a reasonable expectation of privacy in the residence. In *United States v. Torres*,[31] the Eleventh Circuit court held that two house guests who enjoyed unrestricted access to all parts of the house, ate, slept, stored their belongings there, and had been there for two days had a legitimate expectation of privacy in the house. The court said, "When an owner invites someone to his home as his overnight house guest, the expectation of privacy the guest has is akin to that enjoyed by an occupant of a hotel room. The expectation of privacy in a private residence and its appurtenant area is one that society has long recognized as justifiable and legitimate." However, the *Torres* court concluded that these two guests had no expectation of

---

[27]Lester v. State, 163 Ga. App. 604 (1), 295 S.E.2d 566 (1982). Accord, Duque v. State, 228 Ga. App. 391, 392, 491 S.E.2d 841 (1997). See Ferron v. State, 216 Ga. App. 456, 454 S.E.2d 637 (1995). In United States v. Meyer, 656 F.2d 979 (5th Cir. 1981), *Meyer* was held to have no standing where he was in an apartment less than an hour as a casual visitor before agents forced their way in and discovered cocaine in a cabinet under the sink.

In United States v. Garcia, 741 F.2d 363 (11th Cir. 1984), the court held that a defendant had no expectation of privacy in an apartment in which he had met three times to discuss business even though he had given the phone number of the apartment to one person, was in control on the day of the search, had invited two of those present and had answered the phone that afternoon.

[28]Cherry v. State, 230 Ga. App. 443, 496 S.E.2d 764 (1998). Accord, Floyd v. State, 237 Ga. App. 586, 587, 516 S.E.2d 96 (1999).

[29]Smallwood v. State, 171 Ga. App. 784, 321 S.E.2d 118 (1984); Morrill v. State, 216 Ga. App. 468, 472 (5), 454 S.E.2d 796 (1995).

[30]Minnesota v. Olson, 495 U.S. 91, 110 S.Ct. 1684, 109 L.Ed.2d 85 (1990). Unregistered but overnight guests in a hotel room also enjoy a constitutionally protected reasonable expectation of privacy. Snider v. State, 292 Ga. App. 180, 663 S.E.2d 805 (2008). The rule is different in the case of unregistered guests who can only demonstrate mere presence in the hotel room of another. Crisp v. State, 195 Ga. App. 786, 395 S.E.2d 47 (1990). See State v. Delvechio, 301 Ga. App. 560, 687 S.E.2d 845 (2009) (one who obtains a hotel room by fraudulent use of another's credit card can have no reasonable expectation of privacy in the room).

[31]United States v. Torres, 705 F.2d 1287 (11th Cir. 1983). Cf. State v. Brown, 212 Ga. App. 800, 803, 442 S.E.2d 818 (1994).

privacy in a van parked in the driveway of the house. Likewise, persons in possession of a stolen car, as well as those who obtain a hotel room by means of fraud, cannot have a reasonable expectation of privacy.[32]

In *United States v. Bent*,[33] the Eleventh Circuit said that "neither captain nor crew has a legitimate expectation of privacy protected by the fourth amendment in an area which is subject to the common access of those legitimately aboard the vessel. The ice hold or fish hold . . . is such an area."

In *Hudson v. Palmer*,[34] the United States Supreme Court held that a prisoner has no reasonable expectation of privacy in his prison cell which will protect him against unreasonable searches and seizures.

In *State v. Jackson*,[35] the court held that the owner of a house had no expectation of privacy in a car parked on the lawn of her property and from which she had just exited.

In *California v. Greenwood*,[36] the United States Supreme Court held that there was no expectation of privacy in garbage left for collection outside the curtilage of a house. In *United States v. Hall*,[37] the Eleventh Circuit held that there was no reasonable expectation of privacy in discarded documents even though the documents had been shredded and placed in an opaque bag inside a garbage dumpster within the "commercial curtilage" of the business. The dumpster was located about 40 yards up a private drive. The court pointed out that the immediate vicinities of commercial buildings and homes are treated differently for privacy purposes. The court also pointed out that the concept of "commercial curtilage" does not apply when the business has not taken affirmative steps to exclude the public, and that it was unimportant that the company used a private trash collection service.

See § 4:1, supra, for the definition of a "search" and a "seizure," and § 4:2, supra, on protected areas and interests. See § 4:37,

---

[32]Thomas v. State, 274 Ga. 156, 549 S.E.2d 359 (2001) (stolen car); State v. Delvechio, 301 Ga. App. 560, 687 S.E.2d 845 (2009) (hotel room).

[33]United States v. Bent, 707 F.2d 1190 (11th Cir. 1983).

In United States v. Pinto-Mejia, 720 F.2d 248 (2d Cir. 1983), the court held that the members of the crew had no legitimate expectation of privacy in the cargo of a vessel absent some proprietary interest in the cargo.

[34]Hudson v. Palmer, 468 U.S. 517, 104 S.Ct. 3194, 82 L.Ed.2d 393 (1984). In *Hudson* the case also held that

where there is an adequate state remedy, an inmate may not recover in an action under 42 U.S.C.A. § 1983 for the intentional destruction of his property by a prison official.

[35]State v. Jackson, 201 Ga. App. 810, 812 (1), 412 S.E.2d 593 (1991).

[36]California v. Greenwood, 486 U.S. 35, 108 S.Ct. 1625, 100 L.Ed.2d 30 (1988). Cf. Perkins v. State, 197 Ga. App. 577, 579 (1), 398 S.E.2d 702 (1990).

[37]United States v. Hall, 47 F.3d 1091 (11th Cir. 1995).

supra, on abandonment. See § 4:57, supra, on expectation of privacy and controlled deliveries. See § 4:47, supra, on expectation of privacy as to vehicles.

§ 14:84 Motion to suppress—Illegally obtained tangible evidence—Requirements of the motion

A motion to suppress must be in writing[1] and should be promptly filed. Rule 31.1 of the Uniform Rules for the Superior Courts requires all motions to be "at or before the time set by law (ten days after arraignment, O.C.G.A. § 17-7-110) unless time therefor is extended by the judge in writing prior to trial." The failure to timely file the motion amounts to a waiver[2] if the defendant has knowledge of the search.[3] However, there has been some indication that an oral motion to suppress at trial may be adequate if the defendant did not become aware of the illegal seizure until that time.[4] Generally, the defendant must file a motion to suppress before he enters his written plea to the indictment.[5] However, it has been held that a motion to suppress filed on the day of trial but prior to the joining of the issue is timely filed.[6] On the other hand, in *Holton v. State*,[7] the court concluded that the trial judge did not err in denying a motion to suppress as not having been timely filed, where the motion was filed on the Thursday before the trial was scheduled to begin on

---

[Section 14:84]

[1]O.C.G.A. § 17-5-30(b); Graves v. State, 135 Ga. App. 921, 219 S.E.2d 633 (1975); Miller v. State, 238 Ga. 560, 563, 233 S.E.2d 793 (1977). In Hawkins v. State, 117 Ga. App. 70, 72, 159 S.E.2d 440 (1967), the court said it was unnecessary to determine whether the motion to suppress was defective when "it was made orally even though [it had been] stipulated that it be treated as if filed in writing." State v. Hodge, 154 Ga. App. 293, 267 S.E.2d 906 (1980).

[2]Van Huynh v. State, 258 Ga. 663, 664 (2), 373 S.E.2d 502 (1988).

[3]In Thomas v. State, 118 Ga. App. 359, 361, 163 S.E.2d 850 (1968), the defendant did not know about the search until the State was introducing its evidence. The court permitted the defendant to file the motion during trial. The Court of Appeals said that the trial court may, in its discretion, permit the filing of the motion during trial. The same rule is followed in

federal court. Jones v. United States, 362 U.S. 257, 264, 80 S.Ct. 725, 4 L.Ed.2d 697 (1960).

[4]Rucker v. State, 250 Ga. 371, 375, 297 S.E.2d 481 (1982) (dicta).

[5]Waller v. State, 251 Ga. 124 (5), 303 S.E.2d 437 (1983), rev'd on other grounds, 467 U.S. 39, 104 S.Ct. 2210, 81 L.Ed.2d 31 (1984).

[6]Perryman v. State, 149 Ga. App. 54, 55 (3), 253 S.E.2d 444 (1979); Collier v. State, 171 Ga. App. 214, 319 S.E.2d 51 (1984). In State v. Mathiesen, 27 Wash.App. 257, 616 P.2d 1255 (1980), the court held that a defendant is entitled to see an affidavit which is the basis of a search warrant, even if it contains an informer's name, but the state is entitled to excise the name of a confidential informer if one was named in the affidavit.

[7]Holton v. State, 243 Ga. 312, 316 (3), 253 S.E.2d 736 (1979). Cf. Baseler v. State, 213 Ga. App. 822 (1), 446 S.E.2d 250 (1994).

the following Monday, and the defendant had known of the search for over two weeks before the motion was filed.

A motion to suppress may not be a skeleton motion nor set out in a boiler plate form. Rather, the motion must state *facts* showing why the search and seizure was illegal.[8] If the affidavit of the search warrant is inadequate, the motion must state the particular insufficiencies of the affidavit.[9] However, in *Stanley v. State*,[10] the court held that the statements contained in a brief could be considered in conjunction with a motion to suppress in determining the sufficiency of the facts alleged by movant. Also, in the case of "warrantless searches many of the necessary allegations are negative facts (e.g., the search was conducted without a warrant, the movant did not consent to the search) and conclusions based upon mixed questions of law and negative fact (e.g., the officer lacked probable cause to arrest or search)."[11] Where this is the situation, a motion to suppress is sufficient if it "shows the date of the search, the location of the search (albeit a general location as opposed to a specific location), the identity of the person searched, the number of officers making the search (albeit not their identities or the organization with which they were affiliated), the identity of the material seized, the fact that the search was conducted without a warrant being exhibited to the defendant, the fact that defendant did not consent to the search, and the conclusion that there was no probable cause for the search. . . ."[12]

A motion is insufficient where it merely states the following: "The affidavit was illegally executed in that it contains materially false allegations or information; that the place to be searched is vaguely and inaccurately described; the procedures for effectuating and reporting searches were not duly followed; and that the search was without probable cause and not supported by

---

[8]Cadle v. State, 131 Ga. App. 175, 205 S.E.2d 529 (1974). See Watts v. State, 261 Ga. App. 230, 582 S.E.2d 186 (2003) (before state's burden of proving lawful seizure arises, defendant must set forth a factual basis for finding search and seizure were unlawful).

[9]In Cadle v. State, 131 Ga. App. 175, 205 S.E.2d 529 (1974), the court said that a motion to suppress is subject to dismissal before a suppression hearing if it does not allege facts showing why the search and seizure was invalid.

[10]Stanley v. State, 206 Ga. App. 125, 424 S.E.2d 90 (1992).

[11]Lavelle v. State, 250 Ga. 224, 227, 297 S.E.2d 234 (1982).

In State v. Goodman, 220 Ga. App. 169 (1), 469 S.E.2d 327 (1996), the motion to suppress simply stated that the defendant "was lawfully operating his motor vehicle when he was pulled over by" a named officer of the Clayton County Police. The court held that this was adequate.

[12]Hill v. State, 222 Ga. App. 839 (2), 476 S.E.2d 634 (1996). Cf. Dean v. State, 246 Ga. App. 263, 540 S.E.2d 246 (2000).

warrant. The affidavit is facially insufficient."[13] At a minimum, "the suppression motion must be sufficient to put the State on notice as to the type of search [or seizure] involved[,] . . . which witness to bring to the hearing on the motion and *the legal issues to be resolved at the hearing.*"[14]

In *Wallin v. State,*[15] the court held that a motion to suppress was subject to an oral motion to dismiss where the motion simply stated that the search was without probable cause, was made without the defendant's permission, was not incident to a lawful arrest, was totally without any legal justification whatsoever, and was made without a warrant.

In *Cadle v. State,*[16] the court concluded that as a matter of right, a defendant may amend his motion to suppress. However, in *Williams v. State,*[17] the court held that it was not error for the trial judge to refuse to permit the defense to amend an oral motion to suppress. In the 1992 case of *Davis v. State,*[18] the court pointed out that *Cadle* was decided before the enactment of U.S.C.R. 31.1. At the time the case was decided, the rule provided that all motions must be filed at or before arraignment "unless a written extension of time is given by the trial court before trial." U.S.C.R. 31.1 now provides that such motions must be filed within ten days after arraignment unless such time is extended by the court. In *Davis,* a motion to suppress was timely filed before arraignment. At the suppression hearing, after arraignment, the state orally moved to dismiss on the ground that the motion "failed to state reasons or facts showing the search was illegal." After the motion to dismiss had been granted, the defendant moved to amend. The appellate court affirmed the action of the trial judge in refusing to permit the amendment and pointed out that it is discretionary with a trial judge to permit or reject an untimely motion to suppress.

It appears that the Court of Appeals in *Davis* is limiting their holding in *Cadle* by narrowing the time frame in which a defendant may amend a motion to suppress as a matter of right. Prior to *Davis,* and according to *Cadle,* a defendant could file

---

[13]Cadle v. State, 131 Ga. App. 175, 205 S.E.2d 529 (1974). However, in State v. Thomas, 150 Ga. App. 170, 257 S.E.2d 28 (1979), the court held that an appellate court may not consider the question of whether or not a motion to suppress was facially defective unless that question was raised in the trial court.

[14]State v. Roddy, 231 Ga. App. 91, 93, 497 S.E.2d 653 (1998) (citations and punctuation omitted) (emphasis in original). See State v. Allen, 256 Ga. App. 798, 570 S.E.2d 34 (2002).

[15]Wallin v. State, 248 Ga. 29, 279 S.E.2d 687 (1981).

[16]Cadle v. State, 136 Ga. App. 232, 233 (1), 221 S.E.2d 59 (1975).

[17]Williams v. State, 199 Ga. App. 122, 124 (4), 404 S.E.2d 296 (1991).

[18]Davis v. State, 203 Ga. App. 315, 316 (3), 416 S.E.2d 789 (1992).

amendments as a matter of right up until the time of the trial. Following *Davis,* however, it appears that a defendant may only file amendments, as a matter of right, up until the time provided by U.S.C.R. 31.1. However, *Davis* concludes that the trial court in its discretion may permit the filing of an amendment to a motion to suppress up until the time of trial.[19] Provided defense counsel is proceeding in good faith and with all due diligence, a trial court would be hard pressed to decline a request by the defense to amend a motion to suppress based upon facts developed subsequent to the time normally allowed for filing motions.

For motions to suppress, see Studdard, *Daniel's Georgia Criminal Trial Practice Forms* (2018–2019 ed.), §§ 2:4, 3:6 et seq., 4:10, et seq., and Chapter 5.

§ 14:85 Motion to suppress—Illegally obtained tangible evidence—Hearing on motion

A defendant is generally entitled to an evidentiary hearing unless there is a stipulation of facts, in which case the judge may pass upon the motion to suppress as a matter of law.[1] However, in *Quinn v. State,*[2] the court held that a defendant is not entitled to a hearing on a motion to suppress unless the motion is timely filed and unless the motion "state[s] *facts* showing that the search and seizure were unlawful. . . . [M]ere conclusions unsupported by facts . . . do not satisfy this requirement. . . ." Harm or prejudice must be demonstrated before the failure to have a hearing amounts to reversible error.[3]

It is error for the trial judge, over objection, to conduct the hearing in the presence of the jury.[4] However, in a probation revocation proceeding a defendant is not entitled to a separate

---

[19]Cf. State v. Roddy, 231 Ga. App. 91, 497 S.E.2d 653 (1998).

[Section 14:85]

[1]In Gray v. State, 145 Ga. App. 293, 243 S.E.2d 687 (1978), the court held that on the filing of a motion to suppress, it is mandatory that a hearing on the motion be held out of the presence of the jury.

In State v. Ross, 155 Ga. App. 659, 272 S.E.2d 524 (1980), the court pointed out that the state is also entitled to a hearing at which it can present evidence.

In Hartline v. State, 161 Ga. App. 847, 849 (3), 288 S.E.2d 902 (1982), the court seems to hold that

the failure of the trial judge to have a hearing on a motion to suppress is not error, or at least not reversible error, when the record shows that the seized contraband was in plain view.

[2]Quinn v. State, 221 Ga. App. 399, 400 (1), 471 S.E.2d 337 (1996) (emphasis added).

[3]Eidson v. State, 182 Ga. App. 321, 323 (3), 355 S.E.2d 691 (1987).

[4]Yarbrough v. State, 151 Ga. App. 474, 475 (2), 260 S.E.2d 369 (1979). In State v. Peabody, 247 Ga. 580, 277 S.E.2d 668 (1981), rev'g 156 Ga. App. 853, 854 (2), 276 S.E.2d 47 (1980), the court held that while it was error to hear evidence on a motion to suppress in the presence of the jury, when de-

hearing on a motion to suppress.[5] In *McGinnis v. State*,[6] the court held that a defendant has a right to be present at the hearing on a motion to suppress. Of course, this right can be waived "if the waiver is made in the defendant's presence, or with the defendant's express authority, or if the defendant subsequently acquiesces to the waiver made by counsel."

There is no right to a jury trial on a motion to suppress.[7] In *Caldwell v. State*,[8] the court held a defendant at trial has no right to develop new facts related to a motion to suppress since the jury has "no role in deciding factual issues for the motion to suppress." The trial judge passes on both the questions of law and fact.[9] Indeed, the court may consider hearsay evidence which might otherwise be subject to exclusion at trial on issues related to, for example, a third party's consent to search a defendant's premises.[10] It has been held in a foreign jurisdiction that the fact that a judge issued a search warrant does not require the judge to disqualify himself from presiding over a suppression hearing involving the validity of that warrant.[11]

It is not necessary for the trial judge to make findings of fact in support of its order on a motion to suppress.[12] Generally, the burden of proof is on the state to prove that the search and seizure were lawful.[13] In *Watts v. State*,[14] the Court ruled that a defendant has no evidentiary burden or special pleading requirement so long as the motion to suppress puts the state on notice that "it would have to meet its burden of proving that the search and seizure were valid by showing that no material information was omitted or that any such omissions were not deliberate or

---

fense counsel fails to object, this constitutes a waiver.

[5]Davenport v. State, 172 Ga. App. 606, 607, 324 S.E.2d 201 (1984).

[6]McGinnis v. State, 208 Ga. App. 354, 357 (4), 430 S.E.2d 618 (1993). Accord, Hill v. State, 222 Ga. App. 839 (1), 476 S.E.2d 634 (1996).

[7]Ellis v. State, 216 Ga. App. 232, 233 (1), 453 S.E.2d 810 (1995). Cf. Aycock v. State, 142 Ga. App. 755, 236 S.E.2d 863 (1977).

[8]Caldwell v. State, 249 Ga. App. 885, 889 (6), 549 S.E.2d 449 (2001).

[9]O.C.G.A. § 17-5-30(b). The question of the credibility of the witnesses is generally for the determination of the trial judge. State v. Brassell, 144 Ga. App. 279, 241 S.E.2d 57 (1977).

[10]United States v. Matlock, 415 U.S. 164, 94 S.Ct. 988, 39 L.Ed.2d 242 (1974); State v. Gay, 269 Ga. App. 331, 604 S.E.2d 572 (2004); Durden v. State, 209 Ga. App. 205 (1), 433 S.E.2d 128 (1993).

[11]Trussell v. State, 67 Md.App. 23, 506 A.2d 255 (1986).

[12]Shirley v. State, 166 Ga. App. 456 (3), 304 S.E.2d 468 (1983).

[13]O.C.G.A. § 17-5-30(b). In Bell v. State, 128 Ga. App. 426, 428, 196 S.E.2d 894 (1973), the court said the "burden of proof is upon the state to show what facts constituting probable cause existed and were presented to the magistrate (under oath) before the warrant was issued." See Bowman v. State, 332 Ga. App. 407, 773 S.E.2d 33 (2015). Cf. State v. Johnston, 160 Ga. App. 71, 286 S.E.2d 47 (1981).

[14]Watts v. State, 274 Ga. 373, 375, 552 S.E.2d 823 (2001).

reckless." At a minimum, in cases where the search is conducted pursuant to a warrant, this will require production "of the warrant and its supporting affidavit, and by showing either by those documents or by other evidence that the warrant is not subject to the statutory challenge alleged."[15] From a federal constitutional standpoint, the prosecution is obligated to sustain its burden of proof by a preponderance of the evidence.[16] If the state fails to meet its burden of proof, the defendant is entitled to the granting of his motion.[17] This is true in Georgia regardless of whether or not the search is pursuant to a warrant or without a warrant.[18] However, in *Smith v. Hopper,*[19] the Georgia Supreme Court pointed out that "[b]efore the state's burden of proving a lawful seizure arises, the defendant must set forth ' . . . facts showing wherein the search and seizure were unlawful.' " The court then pointed out that if the defendant failed to comply with this pleading requirement, it is not error for the trial judge to refuse to require the state to present evidence of the validity of a seizure. Nevertheless, in *State v. Slaughter,*[20] the Georgia Supreme Court held that if a search was conducted pursuant to a warrant and the defendant does not contend the search "was illegal because [i] the warrant is insufficient on its face, [ii] there was not probable cause for the issuance of the warrant, or [iii] the warrant was illegally executed," and the state produces the warrant and its supporting affidavit at a hearing, the "defendant must prove the facts upon which he relies." In *Slaughter* the defendant contended that the magistrate was not neutral and detached because he had a conflict of interest. The court concluded that the defendant had the burden of producing evidence showing that the magistrate was not neutral and detached.

If a motion to suppress is overruled, a defendant has no right to submit the suppression question to a jury at a later trial.[21] Thus, the procedure is different where a motion to suppress tangible evidence has been overruled, than that which applies where a confession has not been excluded after a *Jackson v. Denno*

---

[15]Watts v. State, 274 Ga. 373, 375, 552 S.E.2d 823 (2001), citing Davis v. State, 266 Ga. 212, 213, 465 S.E.2d 438 (1996).

[16]United States v. Matlock, 415 U.S. 164, 177, 94 S.Ct. 988, 39 L.Ed.2d 242 (1974).

[17]Cook v. State, 134 Ga. App. 712, 716, 215 S.E.2d 728 (1975).

[18]Davis v. State, 266 Ga. 212, 465 S.E.2d 438 (1996).

[19]Smith v. Hopper, 240 Ga. 93, 95, 239 S.E.2d 510 (1977). See State v. Blosfield, 165 Ga. App. 111, 112(2), 299 S.E.2d 588 (1983).

[20]State v. Slaughter, 252 Ga. 435, 438, 315 S.E.2d 865 (1984).

[21]Rogers v. State, 155 Ga. App. 685 (2), 272 S.E.2d 549 (1980).

hearing.[22]

The defendant may testify at the hearing on the motion to suppress.[23] The defendant's testimony may not be used against him in the prosecution's case-in-chief.[24] However, the United States Supreme Court has declined to decide whether or not such testimony by a defendant can be used for purposes of impeachment.[25] Nevertheless, a number of courts have held that such testimony is admissible for impeachment purposes.[26]

Since a search warrant is to be issued in duplicate, the copy is admissible.[27] In *Russell v. State*,[28] the court held that it was immaterial that the warrant and affidavit were not introduced into evidence where they were read into the record.

In *Parks v. State*,[29] the court held that where physical evidence produced probable cause for a search, it is not necessary for the state to produce the physical evidence at the motion to suppress hearing. In this case, the officer testified that he saw marijuana seeds on the seat of an automobile and that the seeds were not produced at the hearing.

A defendant is obligated to raise all defects of the search and seizure upon which he intends to rely. He waives any defects by failing to assert the particular deficiencies. By way of illustration, in one case a defendant moved to suppress tape recordings of telephone conversations allegedly obtained in violation of a statute. His motion was overruled and later affirmed by the Court of Appeals. When the case went back to the trial court, the defendant could not move to suppress the same evidence on the ground that the statute was unconstitutional.[30]

If a defendant's motion to suppress is granted, the property seized "shall be restored, unless otherwise subject to lawful deten-

---

[22]See § 20:6, infra.

[23]Apparently, the defendant has a right to be present whether he testifies or not. People v. DeLuca, 48 Misc.2d 712, 265 N.Y.S.2d 668 (1965).

[24]Culpepper v. State, 132 Ga. App. 733, 209 S.E.2d 18 (1974) (citing Simmons v. United States, 390 U.S. 377, 394, 88 S.Ct. 967, 19 L.Ed.2d 1247 (1968)).

[25]United States v. Salvucci, 448 U.S. 83, 94, 100 S.Ct. 2547, 65 L.Ed.2d 619 (1980). However, see note 9 on page 94 of the Salvucci opinion, and Harris v. New York, 401 U.S. 222, 91 S.Ct. 643, 28 L.Ed.2d 1 (1971).

[26]United States v. Quesada-Rosadal, 685 F.2d 1281 (11th Cir. 1982); Gray v. State, 43 Md.App. 238, 403 A.2d 853 (1979); People v. Douglas, 66 Cal.App.3d 998, 136 Cal.Rptr. 358 (1977); People v. Sturgis, 58 Ill.2d 211, 317 N.E.2d 545 (1974).

[27]Barrett v. State, 146 Ga. App. 207, 245 S.E.2d 890 (1978). Cf. Cayce v. State, 192 Ga. App. 97, 98 (2), 383 S.E.2d 648 (1989).

[28]Russell v. State, 181 Ga. App. 624, 625 (1), 353 S.E.2d 820 (1987).

[29]Parks v. State, 150 Ga. App. 446, 258 S.E.2d 66 (1979).

[30]Cross v. State, 233 Ga. 960, 214 S.E.2d 374 (1975).

tion, and it shall not be admissible in evidence against the movant in any trial."[31] See § 14:87, infra.

After a trial judge has ruled on a motion to suppress, it is within the sound discretion of the trial judge to vacate the earlier order and enter a different order at the same term of court.[32] See Annotation, "Right of Accused To Be Present At Suppression Hearing or At Other Hearing or Conference Between Court And Attorneys Concerning Evidentiary Questions," 23 A.L.R.4th 955 (1981).

§ 14:86 Motion to suppress—Illegally obtained tangible evidence—Identity of informer

Where an officer's affidavit is based on information obtained from an informer whose identity is questionable the trial court must determine the existence of the informant after the officer has been questioned and cross-examined. If the court finds that there has been a failure to establish the existence of an informer, the motion to suppress should be granted.[1]

In *Miller v. State,*[2] the court rather mechanically concluded that it was not error to compel the state to disclose the name of the informer at a suppression hearing or to identify the informer in camera. However, the refusal of the trial judge to permit the defendant to call the affiant and cross-examine him was error.

If defense counsel is in a situation in which he feels there was no informer, consideration should be given to having the affiant officer present at the suppression hearing and asking him as many specific questions about the informer as defense counsel can think of. These questions might include the following:

(1)   When is the last time the informer gave you information?
(2)   What information did the informer give you on this occasion?
(3)   Where was this information given to you?
(4)   Was anyone present when the information was given?
(5)   If so, who was present?
(6)   How many times has the informer given you information?
(7)   In each case when and where was the information given?

---

[31]O.C.G.A. § 17-5-30(b).

[32]Chastain v. State, 158 Ga. App. 654, 655, 281 S.E.2d 627 (1981); Martin v. State, 201 Ga. App. 716, 717 (1), 411 S.E.2d 910 (1991). See State v. Mojica, 316 Ga. App. 619, 730 S.E.2d 94 (2012) (an exception to this general rule is where the evidentiary posture of the issue has changed).

[Section 14:86]

[1]Keith v. State, 238 Ga. 157, 231 S.E.2d 727 (1977); State v. Little, 560 S.W.2d 403 (Tenn.1978); McAllister v. State, 157 Ga. App. 158, 276 S.E.2d 669 (1981).

[2]Miller v. State, 169 Ga. App. 668, 314 S.E.2d 684 (1984).

(8) Was anyone else present?

(9) Has the informant ever given you any information which proved not to be correct?

(10) How many arrests have you made as a result of information from this informer?

(11) How many of these persons have been convicted?

(12) Who did you arrest as a result of information obtained from this informer?

(13) Who was convicted?

(14) In what court was each of these convicted?

(15) When was each of these convictions? If all those arrested were not convicted, defense counsel might consider trying to find out why.

See § 14:38, supra, on identity of informer.

§ 14:87 Motion to suppress—Illegally obtained tangible evidence—False affidavit for search warrant

Minor "factual inaccuracies which are only peripherally relevant to the showing will not void the warrant where their presence in the affidavit is not such as to reflect on the credibility of the affiant."[1]

In 1974, without overruling the older cases cited in the footnotes, the Georgia Supreme Court, in determining whether or not probable cause existed, in effect excised erroneous material from an affidavit.[2] The court noted that there was no evidence of misrepresentation made with an intent to deceive the magistrate. In the 1987 Court of Appeals case of *Daniels v. State*,[3] the court, as in the *Franks* case discussed in the next paragraph, considered a case in which the affiant knew some of the information contained in the affidavit was false. The Court of Appeals determined the adequacy of the affidavit by setting aside the affidavit's false material and determining whether the remaining contents were sufficient to establish probable cause. In the 1989 case of *Ledbetter v. State*,[4] the court pointed out that where allegations of falsity are established by a preponderance of the evidence at a *Franks* hearing, "if the affidavit is not sufficient without the false statement, . . ." the warrant is void.

[Section 14:87]

[1]Dresch v. State, 125 Ga. App. 110 (4), 186 S.E.2d 496 (1971); Summerville v. State, 226 Ga. 854 (1), 178 S.E.2d 162 (1970); Rugendorf v. United States, 376 U.S. 528, 532, 84 S.Ct. 825, 11 L.Ed.2d 887 (1964).

[2]Williams v. State, 232 Ga. 213, 214, 205 S.E.2d 859 (1974).

[3]Daniels v. State, 183 Ga. App. 651, 652, 359 S.E.2d 735 (1987).

[4]Ledbetter v. State, 190 Ga. App. 843 (1), 380 S.E.2d 313 (1989).

In *Franks v. Delaware*,[5] the United States Supreme Court declared unconstitutional that state's absolute rule preventing a hearing on the falsity of an affidavit at a hearing on a motion to suppress. The court first pointed out that from a federal constitutional standpoint there is a presumption of validity.[6] (It could be argued that the Georgia Statute does not permit this presumption,[7] but the Georgia courts have ruled that there is a presumption of validity of an affidavit supporting a search warrant.)[8] Again, from a federal constitutional standpoint, the *Franks* case makes the following points: (1) In order to be entitled to an evidentiary hearing the defendant's "attack must be more than conclusory and must be supported by more than a mere desire to cross examine"; (2) "There must be allegations of deliberate falsehood or of reckless disregard for the truth" and an offer of proof; (3) The defendant should "point out specifically the portion of the . . . affidavit that is claimed to be false" and a statement of the supporting reasons. Verified statements should be furnished or their absence explained; (4) There must be alleged deliberate falsity or reckless disregard of the truth by the affiant; (5) If "these requirements are met and if, when material that is the subject of the alleged falsity or reckless disregard is set to one side, there remains sufficient content in the warrant affidavit to support a finding of probable cause, no hearing is required. On the other hand, if the remaining content is insufficient, the defendant is entitled, under the Fourth Amendment, to his hearing."

The courts have indicated that exculpatory material does not have to be inserted in an affidavit for a search warrant "if no misconduct on the affiant's part has occurred."[9] However, if misconduct by the affiant has occurred, then the false statements shall be deleted, the omitted truthful material be included, and the affidavit be re-examined to determine whether probable cause exists to issue a warrant.

In a case that has since been overruled, *State v. Mason*,[10] the Georgia Court of Appeals pointed out that the United States Supreme Court in *Franks* "expressly declined to decide 'the dif-

[5]Franks v. Delaware, 438 U.S. 154, 98 S.Ct. 2674, 57 L.Ed.2d 667 (1978). Cf. State v. Longstreet, 619 S.W.2d 97 (Tenn.1981). Generally, see § 4:7, supra.

[6]See generally Ross v. State, 169 Ga. App. 655, 657, 314 S.E.2d 674 (1984), overruled by Watts v. State, 274 Ga. 373, 552 S.E.2d 823 (2001).

[7]In O.C.G.A. § 17-5-30(b), the statute places the burden on the state to prove that the search was lawful.

[8]State v. Slaughter, 252 Ga. 435, 437, 315 S.E.2d 865 (1984).

[9]Redding v. State, 192 Ga. App. 87, 88, 383 S.E.2d 640 (1989).

[10]State v. Mason, 181 Ga. App. 806, 808, 353 S.E.2d 915 (1987), overruled by Watts v. State, 274 Ga. 373, 552 S.E.2d 823 (2001).

ficult question whether a reviewing court must ever require the revelation of the identity of an informant once a substantial preliminary showing of falsity has been made.' " The *Mason* case also quoted the following from *Colorado v. Nunez:*[11] "The decision in *Franks* neither required nor contemplated routine disclosure of informants' identities." Generally, see § 14:38, supra, on discovery of an informer.

While the federal constitution prescribes a minimum safeguard for a defendant, this standard does not prevent a state from establishing a standard which gives a defendant greater protection.[12] Initially, the Georgia Courts appeared to follow *Franks*.

In the 1982 case of *Nutter v. State,*[13] the Georgia Court of Appeals ruled on a search warrant issued based on an affidavit which in part alleged that the reliable informer told the affiant that he "was present at the above address between the dates of 11-26-78 and 11-30-78," and he saw the defendant and another man store and use marijuana. The defendant testified at a suppression hearing "that at no time on those dates was anyone else in the house with him." The Court of Appeals decided the case on the basis of *Franks* and concluded that the defendant was not entitled to an evidentiary hearing on the truthfulness of the affidavit since there was no alleged misconduct or deliberate falsehood on the part of the officer.

In a two-judge opinion by the Georgia Court of Appeals in *Cantrell v. State,*[14] in which an affidavit was attacked for want of probable cause, the court said "the question must be determined

---

[11]Colorado v. Nunez, 465 U.S. 324, 104 S.Ct. 1257, 79 L.Ed.2d 338 (1984).

[12]See §§ 4:48, 4:55, 4:59, 5:13, 14:70, supra.

In People v. Cook, 22 Cal.3d 67, 148 Cal.Rptr. 605, 583 P.2d 130 (1978), the court declined to follow Franks v. Delaware and concluded that the "excision" procedure was proper only when the mistake was negligently made. Even an immaterial but intentionally false statement voids the search warrant.

In Waller v. State, 251 Ga. 124 (9), 303 S.E.2d 437 (1983), rev'd on other grounds, 467 U.S. 39, 104 S.Ct. 2210, 81 L.Ed.2d 31 (1984), the court held that where there was sufficient information in an affidavit to establish probable cause even without the mis-

takes set out in the affidavit, it was not error to deny the motion to suppress.

See Annot., "Sufficiency of Information Provided by Confidential Informant, Whose Identity is Known to Police, to Provide Probable Cause for Federal Search Warrant Where There Was Indication That Informant Provided Reliable Information to Police in Past-Cases Decided after Illinois v. Gates," 196 A.L.R. Fed. 1, § 1b (2004); Annot., "Disputation of Truth of Matters Stated in Affidavit in Support of Search Warrant—Modern Cases," 24 A.L.R.4th 1266 (1983).

[13]Nutter v. State, 162 Ga. App. 349, 291 S.E.2d 423 (1982) overruled by Watts v. State, 274 Ga. 373, 552 S.E.2d 823 (2001).

[14]Cantrell v. State, 188 Ga. App.

as of the time the warrant issued, and nothing here suggests that the issuing magistrate had reason to suspect that certain facts included in the affidavit were untrue."

In *Williams v. State*,[15] the Georgia Supreme Court cited and quoted from *Franks* and said the defendant's allegations "fail[ed] to raise an issue of intentional or reckless falsehood under *Franks v. Delaware*" and also pointed out that even without the alleged misrepresentations the "affidavits were sufficient to establish probable cause. This cured any possible error."

It has been held that where officers obtain additional information, after the issuance of a search warrant but before its execution, the officers have a duty to relay this information to the issuing magistrate before executing the warrant if the "new or correcting information . . . is material to the magistrate's determination of probable cause."[16]

In *Rimmer v. State*,[17] the Georgia Court of Appeals did not cite *Franks*, but concluded that "[i]f an affidavit is insufficient to establish probable cause once its false material is set aside, then evidence obtained by means of a search warrant issued in reliance on the affidavit is inadmissible. . . . However, where the remaining information is sufficient to show probable cause, the search warrant is valid."

The Georgia Supreme Court has now overruled *Nutter* and the cases that applied *Franks* in a similar style.[18] In *Watts v. State*,[19] the court ruled that a defendant has no evidentiary burden or special pleading requirement so long as the motion to suppress puts the State on notice that "it would have to meet its burden of proving that the search and seizure were valid by showing that no material information was omitted or that any such omissions were not deliberate or reckless." At a minimum, this will require production "of the warrant and its supporting affidavit, and by showing either by those documents or by other evidence that the warrant is not subject to the challenge alleged."[20]

734, 735, 374 S.E.2d 227 (1988).

[15]Williams v. State, 251 Ga. 749, 796, 312 S.E.2d 40 (1983).

[16]United States v. Marin-Buitrago, slip opinion #183-1339 (2nd Cir. 1984).

[17]Rimmer v. State, 197 Ga. App. 294, 295 (1), 398 S.E.2d 282 (1990).

[18]Watts v. State, 274 Ga. 373, 375 (1), 552 S.E.2d 823 (2001), overruling Bowe v. State, 201 Ga. App. 127, 130 (3), 410 S.E.2d 765 (1991), Ferrell v. State, 198 Ga. App. 270–271 (1), 401 S.E.2d 301 (1991), State v. Mason, 181 Ga. App. 806, 812 (4), 353 S.E.2d 915 (1987), Ross v. State, 169 Ga. App. 655, 657, 314 S.E.2d 674 (1984), and Nutter v. State, 162 Ga. App. 349, 350, 291 S.E.2d 423 (1982).

[19]Watts v. State, 274 Ga. 373, 375, 552 S.E.2d 823 (2001).

[20]Watts v. State, 274 Ga. 373, 375, 552 S.E.2d 823 (2001), citing Davis v. State, 266 Ga. 212, 213, 465 S.E.2d 438 (1996).

In *United States v. Reinholz,*[21] the Eighth Circuit held that a Franks claim will invalidate a search warrant based on an affidavit containing either false statements or omissions where the defendant can show "(1) that a false statement knowingly and intentionally, or with reckless disregard for the truth, was included in the affidavit; and (2) that the affidavit's remaining content is insufficient to establish probable cause . . . [or] (1) that facts were omitted with the intent to make, or in reckless disregard of whether they make, the affidavit misleading; and (2) that the affidavit, if supplemented by the omitted information, could not support a finding of probable cause."

§ 14:88 Motion to suppress—Illegally obtained tangible evidence—Judicial review and binding effect of order

In *Shirley v. State,*[1] the court held that it was not necessary for the trial judge to make a finding of facts in ruling on a motion to suppress, and in *State v. Peacock,*[2] the court said if the record contains conflicting testimony and the trial court simply grants the motion to suppress, the appellate court will affirm. The court then referred to the fact that "the record shows that the court did not really make any findings of fact, articulated or not." The court then remanded the *Peacock* case "to the trial court for determination of the relevant issues after consideration of all of the evidence."

In *Atkins v. State,*[3] the Georgia Supreme Court held that where a motion to suppress is denied by a trial judge and that decision is appealed, and where the appellate court found the consent relied upon by the state was not sufficiently established at the hearing on the motion, the appellate court may remand the case to the trial court for a further "hearing on the validity of the search" to see if the state can "establish the necessary elements" of a valid consent.

In *State v. Akinsonwon,*[4] the case was remanded to the trial court to determine whether the defendant was initially seized, and if seized, whether or not the seizure was justified by at least an articulable suspicion.

Where a case is remanded to the trial court "inasmuch as the

---

[21]United States v. Reinholz, 245 F.3d 765 (8th Cir. 2001).

[Section 14:88]

[1]Shirley v. State, 166 Ga. App. 456, 458 (3), 304 S.E.2d 468 (1983).

[2]State v. Peacock, 178 Ga. App. 96, 97, 342 S.E.2d 364 (1986).

[3]Atkins v. State, 254 Ga. 641, 331 S.E.2d 597 (1985). See particularly the vigorous dissent of Justice Smith.

[4]State v. Akinsonwon, 200 Ga. App. 287, 289, 407 S.E.2d 434 (1991).

question of the magistrate's impartiality was not fully explored," the defendant is not entitled to a de novo suppression hearing at which he can raise issues other than the impartiality of the magistrate.[5]

On appeal after a conviction, the reviewing court, in considering the motion to suppress, may consider not only the evidence presented at the suppression hearing, but also the testimony introduced at the preliminary hearing and the trial of the case.[6] Therefore, if the evidence at the suppression hearing showed that the search was unlawful, there is still no reversible error if the evidence at the suppression hearing and trial demonstrated that the search was lawful.[7] If the evidence which was the subject matter of a motion to suppress is not introduced in evidence at the trial, an erroneous overruling of a motion to suppress is harmless error.[8] If a motion to suppress is denied, the appellate court will assume that the order is correct "absent the availability to . . . [the appellate court] of whatever material the trial court considered. . . ."[9] If an appellate court reviews a motion to suppress, the "any evidence" rule apparently still applies.[10] However, if on appeal the record does not include the affidavit, search warrant or the transcript of the trial but only includes the transcript of the hearing on the motion to suppress and this does not show probable cause, the state fails to sustain its burden of proof.[11] An appellate court is limited to a consideration of the grounds

---

[5]Slaughter v. State, 175 Ga. App. 183, 333 S.E.2d 30 (1985).

[6]Rowe v. State, 184 Ga. App. 437, 438 (1), 361 S.E.2d 705 (1987).

[7]Sanders v. State, 235 Ga. 425, 430 (II), 219 S.E.2d 768 (1975); Carpenter v. State, 177 Ind.App. 161, 378 N.E.2d 908 (1978); People v. Sakalas, 85 Ill.App.3d 59, 40 Ill.Dec. 29, 405 N.E.2d 1121, 1127 (Ill.App. 1980). However, there may be a double jeopardy violation in this rule. DiGiangiemo v. Regan, 528 F.2d 1262 (2d Cir. 1975).

[8]Jackson v. State, 146 Ga. App. 736, 247 S.E.2d 512 (1978). Cf. Yarbrough v. State, 151 Ga. App. 474, 475 (2), 260 S.E.2d 369 (1979).

In Gainous v. State, 171 Ga. App. 157, 158, 319 S.E.2d 62 (1984), the court held that the "overruling of a motion to suppress evidence becomes moot when such evidence is not introduced at trial."

[9]Myrick v. State, 168 Ga. App. 223, 224, 308 S.E.2d 563 (1983).

[10]State v. Swift, 232 Ga. 535, 207 S.E.2d 459 (1974). In State v. Watts, 154 Ga. App. 789, 790 (4), 270 S.E.2d 52 (1980), the court said that the trial judge hearing the suppression motion is the trier of fact; his factual conclusions, if supported by evidence, are controlling. Cf. State v. Mohs, 156 Ga. App. 480, 274 S.E.2d 825 (1980).

[11]Bland v. State, 141 Ga. App. 858, 234 S.E.2d 692 (1977). Likewise, in Liskey v. State, 156 Ga. App. 45, 46, 274 S.E.2d 89 (1980), the court pointed out that where a motion to suppress is filed, alleging that the warrant was issued without probable cause, that the seizure was greater than that authorized in the warrant, and that neither the affidavit nor warrant are in the record, the appellate court must conclude that the state did not carry its burden and the motion must be granted.

contained in the defendant's motion.[12]

In *State v. Slater,*[13] the trial judge held that a stop for a traffic violation was pretextual and suppressed cocaine which was discovered. The state appealed and the court of appeals reversed the suppression. No motion for reconsideration was filed in the appellate court, but after the remittitur was returned, the defendant moved in the trial court for reconsideration of the suppression motion. The trial judge heard no new evidence, but again granted the motion to suppress after concluding that defendant had committed no traffic violation and the officer's stop was pretextual. The state again appealed. The defendant contended that the trial judge had "the right to reconsider a motion to suppress evidence where the 'goal is to secure the ends of justice . . . [if] . . . intervening matters . . . have cast doubt on previous rulings. . . .' " The appellate court held that "this issue has been appealed and decided adversely to defendant[;] . . . relitigation of this very same issue is precluded by res judicata."

In the 1994 case of *Tate v. State,*[14] the Georgia Supreme Court summarized the law guiding an appellate court review of a motion to suppress as follows:

"First, . . . the trial judge . . . sits as the trier of facts. The trial judge 'hears the evidence, and his findings based on conflicting evidence are analogous to the verdict of a jury and should not be disturbed . . . if there is any evidence to support it.' "

"Second, the trial court's decision with regard to questions of fact and *credibility* must be accepted unless clearly erroneous . . . ."

"Third, the reviewing court must construe the evidence most favorably to the upholding of the trial court's findings and judgment."

In *Vansant v. State,*[15] the Georgia Supreme Court summarized by holding that a trial judge's "findings as to disputed facts in a ruling on a motion to suppress will be reviewed to determine whether the ruling was clearly erroneous. . . . [However,] where the evidence is uncontroverted and no question regarding the

---

However, in Ledesma v. State, 251 Ga. 885, 891 (8), 311 S.E.2d 427 (1984), the court held that where the trial judge considered search warrants and supporting affidavits in determining probable cause, the failure to put the search warrant in evidence is not reversible error where appellants have not shown that they were harmed.

[12]Reed v. State, 126 Ga. App. 323, 324 (3), 190 S.E.2d 587 (1972).

[13]State v. Slater, 214 Ga. App. 119, 446 S.E.2d 771 (1994).

[14]Tate v. State, 264 Ga. 53, 54 (1), 440 S.E.2d 646 (1994). Accord, Dickson v. State, 241 Ga. App. 575, 527 S.E.2d 246 (1999).

[15]Vansant v. State, 264 Ga. 319, 320 (1), 443 S.E.2d 474 (1994). See Williams v. State, 301 Ga. 60, 799 S.E.2d 779 (2017).

credibility of witnesses is presented, the trial court's application of the law to undisputed facts is subject to de novo appellate review."

Where a trial judge grants a motion to suppress, the trial judge in his discretion may within the same term vacate the prior suppression order and permit the state to introduce additional evidence. If, based on all the evidence, the motion to suppress should be denied, the trial judge may then deny the motion to suppress.[16] In *State v. Marcus,*[17] the court held that where a judge denied a motion to suppress, it was not an abuse of discretion for another judge of the same circuit to grant the defendant's motion for a rehearing and on the same evidence, grant the motion to suppress.

§ 14:89 Motion to suppress—Illegally obtained tangible evidence—Collateral estoppel

If a defendant and his counsel fail to appear at a hearing on the motion to suppress, the court dismisses the motion as being abandoned, and the evidence is admitted without objection at trial. The defendant may not then seek habeas corpus relief after conviction on grounds of an illegal search.[1] Where contraband has been suppressed in one case against a defendant, it is inadmissible against the same defendant in another case, even though it may be relevant in the second case.[2]

See § 14:57, supra, on collateral estoppel; and § 4:7, supra, on probable cause for a search warrant.

---

[16]Chastain v. State, 158 Ga. App. 654, 281 S.E.2d 627 (1981).

[17]State v. Marcus, 206 Ga. App. 385 (1), 425 S.E.2d 351 (1992).

[Section 14:89]

[1]Jacobs v. Hopper, 238 Ga. 461, 462, 233 S.E.2d 169 (1977). The Fifth Circuit has held that Stone v. Powell, 428 U.S. 465, 96 S.Ct. 3037, 49 L.Ed.2d 1067 (1976), prevents a federal district court in a habeas corpus action from considering an alleged illegal search, where the defendant did not raise the issue in the state trial court. The court said that even though the issue was not considered, the defendant had a "full and fair" opportunity to present the issue and did not do so. O'Berry v. Wainwright, 546 F.2d 1204, 1213-14 (5th Cir. 1977).

However, in Gamble v. Oklahoma, 583 F.2d 1161 (10th Cir. 1978), the court held that Stone v. Powell does not apply where the state court failed to consider a United States Supreme Court decision which was almost directly on point. See Robbins and Sanders, "Judicial Integrity, the Appearance of Justice, and the Great Writ of Habeas Corpus: How to Kill Two Thirds (or More) With One Stone," 15 Am. Crim. L. Rev. 63 (1977). See § 28-19, infra.

In Kimmelman v. Morrison, 477 U.S. 365, 106 S.Ct. 2574, 91 L.Ed.2d 305 (1986), the court held that Stone v. Powell does not prevent a federal petitioner for habeas corpus from asserting that counsel was ineffective in failing to seek the suppression of evidence.

[2]Cook v. State, 141 Ga. App. 241, 233 S.E.2d 60 (1977).

§ 14:90 Reclaiming non-contraband items

O.C.G.A. § 17-5-50 "provides a comprehensive method by which ownership of property seized or utilized as evidence may be determined"[1] as well as a method to determine claims between competing persons, including a claim between a defendant and another person.[2]

Any person claiming any property unlawfully obtained may make application to the law enforcement agency which obtained the property and ask for its return. When such an application is filed, the person in charge of the property section shall serve upon the person from whose custody the property was taken a copy of the application. The person from whom custody of the property was taken shall have a reasonable opportunity to claim ownership of such property and to request a hearing on forms provided by the person in charge of the property section.

If the person from whom custody of the property was taken fails to assert a claim to the property, the property shall be returned to the party filing the application upon a sufficient proof of ownership of the property and presentation of personal identification. The person to whom the property is delivered shall sign (under penalty of false swearing) a declaration of ownership which shall be retained by the person in charge of the property section. Such declaration of ownership in the absence of any other proof of ownership shall be sufficient proof of ownership except in the case of motor vehicles, trailers, tractors or motorcycles which are required to be registered with the State Revenue Commissioner. Any such vehicle shall be returned to the person evidencing ownership of the vehicle through a certificate of title, tag receipt, bill of sale, or other such evidence.

If the person from whom custody of the property was taken asserts a claim of such property and requests a hearing, the court which examines the charge against the person accused of unlawfully obtaining the property, or the court before whom the trial is had for unlawfully obtaining the property shall conduct the hearing to determine the ownership of such property.

The statute expressly provides that it does not apply to any contraband or property which is subject to forfeiture.

At a hearing or trial, photographs, video tapes, or other identification or analysis of properties involved, duly identified in writing by the law enforcement officer originally taking custody of the property as accurately representing such property, shall be

---

[Section 14:90]

[1]State v. Collins, 171 Ga. App. 225, 226, 319 S.E.2d 84 (1984).

[2]Recoba v. State, 167 Ga. App. 447, 449, 306 S.E.2d 713 (1983).

admissible in lieu of the original property.

In the case of an unknown or unapprehended defendant who willfully absents himself from the jurisdiction, the court shall have discretion to appoint a guardian ad litem to represent his interest.

Any statements by a defendant or a person representing a defendant at a hearing provided for under this statute "shall not be admissible for use against the defendant at trial."

In *Baez v. State*,[3] the defendant sought to recover guns, a scale, and other articles contained in a suitcase. During defendant's trial, he testified that he had never seen the guns before and that he did not know what the scale was. The defendant claimed that since he was at least in control of these objects, he was entitled to them. However, the court held that "[t]he law will not allow a defendant to deny ownership in a criminal proceeding where it is proof of guilt, in order to avoid conviction, and then prove ownership so as to regain it."

In *Gunter v. State*,[4] the court held that Gunter was entitled to have a firearm returned to him where it was not stolen or used in the commission of the crime even though he had been "sentenced" under the first offender act.

The case of *State v. Collins*[5] emphasizes the fact that if the state erroneously delivers property to a party not entitled to receive it, even if the property involved is currency, the state is not liable to the lawful owner of such property because of the doctrine of sovereign immunity.

§ 14:91 Motion to transfer to federal court

Upon petition, a defendant's case may be transferred from state to federal court in certain limited civil rights situations. The federal statute authorizing such transfers is found in 28 U.S.C.A. § 1443 and states the following:

"Any of the following civil actions or criminal prosecutions, commenced in a State court may be removed by the defendant to the district court of the United States for the district and division embracing the place wherein it is pending:

"(1) Against any person who is denied or cannot enforce in the courts of such State a right under any law providing for the equal civil rights of citizens of the United States, or of all persons within

---

[3]Baez v. State, 231 Ga. App. 375, 376, 500 S.E.2d 339 (1998).

[4]Gunter v. State, 182 Ga. App. 548, 356 S.E.2d 276 (1987). Cf. Baez v. State, 231 Ga. App. 375, 500 S.E.2d

339 (1998). See also Warren v. State, 297 Ga. 810, 778 S.E.2d 749 (2015).

[5]State v. Collins, 171 Ga. App. 225, 226, 319 S.E.2d 84 (1984).

the jurisdiction thereof;

"(2) For any act under color of authority derived from any law providing for equal rights, or for refusing to do any act on the ground that it would be inconsistent with such law."

The courts have been very reluctant to grant removal to federal court.[1] A removal petition under subsection (1) must satisfy a two-prong test which has been summarized by the United States Supreme Court as follows:

"First, it must appear that the right allegedly denied the removal petitioner arises under a federal law 'providing for specific civil rights stated in terms of racial equality.' Claims that prosecution and conviction will violate rights under constitutional or statutory provisions of general applicability or under statutes not protecting against racial discrimination, will not suffice. That a removal petitioner will be denied due process of law because the criminal law under which he is being prosecuted is allegedly vague or that the prosecution is assertedly a sham, corrupt, or without evidentiary basis does not, standing alone, satisfy the requirements of § 1443(1).

"Second, it must appear, in accordance with the provisions of § 1443(1), that the removal petitioner is 'denied or cannot enforce' the specified federal rights 'in the courts of [the] State.' This provision normally requires that the 'denial be manifest in a formal expression of state law,' . . . such as a state legislative or constitutional provision, 'rather than a denial first made manifest at the trial of the case.' . . . Except in the unusual case where 'an equivalent basis could be shown for an equally firm prediction that the defendant would be' denied or cannot enforce 'the specified federal rights in the state court,' . . . it was to be expected that the protection of federal constitutional or statutory rights could be effected in the pending state proceedings . . . ."[2]

The procedure used in a removal proceeding is outlined in 28 U.S.C.A. § 1446.

In addition to a transfer to federal court under 28 U.S.C.A. § 1443 as discussed above, the United States, any agency thereof, or any officer (or any person acting under that officer) has a right to have a civil or criminal case against him transferred to federal court for any act committed by such person "under color of such office or on account of any right, title or authority claimed under any Act of Congress for the apprehension or punishment of

[Section 14:91]

[1]See Georgia v. Rachel, 384 U.S. 780, 86 S.Ct. 1783, 16 L.Ed.2d 925 (1966), which approved removal of a prosecution for trespass in public restaurants in Atlanta (to U.S. District Court).

[2]Johnson v. Mississippi, 421 U.S. 213, 219, 95 S.Ct. 1591, 44 L.Ed.2d 121, 128 (1975).

criminals or the collection of the revenue."[3] Likewise, there is a statute authorizing the transfer of any civil or criminal case against a member of the armed forces from a state to a federal court if the case arises out of an act done under color of his office or status.[4]

See Annotation, "What is 'Separate and Independent' Cause of Action Within 28 U.S.C.A. § 1441(c) as Amended in 1990, Which Permits Removal From State to Federal Court," 162 A.L.R.Fed. 527 (2000).

§ 14:92   General insanity issues

Historically two kinds of insanity have been recognized in Georgia: insanity at the time of the commission of the alleged crime and incompetency to stand trial.[1]

A plea of mental incompetency to stand trial, previously referred to as a special plea of insanity, is provided for in O.C.G.A. § 17-7-130. This plea relates to the competency at the time of trial. Thus, if the issue is raised, it must be determined whether at the time of trial (1) the defendant understands "the nature and object of the proceedings going on against him," (2) "rightly comprehends his own condition in reference to such proceedings," and (3) "is capable of rendering his attorneys such assistance as a proper defense to the indictment preferred against him demands."[2] "In connection with the last criterion, . . . the relevant inquiry is not whether the defendant *would* assist in his defense, but whether he *could* do so."[3] Hence, it is error for the court to charge that the "right-and-wrong" test is the method of determining the competency of the defendant to stand trial.[4] See Rule 31.4 of the Uniform Rules for the Superior Courts on Mo-

---

[3]See 28 U.S.C.A. § 1442(a)(1); United States v. Charters, 829 F.2d 479 (4th Cir. 1987); § 9:3, supra.

[4]See 28 U.S.C.A. § 1442a.

[Section 14:92]

[1]Danforth v. State, 75 Ga. 614, 615 (3)(c) (1886). In Echols v. State, 149 Ga. App. 620 (2), 255 S.E.2d 92 (1979), Presiding Judge Quillian interestingly traces the history in Georgia of a plea of incompetency to stand trial.

[2]Smalls v. State, 153 Ga. App. 254, 256, 265 S.E.2d 83 (1980) ("a person's mental condition is at best an 'educated guess except in the most extreme cases.' "). See Traylor v. State,

280 Ga. 400, 627 S.E.2d 594 (2006).

See Annot., "Competency to Stand Trial of Criminal Defendant Diagnosed as 'Schizophrenic'-Modern State Cases," 33 A.L.R. 4th 1062, § 1b (1984); See Annot., "Competency to Stand Trial of Criminal Defendant Diagnosed as 'Schizophrenic'—Modern Federal Cases," 63 A.L.R.Fed. 696 (1983).

[3]Levitt v. State, 170 Ga. App. 32, 33, 316 S.E.2d 6 (1984).

[4]Brown v. State, 215 Ga. 784 (1), 113 S.E.2d 618 (1960).

A defendant is not per se incompetent to stand trial because he is suffering from amnesia regarding the facts of the crime. Jackson v. State,

tions and Orders for Mental Examination at Public Expense.

The United States Supreme Court has held that "the criminal trial of an incompetent defendant violates due process."[5] However, the burden of proving incompetency is on the defendant to prove that condition by a preponderance of the evidence and the due process clause of the Fourteenth Amendment does not permit a state to require a defendant to prove his incompetence by clear and convincing evidence.[6] In weighing evidence regarding a defendant's competency, the trial court is not bound by the testimony of an expert and may "rely on its own observations and the basic presumptions permitted by law."[7]

The Georgia statutory theory seems to be that a plea of mental incompetency to stand trial must be filed by the defendant in order to have a trial on the question of the competency of the

---

149 Ga. App. 253, 256, 253 S.E.2d 874 (1979); Aldridge v. State, 247 Ga. 142, 146 (4), 274 S.E.2d 525 (1981); Sanders v. State, 250 Ga. 514, 515 (2), 299 S.E.2d 719 (1983). The test is one of fundamental fairness. United States v. Swanson, 572 F.2d 523 (5th Cir. 1978); Commonwealth v. Barky, 476 Pa. 602, 383 A.2d 526 (1978). In Wilson v. United States, 391 F.2d 460 (D.C.Cir. 1968), the court said a trial judge should consider the following factors in determining whether or not a defendant is competent to be tried:

"(1) The extent to which the amnesia affected the defendant's ability to consult with and assist his lawyer.

"(2) The extent to which the amnesia affected the defendant's ability to testify in his own behalf.

"(3) The extent to which the evidence in suit could be extrinsically reconstructed in view of the defendant's amnesia. Such evidence would include evidence relating to the crime itself as well as any reasonably possible alibi.

"(4) The extent to which the government assisted the defendant and his counsel in that reconstruction.

"(5) The strength of the prosecution's case. Most important here will be whether the government's case is such as to negate all reasonable hypotheses of innocence. If there is any substantial possibility that the ac-

cused could, but for his amnesia, establish an alibi or other defense, it should be presumed that he would have been able to do so.

"(6) Any other facts and circumstances which would indicate whether or not the defendant had a fair trial."

Cf. Commonwealth v. Lombardi, 378 Mass. 612, 393 N.E.2d 346 (1979). See Annot., "Amnesia as Affecting Capacity to Commit Crime or Stand Trial," 46 A.L.R.3rd 544 (1972).

[5]Medina v. California, 505 U.S. 437, 453, 112 S.Ct. 2572, 120 L.Ed.2d 353 (1992).

[6]Cooper v. Oklahoma, 517 U.S. 348, 116 S.Ct. 1373, 134 L.Ed.2d 498 (1996) (unanimous decision).

[7]Flesche v. State, 254 Ga. App. 3, 561 S.E.2d 160 (2002). See In Interest of L. L., 340 Ga. App. 445, 455–56, 798 S.E.2d 1 (2017), citing Strickland v. Francis, 738 F.2d 1542, 1152 (111)(B) (11th Cir. 1984) (four factors court can consider which might "reasonably lead a factfinder to disregard expert testimony on the defendant's mental condition . . . are (1) the correctness or adequacy of the factual assuptions on which the expert opinion is based; (2) possible bias in the expert's appraisal of the defendant's condition; (3) inconsistencies in the expert's testimony, or material variations between experts; and (4) the relevance and strength of the contrary lay testimony).

defendant to stand trial.[8] However, it has been held that the trial judge has inherent authority to satisfy himself "through [a] special jury trial, personal examination or the opinion of experts" that the defendant has sufficient mental capacity to go to trial.[9] In *Rattansay v. State*,[10] the court ruled that "[a]lthough the trial court is authorized to order a mental health expert to examine the defendant in order to determine whether his sanity is likely to be a significant factor at trial, it is the defendant who bears the burden of making that preliminary showing. . . . The mere filing of a motion does not constitute a preliminary showing that sanity at the time of the offense is likely to be a significant factor at trial." Nonetheless, the Court of Appeals has held that a trial court "must conduct *sua sponte*, a competency hearing when the information known to the trial court at the time of trial or plea bargain is sufficient to raise a bona fide doubt regarding the defendant's competence. [cites omitted.]"[11] The Georgia statutory theory now provides that pursuant to O.C.G.A. § 17-7-129, "[w]hen information becomes known to the court sufficient to raise a bona fide doubt regarding the accused's mental competency to stand trial, the court has a duty, sua sponte, to inquire into the accused's mental competency to stand trial."[12]

Rule 31.5 of the Uniform Rules for the Superior Courts provides

---

[8]But see Smalls v. State, 153 Ga. App. 254, 257, 265 S.E.2d 83 (1980).

[9]Griggs v. State, 241 Ga. 317, 245 S.E.2d 269 (1978). The Griggs case says that the trial judge also has this statutory authority. In Beardsley v. State, 149 Ga. App. 531, 532, 254 S.E.2d 715 (1979), the court said that while a trial judge has authority to have a psychiatric examination conducted at the expense of the state, such an examination, on motion, is not generally mandatory but a matter of sound discretion. But see Estelle v. Smith, 451 U.S. 454, 101 S.Ct. 1866, 68 L.Ed.2d 359 (1981).

[10]Rattansay v. State, 240 Ga. App. 165, 167 (2), 523 S.E.2d 36 (1999).

[11]White v. State, 202 Ga. App. 424, 425, 414 S.E.2d 328 (1992). See Traylor v. State, 280 Ga. 400, 404, 627 S.E.2d 594 (2006) (test is whether trial court had enough information "which, objectively considered, should reasonably have raised a doubt about the defendant's competency and alerted the trial court to the possibility that the defendant could [not] understand the proceedings, appreciate their significance, nor rationally aid his attorney in his defense"). See also Duckett v. State, 331 Ga. App. 24, 769 S.E.2d 743 (2015) (fact that trial court became aware during trial that defendant suffered from some mental instability did not *require* that court stop trial and order an evaluation).

[12]An issue that has never been addressed in Georgia courts is that of whether defense counsel may pursue a defense of insanity over the objection of the defendant. The U.S. Supreme Court has recognized that the accused has the ultimate authority to make certain fundamental decisions regarding the case, including plea decisions. Jones v. Barnes, 463 U.S. 745, 751, 103 S. Ct. 3308, 77 L. Ed. 2d 987 (1983). This is consistent with Georgia Rules of Professional Conduct, Rule 1.2(a) (2001). Most of the jurisdictions which have considered the question have concluded that the decision of whether to raise the defense of insanity belongs to the defendant. See State v. Bean,

as follows:

"31.5 Notice of Intention of Defense to Raise Issue of Insanity, Mental Illness, Mental Retardation or Mental Competency

"(A) If, in any criminal proceeding, the defense intends to raise the issue that the defendant or accused was insane, mentally ill or mentally retarded at the time of the act or acts charged against the accused, such intention must be stated, in writing, in a pleading denominated as "Notice of Intent of Defense to Raise Issue of Insanity, Mental Illness or Mental Retardation." This notice shall be filed and served upon the prosecuting attorney in accordance with section 31.1 of these rules. Upon the filing of such notice, the judge shall determine from the prosecuting attorney and the defense attorney whether such issue requires any further mental examination of the accused *or* any further non-jury hearing relative to this issue.

Upon defense motion, the judge may enter an order requiring a mental evaluation of the defendant for the purposes of evaluating the degree of criminal responsibility or insanity at the time of the act in question. The judge may direct the Department of Human Resources to perform the evaluation at a time and place to be set by the department in cooperation with the county sheriff. A copy of the order shall be forwarded to the department accompanied by a copy of the indictment, accusation or specification of charges, a copy of the police arrest report, where available, a copy of the defendant's Notice of Intent to Raise Issues of Insanity if filed, and a brief summary of any known or alleged previous mental health treatment or hospitalization involving this particular person. Any background information available to the court shall also be forwarded to the evaluating department to assist in performing adequately the requested services. Unless otherwise ordered by the court the department shall submit its report to the requesting judge and the defendant's attorney. Contemporaneous with filing the Notice of Intent of Defense to Raise Issue of Insanity, defendant's attorney shall provide a copy of the Report to the prosecuting attorney and shall so certify in writing attached to the Notice of Intent of Defense to Raise Issue of Insanity.

"(B) Except for good cause shown, the issue of insanity shall not be raised in the trial on the merits unless notice has been

---

171 Vt. 290, 762 A.2d 1259 (2000). A minority of such jurisdictions have concluded the decision is one of the strategy, the means of representations and as such, belongs to defense counsel. See People v. Cundiff, 255 Ill. Dec. 608, 749 N.E.2d 1090 (App. Ct. 5th Dist. 2001).

filed and served ahead of trial as provided in these rules."[13]

Rule 31.1 of the Uniform Rules for the Superior Court requires that notice of intent to raise the defense of insanity must be filed at least ten days before trial. Failure to file within that time can serve as a basis for denying an indigent defendant's request for a court ordered psychiatric examination. Indeed, the Georgia Court of Appeals has ruled that a trial court's denial of such a motion was proper despite defense counsel's claim that the motion was filed immediately upon his discovery that a good faith basis existed for the motion.[14]

However, the pre-trial notice requirements of Rule 31.5 are not required when the defendant uses lay, as opposed to expert witnesses, to present mental health evidence, and the state "may not obtain or use the results of an independent mental health evaluation to rebut purely lay testimony."[15] See Studdard, *Daniel's Georgia Handbook on Criminal Evidence* (2018 ed.), § 6:29.

In *Johnson v. State,*[16] the Georgia Supreme Court reversed a conviction where the trial judge refused to permit "the defendant to present any mental issue or evidence at the guilt phase of the trial" where the state had ample notice that defendant's mental condition might be a factor in the case and the notice, although late, was filed two days before the presentation of any evidence.

In *Hudson v. State,*[17] the court held that the defense of insanity and the defendant's competence to stand trial are separate issues and it was error for the court, over objection, to admit evidence of competency to stand trial where there is no showing that such testimony was relevant to the defendant's plea of not guilty by reason of insanity.

In *Cox v. State,*[18] the defendant was mentally retarded and sought to show self-defense in that "he reasonably believed" that threat or force was necessary. The appellate court affirmed the refusal of the trial judge to permit testimony from two mental health professionals where the defendant failed to comply with former Rule 31.4 [now Rule 31.5] of the Uniform Rules for the Superior Courts.

---

[13]Cf. Jackson v. State, 267 Ga. 130, 132 (7), 475 S.E.2d 637 (1996). Rule 31.5(C) provides a copy of a suggested Order for Mental Evaluation re: Degree of Criminal Responsibility or Insanity at the Time of the Act. See also, Studdard, *Daniel's Georgia Criminal Trial Practice Forms* (2018–2019 ed.), §§ 20:7, 20:8.

[14]Gardner v. State, 261 Ga. App. 188(1), 582 S.E.2d 167 (2003).

[15]Abernathy v. State, 265 Ga. 754, 462 S.E.2d 615, 617 (1995). See Otis v. State, 298 Ga. 544, 782 S.E.2d 654 (2016).

[16]Johnson v. State, 262 Ga. 527, 528 (1), 422 S.E.2d 648 (1992).

[17]Hudson v. State, 273 Ga. 124, 127 (4), 538 S.E.2d 751 (2000).

[18]Cox v. State, 216 Ga. App. 86 (2), 453 S.E.2d 471 (1995).

In *Denny v. State,*[19] the court held that the fact the defendant could not remember committing the offense would not require an insanity instruction.

But, in *Pugh v. State,*[20] the court held that expert testimony on the battered woman syndrome was admissible even though no notice was given to the state pursuant to former Rule 31.4 [now rule 31.5]. However, the court also emphasized "the fact that such evidence is admissible in connection with an issue of self-defense, does not mean that it can be used to raise the issues of insanity, mental illness, or mental incompetency—without prior compliance with Rule 31.4."

O.C.G.A. § 17-7-130.1 provides that when such a notice of the defense is filed, "the court shall appoint at least one psychiatrist or licensed psychologist to examine the defendant and to testify at the trial." See § 22:1, infra. *Motes v. State*[21] points out that if the defendant wants to introduce expert testimony, then the state must be allowed to have a psychiatrist examine the defendant and the defendant must cooperate in the examination. However, if the defendant chooses to prove insanity by means other than expert testimony, the case may proceed and the defendant can decide whether to talk with the court-appointed expert.

See sections 21:10, 21:12, and 21:15, infra, on verdicts which may be returned when a general plea of insanity has been entered.

§ 14:93 Special plea of mental incompetency to stand trial—General

In *Baker v. State,*[1] the court said, "The constitutional guarantees require the trial court to inquire into competency, even where

---

[19]Denny v. State, 226 Ga. App. 432, 434 (3), 486 S.E.2d 417 (1997).

[20]Pugh v. State, 191 Ga. App. 394, 396, 382 S.E.2d 143 (1989).

[21]Motes v. State, 256 Ga. 831, 833 (2), 353 S.E.2d 348 (1987); Tolbert v. State, 260 Ga. 527, 528 (2)(b), 397 S.E.2d 439 (1990).

[Section 14:93]

[1]Baker v. State, 250 Ga. 187, 190, 297 S.E.2d 9 (1982). See, Flesche v. State, 254 Ga. App. 3, 4, 5(1), 561 S.E.2d 160 (2002), where the court observed: "A trial court must conduct, *sua sponte*, a competency hearing when the information known to the trial court at the time of the trial or plea bargain is sufficient to raise a bona fide doubt regarding the defendant's competence. The question is: Did the trial judge receive information which objectively considered, should reasonably have raised a doubt about the defendant's competency and alerted him to the possibility that the defendant could neither understand the proceedings or appreciate their significance, nor rationally aid his attorney in his defense? To answer this question an appellate court focuses on three factors: (1) evidence of the defendant's irrational behavior; (2) defendant's demeanor at trial; and (3) prior medical opinion regarding the defendant's competence to stand trial. The defendant bears the burden of

state procedures for raising competency are not followed, if evidence of incompetence comes to the court's attention. . . . [T]he trial court has the inherent authority and duty to question competency before or during trial and 'if at any time while criminal proceedings are pending, the court observes facts which raise doubt as to the sanity of the accused, or such facts are brought to its attention by counsel, the question of his sanity should be settled before further steps are taken.' " O.C.G.A. § 17-7-129(a) now provides: "[w]hen information becomes known to the court sufficient to raise a bona fide doubt regarding the accused's mental competency to stand trial, the court has a duty, sua sponte, to inquire into the accused's mental competency to stand trial." But see § 21:10, infra, on insanity defense.

If the defendant's conduct at his trial is sufficiently bizarre, the defendant's right to a fair trial under the Fourteenth Amendment is denied if the trial judge fails to suspend the trial for a competency evaluation,[2] and if the defendant's mental condition is a "significant" issue, he is "entitled to the kind of independent psychiatric assistance contemplated in *Ake v. Oklahoma*."[3] In *Brogdon v. State*,[4] the court held that a defendant has a constitutional right not to be tried while he is incompetent. Hence, courts "must inquire into competency and hold a hearing on the issue, even during trial, if evidence raising the issue of incompetence becomes apparent. . . . Upon receiving information which, objectively considered, should reasonably raise a doubt about the defendant's competence, trial courts should conduct a civil proceeding before a special jury, even where state procedures for raising the issue are not followed. . . . The proceeding should focus on the determinative factors of competence: whether the defendant (1) understands the nature and object of the proceedings against him; (2) comprehends his own position in relation to the proceedings; and (3) is capable of assisting in his defense." As

---

proving incompetence by a preponderance of the evidence." (Citations and punctuation omitted.) See Phelps v. State, 296 Ga. App. 362 (1), 674 S.E.2d 620 (2009). Cf. Williams v. Newsome, 254 Ga. 714, 334 S.E.2d 171 (1985); Callaway v. State, 208 Ga. App. 508, 510 (1), 431 S.E.2d 143 (1993).

[2]Drope v. Missouri, 420 U.S. 162, 95 S.Ct. 896, 43 L.Ed.2d 103 (1975). But cf. Morrow v. State, 162 Ga. App. 183, 184 (2), 290 S.E.2d 137 (1982); Norris v. State, 250 Ga. 38, 40 (3), 295 S.E.2d 321 (1982). In Lingo v. State,

224 Ga. 333, 341, 162 S.E.2d 1 (1968), the court recognized the right of the trial judge to investigate the question of the present sanity of the defendant where facts come to his attention which raise a question as to defendant's sanity.

[3]Holloway v. State, 257 Ga. 620, 361 S.E.2d 794 (1987). *Ake v. Oklahoma* is discussed in § 21:10, infra.

[4]Brogdon v. State, 220 Ga. App. 31, 33 (1), 467 S.E.2d 598 (1996) (citations omitted).

the Georgia Supreme Court observed in *Sims v. State*,[5] "[t]he factors to consider in determining a defendant's capability to assist in his defense include whether the defendant can adequately consult with others, knows the names and functions of those involved with the case, and reasonably understands the rules, the specific charges, the penalties and the consequences of the proceedings." In *Sims* the Court reversed a trial court's finding of competency in the case of a moderately retarded defendant. Although noting that retardation and IQ are only one element to consider in making a competency determination, the Court implied that a low IQ might be the dominant feature in such a finding.

It has been held that an inmate may be forced to take medication to "normalize" him during a trial.[6] However, in *Riggins v. Nevada*,[7] the United States Supreme Court held that a defendant was subjected to an unacceptably high risk where he was forced to take an antipsychotic medication where there was no judicial finding of the need and appropriateness of such medication. In *Lawrence v. State*,[8] the court pointed out that *Riggins* also stated that "a state satisfies due process if it is demonstrated by the prosecution and found by the trial court 'that treatment with antipsychotic medication was medically appropriate and, considering less intrusive alternatives, essential for the sake of [the accused's] own safety or the safety of others.'" The *Lawrence* case also recognized "that the demeanor at trial of a criminal defendant is of probative value with respect to the defense of insanity," but concluded that "a defendant is not entitled to have the jury view him or her in an unaltered, undrugged state in those instances where the requirements of *Riggins* are met. . . . [However, on and after June 15, 1995] a defendant, who is under medication that may affect his demeanor is entitled, upon motion . . . to have the jury informed by the court at the beginning of the trial and in the charge to the jury that the defendant is under the influence of medication, that the defendant's behavior in their presence is conditioned by the medication, and that the insanity asserted as defendant's defense is to be evaluated as of the time the alleged criminal acts were committed."

---

[5]Sims v. State, 279 Ga. 389 (2), 614 S.E.2d 73 (2005) (citations omitted).

[6]Ake v. State, 1983 OK CR 48, 663 P.2d 1 (App. 1983), rev'd on other grounds, 470 U.S. 68, 105 S.Ct. 1087, 84 L.Ed.2d 53 (1985). Contra, Commonwealth v. Louraine, 390 Mass. 28, 453 N.E.2d 437 (1983).

[7]Riggins v. Nevada, 504 U.S. 127, 112 S.Ct. 1810, 118 L.Ed.2d 479 (1992).

[8]Lawrence v. State, 265 Ga. 310, 314 (3), 454 S.E.2d 446 (1995).

In the 2000 case of *Head v. Taylor*,[9] the Georgia Supreme Court held that counsel has a "duty to seek medication and treatment" for the defendant before trial where there has been a long history of mental problems, the defendant has requested mental health treatment, and counsel knew of the defendant's increasing paranoia that counsel was part of a conspiracy and the defendant refused to cooperate with a psychologist hired to evaluate him.

It is contradictory to contend that a defendant is incompetent and yet contend that he knowingly and intelligently waived his right to have a determination of his capacity to stand trial.[10] The court may take into consideration the defense counsel's opinion regarding the defendant's competency to stand trial.[11]

A defendant is not entitled to file a plea of incompetency to stand trial until he is indicted.[12] He has, however, the right to a separate jury trial by a special jury on the issue of his competency to stand trial. This is treated as a civil trial and "[t]here is no requirement to sequester a competency-trial jury, even in a death penalty case."[13] If he files a plea of mental incompetency to stand trial, the trial judge may also order a psychiatric examination of the defendant to determine his condition at the time of the acts charged.[14] In any event, if there is a valid order for psychiatric examination, defense counsel does not have a right to be present during the examination.[15] However, if a defendant has not raised the question of competency to stand trial or insanity and he is examined by a psychiatrist pursuant to a court order, the testimony of the doctor will not be admissible unless: (1) the defendant has been given Miranda warnings, and (2) he is given

---

[9]Head v. Taylor, 273 Ga. 69, 538 S.E.2d 416 (2000).

[10]Pate v. Robinson, 383 U.S. 375, 384, 86 S.Ct. 836, 15 L.Ed.2d 815 (1966). In this case, the court concluded that *Robinson's* due process rights under the Fourteenth Amendment had been violated, even though he failed to request a hearing on his competency to stand trial.

[11]Drope v. Missouri, 420 U.S. 162, 95 S.Ct. 896, 43 L.Ed.2d 103 (1975).

[12]Chenault v. State, 234 Ga. 216, 218, 215 S.E.2d 223 (1975).

[13]Stripling v. State, 261 Ga. 1, 7 (10), 401 S.E.2d 500 (1991).

[14]Presnell v. State, 241 Ga. 49, 56 (6), 243 S.E.2d 496, rev'd on other grounds, 439 U.S. 14, 99 S.Ct. 235, 58 L.Ed.2d 207 (1978). This case also holds that he has no right to have

counsel present at the time of such a psychiatric examination. Strickland v. State, 247 Ga. 219, 220 (1), 275 S.E.2d 29 (1981). See Annot., "Validity, Construction, and Application of Statute Limiting Physician-Patient Privilege in Judicial Proceedings Relating to Child Abuse or Neglect," 44 A.L.R. 4th 649 § 1 (1986); Generally, see Annot., "Applicability in Criminal Proceedings of Privilege as to Communications Between Physician and Patient," 7 A.L.R.3d 1458 (1966).

[15]Godfrey v. Francis, 251 Ga. 652, 657 (5), 308 S.E.2d 806 (1983). See § 21:10, infra. However, the trial court may always allow counsel to observe the evaluation. See e.g., Hittson v. State, 264 Ga. 682 (2), 449 S.E.2d 586 (1994), overruled on other grounds, Nance v. State, 272 Ga. 217 (2), 526 S.E.2d 560 (2000).

an opportunity to consult with counsel prior to such examination.[16] If a defendant raises a question as to his competency to stand trial or his sanity at the time of the offense, he may apparently be required to submit to a psychiatric examination.[17] However, in *Moss v. State,*[18] the majority opinion indicates that Miranda warnings may have to be given to a defendant before a psychiatric examination, even where the defendant has requested such an examination. The federal constitution does not seem to require this.

In *Porter v. State,*[19] testimony by a psychologist that defendant suffered from a condition in which she "blocked out" and essentially denied excessively painful experiences was admissible in prosecution for cruelty to children on the issue of defendant's knowledge of her husband's abusive behavior toward her child. Because the evidence was being offered on an element of the state's case, i.e. the defendant's knowledge of her husband's actions and not on her sanity at the time of the offense, compliance with Uniform Superior Court Rules 31.1 and 31.4 was not necessary.

In *Hammock v. State,*[20] the court pointed out that " '[a] criminal defendant, who neither initiates a psychiatric evaluation nor attempts to introduce any psychiatric evidence, may not be compelled to respond to a psychiatrist if his statements can be used against him at a capital sentencing proceeding.' . . . [But] if a defendant requests such an evaluation or presents psychiatric evidence, then . . . the prosecution may rebut this presentation with evidence from the reports of the examination that the defendant requested." Further, *Miranda* warnings at the time of arrest are sufficient. The defendant need not be Mirandized again immediately before the psychiatric evaluation.

It has been held that where a defendant is examined and transferred to the Department of Human Resources after an incompetency to stand trial plea is filed, it is mandatory that his

---

[16]Estelle v. Smith, 451 U.S. 454, 101 S.Ct. 1866, 68 L.Ed.2d 359 (1981). Battie v. Estelle, 655 F.2d 692 (5th Cir. 1981). Cf. Spivey v. State, 253 Ga. 187, 202, 319 S.E.2d 420 (1984).

[17]United States v. Cohen, 530 F.2d 43, 47 (5th Cir. 1976); Karstetter v. Cardwell, 526 F.2d 1144 (9th Cir. 1975); United States v. Bohle, 445 F.2d 54 (7th Cir. 1971); United States v. Weiser, 428 F.2d 932 (2d Cir. 1969); United States v. Albright, 388 F.2d 719 (4th Cir. 1968); Pope v. United States,

372 F.2d 710 (8th Cir. 1967) (en banc), vacated and remanded on other grounds, 392 U.S. 651, 88 S.Ct. 2145, 20 L.Ed.2d 1317 (1968).

[18]Moss v. State, 250 Ga. 368, 369 (6), 297 S.E.2d 459 (1982).

[19]Porter v. State, 243 Ga. App. 498, 532 S.E.2d 407 (2000). See Pickle v. State, 280 Ga. App. 821, 635 S.E.2d 197 (2006).

[20]Hammock v. State, 210 Ga. App. 513, 514 (1), 436 S.E.2d 571 (1993).

special plea be resolved at trial when he is returned to the court.[21] After a plea of incompetency to stand trial has been filed, a defendant may not enter a guilty plea until the incompetency plea has been disposed of.[22]

In the interesting case of *Baker v. State*,[23] the trial judge erroneously dismissed a plea of incompetency to stand trial because it was allegedly not timely filed. The defendant was tried and convicted. The Georgia Supreme Court found no error in the actual criminal trial. The court reversed and remanded the case under the following instructions: [1] "[T]he burden first falls upon the state to show there is sufficient evidence to make a meaningful determination of competency at the time of trial. If the court rules that a determination of appellant's competency at the time of trial is not presently possible, then a new trial must be granted. [2] If the court decides such a determination is possible, the issue of competency to stand trial must be tried and the appellant shall have the burden to show incompetency by a preponderance of the evidence. . . . If the jury finds that the appellant was not mentally competent at the time of his [original] trial, the verdict in the main case must be set aside. On the other hand, if the appellant fails . . . to prove incompetence at the time of his [original] trial, the verdict of guilty shall stand. [3] In the event the verdict of guilty is set aside and a new trial ordered as to guilt and innocence, the appellant may again raise the issue of competency by special plea pursuant to Code Ann., § 27-1502 [O.C.G.A. § 17-7-130]."

Generally, an appeal from an adverse determination is regarded as interlocutory in nature and thus requiring a certificate of immediate review.[24] See § 14:99, infra. Until *Sims v. State*,[25] the standard of review from a verdict of competency was "any evidence."[26] In *Sims*, the Georgia Supreme Court ruled that because there is a presumption of competency to stand trial, the "any evidence" standard would effectively thwart any meaningful review of a verdict of competency. The Court then determined

---

[21]Cronch v. State, 141 Ga. App. 851, 852 (1), 235 S.E.2d 40 (1977). See § 14:94, infra, on competency trial and O.C.G.A. § 17-7-130.

[22]Martin v. State, 147 Ga. App. 173, 248 S.E.2d 235 (1978). However, where the defendant has only filed a request for a competency evaluation, the case is different and the court may accept a guilty plea without first conducting a competency hearing. Jones v. State, 282 Ga. 568(2), 651 S.E.2d 728 (2007).

[23]Baker v. State, 250 Ga. 187, 193, 297 S.E.2d 9 (1982).

[24]Pope v. State, 184 Ga. App. 547, 362 S.E.2d 123 (1987), overruled on other grounds by Sims v. State, 279 Ga. 389, 614 S.E.2d 73 (2005).

[25]Sims v. State, 279 Ga. 389, 614 S.E.2d 73 (2005).

[26]Pope v. State, 184 Ga. App. 547 (1), 362 S.E.2d 123 (1987), overruled by Sims v. State, 279 Ga. 389, 614 S.E.2d 73 (2005).

that the correct measure for review of a competency verdict is that of a preponderance of the evidence, i.e., "whether after reviewing the evidence in the light most favorable to the State, a rational trier of fact could have found that the defendant failed to prove by a preponderance of the evidence that he was incompetent to stand trial."[27]

In *Thompson v. State,*[28] the Georgia Supreme Court held that expert evidence of the defendant's low IQ was properly excluded when offered in support of the defense of accident "because his mental disability prevented him from understanding how to use [the murder weapon] properly." The court noted that "[e]vidence of a criminal defendant's mental disability may be presented in support of a defense of insanity or delusional compulsion (see O.C.G.A. §§ 16-3-2 and 16-3-3); a claim of incompetency to stand trial (see O.C.G.A. § 17-7-130); or, since such pleas were authorized, a plea of guilty but mentally ill or guilty but mentally retarded (see O.C.G.A. § 17-7-131)—none of which Appellant raised in this case. . . . For more than 150 years, however, this Court has consistently upheld the exclusion of evidence of a defendant's diminished mental condition when offered to support other defenses or to negate the intent element of a crime."

See §§ 21:10 et seq., infra, on insanity as a defense. For motions related to psychiatric examinations, see Studdard, *Daniel's Georgia Criminal Trial Practice Forms* (2018–2019 ed.), §§ 20:6, 20:10, 20:12.

§ 14:94 Special plea of mental incompetency to stand trial—The trial

O.C.G.A. § 17-7-130 sets out the procedure to be followed by the court when a defendant files a special plea of incompetency to stand trial. The trial of the plea of incompetency to stand trial is civil in nature, with the burden of proof on the defendant[1] or movant to prove by a preponderance of the evidence that he is

---

[27]Sims v. State, 279 Ga. 389, 614 S.E.2d 73 (2005), overruling Pope v. State, 184 Ga. App. 547 (1), 362 S.E.2d 123 (1987).

In Traylor v. State, 280 Ga. 400(4), 627 S.E.2d 594 (2006) the court held that after trial and conviction, a defendant who chooses to raise his or her incompetence to stand trial for the first time must first demonstrate by a preponderance of the evidence that there was a real doubt as to defendant's competence to stand trial. A case of first impression, Traylor sets

the defendant's burden on the issue at the preponderance level while other jurisdictions that have considered the issue ruled that the burden was one of clear and convincing evidence.

[28]Thompson v. State, 295 Ga. 96, 757 S.E.2d 846 (2014). See State v. Abernathy, 289 Ga. 603, 715 S.E.2d 48 (2011) (mental abnormality, unless it amounts to insanity, is not a defense to a crime).

[Section 14:94]

[1]Buttrum v. State, 249 Ga. 652,

not mentally competent to stand trial.[2]

The issue is to be decided by bench trial, unless the state or the accused demands a special jury trial, in which case a jury is selected to determine the defendant's competency at that time, and a different jury is later selected to determine the question of innocence or guilt if the defendant is found competent to stand trial.

The presumption of sanity is admissible as evidence and may be relied on by the jury to find the defendant guilty, even if expert witnesses testify as to his insanity.[3]

In *Waldrip v. State*,[4] the court pointed out that "[s]ince a competency trial is in the nature of a civil proceeding, evidence that may place . . . [defendant's] character in issue is admissible, if it is relevant to the issues to be decided."

If the defendant introduces no evidence in support of his plea, the judge may properly direct a verdict for the state on the issue of competency.[5] Since the proceeding is regarded as civil in nature, the state, over objection, may call the defendant for purposes of cross-examination, although generally no questions may be asked concerning the accused's guilt or innocence.[6] Defense witnesses may not be examined on facts of the crime. The defendant's innocence or guilt of the crime is not relevant, and apparently his sanity or insanity at the time of the crime may be excluded,[7] except as this may relate to his competence to

---

654 (3), 293 S.E.2d 334 (1982); Keener v. State, 97 Ga. 388, 389 (3), 24 S.E. 28 (1895) (defendant must establish his insanity by a preponderance of the evidence); Davenport v. State, 170 Ga. App. 667, 317 S.E.2d 895 (1984). In May v. State, 146 Ga. App. 416 (1), 246 S.E.2d 432 (1978), the court at least implies that since a plea of mental incompetence to stand trial is civil in nature, there can be no due process violation if the trial judge refuses to appoint a psychiatrist to examine the defendant. The court cites Taylor v. State, 229 Ga. 536 (1), 192 S.E.2d 249 (1972) as authority. However, the *Taylor* case is not on point.

[2]Baker v. State, 250 Ga. 187, 189, 297 S.E.2d 9 (1982). Cf. Medina v. California, 505 U.S. 437, 112 S.Ct. 2572, 120 L.Ed.2d 353 (1992).

[3]Fields v. State, 221 Ga. 307, 308 (1), 144 S.E.2d 339 (1965).

[4]Waldrip v. State, 267 Ga. 739, 742 (3), 482 S.E.2d 299 (1997).

[5]Williams v. State, 238 Ga. 298, 304 (3), 232 S.E.2d 535 (1977); Davenport v. State, 170 Ga. App. 667, 317 S.E.2d 895 (1984). Cf. Chaney v. State, 153 Ga. App. 882 (3), 267 S.E.2d 300 (1980).

In Banks v. State, 246 Ga. 178, 181 (3), 269 S.E.2d 450 (1980), the court held that the trial judge could properly direct a verdict against the defendant where there was no evidence (or reasonable deductions therefrom) showing that he was incompetent to stand trial, even if he could not remember the event.

[6]Bacon v. State, 222 Ga. 151, 149 S.E.2d 111 (1966).

[7]Crawford v. State, 240 Ga. 321, 326, 240 S.E.2d 824 (1977). However, Pierce v. State, 243 Ga. 454, 455 (2), 254 S.E.2d 838 (1979) points out that

stand trial.[8] However, evidence "is not inadmissible at a competency proceeding simply because it might also be relevant to the issue of guilt; as long as the evidence is sufficiently relevant and material to the issue of mental incompetence, it is properly admitted at a competency trial."[9] A lay witness may testify as to his opinion of the mental condition of the defendant if he gives his reasons for that opinion.[10] However, the state apparently has no right to call defense counsel as a witness to establish the competency of the defendant.[11]

It has been held that it is not error for the trial judge, at a hearing to determine the mental competency of the defendant to stand trial, to limit evidence to the mental state of the defendant after his arrest, even though such evidence seems somewhat contrary to his apparent condition prior to arrest, where it appeared that there was a gradual deterioration of his condition.[12]

In *Strickland v. State*,[13] the court pointed out (1) that since the special plea was civil in nature, it was not error for the trial judge to fail on his own motion to order a transcript of opening statements, and (2) it was not error to refuse to permit defense counsel to explain during his opening statement and closing argument the consequences of finding the defendant incompetent to stand trial.

A verdict of incompetence to stand trial is not appealable without a certificate for immediate review from the trial judge.[14]

It has been held that even after a defendant is tried on a plea of incompetency to stand trial, and is determined to be competent by the jury, if he is not immediately tried for the crime, the trial judge, in his discretion, may refuse to permit the defendant to stand trial again on the question of his competence to stand trial.[15] See § 14:5, supra, and § 21:10, infra, on the state employing an

---

there is no patient-psychiatrist privilege where a defendant is sent to Central State Hospital for evaluation. Justice Hill in his concurring opinion pointed out that the majority opinion does not hold that the doctor's testimony as to the defendant's description of the crime is admissible if there is an objection to it on the ground that *Miranda* was not complied with. Moody v. State, 244 Ga. 247, 250 (5), 260 S.E.2d 11 (1979).

[8]Brown v. State, 256 Ga. 387, 389, 349 S.E.2d 452 (1986).

[9]Velasquez v. State, 282 Ga. 871(4), 655 S.E.2d 806 (2008).

[10]Leonard v. State, 157 Ga. App. 37, 38 (1), 276 S.E.2d 94 (1981).

[11]Almond v. State, 180 Ga. App. 475, 349 S.E.2d 482 (1986).

[12]Wallace v. State, 248 Ga. 255, 259 (3), 282 S.E.2d 325 (1981).

[13]Strickland v. State, 247 Ga. 219, 222 (10), 275 S.E.2d 29 (1981).

[14]Spell v. State, 120 Ga. App. 398, 170 S.E.2d 701 (1969).

[15]Hardwick v. State, 231 Ga. 181 (4), 200 S.E.2d 728 (1973); Flanagan v. State, 103 Ga. 619 (1), 30 S.E. 550 (1898).

expert for the defendant. Nevertheless, in *Stevens v. State*,[16] the court held that where a special jury has found the defendant competent and there is no evidence of a lapse in the defendant's mental state, it is not necessary to make another competency inquiry before he is put on trial for a criminal offense 19 days later. However, if the jury finds the defendant incompetent to stand trial, then the court shall retain jurisdiction over the defendant and transfer the person to the Department of Behavioral Health and Developmental Disabilities.[17]

§ 14:95   Special plea of mental incompetency to stand trial—Confinement by Department of Behavioral Health and Developmental Disabilities

O.C.G.A. § 17-7-130(c) provides that the Department shall determine within 90 days the probability of the defendant becoming competent. Should the defendant become competent within the 90 days, he shall be returned to the court.

If a defendant is found by a jury to be incompetent to stand trial, he must be transferred to the Department of Behavioral Health and Developmental Disabilities and remain there until it is determined that he may be tried. Either the superior court where the defendant was found to be incompetent to stand trial or the probate court has authority to determine whether a pretrial detainee meets the criteria for civil commitment.[1]

The United States Supreme Court held in *Jackson v. Indiana*[2] that "[u]nder the due process clause of the Fourteenth Amendment, a person charged by a state with a criminal offense who is committed solely on account of his incapacity to proceed to trial, cannot be held more than a reasonable time necessary to determine whether there is a substantial probability that he will attain that capacity in the foreseeable future; if it is determined that he will probably soon be able to stand trial, his continued commitment must be justified by progress toward that goal, while if it is determined that there is no substantial probability that he will attain that capacity in the foreseeable future, the state must either release him or institute the customary civil commitment

---

[16]Stevens v. State, 267 Ga. 36, 37 (3), 472 S.E.2d 426 (1996).

[17]O.C.G.A. § 17-7-130(c).

[Section 14:95]

[1]Department of Human Resources v. Long, 217 Ga. App. 763, 458 S.E.2d 914 (1995).

[2]Jackson v. Indiana, 406 U.S. 715, 758, 92 S.Ct. 1845, 32 L.Ed.2d 435 (1972). The appellant in *Jackson* was a deaf mute but the procedure to determine competency to stand trial set down by the court is used for all petitioners. People v. Lang, 76 Ill.2d 311, 29 Ill.Dec. 87, 391 N.E.2d 350 (1979). O.C.G.A. § 17-7-130 is similar to the standard set down by the Supreme Court.

proceeding that would be required to commit indefinitely any other citizen."

In *Carr v. State*,[3] the Georgia Supreme Court noted that O.C.G.A. § 17-7-130(c) may be subject to a due process challenge because it does not provide direction regarding the amount of time each step in the process should take and how soon the defendant must be returned to court. As a result, the time to complete a competency evaluation is indefinite. In addition, the court held that the statute is unconstitutional to the extent it requires the detention of every person charged with a violent offense whose competency is to be evaluated without regard to whether they pose a danger to themselves or others. The Court noted that due process requires an "individualized" rather than an "automatic" determination as to whether the detention of a defendant is necessary to make a finding as to competency.

In *Sell v. United States*,[4] the Supreme Court ruled that under certain circumstances the state may involuntarily administer psychiatric medication in order to render a defendant competent to stand trial. The Court noted that such instances would be rare and would depend upon a four-tiered standard which required the trial court to make the following findings: (1) Important governmental interests are at stake, (2) involuntary medication will significantly further those governmental interests, (3) involuntary medication is necessary to further those governmental interests, and (4) the administration of the drugs to be used is medically appropriate for the defendant.

If there is not a substantial probability of the defendant becoming competent, the person shall be civilly committed if the person meets the criteria set out under O.C.G.A. §§ 37-3-1 et seq. or O.C.G.A. §§ 37-4-1 et seq.[5]

In *Department of Human Resources v. Long*,[6] the court pointed out that O.C.G.A. § 15-9-30 gives probate court the exclusive jurisdiction to determine matters of civil commitment. However, the court held that in cases involving criminal felonies, a superior court that finds a pre-trial detainee incompetent to stand trial

---

[3]Carr v. State, 303 Ga. 853, 815 S.E.2d 903 (2018). See McGouirk v. State, 303 Ga. 881, 815 S.E.2d 825 (2018).

[4]Sell v. United States, 539 U.S. 166, 123 S.Ct. 2174, 156 L.Ed.2d 197 (2003) (citations omitted). For examples of cases applying *Sell*, see United States v. Gomes, 387 F.3d 157 (2nd Cir. 2004); United States v. Marin, 338 F.3d 838 (8th Cir. 2003); and United States v. Ghane, 392 F.3d 317 (8th Cir.

2004). See also Johnson v. State, 341 Ga. App. 384, 801 S.E.2d 82 (2017) (trial court order directing that defendant be involuntarily medicated to make him competent to stand trial reversed based upon noncompliance with *Sell*).

[5]O.C.G.A. § 17-7-130(c).

[6]Department of Human Resources v. Long, 217 Ga. App. 763, 458 S.E.2d 914 (1995).

has the authority to determine whether the criteria for civil commitment has been met and, in the interest of judicial economy, need not transfer the case to probate court.

Providing there is a substantial probability that the defendant will become competent in the foreseeable future, the Department shall within the 90-day period notify the committing court and it will retain custody over the individual for purposes of continued treatment for an additional period, not to exceed nine months. At the end of the nine-month period, if the person is still incompetent, he shall be civilly committed if he meets the criteria set down under O.C.G.A. §§ 37-3-1 et seq. or O.C.G.A. §§ 31-30-1 et seq. If they are not found incompetent or not civilly committable, then they shall be returned to the committing court.[7]

If a person in the custody of the Department of Behavioral Health and Developmental Disabilities is found mentally competent to stand trial, he is normally to be released to law enforcement officials of the jurisdiction of the committing court's detention facilities for trial, unless the charges have been dismissed.[8]

§ 14:96 Uniform Act to secure the attendance of witnesses from without the state[1]

In the absence of a statute, a state court cannot require the attendance of a witness who is a non-resident of and is absent from the state.[2] To remedy this situation, Georgia enacted the Uniform Act[3] in 1976. Pursuant to the Uniform Act, persons in another

---

[7]O.C.G.A. § 17-7-130(c)(3).

[8]O.C.G.A. § 17-7-130(d)(1).

[Section 14:96]

[1]O.C.G.A. §§ 24-13-90 et seq. See Annot., 44 A.L.R.2d 732 (1955) for a general discussion of the Uniform Act; New York v. O'Neill, 359 U.S. 1, 79 S.Ct. 564, 3 L.Ed.2d 585 (1959).

[2]See 58 Am. Jur. 31 Witnesses § 16. Nor does the Georgia or United States Constitution obligate the state to provide such a statute. Mafnas v. State, 149 Ga. App. 286, 254 S.E.2d 409 (1979) (disapproved of on other grounds by, Davenport v. State, 289 Ga. 399, 711 S.E.2d 699 (2011)); Minder v. State, 113 Ga. 772 (1), 39 S.E. 284 (1901), aff'd, 183 U.S. 559, 22 S.Ct. 224, 46 L.Ed. 328 (1902). Actually, the Uniform Act does not give the demand-ing state the power to subpoena a witness beyond its borders, but merely provides a process for obtaining a court order for the production of the witness, who may then appear in the jurisdiction where he is found and move the court to deny or quash it. Mafnas v. State, 149 Ga. App. 286, 254 S.E.2d 409 (1979); O.C.G.A. § 24-13-92. For a good discussion of the dangers inherent in the inability to obtain witnesses in criminal proceedings, see Wilkerson v. State, 139 Ga. App. 725, 726 (b), 229 S.E.2d 529 (1976).

In Wilkerson v. Turner, 693 F.2d 121 (11th Cir. 1982), the court held that it was error for the district judge to deny the same Wilkerson's petition for federal habeas corpus.

[3]Former O.C.G.A. §§ 24-10-90 et seq. [Effective January 2013, §§ 24-

state may be summoned to testify in Georgia,[4] while persons in this state may be delivered to another state to testify.[5] The Georgia Supreme Court has also held that such "persons" include out-of-state corporate entities, and it is sufficient to subpoena the corporation itself rather than name a human agent. The corporation is responsible for designating that agent.[6] The Uniform Act has been interpreted as also implicitly authorizing the issuance of a subpoena duces tecum.[7] There are special provisions to secure the attendance of prisoners.[8]

It should be noted that all fifty states have enacted the Uniform Act.

In *Davenport v. State*,[9] the court held the appropriate statutory scheme to be employed to analyze a party's request for a certificate requesting the attendance in Georgia of an out-of-state witness is whether the out-of-state witness is a "material witness" pursuant to former O.C.G.A. § 24-10-94 (repealed and replaced by § 24-13-94 effective January 1, 2013). A material witness is one who can "testify about matters having some logical connections with the consequential facts especially if few others, if any, know about these matters." Once the Georgia court determines that the witness is a "material witness" and that the state where the witness is located has laws "for commanding persons within its borders to attend and testify in criminal prosecutions . . . in this state . . .," the court may then issue a certifiate under seal which may then be presented to the appropriate court in the state where the witness is located. That court is then required to hold a hearing to determine "whether the witness is material and necessary to the Georgia criminal proceeding, that compelling the witness to attend the Georgia proceeding and testifying would not cause an undue hardship to the witness and that Georgia will give the witness protection from arrest and the service of civil or criminal process."[10]

10-90 et seq. was replaced by §§ 24-13-90 et seq.] See Annot., "Uniform Act to Secure Attendance of Witnesses from Without a State in Criminal Proceedings," 62B Am. Jur. Process § 41 (2004). See Annot., "Availability Under Uniform Act to Secure the Attendance of Witnesses from Without a State in Criminal Proceedings of Subpoena Duces Tecum," 7 A.L.R.4th 836 (1981).

[4]O.C.G.A. § 24-13-94.

[5]O.C.G.A. § 24-13-92.

[6]Yeary v. State, 289 Ga. 394, 711 S.E.2d 694 (2011).

[7]Wollesen v. State of Georgia, 242 Ga. App. 317, 321 (3), 529 S.E.2d 630 (2000).

[8]O.C.G.A. §§ 24-13-93, 24-13-95.

[9]Davenport v. State, 289 Ga. 399, 711 S.E.2d 699 (2011). See Young v. State, 324 Ga. App. 127, 749 S.E.2d 423 (2013).

[10]Davenport v. State, 289 Ga. 399, 401–02, 711 S.E.2d 699 (2011). See Parker v. State, 296 Ga. 586, 595(b), 769 S.E.2d 329 (2015) (because a proceeding to determine whether a re-

In *Wollesen v. State of Georgia*,[11] the court held a Georgia superior court is entitled to rely on a foreign certificate and supplemental affidavits as "prima facie evidence of materiality and necessity." Also, if the evidence sought from the out-of-state witness is not admissible in Georgia, it is not error for the trial judge to deny the petition.[12]

A judge [of such court] in this state may issue a certificate stating the above facts and designating the number of days the person is required.[13] There may also be a recommendation included in the certificate that the person "be taken into immediate custody and delivered to an officer of this state to assure his attendance in this state."[14] The certificate is then presented to "a judge of a court of record in the county in which the witness is found."[15]

Unless otherwise ordered by the court, the summoned witness is not required to stay in Georgia for any period of time longer than that stated in the certificate.[16] After arriving in Georgia, should the witness fail without good cause to appear and testify as required by the summons, "the witness shall be punished in the manner provided for in Code Section 24-13-26."[17] The out-of-state witness is entitled to certain expenses.[18]

Similar provisions exist for bringing an out-of-state prisoner into this state to testify.[19] If a material witness for "a criminal action pending in a court of record or in a grand jury investigation in this state" is a prisoner in a penal institution in another state, he may be summoned to Georgia to testify.[20] The judge of the Georgia court shall present a certificate "to a judge of a court of record in the other state having jurisdiction over the prisoner confined, and a notice shall be given to the attorney general of the state in which the prisoner is confined."[21] The certificate shall state that the prisoner is a material witness; the specified time the prisoner is required; and that there is pending in the court a

---

quested out-of-state witness is material and necessary under O.C.G.A. § 24-13-94 is a preliminary question "concerning the qualification of a person to be a witness" within the scope of O.C.G.A. § 24-1-104(a), the rules of evidence, other than those relating to privileges, do not apply). See also, Cronkite v. State, 293 Ga. 476, 745 S.E.2d 591 (2013).

[11]Wollesen v. State of Georgia, 242 Ga. App. 317, 320 (1), 529 S.E.2d 630 (2000).

[12]Cf. Arp v. State, 249 Ga. 403 (2), 291 S.E.2d 495 (1982).

[13]O.C.G.A. § 24-13-94(a).

[14]O.C.G.A. § 24-13-94(a).

[15]O.C.G.A. § 24-13-94(a).

[16]O.C.G.A. § 24-13-94(b).

[17]O.C.G.A. § 24-13-94(b).

[18]O.C.G.A. § 24-13-94(b). Presently the witness is entitled to 12 cents a mile for each mile traveled by the ordinary route to and from the court where the prosecution is pending and $25 for each day that he is required to travel and attend as a witness.

[19]O.C.G.A. § 24-13-95.

[20]O.C.G.A. § 24-13-95(a).

[21]O.C.G.A. § 24-13-95(a).

criminal action or "a criminal proceeding or investigation by a grand jury."[22]

Persons coming into Georgia to testify or passing through Georgia to testify in another state, in compliance with a summons directing them to appear and testify, shall not while in Georgia "be subject to arrest or the service of process, civil or criminal, in connection with matters which arose before such person's entrance into this state under the summons."[23]

A material witness in Georgia may be compelled to testify in another state.[24] In addition, a prisoner incarcerated in Georgia may be summoned to testify in another state.[25]

For a person in this state to be summoned to another state to testify, several requirements must be met.[26] The judge of a court of another state ("which by its laws has made provision for commanding persons within that state to attend and testify in this state") must present a certificate in Georgia "to any judge of a court of record in the county in which the person is found."[27] The certificate shall state that the person sought to be summoned is a material witness; that there is pending in the court a "criminal prosecution" or an investigation by a grand jury has begun or will begin; and the specified time the witness is required.[28] The judge in Georgia then sets the place and time for a hearing and orders the witness to attend.[29]

The judge shall conduct a hearing in order to decide whether to issue a summons (attached to a copy of the certificate) requiring the witness to appear and testify in another state at the designated place and time.[30] In making this decision, the judge must find that the laws of the other state will provide the witness with "protection from arrest and the service of civil and criminal process"; and it will not be an "undue hardship" for the person to be required to appear and testify in another state; and that the person is a necessary and material witness.[31] At all times the witness shall be entitled to an attorney.[32]

In certain circumstances, a witness may be placed in immediate custody (as recommended in the certificate of the judge in the requesting state).[33] The witness may be brought to the hearing and the judge "may, in lieu of issuing subpoena or summons, order that the witness be forthwith taken into custody and

---

[22]O.C.G.A. § 24-13-95(a).

[23]O.C.G.A. § 24-13-96(a).

[24]O.C.G.A. § 24-13-92.

[25]O.C.G.A. § 24-13-93.

[26]O.C.G.A. § 24-13-92.

[27]O.C.G.A. § 24-13-92(a).

[28]O.C.G.A. § 24-13-92(a).

[29]O.C.G.A. § 24-13-92(a).

[30]O.C.G.A. § 24-13-92(b).

[31]O.C.G.A. § 24-13-92(b).

[32]O.C.G.A. § 24-13-92(a).

[33]O.C.G.A. § 24-13-92(c).

delivered to an officer of the requesting state."[34] The witness is entitled to certain expenses.[35] After such payment should the witness fail to appear and testify without good cause (as the summons requires), "the witness shall be punished in the manner provided for in Code Section 24-13-26."[36]

Prisoners in this state may be summoned to another state to testify.[37] A judge of another state (which under its law authorizes the summoning of prisoners incarcerated in that state to appear and testify in Georgia) shall present a certificate to a judge who has jurisdiction over the prisoner.[38] The certificate should state that the prisoner is a material witness; "that there is a criminal proceeding or investigation by a grand jury or a criminal action pending in the court"; and the specified time the prisoner is required.[39] The judge in Georgia sets a place and time for a hearing and notice is given to the Attorney General.[40] The prisoner is ordered to be produced at the hearing by the person having custody over him.[41]

Should the judge, during the hearing decide: that requiring the prisoner to appear and testify would not be detrimental to the prisoner's health or legal rights nor adversely affect the interests of the State of Georgia; that the prisoner is a necessary and material witness; "that the laws of the state in which he is required to testify will give him protection from arrest and the service of civil and criminal process because of any act committed prior to his arrival in the state under the order, and that as a practical matter the possibility is negligible that the witness may be subject to arrest or to the service of civil or criminal process in any state through which he will be required to pass," the Georgia prisoner may be required to appear and testify in another state.[42]

A copy of the certificate is attached to the judge's order.[43] The judge shall direct the prisoner to appear and testify; order the person having custody over him to produce him in the other state's court at the specified place and time and prescribe "such conditions as the judge shall determine."[44] The judge may direct the requesting state to take custody of the prisoner in Georgia, and provide "proper safeguards on the witness's custody while in

---

[34]O.C.G.A. § 24-13-92(c).

[35]O.C.G.A. § 24-13-92(d). See n. 18, supra, for the expenses the witness is entitled to.

[36]O.C.G.A. § 24-13-92(d).

[37]O.C.G.A. § 24-13-93.

[38]O.C.G.A. § 24-13-93(a).

[39]O.C.G.A. § 24-13-93(a).

[40]O.C.G.A. § 24-13-93(a).

[41]O.C.G.A. § 24-13-93(a).

[42]O.C.G.A. § 24-13-93(b).

[43]O.C.G.A. § 24-13-93(b).

[44]O.C.G.A. § 24-13-93(b).

transit."[45] The order shall also provide for the prisoner to be returned to a penal institution in Georgia, after he has testified and that the requesting state pay the expenses of the delivery and return of the prisoner.[46] The order of the judge of the Georgia court shall become effective when the judge of the requesting state issues an order requiring compliance with the conditions specified in the Georgia order.[47] However, O.C.G.A. § 24-13-93 is not applicable to prisoners who have received the death sentence or those incarcerated as mentally ill.[48]

See § 14:71, supra, on Interstate Agreement on Detainers and § 17:10, infra, on subpoenas.

For pleadings and orders relating to obtaining out-of-state witnesses, see Studdard, *Daniel's Georgia Criminal Trial Practice Forms* (2018–2019 ed.), §§ 19:8 and 23:41, et seq.

§ 14:97 Oral motion

An oral motion to dismiss or quash, as it is sometimes called, is in the nature of a general demurrer.[1] It is good only if the indictment or accusation is so defective that a motion in arrest of judgment would be valid.

An oral motion may be made at any time during trial[2] and presumably at any time prior to trial.

Under normal circumstances, the defendant is best served by filing a demurrer where the defect is discovered before arraignment.

§ 14:98 Rulings, orders, decisions of trial judge

Generally, the pretrial rulings and orders of the trial judge are regarded as interlocutory in nature and may be changed at the trial judge's discretion.[1] A final order or judgment of the trial court such as an order of discharge based upon speedy trial grounds can be reviewed by the trial court on its own motion, sometimes referred to as the court's "plenary power,"[2] or on a motion seeking reconsideration, provided it is filed within the same term of court as that in which the judgment was rendered. A

---

[45]O.C.G.A. § 24-13-93(b).
[46]O.C.G.A. § 24-13-93(b).
[47]O.C.G.A. § 24-13-93(c).
[48]O.C.G.A. § 24-13-93(d).

[Section 14:97]

[1]See Barton v. State, 79 Ga. App. 380, 387, 53 S.E.2d 707 (1949).

[2]Gilmore v. State, 118 Ga. 299 (1), 45 S.E. 226 (1903); Sheppard v. State, 95 Ga. App. 507, 98 S.E.2d 169 (1957).

[Section 14:98]

[1]Buice v. State, 272 Ga. 323, 324, 528 S.E.2d 788 (2000). Cf. Tucker v. State, 231 Ga. App. 210, 211 (1), 498 S.E.2d 774 (1998).

[2]See Pestana v. State, 328 Ga. App. 454, 762 S.E.2d 178 (2014).

timely filed motion for reconsideration will assure the court's authority to modify or change its judgment even beyond the term in which it was entered. However, a motion filed outside the term of court in which the judgment was entered divests the court of any authority to change its judgment.[3] One exception to this general rule is where the evidentiary posture of the issue has changed.[4]

§ 14:99 Interlocutory appeals

Georgia has made it clear that there is general policy against interlocutory appeals. However, it may be possible for a defendant before trial to obtain an appellate review of some adverse ruling of the trial court by following the appropriate statute. In order to do so, the defendant must ordinarily obtain a certificate from the trial judge within 10 days of the entry of the order, certifying that the decision is of such importance to the case that an immediate review should be had. If such a certificate is obtained, then an application shall be filed with the appropriate court, setting out the need for immediate review and the issues involved. The applicant may include copies of such parts of the records as he deems appropriate. A copy must be served on the district attorney, who may respond. The appellate court may exercise its discretion in permitting or rejecting the appeal. If the appeal is permitted, a notice of appeal is to be filed, and this acts as a supersedeas.[1] In 2005, O.C.G.A. § 5-6-34(b) was amended to specifically provide that a defendant who files a motion to recuse

---

[3]Chishti v. State, 288 Ga. App. 230, 653 S.E.2d 830 (2007).

[4]State v. Mojica, 316 Ga. App. 619, 730 S.E.2d 94 (2012) (additional evidence obtained after denial of motion to suppress warranted court's granting motion for reconsideration well after term of court in which original order was entered).

[Section 14:99]

[1]O.C.G.A. § 5-6-45.

If the order complained of involves the overruling of a plea of double jeopardy, there may be a constitutional right to have the issue determined before trial, since the double jeopardy clause of the Fifth Amendment is intended to prevent a defendant from twice being tried for the same offense. "Because of this focus on the 'risk' of conviction, the guarantee against double jeopardy assures an in-

dividual that, among other things, he will not be forced, with certain exceptions, to endure the personal strain, public embarrassment, and expense of a criminal trial more than once for the same offense. It thus protects interests wholly unrelated to the propriety of any subsequent conviction. . . . Consequently, if a criminal defendant is to avoid exposure to double jeopardy and thereby enjoy the full protection of the clause, his double jeopardy challenge to the indictment must be reviewable before that subsequent exposure occurs." Abney v. United States, 431 U.S. 651, 97 S.Ct. 2034, 52 L.Ed.2d 651 (1977), 3084-3085.

In Stack v. Boyle, 342 U.S. 1, 72 S.Ct. 1, 96 L.Ed. 3 (1951), the court apparently held that there is a pretrial right of appeal from the denial of a bond or the fixing of excessive bail. However, there is no federal constitutional right to a pre-trial appeal based

the trial judge in a criminal case may seek interlocutory review of an order denying the motion.[2]

In a multi-count indictment, a court order sustaining a plea or a demurrer is not considered "final" and thus is outside the ambit of O.C.G.A. § 5-7-1(a). If the state wants to appeal such an order, it must apply for a certificate of immediate review pursuant to O.C.G.A. § 5-7-2.[3]

In *Hayes v. State*,[4] the court held that a certificate of immediate review must be obtained before an interlocutory appeal will lie for the review of an order denying discovery.

However, the Georgia Supreme Court has concluded that an order denying a plea of double jeopardy is appealable under O.C.G.A. § 5-6-34, apparently without a certificate of immediate review, where the plea is filed sufficiently in advance of trial so as not to constitute a delaying device.[5] But where a plea of double jeopardy is denied and the denial of the plea recites "that the plea was frivolous and dilatory," an appeal does not act as a supersedeas, and the defendant can be tried while the appeal is pending.[6] However, generally the trial court loses jurisdiction of a

---

on a denial of speedy trial. United States v. MacDonald, 435 U.S. 850, 98 S.Ct. 1547, 56 L.Ed.2d 18 (1978). The court pointed out in MacDonald that (1) the denial of his speedy trial claim was not a final rejection and could be best considered after trial when the prejudice to the defendant would be more obvious, and (2) the speedy trial defense does not encompass a right not to be tried which must be upheld prior to trial.

In United States v. Dunbar, 611 F.2d 985 (5th Cir. 1980) (en banc), the court acting under its supervisory power said that the filing of an appeal on double jeopardy grounds does not prevent a trial pending appeal if the appeal is frivolous. The court then pointed out that the trial judge should make a finding of fact and conclude whether the appeal is frivolous.

[2]O.C.G.A. § 5-7-1(a) was also amended in 2005 to provide the state with the *right* to appeal an adverse order on a motion to recuse, as well as an order granting a defendant's motion for new trial. O.C.G.A. § 5-7-2 was amended in 2011 to provide that the granting of a motion for new trial is a

final order and subject to direct appeal by the state pursuant to O.C.G.A. § 5-7-1.

[3]State v. Outen, 289 Ga. 579, 714 S.E.2d 581 (2011) (abrogating State v. Tuzman, 145 Ga. App. 481, 243 S.E.2d 675 (1978), and all other authority to the contrary).

[4]Hayes v. State, 207 Ga. App. 520, 428 S.E.2d 425 (1993).

[5]Patterson v. State, 248 Ga. 875, 287 S.E.2d 7 (1982); Nave v. State, 166 Ga. App. 466, 304 S.E.2d 491 (1983). In Young v. State, 251 Ga. 153 (1), 303 S.E.2d 431 (1983), the court made it clear that a denial of a double jeopardy plea "may be appealed without application and certification, which otherwise would be required" under O.C.G.A. § 5-6-34(b).

[6]Rielli v. Oliver, 170 Ga. App. 699, 318 S.E.2d 173 (1984). Accord, Harvey v. State, 296 Ga. 823, 770 S.E.2d 840 (2015); DeSouza v. State, 285 Ga. App. 201, 645 S.E.2d 684 (2007). In Reed v. State, 205 Ga. App. 209, 211 (3), 422 S.E.2d 15 (1992), the same result was reached where a notice of appeal was filed after jury selec-

case when a notice of appeal has been filed.[7]

In *Strickland v. State*,[8] the court held "that a trial court may amend its order denying a plea of former jeopardy, nunc pro tunc, to find the plea dilatory and frivolous, even though a notice of appeal has been filed."

In *Gilliam v. Foster*,[9] the Fourth Circuit, en banc, held that a federal court may enjoin the continuation of a retrial of defendants in state court where their first trial ended in a mistrial, allegedly for "manifest necessity." However, the court stated that the stay was for the purpose of determining the validity of the claim of manifest necessity and should be used only when necessary to protect the defendants against double jeopardy.

The same right of interlocutory appeal without a certificate of immediate review applies where a defendant contends that he is entitled to be discharged[10] pursuant to O.C.G.A. § 17-7-170, providing for a discharge under certain circumstances when the defendant has filed a demand for trial.

In *State v. Vansant*,[11] the court held that the state may appeal "from an order, decision, or judgment sustaining a motion to suppress evidence illegally seized in the case of motions made and ruled upon prior to the impaneling of a jury."

After an appellate court rules on a valid appeal, the trial court does not again acquire jurisdiction to try the defendant until the remittitur has been filed in the trial court.[12] In addition, the "law of the case" doctrine applies in criminal cases just as it does in civil cases. Thus, when an issue is presented to an appellate court by way of an interlocutory appeal and resolved as a result, that disposition is binding in connection with any subsequent appeal.[13] Another form of interlocutory appeal is the collateral or-

---

tion, even though the order did not specify that the plea was "frivolous and dilatory."

[7]State v. Vansant, 208 Ga. App. 772, 776 (2), 431 S.E.2d 708 (1993), rev'd in part on other grounds and aff'd in part, 264 Ga. 319, 443 S.E.2d 474 (1994).

[8]Strickland v. State, 247 Ga. 219, 275 S.E.2d 29 (1981).

[9]Gilliam v. Foster, 61 F.3d 1070 (4th Cir. 1995).

[10]Smith v. State, 169 Ga. App. 251 (1), 312 S.E.2d 375 (1983), overruled on other grounds by State v. Collins, 201 Ga. App. 500, 411 S.E.2d 546 (1991); Hubbard v. State, 254 Ga. 694,

333 S.E.2d 827 (1985).

[11]State v. Vansant, 208 Ga. App. 772, 776 (2), 431 S.E.2d 708 (1993), rev'd in part on other grounds and aff'd in part, 264 Ga. 319, 443 S.E.2d 474 (1994). See Moon v. State, 287 Ga. 304, 696 S.E.2d 55 (2010).

[12]Nave v. State, 171 Ga. App. 165, 167 (3), 318 S.E.2d 753 (1984).

[13]Roulain v. Martin, 266 Ga. 353 (1), 466 S.E.2d 837 (1996); Perez v. State, 263 Ga. App. 411, 588 S.E.2d 269 (2003); Schwindler v. State, 261 Ga. App. 30 (1), 581 S.E.2d 619 (2003). See State v. Stone, 304 Ga. App. 695, 697 S.E.2d 852 (2010) (appellate decision in case later found to be incorrect will still apply to case in which it was

der exception to finality rule. The Supreme Court in *Fulton County v. State*[14] explained it as a rule that is to be applied "if the order (1) resolves an issue that is 'substantially separate' from the basic issues to be decided at trial, (2) would result in the loss of an important right if review had to await final judgment, and (3) completely and conclusively decides the issue on appeal such that nothing in the underlying action can affect it." In the *Fulton County* case, the order involved the payment of expenses associated with the defense of an indigent defendant. The Supreme Court held that the exception applied and that the order was directly appealable since it concerned matters unrelated to the basic issues to be decided at trial. *In re Paul*,[15] is another example of the collateral order exception. There, a trial court order directing non-party news reporters to divulge privileged information was deemed by the Supreme Court to be sufficiently collateral to the trial issues and thus subject to direct appeal.

On appeals by the state, see § 28:4, infra. See sections 28:22 and 28:26, infra, on the right of pre-trial review in death penalty cases.

---

decided even though no longer good authority for future cases). See Gilmore v. State, 341 Ga. App. 585, n.1, 802 S.E.2d 27 (2017) ("There is an exception to this rule when the evidentiary posture of the case changes such that the original evidence submitted is found to be insufficient, and the defi- cient evidence is later supplemented.").

[14]Fulton County v. State, 282 Ga. 570(3), 651 S.E.2d 679 (2007). See Britt v. State, 282 Ga. 746, 653 S.E.2d 713 (2007).

[15]In re Paul, 270 Ga. 680, 513 S.E.2d 219 (1999).

Chapter 15

Plea Bargaining

> **KeyCite®:** Cases and other legal materials listed in KeyCite Scope can be researched through the KeyCite service on Westlaw®. Use KeyCite to check citations for form, parallel references, prior and later history, and comprehensive citator information, including citations to other decisions and secondary materials.

§ 15:1   General

Plea discussion is both an essential and desirable part of the criminal process.[1] It leads to prompt and usually final disposition of most criminal cases, avoids much of the corrosive impact of idleness during pre-trial confinement for those who are denied release pending trial, and protects the public from accused persons who are prone to criminal conduct even while on pre-trial release. Plea discussions also enhance the rehabilitative prospects of the accused when they are ultimately imprisoned by shortening the time between charge and disposition.[2] The importance of plea bargaining has been demonstrated by a recognition of an ineffective assistance of counsel where defense

---

[Section 15:1]

[1]See Note, "Should We Really 'Ban' Plea Bargaining?; The Core Concerns of Plea Bargaining Critics," 47 Emory L.J. 753, 783 (1998); Lucian E. Dervan, "Bargained Justice: Plea-Bargaining's Innocence Problem and the Brady Safety-Valve," 2012 Utah L.Rev. 51 (2012).

[2]Santobello v. New York, 404 U.S. 257, 261, 92 S.Ct. 495, 30 L.Ed.2d 427 (1971); Rule 11 of the Federal Rules of Criminal Procedure.

See Annot., "Adequacy of Defense Counsel's Representation of Criminal Client Regarding Plea Bargaining," 8 A.L.R.4th 660 (1981). See Annot., "Supreme Court's Views as to Plea Bargaining and Its Effects," 50 L.Ed.2d 876 (1978). See Annot., "Choice of Remedies Where Federal Prosecutor Has Breached Plea Bargain—Post-Santobello v. New York . . . Cases," 120 A.L.R.Fed. 501 (1994).

counsel fails to convey a plea offer to the defendant.[3] O.C.G.A. § 24-4-410 prohibits the introduction of evidence regarding plea discussions between the defense and the prosecutor or statements regarding such in connection with court proceedings in which a plea was entered and later withdrawn in any subsequent "judicial or administrative proceeding," including the use of a defendant's withdrawn plea in any trial, civil or criminal, which may occur thereafter. Rule 410 also applies to a plea of nolo contendere.

Plea bargaining, or plea negotiating, gives both prosecution and defense counsel an opportunity to talk about the case informally and hopefully unhurriedly. Both parties may obtain informal discovery and gain other insights into the case.

Plea bargaining is of importance to the prosecuting attorney because of time limitations and the impossibility of having a jury trial in every case. Defense counsel should be interested in plea bargaining for the same reasons, although the time pressures are not, ordinarily, as great.[4] The participation of the trial judge is prohibited as a constitutional matter when it is so great as to render a guilty plea involuntary.[5] This includes comments "by the trial judge that reinforce the unmistakable reality that a defendant who rejects a plea offer and instead opts to go to trial will likely face a greater sentence."[6]

From the defendant's standpoint, plea bargaining may result in a prompt disposition of his case, diminishing the uncertainty of having criminal charges "hanging over him." More importantly, if an agreement is reached between the prosecutor and defense attorney, the defendant is likely to receive a lesser sentence than if found guilty and sentenced by the court. While it is improper for a trial judge to impose a harsher sentence simply because a defendant insisted on being tried,[7] the accused always runs the risk that damaging testimony will come out at trial which will give the judge a better insight into the whole situation than the summary of the facts brought out at the time of the entering of a guilty plea.

Despite the beneficial aspects of plea bargaining, a defendant has no right to engage in plea bargaining unless the district at-

---

[3]Lyles v. State, 178 Ind.App. 398, 382 N.E.2d 991 (1978). See Lloyd v. State, 258 Ga. 645, 646, 373 S.E.2d 1 (1988).

[4]In the case entitled "In Re Conduct of Rook," 276 Or. 695, 556 P.2d 1351 (1976), the court held that the prosecuting attorney was guilty of unethical conduct in refusing to plea bargain with a group of Elks charged with gambling as long as they were represented by certain counsel.

[5]Skomer v. State, 183 Ga. App. 308, 310, 358 S.E.2d 886 (1987).

[6]Gibson v. State, 281 Ga. App. 607(1), 636 S.E.2d 767 (2006).

[7]See § 26:43, infra, on judicial considerations in sentencing.

torney agrees to the plea.[8]

Nevertheless, in *Whitehead v. State,*[9] the court pointed out that, absent extenuating circumstances, a defendant is entitled to be told that an offer has been made by the district attorney in exchange for a guilty plea and to be advised of the consequences of the choices confronting the defendant. Consequently, if the district attorney does make a proposed offer to defense counsel which is not relayed to the defendant, this may amount to ineffective assistance of counsel.[10] See § 7:4, supra, on ineffective assistance of counsel.

In *Sartin v. State,*[11] the court pointed out that a trial judge is not required to accept a plea agreement between the defense and the state. However, in *Lewis v. State,*[12] the court held that the reasoning in *Santobello v. New York,*[13] which compels the state to keep the promises it makes in return for a defendant's plea of guilty, can, under the right circumstances, apply to a trial court. In *Lewis*, the defendant understood that in exchange for his plea and his agreement to testify for the state at the trial of his co-defendants, he would receive a probated sentence. Following the trial, the court refused to impose the recommended sentence, implying tha the defendant had not testified truthfully. Because the state and the defense were in agreement that the defendant had testified truthfully, the case was remanded to the trial court in order to give it the opportunity to identify those parts of the defendant's testimony which were of concern to the sentencing judge.

Generally, on plea bargaining, see 21 Am. Jur. Criminal Law §§ 481 et seq. and Rule 33.3 of the Uniform Rules for the Superior Courts.

§ 15:2   Legal aspects

An agreement by a prosecuting attorney to make a certain recommendation to the court if the defendant pleads guilty, is bind-

---

[8]Harris v. State, 167 Ga. App. 153, 155 (6), 306 S.E.2d 79 (1983); Bostic v. State, 184 Ga. App. 509, 511 (4), 361 S.E.2d 872 (1987).

[9]Whitehead v. State, 211 Ga. App. 121, 122, 438 S.E.2d 128 (1993).

[10]United States v. Blaylock, 20 F.3d 1458 (9th Cir. 1994). See Johnson v. State, 289 Ga. 532, 712 S.E.2d 811 (2011).

[11]Sartin v. State, 201 Ga. App. 612 (1), 411 S.E.2d 582 (1991).

[12]Lewis v. State, 330 Ga. App. 412, 767 S.E.2d 771 (2014) (trial court's determination that a state's witness testified falsely might be basis for post-conviction relief for co-defendants of witness), aff'd State v. Lewis, 298 Ga. 126, 779 S.E.2d 643 (2015) (trial court clearly authorized to set aside plea agreement premised on defendant's cooperation and truthful testimony at trial if court finds that defendant failed to testify truthfully).

[13]Santobello v. New York, 404 U.S. 257, 92 S. Ct. 495, 30 L. Ed. 2d 427 (1971).

ing on him and his office.[1] If the attorney or some other attorney lacking knowledge of the negotiations breaches the agreement, the plea is not binding.[2] Some courts have used a contract analogy of offer and acceptance in determining whether a plea offer of the state may be withdrawn by the state before it is accepted.[3] In *Martin v. State,*[4] the Georgia Court of Appeals held that a plea "agreement may be considered as a contract." "If no time is prescribed for accepting an offer, it must be done within a reasonable time."[5] There is no binding agreement until the offer has been accepted. An offer may be withdrawn prior to acceptance even if the offer provides that it will remain open for a stated time. Other states have pointed out that plea bargains are to be encouraged, and, even though they may be somewhat tentative in that the trial judge may not approve the agreement, still the state should not be permitted to withdraw the agreement with impunity.[6]

In *Mabry v. Johnson,*[7] the United States Supreme Court considered a case where a district attorney offered to make a certain recommendation as to sentence if the defendant pled guilty. Three days later defense counsel called the prosecuting attorney to accept the offer and was told that the offer resulted from a mistake and was withdrawn. The court held that the district attorney could withdraw his offer. The defendant had no constitutional right to have the bargain specifically enforced. In

---

[Section 15:2]

[1]Puckett v. U.S., 129 S. Ct. 1423, 173 L. Ed. 2d 266 (2009); Santobello v. New York, 404 U.S. 257, 92 S. Ct. 495, 30 L. Ed. 2d 427 (1971); Syms v. State, 331 Ga. App. 225, 770 S.E.2d 305 (2015); Sumner v. State, 284 Ga. App. 308(8), 643 S.E.2d 831 (2007).

However, in United States v. Avery, 621 F.2d 214, 216 (5th Cir. 1980), where the government attorney agreed to "remain mute and make no recommendation of sentencing," the court concluded that this agreement did not prevent the United States Attorney from providing information on the defendant's background and character to a probation officer.

See Annot., "When Is Federal Prosecutor Bound by Promises of Immunity or Plea Bargains Made by Another Federal Agent," 55 A.L.R.Fed. 402 (1981).

[2]Santobello v. New York, 404 U.S. 257, 92 S.Ct. 495, 30 L.Ed.2d 427

(1971).

[3]Government of Virgin Islands v. Scotland, 614 F.2d 360 (3d Cir. 1980); United States v. Aguilera, 654 F.2d 352 (5th Cir. 1981).

See Annot., "Right of Prosecutor to Withdraw from Plea Bargain Prior to Entry of Plea," 16 A.L.R.4th 1089 (1982).

[4]Martin v. State, 207 Ga. App. 861, 429 S.E.2d 332 (1993). See McClam v. State, 304 Ga. App. 844, 698 S.E.2d 358 (2010). Cf. United States v. Hyde, 520 U.S. 670, 117 S.Ct. 1630, 137 L.Ed.2d 935 (1997).

[5]Sparks v. State, 232 Ga. App. 179, 182 (3)(c), 501 S.E.2d 562 (1998).

[6]Ex parte Yarber, 437 So.2d 1330 (Ala.1983); State v. Brockman, 277 Md. 687, 357 A.2d 376 (1976).

[7]Mabry v. Johnson, 467 U.S. 504, 104 S.Ct. 2543, 81 L.Ed.2d 437 (1984). Cf. Rowland v. State, 257 Ga. 25, 26 (2), 354 S.E.2d 145 (1987).

Brown v. State,[8] a district attorney entered into a plea agreement with a defendant in which the district attorney agreed that if the defendant would plead guilty to armed robbery and accept a 20 year sentence, the charge pending against the defendant in another circuit would be dismissed. The defendant accepted the plea agreement. The district attorney had not communicated with his counterpart in the other circuit. The defendant was then prosecuted in the other circuit. The court held that the plea agreement did not prevent his prosecution in the other circuit since a district attorney in one circuit cannot bind a district attorney in another circuit, but the breached agreement may be used on the question of the voluntariness of the earlier plea.

In *Ricketts v. Adamson,*[9] the defendant, Adamson, had entered into a plea agreement in which it was agreed that he would plead guilty to murder in the second degree and would testify against others involved in the death. He pled guilty, was sentenced, and was serving time. Then he refused to testify at the re-trial of the other parties after the reversal of their convictions. The United States Supreme Court held that the double jeopardy clause of the Fifth Amendment did not bar the prosecution of the defendant for murder in the first degree.

The significance of plea agreements is also demonstrated by the fact that even if a defendant denied a plea agreement at the time of entering a guilty plea, this does not serve to automatically prevent a post-sentencing inquiry into the question of whether in fact a bargain had been made.[10]

In *Brady v. United States,*[11] the court held that a guilty plea is not invalid under the Fifth Amendment where a prosecutor agrees to accept a plea to a selected count or counts, or to reduce a charge.

In *People v. Seaberg,*[12] the court held that it is proper for a prosecutor to insist that a defendant waive his right to an appeal as a condition of a plea bargain. However, such a waiver does not prevent a defendant from challenging the voluntariness of the plea.

---

[8]Brown v. State, 201 Ga. App. 473, 474 (1), 411 S.E.2d 360 (1991).

[9]Ricketts v. Adamson, 483 U.S. 1, 107 S.Ct. 2680, 97 L.Ed.2d 1 (1987). See Brown v. State, 261 Ga. App. 115, 582 S.E.2d 13 (2003). See also Simmons v. State, 292 Ga. 265, 736 S.E.2d 402 (2013) (state could withdraw plea agreement where defendant made statements while in jail which contradicted testimony she had agreed to provide at trial of co-defendants).

[10]Blackledge v. Allison, 431 U.S. 63, 97 S.Ct. 1621, 52 L.Ed.2d 136 (1977).

[11]Brady v. United States, 397 U.S. 742, 751, 90 S.Ct. 1463, 25 L.Ed.2d 747 (1970).

[12]People v. Seaberg, 74 N.Y.2d 1, 543 N.Y.S.2d 968, 541 N.E.2d 1022 (1989). Accord, Allen v. Thomas, 265 Ga. 518, 519 (2), 458 S.E.2d 107 (1995).

In *Allen v. Thomas*,[13] the court held that a defendant can waive the right to seek relief from a sentence of life imprisonment as a part of an agreement to plead guilty.

In *State v. Hanson*,[14] the court held that, in the future, an agreement not to prosecute a defendant in exchange for his testimony is not binding in Georgia unless the agreement is in writing. Further, the writing must "specifically set forth the transactions to which the promise relates," and it must be approved by the court. See sections 12:14 and 12:15, supra, on witness immunity.

In *State v. Barrett*,[15] the defendant agreed not to run for public office in exchange for a negotiated plea of first offender on some charges and the promise of the State to nolle pross other charges. After completing the first offender probation, the defendant ran for and was elected to public office. The court approved the prosecution of the defendant on the charges which had been nolle prossed even though the statute of limitations had expired. The court enforced the sentencing "deal" because of the valuable consideration received by each of the parties and because the defendant voluntarily and knowingly waived any rights he may have had.

In *Ellison v. State*,[16] the defendant entered into a plea agreement which provided that he would not be eligible for parole for a period of 25 years. At the time the plea agreement was entered, the defendant would have been eligible for parole after 7 years. The court held that the plea agreement was contrary to established law and was therefore void.

See § 5:5, supra, on induced confessions; and § 14:34, supra, on promises of leniency to a prosecution witness. See also sections 16:2, 16:14 and 16:15, infra, on guilty pleas.

§ 15:3 Prosecutorial vindictiveness

In *Bordenkircher v. Hayes*,[1] the defendant refused to plead guilty to a charge of uttering a forged instrument, which would

---

[13]Allen v. Thomas, 265 Ga. 518, 519, 458 S.E.2d 107 (1995).

[14]State v. Hanson, 249 Ga. 739, 747 (3), 295 S.E.2d 297 (1982).

[15]State v. Barrett, 215 Ga. App. 401, 451 S.E.2d 82 (1994) (abrogated on other grounds by, State v. Outen, 289 Ga. 579, 714 S.E.2d 581 (2011)). Compare State v. Young, 260 Ga. App. 44, 579 S.E.2d 16 (2003) where the Court of Appeals reversed a trial court order dismissing an indictment be-

cause the state reneged on agreement to permit defendant to testify before grand jury. The court's ruling was premised on finding that there was no "significant consideration" to support the agreement.

[16]Ellison v. State, 299 Ga. 779, 792 S.E.2d 387 (2016).

[Section 15:3]

[1]Bordenkircher v. Hayes, 434 U.S. 357, 98 S.Ct. 663, 54 L.Ed.2d 604 (1978).

have been punishable by a sentence of two to ten years. The prosecutor said that if the defendant did not plead guilty, he would have the defendant re-indicted as a habitual offender. The defendant refused to plead guilty. The prosecutor obtained a habitual offender indictment which carried a mandatory life sentence. The defendant was tried, convicted and sentenced to life. The United States Supreme Court found no violation of the due process clause of the Fourteenth Amendment and refused to give Hayes relief.

In *Hitchcock v. Wainwright,*[2] the court found no due process violation where a defendant rejected a plea bargain for a life sentence and after conviction was sentenced to death. The court pointed out that the decision to impose the death sentence can be explained by reasons other than vindictiveness, such as the fact that the state has a valid reason for being more lenient with those who pled guilty thus saving the state's resources. Also, a trial judge can learn of other aggravating circumstances at a trial not known at the time of the plea bargain.

In 1982, in *United States v. Goodwin,*[3] the court said "[t]o punish a person because he has done what the law plainly allows him to do is a due process violation 'of the most basic sort.' . . . ." Nevertheless, since the objective of criminal proceedings is to bring about imposition of punishment, the presence or absence of a punishment motivation provides no adequate basis to distinguish legitimate from non-legitimate governmental action.

In *North Carolina v. Pearce,*[4] the court considered a case in which a defendant had been convicted, appealed, obtained a new trial and was then given a greater sentence than after the first trial. Here the court created a presumption of vindictiveness which may be overcome only by some objective evidence in a trial court record justifying an increased sentence. *Pearce* was subsequently overruled in *Alabama v. Smith.*[5] *Smith* restricted the presumption of vindictiveness created in *Pearce* to those cases where the evidence shows a "reasonable likelihood" that the increased sentence was "the product of actual vindictiveness on the part of the sentencing authority."

In *Blackledge v. Perry,*[6] the defendant was convicted in an inferior court having exclusive jurisdiction of misdemeanors. The

---

[2]Hitchcock v. Wainwright, 770 F.2d 1514 (11th Cir. 1985), judgment rev'd on other grounds, 481 U.S. 393, 107 S.Ct. 1821, 95 L.Ed.2d 347 (1987).

[3]U. S. v. Goodwin, 457 U.S. 368, 102 S. Ct. 2485, 73 L. Ed. 2d 74 (1982).

[4]North Carolina v. Pearce, 395 U.S. 711, 89 S.Ct. 2072, 23 L.Ed.2d 656 (1969).

[5]Alabama v. Smith, 490 U.S. 794, 109 S. Ct. 2201, 104 L. Ed. 2d 865 (1989).

[6]Blackledge v. Perry, 417 U.S. 21, 94 S.Ct. 2098, 40 L.Ed.2d 628 (1974). In Thigpen v. Roberts, 468 U.S. 27, 104 S.Ct. 2916, 82 L.Ed.2d 23 (1984), the

court imposed a six-month sentence. The defendant appealed to a higher court having jurisdiction to give him a de novo trial. This court also had jurisdiction to try felony cases. After Perry filed a notice of appeal the prosecuting attorney obtained a felony indictment against him for a more serious offense arising out of the same incident. The court emphasized that it did not matter that there was no evidence of bad faith or malice on the part of the prosecutor. "[T]he likelihood of vindictiveness justified a presumption that would free defendant of apprehension of such a retaliatory motivation on the part of the prosecutor."

In both *Perry* and *Pearce,* the defendant had exercised the right in question after once having been tried and convicted. In *Bordenkircher* and *Goodwin,* the court was concerned with a pre-trial decision to modify the charges against the defendant. "In the course of preparing a case for trial the prosecutor may uncover additional information that suggests a basis for further prosecution or he may come to realize that information possessed by the state has a broader significance. At this stage of the proceeding the prosecutor's assessment of the proper extent of prosecution may not have crystallized. In contrast, once a trial begins—and certainly by the time a conviction has been obtained—it is much more likely that the state has discovered and assessed all information against the accused and has made a determination, on the basis of that information, of the extent to which he should be prosecuted. Thus, a change in the charging decision made after the initial trial is completed is much more likely to be improperly motivated."[7]

Thus, in *Goodwin,* the timing of the prosecutor's action suggests that a presumption of vindictiveness is not warranted. "A prosecutor should remain free before trial to exercise the broad discretion entrusted to him to determine the extent of the societal interest in prosecution."[8] This rule is the basis of *Bordenkircher v. Hayes,* supra. A change in charges during or after plea bargaining is no suitable measure of improper prosecutorial vindictiveness. That was true in *Goodwin* as it had been in *Hayes.* Nothing in the *Goodwin* record supported a finding of actual vindictiveness. Therefore, Goodwin's conviction could be reversed only through invoking a presumption of vindictiveness applicable to all cases. "[A] mere opportunity for vindictiveness is insuf-

---

court reemphasized that (1) in a situation like that of *Perry* and *Roberts,* there is a presumption of unconstitutional vindictiveness in the circumstances and (2) its decision was based on due process. The court found no material distinction in the facts in *Perry* and *Roberts.*

[7]United States v. Goodwin, 457 U.S. 368, 381, 102 S.Ct. 2485, 73 L.Ed.2d 74, 85 (1982).

[8]United States v. Goodwin, 457 U.S. 368, 382, 102 S.Ct. 2485, 73 L.Ed.2d 74, 86 (1982).

ficient to justify" such a rule.[9]

In *Allen v. State*,[10] the court stated that a criminal defendant should not be allowed to reject a sentence concession that is offered in return for a guilty plea and then bind the state to that rejected lenient sentence when he is later convicted at trial. To hold otherwise would allow a criminal defendant to go to trial and seek an acquittal knowing that even if unsuccessful, his sentence would not exceed the one originally offered. The court further stated that "the underlying reason for the [lenient] sentence— [the defendant's acceptance of the plea bargain]—was eliminated when [that plea bargain was rejected] and [the defendant] elected to exercise [his] constitutional right to trial by jury."

In *Dupont v. State*,[11] the court said that where a defendant fails to plead guilty and is sentenced after a conviction to a harsher sentence than that recommended earlier, this does not reflect constitutional "vindictiveness but rather the risk inherent in electing to go to trial instead of plea bargaining."

See § 26:43, infra, on vindictiveness in sentencing.

§ 15:4 Practice of plea bargaining

Once a defense counsel is employed, he should soon speak with the prosecutor. The prosecutor should encourage such meeting.[1] The conference should be held at a time when neither attorney is rushed. The burden of arranging the meeting is on the defense counsel. Defense counsel should not be reluctant to approach the prosecutor about the case. The practice of plea bargaining is no more a sign of weakness than discussing the settlement of a civil case with the opposing counsel. While there are cases which may not be resolved by plea bargaining, attorneys should not hesitate to discuss their case with each other.

Counsel vary in the practice of plea bargaining. Some approach it with the idea of giving the opposing lawyer no information about their side of the case. Others are more willing to tell the opponent about their side of the case. In reality, the opponent

---

[9]United States v. Goodwin, 457 U.S. 368, 384, 102 S.Ct. 2485, 73 L.Ed.2d 74, 87 (1982). See Brandenburg v. State, 292 Ga. App. 191(4), 663 S.E.2d 844 (2008).

[10]Allen v. State, 193 Ga. App. 670, 672, 388 S.E.2d 889 (1989) (quoting Thompson v. State, 154 Ga. App. 704, 269 S.E.2d 474 (1980)).

[11]Dupont v. State, 204 Ga. App. 262, 265 (5), 418 S.E.2d 803 (1992).

[Section 15:4]

[1]See A.B.A. Criminal Justice Standards for the Prosecution Function, Standard 3-5.6(a), which states that a prosecutor should "be open, at every stage of a criminal matter, to discussions with defense counsel concerning . . . [a] negotiated disposition."

always knows something about "your side" of the case.

If an attorney expects to obtain information, he will probably have to give information in exchange. If there is a basic obstacle to the state's case, and the prosecutor is not aware of the problem, from a defense standpoint he is not very likely to be reasonable in plea negotiations. However, if defense counsel is willing to point out the problem in the state's case, he may be able to dispose of the case without a plea, or trial or on the basis of a reasonable plea. Nevertheless, in such a situation, the defense counsel may want to sit back and wait for an acquittal or directed verdict.

Plea bargaining should not be regarded as a procedure which takes place at only one meeting. Negotiations may continue over a series of meetings.

As a matter of practice, a district attorney will frequently dead docket or nolle prosequi a case if the defendant agrees to take a polygraph test and the results are favorable to the defendant.

Defense counsel should never agree to any plea bargaining until his client has agreed to it.[2] Likewise, of course, defense counsel has a duty to notify the defendant of all offers of a negotiated plea made by the district attorney.[3] In *Lloyd v. State*,[4] the court pointed out the duty of counsel to communicate fully to the defendant the substance of discussions between defense counsel and the district attorney and held that the decision of whether or not to accept an offer by the district attorney "is one to be made by the defendant with the best advice of his counsel, and that the failure to communicate the offer of the prosecutor for the defendant's consideration falls below the standard of care expected in the legal profession." If an agreement is reached, the defense counsel must also make sure his client fully understands that the agreement is between the prosecuting attorney and defense counsel and not legally binding on the court.

"Judicial participation in the plea negotiation process is prohibited by court rule in this state and in the federal system."[5] Nonetheless, should the parties "negotiate a tentative plea agreement, a trial court may indicate whether it will concur with the agreement. What is prohibited is when a trial court involves itself in plea negotiations so as to render a guilty plea

---

[2]See Unif. Sup. Ct. R. 33.4.

[3]Rasmussen v. State, 280 Ark. 472, 658 S.W.2d 867 (1983).

[4]Lloyd v. State, 258 Ga. 645, 647 (2)(a), 373 S.E.2d 1 (1988). See Johnson v. State, 289 Ga. 532, 712 S.E.2d 811 (2011) (failure to communicate pros-

ecutor's plea deadline policy).

[5]McDaniel v. State, 271 Ga. 552, 553 (2), 522 S.E.2d 648 (1999); Pride v. Kemp, 289 Ga. 353, 711 S.E.2d 653 (2011). See Rule 33.5(A) of the Uniform Rules for the Superior Courts; Rule 11(e)(1) of the Federal Rules of Criminal Procedure.

involuntary."[6] It is never appropriate for a trial judge to even suggest to a defendant that rejection of a plea offer may result in a harsher punishment in the event of conviction by a jury.[7] However, in the Colorado case of *People v. Jasper*,[8] the court held that a trial court may enforce a deadline for tendering a guilty plea if the parties have adequate notice of the deadline.

See § 16:2, infra, on entering a guilty plea.

§ 15:5 The ten commandments of defense plea bargaining

The following "rules" or "commandments" have been suggested:[1]

(1) Remember that you can't lose your case by plea bargaining, if properly done.

(2) Don't wait—The first defendant to squeal usually gets the deal.

(3) Know where you are. Know your case, the defendant, and his family.

(4) Know where you want to go. You may not know your exact destination, but know it as precisely as possible. Be reasonable. Show the edges of your cards.

(5) Know your case—If you have a defense you need to know it.

(6) Learn and know the state's case.

(7) Know the district attorney, the judge, and the system.

(8) You can lose if you lose your objectivity—Don't be a bull in a china shop. Keep your sense of humor.

(9) Be flexible, be innovative, and look at the whole picture.

(10) Be persistent, be polite, and keep coming back. Don't take "no" for an answer to a reasonable proposition which you suggest unless you or the district attorney suggests an

---

[6]Works v. State, 301 Ga. App. 108, 111, 686 S.E.2d 863 (2009). See State v. Hayes, 301 Ga. 342, 801 S.E.2d 50 (2017) (trial court did not impermissibly participate in plea discussions when it informed defendant of potential maximum sentence if he were found guilty, and thus did not render defendant's plea involuntary).

[7]Skomer v. State, 183 Ga. App. 308, 358 S.E.2d 886 (1987). See U.S. v. Davila, 133 S. Ct. 2139, 186 L. Ed. 2d 139, 111 A.F.T.R.2d 2013-2213 (2013) (magistrate's participation in plea discussions did not require automatic vacatur of the plea without consideration of the error's impact in light of the full record). Compare, Winfrey v. State, 304 Ga. 94, 816 S.E.2d 613 (2018) (trial court's participation in plea discussion violated USCR 33.5(A)).

[8]People v. Jasper, 17 P.3d 807 (Colo.2001).

[Section 15:5]

[1]The material contained in this section has been renamed, summarized, and rearranged, but it has been largely taken from an address by Robert Wilson, former District Attorney, Stone Mountain Judicial Circuit, at a seminar sponsored by the Georgia Association of Criminal Defense Lawyers, King and Prince Hotel, St. Simons Island, Georgia, on May 8, 1981.

equally attractive alternative.

Chapter 16

Arraignment

KeyCite®: Cases and other legal materials listed in KeyCite Scope can be researched through the KeyCite service on Westlaw®. Use KeyCite to check citations for form, parallel references, prior and later history, and comprehensive citator information, including citations to other decisions and secondary materials.

---

§ 16:1   Background

Arraignment is that initial step in a criminal prosecution whereby the defendant is brought before the court to hear the charges and to enter a plea.[1] It consists of reading the indictment to the prisoner and asking him, in open court, whether he is guilty or not guilty.[2] It has been held that the defendant must be

---

[Section 16:1]

[1]Black's Law Dictionary (10th ed. 2014).

[2]Harris v. State, 11 Ga. App. 137, 139, 74 S.E. 895 (1912). See O.C.G.A. § 17-7-93. See Unif. Sup. Ct. Rule 33.2 which provides that a defendant "shall

not be called upon to enter a plea" until he or she has been afforded a reasonable time to retain counsel or have one appointed as well as time to confer with counsel. Also to the same effect, see A.B.A. Standards, Pleas of Guilty, **Standard 14-1.3, Aid of Counsel; Time for Deliberations**.

present at the time of arraignment.[3] An arraignment is to be regarded as a critical stage in a criminal proceeding.[4] If there is a dispute on whether the defendant has been arraigned the minutes of the clerk seem to control.[5]

If a defendant at arraignment requests appointment of counsel, officers may not thereafter initiate interrogation of the defendant. See § 5:20, supra, on *Miranda* right to counsel.

The purpose of arraignment is to put the defendant on notice of the charges against him[6] and give him an opportunity to plead to the indictment.[7] The arraignment serves to form the issues to be tried[8] and to identify the person indicted.[9] The time of arraignment also fixes the time for filing some demurrers and many pleas.[10]

Also, Rule II(C)(1) of the Unified Appeal Procedure requires the district attorney to announce prior to arraignment whether or not he intends to seek the death penalty, but if the prosecuting attorney fails to so notify the defendant before arraignment, this does not prevent the district attorney from then announcing his decision to seek the death penalty and then having the defendant re-arraigned.[11]

The issue is said to be joined when the defendant signs the plea at the time of arraignment.[12] The defendant cannot be considered to have been placed in jeopardy until after the issue has been joined.[13] See § 14:51, supra, on when jeopardy attaches.

If a prisoner, upon being arraigned, fails to plead, the clerk has the responsibility of entering a "not guilty" plea on the minutes with the arraignment.[14] The district attorney has the responsibility of entering the plea of the defendant on the indictment.[15] A defendant, with the consent of the court in all cases except capital

---

[3]Wells v. Terrell, 121 Ga. 368 (3), 49 S.E. 319 (1904). See 2 Torcia, Wharton's Criminal Procedure, §§ 336 et seq. (12th Ed. 1976).

[4]See Hamilton v. State of Ala., 368 U.S. 52, 82 S. Ct. 157, 7 L. Ed. 2d 114 (1961); Carswell v. State, 244 Ga. App. 516, 534 S.E.2d 568 (2000).

[5]E.g., Birt v. State, 127 Ga. App. 532, 194 S.E.2d 335 (1972).

[6]Clark v. State, 138 Ga. App. 266, 271 (7), 226 S.E.2d 89 (1976).

[7]Tarver v. State, 95 Ga. 222, 227 (1), 21 S.E. 381 (1894).

[8]Bryans v. State, 34 Ga. 323, 324 (1866).

[9]Wells v. Terrell, 121 Ga. 368, 49

S.E. 319 (1904).

[10]Rule 31.1 of the Uniform Rules for the Superior Courts, which is largely quoted in § 14:2, supra. See also O.C.G.A. § 17-7-110.

[11]State v. Terry, 257 Ga. 473, 474, 360 S.E.2d 588 (1987).

[12]Cf. Hardwick v. State, 231 Ga. 181, 183 (6), 200 S.E.2d 728 (1973); Waller v. State, 251 Ga. 124 (5), 303 S.E.2d 437 (1983), rev'd on other grounds, 467 U.S. 39, 104 S.Ct. 2210, 81 L.Ed.2d 31 (1984).

[13]Bryans v. State, 34 Ga. 323 (1866).

[14]O.C.G.A. § 17-7-94.

[15]O.C.G.A. § 17-7-96.

felonies, may enter a plea of nolo contendere rather than guilty or not guilty.[16]

It is the responsibility of the court to fix the time of arraignment. There is no provision of law requiring that a defendant be arraigned within a specified period of time.[17] However, a jury cannot be impaneled and sworn until a defendant has been arraigned or waived arraignment.[18] When the time of arraignment has been set, it is the duty of the clerk to notify both the defendant and his counsel of the date set for arraignment.[19] This notice must be sent at least five days before arraignment and may be mailed or served by the sheriff or his deputy.[20] The five-day provision does not require that the notice be received 120 hours before the time of arraignment. Rule 30.1 of the Uniform Rules for the Superior Courts provides for a notice of arraignment to be given to "attorneys of record, defendants, and bondsmen." However, the defendant waives the notice requirements if he appears and enters a plea at the arraignment.[21] In the absence of a waiver, a defendant is entitled to five days notice of arraignment even where there is a material "amendment" to an accusation or a new accusation resulting from the sustaining of a demurrer.[22] Even in the absence of a waiver, procedural irregularities such as the lack of an arraignment or insufficient notice of arraignment are deemed harmless in the absence of some articulable evidence of prejudice as a result.[23] However, "it is reversible error for a trial court to require a defendant to go to trial on an indictment when [she] was not formally arraigned and

---

[16]O.C.G.A. § 17-7-95. However, in Fortson v. Hopper, 242 Ga. 81, 247 S.E.2d 875 (1978), the court said that if a nolo contendere sentence is accepted in a capital case, it is harmless error and the sentence is still valid. See Weaver, "The Effect in Georgia of a Plea of Nolo Contendere Entered in a Georgia Court," 13 Ga. L. R. 723 (1979). See A.B.A. Standards, Pleas of Guilty, §§ 14-1.1 and 14-1.2.

[17]Brand v. Wofford, 230 Ga. 750, 751 (3), 199 S.E.2d 231 (1973).

[18]Hardwick v. State, 231 Ga. 181, 183 (6), 200 S.E.2d 728 (1973).

[19]However, if timely notice is received by defense counsel from the office of the district attorney, he is not entitled to a continuance as a matter or right if he is ready for trial and is not prejudiced by the method of the notice. Dixon v. State, 224 Ga. 636, 163 S.E.2d 737 (1968).

[20]O.C.G.A. § 17-7-91. In Hicks v. State, 145 Ga. App. 669, 244 S.E.2d 597 (1978), the court held that it was reversible error to arraign the defendant where he had not received the notice and his counsel stated at the time that the defendant was not waiving the notice. In Jones v. State, 135 Ga. App. 893, 897 (4), 219 S.E.2d 585 (1975), the court held that the indictment was not subject to a motion to quash simply because the notice of arraignment was sent prior to indictment.

[21]O.C.G.A. § 17-7-91; Huff v. State, 197 Ga. App. 233, 234, 398 S.E.2d 258 (1990).

[22]Hicks v. State, 147 Ga. App. 814, 250 S.E.2d 558 (1978).

[23]Flores v. State, 308 Ga. App. 368, 707 S.E.2d 578 (2011).

refused specifically to waive such arraignment."[24] See § 17:15, infra, on notice of time of trial.

Every defendant is entitled to be arraigned unless he waives this right.[25] If a defendant files a demurrer, a plea in abatement, or a plea in bar to an indictment, he will have waived arraignment unless the right has been expressly reserved.[26] Likewise, a defendant may waive his right to an arraignment by failure to call the court's attention to the defect at the proper time.[27] In *Frazier v. State*,[28] the court held that "[t]he right of formal arraignment and plea will be conclusively considered as waived, where the defendant goes to trial before the jury on the merits, and fails, until after verdict, to bring to the attention of the court that he has not been formally called upon to enter a plea to the indictment." In *Baker v. State*,[29] the court held that the defendant's signature was not required on an indictment where the district attorney signed a statement on the indictment stating, "The defendant . . . [the defendant's name] waives being formally arraigned and pleads not guilty." *Baker* also holds that where the defendant has not signed the indictment until after the jury had been charged, it is not error to refuse to permit the defendant to sign the indictment at that point. Also, it is immaterial that a defendant signs a guilty plea by signing below rather than above the line labeled "Defendant" on the jacket of the accusation.[30]

It has been held that an arraignment cannot be waived in the absence of the defendant.[31] If a plea of not guilty is entered by the defendant, there is a presumption that he has been properly

---

[24]Sapp v. State, 338 Ga. App. 628, 631, 791 S.E.2d 201 (2016) (citing Presnell v. State, 159 Ga. App. 598, 284 S.E.2d 106 (1981)).

[25]Kincade v. State, 14 Ga. App. 544, 81 S.E. 910 (1914). In Moore v. State, 153 Ga. App. 511, 512, 265 S.E.2d 821 (1980), the court said that even if the defendant has not been properly arraigned, "he may waive arraignment and plea by failure to call the attention of the trial judge to the defect at the proper time, and when it does not appear that he made any mention of the fact until after verdict, he is conclusively presumed" to have waived arraignment and plea. But see Sapp v. State, 338 Ga. App. 628, 791 S.E.2d 201 (2016) (proceeding to trial over defendant's objection that she had neither been arraigned nor waived arraignment was reversible error).

[26]See Baskin v. State, 137 Ga.

App. 840, 841, 225 S.E.2d 77 (1976); Callahan v. State, 148 Ga. App. 555, 557 (6), 251 S.E.2d 790 (1978). Cf. Shivers v. State, 188 Ga. App. 21, 22 (1), 372 S.E.2d 2 (1988).

[27]Lyons v. State, 94 Ga. App. 570, 572, 95 S.E.2d 478 (1956). The question cannot be raised after verdict [Hudson v. State, 117 Ga. 704 (1), 45 S.E. 66 (1903)] nor after evidence has been closed [Gravitt v. State, 53 Ga. App. 353, 185 S.E. 594 (1936)].

[28]Frazier v. State, 204 Ga. App. 795, 420 S.E.2d 824 (1992).

[29]Baker v. State, 202 Ga. App. 892, 893, 416 S.E.2d 295 (1992).

[30]Brown v. State, 214 Ga. App. 733, 736 (3), 449 S.E.2d 136 (1994).

[31]Wells v. Terrell, 121 Ga. 368 (2), 49 S.E. 319 (1904). But see dicta in Davis v. State, 135 Ga. App. 203, 205 (2), 217 S.E.2d 343 (1975).

arraigned.[32] In *Loggins v. State*,[33] the court held that a "defendant's right to be present at the arraignment is waived if counsel does not object to proceeding in the defendant's absence" and counsel may plead not guilty in his client's absence.

If a "not guilty" plea is entered at the arraignment, it is the responsibility of the court immediately following arraignment[34] to announce when the case shall be set for trial,[35] and it is not per se error to place the defendant on trial immediately after he is arraigned.[36]

Arraignment is a critical time in the trial because O.C.G.A. § 17-7-110 requires that all pretrial motions, including demurrers and special pleas, shall be filed within ten days after the date of the arraignment, unless the court extends this time for filing.

Generally, see Bond, *Plea Bargaining and Guilty Pleas* (Clark Boardman 1978). On arraignment see 21 Am. Jur. Criminal Law § 433 (1981).

§ 16:2 Guilty plea—General

"A plea of guilty is more than a mere confession of certain acts, 'it is itself a conviction; nothing remains but to give judgment and determine punishment.' "[1]Hence, by pleading guilty to a crime, the defendant waives his later asserted double jeopardy claim involving the charges to which he pled guilty.[2] A superior court judge may accept a guilty plea and impose sentence on a defendant in one county within his circuit even though the indict-

---

[32]Sisson v. State, 141 Ga. App. 559, 560 (4), 234 S.E.2d 146 (1977).

[33]Loggins v. State, 225 Ga. App. 713, 714 (2), 484 S.E.2d 758 (1997).

[34]Clark v. State, 138 Ga. App. 266, 271 (7), 226 S.E.2d 89 (1976).

[35]O.C.G.A. § 17-7-91.

[36]Clark v. State, 138 Ga. App. 266, 271, 226 S.E.2d 89 (1976).

On the contrary, in federal courts the Speedy Trial Act requires a waiting period of a minimum of 30 days. The time period begins to run when "the defendant first appears through counsel." United States v. Daly, 716 F.2d 1499 (9th Cir. 1983).

[Section 16:2]

[1]Bowers v. Moore, 266 Ga. 893, 894 (1), 471 S.E.2d 869 (1996) (quot-

ing Boykin v. Alabama, 395 U.S. 238, 242, 89 S.Ct. 1709, 23 L.Ed.2d 274 (1969)), overruled on other grounds, Lejeune v. McLaughlin, 296 Ga. 291, 766 S.E.2d 803 (2014). Cf. Farist v. State, 249 Ga. App. 320 (1), 547 S.E.2d 618 (2001).

Taken literally, the cited language is misleading. A conviction "is not the verdict; it is the judgment on the verdict or guilty plea. O.C.G.A. § 16-1-3(4)." Leslie v. State, 211 Ga. App. 871, 872, 440 S.E.2d 757 (1994). Until judgment is entered and sentence passed, a guilty plea may be withdrawn. O.C.G.A. § 17-7-93(b). See also Dorsey v. State, 259 Ga. App. 254, 576 S.E.2d 637 (2003).

[2]Manry v. State, 226 Ga. App. 445, 446, 487 S.E.2d 80 (1997).

ment was returned in another county within the circuit.[3]

A guilty plea, like a confession, must be scanned with care and received with caution.[4] In *Edmond v. State*,[5] the court pointed out that "a plea of guilty generally waives all defenses except that based on the knowing and voluntary nature of the plea." In *Smith v. Hardrick*,[6] the court held that a guilty plea waives all defenses other than that the "indictment charges no crime." A plea of guilty is not valid unless the defendant understands the rights he is waiving and the possible consequences of his plea.[7] Hence, the defendant must be present except in the case of a corporation.[8] It is preferable to have "a knowing and intelligent plea of guilty shown on the record of the guilty plea hearing so as to terminate the issue once and for all."[9]

If the voluntariness of a plea is raised on *direct appeal*, the burden is on the state to affirmatively show that the guilty plea was intelligently and voluntarily given. The rule is different when the issue is presented by way of *habeas corpus* petition. In *Lejeune*

---

[3]Cf. McElreath v. State, 163 Ga. App. 826 (2), 296 S.E.2d 622 (1982).

[4]Hamm v. State, 123 Ga. App. 10, 11, 179 S.E.2d 272 (1970). However, in Evans v. State, 148 Ga. App. 422, 424, 251 S.E.2d 325 (1978), the court said that a guilty plea may be valid even though the defendant does not sign such a written plea.

[5]Edmond v. State, 214 Ga. App. 707, 708 (1), 448 S.E.2d 775 (1994).

[6]Smith v. Hardrick, 266 Ga. 54, 56 (3), 464 S.E.2d 198 (1995).

[7]Johnson v. State, 227 Ga. App. 390, 391 (1), 489 S.E.2d 138 (1997).

It must affirmatively appear that the defendant voluntarily and knowingly waived his right (1) against self-incrimination, (2) to a jury trial, and (3) to confront his accusers. Boykin v. Alabama, 395 U.S. 238, 243, 89 S.Ct. 1709, 23 L.Ed.2d 274 (1969). Likewise, due process is violated if the defendant pleads guilty without understanding the sentence which may or must be imposed. United States v. Finkbeiner, 551 F.2d 180 (7th Cir. 1977). However, in People v. Jones, 44 N.Y.2d 76, 404 N.Y.S.2d 85, 375 N.E.2d 41 (1978), the court held that if a defendant admits his guilt there is no due process violation where the district attorney fails to inform him of the death of a crucial prosecution witness before the guilty plea is entered.

[8]Rule 33.1(A) of the Uniform Rules for the Superior Courts.

Cf. Zenlenski v. State, 257 Ga. 381, 359 S.E.2d 676 (1987), in which the court considered the conducting "of arraignments and other non-jury hearings without the physical presence of the defendant but with the use of a closed circuit television system. . . ."

See Studdard, *Daniel's Georgia Handbook on Criminal Evidence* § 1:28 (2018 ed.), on the right of a defendant to have a witness for the state "present" for cross-examination.

[9]Roberts v. Greenway, 233 Ga. 473, 475, 211 S.E.2d 764 (1975) (citing Boykin v. Alabama, 395 U.S. 238, 242, 89 S.Ct. 1709, 23 L.Ed.2d 274 (1969)), overruled on other grounds, Lejeune v. McLaughlin, 296 Ga. 291, 766 S.E.2d 803 (2014). See U. S. ex rel. Hughes v. Rundle, 419 F.2d 116, 118 (3d Cir. 1969). However, in the Roberts case the court said that while it is preferable to have a knowing and intelligent waiver on the record of the plea hearing, it is possible to "fill a silent record by the use of extrinsic evidence that affirmatively shows that the guilty plea was knowing and voluntary."

v. McLaughlin,[10] the Georgia Supreme Court overruled all authority to the contrary and held that thereafter, in habeas proceedings the burden would be on the petitioner to show that the plea was not voluntary.

In *Wilson v. Reed*,[11] the defendant was indicted for burglary. At the time of arraignment he entered a guilty plea to the crime of "theft by taking," and the term "burglary" on the face of the indictment was changed to "theft by taking." At the time it was admitted that the defendant took "some plumbing fixtures and other stuff" but the defendant denied entering the building. The defendant was sentenced for the felony "theft by taking." Later the defendant contended that "theft by taking" is not necessarily a lesser included offense of burglary and that the indictment did not set out the elements of "theft by taking." The appellate court pointed out that the original indictment properly charged burglary by describing an entry to commit theft. Defense counsel asked the trial judge to accept the plea bargain, and all were aware that the plea was a result of the plea bargain. Where the original indictment is valid and through a plea bargain the defendant knowingly enters a plea to a lesser offense, the plea is valid and binding.

A guilty plea, once voluntarily and intelligently given, is valid even if the defendant is not advised of every conceivable constitutional plea that could be raised.[12]

Formerly it was possible for a defendant to enter a guilty plea and reserve his right to attack the constitutionality of the proceeding. However, this is no longer permitted. Even when a defendant does not reserve his right to attack the indictment, he may nevertheless do so if the indictment is void or fails to adequately charge a crime.[13]

In *Waire v. State*,[14] the court pointed out that "[a]n appellate court reviewing a guilty plea must 'determine whether (1) the defendant freely and voluntarily entered his guilty plea with (2) an understanding of the nature of the charges against him and

---

[10]Lejeune v. McLaughlin, 296 Ga. 291, 307, n.8, 766 S.E.2d 803 (2014) (the Court expressed "no opinion" as to the sort of evidence necessary for a petitoner to carry this burden and also hinted that precedent to the effect that the failure of a sentencing court to advise the defendant of his *Boykin* rights can never be deemed harmless error, may be an issue to be addressed in a future case where there is other evidence suggesting that the defendant's plea was voluntary).

[11]Wilson v. Reed, 246 Ga. 743, 272 S.E.2d 699 (1980).

[12]Tollett v. Henderson, 411 U.S. 258, 93 S.Ct. 1602, 36 L.Ed.2d 235 (1973).

[13]Wilson v. Reed, 246 Ga. 743, 272 S.E.2d 699 (1980).

[14]Waire v. State, 211 Ga. App. 69, 70, 438 S.E.2d 142 (1993). Accord, Green v. State, 265 Ga. 263 (1), 454 S.E.2d 466 (1995); Holland v. State, 218 Ga. App. 744, 463 S.E.2d 169 (1995).

(3) an understanding of the consequences of his plea.' "

In *Richards v. State*,[15] the court concluded that the defendant entered a valid guilty plea even though the defendant, his counsel and the district attorney did not sign the plea. The defendant signed an application to enter a guilty plea, signed a probation order and paid a prescribed fine. The court concluded that the defendant "either is estopped to contest the validity of the conviction and sentence or has waived any irregularity by his acceptance and undertaking to complete the sentence."

In *Wilcox v. State*,[16] the court pointed out that "[p]arole eligibility may be a factor which the defendant should consider in bargaining for a recommended sentence, but the trial court is entitled to presume that a defendant has apprised himself of such collateral consequences. . . ." However, an attorney's failure to inform a defendant regarding his ineligibility for parole does not constitute ineffective assistance of counsel. "[E]ligibility or ineligibility [in such a case] is not a consequence of a plea of guilty, but rather is a matter of legislative grace. . . ."[17]

See § 26:14, infra, on admissibility of a conviction at sentencing hearing for recidivism punishment.

§ 16:3   Guilty plea—Counsel

If a defendant is not represented by counsel, the record must show that he was advised of his right as an indigent to have counsel appointed for him, and the record must show whether or not the defendant was indigent. If a non-indigent defendant understands his right to counsel and enters a plea of guilty, without counsel, knowingly and voluntarily, this constitutes a waiver of counsel.[1] In *Jones v. Terry*,[2] the plea of a pro se defendant who was advised by the court that he would have a

---

[15]Richards v. State, 169 Ga. App. 870, 315 S.E.2d 304 (1984). Cf. Price v. State, 223 Ga. App. 185, 186 (1), 477 S.E.2d 353 (1996).

[16]Wilcox v. State, 236 Ga. App. 235, 237 (2), 511 S.E.2d 597 (1999).

[17]King v. State, 246 Ga. App. 100, 102 (3), 539 S.E.2d 614 (2000). In Padilla v. Kentucky, 130 S. Ct. 1473, 176 L. Ed. 2d 284 (2010), the Supreme Court held that because the consequences of deportation are so drastic, the failure of counsel to advise the client that a plea could result in deportation is ineffective counsel. See Smith v. State, 304 Ga. App. 846, 698 S.E.2d 355 (2010), where the Georgia Supreme Court follows *Padilla*, holding that failure to advise a non-citizen that a guilty plea may result in deportation is ineffective assistance and satisfies the first prong of *Strickland*. See also Taylor v. State, 304 Ga. App. 878, 698 S.E.2d 384 (2010) (failure to advise defendant of sex offender registry requirements mandated by plea was deficient representation).

[Section 16:3]

[1]Ward v. State, 248 Ga. 60, 64 (3), 281 S.E.2d 503 (1981); Clowers v. Sikes, 272 Ga. 463, 532 S.E.2d 98 (2000); Iowa v. Tovar, 541 U.S. 77(a), 124 S.Ct. 1379, 158 L.Ed.2d 209 (2004).

"continuing right to the assistance of an attorney throughout the jury trial" was deemed not knowing and voluntary because the defendant, who was indigent and not represented, was never informed that he had a right to counsel for purposes of entering the plea.

§ 16:4 Guilty plea—The record

In *Parks v. State*,[1] the court held that the record must show that the defendant knew he had (1) a right to a jury trial, (2) the right to confront witnesses, and (3) the right not to incriminate himself. The declaration of counsel that the defendant knew the defendant was waiving these three rights is insufficient.

In *David v. State*,[2] the Court of Appeals held that "a plea statement form signed by a defendant . . . can be used to show that a guilty plea is knowingly and voluntarily entered, when the plea statement is placed into the record and combined with a colloquy [concerning the defendant's understanding of the form, etc.]."[3]

In *King v. State*,[4] the court held that the pre-printed plea form standing alone fails to constitute an adequate record of the guilty plea hearing, and that permitting a "withdrawal of [the defendant's] guilty plea [was] necessary to correct a manifest injustice." *King v. State* was a 5 to 2 decision of the Georgia Supreme Court. The court held that the requirement for a "record of the proceeding" set forth under Rule 33.11 of the Uniform Rules for the State Courts requires a "verbatim" record of the guilty plea hearing if a defendant is sentenced to a term of imprisonment. This interpretation is consistent with the express requirement for a "verbatim" record already established under Rule 33.11 of the Uniform Rules for the Superior Courts.[5] According to *King*, if a "verbatim" record of the plea hearing is not retained, the court will declare the

---

[2]Jones v. Terry, 279 Ga. 623, 619 S.E.2d 601 (2005). See Fullwood v. State, 290 Ga. 335, 720 S.E.2d 642 (2012).

[Section 16:4]

[1]Parks v. State, 223 Ga. App. 694, 479 S.E.2d 3 (1996) (holding was premised upon Boykin v. Alabama, 395 U.S. 238, 89 S. Ct. 1709, 23 L. Ed. 2d 274 (1969)).

[2]David v. State, 279 Ga. App. 582, 631 S.E.2d 714 (2006).

[3]David v. State, 279 Ga. App. 582, 631 S.E.2d 714 (2006) citing Gainer v. State, 267 Ga. App. 408, 409, 599 S.E.2d 359 (2004).

[4]King v. State, 270 Ga. 367, 509 S.E.2d 32 (1998). See Foskey v. Battle, 277 Ga. 480, 481 (1), 591 S.E.2d 802 (2004) (overruled on other grounds, Lejeune v. McLaughlin, 296 Ga. 291, 766 S.E.2d 803 (2014)), where pre-printed form reciting rights which defendant waived by his signature was not adequate record to show that plea was intelligent and voluntary.

[5]Wharton v. Henry, 266 Ga. 557, 469 S.E.2d 27 (1996). However, in Taylor v. State, 248 Ga. App. 715 (1), 548 S.E.2d 414 (2001), the court held that "there is no requirement that there be such a recording of a pre-trial conference."

record "inadequate." However, "[e]ven when a defendant proves the record inadequate, [he or] she may withdraw a guilty plea after sentence is imposed only if [he or] she proves withdrawal is necessary to correct a manifest injustice. In conducting the manifest injustice analysis, the reviewing court is not limited to the record of the guilty plea hearing but may also consider subsequent evidence presented to it."[6] Thus, while failure to retain a "verbatim" record of the plea hearing itself will not per se invalidate the conviction, nevertheless if there is no additional evidence in the appellate court record for that court to consider, the inadequate record will prevent the court from determining whether the trial court abused its discretion in ruling that the defendant voluntarily entered the plea and may result in remand to the trial court for further deliberation.

A unanimous court in *State v. Cooper*,[7] without any reference to *King*, found that a defendant's plea was knowing and voluntary where the trial court inquired as to whether the defendant had read and understood the guilty plea form which he had signed. The form involved asked a number of *Boykin* related questions and required the defendant to check "yes" or "no" to each. Even though the defendant did not check several of the boxes, he did check the final "yes" indicating that he had read and understood the rights he was waiving.

The state can show that a defendant was properly advised of his constitutional rights at sentencing through the testimony of defense counsel in a case where there is no record.[8] Counsel's testimony regarding his/her standardized practice and routine in connection with advising criminal defendants of their *Boyken* rights at sentencing can satisfy this burden even though counsel does not have a specific recollection of the case before the court, provided it appears that counsel's conduct at guilty plea hearings is so "fixed and customary as to be habitual."[9]

---

[6]King v. State, 270 Ga. 367, 509 S.E.2d 32 (1998). Compare Moore v. State, 285 Ga. 855, 684 S.E.2d 605 (2009) (plea form signed by and certified by both defense counsel and court is sufficient to show voluntary plea where form indicates it was reviewed by defendant with counsel and responses on form were true, correct and consistent with those given in court).

[7]State v. Cooper, 281 Ga. 63(1), 636 S.E.2d 493 (2006). In a concurring opinion, Justice Sears reminded trial courts that the better practice is for the judge to establish on the record that the defendant is aware of the rights being waived by a guilty plea.

[8]Bazemore v. State, 273 Ga. 160, 535 S.E.2d 760 (2000).

[9]Compare Green v. State, 279 Ga. 687, 620 S.E.2d 788 (2005), overruled on other grounds, Lejeune v. McLaughlin, 296 Ga. 291, 766 S.E.2d 803 (2014); and Baisden v. State, 279 Ga. 702, 620 S.E.2d 369 (2005) (overruled on other grounds by, Lejeune v. McLaughlin, 296 Ga. 291, 766 S.E.2d 803 (2014)).

In *Motley v. State*,[10] the court affirmed the trial court in finding that the defendant's plea was knowingly, intelligently, and voluntarily entered where the defendant nodded affirmative responses when asked if he understood the rights he was giving up by pleading guilty. Because the record shows that he answered affirmatively, either by words or actions, failure to give an oral response did not invalidate the guilty plea.

In *Wilson v. Kemp*,[11] the trial court limited its *Boykin* admonition to the guilty plea hearing only and, thus, upon review by the Supreme Court, the defendant's plea was deemed uninformed. However, it is not necessary that the trial court advise the defendant at the time a plea is entered of his or her *Boykin* rights with any specific words but only what those rights are; that they exist; and, that upon a plea of guilty, they are waived.[12]

§ 16:5 Guilty plea—Competence

In *Godinez v. Moran*,[1] the United States Supreme Court held that a person who is competent to stand trial is competent to plead guilty and to waive the right to counsel.

"A plea of guilty but mentally ill at the time of the crime or a plea of guilty but mentally retarded shall not be accepted until the defendant has undergone examination by a licensed psychologist or psychiatrist and the court has examined the psychological or psychiatric reports, held a hearing on the issue of the defendant's mental condition, and is satisfied that there is a factual basis that the defendant was mentally ill at the time of the offense or mentally retarded to which the plea is entered."[2]

§ 16:6 Guilty plea—Factual basis

Rule 33.9 of the Uniform Rules for the Superior Courts provides as follows:

"33.9 Determining Accuracy of Plea

"Notwithstanding the acceptance of a plea of guilty, judgment should not be entered upon such plea without inquiry on the record as may satisfy the judge that there is a factual basis for the

---

[10]Motley v. State, 273 Ga. 732, 734, 546 S.E.2d 468 (2001).

[11]Wilson v. Kemp, 288 Ga. 779, 727 S.E.2d 90 (2011), overruled on other grounds, Lejeune v. McLaughlin, 296 Ga. 291, 766 S.E.2d 803 (2014).

[12]Phelps v. State, 293 Ga. 873, 750 S.E.2d 340 (2013).

[Section 16:5]

[1]Godinez v. Moran, 509 U.S. 389, 113 S.Ct. 2680, 125 L.Ed.2d 321 (1993).

[2]O.C.G.A. § 17-7-131(b)(2); Cullers v. State, 247 Ga. App. 155, 156, 543 S.E.2d 763 (2000).

plea."[1] Although U.S.C.R. 33.9 applies in a guilty plea hearing, it has no application to a habeas case because the rule is not of a constitutional magnitude.[2]

In *State v. Evans,*[3] the Georgia Supreme Court declared Rule 33.9 of the Uniform Rules for the Superior Courts mandatory and required the trial court judge to determine the factual basis for the defendant's plea on the record. This is done to ensure that the defendant knows that the acts he committed constitutes the crime with which he is charged. The court left the manner in which the trial court "subjectively satisf[ies] itself that there is a factual basis for the plea" within the discretion of the trial court. Although a colloquy on the record is preferred, the court stated that a factual basis may be established by "the prosecutor stating what he expect[s] the evidence to show at trial" or through "parts of the record other than the guilty plea hearing" as long as that is made clear on the record and the parts relied on are "made a part of the record for appeal." However, "not every violation of Rule 33.9 mandates the grant of a motion to withdraw a plea." But if a reviewing court ascertains that "the record does not demonstrate a factual basis for the plea, the reviewing court is then required to determine whether withdrawal of the defendant's guilty plea is necessary to correct a manifest injustice. . . . In undertaking the manifest injustice analysis, the reviewing court is authorized to examine evidence that was not part of the guilty plea hearing."[4]

Even though the rule requires the trial judge to satisfy himself that there is a "factual basis" for the plea, there is no requirement that the judge affirmatively state on the record that he finds a factual basis so long as there is evidence that the trial judge is aware of the factual basis.[5]

The trial judge is only obligated to make himself aware of the factual basis of the plea. "A trial court need not make itself aware of evidence establishing the pleader's guilt beyond a reasonable doubt"; it is sufficient under Uniform Superior Court Rule 33.9

[Section 16:6]

[1]Brownlee v. City of Atlanta, 212 Ga. App. 174, 441 S.E.2d 492 (1994); Caldwell v. State, 213 Ga. App. 531 (1), 445 S.E.2d 560 (1994).

[2]State v. Cooper, 281 Ga. 63, 636 S.E.2d 493 (2006).

[3]State v. Evans, 265 Ga. 332, 334 (1), (2), 454 S.E.2d 468 (1995). Accord, Wharton v. Henry, 266 Ga. 557, 558 (1), 469 S.E.2d 27 (1996).

[4]Craft v. State, 234 Ga. App. 305, 308 (3), 506 S.E.2d 663 (1998) (quot-ing Wharton v. Henry, 266 Ga. 557, 469 S.E.2d 27 (1996)). Thus, in Moore v. State, 304 Ga. App. 198, 695 S.E.2d 717 (2010), the court considered testimony presented on the defendant's motion to withdraw his plea and found in that evidence a factual basis for the plea which alleviated the asserted "manifest injustice."

[5]Holland v. State, 209 Ga. App. 821, 822, 434 S.E.2d 808 (1993); Brown v. State, 216 Ga. App. 312, 315 (2), 454 S.E.2d 596 (1995).

for a term judge to ascertain the factual basis of the plea.[6] However, in *Watt v. State*,[7] the court said, "Since the record fails to show that appellant was cognizant of all the rights he was waiving or that the trial court ascertained the factual basis for the plea, we hold the record does not affirmatively show that appellant's guilty plea was entered knowingly and voluntarily." In *Evans v. State*,[8] the court held that a defendant could timely withdraw a guilty plea when the record failed to affirmatively establish that the trial judge had ascertained the factual basis for the plea.

In *Robinson v. State*,[9] the court said, "[W]e strongly caution . . . courts, in the interests of judicial economy, to comply in spirit and in letter with the requirements of Uniform Superior Court Rules 33.7—33.9. . . ." These rules are set out in the following sections.

§ 16:7 Guilty plea—Elements of crime

In connection with the requirement that the defendant know and understand the nature of the charges to which he is pleading guilty, the case of *Breland v. Smith*[1] must be considered. *Breland* cites the United States Supreme Court case of *Henderson v. Morgan*[2] and at least suggests that a guilty plea is not considered voluntary unless the elements of the crime to which the defendant pled guilty were explained to him on the record. In *Morgan,* the court said that a guilty plea could not be voluntary in a federal constitutional sense unless the defendant received real notice of the nature of the charge against him, i.e., he should have been informed that "intent" was an essential element of the crime to which he pled guilty. However, the court continued by saying:

"Normally the record contains an explanation of the charge by the trial judge or at least a representation by defense counsel that the nature of the offense has been explained to the accused. Moreover even without such an express representation, it may be

---

[6]King v. Hawkins, 266 Ga. 655, 656, 469 S.E.2d 30 (1996).

[7]Watt v. State, 204 Ga. App. 839, 840, 420 S.E.2d 769 (1992).

[8]Evans v. State, 212 Ga. App. 805, 806, 443 S.E.2d 296 (1994), rev'd on other grounds, 265 Ga. 332, 454 S.E.2d 468 (1995); Warner v. State, 214 Ga. App. 343, 344, 447 S.E.2d 692 (1994).

[9]Robinson v. State, 212 Ga. App. 613, 615 (1), 442 S.E.2d 901 (1994), overruled on other grounds by Felix v. State, 271 Ga. 534, 523 S.E.2d 1 (1999). Cf. McKibben v. State, 212 Ga. App. 866, 867, 443 S.E.2d 640 (1994).

[Section 16:7]

[1]Breland v. Smith, 247 Ga. 690, 691, 279 S.E.2d 204 (1981).

[2]Henderson v. Morgan, 426 U.S. 637, 647, 96 S.Ct. 2253, 49 L.Ed.2d 108 (1976). In Morgan, the plea was vacated because the defendant was not informed that intent to cause death was an essential element of second degree murder.

appropriate to presume that in most cases defense counsel routinely explain the nature of the offense in sufficient detail to give the accused notice of what he is being asked to admit. This case is unique because the trial judge found as a fact that the element of intent was not explained to respondent."

Morgan did not establish a per se rule requiring the trial judge to inform a defendant of every element of every offense before a guilty plea could be accepted. However, even before *Morgan* some courts required an explanation of the elements of an offense to a defendant.[3]

In *Green v. State,*[4] the court held that "the indictment provided ample information from which the trial court could discern that the facts alleged by the state actually satisfied the elements of the charges to which [the defendant] was pleading. . . ." In *Green,* the trial judge "read the particulars of the charges from the indictment and asked the accused whether it was to those charges that he wished to enter a plea."

In *Ezzard v. State,*[5] the error was assigned to the failure of the trial judge, in the absence of a request, to charge the jury that intent was an element of the crime of robbery. The court concluded that since the trial judge instructed the jury in the language of the code section defining robbery, it was not error to fail to charge on intent. If there is any doubt about whether a defendant who is pleading guilty understands the nature of the offense, would not the reading of the statute to the defendant and asking if he understands it satisfy the requirement that a guilty plea must be knowingly and intelligently entered?

§ 16:8   Guilty plea—Freely and voluntarily entered

Rule 33.7 of the Uniform Rules for the Superior Courts provides as follows:

"33.7 Determining Voluntariness of Plea

"The judge shall not accept a plea of guilty or *nolo contendere* without first determining, on the record, that the plea is voluntary. By inquiry of the prosecuting attorney and defense

---

[3]People v. Colosacco, 177 Colo. 219, 493 P.2d 650 (1972); United States v. Thomas, 468 F.2d 422 (10th Cir. 1972). Contra, Watson v. State, 538 S.W.2d 69 (Mo.App. 1976).

[4]Green v. State, 265 Ga. 263, 265, 454 S.E.2d 466 (1995). Accord, Battle v. Williams, 268 Ga. 35 (1), 485 S.E.2d 204 (1997). See Smith v. Magnuson, 297 Ga. 210, 773 S.E.2d

205 (2015) (defendant's history of mental health problems story suggested susceptibility to conformity when presented with group environment and that his plea entered during a group plea might have been entered without an understanding of the consequences thereof).

[5]Ezzard v. State, 229 Ga. 465, 466 (5), 192 S.E.2d 374 (1972).

counsel, the judge should determine whether the tendered plea is the result of prior plea discussions and a plea agreement, and, if it is, what agreement has been reached. If the prosecuting attorney has agreed to seek charge or sentence leniency which must be approved by the judge, the judge must advise the defendant personally that the recommendations of the prosecuting attorney are not binding on the judge. The judge should then address the defendant personally and determine whether any other promises or any force or threats were used to obtain the plea."

In *McCarthy v. United States*,[1] the U.S. Supreme Court stressed that an intelligent and voluntary plea is dependent on a defendant's awareness of its likely circumstances and consequences:

[I]f a defendant's guilty plea is not equally voluntary and knowing, it has been obtained in violation of due process and is therefore void. Moreover, because a guilty plea is an admission of all the elements of a formal criminal charge, *it cannot be truly voluntary unless the defendant possesses an understanding of the law in relation to the facts.*

In *Kennedy v. Primack*,[2] the Georgia Supreme Court held that because the record reflected that defendant did not possess a sufficient understanding of the criminal charge to which he pled and its relation to the underlying facts in the case, his plea was not voluntary.

In *State v. Cooper*,[3] the Georgia Supreme Court found that a defendant's plea was knowing and voluntary where the trial court inquired as to whether the defendant had read and understood the guilty plea form which he had signed. The form involved asked a number of *Boykin* related questions and required the defendant to check "yes" or "no" to each. Even though the defendant did not check several of the boxes, he did check the

---

[Section 16:8]

[1]McCarthy v. U.S., 394 U.S. 459, 466 (1), 89 S. Ct. 1166, 22 L. Ed. 2d 418 (1969) (internal quotations and citations omitted) (emphasis added).

[2]Kennedy v. Primack, 299 Ga. 698, 791 S.E.2d 819 (2016).

[3]State v. Cooper, 281 Ga. 63(1), 636 S.E.2d 493 (2006) (abrogated by Lejeune v. McLaughlin, 296 Ga. 291, 766 S.E.2d 803 (2014), to extent case places burden on state to show voluntariness of plea in habeas proceeding). In Hawes v. State, 281 Ga. 822, 642 S.E.2d 92 (2007), overruled on other grounds, Lejeune v. McLaughlin, 296 Ga. 291, 766 S.E.2d 803 (2014), the defendant's conviction was set aside because the trial court failed to advise the defendant about his right against self-incrimination. In Beckworth v. State, 281 Ga. 41, 635 S.E.2d 769 (2006), overruled on other grounds, Lejeune v. McLaughlin, 296 Ga. 291, 766 S.E.2d 803 (2014), the only evidence of the defendant's waiver was a plea questionnaire which did not make any reference to the defendant's right against self-incrimination and his right to confront his accusers.

final "yes" indicating that he had read and understood the rights he was waiving.

In *Britt v. Smith*,[4] the Georgia Supreme Court concluded that a defendant's guilty plea was voluntary where the trial court advised only that by pleading guilty, he would give up his right to remain silent, the right to confront witnesses and the right to a trial by jury. Although Rule 33.8 of the Uniform Rules for the Superior Courts (USCR) details at least eight (8) fundamental rights which the sentencing court should review with the defendant before accepting a guilty plea as voluntary, the court held that a challenge to the voluntariness of a plea in a habeas action required only an examination of the record as a whole and a determination as to whether it shows that the plea was "knowing and voluntary." The court was satisfied that the state had met its burden and expressly declined to engraft on that burden the additional duty of showing that the defendant knowingly and voluntarily waived each of the rights detailed in USCR 33.8.[5]

In *Rooks v. State*,[6] the court held that "[w]here the voluntariness of the guilty plea is challenged, there must be a record of the guilty plea hearing adequate for the reviewing court to determine whether (1) the defendant has freely and voluntarily entered the plea with (2) an understanding of the nature of the charges against him and (3) an understanding of the consequences of his plea."

---

[4]Britt v. Smith, 274 Ga. 611, 556 S.E.2d 435 (2001), overruled on other grounds, Lejeune v. McLaughlin, 296 Ga. 291, 766 S.E.2d 803 (2014). In Hawes v. State, 281 Ga. 822, 642 S.E.2d 92 (2007), overruled on other grounds, Lejeune v. McLaughlin, 296 Ga. 291, 766 S.E.2d 803 (2014), the defendant's conviction was set aside because the trial court failed to advise the defendant about his right against self-incrimination. In Beckworth v. State, 281 Ga. 41, 635 S.E.2d 769 (2006), overruled on other grounds, Lejeune v. McLaughlin, 296 Ga. 291, 766 S.E.2d 803 (2014), the only evidence of the defendant's waiver was a plea questionnaire which did not make any reference to the defendant's right against self-incrimination and his right to confront his accusers. See Adams v. State, 285 Ga. 744, 745–46(1), 683 S.E.2d 586 (2009) (when entering plea, defendant must be advised that

he is giving up the right to remain silent at trial).

[5]Britt v. Smith, 274 Ga. 611, 614, 556 S.E.2d 435 (2001), overruled on other grounds, Lejeune v. McLaughlin, 296 Ga. 291, 766 S.E.2d 803 (2014). See Foskey v. Battle, 277 Ga. 480, 591 S.E.2d 802 (2004), overruled on other grounds, Lejeune v. McLaughlin, 296 Ga. 291, 766 S.E.2d 803 (2014).

[6]Rooks v. State, 245 Ga. App. 655, 656 (3), 538 S.E.2d 555 (2000). See Lejeune v. McLaughlin, 299 Ga. 546, 789 S.E.2d 191 (2016); Foskey v. Battle, 277 Ga. 480, 481 (1), 591 S.E.2d 802 (2004), overruled on other grounds, Lejeune v. McLaughlin, 296 Ga. 291, 766 S.E.2d 803 (2014), where a pre-printed form reciting rights which the defendant waived by his signature was not an adequate record to show that his plea was intelligent and voluntary.

In *Burruss v. State,*[7] the court held that in a guilty plea situation a defendant may be sentenced as a recidivist under O.C.G.A. § 17-10-7 even though there has been no notice prior to the entry of a guilty plea of such a sentence.

In *Thompson v. Greene,*[8] the court held that a guilty plea had not been freely and voluntarily entered where the defendant expected to be re-sentenced and given a lighter sentence after the defendant cooperated with the District Attorney's office. The court pointed out that "[a] guilty plea should not be allowed to stand where 'influenced by the slightest hope of benefit or the remotest fear of injury.' "

In *Autry v. State,*[9] the court held that even if a defendant relied, in good faith, on his attorney's advice in deciding to plead guilty, he cannot avoid the legal consequences of his plea, notwithstanding the actual outcome. " 'A defendant's subjective hopes and unfulfilled desires, not induced by the court or state, are not good grounds for attacking the resulting plea and sentence.' "

A good faith mistake of the defendant and his attorney about where sentence may be served does not render the plea involuntary when the hopes and unfulfilled desires of the defendant were not induced by the state or the court.[10] Likewise, entering a guilty plea in the hope of obtaining a lesser sentence does not prevent the voluntary entry of a guilty plea.[11]

In *Swan v. State,*[12] the court pointed out that "[a] knowing and voluntary plea of guilty acts as a waiver of all defenses known or unknown."

In *Beck v. State,*[13] the defendant contended that his plea was not voluntary in that he was coerced by the threat of a sentence of life without parole. The appellate court affirmed the trial judge's refusal to permit the defendant to withdraw the guilty plea and held that the determination of voluntariness "is whether the plea represents a voluntary and intelligent choice among the alternative courses of action available to defendant." A trial court's refusal to allow a defendant to withdraw a plea after it has been entered will not be upset in the absence of a "manifest"

---

[7]Burruss v. State, 242 Ga. App. 241, 243 (2), 529 S.E.2d 375 (2000).

[8]Thompson v. Greene, 265 Ga. 782, 783-84 (1), 462 S.E.2d 747 (1995) (quoting Rowland v. State, 72 Ga. App. 793, 802, 35 S.E.2d 372 (1945)). See Brown v. State, 324 Ga. App. 194, 749 S.E.2d 781 (2013). See also Missouri v. Frye, 132 S. Ct. 1399, 182 L. Ed. 2d 379 (2012), and § 16:10, infra, on guilty pleas.

[9]Autry v. State, 250 Ga. App. 107, 109 (2), 549 S.E.2d 769 (2001).

[10]Jeffares v. Defrancis, 244 Ga. 183, 259 S.E.2d 444 (1979).

[11]Manues v. State, 232 Ga. App. 454, 455, 501 S.E.2d 826 (1998).

[12]Swan v. State, 251 Ga. App. 80, 81 (3), 553 S.E.2d 383 (2001).

[13]Beck v. State, 222 Ga. App. 168, 169, 473 S.E.2d 263 (1996).

abuse of discretion.[14]

A court must determine whether a defendant is freely entering a plea with an understanding that if he or she is not a United States citizen, then the plea may have an impact on his or her immigration status. This applies with respect to acceptance of any plea of guilty to any state offense in any court of this state or any political subdivision of this state.[15]

In *Cazanas v. State*,[16] the excellent concurring opinion of Justice Sears suggested that it is a good practice for the trial judge in considering a guilty plea from a non-English speaking defendant who is assisted by an interpreter "to inquire on the record, at the end of the plea colloquy . . . , whether the defendant has been able to effectively communicate with the interpreter, and whether there have been any communications with the interpreter that the defendant did not understand." See, Studdard, *Daniel's Georgia Handbook on Criminal Evidence* (2018 ed.) § 6:6 on use of interpreter.

§ 16:9 Guilty plea—*State v. Germany*

In *State v. Germany*,[1] the Georgia Supreme Court held that a defendant has the right to withdraw his guilty plea any time prior to the time the court orally announces what sentence the trial judge is imposing. However, at the time a plea is offered, the court shall, on the record, require the disclosure of any plea agreement which has been reached between the state and the defendant. If "the trial court intends to reject said plea agree-

---

[14]Ramsey v. State, 267 Ga. App. 452, 600 S.E.2d 399 (2004).

[15]O.C.G.A. § 17-7-93(c). This Code section applies only to pleas entered *after* July 1, 2000. See Palacios v. State, 250 Ga. App. 794, 554 S.E.2d 498 (2001). A defendant does not have the constitutional "right" to plead guilty. Sanders v. State, 280 Ga. 780(2), 631 S.E.2d 344 (2006). A court in its discretion may refuse to accept such a plea because, for example, of concerns about whether it is offered knowingly and voluntarily. The state, however, may confer such a right. See e.g., North Carolina v. Alford, 400 U.S. 25, 91 S. Ct. 160, 27 L. Ed. 2d 162 (1970).

[16]Cazanas v. State, 270 Ga. 130, 134, 508 S.E.2d 412 (1998). See Ling v. State, 288 Ga. 299, 702 S.E.2d 881 (2010) (trial court must make findings on the record when it denies request

for interpreters). See also Use of Interpreters for Non-English Speaking Persons, 2003 Georgia Court Order 0.1 (C.O.01), Court Rules, State of Ga., Supreme Court of Ga. (2003).

[Section 16:9]

[1]State v. Germany, 246 Ga. 455, 271 S.E.2d 851 (1980); Lawrence v. State, 234 Ga. App. 603, 507 S.E.2d 490 (1998); Sanders v. State, 169 Ga. App. 125, 312 S.E.2d 160 (1983); Jackson v. State, 172 Ga. App. 874, 324 S.E.2d 816 (1984). Cf. Stapp v. State, 249 Ga. 289, 292, 290 S.E.2d 439 (1982); Vanvelsor v. State, 162 Ga. App. 467, 470, 291 S.E.2d 772 (1982); *State v. Germany* is now codified in Uniform Superior Court Rule 33.10. Accord, Rules 11(e) and 32(d) of the Federal Rules of Criminal Procedure; A.B.A. Standards, Pleas of Guilty, § 14-2.1.

ment the trial court shall, on the record, inform the defendant personally that (1) the trial court is not bound by any plea agreement, (2) the trial court intends to reject the plea agreement presently before it, (3) the disposition of the present case may be less favorable to the defendant than that contemplated by the plea agreement, and (4) that the defendant may then withdraw his or her guilty plea as a matter of right . . . . [2] If the plea is not then withdrawn, sentence may be pronounced and the plea cannot thereafter be withdrawn except upon the sound legal discretion of the court."[3]

State v. Germany is now incorporated in Unif. Sup. Crt. R. 33.10. The Rule requires the court to inform a defendant upon the entry of a negotiated plea that the court might impose a harsher sentence than the one recommended and if the plea is not withdrawn "sentence may be pronounced." It does not provide the state with the right to withdraw from a plea agreement in the event the court imposes a sentence other than the one recommended by the state. Likewise, in the event the plea agreement provides for a plea to a charge not included in the indictment, the state can withdraw from the agreement upon timely objection should the court impose a sentence other than the one recommended in the agreement.[4]

In *Hamm v. Weldon*,[5] the court pointed out that where the trial judge made it clear before sentencing that he did not intend to be bound by a recommendation of the district attorney, a defendant has no right to withdraw his guilty plea after sentencing. In *Bice v. State*,[6] the court held that where the prosecutor announced that the plea was non-negotiated and, thus, he had no recommendation of sentence by the state, and the court concluded that the plea was intelligently and voluntarily entered, the defendant had no statutory right to withdraw the guilty plea following pronouncement of the sentence.

Germany does not apply to guilty pleas entered in a capital

---

[2]Stephens v. State, 162 Ga. App. 578, 292 S.E.2d 420 (1982); Rule 33.10 of the Uniform Rules for the Superior Courts.

[3]Freeman v. State, 211 Ga. App. 716, 718 (2), 440 S.E.2d 490 (1994). Accord, Holman v. State, 236 Ga. App. 111, 114 (2), 511 S.E.2d 240 (1999).

[4]State v. Kelley, 298 Ga. 527, 783 S.E.2d 124 (2016) (disapproving State v. Harper, 279 Ga. App. 620(2), 631 S.E.2d 820 (2006), overruled on other grounds by State v. King, 325 Ga. App. 445, 750 S.E.2d 756 (2013), to the extent it held that in the absence of consent state could not withdraw from plea agreement where court imposes lesser sentence than one negotiated by parties). See State v. Bankston., 337 Ga. App. 601, 788 S.E.2d 506 (2016).

[5]Hamm v. Weldon, 252 Ga. 213, 215, 312 S.E.2d 335 (1984).

[6]Bice v. State, 212 Ga. App. 184 (1), 441 S.E.2d 507 (1994). Accord, Brassfield v. State, 242 Ga. App. 747, 748, 531 S.E.2d 148 (2000).

case.[7] But in a death penalty case "a defendant should be informed of the trial court's decision regarding . . . sentence before entering his guilty plea."[8]

In *Smith v. State*,[9] even where the trial judge told the defendant "regardless of any joint recommendation between your attorney and the District Attorney . . . this Court and this Court alone will impose a sentence . . . within the limits set by law . . . ," the court found that this record did not demonstrate compliance with the requirement of Rule 33.10. The court explained, "We find nothing in the record which clearly informed . . . [the defendant] that the trial court intended to reject the sentence recommendation made by the State pursuant to the plea agreement . . . ."

In *Forrest v. State*,[10] the failure of the trial judge to inform the defendant that a sentence was being imposed on a guilty plea without first informing her that her negotiated plea of nolo contendere was rejected provided the grounds for her motion to withdraw her "plea". The fact that the defendant did not object to the imposition of sentence was not relevant since the trial court has the duty to inform a defendant that one or more elements of a negotiated plea has been rejected.

O.C.G.A. § 17-7-93(b), the statutory authority for a defendant's right to withdraw a plea of guilty "at any time before judgement is pronounced", applies to pleas of nolo contendere but not to pleas entered under the First Offender Act.[11] For purposes of this code section a plea of nolo contendere is deemed the equivalent of a guilty plea.[12] Extending the right to withdraw a plea to a first offender could seriously undermine final case dispositions as for example in the case of a defendant who seeks to withdraw a plea after the revocation of a probated first offender sentence.[13]

§ 16:10   Guilty plea—Waivers of defendant

Rule 33.8 of the Uniform Rules for the Superior Courts provides as follows:

33.8 Defendant to Be Informed

---

[7]Browner v. State, 257 Ga. 321, 357 S.E.2d 559 (1987).

[8]Browner v. State, 257 Ga. 321, 323 (4), 357 S.E.2d 559 (1987).

[9]Smith v. State, 239 Ga. App. 776, 777, 521 S.E.2d 911 (1999). See Underwood v. State, 338 Ga. App. 670, 791 S.E.2d 436 (2016).

[10]Forrest v. State, 251 Ga. App. 487, 554 S.E.2d 735 (2001).

[11]Fair v. State, 245 Ga. 868, 877(8), 268 S.E.2d 316 (1980).

[12]Wright v. State, 75 Ga. App. 764, 44 S.E.2d 569 (1947).

[13]Johnson v. State, 260 Ga. App. 897(1), 581 S.E.2d 407 (2003); Heath v. State, 148 Ga. App. 559, 252 S.E.2d 4 (1978); Davenport v. State, 136 Ga. App. 913(2), 222 S.E.2d 644 (1975).

The judge should not accept a plea of guilty or nolo contendere from a defendant without first:

(A) Determining on the record that the defendant understands the nature of charge(s);

(B) Informing the defendant on the record that by entering a plea of guilty or nolo contendere one waives:

    (1) the right to trial by jury;

    (2) the presumption of innocence;

    (3) the right to confront witnesses against oneself;

    (4) the right to subpoena witnesses;

    (5) the right to testify and to offer other evidence;

    (6) the right to assistance of counsel during trial;

    (7) the right not to incriminate oneself; and that by pleading not guilty or remaining silent and not entering a plea, one obtains a jury trial; and

(C) Informing the defendant on the record:

    (1) of the terms of any negotiated plea;

    (2) that a plea of guilty may have an impact on his or her immigration status if the defendant is not a citizen of the United States;

    (3) of the maximum possible sentence on the charge, including that possible from consecutive sentences and enhanced sentences where provided by law; and/or

    (4) of the mandatory minimum sentence, if any, on the charge.[1] This information may be developed by questions from the judge, the district attorney or the defense attorney, or a combination of any of these."[2]

In *Moore v. State*,[3] the court held that where a defendant seeks to withdraw his guilty plea "[t]he question is not whether the trial court followed the letter of [USCR 33.8] but whether the record, as a whole, affirmatively shows [the defendant's] plea was knowing and voluntary." Accordingly, "a plea statement form signed by a defendant . . . can be used to show that a guilty plea is knowingly and voluntarily entered, when the plea statement is placed into the record and combined with a colloquy [concerning

---

[Section 16:10]

[1]In Smith v. State, 174 Ga. App. 238, 329 S.E.2d 507 (1985), the court held that a defendant is not entitled to withdraw his guilty plea because he was not informed of the adverse parole consequences of the sentence.

[2]In addition, the court is required to inform a defendant at sentencing of the periods of limitation applicable to a habeas petition. In the case of a

felony the applicable period is four years and one year in the case of a misdemeanor. O.C.G.A. § 9-14-42.

[3]Moore v. State, 225 Ga. App. 860(1), 485 S.E.2d 552 (1997), quoting Johns v. State, 223 Ga. App. 553, 554, 479 S.E.2d 388 (1996); Wiggins v. State, 245 Ga. App. 527, 528, 538 S.E.2d 180 (2000); Thompson v. State, 240 Ga. App. 539, 541(4), 524 S.E.2d 239 (1999).

the defendant's understanding of the form, etc.]."[4]

Once a defendant has been sentenced, his guilty plea may only be withdrawn if the defendant "establishes that such withdrawal is necessary to correct a manifest injustice—ineffective assistance of counsel or an involuntary or unknowingly entered guilty plea."[5] As the Supreme Court of Georgia explained in *Smith v. State*,[6] "[a]s a matter of constitutional due process, before a defendant pleads guilty, the trial court must advise him of the 'direct' consequences of entering the plea." However, the court need not advise a defendant of all of the possible "collateral" consequences in order for the guilty plea to be considered knowing and voluntary. "Direct consequences" are those that are "within the sentencing authority of the trial court,"[7] as opposed to the many other potential collateral consequences that may result from a criminal conviction but which "do not lengthen or alter the pronounced sentence."[8] Thus, in *Brantley v. State*,[9] where the defendant claimed that counsel failed to advise him that upon entering a non-negotiated plea his right to withdraw that plea was lost, the court found that the failure to advise of such a collateral effect of the plea did not constitute ineffective assistance of counsel.

However, when counsel affirmatively misrepresents the collateral consequences of a guilty plea in response to the client's specific inquiry, such may amount to constitutional ineffective assistance of counsel. In *Rollins v. State*,[10] when counsel mistakenly advised the defendant that her plea of guilty under the First Offender Act would not adversely affect her immigration status or her opportunity to become a lawyer in the future, the court concluded that her plea was entered improvidently and without the effective assistance of counsel. The court distinguished situations in which trial counsel simply fails to inform a client of the collateral consequences attending a guilty plea, which generally does not amount to deficient performance, from Rollins's lawyer's

---

[4]David v. State, 279 Ga. App. 582, 584-85, 631 S.E.2d 714 (2006), citing Gainer v. State, 267 Ga. App. 408, 409, 599 S.E.2d 359 (2004).

[5]Green v. State, 324 Ga. App. 133, 133, 749 S.E.2d 419 (2013) (quoting Wilson v. State, 302 Ga. App. 433, 434, 691 S.E.2d 308 (2010)).

[6]Smith v. State, 287 Ga. 391, 394, 697 S.E.2d 177 (2010).

[7]Smith v. State, 287 Ga. 391, 394, 697 S.E.2d 177 (2010).

[8]Brantley v. State, 290 Ga. App. 764, 766, 660 S.E.2d 846 (2008).

[9]Brantley v. State, 290 Ga. App. 764, 660 S.E.2d 846 (2008). See also Hermann v. State, 249 Ga. App. 535, 548 S.E.2d 666 (2001) (statutorily mandated fees and costs of probation and drug treatment found to be a collateral effect of plea insofar as they did not lengthen or alter defendant's sentence).

[10]Rollins v. State, 277 Ga. 488, 591 S.E.2d 796 (2004). See State v. Patel, 280 Ga. 181, 626 S.E.2d 121 (2006) (affirmative misrepresentation of the effect nolo plea would have on physician's ability to practice medicine was ineffective and plea should be set aside).

"affirmative act of giving misinformation to his client which the client then relied upon in entering her plea."[11]

Prior to *Padilla v. Kentucky*,[12] the fact that a guilty plea could subject a defendant to automatic deportation was regarded as a collateral consequence of the plea such that the failure of counsel to so advise the client was not considered ineffective assistance of counsel.[13] However, in *Padilla* the Supreme Court found that because the consequences of deportation are so severe, the failure of counsel to advise a client of his or her exposure to deportation as a result of a guilty plea is ineffective assistance of counsel and abrogated all case authority to the contrary.[14] Based in part on *Padilla*, in *Missouri v. Frye*[15] the United States Supreme Court held that defense counsel has a duty to accurately communicate formal offers of a plea made by the prosecution. If such an offer is not communicated in a timely fashion and as a result the defendant either goes to trial or accepts a plea which results in terms and conditions more harsh than the prior plea offer, the defendant may be entitled to relief based upon a claim of ineffective assistance of counsel. See § 14-64, supra, on retroactive application of new rules of criminal law.

In *Alexander v. State*,[16] the court held that the failure to inform the client that his plea to a recidivist sentence eliminated his eligibility for parole constituted ineffective assistance and overruled authority to the contrary. The court noted that when evaluating whether the failure to advise a client about the collateral consequences of a plea amounted to constitutionally deficient performance, the trial court should take into consideration the

---

[11]See also Taylor v. State, 304 Ga. App. 878, 698 S.E.2d 384 (2010) (failure to advise defendant of sex offender registry requirements mandated by plea was deficient representation).

[12]Padilla v. Kentucky, 559 U.S. 356, 130 S. Ct. 1473, 176 L. Ed. 2d 284 (2010).

[13]See, e.g., U.S. v. Campbell, 778 F.2d 764 (11th Cir. 1985).

[14]See Smith v. State, 287 Ga. 391, 697 S.E.2d 177 (2010) (Georgia Supreme Court follows *Padilla*, holding that failure to advise non-citizen that guilty plea may result in deportation may constitute ineffective assistance); Lopez v. State, 309 Ga. App. 756, 711 S.E.2d 345 (2011) (court notes that where law is unclear, *Padilla* only requires that defense counsel advise client that guilty plea may carry a risk

of adverse immigration consequences). Cf. Chaidez v. U.S., 133 S. Ct. 1103, 185 L. Ed. 2d 149 (2013) (*Padilla* is a "new rule" of procedure and does not apply retroactively to cases which were final at the time *Padilla* was announced).

[15]Missouri v. Frye, 132 S. Ct. 1399, 182 L. Ed. 2d 379 (2012). See Harris v. Upton, 292 Ga. 491, 739 S.E.2d 300 (2013); Lloyd v. State, 258 Ga. 645, 373 S.E.2d 1 (1988).

[16]Alexander v. State, 297 Ga. 59, 772 S.E.2d 655 (2015) (overruled by Williams v. Duffy, 270 Ga. 580, 513 S.E.2d 212 (1999)). See Kennedy v. Kohnle, 303 Ga. 95, 810 S.E.2d 543 (2018) (*Alexander* created a "new rule" and is not to be applied retroactively). See also § 7:4, supra, on ineffective assistance.

guidelines suggested by the United States Supreme Court in *Padilla*:

> In addition to professional guidelines, our courts can look to these factors when weighing advice concerning a collateral consequence: (1) whether the collateral consequence is intimately related to the criminal process and is "nearly an automatic result" flowing from the conviction; (2) whether the consequence is a "drastic measure" or a penalty with harsh ramifications for the client; and (3) whether the law imposing the consequence is "succinct, clear and explicit."[17]

In *Syms v. State*,[18] the court held that a trial judge has no duty to inform a defendant of his qualified right to appeal from a conviction resulting from his guilty plea. In cases where the defendant enters a non-negotiated plea of guilty, the trial court is not required to inform defendant of his right to withdraw his plea before sentencing.[19]

In *Washington v. City of Atlanta*,[20] the court held that "it is difficult to imagine a mass arraignment procedure which could satisfy the trial court's burden" of examining the particular circumstances of a defendant's waiver of counsel. Similarly, in *Shabazz v. State*,[21] the Court of Appeals was highly critical of one trial court's use of a mass guilty plea hearing, noting that generally questioning a group of defendants charged under different indictments with different crimes as to whether their pleas were entered voluntarily and also with respect to other waiver related issues was unlikely to produce an environment conducive to a proper plea. However, the Court of Appeals has more recently held that mass plea hearings are not impermissible per se, and will not be considered improper "so long as defendants are informed of their constitutional rights, and are individually advised regarding the charges against each as well as the possible sentences."[22]

Also, perhaps it should be pointed out that a guilty plea does not amount to a waiver of the defendant's Fifth Amendment right

---

[17]Alexander v. State, 297 Ga. 59, 64-65, 772 S.E.2d 655 (2015), citing Padilla v. Kentucky, 559 U.S. 356, 365-69, 130 S. Ct. 1473, 176 L. Ed. 2d 284 (2010).

[18]Syms v. State, 240 Ga. App. 440, 441, 523 S.E.2d 42 (1999).

[19]James v. State, 326 Ga. App. 231, 232, 756 S.E.2d 312 (2014).

[20]Washington v. City of Atlanta, 201 Ga. App. 876, 412 S.E.2d 624 (1991). But see Isaac v. State, 237 Ga. App. 723, 726(2), 516 S.E.2d 575 (1999).

[21]Shabazz v. State, 259 Ga. App. 339, 577 S.E.2d 45 (2003) (overruled on other grounds by Adams v. State, 285 Ga. 744, 683 S.E.2d 586 (2009)).

[22]Lamb v. State, 278 Ga. App. 97, 100, 628 S.E.2d 165 (2006), citing Isaac v. State, 237 Ga. App. 723, 726(2), 516 S.E.2d 575 (1999). Cf. Smith v. Magnuson, 297 Ga. 210, 773 S.E.2d 205 (2015) (group plea will, in most circumstances, be inappropriate in cases involving serious crimes).

to silence if the prosecution subpoenas him in the trial of a co-defendant, unless it is perfectly clear that his testimony could not be used to connect him with other crimes to which he has not pled guilty.[23] In addition, a negotiated plea of guilty does not bar a defendant from contesting on direct appeal the constitutionality of the statute of conviction.[24]

§ 16:11 Guilty plea—*North Carolina v. Alford*

In *North Carolina v. Alford*,[1] the United States Supreme Court held that from a federal constitutional standpoint, a court may accept a guilty plea even if the defendant insists that he is innocent. However, because "of the importance of protecting the innocent and of insuring that guilty pleas are a product of free and intelligent choice . . . pleas coupled with claims of innocence should not be accepted unless there is a factual basis for the plea . . . and until [after] the judge taking the plea has inquired into and sought to resolve the conflict between the waiver of trial and the claim of innocence."[2] In *Minchey v. State*,[3] the court concluded that the judge had not resolved the conflict adequately and the plea of guilty of possession of cocaine was not valid where the defendant denied possession but said that the cocaine was found in a jacket on his premises. The defendant said, "I understand the law enough to know I am responsible for it." The judge said, "Do you still intend to plead guilty to the possession of cocaine?" The defendant said, "I have no choice, yes, sir." Nevertheless, as a matter of right, a defendant is not entitled to enter a plea of guilty.[4] Rather, it is within the discretion of the court to accept or

---

[23]U.S. v. Yurasovich, 580 F.2d 1212 (3d Cir. 1978).

[24]See Hammock v. Zant, 243 Ga. 259, 253 S.E.2d 727 (1979). See also, Class v. U.S., 138 S. Ct. 798, 200 L. Ed. 2d 37 (2018).

[Section 16:11]

[1]North Carolina v. Alford, 400 U.S. 25, 91 S.Ct. 160, 27 L.Ed.2d 162 (1970); McGuyton v. State, 298 Ga. 351, 782 S.E.2d 21 (2016); Freeman v. State, 211 Ga. App. 716, 717 (1), 440 S.E.2d 490 (1994). However, in some states a guilty plea may not be accepted until the trial judge makes certain that facts exist from which the guilt of the defendant may be reasonably inferred. E.g., State v. Neumann, 262 N.W.2d 426 (Minn.1978).

[2]Willett v. Georgia, 608 F.2d 538, 540 (5th Cir. 1979) (quoted with approval in Minchey v. State, 155 Ga. App. 632, 633, 271 S.E.2d 885 (1980)); Wallace v. Turner, 695 F.2d 545 (11th Cir. 1983).

[3]Minchey v. State, 155 Ga. App. 632, 633, 271 S.E.2d 885 (1980).

[4]Burkett v. State, 131 Ga. App. 177, 178, 205 S.E.2d 496 (1974); Shearer v. State, 128 Ga. App. 809 (2), 198 S.E.2d 369 (1973); Echols v. State, 167 Ga. App. 307, 308, 306 S.E.2d 324 (1983). A defendant also has no constitutional right to have a tendered guilty plea accepted. See North Carolina v. Alford, 400 U.S. 25, 39, 91 S.Ct. 160, 27 L.Ed.2d 162 (1970), n. 11. This footnote also says that under Rule 11 of the Federal Rules of Criminal Proce-

reject the guilty plea.[5] A guilty plea is not held to be "compelled" where it is entered to avoid a possible death sentence which might result from a trial.[6]

An *Alford* plea is a guilty plea and carries the same consequences for the defendant as a verdict of guilty entered by a jury after a trial.[7] Thus, in *Wynn v. State*,[8] the Georgia Court of Appeals expressly rejected the notion that an *Alford* plea could not be considered for purposes of sentencing a defendant as a recidivist.

In the case of *In the Interest of B.C.*,[9] the Georgia Court of Appeals held that a juvenile can enter an *Alford* plea pursuant to O.C.G.A. § 15-11-580.

§ 16:12 Guilty plea—Appeal

In *Smith v. State*,[1] the Georgia Supreme Court held that a direct appeal from a judgment of conviction and sentence entered on a guilty plea will lie "only if the issue on appeal can be resolved by the facts appearing in the record."

By way of illustration, the following would constitute claims that would not be of record and therefore not subject to direct appeal: the plea was entered only after coercion by the defendant's trial attorney; illegal evidence was presented to the grand jury; insufficient evidence in the State's case; and, ineffective assistance of counsel. However, these are the sort of claims which would properly be the subject a writ of habeas corpus.[2]

In resolving a motion for an out-of-time appeal from a guilty plea, the court should determine if the issues the defendant seeks to raise on appeal can be resolved from the existing record. If the issue(s) cannot be so resolved, he has no right to file a direct ap-

---

dure, the trial judge has discretion to "refuse to accept a plea of guilty."

[5]United States v. Crosby, 739 F.2d 1542 (11th Cir. 1984); Bowen v. State, 191 Ga. App. 760, 382 S.E.2d 694 (1989).

[6]Miller v. State, 237 Ga. 823, 824, 229 S.E.2d 648 (1976); and see North Carolina v. Alford, 400 U.S. 25, 91 S.Ct. 160, 27 L.Ed.2d 162 (1970). The same rule applies where a defendant says he enters a guilty plea to avoid receiving a longer sentence after a trial. Shakur v. State, 239 Ga. 548, 549, 238 S.E.2d 85 (1977); Brady v. United States, 397 U.S. 742, 747, 90 S.Ct. 1463, 25 L.Ed.2d 747 (1970).

[7]Argot v. State, 261 Ga. App. 569 (2), 583 S.E.2d 246 (2003).

[8]Wynn v. State, 271 Ga. App. 10 (2), 609 S.E.2d 97 (2004).

[9]In re B.C., 333 Ga. App. 763, 777 S.E.2d 52 (2015).

[Section 16:12]

[1]Smith v. State, 266 Ga. 687, 470 S.E.2d 436 (1996). Cf. Campbell v. State, 240 Ga. App. 218, 522 S.E.2d 277 (1999).

[2]Shumake v. State, 257 Ga. App. 209, 210(1), 570 S.E.2d 648 (2002) citing Burroughs v. State, 239 Ga. App. 600, 602(2), 521 S.E.2d 652 (1999).

peal and, thus, no right to an out-of-time appeal.[3]

If he raises issues which can be resolved from the existing record, he must then show that his counsel was ineffective in not filing a timely appeal. However, if the claims can be resolved against him on the face of the plea record so that a timely appeal would not have succeeded, then plea counsel's failure to file an appeal was not deficient nor prejudicial to the defendant.[4]

§ 16:13 Entering a nolo contendere plea

The plea of nolo contendere has been recognized in Georgia since 1946.[1] This plea has been described as "a mild form of pleading guilty."[2] The plea, which means "I do not wish to contend," is said "to stand upon the same footing as a plea of guilty in all respects except where otherwise specifically provided."[3]

In *Wright v. State,*[4] the Georgia Court of Appeals pointed out that a guilty plea to a crime involving moral turpitude would prevent a person from "holding public office, voting and serving on juries." The court concluded that the legislature felt that in some cases this collateral situation is too drastic where the defendant's guilt is largely technical or where the defendant has a good character. The court concluded that the nolo contendere statute was enacted to take care of these situations.

The Georgia statute provides in part as follows: "Except as otherwise provided by law, a plea of nolo contendere shall not be used against the defendant in any other court or proceedings as an admission of guilt or otherwise or for any purpose; and the plea shall not be deemed a plea of guilty for the purpose of effecting any civil disqualification of the defendant to hold public office, to vote, to serve upon any jury, or any other civil disqualification. . . ."[5] The statutes related to habitual violators treat the plea of nolo contendere in much the same way as a plea

---

[3]Stephens v. State, 291 Ga. 837, 733 S.E.2d 266 (2012).

[4]Hagan v. State, 294 Ga. 716, 755 S.E.2d 734 (2014).

[Section 16:13]

[1]Ga. Laws 1946, p. 142.

[2]U. S. ex rel. Collins v. Claudy, 106 F. Supp. 367 (W.D. Pa. 1952), judgment rev'd on other grounds, 204 F.2d 624 (3d Cir. 1953).

[3]Wright v. State, 75 Ga. App. 764, 767 (1), 44 S.E.2d 569 (1947).

[4]Wright v. State, 75 Ga. App.

764, 766, 44 S.E.2d 569 (1947).

[5]O.C.G.A. § 17-7-95. See Hardin v. Brookins, 275 Ga. 477, 569 S.E.2d 511 (2002), where the court reviewed the application of O.C.G.A. § 17-7-95(c) in the context of an elected official who had entered a nolo contendere plea in Florida to a charge of a controlled substance several years earlier. The court concluded that as long as the offense in Florida was one which would also be a violation of Georgia law, the individual would not be barred from holding public office because of the nolo plea.

of guilty to those offenses.[6] In *Blackmon v. State,*[7] the court concluded that it was error to allow a prior conviction of burglary based upon a plea of nolo contendere to serve as the basis for a violation of O.C.G.A. § 16-11-131(b), possession of a firearm by a convicted felon. The court explained that because the statute does not explicitly state that a plea of nolo contendere may be used to prove possession of a firearm by a convicted felon and because the general definition of "conviction" provided in O.C.G.A. § 16-1-3(4) makes no reference to a nolo plea, to hold otherwise would violate general principles of statutory construction which construe criminal statutes most strictly against the state.

The Georgia statute provides that this plea may only be entered in non-capital cases with the consent and approval of the trial judge.[8] One example of when a court may properly consider a defendant's former plea of nolo contendere is in connection with a defendant's pre-sentence hearing. O.C.G.A. § 17-10-2 explicitly provides that a judge may consider a defendant's past history of "criminal convictions and pleas of guilty or nolo-contendere."[9]

In the civil case of *Tilley v. Page,*[10] the Georgia Court of Appeals held that the plaintiff's nolo contendere plea to a shoplifting charge was admissible for purposes of impeachment. However, in *State v. Rocco,*[11] the Georgia Supreme Court held that a nolo contendere plea could not be used for impeachment purposes in a criminal case against the defendant. In *Pitmon v. State,*[12] the Georgia Court of Appeals overruled *Tilley v. Page.* O.C.G.A. § 24-6-609(d) expressly now prohibits the use for impeachment of a case resolved by a plea of nolo contendere.

In 1994, Georgia amended O.C.G.A. § 40-6-391(k) so as to provide that no nolo contendere plea shall be accepted from a person under the age of 21 who is charged with a violation of said statute. Also in 1994, O.C.G.A. § 40-6-391.1(a) was amended so as to provide that no plea of nolo contendere shall be accepted if the defendant is charged with driving under the influence and "had an alcohol concentration of more than 0.15. . . ." Subsection (b) of O.C.G.A. § 40-6-391.1 now provides that a nolo contendere plea may be accepted only if (1) the defendant filed a verified petition requesting acceptance of such plea and sets out special cir-

---

[6]See O.C.G.A. § 40-5-58.

[7]Blackmon v. State, 266 Ga. App. 877, 598 S.E.2d 542 (2004).

[8]O.C.G.A. § 17-7-95; Nelson v. State, 87 Ga. App. 644, 649, 75 S.E.2d 39 (1953); Robinson v. State, 173 Ga. App. 285, 326 S.E.2d 245 (1985).

[9]See Beasley v. State, 345 Ga. App. 247, 812 S.E.2d 561 (2018).

[10]Tilley v. Page, 181 Ga. App. 98, 100 (4), 351 S.E.2d 464 (1986).

[11]State v. Rocco, 259 Ga. 463, 467 (1), 384 S.E.2d 183 (1989).

[12]Pitmon v. State, 265 Ga. App. 655, 595 S.E.2d 360 (2004).

cumstances to show the judge that acceptance of the plea is in the interest of justice, (2) the judge has reviewed the defendant's driving record, and (3) the judge sets out his reasons for accepting the plea. The statute also requires that the reasons for accepting the plea be sent to the Department of Motor Vehicle Safety and if a plea of nolo contendere is entered under subsection (b), the defendant's driver's license shall be sent to the Department of Motor Vehicle Safety.

O.C.G.A. § 40-5-63 was changed in 1991 so as to provide that in a DUI case a nolo contendere plea shall not be accepted if the defendant has had a conviction of or has entered a guilty plea to a DUI case within the previous five years "as measured from the dates of previous arrests."

The trial judge may impose the same sentence pursuant to a plea of nolo contendere as to a plea of guilty.[13] Rule 33.1(B) of the Uniform Rules for the Superior Courts provides in part as follows: "A defendant may plead *nolo contendere* only with the consent of the judge. Such a plea should be accepted by the judge only after due consideration of the views of the parties and the interest of the public in the effective administration of justice." In *Vanegas v. State*,[14] the court pointed out that a trial court's refusal to consider "such a plea in all cases . . . abdicat[es] its judicial responsibility."

See Weaver, "The Effect in Georgia of a Plea of Nolo Contendere Entered in a Georgia Court," 13 Ga. L. Rev. 723 (1979).

§ 16:14   Withdrawal of guilty plea under state law

In O.C.G.A. § 17-7-93(b), it is provided in part that "any time before judgment is pronounced, the accused person may withdraw the plea of 'guilty' and plead 'not guilty'; and the former plea shall not be admissible as evidence against him at his trial."[1] The word "pronounced" as used in Code section 17-7-93(b) means the trial court's oral pronouncement of the sentence.[2]

Rules 33.5 and 33.10 of the Uniform Rules for the Superior

---

[13]O.C.G.A. § 17-7-95(b). Cf. Connelly v. Balkcom, 213 Ga. 491, 492 (3), 99 S.E.2d 817 (1957).

[14]Vanegas v. State, 249 Ga. App. 76, 77 (1), 547 S.E.2d 718 (2001).

[Section 16:14]

[1]In Shoemake v. State, 213 Ga. App. 528, 445 S.E.2d 558 (1994), the court noted that calling the jury's attention to the fact that the defendant previously pled guilty to the same charge for which he was on trial is so

harmful that it cannot be corrected by a jury instruction and will generally require a mistrial where the evidence of guilt is not overwhelming.

[2]State v. Germany, 246 Ga. 455, 271 S.E.2d 851 (1980). See Browner v. State, 257 Ga. 321, 357 S.E.2d 559 (1987) (*Germany* does not apply to pleas entered in capital cases where defendant is informed that the state is seeking the death penalty). See § 16:9, supra, on *State v. Germany*.

Courts provide in part as follows:

"33.05 Responsibilities of the Trial Judge

"(A) The trial judge should not participate in plea discussions.

"(B) If a tentative plea agreement has been reached, upon request of the parties, the trial judge may permit the parties to disclose the tentative agreement and the reasons therefor in advance of the time for the tendering of the plea. The judge may then indicate to the prosecuting attorney and defense counsel whether the judge will likely concur in the proposed disposition if the information developed in the plea hearing or presented in the presentence report is consistent with the representations made by the parties. If the trial judge concurs but the final disposition differs from that contemplated by the plea agreement, then the judge shall state for the record what information in the presentence report or hearing contributed to the decision not to sentence in accordance with the plea agreement."

"33.10 Stating Intention to Reject the Plea Agreement

"If the trial court intends to reject the plea agreement, the trial court shall, on the record, inform the defendant personally that (1) the trial court is not bound by any plea agreement; (2) the trial court intends to reject the plea agreement presently before it; (3) the disposition of the present case may be less favorable to the defendant than that contemplated by the plea agreement; and (4) that the defendant may then withdraw his or her guilty plea as a matter of right. If the plea is not then withdrawn, sentence may be pronounced."

Rule 33.11 of the Uniform Rules for the Superior Courts provides that a verbatim record of the proceeding shall be made and preserved.

Rule 33.12 of the Uniform Rules for the Superior Courts provides as follows:

"33.12 Plea Withdrawal

"(A) After sentence is pronounced, the judge should allow the defendant to withdraw a plea of guilty or *nolo contendere* whenever the defendant, upon a timely motion for withdrawal, proves that withdrawal is necessary to correct a manifest injustice.

"(B) In the absence of a showing that withdrawal is necessary to correct a manifest injustice, a defendant may not withdraw a plea of guilty or *nolo contendere* as a matter of right once sentence has been pronounced by the judge."

In cases where the defendant enters a non-negotiated plea of guilty, the trial court is not required to inform defendant of his right to withdraw his plea before sentencing.[3]

"Once a petitioner raises a question about the validity of a guilty plea, the State has the burden to show that the plea was voluntarily, knowingly, and intelligently made."[4]

In *Blackwell v. State*,[5] defendant entered a negotiated plea which required that he testify at the trial of his co-defendants. Before sentencing, the defendant moved to withdraw his plea. Overruling all authority to the contrary, the court found that the defendant's right to withdraw a plea under O.C.G.A. § 17-9-93(b) is subject to waiver and that the trial court properly denied the defendant's motion. The court's holding was premised on the nature of the plea bargain and that the defendant's motion came on the eve of the co-defendants' trial.

Generally, during the term at which sentence is imposed it is within the discretion of the trial court to determine whether or not to permit a guilty plea to be withdrawn after sentencing "and [his ruling] will not be disturbed on appeal absent a manifest abuse of such discretion."[6] However, in *Kaiser v. State*,[7] the Court of Appeals determined that a defendant may move to withdraw a plea following the imposition of a void sentence at any time prior to resentencing.

It has been held that one who has entered a guilty plea cannot move for a new trial, and a motion for a new trial cannot be used as a motion to withdraw a guilty plea.[8] But see § 28:10, infra, on motion for new trial. In *Atkinson v. State*,[9] the court held that "an appeal will lie from a judgment entered on a guilty plea only if the issue on appeal can be resolved by facts appearing in the

---

[3]James v. State, 326 Ga. App. 231, 232, 756 S.E.2d 312 (2014).

[4]Lejeune v. McLaughlin, 296 Ga. 291, 766 S.E.2d 803 (2014) (when the issue is raised on direct appeal, the burden is on the state; the burden is on the petitioner when the issue is raised by way of a habeas corpus case).

[5]Blackwell v. State, 299 Ga. 122, 786 S.E.2d 669 (2016).

[6]Thornton v. State, 180 Ga. App. 274, 275, 349 S.E.2d 23 (1986). There is no statutory procedure governing the withdrawal of a plea after sentence has been imposed. In Kaiser v. State, 285 Ga. App. 63, 65, 646 S.E.2d 84 (2007), the court observed: "[t]his is a judicially created rule, which evolved

from the established common law tenet that a court cannot set aside or alter a judgment after the expiration of the term at which it was entered, unless the proceeding for that purpose was begun during the original term. [cits.]"

[7]Kaiser v. State, 285 Ga. App. 63(1), 646 S.E.2d 84 (2007).

[8]Amos v. State, 161 Ga. App. 281, 283 (2), 287 S.E.2d 743 (1982).

[9]Campbell v. State, 240 Ga. App. 218 (1), 522 S.E.2d 277 (1999); Atkinson v. State, 219 Ga. App. 366, 466 S.E.2d 32 (1995). Accord, Flanigan v. State, 238 Ga. App. 296, 517 S.E.2d 569 (1999).

record." In *Caine v. State*,[10] the Georgia Supreme Court held that a defendant must file a motion to withdraw his guilty plea in the trial court and have a hearing in that court before filing a direct appeal.

In a felony case, a trial judge has no jurisdiction to consider a motion to withdraw a guilty plea when the motion is filed after the term of court at which the guilty plea was entered.[11] The motion must be filed within the term of court that the plea is entered even if there is less than thirty days remaining in the term at the time the plea is entered.[12] Likewise, a motion in arrest of judgment may not be considered unless it is filed within the term.[13] Thus, after the term the only method of challenging the validity of a guilty plea is through a habeas corpus proceeding[14] or by a direct appeal if the issue is one which may be resolved by facts appearing in the record.[15] If a defendant seeks in an untimely manner to withdraw his guilty plea, the trial judge should dismiss the motion for lack of jurisdiction.[16]

However, any person imprisoned by virtue of a sentence imposed as a result of his conviction where "there was a substantial denial of his rights under the Constitution . . . or of this state may institute" a habeas corpus action.[17]

In *Smith v. State*,[18] the Georgia Supreme Court upheld the constitutionality of the rule prohibiting a trial court from entertaining a defendant's motion to withdraw a guilty plea filed after the expiration of the term in which the defendant was sentenced under the plea. The defendant in *Smith* sought to withdraw a guilty plea from a previous term, arguing that his right to equal protection had been violated because he could not withdraw his plea in a later term, whereas defendants convicted at trial could challenge their convictions by way of an appeal after the expiration of the term in which they were sentenced

---

[10]Caine v. State, 266 Ga. 421, 467 S.E.2d 570 (1996).

[11]Gipson v. State, 269 Ga. 26, 494 S.E.2d 669 (1998); Worle v. State, 227 Ga. App. 575, 489 S.E.2d 374 (1997); State v. Johnson, 222 Ga. App. 156, 473 S.E.2d 593 (1996); Stuckey v. State, 204 Ga. App. 793, 420 S.E.2d 655 (1992); State v. James, 211 Ga. App. 149, 150, 438 S.E.2d 399 (1993). Cf. Cabell v. State, 221 Ga. App. 192, 471 S.E.2d 222 (1996).

[12]Smith v. State, 283 Ga. 376, 659 S.E.2d 380 (2008).

[13]Worle v. State, 227 Ga. App. 575, 489 S.E.2d 374 (1997).

[14]Grice v. State, 236 Ga. App. 379, 380, 511 S.E.2d 909 (1999); Harden v. State, 177 Ga. App. 531, 339 S.E.2d 793 (1986).

[15]Smith v. State, 253 Ga. 169, 316 S.E.2d 757 (1984).

[16]Foskey v. State, 232 Ga. App. 303, 304, 501 S.E.2d 856 (1998).

[17]O.C.G.A. § 9-14-42(a).

[18]Smith v. State, 283 Ga. 376, 659 S.E.2d 380 (2008).

provided they did so within thirty days of their conviction.[19] The court held that the term-of-court rule did not violate the *Equal Protection Clause of the Fourteenth Amendment to the U.S. Constitution* or Art. I, Sec. I, Par. II of the Georgia Constitution because the defendant failed to show that the class of defendants pleading guilty was similarly situated to the class of defendants convicted at trial.

In *Tripp v. State*,[20] the Court of Appeals observed that "judgments of conviction are not entered in cases proceeding under the First Offender Act unless the defendant violates the terms of his probation. . . . [Hence] jurisdiction to consider a motion to withdraw is also retained." Nonetheless, it is clear that O.C.G.A. § 17-7-93(b) has no application to a plea entered under the First Offender Act. Extending that right to such pleas would frustrate the purpose of the Act.[21]

In *State v. Stinson*,[22] the Georgia Supreme Court determined that a plea entered as a condition for entry into a Drug Court program was not subject to withdrawal. As the court observed: "[a] defendant . . . who has pled guilty and utilized the benefits of a rehabilitative option in order to avoid an adjudication of guilt may not withdraw the plea as a matter of right under O.C.G.A. § 17-7-93(b)."

In *Jefferson v. State*,[23] the clerk received the defendant's motion to withdraw his guilty plea on October 27, 1993, two days before the end of the term, but it was not marked filed until November 1, 1993. The appellate court concluded that the motion should be treated as being filed on October 27.

Since there is no statutory provision for the filing of a motion to withdraw a guilty plea, a local rule requiring that such a motion be filed with a rule nisi is valid and enforceable. In *Vaughan v. State*,[24] the court concluded that where there is such a rule, the failure to file a rule nisi for 18 months after the filing of the motion to withdraw the plea amounted to a waiver of the motion.

---

[19]*See* O.C.G.A. § 5-6-38; *see* § 28:11, infra, on notice of appeal.

[20]Tripp v. State, 223 Ga. App. 73, 74, 476 S.E.2d 844 (1996).

[21]State v. Stinson, 278 Ga. 377, 602 S.E.2d 654 (2004). See Davenport v. State, 136 Ga. App. 913, 222 S.E.2d 644 (1975).

[22]State v. Stinson, 278 Ga. 377, 602 S.E.2d 654 (2004). Compare Evans v. State, 293 Ga. App. 371, 667 S.E.2d 183 (2008), where defendant's efforts to plead double jeopardy after he was rejected by drug court because of his physical and mental condition was denied.

[23]Jefferson v. State, 216 Ga. App. 442 (1), 454 S.E.2d 632 (1995).

[24]Vaughan v. State, 161 Ga. App. 265, 287 S.E.2d 728 (1982). In *Vaughn*, while the motion to withdraw the guilty plea was pending, the defendant's probated sentence was revoked and then reinstated.

In *Nash v. State*,[25] the court stated, "[T]he burden in non-death penalty cases is on the recidivism defendant rather than the State to prove by a preponderance of the evidence that a previous guilty plea was not knowingly and voluntarily entered."

The fact that a guilty plea was entered and then is withdrawn is not admissible in evidence at the defendant's trial.[26] See Studdard, *Daniel's Georgia Handbook on Criminal Evidence* (2018 ed.), § 8:2.

In 1986, Georgia imposed a time limitation in which any challenge could be made to "a misdemeanor conviction of any of the traffic laws of [the] state or the traffic laws of any county or municipal government" in a state habeas corpus proceeding. That time limit provides that the case must be filed within 180 days from the date the conviction becomes final.[27] In the 1991 case of *Brown v. Earp*,[28] the court held that the 180 day limitation "applies to any challenge which could be brought by means of a petition for habeas corpus, regardless" of how raised. In *Grant v. State*,[29] the court affirmed the trial judge in considering a prior DUI while setting a sentence without first considering the voluntariness of the earlier guilty plea. The court pointed out that "any challenge to a misdemeanor traffic conviction must be filed within 180 days." However, in *Cunningham v. State*,[30] the defendant erroneously represented to the court that he had no prior felony convictions and thus was sentenced as a first offender. The defendant then challenged the validity of his first offender treatment and moved to withdraw his guilty plea. The appellate court affirmed the trial court's decision denying the defendant's motion based on the defendant's attempt to defraud the court.

The plea withdrawal process is a "critical stage of the criminal prosecution" and in the absence of a valid waiver, a defendant is entitled to counsel.[31] In addition, the defendant is entitled to a

---

[25]Nash v. State, 271 Ga. 281, 519 S.E.2d 893 (1999).

[26]Mathis v. State, 145 Ga. App. 754, 245 S.E.2d 41 (1978). See White v. State, 51 Ga. 285, 289 (1874). See Annot., 86 A.L.R.2d 326 (1962).

[27]O.C.G.A. § 40-13-33. This statute seems to have been enacted to prevent the result reached by the court in Hardison v. Martin, 254 Ga. 719, 334 S.E.2d 161 (1985).

[28]Brown v. Earp, 261 Ga. 522, 407 S.E.2d 737 (1991).

[29]Grant v. State, 231 Ga. App. 868, 501 S.E.2d 27 (1998).

[30]Cunningham v. State, 239 Ga. App. 889, 890 (1), 522 S.E.2d 480 (1999).

[31]The right to counsel in connection with the withdrawal of a guilty plea was first recognized in Fortson v. State, 272 Ga. 457 (1), 532 S.E.2d 102 (2000). However, it will not be applied retroactively since it is not a "watershed" rule. Carter v. Johnson, 278 Ga. 202, 599 S.E.2d 170 (2004). See § 14:63, supra, on Retroactive applica-

hearing on the motion.[32]

In *Carter v. Johnson*,[33] the Georgia Supreme Court recognized that a defendant has the right to appeal directly from the denial of a motion to withdraw a guilty plea. In addition, the Court held that where the right is frustrated either through counsel's negligence or through the trial court's failure to inform the defendant of his right to appeal, the remedy is an out of time appeal.

See § 15:4, supra, on plea bargaining and § 16:2, supra, on entering a guilty plea. See section § 16:15, infra, on withdrawing a guilty plea on federal constitutional grounds.

§ 16:15   Withdrawal of guilty plea on federal constitutional grounds

From a federal constitutional standpoint, unless it affirmatively appears that the defendant intelligently and voluntarily entered his guilty plea, he may as a matter of right withdraw his guilty plea even if represented by counsel when it was entered.[1] On direct appeal, the burden is on the state to show that the plea was intelligently and voluntarily entered.[2] Thus, if the defendant seeks to withdraw his guilty plea on the ground that it was not intelligently and voluntarily entered, there is no burden on the defendant to establish these facts, but the burden is on the state to prove they are not true.[3]

---

tion of new rules of criminal law.

[32]Banhi v. State, 252 Ga. App. 475, 555 S.E.2d 513 (2001). See White v. State, 302 Ga. 315, 806 S.E.2d 489 (2017) (counsel who represents defendant through entry of guilty plea is counsel of record at a minimum through end of term in which sentence was entered unless trial court enters order allowing defense counsel to withdraw; motion to withdraw guilty plea filed by defendant while represented by counsel is considered a nullity).

[33]Carter v. Johnson, 278 Ga. 202 (2), 599 S.E.2d 170 (2004).

[Section 16:15]

[1]Hamm v. State, 123 Ga. App. 10, 12-14, 179 S.E.2d 272 (1970); Capps v. Ault, 229 Ga. 873, 195 S.E.2d 22 (1972). However, in Jones v. Lee, 244 Ga. 837, 262 S.E.2d 130 (1979), the court pointed out that the transcript

of the sentencing does not have to be typed up and entered on the minutes of the court as provided for in O.C.G.A. § 17-8-5 for trial testimony.

[2]Lejeune v. McLaughlin, 296 Ga. 291, 766 S.E.2d 803 (2014) (where the issue is raised in a writ for habeas corpus, the burden is on the petitioner).

[3]Cook v. State, 153 Ga. App. 362, 265 S.E.2d 323 (1980). In Roberts v. Greenway, 233 Ga. 473, 476 (3), 211 S.E.2d 764 (1975), overruled on other grounds by Lejeune v. McLaughlin, 296 Ga. 291, 766 S.E.2d 803 (2014), the court held that where a defendant asserts that his guilty plea was not knowingly and voluntarily entered in that his counsel had not informed him of the possible consequences of a guilty plea, he waived the attorney-client privilege and the attorney may testify to what he told the defendant. Accord,

However, in *Hill v. Lockhart,*[4] the United States Supreme Court reviewed a federal habeas corpus. In this case, the prisoner contended that he had involuntarily entered his guilty plea in that his counsel had misinformed him that if he pled guilty he would be eligible for parole after serving one-third of his sentence whereas under state law such an offender was required to serve one-half of his sentence to be eligible for parole. The Supreme Court held that where the prisoner failed to allege that he was prejudiced by the misinformation in that he would not have pled guilty had it not been for the misinformation, and he did not contend his plea was involuntary or unintelligent because the State did not supply him with the information, the prisoner was not entitled to a habeas corpus hearing. In other words, the court held that the test "enunciated in *Strickland v. Washington*[5] applies when guilty pleas are challenged based on ineffectiveness of counsel. Under these circumstances, to satisfy the second prong of the Strickland test a defendant must show there is a reasonable probability that but for counsel's deficiency he would not have pled guilty, but would have insisted upon going to trial."[6] See § 7:4, supra, on ineffective assistance of counsel.

In *Fortson v. State,*[7] the Georgia Supreme Court held that the right to counsel attaches when a defendant seeks to withdraw a guilty plea and it is error if the court fails to inform the defendant of this right during plea withdrawal proceedings.

See § 16:2, supra, on entering a guilty plea; § 16:10, infra, on waivers of defendant and collateral consequences doctrine; and § 16:14, supra, on withdrawal of a guilty plea. On time limitations on withdrawal of misdemeanor traffic convictions, see § 16:14, supra.

Bailey v. Baker, 232 Ga. 84, 85-86, 205 S.E.2d 278 (1974) (citing with approval United States v. Woodall, 438 F.2d 1317 (5th Cir. 1970)).

[4]Hill v. Lockhart, 474 U.S. 52, 106 S.Ct. 366, 88 L.Ed.2d 203 (1985). Compare Smith v. Williams, 277 Ga. 778, 779 (2), 596 S.E.2d 112 (2004) where the Georgia Supreme Court reversed and remanded to the habeas court for a specific finding on the second prong of the *Hill* test, prejudice, in a case where the petitioner's trial counsel misrepresented the petitioner's parole eligibility. The court explained that counsel's failure to advise a defendant about the parole consequences of a plea did not constitute ineffective assistance of counsel,

while providing erroneous information about parole consequences did constitute ineffective assistance. See also Johnson v. Roberts, 287 Ga. 112, 694 S.E.2d 661 (2010) (ineffective assistance established where counsel provided erroneous advice regarding parole eligibility).

[5]Strickland v. Washington, 466 U.S. 668, 104 S.Ct. 2052, 80 L.Ed.2d 674 (1984).

[6]Murray v. State, 216 Ga. App. 593, 595 (1), 455 S.E.2d 79 (1995). See Missouri v. Frye, 132 S. Ct. 1399, 182 L. Ed. 2d 379 (2012), and § 16:10, supra, on guilty pleas.

[7]Fortson v. State, 272 Ga. 457, 460, 532 S.E.2d 102 (2000).

Part IV

THE TRIAL

Chapter 17

Preliminary Matters and General Requirements

> **KeyCite®**: Cases and other legal materials listed in KeyCite Scope can be researched through the KeyCite service on Westlaw®. Use KeyCite to check citations for form, parallel references, prior and later history, and comprehensive citator information, including citations to other decisions and secondary materials.

§ 17:1   The trial—General

Every person accused of a crime has a right to a fair and impartial trial free from any demonstration or disorder which may prejudicially influence the jury trying the case.[1] Thus, the West Virginia Supreme Court held that a defendant on trial for driving under the influence was deprived of an impartial jury where MADD members showed up in the courtroom wearing MADD buttons and led by the sheriff.[2] Likewise, in Georgia it has been held that a defendant was denied a right to an impartial jury where a sheriff "had packed the courtroom with law enforcement officials . . ." in uniform.[3] However, it is frequently stated that a defendant is entitled to a fair trial, but not a perfect one.[4]

The United States Constitution provides for a public trial of criminal cases under the Sixth Amendment, which is made applicable to the states through the due process clause of the Fourteenth Amendment.[5] In *Vescuso v. Commonwealth,*[6] the court held that the two defendants' rights to a public trial were violated when they were tried in a "courtroom" inside a prison. The Georgia Constitution also provides for the public trial of criminal cases.[7] In *Kilgore v. R. W. Page Corp.,*[8] the court held that a coroner's inquest must be open to the public under the Open Meet-

---

[Section 17:1]

[1]Glenn v. State, 205 Ga. 32, 34, 52 S.E.2d 319 (1949). See Annot., "Emotional Manifestations by Victim or Family of Victim During Criminal Trial as Ground for Reversal, New Trial, or Mistrial," 31 A.L.R.4th 229, § 1b (1984); Annot., "Sufficiency of Courtroom Facilities as Affecting Rights of Accused," 85 A.L.R.3d 918 (1978); Price v. State, 149 Ga. App. 397, 254 S.E.2d 512 (1979) (overruled on other grounds by, State v. Clements, 289 Ga. 640, 715 S.E.2d 59 (2011)) (mother's emotional outbursts).

[2]State v. Franklin, 174 W.Va. 469, 327 S.E.2d 449 (1985).

[3]See Lemley v. State, 258 Ga. 554, 372 S.E.2d 421 (1988).

[4]See Mingo v. State, 133 Ga. App.

385, 387, 210 S.E.2d 835 (1974).

[5]Argersinger v. Hamlin, 407 U.S. 25, 28, 92 S.Ct. 2006, 32 L.Ed.2d 530 (1972). See Globe Newspaper Co. v. Superior Court for Norfolk County, 457 U.S. 596, 102 S. Ct. 2613, 73 L. Ed. 2d 248 (1982).

[6]Vescuso v. Commonwealth, 5 Va.App. 59, 360 S.E.2d 547 (1987) (en banc). In *Vescuso*, the defendants were tried for escape. The Appellate Court held that "before the constitutional right of a defendant to a public trial can be jeopardized, the record must contain findings of fact showing some clear and present overriding public interest or justification."

[7]Ga. Const. 1983, Art. I, § I, ¶ XI. See Purvis v. State, 288 Ga. 865, 708 S.E.2d 283 (2011) (defendant's right to public trial violated when trial

ings Act. However, Georgia has a statute which allegedly gives the trial judge discretion to clear the courtroom of spectators if he feels that the testimony is vulgar and obscene, or relates to the improper acts of the sexes, and tends to debauch the morals of the young,[9] or where a witness fears bodily harm if he testifies in open court,[10] or if there are so many spectators present that they impede the progress of the trial or otherwise interfere with the conduct of a fair trial.[11] The discretion of a trial judge to close the courtroom has been tempered by the United States Supreme Court in *Presley v. Georgia*,[12] where the court held that it was error to close the courtroom without considering other alternatives.

The power of the judge to exclude spectators is intended to extend to certain classes of persons in the courtroom only and does not permit the judge, over objection, to exclude everyone not

---

was conducted in a courtroom located within county jail). See O.C.G.A. § 15-6-18(c), as amended in 2012, providing that in counties with a population of less than 50,000, court may be conducted in a facility which is open to the public where it is impractical to do so in the courthouse provided the facility is designated by county authorities as an alternate venue to the courthouse and in the case of criminal proceedings, the facility is owned or leased by the county.

[8]Kilgore v. R. W. Page Corp., 261 Ga. 410, 405 S.E.2d 655 (1991).

[9]O.C.G.A. § 17-8-53.

[10]Lowe v. State, 141 Ga. App. 433, 435, 233 S.E.2d 807 (1977). A.B.A. Standards, Standard 6-3.10, reads as follows:

(a) Any person who engages in conduct which disturbs the orderly process of the trial may be admonished or excluded, and, if such conduct is intentional, may be punished for contempt. Any person whose conduct in a criminal proceeding tends to menace a defendant, an attorney, a victim, a witness, a juror, a court officer, the judge, or a member of the defendant's or victim's family may be removed from the courtroom.

(b) When a victim or a member of a victim's or a defendant's family is removed from the courtroom during trial, he or she should ordinarily be al-

lowed to return upon assurance of good behavior.

In United States v. Sielaff, 561 F.2d 691 (7th Cir. 1977), the court said that the defendant's right to a public trial is not absolute and a trial judge may take steps to minimize the alleged trauma suffered by a rape victim. In this case, the court approved the action of the trial judge in excluding from the courtroom all persons other than court personnel, lawyers, the press, and a minister during the testimony of the victim.

21A Am. Jur. 2d Criminal Law § 1066, Protection of Witnesses, (2004); See Annot., "Exclusion of Public From State Criminal Trial in Order to Avoid Intimidation of Witness," 55 A.L.R.4th 1196 (1987).

[11]Myers v. State, 97 Ga. 76, 77 (5), 25 S.E. 252 (1895). In Commonwealth v. Stetson, 384 Mass. 545, 427 N.E.2d 926 (1981), the court affirmed the action of the trial judge in excluding the public from a trial for a short period because a witness was afraid to testify.

See Annot., "Exclusion of Public From State Criminal Trial in Order to Prevent Disturbance by Spectators or Defendant," 55 A.L.R.4th 1170 (1987).

[12]Presley v. Georgia, 558 U.S. 209, 130 S. Ct. 721, 175 L. Ed. 2d 675, 38 Media L. Rep. (BNA) 1161 (2010).

connected with the case.[13] In obscenity cases, the closing of the courtroom to all spectators except those who are members of the press, members of the bar, or relatives or close friends of the defendant or a witness has been approved.[14] O.C.G.A. § 17-8-54 requires the court to clear the courtroom "when any person under the age of 16 is testifying concerning any sexual offense." In such cases, "the court shall clear the courtroom of all persons except parties to the cause and their immediate families or guardians, attorneys and their secretaries, officers of the court, victim assistance coordinators, victims' advocates, and such other victim assistance personnel as provided for by Code Section 15-18-14.2, jurors, newspaper reporters or broadcasters, and court reporters." O.C.G.A. § 17-8-55(c) provides that the court on its own motion, or that of the parents or guardian of a victim or witness in a case involving a sexual offense, "shall hold an evidentiary hearing to determine whether a child shall testify outside the physical presence of the accused." Should the court determine by a preponderance of the evidence that testifying in the presence of the accused could cause the child to suffer emotional distress, the court may make provisions to allow the child's testimony to be observed by the accused through closed circuit television. The code section provides a number of factors which the court may consider and it requires that the court's findings of fact and conclusions of law be made on the record. The court must also set out the provision to be made for the child's testimony and the manner in which it will be observed by the defendant. The motion requesting the relief must be made at least 10 days prior to trial, unless that time is shortened by the court. O.C.G.A. § 15-6-18 provides that in counties where the population exceeds 50,000, the governing authority may designate an alternate location in which to hold court where circumstances make the use of the regularly designated court impractical.[15]

Generally, it is within the discretion of the trial judge to conduct a part of a trial at night.[16]

Certain matters, some of which are pre-trial and some of which are post-trial, may be conducted by video conference under

---

[13]Benson v. State, 294 Ga. 618, 754 S.E.2d 23 (2014); State v. Abernathy, 289 Ga. 603, 611, 715 S.E.2d 48 (2011) (failure to raise timely objection to closure waives the issue except in context of an ineffective assistance claim); Tilton v. State, 5 Ga. App. 59, 62 S.E. 651 (1908). Generally, see Annot., "Right of Accused to Have Press or Other Media Representatives Excluded from Criminal Trial," 49 A.L.R.3d 1007 (1973).

[14]Lowe v. State, 141 Ga. App. 433, 436, 233 S.E.2d 807 (1977).

[15]The Code section has slightly different requirements for the use of alternate courtroom facilities for smaller counties. See, e.g., Purvis v. State, 288 Ga. 865, 708 S.E.2d 283 (2011).

[16]See Bloodworth v. State, 161 Ga. 332, 334 (5), 131 S.E. 80 (1925).

Uniform Superior Court Rule 9.2, such as: appointment of counsel for indigent defendants; initial appearance hearings; probable cause hearings; applications for search warrants; arraignment or waiver of arraignment; entry of pleas in criminal cases; and testimony of youthful witnesses.

In *Walker v. State,*[17] the court held that it is an abuse of discretion for a trial judge to permit the mother of the deceased victim to sit at counsel table with the district attorney when her presence is not necessary for the presentation of the case. However, in *Jackson v. State,*[18] the court held that it was not error to permit a victim to testify from a stretcher in the courtroom.

Religious invocation or the saying of prayer at jury assembly or the start of trial is not a *per se* violation of the state or U. S. constitutions.[19] However, references which invite jurors to base their verdicts on religious issues not in evidence might arguably provide grounds for reversible error.[20]

Other matters concerning the trial, such as the right to a speedy trial,[21] counsel,[22] and change of venue because of pre-trial publicity,[23] have been discussed previously.

See § 17:2, infra, on fair trial and free press. See § 24:2, infra, on locking a courtroom during jury instructions.

§ 17:2 The trial—Fair trial and free press

In *Richmond Newspapers, Inc. v. Virginia,*[1] the United States Supreme Court in 1980 said that the press and the public have a

---

[17]Walker v. State, 132 Ga. App. 476, 208 S.E.2d 350 (1974). See Nunnally v. State, 235 Ga. 693, 699 (2), 221 S.E.2d 547 (1975). Generally, see Annot., 75 Am. Jur. 2d Trial § 185, Arrangements in Courtroom—Seating of Nonparty at Counsel's Table, (2004); "Propriety and Prejudicial Effect of Permitting Nonparty to Be Seated at Counsel Table," 87 A.L.R.3d 238 (1978). However, in Tatum v. State, 151 Ga. App. 602, 603 (2), 260 S.E.2d 747 (1979), the court pointed out that in an abandonment case it is proper for the mother to hold the baby in the courtroom during the trial.

[18]Jackson v. State, 149 Ga. App. 496, 499 (3), 254 S.E.2d 739 (1979).

[19]Isaacs v. State, 259 Ga. 717 (18), 386 S.E.2d 316 (1989); Isaacs v. Head, 300 F.3d 1232, 1252 (11th Cir. 2002).

[20]Jones v. State, 270 Ga. 25 (9), 505 S.E.2d 749 (1998) (overruled on other grounds by, Hamm v. State, 294 Ga. 791, 756 S.E.2d 507 (2014)); Carr v. State, 267 Ga. 547, 480 S.E.2d 583 (1997).

[21]See § 14:70, supra, on constitutional right to a speedy trial.

[22]See § 7:1, supra, on defendant's right to counsel.

[23]See § 14:74, supra, on change of venue.

[Section 17:2]

[1]Richmond Newspapers, Inc. v. Virginia, 448 U.S. 555, 100 S.Ct. 2814, 65 L.Ed.2d 973 (1980). In Lexington Herald Leader Co. v. Tackett, 601 S.W.2d 905 (1980), the court held that trauma to witnesses in a sodomy trial is insufficient to close the trial to the press.

In Detroit Free Press, Inc. v.

federal constitutional right to be able to attend criminal trials unless the trial judge makes a finding which supports closure. There is a presumption in favor of open trials even in cases where the defense and the prosecution agree that a non-public trial may be conducted. Should either party, or the court itself, feel that there is a good reason to close any part of the trial to the public, the trial court has an independent duty to "consider all reasonable alternatives" that could ensure a fair and open trial even if neither party suggests an alternative to closure.[2]

In *Globe Newspaper Co. v. Superior Court for the County of Norfolk*,[3] the United States Supreme Court considered a Massachusetts statute which provided that in a rape case where the victim is a minor under 18 years of age, the trial judge "shall exclude the general public from the courtroom." The highest court of the state concluded that the statute was too broad and that it should be applied only when the victim was testifying and during other portions of the trial that the judge in his discretion determined should be closed. The Supreme Court reversed, holding that the mandatory closure rule violated the First Amendment and pointing out that (1) criminal trials have historically been open to the press and the general public, and that (2) public scrutiny of a criminal trial enhances the quality and safeguards of the fact-finding process, gives the appearance of fairness, and heightens public respect for the judicial process. "[T]he circumstances under which the press and the public can be barred from a criminal trial are limited; the State's justification in denying access must be a weighty one . . . . [I]t must be shown that the denial is necessitated by a compelling governmental interest, and is narrowly tailored to serve that interest . . . . A trial court can determine on a case-by-case basis whether closure is necessary to protect the welfare of a minor victim. Among the factors to be weighed are the minor victim's age, psychological maturity and understanding, the nature of the crime, the desires of the victim, and the interests of parents and relatives." In this case, if the trial judge had been permitted to exercise his discretion, closure might have been deemed unnecessary.

Recorder's Court Judge, 409 Mich. 364, 294 N.W.2d 827, 834-838 (1980), the court held that the press and the public have a right to access to criminal trials. Generally, see Annot., "Federal Constitutional Right to Public Trial in Criminal Cases—Federal Cases," 61 L.Ed.2d 1018 (1980).

[2]Presley v. Georgia, 130 S. Ct. 721 (2010), reversing 285 Ga. 270, 674

S.E.2d 909 (2009), which had held that the court has no independent duty where the parties fail to suggest an alternative to closure. See Waller v. Georgia, 467 U.S. 39, 104 S. Ct. 2210, 81 L. Ed. 2d 31 (1984).

[3]Globe Newspaper Co. v. Superior Court for the County of Norfolk, 457 U.S. 596, 102 S.Ct. 2613, 73 L.Ed.2d 248 (1982).

In the 1986 case of *Press-Enterprise Co. v. Superior Court*,[4] the United States Supreme Court held that there is a public right to access to preliminary or commitment hearings, unless the judge specifically finds (1) that there is a "substantial probability" the defendant's right to a fair trial would be prejudiced and (2) that reasonable alternatives to closure cannot adequately protect a defendant's right to a fair trial.

In *Waller v. Georgia*,[5] the Court held that the right to a public trial provided for in the Sixth Amendment applies to a pre-trial suppression hearing. "[T]he party seeking to close . . . [a] hearing must [1] advance an overriding interest that is likely to be prejudiced, [2] the closure must be no broader than necessary to protect that interest, [3] the trial court must consider reasonable alternatives to closing the proceeding, and [4] it must make findings adequate to support the closure." *Waller* applies to requests for closure at the trial of the case as well.[6] However, in *Rockdale Citizen Publishing Co., Inc. v. State*,[7] the court held that assumptions and speculation cannot provide the clear and convincing proof required to justify closure. " 'Clear and convincing proof' necessarily involves concrete, tangible evidence that can be made part of and attached to the record . . . ."

In *Chandler v. Florida*,[8] the United States Supreme Court held that there was no per se due process violation of the defendant's rights where the trial court, pursuant to the revised Canons of Ethics adopted in Florida, permitted televised coverage of the trial over defense objections.

In the landmark unanimous Georgia Supreme Court case of *R. W. Page Corp. v. Lumpkin*,[9] the court considered whether, and when, the pre-trial hearings in criminal cases and the criminal

---

[4]Press-Enterprise Co. v. Superior Court, 478 U.S. 1, 106 S.Ct. 2735, 92 L.Ed.2d 1 (1986).

[5]Waller v. Georgia, 467 U.S. 39, 104 S.Ct. 2210, 81 L.Ed.2d 31 (1984). In Berry v. State, 282 Ga. 376(2), 651 S.E.2d 1 (2007), the Supreme Court declined to apply *Waller* in a case where a juror asked to speak out of the presence of spectators and particularly the defendant's family. However, defense counsel made no objection at trial when the court cleared the courtroom of everyone save counsel and the defendant.

[6]See, e.g., Presley v. Georgia, 130 S. Ct. 721 (2010), where the United States Supreme Court ruled that it was error for the trial court to close

courtroom without considering alternatives. Compare Reid v. State, 286 Ga. 484, 690 S.E.2d 177 (2010), where the Georgia Supreme Court held that ineffective assistance claim based upon failure of defense counsel to object to closure required demonstration of prejudice unlike case where closure is objected to at trial and assigned as error on direct appeal.

[7]Rockdale Citizen Publishing Co., Inc. v. State, 266 Ga. 579, 468 S.E.2d 764 (1996).

[8]Chandler v. Florida, 449 U.S. 560, 101 S.Ct. 802, 66 L.Ed.2d 740 (1981).

[9]R. W. Page Corporation v. Lumpkin, 249 Ga. 576, 292 S.E.2d 815 (1982).

trials themselves may be closed to the public and the news media. In its decision, the court made the following points:

(1) The Georgia Constitution provides that criminal trials *shall* be public. This right applies to pre-trial, trial, and post-trial proceedings. The concept of open courtrooms during hearings in criminal cases is greater in Georgia than under federal law.

(2) "[T]he fact of many possible exceptions allowing closure should not be allowed to obscure the extreme importance of the strong presumption favoring the general rule, which is that in Georgia, the criminal trial itself, and all its consequent hearings on motions (pre-trial, mid-trial, and post-trial) shall be open to the press and public on equal terms unless the defendant or other movant is able to demonstrate on the record by 'clear and convincing proof' that closing the hearing to the press and public is the only means by which a 'clear and present danger' to his right to a fair trial or other asserted right can be avoided. A Georgia trial court judge must approach these issues possessed of less discretion than his federal counterpart because our constitution commands that open hearings are the nearly absolute rule and closed hearings the very rarest of exceptions."

(3) "In most instances when these rights of the public and the defendant seem to be on a collision course, Georgia trial judges will discover that postponing the hearing on an issue (such as a suppression question) until the jurors are sworn and sequestered for the duration of the trial will prove to be entirely adequate to protect the defendant from prejudice that might result from information reaching the empaneled jurors through the news media."

(4) "While federal trial court judges are admonished to *consider* jury sequestration (or some other remedy) as an alternative to the closing of hearings to the public and the press, we now hold that a Georgia trial court judge shall *use* jury sequestration (or some other means) to exclude prejudicial matters from the jury's knowledge and consideration unless for some reason fully articulated in his findings of fact and conclusions of law jury sequestration (or another remedy) would not adequately protect the defendant's right to a fair trial" (footnotes omitted).

(5) "A motion for closure shall receive no consideration by a trial court unless it is in writing, has been served upon the opposing party, has been filed with the clerk of the court and posted on the case docket (as notice to the press and the public) for at least one twenty-four hour period in advance of the time when the motion will be heard, and unless it alleges grounds for relief with that degree of particularity required under Code Ann. § 81A-107(b)(1) [O.C.G.A. § 9-11-7]. The motion must be supported at the hearing by the movant by evidence constituting 'clear and

convincing proof' that no means available other than closure of the hearing will serve to protect the right of the movant. The hearing on the motion shall be open, reported and transcribed. The movant need not be a formal party to the criminal proceedings" (footnotes omitted).

(6) "Closure orders shall be narrowly drawn and strictly construed in favor of open hearings. Such an order shall only be entered pursuant to written findings of fact fully articulating the alternatives to closure considered by the trial court and the reason or reasons why such alternative would not afford the movant an adequate remedy. These requirements cannot be avoided by agreement between the state and the defendant that the media and public should be barred from the hearing."

(7) "Any closure order shall provide that the portion of the hearing closed shall be reported and transcribed and made available to the media and public as soon as the prejudicial effect which caused the closure no longer exists."

(8) "The right of access of the news media representatives is no greater and no less than any other member of the general public" (citations omitted).

(9) "The authority to exclude the public from a hearing in which vulgar evidence is to be presented, Code Ann. § 81-1006 [O.C.G.A. §§ 9-10-3, 17-8-53], and the traditional right and obligation of the trial court to maintain dignity and decorum in the courtroom, as by excluding from the courtroom overflow audiences or unruly spectators, are not drawn in question in, or affected by, the present case. Georgia courts and the United States Supreme Court have given little credence to contentions that a hearing was not 'public' where, in the interest of fair administration of justice, the trial court has cleared a part of the spectators from the courtroom but has allowed representatives of the news media to remain . . . . The presence of news media representatives in a courtroom from which, in the interest of justice, some members of the general public have been excluded, usually will assure that the proceedings will be conducted fairly to all concerned, and discourages perjury and other misconduct by participants, including decisions based on secret bias and partiality" (citations omitted).

(10) "[The Georgia Supreme Court] will expedite on its calendar to the maximum extent feasible appeals and applications pertaining to orders granting closure motions in criminal cases."

In *Georgia Television Co. v. State*,[10] the court emphasized that in *R. W. Page* the courtroom was closed to the public and the press. In *Georgia Television*, the appellate court found that the

---

[10]Georgia Television Co. v. State,   257 Ga. 764, 363 S.E.2d 528 (1988).

specific findings of the trial judge and the facts of that case were sufficient to deny a motion of the media to televise pre-trial proceedings.

The *Lumpkin* case may fail to consider sufficiently the right of a defendant to a fair trial. In *United States v. Chagra*,[11] the Fifth Circuit pointed out that the "right of courtroom access is limited by the constitutional right of defendants to a fair trial."

"A request for installation and use of electronic recording, transmission, videotaping or motion picture or still photography of any judicial proceeding shall be evaluated pursuant to the standards set forth in OCGA § 15-1-10.1."[12]

However, in *Harris v. State*,[13] there was no prior notice to the parties that media wanted to use cameras in the courtroom, and no hearing was conducted until immediately before trial. The Georgia Supreme Court affirmed the use of cameras over a defendant's objection in view of the defendant's inability to show harm.

In *Rockdale Citizen Publishing Co. v. State*,[14] the court remanded the case for consideration of the alternatives to closure. The court pointed out that "[t]he burden is on the defendant, or other movant, to present clear and convincing proof of the need for closure. The burden can be carried more easily, however, where closure of a pretrial hearing is sought because, at that stage of the proceedings, some of the alternatives to closure are absent . . . . However, a closure order must fully articulate the alternatives to closure and the reasons why the alternatives would not protect the movant's rights."

O.C.G.A. §§ 17-8-53 and 17-8-54 authorize the closure of the courtroom to the public in cases where the subject matter of the proceeding involves evidence which relates to "the improper acts of the sexes and tends to debauch the morals of the young" or in the case of a child under the age of 16 who is testifying in a criminal case involving a sexual offense. However, the trial court must still consider the *Waller* factors in the exercise of its discretion and should limit the public's right to attend the trial to a minimum. In *Mullis v. State*,[15] a trial court's order limiting access to the courtroom during the testimony of a fragile 17 year old who was a child abuse victim when he was nine was affirmed in

---

[11]United States v. Chagra, 701 F.2d 354 (5th Cir. 1983).

[12]Rule 22 of the Uniform Rules for the Superior Courts; WALB-TV, Inc. v. Gibson, 269 Ga. 564, 565, 501 S.E.2d 821 (1998). O.C.G.A. § 15-1-10.1 is set out in § 17:3, infra.

[13]Harris v. State, 260 Ga. 860, 866 (7), 401 S.E.2d 263 (1991).

[14]Rockdale Citizen Publishing Co. v. State, 266 Ga. 92, 93 (1), 463 S.E.2d 864 (1995).

[15]Mullis v. State, 292 Ga. App. 218(5), 664 S.E.2d 271 (2008).

light of the court's finding that the concern was the shame to which the witness would be exposed, and given his psychological history, actual harm.

"Gag orders" may be appropriate in highly publicized cases. In *Sheppard v. Maxwell*,[16] the United States Supreme Court pointed out that the trial judge may proscribe "extrajudicial statements by any lawyer, party, witness, or court official which [divulges] prejudicial matters, such as the refusal . . . to submit to interrogation or take any lie detector tests; any statement made by [the defendant] to officials; the identity of prospective witnesses or their probable testimony; any belief in guilt or innocence; or like statements concerning the merits of the case . . . . [T]he court could also . . . [request] appropriate city and county officials to promulgate a regulation with respect to dissemination of information about the case by their employees . . . . [R]eporters . . . could . . . [be] warned as to the impropriety of publishing material not introduced in the proceedings . . . . [T]he interest of justice [must be placed] first . . . . [W]e note that unfair and prejudicial news comment on pending trials has become increasingly prevalent. Due process requires that the accused receive a trial by an impartial jury free from outside influences. . . . . The courts must take such steps by rule and regulation that will protect their processes from prejudicial outside interferences. Neither prosecutors, counsel for defense, the accused, witnesses, court staff nor enforcement officers coming under the jurisdiction of the court should be permitted to frustrate its function. Collaboration between counsel and the press as to information affecting the fairness of a criminal trial is not only subject to regulation, but is highly censurable and worthy of disciplinary measures."

A gag order is a prior restraint of those to whom it applies and as such is presumptively unconstitutional.[17] "[P]rior restraints on speech and publication are the most serious and the least tolerable infringement on First Amendment rights."[18] Accordingly, the proponent of a prior restraint bears a heavy burden of showing

---

[16]Sheppard v. Maxwell, 384 U.S. 333, 361, 86 S.Ct. 1507, 16 L.Ed.2d 600, 619 (1966). See WXIA-TV v. State, 303 Ga. 428, 811 S.E.2d 378 (2018) (modified gag order which restrained lawyers, parties, court personnel, and law enforcement from making extrajudicial comments in highly publicized case was vacated in absence of any evidence that parties restrained had disclosed sensitive or confidential information or had said or done anything that could be deemed prejudicial to defendant).

[17]See New York Times Co. v. U.S., 403 U.S. 713, 714, 91 S. Ct. 2140, 29 L. Ed. 2d 822 (1971).

[18]See Nebraska Press Ass'n v. Stuart, 427 U.S. 539, 559, 96 S. Ct. 2791, 49 L. Ed. 2d 683 (1976).

justification for the imposition of such a restraint.[19] This sort of order must be narrowly drawn "to avoid a clear and present danger or serious and imminent threat and only to the extent that no alternatives less restrictive to a prior restraint are reasonably available."[20]

There is a distinction that can be made between a gag order which amounts to a prior restraint of the media and one that is limited to the parties, counsel, and court personnel. Courts apply a less rigid standard when an order is restricted to the case-related actors.[21] Nonetheless, once the order extends to witnesses and prospective witnesses not yet subpoenaed, the burden is likely higher than when it is restricted to the parties and their attorneys.[22]

See 21A Am. Jur. 2d Criminal Law § 1009, Broadcast or Television of Proceedings (2004). See Annotation, "Validity, Propriety, and Effect of Allowing or Prohibiting Media's Broadcasting, Recording, or Photographing Court Proceedings," 14 A.L.R.4th 121 (1982). Also see 14 A.L.R.4th 108 et seq. (1982), on rules relating to the use of cameras in court. See § 18:15, infra, on the right of a public voir dire examination of prospective jurors. See *Florida Publishing Co. v. Morgan*, 253 Ga. 467, 472, 322 S.E.2d 233 (1984), on public trials in juvenile court. See Rule 22 of the Uniform Rules for the Superior Courts on Electronic and Photographic News Coverage of Judicial Proceedings.

§ 17:3   Electronic and photographic coverage of proceedings

O.C.G.A. § 15-1-10.1 provides:

"(a) It is declared to be the purpose and intent of the General Assembly that certain standards be considered by the courts in determining whether to grant requests for the televising, videotaping, or motion picture filming of judicial proceedings. Such standards are intended to provide an evaluation of the impact on the public interest and the rights of the parties in open judicial proceedings, the impact upon the integrity and dignity of the court, and whether the proposed activity would contribute to the enhancement of or detract from the ends of justice.

"(b) In considering a request for the televising, videotaping, or

---

[19]Organization for a Better Austin v. Keefe, 402 U.S. 415, 419, 91 S. Ct. 1575, 29 L. Ed. 2d 1 (1971); WXIA-TV v. State, 303 Ga. 428, 811 S.E.2d 378 (2018).

[20]See Nebraska Press Ass'n v. Stuart, 427 U.S. 539, 568-569, 96 S. Ct. 2791, 49 L. Ed. 2d 683 (1976); WXIA-TV v. State, 303 Ga. 428, 811 S.E.2d 378 (2018).

[21]WXIA-TV v. State, 303 Ga. 428, 811 S.E.2d 378 (2018).

[22]WXIA-TV v. State, 303 Ga. 428, 811 S.E.2d 378 (2018).

motion picture filming of judicial proceedings, the court shall consider the following factors in determining whether to grant such request:

"(1) The nature of the particular proceeding at issue;

"(2) The consent or objection of the parties or witnesses whose testimony will be presented in the proceedings;

"(3) Whether the proposed coverage will promote increased public access to the courts and openness of judicial proceedings;

"(4) The impact upon the integrity and dignity of the court;

"(5) The impact upon the administration of the court;

"(6) The impact upon due process and the truth finding function of the judicial proceeding;

"(7) Whether the proposed coverage would contribute to the enhancement of or detract from the ends of justice;

"(8) Any special circumstances of the parties, victims, witnesses, or other participants such as the need to protect children or factors involving the safety of participants in the judicial proceeding; and

"(9) Any other factors which the court may determine to be important under the circumstances of the case.

"(c) The court may hear from the parties, witnesses, or other interested persons and from the person or entity requesting coverage during the court's consideration of the factors set forth in this Code section.

"(d) This Code section shall not apply to the use of electronic or photographic means for the presentation of evidence or the perpetuation of a record.

"(e) The court in its discretion may grant requests made under this Code section for all or portions of judicial proceedings."[1]

Rule 22 of the Uniform Rules for the Superior Courts sets forth the requirements which a party seeking to photograph or record proceedings in court must satisfy in order to bring a camera or other recording device into a courtroom. The rule has been amended effective May 1, 2018 to provide greater access and understanding of court proceedings by the participants as well as the general public and the media who report on such proceedings. The rule also governs the use in court of electronic devices, to include phones and computers, for purposes other than recording sounds and images. Exhibit "A" to Rule 22 is the official form

---

[Section 17:3]

[1]See Morris Communications, LLC v. Griffin, 279 Ga. 735, 620 S.E.2d 800 (2005) for a thorough review of the factors to be considered in connection with an application to video record a trial.

which should be filed under the Rule.[2]

§ 17:4 The trial—Fair trial and the right of parties and attorneys to comment

Court ordered restrictions directed at parties, counsel, witnesses and others associated with the prosecution of a case such as investigators and experts are measured by a different standard than those orders which can be characterized as a restraint on the ability of the press to see and report on the trial of a case and all related proceedings. In *Gentile v. State Bar of Nevada*,[1] the United States Supreme Court was presented with a Nevada Supreme Court rule which restricted lawyers from making comments outside of court which would substantially prejudice the ability of the parties to obtain a fair trial. According to the Court, the "substantial likelihood of material prejudice standard constitutes a constitutionally permissible balance between the First

---

[2]

EXHIBIT A
IN THE SUPERIOR COURT OF ___
COUNTY
STATE OF GEORGIA

(STYLE OF CASE/   CASE
CALENDAR)   NO.
                          ———

REQUEST TO USE A RECORDING
DEVICE PURSUANT TO RULE 22
ON
RECORDING OF JUDICIAL
PROCEEDINGS.

Pursuant to Rule 22 of the Uniform Rules for Superior Court regarding Use of Electronic Devices in Courtrooms and Recording of Judicial Proceedings, the undersigned hereby requests permission to use a recording device in Courtroom in order to record images and/or sound during (all) (the following portions) of the proceedings in the above captioned case/calendar.

Consistent with the provisions of the rule, the undersigned desires to use the following described recording device(s): _____. The proceedings that the undersigned desires to record commence on *(date)*. Subject to direction from the court regarding possible pooled coverage, the undersigned wishes to use this device in the courtroom on *(date)*. The personnel who will be responsible for the use of this recording device are: (identify appropriate personnel).

The undersigned hereby certifies that the device to be used and the locations and operation of such device will be in conformity with Rule 22 and any guidelines issued by the court.

The undersigned understands and acknowledges that a violation of Rule 22 and any guidelines issued by the court may be grounds for removal or exclusion from the courtroom and a willful violation may subject the undersigned to penalties for contempt of court.

This _____ day of _____, 20__.

_____ *(Individual Signature)*

_____
(Representing / Firm)

_____ *(Position)*

APPROVED: _____

_____
Judge, Superior Court _____
Judicial Circuit

[Section 17:4]

[1]Gentile v. State Bar of Nevada, 501 U.S. 1030, 111 S.Ct. 2720, 115 L.Ed.2d 888 (1991).

Amendment rights of attorneys in pending cases and the state's interest in fair trials." The Court explained that because the right to a fair trial by impartial jurors is so fundamental, the Nevada bar rule was a reasonable restriction on the sort of comment by counsel which could jeopardize that right.

Georgia has a similar rule to the one in *Gentile*. Rule 3.6 of the State Bar of Georgia Rules of Professional Conduct prohibits a lawyer that "is participating or has participated in the investigation or litigation of a matter" from making any extrajudicial statement that a person "would reasonably believe to be disseminated" by public communication if the lawyer knows or reasonably should know that the statement will "have a substantial likelihood of materially prejudicing an adjudicative proceeding in the matter." Disciplinary Rule 7-107 requires that a trial court make findings that extrajudicial statements to the media by counsel and others would have a substantial likelihood of materially prejudicing the trial before entering an order restricting the parties and counsel from making comments to the media.

The Georgia Court of Appeals in *Atlanta Journal-Constitution and WSB-TV v. State*,[2] found that a trial court's order which prohibited parties, counsel, experts and investigators from making any statement to the press concerning the proceedings in a criminal case other than "no comment" or a general reference to in-court testimony was overbroad in the absence of a specific finding by the trial participants as required by the State Bar Rule and *Gentile* that there exists a substantial likelihood that extrajudicial statements could prejudice the defendant's right to a fair trial by impartial jurors.

§ 17:5 The judge

Rule 3.2 of the Uniform Rules for the Superior Courts provides that actions involving substantially the same parties, subject matter, or factual issues shall be assigned to the same judge. However, where there are two or more defendants in a death penalty case, the cases may be assigned to different judges.[1] The trial judge may dismiss the charges against a defendant if the state is not ready for trial when the calendar is called.[2] The trial judge has the responsibility of being impartial[3] and insuring that the defendant and the state get a fair trial with no interference

---

[2]Atlanta Journal-Constitution and WSB-TV v. State, 266 Ga. App. 168, 596 S.E.2d 694 (2004).

[Section 17:5]

[1]Tokars v. Superior Court of Cobb County, 264 Ga. 180, 442 S.E.2d 454 (1994).

[2]State v. Grimes, 194 Ga. App. 736, 392 S.E.2d 727 (1990).

[3]Due process requires an impartial judge. Hence, where a substantial portion of the funds of a city are de-

from either party or other individuals.[4] In order to perform his duty, the trial judge must be present at all times so as to be aware of situations needing his attention.[5] "A trial judge is responsible for the security of his courtroom, but a defendant has a right to be tried in an atmosphere free of partiality and innuendo created by the use of excessive security precautions."[6] The judge must prevent physical attacks on the defendant and his counsel. If he fails to perform this fundamental duty and shows that his sympathies are with the attacker, he is disqualified from presiding in the case.[7] In addition, the trial judge should exercise control over the general demeanor and behavior of the parties and their attorneys.[8]

The purpose of this rule "is to prevent the jury from being influenced," and there is no violation of the basis of the rule if the jury is not present at the time of such remarks.[9] Also, the better practice is for the trial judge to avoid all ex parte conversations, before the jury with one counsel.[10] "The trial judge has the right to propound a question or a series of questions to any witness for the purpose of developing fully the truth of the case; and . . ." it is said that the extent of such examination is a matter of the judge's discretion.[11] In *Ashley v. State*,[12] the court held that a judge may call a witness and examine the witness to develop the truth. Also, the trial judge "may address a leading question to a

---

rived from traffic fines, the mayor who is responsible for revenue production is not disinterested and may not preside even if there is a right to a de novo trial in a higher court. Ward v. Monroeville, 409 U.S. 57, 93 S.Ct. 80, 34 L.Ed.2d 267 (1972).

[4]See Dyke v. State, 232 Ga. 817, 209 S.E.2d 166 (1974). See A.B.A. Standards, Special Functions of the Trial Judge, Vol. I, Standards 6-3.1 and 6-3.3.

[5]Hayes v. State, 58 Ga. 35, 49 (12) (1877). But if the judge leaves during argument for a few minutes for a necessary cause, this is not reversible error, Pritchett v. State, 92 Ga. 65, 67, 18 S.E. 536 (1893). Cf. Koza v. State, 158 Ga. App. 709, 710 (4), 282 S.E.2d 131 (1981). But see Moore v. State, 29 Ga. App. 274, 115 S.E. 25 (1922). Where no objection is made, temporary absence is not reversible error. Sheppard v. State, 167 Ga. 326, 334 (2), 145 S.E. 654 (1928). But the judge is to remain available while the

jury is deliberating, Martin v. State, 10 Ga. App. 455, 73 S.E. 686 (1912).

[6]Robinson v. State, 164 Ga. App. 379, 380 (2), 296 S.E.2d 225 (1982); Welch v. State, 251 Ga. 197 (7), 304 S.E.2d 391 (1983).

[7]Smith v. State, 239 Ga. 477, 481, 238 S.E.2d 116 (1977).

[8]See Smith v. State, 288 Ga. 348, 703 S.E.2d 629 (2010).

[9]Flantroy v. State, 231 Ga. App. 744, 746 (3), 501 S.E.2d 10 (1998).

[10]Chambers v. State, 224 Ga. App. 245, 246 (3), 480 S.E.2d 288 (1997).

[11]Grayer v. State, 181 Ga. App. 845, 846 (3), 354 S.E.2d 191 (1987).

In Parrish v. State, 182 Ga. App. 247, 249 (4), 355 S.E.2d 682 (1987), the court held that the trial judge may ask leading questions to clarify an issue.

[12]Ashley v. State, 263 Ga. 820, 822 (3)(a), 439 S.E.2d 914 (1994).

witness in order to elicit the truth or clarify an issue."[13] But, while the judge may ask questions of witnesses, he may not intimate an opinion or become argumentative.[14] He may not question a defendant in such a way as to impair his credibility,[15] or question any witness in such a way as to express or intimate an opinion on the facts of the case as to what has or has not been proven.[16] Where a defendant testifies and states that he is willing to take a polygraph on an issue, it is error for the trial judge to ask him if he will take a polygraph on the question of guilt or innocence.[17] However, the extent of a trial judge's examination of a witness is generally said to be a matter within the sound discretion of the court.[18] He may not compliment a witness[19] or make a disparaging remark[20] about a witness. Thus, it is error for the judge in cross-examining a witness to state, "We don't want any perjury, you're already charged with theft."[21] Likewise, a judge is prohibited from intimating in any way some concern about the

---

[13]Barker v. State, 191 Ga. App. 451, 453 (3), 382 S.E.2d 115 (1989).

[14]See DeFreese v. State, 232 Ga. 739, 744 (9), 208 S.E.2d 832 (1974). The judge may not comment on a witness' testimony in such a manner as to indicate an opinion. United States v. Martinez, 496 F.2d 664, 668 (5th Cir. 1974).

[15]Paul v. State, 272 Ga. 845, 846 (1), 537 S.E.2d 58 (2000). See Brundage v. State, 143 Ga. App. 1, 2, 237 S.E.2d 473 (1977); Anderson v. Warden, 696 F.2d 296 (4th Cir. 1982).

[16]Perdue v. State, 147 Ga. App. 648, 652 (9), 249 S.E.2d 657 (1978).

[17]Crane v. State, 164 Ga. App. 638, 298 S.E.2d 619 (1982).

[18]Whiddon v. State, 160 Ga. App. 777, 779 (3), 287 S.E.2d 114 (1982).

[19]See Murphy v. State, 290 Ga. 459, 722 S.E.2d 51 (2012) (court referred to witness as a "good detective" who will assist jury in finding the "truth of the matter"). Generally, see Brooks v. State, 141 Ga. App. 725, 738, 234 S.E.2d 541 (1977), for examples of comments of a judge held not to constitute error.

In Futch v. State, 151 Ga. App. 519, 521 (4), 260 S.E.2d 520 (1979), the court pointed out that the trial judge should not appear to approve a witness by saying to him when he leaves the jury stand, "Good to see you."

[20]Cole v. State, 6 Ga. App. 798, 65 S.E. 839 (1909).

[21]Griffin v. State, 142 Ga. App. 362, 235 S.E.2d 724 (1977), vacated on other grounds, 240 Ga. 470, 241 S.E.2d 230 (1978). A judge's admonition to the sole defense witness that he was not required to testify but if he lied under oath he would see that he was prosecuted, which resulted in the witness refusing to testify, was held to deprive the defendant of his due process right to present witnesses. Webb v. Texas, 409 U.S. 95, 93 S.Ct. 351, 34 L.Ed.2d 330 (1972). In Johnson v. United States, 404 A.2d 162 (D.C.App.1979), the trial judge thought the defendant's testimony would have been perjurious. Defense counsel was told that, if defendant testified, he would not be able to question him about the facts or to argue the defendant's testimony to the jury. The defendant decided not to testify. The conviction was reversed because of the judge's interjection of himself into the case which resulted in the denial of the right of the defendant to testify and the denial of effective assistance of counsel.

credibility of a witness.[22] A judge should not attempt, either in the presence or absence of the jury, to intimidate a witness to testify[23] or threaten a witness with a perjury prosecution if he lies on the stand.[24] However, in the absence of an audio or video tape, the tone of the trial judge's comments or facial expressions is not subject to review.[25] It has likewise been held that a judge has no authority to invoke the Fifth Amendment privilege for a witness.[26] Nor may a judge comment on a defendant's election to exercise his right to remain silent at the time of arrest.[27] However, it has been held that it was not error for a trial judge, in the presence of the jury, to question a witness and instruct him of "his right to refuse to testify and say anything which might tend to incriminate him."[28]

As part of the inherent power to control the proceedings which come before it, a trial court has the authority to regulate the conduct of the parties as well as the attorneys as officers of the court and to control and supervise the practice of law generally, whether in or out of the court. In addition, each court in the state is authorized, pursuant to O.C.G.A. § 15-1-3(1), (3), and (4):

> to preserve and enforce in its immediate presence . . . to prevent interruption, disturbance, or hindrance to its proceedings; . . . [t]o compel obedience to its judgements, orders, and process and to the orders of a judge out of court in an action or proceeding therein; [and] [t]o control, in the furtherance of justice, the conduct of its officers and all other persons connected with a judicial proceeding before it, in every matter appertaining thereto . . ..[29]

Pursuant to O.C.G.A. §§ 15-1-4 and 15-6-8(5), courts are also provided with the power to punish by contempt.

---

[22]Price v. State, 310 Ga. App. 132, 712 S.E.2d 135 (2011) (court's inquiry of witness as to whether he was being truthful suggested to jury that the judge did not believe the witness). See Green v. State, 299 Ga. 337, 788 S.E.2d 380 (2016) (judge is prohibited from informing jury that a witness was held in criminal contempt for lying).

[23]See Dunn v. State, 123 Ga. App. 607, 182 S.E.2d 317 (1971); Anderson v. Maryland Penitentiary, 696 F.2d 296 (4th Cir. 1982).

[24]If such conduct causes the sole defense witness to refuse to testify, this is a violation of the defendant's due process rights. Webb v. Texas, 409 U.S. 95, 93 S.Ct. 351, 34 L.Ed.2d 330 (1972). See Marshall v. State, 291 Md. 205, 434 A.2d 555 (1981).

[25]Goodrum v. State, 269 Ga. App. 397, 604 S.E.2d 251 (2004); Perdue v. State, 147 Ga. App. 648 (9), 249 S.E.2d 657 (1978).

[26]United States v. Colyer, 571 F.2d 941 (5th Cir. 1978). This case does state that the better practice is to ask the witness if he wished to claim the privilege or to consult with his counsel.

[27]Wright v. State, 287 Ga. App. 593, 651 S.E.2d 852 (2007).

[28]Jones v. State, 162 Ga. App. 502, 291 S.E.2d 103 (1982). In *Jones* the witness was already in jail for another offense and was apparently called by the state.

[29]See Villanueva v. First American Title Ins. Co., 292 Ga. 630, 740 S.E.2d 108 (2013).

The court's control in this regard is subject to the proviso that the judge does not abridge the rights of a party under the law. Accordingly, even in the course of supervising courtroom proceedings, a trial judge may not order a warrantless Fourth Amendment search of an attorney or a party that does not otherwise fall under a well-established exception to the requirement of a warrant.[30]

Generally, it is improper for the trial judge to comment on the appellate process. The concern is that the reference to the possibility of appeal intimates that the judge believes that the defendant will be convicted.[31]

Even in the absence of the jury, it is improper for the judge to state in open court "that the law is too lenient and had too many loopholes permitting escape of criminal defendants from justice." However, such a statement is not generally regarded as a basis for reversal of the case on trial, but it has been regarded as possibly tainting jurors who will serve on future cases.[32]

It has been held that a defendant is deprived of a fair trial where the trial judge asks a large number of questions, the tenor of which is prosecutorial.[33] In order to avoid such errors, the better practice is to leave the examination of witnesses to the attorneys trying the case.[34] However, in *Mullins v. State*,[35] the Georgia Supreme Court held that "a trial judge may propound

---

[30]Csehy v. State, 816 S.E.2d 833 (Ga. Ct. App. 2018) (court ordered warrantless search of an attorney in the form of a urine sample was improper in absence of circumstances supporting an except to warrant requirement).

[31]Gibson v. State, 288 Ga. 617 (2), 706 S.E.2d 412 (2011) (mere reference to appellate process in the abstract is not harmful but judicial comment that allowing jurors to see certain exhibits could lead to appeal and retrial was prejudicial). Compare State v. Clements, 289 Ga. 640, 715 S.E.2d 59 (2011). See Mitchell v. State, 293 Ga. 1, 742 S.E.2d 454 (2013).

[32]Harkey v. State, 159 Ga. App. 112, 113 (3), 282 S.E.2d 648 (1981). 75 Am. Jur. 2d Trial § 311, Disparaging Accused (2004). See Annot., "Prejudicial Effect of Trial Judge's Remarks, During Criminal Trial, Disparaging Accused," 34 A.L.R.3d 1313 (1970).

[33]United States v. Hoker, 483 F.2d 359 (5th Cir. 1973); Petway v. United States, 391 A.2d 798 (D.C.Ct.App.

1978); United States v. Hickman, 592 F.2d 931 (6th Cir. 1979). However, in Daniels v. State, 154 Ga. App. 323, 324, 268 S.E.2d 376 (1980), the court said that a lengthy examination of a witness, even using some leading questions, is not error unless the court expresses or intimates an opinion on the case or unless the questioning becomes argumentative.

[34]Spivey v. State, 38 Ga. App. 213, 215, 143 S.E. 450 (1928). This case also says: "It is almost an intellectual impossibility for a judge to engage in an examination of a witness on vital questions of the case on trial, without in some manner and to some extent indicating his own opinion. Every practitioner knows how eagerly alert jurors are to every utterance from the bench, and how sensitive is the mind of the juror to the slightest judicial expression. Therefore, while the trial judge has the right to ask questions of the witnesses whenever necessary to bring out the truth of the case, we are not prepared to say that it is his duty

questions . . . for the purpose of developing fully the truth of the case, and the extent of such an examination is a matter for the trial court's discretion." A defendant will also be deprived of a fair trial where a judge becomes extremely bothered with the manner in which both sides of the case are conducting the trial and interferes so as to force his will on counsel.[36] See 46 Am. Jur. 2d Judges § 249, When Substitution May be Made, (2004). See Annot., "Substitution of Judges Under Rule 25 of the Federal Rules of Criminal Procedure," 73 A.L.R.Fed. 833 (1985); "Substitution of Judge in State Criminal Trial," 45 A.L.R.5th 591 (1997). See Annotation, "Gestures, Facial Expressions or Other Nonverbal Communication of Trial Judge in Criminal Case as Ground for Relief," 45 A.L.R.5th 531 (1997).

O.C.G.A. § 17-8-57 prohibits a trial judge from stating in the presence of the jury an opinion as to what has or has not been proved as to the guilt of the accused.[37] "The purpose of this limitation, in part, is to prevent the jury from being influenced by any disclosure as to the judge's opinion of a witness's credibility. [cits.]"[38] Thus, in *Patel v. State*,[39] reversal was required, despite curative instructions, where the trial court stated in the presence of the jury that "[v]enue is proper [in this county] or we wouldn't be here now," because the court expressed its opinion on the

---

to do so; and, in exercising the right, he should be careful not to intimate any opinion upon the facts, or use any expression calculated to prejudice the rights of either party."

[35]Mullins v. State, 269 Ga. 157, 159 (3), 496 S.E.2d 252 (1998). See State v. Nickerson, 324 Ga. App. 576, 749 S.E.2d 768 (2013).

[36]Dunn v. State, 123 Ga. App. 607, 182 S.E.2d 317 (1971). In Johnson v. State, 278 Ga. 344, 602 S.E.2d 623 (2004), there is a fairly comprehensive analysis and discussion of the features of a case which give rise to a motion for judicial recusal based upon the appearance that the trial judge is not impartial.

[37]Judge Mikell dissenting in Craft v. State, 274 Ga. App. 410, 618 S.E.2d 104 (2005), explained that O.C.G.A. § 17-8-57 prohibits a trial judge from doing four things: "a. expressing his opinion as to what has or has not been proved; b. intimating his opinion as to

what has or has not been proved; c. expressing his opinion as to the guilt of the accused; or d. intimating his opinion as to the guilt of the accused."

[38]O'Hara v. State, 241 Ga. App. 855, 859(3), 528 S.E.2d 296 (2000). However, not every comment by a trial judge which tends to show some bias towards a witness will rise to the "level of advocacy" which tends to undermine the integrity of the jury trial process. See e.g. Jordan v. State, 259 Ga. App. 551, 578 S.E.2d 217 (2003).

[39]Patel v. State, 282 Ga. 412, 413, 651 S.E.2d 55 (2007). Compare State v. Gardner, 286 Ga. 633, 690 S.E.2d 164 (2010), where court found that judicial inquiry in presence of jury as to whether venue had been proved and, if not, to "go ahead and do it before we forget" was not an improper expression of trial court's opinion. The decision drew a sharp dissent from Justice Hines.

proof of a necessary element of the offense. In *Ledford v. State*,[40] the court held that a defendant would no longer be required to move for a mistrial in order to obtain appellate review of a trial judge's alleged improper comment on the evidence and disapproved of authority to the contrary. The court concluded that a trial judge's comment which runs contrary to O.C.G.A. § 17-8-57 will "always" constitute plain error. Section 17-8-57 has since been amended to require that a party who alleges the trial court has made an improper comment to make a "timely objection" specifying the grounds therefor and if the objection is sustained, the trial court is required to give the jury a curative instruction or declare a mistrial, if appropriate. The failure to make such an objection precludes appellate review of the issue unless "such violation constitutes plain error which affects substantial rights of the parties." Accordingly, even in the absence of a timely objection, error involving statutorily prohibited judicial comment at trial can now be reviewed on appeal.[41]

Where the trial judge has expressed such an opinion, the error is not eradicated by a statement in the charge that nothing the court had said or done during the trial was intended to suggest which party should prevail in the case.[42] In addition, the Court may never comment upon the failure of the defendant to testify.[43] Likewise, it is improper for the court to disclose to the jury that it has made a pretrial determination that a defendant's statement to the police was voluntary.[44]

"Where . . . a defendant contends that he did not participate in a crime, but there is no assertion that the crime did not occur, a trial court's assumption that a crime has occurred does not violate the prohibition . . . against an expression of opinion by the trial court."[45] Likewise, a trial court's reference to the complaining witnesses in a criminal proceeding as "victims" did not amount to an improper expression of the guilt of the accused as proscribed by O.C.G.A. § 17-8-57 since that statute only prohibits comments that suggest to the jury what the court believes the evidence to be.[46]

---

[40]Ledford v. State, 289 Ga. 70, 709 S.E.2d 239 (2011). See Rouse v. State, 296 Ga. 213, 765 S.E.2d 879 (2014) (majority decision that remark by trial judge during voir dire that murder happened in Muscogee County was improper and reversal was required drew sharp dissent).

[41]See Willis v. State, 304 Ga. 122, 816 S.E.2d 656 (2018); Quiller v. State, 338 Ga. App. 206, 789 S.E.2d 391 (2016)

(O.C.G.A. § 17-8-57(b) is retroactive).

[42]Brundage v. State, 143 Ga. App. 1, 2, 237 S.E.2d 473 (1977).

[43]Scott v. State, 233 Ga. 815, 213 S.E.2d 676 (1975).

[44]Chumley v. State, 282 Ga. 855 (2), 655 S.E.2d 813 (2008).

[45]Victorine v. State, 264 Ga. 580, 581 (3), 449 S.E.2d 91 (1994).

[46]Morris v. State, 280 Ga. 179(2),

In *Brimidge v. State*,[47] the Court of Appeals set out a three part test for determining the propriety of a judicial comment on the evidence in a case. The comment should be examined to determine whether: (1) the trial court's comment issued from contested evidence; (2) more than one inference could arise from the evidence; and (3) the court's statement assumed as a fact undisputed, but not admitted, evidence which went to the essential element of guilt or innocence. Because the comment made by the court in *Brimidge* was susceptible to multiple inferences and did assume as fact evidence which went to the heart of guilt or innocence, the trial court's remark was found to be harmful error.

A gratuitous remark by the trial court, most probably by oversight, included in its final charge to the jury can rise to the level of an improper comment by the court on the credibility of a witness. In *Starr v. State*,[48] the court included in its final charge an almost literal recitation of the child hearsay statute and included the language "and the court finds the circumstances of the statement provides [sic] sufficient indicia of reliability." The Court of Appeals concluded that the charge as given, represented an opinion by the Court as to what had been proved at trial.

Remarks made by a "judge assigning a reason for his ruling" are not normally regarded as an expression of opinion nor as a comment on the evidence.[49] Likewise, a statement by the trial judge as to what the adverse parties contend is not a statement of opinion by the court.[50]

O.C.G.A. § 17-8-75 provides: [w]here counsel in the hearing of the jury make statements of prejudicial matters which are not in evidence, it is the duty of the court to interpose and prevent the

---

626 S.E.2d 123 (2006). See Linson v. State, 287 Ga. 881 (2), 700 S.E.2d 394 (2010) (comments by trial judge that state may not use all of its witnesses if it feels they are not necessary and that court directed a verdict in favor of co-defendant did not constitute impermissible comment on the evidence).

[47]Brimidge v. State, 287 Ga. App. 22, 651 S.E.2d 344 (2007). See Callaham v. State, 305 Ga. App. 626, 700 S.E.2d 624 (2010). See Murphy v. State, 290 Ga. 459, 722 S.E.2d 51 (2012) (improper expression of opinion for trial judge to refer to police officer witness as a "good detective").

[48]Starr v. State, 269 Ga. App. 466 (1), 604 S.E.2d 297 (2004) (overruled on other grounds by, Hatley v. State,

290 Ga. 480, 722 S.E.2d 67 (2012)). See Wilson v. State, 325 Ga. App. 859, 755 S.E.2d 253 (2014) (judge's instruction to defense counsel during closing that she should not suggest that police were "lying or covering up" was improper comment on credibility of witnesses and required new trial).

[49]Colsson v. State, 177 Ga. App. 840, 842 (4), 341 S.E.2d 318 (1986) (citing Johnson v. State, 246 Ga. 126, 128 (V), 269 S.E.2d 18 (1980)). See Ridley v. State, 290 Ga. 798, 725 S.E.2d 223 (2012) (no error when court stopped expert from testifying after finding witness lacked necessary expertise).

[50]Harper v. State, 213 Ga. App. 444, 447 (3), 445 S.E.2d 303 (1994).

same. On objection made, the court shall also rebuke the counsel and by all needful and proper instructions to the jury endeavor to remove the improper impression from their minds; or, in his discretion, he may order a mistrial if the prosecuting attorney is the offender.[51]

In *Lassic v. State,*[52] the trial judge sua sponte dismissed the jury during closing argument and rebuked counsel out of their presence for misstating the evidence. When the jury was brought back, the court instructed them as to why they had been sent out of court, including the fact that counsel had been rebuked for misstating the evidence, and reminded them that it was their obligation to find the facts as they recalled the evidence from the trial. The Supreme Court found that this did not constitute improper comment and was consistent with the trial judge's duties under O.C.G.A. § 17-8-75.

The trial judge may determine where the district attorney and where the defense counsel will sit in the courtroom.[53]

In *Hill v. State,*[54] the court held that the trial judge "retains the discretion to determine how late to hold court before recessing for the evening."

In *Strickland v. State,*[55] the trial judge became ill after one day of trial. By agreement of the district attorney, defense counsel and the defendant, it was agreed that another judge would serve until the conclusion of the trial. After conviction no evidence was presented in aggravation or mitigation, and the judge completing the trial agreed to impose sentence on a specified date. On that date the original judge imposed sentence. On appeal the sentence was set aside. In *Noble v. State,*[56] a different judge pronounced sentence from the judge who presided over the trial. At the sentencing hearing the defendant did not object to the "new" judge taking over the case. The appellate court held that the defendant's failure to object waived his right to do so. In *Speed v. State,*[57] the Supreme Court found no error where one judge conducted the trial, but because of illness of a member of his fam-

---

[51]See e.g., Arrington v. State, 286 Ga. 335, 687 S.E.2d 438 (2009). See O'Neal v. State, 288 Ga. 219, 702 S.E.2d 288 (2010) (trial court has an "independent" duty on objection to improper statements made in closing by state to rebuke prosecutor and give curative instruction or declare mistrial).

[52]Lassic v. State, 278 Ga. 701 (2), 606 S.E.2d 266 (2004).

[53]Bryan v. State, 148 Ga. App. 428 (1), 251 S.E.2d 338 (1978).

[54]Hill v. State, 263 Ga. 37, 38 (1)(b), 427 S.E.2d 770 (1993).

[55]Strickland v. State, 156 Ga. App. 475, 476, 274 S.E.2d 823 (1980).

[56]Noble v. State, 220 Ga. App. 155, 157 (2), 469 S.E.2d 307 (1996).

[57]Speed v. State, 270 Ga. 688, 698 (43), 512 S.E.2d 896 (1999). All the facts set out above do not appear in the opinion of the case, but they appear on pages 1526 and 1527 of the record.

ily, another judge actually charged the jury giving the charge of the original judge. Rule 25 of the Federal Rules of Criminal Procedure provides for a substitution of judges during a trial in the event of death, illness, or other disability.[58] The rule provides that the substitute judge must first certify that he has read the transcript of the trial. In the absence of such a rule or statutory provision, it seems that there can be no substitution of judges, over objection, during the trial of a criminal case.[59]

In *Potts v. Zant*,[60] the court held that where a judge retires before ruling on an assigned death penalty habeas corpus case, the case should be returned to the president of the Council of Superior Court Judges for reassignment.

Overcrowded courts often require the assistance of judges from outside their own circuit. The order appointing such judges must be specific. O.C.G.A. § 15-1-9.1(f) requires that the order identify "the court in need of assistance, the county where located, the time period covered, the specific case or cases for which assistance is sought if applicable, and the reason that assistance is needed." If the order is not in proper form, the appointed judge is without authority and any other action taken by the judge is void.[61]

See § 14:77, supra, on motion to recuse or disqualify a judge and § 24:20, infra, on communications between court and jury during deliberations. See Annotation, "Substitution of Judge in State Criminal Trial," 45 A.L.R.5th 591 (1997).

§ 17:6   The district attorney

The district attorney or solicitor is a representative of the executive branch of government. He serves as a link between law

---

[58]In United States v. Sisk, 629 F.2d 1174, 1179 (6th Cir. 1980), the court concluded that under the Federal Rules, the substitute judge could not sit in appellate review of the prior actions of his predecessor.

[59]See Annot., "Substitution of Judge in Criminal Case," 83 A.L.R.2d 1032 (1962); A.B.A. Standards, Trial by Jury, Vol. III, Standard 15-3.3.

[60]Potts v. Zant, 263 Ga. 634, 636, 437 S.E.2d 325 (1993). At a minimum, it is bad form for a judge to simply leave the bench during any stage of a trial even for a brief period rather than simply calling a recess. Should the judge leave the bench during a critical stage of a trial and the judge's absence results in structured error, the Supreme Court has stated that it "will not hesitate" to reverse a conviction coming out of such a trial. Berry v. State, 282 Ga. 376(4), 651 S.E.2d 1 (2007).

[61]State v. Kelley, 302 Ga. App. 850, 691 S.E.2d 890 (2010). O.C.G.A. § 15-1-9.1(f) applies only to *inter*-county requests and not to *intra*-county requests. An intra-county request for assistance such as the temporary appointment of a magistrate to act as a superior court judge requires nothing more than the request and appointment by the chief judge of the circuit. O.C.G.A. § 15-1-9.1(b)(2). See Lewis v. McDougal, 276 Ga. 861, 583 S.E.2d 859 (2003).

enforcement officers and the trial of cases. He has the duty to see that the law is enforced, but this duty is to seek justice and not merely to convict.[1] See § 7:12, supra, where one assistant district attorney in an office is disqualified. Of course, he is bound by the ethics of the legal profession.[2] In *Jackson v. Wainwright,*[3] the Fifth Circuit stated: "A weakness in the adversary system of administering justice is the possibility of unfairness arising (sometimes) from the prosecution's superior resources and special access to information and witnesses. To protect the innocent who might suffer from this unequal contest, Canon 5 of the American Bar Association Canons of Professional Ethics commands: 'The primary duty of a lawyer engaged in public prosecution is not to convict, but to see that justice is done. [4] "As an officer of the court, the . . . district attorney has an obligation to ensure that proceedings are conducted in accordance with the rules of evidence and the laws of this state."[5] The suppression of facts or the secreting of witnesses capable of establishing the innocence of the accused is highly reprehensible.' So also commands the due process clause of the Constitution."

The district attorney necessarily has discretion in which cases are to be tried.[6] For example, this discretion is demonstrated in the non-criminal disposition of some cases and in his action in connection with the placing of a case on the dead docket or a

---

[Section 17:6]

[1] See Annot., "Failure of State Prosecutor to Disclose Exculpatory Photographic Evidence as Violating Due Process," 93 A.L.R.5th 527 (2001); Annot., "Failure of State Prosecutor to Disclose Fingerprint Evidence as Violating Due Process," 94 A.L.R.5th 393 (2001); Annot., "Failure of State Prosecutor to Disclose Exculpatory Ballistic Evidence as Violating Due Process," 95 A.L.R.5th 611 (2002); Annot., "Failure of State Prosecutor to Disclose Exculpatory Medical Reports and Tests as Violating Due Process," 101 A.L.R.5th 187 (2002); and Annot, "Failure of State Prosecutor to Disclose Pretrial Statements made by Crime Victim as Violating Due Process," 102 A.L.R.5th 327 (2004). Carr v. State, 267 Ga. 701, 710 (10), 482 S.E.2d 314 (1997), overruled on other grounds by, 270 Ga. 151, 510 S.E.2d 802 (1998).

[2] See A.B.A. Standards, The Prosecution Function, Vol. I, Standard 3-1.1(d).

[3] Jackson v. Wainwright, 390 F.2d 288, 294-95 (5th Cir. 1968). Cf. Thompson v. State, 163 Ga. App. 35, 36 (4), 292 S.E.2d 470 (1982).

[4] Cf. Johnson v. State, 258 Ga. 506, 508 (4)(a), 371 S.E.2d 396 (1988).

[5] McAlister v. State, 204 Ga. App. 259, 260 (1), 419 S.E.2d 64 (1992).

[6] State v. Rish, 222 Ga. App. 729, 731 (1), 476 S.E.2d 50 (1996). But see Annot., "What Constitutes Such Discriminatory Prosecution or Enforcement of Laws as to Provide Valid Defense in State Criminal Proceedings," 95 A.L.R.3d 280 (1979); and Annot., "What Constitutes Such Discriminatory Prosecution or Enforcement of Laws as to Provide Valid Defense in Federal Criminal Proceedings," 45 A.L.R.Fed. 732 (1979). See § 21:28, infra, on selective prosecution.

nolle prosequi, or in dismissal prior to indictment.[7] But see § 17:15, infra, on requirements for calendar preparation. However, his discretion in the prosecution of a criminal case starts long before the steps in a criminal prosecution mentioned before and continues to some extent even after a defendant is sentenced. However, there are limitations placed on the authority. For example, Georgia provides no statutory authority to the prosecutor to dismiss criminal charges before indictment.[8] Also, a nolle prosequi cannot be entered without the consent of the trial judge.[9]

In *Walker v. State*,[10] the court held that the prosecuting attorney "is under a duty to reveal any understanding or agreement with a witness concerning criminal charges pending against that witness. . . . This duty extends to even informal agreements . . . and . . . regardless of how non-promising the agreement was in terms of its prospects for the witness."

The district attorney may not knowingly permit perjurious testimony of a state's witness to go uncorrected,[11] and this seems to be particularly true where the district attorney has made a promise of leniency to a prosecution witness which is denied by the witness while testifying.[12] In *Kitchens v. State*,[13] the court held that the district attorney is charged with the knowledge of perjured testimony if it is shown that police officers, acting on behalf of the state and in connection with the prosecution, had knowledge of the perjured character of the testimony given by a witness for the state. In *Williams v. State*,[14] the court pointed out that "a conviction obtained by the knowing use of perjured testimony is fundamentally unfair, and must be set aside if there is any reasonable likelihood that the false testimony could have

---

[7]State v. Hanson, 249 Ga. 739, 744, 295 S.E.2d 297 (1982). Cf. Noeske v. State, 181 Ga. App. 778, 779 (1), 353 S.E.2d 635 (1987). In State v. Perry, 261 Ga. App. 886, 583 S.E.2d 909 (2003), the court of appeals held that it was an abuse of the court's discretion to dismiss a case *sua sponte* over the state's objection.

[8]State v. Hanson, 249 Ga. 739, 743 (2), 295 S.E.2d 297 (1982).

[9]Williams v. State, 126 Ga. App. 302 (1), 190 S.E.2d 807 (1972).

[10]Walker v. State, 214 Ga. App. 691, 693 (2), 448 S.E.2d 924 (1994).

[11]Miller v. Pate, 386 U.S. 1, 87 S.Ct. 785, 17 L.Ed.2d 690 (1967).

[12]Allen v. State, 128 Ga. App. 361, 196 S.E.2d 660 (1973) (citing Giglio v. United States, 405 U.S. 150, 92 S.Ct. 763, 31 L.Ed.2d 104 (1972)).

[13]Kitchens v. State, 160 Ga. App. 492 (1), 287 S.E.2d 316 (1981). See § 14:34, supra, on *Brady* motions.

However, if the defense knows that testimony is perjured and he does nothing to bring it to the attention of the court or jury, this may amount to a waiver of his denial of due process claim. Kitchens v. State, 160 Ga. App. 492, 493 (2), 287 S.E.2d 316 (1981) (citing Evans v. United States, 408 F.2d 369 (7th Cir. 1969)).

[14]Williams v. State, 250 Ga. 463, 465, 298 S.E.2d 492 (1983) (quoted in Varnadoe v. State, 227 Ga. App. 663, 666, 490 S.E.2d 517 (1997)).

affected the judgment of the jury." However, in *Arnold v. State*,[15] the court held that where a prosecution witness testifies untruthfully about a material matter and the district attorney does not knowingly use the perjured testimony, this does not automatically prevent the conviction from standing.

A prosecutor must be careful to avoid "the appearance or reality of a conflict of interest."[16] Thus, it was held that where the district attorney had formerly represented the victim of an aggravated assault in a divorce case between the victim and the defendant, the district attorney is disqualified from prosecuting the case.[17] This has long been recognized as the public policy of Georgia.[18] It has been said that this rule is intended to prevent a district attorney with a personal interest in a case from working with the grand jury which will be considering the case.[19] A decision by a prosecuting attorney to recuse his or her office from a case because of a conflict of interest is not subject to objection by the defendant.[20]

In *Billings v. State*,[21] the court pointed out that "[i]t would clearly be improper for an attorney to change roles from the prosecution to the defense (and vice versa) in the same case." However, the court held that it was not error for the trial judge to deny the defendant's motion to disqualify the district attorney's office from prosecuting the case inasmuch as an assistant district attorney, who did not participate in the prosecution of the case directly or indirectly while in the public defender's office, had represented the co-defendant in negotiating his plea.

As a general proposition, the court will not inquire into a prosecutor's election to seek the death penalty. "A prosecutor's discretion in seeking a death sentence is limited by statute. See O.C.G.A. § 17-10-30. The prosecutor's discretion is also 'limited by the jury's ultimate decision' and the 'strength of the evidence' in any given case." Accordingly, a challenge to a prosecutor's decision to seek the death penalty must be predicated upon "a prima

---

[15]Arnold v. State, 163 Ga. App. 10, 11 (1)(b), 293 S.E.2d 501 (1982).

[16]A.B.A. Standards, The Prosecution Function, Vol. I, Standard 3-1.2. However, in Chafin v. State, 246 Ga. 709, 712 (2), 273 S.E.2d 147 (1980), the court held that it was not error for the trial judge to refuse to disqualify an assistant district attorney who had been a law assistant for another judge of the circuit while another defendant was tried for the same crime with which the defendant was to be tried.

[17]Davenport v. State, 157 Ga. App.

704, 704-706, 278 S.E.2d 440 (1981). Cf. State v. Tippecanoe County Court, 432 N.E.2d 1377 (Ind.1982).

[18]Gaulden v. State, 11 Ga. 47 (1852).

[19]Brown v. State, 145 Ga. App. 530, 244 S.E.2d 68 (1978), judgment rev'd on other grounds, 242 Ga. 536, 250 S.E.2d 438 (1978).

[20]State v. Mantooth, 337 Ga. App. 698, 788 S.E.2d 584 (2016).

[21]Billings v. State, 212 Ga. App. 125, 129 (4), 441 S.E.2d 262 (1994).

facie case of unconstitutional conduct with respect to his or her case."[22]

See § 7:11, supra, on conflicts of interest. See Annotation, "Disqualification of Prosecuting Attorney in State Criminal Cases on Account of Relationship with Accused," 42 A.L.R.581 (1996).

A district attorney has authority to employ assistants as well as "Special Assistant District Attorneys" for the handling of a particular case. The district attorney may appoint one or more of the employees or members of the Criminal Justice Council, and it is not necessary that the district attorney be physically present when such special assistants exercise the authority they have been given.[23] Assistant district attorneys serve at the pleasure of the district attorney.[24]

When the district attorney is unable to perform his or her duties due to reasons of absence or health, the Chief Assistant in the office shall assume those duties until the district attorney is able to do so, pursuant to O.C.G.A. § 15-18-15. There are cases, however, when the elected district attorney may be completely disqualified from a case.[25] Such is the case when the district attorney is a "necessary witness" for the prosecution, that is, the district attorney's testimony is substantive and not merely technical, e.g., as a custodian of records. In that event, the assistant prosecutors in that office will be disqualified as well. O.C.G.A. § 15-18-5(a) provides:

> When a district attorney's office is disqualified from interest or relationship to engage in a prosecution, the district attorney shall notify the Attorney General of the disqualification. Upon receipt of such notification, the Attorney General shall:
> 1. Request the services of and thereafter appoint a district attorney, a solicitor-general, or a retired prosecuting attorney . . .
> 2. Designate an attorney from the Department of Law; or
> 3. Appoint a competent attorney to act as district attorney pro tempore in place of the district attorney.

A district attorney has a very limited role, if any, in a habeas corpus or other civil action. The state attorney general has been appointed to represent the state where a person has been convicted and is in custody of the Department of Corrections. If "the prisoner is held under some authority other than the DOC, the district attorney of the circuit in which the petitioner is being detained, not the circuit where he was convicted, must defend the

---

[22]Wagner v. State, 282 Ga. 149, 152, 646 S.E.2d 676 (2007); Jenkins v. State, 269 Ga. 282 (2), 498 S.E.2d 502 (1998).

[23]State v. Cook, 172 Ga. App. 433, 440, 323 S.E.2d 634 (1984).

[24]Clark v. Head, 272 Ga. 104 (1), 526 S.E.2d 859 (2000).

[25]See McLaughlin v. Payne, 295 Ga. 609, 761 S.E.2d 289 (2014).

state's interest."[26]

In 1998, Congress enacted a "Citizens Protection Act" for federal prosecutors, which provides that "[a]n attorney for the Government shall be subject to State laws and rules, and local Federal court rules, governing attorneys. . . ."[27]

On prosecutorial vindictiveness, see §§ 14:58 and 15:3, supra. See Studdard, *Daniel's, Georgia Handbook on Criminal Evidence* (2018 ed.), § 6:10, on perjury.

§ 17:7 The defendant—General

The defendant has a right to appear at trial dressed in civilian clothing rather than prison garb.[1] Forcing a defendant to wear prison clothing in court is a denial of his presumption of innocence[2] and violation of the due process clause of the Fourteenth Amendment.[3] However, if the defendant does not object to wearing prison garb or move for a continuance until he can be supplied proper civilian clothing, his action amounts to a waiver of his right[4] and a negation of the presence of unconstitutional compulsion.[5] In *Slade v. State*,[6] the court held that the failure to obtain a ruling on a pre-trial motion to have the defendant wear civilian clothing until the defendant appears before the potential jurors in prison uniform amounts to a waiver of his right. The situation is said to be different when a person is tried for escape,

---

[26]Wiggins v. Lemley, 256 Ga. 152, 345 S.E.2d 584 (1986).

[27]28 U.S.C.A. § 530B(a).

[Section 17:7]

[1]Johnson v. State, 243 Ga. App. 891, 892 (1), 534 S.E.2d 563 (2000). Accord, Sharpe v. State, 119 Ga. App. 222 (1), 166 S.E.2d 645 (1969). See 21A Am. Jur. 2d Criminal Law § 1011, Trial of Accused in Prison Clothing (2004). See Annot., "Propriety and Prejudicial Effect of Compelling Accused to Wear Prison Clothing at Jury Trial—Federal Cases," 26 A.L.R.Fed. 535 (1976).

[2]Hernandez v. Beto, 443 F.2d 634 (5th Cir. 1971). However, in Whittington v. State, 155 Ga. App. 667, 272 S.E.2d 532 (1980), the court held that the defendant had not been prejudiced where he was tried in blue jeans and a tan shirt issued by the sheriff where there were no markings on the clothing.

[3]Sharpe v. State, 119 Ga. App. 222 (1), 166 S.E.2d 645 (1969). However, in Hayslip v. State, 154 Ga. App. 835, 270 S.E.2d 61 (1980), the court held that the overruling of defendant's motion to be tried in his own clothing was harmless error where he was tried in blue coveralls (issued him by the sheriff) which "bore no numbers or other marks commonly associated with prison uniforms." See Pike v. State, 169 Ga. App. 358, 312 S.E.2d 808 (1983), rev'd, 253 Ga. 304, 320 S.E.2d 355 (1984).

[4]Sharpe v. State, 119 Ga. App. 222, 166 S.E.2d 645 (1969); Spurlin v. State, 228 Ga. 763, 765 (4), 187 S.E.2d 856 (1972); Wilkes v. State, 221 Ga. App. 390, 392 (2), 471 S.E.2d 332 (1996).

[5]Estelle v. Williams, 425 U.S. 501, 96 S.Ct. 1691, 48 L.Ed.2d 126 (1976).

[6]Slade v. State, 267 Ga. 868, 869 (3), 485 S.E.2d 726 (1997).

and in this situation no harm is said to result if he wears prison clothing at his trial.[7] In *Culbertson v. State*,[8] the court held that the defendant is not entitled to a reversal for wearing prison clothes if evidence is introduced at trial that the defendant was a prisoner.

In *Choi v. State*,[9] the Georgia Supreme Court held that a defendant has no absolute right to appear in prison clothing, and it was not an abuse of discretion for the trial judge to direct the defendant to wear civilian clothes.

"[W]hile in the presence of the jury . . . [the accused] should be free of indicia of guilt. . . ."[10] Generally, both at common law and under Georgia case law, a defendant has the right to appear in court free from shackles, bonds, and handcuffs. This right is an integral part of a fair and impartial trial[11] and extends to the penalty phase of a capital case.[12] However, in the sound discretion of the trial judge, in extreme situations a defendant may be required to wear shackles to prevent disruptive conduct or to insure the safety of those in the courtroom[13] or perhaps to prevent his escape.[14] In *Weldon v. State*,[15] the court emphasized the importance of the trial judge discussing the situation out of the presence of the jury. Before a trial court requires a criminal defendant to wear an electronic shock device as a security mea-

---

[7]Ingram v. State, 237 Ga. 613, 229 S.E.2d 416 (1976).

[8]Culbertson v. State, 193 Ga. App. 9 (1), 386 S.E.2d 894 (1989).

[9]Choi v. State, 269 Ga. 376, 378 (4), 497 S.E.2d 563 (1998).

[10]Allen v. State, 248 Ga. App. 79, 81 (2), 545 S.E.2d 629 (2001).

[11]McKenzey v. State, 138 Ga. App. 88, 89 (1)(b), 225 S.E.2d 512 (1976).

[12]Deck v. Missouri, 544 U.S. 622, 125 S. Ct. 2007, 161 L. Ed. 2d 953 (2005).

[13]Corbin v. State, 240 Ga. App. 788 (1), 525 S.E.2d 365 (1999); Collins v. State, 164 Ga. App. 482, 484 (4), 297 S.E.2d 503 (1982); Zygadlo v. Wainwright, 720 F.2d 1221, 1223 (11th Cir. 1983); Dennis v. State, 170 Ga. App. 630, 631 (3), 317 S.E.2d 874 (1984); Pace v. State, 212 Ga. App. 489, 442 S.E.2d 307 (1994).

A.B.A. Special Functions of the Trial Judge, "**Standard 6-3.8. The Disruptive Defendant**" provides:

A defendant may be removed from the courtroom during trial when the defendant's conduct is so disruptive that the trial cannot proceed in an orderly manner. Removal is preferable to gagging or shackling the disruptive defendant. The removed defendant ordinarily should be required to be present in the court building while the trial is in progress. The removed defendant should be afforded an opportunity to hear the proceedings and, at appropriate intervals, be offered on the record an opportunity to return to the courtroom upon assurance of good behavior. The offer to return need not be repeated in open court each time. A removed defendant who does not hear the proceedings should be given the opportunity to learn of the proceedings from defense counsel at reasonable intervals.

[14]Thomas v. State, 171 Ga. App. 306, 308 (4), 319 S.E.2d 511 (1984); Hicks v. State, 256 Ga. 715, 719 (9), 352 S.E.2d 762 (1987).

[15]Weldon v. State, 247 Ga. App. 17, 19 (1), 543 S.E.2d 56 (2000).

sure in the courtroom, "the court must: (1) explain why such an extraordinary security measure is needed to protect the safety and decorum of the proceeding and those participating in it; (2) consider alternative ways to address that need; (3) ensure that the defendant is aware of the operation of the device and, in particular, what conduct by him may lead to a shock; and (4) provide an opportunity for the defendant to address these matters and present any other concerns about use of the shock device."[16] In *Mapp v. State,*[17] *the court said that even if the trial judge determines that a defendant must be shackled during a trial, it may be the duty of the trial judge to give curative instructions when the jury sees the defendant shackled. In* Hicks v. State,[18] the court held that when the defendant is shackled during trial, the trial judge "must instruct the jury that the use of physical restraints on the defendant has no bearing on the defendant's guilt or innocence and should not be considered by them during their deliberations." However, in the absence of a request by the defendant to instruct the jury that the use of restraints should not be considered in assessing guilt or innocence, failure to do so is not reversible error.[19] Most of the decisions in Georgia, however, have failed to find reversible error where a defendant, while handcuffed, is seen on an occasion by a juror or jurors.[20] It has been pointed out that where some jurors see the defendant wearing handcuffs, it is proper for the trial judge to give defense counsel an opportunity to question the jurors on whether or not seeing the defendant in handcuffs would cause any bias, prejudice, or leaning in the case, or prevent the defendant from receiving a fair trial. However, the failure of defense counsel to take

---

[16]Weldon v. State, 297 Ga. 537, 775 S.E.2d 522 (2015) (Nahmias, J. concurring). See Nance v. State, 280 Ga. 125, 126-127, 623 S.E.2d 470 (2005).

[17]Mapp v. State, 197 Ga. App. 7, 8, 397 S.E.2d 476 (1990).

[18]Hicks v. State, 200 Ga. App. 602, 604, 409 S.E.2d 82 (1991). See Kitchen v. State, 263 Ga. 629, 436 S.E.2d 645 (1993), concurring opinion of Justice Sears-Collins, and 3 A.B.A. Standards of Criminal Justice, § 15-3.1(c) (2d Ed., 1980).

[19]Pace v. State, 212 Ga. App. 489, 490, 442 S.E.2d 307 (1994).

[20]Haden v. State, 176 Ga. 304, 308 (6), 168 S.E. 272 (1933); Morris v. State, 228 Ga. 39, 40 (18), 184 S.E.2d 82 (1971); Brand v. Wofford, 230 Ga. 750, 752 (6), 199 S.E.2d 231 (1973). In Howard v. State, 144 Ga. App. 208, 212 (8), 240 S.E.2d 908 (1977), some of the jurors had seen the defendant in handcuffs while being taken to the detention room for lunch. After the verdict, each juror was examined by the court. The jurors who had seen the defendant handcuffed testified that this did not influence their verdict. The appellate court affirmed the conviction. Contra, McKenzey v. State, 138 Ga. App. 88, 89 (1)(b), 225 S.E.2d 512 (1976).

In Carter v. State, 155 Ga. App. 840, 841, 273 S.E.2d 417 (1980), the court held that the mere fact that prospective jurors had seen the defendant brought to court in handcuffs does not require the automatic grant of a challenge to the array or motion for a mistrial.

advantage of such an offer would normally seem to amount to a waiver.[21]

"[A] defendant has a right to be tried in an atmosphere free of partiality created by the use of excessive guards except where special circumstances [exist], which in the discretion of the trial judge, dictate added security precautions."[22]

In *Young v. State*,[23] the defendant's conviction was affirmed where the defendant "was equipped with a 'RACC belt,' an electronic security device worn under clothing and activated by a remote transmitter which enables law enforcement personnel to administer an electric shock to control courtroom behavior" because the defendant had been guilty of disruptive behavior and the trial court agreed that the circumstances dictated additional security precautions.

In *Gentry v. State*,[24] the defendant attacked the prosecutor during the course of the trial. His motion for a mistrial was denied. In affirming, the appellate court held that the defendant's actions did not prevent him from receiving a fair trial and pointed out that "[t]o hold otherwise would encourage defendants to engage in tactical courtroom outbursts."

---

[21]Smith v. State, 267 Ga. 502, 480 S.E.2d 838 (1997). Cf. Darling v. State, 248 Ga. 485, 487, 284 S.E.2d 260 (1981).

[22]McKenzey v. State, 138 Ga. App. 88, 89 (1)(b), 225 S.E.2d 512 (1976) (quoting Allen v. State, 235 Ga. 709, 711, 221 S.E.2d 405 (1975)). Accord, Holbrook v. Flynn, 475 U.S. 560, 106 S.Ct. 1340, 89 L.Ed.2d 525 (1986). *Holbrook* seems to suggest that the use of extra guards as a regular practice would not be unconstitutional, unless done in such an outrageous manner as to prevent fair trial. Cf. Rose v. State, 177 Ga. App. 55, 56 (2), 338 S.E.2d 510 (1985); Young v. State, 269 Ga. 478 (2), 499 S.E.2d 60 (1998).

[23]Young v. State, 269 Ga. 478, 499 S.E.2d 60 (1998). Citing *Young*, the court in Stanford v. State, 272 Ga. 267, 528 S.E.2d 246 (2000), held that since the stun belt was shielded from the jury's view and the defendant was not "prejudiced by it in any way," the use of the stun belt was permissible. Compare United States v. Durham, 287 F.3d 1297 (11th Cir. 2002) where the 11th Circuit expressed serious concern

regarding the use of such restraints and the extent to which they may impair a defendant's ability to assist in his own defense. Citing *Durham*, the Georgia Court of Appeals in Scieszka v. State, 259 Ga. App. 486 (1), 578 S.E.2d 149 (2003), suggested that it might be the better practice in jurisdictions where restraints of some sort are employed in the courtroom as a matter of policy in cases involving serious offenses, for the court to make specific findings as to why the restraints are necessary should the defendant object. In such cases, the court may consider the gravity of the offense charged as well as the general policy considerations of the defendant's custodian, but factors such as the defendant's propensity for violence or the risk of escape posed by the defendant are more compelling. In Hawkins v. Comparet-Cassani, 33 F.Supp.2d 1244 (C.D. Cal. 1999), the court enjoined the placement of "stun belts" on potentially disruptive defendants during appearances in court.

[24]Gentry v. State, 226 Ga. App. 216, 219 (2), 485 S.E.2d 824 (1997).

In *Dryer v. State*,[25] the court pointed out that "[g]enerally, a statement by defense counsel made in the presence of the defendant relating to the defendant's conduct is considered a statement by the defendant himself if the defendant does not repudiate counsel's authority to make the statement."

Even if a defendant is represented by counsel, the defendant may generally conduct some part or all of the defense.[26] However, it is not error for the trial judge to refuse to let both defense counsel and the defendant question the same witness.[27]

If a defendant elects to testify, he should normally be permitted to testify from the witness stand. However, in the discretion of the trial judge, he may be required to sit at counsel table, if he testifies, and the court feels that this is necessary for security reasons.[28]

The United States Supreme Court has held that even where a competent defendant has been sentenced to death, he may dismiss his petition to have that court review his case if his decision has been made voluntarily and with full knowledge of the consequences.[29]

See § 7:1, supra, on the right of the defendant to have access to his counsel. See § 17:17, infra, on motions for continuance. See § 14:7, supra, and § 19:3, infra, on the use of depositions in criminal cases.

§ 17:8 The defendant—Presence

"A criminal defendant has a right to be present during all portions of his or her trial, and a defendant's absence during a critical stage of those trial proceedings, absent a waiver of the defendant's right to be present, is not subject to harmless error analysis."[1] However, before a defendant's right to be present in court will be deemed to have been violated, it must first appear

---

[25]Dryer v. State, 205 Ga. App. 671, 672 (1), 423 S.E.2d 297 (1992).

[26]Jackson v. State, 149 Ga. App. 496, 499 (1), 254 S.E.2d 739 (1979); Hiatt v. State, 144 Ga. App. 298, 300 (6), 240 S.E.2d 894 (1977).

[27]Johnson v. State, 246 Ga. 126, 127, 269 S.E.2d 18 (1980). Generally, see § 7:3, supra, on the right of a defendant to represent himself.

[28]Lee v. State, 166 Ga. App. 644 (3), 305 S.E.2d 175 (1983).

[29]Hammett v. Texas, 448 U.S. 725, 100 S.Ct. 2905, 65 L.Ed.2d 1086 (1980).

[Section 17:8]

[1]King v. State, 273 Ga. 258, 264 (15), 539 S.E.2d 783 (2000). See Goodrum v. State, 303 Ga. 414, 812 S.E.2d 220 (2018) (proceedings regarding juror's qualifications to serve are a "critical stage" at which defendant is entitled to be present, but presence at in-chambers conference regarding same may be waived absent objection after being informed about juror's removal). Compare Sammons v. State, 279 Ga. 386, 388, 612 S.E.2d 785 (2005). See § 24:19, infra, on communicating with the jury.

that his presence would have contributed to the fairness of the procedure.[2] Thus, the absence of the defendant at routine bench conferences,[3] charge conferences,[4] or any aspect of the case at which the defendant's presence would not as a practical matter thwart the fundamental fairness of the proceeding will not infringe on the right of the defendant to be present at every critical stage of the case.[5]

Not only does a defendant have a right to be in court dressed in civilian clothing and free from restraint,[6] but he may be present at all times during the course of the trial.[7] But it has been said that "[s]o far as the Fourteenth Amendment is concerned, the presence of a defendant is a condition of due process to the extent that a fair and just hearing would be thwarted by his absence, and to that extent only."[8] However, where motions are argued in the defendant's presence and the trial judge takes

---

[2]Huff v. State, 274 Ga. 110, 549 S.E.2d 370 (2001). See Lyde v. State, 311 Ga. App. 512, 716 S.E.2d 572 (2011) (legal argument discussed outside presence of defendant is not one in which defendant's rights to fair trial are at risk).

[3]Parks v. State, 275 Ga. 320, 565 S.E.2d 447 (2002). See Leeks v. State, 296 Ga. 515, 769 S.E.2d 296 (2015). Cf. Phillips v. Harmon, 297 Ga. 386, 774 S.E.2d 596 (2015) (structural error for court to respond to a jury note without notifying counsel).

[4]Huff v. State, 274 Ga. 110, 549 S.E.2d 370 (2001). See Murphy v. State, 299 Ga. 238, 241 (2), 787 S.E.2d 721 (2016) (defendant does have right to be present unless waived at bench conferences wherein jury strikes are discussed).

[5]See Goodrum v. State, 303 Ga. 414, 812 S.E.2d 220 (2018) (presence of defendant not required for in-chambers conference regarding a juror's qualifications to serve).

[6]Of course, if there are threats on the life of those participating in the trial, the court may provide reasonable security precaution, including, for example, having the defendant brought into court in handcuffs and searching all who enter the courtroom for weapons. Allen v. State, 235 Ga. 709, 711, 221 S.E.2d 405 (1975).

See Annot., "Disruptive Conduct of Accused in Presence of Jury as Ground for Mistrial or Discharge of Jury," 89 A.L.R.3d 960 (1979), 5 Am. Jur. 2d Appellate Review § 731, Requiring Accused to Stand Trial in Prison Clothes or In Shackles (2004); and Annot., "Restraining Accused: Propriety and Prejudicial Effect of Gagging, Shackling or Otherwise Physically Restraining Accused During Course of State Criminal Trial," 90 A.L.R.3d 17 (1979).

[7]In Palmer v. State, 155 Ga. App. 368, 271 S.E.2d 24 (1980), the conviction was reversed where the jury, pursuant to the defendant's request, was permitted to view a truck but the trial judge stated "No lawyers, no witnesses, no parties are to go with the jury." Defense counsel's request to go with the jury was denied. The decision reviewed a number of cases involving the right of a defendant to be present at such an inspection and pointed out that even defense counsel cannot waive the right of the defendant to be present "at every stage of the trial" unless the defendant has expressly authorized his counsel to waive the defendant's presence.

[8]Riley v. State, 180 Ga. App. 409, 411, 349 S.E.2d 274 (1986) (quoting Snyder v. Massachusetts, 291 U.S. 97, 108, 54 S.Ct. 330, 78 L.Ed. 674 (1934)).

them under advisement, the defendant has no right to be present when the judge signs the order.[9] Generally, the defendant has the right to be seated at the defense table with his counsel.[10] A defendant's Sixth Amendment right[11] to be present at trial extends to nearly all trial proceedings from arraignment to acquittal or sentencing.[12] In *Fisher v. Roe,*[13] the Ninth Circuit held that the defendant's right to be present was violated when the court ordered a "read back" and conducted it without notice to the defense. However, in *Keen v. State,*[14] the court concluded that the right of the defendant to be present was not violated where his counsel, with the defendant's knowledge, went to the judge's chambers before the trial began to ask for a continuance. Likewise, colloquy among state counsel, defense counsel, and court prior to trial about the defendant's request for production of documents and pictures was found not to be a "critical stage of the proceedings" entitling him to be present.[15] In *Williams v. State,*[16] the court held that the defendant's right to be present can be waived if defendant's counsel in his presence or with the defendant's express authority waives the defendant's presence or if the accused subsequently acquiesces to the waiver made by counsel. In *Lonchar v. State,*[17] the court held that a defendant may waive his right to be present even in a death penalty case.

If a defendant does not speak English, he has a right to have an interpreter.[18] Mere physical presence is not enough. The defendant must know what is going on and have an opportunity

---

[9]Pfeiffer v. State, 173 Ga. App. 374, 375 (4), 326 S.E.2d 562 (1985).

[10]Young v. Callahan, 700 F.2d 32 (1st Cir. 1983).

[11]People v. Parker, 57 N.Y.2d 136, 454 N.Y.S.2d 967, 440 N.E.2d 1313 (1982). However, the right may be lost if the defendant conducts himself in a disruptive manner, and as an alternative to exclusion under this circumstance, the defendant may be bound and gagged. Illinois v. Allen, 397 U.S. 337, 90 S.Ct. 1057, 25 L.Ed.2d 353 (1970). See Rogers v. Hall, 567 Fed. Appx. 873 (11th Cir. 2014).

[12]See Ward v. State, 288 Ga. 641 (4), 706 S.E.2d 430 (2011) (reversible error for court to excuse juror out of presence of defendant in the absence of waiver); Johnson v. State, 136 Ga. App. 719, 222 S.E.2d 181 (1975) (a defendant has a right to be present when evidence is discussed by judge with lawyers).

[13]Fisher v. Roe, 263 F.3d 906 (9th Cir. 2001), overruled on other grounds by Payton v. Woodford, 346 F.3d 1204 (9th Cir. 2003).

[14]Keen v. State, 164 Ga. App. 81, 85 (3), 296 S.E.2d 91 (1982).

[15]Stone v. State, 177 Ga. App. 750 (1), 341 S.E.2d 280 (1986).

[16]Williams v. State, 251 Ga. 749, 798, 312 S.E.2d 40 (1983). Accord, Brooks v. State, 271 Ga. 456, 457 (2), 519 S.E.2d 907 (1999). Cf. Pennie v. State, 271 Ga. 419, 421 (2), 520 S.E.2d 448 (1999).

[17]Lonchar v. State, 258 Ga. 447, 452, 369 S.E.2d 749 (1988).

[18]Drope v. Missouri, 420 U.S. 162, 95 S. Ct. 896, 43 L. Ed. 2d 103 (1975). See Ling v. State, 288 Ga. 299, 702 S.E.2d 881 (2010) (trial court must make findings on the record when it denies request for interpreters). See also Georgia Uniform Superior Court Rule 7.3; see also Rules for Use of

to meaningfully participate in the trial.[19] However, the use and extent to which an interpreter is used "must necessarily lie within the sound discretion of the trial judge."[20] Thus, in *Hersi v. State*,[21] the Court of Appeals found no error in the failure of the trial court to appoint an official interpreter in a case where the defendant had a working knowledge of the English language and his brother, who was fluent in English as well as his native Somali, was allowed to sit at counsel table and assist in the translation. See Studdard, *Daniel's Georgia Handbook on Criminal Evidence* (2018 ed.), § 6:6, on interpreters.

In *Bishop v. State*,[22] the court stated that a "defendant has the privilege under the Fourteenth Amendment to be present . . . whenever his presence has a relation, reasonably substantial, to the fullness of his opportunity to defend against the charge. . . ." Accordingly, the law requires that all communications between the trial judge and the jury take place in open court and in the presence of the defendant.[23] But under the Fourteenth Amendment a defendant has no right to be present "when presence would be useless, or the benefit but a shadow. . . ." Thus, in *Smith v. State*,[24] the court held that the presence of the defendant was not essential at the time of considering a demand for a copy of the indictment, list of witnesses, a motion for discovery of the defendant's in-custody statement, or a motion for full reconciliation and further held any error harmless beyond a reasonable doubt in light of the overwhelming evidence of the defendant's guilt. Likewise, a defendant has no right to be present for "a conference in chambers dealing solely with questions of law or

---

Interpreters, Ga. Court Rules and Practice (West 2002). In Ramos v. Terry, 279 Ga. 889, 622 S.E.2d 339 (2005), the Supreme Court concluded that the trial court abused its discretion by failing to provide a certified court approved interpreter subject to the interpreter's code of professional responsibility. However, the error is waived in the absence of a timely objection.

[19]In Ferrell v. Estelle, 568 F.2d 1128 (5th Cir. 1978), the court held that where a defendant is deaf, some means must be worked out so that he will be informed of and understand the testimony of witnesses as they testify so that he can assist in his defense. In Baltierra v. State, 586 S.W.2d 553 (Tex.Crim.App. 1979), the defendant

could not speak or understand English, but no interpreter was requested. A bilingual lawyer was appointed to represent the defendant. The conviction was reversed because of the denial of confrontation.

[20]Gonzales v. State, 182 Ga. App. 594, 356 S.E.2d 545 (1987).

[21]Hersi v. State, 257 Ga. App. 63, 65 (1), 570 S.E.2d 365 (2002).

[22]Bishop v. State, 179 Ga. App. 606, 609 (2), 347 S.E.2d 350 (1986) (quoting Snyder v. Massachusetts, 291 U.S. 97, 105-108, 54 S.Ct. 330, 78 L.Ed. 674 (1934)).

[23]Dill v. State, 277 Ga. 150, 152 (7), 587 S.E.2d 56 (2003).

[24]Smith v. State, 182 Ga. App. 623 (1), 356 S.E.2d 702 (1987).

preliminary matters of procedure."[25] Further, in *Goodroe v. State,*[26] the court pointed out that a defendant did not have a right to be present when the voir dire oath is administered, but has a right to be present during the voir dire of prospective jurors, which is a critical stage of the proceeding. In *Fictum v. State,*[27] the court held that counsel "cannot waive the right of the accused to be present unless waiver is made in defendant's presence, by defendant's express authority or unless the defendant subsequently acquiesces to counsel's waiver. . . . The right to be present . . . is not waived by counsel's failure to raise an objection." The court also pointed out that the "right exists in misdemeanor cases as well as felonies." In *Zamora v. State,*[28] the Georgia Supreme Court held that a defendant's right to be present was violated when the trial court decided to remove a juror during a bench conference with counsel. The case illustrates the importance of the defendant's right to be present during all critical stages of a trial as well as the limitations of a bench conference which addresses matters other than scheduling or legal issues. If the bench conference involves concerns about which the defendant could provide a meaningful contribution, such as the decision to remove a juror, the defendant must have the opportunity to be involved. The Court noted that while the defendant was "present" in the courtroom, he was not "present." See § 14:85, supra, on the right of the defendant to be present at a hearing on a motion to suppress.

Generally, the defendant does not have a right to be present at "post-verdict procedures such as a motion for a new trial, at which only questions of law, not questions of fact are determined."[29] But under the Georgia Unified Appeal Procedure, in a death case the defendant does have a right to be present during the entire hearing on a motion for a new trial unless he knowingly, voluntarily, and intelligently waives this right in writing.[30]

Nevertheless, if a defendant is on trial and voluntarily leaves

---

[25]Ferrell v. State, 261 Ga. 115, 122 (12), 401 S.E.2d 741 (1991).

[26]Goodroe v. State, 224 Ga. App. 378, 380 (1), 480 S.E.2d 378 (1997).

[27]Fictum v. State, 188 Ga. App. 348, 349 (2)(b), 373 S.E.2d 54 (1988).

[28]Zamora v. State, 291 Ga. 512, 731 S.E.2d 658 (2012) (defendant acquiesced to trial court's ruling because he saw the bench conferences and the juror's removal and never objected, either at trial or during the motion for new trial when he was represented by new counsel, choosing only to raise the issue on appeal). See Gillespie v. State, 333 Ga. App. 565, 774 S.E.2d 255 (2015) (reversal required where counsel was unable to recall whether he advised client that during course of several bench conferences with court and counsel jurors were discussed and excused).

[29]Rosser v. State, 284 Ga. 335 (2), 667 S.E.2d 62 (2008); Moore v. State, 254 Ga. 525(4)(c), 330 S.E.2d 717 (1985); Dobbs v. State, 245 Ga. 208, 209 (2), 264 S.E.2d 18 (1980).

[30]Brown v. State, 250 Ga. 66, 75 (7), 295 S.E.2d 727 (1982).

after the jury has been selected, he may be tried and sentenced even though not present.[31] In *Pollard v. State,*[32] the court concluded that a defendant waives his Sixth Amendment right to be present and right of confrontation where he voluntarily leaves after the jury has been impaneled and sworn and in a non-jury trial when the trial judge "receives the first evidence." See Annotation, "Sufficiency of Showing Defendant's 'Voluntary Absence' from Trial for Purposes of Criminal Procedure Rule 43, Authorizing Continuance of Trial Notwithstanding Such Absence," 141 A.L.R.Fed. 569 (1997).

A defendant has the right to be present at any time that the court changes the composition of the jury by removing or excusing a juror from further duty. In the absence of an explicit waiver by the defendant, a unilateral decision by the court, even with the consent of counsel, is prejudicial error.[33]

Also, "a defendant [in a criminal case] can lose his right to be present at trial if, after he has been warned by the trial judge that he will be removed if he continues his disruptive behavior, he nevertheless insists on conducting himself in a manner so disorderly, disruptive, and disrespectful of the court that his trial cannot be carried on with him in the courtroom."[34] In *Illinois* v.

---

[31]Byrd v. Ricketts, 233 Ga. 779, 213 S.E.2d 610 (1975); Croy v. State, 168 Ga. App. 241 (1), 308 S.E.2d 568 (1983). In Taylor v. United States, 414 U.S. 17, 20, 94 S.Ct. 194, 38 L.Ed.2d 174 (1973), the defendant was present on the morning his case began. He was on bond and failed to return after lunch. The court unanimously held that the continuation of his trial in his absence did not violate his constitutional right to be present and confront witnesses since his voluntary absence constituted a waiver of those rights. It is not necessary to show that the defendant knew or had been told that his trial would continue in his absence.

See Annot., "Necessity and Content of Instructions to Jury Respecting Reasons for or Inferences from Accused's Absence from State Criminal Trial," 31 A.L.R.4th 676 (1984). See Also Annot., "Am.Jur.2d Trial § 1330, Absence of Defendant From Trial (2004).

In Crosby v. United States, 506 U.S. 255, 113 S.Ct. 748, 122 L.Ed.2d 25 (1993), when a defendant failed to appear for trial after appearing at pretrial conferences and hearings with counsel and after being told when the trial was scheduled to begin, he was tried in his absence. One of his codefendants was acquitted and two were convicted. The court reversed the defendant's convictions.

[32]Pollard v. State, 175 Ga. App. 269, 270, 333 S.E.2d 152 (1985). See Cesari v. State, 334 Ga. App. 605, 780 S.E.2d 56 (2015) (trial court erred in refusing to halt examination of witness in order to allow defense counsel to determine if defendant who had failed to return on time after recess was impaired before coming into courtroom). Cf. Estep v. State, 238 Ga. App. 170, 172, 518 S.E.2d 176 (1999).

[33]See Ward v. State, 288 Ga. 641, 706 S.E.2d 430 (2011).

[34]Smith v. State, 161 Ga. App. 512, 513, 288 S.E.2d 754 (1982) (quoting Illinois v. Allen, 397 U.S. 337, 344, 90 S.Ct. 1057, 25 L.Ed.2d 353 (1970)); West v. State, 271 Ga. App. 522, 610 S.E.2d 159 (2005); Williams v. State, 183 Ga. App. 373, 374, 358 S.E.2d 914

Allen,[35] the court pointed out that there are three constitutional ways to handle a disruptive defendant: (1) bind and gag him and keep him in the courtroom, (2) cite him for contempt, or (3) remove him from the courtroom until he promises to conduct himself properly. However, a defendant may not be excluded from the courtroom without "giving him the opportunity to remain, at the first instance, upon his agreement to act in a proper manner, and to refrain from any similar conduct."[36] See Annotations, "Giving, In Accused's Absence, Additional Instruction to Jury After Submission of Felony Case," 94 A.L.R.2d 270 (1964); "Sufficiency of Showing Defendant's 'Voluntary Absence' From Trial for Purposes of Criminal Procedure Rule 43, Authorizing Continuance of Trial Notwithstanding Such Absence," 141 A.L.R.Fed. 569 (1997); and "Necessity and Content of Instructions to Jury Respecting Reasons For or Inferences From Accused's Absence From State Criminal Trial," 31 A.L.R.4th 676 (1984); "Voluntary Absence of Accused When Sentence Is Pronounced," 59 A.L.R.5th 135 (1998).

The defendant is said to have the right to be present at every stage of a trial unless he has waived that right.[37] The "courts indulge every reasonable presumption against waiver" of fundamental constitutional rights and "do not presume acquiescence in the loss of fundamental rights."[38] Thus, in *Martin v. State*,[39] the trial court granted the state's motion to view a car with an altered serial number, which the defendant was charged with possessing. The order provided that only the jury and bailiffs were to be present. The Court of Appeals reversed the conviction even though the defendant did not object to his absence until he filed a motion for a new trial. See § 14:85, supra, on the right of a defendant to be present at a hearing on a motion to suppress. See Studdard, *Daniel's Georgia Handbook on Criminal Evidence*

(1987).

See Annot., "Propriety and Prejudicial Effect of Gagging, Shackling, or Otherwise Physically Restraining Accused During Course of State Criminal Trial," 90 A.L.R.3d 17 (1977). See Annot., 5 Am. Jur. 2d Appellate Review § 731, Requiring Accused to Stand Trial in Prison Clothes or in Shackles (2004).

[35]Illinois v. Allen, 397 U.S. 337, 344, 90 S.Ct. 1057, 25 L.Ed.2d 353 (1970). Accord, Simmons v. State, 161 Ga. App. 527, 288 S.E.2d 868 (1982); Raymond v. State, 168 Ga. App. 487, 309 S.E.2d 669 (1983).

[36]Fletcher v. State, 168 Ga. App. 521, 523, 309 S.E.2d 824 (1983), aff'd, 252 Ga. 498, 314 S.E.2d 888 (1984). See Weaver v. State, 288 Ga. 540, 705 S.E.2d 627 (2011) (court may direct counsel to consult with client about whether he wishes to return to courtroom and act properly without necessity of court making inquiry of defendant directly).

[37]Chance v. State, 156 Ga. 428, 119 S.E. 303 (1923).

[38]Johnson v. Zerbst, 304 U.S. 458, 464, 58 S.Ct. 1019, 82 L.Ed. 1461 (1938).

[39]Martin v. State, 160 Ga. App. 275, 277, 287 S.E.2d 244 (1981).

(2018 ed.), § 7:35, on the absence of a defendant during the conducting of an experiment.

The Georgia Supreme Court in 1981 in *Jordan v. State*[40] said that there are "at least two types of jury view. One, an 'evidentiary view,' is to permit the jury to view evidence introduced in the case which evidence is so large or affixed that it cannot be brought into the courtroom. . . . Another, 'the scene view,' is to permit the jury to view the premises relevant to the case to enable the jury to better understand the testimony and other evidence introduced in court (e.g., a jury view of the scene of the alleged crime.)" The court concluded "that a jury view of the premises relevant to the case made for the purpose of enabling the jury to better understand the testimony and not made for the purpose of allowing the jury to see evidence introduced in the case" does not *require* the presence of the defendant. However, the trial judge in his discretion may allow the defendant to be present. See Studdard, *Daniel's Georgia Handbook on Criminal Evidence* (2018 ed.), § 4:26.

In *Esposito v. State,*[41] the Georgia Supreme Court summarized some of the factors to be considered in any planned viewing of a crime scene. "[A] trial judge should attend any planned jury view. Taking a jury from the controlled environment of a courtroom to a place that has some relevance to the trial always involves the risk that something unexpected might arise requiring the trial judge's intervention. A court reporter should also attend any jury view so that any important statements or events may be thoroughly reviewed on appeal. The attorneys should also attend, unless their presence is affirmatively waived. While a defendant's presence at a jury view that involves merely the transportation of the jury to a crime scene is not absolutely required, trial courts should note that a defendant's presence is mandatory, if not waived by the defendant himself, whenever testimony or other evidence is presented to the jury. Special dangers exist whenever a witness at trial, particularly a law enforcement officer, attends a jury view, and a trial court should avoid those dangers by excluding such persons. Finally, because jury views have proved to be fertile ground for irregularity and, at times, reversible error, the parties to criminal trials and trial courts should carefully weigh the real benefits of a jury view before planning one." See Studdard, *Daniel's Georgia Handbook on Criminal Evidence* (2018 ed.), § 4:14.

---

[40]Jordan v. State, 247 Ga. 328, 345, 276 S.E.2d 224 (1981).

[41]Esposito v. State, 273 Ga. 183, 187 (4), 538 S.E.2d 55 (2000).

In *Lewis v. State*,[42] the court held that it was not error for the trial judge to refuse to allow the defendant to absent himself from the courtroom during the testimony of the victim who later identified the defendant as one of his assailants. The court said, "Where identification of defendant by a witness is contemplated by the prosecution, the state is entitled to demand the presence of the defendant." See § 19:3, infra, on the right of the victim to be present. See § 18:35, infra, on excusal of a juror in the defendant's absence.

§ 17:9 The transcript

In the trial of felony cases, the judge has the responsibility and duty of having a court reporter present who shall take down all testimony.[1] It has been held that all testimony and proceedings in a felony case must be reported except the argument of counsel.[2] However, if the arguments and objections thereto are not recorded, there is a presumption that nothing improper took place.[3] It has also been held that in a felony case if a recording device does not function during the testimony of a material witness and the transcript shows only that he testified, or there is no transcript, the defendant is entitled to a new trial.[4] However, this does not relieve the defendant of his responsibility to exercise diligence in trying to obtain a transcript or a substitute if he appeals the case.

In the case of an appeal the appellant has the duty to cause a transcript to be prepared and if a defendant who files a notice of appeal fails to order a transcript and no transcript is filed within the time fixed by law, the trial judge may, "after notice and opportunity for hearing, order the appeal dismissed where there has been an unreasonable delay . . . and it is shown that the

---

[42]Lewis v. State, 164 Ga. App. 549, 550, 297 S.E.2d 303 (1982); Tilley v. State, 201 Ga. App. 360 (1), 411 S.E.2d 100 (1991).

[Section 17:9]

[1]Hatcher v. State, 18 Ga. 460(3) (1855); O.C.G.A. § 17-8-5. In Wilson v. State, 246 Ga. 672, 273 S.E.2d 9 (1980), the case was reversed because the trial judge used a court reporter with a serious hearing defect, there were numerous errors in the transcript, and ultimately the tapes of the testimony were lost.

[2]Aiken v. State, 226 Ga. 840, 842, 178 S.E.2d 202 (1970).

[3]Aiken v. State, 226 Ga. 840, 842-43, 178 S.E.2d 202 (1970).

[4]McElwee v. State, 147 Ga. App. 84, 248 S.E.2d 162 (1978). Cf. Hart v. State, 153 Ga. App. 53, 264 S.E.2d 542 (1980), rev'd, 246 Ga. 212, 271 S.E.2d 133 (1980); Montford v. State, 164 Ga. App. 627, 629, 298 S.E.2d 319 (1982).

In Smith v. State, 251 Ga. 229 (2), 304 S.E.2d 716 (1983), the court pointed out that the defendant must show how he was harmed or show that a reviewing court would be unable to adequately review a case because of skips in the record.

delay was inexcusable."[5] It is clear that the absence of a complete transcript in a collateral post-conviction proceeding does not in itself require a new trial. However, at least if the defendant in the criminal case was diligent and if the merits of the habeas petition cannot be reached based upon the available record, a new trial is appropriate if a resolution of the point involved in petitioner's favor would require a new trial.[6] However, where a tape played during a trial is not transcribed, a reversal is not required where the tape is "cumulative rather than critical" to the case.[7]

In capital felony cases, it is mandatory that there be a transcript of the voir dire examination of jurors.[8] Except in a capital case,[9] if counsel wishes to have the argument recorded, there must be a timely request,[10] and it is counsel's duty to see that the reporter takes down the argument.[11] However, it has been held that where an attorney in a motion for a continuance says that he is stating facts "as an officer of the court under oath," it is error for the court to refuse counsel for an indigent defendant a transcript of such remarks where the motion is denied.[12] In the capital case of *Thomason v. State,*[13] the court held that there was no error in denying a motion for a daily transcript.

Even in a misdemeanor case, it is error for the court to deny a motion for a continuance because of the absence of a court reporter when the defendant wishes to have the proceedings transcribed.[14] In the trial of a misdemeanor case the trial judge in his discretion may require the reporting and transcribing of

---

[5]State v. Hart, 246 Ga. 212, 213-14, 271 S.E.2d 133 (1980).

[6]Montgomery v. Tremblay, 249 Ga. 483, 292 S.E.2d 64 (1982). See Sheard v. State, 300 Ga. 117, 793 S.E.2d 386 (2016); Johnson v. State, 302 Ga. 188, 805 S.E.2d 890 (2017) (new trial warranted where trial transcript had been destroyed in fire and recreated transcript was not sufficient to allow for a fair review).

[7]Graham v. State, 171 Ga. App. 242, 249, 319 S.E.2d 484 (1984).

[8]Owens v. State, 233 Ga. 869, 871 (2), 214 S.E.2d 173 (1975).

[9]See § 28:22, infra, on requirements of the Georgia Unified Appeal Procedure.

[10]Montgomery v. State, 140 Ga. App. 286, 288 (4), 231 S.E.2d 108 (1976).

[11]Harris v. State, 237 Ga. 718, 726, 230 S.E.2d 1 (1976). In Lewis v. State, 147 Ga. App. 794, 796-97, 250 S.E.2d 522 (1978), the defendant requested a transcript of the voir dire examination of potential jurors and offered to pay for it. The trial judge denied the motion. The appellate court affirmed, stating that the defendant failed to show that prejudice resulted from the absence of a verbatim transcript of the voir dire. The court pointed out that error had not been assigned to the refusal of the trial judge to order a transcript.

[12]Miller v. State, 165 Ga. App. 487, 489 (3), 299 S.E.2d 174 (1983).

[13]Thomason v. State, 268 Ga. 298, 312 (12), 486 S.E.2d 861 (1997).

[14]Massey v. State, 127 Ga. App. 638, 194 S.E.2d 582 (1972).

evidence.[15] However, if a defendant wishes to have a reporter for a misdemeanor case, he is entitled to one at his own expense, and it is not necessary for the defendant in advance of trial to make arrangements to have a court reporter available for the reporting of the trial.[16] Also if a defendant desires a reporter and one is not available, he should move for a continuance.[17] The failure to move for a continuance might be a waiver of the right to have a reporter.[18]

A request to have an unofficial court reporter present in addition to the regular court reporter should normally be granted.[19] Generally, an attorney should be permitted to use a tape recorder if it will not interfere with the dignity of the court.[20]

Either party, as a matter of right, is entitled to have the arguments reported at his own expense.[21] See § 28:7, infra, on transcripts for an appeal. See Studdard, *Daniel's Georgia Handbook on Criminal Evidence* (2018 ed.), § 9:16, on transcription of video and audio tapes.

In *Robinson v. State*,[22] the court held that the foregoing rules set out in this section apply to transcripts of preliminary hearings and arraignments.

In *Kier v. State*,[23] the court held that it is within the discretion of the trial judge to provide a free transcript of an earlier trial of the same case to an indigent defendant. Relying on *Britt v. North Carolina*,[24] the court makes such a decision by evaluating two factors: "(1) the transcript's value in connection with the

---

[15]O.C.G.A. § 5-6-41(b).

[16]Thompson v. State, 240 Ga. 296, 240 S.E.2d 87 (1977).

[17]Massey v. State, 127 Ga. App. 638, 194 S.E.2d 582 (1972). This case holds that it is reversible error for the trial judge in a misdemeanor case to overrule such a motion.

[18]Thompson v. State, 142 Ga. App. 888, 891, 237 S.E.2d 419 (1977), rev'd on other grounds, 240 Ga. 296, 240 S.E.2d 87 (1977). In Parker v. State, 154 Ga. App. 668, 269 S.E.2d 518 (1980), where an indigent defendant failed to request that a transcript of a trial be made and one was not made, this is not a basis for reversal. In Holzmeister v. State, 156 Ga. App. 94, 274 S.E.2d 109 (1980), the court affirmed the conviction after pointing out that the defendant cannot, after conviction, object to the fact that the trial judge had not appointed an of-

ficial court reporter as required. See Frasier v. State, 160 Ga. App. 812, 287 S.E.2d 669 (1982).

[19]Estep v. State, 129 Ga. App. 909, 913 (3), 201 S.E.2d 809 (1973). Cf. United States v. Cabra, 622 F.2d 182 (5th Cir. 1980).

[20]King v. State, 176 Ga. App. 137 (1), 335 S.E.2d 439 (1985); Davey v. City of Atlanta, 130 Ga. App. 687, 688 (1), 204 S.E.2d 322 (1974). But cf. Rutledge v. State, 245 Ga. 768, 771 (4), 267 S.E.2d 199 (1980).

[21]Dumas v. State, 131 Ga. App. 79, 83, 205 S.E.2d 119 (1974).

[22]Robinson v. State, 182 Ga. App. 423, 424 (1)(a), 356 S.E.2d 55 (1987). Also see § 28:7, n. 1, infra, on transcripts for appeal.

[23]Kier v. State, 240 Ga. App. 152, 153, 525 S.E.2d 102 (1999).

[24]Britt v. North Carolina, 404

defendant's trial or appeal, and (2) the accessibility of other means that would fulfill the same functions as a transcript."

In cases where there is no trial transcript or where some aspect of the case is not reported, the parties by agreement may prepare a transcript in narrative form.[25] The parties may also stipulate to matters which they agree were either omitted from the record or misstated in the official transcript.[26] In the absence of agreement or stipulation, the trial court on its own or on the motion of one of the parties may direct that the record be supplemented.[27]

In the event the parties are unable to agree as to the correctness of what a proper transcript would state, it will be the duty of the trial court to determine the contents thereof and its decision "shall be final and not subject to review."[28] In the event the trial court can not recall what transpired, it will be incumbent upon the court to enter an order to that effect.[29]

In *Merchant Law Firm, P.C. v. Emerson*,[30] the Court considered whether the remedy of mandamus was available to a non-party to obtain access to a court reporter's audio recordings of trial proceedings used by the court reporter to prepare transcripts. Although the court did not rule that such recordings must be made available upon demand by a party or a non-party, it did hold that Uniform Superior Court Rule 21 is the proper vehicle to make such a request. Subsequently, in *Undisclosed LLC v. State*,[31] the court held that Georgia Uniform Superior Court Rule 21 and O.C.G.A. § 5-6-41(e) apply only to those materials which are filed with the trial court. Thus, a non-party was not entitled to the unfiled audio recordings of the court reporter in a case where an official transcript had been filed with the court.

§ 17:10   Subpoenas—General

A criminal defendant has a constitutional right to obtain the testimony of witnesses who may be helpful to his defense.[1] The guarantee of compulsory process exists under the Georgia Consti-

---

U.S. 226, 92 S.Ct. 431, 30 L.Ed.2d 400 (1971).

[25]O.C.G.A. § 5-6-41(d).

[26]O.C.G.A. § 5-6-41(f).

[27]O.C.G.A. § 5-6-41(g).

[28]O.C.G.A. § 5-6-41(g).

[29]O.C.G.A. § 5-6-41(g).

[30]Merchant Law Firm, P.C. v. Emerson, 301 Ga. 609, 800 S.E.2d 557 (2017).

[31]Undisclosed LLC v. State, 302 Ga. 418, 807 S.E.2d 393 (2017).

[Section 17:10]

[1]Of course, this right is limited by the capacity of the trial court to enforce it. In other words, a defendant cannot complain to the trial court if the witness he seeks to subpoena is not within the jurisdiction. Mafnas v. State, 149 Ga. App. 286, 287, 254 S.E.2d 409 (1979) (disapproved of on other grounds by, Davenport v. State, 289 Ga. 399, 711 S.E.2d 699 (2011)). See Poole v. State, 291 Ga. 848, 734 S.E.2d 1 (2012) (no violation of compulsory process where unreasonable and

tution of 1983[2] and under the Sixth Amendment[3] of the federal Constitution, as made applicable to the states through the due process clause of the Fourteenth Amendment.[4] In Georgia, the defendant is entitled to have the sheriff of the county serve the subpoenas without cost to him.[5]

The defendant may waive or forfeit his right to subpoena a witness,[6] or gain a continuance,[7] by failing to make a timely request. Generally, if a defendant is indigent and some expense is connected with securing the witness, the defendant is entitled to have the expense for necessary witnesses paid by the state.[8] However, a state is not required to do anything more than exercise ordinary diligence in subpoenaing a witness.[9] Finally, it is not error to deny or quash the subpoena where it is frivolous or of little value,[10] or unreasonable and oppressive.[11]

A Georgia statute provides that a subpoena must be issued by

---

oppressive subpoenas quashed).

In Hurst v. State, 160 Ga. App. 830, 287 S.E.2d 677 (1982), the trial judge refused to permit the defendant to call a reporter as an impeachment witness to show that the eyewitness had made inconsistent statements before trial unless the defendant first called two other witnesses. The Court of Appeals held that there was no acceptable reason for restricting the defendant's right to compulsory process.

[2]Ga. Const. 1983, Art. I, § I, ¶ XIV; Murphy v. State, 132 Ga. App. 654, 655 (1), 209 S.E.2d 101 (1974); Pullen v. Cleckler, 162 Ga. 111, 132 S.E. 761 (1926).

[3]However, in United States v. Valenzuela-Bernal, 458 U.S. 858, 102 S.Ct. 3440, 73 L.Ed.2d 1193 (1982), the court stated that a defendant cannot establish a violation of his Sixth Amendment right to compulsory process to obtain witnesses "in his favor" merely by showing that deportation of aliens deprived him of their testimony. He must make a reasonable showing of how their testimony would have been material and favorable to him.

See § 14:4, supra, on discovery, generally.

[4]Washington v. Texas, 388 U.S. 14, 87 S.Ct. 1920, 18 L.Ed.2d 1019 (1967).

[5]Harpe v. State, 134 Ga. App. 493, 497, 214 S.E.2d 738 (1975).

[6]Crumpton v. United States, 138 U.S. 361, 11 S.Ct. 355, 34 L.Ed. 958 (1891).

[7]Eady v. State, 129 Ga. App. 656 (1), 200 S.E.2d 767 (1973).

[8]United States v. Barker, 553 F.2d 1013, 1019, 1020 (6th Cir. 1977); cf. United States v. Romano, 482 F.2d 1183, 1194 (5th Cir. 1973), and Annot., 42 A.L.R.Fed. 233 (1979). In Georgia, witnesses do not have to be paid in advance in criminal cases. O.C.G.A. § 24-13-25.

[9]Gilmore v. State, 154 Ga. App. 429, 431, 268 S.E.2d 693 (1980).

[10]Crumpton v. United States, 138 U.S. 361, 11 S.Ct. 355, 34 L.Ed. 958 (1891); Goldsby v. United States, 160 U.S. 70, 16 S.Ct. 216, 40 L.Ed. 343 (1895); Heard v. State, 135 Ga. App. 685, 218 S.E.2d 866 (1975). In Dodd v. State, 236 Ga. 572, 574, 224 S.E.2d 408 (1976), the court upheld the quashing of a subpoena where the subpoenaed witness was a co-indictee of the defendant who at the motion to quash vowed to invoke his privilege against self-incrimination if forced to take the stand.

[11]O.C.G.A. § 24-13-23; Kamensky v. Southern Oxygen Supply Co., 127 Ga. App. 343, 343-44, 193 S.E.2d 164

the clerk of the court and command the person to whom it is directed to attend and give testimony at a time and place specified therein.[12] In addition, courts are required to make subpoenas available in blank online and an attorney of record may complete, sign and issue such a subpoena without the necessity of the signature of the clerk.[13]

A subpoena may be served personally by any adult, or by registered or certified mail or statutory overnight delivery.[14] Today, a subpoena may be served anywhere within the state.[15] "A Georgia court has authority to compel the attendance at a Georgia criminal trial of persons anywhere within Georgia; however, process issued by Georgia courts does not have extraterritorial power. The Uniform Act to Secure the Attendance of Witnesses from Without the State in Criminal Proceedings . . . 'is intended to provide a means for state courts to compel the attendance of out-of-state witnesses at criminal proceedings.' "[16]

See § 17:17, infra, on requirement of counsel to file a list of witnesses and their addresses with the clerk not less than six hours before witnesses are directed to appear where subpoenas were issued by the clerk in blank.

Subpoenas may be enforced by attachment for contempt, by a fine not greater than $300, and by imprisonment not exceeding 20 days.[17] However, the court is under a statutory duty to consider whether under the circumstances of each case the subpoena was served within a reasonable time.[18] It is conclusively presumed that service of the subpoena less than 24 hours prior to the time that attendance thereunder is required is not within a reasonable time.[19] Finally, the court may, in any appropriate case, grant a

---

(1972).

[12]O.C.G.A. §§ 24-13-21 and 24-13-22. However, in Reiman v. Breslin, 175 N.J.Super. 353, 418 A.2d 1293, 1298 (1980), the court held that an "on call" subpoena requiring a witness to appear only when and if he is called was valid.

[13]O.C.G.A. § 24-13-21(c) and (d).

[14]O.C.G.A. § 24-13-24.

[15]O.C.G.A. § 24-13-22; Jones v. Caldwell, 230 Ga. 775, 776 (4), 199 S.E.2d 248 (1973). The constitutionality of this provision was questionable, especially in light of Washington v. Texas, 388 U.S. 14, 87 S.Ct. 1920, 18 L.Ed.2d 1019 (1967), which held unconstitutional a Texas statute which

prevented a defendant from calling an accomplice to testify in his behalf. However, in Hooten v. State, 245 Ga. 250, 264 S.E.2d 192 (1980), the court upheld the constitutionality of the 150 mile rule in a civil (habeas corpus) proceeding.

[16]Davenport v. State, 289 Ga. 399, 711 S.E.2d 699 (2011) (citation omitted). See § 14:96, supra, on the Uniform Act to compel attendance of out-of-state witnesses in criminal cases.

[17]O.C.G.A. § 24-13-26.

[18]Byron v. State, 229 Ga. App. 795, 495 S.E.2d 123 (1997); O.C.G.A. § 24-13-26.

[19]O.C.G.A. § 24-13-26.

continuance in order to assure a witness' appearance.[20]

Members of the Georgia General Assembly are immune from subpoenas entirely whenever that body is in regular or extraordinary session.[21] Furthermore, a witness under subpoena is immune from arrest and service of process while attending the trial, and in going to or returning from the courthouse.[22]

O.C.G.A. § 24-13-25 contains provisions for witness fees and mileage allowances.[23]

There is a statutory procedure available in Georgia by which a defendant can summon a prisoner who is confined anywhere in the state to testify in his behalf.[24] Also, the writ of habeas corpus ad testificandum may be issued by the superior court to cause the production of any witness under imprisonment.[25] If there is an order of the superior court commanding the presence of an inmate witness, no subpoena is needed.[26] There are also methods of obtaining witnesses who are in federal custody[27] and witnesses outside of the state.[28] In connection with witnesses who are in custody, it should be remembered that the defendant is generally entitled to have any such witness appear in court in civil clothing and free from handcuffs and restraints.[29]

See § 14:96, supra, on the Uniform Act to Secure the Atten-

---

[20]O.C.G.A. § 24-13-26.

[21]O.C.G.A. § 24-13-29.

[22]O.C.G.A. § 24-13-1. This is the common law rule also. Ewing v. Elliott, 51 Ga. App. 565, 181 S.E. 123 (1935). However, the defendant in a criminal case is not privileged under this section. Warren v. Hiers, 105 Ga. App. 202, 205, 124 S.E.2d 445 (1962); Rogers v. Rogers, 138 Ga. 803, 76 S.E. 48 (1912).

[23]The witness fee is $25 per day and the mileage fee is 45 cents per mile for each mile between the witness' residence and the courthouse. When the witness resides outside the county where the testimony is to be given, the witness fee for one day and the round trip mileage allowance must be tendered unless the subpoena is issued on behalf of the state or a political subdivision thereof or an accused in a criminal case. The payment of fees is not a condition precedent to the witness' attendance.

[24]O.C.G.A. § 24-13-60. Brand v. State, 154 Ga. App. 781, 784, 270 S.E.2d 206 (1980) (the court indicated

that the accused must make a preliminary showing of need before an incarcerated witness will be produced; but where the ends of justice require the prisoner's presence, he must be produced). This seems to be the general rule. See Owens v. State, 427 N.E.2d 880, 882 (Ind.1981) and the cases cited therein; Edwards v. State, 144 Ga. App. 665, 242 S.E.2d 326 (1978). This statute by its own terms does not apply where the person sought as a witness is being held under a death sentence.

[25]O.C.G.A. § 24-13-62.

[26]Grant v. State, 212 Ga. App. 565, 566 (1)(b), 442 S.E.2d 898 (1994).

[27]Barber v. Page, 390 U.S. 719, 88 S.Ct. 1318, 20 L.Ed.2d 255 (1968). This case outlines the procedure for obtaining a federal prisoner as a witness in a state criminal prosecution.

[28]See § 14:96, supra, on the Uniform Act to Secure the Attendance of Witnesses From Without the State.

[29]Kennedy v. Cardwell, 487 F.2d 101, 105 (n. 5) (6th Cir. 1973). While there is room for some judicial discre-

dance of Witnesses From Without the State,[30] which provides a procedure to secure out of state witnesses if the witness is located in a state which has enacted the same statute. See O.C.G.A. § 24-13-60, O.C.G.A. § 24-13-93, and O.C.G.A. § 24-13-95 on requiring a prisoner to appear as a witness.

§ 17:11   Subpoena for the production of documentary evidence and tangible objects

In *Bazemore v. State*,[1] the court pointed out that "[w]hen a motion to quash [a subpoena for the production of documents] is filed, [1] the party serving the subpoena has the initial burden of showing the documents sought are relevant. . . . [2] If that is done, the party moving to quash has the burden of showing that the subpoena is unreasonable and oppressive."

The subpoena for the production of documentary evidence, formerly known as the subpoena duces tecum,[2] is issued and served in the same manner as is the subpoena for the attendance of witnesses.[3] The party requesting the subpoena for the production of documentary evidence is responsible for filling in the subpoena with the materials he wishes produced before he has the subpoena served.[4] The party to whom the subpoena is directed may move to deny, modify, or quash the subpoena on the grounds that it is unreasonable and oppressive.[5] In Georgia, by statute the court may order production conditioned on the advancement by the person on whose behalf the subpoena is issued of the reasonable costs of producing the books, papers, documents, or tangible things.[6]

A subpoena for the production of evidence is enforced in the same manner as is the subpoena for the attendance of witnesses, discussed in § 17:10, supra.[7] In addition, where books, papers, documents, or tangible things are unsuccessfully sought, second-

---

tion, in State v. Coursolle, 255 Minn. 384, 97 N.W.2d 472, 476 (1959), the court said that in exercising this discretion there must be "reason based on the conduct [that] . . . there must be some immediate necessity for the use of the shackles." See Annot., "Right of Accused to Have His Witnesses Free From Handcuffs, Manacles, Shackles, or the Like," 75 A.L.R.2d 762 (1961).

[30]O.C.G.A. §§ 24-13-60 et seq.

[Section 17:11]

[1]Bazemore v. State, 233 Ga. App. 892, 893 (2), 506 S.E.2d 177 (1998).

[2]See O.C.G.A. § 24-13-23.

[3]O.C.G.A. §§ 24-13-21, 24-13-23. See § 17:10, supra, for the provisions governing the issuance and service of subpoenas in general.

[4]O.C.G.A. § 24-13-21.

[5]O.C.G.A.   § 24-13-23.   See § 17:12, infra on motion to quash subpoena.

[6]O.C.G.A. § 24-13-23.

[7]O.C.G.A. § 24-13-26 provides that subpoenas may be enforced by attachment for contempt, by fine not exceeding $300, and by imprisonment not exceeding 20 days. The court may also grant continuances under ap-

ary evidence thereof is said to be admissible in evidence.[8]

In *Jinks v. State*,[9] the defendant was charged with simple battery on a police officer. The Georgia Court of Appeals affirmed the action of the trial judge in refusing the defense access to the arresting officer's personnel file and pointed out that the defendant did not show that there was anything in the file which was favorable to the defendant or of probative value or exculpatory. The court referred to the defendant's efforts to obtain the material as a fishing expedition. However, the general rule seems to be that where the officer is alleged to be the aggressor, his personnel file may be obtained by the defendant, or, at least, the defendant is entitled to have the trial judge examine the file in camera and determine whether the file contains anything favorable to the defendant which is not already known to the defendant. The defendant's opportunity to obtain an officer's personnel file is considerably limited, however, where it is not contended that the officer was the aggressor.[10]

In *State v. Lucious*,[11] the court held that a defendant must invoke the Criminal Procedure Discovery Act[12] in order to obtain discovery of scientific reports. "Because there is no general constitutional right to discovery in a criminal case, the election not to invoke the discovery provisions of the Act necessarily entitles a defendant to only that discovery specifically afforded by the Georgia and United States Constitutions, statutory excep-

---

propriate circumstances.

[8]O.C.G.A. § 24-13-26. There is a Georgia statute providing that when a person served with a subpoena duces tecum swears that he cannot produce the evidence required without suffering a material hardship or injury, he may make a full transcript of the requested material, have that transcript examined and sworn to by an impartial observer, and produce the transcript in compliance with the subpoena. O.C.G.A. § 24-13-5. If the party requesting production believes the transcript to be false or incomplete, the court may order the production of the material to an impartial person appointed by the court, who will make a full and fair transcript thereof. O.C.G.A. § 24-13-6. Although these provisions were enacted in 1919, there are only three annotations thereunder. It is unclear whether or not these provisions are intended to apply to crimi-

nal cases.

[9]Jinks v. State, 155 Ga. App. 925, 274 S.E.2d 46 (1980). Accord, Wise v. State, 321 Ga. App. 39, 740 S.E.2d 850 (2013).

[10]See Annot., "Accused's Right to Discovery or Inspection of Records of Prior Complaints Against, or Similar Personnel Records of, Peace Officer Involved in the Case," 86 A.L.R.3d 1170 (1978). See Annot., 23 Am. Jur. 2d Depositions and Discovery § 265, Police Officer's Personnel Records; Records of Other Arrests by Officer (2004).

[11]State v. Lucious, 271 Ga. 361, 518 S.E.2d 677 (1999), overruling Eason v. State, 260 Ga. 445, 396 S.E.2d 492 (1990), to the extent that *Eason* allows a defendant to unilaterally obtain evidence of scientific work product.

[12]O.C.G.A. §§ 17-16-1 et seq.

tions to the Act, and non-conflicting rules of court."[13]

In *Pennsylvania v. Ritchie*,[14] the United States Supreme Court held that a convicted defendant, who was charged with sexual assault of his minor daughter, was entitled under the Sixth and Fourteenth Amendments to have the trial judge conduct an in camera review of records of a state welfare agency to determine whether the records contained information that could have changed the outcome of the trial where the defendant had attempted without success to obtain the records prior to trial.

If counsel is considering obtaining records of the federal government by subpoena for use in a state case, he should study Title 28, sections 16.21—16.29 of the Code of Federal Regulations. In summary, section 16.22 provides that no materials or information are to be produced or disclosed without prior approval of the proper Department official. Factors to be considered in determining whether production or disclosure should be made are set out in section 16.26 and include (1) whether the disclosure would be appropriate under the relevant rules of procedure; and (2) whether the disclosure would be appropriate under the relevant substantive law concerning privilege. In addition, the section provides that disclosure will not be made if the effect of such would violate a statute or a specific regulation; reveal classified information, trade secrets, confidential sources or informants, or investigatory records compiled for law enforcement purposes; interfere with enforcement proceedings; or impair the effectiveness of investigatory techniques or procedures. However, where disclosure would not have the effect of violating a statute or specific regulation or revealing classified information, and where a determination is made that the administration of justice requires disclosure, the desired records may be produced. See § 17:12, infra, on motion to quash subpoenas. See also *Smith v. Cromer*,[15] on authority of a state court to evaluate the regulations of the Justice Department which prevents disclosure of certain records.

As is the case with a subpoena for the attendance of witnesses, members of the Georgia General Assembly are exempt from subpoenas for the production of documentary evidence and from notices to produce whenever the General Assembly is in session.[16]

In an interesting Colorado case,[17] it was held that a subpoena duces tecum was properly used to have an arresting officer

---

[13]State v. Lucious, 271 Ga. 361, 364, 518 S.E.2d 677 (1999).

[14]Pennsylvania v. Ritchie, 480 U.S. 39, 107 S.Ct. 989, 94 L.Ed.2d 40 (1987).

[15]Smith v. Cromer, 159 F.3d 875 (4th Cir. 1998).

[16]O.C.G.A. § 24-13-28(d).

[17]People v. Poole, 192 Colo. 56, 555 P.2d 980, 983 (1976). In this case,

"produced" in court appearing as he was at the time he arrested the defendant.

See § 17:10, supra, on subpoenas in general. See sections 14:4 to 14:32, supra, on criminal discovery in general, and particularly § 14:8, supra, on notice to produce. See § 4:2, supra, on production of incriminating documents.

§ 17:12   Motion to quash subpoena

A subpoena or notice to produce may be quashed (dismissed) when it is unreasonable and oppressive.[1] This rule applies to the subpoena for the attendance of witnesses as well as to the subpoena for the production of documentary evidence.[2] It has been held that a hearing on the motion to quash may be ex parte and conducted out of the presence of the defendant and his attorney.[3] However, it has also been held that it is not an abuse of discretion for the trial judge to refuse to permit defense counsel "to make an in-camera showing of relevancy . . . outside the presence of the district attorney."[4] To determine whether a subpoena is unreasonable and oppressive, it is necessary to look at the peculiar facts arising under the particular subpoena.[5]

A motion to quash must be in writing and made at or before the time specified in the subpoena for compliance therewith.[6] Apparently a motion to quash may be filed by defense counsel or the district attorney even if the subpoena is directed to a third person

---

the defendant was charged with assault when he drew and aimed a pistol at an undercover officer who entered his residence. The defendant said that he did not know that the person was an officer. At the time the officer had long hair and whiskers and was dressed in jeans and a fatigue jacket. The subpoena directed the officer to appear in court as he did at the time of the incident in question. Because the officer had shaved his whiskers before he appeared in court, the charge against the defendant was held to have been properly dismissed because of the destruction of the evidence.

[Section 17:12]

[1]O.C.G.A. § 24-13-23.

[2]Dodd v. State, 236 Ga. 572, 574-76, 224 S.E.2d 408 (1976); Clark v. Board of Dental Examiners, 240 Ga. 289, 291, 240 S.E.2d 250 (1977). In Dodd, it was held that the trial court did not err in granting a motion to

quash a subpoena for the attendance of a witness, where the witness was a co-indictee of the defendant who testified at the motion to quash that he would claim his Fifth Amendment privilege if called as a witness at trial. In Clark it was held that the court was correct in granting a motion to quash a subpoena for the attendance of witnesses in a civil case where the witnesses, who were from without the county, were not tendered their witness fees in advance, as is required for out-of-county witnesses by former O.C.G.A. § 24-10-24 (now § 24-13-25).

[3]Park v. State, 154 Ga. App. 348, 349, 268 S.E.2d 401 (1980).

[4]Johnson v. State, 170 Ga. App. 71, 72 (3), 316 S.E.2d 160 (1984).

[5]Aycock v. Household Finance Corp., 142 Ga. App. 207, 209-11, 235 S.E.2d 578 (1977).

[6]O.C.G.A. § 24-13-23.

or the victim of the crime.[7]

It has been held that a motion to quash should be granted in the following situations: (1) where the evidence requested is too extensive, broad, or indefinite;[8] (2) where a production of the requested evidence would cause undue inconvenience, hardship or expense;[9] (3) where the evidence requested is not in the possession, custody or control of the person to whom the request is directed;[10] (4) where the person to whom the notice or subpoena is directed claims that the evidence requested is non-existent and the requesting party makes no showing to the contrary;[11] (5) where the evidence requested is privileged;[12] and (6) where the material requested would tend to incriminate the person to whom the request is directed within the meaning of the Fifth Amendment.[13]

In *Buford v. State*,[14] the court held that it was error to quash a subpoena duces tecum for DEA long distance telephone records involving alleged telephone calls between DEA agents and the defendant. The state had contended that the information was privileged and also would violate 28 CFR §§ 16.21 et seq. The court concluded that the quashing of the subpoena denied the defendant his constitutional right to obtain witnesses in his favor.

In *Henderson v. State*,[15] the defendant was charged with murder, arson and rape. His defense was that a former police officer, Hinton, had committed the crimes. The defendant filed a subpoena duces tecum on the city chief of police to obtain Hinton's personnel file. The "defendant argued that knowledge of the train-

---

[7]Johnson v. State, 170 Ga. App. 71, 72 (3), 316 S.E.2d 160 (1984).

[8]Hill v. Willis, 224 Ga. 263, 267, 161 S.E.2d 281 (1968). In this case, the court held that a notice to produce "all income tax records" for a three year period was too broad, indefinite and extensive.

[9]Jewell v. Franklin Life Insurance Co., 138 Ga. 576, 578, 75 S.E. 592 (1912).

[10]Ferrell v. State, 149 Ga. App. 405, 408 (8), 254 S.E.2d 404 (1979); Patterson v. State, 154 Ga. App. 877 (2), 270 S.E.2d 86 (1980). It is irrelevant that the person to whom the notice to produce or the subpoena is directed had possession, custody or control in the past. Parish v. Weed Sewing-Machine Co., 79 Ga. 682, 686 (3), 7 S.E. 138 (1887).

[11]Patterson v. State, 154 Ga. App. 877 (2), 270 S.E.2d 86 (1980).

[12]Cf. Cranford v. Cranford, 120 Ga. App. 470, 474 (4), 170 S.E.2d 844 (1969); Morris v. State, 246 Ga. 510 (1), 272 S.E.2d 254 (1980).

[13]Wilson v. State Bar of Georgia, 225 Ga. 343, 345-346, 168 S.E.2d 584 (1969).

[14]Buford v. State, 158 Ga. App. 763, 282 S.E.2d 134 (1981). See § 17:11, supra, on 28 C.F.R. § 16.21.

[15]Henderson v. State, 255 Ga. 687, 690 (3), 341 S.E.2d 439 (1986). But cf. Taylor v. State, 182 Ga. App. 494, 496 (1), 356 S.E.2d 216 (1987), where production of files of officers were sought and the defendant sought to defend an obstruction of justice charge on the basis that the officers had been the aggressors.

ing in murder, arson and rape cases Hinton received . . . would be critical to his defense." The appellate court held that it was error for the trial judge to have quashed the subpoena on the grounds of relevancy.[16] In *Davis v. State*,[17] the defendant was convicted of aggravated assault on a police officer. The court held that it was not error for the trial judge to quash a subpoena for the victim's personnel file since it would have no relevance and was a fishing expedition.

In *Tuttle v. State*,[18] the defendant was charged with driving under the influence. The defendant served a subpoena for production of documents on the arresting officer seeking "(a) any and all videotapes made of . . . [defendant] before, during, and after his arrest, and any and all documents the officer produced as a result of the stop and arrest; (b) any and all training materials the officer used while receiving training in DUI detection and testing; (c) any and all books he read relating to DUI detection and testing; and (d) copies of the reports of the five incidents written up immediately before and the five incidents immediately after . . . [defendant's] arrest." The trial judge granted the state's motion to quash the subpoena, which claimed the subpoena "sought irrelevant information and was overly broad, unreasonable and oppressive." In affirming the appellate court, in an admirable opinion, Judge Johnson discussed why each category of requested information should not be made available to the defendant.

In a criminal case, the trial judge is not authorized to award attorney's fees and expenses of litigation in conjunction with quashing a subpoena for production of documents.[19]

It has been held that a motion to dismiss should not be used against a motion to quash, as the same purpose would be accomplished by merely opposing the motion.[20] See § 17:11, supra, for material on subpoenas for production of documents of the federal government.

For motions to quash subpoenas, see Studdard, *Daniel's Georgia Criminal Trial Practice Forms* (2018–2019 ed.), §§ 23:28, et seq. On motion to quash a grand jury subpoena for production of documents, see § 12:13, supra.

---

[16]See Gregg v. State, 331 Ga. App. 833, 835, 771 S.E.2d 486 (2015) ("[w]here the evidence sought in a subpoena duces tecum is demonstrably relevant and material to the defense, it is error for a trial court to quash the subpoena").

[17]Davis v. State, 209 Ga. App. 187, 190 (5), 433 S.E.2d 366 (1993).

[18]Tuttle v. State, 232 Ga. App. 530, 531(2), 502 S.E.2d 355 (1998).

[19]Garcia v. Allen, 202 Ga. App. 529, 530, 414 S.E.2d 742 (1992).

[20]Howland v. Weeks, 133 Ga. App. 843, 844-845, 212 S.E.2d 487 (1975).

§ 17:13   Enforcement of subpoena

Subpoenas must be served within a reasonable time before the witness is to appear. However, in no event is a subpoena to be served less than 24 hours before the time that appearance is to be required.[1] "[I]n deciding whether to enforce a subpoena, a trial court must consider 'whether under the circumstances of each case the subpoena was served within a reasonable time. . . .' "[2]

§ 17:14   Jury trial versus trial by judge

Article I, Section I, Paragraph XI of the Georgia Constitution of 1983 guarantees a defendant in a criminal case the right to a jury trial where the jury shall be the "judges of the law and the facts." In *Geng v. State*,[1] the Supreme Court ruled that this right extends to traffic violations which are charged as misdemeanors under state law. The right does not exist where the offense is premised solely upon a local or municipal ordinance.

Normally, little consideration is given to the trial of a serious criminal case by a judge as opposed to a jury. This attitude may be well justified. However, in less serious cases a defendant may fare as well or better with a judge than with a jury, especially when defense counsel has a solid "technical" defense. For example, if the defendant's sole defense is entrapment, a judge may be as likely to find the defendant not guilty as a jury.

However, the likelihood of obtaining a reversal of the case is generally reduced if a jury is waived. For example, in ruling on the admissibility of evidence it is presumed that a judge considers "only legal evidence."[2] Also, since no charge is given, a defendant does not have an opportunity to seek a new trial because of an erroneous jury instruction. Additionally, a defendant cannot be convicted by a jury unless all 12 jurors agree on the guilt of the defendant.

While judges, at least generally, do not have to try cases without a jury,[3] they are normally willing to do so in the interest of time. Such a non-jury trial will normally also result in a sav-

[Section 17:13]

[1]O.C.G.A. § 24-13-26(a).

[2]Byron v. State, 229 Ga. App. 795, 799 (6), 495 S.E.2d 123 (1997).

[Section 17:14]

[1]Geng v. State, 276 Ga. 428, 578 S.E.2d 115 (2003). See Smith v. State, 270 Ga. App. 759, 608 S.E.2d 35 (2004).

[2]Simmons v. State, 249 Ga. 860,

861(2), 295 S.E.2d 84 (1982).

[3]Sammons v. State, 53 Ga. App. 369, 370, 185 S.E. 923 (1936) (the district attorney objected to a non-jury trial). But cf. State v. Carpenter, 181 Neb. 639, 150 N.W.2d 129, 131 (1967), in which the court concluded that the right to a jury trial was a personal right of the defendant, not the state, and that the prosecuting attorney is without power to require a jury trial when the defendant waives it.

ing of time to both the district attorney and defense counsel.

The trial judge should not accept a waiver of a jury trial unless the defendant fully understands he is waiving this right.[4] The defendant's understanding that he will be "allowed" a bench trial certainly does not amount to a voluntary waiver of a jury trial.[5] "When an accused questions the purported waiver of his right to a jury trial, the State must show on the record that the defendant 'personally, knowingly, voluntarily, and intelligently waived his right to a jury trial.' "[6] The state may prove this "by two means, (1) showing on the record of the guilty plea hearing that the defendant was cognizant of all the rights he was waiving and the possible consequences of his plea; or (2) fill(ing) a silent record by use of extrinsic evidence that affirmatively shows that the guilty plea was knowing and voluntary."[7] In *Jones v. State*,[8] the court noted that such extrinsic evidence may include "testimony by defense counsel in the motion for new trial hearing about his specific recollections, *routine, or standard practices;* an affidavit from trial counsel about his specific recollections; and evidence regarding the defendant's intelligence and cognitive ability." Whether a defendant is capable of making a knowing and intelligent waiver of the right to trial by jury is "to be answered by the trial judge and will be accepted by this court unless such determination is clearly erroneous."[9]

In *Pirkle v. State*,[10] the Georgia Court of Appeals held that the fact that the defendant signed a form entitled "Waiver of Formal Arraignment/Acknowledgement of Court Date" which included a statement: "The defendant waives Formal Arraignment, list of witnesses and Jury Trial and pleads Not Guilty" was insufficient to show that the defendant knowingly and intelligently waived

---

[4]A.B.A. Standards, Trial by Jury, Vol. III, Standard 15-1.2(b) states as follows:

"Standard 15-1.2. Waiver of trial by jury

"(b) The court should not accept a waiver unless the defendant, after being advised by the court of his or her right to trial by jury, personally waives the right to trial by jury, either in writing or in open court for the record."

[5]McCormick v. State, 222 Ga. App. 753, 754 (1), 476 S.E.2d 271 (1996).

[6]Pirkle v. State, 221 Ga. App. 657, 472 S.E.2d 478 (1996) (citing and relying on Jones v. State, 212 Ga. App. 676, 679 (2), 442 S.E.2d 908 (1994)).

[7]Pirkle v. State, 221 Ga. App. 657, 472 S.E.2d 478 (1996) (quoting Bowens v. State, 194 Ga. App. 391, 392 (2), 390 S.E.2d 634 (1990)).

[8]Jones v. State, 294 Ga. App. 169, 170(1), 670 S.E.2d 104 (2008) (emphasis supplied). See Balbosa v. State, 275 Ga. 574, 571 S.E.2d 368 (2002); Oliver v. State, 325 Ga. App. 649, 753 S.E.2d 468 (2014).

[9]Seitman v. State, 320 Ga. App. 646, 740 S.E.2d 368 (2013) (citations and punctuation omitted).

[10]Pirkle v. State, 221 Ga. App. 657, 472 S.E.2d 478 (1996) (citing and relying on Payne v. State, 217 Ga. App. 386, 460 S.E.2d 297 (1995)).

his right to a jury trial. However, in *Gardner v. State*,[11] the Court of Appeals allowed that a pretrial waiver form which referenced the defendant's right to a trial by jury constituted a valid waiver where the defendant specifically initialed that portion of the form. The court did state that the better practice was to make the waiver through a colloquy with the court.

In *Bales v. State*,[12] the defendant for the first time demanded a jury trial in state court when the case was called for trial, and the state did not oppose the request. The trial court denied the defendant's request for jury trial because the enabling statute that created the court provides that in all criminal cases jury trials are automatically waived unless the defendant requests a jury trial "before pleading to the charge," which the trial court interpreted to mean before arraignment. The Court of Appeals reversed, holding that the defendant's demand constituted a revocation of his previous waiver of right to jury trial and the defendant's request must be granted where there is no evidence that the revocation would "substantially delay or impede the cause of justice."

A defendant has no federal constitutional right to a non-jury trial unless both the trial judge and the prosecuting attorney also agree to have the case tried without a jury.[13] In *Palmer v. State*,[14] the Georgia Supreme Court held that it was not error for the trial court to deny a defendant's request for a non-jury trial. There is nothing in the case to suggest that the State objected to the defendant's request. In *Howard v. Lane*,[15] the Supreme Court refused on jurisdictional grounds to hear the State's appeal from an order denying it's request for a writ prohibiting a trial court from giving a defendant a non-jury trial over the objection of the State. In a concurring opinion, Justice Carley opined that the trial court's ruling was clearly erroneous but because of limitations on the State's right to appeal under O.C.G.A. § 5-7-1, suggested that the legislature give the criminal justice system direction with respect to the State's right to insist on a jury trial in a

---

[11]Gardner v. State, 261 Ga. App. 425 (2), 582 S.E.2d 566 (2003). See Stanley v. State, 267 Ga. App. 656, 601 S.E.2d 141 (2004).

[12]Bales v. State, 227 Ga. App. 20, 488 S.E.2d 95 (1997). See Bennett v. State, 262 Ga. App. 800, 586 S.E.2d 704 (2003) where the court concluded that an attempt to revoke waiver of jury trial coming only after the case was called was nothing more than ineffective dilatory tactic.

[13]Patton v. U.S., 281 U.S. 276, 50 S. Ct. 253, 74 L. Ed. 854, 70 A.L.R. 263 (1930) (abrogated on other grounds by Williams v. Florida, 399 U.S. 78, 90 S. Ct. 1893, 26 L. Ed. 2d 446 (1970)).

[14]Palmer v. State, 195 Ga. 661, 25 S.E.2d 295 (1943). Because a defendant has no right to demand a trial without a jury, a trial court is not required to consider such a request. Lindo v. State, 278 Ga. App. 228(1), 628 S.E.2d 665 (2006).

[15]Howard v. Lane, 276 Ga. 688, 581 S.E.2d 1 (2003).

criminal case. However, in *Zigan v. State*,[16] the Supreme Court revisited the issue and concluded that a defendant may waive a jury and proceed to trial before the court *only* with the consent of the state.

In order to have a valid waiver of the right to a jury trial, a defendant must expressly, intelligently,[17] and personally participate in the waiver of his right to a jury trial.[18] In *Jackson v. State*,[19] the Court of Appeals concluded that waiver is best demonstrated when the defendant announces his intention in open court. Thus, the court found that the record failed to indicate a voluntary waiver where defense counsel, after conferring with his client, responded that his client wanted a bench trial to the trial court's inquiry as to whether the defendant wanted a bench or

---

[16]Zigan v. State, 281 Ga. 415, 638 S.E.2d 322 (2006). See State v. Evans, 282 Ga. 63, 646 S.E.2d 77 (2007), where the Georgia Supreme Court held that the state has no right to appeal an acquittal following a bench trial conducted over the objection of the state. Compare Wadkins v. State, 127 Ga. 45, 56 S.E. 74 (1906) where the court held that it was error for the judge to deny a bench trial to a defendant in that court. In *Wadkins* the act creating the court provided that "all criminal cases . . . shall be tried by the judge . . . without a jury, except when the accused . . . shall demand a jury."

[17]Patton v. U.S., 281 U.S. 276, 50 S. Ct. 253, 74 L. Ed. 854, 70 A.L.R. 263 (1930) (abrogated on other grounds by Williams v. Florida, 399 U.S. 78, 90 S. Ct. 1893, 26 L. Ed. 2d 446 (1970)); Johnson v. State, 157 Ga. App. 155, 276 S.E.2d 667 (1981).

In Wooten v. State, 162 Ga. App. 719, 720, 293 S.E.2d 11 (1982), the court said that "it would be preferable to have the defendant's personal participation spread on the record in open court, to forestall subsequent claims of lack of participation or an intelligent or knowing waiver. . . . We have found no legal precedent requiring an 'in-court' waiver of the right of a jury trial. . . . [I]n as much as the record indicates a valid waiver may have occurred but the record does not reflect

whether the defendant personally, knowingly, voluntarily, and intelligently participated in such a waiver, this case is remanded to the trial court for a hearing on this issue."

[18]Hill v. State, 181 Ga. App. 473, 352 S.E.2d 651 (1987).

[19]Jackson v. State, 253 Ga. App. 559, 561, 560 S.E.2d 62 (2002). See, Balbosa v. State, 275 Ga. 574, 571 S.E.2d 368 (2002) where the Supreme Court concluded that an inadequate waiver of trial by jury could never pass as harmless error. See also Bostic v. State, 252 Ga. App. 242, 243(1), 555 S.E.2d 894 (2001). In Stanley v. State, 267 Ga. App. 379, 599 S.E.2d 331 (2004), a written waiver contained in an affidavit signed by defendant and counsel was adequate. Compare Odum v. State, 255 Ga. App. 70, 564 S.E.2d 490 (2002) State was able to show that the waiver was knowing and voluntary where the defendant initialed statements on a form detailing that he entered a plea of not guilty and that he "knowingly and willfully" waived the right to a jury trial which he, his attorney and the prosecutor then signed. But see, Jenkins v. State, 259 Ga. App. 47 (1), 576 S.E.2d 300 (2002), one sentence waiver form stating defendant waives trial by jury and requests trial by the court signed by defendant and counsel is insufficient to establish knowing and voluntary waiver.

jury trial. In *Balbosa v. State*,[20] the Supreme Court went further and ruled that trial counsel's waiver of a trial by jury made in open court and in the presence of the defendant was not sufficient to show that the waiver was knowing and intelligent. "To ensure that [the defendant] waived his right to a jury trial voluntarily, knowingly and intelligently, the trial court should have conducted a colloquy with [the defendant] . . . ." While the burden is on the state to show that the waiver was personally and intelligently made, there is no requirement that the waiver be made in court.[21] O.C.G.A. § 40-13-23 provides that in the case of a traffic misdemeanor the defendant must "waive in writing a trial by jury" if the proceeding is in a probate court or a municipal court.[22]

Action by the state can interfere with the defendant's ability to knowingly and voluntarily waive the right to a jury trial. In *Byrd v. Owen*,[23] the court held that the state's failure to disclose that three of its witnesses had been immunized nullified the voluntariness of the defendant's waiver of a trial by jury.

In *Leggett v. State*,[24] the court held that a waiver of trial by jury may be withdrawn if the defendant "acts timely and in such a season as not substantially to delay or impede the cause of justice." In *Mojica v. State*,[25] the court affirmed the trial judge's refusal to permit the defendant to revoke her waiver of trial by jury on the eve of her re-trial. In *Hansen v. State*,[26] the court pointed out that if there is an effective waiver of a jury trial and defendant wishes to withdraw, it is his "burden to revoke the waiver in such fashion so as not to delay the trial or impede the

---

[20]Balbosa v. State, 275 Ga. 574, 575(1), 571 S.E.2d 368 (2002) (citing United States v. Duante-Higareda, 113 F.3d 1000 (9th Cir. 1997). One such colloquy approved by the Supreme Court is set out in its decision in Brown v. State, 277 Ga. 573 (2), 592 S.E.2d 666 (2004), where the trial court advised the defendant that a trial by the court without a jury meant that the court was the judge of the facts and the law but that the defendant still had a right to appeal any rulings made by the court. The defendant then acknowledged that with the advice of counsel he wished to proceed.

[21]Sims v. State, 167 Ga. App. 479 (1), 306 S.E.2d 732 (1983).

[22]Cf. Snellings v. State, 194 Ga. App. 552, 391 S.E.2d 36 (1990). The fact that a defendant may have an extensive criminal background and

been sentenced previously on guilty pleas cannot be substituted for proof that defendant voluntarily waived his rights at sentencing in the case at issue. Any suggestion to the contrary in cases such as McCollum v. State, 201 Ga. App. 493(1), 411 S.E.2d 328 (1991), was disapproved in Allison v. State, 288 Ga. App. 482(2a), 654 S.E.2d 628 (2007).

[23]Byrd v. Owen, 272 Ga. 807, 536 S.E.2d 736 (2000).

[24]Leggett v. State, 184 Ga. App. 398 (1), 361 S.E.2d 546 (1987).

[25]Mojica v. State, 210 Ga. App. 826, 827 (1), 437 S.E.2d 806 (1993).

[26]Hansen v. State, 222 Ga. App. 537, 539 (3), 474 S.E.2d 735 (1996). See Brumbalow v. State, 128 Ga. App. 581, 197 S.E.2d 380 (1973).

cause of justice."

A trial court is well-advised not to offer any advice to a defendant on whether to proceed to trial without a jury. If it appears from the record that the judge participated in the "decision-making process" on this issue, a defendant's waiver of a jury trial may later be found to be involuntary and not valid.[27]

See § 18:1, infra, on jury trials. See § 7:3, supra, on waiver of counsel, and § 16:2, supra, on entering a guilty plea.

§ 17:15   Calendar preparation

Rule 32.1 of the Uniform Rules for the Superior Courts provides as follows:

"32.1 Calendar Preparation

"All indictments and special presentments shall be set for trial within a reasonable time after arraignment. The judge or designee shall prepare a trial calendar, shall deliver a copy thereof to the clerk of court, and shall give notice in person or by mail to each counsel of record, the bondsman (if any) and the defendant at the last address indicated in court records, not less than 7 days before the trial date or dates. The calendar shall list the dates that cases are set for trial, the cases to be tried at that session of court, the case numbers, the names of the defendants and the names of the defense counsel."

In *Wooten v. State*,[1] the court held that the "precise method of assigning and calendaring cases . . . must comport with the notion of due process . . . as well as the spirit and purpose of the uniform rules and applicable statutes. . . ." Further, the court held that a system in which the district attorney makes the case assignments to the judges and sets the trial calendar violates Rule 3.1 of the Uniform Rules for the Superior Courts and abuses the inherent discretion of O.C.G.A. § 17-8-1. However, on certiorari the Georgia Supreme Court reversed the Court of Appeals and held that "the case assignment system is not unconstitutional and it is highly improbable that it contributed to the jury's verdict."[2]

In *Clark v. State*,[3] the court found that notice of trial provided by telephone to the pro se defendant's answering machine was insufficient and did not comply with the calendar requirements of

---

[27]See Ealey v. State, 310 Ga. App. 893, 714 S.E.2d 424 (2011).

[Section 17:15]

[1]Wooten v. State, 244 Ga. App. 101, 533 S.E.2d 441 (2000), rev'd, 273 Ga. 529, 543 S.E.2d 721 (2001).

[2]State v. Wooten, 273 Ga. 529, 530, 543 S.E.2d 721 (2001); Miners v. State, 250 Ga. App. 443, 447, 550 S.E.2d 725 (2001).

[3]Clark v. State, 259 Ga. App. 573, 578 S.E.2d 184 (2003).

U.S.C.R. 32.1. As a result, the Court of Appeals reversed the trial court's order denying the defendant's motion for discharge and acquittal due to a violation of the right to a speedy trial demand.

See § 16:1, supra, on notice of arraignment.

§ 17:16   Call of the case

Though rarely followed, Georgia law provides that the state shall announce "ready" or "not ready" for trial before the defendant is called upon to state whether he is ready for trial.[1] Cases are normally to be called in the order in which they stand on the docket unless the defendant is in jail.[2] However, the judge may, in his discretion, vary the order of the call of the cases on the docket for the purpose of facilitating the proceedings of the court.[3]

Both the district attorney and the defense counsel have the duty to prepare their cases for trial. If either the district attorney or defense counsel is not ready, he should move for a continuance for cause.[4]

[Section 17:16]

[1]O.C.G.A. § 17-7-172. It should be noted that this section says its provisions do not apply to "those cases where the defendant is entitled by law to demand a trial. . . ."

[2]O.C.G.A. § 17-8-1.

[3]Wilkins v. State, 246 Ga. App. 667 (1), 541 S.E.2d 458 (2000); O.C.G.A. § 17-8-1. A.B.A. Standards, Speedy Trial, Vol. II, Standards 12-1.1 and 12-1.2, state as follows:

"Standard 12-1.1. Priorities in scheduling criminal cases

"To effectuate the right of the accused to a speedy trial and the interest of the public in prompt disposition of criminal cases, insofar as is practicable:

"(a) the trial of criminal cases should be given preference over civil cases; and

"(b) the trial of defendants in custody and defendants whose pretrial liberty is reasonably believed to present unusual risks should be given preference over other criminal cases."

"Standard 12-1.2. Court control; prosecutor's duty to report; individual calendar

"(a) Control over the trial calendar should be vested in the court. The prosecuting attorney should be required to file as a public record periodic reports with the court setting forth the reasons for delay as to each case for which the prosecuting attorney has not requested trial within a prescribed time following charging. The prosecuting attorney should also advise the court of facts relevant in determining the order of cases on the calendar.

"(b) Whenever feasible, there should be individual dockets for each trial judge, with the judge having continuing responsibility for cases on his or her docket from the filing of the indictment or information."

Cf. Arnsdorff v. State, 152 Ga. App. 515, 516 (2), 263 S.E.2d 176 (1979). The court has the right to obtain from the district attorney statistical information about pending criminal cases. In re Pending Cases, Augusta Judicial Circuit, 234 Ga. 264, 266, 215 S.E.2d 473 (1975).

[4]In re Brookins, 153 Ga. App. 82, 87, 264 S.E.2d 560 (1980).

In *State v. Luttrell,*[5] the court held that a trial judge has no authority to dismiss a case with prejudice where the state's witnesses fail to appear for trial.

§ 17:17 Continuances

Continuances are frequently requested for a variety of reasons. Some grounds for continuance which have been recognized in Georgia include (1) where counsel has not had sufficient time to prepare the case,[1] (2) absence of a witness,[2] (3) illness of a witness,[3] (4) illness of the accused,[4] (5) illness of counsel,[5] (6) where leading counsel is engaged in trial of another case,[6] (7) publicity concerning case,[7] (8) newly discovered evidence,[8] (9) withdrawal of counsel immediately before trial,[9] (10) where the defendant requests a court reporter and one is not available,[10] (11) where the district attorney has not complied with a demand for a list of witnesses,[11] (12) where an alibi defense is relied upon and the prosecution seeks to show that the offense occurred on a date other than that set out in the indictment,[12] and (13) where a party has been misled by a witness to rely on his giving testimony and thus kept from having other witnesses present who would testify to the same matter.[13]

A number of other special situations justifying a continuance are set out in O.C.G.A. §§ 17-8-20 et seq., including, for example,

---

[5]State v. Luttrell, 207 Ga. App. 116, 427 S.E.2d 95 (1993).

[Section 17:17]

[1]McArver v. State, 114 Ga. 514, 40 S.E. 779 (1902); Cannon v. State, 136 Ga. App. 479, 482, 221 S.E.2d 674 (1975).

[2]Harris v. State, 142 Ga. App. 37, 38 (3), 234 S.E.2d 798 (1977).

[3]O.C.G.A. § 17-8-25, O.C.G.A. § 17-8-32.

[4]O.C.G.A. § 17-8-23.

[5]O.C.G.A. § 17-8-24. This section applies where there is only one counsel or where lead counsel is sick. The party making the application shall swear that (1) he cannot go safely to trial without the services of such absent counsel and (2) he expects to have his services at the next term of court.

[6]Even in a civil case, there is an absolute right to a continuance if counsel is arguing a case in the Georgia Supreme Court, Hill v. Clark, 51

Ga. 122 (1874) or Court of Appeals, Waxelbaum Co. v. Atlantic Coast Line R. Co., 3 Ga. App. 394, 59 S.E. 1129 (1908). Contra, Smith v. Greek, 226 Ga. 312, 317, 175 S.E.2d 1 (1970).

[7]Dutton v. State, 228 Ga. 850, 852, 188 S.E.2d 794 (1972). This case holds that a motion for a continuance on the ground of inflammatory publicity stands on the same footing as a motion for a change of venue.

[8]Monday v. State, 32 Ga. 672, 676 (1861).

[9]Smith v. Greek, 226 Ga. 312, 317, 175 S.E.2d 1 (1970).

[10]Massey v. State, 127 Ga. App. 638, 194 S.E.2d 582 (1972).

[11]Hunnicutt v. State, 135 Ga. App. 774, 219 S.E.2d 22 (1975).

[12]Caldwell v. State, 139 Ga. App. 279, 287, 228 S.E.2d 219 (1976).

[13]Interstate Life v. Wilmont, 123 Ga. App. 337, 339 (5), 180 S.E.2d 913 (1971).

attendance at the General Assembly[14] and various State Board meetings. Likewise, attendance at a meeting of the State Board of Education or the Board of Regents of the University System of Georgia of counsel or a party to any case is a statutory basis for a continuance.[15] Also see § 17:10, supra, on witnesses who are members of the General Assembly. Also pursuant to O.C.G.A. § 17-8-31, the court shall grant a continuance, on or without a motion if either the leading attorney, any party, or material witness, is absent due to service in the National Guard, or a reserve or on active duty in the armed forces of the United States. If a demand is made for a speedy trial under O.C.G.A. § 17-7-170 or O.C.G.A. § 17-7-171 the court shall grant a continuance if the moving party establishes that a witness is material and necessary, the witness is located outside the state, the party has submitted a request with the military for the testimony of the witness, and the witness will not be available in the pre-allotted time period granted by the demand. The continuance shall toll the running of the demand for trial and shall remain in effect until the witness is released from active duty or is allowed to testify. In such cases where a continuance is granted the defendant will be eligible for bail except in cases punishable by death or life imprisonment without the possibility of parole.

A legal showing must be made as to why a motion for continuance should be granted if the defendant hopes to obtain a reversal if the motion is overruled.[16] For example, where a continuance is sought because of the illness of a witness, there are eight statutory requirements which must be met.[17]

O.C.G.A. § 17-8-25 provides in part as follows:

"In all applications for continuances upon the ground of the absence of a witness, it shall be shown . . . that [1] the witness is absent; that [2] he has been subpoenaed; that [3] he does not reside more than 100 miles from the place of trial by the nearest practical route; that [4] his testimony is material; that [5] the witness is not absent by the permission, directly or indirectly, of the applicant; that [6] the applicant expects he will be able to procure the testimony of the witness at the next term of court; that [7] the application is not made for the purpose of delay but to enable the applicant to procure the testimony of the absent witness; and [8] the application must state the facts expected to be proved by the absent witness."

---

[14]Also see O.C.G.A. § 9-10-150.

[15]O.C.G.A. §§ 9-10-151, 17-8-29.

[16]Chandler v. State, 143 Ga. App. 608, 609 (1), 239 S.E.2d 158 (1977); Halthon-Howard v. State, 234 Ga. App. 229 (1), 506 S.E.2d 415 (1998).

[17]Beasley v. State, 115 Ga. App. 827, 156 S.E.2d 128 (1967); Watts v. State, 142 Ga. App. 857, 237 S.E.2d 231 (1977).

The 1992 case of *Garrett v. State*[18] reaffirmed the statutory requirement that the witness must live not more than 100 miles from the place of trial even though subpoenas may now be served anywhere in the state. See § 17:10, supra, on subpoenas generally. In *McCullough v. State,*[19] the court held that it is not error for the trial judge "to refuse to continue a case in order to procure the testimony of a witness who resides" outside the State of Georgia. (But see § 14:96, supra, on the interstate act to obtain witnesses outside the state.) If a witness, living within the jurisdiction of the court, is temporarily in another state and a party has delivered a subpoena to an officer to serve on the witness, a motion for a continuance should be granted where it is alleged that the motion is made in good faith and not for delay and that the witness is not absent by the defendant's procurement or consent and what his testimony is expected to be.[20] However, no continuance is generally to be allowed because of the absence of a witness if the opposite party admits to the truth of the facts expected to be proved by the witness.[21]

In addition to the requirement set out above, it must be kept in mind that where subpoenas are issued by the clerk in blank, the names and addresses of the witnesses subpoenaed must be filed with the clerk not less than six hours before their appearance is directed. If counsel fails to timely file such a list, he forfeits his right to ask for a continuance because of the failure of a subpoenaed witness to appear.[22]

O.C.G.A. § 17-8-24 provides as follows:

"The illness or absence, from providential cause, of counsel where there is but one, or of the leading counsel where there are more than one, shall be a sufficient ground for continuance: Provided, the party making the application will swear that he cannot go safely to trial without the services of such absent counsel, and that he expects his services at the next term, and

---

[18]Garrett v. State, 202 Ga. App. 463, 414 S.E.2d 693 (1992).

[19]McCullough v. State, 230 Ga. App. 98, 101 (2), 495 S.E.2d 338 (1998) (quoting Smith v. State, 193 Ga. App. 208, 387 S.E.2d 419 (1989)).

[20]Pyburn v. State, 84 Ga. 193, 10 S.E. 733 (1890). A showing that the witness had said his testimony would not do the defendant any good was not a counter-showing. Paulk v. State, 5 Ga. App. 567 (1), 63 S.E. 659 (1909), is generally in accord with *Pyburn*. In this case, the witness had not been subpoenaed, but the court said, "A continuance (or a postponement at least) should be granted where it appears that a witness is absent whose testimony in behalf of the defendant is material, if in addition it is made to appear that the defendant has used all the diligence within his power and all means at his command to procure the attendance of the absent witness, and the witness is within the power of the court's subpoena."

[21]O.C.G.A. § 17-8-32. This section also provides that any such admission shall be reduced to writing.

[22]O.C.G.A. § 24-13-26.

that said application is not made for delay only."

The requirements of this Code section have been summarized by saying that such a motion for continuance must show that counsel "is sick; that the motion is not made for delay only; and that movant expects to secure his services at next term."[23]

As a general proposition if a defendant is without fault and his counsel is not present, he is entitled to a continuance.[24] This position finds support in the constitutional right to be represented by counsel who has had a reasonable amount of time after employment in which to prepare to defend the case.[25] In this connection, the Georgia Supreme Court has said that "[u]ndue haste in the administration of the criminal law is as much to be condemned as unnecessary delay."[26] Thus, generally if a defendant's counsel has not had an opportunity to prepare to defend the case, it is error for the trial judge to overrule a motion for a continuance.[27] See § 7:1, supra, on time to prepare a defense. However, a

---

[23]Williams v. Gooding, 226 Ga. 549, 552, 176 S.E.2d 64 (1970). In Scott v. State, 151 Ga. App. 840, 841, 262 S.E.2d 198 (1979), the court pointed out that a defendant is not entitled to a continuance because of illness of his counsel if his attorney was ill when employed.

[24]Shaw v. State, 251 Ga. 109, 303 S.E.2d 448 (1983). See § 7:1, supra. E.g., Wallis v. State, 137 Ga. App. 457, 459, 224 S.E.2d 91 (1976). A defendant is also deprived of his due process rights under the Fourteenth Amendment when counsel is not present for the trial. Gandy v. Alabama, 569 F.2d 1318 (5th Cir. 1978).

In Miller v. State, 156 Ga. App. 469, 274 S.E.2d 818 (1980), the defendant's original counsel withdrew after arraignment, and the defendant requested a continuance to obtain new counsel. Defendant did not notify the trial judge or try to employ new counsel until the time set for trial. He was tried and convicted without counsel (or a valid waiver of counsel), but his conviction was subsequently reversed. Cf. Robertson v. State, 162 Ga. App. 873, 876, 293 S.E.2d 477 (1982).

[25]See Kimbrough v. State, 352 So.2d 925 (Fla.App.1977).

[26]Smith v. Greek, 226 Ga. 312, 317, 175 S.E.2d 1 (1970).

[27]Tucker v. State, 136 Ga. App. 456 (1), 221 S.E.2d 664 (1975). In this case, a public defender was appointed to represent the defendant at 3:00 p.m. and was engaged in other matters. The following morning the defendant's motion for a continuance was denied and 10 minutes later the defendant's trial started. The appellate court reversed. See Ware v. State, 137 Ga. App. 673, 675 (3), 224 S.E.2d 873 (1976), a probation revocation proceeding. The defendant had six days' notice of the hearing but employed counsel just before hearing. Counsel asked for a continuance of one day to prepare. The refusal to grant the continuance was reversed.

In Forehand v. State, 130 Ga. App. 801, 204 S.E.2d 516 (1974), the court held that where counsel was employed on Friday and had no opportunity to interview the witnesses, it is error to force him to trial on the following Monday. In Bacon v. State, 146 Ga. App. 468, 246 S.E.2d 475 (1978), the court reversed the overruling of a motion for continuance where the public defender was appointed one afternoon and the trial started the next morning. Cf. Spillers v. State, 145 Ga. App. 809 (1), 245 S.E.2d 54 (1978).

In Cooper v. State, 148 Ga. App. 301, 251 S.E.2d 157 (1978), the court said that the lack of preparation of a

defendant is not automatically entitled to a continuance if it appears that he discharged counsel just before trial so as to obtain a continuance.[28] In *Turman v. State*,[29] the trial court denied defendant's request for a continuance where defendant had retained counsel who was ill and unable to come to the trial calendar. Weeks earlier, defendant had been appointed counsel but had informed the court then that he wanted to retain counsel. The court ordered defendant to proceed to trial with appointed counsel despite counsel's protests that he was wholly unprepared. Reversing, the Court of Appeals concluded that the trial court had a duty to determine whether it was satisfied that retained counsel's absence was due to circumstances beyond defendant's control.

There are a number of reported cases in which a number of motions for continuance have been based on the defendant's desire to obtain a copy of a transcript of an earlier trial or a preliminary hearing so that the testimony may be used for cross-examination and impeachment.[30] Generally, if a defendant exercises due diligence in acquiring the transcript and he has not been able to obtain it, this is a valid basis on which to obtain a

---

new counsel is not alone a ground for a continuance.

In Hill v. State, 161 Ga. App. 346 (1), 287 S.E.2d 779 (1982) (quoting Brown v. State, 140 Ga. App. 160, 161, 230 S.E.2d 128 (1976)), the court stated that "[t]here is no fixed rule as to the number of days that should, of right, be allowed counsel in a criminal case to prepare the case for trial. . . . A statement by counsel for the defendant that he has not had sufficient time to investigate and prepare the defense is a mere conclusion. Questions of this nature must of necessity be entrusted to the discretion of the trial judge." (Citations omitted.) Accord, Miller v. State, 165 Ga. App. 487 (1), 299 S.E.2d 174 (1983).

[28]Huckaby v. State, 127 Ga. App. 439, 440, 194 S.E.2d 119 (1972). Cf. Wills v. State, 216 Ga. App. 157, 158 (1), 453 S.E.2d 762 (1995).

In the Huckaby case, the defendant changed counsels several times. She was finally forced to go to trial with a counsel who had been employed two hours before the trial started. This case was in effect reversed in a federal habeas corpus proceeding entitled Lillian Huckaby v. Leroy Stynchcombe, CA 17822 (1973), U. S. Dist. Ct., Northern Dist. of Ga., Atlanta, Ga. Div. See Annot., "Withdrawal, Discharge or Substitution of Counsel in Criminal Case as Ground for Continuance," 73 A.L.R.3d 725 (1976). See Annot., 17 Am. Jur. 2d Continuances § 69, Withdrawal, Discharge or Substitution of Counsel; Constitutional Limitations (2004). In United States v. Burton, 584 F.2d 485 (D.C.Cir. 1978), the court said that the right to counsel of one's choice must be weighed against the public's interest in the prompt, efficient administration of justice.

Cf. Hughes v. State, 168 Ga. App. 413, 414 (2), 309 S.E.2d 409 (1983); Hobson v. State, 266 Ga. 638 (2), 469 S.E.2d 188 (1996).

[29]Turman v. State, 272 Ga. App. 570 (1), 613 S.E.2d 126 (2005).

[30]E.g., Carter v. State, 156 Ga. App. 633, 634 (5), 275 S.E.2d 716 (1980).

continuance.[31] However, in *Gann v. State*,[32] the court found no error in the refusal of the trial judge to supply the defendant with the transcript of his previous trial which had ended in a mistrial.

Whenever a party moves for a continuance, he must show that he has used due diligence in trying to be ready for the trial.[33] If a continuance is to be sought because of the illness of a witness or the defendant, the party should present an affidavit from a physician, stating the nature of the illness. If a witness is in ill health, the affidavit should state that in the opinion of the physician the witness will be able to be present at the next term of the court but that the witness is unable to attend the present term, or that the witness' health will be adversely affected by attending the present term but he will be able to attend the next term. If the illness of the defendant is the basis of the motion, the affidavit should state that the defendant is not able to attend the present term of court.[34] The opposite party may make a counter-showing.[35]

In *Dasher v. State*,[36] the defendant was charged with conspiracy to commit murder. The defendant was indicted in 1974 and was not tried until 1978 or thereafter. A number of continuances had been granted at the defendant's request. The evidence was undisputed that the defendant was ill, would never recover, and his condition would further deteriorate. All medical witnesses said that if the defendant attended a trial, the strain would likely kill him. The trial judge refused to grant a further continuance. The defendant was tried over his objection and he was not present. The court concluded that the trial judge did not abuse his discretion in denying a further continuance and affirmed the conviction. However, on petition for federal habeas corpus Dasher's conviction and sentence were vacated (1) because of his right to be present at his trial and the fact that he "obviously did have 'good cause' to remain away from the trial" and (2) because his physical condition has so impaired his mental capacity that he was prevented from having effective assistance of counsel.[37] However, on appeal to the Eleventh Circuit, the decision of the district court was vacated and the case remanded since the

---

[31]Martin v. State, 151 Ga. App. 9, 15, 258 S.E.2d 711 (1979); Coaxum v. State, 146 Ga. App. 370, 371 (4), 246 S.E.2d 403 (1978); Murphy v. State, 212 Ga. App. 153, 154 (3), 442 S.E.2d 2 (1994).

[32]Davis v. State, 190 Ga. App. 178, 378 S.E.2d 519 (1989); Moreland v. State, 213 Ga. App. 75, 76 (2), 443 S.E.2d 701 (1994).

[33]O.C.G.A. § 17-8-20; Brown v. State, 214 Ga. App. 733, 735 (2), 449 S.E.2d 136 (1994).

[34]In Frain v. State, 40 Ga. 529 (4) (1869), the court said that a defendant is deprived of a fair trial if he is forced to trial when he is too sick to have the use of his faculties.

[35]O.C.G.A. § 17-8-22.

[36]Dasher v. State, 157 Ga. App. 664, 664-65, 278 S.E.2d 465 (1981).

[37]Dasher v. Stripling, 685 F.2d 385 (11th Cir. 1982).

defendant did not show that he had been prejudiced by not being able to attend the trial.[38]

All motions for a continuance are said to be addressed to the sound discretion of the trial judge,[39] and an abuse of discretion must be clear before an appellate court will reverse the trial court.[40] O.C.G.A. § 17-8-33(a) provides in part that the trial judge "shall have power to allow the continuance of criminal cases . . . as often as the principles of justice may require, upon sufficient cause shown under oath." In *Hicks v. State*,[41] the court affirmed the action of the trial judge in granting the state's motion for a continuance due to the absence of an unsubpoenaed witness.

In *State v. Colquitt*,[42] the court indicated that counsel may rely on the local practice in a particular court. Also, it must be kept in mind that a refusal to grant a continuance is not generally reversible error if defense counsel thereafter announces "ready."[43]

The foregoing material has largely discussed continuance in a general context, but there are some special rules which apply to criminal procedure. In theory at least, defendants are to be tried at the term in which indictments are returned, but postponements may be permitted as "the principles of justice" require, and courts have the power to allow the continuance from term to term, but where a court is in continuous session, no postponement shall be granted for 30 days or more over the objection of the opposite party.[44] It has also been pointed out that "each motion for a continuance must stand or fall on its own merits" and the fact that the state had met its burden on five previous occasions does not relieve the defendant of his burden when he moved for a continuance.[45] In *Kendrix v. State*,[46] the defendant moved for a continuance 10 days before a trial involving rape in order to

---

[38]Dasher v. Stripling, 685 F.2d 385 (11th Cir. 1982).

[39]O.C.G.A. § 17-8-22; Wellons v. State, 144 Ga. App. 218, 219 (2), 240 S.E.2d 768 (1977).

[40]Pulliam v. State, 236 Ga. 460, 462, 224 S.E.2d 8 (1976) (citing O.C.G.A. § 17-8-33); Hilton v. Haynes, 147 Ga. 725, 95 S.E. 220 (1918); Pope v. State, 42 Ga. App. 680 (8), 157 S.E. 211 (1931).

In Morris v. Slappy, 461 U.S. 1, 103 S.Ct. 1610, 75 L.Ed.2d 610, 620 (1983), the court said that "broad discretion must be granted trial courts on matters of continuances; only an unreasoning and arbitrary 'insistence upon expeditiousness in the face of a justifiable request for delay' violates the right to the assistance of counsel."

[41]Hicks v. State, 221 Ga. App. 735, 736 (2), 472 S.E.2d 474 (1996). But cf. Sosebee v. State, 190 Ga. App. 746, 750 (7), 380 S.E.2d 464 (1989).

[42]State v. Colquitt, 147 Ga. App. 627, 249 S.E.2d 680 (1978).

[43]Raines v. State, 186 Ga. App. 239, 240 (1), 366 S.E.2d 841 (1988); Whatley v. State, 162 Ga. App. 106 (1), 290 S.E.2d 316 (1982). Cf. Walton v. State, 242 Ga. App. 639, 640 (1), 530 S.E.2d 531 (2000).

[44]O.C.G.A. § 17-8-33.

[45]Eze v. State, 195 Ga. App. 503 (2), 393 S.E.2d 758 (1990).

[46]Kendrix v. State, 206 Ga. App. 627, 628, 426 S.E.2d 251 (1992).

obtain a DNA analysis by the State Crime Lab. The court concluded that a defendant has no right to have such a test performed at the Crime Lab, and it affirmed the refusal to grant the continuance.

The foregoing material has been directed toward a motion for a continuance made before trial. However, in *Dempsey v. State*,[47] the court pointed out that there may be extreme circumstances which arise during the course of a trial which require a trial judge to grant the defendant a continuance to rebut unexpected testimony of a key witness.

If a case is called and the state is not ready but does not move for a continuance, it seems that the trial judge may dismiss the case.[48]

A defendant is not automatically entitled to a continuance simply because his counsel has been called for jury duty.[49]

See Studdard, *Daniel's Georgia Handbook on Criminal Evidence* (2018 ed.), § 1:35, on motion for continuance based on evidence of commission of crime on date other than that set out in the indictment. Also see § 21:8, infra, on alibi as a defense.

See Rule 17.1 of the Uniform Rules for the Superior Courts on the method of resolving conflicts of counsel in two or more courts.[50]

For motions for continuances, see Studdard, *Daniel's Georgia Criminal Trial Practice Forms* (2018–2019 ed.), §§ 23:65 et seq.

§ 17:18   Placing case on dead docket

One of the duties of a clerk of the superior court is to maintain a dead docket. The Georgia Code provides that cases may be transferred to the dead docket at the discretion of the judge and thereafter called only at his pleasure.[1]

The placing of a case on the dead docket postpones the prosecution indefinitely but does not constitute a dismissal nor termination of the case in the defendant's favor. The case need not be reinstated nor the defendant re-indicted before he may be tried. The defendant may be brought to trial at the pleasure of the judge or upon the demand of the accused.[2] A court-ordered dead docket does not constitute a dismissal of the case and hence is

---

[47]Dempsey v. State, 151 Ga. App. 784 (2), 261 S.E.2d 733 (1979).

[48]State v. Finkelstein, 170 Ga. App. 608, 609, 317 S.E.2d 648 (1984).

[49]Riley v. State, 174 Ga. App. 607, 608, 330 S.E.2d 808 (1985).

[50]Baker v. State, 190 Ga. App. 219, 378 S.E.2d 525 (1989).

[Section 17:18]

[1]O.C.G.A. § 15-6-61(a)(4)(B).

[2]Courtenay v. Randolph, 125 Ga. App. 581, 582-83, 188 S.E.2d 396 (1972). See Newman v. State, 121 Ga. App. 692, 175 S.E.2d 144 (1970), on the right of defendant to demand trial even though his case has been placed

not subject to appeal by the state.[3]

In *Wilson v. State*,[4] the case was placed on the dead docket after which the defendant entered a nolo contendere plea. The trial court denied the defendant's motion to modify the sentence which the appellate court affirmed pointing out that the case was still pending even though it had been placed on dead docket.

A case is still pending, even though on the dead docket, and the defendant can make a demand for trial.[5]

Placing a case on the dead docket cannot be used to delay the trial over the defendant's objection, or violate the accused's right to a speedy trial under the Sixth Amendment.[6] However, if the defendant does not demand trial and show prejudice, it appears that a substantial period of time may elapse before a violation of his Sixth Amendment right to a speedy trial occurs.[7]

When an individual's case has remained on the dead docket for longer than twelve months, the individual may petition the court in the county where the case is pending to restrict access to the criminal history record of the offense, pursuant to O.C.G.A. § 35-3-37(j)(3). The petition must be served on the prosecuting attorney and a hearing (if requested) must be held within 90 days of the filing of the petition. The court "shall hear evidence" and—in giving consideration to the reason the case was placed on the dead docket—"shall determine" whether the order is appropriate. However, if an active warrant is pending for the individual, the court "shall not" grant the motion.

For a motion and order to place a case on dead docket, see Studdard, *Daniel's Georgia Criminal Trial Practice Forms* (2018–2019 ed.), §§ 23:71 et seq.

§ 17:19 Entering a nolle prosequi

Prior to indictment the district attorney in his sole discretion

---

on the docket.

[3]State v. Creel, 216 Ga. App. 394, 454 S.E.2d 804 (1995).

[4]Wilson v. State, 240 Ga. App. 681, 523 S.E.2d 613 (1999).

[5]McCord v. Jones, 168 Ga. App. 891, 311 S.E.2d 209 (1983).

[6]Underhill v. State, 129 Ga. App. 65, 66, 198 S.E.2d 703 (1973).

[7]See § 14:70, supra, on constitutional right to a speedy trial. State v. Redding, 274 Ga. 831, 561 S.E.2d 79 (2002) (fact that case is placed on dead docket does not affect defendant's right to speedy trial). Georgia dead docket has been compared with the North Carolina nolle prosequi with leave to reinstate. See Newman v. State, 121 Ga. App. 692, 694, 175 S.E.2d 144 (1970). In Klopfer v. North Carolina, 386 U.S. 213, 87 S.Ct. 988, 18 L.Ed.2d 1 (1967), the court held the North Carolina procedure violative of the Sixth Amendment, but in North Carolina the defendant did not have the right to demand trial after a nolle prosequi with leave to reinstate.

may dismiss a case.[1] Even after indictment, with the consent of the court, the district attorney may enter a nolle prosequi, or "nol pros" the case, before the jury is sworn and after an examination of a case in open court.[2] After the jury is sworn, a nolle prosequi may not be entered unless the defendant consents to it.[3] The pendency of a motion to quash does not preclude a trial court from entering a nolle prosequi.[4] The prosecuting attorney must notify the defendant and the defendant's attorney, either personally or by mail in writing, within 30 days of the entry of a nolle prosequi.[5]

Unlike the situation where a case is placed on the dead docket, prosecution under the indictment terminates when a nolle prosequi has been entered.[6] "The entry of the nolle prosequi render[s] the charge dead."[7] Nevertheless, entering a nolle prosequi does not prevent the return of a new indictment[8] or the framing of another accusation for the same offense[9] if this is done within six months from the time the nolle prosequi was entered or within the statute of limitations for the particular offense.[10] Also, where a court enters a nolle prosequi, the court, during the same term,

---

[Section 17:19]

[1]State v. Hanson, 249 Ga. 739, 744, 295 S.E.2d 297 (1982).

[2]Martin v. State, 73 Ga. App. 573, 575 (1), 37 S.E.2d 411 (1946). The term nolle prosequi means a "formal entry upon the record by the prosecuting officer in a criminal action by which he declares that he will no further prosecute the case, either as to some of the counts, or some of the defendants or altogether." See Williams v. State, 244 Ga. 485, 486-487(2), 260 S.E.2d 879 (1979). See also Layman v. State, 280 Ga. 794, 631 S.E.2d 107 (2006) (defendant who does not consent to nolle prosequi has standing to appeal its entry as a final order).

The trial judge has no authority to enter a nolle prosequi in the absence of a motion therefore by the district attorney. Price v. Cobb, 60 Ga. App. 59, 61, 3 S.E.2d 131 (1939). See Williams v. State, 126 Ga. App. 302, 305, 190 S.E.2d 807 (1972).

[3]O.C.G.A. § 17-8-3; State v. Jackson, 290 Ga. App. 250(1), 659 S.E.2d 679 (2008); Rhear v. State, 171 Ga. App. 435, 436 (1), 319 S.E.2d 895 (1984).

[4]State v. LeJeune, 276 Ga. 179, 576 S.E.2d 888 (2003).

[5]O.C.G.A. § 17-8-3.

[6]O.C.G.A. § 17-3-3.

[7]State v. Sheahan, 217 Ga. App. 26, 28 (2), 456 S.E.2d 615 (1995).

[8]Jones v. State, 115 Ga. 814 (5), 42 S.E. 271 (1902); Earlywine v. Strickland, 145 Ga. App. 626, 627, 244 S.E.2d 118 (1978).

In Richards v. State, 222 Ga. App. 853, 855 (2), 476 S.E.2d 598 (1996), the court pointed out that "[t]he mere entry of [a] nolle prosequi does not indicate an absence of the commission of a criminal act or forever clear one of the charges brought against him. A nolle prosequi is a cessation of prosecution for the . . . [moment], but it may spring into life again and be continued . . . ."

[9]Mitchell v. State, 126 Ga. 84, 54 S.E. 931 (1906).

[10]Kyles v. State, 254 Ga. 49, 50, 326 S.E.2d 216 (1985); State v. Davis, 201 Ga. App. 533, 534, 411 S.E.2d 555 (1991).

may grant an order rescinding the order of nolle prosequi.[11] However, where the nolle prosequi is entered pursuant to a plea agreement, from which the defendant subsequently withdraws, the case may be reinstated outside the term of court in which it was entered.[12]

However, if the defendant has filed a demand for trial and a nolle prosequi is entered thereafter the defendant may move for discharge and acquittal pursuant to O.C.G.A. § 17-7-170 if that statute is not complied with.[13] See § 14:67, supra. But in *Knight v. State*,[14] the court held that there was no automatic right to an acquittal where there has been a nol pros entered and the defendant has waived his right to a discharge by the request of his counsel for a continuance. After the jury has been sworn in, if a nolle prosequi is entered without the defendant's consent, an acquittal[15] will result in that case and a later indictment may not be returned against the defendant for the same offense.[16] A defendant has no right to object to the entering of a nolle prosequi unless it is entered after the jury has been sworn.[17]

In *Rhyne v. State*,[18] the court held that, after a mistrial has been entered because of the inability of the jury to agree on a verdict, a nolle prosequi can be entered without the consent of the defendant.

Where a count in an indictment charges two or more defendants with the commission of a crime, a nolle prosequi may be entered as to one of the defendants without impairing the validity of the

---

[11]Buice v. State, 239 Ga. App. 52, 53 (1), 520 S.E.2d 258 (1999), aff'd, 272 Ga. 323, 327, 528 S.E.2d 788 (2000).

[12]In a case of first impression, the Supreme Court ruled in Carlisle v. State, 277 Ga. 99, 586 S.E.2d 240 (2003) that the limitations imposed on the jurisdiction of the trial court to vacate an order of *nolle prosequi* or the time within which the State may re-indict the case are not changed even when the defendant obtains *habeas* relief from a sentence that was entered pursuant to a plea bargain which involved the *nolle prosequi* of several charges. See Hicks v. State, 315 Ga. App. 779, 728 S.E.2d 294 (2012) (state may re-indict the defendant within six months of *nolle prosequi* regardless of intervening statute of limitations based on the date of the first indictment).

[13]Bond v. State, 212 Ga. App. 608, 442 S.E.2d 482 (1994); Coker v. State, 181 Ga. App. 559, 353 S.E.2d 56 (1987); Ciprotti v. State, 187 Ga. App. 61, 63 (2), 369 S.E.2d 337 (1988). In Day v. State, 216 Ga. App. 29, 30 (2), 453 S.E.2d 73 (1994), the court held that the same rule applies in capital cases under O.C.G.A. § 17-7-171.

[14]Knight v. State, 197 Ga. App. 250, 251 (1), 398 S.E.2d 202 (1990).

[15]Jones v. State, 55 Ga. 625 (2) (1876).

[16]Lamp v. Smith, 56 Ga. 589 (1876).

[17]Jackson v. State, 76 Ga. 551 (2) (1886).

[18]Rhyne v. State, 209 Ga. App. 548, 549 (1), 434 S.E.2d 76 (1993).

indictment as to the remaining defendant(s).[19] In *Broomfield v. State,*[20] the court held that the remaining defendant or defendants do not have standing to object to the grant of a motion to nol pros the case of one defendant, where the trial judge instructs the jury that the jurors are not to regard this action as an inference of guilt for the remaining defendant or defendants and that the reason for this action is not important to the jury's considerations, and there is no other showing of prejudice.

See § 14:65, supra, on a second quashing of an indictment as barring further prosecution. For a motion and order to enter nolle prosequi, see Studdard, *Daniel's Georgia Criminal Trial Practice Forms* (2018–2019 ed.), §§ 23:77 et seq.

§ 17:20 Settlements in criminal cases

O.C.G.A. § 17-8-2 provides that all indictments or presentments may be settled prior to trial by the prosecutor and defendant, and that such a settlement is valid only upon order of the court after an examination of the merits of the case. There is an assumption that the trial judge did, in fact, make a preliminary examination of the merits of the case before passing upon the validity of the settlement.[1]

Georgia case law appears to hold that before indictment, parties may settle cases involving private property and debtor-creditor disputes.[2] Conversely, Georgia law appears to hold that in crimes including wrongs "against society or good morals" the parties may not settle even pre-indictment.[3] This rule is consistent with the idea that the state is the offended party in any crime, having a greater interest in prosecuting and being the party who should decide whether or not a case should be settled.

In indictment or special presentment cases, O.C.G.A. § 17-8-2 comes into play and prohibits all settlement except with the consent of the prosecutor and defendant and with the approval of the judge and a court order upon an examination of the merits of the case.[4]

It is still advisable to seek judicial authorization of settlements in criminal cases; however, since a person is guilty of compound-

---

[19]Williams v. State, 244 Ga. 485, 486 (2), 260 S.E.2d 879 (1979).

[20]Broomfield v. State, 264 Ga. 145, 148 (3), 442 S.E.2d 242 (1994).

[Section 17:20]

[1]Griffin v. State, 12 Ga. App. 615, 627, 77 S.E. 1080 (1913).

[2]Holsey v. State, 4 Ga. App. 453, 454-55, 61 S.E. 836 (1908); Childs v. State, 118 Ga. App. 706, 707-10, 165 S.E.2d 577 (1968); Goolsby v. Bush, 53 Ga. 353, 356 (1874).

[3]Holsey v. State, 4 Ga. App. 453, 454-55, 61 S.E. 836 (1908); Childs v. State, 118 Ga. App. 706, 707-10, 165 S.E.2d 577 (1968); Goolsby v. Bush, 53 Ga. 353, 356 (1874).

[4]Pratt v. State, 167 Ga. App. 819, 307 S.E.2d 714 (1983).

ing a crime when, after instituting criminal proceedings and without leave of the court or of the solicitor of the court having the pending criminal proceedings, he accepts or agrees to accept any benefit in consideration of a promise, expressed or implied, not to prosecute or assist in the prosecution of a criminal offense.[5] Where a crime amounts to a tort, the injured party may agree upon and receive compensation for his personal injury; any attempt, however, to satisfy the public offense, or to suppress a prosecution therefor, is illegal and vitiates the entire agreement except in cases where the law expressly authorizes such a settlement.[6] Where the offense sought to be satisfied or the prosecution sought to be suppressed amounts to a felony, the agreement itself is illegal and constitutes no defense to an action for the tort, but if the offense if not a felony and the agreement is fully executed, it shall constitute a defense to the tort.[7]

It should be remembered that Standard 49 of Rule 4-102 of the Rules and Regulations of the State Bar of Georgia prohibits an attorney from presenting or threatening to present criminal charges solely to obtain an advantage in a civil matter.

§ 17:21   Record restriction; expungement of record

O.C.G.A. § 35-3-36(c) provides in part that "[a]ny person arrested or taken into custody and subsequently released without charge or cleared of the offense through court proceedings shall have any fingerprint record taken in connection therewith returned if required by statute or upon court order. . . ." However, this statute seems to apply only to fingerprint records and not to arrest records,[1] and the statute has been held not to apply where a case is "disposed of" by the entry of a nolle prosequi order.[2] In *Meinken v. Burgess*,[3] Meinken's record showed that he had been arrested for child molestation. After the arrest, he had made a demand for trial which the state did not comply with, and he was

---

[5]O.C.G.A. § 16-10-90. A person convicted of compounding a felony may be fined up to $1000 or imprisoned from one to five years, or both. A person convicted of compounding a misdemeanor shall be punished as for a misdemeanor. In order to convict a defendant of compounding a crime, the state must prove the actual crime for which the defendant is charged with compounding. Hays v. State, 142 Ga. 592 (1), 83 S.E. 236 (1914).

[6]O.C.G.A. § 51-11-20. The intention of the parties in making the agreement controls; if the parties intended to settle only civil liability, the agree-

ment is binding; but if the parties intended to thwart the criminal prosecution, the agreement is null and void. Godwin v. Crowell, 56 Ga. 566 (1876). This issue, of course, is for the jury. McConnell v. Cherokee National Bank, 18 Ga. App. 52 (2), 88 S.E. 824 (1916).

[7]O.C.G.A. § 51-11-20.

[Section 17:21]

[1]Ga. Atty. Gen. 82-8.

[2]Drake v. State, 170 Ga. App. 846, 318 S.E.2d 721 (1984).

[3]Meinken v. Burgess, 262 Ga. 863, 426 S.E.2d 876 (1993).

acquitted pursuant to O.C.G.A. § 17-7-170(b). See § 14:67, supra, on statutory speedy trial demand. Meinken's request to have his arrest record expunged was denied. The Supreme Court in effect affirmed and pointed out that "expungement should be reserved for exceptional cases. . . . The fact that the arrest record did not reflect that Meinken was acquitted by operation of law does not constitute an exceptional circumstance warranting the remedy of expungement instead of modification or supplementation."

O.C.G.A. § 35-3-37, to some extent, ameliorates the foregoing. This statute enables a petitioner or the petitioner's attorney on written application to obtain the petitioner's criminal history record information.[4] Prior to July 1, 2013, § 35-3-37 provided that if a person contested the accuracy of his criminal record, it was mandatory for the Crime Information Center, upon application, to make available a copy of the contested record identifying the portion contested and showing the reason for the contest of accuracy. Effective July 1, 2013,[5] this part of the statute was amended in three ways. First, an individual can now address not only information he believes to be inaccurate or incomplete but also misleading, by requesting the Center to modify, supplement, or correct the information. Second, a 60-day window following such a request has been created for the entity to respond. Finally, if the entity declines to respond within the 60 days or if the individual believes the entity's decision is unsatisfactory, petitioner must appeal within 30 days of whichever occurs later to the court with original jurisdiction of the criminal charges in the county where the entity is located. This is in contrast to appealing to the superior court of the county of petitioner's residence, which was previously provided for under the statute.

O.C.G.A. § 35-3-37 provides a method of restricting access to an individual's criminal history record information,[6] including any fingerprints or photographs of the individual. Amendments to the statute, effective July 1, 2013,[7] added new circumstances in which access to an individual's criminal history record information shall be restricted. The amendments delineated these into prior to and after the indictment or accusation. For example,

---

[4]Formerly referred to as "criminal record."

[5]"[This part] of this Act shall become fully effective on July 1, 2013; provided, however, that for the purposes of preparing for implementation of [this part] of this Act, said part shall become effective on July 1, 2012." The amended statute applies to arrests made prior to July 1, 2013 pursuant to § 35-3-37(n)(1). See Woodhouse v. State, 336 Ga. App. 880, 785 S.E.2d 429 (2016).

[6]Formerly referred to as "expunging one's record."

[7]"[This part] of this Act shall become fully effective on July 1, 2013; provided, however, that for the purposes of preparing for implementation of [this part] of this Act, said part shall become effective on July 1, 2012."

prior to indictment or accusation, the record may be restricted: (1) where an individual was arrested and released by the arresting agency without either: (A) the offence being referred to the prosecuting attorney; or (B) the Center receiving notice from the arresting agency that the offence had been referred to the prosecuting attorney after the determined period of time for that type of crime has passed after the arrest; (2) where the case is referred to the prosecuting attorney but later dismissed; or (3) where the grand jury returned two no bills.[8]

After the indictment or accusation, the record may be restricted: (1) where all charges were dismissed or nolle prossed; (2) where an individual was found or pled guilty to possession of a narcotic drug, marijuana, depressant, or hallucinogenic, was sentenced under Code section 16-13-2, and the individual successfully completed the terms and conditions of probation; (3) where an individual is required to complete a drug court, mental health court, veterans court, or family treatment court division program, prior to the entry of judgment, and in contemplation that the defendant's case will be dismissed or nolle prossed;[9] or (4) where an individual was acquitted of all charges, unless the prosecuting attorney can show the public interest in the individual's criminal history record information being publicly available clearly outweighs the harm to the individual because: (A) the prosecuting attorney was barred from introducing material evidence; or (B) the individual had been charged with a similar offense within the previous 5 years.[10] Because the imposition of a sentence upon a plea of nolo contendere is not a dismissal or nolle prosse, record restriction is not available pursuant to O.C.G.A. § 35-3-7 for persons who enter a plea of nolo contendere.[11]

Further, O.C.G.A. § 35-3-37(j) now provides that an individual may petition the superior court to restrict access to his criminal history record information: (1) where the individual's case has been dead docketed for more than 12 months; (2) where the individual's conviction of an offense, other than the death penalty, was vacated by the trial court or reversed by an appellate court; (3) where the individual had felony charges dismissed, nolle prossed or was found not guilty of them but was convicted of a misdemeanor offense arising out of the same transaction or occurrence; or (4) where the individual was a youthful offender, convicted of a misdemeanor, completed the terms of his sentence, and has not been arrested for five years. If the state opposes the request for record restrictions, the court must consider the indi-

---

[8]O.C.G.A. § 35-3-37(h)(1).

[9]O.C.G.A. § 15-1-20.

[10]O.C.G.A. § 35-3-37(h)(2).

[11]Nasir v. Gwinnett County State Court, 341 Ga. App. 63, 798 S.E.2d 695 (2017).

vidual's conduct and whether record restriction is in the best interest of the public.[12] However, O.C.G.A. § 35-3-37(j)(4)(B) notes that these record restrictions are not available if an individual is convicted of certain crimes.[13]

O.C.G.A. § 35-3-37(j)(2) provides that a person may seek to have his record restricted when that person's conviction is reversed on appeal or another "post-conviction court" and a period of two years has passed since the date the order vacating or reversing the conviction. The petition must be filed in the superior court of the county where the conviction was rendered. In passing on the petition, the court "shall determine whether granting an order restricting such criminal history record information is appropriate," giving due consideration to (1) the reason the judgment was reversed or vacated, (2) the reason the prosecutor has not retried the case, and (3) the public's interest in the criminal history record information being publicly available. In *Gibbs v. Bright*,[14] the petitioner had been tried twice on numerous counts of sexual offenses. The first trial ended in a mistrial and a guilty verdict in the second. On appeal, the conviction was reversed due to ineffective assistance of counsel. The court ruled that record restriction was not warranted after hearing that the case was not retried only because the alleged victims were unwilling to go forward with a third trial. The court found that the public's interest in access to the petitioner's criminal history outweighed any

---

[12]See Gibbs v. Bright, 330 Ga. App. 851, 769 S.E.2d 590 (2015).

[13]The statute provides that the following crimes are not appropriate for restriction:

(i) Child molestation in violation of Code Section 16-6-4;

(ii) Enticing a child for indecent purposes in violation of Code Section 16-6-5;

(iii) Sexual assault by persons with supervisory or disciplinary authority in violation of Code Section 16-6-5.1;

(iv) Keeping a place of prostitution in violation of Code Section 16-6-10;

(v) Pimping in violation of Code Section 16-6-11;

(vi) Pandering by compulsion in violation of Code Section 16-6-14;

(vii) Masturbation for hire in violation of Code Section 16-6-16;

(viii) Giving massages in a place used for lewdness, prostitution, assignation, or masturbation for hire in violation of Code Section 16-6-17;

(ix) Sexual battery in violation of Code Section 16-6-22.1;

(x) Any offense related to minors generally in violation of Part 2 of Article 3 of Chapter 12 of Title 16;

(xi) Theft in violation of Chapter 8 of Title 16; provided, however, that such prohibition shall not apply to a misdemeanor conviction of shoplifting in violation of Code Section 16-8-14; or

(xii) Any serious traffic offense in violation of Article 15 of Chapter 6 of Title 40.

[14]Gibbs v. Bright, 330 Ga. App. 851, 769 S.E.2d 590 (2015).

potential harm to the petitoner.

In *Warren v. State,*[15] the court held that an appeal from an order "entered pursuant to the superior court's de novo review authority under O.C.G.A. § 35-3-37(c) must be made via O.C.G.A. § 5-6-35's discretionary appeal procedures." [Effective July 2013, § 35-3-37(c) was replaced by § 35-3-37(f)]. In addition, as a general rule, O.C.G.A. § 35-3-37(n)(1) provides that the statute does apply to arrests made prior to its effective date of July 1, 2013).

See Annotation, "Expunction of Federal Arrest Records in Absence of Conviction," 97 A.L.R.Fed. 653 (1990).

O.C.G.A. § 42-8-62.1 provides persons sentenced as first offenders with a method of restricting access to their records. See § 26:24, infra, on first offender sentences.

§ 17:22 Requests to charge

Rule 10.3 of the Uniform Rules for the Superior Courts provides as follows:

"10.3 Requests and Exceptions to Charge

"All requests to charge shall be numbered consecutively on separate sheets of paper and submitted to the court in duplicate by counsel for all parties at the commencement of trial, unless otherwise provided by pre-trial order; provided, however, that additional requests may be submitted to cover unanticipated points which arise thereafter."

From the foregoing, it is obvious that a valid request to charge must be in writing.[1]

See also sections 22:7 and 24:1, infra, on requests to charge.

§ 17:23 Notice to defense of evidence in extenuation, mitigation and aggravation of punishment

Prior to 2005, the state did not have to provide the defense with evidence which it intended to introduce at sentencing in aggravation of punishment until the start of trial.[1] That deadline was deleted by the legislature and a new one provided by O.C.G.A. § 17-16-4(a)(5). The state is now required to provide the defendant with notice of any evidence in aggravation of punishment which it intends to introduce at sentencing at least ten days prior to trial or at such time as the court directs, but in no

---

[15]Warren v. State, 239 Ga. App. 468, 521 S.E.2d 424 (1999).

App. 313, 315 (2), 485 S.E.2d 837 (1997).

[Section 17:22]

[1]Cf. Williams v. State, 226 Ga.

[Section 17:23]

[1]O.C.G.A. § 17-10-2.

event later than the start of trial.[2] Under prior law it was required that the notice make it clear in advance that the conviction will be used against the defendant at sentencing; thus, merely giving notice of intent to present a similar transaction did not authorize the use of the earlier conviction against defendant at sentencing.[3] The statutory requirement of "clear notice" to the accused under the prior law did not necessarily require written notice.[4] In *Thornton v. State*,[5] the court held that "notice of unproven criminal charges must be described with enough particularity to alert the accused to what he must defend against. . . . [Likewise,] notice of the state's intention to prove prior convictions must be specific." One of the purposes of this rule was "to allow a defendant to examine [the record presented] to determine if the convictions are in fact his and if he was represented by counsel, and any other defect which would render such documents inadmissible during the pre-sentencing phase of the trial."[6] Also, if the judge intended to consider in aggravation that which was ruled inadmissible at the guilt-innocence phase of the trial, he must inform defense counsel and the state of his intention to do so *before* the beginning of the pre-sentence hearing.[7]

Under the prior law this requirement of pretrial notice,

---

[2]O.C.G.A. § 17-16-4(a)(5).

[3]Boyd v. State, 230 Ga. App. 314, 315(2), 497 S.E.2d 3 (1998). In Washington v. State, 238 Ga. App. 561, 563 (4), 519 S.E.2d 234 (1999), the court emphasized that the state must provide "clear notice."

[4]Graham v. State, 171 Ga. App. 242, 256 (17), 319 S.E.2d 484 (1984). Accord, Powell v. State, 229 Ga. App. 52, 53 (1), 494 S.E.2d 200 (1997).

[5]Thornton v. State, 264 Ga. 563, 576 (22)(a), 449 S.E.2d 98 (1994).

[6]Herring v. State, 238 Ga. 288, 290 (4), 232 S.E.2d 826 (1977). In Jones v. Francis, 252 Ga. 60, 65 (11), 312 S.E.2d 300 (1984), the court said that it is doubtful that a conviction in another state is subject to collateral attack in Georgia on the ground the defendant received ineffective assistance of counsel in the earlier case.

In Nash v. State, 271 Ga. 281, 285, 519 S.E.2d 893 (1999), the Georgia Supreme Court held that when the state wishes to present evidence of prior convictions for purposes of recidivist punishment, the state has the burden "to prove both the existence of the prior guilty pleas and that the defendant was represented by counsel in all felony cases and those misdemeanor proceedings where imprisonment resulted. . . .. 'If the record does not so show, the State bears the burden of showing waiver.' Upon such a showing, the presumption of regularity is then applied and the burden shifts to the defendant to produce some affirmative evidence showing an infringement of his rights or a procedural irregularity in the taking of the plea. 'Defendant can attempt to meet his burden of production with a transcript, with testimony regarding the taking of the plea, or with affirmative evidence.' . . . 'A silent record or the mere naked assertion by an accused that his prior counseled plea was not made knowingly and intelligently is insufficient.' . . . If the defendant is able to present evidence that a constitutional infirmity exists, then the burden of proving the constitutionality of the plea shifts to the State." (Citations omitted).

[7]Dorsey v. Willis, 242 Ga. 316, 318, 249 S.E.2d 28 (1978).

however, may be deemed waived if a prior conviction of the defendant is presented as a factor in aggravation of sentence and considered by the court without objection.[8]

These cases should continue to have some application even though they were decided under former O.C.G.A. § 17-10-2(a)(1). See §§ 26:11 to 26:14, infra, on pre-sentence hearings and aggravating circumstances used at sentencing in capital and non-capital cases. See § 26:26, infra, on release from sex offender registration requirements. See O.C.G.A. §§ 49-5-183 and 49-5-184 on appeal and expungement of designation as a sex offender by Department of Family and Children Services.

§ 17:24 Bifurcation of trial

In *Head v. State,*[1] the defendant was indicted for armed robbery and possession of a firearm by a convicted felon. The court pointed out that three prior convictions were not material to the robbery charge, and that they were admitted without limiting instructions; the court concluded that the robbery conviction must be reversed. The court then outlined the following procedure to be used in such cases.

First, if the possession charge is unrelated to the other count, upon motion, the trial judge shall bifurcate the trial so that the jury shall hear and determine first the more serious charge, while the jury remains unaware of the pendency of the possession charge.[2] Thus, the jury will first determine guilt or innocence as to the more serious charge; and then, regardless of conviction or acquittal of the more serious charge, it shall determine the possession charge.[3] However, the trial court must bifurcate the trial only if such action is requested. The trial court is under no duty to do so on its own motion.[4]

Second, if an accused during voir dire discloses anything relative to the possession charge, "the trial court at that time shall

---

[8]Turner v. State, 259 Ga. App. 902 (1), 578 S.E.2d 570 (2003), overruling Eason v. State, 215 Ga. App. 614, 451 S.E.2d 820 (1994) which had held that the notice requirement by O.C.G.A. § 17-10-2(a) was mandatory and not subject to waiver.

[Section 17:24]

[1]Head v. State, 253 Ga. 429, 322 S.E.2d 228 (1984).

[2]Head v. State, 253 Ga. 429, 322 S.E.2d 228 (1984). See also Graham v. State, 185 Ga. App. 617, 365 S.E.2d 482 (1988), concluding that the trial

court should have bifurcated the trial because proof of the firearm possession was not material to proof of the burglary charge; however, holding that the error was harmless in light of the overwhelming evidence against the defendant as to the burglary charge. Cf. Jones v. State, 265 Ga. 138(2), 454 S.E.2d 482 (1995).

[3]Head v. State, 253 Ga. 429, 430, 322 S.E.2d 228 (1984).

[4]Pyburn v. State, 175 Ga. App. 158, 332 S.E.2d 899 (1985).

issue limiting instructions, admonishing the jury that they are to consider nothing relative to any prior convictions during the trial of the more serious charge, nor are they to draw any inference unfavorable to the accused from the fact that implications relative to any prior convictions have been placed before them in voir dire."[5]

Third, if the jury acquits on the non-possession charge, this will not prevent a trial on the possession charge. Likewise, when a trial is bifurcated as required by *Head v. State,* and the defendant is acquitted on the more serious charge, double jeopardy does not bar the possession by a convicted felon charge. A jury could conclude that the defendant had the gun but did not commit the other crime. Further, intentional possession is sufficient for the firearm possession charge.[6]

Finally, in cases where the count charging possession of a firearm by a convicted felon might be material to a more serious charge, such as where the offenses of murder and possession are charged in one indictment, and the possession count might conceivably become the underlying felony to support a felony murder conviction on the malice murder count of the indictment, the trial need not be bifurcated.[7] Upon request, the trial judge shall carefully instruct the jury as to the proper limitations upon their consideration of any evidence of prior convictions.[8] Specifically, the trial court shall instruct the jury that the only purpose for which they are permitted to receive evidence of prior convictions is relative to the charge of possession; and that they may not consider evidence of prior convictions in determining guilt or innocence on the more serious charge, except as such evidence might be material in considering a lesser included offense. If the defendant does not object and ask the court for a limiting instruction, nor submit a written charge as to the consideration of the prior felony charged against him, the possibility of error is waived.[9] Therefore, the failure of the court to instruct the jury is

---

[5]Head v. State, 253 Ga. 429, 432 (3)(b), 322 S.E.2d 228 (1984).

[6]Clark v. State, 194 Ga. App. 280, 390 S.E.2d 425 (1990).

[7]Head v. State, 253 Ga. 429, 322 S.E.2d 228 (1984); Jones v. State, 265 Ga. 138(2), 454 S.E.2d 482 (1995); Haynes v. State, 269 Ga. 181, 182 (3), 496 S.E.2d 721 (1998); Reeves v. State, 258 Ga. 619, 620, 373 S.E.2d 16 (1988); Roberts v. State, 212 Ga. App. 607 (1), 443 S.E.2d 4 (1994).

[8]Head v. State, 253 Ga. 429, 430,

322 S.E.2d 228 (1984); Head v. State, 262 Ga. 795, 798 (4), 426 S.E.2d 547 (1993), holding a judge's instruction is required upon request from the defendant, and overruling Kellum v. State, 258 Ga. 536, 371 S.E.2d 405 (1988), to the extent *Kellum* appears to negate the requirement of a defendant's request to charge.

[9]Williams v. State, 262 Ga. 422, 423 (4), 420 S.E.2d 301 (1992); Williams v. State, 263 Ga. 135, 429 S.E.2d 512 (1993), holding that it is up to the defendant to object or request a limit-

not error where no request was made by the defendant.[10] In *Appling v. State*,[11] the court held that where "the possession of a firearm charge may be the supporting felony in felony murder, it is proper to try the counts together as long as the jury is carefully charged that the prior felony conviction may not be considered by them in deciding the murder count." Further, if the prior felony was relevant to the possession count as well as to the murder count as a "similar transaction," the limiting instruction as to the felony record would be confusing. Thus, the court in *Kellum v. State*[12] held that "where evidence of a prior conviction is otherwise admissible under a legally recognized theory, then the limiting instructions required under *Head v. State* . . . are inapplicable."

If under *Head v. State* "there was no requirement that the count charging appellant only with possession of a firearm by a convicted felon be tried separately, it necessarily follows that there was no requirement that the alternative count charging appellant with felony murder be tried separately."[13]

In *Griffith v. State*,[14] the court concluded that the better practice is to require the trial court to instruct the jury comprehensively on the law applicable to the case after arguments are completed on the second phase of the trial.

---

ing instruction as to the admission of his felony record where it relates to a convicted felon carrying a firearm.

[10]Brown v. State, 263 Ga. 89, 91(2), 428 S.E.2d 78 (1993).

[11]Appling v. State, 256 Ga. 36, 38(1), 343 S.E.2d 684 (1986). Accord, Robinson v. State, 263 Ga. 424, 425(2)(a), 435 S.E.2d 207 (1993); Williams v. State, 214 Ga. App. 784, 449 S.E.2d 333 (1994).

[12]Kellum v. State, 258 Ga. 536, 537(2), 371 S.E.2d 405 (1988), overruled on other grounds by Head v. State, 262 Ga. 795, 426 S.E.2d 547 (1993).

[13]Willis v. State, 263 Ga. 70, 428 S.E.2d 338 (1993).

[14]Griffith v. State, 264 Ga. 326, 327(2), 444 S.E.2d 794 (1994).

Chapter 18

The Jury

KeyCite®: Cases and other legal materials listed in KeyCite Scope can be researched through the KeyCite service on Westlaw®. Use KeyCite to check citations for form, parallel references, prior and later history, and comprehensive citator information, including citations to other decisions and secondary materials.

---

§ 18:1   Background

In *Duncan v. Louisiana,*[1] the United States Supreme Court held that under the Sixth Amendment to the United States Constitution, as made applicable to the states through the Fourteenth Amendment, a defendant is entitled to a jury trial in any serious criminal case. In *Baldwin v. New York,*[2] the same court held that the federal constitutional right to a jury trial in criminal cases covers any situation where a defendant faces potential imprisonment of more than six months. In 1989 in *Blanton v. City of North Las Vegas, Nevada,*[3] the United States Supreme Court held that there is a presumption that an offense with punishment of 6 months or less is a "petty" offense and there is no federal constitutional right to a jury trial. But, the court indicated that a defendant is entitled to a jury trial in such a case "if he can demonstrate that any additional statutory penalties, viewed in conjunction with the maximum authorized period of incarceration are so severe that they clearly reflect a legislative determination that the offense is a 'serious' one." In the 1996 United States Supreme Court case of *Lewis v. United States,*[4] the Court held that a defendant "in a single proceeding for multiple petty offenses does not have a [constitutional] right to a jury trial where

---

[Section 18:1]

[1] Duncan v. Louisiana, 391 U.S. 145, 88 S.Ct. 1444, 20 L.Ed.2d 491, 493 (1968).

[2] Baldwin v. New York, 399 U.S. 66, 90 S.Ct. 1886, 26 L.Ed.2d 437 (1970). See Annot., "Right to Jury Trial under Federal Constitution Where Two or More Petty Offenses, Each Having Penalty of Less than Six Months' Imprisonment, Have Potential Aggregate Penalty in Excess of Six Months When Tried Together," 26 A.L.R.Fed. 736 (1976).

[3] Blanton v. City of North Las Vegas, Nevada, 489 U.S. 538, 109 S.Ct. 1289, 103 L.Ed.2d 550 (1989).

[4] Lewis v. United States, 518 U.S. 322, 116 S.Ct. 2163, 135 L.Ed.2d 590 (1996).

the [maximum] aggregate prison term authorized for the offenses exceeds six months' imprisonment."

In *Jones v. Wharton*,[5] the Georgia court pointed out that while a defendant may waive his right to a jury trial, where he "is proceeding pro se, a valid waiver . . . cannot be found on the sole ground that the defendant failed to request one."

Similarly, Georgia provides for a jury trial in all criminal cases.[6] Formerly under the Georgia Constitution it was possible to have as few as five jurors in all cases except those tried in superior court.[7] However, the 1983 Georgia Constitution was changed so as to provide that the General Assembly may authorize criminal jury trials with not less than six jurors in "courts of limited jurisdiction and in superior courts in misdemeanor cases."[8] Under the federal Constitution a defendant is entitled to a trial by not less than six jurors even in a misdemeanor case.[9] In a number of inferior courts, special legislative acts have been enacted which provide that, in a misdemeanor case, a defendant may waive his right to a jury trial unless he demands one when the case is called. Generally, such statutes are regarded as valid and binding upon the defendant if he is represented by counsel.[10] However, a defendant may waive his right to a trial by the prescribed number of jurors if the state also agrees to a trial by a lesser number.[11] "Counsel for the accused may validly waive this right for . . . [the defendant] if (1) the waiver is made without objection, in the accused's presence or (2) the accused otherwise acquiesces in the waiver."[12]

The constitutional right to a jury trial applies only to actions which, at common law, entitled the litigant to a jury trial.[13] Consequently, there is no constitutional right to a jury trial at a hearing to determine if a defendant is an "habitual violator" of

---

[5]Jones v. Wharton, 253 Ga. 82, 84, 316 S.E.2d 749 (1984).

[6]Ga. Const. 1983, Art. I, § I, ¶ XI.

In McSears v. State, 247 Ga. 48, 49 (2), 273 S.E.2d 847 (1981), the court held that where a misdemeanor was committed in 1979 and a statute enacted in 1980 authorizing a trial in state court by a six person jury, a six person jury could not be used in the trial. This was considered to be an ex post facto law.

[7]Anderson v. State, 142 Ga. App. 85, 235 S.E.2d 604 (1977).

[8]Ga. Const. 1983, Art. I, § I, ¶ XI.

[9]Ballew v. Georgia, 435 U.S. 223, 98 S.Ct. 1029, 55 L.Ed.2d 234 (1978); Ballew v. State, 145 Ga. App. 829, 245 S.E.2d 169 (1978); Robinson v. State, 146 Ga. App. 318, 246 S.E.2d 518 (1978).

[10]E.g., see Fleming v. State, 139 Ga. App. 849, 229 S.E.2d 800 (1976), and cases cited therein.

[11]Blount v. State, 169 Ga. App. 215, 216, 312 S.E.2d 197 (1983).

[12]Hudson v. State, 250 Ga. 479, 484 (3), 299 S.E.2d 531 (1983).

[13]Gaston v. Shunk Plow Co., 161 Ga. 287, 299, 130 S.E. 580 (1925).

the traffic laws.[14] Likewise, a jury trial is not constitutionally required in delinquency proceedings in juvenile court.[15]

In *Dossett v. State*,[16] the court held that a defendant's failure to raise in probate court the absence of a waiver of a jury trial prevents an appellate court from reviewing the issue.

All experienced counsel recognized the great importance of the proper "selection" of a jury for the case which is about to be tried. "A big part of the battle is the selection of the jury, and an impartial jury is the cornerstone of the fairness of trial by jury."[17] Counsel for each side have three general methods of obtaining a legally qualified, fair and impartial trial jury: (1) a challenge to the array (§ 18:11, infra); (2) a challenge for cause (§§ 18:16 to 18:23, infra); and (3) a peremptory challenge (§§ 18:30 and 18:31, infra).

See § 25:1, infra, on unanimous verdicts. Also see § 17:14, supra, on a jury trial as compared with a trial before the judge.

§ 18:2　Jurors drawn to serve

The method of making up the jury list has been previously discussed.[1] In summary, a defendant has a right to select a jury from a list of jurors which represents a fair cross section of the community.[2] The clerk is tasked with the responsibility of choosing a random list of persons from the county's master jury list to compose the venire.[3]

In *Pope v. State*,[4] the Court held that "[d]rawing the venire was not a 'critical stage' of the proceeding requiring [the defendant's]

---

[14]Williams v. State, 138 Ga. App. 662, 663, 226 S.E.2d 816 (1976).

[15]McKeiver v. Pennsylvania, 403 U.S. 528, 545-550, 91 S.Ct. 1976, 29 L.Ed.2d 647 (1971).

[16]Dossett v. State, 261 Ga. 362, 404 S.E.2d 548 (1991).

[17]Melson v. Dickson, 63 Ga. 682, 686 (1) (1879).

[Section 18:2]

[1]See §§ 12:3 and 12:4, supra, on the make-up and composition of the grand jury. The same procedures are generally employed in the make-up of trial juries.

[2]Taylor v. Louisiana, 419 U.S. 522, 95 S.Ct. 692, 42 L.Ed.2d 690 (1975). Under the Louisiana statute involved here, the names of women were not put on the jury list unless a

woman requested in writing to be placed on the jury list. The general Georgia statute exempting certain persons from jury duty is found in O.C.G.A. § 15-12-1.1.

There is no constitutional guarantee that grand or petit juries will represent a fair cross-section of the community. Rather, the defendant is only guaranteed that the jury pool from which the venire is randomly selected, in a particular case, will be representative of the community. Watson v. State, 261 Ga. App. 562(1), 583 S.E.2d 228 (2003).

[3]O.C.G.A. § 15-12-40.1.

[4]Pope v. State, 256 Ga. 195, 345 S.E.2d 831 (1986), overruled on other grounds by Nash v. State, 271 Ga. 281, 519 S.E.2d 893 (1999).

. . . presence."

Under O.C.G.A. § 15-12-4(a), a person "who has served as a juror at any session of the superior or state courts shall be ineligible for duty as a juror until the next succeeding county master jury list has been received by the clerk." However, this statute does not prevent a juror from serving for a different level of court at the next term.[5] When the name of the juror who is disqualified under this statute is drawn, the name is not to be recorded as that of a juror, but shall be returned to the box.

In *Morgan v. State*,[6] the Georgia Supreme Court held that "the mere fact that jurors were excused previously does not mean that they were not selected randomly . . . [where the] trial court [had a] practice of placing jurors who had been excused during the previous term of court at the top of the jury list."

After the jurors have been summoned, the judge of the court may excuse anyone "who shows that he or she will be engaged during his or her term of jury duty in work necessary to the public health, safety, or good order or who shows other good cause why he or she should be exempt from jury duty . . .". Also exempt from jury duty are: any person who is a full-time student; any person who is the primary caregiver of a child six years of age or younger; any person who is a "primary teacher in a home study program;" and, persons over the age of 70.[7]

Likewise, the chief judge may designate some other person to excuse jurors under such circumstances if the chief judge establishes "guidelines governing excuses."[8] However, all orders of appointment must "provide that, except for permanently mentally or physically disabled persons, all excuses shall be deferred to a date and time certain within that term or the next succeeding term or shall be deferred as set forth in the court order."[9] If there is a disregard of the essential and substantial provisions of this statute, the array will be rendered invalid.[10]

---

[5]O.C.G.A. § 15-12-4(a)

[6]Morgan v. State, 271 Ga. 885, 886 (2), 525 S.E.2d 691 (2000).

[7]O.C.G.A. § 15-12-1.1(a). In Thornton v. State, 264 Ga. 563, 575 (19), 449 S.E.2d 98 (1994), the court held that excusal of a college student was proper where jury service would impose undue hardship on the student.

[8]O.C.G.A. § 15-12-1.1(a). See Hendrick v. State, 257 Ga. 17, 354 S.E.2d 433 (1987).

[9]O.C.G.A. § 15-12-1.1(a).

[10]Hampton v. State, 158 Ga. App. 324 (1), 280 S.E.2d 158 (1981). In Joyner v. State, 251 Ga. 84, 303 S.E.2d 106 (1983), the defendant filed a challenge to the array. Of the jurors summoned the clerk had excused 22 and the sheriff had excused 5. There was some testimony that the district attorney excused one. There was no written order setting out guidelines. The court reversed, saying (1) that " 'a disregard of the essential and substantial provisions of the statute will have the effect of vitiating the array.' . . . [and]

Thus, in *Yates v. State*,[11] the trial court committed error when the clerk of the court excused all potential jurors who proffered a medical excuse without any inquiry and without written order from the court authorizing the clerk to excuse potential jurors according to the guidelines set forth in O.C.G.A. § 15-12-11(a). The rule is otherwise where a duly authorized clerk makes proper inquiry into a potential juror's request for excusal and does not otherwise "deliberately or inadvertently" alter the representative nature of the jury list.[12]

Under the provisions of O.C.G.A. § 15-12-11(b), all prospective trial and grand jurors "may be required to answer written questionnaires, as may be determined and submitted by the judges . . . concerning their qualifications. . . ."

See § 12:9, supra, on the proper makeup of the jury list. See § 18:22, infra, on jury qualifications.

§ 18:3   Investigation of potential jurors

In *Sears v. State*,[1] the court held that there was no reason to prohibit the state from checking the criminal records of potential jurors. This includes the use of GCIC reports which prosecutors, as law enforcement agents, are entitled to access under O.C.G.A. §§ 35-3-30(3), 35-3-30(6) and O.C.G.A. § 35-3-33(a)(10). Criminal defense lawyers are not considered law enforcement agents under the law and as private individuals are not allowed to receive GCIC reports either directly or from the prosecutor unless they have the express written consent or the fingerprints of the jurors. O.C.G.A. §§ 35-3-34(a)(1) and 35-3-34(d).[2]

§ 18:4   Juror orientation and custody before being called for a case

Juror orientation has been recommended by the American Bar Association by means of a juror handbook.[1] However, in *Bowden*

---

(2) that [t]he excusal of five prospective jurors by the sheriff . . . a direct participant in the trial . . . deprive[s] this defendant of her proportional share of peremptory strikes."

[11]Yates v. State, 274 Ga. 312, 315 (2), 553 S.E.2d 563 (2001).

[12]Johnson v. State, 293 Ga. 641, 748 S.E.2d 896 (2013).

[Section 18:3]

[1]Sears v. State, 262 Ga. 805, 808(b), 426 S.E.2d 553 (1993); see

Holmes v. State, 273 Ga. 644, 646(2), 543 S.E.2d 688 (2001).

[2]See generally, Williams v. State, 255 Ga. App. 177, 564 S.E.2d 759 (2002), 255 Ga. App. 177, 564 S.E.2d 759 (2002) for a discussion of issues related to the availability and uses to which a juror's GCIC report may be put.

[Section 18:4]

[1]Mention v. State, 171 Ga. App. 116 (1), 318 S.E.2d 765 (1984).

v. State,[2] the court held that an orientation session is not a "critical stage of the proceeding," and defense counsel has no right to be present. Where a trial judge attempts to orally orient jurors before they are called for a case, a general reference to the right of appeal was found not to require reversal where the instructions were found not to intimate an opinion of the trial judge nor lessen the sense of responsibility of the jurors.[3]

It is not necessarily improper for prospective jurors to be led in prayer by a Christian minister before the jury selection process. In *Morgan v. State,*[4] the Georgia Supreme Court did not approve of such a procedure but stated that in the absence of a record as to what was said to the jurors it would not assume that they were told anything prejudicial.

If the persons selected to serve as jurors are present in the courtroom while other matters are being disposed of, it is important that nothing take place in the presence of the panels which might cause the jurors to form an opinion as to the guilt or innocence of any defendant.[5] If any improper remarks are made before the jury, the remedy is by a challenge to the poll or a motion for a continuance, not by a challenge to the array.[6]

See § 18:36, infra, on pre-trial instructions to jurors.

§ 18:5   Jury bailiffs

Georgia statutes provide an oath which must be administered to all bailiffs who will have charge of a jury,[1] to wit:

> You shall take all juries committed to your charge to the jury room or some other private and convenient place designated by the court and you shall not allow the jurors to receive any books, papers, nourishment, or hydration other than water, or to use any electronic communication device except as directed and approved by the court. You shall make no communication with the jurors nor permit anyone to communicate with the jurors except as specifically authorized by the court. You shall discharge all other duties which may devolve upon you as bailiff to the best of your skill and power. So help you God.

---

[2]Bowden v. State, 202 Ga. App. 802, 803 (1), 415 S.E.2d 527 (1992).

[3]Mention v. State, 171 Ga. App. 116 (1), 318 S.E.2d 765 (1984).

[4]Morgan v. State, 276 Ga. 72 (2), 575 S.E.2d 468 (2003).

[5]See Gaines v. State, 142 Ga. App. 181, 182 (1), 235 S.E.2d 640 (1977), where the district attorney announced in the presence of prospective jurors that the defendant tendered a plea of guilty. This plea was later withdrawn and the defendant was put on trial.

[6]Hill v. State, 221 Ga. 65, 66, 142 S.E.2d 909 (1, 2) (1965); Fields v. State, 190 Ga. 642 (2), 10 S.E.2d 33 (1940). See Finch v. State, 138 Ga. App. 668, 681 (9), 226 S.E.2d 779 (1976).

[Section 18:5]

[1]O.C.G.A. § 15-12-140.

Generally, there is a presumption that the bailiff was properly sworn.[2] The defendant bears the burden of showing affirmatively that the bailiffs were not sworn.[3] It is reversible error to permit a deputy acting as a bailiff who has not been sworn to have charge of the jury.[4] However, in *Arnold v. State*,[5] the court held that the statute requiring the swearing of a bailiff "does not require that the oath be administered before each trial." It is sufficient if the bailiff and the other bailiffs were sworn by a judge at the beginning of each new term of court.

The bailiff should always be disinterested in the case. Thus, it is a violation of the defendant's basic right to a jury trial to have deputy sheriffs, who are two principal prosecution witnesses, in charge of the jury where they have also spent considerable time with the jury.[6]

A "bailiff must not act as an interpreter of juror's questions and the trial judge's answers. . . . [Also] the bailiff must not answer questions posed by the jurors based upon her own perception of the questions, or, for that matter, of the law or of the evidence. Any inquiries by the jurors ultimately related to their decision process must be directed to the judge without interpretation by the bailiff or by any other court personnel."[7]

Generally, see § 18:37, infra, on sequestration of jurors.

§ 18:6   Transcript of jury voir dire

Before jurors are called, defense counsel should consider whether he or she wishes to have the jury selection process taken down by the court reporter. Normally, a defense counsel should have all material taken down from the time he announces ready until the end of the case. If defense counsel wishes to use a court reporter, he or she must make sure the reporter is present before any jurors are called in connection with the case.

In a capital case, failure to record voir dire questions and answers as to capital punishment is reversible error if the death

---

[2]Jackson v. State, 152 Ga. 210, 213, 108 S.E. 784 (1921). Mere testimony of the bailiff that he does not remember being sworn does not necessarily overcome the presumption.

[3]Wilson v. State, 227 Ga. App. 59, 63 (4), 488 S.E.2d 121 (1997).

[4]Roberts v. State, 72 Ga. 673, 678 (2) (1884).

[5]Arnold v. State, 250 Ga. App. 461, 552 S.E.2d 454 (2001).

[6]Turner v. Louisiana, 379 U.S. 466, 85 S.Ct. 546, 13 L.Ed.2d 424 (1965).

[7]Lindsey v. State, 277 Ga. App. 18, 625 S.E.2d 431 (2005); Turpin v. Todd, 271 Ga. 386, 519 S.E.2d 678 (1999); Morris v. State, 257 Ga. 781 (4), 364 S.E.2d 571 (1988).

sentence is imposed.[1] Thus, both the district attorney and defense counsel will normally want all questions and answers related to capital punishment recorded. This would include the actual striking of the jurors so that on review the Supreme Court can determine the order in which jurors were struck.[2] In order to insure that all statements are placed into record, it is advisable for defense counsel to file a pre-trial motion describing the material he wishes the court reporter to transcribe.[3]

In *Roper v. State,*[4] the court held that where a motion for complete recordation of voir dire is made in a non-death case, "by far the better practice is to order complete recordation."

In a non-capital case, even if the defense counsel requests that a transcript be made of the voir dire examination and even if he agrees to pay for it, this does not require a reversal where no transcript is made unless it appears that the defendant was harmed.[5]

In *State v. Graham,*[6] the Georgia Supreme Court held that Georgia law does not require that a transcript of voir dire examination be prepared in a non-capital case, and, if a defendant makes objection to anything taking place during such an examination, the defendant must move at that time to have the questions and answers made a part of the record.

§ 18:7 Call of jurors for particular case

As of July 1, 2012, O.C.G.A. § 15-12-160.1 provides that when any person stands indicted for a felony, the court "shall have impaneled 30 jurors from which the defense and prosecution may strike jurors; provided, however, that in any case in which the state announces its intention to seek the death penalty, the court shall have impaneled 42 jurors from which the defense and the state may strike jurors. The Code section further provides: "[i]f for any reason after striking the panel there remain fewer than 12 qualified jurors to try the case, the clerk shall choose and cause to be summoned such numbers of persons who are competent prospective jurors as may be necessary to provide a full panel or successive panels. In making up the panel or succes-

[Section 18:6]

[1]Owens v. State, 233 Ga. 869, 873 (2), 214 S.E.2d 173 (1975).

[2]O'Kelley v. State, 284 Ga. 758 (2)(c), 670 S.E.2d 388 (2008).

[3]In Watts v. State, 141 Ga. App. 127, 128, 232 S.E.2d 590 (1977), defendant moved to have all voir dire questions to the jury and the answers taken down at state expense. The ap-

pellate court held that this was within the discretion of the trial judge.

[4]Roper v. State, 251 Ga. 95 (5), 303 S.E.2d 103 (1983).

[5]Marshall v. State, 239 Ga. 101, 103 (2), 236 S.E.2d 58 (1977).

[6]State v. Graham, 246 Ga. 341, 271 S.E.2d 627 (1980), rev'g 153 Ga. App. 658, 266 S.E.2d 316 (1980).

sive panels, the clerk shall choose the names of prospective trial jurors in the same manner as prospective trial jurors are chosen and cause such persons to be summoned." See § 18:31, infra, on striking a jury. The sole remedy of a person who wishes to object to a panel of jurors having less than the number fixed by law is by a challenge to the array, which generally must be in writing.[1] In *Larmon v. State*,[2] the Court of Appeals held that there was no constitutional violation where jurors set out for a specific case were selected on the basis of their voter registration number, and hence by the date they registered to vote, when a master list of all jurors had been randomly selected, and the defendant did not show different registration times yielded "distinct and identifiable" groups.

Alternate jurors may be called if, in the opinion of the trial judge, any felony case is likely to be a protracted one.[3] It is the trial judge's responsibility to determine whether alternate jurors are needed, and if so, to call the additional persons after the jury has been impaneled.[4] If alternate jurors are selected, they shall remain with the regular jurors until the time when the jury retires to begin deliberations.[5] See § 18:35, infra.

The clerk has the duty of providing the prosecuting attorney and the accused "with names and identifying information relative to prospective jurors for the case being tried."[6] The clerk has the responsibility of then reading the names on the panel.[7]

It is not error for the trial judge to instruct proposed jurors that the state has waived the death penalty.[8]

§ 18:8　Putting the panel on the defendant

Putting the panel on the defendant is said to have been the

[Section 18:7]

[1]Cauley v. State, 130 Ga. App. 278 (1)(a), 203 S.E.2d 239 (1973); Williams v. State, 31 Ga. App. 173 (3), 120 S.E. 131 (1923). See Ivey v. State, 4 Ga. App. 828, 831, 62 S.E. 565 (1908). But there is authority that the written challenge to the array may be filed later after there is a timely oral challenge to the array. McKenzey v. State, 138 Ga. App. 88 (1), 225 S.E.2d 512 (1976).

[2]Larmon v. State, 177 Ga. App. 763, 764 (2), 341 S.E.2d 237 (1986), aff'd, 256 Ga. 228, 345 S.E.2d 587 (1986).

[3]O.C.G.A. §§ 15-12-168, et seq. In the selection of alternate jurors, the

state and the defendant shall be entitled to as many peremptory challenges to alternate jurors as there are jurors called. O.C.G.A. § 15-12-169.1.

[4]O.C.G.A. § 15-12-168.

[5]O.C.G.A. § 15-12-170 and O.C.G.A. § 15-12-171. This last section provides that the court in its discretion may direct that one or more of the alternate jurors be kept in custody by the sheriff separated from the other jurors until a verdict has been reached.

[6]O.C.G.A. § 15-12-161.

[7]E.g., Cumming v. State, 155 Ga. 346 (2), 117 S.E. 378 (1923).

[8]Waters v. State, 169 Ga. App. 290, 292 (2), 312 S.E.2d 812 (1983).

ancient method of commanding the defendant's attention to the persons on the panel and warning him to exercise the right of challenge.[1] However, the right to have the panel put upon the defendant may be waived, expressly or impliedly. The right is waived where the accused does not object to the omission and proceeds to take part in the selection of the jury.[2] The defendant will also be deemed to have waived his right to have the jury put upon him where pursuant to a request from the court he agrees to accept a panel of 11 jurors instead of 12.[3] If counsel gives notice that he "waives nothing" and a panel is not put upon the accused, it has been held that this is a ground for a new trial.[4] However, in *Walls v. State*,[5] the Georgia Court of Appeals stated that there is no particular ceremony or form required to "put the jury upon the defendant" and concluded that there was no error even though, after completion of the individual voir dire of all prospective jurors, defense counsel stated to the court that the defense waived nothing and would insist that all formalities be followed. The court pointed out that (1) when this statement was made, no mention was made of anything the trial judge failed to do; (2) a jury list had been presented to defense counsel (apparently before the voir dire examination began); (3) the jurors were sworn pursuant to O.C.G.A. § 15-12-132; (4) the jurors had been qualified pursuant to O.C.G.A. § 15-12-135, as to the relationship to the parties and interest in the case; (5) the statutory questions were asked pursuant to O.C.G.A. § 15-12-164; (6) the jurors were put in the jury box in panels of 12 each. In *Walls*, the statement by defense counsel that the defendant would waive nothing was not made in a timely manner. However, the Court of Appeals seemed to, at least, indicate that the nineteenth century Supreme Court case of *Cochran v. State*[6] is unsound and that it would not have been followed even if the announcement of defense counsel had been timely. Likewise, a defendant must raise any challenge he has to the jury list when the jury is put upon him. If he fails to do so he is said to have waived his right to object.[7]

In a misdemeanor case, it is not necessary for the jurors to be put upon the defendant.[8]

[Section 18:8]

[1]Cochran v. State, 62 Ga. 731, 733 (1879).

[2]Vaughn v. State, 88 Ga. 731 (1), 16 S.E. 64 (1892).

[3]Inman v. State, 72 Ga. 269, 277 (2) (1884).

[4]Cochran v. State, 62 Ga. 731 (1) (1879).

[5]Walls v. State, 161 Ga. App. 235, 237, 291 S.E.2d 15 (1982).

[6]Cochran v. State, 62 Ga. 731 (1879).

[7]Young v. State, 232 Ga. 285, 286, 206 S.E.2d 439 (1974).

[8]Fears v. State, 125 Ga. 740 (3), 54 S.E. 661 (1906).

The interesting case of *United States v. Scarfo*[9] involved the trial of a reputed La Cosa Nostra boss. The court concluded that in order to protect the safety of jurors and to minimize the chance of jury tampering, it was not an abuse of discretion for the trial judge to resort to an anonymous list of jurors whose addresses were not given. However, a detailed and personal written questionnaire was completed by the jurors and the trial judge and counsel were permitted to question jurors individually.

§ 18:9   Location of potential jurors during voir dire

It has been held that upon request of either party, it is the duty of the trial judge "to place the jurors in the jury box in panels of 12 at a time, so as to facilitate their examination by counsel."[1] It has been said that there is no room for judicial discretion where such a request has been made and that the failure of the trial court to comply is erroneous as a matter of law.[2]

Also, the preliminary oath is to be administered to each panel before voir dire of that panel.[3] However, in *Hammond v. State*,[4] the court held that the trial court may exercise discretion in determining whether voir dire questions are to be asked to all the jurors sent for the trial or to each panel of 12 or to each juror individually. The trial court's decision to have counsel direct general voir dire questions to a panel as a whole is not an abuse of discretion.

§ 18:10   Challenge to jurors—General

There are two general kinds of challenges to a jury panel:

(1) Challenge to the array and (2) challenge to the poll.[1] Challenges to the array go to the form and manner of making up the entire panel without regard to objection to the individual jurors.

A challenge to the poll is directed to an individual or individuals who make up a panel. The two types of challenges to a jury

---

[9]United States v. Scarfo, 850 F.2d 1015 (3d Cir. 1988). See Annot., "Propriety of, and Procedure for, Ordering Names and Identities of Jurors to Be Withheld From the Accused in Federal Criminal Trial—'Anonymous Juries,' " 93 A.L.R.Fed. 136 (1989), and "Propriety of Using Anonymous Juries in State Criminal Cases," A.L.R.5th 39 (1998). See Annot., 47 Am. Jur. 2d Jury § 197, Maintaining Anonymity of Jury Panel (2004).

[Section 18:9]

[1]O.C.G.A. § 15-12-131.

[2]Lett v. State, 160 Ga. App. 476 (1), 287 S.E.2d 384 (1981).

[3]Lahr v. State, 239 Ga. 813, 814 (4), 238 S.E.2d 878 (1977).

[4]Hammond v. State, 273 Ga. 442, 444 (2), 542 S.E.2d 498 (2001).

[Section 18:10]

[1]Jordan v. State, 247 Ga. 328, 338 (6), 276 S.E.2d 224 (1981).

panel will be discussed subsequently.[2]

§ 18:11   Challenge to the array

"A challenge to the array is an objection to the jurors collectively because of some defect in the panel as a whole."[1] O.C.G.A. § 15-12-162 provides the sole remedy of objecting to the entire panel.[2] Where some of the trial jurors are served at the last term of court, a challenge to the array does not lie for this reason.[3]

In *Lysfjord v. State*,[4] the court pointed out that "[w]here the panel put upon a defendant does not contain the requisite number of jurors, the sole remedy is a challenge to the array . . . [a]nd . . . a challenge to the . . . array must be in writing."

In *Whitt v. State*,[5] the court held that it was not error for a trial judge to take a guilty plea in another case in the presence of the jury panels.

As soon as the panel has been placed upon the defendant, he "may, in writing, challenge the array for any cause going to show that it was not fairly or properly impaneled or ought not to be put upon him. The court shall determine the sufficiency of the challenge at once. If sustained, a new panel shall be ordered; if not sustained, the selections of jurors shall proceed."[6] In *Pugh v. State*,[7] the court held that the defendant's challenge of the jury was untimely when he challenged the array after the state had conducted a portion of its voir dire.

However, it has been held that an oral challenge to the array is sufficient if it is followed by a written challenge.[8] In *Anthony v. State*,[9] the court held that an oral challenge to the array followed by a written challenge in a motion for a new trial is sufficient to comply with the "requirement" of a written challenge. In the case of a charge that a district attorney systematically struck all black jurors (where the defendant is black), it has been held that no written challenge or motion is required.[10] See § 18:31, infra, on limitations on peremptory challenges.

---

[2]Generally, see §§ 18:11 and 18:12, infra.

[Section 18:11]

[1]Bryan v. State, 124 Ga. 79, 80, 52 S.E. 298 (1905).

[2]Williams v. State, 31 Ga. App. 173 (3), 120 S.E. 131 (1923).

[3]Green v. State, 246 Ga. 598, 599 (2), 272 S.E.2d 475 (1980).

[4]Lysfjord v. State, 208 Ga. App. 811, 812 (2), 432 S.E.2d 247 (1993).

[5]Whitt v. State, 215 Ga. App. 704, 452 S.E.2d 125 (1994).

[6]O.C.G.A. § 15-12-162.

[7]Pugh v. State, 214 Ga. App. 470, 471 (2), 448 S.E.2d 16 (1994).

[8]McKenzey v. State, 138 Ga. App. 88 (1), 225 S.E.2d 512 (1976).

[9]Anthony v. State, 213 Ga. App. 303 (1), 444 S.E.2d 393 (1994).

[10]Mincey v. State, 180 Ga. App. 263, 264, 349 S.E.2d 1 (1986), aff'd, 256 Ga. 636, 353 S.E.2d 814 (1987).

The material included in Chapter 12, supra, on the grand jury contains information relating to challenges to the array and § 12:9, supra, relates particularly to challenges based on under-representation of blacks, women and other cognizable groups. This material generally applies as much to petit juries as grand juries. However, "[w]hile traverse jury lists must consist of a representative and fair cross-section of the community to the fullest extent possible, *the same is not true of an array.* Provided that persons are not systematically excluded on the basis of race or other cognizable grouping, and provided that the jurors comprising a panel are randomly selected from a representative pool, the selection process is not inherently defective. *Kent v. State,* 245 Ga. App. 531, 538 S.E.2d 185 (2000). The defendant has the burden of proving purposeful discrimination in the jury array. *Pruitt v. State,* 279 Ga. 140, 142, 611 S.E.2d 47 (2005)."[11]

In *Jewell v. State,*[12] the court held that where blacks were not systematically excluded from a panel, the jury pool was representative, and jurors making up a panel were randomly selected the defendant was not deprived of a fair trial or equal protection. Jewell did not contend that blacks were systematically excluded from the panel of 48. He contended that the random method of choosing the panel from the larger pool produced an unrepresentative panel. "Random selection safeguards the selection process from manipulation and ensures the jury's independence."

In *Pryor v. State,*[13] the court held that a "de facto discrimination is not shown by evidence that a single jury panel contained a disproportionately small percentage of African-Americans compared to the population at large." In *Porter v. State,*[14] the court held that the exclusion of prospective jurors with scruples against the death sentence did not constitute the exclusion of a recognizable class.

If a challenge to the array is filed, it is the duty of the court to hear such evidence as is necessary in order to determine the validity of the challenge[15] and then sustain or deny the challenge.

---

[11]Fisher v. State, 317 Ga. App. 761, 768(7), 732 S.E.2d 821 (2012) (punctuation omitted; emphasis supplied).

[12]Jewell v. State, 261 Ga. 861, 862 (3), 413 S.E.2d 201 (1992); Williams v. State, 213 Ga. App. 458, 459 (1), 444 S.E.2d 831 (1994).

[13]Pryor v. State, 231 Ga. App. 136, 137, 497 S.E.2d 805 (1998).

[14]Porter v. State, 237 Ga. 580(1), 229 S.E.2d 384 (1976).

[15]O.C.G.A. § 15-12-162.

§ 18:12 Challenge to the poll

A challenge to an individual or certain individuals on the panel is called a challenge to the poll.[1] A challenge of the individual jurors or to the poll may be:

(1) Peremptory or without cause. It is not necessary to give any reason for such a challenge. Normally, it is felt that a party is entitled to exercise these peremptory challenges which are given him in any way he wishes.[2]

(2) A challenge to an individual juror or to the poll for cause, and may be (a) for principal cause or (b) for favor. See § 18:19, infra.

(a) A challenge for principal cause is based on facts from which, if proved, the juror is conclusively presumed to be incapable of serving,[3] i.e., such a challenge "is based on facts which if proved automatically disqualify the juror from serving."[4]

(b) A challenge for favor is based on circumstances raising a suspicion of the existence of actual bias in the mind of the individual juror for or against one of the parties.[5] Such a juror might be challenged for prejudice in the particular case.

Except in the case of peremptory challenges, regardless of the nature of the challenge, it is the duty of the trial court to determine whether or not the challenge should be sustained.[6] However, it has been held that it is not error for the judge to overrule a challenge for favor unless it appears that "the juror's opinion was . . . so firm or fixed as to be unyielding."[7] See § 18:15, infra.

Potential jurors excused by the court because of a challenge other than peremptory challenges do not decrease the peremptory challenges or strikes allowed to each side by law.[8]

Formerly the Georgia courts held that the failure of the trial

---

[Section 18:12]

[1]Bryan v. State, 124 Ga. 79, 52 S.E. 298 (1905).

[2]See § 18:30, infra.

[3]O.C.G.A. § 15-12-163, which provides for a challenge for cause, is set out in §§ 18:19 et seq., infra. O.C.G.A. § 15-12-135 provides for a disqualification of a juror where he is related by consanguinity or affinity within the third degree.

[4]Jordan v. State, 247 Ga. 328, 338 (6), 276 S.E.2d 224 (1981).

[5]Bullard v. State, 14 Ga. App. 478, 480, 81 S.E. 369 (1914).

[6]Hagans v. State, 77 Ga. App. 513, 514, 48 S.E.2d 700 (1948).

[7]Holloway v. State, 137 Ga. App. 124, 125 (2), 222 S.E.2d 898 (1975). In Murphy v. Florida, 421 U.S. 794, 95 S.Ct. 2031, 44 L.Ed.2d 589 (1975), the court said that the due process clause of the Fourteenth Amendment does not raise a presumption that jurors are prejudiced because of learning of a defendant's prior criminal record from news sources when the defendant is a nationally known criminal figure.

[8]O.C.G.A. § 15-12-165 expressly refers to peremptory challenges and has no application to challenges for

court to excuse a juror for cause, even if error, is harmless if the defendant failed to exhaust the strikes he has in the selection process.[9] However, the exhaustion of all strikes is no longer a requirement of assigning error to the refusal of the trial court to strike a juror for cause.[10]

§ 18:13　Preliminary oath

Before commencing voir dire, each panel shall be administered the following oath by the trial judge or the clerk of the court:

> **You shall give true answers to all questions as may be asked by the court and its authority, including all questions asked by the parties or their attorneys, concerning your qualifications as jurors in the case of _____ (herein state the case). So help you God.[1]**

Prior to the 1982 change in the statute, the oath had to be administered by the trial judge.[2] However, under the prior statute it was held that if the preliminary oath was not administered and there was no objection, there was no valid basis of reversal in the absence of a showing of harm.[3] The rule is still the same. Unless the defendant can show some prejudice, the trial court's failure to administer the oath will be deemed harmless and in the absence of a timely objection, the error is waived.[4] Also, under that statute it was held that it was not necessary for the defendant to be present when the preliminary oath was administered even in a case in which the death penalty was being sought.[5]

See § 18:34, infra, on final oath after selection.

---

cause which are provided for in O.C.G.A. § 15-12-163, O.C.G.A. § 15-12-164, and O.C.G.A. § 15-12-167. See Melson v. Dickson, 63 Ga. 682, 686 (1) (1879); Jones v. Cloud, 119 Ga. App. 697, 708, 168 S.E.2d 598 (1969).

[9]Gee v. State, 239 Ga. 583 (1), 238 S.E.2d 356 (1977); Foster v. State, 240 Ga. 858, 859 (2), 242 S.E.2d 600 (1978). See also Hopt v. People of Utah, 120 U.S. 430, 7 S.Ct. 614, 30 L.Ed. 708, 710 (1887).

[10]See § 18:19, infra.

[Section 18:13]

[1]O.C.G.A. § 15-12-132.

[2]Ates v. State, 155 Ga. App. 97, 98, 270 S.E.2d 455 (1980).

[3]Gober v. State, 247 Ga. 652, 654 (2), 278 S.E.2d 386 (1981); Gilreath v. State, 247 Ga. 814, 823 (3), 279 S.E.2d 650 (1981).

[4]Hill v. State, 268 Ga. App. 642 (2), 602 S.E.2d 348 (2004); Lowery v. State, 264 Ga. App. 655 (1), 592 S.E.2d 102 (2003). See also Gober v. State, 247 Ga. 652 (2), 278 S.E.2d 386 (1981).

[5]Gilreath v. State, 247 Ga. 814, 823 (3), 279 S.E.2d 650 (1981).

§ 18:14 Pre-voir dire charge

In *Bishop v. State*,[1] the Georgia Supreme Court pointed out that "[w]hether to give pre-voir dire instructions is within the discretion of the trial court. . . . If, however, the trial court determines to give a pre-voir dire charge, the better practice . . . is to do so in accordance with the established procedure and formality applicable to the giving of the jury charge at the conclusion of the guilt-innocence phase." See § 18:36, infra, on pretrial instructions, and § 24:22, infra, on presence of defendant for a recharge of the jury.

§ 18:15 Hearings on challenges

In *Press-Enterprises Co. v. Superior Court*,[1] the United States Supreme Court held that voir dire examinations in criminal cases are presumptively open to the public in the absence of some overriding interest. If a part of the examination is to be closed, the trial judge must first make a finding that closure is essential and that available alternatives have been considered. Any closure of voir dire must be narrowly tailored to fit the circumstances. In addition, "[a]ll voir dire should take place in the courtroom in the presence of all parties."[2]

The trial judge has the duty to immediately hear challenges based on juror qualifications, answers to statutory questions and other challenges for cause. The parties are entitled to present evidence relating to the truth of objections. If the trial judge is satisfied that a juror is disqualified, he shall be excused for cause.[3] See § 18:11, supra, on challenge to the jury.

If a juror answers a question falsely or perhaps inaudibly and counsel does not know of the false answer, this may be a ground for a mistrial after the jury is sworn and before the introduction of evidence begins.[4] See § 18:24, infra, on untruthful answers from jurors.

If any one of these objections shall be true in fact, but the fact shall be unknown to either party or the counsel of such party at the time the juror is under investigation, and is subsequently

---

[Section 18:14]

[1]Bishop v. State, 268 Ga. 286, 292 (9), 486 S.E.2d 887 (1997).

[Section 18:15]

[1]Press-Enterprise Co. v. Superior Court, 464 U.S. 501, 104 S.Ct. 819, 78 L.Ed.2d 629 (1984). See § 17:2, supra, on coverage by news media.

[2]Robertson v. State, 268 Ga. 772, 774 (4), 493 S.E.2d 697 (1997); Russell v. State, 230 Ga. App. 546, 497 S.E.2d 36 (1998).

[3]O.C.G.A. §§ 15-12-163, 15-12-164, 15-12-167.

[4]Jones v. State, 232 Ga. 324, 206 S.E.2d 481 (1974); O.C.G.A. § 15-12-163, O.C.G.A. § 15-12-167. See § 18:24, n. 30, infra, on setting aside juror impartiality.

discovered, such objection may be made and the proof heard at any time before the prosecuting counsel submits to the jury any of his evidence in the case; but if known to the party or his counsel, the objection shall be made before the juror is sworn in the case.[5] Also, untruthful answers by a potential juror during jury selection may be a basis of a new trial.[6] See § 18:24, infra, on untruthful answers from jurors.

Normally, the only question which the court will ask in addition to the statutory questions is whether the juror is related to the prosecutor, the accused or the deceased.

See § 18:24, infra, on the results of untruthful answers from jurors. Also see § 18:34, infra, on determining competency after selection. See § 17:8, supra, on the right of a defendant to be present during voir dire examination.

§ 18:16 Challenge for cause—Statutory questions in felony cases

Challenges for cause generally have either an "actual" or "implied" basis. For example, if a potential juror states that he is biased or prejudiced either for the state or the defendant, this is an "actual" disqualification of the juror for the particular case, and he may be excused for cause. On the other hand, if a potential juror is related by blood or marriage to the defendant within the prohibited degree, he is "impliedly" disqualified and may be stricken for cause. First, the statutory questions and death penalty questions will be discussed. Then challenges for cause will be discussed generally. Next, legal qualifications of jurors are discussed. Lastly, family relationships as related to challenges for cause are discussed. However, a basis for challenge for cause may come to light at any time during the jury selection process.

Normally the district attorney will read the indictment to the potential jurors before he asks the statutory questions.[1] However, it is not necessary that the indictment be read to them while they are being qualified.[2]

In the trial of all felony cases, jurors are asked the following

---

[5]O.C.G.A. §§ 15-12-163, 15-12-167. See Jones v. State, 232 Ga. 324, 206 S.E.2d 481 (1974).

[6]Thomas v. State, 249 Ga. 339, 290 S.E.2d 462 (1982).

[Section 18:16]

[1]Cf. Robertson v. State, 268 Ga. 772, 774 (5), 493 S.E.2d 697 (1997).

[2]Wiggins v. State, 172 Ga. App. 433, 323 S.E.2d 290 (1984); Leverenz

v. State, 140 Ga. App. 632, 638 (7), 231 S.E.2d 513 (1976). At least in the absence of objection, it is not error if the jurors are not informed of the nature of the crime and the parties involved before being asked the statutory questions. Robinson v. State, 238 Ga. 291, 292 (2), 232 S.E.2d 561 (1977).

statutory questions:[3]

1. "Have you, for any reason, formed and expressed any opinion in regard to the guilt or innocence of the accused?" [The result of an affirmative answer is discussed after question #4.]

If the juror answers in the negative, the following question shall be propounded to him:

2. "Have you any prejudice or bias resting on your mind either for or against the accused?"[4]

If the juror answers in the negative, the following question shall be propounded to him:

3. "Is your mind perfectly impartial between the state and the accused?"[5]

If the juror answers the above question in the affirmative, he shall be adjudged and held a competent juror in all cases where the offense does not involve the life of the accused; where the offense does involve the life of the accused, the following additional question shall be put to him:

4. "Are you conscientiously opposed to capital punishment?"[6] See § 18:17, infra.

If the juror answers question number 4 in the negative, he may be held a competent juror unless he has some other disability.

On the surface it would seem that if a juror answers question number 1 in the affirmative he should be automatically excused for cause. However, an affirmative answer does not require

---

[3]O.C.G.A. § 15-12-164.

[4]In Jenkins v. State, 146 Ga. App. 458 (1), 246 S.E.2d 466 (1978), the court pointed out that prejudice in favor of the victim does not disqualify a juror if the juror was not prejudiced against the defendant, just as prejudice against crime does not disqualify a juror if he can deal fairly with the defendant. See Parker v. State, 34 Ga. 262, 266 (1866).

[5]In Bennett v. State, 153 Ga. App. 21, 25, 264 S.E.2d 516 (1980), the court indicated that there is no rule which requires that a jury be selected from an impartial panel.

[6]See § 18:17, infra, on the constitutionality of this provision after Witherspoon v. Illinois, 391 U.S. 510, 88 S.Ct. 1770, 20 L.Ed.2d 776 (1968).

In Blankenship v. State, 247 Ga. 590, 593 (4), 596, 277 S.E.2d 505 (1981), overruled on other grounds by Thompson v. State, 263 Ga. 23, 426 S.E.2d 895 (1993), the court held that in cases where the death penalty is imposed, the improper exclusion from the initial panel of an otherwise qualified juror in violation of Witherspoon is harmful error regardless of whether the state utilized all its peremptory strikes. In the opinion, the court disapproved Alderman v. State, 241 Ga. 496, 246 S.E.2d 642 (1978), and Ruffin v. State, 243 Ga. 95, 252 S.E.2d 472 (1979). See Davis v. Georgia, 429 U.S. 122, 123, 97 S.Ct. 399, 50 L.Ed.2d 339 (1976), and Harris v. Texas, 403 U.S. 947, 91 S.Ct. 2291, 29 L.Ed.2d 859 (1971).

"automatic excusal of the juror." In *Childs v. State,*[7] the court held that despite the statutory change in 1979, "the test for disqualification remains: 'When a prospective juror has formed an opinion based on hearsay (as opposed to being based on his having seen the crime committed or having heard the testimony under oath), to disqualify such individual as a juror on the ground that he has formed an opinion on the guilt or innocence of a defendant, the opinion must be so fixed . . . that it would not be changed by the evidence or charge of the court. . . .' "

In *Lee v. State,*[8] the court held that it was not error for the trial judge to refuse to strike a juror for cause where he knew the victim or had some knowledge of the case from pre-trial publicity when the juror said he could be fair and impartial.

Generally, the statutory questions set out above, with the exception of question number 4, are used in misdemeanor cases. However, in misdemeanor cases the judge has broad discretion in determining whether to use these or other questions.[9]

It is not mandatory that the statutory questions be asked unless the defendant requests them.[10] Nevertheless, these questions are usually asked.

Historically these questions were asked jurors individually.[11] However, this is no longer required.[12]

In *Harris v. State,*[13] a non-capital case, the court stated that when jurors are qualified by the court under these statutory questions they are "deemed prima facie competent."

§ 18:17 Challenge for cause—Death cases

The Georgia Supreme Court[1] and the Eleventh Circuit[2] have concluded that there is no constitutional requirement that *Witherspoon* questions are to be asked individually. However, Uniform

---

[7]Childs v. State, 257 Ga. 243, 250, 357 S.E.2d 48 (1987) (quoting Waters v. State, 248 Ga. 355, 283 S.E.2d 238 (1981)). Accord, Johnson v. State, 219 Ga. App. 547, 549 (2), 466 S.E.2d 63 (1995), rev'd on other grounds, 267 Ga. 77, 475 S.E.2d 595 (1996); Gilstrap v. State, 199 Ga. App. 223 (1), 404 S.E.2d 629 (1991), rev'd on other grounds, 261 Ga. 798, 410 S.E.2d 423 (1991).

[8]Lee v. State, 258 Ga. 762, 763 (2), 374 S.E.2d 199 (1988).

[9]Jones v. State, 221 Ga. App. 374 (1), 471 S.E.2d 318 (1996). See Nobles v. State, 127 Ga. 212, 215 (1), 56 S.E. 125 (1906).

[10]See Smith v. State, 168 Ga. 611, 615 (4), 148 S.E. 531 (1929).

[11]Williams v. State, 60 Ga. 367 (1878); Wilkerson v. State, 74 Ga. 398 (1884). But cf. Whittington v. State, 252 Ga. 168, 172 (1), 313 S.E.2d 73 (1984).

[12]Ivester v. State, 252 Ga. 333, 334 (1), 313 S.E.2d 674 (1984).

[13]Harris v. State, 178 Ga. App. 735, 736, 344 S.E.2d 528 (1986).

[Section 18:17]

[1]Arnold v. State, 236 Ga. 534, 539, 224 S.E.2d 386 (1976). Accord, Uniform Superior Court Rule 10.1.

Superior Court Rule 10.1 provides that "[i]n cases in which the death penalty is sought, the trial judge shall address all *Witherspoon* and reverse-*Witherspoon* questions to prospective jurors individually."[3]

It has been previously pointed out that the last of the four statutory questions which must be asked potential jurors in a felony case pursuant to O.C.G.A. § 15-12-164, is as follows: "4. Are you conscientiously opposed to capital punishment?"[4] However, under the United States Supreme Court's decision in *Witherspoon v. Illinois*,[5] it is unconstitutional to excuse a juror simply because he says he is conscientiously opposed to capital punishment. *Witherspoon* held that a death sentence "cannot be carried out if the jury that imposed it, or recommended it, was chosen by excluding veniremen for cause simply because they voiced general objections to the death penalty or expressed conscientious or religious scruples against its infliction."[6]

In *Adams v. Texas*,[7] the United States Supreme Court held "that a juror may not be challenged for cause based on his views about capital punishment unless those views would prevent or substantially impair the performance of his duties as a juror in accordance with his instructions and his oath. The State may insist, however, that jurors will consider and decide the facts impartially and conscientiously apply the law charged by the court."

In *Crowe v. State*,[8] the court pointed out that "[j]urors who merely state a strong preference for a death sentence when presented with a hypothetical situation are not subject to being stricken for cause in a capital case." The court further stated that it is not appropriate for counsel to outline the facts of the case and then ask a juror what his vote would be.

---

[2]McCorquodale v. Balkcom, 721 F.2d 1493 (11th Cir. 1983).

[3]See Cargill v. State, 255 Ga. 616, 625, n. 7, 340 S.E.2d 891 (1986), rev'd on other grounds, Manzano v. State, 282 Ga. 557, 651 S.E.2d 661 (2007); Curry v. State, 255 Ga. 215, 219 (1)(d), 356 S.E.2d 762 (1985).

[4]See § 18:16, supra.

[5]Witherspoon v. Illinois, 391 U.S. 510, 88 S.Ct. 1770, 20 L.Ed.2d 776 (1968), reh. denied, 393 U.S. 898, 89 S.Ct. 67, 21 L.Ed.2d 186 (1968).

[6]Such a jury, according to the United States Supreme Court in *Witherspoon*, falls "woefully short of that impartiality to which the petitioner was entitled under the Sixth and Fourteenth Amendments," as discussed in Glasser v. United States, 315 U.S. 60, 62 S.Ct. 457, 86 L.Ed. 680 (1942); Irvin v. Dowd, 366 U.S. 717, 81 S.Ct. 1639, 6 L.Ed.2d 751 (1961); Turner v. Louisiana, 379 U.S. 466, 85 S.Ct. 546, 13 L.Ed.2d 424 (1965). For this reason, *Witherspoon* applies retroactively (see n. 22 of the opinion).

[7]Adams v. Texas, 448 U.S. 38, 44, 100 S.Ct. 2521, 65 L.Ed.2d 581 (1980). Accord, Pruitt v. State, 270 Ga. 745, 750 (12), 514 S.E.2d 639 (1999); Jenkins v. State, 269 Ga. 282, 287 (8), 498 S.E.2d 502 (1998).

[8]Crowe v. State, 265 Ga. 582, 588 (9)(a), 458 S.E.2d 799 (1995).

In *Wainwright v. Witt,*[9] the United States Supreme Court approved the Adams test, disapproved a stricter standard and pointed out that the trial judge in a federal habeas corpus action is generally presumed to be correct and concluded that a trial judge did not have to make an oral or written finding of fact on whether or not a juror should be excused.

In order to comply with *Witherspoon,* potential jurors in Georgia capital cases may be asked one or more of the following questions:[10]

(1) "Are you so conscientiously opposed to capital punishment that you would not vote for the death penalty under any circumstances?"

(2) "Would your reservations about capital punishment prevent you from making an impartial decision on the issue of punishment for the defendant's conviction of murder according to the evidence and the instructions of the court?"

(3) "Are your reservations about capital punishment such that you could never vote to impose the death penalty regardless of the evidence and the instructions of the court?"

(4) "Are your reservations about capital punishment such that you would refuse even to consider its imposition in the case before you regardless of the evidence and instructions of the court?"

(5) "Are you irrevocably committed before the trial has even begun on the issue of punishment for the conviction of murder to vote against the penalty of death regardless of the evidence, facts, and circumstances that emerge in the course of the proceedings and instructions of the court?"[11]

---

[9]Wainwright v. Witt, 469 U.S. 412, 105 S.Ct. 844, 83 L.Ed.2d 841 (1985). See Greene v. State, 268 Ga. 47, 485 S.E.2d 741 (1997).

[10]Redd v. State, 242 Ga. 876, 878 (2), 252 S.E.2d 383 (1979). Cf. Goodwin v. Hopper, 243 Ga. 193, 253 S.E.2d 156 (1979). In Banks v. State, 246 Ga. 178, 182, 269 S.E.2d 450 (1980), the court said that a defendant who is not sentenced to death does not have standing to object to the statutory questions relating to the death penalty.

[11]In Lewis v. State, 246 Ga. 101, 103 (2), 268 S.E.2d 915 (1980), the court held that it was error to excuse jurors for cause who stated that they would not vote for the death penalty because the defendant was 16 years of age. The court, quoting *Witherspoon,* said "Veniremen . . . cannot be excluded simply because they indicate that there are some kinds of cases in which they would refuse to recommend capital punishment."

In Griggs v. State, 241 Ga. 317, 317-19, 245 S.E.2d 269 (1978), a potential juror was excused for stating that he was conscientiously opposed to the death penalty "if only certain kinds of evidence were presented." He did not state that he was opposed to the death penalty in all situations. The court said that the juror's uncertainty or equivocation based on the quality of the evidence did not justify his excusal for cause.

In *Morgan v. Illinois,*[12] the United States Supreme Court held that it was error for the trial judge to refuse to ask prospective jurors if they would automatically impose a death sentence following a verdict of guilty even though the jurors had said they could be fair and follow the law. In *Tollette v. State,*[13] the Georgia Supreme Court concluded that *Morgan* requires only "that such questioning occur on request, and does not specify whether the trial court or the parties actually conduct the questioning."

Rule 10.1 of the Uniform Rules for the Superior Courts provides in part that "[p]rior to ruling upon any motion to strike a juror under *Witherspoon,* the trial judge shall confer with counsel for the state and for the accused as to any additional inquiries. Failure to object to the court's ruling on whether or not a juror is qualified shall be a waiver of any such objection."

In *Davis v. Georgia,*[14] the United States Supreme Court held that when just one potential juror was excluded for having expressed a general objection to the death penalty, the death penalty could not be imposed in that case. And in *Blankenship v. State,*[15] the court held that where a potential juror is excluded for cause in violation of the Witherspoon rules, the error is harmful regardless of whether the state had peremptory challenges remaining which it could have used to challenge the juror.[16] In the 1987 case of *Gray v. Mississippi,*[17] the United States Supreme Court held that the "harmless error analysis cannot apply" to a Witherspoon violation "because the impartiality of the adjudicator goes to the very integrity of the legal system."

In *Zellmer v. State,*[18] the Georgia Supreme Court in 2000 concluded that the following voir dire questions are proper:

"(a) If the defendant is found guilty of murder, and it becomes your duty to choose and impose one of the three sentencing options of death, life without parole, and life with the possibility of parole, and you do not feel death is the appropriate sentence,

---

[12]Morgan v. Illinois, 504 U.S. 719, 112 S.Ct. 2222, 119 L.Ed.2d 492 (1992).

[13]Tollette v. State, 280 Ga. 100, 102(2), 621 S.E.2d 742 (2005).

[14]Davis v. Georgia, 429 U.S. 122, 97 S.Ct. 399, 50 L.Ed.2d 339 (1976), rev'g 236 Ga. 804, 807, 225 S.E.2d 241 (1976).

[15]Blankenship v. State, 247 Ga. 590, 593 (4), 277 S.E.2d 505 (1981), overruled on other grounds by Thompson v. State, 263 Ga. 23, 426 S.E.2d 895 (1993).

[16]The *Blankenship* court expressed disapproval of contrary holdings in Alderman v. State, 241 Ga. 496, 246 S.E.2d 642 (1978), and Ruffin v. State, 243 Ga. 95, 252 S.E.2d 472 (1979). See Davis v. Georgia, 429 U.S. 122, 123, 97 S.Ct. 399, 50 L.Ed.2d 339 (1976); Harris v. Texas, 403 U.S. 947, 91 S.Ct. 2291, 29 L.Ed.2d 859 (1971).

[17]Gray v. Mississippi, 481 U.S. 648, 107 S.Ct. 2045, 95 L.Ed.2d 622 (1987).

[18]Zellmer v. State, 272 Ga. 735, 736, 534 S.E.2d 802 (2000).

would you automatically choose and impose life without parole, without giving any consideration to a sentence of life with the possibility of parole?

"Are you conscientiously opposed to a sentence of life with the possibility of parole for one who has been found guilty of murder?

"(b) If the defendant is found guilty of murder, and it becomes your duty to choose and impose one of the three sentencing options of death, life without parole, and life with the possibility of parole, and you do not feel death is the appropriate sentence, would you automatically choose and impose life with the possibility of parole, without giving any consideration to a sentence of life without parole?

"Are you conscientiously opposed to a sentence of life without parole for one who has been found guilty of murder?"

It has been held that it is not error for the district attorney to ask the Witherspoon questions even if the state announces that it will not insist on the death penalty.[19] In *Harper v. State*,[20] the court held that even if potential jurors were erroneously excluded under *Witherspoon,* the defendant has no standing to raise the Witherspoon issue if the defendant did not receive a death sentence.

In a case in which the death penalty is being sought, if a potential juror states that if the defendant is found guilty of the charge he would vote for the death penalty, it is error for the trial judge to refuse to excuse the juror for cause.[21] However, in the 2000 case of *Heidler v. State*,[22] the Georgia Supreme Court said that "[t]he proper standard for determining the disqualification of a prospective juror based upon his views on capital punishment 'is whether the juror's views would "prevent or substantially impair the performance of his duties as a juror in accordance with his instructions and his oath."' "

Lastly, it should be pointed out that some studies have indicated that jurors without scruples against the death penalty are more conviction prone.[23] However, in *Mincey v. State*,[24] the Georgia Supreme Court held (1) that a defendant is not entitled

---

[19]Brown v. State, 228 Ga. 215, 217, 184 S.E.2d 655 (1971).

[20]Harper v. State, 249 Ga. 519, 530 (7), 292 S.E.2d 389 (1982).

[21]Pope v. State, 256 Ga. 195, 345 S.E.2d 831 (1986), overruled on other grounds by Nash v. State, 271 Ga. 281, 519 S.E.2d 893 (1999).

[22]Heidler v. State, 273 Ga. 54, 56 (3), 537 S.E.2d 44 (2000).

[23]Bronson, "On the Conviction Proneness and Representativeness of the Death-Qualified Jury: An Empirical Study of Colorado Veniremen," 42 Col. L. R. (1970). Also see Case Comment, "Grigsby v. Mabry: A New Look at Death-Qualified Juries," 18 Am. Crim. L. R. 145 (1980).

[24]Mincey v. State, 251 Ga. 255 (2), 304 S.E.2d 882 (1983) (citing Smith v. Balkcom, 660 F.2d 573, 578 (5th Cir.

to an evidentiary hearing on the "contention that death-qualified juries are more likely to convict than non-death qualified juries," and (2) even if it is assumed that death-qualified juries are more likely to convict, "the practice of excluding for cause those potential jurors so unequivocally opposed to the death penalty that they would automatically vote against it . . . does not deny a defendant his constitutional right to an impartial jury." In *Lockhart v. McCree*,[25] the United States Supreme Court rejected a claim that death-qualified jurors were more likely to convict, and that striking such jurors does not violate either the fair cross-section requirement or the Sixth Amendment or the defendant's right to an impartial jury.

For a general discussion of the *Witherspoon* decision, see 3 Georgia Law Review 238 (1968).

§ 18:18   Individual examination of jurors

After the statutory questions have been asked, both the state and the defendant have a right to an individual examination of each juror.[1] However, even though "a defendant has a right to individualized responses from each member of the panel, he is not entitled to question each juror individually. . . . Thus, a trial court can . . . require . . . [both counsel] to address general questions to the entire panel rather than allowing him to question each juror seriatim."[2]

See also § 18:24, infra, regarding voir dire generally.

§ 18:19   Challenge for cause—General[1]

A challenge for cause is a challenge to a juror for which some cause or reason is alleged, or is an objection to a juror on the ground that he is not qualified under the provisions of the statute

---

1981)).

[25]Lockhart v. McCree, 476 U.S. 162, 106 S.Ct. 1758, 90 L.Ed.2d 137 (1986). Accord, Catchings v. State, 256 Ga. 241, 243 (3), 347 S.E.2d 572 (1986).

In Walker v. State, 281 Ga. 157, 162, 635 S.E.2d 740 (2006), the court held that "qualifying prospective jurors based upon their death penalty views does not deny capital defendants their right to an impartial jury drawn from a representative cross section of the community and is not otherwise unconstitutional   [cits.]".   See

Wainwright v. Witt, 469 U.S. 412, 418-426, 105 S. Ct. 844, 83 L. Ed. 2d 841 (1985).

[Section 18:18]

[1]O.C.G.A. § 15-12-133.

[2]Walker v. State, 271 Ga. 328, 329 (2), 519 S.E.2d 670 (1999).

[Section 18:19]

[1]See generally 50 C.J.S. Juries §§ 267 et seq. See also A.B.A. Standards for Criminal Justice, Trial by Jury and Right of Fair Trial and Free Press.

fixing the qualifications of jurors,[2] or on some other ground which, in the opinion and discretion of the trial court,[3] renders him unfit to serve as a juror.[4]

Under Georgia practice the substance of a challenge for cause is generally regarded as a challenge to the poll[5] although strictly speaking, a challenge to the poll refers generally to any challenge to an individual juror, whether peremptory or for cause.[6]

At common law and under current Georgia practice, challenges for cause are divided into challenges for principal cause and challenges for favor. A challenge for principal cause is based on grounds which, if shown to exist, would disqualify the juror as a matter of law, and a challenge for favor merely raises a suspicion of bias in that particular case, to be determined as a question of fact.[7] See §§ 18:12 and 18:15, supra, on challenges to the poll and hearings on challenges.

Both parties to a trial have a constitutional right to challenge jurors for cause,[8] that right being implicit in the Sixth Amendment's requirement of an impartial jury and a fair trial.[9] "Whether to strike a juror for cause lies within the sound discretion of the trial court."[10]

In *Hart v. State,*[11] the court held that the trial judge is not required to make a factual finding on the record in support of his decision that a juror should not be excused for cause.

Some Georgia cases have held that jurors should be free from

---

[2]See O.C.G.A. §§ 15-12-163 and 15-12-164 for provisions regarding the qualification of jurors and for the mandatory questions which must be asked jurors in felony cases. See also § 18:16, supra, on statutory juror questions in felony cases.

[3]It is the duty of the trial court to determine whether or not the challenge should be sustained. Hagans v. State, 77 Ga. App. 513, 514, 48 S.E.2d 700 (1948).

[4]E.g., Jesse v. State, 20 Ga. 156 (1856) (deafness); Thomas v. State, 27 Ga. 287 (1859) (intoxication); Crews v. Flanders, 101 Ga. App. 914, 115 S.E.2d 628 (1960) (ambiguous answers to voir dire questions).

[5]See § 18:12, supra, on challenges to the poll.

[6]Hagans v. State, 77 Ga. App. 513, 48 S.E.2d 700 (1948); Garner v. State, 67 Ga. App. 772, 21 S.E.2d 656 (1942).

[7]Jordan v. State, 247 Ga. 328-338, 276 S.E.2d 224 (1981); Hagans v. State, 77 Ga. App. 513, 48 S.E.2d 700 (1948). See § 18:16, supra.

[8]Hall v. State, 64 Ga. App. 644, 13 S.E.2d 868 (1941).

[9]Irvin v. Dowd, 366 U.S. 717, 81 S.Ct. 1639, 6 L.Ed.2d 751 (1961).

[10]Somchith v. State, 272 Ga. 261, 262 (2), 527 S.E.2d 546 (2000).

[11]Hart v. State, 238 Ga. App. 325, 328 (3), 517 S.E.2d 790 (1999). Accord, Clark v. State, 246 Ga. App. 842, 844, 542 S.E.2d 588 (2000). But see Thompson v. State, 294 Ga. 693, 755 S.E.2d 713 (2014) (questions why trial courts have discretion to excuse jurors for cause without a request from the parties and without a stated basis for the excusal) (Nahmias, J. concurring).

even a suspicion of prejudgment.[12] In *Pope v. State*,[13] a juror indicated she knew the victim well and "would be 'more inclined' to believe him than an inmate. However, this prospective juror . . . [also] indicated that she would give consideration to all the evidence before reaching a decision in the case." The court held that it was not error for the trial judge to refuse to strike the juror for cause. In *Davis v. State*,[14] the court held that "[t]he fact that a juror knows a victim does not require dismissal for cause if the juror indicates that he can be fair and impartial. . . ." In *Mosely v. State*,[15] the appellate court affirmed the trial judge's decision not to exclude a juror who had served on a church deacon board along with the defendant. The trial court retained the juror because the juror stated that he could be fair and impartial in reaching a decision on the case.

In *Robertson v. State*,[16] the Georgia Supreme Court held that "[t]here is no requirement that a juror be ignorant of every fact and issue involved in a case. The question is whether the juror can lay aside any impressions he may have and reach a verdict based on the evidence presented at trial." In *Greenway v. State*,[17] the court pointed out that "to disqualify a juror for cause, it must be established that the juror's opinion [is] so fixed and definite that it would not be changed by the evidence or the charge of the court. . . . The fact that a potential juror may have some doubt as to his impartiality, or complete freedom from all bias, does not demand, as a matter of law that the juror be excused for cause. . . . When the venireman indicates that he can render a fair and impartial verdict based solely upon the evidence at trial, he is prima facie competent to serve."

In *Thomas v. State*,[18] the Court of Appeals observed: "[t]here is a legal difference between (a) a potential juror who, because of

---

[12]Edwards v. Griner, 42 Ga. App. 282 (1), 155 S.E. 789 (1930). In Justus v. Commonwealth, 220 Va. 971, 266 S.E.2d 87, 93 (1980), a prospective juror stated that she believed the defendant was guilty based on what she had learned from the newspapers and television. She stated that she would give the defendant a fair trial but she also said that the defendant would have to produce evidence to change her mind about his guilt. The court held that it was error for the trial judge to fail to excuse her for cause.

[13]Pope v. State, 170 Ga. App. 799 (1), 318 S.E.2d 223 (1984); Sanders v. State, 211 Ga. App. 859, 862 (1), 440 S.E.2d 745 (1994).

[14]Davis v. State, 229 Ga. App. 787, 788 (1), 494 S.E.2d 702 (1997).

[15]Mosely v. State, 269 Ga. 17, 495 S.E.2d 9 (1998).

[16]Robertson v. State, 268 Ga. 772, 774, 493 S.E.2d 697 (1997).

[17]Greenway v. State, 207 Ga. App. 511, 513 (3), 428 S.E.2d 415 (1993). See Ellis v. State, 292 Ga. 276, 284(4) (b), 736 S.E.2d 412 (2013); Jones v. State, 338 Ga.App. 505, 790 S.E.2d 301 (2016). Cf. Wilson v. State, 220 Ga. App. 487 (1), 469 S.E.2d 516 (1996).

[18]Thomas v. State, 257 Ga. App. 350, 571 S.E.2d 178 (2002).

life experiences, expresses doubt that he or she can be impartial *if evidence* triggers those experiences, and (b) a juror who, because of life experiences, cannot listen to the evidence before forming a judgment. While the former category may or may not merit a peremptory strike, the latter category does merit a strike for cause." (cite omitted) (emphasis in original).

In *Edenfield v. State*,[19] the Georgia Supreme Court emphasized that "a prospective juror is not unqualified simply because he is inclined to give substantial weight to a specific fact or circumstance—such as the sexual abuse of a child—in his consideration of an appropriate sentence. . . . [T]he issue is not whether the prospective juror will consider a critical fact to be very important . . . [or] . . . that only that fact matters." Instead, the Court noted "the problem lies with a prospective juror who already has made up his mind about the appropriate sentence—either conditionally upon proof of some critical fact or absolutely—before the evidence is in, and who simply will not listen to the full range of evidence or heed the charge of the court."

In *Irvin v. Dowd*,[20] the United States Supreme Court said: "The theory of the law is that a juror who has formed an opinion cannot be impartial. . . . It is not required, however, that the jurors be totally ignorant of the facts and issues involved. In these days of swift, widespread and diverse methods of communication, an important case can be expected to arouse the interest of the public in the vicinity, and scarcely any of those best qualified to serve as jurors will not have formed some impression or opinion as to the merits of the case. This is particularly true in criminal cases. To hold that the mere existence of any preconceived notion as to the guilt or innocence of an accused, without more, is sufficient to rebut the presumption of a prospective juror's impartiality would be to establish an impossible standard. It is sufficient if a juror can lay aside his impression or opinion and render a verdict based on the evidence presented in court."[21]

---

[19]Edenfield v. State, 293 Ga. 370, 744 S.E.2d 738 (2013). See Ellington v. State, 292 Ga. 109, 735 S.E.2d 736 (2012).

[20]Irvin v. Dowd, 366 U.S. 717, 722, 81 S.Ct. 1639, 6 L.Ed.2d 751 (1961). In *Irvin*, the court also said that the adoption of the rule set out in the text "cannot foreclose inquiry as to whether, in a given case, the application of that rule works a deprivation of the prisoner's life or liberty without due process of law. . . . [T]he test is

'whether the nature and strength of the opinion formed are such as in law necessarily . . . raise the presumption of partiality. . . .' Unless [the challenger] . . . shows the actual existence of such an opinion in the mind of the juror as will raise the presumption of partiality, the juror need not necessarily be set aside. . . . If a positive and decided opinion had been formed, he would have been incompetent even though it had not been expressed."

[21]Moss v. State, 250 Ga. 368, 369

Nevertheless, in *Lively v. State*,[22] the court pointed out that a "juror may be found disqualified even though he insists he is not biased; therefore, the juror's opinion of his qualification is by no means determinative. . . ." When ruling on a potential juror's qualifications, the trial court must make a factual determination based on all the circumstances known to the court, including, but not limited to, the juror's own opinion of his impartiality. In *Garland v. State*,[23] the court clarified *Lively* by noting that the decision in that case was based on facts that compelled the disqualification of a potential juror, such that the failure to disqualify could not be supported absent a factual determination. However, the court said they did "not hold that the trial court must make a factual determination part of the record in every case in which a motion to strike a juror for cause is made. Rather, the application of *Lively* comes into play where the record shows on its face circumstances indicating that a potential juror has a compelling interest . . . in the case."

The court noted in *Gilstrap v. State*,[24] "[t]he fact that a potential juror may have some doubt as to his impartiality, or complete freedom from all bias, does not demand as a matter of law that the juror be excused for cause."

In the 1981 case of *Jordan v. State*,[25] the Supreme Court of Georgia pointed out that juror disqualifications for cause are not favored in Georgia and that a trial judge's decision to overrule challenges for cause will rarely be disturbed. The *Jordan* court said that Georgia's strict requirements as to juror disqualification are offset, however, by the large number of peremptory strikes allowed each side in felony cases.[26]

O.C.G.A. § 15-12-133 provides that in all criminal cases, both

---

(4), 297 S.E.2d 459 (1982); Williams v. State, 251 Ga. 749, 804, 312 S.E.2d 40 (1983); Chancey v. State, 256 Ga. 415, 425 (3)(B)(a), 349 S.E.2d 717 (1986).

[22]Lively v. State, 262 Ga. 510, 511, 421 S.E.2d 528 (1992); Matthews v. State, 268 Ga. 798, 799 (2), 493 S.E.2d 136 (1997); Walker v. State, 262 Ga. 694, 696 (2), 424 S.E.2d 782 (1993); McCrary v. State, 191 Ga. App. 336, 337, 381 S.E.2d 579 (1989) (quoting Jones v. State, 232 Ga. 324, 206 S.E.2d 481 (1974)). Cf. Carr v. State, 267 Ga. 547 (5), 480 S.E.2d 583 (1997).

[23]Garland v. State, 263 Ga. 495, 497 (1), 435 S.E.2d 431 (1993).

[24]Gilstrap v. State, 199 Ga. App. 223 (1), 404 S.E.2d 629 (1991), rev'd on other grounds, 261 Ga. 798, 410

S.E.2d 423 (1991) (quoting Harris v. State, 178 Ga. App. 735, 344 S.E.2d 528 (1986)). Accord, Clark v. State, 309 Ga. App. 749, 711 S.E.2d 339 (2011); Somchith v. State, 272 Ga. 261, 262 (2), 527 S.E.2d 546 (2000); Nobles v. State, 201 Ga. App. 483, 487 (7), 411 S.E.2d 294 (1991); Nichols v. State, 221 Ga. App. 600, 601 (2), 473 S.E.2d 491 (1996); Carter v. State, 224 Ga. App. 217 (2), 480 S.E.2d 266 (1997).

[25]Jordan v. State, 247 Ga. 328, 340, 276 S.E.2d 224 (1981).

[26]In most felony cases, both the criminal defendant and the state have nine peremptory challenges. However, where the state announces its intention to seek the death penalty, the defendant and the state are each allowed 15 peremptory challenges.

parties have the right to examine the individual jurors about "any matter or thing which would illustrate any interest of the prospective juror in the case, including any opinion as to which party ought to prevail, the relationship or acquaintance of the prospective juror with the parties or counsel therefor, any fact or circumstance indicating any inclination, leaning, or bias which the prospective juror might have respecting the subject matter of the action or the counsel or parties thereto. . . ." However, it is not error to overrule a challenge for favor where it is not established that the juror's opinion was so fixed and definite that it could not be changed by the evidence or by proper instructions from the court.[27]

In *Harris v. State,*[28] the Georgia Supreme Court held that in all trials commencing after April 17, 1986, it is reversible error for a trial judge to refuse to strike an unqualified juror even if the defendant fails to exhaust his peremptory strikes. In *Cross v. State,*[29] defense counsel asked that a potential juror be excused. The trial court refused but the state struck the juror. The appellate court held that the defendant could not complain. In addition, where the trial court erroneously allows a challenge for cause, the opposing party has no grounds to complain "if a competent and unbiased jury is finally seated."[30]

Even in the absence of a challenge of a potential juror by a party, it has been said that the trial judge "may on its own motion and in the exercise of sound discretion, excuse an incompetent

---

O.C.G.A. § 15-12-165. See § 18:17, supra, on challenges for cause in death penalty cases.

[27]Westbrook v. State, 242 Ga. 151, 154, 249 S.E.2d 524 (1978); Foster v. State, 240 Ga. 858 (2), 242 S.E.2d 600 (1978); Sullens v. State, 239 Ga. 766 (1), 238 S.E.2d 864 (1977).

[28]Harris v. State, 255 Ga. 464, 465 (2), 339 S.E.2d 712 (1986). See also Bass v. State, 183 Ga. App. 349, 352, 358 S.E.2d 837 (1987). Cf. Hayles v. State, 180 Ga. App. 860 (1), 350 S.E.2d 793 (1986).

Subsequent to *Harris*, a number of Court of Appeals' decisions continued to consider whether the defense had exhausted its preemptory strikes as determinative of whether the defendant was prejudiced by the trial court's improper failure to excuse a juror for cause. See e.g., McGriff v. State, 232 Ga. App. 546(1), 502 S.E.2d 482 (1998). Then in Wallace v. State, 275 Ga. 879(3), 572 S.E.2d 579 (2002), the Supreme Court reiterated *Harris* and took the occasion to expressly overrule *McGriff* and other similar cases from the Court of Appeals. See Goulding v. State, 334 Ga. App. 349, 780 S.E.2d 1 (2015) (disapproved of on other grounds by Quiller v. State, 338 Ga. App. 206, 789 S.E.2d 391 (2016)) (see concurring opinion of Judge Ray which is critical of *Harris*).

[29]Cross v. State, 271 Ga. 427, 429 (2), 520 S.E.2d 457 (1999).

[30]Wells v. State, 261 Ga. 282, 282-83, 404 S.E.2d 106 (1991). See Humphreys v. State, 304 Ga. App. 365, 696 S.E.2d 400 (2010).

juror at any time before evidence is given."[31] Likewise, the trial judge may excuse a juror for cause where the juror has stated that "she would not base her decision on the evidence and the law if to do so would result in the defendant's imprisonment."[32] See § 18:34, infra, on the oath of the jury. In *Wells v. State*,[33] the court held that there was no abuse of discretion where the trial judge excused a potential juror for relationship to the defendant even though the extent of relationship was not shown. The court pointed out that "[a] party to a lawsuit has no vested interest in having any particular juror to serve; he is entitled only to a legal and impartial jury."[34]

In 2005, the legislature provided an additional basis to strike a juror for cause. O.C.G.A. § 15-12-164(d) now states that trial courts "shall excuse for cause" any juror whose answers on voir dire demonstrate an inability to be fair. The amendment affords counsel with a compelling basis for a motion to strike in an appropriate case since it also provides that a juror's self serving statement that the juror can be fair is "to be considered by the court but is not determinative."

§ 18:20 Challenge for cause—Situations in which it has been held it is not error for judge to overrule challenge

In the following situations, it was held not to be error for the judge to overrule the challenge for cause: (1) where the juror stated on voir dire that blacks have inherent criminal propensities;[1] (2) where the juror stated on voir dire that he would tend to give greater weight and credibility to the testimony of a policeman;[2] (3) where the potential juror was interim city manager of the city where trial was to be conducted and the case had been

---

[31]Hatten v. State, 253 Ga. 24, 26 (5), 315 S.E.2d 893 (1984). In *Hatten*, the juror was excused before voir dire because he had said that "he would never vote to convict any criminal defendant." Cf. Nichols v. State, 186 Ga. App. 314, 315, 367 S.E.2d 266 (1988).

[32]Brown v. State, 261 Ga. 184, 185 (2), 402 S.E.2d 725 (1991).

[33]Wells v. State, 261 Ga. 282 (2), 404 S.E.2d 106 (1991) (quoting Grasham v. Southern Railway Co., 111 Ga. App. 158, 141 S.E.2d 189 (1965)).

[34]Quoted with approval in Scott v. State, 219 Ga. App. 906, 907 (1), 467 S.E.2d 348 (1996).

[Section 18:20]
[1]Tennon v. State, 235 Ga. 594, 595, 220 S.E.2d 914 (1975).

[2]Tennon v. State, 235 Ga. 594, 595, 220 S.E.2d 914 (1975).

However, in Bradham v. State, 243 Ga. 638, 639 (3), 256 S.E.2d 331 (1979), the court reversed the conviction where the defendant had used all his peremptory challenges and the trial judge had refused to excuse for cause a juror who stated that he had three sons who were in law enforcement in another county and that "he would be inclined to give more credence to a police officer's testimony than a nonpolice witness." The court also stated that in the future it would

handled by the police of that city;[3] (4) where the juror said on voir dire that he believed from pre-trial publicity that the defendant was at the scene of the crime;[4] (5) where the juror had seen the defendant and his counsel in the courtroom on an unrelated matter the previous day;[5] (6) where the juror had contributed money to a fund raising for the family of the deceased victim;[6] (7) where the juror expressed an opinion as to the guilt of the principal at the voir dire of the accessory;[7] (8) where the juror purposely made statements tending to show bias in order to avoid jury duty;[8] (9) where the juror admitted on voir dire that the fact that he had been a victim of a crime similar to the crime for which the defendant was charged could have an "unconscious" influence upon him, but he would not be consciously affected by it;[9] (10) where the juror on voir dire referred to the defendant as an "ex-con";[10] (11) where the juror heard the prosecutor refer to the defendant as a "prisoner";[11] (12) where the juror had met the district attorney on one occasion;[12] (13) where the juror was an honorary deputy sheriff and a part-time volunteer police officer[13] or other part-time police officer;[14] (14) where the juror was a full-time correctional employee who was certified as a peace officer but had no arrest power and who would have had to have additional training to become a law enforcement officer;[15] (15) where a prospective juror had been a police officer but he had retired,

---

not follow Kemp v. State, 226 Ga. 506, 507 (2), 175 S.E.2d 869 (1970), and Patterson v. State, 239 Ga. 409, 411 (1), 238 S.E.2d 2 (1977).

[3]Taylor v. State, 164 Ga. App. 660, 661 (1), 297 S.E.2d 755 (1982).

[4]Taylor v. State, 243 Ga. 222, 224, 253 S.E.2d 191 (1979). This case also held that it was not error to overrule a challenge for cause where the juror's son was a state's witness.

[5]Hiatt v. State, 132 Ga. App. 289, 291, 208 S.E.2d 163 (1974).

[6]Thacker v. State, 226 Ga. 170 (7), 173 S.E.2d 186 (1970).

[7]Loyd v. State, 45 Ga. 57, 73-74 (1872).

[8]Cornwall v. State, 91 Ga. 277 (9), 18 S.E. 154 (1893).

[9]Williams v. State, 146 Ga. App. 543 (3), 246 S.E.2d 729 (1978).

[10]Pierce v. State, 231 Ga. 731 (2), 204 S.E.2d 159 (1974).

[11]Marable v. State, 154 Ga. App. 426 (2), 268 S.E.2d 720 (1980); Collier

v. State, 232 Ga. 282, 206 S.E.2d 445 (1974).

[12]Cruver v. State, 131 Ga. App. 127, 128, 205 S.E.2d 528 (1974).

[13]Welch v. Dunham, 125 Ga. App. 141 (6), 147, 186 S.E.2d 559 (1971). But cf. Hutcheson v. State, 246 Ga. 13, 268 S.E.2d 643 (1980). See § 18:21, infra.

In Wilson v. State, 250 Ga. 630, 635 (4)(a), 300 S.E.2d 640 (1983), the court held that it was not error for the trial judge to refuse to strike for cause a once part-time officer who was a member of the inactive police reserves where he had no uniform and had not worked on the case.

[14]Denison v. State, 258 Ga. 690, 692 (4), 373 S.E.2d 503 (1988). See Clark v. State, 265 Ga. App. 112, 593 S.E.2d 28 (2003) for a review of cases involving challenges to jurors based upon some association with a law enforcement agency.

[15]Thompson v. State, 212 Ga. App. 175 (1), 442 S.E.2d 771 (1994). See §§ 18:21, 18:22, infra. In Mosher v.

no longer had any connection with a law enforcement agency and "no longer exercis[ed] any 'rights' under his certification [as a police officer]";[16] (16) where the juror was the wife of the police chief;[17] (see §§ 18:21 and 18:22, infra) (17) where the juror worked as a clerk in the office which issued an arrest warrant;[18] (18) where the juror was employed as a federal prosecutor;[19] (19) where the juror purposely answered the voir dire falsely, but without "evil motive";[20] (20) where the juror mingled freely with the general public during a recess;[21] (21) where the juror had sent a sympathy card to the family of the victim;[22] (22) where the juror admitted that she believed that the defendant was guilty and that she would not wish to be tried by someone with her state of mind, but that she could nevertheless give the defendant a fair trial;[23] (23) where a "potential juror may have some doubt as to his impartiality";[24] (24) where the juror's brother was to be a state's witness;[25] (25) where jurors were in the courtroom when the calendar was called and the defendant had three felony

---

State, 268 Ga. 555, 557 (2), 491 S.E.2d 348 (1997), the court pointed out that it had previously refused to extend the rule, that full-time police officers who are challenged for cause in a criminal case are automatically disqualified, "to those less connected with law enforcement than full-time police officers."

[16]Smith v. State, 201 Ga. App. 82 (1), 410 S.E.2d 202 (1991); Chavarria v. State, 248 Ga. App. 398, 399 (1), 546 S.E.2d 811 (2001).

[17]Adams v. State, 180 Ga. App. 546, 547 (2), 349 S.E.2d 789 (1986). Cf. Jones v. State, 184 Ga. App. 4 (2), 360 S.E.2d 599 (1987) (daughter of deputy); Carr v. State, 267 Ga. 547, 553 (5), 480 S.E.2d 583 (1997) (sheriff's mother).

[18]Roberts v. State, 261 Ga. 813 (1), 411 S.E.2d 496 (1992).

[19]Floyd v. State, 272 Ga. 65, 67 (2), 525 S.E.2d 683 (2000).

[20]Geiger v. State, 129 Ga. App. 488 (2), 492-95, 199 S.E.2d 861 (1973).

[21]Compton v. State, 179 Ga. 560, 563, 176 S.E. 764 (1934).

[22]Butler v. State, 231 Ga. 276, 201 S.E.2d 448 (1973).

[23]Butler v. State, 231 Ga. 276, 201 S.E.2d 448 (1973).

In Waters v. State, 248 Ga. 355, 362, 283 S.E.2d 238 (1981), five jurors stated that they had formed a belief as to the defendant's guilt based on news coverage. None had seen the crime committed or heard any sworn testimony. One juror initially stated that the defendant would have to put up evidence to overcome her belief of his guilt. However, they all stated that they could put aside any preconceived notions they might have and decide the case on the evidence presented and the law as charged by the court. The court affirmed the refusal of the trial judge to excuse the jurors for cause. The court said, "When a prospective juror has formed an opinion based on hearsay (as opposed to being based on his having seen the crime committed or having heard the testimony under oath), to disqualify such individual as a juror on the ground that he has formed an opinion on the guilt or innocence of a defendant, the opinion must be so fixed and definite that it would not be changed by evidence or charge of the court. . . ."

[24]Holmes v. State, 269 Ga. 124, 125 (2), 498 S.E.2d 732 (1998). Accord, Dorillas v. State, 224 Ga. App. 336 (1)(a), 480 S.E.2d 351 (1997).

[25]Hughes v. State, 161 Ga. App. 824 (2), 288 S.E.2d 916 (1982).

charges against him on the calendar;[26] (26) where a juror initially expressed belief that 99.9% of defendants are guilty.[27]

In *Sinyard v. State*,[28] the court held that remarks of one juror made during jury selection may taint the entire jury panel where "the remarks were 'inherently prejudicial and deprived [the defendant] of his right to begin his trial with a jury "free from even a suspicion of prejudgment or fixed opinion . . . ." ' "

In an outstanding opinion authored by Judge, later Justice, George T. Smith in *Jenkins v. State*,[29] the court held that the trial judge did not err in refusing to excuse a juror for cause where the juror said she was prejudiced in favor of the victim but not prejudiced against the defendant—she was simply prejudiced against crime. The court held that where the prejudice is not against the accused, but against the offense to which the defendant is indicted, it is not necessary that the juror be excused; "[o]therwise, all good men would be disqualified to sit as jurors in all criminal cases. For, if they feel as they should do, they should desire the suppression of crime. . . . This feeling may serve to stimulate their zeal to bring delinquents to punishment. But it does not follow . . . that it will so warp their judgment as to render them incapable of doing justice to the parties. . . ." See § 18:25, infra, on "rehabilitating" a juror.

§ 18:21   Challenge for cause—Situations where it has been held challenges were proper

In the following situations, a challenge for cause was held to be proper: (1) where the juror had been convicted or had pled guilty to a crime of moral turpitude[1] unless his civil rights have been restored; (2) where the juror's name did not appear on the jury

---

[26]Anderson v. State, 165 Ga. App. 885, 886 (2), 303 S.E.2d 57 (1983), rev'd on other grounds, 252 Ga. 103, 312 S.E.2d 113 (1984).

[27]Ellis v. State, 292 Ga. 276, 736 S.E.2d 412 (2013).

[28]Sinyard v. State, 243 Ga. App. 218, 221 (2), 531 S.E.2d 140 (2000).

[29]Jenkins v. State, 146 Ga. App. 458, 459, 246 S.E.2d 466 (1978) (citing and relying on Parker v. State, 34 Ga. 262, 266 (1866)). Accord, Malone v. State, 240 Ga. App. 732, 735, 524 S.E.2d 770 (1999).

[Section 18:21]

[1]See Ga. Const. 1983, Art. I, § I, ¶ XI. In Williams v. State, 12 Ga. App. 337 (3), 77 S.E. 189 (1913), the court held that "[o]ne convicted of larceny was infamous at common law, and not qualified to serve as a juror." The right to a jury trial means a right to be "tried by upright jurors." See Humphreys v. State, 287 Ga. 63, 694 S.E.2d 316 (2010) (a person sentenced under the First Offender Act either before or after discharge without an adjudication of guilt is not incompetent to serve as a juror).

list;[2] (3) where the juror is intoxicated;[3] (4) where the juror is mentally incompetent;[4] (5) where the juror is ill;[5] (6) where the juror says on voir dire that the indictment must mean that the state has a "good case";[6] (7) where the juror is the defendant's bail;[7] (8) where a law enforcement officer is challenged for cause;[8] (9) where the juror is a full-time employee of the district attorney's office;[9] [but see § 18:22, infra, on challenges for cause based on juror qualifications] (10) where the proposed juror is not a citizen of the United States;[10] (11) where the proposed juror is not a resident of the county;[11] (12) where the proposed juror is

---

[2]Faulkner v. Snead, 122 Ga. 28, 49 S.E. 747 (1905).

[3]See Jackson v. Jackson, 40 Ga. 150 (1869); Thomas v. State, 27 Ga. 287 (6) (1859). See O.C.G.A. § 15-12-163(b)(3).

[4]See Wall v. State, 126 Ga. 549 (3), 552-53, 55 S.E. 484 (1906); Jordan v. Massachusetts, 225 U.S. 167, 176, 32 S.Ct. 651, 56 L.Ed. 1038 (1912). See O.C.G.A. § 15-12-163(b)(3).

[5]See Cason v. State, 134 Ga. 786 (3), 68 S.E. 554 (1910).

[6]Bennett v. State, 153 Ga. App. 21, 26, 27, 264 S.E.2d 516 (1980).

[7]Anderson v. State, 63 Ga. 675 (1879).

[8]Harris v. State, 255 Ga. 464, 465 (2), 339 S.E.2d 712 (1986) (state patrolman); Hutcheson v. State, 246 Ga. 13, 14, 268 S.E.2d 643 (1980). However, in Kent v. State, 179 Ga. App. 131, 345 S.E.2d 669 (1986), the court held that the correctional officers are not automatically to be excused for cause. Accord, Scruggs v. State, 227 Ga. App. 35 (1), 488 S.E.2d 110 (1997).

In Dixon v. State, 180 Ga. App. 222, 225 (5), 348 S.E.2d 742 (1986), the court affirmed the refusal to strike a security guard for cause.

In Stocks v. State, 182 Ga. App. 162, 355 S.E.2d 103 (1987), the court held that it was not error for the trial judge to refuse to strike a man employed by the State Patrol who has no arresting power and has not been certified by the Georgia Peace Officers As-

sociation, but whose "sole function is administrative and his duties are to give written tests, eye tests, and driver's tests."

In Woods v. State, 224 Ga. App. 52, 53 (1), 479 S.E.2d 414 (1996), the court pointed out that the following persons are not to be automatically excused: (1) part-time police officers, (2) reserve police officers, (3) full-time correction officers without arrest powers, (4) retired police officers, (5) security guards, (6) Crime Lab forensic experts, and (7) driver's license examiners with the State Patrol.

However, in Terrell v. State, 271 Ga. 783 (1), 523 S.E.2d 294 (1999), the court held that it was error for the trial court to fail to strike for cause a "full-time military policeman with the Georgia National Guard . . . [who had] arrest power."

[9]Beam v. State, 260 Ga. 784, 400 S.E.2d 327 (1991). See Berry v. State, 302 Ga. App. 31, 34, 690 S.E.2d 428 (2010), the "rule in Beam has not been extended beyond full-time employees of the prosecuting authority." In Berry, the Court of Appeals upheld the trial court's decision allowing an I.T. consultant to the district attorney's office to serve as a juror.

[10]See Johnson v. State, 58 Ga. 491 (2) (1877); Jordan v. State, 22 Ga. 545, 546 (5), 556 (5) (1857); O.C.G.A. § 15-12-163(b)(1).

[11]Cf. Brown v. State, 105 Ga. 640 (1), 642 (1), 31 S.E. 557 (1898).

under the legal age;[12] (13) where the juror is disqualified by kinship; (14) where the proposed juror was a corrections officer in
the facility where the defendant was incarcerated for the pending
charges at trial;[13] and (15) where prospective jurors expressed
doubt about impartiality should defendant elect not to testify.[14]

See § 18:23, infra, on challenges for cause based on kinship and
employment.

§ 18:22 Challenge for cause—Juror qualifications

While O.C.G.A. § 15-12-163 does not purport to set out specific
questions relating to the statutory disqualifications of jurors
which may be raised by either party, this statute provides that
each juror "shall be presented to the accused in such a manner
that he can be distinctly seen." The statute also provides that the
State, or the accused, may make any of the following objections,
viz.:

"(1) That he is not a citizen, resident in the county;[1]

"(2) That he is under 18 years of age;[2]

"(3) That he is incompetent to serve as a juror because of
mental illness or mental retardation, or that he is intoxicated;[3]

"(4) That he is so near of kin to the prosecutor, the accused, or
the victim as to disqualify him by law from serving on the jury;

"(5) That the juror has been convicted of a felony in a federal
court or any court of a state of the United States and the juror's
civil rights have not been restored;[4] or

"(6) That the juror is unable to communicate in the English

---

[12]See Jordan v. State, 119 Ga.
443, 46 S.E. 679 (1904); O.C.G.A. § 15-
12-163(b)(2) has never been expressly
changed from 21 years of age to 18.
However, it has probably been changed
by implication. Also the Code uses the
age of 18.

[13]Kier v. State, 263 Ga. App. 347
(1), 587 S.E.2d 841 (2003). Compare
Prince v. State, 277 Ga. 230 (2), 587
S.E.2d 637 (2003).

[14]Rouse v. State, 296 Ga. App.
330, 674 S.E.2d 389 (2009).

[Section 18:22]

[1]See § 18:21, n. 10, supra, on
challenge for cause where a juror is
not a citizen of the United States.

[2]The statute referred to was
never individually changed from 21
years of age. However, the statute was

probably changed to 18 by implication.
Also the Code uses the age of 18.

[3]In Jordan v. Massachusetts, 225
U.S. 167, 176, 32 S.Ct. 651, 56 L.Ed.
1038 (1912), in referring to a conviction by a jury having an incompetent
member, the court said that due process implies a tribunal both impartial
and mentally competent to afford a
hearing. However, in Caldwell v. State,
249 Ga. App. 885, 889, 549 S.E.2d 449
(2001), the court pointed out that "the
fact that a person has been treated for
mental illness does not render a person
incompetent to serve as a juror." However, "[w]hether a potential juror is
competent to serve because of mental
illness is a proper inquiry on voir dire."

[4]Provisions (4) and (5) of the
statute were added by an amendment
in 1995. See § 10:8, supra, on restoration of civil rights. In Humphreys v.

language."

In 1984, the Georgia legislature abolished all exemptions from jury service except the requirements set out above.[5] O.C.G.A. § 15-12-4(b) provides that only citizens of the United States shall be qualified to serve as jurors.

Generally law enforcement officers are eligible to serve as jurors.[6] However, if such an officer is challenged for cause in a criminal case, the officer must be excused.[7] Likewise, a former superior court judge who issued two pre-trial orders should be stricken for cause on motion.[8] Nevertheless, a juror is not subject to challenge for cause simply because he is an honorary deputy sheriff,[9] and it has been held not to be error for the trial judge to refuse to strike for cause the brother of a deputy sheriff who is listed as a witness and a brother of the bailiff who is to be in charge of the jury.[10] Likewise, a person is not disqualified because his or her spouse served on the grand jury which indicted the defendant.[11] While a person serving on the grand jury which indicted a defendant is generally not eligible for jury duty, "until the next succeeding county master jury list has been received by the clerk,"[12] the spouse of such person is not disqualified from serving as a trial juror.[13] The sheriff's wife is not disqualified per se from serving on a criminal jury even though the sheriff assisted the district attorney with jury selection.[14] A person who signed the defendant's bond is disqualified from serving as a juror.[15] See §§ 18:20 and 18:21, supra.

In connection with the challenge of an individual juror for cause, the parties are not limited to the situations set out in

---

State, 287 Ga. 63, 694 S.E.2d 316 (2010), the court held that a juror who has been placed on probation or sentenced to a term of confinement pursuant to the First Offender Act is not incompetent to serve under O.C.G.A. § 15-12-163(b)(5).

[5]O.C.G.A. § 15-12-1.1.

[6]O.C.G.A. § 15-12-1.1. See § 12:4, supra.

[7]Hutcheson v. State, 246 Ga. 13, 268 S.E.2d 643 (1980); King v. State, 173 Ga. App. 838, 328 S.E.2d 740 (1985); Davis v. State, 236 Ga. App. 32, 35 (5), 510 S.E.2d 889 (1999). However, law enforcement officers are not automatically excluded from grand jury duty. Stinski v. State, 281 Ga. 783, 642 S.E.2d 1 (2007). See §§ 12:4, 18:20, n. 15, and § 18:21, n. 8, supra.

[8]McKinney v. State, 174 Ga. App.

78 (1), 329 S.E.2d 258 (1985). However, the Court of Appeals found the error to be harmless. But in McKinney v. State, 254 Ga. 503, 330 S.E.2d 884 (1985), the court concluded that the error was not harmless and reversed.

[9]Neese v. State, 183 Ga. App. 773, 776, 360 S.E.2d 1 (1987).

[10]Edwards v. State, 161 Ga. App. 18 (1), 289 S.E.2d 282 (1982).

[11]Walker v. State, 254 Ga. 149, 155 (6), 327 S.E.2d 475 (1985).

[12]O.C.G.A. § 15-12-4.

[13]Walker v. State, 254 Ga. 149, 155 (6), 327 S.E.2d 475 (1985).

[14]Brantley v. State, 262 Ga. 786, 788 (2)(e), 427 S.E.2d 758 (1993).

[15]Hart v. State, 157 Ga. App. 716, 717 (2), 278 S.E.2d 419 (1981). See § 18:21, n. 7, supra.

O.C.G.A. § 15-12-163.

In the interesting case of *Carter v. State,*[16] the defendant moved to disqualify a juror because she allegedly could not hear. In affirming the trial court's refusal to disqualify the juror, the Court of Appeals pointed out that "striking for cause a juror based upon a physical disability which is cognizable under the Americans with Disabilities Act of 1990, 42 U.S.C.A. §§ 12101 et seq., without making an attempt at a reasonable accommodation for the disability, may constitute a violation of the Act, if, as in the case sub judice, the juror wanted to serve." However, the Georgia Supreme Court, in *Jenkins v. State,*[17] affirmed the excusing of a prospective juror due to a hearing disability.

In *Kirkland v. State,*[18] the Supreme Court of Georgia concluded that defense counsel provided ineffective assistance when he failed to challenge for cause those jurors who owned stock in the corporation which was the named victim in an indictment charging the defendant with, inter alia, burglary. Because such jurors are considered "related" to one of the parties in the case, bias on their part is "presumed" and the error by the attorney is harmful "per se."[19] Likewise, in *Fortson v. State,*[20] the Georgia Supreme Court concluded that the defendant received ineffective assistance with the apparent oversight of the trial court and the prosecutor when his attorney used a peremptory strike to remove a juror whom the court had already struck for cause. The court concluded that counsel's error was harmful per se.

See § 18:2, supra, on ineligibility to serve at succeeding terms. See § 18:6, supra, on transcript of voir dire examination of prospective jurors. See § 10:8, supra, on restoration of civil rights.

§ 18:23   Challenge for cause—Relationship

Sir Edward Coke said that the relationship of a potential juror in any degree to a party disqualified the juror, but Blackstone writing later said that a juror was disqualified if he was related to either party within the ninth degree, as calculated according to the civil law.[1] The rule as given by Blackstone was recognized

---

[16]Carter v. State, 228 Ga. App. 335, 338, 491 S.E.2d 525 (3, n. 1) (1997).

[17]Jenkins v. State, 269 Ga. 282, 289 (10), 498 S.E.2d 502 (1998). But see Jones v. State, 249 Ga. App. 327 (1), 548 S.E.2d 75 (2001).

[18]Kirkland v. State, 274 Ga. 778, 560 S.E.2d 6 (2002).

[19]Kirkland v. State, 274 Ga. 778, 780, 560 S.E.2d 6 (2002).

[20]Fortson v. State, 277 Ga. 164, 165 (2), 587 S.E.2d 39 (2003).

[Section 18:23]

[1]See Crawley v. State, 151 Ga. 818, 822, 108 S.E. 238 (1921). In Churchill v. Churchill, 12 Vt. 661, 666 (1839), the court pointed out that by

in Georgia[2] until it was changed in 1935 by statute to the sixth degree as computed according to the civil law. In 2016, O.C.G.A. § 15-12-135(a) was amended to provide that the threshold is the third degree.

Thus, while a husband or a wife is said to be related to the relations of the other, their marriage does not cause the relatives of the husband to be relatives of the family of the wife. Hence, if the prosecutor and the potential juror married second cousins, the prosecutor is not regarded as being related to the juror, but the wife of the potential juror would be disqualified from serving on the jury.[3] A husband is regarded as being related to the kindred of the wife in the same degree as the wife, and there is not a step or degree between the husband and the wife. Hence, the wife of a third cousin of the defendant is related to the defendant within the third degree.[4] A prospective juror's brother who is the stepfather of the victim is not within the prohibited degree.[5] The wife of an uncle of the defendant is not disqualified.[6] A juror is not disqualified where her father-in-law was a first cousin of the defendant's grandfather.[7]

In Georgia, a potential juror may be challenged for cause because of the relationship of the juror to (1) the defendant,[8] (2) a co-defendant (who is not on trial),[9] (3) the prosecuting witness,[10]

---

canon law persons were considered as nearly related to each other as they were to a common ancestor, and the number of degrees from the common ancestor established the degree of relationship. The civil law method of computation is discussed in the body later. On both methods of computation, see generally Crawley v. State, 151 Ga. 818, 821, 108 S.E. 238 (1921).

[2]O'Berry v. State, 153 Ga. 644, 113 S.E. 2 (1922).

[3]Baldwin v. State, 120 Ga. 188, 190, 47 S.E. 558 (1904). In Smith v. Smith, 119 Ga. 239 (3), 46 S.E. 106 (1903), the court held that the brother of the wife of the defendant's brother was not disqualified.

[4]Eaton v. Grindle, 236 Ga. 324, 325, 223 S.E.2d 670 (1976).

[5]Day v. State, 188 Ga. App. 648, 649 (4), 374 S.E.2d 87 (1988).

[6]Alexander v. State, 260 Ga. 870, 871 (2), 401 S.E.2d 7 (1991).

[7]Jones v. State, 139 Ga. App. 824

(2), 229 S.E.2d 789 (1976).

[8]O.C.G.A. §§ 15-12-163(b)(4), 15-12-135; Burns v. State, 89 Ga. 527 (1), 15 S.E. 748 (1892) (implication).

[9]Banfield v. State, 221 Ga. App. 156, 471 S.E.2d 16 (1996).

[10]O.C.G.A. § 15-12-163(b)(4); Kennedy v. State, 191 Ga. 22, 31 (6), 11 S.E.2d 179 (1940); Merritt v. State, 152 Ga. 405, 110 S.E. 160 (1921). The prosecutor or prosecuting witness has been said to be one who instigates a prosecution by making an affidavit, charging the defendant with a crime, upon which a warrant is issued or an indictment or accusation is based. Spence v. State, 238 Ga. 399, 400, 233 S.E.2d 363 (1977). However, in McKenzie v. State, 28 Ga. App. 33, 110 S.E. 248 (1921), the court said that a juror was not disqualified even though he was related to a town marshal who arrested the defendant and signed a warrant at the direction of someone and was not partisan. In Taylor v. State, 243 Ga. 222, 224 (2), 253 S.E.2d 191

(4) the victim,[11] (5) a person who contributes to a fund to hire a special prosecutor in the case,[12] or (6) where the potential juror is the wife of the detective who questioned the defendant and swore out a warrant for him.[13] Generally, a juror may not be excused for cause because of his relationship to the district attorney,[14] defense counsel,[15] or sheriff because of the office he holds.[16] Also, a juror is not disqualified because of his relationship to a witness who is to testify for the state[17] even if the witness has been jointly indicted with the defendant.[18] However, a juror is disqualified if he is related to a policy holder in a mutual insurance company which insured the deceased if the company paid an attorney to assist the district attorney with the murder case,[19] or if the juror is related to a stockholder or employee of a corporation from which the defendant is charged with having taken money or property.[20] Likewise, where a Rural Electric Membership Corporation is the victim of the crime charged, its members and those related to members within the prohibited degree are disqualified.[21] But in *Willingham v. State*,[22] the court affirmed the refusal of the trial judge to excuse for cause an employee of the

---

(1979), the court said the "fact a juror is related to a witness for the state . . . does not render the juror incompetent. . . ."

[11]Ethridge v. State, 163 Ga. 186, 189, 136 S.E. 72 (1926); Leadingham v. Commonwealth, 182 Ky. 291, 206 S.W. 483 (1918) (implication); State v. Byrd, 72 S.C. 104, 51 S.E. 542 (1905).

[12]Tatum v. State, 206 Ga. 171 (3), 56 S.E.2d 518 (1949). Of course, a person who contributes to a fund to hire a special prosecutor or to assist in the prosecution of the defendant is disqualified since he is regarded as a voluntary prosecutor. O'Berry v. State, 153 Ga. 644 (2), 113 S.E. 2 (1922).

[13]McKee v. State, 168 Ga. App. 214, 308 S.E.2d 574 (1983).

[14]Ferguson v. State, 215 Ga. 117, 120 (5)(a), 109 S.E.2d 44 (1959).

[15]Howard v. State, 9 Ala.App. 74, 63 So. 753 (1913).

[16]Davis v. State, 194 Ga. App. 482, 485 (3), 391 S.E.2d 124 (1990). Here the court said, "A prosecutor is one who institutes a prosecution." Assisting in the arrest, sitting at the table with the district attorney, and assisting in striking a jury does not

alone make the sheriff a prosecutor.

[17]Spence v. State, 238 Ga. 399, 233 S.E.2d 363 (1977).

[18]Jones v. State, 68 Ga. App. 210 (2), 22 S.E.2d 671 (1942).

[19]See Gossett v. State, 201 Ga. 809, 41 S.E.2d 308 (1947).

[20]Cf. McElhannon v. State, 99 Ga. 672 (1), 26 S.E. 501 (1896); Temples v. Central of Georgia Railway Co., 15 Ga. App. 115, 82 S.E. 777 (1914); Manry v. First National Bank, 195 Ga. 163, 166 (6), 23 S.E.2d 662 (1942) (implication). But a juror related to a depositor in bank is not automatically disqualified. Heaton v. State, 37 Ga. App. 195 (5), 139 S.E. 103 (1927), rev'd on other grounds, 167 Ga. 147, 144 S.E. 782 (1928); Smith v. State, 124 Ga. App. 581, 184 S.E.2d 681 (1971). Likewise, a relationship to an employee of a corporation does not ordinarily disqualify a juror. Wilson v. Atlantic Coast Line Railroad Co., 116 Ga. App. 193, 156 S.E.2d 463 (1967).

[21]Lowman v. State, 197 Ga. App. 556, 557 (2), 398 S.E.2d 832 (1990).

[22]Willingham v. State, 198 Ga. App. 178, 401 S.E.2d 63 (1990).

University of Georgia in a case involving a theft from the University of Georgia library.

A party cannot successfully object to a potential juror because the juror is related to the objecting party.[23]

In *Croom v. State*,[24] the court pointed out that a juror is not disqualified because she is related to a police officer who had been involved in the case or to a witness who is to testify for the state.

A defendant may waive his right to challenge a potential juror,[25] but if a juror is related to prosecuting witness within the prohibited degree and the defendant does not know this until after conviction, he is entitled to a new trial,[26] if he can show that neither the defendant or his counsel knew of the relationship nor could have discovered it before the verdict by the exercise of ordinary care.[27] If during the course of a trial a party learns of the relationship of a juror to a party or the prosecutor, it is the duty of the party making such discovery to call it to the attention of the trial judge at that time, otherwise a waiver is likely to result.[28] However, in *Gribble v. State*,[29] the defendant, after conviction, presented affidavits stating that a juror's grandfather was also the victim's great-grandfather. The juror testified that she was fair and impartial and that she had no knowledge of a relationship to the victim. The court affirmed the denial of the motion for a new trial.

In *Wells v. State*,[30] the court held that the trial judge may excuse a juror for cause who is related to the defendant but not within the sixth degree (decided prior to 2016 amendment), since a party has no vested interest in having a particular juror serve.

See § 18:19, supra, on challenges for cause.

---

[23]Sikes v. State, 105 Ga. 592, 31 S.E. 567 (1898); Finger v. State, 112 Ga. App. 188 (2), 144 S.E.2d 479 (1965).

[24]Croom v. State, 217 Ga. App. 596, 597 (2), 458 S.E.2d 679 (1995).

[25]Miller v. State, 139 Ga. 716, 719 (2), 78 S.E. 181 (1913); Manry v. First National Bank of Barnesville, 195 Ga. 163, 166 (6), 23 S.E.2d 662 (1942).

In McKenzie v. State, 248 Ga. 294, 298 (15), 282 S.E.2d 95 (1981), defense counsel was present during the entire voir dire, but did not object to the failure to qualify the jury as to relationship to the victim. The court stated that this amounted to a waiver or induced error.

[26]Harris v. State, 188 Ga. 745 (2), 4 S.E.2d 651 (1939).

[27]Williams v. State, 206 Ga. 107 (2), 55 S.E.2d 589 (1949).

[28]Shields v. State, 162 Ga. App. 388, 389 (3), 291 S.E.2d 448 (1982); Everett v. Clegg, 94 Ga. App. 725, 96 S.E.2d 382 (1956), judgment rev'd on other grounds, 213 Ga. 168, 97 S.E.2d 689 (1957); Lampkin v. State, 87 Ga. 516, 517 (7), 13 S.E. 523 (1891).

[29]Gribble v. State, 248 Ga. 567, 570 (4), 284 S.E.2d 277 (1981).

[30]Wells v. State, 261 Ga. 282 (2), 404 S.E.2d 106 (1991).

§ 18:24   Voir dire examination—General

Perhaps it should first be pointed out that a defendant has an absolute right to be present during voir dire.[1] But the right to be present may be waived expressly or impliedly by the defendant if he remains silent as his counsel states in open court that the defendant has in fact waived this right. Consequently, it has been pointed out that "[a]ll voir dire should take place in the courtroom in the presence of all parties."[2]

Rule 10.1 of the Uniform Rules for the Superior Courts provides in part as follows:

"10.1 Voir Dire

"The court may propound, or cause to be propounded by counsel, such questions of the jurors as provided in OCGA § 15-12-133; however, the form, time required and number of such questions is within the discretion of the court. The court may require that questions be asked once only to the full array of the jurors, rather than to every juror—one at a time—provided that the question be framed and the response given in a manner that will provide the propounder with an individual response prior to the interposition of challenge. Hypothetical questions are discouraged, but may be allowed in the discretion of the court. It is improper to ask how a juror would act in certain contingencies or on a certain hypothetical state of facts. No question shall be framed so as to require a response from a juror which might amount to a prejudgment of the action. Questions calling for an opinion by a juror on matters of law are improper. The court will exclude questions which have been answered in substance previously by the same juror. It is discretionary with the court to permit examination of each juror without the presence of the remainder of the panel. Objections to the mode and conduct of voir dire must be raised promptly or they will be regarded as waived."[3]

The right of voir dire examination was expanded in Georgia in 1951 with the enactment of O.C.G.A. § 15-12-133, which provides in part as follows: "In all criminal cases both the state and the defendant shall have the right to an individual examination of each prospective juror from which the jury is to be selected prior to interposing a challenge. The examination shall be conducted after the administration of a preliminary oath to the panel or in

---

[Section 18:24]

[1]Goodroe v. State, 224 Ga. App. 378, 380 (1), 480 S.E.2d 378 (1997); Register v. State, 229 Ga. App. 648, 494 S.E.2d 555 (1997).

[2]Robertson v. State, 268 Ga. 772,

774 (4), 493 S.E.2d 697 (1997).

[3]In Watkins v. State, 191 Ga. App. 87, 90 (5), 381 S.E.2d 45 (1989), the court discussed hypothetical questions in the light of Rule 10.1.

criminal cases after the usual voir dire questions have been put by the court. [See § 18:13, supra, on preliminary oath.] In the examination, the counsel for either party shall have the right to inquire of the individual prospective jurors examined touching any matter or thing which would illustrate any interest of the prospective juror in the case, including any opinion as to which party ought to prevail, the relationship or acquaintance of the prospective juror with the parties or counsel therefor, any fact or circumstance indicating any inclination, leaning, or bias which the prospective juror might have respecting the subject matter of the action or the counsel or parties thereto, and the religious, social, and fraternal connections of the prospective juror."[4] In *Legare v. State,*[5] the court pointed out that a defendant "has an absolute right to have his prospective jurors questioned as to those matters specified in OCGA § 15-12-133."

It should be noted that whereas the statute above provides for "individual examination of each juror," Rule 10.1 provides that the judge "may require that questions be asked once only to the full array of the jurors, rather than to every juror—one at a time."[6]

In *Peters v. State,*[7] the court emphasized the fact that it is error for the trial judge over objection to cause the parties to begin striking jurors before all the potential jurors have been individually questioned. In *Peters* the parties were permitted to voir dire and then caused to strike jurors in the first panel of 12 before the voir dire of the remaining potential jurors.

Defense counsel and the district attorney may give up their right to conduct voir dire examinations of prospective jurors and permit the court to ask all such questions.[8]

The Georgia statute provides for an individual examination of jurors.[9] However, in *State v. Hutter,*[10] the Georgia Supreme Court held that a defendant was not deprived of his individual examination of prospective jurors where the trial judge refused to permit defense counsel to ask each juror whether or not he or she had children. The trial judge had permitted defense counsel to ask each member of the entire panel who had children to raise his or her hand. Apparently when a hand was raised, counsel

---

[4]Of course, counsel generally has the right to ask prospective jurors individually the questions provided for in O.C.G.A. § 15-12-133.

[5]Legare v. State, 256 Ga. 302, 303 (1), 348 S.E.2d 881 (1986).

[6]Shadix v. State, 179 Ga. App. 644, 645 (4), 347 S.E.2d 298 (1986).

[7]Peters v. State, 261 Ga. 373, 375 (2), 405 S.E.2d 255 (1991). Accord,

Thomas v. State, 247 Ga. 7, 273 S.E.2d 396 (1981).

[8]Tucker v. State, 249 Ga. 323, 327, 290 S.E.2d 97 (1982).

[9]Reid v. State, 129 Ga. App. 657 (1), 200 S.E.2d 454 (1973).

[10]State v. Hutter, 251 Ga. 615, 307 S.E.2d 910 (1983). See Lawrence v. State, 267 Ga. App. 515, 600 S.E.2d 444 (2004).

was permitted to ascertain the person's name and individually determine whether the proposed juror would have any prejudice against the defendant. Nevertheless, in *Craig v. State*,[11] the court held that O.C.G.A. § 15-12-133 should not be "limited simply because more general questions dealing with the same subject matter have been previously addressed to the entire panel."

In *Allen v. State*,[12] the court held that a defendant has no *right* to question jurors via a written questionnaire. "Whether voir dire questions are propounded in writing or orally is a matter that falls within the sound discretion of the trial court." In *Thompson v. State*,[13] the trial judge ordered defense counsel to submit a list of proposed voir dire questions and informed counsel that only questions on the list could be asked, and further informed counsel that prior to trial the judge would inform counsel which of these questions could be asked and which could not be. Before trial the judge entered an order designating which questions could be asked and reworded some questions. On appeal the court concluded that the defendants were afforded a thorough examination of prospective jurors and the conviction was affirmed.

The purpose of examining potential jurors is to ascertain their impartiality and their ability to determine the case objectively and free from bias or inclination.[14] In *Jefferson v. State*,[15] the court said that the "determination of juror bias cannot be reduced to question-and-answer sessions which obtain results in the manner of a catechism. . . . Often, the answers of a prospective juror will to some degree be contradictory."

The scope of voir dire examination is frequently said to lie within the discretion of the trial judge, but it has been held to be reversible error for the court to announce that it would permit counsel for the defendant to ask only two more questions during voir dire.[16] Since the control of voir dire is vested in the trial judge, it has been held that it is not error for the trial judge to refuse to permit counsel to submit a questionnaire to potential

---

[11]Craig v. State, 165 Ga. App. 156, 299 S.E.2d 745 (1983).

[12]Allen v. State, 239 Ga. App. 899, 900, 522 S.E.2d 502 (1999). Accord, Wilkins v. State, 246 Ga. App. 667 (2), 541 S.E.2d 458 (2000).

[13]Thompson v. State, 154 Ga. App. 704, 705 (2), 269 S.E.2d 474 (1980). Cf. McGraw v. State, 199 Ga. App. 389, 390 (2)(b), 405 S.E.2d 53 (1991).

[14]Reynolds v. State, 231 Ga. 582, 583 (2), 203 S.E.2d 214 (1974). Cf. Waters v. State, 248 Ga. 355, 363, 283 S.E.2d 238 (1981).

Annot., "Religious Belief, Affiliation and Prejudice of Prospective Juror as Proper Subject of Inquiry or Ground for Challenge on Voir Dire," 95 A.L.R.3d 172 (1979). See Annot., 47 Am. Jur. 2d Jury § 272, Religious Beliefs, Prejudices, and Membership (2004).

[15]Jefferson v. State, 256 Ga. 821, 823 (2), 353 S.E.2d 468 (1987).

[16]Lane v. State, 126 Ga. App. 375, 377 (6), 190 S.E.2d 576 (1972).

jurors.[17] However, in *Jones v. State*,[18] the Georgia Supreme Court pointed out that a trial judge may have a juror questionnaire sent out with the juror summons.

In *Henderson v. State*,[19] the court concluded that the burden of showing harm as a result of a trial court's limitations of voir dire is upon the defendant. After showing error, the defendant is "under no burden to show prejudice." The burden of showing that a defendant was not harmed by any deprivation of his rights under O.C.G.A. § 15-12-133 is upon the state.

Nevertheless, the trial judge should exclude hypothetical questions involving evidence or requiring a juror to prejudge the case.[20] "Neither party has the right simply to outline the case and then ask a prospective juror his opinion of that evidence."[21] Jurors are not to be "invited to place themselves in the victim's place in regard to the crime itself" and it is improper to ask a juror what he would have done in the victim's place.[22] Nonetheless, the Georgia Supreme Court in *Ellington v. State*[23] emphasized that counsel should be allowed to inquire during voir dire about "critical facts of the case that experience, reason and common sense indicate will be so influential for at least some prospective jurors that they will be unable to consider all of the evidence in the case in light of the court's instructions on the law and render a fair and impartial verdict." The Court noted that such questions would be the exception and appropriate "only when *not* asking them runs a real risk that juror partiality driven by the fact at issue will not otherwise be identified in voir dire."

It has been held that a person called as a juror cannot be compelled to disclose under oath whether he has committed a speci-

---

[17]Baxter v. State, 254 Ga. 538, 542 (5), 331 S.E.2d 561 (1985).

[18]Jones v. State, 263 Ga. 904, 907 (9)(b), 440 S.E.2d 161 (1994).

[19]Henderson v. State, 251 Ga. 398, 400, 306 S.E.2d 645 (1983). See Reynolds v. State, 334 Ga. App. 496, 779 S.E.2d 712 (2015) (no abuse of discretion where trial court limited each side to 10 general questions but did not limit specific questions to individual jurors).

[20]Pinion v. State, 225 Ga. 36, 37 (4), 165 S.E.2d 708 (1969).

However, in Lamb v. State, 241 Ga. 10, 11 (1), 243 S.E.2d 59 (1978), the court held that the trial judge did not abuse his discretion in permitting the district attorney to state "to pro-

spective jurors that the state expected to introduce demonstrative evidence that the victim was shot, beaten and stabbed" and to inquire "if this aggravated situation would cause any reluctance on the part of any of them to serve as a juror."

[21]Shields v. State, 202 Ga. App. 659, 660, 415 S.E.2d 478 (1992).

[22]Greene v. State, 266 Ga. 439, 446 (19)(c), 469 S.E.2d 129 (1996), rev'd on other grounds, 519 U.S. 145, 117 S.Ct. 578, 136 L.Ed.2d 507 (1996).

[23]Ellington v. State, 292 Ga. 109, 135–136, 735 S.E.2d 736 (2012) (involved questions regarding possible juror bias in a case where the victim was a child).

fied crime which would disqualify him.[24] The United States Supreme Court has held that the discretion of a trial judge is limited to the demands of fairness.[25] Even on his own motion the trial judge may excuse a prospective juror who does not understand questions of a most elementary nature.[26]

During voir dire examination the jurors must be placed so that they can plainly see the defendant.[27] On motion, the jurors must be placed in the jury box so that they can both be seen and see clearly.[28]

Of course counsel has a right to truthful answers from potential jurors. It has been said that this is as important as getting truthful answers from a witness. Failure of a juror to answer a material question truthfully has been held to be a basis for reversal.[29] However, in *Calloway v. State*,[30] the court held that "[i]n order to obtain a new trial . . . [the defendant] must show that the juror failed to answer honestly a material question and that the correct response would have provided a valid basis for a challenge

---

[24]Burt v. Panjaud, 99 U.S. (9 Otto) 180, 25 L.Ed. 451 (1878).

[25]Aldridge v. United States, 283 U.S. 308, 51 S.Ct. 470, 75 L.Ed. 1054 (1931).

[26]High v. State, 247 Ga. 289, 291 (6), 276 S.E.2d 5 (1981).

[27]See O.C.G.A. § 15-12-163.

[28]See O.C.G.A. § 15-12-131.

[29]Pierce v. Altman, 147 Ga. App. 22, 248 S.E.2d 34 (1978).

However, in Jones v. State, 247 Ga. 268, 270, 275 S.E.2d 67 (1981), the court said that every incorrect answer given on voir dire does not require a new trial. If a good faith answer is given, "with no deliberate intent to mislead the trial judge may well find that no prejudice resulted, even though the lack of disclosure might have impaired defendant's right to exercise a knowledgeable peremptory challenge. . . . Although the question of juror impartiality is a mixed question of law and fact, the trial court's finding of impartiality will be set aside only where 'manifest prejudice' to the defendant has been shown."

In Thomas v. State, 249 Ga. 339, 341, 290 S.E.2d 462 (1982), the trial judge read the names of the jurors who had served on the grand jury which indicted the defendant and asked them to stand if they were in the courtroom. Two potential jurors stood, but after conviction it appeared that one potential juror who had served on the grand jury did not stand. This same person failed to answer in the affirmative when asked the statutory question, "Have you, for any reason, formed and expressed any opinion in regard to the guilt or innocence of the accused?" This person was on the jury selected. The state contended that the defendant had waived his right to object by failing to exercise proper diligence. The Supreme Court, in reversing the conviction, stated that the defendant "was entitled to rely on the juror's answers absent actual knowledge of the incorrectness of those answers."

[30]Calloway v. State, 232 Ga. App. 265, 266 (2), 501 S.E.2d 602 (1998) (quoting Gardiner v. State, 264 Ga. 329, 444 S.E.2d 300 (1994)). See Green v. State, 295 Ga. 108, 757 S.E.2d 856 (2014). Accord, Wright v. State, 233 Ga. App. 358, 360 (2), 504 S.E.2d 261 (1998); Sears v. State, 270 Ga. 834, 839 (2), 514 S.E.2d 426 (1999).

for cause." In *Mosley v. State*,[31] the court held that "a juror's inaccuracy in answering a question . . . concerning whether he knew the victim's wife" does not require the grant of a new trial "[i]n the absence of a showing of some prejudice other than the possible opportunity to exercise a knowledgeable peremptory challenge. . . . " In *Poole v. State*,[32] a juror stated that she attended school with the victim but otherwise had not been associated with him. In support of a motion for a new trial, a witness testified that the victim and the juror had both been present at a party and another witness testified he had seen the victim and juror conversing several times at the juror's place of work. The court affirmed the refusal to grant a new trial and said that under these circumstances, "the defendant must show that the juror 'failed to answer honestly a material question on voir dire, and then further show that *a correct response would have provided a valid basis for a challenge for cause.*' " (Emphasis added.) Also, if the defense knows a juror has not answered a question truthfully and knows what the truth of the matter is and if the defense accepts a juror under these circumstances, he waives his right to complain about the untruthful answer.[33] See § 18:15, supra, on results of untruthful answers from jurors.

If during voir dire a potential juror says something in the presence of the other potential jurors which is so prejudicial to the defendant as to brand him as a criminal, instructions from the court to disregard such comments may not be sufficient.[34] It has been said that where this happens the defense counsel should challenge the poll.[35] However, in *Giles v. State*,[36] the court held that the better practice may be to excuse the panel. Of course, the defendant may also move for a postponement to impanel

---

[31]Mosley v. State, 257 Ga. 382, 384 (4), 359 S.E.2d 653 (1987).

[32]Poole v. State, 262 Ga. 668, 670, 424 S.E.2d 275 (1993). Accord, Stiles v. State, 264 Ga. 446, 448 (3), 448 S.E.2d 172 (1994); Maxwell v. State, 218 Ga. App. 780, 781 (1), 463 S.E.2d 517 (1995).

[33]Sanders v. State, 246 Ga. 42, 43 (3), 268 S.E.2d 628 (1980).

[34]Lingerfelt v. State, 147 Ga. App. 371, 372 (1), 249 S.E.2d 100 (1978). In *Lingerfelt*, the court said that the remark by the juror branded the defendant as a sex deviate before the trial started and instructions to disregard the statement could not have been sufficient to remove the potential harm. Cf. Moore v. State, 156 Ga. App. 92, 274 S.E.2d 107 (1980) (potential juror said he heard defendant was a "firebug" in a case where the charge was arson). But cf. Ford v. State, 154 Ga. App. 506, 268 S.E.2d 788 (1980); Stone v. State, 170 Ga. App. 234 (1), 316 S.E.2d 836 (1984). See § 18:38, n. 2, infra; cf. Hughey v. State, 180 Ga. App. 375, 377 (2), 348 S.E.2d 901 (1986).

[35]Hill v. State, 221 Ga. 65 (1), (2), 142 S.E.2d 909 (1965).

[36]Giles v. State, 253 Ga. 144, 145 (2), 317 S.E.2d 527 (1984).

other jurors who have not heard the comment.[37] When a prospective juror makes a statement which would make it difficult for the jurors to reach a fair verdict, this is not a basis for a motion for mistrial but is a basis for a motion to disqualify the jury.[38] A motion for "[a] mistrial is not a viable remedy before a jury has been impaneled and sworn."[39]

Where defense counsel, pursuant to a demand for a list of witnesses, learns that the state is planning to call a witness whose name does not appear on the list he has received and some of the jurors have already undergone voir dire, he may move to reexamine the jurors, previously examined, as to the "new" witness.[40]

Georgia appellate courts have been critical of defense attorneys and district attorneys asking questions of jurors about technical provisions of the law during voir dire.[41] However, it may not be objectionable to ask a potential juror if he would have any reluctance in returning a "not guilty" verdict where he has a reasonable doubt as to the defendant's guilt.

It has been held that it is not error for the trial judge to permit a district attorney to question a rabbi on voir dire as follows: "[S]ince you deal with counseling those that are in trouble, you would feel more inclined to help someone that was in trouble as a result of your job."[42]

As a general rule, "a new trial will not be granted based upon a voir dire error unless the movant proves that a juror failed to answer (or to answer honestly) a material question on voir dire and then shows that a correct response would have established a valid basis for a challenge for cause."[43]

On voir dire questions relating to capital punishment, see § 18:17, supra. See § 14:76, supra, on the right of the defendant to an impartial jury. See § 18:6, supra, on transcript of voir dire examination of prospective jurors. See § 18:23, supra, and § 18:34 and § 24:15, infra, on replacing an incompetent juror who has been chosen. See § 18:19, supra, on challenges for cause. See § 18:25, infra, on "rehabilitating" a juror.

---

[37]Ferguson v. State, 219 Ga. 33 (3), 131 S.E.2d 538 (1963).

[38]Nelson v. State, 199 Ga. App. 487, 488 (4), 405 S.E.2d 310 (1991).

[39]Baker v. State, 230 Ga. App. 813, 815 (1)(c), 498 S.E.2d 290 (1998); Mitchell v. State, 284 Ga. App. 209, 644 S.E.2d 147 (2007).

[40]Cf. Brown v. State, 161 Ga. App. 729, 730 (2), 288 S.E.2d 866 (1982).

[41]Lundy v. State, 130 Ga. App. 171, 172 (2), 202 S.E.2d 536 (1973); Mills v. State, 137 Ga. App. 305, 306 (2), 223 S.E.2d 498 (1976).

[42]Creamer v. State, 168 Ga. App. 790 (1), 310 S.E.2d 560 (1983).

[43]Roebuck v. State, 261 Ga. App. 679, 680, 583 S.E.2d 523 (2003).

§ 18:25 Rehabilitating a juror

As pointed out in §§ 18:20 and 18:24, supra, the general rule is that the trial judge generally determines whether a juror is perfectly impartial between the state and the accused and whether or not a juror should be excused for cause. Of course, a potential juror who is inclined toward either party is not to be disqualified if she or he will be able to set aside her or his opinion and decide the case upon the evidence and the court's charge.[1] Decisions in the Court of Appeals, however, make clear that any effort at juror rehabilitation by the trial court will be met with careful scrutiny. For example, in *Cannon v. State*,[2] the court held that when ruling on the potential juror's qualification, a "court may not rely on a prospective juror's assurance of his impartiality where the record shows on its face that a juror has a compelling bias or interest in the outcome of the case." The court suggested that the better course might be to simply excuse a juror who appears sympathetic to one side or the other. "A trial judge should err on the side of caution by dismissing rather than trying to rehabilitate. . . ."[3] However, it is not coercive rehabilitation for a trial court to instruct a juror, who initially expresses some doubt about his ability to listen to certain evidence because of a prior experience, that a juror's role is not whether he wants to listen to evidence, but whether he can evaluate it with impartiality and fairness.[4]

In *Kim v. Walls*,[5] the Supreme Court found that the trial court had abused its discretion in failing to allow counsel wide latitude in examining a potential juror who had an employment relationship with one of the parties. Although *Kim* is a civil case, its instruction is clear. Once a potential juror discloses a basis for partiality, the trial judge must allow counsel a full and fair opportunity to develop the existence, if any, of bias.

[Section 18:25]

[1]Johnson v. State, 262 Ga. 652, 653 (2), 424 S.E.2d 271 (1993).

[2]Cannon v. State, 250 Ga. App. 777, 779, 552 S.E.2d 922 (2001). Compare Torres v. State, 253 Ga. App. 318, 320 (2), 558 S.E.2d 850 (2002), where the Court of Appeals found the trial court's inquiry regarding a potential juror's ability to be fair and impartial not to constitute coercive rehabilitation.

[3]See Walls v. Kim, 250 Ga. App. 259, 260, 549 S.E.2d 797 (2001), aff. Kim v. Walls, 275 Ga. 177, 563 S.E.2d 847 (2002).

[4]Kim v. Walls, 275 Ga. 177, 563 S.E.2d 847 (2002). See Park v. State, 260 Ga. App. 879, 581 S.E.2d 393 (2003) for an illustration of a trial court's abuse of discretion in refusing to strike for cause a juror who, after candidly admitting that he would not be able to be impartial because of the defendant's race, stated that he could in fact be impartial in response to the court's cursory rehabilitation effort. See Powell v. Amin, 256 Ga. App. 757(1), 569 S.E.2d 582 (2002).

[5]Kim v. Walls, 275 Ga. 177, 563 S.E.2d 847 (2002).

The Court of Appeals has now applied *Walls,* in the context of a criminal case. In *Ivey v. State,*[6] the court found that a trial judge's efforts to rehabilitate a prospective juror went too far. "Where a prospective juror, who has been asked whether he or she can be fair and impartial in the case answers under oath a plain, 'no,' and provides an explanation for the inability to be fair and impartial, the court should limit further questions to clarification of the answer. Neither the court nor the parties should incessantly interrogate the juror in a manner calculated only to elicit a response contrary to the one originally given. Interrogation for that purpose is nothing more than a effort to justify finding a biased juror qualified."[7]

Since deciding *Walls v. Kim,*[8] the Court of Appeals has issued a number of decisions regarding the proper exercise of a trial court's discretion in its consideration of a motion to strike a juror for cause. In *Doss v. State,*[9] the court took the occasion to summarize them as follows:

"a. When some hint of juror bias or partiality appears, it is an abuse of discretion to cut off inquiry and rely on an affirmative answer to a rehabilitative question from the bench as a talisman to show that the juror has magically, suddenly become unbiased and impartial.

"b. On the other hand, there is no per se rule disqualifying a class of persons from jury duty based, for example, on employment relationships or doctor-patient relationships. Jurors are presumed to be impartial. And trial courts continue to have 'extremely broad discretion . . . *once an adequate inquiry has been conducted.*'

"c. In conducting the adequate inquiry mandated by *Walls v. Kim,* and *Kim v. Walls,* it is completely improper for counsel, and especially for the trial court, to browbeat the juror into affirmative answers to rehabilitative questions by using multiple, leading questions.

"d. '[L]engthy and repeated questioning . . . about laying aside . . . bias and deciding the case solely on the evidence [can become] more an instruction on the desired answer than a neutral attempt to determine the juror's impartiality.'[10]

"e. During the adequate (but not lengthy or repeated) question-

[6]Ivey v. State, 258 Ga. App. 587(2), 574 S.E.2d 663 (2002).

[7]Ivey v. State, 258 Ga. App. 587, 592, 574 S.E.2d 663 (2002).

[8]Walls v. Kim, 250 Ga. App. 259, 260, 549 S.E.2d 797 (2001), aff'd Kim v. Walls, 275 Ga. 177, 563 S.E.2d 847 (2002).

[9]Doss v. State, 264 Ga. App. 205, 210, 590 S.E.2d 208 (2003) (citations omitted).

[10]Howell v. State, 278 Ga. App. 634 (9), 629 S.E.2d 398 (2006) (overruled on other grounds by, Hatley

ing required by *Walls v. Kim* and *Kim v. Walls*, a trial court is allowed by Supreme Court precedent to ask questions of jurors 'which might lead to their rehabilitation.'

"f. Nothing in *Walls v. Kim*, or its progeny, changed the traditional Georgia rules that a prospective juror's doubt about his or her impartiality does not demand as a matter of law that he or she be excused for cause. Nor is excusal required when a potential juror expresses reservations about his or her ability to put aside personal experiences. And in *Garland* the trial court did not abuse its discretion in refusing to excuse a prospective juror who stated that she would 'try' to put aside her emotions and consider the case based upon the evidence."

In *Valentine v. State*,[11] the court observed that *Kim* was not limited to those cases in which juror bias might be apparent because of a juror's knowledge regarding an actual party. Rather, the proper inquiry is whether a juror has a relationship with a party that is merely suggestive of bias. Thus, the trial court in that case was reversed because a juror was not properly rehabilitated after admitting that she knew the victim's mother who was also to be a witness in the case.

In *Poole v. State*,[12] the Georgia Supreme Court noted that while a trial court is "authorized to pose questions during the voir dire of a venireperson who is the subject of a challenge for cause . . . *Kims v. Walls* should not be read as imposing upon a trial court the duty and responsibility to independently question a member of the venire when counsel for the parties do not wish to question the person further." The burden of showing cause to strike a proposed juror rests with the party seeking to have the person disqualified and the court disapproved authority to the contrary. However, "the erroneous allowing of a [strike] for cause [ordinarily] affords no grounds of complaint if a competent and unbiased jury is finally selected."[13]

---

v. State, 290 Ga. 480, 722 S.E.2d 67 (2012)) (trial court does not abuse its discretion when it questions a prospective juror after the parties have concluded their questioning provided the court does not unduly restrict their opportunity for voir dire).

[11]Valentine v. State, 265 Ga. App. 139 (2), 592 S.E.2d 918 (2004) (disap-

proved of by, Poole v. State on other grounds, 291 Ga. 848, 734 S.E.2d 1 (2012)).

[12]Poole v. State, 291 Ga. 848, 854, 734 S.E.2d 1 (2012).

[13]Bryant v. State, 288 Ga. 876, 881 (4)(e), 708 S.E.2d 362 (2011) (citing Wells v. State, 261 Ga. 282, 282-83 (2), 404 S.E.2d 106 (1991)).

§ 18:26   Voir dire examination—Examples of questions which it has been held that trial judge may refuse to permit

In *Harper v. State,*[1] while not stating the exact questions which counsel for defendant wished to ask, the court held that "[i]t is not within the purview of voir dire to inquire into technical legal questions, such as those ultimately involving the presumption of innocence. . . . Generally, juror examination should be confined to questions designed to elicit the possible prejudice of jurors against the accused or juror bias or interest in the outcome. . . . [Q]uestions of a legal nature about an indictment as evidence of guilt, the function of grand jury proceedings, and the role of jurors as factfinders . . . [are] not proper subjects for voir dire questioning."

Georgia appellate courts have affirmed decisions where the trial court refused to permit defense counsel to ask (1) "If you were asked right now to return a verdict without hearing any evidence from either side, what would your verdict be?"[2] (2) "Do any of you believe the defendant must be guilty since he is charged with two different offenses?"[3] (3) "Could you keep an open mind until all the evidence is in?"[4] (4) "Do you believe . . . [the defendant] innocent, an innocent man?"[5] (5) whether a juror would be willing to consider the presumption of innocence if the defendant exercised his right not to testify,[6] (6) "Have you ever expressed an opinion about other criminal cases?"[7] (7) "If you should believe that the defendant might be guilty, but the state has not proven this beyond a reasonable doubt, would your

---

[Section 18:26]

[1]Harper v. State, 222 Ga. App. 393, 394, 474 S.E.2d 288 (1996).

[2]McNeal v. State, 228 Ga. 633, 635 (3), 187 S.E.2d 271 (1972), held that this question called for a conclusion. See also, Gonzales v. State, 345 Ga. App. 334, 812 S.E.2d 638 (2018) (physical precedent).

In Calloway v. State, 144 Ga. App. 457, 241 S.E.2d 575 (1978), the trial judge refused to permit defense counsel to ask prospective jurors if they recognized that a defendant is presumed innocent until proven guilty beyond a reasonable doubt. On appeal the case was affirmed apparently on the theory that this was a technical legal question. Accord, Banks v. State, 144 Ga. App. 471, 472 (5), 241 S.E.2d 587 (1978).

[3]Anderson v. State, 236 Ga. App. 679, 682 (3), 513 S.E.2d 235 (1999).

[4]Walker v. State, 179 Ga. App. 782, 784 (2), 347 S.E.2d 711 (1986).

[5]Evans v. State, 222 Ga. 392, 400 (13), 150 S.E.2d 240 (1966), overruled on other grounds, Harris v. State, 255 Ga. 464, 339 S.E.2d 712 (1986).

In Boyer v. State, 178 Ga. App. 372, 374 (3)(b), 343 S.E.2d 146 (1986), the court held that it was not error for the trial judge to refuse to permit the defense to ask a prospective juror whether the defendant's presence in the courtroom would require defendant to prove he was not guilty.

[6]Simmons v. State, 282 Ga. 183(7), 646 S.E.2d 55 (2007); Moak v. State, 222 Ga. App. 36, 38 (2), 473 S.E.2d 576 (1996).

[7]Alderman v. State, 254 Ga. 206, 207 (3), 327 S.E.2d 168 (1985).

verdict be guilty or not guilty?"[8] (8) Would any of you have any reluctance in returning a not guilty verdict when you have a reasonable doubt as to the defendant's guilt?[9] (9) "whether or not they could 'follow two basic rules of law . . . the presumption of innocence [[10]] and the duty to not find the defendant guilty unless they believe his guilt beyond a reasonable doubt,' "[11](10) whether a juror would be able to follow the instructions of the trial judge,[12] (11) whether they had ever read anything about the reliability of hypnosis,[13] (12) about "previous jury service on any jury that had returned a death penalty verdict,"[14] (13) whether a juror who had previously served on a grand or trial jury had ever served as foreperson,[15] (14) whether the prospective juror had ever served on a grand or petit jury,[16] (15) whether a prospective juror had been able to reach a verdict in an earlier case in which he had served as a juror,[17] (16) the age of each juror, unless it appeared that the age of prospective jurors was relevant as an indication of bias,[18] (17) "Have you read any of the President's [Crime] Commission Report [which] recommended decriminalization of marijuana?"[19] (18) "Have you formed an opinion as to whether or not marijuana is an addictive drug?"[20] (19) "Would you expect one accused of burglary and entering a plea of not guilty to make an explanation to the jury?"[21] (20) "Does everyone in this panel understand that you would be enforcing the law just as vigorously by voting not guilty in the event the State fails to prove its case beyond reasonable doubt than [sic] you would by voting

---

[8]Stack v. State, 234 Ga. 19, 26 (2), 214 S.E.2d 514 (1975).

[9]Chastain v. State, 255 Ga. 723, 724 (1), 342 S.E.2d 678 (1986).

[10]Harper v. State, 222 Ga. App. 393, 394, 474 S.E.2d 288 (1996).

[11]Frazier v. State, 195 Ga. App. 109 (1), 393 S.E.2d 262 (1990).

[12]Shields v. State, 202 Ga. App. 659, 660, 415 S.E.2d 478 (1992).

[13]Alderman v. State, 254 Ga. 206, 207 (3), 327 S.E.2d 168 (1985).

[14]Thacker v. State, 226 Ga. 170, 171 (6), 173 S.E.2d 186 (1970). In State v. McGhee, 350 So.2d 370 (La.1977), the court held that defense counsel not only had the right to ask about prior jury service, but also to ask whether the jury had convicted the defendant in the earlier trial.

[15]Alderman v. State, 254 Ga. 206, 207 (3), 327 S.E.2d 168 (1985).

[16]Frazier v. State, 138 Ga. App. 640, 643 (2)(b), 227 S.E.2d 284 (1976); Wiggins v. State, 252 Ga. 467, 314 S.E.2d 212 (1984). In *Wiggins*, the court also affirmed the action of the trial judge in refusing to permit defense counsel to ask a prospective juror if he had ever served as a juror in that particular courtroom.

[17]Jackson v. State, 172 Ga. App. 359, 363 (7), 323 S.E.2d 198 (1984).

[18]White v. State, 230 Ga. 327, 336 (a), 196 S.E.2d 849 (1973).

[19]Merrill v. State, 130 Ga. App. 745, 750 (3)(c), 204 S.E.2d 632 (1974).

[20]Merrill v. State, 130 Ga. App. 745, 750 (3)(c), 204 S.E.2d 632 (1974).

[21]Young v. State, 131 Ga. App. 553, 554 (2), 206 S.E.2d 536 (1974). Cf. Henderson v. State, 173 Ga. App. 302 (1), 326 S.E.2d 246 (1985).

guilty under these charges?"[22] (21) about the attitudes or knowledge of the prospective jurors on matters of law,[23] (22) "Questions seeking to test the prospective jurors' willingness to accept" a defense anticipated in the case,[24] (23) "Do you have an understanding what the term presumption of innocence means to you?" "What does the term reasonable doubt mean to you?"[25] (24) "If you were not personally agreeable with certain laws, would you attach any less importance to that law than you would to laws that you agree with?"[26] (25) Are you "conscientiously opposed to the defense of self defense"?[27] (26) Do any of you have "the opinion that simply because you own a gun . . . that you are ultimately responsible for anything that that gun is used for?"[28] (27) "Have you got any fixed opinions in your mind as to whether or not our criminal system works?"[29] (28) "Do you feel that criminals generally get treated too leniently?"[30] or whether they thought life imprisonment would allow the possibility of parole,[31] (29) in a capital case, refusing to permit defense counsel to ask jurors if they felt the death penalty was a deterrence to crime,[32] or what would they want to know before deciding on the death penalty, or what went through their minds when they learned they might be serving on a death penalty case,[33] or "to ask a juror to describe the *kind* of case" which would in his opinion warrant a death sentence,[34] or "what they felt imposition of the death penalty accomplished" or "whether they felt they owed anything to the victim's family,"[35] (30) whether they could give Adolph Hitler the death penalty for killing 6,000,000 Jews,[36] (31) whether they

---

[22]Hall v. State, 135 Ga. App. 690, 692, 218 S.E.2d 687 (1975).

[23]Frazier v. State, 138 Ga. App. 640, 642 (2)(a), 227 S.E.2d 284 (1976).

[24]Meeks v. State, 216 Ga. App. 630, 632 (4), 455 S.E.2d 350 (1995).

[25]Baxter v. State, 254 Ga. 538, 543 (7), 331 S.E.2d 561 (1985).

[26]Williams v. State, 249 Ga. 6, 7, 287 S.E.2d 31 (1982).

[27]Parker v. State, 172 Ga. App. 540, 541 (2), 323 S.E.2d 826 (1984); Kyles v. State, 243 Ga. 490 (1), 255 S.E.2d 10 (1979), disapproving Adams v. State, 139 Ga. App. 670 (1), 229 S.E.2d 142 (1976).

[28]McGinnis v. State, 258 Ga. 673, 674 (3), 372 S.E.2d 804 (1988).

[29]Williams v. State, 165 Ga. App. 69, 70 (2), 299 S.E.2d 402 (1983). In *Williams* the court treated the question as being too broad.

[30]Williams v. State, 165 Ga. App. 69, 70 (2), 299 S.E.2d 402 (1983).

[31]Spivey v. State, 253 Ga. 187, 193, 319 S.E.2d 420 (1984).

[32]Roberts v. State, 252 Ga. 227, 237 (f), 314 S.E.2d 83 (1984).

[33]Spivey v. State, 253 Ga. 187, 193, 319 S.E.2d 420 (1984).

[34]Isaacs v. State, 259 Ga. 717, 731, 386 S.E.2d 316 (1989); Hall v. State, 261 Ga. 778, 781 (4), 415 S.E.2d 158 (1991).

[35]Beck v. State, 255 Ga. 483, 484 (1), 340 S.E.2d 9 (1986).

[36]Alderman v. State, 254 Ga. 206, 207 (3), 327 S.E.2d 168 (1985).

were members of any political organization,[37] (32) or the extent of political activity of jurors,[38] (33) what kinds of bumper stickers they have on their automobiles,[39] (34) the employment of prospective juror's children,[40] (35) whether the potential jurors smoked cigarettes[41] or drank alcohol[42] and the names of the newspapers or magazines they regularly read,[43] or what kinds of television programs they watched,[44] (36) "Do you feel that because the State has brought charges against . . . that he is in fact guilty?"[45] (37) "If there is any conflict in the testimony between a police officer and another witness, would you tend to give more weight to the officer's testimony simply because he is a police officer?"[46] (38) oddly, in a trial to determine competency to stand trial, it has been held that it is not error for a trial judge to refuse to permit defense counsel to ask a prospective juror if he would follow a charge of the court as to mental competency,[47] (39) "Whether the juror could set aside any evidence which might be elicited pertaining to guilt or innocence of the actual charges." [Both of these questions (numbers 37 & 39) were said to be of a technical legal nature[48] and therefore not a proper area for voir dire examination.] (40) "Do you think that places such as the Fifth

---

[37]Alderman v. State, 254 Ga. 206 (3), 327 S.E.2d 168 (1985).

[38]Samples v. State, 217 Ga. App. 509 (2), 460 S.E.2d 795 (1995).

[39]Alderman v. State, 254 Ga. 206 (3), 327 S.E.2d 168 (1985).

[40]Frazier v. State, 138 Ga. App. 640, 643 (2)(c), 227 S.E.2d 284 (1976).

[41]Frazier v. State, 138 Ga. App. 640, 643 (2)(c), 227 S.E.2d 284 (1976).

[42]Frazier v. State, 138 Ga. App. 640, 643 (2)(c), 227 S.E.2d 284 (1976).

[43]Frazier v. State, 138 Ga. App. 640, 643 (2)(c), 227 S.E.2d 284 (1976); Spivey v. State, 253 Ga. 187, 193, 319 S.E.2d 420 (1984); Alderman v. State, 254 Ga. 206 (3), 327 S.E.2d 168 (1985).

[44]Spivey v. State, 253 Ga. 187, 193, 319 S.E.2d 420 (1984).

[45]Todd v. State, 243 Ga. 539, 544 (7), 255 S.E.2d 5 (1979). Cf. Baxter v. State, 254 Ga. 538, 543 (7), 331 S.E.2d 561 (1985). See also Harper v. State, 222 Ga. App. 393, 394, 474 S.E.2d 288 (1996).

[46]Patterson v. State, 154 Ga. App. 877, 270 S.E.2d 86 (1980); Blanco v. State, 185 Ga. App. 535, 364 S.E.2d 903 (1988).

In Eafford v. State, 155 Ga. App. 865, 274 S.E.2d 37 (1980), the court affirmed the trial judge's refusal to permit defense counsel to ask prospective jurors whether they would tend to believe the testimony of the police officer who was to testify for the state in preference to that of the defendant, an African American. The court concluded that this question called for a prejudgment of the case and is different from a question directed to whether a juror would generally believe a white police officer rather than an African American. Cf. Boyer v. State, 178 Ga. App. 372, 373 (3)(a), 343 S.E.2d 146 (1986) (fact that police officer was white and defendant was black did not give the question validity).

[47]Wallace v. State, 248 Ga. 255, 259 (2), 282 S.E.2d 325 (1981). In Head v. State, 160 Ga. App. 4, 6 (6), 285 S.E.2d 735 (1981), the court stated that the defense was not entitled to ask whether or not the jury would be able to follow the instructions of the trial judge.

[48]Wallace v. State, 248 Ga. 255, 259 (2), 282 S.E.2d 325 (1981). See n.

Inn should be closed . . . .?"[49] (41) Questions about what the prospective juror thought would happen to the victim,[50] (42) "[Q]uestions about the feelings of persons other than the prospective juror, or how those assumed feelings of other persons would affect a prospective juror,"[51] (43) "a general question asking whether defense counsel had failed to touch upon any matter bothering any prospective juror which would make it difficult for him to serve,"[52] (44) where a potential juror states that he is "leaning" but he believes he could be fair, it is not error for the trial judge to refuse to let defense counsel ask whether the juror is leaning toward the defendant or the state,[53] (45) in a robbery case defense counsel was not permitted to ask about previous military service,[54] (46) in a murder case it was held not to be error to refuse to permit defense counsel to ask for prospective jurors' views on abortion,[55] (47) "If the judge's charge is contrary to the Bible, which would you follow?"[56] (48) In a rape case it was held not to be error for the trial judge to refuse to permit jurors to be asked "if any of them had an opinion as to whether sex offenses were being handled adequately by the courts."[57] (49) In a feticide case it was found not to be error for the trial judge to refuse to allow defense counsel to question prospective jurors about their views regarding abortion,[58] (50) in a cruelty to children case, "Is there anyone here that believes that in disciplining a child that sometimes it would be necessary to use a belt, a stick or an antenna cord and beat them from their head to their toes?"[59] (51) inquiring about the phrase "guilt by association" and what it means to those jurors who had heard of the expression;[60] (52) questions designed to find jurors willing to accept a particular

---

2, supra.

[49]Williams v. State, 249 Ga. 6, 7, 287 S.E.2d 31 (1982).

[50]Berryhill v. State, 249 Ga. 442, 291 S.E.2d 685 (1982) (abrogated on other grounds by Jones v. State, 261 Ga. 665, 409 S.E.2d 642 (1991)).

[51]Berryhill v. State, 249 Ga. 442, 291 S.E.2d 685 (1982) (abrogated on other grounds by Jones v. State, 261 Ga. 665, 409 S.E.2d 642 (1991)).

[52]Berryhill v. State, 249 Ga. 442, 291 S.E.2d 685 (1982) (abrogated on other grounds by Jones v. State, 261 Ga. 665, 409 S.E.2d 642 (1991)).

[53]Wilcox v. State, 250 Ga. 745, 758, 301 S.E.2d 251 (1983).

[54]Brown v. State, 170 Ga. App. 398, 399 (1), 317 S.E.2d 207 (1984). In

Brown, the court concluded that the question "does not relate to any fact or circumstance indicating an inclination, leaning or bias which the juror might have respecting the *subject matter of the action*." (Emphasis added.)

[55]Baxter v. State, 254 Ga. 538, 543 (7), 331 S.E.2d 561 (1985).

[56]Martin v. State, 195 Ga. App. 548, 551 (7), 394 S.E.2d 551 (1990).

[57]Hunter v. State, 170 Ga. App. 356 (1), 317 S.E.2d 332 (1984).

[58]Brinkley v. State, 253 Ga. 541, 545 (3), 322 S.E.2d 49 (1984).

[59]Cherry v. State, 174 Ga. App. 145 (1), 329 S.E.2d 580 (1985).

[60]Hubbard v. State, 274 Ga. App. 184(2), 617 S.E.2d 167 (2005).

defense, e.g., self-defense;[61] and (53) in a child molestation case, inquiring about whether jurors felt that children lack the "worldly knowledge" to make the kind of allegations made in the case.[62]

See § 18:17, supra, on voir dire in death cases.

§ 18:27 Voir dire examination—Examples of questions which it has been held the trial judge must permit

It has been held to be an abuse of discretion for the judge to refuse (1) questioning of jurors as to whether they have any racial bias where the defendant is black,[1] and in a capital case, it is error for the trial judge to refuse to permit prospective jurors to be informed of the race of the victim and questioned as to racial bias in an interracial crime,[2] and (2) to permit defense counsel to ask if prospective jurors or any members of their immediate family have ever been the victim of any crime.[3] Also, (3) it has been held to be error for the trial judge to refuse to permit questions on "juror's membership in fraternal,[4] social or church organizations."[5]

---

[61]Stewart v. State, 262 Ga. App. 426, 585 S.E.2d 622 (2003).

[62]Carver v. State, 331 Ga. App. 120, 769 S.E.2d 722 (2015).

[Section 18:27]

[1]Walker v. State, 215 Ga. App. 790, 792 (4), 452 S.E.2d 580 (1994); Ham v. South Carolina, 409 U.S. 524, 93 S.Ct. 848, 35 L.Ed.2d 46 (1973); but see Ristaino v. Ross, 424 U.S. 589, 96 S.Ct. 1017, 47 L.Ed.2d 258 (1976), and Rosales-Lopez v. United States, 451 U.S. 182, 101 S.Ct. 1629, 68 L.Ed.2d 22 (1981) (where racial issues are integral to case and there exist strong indications that racial prejudice could affect jurors, voir dire regarding such is proper).

In Bowens v. State, 116 Ga. App. 577, 579 (5), 158 S.E.2d 420 (1967), the court held that if a prospective juror testifies that he would believe any police officer in preference to an African American and the defendant is black, the juror is disqualified. In Hernandez v. State, 563 S.W.2d 947 (Tex.Crim.App. 1978), the court held that the juror's predisposition to believe police officers is a basis for challenge for cause. In Powers v. State, 150 Ga. App. 25, 27 (2), 256 S.E.2d 637 (1979), the court held that it was not error to refuse to strike a juror for cause even if the juror says he would give more credibility to the testimony of a police officer than other witnesses. The court said that this is different from a juror saying he would believe one particular party in the case over another, "such opinion is not one relating to the matter at issue or the particular parties to the case or the particular witnesses." See Annot., "Racial or Ethnic Prejudice of Prospective Jurors as Proper Subject of Inquiry or Ground of Challenge on Voir Dire in State Criminal Case," 94 A.L.R.3d 15 (1979); Bennett v. State, 153 Ga. App. 21, 26, 264 S.E.2d 516 (1980).

[2]Turner v. Murray, 476 U.S. 28, 106 S.Ct. 1683, 90 L.Ed.2d 27 (1986); but see Mitchell v. State, 176 Ga. App. 32, 33 (2), 335 S.E.2d 150 (1985).

[3]Commonwealth v. Davis, 264 Pa.Super. 574, 400 A.2d 1320 (1979).

[4]Dunn v. State, 251 Ga. 731, 732 (1), 309 S.E.2d 370 (1983).

[5]Cowan v. State, 156 Ga. App. 650, 275 S.E.2d 665 (1980); Perry v. State, 216 Ga. App. 661 (1), 455 S.E.2d

In *Sanders v. State*,[6] it was held that it was error for the trial judge to refuse to permit defense counsel to ask (4) "Do any of you have any bias against me because I am a criminal defense lawyer? (5) Do any of you think I would trick you?" In a case where the defendant was indicted for trafficking in cocaine, it has been held to be error for the trial judge to refuse to permit defense counsel to ask (6) "Have you or any of your children ever been a victim of a drug transaction?" (7) "Has any member of your family ever had any problems with drugs?"[7] The trial judge erred (8) in refusing to permit defense counsel "to ask the panel whether members of the jurors' immediate families had ever worked for law enforcement agencies."[8] In *Meeks v. State*,[9] the Court of Appeals found that the trial court abused its discretion by restricting defense counsel's voir dire of prospective jurors regarding their feelings about the sort of conduct alleged in the indictment, child molestation, and whether those feelings would impair their ability to be fair and impartial. It has been held that it is not error to permit the district attorney to ask a prospective juror if he believed "that a person had the right for peaceful enjoyment of his property without the intervention from the outside of other persons."[10] In *Berthiaume v. Smith*,[11] the Eleventh Circuit held that voir dire about whether a potential juror's impartiality could be influenced by the sexual orientation of the defendant or the witnesses is proper provided such is relevant to the issue in the case.

§ 18:28 Voir dire examination—Examples of questions which trial judge in his discretion may permit

It has been held that it is not an abuse of discretion for a trial judge to permit counsel to ask the following questions: (1) whether a prospective juror had ever been the victim of a crime,[1] (2) in a case involving the sale of illegal drugs, the experience of a prospective juror with children or students who had taken

---

607 (1995).

[6]Sanders v. State, 204 Ga. App. 37 (1), 419 S.E.2d 24 (1992).

[7]Craig v. State, 165 Ga. App. 156, 299 S.E.2d 745 (1983).

[8]Henderson v. State, 251 Ga. 398, 399 (1), 306 S.E.2d 645 (1983). Chief Justice Hill was the author of the excellent opinion in *Henderson*. This case contains a veritable annotation of Georgia cases on the question involved and on related voir dire questions.

[9]Meeks v. State, 269 Ga. App. 836 (1), 605 S.E.2d 428 (2004).

[10]Harris v. State, 120 Ga. App. 359 (2), 170 S.E.2d 743 (1969).

[11]Berthiaume v. Smith, 875 F.3d 1354 (11th Cir. 2017). See U.S. v. Bates, 590 Fed. Appx. 882 (11th Cir. 2014).

[Section 18:28]

[1]Lamb v. State, 241 Ga. 10, 12 (1), 243 S.E.2d 59 (1978).

drugs,[2] and (3) in a case involving a member of the Ku Klux Klan, whether any of the jurors are members of the KKK or any such club or organization.[3]

In *Childers v. State,*[4] the defendant was tried for aggravated battery growing out of domestic violence in which the defendant beat his girlfriend. The trial judge permitted the state to make the following inquiry: "if . . . [any potential juror] agrees with the following please raise your hand: (1) some women want to be hit; (2) some women ask to be hit; (3) the only way to get the attention of some women is to hit them; (4) hitting, punching, or kicking someone is an acceptable way to vent anger or frustration; and (5) the State should not get involved in domestic and/or family violence situations."

§ 18:29 Excusal of potential juror by court

There are five statutory bases for the excusal of a potential juror by the court. O.C.G.A. § 15-12-1.1(a) provides that the judge may excuse a potential juror if (1) he or she is engaged "in work necessary to the public health, safety, or good order," (2) is a full-time student, (3) is the primary caregiver of a child six years of age or younger, (4) is a "primary teacher in a home study program," or (5) is the primary unpaid caregiver of a disabled person over the age of six who executes an affidavit that such person cannot be left unattended.[1]

In *Dorillas v. State,*[2] the court held that a potential trial or grand juror could be excused for hardship because of health problems. In *McMichen v. State,*[3] the court held that the trial judge could similarly excuse a primary caregiver of young children. In *Gulley v. State,*[4] the court held that "whether to excuse a juror for hardship lies within the trial court's discretion."

---

[2]Ridgeway v. State, 174 Ga. App. 663, 665 (3), 330 S.E.2d 916 (1985).

[3]Mize v. State, 190 Ga. App. 166, 378 S.E.2d 392 (1989).

[4]Childers v. State, 228 Ga. App. 214, 215 n. 2, 491 S.E.2d 456 (1997).

[Section 18:29]

[1]The Supreme Court requires that superior courts provide a jury management order which, inter alia, provides guidelines for the deferral, excusal and inactivation of jurors.

[2]Dorillas v. State, 224 Ga. App. 336, 337 (1)(b), 480 S.E.2d 351 (1997).

[3]McMichen v. State, 265 Ga. 598, 612 (33)(a), 458 S.E.2d 833 (1995).

[4]Gulley v. State, 271 Ga. 337, 344 (7), 519 S.E.2d 655 (1999).

§ 18:30 Number of peremptory strikes—Generally

Challenges for cause are not counted against the number of peremptory strikes or challenges to which a party is entitled.[1] In the case of a strike for cause, the potential juror is excused because the court has concluded that he is not competent to serve in a particular case. On the other hand, a peremptory challenge is generally regarded as an arbitrary or capricious strike or challenge. Peremptory challenges are sometimes referred to as "hunch" challenges. That is, a potential juror is excused just because counsel "feels" that this juror will not respond favorably to his side of the case. Generally, the party exercising a peremptory challenge is not obligated to justify or explain his reasons for the challenge.[2] But see § 18:31, infra, on cases following *Batson v. Kentucky*.[3]

In 2005, O.C.G.A. § 15-12-165 was changed so as to provide as follows:

"Every person accused of a felony may peremptorily challenge nine of the jurors impaneled to him or her. The state shall be allowed the same number of peremptory challenges allowed to the defendant; provided, however, that in any case in which the state announces its intention to seek the death penalty, the defendant may peremptorily challenge 15 jurors and the state shall be allowed the same number of peremptory challenges."[4]

Thus, where a defendant has been indicted and the state is not seeking the death penalty, under O.C.G.A. § 15-12-165 there must be at least 30 qualified jurors. In the selection of a jury of 12, both the defendant and the state are entitled to peremptorily strike or excuse nine of the 30 jurors, meaning a maximum of 18 jurors may be struck and 12 remain. The code section, as amended, applies to all trials that commence on or after July 1,

---

[Section 18:30]

[1]Jones v. Cloud, 119 Ga. App. 697, 708, 168 S.E.2d 598 (1969).

In State v. Arbeitman, 131 Vt. 596, 313 A.2d 17 (1973), the court said that there is no limit to the number of challenges for cause which a defendant has. In Cluverius v. Commonwealth, 81 Va. 787 (1886), in a murder trial which lasted 30 days (p. 789), about 900 persons were excused for cause (p. 798).

In Irvin v. Dowd, 366 U.S. 717, 727, 81 S.Ct. 1639, 6 L.Ed.2d 751 (1961), the trial judge excused 268 potential jurors for cause.

[2]People v. McCray, 57 N.Y.2d 542, 457 N.Y.S.2d 441, 443 N.E.2d 915 (1982). But see § 18:31, infra.

[3]Batson v. Kentucky, 476 U.S. 79, 106 S.Ct. 1712, 90 L.Ed.2d 69 (1986).

[4]As amended, O.C.G.A. § 15-12-165 applies retroactively to cases pending at the time of its enactment. Madison v. State, 281 Ga. 640(2c), 641 S.E.2d 789 (2007). Prior to 2005, O.C.G.A. § 15-12-165 provided the defendant 12 peremptory challenges and the state one-half that number. In cases where the state sought the death penalty, the defendant had 20 peremptory challenges and the state had one-half that number.

2005.

In the event two or more defendants are tried jointly, the court, upon request of the defendants, shall allow an equal number of strikes to the defendants not to exceed five each, as the court shall deem necessary. The court may allow the state additional strikes not to exceed the number of additional strikes as are allowed to the defendants.[5] See § 18:33, infra, on the order of exercising strikes where there are two or more defendants. If a defendant is tried on two or more indictments[6] at the same time, or if there is more than one count in the indictment,[7] he is not entitled to additional challenges. See § 18:35, infra, on the number of peremptory challenges allowed in the selection of alternate jurors.

Generally in a misdemeanor case, either party may demand a full panel of 12 competent jurors from which to select a jury of six pursuant to O.C.G.A. § 15-12-125. The defendant and the state both have the right to strike three jurors peremptorily.[8]

Historically, it has been felt that a defendant may not complain that a prospective juror was not stricken for cause unless he exhausted all his peremptory challenges in the jury selection process.[9] See § 18:33, infra, on methods of striking a jury.

§ 18:31 Peremptory challenges—Limitations—*Batson v. Kentucky*

In *Batson v. Kentucky*,[1] the United States Supreme Court held that the equal protection clause of the Fourteenth Amendment guarantees the defendant that the state will not exclude members of his race from the jury venire on account of race, or on the false assumption that members of his race, as a group, are not quali-

---

[5]O.C.G.A. § 17-8-4. The fact that two or more defendants tried together receive less strikes than a defendant in a solo trial does not amount to a denial of equal protection of the law. Dixon v. State, 285 Ga. 312 (2), 677 S.E.2d 76 (2009).

[6]Callahan v. State, 229 Ga. 737, 739, 194 S.E.2d 431 (1972). See Annot., "Additional Peremptory Challenges Because of Multiple Criminal Charges," 5 A.L.R.4th 533 (1981).

[7]Reynolds v. State, 101 Ga. App. 715, 716 (2), 115 S.E.2d 214 (1960).

[8]Prior to 2005, O.C.G.A. § 15-12-125 allowed the defendant four peremptory challenges and the state was allowed two.

[9]Finney v. State, 242 Ga. 582, 587 (7), 250 S.E.2d 388 (1978). But see Henderson v. State, 251 Ga. 398, 306 S.E.2d 645 (1983). See § 18:17, supra, on *Witherspoon* violations.

[Section 18:31]

[1]Batson v. Kentucky, 476 U.S. 79, 106 S.Ct. 1712, 90 L.Ed.2d 69 (1986). See Justice Benham's concurring opinion in Flanders v. State, 279 Ga. 35, 609 S.E.2d 346 (2005) for an elegant discussion of the significance of *Batson*.

fied to serve as jurors.[2] Writing for the majority, Justice Powell established a three-step test to determine if the state violated the defendant's equal protection rights in the jury selection process. First, the defendant must establish a prima facie case of purposeful discrimination in selection of the trial[3] jury.[4] To do so, a defendant must show that (1) he is a member of a cognizable racial group, and (2) the prosecutor used race to exclude veniremen from the petit jury in his case. Second, when the defendant makes a prima facie showing, the burden shifts to the state to come forward with a race-neutral explanation for challenging the juror(s).[5] Third, the trial court must then decide whether the opponent of the strike has proved purposeful racial discrimination.[6] It is important to note that while the burden of production shifts throughout the Batson analysis, "the ultimate burden of persuasion regarding racial motivation rests with, and never shifts from, the opponent of the strike."[7]

Since 1986 the United States Supreme Court has explained and expanded its holdings in *Batson*. In *Powers v. Ohio*,[8] the Court abandoned the requirement that the defendant challenging a strike must share the same race as the excluded juror(s). Then in *Georgia v. McCollum*,[9] the Court held that *Batson* applies to the use of peremptory challenges by a criminal defendant as well as the prosecution. The court also extended the scope of *Batson*— now neither party may use its peremptory strikes to exclude

---

[2]Batson v. Kentucky, 476 U.S. 79, 85-88, 106 S.Ct. 1712, 90 L.Ed.2d 69 (1986). However, the defendant does *not* have a right to a petit jury composed in whole or in part of persons of his own race. Strauder v. West Virginia, 100 U.S. (10 Otto) 303, 305, 25 L.Ed. 664 (1880).

[3]The "petit jury" is the jury for trial. Black's Law Dictionary 768 (5th ed. 1979).

[4]Batson v. Kentucky, 476 U.S. 79, 96, 106 S.Ct. 1712, 90 L.Ed.2d 69 (1986). See Miller-El v. Cockrell, 537 U.S. 322, 123 S.Ct. 1029, 154 L.Ed.2d 931 (2003), where Supreme Court engaged in an in-depth evaluation of a habeas petitioner's *Batson* challenge.

[5]O.C.G.A. § 17-8-4 (GCA § 27-2101), as amended April 5, 2005.

[6]Hernandez v. New York, 500 U.S. 352, 358-59, 111 S.Ct. 1859, 114 L.Ed.2d 395 (1991) (plurality opinion).

[7]Jackson v. State, 265 Ga. 897, 898, 463 S.E.2d 699 (1995) (citing Purkett v. Elem, 514 U.S. 765, 115 S.Ct. 1769, 131 L.Ed.2d 834 (1995)); Chandler v. State, 266 Ga. 509, 510, 467 S.E.2d 562 (1996); Gilbert v. State, 226 Ga. App. 230, 486 S.E.2d 48 (1997).

[8]Powers v. Ohio, 499 U.S. 400, 111 S.Ct. 1364, 113 L.Ed.2d 411 (1991). Larry Joe Powers was a white male who contested the state's use of peremptory challenges to exclude seven black venirepersons. Georgia followed the Powers decision in Congdon v. State, 261 Ga. 398, 405 S.E.2d 677 (1991). However, in the 1998 decision of Smith v. State, 231 Ga. App. 677, 683 (5), 499 S.E.2d 663 (1998), the court did not follow Powers.

[9]Georgia v. McCollum, 505 U.S. 42, 112 S.Ct. 2348, 120 L.Ed.2d 33 (1992), followed in Chandler v. State, 266 Ga. 509, 510, 467 S.E.2d 562 (1996). Cf. Pickren v. State, 272 Ga. 421, 424 (4), 530 S.E.2d 464 (2000).

potential jurors based on race,[10] gender[11] and probably ethnicity.[12] Striking venirepersons based on their religion has not yet been addressed by the United States Supreme Court except to deny a petition for certiorari in *Davis v. Minnesota*,[13] where the Minnesota Supreme Court held that the equal protection clause was not violated where a party used its peremptory strikes to remove jurors based on their religious beliefs.

Counsel should note that "*Batson* applies only to the use of peremptory strikes, not strikes for cause, such as a prospective juror's admitted inability to decide the case solely on the evidence . . . [A] strike 'for cause'—which is based on a juror's lack of impartiality or other good cause—is by definition not a strike based on the juror's race."[14]

A. STEP 1—THE PRIMA FACIE CASE

Part of the significance of *Batson* was the Court's holding that a defendant may establish a prima facie case of purposeful discrimination solely on evidence of the prosecutor's use of peremptory strikes at the defendant's trial.[15] Previously, courts applying *Swain v. Alabama*[16] required the defendant to show that the prosecution repeatedly struck black jurors over a number of cases to establish a violation of the equal protection clause in his case.[17]

In Georgia, a *Batson-McCollum*[18] motion must be made after the selection process is finished[19] but before the jury is sworn.[20] **The party challenging a strike has the burden of perfect-**

---

[10]Batson v. Kentucky, 476 U.S. 79, 106 S.Ct. 1712, 90 L.Ed.2d 69 (1986).

[11]J. E. B. v. Alabama, 511 U.S. 127, 114 S.Ct. 1419, 128 L.Ed.2d 89 (1994).

[12]See Hernandez v. New York, 500 U.S. 352, 360, 111 S.Ct. 1859, 114 L.Ed.2d 395 (1991) (plurality opinion). See also Annot., "Use of Peremptory Challenges to Exclude Ethnic and Racial Groups, Other than Black Americans, from Criminal Jury—Post Batson State Cases," 20 A.L.R.5th 398 (1994).

[13]Davis v. Minnesota, 511 U.S. 1115, 114 S.Ct. 2120, 128 L.Ed.2d 679 (1994). See Bryant v. State, 288 Ga. 876, 708 S.E.2d 362 (2011) (court was skeptical of effort by defense to apply *Batson* to religious beliefs of jurors). See also Annot., "Use of Peremptory Challenges to Exclude Persons from Criminal Jury Based on Religious Affiliation—Post-Batson State Cases," 63 A.L.R.5th 375 (1998).

[14]Anthony v. State, 303 Ga. 399, 811 S.E.2d 399 (2018).

[15]Batson v. Kentucky, 476 U.S. 79, 95, 106 S.Ct. 1712, 90 L.Ed.2d 69 (1986).

[16]Swain v. Alabama, 380 U.S. 202, 85 S.Ct. 824, 13 L.Ed.2d 759 (1965).

[17]See Batson v. Kentucky, 476 U.S. 79, 92-93, 106 S.Ct. 1712, 90 L.Ed.2d 69 (1986).

[18]A *Batson* motion challenges the state's peremptory strikes, but when the state objects to the defendant's use of his strikes, the motion is properly made under *McCollum*.

[19]Bright v. State, 265 Ga. 265, 282-83 (10), 455 S.E.2d 37 (1995).

[20]State v. Sparks, 257 Ga. 97, 98,

ing the record with information revealing (1) the racial composition of the original panel, (2) the breakdown of the strikes of both parties, and (3) the makeup of the jury selected.[21] A colloquy between defense counsel, the prosecutor and the trial judge, even if on the record, is not "competent evidence of the facts observed therein and do[es] not suffice to make a proper record of facts required to establish a prima facie case of discrimination."[22]

In deciding whether the party opposing a peremptory strike established a prima facie case of discrimination, courts generally look at how many strikes were used to exclude members of a cognizable group[23] in relation to that group's representation in the qualified venire.[24] When the racial makeup of the group excluded closely parallels the racial makeup of the venire, the laws of probability may tend to support the striking party's claim that none of the jurors were excluded because of their race.[25] However, the fact that the trial jury ultimately contained a greater percentage of a certain group of jurors than were available in the qualified venire is not itself sufficient to rebut a prima facie case

---

355 S.E.2d 658 (1987); Greene v. State, 260 Ga. 472, 473, 396 S.E.2d 901 (1990).

[21]Aldridge v. State, 258 Ga. 75, 77, 365 S.E.2d 111 (1988); Woods v. State, 208 Ga. App. 565, 566, 431 S.E.2d 167 (1993).

[22]Shaw v. State, 201 Ga. App. 438, 439-40, 411 S.E.2d 534 (1991); Thomas v. State, 208 Ga. App. 367, 367-68, 430 S.E.2d 768 (1993); Woods v. State, 208 Ga. App. 565, 566, 431 S.E.2d 167 (1993).

[23]See Rose v. State, 287 Ga. 238, 695 S.E.2d 261 (2010) (defense used all of its strikes to exclude Caucasians); Slade v. State, 267 Ga. 868, 870 (4), 485 S.E.2d 726 (1997) (trial judge erred in not finding prima facie case of discrimination where prosecutor used 100% of peremptory strikes against black jurors); Malone v. State, 225 Ga. App. 315, 484 S.E.2d 6 (1997) (state established prima facie case where defendant used 10 of 11 peremptory challenges to strike whites from jury); Gardner v. State, 225 Ga. App. 427, 483 S.E.2d 912 (1997) (defendant used all 10 peremptory strikes to remove

white jurors); Miller-El v. Cockrell, 537 U.S. 322, 123 S.Ct. 1029, 154 L.Ed.2d 931 (2003) (prosecutor used peremptory strikes to exclude 91% of prospective black jurors but only 13% of prospective white jurors).

[24]In Griffeth v. State, 224 Ga. App. 462, 464-65 (2), 480 S.E.2d 889 (1997), it was error for the trial judge to not find a prima facie case of racial discrimination where the state used 3 (½ of its) peremptory strikes against black potential jurors where there were only 6 blacks in the 30-person venire. In Staples v. State, 209 Ga. App. 802 (1), 434 S.E.2d 757 (1993), the Court of Appeals held that the defendant made a prima facie case of racial discrimination where the prosecutor used peremptory strikes to exclude 5 of the 8 prospective black jurors out of a 42-person venire. In Ford v. State, 262 Ga. 558, 560, 423 S.E.2d 245 (1992), the Court of Appeals reversed the conviction where the prosecutor struck 9 out of 10 blacks on a 42-person jury panel.

[25]See Ford v. State, 262 Ga. 558, 560, 423 S.E.2d 245 (1992).

of intentional discrimination.[26] As the court observed in *Lane v. State*,[27] "[T]he Constitution does not guarantee that the jury impaneled in a particular case will be a representative cross-section of the community. The correct inquiry concerns the procedures for compiling the jury lists and not just the composition of a particular jury." (Citations omitted.)

In *Whitaker v. State*,[28] the Georgia Supreme Court held that "numbers alone did not establish a disproportionate exercise of strikes sufficient to raise a prima facie inference that the strikes were exercised with discriminatory intent under *Batson*."

However, in *Beasley v. State*,[29] the trial court failed to conduct a hearing to determine whether the prosecution purposely discriminated against two groups. Instead, it directly asked the prosecution to explain the reasons for its strikes. The prosecution articulated explanations which the court found legitimate. The appellate court affirmed.

In *Johnson v. California*,[30] the United States Supreme Court found California's "more likely than not" standard to be "an inappropriate yardstick by which to measure the sufficiency of a prima facie case" of purposeful discrimination. The defendant is only required to show facts which would allow the trial judge to draw an inference that purposeful discrimination has occurred.

B. STEP 2—THE NEUTRAL EXPLANATION

The initial question is whether the opponent of the strike established a prima facie case of intentional[31]

---

[26]In Davis v. State, 263 Ga. 5, 7, n. 3, 426 S.E.2d 844 (1993); Berry v. State, 263 Ga. 493, 435 S.E.2d 433 (1993); Weems v. State, 262 Ga. 101 (2), 416 S.E.2d 84 (1992).

[27]Lane v. State, 239 Ga. App. 230, 230 (2) (b), 520 S.E.2d 705 (1999). See Tyre v. State, , 323 Ga.App. 37, 747 S.E.2d 106 (2013).

[28]Whitaker v. State, 269 Ga. 462, 464 (3), 499 S.E.2d 888 (1998). Accord, Livingston v. State, 271 Ga. 714, 718, 524 S.E.2d 222 (1999). Compare Rakestrau v. State, 278 Ga. 872, 608 S.E.2d 216 (2005), prima facie case of discrimination found where the panel was evenly divided between whites and African-Americans and the state used all four of its strikes against African-Americans.

[29]Beasley v. State, 269 Ga. 620, 625 (12), 502 S.E.2d 235 (1998).

[30]Johnson v. California, 545 U.S. 162, 125 S. Ct. 2410, 162 L. Ed. 2d 129 (2005).

[31]In Hernandez v. New York, 500 U.S. 352, 362, 111 S.Ct. 1859, 114 L.Ed.2d 395 (1991) (plurality opinion), the Court held that although "disparate impact should be given appropriate weight in determining whether the [striking party] acted with a forbidden intent, . . . it will not be conclusive in the preliminary race-neutrality step of the Batson inquiry. . . . Unless the [striking party] adopted a criterion with the intent of causing the impact asserted, that impact itself does not violate the principle of race neutrality."

discrimination based on "a totality of the relevant facts."[32] If the answer is yes, the trial court should require the striking party to provide neutral reasons that support the strike. In *Batson,* the court held that at Step 2 the proponent's explanation for the challenged peremptory strike need not rise to the level justifying a challenge for cause[33]—but the reasons for the strike must be legitimate (nondiscriminatory), clear, reasonably specific and related to the particular case to be tried.[34] A "legitimate reason is not a reason that makes sense, but a reason that does not deny equal protection."[35]

However, in *Purkett v. Elem*[36] the United States Supreme Court clarified that the race-neutral reason for the strike does not have to be "persuasive, or even plausible." "At this [second] step of the inquiry, the issue is the facial validity of the prosecutor's explanation. Unless a discriminatory intent is inherent in the prosecutor's explanation, the reason offered will be deemed race neutral."[37] Put simply, at Step 2 the trial court *must* accept the given explanation so long as it is not itself discriminatory.[38]

In *Curry v. State,*[39] the court held that "it is not necessary for the trial court to make an explicit finding that the offered explanation is valid at the conclusion of step two. . . ."

It is important to recognize that Steps 2 and 3 of the Batson inquiry are different because the burden of production shifts from Step 2 to Step 3. The combining of the two steps "impermissibly transforms the *opponent's* burden of providing purposeful discrimination into the *proponents'* burden of disproving discrimination."[40] In other words, it has been held that if the trial court merges Steps 2 and 3 of the Batson analysis, it will be

---

[32]Batson v. Kentucky, 476 U.S. 79, 94, 106 S.Ct. 1712, 90 L.Ed.2d 69 (1986); Whatley v. State, 266 Ga. 568, 570, 468 S.E.2d 751 (1996).

[33]Batson v. Kentucky, 476 U.S. 79, 97, 106 S.Ct. 1712, 90 L.Ed.2d 69 (1986).

[34]Batson v. Kentucky, 476 U.S. 79, 98, 106 S.Ct. 1712, 90 L.Ed.2d 69 (1986). The explanation should be concrete, tangible, race-neutral, and neutrally applied. Ford v. State, 262 Ga. 558, 560, 423 S.E.2d 245 (1992). See Lingo v. State, 263 Ga. 664(1)(c), n.4, 437 S.E.2d 463 (1993) (jury selection is invalid where it appears racially neutral explanation is pretextual because of apparent racially motivated reason for strike). See also Minor v. State, 328 Ga. App. 128, 761 S.E.2d

538 (2014).

[35]Purkett v. Elem, 514 U.S. 765, 115 S.Ct. 1769, 1771, 131 L.Ed.2d 834 (1995).

[36]Purkett v. Elem, 514 U.S. 765, 115 S.Ct. 1769, 1771, 131 L.Ed.2d 834 (1995). See Toomer v. State, 292 Ga. 49, 734 S.E.2d 333 (2012).

[37]Hernandez v. New York, 500 U.S. 352, 360, 111 S.Ct. 1859, 114 L.Ed.2d 395 (1991) (plurality opinion).

[38]Leeks v. State, 226 Ga. App. 227, 229, 483 S.E.2d 691 (1997).

[39]Curry v. State, 238 Ga. App. 511, 514 (1)(a), 519 S.E.2d 269 (1999).

[40]Malone v. State, 225 Ga. App. 315, 319, 484 S.E.2d 6 (1997) (emphasis added). Accord, Smith v. State, 232 Ga. App. 458, 459 (1), 501 S.E.2d 622

reversed.[41] Accordingly a trial court should not, at Step 2, determine both the *neutrality* and *credibility* of the proffered reasons for the strike. It is not until Step 3 that the trial court decides whether the proffered explanation is persuasive or merely a pretext for intentional discrimination.

In *Byron v. State,*[42] the court pointed out that "[u]nless a discriminatory intent is inherent in the proponent's explanation, the reason offered will be deemed race[-]neutral."

In *Williams v. State,*[43] the trial court was affirmed in denying the request of defense counsel to question the assistant district attorney and law enforcement officers about investigatory information upon which the state based its strikes.

1. Explanations for Peremptory Strikes that Georgia Courts Accepted as Neutral[44]

a. Impartiality—Generally

"A reasonable suspicion about a prospective juror's impartiality [justifying an excusal under *Batson*] that falls short of justifying an excusal for cause might well justify the exercise of a peremptory strike."[45] However, in *Ridley v. State,*[46] the court pointed out that the reasons cannot be "too vague, too subjective . . . nonspecific [or] non-case related." In this connection, the court pointed out that striking a juror based solely on the similarity between the juror's name and the name of a defendant or defendants in prior actions is probably improper.[47]

b. Impartiality—the State—Generally

There is no requirement that the state's racially neutral explanation for its use of peremptory strikes be supported by a transcript of voir dire.[48] A prosecutor's explanation may be based

---

(1998).

[41]See Pickett v. State, 226 Ga. App. 743, 744 (1), 487 S.E.2d 653 (1997); Malone v. State, 225 Ga. App. 315, 484 S.E.2d 6 (1997); Leeks v. State, 226 Ga. App. 227, 228 (3), 483 S.E.2d 691 (1997); O'Neal v. State, 226 Ga. App. 224, 482 S.E.2d 478 (1997); Smith v. State, 229 Ga. App. 765, 494 S.E.2d 757 (1997). Cf. Mitchell v. State, 230 Ga. App. 149, 495 S.E.2d 626 (1998).

[42]Byron v. State, 229 Ga. App. 795, 798 (5), 495 S.E.2d 123 (1997) (quoting Jackson v. State, 265 Ga. 897, 463 S.E.2d 699 (1995)).

[43]Williams v. State, 271 Ga. 323, 324 (2), 519 S.E.2d 232 (1999).

[44]While the following reasons for striking prospective jurors are divided into subsections, the reader should note that there is significant overlap between them. Standing alone, some of these explanations for the peremptory strikes might not be sufficient to rebut a strong prima facie case.

[45]Hall v. State, 261 Ga. 778, 780, 415 S.E.2d 158 (1991).

[46]Ridley v. State, 235 Ga. App. 591, 592 (1), 510 S.E.2d 113 (1998).

[47]But see Trammel v. State, 265 Ga. 156, 157 (2), 454 S.E.2d 501 (1995); Rakestrau v. State, 278 Ga. 872, 875, 608 S.E.2d 216 (2005).

[48]Burgess v. State, 194 Ga. App. 179, 180, 390 S.E.2d 92 (1990).

on mistake, ignorance or idiosyncracy[49] so long as it is neutral. As the Georgia Supreme Court observed in *Taylor v. State*,[50] the ultimate inquiry in a *Batson* challenge is not whether the prosecutor's explanation for the strike is suspect, but whether the prosecutor "is telling the truth in his or her assertion that the challenge is not race based." However, the state does not fulfill its burden to provide race-neutral reasons simply because its peremptory challenges were exercised in deference to the wishes of an individual connected with the case.[51] In *Barnes v. State*,[52] the Georgia Supreme Court held that "the state may rely on information and advice provided by others so long as this input is not predicated upon . . . race . . . ." In such a situation, the state must set forth a race-neutral, case-related reason underlying the decision of the person to whom the prosecutor deferred.[53] In *Odom v. State*,[54] the state was allowed to strike a juror because he was a single father.

c. Impartiality—the State—Bias in Favor of

In *Cooper v. State*,[55] where the defendant struck a white female because she previously served on a jury and "looked at the prosecution in a very accepting way during questioning on voir dire," the court found this to represent a race-neutral reason for a peremptory strike. In a case where the defense's theory was "the government screwed up," striking a white female government employee who thought the government did a good job most of the time was found to be a "concrete, tangible, and non-racial reason" for a peremptory strike.[56]

d. Impartiality—the State—Bias Against

The state's concern that a prospective juror is hostile to the state or will not seriously consider the state's evidence are race-neutral reasons for a peremptory strike. In *Russell v. State*,[57] the prosecutor struck a black female who was involved in a shooting

---

[49]Gamble v. State, 257 Ga. 325, 326 (2), 357 S.E.2d 792 (1987). See also Bess v. State, 187 Ga. App. 185, 369 S.E.2d 784 (1988) (prosecutor struck a black female upon belief that she was single and childless; on appeal, the court upheld the strike even though there was no indication in the record that that prospective juror was in fact not married or did not have children).

[50]Taylor v. State, 279 Ga. 706, 708(3), 620 S.E.2d 363 (2005).

[51]Lewis v. State, 262 Ga. 679 (2), 424 S.E.2d 626 (1993).

[52]Barnes v. State, 269 Ga. 345, 350 (5), 496 S.E.2d 674 (1998).

[53]Lewis v. State, 262 Ga. 679, 681 (2), 424 S.E.2d 626 (1993). Compare Congdon v. State, 262 Ga. 683, 424 S.E.2d 630 (1993).

[54]Odom v. State, 241 Ga. App. 361, 362, 526 S.E.2d 646 (1999).

[55]Cooper v. State, 220 Ga. App. 531, 532, 469 S.E.2d 790 (1996).

[56]Malone v. State, 225 Ga. App. 315, 316, 484 S.E.2d 6 (1997).

[57]Russell v. State, 267 Ga. 865, 867, n. 2, 485 S.E.2d 717 (1997).

incident involving the local police department. In *Jones v. State*,[58] a black male, who was the victim of a crime in another state, was struck because he was unhappy with the manner in which police handled the investigation. Another juror was struck in *Jones* because the prosecutor sensed "bad vibes" after the black female "cut her eyes" at him.[59] Both of these strikes were upheld. In *Dixon v. State*,[60] the prosecutor used a peremptory challenge to excuse a black male who had been discharged from a law enforcement position because of substance abuse. This was held valid. In *Rakestrau v. State*,[61] the court upheld the prosecutor's strike of a prospective black juror because of her "observed camaraderie with a fellow prospective juror who had previously served as a witness in an unrelated murder trial in which both prosecutors had participated." The prosecutor also expressed concern that the juror would have difficulty "understanding the scientific evidence in the case." In *George v. State*,[62] the prosecutor legitimately struck a black male because he knew something about the case, had counseled inmates in jail and also had a suit pending against a police officer. In *Alford v. State*,[63] a black female was validly struck by the prosecutor on advice from a police officer that the prospective juror was "very anti-law enforcement." In *Ellerbee v. State*,[64] the prosecutor legitimately struck a white male because he was "unemployed [and] might be a little prejudice[d] against the State." In *Berry v. State*,[65] it was found not discriminatory for the state to strike a panel member who had recently been the subject of an investigation by the district attorney's office. In *Brown v. State*,[66] the Court of Appeals ruled that it was error to allow the prosecution to strike an African American juror who expressed a belief that the justice system was prejudiced against African Americans in a case where the juror and the defendant were the same race. The Court rejected the argument that the juror's professed suspicions of the justice system provided a race-neutral reason for the strike because of the statement by the prosecutor that the juror's race was "particularly relevant" to her decision to exercise the strike.

See Jason J. Carter and Edward D. Tolley, *Striking out in the*

---

[58]Jones v. State, 226 Ga. App. 428 (1)(c), 487 S.E.2d 62 (1997).

[59]Jones v. State, 226 Ga. App. 428 (1)(b), 487 S.E.2d 62 (1997).

[60]Dixon v. State, 214 Ga. App. 374, 376-77 (3), 448 S.E.2d 40 (1994).

[61]Rakestrau v. State, 278 Ga. 872, 608 S.E.2d 216 (2005).

[62]George v. State, 262 Ga. 436, 437 (2), 421 S.E.2d 67 (1992).

[63]Alford v. State, 224 Ga. App. 451, 458 (6), 480 S.E.2d 893 (1997).

[64]Ellerbee v. State, 215 Ga. App. 102, 106-108 (9), 449 S.E.2d 874 (1994), overruled on other grounds, Felix v. State, 271 Ga. 534, 523 S.E.2d 1 (1999).

[65]Berry v. State, 267 Ga. 605, 608-609 (5), 481 S.E.2d 203 (1997).

[66]Brown v. State, 256 Ga. App. 209, 210(1), 568 S.E.2d 62 (2002).

Batson Box: A Guide to Non-discriminatory Jury Selection in Georgia. Georgia Bar Journal, Vol. 8, No. 3 (December 2002): pps. 12-18.

e. Impartiality—the State—Bias Against—Prior Arrests and Convictions

In *Jones v. State,*[67] the court affirmed the striking of a black male by the prosecutor after stating he had been unfairly arrested by police. Also affirmed in *Green v. State*[68] was the prosecution's striking of a black female from the jury pool because she had been prosecuted for felony welfare fraud. Likewise, in *Dixon v. State,*[69] the prosecutor's explanation that jurors were excused based upon their commission of criminal offenses in the past was deemed sufficiently race-neutral. In *Lingo v. State,*[70] the prosecutor used peremptory strikes against prospective jurors who had a DUI conviction, shoplifting conviction and a "bad check problem." The court held that these were legitimate race-neutral reasons to strike prospective jurors.

f. Impartiality—the State—Bias Against—Prior Arrests and Convictions of Family Members

Prior convictions or arrest histories of a family member are also sufficiently race-neutral reasons to exercise a peremptory strike.[71] In *Jones v. State,*[72] the prosecutor validly struck a black male who stated his brother had been treated unfairly by police. In *Henry v. State,*[73] the prosecutor used a peremptory challenge to strike two prospective jurors, both black females. One was struck because her cousin had been prosecuted for several offenses, including murder, and that same cousin was a shooting victim in a case that was dismissed by the state. The other black female was struck because her son had been prosecuted for a felony offense. Both of these strikes were held to be race neutral. In *Chunn v. State,*[74] the prosecutor legitimately struck a black male because his son had been charged with a crime. In *Height v. State,*[75] the prosecutor legitimately struck a black female because she knew the defendant and that same state's attorney person-

---

[67]Jones v. State, 226 Ga. App. 428 (1)(f), 487 S.E.2d 62 (1997).

[68]Green v. State, 219 Ga. App. 24, 25 (2), 464 S.E.2d 21 (1995).

[69]Dixon v. State, 214 Ga. App. 374, 377 (3), 448 S.E.2d 40 (1994).

[70]Lingo v. State, 263 Ga. 664, 666 (2), (9), (10), 437 S.E.2d 463 (1993).

[71]Davis v. State, 263 Ga. 5 (10), 426 S.E.2d 844 (1993); LeMon v. State, 290 Ga. App. 527 (1), 660 S.E.2d 11 (2008).

[72]Jones v. State, 226 Ga. App. 428 (1)(a), 487 S.E.2d 62 (1997). Accord, Dennis v. State, 238 Ga. App. 343, 347 (5)(f), 518 S.E.2d 745 (1999).

[73]Henry v. State, 265 Ga. 732, 733 (2), 462 S.E.2d 737 (1995).

[74]Chunn v. State, 210 Ga. App. 209, 210 (2), 435 S.E.2d 728 (1993).

[75]Height v. State, 221 Ga. App. 647, 648 (2), 472 S.E.2d 485 (1996).

ally prosecuted her brother for murder. In *Davis v. State*,[76] a juror was validly struck because her son was arrested for burglary and her daughter "got into a rash of shoplifting." In *Foster v. State*,[77] the prosecution used peremptory strikes against a black female social worker whose cousin lost his job after he was arrested for serious drug charges and another black female who denied having a friend or relative accused or convicted of a crime, even though her brother was a repeat offender and her husband had been convicted for carrying a concealed weapon. Both of these strikes were held to be non-discriminatory. In *Batton v. State*,[78] a black female was validly struck because she had relatives who had "trouble with the law." In *Rector v. State*,[79] the prosecutor validly used a peremptory challenge to strike a black female whose brother was charged with murder in another county. However, in that case the trial court also found that the prosecutor's alternative basis for the strike, that the juror had a gold tooth, amounted to racist stereotyping and was improper. Nonetheless, the court allowed the strike to stand because it was supported by a race-neutral reason. The Court of Appeals reversed, finding that any race-based rationale invalidates a strike even though there may be other proffered race-neutral reasons to support it.

g. Impartiality—the Defendant—in Favor of—Generally

In *Parker v. State*,[80] the court affirmed the prosecutor's strike of a female student majoring in criminal justice because he believed that someone with her background would take a "microscopic view of the evidence" and have "an extremely narrow perspective of reasonable doubt."

h. Impartiality—the Defendant—in Favor of—Prospective Juror Related to or Acquainted with Defendant, His Family, an Accomplice or a Defense Witness; Defense Counsel; or Familiar with Case

In *Russell v. State*,[81] the court allowed a peremptory strike where a black male knew the defendant, his entire family, and was the grandfather of two defense witnesses. Accordingly, the

---

[76]Davis v. State, 263 Ga. 5, 8-9, 426 S.E.2d 844 (1993).

[77]Foster v. State, 258 Ga. 736, 739 (2), 374 S.E.2d 188 (1988).

[78]Batton v. State, 260 Ga. 127, 129 (2), 391 S.E.2d 914 (1990).

[79]Rector v. State, 213 Ga. App. 450 (2), 444 S.E.2d 862 (1994) (strike based on juror's gold tooth was ruled racial stereotyping and a discriminatory reason for strike).

[80]Parker v. State, 219 Ga. App. 361, 362, 464 S.E.2d 910 (1995) (disapproved on other grounds, Toomer v. State, 292 Ga. 49, 734 S.E.2d 333 (2012)).

[81]Russell v. State, 267 Ga. 865, 867 n. 2, 485 S.E.2d 717 (1997).

court in *Evans v. State*[82] held that a proper and racially-neutral basis exists for a peremptory strike where a black female knew the defendant "all her life." In *Aldridge v. State,*[83] the prosecutor struck one black woman because she knew the defendant and his friends and struck another because she missed the first day of jury duty and knew the defendant's family. The Georgia Supreme Court upheld both strikes. Likewise, in *Height v. State,*[84] the court found a strike had legitimate, race-neutral reasons where the juror was a friend of the defendant, knew the defendant's mother, was related to an accomplice, and stated that these relationships would affect her ability to decide the case fairly and impartially. In *Hightower v. State,*[85] the prosecutor validly struck six prospective jurors because they knew either the defendant or a member of his family. Similarly, in *Marshall v. State,*[86] the prosecutor legitimately struck four prospective jurors because they were related to or closely associated with the defendant and his family. In *Lingo v. State,*[87] the court allowed a strike against a black man who was familiar with the defendant and with a witness and against a black woman who also knew a witness. In *Rakestrau v. State,*[88] the court upheld the strike of a prospective black juror where the juror "was employed by the Department of Family and Children's Services and there was information that defendant's mother may have known either [the juror] or her co-workers." In *George v. State,*[89] the court held that strikes against eight of nine potential black jurors were sufficiently race-neutral where all were well acquainted with the defendant, his relatives, and defense witnesses. Similarly, in *Batton v. State,*[90] the prosecutor validly struck three black women where all three knew the defendant and his family. The court in *Davis v. State*[91] affirmed the striking of a potential black juror after he stated that he used to work with the defendant's mother and aunt and that this would affect his "ability to reach a fair decision in the case."

The court in *Berry v. State*[92] found the fact that two black prospective jurors were represented in other litigation by defense

---

[82]Evans v. State, 225 Ga. App. 589, 590-91 (2), 484 S.E.2d 320 (1997).

[83]Aldridge v. State, 222 Ga. App. 437 (1), 475 S.E.2d 195 (1996).

[84]Height v. State, 221 Ga. App. 647, 648 (2), 472 S.E.2d 485 (1996).

[85]Hightower v. State, 220 Ga. App. 165, 166 (1), 469 S.E.2d 295 (1996).

[86]Marshall v. State, 266 Ga. 304 (2), 466 S.E.2d 567 (1996).

[87]Lingo v. State, 263 Ga. 664, 665

(1)(b)(6), (1)(b)(9), 437 S.E.2d 463 (1993).

[88]Rakestrau v. State, 278 Ga. 872, 608 S.E.2d 216 (2005).

[89]George v. State, 262 Ga. 436, 437 (2), 421 S.E.2d 67 (1992).

[90]Batton v. State, 260 Ga. 127, 129 (2), 391 S.E.2d 914 (1990).

[91]Davis v. State, 263 Ga. 5, 7 (10), 426 S.E.2d 844 (1993).

[92]Berry v. State, 267 Ga. 605, 608 (5), 481 S.E.2d 203 (1997).

counsel to be a legitimate and race-neutral reason for use of peremptory strikes by the prosecutor. Likewise, past representation by defense counsel was found to legitimately support striking of black jurors in *Dixon v. State*.[93] In *Gilbert v. State*,[94] the court stated that "[a] strike based on a party's employment status . . . is not, on its face, racially discriminatory," and found that striking a juror because he worked for a business with which defense counsel had had "several run-ins" and another juror because defense counsel thought he knew the juror from the post office or the bank were legitimate and race neutral.

i. Impartiality—the Defendant—in Favor of—Sympathy for or Similarity To

In *Berry v. State*,[95] the court affirmed the prosecutor's use of peremptory strikes to exclude women over 50 because the defendant was young and the state's attorney perceived that older women would take pity on the defendant and would not believe the "jailbird witnesses." In *Jones v. State*,[96] the prosecutor validly used a peremptory strike to excuse a black female who had "forgiven" those who shot her husband. In *Scott v. State*,[97] the prosecutor legitimately struck a black female who had three children close in age to the defendant. In *Ledford v. State*,[98] the court accepted as race neutral the prosecutor's strikes against two black jurors because they had sons near the same age as the defendant. The court in *Ware v. State*[99] held that a black female was legitimately struck in part because she was similar in age to the defendant. Similarly, in *Green v. State*,[100] a black male was validly struck by the state because he had been a defense witness in another case and appeared to be the same age as this defendant. In *Woods v. State*,[101] the defendant was charged with possession of cocaine with intent to distribute. The court affirmed the state's strike of a young male student because the prosecutor perceived that the juror's young age and field of study (drafting) might make him more tolerant of drug use.[102] Likewise, in *Hig-*

---

[93]Dixon v. State, 214 Ga. App. 374, 376 (3), 448 S.E.2d 40 (1994).

[94]Gilbert v. State, 226 Ga. App. 230, 486 S.E.2d 48 (1997) (quoting O'Neal v. State, 226 Ga. App. 224, 482 S.E.2d 478 (1997)).

[95]Berry v. State, 263 Ga. 493, 435 S.E.2d 433 (1993).

[96]Jones v. State, 226 Ga. App. 428, 429 (1)(e), 487 S.E.2d 62 (1997).

[97]Scott v. State, 225 Ga. App. 729, 730 (1), 484 S.E.2d 780 (1997).

[98]Ledford v. State, 207 Ga. App. 705, 706 (1), 429 S.E.2d 124 (1993).

[99]Ware v. State, 191 Ga. App. 896 (1), 383 S.E.2d 368 (1989).

[100]Green v. State, 219 Ga. App. 24, 25-26 (2), 464 S.E.2d 21 (1995).

[101]Woods v. State, 224 Ga. App. 52, 53-54 (2), 479 S.E.2d 414 (1996).

[102]Woods v. State, 224 Ga. App. 52, 53-54 (2), 479 S.E.2d 414 (1996). See O'Connell v. State, 294 Ga. 379, 754 S.E.2d 29 (2014) (strike of black ve-

ginbotham v. State,[103] the prosecutor legitimately used a peremptory strike against a prospective juror who lived in the same general area as the defendant and was approximately the same age. The court did not require proof that the defendant and the prospective juror were personally acquainted. In *Smith v. State*,[104] where the defendant was charged with gang-related murder, the court affirmed the action of the prosecutor in striking two black males because they were residents of a particular housing project where gang activity was prevalent. The court in *Ellerbee v. State*[105] affirmed that the prosecutor in a DUI case validly struck a real estate agent from the jury pool on advice from a police officer that "most [R]ealtors drink." In *Foster v. State*,[106] where the defendant's mental health and upbringing were at issue, the prosecutor validly struck a black male whose son was the same age as the defendant and had been convicted of misdemeanor theft, and whose wife was employed by a mental health facility. The state's use of a peremptory strike to excuse a black female who worked as a social worker with underprivileged children was also affirmed.[107] In *Russell v. State*,[108] the prosecutor legitimately struck a black female whose husband was a local politician out of concern that his constituency might influence her in favor of the defendant.

j. Impartiality—the Defendant—Bias Against

In *Jackson v. State*,[109] the court granted a new trial to the defendant where the trial court had refused to allow the strike of a white female because she worked for her husband's bonding company, and because the defendant had "jumped bond." Similarly, in *Chandler v. State*,[110] the Georgia Supreme Court granted a new trial to the defendant where the trial court had denied him use of his peremptory strikes to exclude two white jurors because they were in managerial positions and had authoritarian personalities.

k. Nature of Employment

---

nire member who was full-time student and appeared "bucking to get on trial" was race-neutral).

[103]Higginbotham v. State, 207 Ga. App. 424, 425 (3), 428 S.E.2d 592 (1993).

[104]Smith v. State, 264 Ga. 449 (1), 448 S.E.2d 179 (1994). Cf. Congdon v. State, 262 Ga. 683, 658, 424 S.E.2d 630 (1993).

[105]Ellerbee v. State, 215 Ga. App. 102, 107, 449 S.E.2d 874 (1994), overruled on other grounds, Felix v.

State, 271 Ga. 534, 523 S.E.2d 1 (1999).

[106]Foster v. State, 258 Ga. 736, 737-38 (2), 374 S.E.2d 188 (1988).

[107]Foster v. State, 258 Ga. 736, 739 (2), 374 S.E.2d 188 (1988).

[108]Russell v. State, 267 Ga. 865, 867, n. 2, 485 S.E.2d 717 (1997).

[109]Jackson v. State, 265 Ga. 897, 463 S.E.2d 699 (1995).

[110]Chandler v. State, 266 Ga. 509, 510 (2), 467 S.E.2d 562 (1996).

In *Trice v. State,*[111] the court held that the nature of a prospective juror's employment is not a characteristic peculiar to any race. In *Trice,* the prosecutor struck a prospective juror who was employed by Job Corps because of the prosecutor's experience with lack of cooperation by Job Corps employees. The state used a peremptory strike in *Higginbotham v. State*[112] against a black prospective juror because he was a pastor. The court upheld the strike, noting that the state may "secure jurors who are in a less . . . judgmental line of work." In *Minor v. State,*[113] the court affirmed the strike by the prosecutor of a black female who was an unemployed nightclub singer because her profession, or lack thereof, showed "a lack of commitment and dedication to the community."

l. Expressed Unwillingness or Hesitancy to Impose Death Penalty[114]

m. Unkempt Physical Appearance

In *Purkett v. Elem,*[115] the United States Supreme Court held that the prosecutor's explanation for striking a potential juror because he had "long, unkempt hair, a mustache, and a beard" was race neutral.

n. Perceived Immaturity,[116] Inattention, Nonresponsiveness and Reluctance or Hostility Toward Jury Service[117]

o. Prior Jury Service

In *Crawford v. State,*[118] the Court of Appeals upheld the prosecutor's strike of a black female because of her previous ser-

---

[111]Trice v. State, 266 Ga. 102, 103 (2), 464 S.E.2d 205 (1995).

[112]Higginbotham v. State, 207 Ga. App. 424, 426 (3), 428 S.E.2d 592 (1993).

[113]Minor v. State, 264 Ga. 195, 197 (5), 442 S.E.2d 754 (1994).

[114]Whatley v. State, 266 Ga. 568, 569-70 (3), 468 S.E.2d 751 (1996); Wellons v. State, 266 Ga. 77, 83 (3), 463 S.E.2d 868 (1995); Burgess v. State, 264 Ga. 777, 781 (9), 450 S.E.2d 680 (1994); Davis v. State, 263 Ga. 5, 8 (10), 426 S.E.2d 844 (1993); Lingo v. State, 263 Ga. 664, 666-68 (1), (4), (6), (7), (11), 437 S.E.2d 463 (1993); Tharpe v. State, 262 Ga. 110, 112 (6), 416 S.E.2d 78 (1992); Batton v. State, 260 Ga. 127, 129 (2), 391 S.E.2d 914 (1990); Foster v. State, 258 Ga. 736, 374 S.E.2d 188 (1988).

[115]Purkett v. Elem, 514 U.S. 765, 115 S.Ct. 1769, 1771, 131 L.Ed.2d 834 (1995).

[116]Alford v. State, 224 Ga. App. 451, 457-58 (6), 480 S.E.2d 893 (1997); Jones v. State, 226 Ga. App. 428, 429 (1)(d), 487 S.E.2d 62 (1997).

[117]Lingo v. State, 263 Ga. 664, 667 (1)(b)(5), (8), 437 S.E.2d 463 (1993); Moak v. State, 222 Ga. App. 36, 39 (3), 473 S.E.2d 576 (1996); Sorrells v. State, 218 Ga. App. 413, 424 (2), 461 S.E.2d 904 (1995); Berry v. State, 263 Ga. 493, 494, 435 S.E.2d 433 (1993); Dixon v. State, 214 Ga. App. 374, 376-77 (3), 448 S.E.2d 40 (1994); Evans v. State, 183 Ga. App. 436, 440 (3), 359 S.E.2d 174 (1987); Rakestrau v. State, 278 Ga. 872, 608 S.E.2d 216 (2005).

[118]Crawford v. State, 220 Ga. App. 786, 788 (1), 470 S.E.2d 323 (1996).

vice on a jury which returned a not guilty verdict in a felony case. Similarly, in *Richard v. State*,[119] the prosecutor validly used a peremptory strike to excuse a black panel member who served on a jury that acquitted a defendant prosecuted by the same attorney. In *Tharpe v. State*,[120] a death penalty case, the court held that it was not discriminatory for the prosecutor to strike a black female who had recently served on a jury in another murder case and voted to acquit the defendant who was represented by the same defense counsel as Tharpe. The courts have also held that strikes based on a panel member's service on a prior "hung jury" were not discriminatory.[121]

2. Explanations for Peremptory Strikes that Georgia Courts Rejected as Non-Neutral[122]

a. Failure to Connect Reason for Strike to Aspect of Case[123]

In *Blair v. State*,[124] the court held that the defendant failed to offer "race and gender neutral, case-related, specific explanations" for three of his strikes against white female jurors and, therefore, the trial court did not err in returning the jurors to the panel. In *Walton v. State*,[125] the prosecutor struck a black female who stated that she believed there "was a dual system of justice . . . against black people who are tried by the court in this country." The Georgia Supreme Court reversed the conviction, stating that the prosecutor's explanation was not "case related, clear and reasonably specific" and warned that trial judges should not provide "the very rationale [for the peremptory strike] which the judge must then adjudicate as racially neutral or racially

---

Compare Bethune v. State, 291 Ga. App. 674 (2), 662 S.E.2d 774 (2008), where the Court of Appeals upheld the state's strike of the sole African American on the jury venire based upon her response, "I don't know what a juror is," to the question on a jury questionnaire about prior jury service.

[119]Richard v. State, 223 Ga. App. 98, 476 S.E.2d 849 (1996).

[120]Tharpe v. State, 262 Ga. 110, 112 (6), 416 S.E.2d 78 (1992).

[121]See Aldridge v. State, 222 Ga. App. 437, 475 S.E.2d 195 (1996); Jackson v. State, 220 Ga. App. 98, 469 S.E.2d 264 (1996).

[122]See generally Gamble v. State, 257 Ga. 325, 357 S.E.2d 792 (1987).

[123]Concurring specially in Parker v. State, 219 Ga. App. 361, 364-65, 464 S.E.2d 910 (1995), Presiding Judge Pope opined that whether the reasons given for a peremptory strike must be related to the specifics of the case is "in a state of flux" after Purkett v. Elem, 514 U.S. 765, 115 S.Ct. 1769, 1771, 131 L.Ed.2d 834 (1995), where the United States Supreme Court did not require the race-neutral reason for a strike (the juror had "long, unkempt hair, a moustache, and a beard") to be case related.

[124]Blair v. State, 267 Ga. 166, 167 (2), 476 S.E.2d 263 (1996).

[125]Walton v. State, 267 Ga. 713, 718-20 (5), 482 S.E.2d 330 (1997).

based." However, in *Toomer v. State*,[126] the court disapproved *Blair* holding that "to carry the burden of production at step two, the proponent of the strike need not offer an explanation that is 'concrete,' 'tangible,' or 'specific.' The explanation need not even be 'case related.' The explanation for the strike only needs to be facially race-neutral."

b. Peremptory Strike Based on Prospective Juror's Demeanor

In *Parker v. State*,[127] the prosecutor struck three black females based almost entirely on their demeanor. The court held that the prosecutor's "bare hunches" without any inquiry as to potential biases "reflected unacceptable stereotypical attitudes as to particular groups which cannot serve as a basis for exercising peremptory strikes." In *Tharpe v. State*,[128] the court noted that striking a juror because he "allegedly ma[d]e minor mistakes on the jury questionnaire; or show[ed] signs of immaturity; or demonstrate[d] certain aspects of eye contact—reflect[ed] certain stereotypical attitudes as to particular groups. Any [strikes based on] such explanations should be given additional scrutiny by the trial court before they are found acceptable." The court in *Tharpe* went on to uphold the prosecutor's strike of a black female who "kept making close eye contact with the defendant all through questioning." Then in *McKibbons v. State*,[129] the Court of Appeals held that excusing a juror because he "avoided eye contact" impermissibly reflected stereotypical attitudes as to particular groups. But in *Jones v. State*,[130] the Court of Appeals upheld the state's use of peremptory strikes based on the demeanor of prospective jurors. In doing so, the Court of Appeals deferred to the trial judge's observations during voir dire while noting that whether a juror "cut her eyes" or used a hostile tone of voice does not show up in a trial transcript.

The United States Supreme Court recognized in *Snyder v. Louisiana*[131] that while the trial court's "firsthand observations" are of great importance when considering a challenge to a demeanor-based strike, there is no categorical rule mandating rejection of such a challenge when the judge either does not recall the juror's demeanor or was not present during voir dire.[132]

c. Stereotype

---

[126]Toomer v. State, 292 Ga. 49, 734 S.E.2d 333 (2012).

[127]Parker v. State, 219 Ga. App. 361, 464 S.E.2d 910 (1995).

[128]Tharpe v. State, 262 Ga. 110 (6), 416 S.E.2d 78 (1992).

[129]McKibbons v. State, 216 Ga. App. 389, 455 S.E.2d 293 (1995), rev.

denied.

[130]Jones v. State, 226 Ga. App. 428, 430, 487 S.E.2d 62 (1997).

[131]Snyder v. Louisiana, 552 U.S. 472, 128 S. Ct. 1203, 170 L. Ed. 2d 175 (2008).

[132]Thaler v. Haynes, 130 S. Ct. 1171 (2010).

In *Congdon v. State*,[133] the prosecutor struck two black members of the venire based solely upon the belief that, as the result of an unrelated criminal investigation, all black residents of a particular neighborhood were prejudiced against the white county sheriff who was the state's primary witness. The Georgia Supreme Court reversed, stating that such a belief was racially stereotypical and would not support a peremptory strike. In *Randolph v. State*,[134] the prosecutor struck a black prospective juror because he was a member of certain all-black professional or social organizations and expressed a general opinion that racism is present "everywhere," including the judicial system. The court held that such a strike was based on an "impermissible assumption ultimately arising solely from the juror's race" and granted the defendant a new trial. Likewise, the court in *Rector v. State*,[135] held that the prosecutor improperly used stereotypical reasoning in striking a black female based mainly on the fact that she had a monogrammed gold tooth in the front of her mouth.

d. Failure to Strike Similarly Situated Jurors of Different Race

In *Blair v. State*,[136] the court affirmed the trial judge in finding that the defendant's explanation for striking a white prospective juror was pretextual where similarly situated non-whites were not challenged. In *Ford v. State*,[137] the Court reversed the lower court which had allowed the prosecutor to strike a black prospective juror who was related to a minister, a juror who worked in Fulton County, and another juror who stated that he would automatically impose the death penalty, even though the prosecutor had declined to excuse white venirepersons with the same attributes. In a footnote, the court pointed out that the failure of a prosecutor "to explain the [apparent] disparate treatment of similarly situated white and black jurors certainly diminishes the force of his explanation for striking a black juror." However, this rule does not apply unless the situations of the two

---

[133]Congdon v. State, 262 Ga. 683, 424 S.E.2d 630 (1993).

[134]Randolph v. State, 203 Ga. App. 115, 116-17, 416 S.E.2d 117 (1992).

[135]Rector v. State, 213 Ga. App. 450 (2), 444 S.E.2d 862 (1994). See Clayton v. State, 341 Ga. App. 193, 797 S.E.2d 639 (2017).

[136]Blair v. State, 267 Ga. 166, 167 (2), 476 S.E.2d 263 (1996) (disapproved on other grounds, Toomer v. State, 292 Ga. 49, 734 S.E.2d 333 (2012)); see also George v. State, 263 Ga. App. 541, 588 S.E.2d 312 (2003).

[137]Ford v. State, 262 Ga. 558, 559-60, n. 1, 423 S.E.2d 245 (1992). Accord, Wilcher v. State, 231 Ga. App. 641, 642 (1), 500 S.E.2d 397 (1998). Cf. Osborne v. State, 263 Ga. 214, 216-17, 430 S.E.2d 576 (1993) (holding where the state accepted no similarly situated white prospective jurors undercuts any purported motive to exclude blacks).

venirepersons are almost identical.[138] In *Freeman v. State*,[139] the defendant argued that the prosecutor used his peremptory challenges in a racially discriminatory way by striking two black prospective jurors for reasons that were not applied to similarly situated jurors of other races. However, the Georgia Supreme Court upheld the state's use of its strikes and found that those persons who were not struck had "features" which distinguished them from the black venirepersons who were excused and made them more favorable to the state. In *Williams v. State*,[140] the Georgia Supreme Court reversed the conviction and granted the defendant a new trial where the prosecutor used peremptory strikes to exclude blacks who expressed hesitancy to impose the death penalty and who were related to or knew mentally ill persons even though these characteristics applied with equal force to white jurors whom the state accepted. In *Taylor v. State*,[141] the defendant accepted black venirepersons, but struck their white counterparts, who had friends on the jury or ties to law enforcement. The trial court held, and the appellate court affirmed, that these "strikes were not exercised in a race-neutral fashion." In *Ellerbee v. State*,[142] the court affirmed the trial judge in disallowing the defendant to use a peremptory strike against a white female because she was a crime victim and worked for Delta. The court had disallowed the strike and seated the white juror because the defendant accepted black jurors who had also been crime victims or had worked for Delta. But in *Byron v. State*,[143] the Court of Appeals upheld the trial judge's finding that the prosecutor's strike of a black male who went to school with the defendant was not discriminatory even though the state did not strike a similarly situated white male. The appellate court affirmed the trial judge's determination "even though [this court] may have reached a different conclusion. . . ."

C. STEP 3—THE TRIAL COURT'S DETERMINATION

Once a race-neutral explanation has been tendered, the trial court must then decide whether purposeful racial discrimination has been proven. At Step 3 the burden shifts back to the opponent of the strike to prove discrimi-

[138]Freeman v. State, 268 Ga. 181, 182 (1), 486 S.E.2d 161 (1997).

[139]Freeman v. State, 268 Ga. 181, 182 (1), 486 S.E.2d 161 (1997).

[140]Williams v. State, 262 Ga. 732, 733-34 (1), n. 3, 426 S.E.2d 348 (1993).

[141]Taylor v. State, 219 Ga. App. 475, 477 (2), 465 S.E.2d 473 (1995), rev. denied.

[142]Ellerbee v. State, 215 Ga. App. 312, 315-16 (7), 450 S.E.2d 443 (1994), overruled on other grounds, Felix v. State, 271 Ga. 534, 523 S.E.2d 1 (1999). See also, Nelson v. State, 271 Ga. App. 870, 611 S.E.2d 147 (2005).

[143]Byron v. State, 229 Ga. App. 795, 798 (5), 495 S.E.2d 123 (1997).

natory intent.[144] However, "[t]he opponent of a strike is not required to submit evidence which proves discriminatory intent during step three. Instead, the opponent may carry its burden of persuasion by reference to the facts and circumstances surrounding the proponent's use of its peremptory strikes."[145] Nevertheless "numbers alone may not . . . raise a prima facie inference that the strikes were exercised with discriminatory intent."[146] It is at this stage that implausible or fantastic justifications may (and probably will) be found to be pretexts for purposeful discrimination.[147]

In *McGlohon v. State*,[148] the court pointed out that "the number of . . . [the defendant's] strikes against women, the fact that . . . [the defendant] proffered a 'laundry list' of reasons for almost every strike, only some of which were facially neutral, and the indication that counsel was engaging in post hoc rationalization" raised some question as to the validity of the explanation. The court held that "the trial court's decision [to set aside two of his peremptory jury strikes] was well supported by the record."

"The ultimate inquiry for the [trial court] is not whether counsel's reason[s are] suspect, or weak, or irrational; but whether counsel is telling the truth in his or her assertion that the challenge is not race-based."[149] "There will seldom be much evidence bearing on that issue, and the best evidence often will be the demeanor of the attorney who exercises the challenge. As with the state of mind of a juror, evaluation of the prosecutor's state of mind based on demeanor and credibility lies peculiarly within a trial judge's province."[150]

---

[144]O'Neal v. State, 226 Ga. App. 224, 225, 482 S.E.2d 478 (1997); Burkett v. State, 230 Ga. App. 676, 677 (1), 497 S.E.2d 807 (1998); Mitchell v. State, 230 Ga. App. 149, 151, 495 S.E.2d 626 (1998). See Minor v. State, 328 Ga. App. 128, 761 S.E.2d 538 (2014) (error for trial court to refuse opponent of strike an opportunity to address proponent's race-neutral explanation for strike).

[145]Curry v. State, 238 Ga. App. 511, 514 (1)(b), 519 S.E.2d 269 (1999).

[146]Jones v. State, 246 Ga. App. 596 (1), 539 S.E.2d 602 (2000).

[147]Purkett v. Elem, 514 U.S. 765, 115 S.Ct. 1769, 131 L.Ed.2d 834 (1995).

[148]McGlohon v. State, 228 Ga. App. 726 (1), 492 S.E.2d 715 (1997) (implication).

[149]Smith v. State, 264 Ga. 449, 454, 448 S.E.2d 179 (1994) (quoting with approval United States v. Bentley-Smith, 2 F.3d 1368, 1375 (5th Cir. 1993)). Cf. Ridley v. State, 235 Ga. App. 591, 595 (1), (3), 510 S.E.2d 113 (1998).

[150]Hernandez v. New York, 500 U.S. 352, 365, 111 S.Ct. 1859, 114 L.Ed.2d 395 (1991) (plurality opinion); Gardner v. State, 225 Ga. App. 427, 428, 483 S.E.2d 912 (1997); Hightower v. State, 220 Ga. App. 165, 166, 469 S.E.2d 295 (1996); Smith v. State, 264 Ga. 449, 454, 448 S.E.2d 179 (1994).

In *McKenzie v. State*,[151] the court pointed out that "the trial court in most cases must infer discriminatory intent [if it is to be found] from circumstantial evidence. 'The factfinder's disbelief of the reasons put forward by the defendant (particularly if disbelief is accompanied by a suspicion of mendacity) may, together with the elements of the prima facie case, suffice to show intentional discrimination. Thus, rejection of the defendant's proffered reasons . . . will *permit* the trier of fact to infer the ultimate fact of intentional discrimination. . . .'" (Emphasis in original.)

In *Williams v. State*,[152] the court pointed out that "'[w]here . . . the [trial] court combines steps two and three of *Batson,* it prematurely evaluates the persuasiveness of counsel's explanation [and] thereby impermissibly . . . [places] the ultimate burden of persuasion upon the proponent of the strike. . . . The ultimate burden of persuasion regarding . . . motivation rests with, and never shifts from, the opponent of the strike.'"

In *Ruffin v. State*,[153] the court pointed out that the decision of the trial judge "rests largely upon assessment of the prosecutor's state of mind and credibility. . . . The trial court's factual findings must be given great deference and may be disregarded only if clearly erroneous." Recognizing this evidentiary problem, then Justice Benham suggested that trial judges use the following criteria to evaluate the striking party's explanation for a suspect peremptory challenge:[154]

(1) susceptibility of the particular case to racial influences;[155]

(2) statements made during voir dire;

(3) race of victim and primary witnesses;

(4) the prosecutor's demeanor;

(5) patterns, if any, of discrimination by the prosecutor's office[156] (lack of pattern alone should not exempt the explanation from rigorous scrutiny); and

(6) the method of questioning and treatment of similarly situated jurors of a different race.

---

[151]McKenzie v. State, 227 Ga. App. 778, 779, 490 S.E.2d 522 (1997).

[152]Williams v. State, 249 Ga. App. 292, 295, 548 S.E.2d 63 (2001).

[153]Ruffin v. State, 232 Ga. App. 614, 615 (2), 502 S.E.2d 551 (1998) (quoting Byron v. State, 229 Ga. App. 795, 495 S.E.2d 123 (1997)).

[154]Mallory v. State, 261 Ga. 625, 635, 409 S.E.2d 839 (1991) (Benham, J., concurring), overruled on other grounds, Clark v. State, 271 Ga. 6, 515 S.E.2d 155 (1999).

[155]Gardner v. State, 225 Ga. App. 427, 429, 483 S.E.2d 912 (1997) (trial court can rely on its knowledge of the community in relation to the explanations offered).

[156]Gardner v. State, 225 Ga. App. 427, 429, 483 S.E.2d 912 (1997) (trial court can rely on its knowledge of the party utilizing the strike in relation to the explanations offered).

In *McBride v. State*,[157] the court emphasized that in these cases the question is not whether the person striking gave a "sufficient" or "sufficient race neutral reason," the question "is whether the strike was motivated by discriminatory intent." Thus it is error for the trial court to focus simply on the sufficiency of the reason given for the strike in determining the ultimate issue of whether the state had proven intentional discrimination.

In *Chavarria v. State*,[158] the court held that there "is no requirement that the State's racially neutral explanation . . . be supported by" facts revealed during voir dire. The court then affirmed the trial court in refusing to permit defense counsel to cross-examine the district attorney about the source of his information and allowing him to introduce evidence.

However, the persuasiveness of a proffered explanation may be magnified or diminished by the persuasiveness of companion explanations, and by the strength of the prima facie case.[159] "A court . . . may be less troubled by one relatively weak explanation for striking a black juror when all the remaining explanations are persuasive than where several of the prosecutor's proffered justifications are questionable."[160] Where multiple racially-neutral reasons are given for the peremptory strike of a black juror, a Batson violation does *not* exist simply because one or more of those racially-neutral reasons was not used to strike white potential jurors.[161] The trial court's findings are entitled to great deference and will be affirmed unless clearly erroneous.[162]

In *Miller-El v. Cockrell*,[163] the United States Supreme Court clarified the third stage of a Batson challenge in stating that "the critical question in determining whether an [individual] has proved purposeful discrimination . . . is the persuasiveness of the prosecutor's justification for his peremptory strike." In the

---

[157]McBride v. State, 247 Ga. App. 767, 769, 545 S.E.2d 332 (2001).

[158]Chavarria v. State, 248 Ga. App. 398, 402 (2), 546 S.E.2d 811 (2001).

[159]Gamble v. State, 257 Ga. 325, 327 (5), 357 S.E.2d 792 (1987).

[160]Gamble v. State, 257 Ga. 325, 327 (5), 357 S.E.2d 792 (1987). In this regard the Georgia Court of Appeals, in Gay v. State, 258 Ga. App. 634(1), 574 S.E.2d 861 (2002), overruled Ayiteyfio v. State, 254 Ga. App. 1, 561 S.E.2d 157 (2002) to the extent it prohibits a trial judge from inferring racial motivation from the totality of the circumstances surrounding the voir dire conducted in a case and in doing so was sharply critical of the

"multiple reasons" analysis of *Batson / McCollum* challenges.

[161]Smith v. State, 264 Ga. 449, 452, 448 S.E.2d 179 (1994) (citing Lingo v. State, 263 Ga. 664, 667-68 (1), 437 S.E.2d 463 (1993)). Compare Rector v. State, 213 Ga. App. 450, 454-55, 444 S.E.2d 862 (1994) (one racially-motivated reason vitiates multiple racially-neutral reasons).

[162]Batson v. Kentucky, 476 U.S. 79, 98, n. 21, 106 S.Ct. 1712, 90 L.Ed.2d 69 (1986); Gamble v. State, 257 Ga. 325, 327 (5), 357 S.E.2d 792 (1987).

[163]Miller-El v. Cockrell, 537 U.S. 322, 123 S.Ct. 1029, 154 L.Ed.2d 931 (2003).

event that a prosecutor's justifications seem "implausible," the issue becomes whether or not the trial court finds the prosecutor to be credible.[164] The *Cockrell* opinion went on to explain that "[c]redibility can be measured by . . . the prosecutor's demeanor; by how reasonable or how improbable the explanations are; and by whether the proffered rationale has some basis in accepted trial strategy."[165]

In 2005, following a finding by the Fifth Circuit that *Miller-El* failed to show by clear and convincing evidence that the state court's finding of no discrimination was wrong, *Miller-El v. Cockrell* was again accepted for review by the United States Supreme Court, this time as *Miller-El v. Dretke*.[166] In *Dretke*, the Supreme Court again found the prosecution's explanations for the striking of prospective black jurors unpersuasive. Writing for the Court, Justice Souter commented on the appeals court's "substitution of [its own] reasoning" for that of the prosecutor, stating, ". . . [W]hen legitimate grounds like race are in issue, a prosecutor simply has got to state his reasons as best he can and stand or fall on the plausibility of the reasons he gives. A *Batson* challenge does not call for a mere exercise in thinking up any rational basis. If the stated reason does not hold up, its pretextual significance does not fade because a trial judge, or an appeals court, can imagine a reason that might not have been shown up as false." In so holding, the court found the Fifth Circuit's conclusion "as unsupportable as the 'dismissive and strained interpretation' of his evidence that we disapproved when we decided Miller-El was entitled to a certificate of appealability."[167] Thus, because the Court found that the prosecution's proffered reasons for striking prospective black jurors were equally applicable to white jurors who were not struck, the case was remanded for entry of judgment for the petitioner.[168]

---

[164]Miller-El v. Cockrell, 537 U.S. 322, 123 S.Ct. 1029, 154 L.Ed.2d 931 (2003). See Stokes v. State, 281 Ga. 825, 642 S.E.2d 82 (2007), where the Georgia Supreme Court noted in the context of a *McCollum* challenge that the trial court's determination of the credibility of a racially-neutral reason for a strike is to be given great deference.

[165]Miller-El v. Cockrell, 537 U.S. 322, 123 S.Ct. 1029, 154 L.Ed.2d 931 (2003). See Foster v. Chatman, 136 S. Ct. 1737, 195 L. Ed. 2d 1 (2016) (shifting explanations offered by prosecutors to justify strikes of two black

jurors led to conclusion that the real basis for the strikes was race).

[166]Miller-El v. Dretke, 545 U.S. 231, 125 S. Ct. 2317, 162 L. Ed. 2d 196 (2005).

[167]Miller-El v. Dretke, 545 U.S. 231, 125 S. Ct. 2317, 162 L. Ed. 2d 196 (2005), quoting Miller-El v. Cockrell, 537 U.S. 322, 123 S.Ct. 1029, 154 L.Ed.2d 931 (2003).

[168]In his dissent, Justice Breyer suggested that peremptory challenges should be eliminated altogether, writing that the *Batson* analysis fails to ferret out racial discrimination in jury selection, essentially requiring judges

D. THE REMEDY FOR A SUCCESSFUL *BATSON* CHALLENGE

Although the United States Supreme Court expressly declined in *Batson* to dictate procedures to remedy a violation discovered at the trial level, the Court did identify two possible solutions: (1) to discharge the venire and select a new jury from a panel not previously associated with the case, or (2) to disallow the discriminatory challenges and resume selection with the improperly challenged jurors reinstated on the venire.[169] A third possibility is substituting an alternate juror or jurors for the improperly excused juror or jurors if there are sufficient alternates.[170]

It appears that the trend among Georgia trial courts is to seat an improperly challenged panel member on the jury for trial. This approach should be consistent with *Batson's* directive to fashion appropriate methods because an individual juror has the right not to be discriminated against in the selection process.[171] In *Brown v. State*,[172] the trial judge used a silent strike for jury selection. After the state made out a prima facie case of discrimination, the court implicitly rejected the defendant's race-neutral explanations and "reinstated" three of the white jurors. The Court of Appeals affirmed and held that "[w]hen a Batson challenge results in a finding that jury selection was not racially neutral and when . . . the jurors remain unaware of the party

---

to engage in "the awkward, sometimes hopeless, task of second-guessing a prosecutor's instinctive judgment-the underlying basis for which may be invisible even to the prosecutor exercising the challenge."

There is no federal constitutional right to peremptory challenges. United States v. Martinez-Salazar, 528 U.S. 304, 120 S.Ct. 774, 145 L.Ed.2d 792 (2000). Thus, if a defendant loses a peremptory strike because a state trial court improperly, but in good faith, grants the prosecutor's *McCollum* challenge and reseats a juror struck by the defense, it is for each state to decide whether the error is harmless or error per se. Rivera v. Illinois, 556 U.S. 148, 129 S.Ct. 1446, 173 L.Ed.2d 320 (2009).

[169]Batson v. Kentucky, 476 U.S. 79, 99-100, n. 24, 106 S.Ct. 1712, 90 L.Ed.2d 69 (1986). Accord, Eppinger v. State, 231 Ga. App. 614, 616 (5), 500 S.E.2d 383 (1998).

[170]The third possibility may be less

acceptable since in Powers v. Ohio, 499 U.S. 400, 111 S.Ct. 1364, 113 L.Ed.2d 411, 422 (1991), the court referred to the right of a juror not to be excluded from the jury on account of race.

[171]See Batson v. Kentucky, 476 U.S. 79, 86-87, 106 S.Ct. 1712, 90 L.Ed.2d 69 (1986); Ellerbee v. State, 215 Ga. App. 312, 316, 450 S.E.2d 443 (1994), overruled on other grounds, Felix v. State, 271 Ga. 534, 523 S.E.2d 1 (1999); Lewis v. State, 262 Ga. 679, 680, 424 S.E.2d 626 (1993); Eppinger v. State, 231 Ga. App. 614, 616 (5), 500 S.E.2d 383 (1998).

[172]Brown v. State, 218 Ga. App. 469, 471 (3), 462 S.E.2d 420 (1995). In a paper delivered at the Superior Court Judges Summer Seminar of 1994, Judge Coursey suggested that trial judges should use the "silent strike" method of civil jury selection in criminal trials. In 1997 Update and Revision to Judge Coursey's paper, Judge Dempsey joined in this recommendation.

who struck them, reinstating improperly challenged jurors does not abridge the defendant's right to a fair and impartial jury."[173] However, the opposite result is obtained where jurors are present when the parties announce their strikes. In such a case, it would be reversible error to reseat a juror who is aware that he or she had been the subject of a challenge by one of the parties.[174]

In *McKibbons v. State*,[175] it was not error for the trial judge to seat as jurors the five white panel members that defendant struck through discriminatory use of peremptory challenges. In *Ellerbee v. State*,[176] the defendant exercised a peremptory strike against juror no. 70, a white female. After the trial judge determined that the reason for the strike was discriminatory, the parties were ordered to "restrike" the jury. When the defendant again tried to strike juror no. 70, the trial judge seated her on the jury. The Georgia Court of Appeals affirmed. In *Gardner v. State*,[177] the trial court granted the state's McCollum motion and placed two white panel members on the jury after the black defendant improperly used his peremptory strikes against them. In *Ledford v. State*,[178] the trial court refused to accept the prosecutor's explanation for striking a black male from the venire and sat the improperly challenged juror.

§ 18:32 Points for consideration in jury selection

In a sense, a party does not select a jury but rather tries to excuse those persons whom he feels will be biased against his client. Each side wants as many jurors on the panel as possible who will be favorable to "his side of the case."

In determining which jurors a defendant or the state wishes to leave on the jury, a number of factors warrant consideration. A good approach is to try to determine the characteristics of the ideal juror for your side of the case. Consideration should be given to age, sex, occupation, education, religion, military service, relation to law enforcement, and past experience with crime, particularly whether the juror has ever been the victim of a crime similar to the one charged in the indictment. Former jury experience is also important. The juror should then be rated as to each

---

[173]Brown v. State, 218 Ga. App. 469, 472, 462 S.E.2d 420 (1995). See Holmes v. State, 273 Ga. 644 (2), 543 S.E.2d 688 (2001).

[174]Gaines v. State, 258 Ga. App. 902(3), 575 S.E.2d 704 (2002).

[175]McKibbons v. State, 216 Ga. App. 389, 391, 455 S.E.2d 293 (1995), rev. denied.

[176]Ellerbee v. State, 215 Ga. App. 312, 315-16 (7), 450 S.E.2d 443 (1994), overruled on other grounds, Felix v. State, 271 Ga. 534, 523 S.E.2d 1 (1999).

[177]Gardner v. State, 225 Ga. App. 427, 429, 483 S.E.2d 912 (1997) (physical precedent).

[178]Ledford v. State, 207 Ga. App. 705, 706 (1), 429 S.E.2d 124 (1993).

criterion. After being weighed in the light of the particular case, a juror will probably have some pluses and some minuses. If he is completely unsuitable, you will naturally want to strike him, and if he is completely ideal for your side of the case, the opposition will strike him anyway. While the process may be overly complicated for the run-of-the-mill case, it helps to get the attorney thinking of the kind of juror he wants in the case.

It must be kept in mind that at least most of the time no one characteristic or factor will determine whether or not a person will be a good juror for a particular case. It is normally a weighing of the pluses and minuses together with consideration of the next person who is to be considered as a juror if the first is excused.

Besides the factors listed above, thought must be given to the ability of the district attorney, defense counsel, defendant or an important prosecution witness to relate to the juror. Investigation of venire in advance of trial can also bring to light background information which may be helpful in determining whether to excuse a particular juror.

The importance of voir dire examination, discussed subsequently, cannot be overemphasized in selecting a jury. It should always be remembered that the manner in which a juror thinks is probably of more importance than which one of the opposing attorneys he knows. Of course, if the relationship between the juror and the opposing attorney is so close that it will alter the juror's thinking, then he will probably have to be excused.

In the most general terms, accountants, bankers, military officers, and those related to law enforcement are usually thought of as good prosecution jurors. Property owners are normally good prosecution jurors in burglary cases. The artist, actor, salesman, and the individual who has traveled extensively or lived in a number of different locations, are usually thought to be good defense jurors.

The race of the juror may be important. If the defendant is black and the juror is black, the juror may well identify better with the defendant. But if the crime was committed against another black, the black juror may regard it more seriously than a white juror. Also, in general terms, the idea exists that blacks, Italians, and those of Spanish descent make good defense jurors, whereas the Swiss, the English and particularly the Germans make better prosecution jurors.

§ 18:33 Methods of striking a jury

Rule 11 of the Uniform Rules for the Superior Courts provides as follows:

"After completion of the examination of jurors upon their voir dire, the parties and their counsel shall be entitled, upon request, to 15 minutes to prepare for jury selection; thereafter, during the selection of jurors, the court in its discretion, upon first warning counsel, may restrict to not less than 1 minute the time within which each party may exercise a peremptory challenge; a party shall forfeit a challenge by failing to exercise it within the time allowed."

There are two general methods of striking a jury in a criminal case. If either party insists upon it, an individual voir dire examination of all the jurors on the panel must be conducted before any jurors are stricken.[1] This practice applies to both felony and misdemeanor cases.[2] Where this method is used, the actual striking is done in the same manner as that described below with the exception that all voir dire questions are asked before the striking begins.

The second way of striking a jury is to have the name of a potential juror called and for the state, followed by the defendant, to ask the juror voir dire questions. The state then decides whether to reject or accept the juror. If the juror is rejected, he is excused; but if he is accepted by the state, he is then passed on by the defendant, who either accepts or excuses him. If the defendant accepts a juror, the state may not strike or excuse him.[3] The process continues until 12 jurors, plus such alternates as the judge may determine, are accepted.[4]

In *Blair v. State*,[5] the Georgia Supreme Court held that when the trial judge finds a Batson violation in the case of one or more jurors, the trial court may return such juror or jurors to the jury panel. In view of *Batson* (§ 18:31, supra) it has been suggested that courts use a "silent strike" procedure in criminal cases as well as in civil cases to avoid prejudicing any of the potential jurors against either party. This method may be useful if there is

---

[Section 18:33]

[1]Ladd v. State, 228 Ga. 113 (1), 184 S.E.2d 158 (1971); Blount v. State, 214 Ga. 433, 434 (3), 105 S.E.2d 304 (1958).

[2]Thomas v. State, 247 Ga. 7, 273 S.E.2d 396 (1981); Reid v. State, 129 Ga. App. 657 (1), 200 S.E.2d 454 (1973).

[3]O.C.G.A. § 15-12-166; Sakobie v. State, 115 Ga. App. 460 (2), 154 S.E.2d 830 (1967). However, where a prosecutor overlooked a remaining strike or was misinformed by the clerk regarding the number of strikes remaining and in the absence of any harm to the

defense, a trial court may allow the state to use a remaining strike to remove a juror previously noted as acceptable to both parties. See e.g., Cox v. State, 293 Ga. App. 98 (2), 666 S.E.2d 379 (2008); Thompkins v. State, 181 Ga. App. 158 (2), 351 S.E.2d 475 (1986).

[4]Denham v. State, 218 Ga. App. 191, 192 (2)(b), 460 S.E.2d 869 (1995).

[5]Blair v. State, 267 Ga. 166, 167 (2), 476 S.E.2d 263 (1996) (disapproved on other grounds, Toomer v. State, 292 Ga. 49, 734 S.E.2d 333 (2012)).

a Batson objection and one or more of the peremptory strikes are later denied by the trial judge. This procedure provides that a list of all potential jurors be prepared and that the list be passed first to the prosecutor allowing him or her to silently indicate whether a particular juror is accepted or excused and then passed to the defense counsel to allow him or her to silently indicate the same. The process of passing the list would be repeated until the jury and desired number of alternates have been selected.

After the jury is selected, the trial judge may conduct a bench conference to determine if there are any objections to the jury as selected. The trial judge may have the venire removed from the courtroom before hearing and ruling on any Batson challenge.[6]

In *Henry v. State,*[7] the court approved the following method of striking jurors where two defendants are being tried together: "The first juror should be placed on the State and if accepted, then on defendant A. If accepted by defendant A, then [the juror should be placed] on defendant B. The second juror should be placed on the State and if accepted, then [the second juror should be placed] on defendant B. If accepted by defendant B, then [the second juror should be placed] on defendant A. Defendants A and B should be alternated in this manner and this procedure followed until the jury is selected."

Regardless of the procedure utilized, either party may move for an individually sequestered voir dire examination of each person on the panel. The granting or denying of the motion lies in the sound discretion of the trial judge.[8] An individual examination of each of the jurors normally takes longer but tends to largely eliminate the danger of one potential juror making statements which might bias others on the panel.[9] In *Wallace v. State,*[10] the defendant's written motion for individual voir dire had been granted. However, another judge presided at the trial. His refusal to permit individual voir dire was reversible error.

"For the trial of misdemeanors in all courts, each party may demand a full panel of 12 competent and impartial jurors from which to select a jury . . . ." O.C.G.A. § 15-12-125.

Prior to July 1, 2005, the defense had four and the state had

---

[6]The "silent strike" was suggested by Judge Daniel M. Coursey, Jr., of the DeKalb Superior Court at the Summer 1994 Seminar of the Council of Superior Court Judges at St. Simons Island, Georgia.

[7]Henry v. State, 256 Ga. 313, 314, 348 S.E.2d 640 (1986).

[8]See Parham v. State, 135 Ga. App. 315, 319 (4), 217 S.E.2d 493 (1975); Pass v. State, 227 Ga. 730, 735

(8), 182 S.E.2d 779 (1971).

[9]In the event of such an outburst, which may result in influencing other jurors, a challenge to the array should be filed, since a motion for a mistrial may not be made before the jury is sworn. Ferguson v. State, 219 Ga. 33, 34 (3), 131 S.E.2d 538 (1963).

[10]Wallace v. State, 164 Ga. App. 642, 298 S.E.2d 627 (1982).

two peremptory strikes. After that date, however, the defendant and the state each have three strikes.[11] The state strikes first, giving the defendant the last opportunity for a strike.

See § 18:24, supra, on prejudicial remark of juror during selection. See § 18:30, supra, on number of strikes.

§ 18:34 Swearing a jury—The oath

As soon as the jury is selected, the jurors should be sworn[1] by the *judge* or the *clerk*.[2] However, even in a death penalty case, if the oath is administered by the district attorney without objection, this does not constitute reversible error.[3]

O.C.G.A. § 15-12-139 prescribes the use of the following oath:

You shall well and truly try the issue formed upon this bill of indictment (or accusation) between the State of Georgia and (name of accused), who is charged with (here state the crime or offense), and a true verdict give according to the evidence. So help you God.

The same oath is given to alternate jurors if they have been selected.[4]

It has been held that the failure to administer the oath cannot be waived.[5] Indeed, a verdict of acquittal rendered by an unsworn jury is a nullity and will not bar a retrial since jeopardy never at-

---

[11]O.C.G.A. § 15-12-125.

[Section 18:34]

[1]However, it is not error to let the jury disperse after being selected but before being sworn. Gamble v. State, 141 Ga. App. 304 (1), 233 S.E.2d 264 (1977). The failure of the court to swear the jury prior to some preliminary instructions is not error. The oath need only be administered prior to the presentation of evidence. Thomas v. State, 282 Ga. App. 522(2), 639 S.E.2d 531 (2006).

[2]Ates v. State, 155 Ga. App. 97, 98, 270 S.E.2d 455 (1980).

[3]Gilreath v. State, 247 Ga. 814, 824 (4), 279 S.E.2d 650 (1981).

[4]O.C.G.A. § 15-12-170.

[5]Adams v. State, 286 Ga. 496, 690 S.E.2d 171 (2010); Keller v. State, 261 Ga. App. 769, 583 S.E.2d 591 (2003); Smith v. State, 122 Ga. App. 98(1), 176 S.E.2d 284 (1970). However,

in another Smith v. State, 235 Ga. 852, 221 S.E.2d 601 (1976), the court pointed out that if the record fails to show that the jury was sworn, the district attorney may move to amend the transcript and after a hearing and introduction of evidence, the trial judge may determine whether or not it was sworn. The record may be supplemented by such a hearing and the conclusion of the court.

In Fedd v. State, 298 Ga. App. 508 (1), 680 S.E.2d 453 (2009), the court held that an oath administered *after* the presentation of the evidence but before jury deliberations commenced was sufficient in the absence of any showing of harm as a result thereof.

In State v. Desai, 337 Ga. App. 873, 789 S.E.2d 222 (2016) (failure of the trial court to administer the oath after deliberations begin but before verdict is not timely and renders the verdict "a mere nullity").

tached to the first trial in the absence of a properly sworn jury.[6] However, in *Stokes v. State,*[7] the court stated that "[t]he courts of this State have consistently held that the failure of the record to reflect whether the jury is sworn does not constitute reversible error." In *Grant v. State,*[8] the court pointed out that to establish that a "verdict" is void, "[i]t must appear affirmatively that the jury was not sworn. If an appellant claims that the jury was not sworn, his or her remedy is to have the record corrected by following the provisions of O.C.G.A. § 5-6-41(f)," which provides for the correction of a transcript, *i.e.,* the official notation that the jury was not sworn. The administration of a defective oath may be waived by the defendant's acquiescence until after the verdict.[9] The better practice is to administer the oath before the opening statements of counsel, however, failure to administer the oath until after the presentation of the evidence is not error in the absence of an actual showing of prejudice.[10]

O.C.G.A. § 15-12-167 contains a provision which enables the trial judge, before the introduction of evidence, to hold a hearing to determine the competency of a juror or to disprove an answer he gave on voir dire. If the juror is found to be incompetent, the judge may remove him and permit the selection of another juror. Thus, in *Norris v. State,*[11] the court held that the trial judge did not err in excusing a juror because he was a convicted felon and replacing the juror with the first alternate juror. See § 10:9, supra, on whether a convicted juror may serve on a jury. In *White v. State,*[12] the court held that the same procedure was authorized if it was determined that a juror had not answered material ques-

---

[6]Spencer v. State, 281 Ga. 533, 640 S.E.2d 267 (2007).

[7]Stokes v. State, 206 Ga. App. 781 (1), 426 S.E.2d 573 (1992).

[8]Grant v. State, 237 Ga. App. 892, 893 (1), 515 S.E.2d 872 (1999), rev'd, 272 Ga. 213, 528 S.E.2d 512 (2000), "because the State [concedes] . . . that the jury oath . . . was never administered."

[9]Smith v. State, 63 Ga. 168, 169 (9) (1879); Colbert v. State, 178 Ga. App. 657, 658, 344 S.E.2d 479 (1986).

[10]Adams v. State, 286 Ga. 496, 690 S.E.2d 171 (2010).

[11]Norris v. State, 250 Ga. 38 (1), 295 S.E.2d 321 (1982).

[12]White v. State, 154 Ga. App. 527, 268 S.E.2d 790 (1980).

In Baxter v. State, 159 Ga. App.

632 (1), 284 S.E.2d 649 (1981), after the jury had been selected but before it was sworn, a juror informed the trial judge that he knew the defendant's brother. The state was permitted to peremptorily strike this juror. The Court of Appeals affirmed the defendant's conviction.

In Neal v. State, 160 Ga. App. 834, 836 (2), 288 S.E.2d 241 (1982), after the jury had been sworn but before the introduction of evidence, the judge received a note from a juror stating that the juror "could not conscientiously find a person guilty irrespective of the quality or quantum of evidence if the defendant continued to protest his innocence. . . ." The judge conducted a hearing, excused the juror, and caused the alternate to be seated on the jury. The Court of Appeals affirmed and pointed out that the trial

tions correctly.

In *Rhodes v. State*,[13] the Supreme Court approved the trial court's decision to re-open voir dire to inquire about a juror's possible bias after the jury had been selected but before it had been sworn. The court declined to find that the trial court had abused its discretion by denying the defense's request to question the juror outside the presence of the other jurors.

See § 18:19, supra, and § 18:35, infra, on excusal of a juror by the judge. See § 18:13, supra, on preliminary oath.

§ 18:35   Alternate jurors

O.C.G.A. § 15-12-168 provides that in a felony case which, in the opinion of the trial judge, is likely to be protracted, after the jury has been sworn one or more additional alternate jurors may be called. Alternate jurors must be drawn from the same source and in the same manner and have the same qualifications as the jurors previously sworn. They are subject to the same voir dire examination and challenges. The state and the defendant are entitled to as many peremptory challenges to the alternates as there are alternate jurors to be selected. "The peremptory challenges allowed to the state and to the defendant in such event shall be in addition to the regular number of peremptory challenges allowed in criminal cases to the defendant and to the state. . . . When two or more defendants are tried jointly, the number and manner of exercising peremptory challenges shall be determined as provided in Code Section 17-8-4."[1] See § 18:30, supra, on number of peremptory strikes.

As previously pointed out, the alternate jurors take the same oath as the one already administered to the jury. They are to "be seated near the jury, with equal opportunity for seeing and hearing the proceedings, and shall attend at all times upon the trial with the jury. They shall obey all orders and admonitions of the court to the jury."[2]

In *Perry v. State*,[3] the court held that it was not error for a trial

---

judge for good cause could excuse a juror at any time and substitute an alternate juror.

[13]Rhodes v. State, 264 Ga. 123, 441 S.E.2d 748 (1994). See Wilmore v. State, 268 Ga. App. 646, 602 S.E.2d 343 (2004); Kelly v. State, 255 Ga. App. 813, 567 S.E.2d 36 (2002).

[Section 18:35]

[1]O.C.G.A. § 15-12-169.1. Prior to 2005, the state was entitled to as

many peremptory challenges to alternates as there were alternate jurors called. A single defendant was entitled to twice that number.

[2]O.C.G.A. § 15-12-170.

[3]Perry v. State, 255 Ga. 490, 493 (5), 339 S.E.2d 922 (1986).

judge to recall an alternate juror to replace a juror who was disqualified to serve because he had served on the grand jury which
had indicted the defendant. Here the jury had retired to deliberate and the alternate had gone home.

In *Darden v. State*,[4] a juror was seen talking with the defendant
during a recess. The trial judge determined that nothing improper
had taken place, but excused the juror and replaced her with an
alternate. The court held that the judge had discretion to discharge a juror and replace him or her at any time if there was a
sound legal basis for the action.

In *Payne v. State*,[5] after the close of the evidence, the district
attorney moved to have a juror removed because defense counsel
had briefly represented the juror. The district attorney failed to
see the juror raise his hand when the jurors were asked if any of
them had been represented by counsel. The court found no error
in the removal of the juror and substitution of an alternate. In
Smith v. State,[6] the trial judge excused a juror on the second day
of trial because she informed the judge she had to undergo emergency dental surgery. Over defense objection that the judge
should have further investigated the request for excusal, an
alternate was substituted. The appellate court affirmed and
pointed out that the judge was "under no obligation to consult
with a doctor to confirm the need to excuse an ill juror."

In *Scott v. State*,[7] about two and one-half hours after jury
deliberations began and while the trial judge had begun trying
another case, the foreperson notified the trial judge, "in writing,
'We have an ill juror.' The court responded, 'Does it appear that
the juror is unable to continue on the case?' To which the foreman responded, 'Yes.' At that point the court replaced the sick
juror with the alternate, without consulting the State or Scott."
The appellate court pointed out that the judge "did not make . . .
[an] independent determination that the juror was in fact ill and
could not complete deliberations [as the court should have done]."
The defendant and his attorney were not present when the juror
was excused. Also, the appellate court pointed out that the
excusal of the juror in the absence of the defendant cannot be
regarded as harmless. See § 17:8, supra, on the necessity of the
defendant's presence.

---

[4]Darden v. State, 212 Ga. App. 345, 347 (4), 441 S.E.2d 816 (1994).

[5]Payne v. State, 195 Ga. App. 523, 524 (2), 394 S.E.2d 781 (1990).

[6]Smith v. State, 266 Ga. 827, 829 (2), 470 S.E.2d 674 (1996). See also Harris v. State, 278 Ga. 596, 604 S.E.2d 788 (2004) (finding trial court did not abuse its discretion in seating an alternate juror when one of the original jurors failed to report for duty on the second day of trial.)

[7]Scott v. State, 219 Ga. App. 798, 799 (2), 466 S.E.2d 678 (1996).

In *Wooten v. State,*[8] the court affirmed the dismissal of a juror during deliberations where the juror indicated he knew the defendant and had no intention of considering the testimony of the alleged victim.

In *Stokes v. State,*[9] the trial court replaced two jurors with alternates when the two jurors would not decide whether the defendant was guilty or innocent "because they fe[lt] that there ha[d] not been enough evidence either way." This was found to be error and prejudicial to the defendant when the "court made no attempt to inquire into the jurors' reasons for not voting" and there had been no "showing that the jurors were in any way incapacitated."

A defendant has the right to be present at any time that the court changes the composition of the jury by removing or excusing a juror from further duty. In the absence of an explicit waiver by the defendant, a unilateral decision by the court, even with the consent of counsel, is prejudicial error.[10]

See § 18:7, supra, on call of jurors for a particular case. Also see § 24:15, infra, on alternate jurors during deliberations. See § 18:34, supra, on substituting an alternate juror for one of the original 12. See § 24:24, infra, on replacement of a juror.

§ 18:36 Pre-trial instructions

It is not error for a trial judge, prior to the introduction of evidence, to inform the jury of the procedural aspects of the trial insofar as the attorneys, jury, and court are concerned.[1] A 1976 case encouraged a "pre-evidentiary" charge given to the jury covering the definition of reasonable doubt, conflicts in evidence, the necessity of objections, the purpose of closing arguments, and the charge of the court.[2] The appellate court stated that the procedure was not error, but rather a commendable effort to educate lay persons as to trial procedures.[3] Similar "pre-evidentiary" charges to the jury are presently being adopted by many able trial jurists.[4] However, it is not error for the trial judge to refuse

---

[8]Wooten v. State, 250 Ga. App. 686, 552 S.E.2d 878 (2001).

[9]Stokes v. State, 204 Ga. App. 141, 418 S.E.2d 419 (1992).

[10]See Ward v. State, 288 Ga. 641, 706 S.E.2d 430 (2011).

[Section 18:36]

[1]Paulhill v. State, 229 Ga. 415, 416 (1), 191 S.E.2d 842 (1972).

[2]Decker v. State, 139 Ga. App. 707, 708 (4), 229 S.E.2d 520 (1976).

[3]Cf. Oliver v. State, 168 Ga. App. 477, 478 (4), 309 S.E.2d 627 (1983); Edmonds v. State, 196 Ga. App. 190, 195 (1), 395 S.E.2d 566 (1990); Blandburg v. State, 209 Ga. App. 752, 753 (2), 434 S.E.2d 510 (1993).

[4]Rule 513(b) of the Uniform Rules of Criminal Procedure provides as follows:

"Rule 513. [Trial Jurors.]

to give a pre-evidentiary charge even when requested.[5]

It has been said that pre-trial instructions may to some extent be relied upon by the court and perhaps not be repeated in the final charge.[6] However, in *Farmer v. State*,[7] the court held that "a pre-evidentiary statement is not the equivalent of a jury charge; even if a portion thereof had been incorrect, where the principles of law were thoroughly covered in the main charge, the initial statement would not have misled the jury and would be harmless error." In *Blandburg v. State*,[8] the court held that preliminary instructions before the introduction of evidence "cannot serve as a substitute for a complete jury charge . . . after the evidence is closed. . . ."

In *Honeycutt v. State*,[9] the court pointed out that the "[t]rial court's failure to reiterate after closing arguments its preliminary charge on the standard of proof and definition of 'beyond a reasonable doubt' was reversible error."

See § 18:4, supra, on orientation of jurors. See § 18:14, supra, on pre-voir dire instructions. See § 24:2, infra, on the necessity of repeating pre-trial instructions at the end of the case after arguments have been completed.

§ 18:37 Sequestration of jury

In a case in which the death penalty is not being sought, it has been held that generally it is not error for the trial judge with proper instructions to excuse a jury after it has been selected and sworn and to have the jury report back for the commencement of

---

"**(b) Admonitions.** The court shall give the jurors appropriate admonitions regarding their conduct during the case. These shall include admonitions:

"(1) Not to communicate with other jurors or anyone else upon any subject connected with the trial nor form or express any opinion thereon until the case is finally submitted to the jury;

"(2) To report promptly to the court any incident involving an attempt by any person improperly to influence any member of the jury or a violation by any juror of any of the court's admonitions; and

"(3) Not to read, listen to, or view any news reports concerning the case; the court shall explain the reasons for this admonition."

[5]See Cagle v. State, 160 Ga. App. 803, 287 S.E.2d 660 (1982).

[6]See Bigby v. State, 146 Ga. App. 500, 246 S.E.2d 496 (1978). Contra, People v. Cardinale, 35 A.D.2d 1073, 316 N.Y.S.2d 369 (1970).

[7]Farmer v. State, 180 Ga. App. 720, 721 (1), 350 S.E.2d 583 (1986); Massey v. State, 270 Ga. 76, 77 (2)(b), 508 S.E.2d 149 (1998).

[8]Blandburg v. State, 209 Ga. App. 752, 753 (2), 434 S.E.2d 510 (1993). Accord, Little v. State, 230 Ga. App. 803, 805 (2), 498 S.E.2d 284 (1998).

[9]Honeycutt v. State, 245 Ga. App. 819, 821 (3), 538 S.E.2d 870 (2000).

the trial several days later.[1]

Under present Georgia law, the trial judge may, in his discretion, permit the jury to disperse under proper instructions either before or during their deliberations, except in cases in which the district attorney is seeking the death penalty.[2] The above rule applies after the jury has been selected and before they are sworn as set out in O.C.G.A. § 15-12-139.[3] Even in a capital case, the trial judge may allow prospective jurors to disperse under proper instructions during voir dire and before being selected. However, after a jury has been selected in a capital case, the jurors must be sequestered,[4] unless the defendant[5] or perhaps defense counsel[6] consents to their dispersal. See § 14:93, supra, on sequestration of a jury to determine competency to stand trial.

However, in *Perault v. State,*[7] the court said that where the jury is improperly allowed to disperse in a case in which the death penalty is being sought, the dispersal is rendered harmless if the death penalty is not imposed by the jury. The problem with *Perault* is that it fails to recognize that the trial judge may in the exercise of his discretion have a jury sequestered in a non-capital case; it seems that he must exercise this discretion. The rule is that when the union and isolation of a sequestered jury has been broken, there is a presumption that the defendant has been injured and the burden is on the state to show that the juror did not speak to anyone nor did anyone speak to him about the case and that he did not hear anyone discuss the case.[8] In *Huey v. State,*[9] the court held that generally there is a presumption of prejudice if some of the jurors are separated from the others. However, if the defendant consents to the separating, he has the burden of showing how the separation harmed him.

The same rules of sequestration apply to alternate jurors, if any are selected. Alternate jurors are to be seated near or with

---

[Section 18:37]

[1]Cf. Roper v. State, 251 Ga. 95 (4), 303 S.E.2d 103 (1983). In the Roper opinion it does not appear that the jury was sworn after selection and before dispersal, but the transcript makes it clear that the jury was sworn before it was dispersed.

[2]See O.C.G.A. § 15-12-142; Harrison v. State, 236 Ga. 355, 223 S.E.2d 715 (1976); Jordan v. State, 235 Ga. 732, 735 (3), 222 S.E.2d 23 (1975); Whitaker v. State, 246 Ga. 163, 168 (14), 269 S.E.2d 436 (1980).

[3]Gamble v. State, 141 Ga. App. 304 (1), 233 S.E.2d 264 (1977).

[4]Willis v. State, 243 Ga. 185, 188 (5), 253 S.E.2d 70 (1979).

[5]Williams v. State, 286 Ga. 884, 692 S.E.2d 374 (2010); Bailey v. State, 249 Ga. 535, 538 (3), 291 S.E.2d 704 (1982).

[6]Mason v. State, 239 Ga. 538, 540, 238 S.E.2d 79 (1977).

[7]Perault v. State, 162 Ga. App. 294 (1), 291 S.E.2d 122 (1982).

[8]Legare v. State, 243 Ga. 744, 752 (11), 257 S.E.2d 247 (1979).

[9]Huey v. State, 263 Ga. 840, 842 (6), 439 S.E.2d 656 (1994).

the regular jurors. They are to remain with the other jurors when they are kept together[10] until deliberations begin.[11]

The current attitude toward the separation and conduct of jurors is more lax than it formerly was.[12] However, before dispersal the jury must be charged (1) not to communicate with anyone about the case, (2) nor permit anyone to communicate with them about it, (3) nor read newspaper articles or listen to radio or television broadcasts about the case.[13]

However, in *Thomas v. State*,[14] the court held that it was not error for the trial judge to refuse to ask jurors individually if they had had any inadvertent contact with anyone about the case during an overnight recess or whether they had access to any news reports about the case or any conversations about the case, where the judge "asked the full panel if they failed to understand and follow his precautionary instructions prior to the recess; [and] no juror responded."

After a jury is selected it is placed in the custody of a bailiff during the period of time the jury is kept together or sequestered. A sheriff or deputy sheriff who is a prosecutor is disqualified to act as a bailiff.[15] However, a deputy sheriff's eligibility to serve as a bailiff is to be determined by his involvement in the trial and he is not disqualified simply because the sheriff is disqualified.[16] Nevertheless, it has been held that where a disqualified sheriff or deputy serves as bailiff and no objection is made at trial, this is not a sufficient ground for a new trial.[17]

It has been held to be reversible error, where jurors were sequestered, for the bailiff to take the jury to a prayer meeting conducted by a pastor who assisted the state in selecting the jury and then testified for the prosecution,[18] or to tell a juror that the defendant is guilty.[19]

In *Radford v. State*,[20] a deputy sheriff was an important witness for the state. After he testified, he was assigned to serve as

---

[10]O.C.G.A. § 15-12-170.

[11]O.C.G.A. § 15-12-171.

[12]Maltbie v. State, 139 Ga. App. 342, 343, 228 S.E.2d 368 (1976).

[13]Atlanta Newspapers v. State, 216 Ga. 399, 400 (4), 116 S.E.2d 580 (1960).

[14]Thomas v. State, 171 Ga. App. 306, 308 (5), 319 S.E.2d 511 (1984).

[15]Cf. Hudson v. State, 250 Ga. 479, 484 (5), 299 S.E.2d 531 (1983).

[16]Reaves v. State, 242 Ga. 542, 550 (5), 250 S.E.2d 376 (1978).

[17]Hudson v. State, 250 Ga. 479, 484 (5), 299 S.E.2d 531 (1983).

[18]Shaw v. State, 83 Ga. 92, 98, 9 S.E. 768 (1889). Cf. § 18:38, infra, and Turner v. Louisiana, 379 U.S. 466, 85 S.Ct. 546, 13 L.Ed.2d 424 (1965).

[19]Lockridge v. State, 260 Ga. 528, 397 S.E.2d 695 (1990).

[20]Radford v. State, 263 Ga. 47, 426 S.E.2d 868 (1993). See Bass v. State, 285 Ga. 89, 674 S.E.2d 255 (2009), failure to object to allowing deputy sheriff to serve as bailiff who was also a key witness in the case was

a bailiff for the sequestered jury. He had contact with all the jurors, rode with them to and from their motel and to meals, dined with them, and stood guard on the jury where they congregated in the evenings. The state argued that the bailiff was not a "key" witness, but his testimony was not "confined to uncontroverted or merely formal aspect of the case." In reversing the conviction, the court pointed out that the bailiff had "substantial and continuing contact with and authority over" the jurors during much of the trial.

See § 18:38, § 24:23 and § 25:7, infra, on improper jury conduct, and § 24:19, infra, on the communication of a bailiff with the jury.

§ 18:38 Improper influence or conduct[1]

It has been held that it is error for the trial court to take a guilty plea of a co-defendant in the presence of the venire.[2]

Where an irregularity in the conduct of a juror is shown, there is a presumption that the defendant has been prejudiced.[3] In order to avoid reversal, the state must disprove prejudice beyond a reasonable doubt. That presumption has not changed under the 2013 Evidence Code.[4] However, "[w]hen the trial court 'has discovered facts during a trial which indicated that one or more members of a jury *might* be biased . . . the duty of the judge in this event is to discharge the jury and direct a retrial.' "[5] (emphasis in original). Thus, in *Martin v. State*,[6] where a juror communicated to a witness that the defendant was going to be acquitted unless the state shored up its case in a certain manner, the court held that such communication gave rise to a presump-

---

ineffective assistance of counsel.

[Section 18:38]

[1]For a splendid annotation of improper communications with jurors, see the Appendix by Judge Stolz in Maltbie v. State, 139 Ga. App. 342, 345, 228 S.E.2d 368 (1976).

[2]Hayes v. State, 136 Ga. App. 746, 222 S.E.2d 193 (1975). See § 18:24, n. 34, supra, on prejudicial statements in presence of the jury.

[3]Lamons v. State, 255 Ga. 511, 512, 340 S.E.2d 183 (1986). See Edge v. State, 345 Ga. App. 794, 815 S.E.2d 146 (2018) (state failed to overcome presumption of prejudice where two or three jurors referred to cell phones for sight and distance detail about witness view of crime scene).

[4]Lloyd v. State, 339 Ga. App. 1, 792 S.E.2d 445 (2016) (state could not overcome prejudice caused by juror's research of facts and law which was shared with other jurors during deliberations).

[5]Smith v. State, 278 Ga. App. 315, 320, 628 S.E.2d 722 (2006) (punctuation omitted) quoting McCrary v. State, 191 Ga. App. 336, 337, 381 S.E.2d 579 (1989).

[6]Martin v. State, 242 Ga. 699, 701, 251 S.E.2d 240 (1978).

tion of prejudice. However, in *Clark v. State,*[7] the court concluded that an unauthorized communication between a witness and a juror does not vitiate an otherwise valid conviction unless defendant was actually prejudiced. In *Sims v. State,*[8] the court held that "a jury verdict will not be upset solely because of such conduct, unless 'the statements are so prejudicial that the verdict must be deemed "inherently lacking in due process."' "

It has been held that grounds for a new trial exist where the widow of the deceased is seen shaking hands with a juror after he was selected to try the case involving the alleged murder of her husband.[9] It has been held that where it is alleged that there was an improper conversation between a juror and a prosecution witness, it is error for the court to fail to conduct an inquiry,[10] including hearing from the juror.[11] However, in *Reed v. State,*[12] the court held that "[w]hen a trial court determines that a juror has received an improper communication it may, but is not required to, determine whether the communication had in fact prejudiced the juror before granting a mistrial." If a jury is not sequestered and a highly prejudicial news story appears, the court has a duty to determine if any of the jurors have learned of the story even though the jurors had been instructed not to read anything about the case.[13] It has also been held that the court should interrogate each juror separately who has admitted contact with prejudicial publicity.[14] Likewise, the trial judge should conduct a voir dire examination after a newspaper reported that the life of a star witness had been threatened.[15]

In *Smith v. Phillips,*[16] the United States Supreme Court concluded that it was not violative of the due process clause of the Fourteenth Amendment for a juror to submit an employment application to the district attorney's office during a criminal trial.

---

[7]Clark v. State, 153 Ga. App. 829 (1), 266 S.E.2d 577 (1980).

[8]Sims v. State, 266 Ga. 417, 419 (3), 467 S.E.2d 574 (1996). Accord, Huff v. State, 239 Ga. App. 83, 87 (3), 519 S.E.2d 263 (1999). See Causey v. State, 319 Ga. App. 841, 738 S.E.2d 672 (2013).

[9]Golden v. State, 63 Ga. App. 765, 766, 12 S.E.2d 108 (1940).

[10]Richardson v. United States, 360 F.2d 366, 369 (5th Cir. 1966).

[11]Castro v. State, 186 Ga. App. 248, 249 (2), 367 S.E.2d 42 (1988).

[12]Reed v. State, 267 Ga. 482, 484 (1), 480 S.E.2d 27 (1997).

[13]United States v. Perrotta, 553 F.2d 247 (1st Cir. 1977). Cf. Bell v. State, 163 Ga. App. 672, 295 S.E.2d 147 (1982). See Annot., "Juror's Reading of Newspaper Account of Trial in State Criminal Case During Its Progress as Ground for Mistrial, New Trial, or Reversal," 46 A.L.R.4th 11 (1986). See Annot., 75B Am. Jur. 2d Trial § 1730, Jurors' Reading of General Newspaper Account (2004).

[14]Margoles v. United States, 407 F.2d 727, 735 (7th Cir. 1969).

[15]United States v. Herring, 568 F.2d 1099 (5th Cir. 1978).

[16]Smith v. Phillips, 455 U.S. 209, 102 S.Ct. 940, 71 L.Ed.2d 78 (1982).

There had been extensive voir dire examination during jury selection, and the trial judge had found beyond a reasonable doubt that the event did not influence the verdict. Additionally, there was no proof of actual bias on the part of the juror. The court pointed out that the preservation "of the opportunity to prove actual bias is a guarantee of a defendant's right to an impartial jury" and that this could be provided in a post-trial hearing as had been conducted in this case.

In *Mason v. State*,[17] the prosecution sought the death penalty. The court said that with the consent of defense counsel the jury may be allowed to disperse overnight. Where there is such a dispersal with consent of defense counsel, there is no burden on the state to show that no harm accrued to the defendant by reason of a newspaper article disclosing his former conviction of murder.

Generally, jurors may take notes of any or all of the evidence and take those notes to the jury room unless the trial judge prevents this.[18] As a general matter, jurors may not directly question witnesses.[19] However, under proper instruction from the court, jurors may be allowed to submit questions they may have in writing to the court at the conclusion of the witness' testimony.[20]

In *Tankersley v. State*,[21] the court held that it was proper for the state to supply each juror with a copy of the indictment to be referred to by the juror during the trial of a complex case.

There is some indication that a defendant may not in a motion for a new trial raise for the first time his contention that a juror was asleep or dozing during a trial when he made no complaint at the time of the occurrence.[22] The Georgia Supreme Court has said that if a juror should "fall asleep during the course of a trial it is the duty of the trial judge to awaken him. Should counsel or

---

[17]Mason v. State, 239 Ga. 538, 540, 238 S.E.2d 79 (1977).

[18]Holcomb v. State, 130 Ga. App. 154, 156 (4), 202 S.E.2d 529 (1973); Denson v. State, 149 Ga. App. 453, 455 (3), 254 S.E.2d 455 (1979). See Annot., "Taking and Use of Trial Notes by Jury," 36 A.L.R.5th 255 (1996).

[19]Matchett v. State, 257 Ga. 785, 786 (2), 364 S.E.2d 565 (1988).

[20]See Hernandez v. State, 299 Ga. 796, 792 S.E.2d 373 (2016); Allen v. State, 286 Ga. 392, 687 S.E.2d 799 (2010). See also Hoehn v. State, 293 Ga. 127, 744 S.E.2d 46 (2013) (improper for juror to directly ask witness a question).

[21]Tankersley v. State, 155 Ga. App. 917, 920 (6), 273 S.E.2d 862 (1980). In the *Tankersley* case, the court also approved the action of the state in providing each juror with a note pad.

[22]Adkins v. State, 164 Ga. App. 273, 275, 297 S.E.2d 47 (1982). See § 18:1, n. 1, supra; Trenor v. State, 252 Ga. 264, 266 (5), 313 S.E.2d 482 (1984). Generally, see Annot., 38 A.L.R.Fed. 148 (1978), relating to replacement of a sleeping juror by an alternate in federal court.

the parties in a trial observe a sleeping juror it is their duty to bring it to the attention of the court. What a litigant may not do is observe a juror sleeping, fail to bring this to the judge's attention at a time when corrective action may be had, take a chance on a favorable verdict and then when the verdict is unfavorable have a mistrial or new trial because of the otiose juror."[23] See Annotation, "Inattention of Juror From Sleepiness or Other Cause as Ground for Reversal or New Trial," 59 A.L.R. 5th (1998).

In the same vein, the failure of defense counsel to request the removal of a juror who had been the subject of a bribery attempt during deliberations was fatal to a post conviction motion for a mistrial in *Thompson v. State*.[24] Although the juror had discussed the bribe attempt with other jurors before informing the court, the trial judge denied the defendant's motion for mistrial after a verdict was reached because the defendant had failed to request either that the juror be removed or that a curative instruction be given. The Court of Appeals affirmed noting that any other result might promote improper jury contact in future trials where a conviction was likely.

In *Parker v. State*,[25] the court held that if defense counsel "knew of possible misconduct and did not bring it to the attention of the court . . . this issue . . . [is] waived."

Also see § 18:37, supra, on sequestration; § 24:23, infra, on jury misconduct; and § 25:7, infra, on impeaching the verdict. See § 24:24, infra, on replacing a juror.

---

[23]Foster v. State, 255 Ga. 425 (2), 339 S.E.2d 256 (1986), quoted in Yount v.State, 249 Ga. App. 563, 566 (2), 548 S.E.2d 674 (2001). See Smith v. State, 284 Ga. 17 (4), 663 S.E.2d 142 (2008), for illustration of court instructions for the sleepy juror.

[24]Thompson v. State, 260 Ga. App. 253(3), 581 S.E.2d 596 (2003).

[25]Parker v. State, 249 Ga. App. 509, 511 (2), 548 S.E.2d 475 (2001).

Chapter 19

Opening Statements

KeyCite®: Cases and other legal materials listed in KeyCite Scope can be researched through the KeyCite service on Westlaw®. Use KeyCite to check citations for form, parallel references, prior and later history, and comprehensive citator information, including citations to other decisions and secondary materials.

---

§ 19:1   General considerations

Most attorneys fail to give opening statements the attention they deserve. Some psychologists who have studied the jury process have concluded that most jurors make up their minds about a case by the time opening statements have been completed and subsequently never change their minds.[1] Even if it is only possible that the conclusions of psychologists are correct, there is a need to give careful attention to opening statements.

An opening statement is intended to further educate the juror about the facts of the particular case. Hopefully, the jury will have learned something about the facts of the case during voir dire examination. The opening statement gives counsel an opportunity to review the entire case and thus fill in facts which may not have been previously brought out.

Rule 10.2 of the Uniform Rules for the Superior Courts provides as follows:

[Section 19:1]

[1]Address by Dr. Helen Singer, Psychologist from New York, N.Y., at a P.L.I. Seminar held at the Hyatt Regency, Atlanta, Georgia, January 14, 1977. See Owen, Defending Criminal Cases Before Juries: A Common Sense Approach, p. 148, Prentice Hall, Inc.

(1973).

Some studies of civil cases have shown that 80 percent of the jurors make up their minds on liability irrevocably on opening statements. Spangenberg, "Basic Values and Techniques of Persuasion," 3 Litigation No. 4, pp. 13-14 (Summer 1977).

"10.2 Opening Statements in Criminal Matters

"The district attorney may make an opening statement prior to the introduction of evidence. This statement shall be limited to expected proof by legally admissible evidence. Defense counsel may make an opening statement immediately after the state's opening statement and prior to introduction of evidence, or following the conclusion of the state's presentation of evidence. Defense counsel's statement shall be restricted to expected proof by legally admissible evidence, or the lack of evidence."

The rule makes it clear that defense counsel may make an opening statement immediately after that of the state *or* after the conclusion of the state's evidence.[2]

When an attorney makes an opening statement, he should tell the jury that he expects the evidence to show certain facts. He should not, however, preface each sentence or paragraph with words such as "We expect to show you. . . . " The opening statement should be complete but not boring. The attorney needs to capture the attention of the jurors with the first sentence. Yet, he must not oversell his case in the opening statement. Do not tell the jury that you will prove a certain point unless you are reasonably certain you can do so. It is a good idea for the attorneys to make notes on the representations the opposing counsel tells the jury he will prove. The opposing attorney's failure to prove these points may be noted in the closing argument.

In general terms, an attorney may state fully that which he expects to show[3] as long as the matters may be proved by admissible evidence.[4] Statements "should not refer to anything that may tend to arouse feeling or to prejudice the cause of the opposite party in the eyes of the jury."[5] In addition, counsel should not display documents or read from papers or letters before the same have been admitted into evidence.[6]

§ 19:2 "Invoking the rule"—Sequestration of witnesses

The purpose of the sequestration rule is to prevent a witness who has not testified or completed his testimony from overhearing another witness' testimony and thus having his testimony affected by that of another witness.[1] However, while either party has the right to invoke the rule, the statutory sequestration rule

---

[2]Mason v. State, 197 Ga. App. 534, 535 (1), 398 S.E.2d 822 (1990).

[3]Dowda v. State, 74 Ga. 12, 15 (3) (1885).

[4]Green v. State, 172 Ga. 635 (3), 158 S.E. 285 (1931).

[5]Green v. State, 172 Ga. 635 (3), 158 S.E. 285 (1931).

[6]See Montross v. State, 72 Ga. 261, 267, 1884 WL 2156 (1884).

[Section 19:2]

[1]See Annot., "Effect of Witness' Violation of Order of Exclusion," 16 A.L.R.3d 16, 21 (1967).

does not apply unless it is invoked by one or both parties.[2]

The rule has also been held to apply to communications between witnesses outside the courtroom.[3] It has been pointed out that the statute is intended "to preserve the integrity of testimony" and " 'the rule extends to communications, direct and indirect, between witnesses outside the courtroom, . . .' Consequently, when the rule is invoked, the court . . . should instruct all witnesses not only to remain outside the courtroom but also to not discuss the case with the other witnesses or parties until the evidence is concluded or both have been excused. . . . "[4] However, the "rule does not prohibit discussions between an attorney to the case and a prospective witness, at least so long as the attorney talks to him separately from the other witnesses and does not inform him of previous testimony."[5]

With the exception of the victim of the offense being tried, at the request of a party or on its own motion, "the court shall order witnesses excluded so that each witness cannot hear the testimony of other witnesses," and the court has the duty to enforce such sequestration.[6] It should be noted that the statute, as used in criminal cases, provides that the state can have defense witnesses excluded on motion of the state. It also provides that the defendant can have the witnesses for the state excluded on motion of the defendant. It does not provide that the state has

---

[2]Watson v. State, 222 Ga. App. 158, 159 (2), 473 S.E.2d 262 (1996).

[3]Lackey v. State, 246 Ga. 331, 334 (5), 271 S.E.2d 478 (1980). However, in Boyd v. State, 168 Ga. App. 246, 250 (5), 308 S.E.2d 626 (1983), the court said that the statutory rule of sequestration was not violated where witnesses discuss their testimony out of court. The court did point out that such a discussion could be a violation of a court order if such an instruction had been given.

[4]O'Kelley v. State, 175 Ga. App. 503, 504, 333 S.E.2d 838 (1985). See Childress v. State, 266 Ga. 425, 467 S.E.2d 865 (1996) (error to exclude evidence that state witness clearly violated the rule by discussing testimony with another state witness out of court because such evidence bears not only on the recipient's credibility as a witness, but also speaks to the bias and motivation of the witness who divulges the information); cf. Askew v. State, 254 Ga. App. 137, 564 S.E.2d 720 (2002).

[5]Jones v. State, 271 Ga. 516, 518 (3), 520 S.E.2d 454 (1999); Ross v. State, 254 Ga. 22, 28, 326 S.E.2d 194 (1985), overruled on other grounds by O'Kelley v. State, 278 Ga. 564, 604 S.E.2d 509 (2004); Norman v. State, 212 Ga. App. 105, 109 (4), 441 S.E.2d 94 (1994). Cf. Fowler v. State, 179 Ga. App. 492, 494 (3), 347 S.E.2d 322 (1986).

[6]O.C.G.A. § 24-6-615 provides as follows: "Except as otherwise provided in Code Section 24-6-616, at the request of a party the court shall order witnesses excluded so that each witness cannot hear the testimony of other witnesses, and it may make the order on its own motion." Cf. Rule 615 of the Federal Rules of Evidence. In the puzzling majority opinion of Smith v. State, 244 Ga. 814, 816, 262 S.E.2d 116 (1979), the court indicates that if witnesses are sequestered, opposing counsel has no right to talk to them without the permission of the court.

an automatic right to have the judge exclude the state's witnesses. Likewise, the statute does not provide that the defendant has an automatic right to have the trial judge exclude the defense witnesses.[7] However, there is a longstanding practice, approved by the Georgia Court of Appeals, to exclude *all* witnesses when a party moves for sequestration.[8] However, O.C.G.A. § 24-6-616 provides that pursuant to O.C.G.A. § 17-17-9, the victim of a criminal offense "shall be entitled to be present" at all criminal proceedings in which the accused has a right to be present.

Exclusion of witnesses from the courtroom while other witnesses are testifying has been said to be mandatory after request by either party, subject only to the sound discretion of the judge in permitting one or more witnesses, such as law enforcement officers, to remain in the courtroom to assist counsel in the presentation of the case.[9] "Generally, this discretion should be exercised only if the party requesting the exception can demonstrate a need for the presence of the witness"[10] or witnesses.[11] The discretion of the judge must be exercised at the time the rule is invoked. If either party wishes to keep a witness in the courtroom, it should be called to the attention of the court and an explanation given at that time, as the burden of excepting a witness from a sequestration order is on the party seeking the exception.[12] The notion that the prosecution requires the assistance of a law enforcement witness in the courtroom throughout the trial because of a generalized "need" has been criticized. In *Carter v. State*,[13] the Court of Appeals recommended that trial courts should require a demonstration of some particularized necessity

---

[7]The examples used in the body and the explanation of the statute are a result of a discussion of the author with Judge Walter McMillan of Sandersville, Georgia.

[8]McNeil v. State, 229 Ga. App. 149, 150, 493 S.E.2d 570 (1997).

[9]Cornett v. State, 218 Ga. 405, 407, 128 S.E.2d 317 (1962). There, the court concluded that it was not an abuse of discretion in that case for a sheriff or prosecutor to be allowed to remain in the courtroom over objection and then testify for the state. Accord, Durham v. State, 129 Ga. App. 5 (2), 198 S.E.2d 387 (1973). But in Bush v. State, 129 Ga. App. 160, 199 S.E.2d 121 (1973), where the defendant invoked the rule and a deputy sheriff remained in the courtroom with no request that he be permitted to stay or explanation of why he was needed, it was held to be error to permit him to testify after another officer had testified. In James v. State, 143 Ga. App. 696 (2), 240 S.E.2d 149 (1977), the court said that the burden of showing an exception (as where the district attorney needs the witness) is on the state and if that witness does not testify first, sufficient reason must be shown to the trial judge.

[10]Herreras v. State, 190 Ga. App. 359, 379 S.E.2d 12 (1989).

[11]Spurlin v. State, 222 Ga. 179, 180 (2), 149 S.E.2d 315 (1966).

[12]Parham v. State, 135 Ga. App. 315, 319 (8), 217 S.E.2d 493 (1975).

[13]Carter v. State, 271 Ga. App. 588 (2), 610 S.E.2d 181 (2005). But cf., Warner v. State, 281 Ga. 763(2), 642 S.E.2d 821 (2007).

and that even then the presence of such witnesses should be the exception rather than the rule.

In *Gray v. State*,[14] the court held that "[e]ven when an expert witness would be assisted by hearing the testimony of preceding witnesses instead of answering a hypothetical question and could assist counsel in conducting the cross-examination, the grant or denial of such exemption lies within the sound discretion of the trial court. . . ."

When the judge grants a request to allow a sequestered witness to remain in the courtroom, the party calling that witness should present him as his first witness, or explain to the satisfaction of the trial judge why this cannot be done.[15] However, if the opposing party does not request the trial judge to have the witness testify first, he may allow the witness to testify after other witnesses have testified.[16] However, this order of witnesses does not apply to the defendant, who has a constitutional right to testify as the last defense witness.[17]

In 1981, the Georgia Supreme Court decided two cases dealing with the consequences of a violation of a sequestration order. In *Jordan v. State*,[18] the court held that where a defense witness in a criminal case violates the sequestration rule, the witness is not rendered incompetent to testify, but the jury may be instructed that the presence of the witness in the courtroom in violation of the rule should be considered in determining the weight and credit to be given to the testimony of the witness.[19] However, in the absence of a timely request, the trial judge does not err in failing to instruct the jury on the credibility of a witness who heard the testimony of another witness.[20] In *Rakestrau v. State*,[21] the court noted that generally a violation of the rule "does not affect the admissibility of the testimony, but may impact the offending witness' credibility."

---

[14]Gray v. State, 222 Ga. App. 626, 631, 476 S.E.2d 12 (1996).

[15]Parham v. State, 135 Ga. App. 315, 321, 217 S.E.2d 493 (1975); Whitfield v. State, 143 Ga. App. 779 (2), 240 S.E.2d 189 (1977). In James v. State, 143 Ga. App. 696, 697 (2), 240 S.E.2d 149 (1977), the court said that "save in very exceptional circumstances," a witness should not be allowed to remain in the courtroom, after the rule has been invoked, while other witnesses testify. However, the court found no reversible error where the district attorney explained that this was necessary to have the testimony presented in sequence. McKen-

zie v. State, 249 Ga. 582 (1), 292 S.E.2d 692 (1982).

[16]Hill v. State, 250 Ga. 277, 286, 295 S.E.2d 518 (1982).

[17]Brooks v. Tennessee, 406 U.S. 605, 607-12, 92 S.Ct. 1891, 32 L.Ed.2d 358 (1972).

[18]Jordan v. State, 247 Ga. 328, 346 (10), 276 S.E.2d 224 (1981).

[19]Jordan v. State, 247 Ga. 328, 347, 276 S.E.2d 224 (1981).

[20]Mitchell v. State, 223 Ga. App. 319, 322 (7), 477 S.E.2d 612 (1996).

[21]Rakestrau v. State, 278 Ga. 872, 876, 608 S.E.2d 216 (2005).

Of course, the witness, and perhaps the party calling him, may be found in contempt of court for a willful violation of the sequestration order.[22] In *Wessner v. State,*[23] the same court had held that the trial judge could exercise discretion in determining whether or not to permit a witness to testify where he had violated such an order. *Jordan* overrules *Wessner* to the extent *Wessner* is inconsistent with *Jordan.*[24] Thus, the present rule seems to be that a defense witness' violating sequestration orders may testify, and the trial judge has no discretionary authority to disqualify a witness for violating the rule. Although the refusal of the court in *Jordan v. State* to disqualify a defense witness who violated the sequestration order may have been grounded on the defendant's Sixth Amendment right to present witnesses in his behalf,[25] still the same court in *Blanchard v. State*[26] held that in all criminal cases, a violation of the rule of sequestration by *any* (court's emphasis) witness, either for the defense or for the prosecution, affects only the weight and credibility, and not the admissibility, of the witness' testimony. However, in *Scott v. State,*[27] the court pointed out that the trial judge "has discretion to grant or deny a motion for mistrial based on an alleged violation of a sequestration order."

In *Dunbar v. State,*[28] the Georgia Court of Appeals held "[i]n the absence of a timely request, the trial court [does] not err in failing to instruct the jury on the credibility of a witness who has heard the testimony of other witnesses."

However, most other jurisdictions hold that it is within the sound discretion of the trial court to exclude the testimony of a witness who violates a sequestration order, and that an appellate court will only interfere with the trial court's decision in the case of an abuse of discretion,[29] and in the 1987 Georgia Supreme Court case of *Hicks v. State,*[30] the court indicated that there may be cases in which the conduct is so egregious and deliberate that a violation of the rule of sequestration might necessitate a mistrial. While most of the cases hold that a mere violation of a

---

[22]Baker v. State, 131 Ga. App. 48, 51-52, 205 S.E.2d 79 (1974). See also 14 A.L.R.3d 16, 22 (1967).

[23]Wessner v. State, 236 Ga. 162, 166-167, 223 S.E.2d 141 (1976).

[24]Jordan v. State, 247 Ga. 328, 347, 276 S.E.2d 224 (1981).

[25]Jordan v. State, 247 Ga. 328, 347, 276 S.E.2d 224 (1981).

[26]Blanchard v. State, 247 Ga. 415, 416, 417, 276 S.E.2d 593 (1981). Ac-

cord, Tiller v. State, 267 Ga. 888, 891 (5), 485 S.E.2d 720 (1997); Cook v. State, 221 Ga. App. 831 (2), 472 S.E.2d 686 (1996).

[27]Scott v. State, 227 Ga. App. 900, 903 (5), 490 S.E.2d 208 (1997).

[28]Dunbar v. State, 209 Ga. App. 97 (1), 432 S.E.2d 829 (1993).

[29]14 A.L.R.3d 16, 22 (1967).

[30]Hicks v. State, 256 Ga. 715, 720 (12), 352 S.E.2d 762 (1987).

sequestration order does not, of itself, disqualify the witness,[31] the following circumstances tend to justify a disqualification:[32] (1) where the party or counsel calling the witness aided or abetted the violation; (2) where the witness willfully violated the order; (3) where the testimony overheard by the witness is related to the testimony which the witness can be expected to proffer; and (4) where the testimony expected to be elicited from the witness is merely cumulative. However, even in those jurisdictions where a witness may be disqualified at the discretion of the trial court, the refusal to permit a defense witness to testify is more limited than in the case of a state's witness, since a criminal defendant has a Sixth Amendment right to present witnesses in his behalf, and hence it is said that a defendant cannot be deprived of their testimony merely because they violated a sequestration order, where neither the defendant nor his counsel was at fault.[33]

In *United States v. Gibson*,[34] the Sixth Circuit held that the trial judge did not abuse his discretion by excluding a witness for the defendant for failing to obey the sequestration order. The defendant did not show that he was prejudiced, and, as a matter of fact, he was able to present another witness who could present substantially the same testimony. The United States Supreme Court denied certiorari.

As pointed out previously,[35] the defendant generally has a right to be present at all times during the trial, regardless of when he testifies. However, it has been held that it is not error to sequester the defendant while his wife testifies in support of his change of venue.[36]

Finally, it is within the discretion of the trial judge to have the witnesses sequestered during opening statements.[37] Counsel should normally exert every effort to have witnesses sequestered

---

[31] 14 A.L.R.3d 16, 22 (1967).

[32] 14 A.L.R.3d 16, 23 (1967).

[33] 14 A.L.R.3d 16, 55 (1967). See also Braswell v. Wainwright, 463 F.2d 1148, 1155-57 (5th Cir. 1972). Cf. Baker v. State, 131 Ga. App. 48, 51 (2), 205 S.E.2d 79 (1974); Best v. State, 176 Ga. 46, 166 S.E. 772 (1932); Lockleer v. State, 144 Ga. App. 493, 494 (2), 241 S.E.2d 613 (1978); Jordan v. State, 247 Ga. 328, 346 (10), 276 S.E.2d 224 (1981). See § 17:8, supra.

[34] United States v. Gibson, 675 F.2d 825, 835 (6th Cir. 1982). In Holder v. United States, 150 U.S. 91, 14 S.Ct. 10, 37 L.Ed. 1010 (1893), the court said, "If a witness disobeys the order of withdrawal, while he may be proceeded against for contempt and his testimony is open to comment to the jury by reason of his conduct, he is not thereby disqualified, and the weight of authority is that he cannot be excluded on that ground merely, although the right to exclude under particular circumstances may be supported as within the sound discretion of the trial court."

[35] See § 17:8, supra.

[36] Cochran v. State, 151 Ga. App. 478, 483 (10), 260 S.E.2d 391 (1979). Generally, see § 17:8, supra, on the right of the defendant to be present.

[37] Hughes v. State, 128 Ga. 19, 20

during opening statements as well as during the introduction of all evidence.

See § 14:22, supra, on requiring a defendant to identify defense witnesses. See § 19:3, infra, on the right of a victim to be present.

For a written motion to sequester witnesses, see Studdard, *Daniel's Georgia Criminal Trial Practice Forms* (2018–2019 ed.), §§ 25:1 et seq.

§ 19:3   The right of the victim and the defendant to be present

O.C.G.A. § 24-6-615 provides that pursuant to O.C.G.A. § 17-17-9, the victim of a criminal offense "shall be entitled to be present" at all criminal proceedings in which the accused has a right to be present.

On the other hand, it has been held that an accused's right to confrontation is not violated by the use of a videotape of the testimony of a child where the defendant, his counsel, the judge, a reporter, the prosecuting attorney and the child and his mother were present at the taping.[1] See Annotation, "Closed-Circuit Television Witness Examination," 61 A.L.R.4th 1155 (1988). See Annot., 81 Am. Jur. 2d Witnesses § 695, Constitutionality of Televised or Videotaped Testimony (2004). See Studdard, *Daniel's Georgia Handbook on Criminal Evidence* (2018 ed.), § 8:33, on hearsay statements of children. See § 14:7, supra, on use of depositions. See § 17:8, supra, on the right of the defendant to be present.

§ 19:4   Purpose of opening statement

In *Franks v. State*,[1] the court said that the "purpose of the opening statement is to inform the jury and the court of the nature of the case, and to give an outline of the proof the party anticipate[s] presenting. Recounting the evidence already presented and suggesting the conclusion demanded by that evidence is the subject matter of closing argument." See Chapter 23, infra, on argument.

§ 19:5   State's opening

The district attorney is entitled to make an opening statement

---

(1), 57 S.E. 236 (1907).

[Section 19:3]

   [1]State v. Cooper, 291 S.C. 351, 353 S.E.2d 451 (1987).

[Section 19:4]

   [1]Franks v. State, 188 Ga. App.

263 (1), 372 S.E.2d 831 (1988); Clark v. State, 271 Ga. 6, 8 (2), 515 S.E.2d 155 (1999). See L. Timothy Perrin, From O.J. to McVeigh: The Use of Argument in the Opening Statement, 48 Emory L.J. 107 (1999) (an article well worth the time of any litigator regardless of how experienced).

first. In some cases he may choose to waive this right, although this ordinarily should not be done.[1] There are two conceivable situations in which the district attorney may not want to make an opening statement: (1) where his refusal to make an opening statement might lead the defense counsel not to make one; and (2) where he thinks that the defense counsel knows very little about the case.

Generally, counsel may state what he expects his witnesses to testify to,[2] but he may not refer to testimony which is inadmissible.[3] However, the " 'trial court has a sound discretion to control the content on the opening statement of either party, particularly with regard to matters of questionable admissibility.' "[4]

It has been held to be reversible error for the prosecuting attorney to refer in his opening statement to the drug problem in the county and to make remarks about how the state's principal witness came forward to help stamp out the drug evil because these matters were not admissible in evidence.[5] In addition, while not error *per se*, because a criminal defendant has no obligation of proof at the trial of a case, it is at the very least "inappropriate for a prosecutor in a criminal case to discuss in opening statement the evidence she anticipates the defense will present at trial."[6] A prosecutor should not refer to an assertion of fact which the prosecutor either knows can not be presented during the trial of the case or for which the prosecutor does not at least hold a good faith belief that the evidence needed to support the asserted fact is available and will be presented.[7] The long-standing rule is that a prosecutor may not express to the jury his or her personal

---

[Section 19:5]

[1]In federal court, the United States Attorney may waive his right to make an opening statement. United States v. Yaughn, 493 F.2d 441 (5th Cir. 1974).

[2]Jordan v. State, 78 Ga. App. 879 (6), 52 S.E.2d 505 (1949). See Annot., "Prosecutor's Reference in Opening Statement to Matters Not Provable or Which He Does Not Attempt to Prove as Ground for Relief," 16 A.L.R.4th 810 (1982). See Annot., 58 Am. Jur. 2d New Trial § 148, Reference in Opening Statement to Matters Counsel Does Not Attempt to Prove (2004).

[3]Green v. State, 172 Ga. 635 (3), 158 S.E. 285 (1931). See Hall v. State, 138 Ga. App. 20 (1), 225 S.E.2d 705 (1976). In Watson v. State, 137 Ga.

App. 530 (1), 224 S.E.2d 446 (1976), the court said, "Where matters are stated which relate to evidence that is not admissible in evidence, it constitutes harmful error."

[4]Yarborough v. State, 183 Ga. App. 198, 200 (3), 358 S.E.2d 484 (1987) (quoting Sims v. State, 251 Ga. 877, 879 (3), 311 S.E.2d 161 (1984)).

[5]Watson v. State, 137 Ga. App. 530 (1), 224 S.E.2d 446 (1976).

[6]Parker v. State, 277 Ga. 439 (2), 588 S.E.2d 683 (2003).

[7]See e.g. Alexander v. State, 270 Ga. 346, 349, 509 S.E.2d 56 (1998). Conviction reversed where no evidence introduced to support prosecutor's assertions in opening that the murder was gang related. Court observed "a conviction will not be reversed if the

belief about the veracity of a witness.[8] Thus, in *Bell v. State*,[9] the court held that questions by the prosecutor about whether his "star" witness had ever been "accused" of lying or "changing" his story amounted to an improper attempt to bolster the credibility of the witness.

It is error for the district attorney to tell the jury that co-defendants named in the indictment had previously entered guilty pleas.[10]

§ 19:6   Defendant's opening

Counsel for the defendant must decide whether he wishes to make an opening statement before the introduction of any evidence or whether he would like to reserve the right to make an opening statement until the state has closed its evidence. Defense counsel may have reservations about making an opening statement before the state introduces its evidence since he may not know the exact evidence that will be presented. Thus, defense counsel may prefer to wait until the close of the state's evidence. On the other hand, if a jury makes up its mind without ever hearing the defendant's side of the case, the verdict will probably be "guilty." Also, it has been held that it is not error for the district attorney in his concluding argument to point out that defense counsel failed to state his theory of the case in his opening statement.[1]

If there are two or more defendants represented independently of each other and there is cooperation between the defense attorneys, one counsel may be permitted to make an opening statement immediately after the district attorney's statement while the other counsel reserves his right to make an opening statement until the close of the state's evidence. In the case of a single defendant, it is probably generally advantageous for defense counsel to make the best opening statement he can immediately

---

prosecutor acted in good faith and if the trial court instructs the jury that the prosecutor's opening statement is not evidence and has no probative value."

See also Ramirez v. State, 276 Ga. 249(3), 577 S.E.2d 558 (2003); Ballamy v. State, 272 Ga. 157, 160, 527 S.E.2d 687 (2002).

[8]Woods v. State, 275 Ga. 844, 573 S.E.2d 394 (2002).

[9]Bell v. State, 294 Ga. 443, 754 S.E.2d 327 (2014).

[10]Middlebrooks v. State, 169 Ga.

App. 507, 509, 313 S.E.2d 764 (1984).

[Section 19:6]

[1]Morris v. State, 228 Ga. 39, 52 (21), 184 S.E.2d 82 (1971). The objection which was raised in the Morris case was that the remarks of the district attorney violated the defendant's right to remain silent and his due process and fair trial rights under the Sixth and Fourteenth Amendments. Eubanks v. State, 240 Ga. 544, 547 (3a), 242 S.E.2d 41 (1978). Cf. Crayton v. State, 145 Ga. App. 365, 366 (3), 243 S.E.2d 738 (1978).

after the district attorney has made his opening statement. However, even a complete waiver of the right to make an opening statement may be regarded as a trial tactic "which cannot be equated to ineffective assistance of counsel."[2]

Defense counsel has no right in his opening statement to make argumentative statements related to irrelevant matters.[3] Hence, it is improper for him to state that it is his duty to represent the innocent.[4] Statements of counsel are not evidence nor technically binding admissions,[5] but where the district attorney outlines the evidence he intends to present and defense counsel in his opening statements admits such facts are true, it is not error for the trial judge to overrule an objection to such evidence when it is offered by the state.[6]

Generally, see State's opening, § 19:5, supra.

---

[2]Futch v. State, 151 Ga. App. 519, 520 (1), 260 S.E.2d 520 (1979).

[3]Perry v. State, 102 Ga. 365, 367 (13), 30 S.E. 903 (1897).

[4]Hayes v. State, 138 Ga. App. 223 (1), 225 S.E.2d 749 (1976).

[5]Brown v. State, 129 Ga. App. 743, 746 (4), 201 S.E.2d 14 (1973).

[6]Chapman v. State, 90 Ga. App. 564 (1), 83 S.E.2d 572 (1954).

Chapter 20

Presenting the State's Case and Attacks Thereon

KeyCite®: Cases and other legal materials listed in KeyCite Scope can be researched through the KeyCite service on Westlaw®. Use KeyCite to check citations for form, parallel references, prior and later history, and comprehensive citator information, including citations to other decisions and secondary materials.

---

§ 20:1   Presumption of innocence[1]

The district attorney must be prepared to overcome the presumption of innocence which surrounds the defendant. The Criminal Code of Georgia provides that "[e]very person is presumed innocent until proved guilty."[2] The defendant enters a trial with the presumption of innocence in his favor. The presumption remains with him throughout the trial until his guilt is established by evidence beyond all reasonable doubt.[3]

The presumption of innocence is not the equivalent of proof beyond a reasonable doubt. The term "presumption of innocence" refers to a substantive right in the nature of evidence while the term "reasonable doubt" applies to the degree of proof necessary

---

[Section 20:1]

[1]See Sherman, "Pretrial Police Procedures and the Presumption of Innocence," 15 Crim. L. R. 577 (1979).

[2]O.C.G.A. § 16-1-5.

[3]Anderson v. State, 196 Ga. 468 (7), 26 S.E.2d 755 (1943). The presumption of innocence is with the defendant throughout the trial and applies to every fact which must be proved by the state. Kirby v. United States, 174 U.S. 47, 55, 19 S.Ct. 574, 43 L.Ed. 890 (1899).

to produce a mental and moral conclusion.[4]

Even in the absence of a request, it is error for the trial court to fail to charge on the presumption of innocence.[5]

See Studdard, *Daniel's Georgia Handbook on Criminal Evidence* (2018 ed.), § 1:9.

§ 20:2 Presumptions and inferences—General

While the state has the burden of proof and must be prepared to overcome the defendant's presumption of innocence by proof of guilt beyond a reasonable doubt, the state may be aided by certain presumptions and inferences.[1]

See Studdard, *Daniel's Georgia Handbook on Criminal Evidence* (2018 ed.), § 3:2.

§ 20:3 Presumptions and inferences—Examples—General

There are numerous presumptions and a few inferences in Georgia law created by statute or judicial decision. The following are examples of presumptions and inferences:

The court has approved a charge that all witnesses are presumed to speak the truth, even when the defendant has not testified.[1] However, in *Noggle v. State*,[2] the Georgia Supreme Court disapproved of the giving of such a charge.

An inference of guilt may arise from a trial, or bond forfeiture.[3] The United States Supreme Court has approved a charge that the flight of an accused, if not satisfactorily explained, is a fact which may be taken into consideration as having a tendency to

---

[4]Coffin v. United States, 156 U.S. 432, 15 S.Ct. 394, 39 L.Ed. 481 (1895); Butts v. State, 13 Ga. App. 274 (2), 275 (2), 79 S.E. 87 (1913).

[5]Ealey v. State, 141 Ga. App. 94, 95, 232 S.E.2d 620 (1977).

[Section 20:2]

[1]See Nesson, "Reasonable Doubt and Permissive Inferences: The Value of Complexity," 92 Harv. L. Rev. 1187 (1979).

[Section 20:3]

[1]Cupp v. Naughten, 414 U.S. 141, 94 S.Ct. 396, 38 L.Ed.2d 368 (1973).

[2]Noggle v. State, 256 Ga. 383, 385 (4), 349 S.E.2d 175 (1986).

[3]Strickland v. State, 137 Ga. App. 628, 224 S.E.2d 809 (1976). However, in Denham v. State, 144 Ga. App. 373, 374 (1), 241 S.E.2d 295 (1977), the court pointed out that the presence of the defendant at the scene of a crime (possession of drugs) and flight from officer are not sufficient to support a conviction. In Crass v. State, 150 Ga. App. 374, 378 (8), 257 S.E.2d 909 (1979), an argumentative charge on lack of flight as indicating innocence was held properly rejected.

In Hudson v. State, 150 Ga. App. 126 (2), 257 S.E.2d 312 (1979), it was held permissible for the district attorney to ask a state's witness how long he had to look for defendant after he obtained an arrest warrant for him.

establish guilt.[4] However, the Supreme Court disapproved a charge stating that the law recognizes as true that the wicked flee when no man pursues.[5]

The presumption of intoxication from a chemical test, created by O.C.G.A. § 40-6-392, was rebuttable and has been held not to constitute a violation of due process or equal protection.[6] However, the statute as amended in 2001 provides that a person driving with "an alcohol concentration of 0.08 or more grams in the person's blood, breath, or urine" shall be in violation of O.C.G.A. § 40-6-391(a)(5).[7]

The more detailed and specific material on presumptions and inferences previously contained in this Chapter have been transferred to Studdard, *Daniel's Georgia Handbook on Criminal Evidence* (2018 ed.), §§ 3:15 et seq.

§ 20:4 Jurisdiction and venue

O.C.G.A. § 17-2-1 provides as follows:

(a) It is the policy of this state to exercise its jurisdiction over crime and persons charged with the commission of crime to the fullest extent allowable under, and consistent with, the Constitution of this state and the Constitution of the United States.

(b) Pursuant to this policy, a person shall be subject to prosecution in this state for a crime which he commits, while either within or outside the state, by his own conduct or that of another for which he is legally accountable, if:

(1) The crime is committed either wholly or partly within the state;

(2) The conduct outside the state constitutes an attempt to commit a crime within the state; or

(3) The conduct within the state constitutes an attempt to commit in another jurisdiction a crime under the laws of both this state and the other jurisdiction.

(c) A crime is committed partly within this state if either the conduct which is an element of the crime or the result which is such an element occurs within the state. In homicide, the "result" is either the act which causes death or the death itself; and, if the body of a homicide victim is found within this state, the death is presumed to have occurred within the state.

(d) A crime which is based on an omission to perform a duty imposed by the law of this state is committed within the state, regardless of the location of the accused at the time of the omission.

Generally, a person accused of a crime shall be tried in the county

---

[4]Allen v. United States, 164 U.S. 492, 17 S.Ct. 154, 41 L.Ed. 528 (7) (1896).

[5]Hickory v. United States, 160 U.S. 408, 16 S.Ct. 327, 40 L.Ed. 474

(4) (1896).

[6]Olsen v. State, 168 Ga. App. 296 (1), 308 S.E.2d 703 (1983).

[7]O.C.G.A. § 40-6-392(c)(1), effective July 1, 2001.

where the crime was alleged to have been committed, unless the trial judge determines that an impartial jury cannot be obtained in the county.[1] In *Schiefelbein v. State*,[2] the court pointed out that "[t]he constitutional and statutory law of this State require that all criminal cases be tried in the county where the crime was committed unless otherwise provided by law." "Venue is proper in the location where all *elements* of the crime are committed." (Emphasis added.)[3] At trial the state must establish venue of the alleged offense beyond a reasonable doubt.[4] In criminal cases, proof of venue is a jurisdictional fact[5] which must be proved as part of the district attorney's case-in-chief.[6]

The Criminal Code of Georgia, in O.C.G.A. § 17-2-2, enacted in 1968, contains provisions for determining venue where a crime was committed on a county line, in homicide cases, in crimes commenced outside the state, in crimes committed in transit or on water boundaries of a county or the state, and in crimes where it cannot be determined in which county the offense was committed.[7] These provisions simplify venue requirements for the

---

[Section 20:4]

[1]Ga. Const. 1983, Art. VI, § II, ¶ VI. Where there has been a change of venue, of course, the state does not have to prove that the crime was committed in the county where the defendant is being tried. In such a case, it is said that the trial judge determines the question of venue rather than the jury. Howell v. State, 162 Ga. 14 (1), 134 S.E. 59 (1926); Harris v. State, 191 Ga. 243, 257 (12), 12 S.E.2d 64 (1940).

See State v. Mayze, 280 Ga. 5, 622 S.E.2d 836 (2005), where Supreme Court held that prosecution of identity theft under O.C.G.A. § 16-9-125 in the county of victim's residence was constitutional because the victim's "identity" was located and hence misappropriated there. In a strong dissent three justices expressed their concern that the decision was a result-oriented outcome with no constitutional support.

Under the Georgia Constitution, this general rule applies to *uniform* courts. Non-uniform courts, such as the City Court of Atlanta, are not subject to the constitutional venue requirements of Art. VI, Sec. 1, Par. 1. See O.C.G.A. § 17-2-2(a) (Criminal

cases to be tried in county where crime committed "except as otherwise provided by law"). Because the City of Atlanta is located in both Fulton and DeKalb counties, proof of either would be meaningless for purposes of venue. It is proof that the offense occurred within the city limits which is required. State v. Walker, 276 Ga. 756, 585 S.E.2d 77 (2003).

[2]Schiefelbein v. State, 258 Ga. 623, 373 S.E.2d 354 (1988).

[3]Bradley v. State, 272 Ga. 740, 742 (2), 533 S.E.2d 727 (2000).

[4]Toland v. State, 115 Ga. App. 786, 156 S.E.2d 215 (1967); Murphy v. State, 121 Ga. 142, 48 S.E. 909 (1904); Carter v. State, 146 Ga. App. 681, 247 S.E.2d 191 (1978). See State v. Wallace, 338 Ga. App. 611, 791 S.E.2d 187 (2016) (venue as a jurisdictional issue is not relevant to a motion to suppress).

[5]Patterson v. State, 157 Ga. App. 233, 276 S.E.2d 900 (1981).

[6]Dempsey v. State, 52 Ga. App. 35, 182 S.E. 56 (1935).

[7]See Drake v. State, 238 Ga. App. 584, 519 S.E.2d 692 (1999) (evidence was sufficient to prove beyond a reasonable doubt that offense may have

prosecution, thus making it easier to obtain a conviction.[8] However, in *Bundren v. State*,[9] the Georgia Supreme Court held that the statute does not violate the state constitution.

When it cannot be ascertained in what county an offense was allegedly committed, the trial court shall charge that the crime should be considered to have been committed in that county which the evidence shows beyond a reasonable doubt that it might have been committed.[10] Moreover, if a crime is committed on, or immediately adjacent to, the boundary line between two counties, the crime shall be considered as having been committed in either county.[11]

In such cases, however, it is incumbent upon the state to show that the county in which the crime occurred, in fact, cannot be readily determined.[12] In *Owens v. McLaughlin*,[13] the 11th Circuit held that a charge which instructs the jury where venue "shall be considered" to lie pursuant to O.C.G.A. § 17-2-2 impermissibly shifts the burden of proof.

In a conspiracy case, venue is properly laid either in the jurisdiction where "the conspiracy was formed or in any jurisdiction

---

been committed in DeKalb County).

[8]See Maddox v. State, 145 Ga. App. 363, 364 (4), 243 S.E.2d 740 (1978); Bundren v. State, 155 Ga. App. 265 (1), 270 S.E.2d 807 (1980), rev'd, 247 Ga. 180, 274 S.E.2d 455 (1981).

[9]Bundren v. State, 247 Ga. 180, 181, 274 S.E.2d 455 (1981).

[10]Hendrix v. State, 242 Ga. App. 678, 680 (1), 530 S.E.2d 804 (2000); Bundren v. State, 247 Ga. 180, 274 S.E.2d 455 (1981); Melton v. State, 204 Ga. App. 103, 104 (2), 418 S.E.2d 428 (1992).

See Napier v. State, 276 Ga. 769, 771 (2), 583 S.E.2d 825 (2003), where the court disapproved a charge literally based upon O.C.G.A. §§ 17-2-2(c) and (h) because language in statute may create a burden shifting presumption regarding venue when only a permissive inference is warranted. The court suggested that in the future, trial courts would do better to give the following charge in those cases where venue is an issue:

A homicide shall be considered as having been committed in the county in which the cause of death was inflicted. It if cannot be determined in which county the cause of death was

inflicted, the jury may consider whether it was inflicted in the county in which the death occurred.

If a dead body is discovered in this state and it cannot be readily determined in which county the cause of death was inflicted, the jury may consider whether the cause of death was inflicted in the county in which the dead body was discovered.

If, in any case, it cannot be determined in which county a crime was committed, the jury may consider whether it was committed in any county in which the evidence shows beyond a reasonable doubt that it might have been committed.

See also Coleman v. State, 301 Ga. 753, 804 S.E.2d 89 (2017).

[11]O.C.G.A. § 17-2-2(b).

[12]Stockard v. State, 327 Ga. App. 184, 761 S.E.2d 351 (2014) (failure of state to offer any evidence as to where crime occurred, or that the county in which the crime occurred, was not subject to ready determination and was the equivalent of not proving venue).

[13]Owens v. McLaughlin, 733 F.3d 320 (11th Cir. 2013).

wherein a conspirator committed an overt act in furtherance of the conspiracy."[14] In cases involving the use of computers in connection with pornography and child exploitation, venue is properly laid in either the county where the defendant used the computer or the county in which the online service was received.[15]

In *Brown v. State*,[16] the court found that defendant's participation in online "chats" with a Georgia officer posing as a 14-year-old from Tennessee and thereafter traveling to Georgia for the purpose of meeting and engaging in sexual activities with "Brittany," the Georgia officer, was sufficient to warrant prosecution in Georgia for attempted child molestation. In addition, the court held that venue for the crime of computer child exploitation was proper in the county where the recipient of the computer messages resides even though defendant resides elsewhere. In such cases, the defendant is deemed to have used computer online services in the recipient's county.

Until *Jones v. State*,[17] the general rule regarding venue was that only when evidence of venue was not conflicting and no challenge to venue was raised at trial, "slight evidence" would suffice for the state's burden on venue. However, in *Jones*, the court observed that venue is always challenged by a plea of not guilty. The court expressly disapproved of the "slight evidence" exception and reaffirmed that venue must be established by the same standard of proof beyond a reasonable doubt that the state must meet as to every other element of a criminal offense.

In *Chapman v. State*,[18] the Supreme Court found venue proper where the state presented the testimony of the police officer who

---

[14]Davis v. State, 225 Ga. App. 564, 566(3), 484 S.E.2d 284 (1997). See Shelton v. Lee, 299 Ga. 350, 788 S.E.2d 369 (2016) (jury instruction that in case where it can not be readily determined in which county the cause of death was inflicted, "it shall be considered that the cause of death was inflicted in the county in which the dead body was discovered," did not shift burden of proof to defendant).

[15]Selfe v. State, 290 Ga. App. 857 (2), 660 S.E.2d 727 (2008).

[16]Brown v. State, 321 Ga. App. 798, 743 S.E.2d 474 (2013).

[17]Jones v. State, 272 Ga. 900 (2), 537 S.E.2d 80 (2000). Here venue was not established where the only proof of venue in Fulton County was that investigating officers worked for the City of Atlanta police, who patrol both Fulton and DeKalb counties. See Thompson v. State, 277 Ga. 102, 586 S.E.2d 231 (2003), a child molestation case where burden of venue was satisfied as to one count but not another. See also O'Donnell v. Smith, 294 Ga. 307, 751 S.E.2d 324 (2013) (concurring opinion of Justice Nahmias is critical of "erroneous logic" in *Jones* and suggests it may be overruled in the future).

[18]Chapman v. State, 275 Ga. 314, 565 S.E.2d 442 (2002). In Starling v. State, 242 Ga. App. 685, 530 S.E.2d 757 (2000), the court found that venue was not proved and the state was not entitled to inference that officer was acting within the territorial jurisdiction of his office when he made the arrest on his way to work.

responded to the call for emergency help, coupled with the testimony of the deputy chief medical examiner of Fulton County. Both of the aforementioned persons testified that they were employed by Fulton County on the night in question. As such, because of "the well-settled principle that public officials are believed to have performed their duties properly and not to have exceeded their authority unless clearly proven otherwise," the court found that the jury could conclude beyond a reasonable doubt that the crimes were committed in Fulton County, thus making venue in Fulton County proper.[19] However, in *In re: B.R.*,[20] the Georgia Court of Appeals ruled that where the *only* evidence of venue was the testimony of the responding officers as to the county for whom they were employed, venue was not established by proof beyond a reasonable doubt. The court reached a similar result in *In the interest of D.D.*[21] Both cases indicate a retreat from *Chapman* although neither acknowledges that trend.

In *Wright v. State*,[22] the court pointed out that in determining where venue existed that "it is difficult to imagine how an investigator, who has no personal or independent knowledge of the crime, could conclude that the armed robbery occurred in one county when there is absolutely no physical evidence indicating where it occurred and the only witness to the crime states positively that it occurred in another county." The court then reversed the conviction. In a theft by taking case, venue is proper in any county where the defendant exercised control over the property at issue. In *Davis v. State*,[23] the state claimed that the defendant had defrauded the victim in connection with a business loan. The victim resided in Dodge County and the negotiations for the transaction occurred there. However, because the funds were wired to the defendant in Atlanta, the defendant never exercised control over the money in Dodge County and, hence, venue there was not proper.

Georgia has some special laws relating to offenses involving theft. O.C.G.A. § 16-8-11 provides as follows: "In a prosecution under O.C.G.A. §§ 16-8-2 through 16-8-9 and O.C.G.A. §§ 16-8-13 through 16-8-15, the crime shall be considered as having been committed in any county in which the accused exercised control over the property which was the subject of the theft. In addition, in any prosecution under O.C.G.A. § 16-8-4 in which there is a

---

[19]But see King v. State, 271 Ga. App. 384, 609 S.E.2d 725 (2005).

[20]In re: B.R., 289 Ga. App. 6(3), 656 S.E.2d 172 (2007).

[21]In re D.D., 287 Ga. App. 512(2), 651 S.E.2d 817 (2007).

[22]Wright v. State, 219 Ga. App. 119, 120 (2), 464 S.E.2d 216 (1995).

[23]Davis v. State, 326 Ga. App. 279, 754 S.E.2d 815 (2014).

written rental agreement for personal property, the crime shall also be considered to have been committed in the county in which the accused signed the rental agreement." Accordingly, in cases involving theft by conversion the state has two options regarding venue. "First the state can proceed in the county where the accused received the money. There is sound authority that the accused exercised control over the money there. [Cits.] Second, the state can produce evidence tracing funds disbursed [i.e. spent] in one county (where the case is being prosecuted) back to the account or other source in the origin county, showing further that the funds were not disbursed in accordance with the contract provisions regarding the use of the funds."[24]

McCarty v. State[25] pointed out that venue may not be artificially created by officers. In this case, an undercover officer drove the defendant (in possession of marijuana) through several counties before arresting the defendant in Muscogee County, where he was tried. In *Griffin v. State,*[26] the defendant was indicted for murder in McIntosh County. The state did not seek the death penalty. The trial ended in a mistrial. He was re-indicted in McIntosh County, pled double jeopardy, and appealed. While the appeal was pending, he was indicted in Thomas County for kidnapping and the same murder. In Thomas County, the state sought the death penalty. The defendant appealed and the Supreme Court held that the Thomas County indictment must be quashed as to the count of murder because that county lacked the right to exercise jurisdiction. Further, the Georgia Supreme Court found the defendant could be tried for kidnapping in Thomas County, and, if re-indicted, the state could prosecute the murder charge in Thomas County as well.

The court pointed out that "[w]here two or more courts have concurrent jurisdiction of the same offense, the court which first acquires jurisdiction of the prosecution retains it to the exclusion of others while that case is pending." Although McIntosh County held exclusive jurisdiction of the murder charge at the time Thomas County originally indicted the defendant, McIntosh County dismissed the second indictment through nolle prosequi,

---

[24]Stowe v. State, 163 Ga. App. 535, 295 S.E.2d 209 (1982). Compare, Naylor v. State, 257 Ga. App. 899 572 S.E.2d 410 (2002), where the defendant, a Florida resident, was charged with theft by taking. The victim, a Fayette County, Georgia, resident, wire transferred the sum of $125,000 from a bank account in Fayette County, Georgia, to the defendant in Florida. Reversing the conviction, the Court of Appeals found that there was no evidence that the defendant either received the funds or spent them in Fayette County.

[25]McCarty v. State, 152 Ga. App. 726, 263 S.E.2d 700 (1979).

[26]Griffin v. State, 266 Ga. 115, 116-118, 464 S.E.2d 371 (1995) (quoting Brown v. Ohio, 432 U.S. 161, 164 n. 4, 97 S.Ct. 2221, 53 L.Ed.2d 187 (1977)).

thereby opening jurisdiction to Thomas County over the murder charge if they re-indicted the defendant. Thus, the court quashed Thomas County's original murder charge because of lack of jurisdiction, but noted that "[n]othing bars the State from reindicting [the defendant] for murder."

"Prosecutions of the same defendant in different counties of the same state 'must be viewed as the act of a single sovereign under the Double Jeopardy Clause.' " While this principle applies to the murder charge in *Griffin,* venue over the kidnapping charge lies solely in Thomas County. Under these circumstances there is no violation of Georgia procedural aspects as set out in O.C.G.A. § 16-1-7(b), which "requires that prosecution of a 'dual venue' criminal charge must occur in that one county where other criminal charges arising out of the same multi-county crime spree must be prosecuted."

Cases involving schemes to defraud the Georgia Medical assistance authorities present special problems. Where the criminal act involves the knowing and willful receipt of medical assistance payments to which one is not entitled through the use of a fraudulent scheme pursuant to O.C.G.A. § 49-4-146.1(b)(1)(C), venue is proper in any county in which one act in furtherance of the crime took place.[27] When the prosecution is based upon a provider's knowing and willful acceptance of "medical assistance payments to which he is not entitled or in an amount greater than that to which he is entitled" or a provider's intentional falsification of a required medical assistance document pursuant to O.C.G.A. § 49-4-146.1(b)(2), venue is proper in the county where the medical assistance document was falsified.[28]

In *Perkinson v. State,*[29] the Georgia Supreme Court held: "(1) If a defendant is convicted of felony murder in one county with an underlying felony committed in a second county, and the felony murder conviction is vacated by operation of *Malcom v. State,*[30] . . . the defendant [cannot] be tried and convicted of the underly-

---

[27]State v. Kell, 276 Ga. 423, 577 S.E.2d 551 (2003).

[28]State v. Barber, 193 Ga. App. 397, 388 S.E.2d 350 (1989). The venue distinction between O.C.G.A. §§ 49-4-146.1(b)(2) and 49-4-146.1(b)(1)(C) do not seem necessary. In State v. Kell, 276 Ga. 423, 577 S.E.2d 551 (2003), the Supreme Court took note of Barber but expressly restricted its holding to venue for cases brought under O.C.G.A. § 49-4-146.1(b)(1)(C). Compare McKinney v. State, 282 Ga. 230, 647 S.E.2d 44 (2007) (venue for misde-meanor violations of Georgia Ethics in Government Act involving failure to register campaign committee and file reports lay in Fulton County since State Commission which registered campaign committees and received their reports was located exclusively in Fulton County).

[29]Perkinson v. State, 273 Ga. 491, 493, 542 S.E.2d 92 (2001). See Sallie v. State, 216 Ga. App. 502, 455 S.E.2d 315 (1995).

[30]Malcolm v. State, 263 Ga. 369, 372 (4), 434 S.E.2d 479 (1993).

ing felony in the second county. . . . (2) If a defendant kidnaps a victim in one county and abducts the victim to a second county where he inflicts bodily injury on the victim, and the defendant is subsequently convicted of false imprisonment in the second county, . . . the defendant [cannot] then be tried and convicted of kidnapping with bodily injury in the first county."

Generally, venue is to be determined by the jury, and its decision will not be set aside as long as there is any evidence to support it.[31] However, in *State v. Wilson*,[32] a motion to dismiss for improper venue was filed and granted by the trial judge. Consequently, if there is testimony to the fact that a crime was committed on a certain street in a named city, an appellate court will take judicial notice of the county in which the city is located[33] if it is located in only one county.[34] In *Perry v. State*,[35] the court held that the state did not establish venue in Sumter County based solely on the defendant's unspecified street address, the affiliation of officers involved in the investigation, and the fact that the defendant was taken to Sumter County Sheriff's Department.

In *Graham v. State*,[36] the Supreme Court reversed a defendant's conviction for felony murder and aggravated assault after finding that the state failed to prove venue in Clayton County. Although the trial court properly took judicial notice that the city of Riverdale was located entirely within Clayton County, it failed to instruct the jury that it had taken such notice. Thus, the jury had no evidence as to the county in which the crimes had occurred. The court recommended that in the future when a trial court elects to take judicial notice of a fact that it follow Federal Rules of Evidence 201 (g) "by instructing the jury that it 'may, but is not required to, accept as conclusive any fact judicially noticed.' "[37]

---

[31]Jones v. State, 245 Ga. 592, 266 S.E.2d 201 (1980); Johns v. State, 239 Ga. 681, 682, 238 S.E.2d 372 (1977). See Wilkes v. State, 238 Ga. 57, 58 (1), 230 S.E.2d 867 (1976). In *Wilkes*, the court was actually confronted with the question of whether the trial judge erred in overruling a motion for a directed verdict.

[32]State v. Wilson, 220 Ga. App. 538, 469 S.E.2d 804 (1996).

[33]Landy v. State, 155 Ga. App. 763, 272 S.E.2d 735 (1980).

[34]But cf. Melton v. State, 252 Ga. 97, 311 S.E.2d 471 (1984).

[35]Perry v. State, 154 Ga. App. 559

(1), 269 S.E.2d 63 (1980), overruled by Joiner v. State, 231 Ga. App. 61, 497 S.E.2d 642 (1998), "to the extent that . . . [it] provide[s] authority for the proposition that venue can never be shown by evidence concerning an investigating officer's affiliation with a county or city law enforcement unit . . . ."

[36]Graham v. State, 275 Ga. 290, 565 S.E.2d 467 (2002).

[37]Graham v. State, 275 Ga. 290, 565 S.E.2d 467 (2002). In Robinson v. State, 260 Ga. App. 186, 581 S.E.2d 285 (2003), the defendant's conviction was reversed when the State proved only that the offense occurred in Jones-

In *Dowdell v. State*,[38] the Georgia Supreme Court held that where the defendant voluntarily pointed out to a person the place where the crime was committed and that person testified where that place was located, venue was sufficiently proved when another witness testified that the location was entirely in the county where the case was being tried. However, the validity of this case may be questioned in view of *Jones v. State*,[39] which is discussed above.

When a case is tried and, on appeal, it is determined that venue was not established by the state, the conviction is reversed; however, this does not prevent the re-trial of the defendant "in a court where venue is proper."[40] A reversal of a conviction due to the insufficiency of evidence concerning the procedural propriety of laying venue within a particular county and not because of an evidentiary insufficiency concerning the defendant's guilt does not raise the bar of double jeopardy to a retrial.[41]

In 1995, Georgia enacted O.C.G.A. § 17-2-4, which provides in part that a defendant in custody or present in a county other than that in which an indictment, accusation, complaint or arrest warrant is pending against him "may state in writing a wish to plead guilty, guilty but mentally ill, guilty but mentally retarded, or nolo contendere . . . and . . . consent to disposition of the case in the county in which the defendant" is being held. If the prosecuting attorney in each county approves, the clerk of the county where the indictment, complaint or arrest warrant is pending shall transfer the papers to the clerk of the court for the county where the defendant is being held, or is present and the "prosecution shall continue in that county." However, if "after the proceeding has been transferred pursuant [to the defendant's writing], the defendant pleads not guilty or not guilty by reason of insanity, the clerk shall return the papers to the court in which the prosecution was commenced and the proceeding shall be restored to the docket of that court."

Generally, see 21 Am. Jur. Criminal Law §§ 365 et seq. (1981).

---

boro, Georgia, but failed to establish that Jonesboro is located in Clayton County.

[38]Dowdell v. State, 200 Ga. 775 (1), 38 S.E.2d 780 (1946).

[39]Jones v. State, 272 Ga. 900, 537 S.E.2d 80 (2000).

[40]Hernandez v. State, 182 Ga. App. 797, 798, 357 S.E.2d 131 (1987).

[41]See Lynn v. State, 275 Ga. 288, 565 S.E.2d 800 (2002). See Twitty v. State, 298 Ga. 204, 779 S.E.2d 298 (2015).

§ 20:5   General requirements of proof—Variance

In *Prater v. State,*[1] the Georgia Supreme Court pointed out that unless a jury is charged on a particular crime, no verdict may be rendered on that crime.

The material on variance previously included in this chapter has been transferred to Studdard, *Daniel's Georgia Handbook on Criminal Evidence* (2018 ed.), §§ 1:40 et seq.

§ 20:6   *Jackson-Denno* hearings

In *Jackson v. Denno,*[1] the United States Supreme Court said that the due process clause of the Fourteenth Amendment requires the trial judge to determine that a confession was voluntary before permitting the jury to hear it. However, 22 years later in *Colorado v. Connelly,*[2] the United States Supreme Court held that coercive police or government activity "is a necessary predicate to the finding that a confession is not 'voluntary' within the meaning of the Due Process Clause of the Fourteenth Amendment." In *Sims v. Georgia,*[3] the court said that even when there is a conflict in the testimony on the question of voluntariness, the trial judge must first determine the issue of voluntariness before submitting the confession to the jury. The judge need not make a formal finding of fact, but his conclusion must clearly appear in the record.[4] In *Parrish v. State,*[5] the court held that a defendant is not entitled to a *Jackson v. Den*no hearing prior to trial. See § 5:26, supra, on defendant's right under Georgia law to a voluntariness hearing before a jury is permitted to hear a confession made to a private person.

In Georgia, it has been stated that a defendant is not entitled to a *Jackson-Denno* hearing unless he challenges the confession as not having been voluntarily made.[6] Based on the above rationale, the Georgia Supreme Court refused to overrule the trial

---

[Section 20:5]

[1]Prater v. State, 273 Ga. 477, 482 (5), 545 S.E.2d 864 (2001).

[Section 20:6]

[1]Jackson v. Denno, 378 U.S. 368, 84 S.Ct. 1774, 12 L.Ed.2d 908 (1964).

[2]Colorado v. Connelly, 479 U.S. 157, 167, 107 S.Ct. 515, 93 L.Ed.2d 473 (1986).

[3]Sims v. Georgia, 385 U.S. 538, 87 S.Ct. 639, 17 L.Ed.2d 593 (1967). In Pinto v. Pierce, 389 U.S. 31, 88 S.Ct. 192, 19 L.Ed.2d 31 (1967), the court said that it was prudent to have the hearing outside of the presence of the jury, but if a hearing is conducted in the presence of the jury, this is not reversible error if the court finds that the confession was freely and voluntarily given. The implication is that if the court found it was not voluntarily given, then a mistrial would have to be declared.

[4]Walraven v. State, 250 Ga. 401, 407 (4)(a), 297 S.E.2d 278 (1982).

[5]Parrish v. State, 194 Ga. App. 760, 761 (2), 391 S.E.2d 797 (1990).

[6]Day v. Mills, 224 Ga. 741, 744, 164 S.E.2d 828 (1968). However, in

court in *Sims v. State*, but the United States Supreme Court reversed the case.[7] In 1977, the Georgia Supreme Court held that where there was no objection to foundation evidence relating to the admissibility of a confession, and the first objection was made when the taped confession was offered, the defense could not object for the first time on appeal that a *Jackson-Denno* hearing was not held.[8] Likewise, in *McNair v. State*,[9] the court held that "[i]n the absence of a proper objection . . . there is no requirement" of a *Jackson v. Denno* hearing.

Also, there appears to be some change in attitude of the United States Supreme Court in regard to collateral relief and *Jackson-Denno* hearings as demonstrated in *Wainwright v. Sykes*.[10] In *Wainwright*, the Supreme Court stated that where there was no *Jackson-Denno* hearing on whether a defendant waived his *Miranda* rights and no contemporaneous objection was made, as required by Florida law, to the admission of an inculpatory statement, federal habeas corpus relief was not available to a defendant in the absence of a showing of the cause for noncompliance and of actual prejudice.[11] Of even more significance is the statement by the United States Supreme Court that there is no right to a *Jackson-Denno* hearing in the absence of an objection of the defendant and the disapproval of the contrary language contained in *Fay v. Noia*.[12]

On the state level, in *Watson v. State*,[13] the court held that, absent a proper objection and evidence of involuntariness, the

---

United States v. Powe, 591 F.2d 833 (D.C.Cir. 1978), the court held that a trial judge may, on its own motion, have a Jackson v. Denno hearing conducted.

[7]Sims v. State, 221 Ga. 190, 191 (5)(c), 144 S.E.2d 103 (1965), rev'd, 385 U.S. 538, 87 S.Ct. 639, 17 L.Ed.2d 593 (1967), remanded, 223 Ga. 126, 153 S.E.2d 567 (1967).

[8]Pierce v. State, 238 Ga. 682, 235 S.E.2d 374 (1977). Cf. Taylor v. State, 143 Ga. App. 881, 883 (2), 240 S.E.2d 236 (1977); Dent v. State, 243 Ga. 854, 257 S.E.2d 241 (1979).

In Craver v. State, 246 Ga. 467, 468, 271 S.E.2d 862 (1980), the court said that a hearing on the issue of voluntariness is required only if the evidence presents a question as to the voluntariness of a statement. Accord, Cook v. State, 269 Ga. 460, 461 (3), 499 S.E.2d 887 (1998).

[9]McNair v. State, 190 Ga. App. 412, 413 (2), 379 S.E.2d 424 (1989).

[10]Wainwright v. Sykes, 433 U.S. 72, 97 S.Ct. 2497, 53 L.Ed.2d 594 (1977), reh. denied, 434 U.S. 880, 98 S.Ct. 241, 54 L.Ed.2d 163 (1977).

[11]In Barrett v. State, 146 Ga. App. 207, 208 (3), 245 S.E.2d 890 (1978), the court said that where there was no objection to the introduction of evidence of defendant's incriminating statements, it was not necessary to have a hearing to determine whether or not the statements were voluntarily given. Accord, Elder v. State, 162 Ga. App. 425, 426, 291 S.E.2d 565 (1982).

[12]Fay v. Noia, 372 U.S. 391, 83 S.Ct. 822, 9 L.Ed.2d 837 (1963).

[13]Watson v. State, 227 Ga. 698, 182 S.E.2d 446 (1971). In Anderson v. State, 153 Ga. App. 401, 402 (2), 265 S.E.2d 299 (1980), the court implied that there is no error in not having a

admission of a statement was not error. However, on the next page of the decision, the court stated that where the voluntariness of a confession is questioned, it is necessary to have a separate hearing as to voluntariness.[14] In *Helton v. State*,[15] the defendant alleged that his pre-trial statement should have been inadmissible because it was not given freely and voluntarily; rather he gave the statement because police threatened to bring allegations of child abuse against him and because the police gave him hope of benefit by promising to tell the district attorney of his cooperation. Although Helton's testimony during the *Jackson-Denno* hearing, which was conducted to determine the admissibility of his pre-trial statement, mentioned these subjects, Helton did not claim that he made the statements due to promise of hope of benefit or coercion. Instead, Helton denied making the statements altogether. Thus, the court determined this was not a voluntariness violation. If the voluntariness of a statement is not what is challenged, no *Jackson-Denno* hearing is required.[16]

In *Schneider v. State*,[17] it was stated that where the state wishes to offer a statement in evidence, the court must offer the defendant a hearing outside the presence of the jury. Since the law is not clear on this point, the prosecuting attorney, in order to avoid possible error, should ask the trial court, out of the presence of the jury, for a *Jackson-Denno* hearing before attempting to introduce a statement in evidence.[18] The district attorney should also insure that the trial court clearly makes a finding that the statement was voluntarily given before the jury is permitted to hear the statement. In *Parker v. State*,[19] the court remanded the case where the trial judge at the end of a *Jackson-Denno* hearing "simply denied the [defendants'] motion" where

Jackson-Denno hearing unless the defendant requests one.

In Hudson v. State, 250 Ga. 479, 485, 299 S.E.2d 531 (1983), the court said, "[T]here is no constitutional requirement that the trial court conduct, sua sponte, a *Jackson v. Denno* hearing on voluntariness absent a contemporaneous challenge to the use of the confession in evidence."

[14]Watson v. State, 227 Ga. 698, 699, 182 S.E.2d 446 (1971). Cf. Cardell v. State, 119 Ga. App. 848, 168 S.E.2d 889 (1969); Strickland v. State, 226 Ga. 750, 177 S.E.2d 238 (1970).

[15]Helton v. State, 206 Ga. App. 600, 601, 426 S.E.2d 172 (1992) ("hope of benefit" has generally referred to promises of lighter sentence, reduced

charge or no charge at all).

[16]Henderson v. State, 204 Ga. App. 884, 888 (4), 420 S.E.2d 813 (1992).

[17]Schneider v. State, 130 Ga. App. 3, 5 (3), 202 S.E.2d 238 (1973); Pierce v. State, 238 Ga. 126, 128, 231 S.E.2d 744 (1977).

[18]Hall v. State, 176 Ga. App. 498, 503, 336 S.E.2d 604 (1985). See Jackson v. State, 124 Ga. App. 488, 489 (2), 184 S.E.2d 185 (1971). Both the state and the defense have a right to a full evidentiary hearing to determine the factual context of a statement which has been made.

[19]Parker v. State, 255 Ga. 167, 168 (1), 336 S.E.2d 242 (1985).

there was no "showing that the trial judge determined the voluntariness of the confession."

It has been held that where a defendant is asked about a former statement for the purpose of impeaching his earlier exculpatory testimony at the trial, no *Jackson-Denno* hearing is required.[20]

In *Crutchfield v. State*,[21] the defendant who was in custody on the charge of driving on a suspended license agreed to testify for an old acquaintance in an upcoming trial unrelated to the defendant. The testimony he provided implicated him in drug related offenses. The state later used the testimony to indict the defendant with drug charges. The court held that the defendant was not entitled to a *Jackson-Denno* hearing since his testimony was voluntarily provided and because he was not in custody on the drug related charges at the time of his testimony but on the unrelated suspended license charge.

In the absence of a valid waiver, a defendant is entitled to be present at a *Jackson-Denno* hearing.[22] At the hearing, the state first introduces its evidence to show voluntariness; then the defendant is entitled to introduce rebuttal evidence.[23] It has been held that where an officer testifies to all "the circumstances surrounding the confession, showing clearly that it was voluntary," it is not error for the trial judge to permit the officer to testify that the "statement was freely and voluntarily made."[24] The defendant may testify if he wishes,[25] but the court cannot call him as a witness.[26] In *Brown v. State*,[27] the Georgia Court of Appeals held that if a defendant does testify at a *Jackson v. Denno* hearing, the testimony is admissible at the trial of the case for purposes of impeachment and as substantive evidence.

---

[20]Anderson v. State, 153 Ga. App. 841, 842, 267 S.E.2d 259 (1980). But cf. Hill v. State, 246 Ga. 402, 407, 271 S.E.2d 802 (1980).

[21]Crutchfield v. State, 291 Ga. App. 24 (1), 660 S.E.2d 878 (2008).

[22]Deal v. State, 213 Ga. App. 131, 443 S.E.2d 713 (1994).

[23]See Hunsinger v. State, 225 Ga. 426 (1), 169 S.E.2d 286 (1969).

[24]Owens v. State, 161 Ga. App. 184, 288 S.E.2d 262 (1982).

[25]Stone v. State, 155 Ga. App. 357 (2), 271 S.E.2d 22 (1980).

[26]Shepherd v. State, 236 Ga. 787, 788, 225 S.E.2d 312 (1976). Apparently the defendant may be sworn and testify at the Jackson-Denno hearing without testifying before the jury. However, if a defendant elects to testify before the jury on the admissibility of the statement, he subjects himself to the usual cross-examination and not just to the facts surrounding the giving of the statement. Williams v. State, 231 Ga. 508, 509 (2), 202 S.E.2d 433 (1973). Cf. Hewell v. State, 136 Ga. App. 420, 221 S.E.2d 219 (1975).

[27]Brown v. State, 226 Ga. App. 140, 144, 486 S.E.2d 370 (1997). Accord, Wingfield v. State, 229 Ga. App. 75, 82 (4)(b), 493 S.E.2d 235 (1997), overruled on other grounds by Felix v. State, 271 Ga. 534, 523 S.E.2d 1 (1999).

The judge should consider the totality of the circumstances surrounding the giving of the statement.[28] "The standard for determining the admissibility of confessions is the preponderance of the evidence."[29] Hence, it is error to limit the defendant's testimony to whether he received the *Miranda* warnings.[30]

If a defendant testifies that he did not understand his *Miranda* warnings which were given him, on cross-examination he may be asked if he has ever been advised of his *Miranda* rights before if there is a factual basis for the question.[31] In *Nelson v. State,*[32] the court pointed out that "[g]enerally, when a trial court denies a motion to suppress a custodial statement without explanation, remand is necessary for clarification. . . . However, where 'there is *no* evidence which would authorize the trial court to find that appellant's statement was *not* voluntarily given . . . there is no reason to remand for findings of fact. . . .' "

A defendant is entitled to have all witnesses testify at the *Jackson-Denno* hearing who were present when a confession was given, otherwise the defendant is denied his right to fully investigate all the circumstances surrounding the confession.[33] In *Daniel v. State,*[34] *the court held that the state was not required to corroborate the officer's testimony by proffering a videotape of the session at which the statement was made.* In *Eagle v. State,*[35] the court held that a trial judge has discretion to re-open the evidence at a *Jackson-Denno* hearing to hear testimony from another witness.

The trial judge must be satisfied by a preponderance of the evidence that the confession was freely and voluntarily given,[36] and, where *Miranda* applies, that the defendant knowingly and intelligently waived his *Miranda* rights.[37] In *Jordan v. State,*[38] the court pointed out that a resolution of "the *Miranda* issue, when

[28]Lee v. State, 145 Ga. App. 369, 371 (2), 243 S.E.2d 734 (1978).

[29]Martin v. State, 271 Ga. 301, 304 (2), 518 S.E.2d 898 (1999).

[30]Pierce v. State, 238 Ga. 126, 129, 231 S.E.2d 744 (1977).

[31]Bowles v. State, 155 Ga. App. 753, 272 S.E.2d 595 (1980).

[32]Nelson v. State, 208 Ga. App. 686, 687 (1), 431 S.E.2d 464 (1993).

[33]See Porter v. State, 143 Ga. App. 640, 642, 239 S.E.2d 694 (1977).

[34]Daniel v. State, 268 Ga. 9 (2), 485 S.E.2d 734 (1997).

[35]Eagle v. State, 264 Ga. 1, 2 (1), 440 S.E.2d 2 (1994).

[36]Lego v. Twomey, 404 U.S. 477, 92 S.Ct. 619, 30 L.Ed.2d 618 (1972); High v. State, 233 Ga. 153, 210 S.E.2d 673 (1974); LaRue v. State, 171 Ga. App. 371, 372, 319 S.E.2d 468 (1984). In Brooks v. State, 244 Ga. 574, 581 (2), 261 S.E.2d 379 (1979), the court said that the state must prove by a preponderance of the evidence (1) that the confession was voluntary and (2) if it was the product of custodial interrogation by officers, that the confession was preceded by the appellant's knowing and voluntary waiver of his *Miranda* rights.

[37]Lane v. State, 247 Ga. 19, 20 (3), 273 S.E.2d 397 (1981). See Annot., "Duty of Court, in Federal Criminal

there is one, does not dispense with the mandate that 'a jury is not to hear a confession unless and until the trial judge has determined that it was freely and voluntarily given.' " The trial judge does not have to make a formal finding of fact,[39] but a mere ruling that he finds the issue in dispute and will let it go to the jury is insufficient.[40] The judge must rule that he will admit or reject the confession for the consideration of the jury.[41] The judge's failure to make a preliminary finding as to voluntariness before submitting the confession to the jury violates the defendant's Fourteenth Amendment rights.[42] The Georgia Supreme Court has said that it prefers rather "complete findings of fact, if the evidence warrants them, substantially as follows: I find from a preponderance of the evidence that the defendant was advised of each of his *Miranda* rights, that he understood them, that he voluntarily waived them, and that he thereafter gave his statement freely and voluntarily without any hope of benefit or fear of injury. (If the defendant denies having been advised of any one of his *Miranda* rights or says that he requested an attorney, specific findings as to the point in controversy should also be made.)"[43] However, in *Bryant v. State*,[44] the court pointed out that if there is no such findings of fact, a remand for clarification would generally be required. Some older Georgia Court of Appeal decisions have held that on appellate review the decision of the trial judge will be upheld unless there is an obvious error,[45] or the decision

---

Prosecution, to Conduct Inquiry into Voluntariness of Accused's Statement—Modern Cases," 132 A.L.R.Fed. 415 (1996).

[38]Jordan v. State, 207 Ga. App. 710, 713 (3), 429 S.E.2d 97 (1993).

[39]Brazell v. State, 140 Ga. App. 340, 231 S.E.2d 105 (1976).

[40]Jackson v. State, 124 Ga. App. 488, 489 (2), 184 S.E.2d 185 (1971); Richardson v. State, 143 Ga. App. 846, 847, 240 S.E.2d 217 (1977); Lee v. State, 145 Ga. App. 369, 371 (2), 243 S.E.2d 734 (1978). In Jones v. State, 146 Ga. App. 88, 245 S.E.2d 449 (1978), a majority of the court applied the "any evidence" rule to conflicting evidence concerning the voluntariness of a confession. Judge Smith, in a well-presented and documented dissent, emphasized that the "clearly erroneous" test should be applied. It should be kept in mind that if there is a question about a compliance with *Miranda*,

there is a "heavy burden" on the state. See § 5:19, supra.

[41]Schneider v. State, 130 Ga. App. 3, 5, 202 S.E.2d 238 (1973).

[42]Schneider v. State, 130 Ga. App. 3, 4 (1), 202 S.E.2d 238 (1973). If it is unclear as to the trial judge's ruling on voluntariness, an appellate court may under O.C.G.A. § 5-6-48(d) have the trial judge clarify the point and if it is so clarified as to show that the statement was voluntarily made, the case will not be reversed on this point. Ward v. State, 239 Ga. 205 (1), 236 S.E.2d 365 (1977); Stone v. State, 155 Ga. App. 357, 271 S.E.2d 22 (1980).

[43]Berry v. State, 254 Ga. 101, 104 n. 6, 326 S.E.2d 748 (1985). See Brown v. State, 294 Ga. 677, 755 S.E.2d 699 (2014).

[44]Bryant v. State, 268 Ga. 664, 492 S.E.2d 868 (1997).

[45]Ingram v. State, 137 Ga. App. 412, 413 (2), 224 S.E.2d 527 (1976);

is clearly erroneous.[46] Existence of conflicting evidence at a *Jackson-Denno* hearing does not automatically cause the trial court's finding, that the confession was freely and voluntarily given, to be clearly erroneous. In determining whether the trial court's ruling was clearly erroneous, an appellate court may look to all the evidence contained in the record.[47]

The "totality of the circumstances" test applies in determining whether or not a confession was freely and voluntarily given.[48] The Georgia Supreme Court has said that it is proper to consider the following factors in determining whether the "totality of the circumstances" test has been met: (1) the age of the defendant; (2) his education; (3) the knowledge of the defendant as to both the substance of the charge and the nature of his right to consult an attorney and his right to remain silent; (4) whether the accused is held incommunicado or allowed to consult with relatives, friends or an attorney; (5) whether the accused was interrogated before or after formal charges had been filed; (6) methods used in interrogation; (7) length of interrogation; (8) whether or not the accused refused to voluntarily give a statement(s) on (a) prior occasion(s); and (9) whether the accused repudiated the extrajudicial statement at a later date.[49]

However, to establish a waiver of rights under *Miranda,* there must be a knowing and intelligent relinquishment of a known right or privilege,[50] a matter which depends in each case "upon the particular facts and circumstances surrounding that case, including the background, experience and conduct of the accused."[51] For example, in *Clay v. State,*[52] the court held that *Miranda* warnings which were read to the defendant at "super speed" amounted to "gibberish" and were properly excluded since the defendant was never provided with an intelligible statement of his rights.

Johnson v. State, 233 Ga. 58, 209 S.E.2d 629 (1974); Smith v. State, 159 Ga. App. 20, 21, 282 S.E.2d 677 (1981); Stephens v. State, 170 Ga. App. 342, 343, 317 S.E.2d 627 (1984).

[46]Evans v. State, 248 Ga. App. 99, 545 S.E.2d 641 (2001); Stephens v. State, 170 Ga. App. 342, 343, 317 S.E.2d 627 (1984). See n. 44, supra, and n. 54, infra.

[47]Bowen v. State, 203 Ga. App. 371, 373 (2), 417 S.E.2d 18 (1992).

[48]Schneckloth v. Bustamonte, 412 U.S. 218, 93 S.Ct. 2041, 36 L.Ed.2d 854 (1973); LaRue v. State, 171 Ga. App. 371, 372, 319 S.E.2d 468 (1984).

[49]Riley v. State, 237 Ga. 124, 128, 226 S.E.2d 922 (1976) (citing West v. United States, 399 F.2d 467, 469 (5th Cir. 1968)). Accord, Henry v. State, 264 Ga. 861, 862 (2), 452 S.E.2d 505 (1995).

[50]Miranda v. Arizona, 384 U.S. 436, 86 S.Ct. 1602, 16 L.Ed.2d 694 (1966).

[51]Edwards v. Arizona, 451 U.S. 477, 101 S.Ct. 1880, 68 L.Ed.2d 378 (1981).

[52]Clay v. State, 290 Ga. 822, 725 S.E.2d 260 (2012).

Edwards v. Arizona[53] illustrates this distinction, emphasizing that where *Miranda* applies, an admission may not be received in evidence unless there was a knowing and intelligent waiver; but where *Miranda* does not apply, an admission may be received in evidence if it was freely and voluntarily given. Therefore, unless a defendant understands his *Miranda* rights and knowingly and intelligently relinquishes them, a statement obtained from him pursuant to custodial interrogation, or its functional equivalent, is inadmissible.[54]

The test for voluntariness of admissions under the Fifth Amendment is stricter than the test for consent to search cases under the Fourth Amendment, as in the latter situation it is not necessary to show that the person consenting to the search was informed of or knew that he had a right to refuse to consent in order to show that the consent was voluntary.[55]

If the judge finds that the confession was voluntarily made (and if *Miranda* applies, that the defendant knowingly and intelligently waived his *Miranda* rights), then after presenting before the jury the same evidence as that at the *Jackson v. Denno* hearing, the state may offer the confession before the jury without further proof of its voluntary character (or proof of a waiver of *Miranda* rights if that is involved). However, in *Crane v. Kentucky*,[56] the United States Supreme Court held that the defendant is still entitled to introduce evidence before the jury to show that the confession was not made or that it was not voluntarily given[57] and to show "the environment in which the police secured his confession." This evidence is admissible if it relates to voluntariness and hence to the weight to be given the statement. The State has the right to rebut such evidence before the jury if it wishes.[58]

Even if the court determines that the confession was voluntarily made, the defendant may still have the jury pass on the issue by making a timely written request to charge.[59] However, the trial judge is not obligated to charge the jury to return a special

---

[53]Edwards v. Arizona, 451 U.S. 477, 101 S.Ct. 1880, 68 L.Ed.2d 378 (1981).

[54]Miranda v. Arizona, 384 U.S. 436, 86 S.Ct. 1602, 16 L.Ed.2d 694 (1966); Edwards v. Arizona, 451 U.S. 477, 101 S.Ct. 1880, 68 L.Ed.2d 378 (1981).

[55]Schneckloth v. Bustamonte, 412 U.S. 218, 93 S.Ct. 2041, 36 L.Ed.2d 854 (1973).

[56]Crane v. Kentucky, 476 U.S. 683, 106 S.Ct. 2142, 90 L.Ed.2d 636 (1986).

[57]Young v. State, 149 Ga. App. 78, 80, 253 S.E.2d 410 (1979).

[58]Cardell v. State, 119 Ga. App. 848 (2), 168 S.E.2d 889 (1969).

[59]In Murray v. State, 151 Ga. App. 122, 258 S.E.2d 919 (1979), the court held that it was proper to have the jury determine whether the defendant's confession had been "given voluntarily and after he had knowingly

verdict concerning the voluntariness of an incriminating statement.[60] In a case in which the defense wishes to have the jury pass on the question of voluntariness and/or the adequacy of the compliance with *Miranda,* it is error for the court to inform the jury that the judge has found that the statement is admissible.[61] In the absence of such a request, it is not necessary for the court to charge on the question of voluntariness or to submit the issue to the jury.[62]

If a defendant makes a valid oral confession or admission, the person to whom it is made may testify as to what was said.[63] If a defendant makes a valid written, signed confession, the confession may be read to the jury, but it is not admissible in evidence to the extent that the document may be carried to the jury room. The actual written confession in the hands of the jurors is regarded as giving the confession undue weight and importance.[64] However, it has been held that permitting a signed, written statement of the defendant to go to the jury is not reversible error where it is consistent with the theory of the defense,[65] and even where a statement is found to be voluntarily made, it may still be inadmissible if there is some other reason for excluding it, such as the fact that it is hearsay.[66]

If a defendant signs a *Miranda* waiver form, apparently this is admissible in evidence and may be carried to the jury room with the other evidence.[67]

---

waived his constitutional rights."

[60]McKenzie v. State, 249 Ga. 582, 583 (3), 292 S.E.2d 692 (1982).

[61]Dean v. State, 168 Ga. App. 172, 174 (3), 308 S.E.2d 434 (1983).

[62]Serrano v. State, 146 Ga. App. 781, 783, 247 S.E.2d 593 (1978); Batts v. State, 238 Ga. 664, 235 S.E.2d 377 (1977), and see particularly the concurring opinion beginning on page 665.

[63]Hayes v. State, 152 Ga. App. 858, 859 (3), 264 S.E.2d 307 (1980).

[64]Royals v. State, 208 Ga. 78 (2), 65 S.E.2d 158 (1951). But if a written confession is admitted into evidence and taken into the jury room without objection, this is not error. Smithwick v. State, 199 Ga. 292, 293 (10), 34 S.E.2d 28 (1945). Also, if a statement is admitted over objection, this does not entitle the defendant to a reversal unless he was prejudiced by its admission. This is particularly true where

the statement actually supports the defendant's theory of the case. Proctor v. State, 235 Ga. 720, 724, 221 S.E.2d 556 (1975); Laster v. State, 163 Ga. App. 294 (2), 293 S.E.2d 75 (1982).

[65]Proctor v. State, 235 Ga. 720, 724, 221 S.E.2d 556 (1975); Laster v. State, 163 Ga. App. 294 (2), 293 S.E.2d 75 (1982).

[66]Lane v. State, 247 Ga. 19, 21 (4), 273 S.E.2d 397 (1981).

In Owens v. State, 248 Ga. 629, 630, 284 S.E.2d 408 (1981), a taped statement of the defendant was played before the jury and, over objection, the jury was allowed to take the tape to the jury room. The court concluded that this was error, but concluded it was highly probable that it did not contribute to the verdict and that the error was harmless.

[67]Hill v. State, 144 Ga. App. 259, 260 (5), 241 S.E.2d 44 (1977); Davis v. State, 162 Ga. App. 190 (1), 290 S.E.2d

In *Gates v. State,*[68] the court affirmed the showing of a videotaped confession after a *Jackson-Denno* hearing.

At a joint trial, if a confession of one defendant is considered, great care must be used to be sure that the identity of the person or persons (other than the confessing defendant) is or are not identified.[69] See § 14:72, supra, on severance of parties.

It must be remembered that statements made by a defendant which are not incriminating on their face, but which are contradictory to statements made by a defendant to an officer, may become incriminating and their admissibility in evidence is determined by the same rules governing the admissibility of a confession.[70] However, self-serving declarations made by a defendant to an arresting officer are not admissible and may not be developed by defense counsel while cross-examining a witness called by the state.[71] Nevertheless, it must be remembered that where a defendant's confession is admitted it is deemed to be admitted in its entirety including any portions which are exculpatory.[72]

Generally, see § 14:72, supra, on severance of parties. Also see §§ 5:3 et seq., supra, on admissibility of confessions and admissions. See §§ 14:79 et seq., supra, on a hearing to suppress tangible evidence.

§ 20:7 Evidence—general

Over 60 years ago, Mr. Molnar, in his treatise on Georgia criminal law, said that "the subject of Evidence is one of the most extensive and voluminous in the criminal law. It is impossible to embrace this subject within the limits of a general brief, which is intended, primarily, to be used for quick reference in the courtroom."[1] With the continued growth in the field of evidence since that time, the above statement is even more applicable today.

In view of space limitations, only the most important rules of evidence which relate particularly to criminal cases will be discussed. Some aspects of the subject have already been

---

124 (1982).

[68]Gates v. State, 244 Ga. 587, 588 (1), 261 S.E.2d 349 (1979).

[69]In Edge v. State, 144 Ga. App. 213, 214 (1), 240 S.E.2d 765 (1977), the court held that the deletion of the names of the other three defendants was not sufficient since the confession clearly implicated the other defendants.

[70]Hill v. State, 246 Ga. 402, 407, 271 S.E.2d 802 (1980). See § 5:14, supra.

[71]Thomas v. State, 248 Ga. 247, 252 (10), 282 S.E.2d 316 (1981).

[72]Spencer v. State, 180 Ga. App. 498, 500 (2), 349 S.E.2d 513 (1986).

[Section 20:7]

[1]Molnar, Georgia Criminal Law, 140 (Harrison Co., 1935).

discussed and will not be repeated here. For example, "confessions" were discussed in Chapter 5, supra, from the investigative standpoint and in § 20:6, supra, under the title of *"Jackson-Denno* hearings."

Generally, if there is doubt as to the admissibility of evidence, the evidence should be admitted and its weight left to the jury.[2]

A distinction is drawn between positive and negative evidence.[3] Positive testimony is testimony that a particular event took place. Negative testimony is testimony of a witness that he did not see or hear the particular event.[4] The idea that if witnesses are equally credible and have the same opportunity of observation, positive testimony should outweigh that which is negative and such a charge to the jury is proper,[5] if the facts justify it. However, the positive and negative evidence rule does not apply "when two parties have equal facilities for seeing or hearing a thing and one swears that it occurred while the other swears that it did not."[6]

Courts may take judicial notice of facts of common knowledge that are certain or are subject to verification.[7] Thus, a judge may take judicial notice of the contents of an official census.[8] The Georgia Supreme Court may take judicial notice of the contents of other records on file with that court,[9] but a superior court may not take judicial notice of the record of another case in the same court,[10] nor of municipal ordinances.[11]

Generally, a non-expert witness may give his opinion or belief if this is material and if he states his reasons for his opinion, but he may not give his opinion of the ultimate issue to be determined by the jury.[12]

The testimony of a witness is not to be rejected merely because he refuses to testify to a certain thing positively.[13] It is sufficient

---

[2]Green v. State, 112 Ga. App. 329 (4), 145 S.E.2d 80 (1965); Central of Georgia Railway Co. v. Bernstein, 113 Ga. 175, 177, 38 S.E. 394 (1901); Allanson v. State, 144 Ga. App. 450, 453 (2), 241 S.E.2d 314 (1978). In Miller v. State, 150 Ga. App. 597, 601, 258 S.E.2d 279 (1979), the court said that generally "every fact or circumstance serving to throw light on the issue being tried constitutes proper evidence."

[3]O.C.G.A. § 24-14-7.

[4]See Lyens v. State, 133 Ga. 587, 594 (2), 66 S.E. 792 (1909), limited by Hewitt v. State, 27 Ga. App. 676, 109 S.E. 679 (1921).

[5]Wood v. State, 9 Ga. App. 365, 71 S.E. 500 (1911).

[6]O.C.G.A. § 24-14-7.

[7]See O.C.G.A. § 24-2-201 and O.C.G.A. § 24-2-220.

[8]Tift v. Bush, 209 Ga. 769, 771, 75 S.E.2d 805 (1953).

[9]Stynchcombe v. Clements, 227 Ga. 244, 245, 179 S.E.2d 917 (1971).

[10]Kazakos v. Baranan, 122 Ga. App. 594, 595, 178 S.E.2d 222 (1970).

[11]McAllister v. State, 7 Ga. App. 541, 67 S.E. 221 (1910).

[12]O.C.G.A. § 24-7-701.

[13]Holcombe v. State, 5 Ga. App. 47, 48 (6), 62 S.E. 647 (1908); Fletcher v. Gillespie, 201 Ga. 377, 390, 40

if he testifies to the best of his recollection.[14] "Although a witness may have no distinct and independent recollection of the details of a fact occurring in the course of the routine of his business, he may testify . . . to his fixed and uniform habit in such cases, and state that he knows that what he did in a given transaction was in accordance with that habit."[15]

In *Thomas v. Lockwood*,[16] the court said, "Direct and positive testimony . . . which is given by an unimpeached witness as to the existence of facts apparently within his own knowledge, which is not in itself incredible, impossible, or inherently improbable, and which is not contradicted directly or indirectly by proof of facts or circumstances that could be taken as incompatible with such testimony, cannot be arbitrarily rejected by a . . . trier of the facts upon the mere surmise that it perhaps might not be in accord with the truth." This notion, however, has been rejected by the Court of Appeals which found that it is appropriate if at all, only in civil cases.[17] Instead, the court endorsed the rule expressed in *Tate v. State*,[18] to the effect that the trier of fact "is not obligated to believe a witness even if the testimony is uncontradicted and may accept or reject any portion of the testimony." Thus, a number of cases have held that "courts and juries are not bound to believe testimony as to facts incredible, impossible, or inherently improbable."[19]

When evidence is admitted for one purpose, it is not error for the trial judge to fail to instruct the jury to limit its consideration of that evidence to the one purpose for which it was admitted in the absence of a request to so instruct the jury.[20] It has been held that when the trial court does instruct the jury that evidence is admitted for a limited purpose, it is immaterial whether such an instruction is given before or after the testimony.[21]

It is not necessary for the state to have a victim testify if the prosecution can prove the defendant's guilt without the testimony

S.E.2d 45 (1946). E.g., Lyons v. State, 247 Ga. 465, 277 S.E.2d 244 (1981).

[14]Holcombe v. State, 5 Ga. App. 47, 48 (6), 62 S.E. 647 (1908).

[15]Green v. State, 165 Ga. App. 702 (2), 302 S.E.2d 604 (1983) (crime lab expert did not specifically remember marijuana involved).

[16]Thomas v. Lockwood, 198 Ga. 437, 446, 31 S.E.2d 791 (1944).

[17]State v. Hester, 268 Ga. App. 501, 602 S.E.2d 271 (2004) expressly overruled State v. Stokes, 185 Ga. App. 718, 719, 365 S.E.2d 477 (1988) and

the statement taken from Thomas v. Lockwood quoted in text above.

[18]Tate v. State, 264 Ga. 53, 56 (3), 440 S.E.2d 646 (1994).

[19]Thornton v. State, 161 Ga. App. 296, 298, 287 S.E.2d 749 (1982); Howell v. State, 179 Ga. App. 632, 633 (1), 347 S.E.2d 358 (1986).

[20]Shields v. State, 147 Ga. App. 131, 248 S.E.2d 205 (1978); Bettis v. State, 160 Ga. App. 109 (2), 286 S.E.2d 759 (1981).

[21]Hurst v. State, 166 Ga. App. 852, 305 S.E.2d 663 (1983).

of the victim, unless the defense seeks to have the victim testify.[22]

Documents or pictures which are not formally tendered in evidence but are shown to the jury and treated as though they have been admitted in evidence are treated as having been admitted.[23]

The counsel asking a question of a witness cannot object to the answer if it is a direct and pertinent response to the question asked.[24]

In *Cody v. State*,[25] the court reviewed the procedure to follow when a witness invokes the privilege against self incrimination as follows:

"First, the trial court is required to decide whether there is a real and appreciable danger that the answer *could* incriminate the witness. If so, then the decision on whether to answer must be left to the witness. If the trial court determines that the answers could not incriminate the witness, the witness is required to answer or face the court's sanction. If the witness's refusal to answer (whether because the answer could incriminate or because the witness violates the court's order to answer) denies a party a thorough and sifting cross-examination of the specific of the witness's testimony on direct, then the trial court is authorized to strike that witness's direct testimony. However, if the invocation of the privilege relates to a collateral issue or to his general credibility, then the testimony need not be stricken." [citations omitted].

Georgia courts,[26] as well as those of other states,[27] have recognized that a question which is asked of a witness may constitute a statement of some prejudicial matter. Thus, it is error for the district attorney to ask an officer whether he is familiar with the defendant's reputation where his character has not been put in evidence.[28] A district attorney must act in good faith when he asks about specific events, even if the events are admissible

---

[22]White v. State, 193 Ga. App. 428, 431 (6), 387 S.E.2d 921 (1989).

[23]Clayton v. State, 149 Ga. App. 374, 375 (1), 254 S.E.2d 495 (1979).

[24]Rice v. State, 159 Ga. App. 641 (2), 284 S.E.2d 657 (1981); Jackson v. State, 180 Ga. App. 363, 364 (2), 349 S.E.2d 252 (1986).

[25]Cody v. State, 278 Ga. 779, 780 (2), 609 S.E.2d 320 (2004).

[26]Bowers v. State, 153 Ga. App. 894(1)[0], 267 S.E.2d 309 (1980) (citing former O.C.G.A. § 24-9-67 [effec-
tive January 1, 2013, § 24-9-67 was replaced by § 24-7-702 and § 24-7-703.]; Gamble v. State, 141 Ga. App. 304, 305, 233 S.E.2d 264 (1977); Watson v. State, 137 Ga. App. 530, 224 S.E.2d 446 (1976).

[27]Richardson v. United States, 150 F.2d 58, 64 (6th Cir. 1945); People v. Di Paolo, 366 Mich. 394, 115 N.W.2d 78 (1962); State v. Flowers, 262 Minn. 164, 114 N.W.2d 78 (1962).

[28]Stanley v. State, 94 Ga. App. 737 (1), 96 S.E.2d 195 (1956).

and they in fact took place.[29] Thus, in questioning a witness, it is error for counsel to make prejudicial insinuations which have no factual basis.[30]

In *Crawford v. Washington*,[31] the United States Supreme Court held that a defendant's right to confront a witness against him could not be abridged simply because the witness was unavailable and his or her out-of-court statements could be characterized as trustworthy. Accordingly, the question of whether the out-of-court statements of a witness are of a "testimonial" character, such as that made during the course of a police investigation or in front of a grand jury, is a critical one. *Crawford* and related issues to a defendant's right of confrontation are discussed in Studdard, *Daniel's Georgia Handbook on Criminal Evidence*, § 1:28 on cross examination.

If an objection is sustained some of the testimony of a witness on direct examination, the party attempting to introduce the evidence must make an offer of proof to show what the testimony would have been. In the absence of such an offer of proof, there can be no reversal because of the ruling of the court.[32]

The material formerly contained in this volume on witnesses and evidence in Chapters 20 and 21 has been removed because of space limitations. That material has been updated and republished in Studdard, *Daniel's Georgia Handbook on Criminal Evidence* (2018 ed.).

§ 20:8   Resting the state's case

Many attorneys feel that the first and last witnesses have the

---

[29]See Sherman v. State, 141 Ga. App. 632, 633 (1), 234 S.E.2d 175 (1977). In Douglas v. Alabama, 380 U.S. 415, 85 S.Ct. 1074, 13 L.Ed.2d 934 (1965), the defendant was on trial for murder. Previously an accomplice named Lloyd had been convicted of the murder. Lloyd was called as a prosecution witness and invoked the Fifth Amendment. The prosecuting attorney, over objection, then used a confession signed by Lloyd and, in the guise of refreshing the witness's recollection, read it a sentence or two at a time to the witness asking after each excerpt if he made that statement. The Supreme Court held that this was a violation of the confrontation clause of the Sixth Amendment.

[30]People v. Nuccio, 43 Ill.2d 375, 253 N.E.2d 353 (1969); Boggs v. State, 268 Ala. 358, 106 So.2d 263 (1958).

A.B.A. Standards, The Prosecution Function, Vol. I, Standard 3-5.7(d) states, "A prosecutor should not ask a question which implies the existence of a factual predicate for which a good faith belief is lacking." A.B.A. Standards, The Defense Function, Vol. I, Standard 4-7.6 contains an identical provision.

[31]Crawford v. Washington, 541 U.S. 36, 124 S. Ct. 1354, 158 L. Ed. 2d 177, 63 Fed. R. Evid. Serv. 1077 (2004).

[32]See Smith v. State, 142 Ga. App. 810, 812 (4), 237 S.E.2d 216 (1977). However, in Wesley v. State, 166 Ga. App. 28 (2), 303 S.E.2d 124 (1983), the court held that it was not error for the trial judge to refuse a tender of evidence if it is clear that the judge knew the evidence was not admissible.

greatest impact on the jury and thought should be given to ending on a high note. In theory, the prosecuting attorney should present all the direct testimony available to him in his case-in-chief before the defense puts up any of its evidence. If he fails to put up all his direct testimony, he may run an unnecessary risk of having a directed verdict of acquittal granted against him. However, the district attorney may correctly feel that he has made out a sufficiently strong case without the use of all his witnesses or that to put up other witnesses would unduly prolong the case. In addition, there is always the chance that another witness might damage the prosecution's case.

The district attorney may also feel that it may be advantageous to hold a witness back if he feels he can use the witness in rebuttal. The obvious danger in employing such a strategy is the possibility that neither the defendant nor any other defense witness will take the stand to testify, in which case the prosecuting attorney will not be able to use his witnesses unless the court agrees to allow him to reopen the evidence.[1] Thus, the state's counsel must determine whether to put up all of the witnesses and evidence he has initially to take a chance with the hope that he does not need them or can use them later. The conservative practice is for the district attorney to present the best and most complete evidence in his case-in-chief.

§ 20:9   Continuances during course of trial

The trial judge has authority to continue a case during a trial by jury. However, a "lengthy continuance, absent exceptional circumstances or consent of the parties, is improper."[1]

[Section 20:8]
[1]"Reopening the evidence" is discussed in § 22:6, infra.

[Section 20:9]
[1]Morris v. State, 264 Ga. 823, 825 (4), 452 S.E.2d 100 (1995).

Chapter 21

Presenting the Defendant's Case and Attacks Thereon

§ 21:31   — —Sudden emergency
§ 21:32   — —Proximate cause
§ 21:33   — —Gender discrimination by district attorney in
                 death case
§ 21:34   — —Reverse sting operations
§ 21:35   — —Involuntariness of confession

KeyCite®: Cases and other legal materials listed in KeyCite Scope can be researched through the KeyCite service on Westlaw®. Use KeyCite to check citations for form, parallel references, prior and later history, and comprehensive citator information, including citations to other decisions and secondary materials.

---

§ 21:1   Motion for directed verdict of acquittal

At the conclusion of the state's evidence, the defendant may move for a directed verdict of acquittal. If the motion is overruled, the defendant may then submit any evidence he wishes in the defense of the case. If the motion is granted, it effectively terminates the case[1] regardless of whether the jury agrees to the action. If the motion is overruled and the defendant presents evidence, he may again move for a directed verdict after both prosecution and defense have rested.[2]

O.C.G.A. § 17-9-1(a) provides for a directed verdict as follows:

"(a) Where there is no conflict in the evidence and the evidence introduced with all reasonable deductions and inferences therefrom shall demand a verdict of acquittal or 'not guilty' as to the entire offense or to some particular count or offense, the court may direct the verdict of acquittal to which the defendant is entitled under the evidence and may allow the trial to proceed only as to the counts or offenses remaining, if any."

In the 1981 case of *Lee v. State*,[3] the court pointed out that a trial judge must grant a motion for a directed verdict of acquittal "unless viewing the evidence in the light most favorable to the prosecution, a rational trier of fact could find the essential elements of the crime beyond a reasonable doubt."

The words in the statute referring to "no conflict in the evi-

---

[Section 21:1]

[1]In Fong Foo v. United States, 369 U.S. 141, 82 S.Ct. 671, 7 L.Ed.2d 629 (1962), the court held that even if the trial judge erred in directing a verdict of acquittal, the double jeopardy clause prevents a retrial. See § 14:61, supra.

[2]O.C.G.A. § 17-9-1(b). See § 22:5, infra. A motion for a directed verdict of acquittal may not be filed prior to trial. Carlile v. State, 132 Ga. App. 787, 209 S.E.2d 241 (1974).

[3]Lee v. State, 247 Ga. 411, 412 (6), 276 S.E.2d 590 (1981); Rautenberg v. State, 178 Ga. App. 165, 167 (1), 342 S.E.2d 355 (1986).

dence . . . with all reasonable deductions and inferences" mean that a motion for a directed verdict of acquittal should be granted if the evidence is insufficient as a matter of law to authorize a conviction. Even where there is a conflict in the evidence, it is the duty of the trial judge to grant a motion for a directed verdict of acquittal if the evidence will not support a conviction. Thus, in a felony trial where the only evidence against the defendant is the testimony of an accomplice, it is error for the trial court to refuse to grant a motion for a directed verdict of acquittal.[4] In determining whether to grant a motion for directed verdict, the trial judge may properly consider inferences and presumptions found in our law.[5]

If a defendant fails to make a motion for a directed verdict of acquittal, he will be deemed to have waived his right to the motion.[6] While normally a defendant will not wish to waive his right to make a motion for a directed verdict, there may be circumstances in which he should consider not making the motion. For example, if the state overlooks some essential element of the offense which leads the defendant to move for a directed verdict of acquittal at the close of the state's case, the trial judge may agree to reopen the evidence at that point in time in order to permit the prosecution to supply the missing evidence. On the other hand, if the trial judge overrules a motion for a directed verdict at the conclusion of the evidence and on appeal this ruling is reversed, the appellate court will direct the trial court to enter a judgment of acquittal,[7] thus terminating the case.

---

[4]Boggus v. State, 136 Ga. App. 917, 920 (7), 222 S.E.2d 686 (1975). Merino v. State, 230 Ga. 604, 198 S.E.2d 311 (1973), emphasizes that under the present Georgia statute, it is error for the trial judge to refuse to grant a motion for a directed verdict of acquittal when the evidence is insufficient to support a conviction, and disapproved cases holding the contrary, such as Pritchard v. State, 224 Ga. 776, 779 (2), 164 S.E.2d 808 (1968), Carter v. State, 227 Ga. 788, 795 (7), 183 S.E.2d 392 (1971), and Allen v. State, 228 Ga. 859, 860 (2), 188 S.E.2d 793 (1972).

[5]Lingold v. State, 162 Ga. App. 486, 487, 292 S.E.2d 193 (1982).

[6]See Smith v. State, 205 Miss. 170, 38 So.2d 698 (1949), and Palos v. United States, 416 F.2d 438 (5th Cir.

1969). If there is insufficient evidence to support a conviction, a defendant should be able to obtain a new trial, but if a motion for a directed verdict is made and after conviction a motion for judgment not withstanding the verdict is made and this is sustained either in the trial or appellate courts, this terminates the case.

[7]See Granger v. State, 142 Ga. App. 612, 614, 236 S.E.2d 762 (1977).

In Bethay v. State, 235 Ga. 371, 219 S.E.2d 743 (1975), the court said in determining whether or not the trial judge committed error in refusing to grant a motion for a directed verdict of acquittal, the appellate court must consider all the evidence introduced in the trial court by the state and the defendant—not just the state's evidence.

In *Lam v. State*,[8] the court held that while "[a] RICO conviction requires proof that a defendant has committed two or more offenses of the kind included in the RICO statute; it does not require the State to prove all of the alleged predicate offenses."

It should also be kept in mind that the constitutionality of a criminal statute which the defendant is charged with violating or one which provides for exceptions to such a statute, may be raised by a motion for directed verdict.[9] On the other hand, in *Tibbs v. State*,[10] the court held that a "motion for a directed verdict of acquittal is not the proper way to contest the sufficiency of an indictment." Thus, a motion for directed verdict must be addressed to the sufficiency of the evidence and not to the adequacy of the indictment.[11]

The oral statement of the trial judge that he is granting a motion for a directed verdict of acquittal does not amount to a judgment until he signs an order.[12] However, if a trial judge in the trial of a multi-count indictment orally indicates that he will grant a motion for directed verdict as to one count and the trial continues on the remaining count or counts and later the judge changes his mind about the grant of the directed verdict, if the defense has been misled, counsel has a right to request or move to have the evidence reopened.[13]

See § 22:5, infra, on a motion for a directed verdict of acquittal after the evidence has been closed.

§ 21:2   General consideration of defendant's case

From a purely technical point of view, a defendant need not "put up any case."[1] A defense lawyer must be sure the jury thoroughly understands this fact. If from the presence or lack of evidence, there is a reasonable doubt as to the defendant's guilt,

---

[8]Lam v. State, 208 Ga. App. 324, 325 (4), 430 S.E.2d 775 (1993).

[9]Simmons v. State, 246 Ga. 390, 271 S.E.2d 468 (1980).

[10]Tibbs v. State, 211 Ga. App. 250, 251 (1), 438 S.E.2d 706 (1993).

[11]Williams v. State, 162 Ga. App. 350, 351, 291 S.E.2d 425 (1982).

[12]Harden v. State, 160 Ga. App. 514, 515, 287 S.E.2d 329 (1981).

[13]Harden v. State, 160 Ga. App. 514, 517, 287 S.E.2d 329 (1981).

[Section 21:2]

[1]In United States v. Frank, 494 F.2d 145 (2d Cir. 1974), the court said,

"To be sure, the defendants were not required to testify or to present any case at all, and the jury could not permissibly draw an adverse inference simply from their failure to take the stand. But the self-incrimination clause does not elevate a defendant's silence, much less the failure to present any defense case, to the level of a convincing reputation." See State v. Moore, 237 Ga. 269, 270, 227 S.E.2d 241 (1976); Davis v. United States, 160 U.S. 469, 487, 16 S.Ct. 353, 40 L.Ed. 499 (1895).

he is entitled to an acquittal regardless of whether he introduces any evidence.[2] However, from a practical standpoint, the jury may still feel that the defendant should be convicted unless he can give an explanation of his actions.[3] This possible attitude on the jury's part must be weighed against the possibility of perjury if the defendant takes the stand.[4]

After evidence is closed on both sides, the prosecuting attorney shall open and conclude the argument to the jury regardless of whether or not the defendant presented any evidence.[5] The defendant shall be entitled to make a closing argument prior to the concluding argument of the prosecuting attorney.[6]

From a technical standpoint, a defendant may raise inconsistent defenses,[7] but from a practical standpoint this is rarely, if ever, desirable.

Since the defendant is entitled to remain in the courtroom at all times during the trial,[8] it may be preferable to have him testify as the last defense witness, if he is to testify at all. The defendant will thus have an opportunity, after hearing all the other witnesses, to explain any discrepancies, conflicts, or questions which may have arisen and in a sense tie the loose ends of the case together.

§ 21:3   The defendant as a witness

As previously pointed out, a defendant need not testify at trial.[1] If he fails to testify, the prosecution may not refer to his failure

---

[2]Williamson v. State, 9 Ga. App. 442, 445, 71 S.E. 509 (1911).

[3]In the unanimous opinion of Wilson v. Zant, 249 Ga. 373, 385 (4), 290 S.E.2d 442 (1982), disapp. on other grounds, Morgan v. State, 267 Ga. 203, 476 S.E.2d 747 (1996), the court stated: "Notwithstanding the fact that the burden of proof is upon the state, it is merely a truism to say that a person charged with a criminal offense will put before the jury evidence to corroborate his innocence or create a reasonable doubt if such evidence is available. Thus, when the prosecution comments on the defendant's failure to produce purportedly favorable evidence, it is urging the jury to make the reasonable deduction that there exists no such favorable evidence."

[4]See Zolun v. State, 169 Ga. App. 707, 708 (2), 314 S.E.2d 672 (1984) (af-

ter defendant's acquittal in murder case, he was convicted of perjury in connection with his trial testimony with the court finding that other evidence presented at the murder trial could have been basis for jury's verdict rather than defendant's testimony, precluding application of collateral estopped in the perjury case).

[5]O.C.G.A. § 17-8-71.

[6]O.C.G.A. § 17-8-71.

[7]Green v. State, 7 Ga. App. 803, 68 S.E. 318 (1910).

[8]See § 17:8, supra, on defendant's presence during court proceedings.

[Section 21:3]

[1]See § 21:2, supra; Fifth Amendment to the United States Constitution; Ga. Const. 1983, Art. I, § I, ¶ XVI; O.C.G.A. § 24-5-506.

In Young v. Ricketts, 242 Ga. 559, 250 S.E.2d 404 (1978), the court

to take the stand.[2] However, in the absence of a request to charge, if a defendant does not testify, it is not error for the trial judge to fail to instruct the jury that the defendant's failure to testify does not create a presumption against the accused.[3]

In *Bell v. State*,[4] the court found no error where the trial judge, in the presence of the jury, told the defendant that he was not obligated to testify and the defendant did testify.

In *Barron v. State*,[5] the Georgia Supreme Court found that an on-the-record colloquy between the court and a defendant who elects not to testify regarding the defendant's waiver of the right to testify is not necessary. The court did, however, "acknowledge" that such a discussion would be the better practice in order to avoid post-conviction challenges to the voluntariness of the defendant's election not to testify at trial and the effectiveness of trial counsel on the issue.

Prior to July 1, 2005, no evidence of general bad character or prior convictions could be admitted against a defendant who chose to testify unless the defense first put his or her character in issue. Moreover, evidence of prior felony convictions could only be admitted in those cases where the prior felony convictions were alleged in the indictment. In 2005, however, the Georgia Legislature eliminated the aforementioned provisions and those changes were incorporated into the 2013 revision of the rules of evidence. O.C.G.A. § 24-5-506(b) now provides as follows:

"If a defendant in a criminal case wishes to testify and announces in open court his or her intention to do so, the defendant may so testify in his or her own behalf. If a defendant testifies, he or she shall be sworn as any other witness and may be examined and cross-examined as any other witness. The failure of a defendant to testify shall create no presumption against him or her, and no comment shall be made because of such failure."

---

indicated that counsel may unilaterally waive the right of the defendant to testify. But cf. Winters v. Cook, 489 F.2d 174, 179 (6) (5th Cir. 1973).

[2]Griffin v. California, 380 U.S. 609, 85 S.Ct. 1229, 14 L.Ed.2d 106 (1965); Ex parte Yarber, 375 So. 2d 1231 (Ala. 1979). In *Yarber*, the court pointed out that an indirect reference to defendant's failure to testify is cause for a reversal.

[3]Lay v. State, 242 Ga. 225, 227 (2), 248 S.E.2d 611 (1978); Williams v. State, 249 Ga. 822, 826 (6), 295 S.E.2d 293 (1982); Jones v. State, 250 Ga. 166, 170, 296 S.E.2d 598 (1982). Cf.

Stephens v. State, 157 Ga. App. 414, 278 S.E.2d 70 (1981).

[4]Bell v. State, 226 Ga. App. 271, 272 (3), 486 S.E.2d 422 (1997).

[5]Barron v. State, 264 Ga. 865(2), 452 S.E.2d 504 (1995). See Feaster v. State, 283 Ga. App. 417(4), 641 S.E.2d 635 (2007). The duty to inform the defendant of the right to testify rests with counsel but the right itself is personal to the defendant and may not be waived by counsel or the court. U.S. v. Teague, 953 F.2d 1525 (11th Cir. 1992); State v. Nejad, 286 Ga. 695, 690 S.E.2d 846 (2010).

Thus, if a defendant elects to testify, prior convictions are admissible regardless of whether the defense first puts his or her character in issue. However, pursuant to O.C.G.A. § 24-6-609(a), the rules of evidence have also been modified to provide that the credibility of the defendant may only be impeached with a prior conviction if (1) "the crime was punishable by death or imprisonment of one year or more under the law under which the defendant was convicted," and (2) "the court determines that the probative value of admitting the evidence outweighs its prejudicial effect to the defendant. . . ."[6] Also, "[e]vidence that a witness or the defendant has been convicted of a crime shall be admitted if it involved dishonesty or making a false statement, regardless of the punishment that could be imposed for such offense."[7]

Parties seeking to introduce evidence of convictions more than ten years old against a witness or the defendant must provide the adverse party "sufficient advance written notice of intent to use such evidence."[8] Even assuming notice is provided, however, such evidence is inadmissible unless the court determines that the "probative value of the conviction supported by specific facts and circumstances substantially outweighs its prejudicial effect." The remainder of O.C.G.A. § 24-6-609. deals with the effect of pardon/annulment, juvenile adjudication, and pendency of appeal.[9]

In addition, pursuant to O.C.G.A. § 24-6-608, any party may

---

[6]O.C.G.A. § 24-6-609(a). The rule is similar in the case of witnesses other than a criminal defendant. Prior convictions may be used to impeach any other witness so long as the crime "was punishable by death or imprisonment of one year or more," and the probative value of admission outweighs the prejudicial effect to the witness.

[7]O.C.G.A. § 24-6-609(a).

[8]O.C.G.A. § 24-6-609(b).

[9]O.C.G.A. § 24-6-609(c)–(e) provide as follows:

(c) Effect of pardon, annulment, certificate of rehabilitation, or discharge from a first offender program. Evidence of a final adjudication of guilt and subsequent discharge under any first offender statute shall not be used to impeach any witness and evidence of a conviction shall not be admissible under this Code section if:

(1) The conviction has been the subject of a pardon, annulment, certif-

icate of rehabilitation, or other equivalent procedure based on a finding of the rehabilitation of the person convicted, and that such person has not been convicted of a subsequent crime which was punishable by death or imprisonment in excess of one year; or

(2) The conviction has been the subject of a pardon, annulment, or other equivalent procedure based on a finding of innocence.

(d) Nolo contendere pleas and juvenile adjudications. A conviction plea based on a plea of nolo contendere shall not be admissible to impeach any witness under this Code section. Evidence of juvenile adjudications shall not generally be admissible under this Code section. The court may, however, in a criminal proceeding allow evidence of a juvenile adjudication of a witness other than the accused if conviction of the offense would be admissible to attack the credibility of an adult and the court is satisfied that admission in evidence is neces-

impeach the credibility of the witness through evidence of bad character in the form of reputation.[10] The evidence may only refer to the witness's character for truthfulness or untruthfulness, and opinion is only admissible "after the character of the witness for truthfulness has been attacked by opinion or reputation evidence or otherwise."[11] In the case of a criminal defendant who chooses to testify, the character for untruthfulness of the defendant may only be admitted if the defense first puts his or her character for truthfulness in issue.[12]

Finally, the defendant must be sworn before he testifies.

See Studdard, *Daniel's Georgia Handbook on Criminal Evidence* (2018 ed.), § 6:30.

§ 21:4   Attempt as a defense

An "attempt" is now defined under Georgia statutory law as follows: "A person commits the offense of criminal attempt when, with intent to commit a specific crime, he performs any act which constitutes a substantial step toward the commission of that crime."[1] In *English v. State*,[2] the court noted "[t]he 'substantial step' requirement [under the criminal-attempt statute] shifts the emphasis from what remains to be done to what the actor has already done. The fact that further steps must be taken before the crime can be completed does not preclude such a finding that the steps already undertaken are substantial." However, "[m]ere acts of preparation, not proximately leading to the consummation of the intended crime, will not suffice to establish an attempt to commit it."[3]

In *Guzman v. State*,[4] the court reversed a conviction on the ground that the defendant knew she could not have committed the crime of attempted possession of cocaine since she had no

---

sary for a fair determination of the issue of guilt or innocence of the accused.

(e) Pendency of appeal. The pendency of an appeal shall not render evidence of a conviction inadmissible. Evidence of the pendency of an appeal shall be admissible.

[10]O.C.G.A. § 24-6-608.

[11]O.C.G.A. § 24-6-608(a)(1) and (a)(2).

[12]O.C.G.A. § 24-6-608(b). The limitation placed on the state's ability to attack the testifying defendant's character for truthfulness rests on the seemingly incongruous assumption that, by taking the stand and swearing to tell the truth, the defendant has not already put his or her character for truthfulness in issue.

[Section 21:4]

[1]O.C.G.A. § 16-4-1.

[2]English v. State, 301 Ga. App. 842, 843, 689 S.E.2d 130 (2010) (internal punctuation omitted). See Smith v. The State, 340 Ga. App. 457, 797 S.E.2d 679 (2017).

[3]Tucker v. State, 182 Ga. App. 625, 626, 356 S.E.2d 559 (1987) (quoting Groves v. State, 116 Ga. 516, 42 S.E. 755 (1902)).

[4]Guzman v. State, 206 Ga. App. 170, 172, 424 S.E.2d 849 (1992).

PRESENTING THE DEFENDANT'S CASE

money with her to complete the purchase from a dealer. See O.C.G.A. § 16-4-4.

In *State v. Harlacher*,[5] the court determined that a defendant was improperly charged with criminal attempt to commit aggravated assault by alleging that he attempted to place the victim in apprehension of receiving a violent injury with a pistol where it appeared that the victim was unaware that the defendant had pointed the handgun at him. However, a defendant can be convicted of criminal attempt to commit child molestation where the defendant engaged in explicit online communications with a law enforcement officer posing as a 15-year-old girl and went to an arranged meeting place.[6]

In *Neal v. State*,[7] the court held that "the entry of separate convictions and sentences against defendant for both aggravated assault (with intent to rob) and the completed offense of robbery by force is barred. . . ."

Under Georgia law prior to the adoption of the Criminal Code, a defendant could not be convicted of an attempt if the crime attempted was in fact committed. Thus, a criminal charge of attempt could be defended by showing the completion of the crime.[8] However, today a defendant may be convicted of an attempt even if the crime was committed.[9]

Generally, on attempts see 21 Am. Jur. 2d Criminal Law §§ 158 et seq. (1981).

§ 21:5 Abandonment as a defense

In an effort to deter crimes and to reward those who do not complete a criminal undertaking, the Georgia Legislature, in O.C.G.A. § 16-4-5, added a provision to the Criminal Code that has no counterpart in former Georgia law.

O.C.G.A. § 16-4-5 provides as follows:

"(a) When a person's conduct would otherwise constitute an attempt to commit a crime . . ., it is an affirmative defense that he abandoned his effort to commit the crime or in any other manner prevented its commission under circumstances manifesting a voluntary and complete renunciation of his criminal purpose.

"(b) A renunciation of criminal purpose is not voluntary and complete if it results from:

---

[5]State v. Harlacher, 336 Ga. App. 9, 783 S.E.2d 411 (2016).

[6]Brown v. State, 321 Ga. App. 798, 800 (1), 743 S.E.2d 474 (2013). See Lopez v. State, 326 Ga. App. 770, 774, 757 S.E.2d 436 (2014).

[7]Neal v. State, 219 Ga. App. 891, 892 (1), 467 S.E.2d 219 (1996).

[8]Harris v. State, 3 Ga. App. 457, 60 S.E. 127 (1908); Brantley v. State, 132 Ga. 573, 578, 64 S.E. 676 (1909).

[9]O.C.G.A. § 16-4-2.

"(1) A belief that circumstances exist which increase the probability of detection or apprehension of the person or which render more difficult the accomplishment of the criminal purpose; or

"(2) A decision to postpone the criminal conduct until another time."

§ 21:6   Impossibility as a defense

The defense of impossibility of a criminal attempt has plagued the law for centuries.[1] Present Georgia law has put an end to the troublesome problem by providing that neither factual nor legal impossibility prevents a conviction of an attempt "if such crime could have been committed had the attendant circumstances been as the accused believed them to be."[2]

§ 21:7   Mistake of fact as a defense

O.C.G.A. § 16-3-5 provides for "mistake of fact" as a defense of a criminal act. The Code states: "A person shall not be found guilty of a crime if the act or omission to act constituting the crime was induced by a misapprehension of fact which, if true, would have justified the act or omission." A mistake of fact "is a defense to a crime to the extent that the ignorance of some fact negates the existence of the mental state required to establish a material element of the crime."[1]

O.C.G.A. § 16-3-5 must be considered in light of O.C.G.A. § 16-

---

[Section 21:6]

[1]Deusner, "The Doctrine of Impossibility in the Law of Criminal Attempts," 4 Crim. L. Bull. 398 (1968). See Annot., "Impossibility of Consummation of Substantive Crime as Defense in Criminal Prosecution for Conspiracy or Attempt to Commit Crime," 37 A.L.R.3d 375 (1971). There were said to be two kinds of impossibility: (1) legal impossibility and (2) factual impossibility, but it was quite difficult to distinguish between the two. Legal impossibility has been said to be illustrated by the case of State v. Guffey, 262 S.W.2d 152 (Mo.Ct.App.1953), where the defendant was charged with hunting deer out of season. The defendant had stopped while driving on the highway and fired at what he thought was a deer but was actually a "stuffed" hide of a deer which the game officials had placed in the woods. The Court, on appeal, concluded that a person

could not be convicted of an attempt to commit a crime unless he could have been convicted if his attempt had been successful. Since it would have been impossible to kill the fake deer, the charge of attempt did not lie. Factual impossibility, on the other hand, is the concept that the only thing which prevented the committing of a crime was some element which was out of control of the defendant. In this case, the defendant could be convicted of an attempt. Thus, in People v. Moran, 123 N.Y. 254, 25 N.E. 412 (1890), it was held that where a pickpocket put his hand into someone's pocket and found it empty, he could still be convicted of attempted larceny.

[2]O.C.G.A. § 16-4-4.

[Section 21:7]

[1]Jones v. State, 263 Ga. 835, 839(2), 439 S.E.2d 645 (1994). See Windhom v. State, 315 Ga. App. 855, 729 S.E.2d 25 (2012) (error to refuse

2-2, which provides as follows: "A person shall not be found guilty of any crime committed by misfortune or accident where it satisfactorily appears there was no criminal scheme or undertaking, intention, or criminal negligence." See § 21:29, infra.

Other than a few cases involving the defendant's intent as the sole defense,[2] no reported cases have found error in the trial judge's failure to charge on mistake of fact.[3] In all likelihood, O.C.G.A. § 16-3-5 will have little impact on existing practice, and will not apply unless the "mistake of fact" is otherwise covered in Georgia law.[4] In *Turner v. State*,[5] the court held that this statute applies only in cases of mistake of fact and not to a mistake of law.

In *Randall v. State*,[6] the court held that "[m]istake of fact is a defense to a crime to the extent that the ignorance of some *fact* negates the existence of the mental state required to establish a material element of the crime. . . ." (Emphasis in original.) The court then concluded that where a defendant in a burglary case acted on advice of counsel that she had a legal right to sell the victim's property to reimburse the defendant for money allegedly owed the defendant, this was a mistake of law, not of fact.

In *Veasey v. State*,[7] the defendant sought to defend a child molestation case on the ground that he was mistaken about her age. The court held that a mistaken belief about age would not justify a jury charge on a mistake of fact. The court reasoned that the victim's age was not an element of the crime. Similarly, courts have held that the prosecution need not show that a defendant knew a potential victim's occupation when charged with threaten-

---

to charge on mistake of fact in case where defendant drove robbers to shopping center unaware that robbery was planned).

[2]See Price v. State, 289 Ga. 459, 712 S.E.2d 828 (2011) (error to fail to give charge on mistake of fact where defendant charged with burglary asserted that he entered the residence under the impression that the house was for sale and seller was having an "open house"); Duvall v. State, 289 Ga. 540, 712 S.E.2d 850 (2011) (error not to give mistake of fact charge where defendant in VGCSA case denied knowing what the pills he possessed were); Gray v. State, 158 Ga. App. 582 (2), 281 S.E.2d 328 (1981) (error to not give charge on mistake of fact where defendant thought diner he entered

was open and that someone was inside).

[3]E.g., Jordon v. State, 232 Ga. 749 (4), 208 S.E.2d 840 (1974); Treadwell v. State, 129 Ga. App. 573, 574 (4), 200 S.E.2d 323 (1973). Both of these cases involved a refusal to give a request to charge on O.C.G.A. § 16-3-5.

[4]E.g., O.C.G.A. § 16-3-3.

[5]Turner v. State, 210 Ga. App. 303, 304 (1), 436 S.E.2d 229 (1993).

[6]Randall v. State, 234 Ga. App. 704, 705 (1), 507 S.E.2d 511 (1998). See Stillwell v. State, 329 Ga.App. 108, 764 S.E.2d 419 (2014).

[7]Veasey v. State, 234 Ga. App. 795, 507 S.E.2d 799 (1998).

ing to murder a federal judge,[8] or conspiring to murder a DEA agent.[9] However, in *King v. Waters,*[10] the court held that the state must prove that the defendant knew that a victim was a peace officer in a prosecution for aggravated assault of a peace officer. See Studdard, *Daniel's Georgia Handbook on Criminal Evidence* (2018 ed.), § 3:20.

In *Taylor v. State,*[11] the court held that it was not error to fail to charge on identity and misapprehension of fact or mistaken belief "because the charges were not pertinent and material to the issues to be considered by the jury."

O.C.G.A. § 16-3-5 provides that "[a] person shall not be found guilty of a crime if . . . induced by a misapprehension of fact which, if true, would have justified the act or omission."

In *Darty v. State,*[12] the court pointed out that "[s]ince it is . . . [the defendant's] responsibility to produce evidence supporting the affirmative defense . . . he may not rely on the evidence adduced in the state's case unless 'the state's evidence raises the issue. . . .' " Hence, it was not error to fail to charge on the "sole defense" of mistake of fact.

In *Crawford v. State,*[13] the Georgia Supreme Court pointed out that "[g]enerally speaking, ignorance or mistake of fact constitutes a defense to a criminal charge only if it is '. . . not superinduced by the fault [or] negligence of the party doing the wrongful act. . . .' "

In *Allen v. State,*[14] the court held that a mistake as to the legality of an arrest is a mistake of law and it is not error for the court to fail to give a mistake-of-fact charge where a mistake of law has been made.

§ 21:8 Alibi as a defense

The word "alibi" is sometimes used by the layman as an excuse for a charge. The layman's attitude toward the word "alibi" should be kept in mind by both defense and prosecution counsel. The defense will want to emphasize that the defendant is not just "grabbing at straws" seeking to avoid conviction when it may ap-

---

[8]United States v. Berki, 936 F.2d 529 (11th Cir. 1991).

[9]United States v. Benitez, 741 F.2d 1312 (11th Cir. 1984).

[10]King v. Waters, 278 Ga. 122, 598 S.E.2d 476 (2004).

[11]Taylor v. State, 272 Ga. 744, 745 (1), 534 S.E.2d 67 (2000).

[12]Darty v. State, 232 Ga. App. 814, 815 (2), 503 S.E.2d 76 (1998)

(quoting O.C.G.A. 16-1-3).

[13]Crawford v. State, 267 Ga. 543, 544 (2), 480 S.E.2d 573 (1997) (quoting Clark v. State, 192 Ga. App. 718, 386 S.E.2d 378 (1989)).

[14]Allen v. State, 237 Ga. App. 744, 745 (3), 516 S.E.2d 788 (1999) (citing Turner v. State, 210 Ga. App. 303, 436 S.E.2d 229 (1993)).

pear that there is no real defense to the charge. Jurors also need to be reminded that an alibi, in the vast majority of cases, must be established by family members and close friends.

The legal or technical meaning of alibi is "absence from the scene of the alleged crime at the time of its commission," thus making it impossible for the defendant to have committed the crime.[1] In connection with alibi as a defense, the Georgia Code states the following:

"The defense of alibi involves the impossibility of the accused's presence at the scene of the offense at the time of its commission. The range of the evidence in respect to time and place must be such as reasonably to exclude the possibility of presence."[2]

Where the defense testimony tends to show that the defendant was not actually present at the time of a homicide even though he was near the scene of the crime but in no position to have committed the killing, court should charge the jury on alibi even without a request.[3] Thus, it has been held where the only defense is alibi and the evidence tends to show the impossibility of the defendant's presence at the scene of the crime, it is harmful error for the court to fail to charge on alibi.[4] However, in *Newby v. State,*[5] it was held that it is not error for the trial judge to fail to charge on alibi where there is no request for such a charge and a charge is given on identification. In *Rivers v. State,*[6] the Georgia Supreme Court stated "that it is ordinarily not error to fail to charge specifically on alibi absent a request." Likewise, in *Pearson v. State,*[7] the court held that in the absence of a request it is not error to fail to charge on alibi where the defendant "merely testified that he was not present . . . because he was somewhere else

---

[Section 21:8]

[1]Williams v. State, 123 Ga. 138, 141 (3), 51 S.E. 322 (1905).

[2]O.C.G.A. § 16-3-40. In Jones v. State, 150 Ga. App. 645, 646 (2), 258 S.E.2d 297 (1979), the court said that "where the evidence relating to alibi is not clear and of strong probative value, the failure to charge thereon in the absence of a proper request" is not reversible error.

[3]Moseley v. State, 165 Ga. 290, 291 (1), 140 S.E. 754 (1927). But in Callahan v. State, 147 Ga. App. 301, 248 S.E.2d 561 (1978), the court said that where the evidence relating to an "alibi is not clear and of strong probative value, the failure to charge thereon, in the absence of a proper request, will not be cause for reversal."

[4]Tiller v. State, 118 Ga. App. 590 (1), 164 S.E.2d 915 (1968); McCauley v. State, 37 Ga. App. 610, 141 S.E. 85 (1928); Howard v. State, 141 Ga. App. 238, 240 (4), 233 S.E.2d 58 (1977).

[5]Newby v. State, 161 Ga. App. 805, 807 (3), 288 S.E.2d 889 (1982).

[6]Rivers v. State, 250 Ga. 288, 300, 298 S.E.2d 10 (1982). However, in Rivers the trial judge charged completely "on the defendant's presumption of innocence [and] on the state's burden of proving beyond a reasonable doubt that the defendant had committed the crimes at issue." Cf. Ashley v. State, 240 Ga. App. 502, 504 (2), 523 S.E.2d 901 (1999).

[7]Pearson v. State, 164 Ga. App. 337, 338, 297 S.E.2d 98 (1982).

. . . but his testimony as to range of time and place was vague and contradictory . . . and inconclusive . . . and the brother whom . . . [the defendant] claimed to be with did not testify."

It is improper for the district attorney to ask the defendant his reasons for not telling law enforcement officers at the time of his arrest that he was elsewhere when the crime was committed.[8] However, there is no reason to prevent the district attorney from asking alibi witnesses their reasons for not advising law enforcement officers earlier of the defendant's presence elsewhere.[9]

Georgia appellate courts have struggled for some time with a correct alibi charge. Conflict had revolved around the idea that under the due process clause of the Fourteenth Amendment the defendant need not prove anything to be entitled to an acquittal and the notion that an alibi needs to be established to the reasonable satisfaction of the jury.[10] In *Patterson v. State,*[11] the Georgia Supreme Court unanimously approved the following alibi charge:

"Now, the defendant in this case contends that he was not present at the scene of the offense at the time of its commission. In that connection I charge you that alibi as a defense involves the impossibility of the accused's presence at the scene of the offense at the time of its commission. Presence of the defendant at the scene of the crime(s) alleged or his involvement as a co-conspirator is an essential element of the crime(s) set forth in this indictment, and the burden of proof as to such issue rests upon the State as I have instructed you already. Any evidence in the nature of an alibi should be considered by the jury in connection with all other facts in the case, and if, in doing so, the jury should entertain a reasonable doubt as to the guilt of the accused, they should acquit."[12]

The general rule is that the district attorney may prove a crime was committed any time within the statute of limitations.[13] However, if a defendant relies on an alibi defense, such a vari-

---

[8]Clark v. State, 237 Ga. 901, 230 S.E.2d 277 (1976).

[9]Hill v. State, 238 Ga. 354, 233 S.E.2d 182 (1977); United States v. Johns, 734 F.2d 657 (11th Cir. 1984).

[10]In Trimble v. State, 229 Ga. 399, 191 S.E.2d 857 (1972), the court, 4 to 3, approved a charge which said defense should establish an alibi to the reasonable satisfaction of the jury. *Trimble* was later released on federal habeas corpus because of the charge. Trimble v. Stynchcombe, 481 F.2d 1175 (5th Cir. 1973).

In Barfield v. Dampier, 241 Ga. 168, 243 S.E.2d 876 (1978), the court held that it was error for the trial judge to charge that the burden is on the defendant to establish his alibi, not beyond a reasonable doubt, but to the reasonable satisfaction of the jury.

[11]Patterson v. State, 233 Ga. 724, 213 S.E.2d 612 (1975).

[12]Patterson v. State, 233 Ga. 724, 730, 213 S.E.2d 612 (1975).

[13]See § 13:6, supra.

ance might deprive a defendant of his defense. Thus, when a defendant first learns that the state is going to try to establish the commission of the offense at some other time, he should move for a continuance[14] or a mistrial so as to have an opportunity to prepare a defense for the date the district attorney is going to rely on,[15] unless of course the indictment states that the date is an essential averment of the offense in which case the state could not convict the defendant upon proof of the commission of the offense on another date.[16] However, where an indictment contains one date and the defendant knows because of a preliminary hearing that the state will attempt to show that the crime was committed on another date, a failure to grant a continuance or mistrial is not error.[17]

Prior to the 1994 Georgia law (which became effective January 1, 1995) relating to reciprocal discovery, defense counsel was not obligated to supply the state with the names of alibi witnesses whom he planned to call.[18] The same rule continues to apply when a defendant elects not to engage in reciprocal discovery. However, should the defendant elect to participate in reciprocal discovery, the defense will have to provide notice to the state of its intent to rely on an alibi and provide the names of the witnesses in support of the defense as well as the other information required by O.C.G.A. § 17-16-5(a). If the only witness in support of the defense is the defendant, that fact must be disclosed but not the substance of the defendant's testimony.[19] See §§ 14:9 ct seq., supra, on the 1994 Georgia law on discovery and § 14:19, supra, on reciprocal discovery in felony cases involving alibi witnesses.

§ 21:9 Age as a defense—General

The Georgia Criminal Code provides that a person shall not be guilty of a crime "unless he has attained the age of 13 years at the time of the act, omission, or negligence constituting the

---

[14]Bradford v. State, 285 Ga. 1, 673 S.E.2d 201 (2009); Riles v. State, 155 Ga. App. 586, 271 S.E.2d 718 (1980).

[15]Caldwell v. State, 139 Ga. App. 279, 287, 228 S.E.2d 219 (1976).

[16]See § 13:6, supra. In Thomas v. State, 158 Ga. App. 97 (1), 279 S.E.2d 335 (1981), the court affirmed the conviction where the trial judge charged the jury that each allegation of the indictment was material "save only the date of the offense." The

defendant had relied on an alibi defense and the court agreed that it was possibly confusing. However, since both the state and the defendant relied on the date in the indictment, it was held not to be reversible error.

[17]Barton v. State, 161 Ga. App. 591, 592 (2), 288 S.E.2d 914 (1982).

[18]Generally, see § 14:19, supra, on reciprocal discovery, alibi witnesses.

[19]State v. Charbonneau, 281 Ga. 46, 635 S.E.2d 759 (2006).

crime."[1] The age referred to in the Georgia statute is the biological age, not the "mental age," of the defendant.[2]

Age as a defense to a crime should not be confused with the age limitations established in juvenile court proceedings. The juvenile courts have exclusive jurisdiction to try the case of what would otherwise be an adult crime where the child has not reached the age of 18 at the time of the offense[3] and the offense is not a capital felony.[4] However, if the juvenile court has determined that a child cannot be rehabilitated, the case may be transferred to the superior court for trial.[5] Juvenile courts have concurrent jurisdiction with the superior courts where the offense is one for which an adult could be punished by death or life imprisonment.[6] The court which first takes jurisdiction of the prosecution is regarded as having jurisdiction to complete the proceeding.[7]

In a 1993 case, the court pointed out that "a juvenile case 'commences,' and the juvenile court acquires jurisdiction of it only by the filing of a petition of delinquency."[8] The Georgia Supreme Court later clarified its position, in *State v. Whetstone,*[9] by reaffirming *In re C. R.* yet holding that the "filing of a juvenile complaint form does not expand the statutory jurisdictional provisions of the Juvenile Code."

See § 13:27, supra, on transfer of a case to or from juvenile court.

§ 21:10 Insanity as a defense—General

See § 14:92, supra, on the necessity of the defendant giving notice of intention of the defense to raise the issue of insanity or mental competency.

It has been said that the "insanity defense represents societal

---

[Section 21:9]

[1]O.C.G.A. § 16-3-1.

[2]Couch v. State, 253 Ga. 764 (2), 325 S.E.2d 366 (1985).

[3]In W. F. v. State, 144 Ga. App. 523, 524 (1), 241 S.E.2d 631 (1978), the defendant was 19 at the time of trial. The court said that he should still be tried in juvenile court unless it is established that he is not amenable to rehabilitation in the juvenile system.

[4]O.C.G.A. §§ 15-11-2, 15-11-560, 15-11-561; Relyea v. State, 236 Ga. 299, 223 S.E.2d 638 (1976).

In Edmonds v. State, 154 Ga.

App. 650, 269 S.E.2d 512 (1980), the court pointed out that a person reaches the age of seventeen at the first moment of the day before his seventeenth birthday.

[5]J. J. v. State, 135 Ga. App. 660 (2), 218 S.E.2d 668 (1975).

[6]O.C.G.A. § 15-11-560(b); Lincoln v. State, 138 Ga. App. 234, 235 (1), 225 S.E.2d 708 (1976).

[7]See Brown v. State, 235 Ga. 353, 354 (2), 219 S.E.2d 419 (1975).

[8]In re C. R., 263 Ga. 155, 156, 430 S.E.2d 3 (1993).

[9]State v. Whetstone, 264 Ga. 135, 441 S.E.2d 842 (1994).

forgiveness . . . and is exactly what society says that it is—which is stated in a statute."[1]

A plea of "not guilty" encompasses the defense of not guilty by reason of insanity.[2]

In *Kelley v. State*,[3] the court held that insanity is an affirmative defense, i.e., "a defense that admits the doing of the act charged but seeks to justify, excuse or mitigate it . . . ." If a defendant does not admit to committing any act which constitutes the crime charged, he does not establish the required foundation for charging on insanity.

Georgia recognizes four different kinds of mental conditions that may exist at the time of the commission of the act charged: (1) the "right-and-wrong" test of insanity, (2) the delusional compulsion test, (3) in felony cases, the mentally ill test, and (4) in felony cases, the guilty but mentally retarded test.

First, the right-and-wrong test of insanity is set out in O.C.G.A. § 16-3-2, which provides as follows:

"A person shall not be found guilty of a crime if, at the time of the act, omission, or negligence constituting the crime, the person did not have mental capacity to distinguish between right and wrong in relation to such act, omission, or negligence."

The Georgia Supreme Court, over 130 years ago, approved a charge on the right-and-wrong test of insanity which states that a person is not responsible for his acts unless he has "sufficient memory, intelligence, reason, and will to enable him to distinguish between right and wrong, in regard to the particular act about to be done, to know and understand that it will be wrong, and that he will deserve punishment by committing it. In order to constitute a crime, a man must have intelligence and capacity enough to have a criminal intent and purpose; and if his mental powers are either so deficient that he has no will, no consent, or if through the overwhelming power of mental disease his intellectual power is for the time obliterated, he is not a responsible moral agent. . . ."[4]

Second, in addition to the right-and-wrong test of insanity,

[Section 21:10]

[1]Dennis v. State, 170 Ga. App. 630, 631, 317 S.E.2d 874 (1984).

[2]Duck v. State, 250 Ga. 592, 596, 300 S.E.2d 121 (1983).

[3]Kelley v. State, 235 Ga. App. 177, 509 S.E.2d 110 (1998) (quoting Brown v. State, 267 Ga. 350, 478 S.E.2d 129 (1996)).

[4]Roberts v. State, 3 Ga. 310, 326-27 (1847). See Annot., "Construction and Application of 18 U.S.C.A. § 17, Providing for Insanity Defense in Federal Criminal Prosecutions," 118 A.L.R.Fed. 265 (1994). See Annot., "Automatism or Unconsciousness as Defense to Criminal Charges," 27 A.L.R.4th 1067 (1984). See 2 Subst.Crim.L. § 9.4, Automatism (2003).

Georgia follows the delusional compulsion rule. O.C.G.A. § 16-3-3 provides as follows:

"A person shall not be found guilty of a crime when, at the time of the act, omission, or negligence constituting the crime, the person, because of mental disease, injury, or congenital deficiency, acted as he did because of a delusional compulsion as to such act which overmastered his will to resist committing the crime."

It must be emphasized that a person may be suffering from delusional insanity even though he can distinguish between right and wrong. Thus, "although a man has reason sufficient to distinguish between right and wrong as to a particular act about to be committed, yet if, in consequence of some delusion brought about by mental disease, his will was overmastered so that there was no criminal intent with reference to the act in question, he will not be held as criminally responsible . . . yet in order for such defense to be available . . . it must appear, not only that the defendant was actually laboring under a delusion . . . , but that the act itself is connected with the particular delusion . . . and also that the delusion was as to a fact which, if true, would justify the act."[5]

In *Graham v. State,*[6] the court said that the defense of delusional compulsion is not available unless it is shown (1) that the defendant was laboring under a delusion; (2) "that the act itself was connected with the delusion"; and (3) that the delusion (if it were true) would have justified the act. A fourth requirement is that the defendant did not voluntarily induce his delusion.[7] However, as to the third requirement, in *Dutton v.*

---

[5]Brown v. State, 228 Ga. 215, 217 (2), 184 S.E.2d 655 (1971) (quoting Johnson v. State, 226 Ga. 511, 515, 175 S.E.2d 840 (1970), and Barker v. State, 188 Ga. 332, 333, 4 S.E.2d 31 (1939)); Williams v. State, 249 Ga. 839, 843, 295 S.E.2d 74 (1982); Bentley v. State, 162 Ga. App. 755 (1), 293 S.E.2d 36 (1982).

[6]Graham v. State, 236 Ga. 378, 223 S.E.2d 803 (1976); Choisnet v. State, 295 Ga. 568, 761 S.E.2d 322 (2014); VanVoorhis v. State, 234 Ga. App. 749, 507 S.E.2d 555 (1998). Accord, Webb v. State, 270 Ga. 556, 557 (2), 512 S.E.2d 633 (1999).

[7]Bailey v. State, 249 Ga. 535, 537, 291 S.E.2d 704 (1982). In *Bailey,* the court stated "that a chronic paranoid schizophrenic may no more voluntarily and intentionally induce his delusion than a chronic alcoholic voluntarily may induce his drunkenness [and] then expect the homicide to be excused." The court pointed out that the defendant had been warned to avoid highly stressful confrontations. He could have avoided the confrontation that led to the murder, but did not do so. If he had a delusion, he brought it about. Hence, it was held not to be error for the trial judge to refuse to charge the jury on delusion as a defense to the crime.

State,[8] the court held that "justification" means "legal justification" for the defendant's acts. The evidence is to be evaluated in light of the general justification statutes O.C.G.A. § 16-3-20 and O.C.G.A. § 16-3-21 to determine whether the defendant met the justification criterion of the delusional compulsion defense.

However, even if a defendant has the capacity to distinguish right from wrong and even if he is not acting under a delusional compulsion, mental weakness is a factor which may be considered in determining whether the event was induced by a misapprehension of fact. If the act was induced by such a misapprehension, he should be found not guilty.[9]

"A plea of not guilty by reason of insanity at the time of the crime shall not be accepted and the defendant adjudicated not guilty by reason of insanity by the court without a jury until the defendant has undergone examination by a licensed psychologist or psychiatrist and the court has examined the psychological or psychiatric reports, has held a hearing on the issue of the defendant's mental condition, and the court is satisfied that the defendant was insane at the time of the crime according to the criteria of O.C.G.A. § 16-3-2 or O.C.G.A. § 16-3-3."[10]

If a defendant calls a psychiatrist to testify concerning his ability to distinguish right from wrong, he waives his right to object to the cross-examination of the doctor on the ground of a privileged communication.[11] However it has been held that when defense counsel has a psychiatrist examine the defendant in connection with insanity at the time of the commission of the crime, the state has no right to force the doctor to testify for the state. His testimony is deemed to be barred by the attorney-client privilege.[12]

Third, a defendant who does not come within either of the first

---

[8]Dutton v. State, 225 Ga. App. 67, 69 (1), 483 S.E.2d 305 (1997). See Woods v. State, 291 Ga. 804, 733 S.E.2d 730 (2012) (charge on delusional compulsion must be accompanied by instruction on justification/self defense).

[9]Bowers v. State, 153 Ga. App. 894, 897 (2), 267 S.E.2d 309 (1980); State v. Gonzales, Sup. Ct. #6051-PR, Ct. of Appeals No.—2 CA-CR2776, Pima County Sup. Ct. CR04856, Sup. Ct. of Ariz., en banc, slip opinion (3/22/84). However, in State v. Mishne, 427 A.2d 450, 460 (Me.1981), the court held that it was not error to reject testimony of misapprehension or compulsion caused by drug withdrawal.

[10]O.C.G.A. § 17-7-131(b)(2.1).

[11]Fields v. State, 221 Ga. 307 (2), 144 S.E.2d 339 (1965). See Griggs v. State, 241 Ga. 317, 318, 245 S.E.2d 269 (1978); Trammel v. Bradberry, 256 Ga. App. 412, 424, 568 S.E.2d 715 (2002).

[12]Neuman v. State, 297 Ga. 501, 773 S.E.2d 716 (2015). In Smith v. Estelle, 602 F.2d 694 (5th Cir. 1979), aff'd, 451 U.S. 454, 101 S.Ct. 1866, 68 L.Ed.2d 359 (1981), the court held that a defendant may not be forced to speak to a psychiatrist who can use such statements against him in the sentencing phase of a capital case. However, in United States v. Cohen, 530 F.2d 43

two categories may be found "mentally ill" and consequently be entitled to different treatment than provided by either of the traditional insanity situations. O.C.G.A. § 17-7-131(a), as amended, states, in part, as follows:

"(2) 'Mentally ill' means having a disorder of thought or mood which significantly impairs judgment, behavior, capacity to recognize reality, or ability to cope with the ordinary demands of life. However, the term 'mental illness' shall not include a mental state manifested only by repeated unlawful or antisocial conduct."

Fourth, a defendant who does not come within either of the first three categories may be found guilty but mentally retarded if he is charged with a felony.

O.C.G.A. § 17-7-131(a)(3) states that " '[m]entally retarded' means having significantly subaverage general intellectual functioning resulting in or associated with impairments in adaptive behavior which manifested during the developmental period."

O.C.G.A. § 17-7-131 deals with types of verdicts which may be rendered and provides in part:

"(b)(1) In all cases in which the defense of insanity is interposed, the jury, or the court if tried by it, shall find whether the defendant is:

"(A) Guilty;

"(B) Not guilty;

"(C) Not guilty by reason of insanity at the time of the crime;

"(D) Guilty but mentally ill at the time of the crime, but the finding of guilty but mentally ill shall be made only in felony cases; or

"(E) Guilty but mentally retarded but the finding of mental retardation shall be made only in felony cases."[13]

In *Stripling v. State,*[14] the Georgia Supreme Court noted that a trial court may not accept a plea of guilty but mentally retarded over the objection of the state and the issue must then be resolved by a jury.

(5th Cir. 1976), the court held that if a defendant raises the defense of insanity, he may be compelled to undergo an examination by a prosecution-selected psychiatrist. In Smith the court pointed out that in the Cohen situation the psychiatrist's conclusion may be based on "non-testimonial aspects of defendant's conduct."

[13]In Taylor v. State, 440 N.E.2d

1109 (Ind.1982), the court held the Indiana guilty but "mentally ill" statute constitutional.

In Kirkland v. State, 166 Ga. App. 478 (2), 304 S.E.2d 561 (1983), the court held that the "guilty but mentally ill" statute applied to a crime committed before its enactment.

[14]Stripling v. State, 289 Ga. 370, 711 S.E.2d 665 (2011).

In *Mack v. State,*[15] the court emphasized that when a trial judge charges on the defense of "insanity" and on "guilty but mentally ill" at the time of the crime, *"the trial court must make clear to the jury in its charge that if they find the defendant did not have the mental capacity to distinguish between right and wrong (or acted because of delusional compulsion) they must find the defendant not guilty by reason of insanity and must not find the defendant guilty but mentally ill."*

See § 21:12, infra, on statutory charge of the trial judge.

In *Shifflett v. Commonwealth,*[16] the court held that a trial judge has inherent authority to have a defendant examined to determine his sanity at the time of the offense. In *Strickland v. State,*[17] the Georgia Supreme Court held that a trial judge may order a defendant to submit to a psychiatric examination in order for the psychiatrist to testify as a state's witness. The court further pointed out that such an order is not a violation of the defendant's privilege against self-incrimination, and held that a trial judge may impose "the sanction of striking the defendant's expert testimony on insanity should the defendant refuse to submit to the examination sought by the state." In *Lynd v. State,*[18] the court held that the trial judge "did not err by excluding testimony of the defendant's mental health experts where the defendant refused to submit to an examination by mental health experts chosen by the state."

When the defendant refuses to be examined by *any* expert including one employed by the defense, it would be proper for a psychological expert to opine upon the competency of the accused to stand trial based upon the observations of the accused by third parties, letters written by the accused, and other documentary evidence which is equally available to the state.[19] In *Kansas v.*

---

[15]Mack v. State, 206 Ga. App. 402, 403 (1), 425 S.E.2d 671 (1992); Foote v. State, 265 Ga. 58, 59 (2), 455 S.E.2d 579 (1995).

[16]Shifflett v. Commonwealth, 221 Va. 760, 274 S.E.2d 305 (1981).

[17]Strickland v. State, 257 Ga. 230, 233 (5), 357 S.E.2d 85 (1987).

[18]Lynd v. State, 262 Ga. 58 (11), 414 S.E.2d 5 (1992). See State v. Johnson, 276 Ga. 78, 576 S.E.2d 831 (2003) where the court observed that when the defense wants to make an issue of the defendant's mental status there are several competing interests at stake consisting of: the court's inter-est in the integrity of the justice system; the defendant's constitutionally protected interest against self-incrimination; and, the state's interest in being able to respond to the defendant's mental health expert. In this case, because the defendant did not intend to offer the evidence until the penalty phase, the court ordered the report sealed until that time. See also, Nance v. State, 272 Ga. 217(2), 526 S.E.2d 560 (2000).

[19]Humphrey v. Walker, 294 Ga. 855, 757 S.E.2d 68 (2014) (Court expressed no opinion on whether such testimony would be admitted at the guilt-innocence stage of trial or at sen-

Cheever,[20] the United States Supreme Court held that: "where a defense expert who has examined the defendant testifies that the defendant lacked the requisite mental state to commit a crime, the prosecution may offer evidence from a court-ordered psychological examination for the limited purpose of rebutting the defendant's evidence."

The court in *Presnell v. State*[21] held that a defendant has no constitutional right to have an attorney present during the psychiatric examination. But in *Estelle v. Smith,*[22] where an accused neither initiated a psychiatric evaluation nor attempted to introduce any psychiatric evidence, the court held that the defendant may not be compelled to respond to a psychiatrist if his statement can be used against him in a capital sentencing proceeding, thus giving the accused the same Fifth Amendment rights against self-incrimination in the pre-trial psychiatric examination setting as he already has in a custodial interrogation setting. However, in *Satterwhite v. Texas*[23] and *Powell v. Texas,*[24] the court held that while a defendant may waive his Fifth Amendment privilege by raising a mental status defense, this does not resolve the defendant's separate Sixth Amendment claim. In *Powell*, the court reasoned that "[w]hile it may be unfair to the State to permit a defendant to use psychiatric testimony without allowing the State a means to rebut that testimony, it certainly is not unfair to require the State to provide counsel with notice before examining the defendant concerning future dangerousness." Since the court found no basis for concluding that the defendant had waived his Sixth Amendment rights, it reversed the Court of Criminal Appeals and the defendant's death sentence. See § 14:93, supra, on forcing a defendant to take medication during trial to "normalize" him.

In *Duck v. State,*[25] the court said that "[i]n the absence of a special plea of insanity, an accused's request for a psychiatric evaluation lies within the sound discretion of the trial court."

As explained in § 14:92, supra, generally the issue of insanity may not be raised at trial unless prior notice has been given.

However, in *Ake v. Oklahoma,*[26] the United States Supreme Court held that an indigent defendant who makes a preliminary

---

tencing).

[20]Kansas v. Cheever, 134 S. Ct. 596, 603, 187 L. Ed. 2d 519 (2013).

[21]Presnell v. State, 241 Ga. 49, 243 S.E.2d 496 (1978), judgment rev'd in part on other grounds, 439 U.S. 14, 99 S.Ct. 235, 58 L.Ed.2d 207 (1978).

[22]Estelle v. Smith, 451 U.S. 454, 101 S.Ct. 1866, 68 L.Ed.2d 359 (1981).

[23]Satterwhite v. Texas, 486 U.S. 249, 108 S.Ct. 1792, 100 L.Ed.2d 284 (1988).

[24]Powell v. Texas, 492 U.S. 680, 109 S.Ct. 3146, 106 L.Ed.2d 551 (1989).

[25]Duck v. State, 250 Ga. 592, 596, 300 S.E.2d 121 (1983).

[26]Ake v. Oklahoma, 470 U.S. 68,

showing that his sanity at the time of the crime will likely be a significant factor at trial is entitled under the due process clause of the Fourteenth Amendment to a psychiatrist provided at state expense to assist the defendant in the preparation and presentation of his defense. Likewise, in a capital case an indigent defendant is entitled to help at the sentencing phase of his trial if the state presents psychiatric evidence as to the defendant's future dangerousness. See § 14:92, supra, on appointing an expert for a defendant.

In *Bright v. State,*[27] the court pointed out that a "motion on behalf of an indigent criminal defendant for funds . . . for a scientific expert should disclose to the trial court, with a reasonable degree of precision, why certain evidence is critical, what type of scientific testimony is needed, what that expert proposes to do regarding the evidence, and the anticipated costs for services." In *Bright* the court held that the refusal of the defendant to cooperate with the court psychiatrist does not amount to a waiver of his right to funds pursuant to *Ake.*

In *Lindsey v. State,*[28] the court, in applying *Ake,* said that where the defendant first makes a showing "that the defendant's sanity is likely to be a significant factor at trial, the state is required to provide an indigent defendant with access to the assistance of a competent psychiatrist in preparing the defense. . . . 'The assistance of a psychiatrist may well be crucial to the defendant's ability to marshal his defense. . . .' [I]n addition to examining the defendant, the psychiatrist must assist the defense by aiding defense counsel in the cross-examination and rebuttal of the state's medical experts." (Emphasis in original.) In *Brooks v. State,*[29] the court pointed out that such a request for funds may be made to the judge without the knowledge or presence of the district attorney. However, district attorney can be present for any hearing dealing solely with the indigency. *Brooks* also provides that the ex parte proceeding involving why the evidence is critical, the type of scientific testimony needed, what the expert

---

105 S.Ct. 1087, 84 L.Ed.2d 53 (1985). Cf. Williams v. Newsome, 254 Ga. 714, 334 S.E.2d 171 (1985); State v. Grant, 257 Ga. 123, 126, 355 S.E.2d 646 (1987); Scott v. State, 177 Ga. App. 474, 475, 339 S.E.2d 718 (1985).

[27]Bright v. State, 265 Ga. 265, 270, 455 S.E.2d 37 (1995).

[28]Lindsey v. State, 254 Ga. 444, 448, 330 S.E.2d 563 (1985). See also Eddy v. State, 255 Ga. 321, 322 (2), 338 S.E.2d 262 (1986) (preliminary showing not satisfied by mere inexpli-cability of the crime).

[29]Brooks v. State, 259 Ga. 562, 566 (2), 385 S.E.2d 81 (1989). See Putnal v. State, 303 Ga. 569, 814 S.E.2d 307 (2018) (court violated defendant's due process right to communicate ex parte with court when it entered an order on the public record rather than under seal as requested by the defense denying motion to allow mental health experts to have access to defendant while in custody).

proposes to do and the anticipated costs shall be reported, and a transcription for the record shall be incorporated in the record, "but shall be sealed in the same manner as are those items examined in camera."

In *Harris v. State*,[30] the court held that where an indigent defendant represents "to the court [prior to trial] that his only defense was temporary insanity," it is error for the trial judge to refuse funds "necessary to enable him to prepare and present the defense" and to fail to have him "examined by a mental health expert so that a threshold determination could be made as to whether his sanity or lack thereof was likely to be a significant factor at trial." This is true even if there has been no compliance with Rule 31.4 of the Uniform Rules for the Superior Courts, which is set out in § 14:92, supra.

Also see §§ 14:92 et seq., supra.

§ 21:11 Insanity as a defense—Evidence, presumptions, and burden of proof

If a defendant intends to raise the issue of insanity or mental illness at the time of the act charged, he must, in writing, give "Notice of Intent to Raise Issue of Insanity or Mental Incompetence." See § 14:92, supra, on defense of insanity, mental illness, mental retardation or mental competency.[1]

The Georgia Code provides that every "person is presumed to be of sound mind and discretion," but the presumption may be rebutted.[2] Thus, it was held in *Handspike v. State*[3] that where a defendant claims insanity at the time of the offense, "and intro-

---

[30]Harris v. State, 181 Ga. App. 358, 352 S.E.2d 226 (1986).

[Section 21:11]

[1]See Porter v. State, 243 Ga. App. 498, 532 S.E.2d 407 (2000), where testimony by a psychologist that defendant suffered from a condition in which she "blocked out" and essentially denied excessively painful experiences was admissible in prosecution for cruelty to children on the issue of defendant's knowledge of her husband's abusive behavior toward her child. Because the evidence was being offered on an element of the state's case, i.e. the defendant's knowledge of her husband's actions and not on her sanity at the time of the offense, compliance with Uniform Superior Court Rules 31.1 and 31.4 was not necessary.

See also Pickle v. State, 280 Ga. App. 821, 635 S.E.2d 197 (2006).

[2]O.C.G.A. § 16-2-3. But in United States v. Lawrance, 480 F.2d 688 (5th Cir. 1973), the court held that it was error to charge on the presumption of sanity if there was any evidence of insanity. See Eule, "The Presumption of Sanity: Bursting the Bubble," 25 U.C.L.A. Rev. 637 (1978). It is also error to charge on the issue of insanity where the defense is premised upon an unconsciousness disorder such as sleepwalking. As the Georgia Supreme Court observed in Smith v. State, 284 Ga. 33 (2), 663 S.E.2d 155 (2008) persons who commit potentially criminal acts while in such a state should not be regarded as criminally responsible because they "are not acting voluntarily and with criminal intent."

duces evidence sufficient to overcome the presumption of sanity, and there is no evidence that he was sane at the time of the" homicide, a guilty verdict is not authorized. Although the *Handspike* case was not overruled until 1981, it does not seem that it was followed for some time before that.[4]

The Georgia Supreme Court leans toward the view that there is always a factual question as to insanity where that issue is raised.[5] Jurors may reject the testimony of experts and rely on the presumption.[6]

"Admission to a mental institution will not give rise to a presumption of insanity absent an adjudication of insanity."[7]

Where a person has been adjudicated insane, it is presumed that the insanity continues until there is an adjudication to the contrary,[8] but such presumption is rebuttable.[9] For example, it has been held that an administrative release from Central State Hospital rebuts the continuing presumption of insanity[10] and leaves a presumption of sanity.[11] However, in *State v. Vosler*,[12] the court held that a trial judge has no authority to have a psychiatrist examine the defendant where the defendant is not relying on an insanity defense but on a lack of intent. Nevertheless, it is error for a trial judge to exclude evidence of a prior adjudication of insanity.[13] However, while the presumption is rebuttable,[14] the presumption of sanity need not dissipate with the presenta-

---

[3]Handspike v. State, 203 Ga. 115, 119, 45 S.E.2d 662 (1947), overruled by Brooks v. State, 247 Ga. 744, 279 S.E.2d 649 (1981).

[4]Cf. Brooks v. State, 157 Ga. App. 650, 278 S.E.2d 463 (1981), aff'd, 247 Ga. 744, 279 S.E.2d 649 (1981).

[5]However, there is dicta in Brown v. State, 250 Ga. 66, 71, 295 S.E.2d 727 (1982), stating that "[i]nsanity may be so clear and the proof so overwhelming that a jury finding of sanity cannot be upheld."

[6]Boswell v. State, 275 Ga. 689, 691 (2), 572 S.E.2d 565 (2002); Murphy v. State, 263 Ga. App. 62, 64 (2), 587 S.E.2d 223 (2003); Peek v. State, 250 Ga. 50, 51 (1), 295 S.E.2d 834 (1982).

In Brown v. State, 250 Ga. 66, 71, 295 S.E.2d 727 (1982), the court said that since "jurors are not bound by the opinions on sanity of either lay or expert witnesses, the jury may reject defense testimony on insanity even if uncontradicted."

[7]Brown v. State, 250 Ga. 66, 71, 295 S.E.2d 727 (1982); Heaton v. State, 175 Ga. App. 735, 334 (3), 334 S.E.2d 334 (1985).

[8]Gary v. State, 122 Ga. App. 151, 176 S.E.2d 478 (1970). See Durrence v. State, 287 Ga. 213, 695 S.E.2d 227 (2010).

[9]Guest v. State, 230 Ga. 569, 572, 198 S.E.2d 158 (1973).

[10]Gilbert v. State, 235 Ga. 501, 502, 220 S.E.2d 262 (1975); Brackett v. State, 227 Ga. 493 (1), 181 S.E.2d 380 (1971); Cantwell v. State, 153 Ga. App. 717, 718 (2), 266 S.E.2d 354 (1980); Fulghum v. State, 246 Ga. 184, 186, 269 S.E.2d 455 (1980).

[11]Salter v. State, 257 Ga. 88, 89 (1), 356 S.E.2d 196 (1987).

[12]State v. Vosler, 216 Neb. 461, 345 N.W.2d 806 (1984).

[13]Newman v. State, 258 Ga. 428, 430 (2), 369 S.E.2d 902 (1988).

[14]Guest v. State, 230 Ga. 569, 572,

tion of evidence to the contrary; the jury is free to reject the evidence and accept the presumption.[15]

In *Keener v. State*,[16] the court pointed out that the guilty but mentally ill statute, O.C.G.A. § 17-7-131 "places no burden on a defendant to prove that he is not mentally ill, or that he is guilty but mentally ill. The burden is on the state to prove that the defendant is guilty of the crime charged, including the requisite element of intent, beyond a reasonable doubt. The burden is on the defendant to prove he is not guilty by reason of insanity by a preponderance of the evidence."

In *Kirk v. State*,[17] the court said "a defendant's sanity is presumed; a defendant has the burden of proving insanity by a preponderance of the evidence; the presentation by a defendant of evidence contrary to the presumption does not as a matter of law dissipate it; jurors are permitted to reject the testimony of lay or expert witnesses as to sanity of the accused, and to rely upon the presumption of sanity."

Lay testimony on the issue of insanity is admissible if the witnesses state the facts upon which their opinions are based.[18] It has been said that in order to lay a sufficient factual basis for such testimony, it should appear that the witness knew the defendant "had been in his presence, and had observed his conduct."[19] However, a non-expert may not give an opinion as to the sanity of a person at the time of the crime based solely on observations of the accused months after the commission of the crime.[20]

Georgia courts also recognize that insanity may be established by testimony of the bizarre circumstances of the crime,[21] but not by reputation in the community. Likewise, where a witness testifies to the insanity of a defendant based on personal observation at a specific time and place, the testimony cannot be impeached

---

198 S.E.2d 158 (1973).

[15]See generally Potts v. State, 241 Ga. 67, 82, 243 S.E.2d 510 (1978), vacated by Potts v. Zant, 575 F.Supp. 374 (N.D.Ga.1983).

[16]Keener v. State, 254 Ga. 699 (2), 334 S.E.2d 175 (1985); Holder v. State, 194 Ga. App. 790, 793 (3), 391 S.E.2d 808 (1990).

[17]Kirk v. State, 252 Ga. 133 (2), 311 S.E.2d 821 (1984); Murray v. State, 253 Ga. 90, 91, 317 S.E.2d 193 (1984); Harris v. State, 181 Ga. App. 358, 352 S.E.2d 226 (1986).

[18]See Compton v. Porterfield, 155 Ga. 480 (1), 117 S.E. 464 (1923); Davis v. United States, 413 F.2d 1226 (5th Cir. 1969). In Ryder v. State, 100 Ga. 528, 529, 28 S.E. 246 (1897), the court held that it was error to charge that the testimony of an expert witness as to sanity was entitled to greater weight than that of lay witnesses. See O.C.G.A. § 24-7-701.

[19]Chancellor v. State, 165 Ga. App. 365, 369, 301 S.E.2d 294 (1983).

[20]Smith v. State, 141 Ga. App. 720, 722, 234 S.E.2d 385 (1977).

[21]Wilson v. State, 9 Ga. App. 274, 281 (1), 70 S.E. 1128 (1911). See Brown v. State, 228 Ga. 215, 219 (3), 184 S.E.2d 655 (1971).

by showing the general opinion in the witness' family or community which is contrary to the witness' stated opinion.[22]

However, under a 1982 Georgia statute, a defendant may not be found to be mentally ill if such "mental state [is] manifested only by repeated unlawful or antisocial conduct."[23]

In federal court, when a defendant introduces evidence of insanity, the burden shifts to the government to prove his sanity.[24] However, the Constitution does not require this rule,[25] and this is not the Georgia rule.

In weighing the evidence to determine whether or not it supports a guilty verdict, the Georgia Supreme Court continues to stress the fact that because of the Georgia statute providing for a presumption of sanity,[26] the burden is said to be on the defendant to show by a preponderance of the evidence that he was insane even though expert and lay testimony show insanity.[27] This burden of proof requires a defendant to show that a "[m]ental abnormality, such as . . . [a] psychosis . . . amounts to insanity."[28] However, once the defendant has "illustrated his insanity," then "the state is required to rebut that showing beyond a reasonable doubt."[29] Thus, "when the proof of insanity is overwhelming, juries may no longer rely solely on the presumption of sanity."[30] The standard for appellate review of the sufficiency of the evidence in regard to a jury's finding of sanity "is whether after reviewing the evidence in the light most favorable to the state, a rational trier of fact could have found that the defendant failed to prove by a preponderance of the evidence that he was insane at the time of the crime."[31]

To establish mental retardation of a defendant, the question of whether he must prove that condition by a preponderance of the

[22]Cooper v. State, 238 Ga. 502, 503, 233 S.E.2d 762 (1977).

[23]O.C.G.A. § 17-7-131.

[24]United States v. Faulkner, 35 Fed. 730, 731 (1888); Taylor v. United States, 329 F.2d 384 (5th Cir. 1964).

[25]Grace v. Hopper, 566 F.2d 507 (5th Cir. 1978), rev'g 425 F.Supp. 1355 (M.D.Ga.1977); cf. Wilson v. State, 9 Ga. App. 274, 286, 70 S.E. 1128 (1911), disapproved of in Terhune v. State, 117 Ga. App. 59, 60 (3), 159 S.E.2d 291 (1967).

[26]O.C.G.A. § 16-2-3.

[27]Durham v. State, 239 Ga. 697, 698 (1), 238 S.E.2d 334 (1977); Longshore v. State, 242 Ga. 689, 691 (1), 251 S.E.2d 280 (1978).

[28]Dennis v. State, 170 Ga. App. 630, 631, 317 S.E.2d 874 (1984).

[29]Moses v. State, 245 Ga. 180, 183 (b), 263 S.E.2d 916 (1980), overruled on other grounds by Nagel v. State, 262 Ga. 888, 427 S.E.2d 490 (1993); Cooper v. State, 163 Ga. App. 482, 484 (4), 295 S.E.2d 161 (1982). But cf. Williams v. State, 249 Ga. 839, 842 (5), 295 S.E.2d 74 (1982); Dollar v. State, 168 Ga. App. 726 (2), 310 S.E.2d 236 (1983).

[30]Stevens v. State, 256 Ga. 440, 442, 350 S.E.2d 21 (1986).

[31]Brown v. State, 250 Ga. 66, 71, 295 S.E.2d 727 (1982).

evidence or beyond a reasonable doubt depends on when the trial is held. If he is tried after the enactment of O.C.G.A. § 17-7-131(c)(3), (j), which occurred on July 1, 1988, he is required to prove mental retardation beyond a reasonable doubt. If he is tried before that time, he would only be required to prove mental retardation by a preponderance of the evidence.[32]

But see § 21:12, infra, on the charge of the court. See § 5:21, supra, on evidence of sanity by refusal to speak after *Miranda* warnings. Other aspects of the insanity defense are discussed in greater depth in the next section.

§ 21:12　Insanity as a defense—Jury instructions

The facts contained in this section were true prior to the 1985 requirement that the defendant give notice that he plans to present an insanity defense. See § 14:92, supra, on defense of insanity, mental illness, mental retardation or mental competency. It is difficult to now determine how much of this section still applies.

In *Kelley v. State*,[1] the court held that insanity is an affirmative defense. If a defendant does not admit to committing the act, he is not entitled to a charge on insanity. See § 21:17, infra, on affirmative defenses.

Where there is testimony on insanity, whether it pertains to the right-and-wrong test or the delusional compulsion rule, it is the duty of the trial judge to charge on insanity.[2] Also, in all felony cases in which "an accused shall contend that he was insane or otherwise mentally incompetent under the law at the time of the act or acts charged against him were committed, the trial judge shall instruct the jury that they may consider, in addition to verdicts of 'guilty' and 'not guilty,' the additional verdicts of 'not guilty by reason of insanity at the time of the crime' and 'guilty but mentally ill at the time of the crime.' "[3] Yet, it has been held that where a defendant does not remember his allegedly criminal activity, a charge of insanity is not required.[4] At this time, there are no Georgia cases on the question of whether a charge on being mentally ill is required where the defendant does not remember the events related to the crime charged.

If the evidence justifies it, the trial judge is to first charge on "insanity" as has been done in the past. However, the trial judge

---

[32]Stephens v. State, 270 Ga. 354, 355 (2), 509 S.E.2d 605 (1998).

[Section 21:12]

[1]Kelley v. State, 235 Ga. App. 177, 179 (1), 509 S.E.2d 110 (1998).

[2]Sanders v. State, 140 Ga. App. 101, 103 (2), 230 S.E.2d 20 (1976).

[3]O.C.G.A. § 17-7-131.

[4]Williams v. State, 237 Ga. 399, 400, 228 S.E.2d 806 (1976); Gooch v. State, 259 Ga. 301, 302 (2), 379 S.E.2d 522 (1989).

must make it clear to the jury that if the defendant is found insane they must find the defendant not guilty by reason of insanity.[5] Second, the judge must instruct the jury that if the defendant is not found to be insane, then the jury is to consider whether the defendant is guilty but mentally ill, as has been done in the past. Third, if the jury does not find the defendant to be insane at the time of the crime or guilty but mentally ill at the time of the crime, then the jury is to be charged on the general finding of guilt. Fourth, if the jury does not find the defendant to be insane or mentally ill at the time of the crime and does not find the defendant to be guilty of any offense charged, then the jury is to return a verdict of not guilty.

It is error for the trial judge to refuse to charge on the presumption of continuing insanity, if the facts justify such a charge.[6] See § 21:10, supra, on insanity defense.

A defendant claiming insanity has the burden of proving the defense by a preponderance of the evidence.[7] Under Georgia law, a person is insane, and shall not be guilty of a crime, if at the time of the act, omission, or negligence constituting the crime, the person did not have mental capacity to distinguish between right and wrong in relation to the criminal act or acted because of a delusional compulsion which overmastered his will to resist committing the crime.[8]

Because Georgia law presumes every person is of sound mind and discretion, criminal trials begin with the rebuttable presumption that the defendant is sane and this presumption is evidence.[9]

It is also true, however, that our law presumes the continued existence of a mental state once it is proved to exist.[10] It is for this reason that where a defendant previously has been adjudicated insane, introduction into evidence of the insanity order raises a counter-presumption.[11] In such cases, the burden shifts to the State to prove the defendant was sane at the time of the crimes.[12] The counter-presumption does not survive once the defendant is properly released from the hospital or institution, but instead the presumption of sanity is restored.[13]

---

[5]Price v. State, 179 Ga. App. 598, 601 (1), 347 S.E.2d 608 (1986).

[6]Hankinson v. State, 129 Ga. App. 568, 570, 200 S.E.2d 315 (1973).

[7]Durrence v. State, 287 Ga. 213, 695 S.E.2d 227 (2010).

[8]O.C.G.A. §§ 16-3-2, 16-3-3; Foster v. State, 283 Ga. 47, 656 S.E.2d 838 (2008).

[9]O.C.G.A. § 16-2-3; Gilbert v. State, 235 Ga. 501, 220 S.E.2d 262 (1975).

[10]O.C.G.A. § 24-14-21; Gilbert v. State, 235 Ga. 501, 501–502, 220 S.E.2d 262 (1975).

[11]Durham v. State, 239 Ga. 697(1), 238 S.E.2d 334 (1977).

[12]Durham v. State, 239 Ga. 697(1), 238 S.E.2d 334 (1977).

[13]Durham v. State, 239 Ga. 697(1),

In *Powell v. State*,[14] the Georgia Supreme Court, in regard to the burden of proof as to insanity, held that where the charge of the court includes instruction as to insanity but places the burden of proof as to each essential element of the crime, including intent, upon the state beyond a reasonable doubt, it is not error for the court not to instruct the jury more specifically as to the burden of proof in the absence of a request.[15] It has been held error for the trial judge to instruct the jury that "the law presumes that a person intends the ordinary consequences of his voluntary acts" because this presumption shifts the burden of proof to the defendant.[16] See Studdard, *Daniel's Georgia Handbook on Criminal Evidence* (2018 ed.), § 3:20.

In *Boswell v. State*,[17] the court approved a charge providing as follows: "The burden is on the defendant to establish by this preponderance of the evidence . . . that at the time of the alleged offense, he was mentally irresponsible under tests that have been recognized by the law of Georgia. . . . [I]f you have a reasonable doubt as to his sanity at the time of the alleged murder charged against him was committed, you are to give him the benefit of the doubt and acquit him on those grounds." However, in *Spivey v. State*,[18] the court affirmed a charge which stated that if the jury "believed 'beyond a reasonable doubt . . . that the defendant is guilty and mentally ill at the time of the commission of the offense' then the jury would be authorized to find Spivey guilty but mentally ill." The same burden of proof is on a defendant if he is to be found guilty but mentally retarded.[19] See O.C.G.A. § 17-7-131(b)(3), on sequence of charge.

It has been held that if a defendant testifies that he did not know what he was doing, this raises the issue of insanity, and it

---

238 S.E.2d 334 (1977); Nelson v. State, 254 Ga. 611(1), 331 S.E.2d 554 (1985); Brown v. State, 250 Ga. 66, 295 S.E.2d 727 (1982).

[14]Powell v. State, 237 Ga. 490, 492, 228 S.E.2d 875 (1976). Cf. Myers v. State, 143 Ga. App. 195, 237 S.E.2d 662 (1977).

[15]From a federal constitutional standpoint, Patterson v. New York, 432 U.S. 197, 97 S.Ct. 2319, 53 L.Ed.2d 281 (1977) should be considered. In this case, the United States Supreme Court held that it was not unconstitutional to require a defendant to prove by a preponderance of the evidence that he was acting under the influence of extreme emotional disturbance in order to reduce a charge of second degree murder to manslaughter. The court further reaffirmed Leland v. Oregon, 343 U.S. 790, 72 S.Ct. 1002, 96 L.Ed. 1302 (1952), which held that due process is not violated by requiring a defendant to prove his insanity.

[16]Sandstrom v. Montana, 442 U.S. 510, 99 S.Ct. 2450, 61 L.Ed.2d 39 (1979).

[17]Boswell v. State, 243 Ga. 732, 256 S.E.2d 470 (1979).

[18]Spivey v. State, 253 Ga. 187, 188 (2), 319 S.E.2d 420 (1984).

[19]Palmer v. State, 271 Ga. 234, 237 (3), 517 S.E.2d 502 (1999). *Palmer* also holds that this burden on the defendant is constitutional.

is not error for the court to charge on insanity.[20] However, it has been held that where one witness was asked the single question "Did it look like . . . [the defendant] lost his mind?" and she responded "I'll say he's crazy. Cause you don't just go doing things like that," this alone does not require the trial judge to charge on insanity.[21] However, in light of the 1985 requirement of prior notice of an insanity defense, only the prosecution can raise an insanity plea after hearing such testimony from a defendant. If the defense intends to raise the issue of insanity or mental illness, notice must be given and filed "at or before the time set by law unless time therefor is extended by the judge in writing prior to trial."[22]

Prior to the 1982 statutory enactment, the Georgia courts held that it was mandatory to charge the provisions of the first part of O.C.G.A. § 17-7-131 when the defendant pled insanity as a defense. Although it was considered better practice not to inform the jury as to the disposition which would be made of a defendant if he were found not guilty by reason of insanity, it was not error to charge the entire Code section.[23] Nevertheless, it was recognized, even prior to the 1982 enactment, that the failure to inform the jury on the disposition of the defendant might result in the jury's being unwilling to find him not guilty by reason of insanity if the jury thought that the accused would simply be turned loose if such a verdict were returned.[24]

O.C.G.A. § 17-7-131, in connection with the charge provides as

---

[20]Lewis v. State, 239 Ga. 732, 733 (4), 238 S.E.2d 892 (1977).

[21]McClendon v. State, 157 Ga. App. 435, 278 S.E.2d 96 (1981).

[22]Ga. Unif. Super. Ct. R. 31.1, 31.5.

[23]Printup v. State, 142 Ga. App. 42, 43 (4), 234 S.E.2d 840 (1977). This seems to be the majority rule. See Annot., 11 A.L.R.3d 737 (1967). In Dubose v. State, 148 Ga. App. 9, 251 S.E.2d 15 (1978), the court pointed out that a defendant committed as a result of a finding of not guilty by reason of insanity is entitled to be released if he (1) is not likely to injure himself or others and (2) is capable of caring for his physical health and safety. However, even when there is expert testimony saying he meets there requirements, he does not have to be released if there is evidence that he is likely to violate the criminal laws if he is released.

In Neal v. State, 160 Ga. App. 498, 501 (3), 287 S.E.2d 399 (1981), rev'd on other grounds, Bangs v. State, 198 Ga. App. 404, 406, 401 S.E.2d 599 (1991), the district attorney argued, without objection, that the defendant would be released if she were found not guilty by reason of insanity. The defendant then contended that she was entitled to have the entire contents of O.C.G.A. § 17-7-131 charged in view of the improper argument. The Court of Appeals found no error in the refusal to give the requested instruction and stated that the defense should have objected or moved for a mistrial during the argument.

[24]Some cases from other jurisdictions have held that it is necessary for the trial judge to inform the jury of the disposition of the defendant if he is found not guilty by reason of insanity. Taylor v. United States, 222 F.2d 398 (D.C.Cir. 1955); contra, State v.

follows:

"(c) In all criminal trials in any of the courts of this state wherein an accused shall contend that he was insane or otherwise mentally incompetent under the law at the time the act or acts charged against him were committed, the trial judge shall instruct the jury that they may consider, in addition to verdicts of 'guilty' and 'not guilty,' the additional verdicts of 'not guilty by reason of insanity at the time of the crime'; 'guilty but mentally ill at the time of the crime,' and 'guilty but mentally retarded.' "[25]

In 2006, the Legislature amended O.C.G.A. § 17-7-131(b)(3) to make the psychiatric evaluation of a defendant found guilty but mentally ill/retarded the sole responsibility of the Department of Behavioral Health and Developmental Disabilities.[26] Beginning July 1, 2006, § 17-7-131(b)(3) requires the trial judge to charge the jury as follows:

"(A) I charge you that should you find the defendant not guilty by reason of insanity at the time of the crime, the defendant will be committed to a state mental health facility until such time, if ever, that the court is satisfied that he or she should be released pursuant to law.

"(B) I charge you that should you find the defendant guilty but mentally ill at the time of the crime, the defendant will be placed in the custody of the Department of Corrections which will have responsibility for the evaluation and treatment of the mental health needs of the defendant, which may include, at the discretion of the Department of Corrections, referral for temporary hospitalization at a facility operated by the Department of Behavioral Health and Developmental Disabilities.

"(C) I charge you that should you find the defendant guilty but mentally retarded, the defendant will be placed in the custody of

---

Bracy, 215 N.C. 248, 1 S.E.2d 891 (1939); Pope v. United States, 298 F.2d 507 (5th Cir. 1962). Also, it has been held that such a request for charge must be given. Bean v. State, 81 Nev. 25, 398 P.2d 251 (1965). Contra, Commonwealth v. Gable, 323 Pa. 449, 187 A. 393 (1936).

In Bell v. State, 244 Ga. 211, 259 S.E.2d 465 (1979), the court at least implied that a defendant sentenced under O.C.G.A. § 17-7-131 is not entitled to be released if he meets the civil commitment criterion of O.C.G.A. § 37-3-1(12), O.C.G.A. §§ 37-3-1 et seq. or O.C.G.A. §§ 37-4-1 et seq., as now or hereafter amended.

[25]In State v. Ball, 251 Ga. 840, 310 S.E.2d 516 (1984), the court held that when a trial judge charges on "guilty but mentally ill at the time of the crime" it is not necessary for him to charge on "not guilty by reason of insanity at the time of the crime" when there is no evidence to support a charge of "not guilty by reason of insanity." See Choisnet v. State, 295 Ga. 568, 761 S.E.2d 322 (2014) (where defense is insanity, court *must* charge on verdict of guilty but mentally ill and/or mentally retarded).

[26]See also O.C.G.A. § 17-7-131(g) and (i), as amended July 1, 2006.

the Department of Corrections which will have responsibility for the evaluation and treatment of the mental health needs of the defendant, which may include, at the discretion of the Department of Corrections, referral for temporary hospitalization at a facility operated by the Department of Behavioral Health and Developmental Disabilities."

The defendant may be found "not guilty by reason of insanity at the time of the crime" if he meets the criteria of O.C.G.A. § 16-3-2 or O.C.G.A. § 16-3-3 at the time of the commission of the crime. If the court or jury should make such finding, it shall so specify in its verdict. However, both guilt and mental illness must be proved beyond a reasonable doubt.[27]

In *Stripling v. State*,[28] the Georgia Supreme Court noted that a trial court may not accept a plea of guilty but mentally retarded over the objection of the state and the issue must then be resolved by a jury.

The defendant may be found "guilty but mentally ill at the time of the crime" if the jury or court acting as trier of facts finds beyond a reasonable doubt that the defendant is guilty of the crime charged and was mentally ill or mentally retarded at the time of the commission of the crime. If the court or jury should make such finding, it shall so specify in its verdict.[29] However, it has been held that a defendant has the burden of proving mental retardation beyond a reasonable doubt.[30]

O.C.G.A. § 17-7-131(g)(1) provides that a defendant who has been found "guilty but mentally ill at the time of a felony or guilty but mentally retarded, or enters a plea to that effect that is accepted by the court" shall be sentenced as a defendant who has been found guilty.

See §§ 14:93 et seq., supra, on a special plea of insanity to establish a defendant's inability to stand trial.

§ 21:13 Insanity as a defense—Georgia's statutory procedure for release when defendant is found not guilty by reason of insanity at the time of the crime

O.C.G.A. § 17-7-131(c) provides that the jury verdict must specify when a defendant is found "not guilty by reason of insan-

---

[27]Hood v. State, 187 Ga. App. 88, 369 S.E.2d 348 (1988).

[28]Stripling v. State, 289 Ga. 370, 711 S.E.2d 665 (2011).

[29]O.C.G.A. §§ 17-7-131(c)(1), (2).

[30]Williams v. State, 265 Ga. 351, 352 (3), 455 S.E.2d 836 (1995); Jenkins v. State, 269 Ga. 282, 292 (17), 498 S.E.2d 502 (1998). Accord, O.C.G.A. § 17-7-131(c)(3).

ity at the time of the crime."[1] See § 21:15, infra.

If such a verdict is returned, the court retains jurisdiction over the person so acquitted and shall order him detained in a mental health facility for a period not exceeding 30 days from the date of acquittal for evaluation of his mental condition. This is to be regarded as a state-initiated commitment hearing. A copy of the report of the defendant shall be sent to the trial judge, the district attorney, and defense counsel.[2]

At the time a defendant is admitted for evaluation, he shall be notified in writing of certain statutory rights. These rights are:

(A) A notice that a hearing will be held and the time and place thereof;

(B) A notice that the defendant has the right to counsel and that the defendant or his representatives may apply immediately to the court to have counsel appointed if the defendant cannot afford counsel and that the court will appoint counsel for the defendant unless he indicates in writing that he does not desire to be represented by counsel;

(C) The right to confront and cross-examine witnesses and to offer evidence;

(D) The right to subpoena witnesses and to require testimony before the court in person or by deposition from any person upon whose evaluation the decision of the court may rest;

(E) Notice of the right to have established an individualized service plan or individualized program plan specifically tailored to the person's treatment needs, as such plans are defined in Chapter 3 of Title 37 and Chapter 4 of Title 37; and

(F) A notice that the defendant has the right to be examined by a physician or a licensed clinical psychologist of his own choice at his own expense and to have that physician or psychologist submit a suggested service plan for the patient which conforms to the requirements of Chapter 3 of Title 37 or Chapter 4 of Title 37, whichever is applicable.[3]

After the expiration of the 30-day evaluation period, if the report indicates that the defendant does not meet the commitment criteria of O.C.G.A. §§ 37-3-1 et seq. or O.C.G.A. §§ 37-4-1 et seq., the trial judge may issue an order discharging the

---

[Section 21:13]

[1]An acquittal by reason of insanity constitutes a finding that the defendant is not guilty because the defendant was insane at the time of the commission of the crime. See O.C.G.A.

§ 16-3-2 and O.C.G.A. § 16-3-3 and Clark v. State, 245 Ga. 629, 266 S.E.2d 466 (1980).

[2]O.C.G.A. § 17-7-131(d).

[3]O.C.G.A. § 17-7-131(e)(4).

defendant from custody without a hearing.[4] However, once a person is found not guilty by reason of insanity and committed to a mental hospital, the person is presumed to be unfit for release.[5]

On the other hand, if the defendant is not released without a hearing as set out above, the trial judge shall order a hearing to determine whether the defendant should be committed to the Department of Human Resources. The hearing shall be conducted at the earliest opportunity after the 30-day evaluation period and not later than 30 days after receipt by the district attorney of the evaluation report.[6]

At the hearing, the trial judge may take judicial notice of the evidence introduced at the trial of the defendant. The defendant "may call for testimony from any person with knowledge concerning whether the defendant is currently a mentally ill person in need of involuntary treatment as defined by paragraph (12) of Code Section 37-1-1, or a person with a developmental disability as defined in paragraph 8 of Code Section 37-1-1 who presents a substantial risk of imminent harm to himself or herself or others." At the hearing, the district attorney may cross-examine witnesses called by the court and the witnesses of the defendant. Also, he may present relevant evidence.[7] The defendant has the same rights with respect to calling and cross-examining witnesses as the district attorney.[8]

The statute provides that at such a hearing the burden of proof is "upon the applicant,"[9] and there is a continuing presumption of insanity at the time of the release hearing.[10] In *Jones v. State*[11] the court pointed out that the trial judge is not bound by expert testimony that applicant is not mentally ill. In *Butler v. State*,[12] the court held that the "[t]rial judge as finder of fact is not bound by the opinions of either lay or expert witnesses and may rely upon the basic presumptions permitted by law."

If the trial judge at the hearing finds that the defendant meets

---

[4]O.C.G.A. § 17-7-131(e)(1).

[5]Butler v. State, 225 Ga. App. 288, 289, 483 S.E.2d 385 (1997).

[6]O.C.G.A. § 17-7-131(e)(3).

[7]O.C.G.A. § 17-7-131(e).

[8]O.C.G.A. § 17-7-131(f)(2).

[9]O.C.G.A. § 17-7-131(f)(2); Arnold v. State, 173 Ga. App. 839, 328 S.E.2d 572 (1985).

In Jones v. United States, 463 U.S. 354, 103 S.Ct. 3043, 77 L.Ed.2d 694 (1983), the court appears to say that the burden is on the defendant to show that he was no longer mentally ill or dangerous.

[10]Moses v. State, 167 Ga. App. 556, 558, 307 S.E.2d 35 (1983), overruled on other grounds by Nagel v. State, 262 Ga. 888, 427 S.E.2d 490 (1993); Cox v. State, 171 Ga. App. 550, 320 S.E.2d 611 (1984).

[11]Jones v. State, 191 Ga. App. 561, 382 S.E.2d 612 (1989). See Newman v. State, 314 Ga. App. 99, 722 S.E.2d 911 (2012). Cf. Nelor v. State, 309 Ga. App. 165, 709 S.E.2d 904 (2011).

[12]Butler v. State, 225 Ga. App. 288, 291, 483 S.E.2d 385 (1997).

the criteria for commitment, the judge shall order the defendant committed to the Department of Human Resources to receive involuntary treatment under O.C.G.A. §§ 37-3-1 et seq. or to receive services pursuant to O.C.G.A. §§ 37-4-1 et seq.

Once it has been established that a defendant meets the criteria of civil commitment, it is presumed that this condition continues to exist, and the burden is on the defendant to establish that he does not meet the criteria for involuntary commitment. At such a hearing the trial judge is not bound by the testimony of either lay or expert witnesses and may rely on the basic presumption.[13]

The criteria for civil commitment under O.C.G.A. §§ 37-3-1 et seq. is met if a person "is mentally ill and . . . presents a substantial risk of imminent harm to that person or others, as manifested by either recent overt acts or recent expressed threats of violence which present a probability of physical injury to that person or other persons, or . . . is so unable to care for that person's own physical health and safety as to create an imminently life-endangering crisis."[14] However, in *Gates v. State*,[15] the Georgia Court of Appeals concluded that a defendant is not entitled to be released if it is found upon a totality of the evidence that he is mentally ill "even if because of the controlled environment in which he had been living" he no longer suffers from all of his former problems if it is concluded that if he is not living in a structured environment he is likely to regress and might "pose a danger to others."

O.C.G.A. § 17-7-131(a)(3) defines mentally retarded as a person "having significantly subaverage general intellectual functioning resulting in or associated with impairments in adaptive behavior which manifested during the developmental period."

O.C.G.A. § 17-7-131(f) provides in part as follows:

"A defendant who has been found not guilty by reason of insanity at the time of the crime and is ordered committed to the Department of Behavioral Health and Developmental Disabilities under subsection (e) of this Code section may only be discharged from that commitment by order of the committing court in accordance with the procedures specified in this subsection:

"(1) Application for the release of a defendant who has been committed to the Department of Behavioral Health and Developmental Disabilities under subsection (e) of this Code section upon the ground that he does not meet the civil commitment criteria under Chapter 3 of Title 37 or Chapter 4 of Title 37 may be made

---

[13]Haugebrooks v. State, 196 Ga. App. 5, 395 S.E.2d 348 (1990); Crawford v. State, 202 Ga. App. 653, 415 S.E.2d 300 (1992).

[14]O.C.G.A. § 37-3-1.

[15]Gates v. State, 167 Ga. App. 353, 306 S.E.2d 411 (1983).

to the committing court, either by such defendant or by the superintendent of the state hospital in which the said defendant is detained."

In *Sikes v. State*,[16] the Georgia Supreme Court held that when a defendant who has been found not guilty by reason of insanity and who has been ordered to undergo involuntary inpatient treatment successfully completes a conditional release program ordered by the trial court under O.C.G.A. § 17-7-131(e)(5)(A), the trial court must find whether the defendant successfully completed his conditional release plan, and if the court so finds, the defendant must be discharged from the order requiring his hospitalization. However, the court may order the defendant committed to involuntary outpatient treatment if the court determines that the defendant meets the requirements for such treatment. If the trial court determines that the defendant did not successfully complete his conditional release program, the court may take either of the actions authorized by O.C.G.A. § 17-7-131(e)(5)(C)(i) or O.C.G.A. § 17-7-131(e)(5)(C)(ii), i.e., revoke the period of conditional release and return the defendant to a state hospital for inpatient services or impose additional or revise existing conditions on the defendant as appropriate to continue the period of conditional release.

O.C.G.A. § 17-7-131(f) also provides that if the trial judge rules against a release for the defendant, another release application shall not be heard until 12 months have elapsed from the date of the last hearing.[17]

Pursuant to O.C.G.A. § 37-3-148(b) a patient may petition the "appropriate" court for relief if the patient contends that he or she has been deprived of some right provided by the civil commitment statutory scheme. In *Ledbetter v. Cannon*,[18] the court held that the only appropriate court to entertain a petition under O.C.G.A. § 37-3-148(b) is the court which ordered the insanity acquittee committed and the probate court has no jurisdiction in such matters. In addition, habeas corpus relief is available pursuant to O.C.G.A. § 37-3-148(a) at any time and without notice to a person detained pursuant to the commitment statute.[19]

In the 1993 case of *Nagel v. State*,[20] the Georgia Supreme Court considered the presumption of insanity which must be overcome by an insanity acquittee in order to obtain release. The court

[16]Sikes v. State, 268 Ga. 19, 485 S.E.2d 206 (1997).

[17]O.C.G.A. § 17-7-131(f)(3).

[18]Ledbetter v. Cannon, 192 Ga. App. 392, 384 S.E.2d 875 (1989).

[19]See Fullwood v. Sivley, 271 Ga. 248, 517 S.E.2d 511 (1999). See also Hogan v. Nagel, 273 Ga. 577, 543 S.E.2d 705 (2001).

[20]Nagel v. State, 262 Ga. 888, 890 (2), 427 S.E.2d 490 (1993). See Gibson v. State, 335 Ga. App. 569, 782 S.E.2d 472 (2016); Nelor v. State, 309 Ga. App. 165, 709 S.E.2d 904 (2011).

pointed out that this presumption may be rebutted, and "[w]hen proof of [sanity] is overwhelming, [judges] may not rely solely on the rebuttable presumption of [insanity]." The standard of review by an appellate court may not be based on the "any evidence" test.

> "[T]he trial court must supply specific findings regarding the evidence of sanity and insanity, and his conclusions based on that evidence. The court must consider expert and other evidence presented at the release hearing, and contained in the trial record, on the issue of sanity or insanity. Regarding expert evidence, the court must carefully consider *all* credible relevant evidence on either side. Finally, the court must weigh the evidence in light of the defendant's burden to overcome the presumption by a preponderance of the evidence."

The court's 1993 *Nagel* decision resulted in a remand. The case was appealed again in 1994,[21] and the court held that evidence that the defendant has never been mentally ill or insane is not admissible at a hearing for release from civil commitment because the jury's "verdict of not guilty by reason of insanity [NGRI] *establishes* two facts: (i) the defendant committed an act that constitutes a criminal offense, and (ii) he committed the act because of *mental illness*." Thus, the issue of the defendant's sanity is res judicata.

In *Butler v. State*,[22] the court held that the trial judge may consider whether or not a defendant will continue to take his medication if he is conditionally released where there is testimony he is no longer a danger to himself or others because his mental condition is controlled by medicine.

In *O'Neal v. State*,[23] the court held that a trial judge has authority to allow an insanity acquittee to pursue treatment, educational or other goals outside the confines of the treating facility. See § 21:15, infra.

§ 21:14   Insanity as a defense—Constitutional considerations relating to the release of a defendant who has been found not guilty by reason of insanity at the time of the crime

The Georgia statutory procedure for the release hearing for insanity-acquittees differs from the release hearing for civil com-

---

[21]Nagel v. State, 264 Ga. 150, 151 (2), 442 S.E.2d 446 (1994).

[22]Butler v. State, 225 Ga. App. 288, 290, 483 S.E.2d 385 (1997).

[23]O'Neal v. State, 185 Ga. App. 838, 840, 365 S.E.2d 894 (1988).

mittees in a number of ways:[1] (1) insanity-acquittees are under a continuing presumption of mental illness;[2] (2) the insanity-acquittee has the burden of proof in release hearings;[3] (3) the state is not required to prove by clear and convincing evidence that the insanity-acquittee meets the criteria for continued commitment;[4] (4) the release of an insanity-acquittee must be ordered by the committing court;[5] and (5) once an application for a release has been denied, another cannot be filed for a year.[6] Due to these and other procedural and substantive differences between the rights afforded the criminally and civilly insane, O.C.G.A. § 17-7-131 has been attacked on equal protection and due process grounds.[7]

One such attack on the constitutionality of O.C.G.A. § 17-7-131 arose in a United States District Court class action, *Benham v. Edwards*.[8] In that case, Judge Harold Murphy concluded that the Georgia statutes failed to pass constitutional muster on equal protection and due process grounds. This decision was generally affirmed by the Fifth Circuit Court of Appeals.[9] However, while review of this case was pending in the United States Supreme Court, that court handed down an opinion in *Jones v. United States*.[10] In *Jones,* the defendant had been found not guilty by reason of insanity, the United States Supreme Court said "[1] The fact that a person has been found, beyond a reasonable doubt,

---

[Section 21:14]

[1]The Georgia procedure for release hearings for insanity acquittees is set out in O.C.G.A. § 17-7-131 and discussed in § 21:13, supra. The Georgia involuntary civil commitment provisions are set out in O.C.G.A. §§ 37-3-1 et seq. and O.C.G.A. §§ 37-4-1 et seq.

[2]Clark v. State, 245 Ga. 629, 631, 266 S.E.2d 466 (1980). See Coogler v. State, 324 Ga. App. 796, 751 S.E.2d 584 (2013) (trial court may not deny an insane acquittee's petition for release from civil commitment solely on the basis of the presumption of insanity where there is unrebutted competent evidence that he no longer meets the criteria for civil commitment).

[3]Benham v. Edwards, 501 F.Supp. 1050, 1056 (N.D.Ga.1980). See also Corn v. State, 240 Ga. 130, 139-40, 240 S.E.2d 694 (1977) and May v. State, 146 Ga. App. 416, 246 S.E.2d 432 (1978) (both cases involve a special plea of insanity); Pope v. State, 172 Ga. App. 396, 397 (1), 323 S.E.2d 268 (1984).

[4]Benham v. Edwards, 501 F.Supp. 1050 (N.D.Ga.1980).

[5]O.C.G.A. § 17-7-131(b).

[6]O.C.G.A. § 17-7-131(b).

[7]In Baxstrom v. Herold, 383 U.S. 107, 86 S.Ct. 760, 15 L.Ed.2d 620 (1966), the United States Supreme Court held that while there is a difference between civil and criminal committees (the latter having been charged with a crime), and although that difference may justify a difference in care and treatment, it does not justify diluted procedural safeguards for the insanity-acquittee.

[8]Benham v. Edwards, 501 F.Supp. 1050 (N.D.Ga.1980).

[9]Benham v. Edwards, 678 F.2d 511 (5th Cir. 1982), judgment vacated by Ledbetter v. Benham, 463 U.S. 1222, 103 S.Ct. 3565, 77 L.Ed.2d 1406 (Ga.1983).

[10]Jones v. United States, 463 U.S. 354, 103 S.Ct. 3043, 77 L.Ed.2d 694 (1983).

to have committed a criminal act certainly indicates dangerousness. . . . [2] The fact that the accused was found to have committed a criminal act is 'strong evidence that his continued liberty could imperil" the preservation of the peace ". . . Indeed, this concrete evidence generally may be at least as persuasive as any predictions about dangerousness that might be made in a civil-commitment proceeding. [3] We do not agree . . . that the requisite dangerousness is not established by proof that a person committed a non-violent crime against property. . . . [4] Nor can we say that it was unreasonable for Congress to determine that the insanity acquittal supports an inference of continuing mental illness. . . . The precise evidentiary force of the insanity acquittal, of course, may vary from case to case, but the Due Process Clause does not require Congress to make classifications that fit every individual with the same degree of relevance. . . . [5] [Jones] also argues that . . . the Government lacks a legitimate reason for committing insanity acquittees automatically because it can introduce the insanity acquittal as evidence in a subsequent civil proceeding. This argument fails to consider the Government's strong interest in avoiding the need to conduct a *de novo* commitment hearing following every insanity acquittal. . . . We therefore conclude that a finding of not guilty by reason of insanity is a sufficient foundation for commitment of an insanity acquittee for the purpose of treatment and the protection of society. [6] The Government at a hearing on a petition for release of an insanity acquittee is only obligated to show continuing insanity by a preponderance of the evidence. [7] There is simply no necessary correlation between severity of the offense and length of time necessary for recovery." Thus, an insanity-acquittee may be kept in custody for a longer period than the maximum sentence the defendant could have received for the crime with which he was charged.

As an aftermath of *Jones,* the United States Supreme Court reversed *Benham* and remanded it for consideration in light of *Jones.*[11] On remand, Judge Murphy handed down an order on April 22, 1985, finding no constitutional violations in the Georgia statutes.[12] On March 23, 1986, the Eleventh Circuit in *Benham v. Ledbetter*[13] held that the Georgia statutory scheme for releasing insanity-acquittees is constitutional.

In the 1992 case of *Foucha v. Louisiana,*[14] the United States Supreme Court in a plurality decision again pointed out that a

---

[11]Ledbetter v. Benham, 463 U.S. 1222, 103 S.Ct. 3565, 77 L.Ed.2d 1406 (1983).

[12]Benham v. Ledbetter, 609 F.Supp. 125 (N.D.Ga.1985).

[13]Benham v. Ledbetter, 785 F.2d 1480 (11th Cir. 1986).

[14]Foucha v. Louisiana, 504 U.S. 71, 112 S.Ct. 1780, 118 L.Ed.2d 437 (1992).

defendant who has been found not guilty by reason of insanity is entitled to be released when he has recovered his sanity and is not dangerous.

In *Hogan v. Nagel*,[15] the Georgia Supreme Court held that it was not necessary that a defendant must first exhaust remedies under the criminal code before seeking habeas corpus relief.

§ 21:15 Insanity as a defense—Release of defendant found guilty but mentally ill or guilty but mentally retarded

Under O.C.G.A. § 17-7-131(b)(1), in all felony cases "in which the defense of insanity is interposed," the jury (or the court in a bench trial) shall find whether the defendant is guilty, not guilty, not guilty by reason of insanity at the time of the crime, guilty but mentally ill at the time of the crime, or guilty but mentally retarded. Moreover,

[i]n all criminal trials in any of the courts of this state wherein an accused shall contend that he was insane or otherwise mentally incompetent under the law at the time of the act or acts charged against him were committed, the trial judge shall instruct the jury that they may consider, in addition to verdicts of "guilty" and "not guilty," the additional verdicts of "not guilty by reason of insanity at the time of the crime," "guilty but mentally ill at the time of the crime," and "guilty but mentally retarded."[1]

Under O.C.G.A. § 17-7-131(a)(2), " '[m]entally ill' means having a disorder of thought or mood which significantly impairs judgment, behavior, capacity to recognize reality, or ability to cope with the ordinary demands of life. However, the term 'mental illness' shall not include a mental state manifested only by repeated unlawful or antisocial conduct."

Accordingly, mental illness which is not the equivalent of legal insanity or incompetency at the time of the crime is not a defense to the crime.[2]

O.C.G.A. § 17-7-131 provides in part as follows:

"(g)(1) Whenever a defendant is found guilty but mentally ill at the time of a felony or guilty but mentally retarded, or enters a plea to that effect that is accepted by the court, the court shall sentence him or her in the same manner as a defendant found guilty of the offense, except as otherwise provided in subsection (j) of this Code section. A defendant who is found guilty but

---

[15]Hogan v. Nagel, 273 Ga. 577, 543 S.E.2d 705 (2001).

[Section 21:15]

[1]O.C.G.A. § 17-7-131(c).

[2]State v. Abernathy, 289 Ga. 603, 608-09, 715 S.E.2d 48 (2011).

mentally ill at the time of the felony or guilty but mentally retarded shall be committed to an appropriate penal facility and shall be evaluated then treated, if indicated, within the limits of state funds appropriated therefor, in such manner is as psychiatrically indicated for his or her mental illness or mental retardation.

"(2) If at any time following the defendant's conviction as a guilty but mentally ill or guilty but mentally retarded offender it is determined that a temporary transfer to the Department of Behavioral Health and Developmental Disabilities is clinically indicated for his or her mental illness or mental retardation, then the defendant shall be transferred to the Department of Behavioral Health and Developmental Disabilities pursuant to procedures set forth in regulations of the Department of Corrections and the Department of Behavioral Health and Disabilities. In all such cases, the legal custody of the defendant shall be retained by the Department of Corrections. Upon notification from the Department of Behavioral Health and Developmental Disabilities to the Department of Corrections that hospitalization at a Department of Behavioral Health and Developmental Disabilities facility is no longer clinically indicated for his or her mental illness or mental retardation, the Department of Corrections shall transfer the defendant back to its physical custody and shall place such individual in an appropriate penal institution."

"(h) If a defendant who is found guilty but mentally ill at the time of a felony or guilty but mentally retarded is placed on probation under the 'State-wide Probation Act,' [O.C.G.A. §§ 42-8-20 et seq.], the court may require that the defendant undergo available outpatient medical or psychiatric treatment or seek similar available voluntary inpatient treatment as a condition of probation. Persons required to receive such services may be charged fees by the provider of the services."

In *Senior v. State*,[3] the court held that a trial judge does not have to approve a plan from an institution providing for a conditional release or "off-campus privileges." The trial judge "is entirely free to reject the recommendation." See § 21:13, supra.

In *Lewis v. State*,[4] the Georgia Supreme Court held that O.C.G.A. § 17-7-131 does not preclude the imposition of the death penalty in the case of a defendant who is found guilty but mentally ill.

See §§ 21:10 and 21:12, supra, on charge in insanity cases.

---

[3]Senior v. State, 186 Ga. App. 861, 862, 369 S.E.2d 49 (1988).

[4]Lewis v. State, 279 Ga. 756(12), 620 S.E.2d 778 (2005).

§ 21:16 Intoxication as a defense[1]

It is generally held that voluntary intoxication or drunkenness is not a defense to a crime.[2] In *Montana v. Egelhoff*,[3] the United States Supreme Court held that a state statute did not violate the due process clause when it provided that the jury could not consider the defendant's intoxicated condition in determining the existence of a mental state which is an element of a criminal offense. The defendant was charged and convicted of "purposely" and "knowingly" causing the death of another human being.

However, in Georgia if prolonged drunkenness causes a permanent mania or insanity, then an insanity defense may be used.[4]

O.C.G.A. § 16-3-4 provides as follows:

"(a) A person shall not be found guilty of a crime when, at the time of the act, omission, or negligence constituting the crime, the person, because of involuntary intoxication, did not have sufficient mental capacity to distinguish between right and wrong in relation to such act.

"(b) Involuntary intoxication means intoxication caused by:

"(1) Consumption of a substance through excusable ignorance; or

"(2) The coercion, fraud, artifice, or contrivance of another person.

"(c) Voluntary intoxication shall not be an excuse for any criminal act or omission."[5]

The Committee Notes state that O.C.G.A. § 16-3-4 generally conforms to the status of the law before the statute was enacted. The reported cases decided after the effective date of the statute (July 1, 1969) do not indicate a change in the former law. Cases

---

[Section 21:16]

[1]Generally, on background of the subject, see Lunter, "The Effect of Drug-Induced Intoxication on Issue of Criminal Responsibility," 8 Crim. L. Bull. 731 (1972); Kaplan, "Powell v. Texas [392 U.S. 514, 88 S.Ct. 2145, 20 L.Ed.2d 1254 (1968)]: Alcoholics Anomalous Chapter I" or "Chronic Alcoholism and Criminal Responsibility," 5 Crim. L. Bull. 191 (1969); and Annot., 8 A.L.R.3d 1236 (1966).

[2]Brown v. State, 148 Ga. 264, 265, 96 S.E. 435 (1918); Stephens v. State, 139 Ga. 594 (1), 77 S.E. 875 (1913) (voluntary drunkenness alone is no defense to murder); Dickens v. State, 137 Ga. 523 (5), 529, 73 S.E. 826

(1912) (dicta, and court pointed out that defendant could have requested a fuller charge); and see Bonner v. State, 26 Ga. App. 185, 186 (4), 105 S.E. 863 (1921).

[3]Montana v. Egelhoff, 518 U.S. 37, 116 S.Ct. 2013, 135 L.Ed.2d 361 (1996).

[4]Peek v. State, 155 Ga. 49, 52 (7), 116 S.E. 629 (1923); Strickland v. State, 137 Ga. 115 (1), 116 (1), 72 S.E. 922 (1911); Beck v. State, 76 Ga. 452 (1)(a), 470-71 (1886).

[5]See Koldewey v. State, 310 Ga. App. 788, 714 S.E.2d 371 (2011) (the burden of proving the defense of mistake of fact by a preponderance of the evidence is on the defendant).

decided after the effective date of the statute still rely on decisions rendered before the statute's enactment.[6]

In *Wayne v. State,*[7] Judge Pope precisely summarized the defense of intoxication as follows: "In the case of involuntary intoxication, the issue is whether alcohol or drugs impaired the actor's moral judgment. However, in the case of voluntary intoxication, the issue is whether the actor was so intoxicated "as to render whatever acts he may have committed . . .'unintentional.' [I]f the intention to commit the act in controversy is present, intoxication is no excuse . . . ." *Hardy v. State,* 242 Ga. 702, 706 (251 S.E.2d 289) (1978). Thus, unless the actor was so intoxicated as to be unable to know, understand and intend to do the act, it cannot be said his act was not intentional.' " In *Height v. State,*[8] the court held that "[v]oluntary intoxication is not a defense to a crime unless such intoxication has resulted in the alteration of [the] brain function so as to negate intent. Even then, the brain function alteration must be more than temporary." In *Carsner v. State,*[9] the court held that "[m]ere presence, where one is in a comatose condition or otherwise completely unaware of what was going on, is what is meant by being so intoxicated at the time that [he] could not form the requisite intent."

It has been said that temporary insanity caused by drunkenness is no defense to a criminal charge if the accused knows the difference between right and wrong when he is sober.[10] Also, it has been said that a drunk man intends the natural consequences of his acts,[11] and that in order to use intoxication as a defense, the accused must be so drunk that he is incapable of forming the intent to shoot.[12] However, despite the foregoing, if intent is a necessary element of the crime, and the accused is so intoxicated that he cannot form the requisite intent, then drunkenness is a

---

[6]E.g., Barrett v. State, 129 Ga. App. 72, 199 S.E.2d 116 (1973); Cochran v. State, 136 Ga. App. 125, 127, 220 S.E.2d 477 (1975); McLaughlin v. State, 236 Ga. 577, 578 (4), 224 S.E.2d 412 (1976); Johnson v. State, 235 Ga. 486, 489, 220 S.E.2d 448 (1975); Pitts v. State, 128 Ga. App. 827 (4), 198 S.E.2d 377 (1973).

[7]Wayne v. State, 184 Ga. App. 160, 161, 361 S.E.2d 39 (1987). Cf. Foster v. State, 258 Ga. 736, 743 (4), 374 S.E.2d 188 (1988).

[8]Height v. State, 214 Ga. App. 570, 572 (4); 448 S.E.2d 726 (1994); Horton v. State, 258 Ga. 489, 491 (8), 371 S.E.2d 384 (1988). Accord, Burgos v. State, 233 Ga. App. 897, 900 (1), 505 S.E.2d 543 (1998).

[9]Carsner v. State, 190 Ga. App. 141, 378 S.E.2d 181 (1989).

[10]Choice v. State, 31 Ga. 424 (7), 454-56 (1860); Beck v. State, 76 Ga. 452 (1)(a), 470-71 (1886); Barrett v. State, 129 Ga. App. 72, 199 S.E.2d 116 (1973).

[11]Knight v. State, 12 Ga. App. 111, 112 (3), 76 S.E. 1047 (1913); Willis v. State, 162 Ga. App. 420, 421 (3), 291 S.E.2d 736 (1982).

[12]Hanvey v. State, 68 Ga. 612, 614 (2) (1882).

defense.[13] But in *Haywood v. State,*[14] the Georgia Supreme Court held that it was not error for a trial judge to refuse to give such a charge.

The Georgia Supreme Court has seemed to develop a rule relating only to voluntary intoxication in a homicide case. It has indicated that because of the presumption of malice in such a case, intent does not have to be established; thus, in *Young v. State,*[15] the court held that intoxication is not a defense in a murder case. This theory conflicts with the principle that the state must prove beyond a reasonable doubt every fact necessary to constitute the crime.[16]

---

[13]Griffin v. State, 204 Ga. App. 270 (1), 419 S.E.2d 115 (1992); Greeson v. State, 90 Ga. App. 57, 59, 81 S.E.2d 839 (1954); Walker v. State, 9 Ga. App. 863 (2), 864 (2), 72 S.E. 446 (1911); Hayes v. State, 57 Ga. App. 801, 196 S.E. 926 (1938); Vickers v. State, 55 Ga. App. 163, 189 S.E. 377 (1937); Cochran v. State, 136 Ga. App. 125, 126 (2), 220 S.E.2d 477 (1975); Hanvey v. State, 68 Ga. 612 (1882); Miley v. State, 118 Ga. 274, 275, 45 S.E. 245 (1903); Smith v. State, 181 Ga. App. 595, 596 (2), 353 S.E.2d 35 (1987). But see State v. Stasio, 78 N.J. 467, 396 A.2d 1129 (1979). In Fouts v. State, 374 So.2d 22 (Fla.App.1979), the court held that LSD intoxication is a defense to a crime requiring a specific intent.

See Johnson v. State, 235 Ga. 486, 490 (1), 220 S.E.2d 448 (1975). However, in Butler v. State, 161 Ga. App. 251, 253, 288 S.E.2d 306 (1982), the court stated that being so intoxicated that a person could not form the requisite intent means the person "is in a comatose condition or otherwise completely unaware of what was going on."

See Annots., "Modern Status of the Rules as to Voluntary Intoxication as a Defense to Criminal Charge," 8 A.L.R.3d 1236 (1966); "Effect of Voluntary Drug Intoxication upon Criminal Responsibility," 73 A.L.R.3d 98 (1976). See Annot., 21 Am. Jur. 2d Criminal Law § 168, Voluntary Intoxication; Generally (2004).

In the child molestation case of Hutter v. State, 166 Ga. App. 608 (3), 305 S.E.2d 124 (1983), rev'd on other grounds, 251 Ga. 615, 307 S.E.2d 910 (1983), the court affirmed the refusal of the trial judge to charge that voluntary intoxication to such an extent that the defendant cannot form the requisite intent is a defense. The court relied on Gilreath v. State, 247 Ga. 814, 279 S.E.2d 650 (1981), which was a murder case. The Court of Appeals failed to recognize the distinction between murder cases and other criminal cases as discussed in this section. The Hutter opinion also stated, "The pattern charge is misleading to the extent that it implies that voluntary intoxication in and of itself may be a defense to a crime."

[14]Haywood v. State, 256 Ga. 694, 696 (1), 353 S.E.2d 184 (1987).

In Franklin v. State, 183 Ga. App. 58, 59, 357 S.E.2d 879 (1987), the court held that it was not error for the trial judge to refuse to charge that the defendant should be acquitted if he was intoxicated to the point that he could not form the requisite intent for the crimes of attempted armed robbery and aggravated assault.

[15]Young v. State, 239 Ga. 53, 59, 236 S.E.2d 1 (1977) (citing Wiggins v. State, 221 Ga. 609, 146 S.E.2d 294 (1965) and Meadows v. State, 230 Ga. 471, 472, 197 S.E.2d 698 (1973)). Cf. Harris v. State, 250 Ga. 889, 302 S.E.2d 104 (1983).

[16]Mullaney v. Wilbur, 421 U.S. 684, 95 S.Ct. 1881, 44 L.Ed.2d 508 (1975). Also, there is abundant authority in other states holding that the pre-

In *Pickstock v. State*,[17] the court held that it was not error to charge on voluntary intoxication even though the defendant did not claim this as a defense where he had "offered intoxication as an explanation for his lack of memory."

§ 21:17   Affirmative statutory defenses—Immunity from prosecution

In *Bacon v. State*,[1] the court pointed out that "[a]n 'affirmative defense' is one in which a defendant admits the act but seeks to justify, excuse, or mitigate it. With an 'affirmative defense' the focus no longer becomes the act itself, since such is admitted. Instead, the state's burden becomes 'the introduction of evidence that disputes,' i.e. disproves, 'the defendant's alleged justification/excuse for the act.' "

The Criminal Code of Georgia sets out six basic "affirmative defenses" to crimes:[2] (1) justification,[3] (2) defense of self or others,[4] (3) defense of habitation,[5] (4) defense of property,[6] (5) entrapment,[7] and (6) coercion.[8] O.C.G.A. § 20-2-1001 also provides an "educator" with immunity from criminal prosecution "for any act or omission" relating to the "discipline of any student" provided that the educator "acted in good faith." Under that statute, the term "educator" includes a wide variety of the personnel in a school who have contact with a student, including teachers, bus

---

meditation required for murder or first degree murder may be negated by showing voluntary intoxication. However, these cases generally hold that the intoxication has the result of reducing the crime to manslaughter or second degree murder. People v. Garcia, 398 Mich. 250, 247 N.W.2d 547, 550 (1976); People v. Horn, 12 Cal.3d 290, 115 Cal.Rptr. 516, 524 P.2d 1300, 1306 (1974); Commonwealth v. Reid, 432 Pa. 319, 247 A.2d 783, 785 (1968); State v. Tansimore, 3 N.J. 516, 71 A.2d 169, 176 (1950).

[17]Pickstock v. State, 235 Ga. App. 451, 453 (3), 509 S.E.2d 717 (1998).

[Section 21:17]

[1]Bacon v. State, 249 Ga. App. 347, 349, 548 S.E.2d 78 (2001). See Pierre v. State, 330 Ga. App. 782, 769 S.E.2d 533 (2015) (failure to admit to the crime precludes assertion of defense); McClure v. State, 347 Ga. App. 68, 815 S.E.2d 313 (Ga. Ct. App. 2018) (physical precedent) (in concurring opinion, Judge McFadden questions

the soundness of the rule which precludes defendant from claiming justification unless he admits to all elements of charged offense except intent, reasoning that in civil matters parties are allowed to plead alternative theories of recovery or defense).

[2]O.C.G.A. § 16-3-28.

[3]O.C.G.A. § 16-3-20.

[4]O.C.G.A. § 16-3-21.

In Means v. Solem, 646 F.2d 322 (8th Cir. 1980), aff'g 480 F.Supp. 128 (8th Cir. 1979), the court held that there was a due process violation where the trial judge refused to charge the jury on defendant's theory of self-defense when there was substantial evidence supporting such a charge.

[5]O.C.G.A. § 16-3-23.

[6]O.C.G.A. § 16-3-24.

[7]O.C.G.A. § 16-3-25. See § 21:25, infra, on entrapment defense.

[8]O.C.G.A. § 16-3-26. See § 21:24, infra, on coercion defense.

drivers and school counselors.[9] In 2016, the legislature extended the defense of "justification and excuse" to include a person who, in 72 hours, comes into possession of pornography and other materials in violation of O.C.G.A. § 16-12-80 et seq. See § 21:20, infra, on justification and excuse. In theft cases there are three additional statutory affirmative defenses which are set out in a later section. The more general defenses of entrapment and coercion are treated in later sections in this chapter.

O.C.G.A. § 16-3-23.1 provides:

"A person who uses threats or force in accordance with Code Section 16-3-21, relating to the use of force in defense of self or others, Code Section 16-3-23, relating to the use of force in defense of a habitation, or Code Section 16-3-24, relating to the use of force in defense of property other than a habitation, has no duty to retreat and has the right to stand his or her ground and use force as provided in said Code sections, including deadly force."

In addition, O.C.G.A. § 16-3-24.2 provides:

"A person who uses threats or force in accordance with Code Section 16-3-21, 16-3-23, 16-3-23.1 or 16-3-24 shall be immune from criminal prosecution therefore unless in the use of deadly force, such person utilizes a weapon the carrying of or possession of which is unlawful by such person under part 2 or 3 of Article 4 of Chapter 11 of this title."[10]

In *Fair v. State*,[11] the Georgia Supreme Court held that once a defendant seeks immunity from prosecution pursuant to O.C.G.A. § 16-3-24.2, the trial court is required to resolve the issue prior to trial.

In *Kelley v. State*,[12] the court held that "[a]n affirmative defense is a defense that admits the doing of the act charged but seeks to justify, excuse or mitigate it. . . ." Hence, as a general proposition in order to get a charge on an affirmative defense, the defendant

---

[9]See State v. Pickens, 330 Ga. App. 862, 769 S.E.2d 594, 315 Ed. Law Rep. 1099 (2015) (motion asserting immunity must be resolved prior to trial); State v. Cohen, 309 Ga. App. 868, 711 S.E.2d 418, 269 Ed. Law Rep. 376 (2011) (burden of proving immunity is by preponderance of evidence).

[10]See also O.C.G.A. § 51-11-9, providing that a person justified in threatening or using force against another in accordance with Code Sections 16-3-21, 16-3-23, or 16-3-24 "has no duty to retreat from the use of such force and shall not be held liable to the person against whom the use of force was justified or to any person acting as an accomplice or assistant to such person in any civil action brought as a result of the threat or use of such force."

[11]Fair v. State, 284 Ga. 165, 664 S.E.2d 227 (2008).

[12]Kelley v. State, 235 Ga. App. 177, 179 (1), 509 S.E.2d 110 (1998) (quoting Brown v. State, 267 Ga. 350, 478 S.E.2d 129 (1996)). See Manders v. State, 281 Ga. App. 786(3), 637 S.E.2d 460 (2006).

must admit all elements of the offense charged except that of intent.[13]

In dealing with affirmative defenses, consideration must be given to the burden of proof. Traditionally, the burden has been on the defendant to establish any affirmative defense.[14] When the statutory affirmative defenses were set out, it was probably thought that the burden of proof as to these defenses would be placed on the defendant. The Georgia appellate courts have placed the burden on the defendant in the case of some specific defenses.[15] However, the Council of Superior Court Judges, in its Criminal Charge Book,[16] has eliminated instructions placing the burden of proof on the defendant to establish an affirmative defense.

In 1976, in *State v. Moore*,[17] the Georgia Supreme Court handed down a landmark decision in which it concluded "that henceforth charges which place any burden of persuasion upon the defendant in criminal cases shall not be given and such charges will be deemed erroneous and subject to reversal, absent harmless error and invited error. We point out that usual charges on presumptions are not considered 'burden shifting' charges, nor are charges that such presumptions may be rebutted. We reiterate that this conclusion is prospective and applies only to cases tried after the final date of this decision." It thus appears clear that the defendant no longer has the burden of proof when he relies on an affirmative defense despite a number of older cases holding the contrary which have not been specifically overruled.[18] For

---

[13]Maxey v. State, 272 Ga. App. 800(1), 613 S.E.2d 236 (2005).

[14]State v. McNeill, 234 Ga. 696, 697, 217 S.E.2d 241 (1976). See Cowart v. State, 136 Ga. App. 528, 529, 221 S.E.2d 649 (1975).

In Martin v. Ohio, 480 U.S. 228, 107 S.Ct. 1098, 94 L.Ed.2d 267 (1987), the court held that the Fourteenth Amendment due-process clause does not prevent a state from placing the burden of proving self-defense on a defendant when he was tried for murder.

[15]E.g., State v. McNeill, 234 Ga. 696, 217 S.E.2d 281 (1975) (entrapment). See also Chandle v. State, 230 Ga. 574, 576, 198 S.E.2d 289 (1973), which involved the defense of "accident."

See Allen, "The Restoration of

In Re Winship: A Comment on Burdens of Persuasion in Criminal Cases after Patterson v. New York," 76 Mich. L. R. 30 (1978).

[16]See State v. Moore, 237 Ga. 269, 270, 227 S.E.2d 241 (1976).

[17]State v. Moore, 237 Ga. 269, 270, 227 S.E.2d 241 (1976); Pope v. State, 167 Ga. App. 328, 330 (3), 306 S.E.2d 326 (1983); Lett v. State, 160 Ga. App. 476, 477 (2), 287 S.E.2d 384 (1981). See Note, "The Constitutionality of Affirmative Defenses after Patterson v. New York," 78 Col. L. R. 655 (1978); and McLane, "The Burden of Proof in Criminal Cases: Mullaney and Patterson Compared," 15 Crim. L. Bull. 346 (1979).

[18]From the standpoint of the due process clause of the federal Constitution, it is permissible to require the

example, in *Hill v. State*,[19] the Georgia Supreme Court pointed out that "[a]fter a defendant presents a prima facie case of entrapment, the burden is on the state to disprove entrapment beyond a reasonable doubt."

In *Austin v. State*,[20] the defendant was charged with simple battery. The defendant claimed justification. The court reversed the conviction because the trial judge did not charge that "the burden is on the State to disprove the defense beyond a reasonable doubt." However, in *Jordan v. State*,[21] the court held that it was not error for the trial judge to refuse to charge "that the State has the additional burden of proving beyond a reasonable doubt the absence of justification" where the defense is justification.

In *Bunn v. State*,[22] the Supreme Court took the opportunity to clarify the standard of review a trial court should employ when a defendant raises an affirmative defense. Similar to the burden required of defendants in cases where the defense is mental incompetency, the Court held that "to avoid trial, a defendant bears the burden of showing that he is entitled to immunity under O.C.G.A. § 16-3-24.2 by a preponderance of the evidence."[23] If the defendant does not prevail at a pre-trial hearing on the claim of immunity, the defendant may still raise the defense at trial, at which time the state would have the burden of disproving the defense by proof beyond a reasonable doubt. If the defendant does prevail, the charges in the indictment are effectively dismissed subject to the state's appeal rights.[24]

Special care should be taken in those cases where an affirmative defense is the sole defense. In such cases, failure to charge on an affirmative defense even without a request constitutes error.[25]

In addition to the foregoing, there are specific kinds of excep-

---

establishment of some affirmative defense by a preponderance of the evidence. Patterson v. New York, 432 U.S. 197, 97 S.Ct. 2319, 53 L.Ed.2d 281 (1977). Generally, see Note, "Burden of Proving Affirmative Defense Can Be Placed on Defendant," 29 Mercer L. Rev. 875 (1978). See also Hill v. State, 197 Ga. App. 260, 262, 398 S.E.2d 226 (1990), rev'd on other grounds, 261 Ga. 377, 405 S.E.2d 258 (1991); Bentley v. State, 261 Ga. 229, 230 (2), 404 S.E.2d 101 (1991).

[19]Hill v. State, 261 Ga. 377, 405 S.E.2d 258 (1991).

[20]Austin v. State, 218 Ga. App. 90, 91 (2), 460 S.E.2d 310 (1995).

[21]Jordan v. State, 171 Ga. App. 558 (1), 320 S.E.2d 395 (1984).

[22]Bunn v. State, 284 Ga. 410, 667 S.E.2d 605 (2008).

[23]Bunn v. State, 284 Ga. 410, 413, 667 S.E.2d 605 (2008).

[24]See O.C.G.A. § 5-7-1(a)(1); State v. Burks, 285 Ga. 781, 684 S.E.2d 269 (2009); State v. Yapo, 296 Ga. App. 158 (1), 674 S.E.2d 44 (2009).

[25]Tarvestad v. State, 261 Ga. 605, 409 S.E.2d 513 (1991); James v. State, 275 Ga. 387 (6), 565 S.E.2d 802 (2002).

tions to some criminal statutes. For example, it has been held that it is not illegal for certain pharmacists to sell marijuana. However, it is not necessary for the state to prove that a defendant charged with selling marijuana is not a pharmacist until the defendant first produces evidence to support such a defense.[26] O.C.G.A. § 16-13-5, Georgia's Medical Amnesty Law, provides that a person "who in good faith seeks medical assistance for a person experiencing or believed to be experiencing a drug overdose shall not be arrested, charged or prosecuted for a drug violation if the evidence for the arrest, charge or prosecution of such drug violation resulted solely from seeking such medical assistance." The same rule applies to a person who is experiencing an overdose and seeks to obtain medical assistance for himself or others or is a person for whom such a request is made. See §§ 12:14, 12:15, supra, on witness immunity; § 2:3, supra, on immunity from arrest.

See § 13:13, supra, on an indictment alleging exceptions.

§ 21:18   Affirmative statutory defenses—Self-defense

In *Jackson v. State*,[1] the court held that where self-defense is the sole defense and retreat is raised by the evidence, the defendant is entitled to a charge on retreat.

In *Hodges v. State*,[2] the court questioned whether a number of cases as well as the pattern charge on justification which require a showing that the defendant didn't act "in a spirit of revenge" are still good law. Since the issue was not raised by the appeal, the court did not resolve it but noted the requirement that the defendant show that he did not act from revenge had been previously removed from the statute and is no longer a part of O.C.G.A. § 16-3-21(a). The defense is not available to a person who uses force in self-defense if that person "[i]s attempting to commit, [is] committing, or [is] fleeing after the commission or attempted commission of a felony."[3]

Often associated, incorrectly, with the affirmative defenses of self-defense and justification is the concept of "mutual combat." A determination that a defendant was engaged in mutual combat at the time the victim was killed may authorize a jury to find the

---

[26]May v. State, 179 Ga. App. 736 (2), 348 S.E.2d 61 (1986).

[Section 21:18]

[1]Jackson v. State, 237 Ga. App. 746, 516 S.E.2d 792 (1999); Ellis v. State, 245 Ga. App. 807, 808 (3), 539 S.E.2d 184 (2000).

[2]Hodges v. State, 319 Ga. App. 657, 738 S.E.2d 111 (2013).

[3]O.C.G.A.§ 16-3-21(b)(2).   See Woodard v. State, 296 Ga. 803, 771 S.E.2d 362 (2015) (overruling Heard v. State, 261 Ga. 262, 403 S.E.2d 438 (1991), which held that O.C.G.A. § 16-3-21(b)(2) applied only "where it makes sense to do so").

defendant guilty of voluntary manslaughter and not malice murder.[4] Where there exists some evidence from which a jury could have found both parties intended to resolve their differences by fighting with each other with deadly weapons, a defendant is entitled to a charge on voluntary manslaughter.[5] However, as the court noted in the oft cited *Mathis v. State*,[6] "[t]he essential ingredient, mutual intent, in order to constitute mutual combat, must be a willingness, a readiness, and an intention on the part of both parties to fight. Reluctance, or fighting to repel an unprovoked attack, is self-defense, and is authorized by the law, and should not be confused with mutual combat."

See § 21:17, supra, regarding the use of deadly force in defense of self or others, and § 21:20, infra, on justification.

§ 21:19 Affirmative statutory defenses—Habitation

O.C.G.A. § 16-3-23 provides the affirmative defense of habitation or the use of such reasonable force necessary to repel or terminate another's unlawful entry or attack upon one's residence or place of habitation.[1] O.C.G.A. § 16-3-24.1 defines the term "habitation" to include "any dwelling, motor vehicle or place of business . . . ."[2] The entry upon one's residence must, in fact, be *unlawful*. In *Fair v. State*,[3] a pair of defendants used deadly force to repel what they claimed to believe at the time was an attack upon their residence. In fact, the defendants shot and killed a sheriff's deputy attempting to execute a "no knock" warrant in connection with a drug task force investigation. The Georgia Supreme Court rejected the application of a reasonable belief standard and ruled that prior case law, common law and O.C.G.A. § 16-3-23 required that the entry, in fact, be unlawful before the defendant can raise the defense.

---

[4]Sanders v. State, 283 Ga. 372, 375, 659 S.E.2d 376 (2008).

[5]Carreker v. State, 273 Ga. 371(2), 541 S.E.2d 364 (2001).

[6]Mathis v. State, 196 Ga. 288, 26 S.E.2d 606 (1943). See Berrian v. State, 297 Ga. 740, 743, 778 S.E.2d 165 (2015).

[Section 21:19]

[1]See Salazar-Balderas v. State, 343 Ga. App. 201, 806 S.E.2d 644 (2017) (unlike defense of justification, defense of habitation "in recognition of the sanctity of a person in his home or motor vehicle or place of business" allows the use of deadly force even if such person is not in fear of great bodily injury or death).

[2]In Benham v. State, 277 Ga. 516, 591 S.E.2d 824 (2004), the Supreme Court concluded that the tactical decision by counsel to forego requesting a charge on the defense of habitation and rely only on the defense of self-defense was not a reasonable decision a competent counsel would have made under the facts in that case and constituted ineffective assistance.

[3]Fair v. State, 288 Ga. 244, 702 S.E.2d 420 (2010).

In *Huff v. State*,[4] the Court of Appeals concluded that the designation of "habitation" for purposes of the defense could be applied to a boarder's bedroom in a boarding house.

In *State v. Burks*,[5] the Georgia Supreme Court noted that a convicted felon who uses a firearm in defense of his residence is not entitled to seek immunity from prosecution because O.C.G.A. § 16-3-24.2 by its own terms excludes from immunity persons whose possession of a firearm is unlawful. However, the defendant can still pursue the defense of justification at trial.

In *Kendrick v. State*,[6] the court held that a defendant could not defend against a malice murder charge by claiming justification in the defense of habitation where the defendant did not use deadly force until after the event justifying the use of deadly force was over. The defendant shot the victim while in pursuit of the victim who had stolen the defendant's motor vehicle.

See § 21:17, supra, regarding the use of deadly force in defense of habitation or other property.

§ 21:20 Affirmative statutory defenses—Justification and excuse

Beginning July 1, 2006, under the affirmative defense of justification, a person is immune from criminal prosecution if they use justifiable force, including deadly force, in self-defense, defense of habitation, or defense of non-habitation property.[1] According to *Boggs v. State*,[2] "the decision as to whether a person is immune under O.C.G.A. § 16-3-24.2 must be determined by the trial court before the trial of that person commences." If that is-

---

[4]Huff v. State, 113 Ga. App. 257, 147 S.E.2d 840 (1966). See Hammock v. State, 277 Ga. 612, 614 (3), 592 S.E.2d 415 (2004) where court refused to allow defense in the context of a jointly occupied dwelling in the absence of a clear agreement or court order which acknowledged the right of the defendant to exclusively occupy some part of the premises.

[5]State v. Burks, 285 Ga. 781, 684 S.E.2d 269 (2009).

[6]Kendrick v. State, 287 Ga. 676, 699 S.E.2d 302 (2010). See Coleman v. State, 286 Ga. 291, 687 S.E.2d 427 (2009).

[Section 21:20]

[1]O.C.G.A. § 16-3-24.2, as amended July 1, 2006. Note also that, pursuant to O.C.G.A. § 51-11-9, such persons shall not be held civilly liable for the use of justifiable force in defense of self or others, in defense of a habitation, or in defense of non-habitation property. See State v. Burks, 285 Ga. 781, 684 S.E.2d 269 (2009) (convicted felon prohibited by law from carrying a firearm not entitled to immunity from prosecution as a person using force in defense of habitation).

[2]Boggs v. State, 261 Ga. App. 104, 106, 581 S.E.2d 722 (2003). In Fair v. State, 284 Ga. 165 (1), 664 S.E.2d 227 (2008), the Georgia Supreme Court ruled that *Boggs* was correctly decided and that a trial court is required to decide whether a defendant is immune from prosecution based upon the defense of habitation prior to trial.

sue is decided adversely to the defendant, the defense is not entitled to a jury instruction on immunity.[3] However, the defendant can still raise the affirmative defense of justification at trial. An affirmative defense is different than a plea of immunity. If a defendant can prevail prior to trial on the basis of immunity, then that ends the case. An affirmative defense may be raised during trial but it will not prevent a trial from going to verdict.[4]

In *Porter v. State*,[5] the Georgia Supreme Court held that "[w]hen a defendant raises the affirmative defense of justification, he must present evidence that he was justified in using deadly force. . . . The burden then shifts to the State to disprove that defense beyond a reasonable doubt." However, this defense is inconsistent with the theory of involuntary manslaughter since it is premised upon the use of force under circumstances which make such force justified, such as self-defense. Accordingly, a defendant at trial may not employ justification as a defense and also request a charge on involuntary manslaughter.[6] A charge on justification and a charge on voluntary manslaughter "are not mutually exclusive, and only slight evidence is necessary to entitle a defendant to a charge on voluntary manslaughter."[7] However, the provocation necessary to support a charge of voluntary manslaughter is different from that necessary to support the defense of justification. The principal difference is "whether the accused was so influenced and excited that he reacted pas-

---

[3]Campbell v. State, 297 Ga. App. 387 (3), 677 S.E.2d 312 (2009). See Mullins v. State, 287 Ga. 302, 695 S.E.2d 621 (2010) (no direct appeal from denial of an immunity claim).

[4]Bunn v. State, 284 Ga. 410, 667 S.E.2d 605 (2008). See Hipp v. State, 293 Ga. 415, 746 S.E.2d 95 (2013) (reversing Court of Appeals, Supreme Court holds that trial court, after guilty plea, may reconsider pretrial order denying immunity by way of motion for new trial).

[5]Porter v. State, 272 Ga. 533, 534 (3), 531 S.E.2d 97 (2000). In Preston v. State, 282 Ga. 210(3), 647 S.E.2d 260 (2007) the trial court instructed the jury on the state's burden to disprove the defense of justification and then proceeded to charge the jury "[w]here the defense of justification is offered, it is the duty of the jury to consider it along with all the testimony in the case, and if the evidence, taken as a whole, raises a reasonable doubt in the mind of the jury of the defendants guilt, then you should acquit him." The Supreme Court disapproved the charge as "confusing." The concurring opinion was sharply critical of the ruling.

See Henry County Board of Education v. S.G., 301 Ga. 794, 804 S.E.2d 427, 347 Ed. Law Rep. 1232 (2017) (O.C.G.A. § 16-3-21(c) provides that state, county, and city rules, regulations, and ordinances in conflict with legal defense of justification will not prevent assertion of justification defense in civil proceedings, but proponent bears the burden of proof).

[6]Paul v. State, 274 Ga. 601, 604 (3), 555 S.E.2d 716 (2001); Saylors v. State, 251 Ga. 735, 737 (3), 309 S.E.2d 796 (1983).

[7]Woody v. State, 262 Ga. 327, 328 (2), 418 S.E.2d 35 (1992); Webb v. State, 284 Ga. 122 (4), 663 S.E.2d 690 (2008).

sionately rather than simply in an attempt to defend himself."[8] Likewise, when two parties who are armed and intend to resolve their differences by fighting each other, a defendant can be convicted for voluntary manslaughter in lieu of murder. This is commonly referred to as "mutual combat" and may apply regardless of who struck the first blow.[9]

In *Moore v. State*,[10] the defendant was charged with interference with government property by kicking out a window of a police cruiser. He requested the following charge: "If you find that the defendant's conduct was justified, this is a defense for prosecution for any crime based on that conduct." In reversing the trial court for refusing to give the foregoing charge, the appellate court pointed out that the defendant "had high blood pressure and allergies and the pepper spray caused . . . [the defendant] acute respiratory distress. . . . [H]e screamed for air, gagged, and bodily secretions streamed down his face."

"The critical factor in a justification defense is whether a defendant acted with the fear of a reasonable person. . . . Because justification is based upon the fears of a *reasonable* person, the *subjective* fears of a particular defendant are irrelevant in the evaluation of this defense."[11] Thus, the fact that a defendant has been the subject of violent acts or abuse by someone other than the victim is generally considered inadmissible.[12]

In *State v. Green*,[13] the court held that the defense of justification does not require that the defendant actually use force or even intend to use force in defense of himself or others. It is sufficient if the defendant simply threatens to use force in response to another's imminent use of force. In *Green*, the defendant was using a knife to deter his assailant, and when attacked, the knife entered the victim without any intention of the defendant that it do so.

In *United States v. Oakland Cannabis Buyers' Cooperative and Jeffery Jones*,[14] the United States Supreme Court held that the medical necessity defense is not a valid defense to the manufacture and distribution of marijuana under the Controlled Substances Act.

---

[8]Walker v. State, 281 Ga. 521, 524, 640 S.E.2d 274 (2007), citing Yates v. State, 274 Ga. 312, 317(3), 553 S.E.2d 563 (2001).

[9]Sanders v. State, 283 Ga. 372, 375, 659 S.E.2d 376 (2008); Platt v. State, 335 Ga. App. 49, 778 S.E.2d 416 (2015).

[10]Moore v. State, 234 Ga. App. 332, 333 (1), 506 S.E.2d 685 (1998).

[11]O'Connell v. State, 294 Ga. 379, 382, 754 S.E.2d 29 (2014).

[12]See Lewis v. State, 270 Ga. 891, 515 S.E.2d 382 (1999).

[13]State v. Green, 289 Ga. 802, 716 S.E.2d 194 (2011).

[14]United States v. Oakland Cannabis Buyers' Cooperative, 532 U.S. 483, 121 S.Ct. 1711, 149 L.Ed.2d 722 (2001).

In *Carter v. State*,[15] the court held that "[t]he doctrine of reasonable fear does not apply to any case of homicide where the danger apprehended is not urgent and pressing, or apparently so, at the time of the killing." Accordingly, where a deadly assault has terminated, the defense of justification is not available "unless the assailant has some further apparent ability to continue it."[16] Likewise, "verbal insults and taunts are insufficient, without more, to warrant a justification charge."[17]

An issue related to the defense of justification is that of "transferred justification." That principle holds that "no guilt attaches if an accused is justified in shooting to repel an assault, but misses and kills an innocent bystander."[18]

In 2016, the legislature created the new affirmative statutory defense of "justification and excuse by adding new Code section 16-3-22.1." This defense is available to persons who in good faith came into possession of child pornography and other materials the possession of which is prohibited by O.C.G.A. §§ 16-12-80 et seq. Provided such persons report this discovery to law enforcement authorities within 72 hours of discovery, they are immune from criminal prosecution. The purpose of the immunity provided by the statute is to "provide for those persons that act in good faith to assist law enforcement officers . . . when the health and safety of a child are being adversely affected and threatened by the conduct of another."

§ 21:21 Affirmative statutory defenses—Accident

In *Griffin v. State*,[1] the Georgia Supreme Court held that the defense of accident is to be treated as an affirmative statutory defense even though it is not designated by statute as an affirmative defense. It admits "the doing of the act charged but seeks to justify, excuse or mitigate it. Thus, if a defendant does not admit to committing any act which constitutes the offered charge, [he]

---

[15]Carter v. State, 285 Ga. 565, 566 (2), 678 S.E.2d 909 (2009) (quoting Short v. State, 140 Ga. 780, 780 (3), 80 S.E. 8 (1913)).

[16]Collier v. State, 288 Ga. 756, 707 S.E.2d 102 (2011) (quoting Cochran v. State, 9 Ga. App. 824, 825(1), 72 S.E. 281 (1911)).

[17]Boutier v. State, 328 Ga.App. 869, 763 S.E.2d 255 (2014). See Carter v. State, 150 Ga. App. 119, 257 S.E.2d 11 (1979). Compare Lynn v. State, 296 Ga. 109, 765 S.E.2d 322 (2014) ("words

that disclose adulterous conduct of a spouse are not *just* words [and] can amount to sufficient provocation") (emphasis in original).

[18]Crawford v. State, 267 Ga. 543, 544(1), 480 S.E.2d 573 (1997). See Springer v. State, 335 Ga. App. 462, 781 S.E.2d 575 (2016).

[Section 21:21]

[1]Griffin v. State, 267 Ga. 586 (1), 481 S.E.2d 223 (1997).

is not entitled to a charge of accident."[2]

The essential difference between the defenses of justification and accident is the element of intent. A defendant who asserts the justification defense admits committing the conduct involved, "but argues that under the circumstances he was justified in so acting and that he therefore lacked the requisite criminal intent. . . . [T]he defense of accident is premised on the defendant's assertion that he did not intend to commit the act which constitutes the crime."[3]

In strict liability cases, such as traffic offenses, which require no specific criminal intent but do require proof that the defendant voluntarily committed the prohibited act, the defense of accident is available only where there is at least some evidence that the defendant did not voluntarily commit the act. Accordingly, in *State v. Ogilvie*,[4] where the defendant was charged with second degree vehicular manslaughter and failure to yield to a pedestrian, a charge on accident would not be appropriate unless there was some evidence that the defendant did not intend to drive into the crosswalk. The claim that the victim darted in front of the defendant's vehicle went to the issue of proximate cause, not the defense of accident.

In *Smith v. State*,[5] the appellate court declined to reverse the trial court in failing "to instruct the jury, sua sponte, that the state had the burden to disprove the defense of accident beyond a reasonable doubt."

§ 21:22   Affirmative statutory defenses—Battered person syndrome

In the Georgia Court of Appeals case of *Smith v. State*,[1] the court held that Georgia "cases construing the battered person syndrome consistently hold" that the battered person syndrome "is not a separate defense but falls within the ambit of the justification defense" and no other charge on the battered person syndrome need be given. However, when this case was considered by the Georgia Supreme Court in 1997, it reversed the Court of Appeals decision.[2] The Supreme Court concluded that a "[m]odifi-

---

[2]Sevostiyanova v. State, 313 Ga. App. 729, 736 (9), 722 S.E.2d 333 (2012).

[3]Jackson v. State, 329 Ga. App. 240, 241-42, 764 S.E.2d 569 (2014).

[4]State v. Ogilvie, 292 Ga. 6, 734 S.E.2d 50 (2012). See Sapp v. State, 179 Ga. App. 614, 347 S.E.2d 354 (1986).

[5]Smith v. State, 234 Ga. App. 314, 315 (2), 506 S.E.2d 659 (1998).

[Section 21:22]

[1]Smith v. State, 222 Ga. App. 412, 413 (2), 474 S.E.2d 291 (1996).

[2]Smith v. State, 268 Ga. 196, 486 S.E.2d 819 (1997). Accord, Freeman v. State, 269 Ga. 337 (1), 496 S.E.2d 716 (1998).

cation of the justification by self-defense charge is necessary both to comport with O.C.G.A. § 16-3-21(d), and 'to permit juries to consider the reasonableness of the defendant's belief that the use of force was necessary in light of both . . . [the defendant's] circumstances at the time . . . [defendant] used force, and any psychological condition resulting from the circumstances.' "Hence a modified jury instruction must be given in all battered person syndrome cases when authorized by the evidence and requested by the defendant. The court suggested that in these cases, "[i]n addition to the pattern instruction in the language of O.C.G.A. § 16-3-21(a) it is suggested that such modified instruction read as follows:

"I charge you that the evidence that the defendant suffers from battered person syndrome was admitted for your consideration in connection with the defendant's claim of self-defense and that such evidence relates to the issue of the reasonableness of the defendant's belief that the use of force was immediately necessary, even though no use of force against the defendant may have been, in fact, imminent. The standard is whether the circumstances were such as would excite the fears of a reasonable person possessing the same or similar psychological and physical characteristics as the defendant, and faced with the same circumstances surrounding the defendant at the time the defendant used force."

In concluding, the Supreme Court decision pointed out that the rule it had reached in *Smith* "is to be applied to all cases now in 'the pipeline,' i.e., those on direct review or in which a judgment has not yet been rendered." However, in *Alexis v. State*,[3] the court held that where a defendant does not request a charge that the state has the burden of disproving an affirmative defense, the trial court is not required to so instruct the jury.

In *Adame v. State*,[4] the court held that "[t]he battered person syndrome describes a series of common characteristics that appear in women who are abused physically and psychologically over an extended period of time by the dominate male figure in their lives."

However, in *Mobley v. State*,[5] the court held that before the defendant is entitled to a battered person syndrome defense, the evidence must be more than an expert's opinion that the defendant suffers from the battered person syndrome. "Among the factors to [be] consider[ed] are evidence of [1] a close personal

---

[3]Alexis v. State, 273 Ga. 423, 425 (3), 541 S.E.2d 636 (2001).

[4]Adame v. State, 244 Ga. App. 257, 258 (1), 534 S.E.2d 817 (2000)

(citing Johnson v. State, 266 Ga. 624, 626, 469 S.E.2d 152 (1996)).

[5]Mobley v. State, 269 Ga. 738, 740 (1), 505 S.E.2d 722 (1998).

relationship between the defendant and victim; [2] a pattern of physical, sexual, or psychological abuse, and [3] a reasonable apprehension of harm."

In *Bishop v. State*,[6] a majority of the court held that "[t]o make a prima facie showing of self-defense based upon the battered person syndrome, a defendant should present the opinion testimony of an expert as well as independent testimony regarding the historical facts upon which the expert relies." Since the defendant "presented no expert testimony . . . he failed to make a prima facie showing of the battered person syndrome. . . ."

The battered person syndrome has also been used in certain cases to explain the actions of victims of crimes. For example, in *Alvarado v. State*,[7] the prosecution was allowed to show through expert testimony that a victim of domestic abuse would not be expected to report the defendant to the police because she suffered from battered person syndrome.

In *Nguyen v. State*,[8] the Georgia Supreme Court held that "the psychological abuse inflicted on the accused must have been of such an extreme nature that it engendered in the accused 'a 'reasonable belief in the imminence of the victim's use of unlawful force.' . . . Psychological abuse which humiliates, embarrasses or abases an individual is deplorable, but such abuse, when unaccompanied by other acts or verbal statements giving rise to a reasonable fear of imminent physical harm, cannot alone justify the admission of expert evidence on the battered person syndrome."

See Studdard, *Daniel's Georgia Handbook on Criminal Evidence* (2018 ed.), § 7:9.

§ 21:23 Affirmative statutory defenses in theft cases

O.C.G.A. § 16-8-10 provides as follows:

"It is an affirmative defense to a prosecution for violation of O.C.G.A. §§ 16-8-2 through 16-8-7 that the person:

"(1) Was unaware that the property or service was that of another;

"(2) Acted under an honest claim of right to the property or ser-

---

[6]Bishop v. State, 271 Ga. 291, 293 (3), 519 S.E.2d 206 (1999). See McLaughlin v. State, 338 Ga. App. 1, 789 S.E.2d 247 (2016).

[7]Alvarado v. State, 257 Ga. App. 746, 572 S.E.2d 18 (2002). See Parrish v. State, 237 Ga. App. 274, 514 S.E.2d 458 (1999). See also Pickle v. State, 280 Ga. App. 821(1), 635 S.E.2d 197 (2006). A divided panel on the Court of Appeals found that trial court erroneously excluded battered person syndrome evidence offered by defendant to negate intent element of child cruelty charge.

[8]Nguyen v. State, 271 Ga. 475, 476, 520 S.E.2d 907 (1999). See "Taking Bullies at Their Words," ABA Journal, Dec. 1999, p. 34.

vice involved or under a right to acquire or dispose of it as he did; or

"(3) Took property or service exposed for sale intending to purchase and pay for it promptly or reasonably believing that the owner, if present, would have consented."

§ 21:24 Affirmative statutory defenses—Coercion

It is generally recognized that a person is excused from the commission of a crime if he committed the offense while acting under the duress, coercion, or compulsion of another. O.C.G.A. § 16-3-26 provides as follows:

"A person is not guilty of a crime, except murder, if the act upon which the supposed criminal liability is based is performed under such coercion that the person reasonably believes that performing the act is the only way to prevent his imminent death or great bodily injury."

In order for coercion or compulsion to be a valid defense, it must be shown from the facts and circumstances that the defendant was in danger of present and immediate violence and that he acted based on such fear.[1] The fear of injury must be reasonable under the circumstances. If the defendant has a reasonable way to escape or avoid committing the crime, coercion is no defense.[2] "The defense of coercion is predicated on the reasonable person standard, not the subjective situation of the defendant."[3]

The Georgia statute excludes coercion as a defense where the crime involved is murder. Several other state statutes contain the same exception.[4] Nevertheless, there are some Georgia murder cases in which coercion has been charged as a defense.[5]

After evidence of coercion is presented, the burden of proof is on the state to prove that no coercion existed in the particular case and not on the defendant to show that it did.[6]

[Section 21:24]

[1]See Bush v. State, 317 Ga. App. 439, 731 S.E.2d 121 (2012).

[2]Barnes v. State, 178 Ga. App. 205 (1), 342 S.E.2d 388 (1986); Vowell v. State, 174 Ga. App. 426, 427 (2), 330 S.E.2d 167 (1985); Hill v. State, 135 Ga. App. 766, 767, 219 S.E.2d 18 (1975). But cf. Perryman v. State, 63 Ga. App. 819, 12 S.E.2d 388 (1940).

[3]Allen v. State, 296 Ga. 785, 791, 770 S.E.2d 824 (2015).

[4]Illinois Criminal Code, § 7-11; Wisconsin Criminal Code, § 939.46. It has been said that at common law, the defense of coercion was not available in a murder case. See Perkins, Criminal Law 842 (1957).

[5]Spikes v. State, 183 Ga. 279, 188 S.E. 454 (1936); Tucker v. State, 180 Ga. 87, 178 S.E. 152 (1935); Henderson v. State, 5 Ga. App. 495 (2), 63 S.E. 535 (1909).

[6]Graham v. State, 239 Ga. App. 429, 432 (1)(b), 521 S.E.2d 249 (1999); Davis v. State, 232 Ga. App. 882, 883 (1), 502 S.E.2d 779 (1998); Norris v. State, 227 Ga. App. 616, 618 (2), 489 S.E.2d 875 (1997). See Hines v. State,

In *Palmer v. State,*[7] the Georgia Court of Appeals affirmed the trial court's failure to charge the jury on the state's burden to disprove coercion when the defendant only requested a charge on the general defense of coercion and not on the charge of the state's burden where the trial court gave a thorough charge on the law of coercion as requested.

See Annotation, "Duress, Necessity, or Conditions of Confinement as Justification for Escape From Prison," 54 A.L.R.5th 141 (1997).

§ 21:25 Affirmative statutory defenses—Entrapment

Entrapment is a defense to a crime under O.C.G.A. § 16-3-25, which provides as follows:

"A person is not guilty of a crime if, by entrapment, his conduct is induced or solicited by a government officer or employee, or agent of either, for the purpose of obtaining evidence to be used in prosecuting the person for commission of the crime. Entrapment exists where the idea and intention of the commission of the crime originated with a government officer or employee, or with an agent of either, and he, by undue persuasion, incitement, or deceitful means, induced the accused to commit the act which the accused would not have committed except for the conduct of such officer."[1]

If the alleged entrapper is a confidential informant and "the defendant can show that he has an arguably persuasive defense of entrapment—the state might have a duty to produce such a witness."[2] Where the informant is the only participant other than the defendant in the transaction, the informant is "the only witness to *amplify* or *contradict* the testimony of government witnesses."[3]

In *Keaton v. State,*[4] the court stated that "the entrapment defense consists of three distinct elements: (1) the idea of the

---

308 Ga. App. 299, 707 S.E.2d 534 (2011). See also § 21:17, supra.

[7]Palmer v. State, 247 Ga. App. 586, 544 S.E.2d 215 (2001).

[Section 21:25]

[1]This Code section has been summarized as follows: "There is no criminal responsibility where (1) the idea and intention of the crime originated with a state agent; (2) the criminal act was induced by the agent's undue persuasion, incitement, or deceit; and (3) the crime would not have been committed but for the agent's conduct."

Schaffer v. State Board of Veterinary Medicine, 143 Ga. App. 68, 71 (2), 237 S.E.2d 510 (1977).

[2]Boatright v. State, 260 Ga. 534, 536, 397 S.E.2d 689 (1990). See Hampton v. State, 338 Ga. App. 864, 792 S.E.2d 124 (2016).

[3]Roviaro v. U.S., 353 U.S. 53, 64, 77 S. Ct. 623, 1 L. Ed. 2d 639 (1957).

[4]Keaton v. State, 253 Ga. 70, 71, 316 S.E.2d 452 (1984). Accord, Wagner v. State, 220 Ga. App. 71, 467 S.E.2d 385 (1996); Byrd v. State, 211 Ga. App. 881 (1), 440 S.E.2d 764 (1994); Hill v. State, 261 Ga. 377, 405 S.E.2d 258

commission of the crime must originate with the state agent; (2) the crime must be induced by the agent's undue persuasion, incitement, or deceit; and (3) the defendant must not be predisposed to commit the crime."

Entrapment occurs only "when the criminal conduct was 'the product of the creative activity' of law enforcement officials."[5] In *Hill v. State*,[6] the Georgia Supreme Court held that "if the 'creative activity' . . . of the law-enforcement official generates criminal acts that are 'not independent acts subsequent to the inducement but part of a course of conduct which was the product of the inducement,' . . . those criminal acts cannot be used to show predisposition." If the state fails to introduce evidence to rebut a defendant's affirmative defense of entrapment, the defendant is entitled to a directed verdict of acquittal.

The lack of "predisposition of a defendant toward [the] crime is the key element of the defense."[7] There is no entrapment where the officer merely furnishes the facilities for the commission of an offense or an opportunity to a defendant who is ready to commit

---

(1991); Brooks v. State, 224 Ga. App. 829, 830, 482 S.E.2d 725 (1997).

[5]Jones v. State, 101 Ga. App. 851, 863, 115 S.E.2d 576 (1960); Sorrells v. United States, 287 U.S. 435, 53 S.Ct. 210, 77 L.Ed. 413 (1932); Hall v. State, 136 Ga. App. 622, 222 S.E.2d 140 (1975). In Sherman v. United States, 356 U.S. 369, 78 S.Ct. 819, 2 L.Ed.2d 848 (1958), a government informer first met the defendant at a doctor's office where both were apparently being treated for narcotics addiction. Several accidental meetings followed at the doctor's office and at the pharmacy where both had their prescriptions filled. Conversations progressed to discussion of mutual experiences and problems, including their attempts to overcome their addictions. The informer finally asked the defendant if he knew of a source for narcotics because he was not responding to treatment and needed a source. From the first, the defendant tried to avoid the issue, but finally gave in after a number of requests based on the informer's presumed suffering and obtained narcotics several times for the informer and himself. Each time, the defendant told the informer the cost of the drugs

was $25 and that the informer owed him $15. After several transactions the informer notified an agent of the Bureau of Narcotics, and three times during November of 1951 government agents observed the defendant giving drugs to the informer in exchange for money supplied by the government. The defendant, who had been convicted of the sale of narcotics in 1942 and possession in 1946, was arrested. At trial the issue of entrapment was submitted to the jury and the defendant was convicted. The United States Supreme Court reversed the conviction and held that the defendant had been entrapped as a matter of law. Sherman was followed in Jacobson v. United States, 503 U.S. 540, 112 S.Ct. 1535, 118 L.Ed.2d 174 (1992).

In Wagner v. State, 220 Ga. App. 71, 467 S.E.2d 385 (1996), the court pointed out that the facts in *Wagner* "substantially track those in Sherman."

[6]Hill v. State, 261 Ga. 377, 405 S.E.2d 258 (1991).

[7]Hattaway v. State, 185 Ga. App. 607, 608, 365 S.E.2d 480 (1988).

the crime.[8] Put another way, it has been said that the defense of entrapment is invalid when the conduct of the officer toward the defendant "would not likely have enticed into crime an unwary innocent who would otherwise have struggled with himself and resisted ordinary temptations, but would be likely to induce only those ready and willing to commit a crime."[9] The "mere fact that the defendant was persuaded . . . by a friend to engage in practices he knew to be criminal simply to 'make a lot of money' does not constitute entrapment."[10] "Even repeated requests and offers of money do not make out an entrapment situation as a matter of law."[11] Likewise, even if the defendant's motive in selling the drugs was merely to help the seller, this does not relieve the defendant of his criminal responsibility.[12]

In *Ordonez v. State*,[13] the court pointed out that it "may well be true that normally predisposition refers to the state of mind of a defendant [immediately] before government agents make any suggestion that he should commit a crime. . . . Nevertheless . . . [we] do not think that if [the defendant] was not initially disposed to [deal] drugs, he could not, as a matter of law, develop such a disposition during the later course of dealing. He might well have found such dealing so profitable and easy that he thereafter willingly continued it regardless of [the] original inducement. The initial entrapment, assuming it existed [would] not immunize [the defendant] from criminal liability for subsequent transactions that he readily and willingly undertook."

In *Keaton v. State*,[14] the Georgia Supreme Court reversed a charge which included the following statement: *"If an officer acts in good faith in the honest belief that the defendant is engaged in unlawful conduct of which the offense charged is a part, and the*

---

[8]Hill v. State, 225 Ga. 117, 166 S.E.2d 338 (1969); Philmore v. State, 142 Ga. App. 507, 508 (3), 236 S.E.2d 180 (1977). In Seabrooks v. State, 164 Ga. App. 747, 748 (1), 297 S.E.2d 745 (1982), aff'd, 251 Ga. 564, 308 S.E.2d 160 (1983), the court said that entrapment "means something more than the request to purchase."

    See U.S. v. Russell, 411 U.S. 423, 93 S. Ct. 1637, 36 L. Ed. 2d 366 (1973) (conduct of government cannot be so outrageous as to violate due process).

[9]Huskey v. State, 139 Ga. App. 752, 753 (1), 229 S.E.2d 547 (1976).

    In United States v. Hill, 655 F.2d 512 (3d Cir. 1981), the defendant was tried for distribution of heroin. His defense was entrapment, and he sought to introduce testimony showing that he was particularly susceptible to persuasion and psychological pressure. The court concluded that it was error to reject the testimony in view of the Federal Rules of Evidence.

[10]Ellis v. State, 164 Ga. App. 366, 367 (1), 296 S.E.2d 726 (1982).

[11]Pennyman v. State, 175 Ga. App. 405, 407, 333 S.E.2d 659 (1985) (quoting Paras v. State, 247 Ga. 75, 77 (2), 274 S.E.2d 451 (1981)).

[12]Roden v. State, 181 Ga. App. 287, 293 (3), 351 S.E.2d 713 (1986).

[13]Ordonez v. State, 202 Ga. App. 623, 624, 415 S.E.2d 179 (1992).

[14]Keaton v. State, 253 Ga. 70, 71, 316 S.E.2d 452 (1984).

purpose of the officer is not to induce an innocent man to commit a crime, but to secure evidence upon which a guilty man can be brought to justice, the defense of entrapment is without merit." The court held that the emphasized material was erroneous in that it "caused the jury to focus on the subjective state of mind of the police officer, [and] in effect . . . [created] a 'good faith' exception to the entrapment defense." Perhaps the most significant thing about the charge is that it has been included in the Pattern Charge book prepared by the Council of Superior Court Judges. The instruction has now been changed by the Council, but the erroneous charge is likely to be given unless the judge involved uses care.

Georgia courts have been very reluctant to find entrapment as a matter of law.[15] It has been held that there is no entrapment as a matter of law "where a defendant approaches a police officer with an offer to commit a crime, if that officer then plays a role in order to provide the defendant with an opportunity to commit the intended offense."[16] In another case, where the defendant sold marijuana to an acquaintance, who turned out to be an informer, the court found no entrapment as a matter of law.[17]

However, in the 1991 case of *Hill v. State*,[18] the Georgia Supreme Court stated that "[a]fter a defendant presents a prima facie case of entrapment, the burden is on the state to disprove entrapment beyond a reasonable doubt. . . . [W]here there is no conflict in the evidence, and all the evidence prior to the entrapment that is introduced, with all reasonable deductions and inferences, demands a verdict of acquittal, the trial judge must direct a verdict of acquittal. The government's burden is far greater than merely impeaching the accused, it 'must go further and contradict this witness' testimony as to the affirmative defense.' "

Until 1982, if a defendant wished to rely on an entrapment defense in Georgia, it was said that he must admit the commis-

---

[15]Cf. Connell v. State, 163 Ga. App. 53, 293 S.E.2d 367 (1982). See also Curtis v. State, 172 Ga. App. 473, 323 S.E.2d 684 (1984).

[16]Orkin v. State, 236 Ga. 176, 195 (8), 223 S.E.2d 61 (1976). This decision actually said that the conduct described did not constitute entrapment, but the question which had been raised by the defendant was whether or not it was entrapment as a matter of law.

[17]Huskey v. State, 139 Ga. App. 752, 753 (2), 229 S.E.2d 547 (1976).

Cf. Brooks v. State, 125 Ga. App. 867, 189 S.E.2d 448 (1972); Parker v. State, 155 Ga. App. 617, 271 S.E.2d 871 (1980).

Generally, see Annot., 62 A.L.R.3d 110 (1975).

[18]Hill v. State, 261 Ga. 377, 405 S.E.2d 258 (1991) (citations omitted), quoted with approval in Wilkey v. State, 203 Ga. App. 1, 416 S.E.2d 350 (1992). Accord, Brooks v. State, 224 Ga. App. 829, 830 (1), 482 S.E.2d 725 (1997); Wilcox v. State, 229 Ga. App. 227, 229 (1), 493 S.E.2d 724 (1997).

sion of the crime.[19] Hence, it was held in a case that was later overruled, that if a defendant denied the commission of the act charged, it was not error or reversible error for the trial judge to refuse to charge on entrapment.[20] However, in the 1982 case of *Gregoroff v. State,*[21] the Georgia Supreme Court modified this rule slightly. *Gregoroff* held that "when the State's case shows evidence of entrapment, and the defendant offers no evidence of entrapment inconsistent with his defense that he did not commit the crime, the defendant is not required to admit the commission of the crime in order to be entitled to a charge on entrapment."

In *Mathews v. United States,*[22] the United States Supreme Court held "that a defendant may both deny the acts and other elements necessary to constitute the crime charged and at the same time claim entrapment. . . ."

In considering an entrapment defense, it must be remembered that if such a defense is relied upon, crimes of a similar nature are admissible on the issue of intent,[23] and to show plan, scheme, or design.[24] Nevertheless, proof of the prior commission of the

---

[19]Roberts v. State, 140 Ga. App. 21, 22 (1), 230 S.E.2d 84 (1976); Myers v. State, 140 Ga. App. 641 (2), 231 S.E.2d 496 (1976); Rodriguez v. United States, 227 F.2d 912 (5th Cir. 1955). Contra, People v. Perez, 62 Cal.2d 769, 44 Cal.Rptr. 326, 401 P.2d 934, 937 (1965); United States v. Demma, 523 F.2d 981 (9th Cir. 1975); State v. McBride, 287 Or. 315, 599 P.2d 449 (1979).

[20]Sutton v. State, 59 Ga. App. 198 (4), 200 S.E. 225 (1938), overruled by Keaton v. State, 253 Ga. 70, 316 S.E.2d 452 (1984). However, in Sears v. United States, 343 F.2d 139, 143 (5th Cir. 1965), the court held that "if the government injects evidence of entrapment into the case, the defendant is entitled to have the jury instructed that if they find he committed the acts charged, they must further consider whether he was entrapped into committing them." Accord, White v. State, 146 Ga. App. 810, 811 (1), 247 S.E.2d 536 (1978).

[21]Gregoroff v. State, 248 Ga. 667, 672, 285 S.E.2d 537 (1982); Ellzey v. State, 272 Ga. App. 253(1), 612 S.E.2d 77 (2005).

In Menefield v. State, 165 Ga.

App. 545, 546 (1), 301 S.E.2d 902 (1983), the court pointed out that "if a reasonable inference of entrapment may be drawn by a rational jury from the state's evidence, the defendant is entitled to a jury charge on entrapment unless he has presented evidence of entrapment inconsistent with his denial of the commission of the crime." See Hastings, "Entrapment and Denial of the Crime: A Defense of the Inconsistency Rule," 1986 Duke L. J. 866 (1986).

[22]Mathews v. United States, 485 U.S. 58, 108 S.Ct. 883, 99 L.Ed.2d 54 (1988).

[23]East v. State, 135 Ga. App. 291, 292, 217 S.E.2d 490 (1975); United States v. Crawford, 438 F.2d 441, 446 (8th Cir. 1971); Annot., 93 A.L.R.2d 1097 (1964); Medrano v. United States, 285 F.2d 23 (9th Cir. 1960). However, in United States v. Webster, 649 F.2d 346 (5th Cir. 1981), where the defendant claimed entrapment to a charge of distribution of cocaine, the court held that it was error for the trial judge to admit hearsay evidence that the defendant had sold cocaine on several occasions.

[24]Marshall v. State, 143 Ga. App.

same type of offense is not automatically admissible.[25]

However, the burden is not on the defendant to establish entrapment; but after the defendant presents a prima facie case of entrapment, the burden is on the state to show that there was no entrapment.[26] Thus, if the defendant testifies to entrapment by an identified informer and the state in rebuttal merely challenges the defendant's credibility, it is error for the court to overrule a motion for directed verdict of acquittal.[27] However, a defendant's testimony as to entrapment, even if unrebutted, will not entitle him to a directed verdict unless the unrebutted testimony together with all reasonable deductions and inferences therefrom demands a finding that entrapment occurred.[28] In the absence of a timely request to charge, it is generally not error for

---

249, 253 (3), 237 S.E.2d 709 (1977); People v. Ballard, 145 Cal.App.2d 94, 302 P.2d 89 (1956); United States v. Smith, 283 F.2d 760 (2d Cir. 1960); Annot., 61 A.L.R.3d 293.

[25]Johns v. State, 164 Ga. App. 133, 134 (2), 296 S.E.2d 638 (1982).

[26]Haralson v. State, 223 Ga. App. 787, 789 (1), 479 S.E.2d 115 (1996). In Coleman v. State, 141 Ga. App. 193, 194 (2), 233 S.E.2d 42 (1977), the court held that where the defendant raises the defense of entrapment in his testimony, then the burden shifts to the state to rebut the defendant's testimony. If the prosecution fails to do so, a directed verdict is proper. See also § 21:17, supra.

In Griffin v. State, 154 Ga. App. 261, 264, 267 S.E.2d 867 (1980), the court pointed out that the defendant must make out a prima facie case that the agent induced him to commit the offense charged. When this has been done, the burden is then on the state to prove beyond a reasonable doubt that the defendant was predisposed to commit the offense, i.e., "that he was ready and willing without persuasion and awaiting a propitious opportunity to commit the crime."

[27]Perry v. State, 143 Ga. App. 227, 228 (1), 237 S.E.2d 705 (1977). In this case, the court said that if the informer's testimony would disprove the defendant's testimony, the state should have produced him. Cf. Hughes v. State, 152 Ga. App. 80, 262 S.E.2d 245

(1979). However, in Marshall v. State, 143 Ga. App. 249, 252, 237 S.E.2d 709 (1977), the court said that if the defendant's testimony on entrapment is conflicting, it is not necessary for the state to rebut it by using the informer. In Robinson v. State, 145 Ga. App. 17 (1), 243 S.E.2d 257 (1978), the court held that where a defendant testifies to persistent and repeated requests on different occasions and he finally agrees to buy heroin for "friends" of informer and he denies having used heroin or being a dealer and there is no evidence that defendant had been regularly engaged in selling heroin, defendant is entitled to a directed verdict if his testimony is not rebutted.

[28]In State v. Royal, 247 Ga. 309, 275 S.E.2d 646 (1981), rev'g 155 Ga. App. 691, 272 S.E.2d 556 (1980), there was no evidence that the defendant was a seller of marijuana or other controlled substances or that he had a predisposition to do so, and the defendant testified that he did not want to purchase the marijuana he was convicted of selling but that he was induced to do so over his objections by persistent solicitations of a confidential police informant by undue persuasion. The informant selected the source. The undercover officer supplied the defendant with the money to make the purchase after the informer brought the defendant to the officer. They all drove to the supplier's house, and the defendant went into the house

the trial judge to fail to charge that the burden of proof is on the state to show that the defendant was not entrapped.[29]

Generally, see 21 Am. Jur. Criminal Law §§ 202 et seq.; Annotation, "Adequacy of Defense Counsel's Representation of Criminal Client Regarding Entrapment Defense," 8 A.L.R.4th 1160 (1981). See Annotation, "Burden of Proof as to Entrapment Defense—State Cases," 52 A.L.R.4th 775 (1987). See Annotation, "Entrapment as Defense to Charge of Selling or Supplying Narcotics Where Governmental Agents Supplied Narcotics to Defendant and Purchased Them From Him," 9 A.L.R.5th 464 (1993). See § 21:26, infra, on the defendant acting as an agent or conduit. See Annotation, "Right of Criminal Defendant to Raise Entrapment Defense Based on Having Dealt with Other Party Who Was Entrapped," 15 A.L.R.5th 39 (1993).

§ 21:26 Defenses—Miscellaneous—Defendant as agent of or conduit between government informer or officer

O.C.G.A. § 16-2-20(a) provides that every person "concerned" in the commission of a crime is a party thereto. A person is "concerned" in the commission of a crime only if he (1) directly commits the crime; or (2) intentionally causes some other person to commit the crime under such circumstances that the other person is not guilty either in fact or because of legal incapacity; or (3) intentionally aids or abets in the commission of the crime; or (4) intentionally advises, encourages, hires, counsels, or procures another to commit the crime.[1] Questions have arisen as to whether a defendant can be convicted under these provisions where (1) the defendant purchased contraband from a government agent and is charged under O.C.G.A. § 16-2-20 with the purchase;[2] or (2) the defendant sold contraband to a government agent and is charged under O.C.G.A. § 16-2-20 with the sale;[3] or (3) the defendant purchased contraband from one government agent in order to sell it to another, and is charged under O.C.G.A. § 16-2-20 with the purchase, the sale, or both.

---

and purchased for the agent the marijuana. The informer did not testify. However Royal admitted that he was not threatened or coerced to obtain the marijuana and admitted that he had smoked marijuana on the same evening both before and after the incident. The court concluded that the evidence did not demand a finding of entrapment.

Cf. Connell v. State, 163 Ga. App. 53, 293 S.E.2d 367 (1982); Armand

v. State, 164 Ga. App. 350, 296 S.E.2d 734 (1982).

[29]McDonald v. State, 156 Ga. App. 143, 149 (6), 273 S.E.2d 881 (1980).

[Section 21:26]

[1]O.C.G.A. § 16-2-20(b).

[2]Cf. Brooks v. State, 125 Ga. App. 867, 868 (1), 189 S.E.2d 448 (1972).

[3]Diana v. State, 164 Ga. App. 779, 780 (1), 298 S.E.2d 281 (1982).

It has been previously pointed out that the defense of entrapment does not lie merely because government agents either supplied, purchased, or supplied and purchased the contraband with which the defendant was charged.[4] Likewise, the fact that the defendant made no profit on the transaction and that he procured the drug on request does not require a finding of entrapment.[5] Similarly, Georgia case law uniformly holds that the fact that the defendant was the agent of or a conduit between government agents will not prevent the conviction of the defendant as a party to a crime under O.C.G.A. § 16-2-20.[6] The apparent rationale of these decisions is that the phrase "concerned in the commission of a crime," as it appears in O.C.G.A. § 16-2-20, encompasses any situation where the defendant intentionally aided or abetted in the commission of a crime or intentionally procured another person to commit a crime,[7] regardless of the legal capacity of that other person.[8]

Other jurisdictions, however, focus on the conduct of the government rather than on the conduct of the defendant, and thus invalidate convictions for crimes which would not or could not have taken place but for the agents' conduct.[9] In *People v. Spahr*,[10] the Illinois Court of Appeals held that a conviction for selling a controlled substance cannot be sustained where the substance is supplied by the state.[11] It has also been held that one who acts solely as the agent of a purchaser in a narcotics case cannot be convicted of a sale.[12] Although these cases turn to some extent on a technical application of agency law, there is respectable authority advocating a due process test based upon the outrageous conduct of law enforcement officials.[13]

---

[4]See § 21:25, supra.

[5]Roden v. State, 181 Ga. App. 287, 291, 351 S.E.2d 713 (1986).

[6]Royal v. State, 158 Ga. App. 405, 280 S.E.2d 427 (1981); Loder v. State, 140 Ga. App. 166 (2), 230 S.E.2d 124 (1976), vacated on other grounds, 238 Ga. 200, 232 S.E.2d 71 (1977), reaffirmed, 141 Ga. App. 665, 234 S.E.2d 132 (1977); Zinn v. State, 134 Ga. App. 51 (3), 213 S.E.2d 156 (1975); Brooks v. State, 125 Ga. App. 867 (1), 189 S.E.2d 448 (1972); Green v. State, 124 Ga. App. 469, 184 S.E.2d 194 (1971).

Accord, State v. Mansir, 440 A.2d 6 (Me.1982); Lucas v. State, 165 Ga. App. 468, 302 S.E.2d 121 (1983).

[7]Holiday v. State, 128 Ga. App. 817, 198 S.E.2d 364 (1973).

[8]See O.C.G.A. § 16-2-20(b)(2).

[9]This decision of whether to focus upon the predispositions of the defendant or upon the conduct of the government agent has been discussed previously with regard to the entrapment defense, § 21:25, supra.

[10]People v. Spahr, 56 Ill.App.3d 434, 14 Ill.Dec. 208, 371 N.E.2d 1261, 1265 (1978).

[11]Accord, State v. Johnson, 268 N.W.2d 613 (S.D.1978).

[12]People v. Roche, 45 N.Y.2d 78, 407 N.Y.S.2d 682, 379 N.E.2d 208 (1978).

[13]See State v. Mullen, 216 N.W.2d 375 (Iowa 1974); State v. Sainz, 84

§ 21:27   Defenses—Miscellaneous—Possession of de minimis amount in possession of unlawful substance cases

Prior to 1976, the Georgia courts had left unanswered the question of whether there is "a minimum amount of an illegal substance below which no claim of intentional possession is sustainable."[1] However, in the 1976 decision of *Partain v. State,*[2] both the Georgia Court of Appeals and the Georgia Supreme Court answered the question in the negative, holding that "regardless of the amount, however minute, if it is enough for the officers to recover, as small as it may be, and capable of being identified by expert chemical analysis, such testimony would be sufficient . . ." to sustain a conviction for unlawful possession.[3] This rule is true even where the state crime lab uses the entire sample in making its analysis, resulting in the defendant's inability to obtain an independent analysis of the sample.[4]

Other jurisdictions, including Hawaii,[5] California,[6] Nevada,[7] Texas,[8] and Arizona[9] adhere to the so-called "usable quantity standard," by which a defendant can be found guilty of unlawful possession of a narcotic only where the quantity possessed is in

---

N.M. 259, 501 P.2d 1247 (Ct. App. 1972); Batson v. State, 568 P.2d 973 (Alaska 1977); Grossman v. State, 457 P.2d 226 (Alaska 1969); People v. Benford, 53 Cal.2d 1, 345 P.2d 928 (1959); People v. Turner, 390 Mich. 7, 210 N.W.2d 336 (1973); Williamson v. United States, 311 F.2d 441 (5th Cir. 1962). In United States v. Twigg, 588 F.2d 373 (3d Cir. 1978), the government agent originated the scheme, employed a man who had a prior conviction for manufacturing narcotics as a go-between, and contacted the defendants. When problems were encountered, the agent would help solve them, with the defendants being nothing more than errand-boys. The court held that the conduct of the agent was so outrageous that due process required the conviction to be overturned.

[Section 21:27]

[1]Wallace v. State, 131 Ga. App. 204, 205 (2), 205 S.E.2d 523 (1974); Partain v. State, 139 Ga. App. 325 (5), 228 S.E.2d 292 (1976), aff'd, 238 Ga. 207, 232 S.E.2d 46 (1977).

[2]Partain v. State, 139 Ga. App. 325 (5), 228 S.E.2d 292 (1976), aff'd,

238 Ga. 207, 232 S.E.2d 46 (1977).

[3]The Georgia Court of Appeals reconsidered and reaffirmed this holding in Rogers v. State, 155 Ga. App. 685, 687 (4), 272 S.E.2d 549 (1980), where the defendant was convicted on the basis of "white powder residue" found in three plastic bags, three syringes, a razor blade, and a pill-crusher.

[4]Partain v. State, 139 Ga. App. 325 (5), 228 S.E.2d 292 (1976), aff'd, 238 Ga. 207, 232 S.E.2d 46 (1977). In Patterson v. State, 138 Ga. App. 290, 226 S.E.2d 115 (1976), the court held that the inability of the defendant to obtain an independent analysis of such a sample does not violate due process.

[5]State v. Vance, 61 Haw. 291, 602 P.2d 933 (1979).

[6]People v. Leal, 64 Cal.2d 504, 50 Cal.Rptr. 777, 413 P.2d 665 (1966).

[7]Watson v. State, 88 Nev. 196, 495 P.2d 365 (1972).

[8]Pelham v. State, 164 Tex.Crim. 226, 298 S.W.2d 171 (1957).

[9]State v. Junkin, 123 Ariz. 288, 599 P.2d 244 (App.1979).

sufficient amounts to be usable or saleable "under the known practices of addicts."[10] Pursuant to this rule, possession of a microscopic trace of a narcotic in combination with other factors, such as adulteration, which indicate an inability for the drug to produce a narcotic effect, requires the dismissal of any charge requiring that the drug sold or possessed be "dangerous" or a "narcotic."[11] See Annotation, 4 A.L.R.5th 1 (1992).

Hawaii has a statutory procedure specifically regulating the use, sale, and possession of narcotics in de minimis amounts.[12]

§ 21:28 Defenses—Miscellaneous—Selective prosecution

Some selectivity in enforcement is not in itself a constitutional violation.[1] "To be a constitutional violation, the selective enforcement must represent an intentional and purposeful discrimination based upon some unjustifiable standard such as race, religion, or other arbitrary classification."[2] In *United States v. Berrios,*[3] the court said, "To support a defense of selective or discriminatory prosecution, a defendant bears the heavy burden of establishing at least prima facie, (1) that, while others similarly situated have not generally been proceeded against because of conduct of the type forming the basis of the charge against him, he has been singled out for prosecution, and (2) that the government's discriminatory selection of him for prosecution has been invidious or in bad faith, i.e., based upon such impermissible considerations as race, religion, or the desire to prevent his exercise of constitutional rights.[4] These two essential elements are sometimes referred to as 'intentional and purposeful discrimination.' . . . Mere 'conscious exercise of some selectivity in enforcement is not in itself a federal constitutional violation.' "

In *Reed v. State,*[5] the court concluded that "[t]he applicable standard is the intent of the prosecutor in the misconduct, and

[10]State v. Junkin, 123 Ariz. 288, 599 P.2d 244 (App.1979).

[11]State v. Vance, 61 Haw. 291, 602 P.2d 933 (1979).

[12]See State v. Vance, 61 Haw. 291, 602 P.2d 933 (1979); H.R.S. §§ 712-236, 712-1248.

[Section 21:28]

[1]Oyler v. Boles, 368 U.S. 448, 456, 82 S.Ct. 501, 7 L.Ed.2d 446 (1962).

[2]Sabel v. State, 250 Ga. 640, 643, 300 S.E.2d 663 (1983), overruled by Massey v. Meadows, 253 Ga. 389, 321 S.E.2d 703 (1984), only to the extent

that they are in conflict in regard to fines as a condition precedent to probation; Lee v. State, 177 Ga. App. 698, 700, 340 S.E.2d 658 (1986). See § 17:6, n. 7, supra, on district attorney's discretion in non-criminal disposition of cases.

[3]United States v. Berrios, 501 F.2d 1207 (2d Cir. 1974). See Mooney v. State, 266 Ga. App. 587, 589, 597 S.E.2d 589 (2004).

[4]Quoted with approval in Carver v. State, 185 Ga. App. 436, 438 (2), 364 S.E.2d 877 (1987).

[5]Reed v. State, 222 Ga. App. 376, 378 (1), 474 S.E.2d 264 (1996). In

such intent is a fact question for the court to resolve."

In *Mooney v. State*,[6] the court noted:

A defendant has the burden of proving, by the weight of the evidence, that his prosecution represents an intentional or purposeful discrimination which is deliberately based upon an unjustifiable standard, such as race, religion, or other arbitrary classification. A showing that others were not prosecuted for doing what the defendant allegedly did is not, in itself, sufficient to establish selective prosecution.

Thus, in *United States v. Wayte*,[7] the Ninth Circuit held that the prosecution of only vocal non-registrants of the draft was not unlawful.

See § 17:6, supra, on prosecutorial discretion and § 26:4, infra, on equal protection as related to sentencing. See § 21:33, infra, on defense of gender discrimination in a death penalty case. See Studdard, *Daniel's Georgia Handbook on Criminal Evidence* (2018 ed.), §§ 1:6 and 5:14, on federal constitutional requirements where a defendant claims selective prosecution.

§ 21:29 Defenses—Miscellaneous—Misfortune or accident

O.C.G.A. § 16-2-2 provides as follows: "A person shall not be found guilty of any crime committed by misfortune or accident where it satisfactorily appears that there was no criminal scheme or undertaking, intention or criminal negligence." In *Mills v. State*,[1] the Georgia Supreme Court explained "[t]o succeed on an affirmative defense of accident the defendant must show that he acted without criminal intent, was not engaged in a criminal scheme, and was not criminally negligent, that is he did not act in a manner showing an utter disregard for the safety of others who might reasonably be expected to be injured thereby."

In *Sampson v. State*,[2] the court considered a case in which the state sought to show that the defendant was in possession of drugs found in his home. The defendant contended that his sister accidentally left the substance. The court held that a charge on

---

Morrison v. State, 272 Ga. 129, 130 (2), 526 S.E.2d 336 (2000), the court pointed out that "selective prosecution was not a matter for the jury . . ." but rather may be raised "by means of a motion to dismiss. . . ."

[6]Mooney v. State, 266 Ga. App. 587, 588, 597 S.E.2d 589 (2004) (citations and punctuation omitted). See Randolph v. State, 334 Ga. App. 475, 780 S.E.2d 19 (2015).

[7]United States v. Wayte, 710 F.2d 1385 (9th Cir. 1983), aff'd, 470 U.S. 598, 105 S.Ct. 1524, 84 L.Ed.2d 547 (1985).

[Section 21:29]

[1]Mills v. State, 287 Ga. 828, 700 S.E.2d 544 (2010). See Wilson v. State, 279 Ga. 104, 105(2), 610 S.E.2d 66 (2005).

[2]Sampson v. State, 165 Ga. App. 833, 834 (4), 303 S.E.2d 77 (1983).

accident was not required, since the "accident" was not that of the defendant but of his sister.

In *Grude v. State*,[3] the defendant's testimony showed "that his criminal attempt to commit an aggravated assault upon the victim was 'accidentally' completed in a manner other than he had intended. At the time the gun discharged . . . [the defendant] was engaged in an attempt to commit aggravated assault . . . by drawing the gun and pointing it at her . . . . He would not be entitled to a charge on the defense of accident simply because his criminal attempt had the unintended consequence of completing the offense by actually" shooting the victim.

In *Turner v. State*,[4] the court held that both the defense of accident and of self-defense may be appropriate "[w]here the court finds evidence of the involvement of both . . . ." Indeed, in *Turner*, the Court held that the trial court committed reversible error by failing to charge on both self defense and accident where the charges were requested and there was evidence to support both charges. The charges are not per se mutually exclusive.

In *Griffin v. State*,[5] the court held that it is error for the trial judge, on proper written request, to decline to charge the jury that the state has the burden of disproving the defense of accident beyond a reasonable doubt, where the defendant has raised that defense. In cases where the state need only prove the general intent of the defendant, i.e., to commit the act which the law forbids rather than the specific intent to commit the crime itself, the defense of accident is only available "where there is evidence, however slight, that the defendant did not voluntarily commit the prohibited act." Accordingly, the defense of accident would not be available to a defendant charged with second degree vehicular homicide based on her failure to stop for a pedestrian in a crosswalk, where the defendant claimed that the victim darted suddenly in front of her car thereby depriving the defendant of an opportunity to stop her vehicle. In such a case, the issue would be one of proximate cause since the defendant had the general intent to drive her vehicle through the crosswalk.[6]

---

[3]Grude v. State, 189 Ga. App. 901, 902 (1), 377 S.E.2d 731 (1989).

[4]Turner v. State, 262 Ga. 359, 361 (2)(c), 418 S.E.2d 52 (1992). Accord, Williams v. State, 239 Ga. App. 30, 33 (6), 521 S.E.2d 27 (1999).

[5]Griffin v. State, 267 Ga. 586 (1), 481 S.E.2d 223 (1997).

[6]State v. Ogilvie, 292 Ga. 6, 734 S.E.2d 50 (2012) (had defendant been charged with "intentionally" or "maliciously" hitting the victim with her vehicle, the defense of accident would have been available on these facts to negate the specific intent alleged). See Sapp v. State, 179 Ga. App. 614, 347 S.E.2d 354 (1986) (accident defense available in prosecution for police obstruction where defendant claimed that she obstructed officer when she fell due to illness).

§ 21:30   Defenses—Miscellaneous—Crimes committed on United States property

"Under O.C.G.A. § 50-2-23 the state retains criminal jurisdiction over persons for state offenses committed on property that has been acquired by the United States, except for property used by the Department of Defense and the Department of Justice. Even where the latter type of federal property is involved, the state retains jurisdiction unless the criminal defendant shows that the United States has accepted such jurisdiction by its filing a notice with the governor of the state. . . ."[1]

§ 21:31   Defenses—Miscellaneous—Sudden emergency

A "charge of sudden emergency is 'not appropriate in a criminal case. . . .' "[1]

§ 21:32   Defenses—Miscellaneous—Proximate cause

In *Franklin v. State,*[1] the Georgia Supreme Court noted:

When construing Georgia's felony murder statute, this Court has held that causing the death of another human being means *proximate* causation. *State v. Jackson*, 287 Ga. 646(2), 697 S.E.2d 757 (2010). "Proximate causation imposes liability for the reasonably foreseeable results of criminal . . . conduct if there is no sufficient, independent, and unforeseen intervening cause." *Id.* at 654. We consider the elements of the felony not in the abstract, but in the actual circumstances in which the felony was committed. *Davis v. State*, 290 Ga. 757, 760(4), 725 S.E.2d 280 (2012).

In *Franklin,* the Court held that the accidental dislodgement of the victim's tracheal tube that had been surgically fitted following a beating inflicted by the defendant three months earlier was not an unforeseen intervening cause of the victim's death that relieved defendant of liability for felony murder. Likewise, in *Dupree v. State,*[2] the defendant's actions in robbing the victim at gunpoint and hitting the victim were considered to be the proximate cause of the victim's death by cardiac arrest. In *Walker v. State,*[3] however, the court found that the predicate felonies alleged in the felony murder counts involving a child victim which

---

[Section 21:30]

[1]Jackson v. State, 183 Ga. App. 594, 595, 359 S.E.2d 457 (1987). Cf. Harris v. State, 186 Ga. App. 756, 757 (1), 368 S.E.2d 527 (1988).

[Section 21:31]

[1]Meeks v. State, 216 Ga. App. 630, 631 (1), 455 S.E.2d 350 (1995).

[Section 21:32]

[1]Franklin v. State, 295 Ga. 204, 205, 758 S.E.2d 813 (2014).

[2]Dupree v. State, 247 Ga. 470, 277 S.E.2d 18 (1981). See Skaggs v. State, 278 Ga. 19, 596 S.E.2d 159 (2004).

[3]Walker v. State, 296 Ga. 161,

consisted of the murder of the child's mother and the concealment of her death, did not provide the proximate cause necessary
to support the charges.

In *Billingsley v. State*,[4] the defendant was tried for vehicular
homicide. The appellate court held that the trial judge did not err
in failing to charge on proximate cause in the absence of a request
where the trial judge did specifically charge the jury that causation was a material element of the offense. However, in *Johnson
v. State*,[5] the court upheld the giving of a proximate cause charge
in a homicide by vehicle case.

In *Castro v. State*,[6] the court held that an injury can constitute
the proximate cause of a victim's death if it "materially accelerated the death, although proximately occasioned by a pre-existing
cause." In that case, the defendant was convicted of the felony
murder of a two-year-old victim for whom she and her co-
defendant were the primary caretakers. The felony murder
charge was predicated on the defendant's refusal to seek medical
treatment for the child for a week and that her failure to act
materially accelerated the child's death, even though the beat-
ings were a pre-existing condition.

§ 21:33 Defenses—Miscellaneous—Gender discrimination by district attorney in death case

In *Perkins v. State*,[1] the defendant filed a plea in bar to prevent
the district attorney's office from seeking the death penalty
because of gender discrimination in the district attorney's office.
The court declined to "create a *Batson* . . . like rule that would
require the state to explain its reasons for seeking the death
penalty. . . ." The court also pointed out that in order to prevail,
the defendant must show a purposeful discrimination by the decision makers in his case.

---

766 S.E.2d 28 (2014).

[4]Billingsley v. State, 183 Ga.
App. 850, 853 (5), 360 S.E.2d 451
(1987). Cf. Mote v. State, 212 Ga. App.
551, 553 (2), 442 S.E.2d 799 (1994).

[5]Johnson v. State, 170 Ga. App.
433 (1), 317 S.E.2d 213 (1984).

[6]Castro v. State, 295 Ga. 105,
107, 757 S.E.2d 853 (2014). See Chua
v. State, 289 Ga. 220, 229(1)(b), 710
S.E.2d 540 (2011); State v. Jackson,
287 Ga. 646, 654(3), 697 S.E.2d 757
(2010).

[Section 21:33]

[1]Perkins v. State, 269 Ga. 791,
794 (2), 505 S.E.2d 16 (1998).

§ 21:34   Defenses—Miscellaneous—Reverse sting operations

In *Gober v. State,*[1] the defendant was convicted of drug possession. He attempted to defend contending that former O.C.G.A. § 16-13-49(u)(1) required officers to destroy the substance sold to him. The court affirmed the conviction holding that the conduct of police was not so outrageous as to constitute a violation of the defendant's due process right.

§ 21:35   Defenses—Miscellaneous—Involuntariness of confession

Involuntariness of a confession may not be used as a defense to a criminal charge. The voluntariness aspect of a confession strictly relates to admissibility as evidence at trial and not as to why the defendant believes the prosecutor does not have a valid case.[1]

[Section 21:34]

[1]Gober v. State, 249 Ga. App. 168, 547 S.E.2d 656 (2001). Cf. Giraldo v. State, 249 Ga. App. 178, 547 S.E.2d 651 (2001).

[Section 21:35]

[1]Robinson v. State, 272 Ga. 752, 754 (2), 533 S.E.2d 718 (2000).

Chapter 22

From Rebuttal to Request to Charge

KeyCite®: Cases and other legal materials listed in KeyCite Scope can be researched through the KeyCite service on Westlaw®. Use KeyCite to check citations for form, parallel references, prior and later history, and comprehensive citator information, including citations to other decisions and secondary materials.

---

§ 22:1 Insanity—Testimony of psychiatrist or psychologist appointed

In 1985, Georgia enacted O.C.G.A. § 17-7-130.1. This statute provides that testimony of a psychiatrist or psychologist appointed by the trial judge follows "the presentation of the evidence for the prosecution and for the defense, including testimony of any medical experts employed by the state or by the defense.

In *Moore v. State*,[1] the court pointed out that such an appointment is to be made *when* the defendant notifies the state and the court that insanity will be an issue. If the court observes facts that raise doubts as to the sanity of the accused, or if such facts are brought before the court by counsel, then the issue of the accused's sanity should be settled before the court moves forward with the case. Factors such as reports of the defendant's irrational behavior, the defendant's demeanor at trial, or expert medical opinion regarding the defendant's competency, should all be considered when determining whether the defendant is competent. In *Villegas v. State*,[2] the court held that if no such ev-

---

[Section 22:1]

[1]Moore v. State, 220 Ga. App. 434, 436 (2), 469 S.E.2d 211 (1996).

[2]Villegas v. State, 262 Ga. App. 55, 584 S.E.2d 666 (2003).

idence is presented the court may deny a motion for the appointment of a psychiatrist. "The medical witnesses appointed by the court may be cross-examined by both the prosecution and the defense, and each side may introduce evidence in rebuttal to the testimony of such a medical witness." See § 14:92, supra.

In *Lynd v. State*,[3] the court held that a "defendant can no more present psychiatric testimony without submitting to an examination by a state-selected psychiatrist than he may testify at trial without submitting to a cross-examination."

In *Hittson v. State*,[4] the court held that custodial communications made between a court appointed mental health expert and a defendant are testimonial and if *Miranda* warnings are given, the defendant's statements are admissible during the state's case-in-chief or at the sentencing phase of the trial.

In *Abernathy v. State*,[5] the court held that pre-trial notice of the defendant's intent to present mental health evidence applies only when the evidence is presented through experts. "[T]he State may not obtain or use the results of an independent mental health evaluation to rebut purely lay testimony." The court declined to place a limit on the scope of the independent evaluation. However, "the State may offer expert mental health testimony only in the sentencing phase and strictly in rebuttal of expert mental health evidence. . . ."

In *Henry v. State*,[6] the defendant filed a notice of intent to raise the issue of insanity. A psychiatrist was appointed. The defendant withdrew his notice of insanity before trial but presented mental health witnesses during the sentencing phase of this death penalty case. These defense witnesses testified that the defendant suffered from various mental illnesses. After the state presented expert witnesses in rebuttal, the court called the psychiatrist appointed earlier. The Georgia Supreme Court affirmed and pointed out that the trial judge may call a witness of his or her own choosing.

§ 22:2 Calling witnesses by the court

Generally, the "trial court has the right to develop fully the

---

[3]Lynd v. State, 262 Ga. 58, 64 (11), 414 S.E.2d 5 (1992). Cf. Daniel v. State, 268 Ga. 9, 10 (3), 485 S.E.2d 734 (1997).

[4]Hittson v. State, 264 Ga. 682, 684 (2), 449 S.E.2d 586 (1994), overruled on other grounds, Nance v. State, 272 Ga. 217 (2), 526 S.E.2d 560 (2000).

[5]Abernathy v. State, 265 Ga. 754, 462 S.E.2d 615 (1995). See Otis v. State, 298 Ga. 544, 782 S.E.2d 654 (2016) (Ga. Unif. Super. Ct. R. 31.1 does not apply where insanity defense is supported only by lay testimony and expert opinion is not involved).

[6]Henry v. State, 265 Ga. 732, 739 (9), 462 S.E.2d 737 (1995).

truth of a case, and may exercise this right by examining witnesses called by the parties, or by calling its own witnesses. . . . [Nevertheless] whenever a court calls its own witness, the better practice is to instruct the jury that by calling a witness, the court suggests nothing about credibility and that this witness is to be assessed like all other witnesses."[1]

§ 22:3 Rebuttal by state

After the defense has rested, the state has the right to call rebuttal witnesses in an attempt to refute or explain any or all of the testimony introduced by the defendant.[1] For example, if the defense introduced evidence in a murder case inferring that the victim had a bad reputation, the state may present rebuttal evidence showing that the victim had a good reputation.[2] If defense testimony as to the indigency of the defendant was introduced, the state may, in rebuttal, call witnesses to testify that the accused wore expensive clothes and owned an automobile.[3]

In rebuttal of defense evidence, the state may recall a witness who had previously testified in order to bring out some additional evidence which is contrary to the defense testimony.[4] The fact that a witness has been excused by the state after he testified does not prevent the witness from being recalled for rebuttal testimony.[5] Even where the state has established a certain fact in its case-in-chief, the trial judge may, in his discretion, permit the state to call a witness who has not previously testified for the purpose of showing that the defense testimony on the point was incorrect.[6] After the defense testimony, it is within the discretion of the trial judge to admit relevant evidence even where it is not actually in rebuttal of the defense testimony.[7]

It would seem that if a defendant offers no evidence, the state has nothing to rebut and cannot put up rebuttal evidence, but the trial judge, in his discretion, may permit the state to

---

[Section 22:2]

[1]O'Hara v. State, 241 Ga. App. 855, 858, 528 S.E.2d 296 (2000).

[Section 22:3]

[1]See Barnes v. State, 24 Ga. App. 372, 373 (4), 100 S.E. 788 (1919).

[2]Taylor v. State, 229 Ga. 536 (4), 540 (4), 192 S.E.2d 249 (1972).

[3]Wilson v. State, 126 Ga. App. 145, 148 (2), 190 S.E.2d 128 (1972).

[4]Thomas v. State, 27 Ga. 287, 288 (12) (1859).

[5]Butler v. State, 163 Ga. App. 475, 476 (2), 294 S.E.2d 700 (1982).

[6]Johnson v. State, 164 Ga. 47 (2), 137 S.E. 553 (1927); Leatherwood v. State, 212 Ga. App. 342, 343 (3), 441 S.E.2d 813 (1994).

[7]See Cooper v. State, 103 Ga. 63 (1), 29 S.E. 439 (1897); Smith v. State, 126 Ga. 803, 804 (3), 55 S.E. 1024 (1906); Williams v. State, 254 Ga. 6, 10 (5), 326 S.E.2d 444 (1985).

introduce additional evidence at this time.[8]

In *Thompson v. State*,[9] the court held that "[r]ebuttal testimony should not be excluded merely because the state could have introduced it during its main case. Each case must be decided on its own merits. It is the importance of the evidence to the state's main case and whether the withholding was intended or designed to deny the defendant an opportunity to prepare his defense in relation to that evidence which will determine if reversible error has occurred." In this case, the appellate court affirmed the trial court in permitting witnesses to testify in rebuttal "who had not been listed on the state's witness list."

§ 22:4   Rebuttal by defendant, further rebuttal and testimony

After the state has completed its rebuttal, the defendant may rebut any rebuttal evidence of the state.[1] The trial judge may, within his discretion, permit the defendant to introduce other testimony not strictly in rebuttal.[2]

If the defense, in rebuttal is permitted to offer any new evidence, the state has the right, in a surrebuttal, to try to rebut the defendant's rebuttal testimony.[3] Thereafter, it seems the defense has the same right of surrebuttal.

It has been held that where a defendant testifies that he was not at the scene of the crime and a state rebuttal witness claims otherwise, if the defendant does not again take the stand in surrebuttal, it is not error for the prosecuting attorney to comment on the defendant's failure to testify to his alibi in surrebuttal.[4] The unfortunate aspect about the above-cited case is that it encourages both the prosecution and the defense to seek the "last word" rather than be concerned with matters actually in rebuttal.

In *Evans v. State*,[5] the court held that a trial judge has discretion to permit the state to introduce evidence after the defendant has closed his testimony, even if it is not strictly in rebuttal and even if such evidence tends to bolster the state's case more than to directly impeach defense evidence.

---

[8]See Hobbs v. State, 229 Ga. 556, 559 (4), 192 S.E.2d 903 (1972). In this case, the admission of a former indictment was permitted after the evidence had been reopened. The court held this was not error.

[9]Thompson v. State, 237 Ga. App. 91, 93 (2), 514 S.E.2d 870 (1999).

[Section 22:4]

[1]See Timmons v. State, 13 Ga. App. 376, 79 S.E. 216 (1913).

[2]See Burden v. State, 182 Ga. 533, 534 (3), 186 S.E. 555 (1936).

[3]Simmons v. State, 118 Tex.Crim. 519, 40 S.W.2d 804, 806 (1931).

[4]Gosha v. State, 239 Ga. 37, 235 S.E.2d 527 (1977).

[5]Evans v. State, 225 Ga. App. 589, 591, 484 S.E.2d 320 (1997).

See § 22:6, infra, on reopening the case and § 24:21, infra, on reopening the evidence.

§ 22:5   Motion for directed verdict of acquittal

A motion for a directed verdict of acquittal does not lie in a bench trial. A motion for a directed verdict "has no meaning when a case is tried without a jury."[1]

Once the state and the defense have rested, the defendant may move for a directed verdict of acquittal.[2] If there is no conflict in the credible evidence,[3] "and the evidence introduced, with all reasonable deductions and inferences therefrom, shall demand a verdict of . . . 'not guilty' . . . , the court may direct the verdict of acquittal."[4]

Despite the words "may direct" which appear in the statute, it is error for the trial judge to refuse to grant a motion for acquittal if the evidence is insufficient to support a conviction,[5] of the offense charged or a lesser included offense.[6] "A trial judge must grant a motion for directed verdict unless, viewing the evidence in the light most favorable to the prosecution, a rational trier of fact could find the essential elements of the crime beyond a reasonable doubt."[7] However, as stated in a case that was later overruled "a defendant is not entitled to a directed verdict [of acquittal] simply because the offenses charged may merge [with another charge]."[8] In *Garrett v. State,*[9] the court held that "[t]he standard of review for the denial of a motion for a directed verdict of acquittal is the same as that for reviewing the sufficiency of the evidence to support a conviction." If a motion for directed verdict of acquittal is granted, the state has no right to appeal.[10]

[Section 22:5]

[1]Poole v. State, 249 Ga. App. 409, 410 (1), 548 S.E.2d 113 (2001).

[2]O.C.G.A. § 17-9-1(b). See generally § 21:1, supra.

[3]See Boggus v. State, 136 Ga. App. 917, 921 (7), 222 S.E.2d 686 (1975).

[4]O.C.G.A. § 17-9-1(a).

[5]Phillips v. State, 133 Ga. App. 461, 464, 211 S.E.2d 411 (1974); Bethay v. State, 235 Ga. 371, 373, 219 S.E.2d 743 (1975). Contra, Grant v. State, 161 Ga. App. 403, 404 (3), 288 S.E.2d 118 (1982).

[6]Hack v. State, 168 Ga. App. 927, 928 (3), 311 S.E.2d 211 (1983).

[7]Lee v. State, 247 Ga. 411, 412 (6), 276 S.E.2d 590 (1981); Adams v. State, 164 Ga. App. 295, 296 (1), 297 S.E.2d 77 (1982).

However, in Taylor v. State, 252 Ga. 125, 127, 312 S.E.2d 311 (1984), without discussion the court lapsed back to the rule existing before Lee v. State, 247 Ga. 411, 412 (6), 276 S.E.2d 590 (1981).

[8]Williams v. State, 233 Ga. App. 217, 220 (4), 504 S.E.2d 53 (1998), overruled by Curtis v. State, 275 Ga. 576, 571 S.E.2d 376 (2002).

[9]Garrett v. State, 184 Ga. App. 715, 716 (3), 362 S.E.2d 423 (1987).

[10]State v. Sykes, 137 Ga. App. 297, 223 S.E.2d 491 (1976). The *Sykes*

In *McArthur v. State,*[11] the defendant was charged with obstructing an officer and public drunkenness. The defendant moved for a directed verdict of acquittal on the obstruction charge. The motion was denied. The jury returned a verdict of not guilty on the obstruction charge but guilty of public drunkenness. The defendant appealed, urging a reversal because his motion for a directed verdict on the obstruction charge had been denied. He contended that it placed "an undue burden" on him in his defense of the drunkenness charge to also have to defend against the other charge. The court referred to the defendant's contention as "novel but non-meritorious."

It is reversible error for a trial judge to direct a verdict of guilty even "where the defendant and his attorney in effect plead guilty in open court before the judge and jury." A defendant in a criminal case "is entitled to have a jury weigh and consider the evidence presented in the case and the right to the presumption of innocence until the jury decides that he is guilty."[12]

It has been held that it is permissible for the trial judge to reserve a ruling on a motion for a directed verdict of acquittal until after a jury returns its verdict and has been dispersed.[13]

If a motion for a directed verdict of acquittal is granted to a count of the indictment, the indictment does not have to be redacted in such a fashion as to obscure the fact that the count was originally in the indictment.[14] In addition, when a motion for directed verdict is granted, a lesser included offense of the named and charged offense may still be submitted to the jury, provided the greater offense sets out all the essential elements of the lesser included offense.[15]

See § 21:1, supra, on the amount of evidence required to withstand a motion for a directed verdict of acquittal.

---

case is based on a Georgia statute. However in United States v. Scott, 437 U.S. 82, 98 S.Ct. 2187, 57 L.Ed.2d 65 (1978), the court held that the double jeopardy clause of the Fifth Amendment does not prevent the state from appealing the granting of a directed verdict.

[11]McArthur v. State, 169 Ga. App. 263 (2), 312 S.E.2d 358 (1983).

[12]Bryant v. State, 163 Ga. App. 872, 874, 296 S.E.2d 168 (1982). The *Bryant* case is an excellent opinion of Judge Carley in which he also discusses how jurors serve as the judges of the law and the facts.

In Connecticut v. Johnson, 460 U.S. 73, 103 S.Ct. 969, 74 L.Ed.2d 823, 832 (1983), a plurality opinion, the court said a trial "judge may not direct a verdict of guilty no matter how conclusive the evidence." Accord, United States v. Martin Linen Supply Co., 430 U.S. 564, 572, 97 S.Ct. 1349, 51 L.Ed.2d 642 (1977).

[13]State v. Seignious, 197 Ga. App. 766, 767, 399 S.E.2d 559 (1990).

[14]Anderson v. State, 236 Ga. App. 679, 684 (6), 513 S.E.2d 235 (1999).

[15]Martinez v. State, 318 Ga. App. 254, 735 S.E.2d 785 (2012).

§ 22:6 Reopening the case

It is within the sound discretion of the trial judge to permit either the state or the defense to reopen the case after the close of the evidence[1] and within a short period of time subsequent to the jury's retiring to reach a verdict.[2] Thus, where the evidence has been closed and the defendant moves for a directed verdict of acquittal, it is not error for the trial judge to permit the district attorney to reopen his case in order to bring out a point which was previously overlooked.[3] In *Carter v. State,*[4] where the defendant was being re-tried and the defense introduced no evidence, the trial judge allowed the state to reopen the case in order to permit the state to present the defendant's testimony from the original trial. The appellate court affirmed. It has also been held that it is permissible for the evidence to be reopened during arguments,[5] or after argument and charge but before the commencement of deliberation.[6] In addition, a judge in the sound exercise of his or her discretion may reopen and admit evidence upon the request of the jury after deliberations have begun.[7]

The discretion of the trial judge in refusing to reopen the evidence may be abused. Thus, it has been held reversible error for the court to refuse to reopen the evidence after the charge had

---

[Section 22:6]

[1]Leach v. State, 143 Ga. App. 598, 601, 239 S.E.2d 177 (1977); Brawner v. State, 161 Ga. App. 120 (4), 289 S.E.2d 277 (1982). In Traylor v. State, 163 Ga. App. 473, 474, 294 S.E.2d 707 (1982), the court pointed out the discretionary power of the trial judge to allow another witness to be sworn and to testify after the evidence has been closed and argument has begun and noted that "a liberal practice in this respect is most favorable to the ends of justice."

[2]Merritt v. State, 168 Ga. 753 (4), 149 S.E. 46 (1929). Here the jury had been out four or five minutes when they were recalled and evidence on venue was heard. In Judge v. State, 8 Ga. 173 (5) (1850), the court held that after the case is submitted to the jury, the state may not introduce any further evidence against the defendant. See Hurt v. State, 239 Ga. 665, 672 (8), 238 S.E.2d 542 (1977); Chancellor v. State, 165 Ga. App. 365, 373 (27), 301 S.E.2d 294 (1983).

[3]McFarland v. State, 137 Ga. App. 354, 357 (5), 223 S.E.2d 739 (1976); Miller v. State, 156 Ga. App. 690, 275 S.E.2d 663 (1980).

[4]Carter v. State, 263 Ga. 401, 402 (2), 435 S.E.2d 42 (1993).

[5]O'Brien v. State, 50 Ga. App. 189, 177 S.E. 351 (1934).

[6]Pennington v. State, 42 Ga. App. 377 (2), 382-83, 156 S.E. 286 (1930). Strickland v. State, 115 Ga. 222, 224 (2), 41 S.E. 713 (1902), reviews a number of older cases in which the trial judge, at various times after the close of the evidence, permitted the evidence to be reopened. The case actually holds that it was not an abuse of discretion for the court to permit the evidence to be reopened after the jury had been unable to reach a verdict because the jurors said they could not remember any evidence on a particular point.

[7]State v. Roberts, 247 Ga. 456, 277 S.E.2d 644 (1981) (documents used to refresh recollection of witness but not admitted during trial).

begun where the state's primary witness states that he then wanted to tell the truth.[8] Also, where both the state and the defense have rested, it was held reversible error to permit a co-defendant who had earlier admitted guilt to take the stand, over objection of defense counsel who represented both defendants. Here the defendant had made an out-of-court statement to the trial judge not revealed to either the district attorney or defense counsel about the participation of the other defendant.[9]

In connection with the reopening of the evidence, it has been held that prior knowledge of a police officer concerning a witness is not imputed to the district attorney.[10]

It is generally within the discretion of the trial judge to rehear requested parts of the testimony after deliberation has begun, and it is generally proper for the trial judge to reopen the evidence and to permit *new* evidence to be introduced (where requested by the jury) after deliberations have begun.[11]

See § 22:4, supra, on rebuttal and further testimony. See § 24:19, infra, on communicating with the jury after deliberations have commenced, and see § 24:21, infra, on the admission of additional evidence after commencement of jury deliberations. See § 24:20, infra, on having testimony read to the jury.

§ 22:7   Requests to charge

As pointed out in § 17:22, supra, requests to charge must generally be filed in writing and in duplicate at the commencement of the trial. Copies of the requests must be given to the opposing counsel prior to the charge. An attempted oral adoption of the request to charge of a co-defendant is insufficient.[1] It is the duty of the court to inform counsel of "its proposed action upon the requests prior to their arguments to the jury."[2] However, a defendant has no right to have an oral discussion with the trial

---

[8]Hollins v. State, 133 Ga. App. 183 (1), 210 S.E.2d 354 (1974).

[9]Smith v. State, 156 Ga. App. 563, 564 (1), 275 S.E.2d 140 (1980).

[10]Payne v. State, 168 Ga. App. 485, 486 (2), 309 S.E.2d 667 (1983).

[11]State v. Roberts, 247 Ga. 456, 277 S.E.2d 644 (1981); Childs v. State, 257 Ga. 243, 255 (18), 357 S.E.2d 48 (1987); State v. Shutt, 279 N.C. 689, 185 S.E.2d 206, 209 (1971); Annot., 87 A. L. R. 2d 849 (1963).

[Section 22:7]

[1]Valdez-Hardin v. State, 201 Ga. App. 126, 410 S.E.2d 354 (1991).

[2]O.C.G.A. § 5-5-24(b); Thompson v. State, 173 Ga. App. 566, 327 S.E.2d 236 (1985). However, in Benson v. State, 164 Ga. App. 19 (2), 295 S.E.2d 579 (1982), the court concluded that the failure of the trial judge to inform counsel of which requests to charge would be given was harmless where he gave in substance all requested charges supported by the evidence.

judge about the proposed charges.[3] If the trial judge conducts an optional pre-charge conference, it has been held that the defendant does not have an unequivocal right to be present.[4] However, if the defendant requests to be present, the better practice is to permit him to be present.[5]

If the court, in its charge, includes a request to charge which the court stated it would not give, the party affected should call this to the attention of the judge and request the right to argue that particular matter to the jury.[6] If a judge charges a jury contrary to his earlier ruling, the error is not cured by giving counsel an opportunity for further argument in cases where the defense counsel relied on the court's ruling.[7]

Requests to charge are important in the trial of any case. Requests give each party the opportunity to submit to the court the theory of law he believes applicable to the case on trial. A party has the opportunity to submit his contention to the court in lay language rather than the more legalistic language which is likely to come from the court.[8] However, the failure of the trial judge to charge in the exact language requested is not error where the charge given substantially covered the same principles of law.[9]

Requests to charge are also advantageous in that a party may be able to get the court to charge on principles of law which otherwise might not be covered. Numerous Georgia appellate decisions have held that it is not error to fail to charge, or to charge more fully, on a certain matter in the absence of a timely written

---

[3]Simmons v. State, 172 Ga. App. 695, 696, 324 S.E.2d 546 (1984), rev'd on other grounds, Heard v. State, 261 Ga. 262, 263, 403 S.E.2d 438 (1991).

[4]Aleman v. State, 227 Ga. App. 607, 613 (3)(e), 489 S.E.2d 867 (1997).

[5]McBride v. State, 213 Ga. App. 857, 861 (11), 446 S.E.2d 193 (1994).

[6]Daniels v. State, 137 Ga. App. 371, 375, 224 S.E.2d 60 (1976). However, in Miller v. State, 163 Ga. App. 889, 892, 296 S.E.2d 182 (1982), the court pointed out that a defendant is not entitled to a reversal where the error was harmless.

[7]Chase v. State, 148 Ga. App. 690 (3), 252 S.E.2d 194 (1979). In the Chase case the trial judge had told defense counsel he would charge that

driving under the influence was a lesser included offense of automobile homicide. Defense counsel had argued that defendant should be convicted of driving under the influence. Then the court declined to charge that driving under the influence was a lesser included offense.

[8]However, the refusal of the judge to give a charge in the exact language requested is not ordinarily error. Seagraves v. Abco Manufacturing Co., 121 Ga. App. 224, 226 (3), 173 S.E.2d 416 (1970).

[9]Kelly v. State, 241 Ga. 190, 191 (4), 243 S.E.2d 857 (1978); Payne v. State, 248 Ga. App. 158, 161 (3), 545 S.E.2d 336 (2001); Cohran v. State, 141 Ga. App. 4, 5 (2), 232 S.E.2d 355 (1977).

request.[10] If a party wishes to have certain matters covered in the judge's instructions, it is best to submit the point to the court in a timely request to charge. It is also to the defendant's advantage[11] to submit requested instructions since the court may commit reversible error if the trial judge refuses to give a requested charge[12] and there is, "at trial, slight evidence supporting the theory of the charge."[13]

A request to charge which is irrelevant to all issues to be determined by the jury may be rejected.[14] A request for jury instruction must relate to some issue to be determined in the case.[15] The charge should not be argumentative[16] and must be a correct statement of law.[17]

In *Clarke v. Cotton*,[18] the court pointed out that a request to charge should be refused "unless the charge ought to be given in the very terms in which requested. . . . The trial court is not under any obligation to rewrite an instruction which either party requests. . . ." In *Davis v. State*,[19] the court pointed out that a "request to charge . . . must be correct, legal, apt, and precisely adjusted to some principle involved in the case. If any portion of the request is inapt or incorrect, denial of the request is proper."

If a series of propositions are presented in block without separate requests to charge, it is not error for the court to refuse to give any of the requests if one or more are unsound or inapplicable to the case.[20]

In *Andrews v. State*,[21] the court pointed out that a jury has the power to acquit the defendant regardless of the strength of the

---

[10]E.g., Scudiere v. State, 130 Ga. App. 477, 478 (2), 203 S.E.2d 581 (1973); Barner v. State, 263 Ga. 365, 367 (3), 434 S.E.2d 484 (1993).

[11]O.C.G.A. §§ 5-5-24(a) and 5-7-1 do not give the state the right to appeal for the failure to give a requested charge to the jury.

[12]See Redding v. State, 214 Ga. 524, 106 S.E.2d 5 (1958).

[13]McBurnette v. State, 236 Ga. App. 398, 512 S.E.2d 298 (1999).

[14]White v. State, 230 Ga. 327 (7), 338 (7), 196 S.E.2d 849 (1973).

[15]Birt v. State, 236 Ga. 815, 828 (5), 225 S.E.2d 248 (1976).

[16]See Johnson v. State, 148 Ga. 546, 547 (4), 97 S.E. 515 (1918).

[17]Green v. State, 124 Ga. 343, 344 (8), 52 S.E. 431 (1905).

[18]Clarke v. Cotton, 207 Ga. App. 883, 885 (2), 429 S.E.2d 291 (1993) (citing and relying on Tatum v. State, 57 Ga. App. 849, 853 (3), 197 S.E. 51 (1938)). Cf. Harmon v. State, 208 Ga. App. 271, 274 (5), 430 S.E.2d 399 (1993).

[19]Davis v. State, 266 Ga. 801, 803 (7), 471 S.E.2d 191 (1996). Accord, Carlson v. State, 240 Ga. App. 589, 590 (3), 524 S.E.2d 283 (1999); Scott v. State, 227 Ga. App. 625, 628 (2), 490 S.E.2d 104 (1997). Cf. Scruggs v. State, 227 Ga. App. 35, 37 (3), 488 S.E.2d 110 (1997).

[20]See May v. State, 24 Ga. App. 379, 380 (10), 100 S.E. 797 (1919); and see Conley v. State, 21 Ga. App. 134, 135 (6), 94 S.E. 261 (1917).

[21]Andrews v. State, 222 Ga. App. 129, 130 (1)(b), 473 S.E.2d 247 (1996). Accord, Duggan v. State, 225 Ga. App.

evidence. However, it is not error for the trial judge to refuse to charge on jury nullification. See § 24:24, infra, on removal of a jury because the jury would not follow the law.

Where a party requests a certain charge which the court gives to the jury, he may not later assign error to the giving of the charge.[22]

Also on requests to charge, see § 24:1, infra. On jury instructions, generally see §§ 24:2 et seq., infra.

291, 295 (3), 483 S.E.2d 373 (1997).

[22]Meyers v. State, 169 Ga. 468 (3), 151 S.E. 34 (1929); Wright v. State,

162 Ga. App. 60, 290 S.E.2d 163 (1982).

Chapter 23

Argument

KeyCite®: Cases and other legal materials listed in KeyCite Scope can be researched through the KeyCite service on Westlaw®. Use KeyCite to check citations for form, parallel references, prior and later history, and comprehensive citator information, including citations to other decisions and secondary materials.

---

§ 23:1   General considerations

Argument, or summation, gives counsel for both sides the last opportunity to present their side of the case. Most experienced lawyers feel that argument, particularly closing argument, is one of the most important phases of the trial.[1] While some of the oratory which was of so much importance in earlier generations may not be as successful today, there is still room for a well-reasoned and effectively presented argument.

In regard to argument, O.C.G.A. § 17-8-70 provides as follows: "Not more than two counsel shall be permitted to argue any case for each side, except by express leave of the court. In no case shall more than one counsel for each side be heard in conclusion."[2]

[Section 23:1]

[1]Under the Sixth Amendment, a defendant, even in a non-jury trial, has a right to have his counsel argue his case. Herring v. New York, 422 U.S. 853, 95 S.Ct. 2550, 45 L.Ed.2d 593 (1975). But in Lewis v. State, 11 Ga. App. 14 (1), 74 S.E. 442 (1912), the court said that if a case is tried before a judge without a jury, it is discretionary for the court to permit or refuse to permit argument.

[2]Also see Rule 13.3 of the Uniform Rules for the Superior Courts; Little v. State, 157 Ga. App. 462, 463 (3), 278 S.E.2d 17 (1981).

The "final portion of § 17-8-70 is a limitation on the number of attorneys who may present closing arguments on behalf of any *one* defendant tried jointly."

Before argument begins, counsel needs to obtain a ruling from the court on whether the judge will give each of his requests to charge.[3]

On motion, the defendant is entitled to have arguments reported at his expense.[4] In *Stephens v. Hopper*,[5] the court pointed out that in a case in which the state is seeking the death penalty, arguments of counsel should be taken down by a court reporter. However, the failure to have closing arguments transcribed is not reversible error unless the defendant is prejudiced by the failure to do so.[6]

The proper time to object to statements made by opposing counsel during argument is at the time they are made. This gives the court an opportunity to take any necessary action. Waiting until the end of closing argument to move for a mistrial because of statements made by the prosecutor during closing has been held untimely.[7]

In *Hall v. State*,[8] the court concluded that "a mere objection to alleged improper argument . . . raises on appeal *only* the issue of whether the trial court erred in failing to sustain the objection so as to require . . . counsel to desist from the argument, not whether the trial court erred in failing to take any other additional curative actions."

See § 23:2, infra, on who is entitled to make a closing argument.

§ 23:2 Opening argument and concluding argument

Prior to July 1, 2005, O.C.G.A. § 17-8-71 provided that the prosecution is entitled to opening and concluding argument only if the defense presents evidence other than the testimony of the

---

[3]It is error for the trial judge to refuse to inform counsel of which of his requests to charge will be given. Evans v. State, 146 Ga. App. 480, 246 S.E.2d 482 (1978). Also see United States v. Bass, 425 F.2d 161 (7th Cir. 1970); United States v. Mendoza, 473 F.2d 697, 700 (5th Cir. 1973).

[4]Dumas v. State, 131 Ga. App. 79, 83, 205 S.E.2d 119 (1974). Where the district attorney makes improper remarks in argument after motion to have argument taken down at defendant's expense has been denied, the case should be reversed. Carson v. State, 136 Ga. App. 572 (1), 222 S.E.2d 120 (1975).

[5]Stephens v. Hopper, 241 Ga. 596, 600 (2), 247 S.E.2d 92 (1978).

[6]E.g., Ellis v. State, 137 Ga. App. 834, 836 (1), 224 S.E.2d 799 (1976).

[7]Butler v. State, 273 Ga. 380 (8), 541 S.E.2d 653 (2001). In the absence of a timely objection, the issue is deemed waived on appeal. See e.g., Carson v. State, 259 Ga. App. 21(3), 576 S.E.2d 12 (2002) (overruled on other grounds by, Watson v. State, 297 Ga. 718, 777 S.E.2d 677 (2015)).

[8]Hall v. State, 180 Ga. App. 881, 883 (3), 350 S.E.2d 801 (1986).

defendant. After that date, however, the law was amended to provide that the prosecuting attorney shall open and conclude the argument to the jury regardless of whether or not the defense has presented any evidence.[1] The defendant shall be entitled to make a closing argument prior to the concluding argument of the prosecuting attorney.[2] In cases where the death penalty may be imposed, the prosecuting attorney shall open and the defendant shall conclude the argument presented during the sentencing stage of trial.[3]

If a defendant is not a lawyer and is represented by counsel, he or she has no right to make a closing argument.[4]

Rule 13.3 of the Uniform Rules for the Superior Courts provides as follows:

"13.3 Number of Arguments

"Not more than two attorneys shall be permitted to argue any case for any party except by leave of court; in no event shall more than one attorney for each party be heard in concluding argument."[5]

In *Wakily v. State,*[6] the court held that the word "concluding" in the rule and the statute refers "to the concluding portion of final argument." In *Goforth v. Wigley,*[7] the court explained that closing arguments to a jury following the presentation of the evidence by the parties "generally include an 'opening' and a 'conclusion' and an argument in between." Adopting the reasoning of the Court of Appeals in *Limbrick v. State,*[8] the Supreme Court in *Sheriff v. State*[9] held that the limitation of one attorney in closing argument applied only to the side having the "last say". Accordingly, the court reversed a trial court's order which prohibited the defense from dividing its portion of closing argument, the "argument in between," between two lawyers. The court stated: "The right to make a closing argument to the jury is an important one, and abridgment of this right is not to be tolerated. Harm requiring that a defendant be given a new trial is presumed when the right is erroneously denied, and the presumption of harm, though not absolute, is not readily overcome. [Cits.] The presump-

---

[Section 23:2]

[1]O.C.G.A. § 17-8-71.

[2]O.C.G.A. § 17-8-71.

[3]O.C.G.A. § 17-10-2(a)(2).

[4]Vick v. State, 237 Ga. App. 762(2), 516 S.E.2d 815 (1999).

[5]O.C.G.A. § 17-8-70 contains a like provision. Also see Rule 13.1 of the Uniform Rules for the Superior Courts; Little v. State, 157 Ga. App. 462, 463 (3), 278 S.E.2d 17 (1981).

[6]Wakily v. State, 225 Ga. App. 56, 59 (6), 483 S.E.2d 313 (1997).

[7]Goforth v. Wigley, 178 Ga. App. 558, 561 (3), 343 S.E.2d 788 (1986).

[8]Limbrick v. State, 152 Ga. App. 615, 263 S.E.2d 502 (1979).

[9]Sheriff v. State, 277 Ga. 182 (2), 587 S.E.2d 27 (2003).

tion of harm may fall when the denial of the right is not complete and only in those extreme cases in which the evidence of a defendant's guilt is so overwhelming that it renders any other version of events virtually without belief. [Cits.]"[10] Because the evidence in *Sheriff* was not "so overwhelming" as to render "any other version of events virtually without belief," the court concluded that the harm done to the defense required a new trial.[11]

In *Bradham v. State*,[12] the Georgia Supreme Court held that a trial court does not abuse its discretion when it allows the state to waive its opening portion of closing argument and reserve to its final argument the entire presentation of both fact and law. Apparently, the amendment to O.C.G.A. § 17-8-71 will not change the rule announced in *Bradham*. In *Warren v. State*,[13] the Georgia Court of Appeals, while critical of the disadvantage a defendant faces when trying to conduct a closing argument without having first heard the basic position of the state, concluded nonetheless that it was bound to follow *Bradham*. However, there is nothing in *Bradham* which suggests that the state has the *right* to waive its opening portion of final argument. It would certainly seem to be the better and fairer practice to require the state on a proper motion by the defense to make a full and fair opening and devote its concluding portion of final argument to rebuttal. This is the rule in federal court.[14]

---

[10]Sheriff v. State, 277 Ga. 182 (2), 587 S.E.2d 27 (2003) citing Hayes v. State, 268 Ga. 809, 813 (7), 493 S.E.2d 169 (1997). Although in Willis v. State, 243 Ga. 185 (12) 253 S.E.2d 70 (1979) the court held that the defendant's rights were not violated where the trial court allowed only one attorney for each side to argue, it appears that in light of Sheriff any restriction on the use of counsel during final argument which conflicts with either the Uniform Rules or O.C.G.A. § 17-8-70 will be subject to close scrutiny.

[11]Sheriff v. State, 277 Ga. 182, 188, 587 S.E.2d 27 (2003) (quoting Hayes v. State, 268 Ga. 809, 813 (7), 493 S.E.2d 169 (1997)). See Brown v. State, 288 Ga. 902, 708 S.E.2d 294 (2011).

[12]Bradham v. State, 243 Ga. 638(2), 256 S.E.2d 331 (1979). At the time *Bradham* was decided there was case law which said that in those cases

where counsel chose to waive the opening portion of concluding argument, counsel was required to outline for opposing counsel the legal authorities upon which the argument was to be based and, if in concluding argument counsel raised new points, opposing counsel could ask for rebuttal. Fort v. State, 3 Ga. App. 448(2), 60 S.E. 282 (1908). See Hill v. State, 73 Ga. App. 293, 36 S.E.2d 191 (1945).

[13]Warren v. State, 281 Ga. App. 490, 636 S.E.2d 671 (2006). The Georgia Supreme Court has declined to adopt the federal practice and has ruled that a trial court may permit the state to waive its initial closing argument. Lewis v. State, 283 Ga. 191(3), 657 S.E.2d 854 (2008).

[14]Fed. R. Crim. P. 29.1. See e.g., U.S. v. Garcia, 94 F.3d 57 (2d Cir. 1996); U.S. v. Byrd, 834 F.2d 145 (8th Cir. 1987); U.S. v. Sarmiento, 744 F.2d 755 (11th Cir. 1984).

§ 23:3 Time limit on argument

O.C.G.A. § 17-8-72 provides that in misdemeanor cases neither the prosecuting attorney nor the defense counsel shall be entitled to more than one-half hour for argument. In non-capital felonies, each side is limited to one hour; in capital felonies, counsel for each side is limited to two hours. Rule 13 of the Uniform Rules for the Superior Courts provides that in felony cases in which the death penalty is sought, each side is given two hours. In all other felony cases, each side has one hour. In misdemeanor cases each side is given 30 minutes. However, in *Hayes v. State*,[1] the Georgia Supreme Court held that whenever, by statute, a defendant could be given a death sentence, the defendant is entitled to two hours for closing argument, even though the district attorney is not seeking the death sentence. In *Hayes* the court affirmed the conviction of three defendants for murder where the trial judge limited the total time of defense's argument to 30 minutes for each defendant. The majority concluded that the error was harmless. In *Chapman v. State*,[2] the Georgia Supreme Court held that it is error as a matter of law for the trial court to limit each of two defendants, being tried jointly for murder, to 45 minutes where the death penalty was not being sought. The court reasoned that O.C.G.A. § 17-8-73 requires that "in cases involving capital felonies, counsel shall be limited to two hours for each side." For purposes of that Code section, malice murder and felony murder (charges the defendant faced) are capital felonies even when the death penalty is not sought. In *Monroe v. State*,[3] the court held that "capital felony" as used in O.C.G.A. § 17-8-73 includes those cases in which the defendant is being tried for murder even though the death penalty is not being sought.

Nevertheless, counsel may be able to obtain an extension of time where the request is properly made before argument begins, under O.C.G.A. § 17-8-74, which provides as follows:

"If, before argument begins, counsel on either side applies to the court for an extension of the time prescribed for argument and states in his place or on oath, in the discretion of the court, that he cannot do the case justice within the time prescribed and that it will require for that purpose, additional time, stating how much additional time will be necessary, the court shall grant such extension of time as may seem reasonable and proper,

---

[Section 23:3]

[1]Hayes v. State, 268 Ga. 809, 813 (7), 493 S.E.2d 169 (1997). Accord, Massey v. State, 270 Ga. 76, 78 (3), 508 S.E.2d 149 (1998); Monroe v. State, 272 Ga. 201 (2), 528 S.E.2d 504 (2000).

See Brown v. State, 288 Ga. 902, 708 S.E.2d 294 (2011).

[2]Chapman v. State, 273 Ga. 865, 869 (3), 548 S.E.2d 278 (2001).

[3]Monroe v. State, 272 Ga. 201 (2), 528 S.E.2d 504 (2000).

provided that the extension of time granted in misdemeanor cases or cases brought up from inferior judicatories shall not exceed 30 minutes."[4]

Counsel must be careful to comply with O.C.G.A. § 17-8-74 if he expects to obtain additional time for argument.[5] However, in *Carter v. State*,[6] the Georgia Supreme Court held that the Uniform Rules for the Superior Courts do not prevent the trial judge "from exercising [his] discretion [in granting] a short period of additional time to counsel who has failed to make a pre-argument request, when . . . the purpose is merely to allow counsel to reach the logical conclusion of his closing argument."

§ 23:4 Reading law

In *Conklin v. State*,[1] the Georgia Supreme Court held that in future criminal cases, as well as civil cases, "the jury shall receive the law *exclusively* from the trial judge," and reading law to the court in the presence of the jury during the time for argument of the case constitutes reversible error. However, this rule does not prevent counsel from citing and discussing relevant law which the court is going to give in charge, and counsel has a right to state his legal position to the jury so long as he does not misstate the law.[2]

§ 23:5 Scope of argument—General (background)

In making his argument, counsel can use figurative speech.[1] Flights of oratory are proper as well as the use of well-established historical facts and principles of divine law[2] "relating to transactions of men as may be appropriate to the case."[3] The use of false logic does not require rebuke.[4] Counsel's illustrations may be as various as the resources of his genius and his argument as full

---

[4]Rule 13.2 of the Uniform Rules for the Superior Courts.

[5]Bloodworth v. State, 161 Ga. 332, 333 (4), 131 S.E. 80 (1925); Hand v. State, 88 Ga. App. 775 (2)(a), 77 S.E.2d 746 (1953).

[6]Carter v. State, 263 Ga. 401, 402 (3), 435 S.E.2d 42 (1993).

[Section 23:4]

[1]Conklin v. State, 254 Ga. 558, 570, 331 S.E.2d 532 (1985). Accord, Whitsell v. State, 179 Ga. App. 358 (1), 346 S.E.2d 130 (1986).

[2]Freels v. State, 195 Ga. App. 609, 611 (2), 394 S.E.2d 405 (1990).

[Section 23:5]

[1]Patterson v. State, 124 Ga. 408, 409, 52 S.E. 534 (1905). Here the district attorney argued that the "blood of this dead man calls upon you to punish this man and protect his family." The case was affirmed.

[2]Western & Atlantic R. Co. v. York, 128 Ga. 687, 689, 58 S.E. 183 (1907).

[3]Hicks v. State, 256 Ga. 715, 731 (23), 352 S.E.2d 762 (1987).

[4]Johnson v. State, 187 Ga. App. 803, 804 (4), 371 S.E.2d 419 (1988); Reeves v. State, 192 Ga. App. 12, 13, 383 S.E.2d 613 (1989).

and profound as his learning can make it.[5] He may quote from memory or read brief extracts from literary or historical matter to illustrate the points of his argument[6] or refer to "well-established historical facts . . . [so] long as he does not introduce 'extrinsic and prejudicial matters' which have no basis in the evidence in the case."[7] Likewise, counsel may refer to facts of well-known cases in considering evidence of the case being tried.[8] Counsel may draw deductions from the evidence, and there is no basis for objection if the deductions are illogical or unreasonable, but this is a matter for reply by adverse counsel.[9] So long as testimony, to which no objection has been made, remains in the record, it is the privilege of counsel to comment upon it, regardless of its impropriety.[10] Also, the Georgia Court of Appeals has held that counsel may argue that all potential jurors of a certain kind were stricken.[11] However, in *Joseph v. State*,[12] the court held that "what occurred during voir dire is not evidence and therefore should not be raised in closing argument."

It is improper for counsel to inform the jury that the action was originally instituted against two defendants and that a motion for a directed verdict has been granted to one and the case has proceeded against the other.[13] In *Luke v. State*,[14] the court held that it was improper for the prosecution to argue that if a case had not been made out against a defendant, the court would have directed a verdict of not guilty.

---

[5]Mitchum v. State, 11 Ga. 615, 631 (1852). This includes references to notorious defendants in well publicized cases such as Charles Manson as well as historical facts provided the argument does not seek to introduce "extrinsic and prejudicial matters". Robinson v. State, 257 Ga. 194, 196 (4), 357 S.E.2d 74 (1987); Dixon v. State, 285 Ga. 312 (5)(a), 677 S.E.2d 76 (2009).

[6]Quattlebaum v. State, 119 Ga. 433, 435, 46 S.E. 677 (1904). He may quote from the Bible. Ferrell v. State, 149 Ga. App. 405, 409, 254 S.E.2d 404 (1979).

[7]Robinson v. State, 257 Ga. 194, 196 (4), 357 S.E.2d 74 (1987).

[8]Jordan v. State, 172 Ga. App. 496, 497 (2), 323 S.E.2d 657 (1984).

[9]Morgan v. State, 267 Ga. 203, 204 (1), 476 S.E.2d 747 (1996); Owens v. State, 120 Ga. 209, 210 (3), 47 S.E. 545 (1904). In Clark v. State, 146 Ga. App. 697 (3), 247 S.E.2d 221 (1978), it was said that since defendant on cross-examination strongly contradicted some of his direct testimony, the district attorney could refer to him as a "liar."

[10]McCluskey v. American Oil Co., 225 Ga. 63, 64, 165 S.E.2d 830 (1969).

[11]Giddens v. State, 156 Ga. App. 258, 260 (2), 274 S.E.2d 595 (1980).

[12]Joseph v. State, 231 Ga. App. 399, 403 (2), 498 S.E.2d 808 (1998). Accord, Sterling v. State, 267 Ga. 209, 212 (8), 477 S.E.2d 807 (1996).

[13]Uhls v. Old Ben Coal Corporation, 281 Ill. App. 254, 1935 WL 3655 (4th Dist. 1935), appeal denied; C.J.S. Trial § 179 (1955), points out that earlier events in the history of the case in court, not included in the evidence admitted, are not to be used by counsel in arguing to the jury.

[14]Luke v. State, 236 Ga. App. 543, 545 (4), 512 S.E.2d 39 (1999).

While Georgia courts have permitted a broad latitude in argument, certain matters may not be argued.[15] It is improper for either counsel to urge his personal beliefs as to the defendant's guilt or the truthfulness of a witness.[16]

It is error for counsel to relate to the jury comments that a witness made to him privately.[17] It is also error for counsel to argue that a witness is not worthy of belief because she is living with a man to whom she is not married.[18]

It is improper for an attorney to minimize the jury's sense of responsibility in reaching a verdict.[19]

In *Williams v. State*,[20] the court stated that when "an improper argument is made, whether substantive or procedural, opposing counsel has a duty to act by interposing an objection" and contemporaneously moving for a mistrial if it is to serve as a basis for reversal[21] in order to afford the trial judge the opportunity to take remedial action.[22] In *Sears v. State*,[23] the court pointed out that when "no timely objection is interposed, the test

---

[15]Former Superior Court Rule 19 stated that parties were limited to a discussion of the law and facts involved. See A.B.A. Standards, The Defense Function, Vol. I, Standards 4-7.8 and 4-7.9.

The same rules are found in A.B.A. Standards, The Prosecution Function, Vol. I, Standards 3-5.8 and 3-5.9. See also A.B.A. Standards, Special Functions of the Trial Judge, Vol. I, Chapter 6. Griffin v. California, 380 U.S. 609, 85 S.Ct. 1229, 14 L.Ed.2d 106 (1965). The Griffin case is criticized in Ayer, "The Fifth Amendment and the Inference of Guilt From Silence: Griffin v. California After Fifteen Years," 78 Mich. L. R. 841 (1980).

[16]Metts v. State, 270 Ga. 481, 484 (4), 511 S.E.2d 508 (1999); Broznack v. State, 109 Ga. 514(3), 35 S.E. 123 (1900); Johnson v. State, 150 Ga. 67(1), 102 S.E. 439 (1920); Wells v. State, 194 Ga. 70 (5), 20 S.E.2d 580 (1942); United States v. Brown, 451 F.2d 1231 (5th Cir. 1971); United States v. Lamerson, 457 F.2d 371 (5th Cir. 1972); Burnett v. State, 240 Ga. 681, 686(5), 242 S.E.2d 79 (1978); United States v. Butera, 677 F.2d 1376 (11th Cir. 1982).

[17]Johnson v. State, 238 Ga. 59, 60, 230 S.E.2d 869 (1976).

See Annot., "Propriety and Prejudicial Effect of Prosecutor's Argument to Jury Indicating His Belief or Knowledge as to Guilt of Accused," 88 A.L.R.3d 449 (1978); and see also 41 A.L.R.Fed. 10 (1979); Annot., "Propriety and Prejudicial Effect of Prosecutor's Argument to Jury Indicating That He Has Additional Evidence of Defendant's Guilt Which He Did Not Deem Necessary to Present," 90 A.L.R.3d 646 (1979).

[18]Smith v. State, 235 Ga. 327, 328 (2)(a), 219 S.E.2d 440 (1975).

[19]Smith v. State, 270 Ga. 240, 247 (11), 510 S.E.2d 1 (1998).

[20]Williams v. State, 251 Ga. 749, 801, 312 S.E.2d 40 (1983). See Ellington v. State, 292 Ga. 109, 735 S.E.2d 736 (2012).

[21]Kyler v. State, 270 Ga. 81, 508 S.E.2d 152 (1998) (abrogated on other grounds by Mann v. State, 273 Ga. 366, 541 S.E.2d 645 (2001)).

[22]Mullins v. State, 270 Ga. 450 (2), 511 S.E.2d 165 (1999).

[23]Sears v. State, 268 Ga. 759, 765(15), 493 S.E.2d 180 (1997). Accord, Elam v. State, 211 Ga. App. 739, 740(3), 440 S.E.2d 511 (1994); Barnes v. State, 269 Ga. 345, 496 S.E.2d 674 (1998).

for reversible error is not simply whether or not the argument is objectionable, or even if it might have contributed to the verdict; the test is whether the improper argument in reasonable probability changed the result of the trial." An exception to this general rule exists in cases where the death penalty is sought. As explained by the Georgia Supreme Court in *Sears v. State*,[24] its application is appropriate "only in the context of appellate review of a criminal case in which the death penalty was imposed. [cits.]"

If a party wishes to object to the opposing party's argument, the objection must be made "when the impropriety occurs at trial, when the trial judge may take remedial action to cure any possible error."[25] In *Bolden v. State*,[26] the court pointed out that "[w]hen an improper argument is made, opposing counsel may obtain appellate review of the trial court's ruling simply by objecting. . . . [T]he defendant is not required to renew his objection or move for a mistrial after the trial court overrules the objection." Counsel should also note that "there is no authority for the application of plain error review to comments made by the lawyers during opening statements [or closing argument]."[27]

In *Hayes v. State*,[28] the court pointed out that it is improper for either the prosecution or the defendant to make the classic "golden rule" argument which invites jurors to place themselves in the victim's or the defendant's place with regard to the crime itself. However, the court held that an argument asking jurors to put themselves in the place of a witness (who took a statement of the defendant) is not a violation of the golden rule ban. More recently, in *Shaw v. State*,[29] the court found the prosecution's statement that a conviction would allow Hall County citizens to "take the first step toward being free of drugs" to be an "appeal to the jury to convict for the safety of the community," and therefore not in violation of the golden rule ban.

---

[24]Sears v. State, 268 Ga. 759, 765(15), 493 S.E.2d 180 (1997); Barnes v. State, 269 Ga. 345, 496 S.E.2d 674 (1998). The Court of Appeals had applied the "reasonable probability" test in several non-capital cases. In Mullins v. State, 270 Ga. 450(2), 511 S.E.2d 165 (1999), the Supreme Court overruled those cases.

[25]Richards v. State, 232 Ga. App. 584, 588 (4), 502 S.E.2d 519 (1998).

[26]Bolden v. State, 272 Ga. 1, 2, 525 S.E.2d 690 (2000). However, if a defendant objects and moves for a mistrial, should the court deny the motion but provide some curative instruction, the issue can only be preserved for appeal if the defense renews its objection. Wells v. State, 243 Ga. App. 629, 631(3), 534 S.E.2d 106 (2000).

[27]Crayton v. State, 298 Ga. 792, 794, 784 S.E.2d 343 (2016).

[28]Hayes v. State, 236 Ga. App. 617, 619(3), 512 S.E.2d 294 (1999). But cf. Hines v. State, 246 Ga. App. 835, 837 (3), 541 S.E.2d 410 (2000).

[29]Shaw v. State, 265 Ga. App. 451, 453, 594 S.E.2d 393 (2004). Accord, Navarro v. State, 279 Ga. App. 311, 630 S.E.2d 893 (2006). See United States v. Durham, 659 Fed. Appx. 990 (11th Cir. 2016).

In *Mize v. State*,[30] the court pointed out that "[a]nalogizing a defendant or a defendant's case to a well-known defendant or case is permissible during argument if the analogy is supported by facts in evidence." However, in *Bell v. State*,[31] the Georgia Supreme Court held that references to extraneous and "prejudicially inflammatory material" not in the evidence exceed the wide latitude generally afforded during closing arguments.

In *Kirkland v. State*,[32] in a four to three decision, the Georgia Supreme Court approved of counsel showing visual aids on which were written the text of expected legal instructions.

§ 23:6   Scope of argument—Possibility of clemency, probation, parole, pardon—Mandatory mistrial

Except as hereinafter set out below, O.C.G.A. § 17-8-76 provides that "[n]o attorney in a criminal case shall argue to or in the presence of the jury that a defendant, if convicted, may not be required to suffer the full penalty imposed by the court or jury because [of] pardon, parole, or clemency. . . . If counsel for either side in a criminal case . . . [violates this rule] opposing counsel shall have the right immediately to request the court to declare a mistrial, in which case it shall be mandatory upon the court to declare a mistrial." However, in *Freeman v. State*,[1] the court held that the trial court did not err in permitting the prosecutor to argue "to the jury that it was *not* to consider punishment, including whether . . . [the defendant] received 'prison time or probation.' " (Emphasis in original.)

Nevertheless, O.C.G.A. § 17-10-31(b) provides that during the sentencing phase of a death case, "counsel for the state and the accused may present argument and the trial judge may instruct the jury" on the definitions of life without parole and life imprisonment.

§ 23:7   Scope of argument—Prosecutor—Permissible scope

The Georgia courts have demonstrated an almost unbelievable reluctance to condemn some material in arguments which seems so prejudicial as to perhaps violate the defendant's right to a fair

---

[30]Mize v. State, 269 Ga. 646, 654 (8), 501 S.E.2d 219 (1998) (quoting Carr v. State, 267 Ga. 547, 480 S.E.2d 583 (1997)).

[31]Bell v. State, 263 Ga. 776, 439 S.E.2d 480 (1994).

[32]Kirkland v. State, 271 Ga. 217, 219 (3), 518 S.E.2d 687 (1999).

[Section 23:6]

[1]Freeman v. State, 245 Ga. App. 384, 385 (3), 537 S.E.2d 776 (2000).

trial as guaranteed by the Constitution.[1] For example, in *Martin v. State*,[2] comparing the defendant with the Viet Cong and saying that the possibility of the defendant returning to society would be a greater danger than the threat of communism was not held to be error in the absence of a motion for mistrial. In other cases it has been held not to be error for the district attorney to compare the murder involved in a case to the Nazi extermination of Jews,[3] to argue that a rapist should be convicted for the protection of women,[4] or to state that the "world must know how we deal with murderers who come into our county for the express purpose of assassination."[5]

In *Scott v. State*,[6] the court held there was no error in permitting the prosecutor to argue to the jury to "stomp . . . drug abuse out now," or to refer to cocaine as a "slow killer" and analogizing the presence of cocaine to the "Black Plague."

Georgia is not alone in the broad scope of argument permitted. The Fifth Circuit has said that the unflattering "characterization of a defendant does not require a new trial when such descriptions are supported by the evidence."[7] Thus, it has been held that the characterization of a defendant as a "dope pusher" may be proper.[8]

In *Laney v. State*,[9] the court held that the trial court did not err in permitting the prosecutor to use the word "murder" instead of "homicide."

It has been held that a prosecutor can characterize the defendant as a brute, a beast, an animal, or a mad dog who does not deserve to live, or argue that if the defendant is found not guilty by reason of insanity, he can only be kept in the hospital for a year and warn the jury they had better spend that year fortifying their homes "because you will have turned loose a

---

[Section 23:7]

[1]Generally, see Annot., 40 L.Ed.2d 886 (1975).

[2]Martin v. State, 223 Ga. 649, 650 (2), 157 S.E.2d 458 (1967).

[3]Forehand v. State, 235 Ga. 295 (1), 219 S.E.2d 378 (1975).

[4]Powell v. State, 179 Ga. 401, 411 (4), 176 S.E. 29 (1934). In Shelton v. State, 146 Ga. App. 763, 247 S.E.2d 580 (1978), an assault with intent to rape case, the district attorney argued that there would be another victim, "we just don't know her name yet." There had been evidence of two prior

charges for the same offense as well as a rape charge and some other offenses. The conviction was affirmed.

[5]Chenault v. State, 234 Ga. 216, 223 (7), 215 S.E.2d 223 (1975).

[6]Scott v. State, 240 Ga. App. 50, 51 (3), 522 S.E.2d 535 (1999); Jennings v. State, 282 Ga. 679(4), 653 S.E.2d 17 (2007).

[7]United States v. Malatesta, 583 F.2d 748, 759 (5th Cir. 1978).

[8]United States v. Metz, 608 F.2d 147, 158 (5th Cir. 1979).

[9]Laney v. State, 271 Ga. 194, 196 (7), 515 S.E.2d 610 (1999).

sociopath."[10] The district attorney can further state that "if you turn him loose, who's going to be the next victim—one of your relatives, one of your mothers, grandmothers?"[11]

In *Boyle v. State*,[12] defense counsel's opening statement listed the evidence which would be presented. After the state rested, the defendant "took the stand . . . and testified as defense counsel had outlined in opening." The defendant also testified that he saw the victim being robbed. In closing, the state commented on defense counsel's failure to include the last statement in opening. The state concluded, "Could it be that nobody knew except this defendant what was going to come out of his mouth?" The appellate court found no error. If a defendant testifies, it has been held proper for the district attorney to comment on the defendant's failure to refute the testimony of a state's witness.[13] Where a defendant offers no evidence and a conviction is authorized, unless the defendant explains his recent possession of stolen property, it is permissible for the district attorney to argue that the defendant did not explain how he came into possession of the property belonging to victims.[14] Also, in the 1981 case of *Montgomery v. State*,[15] the court held that where the defendant did not testify, it was not error for the district attorney to argue that "there is no evidence other than the evidence presented by the state." If a defendant testifies that a person present in the courtroom could contradict certain evidence of the state, it is

---

[10]Berryhill v. State, 235 Ga. 549, 552 (7), 221 S.E.2d 185 (1975). See Bruce v. State, 142 Ga. App. 211, 215, 235 S.E.2d 606 (1977).

[11]Lumpkin v. State, 136 Ga. App. 828, 829, 222 S.E.2d 669 (1975).

[12]Boyle v. State, 241 Ga. App. 883, 885 (2), 528 S.E.2d 303 (2000).

[13]Gosha v. State, 239 Ga. 37, 235 S.E.2d 527 (1977). Here the defendant testified to an alibi; in rebuttal the state put up two additional witnesses who testified to seeing the defendant at scene of the crime. The defendant did not retake the stand and deny his presence. Accord, Mention v. State, 171 Ga. App. 116, 117 (3), 318 S.E.2d 765 (1984). See Berry v. State, 123 Ga. App. 616 (1), 182 S.E.2d 166 (1971); Felker v. State, 144 Ga. App. 458 (1), 241 S.E.2d 576 (1978).

In Head v. State, 160 Ga. App. 4, 8 (8), 285 S.E.2d 735 (1981), the court held that it was not error for the district attorney to state that "an in-nocent person would have contacted the prosecution to say that he could not have committed the crime because he was elsewhere."

See Perry v. State, 232 Ga. App. 484, 487 (1)(b), 500 S.E.2d 923 (1998).

[14]Valenzuela v. State, 157 Ga. App. 247, 250 (3), 277 S.E.2d 56 (1981).

In Brown v. State, 157 Ga. App. 473, 476, 278 S.E.2d 31 (1981), the court in a case involving stolen property stated that it is not error for the district attorney to reflect on the failure of the defense to present any evidence to rebut the proof presented by the state.

In Davis v. State, 161 Ga. App. 358 (2), 288 S.E.2d 631 (1982), the court applied the same rule to a burglary case.

[15]Montgomery v. State, 159 Ga. App. 446, 448 (6), 283 S.E.2d 663 (1981). Accord, Miller v. State, 240 Ga. App. 18, 19 (2), 522 S.E.2d 519 (1999).

proper for the district attorney to ask why the witness was not called to rebut the state's evidence.[16] However, it is improper for the state during closing to ask the defendant's girlfriend to stand up and make her presence known even though she had not testified at trial. Although the defendant had identified her as someone who could have provided exculpatory evidence during his testimony at trial, by choosing to make a demonstration of the witness's availability during closing, the prosecutor had, in effect, introduced evidence at a time when the defendant was unable to confront it.[17]

In cases where the defendant has not testified, it has been held that it is not error for the district attorney to argue that the defendant has not presented any evidence in rebuttal of that presented by the state.[18] It has been emphasized that "[w]hat is prohibited is a comment that the defendant could have 'denied,' 'explained,' or otherwise 'disputed' the state's case against him."[19]

In *United States v. Robinson*,[20] the United States Supreme Court held that the prosecuting attorney did not err in telling the jury that the defendant could have taken the stand and explained things to you, where defense counsel commented during closing argument that the government had not permitted the defendant to explain his actions.

In the 1982 case of *Ranger v. State*,[21] the Georgia Supreme Court held that the trial judge did not err in overruling an objection to the district attorney's argument. Apparently the defendant did not testify. The district attorney argued that defense counsel "is going to argue a whole lot of facts . . . , but the defense has put forward no explanation of any accident. . . . [T]here is no evidence before you in this case of any accident." The defendant contended that these comments violated his Fifth Amendment right not to incriminate himself and his statutory right not to have any comment made on his failure to testify. The Georgia Supreme Court found the Fifth Circuit case of *United States v.*

---

[16]Weaver v. State, 145 Ga. App. 194, 196 (4), 243 S.E.2d 560 (1978). Cf. Franklin v. State, 208 Ga. App. 740, 741 (3), 431 S.E.2d 733 (1993).

[17]Mowoe v. State, 328 Ga. App. 536, 759 S.E.2d 663 (2014). See also Luke v. State, 324 Ga. App. 531, 751 S.E.2d 180 (2013) (improper for prosecutor to make reference to a co-defendant's involvement in an unrelated gang shooting which had not been brought up during trial).

[18]McCord v. State, 268 Ga. 842,

843 (3), 493 S.E.2d 129 (1997); Lowe v. State, 245 Ga. App. 659, 661 (3), 538 S.E.2d 552 (2000); Gilstrap v. State, 162 Ga. App. 841, 845 (9), 292 S.E.2d 495 (1982); Lowe v. State, 253 Ga. 308, 310 (1), 319 S.E.2d 834 (1984).

[19]Smith v. State, 170 Ga. App. 673, 674, 317 S.E.2d 626 (1984).

[20]United States v. Robinson, 485 U.S. 25, 108 S.Ct. 864, 99 L.Ed.2d 23 (1988).

[21]Ranger v. State, 249 Ga. 315, 319 (3), 290 S.E.2d 63 (1982).

Rochan[22] to be directly in point. In *Rochan,* the court said that to "reverse for improper comment . . . we must find one of two things: [1] that 'the prosecutor's manifest intention was to comment upon the accused's failure to testify' or [2] that the remark was 'of such a character that the jury would naturally and necessarily take it to be a comment on the failure of the accused to testify.' "In explanation of the first point the court said, "We cannot find that the prosecutor manifestly intended to comment on the defendant's failure to testify, if some other explanation for his remark is equally plausible." In discussing the second point, the court said "that a prosecutor's comment on the uncontradicted state of the evidence would not necessarily be construed by the jury as a comment on the defendant's failure to testify." The *Rochan* case then found no error where the United States Attorney had argued, "Now ladies and gentlemen of the jury, what did we hear from the defense in this case? Well, we heard that Mr. Rochan was a model prisoner." The *Rochan* case does make the point that a closer question would have been presented if the prosecutor had used the word "defendant" rather than the word "defense." The *Ranger* opinion pointed out that, in this case, the district attorney had used the word "defense" and not "defendant." The court attached no importance to the fact that since the defendant was the only surviving eyewitness, any such evidence would, of necessity, have come from the defendant.

In a later 1982 case of *Hall v. State,*[23] the Georgia Court of Appeals found no error where the defendant had not testified and the district attorney "remarked several times that the defendant had presented no evidence." Likewise, it has been held that it is not error for the district attorney to state in argument that the state's evidence has not been rebutted or that the state's evidence is uncontradicted and unrefuted.[24] Where a defendant testifies, "the prosecutor may comment on the defendant's failure to explain incriminating evidence."[25] It is permissible for the prosecuting attorney to ask the jury to "make them [the defense] explain" various pieces of circumstantial evidence.[26]

Apparently, if there is evidence that a defendant employs a fingerprint expert, the district attorney may argue that the defendant would have called the expert to testify if the results of

---

[22]United States v. Rochan, 563 F.2d 1246, 1249 (5th Cir. 1977). Accord, Russell v. State, 184 Ga. App. 657, 362 S.E.2d 392 (1987).

[23]Hall v. State, 163 Ga. App. 515, 517 (4), 295 S.E.2d 194 (1982).

[24]Jones v. State, 168 Ga. App. 652, 653 (2), 310 S.E.2d 17 (1983).

[25]Wells v. State, 200 Ga. App. 104, 106 (2), 407 S.E.2d 86 (1991).

[26]Johnson v. State, 271 Ga. 375, 383 (15)(a), 519 S.E.2d 221 (1999).

his testing had been beneficial to the defendant.[27]

In *Wynn v. State,*[28] the court held that it was not error for the district attorney to point out in argument generally, without direct reference to the exercise of the spousal privilege, that the state had no power to call the spouse of the defendant.

In *Tucker v. Francis,*[29] the Eleventh Circuit held that the Fifth Amendment did not prevent a district attorney from commenting, during closing argument, in a capital case, on the failure of the defendant to testify at the innocence-guilt phase of the case, and it is proper for the district attorney to inform the jury that it would be concerned only with the guilt or innocence of the defendant and not with punishment.[30] In *Hance v. State,*[31] the court approved a statement by the district attorney "that if they returned a verdict recommending death they [the jury] would not be responsible for Hance's execution any more than would be the police officers involved, the grand jurors, the prison officials, the DA himself or the trial judge. Rather, . . . Hance himself bore the ultimate responsibility because it was he who committed the crime which authorized imposition of the death sentence." In *Potts v. State,*[32] the court held that the "prosecutor did not impermissibly trivialize the task of the sentencing jury by arguing that Potts himself—not the jury—was ultimately responsible for the crimes he committed and for whatever punishment he received."

The district attorney may call the attention of the jury to the fact that they have an interest in proper law enforcement[33] and may appeal to the jury to convict for the safety of the community.[34] In *Waters v. State,*[35] the court, in an arson case, held that the district attorney could argue that arson increases insurance rates.

---

[27]Blige v. State, 263 Ga. 244, 430 S.E.2d 761 (1993).

[28]Wynn v. State, 168 Ga. App. 132, 135, 308 S.E.2d 392 (1983). The state may never ask the jury to draw a negative inference from a defendant's assertion that certain communications with a spouse or a physician are privileged. Willett v. State, 223 Ga. App. 866(1), 479 S.E.2d 132 (1996).

[29]Tucker v. Francis, 723 F.2d 1504 (11th Cir. 1984).

[30]Mitchell v. State, 167 Ga. App. 306, 307, 306 S.E.2d 322 (1983).

[31]Hance v. State, 254 Ga. 575, 578 (5), 332 S.E.2d 287 (1985). Cf. Hicks v. State, 256 Ga. 715, 731 (23), 352 S.E.2d 762 (1987).

[32]Potts v. State, 261 Ga. 716, 725 (27), 410 S.E.2d 89 (1991).

[33]Demps v. State, 140 Ga. App. 90, 91 (2), 230 S.E.2d 97 (1976). Cf. Davis v. State, 266 Ga. 801, 804 (8), 471 S.E.2d 191 (1996).

[34]Cummings v. State, 233 Ga. App. 806, 809 (5), 505 S.E.2d 73 (1998). See Jowers v. State, 272 Ga. App. 614, 617(3), 613 S.E.2d 14 (2005) where the Court of Appeals found no harm in prosecutor's argument to jury "send a message to the people in Columbus, Georgia that we're not going to tolerate the brutal shootings."

[35]Waters v. State, 174 Ga. App. 916, 918 (4), 331 S.E.2d 893 (1985).

Likewise, it has been held that it was not error to argue "that it was the jury's duty to convict to stem the drug problem in the area."[36] In *Burke v. State,*[37] the court held that it is proper for the district attorney to "appeal to the safety of the community and general prevention of crime." In *Blackston v. State,*[38] the court held that a district attorney may also refer to the necessity for enforcement of the law. In *Philmore v. State,*[39] the court upheld a prosecutor's appeal to the jury "to convict so as to send a message to others that criminal activities will not go unpunished."

In *O'Neal v. State,*[40] the court held that, where a prior conviction of the defendant was properly admitted, the district attorney could argue that such evidence could be considered in establishing guilt. With this background the court seems to approve an argument "that what a man does in the past can help you predict what he will do in the future."

Generally, the prosecuting attorney may refer "to the victim's family circumstances," such as the number of children in the victim's family, if supported by the evidence.[41] In *Ward v. State,*[42] the court held that it was permissible for the prosecuting attorney "to tell the jury that the victim's daughter no longer had a mother, her husband no longer had a wife and her mother had lost her daughter."

In *Williams v. State,*[43] the court held that "the prosecutor did not exceed the bounds of permissible argument by asserting that . . . [the defendant] did not deserve to have his life spared so he could go to the penitentiary and get free food, housing and medical attention, while the victim lay in her grave."

In *Stroud v. State,*[44] the court held that the "argument that a defendant represents a future danger to society is impermissible

---

[36]Head v. State, 160 Ga. App. 4, 8 (8), 285 S.E.2d 735 (1981).

[37]Burke v. State, 153 Ga. App. 769, 771 (8), 266 S.E.2d 549 (1980). Cf. Boone v. State, 234 Ga. App. 373, 374 (2), 506 S.E.2d 884 (1998). See Annot., "Propriety, under Federal Constitution, of Evidence or Argument Concerning Deterrent Effect of Death Penalty," 78 A.L.R.Fed. 553 (1986).

[38]Blackston v. State, 172 Ga. App. 172, 175 (5), 322 S.E.2d 300 (1984).

[39]Philmore v. State, 263 Ga. 67, 69 (3), 428 S.E.2d 329 (1993). See Poellnitz v. State, 296 Ga. 134, 765 S.E.2d 343 (2014). Accord, Carr v. State, 267 Ga. 547, 556 (7)(c), 480 S.E.2d 583 (1997).

[40]O'Neal v. State, 170 Ga. App. 637, 638 (2), 318 S.E.2d 66 (1984).

[41]Cargill v. State, 255 Ga. 616, 640 (26), 340 S.E.2d 891, 912-13 (1986) (citing Annot., "Propriety and Prejudicial Effect of Prosecutor's Remarks as to Victim's Age, Family Circumstances, or the Like," 50 A.L.R.3d 8 (1973)). See Goger, *Daniel's Georgia Handbook on Criminal Evidence* (2017 ed.), § 4:2, on admissibility of such evidence.

[42]Ward v. State, 262 Ga. 293, 297 (6)(g), 417 S.E.2d 130 (1992).

[43]Williams v. State, 258 Ga. 281, 288, 368 S.E.2d 742 (1988).

[44]Stroud v. State, 272 Ga. 76, 77 (2), 526 S.E.2d 344 (2000).

when a jury is determining guilt or innocence." The prosecutor may argue the future dangerousness of the defendant in the sentencing phase of a death penalty case.[45] Such an argument must be premised on evidence of future dangerousness in the record and not simply on the basis of the murder for which the defendant is on trial.[46] However, future behavior of a defendant may not be argued in a case in which a death sentence is not being sought by the state.[47] Both the Georgia Supreme Court and the Court of Appeals have concluded failure to object to such an argument constitutes deficient performance by defense counsel.[48]

It has been held that it is not error for the district attorney to remark that a defense *witness* will soon be released from prison under the guidelines of the Pardon and Parole Board.[49] In *White v. State*,[50] the court found no error where "the State's attorney . . . reasoned during his closing argument that defendant's flight from the crime scene is evidence of . . . guilt."

It is proper for the district attorney to refer to the conduct and appearance of the defendant during the trial.[51] Additionally, the district attorney is not prohibited from discussing a defendant's lack of remorse.[52]

In *Martin v. State*,[53] the defendant contended that he accidentally shot the victim. The pistol the defendant allegedly used was introduced in evidence. The appellate court affirmed the trial judge in permitting the prosecutor to invite the jurors to pull the trigger to see how difficult it is to pull it. In *Laney v. State*,[54] the court held that it was not error, during closing argument, for the prosecutor to use a five-pound bag of sugar to illustrate how much pressure it took to pull the trigger of the weapon used to kill the victim.

Also in *Laney v. State*,[55] the court found the prosecutor's argument proper when he told the jurors "this is your community"; that defense counsel had done "an excellent job" and was a very

[45]Hill v. State, 263 Ga. 37, 46 (19), 427 S.E.2d 770 (1993).

[46]Henry v. State, 278 Ga. 617 (1), 604 S.E.2d 826 (2004).

[47]Sterling v. State, 267 Ga. 209, 210 (2), 477 S.E.2d 807 (1996).

[48]Mason v. State, 274 Ga. 79(2)(c), 548 S.E.2d 298 (2001); Nickerson v. State, 248 Ga. App. 829 (2) (a), 545 S.E.2d 587 (2001). A number of cases in which prosecutors argued the "future dangerousness" of the defendant are discussed in Fulton v. State, 278 Ga. 58 (8), 597 S.E.2d 396 (2004).

[49]Cave v. State, 171 Ga. App. 22 (1), 318 S.E.2d 689 (1984).

[50]White v. State, 226 Ga. App. 822, 823 (2), 488 S.E.2d 83 (1997).

[51]E.g., Johnson v. State, 256 Ga. 588, 591, 351 S.E.2d 202 (1987).

[52]DeYoung v. State, 268 Ga. 780, 791 (15), 493 S.E.2d 157 (1997).

[53]Martin v. State, 268 Ga. 682, 686 (9), 492 S.E.2d 225 (1997).

[54]Laney v. State, 271 Ga. 194, 198 (9), 515 S.E.2d 610 (1999).

[55]Laney v. State, 271 Ga. 194, 198 (10), 515 S.E.2d 610 (1999).

good attorney; that the defendant had a "smirk" on his face during trial; and called the jury to convict for safety.

The Georgia Supreme Court did note, however, in *Bell v. State*,[56] "[a]rgument of counsel is a valuable privilege, and may not be unduly restricted. On the other hand, the court must not allow such latitude as will defeat the justice of the cause, such as introduce prejudicial matters not in evidence. The dignity of the court, and the public interest in having its courts properly conducted are involved." In *Bell*, the court reversed the defendant's conviction, because the state in closing referred to cases involving a serial rapist and a triple murder which were in no way related to the defendant or his case.

Generally, on the scope of district attorney argument, see 23A C.J.S. Criminal Law § 1081(a) (1961). See Studdard, *Daniel's Georgia Handbook on Criminal Evidence* (2018 ed.), §§ 3:4 and 4:24, on referring to the failure of the defendant to have a witness testify.

§ 23:8　Scope of argument—Limitations on prosecutor's argument

It is error for the district attorney to comment on a defendant's failure to testify,[1] or to argue that the accused did not tell the court about certain facts relating to the evidence,[2] or argue that

---

[56]Bell v. State, 263 Ga. 776, 777, 439 S.E.2d 480 (1994). See Cantrell v. State, 290 Ga. App. 651, 660 S.E.2d 468 (2008) (prosecutor's reference to the funeral of a police officer killed in the line of duty improper where it had no relation to case).

[Section 23:8]

[1]Graham v. State, 118 Ga. 807 (3), 45 S.E. 616 (1903). In Chapman v. California, 386 U.S. 18, 87 S.Ct. 824, 17 L.Ed.2d 705 (1967), the court held that the charge by the trial court judge that the jury could draw adverse inferences from the failure of the defendants to testify violated the defendants' Fifth Amendment rights as the same were made applicable to the states through the Fourteenth Amendment. However, if a defendant does testify, the prosecuting attorney may apparently point out that he failed to testify to certain facts about certain important points in the case. See Gosha

v. State, 239 Ga. 37, 235 S.E.2d 527 (1977).

But in Lockett v. Ohio, 434 U.S. 889, 98 S.Ct. 261, 54 L.Ed.2d 173 (1977), the court declined to reverse a conviction where the district attorney argued that the evidence was "unrefuted and uncontradicted" where "defense counsel had clearly focused the jury's attention" to the silence of the defendant.

In Shaw v. State, 163 Ga. App. 615, 619 (3), 294 S.E.2d 676 (1982), rev'd on other grounds, 251 Ga. 109, 303 S.E.2d 448 (1983), the court concluded that it was not reversible error for the district attorney to comment on the defendant's failure to testify where the defense had first made reference to the fact that the defendant did not testify.

[2]Salisbury v. State, 221 Ga. 718, 720 (5), 146 S.E.2d 776 (1966); Spann v. State, 126 Ga. App. 370, 371 (2), 190 S.E.2d 924 (1972). But see Mitchell v.

the accused "has no excuse."[3] However, a prosecutor's reference in closing argument to the failure of the defense to contradict evidence does not amount to an objectionable comment on the right to remain silent provided it was not intended as such by the state or a jury would necessarily infer it as such.[4] In *Pinch v. State,*[5] the court noted that it is improper for the prosecutor in a DUI case to tell the jury that had the defendant taken a breath test, "there was a chance to show sobriety." However, in *Portuondo v. Agard,*[6] the United States Supreme Court held that a prosecutor could comment that a testifying defendant's presence at trial gave the defendant an opportunity to tailor his testimony so as to harmonize it with the testimony of the other witnesses. The Georgia Supreme Court, in considering an argument that there was no evidence in support of the defendant's defense, held that the "prosecutor's remarks warrant reversal . . . [only if (1)] the prosecutor's manifest intent was to comment upon the defendant's failure to testify or (2) the remark was such that the jury would naturally and necessarily take it as comment on the defendant's failure to testify."[7] Testimony at the trial elicited by the state from a detective assigned to the case to the effect that in the time between the crime and the trial of the case, he had never been contacted by anyone regarding an alibi, that the defendant was not at the incident location at the time of the crime or that he was somewhere else at that time, was not considered a comment

---

State, 226 Ga. 450, 451 (4), 175 S.E.2d 545 (1970); Floyd v. State, 135 Ga. App. 217, 220, 217 S.E.2d 452 (1975).

Griffin v. California, 380 U.S. 609, 85 S.Ct. 1229, 14 L.Ed.2d 106 (1965), and Fontaine v. California, 390 U.S. 593, 88 S.Ct. 1229, 20 L.Ed.2d 154 (1968), held that comments by the district attorney or judge that the jury could draw adverse inference against the accused because of his failure to testify are a violation of the self-incrimination provision of the Fifth Amendment which is made applicable to the states through the Fourteenth Amendment.

[3]Spann v. State, 126 Ga. App. 370, 371 (2), 190 S.E.2d 924 (1972). But in Delvers v. State, 139 Ga. App. 119, 121, 227 S.E.2d 844 (1976), where the defendant did not testify, the court held that it was not error for the district attorney to ask where certain witnesses are and to ask the jury if the defendant would not have had alibi witnesses present if he were innocent. Cf. Haas v. State, 146 Ga. App. 729, 731 (3), 247 S.E.2d 507 (1978). In Redding v. State, 151 Ga. App. 140, 259 S.E.2d 146 (1979), a conviction was affirmed where the district attorney argued "the testimony of the victim stands unrefuted; there is not testimony to the contrary." Accord, Burgess v. State, 158 Ga. App. 593, 281 S.E.2d 337 (1981).

[4]Kilgore v. State, 300 Ga. 429, 796 S.E.2d 290 (2017).

[5]Pinch v. State, 265 Ga. App. 1, 5(4), 593 S.E.2d 1 (2003). See State v. Mitchell, 326 Ga. App. 370, 756 S.E.2d 609 (2014).

[6]Portuondo v. Agard, 529 U.S. 61, 120 S.Ct. 1119, 146 L.Ed.2d 47 (2000).

[7]Millwood v. State, 191 Ga. App. 659, 660 (2), 382 S.E.2d 430 (1989) (citing Ranger v. State, 249 Ga. 315, 319 (3), 290 S.E.2d 63 (1982)).

on the defendant's failure to testify in *Davis v. State*.[8]

Likewise, where a defendant has not put his character in evidence, it is error for the district attorney in his argument to ask, "How many times has he broken the law? How many times has he gotten away with it?"[9]

Since a defendant cannot force his wife to testify, it has been held that it is error for the district attorney to refer to the fact that the accused's wife did not testify.[10] In *Blige v. State*,[11] the court held that the district attorney could not comment on the failure of a defendant to call a particular expert witness unless there is evidence in the record of the existence of that witness and that he had been provided with material to be examined by the expert.

It is error for counsel to refer to the fact that a pardon, parole, clemency[12] or possible reversal of the case by a higher court[13] may be available. In *Spencer v. State*,[14] the court held that "[w]hile the state may not argue that the defendant might be paroled, . . . the state is permitted to argue that a defendant's probable future

---

[8]Davis v. State, 328 Ga.App. 796, 760 S.E.2d 728 (2014).

[9]Bethea v. State, 149 Ga. App. 312, 313 (2), 254 S.E.2d 468 (1979). Note, however, pursuant to O.C.G.A. § 24-5-506(b), if a defendant elects to testify, he or she "shall be sworn as any other witness and, except as provided in Code Sections 24-6-608 and 24-6-609, may be examined and cross-examined as any other witness." O.C.G.A. § 24-6-608 allows the credibility of a witness to be attacked or supported by opinion or reputation evidence as to the character of the witness for truthfulness. O.C.G.A. § 24-6-609 allows the credibility of a witness to be attacked on the basis of the prior criminal history of the witness.

[10]James v. State, 223 Ga. 677, 682 (5), 157 S.E.2d 471 (1967); Askins v. State, 210 Ga. 532 (1), 81 S.E.2d 471 (1954); Ferry v. State, 161 Ga. App. 795, 797, 287 S.E.2d 732 (1982). Cf. Price v. State, 175 Ga. App. 780 (1), 334 S.E.2d 711 (1985). But see Kessel v. State, 236 Ga. 373, 374 (3), 223 S.E.2d 811 (1976), where the court said that it was within the discretion of the trial court to permit the district attorney to ask the defendant on the stand why he did not call her to testify.

See Goger, *Daniel's Georgia Handbook on Criminal Evidence* (2017 ed.), § 5:2, n. 15. Cf. Annot., "Propriety and Prejudicial Effect of Prosecutor's Argument Commenting on Failure of Defendant's Spouse to Testify," 26 A.L.R.4th 9 (1983). See Annot., 75A Am. Jur. 2d, Trial § 597, Failure to Call Family Members: Spouse (2004).

[11]Blige v. State, 263 Ga. 244, 245 (2), 430 S.E.2d 761 (1993).

[12]O.C.G.A. § 17-8-76; Willingham v. State, 134 Ga. App. 144, 146 (4), 213 S.E.2d 516 (1975); but see Berrian v. State, 139 Ga. App. 571, 572 (1), 228 S.E.2d 737 (1976). Counsel may, however, refer to the significance of life without parole and life with the possibility of parole as provided in O.C.G.A. § 17-10-31(b). Tollette v. State, 280 Ga. 100(10), 621 S.E.2d 742 (2005). Note also that in Tucker v. State, 245 Ga. 68, 72, 263 S.E.2d 109 (1980), the court held that the district attorney's argument about parole was not a basis for reversal where no objection or motion for a mistrial was made.

[13]Faust v. State, 222 Ga. 27, 28 (2), 148 S.E.2d 430 (1966).

[14]Spencer v. State, 260 Ga. 640, 653 (20), 398 S.E.2d 179 (1990).

behavior 'indicates a need for the most effective means of incapacitation, i.e., the death penalty.' "But in a capital case it is reversible error, even in the absence of an objection, for the district attorney to argue that the case will automatically be reviewed by the Supreme Court.[15] However, in *Romine v. State*,[16] the court found no error where the district attorney discussed rehabilitation and then argued that if he were released he would go back to drugs like he has before.

A prosecuting attorney may not state that he tries to prosecute only the guilty.[17] Likewise, it is improper for the prosecuting attorney to argue that officers who testified had no interest in the case "other than . . . upholding . . . the laws" and that people like the defendant should be brought to justice.[18] A prosecutor is not authorized to make comparisons "between the case at hand and other cases with which he is personally familiar, nor imply that he has 'canvassed all murder cases and selected this one as particularly deserving of the death penalty. . . .' "[19]

"[A]lthough it would be improper to argue that 'the jury has no *right* to be merciful,' the state may 'urge vigorously' that mercy is inappropriate [to] ' . . . the case at hand.' "[20]

It is improper for a prosecuting attorney to argue that conviction of the defendant will benefit everyone in the county and state[21] or to ask the jurors to put themselves in the place of the

---

[15]Hawes v. State, 240 Ga. 327, 335, 240 S.E.2d 833 (1977); Caldwell v. Mississippi, 472 U.S. 320, 105 S.Ct. 2633, 86 L.Ed.2d 231 (1985).

[16]Romine v. State, 256 Ga. 521, 532 (10), 350 S.E.2d 446 (1986).

[17]Hall v. United States, 419 F.2d 582 (5th Cir. 1969). See Powell v. State, 291 Ga. 743, 733 S.E.2d 294 (2012). In Head v. State, 160 Ga. App. 4, 8 (8), 285 S.E.2d 735 (1981), the district attorney had asked, "Do you think we want to waste our time charging innocent people?" The court said the question was ill-formed but not error.

In Conner v. State, 251 Ga. 113 (6), 303 S.E.2d 266 (1983), the district attorney argued that he had never before sought the death penalty, but he was seeking it in this case. The court held that the argument was improper.

[18]United States v. Morris, 568 F.2d 396 (5th Cir. 1978).

[19]Conklin v. State, 254 Ga. 558, 572 (11), 331 S.E.2d 532 (1985) (quoting Brooks v. Kemp, 762 F.2d 1383, 1413 (11th Cir. 1985)).

[20]Hicks v. State, 256 Ga. 715, 730 (23), 352 S.E.2d 762 (1987). In Ford v. State, 255 Ga. 81, 335 S.E.2d 567 (1985), rev'd on other grounds, 479 U.S. 1075, 107 S.Ct. 1268, 94 L.Ed.2d 129 (1987), citing Drake v. Kemp, 762 F.2d 1449 (11th Cir. 1985), the Supreme Court of Georgia found, "To argue, however, that the jury has no right to be merciful goes too far, as does the characterization of the exercise of mercy as a 'travesty and a sick joke.' "

[21]Locklear v. Morgan, 129 Ga. App. 763, 764 (5)(c), 767 (5)(c), 201 S.E.2d 163 (1973).

state's witness.[22] Likewise, it is error for the district attorney to ask, "Who wants to prosecute innocent people? What pleasure does the Grand Jury get out of indicting these people?"[23] Additionally, in *Wilson v. Kemp*,[24] the 11th Circuit held it to be improper for the prosecutor to pose the question during closing argument, "Is it reasonable to think that the government would fabricate a case with all the crime in this area?" Where a district attorney is aware of evidence favorable to the defendant's defense, it is error for him to argue that such evidence does not exist.[25] Also, it has been held that it is improper for the district attorney, in the absence of supporting evidence, to tell the jury that drug sellers must be having a great success and that they must make a large number of sales before getting caught or to argue that officers who do this kind of work are risking their lives.[26] In *Tate v. State*,[27] there was no evidence that the defendant used drugs, and the court held that it was error for the district attorney to argue that the robbery was connected with the defendant's use of "dope."

In *Brooks v. Kemp*,[28] the court held that it was impermissible to argue that the death penalty is cheaper than life imprisonment. The court also found it clearly improper for a prosecutor to urge the imposition of the death penalty because of the race, religion, sex or social status of the victim. According to the court in *Larkins v. McNeil*,[29] in order for a prosecutor's remarks during closing to constitute misconduct, "a two-prong test must be satisfied: (1) the prosecutor's comments must have been improper, and (2) the comments must have rendered the trial fundamentally unfair."

In *Hammond v. State*,[30] a death penalty case, the court held that it was improper for the prosecuting attorney to argue as follows:

"He violated the law of God. Thou shalt not kill. Whoever sheds the blood of man by man shall his blood be shed, for God created man in his own image. An eye for an eye; a tooth for a tooth. A life for a life."

---

[22]Com. v. Cherry, 474 Pa. 295, 378 A.2d 800 (1977).

[23]DeNamur v. State, 156 Ga. App. 270, 274 S.E.2d 673 (1980).

[24]Wilson v. Kemp, 777 F.2d 621 (11th Cir. 1985).

[25]State v. Goshea, 137 Vt. 69, 398 A.2d 289 (1979). In *Goshea*, the district attorney had failed to inform the defense counsel of the favorable evidence. The court concluded that the argument amounted to a due process violation as a result of prosecutorial misconduct.

[26]Morris v. State, 160 Ga. App. 505, 287 S.E.2d 405 (1981).

[27]Tate v. State, 191 Ga. App. 727, 728 (3), 382 S.E.2d 688 (1989).

[28]Brooks v. Kemp, 762 F.2d 1383 (11th Cir. 1985), judgment vacated, 478 U.S. 1016, 106 S.Ct. 3325, 92 L.Ed.2d 732 (1986), reinstated 809 F.2d 700 (11th Cir. 1987).

[29]Larkins v. McNeil, 2008 WL 4936489 (N.D. Fla. 2008).

[30]Hammond v. State, 264 Ga. 879, 886 (8)(d), 452 S.E.2d 745 (1995).

The court concluded that the argument was an "inflammatory appeal to the jurors' private religious beliefs" and suggests that all homicides should be punished by death. Likewise, it is error for the prosecutor "to urge the jury to follow the religious mandates of the Bible rather than Georgia law. . . ."[31]

The court held that an error of constitutional dimensions had been committed when the district attorney (1) appealed to the fear of the jurors by trying to convince the jury that if the defendant were given life imprisonment he would be likely to escape, and even if he did not, prison guards and other inmates would be in danger; and (2) exhorted the jury to patriotism and to engage in a war against crime. While the district attorney is not permitted to appeal to the passions or prejudice of the jury, it is his duty to use all of his skill and ability in presenting case.[32]

Of course, it is improper for counsel to do anything in closing argument which amounts to introducing new evidence. Thus, in *Williams v. State*[33] the court found that it was error in final argument for the district attorney to demonstrate by the use of a small man the ease or difficulty he had in firing a pistol which had been introduced in evidence, since the defendant had no opportunity to rebut the prosecutor's demonstration.

In *Watkins v. State*,[34] the Georgia Supreme Court concluded that it was within the sound discretion of the trial court as to whether a prosecutor could deliver part of his closing argument while sitting in the witness chair. However, in concurring with the majority, Chief Justice Fletcher was critical of this part of the holding, noting that in several other jurisdictions this tactic has been disapproved since it has the capacity to blur the distinction between the roles of witness and advocate.

§ 23:9 Scope of argument—Limitations on defense counsel's argument

A defense counsel cannot argue that one of his duties is to represent the innocent of the state.[1]

In *Morgan v. State*,[2] the Georgia Supreme Court held that "defense and prosecuting counsel are equally able to comment on the failure of the other to present certain witnesses as long as

---

[31]Carruthers v. State, 272 Ga. 306, 307, 528 S.E.2d 217 (2000).

[32]Goldsmith v. State, 148 Ga. App. 786, 790 (10), 252 S.E.2d 657 (1979).

[33]Williams v. State, 254 Ga. 508, 511 (3), 330 S.E.2d 353 (1985).

[34]Watkins v. State, 278 Ga. 414 (2), 603 S.E.2d 222 (2004).

[Section 23:9]

[1]Hayes v. State, 138 Ga. App. 223 (1), 225 S.E.2d 749 (1976).

[2]Morgan v. State, 267 Ga. 203, 207 (4), 476 S.E.2d 747 (1996).

that argument is derived from evidence before the fact finder."
However, defense counsel has no right to comment on the absence
of persons just because they appeared on the state's witness list.
See Studdard, *Daniel's Georgia Handbook on Criminal Evidence*
(2018 ed.), §§ 3:4 and 4:24. Neither is defense counsel allowed to
comment on the prosecution's failure to present evidence that has
been successfully suppressed or otherwise excluded.[3]

It is not error for the court to prevent counsel from mentioning
the potential punishment which the defendant could receive if
convicted.[4] In *Towns v. State*,[5] the court held that neither "the
lack of an expert witness . . . nor the lack of funds to pay for
such an expert" is a fact to be argued to the jury.

It has been held proper for the trial court to refuse permission
to defense counsel to read "an extract from a book entitled
'Convicting the Innocent,'[6] relating to other criminal cases which
involved the innocence or sanity of other accused persons, the
methods used to obtain confessions in those cases, and the report
of a federal commission of lawlessness in law enforcement,
together with facts in those extraneous cases . . . and opinions
. . . as to such matters."[7] However, an older Georgia Supreme
Court case holds that it is proper for defense counsel to read from
"Phillips' Remarkable Cases of Circumstantial Evidence."[8] In
Hudson v. State,[9] a 4 to 3 decision of the Georgia Supreme Court,
the court affirmed the trial court in permitting counsel to argue
the facts of well known criminal cases and their similarity or dis-
similarity to the case on trial.

In *Singleton v. State*,[10] the court did not abuse its discretion in
refusing to allow defense counsel to replay the surveillance
videotape during closing argument. It is error for defense counsel
to repeatedly refer to the defendants as "bastards" and "niggers"

---

[3]Ellis v. State, 279 Ga. App. 902, 633 S.E.2d 64 (2006).

[4]Hill v. State, 239 Ga. 799 (1), 239 S.E.2d 15 (1977). In Fleming v. State, 240 Ga. 142, 146 (6), 240 S.E.2d 37 (1977), the court said that if an improper remark is made about a death sentence being reviewed, the trial judge should "explain to the jury that it is the responsibility of each juror to decide whether or not the defendant will be executed, and that they cannot pass this responsibility onto anyone else," and to decide the case as if there were no possibility of any review.

[5]Towns v. State, 191 Ga. App. 229, 230 (2), 381 S.E.2d 405 (1989).

[6]E. Borchard, Convicting the Innocent, Garden City Publishing Co., Inc. (1932).

[7]Bryant v. State, 191 Ga. 686, 687 (5), 13 S.E.2d 820 (1941).

[8]Jones v. State, 65 Ga. 506, 507 (6), 510 (1880).

[9]Hudson v. State, 273 Ga. 124, 127 (5), 538 S.E.2d 751 (2000).

[10]Singleton v. State, 231 Ga. App. 694, 695 (3), 500 S.E.2d 411 (1998).

as this improperly injects race into the case.[11] It is not an abuse of discretion for the trial judge to prevent defense counsel from arguing that an officer should arrest a person who commits a crime in the officer's presence within a reasonable time.[12]

In *Palma v. State*,[13] the Georgia Supreme Court ruled that defense counsel should have been allowed in closing argument to make specific references to the potential term of incarceration which several witnesses for the state avoided as a result of their cooperation with the prosecution.

In *Andrews v. State*,[14] the court pointed out that the trial judge, in his discretion, may prevent "a defendant from making a jury nullification argument to the jury, as such would be inconsistent with their duty to convict in those instances where the evidence proves defendant guilty beyond a reasonable doubt. . . ."

In *Felder v. State*,[15] the court held that where "there is no fatal variance between the allegata and probata," the trial judge does not err in precluding an argument that there is a fatal variance.

Generally, on scope of argument of defense counsel, see 23A C.J.S. Criminal Law § 1081(b) (1961). See Studdard, *Daniel's Georgia Handbook on Criminal Evidence* (2018 ed.), §§ 3:4 and 4:24, on defense counsel arguing that the state failed to call certain witnesses.

---

[11]Kornegay v. State, 174 Ga. App. 279, 329 S.E.2d 601 (1985).

[12]Meaux v. State, 176 Ga. App. 345, 346 (2), 335 S.E.2d 741 (1985).

[13]Palma v. State, 280 Ga. 108, 624 S.E.2d 137 (2005).

[14]Andrews v. State, 222 Ga. App. 129, 130, 473 S.E.2d 247 (1996).

[15]Felder v. State, 270 Ga. 641, 644 (3), 514 S.E.2d 416 (1999).

Chapter 24

Submitting the Case to the Jury

KeyCite®: Cases and other legal materials listed in KeyCite Scope can be researched through the KeyCite service on Westlaw®. Use KeyCite to check citations for form, parallel references, prior and later history, and comprehensive citator information, including citations to other decisions and secondary materials.

---

§ 24:1 Requests to charge

The right to submit requested jury instructions for the trial judge is very important. The district attorney and the defense counsel have an opportunity to present charges which are carefully tailored to fit the facts and law of the case being tried. However, the failure of the trial judge to give a requested charge in the exact language requested is not grounds for reversal where the charge given substantially covers the same principle.[1]

In *Hubbard v. State,*[2] the court pointed out that "[g]enerally, where no written request for a jury charge has been filed, the failure to give a charge is not error. . . . However, failure to charge the sole defense, even without a request, constitutes reversible error" if there is sufficient evidence to support the charge. See § 24:2, infra, on charge to the jury.

Requests to charge are treated in more detail in §§ 17:22 and 22:7, supra. See §§ 24:8 and 24:9, infra, on jury charges.

§ 24:2   Charge—General

After the jury has heard all the evidence, it is the trial judge's duty to instruct or charge the jury on the principles of law which apply to the case.[1] There is foreign authority holding that a trial judge may order the doors of the courtroom locked while the jury is being instructed "to preserve order and decorum" and to enhance the comprehension of the jury.[2]

In *Langston v. State,*[3] the court pointed out that "[i]nstructions to the jury, particularly those explaining difficult concepts, are to be 'the lamp . . . to guide [the jury's] feet in journeying through the testimony in search of a legal verdict.' " Jury instructions should be tailored to the indictment and adjusted to the evidence admitted.[4] The court should refer to the evidence only to the extent necessary to present the most important issues to the jury. It is best for the judge not to state what a witness testified, since such a statement is in effect an expression of opinion.[5] The judge should not express an opinion as to what has or has not

[Section 24:1]

[1]Herring v. State, 224 Ga.App. 809, 815 (8), 481 S.E.2d 842 (1997). Accord, Caldwell v. State, 167 Ga.App. 692, 695 (6), 307 S.E.2d 511 (1983).

[2]Hubbard v. State, 220 Ga.App. 678 (1), 469 S.E.2d 866 (1996).

[Section 24:2]

[1]Crosby v. State, 150 Ga. App. 555, 557, 258 S.E.2d 264 (1979); Pope v. State, 52 Ga. App. 411, 413, 183 S.E. 630 (1936); Morris v. U.S., 156 F.2d 525, 527, 169 A.L.R. 305 (C.C.A. 9th Cir. 1946).

[2]People v. Colon, 71 N.Y.2d 410, 526 N.Y.S.2d 932, 521 N.E.2d 1075 (1988).

[3]Langston v. State, 208 Ga.App. 175, 177, 430 S.E.2d 365 (1993).

[4]Joiner v. State, 163 Ga.App. 521, 523 (5), 295 S.E.2d 219 (1982).

[5]Nelson v. State, 124 Ga. 8, 9, 52 S.E. 20 (1905).

been proved,[6] or whether or not the defendant should be acquitted or convicted.[7]

In the 1994 case of *Griffith v. State*,[8] the Georgia Supreme Court held that it was "error for the trial court to fail to repeat its preliminary instructions on the presumption of innocence and the burden of proof when it gave its general charge following arguments to the jury." The court continued by stating that "the better rule is to require a trial court 'after arguments are completed,' to instruct comprehensively on the law applicable to the case, i.e., those charges which are relevant and necessary to weigh the evidence and enable the jury to discharge its duty. . . ." See section 18-36, supra, on pre-trial instructions.

The instructions from the court must be presented so as to enable the jury to deal with the real issues in the case and properly decide them.[9] It has been held that if the judge undertakes to charge the law on any subject, it is his duty to charge all the law on that subject which is material and applicable to the case on trial.[10]

In *Bridges v. State*,[11] the Georgia Supreme Court emphasized that in a charge "no burden is ever [to be] placed on a criminal defendant to establish [his] innocence."

Instructions are to be plain and clear.[12] However, common terms need not be defined when instructing a jury.[13] The judge should explain to the jury the meaning of technical terms used in his instructions.[14] He should guard against using abstract legal quotations and sententious judicial utterances in such a manner as to make them misleading.[15] Nevertheless "a charge that is suf-

[6]Bedgood v. State, 100 Ga.App. 736, 112 S.E.2d 430 (1959).

[7]Johnson v. State, 69 Ga.App. 440, 26 S.E.2d 121 (1943).

[8]Griffith v. State, 264 Ga. 326, 444 S.E.2d 794 (1994).

[9]Glaze v. State, 2 Ga.App. 704 (2), 58 S.E. 1126 (1907).

[10]Harper v. State, 17 Ga.App. 561 (2), 87 S.E. 808 (1916). An instruction which states what the defendant contends is not regarded as shifting the burden of proof to the defendant. Brown v. State, 142 Ga.App. 247 (1), 235 S.E.2d 671 (1977).

[11]Bridges v. State, 268 Ga. 700, 703 (2)(b), 492 S.E.2d 877 (1997).

[12]Leonard v. State, 133 Ga. 435, 437 (3), 66 S.E. 251 (1909); Langston v. State, 208 Ga.App. 175, 177, 430 S.E.2d 365 (1993). See Charrow, "Making Legal Language Understandable; A Psycholinguistic Study of Jury Instructions," 79 Columbia L. R. 1307 (1979).

[13]Williams v. State, 217 Ga.App. 709, 710 (1), 458 S.E.2d 892 (1995). In *Williams* the court held that the word "assault" is a common term which need not be defined when instructing the jury.

[14]Pickens v. State, 132 Ga. 46, 47, 63 S.E. 783 (1909). However, the failure to define technical terms is not ordinarily a ground for a new trial.

[15]Holland v. State, 3 Ga.App. 465, 466 (5), 60 S.E. 205 (1908); Whitehead v. State, 107 Ga.App. 15 (1), 128 S.E.2d 552 (1962).

ficiently clear to be understood by jurors of ordinary understanding is all that is required."[16] However, it has been held that it is not error for him to refer to the deceased as the "victim" since this word is said to have no criminal connotation.[17]

It is the duty of the trial judge to state the contentions of both the state and the defendant; however, in the absence of a request for more specific instructions, the court is regarded as having stated each side's contention when he charges that the indictment and the defendant's plea of not guilty form the issue to be tried by the jury.[18] The trial judge is not required to read the indictment to the jury.[19] If an affirmative defense is raised by the evidence, the trial judge must charge on the affirmative defense even in the absence of a request, but a charge on such an affirmative defense need not be specifically given if the charge as a whole fairly presents the case to the jury.[20] The trial judge should charge the jury that the indictment is not to be regarded as evidence.[21] If a trial is proceeding on an accusation, the jury should be charged that the accusation is not evidence, and the jury should be charged that the affidavit and accusation are not evidence.[22] In this connection it has been held that it is not error for the judge to charge that the plea of not guilty is not evidence of the defendant's innocence.[23]

Where the trial judge gives a requested instruction, he should not refer to the fact that it was requested by the state or the defense.[24]

Even in the absence of a request to charge, the court should

---

[16]Lovell v. State, 189 Ga.App. 311, 312 (1), 375 S.E.2d 658 (1988); Beck v. State, 211 Ga.App. 125, 128 (3)(d), 438 S.E.2d 391 (1993).

[17]Bradham v. State, 148 Ga. App. 89, 250 S.E.2d 801 (1978), judgment aff'd in part, rev'd in part, 243 Ga. 638, 256 S.E.2d 331 (1979).

[18]Wilensky v. State, 15 Ga.App. 360 (2), 83 S.E. 276 (1914). It has been stated that a defendant is entitled to a charge on inconsistent defenses if it is based on evidence. United States v. Daniels, 437 F.2d 656, 659 n. 6 (D.C.Cir. 1970).

[19]Goss v. State, 255 Ga. 678, 680 (3), 341 S.E.2d 448 (1986).

[20]Booker v. State, 247 Ga. 74, 274 S.E.2d 334 (1981). See Griffin v. State, 267 Ga. 586 (1), 481 S.E.2d 223 (1997) (reversible error for trial court to

decline to give a requested charge on the state's burden of proof in case where there is an affirmative defense).

[21]See Owens v. State, 81 Ga.App. 182, 184 (2), 58 S.E.2d 550 (1950).

[22]Faulkner v. State, 146 Ga.App. 604, 607 (3)(a), 247 S.E.2d 147 (1978).

[23]Ramsey v. State, 145 Ga.App. 60, 62 (6), 243 S.E.2d 555 (1978), rev'd on other grounds, 241 Ga. 426, 246 S.E.2d 190 (1978).

[24]Hamilton v. State, 129 Ga. 747 (1), 59 S.E. 803 (1907); and see Blandon v. State, 6 Ga.App. 782 (3), 65 S.E. 842 (1909). However, in Hubbard v. State, 145 Ga.App. 714, 716 (2), 244 S.E.2d 639 (1978), the court pointed out that informing the jury that a certain charge was given at the request of a certain party does not ordinarily demand a new trial.

give the jury appropriate instructions on every substantial issue in the case presented by the evidence.[25] Thus, it is error for the court to fail to instruct the jury on the sole defense of a defendant, even in the absence of a request to charge,[26] if the evidence supports such an instruction.[27] Of course, it is error for a trial judge to charge on evidence which is not in the record. Thus, it has been held to be reversible error to charge a jury on the use of a deadly weapon in a homicide case when there is no evidence of the use of any weapon which could have caused the death.[28] Nevertheless, it has been held that where a defendant is indicted and tried for robbery by intimidation and is convicted of robbery, a charge on armed robbery is deemed to be harmless error.[29] It seems that a trial judge must charge on the controlling issues and the main theories of the defense.[30] But even when there is evidence that the defendant was present at the time of the commission of a crime, and the defendant relies on an alibi defense, it is not error for the trial judge to refuse to give a charge on criminal trespass.[31]

If supported by the evidence, it is proper to charge the jury that "witnesses are not parties and should be partisans."[32]

It is proper for the judge to impress upon the jury the gravity of the case on trial so long as he is careful not to indicate any opinion as to the proper resolution of the case.[33] In keeping with this rule, it is not error for the court to instruct the jury that it "is not wise to immediately express a determination or insist on a certain verdict."[34]

It is not error for the trial judge to refuse to give a charge informing the jury that "each juror must decide the case based on his own opinion of the evidence. In deciding the question of reasonable doubt, each juror must decide for himself. . . . [J]urors are not to be addressed in the charge in a way to discourage mental harmony and concert." Hence, it is not error to refuse to

[25]Walker v. State, 122 Ga. 747 (2), 50 S.E. 994 (1905).

[26]Arnold v. State, 157 Ga.App. 714 (1), 278 S.E.2d 418 (1981). See Harris v. State, 145 Ga.App. 675, 244 S.E.2d 620 (1978); Smith v. State, 147 Ga.App. 549, 553, 249 S.E.2d 353 (1978).

[27]Young v. State, 163 Ga.App. 507, 508, 295 S.E.2d 175 (1982). Accord, Priester v. State, 249 Ga.App. 594, 596 (1), 549 S.E.2d 429 (2001); Williams v. State, 227 Ga.App. 147, 148 (2), 488 S.E.2d 708 (1997).

[28]Stanley v. State, 153 Ga.App. 42, 45 (6), 264 S.E.2d 533 (1980).

[29]Bennett v. State, 153 Ga.App. 210, 264 S.E.2d 688 (1980).

[30]Kimbrell v. State, 148 Ga.App. 302, 304, 250 S.E.2d 883 (1978) (implication).

[31]Wilson v. State, 168 Ga.App. 269, 270 (5), 308 S.E.2d 572 (1983).

[32]Conyers v. State, 260 Ga. 506, 508 (6)(a), 397 S.E.2d 423 (1990).

[33]Lyles v. State, 130 Ga. 294 (5), 60 S.E. 578 (1908).

[34]Spraggins v. State, 243 Ga. 73, 75 (4), 252 S.E.2d 620 (1979).

charge "[t]hat each juror must be satisfied for himself, from the evidence, of the guilt of the defendant, before he can lawfully agree to a verdict of guilty."[35]

The trial judge should explain the bifurcated trial procedure to the jury by instructing them in his charge that at this stage of the trial the jury is to determine the question of innocence or guilt, and that at a later stage the severity of punishment, if the defendant is found guilty, is to be determined.[36] As it is sometimes put, the jury is not to be concerned at this point in the proceeding with what sentence is to be imposed if the defendant is convicted. It is not error for the trial judge to charge that the jury is not responsible for the consequences of its verdict, but only its truthfulness.[37]

Also, generally the trial judge, in his charge to the jury, may exclude previously admitted evidence from the jury's consideration by instructing the jury to disregard it.[38]

Repetition "of a principle of law . . . will not require reversal unless it appears from the charge as a whole that there was such undue emphasis as to result in an unfair statement of the law in relation to the defendant's rights. . . ."[39]

Historically, courts have frowned upon sending a written charge to the jury room with the jury.[40] However, in the absence of objection, it was held that it is not reversible error for the trial court, on request, to permit a secretary who is on the jury to take down a part of the charge in shorthand.[41] Also, the Georgia Supreme Court, in the 1992 case of *Anderson v. State*,[42] said, "[W]e think it is frequently desirable that instructions which

---

[35]Felker v. State, 252 Ga. 351, 314 S.E.2d 621 (1984), overruled on other grounds by Fleming v. State, 265 Ga. 541, 458 S.E.2d 638 (1995).

[36]Shepherd v. State, 234 Ga. 75, 79, 214 S.E.2d 535 (1975). Cf. Putnam v. State, 250 Ga. 418, 419 (2), 297 S.E.2d 286 (1982).

[37]Hicks v. State, 256 Ga. 715, 727 (18), 352 S.E.2d 762 (1987).

[38]Underwood v. State, 144 Ga.App. 684, 689, 242 S.E.2d 339 (1978).

[39]Payne v. State, 248 Ga.App. 158, 162 (3), 545 S.E.2d 336 (2001).

[40]Gholston v. Gholston, 31 Ga. 625, 638 (11) (1860). Cf. The Chattahoochee Brick Co. v. Sullivan, 86 Ga. 50, 67 (6), 12 S.E. 216 (1890). See Annot., "Propriety and Prejudicial Effect of Sending Written Instructions with

Retiring Jury in Criminal Case," 91 A.L.R.3d 382 (1979). See Annot., 75A Am. Jur. 2d Trial § 1156, Propriety of Sending Written Instructions with Jury in Criminal Cases (2004).

[41]White v. State, 137 Ga.App. 9 (1), 223 S.E.2d 24 (1975). In Llewellyn v. State, 241 Ga. 192, 194 (2), 243 S.E.2d 853 (1978), on the third day of jury deliberations and just before the verdict, it was discovered that two charges given by the court and one of the defendant's requests had been mixed with the documentary evidence and were in the possession of the jury. The defendant had made no objection to the charge. There was no contention that the instructions were incorrect. The court held that if this amounted to error, it was harmless.

[42]Anderson v. State, 262 Ga. 26,

have been reduced to writing be not only read to the jury but also be handed over to the jury. This course is required in some states and is widely practiced. . . . *We see no good reason why the members of the jury should always be required to . . . rely upon their several recollections of what a judge said when proof of what he said is readily available.*" (Emphasis by the court.)

It is within the discretion of the trial court to give recharges requested by the jury in writing even though the balance of the charge was provided orally. However, a written recharge should be accompanied by a cautionary instruction which reminds the jury not to put undue emphasis on the recharge, and that they should consider it only in the context of the charge as a whole.[43]

Under Georgia capital punishment procedure, after the question of guilt has been determined, the applicable provisions of O.C.G.A. § 17-10-30 must be given to the jury orally and in writing.

The Massachusetts Supreme Judicial Court in 1995 approved the sending of a tape recording of the entire jury instructions to the jury for use during deliberations and outlined a procedure for doing so.[44]

See § 22:7, supra, on requests to charge; § 24:16, infra, on objections to charges; § 26:10, infra, on charges in capital cases; § 24:4, infra, on instructing a jury on definition of crime charged; § 24:9, infra, on matters which do not have to be charged; and § 24:13, infra, on errors in charges requiring reversal. See § 21:3, supra, on instructions to jury where the defendant does not testify. See § 21:12, supra, on instructions to be given where insanity is involved.

§ 24:3 Charge—Opinion of judge

O.C.G.A. § 17-8-57(a)(1) prohibits a judge "during any phase of any criminal case" from expressing an opinion as to "whether a fact at issue has or has not been proved or as to the guilt of the accused." However, § 17-8-57 (a)(2) requires that a party who has an objection to such a comment must raise it in a timely fashion. The failure to do so will preclude review of the issue unless it amounts to plain error. See § 17:5, supra, on the judge.

28, 413 S.E.2d 732 (1992); Gidden v. State, 205 Ga.App. 245, 247 (2), 422 S.E.2d 30 (1992); Miner v. State, 268 Ga. 67 (2), 485 S.E.2d 456 (1997); Pullins v. State, 232 Ga.App. 267, 501 S.E.2d 612 (1998). But cf. Spitzberg v. State, 233 Ga.App. 848, 850 (2), 506 S.E.2d 143 (1998).

[43]Rickman v. State, 277 Ga. 277, 279 (2), 587 S.E.2d 596 (2003).

[44]Commonwealth v. Baseler, 419 Mass. 500, 645 N.E.2d 1179 (1995).

§ 24:4   Charge—Instructions defining offense charged

In *Gardner v. State,*[1] the court held that "[t]he trial judge *must* charge the jury on each crime specified in the indictment or accusation, unless the evidence does not warrant a conviction of such crime, or unless the state has affirmatively withdrawn a crime or stricken it from the indictment or accusation."

Generally, if a part of a section of the Georgia Code may be charged, the entire section may be given.[2] This rule applies even though a part of the charge may be inapplicable under the facts in evidence.[3] A charge given in substantially the same language as a code section is generally sufficient[4] and "a mere slip of the tongue" may be considered harmless when considered in the light of the entire charge.[5] However, if a code section states that an offense may be committed in more than one way, and an indictment charges that the offense was committed in one way, the charge of the code section *must* be followed by a charge that the jury is not authorized to convict unless the jury finds that the offense was committed in the manner charged in the indictment.[6] Thus, it is "reversible error to charge that a crime may be committed by either of two methods, when the indictment charges it was committed by one specific method, and then charge the jury that they may convict the defendant if they find he committed the offense by a method other than the specific type charged in the indictment."[7] However, in *Mikell v. State,*[8] the Georgia Supreme Court held that this defect in a charge "is cured . . . where the court provides the jury with the indictment and instructs jurors that the burden of proof rests upon the State to

---

[Section 24:4]

[1]Gardner v. State, 185 Ga.App. 184, 363 S.E.2d 843 (1987).

[2]Keller v. State, 245 Ga. 522, 265 S.E.2d 813 (1980); Bagley v. State, 153 Ga.App. 777, 266 S.E.2d 804 (1980).

[3]Slack v. State, 159 Ga.App. 185, 188, 283 S.E.2d 64 (1981); Rains v. State, 161 Ga.App. 361, 363 (7), 288 S.E.2d 626 (1982).

[4]Cf. Johnston v. State, 232 Ga. 268, 272 (5), 206 S.E.2d 468 (1974); Carter v. State, 137 Ga.App. 824, 827 (5), 225 S.E.2d 73 (1976).

[5]Mathis v. State, 153 Ga.App. 587 (1-a), 266 S.E.2d 275 (1980).

[6]Walker v. State, 146 Ga.App. 237, 243, 246 S.E.2d 206 (1978); Searcy v. State, 168 Ga.App. 233 (1), 308 S.E.2d 621 (1983); Hunley v. State, 227

Ga.App. 234, 235 (1), 488 S.E.2d 716 (1997). See Goss v. State, 289 Ga. App. 734, 737, 658 S.E.2d 168 (2008) (one exception is where "under the evidence there is no reasonable possibility that the jury convicted the defendant of the commission of the crime in a manner not charged in the indictment").

[7]Lumpkin v. State, 249 Ga. 834, 836, 295 S.E.2d 86 (1982); Griffin v. State, 214 Ga.App. 813, 815(2), 449 S.E.2d 341 (1994); Zinnamon v. State, 261 Ga.App. 170(3), 582 S.E.2d 146 (2003). Cf. Caithaml v. State, 163 Ga.App. 429, 430 (2), 294 S.E.2d 674 (1982). See Owens v. State, 173 Ga.App. 309, 312(4), 326 S.E.2d 509 (1985).

[8]Mikell v. State, 286 Ga. 722, 724, 690 S.E.2d 858 (2010).

prove every material allegation of the indictment and every essential element of the crime charged beyond a reasonable doubt." However, "[w]here two or more jury instructions directly conflict with one another, a new trial is required."[9]

In *Travitt v. State*,[10] the court pointed out that when an indictment properly charged conjunctively that the defendant took property "from the person and immediate presence" of the victim, the trial judge's charge using the disjunctive "or" was not error.

Where the court in charging the jury reads an indictment which incorrectly attempts to charge a crime and the defendant has not demurred to the indictment, this is not a ground for reversal in that this is regarded as an error induced by the defendant.[11]

Generally, the court should not instruct the jury that an offense for which the defendant is being tried is a felony or a misdemeanor.[12]

§ 24:5 Charge—Lesser included offenses

Under Georgia law as it existed for more than a century, if evidence introduced in the trial of a case showed that the defendant could be found guilty of a lesser included offense, the trial judge was obligated to charge on the lesser offense.[1] However, in 1976, the Georgia Supreme Court stated that it would no longer follow those cases holding that the judge must charge on the lesser offense and in its words, "set forth the following rules:

"(1) The trial judge must charge the jury on each crime specified in the indictment or accusation unless the evidence does not warrant a conviction of such crime or unless the state has affirmatively withdrawn a crime or stricken it from the indictment or accusation.

"(2) The trial judge may, in his discretion, charge on a lesser crime of that included in the indictment. However, his failure to do so, without a written request by the state or the accused, is not error.[2]

"(3) The state or the accused may, by written application to the

---

[9]Able v. State, 312 Ga. App. 252, 718 S.E.2d 96 (2011).

[10]Travitt v. State, 228 Ga.App. 711, 712 (3), 492 S.E.2d 574 (1997).

[11]Mahomet v. State, 151 Ga.App. 462, 463 (1), 260 S.E.2d 363 (1979).

[12]E.g., Johnson v. State, 261 Ga. 236, 239 (5), 404 S.E.2d 108 (1991).

[Section 24:5]

[1]See Stonaker v. State, 137 Ga.App. 830, 224 S.E.2d 818 (1976).

[2]Hawkins v. State, 267 Ga. 124, 125 (3), 475 S.E.2d 625 (1996); Brooks v. State, 143 Ga.App. 523, 524 (2), 239 S.E.2d 207 (1977). In Comer v. State, 247 Ga. 167, 275 S.E.2d 309 (1981), the court said it is never error for a trial judge to refuse to give a charge on a lesser included offense in the absence of a timely written request.

trial judge at or before the close of the evidence, request him to charge on lesser crimes that are included in the offenses set forth in the indictment or accusation. The trial judge's failure to charge as requested, if the evidence warrants such requested charge, shall be error.[3]

"(4) An erroneous charge on a lesser crime to that set forth in the indictment or accusation does not rise to the level of reversible error unless the charge was harmful to the accused as a matter of law."[4]

In *Hancock v. State*,[5] the court held that a lesser included offense is one which falls within the parameters of O.C.G.A. § 16-1-6(1). See § 14:52, supra, on double jeopardy implication for lesser included offense.

In *Henson v. State*,[6] where there was no request to charge on a lesser included offense, the court held that the trial judge is not required to give defense counsel notice of his intent to charge on an included offense. In *Tucker v. State*,[7] the court held that in the absence of a *written* request to charge, it is never error to fail to charge on the lesser included offense. But *Gagnon v. State*,[8] held that "a trial court, sua sponte, may charge . . . on a lesser included offense if" justified by the evidence even though not requested in writing before the commencement of the trial.

However, in *Beck v. Alabama*,[9] the United States Supreme Court held that a death sentence may not be constitutionally

---

[3]Jackson v. State, 213 Ga.App. 170 (2)(a), 444 S.E.2d 126 (1994); Malone v. State, 142 Ga.App. 47, 48, 234 S.E.2d 844 (1977); Prince v. State, 142 Ga.App. 734, 735 (1), 236 S.E.2d 918 (1977); King v. State, 214 Ga.App. 311, 312 (2), 447 S.E.2d 645 (1994).

[4]State v. Stonaker, 236 Ga. 1, 2, 222 S.E.2d 354 (1976). In Edwards v. State, 264 Ga. 131, 133, 442 S.E.2d 444 (1994), the Georgia Supreme Court stated: "[t]he complete rule with regard to giving a defendant's requested charge on a lesser included offense is: where the state's evidence establishes all of the elements of an offense and there is no evidence raising the lesser offense, there is no error in failing to give a charge on the lesser offense." Where the evidence shows either the commission of the completed offense as charged, or the commission of no offense, the trial court is not required to charge the jury on a lesser included offense. Peebles v. State, 260

Ga. 430, 432 (4), 396 S.E.2d 229 (1990). In Huckeba v. State, 217 Ga.App. 472, 458 S.E.2d 131 (1995), the Court of Appeals found that a lesser included offense charge wasn't required where the evidence showed the commission of the completed offense of aggravated assault with intent to rape or showed, because the defendant's defense was alibi, the commission of no offense.

[5]Hancock v. State, 210 Ga.App. 528, 532 (3)(b), 437 S.E.2d 610 (1993).

[6]Henson v. State, 258 Ga. 600, 602 (5), 372 S.E.2d 806 (1988).

[7]Tucker v. State, 238 Ga.App. 645, 646, 519 S.E.2d 745 (1999).

[8]Gagnon v. State, 240 Ga.App. 754, 755 (1), 525 S.E.2d 127 (1999).

[9]Beck v. Alabama, 447 U.S. 625, 100 S.Ct. 2382, 65 L.Ed.2d 392 (1980). The *Beck* case resulted from an Alabama statute which "specifically prohibited [the trial judge] from giving

imposed when the jury was not permitted to consider a verdict of guilt of a lesser included offense when the evidence would have supported such verdict. At least in a capital case and perhaps in all criminal cases all of the foregoing material must be considered in the light of *Beck*. But the Georgia Supreme Court has held that a "trial judge never errs in failing to include a charge on a lesser included offense unless there is a written request to charge."[10]

The *Beck* case points out that (1) in federal courts a defendant is entitled to an instruction on a lesser included offense; (2) "the state courts that have addressed the issue have unanimously held that a defendant is entitled to a lesser included offense instruction where the evidence warrants it";[11] and (3) "as a matter of due process, the nearly universal acceptance of the rule in both state and federal courts establishes the value to the defendant of this procedural safeguard." Also, the decision in *Beck* in footnote 14 stated that the court was not deciding the question of whether there is a due process violation in a non-capital case if the trial judge fails to charge on a lesser included offense.

In connection with charging on a lesser included offense, it must be kept in mind that, at least where there is a proper request, the trial judge is obligated to give such a charge even if the defendant's testimony, taken as a whole, does not justify it, if from the evidence as a whole the charge is justified.[12] It has been held that the any evidence rule continues to apply to a request to

---

the jury the option of convicting the defendant of a lesser included offense. . . . Instead the jury is given the choice of either convicting the defendant of the capital crime, . . . or acquitting him."

[10]Gadson v. State, 264 Ga. 280, 281 (2), 444 S.E.2d 305 (1994); Mosley v. State, 257 Ga. 382, 383 (2), 359 S.E.2d 653 (1987).

[11]In Hopper v. Evans, 456 U.S. 605, 102 S.Ct. 2049, 72 L.Ed.2d 367 (1982), the court stated that in a capital case it was not error to fail to charge on a lesser included offense when the evidence negates the possibility that such a charge was warranted. However, certiorari was granted in the case "to determine whether, after invalidation of a state law which precluded instructions on

lesser included offenses in capital cases [the *Beck* case], a new trial is required in a capital case in which the defendant's own evidence negates the possibility that such an instruction might have been warranted." The opinion seemed to go further than the question presented and discussed the alleged error without drawing a distinction between whether the evidence requiring a lesser included charge is that of the state or of the defendant, or a combination of the state's and the defendant's.

[12]Henderson v. State, 234 Ga. 827, 831 (2), 218 S.E.2d 612 (1975); Raines v. State, 247 Ga. 504, 277 S.E.2d 47 (1981). Cf. Robinson v. State, 248 Ga. 627, 628, 284 S.E.2d 400 (1981).

charge a jury on a lesser included offense.[13] However, in *Santone v. State*,[14] the court said that "[e]ven when an instruction is requested in writing, the trial court can refuse to charge on a lesser included offense when the evidence does not reasonably raise the issue that the defendant may be only guilty of the lesser crime." But in *State v. Alvarado*,[15] the Georgia Supreme Court disapproved the *Santone* language and said that "[t]he correct rule is that a written request to charge a lesser included offense must be always given if there is any evidence that the defendant is guilty of the lesser included offense."

Nevertheless, the failure to charge on a lesser included offense does not prevent an appellate court from reversing a conviction where the omission was "clearly harmful and erroneous as a matter of law in that . . . [the charge] fails to provide the jury with the proper guidelines for determining guilt or innocence."[16]

However, "[w]here the evidence shows either the completed offense as charged or no offense, . . . the court should not charge on the lesser grades of the offense."[17] In *Hambrick v. State*,[18] the court held that "where the evidence shows completion of the greater offense, . . . it is not necessary for the court to charge on a lesser included offense." In *Dickerson v. State*,[19] the court held that where "the undisputed evidence shows that the assault was committed with a deadly weapon, it is not error to refuse to . . . charge on simple assault as a lesser included offense." In *Mitchell v. State*,[20] the defendant was charged with sale of cocaine and possession with intent to distribute. The defendant was found guilty of the sale of cocaine and an appeal asserted error in the

---

[13]State v. Clay, 249 Ga. 250 (1), 290 S.E.2d 84 (1982). But see Cooper v. State, 180 Ga.App. 37, 39 (2), 348 S.E.2d 486 (1986), overruled as to Division (1) by Brewer v. State, 271 Ga. 605, 523 S.E.2d 18 (1999). See § 28:8, infra, on Jackson v. Virginia, 443 U.S. 307, 99 S.Ct. 2781, 61 L.Ed.2d 560 (1979).

[14]Santone v. State, 187 Ga.App. 789, 791 (2), 371 S.E.2d 428 (1988); Leeks v. State, 188 Ga.App. 625, 628 (3), 373 S.E.2d 777 (1988).

[15]State v. Alvarado, 260 Ga. 563, 564, 397 S.E.2d 550 (1990). Accord, Brewer v. State, 219 Ga.App. 16, 19 (5), 463 S.E.2d 906 (1995).

[16]Jackson v. State, 239 Ga. 40, 42, 235 S.E.2d 477 (1977) (concurring opinion of Justice Hall).

[17]Burley v. State, 172 Ga.App. 34, 35, 321 S.E.2d 783 (1984); Dean v. State, 215 Ga.App. 23 (1), 449 S.E.2d 622 (1994); Cotton v. State, 274 Ga. 26 (2), 549 S.E.2d 71 (2001).

[18]Hambrick v. State, 174 Ga.App. 444, 447 (2), 330 S.E.2d 383 (1985).

[19]Dickerson v. State, 207 Ga.App. 241 (1), 427 S.E.2d 591 (1993).

[20]Mitchell v. State, 221 Ga.App. 183, 184 (3), 470 S.E.2d 771 (1996) (citing and relying on Edwards v. State, 264 Ga. 131, 133, 442 S.E.2d 444 (1994)) (emphasis in original). See Daniel v. State, 301 Ga. 783, 804 S.E.2d 61 (2017) (fact that a jury is permitted to infer specific intent to steal in a burglary case does not mean that "defendant has any obligation to testify or otherwise contest that inference").

trial judge's refusal to charge on possession of cocaine. In affirming the conviction, the court pointed out that "where the state's evidence establishes all of the elements of an offense *and there is no evidence raising the lesser offense*, there is no error in failing to give a charge on the lesser offense."

In *Greene v. State*,[21] the court held that when the state's evidence demonstrates that the offense of armed robbery was committed, "and the only evidence to the contrary is the defendant's denial that he participated in the crime, it is not error" for the trial judge to refuse to charge on a lesser included offense. In *Hawkins v. State*,[22] the court held that "theft by receiving stolen property is not a lesser included offense of armed robbery. . . ."

In *Johnson v. State*,[23] the defendant was tried for burglary. He contended that he had not been in or near the building, attacked the identification evidence and presented an alibi defense. The court concluded that it was not error for the trial judge to refuse to charge on criminal trespass.

If the trial judge improperly charges on a lesser included offense, this does not amount to reversible error "unless the charge was harmful to the accused as a matter of law."[24] Thus, in *Thompkins v. State*,[25] the court held that "if in a trial for murder the evidence does not involve the law of voluntary manslaughter, but the trial judge instructs on voluntary manslaughter and the jury convicts of voluntary manslaughter, it is not cause for a new trial if the evidence demanded a verdict of murder." Also, in *Griffith v. State*,[26] the court held that when a defendant specifically requests a charge on a lesser included offense he may not complain if a jury convicts him of that offense.

The Georgia Supreme Court in *Edge v. State*[27] held that it was error for the trial judge to give a sequential charge that required the jury to consider voluntary manslaughter only if it found the defendant not guilty of felony murder. The concern of the court "was to ensure that persons are not convicted of felony murder in cases where the facts warrant [a conviction for] voluntary

---

[21]Greene v. State, 263 Ga. 466, 467 (1), 435 S.E.2d 607 (1993).

[22]Hawkins v. State, 242 Ga.App. 603, 604 (1), 528 S.E.2d 853 (2000).

[23]Johnson v. State, 164 Ga.App. 429 (1), 296 S.E.2d 775 (1982). Accord, O'Neal v. State, 171 Ga.App. 582, 320 S.E.2d 612 (1984).

[24]Weeks v. State, 152 Ga.App. 629 (1), 263 S.E.2d 513 (1979). In *Weeks*, the court affirmed a conviction where simple battery was charged as a lesser included offense of child molestation.

[25]Thompkins v. State, 180 Ga.App. 473, 474 (1), 349 S.E.2d 768 (1986).

[26]Griffith v. State, 188 Ga.App. 789, 374 S.E.2d 359 (1988).

[27]Edge v. State, 261 Ga. 865, 414 S.E.2d 463 (1992) (cited with approval in Green v. State, 266 Ga. 758, 759 (2)(a), 470 S.E.2d 884 (1996)).

manslaughter." Subsequently, in *Lajara v. State*,[28] the Supreme
Court held that this purpose is met when the jury considers voluntary manslaughter, even though a sequential charge is given.
A proper charge under *Edge clearly* informs the jury that they
are not to consider the crimes in any particular order.[29]

If a trial judge charges on a lesser included offense, he should
charge the jury to first consider the offense charged in the indictment, and if the jury has a reasonable doubt as to the guilt of the
defendant of that offense then it could consider the lesser
offense.[30] In *Paradise v. State*,[31] the court held that "jury instructions on consideration of a lesser included offense should be
couched in terms of what a jury is *authorized to do . . . and not
in terms of what a jury would be* forced to do." (Emphasis in
original.) It is proper for the trial judge to charge the jury to find
the defendant not guilty if the jury does not find him guilty of
any of the crimes about which the jury has been charged.[32]

In *Williams v. State*,[33] the court held that it is not error for the
trial judge to fail to inform a jury that a lesser included offense is
a misdemeanor.

In *Walls v. State*,[34] the defendant was charged with aggravated
assault on a police officer in the execution of his duties. The trial
judge failed to charge the jury that it must find that the officer
was acting in the execution of his duties at the time of the assault.
The evidence supported a finding of guilt of the offense charged.
The trial judge, after conviction and without objection from the
state, sentenced the defendant for aggravated assault, a lesser
included offense. The appellate court affirmed.

In *Collins v. State*,[35] the court held that it was not error for the
trial judge to refuse to charge on possession of marijuana where
the evidence "clearly showed that the appellant sold marijuana to
an undercover agent."

In *Manbeck v. State*,[36] the defendant was charged with possession of marijuana. The trial judge declined to give a charge on
possession of less than an ounce. In affirming the conviction, the

---

[28]Lajara v. State, 263 Ga. 438,
439, 435 S.E.2d 600 (1993) (cited with
approval in Green v. State, 266 Ga.
758, 759 (2)(a), 470 S.E.2d 884 (1996)).

[29]Walker v. Williams, 282 Ga. 409,
651 S.E.2d 59 (2007).

[30]Leslie v. State, 211 Ga.App. 871,
872, 440 S.E.2d 757 (1994); Brownlee
v. State, 155 Ga.App. 875, 877, 273
S.E.2d 636 (1980).

[31]Paradise v. State, 212 Ga.App.
166, 170 (4)(b), 441 S.E.2d 497 (1994).

[32]Scott v. State, 170 Ga.App. 409,
412 (5), 317 S.E.2d 282 (1984).

[33]Williams v. State, 267 Ga. 771,
774 (2)(b), 482 S.E.2d 288 (1997).

[34]Walls v. State, 161 Ga.App. 625,
628 (3), 288 S.E.2d 769 (1982).

[35]Collins v. State, 146 Ga.App.
138, 245 S.E.2d 488 (1978).

[36]Manbeck v. State, 165 Ga.App.
625 (2), 302 S.E.2d 361 (1983).

court pointed out that the requested charge was not supported by the evidence where the defendant was the sole occupant of the house and 25 small bags of marijuana were found together in a garbage bag even though traces of residue were found throughout the house.

In *Adorno v. State*,[37] the court held that simple possession of cocaine is a lesser included offense of trafficking in cocaine.

In *Metts v. State*,[38] the defendant was convicted of felony murder with the underlying felony being possession of a firearm by a convicted felon. The court held that "the underlying felony . . . had to be dangerous per se or had to create a foreseeable risk of death when attendant circumstances were taken into account."

Although a trial court may accept a "partial verdict" on felony murder and related charges without also resolving the malice murder charge, it may do so only after the jury has indicated that it is unable to resolve certain counts. Thus, in *Marshall v. State*,[39] the court's decision to accept a partial verdict and enter a *nolle prosequi* as to the malice murder count on which the jury had not decided was reversed because the defendant had not consented to the disposition and the jury had not indicated they were deadlocked. In *Byrd v. State*,[40] a jury which was unable to resolve the malice murder charge returned a partial verdict which was acceptable since the trial court determined that the jury was deadlocked. The concern presented by the partial verdict is that of whether the jury fully considered the lesser included charge of "involuntary manslaughter and a possible finding that the killing was done without intent but during an act of reckless conduct."[41]

See § 25:2, infra, on verdicts involving a lesser included offense.

§ 24:6 Charge—Lesser included offenses—When predicate of felony murder; murder in the second degree

In *Prater v. State*,[1] the defendant was charged with felony murder predicated on armed robbery. The Georgia Supreme Court reversed because the evidence was insufficient to establish robbery. The Court found the evidence insufficient to show an attempt to commit armed robbery because there had not been a jury instruc-

[37]Adorno v. State, 236 Ga.App. 588, 592 (4), 512 S.E.2d 703 (1999).

[38]Metts v. State, 270 Ga. 481, 482 (1), 511 S.E.2d 508 (1999).

[39]Marshall v. State, 275 Ga. 218, 563 S.E.2d 868 (2002).

[40]Byrd v. State, 277 Ga. 554, 556 (3), 592 S.E.2d 421 (2004).

[41]Byrd v. State, 277 Ga. 554, 558, 592 S.E.2d 421 (2004).

[Section 24:6]

[1]Prater v. State, 273 Ga. 477 (1), (2), 545 S.E.2d 864 (2001).

tion identifying the included offense as a felony and setting out its essential elements.

In *State v. Crane*,[2] the Supreme Court held that a defendant is not criminally liable for felony murder where the murder victim was killed by someone other than the defendant, e.g. where the victim shoots and kills a cohort of the defendant in self-defense. However, in *State v. Jackson*,[3] the court overruled *Crane* and held that the felony murder statute requires only that the defendant's felonious conduct proximately cause the death of the victim.

In *Ford v. State*,[4] the Georgia Supreme Court held that before a felony may serve as the predicate for the offense of felony murder, the felony charged must be one which is "inherently dangerous" or committed under such circumstances so as to create a reasonably foreseeable risk of death. In *Ford,* the underlying felony was possession of a firearm by a convicted felon. The defendant accidentally discharged the weapon and shot the victim who was, at the time, in a different apartment. However, in *Shivers v. State*,[5] the court noted that a status felony such as possession of a firearm by a convicted felon, under the right circumstances, may constitute an inherently dangerous felony. In *Crayton v. State*,[6] the Court explained: "Under *Ford* and its progeny, to show that a defendant possessed a firearm in circumstances that posed a foreseeable risk of death, the State has to prove that the defendant used the firearm intentionally to make an assault, that he used the firearm intentionally for some other criminal purpose, that he possessed it in a manner that was criminally reckless or negligent, or that he possessed it in some other criminally culpable and dangerous way."

The purpose of the felony murder rule is "to furnish an added deterrent to the perpetration of felonies which, by their nature or by the attendant circumstances, create a foreseeable risk of death."[7] However, a statute enacted by the legislature specifically designed to prosecute a particular form of conduct which creates

---

[2]State v. Crane, 247 Ga. 779, 279 S.E.2d 695 (1981).

[3]State v. Jackson, 287 Ga. 646, 697 S.E.2d 757 (2010).

[4]Ford v. State, 262 Ga. 602, 423 S.E.2d 255 (1992). Compare Hines v. State, 276 Ga. 491, 578 S.E.2d 868, 872 (2003).

[5]Shivers v. State, 286 Ga. 422, 688 S.E.2d 622 (2010) (see Nahmias, J., concurring opinion advocating that the issue of "inherently dangerous

felony" should be a jury question and the subject of jury instruction unless, under *Ford*, the felony is among a class of felonies previously determined to be inherently dangerous as a matter of law). See also Chance v. State, 291 Ga. 241, 728 S.E.2d 635 (2012).

[6]Crayton v. State, 298 Ga. 792, 784 S.E.2d 343 (2016).

[7]Chapman v. State, 266 Ga. 356, 358, 467 S.E.2d 497 (1996) (citing Ford v. State, 262 Ga. 602, 423 S.E.2d 255 (1992)).

a "foreseeable risk of death" cannot be used as the felony for purposes of a felony murder accusation. Thus, in *Williams v. State*,[8] the Court held that the felony of contributing to the delinquency or dependence of a child cannot serve as a predicate to a felony murder charge. O.C.G.A. § 16-12-(d.1)(1) specifically proscribes conduct which culminates in the conviction of the defendant "[for] an offense which resulted in the serious injury or death of a child" and provides a sentencing scheme for such offenses while the felony murder statute criminalizes general felony conduct resulting in the death of another.

In 2014, the legislature created the offense of "murder in the second degree." O.C.G.A. § 16-5-1 now provides that the offense of murder in the second degree occurs "when, in the commission of cruelty to children in the second degree" the defendant causes the death of another human being irrespective of malice.

§ 24:7 Charge—Different counts and/or different defendants

"The Supreme Court of Georgia has recognized that 'it is the "better practice" for a trial court to give a separate instruction which details the jury's duty to consider each charge in the indictment against each defendant separately and which reminds the jury that the guilt of one defendant does not require the return of a guilty verdict against the other defendant. . . . To determine whether the failure to give such an instruction was harmful error, we must consider the charge as a whole.' "[1]

§ 24:8 Charge—Matters that must be charged

Even in the absence of a request to charge, certain basic matters must be covered by the instructions given to the jury. However, according to Georgia appellate courts' decisions, the list is surprisingly short. The following omissions in instructions have been held to be error: (1) failure to charge on the presump-

---

[8]Williams v. State, 299 Ga. 632, 791 S.E.2d 55 (2016) (Court noted that O.C.G.A. § 16-12-1, child deprivation, was enacted after the felony murder statute, O.C.G.A. § 16-5-1(c) and that the legislature is presumed to know the condition of the laws and to enact statutes with reference to it, citing State v. Tiraboschi, 269 Ga. 812, 814, 504 S.E.2d 689 (1998), and the gen-

eral principle that "a specific statute will prevail over a general statute absent any indication of a contrary legislative intent," citing State v. Nankervis, 295 Ga. 406, 409 (2), 761 S.E.2d 1 (2014)).

[Section 24:7]

[1]Overstreet v. State, 250 Ga.App. 336, 339 (3), 551 S.E.2d 748 (2001).

tion of innocence;[1] (2) failure "to charge . . . that the defendant enters upon his trial with a presumption of innocence in his favor, and that this presumption remains with him, in the nature of evidence, until rebutted by proof satisfying the jury of his guilt to the exclusion of reasonable doubt";[2] (3) failure to instruct the jury on every substantial issue presented by the evidence;[3] (4) failure to instruct the jury that the defendant's guilt must be proved beyond a reasonable doubt;[4] (5) failure to charge on circumstantial evidence where the guilt of the defendant is based wholly on such evidence;[5] (6) failure to charge on circumstantial evidence where the state's case depends in whole or in part[6] on such evidence and there is a timely written request to give such a charge;[7] and (7) failure to call the jury's attention to a defense, supported by evidence which has been primarily relied upon by the defendant.[8] Indeed, the failure of the defense to request a charge on the defendant's sole defense is still subject to review on appeal since O.C.G.A. § 5-5-24(c) provides that erroneous charges must be reviewed if there has been a substantial error as a matter of law.[9] Although written requests to charge are ordinarily required, a defendant "is relieved of this duty 'where the omission is clearly harmful and erroneous as a matter of law in that it fails to

---

[Section 24:8]

[1]Bird v. State, 89 Ga.App. 37, 38, 78 S.E.2d 551 (1953); Foster v. State, 240 Ga. 858, 860 (4), 242 S.E.2d 600 (1978). In Kentucky v. Whorton, 441 U.S. 786, 99 S.Ct. 2088, 60 L.Ed.2d 640 (1979), the court indicated, that from a federal constitutional standpoint, the failure to charge on the presumption of innocence may deprive a defendant of his due process rights under the Fourteenth Amendment. Cf. Taylor v. Kentucky, 436 U.S. 478, 98 S.Ct. 1930, 56 L.Ed.2d 468 (1978). Cf. Ford v. State, 164 Ga.App. 620 (2), 298 S.E.2d 327 (1982).

[2]Blair v. State, 179 Ga.App. 519, 347 S.E.2d 337 (1986).

[3]Walker v. State, 122 Ga. 747 (2), 50 S.E. 994 (1905).

[4]See Cain v. State, 41 Ga.App. 333, 337, 153 S.E. 79 (1930).

[5]Daniel v. State, 59 Ga.App. 454 (1), 1 S.E.2d 229 (1939), but it is not error to fail to charge on circumstantial evidence, absent a request, if there is some direct evidence of guilt. Sheffield v. State, 188 Ga. 1, 12 (11), 2 S.E.2d 657 (1939).

[6]Robinson v. State, 261 Ga. 698, 699, 410 S.E.2d 116 (1991).

[7]Manning v. State, 207 Ga.App. 181, 182 (2), 427 S.E.2d 521 (1993).

[8]See Reed v. State, 15 Ga.App. 435 (1), 83 S.E. 674 (1914); Nix v. State, 135 Ga.App. 672, 674, 219 S.E.2d 6 (1975); McRoy v. State, 131 Ga.App. 307, 308 (3), 205 S.E.2d 445 (1974); Jackson v. State, 154 Ga.App. 867, 868 (2), 270 S.E.2d 76 (1980). Bailey v. State, 294 Ga. App. 437(2), 669 S.E.2d 453 (2008) (failure to give equal access charge reversible error even without request as it was the defendant's sole defense). However, if a defendant has an undisclosed theory of defense, with evidence to support it, and the court does not charge on it but at the conclusion of the charge asks counsel for defendant if the court has left anything out and counsel says "no," this is regarded as induced error and is not a basis for reversal. Hill v. State, 237 Ga. 523, 525, 228 S.E.2d 898 (1976).

[9]Harris v. State, 294 Ga.App. 668, 669 S.E.2d 706 (2008).

provide the jury with the proper guidelines for determining guilt or innocence.' "[10]

Up until 1981 it was commonly thought that it was error for a trial judge to fail to charge, where applicable, former O.C.G.A. § 24-9-85(b), which provided, "If a witness shall willfully and knowingly swear falsely, his testimony shall be disregarded entirely, unless corroborated. . . ."[11] However, effective January 2013 § 24-9-85(b) was replaced by § 24-6-620, which broadens this language, only stating that "the court shall give the jury proper instructions as to the credibility of a witness."

The same attitude evidenced by the Georgia appellate courts on the failure to charge on specific matters in the absence of a request appears to exist in the United States Supreme Court. That court has said in a habeas corpus context, that an "omission or an incomplete instruction is less likely to be prejudicial than a misstatement of the law."[12]

§ 24:9 Charge—Matters which do not have to be charged

"[A] . . . defendant is ordinarily required to present written requests for any desired jury instructions. . . . He is relieved of this duty only 'where the omission is clearly harmful and erroneous as a matter of law in that it fails to provide the jury with the proper guidelines for determining guilt or innocence.' "[1]

In the absence of a proper request, it is not the duty of the trial judge to charge on any collateral matter.[2] Likewise, in the absence of a proper request, it is not necessary for the court to charge on the necessity of a unanimous verdict,[3] or to charge that in a crime there must be a joint operation of act and intention,[4] or to read the indictment to the jury or to instruct the jury that they may read the indictment where the jury has the indictment and where the judge has charged fully on the offense charged.[5] Also, in the absence of a request to charge, or the matter being called to the court's attention, it is not error for the judge to fail to charge on the duty to reconcile the testimony of witnesses, or on the effects

---

[10]Camphor v. State, 272 Ga. 408, 414, 529 S.E.2d 121 (2000).

[11]Cf. Martin v. State, 93 Ga.App. 580, 581 (2), 92 S.E.2d 233 (1956).

[12]Henderson v. Kibbe, 431 U.S. 145, 97 S.Ct. 1730, 52 L.Ed.2d 203 (1977).

[Section 24:9]

[1]Camphor v. State, 272 Ga. 408, 414 (6), 529 S.E.2d 121 (2000) (citation omitted).

[2]Watson v. State, 136 Ga. 236, 240 (6), 71 S.E. 122 (1911).

[3]Porter v. State, 141 Ga.App. 602, 603 (4), 234 S.E.2d 100 (1977); Hamilton v. State, 166 Ga.App. 328, 304 S.E.2d 473 (1983).

[4]Barrett v. State, 146 Ga.App. 207, 208 (2), 245 S.E.2d 890 (1978); O.C.G.A. § 16-2-1.

[5]Benefield v. State, 148 Ga.App. 211, 251 S.E.2d 78 (1978).

of contradictory or equivocal testimony, or on impeachment of a witness, or on the credit to be given an impeached witness.[6] However, while there is generally no error where a court, in the absence of a request, fails to instruct the jury that evidence admitted for one purpose is to be considered only for that purpose, it is error for a judge to fail to give such a requested instruction.[7]

In the absence of a timely written request, it is not error for the trial judge to fail to charge that the defendant's failure to testify does not create a presumption against him.[8]

Since the trial judge now sets the punishment and determines the sentence, the court is not required to instruct the jury that it can recommend misdemeanor punishment.[9]

In *Austin v. State*,[10] the court held that there was no error for the trial judge to fail to charge the jury that the defendant could not be convicted of both a count on malice murder and a count on felony murder as long as only one sentence was imposed.

§ 24:10   Charge—Matters that cannot be charged

It is error for the trial judge to give certain instructions to the jury. The following are examples of matters which have been held improper to include in jury instructions: (1) a reminder to the jury of the existence of the Supreme Court and the right of the defendant to appeal his case;[1] (2) references to probation, pardons, or paroles;[2] (3) instructions as to the possible sentences which could be imposed if the defendant is found guilty;[3] (4) appointment of a foreman of the jury;[4] (5) instruction to the jury

---

[6]Floyd v. State, 149 Ga.App. 164, 253 S.E.2d 780 (1979).

[7]Harrell v. State, 241 Ga. 181, 186, 243 S.E.2d 890 (1978).

[8]Mauldin v. State, 167 Ga.App. 789, 790 (4), 307 S.E.2d 689 (1983).

[9]Wallace v. State, 188 Ga.App. 77, 78 (2), 371 S.E.2d 914 (1988).

[10]Austin v. State, 261 Ga. 550, 551 (2), 408 S.E.2d 105 (1991).

[Section 24:10]

[1]Monroe v. State, 5 Ga. 85, 86 (5) (1848). See Gibson v. State, 288 Ga. 617, 706 S.E.2d 412 (2011) (remark by court to jury that "it would be reversible error" for them to receive certain exhibits deemed prejudicial because of possible inference that the exhibits were harmful to defendant and that

court believed that defendant was guilty). But cf. United States v. Dunbar, 591 F.2d 1190 (5th Cir. 1979). But in Corn v. Hopper, 244 Ga. 28, 31 (7), 257 S.E.2d 533 (1979), the court said that it was not error for the trial judge to inform the jury that there would be an automatic appeal of a death sentence.

[2]See O.C.G.A. § 17-8-76; Cash v. State, 231 Ga. 285, 286 (5), 201 S.E.2d 625 (1973).

[3]Moore v. State, 228 Ga. 662, 665 (5), 187 S.E.2d 277 (1972); Lewis v. State, 158 Ga.App. 575, 281 S.E.2d 318 (1981).

[4]Maynard v. Readdick, 128 Ga.App. 368, 369 (4), 196 S.E.2d 688 (1973).

that the defendant should be found guilty;[5] (6) charge to jury in capital case that the judge will fix the punishment for the defendant if the jury cannot agree;[6] (7) statement of judge to jury that "you may retire, and the quicker you get through the quicker we'll all go home";[7] (8) charge to the jury that it may recommend misdemeanor punishment;[8] (9) in a recidivist case the trial judge may not refer to the prior felony or the fact that the defendant is being tried as a recidivist.[9]

In *Quick v. State*,[10] the court held that a jury should not be encouraged to add stipulations, conditions, or recommendations of no parole. "Nor should the jury be instructed, implicitly or explicitly, that a defendant's release on parole is a matter governed solely by . . . the Board of Pardons and Paroles. If, and only if, the jury asks to be instructed about the possibility of parole, the court should mention the issue only to the extent of telling the jury in no uncertain terms that such matters are not proper for the jury's consideration."

§ 24:11   Sequential charges

In *Edge v. State*,[1] the trial judge first charged on malice murder, then on felony murder, and still later on voluntary manslaughter. The Georgia Supreme Court reversed. In *Miner v. State*,[2] the court held that "[n]othing in *Edge* requires the trial court to instruct a jury according to an exact formula; the intent of *Edge* was to preclude a sequential charge which could allow juries to find a defendant guilty of murder without consideration of evidence of provocation or passion which might authorize a verdict of voluntary manslaughter." In brief, the trial judge should charge on malice murder, then voluntary manslaughter and thereafter on felony murder if such a charge is appropriate in the case.

---

[5]Johnson v. State, 69 Ga.App. 440, 26 S.E.2d 121 (1943); United States v. Skinner, 437 F.2d 164, 165 (5th Cir. 1971).

[6]See Morrison v. State, 126 Ga.App. 1, 4 (5), 189 S.E.2d 864 (1972).

[7]Foushi v. State, 144 Ga.App. 608, 609 (3), 244 S.E.2d 14 (1978).

[8]Goodrum v. State, 158 Ga.App. 602, 604 (6), 281 S.E.2d 254 (1981).

[9]Jolly v. State, 164 Ga.App. 240 (1), 296 S.E.2d 784 (1982). See § 13:8, supra, on requirement of grand juror's names in the indictment, and § 24:18, infra, on sending the indictment and evidence to the jury room.

[10]Quick v. State, 256 Ga. 780, 787, 353 S.E.2d 497 (1987).

[Section 24:11]

[1]Edge v. State, 261 Ga. 865 (2), 414 S.E.2d 463 (1992).

In Battles v. Chapman, 269 Ga. 702, 506 S.E.2d 838 (1998), the court held that the defendant in an appeal was denied effective assistance of counsel where appellate counsel failed to raise as error the failure of the trial court to follow *Edge*.

[2]Miner v. State, 268 Ga. 67, 68 (4), 485 S.E.2d 456 (1997).

In *Harrison v. State*,[3] the court said, "In *Edge* we adopted the 'modified merger rule,' which provides that a felony murder conviction is precluded only where it would prevent an otherwise warranted verdict of voluntary manslaughter. . . ." *Edge* has no application to cases where the defendant is found guilty of murder and involuntary manslaughter.[4]

In *Akins v. State*,[5] the Georgia Supreme Court held that it was not error for the trial judge to instruct "the jury that it had to determine malice murder before it considered the lesser-included offense of voluntary manslaughter." Furthermore, in *Bellamy v. State*,[6] the court held that where a defendant was convicted of malice murder, there can be no harmful Edge violation. Indeed, *Edge* is essentially restricted to the context of felony murder and voluntary manslaughter.[7] In a case where the defendant is charged with armed robbery and aggravated assault, *Edge* would have no application since the elements of any lesser included offense would be included in the greater offense.[8] In *Parks v. State*,[9] the court approved an instruction providing that "should you find the defendant not guilty of . . . [the greater offense] or should you have a reasonable doubt as to his guilt of that offense, you would be authorized to determine whether he is guilty of the lesser included offense. . . ."

A trial court may instruct a jury to consider a lesser offense. "A trial court may not, however, instruct the jury that it must reach a unanimous verdict on the greater offense before considering the lesser offense."[10]

§ 24:12   Charge—Defenses

As previously pointed out, if an affirmative defense is raised by the evidence, the trial judge must charge on the defense even in

---

[3]Harrison v. State, 268 Ga. 574, 575 (2), 492 S.E.2d 218 (1997).

[4]Jones v. State, 263 Ga. 835, 840, 439 S.E.2d 645 (1994). See Kipp v. State, 296 Ga. 250, 252, 765 S.E.2d 924 (2014) (unlike voluntary manslaughter, offense of involuntary manslaughter does not contain the mitigating factor of "provoked passion").

[5]Akins v. State, 269 Ga. 838, 839 (2), 504 S.E.2d 196 (1998). Cf. Camphor v. State, 272 Ga. 408, 415 (6)(b), 529 S.E.2d 121 (2000).

[6]Bellamy v. State, 272 Ga. 157, 160 (6), 527 S.E.2d 867 (2000).

[7]Grimes v. State, 293 Ga. 559, 748 S.E.2d 441 (2013); Kirk v. State, 210 Ga.App. 440, 436 S.E.2d 553 (1993).

[8]Davis v. State, 264 Ga.App. 221, 226 (5), 590 S.E.2d 192 (2003).

[9]Parks v. State, 241 Ga.App. 381, 384 (5), 526 S.E.2d 893 (1999).

[10]Armstrong v. State, 277 Ga. 122, 123 (2), 587 S.E.2d 5 (2003). See Watson v. State, 329 Ga. App. 334, 765 S.E.2d 24 (2014), opinion vacated in part on other grounds, 335 Ga. App. 227, 780 S.E.2d 822 (2015).

the absence of a request. See § 24:2, supra. In *Jones v. State,*[1] the court pointed out that "[w]here an affirmative defense is raised by the evidence, including a defendant's own statement, the trial court must present that defense to the jury as part of its charge, even absent a request and even absent a reservation of right to later object."

The trial court cannot "arbitrarily reject the defense theory raised by the accused's testimony as unworthy of belief and refuse to charge upon the issue raised."[2] If some evidence exists to support the defense, the charge is required regardless of the court's opinion of the credibility of that evidence.[3]

Nonetheless, an affirmative defense need not be specifically charged "if the case as a whole is fairly presented to the jury."[4] For example, where the defense is justification and the charge as a whole fairly explains that the jury may not find the defendant guilty should it believe that the defendant's actions were justified, a specific charge on justification is not required.

Generally a defendant is not entitled to a charge on both self-defense and accident since the defenses are deemed to be inconsistent, due to the fact that in self-defense the defendant admits that the act was intentional.[5]

However, it is error for the trial judge to refuse to give a charge on self-defense and accident where there is evidence which shows that the victim was killed while the defendant was using force he reasonably believed was necessary to prevent the victim from killing or inflicting great bodily harm on the defendant.[6]

In *Seckinger v. State,*[7] the court held that there was no error where the trial judge failed to charge on "guilty but mentally ill" where the defendant "did not give notice of his intention to raise the defense of mental illness and offered no evidence that at the time of the crime he had a disorder that significantly impaired his judgment, behavior, capacity to recognize reality, or ability to cope with ordinary demands of life." See § 14:92, supra, on notice required of the defendant to raise the issue of insanity, mental illness or mental competency.

[Section 24:12]

[1]Jones v. State, 226 Ga.App. 619, 621 (1), 487 S.E.2d 371 (1997).

[2]Booker v. State, 247 Ga. 74, 274 S.E.2d 334 (1981).

[3]Jones v. State, 220 Ga.App. 784, 470 S.E.2d 326 (1996). See Ellzey v. State, 272 Ga.App. 253, 612 S.E.2d 77 (2005) (citations omitted).

[4]Owens v. State; 173 Ga.App. 309, 313 (5), 326 S.E.2d 509 (1985)

(citations omitted).

[5]Koritta v. State, 206 Ga.App. 228, 229 (1), 424 S.E.2d 799 (1992), rev'd on other grounds, 263 Ga. 703, 438 S.E.2d 68 (1994).

[6]Koritta v. State, 263 Ga. 703, 438 S.E.2d 68 (1994); Turner v. State, 262 Ga. 359, 418 S.E.2d 52 (1992).

[7]Seckinger v. State, 267 Ga. 260, 261 (2), 477 S.E.2d 129 (1996).

§ 24:13   Charge—Errors requiring reversal

Where there is an error in jury instructions, it is presumed to be prejudicial and harmful, and the appellate courts so hold unless it appears from the entire record that the error was harmless.[1] However, even when instructions are not technically perfect, it "is not necessary, in considering a charge, to assume a possible adverse construction, for a charge that is sufficiently clear to be understood by jurors of ordinary capacity."[2] As far as reversal is concerned, an error in a charge must be considered in the light of the rule that "[s]ubstantial correctness, rather than mathematical accuracy is required of the trial judge in instructing the jury."[3] "A mere verbal inaccuracy . . . which results from a palpable 'slip of the tongue' and clearly could not have misled or confused the jury, is not reversible error."[4]

If the trial court charges the jury correctly on a certain point and elsewhere in the instructions he charges incorrectly on the same point, this constitutes error since the jury cannot be expected to select and be guided by the correct portion and to disregard the incorrect.[5] "Where two or more jury instructions directly conflict with one another, a new trial is required."[6] If the court gives an erroneous instruction, it can be corrected only by having the judge expressly withdraw it and tell the jury to disregard it.[7]

A repetition of a principle of law is not reversible error unless it appears, from the charge as a whole, that there is such undue emphasis as to relate to an unfair statement of the law.[8]

An erroneous charge on a theory not in issue does not require a reversal unless it is shown to be prejudicial and harmful in the light of the entire record.[9]

In *Victorine v. State*,[10] the court held that where "trial counsel

---

[Section 24:13]

[1]Barton v. State, 79 Ga.App. 380, 387, 53 S.E.2d 707 (1949). See Muir v. State, 248 Ga. App. 49, 545 S.E.2d 176 (2001).

[2]Murdix v. State, 250 Ga. 272, 275 (2), 297 S.E.2d 265 (1982); Feblez v. State, 181 Ga.App. 567, 568, 353 S.E.2d 64 (1987).

[3]Tuggle v. State, 165 Ga.App. 53, 54, 299 S.E.2d 121 (1983).

[4]Caldwell v. State, 167 Ga.App. 692, 695 (4), 307 S.E.2d 511 (1983).

[5]Gill v. Willingham, 156 Ga. 728, 729 (4), 120 S.E. 108 (1923); Bryant v. State, 191 Ga. 686, 720 (13), 13 S.E.2d 820 (1941).

[6]Dodd v. State, 324 Ga. App. 827, 834, 752 S.E.2d 29 (2013).

[7]Burnett v. State, 152 Ga.App. 738, 264 S.E.2d 33 (1979).

[8]Brown v. State, 142 Ga.App. 247, 248 (2), 235 S.E.2d 671 (1977). Accord, Key v. State, 226 Ga.App. 240, 242, 485 S.E.2d 804 (1997).

[9]Davis v. State, 167 Ga.App. 701, 702 (1), 307 S.E.2d 272 (1983).

[10]Victorine v. State, 264 Ga. 580, 581 (4)(a), 449 S.E.2d 91 (1994); Burk v. State, 223 Ga.App. 530, 531 (1), 478

[for the defendant] specifically requests that a portion of the charge be omitted and the trial court acquiesces," the defendant may not object to the charge as given. Likewise, a defendant cannot complain of the giving of a charge which he requested.[11] Conversely, the failure to give an unrequested charge will only constitute reversible error where "the omission is clearly harmful and erroneous as a matter of law in that [the charge as given] fails to provide the jury with the proper guidelines for determining guilt or innocence."[12]

§ 24:14 Custody, conduct, and deliberations of jury

After the charge is given, the jury is taken to the jury room with the admonition not to begin deliberations until they receive the indictment as well as any documentary or real evidence which may have been introduced at the trial. The trial judge, in all cases except capital cases where the prosecution is seeking the death penalty,[1] may in his discretion allow the jury to be separated before or during deliberations under appropriate instructions.[2] It appears that the jury may still not deliberate about the case unless all jurors are together.[3]

In *Sears v. State*,[4] the court pointed out that jurors are expected to bring their life experiences into the jury room and that "threats and belligerent exchanges in the course of deliberations often accompany the heightened atmosphere in the jury room and are insufficient to upset the verdict."

The trial court has discretion to allow a jury in deliberation to rehear testimony provided the defendant is present.[5] In *Tuff v.*

S.E.2d 416 (1996).

[11]Woods v. State, 224 Ga.App. 52, 56 (6), 479 S.E.2d 414 (1996).

[12]Seay v. State, 276 Ga. 139, 140 (2), 576 S.E.2d 839 (2003); see Kennedy v. State, 277 Ga. 588, 591 (3), 592 S.E.2d 830 (2004); see also, Kitchen v. State, 263 Ga. 629 (1), 436 S.E.2d 645 (1993).

[Section 24:14]

[1]Harrison v. State, 236 Ga. 355 (3), 223 S.E.2d 715 (1976).

[2]O.C.G.A. § 15-12-142. Rule 532 of the Uniform Rules of Criminal Procedure provides as follows:

"Rule 532. [Jury Deliberations.]

"The jurors shall be kept together for deliberations as the court reasonably directs. If the court permits the jury to recess its deliberations, it shall admonish the jurors not to discuss the case until they reconvene in the jury room. If the deliberations are recessed, the jurors shall be sequestered unless, upon consent of the parties, the court otherwise orders."

[3]See Norton v. State, 137 Ga. 842 (6), 74 S.E. 759 (1912).

[4]Sears v. State, 270 Ga. 834, 840 (3), 514 S.E.2d 426 (1999) (citing People v. Redd, 164 A.D.2d 34, 561 N.Y.S.2d 439 (1990)).

[5]Johns v. State, 239 Ga. 681, 238 S.E.2d 372 (1977).

State,[6] the "testimony" which the jury was properly allowed to hear was an audiotape of a witness's 911 call.

The trial court has broad discretion in determining how late to keep jurors during the evidentiary phase of a trial and after the jury has started its deliberations. However, a judge's threat to hold a jury over a weekend unless it reaches a verdict may amount to intimidation and coercion.[7]

§ 24:15   Alternate jurors during deliberations

At this time alternate jurors may be discharged by the court or, in the judge's discretion, kept in the custody of the sheriff or some other court officer separate[1] from the regular jurors until a verdict has been reached.[2] O.C.G.A. § 15-12-172 provides:

"If at any time, whether before or after final submission of the case to the jury, a juror dies, becomes ill, upon other good cause shown to the court is found to be unable to perform his duty, or is discharged for other legal cause, the first alternate juror shall take the place of the first juror becoming incapacitated. Further replacements shall be made in similar numerical sequence provided the alternate jurors have not been discharged. An alternate juror taking the place of any incapacitated juror shall thereafter be deemed to be a member of the jury of 12 and shall have full power to take part in the deliberations of the jury and the finding of the verdict. Any verdict found by any jury having thereon alternate jurors shall have the same force, effect, and validity as if found by the original jury of 12."

The Georgia Supreme Court has upheld O.C.G.A. § 15-12-172 against an attack asserting that it violated the constitutional right to an impartial jury where an alternate juror was substituted after deliberations had begun.[3]

In *Perry v. State,*[4] the Georgia Supreme Court concluded that there was no error in recalling an alternate juror who had been discharged and had gone home after the charge to the jury.

The federal rule provides that an alternate juror may be

---

[6]Tuff v. State, 278 Ga. 91 (6), 597 S.E.2d 328 (2004).

[7]State v. Jones, 292 N.C. 513, 234 S.E.2d 555 (1977).

[Section 24:15]

[1]In Bullock v. State, 150 Ga.App. 824, 825 (2), 258 S.E.2d 610 (1979), the court held that it was error to allow the alternate juror to retire with the other 12 jurors for deliberations in the face of defense counsel's objections.

[2]O.C.G.A. § 15-12-171.

[3]Tanner v. State, 242 Ga. 437 (1), 249 S.E.2d 238 (1978). Generally, see Annot., 84 A.L.R.2d 1288 (1962), and see the commentary following A.B.A. Standards, Trial by Jury, Vol. III, Standard 15-2.7; Green v. State, 246 Ga. 598, 603 (16), 272 S.E.2d 475 (1980).

[4]Perry v. State, 255 Ga. 490, 493 (5), 339 S.E.2d 922 (1986).

substituted for one of the regular jurors after the jury retires for the purpose of reaching a verdict, but if an alternate does replace a juror after deliberations have begun, the jury must begin its deliberations anew.[5]

If an alternate juror goes to the jury room with the other jurors when they begin their deliberations, there seems to be a presumption that the defendant has been injured. However, when this fact has been discovered, if the alternate juror is immediately removed and the trial judge determines that his presence in the jury room will not influence the members of the jury, the presumption of harm is overcome.[6] In *Weaver v. State,*[7] an alternate juror remained in the jury room during all the deliberations. The state obtained affidavits from all the jurors stating that their decisions were not influenced at all by the alternate's presence. The court concluded that the state had met its burden of showing harmlessness.

Even after a jury begins deliberations, the trial judge may excuse a juror if the judge learns that the juror is disqualified[8] and continue the trial with an alternate juror if there is an alternate juror or if the parties agree to a verdict of a jury of less than 12 jurors. Indeed "[c]ounsel for an accused can validly waive the accused's right to a jury of twelve 'if (1) the waiver is made without objection, in the accused's presence or (2) the accused

---

[5]Rule 24(c) of the Federal Rules of Criminal Procedure.

[6]Duncan v. State, 155 Ga.App. 624, 626 (4), 271 S.E.2d 878 (1980). In *Duncan*, the alternate juror remained in the jury room for about 55 minutes before the trial judge discovered what had happened. The jury was immediately called in and the foreman when questioned said that the jury had not reached a verdict and was not close to doing so. The judge then asked each juror if the fact that the alternate had been in the jury room would cause him or her to vote any differently than he or she would have voted. Each juror answered no. The foreman was then asked what the alternate had said and this was related to the judge. The jury was instructed to disregard anything the alternate had said.

Most of the federal cases have held that the presence of an alternate juror in the jury room during delibera-

tions is per se reversible error. United States v. Chatman, 584 F.2d 1358 (4th Cir. 1978); United States v. Beasley, 464 F.2d 468 (10th Cir. 1972). Contra, United States v. Allison, 481 F.2d 468 (5th Cir. 1973). See U.S. v. Olano, 507 U.S. 725, 113 S. Ct. 1770, 123 L. Ed. 2d 508 (1993) (in absence of prejudice, presence of alternate jurors during deliberations with instructions not to deliberate did not violate substantive rights of defendant and was not plain error). See Annot., "Presence of Alternate Juror in Jury Room as Ground for Reversal of State Criminal Conviction," 15 A.L.R.4th 1127 (1982).

[7]Weaver v. State, 170 Ga.App. 731, 733(6), 318 S.E.2d 196 (1984); London v. State, 260 Ga.App. 780, 580 S.E.2d 686 (2003). Accord, State v. Newsome, 259 Ga. 187, 188(2), 378 S.E.2d 125 (1989).

[8]Hart v. State, 157 Ga.App. 716, 718 (2), 278 S.E.2d 419 (1981).

otherwise acquiesces in the waiver.' "[9]

Generally, on alternate jurors, see section 18-35, supra.

§ 24:16　Objections to charge

As soon as the jury is taken to the jury room, counsel for each side is normally given an opportunity to object to the charge.[1] If objections are made and the trial judge decides that he made an error in the charge, he may recall the jury and attempt to correct the mistake. However, in a criminal case, it has been held that the trial judge "is not obligated to ask counsel whether they have any charge objections before the jury returns its verdict"[2] and "a trial court's failure to inquire of counsel whether there are exceptions to the charge does not result in reversible error."[3]

Although O.C.G.A. § 5-5-24 relating to the necessity of making exceptions to the charge of the court for errors in the charge does not apply to criminal cases, effective July 1, 2007, counsel in criminal cases must put on the record specific objections to the jury charge before deliberations begin pursuant to O.C.G.A. § 17-8-58. Any objection to the charge not made of record, save those involving plain error, are waived under O.C.G.A. § 17-8-58. Previously, counsel could generally reserve objections to the charge pending a motion for new trial or appeal.[4] This represents a major change in the manner by which error in a charge is presented and counsel should be prepared to state objections with sufficient specificity to allow the trial court an opportunity to rule intelligently.[5] However, after the enactment of O.C.G.A. § 17-8-58, there were a number of cases which did not restrict appellate review of jury charges to those which involved plain error and which also were not the subject of an objection at trial. In *State v.*

---

[9]Reed v. State, 318 Ga. App. 412, 414, 734 S.E.2d 113 (2012) (citing Davis v. State, 192 Ga. App. 47, 48, 383 S.E.2d 615 (1989)).

[Section 24:16]

[1]See Daniels v. State, 230 Ga. 126, 195 S.E.2d 900 (1973), holding that there is no statute in Georgia giving counsel an opportunity to object to a charge in a criminal case.

In United States v. Schartner, 426 F.2d 470, 478 (3d Cir. 1970), the court said that under Rule 30 it is mandatory that counsel be given an opportunity to except to the charge out of the presence of the jury.

[2]Garrett v. State, 184 Ga.App. 593, 594 (3), 362 S.E.2d 150 (1987).

[3]Crenshaw v. State, 237 Ga.App. 511, 515 (3), 515 S.E.2d 642 (1999).

[4]Gaither v. State, 234 Ga. 465, 216 S.E.2d 324 (1975); McCoy v. State, 262 Ga. 699, 425 S.E.2d 646 (1993).

[5]See Collier v. State, 288 Ga. 756, 707 S.E.2d 102 (2011) (dissent by Justice Nahmias is critical of several appellate decisions which have failed to restrict the review of jury charges to plain error in those cases where counsel did not object to the charge at trial).

Kelly,[6] the Georgia Supreme Court held that "appellate review for plain error is required whenever an appealing party properly asserts an error in jury instruction." The court overruled all authority to the contrary.

The court reiterated that the definition in Georgia for plain error is the same as that in federal courts. "Plain error" is "that which is 'so clearly erroneous so as to result in a likelihood of a grave miscarriage of justice' or which seriously affects the fairness of the proceedings."[7] In order to meet that standard, the court adopted a four-prong test:

> First, there must be an error or defect—some sort of "[d]eviation from a legal rule"—that has not been intentionally relinquished or abandoned, i.e., affirmatively waived, by the appellant. Second, the legal error must be clear or obvious, rather than subject to reasonable dispute. Third, the error must have affected the appellant's substantial rights, which in the ordinary case means he must demonstrate that it "affected the outcome of the [trial] court proceedings." Fourth and finally, if the above three prongs are satisfied, the [appellate court] has the *discretion* to remedy the error—discretion which ought to be exercised only if the error " 'seriously affect[s] the fairness, integrity or public reputation of judicial proceedings.' "[8]

The court went on to note that while it would "review properly enumerated and argued claims of jury instruction error regardless of whether the appealing party specifically casts the alleged infirmity as plain error" it warned that "the hurdle to establishing plain error is high . . . and therefore that the failure to specifically articulate how the alleged error satisfies the high standard increases the likelihood that their claims . . . will be denied."[9] Whether an instruction constitutes "plain error" for purposes of O.C.G.A. § 17-8-58(b) is determined by what the law is at the time the issue is under review on appeal, not the law in effect at the time the trial court made its ruling at trial.[10]

O.C.G.A. § 5-5-24(c) provides that "appellate courts shall consider and review erroneous charges where there has been a *substantial* error in the charge which was harmful as a matter of law, regardless of whether objection was made. . . ." (Emphasis

---

[6]State v. Kelly, 290 Ga. 29, 32–33, 718 S.E.2d 232 (2011).

[7]State v. Kelly, 290 Ga. 29, 32–33, 718 S.E.2d 232 (2011), citing U.S. v. Fuentes-Coba, 738 F.2d 1191, 1196, 16 Fed. R. Evid. Serv. 50 (11th Cir. 1984).

[8]State v. Kelly, 290 Ga. 29, 32–33,

718 S.E.2d 232 (2011), citing Puckett v. U.S., 556 U.S. 129 (II)(a), 129 S. Ct. 1423, 173 L. Ed. 2d 266 (2009).

[9]State v. Kelly, 290 Ga. 29, 32 n.2, 718 S.E.2d 232 (2011).

[10]Lyman v. State, 301 Ga. 312, 800 S.E.2d 333 (2017).

added.)[11] Thus, in *Essuon v. State*,[12] despite the failure of the defense to object to the charges, the defendant's conviction was reversed because the trial court failed to define "felony" and "murder" under elements of the offense charged.

In *Woodard v. State*,[13] the Court noted:

> [W]hen a defendant fails to object to an alleged instructional error before the jury begins its deliberations, appellate review is precluded unless the alleged defect amounts to "plain error" O.C.G.A. § 17-8-58(b), and there is no plain error where the defendant "affirmatively waived" the alleged error. The concept that even a plain error can be waived is often referred to as "invited" error. However, looking to the federal plain-error decisions on which this court has relied in articulating the scope of plain error review under O.C.G.A. § 17-8-58, we have cautioned that a "waiver" in this context differs from the "forfeiture" that results from the mere failure to timely assert a legal right. An affirmative waiver requires the "*intentional* relinquishment or abandonment of a *known* right." Id. (emphasis added) (quoting *United States v. Olano*, 507 U.S. 725, 733, 113 S.Ct. 1170, 123 L.Ed.2d 508) (1993)). [Internal citations omitted.]

Thus, in *Cheddersingh v. State*,[14] the failure of defense counsel to object, even when asked by the court, as to whether he had an objection to a verdict form which contained wording which stated "we the jury unanimously and beyond a reasonable doubt find the Defendant _____," providing the choices of guilty or not guilty was considered a forfeiture rather than an affirmative waiver. Unable to find an intent to waive a known right in the dialogue between counsel and the court or discern "any tactical reason on the part of the defense to embrace such a burden-shifting verdict form," the Georgia Supreme Court proceeded to reverse the lower court on the basis of plain error.

If the trial judge, prior to argument, tells counsel that he will reject a specified charge and then gives it, counsel should call the

---

[11]See Young v. State, 238 Ga.App. 555, 556 (2), 519 S.E.2d 481 (1999).

[12]Essuon v. State, 286 Ga. App. 869, 650 S.E.2d 409 (2007). See Powell v. State, 304 Ga. App. 221, 695 S.E.2d 736 (2010) (error not waived by failure to object to charge where court charged entire battery statute when indictment only charged one means for committing offense but evidence supported conviction by another means).

[13]Woodard v. State, 296 Ga. 803, 809(a), 771 S.E.2d 362 (2015). The Court did note that cases decided prior to the enactment of O.C.G.A. § 17-8-58 which broadly applied the invited error doctrine to preclude review of jury instructions requested by the defense may no longer be viable. The issue would be whether the defense would now be deemed to have waived all error related to a charge it requests or only error related to specific language "that the record shows the defendant included or omitted after considering the controlling law." The court did not need to resolve that question but the latter approach is the likely direction that the court will one day take.

[14]Cheddersingh v. State, 290 Ga. 680, 684, 724 S.E.2d 366 (2012).

fact to the court's attention and request the right to argue the particular point to the jury after the charge.[15] Where the trial judge agrees to give a defense instruction, and the defendant excepts to the failure to give such a charge, the failure of defense counsel to request an opportunity to re-argue the case is not a waiver of his objection.[16]

In *Stynchcombe v. Floyd,*[17] the Georgia Supreme Court held that the express waiver of counsel of objections to a charge does not apply at the sentencing phase of a death case. Thus, the fact that defense counsel stated that he had no objections to a charge at the sentencing phase of a case did not prevent the reversal of the death sentence where the jury was not charged that it could recommend a life sentence even if it found statutory aggravating circumstances. O.C.G.A. § 24-1-103(d) (effective January 1, 2013) now allows a court to consider plain errors "affecting substantial rights although such errors were not brought to the attention of the court."[18]

§ 24:17   Right of counsel to further argument

When the trial judge gives a charge which he previously indicated he would not give, counsel may have a right to further argument if it is necessary for him to cover the point unexpectedly charged by the trial judge. See § 24:16, supra.

§ 24:18   Sending the indictment and the evidence to jury room

After objections to the charge have been raised and heard, real and documentary evidence as well as the indictment are taken to the jury room.[1] Before the evidence is carried to the jury room, counsel should carefully check it to be sure that the only items

---

[15]Jones v. State, 177 Ga.App. 531, 532 (2), 339 S.E.2d 786 (1986); Daniels v. State, 137 Ga.App. 371, 374, 224 S.E.2d 60 (1976); Blackmon v. State, 158 Ga.App. 665, 667 (2), 281 S.E.2d 634 (1981).

[16]Goins v. State, 177 Ga.App. 536 (1), 339 S.E.2d 790 (1986).

[17]Stynchcombe v. Floyd, 252 Ga. 113, 114, 311 S.E.2d 828 (1984).

[18]See Durham v. State, 292 Ga. 239, 734 S.E.2d 377 (2012). See also, O.C.G.A. § 17-8-57 (judge's opinion on what has or has not been proven or defendant's guilt); O.C.G.A. § 17-8-58(b) (plain error in charge subject to

review on appeal of timely objection).

[Section 24:18]

[1]In Salem v. State, 228 Ga. 186, 188 (5), 184 S.E.2d 650 (1971), the court said it is the practice in Georgia to permit the jury to have the indictment in the jury room. McCormick, Evidence § 217. A.B.A. Standards, Trial by Jury, Vol. III, Standard 15-4.1 provides as follows:

"**Standard 15-4.1. Materials to jury room**

"(a) The court in its discretion may permit the jury, upon retiring for deliberation, to take to the jury room a copy of the charges against the

going out to the jury are the indictment, evidence properly admitted in court, and specimen verdicts if they are being used.

Where the trial judge has carefully instructed the jury as to the law and the various forms of verdicts, it is not error to permit the jury to have with the evidence a form verdict for every verdict which could legally be returned under the evidence, provided this is not done in such a way as to influence the jury but merely to help them in putting the verdict they reach in the proper form.[2]

In connection with an indictment in which the defendant is charged as an habitual offender or a recidivist, it is error to permit the indictment to go to the jury unless the part relating to prior convictions and recidivism is so obscured[3] or eliminated that the jury will not be advised of such fact.[4] Likewise, where a defendant is charged with murder and possession of a firearm as a convicted felon, it is error to submit an indictment to the jury setting out the earlier felony if the defendant has entered a guilty plea to the latter count.[5] In a case not involving possession of a firearm by a convicted felon, the better practice is probably to send a "dummy" indictment to the jury room from which all references to prior offenses and recidivism have been deleted.[6] The same rule applies to an indictment, when there is a notation of a prior mistrial on it. But if the defendant fails to object and the indictment is sent to the jury room, the defendant may not later object.[7] Likewise, where a verdict, finding a co-indictee guilty, has been written on the indictment, the verdict should be con-

defendant and exhibits and writings which have been received in evidence, except depositions, and with the consent of both parties copies of instructions previously given.

"(b) Among the considerations the court should take into account in making this determination are:

"(i) whether the material will aid the jury in proper consideration of the case;

"(ii) whether any party will be unduly prejudiced by submission of the material; and

"(iii) whether the material may be subjected to improper use by the jury."

[2]Park v. State, 126 Ga. 575, 576 (13), 55 S.E. 489 (1906).

[3]Tankersley v. State, 155 Ga.App. 917, 920 (5), 273 S.E.2d 862 (1980).

[4]Clemmons v. State, 233 Ga. 187, 210 S.E.2d 657 (1974). In Starks v.

State, 157 Ga.App. 579, 278 S.E.2d 156 (1981), the court pointed out that where a defendant makes no objection to giving a masked indictment to the jury, he waives any objection which he may have as to the form of the indictment.

See § 13:18, supra, on contents of a recidivist indictment, and § 26:11, infra, on recidivism punishment.

[5]Evans v. State, 253 Ga. 331, 320 S.E.2d 168 (1984).

[6]In Chandler v. State, 143 Ga.App. 608, 610 (6), 239 S.E.2d 158 (1977), the court concluded that under the facts of that case it was not error to permit a copy of the indictment with a deletion of the name and plea of the co-defendant to go out with the jury.

[7]Page v. State, 120 Ga.App. 709 (1), 172 S.E.2d 207 (1969). The *Page* case actually says that the request to conceal the notation should be made before the jury retires. Cf. Salem v.

cealed unless a "dummy indictment" is used as suggested above, but the defendant may waive this right.[8] In *Gilstrap v. State*,[9] the court held that the trial judge did not err in permitting an indictment to go to the jury room without excising the guilty plea of a co-indictee, where defense counsel had been given an opportunity to inspect the indictment and no objection was made until after verdict.

As previously pointed out in § 20:6, supra, a written confession may not be carried to the jury room over proper objection even if the document has been previously read to the jury.

Where a defendant has been convicted on a lesser included offense and he obtains a new trial, see § 14:61, supra, on the handling of the indictment at the second trial. See § 26:28, infra, on recidivism punishment and former convictions.

§ 24:19 Communicating with jury

Unless the trial judge permits the jury to disperse during deliberation, as is permissible in cases where the death penalty is not sought,[1] the jury "shall be entirely separated from the world, and . . . . no communication whatever shall be had with them from the beginning of the trial until the verdict is rendered, unless by leave of the court. It [the law] contemplates that no outside influence shall be brought to bear on the minds of the jury, and that nothing shall occur outside of the trial which shall disturb their minds in any way; that the minds of the jury shall be entirely occupied with the consideration of the cases which they are sworn to try."[2] If there is any communication between sequestered jurors and outsiders, there is a presumption that the defendant has been injured and the burden is on the state to rebut the presumption.[3] For purposes of this rule, the jury bailiff is deemed to be an outsider, and the burden is on the state to

---

State, 228 Ga. 186, 188 (5), 184 S.E.2d 650 (1971). In Harrison v. State, 143 Ga.App. 883, 885, 240 S.E.2d 263 (1977), the court said that generally in Georgia it has been held that "masking, detaching or erasure of former verdicts and damaging evidence" has been permitted.

[8]Johnson v. State, 246 Ga. 474, 271 S.E.2d 789 (1980). In Pope v. State, 157 Ga.App. 154 (2), 276 S.E.2d 666 (1981), the court held that it was error for the trial judge, over objection, to permit a special presentment to go to the jury room when it contained a guilty plea of a co-defendant and notes

written by the district attorney.

[9]Gilstrap v. State, 162 Ga.App. 841, 845 (8), 292 S.E.2d 495 (1982).

[Section 24:19]

[1]O.C.G.A. § 15-12-142.

[2]Shaw v. State, 83 Ga. 92, 100, 9 S.E. 768 (1889) (quoted with approval in Battle v. State, 234 Ga. 637, 638, 217 S.E.2d 255 (1975)); Owens v. State, 251 Ga. 313 (9), 305 S.E.2d 102 (1983). Cf. Recoba v. State, 179 Ga.App. 31, 33, 345 S.E.2d 81 (1986).

[3]Whitlock v. State, 230 Ga. 700, 701 (1), 198 S.E.2d 865 (1973). In Stewart v. State, 165 Ga.App. 428,

rebut the presumption of harm where a communication takes place between a bailiff and a juror.[4] Thus, where the sheriff testified at the trial, and during deliberations took the indictment inside the jury room, placed it on the table and left without speaking, the court held that it was error to overrule the defendant's motion for mistrial where the state did not show the error to be harmless. The court said "the presence of the county's chief law enforcement in the jury room, bringing in the indictment, itself constitutes a communication."[5]

In *Hanifa v. State*,[6] the court pointed out that "the trial judge should not in any manner communicate with the jury about the case in the absence of the accused and his counsel." Thus, in *Sammons v. State*,[7] the Georgia Supreme Court reversed a defendant's conviction where the trial court excused a juror and replaced her with an alternate after an ex-parte conference with the juror. The court's holding was premised upon the well established notion that "[p]roceedings at which the jury composition is selected or changed are a critical stage at which the defendant is entitled to be present."

Although there is no burden on the state to rebut the presumption of harm to the defendant because a jury is not sequestered during deliberations, if there is any evidence of a communication between a juror and another individual about the case, the same presumption of harm to the defendant referred to above appears to be applicable, even though the jurors were not sequestered.[8]

However, where there has been such an improper communication, the trial judge may examine the juror or jurors and the third person or persons one by one (outside the presence of each

---

430, 300 S.E.2d 331 (1983), the court said that "unless the character of the communication clearly shows that it could not have been prejudicial to the accused, the presumption of law would be that it was prejudicial."

[4]Vick v. State, 166 Ga.App. 572 (4), 305 S.E.2d 17 (1983) (citing Battle v. State, 234 Ga. 637, 639, 217 S.E.2d 255 (1975)).

[5]McMichael v. State, 252 Ga. 305, 308 (4), 313 S.E.2d 693 (1984).

[6]Hanifa v. State, 269 Ga. 797, 807 (6), 505 S.E.2d 731 (1998). See Vaughn v. State, 281 Ga. App. 475, 636 S.E.2d 163 (2006), defendants absence deemed prejudicial where court, with counsel present, considered and denied a motion to excuse a juror after talking with juror about suspicious

hang-up calls juror had received during trial.

[7]Sammons v. State, 279 Ga. 386, 387 (2), 612 S.E.2d 785 (2005) (citations omitted). Only after the juror was excused did the trial court inform counsel of its decision to replace the juror. The defendant first learned of the court's action when it was put on the record following the in-chambers conference with counsel. Compare Fuller v. State, 277 Ga. 505 (2), 591 S.E.2d 782 (2004) and Berry v. State, 274 Ga.App. 366, 618 S.E.2d 72 (2005) to avoid waiver, defendant must make timely objection to communication with jury made out of the presence of the defendant.

[8]United States v. Williams, 568 F.2d 464 (5th Cir. 1978).

other) in court to determine the contents of the communication, whether the juror or jurors have passed the information on to other jurors, and whether there is any evidence that the communication has or will exert any influence on any juror.[9]

It is improper for the bailiff to communicate with the jury about the case[10] or for other persons to communicate with the jurors outside the presence of the defendant, his counsel, and the judge.[11] In other words, all communications between the jurors and other persons should be in open court[12] in the presence of the defendant and his counsel. "[T]he better practice is for the judge to have no communication with the jury . . . except through the medium of the sworn bailiff in charge of the jury[,] and the communication should be restricted, in the absence of the accused and his counsel, to matters relating to the comfort and convenience of the

---

[9]Cf. Head v. State, 191 Ga.App. 262, 264 (4), 381 S.E.2d 519 (1989); Arnold v. State, 243 Ga.App. 118, 122 (2), 532 S.E.2d 458 (2000).

[10]See Battle v. State, 234 Ga. 637, 217 S.E.2d 255 (1975). Where the bailiff in charge of a jury states to a juror that a defendant is guilty and to another juror that if there is anything wrong in finding the defendant guilty, the Supreme Court will correct it, this violates the confrontation clause of the Sixth Amendment made applicable to the states through the due process clause of the Fourteenth Amendment. Parker v. Gladden, 385 U.S. 363, 87 S.Ct. 468, 17 L.Ed.2d 420 (1966).

In Mercer v. State, 169 Ga.App. 723, 728 (6), 314 S.E.2d 729 (1984), a juror believed to be the foreman asked the bailiff "if the jury could have a portion of a witness's testimony repeated." The bailiff told the juror that the jury "would have to go with what they had" but also asked if the juror would like to see the judge. The juror declined. The court reversed the conviction since the state failed to rebut the "presumption of harm." Accord, Turpin v. Todd, 268 Ga. 820, 821 (1), 493 S.E.2d 900 (1997).

[11]See Rogers v. United States, 422 U.S. 35, 95 S.Ct. 2091, 45 L.Ed.2d 1 (1975) (citing Shields v. United States, 273 U.S. 583, 47 S.Ct. 478, 71 L.Ed. 787 (1927)). Both of these cases condemn written communications be-

tween the judge and jury when the defendant and defense counsel are not present.

[12]Rogers v. United States, 422 U.S. 35, 95 S.Ct. 2091, 45 L.Ed.2d 1 (1975). In United States v. Glick, 463 F.2d 491 (2d Cir. 1972), the court held that it was error for the judge to communicate with the jury out of the presence of the defendant by answering in writing a question sent to the judge by the jury without counsel having knowledge of what was being done. Cf. Barraza v. State, 149 Ga.App. 738, 739 (2), 256 S.E.2d 48 (1979), in which the court stated that the judge should not speak to one or more of the jurors "out of the hearing of the parties and their attorneys." See generally, Annot., "Propriety and Prejudicial Effect, in Criminal Case, of Placing Jury in Charge of Officer Who is a Witness in the Case," 38 A.L.R.3d 1012 (1971); Annot., "Communication Between Court Officials or Attendants and Jurors in Criminal Trial as Grounds for Mistrial or Reversal-Post Parker Cases," 35 A.L.R.4th 890 (1985); and Annot., "Postretirement Out-of-Court Communications Between Jurors and Trial Judge as Grounds for New Trial or Reversal in Criminal Case," 43 A.L.R.4th 410 (1986).

See 4 Torcia, Wharton's Criminal Procedure, 87, § 561 (12th Ed. 1976).

jury."[13] It may be that this should be stressed to the jury in the charge. If, during deliberations, a note is received by the trial judge, both the district attorney and defense counsel should read it, and the judge should respond to it in open court in the absence of an agreement to the contrary and with the acquiescence of the defendant.[14] However, after requesting a recharge, if the jury returns a verdict before the trial judge has time to recharge, the failure to recharge before the verdict is not error.[15]

It is improper for the trial judge to call the foreman and ask him if the jury desires any further instructions.[16] See § 24:22, infra, on recharge of the jury. If the defendant alleges an improper communication between a juror and a prosecution witness or improper publicity during a trial,[17] the court should

---

[13]Collins v. State, 191 Ga.App. 289, 290 (2), 381 S.E.2d 430 (1989). Cf. Waldrip v. State, 266 Ga. 874, 878, 471 S.E.2d 857 (1996); Burtts v. State, 269 Ga. 402, 403 (3), 499 S.E.2d 326 (1998).

[14]In United States v. Ronder, 639 F.2d 931 (2d Cir. 1981), the court found under the facts of that case that it was reversible error for the trial judge to fail to disclose to counsel inquiries from the jury before responding to them in open court. Note, however, that the Court of Appeals has held that, where the trial judge reads the "material contents" of a jury note in open court, it is not error to exclude the numerical information regarding the exact split between guilt and innocence. Youmans v. State, 270 Ga.App. 832, 608 S.E.2d 300 (2004).

[15]Stevens v. State, 206 Ga.App. 418, 420 (4), 425 S.E.2d 373 (1992).

[16]Mosley v. State, 145 Ga.App. 651, 244 S.E.2d 610 (1978). In footnote 1 the court said that the calling of a single juror by the judge "is an unwise practice fraught with possibilities of inviting trouble." This case also takes a dim view of the trial judge taking a juror during deliberation to a hospital when her brother became suddenly ill. In United States v. U. S. Gypsum Co., 438 U.S. 422, 98 S.Ct. 2864, 57 L.Ed.2d 854 (1978), the trial judge with the consent of counsel, met alone with the foreman of the jury "to discuss the condition of the jury and further guidance." A transcript was made of the meeting but it was impounded until the case was appealed. The court said any "ex parte meeting or communication between the judge and the foreman of a deliberating jury is pregnant with possibilities of error." First, it is difficult to anticipate the direction of the conversation. Unexpected questions may generate unexpected and misleading answers. Second, anything to be communicated to the jury as a whole through one juror risks innocent misstatements and misinterpretations. Third, absence of counsel and unavailability of a transcript compounds the problem. In the Gypsum case the court reversed the conviction since it concluded that the foreman understood the judge to tell him he wanted a definite verdict "one way or the other." Cf. Brannon v. State, 163 Ga.App. 340 (1), 295 S.E.2d 110 (1982).

See Annot., "Propriety and Prejudicial Effect, in Federal Criminal Cases, of Communications Between Judge and Jury Members Made in Absence of Counsel, Regarding the Ability of Jury Members to Continue Deliberations," 64 A.L.R.Fed. 874 (1983).

[17]Margoles v. United States, 407 F.2d 727 (7th Cir. 1969). The court held that where press published inadmissible testimony on the fourth day of trial, collective questioning of jurors of whether they read the articles was

conduct an inquiry into the alleged incident.[18]

The Georgia Supreme Court held in *Gibson v. State*[19] that it is not per se reversible error for the trial judge to inquire into the numerical division of a deadlocked jury. Likewise, it is not improper for the judge to ask the jury in open court whether there is any likelihood of their reaching a verdict.[20] If a trial judge wants to determine the numerical standing of the jurors, it has been suggested that the following language be used: "Tell me how you stand numerically—that is whether you are 6 and 6, 8 to 4, etc., but do not tell me whether that number is for guilt or innocence. Do you understand my question?"[21] However, even when a trial judge asks for the numerical division of the jury without stating how many are for "guilty" and how many are for "not guilty" and the foreman answers "8 guilty and 4 not guilty," reversal is not required when the defendant is later convicted.[22] The United States Supreme Court held in *Lowenfield v. Phelps*[23] that it was not improper for a trial judge to poll the jurors to determine whether they felt that further deliberations would be helpful.

If the jury is unable to recall certain evidence, in his discretion the trial judge may in the courtroom (1) direct the jury to decide as best it can what the evidence was; (2) permit counsel on each side to state his recollection of the evidence; or (3) have the court reporter read back the evidence.[24]

Likewise, it is generally within the discretion of the trial judge

---

proper. See United States v. McKinney, 429 F.2d 1019 (5th Cir. 1970).

[18]Richardson v. United States, 360 F.2d 366 (5th Cir. 1966), holding this error.

[19]Gibson v. State, 272 Ga. 801, 803 (2), 537 S.E.2d 72 (2000).

[20]Jones v. State, 117 Ga. 710 (1), 44 S.E. 877 (1903).

[21]Wilson v. State, 145 Ga.App. 315, 320, 244 S.E.2d 355 (1978). The opinion of Judge Quillian in the *Wilson* case contains an excellent discussion of cases relating to the material referred to in the body. Also see Annot., "Propriety and Prejudicial Effect of Trial Court's Inquiry as to Numerical Division of Jury," 77 A.L.R.3d 769 (1977). See Annot., 75B Am. Jur. 2d Trial § 1583, Inquiries Into or Comments Regarding Numerical Division of Jurors (2004). In Brasfield v. United States, 272 U.S. 448, 47 S.Ct. 135, 71

L.Ed. 345 (1926), the court established a per se rule which prevents a judge from asking a deadlocked jury for its numerical division. However, in Ellis v. Reed, 596 F.2d 1195 (4th Cir. 1979), the court held that *Brasfield* was based on non-constitutional grounds. Accord, Muhammad v. State, 243 Ga. 404, 408, 254 S.E.2d 356 (1979).

[22]Tutt v. State, 165 Ga.App. 715, 716 (2), 302 S.E.2d 580 (1983).

[23]Lowenfield v. Phelps, 484 U.S. 231, 108 S.Ct. 546, 98 L.Ed.2d 568 (1988). In *Lowenfield*, the court also found that, after most of the jurors had indicated that further deliberations would be helpful, there was no impropriety in the trial judge then giving a modified *Allen* charge and instructing the jury that, if they did not reach a unanimous verdict, that a life sentence would be imposed.

[24]Lindsey v. State, 135 Ga.App. 122, 123 (3), 218 S.E.2d 30 (1975).

to permit the testimony of a witness or witnesses to be read back to the jury in the courtroom if it is requested by the jury.[25]

With specific respect to the subject of questions from a jury to the trial court, the Georgia Supreme Court offered this advice in *Lowery v. State*:[26] "In an exercise of this Court's inherent power to maintain a court system capable of providing for the administration of justice in an orderly and efficient manner . . ., we take this opportunity to require trial courts to have jurors' communications submitted to the court in writing; to mark the written communication as a court exhibit in the presence of counsel; to afford counsel a full opportunity to suggest an appropriate response; and to make counsel aware of the substance of the trial court's intended response in order that counsel may seek whatever modifications counsel deems appropriate before the jury is exposed to the instruction."

See § 22:6, supra, on reopening the case, and § 24:14, supra, on custody, conduct, and deliberations of the jury.

§ 24:20   Reading testimony to jury

After deliberations begin, it is in the discretion of the trial judge to grant or refuse to grant a request of the jury to rehear a portion of the testimony, in the presence of the defendant, either by having the court reporter read it to the jury or by replaying a recording of it where this is done in the courtroom,[1] or by replaying a videotape of the crime.[2] Where jurors request to rehear a certain portion of the testimony, it is generally proper for the trial judge to limit what they rehear to what has been requested "absent special circumstances which might work an injustice."[3] Thus, it has been held that it is not error for the trial judge to fail to ask the jury if they want to hear any other part of the evidence.[4]

See § 22:6, supra, on re-opening the evidence.

---

[25]Byrd v. State, 237 Ga. 781, 782, 229 S.E.2d 631 (1976). In the *Byrd* case the court held that if the jury asks to hear the taped direct examination of a state's witness, it was not error to also let the jury hear the recording of the cross-examination.

[26]Lowery v. State, 282 Ga. 68(4)(b) (1), 646 S.E.2d 67 (2007) (citations omitted).

[Section 24:20]

[1]Johns v. State, 239 Ga. 681, 683 (2), 238 S.E.2d 372 (1977); Davis v. State, 266 Ga. 801, 802 (4), 471 S.E.2d

191 (1996). See § 24:19, supra.

[2]Barnett v. State, 204 Ga.App. 588, 589 (1), 420 S.E.2d 96 (1992). Cf. Davis v. State, 246 Ga.App. 877, 878 (1), 542 S.E.2d 626 (2000).

[3]In Wilkerson v. State, 165 Ga.App. 14, 299 S.E.2d 67 (1983), the court said, "[T]he jury should be permitted to limit what they rehear to what they desire to rehear, absent special circumstances which might work an injustice."

[4]Pontoon v. State, 177 Ga.App. 868 (1), 341 S.E.2d 505 (1986).

§ 24:21 Reopening evidence

In *Beasley v. State,*[1] a photograph was admitted in evidence, pursuant to agreement of counsel, after the jury had been deliberating for some time. Thereafter defense counsel requested that he be permitted to argue about the picture. The Court of Appeals affirmed the trial judge's refusal to permit further argument.

In *Dandy v. State,*[2] the court held that "[i]t is within the trial court's discretionary power to permit the state to reopen its case after the close of evidence and to introduce further evidence."

See § 22:4, supra, on rebuttal. See § 22:6, supra, on reopening the evidence and § 24:20, supra, on reading testimony to jury.

§ 24:22 Recharge

In *Miller v. State,*[1] the court pointed out that as a general rule "[t]he need, breadth, and formation of additional jury instructions are left to the sound discretion of the trial court. . . . After a jury commences to deliberate, the trial court has inherent authority to call the jury back into the courtroom to give further instructions which may have been omitted for any reason . . . and on receiving a request [for further instruction] from the jury . . . to give such reply as the facts may warrant." A corrective re-charge may be given up until the time the verdict is published in open court. Therefore, a re-charge may be given even though the jury has notified the judge that it has reached a verdict.[2]

If the jury asks to be recharged on a question in the case, it is the duty of the trial judge to do so,[3] and if it is apparent from a question asked by the jury that the jurors are confused, it is the duty of the court to further instruct them and not merely tell the jury to consider the evidence and the charge previously given.[4] However, in *Kimmel v. State,*[5] the Court held that a judge need not "engage in a question and answer session with the jury or instruct the jurors individually on how to apply the law to the

---

[Section 24:21]

[1]Beasley v. State, 168 Ga.App. 255, 257 (3), 308 S.E.2d 560 (1983).

[2]Dandy v. State, 238 Ga.App. 435 (2), 518 S.E.2d 907 (1999).

[Section 24:22]

[1]Miller v. State, 221 Ga.App. 718, 719 (1), 472 S.E.2d 697 (1996).

[2]Altman v. State, 229 Ga.App. 769, 771 (6), 495 S.E.2d 106 (1997).

[3]Edwards v. State, 233 Ga. 625, 626 (2), 212 S.E.2d 802 (1975); Hubert v. City of Marietta, 224 Ga. 706, 707 (4), 164 S.E.2d 832 (1968); Carter v. State, 142 Ga.App. 351, 352 (5), 235 S.E.2d 750 (1977); Rule 534 of the Uniform Rules of Criminal Procedure. But cf. Finney v. State, 150 Ga.App. 874, 258 S.E.2d 670 (1979).

[4]Freeman v. State, 142 Ga.App. 293, 294 (4), 235 S.E.2d 560 (1977).

[5]Kimmel v. State, 261 Ga. 332, 335, 404 S.E.2d 436 (1991).

facts." Thus, in *Redding v. State*,[6] it was proper for the judge not to provide a direct answer to a question from the jury which asked, in effect, if the defendant could be found guilty if he was not the person who actually committed the act but was part of the group that did. The judge had already decided not to charge on party to a crime and answered the jury's question by directing them to the specific counts in the indictment with the instruction that their duty was to consider whether the state had met its burden as to each count.

The defendant must generally be present when the trial judge re-charges the jury or answers a question submitted by the jury, even though defense counsel does not object to the absence of his client. However, the right of the defendant to be present may be waived if done by his attorney in the defendant's presence and with the defendant's express authority or subsequent acquiescence.[7] See § 18:14, supra, on presence of defendant at a pre-voir dire charge.

In recharging the jury, care must be taken not to overemphasize the particular point which the judge is trying to cover.[8] In *United States v. Carter*,[9] the Fifth Circuit said that "when the jury requests further instructions on points which are favorable to the Government, the trial judge should repeat instructions favorable to the defense where the requested instructions taken alone might leave an erroneous impression in the mind of the jury." The Georgia Court of Appeals has commended this rule to trial courts,[10] but generally it is within the discretion of the judge to recharge the jury fully or only on the point or points requested.[11] However, the Georgia Court of Appeals has emphasized that an instruction on a specific point only does not amount to error unless the "instruction taken alone might leave an erroneous impression in the minds of the jury."[12] In *Taylor v. State*,[13] the court held that where a jury requested a charge or recharge on a

---

[6]Redding v. State, 296 Ga. 471, 473(2), 769 S.E.2d 67 (2015).

[7]Locklin v. State, 228 Ga.App. 696, 697 (2), 492 S.E.2d 712 (1997).

[8]Brannon v. State, 163 Ga.App. 340, 341 (2), 295 S.E.2d 110 (1982). See United States v. Carter, 491 F.2d 625 (5th Cir. 1974). In this case, supplemental instructions on circumstantial evidence were held to constitute reversible error where trial court repeated distinction between direct and circumstantial evidence and recited two illustrations which pointed to the guilt of the defendant.

[9]United States v. Carter, 491 F.2d 625, 634 (5th Cir. 1974).

[10]Brannon v. State, 163 Ga.App. 340, 341 (2), 295 S.E.2d 110 (1982).

[11]Demps v. State, 140 Ga.App. 90, 91 (1), 230 S.E.2d 97 (1976); Williams v. State, 151 Ga.App. 765, 766, 261 S.E.2d 487 (1979); Dyson v. State, 155 Ga.App. 297, 299, 270 S.E.2d 711 (1980).

[12]Dyer v. State, 167 Ga.App. 310, 311 (3), 306 S.E.2d 313 (1983).

[13]Taylor v. State, 169 Ga.App. 842, 844, 315 S.E.2d 661 (1984). Accord, Hemidi v. State, 245 Ga.App.

particular point, it is within the discretion of the judge to also give or not give additional instructions. It is not error for the trial judge, in response to a request for a recharge, to do so orally or in writing or partially in writing.[14] See § 24:19, supra.

In *Childs v. State*,[15] the trial judge did not err in "refusing to tell the jury that it could make a non-binding recommendation of life without parole." In *Potts v. State*,[16] the court held that it was not reversible error for the trial judge to refuse to answer questions about the possibility of parole, but that the better practice is to respond to such questions by "telling the jury in no uncertain terms that such matters are not proper for the jury's consideration." In *Quick v. State*,[17] the Georgia Supreme Court set out a suggested charge to be given at the end of the sentencing phase of a death case if a question is asked about parole. That suggestion is as follows:

> "You shall not consider the question of parole. Your deliberations must be limited to whether this defendant shall be sentenced to death or whether he shall be sentenced to life in prison. You should assume that your sentence, whichever it may be, will be carried out."

The trial judge, on his own motion, may call a jury back and give further instructions which he had omitted.[18] In the foreign case of *State v. Fletcher*,[19] the court said that an individual juror has a right to ask the foreperson to apply to the trial judge for a clarification of the charge even if other jurors do not agree to the submission of the question.

In *Mobley v. State*,[20] the court pointed out that in determining whether a recharge was erroneous "we must look at not only the recharge but the original charge as well, as jury instructions must be read and considered as a whole in determining whether the charges contain error."

§ 24:23 Jury misconduct

A visit by a juror to the scene of an alleged crime and subsequent reports to other jurors as to his observations consti-

---

417, 419 (3), 537 S.E.2d 804 (2000).

[14]Caldwell v. State, 245 Ga.App. 630, 632 (3), 538 S.E.2d 531 (2000).

[15]Childs v. State, 257 Ga. 243, 256 (20), 357 S.E.2d 48 (1987).

[16]Potts v. State, 261 Ga. 716, 725 (24), 410 S.E.2d 89 (1991).

[17]Quick v. State, 256 Ga. 780, 787, n. 3, 353 S.E.2d 497 (1987).

[18]Barraza v. State, 149 Ga.App. 738, 739 (2), 256 S.E.2d 48 (1979).

[19]State v. Fletcher, 10 Conn.App. 697, 525 A.2d 535 (1987).

[20]Mobley v. State, 218 Ga.App. 739, 740 (2), 463 S.E.2d 166 (1995).

tutes misconduct.[1] However, even when there is such misconduct, a new trial is not required if there is no "reasonable possibility" that this activity contributed to the conviction,[2] and the court in *Maxwell v. State*[3] seems to go even further protecting such activity. In *Maxwell* the court, in affirming a conviction, pointed out that "there is no indication as to the nature of the evidence gathered, what was discussed, or that the verdict was influenced by this misconduct. . . . [T]here is no showing . . . that the information discussed was highly prejudicial." It seems that the burden should be on the state to establish that the activity was harmless,[4] but *Maxwell* seems to put the burden on the defendant to show injury. In *Newson v. Foster*,[5] a case where the foreperson visited the crime scene, the court overruled the order of the trial court granting a new trial. The Court of Appeals held that the trial court's decision was based solely on evidence that it had no power to receive i.e. affidavits of jurors. Generally, affidavits of jurors may only be used by the court to sustain, not impeach, the verdict. O.C.G.A. § 24-6-606(b), however, provides an exception to this general rule and allows that "a juror may testify on the question of whether extraneous prejudicial information was improperly brought to the juror's attention, whether any outside influence was improperly brought to bear upon any juror, or

---

[Section 24:23]

[1]Watkins v. State, 237 Ga. 678, 683, 229 S.E.2d 465 (1976); Bobo v. State, 254 Ga. 146, 327 S.E.2d 208 (1985); Gaines v. State, 274 Ga. App. 575, 618 S.E.2d 197 (2005). See, Hammock v. State, 277 Ga. 612, 613 (2), 592 S.E.2d 415 (2004), juror misconduct found where juror obtained information from her home which helped explain conclusions reached by expert. Key to court's reasoning was that previously undecided jury reached unanimous verdict on the day the information was provided. But cf. Moore v. State, 179 Ga.App. 125, 127, 345 S.E.2d 631 (1986). See Annot., "Unauthorized View of Premises by Juror or Jury in Criminal Case as Ground for Reversal, New Trial, or Mistrial," 50 A.L.R.4th 995 (1986). In People v. Brown, 48 N.Y.2d 388, 423 N.Y.S.2d 461, 399 N.E.2d 51 (1979), an experiment by a juror alone about visibility afforded by a van resulted in a reversal.

[2]Chadwick v. State, 164 Ga.App. 102 (2), 296 S.E.2d 398 (1982). In *Chadwick*, a juror went to the scene of the crime the night before the verdict and reported his observation to the others the next morning prior to the reaching of the verdict. "Another juror commented, assertedly on the basis of a personal experiment, or defense evidence that the revolver had slipped off the automobile seat." The testimony of the eight available jurors at "the motion for a new trial hearing showed that none of the jurors could remember which of the jurors had gathered and reported the information or what the jurors had said except in vague generalities. Moreover, each of the jurors testified that the verdict was based entirely on the evidence adduced at trial and was not influenced by any extrajudicial information. We, therefore, find that the contended juror misconduct . . . was not so prejudicial . . . as to constitute reversible error."

[3]Maxwell v. State, 170 Ga.App. 831, 835 (5), 318 S.E.2d 650 (1984).

[4]See § 18:38, supra.

[5]Newson v. Foster, 261 Ga.App. 16, 581 S.E.2d 666 (2003).

whether there was a mistake in entering the verdict onto the verdict form."[6]

In *Holcomb v. State*,[7] the Georgia Supreme Court held that "when irregular juror conduct is shown, there is a presumption of prejudice to the defendant, and the prosecution carries the burden of establishing beyond a reasonable doubt that no harm occurred. However, in order for juror misconduct to upset a jury verdict, it must have been so prejudicial that the verdict is deemed 'inherently lacking in due process.' "[8]

Communications between a juror and outsiders about the case also constitutes misconduct.[9] However, a "verdict may not be impeached by the affidavit of a third person establishing the utterance by a juror of remarks which may impeach his verdict."[10] It has been held improper for jurors to use a dictionary to obtain definitions of the words "reasonable," "doubt," "imaginary," and "vague."[11] However, in *Hardwick v. State*,[12] the jury asked for a charge on the definition of two words. The judge stated he would provide them with a dictionary. The defendant stated that he did not object to the judge handling the question in this manner. The appellate court held that the defendant's acquiescence prevented his later objection. In *Moore v. State*,[13] the court held that a juror's study of a legal point "other than that charged by the trial court . . . [is] misconduct." In *Jones v. Kemp*,[14] the court held that "it was constitutional error for the court to permit the Christian Bible to go to the jury room at the request of the jurors apparently for consultation in connection with their deliberations."

In *Royal v. State*,[15] a juror took a map to the jury room and displayed it to the other jurors. Upon inquiry in chambers, the

---

[6]See Chambers v. State, 321 Ga. App. 512, 739 S.E.2d 513 (2013) (juror's Google search of law relating to defense of habitation was improper).

[7]Holcomb v. State, 268 Ga. 100, 103 (2), 485 S.E.2d 192 (1997); Greer v. Thompson, 281 Ga. 419, 637 S.E.2d 698 (2006).

[8]Turtle v. State, 271 Ga. 440, 445 (5), 520 S.E.2d 211 (1999).

[9]Wellmaker v. State, 124 Ga.App. 37, 38, 183 S.E.2d 62 (1971).

[10]Stroud v. State, 200 Ga.App. 387, 390 (2), 408 S.E.2d 175 (1991).

[11]Alvarez v. State, 653 P.2d 1127 (Colo.1982). See Annot., "Prejudicial Effect of Jury's Procurement or Use of Book During Deliberations in Criminal Cases," 35 A.L.R.4th 626 (1985).

See Annot., 75B Am. Jur. 2d Trial § 1561, Dictionaries; Other Sources of Definitions (2004). Cf. Tate v. State, 198 Ga.App. 276, 277 (1), 401 S.E.2d 549 (1991).

[12]Hardwick v. State, 210 Ga.App. 468, 471 (9), 436 S.E.2d 676 (1993).

[13]Moore v. State, 172 Ga.App. 844, 845, 324 S.E.2d 760 (1984); Steele v. State, 216 Ga.App. 276, 278, 454 S.E.2d 590 (1995). See Chambers v. State, 321 Ga. App. 512, 739 S.E.2d 513 (2013).

[14]Jones v. Kemp, 706 F.Supp. 1534 (N.D.Ga.1989).

[15]Royal v. State, 217 Ga.App. 459, 460 (3), 458 S.E.2d 366 (1995). See Chambers v. State, 321 Ga. App. 512, 739 S.E.2d 513 (2013) (juror's Google search of law relating to defense of

juror said she pulled "the map from her purse when other jurors asked about the location of the road on which the victim lived. The juror stated that the map did not have an effect on any members of the jury. Upon further inquiry of the trial court, all of the jurors indicated that they would disregard any information they received from observing the map and that they each could reach a verdict based solely on the evidence presented from the witness stand. . . ." The court affirmed the trial judge's refusal to grant a mistrial. However, in *Merritt v. State*,[16] the court held that it is not mandatory that in every instance a trial court must question each juror individually whenever there is an allegation of misconduct. "In order to upset a jury verdict because of juror misconduct, the jurors' statements must be 'so prejudicial that the verdict must be deemed inherently lacking in due process.' There must be a reasonable probability that the misconduct contributed to the conviction."

In *Hand v. State*,[17] during the course of the trial a juror called the defendant's wife and asked if the shooting was the result of a drug transaction gone bad. The juror told the wife not to worry, because it should be self-defense. The wife reported this to the defendant, and the defendant informed counsel of the incident. The incident was not called to the attention of the trial judge. After conviction, the defendant sought a new trial on the ground of jury misconduct. The court held that the failure to call the misconduct to the attention of the judge at once amounted to a waiver.

In *Chambers v. State*,[18] a juror admitted that she had performed internet research and shared her findings with fellow jurors during deliberations on the defense of habitation which had been raised at trial by the defendant. The court held that the defendant's right to be present at all critical stages of his trial and to be tried by an impartial jury had been violated, giving rise to a presumption of prejudice which the state was required to overcome.

On improper influence and conduct, see § 18:38, supra. On impeaching the verdict, see § 25:7, infra. See § 24:24, infra, on replacing a juror.

---

habitation was improper).

[16]Merritt v. State, 248 Ga.App. 709, 711 (1), 548 S.E.2d 427 (2001).

[17]Hand v. State, 205 Ga.App. 467 (1), 422 S.E.2d 316 (1992). See Fuller v. State, 313 Ga. App. 759, 722 S.E.2d 453 (2012) (conversation between juror and victim during trial requires that conviction be reversed).

[18]Chambers v. State, 321 Ga. App. 512, 739 S.E.2d 513 (2013). See Edge v. State, 345 Ga. App. 794, 815 S.E.2d 146 (2018) (state failed to overcome presumption of prejudice where two or three jurors referred to cell phones for sight and distance detail about witness view of crime scene).

§ 24:24 Replacement of juror

O.C.G.A. § 15-12-172 authorizes the trial judge at any time "before or after final submission of the case to the jury" to replace the juror with the first or next alternate juror if the replaced juror "dies, becomes ill, upon other good cause shown to the court is found to be unable to perform his duty, or is discharged for other legal cause." The judge must inquire of the juror on the record to establish that the juror is unable to perform his duty. If the juror is replaced during deliberations, the judge must charge the jury to begin anew.[1]

Improper conduct on the part of the juror is not required.[2] In *Darden v. State,*[3] a juror was seen talking with the defendant during a recess. The trial judge determined that nothing improper had taken place, but excused the juror and replaced her with an alternate. The court held that the judge had discretion to discharge a juror and replace him or her at any time if there was a sound legal basis for the action.

However, in *Boler v. State,*[4] the appellate court affirmed the trial court's decision to replace a juror during deliberations after "it was discovered that the replaced juror met with a relative during a lunch break and that this relative stated her opinion as to defendant's innocence."

A trial court may not honor a request from a juror to be discharged if it appears that there is a substantial possibility that the request is premised upon the juror's belief that the evidence offered at trial is not sufficient to support a conviction.[5] However, where it is apparent that a juror is not going to follow the law, the trial judge my dismiss the juror.[6] In *Cornwell v. State,*[7] the court held that it is not error for the trial court to refuse to charge the jury that "the jury shall be the judges of the law and the facts." See § 22:7, supra, on a jury charge on nullification. In *People v. Hightower,*[8] the court held that "the trial court may and must conduct an inquiry into jury deliberations sufficient to resolve claims of misconduct or other cause for

---

[Section 24:24]

[1]Peek v. Kemp, 746 F.2d 672 (11th Cir. 1984).

[2]Darden v. State, 212 Ga.App. 345, 347 (4), 441 S.E.2d 816 (1994).

[3]Darden v. State, 212 Ga.App. 345, 347 (4), 441 S.E.2d 816 (1994). Cf. Worthy v. State, 223 Ga.App. 612, 613 (1), 478 S.E.2d 421 (1996); Ballou v. State, 226 Ga.App. 602, 750 (4), 487 S.E.2d 140 (1997); Mason v. State, 244 Ga.App. 247, 249 (1), 535 S.E.2d 497 (2000).

[4]Boler v. State, 240 Ga.App. 90 (2), 522 S.E.2d 676 (1999).

[5]U.S. v. Brown, 823 F.2d 591, 596(II)(A) (D.C. Cir. 1987).

[6]U.S. v. Thomas, 116 F.3d 606, 614 (II)(B) (2d Cir. 1997).

[7]Cornwell v. State, 246 Ga.App. 686, 687 (1), 541 S.E.2d 101 (2000).

[8]People v. Hightower, 77 Cal.App. 4th 1123, 1150, 92 Cal.Rptr.2d 497 (2000).

removal. . . . [California case law permits] inquiry into jury deliberations when it is reasonably calculated to ascertain the truth of suggestions that a juror has prejudged the case, is unable or unwilling to deliberate, or otherwise lacks the capability to fulfill his or her duties."

In *Cloud v. State*,[9] a juror wrote the judge a note saying "[I] cannot take this anymore . . . It is making me sick." Upon questioning the juror outside of the other jurors, the juror said he could not say if the defendant was guilty and he did not want to go back into the jury room. The juror then started crying. The appellate court affirmed the removal of this juror.

In *Stokes v. State*,[10] the trial court replaced two jurors with alternates when the two jurors would not decide whether the defendant was guilty or innocent "because they fe[lt] that there ha[d] not been enough evidence either way." This was found to be error and prejudicial to the defendant when the "court made no attempt to inquire into the jurors' reasons for not voting" and there had been no "showing that the jurors were in any way incapacitated." The appellate court pointed out that the trial judge "should have either recharged the jury as to the burden of proof and continued deliberations or declared a mistrial."

In *Byrd v. State*,[11] after an outburst in court by the victim's uncle toward the appellant, the trial judge conducted a voir dire of members of the jury and found that one juror expressed doubts about his ability to be fair. The appellate court affirmed the trial judge's decision to dismiss the juror and replace him with an alternate.

In *McGuire v. State*,[12] the trial judge replaced a juror who, contrary to instructions, visited the crime scene and discussed his observations with the other jurors. The appellate court affirmed even though there had been no showing that the juror was incapable of returning an impartial verdict.

In *Henry v. State*,[13] the defendant contended that a juror's irregular behavior coupled with a statement that he could not make an accurate decision did not reach the level of incapacity required for removal. However, the appellate court found that the foregoing "constituted ample justification for the trial judge to exercise . . . [his] discretion in removing the juror" after the close of the evidence.

---

[9]Cloud v. State, 235 Ga.App. 721 (1), 510 S.E.2d 370 (1998).

[10]Stokes v. State, 204 Ga.App. 141, 418 S.E.2d 419 (1992). But cf. Alford v. State, 244 Ga.App. 234, 237, 534 S.E.2d 103 (2000).

[11]Byrd v. State, 262 Ga. 426, 420 S.E.2d 748 (1992).

[12]McGuire v. State, 200 Ga.App. 509, 510 (3), 408 S.E.2d 506 (1991).

[13]Henry v. State, 265 Ga. 732, 739 (7)(b), 462 S.E.2d 737 (1995).

In *Cleveland v. State,*[14] the Georgia Court of Appeals affirmed the replacement of a juror where the "juror indicted that he had an emergency, in that he had a possible cancerous growth on the back of his ear which . . . was getting larger and needed to be taken care of as soon as possible, and an operation to remove it had been scheduled for that day." The court pointed out that "[h]urrying to a verdict because of anxiety about keeping an important medical appointment . . . could itself infect the verdict."

In *Norris v. State,*[15] the court held that it is "not an abuse of discretion to conclude that the juror's failure to respond truthfully during voir dire, coupled with his admitted actions during jury deliberations, constituted legal cause for removal," and it was not necessary to inquire further as to the juror's ability to be fair.

In *People v. Williams,*[16] the California Supreme Court held that the trial court has authority to remove a juror who expresses an unwillingness to follow the court's instructions. However, the trial court's investigation should be limited to the juror's conduct and not the content of deliberation. A juror who will not deliberate is unable to perform his duty.

In *Reynolds v. State,*[17] the appellate court affirmed the trial court in excusing a juror and substituting an alternate where the juror, after the trial began, became aware of his knowledge of the defendant's family and stated that it would be difficult for him to return a guilty verdict. However, after deliberations have commenced and if the jury has become deadlocked, particular care must be observed to ensure that a juror is not removed improperly. This is especially true when the juror is a holdout. Without more, the fact that one juror does not agree with the others will not constitute cause for removal.[18] However, disruptive behavior, such as insult, slander and humiliation of other jurors that is wholly unrelated to the issues under consideration,

---

[14]Cleveland v. State, 218 Ga.App. 661, 663 (4), 463 S.E.2d 36 (1995).

[15]Norris v. State, 230 Ga.App. 492, 495 (5), 496 S.E.2d 781 (1998) followed and quoted in Wooten v. State, 250 Ga.App. 686, 687 (2), 552 S.E.2d 878 (2001).

[16]People v. Williams, 25 Cal.4th 441, 21 P.3d 1209, 106 Cal.Rptr.2d 295 (2001).

[17]Reynolds v. State, 271 Ga. 174, 175 (2), 517 S.E.2d 51 (1999). See Wallace v. State, 303 Ga. 34, 810 S.E.2d 93 (2018) (recalling and reseating a juror who has been dismissed presents the issue of whether the juror has discussed the case with others between the time of her dismissal and recall). See also Dietz v. Bouldin, 136 S. Ct. 1885, 195 L. Ed. 2d 161 (2016) (federal courts have some discretion to recall a discharged juror in civil cases).

[18]Mason v. State, 244 Ga. App. 247(1), 535 S.E.2d 497 (2000). See Semega v. State, 302 Ga. App. 879, 691 S.E.2d 923 (2010).

is a sound legal basis for removal.[19]

See § 18:35, supra, on alternate jurors and § 18:37, supra on sequestration of a jury. See sections 18:38 and 24:23, supra, on juror misconduct.

§ 24:25   Change of jury foreman

In *Larry v. State*,[1] the court affirmed the trial judge in allowing the jury to change its foreman after deliberations had begun where the defendant does not articulate any harm.

§ 24:26   The Allen charge

The *"Allen* charge," also known as the "dynamite charge," "hung-jury charge," "log-jam charge," or the "hammer instruction" derives its name from the case of *Allen v. United States*[1] in which the United States Supreme Court held it not to be error to charge the jury "that in a large proportion of cases, absolute certainty could not be expected; that although the verdict must be the verdict of each individual juror, and not a mere acquiescence in the conclusion of his fellows, yet they should examine the question submitted with candor and with a proper regard and deference to the opinions of each other; that it was their duty to decide the case if they could conscientiously do so; that they should listen, with a disposition to be convinced, to each other's arguments; that, if much the larger number were for conviction, a dissenting juror should consider whether his doubt was a reasonable one which made no impression upon the minds of so many men, equally honest, equally intelligent with himself. If, upon the other hand, the majority was for acquittal, the minority ought to ask themselves whether they might not reasonably doubt the correctness of a judgment which was not concurred in by the majority."[2] The charge has been severely criticized by the courts[3]

---

[19]State v. Arnold, 280 Ga. 487, 629 S.E.2d 807 (2006).

[Section 24:25]

[1]Larry v. State, 266 Ga. 284, 287 (4), 466 S.E.2d 850 (1996).

[Section 24:26]

[1]Allen v. United States, 164 U.S. 492, 17 S.Ct. 154, 41 L.Ed. 528 (1896).

[2]Allen v. United States, 164 U.S. 492, 501, 17 S.Ct. 154, 41 L.Ed. 528 (1896); Annot., "Instructions Urging Dissenting Jurors in State Criminal Case to Give Due Consideration to Opinion of Majority (*Allen* Charge) Modern Cases," 97 A.L.R.3d 96 (1980).

[3]The concern that has brought about the modifications of the traditional *Allen* charge in some jurisdictions are its potential coercive effects. Factors that are often considered are (1) whether the minority and majority were both asked to re-examine their positions; (2) whether the jury was instructed that they had a right to fail to agree with the jury's majority opinion; and (3) whether the jury was instructed that the burden of proving guilt beyond a reasonable doubt re-

and legal writers.[4] One commentator has suggested that instead of the *Allen* charge or some modification thereof, the trial court employ a "silent charge" which does no more than suggest that the jurors continue to deliberate without any reference to the "deadlock" and avoiding any language which might be construed as coercive.[5]

In an excellent opinion by Justice Clark in *Romine v. State*[6] the court pointed out that "it is somewhat imprecise to refer to a single *Allen* charge. Decades of judicial interpretation have produced a variety of permutations and amplifications of the original wording. . . ."

In *Spaulding v. State*,[7] the Georgia Supreme Court upheld the following *Allen* charge:

"Mr. Foreman and ladies and gentlemen, you have now been deliberating on this case for a considerable period of time, and the court deems it proper to advise you further in regard to the desirability of agreement, if possible. The case has been exhaustively and carefully tried by both sides and has been submitted to you for decision and verdict, if possible, and not for disagreement. It is the law that a unanimous verdict is required and while this verdict must be the conclusion of each juror and not a mere acquiescence of the jurors in order to reach an agreement, it is still necessary for all of the jurors to examine the issues and questions submitted to them with candor and fairness and with a proper regard for, and deference to, the opinion of each other. A proper regard for the judgment of others will greatly aid us in forming our own judgment. This case must be decided by some jury selected in the same manner this jury was selected, and there is no reason to think a jury better qualified than you would ever be chosen. Each juror should listen to the arguments of the other jurors with a disposition to be convinced by them; and if

---

mained with the government. United States v. Manning, 79 F.3d 212 (1st Cir. 1996). See Harrison v. Gillespie, 640 F.3d 888 (9th Cir. 2011).

[4]Samantha P. Bateman, Comment, "Blast it all: Allen Charges and the Dangers of Playing with Dynamite," 32 U. Haw. L. Rev. 323 (2010); Comment, "Instructing Deadlocked Juries," 78 Yale L. J. 100 (1968); Note, "Supplemental Jury Charges Urging a Verdict—The Answer Is Yet to Be Found," 56 Minn. L. Rev. 1199 (1972); Rogers, "Criminal Law—Cushioning the Blow of the 'Dynamite Charge,' " 6 Memphis St. L. Rev. 553 (1976).

[5]George C. Thomas, III & Mark Greenbaum, "Justice Story Cuts the Gordian Knot of Hung Jury Instructions," 15 Wm & Mary Bill Rts. J. 893 (2007).

[6]Romine v. State, 256 Ga. 521, 526, 350 S.E.2d 446 (1986) (quoting People v. Gainer, 19 Cal.3d 835, 139 Cal.Rptr. 861, 566 P.2d 997 (1977)). The *Romine* opinion discusses problems of the *Allen* charge, the A.B.A. Standards, and some of the problems in "the charge."

[7]Spaulding v. State, 232 Ga. 411, 207 S.E.2d 43 (1974).

the members of the jury differ in their views of the evidence, such difference of opinion should cause them all to scrutinize the evidence more closely and to re-examine the grounds of their opinion. Your duty is to decide the issues of fact which have been submitted to you if you can conscientiously do so. In conferring you should lay aside all mere pride of opinion and should bear in mind that the jury room is no place for espousing and maintaining, in a spirit of controversy, for either side of a cause. You should not be advocates for either side. The aim ever to be kept in view is the truth as it appears from the evidence, examined in the light of the instructions of the court."[8]

In *Burchette v. State,*[9] the Georgia Supreme Court disapproved this charge to the extent it instructs the jury that "[t]his case must be decided by some jury selected in the same manner this jury was selected and there is no reason to think a jury better qualified than you would ever be chosen." The court concluded that the phrase "must be decided by some jury" was not an accurate statement since cases which end in a mistrial because of juries which cannot reach a verdict are not always retried for any number of reasons, and further, because there is no legal requirement for the retrial of a case involving a hung jury.

Generally, the decision of when not to give an *Allen* charge[10] and when to give an *Allen* charge[11] is left to the discretion of the trial judge. However, where the jury has been unable to reach a verdict, it is error for the judge to charge that "someone is being a little unreasonable and stubborn" since such comment tends to coerce the jury.[12] However, in *State v. Greeson,*[13] the court held that an *Allen* charge was not erroneous even though it did not inform the jury that no member is required to surrender his or her opinion for the purpose of reaching a unanimous verdict. Nevertheless, if such a charge is given, the trial court should not refer to any additional expense which the county would incur if

[8]Spaulding v. State, 232 Ga. 411, 413 (4), 207 S.E.2d 43 (1974) (punctuation omitted).

[9]Burchette v. State, 278 Ga. 1, 596 S.E.2d 162 (2004). In addition, it would appear that the case is not retroactive. See Burge v. State, 273 Ga. App. 38, 614 S.E.2d 158 (2005) [Unless it appears that the charge had a coercive effect on one or more jurors as demonstrated by a verdict shortly after the instruction or during the poll of the jury, the error would be harmless.]

[10]Caldwell v. State, 167 Ga.App. 692, 695 (5), 307 S.E.2d 511 (1983).

[11]Banks v. State, 169 Ga.App. 571, 572 (2), 314 S.E.2d 235 (1984); Moore v. State, 215 Ga.App. 626, 628 (3), 451 S.E.2d 534 (1994).

[12]Riggins v. State, 226 Ga. 381, 384, 174 S.E.2d 908 (1970).

[13]State v. Greeson, 237 Ga. 193, 227 S.E.2d 324 (1976), rev'g 139 Ga.App. 767, 229 S.E.2d 547 (1976). See Callaham v. State, 317 Ga. App. 513, 732 S.E.2d 88 (2012) (Court of Appeals is critical of *Greeson* decision.).

the jury cannot agree on a verdict.[14] In *Dennis v. State*,[15] the court held that a modified *Allen* charge is not unduly coercive where the trial judge instructed the jury that the jury's failure to agree "would cause a mistrial resulting in another trial by another jury." Likewise, an *Allen* charge is not considered unduly coercive where the jurors indicate that there is a significant numerical divide among them.[16]

In *Gibson v. State*,[17] the Court noted that should a jury indicate that it is deadlocked, it is appropriate for the trial court to "inquire how the jury stands numerically." However, trial courts should not inquire as to the nature of a jury's numerical division. In *Thornton v. State*,[18] the court suggested that when informed of a deadlock, trial judges should take the following steps in determining whether to order a mistrial or to require the jury to deliberate further:

1. Polling the jurors or questioning them as a group to determine whether additional time for deliberation would be helpful in overcoming their current deadlock.

2. Considering whether the jury is so exhausted that the minority might be induced to vote for a verdict which they otherwise would not support.

3. Considering the length of the trial and the complexity of the issues in the case.

4. Consideration of the length of time the jury deliberated before declaring itself deadlocked.

In an *Allen*-type charge, it has been said that the charge is not coercive if it states that no juror is required to surrender his honest opinion for the purpose of reaching a verdict.[19] Likewise, it

---

[14]Taylor v. Murray, 102 Ga.App. 145, 148, 115 S.E.2d 776 (1960). In Driver v. State, 155 Ga.App. 726, 728 (3), 272 S.E.2d 580 (1980), the court said that an "instruction to jurors to consider the expense of the trial as a factor in their deliberations is reversible error." However, the court declined to reverse a conviction in the absence of an objection where an offhand remark was made relating to expense in explanation of the judge's decision to have the jury deliberate further. Cf. Brantley v. State, 190 Ga.App. 642, 644 (3), 379 S.E.2d 627 (1989).

[15]Dennis v. State, 220 Ga.App. 420, 421 (3), 469 S.E.2d 494 (1996).

[16]See Gibson v. State, 272 Ga. 801, 803-804(3), 537 S.E.2d 72 (2000)

(*Allen* charge was not improper where jury split was 11-1). See also Gamble v. State, 291 Ga. 581, 584(5), 731 S.E.2d 758 (2012).

[17]Gibson v. State, 272 Ga. 801, 802(2), 537 S.E.2d 72 (2000).

[18]Thornton v. State, 145 Ga. App. 793, 795, 245 S.E.2d 22 (1978). See Honester v. State, 329 Ga. App. 406, 410, 765 S.E.2d 376 (2014).

[19]Willingham v. State, 134 Ga.App. 603, 607 (5), 215 S.E.2d 521 (1975); Posey v. United States, 416 F.2d 545 (5th Cir. 1969).

In Redeord v. State, 93 Nev. 649, 572 P.2d 219, 220 (1977), the court found an *Allen* charge which did not "remind the individual jurors not to surrender conscientiously held opin-

has been held that it is not error to instruct the jury that each juror must take a stand by saying, "You've got to vote either one way or the other."[20] Nevertheless, it is error for the trial judge to instruct a jury that it will have to continue to deliberate until it reaches a verdict.[21] Likewise, although a case that was later overruled, it has been held to be reversible error for the trial judge to give an *Allen* charge and also state that he feels "like there is enough evidence . . . for you to reach a verdict one way or another."[22]

In *Harris v. State,*[23] the court pointed out that while "a predeliberation charge on unanimity is proper, informing the jury in such a charge of the consequences of a failure to achieve unanimity is disapproved."

The American Bar Association Standards of Criminal Justice rejects the *Allen* charge,[24] but suggests the giving of an instruction as a part of the main charge relating to jury deliberations and deadlocked juries.[25] The proposed substitute is less subject to criticism because the charge is given before the jury retires and, thus, before a minority is established. It also makes no reference to the minority, but instead charges all jurors to consult with one another.[26]

The *Allen* charge must be distinguished from what has been called a "time fuse" instruction. A "time fuse instruction" is one in which the trial judge charges the jury that unless the jury reaches a verdict in a specified short time, the court will declare a mistrial. The arbitrary deadline instructions are generally deemed coercive and deny a defendant a fair trial.[27]

In *Howard v. State,*[28] the jury returned a non-unanimous "verdict." Some 20 to 30 minutes later, a juror was brought in

---

ions for the sake of judicial economy" was coercive and required a reversal.

[20]Pender v. State, 249 Ga. 495, 496 (2), 292 S.E.2d 69 (1982); Thompson v. State, 166 Ga.App. 850 (2), 305 S.E.2d 662 (1983).

[21]Sanders v. State, 162 Ga.App. 175, 290 S.E.2d 516 (1982).

[22]McClinic v. State, 172 Ga.App. 54, 321 S.E.2d 796 (1984), overruled by Wallace v. State, 175 Ga.App. 685, 333 S.E.2d 874 (1985).

[23]Harris v. State, 263 Ga. 526, 528 (6), 435 S.E.2d 669 (1993); Mangum v. State, 274 Ga. 573 (11), 555 S.E.2d 451, 456 (2001).

[24]A.B.A. Standards, Trial by Jury, Vol. III, Commentary, Standard 15-

4.4(a).

[25]Harris v. State, 263 Ga. 526, 528 (6), 435 S.E.2d 669 (1993); The Charge Book of the Superior Court Judges Manual suggests that a limited *Allen* charge be given as a part of the main charge. Part I, section 9, p. 23.

[26]See A.B.A. Standards, Trial by Jury, Vol. III, Commentary, Standard 15-4.4(a).

[27]Allen v. People, 660 P.2d 896 (Colo.1983). In Burroughs v. United States, 365 F.2d 431 (10th Cir. 1966), the court placed a per se ban on time deadlines.

[28]Howard v. State, 218 Ga.App. 346, 347 (1), 461 S.E.2d 274 (1995).

and asked the judge a question. The judge told the juror he could not answer the question and ended by saying, "I'm going to let you stay here till four o'clock, and then I'm going to have to go, but we're not going to mistry this case. . . . [T]hat's all there is to it." Nine minutes later the jury returned a guilty verdict. The appellate court reversed and said the jury should have been given an *Allen* charge.

Despite the foregoing, special problems exist in a capital case at the sentencing phase of the trial. Thus, in *Legare v. State*,[29] the Georgia Supreme Court held that it was reversible error to give an *Allen* charge to a jury at this stage which included the statement that "[t]his case must be decided by some Jury selected in the same manner." The court pointed out that this is not a correct statement of law as applied to that case since under Georgia law if the jury could not reach a verdict as to sentence, the trial judge must impose a sentence of life imprisonment.

§ 24:27 Mistrial

The trial judge has broad discretion in determining whether to declare a mistrial because of the inability of the jurors to reach a verdict.[1] See § 14:58, supra, on manifest necessity.

A motion for a mistrial is premature until such time as a jury is impaneled and sworn.[2] The proper remedy to correct verbal or other improprieties that could taint a panel during voir dire is either a challenge to the poll or a motion for postponement to impanel other jurors who were not exposed to the improper conduct or speech.[3] The failure to object at the time of the objectionable conduct and seek corrective action will constitute a waiver.[4]

In *Warren v. State*,[5] the Court of Appeals concluded that the trial court did not abuse its discretion in denying a motion for

---

[29]Legare v. State, 250 Ga. 875, 302 S.E.2d 351 (1983). However in *Legare* the court held that a charge, such as that referred to in the body which results in a verdict of death, will not prevent a retrial on the question of sentence after reversal.

[Section 24:27]

[1]Williford v. State, 23 Ga. 1 (1857); and see Lovett v. State, 80 Ga. 255, 256 (1), 4 S.E. 912 (1888). See Sears v. State, 270 Ga. 834, 835 (1), 838, 514 S.E.2d 426 (1999), for citations of cases holding that a jury was not deadlocked where a verdict was not reached in four days (more than the time required to try the case) or

even where the jury had been deliberating for seven days.

[2]Sharpe v. State, 272 Ga. 684(5), 531 S.E.2d 84 (2000); Callaway v. State, 208 Ga.App. 508(2), 431 S.E.2d 143 (1993).

[3]Sharpe v. State, 272 Ga. 684(5), 531 S.E.2d 84 (2000); Callaway v. State, 208 Ga.App. 508(2), 431 S.E.2d 143 (1993).

[4]Robertson v. State, 268 Ga. 772(7), 493 S.E.2d 697 (1997).

[5]Warren v. State, 314 Ga. App. 477, 724 S.E.2d 404 (2012). See Berry v. State, 210 Ga. App. 789, 437 S.E.2d 630 (1993).

mistrial where the witness did not answer the question and, upon objection, the prosecution withdrew the question and the trial court instructed the jury to disregard it.

In *Cantrell v. State*,[6] the court pointed out that "(1) Where a jury is unable to agree on a verdict, that disagreement is not itself a verdict; and (2) whether a jury is hopelessly deadlocked is an evaluation (committed) to the sound discretion of the trial court, subject to appellate review for an abuse of discretion."

In determining when to grant a mistrial, the court will consider the length of time the trial has required and likelihood of the jury reaching a verdict.[7]

In *Thornton v. State*,[8] the court said[9] that when the trial judge is informed that the jury is deadlocked he "should consider four factors in making his decision of whether or not to order a mistrial or to require the jury to deliberate further. These factors include:

"1. Polling the jurors or questioning them as a group as to whether additional time for deliberation would be helpful in overcoming their current deadlock.

"2. Considering whether the jury is so exhausted that the minority might be induced to vote for a verdict which they otherwise would not support.

"3. Considering the length of the trial and the complexity of the issues in the case.

"4. Consideration of the length of time the jury deliberated before declaring itself deadlocked."

In *Phillips v. State*,[10] a mistrial was declared after the jury had been deliberating only two hours and fifteen minutes. The court said, "[t]he decisive factor is not the length of deliberations but the inability of the jury to reach a verdict."

In *State v. Archie*,[11] the court held that the trial court's declaration of a mistrial as a result of a "hung jury is not an event that

[6]Cantrell v. State, 217 Ga.App. 641 (1), 459 S.E.2d 564 (1995), rev'd on other grounds, 266 Ga. 700, 469 S.E.2d 660 (1996).

[7]See A.B.A. Standards, Trial By Jury, Vol. III, Standard 15-4.4(b), (c). In Cofield v. State, 247 Ga. 98, 274 S.E.2d 530 (1981), the Supreme Court held that as a general proposition, a motion for mistrial based upon the length of the jury's deliberation was within the sound discretion of the trial court.

[8]Thornton v. State, 145 Ga.App.

793, 795, 245 S.E.2d 22 (1978).

[9]These factors are actually taken from United States v. See, 505 F.2d 845 (9th Cir. 1974).

[10]Phillips v. State, 238 Ga. 632, 634, 235 S.E.2d 12 (1977).

[11]State v. Archie, 230 Ga.App. 253, 495 S.E.2d 581 (1998) (quoting Rower v. State, 267 Ga. 46, 472 S.E.2d 297 (1996)). See Blueford v. Arkansas, 132 S. Ct. 2044, 182 L. Ed. 2d 937, 77 A.L.R. Fed. 2d 737 (2012) (double jeopardy did not bar retrial of murder charge after jury announced it had

terminates the original jeopardy to which (the defendant) was subjected. . . . [Hence, the accused may be tried again] for the same offense."

In *State v. Telenko*,[12] the court held that it was error for the trial judge to grant an earlier motion for mistrial, which had been held in abeyance, based on prosecutorial misconduct. The granting of the mistrial because of prosecutorial misconduct occurred after the jury had deliberated and been dismissed after failing to reach a verdict. The trial court's dismissal of the jury was in effect a declaration of a mistrial. Therefore, the court's subsequent declaration of a mistrial based on the prosecutor's improper argument was a nullity. See § 14:58, supra, on granting a mistrial because of prosecutorial misconduct, double jeopardy, and mistrials. See Studdard, *Daniel's Georgia Handbook on Criminal Evidence* (2018 ed.), § 1:36, on mistrials.

In *Pleas v. State*,[13] the Georgia Supreme Court held that no jurisdictional basis for an appeal exists in regard to an order declaring a mistrial, since a mistrial is not a final judgment. In addition, it seems that there is no requirement that an actual written mistrial order be signed by the trial judge before the second trial begins.[14]

For an order declaring a mistrial, see Studdard, *Daniel's Georgia Criminal Trial Practice Forms* (2018–2019 ed.), §§ 29:2 et seq. and 30:1 et seq. Also see § 14:58, supra, on double jeopardy and mistrials.

---

decided to acquit defendant on that charge but was deadlocked on other charges).

[12]State v. Telenko, 225 Ga.App. 724, 484 S.E.2d 725 (1997).

[13]Pleas v. State, 268 Ga. 889, 890 (1), 495 S.E.2d 4 (1998).

[14]Swafford v. State, 161 Ga.App. 139, 291 S.E.2d 3 (1982).

Chapter 25

The Verdict

KeyCite®: Cases and other legal materials listed in KeyCite Scope can be researched through the KeyCite service on Westlaw®. Use KeyCite to check citations for form, parallel references, prior and later history, and comprehensive citator information, including citations to other decisions and secondary materials.

---

§ 25:1   Background

The word "verdict" has been defined as "the answer of the jury given to the court concerning the matters of fact submitted to them under the issues made by the pleadings and as applied to the legal principles laid down. . . ."[1] Although the word "verdict" comes from the Latin word "veredictum" which means "a true declaration," technically it does not mean truth.[2] Thus, it is a mistake for defense counsel in a criminal case to think of a verdict as speaking the truth.

A verdict of "not guilty" is not intended to establish the fact that the defendant did not commit the act charged. It is simply a finding that the defendant has not been proven guilty beyond a reasonable doubt in the case tried.[3] Defense counsel should impress upon the jury their duty to acquit the defendant if the

---

[Section 25:1]

[1]Doe v. Goetchius, 180 Ala. 381, 61 So. 330, 331 (1913).

[2]In Hyndman v. Hyndman, 208

Ga. 797, 799, 69 S.E.2d 859 (1952), the court indicates that the word "verdict" means "a true saying."

[3]Woody v. State, 10 Okla.Crim. 322, 136 P. 430, 432 (1913).

state fails to prove him guilty beyond a reasonable doubt, even if the jurors think that the accused is guilty as matter of fact of the charges.[4]

As pointed out elsewhere, in Georgia a verdict must generally be agreed to by all jurors.[5] However, a verdict agreed to by less than all of the jurors may be valid, but before such a verdict is valid it must be agreed to by the state, sanctioned by the trial judge, and must be expressly and intelligently agreed to by the defendant.[6]

In *Wellons v. State,*[7] the court held in a death case that it was not error for the trial judge to charge that its sentencing verdict had to be unanimous while failing to charge that its findings as to mitigating circumstances need not be unanimous.

In *Dansby v. State,*[8] the defendant was convicted of four felony counts of theft by deception. The jury returned a general verdict rather than a separate verdict on each count. The trial judge gave a correct form verdict to the foreperson and suggested that it be filled out in the courtroom. The foreperson completed and signed the verdict in open court with the jury still in the box. The defendant raised no objection and did not poll the jury. The appellate court concluded "that verdicts may be reformed in the presence of the jury and even after the jury has been dispersed."

The trial judge may not in open court either directly or indirectly express his approval or disapproval of the verdict.[9]

Once a judgment of not guilty has been entered, the trial judge

---

[4]O.C.G.A. § 24-1-1 states that the object of all legal investigation is the discovery of truth. In Holcomb v. State, 261 Ga. 178, 402 S.E.2d 719 (1991), the court held that it was not error for the trial judge to charge this section. However, it may be argued. The object of the trial of a criminal case is not to discover whether the defendant is or is not guilty; the object is to determine whether or not the state can prove him guilty beyond a reasonable doubt. Actual guilt in a moral sense may exist in a particular case when the state cannot prove the defendant's guilt beyond a reasonable doubt. See Pulaske, "Criminal Trials: 'A Search for Truth or Something Else,' "16 Crim. L. Bull. 41, 44 (1980).

However, in Colorado v. Connelly, 479 U.S. 157, 107 S.Ct. 515, 93 L.Ed.2d 473 (1986), the court said

that the "central purpose of a criminal trial is to decide the factual question of the defendant's guilt or innocence," quoting Delaware v. Van Arsdall, 475 U.S. 673, 106 S.Ct. 1431, 89 L.Ed.2d 674 (1986).

[5]See § 25:2, n. 1, infra.

[6]Glass v. State, 250 Ga. 736, 737 (1), 300 S.E.2d 812 (1983); Copeland v. State, 241 Ga. 370, 371 (4), 245 S.E.2d 642 (1978).

[7]Wellons v. State, 266 Ga. 77, 89 (23), 463 S.E.2d 868 (1995).

[8]Dansby v. State, 165 Ga. App. 41, 42 (2)(b), 299 S.E.2d 579 (1983). Accord, Ledbetter v. State, 234 Ga. App. 380, 382 (2), 506 S.E.2d 699 (1998).

[9]O.C.G.A. § 9-10-8, O.C.G.A. § 17-9-22.

has no authority to vacate or set it aside.[10]

§ 25:2 Mechanics related to verdicts

Generally, a verdict must be freely and voluntarily agreed to by all the jurors[1] and received in open court.[2] But see § 25:1, supra, on an agreement to accept a "verdict" by fewer than all jurors. Where a verdict is defective, the court should instruct the jury to return to the jury room and return a verdict which is proper in form.[3] If the jury returns a verdict finding the defendant "guilty without intent," where intent is an element of the crime, this is a verdict of acquittal; thus, in this situation, the court has no authority to send the jury out for further deliberation.[4] However, in *Fambro v. State*,[5] the defendant was charged with aggravated assault. The jury returned a verdict "Guilty (Criminal Negligence)." The court affirmed, since a conviction is valid if there is a finding of criminal intent or criminal negligence.

In *Westbrook v. State*,[6] the court considered a verdict finding the defendant guilty of murder and recommended "mercy or that defendant's punishment be life imprisonment with the stipulation that it be life without parole." Although the case was eventually overruled, the court held that this was a valid verdict and its " 'stipulation' regarding parole was mere surplusage not affecting its recommendation of mercy." As a general proposition, a jury's recommendation of leniency is considered surplusage and will not

---

[10]See Shuman v. State, 146 Ga. App. 822, 247 S.E.2d 561 (1978).

[Section 25:2]

[1]Maddox v. State, 233 Ga. 874, 875, 213 S.E.2d 654 (1975). See Mitchell v. State, 22 Ga. 211, 236 (16) (1857).

In United States v. Scalzitti, 578 F.2d 507 (3d Cir. 1978), the court held that a defendant could not waive his right to a unanimous verdict in federal court except in accordance with Fed. R. Crim. P. 23(b). Accord, United States v. Pachay, 711 F.2d 488 (2d Cir. 1983). From a federal constitutional standpoint, Johnson v. Louisiana, 406 U.S. 356, 92 S.Ct. 1620, 32 L.Ed.2d 152 (1972) held in a non-capital case that a majority verdict of 9 out of 12 was enough for a conviction. However, in the case of a six-person jury used for non-petty offenses, the verdict must be unanimous under the Sixth and Fourteenth Amendments. Burch v. Louisiana, 441 U.S. 130, 99 S.Ct. 1623, 60 L.Ed.2d 96 (1979).

In the absence of a timely request to charge, it is not error for the trial judge to fail to charge the jury that the verdict must be unanimous. Carter v. State, 137 Ga. App. 824, 827 (5), 225 S.E.2d 73 (1976).

[2]O.C.G.A. § 9-12-3, O.C.G.A. § 17-9-21.

[3]Allison v. State, 110 Ga. App. 266, 267 (3), 138 S.E.2d 335 (1964).

[4]Maltbie v. State, 139 Ga. App. 342, 345, 228 S.E.2d 368 (1976).

[5]Fambro v. State, 164 Ga. App. 359, 297 S.E.2d 111 (1982).

[6]Westbrook v. State, 256 Ga. 776, 778 (5), 353 S.E.2d 504 (1987), overruled by State v. Freeman, 264 Ga. 276, 444 S.E.2d 80 (1994).

disturb the validity of the verdict.[7] However, an exception to this rule can arise where "the circumstances of the jury's recommendation [of leniency] cast doubt upon the unqualified nature of the verdict."[8] As the Georgia Supreme Court observed in *State v. Benton,*[9] ". . . courts have concluded that when a jury asks a trial court if it may recommend leniency, the unqualified nature of the verdict is in doubt, as the judge's response may have induced the jury to reach a unanimous verdict." In *Benton,* the court concluded that the jury's verdict was not so qualified in light of, inter alia, the judge's instruction that the jurors were not to give any consideration to punishment in connection with the verdict they returned.

The jury may not return a verdict finding the defendant guilty of a crime not charged unless it is a lesser included offense of the crime charged. If a jury returns a verdict finding a defendant guilty of a crime not charged and not a lesser included offense of the crime charged, it is a nullity and the court may instruct the jury to retire again and return a verdict in accordance with the charge of the court.[10] In *Stubbs v. State,*[11] the court held that "[i]f the trial court receives a verdict of guilty on a crime that was neither charged nor was a lesser included offense of a crime charged, then the verdict has the legal effect of an acquittal."

In the 4 to 3 decision of the Georgia Supreme Court in *Cantrell v. State,*[12] the defendant was charged with possession of cocaine with intent to distribute it. The majority opinion held that when the jury returns an unanimous verdict of guilty of simple possession of cocaine, this operates as an acquittal of possession with intent to distribute. "Thus, if a jury returns a verdict of guilty on a lesser included offense, further deliberations are precluded." A jury does not have to reach an unanimous agreement on the greater offense before considering and reaching a verdict on a lesser included offense.[13]

When an ambiguous verdict is returned by a jury, the trial court may refuse to accept the verdict and require the jury to

---

[7]See e.g., United States v. Austin, 231 F.3d 1278 (10th Cir. 2000); State v. Benton, 278 Ga. 503, 604 S.E.2d 169 (2004).

[8]State v. Benton, 278 Ga. 503, 604 S.E.2d 169 (2004).

[9]State v. Benton, 278 Ga. 503, 604 S.E.2d 169 (2004).

[10]State v. Freeman, 264 Ga. 276, 278, 444 S.E.2d 80 (1994); Dunn v. State, 141 Ga. App. 853 (2), 234 S.E.2d 687 (1977).

[11]Stubbs v. State, 220 Ga. App. 106, 107 (1), 469 S.E.2d 229 (1996). See Newsome v. State, 323 Ga. App. 15, 747 S.E.2d 99 (2013).

[12]Cantrell v. State, 266 Ga. 700, 469 S.E.2d 660 (1996). Accord, Parker v. State, 226 Ga. App. 462, 465 (6)(b), 486 S.E.2d 687 (1997).

[13]Kunselman v. State, 232 Ga. App. 323, 324 (1), 501 S.E.2d 834 (1998).

continue its deliberations.[14] After a verdict has been received, re-corded, and the jury dispersed, a defendant is entitled to the ben-efit of the doubt in the construction of an ambiguous verdict.[15]

The court should instruct the jury as to the form the verdict should take.[16] If a verdict contains an erasure and substitution of words, but the meaning is clear, it should not be rejected by the court.[17] In *Rucker v. State,*[18] the Georgia Supreme Court in 1999 concluded "that the use of a jury verdict form preprinted with the words 'Guilty' and 'Not Guilty' does not constitute error unless the form would mislead jurors of reasonable understanding. . . ."

In *Moyer v. State,*[19] the defendant was tried for criminal at-tempt to commit theft of a motor vehicle. The jury returned a verdict of guilty of "attempt to steal." The trial judge instructed the foreman to add the words "an automobile." The appellate court affirmed.

In the case of an indictment containing two or more counts, in the absence of an objection, it is not error to permit the jury to publish the verdict on a count, on which the jury had reached agreement, and to continue to deliberate on the remaining count or counts.[20] In *Tyler v. United States,*[21] the court held that "[e]ach count of an indictment is an entity, and each verdict rendered on each count is an entity." The court then affirmed the acceptance of a verdict of guilty to three counts of an indictment and a decla-ration of a mistrial to the remaining counts. In *State v. LeMay,*[22] the court held that in such a case the defendant could be re-tried on the counts on which a mistrial had been ordered. A general verdict of guilty on a two count indictment has been interpreted to mean that the defendant was found guilty of both counts.[23]

A verdict is normally signed by the foreman of the jury, but it

[14]Ingram v. State, 290 Ga. 500, 503 (2), 722 S.E.2d 714 (2012).

[15]O.C.G.A. § 17-9-40. See Washington v. State, 333 Ga. App. 236, 775 S.E.2d 719 (2015).

[16]Lambert v. State, 17 Ga. App. 348 (1), 86 S.E. 782 (1915).

See Dixon v. State, 154 Ga. App. 828, 830 (7), 269 S.E.2d 909 (1980). In Smith v. State, 249 Ga. 228, 232, 290 S.E.2d 43 (1982), the court discussed a form verdict which was sent to the jury. The court pointed out that in such forms it is better practice not to include the words "guilty" or "not guilty" since the sequence of these words on a verdict form may be re-garded as having some significance.

[17]Pippin v. State, 172 Ga. 224, 229 (2), 157 S.E. 185 (1931).

[18]Rucker v. State, 270 Ga. 431 (5), 510 S.E.2d 816 (1999).

[19]Moyer v. State, 164 Ga. App. 629, 298 S.E.2d 308 (1982).

[20]Disby v. State, 238 Ga. 178, 231 S.E.2d 763 (1977).

[21]Tyler v. United States, 397 F.2d 565 (5th Cir. 1968).

[22]State v. LeMay, 186 Ga. App. 146, 367 S.E.2d 61 (1988).

[23]Goodwin v. State, 236 Ga. 339, 345, 223 S.E.2d 703 (1976).

may be signed by some other juror for the foreman.[24] The failure to sign the verdict has been held to be a formality which may be later cured by signing.[25]

It is commonly thought that to have a court there must be present a judge, a sheriff or deputy, and a clerk.[26] However, it has been held that a verdict may be received at night after the clerk has left.[27] Nevertheless, in *Williams v. State*,[28] the court held that it is no longer necessary for a clerk to be present during a trial.

The defendant and his counsel have a right to be present when the verdict is returned.[29] However, the defendant waives his right to be present if he absconds or is out on bond and cannot be located. Likewise, it has been held that the right to have counsel present at the time the verdict is returned may be waived if counsel cannot be located at the time.[30] Still, it is difficult to conceive of a situation in which the defendant can be constitutionally deprived of counsel at the time the verdict is returned unless the accused has in some way acquiesced in his attorney's absence.[31]

Historically, in Georgia the jury may return a verdict of "guilty" or "not guilty"[32] or "not guilty by reason of insanity,"[33] only if that plea was properly made. In 1988, the Georgia legislature enacted a statute which now makes it possible, in a felony case, for the following verdicts:

---

[24]Sullivan v. State, 29 Ga. App. 377, 381, 115 S.E. 290 (1923); and see Murphy v. State, 64 Ga. App. 690, 691 (1), 13 S.E.2d 870 (1941). In a civil case, it has been held that where a verdict is not signed by anyone but is received without objection and entered on the minutes of the court but objected to before the minutes are signed, a motion in arrest of judgment is not good. Patterson v. Murphy, 63 Ga. 281 (1879).

[25]Avera v. Tool, McGarrah & Toudee, 74 Ga. 398 (1884). Sullivan v. State, 29 Ga. App. 377, 381, 115 S.E. 290 (1923), says that an unsigned verdict properly returned is valid and implies that it does not have to be amended, but in fact the case relied on as authority for this rule was *Avera v. Tool* which was in fact amended the next day.

[26]The case of Mealing v. Pace, 14 Ga. 596, 629 (1854), recognized that a court could exist without a clerk. In Robinson v. State, 209 Ga. 650 (2), 75 S.E.2d 9 (1953), the court said that a

mistrial is not required where the clerk was momentarily absent from the courtroom. However, see Zugar v. State, 194 Ga. 285, 21 S.E.2d 647 (1942).

[27]Richards v. State, 136 Ga. 67, 68 (3), 70 S.E. 868 (1911). Generally, see O.C.G.A. § 15-1-6 on the validity of acts of court during absence of clerk.

[28]Williams v. State, 233 Ga. App. 70, 72 (2), 503 S.E.2d 324 (1998).

[29]Parham v. State, 28 Ga. App. 569, 112 S.E. 289 (1922). In Lyons v. State, 7 Ga. App. 50 (1), 66 S.E. 149 (1909), the court said that a verdict returned during the enforced absence of the defendant is a nullity.

[30]Richards v. State, 136 Ga. 67 (2), 70 S.E. 868 (1911).

[31]See Mempa v. Rhay, 389 U.S. 128, 88 S.Ct. 254, 19 L.Ed.2d 336 (1967), and cases cited.

[32]O.C.G.A. § 17-9-2.

[33]O.C.G.A. § 17-7-131.

"(A) Guilty;

"(B) Not guilty;

"(C) Not guilty by reason of insanity at the time of the crime;

"(D) Guilty but mentally ill at the time of the crime . . . ; or

"(E) Guilty but mentally retarded."[34]

If the defendant is found guilty in a case where the death penalty is not sought, sentence is to be imposed by the trial judge after a pre-sentence hearing has been conducted.[35] See §§ 26:13 and 26:14, infra, on pre-sentence hearings. If the defendant has been convicted of a capital offense and the district attorney is seeking the death penalty, where a "guilty" verdict has been returned, the jury at the second phase of the bifurcated trial will have the responsibility of determining whether the defendant is to be sentenced to death or life imprisonment.[36] See §§ 26:6 et seq., infra, on hearings on punishment in capital cases. If the verdict is "not guilty," the defendant is to be released immediately.

In *Matthews v. State,*[37] the court held that where a jury convicts a defendant of a malice murder count and a felony murder count of the same person, it is proper for the court to merge the two counts and sentence the defendant to only one life sentence. See § 26:37, infra, on sentencing on multiple counts of murder.

Any irregularity in the form of a verdict is waived in the absence of an objection at the time of its return.[38] If a verdict in an improper form is returned, the judge may have the jury retire and prepare a verdict in accordance with the instruction of court. Any objection to reformation of a verdict is waived if it is not contemporaneously raised.[39]

See § 24:5, supra, and §§ 26:30 et seq., infra, on lesser included offense.

§ 25:3 Multiple count indictment

In the case of an indictment containing two or more counts, in the absence of an objection, it is not error to permit the jury to publish the verdict on a count on which the jury had reached agreement and to continue to deliberate on the remaining count

---

[34]O.C.G.A. § 17-7-131.

[35]O.C.G.A. § 17-10-2(a). See § 26:13, infra.

[36]O.C.G.A. § 17-10-2(b). See § 26:7, infra.

[37]Matthews v. State, 258 Ga. 144, 145 (4), 366 S.E.2d 280 (1988).

[38]Wilkes v. State, 210 Ga. App. 898, 899 (2), 437 S.E.2d 837 (1993); Bissell v. State, 153 Ga. App. 564, 567 (2), 266 S.E.2d 238 (1980).

[39]Dansby v. State, 165 Ga. App. 41, 42 (2)(b), 299 S.E.2d 579 (1983).

or counts.[1] In *Tyler v. United States*,[2] the court held that "[e]ach count of an indictment is an entity, and each verdict rendered on each count is an entity." The court then affirmed the acceptance of a verdict of guilty to three counts of an indictment and a declaration of a mistrial on the remaining counts. In *State v. LeMay*,[3] the court held that in such a case the defendant could be re-tried on the counts on which a mistrial had been ordered. A general verdict of guilty on a two-count indictment has been interpreted to mean that the defendant was found guilty of both counts.[4]

"The key question in determining whether a merger has occurred is whether the different offenses are proven with the same facts. For example, if one crime is complete before the other takes place, the two crimes do not merge. However, if the same facts are used to prove the different offenses, the different crimes merge."[5]

In *Briscoe v. State*,[6] the defendant was convicted of felony murder, armed robbery, and aggravated assault. The verdict failed to specify whether armed robbery or aggravated assault served as the underlying felony of felony murder. The court held that the trial judge must merge the most severe offense in terms of punishment. Hence, the armed robbery must be merged into the felony murder and the defendant may be sentenced for aggravated assault separately or in addition to the sentence imposed for felony murder.

If a defendant is convicted of murder and felony murder of the same victim, the defendant should be sentenced only on the malice murder count.[7]

In *Mayorga v. State*,[8] the defendant was indicted for false imprisonment and rape. The jury found the defendant guilty of false imprisonment, but deadlocked on the rape charge. "[A] mistrial was declared, and the state . . . nolle prossed the charge." In affirming the conviction, the court held that the conviction of false imprisonment was not inconsistent with the failure to reach

[Section 25:3]

[1]Disby v. State, 238 Ga. 178, 231 S.E.2d 763 (1977).

[2]Tyler v. United States, 397 F.2d 565 (5th Cir. 1968). Cf. Bair v. State, 250 Ga. App. 226, 551 S.E.2d 84 (2001).

[3]State v. LeMay, 186 Ga. App. 146, 367 S.E.2d 61 (1988). Cf. Rower v. State, 267 Ga. 46, 472 S.E.2d 297 (1996).

[4]Goodwin v. State, 236 Ga. 339, 345, 223 S.E.2d 703 (1976).

[5]Reeves v. State, 233 Ga. App. 802, 805 (2), 505 S.E.2d 540 (1998) (quoting Taylor v. State, 219 Ga. App. 475, 465 S.E.2d 473 (1995)).

[6]Briscoe v. State, 263 Ga. 310, 431 S.E.2d 375 (1993). Accord, Robertson v. State, 268 Ga. 772, 780 (22), 493 S.E.2d 697 (1997).

[7]Tiller v. State, 267 Ga. 888, 890 (2), 485 S.E.2d 720 (1997).

[8]Mayorga v. State, 225 Ga. App. 496, 484 S.E.2d 292 (1997).

a verdict on rape. "The outcomes are not mutually exclusive and are based on entirely independent crimes." See §§ 26:33 et seq., infra, on merger of multiple charges on counts.

§ 25:4 Polling the jury

After the verdict has been published and found to be proper in form, on motion of one of the parties[1] or on the initiative of the court,[2] the jury must be polled. Failure to poll the jury, after proper demand, renders the verdict fatally defective.[3] However, in the absence of a timely motion, the right to poll the jury is waived.[4] Also, if there is any defect in the conduct of the poll, it should be objected to at the time.[5] Thus, when one or more jurors are inadvertently omitted during the polling, and the jury then dismissed, and the court discovers the error and sua sponte obtains an affidavit from the omitted juror, with the defense counsel having been present during the polling, there is no reversible error.[6]

A party may demand that the jury be polled any time after the publication of the verdict and before the dispersion of the jury and recording of the verdict.[7] Some cases hold that the demand to

---

[Section 25:4]

[1]McCullough v. State, 10 Ga. App. 403 (6), 73 S.E. 546 (1912). Under the A.B.A. Standards and Uniform Rules of Criminal Procedure polling the jury is required. A.B.A. Standards, Trial by Jury, Vol. III, Standard 15-4.5.

[2]Groves v. State, 162 Ga. 161 (1), 132 S.E. 769 (1926).

[3]Russell v. State, 68 Ga. 785, 788 (1882).

[4]Maddox v. State, 233 Ga. 874, 876, 213 S.E.2d 654 (1975).

In Coleman v. State, 256 Ga. 306, 308 (2), 348 S.E.2d 632 (1986), after returning a verdict of guilty in a murder case, the trial judge immediately sent the jury to lunch before beginning the sentencing phase of the case. After the jury left, defense counsel asked that the jury be polled. The Georgia Supreme Court held that this request was timely.

See Clifford v. State, 266 Ga. 620, 622 (5), 469 S.E.2d 155 (1996).

[5]See Hargett v. State, 151 Ga. App. 532, 260 S.E.2d 406 (1979), which held that where the failure to poll all jurors was not discovered until after the defendant was sentenced and defense counsel could not be located, it was not error for the trial court to poll the remaining jurors in the absence of defense counsel.

[6]Hunter v. State, 177 Ga. App. 326, 327 (2), 339 S.E.2d 381 (1985). See Miller v. State, 302 Ga. 118, 805 S.E.2d 22 (2017) (inadvertent failure to poll one of the jurors did not require reversal in absence of any evidence that the jury failed to reach unanimous verdict).

[7]Taylor v. State, 36 Ga. App. 639, 643, 138 S.E. 83 (1927); Webb v. State, 166 Ga. 218 (1), 142 S.E. 898 (1928).

But if the jury is not polled, a defendant normally loses his right to contend that the verdict was not unanimous since a juror may not generally impeach the verdict. Thus, an affidavit of a juror in which he testifies that he did not vote for conviction may not be considered. Gainer v. State, 142 Ga. App. 871, 237 S.E.2d 235 (1977).

poll the jury must be made before a sentence is imposed,[8] unless sentence is imposed so quickly after the verdict has been published that the defendant has no opportunity to request to have the jury polled.[9] Under Georgia's present bifurcated trial procedure, it seems most unlikely that there could be such a quickly imposed sentence as that referred to.

It has been held that in a capital felony case where the jury has returned a guilty verdict, if defense counsel wishes to have the jury polled, he must make a motion to have it polled before the jury retires again to determine the sentence to be imposed.[10]

However, in a capital case, if the jury returns a verdict of death, at the end of the sentencing phase of the case the trial judge *shall* poll the jury as to its verdict.[11]

A demand to have the jury polled is not complied with by asking the jurors collectively whether they agreed to the verdict.[12] In a proper polling, the jurors are each asked certain questions.[13] The questions most commonly asked are:[14]

"M_____, was that your verdict in the jury room?"

"Was it freely and voluntarily made by you?"[15]

"Is it still your verdict?"

In Rinker v. State, 228 Ga. App. 767, 768, 492 S.E.2d 746 (1997), the court said that a request to have the jury polled was timely if made before the jury was "discharged and sentence had not been passed."

[8]Wooten v. State, 19 Ga. App. 739, 740, 92 S.E. 233 (1917); Robinson v. State, 109 Ga. 506 (8), 34 S.E. 1017 (1900). Cf. Green v. State, 246 Ga. 598, 604, 272 S.E.2d 475 (1980).

[9]McCullough v. State, 10 Ga. App. 403 (7), 73 S.E. 546 (1912).

[10]Plummer v. State, 229 Ga. 749, 750, 194 S.E.2d 419 (1972).

[11]Unified Appeal Procedure, Rule III.B.3. (Georgia Court and Bar Rules Manual).

[12]Favors v. State, 234 Ga. 80, 88 (6), 214 S.E.2d 645 (1975), overruled on other grounds, Matthews v. State, 268 Ga. 798, 493 S.E.2d 136 (1997).

[13]Campbell v. State, 111 Ga. App. 219, 220 (7), 141 S.E.2d 186 (1965).

[14]See Wilson v. State, 93 Ga. App. 375 (2), 91 S.E.2d 854 (1956). In Green v. State, 246 Ga. 598, 605, 272 S.E.2d 475 (1980), the trial judge asked each juror only one question, to-wit: "You have heard the verdict published. Is it your verdict?" The court concluded that this was not error where there was no objection. The court pointed out that there is no uniform way of polling the jury. The object is to determine if the verdict agreed on is still the unanimous verdict of the jury.

Love v. State, 199 Ga. App. 482, 483 (3), 405 S.E.2d 308 (1991), held that there was a sufficient polling where each juror was asked: (1) Is this your verdict? And after receiving an affirmative answer, by asking: (2) Was this your verdict in the jury room?

[15]Hudson v. State, 237 Ga. 241 (3), 227 S.E.2d 257 (1976), holds that it is not error to refuse to permit the juror to be asked if he "voluntarily agreed upon" the verdict. However, Ponder v. State, 11 Ga. App. 60, 74 S.E. 715 (1912) holds that if a juror did not freely and voluntarily agree to a verdict, the verdict should not be received. This case has never been overruled and was not cited in the *Hudson* case.

In Burnett v. State, 240 Ga. 681, 688 (11), 242 S.E.2d 79 (1978), the

The law recognizes that a juror may consent to a verdict in the jury room and change his mind by the time he is polled in the courtroom, but it is not error for the trial judge to refuse to instruct the jury, at the time it is polled, that a juror may change his mind.[16] Where a juror has changed his mind, the verdict must be set aside[17] and the jury sent to the jury room again for further deliberation.[18] However, a juror's statement, upon being polled, that he reluctantly agreed to the verdict, will not invalidate the verdict.[19] A verdict is also valid where a juror states that the verdict was voluntarily made but with reservations.[20] However, if a juror states that the verdict is his "with reasonable doubt" the verdict is not valid.[21] As the court explained in 1912 in *Ponder v. State*,[22] "[T]here is a great difference between agreeing reluctantly to a verdict and so unwillingly consenting to a verdict as to seize the first proper opportunity to declare that fact. . . . [W]hen the juror states that his assent to a verdict of guilty was not freely nor voluntarily given, it is necessarily to be implied that his consent was due to external pressure, and that his concurrence is not due to his own volition, but to the volition of another substituted in place of his own."

---

court said that the asking of the other two questions contained in the body meets "minimum requirements of the defendant's right to a poll of the jurors." Query: Does this indicate that the failure to ask the question footnoted herein would be error if there was a specific request that it be asked?

In Scruggs v. State, 181 Ga. App. 55, 56 (1), 351 S.E.2d 256 (1986), the court said that a verdict was valid even though a juror stated that her verdict was free and voluntary but in her heart she really had some doubts. The court said that "even reluctant agreement is sufficient," quoting Watts v. State, 142 Ga. App. 857, 237 S.E.2d 231 (1977).

[16]Mitchell v. State, 239 Ga. 456, 459, 238 S.E.2d 100 (1977).

[17]See Cooper v. State, 103 Ga. 63, 64 (2), 29 S.E. 439 (1897).

[18]See Hinton v. State, 223 Ga. 174, 154 S.E.2d 246 (1967), judgment rev'd on other grounds, 390 U.S. 206, 88 S.Ct. 902, 19 L.Ed.2d 1039 (1968); United States v. Edwards, 469 F.2d 1362 (5th Cir. 1972).

[19]Terry v. State, 224 Ga. App. 157, 161 (5), 480 S.E.2d 193 (1996); Parker v. State, 81 Ga. 332 (5), 6 S.E. 600 (1888); see Ponder v. State, 11 Ga. App. 60, 61, 74 S.E. 715 (1912).

See Annot., "Juror's Reluctant, Equivocal or Conditional Assent to Verdict, on Polling, as Ground for Mistrial or New Trial in Criminal Case," 25 A.L.R.3d 1149 (1969). See Annot., 21A Am. Jur. 2d Criminal Law § 1299, Effect of Conditional, Equivocal or Inconsistent Responses by Individual Jurors (2004).

[20]Young v. State, 239 Ga. 53, 60, 236 S.E.2d 1 (1977). However, in United States v. Edwards, 469 F.2d 1362 (5th Cir. 1972), the court held that where a juror on being polled says, "It's my verdict, but I am still in doubt," the court must dismiss the jury and declare a mistrial or send the jury back for further deliberations. The trial judge must refrain from trying to make the verdict unanimous.

[21]Sincox v. United States, 571 F.2d 876 (5th Cir. 1978).

[22]Ponder v. State, 11 Ga. App. 60, 74 S.E. 715 (1912).

In *Carter v. State,*[23] the court found there was no error in refusing to permit defense counsel to poll the jury by asking (1) if they had found defendant guilty of trespass based on a feud that had been going on for years and (2) if they felt sorry for the adjoining owner and did not go by evidence presented. The court pointed out that a "defendant's right to poll a jury . . . does not encompass questioning which attempts to impeach the verdict."

If, as a result of the polling of the jury, it is determined that the verdict is not valid, the trial judge may direct the jury to return to the jury room and deliberate further.[24] The fact that a juror or jurors did not agree to a verdict is not a ground for a mistrial. The proper motion is to have the jury retire to the jury room for further deliberations.[25] However, when there is some doubt as to whether a juror's verdict was freely and voluntarily given, the court should require further deliberation without the necessity of a motion by counsel.[26]

§ 25:5 Bifurcated trials

See § 17:24, supra, on bifurcated trials and § 18:36, supra, on pre-trial instructions.

§ 25:6 Consistency of verdict

O.C.G.A. § 17-9-2 provides that jury verdicts are to be given a reasonable interpretation and are to be set aside only out of necessity. The issue of consistency in verdicts arises in two distinct situations. In the first situation, a single defendant is charged with multiple offenses.[1] For example, in *Dunn v. United States,*[2] the petitioner was found guilty of "maintaining a common nuisance by keeping for sale at a specified place intoxicating liquor." However, he was acquitted of unlawful possession of intoxicating liquor and also acquitted of unlawful sale of the liquor. The court stated:

"Consistency in the verdict is not necessary. Each count in an

---

[23]Carter v. State, 231 Ga. App. 42, 43 (3), 497 S.E.2d 812 (1998).

[24]Walker v. State, 159 Ga. App. 50, 282 S.E.2d 697 (1981).

[25]Mills v. State, 160 Ga. App. 49 (2), 286 S.E.2d 55 (1981); Lockleer v. State, 188 Ga. App. 271 (1), 372 S.E.2d 663 (1988).

[26]Benefield v. State, 278 Ga. 464, 602 S.E.2d 631 (2004).

[Section 25:6]

[1]Cf. Martin v. State, 157 Ga.

App. 304, 277 S.E.2d 300 (1981); see Annotation, "Inconsistency of Criminal Verdict With Verdict on Another Indictment or Information Tried at Same Time," 16 A.L.R.3d 866; Annotation, "Inconsistency of Criminal Verdict As Between Different Counts of Indictment or Information," 18 A.L.R.3d 259.

[2]Dunn v. United States, 284 U.S. 390, 52 S.Ct. 189, 76 L.Ed. 356 (1932). Accord, Swofford v. State, 180 Ga. App. 901, 351 S.E.2d 104 (1986).

indictment is regarded as if it was a separate indictment. . . . If separate indictments had been presented against the defendant for possession and for maintenance of a nuisance, and had been separately tried, the same evidence being offered in support of each, an acquittal on one could not be pleaded as res judicata of the other. Where the offenses are separately charged in the counts of a single indictment the same rule must hold."

In 1984, in *United States v. Powell*,[3] the United States Supreme Court approved the rule established in *Dunn* which the court said "has stood without exception in this Court for 53 years." In *Powell*, the defendant was acquitted of conspiracy to possess cocaine and possession of cocaine but she was found guilty of using the telephone to facilitate those offenses. The court concluded that "there is no reason to vacate [the defendant's] conviction merely because the verdicts cannot rationally be reconciled."

In *Thornton v. State*,[4] the Court of Appeals applied the rationale expressed in *Powell* and other cases and applied the inconsistent verdict rule in the context of a case where only one of two alleged co-conspirators was convicted.

In *United States v. Lichenstein*,[5] the court cited *Dunn* and stated: "Juries in criminal cases in this country are free to render verdicts that are inconsistent or even the result of mistake or compromise." The appellants had argued that an acquittal of the substantive count (of "knowingly and willfully submitting a false statement to a government agency . . . by falsely designating as 'vessel supplies' 1,150 cases of bonded scotch whiskey on a United States Customs form") and a finding of guilty on the conspiracy count "were so inconsistent as to require reversal." The court rejected this argument and decided that "any apparent inconsistency between verdicts on the two counts of the indictment does not undermine convictions on the conspiracy count on which appellants were found guilty. 'Each count is separately considered and, if it is supported by the evidence, may stand.' "[6]

When a trial is held at the same time on two separate counts of an accusation or indictment, a guilty verdict on one count alone operates as an acquittal of the other count. However, "such acquittal does not vitiate the conviction although both counts

---

[3]United States v. Powell, 469 U.S. 57, 105 S.Ct. 471, 83 L.Ed.2d 461 (1984).

[4]Thornton v. State, 331 Ga. App. 191, 770 S.E.2d 279 (2015). See U.S. v. Andrews, 850 F.2d 1557 (11th Cir. 1988); U.S. v. Church, 955 F.2d 688, 695(2)(B)(1), 35 Fed. R. Evid. Serv. 445 (11th Cir. 1992) ("[I]nconsistent verdicts on a conspiracy count . . . do not defeat the propriety of a defendant's conviction, even if every defendant but one is acquitted"). See also U.S. v. Collins, 412 F.3d 515 (4th Cir. 2005).

[5]United States v. Lichenstein, 610 F.2d 1272 (5th Cir. 1980).

[6]See also Horne v. United States, 193 F.2d 175 (5th Cir. 1951).

may relate to the same transaction."[7]

In *Milam v. State,*[8] the Georgia Supreme Court abolished the "inconsistent verdict rule in criminal cases." Thus, a defendant cannot attack a jury verdict of guilty on one count and of acquittal on another count. In *Milam,* a defendant was charged with two murders committed at the same time. The jury returned a verdict of not guilty by reason of insanity as to one murder and guilty but mentally ill as to the other. In *King v. Waters,*[9] the court noted that appellate courts "cannot know and should not speculate why a jury acquitted on . . . [one] offense and convicted on . . . [another] offense. The reason could be an error by the jury in its consideration or it could be mistake, compromise, or lenity . . . ."

The case is otherwise in those instances where the jury returns multiple convictions as to crimes which are not merely inconsistent but mutually exclusive of each other. Thus, a person cannot be convicted of both robbery of a vehicle and theft by receiving the same vehicle. Theft by receiving is an offense which can only be committed by one who buys or receives stolen goods, as disntinguished from the person who stole the goods. The essential element of theft by receiving is that the goods were stolen by someone else.[10]

Further, in cases "where there are mutually exclusive convictions, it is insufficient for an appellate court merely to set aside the lesser verdict, because to do so is to speculate about what the jury might have done if properly instructed, and to usurp the functions of both the jury and the trial."[11] In such cases, a new trial is required.[12] "To avoid potentially invalid verdicts, even if 'proper charges are not requested by either side, the trial court

---

[7]Hathcock v. State, 88 Ga. 91 (2), 13 S.E. 959 (1891).

[8]Milam v. State, 255 Ga. 560, 562 (2), 341 S.E.2d 216 (1986). See Thornton v. State, 298 Ga. 709, 784 S.E.2d 417 (2016) (*Milam* applied to case where jury returns inconsistent verdicts to co-conspirators); U.S. v. Andrews, 850 F.2d 1557, 1561 (11th Cir. 1988) (inconsistent verdicts on conspiracy charge will not upset conviction because a co-conspirator was acquitted by the same jury); Lucas v. State, 264 Ga. 840, 452 S.E.2d 110 (1995) (holding that *Milam* is "equally applicable where jury returns inconsistent verdicts against co-defendants").

[9]King v. Waters, 278 Ga. 122,

123, 598 S.E.2d 476 (2004).

[10]See Thomas v. State, 261 Ga. 854, 413 S.E.2d 196 (1992).

[11]Dumas v. State, 266 Ga. 797, 800(2), 471 S.E.2d 508 (1996).

[12]Thomas v. State, 261 Ga. 854, 413 S.E.2d 196 (1992); Ingram v. State, 268 Ga. App. 149, 601 S.E.2d 736 (2004). There is an exception to the abolition of the inconsistent verdict rule. The rule does not apply in cases where there the jury's reasoning is transparent and therefore no speculation exists as to the cause of the inconsistent verdicts. Such is the case where the jury verdict form used by the court demonstrates jury confusion and legal error. In Turner v. State, 282 Ga. 880 (2), 655 S.E.2d 804 (2008), the jury

should give them sua sponte.'"

In *Kimble v. State,*[13] the court clarified *Thomas* and *Milam*. *Thomas* applies in cases where multiple guilty verdicts result in punishment for crimes that are mutually exclusive; while *Milam* adopted *Powell's* analysis of inconsistency among guilty and not guilty verdicts on multiple charges.

In *Darden v. State,*[14] the court held that "[t]he trial court erred in sentencing [the defendant] for felony murder and voluntary manslaughter based on the same underlying aggravated assault . . . [since] a defendant found guilty of voluntary manslaughter lacks the mens rea required to commit felony murder in that any malice which would have been imputed from the underlying felony has been mitigated by the provocation which induced the crime of voluntary manslaughter."

In the 1996 case of *Dumas v. State,*[15] the Georgia Supreme Court followed *Thomas*. Here the defendant was charged with malice murder, felony murder, vehicular homicide, and driving under the influence. The jury "returned verdicts finding Dumas guilty of malice murder, vehicular homicide, and driving under the influence, and not guilty of felony murder. The court told the jury that it had rendered inconsistent guilty verdicts on malice murder and vehicular homicide . . . and sent the jury back for further deliberation, over . . . objection. The jury then returned verdicts of guilty of malice murder and driving under the influence" and not guilty of the other charges. The Georgia Supreme Court said that this case "involves two verdicts of *guilty* that not only were inconsistent, but also were *mutually exclusive*. . . ." (Emphasis in original.) Malice murder is "the killing of another 'with malice aforethought. . . .'" Vehicular homicide is "killing another while operating a car 'without malice aforethought. . . .'" In light of these definitions, the court held that "[o]bviously, the two verdicts were mutually exclusive. . . . [T]he trial court was absolutely correct when it refused to accept the . . . [earlier verdict] and sent the jury back to continue its deliberations."

---

found the defendant not guilty of murder, but convicted on the count of felony murder. However, the verdict form also reflected the jury's finding that the defendant's actions were justified. Since justification is a complete defense to any crime based on the underlying conduct, the conviction was invalid.

[13]Kimble v. State, 236 Ga. App. 391, 512 S.E.2d 306 (1999), overruling

Strong v. State, 223 Ga. App. 434, 477 S.E.2d 866 (1996).

[14]Darden v. State, 271 Ga. 449, 451 (4), 519 S.E.2d 921 (1999).

[15]Dumas v. State, 266 Ga. 797, 471 S.E.2d 508 (1996). See State v. Owens, 296 Ga. 205, 766 S.E.2d 66 (2014); Gutierrez v. State, 235 Ga. App. 878, 880(2), 510 S.E.2d 570 (1998).

In *Knight v. State*,[16] the court held that a verdict for malice murder and felony murder were not mutually exclusive since a verdict for felony murder does not constitute a finding that the murder was committed without malice but rather that the murder was committed while in the commission of another felony "irrespective of malice." In *State v. Springer*,[17] the court considered the issue of whether guilty verdicts on the greater charge of aggravated assault and the lesser included offense of reckless conduct were mutually exclusive given that a finding of aggravated assault pursuant to O.C.G.A. § 16-5-20(a)(1), requires proof of a specific intent to inflict harm and reckless conduct is dependent upon a finding of only a conscious disregard or complete indifference for the consequences of one's actions. Overruling all authority to the contrary,[18] the court held that although the specific intent to cause harm and the conscious disregard of the consequences of one's actions, while distinct and apparently contradictory states of mind, are not incompatible or inconsistent as a matter of law.

The court noted that it had previously held that the criminal intent necessary to prove criminal negligence is not interchangeable with that necessary to prove aggravated assault "in those instances where the mental culpability of the actor is the essential element that distinguishes two separate offenses, with separate penalties, for committing the same behavior."[19] If such were the case, a jury could convict a defendant for aggravated assault under O.C.G.A. § 16-5-20(a)(1) based upon proof of the lesser mens rea of criminal negligence. However, in *Springer* the court concluded "one cannot and should not be allowed to defend against a lesser included charge by proving that he is more culpable." If the state is able to prove the specific intent to harm required by the greater offense, a jury is not precluded from also finding a defendant guilty of the lesser included crime.

In *Lindsey v. State*,[20] the court pointed out that the defendant is entitled to the benefit of the doubt in the construction of an ambiguous verdict.

In the second situation involving inconsistent verdicts, multiple

---

[16]Knight v. State, 271 Ga. 557, 559 (2), 521 S.E.2d 819 (1999).

[17]State v. Springer, 297 Ga. 376, 774 S.E.2d 106 (2015).

[18]These cases include Jackson v. State, 276 Ga. 408, 577 S.E.2d 570 (2003), Allaben v. State, 294 Ga. 315, 751 S.E.2d 802 (2013), Walker v. State, 293 Ga. 709, 749 S.E.2d 663 (2013), Dryden v. State, 285 Ga. 281, 676 S.E.2d 175 (2009), Flores v. State, 277 Ga. 780, 596 S.E.2d 114 (2004), Holcomb v. State, 310 Ga. App. 853, 714 S.E.2d 407 (2011), and Reddick v. State, 264 Ga. App. 487, 591 S.E.2d 392 (2003).

[19]Dunagan v. State, 269 Ga. 590, 592, 502 S.E.2d 726 (1998).

[20]Lindsey v. State, 262 Ga. 665, 666 (1), 424 S.E.2d 616 (1993).

defendants are charged with multiple offenses arising out of the same set of facts.[21]

In *Milner v. United States*,[22] one defendant (Milner) was convicted of receiving stolen goods but the jury could not agree as to the guilt of the other defendant on a larceny count. The court found nothing repugnant nor inconsistent in the verdict. The court stated that to convict Milner it was necessary to prove that the goods were stolen while traveling in interstate commerce, and that he received them knowing that they were stolen. The court pointed out that others had pled guilty to the larceny, and the court decided that it was not necessary to prove any particular defendant committed the larceny in order to convict Milner of receiving stolen goods.

Likewise, inconsistent verdicts for multiple defendants in a bench trial do not offend due process.[23] In *Thompson v. State*,[24] the defendant was charged with felony murder based on three underlying felonies: aggravated assault with a deadly weapon, aggravated assault with the intent to rob, and burglary. The jury returned a general verdict on felony murder without designating the underlying felony. The court set aside the felony murder conviction because the court failed to properly instruct the jury as to the burglary charge. However, as the Supreme Court noted in *Jones v. State*,[25] *Thompson* has never been cited by the court to set aside a felony murder conviction based upon a general verdict where one of several possible predicate offenses is not supported by sufficient evidence. The Court found that in *Thompson* one of the possible basis for a guilty verdict was contrary to law because of the improper jury instruction. In cases where one of the possible predicates for a felony murder conviction is not sufficiently supported by the evidence or a factually inadequate theory, the law should not presume that the verdict rests on a ground that the evidence does support.

See § 26:33, infra, on merger.

---

[21]Cf. Standefer v. United States, 447 U.S. 10, 100 S.Ct. 1999, 64 L.Ed.2d 689 (1980), where a defendant's conviction as an aider and abettor was upheld even though his co-defendant was acquitted as principal. The court stated: "This case does no more than manifest the simple, if discomforting, reality that 'different juries may reach different results under any criminal statute. That is one of the consequences we accept under our jury system.'" See also Annotation, "Inconsistency of Criminal Verdicts as Between Two or More Defendants Tried Together," 22 A.L.R.3d 717.

[22]Milner v. United States, 293 Fed. 590 (5th Cir. 1923).

[23]Harris v. Rivera, 454 U.S. 339, 102 S.Ct. 460, 70 L.Ed.2d 530 (1981). In the *Rivera* case, the court pointed out that judges in bench trials enjoy the same freedom as jurors to render inconsistent verdicts.

[24]Thompson v. State, 271 Ga. 105, 108 (2), 519 S.E.2d 434 (1999).

[25]Jones v. State, 301 Ga. 94, 799 S.E.2d 749 (2017).

§ 25:7 Impeaching the verdict

Generally, jurors are not allowed to impeach their own verdicts. O.C.G.A. § 24-6-606(b) provides an exception to that rule whereby a juror may testify on the question of "whether extraneous prejudicial information was improperly brought to the juror's attention [or] whether any outside influence was improperly brought to bear upon any juror."

O.C.G.A. § 24-6-606(b) was adopted in 2013 but is generally consistent with cases decided prior thereto.

In interpreting Federal Rule of Evidence 606(b) in *Tanner v. United States*,[1] the Supreme Court cited the following examples of extraneous influences about which a juror could testify: a bailiff's comments to the jury about the defendant,[2] a bribe offered to a juror,[3] or that a juror in a criminal trial had submitted an employment application to the district attorney's office.[4] A juror is not allowed to testify about internal jury matters, including whether a juror sufficiently understood the English language, or whether a hearing impairment interfered with a juror's understanding of the evidence. In *Tanner* itself, the Court held that a juror could not testify as to alleged drug and alcohol use by other jurors during the trial because such behavior was not an "outside influence" and therefore the testimony was barred under Rule 606(b).[5] It has been stated that intra-jury comments do not create an extraneous influence unless they carry "the coercive force of threats or bribery."[6]

In federal courts, the inquiry is limited to the contents of the alleged prejudicial information; a juror may not testify as to the impact of such information on the juror's thought process.[7]

In *United States v. Lakhani*,[8] the Third Circuit Court of Appeals identified five policies underlying this narrow exception regarding juror testimony:

(1) discouraging harassment of jurors by losing parties eager

---

[Section 25:7]

[1]Tanner v. U.S., 483 U.S. 107, 107 S. Ct. 2739, 97 L. Ed. 2d 90, 22 Fed. R. Evid. Serv. 1143 (1987).

[2]Parker v. Gladden, 385 U.S. 363, 87 S. Ct. 468, 17 L. Ed. 2d 420 (1966).

[3]Remmer v. U.S., 1954-1 C.B. 146, 347 U.S. 227, 74 S. Ct. 450, 98 L. Ed. 654, 54-1 U.S. Tax Cas. (CCH) P 9274, 46 A.F.T.R. (P-H) P 936 (1954).

[4]Government of Virgin Islands v. Nicholas, 759 F.2d 1073, 17 Fed. R.

Evid. Serv. 1054 (3d Cir. 1985).

[5]Tanner v. U.S., 483 U.S. 107, 107 S. Ct. 2739, 97 L. Ed. 2d 90, 22 Fed. R. Evid. Serv. 1143 (1987).

[6]Government of Virgin Islands v. Gereau, 12 V.I. 213, 523 F.2d 140, 152, 1 Fed. R. Evid. Serv. 1 (3d Cir. 1975).

[7]Haugh v. Jones & Laughlin Steel Corp., 949 F.2d 914, 34 Fed. R. Evid. Serv. 841 (7th Cir. 1991).

[8]U.S. v. Lakhani, 480 F.3d 171, 72 Fed. R. Evid. Serv. 881 (3d Cir. 2007).

to have the verdict set aside;

(2)   encouraging free and open discussions among jurors;

(3)   reducing incentives for jury tampering;

(4)   promoting verdict finality; and

(5)   maintaining viability of the jury as a decision-making body.

In *Gardiner v. State*,[9] juror affidavits were submitted in order to show that "(1) Juror Golden commented on the guilt of the defendants from the outset of the trial contrary to the court's instructions; (2) juror Golden was personally familiar with family members of the victim and with certain witnesses and conversed during the trial with the victim's father who later testified as a witness for the prosecution; (3) certain jurors did not understand instructions regarding reasonable doubt; (4) certain jurors had concerns about their personal safety and the possibility of racial unrest in the community in the event of an acquittal; (5) certain jurors were concerned about the length of the trial and therefore were not impartial; and (6) juror Cooper, an attorney, provided legal information which unfairly influenced other jurors." The trial judge was notified of Golden's conduct before commencement of deliberations. Defense was offered an additional peremptory strike which was exercised to remove Golden and an alternate juror was substituted. The appellate court concluded that any prejudice to the defense as to Golden had been cured with approval. That court then concluded that complaints 3 through 6 did not fall within an exception to the rule against impeachment of verdicts.

In 1998, in *Devoney v. State*,[10] the Florida Supreme Court held that testimony of a juror that other jurors failed to follow the trial judge's charge not to consider certain inadmissible evidence is insufficient to grant a new trial.

In 1984, in *Williams v. State*,[11] the court considered an alleged statement by a juror during deliberations that he had seen one of the defendants in a store attempting to shoplift. This juror said that the incident did not affect his decision to vote for a conviction. The court concluded "that to allow a jury verdict to be upset solely because of such statements goes very far toward impugning the sanctity of jury deliberations, undermining the finality of jury verdicts, and subjecting jurors to post-trial harassment. Therefore, we will not allow a jury verdict to be upset solely because of such statements unless the statements are so prejudicial that the verdict must be deemed 'inherently

---

[9]Gardiner v. State, 264 Ga. 329, 332 (2), 444 S.E.2d 300 (1994).

[10]Devoney v. State, 717 So.2d 501 (Fla.1998).

[11]Williams v. State, 252 Ga. 7, 8, 310 S.E.2d 528 (1984).

lacking in due process.' "

In the 1994 case of *Joachim v. State*,[12] the court followed *Williams* and affirmed the conviction even though a juror "made negative comments about a witness based on knowledge from her employment" to the other jurors.

However, there are constitutional limitations[13] and exceptions[14] to the rule prohibiting a juror from impeaching his verdict. Since evidence against a defendant must be presented at trial so as to protect his right of confrontation,[15] in a case where two jurors made an unauthorized visit to the scene of the crime and presented their findings to other jurors, the jurors were allowed to impeach their verdict since the accused was deprived of a fair trial.[16] These constitutional limitations, in effect, disapprove a great number of older Georgia cases which declined to permit a juror to impeach his verdict in almost any situation.[17] But there is no automatic right to a reversal of a conviction simply because two or more witnesses witnessed the scene of a crime during deliberations and reported to the other jurors.[18]

A verdict may not be impeached simply by showing that some jurors only agreed to murder because one juror said a verdict of voluntary manslaughter would not give the defendant enough punishment[19] or by an affidavit of one juror stating that she only

---

[12]Joachim v. State, 263 Ga. 816, 817 (3), 440 S.E.2d 15 (1994).

[13]Watkins v. State, 237 Ga. 678, 685, 229 S.E.2d 465 (1976).

[14]See Livingston v. Wynne, 147 Ga. 307, 308 (1), 93 S.E. 877 (1917), where the court held that it was error on motion for a mistrial to refuse to consider the affidavit of a juror stating that two of the jurors had been entertained at the home of the defendant's brother during the trial. The affidavit had been objected to on the grounds that it tended to impeach the verdict of the juror. The court pointed out that at the time of the motion there was no verdict.

[15]Parker v. Gladden, 385 U.S. 363, 87 S.Ct. 468, 17 L.Ed.2d 420 (1966). See Annot., "Communication Between Court Officials or Attendants and Jurors in Criminal Trial as Ground for Mistrial or Reversal—Post-Parker Cases," 35 A.L.R.4th 890 (1985).

[16]Watkins v. State, 237 Ga. 678, 684, 229 S.E.2d 465 (1976).

[17]For example, see Redfearn v. Thompson, 10 Ga. App. 550 (5), 73 S.E. 949 (1912), holding that a juror's affidavit that he did not voluntarily assent to the verdict cannot be received.

[18]Boles v. State, 168 Ga. App. 904, 906 (2), 310 S.E.2d 741 (1983).

[19]Aguilar v. State, 240 Ga. 830, 831 (1), 242 S.E.2d 620 (1978). In United States v. Duzac, 622 F.2d 911 (5th Cir. 1980), the court held that jurors would not be permitted to impeach their verdict where there was no evidence of outside influence but a note said there were prejudices among the jury because of prior personal experience. The trial judge then charged the jury that it was their obligation to decide the case on the evidence without regard to prejudice. Shortly thereafter the jury returned a verdict. When polled, all jurors adhered to their verdict. The rule is different where the

voted on one count of the indictment,[20] or by an affidavit of defense counsel in which he sets out what a juror told him after the trial.[21]

Also, a defendant is not entitled to a new trial based on a single affidavit stating that a juror who later served on the jury in the defendant's trial expressed a dislike of the defendant and said he thought he was guilty before he was selected as a juror.[22] In *Spencer v. State*,[23] the court held that it was not error for the trial judge to refuse to consider "a post-trial affidavit from one of the jurors stating she overheard two white jurors making racially derogatory comments about the defendant during the jury's deliberations." When a juror is selected he swears that he had no bias or prejudice and that he is impartial; hence there must be more than an affidavit from a single witness. If this were not the rule there would be simply one oath against one oath.[24]

If a verdict in an improper form is returned, the judge may have the jury retire and prepare a verdict in accordance with the instruction of court. Any objection to reformation of a verdict is waived if it is not contemporaneously raised.[25]

See § 18:38, supra, on improper influence or improper conduct, and see § 24:23, supra, on jury misconduct. See Studdard, *Daniel's Georgia Handbook on Criminal Evidence* § 6:14 (2018 ed.) on impeaching the verdict. For a motion for a new trial based on jury misconduct and supporting affidavits, see Studdard, *Daniel's Georgia Criminal Trial Practice Forms* (2018–2019 ed.), §§ 31:8 et seq.

§ 25:8   Amending the verdict

O.C.G.A. § 17-9-40 provides that "[a] verdict may be amended in mere matter of form after the jury have dispersed; but . . . may not be amended in matter of substance, either by what the

---

juror misconduct complained of occurs during voir dire. A movant may be entitled to a new trial where it appears that a "juror failed to answer [or to answer] honestly a material question on voir dire, and then further show that a correct response would have provided a valid basis for a challenge for cause." Gainesville Radiology Group v. Hummel, 263 Ga. 91, 428 S.E.2d 786 (1993) (citing McDonough Power Equipment, Inc. v. Greenwood, 464 U.S. 548, 556, 104 S. Ct. 845, 78 L. Ed. 2d 663 (1984)). See Glover v. State, 274 Ga. 213, 552 S.E.2d 804 (2001).

[20]Dansby v. State, 165 Ga. App. 41, 42 (2)(a), 299 S.E.2d 579 (1983).

[21]Arnold v. State, 166 Ga. App. 313 (1), 304 S.E.2d 118 (1983).

[22]Barrett v. State, 157 Ga. App. 174 (1), 276 S.E.2d 857 (1981).

[23]Spencer v. State, 260 Ga. 640, 643 (3), 398 S.E.2d 179 (1990).

[24]Coggeshall v. Park, 162 Ga. 78, 79 (3), 132 S.E. 632 (1926); Jones v. State, 247 Ga. 268, 270, 275 S.E.2d 67 (1981).

[25]Dansby v. State, 165 Ga. App. 41, 42 (2)(b), 299 S.E.2d 579 (1983).

jurors say they intended to find or otherwise."

It is the responsibility of the trial court "to insist on a legal verdict, that is, a verdict responsive to the issues as framed by the indictment or accusation and the evidence."[1] The way to correct a verdict which does not conform to this standard "is for the trial court and counsel to review the verdict prior to its publication in open court, and if the verdict is not proper in that it finds the defendant guilty of an offense with regard to which the trial court did not instruct the jury,"[2] the trial court should require the jury to continue its deliberations with instructions to return a verdict consistent with the instructions provided at the close of evidence. If the trial court should fail to intervene in order to secure a proper verdict before dispensing the jury, a new trial is required.[3]

However, a verdict may not be amended so as to effect a substantive change in the verdict even if the change in the verdict would not affect the sentence.[4]

§ 25:9   Interviewing jurors

Generally, jurors have a right to discuss a case after a verdict has been returned and they have been discharged.[1] Likewise, a juror has a right to refuse to talk with a non-juror.[2] Certainly an outsider has no right to harass a former juror.[3] Likewise, it has been held that there are strong policy reasons disfavoring the interrogation of jurors after a verdict has been returned.[4] However, the Fifth Circuit has held that a rule of court which provides that no person shall "interview . . . any juror, relative, friend, or associate thereof . . . with respect to the deliberations . . . except on leave of court" is a violation of the First

---

[Section 25:8]

[1]State v. Freeman, 264 Ga. 276, 277-278, 444 S.E.2d 80 (1994).

[2]State v. Freeman, 264 Ga. 276, 278, 444 S.E.2d 80 (1994).

[3]See Newsome v. State, 323 Ga. App. 15, 747 S.E.2d 99 (2013); Brooks v. State, 311 Ga. App. 857, 717 S.E.2d 490 (2011). See also Robinson v. State, 282 Ga. App. 214, 638 S.E.2d 370 (2006) (verdict which found defendant "guilty with reasonable doubt" not accepted and jury directed to continue deliberating).

[4]Hollis v. State, 215 Ga. App. 35, 36, 450 S.E.2d 247 (1994).

[Section 25:9]

[1]In re Express-News Corp., 695 F.2d 807, 810 (5th Cir. 1982).

[2]Cf. O'Rear v. Fruehauf, 554 F.2d 1304, 1309 (5th Cir. 1977).

[3]Cf. United States v. Harrelson, 713 F.2d 1114 (5th Cir. 1983). See Sharp, "Postverdict Interviews With Jurors," 88 Case & Comment, No. 5, p. 3 (1983).

[4]United States v. Crosby, 294 F.2d 928, 950 (2d Cir. 1961); 24 C.J.S. 103 Criminal Law § 1447.

Amendment.[5] Nevertheless, in *United States v. Cleveland,*[6] the same Court affirmed the issuance of the following order in a case: "I now instruct you that you have no obligation to speak to any person about this case. I also instruct you that, absent a special order by me, no juror may be interviewed by anyone concerning the deliberations of the jury. I also instruct you that the lawyers and the parties are not to attempt to question you without an order from me." The appellate court quoted from *Clark v. United States*[7] where the United States Supreme Court pointed out that "[f]reedom of debate might be stifled and independence of thought checked if jurors were made to feel that their arguments and ballots were to be freely published to the world." The Fifth Circuit held that the order having been issued "was an appropriate measure taken to address the danger, identified in *Clark* that compromises of the secrecy of jury deliberations presents to our criminal justice system's reliance on jury determinations. Thus . . . we find that the order . . . was narrowly tailored to prevent a substantial threat to the administration of justice—namely, the threat presented to freedom of speech within the jury room by the possibility of post-verdict interviews."

In *Sears v. State,*[8] the Georgia Supreme Court reinstated the trial court's order granting funds for an investigator so that the investigator and defense counsel could contact jurors "to investigate the claim of jury misconduct." However, "[a]nyone seeking to speak with a juror must clearly inform that juror that he or she has the right to choose to answer questions and the right to decline the request." Because there was no evidence or even any suggestion that defense counsel had harassed any juror, the questioning of jurors was allowed. Further, the court held that it was error for the trial court to restrict the questioning by demanding that counsel foretell what information would be gained in the process. The court found that the restriction "placed an impossible burden on counsel."

See § 25:4, supra, on polling the jury.

§ 25:10   Recalling jury and giving further instructions after conviction

Where a trial judge fails to instruct the jury on an important matter and does not realize the omission until after the defendant has been found guilty and the jury has dispersed, the judge has

---

[5]In re Express-News Corp., 695 F.2d 807 (5th Cir. 1982); United States v. Harrelson, 713 F.2d 1114 (5th Cir. 1983).

[6]United States v. Cleveland, 128 F.3d 267 (5th Cir. 1997).

[7]Clark v. United States, 289 U.S. 1, 53 S.Ct. 465, 77 L.Ed. 993, 999 (1933).

[8]Sears v. State, 268 Ga. 759, 767, 493 S.E.2d 180 (1997).

no authority to resummon the jury to attempt to correct the situation. When a verdict is agreed upon and the jury dispersed, the trial is at an end.[1]

See Annotation, "Criminal Law: Propriety of Reassembling Jury to Amend, Correct, Clarify or Otherwise Change Verdict After Jury Has Been Discharged or Has Reached or Sealed Its Verdict and Separated," 14 A.L.R.5th 89 (1993).

[Section 25:10]   236, 239, 339 S.E.2d 298 (1985).
[1]Chastain v. State, 177 Ga. App.

Chapter 26

Sentencing

KeyCite®: Cases and other legal materials listed in KeyCite Scope can be researched through the KeyCite service on Westlaw®. Use KeyCite to check citations for form, parallel references, prior and later history, and comprehensive citator information, including citations to other decisions and secondary materials.

---

§ 26:1   General

Where a valid sentence is not imposed at the term of the court at which a defendant is convicted, the court may impose a valid sentence at a later term.[1] However, there is a presumption that a sentence was correctly imposed "and the burden of showing that a sentence was not correctly imposed is with the party who asserts its impropriety."[2]

A sentence which is not authorized by law is a nullity.[3] When a sentence is void, until a new sentence has been entered, the defendant is treated as though he has been convicted but not sentenced.[4] Thus, the court has authority to correct the sentence even if the correction increases the sentence which the defendant has already started serving.[5] A void sentence may be attacked by

---

[Section 26:1]

[1]Sherman v. State, 142 Ga. App. 691, 692, 237 S.E.2d 5 (1977).

[2]Lynn v. State, 236 Ga. App. 600, 604, 512 S.E.2d 695 (1999).

[3]Mullins v. State, 134 Ga. App. 243 (1), 214 S.E.2d 1 (1975); Pruitt v. State, 135 Ga. App. 677, 679 (2), 218 S.E.2d 679 (1975).

[4]Mullins v. State, 134 Ga. App. 243 (1), 214 S.E.2d 1 (1975). See Franks v. State, 323 Ga. App. 813, 748 S.E.2d 291 (2013).

[5]Mullins v. State, 134 Ga. App. 243, 214 S.E.2d 1 (1975). See Annot., "Power of Court to Increase Severity of Unlawful Sentence—Modern Status," 28 A.L.R.4th 147 (1984).

habeas corpus or by a motion for modification of the sentence.[6] In *Gonzalez v. State*,[7] the court pointed out that where a void sentence has been imposed, "then a new and valid sentence can be imposed by the trial judge at any time." When a sentence is ambiguous and doubtful, it should be given the construction which favors the defendant.[8] In *Lockhart v. State*,[9] the court held that a trial judge when re-sentencing a defendant must sentence in accordance with "the sentencing provisions that existed *at the time of his criminal act*." (Emphasis in original.) However, once a defendant enters upon the execution of a felony sentence, the court has no authority to change the sentence by increasing or decreasing the punishment.[10] In *Edge v. State*,[11] the court held "that a defendant enters upon service of a probated sentence by meeting with a probation officer after the sentence is imposed." In the case of a misdemeanor, the trial judge may "amend, modify, alter, suspend, or probate sentences" unless the sentence provided for confinement under the jurisdiction of the Board of Corrections.[12]

In *Curry v. State*,[13] the court pointed out that a "sentence which has been reduced to writing and signed by the judge may not be increased after the defendant has begun to serve that sentence. [But an] oral declaration as to what the sentence shall be is not the sentence of the court" until it is reduced to writing and signed by the judge. Nevertheless, "the oral declaration of the sentence may not be increased after the defendant has begun to serve it." In *Castillo v. State*,[14] the court said the defendant had not begun to serve a probated sentence, which was in writing and filed with the clerk of the court, and the trial court did not err in modifying the sentence, at the same term of the court, by adding time to be

---

[6]McCranie v. State, 157 Ga. App. 110, 111 (3), 276 S.E.2d 263 (1981), overruled on other grounds recognized, Jones v. State, 333 Ga. App. 796, 777 S.E.2d 480 (2015). See Estes v. Chapman, 382 F.3d 1237 (11th Cir. 2004).

[7]Gonzalez v. State, 201 Ga. App. 437, 438, 411 S.E.2d 345 (1991). In Kaiser v. State, 285 Ga. App. 63(1), 646 S.E.2d 84 (2007), the Court of Appeals determined that a defendant may move to withdraw a plea following the imposition of a void sentence at any time prior to re-sentencing.

[8]Jenkins v. Montgomery, 248 Ga. 696, 285 S.E.2d 706 (1982).

[9]Lockhart v. State, 227 Ga. App. 481, 483, 489 S.E.2d 594 (1997).

[10]Jones v. State, 155 Ga. App. 382, 383 (1), 271 S.E.2d 30 (1980); Jones v. State, 154 Ga. App. 581, 584, 269 S.E.2d 77 (1980).

In United States v. Jones, 722 F.2d 632 (11th Cir. 1983), the court held that double jeopardy was violated where a defendant is sentenced, starts serving his sentence and is then re-sentenced.

[11]Edge v. State, 194 Ga. App. 466, 391 S.E.2d 18 (1990).

[12]O.C.G.A. § 17-10-3(b).

[13]Curry v. State, 248 Ga. 183, 185 (4), 281 S.E.2d 604 (1981); cf. Sacchinelli v. State, 161 Ga. App. 763, 766 (5), 288 S.E.2d 894 (1982).

[14]Castillo v. State, 178 Ga. App. 312, 314 (5), 342 S.E.2d 782 (1986).

served. However, a sentence may be corrected to reflect the fact of the recidivism aspect of the sentence.[15] In *Paul v. State*,[16] the court held that a defendant is not regarded as having begun to serve his sentence between oral announcement and the signing of the sentence where the record does not indicate that the written sentence was entered after oral pronouncement.

The case of *Hudson v. State*[17] points out that the result may well be different in an abandonment case. In *Hudson*, the defendant was sentenced in 1975 to 12 months' imprisonment and a $50 fine. The sentence was suspended on the condition that the defendant pay $210 per month support for his minor children until they reach majority. The sentence order provided that the trial judge could, for good cause, modify any of the terms or conditions of the sentence. In 1980, the amount of the payments was increased to $430 per month after notice to the defendant and pursuant to former O.C.G.A. § 42-8-34(d)(4) . The defendant contended that this was double jeopardy. The court denied the defendant's claim for two reasons: First, the payments were not a part of the sentence. The periodic payments are not, strictly speaking, in the nature of a penalty. They are merely the enforcement of a legal obligation which exists separately from the abandonment case. Second, a suspended sentence as opposed to a probated sentence, does not begin to run until the suspension is revoked. Hence, the execution of the sentence had not begun. In connection with a sentence for abandonment, former O.C.G.A. § 42-8-34(d)(4) [now O.C.G.A. § 19-10-1(j)(4)] provides that the trial judge retains the right to modify the amount of payments based on the "ability of the defendant . . . and . . . the adequacy of the present support payments." Nevertheless, a trial judge loses his authority to require a defendant to serve his sentence in abandonment cases when the child or children reach the age of majority.[18]

However, in *Strickland v. State*,[19] the court pointed out that once a "sentence has been actually served (whether in confinement or on probation) jurisdiction over the offender no longer

---

[15]McClinic v. State, 172 Ga. App. 54, 321 S.E.2d 796 (1984), overruled on other grounds by Carter v. State, 238 Ga. App. 632, 519 S.E.2d 717 (1999).

[16]Paul v. State, 170 Ga. App. 746 (3), 318 S.E.2d 200 (1984).

[17]Hudson v. State, 248 Ga. 397, 283 S.E.2d 271 (1981). Cf. Tillman v. State, 249 Ga. 792, 294 S.E.2d 516 (1982). However, in *Tillman*, the court

held that the rule applying in abandonment case did not apply to a defendant who had been sentenced under the former bastardy law.

[18]Moody v. State, 190 Ga. App. 91, 92, 378 S.E.2d 375 (1989).

[19]Strickland v. State, 165 Ga. App. 197, 200, 300 S.E.2d 537 (1983); Jones v. State, 166 Ga. App. 277, 304 S.E.2d 451 (1983).

exists." Likewise, in *Taylor v. State*,[20] the court pointed out that "a sentencing judge is empowered to modify or change a probated sentence at any time during the term of probation."

Finally, a "criminal sentence should be clear and unambiguous" and if it is not the defendant may have to be re-sentenced.[21]

It has been held that where there is a transcript of the actual sentencing and the sentence which is signed fails to have a printed provision for probation stricken from it in accordance with the oral declaration of the judge, the sentencing court has inherent power to correct the written sentence.[22] However, in *Morgan v. Mount*,[23] where the court considered a case in which the trial judge orally announced that the defendant's sentence could run concurrently with a federal sentence, but, the signed sentence did not contain this provision, the appellate court concluded that the written sentence controlled.

However, in *Henderson v. State*,[24] the court recognized that there is a distinction between increasing a sentence and amending a sentence so as to impose the originally intended sentence. Here evidence of three prior felonies was presented after conviction. The trial judge imposed a 30-year sentence, the maximum provided for the offense. The defendant was taken out of the courtroom as the clerk was writing up the sentence. The clerk asked if the sentence should not reflect that the defendant was sentenced as a recidivist. The trial judge called the defendant back and added the suggested clause to the sentence. The defendant contended that he had already commenced serving the sentence and that the judge could not add the suggested provision. The Court of Appeals found no error.

Generally, where consecutive sentences for different "offenses are imposed at the same time, and where the underlying conviction for which the earlier sentence was imposed is reversed or set aside, the time the defendant served under the invalidated sentence will be credited toward the latter sentence so that the latter sentence will be held to have commenced at the date of commencement of the earlier, invalid sentence." However, "if sentences [are] imposed at different times, the defendant may be entitled to some credit for time served under the earlier, invalid sentence, but the latter sentence will not automatically be held to have begun at the commencement of the earlier sentence." Also, "where the earlier sentence is invalidated but the conviction is

---

[20]Taylor v. State, 181 Ga. App. 199 (1), 351 S.E.2d 723 (1986).

[21]Jones v. State, 154 Ga. App. 581, 584, 269 S.E.2d 77 (1980).

[22]Hopper v. Williams, 238 Ga. 612, 234 S.E.2d 525 (1977).

[23]Morgan v. Mount, 195 Ga. 281, 24 S.E.2d 17 (1943).

[24]Henderson v. State, 162 Ga. App. 320, 325, 292 S.E.2d 77 (1982).

upheld and the defendant subsequently is re-sentenced, the latter sentence will not begin to run until termination of the resentence."[25]

See § 26:41, infra, on the lack of authority of the court to impose a more severe sentence where a defendant exercised his right to a trial. Also see § 26:18, infra, on modification of a probated sentence. See § 26:46, infra, on reduction of sentence.

§ 26:2   Cruel or unusual punishment

The Eighth Amendment's proscription against cruel and unusual punishments applies after there has been a formal adjudication of guilt. The Eighth Amendment does not apply to custodial conditions prior to an adjudication of guilt. Prior to a formal adjudication of guilt, the due process clause of the Fourteenth Amendment controls custodial care if the defendant is in custody.[1]

The infliction of cruel or unusual punishment by the state is prohibited by both the Georgia Constitution[2] and the Eighth Amendment to the United States Constitution.[3] Although the exact scope of the phrase "cruel or unusual" has defied precise delineation,[4] it is clear that punishments of torture and other forms of unnecessary cruelty are forbidden.[5] Although it would seem that disproportion, both among punishments and between punishment and crime, is what the cruel or unusual punishment clause addresses,[6] it is also true that the cruel or unusual punishment clause does not bar all forms of retribution or social retalia-

---

[25]Jackson v. Jones, 254 Ga. 127, 128 (1), 129 (1), 327 S.E.2d 206 (1985).

[Section 26:2]

[1]City of Revere v. Massachusetts General Hospital, 463 U.S. 239, 103 S.Ct. 2979, 77 L.Ed.2d 605 (1983).

[2]Ga. Const. 1983, Art. I, § I, ¶ XVII.

[3]Robinson v. California, 370 U.S. 660, 82 S.Ct. 1417, 8 L.Ed.2d 758, reh. denied, 371 U.S. 905, 83 S.Ct. 202, 9 L.Ed.2d 166 (1962).

[4]Trop v. Dulles, 356 U.S. 86, 99, 78 S.Ct. 590, 2 L.Ed.2d 630 (1958).

[5]Wilkerson v. Utah, 99 U.S. (9 Otto) 130, 135, 25 L.Ed. 345 (1878); Weems v. United States, 217 U.S. 349, 30 S.Ct. 544, 54 L.Ed. 793 (1910).

[6]Jackson v. Bishop, 404 F.2d 571, 579 (8th Cir. 1968). See Humphrey v. Wilson, 282 Ga. 520, 652 S.E.2d 501 (2007), where the court held that a mandatory minimum 10-year sentence without parole and permanent registration as a sex offender constituted cruel and unusual punishment for the crime of aggravated child molestation under both the United States and Georgia Constitutions when the fifteen-year-old victim engaged in consensual oral sex with the seventeen-year-old defendant. In finding gross disproportionately between the sentence and the crime, the *Humphrey* court noted that the legislature amended the punishment for defendant's conduct subsequent to his conviction from felony to misdemeanor status in cases of willing teenage participants reflected society's evolving views regarding the seriousness of the crime.

tion against a defendant.[7]

In *Nihart v. State*,[8] the court pointed out that "[l]egislative enactments constitute the clearest and most objective evidence of how contemporary society views a particular punishment. Legislative discretion must be deferred to unless, under the circumstances, the sentence shocks the conscience."

A subsequent repeal or amendment of the statute under which the defendant was convicted does not affect the validity of either the conviction or the punishment.[9] Similarly, a reduction of potential punishment subsequent to the sentencing of the accused need not inure to his benefit.[10]

In *Helling v. McKinney*,[11] the United States Supreme Court reversed the grant of a motion for a directed verdict where the petitioner claimed cruel and unusual punishment resulting from the alleged breathing of "second-hand" cigarette smoke. The petitioner was housed with a prisoner who smoked five packs of cigarettes a day. However, the plaintiff must show he was exposed to unreasonably high levels of such smoke, and he must also "show that the risk of which he complains is not one that today's society chooses to tolerate."

It is not necessarily cruel or unusual punishment to sentence a defendant to life imprisonment without providing for the possibility of parole.[12] Previously in Georgia, the sentencing option of life without the possibility of parole in a capital case could only be imposed as an alternative where the state was seeking the death penalty.[13] In 2009, O.C.G.A. § 16-5-1 was amended to provide that in the case of murder, the state can seek death or life in prison without the possibility of parole or life with the possibility of parole. Life without the possibility of parole may also be

---

[7]Verdugo v. United States, 402 F.2d 599, 617 (9th Cir. 1968).

[8]Nihart v. State, 227 Ga. App. 272, 279 (4), 488 S.E.2d 740 (1997). See Fleming v. Zant, 259 Ga. 687, 386 S.E.2d 389 (1989); Johnson v. State, 276 Ga. 57, 573 S.E.2d 362 (2002); Humphrey v. Wilson, 282 Ga. 520, 652 S.E.2d 501 (2007).

[9]United States v. Rojas-Colombo, 462 F.2d 1091 (5th Cir. 1972); Capuchino v. Estelle, 506 F.2d 440 (5th Cir. 1975).

[10]United States v. Rojas-Colombo, 462 F.2d 1091, 1092 (5th Cir. 1972).

[11]Helling v. McKinney, 509 U.S. 25, 113 S.Ct. 2475, 125 L.Ed.2d 22 (1993).

[12]In Lanier v. State, 635 So.2d 813 (Miss.1994), the court held that a plea bargain for life on condition that the defendant waive parole rights is contrary to public policy. See Lee v. Alabama, 291 F.Supp. 921, 928 (D.C.Ala.1967), aff'd, 406 F.2d 466 (5th Cir. 1968); Moore v. Cowan, 560 F.2d 1298 (6th Cir. 1977).

In Schick v. Reed, 419 U.S. 256, 95 S.Ct. 379, 42 L.Ed.2d 430 (1974), the court upheld a life sentence conditioned on the defendant not being able to obtain parole. Here President Eisenhower had commuted the death sentence of *Schick* conditioned on a no-parole life sentence.

[13]State v. Ingram, 266 Ga. 324, 467 S.E.2d 523 (1996).

imposed pursuant to O.C.G.A. § 17-10-7 in the case of a repeat offender of serious violent felonies. See § 26:45, infra, on sentence of life without possibility of parole. A defendant may be sentenced to life imprisonment for the crime of armed robbery,[14] and, also in Georgia, a defendant sentenced to two or more life terms may be ordered to serve those terms consecutively.[15] Also, the Georgia Supreme Court has rejected the contention that electrocution is a cruel and unusual punishment.[16]

Generally, a sentence for a determinate period less than life will not be subject to attack on cruel or unusual punishment grounds if the sentence falls within the statutory parameters for the given crime.[17] See § 26:17, infra, on length of sentence. Nor will the cumulative impact of consecutive sentences be subject to a similar attack.[18] Sentences of extraordinary length, designed to minimize the possibility or likelihood of parole, are frequently upheld on appeal. For example, in *Yeager v. Estelle*,[19] the Fifth Circuit Court of Appeals upheld a sentence of 500 years for murder. In *Harmelin v. Michigan*,[20] the United States Supreme Court upheld a life sentence without the possibility of parole for possession of more than 650 grams of cocaine.

In *Ewing v. California*,[21] the United States Supreme Court ruled that a sentence of 25 years to life for felony grand theft imposed pursuant to a three strikes sentencing statute in California was not grossly disproportionate under the Eighth Amendment. Justice O'Connor noted that "the primacy of the legislature, the variety of legitimate penological schemes, the nature of our federal system, and the requirement that proportionality review be guided by objective factors inform the final principle that the 'Eighth Amendment does not require strict proportionality between crime and sentence.' "[22]

---

[14]Mydell v. State, 238 Ga. 450, 233 S.E.2d 199 (1977).

[15]Crawford v. State, 236 Ga. 491, 494, 224 S.E.2d 365 (1976).

[16]Mincey v. State, 251 Ga. 255 (4), 304 S.E.2d 882 (1983).

[17]Pollard v. State, 230 Ga. App. 159, 495 S.E.2d 629 (1998); Stuart v. State, 117 Ga. App. 183, 184 (3), 160 S.E.2d 409 (1968); Chappell v. State, 164 Ga. App. 77, 78 (4), 296 S.E.2d 629 (1982).

[18]Dutton v. Smart, 222 Ga. 35, 36 (2), 148 S.E.2d 396 (1966); Hoard v. Dutton, 360 F.2d 673, 674 (5th Cir. 1966). See also § 26:29, infra, on concurrent and consecutive sentencing.

[19]Yeager v. Estelle, 489 F.2d 276 (5th Cir. 1973).

[20]Harmelin v. Michigan, 501 U.S. 957, 111 S.Ct. 2680, 115 L.Ed.2d 836 (1991).

[21]Ewing v. California, 538 U.S. 11, 123 S.Ct. 1179, 155 L.Ed.2d 108 (2003).

[22]Ewing v. California, 538 U.S. 11, 123 S.Ct. 1179, 155 L.Ed.2d 108 (2003); see also Lockyer v. Andrade, 538 U.S. 63, 123 S.Ct. 1166, 155 L.Ed.2d 144 (2003).

In *Davis v. Davis,*[23] the court held that a sentence of 40 years imposed on a defendant convicted of two marijuana charges was so disproportionate as to constitute cruel and unusual punishment. However, the United States Supreme Court, by per curiam order, reversed.[24] Nevertheless, in 1983, the United States Supreme Court in *Solem v. Helm*[25] said, "[W]e hold as a matter of principle that a criminal sentence must be proportionate to the crime for which the defendant has been convicted. Reviewing courts, of course, should grant substantial deference to the broad authority that legislatures necessarily possess in determining the types and limits of punishments for crimes, as well as to the discretion that trial courts possess in sentencing convicted criminals. But no penalty is *per se* constitutional. . . . [A] court's proportionality analysis under the Eighth Amendment should be guided by objective criteria, including (i) the gravity of the offense and harshness of the penalty; (ii) the sentences imposed on other criminals in the same jurisdiction; and (iii) the sentences imposed for commission of the same crime in other jurisdictions." The court then determined that it was a violation of the Eighth Amendment to sentence to life imprisonment without parole a recidivist who had three burglary convictions, a grand larceny conviction and a third offense of driving while intoxicated where the defendant was "charged with uttering a 'no account' check for $100." The defendant said he was intoxicated at the time and had no recollection of writing the check. The court said that the check charge and all his prior offenses were non-violent, relatively minor and none were against a person.

In *Haygood v. State,*[26] the court held that imposing the maximum misdemeanor punishment on the defendant would be viewed by society as "cruel and unusual" in the constitutional sense under the facts of that particular case. Actually, the court seemed to feel that the defendant was being penalized for not pleading guilty and giving up the right to appeal.

In *Campbell v. State,*[27] the Georgia Supreme Court pointed out that "[p]unishment is unconstitutionally excessive if it '(1) makes no measurable contribution to acceptable goals of punishment and hence is nothing more than the purposeful and needless imposition of pain and suffering; or (2) is grossly out of proportion to the severity of the crime. . . .' And '[a] sentence which is not otherwise cruel and unusual does not become so simply

---

[23]Davis v. Davis, 646 F.2d 123 (4th Cir. 1981) (en banc).

[24]Hutto v. Davis, 454 U.S. 370, 102 S.Ct. 703, 70 L.Ed.2d 556 (1982).

[25]Solem v. Helm, 463 U.S. 277, 103 S.Ct. 3001, 77 L.Ed.2d 637 (1983).

[26]Haygood v. State, 225 Ga. App. 81, 83 (2), 483 S.E.2d 302 (1997).

[27]Campbell v. State, 268 Ga. 44, 45 (1), 485 S.E.2d 185 (1997).

because it is "mandatory." ' "

In *Bradshaw v. State*,[28] the Georgia Supreme Court held that a mandatory life sentence in the case of a sex offender twice convicted of failing to timely register his new address constituted cruel and unusual punishment. The court's decision was premised upon its review of other crimes in Georgia which provided for life sentences and noted that each involved violence or conduct that was seriously disruptive of society.

In *Seritt v. Alabama*,[29] the Eleventh Circuit rejected the claim of a federal habeas corpus petition that a sentence of life imprisonment without parole is disproportionate to the crime of armed robbery where the sentence was imposed under a habitual offender statute.

In *Miller v. Alabama*,[30] the court held that "mandatory life without parole for those under the age of 18 at the time of their crimes violates the Eighth Amendment's prohibition on 'cruel and unusual punishments.' " The court reasoned that a juvenile lacks the life experience and often the societal and family support system to fully appreciate the consequences of their actions. However, *Miller* did not absolutely bar a trial court from imposing a sentence of life without parole upon a minor. As the Court pointed out in *Montgomery v. Louisiana*,[31] *Miller* stands for the proposition that such sentences are only proper where the sentencing court first determines that the juvenile defendant is hopelessly corrupt. The Court noted that a life without parole sentence can only be imposed in "exceptional circumstances" for "the *rare* juvenile offender who exhibits such *irretrievable depravity* that rehabilitation is *impossible*."[32]

Prolonged incarceration of several years between trial and direct appeal does not violate the Eighth Amendment's prohibition of cruel and unusual punishment.[33] See § 26:6, infra, for a discussion of the death penalty and cruel and unusual punish-

---

[28]Bradshaw v. State, 284 Ga. 675, 671 S.E.2d 485 (2008).

[29]Seritt v. Alabama, 731 F.2d 728 (11th Cir. 1984).

[30]Miller v. Alabama, 132 S. Ct. 2455, 183 L. Ed. 2d 407 (2012). See Montgomery v. Louisiana, 136 S. Ct. 718, 193 L. Ed. 2d 599 (2016) (*Miller* may be applied retroactively). See also Dennis v. State, 300 Ga. 457, 796 S.E.2d 275 (2017) (juvenile may be resentenced based on *Montgomery v. Louisiana* if trial court failed to determine whether criminal conduct constituted irreparable corruption).

[31]Montgomery v. Louisiana, 136 S. Ct. 718, 733-736, 193 L. Ed. 2d 599 (2016). See Veal v. State, 298 Ga. 691, 784 S.E.2d 403 (2016).

[32]See Veal v. State, 303 Ga. 18, 810 S.E.2d 127 (2018) (*Miller* and *Montgomery* considerations do not apply in case where juvenile receives a "virtual" LWOP sentence, e.g., aggregate sentence of 60 years' prison service).

[33]See Johnson v. Bredesen, 558 U.S. 1067, 130 S. Ct. 541, 175 L. Ed. 2d 552 (2009) (29 years); Thompson v. McNeil, 556 U.S. 1114, 129 S. Ct. 1299

ment, and see § 26:4, infra, on equal protection and the death penalty. See § 26:28, infra, on the validity of recidivist punishment, and see § 26:43, infra, on judicial considerations in sentencing.

§ 26:3 Due process

As previously pointed out in § 26:2, supra, the due process clause of the Fourteenth Amendment governs the custodial conditions of a defendant prior to trial. However, "the due process rights of a [defendant in custody prior to trial] are at least as great as the Eighth Amendment protections available to a convicted prisoner."[1]

A governing authority which holds a defendant in custody prior to trial requires the agency to provide medical attention necessary for his injury. However, the governing authority is not constitutionally obligated to pay for such treatment if such treatment can be obtained without the authority paying for it.[2]

In *Derrer v. Anthony*,[3] Anthony was sentenced in 1986 to three years to serve for aggravated assault. On July 23, 1987, he was sentenced to serve ten years to be followed by seven years on probation. On July 24, 1987, the Parole Board commuted the aggravated assault sentence. Anthony was erroneously released on August 4, 1987, and remained free until he was arrested on May 30, 1994. Pursuant to a habeas petition, Anthony was released. The appellate court affirmed, pointing out that "where a prisoner is discharged from a penal institution, without any contributing fault on his part, and without violation of conditions of parole, ... his sentence continues to run while he is at liberty." Under the due process clause, "a defendant may not be required to serve a sentence of confinement in installments where his premature release was brought about through no fault of his own. . . ." This would be "inconsistent with 'fundamental principles of liberty and justice.' "

Courts in Georgia are vested with broad discretion when determining the appropriate sentence to impose upon a criminal defendant, and it is the duty of the trial court to exercise that discretion as to all aspects of the sentence it imposes. That discre-

---

(2009) (32 years); Thompson v. Secretary for Dept. of Corrections, 517 F.3d 1279, 1284(II) (11th Cir. 2008) (31 years). See also Hulett v. State, 296 Ga. 49, 73(6), 766 S.E.2d 1 (2014) (nine years).

[Section 26:3]

[1]City of Revere v. Massachusetts General Hospital, 463 U.S. 239, 103 S.Ct. 2979, 77 L.Ed.2d 605 (1983).

[2]City of Revere v. Massachusetts General Hospital, 463 U.S. 239, 103 S.Ct. 2979, 77 L.Ed.2d 605 (1983).

[3]Derrer v. Anthony, 265 Ga. 892, 895 (4), 463 S.E.2d 690 (1995).

tion must nonetheless be exercised within the perimeters of the Fourteenth Amendment, which protects all "persons"—including those residing in the country illegally from invidious governmental discrimination based solely upon their immigration status.[4] Nonetheless, a sentencing judge need not "shut his eyes to the reality of the factual situation before him and pretend that the defendant is not an illegal alien."[5] The defendant's alien status may well be a relevant factor in a court's decision, for example, as to whether to impose a probated sentence.[6]

§ 26:4 Equal protection

Although it has been held that the equal protection clause of the Fourteenth Amendment requires that no greater punishment be imposed on one defendant than on all others charged with like offenses,[1] a mere disparity in sentences between parties charged with the same crime is unlikely to raise a constitutional question.[2] In fact, the conscious exercise of some selectivity in sentencing is not in itself a violation of the Fourteenth Amendment where the disparity is not deliberately based upon an unjustifiable standard such as race, religion or other arbitrary classification.[3] Justice Holmes once wrote that an Equal Protection claim "is the usual last resort of constitutional arguments."[4]

In order to mount a successful equal protection challenge to a statute, the claimant must initially establish that he is similarly situated to the members of the class who are treated differently from him.

If a claimant has established that he is similarly situated to members of the class who are treated differently from him, the statute must next be addressed to determine under what analysis it is tested:

---

[4]Trujillo v. State, 304 Ga. App. 849, 852(2), 698 S.E.2d 350 (2010).

[5]U.S. v. Gomez, 797 F.2d 417, 419 (7th Cir. 1986).

[6]Trujillo v. State, 304 Ga. App. 849, 852(2), 698 S.E.2d 350 (2010); People v. Sanchez, 190 Cal. App. 3d 224 (I) (5), 235 Cal. Rptr. 264 (5th Dist. 1987); State v. Zavala-Ramos, 116 Or. App. 220, 840 P.2d 1314 (1992).

[Section 26:4]

[1]Moore v. Missouri, 159 U.S. 673, 16 S.Ct. 179, 40 L.Ed. 301 (1895); Hodgson v. Vermont, 168 U.S. 262, 18 S.Ct. 80, 42 L.Ed. 461 (1897).

[2]United States v. Harbolt, 491 F.2d 78 (5th Cir. 1974).

[3]Oyler v. Boles, 368 U.S. 448, 82 S.Ct. 501, 7 L.Ed.2d 446 (1962). See § 26:43, infra.

[4]Buck v. Bell, 274 U.S. 200, 208, 47 S.Ct. 584, 71 L.Ed. 1000 (1927). See Plyler v. Doe, 457 U.S. 202, 210, 102 S. Ct. 2382, 72 L. Ed. 2d 786, 4 Ed. Law Rep. 953 (1982) ("Aliens, even aliens whose presence in this country is unlawful, have long been recognized as 'persons' guaranteed due process of law by the Fifth and Fourteenth Amendments"). See also Trujillo v. State, 304 Ga. App. 849, 698 S.E.2d 350 (2010).

When assessing equal protection challenges, a statute is tested under a standard of strict scrutiny if it either operates to the disadvantage of a suspect class or interferes with the exercise of a fundamental right . . . . If neither a suspect class nor a fundamental right is affected by the statute, the statute need only bear a rational relationship to some legitimate state purpose.[5]

Judicial review which examines only whether there is a rational basis for the legislation involved has been characterized as the "most lenient" level of judicial scrutiny. It "involves a two prong evaluation of the challenged statute. 'Initially, the claimant must establish that he is similarly situated to members of the class who are treated differently than him. Next, the claimant must establish that there is no rational basis for such different treatment.' " Because legislation is presumed to be valid, "the claimant has the burden of proof as to both prongs."[6] The "relevant inquiry in deciding whether strict scrutiny analysis or rational basis analysis applies to determine whether a criminal statute violates equal protection rights is not whether the punishment the criminal statute prescribes interferes with a fundamental right, but whether the behavior proscribed or regulated by the statute itself involves a fundamental right."[7]

An individual's financial status has been characterized as "suspect clarification."[8] Although that conclusion has been called into question, the basic premise is sound. "To imprison an indigent when in the same circumstances an individual of financial means would remain free constitutes a denial of equal protection of laws."[9] It has therefore been held impermissible to imprison a defendant because he is financially unable to pay a fine,[10] or to imprison a defendant until he "works off" the fine at a specified statutory rate.[11]

---

[5]Barnett v. State, 270 Ga. 472, 472, 510 S.E.2d 527 (1999) (citations and punctuation omitted).

[6]Bunn v. State, 291 Ga. 183, 186, 728 S.E.2d 569 (2012), citing Drew v. State, 285 Ga. 848, 850 n.3, 684 S.E.2d 608 (2009). See Harper v. State, 292 Ga. 557, 738 S.E.2d 584 (2013) (equal protection challenge upon longer statute of limitations period based upon the age of the victim subject to rational basis review).

[7]Fair v. State, 288 Ga. 244, 247 (1)(A), 702 S.E.2d 420 (2010).

[8]San Antonio Independent School Dist. v. Rodriguez, 411 U.S. 1, 93 S. Ct. 1278, 36 L. Ed. 2d 16 (1973).

[9]Barnett v. Hopper, 548 F.2d 550 (5th Cir. 1977), reh. denied, 555 F.2d 1391, vacated as moot, 439 U.S. 1041, 99 S. Ct. 714, 58 L. Ed. 2d 701 (1978).

[10]Williams v. Illinois, 399 U.S. 235, 90 S.Ct. 2018, 26 L.Ed.2d 586 (1970).

[11]Tate v. Short, 401 U.S. 395, 91 S.Ct. 668, 28 L.Ed.2d 130 (1971). *Tate* involved an offense punishable only by fine, unless the defendant cannot pay, in which event it could be worked off at $5 per day; and Williams v. Illinois, 399 U.S. 235, 90 S.Ct. 2018, 26 L.Ed.2d 586 (1970), involved a situation in which the defendant received a maximum sentence as to time plus a fine of $500 which was to be "worked out" at

In *McCleskey v. Kemp,*[12] the United States Supreme Court held that Georgia's capital sentencing process had not violated the equal protection clause. In this case, a black man had killed a white police officer. The court considered a study which indicates that a black defendant who killed a white victim has the greatest likelihood of being sentenced to death. The court said that in order for McCleskey to prevail, he would have to prove that the decisionmakers in his case acted with discriminatory purpose, and he failed to offer such evidence in his case. Since discretion is essential in such cases, exceptionally clear evidence is required before the Supreme Court will infer that discretion has been abused. The court also concluded that there was no violation of the Eighth Amendment's prohibition against cruel and unusual punishment.

A unanimous decision by the United States Supreme Court has held that a Georgia statute[13] which sets a harsher criminal penalty for parents who abandon their children and leave the state than for parents who abandon their children but remain in the state does not violate the equal protection clause.[14] Also see § 21:28, supra, on selective prosecutions and sections 30:1 to 30:8, infra, on revocation of probation.

In *Anderson v. State,*[15] the court pointed out that a statistical showing alone of the number of black persons in a certain county who are sentenced to life imprisonment for a second conviction for selling drugs is insufficient to prove intentional discrimination.

Generally, see § 26:15, infra, on fines.

§ 26:5   Pre-sentence hearings—Victim impact statements

Georgia has two victim impact statutes. The first, O.C.G.A. § 17-10-1.1, applies to written statements, whereas the second, O.C.G.A. § 17-10-1.2, regulates the use of oral victim impact statements. Both statutes require that the defendant be supplied with a copy of the statement prior to any hearing at which sentencing or a determination of restitution will be considered by the court. However, the statutes specifically state that a sentence

---

$5 per day at the end of sentence if it had not been paid. In both of these cases the United States Supreme Court held that the sentences deprived the indigent defendant of his rights under the equal protection clause of the Fourteenth Amendment, since the sentence of an indigent would exceed the maximum sentence fixed for the offense.

[12]McCleskey v. Kemp, 481 U.S. 279, 107 S.Ct. 1756, 95 L.Ed.2d 262

(1987).

[13]O.C.G.A. § 19-10-1.

[14]Jones v. Helms, 452 U.S. 412, 101 S.Ct. 2434, 69 L.Ed.2d 118 (1981). The court noted that the statute applies equally to all parents residing in Georgia and is not arbitrarily or discriminatorily applied.

[15]Anderson v. State, 218 Ga. App. 872 (1), 463 S.E.2d 502 (1995).

imposed will not be invalidated due to a failure to comply with the statute.

O.C.G.A. § 17-10-1.1 was substantially amended in 2005 to provide that alleged victims or, where the victim is no longer living, a member of the victim's family possess an unqualified right to submit a victim impact "form".[1] Moreover, victims are now permitted, rather than required, to submit: (1) an itemization of any economic loss suffered as a result of the offense, (2) identification of any physical injury suffered by the victim as a result of the offense along with its seriousness and permanence, and (3) any change in the victim's personal welfare or familial relationships as a result of the offense. The requirement that the victim identify any request for psychological services initiated by the victim or the victim's family as a result of the offense has been stricken from the statute entirely.

Other provisions include the requirement that, if the defendant engages in pre-trial discussions with the prosecuting attorney for the purpose of reaching a plea agreement or other pre-trial disposition of the case, the prosecuting attorney, upon the request of the defendant, shall provide the defendant with a copy of the victim impact form within a reasonable time prior to such discussions. Moreover, if the prosecuting attorney intends to present information from a victim impact form to the court at any hearing at which sentencing or a determination of restitution will be considered by the court, he or she is required to furnish the defendant with a copy of the form not less than five days prior to any such hearing The defendant shall have the right to rebut the information contained in the form.

Finally, O.C.G.A. § 17-10-1.1 now explicitly requires the court to consider the victim impact form prior to imposing a sentence or making a determination as to the amount of restitution. The Prosecuting Attorneys' Council of Georgia is charged with the responsibility of establishing such "forms," designed to obtain the information specified by § 17-10-1.1. The victim is no longer required to request such "forms," as it is now the duty of the prosecuting attorney to make them available.

The statute was amended again in 2010 to provide that victims of crimes against the person are to be given reasonable notice of all court proceedings. In addition, O.C.G.A. § 17-17-9 now provides that a court cannot exclude victims or members of their

---

[Section 26:5]

[1]Prior to July 1, 2005, § 17-10-1.1 provided certain conditions precedent to the filing of a victim impact statement, to-wit: (1) where the charge is a felony, that the defendant alleg-edly caused physical, psychological, or if restitution is sought, economic injury to the victim, and (2) where the charge is a misdemeanor, that the defendant allegedly caused serious physical injury or death to the victim.

family from courtroom proceedings "based solely on the fact that he or she is subpoenaed to testify unless it is established that such victim or family member is a material and necessary witness." Thus, victims and immediate family members who are or may be witnesses in the case are no longer strictly subject to the rule of sequestration. Counsel and the trial court should be sensitive to this issue and make every effort to call victims and their family members as soon as possible in the case.

A distinction arising from the use of a victim impact statement at pre-sentence hearings turns on whether or not it is a capital case. O.C.G.A. § 17-10-1.2 is further divided into two sections to account for this difference. Subsection (a)(1) applies in cases where the death penalty may be imposed after an adjudication of guilt in conjunction with the procedures set out in O.C.G.A. § 17-10-30, whereas subsection (a)(2) is for those cases where the death penalty may not be imposed. See § 26:14, infra, on pre-sentence hearing in non-capital cases.

In *Payne v. Tennessee,*[2] the United States Supreme Court overruled older decisions and held that the Eighth Amendment does not per se prevent a jury from considering the character of the victim and the emotional impact on the victim's family in a capital case. Additionally, the court pointed out that a victim impact statement is "simply another form or method of informing the sentencing authority about the specific harm caused by the crime in question."[3] Three years earlier, in *South Carolina v. Gathers,*[4] the United States Supreme Court held that contents of personal papers, a religious tract, religious objects, and a voter registration card in the victim's possession at the time of his death "cannot be said to be directly related to the circumstances of the crime." The contents of the papers the victim was carrying when attacked was "purely fortuitous, and cannot provide any information relevant to the defendant's moral culpability."

When using oral victim impact statements in death penalty cases, O.C.G.A. § 17-10-1.2 procedures permit the trial judge to "allow evidence from the family of the victim, or such other witness having personal knowledge of the victim's personal characteristics and the emotional impact of the crime on the victim, the

[2]Payne v. Tennessee, 501 U.S. 808, 111 S.Ct. 2597, 115 L.Ed.2d 720 (1991). Accord, Livingston v. State, 264 Ga. 402, 444 S.E.2d 748 (1994).

[3]Payne v. Tennessee, 501 U.S. 808, 111 S.Ct. 2597, 115 L.Ed.2d 720 (1991). See Annotation, "Validity Construction and Application of Victim Impact Statutes—Post Payne v. Tennessee," 79 A.L.R.5th 33 (2000).

[4]South Carolina v. Gathers, 490 U.S. 805, 109 S.Ct. 2207, 104 L.Ed.2d 876 (1989).

victim's family, or the community."[5] Such evidence must be given in the presence of the defendant and jury and is subject to cross-examination and rebuttal. In non-capital cases, the use of oral victim impact statements may be used at the discretion of the trial judge "from the victim, the family of the victim, or such other witness having personal knowledge of the impact of the crime on the victim, the family of the victim, or community."[6] Similar to the capital cases, such evidence in non-capital cases must be given in the presence of the defendant and is also subject to cross-examination and rebuttal.

In a capital case, the admissibility of the evidence from the oral victim impact statement is in the sole discretion of the judge and "shall be permitted only in such a manner and to such a degree as not to inflame or unduly prejudice the jury." In *Turner v. State*,[7] a death penalty case, the trial judge allowed victim impact testimony from both the mother and sister of the decedent. On appeal, the Georgia Supreme Court affirmed the trial court and commended the trial judge's procedure for dealing with the victim impact statements. Prior to trial, the defendant was afforded the opportunity to challenge the content of the mother's and sister's statements to remove any language that might inflame passion or prejudice. At trial, the witnesses were asked the same question, "What emotional impact has the murder . . . had on you . . . ?" which was the basis of their written impact statements. The witnesses then responded by reading their prepared statements. The Supreme Court ultimately approved the use of this procedure for future cases, stating that "this procedure best comports with the statute and minimizes undue prejudice. . . ." The court further suggested that the following jury instruction be given regarding victim impact evidence:

> The prosecution has introduced what is known as victim impact evidence. Victim impact evidence is not the same as evidence of a statutory aggravating circumstance. Introduction of victim impact evidence does not relieve the state of its burden to prove beyond a reasonable doubt the existence of a statutory aggravating circumstance. This evidence is simply another method of informing you about the harm caused by the crime in question. To the extent that you find that this evidence reflects on the defendant's culpability you may consider it, but you may not use it as a substitute for proof beyond a reasonable doubt of the existence of a statutory ag-

---

[5]O.C.G.A. § 17-10-1.2(5) provides, "it shall be the duty of the court to inquire of the prosecuting attorney whether or not the victim has been notified of the presentence hearing." If the court finds that reasonable effort to notify the victim has not been made, the presentence hearing shall be recessed to allow the victim the opportunity to attend.

[6]O.C.G.A. § 17-10-30.

[7]Turner v. State, 268 Ga. 213, 214-16 (2), 486 S.E.2d 839 (1997).

gravating circumstance.

In addition, it should be noted that the failure to object to victim impact testimony at sentencing or to the trial court's failure to conduct a full hearing on the admissibility of victim impact testimony results in a waiver of those issues on appeal.[8]

Clarifying the use of oral victim impact statements in noncapital cases, O.C.G.A. § 17-10-1.2(b) allows with permission of the trial judge that the statement may:

(1) describe the nature of the offense;

(2) itemize any economic loss suffered by the victim or family, if restitution is sought;

(3) identify any physical injury, its seriousness and permanence;

(4) describe any change in victim's welfare or familial relationships as a result of the offense;

(5) identify any request for psychological services initiated as a result of the offense; and

(6) include other relevant information of the impact on the victim, the victim's family, or the community.

In *Sermons v. State*,[9] the court concluded that evidence is not admissible to demonstrate the psychological, emotional, and physical impact of the crime on the victim's families and community. However, the state is not prevented from "introducing evidence for purposes other than demonstrating victim impact if that evidence also incidentally conveys that the defendant's crime has had victim impact consequences."

In *Jones v. State*,[10] the court stressed the fact that "victim impact evidence is limited to the impact of the offense upon the victim's family or community." However, victim impact evidence is to be permitted "only in such manner and to such a degree as not to inflame or unduly prejudice the jury, . . . [but] the trial court [has] unusually broad discretion in admitting such evidence." The court held in *McClain v. State*[11] that the father of the deceased victim should not have been permitted to testify to the "anger in the community about . . . the apparent trend" in increasing lawlessness or crime in general.

---

[8]Walker v. State, 282 Ga. 774(11), 653 S.E.2d 439 (2007).

[9]Sermons v. State, 262 Ga. 286, 288, 417 S.E.2d 144 (1992). Cf. Moore v. State, 263 Ga. 11, 13 (8), 427 S.E.2d 766 (1993).

[10]Jones v. State, 267 Ga. 592, 595 (2), 481 S.E.2d 821 (1997).

[11]McClain v. State, 267 Ga. 378, 388 (10)(b), 477 S.E.2d 814 (1996). See Stinski v. State, 286 Ga. 839, 691 S.E.2d 854 (2010) (error to allow relatives of victims to offer opinions and characterizations of the crime, the defendant and the sentence to be imposed).

In *Williams v. State,*[12] the defendant's contention that the trial court erred in failing to allow him to cross-examine the victim pursuant to O.C.G.A. § 17-10-1.2(c) was ruled meritless due to the provision in subsection (d) of that Code section specifically providing that failure to comply with the provisions of that Code section does not invalidate a sentence. Similarly, in the capital case of *Brantley v. State,*[13] the court held that the failure to permit defense counsel to review and rebut the victim impact statements does not invalidate the sentence. See § 26:13, supra, on the necessity of a district attorney's notifying the defense prior to trial of evidence the state plans to present in aggravation.

§ 26:6 Capital cases—General

The United States Supreme Court, in *Coker v. Georgia,*[1] held that the death penalty in the case of rape of an adult female, who is not killed, is grossly out of proportion to the severity of the crime and that such a penalty is violative of the Eighth Amendment to the federal Constitution.[2] While the Court continues to recognize *Gregg v. Georgia*[3] and to point out that the death penalty may be imposed for murder under Georgia's statutory procedure and while it does not say that the death sentence may only be imposed in a murder case, the opinion in *Coker* casts grave doubts on the constitutionality of imposing the death sentence in any case other than one where a life has been taken.[4] See Annotation, "Application of Death Penalty to Non-Homicide Cases," 62 A.L.R.5th 121 (1998).

In *Kennedy v. Louisiana,*[5] a jury found the defendant guilty of brutally raping his 8-year old stepdaughter. Under a state stat-

---

[12]Williams v. State, 226 Ga. App. 720 (2), 487 S.E.2d 470 (1997).

[13]Brantley v. State, 268 Ga. 151, 153 (3), 486 S.E.2d 169 (1997).

[Section 26:6]

[1]Coker v. Georgia, 433 U.S. 584, 97 S.Ct. 2861, 53 L.Ed.2d 982 (1977).

[2]The Georgia Supreme Court has since held that its proportionality review meets all constitutional requirements. See, e.g., McMichen v. State, 265 Ga. 598, 458 S.E.2d 833 (1995). See also Gissendaner v. State, 272 Ga. 704, 532 S.E.2d 677 (2000), explaining that the proper inquiry on proportionality reviews is not limited to whether there have ever been sentences less than death imposed for similar crimes; rather, the court's

review focuses on whether the death penalty is "excessive per se" or "substantially out of line" for the type of offense involved when viewed "against the backdrop of all similar cases in Georgia."

[3]Gregg v. Georgia, 428 U.S. 153, 96 S.Ct. 2909, 49 L.Ed.2d 859 (1976).

[4]See Radin, "The Jurisprudence of Death: Evolving Standards for Cruel and Unusual Punishment Clause," 126 U. Pa. L. R. 989 (1978); Annot., "Supreme Court's Views on Constitutionality of Death Penalty and Procedures Under Which It Is Imposed," 51 L.Ed.2d 886 (1978).

[5]Kennedy v. Louisiana, 128 S. Ct. 2641, 171 L. Ed. 2d 525 (U.S. 2008), as modified (Oct. 1, 2008), and opinion modified on denial of reh'g, Kennedy v.

ute authorizing the death penalty for the rape of a child under 12 years of age, the defendant was sentenced to death. The U.S. Supreme Court held that the Eighth Amendment bars states "from imposing the death penalty for the rape of a child where the crime did not result, and was not intended to result, in the victim's death." The court also noted that the questionable reliability of child victim testimony in some child rape cases produces a "special risk of wrongful execution."

The Georgia Supreme Court, in *Collins v. State,*[6] concluded that under *Coker* the death penalty may no longer be imposed for rape, unless the victim dies.[7] It said that it had previously held that armed robbery alone does not warrant the death penalty.[8] In *Collins,* the court held that the rationale of *Coker* must be applied to armed robbery and kidnapping and, therefore, the death penalty may not be imposed for these crimes either.[9] *Collins* states that aircraft hijacking and treason are still capital felonies. However, in the case of aircraft hijacking the statute relating to mitigating and aggravating circumstances does not apply and the death penalty may be imposed "in any case."[10] Thus, the penalty may be imposed capriciously, and there are no guide lines or criteria fixed by statute.[11] This statutory scheme seems to have the same infirmity as the Georgia law held to be unconstitutional in *Furman v. Georgia.*[12]

Louisiana, 129 S. Ct. 1, 129 S.Ct. 1, 171 L.Ed.2d 932 (2008).

[6]Collins v. State, 239 Ga. 400, 402 (2), 236 S.E.2d 759 (1977).

[7]Moore v. State, 240 Ga. 807, 822 (2), 243 S.E.2d 1 (1978).

[8]Collins v. State, 239 Ga. 400, 402 (2), 236 S.E.2d 759 (1977) (citing Gregg v. State, 233 Ga. 117, 126-127, 210 S.E.2d 659 (1974)).

[9]The court also concluded that appeals from rape, kidnapping and armed robbery convictions should be to the Georgia Court of Appeals rather than to the Georgia Supreme Court. In Thomas v. State, 145 Ga. App. 69 (1), 243 S.E.2d 250 (1978), the court said that since the victim of an armed robbery did not die, the defendant's death sentence must be set aside.

[10]O.C.G.A. § 17-10-30.

[11]Gregg v. Georgia, 428 U.S. 153, 96 S.Ct. 2909, 49 L.Ed.2d 859 (1976).

[12]Furman v. Georgia, 408 U.S. 238, 92 S.Ct. 2726, 33 L.Ed.2d 346 (1972). There are 9 separate opinions as well as a per curiam opinion in this case, and it is difficult to be precise about the basis of the court's holding. However, in Gregg v. Georgia, 428 U.S. 153, 96 S.Ct. 2909, 49 L.Ed.2d 859, 883 (1976), the court said that *Furman* held that the death penalty could not be imposed under a sentencing procedure in which there was a substantial risk that it would be inflicted in an arbitrary and capricious manner. (See also the concurring opinion in Gregg at p. 222.) In *Gregg,* Justices Marshall and Brennan dissented saying that the death penalty violates the Eighth and Fourteenth Amendments. Justice Blackmun is opposed to capital punishment but feels that the courts are not authorized to step in. Chief Justice Burger, Justices White, Rehnquist, Stewart, Powell, and Stevens concluded that the Georgia statutory scheme for murder did not on its face violate the Eighth Amendment since the statute provided guidance to juries

In *Enmund v. Florida*,[13] the defendant seems to have been the driver of the automobile in which two robbers escaped. The two victims were killed in the robbery. The defendant was tried for the murders as an aider and abettor. He was convicted and sentenced to death. The court reversed the death sentence, concluding that the death sentence was an excessive penalty for one who did not kill or intend to kill. "[C]apital punishment can serve as a deterrent only when murder is the result of premeditation and deliberation . . . for if a person does not intend that life be taken or contemplate that lethal force will be employed by others, the possibility that the death penalty will be imposed for vicarious felony murder will not 'enter into the cold calculus that precedes the decision to act.' "Thus, in *Enmund* it seemed that a defendant, who was not the triggerman and who did not intend for a victim to be killed nor for lethal force to be used in the commission of a felony, may not be sentenced to death. However, in the 1987 case of *Tison v. Arizona*,[14] the court in a felony murder case held that the reckless disregard for human life implicit in knowingly engaging in criminal activities known to carry a grave risk of death amounts to a "reckless indifference to human life, [and] is sufficient to satisfy the *Enmund* culpability requirement."

In *Bankston v. State*,[15] the court said that the death sentence is permissible only in homicide cases. In 1993, Georgia changed its statutory law so as to authorize "the imposition of a sentence for

---

in exercising discretion as well as review by the Georgia Supreme Court to compare the facts and circumstances of the particular case with other cases in which the death penalty has been imposed. In Lockett v. Ohio, 438 U.S. 586, 98 S.Ct. 2954, 57 L.Ed.2d 973 (1978), the court said that the Constitution requires the consideration of mitigating circumstances. See Husbands, "New Direction for Capital Sentencing or an About-Face for the Supreme Court?—Lockett v. Ohio," 16 Am. Crim. L. Rev. 317 (1979).

In Woodson v. North Carolina, 428 U.S. 280, 304, 96 S.Ct. 2978, 49 L.Ed.2d 944 (1976), the court said, "A process that accords no significance to relevant facets of the character and record of the individual offender or the circumstances of the particular offense excludes from consideration in fixing the ultimate punishment of death the possibility of compassionate or mitigating factors stemming from the diverse frailties of humankind. It treats all

persons convicted of a designated offense not as uniquely individual human beings, but as members of a faceless, undifferentiated mass to be subjected to the blind infliction of the penalty of death.

"This Court has previously recognized that '[f]or the determination of sentences, justice generally requires consideration of more than the particular acts by which the crime was committed and that there be taken into account the circumstances of the offense together with the character and propensities of the offender.' Pennsylvania ex rel. Sullivan v. Ashe, 302 U.S. 51, 55, 58 S.Ct. 59, 82 L.Ed. 43 (1937)."

[13]Enmund v. Florida, 458 U.S. 782, 102 S.Ct. 3368, 73 L.Ed.2d 1140 (1982).

[14]Tison v. Arizona, 481 U.S. 137, 107 S.Ct. 1676, 95 L.Ed.2d 127 (1987).

[15]Bankston v. State, 258 Ga. 188, 189, 367 S.E.2d 36 (1988).

life without parole" in a death penalty case.[16] However, the sentence of life without parole could only be imposed in cases where the state was seeking the death penalty and then only after the court or the jury finds one or more statutory aggravating circumstances. In 2009, the law was amended so as to allow the state to seek a sentence of life without the possibility of parole without also having to seek the death sentence. Special note should be taken that, as amended, the requirement that the judge or jury must first find a statutory aggravator is no longer required for the imposition of a sentence of life without the possibility of parole.[17] See § 26:45, infra, on sentencing a defendant to life without parole.

A crime which was a capital felony at the time of the enactment of Georgia's death penalty statute remains a capital felony for purposes of aggravation even though it is no longer treated as a capital felony for purposes of punishment under the decisions of the Georgia Supreme Court.[18] Georgia's death penalty statute does not apply to crimes which occurred before its enactment.[19]

Under Georgia law, if a defendant is under 17 at the time of the commission of the offense the death penalty may not be imposed.[20] In *Thompson v. Oklahoma,*[21] the United States Supreme Court said that the cruel and unusual punishment provision of the Eighth Amendment prevents the execution of a defendant who was under 16 years of age at the time of his or her offense unless the legislature has spoken to the contrary. In the 2005 decision of *Roper v. Simmons,*[22] the United States Supreme Court held that execution of individuals who were under 18 years of age at the time of their capital crimes is prohibited by the Eighth and Fourteenth Amendments, thus abrogating *Stanford v. Kentucky.*[23] Likewise, in *Miller v. Alabama,*[24] the Court held that because the Eighth Amendment's prohibition of cruel

---

[16]O.C.G.A. § 17-10-1, O.C.G.A. § 17-10-2.

[17]O.C.G.A. § 16-5-1(e). See Williams v. State, 291 Ga. 19, 727 S.E.2d 95 (2012) (other than the death penalty, there is no constitutional requirement that a court consider mitigating factors before imposing sentence of life without possibility of parole).

[18]Peek v. State, 239 Ga. 422, 432, 238 S.E.2d 12 (1977); Bowden v. State, 239 Ga. 821, 829, 238 S.E.2d 905 (1977).

[19]Akins v. State, 231 Ga. 411, 412 (1), 202 S.E.2d 62 (1973).

[20]Legare v. State, 250 Ga. 875, 878, 302 S.E.2d 351 (1983) (citing O.C.G.A. § 17-10-35). See also Bankston v. State, 258 Ga. 188, 189, 367 S.E.2d 36 (1988). Cf. High v. Kemp, 819 F.2d 988 (11th Cir. 1987).

[21]Thompson v. Oklahoma, 487 U.S. 815, 108 S.Ct. 2687, 101 L.Ed.2d 702 (1988).

[22]Roper v. Simmons, 543 U.S. 551, 125 S. Ct. 1183, 161 L. Ed. 2d 1 (2005).

[23]Stanford v. Kentucky, 492 U.S. 361, 109 S.Ct. 2969, 106 L.Ed.2d 306 (1989). See Moore v. State, 293 Ga. 705, 749 S.E.2d 660 (2013) (*Roper* prohibition against death penalty for

and unusual punishment guarantees individuals the right not to be subjected to excessive sanctions, the punishment of life without the possibility of parole for persons under the age of 18 under a sentencing scheme that makes such a punishment *mandatory* is impermissible. The Court reaffirmed the principle that because the character of a child is not as "well formed" as that of an adult, lacking in maturity and a fully developed sense of responsibility, the mandatory impositions of one of the law's most severe penalties cannot be tolerated when the sentencing authority is not permitted to consider the "mitigating qualities of youth."

In *Foster v. State*,[25] the Georgia Supreme Court held that the imposition of a sentence of life without parole upon a juvenile is not prohibited by the Eighth Amendment provided the sentence is not mandatory by law but may be imposed at the discretion of the judge upon consideration of all the facts in the case, including the defendant's age and any relevant evidence in mitigation.

In 1988, Georgia enacted a statute which prevents the imposition of a death sentence if a defendant has been found guilty but mentally retarded or if he enters a plea of guilty but mentally retarded.[26] At the punishment stage of a death case, the burden is on the defendant to establish beyond a reasonable doubt that he is mentally retarded[27] if he wishes to use this defense to avoid a death sentence. In *Head v. Hill*,[28] the court stated that even in habeas corpus proceedings the burden is on the defendant to prove his mental retardation beyond a reasonable doubt. Further, if the defendant raises mental retardation for the first time during habeas corpus proceedings, he is not constitutionally entitled to a jury determination of his mental retardation.[29] In the event a person was sentenced to death before July 1, 1988, the effective date of this statute, if a habeas corpus is filed and " 'sufficient credible evidence [presented] to create a genuine issue regarding . . . retardation,' then the habeas court must grant the writ and return the case to a trial court 'for the limited purpose of conducting a trial on the issue of retardation only.' " However, at such a trial, absent exceptional circumstances, the jury should not be informed that if it finds the defendant mentally

minors is retroactive).

[24]Miller v. Alabama, 132 S. Ct. 2455, 183 L. Ed. 2d 407 (2012); Montgomery v. Louisiana, 136 S. Ct. 718, 193 L. Ed. 2d 599 (2016) (*Miller* may be applied retroactively).

[25]Foster v. State, 294 Ga. 383, 387(11), 754 S.E.2d 33 (2014). See Bun v. State, 296 Ga. 549, 769 S.E.2d 381 (2015).

[26]O.C.G.A. § 17-7-131(j).

[27]Mosher v. State, 268 Ga. 555, 558(4), 491 S.E.2d 348 (1997).

[28]Head v. Hill, 277 Ga. 255, 587 S.E.2d 613 (2003). See Sims v. State, 279 Ga. 389, 614 S.E.2d 73 (2005) where the court reversed a trial court's finding of competency in the case of a moderately retarded defendant.

[29]Head v. Hill, 277 Ga. 255, 259, 587 S.E.2d 613 (2003).

retarded the death sentence will be vacated.[30]

In *Penry v. Lynaugh*,[31] the United States Supreme Court concluded that the Eighth Amendment does not preclude the execution of a mentally retarded person convicted of a capital offense simply by virtue of their mental retardation. That decision was premised on the notion that whether a particular form of punishment is excessive should be judged by prevailing norms of decency.[32] Thirteen years later, in *Atkins v. Virginia*,[33] the Court concluded that community standards had evolved to the point that execution of a mentally retarded person is unconstitutionally cruel and unusual punishment. Then, in *Hill v. Schofield*,[34] the Eleventh Circuit Court of Appeals held that the reasonable doubt standard in Georgia by which petitioner was required to prove his mental retardation was too heavy a burden and as such "ensures that some, if not many, mentally retarded offenders will be executed in violation of the Eighth Amendment." The court noted that *Atkins* "prohibits the execution of all mentally retarded defendants, not only the severe or profound mentally retarded, and it directs the states to create appropriate procedures that protect all of those individuals."[35] The court concluded that the reasonable doubt burden in Georgia was thus contrary to "clearly established federal law" as pronounced in *Atkins*. However, the decision in *Schofield* was vacated for a hearing en banc.[36] Following a decision by the Georgia Supreme Court reaffirming the reasonable doubt standard on mental retardation claims,[37] the Eleventh Circuit held that the reasonable doubt standard in Georgia was not contrary to clearly established precedent and hence a

---

[30]State v. Patillo, 262 Ga. 259, 417 S.E.2d 139 (1992).

[31]Penry v. Lynaugh, 492 U.S. 302, 109 S.Ct. 2934, 106 L.Ed.2d 256 (1989).

[32]Weems v. United States, 217 U.S. 349, 30 S.Ct. 544, 54 L.Ed. 793 (1910).

[33]Atkins v. Virginia, 534 U.S. 1122, 122 S.Ct. 982, 151 L.Ed.2d 963 (2002). See Graham v. Florida, 130 S. Ct. 2011, 176 L. Ed. 2d 825 (2010) (based on *Atkins*, constitution prohibits imposition of life sentence without parole on juvenile who did not commit homicide). See also Hall v. Florida, 134 S. Ct. 1986, 188 L. Ed. 2d 1007 (2014) (state rule which prohibited consideration of a capital defendant's intellectual disability if his I.Q. was more

than 70 created unreasonable risk that persons with an intellectual disability would be executed in violation of Eighth Amendment, with court noting that I.Q. scores are only one indication of intellectual disability); Moore v. Texas, 137 S.Ct. 1039, 197 L.Ed.2d 416 (2017) (states do not have "unfettered discretion" in application of *Atkins*; constrained by medical community's current standards).

[34]Hill v. Schofield, 608 F.3d 1272 (11th Cir. 2010).

[35]Hill v. Schofield, 608 F.3d 1272 (11th Cir. 2010).

[36]Hill v. Schofield, 608 F.3d 1272 (11th Cir. 2010).

[37]Stripling v. State, 289 Ga. 370, 711 S.E.2d 665 (2011).

federal habeas petitioner was not entitled to relief under *Atkins*.[38]

In passing, it should be noted that Georgia has a statute which prevents a person under a sentence of death from being executed if he is mentally incompetent.[39] Likewise, the Eighth Amendment prohibits the infliction of the death penalty upon a prisoner who is insane.[40]

Since *Gregg* was decided, the Massachusetts Supreme Court has held that in the light of contemporary standards of decency, capital punishment is cruel and unusual.[41] However, the California Supreme Court has upheld that state's death penalty statute.[42]

In *Simmons v. South Carolina*,[43] the trial court held that the defense attorney was forbidden to even mention the subject of parole. The prosecution argued for the death penalty partly because of the future dangerousness of the defendant. However, under South Carolina law the defendant could not be released from prison if sentenced to life. The defendant requested and the trial judge refused to charge the jury that if the defendant was sentenced to life, the defendant would be imprisoned for the rest of the his life. In reversing, the United States Supreme Court held that the due process clause "does not allow the execution of a person 'on the basis of information which he had no opportunity to deny or explain.' " In *Burgess v. State*,[44] the Georgia Supreme Court concluded that *Simmons* "only stands for the relatively narrow proposition that, where the State makes an issue of the defendant's future dangerousness during the sentencing phase of a capital trial and state law *prohibits* the defendant's release on parole, the jury must be informed that the defendant is ineligible for parole." This interpretation of *Simmons* is no longer accurate. In *Kelly v. South Carolina*,[45] the United States Supreme Court held that where the only alternative to death is life in prison with no possibility of parole, due process requires that the jury be clearly informed of the defendant's parole eligibility. As for the

---

[38]Hill v. Humphrey, 662 F.3d 1335 (11th Cir. 2011).

[39]O.C.G.A. § 17-10-61.

[40]Hance v. Kemp, 258 Ga. 649, 660 (8), 373 S.E.2d 184 (1988) (citing Ford v. Wainwright, 477 U.S. 399, 106 S.Ct. 2595, 91 L.Ed.2d 335 (1986) (execution may not be administered if defendant suffers from a mental illness which deprives him of mental ability to understand that he is being executed for a crime he committed)).

[41]District Attorney v. Watson, 381

Mass. 648, 411 N.E.2d 1274, 1283 (1980).

[42]People v. Jackson, 28 Cal.3d 264, 168 Cal.Rptr. 603, 618 P.2d 149, 177 (1980).

[43]Simmons v. South Carolina, 512 U.S. 154, 114 S.Ct. 2187, 129 L.Ed.2d 133 (1994).

[44]Burgess v. State, 264 Ga. 777, 788 (33), 450 S.E.2d 680 (1994).

[45]Kelly v. South Carolina, 534 U.S. 246, 122 S.Ct. 726, 151 L.Ed.2d 670 (2002).

notion of future dangerousness, the court ruled that regardless of whether the State chooses to argue the point, the jury could infer such from the record.[46] See § 23:6, supra, on scope of argument, possibility of clemency, probation, parole or pardon.

In the year 2000, Georgia's death penalty statute was amended to provide for death by lethal injection.[47] In an uncodified provision of the amendment, the legislature allowed that if the Supreme Court of Georgia should at some time declare that death by electrocution was no longer a constitutionally permissible form of punishment, death by lethal injection would be administered to all those persons who had been convicted and sentenced to death by electrocution and who were awaiting the imposition of their sentence.[48]

A majority of the Georgia Supreme Court in *Dawson v. State*[49] held that "the continued use of electrocution for executing death sentences in Georgia violates the Georgia Constitution, [but] sentences of death which previously would have been executed by electrocution are not thereby rendered void. 'Where one portion of a statute is unconstitutional, this court has the power to sever that portion of the statute and preserve the remainder if the remaining portion of the Act accomplishes the purpose the legislature intended.' " The court concluded that "full effect" would now be given to the remaining provisions in the uncodified provisions of the amendment allowing for death by lethal injection to those then under sentence for death by electrocution.[50] The Court has since rejected attempts to have death by lethal injection ruled an unconstitutional form of punishment.[51] In *Baze v. Rees*,[52] the United States Supreme Court took a similar approach, holding that lethal injection as applied in Kentucky did not constitute cruel and unusual punishment in violation of the Eighth Amendment to the U.S. Constitution.

---

[46]In this regard, the Georgia Supreme Court ruled in Henry v. State, 278 Ga. 617, 604 S.E.2d 826 (2004) that future dangerousness can be argued only if there is evidence of such in the record. The court stated that it is improper to argue that the defendant will pose a mortal threat in prison simply because he killed while he was free. See § 23:7, supra, on scope of argument permissible scope of prosecutor.

[47]Ga. L. 2000, p. 947, § 1. See O.C.G.A. § 17-10-38.

[48]Ga. L. 2000, p. 947, § 1. See O.C.G.A. § 17-10-38.

[49]Dawson v. State, 274 Ga. 327, 554 S.E.2d 137 (2001).

[50]Dawson v. State, 274 Ga. 327, 336, 554 S.E.2d 137 (2001).

[51]Williams v. State, 281 Ga. 87(3), 635 S.E.2d 146 (2006); Lewis v. State, 279 Ga. 756, 620 S.E.2d 778 (2005); Riley v. State, 278 Ga. 677(15), 604 S.E.2d 488 (2004).

[52]Baze v. Rees, 553 U.S. 35, 128 S. Ct. 1520, 170 L. Ed. 2d 420 (2008). See O'Kelley v. State, 284 Ga. 758 (5), 670 S.E.2d 388 (2008).

§ 26:7 Capital cases with jury—Overview

The district attorney has the discretion to seek the death penalty. If the district attorney does not seek the death penalty, such a sentence may not be imposed.[1] In all trials by a jury in which the death penalty may be imposed as a result of the finding of guilty, the jury determines whether the defendant will be sentenced to death or life imprisonment.[2] The same jury which convicts the defendant also determines his punishment,[3] unless the case is reversed and there is a new trial.[4] If a defendant is charged with murder and the jury finds him guilty of manslaughter, the judge must impose sentence.[5] If the jury cannot agree on a punishment, then the trial judge must impose a sentence of life imprisonment.[6] Or where a defendant is convicted of murder and there are no aggravating circumstances warranting the death penalty, the trial judge may direct a verdict of life imprisonment.[7]

If a defendant is convicted of murder but the state does not seek the death penalty, the trial judge should excuse the jury and impose a sentence of life imprisonment.[8] But where the death penalty is not waived and the defendant is convicted of murder, a

---

[Section 26:7]

[1]State v. Ingram, 266 Ga. 324, 467 S.E.2d 523 (1996). However, in the case of In re Johnson, 229 A.D.2d 242, 655 N.Y.S.2d 463 (1997), affirmed, 91 N.Y.2d 214, 668 N.Y.S.2d 978, 691 N.E.2d 1002 (1997), the court held that the governor could prevent a prosecutor from trying a case where the district attorney did not seek the death penalty, and have the attorney general handle the case.

[2]O.C.G.A. § 17-10-2(c). The constitutionality of Georgia's capital punishment statute was upheld in Gregg v. Georgia, 428 U.S. 153, 96 S.Ct. 2909, 49 L.Ed.2d 859 (1976), which contains an excellent discussion of Georgia's capital punishment law. In Mulligan v. State, 245 Ga. 266, 264 S.E.2d 204 (1980), the court held that the Georgia statute did not violate the Eighth Amendment by providing that the jury and not the judge fix the sentence after the jury determines the guilt of the defendant.

[3]Miller v. State, 237 Ga. 557, 559, 229 S.E.2d 376 (1976), construing O.C.G.A. § 17-10-2(c); also see O.C.G.A. § 17-10-30. However, when a defen-

dant is convicted and obtains a new trial, a new jury determines the question of guilt and fixes the sentence if it finds the defendant guilty.

[4]Fleming v. State, 243 Ga. 120, 122 (4), 252 S.E.2d 609 (1979).

[5]Lindsey v. State, 135 Ga. App. 122, 123 (4), 218 S.E.2d 30 (1975).

[6]Miller v. State, 237 Ga. 557, 559, 229 S.E.2d 376 (1976); Hill v. State, 250 Ga. 821, 301 S.E.2d 269 (1983). In Bowman v. State, 231 Ga. 220, 200 S.E.2d 880 (1973), the court said that it was not error for the trial judge to discharge the jury after 31 minutes of deliberation and impose sentence himself.

[7]Ford v. State, 232 Ga. 511 (8), 516 (8), 207 S.E.2d 494 (1974).

[8]Brown v. State, 246 Ga. 251, 253 (6), 271 S.E.2d 163 (1980). However, in Birks v. State, 237 Ga. 861, 864, 230 S.E.2d 294 (1976), it was held that the trial judge should conduct a pre-sentence hearing before imposing sentence. There is some question of what the purpose of the pre-sentence hearing is, if the defendant is guilty of murder, since the only thing the judge can do in this situation is to sentence

pre-sentence hearing must be conducted in order to give the jury the necessary evidence to come to an informed punishment decision.[9]

At a sentencing hearing where the death penalty may be imposed, the defendant has the final closing argument. In cases other than where the death penalty may be imposed, the prosecution has the final closing argument.[10]

In *Ford v. Wainwright*,[11] the United States Supreme Court held that the Eighth Amendment prevents the execution of a defendant who is insane at the time of execution. See § 26:6, supra.

In *Morrison v. State*,[12] the Georgia Supreme Court said that in a death case "the trial court . . . *may* have an obligation to conduct an independent investigation into the possible existence of evidence in mitigation." (Emphasis added.)

In *Mize v. State*,[13] the court held that "[w]here a properly-informed, competent defendant insists that he prefers a death sentence to life imprisonment, his attorney does not violate any right of the defendant by attempting to comply with his client's wishes."

See § 26:4, supra, on the equal protection clause.

§ 26:8   Capital cases with jury—The pre-sentence hearing—Evidence

The hearing is conducted in the same general manner as a pre-sentence hearing before a judge in a non-capital case.[1] At the hearing the jury receives any evidence in aggravation of punishment provided to the defendant ten days prior to trial or such time as the court directed, no later than the start of trial.[2] The intention of the state to use the defendant's history of criminal convictions must be "unmistakable."[3] The purpose of the notice is to provide the defendant with ample opportunity to examine his record in order to determine whether the convictions are in fact his or whether there was some defect in the prior cases, such as the absence of defense counsel, which might render them

---

the defendant to life imprisonment.

[9]O.C.G.A. § 17-10-2(c).

[10]O.C.G.A. § 17-10-2(a)(2).

[11]Ford v. Wainwright, 477 U.S. 399, 106 S.Ct. 2595, 91 L.Ed.2d 335 (1986).

[12]Morrison v. State, 258 Ga. 683, 687, 373 S.E.2d 506 (1988).

[13]Mize v. State, 269 Ga. 646, 656

(12), 501 S.E.2d 219 (1998), quoting Morrison v. State, 258 Ga. 683, 373 S.E.2d 506 (1988).

[Section 26:8]

[1]See O.C.G.A. § 17-10-2(a); § 26:13, infra.

[2]O.C.G.A. § 17-16-4(a)(5).

[3]Evans v. State, 290 Ga. App. 746, 748, 660 S.E.2d 841 (2008).

inadmissible during the pre-sentence hearing.[4] The rule about the timing of notice of similar transactions or other acts evidence does not apply to sentencing hearings.[5] In *Payne v. State*,[6] the court held that the words in the statute "prior to his trial" means before the jury is sworn. However, the state "is not limited to proof only of the enumerated statutory aggravating circumstances,"[7] but it is not necessary for the state to introduce any additional evidence at the sentencing hearing in order for the jury to return a death sentence.[8]

A defendant is entitled to testify at his pre-sentence hearing even if he did not take the stand at the guilt-or-innocence phase of the trial.[9] The defendant may testify for the first time about events which took place at the time of the crime.[10] Evidence introduced earlier does not have to be reintroduced. But if a defendant chooses to testify, he may be cross-examined about details of the crime which have not been in evidence before.[11] However, where a defendant entered a plea of not guilty and testified during the sentencing phase that he did commit the act charged, it is not proper for the district attorney to ask the defendant why he pled not guilty.[12] In *Burgess v. State*,[13] the court held that photographs of an earlier "murder victim whom appellant had been convicted of murdering . . . [were] properly admitted in aggravation during the sentencing phase" of the trial.

Georgia decisions further define the purposes of the pre-sentence hearing. In *Dudley v. State*,[14] the Georgia Supreme Court stated: "The issue to be decided at the pre-sentence hearing calls for different evidence from that on the trial which determines guilt or innocence. On the issue of guilt or innocence

---

[4]Hightower v. State, 210 Ga. App. 216, 436 S.E.2d 31 (1993).

[5]Gulley v. State, 271 Ga. 337, 341 (4), 519 S.E.2d 655 (1999).

[6]Payne v. State, 219 Ga. App. 318, 319 (4), 464 S.E.2d 884 (1995).

[7]Hicks v. State, 256 Ga. 715, 727, 352 S.E.2d 762 (1987) (quoting Devier v. State, 253 Ga. 604, 323 S.E.2d 150 (1984)).

[8]Dick v. State, 246 Ga. 697, 707 (18), 273 S.E.2d 124 (1980). In Wainwright v. Torna, 455 U.S. 586, 102 S.Ct. 1300, 71 L.Ed.2d 475 (1982), Torna contended that he was entitled to habeas relief because of ineffective assistance of counsel in that counsel failed to file a timely application for certiorari. The court concluded that since he had no constitutional right to pursue a discretionary appeal "he could not be deprived of effective assistance of counsel by his retained counsel's failure to file the application timely."

[9]The defendant also has a right to refuse to testify. Estelle v. Smith, 451 U.S. 454, 101 S.Ct. 1866, 68 L.Ed.2d 359 (1981).

[10]Brown v. State, 235 Ga. 644, 647 (3), 220 S.E.2d 922 (1975).

[11]Cf. Rockholt v. State, 129 Ga. App. 99, 101, 198 S.E.2d 885 (1973).

[12]Cervi v. State, 248 Ga. 325, 330 (7), 282 S.E.2d 629 (1981).

[13]Burgess v. State, 264 Ga. 777, 784 (17), 450 S.E.2d 680 (1994).

[14]Dudley v. State, 228 Ga. 551, 186 S.E.2d 875 (1972).

the only relevant evidence is that pertaining to the particular offense with which the defendant is charged. In a pre-sentence hearing the jury must make a determination as to the sentence to be imposed, taking into consideration the past criminal record, or lack of criminal record, of the defendant, and his general moral character,"[15] as well as the circumstances of the offense. However, it has been held that a defendant may not present evidence of penalties imposed upon him in other cases,[16] and it has been pointed out that the trial court has authority "to exclude, as irrelevant, evidence not bearing on the defendant's character, prior record, or the circumstances of the offense."[17] Nonetheless, the scope of the evidence which may be submitted in mitigation is wide, described by the Georgia Supreme Court as "anything that might persuade the jury to impose a sentence less than death . . . ."[18] In *Tennard v. Dretke*,[19] the Supreme Court held that evidence of the defendant's low IQ (67) and impaired intellectual functioning could be used as mitigation evidence in the penalty phase. In addition, evidence of organic brain damage might also be used by the defense in mitigation. However, counsel should carefully consider the potential for backlash that could come with such evidence. In *Martinez v. Dretke*,[20] the court stated that "evidence of organic brain injury presents a 'double-edged sword' " because of its association with poor impulse control and a violent propensity which could very well support a finding of future dangerousness. Although the defense is given great latitude regarding evidence that may be submitted in mitigation, the United States Supreme Court in *Oregon v. Guzek*[21] found that the Eighth Amendment does not deprive the state of its authority to limit the "innocence-related evidence" at the pre-sentencing hearing to that introduced by the defendant at his original trial. Noting that the sentencing phase "traditionally concerns *how*, not *whether*, a defendant committed the crime," the *Guzek* court

---

[15]See 21 Am. Jur. 2d 548, Criminal Law § 585, at 561, quoted with approval in Johnson v. State, 126 Ga. App. 757, 760, 191 S.E.2d 614 (1972).

[16]Wilson v. State, 250 Ga. 630, 639, 300 S.E.2d 640 (1983).

[17]Cargill v. State, 255 Ga. 616, 645 (36), 340 S.E.2d 891 (1986) (quoting Franklin v. State, 245 Ga. 141, 152 (7), 263 S.E.2d 666 (1980), and Lockett v. Ohio, 438 U.S. 586, 604, n. 12, 98 S.Ct. 2954, 57 L.Ed.2d 973 (1978)).

[18]Head v. Thomason, 276 Ga. 434, 578 S.E.2d 426, 429 (2003) (citing Head v. Ferrell, 274 Ga. 399, 554 S.E.2d 155

(2001)). See Studdard, *Daniel's Georgia Handbook on Criminal Evidence* (2018 ed.), § 4:12, on testimony that the defendant was a good prisoner at the penalty phase of a capital case.

[19]Tennard v. Dretke, 542 U.S. 274, 124 S.Ct. 2562, 159 L.Ed.2d 384 (2004).

[20]Martinez v. Dretke, 404 F.3d 878, 889-890 (5th Cir. 2005). See Sears v. Humphrey, 294 Ga. 117, 751 S.E.2d 365 (2013).

[21]Oregon v. Guzek, 546 U.S. 517, 126 S. Ct. 1226, 163 L. Ed. 2d 1112 (2006).

specifically held that the defendant could not present live testimony from his mother about his alibi, but was instead limited to the transcript of such evidence from the original trial.[22]

In *Romano v. Oklahoma*,[23] the United States Supreme Court considered whether evidence could be admitted at the sentencing phase of a capital case showing that the defendant had previously been sentenced to death in a separate case. The Supreme Court in a 5 to 4 decision found that the admission of this evidence did not violate the Constitution in view of the instructions given by the trial judge. The earlier death sentence was later overturned. The Supreme Court noted that the earlier sentence was irrelevant as a matter of state law, but the admission of this evidence did not "so . . . [infect] the sentencing proceeding with unfairness as to render the jury's imposition of the death penalty a denial of due process." The alleged problem with the introduction of the earlier death sentence was that the evidence would reduce the jury's sense of responsibility for its verdict in violation of *Caldwell v. Mississippi*.[24]

Similarly, in *Gregg v. Georgia*,[25] the United States Supreme Court, in upholding Georgia's capital punishment statutes, stated:

"The petitioner objects, finally, to the wide scope of evidence and argument allowed at pre-sentence hearing. We think that the Georgia court wisely has chosen not to impose unnecessary restrictions on the evidence that can be offered at such a hearing and to approve open and far-ranging argument.[26] So long as the evidence introduced and the arguments made at the pre-sentence hearing do not prejudice a defendant, it is preferable not to impose restrictions. We think it desirable for the jury to have as much information before it as possible when it makes the sentencing decision."[27] Thus, in *Blankenship v. State*,[28] the court held that where a different jury passes on the question of a sentence,

---

[22]Oregon v. Guzek, 546 U.S. 517, 126 S. Ct. 1226, 163 L. Ed. 2d 1112 (2006) (emphasis in original).

[23]Romano v. Oklahoma, 512 U.S. 1, 114 S.Ct. 2004, 129 L.Ed.2d 1 (1994).

[24]Caldwell v. Mississippi, 472 U.S. 320, 105 S.Ct. 2633, 86 L.Ed.2d 231 (1985).

[25]Gregg v. Georgia, 428 U.S. 153, 96 S.Ct. 2909, 49 L.Ed.2d 859 (1976).

[26]See, e.g., Brown v. State, 235 Ga. 644, 220 S.E.2d 922 (1975). In Simmons v. South Carolina, 512 U.S. 154, 114 S.Ct. 2187, 129 L.Ed.2d 133 (1994), the court held that "[t]he State may not create a false dilemma by advancing generalized arguments regarding the defendant's future dangerousness while . . . preventing the jury from learning that the defendant never will be released on parole." See Lynch v. Arizona, 136 S. Ct. 1818, 195 L. Ed. 2d 99 (2016).

[27]Gregg v. Georgia, 428 U.S. 153, 96 S.Ct. 2909, 49 L.Ed.2d 859, 891 (1976). In Cobb v. State, 244 Ga. 344, 359, 260 S.E.2d 60 (1979), the court said that "the legislature meant to

evidence may not be excluded on the ground that it only relates to the guilt or innocence of the defendant.

It has also been held that the death sentence may be imposed based on circumstantial evidence.[29] In *Cofield v. State*,[30] the court held that it was proper to permit the defendant's mother to take the stand and testify that she loved the defendant and did not want him to die. In *Eddings v. Oklahoma*,[31] a 16-year-old was charged with murder, and the court stated that the Eighth and Fourteenth Amendments require considering as a mitigating factor "any aspect of a defendant's character or record and any of the circumstances of the offense that the defendant" presents. The court concluded that it was error for the sentencer to fail to consider evidence of Eddings' troubled youth, consisting of testimony that he had been raised without proper guidance, that his parents were divorced when he was five, that he lived with his mother until he was 14 without rules or supervision, that his mother was an alcoholic and possibly a prostitute, that by the time he was 14 he could not be controlled by his mother, that Eddings was frightened and bitter, that his father overreacted and used excessive punishment, and that Eddings was emotionally disturbed by the time of the trial. Nevertheless, it has been held that it is not error for the trial judge to refuse to permit a defendant to call a reporter, a prison chaplain, and a professor of religion at the sentencing phase of the case for the purpose of describing executions,[32] life on death row, statistics relating to executions, and religious and philosophical approaches to the

---

empower the jury to consider as mitigating anything they found to be mitigating without limitation or definition." In Collier v. State, 244 Ga. 553, 566, 261 S.E.2d 364 (1979), overruled on other grounds by Thompson v. State, 263 Ga. 23, 426 S.E.2d 895 (1993), the court held that evidence not admissible under the rules of evidence is admissible in mitigation of a capital case; however, the mitigating effect of such testimony must be weighed against the harm resulting from a violation of the rules of evidence, but in close cases doubt should be resolved in favor of admissibility. In Brooks v. State, 244 Ga. 574, 584, 261 S.E.2d 379 (1979), the court said, "The trial court should exercise a broad discretion in allowing any evidence reasonably tending toward mitigation. But the court is authorized to hold witnesses 'within reasonable bounds.'

"However, evidence may not be introduced against a defendant at the sentencing phase if its admission at the guilt-innocence phase would violate a fundamental constitutional guarantee. Estelle v. Smith, 451 U.S. 454, 101 S.Ct. 1866, 68 L.Ed.2d 359 (1981).

[28]Blankenship v. State, 251 Ga. 621, 624, 308 S.E.2d 369 (1983).

[29]Douthit v. State, 239 Ga. 81, 89, 235 S.E.2d 493 (1977).

[30]Cofield v. State, 247 Ga. 98, 112, 274 S.E.2d 530 (1981). Cf. Lockett v. Ohio, 438 U.S. 586, 98 S.Ct. 2954, 57 L.Ed.2d 973 (1978).

[31]Eddings v. Oklahoma, 455 U.S. 104, 102 S.Ct. 869, 71 L.Ed.2d 1 (1982).

[32]Cf. Ingram v. State, 253 Ga. 622, 635 (11), 323 S.E.2d 801 (1984).

death penalty.[33] Thus, in *Godfrey v. Francis*,[34] the court held that it was not error to reject the testimony of "a representative of the ACLU as to the frequency of death sentences in domestic cases." It is error to admit evidence about the psychological effect of the crime on the victim;[35] but it is not error to admit evidence of the defendant's cooperation with the police,[36] and evidence of the future dangerousness of the defendant is admissible.[37] It is not error for the trial judge to exclude evidence of a plea bargain offered by the state and refused by the defendant.[38]

Georgia statutes do not make any distinction between the evidence admissible in a pre-sentence hearing in a death case and the evidence admissible in a pre-sentence hearing before a judge in other cases. However, in a non-capital case, the trial judge may consider a pre-sentence report[39] which would be inadmissible in a death case.[40] A distinction also exists in the admissibility of evidence of the conduct of the defendant while confined. Generally, under Georgia law such evidence is not admissible,[41] but in a capital case such evidence is admissible during the sentencing hearing.[42]

In *Jenkins v. State*,[43] the court held it is not error for the trial judge to exclude testimony of mental health experts as mitigation in the sentencing phase where the defendant has not submitted to "a court-ordered examination by mental health experts, whose report would thereafter be made available to the prosecution." *Jenkins* is premised on "the State's overwhelming difficulty in responding to the defense psychiatric testimony without its own psychiatric examination of the accused."[44] However, the rule is different when the defendant refuses to be examined by *any* expert including one employed by the defense. In that event, it

---

[33]Franklin v. State, 245 Ga. 141, 263 S.E.2d 666 (1980); Childs v. State, 257 Ga. 243, 256 (19), 357 S.E.2d 48 (1987).

[34]Godfrey v. Francis, 251 Ga. 652, 661 (8), 308 S.E.2d 806 (1983).

In Pulley v. Harris, 465 U.S. 37, 104 S.Ct. 871, 79 L.Ed.2d 29 (1984), the court held that the Eighth Amendment does not as a constitutional matter require appellate courts to compare the sentence imposed with penalties imposed in like cases.

[35]Muckle v. State, 233 Ga. 337, 211 S.E.2d 361 (1974).

[36]Boorstine v. State, 126 Ga. App. 90, 92 (11), 190 S.E.2d 83 (1972).

[37]Hicks v. State, 256 Ga. 715, 730 (23), 352 S.E.2d 762 (1987).

[38]Davis v. State, 255 Ga. 598, 614 (24), 340 S.E.2d 869 (1986).

[39]Munsford v. State, 235 Ga. 38, 45, 218 S.E.2d 792 (1975).

[40]Gardner v. Florida, 430 U.S. 349, 97 S.Ct. 1197, 51 L.Ed.2d 393 (1977).

[41]Smalls v. State, 102 Ga. 31, 32 (2), 29 S.E. 153 (1897).

[42]Skipper v. South Carolina, 476 U.S. 1, 106 S.Ct. 1669, 90 L.Ed.2d 1 (1986).

[43]Jenkins v. State, 265 Ga. 539, 540 (3), 458 S.E.2d 477 (1995).

[44]Lynd v. State, 262 Ga. 58(11), 414 S.E.2d 5 (1992).

would be proper for a psychological expert to opine upon the competency of the accused to stand trial based upon observations of the accused by third parties, letters written by the accused, and other documentary evidence which is equally available to the state.[45]

In *Fleming v. State,*[46] the court held that "both the prosecution and the defense have the opportunity to argue the issue [of the deterrent effect of the death penalty] to the jury"; however, "both the prosecution and the defense are precluded from introducing evidence on the issue."

In *Height v. State,*[47] the Georgia Supreme Court held that "Georgia's general ban on the admission of polygraph test results absent the parties' stipulation should not be applied automatically in the sentencing phase of a capital case so as to prevent the defendant from presenting a favorable polygraph test result." The Court noted, however, that "the trial court must exercise its discretion to determine whether those results are sufficiently reliable to be admitted.

As to other evidence admissible at the pre-sentence hearing, it is error to permit the district attorney to question a defendant about a charge on which he was acquitted.[48] Likewise, where a defendant attempts to plead guilty during the course of a trial and the plea is not accepted, it is error for the district attorney to cross-examine the defendant during the sentencing phase about the attempt to plead guilty.[49] However, the Georgia Supreme Court has held that a conviction of the defendant after his murder conviction but before his pre-sentencing hearing is admissible at the pre-sentencing hearing if the defense has been given proper notice.[50] It is generally recognized that no prior conviction, felony or misdemeanor, may be admitted against a defendant at a pre-sentence hearing unless there is a showing that the defendant was represented by counsel or that he intelligently waived his right to counsel.[51]

Where the district attorney gives proper notice of those prior

---

[45]Humphrey v. Walker, 294 Ga. 855, 757 S.E.2d 68 (2014) (Court expressed no opinion upon whether such testimony would be admitted at the guilt-innocence stage of trial or at sentencing).

[46]Fleming v. State, 265 Ga. 541, 543, 458 S.E.2d 638 (1995).

[47]Height v. State, 278 Ga. 592, 604 S.E.2d 796 (2004).

[48]Clark v. State, 138 Ga. App. 266, 270, 226 S.E.2d 89 (1976).

[49]Thomas v. State, 248 Ga. 247, 253 (1), 282 S.E.2d 316 (1981).

[50]Stephens v. Hopper, 241 Ga. 596, 247 S.E.2d 92 (1978). The court said that "prior record of conviction of a capital felony" as set out in O.C.G.A. § 17-10-30(b)(1) means prior conviction at the time of sentencing, not prior conviction at the time of the commission of the crime for which he is being tried.

[51]Morgan v. State, 235 Ga. 632, 221 S.E.2d 47 (1975) (citing Argers-

convictions he intends to use at the pre-sentence hearing, he may, without further notice, use witnesses to identify the defendant as the person named in the prior indictment.[52] A witness may be used by the state to describe how the earlier crime was carried out.[53] Also, at the pre-sentence hearing, a properly authenticated prison record of the defendant may be introduced.[54] However, all extraneous material should, on motion, be deleted from such exhibits.[55] Hence, a certified copy of the Georgia Division of Investigation is admissible if it only contains records of valid convictions, but if it shows arrests for which the defendant was not prosecuted or if it shows a pending case, it is not admissible.[56]

See § 26:5, infra, on admissibility of victim impact statement.

See Studdard, *Daniel's Georgia Handbook on Criminal Evidence* (2018 ed.), § 4:39.

§ 26:9 Capital cases with jury—The pre-sentence hearing—Procedure

The actual procedure at the pre-sentence hearing is rather sketchy. O.C.G.A. § 17-10-2 makes no reference to opening statements. If the state wishes to introduce any evidence in aggravation, apparently it does so first. The defendant then may introduce evidence in mitigation. In *O'Kelley v. State*,[1] the Supreme Court recognized for the first time that the sentencing phase of a death penalty case constituted a "criminal matter" for purposes of Uniform Superior Court Rule 10.2. Thus, the defendant has a right to make an opening statement either immediately after the state's opening or at the conclusion of the state's presentation of evidence. The option of when the defendant exercises that right, the Court stated, belongs to the defense and not to the discretion of the trial court. At the conclusion of the evidence, the state has the right to make a closing argument and

---

inger v. Hamlin, 407 U.S. 25, 92 S.Ct. 2006, 32 L.Ed.2d 530 (1972)). See also Van Voltenburg v. State, 138 Ga. App. 628, 634, 227 S.E.2d 451 (1976); Schamber v. State, 236 Ga. 159, 160, 223 S.E.2d 138 (1976). In Cobb v. State, 244 Ga. 344, 354 (20)(c), 260 S.E.2d 60 (1979), it was held that a prior judgment of conviction is admissible without the copy of the indictment upon which the conviction was predicated.

[52]Davis v. State, 229 Ga. 509 (2), 192 S.E.2d 253 (1972).

[53]Davis v. State, 229 Ga. 509, 510, 192 S.E.2d 253 (1972).

[54]Davis v. State, 229 Ga. 509, 511, 192 S.E.2d 253 (1972).

[55]Phillips v. Stynchcombe, 231 Ga. 430, 436 (6)(b), 202 S.E.2d 26 (1973).

[56]Cowan v. State, 130 Ga. App. 320, 322 (3), 203 S.E.2d 311 (1973).

[Section 26:9]

[1]O'Kelley v. State, 284 Ga. 758 (3), 670 S.E.2d 388 (2008).

defense counsel has a similar right.[2] In 2005, O.C.G.A. § 17-10-2(a)(2) was amended to provide the following: "Except in cases where the death penalty may be imposed, the prosecuting attorney shall open and conclude the argument. In cases where the death penalty may be imposed, the prosecuting attorney shall open and the defendant or the defendant's counsel shall conclude the argument." It is not error to prevent defense counsel from arguing that since the defendant is an "habitual violator he would have to serve 20 years without parole" if the death penalty is not imposed,[3] or to prevent counsel during argument from describing the mechanics of an electrocution.[4] The Georgia statute makes no reference to the length of these arguments or to whether time previously spent in arguing the case[5] is to be considered.

Georgia law provides that a verdict recommending mercy, in all capital cases other than homicide, is regarded as a recommendation of life imprisonment, which is binding on the judge.[6] If a jury recommends the death penalty, it shall designate it in a written verdict, signed by the foreman of the jury,[7] and designating the "aggravating circumstance or circumstances which it found beyond a reasonable doubt."[8] If the jury recommends death,

---

[2]See O.C.G.A. § 17-10-2.

[3]Horton v. State, 249 Ga. 871, 873 (4), 295 S.E.2d 281 (1982).

[4]Horton v. State, 249 Ga. 871, 873 (5), 295 S.E.2d 281 (1982).

[5]See § 23:3, supra, on time limits for arguments.

[6]O.C.G.A. § 17-9-3. Also see O.C.G.A. § 17-10-31.

[7]O.C.G.A. § 17-10-30. Notice that for cases of treason and aircraft hijacking, there does not have to be aggravating circumstances. O.C.G.A. § 17-10-30(a).

[8]See Presnell v. State, 241 Ga. 49, 52 (1), 243 S.E.2d 496 (1978), rev'd on other grounds, 439 U.S. 14, 99 S.Ct. 235, 58 L.Ed.2d 207 (1978), on remand, 243 Ga. 131, 252 S.E.2d 625 (1979); Stevens v. State, 245 Ga. 583, 584, 266 S.E.2d 194 (1980). In Burger v. State, 245 Ga. 458, 462 (4), 265 S.E.2d 796 (1980), the court pointed out that where a jury finds two or more statutory aggravating circumstances, the failure of one does not invalidate a death sentence. But see Stephens v. Zant, 631 F.2d 397 (5th Cir. 1980), which is discussed in § 26:11, infra.

In 2006, the U.S. Supreme Court in Brown v. Sanders, 126 S. Ct. 884, 163 L. Ed. 2d 723 (U.S. 2006), adopted the following rule for use in both "weighing" and "non-weighing" states: "An invalidated sentencing factor (whether an eligibility factor or not) will render the sentence unconstitutional by reason of its adding an improper element to the aggravation scale in the weighing process unless one of the other sentencing factors enables the sentencer to give aggravating weight to the same facts and circumstances." *Brown* does not change the law regarding invalidated sentencing factors in Georgia. Writing for the majority, Justice Scalia claims the new rule is merely an attempt to "clarify the analysis, and simplify the sentence-invalidating factors [the Court has] hitherto applied to non-weighing states," such as Georgia. Brown v. Sanders, 126 S. Ct. 884, 892, 163 L. Ed. 2d 723 (U.S. 2006).

it is the duty of the trial judge to sentence the defendant to death.[9] However, O.C.G.A. § 17-10-35 provides for an automatic appeal and review by the Georgia Supreme Court before the sentence is imposed.[10]

If a defendant is convicted of a capital felony and is given a life sentence but obtains a new trial, at the later trial he may not be given a sentence greater than life imprisonment, as such a greater sentence is regarded as being disproportionate to the life sentence previously given.[11]

If the death penalty is imposed, the trial judge is also obligated to complete a questionnaire[12] which, along with the other records, is transmitted to the Georgia Supreme Court.[13]

§ 26:10 Capital cases with jury—The pre-sentence hearing—Jury instructions

The trial judge is obligated to give the jury proper instructions before the jury retires,[1] and may, in addition, also charge the jury, to the extent warranted by the evidence, on the provisions of O.C.G.A. § 17-10-30 regarding the role of mitigating and aggravating circumstances. See § 26:11, infra, on aggravating circumstances.

The sentencing charge is regarded as being so crucial to the outcome of a death case that the Georgia Supreme Court will review the charge even when the issue first arises in a habeas corpus action without prior objection in the trial court.[2] The applicable provisions of O.C.G.A. § 17-10-30 must be given to the

---

[9]O.C.G.A. § 17-9-3, O.C.G.A. § 17-10-31.

[10]O.C.G.A. § 17-10-35. In Judy v. State, 275 Ind. 145, 416 N.E.2d 95 (1981), the court held that a defendant could not, under the law of that state, relieve the State Supreme Court of its duty to review a death sentence. But see Stephens v. Zant, 631 F.2d 397 (5th Cir. 1980), which is discussed in § 26:11, infra.

[11]Ward v. State, 239 Ga. 205, 208, 236 S.E.2d 365 (1977). In Bullington v. Missouri, 451 U.S. 430, 101 S.Ct. 1852, 68 L.Ed.2d 270 (1981), the court reached the same conclusion on double jeopardy grounds. However, in Patrick v. State, 249 Ga. 708, 709, 293 S.E.2d 329 (1982), the court pointed out that

where a jury imposes the death penalty and the death penalty is vacated on legal grounds, as opposed to grounds that the evidence is insufficient to support the verdict, the state may again seek the death penalty.

[12]In Greene v. State, 240 Ga. 804, 242 S.E.2d 587 (1978), the court held that the completion of the questionnaire was the responsibility of the judge, and defense counsel could not be ordered to complete it.

[13]O.C.G.A. § 17-10-35(a).

[Section 26:10]

[1]O.C.G.A. § 17-10-2(c).

[2]Banks v. Glass, 242 Ga. 518, 520, 250 S.E.2d 431 (1978).

jury orally and a written copy provided for use in the jury room.[3] However, in *Johnson v. State*,[4] the court held that it is not error for the trial judge to fail to give the jury written instructions on mitigating and aggravating circumstances if the jury is properly instructed and given in writing the possible verdicts which can be returned under the evidence. The jury must be charged clearly that it can recommend a life sentence even if statutory aggravating circumstances are found to exist,[5] and failure to so charge has been held to be reversible error even where defense counsel states that he has no objections to the charge.[6] The jury must be instructed on the meaning of life with and without the possibility of parole. In addition, the parties may argue as to the appropriateness of these sentences.[7] Also, the jury must be charged that mitigating circumstances are to be considered in determining whether or not to impose the death sentence.[8] Thus, in *Hitchcock v. Dugger*,[9] the United States Supreme Court found that the death sentence had been improperly imposed where the jury had been instructed that it was to consider only the mitigating factors contained in the state's statute.

In *Smith v. State*,[10] the Georgia Supreme Court held that it is not necessary for the trial judge to define the term "mitigating,"

---

[3]In Collier v. State, 244 Ga. 553, 569, 261 S.E.2d 364 (1979), overruled on other grounds by Thompson v. State, 263 Ga. 23, 426 S.E.2d 895 (1993), the court held that it was not error to give the jury written instructions on aggravating circumstances while failing to give the jury written instructions on mitigating circumstances. Accord, Tucker v. State, 244 Ga. 721, 729, 261 S.E.2d 635 (1979), overruled by Woodard v. State, 269 Ga. 317, 496 S.E.2d 896 (1998), only as it pertains to the admissibility of witnesses' prior consistent statements.

In Cunningham v. State, 248 Ga. 558, 564 (14), 284 S.E.2d 390 (1981), the court declined to reverse where the trial judge in his oral charge did not give the entire written charge that was ultimately sent to the jury room.

[4]Johnson v. State, 242 Ga. 649, 654 (5), 250 S.E.2d 394 (1978); Finney v. State, 242 Ga. 582, 583 (1), 250 S.E.2d 388 (1978).

[5]Fleming v. State, 240 Ga. 142, 146 (7), 240 S.E.2d 37 (1977); Redd v. State, 240 Ga. 753, 757 (7), 243 S.E.2d 16 (1978); Spraggins v. State, 240 Ga. 759, 763, 243 S.E.2d 20 (1978). But cf. the dissenting opinion of Justice Bowles in Morgan v. State, 241 Ga. 485, 489, 246 S.E.2d 198 (1978).

[6]Stynchcombe v. Floyd, 252 Ga. 113, 115, 311 S.E.2d 828 (1984).

[7]Lamar v. State, 278 Ga. 150 (14), 598 S.E.2d 488 (2004).

[8]Hawes v. State, 240 Ga. 327, 334, 240 S.E.2d 833 (1977). In Lockett v. Ohio, 438 U.S. 586, 98 S.Ct. 2954, 57 L.Ed.2d 973 (1978), and Bell v. Ohio, 438 U.S. 637, 98 S.Ct. 2977, 57 L.Ed.2d 1010 (1978), the court held the Ohio death penalty unconstitutional because it limited too strictly mitigating circumstances, preventing an "individualized consideration of mitigating factors that is required of the Eighth and Fourteenth Amendments."

[9]Hitchcock v. Dugger, 481 U.S. 393, 107 S.Ct. 1821, 95 L.Ed.2d 347 (1987).

[10]Smith v. State, 249 Ga. 228, 229 (2), 290 S.E.2d 43 (1982).

and the charge must not limit what the jury can consider as mitigation.[11] Nevertheless, the Eleventh Circuit has held that a trial judge must explain why the law allows "such a consideration and what effect a finding of mitigating circumstances has on the ultimate recommendation of sentence."[12] It is for the jury to determine whether or not certain factors are mitigating, and there is no duty on the part of the trial judge to charge that certain circumstances amount to mitigation.[13] In *Spivey v. State*,[14] a five to two majority held that it is not error for the trial judge to fail to use the exact words "mitigating circumstances" if a reasonable juror would understand from the charge as a whole that he could consider mitigation and recommend life imprisonment.

In *Brantley v. State*,[15] the court pointed out that Georgia law does not require a jury "to list in writing its findings of mitigating circumstances or to agree unanimously on any particular mitigating circumstance. . . ."

There is no presumption that the defendant is innocent of aggravating circumstances. However, the trial judge must charge the jury that the burden is on the state to prove beyond a reasonable doubt that the aggravating circumstances charged do exist.[16]

At the sentencing phase of a capital case it is error for the trial judge to give a charge instructing the jury that it should not render a verdict based on "sympathy for either party."[17]

It is not error for the trial judge to explain the bifurcated trial procedure to the jury during the guilt-innocence phase, and where such an explanation is given, it is not error to omit instructions as to the possible sentences which may be imposed.[18] Generally, on jury instructions see Chapter 24, supra.

In *California v. Brown*,[19] the United States Supreme Court held that there was no violation of the Eighth and Fourteenth

[11]Smith v. State, 249 Ga. 228, 229 (2), 290 S.E.2d 43 (1982) (citing Eddings v. Oklahoma, 455 U.S. 104, 102 S.Ct. 869, 71 L.Ed.2d 1 (1982)). *Eddings* is discussed in § 26:8, supra.

[12]Morgan v. Zant, 743 F.2d 775, 779 (11th Cir. 1984).

[13]Spivey v. State, 241 Ga. 477, 479, 246 S.E.2d 288 (1978); Gates v. State, 244 Ga. 587, 597, 261 S.E.2d 349 (1979). See Kansas v. Carr, 136 S. Ct. 633, 193 L. Ed. 2d 535 (2016) (Court opines that it may not be possible to define a standard of proof to the mitigating factor determination since whether mitigation exists is a judgment or value call for each juror).

[14]Spivey v. State, 241 Ga. 477, 479, 246 S.E.2d 288 (1978). The decision cited and relied upon Jurek v. Texas, 428 U.S. 262, 96 S.Ct. 2950, 49 L.Ed.2d 929 (1976).

[15]Brantley v. State, 262 Ga. 786, 793 (16), 427 S.E.2d 758 (1993).

[16]Finney v. State, 242 Ga. 582, 584 (3), 250 S.E.2d 388 (1978).

[17]Legare v. State, 250 Ga. 875, 877 (2), 302 S.E.2d 351 (1983). Cf. People v. Easley, 34 Cal.3d 858, 196 Cal.Rptr. 309, 671 P.2d 813 (1983).

[18]Nichols v. State, 247 Ga. 534, 277 S.E.2d 50 (1981).

[19]California v. Brown, 479 U.S.

Amendments where a trial judge "instructed the jury to consider the aggravating and mitigating circumstances and to weigh them in determining the appropriate penalty. . . . But the court cautioned the jury that it 'must not be swayed by mere sentiment, conjecture, sympathy, passion, prejudice, public opinion or public feeling.' "

§ 26:11   Capital cases with jury—The pre-sentence hearing—Aggravating circumstances

"In a case in which a death sentence is imposed, the jury is required to set forth in writing the statutory aggravating circumstances which it has found beyond a reasonable doubt. . . . This written finding must show the jury's intent 'with sufficient clarity that [the Georgia Supreme] Court can rationally review the jury findings.' "[1]

In determining aggravating circumstances where a defendant is charged with two connected capital offenses, the jury may not find that each of the offenses so aggravated the other that the defendant may be given two death sentences; however, one of the offenses may so aggravate the other that one death sentence and one life sentence may be returned.[2] Armed robbery may constitute aggravation for felony murder even though it cannot be punished separately.[3] It is not necessary that the aggravating circumstances be directed toward the murder victim; they may be inflicted on another.[4] Also, it is not necessary that the aggravating capital offense actually be performed or completed so long as it was being engaged in at the time of the commission of the other capital offense.[5] Also, the fact that two murders are almost instantaneous will not prevent one from being an aggravating

---

538, 107 S.Ct. 837, 93 L.Ed.2d 934 (1987). See Kansas v. Carr, 136 S. Ct. 633, 193 L. Ed. 2d 535 (2016) (U.S. Constitution does not require that jury be instructed that mitigating circumstances need not be proved beyond a reasonable doubt).

[Section 26:11]

[1]Page v. State, 256 Ga. 191, 345 S.E.2d 600 (1986). See Ellington v. State, 292 Ga. 109, 116(3)(a), 735 S.E.2d 736 (2012) (Georgia death penalty statutes provide sufficient guidance to jury in considering aggravating and mitigating circumstances and whether to vote for a death sentence or a sentence of less than death).

[2]Gibson v. State, 236 Ga. 874,

882 (III), 226 S.E.2d 63 (1976).

[3]Stanley v. State, 240 Ga. 341, 350, 241 S.E.2d 173 (1977); Pryor v. State, 238 Ga. 698, 702, 234 S.E.2d 918 (1977), disapp. on other grounds, Montes v. State, 262 Ga. 473, 421 S.E.2d 710 (1992).

[4]Presnell v. State, 241 Ga. 49, 62, 243 S.E.2d 496 (1978), rev'd on other grounds, 439 U.S. 14, 99 S.Ct. 235, 58 L.Ed.2d 207 (1978), on remand, 243 Ga. 131, 132 (1), 252 S.E.2d 625 (1979).

[5]Amadeo v. State, 243 Ga. 627, 630, 255 S.E.2d 718 (1979). In Fair v. State, 245 Ga. 868, 869 (2), 268 S.E.2d 316 (1980), the court held that a murder in another county for which the defendant had not been tried could be

circumstance for the other,[6] but they may not be regarded as mutually supporting a death sentence. Hence, in such circumstances, the defendant may only be sentenced to death for one of the murders.[7] There is no requirement that the defendant must have already been found guilty of the capital felony which is being used as an aggravating circumstance for the other capital felony.[8]

Those crimes which were capital felonies in 1973 when Georgia Code Annotated section 27-2534.1 (now O.C.G.A. § 17-10-30) was enacted are regarded as "capital felonies" within the meaning of that statute even if such crime is no longer punishable by death.[9] Where two persons participate in a murder and the "trigger man" receives life imprisonment, if the other defendant did not order the killing and was not the "prime mover," generally he may not be sentenced to death.[10] However, there is no general rule that one co-defendant may not be sentenced to death when the other co-defendant has received a lesser penalty.[11]

In *Stephens v. Zant*,[12] the court in effect set aside a death sentence which was imposed by a jury based on three aggravating circumstances, one of which was later set aside as unconstitutional. The court said it was impossible for the reviewing court to determine satisfactorily whether the verdict was decisively affected by the unconstitutional aggravating circumstance. However, in 1983 the United States Supreme Court reversed the Eleventh Circuit opinion in *Stephens*,[13] and the Georgia Supreme Court continues to hold that where "[o]ne statutory aggravating circumstance remains" after one or more circumstances have been invalidated, the death sentence remains valid.[14]

---

used in aggravation.

[6]Godfrey v. State, 248 Ga. 616, 620 (3), 284 S.E.2d 422 (1981).

[7]Godfrey v. State, 248 Ga. 616, 625, 284 S.E.2d 422 (1981).

[8]Jones v. State, 249 Ga. 605, 611 (6), 293 S.E.2d 708 (1982).

[9]Cervi v. State, 248 Ga. 325, 333, 282 S.E.2d 629 (1981).

[10]Baker v. State, 243 Ga. 710, 711, 257 S.E.2d 192 (1979).

[11]Hall v. State, 241 Ga. 252, 258 (8), 244 S.E.2d 833 (1978) (overruled on other grounds by, Hamm v. State, 294 Ga. 791, 756 S.E.2d 507 (2014)). Cf. Bell v. Ohio, 438 U.S. 637, 98 S.Ct. 2977, 57 L.Ed.2d 1010 (1978), and Lockett v. Ohio, 438 U.S. 586, 98 S.Ct. 2954, 57 L.Ed.2d 973 (1978). However, in Green v. State, 246 Ga. 598, 607-608, 272 S.E.2d 475 (1980), the court said that when the "trigger man" receives the death sentence, the other defendant may also receive the death sentence when he had participated in the entire criminal enterprise.

[12]Stephens v. Zant, 631 F.2d 397 (5th Cir. 1980).

[13]Zant v. Stephens, 462 U.S. 862, 103 S.Ct. 2733, 77 L.Ed.2d 235 (1983).

[14]Rivers v. State, 250 Ga. 288, 301, 298 S.E.2d 10 (1982). Cf. Ford v. Strickland, 696 F.2d 804 (11th Cir. 1983).

In the questionable 1981 decision in *Godfrey v. State*,[15] the court concluded that where a defendant is re-tried on the question of sentence, the state is not to be limited to the aggravating circumstances which it relied upon at the earlier pre-sentence hearing. However, Justice Hill in his dissenting opinion felt that this amounted to a double jeopardy violation and cited *Bullington v. Missouri*.[16] He pointed out that at the first trial the trial judge determined that aggravated circumstance, as described in O.C.G.A. § 17-10-30(b)(7), was warranted and erroneously determined that subsection (b)(2) was not warranted. At the first trial, aggravated circumstance, as described in subsection (b)(7), was found by the jury to exist. After reversal the state relied upon subsection (b)(2), and the jury found this aggravating circumstance to exist.

In *Poland v. Arizona*,[17] the United States Supreme Court held that a defendant, who had been sentenced to the death penalty then re-tried and again sentenced to the death penalty, had not been subjected to double jeopardy. The evidence in the first trial had been insufficient to support the original aggravating circumstance, but was sufficient in the second trial to support the death penalty or other aggravating circumstances. The question is "whether the sentencer or reviewing court has 'decided that the prosecution has not proved its case' " for the death penalty and hence has acquitted petitioners.[18]

In *Zant v. Redd*,[19] "three aggravating circumstances were submitted to the jury: (1) The offense of murder was committed while the defendant was engaged in the commission of the capital felony of kidnapping with bodily injury . . . ; (2) the offense of murder was outrageously or wantonly vile or inhuman in that it involved torture, or depravity of mind, or an aggravated battery . . . ; and (3) the offense of murder was committed while the offender was engaged in the commission of the capital felony of armed robbery . . . ."[20] The jury recommended death based on the first circumstance; i.e., the murder was committed while the defendant was engaged in the capital felony of kidnapping with bodily injury. On appeal, the case was reversed because the jury had not been properly instructed on its right to recommend life imprisonment even if it found the existence of an aggravating

---

[15]Godfrey v. State, 248 Ga. 616, 617 (1), 284 S.E.2d 422 (1981).

[16]Bullington v. Missouri, 451 U.S. 430, 101 S.Ct. 1852, 68 L.Ed.2d 270 (1981).

[17]Poland v. Arizona, 476 U.S. 147, 106 S.Ct. 1749, 90 L.Ed.2d 123 (1986).

[18]Poland v. Arizona, 476 U.S. 147, 106 S.Ct. 1749, 90 L.Ed.2d 123 (1986) (quoting Bullington v. Missouri, 451 U.S. 430, 443, 101 S.Ct. 1852, 68 L.Ed.2d 270 (1981)).

[19]Zant v. Redd, 249 Ga. 211, 290 S.E.2d 36 (1982).

[20]Zant v. Redd, 249 Ga. 211, 215, 290 S.E.2d 36 (1982) (concurring opinion of Justice Hill).

circumstance. At the time of the re-sentencing trial, the jury was permitted to consider four aggravating circumstances, the same three as before, plus the fourth aggravating circumstance of murder committed for the purpose of receiving money. The jury again returned a verdict of death, based on aggravating circumstances number one (kidnapping with bodily injury) and number two (outrageously or wantonly vile, horrible, or inhuman in involving torture, depravity of mind, or aggravated battery). The defendant raised a double jeopardy claim in state habeas proceedings contending that at his first trial he had been acquitted of aggravating circumstances numbers two and three and it was therefore error for the trial judge to admit evidence on these circumstances and error to permit the second jury to consider them. The Georgia Supreme Court, finding no error, disagreed and stated: "[I]f a defendant overturns his death sentence on technical grounds, the sentence is nullified and the state and the defense start anew. Consequently, on resentencing the state may again seek the death penalty and may offer any evidence on aggravating circumstances in support thereof. Likewise, the defendant is entitled to bring to the jury any mitigating circumstances available to him, including those not known or utilized at the first sentencing trial. [Thus] . . . if a defendant overturns his death sentence on legal grounds, the death penalty may be sought on resentencing, and the state may offer proof of statutory aggravating circumstances not offered at the first trial. We take that reasoning one step further and hold that on resentencing in this case the state acted properly in offering proof of statutory aggravating circumstances submitted to the first jury but not listed by that jury in support of the death sentence."

In a special concurring opinion in *Redd,* Justice Hill concluded that the death penalty could be imposed since the first sentence was not reversed due to lack of evidence. In *Phillips v. State,*[21] the court held that where a defendant kills the victim by four or five shots in rapid succession, this alone does not amount to torture within the meaning of O.C.G.A. § 17-10-30(b)(7).

There is no requirement that prior to trial the state provide the defendant written notice of the statutory aggravating circumstances which the state intends to rely upon.[22] Indeed, in *Terrell v. State,*[23] the Georgia Supreme Court expressly rejected the notion that any facts (other than prior convictions) upon which the State intends to rely in order to seek an enhancement of what would otherwise be the maximum sentence for the offense com-

---

[21]Phillips v. State, 250 Ga. 336, 342, 297 S.E.2d 217 (1982).

[22]Roberts v. State, 252 Ga. 227, 240 (11), 314 S.E.2d 83 (1984).

[23]Terrell v. State, 276 Ga. 34 (5), 572 S.E.2d 595 (2002).

mitted must be specifically alleged in the indictment. The Court concluded that the federal constitution as interpreted and applied by the U.S. Supreme Court required only that the defendant be given fair notice of every fact upon which the State relies to enhance a criminal defendant's punishment and that such must be proven to the satisfaction of the jury beyond a reasonable doubt.[24]

O.C.G.A. § 17-10-31 provides that the court can only impose a sentence of death where the jury recommends that penalty after finding one of the statutory aggravators. Where the jury does not find a statutory aggravator or where it does find a statutory aggravator but does not recommend death, the jury shall then retire to consider whether the sentence should be life in prison or life in prison without the possibility of parole.

§ 26:12   Capital cases—Without jury

If a person has been indicted for a capital case and enters a plea of guilty, the judge of the superior court in his or her discretion may impose a sentence of life or life without the possibility of parole. In order to impose a sentence of death, except in the case of treason or aircraft hijacking, the court must first find one of the statutory aggravating circumstances.[1]

If the case is tried before a judge without a jury, the introduction of mitigating and aggravating circumstances at the presentence hearing[2] is allowed as in the case of a jury trial. However, it should be emphasized that in a death case the trial judge has no right to obtain or rely on an undisclosed probation or pre-sentence report.[3]

---

[24]The cases discussed by the Court in Terrell v. State, 276 Ga. 34, 572 S.E.2d 595 (2002) are: Jones v. United States, 526 U.S. 227, 119 S.Ct. 1215, 143 L.Ed.2d 311 (1999); Apprendi v. New Jersey, 530 U.S. 466, 120 S.Ct. 2348, 147 L.Ed.2d 435 (2000); Ring v. Arizona, 536 U.S. 584, 122 S.Ct. 2428, 153 L.Ed.2d 556 (2002).

[Section 26:12]

[1]O.C.G.A. §§ 17-10-2(b) and 17-10-30. Merely pleading guilty to the indictment does not preclude the defendant from exercising the right to a jury trial as to punishment.

[2]O.C.G.A. § 17-10-2, which refers to O.C.G.A. § 17-10-30.

[3]Gardner v. Florida, 430 U.S. 349, 97 S.Ct. 1197, 51 L.Ed.2d 393 (1977).

§ 26:13 Pre-sentence hearing in non-capital cases— General

By statute, Georgia has provided, except in death cases and in the case of a misdemeanor,[1] that after a defendant has been found guilty, the judge shall release the jury[2] and conduct a pre-sentence hearing.[3] However, it has been held that it is not error for the judge to allow the jury to remain in the courtroom during the pre-sentence hearing and the sentencing.[4] The trial judge is obligated to hold a pre-sentence hearing at which both sides are permitted to present evidence in aggravation, extenuation, and mitigation. Where a pre-sentence hearing is not waived, the "[f]ailure to follow the mandate of § 27-2503 [O.C.G.A. § 17-10-2] is neither harmless nor waived by failure to object to procedure."[5] However, "a trial court's failure to hold a presentence hearing in a non-death penalty case . . . does not render a sentence void."[6] Also, in *Edwards v. State*,[7] the court held that it is not error for the trial judge to fail to hold a pre-sentence hearing where the judge imposes the minimum statutory sentence which could be imposed for the crime.

The rules of procedure and evidence referred to earlier in regard to a pre-sentence hearing in a capital case tried by a jury generally apply.[8] If a defendant is charged and convicted of several offenses and one or more is not a capital offense, the trial

---

[Section 26:13]

[1]In Robinson v. State, 212 Ga. App. 613, 615 (2), 442 S.E.2d 901 (1994), overruled on other grounds by Felix v. State, 271 Ga. 534, 523 S.E.2d 1 (1999), the court held that the state is "not required to give [the defendant] pretrial notice of the evidence in aggravation of punishment" in a misdemeanor case.

[2]The case of Whitley v. State, 137 Ga. App. 245, 246 (2), 223 S.E.2d 279 (1976), holds that it is not mandatory that the jury be dismissed before the pre-sentence hearing takes place.

[3]O.C.G.A. § 17-10-2. Sentencing by the trial judge is to be used in all non-capital felonies even in cases where the alleged crime was committed before July 1, 1974, the effective date of the judge-sentencing statute. DeLoach v. State, 142 Ga. App. 666, 667 (2), 236 S.E.2d 904 (1977). In Almond v. State, 128 Ga. App. 758, 761 (6), 197 S.E.2d 836 (1973), the court

held that there must be a pre-sentence hearing even if the defendant is tried as a habitual offender and the defendant is to receive the maximum punishment.

[4]Whitley v. State, 137 Ga. App. 245, 246 (2), 223 S.E.2d 279 (1976). However, it seems that allowing the jury to remain in the courtroom during a pre-sentence hearing and/or sentencing may be a violation of O.C.G.A. § 9-10-8, O.C.G.A. § 17-9-22 in some cases. These code sections prevent the judge from expressing approval or disapproval of a verdict.

[5]Sprouse v. State, 242 Ga. 831, 834 (5), 252 S.E.2d 173 (1979).

[6]Williams v. State, 271 Ga. 686, 689 (2), 523 S.E.2d 857 (1999).

[7]Edwards v. State, 219 Ga. App. 239, 240 (1), 464 S.E.2d 851 (1995).

[8]Smith v. State, 156 Ga. App. 419, 420 (2), 274 S.E.2d 703 (1980), rev'd on other grounds, 247 Ga. 612, 277 S.E.2d 678 (1981). In the *Smith*

judge apparently has the responsibility of fixing the punishment for the non-capital offense(s) as though no capital crime were involved.[9] Prior to 2005, the state did not have to provide the defense with evidence which it intended to introduce at sentencing in aggravation of punishment until the start of trial.[10] That deadline was deleted by the legislature and a new one provided by O.C.G.A. § 17-16-4(a)(5). The state is now required to provide the defendant with notice of any evidence in aggravation of punishment which it intends to introduce at sentencing at least ten days prior to trial or at such time as the court directs, but in no event later than the start of trial.[11] Additionally, this notice must make it clear in advance that the conviction will be used against the defendant at sentencing; thus, merely giving notice of intent to present a similar transaction does not authorize the use of the earlier conviction against defendant at sentencing.[12] Under the prior law, the statutory requirement of "clear notice" to the accused did not necessarily require written notice.[13] Thus, in *Beecher v. State*,[14] even when the state notified the defendant of its intention to introduce prior convictions during the sentencing phase of the first trial, and the result is a mistrial, the court found that the state was required to give notice a second time for use of the convictions at the subsequent trial. In *Thornton v. State*,[15] the court held that "notice of unproven criminal charges must be described with enough particularity to alert the accused to what he must defend against. . . . [Likewise,] notice of the state's intention to prove prior convictions must be specific." One of the purposes of this rule "is to allow a defendant to examine [the record presented] to determine if the convictions are in fact his and if he was represented by counsel, and any other defect which would render such documents inadmissible during the pre-sentencing phase of the trial."[16] Also, if the judge intends to consider in aggravation that which was ruled inadmissible at the

---

case the court held that the trial judge properly excluded a report by a psychiatrist, one by a psychologist, a scrap book of family pictures, Bible school reports, school grades and a letter defendant wrote to her family.

[9]Cobb v. State, 244 Ga. 344, 356 (25), 260 S.E.2d 60 (1979).

[10]O.C.G.A. § 17-10-2.

[11]O.C.G.A. § 17-16-4(a)(5).

[12]Boyd v. State, 230 Ga. App. 314, 315 (2), 497 S.E.2d 3 (1998). In Washington v. State, 238 Ga. App. 561, 563 (4), 519 S.E.2d 234 (1999), the court emphasized that the state must provide "clear notice."

[13]Graham v. State, 171 Ga. App. 242, 256 (17), 319 S.E.2d 484 (1984). Accord, Powell v. State, 229 Ga. App. 52, 53 (1), 494 S.E.2d 200 (1997).

[14]Beecher v. State, 240 Ga. App. 457, 460 (5), 523 S.E.2d 54 (1999).

[15]Thornton v. State, 264 Ga. 563, 576 (22)(a), 449 S.E.2d 98 (1994).

[16]Herring v. State, 238 Ga. 288, 290 (4), 232 S.E.2d 826 (1977). In Jones v. Francis, 252 Ga. 60, 65 (11), 312 S.E.2d 300 (1984), the court said that it is doubtful that a conviction in another state is subject to collateral at-

guilt-innocence phase of the trial, he must inform defense counsel and the state of his intention to do so *before* the beginning of the pre-sentence hearing.[17] These cases should continue to have some application even though they were decided under former O.C.G.A. § 17-10-2(a)(1).

This requirement of pretrial notice however, may be deemed waived if a prior conviction of the defendant is presented as a factor in aggravation of sentence and considered by the court without objection.[18] However the failure of counsel to make the proper objection may constitute ineffective assistance of counsel.[19]

Where the trial judge has the duty to impose sentence if the defendant does not object to having the question submitted to the jury, it seems that this will generally be regarded as a waiver of the right to be sentenced by the court.[20]

Apparently there is no right to a formal pre-sentence hearing in a misdemeanor case.[21]

Georgia has special statutes relating to the punishment of misdemeanors[22] and misdemeanors of a high and aggravated nature.[23]

Generally, see the material on pre-sentence hearings in capital cases in §§ 26:8 et seq., supra. See § 14:1, supra, on proof of notice.

§ 26:14 Pre-sentence hearing in non-capital cases— Evidence

The court cannot consider "repeated rumors" about the defendant under O.C.G.A. § 17-10-2.[1] Likewise, a pending indictment against a defendant may not be considered in aggravation

---

tack in Georgia on the ground that the defendant received ineffective assistance of counsel in the earlier case.

[17]Dorsey v. Willis, 242 Ga. 316, 318, 249 S.E.2d 28 (1978).

[18]Turner v. State, 259 Ga. App. 902(1), 578 S.E.2d 570 (2003) (overruling Eason v. State, 215 Ga. App. 614, 451 S.E.2d 820 (1994) which had held that the notice required by O.C.G.A. § 17-10-2(a) was mandatory and not subject to waiver.)

[19]Turner v. State, 259 Ga. App. 902(2), 578 S.E.2d 570 (2003); See West v. Waters, 272 Ga. 591(1), 533 S.E.2d 88 (2000).

[20]McNeese v. State, 236 Ga. 26, 29 (3), 222 S.E.2d 318 (1976); but cf. Wheeless v. State, 135 Ga. App. 406 (10), 218 S.E.2d 88 (1975); Melton v. State, 149 Ga. App. 506, 509 (3), 254

S.E.2d 732 (1979).

[21]O.C.G.A. § 17-10-2.

[22]O.C.G.A. § 17-10-3.

[23]O.C.G.A. § 17-10-4.

[Section 26:14]

[1]Pounds v. State, 136 Ga. App. 852, 853 (6), 222 S.E.2d 629 (1975). However, in Bentley v. Willis, 247 Ga. 461, 463, 276 S.E.2d 639 (1981), the court said that O.C.G.A. § 42-8-34 authorizes a judge to consider investigative reports for the purpose of determining whether to suspend or probate all or a part of a sentence. The court also pointed out that in practice such reports may be considered by the trial judge in reducing the length of the sentence. However there is no requirement that a sentence not be imposed until after such report is prepared and considered. See Alliston v. State, 183

of punishment.[2] The purpose of this last Code section is to allow the defendant's counsel to examine prior convictions or pleas the district attorney plans to introduce to determine if the convictions are his client's, if he was represented by counsel at the time,[3] and to see if there is any other defect which would render them inadmissible.[4] However, O.C.G.A. § 17-10-2(a) does not apply to the use of prior convictions in the sentencing phase of misdemeanor cases.[5] In *Stephens v. State,*[6] the court held that a statement by the district attorney to defense counsel that the state intended to seek a life sentence if the defendant was convicted of possession with intent to distribute is not "any notice of a prior conviction on which the State intended to rely."

In *Burgett v. Texas,*[7] the court also held that an uncounseled felony conviction cannot be used for enhancement of punishment. If a defendant asserts his objection to an earlier conviction, the state bears the burden of establishing the validity of the conviction to argue for recidivist treatment.[8] Likewise, a conviction based upon a plea which was not entered voluntarily cannot be used in aggravation of a defendant's sentence.[9]

However, the Georgia Supreme Court, in *Mathis v. State,*[10] held that where a prior indictment and guilty plea are properly certified and it shows on its face that the defendant was represented by counsel at the time of that case, it is not necessary for the state to go behind the guilty plea and prove that it was voluntarily entered before introducing the document into evidence.

Ga. App. 462, 464 (3), 359 S.E.2d 220 (1987).

[2]Sinkfield v. State, 262 Ga. 239 (2), 416 S.E.2d 288 (1992).

[3]Unless it appears from the record of a former conviction that defendant was represented by counsel, the conviction is not admissible. Ledford v. State, 148 Ga. App. 819, 821, 253 S.E.2d 239 (1979); Hall v. State, 160 Ga. App. 508, 287 S.E.2d 223 (1981).

In United States v. Tucker, 404 U.S. 443, 92 S.Ct. 589, 30 L.Ed.2d 592 (1972), the court held that it was error for the trial judge to consider, for purposes of enhancement of sentence, a prior conviction when the defendant was not represented by counsel. Cf. § 26:28, infra, where it is pointed out that an uncounseled conviction may not be used to enhance punishment under a recidivist statute. Cf. Baldasar v. Illinois, 446 U.S. 222, 100 S.Ct.

1585, 64 L.Ed.2d 169 (1980), which is discussed in § 26:28, infra.

[4]Adams v. State, 142 Ga. App. 252, 255, 235 S.E.2d 667 (1977). This case also points out that if no objection is made at this time, the admissibility of these prior offenses will not be considered by an appellate court if the case is later appealed.

[5]See Wilcoxson v. State, 227 Ga. App. 25 (2), 488 S.E.2d 104 (1997).

[6]Stephens v. State, 219 Ga. App. 881, 883 (2), 467 S.E.2d 201 (1996).

[7]Burgett v. Texas, 389 U.S. 109, 88 S.Ct. 258, 19 L.Ed.2d 319 (1967).

[8]Tanner v. State, 230 Ga. App. 77, 78 (4), 495 S.E.2d 315 (1997).

[9]Donaldson v. State, 244 Ga. App. 89 (5), 534 S.E.2d 839 (2000).

[10]Mathis v. State, 249 Ga. 454, 458 (10), 291 S.E.2d 489 (1982).

In the 1999 case of *Nash v. State*,[11] the Georgia Supreme Court held that when the state wishes to present evidence of prior conviction for purposes of recidivist punishment, the state has the burden

> to prove both the existence of the prior guilty pleas and that the defendant was represented by counsel in all felony cases and those misdemeanor proceedings where imprisonment resulted. . . . "If the record does not so show, the State bears the burden of showing waiver." Upon such a showing, the presumption of regularity is then applied and the burden shifts to the defendant to produce some affirmative evidence showing an infringement of his rights or a procedural irregularity in the taking of the plea. "Defendant can attempt to meet his burden of production with a transcript, with testimony regarding the taking of the plea, or with other affirmative evidence." . . . "A silent record or the mere naked assertion by an accused that his prior counseled plea was not made knowingly and intelligently is insufficient." . . . If the defendant is able to present evidence that a constitutional infirmity exists, then the burden of proving the constitutionality of the plea shifts to the State.[12]

Also if defense counsel is supplied with copies of former convictions in a timely manner and it appears thereon that the defendant was not represented by counsel, and no objection to the consideration of such documents is made at sentencing, the sentencing is not considered invalid.[13] See § 26:28, infra, on recidivist notice.

In *Armstrong v. State*,[14] the Court of Appeals held that where a life sentence is mandated by O.C.G.A. § 16-13-30(d), the prosecution is not required to give the defendant advance notice of a prior drug conviction. However, on appeal,[15] the Georgia Supreme Court held that notice of intent to present a similar transaction does not eliminate the need to give notice that the state plans to use the prior conviction in aggravation of punishment, but apparently the "state's notice that it intend[s] to present evidence of

---

[11]Nash v. State, 271 Ga. 281, 519 S.E.2d 893 (1999). Accord, Cantrell v. State, 210 Ga. App. 218, 222 (3), 435 S.E.2d 737 (1993). See Carswell v. State, 263 Ga. App. 833 (1), 589 S.E.2d 605 (2003), where defendant was able to show through sentencing transcripts that Boykin dialogue did not take place, the court held that the state had the burden to show that prior convictions used in aggravation of sentence to be imposed in pending case were based upon guilty pleas that were entered voluntarily.

[12]Nash v. State, 271 Ga. 281, 285, 519 S.E.2d 893 (1999); Murray v. State, 328 Ga. App. 192, 761 S.E.2d 590 (2014).

[13]Pope v. State, 169 Ga. App. 969, 970 (3), 315 S.E.2d 685 (1984).

[14]Armstrong v. State, 209 Ga. App. 796, 798 (2), 434 S.E.2d 560 (1993).

[15]Armstrong v. State, 264 Ga. 237, 238 (2), 442 S.E.2d 759 (1994). Accord, Miller v. State, 219 Ga. App. 284, 287 (5), 464 S.E.2d 860 (1995).

prior convictions as similar transactions, coupled with oral notice that it intend[s] to seek a life sentence under recidivist statute, fulfill[s] the purpose of [the] notification requirement."

The Georgia Court of Appeals in *Caver v. State*[16] held that "where the State proves a defendant's prior felony convictions for the purpose of convicting him of being a convicted felon in possession of a firearm, it may not also use those prior convictions in aggravation of punishment."

While it is permissible for a trial judge to use a "pre-sentence" or a "post-sentence" report of a probation officer for the purpose of deciding whether to *suspend or probate* all or a part of the sentence, such a "pre-sentence" or "post-sentence" report *may not be used* in fixing the length of the sentence to be imposed.[17] However, whether or not to order such a "report is a matter within the sound discretion of the trial court."[18] However, *Payne* does not *require* that all victim impact evidence be admitted. Thus, in *Muckle v. State,*[19] the court reversed the sentence in a rape case where the state had introduced testimony concerning the psychological effect of a crime on the victim.[20] Although the case was later overruled, in *Brawner v. State,*[21] the court held that as a part of a pre-sentence report it was proper for the trial judge to consider juvenile court adjudications entered, where the defendant was not represented by counsel and no imprisonment was imposed, in determining whether a "subsequent felony

---

[16]Caver v. State, 215 Ga. App. 711, 713 (4), 452 S.E.2d 515 (1994).

[17]Threatt v. State, 156 Ga. App. 345, 274 S.E.2d 734 (1980). In Threatt, the court remanded the case for resentencing where the trial judge imposed the maximum sentence and then intended to use the "post-sentence" report to determine whether or not to reduce the sentence imposed. Watts v. State, 141 Ga. App. 127, 132 (8), 232 S.E.2d 590 (1977). See Munsford v. State, 235 Ga. 38, 45, 218 S.E.2d 792 (1975).

In Jones v. State, 129 Ga. App. 623, 624, 200 S.E.2d 487 (1973), the court held that a pre-sentence report (under O.C.G.A. § 42-8-34) could properly include the defendant's juvenile court record for the consideration of the court. In Mills v. State, 244 Ga. 186, 187, 259 S.E.2d 445 (1979), the court pointed out that where a pre-sentence report is used, the trial judge should reveal to defense counsel any matter adverse to defendant which is

likely to influence his decision on whether or not to suspend or probate a sentence. See Rampley v. State, 166 Ga. App. 521 (4), 304 S.E.2d 574 (1983). See also Rule 32 of the Federal Rules of Criminal Procedure; Saine v. State, 170 Ga. App. 610, 612, 317 S.E.2d 650 (1984); McDuffie v. Jones, 248 Ga. 544, 549, 283 S.E.2d 601 (1981), overruled on other grounds by West v. Waters, 272 Ga. 591, 533 S.E.2d 88 (2000); Chambley v. State, 163 Ga. App. 502, 505 (3), 295 S.E.2d 166 (1982).

[18]Galloway v. State, 165 Ga. App. 536, 301 S.E.2d 894 (1983).

[19]Muckle v. State, 233 Ga. 337, 211 S.E.2d 361 (1974).

[20]Sermons v. State, 262 Ga. 286, 417 S.E.2d 144 (1992).

[21]Brawner v. State, 250 Ga. 125, 126, 296 S.E.2d 551 (1982), overruled by Barnes v. State, 275 Ga. 499, 570 S.E.2d 277 (2002).

conviction should be probated." O.C.G.A. § 15-11-703 provides that a juvenile record may be considered in fixing the conditions of bail and in sentencing in felony cases.[22] Nevertheless, the trial court should exercise its sound discretion in determining whether to reveal the contents of such reports to counsel for the defendant and for the state. If a pre-sentence report contains any matter adverse to the defendant likely to influence the decision to suspend or probate the sentence, it should be revealed to defense counsel by the trial judge in advance of the pre-sentence hearing to give the accused an opportunity for explanation or rebuttal.[23] It should be emphasized that if a trial judge considers evidence which is improper, defense counsel must object at that time since failure to do so would normally amount to a waiver.[24] Likewise, where the court without objection asks a defendant what crimes he has served time for, and the defendant names certain crimes, he may not later object that no prior notice was given of these crimes.[25] Also, where a defendant is convicted and at request of defense counsel and the district attorney sentencing is delayed until the trial judge can get a pre-sentence report, and the report is obtained and used in sentencing without objection, this procedure may not later be attacked.[26]

If the defense has been given proper notice, any prior valid criminal conviction, guilty plea or plea of nolo contendere may be

---

[22]See Taylor v. State, 331 Ga. App. 577, 771 S.E.2d 224 (2015).

[23]Dorsey v. Willis, 242 Ga. 316, 318, 249 S.E.2d 28 (1978); Geyer v. State, 289 Ga. App. 492(2), 657 S.E.2d 878 (2008). Cf. Almon v. State, 151 Ga. App. 863, 865, 261 S.E.2d 772 (1979) (FBI rap sheet contained in presentence report); State v. Byrd, 163 W.Va. 248, 256 S.E.2d 323 (1979) (holding modified by State ex rel. Aaron v. King, 199 W. Va. 533, 485 S.E.2d 702 (1997)).

[24]Cf. Bradshaw v. State, 145 Ga. App. 664, 244 S.E.2d 600 (1978). In Gates v. State, 147 Ga. App. 126, 127 (5), 248 S.E.2d 194 (1978), the court affirmed a conviction where prior offenses were presented during sentencing to the trial judge without certification or prior notification to defendant. The trial court stated that the convictions would not be considered. In Wells v. State, 151 Ga. App. 416, 419, 260 S.E.2d 374 (1979), the court said that

it was improper for the trial judge to consider an unauthenticated copy of defendant's prior record, and where the trial does not indicate whether defendant was properly represented in prior criminal proceedings or was given adequate notice of convictions to be considered, his sentence must be vacated even if no objection was raised at trial. See Arnold v. State, 163 Ga. App. 10, 14 (5), 293 S.E.2d 501 (1982). In McDuffie v. Jones, 248 Ga. 544, 551, 283 S.E.2d 601 (1981), overruled on other grounds by West v. Waters, 272 Ga. 591, 533 S.E.2d 88 (2000), the court concluded that the failure of trial counsel to object to the trial judge's considering a probation report in aggravation does not alone constitute ineffective assistance of counsel.

[25]Black v. State, 146 Ga. App. 226, 246 S.E.2d 133 (1978).

[26]Gary v. State, 158 Ga. App. 327, 328 (2), 280 S.E.2d 378 (1981).

considered.[27] This provision means any such disposition of a criminal case *prior to the sentencing.* Thus, a conviction after the commission of the crime for which the defendant is being sentenced may be considered, and the date of the commission of the other crime does not control.[28] However, it is improper for the trial judge to consider pending untried indictments against the defendant when imposing sentence.[29] Also, it is improper for the trial judge to consider a conviction which is not final and which is on appeal.[30]

However, if a trial judge erroneously considers improperly admitted evidence and the defendant is to be re-sentenced, there is a presumption that the same judge in re-sentencing the defendant considered only admissible evidence, and the trial judge is not prevented from imposing the same sentence again.[31]

In *Brown v. State,*[32] the court pointed out that the defense frequently relies on argument rather than evidence at the sentencing stage, and the failure to present evidence does not automatically establish ineffective assistance of counsel.

§ 26:15   Fines[1]

In 1990, Georgia law was changed so as to provide that when a defendant is placed on probation for a felony, a fine may be imposed which "shall not exceed $100,000.00 or the amount of the maximum fine which may be imposed for conviction of such a felony, whichever is greater."[2] In *State v. Shepherd Construction*

---

[27]O.C.G.A. § 17-16-4(a)(5). See § 14:25, supra.

[28]Clark v. State, 146 Ga. App. 799, 800, 247 S.E.2d 489 (1978).

[29]Cottros v. State, 154 Ga. App. 243, 268 S.E.2d 355 (1980).

[30]Croker v. Smith, 225 Ga. 529 (4), 532 (4), 169 S.E.2d 787 (1969); Dunn v. State, 208 Ga. App. 197, 198 (4), 430 S.E.2d 50 (1993); Covington v. State, 226 Ga. App. 484, 485 (3), 486 S.E.2d 706 (1997).

[31]Richards v. State, 160 Ga. App. 489, 287 S.E.2d 394 (1981).

In United States v. Bunch, 730 F.2d 517 (7th Cir. 1984), the court held that a trial judge who reviewed a defendant's pre-sentence report and rejected a plea agreement was not required to recuse himself when there was no showing of actual prejudice.

[32]Brown v. State, 179 Ga. App. 538, 539 (2), 346 S.E.2d 908 (1986).

[Section 26:15]

[1]Generally, on equal protection and fines, see § 26:4, supra.

[2]O.C.G.A. § 17-10-8. In the case of compounding a crime which is a felony, O.C.G.A. § 16-10-90, the punishment is fixed as a fine of not more than $1,000 and/or imprisonment for not less than one nor more than five years. Certain "deceptive practices," including credit card theft, O.C.G.A. § 16-9-31; forgery of credit cards, O.C.G.A. § 16-9-32; and criminal receipt of goods and services fraudulently obtained, O.C.G.A. § 16-9-35, may be punished by a fine up to $5,000 under O.C.G.A. § 16-9-38(b). O.C.G.A. § 16-13-31 radically changes fines which may be imposed in drug cases. These fines go up to $1 million.

Co.,[3] the court concluded that a corporation could be fined in cases where an individual would be imprisoned. The statute expressly provides that the defendant is not entitled to a rebate or refund of any part of the fine paid in the event that probation is revoked.

In *McClure v. State,*[4] the court pointed out that "O.C.G.A. § 40-6-391(g) permits trial courts, but does not require them, to allow a defendant to pay a fine in installments in order to avoid economic hardship."

In *Taylor v. State,*[5] the court said, "The General Assembly has not seen fit to permit the imposition of both a fine and imprisonment as punishment for a felony, except in specified cases." Thus, in a felony case, where a defendant is sentenced to a term to serve and no part of the sentence is to be served on probation, the trial judge may not generally impose a fine.[6] In *Eason v. State,*[7] the court held that a defendant could be sentenced to a period of incarceration followed by a period of probation and a fine.

In *Hunt v. State,*[8] the court held that there does not have to be a presentation of evidence on the ability to pay before a fine is imposed unless the fine is imposed as a condition precedent of probation or probation is about to be revoked for a failure to pay a fine. However, a person may not be imprisoned for failure to pay a fine solely because he lacks resources to pay. See §§ 26:19 and 30:8, infra, on conditions and violation of probation.

In the case of a misdemeanor, a defendant may ordinarily be fined not more than $1,000 and/or sentenced to serve a total of not more than 12 months.[9] Some years ago Georgia provided by statute that a person convicted of a misdemeanor of a high and aggravated nature may be fined not over $5,000 and/or confined up to 12 months.[10]

In 1983, Georgia enacted a statute intended to provide for the funding of the training of law enforcement and prosecuting officials. O.C.G.A. §§ 15-21-70 et seq. These statutes provide that

---

[3]State v. Shepherd Construction Co., 248 Ga. 1, 281 S.E.2d 151 (1981). Cf. 19 C.J.S. Corporations § 736 (1990).

[4]McClure v. State, 218 Ga. App. 365, 366, 460 S.E.2d 884 (1995).

[5]Taylor v. State, 149 Ga. App. 362, 364 (3), 254 S.E.2d 432 (1979). Accord, Rawls v. State, 210 Ga. App. 408, 436 S.E.2d 527 (1993).

[6]Young v. State, 163 Ga. App. 507, 509 (4), 295 S.E.2d 175 (1982); Hendrix v. State, 199 Ga. App. 599,

601 (3), 405 S.E.2d 576 (1991).

[7]Eason v. State, 215 Ga. App. 614, 616 (5), 451 S.E.2d 820 (1994) rev'd on other grounds, Turner v. State, 259 Ga. App. 902(1), 578 S.E.2d 570 (2003).

[8]Hunt v. State, 222 Ga. App. 66, 70 (3), 473 S.E.2d 157 (1996).

[9]O.C.G.A. § 17-10-3(a).

[10]This provision in former GCA § 27-2506 was not carried forward into the O.C.G.A. However, see § 26:13, supra.

in all traffic and criminal cases when a fine is imposed "which shall be construed to include costs . . . there shall be imposed as an additional penalty a sum equal to the lesser of $50.00 or 10 percent of the original fine. . . . Such sums shall . . . be paid into the Peace Officers' Annuity and Benefit Fund."[11]

In *Huff v. McLarty,*[12] a majority of the Georgia Supreme Court concluded that where a defendant is sentenced to pay a fine and serve time on probation, the payment of the fine is not a condition precedent to serving the probated sentence but is rather a condition of probation.

Where the authorized fine for an offense is increased after the defendant commits that offense, but before he is sentenced for it, the defendant may not be fined in excess of the maximum authorized fine which existed at the time he committed the offense because the new punishment, if applied to the defendant, would operate as an ex post facto law.[13]

At least in a case where there is a provision for probation of all or a part of a sentence, a defendant may be required to pay not only the maximum fine authorized by law but also to pay court costs.[14] In *Ward v. State,*[15] the court held that the trial judge has inherent power "to issue a writ of execution for the purpose of collecting a fine from a criminal defendant." A judgment providing for a fine or restitution as a condition of probation is not dischargeable in bankruptcy.[16]

Georgia has statutory authority, in all felony and misdemeanor cases in which a fine may be imposed, which permits a judge to allow a person to satisfy the fine through community service at the minimum wage for each hour of such service. Before or after sentencing a defendant may request that a part or all of his fine may be satisfied in this manner.[17]

Generally, where payment of a fine is a condition of probation, see § 26:19, infra. See also § 26:4, supra, on equal protection. See § 26:16, infra, on payment of a fine including costs. On "excessive fines" and forfeitures, see sections 10:1 and 10:2, supra.

§ 26:16 Payment of costs

If a defendant is convicted, a judgment may be entered against

---

[11]Phillips v. State, 236 Ga. App. 744, 747 (2), 512 S.E.2d 32 (1999).

[12]Huff v. McLarty, 241 Ga. 442, 246 S.E.2d 302 (1978).

[13]Holley v. State, 157 Ga. App. 863, 867-868 (5), 278 S.E.2d 738 (1981).

[14]Giddens v. State, 156 Ga. App. 258, 260 (4), 274 S.E.2d 595 (1980).

[15]Ward v. State, 195 Ga. App. 166, 168 (4), 393 S.E.2d 21 (1990).

[16]Kelly v. Robinson, 479 U.S. 36, 107 S.Ct. 353, 93 L.Ed.2d 216 (1986).

[17]O.C.G.A. § 17-10-1(d). See also, O.C.G.A. § 42-3-52.

him for all costs accrued in the committing and trial court.[1] Such a judgment shall constitute a lien on all the property of the defendant from the time it is rendered.[2] However, the state must present evidence of the amount of the costs.[3] Witness fees are included in "costs."[4] However, costs do not include the costs of bailiffs and jurors,[5] nor the cost of operating, staffing, or constructing jails.[6] Likewise, the trial court is not authorized in assessing against a defendant expenses for airline tickets and hotel accommodations in connection with the appearance of witnesses for the state.[7]

In *Reid v. State*,[8] the court held that a trial judge may not require a defendant to perform community service to reimburse the county for an attorney's services performed through the public defender's office unless the trial judge conducts a hearing or otherwise determines to what extent the defendant was able to pay. The failure to object to such a sentence at the time of sentencing does not waive the defendant's right to later object.

In 1997, O.C.G.A. § 15-21-131 was enacted to provide:

"(a) In every case in which any court of this state or any municipality or political subdivision of this state shall impose a fine, which shall be construed to include costs, for any criminal offense or any criminal ordinance violation, there shall be imposed as an additional penalty a sum equal to 5 percent of the original fine.

"(b) Such sums shall be in addition to any amount required by O.C.G.A. § 47-17-60 to be paid into the Peace Officers' Annuity and Benefit Fund and in addition to any other amounts provided for in this chapter."

As a condition of probation, a defendant may be required to pay items of cost connected with a prosecution not generally regarded as a part of the costs of a case as long as there is no abuse of discretion.[9]

When the defendant is acquitted and it is properly determined that a prosecution was brought maliciously or the prosecution is abandoned before trial, the prosecutor becomes liable to pay

---

[Section 26:16]

[1]O.C.G.A. § 17-11-1.

[2]Brainard v. State, 246 Ga. 586, 587, 272 S.E.2d 683 (1980).

[3]Holloway v. State, 178 Ga. App. 141, 142 (3), 342 S.E.2d 363 (1986).

[4]Walden v. State, 185 Ga. App. 413 (1), 364 S.E.2d 304 (1987), rev'd in part, 258 Ga. 503, 371 S.E.2d 852 (1988).

[5]Walden v. State, 258 Ga. 503, 371 S.E.2d 852 (1988).

[6]Woods v. State, 204 Ga. App. 415, 417 (2), 419 S.E.2d 513 (1992).

[7]Smith v. State, 272 Ga. 83, 526 S.E.2d 59 (2000).

[8]Reid v. State, 224 Ga. App. 524, 481 S.E.2d 259 (1997).

[9]Giddens v. State, 156 Ga. App. 258, 260 (4), 274 S.E.2d 595 (1980).

costs.[10]

See § 26:21, infra, on causing a defendant to pay for attorneys' fees. See § 26:15, supra, on fines.

§ 26:17 Terms and conditions

In non-capital cases, at the conclusion of the pre-sentence hearing, it is the duty of the trial judge to fix a definite sentence within the limits fixed by the law for the particular offense[1] (1) subject to the court's right to probate or suspend all or a part of the sentence[2] and (2) subject to the right of the trial judge to provide that the defendant may be considered for parole prior to his completing the time normally required for consideration of parole eligibility.[3] It is mandatory for the trial judge "to impose the sentence provided for by the law in force at the time of the commission of the crime."[4]

O.C.G.A. § 16-4-6 provides that in the case of an attempt to commit a felony, the punishment is to be not less than one year nor more than half the maximum time to which the defendant could have been sentenced if he had been convicted of the crime attempted and/or fined up to half the maximum fine. If the felony attempted is punishable by death or life imprisonment, then the punishment shall be not less than one nor more than 30 years. A person convicted of an attempt to commit a misdemeanor shall be punished as for a misdemeanor.[5]

In the case of a person who is sentenced to probation, not to include a split sentence, on his or her first felony offense, the court is required, pursuant to O.C.G.A. § 17-10-1(a)(1)(B), to set a "behavioral incentive date," as part of its sentencing hearing that does not exceed three years from the date sentence is imposed.[6] Provided the person is in compliance with the general and special terms of his or her probation and that any restitution ordered has been paid by the designated date, the Department of Community Supervision is required to provide the court, within 60 days thereof, with an order terminating probation subject to objection by either the prosecutor or the court.[7]

---

[10]O.C.G.A. § 17-11-4.

[Section 26:17]

[1]O.C.G.A. § 17-10-2.

[2]O.C.G.A. § 17-10-1.

[3]O.C.G.A. § 17-10-1(b).

[4]Holtapp v. City of Fayetteville, 208 Ga. App. 606, 608 (3), 431 S.E.2d 403 (1993). Accord, Lloyd v. State, 226 Ga. App. 401, 403 (5), 487 S.E.2d 44

(1997).

[5]See Johnson v. State, 144 Ga. App. 568, 570 (3), 241 S.E.2d 458 (1978).

[6]See Mays v. State, 345 Ga. App. 562, 814 S.E.2d 418 (2018) (court is not required to impose a behavioral release date where defendant is sentenced as a first offender).

[7]O.C.G.A. § 42-8-37(c)(1) requires

In *Davis v. State*,[8] the court held that when a defendant is convicted of two or more misdemeanor offenses, the trial judge may require that the sentences be served one after the other even though the total time to be served exceeds 12 months.

O.C.G.A. § 16-13-33 provides that persons convicted of conspiracy or a criminal attempt to violate any provision of Title 16, Article 13, controlled substances, shall be exposed at sentencing to the maximum prison sentence prescribed for the offense which was the object of the attempt or conspiracy. Accordingly, the general punishment provision applicable to conspiracy and criminal attempt, O.C.G.A. § 16-4-3, is not applicable to cases involving controlled substances.[9] Thus, the punishment for attempted possession of marijuana is the same as that provided in O.C.G.A. § 16-13-30 for possession.[10] However, because O.C.G.A. § 16-13-33 makes no provision for the imposition of a fine, a court may not impose such in connection with a sentence under the statute.[11]

O.C.G.A. § 16-13-33 provides that the punishment for attempted possession of marijuana is the same as that provided in O.C.G.A. § 16-13-30 for possession.[12]

O.C.G.A. § 16-11-129(e) provides that if a person who has a weapons carry license is convicted of a crime or involved in any matter which would make the maintenance of that person's license unlawful, the Superior or State Court judge before whom such matter was pending "shall" notify the probate court which issued or most recently renewed the license accordingly. The probate court will then determine whether license revocation proceedings are in order.[13]

In *Head v. State*,[14] the defendant was indicted for the sale of methaqualone. Under the Controlled Substances Act, the offense is a felony. Under the Dangerous Drug Act, the same offense is a misdemeanor. The defendant had been indicted under the Controlled Substances Act, and the court concluded that the defendant could be sentenced for a felony. The court also pointed

---

that "the case of each person receiving a probated sentence of three years or more shall be reviewed by the officer responsible for such case after service of three years on probation" who will also provide the court with a progress report and a recommendation for early termination.

[8]Davis v. State, 213 Ga. App. 212, 214 (2), 444 S.E.2d 142 (1994).

[9]See Raftis v. State, 175 Ga. App. 893(7), 334 S.E.2d 857 (1985); Gonzalez v. State, 201 Ga. App. 437, 411 S.E.2d 345 (1991).

[10]Davis v. State, 164 Ga. App. 633, 635(6), 298 S.E.2d 615 (1982).

[11]Watson v. State, 276 Ga. 212, 576 S.E.2d 897 (2003).

[12]Davis v. State, 164 Ga. App. 633, 635(6), 298 S.E.2d 615 (1982).

[13]The statute requires the Councils of Superior and State Court Judges to provide by rule for the procedures courts should follow for these purposes.

[14]Head v. State, 160 Ga. App. 4(2), 285 S.E.2d 735 (1981).

out that this is not a situation in which two sections of a statute provide different penalties for the same offense. In that situation, the statute providing the lesser penalty prevails.[15]

In *Jackson v. State*,[16] the court considered the situation where the penalty for possession of cocaine with intent to distribute changed from a mandatory life sentence under a 1980 statute for a second conviction to a sentence of not less than 10 years nor more than 40 years or life under a 1996 statute. The defendant had been convicted before the more lenient statute became effective. After the new statute was enacted, the defendant filed a "motion to correct void sentence." The court in affirming the original sentence pointed out that "[l]aws prescribe only for the future; they cannot . . . ordinarily have a retrospective operation."

O.C.G.A. § 17-10-11(a) provides that when a defendant is sentenced, he must be given credit for time already served. This statute applies only to "each day spent in confinement." Thus, time spent particpating while not in custody in a drug court program during a period where sentencing is deferred is not credited against a sentence imposed after the defendant is sentenced because he or she failed to comply with the rules of the program.[17] In *Addo v. State*,[18] the court held that a judge may not sentence a defendant to a specific term and provide that the defendant is not to receive credit for the time he spent in jail awaiting trial. The computation of the amount of credit due for "time served" prior to conviction is performed by the defendant's presentence custodian and the Department of Corrections is required to apply the credit based upon that calculation. The remedy for an incorrect calculation and application of time served is by way of mandamus or injunction against the commissioner of the Department of Corrections.[19]

In *Johnson v. State*,[20] the court held that a judge in a misdemeanor case may sentence a defendant to serve weekends in jail until there is an opening at a diversion center. However, on such a sentence the defendant cannot be required to serve on weekends for more than 52 weeks. O.C.G.A. § 17-10-3.1 provides that, for first-time violations of O.C.G.A. § 40-6-391(k), the judge may allow the sentence to be served on weekends or nonworking hours of a defendant and served in the county jail segregated from all

---

[15]Aycock v. State, 146 Ga. App. 489, 495, 246 S.E.2d 489 (1978).

[16]Jackson v. State, 223 Ga. App. 471(2), 477 S.E.2d 893 (1996).

[17]Fleming v. State, 297 Ga. 606, 774 S.E.2d 594 (2015).

[18]Addo v. State, 212 Ga. App. 163 (1), 441 S.E.2d 486 (1994).

[19]Cochran v. State, 315 Ga. App. 488, 727 S.E.2d 125 (2012).

[20]Johnson v. State, 226 Ga. App. 503, 487 S.E.2d 90 (1997).

other offenders except those confined for the same violation. Persons who are convicted of a second DUI offense within a period of five years must serve a minimum sentence of 72 hours of "actual" incarceration pursuant to O.C.G.A. § 40-6-391(c)(2)(B). Thus, a sentence which substitutes a period of house arrest for the required incarceration is invalid.[21]

See § 26:29, infra, on consecutive and concurrent sentences. See § 26:28, infra, for recidivism punishment and punishment for the "seven deadly sins."

§ 26:18 Probation and suspended sentences—General

The word "probation" comes from a Latin word meaning "to prove yourself." This is much the meaning which probation is intended to have in our law.

In *Roberts v. United States*,[1] the United States Supreme Court stated that the primary purpose of probation is "[t]o provide an individualized program offering a young or unhardened offender an opportunity to rehabilitate himself without institutional confinement under the tutelage of a probation official and under the continuing power of the Court to impose institutional punishment for his original offense in the event that he abuse this opportunity." The Comprehensive Criminal Justice Reform Bill of 2016 acknowledged probation's utility as a tool to reduce recidivism rates. As part of that Bill, the General Assembly required the Department of Community Supervision to establish an "offender transition and reentry unit within DCS" tasked with reducing recidivism through better reentry services.[2]

Generally, under Georgia law, in its discretion, a court may suspend a defendant's sentence or place him on probation unless the offense is punishable by death or life imprisonment. O.C.G.A. § 17-10-1 generally provides that the judge imposing the sentence has the power and authority to suspend or probate a sentence under such rules and regulations that he deems proper. The judge also has the power to revoke or suspend probation when the defendant has violated any of the rules and regulations prescribed by the court. However, such actions by the judge shall be subject to O.C.G.A. § 17-10-6.1, which provides punishment for the serious violent offenses of (1) murder or felony murder, (2) armed robbery, (3) kidnapping, (4) rape, (5) aggravated child molestation, (6) aggravated sodomy, and (7) aggravated sexual battery.

---

[21]Pierce v. State, 278 Ga. App. 162, 628 S.E.2d 235 (2006).

[Section 26:18]

[1]Roberts v. United States, 320

U.S. 264, 272, 64 S.Ct. 113, 88 L.Ed. 41 (1943).

[2]O.C.G.A. § 42-3-5.

Any person convicted of armed robbery or the kidnapping of an individual 14 years of age or older is required to serve at least ten years in prison. Also, the sentence of any person convicted of (1) kidnapping involving a victim less than 14 years of age, (2) rape, (3) aggravated child molestation, (4) aggravated sodomy, or (5) aggravated sexual battery shall, "unless sentenced to life imprisonment, be a split sentence which shall include a mandatory minimum term of imprisonment of 25 years, followed by probation for life." Neither the sentencing judge nor the Board of Pardons and Paroles has discretion to reduce, suspend or otherwise disturb a mandatory minimum sentence issued under § 17-10-6.1.[3]

O.C.G.A. § 17-10-1.3 specifically authorizes a trial court to consider whether the general purposes of a probated sentence would be frustrated if the person to be sentenced is not legally present in the United States and thus subject to deportation. The statute authorizes the sentencing court to decline to probate or suspend any or all of a sentence in such a case "in furtherance of the state interest in certain and complete execution of sentences." O.C.G.A. § 42-9-43.1 is a parallel statute for similar cases being considered for parole by the Board of Pardons and Parole.

O.C.G.A. §§ 42-3-1 et seq., created the Board and the Department of Community Supervision. The Board "establish[es] the general policy to be followed by the Department of Community Supervision."[4] The Department of Community Supervision has supervisory duties and responsibilities for persons on probation or parole, and for probation of children adjudicated for Class A or B designated felony acts. Prior to the creation of the Department of Community Supervision, the Department of Corrections and Board of Juvenile Justice shared responsibility for these duties and responsibilities. The Department is also responsible for "[r]eviewing the uniform professional standards for private probation officers and uniform contract standards for private probation contracts."[5]

In *Fox v. State*,[6] the sentence was based upon what was told to the defendant by the judge and the district attorney, and not upon what was in the written sentence. The court found the defendant's waiver of his Fourth Amendment rights to be defective because the condition of probation was not discussed with the defendant during plea bargaining even though it was evident from the sentencing form.

---

[3]The complete text of O.C.G.A. § 17-10-6.1 is set out in § 26:28, infra.

[4]O.C.G.A. § 42-3-2.

[5]O.C.G.A. § 42-3-3.

[6]Fox v. State, 272 Ga. 163, 164 (1), 527 S.E.2d 847 (2000).

In *Grant v. State,*[7] the court pointed out that " 'probation and suspension statutes in Georgia vest broad discretion in trial judges. In the absence of express authority to the contrary, we see no logical reason why any reasonable condition imposed for probation or suspension of a sentence . . . should not be approved. . . . [Such] sentences . . . [are] effective tools of rehabilitation and serve a useful purpose in appropriate cases.' "However, in *State v. Barrett,*[8] the court held that a condition of probation must cease when the probated term ends.

The Georgia courts have failed to make any meaningful distinction between a "suspended sentence" and a "probated sentence."[9] Generally, the courts have held that any valid condition of probation may likewise be imposed as a condition of a suspended sentence.[10] However, in *Williams v. State,*[11] the court stated that the "only real distinction between a probated sentence and a suspended sentence is that a probated sentence is served under the supervision of the probation officers[,] . . . whereas a suspended sentence is served without such supervision."

O.C.G.A. § 42-8-35.2 provides that when a trial judge imposes a sentence of imprisonment after a conviction for a drug offense, the judge "shall impose a special term of probation of three years in addition to such term of imprisonment" and upon a second or subsequent such conviction, "the special term of probation shall be six years. . . ."

See § 30:1, infra, on Probation Management Act.

§ 26:19 Probation and suspended sentences—Terms and conditions

All cases may be probated except for the following types: serious violent felonies; "sexual offenses" as defined in O.C.G.A. § 17-10-6.2; some recidivist situations; and cases where the defendant

---

[7]Grant v. State, 176 Ga. App. 460 (1), 336 S.E.2d 354 (1985) (quoting Davis v. State, 172 Ga. App. 787 (6), 324 S.E.2d 767 (1984)).

[8]State v. Barrett, 215 Ga. App. 401, 402, 451 S.E.2d 82 (1994) (abrogated on other grounds by, State v. Outen, 289 Ga. 579, 714 S.E.2d 581 (2011)).

[9]Cross v. State, 128 Ga. App. 774 (1), 197 S.E.2d 853 (1973). However, see O.C.G.A. § 42-8-39.

In Jones v. State, 154 Ga. App. 581, 583, 269 S.E.2d 77 (1980), the court cited O.C.G.A. § 42-8-39 and indicated that a defendant could not receive both a probated sentence and a suspended sentence.

[10]See O'Quinn v. State, 121 Ga. App. 231, 232 (3), 173 S.E.2d 409 (1970), ordering defendant to pay victim's medical expenses as a condition of a suspended sentence. Also see Falkenhainer v. State, 122 Ga. App. 478, 479, 177 S.E.2d 380 (1970).

[11]Williams v. State, 191 Ga. App. 217 (1), 381 S.E.2d 399 (1989) (cited, quoted and relied on in Harp v. State, 228 Ga. App. 473, 475, 491 S.E.2d 923 (1997)).

is sentenced to death or life imprisonment. However, the "active supervision" of a defendant shall terminate after a period of two years from the date of actual commencement in all cases other than those where there remains an outstanding obligation of restitution and those involving charges of street gang violence,[1] "unless specially extended or reinstated by the sentencing court upon notice and hearing and for good cause shown; provided, however, in those cases involving the collection of restitution, the period of active probation supervision shall remain in effect for so long as any such obligation is outstanding, or until termination of the sentence, whichever first occurs. . . ."[2] One other exception to the general rules of supervised probation is in those cases involving a conviction under the "Georgia Street Gang and Terrorism and Prevention Act" which requires that supervised probation remain in effect until the termination of the sentence but not to exceed five years.[3] In *Brady v. State*,[4] the court points out that O.C.G.A. § 42-8-35.4 "authorizes confinement to a probation detention center as a condition of probation for: (1) those convicted of felonies and sentenced to a period of not less than one year on probation; and (2) those who were previously sentenced to probation or probation alternatives for either forcible misdemeanors or misdemeanors of a high and aggravated nature, who have violated probation, and who subsequently are sentenced to a period of not less than one year on probation."[5]

It is the duty of the trial court to set the terms of a defendant's

---

[Section 26:19]

[1]O.C.G.A. § 17-10-1. See § 26:28, infra, for text of the statute governing serious violent felonies (O.C.G.A. § 17-10-6.1). In 2017, this Code section was amended to delete from the categories of cases in which actual supervision terminates after two years those cases in which the defendant had not paid in full any required fines.

[2]O.C.G.A. § 17-10-1(a)(2).

In Ledford v. State, 189 Ga. App. 148, 375 S.E.2d 280 (1988), the defendant was sentenced to 20 years' supervised probation on condition that he pay restitution for counseling for the victim, pay a $1,000 fine, plus $50 to PO & P Training Fund, pay for attending "mental health," that he not reside with a child under 17, and that he not be alone with victims. The court concluded that the conditions of probation invoke the exception to the 4-year rule of supervised probation.

[3]O.C.G.A. § 17-10-1(a)(2).

[4]Brady v. State, 246 Ga. App. 412, 413, 541 S.E.2d 396 (2000). *Brady* was decided before the general sentencing statute applicable to misdemeanors, O.C.G.A. § 17-10-3, was amended. In Anderson v. State, 260 Ga. App. 606(1), 580 S.E.2d 249 (2003), the Court of Appeals construed O.C.G.A. § 17-10-3 and O.C.G.A. § 42-8-35.4 so as to provide that misdemeanors can only be punished by confinement in a probation detention center or diversion center if the defendant's conduct fits the categories of offenses set out in O.C.G.A. § 42-8-35.4. See e.g., Anderson v. State, 261 Ga. App. 716, 583 S.E.2d 549 (2003).

[5]A defendant sentenced to multiple consecutive probated twelve month sentences cannot upon revocation be confined in a probation detention center unless the misdemeanor offenses are forcible or of a high and

probation.[6] The court may not delegate this responsibility to another.[7] However, regardless of the other conditions of probation, it is the duty of the defendant to keep his probation officer informed as to his residence, and the court may also provide that the defendant must keep the probation officer "informed as to his or her whereabouts."[8] Some suggested terms of probation are set out in O.C.G.A. § 42-8-104, which includes such terms and conditions as limitations on where the probationer may reside; restitution; payment of support for dependents; drug and alcohol evaluation; and waiver of extradition.

Further, O.C.G.A. § 35-3-160 provides that any person placed on probation who was convicted of a felony offense must provide the G.B.I. with a DNA sample.

Other conditions not set out in the statute may also be fixed by the court. However, the power of the judge is not unlimited.[9] The conditions must be definite,[10] reasonable,[11] and designed to assist the probationer in leading a law-abiding life. They should be related to his rehabilitation[12] and not unduly restrictive of his liberty or personal expression.[13] Thus, a condition of probation which prohibited the probationer from working in a business that

---

aggravated nature. Wilson v. Windsor, 280 Ga. 576, 630 S.E.2d 367 (2006).

[6]O.C.G.A. § 42-8-34. See O.C.G.A. § 17-10-1.

[7]Simmons v. State, 96 Ga. App. 718, 101 S.E.2d 111 (1957).

[8]O.C.G.A. § 42-8-36.

[9]Clackler v. State, 130 Ga. App. 738, 739(2), 204 S.E.2d 472 (1974). See Annots., "Persons or Entities Entitled to Restitution as 'Victim' Under State Criminal Restitution Statute," 92 A.L.R.5th 35 (2001); "Validity of Requireent That as Condition of Probation, Indigent Defendant Reimburse Defense Costs," 79 A.L.R.3d 1025 (1977); 59 Am. Jur. 2d Pardon and Parole § 97, Propriety of Particular Conditions (2004); "Propriety of Conditioning Probation upon Defendant's Posting of Bond Guranteeing Compliance with Terms of Probation," 79 A.L.R.3d 1068 (1977); "Validity of Requirement That, as Condition of Probation, Defendant Submit to Warrantless Searches," 79 A.L.R.3d 1083 (1977).

In states where there is a valid state statute providing for payment of counsel fees incurred in the defense of an indigent, the court may order payment of such fees as a condition of probation. Fuller v. Oregon, 417 U.S. 40, 94 S. Ct. 2116, 40 L. Ed. 2d 642 (1974); Basaldua v. State, 558 S.W.2d 2 (Tex. Crim. App. 1977).

[10]Ellis v. State, 221 Ga. App. 103 (1), 470 S.E.2d 495 (1996). In Clackler v. State, 130 Ga. App. 738, 739, 204 S.E.2d 472 (1974), the court said that conditions of probation should not be so vague or ambiguous as to give no real guidance. See Grovenstein v. State, 282 Ga. App. 109(1), 637 S.E.2d 821 (2006), condition of probation which prohibited 18 year old defendant from "uniting with any family unit" in which children under the age of 14 resided was vague and overbroad.

[11]Guest v. State, 87 Ga. App. 184, 73 S.E.2d 218 (1952).

[12]Generally, see Annot., "Propriety, as Condition of Probation Granted Pursuant to 18 U.S.C.A. § 3651 of Requiring That Probationer Refrain From Consumption of Alcoholic Beverages," 37 A.L.R.Fed. 843 (1978).

[13]Inman v. State, 124 Ga. App.

provides care or services to children under the age of 18 was considered overbroad and void in the case of a pair of defendants convicted of statutory rape.[14] However the law does not permit imposition of a condition which would result in the probationer being placed in danger.[15] After an accused has been given a suspended sentence, if a condition is added without notice to the defendant, the condition is invalid.[16]

The following conditions have been upheld by the Georgia courts as valid: (1) good behavior;[17] (2) prohibition against further violation of any law;[18] (3) restitution to injured party;[19] (4) child support in a fornication case;[20] (5) prohibition against practicing law;[21] (6) prohibition against driving a motor vehicle;[22] (7) suspension of a driver's license;[23] (8) suspension of hunting and fishing privileges;[24] (9) prohibition against indulging in any unlawful, disrespectful, or disorderly conduct or habits;[25] (10) compliance

190, 194, 183 S.E.2d 413 (1971). See Annot., "Propriety of Conditioning Probation on Defendant's Remaining Childless or Having No Additional Children During Probationary Period," 94 A.L.R.3d 1218 (1976). In Rodriguez v. State, 378 So.2d 7 (Fla.App.1979), in a child abuse case the court held that the trial judge could bar her from having custody of any children but could not bar her from getting married or becoming pregnant.

[14]Harrell v. State, 253 Ga. App. 440, 559 S.E.2d 155 (2002).

[15]Williams v. State, 234 Ga. App. 37, 39, 505 S.E.2d 816 (1998).

[16]Hinton v. State, 127 Ga. App. 853, 854, 195 S.E.2d 472 (1973).

[17]Poss v. State, 114 Ga. App. 609, 611, 152 S.E.2d 695 (1966).

[18]Jackson v. State, 91 Ga. App. 291, 293 (2), 85 S.E.2d 444 (1954).

[19]Marshall v. State, 127 Ga. App. 805 (3), 195 S.E.2d 469 (1972); Henry v. State, 77 Ga. App. 735, 738, 49 S.E.2d 681 (1948). However, restitution may not be imposed as a condition of probation if the amount is in dispute, unless there has been an adjudication of the amount, Bennett v. State, 141 Ga. App. 795, 797 (2), 234 S.E.2d 327 (1977); where the amount is agreed to by the defendant, Biddy v. State, 138 Ga. App. 4, 8 (4), 225 S.E.2d

448 (1976); or where the amount is not in dispute, O.C.G.A. § 42-8-35(a)(7). Also, even though the maximum fine which may be imposed as a condition to probation is $10,000 (O.C.G.A. § 17-10-8), this will not prevent a provision for restitution exceeding $2,000 if otherwise justified. See Biddy v. State, 138 Ga. App. 4, 7 (4), 225 S.E.2d 448 (1976).

Generally, see Annot., "Ability to Pay as Necessary Consideration in Conditioning Probation or Suspended Sentence Upon Reparation or Restitution," 73 A.L.R.3d 1240 (1976).

[20]Swanson v. State, 38 Ga. App. 386, 144 S.E. 49 (1928).

[21]Yarbrough v. State, 119 Ga. App. 46, 47 (2), 166 S.E.2d 35 (1969).

[22]Jones v. State, 27 Ga. App. 631, 110 S.E. 33 (1921).

[23]Falkenhainer v. State, 122 Ga. App. 478, 177 S.E.2d 380 (1970) (dicta). In Brock v. State, 165 Ga. App. 150, 299 S.E.2d 71 (1983), the court held that in a traffic related offense, the trial judge may order probation conditioned on the defendant's surrender of his driver's license for one year.

[24]Quintrell v. State, 231 Ga. App. 268, 271 (2), 499 S.E.2d 117 (1998) (physical precedent).

[25]Rowland v. State, 124 Ga. App.

with an order in a defendant's divorce proceeding;[26] and (11) banishment from several counties within the state for a certain period of time.[27] (12) In *Hardman v. Hardman*,[28] the court found valid a condition which provided that the defendant have no unsupervised contact with females under the age of 14 and a condition requiring that a defendant's visitation with his granddaughter be approved by the Department of Family and Children Services. However, in *Tyler v. State*,[29] with no mention of *Hardman*, the Georgia Court of Appeals ruled that a condition of probation which prohibited defendant from having any contact with a person under the age of 18, was too vague to be applied in a manner consistent with reasonable sentencing objections. (13) A provision preventing the defendant from possessing "sexually

---

494, 495 (2), 184 S.E.2d 494 (1971).

[26]Murray v. State, 135 Ga. App. 344 (1), 217 S.E.2d 448 (1975).

[27]See Thompson v. Eubanks, 557 Fed. Appx. 855 (11th Cir. 2014); State v. Collett, 232 Ga. 668, 671, 208 S.E.2d 472 (1974). Cf. Wilson v. State, 151 Ga. App. 501, 504 (8), 260 S.E.2d 527 (1979); Parrish v. State, 182 Ga. App. 247, 248 (2), 355 S.E.2d 682 (1987); Kerr v. State, 193 Ga. App. 165, 169 (6), 387 S.E.2d 355 (1989). In Sanchez v. State, 234 Ga. App. 809 (1), 508 S.E.2d 185 (1998), the court held that a court may banish a probationer from certain areas of the state, but such a condition must be related logically to the rehabilitative purposes of the sentence and a trial judge may not as a condition of probation order that a defendant be deported from the country.

On April 27, 2006, O.C.G.A. § 42-8-35(a)(6) was amended to provide that a probationer shall not be banished to any area of the state "(A) that does not consist of at least one entire judicial circuit as described by Code Section 15-6-1; or (B) in which any service or program in which the probationer must participate as a condition of probation is not available."

See Regent v. State, 333 Ga. App. 350, 774 S.E.2d 213 (2015), judgment rev'd on other grounds, 299 Ga. 172, 787 S.E.2d 217 (2016) (banishment to only one of several counties within a judicial circuit is not permitted).

See State v. Morgan, 389 So.2d 364 (La.1980). In Parkerson v. State, 156 Ga. App. 440, 274 S.E.2d 799 (1980), the court held that the trial judge had no right to banish both the defendant *and his wife* from the judicial circuit for the term of the probated sentence.

See Annot., "Propriety of Conditioning Probation on Defendant's Not Entering Specified Geographical Area," 28 A.L.R.4th 725 (1984) and see 54 A.L.R.5th 743 (1997) on the same subject.

In Wyche v. State, 197 Ga. App. 148, 397 S.E.2d 738 (1990), one condition of probation was that upon his release he was to immediately leave five designated counties "and not to return into said area at any time." The court pointed out that banishment existed only during defendant's probation and was valid.

In Whitehead v. State, 207 Ga. App. 891, 892 (2), 429 S.E.2d 536 (1993), the court held valid the banishment from the Southern Judicial Circuit for 20 years which was the period of his time to serve plus the probationary time to follow.

[28]Hardman v. Hardman, 185 Ga. App. 519, 521 (5), 364 S.E.2d 645 (1988), overruled on other grounds by Pender v. Witcher, 196 Ga. App. 856, 397 S.E.2d 193 (1990).

[29]Tyler v. State, 279 Ga. App. 809(4), 632 S.E.2d 716 (2006).

explicit" material has been held valid.[30] Also, (14) it has been said that a probationer may be required to take periodic lie detector tests, including polygraph, psychological stress evaluation and/or psychometric tests,[31] or (15) be required to wear "a fluorescent pink plastic bracelet imprinted with the words 'D.U.I. CONVICT.' "[32] (16) Also, a prohibition against consumption of alcohol is proper.[33] (17) In *Cox v. State*,[34] the court impliedly approved as a condition of probation the requirement of having the defendant remain in a specified drug treatment program. (18) In *Toth v. State*,[35] the court affirmed an order requiring the defendant to attend Narcotics Anonymous meetings twice a week. (19) In *Hardman v. Hardman*,[36] the court found valid a condition that the defendant "continue to take any medication prescribed for him." (20) Moreover, a condition has been held valid which provided that a defendant on request from a probation officer or law enforcement officer must submit to a warrantless search.[37] In *Smith v. State*,[38] the court approved a condition of probation which required a probationer upon request by any probation supervisor or officer to "produce a breath, spittle, urine, and/or blood specimen for analysis for . . . the presence" of a controlled substance. In *Allen v. State*,[39] the court approved as a condition for probation a provision that the "defendant shall waive all Fourth Amendment rights and submit to random searches of his

[30]Ellis v. State, 221 Ga. App. 103, 105 (3), 470 S.E.2d 495 (1996).

[31]Mann v. State, 154 Ga. App. 677, 269 S.E.2d 863 (1980). See Annot., "Propriety of Conditioning Probation on Defendant's Submission to Polygraph or Other Lie Detector Testing," 86 A.L.R.4th 709 (1991).

[32]Ballenger v. State, 210 Ga. App. 627, 628 (1), 436 S.E.2d 793 (1993).

[33]Mock v. State, 156 Ga. App. 763, 275 S.E.2d 393 (1980); Ellis v. State, 221 Ga. App. 103, 105 (4), 470 S.E.2d 495 (1996).

[34]Cox v. State, 159 Ga. App. 488, 283 S.E.2d 716 (1981). This case actually holds that where such a condition of probation is imposed the trial judge may revoke probation if the defendant fails to obey the rules of a drug treatment establishment and he is, therefore, dismissed from the program.

[35]Toth v. State, 213 Ga. App. 247, 252 (9), 444 S.E.2d 159 (1994).

[36]Hardman v. Hardman, 185 Ga. App. 519, 521 (5), 364 S.E.2d 645 (1988), overruled on other grounds by Pender v. Witcher, 196 Ga. App. 856, 397 S.E.2d 193 (1990).

[37]Luke v. State, 178 Ga. App. 614, 616 (2), 344 S.E.2d 452 (1986). See Brooks v. State, 292 Ga. App. 445, 664 S.E.2d 827 (2008), judgment aff'd, 285 Ga. 424, 677 S.E.2d 68 (2009).

[38]Smith v. State, 250 Ga. 438, 298 S.E.2d 482 (1983); Green v. State, 260 Ga. 625, 627 (2), 398 S.E.2d 360 (1990) (urine).

[39]Allen v. State, 258 Ga. 424, 369 S.E.2d 909 (1988). See Griffin v. Wisconsin, 483 U.S. 868(II)(A), 107 S. Ct. 3164, 97 L. E. 2d 709 (1987); Jones v. State, 282 Ga. 784 (1), 653 S.E.2d 456 (2007), warrantless search of probationer's home must be grounded upon state law, sentencing order or lawful regulation and not the whim of probation officer. See also Brooks v. State, 285 Ga. 424, 677 S.E.2d 68 (2009).

residence, automobile or any other building in which the defendant is located by law enforcement officers without notice and without probable cause." (But see § 4:31, supra, on waiver of Fourth Amendment.) (21) In a case in which the defendant had harassed his mother and shot his brother, the court found that it was proper to require the defendant to stay away from his mother and brother during the term of his probation.[40] (22) A probation condition was upheld requiring a defendant to pay $3,032.30 for expenses in a marijuana case not considered taxable costs of prosecution. The $3,032.30 was composed of $1,080 juror cost, $132 witness fees, $150 court reporter, $108 bailiff fees, $1,484.30 sheriff's cost for guarding field, harvesting and preserving the evidence, and $78 transcript of evidence.[41] (23) The Georgia Attorney General has ruled that a probationer may be required as a condition of probation to pay a reasonable fee for probation supervision. This fee may apparently be paid into the state treasury or retained by the probation department.[42] (24) In a felony case, if a defendant who is found guilty but mentally ill at the time of a felony is placed on probation under O.C.G.A. §§ 42-8-20 et seq., the "State-wide Probation Act," the court may require that the defendant undergo available outpatient medical or psychiatric treatment or seek similar available voluntary inpatient treatment as a condition of probation. Persons required to receive such services may be charged fees by the provider of the services.[43] (25) The trial judge may require a defendant, as a condition of probation, to perform from 20 to 250 hours of community service (to be completed within one year) for a traffic ordinance or a misdemeanor offense and from 20 to 500 hours of community service (to be completed within three years) in a felony case.[44] (26) A curfew from "10:00 p.m. to 6:00 a.m." has been found a valid condition of probation.[45] (27) Likewise, a provision for "house arrest" is valid.[46] (28) The 1984 enactment of O.C.G.A. § 17-10-1 enables a trial judge sentencing a minor who has not achieved a high school diploma or the equivalent to require a course of study leading to such diploma or equivalent as a condition of probation or suspension of sentence. (29) In *Mangiapane v. State*,[47] the court upheld a condition of probation requiring the defendant to "complete [the] written requirements for Boy Scout merit badges

---

[40]West v. State, 160 Ga. App. 855, 856 (4), 287 S.E.2d 694 (1982).

[41]Giddens v. State, 156 Ga. App. 258, 274 S.E.2d 595 (1980).

[42]Ga. Atty. Gen. 81-100.

[43]O.C.G.A. § 17-7-131(h).

[44]O.C.G.A. § 42-3-52(b).

[45]Johnson v. State, 162 Ga. App. 226, 291 S.E.2d 94 (1982) (implication).

[46]Pitts v. State, 231 Ga. App. 9, 498 S.E.2d 534 (1998). Also see § 26:22, infra.

[47]Mangiapane v. State, 178 Ga. App. 836 (1), 344 S.E.2d 756 (1986).

on the subjects of traffic safety, law, and citizenship in the community." (30) In *Morrison v. State*,[48] the court held that it was not error for a trial judge to order restitution of a specified amount to be paid "jointly and severally" by the defendants as a condition of probation. (31) O.C.G.A. § 42-8-72 provides that community service may be imposed as a condition of probation, and a defendant may be ordered "to perform community service hours in a 40-hour per week work detail in lieu of incarceration." (32) In *Germany v. State*,[49] the court found that a special condition of probation which required that a sex offender submit to lie detector examinations did not violate the probationer's Fifth Amendment rights in the absence of a properly asserted right to privilege against self-incrimination. (33) In *Loya v. State*,[50] the court approved, as a special condition of probation, a requirement that a defendant convicted of indecent exposure be registered as a sex offender.

O.C.G.A. § 42-8-35(a)(6)(A) and (B) permit a court to "banish" or require, as a condition of probation, that a defendant remain in a specific area of the state, provided it consists of at least one judicial circuit or one in which a service or program in which the probationer must participate as a condition of probation is not available. An overriding consideration to a condition of probation which includes banishment is that of reasonableness. The banishment condition must "bear a logical relationship to the rehabilitative scheme of the sentence pronounced."[51]

O.C.G.A. § 42-1-19 provides that a sex offender who has completed all prison, parole and probation for which registration as a sex offender is required may seek release from the registration requirements of O.C.G.A. § 42-1-12 if it appears that the petitioner is confined in a hospice or nursing home; is permanently disabled; or is seriously incapacitated. O.C.G.A. § 42-1-19(a)(4) also authorizes a convicted sex offender who has completed the service of his sentence to petition for release from required registration provided the petitioner can show that: 10 years has elapsed since the offender has completed his sentence; that the victim did not suffer any intentional physical harm during the commission of the offense; that the offender has no prior convictions for sexual offenses; that the offense at issue did not involve the use of a firearm; that the court can find no evidence

---

[48]Morrison v. State, 181 Ga. App. 440, 352 S.E.2d 622 (1987).

[49]Germany v. State, 315 Ga. App. 717, 727 S.E.2d 240 (2012) (court based its decision on Minnesota v. Murphy, 465 U.S. 420, 104 S. Ct. 1136, 79 L. Ed. 2d 409 (1984)).

[50]Loya v. State, 321 Ga. App. 430, 740 S.E.2d 382 (2013).

[51]Terry v. Hamrick, 284 Ga. 24, 26-27(3), 663 S.E.2d 256 (2008). See Mallory v. State, 335 Ga. App. 852, 783 S.E.2d 370 (2016).

of a similar transaction; the offense did not involve the transportation of the victim; and, the victim was not physically harmed during the commission of the offense.[52]

In 1980, Georgia enacted former Georgia Code Annotated, section 27-3001 et seq. (now O.C.G.A. §§ 17-14-1 et seq.),[53] in which it was declared to be the policy of the state that restitution is a primary concern of the criminal justice system. In 2005, the Georgia Legislature expanded the policy to include the juvenile justice system.[54] This chapter provides for a much more comprehensive law governing restitution and should be studied and followed in situations where this announced policy of the state may be carried out. See § 26:21, infra, on restitution.

Pursuant to O.C.G.A. § 42-8-102(d), in misdemeanor cases the court is authorized to "convert fines, statutory surcharges, and probation supervision fees to community service on the same basis as it allows a defendant to pay a fine through community service as set forth in subsection (d) of Code section 17-10-1." The court may also waive such fees and charges in the event the court finds that they pose "a significant financial hardship."[55] A sentencing court has similar authority in felony cases pursuant to O.C.G.A. § 42-8-34(e).

Pursuant to O.C.G.A. § 17-12-51, a court may order as a condition of probation that the defendant pay all or a portion of the cost of legal services provided by a municipality, a county or the state.

It is not a valid condition of probation to require a defendant to keep his hair cut[56] or to "maintain a correct life."[57] Likewise, as a condition of probation a trial judge may not require a defendant to live at home, since this is regarded as requiring the defendant's parents to continue to provide a home for the defendant.[58]

In *Kaiser v. State*,[59] the Georgia Court of Appeals held that a condition of probation which permanently prohibited the defendant from practicing medicine was void since it exceed the term of the defendant's sentence.

---

[52]See State v. Randle, 298 Ga. 375, 781 S.E.2d 781 (2016) ("intentional physical harm" does not include offensive contact, such as an unwanted touching of another, unless there is also physical pain or injury).

[53]O.C.G.A. §§ 17-14-1 et seq.

[54]O.C.G.A. § 17-14-1.

[55]O.C.G.A. § 42-8-102(e).

[56]Inman v. State, 124 Ga. App. 190, 183 S.E.2d 413 (1971).

[57]Morgan v. Foster, 208 Ga. 630, 68 S.E.2d 583 (1952). This was regarded as too indefinite.

[58]Ward v. State, 248 Ga. 60, 63, 281 S.E.2d 503 (1981).

[59]Kaiser v. State, 275 Ga. App. 684(2), 621 S.E.2d 802 (2005).

In the theft by taking case of *Darby v. State*,[60] the appellate court affirmed, as a condition of probation, the requirement to pay child support of $200 per month directly to his ex-wife.

In *State v. Oakley*,[61] the defendant had been convicted of failing to pay child support. The Wisconsin Supreme Court held valid a condition of probation which prevented the defendant from having any more children without demonstrating that he can support them and that he is supporting the children he already has. However, in the Indiana case of *Trammell v. State*,[62] the defendant was convicted of neglect of her child. One of the conditions of her probation was that she should not become pregnant. In disapproving of this condition, the court pointed out that it had no rehabilitative purpose and did nothing to improve her parenting skills.

In the California case of *People v. Josh W.*,[63] the court held that a juvenile court could order probation of an offender conditioned on his naming the others involved in the crime.

The total period of probation and confinement (if any) may not exceed the maximum time provided as punishment for the crime. Hence, a sentence in a misdemeanor case to 30 days in jail as a condition precedent to 12 months probation is invalid.[64]

In *Pitts v. State*,[65] the court held that "incarceration" and "probation" are mutually exclusive concepts. Thus, a "probated" sentence which is conditioned on the defendant's "continuous and uninterrupted *incarceration*" in a named county correctional institution is not valid. However, a probated sentence may require "confinement for intermittent periods, such as weekends, or confinement in a facility other than a jail or penitentiary . . . ."[66] In *Jones v. State*,[67] the court invalidated a sentence to serve six years on probation with a special condition that defendants spend time in a probation boot camp and remain incarcerated until there was room for them in the boot camp. However, in *Gosier v. State*,[68] the court affirmed a ruling that the defendant be held in jail until space became available in the detention center though

---

[60]Darby v. State, 230 Ga. App. 32 (1), 495 S.E.2d 146 (1997).

[61]State v. Oakley, 245 Wis.2d 447, 629 N.W.2d 200 (2001).

[62]Trammell v. State, 751 N.E.2d 283 (Ind.App.2001).

[63]People v. Josh W., 55 Cal.App. 4th 1, 63 Cal.Rptr.2d 701 (1997), citing and relying on People v. Lent, 15 Cal.3d 481, 124 Cal.Rptr. 905, 541 P.2d 545 (1975).

[64]Sherman v. State, 142 Ga. App.

691, 692, 237 S.E.2d 5 (1977).

[65]Pitts v. State, 206 Ga. App. 635, 637, 426 S.E.2d 257 (1992). Accord, Radford v. State, 223 Ga. App. 312, 313 (1), 477 S.E.2d 428 (1996).

[66]Yother v. State, 243 Ga. App. 422, 423, 532 S.E.2d 696 (2000).

[67]Jones v. State, 224 Ga. App. 340, 341 (1), 480 S.E.2d 618 (1997).

[68]Gosier v. State, 249 Ga. App. 379, 380, 548 S.E.2d 107 (2001).

this provision was included in the conditions of probation. The appellate court held that this difference was sufficient to distinguish *Jones*.

If a condition of probation is believed to be illegal, the appropriate remedy is for the defendant to apply for a modification under O.C.G.A. § 42-8-34. A petition for habeas corpus is not an appropriate remedy.[69]

If a defendant violates any of the conditions imposed on a suspended sentence[70] or a probated sentence,[71] the trial judge may revoke or modify the defendant's probation.[72] If a defendant is fined as a condition precedent to probation, the probation does not become operative until the fine is paid.[73] Where a defendant is orally fined, sentenced to probation, and then pays his fine, the judge may not thereafter change the "oral" sentence so as to revoke his probation where the accused has not violated its terms.[74]

While there are numerous decisions stating that a trial court may not change a sentence by increasing the punishment, since no individual shall be put in jeopardy more than once for the same offense, the trial judge may, during the same term at which the sentence was rendered, reduce the confinement portion of the sentence and place the defendant on probation.[75] However, an orally stated sentence of probation which was never reduced to

---

[69]Dean v. Whalen, 234 Ga. 182, 183, 215 S.E.2d 7 (1975).

However, in Owens v. Kelley, unpublished Civil Action No. 78-72 ALB (D. C. M. D. Ga. 1980), the court held that an action could be brought under 42 U.S.C.A. § 1983 for declaratory and injunctive relief where the terms of probation are unconstitutional.

[70]Cross v. State, 128 Ga. App. 774 (1), 197 S.E.2d 853 (1973). In *Cross* the court said that "if a suspended sentence cannot be revoked, it has no existence or meaning in the first instance."

[71]O.C.G.A. § 42-8-38.

[72]O.C.G.A. § 42-8-38. However, due process requires a preliminary and a final revocation hearing before revocation of probation can take place. If the probationer would have difficulty presenting any defense he has to the revocation, he is entitled to counsel. If a request for counsel is refused, the grounds of the refusal must be set out in the record. Gagnon v. Scarpelli, 411 U.S. 778, 93 S.Ct. 1756, 36 L.Ed.2d 656 (1973). In Foskey v. Sapp, 237 Ga. 788, 229 S.E.2d 635 (1976), the court, under the facts of that case, declined to reverse a probation revocation where the defendant requested and was denied counsel. However, there were two concurring and two dissenting opinions and *Gagnon v. Scarpelli* was considered. Generally, on probation revocation, see Chapter 30, infra.

[73]Calhoun v. Couch, 232 Ga. 467, 207 S.E.2d 455 (1974); Barnett v. Hopper, 234 Ga. 694, 217 S.E.2d 280 (1975). But see § 26:4, supra, on equal protection and indigents.

[74]Inman v. State, 124 Ga. App. 190, 183 S.E.2d 413 (1971).

[75]Tyson v. State, 301 Ga. App. 295, 687 S.E.2d 284 (2009); King v. State, 290 Ga. App. 118, 658 S.E.2d 883 (2008).

writing is said to be without effect.[76] In *Garland v. State*,[77] the trial judge announced a 20 year sentence for burglary. Ten years were to be served and ten years served on probation, conditioned on banishment from the circuit. The defendant replied that he was coming back if his mother were sick or needed him. The judge then changed the sentence to 20 years to serve. The action of the trial judge was affirmed.

Pursuant to O.C.G.A. § 42-8-34(g), the court is "empowered to revoke any or all of the probated sentence . . . including order-ing the probationer into the sentencing options system, as provided in Article 6 of Chapter 3 of this title, at any time during the period of time prescribed for the probated sentence to run."

O.C.G.A. § 42-8-37(c) requires probation officers to review the case of each person receiving a probated sentence in excess of three years and, after service of three years on probation, to provide the sentencing court with a written report and recom-mendation as to whether early termination is warranted. Such cases thereafter are to be reviewed annually until the case is terminated or otherwise closed. Similarly, for defendants serving consecutive misdemeanor sentences, the probation officer must review the defendant's case after 12 months of probation and every four months thereafter to determine whether early termina-tion is warranted.[78]

See § 26:22, infra, on alternatives to institutional incarceration. See § 30:1, infra, on Probation Management Act. See sections 30:1 and 30:6 et seq., infra, on revocation of probation.

§ 26:20   Probation—"Special alternative incarceration— Probation boot camp"

In 1991, Georgia enacted O.C.G.A. § 42-8-35.1, providing for a "special alternative incarceration—probation boot camp" for certain probationers. Under this statute a healthy probationer from 17 to not more than 30 years of age who is sentenced to not less than one year on probation may be required to complete a program of confinement in a "special alternative incarceration— probation boot camp" unit of the Department of Corrections for a period of 120 days from the time of initial confinement in the unit.

In *Johnson v. State*,[1] the Georgia Supreme Court held that while a trial judge under certain circumstances may order

---

[76]Sherman v. State, 142 Ga. App. 691, 692, 237 S.E.2d 5 (1977).

[77]Garland v. State, 160 Ga. App. 97, 99 (4), 286 S.E.2d 330 (1981).

[78]O.C.G.A. § 42-8-103.1.

[Section 26:20]

[1]Johnson v. State, 267 Ga. 77, 475 S.E.2d 595 (1996).

confinement in "a probation boot camp for a misdemeanor probationer whose sentence is revoked, this . . . does not confer authority under O.C.G.A. § 42-8-35.1 to order that an original misdemeanor probation be served in boot camp."

An unsatisfactory report from the department is a ground for revocation of the probated sentence as any other violation of a term of probation. Upon receipt of a satisfactory report, "the trial court shall release the individual from confinement in the . . . unit."

§ 26:21 Restitution

According to O.C.G.A. § 17-14-1, "[i]t is hereby declared to be the policy of this state that restitution to their victims by those found guilty of crimes or adjudicated as having committed delinquent acts is a primary concern of the criminal justice system and the juvenile justice system." Over 100 years ago Justice Bleckley wrote, "Restitution before absolution is as sound in law as in theology."[1] The Bible provides that a thief is to make restitution.[2] The amount of restitution ordered "may be equal to or less than, but not more than, the victim's damages."[3] "Damages" in the context of restitution means "all special damages which a victim could recover against an offender in a civil action . . . based on the same act . . . for which the offender is sentenced."[4]

Pursuant to O.C.G.A. § 17-14-3, a judge of any court of competent jurisdiction is required to order the offender, adult or juvenile, to make full restitution to any victim.[5] If the offender is placed on probation, including probation imposed pursuant to Chapter 11 of Title 15 or Article 3 of Chapter 8 of Title 42, or if the sentence is suspended, deferred, or withheld, restitution under Chapter 14 of Title 17 shall be a condition of that probation, sentence, or order.[6] Similarly, the Department of Juvenile Justice, Department of Corrections, and the State Board of Pardons and Paroles shall condition any relief[7] ordered upon the offender making restitution.[8] The sentencing court retains jurisdiction to modify an order of restitution at any time before the

---

[Section 26:21]

[1]Summerall v. Graham, 62 Ga. 729, 731 (1879).

[2]Exodus 22:3.

[3]In re E.W., 290 Ga. App. 95, 97, 658 S.E.2d 854 (2008) (citations and punctuation omitted).

[4]O.C.G.A. § 17-14-2(2).

[5]O.C.G.A. § 17-14-3(a).

[6]O.C.G.A. § 17-14-3(b).

[7]"Relief" means any parole or other conditional release from incarceration; the awarding of earned time allowances' reduction in security status; or placement in prison rehabilitation programs, including, but not limited to, those in which the offender receives monetary compensation.

[8]O.C.G.A. § 17-14-3(c).

expiration of the sentence pursuant to O.C.G.A. § 17-14-12.

For purposes of ensuring compliance with a restitution order, the juvenile courts are authorized to retain jurisdiction over a juvenile subject to such restitution order until the juvenile reaches 21 years of age, at which point the uncompleted restitution order is to be transferred to the superior court.[9] Moreover, if the court determines that a juvenile is unable to comply with a restitution order, after notice to the juvenile's parents and an opportunity for the parents to be heard, the court may order the parents to pay any portion that is outstanding. Such an order may only be entered where the court or a jury finds by clear and convincing evidence that the parents knew or should have known of the juvenile's propensity to commit such acts and the acts are due to the parents' negligence or reckless disregard for the juvenile's propensity to commit such acts. Upon the eighteenth birthday of the juvenile, the parental obligation to pay restitution is terminated.[10]

In *Rider v. State*,[11] the defendant and Smith were tried for aggravated assault. The trial judge directed a verdict for the defendant on aggravated assault. The defendant was convicted of assault. Smith was convicted as charged. The only injury to the victim was from a gunshot wound inflicted by Smith. The appellate court reversed the order requiring the defendant to pay restitution, pointing out that the defendant cannot be held responsible for damages arising out of an act for which he was acquitted.

As provided by O.C.G.A. § 17-14-7, the offender himself may offer the ordering authority a restitution plan. In deciding whether to accept the voluntary plan, the ordering authority considers the factors stated in O.C.G.A. § 17-14-10. If acceptable, the plan is included in the restitution order.

In 2005, the Georgia Legislature amended § 17-14-7 to require a hearing where the parties cannot agree on the proper amount of restitution. The burden of demonstrating the amount of loss suffered by the victim is on the state, with the offender required to demonstrate his or her available financial resources. The ordering authority will resolve the dispute on the preponderance of the evidence, and may apportion payment among the offenders "to reflect the level of contribution to the victim's loss and economic

---

[9]O.C.G.A. § 17-14-5(c). In addition, pursuant to O.C.G.A. § 15-11-607(b) a juvenile probation order may be extended upon notice and hearing for up to two years from the expiration date of the prior order upon the court's finding of good cause.

[10]O.C.G.A. § 17-14-5(e).

[11]Rider v. State, 210 Ga. App. 802, 803 (2), 437 S.E.2d 493 (1993).

circumstances of each offender."[12] In *Gibson v. State*,[13] the court held that a separate hearing conducted in order to determine the proper amount of restitution in those cases where that amount is contested is a "critical stage of proceedings" at which the defendant is entitled to counsel.

The statutory scheme of O.C.G.A. § 17-14-8, O.C.G.A. § 17-14-9 and O.C.G.A. § 17-14-10 "contemplate *a hearing* and specific written findings by the court in determining whether it will order restitution and, if so, the amount thereof."[14] In *Garrett v. State*,[15] the court remanded the case "for preparation of written finding of fact related to the factors in O.C.G.A. § 17-14-10." In *Patterson v. State*,[16] the court held that "evidence adduced during the guilt-innocence phase of the trial" will not satisfy the statutory requirements. A sentence imposing restitution in the absence of such a hearing, wherein the factors set out in O.C.G.A. § 17-14-10 are considered by the trial court, cannot withstand appellate scrutiny.

The provisions of O.C.G.A. §§ 17-14-1 et seq. regarding restitution should not be interpreted to authorize "peonage."[17] The offender shall not surrender any privilege, benefit, or relief which he should otherwise receive solely because he is not "and cannot become financially able to make restitution."[18]

There is no longer any requirement that the court make specific written findings before ordering restitution.[19] However, as set forth in O.C.G.A. § 17-14-10,[20] various factors are considered in determining the amount and nature of the restitution:

"(1) The financial resources and other assets of the offender or person ordered to pay restitution including whether any of the assets are jointly controlled;

---

[12]O.C.G.A. § 17-14-7. Prior to the amendment, written findings of fact supporting the award of restitution were required. That requirement was eliminated with the amendment. McCart v. State, 289 Ga. App. 830 (1), 658 S.E.2d 465 (2008).

[13]Gibson v. State, 319 Ga. App. 627, 737 S.E.2d 728 (2013).

[14]Steele v. State, 270 Ga. App. 488 (1), 606 S.E.2d 664 (2004). Patterson v. State, 161 Ga. App. 85, 86, 289 S.E.2d 270 (1982) (citing Cannon v. State, 246 Ga. 754, 756, 272 S.E.2d 709 (1980)); Williams v. State, 180 Ga. App. 854 (3)(b), 350 S.E.2d 837 (1986); Taylor v. State, 182 Ga. App. 494, 496 (4), 356 S.E.2d 216 (1987); Bridges v. State, 208 Ga. App. 555, 556 (1), 431

S.E.2d 164 (1993); Radford v. State, 223 Ga. App. 312, 313 (2), 477 S.E.2d 428 (1996).

[15]Garrett v. State, 175 Ga. App. 400, 403, 333 S.E.2d 432 (1985); Gould v. State, 190 Ga. App. 611, 381 S.E.2d 442 (1989).

[16]Patterson v. State, 161 Ga. App. 85, 86 (5), 289 S.E.2d 270 (1982); Jarrett v. State, 161 Ga. App. 285, 287 (4), 287 S.E.2d 746 (1982).

[17]O.C.G.A. § 17-14-15(a).

[18]O.C.G.A. § 17-14-15(b).

[19]O.C.G.A. § 17-14-8, as amended April 11, 2005.

[20]O.C.G.A. § 17-14-10, as amended April 11, 2005.

"(2) The earnings and other income of the offender or person ordered to pay restitution;

"(3) Any financial obligations of the offender or person ordered to pay restitution, including obligations to dependents;

"(4) The amount of damages;[21]

"(5) The goal of restitution to the victim and the goal of rehabilitation of the offender;

"(6) Any restitution previously made;

"(7) The period of time during which the restitution order will be in effect; and

"(8) Other factors which the ordering authority deems to be appropriate.

In *Summer v. State*,[22] the Court of Appeals ruled that a sentence which required the defendant to pay restitution while incarcerated was void. Restitution "may not be joined with a prison term."[23]

Moreover, if, subsequent to restitution being ordered pursuant to this article, a victim is convicted of a crime for which restitution is ordered, the ordering authority shall consider the previously ordered restitution as part of the financial resources of such victim.[24]

In *Dukes v. State*,[25] the court held that it "is not sufficient for the trial judge to consider only the amount of the victim's damages." In addition, the court is required to consider the financial circumstances of the defendant, including the defendant's future earning capacity.

In *Zebley v. State*,[26] the court held that factors set out in O.C.G.A. § 17-14-10 "should be considered in cases where restitution has been imposed pursuant to the entry of a *non*-negotiated guilty plea." (Emphasis in original.)

In *Fonseca v. State*,[27] the court held that a defendant does not waive his right to challenge a restitution order on appeal by failing to object to the order, where the order was entered and the trial court did not consider the factors set out in O.C.G.A. § 17-

---

[21]In LaPann v. State, 167 Ga. App. 288, 292 (7), 306 S.E.2d 373 (1983), the court held that as a condition of probation the defendant could be required to repay the salary paid him by the county while he was suspended from office.

[22]Sumner v. State, 284 Ga. App. 308(1), 643 S.E.2d 831 (2007).

[23]Queen v. State, 210 Ga. App. 588, 589, 436 S.E.2d 714 (1993).

[24]O.C.G.A. § 17-14-10(b), as amended April 11, 2005.

[25]Dukes v. State, 213 Ga. App. 701, 446 S.E.2d 190 (1994), judgment aff'd in part, rev'd in part, 265 Ga. 422, 457 S.E.2d 556 (1995).

[26]Zebley v. State, 234 Ga. App. 18, 19, 505 S.E.2d 562 (1998).

[27]Fonseca v. State, 212 Ga. App. 463, 464 (2), 441 S.E.2d 912 (1994).

14-10 or hold a revocation hearing. However, in *Cheeks v. State*,[28] a 5 to 4 decision of the Georgia Court of Appeals, the court held that the defendant waives the right to present evidence on the issue of her ability to pay restitution when she had the opportunity but failed to do so. The court further stated that the defendant is not entitled to a second restitution hearing when the trial court clearly considered the factors enumerated in O.C.G.A. § 17-14-10.

In the absence of a waiver by the defendant, a hearing and written findings supporting an order of restitution are required. Failure to conduct the hearing and make the findings renders the order of restitution deficient.[29]

In *Dorsey v. State*,[30] the court held that there can be more than one proximate cause of an injury causing damages for which restitution may be ordered. The same case also held that the fact that the tort statute of limitations for the injury had run will not prevent restitution from being ordered.

It has been held that restitution may be awarded only to the victim of the crime.[31] If a victim has received partial or total restitution from the offender, O.C.G.A. § 17-14-6(a) requires the ordering authority to set off any such amounts and reduce the amount payable to the victim.[32] In 2005, four additional subsections were added to § 17-14-6:

"(b) The ordering authority shall not order restitution to be paid to a victim or victim's estate if the victim or victim's estate has received or is to receive full compensation for that loss from the offender or as a result of a civil proceeding.

"(c) Any amount paid to a victim or victim's estate under a restitution order shall reduce the amount payable to a victim or a victim's estate by an award from the Georgia Crime Victims Compensation Board made prior to or after a restitution order under this article.

"(d) The ordering authority shall order restitution be [sic] paid to the Georgia Crime Victims Compensation Board, other

---

[28]Cheeks v. State, 218 Ga. App. 212, 213, 460 S.E.2d 860 (1995).

[29]Wiggins v. State, 272 Ga. App. 414, 612 S.E.2d 598 (2005), judgment aff'd in part, rev'd in part on other grounds, 280 Ga. 268, 626 S.E.2d 118 (2006); Nobles v. State, 253 Ga. App. 814, 560 S.E.2d 724 (2002).

[30]Dorsey v. State, 206 Ga. App. 709, 715 (8), 426 S.E.2d 224 (1992).

[31]Pruitt v. State, 230 Ga. App. 334, 335(4), 496 S.E.2d 324 (1998). Note, however, that the Georgia Legislature in 2005 amended the definition of "victim" to include the victim's estate if the victim is deceased. See O.C.G.A. § 17-14-2, as amended April 11, 2005. Note also that, in United States v. Gamma Tech Industries, Inc., 265 F.3d 917 (9th Cir. 2001), the court held that in a federal case a district court could order restitution to be paid to one who had not been named as the victim.

[32]O.C.G.A. § 17-14-6(a), as amended April 11, 2005.

governmental entities, or to any individuals, partnerships, corporations, associations, or other legal entities acting on behalf of a government entity that have compensated the victim or the victim's estate for a loss incurred by the victim to the extent of the compensation paid for that loss. The ordering authority shall also order restitution for the costs of services provided to persons or entities that have provided services to the victim as a result of the crime. Services that are subject to restitution under this subsection include, but are not limited to, shelter, food, clothing, and transportation. However, a restitution order shall require that all restitution to a victim or a victim's estate under the restitution order be made before any restitution to any other person or entity under that restitution order is made.

"(e) In the event the ordering authority provides for a setoff or priority in terms of payment of restitution, the ordering authority shall state on the record with specificity the reasons for its actions."

The amount of restitution ordered shall not exceed the victim's damages.[33] In addition, the state or the victim may, within four years of the date of the crime, institute an action against an offender pursuant to O.C.G.A. § 17-14-17 to set aside a transfer of real, personal, or other property made by the offender on or after the date of the crime committed by the offender.[34] Such a transfer must have been made by the offender with the intent to conceal the crime or fruits of the crime; hinder, delay, or defraud the victim; or to avoid payment of restitution.[35] However, where only the improvements to real property, such as a house or a building, are damaged, the proper amount of restitution is the cost of repair rather than the diminution to the value of the property as a whole.[36]

In *Cardwell v. State*,[37] the court held that "[f]air market value is the measure of such damages and it must be determined

---

[33]O.C.G.A. § 17-14-9, as amended April 11, 2005. See O.C.G.A. § 17-14-2(2), as amended April 11, 2005, which amends the definition of "damages" to mean "special" damages not to be limited by any law which may cap economic damages and to include costs of transportation to and from court proceedings. Cf. Bottoms v. State, 194 Ga. App. 862(2), 392 S.E.2d 59 (1990); Lomax v. State, 200 Ga. App. 233, 234, 407 S.E.2d 462 (1991). See also Vaughn v. State, 324 Ga. App. 289, 750 S.E.2d 375 (2013) (restitution limited to

amount victim could recover in civil action and cannot include amounts which would be subject to the statute of limitations bar).

[34]The Uniform Voidable Transactions Act is set out in O.C.G.A. §§ 18-2-70 et seq.

[35]O.C.G.A. § 17-14-17.

[36]Overby v. State, 315 Ga. App. 735, 728 S.E.2d 278 (2012).

[37]Cardwell v. State, 225 Ga. App. 337, 338, 484 S.E.2d 38 (1997).

exactly." In *Jackson v. State*,[38] the court emphasized that replacement cost is not fair market value. However, where restitution is to be paid over a period of time, the judge may require the defendant to also pay an amount for interest.[39] Also, if an owner has been deprived of the use of certain property, the defendant may be required to pay the rental value or hire of the property.[40]

In *Buchanan v. State*,[41] the defendant was charged with conversion of homeowner's payments for real property improvements involving the building of six houses. The restitution order provided for expenses and legal fees to be paid homeowner victims and to the subcontractors not named in the indictment. In affirming the ordered restitution, the court pointed out that in a civil action the homeowners could recover for the defendant's failing to pay subcontractors.

An order for restitution does not bar the assertion of a civil action against the offender. However, the offender is entitled to a set off for payments made to the victim pursuant to an order for restitution where the civil action is "based on the same facts for which restitution was ordered." In *Crozier v. State*,[42] the court affirmed the trial judge in requiring the defendant to pay restitution so as to cover all medical expenses incurred by the victim even if the victim has filed bankruptcy as to some or all of the medical bills. A restitution order or the fact of restitution shall not be submitted to a jury on the issue of liability.[43]

O.C.G.A. § 17-14-13 covers the enforcement of restitution orders. Should an offender wilfully not comply with the restitution order, upon application of the victim or the district attorney, the restitution order "in the discretion of the court, may be enforced by attachment for contempt." Also, the offender's failure to comply with an order for restitution "may, in the discretion of the ordering authority, be grounds to revoke or cancel the relief at any time the restitution order is in effect. Where the relief is earned time allowances, the Department of Corrections may suspend the offender from earning earned time allowances for a specified period of time." An order for restitution is enforceable "as is a civil judgment by execution as provided in O.C.G.A. § 17-

---

[38]Jackson v. State, 250 Ga. App. 617, 552 S.E.2d 546 (2001).

[39]Patrick v. State, 184 Ga. App. 260, 261 (1), 361 S.E.2d 251 (1987); Corbin v. State, 202 Ga. App. 464, 415 S.E.2d 14 (1992).

[40]Hodges v. State, 201 Ga. App. 729, 731, 411 S.E.2d 775 (1991).

[41]Buchanan v. State, 248 Ga. App. 489, 490, 546 S.E.2d 869 (2001).

[42]Crozier v. State, 233 Ga. App. 831, 832 (2), 506 S.E.2d 139 (1998). See Elsasser v. State, 313 Ga. App. 661, 722 S.E.2d 327 (2011) (trial court is not required to apportion amount of restitution where there may be others responsible for victim's damages).

[43]O.C.G.A. § 17-14-11.

10-20."[44]

In 2005, the Georgia Legislature added new O.C.G.A. § 17-10-20, which provides that, where a fine or restitution is imposed as part of the sentence, such fine and restitution shall constitute a judgment against the defendant. Upon the request of the prosecuting attorney, the clerk of the sentencing court is required to issue a write of fieri facias thereon and enter it on the general execution docket. If the fine or restitution is not paid in full, such judgment may be enforced by instituting any procedure for execution upon the writ of fieri facias through levy, foreclosure, garnishment, etc.

In the absence of a showing that the parties have "agreed on the amount of restitution prior to sentencing," a hearing to determine restitution is required.[45] It has been held that where the state accepts the victim's valuation of damages at face value, and fails to show that valuation to be "fair and reasonable," the trial court must inquire into and adjudicate the amount of the victim's damages or obtain from the defendant an acceptance of the state's valuation before the defendant can be ordered to pay restitution.[46] Nevertheless, the trial judge may defer "the initial decision on the amount of restitution until a later hearing."[47] The general rules of evidence apply in determining the amount of loss or damage suffered by the victim.[48] In *Gaskin v. State*,[49] the court held that the amount of restitution must be based on fair market value, which must be determined exactly, and not on replacement cost. In determining the sufficiency of the evidence used to determine the amount of restitution, the civil standard of preponderance of the evidence applies.[50]

In *Jones v. State*,[51] the court held that "[v]oluntary payments by friends and family of the defendant . . . are not appropriate considerations" for the trial court in determining the amount of

---

[44]O.C.G.A. § 17-14-13, as amended April 11, 2005.

[45]McCart v. State, 289 Ga. App. 830, 832(1), 658 S.E.2d 465 (2008) (written findings of fact no longer required in restitution orders issued after July 1, 2005). See Parker v. State, 320 Ga. App. 319, 741 S.E.2d 159 (2013) (decisions that required defendant to dispute the amount of restitution before a hearing is required were superseded by changes to the statute).

[46]Johnson v. State, 157 Ga. App. 155, 156 (2), 276 S.E.2d 667 (1981); Little v. State, 165 Ga. App. 441, 301 S.E.2d 660 (1983).

[47]Zebley v. State, 234 Ga. App. 18, 19 (2), 505 S.E.2d 562 (1998).

[48]See In the Interest of J. C., 163 Ga. App. 822 (3), 296 S.E.2d 117 (1982).

[49]Gaskin v. State, 221 Ga. App. 142, 145 (3)(b), 470 S.E.2d 531 (1996).

[50]Evans v. State, 204 Ga. App. 458, 419 S.E.2d 532 (1992); Barnes v. State, 239 Ga. App. 495, 500 (2), 521 S.E.2d 425 (1999).

[51]Jones v. State, 246 Ga. App. 857, 860 (2), 542 S.E.2d 584 (2000).

restitution. In *Denny v. State*,[52] the court held that where restitution is not a condition precedent to probation, no hearing on the defendant's ability to pay is required.

Prior to the enactment of the Georgia Indigent Defense Act of 2003, restitution could include attorney fees paid by a county on account of an indigent defendant.[53] Although that statutory authority was repealed with the 2003 law, the Georgia Supreme Court has since ruled that ordering the restitution of attorney fees continues to be a reasonable condition of probation in the absence of an express legislative prohibition to the contrary.[54]

In *Woods v. State*,[55] the court held that a defendant could not be required under the statutory definition of "restitution" to reimburse the county for medical treatment rendered to the defendant, while he was being held in jail, for injuries occurring prior to his arrest, since the payments were not to go to the victim. Nevertheless, the court concluded that it was not error for the trial judge to require such payments as a condition of the defendant's probation. However, in cases where an insurance carrier has paid for crime related losses, the defendant may be ordered to pay restitution to the insurer.[56]

In *Martin v. State*,[57] the court held that two defendants could be jointly and severally liable for the restitution of costs.

A restitution obligation imposed as a condition of probation is not dischargeable in bankruptcy. In *Pennsylvania Department of Public Welfare v. Davenport*,[58] the United States Supreme Court held that restitution payments ordered in a criminal sentencing may be discharged under Chapter 13 of the Bankruptcy Code but the result is not the same in a Chapter 7 proceeding.

In *People v. Peters*,[59] the Supreme Court of Michigan held that fines which are penal in nature are abated upon the death of the defendant. Restitution, however, is not discharged because its purpose is to compensate the victim.

After the defendant begins to serve his sentence, the trial judge has no authority to increase the amount of restitution which had

---

[52]Denny v. State, 226 Ga. App. 432, 436 (14), 486 S.E.2d 417 (1997).

[53]Fowler v. State, 184 Ga. App. 177, 360 S.E.2d 918 (1987). See former O.C.G.A. § 17-12-10(c).

[54]State v. Pless, 282 Ga. 58, 646 S.E.2d 202 (2007).

[55]Woods v. State, 204 Ga. App. 415, 416, 419 S.E.2d 513 (1992).

[56]In the Interest of C. B., 221 Ga. App. 102, 103 (2), 470 S.E.2d 493

(1996).

[57]Martin v. State, 189 Ga. App. 483, 494 (9), 376 S.E.2d 888 (1988).

[58]Pennsylvania Department of Welfare v. Davenport, 495 U.S. 552, 110 S.Ct. 2126, 109 L.Ed.2d 588 (1990).

[59]People v. Peters, 449 Mich. 515, 537 N.W.2d 160 (1995). See U.S. v. Dudley, 739 F.2d 175 (4th Cir. 1984).

been ordered.[60] In *McKerley v. State*,[61] the court pointed out that "if the information necessary to determine an appropriate amount for restitution is not available, the proper procedure is to indicate that restitution will be awarded, and defer the hearing on restitution until that information is available. . . ."

If restitution payments are paid into the probation office and the intended recipient cannot be located, the money should be retained for a seven year period. At the end of that time, the State Revenue Commissioner should be notified and the money transferred to the Commissioner.[62]

Previously, if restitution payments were paid into the probation office and the intended recipient could not be located, the money was to be retained for a seven year period, at the end of which the money was to be transferred to the State Revenue Commissioner. After July 1, 2005, however, where funds are not claimed within two years after the date on which the recipient could have claimed such restitution, the unclaimed funds are to be deposited in the Crime Victims Emergency Fund. However, a person or entity entitled to such restitution may claim such at any time within five years of the date on which he or she could have claimed such restitution by applying in writing to the Georgia Crime Victims Compensation Board.[63] Pursuant to O.C.G.A. § 48-7-161, the Department of Juvenile Justice is now considered a "claimant agency" for purposes of setoff debt collection.[64]

See § 26:19, supra, on terms and conditions of probation. See § 26:15, supra, on imposition of fines. On payment of costs, see § 26:16, supra.

§ 26:22 Alternatives to institutional incarceration

Georgia has a special statute, O.C.G.A. § 42-1-4, which provides for a work-release program for county prisoners. O.C.G.A. § 42-1-9 details a work-release, educational and habilitative program for prisoners. Moreover, O.C.G.A. § 42-1-8 provides for a home arrest program under certain conditions.

In *McKinney v. State*,[1] the court held valid a condition of probation that provided "limited confinement in a detention or diversion center or in the defendant's own home." However, "[s]uch limited confinement does not constitute incarceration, which

---

[60]Harris v. State, 261 Ga. 859, 861 (2), 413 S.E.2d 439 (1992).

[61]McKerley v. State, 214 Ga. App. 529, 530 (1), 448 S.E.2d 85 (1994).

[62]Ga. Atty. Gen. U87-17.

[63]O.C.G.A. § 17-14-18, as amended April 11, 2005.

[64]O.C.G.A. § 48-7-161, as amended July 1, 2015.

[Section 26:22]

[1]McKinney v. State, 240 Ga. App. 812, 814 (2), 525 S.E.2d 395 (1999).

'refers to continuous and uninterrupted custody in a jail or penitentiary.' " In *Pierce v. State*,[2] the Court of Appeals found the trial court to have committed reversible error by sentencing defendant to house arrest in lieu of the mandatory 72 hours incarceration required by O.C.G.A. § 40-6-391(c)(2)(B) for a second DUI conviction within a five year period.

See Annotation, "Effect of Delay in Taking Defendant Into Custody After Conviction and Sentence," 76 A.L.R.5th 485 (2000).

§ 26:23 Youthful offenders

In 1971, Georgia enacted a Youthful Offender Act which is now found in O.C.G.A. §§ 42-7-1 et seq. This act may be available to defendants who are at least 17 but less than 25 years of age at the time of conviction. Such offenders "shall undergo treatment in secure institutions, including training schools, hospitals, farms, and forestry and other camps and including vocational training facilities and other institutions. . . .[1] To the extent possible, such institutions and facilities shall be used only for treatment of youthful offenders who have the potential and desire for rehabilitation."[2]

O.C.G.A. § 42-7-8 provides that the trial judge may *recommend* in his sentence that such a person be given youthful offender treatment. This is an indeterminate sentence and the Department of Corrections determines whether to accept the recommendation of the trial judge.

In *Lazenby v. State*,[3] the court held that a sentence under the provisions of the Youthful Offender Act does not exonerate the defendant and it is to be used in sentencing under O.C.G.A. § 17-10-7(b), the general Georgia recidivist statute.

Apart from the Youthful Offender Act, in case of any person under the age of 17 who "is convicted of a felony and sentenced as an adult to life imprisonment or to a certain term of imprisonment, such person shall be committed to the Department of Juvenile Justice to serve such sentence in a detention center of such department until such person is 17 years of age at which time such person shall be transferred to the Department of Corrections to serve the remainder of the sentence."[4] However, O.C.G.A. §§ 17-10-14 and 49-4A-9 authorize a trial court to reevaluate a juvenile defendant's sentence as his or her 17th birthday ap-

---

[2]Pierce v. State, 278 Ga. App. 162, 166, 628 S.E.2d 235 (2006).

[Section 26:23]

[1]O.C.G.A. § 42-7-3(a).

[2]O.C.G.A. § 42-7-3(c).

[3]Lazenby v. State, 221 Ga. App. 148, 150 (3), 470 S.E.2d 526 (1996).

[4]O.C.G.A. § 17-10-14(a). Cf. Allen v. Ricketts, 236 Ga. 294, 295-296, 223 S.E.2d 633 (1976).

proaches and consider whether such child should be placed on probation, have his or her sentence reduced, or be transferred to the Department of Corrections for the remainder of the original sentence.[5]

In a case where a person is under the age of 21 and is convicted of driving under the influence, the judge may, if this is a case involving the first such violation of O.C.G.A. § 40-6-391(k), permit the sentence to be served on weekends or during non-working hours of the defendant.[6]

Following a dispositional hearing, the court may, in addition to any other treatment or rehabilitation, suspend or prohibit the issuance of a juvenile's driver's license for any period of time not to exceed the date on which the child becomes 18 years of age.[7] If a child is adjudicated for the commission of a delinquent act in cases involving "[a]n offense that would be a felony if committed by an adult; or . . . [a]n offense that would be a misdemeanor if committed by an adult and such child has had at least one prior adjudication for an offense that would be a felony if committed by an adult and at least three other prior adjudications for a delinquent act as defined in subparagraph (A) of paragraph (19) of Code section 15-11-2," the court may order that the child "serve up to a maximum of 30 days in a secure residential facility or, after a risk assessment and with the court's approval, in a treatment program provided by [the Department of Juvenile Justice] or the juvenile court."[8] A child ordered to a secured residential facility shall be given credit for time served while detained in a secure residential facility or nonsecure residential facility pending placement in such a secured residential facility.[9]

§ 26:24   First offender treatment

Defendants who have never been convicted of a felony may, under certain circumstances, be sentenced as a first offender under O.C.G.A. § 42-8-60.[1] Upon completion of their probation or confinement and parole, defendants sentenced as first offenders are exonerated of guilt and stand discharged as a matter of law.[2] Subject only to the state sexual offender registry and O.C.G.A. § 42-8-63.1:

First offender exoneration shall completely exonerate the defendant

---

[5]State v. T. M. H., 339 Ga. App. 628, 794 S.E.2d 201 (2016). See State v. Hudson, 303 Ga. 348, 812 S.E.2d 270 (2018) (discretion given to sentencing court by O.C.G.A. § 49-4A-9(e) is limited by mandatory sentencing requirements of O.C.G.A. § 17-10-6.1).

[6]O.C.G.A. § 17-10-3.1.

[7]O.C.G.A. § 15-11-601(a)(9).

[8]O.C.G.A. § 15-11-601(b).

[9]O.C.G.A. § 15-11-601(c).

[Section 26:24]

[1]O.C.G.A. § 42-8-60(a).

[2]O.C.G.A. § 42-8-60(e).

of any criminal purpose and shall not affect any of his or her civil rights or liberties, and the defendant shall not be considered to have a criminal conviction.[3]

However, the court may still enter an adjudication of guilt if the defendant violates the terms of first offender probation, is convicted of another crime during the period of first offender probation, or the court determines that the defendant was not eligible for first offender sentencing.[4]

A defendant is sentenced as a first offender "upon a guilty verdict or plea of guilty or nolo contendere and before the adjudication of guilt, without entering a judgment of guilt and with the consent of the defendant."[5] Pursuant to O.C.G.A. § 42-8-60(j), a first offender sentence is not allowed for persons convicted of serious violent felonies as defined in O.C.G.A. § 17-10-6.1; certain sexual criminal offenses as defined in O.C.G.A. §§ 17-10-6.2, 16-12-100, 16-12-100.1 and 16-12-100.2; trafficking in persons as prohibited by O.C.G.A. § 16-5-46; certain crimes against disabled adults, elder persons, or residents as prohibited by O.C.G.A. § 16-5-101 and O.C.G.A. § 16-5-102; obstruction and assault charges against a law enforcement officer; or driving under the influence as prohibited by § 40-6-391.[6] In addition to those restrictions, the court must also review the defendant's criminal record before sentencing the defendant as a first offender.[7]

Ultimately, the trial judge may use his sound discretion in determining whether or not to impose first offender punishment on an eligible defendant.[8] Nonetheless, when first offender status is requested, "[the] [r]efusal to consider first offender treatment

---

[3]O.C.G.A. § 42-8-60(i).

[4]O.C.G.A. § 42-8-60(d). In Wilford v. State, 278 Ga. 718, 606 S.E.2d 252 (2004), the court held that the constitutional prohibition against double jeopardy is not offended where a defendant's first offender sentence is revoked after the trial court discovers that the defendant was not eligible to be sentenced as a first offender and proceeds to impose a harsher sentence. The Georgia First Offender Act specifically contemplates the resentencing if a defendant is improperly sentenced as a first offender, so there is no expectation of finality in the original sentence. See U.S. v. DiFrancesco, 449 U.S. 117, 101 S. Ct. 426, 66 L. Ed. 2d 328 (1980).

[5]O.C.G.A. § 42-8-60(a).

[6]O.C.G.A. § 42-8-60(j).

[7]O.C.G.A. § 42-8-60(b). Prior to 1998, a defendant found guilty of a serious violent felony was not precluded from first offender treatment. Fleming v. State, 271 Ga. 587, 523 S.E.2d 315 (1999). Persons convicted of a "sexual offense" were eligible for first offender treatment until 2006, when the General Assembly enacted O.C.G.A. § 17-10-6.2. See Tew v. State, 320 Ga. App. 127, 739 S.E.2d 423 (2013); Planas v. State, 296 Ga. App. 51, 673 S.E.2d 566 (2009).

[8]Welborn v. State, 166 Ga. App. 214, 303 S.E.2d 755 (1983); Todd v. State, 172 Ga. App. 231(2), 323 S.E.2d 6 (1984); Hardman v. Hardman, 185 Ga. App. 519, 520, 364 S.E.2d 645 (1988) (overruled on other grounds by,

as part of a sentencing formula or policy of automatic denial constitutes an abuse of discretion and constitutes reversible error" if the record supports such a finding.[9]

First offender sentencing is available for both felonies and misdemeanor offenders.[10] A defendant can only avail himself as a first offender "on one occasion."[11] In *Higdon v. State*,[12] the Court of Appeals held that "one occasion" "means . . . one or more offenses set forth in multiple charging instruments consolidated or joined for one trial . . ., [i]n other words . . . a single prosecution of related offenses." On appeal, the Supreme Court declined to reach that issue, finding only that first offender treatment was available only on "one occasion" and that occasion occurs upon the entry of the trial court's judgment.[13] The Court acknowledged that a multi-count indictment might qualify as "one occasion" for the purposes of the first offender statute, but declined to go so far as to say that several indictments consolidated for prosecution and trial would also be eligible for first offender treatment. The Court was clear that resolving multiple indictments at one sentencing hearing is not the equivalent of a single judgment and thus would not be eligible for first offender status based solely on that reason.[14]

The trial court must ensure that the defendant is aware of the consequences of entering a first offender plea.[15] Defense attorneys must inform defendants of their eligibility for sentencing as first offenders. If the defendant is pro se, the court has to inquire about the defendant's interest in entering a first offender plea.[16] Persons convicted without being informed of their eligibility for first offender status may petition the superior court in the county where they were convicted for exoneration of guilt and discharge as a matter of law. The court can retroactively grant exoneration if the preponderance of the evidence shows that the defendant was eligible when sentenced and "the ends of justice and the welfare of society are served by granting [the] petition."[17] A trial court may also recommend in the case of a person sentenced as a

---

Pender v. Witcher, 196 Ga. App. 856, 397 S.E.2d 193 (1990)). Cf. Tolliver v. State, 243 Ga. App. 180, 183(3), 531 S.E.2d 383 (2000), aff'd, 273 Ga. 785, 546 S.E.2d 525 (2001).

[9]McCullough v. State, 317 Ga. App. 853, 853, 733 S.E.2d 36 (2012).

[10]See Stafford v. State, 251 Ga. App. 203, 554 S.E.2d 219 (2001), holding that the First Offender Act is available to misdemeanor offenders. See also Ga. Op. Att'y Gen. 2000-1 (Jan. 3, 2000).

[11]O.C.G.A. § 42-8-60(l).

[12]Higdon v. State, 291 Ga. 821, 823, 733 S.E.2d 750 (2012).

[13]Higdon v. State, 291 Ga. 821, 826, 733 S.E.2d 750 (2012).

[14]Higdon v. State, 291 Ga. 821, 825-826, 733 S.E.2d 750 (2012).

[15]O.C.G.A. § 42-8-61.

[16]O.C.G.A. § 42-8-61.

[17]O.C.G.A. § 42-8-66(a)(1). Code section 42-8-66(a)(2) provides that persons sentenced between March 18,

first offender that the State Board of Pardons and Paroles, "acting in its sole discretion" consider parole for such person "at any time prior to the completion of any minimum [sentence] requirement" otherwise mandated by law or regulation.[18]

A defendant sentenced under O.C.G.A. § 42-8-60 may be sentenced to probation or a term of confinement.[19] Fines may also be imposed as a term of probation.[20] In *Penaherrera v. State*,[21] the defendant contended that, under this provision of the statute, he could not be sentenced to both probation and confinement, and that the time he spent in a detention center (90 to 270 days) and a diversion center (from 180 days to the date all money is paid) is confinement. However, the court concluded that such limited confinement does not constitute incarceration, and affirmed the sentence.

The court must state the "prospective effective date of the defendant being exonerated of guilt and discharged as a matter of law, assuming the defendant successfully complies with its sentencing order."[22] Defendants sentenced as first offenders retain all of the rights of appeal that they would if they had been adjudicated as guilty.[23]

At the time of sentencing, the court may, at its discretion, limit access to the defendant's first offender records, criminal file, docket books, final records, record of arrests (including fingerprints and photographs), and all of the defendant's other criminal records. If the court determines that the potential harm to the defendant's privacy outweighs the public's interest in the defendant's criminal history record being publically available, it must issue written findings of fact, and specify the date that the restrictions will take effect.[24] Individuals exonerated before July 1, 2016 can petition the court for restriction of their records in the same manner.[25] Discharge and exoneration as a first offender can only be used as disqualification from employment under a limited set of circumstances enumerated in O.C.G.A. § 42-8-63.1.

1968, and October 31, 1982, and who would have otherwise qualified for sentencing as a first offender may, with the consent of the state, "petition the superior court in the county in which he or she was convicted for exoneration of guilt and discharge." See Bishop v. State, 341 Ga. App. 590, 802 S.E.2d 39 (2017) (retroactive relief not available to persons sentenced on felony conviction prior to July 1, 2015; concurring opinion of McFadden suggests that this limitation may be an oversight on part of legislature).

[18]O.C.G.A. § 17-10-1(b).

[19]O.C.G.A. § 42-8-60(a).

[20]Todd v. State, 172 Ga. App. 231, 323 S.E.2d 6 (1984).

[21]Penaherrera v. State, 211 Ga. App. 162, 163(1), 438 S.E.2d 661 (1993).

[22]O.C.G.A. § 42-8-60(c).

[23]O.C.G.A. § 42-8-64.

[24]O.C.G.A. § 42-8-62.1(b). See Austin v. State, 343 Ga. App. 118, 807 S.E.2d 1 (2017).

[25]O.C.G.A. § 42-8-62.1(c).

After exoneration, the Georgia Crime Information Center "shall not provide records of arrest, charges, or sentences" to private persons or businesses.[26]

"In a strict legal sense, first-offender treatment does not constitute a sentence at all. 'Rather, under the Act, 'sentence' is deferred while the defendant is given an opportunity by the trial court to show that he is capable of comporting himself as a responsible, law-abiding citizen."[27] Accordingly, because a person who successfully completes all conditions of his or her first offender punishment is not "convicted" of an underlying offense, that person's first offender record may not be used for purposes of general impeachment.[28] A first offender record may, however, be used to disprove or contradict a witness's testimony.[29] In addition, the fact that the witness is on probation as a first offender may, however, be admissible to show bias in favor of the state.[30] See Studdard, *Daniel's Georgia Handbook on Criminal Evidence* (2018 ed.) § 6:22, on the use of a first offender guilty plea for impeachment of a witness.

If the defendant is prosecuted for another offense before exoneration of guilt and discharge, "the prior finding of guilt [where the defendant received a first offender sentence] may be pleaded and proven as if an adjudication of guilt had been entered."[31] In *State v. Mills*,[32] the Georgia Supreme Court held that because the state did not file a petition alleging that the defendant had committed a drug offense during his probation period, the state could not contend after the expiration of the probationary period that the defendant had failed to fulfill the terms of his probation. In 2016, the General Assembly modified O.C.G.A. § 42-8-65(b) to allow the Georgia Crime Information Center to modify records showing treatment as a first offender only when a court of competent jurisdiction enters:

(1) An adjudication of guilt for the offense for which the offender has been sentenced as a first offender;

(2) An order modifying the sentence originally imposed; or

(3) An order correcting an exoneration of guilt and discharge entered pursuant to subsection (g) of Code Section 42-8-60.

In spite of these restrictions, a trial judge can consider the

---

[26]O.C.G.A. § 35-3-34.

[27]O'Ree v. State, 172 Ga. App. 51, 322 S.E.2d 89 (1984).

[28]Matthews v. State, 268 Ga. 798, 493 S.E.2d 136 (1997).

[29]Williams v. State, 301 Ga. 829, 804 S.E.2d 398 (2017).

[30]Scott v. State, 242 Ga. App. 850, 527 S.E.2d 210 (1999).

[31]O.C.G.A. § 42-8-65(a).

[32]State v. Mills, 268 Ga. 873, 495 S.E.2d 1 (1998). See Collins v. State, 338 Ga. App. 886, 792 S.E.2d 134 (2016).

defendant's first offender record during sentencing for a later crime.[33]

If a defendant violates the terms of his first offender probation, or is convicted of another crime, the trial judge must first enter an adjudication of guilt before sentencing the defendant.[34] However, in *Mohammed v. State*,[35] the court held that the trial court may change or add conditions to a first offender's sentence without revoking and resentencing for probation violations. The trial court also has discretion to continue a first offender on probation even in those cases where the first offender commits another offense after first weighing the seriousness of the offense involved, the concerns of the public interest and the extent to which it affects the rights of third persons.[36] The trial judge "has a discretion to continue a first offender on probation despite technical violations of conditions of probation."[37] When a defendant's first offender probation is revoked, the court may impose any sentence it was originally authorized to impose provided that the judge made that condition clear to the defendant when the first offender probation was originally imposed.[38] The judge must, however, give the first offender credit for any time already spent on probation.[39]

O.C.G.A. § 16-11-131 provides that a first offender "who is on

---

[33]Williams v. State, 228 Ga. App. 622, 623(3), 492 S.E.2d 290 (1997).

[34]Beasley v. State, 165 Ga. App. 160, 299 S.E.2d 886 (1983).

[35]Mohammed v. State, 226 Ga. App. 387, 486 S.E.2d 652 (1997) (disapproved of on other grounds by, Bliss v. State, 244 Ga. App. 160, 535 S.E.2d 251 (2000)).

[36]Bliss v. State, 244 Ga. App. 160, 162, 535 S.E.2d 251 (2000) (disapproving dicta in Mohammed v. State, 226 Ga. App. 387, 486 S.E.2d 652 (1997)), which stated that the trial court is required to revoke first offender status when a first offender commits another crime.

[37]Mohammed v. State, 226 Ga. App. 387-388, 486 S.E.2d 652 (1997) (disapproved of on other grounds by, Bliss v. State, 244 Ga. App. 160, 535 S.E.2d 251 (2000)).

[38]Austin v. State, 162 Ga. App. 709, 710, 293 S.E.2d 10 (1982). Cf. Puckett v. State, 163 Ga. App. 156, 157(4), 293 S.E.2d 544 (1982); Crawford

v. State, 166 Ga. App. 272, 273(2), 304 S.E.2d 443 (1983). See Otuwa v. State, 303 Ga. App. 410, 693 S.E.2d 610 (2010), where the Court of Appeals noted that when sentencing a defendant on a First Offender to a period of probation under O.C.G.A. § 42-8-60, upon an adjudication of guilt, the defendant may be sentenced to the maximum that the law allows. If the defendant is sentenced to a period of confinement, however, the court noted that the execution of sentence is suspended, thereby implying that the original sentence, upon an adjudication of guilt, cannot be increased. See also Tallant v. State, 187 Ga. App. 138, 369 S.E.2d 789 (1988).

[39]Franklin v. State, 236 Ga. App. 401, 402(1), 512 S.E.2d 304 (1999). See Johns v. State, 223 Ga. App. 553, 479 S.E.2d 388 (1996). See Smith v. State, 322 Ga. App. 549, 745 S.E.2d 771 (2013) (defendant who knew at the time of sentencing that he did not qualify for drug first offender under O.C.G.A. § 16-13-2 could not complain when the court adjudicated him guilty and re-

probation" for a felony may not possess a firearm.[40] However, after discharge "without court adjudication of guilt as a matter of law . . . [he] shall, upon such discharge, be relieved from the disabilities imposed by this Code section."[41]

Georgia has a special statute for first offenders of drug and marijuana laws.[42] O.C.G.A. § 16-13-2(c) also provides that a defendant who is charged with nonviolent property crimes in connection with related drug offenses may be sentenced as a first offender and participate in a court approved drug treatment program on the condition that the defendant make full restitution to the victims as a condition of probation. However, if first offender sentences imposed under § 16-13-2 for drug trafficking and whose mandatory minimum sentences receive a judicial discretionary downward departure pursuant to either §§ 16-13-31(g) or 16-13-31.1(b) they cannot be reduced by "any earned time, early release, work release, leave or other sentence-reducing measures under programs administered by the Department of

---

sentenced him).

[40]It should be noted that in Blackmon v. State, 266 Ga. App. 877, 598 S.E.2d 542 (2004), the court held that a person who enters a nolo contendere plea to a felony is not a "convicted felon" for purposes of O.C.G.A. § 16-11-131(b).

[41]O.C.G.A. § 16-11-131(f).

[42]O.C.G.A. § 16-13-2(a) and (c) provide that conditional discharge and dismissal only applies to first time offenders who have either (1) pled guilty or have been found guilty, for the first time, of possession of a narcotic, marijuana, stimulant, depressant, or hallucinogenic drug, or (2) have been charged, for the first time, with a nonviolent property crime, which the court believes is related to the accused's drug or alcohol addiction, and are eligible for any court-approved drug program. The offender must have no prior state or federal convictions of any drug offenses.

The court may, without entering a judgment of guilt and with the consent of the offender, defer further proceedings and place the offender on probation upon such reasonable terms and conditions as the court may require for up to a period of five years.

The terms and conditions of the probation should preferably include a comprehensive rehabilitation program, not to exceed three years, designed to educate the offender on the negative effects of drug abuse and the positive gains and benefits that can be achieved by being a good member of society.

The court is required to discharge the offender and dismiss any proceedings against him upon fulfillment of the terms and conditions of probation and upon full restitution to all victims of the charged offense. Should any term or condition of the probation be violated, the court may enter an adjudication of guilt and proceed accordingly.

Discharge and dismissal under O.C.G.A. § 16-13-2 shall be without court adjudication of guilt, shall not be deemed a conviction for purposes of O.C.G.A. § 16-13-2, shall not be deemed a conviction for purposes of disqualifications or disabilities imposed by law upon conviction of a crime, and may not be used to disqualify a person in any application for employment or appointment to office in either the public or private sector. See State v. Barrow, 332 Ga. App. 353, 772 S.E.2d 802 (2015) (statute applies only to drug *possession* charges and does not include charge of manufacturing methamphetamine).

Corrections. . . ."

§ 26:25 Special conditions

Over the years, the General Assembly has enacted special sentencing regimes in an effort to combat recidivism for certain types of offenses. Two areas where the law has evolved considerably in this regard are sentencing, reporting, and classification requirements for sexual offenders, and restrictions on gun ownership and possession for convicted felons.

§ 26:26 Special conditions—Sexual offenders

O.C.G.A. § 17-10-6.2 provides that persons convicted of the more serious sexual offenses are subject to a mandatory sentencing scheme that requires a "split sentence which shall include the minimum term of imprisonment . . . applicable to the offense."[1] The Code section does not allow the sentencing court to suspend, stay, probate, or defer any portion of the mandatory minimum sentence and requires as additional punishment at least one year of probation.[2] The law does allow the trial court to deviate from the mandatory sentencing guideline, provided the state and the defense agree, or if it finds that the defendant did not use a deadly weapon during the commission of the offense, had not previously engaged in similar conduct, did not cause intentional harm to the victim, and did not transport or physically restrain the victim in connection with the commission of the offense. Should the court deviate in its sentence, it must state the reasons therefor in a written order.[3]

[Section 26:26]

[1]O.C.G.A. § 17-10-6.2(b). See Duncan v. State, 342 Ga. App. 530, 804 S.E.2d 156 (2017) (failure to sentence defendant convicted of sexual offense to a split sentence as required by O.C.G.A. § 17-10-6.2(b) is "illegal").

[2]See Clark v. State, 328 Ga. App. 268, 761 S.E.2d 826 (2014) (split sentence is mandatory and requires at least one year of probation making void a sentence of 20 years to serve). O.C.G.A. § 17-10-6.2(b) was amended in 2017 to provide that in cases where the defendant is convicted of multiple sexual offenses, the requirement that the court impose a split sentence of at least one year shall only apply to the final consecutive sentence imposed.

The amendment is not retroactive and applies only to cases arising after its July 1, 2017, effective date. See Hardin v. State, 344 Ga. App. 378, 810 S.E.2d 602 (2018).

[3]See Hedden v. State, 288 Ga. 871, 708 S.E.2d 287 (2011) (trial court had authority to deviate from mandatory minimum in child exploitation case where defendant had a pornographic image on his computer of a child being physically restrained during sexually explicit conduct but there was no evidence that defendant was involved in making the photo). See Evans v. State, 300 Ga. 271, 794 S.E.2d 40 (2016) (court discusses the issue of "relevant similar transactions" for purposes of downward departure and also notes a "relevant similar transac-

In *State v. Crossen*,[4] the court noted that the statute is silent as to which party has the burden of establishing the absence of the factors which would authorize a downward departure, thereby creating ambiguity. Construing the penal statute in favor of the defendant, the court held that the burden fell upon the state and in the absence of any evidence to support the finding of any of the factors which would prohibit a downward departure, the trial court was authorized to exercise its discretion and depart from the otherwise mandatory sentence.

After conviction, O.C.G.A. §§ 42-1-12 et seq. govern registration and classification requirements for sexual offenders. For the purposes of this chapter, the term "sexual offender" encompasses persons convicted of enumerated offenses against minors[5] and "dangerous sexual offense[s]."[6] All sexual offenders are required to register their address, along with a photograph, fingerprints, date of birth, height, weight, eye color, and hair color "to the appropriate official before being released from prison or placed on parole, supervised release, or probation."[7] Sexual offenders also must register with the sheriff in the county where they reside within 72 hours of establishing residence in that county. Sexual offenders may not reside within 1,000 feet of a school, church, child care facility, or any other area where minors congregate, and may not work, volunteer, or loiter at such facilities. Sexually dangerous predators may not work or volunteer within 1,000 feet of a school, church, child care facility, or area where minors loiter.[8] These registration requirements are effective for the remainder of the sexual offender's life.[9]

A sexual offender may petition the court for release from the requirements and restrictions imposed by O.C.G.A. §§ 42-1-12 et seq. under certain circumstances. A sexual offender who has "completed all prison, parole, supervised release, and probation for the offense," and is confined to a hospice, nursing home, or residential care facility for the elderly; is totally or permanently disabled; or "otherwise seriously physically incapacitated due to

---

tion" can include two or more like crimes charged in separate courts within the same indictment).

[4]State v. Crossen, 328 Ga. App. 198, 761 S.E.2d 596 (2014) (because the state failed to properly raise the issue, the court did not address the contention that each count to which the defendant pled constituted a "relevant similar transaction" which would preclude downward departure under § 17-10-6.2).

[5]O.C.G.A. § 42-1-12(a)(9).
[6]O.C.G.A. § 42-1-12(a)(10).
[7]O.C.G.A. §§ 42-1-12(a)(16), (f).
[8]O.C.G.A. § 42-1-15. Subsection (d) of § 42-1-15 makes it unlawful "for any person who is or should be registered on another state's sexual offender registry to loiter, as prohibited by Code section 16-11-36, at any child care facility, school or area where minors congregate."
[9]O.C.G.A. § 42-1-12(f)(6).

illness or injury" may qualify for release.[10] Likewise, sexual offenders convicted of crimes that became punishable by misdemeanors, or whose sole basis for being required to register is a kidnapping or false imprisonment charge against a minor that did not include an attempt to commit a sexual offense may also petition for release. Less narrowly, sexual offenders who have "completed all prison, parole, supervised release, and probation" may petition for release from the registration requirements and restrictions if they have been classified as Level I offenders and 10 years or more have elapsed since the completion of their sentences.[11] Such sexual offenders may be considered for relief "if the court finds by a preponderance of the evidence that the individual does not pose a substantial risk of perpetrating any future dangerous sexual offense."[12]

The Sexual Offender Registration Review Board classifies sexual offenders by determining "the likelihood that a sexual offender will engage in another crime against a victim who is a minor or a dangerous sexual offense."[13] The Board renders such classification recommendations within:

(1)   60 days of request for evaluation if the sexual offender is sentenced pursuant to O.C.G.A. § 17-10-6.2(c);

(2)   6 months prior to the sexual offender's proposed date of release from confinement;

(3)   60 days of receipt of required registration information from a sheriff when a sexual offender changes residence into Georgia;

(4)   60 days if the sexual offender is sentenced to a probated or suspended sentence;

(5)   90 days if reclassification is requested by the court pursuant to O.C.G.A. § 42-1-19.[14]

The Board uses a three-level risk classification system. Level I offenders present a low risk of committing a subsequent offense, Level II offenders present an intermediate risk, and sexually dangerous predators present a high risk of recidivism.[15] Sexual offenders classified as sexually dangerous predators are the most likely to commit additional sexual offenses, and face additional requirements. Most notably, sexually dangerous predators must submit to electronic GPS monitoring that "locate[s] and record[s]"

---

[10]O.C.G.A. § 42-1-19.

[11]O.C.G.A. § 42-1-19(c).

[12]O.C.G.A. § 42-1-19(f).

[13]O.C.G.A. § 42-1-14(a)(1).

[14]O.C.G.A. § 42-1-14(a)(2)(A) to (E).

[15]O.C.G.A. § 42-1-12(a)(12) to (13); O.C.G.A. § 42-1-14(a)(2).

their locations for the remainder of their natural lives.[16]

Prior to classification, sexual offenders may provide the Board with information including psychological evaluations, sexual history polygraphs, personal, education, and work history, and any other relevant information. The prosecuting attorney must provide the Board with the sexual offender's criminal history and criminal history records. The Board also has access to Department of Corrections, Department of Community Supervision, and State Board of Pardons and Paroles information.[17]

Sexual offenders classified as Level II offenders or sexually dangerous predators may petition the Board for reevaluation, provided they do so within 30 days of the letter from the Board announcing their classification. Offenders have 60 days from the date of the letter to provide the Board with any information they want the board to consider in the reevaluation.[18] Either within 30 days of the letter from the Board or after the Board denies the sexual offender's request for reevaluation, sexual offenders may petition the superior court in the county where the board is located for judicial review of the Board's classification or denial of reevaluation.[19]

O.C.G.A. § 42-1-14(c) states that on judicial review, the superior court may hold an evidentiary hearing regarding a sexual offender's classification. In *Gregory v. Sexual Offender Registration Review Board*,[20] a sexual offender was classified as a sexually dangerous predator. On review, the Board denied his request for reevaluation, and the superior court affirmed the Board's denial. Neither the Board nor the superior court granted Gregory's requests for evidentiary hearings, even though he submitted evidence to support both petitions. On appeal, the Supreme Court reversed and held that either the Board or the superior court on review must afford persons classified as a sexually dangerous predator "a meaningful opportunity . . . to present favorable evidence and confront the evidence against them."[21] The Court found that the additional tracking, monitoring, and reporting requirements imposed upon sexually dangerous predators falls squarely within the liberties protected by the Due Process Clause of the Fourteenth Amendment. Additionally, evidence regarding classification as a sexually dangerous predator "tends to be subjective in nature. . . . Without an evidentiary hearing to assess

---

[16]O.C.G.A. § 42-1-14(e).

[17]O.C.G.A. § 42-1-14(a)(2).

[18]O.C.G.A. § 42-1-14(b)(2).

[19]O.C.G.A. § 42-1-14(c).

[20]Gregory v. Sexual Offender Registration Review Bd., 298 Ga. 675,

784 S.E.2d 392 (2016).

[21]Gregory v. Sexual Offender Registration Review Bd., 298 Ga. 675, 691, 784 S.E.2d 392 (2016).

that evidence and resolve these disputes, the danger of an erroneous risk classification is substantial."[22] Thus, if the Board has refused to grant a sexual offender classified as a sexually dangerous predator an evidentiary hearing, on review the superior court must either grant such a hearing or remand with instructions for the Board to conduct the hearing.

§ 26:27 Special conditions—Felon in possession of firearms

O.C.G.A. § 16-11-131 prohibits convicted felons or persons on first offender probation for commission of a felony from possessing a firearm. Violation of this statute is a felony, and a violation of this statute during a homicide may render the defendant guilty of felony murder.[1] In *King v. State*,[2] the court held that where a previously convicted felon is charged with the sole offense of being a felon in possession of a firearm, the defendant's prior conviction may not be used to enhance the sentence pursuant to O.C.G.A. § 17-10-7(a) to the maximum punishment of the offense of possession of a firearm by a convicted felon. To hold otherwise would mean that every conviction for the offense of possession of a firearm by a convicted felon would result in the maximum punishment of five years, rendering meaningless the authorized punishment of one to five years. The reasoning in *King* has also been used to prohibit the use of prior convictions, such as rape, to serve as the basis for both a charge of failure to register as a sex offender and for a recidivist sentence under such offense.[3]

King has no application where a defendant with three prior convictions is sentenced under O.C.G.A. § 17-10-7(a), because the court still has no discretion to sentence under that statute within

---

[22]Gregory v. Sexual Offender Registration Review Bd., 298 Ga. 675, 689, 784 S.E.2d 392 (2016).

[Section 26:27]

[1]Scott v. State, 250 Ga. 195, 198, 297 S.E.2d 18 (1982) (holding that the jury could find the defendant guilty of felony murder because of a violation of § 16-11-131, even though the defendant was not represented by counsel in the previous felony conviction for burglary); Lewis v. U.S., 445 U.S. 55, 100 S. Ct. 915, 63 L. Ed. 2d 198 (1980).

[2]King v. State, 169 Ga. App. 444, 313 S.E.2d 144 (1984). See State v. Slaughter, 289 Ga. 344, 711 S.E.2d 651 (2011) (restricting *King's* applicability

in cases where a defendant who has three prior convictions, and in a subsequent prosecution is convicted of possessing a firearm by a convicted felon). See Johnson v. State, 298 Ga. App. 639, 680 S.E.2d 675 (2009) (when the trial court imposes a recidivist sentence based on three prior felony convictions, one of which was also used by the state to establish an element of the offense charged, such as possession of a firearm by a convicted felon, a challenge to the sentence as void is not waived based upon the defendant's failure to object).

[3]Pardon v. State, 322 Ga. App. 393, 745 S.E.2d 658 (2013).

the authorized range of punishment.[4] Where a defendant is charged as a convicted felon in possession of a firearm, the indictment may set out any number of prior felony convictions.[5] Normally, however, the indictment charging prior felonies should not be sent to the jury until the jury has determined the innocence or guilt of the defendant on the non-possession charge.[6]

The court must give special scrutiny to the prior conviction when the prior "felony" conviction was committed and adjudicated in another state under laws which refer to the offense as a misdemeanor even though the sentence imposed may have been in excess of 12 months. In *State v. Langlands*,[7] the Supreme Court concluded that the reference in O.C.G.A. § 16-11-131 failed to provide sufficient notice that it could apply in a case where the predicate offense was involuntary manslaughter—characterized in the sentencing state as a "first degree misdemeanor" punishable by up to five years in prison.[8]

§ 26:28   Recidivism punishment

O.C.G.A. § 17-10-7 is Georgia's historic general recidivist or habitual offender statute. This statute as amended in 2015 provides as follows:

(a) Except as otherwise provided in subsection (b) or (b.1) of this Code section, any person who, after having been convicted of a felony offense in this state or having been convicted under the laws of any other state or of the United States of a crime which if committed within this state would be a felony and sentenced to confinement in a penal institution, commits a felony punishable by confinement in a penal institution shall be sentenced to undergo the longest period of time prescribed for the punishment of the subsequent offense of which he or she stands convicted, provided that, unless otherwise provided by law, the trial judge may, in his or her discretion, probate or suspend the maximum sentence prescribed for the offense.

(b)(1) As used in this subsection, the term 'serious violent felony' means a serious violent felony as defined in subsection (a) of Code section 17-10-6.1.

(2) Except as provided in subsection (e) of Code Section 17-10-6.1, any person who has been convicted of a serious violent felony in this state or who has been convicted under the laws of any other

---

[4]State v. Slaughter, 289 Ga. 344, 711 S.E.2d 651 (2011).

[5]Head v. State, 170 Ga. App. 324, 326, 316 S.E.2d 791 (1984), judgment rev'd on other grounds, 253 Ga. 429, 322 S.E.2d 228 (1984).

[6]Head v. State, 253 Ga. 429, 322 S.E.2d 228 (1984).

[7]State v. Langlands, 276 Ga. 721, 583 S.E.2d 18 (2003).

[8]See Clark v. State, 328 Ga. App. 268, 761 S.E.2d 826 (2014) (split sentence is mandatory and requires at least one year of probation making void a sentence of 20 years to serve).

state or of the United States of a crime which if committed in this state would be a serious violent felony and who after such first conviction subsequently commits and is convicted of a serious violent felony for which such person is not sentenced to death shall be sentenced to imprisonment for life without parole. Any such sentence of life without parole shall not be suspended, stayed, probated, deferred, or withheld, and any such person sentenced pursuant to this paragraph shall not be eligible for any form of pardon, parole, or early release administered by the State Board of Pardons and Paroles or for any earned time, early release, work release, leave, or any other sentence-reducing measures under programs administered by the Department of Corrections, the effect of which would be to reduce the sentence of life imprisonment without possibility of parole, except as may be authorized by any existing or future provisions of the Constitution.

(b.1) Subsections (a) and (c) of this Code section shall not apply to a second or any subsequent conviction for any violation of subsection (a), paragraph (1) of subsection (i), or subsection (j) of Code Section 16-13-30.

(c) Except as otherwise provided in subsection (b) or (b.1) of this Code section and subsection (b) of Code Section 42-9-45, any person who, after having been convicted under the laws of this state for three felonies or having been convicted under the laws of any other state or of the United States of three crimes which if committed within this state would be felonies, commits a felony within this state shall, upon conviction for such fourth offense or for subsequent offenses, serve the maximum time provided in the sentence of the judge based upon such conviction and shall not be eligible for parole until the maximum sentence has been served.

(d) For the purpose of this Code section, conviction of two or more crimes charged on separate counts of one indictment or accusation, or in two or more indictments or accusations consolidated for trial, shall be deemed to be only one conviction.

(e) This Code section is supplemental to other provisions relating to recidivous offenders.[1]

In *State v. Jones*,[2] the Court of Appeals explained how the various subsections of the recidivist statute blend together.

[I]f two of the subsections apply, a trial court must apply them both. This is not to say, however, that a trial court completely lacks

---

[Section 26:28]

[1]Effective July 1, 2015, O.C.G.A. § 42-9-45(b)(3) provides that an inmate sentenced to a term of at least 12 years and up to a life sentence under O.C.G.A. § 16-13-30(d) (manufacture, sale or possession with intent to distribute controlled substances) and O.C.G.A. § 17-10-7(c) (repeat offenders) under certain conditions may become eligible for parole, including: he or she has never been convicted of a serious violent felony or an offense for which registration as a sex offender was required; has served at least 12 years of his or her sentence; has obtained a low risk assessment to reoffend from the DOC; and other benchmarks which reflect little propensity to commit a crime.

[2]State v. Jones, 253 Ga. App. 630, 632, 560 S.E.2d 112 (2002).

discretion in sentencing a recidivist. Under O.C.G.A. § 17-10-7(a), a trial court retains authority to suspend or probate a portion of the sentence. And, under subsection (c), a felon must "serve the maximum time provided in the sentence of the judge." Accordingly, it is conceivable that a felon would not be required to actually serve the maximum sentence if the trial court decided, in its discretion, to suspend or probate a portion of the sentence. But where the maximum penalty is life in prison, a trial court lacks discretion to probate or suspend any part of the sentence. It follows that when a three-time recidivist commits a fourth felony for which the maximum penalty is life in prison, the trial court lacks discretion to sentence such felon to anything other than a life sentence without possibility of parole.[3]

In *Webb v. State*,[4] the Court of Appeals upheld the trial judge's decision to sentence a defendant convicted for child molestation as a recidivist to less than life imprisonment. In distinguishing *State v. Jones*,[5] the court pointed out that the defendant there was convicted of aggravated sodomy under O.C.G.A. § 16-6-2, the maximum punishment for which is, without limitation, life imprisonment. "In contrast, the maximum punishment for conviction of a second offense of child molestation is limited; the State can seek life imprisonment only upon serving a notice of intent to seek this punishment."[6] Thus, because the state failed to timely file the notice of intent to seek life imprisonment required by § 16-6-4 (b), the court was not required to impose life imprisonment.

In *Robinson v. State*,[7] at sentencing, the state presented two prior indictments in aggravation of punishment. The defendant contended that "since the two indictments were pled out at the same time, before the same judge, and resulted in the same sentence to run concurrently, the offenses should be viewed as consolidated and treated as only one offense." The court held that since there were two indictments and separate sentencing orders, the record indicated there was no consolidation.

"In determining whether separate offenses should be considered 'consolidated for trial' for purposes of recidivist sentencing,

---

[3]State v. Jones, 253 Ga. App. 630, 632, 560 S.E.2d 112 (2002). Where the basis for such a sentence is the recidivist statute, there is no right to have the matter considered by a jury under O.C.G.A. § 17-10-7. Shields v. State, 264 Ga. App. 232, 238(5), 590 S.E.2d 217 (2003). See Blackwell v. State, 302 Ga. 820, 809 S.E.2d 727 (2018) (the "longest period of time prescribed for the punishment" for the offense of murder under O.C.G.A. § 17-10-7(a) is

life; parole is not excluded as it is under § 17-10-7(b) and (c)).

[4]Webb v. State, 270 Ga. App. 817, 608 S.E.2d 241 (2004).

[5]State v. Jones, 253 Ga. App. 630, 632, 560 S.E.2d 112 (2002).

[6]Webb v. State, 270 Ga. App. 817, 821, 608 S.E.2d 241 (2004).

[7]Robinson v. State, 232 Ga. App. 280(2), 501 S.E.2d 536 (1998).

[courts] look to the totality of the circumstances."[8] As the Court of Appeals reaffirmed in 2015:[9]

"If separate offenses are charged under separate charging instruments and a defendant is sentenced under separate orders, the offenses are generally not consolidated for trial within the meaning of O.C.G.A. § 17-1007(d)." If the prior offenses "were the result of separate indictments and a separate order of sentence was entered on each indictment," there is no consolidation even if the sentences for the offenses were entered on the same day and were run concurrent to one another.

An exception to these rules exists where the offenses charged in multiple charging instruments refer to the same incident.[10]

In *Davis v. State*,[11] the court held that where one of the defendant's "convictions" was an ongoing sentence of first offender probation, which had not yet been discharged or revoked, the defendant could not be sentenced to life without parole under O.C.G.A. § 17-10-7(a). The court pointed out that, under the first offender statute, the earlier case has been suspended during the period of probation and thus did not qualify as a "conviction." In such a case, only revocation of probation qualifies as a conviction.

In *Woodson v. State*,[12] the court pointed out that the "State bears the burden of showing that the foreign convictions were 'for conduct which would be considered felonious under the laws of this state.'" Thus, certified copies of a defendant's five prior Alabama felony convictions, consisting of burglary, escape and receiving stolen property, do not justify a recidivist punishment without considering evidence that the convictions were for conduct that would have constituted felonies in Georgia. However, in *Smith v. State*,[13] the defendant was charged with robbery and agreed at the sentencing hearing to the admission into evidence of a certified copy of the Florida two-count indictment showing his convic-

---

[8]Stone v. State, 245 Ga. App. 728, 728, 538 S.E.2d 791 (2000) (citations and footnote omitted).

[9]Thompson v. State, 332 Ga. App. 204, 770 S.E.2d 364 (2015) (whole court), quoting Baker v. State, 306 Ga. App. 99, 103(2), 701 S.E.2d 572 (2010); Philmore v. State, 263 Ga. 67, 70(6), 428 S.E.2d 329 (1993).

[10]See Stone v. State, 245 Ga. App. 728, 728, 538 S.E.2d 791 (2000) (citations and footnote omitted).

[11]Davis v. State, 273 Ga. 14, 537 S.E.2d 663 (2000).

[12]Woodson v. State, 242 Ga. App.

67, 70(4), 530 S.E.2d 2 (2000), judgment aff'd, 273 Ga. 557, 544 S.E.2d 431 (2001). See Nordahl v. State, 344 Ga. App. 686, 811 S.E.2d 465 (2018) (when interpreting and applying specific sentencing statutes it is not necessary to apply an "elements only" test); Loveless v. State, 344 Ga. App. 716, 812 S.E.2d 42 (2018) (proper to use federal counterfeiting conviction in sentencing pursuant to §§ 17-10-7(a) and (c) because, while not a felony under Georgia law, counterfeiting is a form of the Georgia felony of forgery).

[13]Smith v. State, 241 Ga. App. 770, 771(1), 527 S.E.2d 608 (2000).

tion for two robbery offenses committed several years earlier. The court held that "[a]lthough the language of the Florida indictment does not track Georgia's armed robbery statute, the Florida indictment's language describes that defendant was in possession of a shotgun when he forcefully and violently took valuables from two victims. This is sufficient to prove that defendant was convicted of two offenses in Florida which would have each been the serious violent felony of armed robbery had the offenses been committed in Georgia."

In *Miller v. State*,[14] the Georgia Court of Appeals held that the defendant's juvenile disposition in North Carolina of an offense which would be a felony for an adult did not amount to a conviction for purposes of O.C.G.A. § 17-10-7(c).

In *Wheeler v. State*,[15] the court reversed a recidivist sentence where the only record of defendant's prior convictions consisted of a colloquy between the trial court and counsel. The decision suggests that, at a minimum, the state should provide the defense with certified copies of the prior convictions and enough detail regarding out-of-state convictions so as to furnish the sentencing court with a basis for finding that the conviction would have constituted a felony in Georgia.

A part of the following material on the "seven deadly sins" or punishment of serious violent offenders actually is not concerned with recidivism, but is a part of the statute, and the whole statute is discussed in this section.

Originally enacted in 1994 and entitled, "Punishment for serious violent offenders," O.C.G.A. § 17-10-6.1 was amended in 2006, 2009, 2011, 2013 and 2014. The law now provides in part as follows:

(a) As used in this Code section, the term "serious violent felony" means:

(1) Murder or felony murder, as defined in Code Section 16-5-1;

(2) Armed robbery, as defined in Code Section 16-8-41;

(3) Kidnapping, as defined in Code Section 16-5-40;

(4) Rape, as defined in Code Section 16-6-1;

(5) Aggravated child molestation, as defined in subsection (c) of Code Section 16-6-4, unless subject to the provisions of paragraph (2) of subsection (d) of Code Section 16-6-4;

(6) Aggravated sodomy, as defined in Code Section 16-6-2; or

(7) Aggravated sexual battery, as defined in Code Section 16-6-22.2.

(b)(1) Except as provided in subsection (e) of this Code section, any

---

[14]Miller v. State, 231 Ga. App. 869, 870(2), 501 S.E.2d 42 (1998).

[15]Wheeler v. State, 270 Ga. App. 363, 606 S.E.2d 612 (2004).

person convicted of the serious violent felony of kidnapping involving a victim who is 14 years of age or older or armed robbery shall be sentenced to a mandatory minimum term of imprisonment of ten years, and no portion of the mandatory minimum sentence imposed shall be suspended, stayed, probated, deferred, or withheld by the sentencing court.

(2) Except as provided in subsection (e) of this Code section, the sentence of any person convicted of the serious violent felony of:

(A) Kidnapping involving a victim who is less than 14 years of age;

(B) Rape;

(C) Aggravated child molestation, as defined in subsection (c) of Code Section 16-6-4, unless subject to the provisions of paragraph (2) of subsection (d) of Code Section 16-6-4;

(D) Aggravated sodomy, as defined in Code Section 16-6-2; or

(E) Aggravated sexual battery, as defined in Code Section 16-6-22.2 shall, unless sentenced to life imprisonment, be a split sentence which shall include a mandatory minimum term of imprisonment of 25 years, followed by probation for life and no portion of the mandatory minimum sentence imposed shall be suspended, stayed, probated, deferred, or withheld by the sentencing court.

(3) No person convicted of a serious violent felony shall be sentenced as a first offender pursuant to Article 3 of Chapter 8 of Title 42, relating to probation for first offenders, or any other provision of Georgia law relating to the sentencing of first offenders. The State of Georgia shall have the right to appeal any sentence which is imposed by the superior court which does not conform to the provisions of this subsection in the same manner as is provided for other appeals by the state in accordance with Chapter 7 of Title 5, relating to appeals or certiorari by the state.

(c)(1) Except as otherwise provided in subsection (c) of Code Section 42-9-39, for a first conviction of a serious violent felony in which the accused has been sentenced to life imprisonment, that person shall not be eligible for any form of parole or early release administered by the State Board of Pardons and Paroles until that person has served a minimum of 30 years in prison. The minimum term of imprisonment shall not be reduced by any earned time, early release, work release, leave, or other sentence-reducing measures under programs administered by the Department of Corrections.

(2) For a first conviction of a serious violent felony in which the accused has been sentenced to death but the sentence of death has been commuted to life imprisonment, that person shall not be eligible for any form of parole or early release administered by the State Board of Pardons and Paroles until that person has served a minimum of 30 years in prison. The minimum term of imprisonment shall not be reduced by any earned time, early release, work release, leave, or other sentence-reducing measures under programs administered by the Department of Corrections.

(3) For a first conviction of a serious violent felony in which the accused has been sentenced to imprisonment for life without parole,

that person shall not be eligible for any form of parole or early release administered by the State Board of Pardons and Paroles or for any earned time, early release, work release, leave, or other sentence-reducing measures under programs administered by the Department of Corrections.

(4) Except as otherwise provided in this subsection, any sentence imposed for the first conviction of any serious violent felony shall be served in its entirety as imposed by the sentencing court and shall not be reduced by any form of parole or early release administered by the State Board of Pardons and Paroles or by any earned time, early release, work release, leave, or other sentence-reducing measures under programs administered by the Department of Corrections, the effect of which would be to reduce the period of incarceration ordered by the sentencing court; provided, however, that during the final year of incarceration an offender so sentenced shall be eligible to be considered for participation in a department administered transitional center or work release program.

(d) For purposes of this Code section, a first conviction of any serious violent felony means that the person has never been convicted of a serious violent felony under the laws of this state or of an offense under the laws of any other state or of the United States, which offense if committed in this state would be a serious violent felony. Conviction of two or more crimes charged on separate counts of one indictment or accusation, or in two or more indictments or accusations consolidated for trial, shall be deemed to be only one conviction.

(e) In the court's discretion, the judge may depart from the mandatory minimum sentence specified in this Code section for a person who is convicted of a serious violent felony when the prosecuting attorney and the defendant have agreed to a sentence that is below such mandatory minimum.

(f) Any sentence imposed pursuant to this Code section shall not be reduced by any earned time, early release, work release, leave, or other sentence-reducing measures under programs administered by the Department of Corrections, the effect of which would be to reduce the period of incarceration ordered by the sentencing court or any form of pardon, parole, or commutation of sentence by the State Board of Pardons and Paroles; provided, however, that during the final year of incarceration, a defendant so sentenced shall be eligible to be considered for participation in a Department of Corrections administered transitional center or work release program.

In *Bryant v. State*,[16] the court held that when a trial judge sentenced the defendant to a term less than the mandatory minimum set forth in O.C.G.A. § 17-10-6.1, the court may vacate the earlier sentence and impose a proper sentence. O.C.G.A. § 17-10-2 provides for a pre-sentence hearing in all felony cases (except in cases in which the death penalty may be imposed). See § 26:14, supra. The trial judge shall hear evidence "of any prior criminal

---

[16]Bryant v. State, 229 Ga. App.   534(1), 494 S.E.2d 353 (1997).

convictions and pleas of guilty or nolo contendere" which "the state has made known to the defendant prior to trial." See § 14:1, supra, on notice. The lack of notice in the indictment of the defendant's recidivism does not prevent a recidivist sentence.[17] See § 13:18, supra. In *Martin v. State*,[18] the court held that where a defendant is served before trial with notice of the State's intention to use felony convictions in aggravation of punishment pursuant to O.C.G.A. § 17-10-7(b), this is "fair notice of its intention to use prior convictions in aggravation of punishment." Based on the above statute, the crimes of murder, armed robbery, kidnapping, rape, aggravated child molestation, aggravated sodomy and aggravated sexual battery are referred to as the "seven deadly sins."[19]

In 1997, the court held in *State v. Allmond*[20] that the mandatory sentencing provisions of O.C.G.A. § 17-10-6.1 do not apply where a defendant is not "convicted" of one of the "seven deadly sins" but was sentenced pursuant to the provisions of the First Offender Act. The Georgia Supreme Court denied certiorari. O.C.G.A. § 17-10-6.1 was amended in 1998 to reflect the express intent of the General Assembly that persons who commit serious violent felonies specified in the Sentence Reform Act of 1994 shall be sentenced to a mandatory term of not less that 10 years and shall not be eligible for first offender treatment.

However, in *Johnson v. State*,[21] the court held that if a defendant is convicted of the "seven deadly sins" and is improperly sentenced, the defendant may be re-sentenced, in keeping with O.C.G.A. § 17-10-6.1, and a longer sentence may be imposed. The court also pointed out that defendants sentenced under recidivist statutes "are not punished a second time for the earlier offense, but the repetition of criminal conduct aggravates their guilt and justifies heavier penalties when they are again convicted." In *Bryant v. State*,[22] the court held that the trial judge in re-sentencing the defendant could sentence him to 20 years confine-

---

[17]Mitchell v. State, 202 Ga. App. 100, 413 S.E.2d 517 (1991); Camaron v. State, 246 Ga. App. 80, 81(1), 539 S.E.2d 577 (2000).

[18]Martin v. State, 205 Ga. App. 200(2), 422 S.E.2d 6 (1992). See Moore v. State, 304 Ga. App. 198, 695 S.E.2d 717 (2010) (written notice that defendant's prior convictions were to be used for aggravation of punishment contradicted by state's oral representation at sentencing following defendant's plea that it was not seeking recidivist punishment was inadequate).

[19]E.g., Fulton County Daily Report, Thursday, September 26, 1996.

[20]State v. Allmond, 225 Ga. App. 509, 484 S.E.2d 306 (1997) (overruled on other grounds by, Fleming v. State, 233 Ga. App. 483, 504 S.E.2d 542 (1998)).

[21]Johnson v. State, 229 Ga. App. 400, 493 S.E.2d 926 (1997) (quoting Fowler v. State, 235 Ga. 535, 221 S.E.2d 9 (1975)).

[22]Bryant v. State, 229 Ga. App. 534, 494 S.E.2d 353 (1997).

ment even though the original sentence had been 20 years to serve five.

In 1996, the Georgia legislature revised the rape and aggravated sodomy statutes. In doing so, they omitted from the two statutes language which provides that "[a]ny person convicted under this Code section shall, in addition, be subject to the sentencing and punishment provisions of O.C.G.A. § 17-10-6.1 and O.C.G.A. § 17-10-7." This situation was changed promptly during the 1997 session of the General Assembly. However, the 1996 revised statutes will remain applicable to sentencing until such time for crimes committed before the effective date of the new statute,[23] and crimes committed before the 1997 revision will continue to be controlled by the law in 1996 since an increase in sentence applied to occurrences before enactment would be invalid as ex post facto law.[24] In an unofficial opinion of the Attorney General of Georgia,[25] he concluded that "the General Assembly has repealed the ten year mandatory minimum sentence for rape and aggravated sodomy formerly applicable to first offenders. The mandatory minimum sentence for these offenses was one year until the 1997 change. The provisions applicable to recidivists [O.C.G.A. § 17-10-7(b) for a second serious violent felony] have never been modified; [and] the mandatory sentence remains life without parole."

O.C.G.A. § 16-11-133 provides in pertinent part:

(b) Any person who has previously been convicted of or who has previously entered a guilty plea to the offense of murder, murder in the second degree, armed robbery, home invasion in any degree, kidnapping, rape, aggravated child molestation, aggravated sodomy, aggravated sexual battery, or any felony involving the use or possession of a firearm and who shall have on or within arm's reach of his or her person a firearm during the commission of, or the attempt to commit:

(1) Any crime against or involving the person of another;

(2) The unlawful entry into a building or vehicle;

(3) A theft from a building or theft of a vehicle;

(4) Any crime involving the possession, manufacture, delivery, distribution, dispensing, administering, selling, or possession with intent to distribute any controlled substance as provided in O.C.G.A. § 16-13-30; or

(5) Any crime involving the trafficking of cocaine, marijuana, or illegal drugs as provided in O.C.G.A. § 16-13-31, and which crime

---

[23]Arnold v. State, 134 Ga. App. 853, 216 S.E.2d 373 (1975).

[24]16 Am. Jur. 2d 598, Constitutional Law § 643; 16A C.J.S. 350, Constitutional Law § 409; cf. Lindsey v. Washington, 301 U.S. 397, 57 S. Ct. 797, 81 L. Ed. 1182 (1937).

[25]Ga. Op. Att'y Gen. U96-20 (Oct. 25, 1996).

is a felony, commits a felony and, upon conviction thereof, shall be punished by confinement for a period of 15 years, such sentence to run consecutively to any other sentence which the person has received.

(c) Upon the second or subsequent conviction of a convicted felon under this Code section, such convicted felon shall be punished by confinement for life. Notwithstanding any other law to the contrary, the sentence of any convicted felon which is imposed for violating this Code section a second or subsequent time shall not be suspended by the court and probationary sentence imposed in lieu thereof.

In 1996, Georgia amended O.C.G.A. § 16-13-30 so as to provide that on a second or subsequent conviction for distribution of Schedule I or II controlled substances the defendant shall be sentenced to not less than 10 years and no more than 40 years or life. However, "the sentencing judge retains the *discretion* either to impose any sentence within the statutory mandatory minimum and maximum sentence range *or* else impose a life sentence." (Emphasis added.)[26] The same statute provides that upon a second or subsequent conviction of possession of a Schedule II drug, the defendant shall be sentenced to not less than five years or more than 30 years.

In *Miller v. State*,[27] the Georgia Court of Appeals held that a plea of nolo contendere constitutes a conviction under O.C.G.A. § 17-10-7. Likewise, in *Spinner v. State*,[28] the court held that a plea of *nolo contendere* may be considered as a "prior conviction" for purposes of O.C.G.A. § 17-10-7. It should be noted, however, that in *Beasley v. State*,[29] the court overruled *Spinner* and was critical of the reasoning in *Miller*. The court found that based upon a literal application of several of Georgia's recidivist statutes, as well as recent case law, a plea of nolo contendere should not be considered for sentencing enhancement or recidivist purposes in the absence of a legislative statement to the contrary.

In *Scott v. State*,[30] the court held that a "prior first offender record may not be used to sentence a defendant as a recidivist for a

---

[26]Scott v. State, 248 Ga. App. 542, 545(2), 545 S.E.2d 709 (2001).

[27]Miller v. State, 162 Ga. App. 730, 292 S.E.2d 102 (1982), overruled by Matthews v. State, 268 Ga. 798, 493 S.E.2d 136 (1997), only as it pertains to the use of a first offender record for impeachment by prior conviction of a crime; 4 Torcia, Wharton's Criminal Procedure, § 631 (12th Ed. 1976).

[28]Spinner v. State, 263 Ga. App.

802, 589 S.E.2d 344 (2003), overruled, Beasley v. State, 345 Ga. App. 247, 812 S.E.2d 561 (2018).

[29]Beasley v. State, 345 Ga. App. 247, 812 S.E.2d 561 (2018). See Jeffrey v. State, 296 Ga. 713, 770 S.E.2d 585 (2015) (physical precedent); Blackmon v. State, 266 Ga. App. 877, 598 S.E.2d 542 (2004).

[30]Scott v. State, 216 Ga. App. 692, 694(4), 455 S.E.2d 609 (1995).

later crime if the conditions of probation under the prior first of-fender treatment have been fulfilled and the defendant has been 'discharged' under O.C.G.A. § 42-8-62." In *Daniels v. State*,[31] the court held that when a defendant is adjudicated under the First Offender Act and he is given probation, then the probation is revoked and he is adjudicated as a felon, he may be sentenced for a later crime under O.C.G.A. § 17-10-7 as a repeat offender.

In *Dunn v. State*,[32] the court held that when a previous convic-tion is relied upon for imposing an enhanced punishment, the conviction must be final and not on appeal.

In *Thomas v. State*,[33] the court held that where a defendant has entered a guilty plea and the "[s]tate . . . initially prove[d] only the existence of the prior guilty plea and that [the] defendant was represented by counsel in all felony cases . . . [t]he burden then shifts to the defendant to produce some affirmative evidence showing an infringement of his rights or a procedural irregular-ity when the plea was taken."

Under Georgia's current law the trial judge alone determines punishment when the death sentence is not involved. "Since re-cidivism is an issue only in the sentencing phase of a trial . . . [the] defendant had no right to a jury determination of this issue."[34] The statute is applicable to capital cases.

In the 1999 case of *Nash v. State*,[35] a majority of the Georgia Supreme Court held that when the state wishes to present prior guilty pleas in aggravation of punishment so as to warrant recid-ivist punishment and the defendant claims that he did not volun-tarily enter the earlier pleas, "the burden is on the State to prove both the existence of the prior guilty pleas and that the defendant was represented by counsel in all felony cases and those misde-meanor proceedings where imprisonment resulted [or] 'a docket entry or other affirmative statement that the defendant waived the right to counsel.' . . . Upon such a showing, the presumption of regularity is then applied and the burden shifts to the defendant to produce some affirmative evidence showing an in-fringement of his rights or a procedural irregularity in the taking of the plea. 'Defendant can attempt to meet his burden of produc-tion with a transcript, with testimony regarding the taking of the plea, or with other affirmative evidence.' . . . 'A silent record or the mere naked assertion by an accused that his prior counseled

---

[31]Daniels v. State, 271 Ga. 167, 517 S.E.2d 66 (1999).

[32]Dunn v. State, 208 Ga. App. 197, 198(4), 430 S.E.2d 50 (1993).

[33]Thomas v. State, 249 Ga. App. 571, 573(5), 549 S.E.2d 408 (2001).

[34]LaPalme v. State, 169 Ga. App. 540(4), 313 S.E.2d 729 (1984).

[35]Nash v. State, 271 Ga. 281, 285, 519 S.E.2d 893 (1999). Accord, Wheeler v. State, 249 Ga. App. 116, 117(2), 547 S.E.2d 746 (2001).

plea was not made knowingly and intelligently is insufficient.'
. . . If the defendant is able to present evidence that a constitutional infirmity exists, then the burden of proving the constitutionality of the plea shifts to the State. 'The State will meet its
burden of proof if it introduces a "perfect" transcript of the taking
of the guilty plea, one which reflects a colloquy between judge
and defendant wherein the defendant was informed of and specifically waived his right to trial by jury, his privilege against self
incrimination, and his right to confront his accusers. If the State
introduces anything less than a "perfect" transcript, . . . the
judge then must weigh the evidence submitted by the defendant
and by the State to determine whether the State has met its
burden of proving that defendant's prior guilty plea was informed
and voluntary, and made with an articulated waiver of the three
Boykin rights.' " Apparently, "the three *Boykin* rights" are as
follows: "First, is the privilege against compulsory self-
incrimination guaranteed by the Fifth Amendment and applicable
to the States by reason of the Fourteenth. . . . Second, is the
right to trial by jury. . . . Third, is the right to confront one's
accusers."[36] The court cited and relied on the United States
Supreme Court case of *Parke v. Raley*,[37] which held there was no
due process violation in a similar case and pointed out that the
defendant in that case "never appealed his earlier convictions.
They became final years ago, and he now seeks to revisit the
question of their validity in a separate recidivism proceeding."
The court pointed out that there is a deeply rooted presumption
in our law that the " 'presumption of regularity' . . . attaches to
final judgments, even when the question is [a] waiver of constitutional rights."

In fact, it has been pointed out that today the only purpose for
including prior offenses in an indictment is to make it clear that
the defendant had notice of prior convictions which were to be
used in sentencing.[38] In *State v. Hendrixson*,[39] the Georgia
Supreme Court held that a defendant may be sentenced under
O.C.G.A. § 16-13-30(d), providing for enhanced punishment for
drug offenses, even though prior offenses were not set out in the
indictment.

In *Baldasar v. Illinois*,[40] the United States Supreme Court held
that an uncounseled plea or conviction, even for a misdemeanor,

---

[36]Boykin v. Alabama, 395 U.S.
238, 243, 89 S. Ct. 1709, 23 L. Ed. 2d
274, 279 (1969).

[37]Parke v. Raley, 506 U.S. 20, 113
S. Ct. 517, 121 L. Ed. 2d 391 (1992).

[38]Mitchell v. State, 202 Ga. App.
100(1), 413 S.E.2d 517 (1991).

[39]State v. Hendrixson, 251 Ga.
853, 310 S.E.2d 526 (1984).

[40]Baldasar v. Illinois, 446 U.S.
222, 100 S. Ct. 1585, 64 L. Ed. 2d 169
(1980). But in Harris v. State, 160 Ga.
App. 47(2), 285 S.E.2d 781 (1981), the
court held that an uncounseled guilty

cannot be used as the basis of punishment under a recidivist or punishment-enhancement statute, at least in the absence of a valid waiver of counsel. However, in the 1994 case of *Nichols v. United States*,[41] the United States Supreme Court overruled *Baldasar*, re-adopted the rule of *Scott v. Illinois*[42] and held that, under the Sixth and Fourteenth Amendments, if there is an uncounseled misdemeanor conviction and the defendant is sentenced only to pay a fine, the conviction may be relied upon in sentencing him for a later offense, even though the latter sentence entails imprisonment.

If the defendant's prior conviction is not valid, he cannot receive enhanced punishment as a recidivist for the later offense.[43] However, in *Parke v. Raley*,[44] the same court held that the due process clause permits a state to impose a burden on the defendant who challenges the validity of a prior plea to show that it was not made knowingly. While a waiver of rights resulting in a guilty plea cannot be presumed, there is a " 'presumption of regularity' that attaches to final judgments, even when the question is waiver of constitutional rights." This is true of any collateral attack.[45]

In *Jones v. State*,[46] where the defendant had pled guilty to a prior felony and the accusation recited that he had been advised "by the Court of his constitutional rights, including the right to counsel and indictment by grand jury, hereby waives arraignment, copy of accusation, list of witnesses, grand jury indictment and pleads guilty" and this plea was signed by the defendant and by his attorney, the Georgia Court of Appeals concluded that there was a sufficient showing that he was represented by counsel, and had been advised of his rights, and freely and voluntarily entered his guilty plea. See § 26:14, supra.

Also, a special situation exists in the application of O.C.G.A. § 40-5-58(c). This statute relates to driving a motor vehicle without a license after a driver has been notified that he has been declared an habitual violator. The offense of driving in such

---

plea to the misdemeanor offense of driving under the influence was admissible at sentencing where the defendant was charged with vehicular homicide. See § 7:1, supra.

In Scott v. State, 250 Ga. 195, 198, n.4, 297 S.E.2d 18 (1982), the court pointed out that an uncounseled felony conviction cannot be used to enhance punishment under a recidivist statute.

[41]Nichols v. U.S., 511 U.S. 738, 114 S. Ct. 1921, 128 L. Ed. 2d 745 (1994).

[42]Scott v. Illinois, 440 U.S. 367, 99 S. Ct. 1158, 59 L. Ed. 2d 383 (1979).

[43]See U. S. v. Tucker, 404 U.S. 443, 92 S. Ct. 589, 30 L. Ed. 2d 592 (1972).

[44]Parke v. Raley, 506 U.S. 20, 113 S. Ct. 517, 121 L. Ed. 2d 391 (1992).

[45]Nash v. State, 233 Ga. App. 75, 77, 503 S.E.2d 23 (1998).

[46]Jones v. State, 161 Ga. App. 620, 623(4), 288 S.E.2d 795 (1982).

a situation is deemed to be "an offense separate and distinct from the offenses which led to the driver being declared a habitual violator." Hence, it is reasoned that this statute "is not a recidivist statute and that in a prosecution under this statute it is not necessary to prove the defendant's prior convictions."[47] It follows that the fact that the defendant was not represented by counsel and did not knowingly and intelligently waive his right to counsel during the previous pleas and/or convictions makes no difference.[48]

In *Custis v. United States*,[49] state convictions were used to enhance the sentence imposed. The defendant contended that the convictions should not have been used (1) because of ineffective assistance of counsel, (2) because his guilty plea was not knowingly and intelligently entered, and (3) because his counsel failed to advise him of an available defense. The United States Supreme Court held that there was no constitutional violation in the denial of the collateral attack on the state convictions and that a defendant has no right to such a collateral attack with the sole exception of convictions obtained in violation of the right to counsel.

Sometimes there are evidentiary problems in the proof of former conviction. In *Glass v. State*,[50] the court held that a certified copy of a conviction of a person with the same name as the defendant on trial is some evidence of identity. The case of *Tankersley v. State*[51] holds that it is not error to admit uncertified copies of "the prior conviction" of the defendant for recidivist purposes.

Where the indictment sets out prior convictions under a recidivist statute, it is not necessary for the state to give the defendant any notice of the prior convictions other than that which is contained in the indictment.[52] Hence, it is not error for the trial judge to admit certified copies of such former convictions without any other prior notice to the defendant.

When a defendant is indicted as a recidivist, it is error for the court to permit the former conviction to become known to the

---

[47]Smith v. State, 248 Ga. 828, 830(3), 286 S.E.2d 709 (1982); Todd v. State, 163 Ga. App. 814(1), 294 S.E.2d 714 (1982).

[48]Rowland v. State, 161 Ga. App. 525, 526, 289 S.E.2d 15 (1982); Love v. Hardison, 166 Ga. App. 677(1), 305 S.E.2d 420 (1983).

[49]Custis v. U.S., 511 U.S. 485, 114 S. Ct. 1732, 128 L. Ed. 2d 517 (1994).

[50]Glass v. State, 181 Ga. App. 448, 352 S.E.2d 642 (1987); Mincey v. State, 186 Ga. App. 839, 841(4), 368 S.E.2d 796 (1988).

[51]Tankersley v. State, 155 Ga. App. 917, 922(14), 273 S.E.2d 862 (1980).

[52]Newton v. State, 154 Ga. App. 98, 100(2), 267 S.E.2d 641 (1980).

jury during the innocence-guilt phase of the trial.[53] However, where a defendant is charged with possession of a firearm, after having been convicted of a felony, and a previous conviction is set out in the indictment, a certified copy of the earlier conviction is admissible since the other offense is an element of the offense charged in the indictment on which the defendant is being tried.[54]

In *Gary v. State*,[55] the court held that it was not error for a trial judge to dismiss a "jury after a verdict has been rendered and making a determination without the intervention of a jury as to the recidivist counts of the indictment."

O.C.G.A. § 17-10-7(b.1) provides: "Subsections (a) and (d) of this Code section shall not apply to second or any subsequent convictions for any violation of subsection (a) . . . of Code section 16-13-30 (purchase or possession of controlled substances)." O.C.G.A. § 16-13-30(d) prohibits the use of the recidivist statute (O.C.G.A. § 17-10-7(a)) for a second conviction of possession of narcotics with intent to distribute under O.C.G.A. § 16-13-30(b), though it does apply to subsequent offenses. This rule does not apply, however, "where a defendant has previous convictions for violating [O.C.G.A. § 16-13-30(i)(1)] (simple possession of a counterfeit substance) or [O.C.G.A. § 16-13-30(j)] (marijuana-related offenses) and is thereafter convicted of simple possession of a controlled substance [O.C.G.A. § 16-13-30(s)].[56] But in *Brooks v. State*,[57] the court held that the fact that the sentence cannot be paroled does not automatically prevent the defendant from receiving a probated sentence in the case of a fourth offender recidivist.[58] Former GCA section 79A-9911 (not carried forward into the O.C.G.A.) was intended to apply to cases where increased punishment was sought for subsequent drug offenses.[59] O.C.G.A. § 16-11-126(i)(2), which relates to carrying a concealed weapon, is also a recidivist statute.[60] There are special recidivist statutes which apply to a subsequent armed robbery,[61] subsequent burglaries,[62]

---

[53]Clemmons v. State, 233 Ga. 187, 210 S.E.2d 657 (1974); Lawrence v. State, 259 Ind. 306, 286 N.E.2d 830 (1972).

[54]Biggers v. State, 162 Ga. App. 163, 165, 290 S.E.2d 159 (1982).

[55]Gary v. State, 186 Ga. App. 231, 366 S.E.2d 833 (1988).

[56]Mathis v. State, 336 Ga. App. 257, 261, 784 S.E.2d 98 (2016).

[57]Brooks v. State, 165 Ga. App. 115, 117(4), 299 S.E.2d 167 (1983).

[58]O.C.G.A. § 16-13-30.

[59]Lloyd v. State, 139 Ga. App. 625, 627(4), 229 S.E.2d 106 (1976); Williams v. State, 130 Ga. App. 418, 419(2), 203 S.E.2d 627 (1973). However, in Hinton v. State, 138 Ga. App. 702(5), 227 S.E.2d 474 (1976), it was held proper to sentence a defendant as a recidivist on a narcotic offense based on prior convictions for non-narcotics offenses under O.C.G.A. § 17-10-7.

[60]Favors v. State, 182 Ga. App. 179(1), 355 S.E.2d 109 (1987).

[61]O.C.G.A. § 16-8-41.

subsequent shopliftings,[63] and subsequent drug offenses.[64] Also, Georgia has a statute making it a separate offense to commit certain felonies while in possession of a knife or firearm. This statute likewise contains a recidivist provision.[65] For example, in *Norwood v. State*,[66] the court held that the general provision for enhanced sentencing of repeat offenders provided for in O.C.G.A. § 17-10-7 does not prevent the trial judge from exercising discretion in a burglary case and sentencing a defendant under O.C.G.A. § 16-7-1(b).

In *Mann v. State*,[67] the court held that the trial court in a drug case has discretion in sentencing a defendant under the specific recidivist provisions of O.C.G.A. § 16-13-30(d) and is not required to sentence the defendant to life in prison under the general recidivist provisions of O.C.G.A. § 17-10-7(a). Likewise, a defendant who is convicted of a fifth shoplifting offense, three of which were felonies, would be exposed at sentencing to the recidivist shoplifting statute rather than the general recidivist sentencing scheme.[68] As the court in *Mann* explained "a specific statute will prevail

---

[62]O.C.G.A. § 16-7-1. In Green v. State, 154 Ga. App. 295, 298(3), 267 S.E.2d 898 (1980), the court held that it was proper to sentence a burglary defendant under O.C.G.A. § 17-10-7 as a fourth offender rather than as a second offender under the burglary recidivist statute.

[63]O.C.G.A. § 16-8-14. See Williams v. State, 261 Ga. App. 176, 582 S.E.2d 141 (2003), where trial court's imposition of maximum sentence under felony shoplifting statute was reversed based upon the court's misunderstanding that maximum sentence was mandatory.

[64]O.C.G.A. § 16-13-30(d), (f), (g), (l).

[65]O.C.G.A. § 16-11-106.

[66]Norwood v. State, 249 Ga. App. 507, 508(2), 548 S.E.2d 478 (2001). O.C.G.A. § 17-10-7 is supplemental to other recidivist sentencing statutes such as O.C.G.A. § 16-7-1(b) (burglary) or O.C.G.A. § 16-13-30(d) (narcotics). It will yield to the more specific recidivist statute when the defendant's felony record consists only of the specific crime such as burglary or narcotics. However, when the defendant's criminal history is not so restricted and includes other types of felony of-

fenses, O.C.G.A. § 17-10-7 will control. As the court explained in Goldberg v. State, 282 Ga. 542, 651 S.E.2d 667 (2007), "the General Assembly intended that a habitual burglar be given the benefit of the trial court's sentencing discretion, but it further intended, that a habitual burglar who is also a habitual felon be subject to the imposition of the longest sentence prescribed for the subsequent offense for which he or she was convicted."

[67]Mann v. State, 273 Ga. 366, 367, 541 S.E.2d 645 (2001). The Court's observation regarding the interplay between O.C.G.A. § 16-13-30(d) and O.C.G.A. § 17-10-7 is worth noting: "we must bear in mind the principle that 'a specific statute will prevail over a general statute, absent any indication of a contrary legislative intent.' . . . . For this reason, the general recidivist scheme of § 17-10-7 will apply to multiple convictions under O.C.G.A. § 16-13-30(b) only if § 16-13-30(d) permits the applicability of O.C.G.A. § 17-10-7." (cits. omitted) *Mann*, 273 Ga. at 368, 541 S.E.2d 645. See Parham v. State, 342 Ga. App. 754, 805 S.E.2d 264 (2017).

[68]Williams v. State, 261 Ga. App. 176(3), 582 S.E.2d 141 (2003).

over a general statute, absent any indication of a contrary legislative intent."[69]

In considering whether a convicted defendant may be subject to enhanced punishment as a recidivist, counsel and the court should be careful to look at the date of the offenses on which the defendant's prior convictions were based. Recidivist punishment is designed to punish the *repetition* of unlawful conduct. Thus, convictions that are prior in time to the one in which the state is seeking an enhanced sentence, but which are based on conduct which occurred subsequent to the pending case, may not be considered for purposes of a recidivist sentence. They may, of course, be considered like that of any other conduct of a defendant as aggravation evidence at a sentencing provided the state has given notice of its intent to rely on such evidence as required by O.C.G.A. § 17-16-4(a)(5).[70]

See § 13:18, supra, on indictment for possession of a firearm by a felon and on contents of an indictment where a defendant is charged as a recidivist and see § 24:18, supra, on sending the indictment to the jury room. See § 26:2, supra, on cruel and unusual punishment. See, Appendix B, infra, "Recidivist Punishment Under O.C.G.A. § 17-10-7," prepared by Marc A. Mallon, Assistant District Attorney, Fulton County, Georgia.

§ 26:29   Concurrent and consecutive sentences

Generally, when there are multiple convictions in a single trial, the sentencing judge may expressly provide whether the sentences are to be served consecutively or concurrently.[1] *Duckworth v. State*[2] held that where the death penalty is not sought, a "court sitting without a jury pursuant to [O.C.G.A. § 17-10-2(a)] was authorized to fix [the defendant's] two life sentences to run either concurrently or consecutively."

However, O.C.G.A. § 16-11-106(b) provides that a defendant convicted of possession of a knife or firearm during the commission of certain crimes must "be punished by confinement for a period of five years [and] such sentence [must] run consecutively to any other sentence which the person has received." Nevertheless, in *Busch v. State*,[3] the Georgia Supreme Court construed the statute "to require that a sentence for the possession offense be served consecutively only to the underlying felony for that of-

---

[69]Mann v. State, 273 Ga. 366, 368, 541 S.E.2d 645 (2001).

[70]Mays v. State, 262 Ga. 90, 414 S.E.2d 481 (1992).

[Section 26:29]

[1]Giles v. State, 211 Ga. App. 618,

441 S.E.2d 101 (1993).

[2]Duckworth v. State, 246 Ga. 631, 633 (2), 272 S.E.2d 332 (1980).

[3]Busch v. State, 271 Ga. 591, 523 S.E.2d 21 (1999).

fense" and not to all sentences being imposed.

If the trial court fails to specify whether or not one sentence is to run concurrently or consecutively with another, O.C.G.A. § 17-10-10 applies. That statute provides in part as follows:

"(a) Where at one term of court a person is convicted on more than one indictment or accusation, or on more than one count thereof, and sentenced to imprisonment, the sentences shall be served concurrently unless otherwise expressly provided therein.

"(b) Where a person is convicted on more than one indictment or accusation at separate terms of court, or in different courts, and sentenced to imprisonment, the sentences shall be served concurrently, one with the other, unless otherwise expressly provided therein.

"(c) This Code section shall apply alike to felony and misdemeanor offenses.

"(d) This Code section shall govern and shall be followed by the Department of Corrections in the computation of time that sentences shall run."

Where a prosecutor seeks the death penalty for two offenses and the jury recommends mercy for both, only the jury has the right to designate that the sentences are to run concurrently. However, where the defendant is serving a life sentence and he is tried for a case in which the death penalty is sought, the trial judge not the jury has the authority to determine whether or not the sentences are to run consecutively regardless of whether the jury in the later case imposes the death penalty.[4] However, where there is a bench trial for two murders and the death penalty is not sought, the trial judge may sentence the defendant to serve consecutive life sentences.[5]

If judgments and probation orders fail to specify the order in which consecutive sentences (imposed by the same court) are to be served, the sequence of service shall correspond to the order of the cases as shown by their numbers.[6]

Georgia sentences do not run concurrently with federal sentences unless it is expressly provided that they do so.[7] It has been held that a federal court cannot order a federal sentence to be served concurrently with a state sentence.[8] Where a defendant has been previously sentenced in a court of another state, the sentence imposed in Georgia may be fixed to run consecutively to

---

[4]Spivey v. State, 253 Ga. 187, 192 (5), 319 S.E.2d 420 (1984).

[5]Duckworth v. State, 246 Ga. 631, 633 (2), 272 S.E.2d 332 (1980).

[6]Jackson v. State, 91 Ga. App. 291, 292, 85 S.E.2d 444 (1954).

[7]Grimes v. Greer, 223 Ga. 628, 157 S.E.2d 260 (1967); Taylor v. Green, 229 Ga. 164, 190 S.E.2d 66 (1972).

[8]Joslin v. Moseley, 420 F.2d 1204 (10th Cir. 1969).

the prior out-of-state sentence.[9]

It has been said that in the case of consecutive sentences, each succeeding sentence begins at the date of the termination of the prior sentence. This is true even if the first sentence is shortened because of good time or lengthened because of an escape.[10] If a defendant is sentenced consecutively to a sentence in another court which is appealed, the defendant may be assigned to the prison system after the finality of the second sentence.[11]

When a defendant is sentenced to 15 years "as to each count" of a three count indictment as a result of a clerical error, the sentence may be amended to provide that the sentences are to be served consecutively.[12]

In *Jones v. Thomas*,[13] the United States Supreme Court considered a case in which the defendant had been improperly sentenced consecutively for both felony murder and the underlying felony. The shorter sentence had been served when the state court sought to remedy the situation by giving Thomas credit for the time served on the longer sentence. The Supreme Court remanded the case for dismissal of Thomas' petition for federal habeas corpus since the state court's action "provided suitable protection for his double jeopardy rights."

§ 26:30 Sentencing on multiple counts or indictments—General limitations

The substantive aspect of double jeopardy, set forth in O.C.G.A. § 16-1-7(a), places limits on the number of convictions and punishments which may be imposed for crimes arising from the same criminal conduct. For an overview of the differences between substantive and procedural aspects of double jeopardy, see § 14:54, supra.

O.C.G.A. § 16-1-7 reads as follows:

"(a) When the same conduct of an accused may establish the commission of more than one crime, the accused may be prosecuted for each crime. He may not, however, be convicted of more than one crime if:

"(1) One crime is included in the other;[¹] or

---

[9]Cobb v. State, 250 Ga. 1, 295 S.E.2d 319 (1982).

[10]Jackson v. State, 91 Ga. App. 291, 292, 85 S.E.2d 444 (1954).

[11]Wise v. Balkcom, 245 Ga. 126, 263 S.E.2d 158 (1980).

[12]Bryant v. Evans, 244 Ga. 673, 261 S.E.2d 620 (1979).

[13]Jones v. Thomas, 491 U.S. 376, 109 S.Ct. 2522, 105 L.Ed.2d 322 (1989).

[Section 26:30]

[1]Rules for determining whether one crime is included in the other are set out in O.C.G.A. § 16-1-6. See also § 14:52, supra.

"(2) The crimes differ only in that one is defined to prohibit a designated kind of conduct generally and the other to prohibit a specific instance of such conduct."

§ 26:31 Sentencing on multiple counts or indictments— What constitutes a conviction?

As the court in *Sartin v. State*,[1] pointed out, a "[c]onviction is not the verdict; [a conviction] is the judgment on the verdict or guilty plea [entered by the court]"[2] while punishment is the actual sentence imposed on the defendant.[3] However, our courts have not always recognized this distinction. In *Wells v. State*,[4] the court stated that it was not proper to "convict" on both counts of an indictment charging possession *and* possession with intent to distribute, and found that "the trial court erred in so charging the jury." By defining conviction as the court did in *Sartin*, the conviction comes after the verdict; so the court's statement in *Wells* that the two separate offenses could not even be sent to the jury for a verdict implies that the court interpreted "conviction" as equal to a verdict.[5]

Likewise, courts often use the term "conviction" as synonymous with "punishment" or "sentencing." Both the conviction and punishment phases of the trial process are discussed herein as they relate to the substantive aspect of double jeopardy. Although an effort has been made to clarify which phase of the trial is actually at issue in the following case examples, a close reading of each case will better identify possible avenues of distinction.

[Section 26:31]

[1]Sartin v. State, 223 Ga. App. 759, 761 (4), 479 S.E.2d 354 (1996).

[2]Sartin v. State, 223 Ga. App. 759, 761 (4), 479 S.E.2d 354 (1996). See also Spence v. State, 233 Ga. 527, 528 (1), 212 S.E.2d 357 (1975), holding where a defendant was charged with possession of a firearm during the commission of a crime and murder, it was not error to dismiss the charge of possession of a firearm after a guilty verdict was entered by the jury on both counts.

[3]Sartin v. State, 223 Ga. App. 759, 761 (4), 479 S.E.2d 354 (1996).

[4]Wells v. State, 126 Ga. App. 130, 132, 190 S.E.2d 106 (1972). But see Rhear v. State, 171 Ga. App. 435, 436 (3), 319 S.E.2d 895 (1984), holding that it was not reversible error for the judge to fail to instruct the jury that they could only convict on either the felony murder charge or the armed robbery charge where he was charged with felony murder and with armed robbery.

[5]Wells v. State, 126 Ga. App. 130, 132, 190 S.E.2d 106 (1972). See also State v. Estevez, 232 Ga. 316, 320 (2), 206 S.E.2d 475 (1974), overruled on other grounds by Drinkard v. Walker, 281 Ga. 211, 636 S.E.2d 530 (2006); Burns v. State, 127 Ga. App. 828, 829, 195 S.E.2d 189 (1973).

§ 26:32 Sentencing on multiple counts or indictments— Included offenses limitations

As noted by the court in *State v. Estevez,*[1] even though the defendant may be prosecuted for more than one crime, he may not be convicted or punished for more than one crime if "one of the crimes is included in the other."[2] "A crime is an included crime, and multiple [conviction and] punishment, therefore, is barred, if it is the same [crime] as a matter of fact *or* as a matter of law." (Emphasis added.)[3] Subsections (1) and (2) of O.C.G.A. § 16-1-6 set out the rules for determining whether an included crime is one as a matter of law or of fact.

A crime is an included crime as a matter of fact if "[i]t is established by proof of the same or less than all the facts or a less culpable mental state than is required to establish commission of the crime charged."[4] Whereas, a crime is an included crime as a matter of law if "[i]t differs from the crime charged only in the respect that a less serious injury or risk of injury to the same person, property, or public interest or a lesser kind of culpability suffices to establish its commission."[5]

In *Drinkard v. Walker,*[6] the Georgia Supreme Court overruled *State v. Estevez*[7] and the "actual evidence" test for determining whether a lesser crime is included in a greater crime under O.C.G.A. § 16-1-6 and adopted the *Blockburger* or "required evidence" test. Under the required evidence test, "where the same act or transaction constitutes a violation of two distinct statutory provisions, the test to be applied to determine whether there are two offenses or only one, is whether each provision requires proof

---

[Section 26:32]

[1]State v. Estevez, 232 Ga. 316, 319 (1), 206 S.E.2d 475 (1974), overruled on other grounds by Drinkard v. Walker, 281 Ga. 211, 636 S.E.2d 530 (2006).

[2]O.C.G.A. § 16-1-7(a)(1); Hewett v. State, 244 Ga. App. 112, 534 S.E.2d 867 (2000).

[3]State v. Estevez, 232 Ga. 316, 320 (1), 206 S.E.2d 475 (1974), overruled on other grounds by Drinkard v. Walker, 281 Ga. 211, 636 S.E.2d 530 (2006).

[4]O.C.G.A. § 16-1-6(1).

[5]O.C.G.A. § 16-1-6(2). See Zamudio v. State, 332 Ga. App. 37, 771 S.E.2d 733 (2015) (trial court incorrectly merged aggravated battery conviction into conviction for criminal attempt to commit murder, rather than the other way around because attempted murder requires a less serious injury to the person).

[6]Drinkard v. Walker, 281 Ga. 211, 636 S.E.2d 530 (2006).

[7]State v. Estevez, 232 Ga. 316, 206 S.E.2d 475 (1974) (overruled by, Drinkard v. Walker, 281 Ga. 211, 636 S.E.2d 530 (2006)). Under the actual evidence test, a lesser crime will be included in a greater crime if "the evidence actually presented at trial to establish the elements of the crime charged also establishes all the elements of the lesser crime." State v. Burgess, 263 Ga. 143, 144-45, 429 S.E.2d 252 (1993).

of a fact which the other does not."[8] Thus, the court held that the crime of rape did not include the crimes of statutory rape and incest because the latter crimes required the state to prove additional facts, e.g., that the victim was thirteen and was the defendant's niece.[9]

Conversely, when "[t]he crimes differ only in that one is defined to prohibit a designated kind of conduct generally and the other to prohibit a specific instance of such conduct"[10] multiple convictions and punishments are prohibited under O.C.G.A. § 16-1-7(a)(2) This prong of the Code has rarely been addressed specifically in the opinions of the courts. However, in *Johnson v. State*,[11] the court held that the defendant could not be convicted for both theft of a motor vehicle and theft of its contents since "Code Ann. § 26-1802 [now O.C.G.A. § 16-8-2] (theft by taking) and § 26-1813 [former O.C.G.A. § 16-8-17] (motor vehicle theft) differ only in that the former is defined to prohibit a designated kind of conduct generally (theft of 'any property') and the latter to prohibit a specific instance of such conduct (theft of a 'motor vehicle')." Thus, conviction of theft by taking a motor vehicle merges into theft by taking (related to the contents). But in *Brown v. State*,[12] the court held that the conviction for possession of a firearm by a convicted felon (a prohibited person) did not merge with the offense of possession of a shotgun (a prohibited weapon). See, Appendix B, *Lesser Included Offenses in Georgia*, a summary prepared by Atlanta attorney, Donald F. Samuel, first published in *The Georgia Defender*, Vol. XXII, No. 1 (2003). See § 26:44, infra.

§ 26:33 Sentencing on multiple counts or indictments— Merger limitations

The required evidence test approved in *Drinkard v. Walker*,[1] i.e., where the same act or transaction constitutes a violation of "two distinct statutory provisions," has no application to those instances where a course of conduct can result in multiple violations of the same statute. In *Gonzales v. State*,[2] the defendant was convicted of two separate counts of aggravated battery based upon a single act of pushing the victim out of a moving car. One count charged that his actions caused disfigurement to the

---

[8]Drinkard v. Walker, 281 Ga. 211, 636 S.E.2d 530 (2006) quoting Blockburger v. U.S., 284 U.S. 299, 304, 52 S. Ct. 180, 76 L. Ed. 306 (1932).

[9]Drinkard v. Walker, 281 Ga. 211, 636 S.E.2d 530 (2006).

[10]O.C.G.A. § 16-1-7(a)(2).

[11]Johnson v. State, 130 Ga. App. 134, 136, 202 S.E.2d 525 (1973).

[12]Brown v. State, 168 Ga. App. 537, 538 (3), 309 S.E.2d 683 (1983).

[Section 26:33]

[1]Drinkard v. Walker, 281 Ga. 211, 636 S.E.2d 530 (2006).

[2]Gonzales v. State, 298 Ga. App. 821, 681 S.E.2d 248 (2009).

victim's buttocks and back. The other charged that his actions rendered useless the victim's legs. The issue is resolved through a determination of "the precise act or conduct that is criminalized under the statute." Although aggravated battery may be committed in more than one way, a defendant cannot be sentenced for two counts of aggravated battery arising out of a single unlawful act toward a single victim. Likewise, if during the course of a criminal transaction, the defendant injures a victim in a manner which would support a charge of aggravated assault and then injures the victim in a manner which would support a charge of aggravated battery and the same weapon is used to cause both injuries, the offenses would be subject to merger for purposes of sentencing provided the wounds were inflicted in quick succession without a deliberate interval between each.[3]

In *Kirkland v. State*,[4] the defendant was charged with one count of driving under the influence and injuring the victim's right foot and another count of driving under the influence and injuring the victim's left foot. The court held that "although [the defendant] could be prosecuted on both of these counts, he could not be convicted and sentenced on both, [because] the single instance of [the defendant's] conduct in driving under the influence was 'used up' in proving one of the counts and could not be used again as the predicate for a conviction and sentence on the other."[5] In *Taylor v. State*,[6] the defendant was charged in separate counts with driving under the influence of alcohol, cocaine and marijuana and was sentenced to three consecutive 12-month sentences. The appellate court held that these three charges merged and the defendant could not be sentenced to three successive 12-month sentences. The court reasoned that the legislative intent was to treat the separate offenses as a single offense and "the subsections 'merely define different modes of committing that one crime.' "The court said that "the question is: What did the legislature intend?" and then reasoned that the legislature intended to treat the separate offenses as a single offense and "the subsections 'merely define different modes of committing that one crime.' "Likewise, in *Gunter v. State*,[7] the court held that because "the evidence relied upon . . . to establish the offense of attempted

---

[3]Regent v. State, 299 Ga. 172, 787 S.E.2d 217 (2016).

[4]Kirkland v. State, 206 Ga. App. 27 (2), 424 S.E.2d 638 (1992).

[5]Kirkland v. State, 206 Ga. App. 27 (2), 424 S.E.2d 638 (1992). See also Gary v. State, 122 Ga. App. 151, 152 (2), 176 S.E.2d 478 (1970), stating that a defendant may not be charged with

possession of a vehicle knowing the identification number had been "removed and falsified" and possession of a vehicle knowing the identification number has been "falsified."

[6]Taylor v. State, 238 Ga. App. 753, 754 (2), 520 S.E.2d 267 (1999).

[7]Gunter v. State, 155 Ga. App. 176 (2), 270 S.E.2d 224 (1980).

livestock theft was precisely the evidence used to establish that appellants had committed criminal trespass, [t]he latter offense is [necessarily] included in the former as a matter of fact."

Where the defendant was convicted of four counts for statements made during one deposition, the court in *Beecher v. State*,[8] held that the four counts "constituted only one offense . . . made under the same oath" and thereby vacated the conviction and punishment for three of the counts.[9] Additionally, the court in *Nave v. State*[10] held that a violation of oath by a public officer is a lesser included offense of bribery as a matter of fact.

In *Withrow v. State*,[11] a child cruelty case, the Court of Appeals concluded that it was error to sentence a defendant on three separate counts where the indictment charged a course of conduct occurring over a period of three consecutive days. In the absence of a clear legislative intent, the court ruled that a continuing course of criminal conduct was not divisible for purposes of sentencing.

In *State v. Williams*,[12] the defendant filed a motion to dismiss because of "multiplicity" where 47 counts in an indictment charged the defendant with possession of a separate and distinct image of child pornography. "Multiplicity is the charging of the same crime in several counts of the charging document."[13] The court noted that it is the legislature's responsibility to determine whether a course of conduct can result in separate violations of the same statute, each of which may be subject to an independent sentence and not be subject to merger. The court held that O.C.G.A. § 16-12-100(b)(8) reflects such an intention and that the trial court was correct in denying the motion.

In *Linson v. State*,[14] the defendant was convicted of sodomy and aggravated child molestation and given concurrent sentences. The trial court merged the sodomy conviction into the aggravated child molestation. On appeal, the conviction of aggravated child molestation was reversed. On remand, the court reinstated the

---

[8]Beecher v. State, 164 Ga. App. 54, 56 (2), 296 S.E.2d 374 (1982).

[9]Beecher v. State, 164 Ga. App. 54, 56 (2), 296 S.E.2d 374 (1982). See McKee v. State, 275 Ga. App. 646(5), 621 S.E.2d 611 (2005) where failure of trial court to merge four counts of child cruelty which occurred over a span of four consecutive days and involved the same victim was error since the acts were part of a course of conduct and there was nothing in the applicable statute which would authorize treating each day of abuse as a separate incident for purposes of punishment.

[10]Nave v. State, 171 Ga. App. 165 (1), 318 S.E.2d 753 (1984).

[11]Withrow v. State, 275 Ga. App. 110(4), 619 S.E.2d 714 (2005).

[12]State v. Williams, 818 S.E.2d 256 (Ga. Ct. App. 2018).

[13]Chancey v. State, 256 Ga. 415, 349 S.E.2d 717 (1986). See § 26:33, infra, on merger limitations.

[14]Linson v. State, 239 Ga. App. 658, 522 S.E.2d 55 (1999).

sodomy conviction and dead docketed the other charge. In affirming the trial court, the court pointed out that the trial court had the power to "unmerge" the sodomy conviction and to re-sentence on sodomy alone. "[O]n remand a trial court may reconsider any merger issues and sentence accordingly."

While "[t]he crimes of aggravated assault or rape and kidnapping do not necessarily merge as a matter of law, . . . they may do so as a matter of fact."[15] Likewise, the court in *Hizine v. State*[16] recognized that the crimes of aggravated assault and armed robbery do not merge as a matter of law, but may as a matter of fact. In *Hizine* the court found that the aggravated assault, as a matter of fact, is a lesser include offense of the armed robbery where "hedge clippers, [a] chair, and [a] knife . . . were . . . used against [the] victim in [an] effort to subdue him prior to taking his money."[17]

Further, in *Lovell v. State*,[18] the court pointed out that "[t]he general rule is that when individual acts are prohibited, each act is punished separately, no matter how close they may be in time to each other." Unless there are separate victims, a defendant may not be convicted of both felony murder and the underlying felony because these charges would merge as a matter of law.[19]

---

[15]Thornton v. State, 144 Ga. App. 595, 241 S.E.2d 478 (1978). See Allen v. State, 233 Ga. 200, 203, 210 S.E.2d 680 (1974); Roberts v. State, 228 Ga. 298, 185 S.E.2d 385 (1971) (holding that auto theft merged into armed robbery as a matter of fact); Holt v. State, 239 Ga. 606, 238 S.E.2d 399 (1977) (holding that auto theft did not merge into armed robbery as a matter of law nor here as a matter of fact). See also Williams v. State, 238 Ga. 244, 246 (7), 232 S.E.2d 238 (1977) (holding that aggravated assault and simple battery merged as a matter of fact into the offense of kidnapping with bodily harm); Chambley v. State, 163 Ga. App. 502, 504 (2), 295 S.E.2d 166 (1982) (holding that neither robbery nor armed robbery merged with kidnapping as a matter of fact or as a matter of law).

[16]Hizine v. State, 148 Ga. App. 375, 251 S.E.2d 393 (1978). Accord, Hambrick v. State, 256 Ga. 148, 344 S.E.2d 639 (1986); Young v. State, 177 Ga. App. 756, 757 (2), 341 S.E.2d 286 (1986); Luke v. State, 171 Ga. App. 201, 202 (2), 318 S.E.2d 833 (1984);

Chitwood v. State, 170 Ga. App. 599, 600 (4), 317 S.E.2d 589 (1984) (holding that aggravated assault merges into armed robbery as a matter of fact, and upholding conviction of mutiny and armed robbery). Cf. Green v. State, 170 Ga. App. 806, 318 S.E.2d 513 (1984) (holding that aggravated assault charge merges into mutiny charge as a matter of fact).

[17]Dunbar v. State, 163 Ga. App. 243, 292 S.E.2d 897 (1982).

[18]Lovell v. State, 235 Ga. App. 140, 143 (2), 508 S.E.2d 771 (1998). See Moore v. State, 285 Ga. 157 (3), 674 S.E.2d 315 (2009) (aggravated assault with a weapon committed minutes before fatal shooting with the same weapon did not merge based upon finding that the aggravated assault, pointing the firearm, was a completed crime before the murder occurred when victim attempted escape).

[19]Brown v. State, 256 Ga. 439 (2), 349 S.E.2d 738 (1986). Accord, Milledge v. State, 266 Ga. 699, 700 (2), 470 S.E.2d 439 (1996) (aggravated assault into felony murder); Mason v. State,

Accordingly, the court in *Brown v. State*[20] vacated the defendant's conviction of the offense of peeping tom (the underlying felony) where the defendant was also convicted of felony murder. Similarly, in *Bolton v. State*,[21] the defendant's conviction for the underlying felony of cruelty to children was vacated where the defendant was also convicted of felony murder. No new trial was required. Likewise, a vehicular homicide charge merges as a matter of law into the felony murder charge where the charges are pertaining to the same victim.[22]

In *Reddick v. State*,[23] the defendant was found guilty of possession of cocaine and possession and use of drug related objects. The appellate court held that it was error to fail to merge the two drug violations. In *Gooch v. State*,[24] the court held that it was error to fail to merge the possession of a methamphetamine count with the count charging possession of methamphetamine with intent to distribute.

In *Curtis v. State*,[25] the Supreme Court overruled those cases which previously had held that the issue of merger of included offenses may be waived by failure to assert the issue in the trial court. The Court reasoned that a conviction and sentence premised upon a count in an indictment which should have merged with another at sentencing was void and its illegality was not subject to waiver. However, in *Nazario v. State*,[26] the Court elaborated on *Curtis* and explained that while the merger issue may not be subject to waiver, an appellate court's consideration of the issue is limited to the record. Accordingly, in cases where the defendant pleads guilty to a multiple count indictment there will often be little support in the record to support a merger

---

267 Ga. 314 (2), 477 S.E.2d 568 (1996) (same); Thomas v. State, 256 Ga. 176, 345 S.E.2d 350 (1986) (escape into felony murder); Gore v. State, 246 Ga. 575, 576 (4), 272 S.E.2d 306 (1980) (same). See also Atkins v. Hopper, 234 Ga. 330, 333 (3), 216 S.E.2d 89 (1975) (holding same but in a habeas corpus proceeding).

[20]Brown v. State, 256 Ga. 439 (2), 349 S.E.2d 738 (1986).

[21]Bolton v. State, 253 Ga. 116, 117 (1), 318 S.E.2d 138 (1984).

[22]Diamond v. State, 267 Ga. 249, 251 (3)(b), 477 S.E.2d 562 (1996).

[23]Reddick v. State, 249 Ga. App. 678, 679 (2), 549 S.E.2d 151 (2001).

[24]Gooch v. State, 249 Ga. App. 643, 648 (5), 549 S.E.2d 724 (2001).

[25]Curtis v. State, 275 Ga. 576(1), 571 S.E.2d 376 (2002) (overruling Howard v. State, 230 Ga. App. 437(3), 496 S.E.2d 532 (1998) and numerous other cases which all had held that the issue of merger at sentencing was subject to waiver.) *Curtis* was overruled on other grounds in Williams v. State, 287 Ga. 192, 695 S.E.2d 244 (2010) (challenge to a conviction as opposed to the sentence cannot be raised by O.C.G.A. § 16-1-7(a), motion to correct illegal sentence).

[26]Nazario v. State, 293 Ga. 480, 746 S.E.2d 109 (2013). See Dixon v. State, 302 Ga. 691, 808 S.E.2d 696 (2017) (court will no longer exercise its discretion to correct future sentencing errors which benefit defendant unless the issue is raised by state on cross-appeal).

claim as compared to the expanded record provided by trial where the factual basis for an included offense is readily apparent.

In *Alleyne v. United States*,[27] the U.S. Supreme Court, building upon *Apprendi v. New Jersey*,[28] held "[a]ny fact that, by law, increases the penalty for a crime is an 'element' that must be submitted to the jury and found beyond a reasonable doubt. Mandatory minimum sentences increase the penalty for a crime. It follows, then, that any fact that increases the mandatory minimum is an 'element' that must be submitted to the jury."

Because an aggravated assault committed as in the context of family violence as defined by O.C.G.A. § 16-5-21(k) enhances the minimum punishment from one to three years, the Georgia Supreme Court, based on *Alleyne*, reversed prior case authority which treated the family violence aspect of the offense "as merely a sentencing factor and not an element of the aggravated assault charge." As a result, the court vacated a sentencing order which had merged four counts of felony murder based upon aggravated assault, domestic violence, into the malice murder charge, finding that the felony murder counts required proof of a fact that the murder count did not, to wit: domestic violence. Instead, the felony murder counts should have been vacated as a matter of law. The aggravated assault charges should have merged into one count for sentencing.[29]

In *Hendrix v. State*,[30] the Georgia Supreme Court held that the defendant was improperly convicted and sentenced on counts of malice and felony murder since there was a single victim. The felony murder count "must be vacated as mere surplusage." In turn, it was error to merge the predicate felony of felon-in-possession into the felony murder as the latter was vacated by operation of law, and appellant was subject to being sentenced on the predicate felony. In addition, because the aggravated assault was based on the same act as malice murder, it was a lesser included offense and should have been merged into the malice murder.

---

[27]Alleyne v. United States, 570 U.S. 99, 133 S. Ct. 2151, 186 L. Ed. 2d 314 (2013), overruling Harris v. U.S., 536 U.S. 545, 122 S. Ct. 2406, 153 L. Ed. 2d 524 (2002).

[28]Apprendi v. New Jersey, 530 U.S. 466, 120 S. Ct. 2348, 147 L. Ed. 2d 435 (2000).

[29]Jeffrey v. State, 296 Ga. 713, 770 S.E.2d 585 (2015) (overruling Durden v. State, 293 Ga. 89, 744 S.E.2d 9 (2013)).

[30]Hendrix v. State, 298 Ga. 60, 779 S.E.2d 322 (2015). See Noel v. State, 297 Ga. 698, 777 S.E.2d 449 (2015) (defendant improperly sentenced to three life sentences where there was only one victim, requiring remand for sentencing on two non-murder felonies which had served as predicates to two of the felony murder counts).

§ 26:34 Sentencing on multiple counts or indictments— Completion of crime limitations on merger

The defendant in *Lowe v. State*,[1] was found guilty by the jury of malice murder, felony murder and the underlying felony of aggravated assault. The reviewing court noted that the trial court correctly merged the offense of felony murder with that of malice murder prior to the sentencing and affirmed the separate conviction of the underlying aggravated assault and malice murder. Because the separate offense of assault occurred and was completed when the defendant fired one single shot into the victim's arm, the court ruled that the aggravated assault and malice murder did not merge as a matter of fact. The malice murder offense occurred after "some time had passed" and the defendant had walked around the car and watched the victim plea for his life before firing a separate fatal shot to his abdomen.

In *Dunbar v. State*,[2] the court found no merger of the aggravated assault and armed robbery where the armed robbery had itself been completed via threat with a rifle prior to the incident of aggravated assault whereby the defendants severely beat the victim with a tire tool. In *Kellibrew v. State*,[3] the court held that the conviction of aggravated assault was completed before the aggravated battery, and therefore the defendant could be sentenced for each crime. Likewise, in *Hug v. State*,[4] the defendant claimed he should not have been convicted of both charges of aggravated assault, but the court affirmed the trial court judge due to the fact that one count was for hitting the victim in the head with an object likely to cause serious bodily harm, while the second charge was for shooting the victim. The evidence showed that the defendant entered the victim's home, sat on her back, and hit her in the head with a blunt object. When the victim tried to escape, the defendant shot her. The crimes were completed one after the other, and thus were not included offenses as a matter of fact.[5]

[Section 26:34]

[1]Lowe v. State, 267 Ga. 410, 412 (1), 478 S.E.2d 762 (1996). Accord, O'Neal v. State, 228 Ga. App. 162, 163 (2), 491 S.E.2d 216 (1997).

[2]Dunbar v. State, 163 Ga. App. 243, 292 S.E.2d 897 (1982).

[3]Kellibrew v. State, 239 Ga. App. 783, 786 (4), 521 S.E.2d 921 (1999).

[4]Hug v. State, 205 Ga. App. 746 (1), 423 S.E.2d 700 (1992).

[5]Hug v. State, 205 Ga. App. 746 (1), 423 S.E.2d 700 (1992). See also Talley v. State, 164 Ga. App. 150, 153 (7), 296 S.E.2d 173 (1982), affirming conviction on two separate counts of aggravated assault where the defendant ran the victim down with a truck, and, after an exchange of words, got out of the vehicle and slashed the victim's throat.

§ 26:35 Sentencing on multiple counts or indictments—Miscellaneous cases where there is no merger

A defendant may be convicted and punished for both armed robbery and burglary as neither are included offenses of the other under O.C.G.A. § 16-1-7(a)(1) as a matter of fact or of law, and each are intended to prohibit a designated kind of conduct generally, O.C.G.A. § 16-1-7(a)(2).[1] Likewise, the court in *Groves v. State*[2] held that since the elements required to prove rape and those required to prove burglary were not the same, the rape charge was not an included offense of burglary as a matter of fact or as a matter of law. Also, the court in *Bailey v. State*[3] held that kidnapping does not merge as a matter of fact or of law into the offense of escape. And, in *Williams v. State,*[4] the court held that enticing a child for indecent purposes and child molestation where the defendant allegedly met the child on the street, accompanied her to a wooded area, and attempted to have intercourse with her were not the same as a matter of fact or law. In *Smith v. State,*[5] the court held that the offense of possession of a firearm during the commission of a felony does not merge into the felony as a matter of law or fact upon conviction of both. Just as the conviction of possession of a firearm by a convicted felon does not merge as a matter of law or fact into a conviction for possession of a firearm during the commission of a felony.[6] O.C.G.A. § 16-5-44.1(d) provides that the offense of motor vehicle hijacking is to

---

[Section 26:35]

[1] Moore v. State, 140 Ga. App. 824, 826 (2), 232 S.E.2d 264 (1976). Accord, Brown v. State, 199 Ga. App. 773, 774, 406 S.E.2d 248 (1991); Luke v. State, 171 Ga. App. 201, 202 (1), 318 S.E.2d 833 (1984). Judge Benham's excellent opinion also discusses a number of other merger situations.

[2] Groves v. State, 152 Ga. App. 606, 607 (2), 263 S.E.2d 501 (1979). See also Sanford v. State, 169 Ga. App. 769, 315 S.E.2d 281 (1984), holding that a defendant can be convicted of hunting game from a motor vehicle, hunting wildlife upon a public road, and hunting game animals at night with a light exceeding six volts, because each rests upon proof of additional distinct elements not shared with the others.

[3] Bailey v. State, 146 Ga. App. 774, 247 S.E.2d 588 (1978).

[4] Williams v. State, 156 Ga. App. 481, 482, 274 S.E.2d 826 (1980).

[5] Smith v. State, 205 Ga. App. 810, 812 (2), 424 S.E.2d 56 (1992). Accord, Miller v. State, 250 Ga. 436, 437, 298 S.E.2d 509 (1983) (stating prior holdings to the contrary are no longer controlling and citing Chumley v. State, 235 Ga. 540, 541 (2), 221 S.E.2d 13 (1975) and Jackson v. State, 143 Ga. App. 406, 238 S.E.2d 752 (1977)); Wilson v. Zant, 249 Ga. 373, 380 (2), 290 S.E.2d 442 (1982), disapp. on other grounds, Morgan v. State, 267 Ga. 203, 476 S.E.2d 747 (1996); Johnson v. State, 209 Ga. App. 632, 634 (3), 434 S.E.2d 169 (1993); Brown v. State, 199 Ga. App. 773, 774, 406 S.E.2d 248 (1991). But see Roberts v. State, 228 Ga. 298, 185 S.E.2d 385 (1971), holding offense of possession of firearm during the commission of a crime necessarily merged into armed robbery.

[6] Smith v. State, 205 Ga. App. 810, 812 (2), 424 S.E.2d 56 (1992). Ac-

be considered as a separate offense, punished as such and not to be merged with any other offense.[7] However, in *Busch v. State*,[8] the court held that where the defendant is convicted of possession of a firearm during the commission of a felony, a five-year sentence shall be imposed to run consecutively to the sentence received for the underlying felony, not to all other sentences he may be given.

In *Washington v. State*,[9] the Court disapproved cases which had suggested that the offenses of malice murder and kidnapping with bodily injury were subject to merger. The Court found that the two crimes do not merge as a matter of law citing *Pryor v. State*.[10] The Court went on to find that there was no merger as a matter of fact since "there was no requirement that the state prove the existence of malice aforethought to establish the charge of kidnapping with bodily injury though malice aforethought had to be proven for the murder charge, and there was no requirement that the State prove the victim was unlawfully abducted to establish the murder charge, though such unlawful abduction had to be proven to establish kidnapping with bodily injury."[11]

Also noteworthy is the holding in *Brown v. State*,[12] that a defendant may be convicted of armed robbery, possession of a firearm by a convicted felon, and possession of a sawed-off shotgun because they do not merge as a matter of fact or as a matter of law. The court in *Buford v. State*[13] held that delivery of marijuana and distribution of marijuana are not included offenses as a matter of fact or as a matter of law, "[t]he difference between them is one of kind and not merely one of degree." A defendant may be convicted of both stealing an item from one person and selling that same item to another person, as the court

---

cord, Bivins v. State, 166 Ga. App. 580 (3), 305 S.E.2d 29 (1983); Coleman v. State, 163 Ga. App. 173, 174, 293 S.E.2d 395 (1982).

In Pace v. State, 239 Ga. App. 506, 509 (4), 521 S.E.2d 444 (1999), the court held that "[t]he legislature intended to impose additional punishment against an individual who uses a firearm during the commission of certain crimes, including aggravated assault. . . ." Hence, there was no merger.

[7]See Mathis v. State, 273 Ga. 508 (1), 543 S.E.2d 712 (2001) and § 14:47, supra, for discussion of double jeopardy implications of O.C.G.A. § 16-5-44.1(d).

[8]Busch v. State, 271 Ga. 591, 523 S.E.2d 21 (1999) (a 4 to 3 decision).

[9]Washington v. State, 276 Ga. 655(3), 581 S.E.2d 518 (2003) (disapproving Griffin v. State, 266 Ga. 115, 118, n. 5, 464 S.E.2d 371 (1995) and Wilson v. State, 264 Ga. 287(4)(b), 444 S.E.2d 306 (1994)).

[10]Pryor v. State, 238 Ga. 698, 701, 234 S.E.2d 918 (1977) (disapproved of, on other grounds, by Montes v. State, 262 Ga. 473, 421 S.E.2d 710 (1992)).

[11]Washington v. State, 276 Ga. 655(3), 581 S.E.2d 518 (2003).

[12]Brown v. State, 168 Ga. App. 537, 538(3), 309 S.E.2d 683 (1983).

[13]Buford v. State, 162 Ga. App. 498, 499(4), 291 S.E.2d 256 (1982).

found in *Stone v. State*[14] because theft of an article and selling a stolen article are not included offenses as a matter of law.

In *Lawson v. State*,[15] the Georgia Supreme Court held that an aggravated assault does not merge with a felony murder premised upon possession of a firearm by a convicted felon.

§ 26:36 Sentencing on multiple counts or indictments— Sentencing when there are different victims

"Where one is charged with the homicide of different people in different counts and is found guilty on each count, he may be sentenced separately on each count to run consecutively for the reason that the killing of different persons constitutes separate crimes even though done at the same time with one stroke of the same death-dealing instrument."[1] In *Pace v. State*,[2] the court affirmed the trial court's holding that when the defendant fired four shots into a crowd of nine people, he committed aggravated assault against each person. The court rejected the argument that the defendant should be charged with only four counts because of the number of shots fired. In *Jordan v. State*,[3] the defendant was convicted of firing a shotgun at and wounding two police officers. The court found no merger where the act affected different persons. In *Biddy v. State*,[4] the court held that murder and aggravated assault upon different victims do not merge as a matter of law. Likewise, a defendant may be convicted and punished for two counts of armed robbery where money was taken from two different people but belonged to only a third individual, the store owner.[5] For instance, in *Nelson v. State*,[6] the defendant robbed two individual bank tellers at the same site. The court

---

[14]Stone v. State, 166 Ga. App. 245, 304 S.E.2d 94 (1983).

[15]Lawson v. State, 280 Ga. 881, 635 S.E.2d 134 (2006). See Crayton v. State, 298 Ga. 792, 784 S.E.2d 343 (2016) (where Justice Blackwell was critical of *Lawson v. State* in a concurring opinion).

[Section 26:36]

[1]Brown v. State, 129 Ga. App. 743, 746 (5), 201 S.E.2d 14 (1973); Cox v. State, 243 Ga. App. 668, 669, 533 S.E.2d 435 (2000). In Carter v. State, 270 Ga. 637, 640 (5), 514 S.E.2d 19 (1999), the court held that "[w]hen the underlying felony is committed upon one victim and the felony murder charged in another count . . . is committed upon another victim, the under-

lying felony does not merge with the felony murder conviction."

[2]Pace v. State, 239 Ga. App. 506, 509 (6), 521 S.E.2d 444 (1999).

[3]Jordan v. State, 242 Ga. App. 408 (2), 530 S.E.2d 42 (2000), physical precedent.

[4]Biddy v. State, 253 Ga. 289, 292 (2), 319 S.E.2d 842 (1984). Accord, Satterfield v. State, 248 Ga. 538, 285 S.E.2d 3 (1981). But see Walker v. State, 254 Ga. 149, 327 S.E.2d 475 (1985), stating that the "rationale of Satterfield is not applicable to a case where . . . 'the count of the indictment alleging felony murder sets forth the underlying felony or felonies supporting the charge of felony murder.' "

[5]Simmons v. State, 174 Ga. App.

held that the robberies did not merge as a matter of fact or law. It follows that, where money belongs to two different people but is taken only from one owner, only one conviction of robbery may stand,[7] and where multiple items are taken from only one owner, only one conviction of armed robbery may stand.[8] However, "the crime of theft is not committed until the act of taking another's property coincides with the intent to deprive him of it."[9]

Therefore, the court in *Cook v. State*[10] held that where a van is stolen containing money the defendant did not know was there and the defendant later finds the money and keeps it, the later offense is separate from that of the taking of the van even though both items belonged to only one person. Additionally, as the court pointed out in *Hardin v. State,*[11] a theft by receiving stolen property case, even where there are four separate counts, or four separate indictments, each with a different car victim, theft which occurred on four different occasions, and the defendant was not privy to the thefts, the defendant obtained all four cars at one time, and the defendant was in possession of all the cars, there is only one offense. The court in *Stancil v. State*[12] affirmed the conviction and punishment of the defendant of two separate offenses where it was shown he sold the same kind of contraband to the same buyer on the same day, but at two different locations.

906, 331 S.E.2d 923 (1985). Accord, Walker v. State, 206 Ga. App. 81, 82 (2), 424 S.E.2d 364 (1992). But see Harris v. State, 165 Ga. App. 249, 252 (5), 299 S.E.2d 924 (1983), holding that a defendant could not be convicted on two counts of impersonating an officer even though he held himself out as such to two people.

[6]Nelson v. State, 242 Ga. App. 63, 64 (2), 528 S.E.2d 844 (2000).

[7]Creecy v. State, 235 Ga. 542, 543 (5), 221 S.E.2d 17 (1975). Accord, Leonard v. State, 218 Ga. App. 369, 370 (4), 461 S.E.2d 309 (1995) (robbing a corporation's clerk of his own money as well as that of the corporation represents only one offense); Deans v. State, 212 Ga. App. 571, 443 S.E.2d 6 (1994).

[8]Bland v. State, 264 Ga. 610, 612 (4), 449 S.E.2d 116 (1994).

[9]Cook v. State, 180 Ga. App. 139, 140, 348 S.E.2d 687 (1986).

[10]Cook v. State, 180 Ga. App. 139, 140, 348 S.E.2d 687 (1986).

[11]Hardin v. State, 141 Ga. App. 115, 117 (4), 232 S.E.2d 631 (1977); Harris v. State, 165 Ga. App. 249, 252 (5), 299 S.E.2d 924 (1983) (holding that defendant could not be punished for four counts of impersonating an officer where he represented himself as such to two separate people); Hall v. State, 155 Ga. App. 724, 272 S.E.2d 578 (1980) (finding two separate and punishable offenses where the defendant bribed two separate officers even though the incident occurred at the same time); Breland v. State, 135 Ga. App. 478, 218 S.E.2d 153 (1975) (holding that "the theft of the two trucks, taken from the same place at the same time from the same owner under the same circumstances, can only constitute one offense").

[12]Stancil v. State, 155 Ga. App. 731 (2), 272 S.E.2d 511 (1980).

In *Russell v. State*,[13] the court affirmed the trial court in imposing three separate sentences where the state showed that the defendant had three separate packages of marijuana delivered to him on three separate occasions. The court in *Maxwell v. State*[14] held that where a defendant is convicted of showing six obscene films in a continuous uninterrupted manner for a single admission price, he may only be punished for one offense. However, in *G & E Business Services, Inc. v. State*,[15] the court upheld 39 separate convictions where police officers entering two adult bookstores on two separate occasions on the same day were able to view obscene films via individual coin-fed booths. The court distinguished *G & E Business, Inc.* from *Maxwell* based on the fact that the officers in *G & E Business, Inc.* had to feed coins into a machine in order to view even one film versus multiple films being shown to a large audience in sequence.

Cases involving obstruction of law enforcement officers are similar to the foregoing. Where the defendant flees from the grasp of two officers, only one charge would be appropriate. If, however, the defendant obstructs two officers in the discharge of their duties in a separate and distinct fashion, two charges might be appropriate.[16]

§ 26:37 Sentencing on multiple counts or indictments— Murder; rule of lenity

"If a jury returns a guilty verdict for both malice murder and felony murder when there is a single victim, 'it is proper for the trial court to treat the felony murder count as merely surplusage,' " because the felony murder verdict stands vacated as a matter of law.[1] However, the court must then proceed "to determine whether the underlying felony [that originally formed the basis for the felony murder] did or did not merge, as a matter

---

[13]Russell v. State, 243 Ga. App. 378, 382 (5), 532 S.E.2d 137 (2000).

[14]Maxwell v. State, 152 Ga. App. 776, 778 (1), 264 S.E.2d 254 (1979).

[15]G & E Business Services, Inc. v. State, 156 Ga. App. 391, 274 S.E.2d 644 (1980).

[16]See Lidy v. State, 335 Ga. App. 517, 782 S.E.2d 302 (2016). See Mobley v. State, 345 Ga. App. 393, 812 S.E.2d 796 (2018).

[Section 26:37]

[1]Diamond v. State, 267 Ga. 249, 251(3), 477 S.E.2d 562 (1996) (quoting Malcolm v. State, 263 Ga. 369, 372(4),

434 S.E.2d 479 (1993)). See Favors v. State, 296 Ga. 842, 847(5), 770 S.E.2d 855 (2015); Hulett v. State, 296 Ga. 49, 53(2), 766 S.E.2d 1 (2014). But see Dampier v. State, 245 Ga. 427, 435(13), 265 S.E.2d 565 (1980), opinion supplemented, 245 Ga. 882, 268 S.E.2d 349 (1980), holding that where jury returned a verdict of guilty on "murder," not specifying whether malice murder or felony murder, and armed robbery, the "[defendant] must be given the benefit of the doubt" and the felony murder must stand, vacating both the malice murder conviction and the armed robbery as an underlying felony to felony murder.

of fact, into the malice murder count."[2] Accordingly, the court in *Dunn v. State*[3] held that where a defendant is found guilty of felony murder with both aggravated assault and theft by taking being the underlying felonies, the most severe felony (in this instance the aggravated assault) merges with the felony murder conviction and the defendant also may be sentenced on the less severe crime. In *Noel v. State*,[4] the defendant was charged with three counts of felony murder of the same victim, with a different predicate felony charged in each and which were also charged separately in a six-count indictment. The Supreme Court held that the trial court improperly sentenced the defendant by imposing three life sentences and then merging the non-murder felonies into the felony murder counts. The Court said that the defendant can only be sentenced on one felony murder count with the predicate felony charged in that count merging into the felony murder. The other felony murder counts are vacated as a result. However, the predicate felonies in those counts which were also separately charged do not merge and remain for sentencing by the trial court, unless the court determines the remaining predicate felonies merge as a matter of fact into the felony murder conviction.

The Supreme Court in *Lumpkins v. State*,[5] criticized the single count indictment of felony murder which alleges two felonies as alternative predicate offenses. "If a verdict of 'not guilty' were returned on a 'malice murder' count and a general verdict of 'guilty' were returned on a single 'felony murder' count which alternatively alleged the underlying felonies, it would not be possible to determine whether the jury had found appellant guilty of felony murder while in the commission of an 'aggravated assault'

---

[2]Diamond v. State, 267 Ga. 249, 251 (3)(b), 477 S.E.2d 562 (1996). Accord, Brown v. State, 129 Ga. App. 743, 746 (5), 201 S.E.2d 14 (1973).

[3]Dunn v. State, 263 Ga. 343, 344 (2), 434 S.E.2d 60 (1993). Accord, Robertson v. State, 268 Ga. 772, 780 (22), 493 S.E.2d 697 (1997) (holding that where defendant was convicted of felony murder, armed robbery and burglary, the more severe offense of armed robbery must merge with the felony murder conviction); Thompson v. State, 263 Ga. 23, 24 (2), 426 S.E.2d 895 (1993) (holding that where it is unclear which of two or more felonies is underlying felony for felony murder conviction, trial court must merge most severe felony in terms of potential punishment); Hawes v. State, 239 Ga.

630, 238 S.E.2d 418 (1977) (holding that where jury simply returned a verdict of "guilty" on charges of malice murder, felony murder, and armed robbery, the felony murder charge necessarily merges with the malice murder offense, but armed robbery is not a lesser included offense of malice murder and may stand); Barrow v. State, 235 Ga. 635, 637 (2), 221 S.E.2d 416 (1975) (holding that armed robbery is not a lesser included offense of malice murder). See Gordon v. State, 334 Ga. App. 633, 780 S.E.2d 376 (2015).

[4]Noel v. State, 297 Ga. 698, 777 S.E.2d 449 (2015). See Smith v. State, 298 Ga. 406, 782 S.E.2d 269 (2016).

[5]Lumpkins v. State, 264 Ga. 255, 257(4), 443 S.E.2d 619 (1994).

or while in the commission of an 'armed robbery.' " The Court concluded that drawing the indictment in separate counts is the better practice since the jury's verdict is explicit as to each of the predicate offenses.

This is generally referred to as the "rule of lenity." The "principle of lenity" provides that a penal statute which allows for two possible grades of punishment or penalty for the same offense is uncertain and for that reason the defendant is entitled to the lesser of the two penalties. There are a number of cases which have held that the rule has no application when the defendant is charged under two statutes both of which are felonies.[6] However, in *McNair v. State*,[7] the Supreme Court reversed those cases and clarified that in determining whether to apply the rule of lenity, the primary consideration "is not whether the statutes in question exact felony and/or misdemeanor punishment but whether there is an ambiguity that would result in varying degrees of punishment for the same offense."

The rule has no application in the case of a defendant who is indicted and convicted on separate counts of the felony murder of the same victim with each count specifying a different predicate felony. In this instance, the trial court has discretion in selecting the count on which the sentence for felony murder is to be imposed and hence the felony count which will merge with that sentence. This may result in exposing the defendant to punishment on the more serious felony offenses charged separately and as the predicate offenses for the other felony murder counts.[8]

In *Banta v. State*,[9] the Georgia Supreme Court summarized the application of the rule in this way:

> The rule of lenity applies when a statute, or statutes, establishes, or establish, different punishments for the same offense, and provides that the ambiguity is resolved in favor of the defendant, who will then receive the lesser punishment . . . . However, the

---

[6]See, e.g., Poole v. State, 302 Ga. App. 464, 691 S.E.2d 317 (2010).

[7]McNair v. State, 293 Ga. 282, 745 S.E.2d 646 (2013). See Chynoweth v. State, 331 Ga. App. 123, 768 S.E.2d 536 (2015).

[8]McClellan v. State, 274 Ga. 819(2), 561 S.E.2d 82 (2002). Compare, Brown v. State, 276 Ga. 606, 581 S.E.2d 35 (2003) where sale of fake crack cocaine constituted a violation of felony and misdemeanor statutes. The rule of lenity requires that the defendant be sentenced under the less severe misdemeanor statute.

[9]Banta v. State, 281 Ga. 615, 617-618, 642 S.E.2d 51 (2007) (citations omitted). See Gordon v. State, 334 Ga. App. 633, 780 S.E.2d 376 (2015); Harrison v. State, 330 Ga. App. 570, 768 S.E.2d 762 (2015) (rule of lenity applied in probation revocation case where probation was violated when defendant admitted to one count of theft by taking pursuant to O.C.G.A. § 16-8-12 but record failed to show the value of the items involved, trial court could only revoke based upon the lowest value assigned for sentencing purposes in statute).

rule does not apply when the statutory provisions are unambiguous. . . . Further, that a single act may, as a factual matter, violate more than one penal statute does not implicate the rule of lenity. For instance, depending upon attendant circumstances, it is possible for the act of striking another person with an object to meet the definitions of each of the crimes of: simple battery, OCGA § 16-5-23, a misdemeanor; aggravated battery, OCGA § 16-5-24, a felony; simple assault, OCGA § 16-5-20, a misdemeanor; aggravated assault, OCGA § 16-5-21, a felony; and malice murder, OCGA § 16-5-1, a felony. In such a circumstance, a defendant may be prosecuted for more than one crime. OCGA § 16-1-7(a). However, the injustice that must be avoided is *sentencing* the defendant for more than one crime following his conviction of multiple crimes based upon the same act. When a defendant is so prosecuted, the principle of factual merger operates to avoid the injustice. [In such cases, the lesser crime is merged into the greater. The defendant is sentenced for only one crime.]

In *Dixon v. State*,[10] the Georgia Supreme Court applied the rule of lenity to provide that where the same conduct can result in the imposition of dramatically different penalties under two different statutes, one a felony and the other a misdemeanor, the defendant must be sentenced under the misdemeanor statute. In this case, the defendant was convicted of misdemeanor statutory rape and aggravated child molestation. The defendant was 18 years old and a high school senior at the time of the incident. The victim was a 15 year old tenth grader. Because the victim was under the age of 16, the state was required to show some sort of physical injury to the victim in addition to the conduct necessary to show statutory rape in order to make the case for aggravated child molestation. Nonetheless, the court concluded that the legislature intended that teenagers who engaged in certain forms of prohibited sexual conduct should only be charged with the misdemeanor offense when the age difference between the victim and the defendant is three years or less.

"[W]here the evidence would authorize a verdict for either voluntary manslaughter or felony murder, the . . . court should instruct the jury on both forms of homicide. However, [if] the jury renders a verdict for voluntary manslaughter, it cannot also find felony murder based on the same underlying [felony]. This can be understood by recognizing the theory of felony murder; that is, that it depends on the transfer or imputation of malice from the mens rea of the felonious assault to the killing. If the jury finds

---

[10]Dixon v. State, 278 Ga. 4 (2), 596 S.E.2d 147 (2004). In Quaweay v. State, 274 Ga. App. 657, 618 S.E.2d 707 (2005), the Georgia Court of Appeals noted that the applicable misdemeanor need not be a lesser included offense of the charged felony provided both crimes can be proved with the same evidence.

voluntary manslaughter, it necessarily finds the felonious assault was mitigated by provocation, and committed without the mens rea essential to impute malice to the killing. Thus, the felony of assault in that instance cannot support a felony murder conviction because there is no malice to be transferred."[11]

The court in *Edge v. State*[12] held that the trial court erred by entering judgment on both verdicts for voluntary manslaughter and felony murder since the basis for both was the same aggravated assault. Accordingly, they stated that "[b]ecause the jury . . . convicted the defendant of both voluntary manslaughter and felony murder, it must be assumed the jurors found the underlying aggravated assault to be the product of provocation and passion. Thus, only the voluntary manslaughter conviction may stand. The felony murder conviction is, accordingly, reversed."[13] The holding in *Edge* is, in effect, a modified merger rule. It applies if the underlying felony is directed against the homicide victim and "is not independent, but rather an integral part of the killing . . . . [T]he defendant cannot be convicted and sentenced for felony murder, because the voluntary manslaughter verdict indicates that the underlying felony is mitigated by provocation and passion . . . . The modified merger rule cannot be waived by a defendant's failure to raise it in the trial court or to enumerate it as error, because a conviction which should have merged into another as a matter of law is void."[14] *Edge* has no application to cases where the defendant is found guilty of murder and involuntary manslaughter.[15] *Edge* has no application to cases where a defendant is found guilty of felony murder and involuntary manslaughter. Unlike voluntary manslaughter, the offense of involuntary manslaughter does not contain the mitigating factor of "provoked passion."

While no Georgia court has directly dealt with the issue, the Georgia Court of Appeals has cited approvingly the practice of merging an aggravated assault conviction into one of voluntary manslaughter where the defendants were charged with murder, or felony murder, but found guilty on the lesser included offense

---

[11]Edge v. State, 261 Ga. 865, 414 S.E.2d 463 (1992).

[12]Edge v. State, 261 Ga. 865, 414 S.E.2d 463 (1992).

[13]Edge v. State, 261 Ga. 865, 414 S.E.2d 463 (1992).

[14]Sanders v. State, 281 Ga. 36, 37(1), 635 S.E.2d 772 (2006) (citations omitted), overruling Dennard v. State, 263 Ga. 453, 435 S.E.2d 26 (1993), Cruz-Padillo v. State, 262 Ga. 629, 630(2), 422 S.E.2d 849 (1992), Wilson v. State, 262 Ga. 588, 590(2)(C), 422 S.E.2d 536 (1992), and Carter v. State, 261 Ga. 740, 741(3), 410 S.E.2d 102 (1991).

[15]Jones v. State, 263 Ga. 835, 839(5), 439 S.E.2d 645 (1994). See Kipp v. State, 296 Ga. 250, 765 S.E.2d 924 (2014) (unlike voluntary manslaughter, offense of involuntary manslaughter does not contain the mitigating factor of "provoked passion").

of voluntary manslaughter.[16] Additionally, the court in *Griffin v. State*[17] held that where the facts in the case show that the same intent is the basis of assault aggravated by intent to rob and criminal attempt to commit a robbery by striking the victim, these offenses must merge as a matter of law and of fact.

§ 26:38 Sentencing on multiple counts or indictments— Sexual offenses

In *Eggleston v. State*,[1] the defendant was charged in Counts 3 through 7 with "engaging in various distinct acts of child molestation. The different counts alleged that Eggleston 'with intent to arouse and satisfy [his] sexual desires': (Count 3) 'placed his penis on the vaginal area of [the victim]'; (Count 4) 'pulled down the pants and underwear of [the victim]'; (Count 5) 'placed his hand and fingers on the breast of [the victim]'; (Count 6) 'placed his mouth on the breast of [the victim]'; and (Count 7) 'forced [the victim] to touch the penis of said accused.' " The court held that "evidence supporting any one count was not 'used up' in proving any other count . . . . Instead the testimony of the victim established that each of these counts was a separate and distinct crime."

§ 26:39 Sentencing on multiple counts or indictments— Possession of a firearm or knife

In the case of a sentence for possession of a firearm or knife during the commission of a crime, a five-year sentence must be imposed to run consecutively to the sentence of the underlying felony. However, such a consecutive sentence is only applicable to the underlying felonies enumerated in O.C.G.A. § 16-11-106.[1] In *Johnson v. State*,[2] the court vacated the defendant's sentence for possession of a weapon on the kidnapping charge because it was not one of the listed crimes.

O.C.G.A. § 16-11-106(b) provides, in pertinent part, that "[a]ny person who shall have on . . . his person a firearm or knife . . . during the commission of . . . :

---

[16]Haynes v. State, 234 Ga. App. 272, 275, 507 S.E.2d 151 (1998); Young v. State, 229 Ga. App. 497, 494 S.E.2d 226 (1997); Gentry v. State, 212 Ga. App. 79, 441 S.E.2d 249 (1994). See Amos v. State, 297 Ga. 892, 778 S.E.2d 203 (2015) (merger of voluntary manslaughter into felony murder is proper where underlying felony is not integral to the homicide, e.g., possession of a firearm by a convicted felon).

[17]Griffin v. State, 168 Ga. App. 696, 698 (4), 310 S.E.2d 278 (1983).

[Section 26:38]

[1]Eggleston v. State, 247 Ga. App. 540, 543 (3), 544 S.E.2d 722 (2001).

[Section 26:39]

[1]Busch v. State, 271 Ga. 591, 523 S.E.2d 21 (1999).

[2]Johnson v. State, 247 Ga. App. 157, 162 (9), 543 S.E.2d 439 (2000).

(1) Any crime against or involving the person of another;

(2) The unlawful entry into a building or vehicle;

(3) A theft from a building or theft of a vehicle;

(4) Any crime involving the possession, manufacture, delivery, distribution, dispensing, administering, selling, or possession with intent to distribute any controlled substance or marijuana as provided in O.C.G.A. § 16-13-30, any counterfeit substance as defined in O.C.G.A. § 16-13-21, or any noncontrolled substance as provided in O.C.G.A. § 16-13-30.1; or

(5) Any crime involving the trafficking of cocaine, marijuana, or illegal drugs as provided in O.C.G.A. § 16-13-31,

and which crime is a felony, commits a felony and, . . . shall be punished by confinement for a period of five years, such sentence to run consecutively to any other sentence which the person has received."

O.C.G.A. § 16-11-106(e) provides that "[a]ny crime committed in violation . . . of this Code section shall be considered a separate offense." Although a weapons possession charge must run consecutive to the underlying felony, it may also run consecutive to other unrelated offenses for which the defendant was convicted.[3] In cases where "multiple crimes are committed together during the course of one continuous crime spree, a defendant may be convicted once for possession of a firearm during the commission of a crime as to every individual victim of the crime spree."[4] However, when a defendant is convicted of both aggravated assault and armed robbery of the same victim, he can only be sentenced once for firearm possession as to that victim, provided the underlying felonies were part of one continuous criminal action.[5] Likewise, "convictions and sentences for aggravated assault and malice murder (or felony murder) 'merged' when a fatal injury preceded the infliction of a non-fatal injury and the injuries were not separated by a 'deliberate interval.' "[6] Similarly, a defendant who is in possession of several firearms at the time he/she commits a felony, is subject to only one prosecution and conviction for the simultaneous possession of multiple firearms.[7]

---

[3]Braithwaite v. State, 275 Ga. 884 (9), 572 S.E.2d 612 (2002); Pennymon v. State, 261 Ga. App. 450 (6), 582 S.E.2d 582 (2003).

[4]Gutierrez v. State, 285 Ga. 878, 880(3), 684 S.E.2d 652 (2009).

[5]Abdullah v. State, 284 Ga. 399(4), 667 S.E.2d 584 (2008). See Ensley v. State, 294 Ga. 200, 751 S.E.2d 396 (2013).

[6]Slaughter v. State, 292 Ga. 573, 575, 740 S.E.2d 119 (2013) (citations omitted).

[7]Coates v. State, 818 S.E.2d 622 (Ga. 2018).

§ 26:40 Sentencing on multiple counts or indictments—Conspiracy sentencing

Treatment of multiple convictions under O.C.G.A. § 16-1-7 with regard to conspiracy charges necessarily depends on the theory of the conspiracy set forth in the indictment (i.e., one overall conspiracy with multiple acts to further that conspiracy versus multiple conspiracies). Accordingly, in *Price v. State*,[1] two defendants were indicted in a 168-count indictment for conspiring to violate the Georgia Controlled Substances Act. They were convicted on 150 counts. The state proceeded under a "special conspiracy statute found at [Code Ann.] § 79A-812 [O.C.G.A. § 16-13-33] of the Act" and "not under the general conspiracy statute codified at Code Ann. § 26-3201 (Ga. L. 1968, pp. 1249, 1335; as amended) [O.C.G.A. § 16-4-8]" (i.e., the indictment included 168 different counts of violation of a specific act). The Georgia Supreme Court held that the defendants could not be convicted on multiple counts of a multi-count conspiracy indictment, but could only be convicted of one offense of conspiracy to violate the Controlled Substances Act, where the evidence showed the commission of multiple substantive offenses that were the object of what was one conspiracy. The court also noted, however, that "when a conspiracy contemplates the commission of more than one substantive offense, and there are separate conspiracy statutes separately punishing a conspiracy to commit each offense, a separate conviction under each conspiracy statute may be authorized . . . [and] that where multiple overt acts are committed pursuant to what is albeit a single conspiracy, and each overt act constitutes a separate substantive offense, there may be multiple convictions for the multiple substantive offenses,"[2] but that this was not one of those cases.

Less than six months after *Price* was decided, the United States Supreme Court issued a ruling in *Albernaz v. United States*,[3] related to multiple convictions in conspiracy cases. In *Albernaz*, the defendants, found to have agreed to import marijuana and then to distribute it domestically, were convicted and given consecutive sentences for the offenses of "conspiracy to import marijuana (Count 1) in violation of 21 U.S.C.A. § 963 and conspiracy to distribute marijuana (Count II) in violation of 21 U.S.C.A. § 846." The court held that Congress intended to permit imposition of consecutive sentences for offenses of conspiracy to import marijuana and conspiracy to distribute marijuana even though

---

[Section 26:40]

[1]Price v. State, 247 Ga. 58, 273 S.E.2d 854 (1981).

[2]Price v. State, 247 Ga. 58, 273 S.E.2d 854 (1981).

[3]Albernaz v. United States, 450 U.S. 333, 101 S.Ct. 1137, 67 L.Ed.2d 275 (1981).

such offenses arose from a single agreement or conspiracy having dual objectives; and imposition of consecutive sentences did not violate the double jeopardy clause of the Fifth Amendment. Prior to *Albernaz* it was thought that the federal constitution imposed some limitation on the right of a state or federal court to impose multiple sentences for the "same conduct." However, under *Albernaz* it seems that the propriety of multiple sentences is one of statutory construction and the intent of the legislature, and the double jeopardy clause will not prevent their imposition on guilty defendants.

However, Georgia courts appear to not have adopted the rule of *Albernaz* in at least some situations. In *Evans v. State*,[4] where the defendant was accused of conspiracy to commit the offenses of theft by receiving stolen goods and of altering vehicle identification numbers, the court held there could only be one conviction for either the conspiracy or the crime, but not both. The court stated that "[a]t common law, and now in the majority of states and the Federal courts, conspiracy to commit a crime is an offense separate and distinct from the crime or crimes which are the object of the conspiracy.[5] However, in Georgia, conspiracy is a statutory crime . . . , and the Supreme Court has held that conspiracy 'clearly is merged into the greater crime where the evidence shows without dispute that the crime charged was actually committed.' . . . Thus, the rule in Georgia is contrary to the Federal and general rule that conspiracy and the completed crime do not merge. . . . Accordingly, it would be improper to convict a defendant of conspiracy to commit a specified crime, and the crime he conspired to commit."

§ 26:41   Re-sentencing

While, chronologically, material on re-sentencing does not precisely fit in at this point in the criminal process, it is so related to sentencing that a few factors need to be mentioned at this point.

Neither the double jeopardy nor equal protection clause prevents a state from imposing a more severe second sentence; however, due process requires that there be a finding of facts justifying a greater sentence if a defendant is re-sentenced by a judge for the crime for which he has previously been sentenced.[1] As the Georgia Supreme Court has stated, "[V]indictiveness must

---

[4]Evans v. State, 161 Ga. App. 468, 470 (2), 288 S.E.2d 726 (1982).

[5]Evans v. State, 161 Ga. App. 468, 470 (2), 288 S.E.2d 726 (1982) citing 16 Am. Jr. 2d 220, Conspiracy § 5;

22 C.J.S. 775, Criminal Law § 288.

[Section 26:41]

[1]North Carolina v. Pearce, 395 U.S. 711, 723, 89 S.Ct. 2072, 23

not be the motivating force behind the increased sentence."[2] From a constitutional standpoint, where vindictiveness is not present and a defendant is re-tried before a jury, the jurors may impose a greater sentence.[3]

Where a judge imposes a more severe sentence upon a defendant after a new trial, *North Carolina v. Pearce*[4] states that "the reasons for his doing so must be based upon objective information concerning identifiable conduct on the part of the defendant occurring after the time of the original sentencing proceeding."[5] In determining whether a re-sentence is more severe than the first sentence, Georgia courts previously analyzed the re-sentence on a count-by-count basis.[6] However, in *State v. Hudson*,[7] the Georgia Supreme Court abandoned this approach in favor of a review of the sentence in the aggregate. Thus, changing a sentence from probation time to prison time constitutes an increased sentence even if the aggregate number of years of the sentence is not changed.[8] In *United States v. Wasman*,[9] the Eleventh Circuit held that an interim conviction for an offense committed before the imposition of the first sentence justified a

---

L.Ed.2d 656 (1969), overruled by Alabama v. Smith, 490 U.S. 794, 109 S. Ct. 2201, 104 L. Ed. 2d 865 (1989); Taylor v. State, 181 Ga. App. 199, 201, 351 S.E.2d 723 (1986). In Blake v. State, 272 Ga. App. 402, 403(1), 612 S.E.2d 589 (2005), the Court of Appeals made the observation that if the trial court plans to impose a more severe penalty upon resentencing it must "affirmatively appear" from the record that the court had an objective basis warranting the increased sentence. See Adams v. State, 287 Ga. 513, 696 S.E.2d 676 (2010), where the court held that unless the new sentence is more severe in the aggregate, as compared to a per count analysis, *Pearce* has no application.

[2]Anthony v. Hopper, 235 Ga. 336, 337(1), 219 S.E.2d 413 (1975), overruled on other grounds, State v. Hudson, 293 Ga. 656, 748 S.E.2d 910 (2013).

[3]Michigan v. Payne, 412 U.S. 47, 93 S.Ct. 1966, 36 L.Ed.2d 736 (1973); Chaffin v. Stynchcombe, 412 U.S. 17, 93 S.Ct. 1977, 36 L.Ed.2d 714 (1973). Of course, where the jury fixes the second sentence, no finding of facts is necessary.

[4]North Carolina v. Pearce, 395 U.S. 711, 89 S.Ct. 2072, 23 L.Ed.2d 656 (1969) (quoted with approval in Hewell v. State, 238 Ga. 578, 579, 234 S.E.2d 497 (1977)). See also Chambers v. State, 213 Ga. App. 414, 418 (5), 444 S.E.2d 820 (1994).

[5]North Carolina v. Pearce, 395 U.S. 711, 726, 89 S.Ct. 2072, 23 L.Ed.2d 656, 670 (1969); Pressley v. State, 158 Ga. App. 638, 639 (3), 281 S.E.2d 364 (1981). However, in Turner v. State, 151 Ga. App. 631, 260 S.E.2d 756 (1979), the court held that where a defendant is sentenced with the knowledge of another case pending in another court and is later re-tried and sentenced, the trial judge can make the second sentence follow the sentence which in the meantime has been imposed in the other court.

[6]Anthony v. Hopper, 235 Ga. 336, 219 S.E.2d 413 (1975), overruled by State v. Hudson, 293 Ga. 656, 748 S.E.2d 910 (2013).

[7]State v. Hudson, 293 Ga. 656, 748 S.E.2d 910 (2013).

[8]State v. Hudson, 293 Ga. 656, 748 S.E.2d 910 (2013).

[9]United States v. Wasman, 700 F.2d 663 (11th Cir. 1983).

greater sentence on the defendant's re-conviction. *Pearce* was subsequently overruled in *Alabama v. Smith*.[10] *Smith* restricted the presumption of vindictiveness created in *Pearce* to those cases where the evidence shows a "reasonable likelihood" that the increased sentence was "the product of actual vindictiveness on the part of the sentencing authority."

In *Mallarino v. State*,[11] the court stated "that resentencing a prisoner to correct an illegal sentence does not implicate double jeopardy rights, even if the prisoner has already served part of his term." In *Howard v. State*,[12] the court pointed out that an illegal sentence could be corrected by a motion to correct and a direct appeal will lie from a denial of the motion to correct. "[I]f the sentence imposed was . . . void . . . , then a new and valid sentence can be imposed by the trial judge at any time." Likewise, a sentence can be corrected by a habeas corpus action.

In *Moore v. Zant*,[13] the court held that where a defendant's conviction is affirmed but a re-sentencing trial is ordered, he is not entitled to be released from the prison system pending his re-sentencing.

The Georgia Supreme Court has held that a defendant has a right to be present whenever it is legally possible for him to receive a greater sentence than that which was originally imposed.[14] Yet, apparently, under Georgia law, he is not entitled to be present unless he could potentially receive an enhanced

---

[10]Alabama v. Smith, 490 U.S. 794, 109 S. Ct. 2201, 104 L. Ed. 2d 865 (1989).

[11]Mallarino v. State, 194 Ga. App. 212, 213, 390 S.E.2d 114 (1990) (quoting Stuckey v. Stynchcombe, 614 F.2d 75 (5th Cir. 1980)). In Wilford v. State, 278 Ga. 718, 606 S.E.2d 252 (2004), the court held that the constitutional prohibition against double jeopardy is not offended where a defendant's sentence as a First Offender is revoked after the trial court discovers that the defendant was not eligible to be sentenced as such and thereafter proceeds to impose a harsher sentence. The Georgia First Offender Act specifically contemplates the prospect of resentencing in the event a person is improperly sentenced as a First Offender and for that reason there is no expectation of finality in the original sentence. See United States v. DiFrancesco, 449 U.S. 117, 101 S.Ct. 426, 66

L.Ed.2d 328 (1980).

[12]Howard v. State, 234 Ga. App. 260, 261(1), 506 S.E.2d 648 (1998). See, e.g., Strickland v. State, 301 Ga. App. 272, 687 S.E.2d 221 (2009), holding the trial court could later amend defendant's sentence for a trafficking conviction when it inadvertently failed to impose a mandatory $200,000 fine because the original sentence was void. See also Williams v. State, 287 Ga. 192, 695 S.E.2d 244 (2010), holding that a challenge to a conviction, as opposed to the sentence, cannot be raised by O.C.G.A. § 16-1-7(a), motion to correct illegal sentence.

[13]Moore v. Zant, 264 Ga. 536(1), 448 S.E.2d 695 (1994).

[14]Anthony v. Hopper, 235 Ga. 336, 339, 219 S.E.2d 413 (1975), rev'd on other grounds, State v. Hudson, 293 Ga. 656, 748 S.E.2d 910 (2013).

punishment.[15]

In a capital case, if a defendant is sentenced to life on the first trial and later re-tried, a death sentence cannot be imposed at the conclusion of the second trial.[16]

In *Wilford v. State,*[17] the Georgia Supreme Court determined that once a defendant begins serving his sentence, it can only be increased at resentencing if "(a) such resentencing is allowed by law, and (b) the defendant had no reasonable expectation in the finality of the original sentence." As the court observed in *Williams v. State,*[18] "[a]bsent these circumstances the resentencing constitutes a double punishment that runs afoul of the Fifth Amendment prohibition against double jeopardy." Thus, in *Williams*, the case was remanded for resentencing where the trial court modified the original sentence to allow for less incarceration but increased the sentence by adding to the amount of time to be served on probation.

See § 14:61, supra, on double jeopardy.

§ 26:42 Practical defense considerations for pre-sentence hearings and sentencing

Aside from the legal niceties of the law, there is much that can be done at a pre-sentence hearing by both the defense and the prosecution. A pre-sentence hearing affords the parties an opportunity to give the judge or jury insight into the case and into the defendant himself.

If the district attorney wants to introduce any evidence in aggravation or in an effort to have a more severe sentence imposed, he must, of course, give the defendant notice of the evidence in advance of trial.[1] However, the failure of a defendant to object at the pre-sentencing hearing to the introduction of such evidence constitutes a waiver of the required notice.[2] Usually district attorneys use certified copies of former convictions but they are not limited by law to evidence of convictions. By statute, a district attorney may introduce other evidence in aggravation of punishment.[3]

From the defense standpoint, it is the responsibility of the defense counsel to present the good in his client in the best pos-

[15]Johnson v. Caldwell, 232 Ga. 200, 201, 205 S.E.2d 857 (1974).

[16]Ward v. State, 239 Ga. 205, 208, 236 S.E.2d 365 (1977); Palmer v. State, 174 Ga. App. 720, 331 S.E.2d 77 (1985).

[17]Wilford v. State, 278 Ga. 718, 720, 606 S.E.2d 252 (2004).

[18]Williams v. State, 273 Ga. App. 42, 46(6), 614 S.E.2d 146 (2005).

[Section 26:42]

[1]O.C.G.A. § 17-16-4(a)(5).

[2]Turner v. State, 259 Ga. App. 902, 903 (1), 578 S.E.2d 570 (2003).

[3]O.C.G.A. § 17-10-2(c).

sible light and to try to minimize the bad. While it may be deflating to the ego of defense counsel to think that the jury might find his client guilty, he should be prepared for such possibility. In advance of trial, defense counsel should consider what witnesses he can have for the pre-sentence hearing if the defendant is convicted. If there is any doubt about having these witnesses present, they should be subpoenaed. In short, witnesses should be available for this part of the trial just as for the "guilt-innocence" phase.

From a statistical standpoint, the vast majority of cases end in a conviction. Hence, the efforts of defense counsel in mitigation may be of much more practical importance than the efforts to obtain an acquittal.

Answers to the following questions may bring out information at the pre-sentence hearing which might favorably influence the determination of the defendant's sentence.[4]

(1)   If the defendant is young, from what kind of family does he come?

(2)   If the defendant is older, what kind of family has he established?

(3)   Does he have a family which is interested in him and who will try to help him if he is "given another chance"?

(4)   What is the defendant's educational background and occupation? Is he doing something useful in life?

(5)   What is the personal character and intelligence of the defendant?

(6)   If the defendant is young, is he still pursuing his education? If given an opportunity, is he willing to go back to school or to a trade school?

(7)   Does the defendant have a prior record? If so, were the offenses minor?

(8)   Is there any *good* explanation which can be made for a prior plea of guilty or nolo contendere?

(9)   Is the present offense one which is likely to reoccur?

(10)   What is the defendant's present attitude?

(11)   Was the defendant simply going along with the wrong crowd? If so, has he learned to leave "that crowd" alone?

(12)   What options are available to the court?

Most judges probably appreciate having more than the facts of the case upon which to base a sentence. Frequently it is well to encourage the judge to get a pre-sentence investigation report.

---

[4]Generally, on this subject, see Vol. IV, No. 1 Ga. Courts Journal 18 (Sept. 1976), where some 12 considerations used by Judge A. Richard Kenyon are listed.

Full cooperation by the defendant and his counsel with probation officers may help to give the judge a better insight into the "real" defendant.

Testimony from others about the virtues of a defendant is always helpful. In the case of a young person, teachers frequently make good witnesses. If the defendant has been a good worker, his employer can speak on his behalf. It may also be possible to use character witnesses who were not used in the earlier phases of the case. In addition, consideration should be given to obtaining letters addressed to the court from anyone who is familiar with the defendant and willing to speak a good word in his behalf.

Generally, the pre-sentence hearing or the time of sentencing is not the time for further declarations of the defendant's innocence.[5]

§ 26:43 Sentencing—Judicial considerations[1]

Except in a capital case, after a criminal defendant is convicted, the trial judge has the power and the duty to pronounce sentence, unless he decides to set the verdict aside.[2] In discharging this duty, the sentencing judge is required to consider all mitigating and aggravating circumstances which have been brought to his attention.[3] The trial judge is in a particularly good position to determine the appropriate sentence, since he has heard the evidence, observed the demeanor of the defendant, and read whatever pre-sentence information that was made available to him.[4] Even where a sentence is being imposed pursuant to a guilty plea rather than a trial conviction, the trial judge is still in a much better position than an appellate court to evaluate the defendant and the crime, and to fix an appropriate sentence. It has been said that the goal of the sentencing judge is to acquire a thorough acquaintance with the character and history of the accused.[5]

O.C.G.A. § 17-10-17 provides that when a crime is found to be a "hate crime," as defined in that Code section, where "the defendant intentionally selected . . . [the] victim . . . because of bias or prejudice . . . ," the judge must increase the sentence.

---

[5]However, if the defense has any idea of getting the conviction reversed, he will not want to admit his guilt.

[Section 26:43]

[1]See American Bar Association Standards for Criminal Justice, "Sentencing Alternatives and Procedures," Vol. III, Chapter 18.

[2]Parks v. State, 206 Ga. 675, 676, 58 S.E.2d 142 (1950). See O.C.G.A. § 17-10-2.

[3]Williams v. New York, 337 U.S. 241, 69 S.Ct. 1079, 93 L.Ed. 1337 (1949); Williams v. Oklahoma, 358 U.S. 576, 79 S.Ct. 421, 3 L.Ed.2d 516 (1959), reh. denied, 359 U.S. 956, 79 S.Ct. 737, 3 L.Ed.2d 763 (1959).

[4]United States v. McCoy, 429 F.2d 739 (C.A.D.C. 1970).

[5]United States v. Doyle, 348 F.2d 715, 721 (2d Cir. 1965).

The Code allows for a 50% increase of the sentence for misdemeanors up to the authorized maximum, and up to 5 years for a felony not to exceed the maximum. This statute has now been declared too vague in its definition of the conduct it seeks to prohibit to satisfy the due process requirements of the state and federal constitutions.[6] Furthermore, the Code prevents parole or early release for this type of felony until the defendant has served at least 90% of his or her time. However, in *Apprendi v. New Jersey,*[7] the United States Supreme Court held that a court may not impose a sentence exceeding the maximum fixed by statute where the defendant was motivated by bias or prejudice or race unless the jury has found beyond a reasonable doubt that the defendant was motivated by bias, prejudice or race. Following *Apprendi,* the Supreme Court in *Ring v. Arizona,*[8] ruled that in death penalty cases the Sixth Amendment requires that the jury, not the judge, make the factual determination that aggravating factors are present in the case which would warrant the imposition of the death penalty after the defendant's guilt has been found. In *Blakely v. Washington,*[9] the defendant was convicted of second-degree kidnapping, an offense carrying a maximum

---

[6]Botts v. State, 278 Ga. 538, 604 S.E.2d 512 (2004).

[7]Apprendi v. New Jersey, 530 U.S. 466, 120 S.Ct. 2348, 147 L.Ed.2d 435 (2000). While the jury must make the factual findings which warrant sentence aggravation, they are not required to find those facts which decrease the punishment for crime. See, e.g., Kolar v. State, 292 Ga. App. 623 (2), 665 S.E.2d 719 (2008) (jury not required to find the age of child where misdemeanor sentence would be proper punishment pursuant to O.C.G.A. § 16-6-4(b)(2) if victim was at least 14 years old and defendant is 18 years or younger.); Hernandez v. State, 300 Ga. App. 792, 686 S.E.2d 373 (2009) (jury not required as to an omitted finding where evidence of finding is uncontested and overwhelming). See Babbage v. State, 296 Ga. 364, 768 S.E.2d 461 (2015) (*Apprendi* has no application to life without parole sentence under O.C.G.A. § 16-5-1 since it is within the statutorily authorized range of punishments in most murder cases).

[8]Ring v. Arizona, 536 U.S. 584, 122 S.Ct. 2428, 153 L.Ed.2d 556 (2002). See Hurst v. Florida, 136 S. Ct. 616, 193 L. Ed. 2d 504 (2016) (Florida death penalty statute which allows judge to impose death penalty over jury recommendation of life is unconstitutional); Morrison v. State, 276 Ga. 829 (7), 583 S.E.2d 873 (2003) (Court determined that *Ring* has no application to the proportionality review conducted on appeal from a conviction in a case where the defendant received a sentence of death since the procedure only allows the Georgia Supreme Court to either affirm or reduce the sentence).

[9]Blakely v. Washington, 542 U.S. 296, 124 S.Ct. 2531, 159 L.Ed.2d 403 (2004). It should be noted that Blakely pled guilty in order to avoid a trial which could have resulted in a conviction for first degree kidnapping. Since he did not stipulate to the aggravating circumstances as found by the court, absent a waiver, he was entitled to a jury determination of those facts. See Alleyne v. United States, 133 S. Ct. 2151, 186 L. Ed. 2d 314 (2013) (any fact other than prior conviction which triggers mandatory minimum sentence is one which jury must find unless stipulated to by defendant).

penalty of 10 years of confinement. However, the trial judge determined that the defendant had acted with "deliberate cruelty," an aggravating circumstance, and sentenced him to 3 years above the maximum prison term. The Supreme Court reversed as to the sentencing and applied their holding in *Apprendi* stating: "[o]ther than the fact of a prior conviction, any fact that increases the penalty for a crime beyond the prescribed statutory maximum must be submitted to a jury, and proved beyond a reasonable doubt."[10] *Blakely* will have limited application to cases prosecuted under Georgia law.[11] It will, however, dictate the manner in which a sentence is imposed under federal law and the laws of other states which allow an otherwise maximum sentence to be enhanced upon the finding of certain aggravating factual circumstances.[12]

There is an unofficial opinion of the Attorney General stating that a superior court judge may order a psychological evaluation of criminal defendants, at county expense, before sentencing if the trial judge finds that competent sentencing requires such information.[13]

It has long been the practice to permit the sentencing judge to exercise a wide discretion as to the sources and types of information used to assist him in determining the sentence to be imposed within the limits fixed by law.[14] Generally, so long as the trial judge's sentencing decision falls within the statutory limits for the offense charged, the reasons for that particular sentence will

---

[10]Blakely v. Washington, 542 U.S. 296, 124 S.Ct. 2531, 159 L.Ed.2d 403 (2004) (quoting Apprendi v. New Jersey, 530 U.S. 466, 490, 120 S.Ct. 2348, 147 L.Ed.2d 435 (2000)). Recidivist sentencing by a court is not prohibited by *Apprendi* since it is based upon prior convictions. Brown v. State, 284 Ga. 727 (3), 670 S.E.2d 400 (2008). In Oregon v. Ice, 555 U.S. 160, 129 S.Ct. 711, 172 L.Ed.2d 517 (2009), the Supreme Court held that *Apprendi* had no application to fact finding conducted by judges rather than juries necessary to the imposition of consecutive sentences.

[11]See Jeffrey v. State, 296 Ga. 713, 718(3), 770 S.E.2d 585 (2015) (aggravated assault, domestic violence does not merge into malice murder charge along with related aggravated assault felony murder charges because of additional element of the offense, i.e., an assault between spouses).

[12]See e.g., United States v. Gonzalez, 2004 WL 1444872 (S.D.N.Y. 2004) noting that the *Blakely* decision "calls into serious question" federal courts' implementation of Sentencing Guidelines. Indeed, in U.S. v. Booker, 543 U.S. 220, 125 S. Ct. 738, 160 L. Ed. 2d 621 (2005), the Supreme Court declared the sentencing guidelines unconstitutional to the extent they required judicial fact finding at sentencing and essentially recast the guidelines as guidelines-something for the trial court to consider at sentencing.

[13]Letter to Judge Asa D. Kelly, Jr., Albany, Ga., from Michael J. Bowers, dated July 3, 1985.

[14]Williams v. New York, 337 U.S. 241, 69 S.Ct. 1079, 93 L.Ed. 1337 (1949).

not be subject to appellate review.[15]

However, where it is clear that the trial judge exercised no sentencing discretion whatsoever, as where he routinely metes out the maximum sentence for a particular offense (often called "mechanical sentencing"),[16] appellate review is proper.[17] The United States Supreme Court, in *Williams v. New York*,[18] held that the sentencing decision must be tailored to fit the offender, not merely the offense:

"[T]he belief no longer prevails that every offense in a like legal category calls for an identical punishment without regard to the past life and habits of a particular offender . . . [I]t is necessary to individualize each case, to give that careful, humane, and comprehensive consideration to the particular situation of each offender which would be possible only in the exercise of a broad discretion . . . [F]or the determination of sentences, justice generally requires consideration of more than the particular acts by which the crime was committed and that there be taken into account the circumstances of the offense together with the character and propensities of the offender."

---

[15]Dorszynski v. United States, 418 U.S. 424, 94 S.Ct. 3042, 41 L.Ed.2d 855 (1974); United States v. Tucker, 404 U.S. 443, 92 S.Ct. 589, 30 L.Ed.2d 592 (1972); Gore v. United States, 357 U.S. 386, 78 S.Ct. 1280, 2 L.Ed.2d 1405 (1958); Hill v. Stynchcombe, 225 Ga. 122, 166 S.E.2d 729 (1969). In Tommie v. State, 158 Ga. App. 216 (1), 279 S.E.2d 510 (1981), the court said that it "will not review for legal error any sentence which is within the statutory limits . . . [a]ny question as to excessiveness of a sentence . . . should be addressed to the sentence review panel."

However, in Terrebonne v. Blackburn, 624 F.2d 1363 (5th Cir. 1980), the court held that a life sentence for the sale of a small amount of heroin to an undercover officer was cruel and unusual punishment.

In Ferguson v. State, 606 P.2d 382 (Alaska 1980), the court found that imposing the maximum statutory sentence on the defendant was error where he had no prior criminal record and a favorable pre-sentence report.

[16]United States v. Hart, 488 F.2d 970 (5th Cir. 1974) (drug offense); United States v. Wardlaw, 576 F.2d 932 (1st Cir. 1978) (drug offense); Woosley v. United States, 478 F.2d 139 (8th Cir. 1973) (draft evasion); United States v. Daniels, 446 F.2d 967 (6th Cir. 1971) (draft evasion).

[17]Dorszynski v. United States, 418 U.S. 424, 94 S.Ct. 3042, 41 L.Ed.2d 855 (1974); Yates v. United States, 356 U.S. 363, 78 S.Ct. 766, 2 L.Ed.2d 837 (1958); United States v. Daniels, 446 F.2d 967 (6th Cir. 1971); United States v. Williams, 407 F.2d 940 (4th Cir. 1969). Although the general rule allows the trial judge wide discretion in determining how much weight, credibility, and probative value to give the various items of information he chooses to rely upon, Scott v. United States, 419 F.2d 264 (C.A.D. C. 1969), an inflexible sentencing policy based solely on the crime charged is not an exercise of informed judicial discretion, as such an approach ignores the rehabilitative purposes of sentencing. United States v. McCoy, 429 F.2d 739 (C.A.D.C. 1970). Cf. United States v. Hartford, 489 F.2d 652, 656 (5th Cir. 1974).

[18]Williams v. New York, 337 U.S. 241, 69 S.Ct. 1079, 93 L.Ed. 1337 (1949).

In *Cottingham v. State,*[19] the court held that a mechanical sentencing formula "is an abdication of judicial responsibility" and "amounts to a refusal to exercise . . . discretion." The court then remanded the case for re-sentencing where the trial judge had followed his policy of imposing any sentence given to be consecutive to any sentence the defendant was then serving. Nevertheless, in *Nation v. Georgia,*[20] the court indicated that a question of mechanical sentencing must be raised on direct appeal. The court then held that where a state trial judge follows a policy of mechanical sentencing "that such an abuse of discretion is not unconstitutional" and is not a basis for a grant of federal habeas corpus. In *Knight v. State,*[21] the court held that in "the absence of any affirmative showing to the contrary, the trial court is presumed to have exercised its discretion in imposing . . ." a sentence.

In *Harrison v. State,*[22] the court held that where a defendant is given a straight sentence to serve for a specified period of time with no probationary period, a condition of preventing the defendant from engaging in the bonding business in Georgia is a nullity at law.

Since 1985, the judge has been authorized to consider any written or oral victim impact statement. It has also been held in Georgia that a defendant's juvenile court record may be considered in sentencing the defendant for a crime committed as an adult.[23] See § 26:14, supra, on evidence considered in pre-sentence hearing.

In *State v. Tew,*[24] the Wisconsin Supreme Court, in an excellent opinion, and a truly leading case, set out a number of factors which a trial judge may properly consider before sentencing the defendant. They are as follows: (1) the amount of time the defendant has already spent in jail prior to sentencing;[25] (2) the

---

[19]Cottingham v. State, 206 Ga. App. 197, 199, 424 S.E.2d 794 (1992). Accord, Jackson v. State, 244 Ga. App. 477, 479 (3), 535 S.E.2d 818 (2000); Jefferson v. State, 209 Ga. App. 859, 863 (3), 434 S.E.2d 814 (1993); Worley v. State, 265 Ga. 251, 253 (2), 454 S.E.2d 461 (1995); Walton v. State, 217 Ga. App. 11, 13 (5), 456 S.E.2d 289 (1995).

[20]Nation v. Georgia, 645 F.Supp. 179 (N.D.Ga. 1986), affirmed without opinion, 822 F.2d 64 (11th Cir. 1987).

[21]Knight v. State, 221 Ga. App. 92, 93, 470 S.E.2d 486 (1996).

[22]Harrison v. State, 201 Ga. App. 577, 583 (5), 411 S.E.2d 738 (1991).

[23]Ruffin v. State, 243 Ga. 95, 101, 252 S.E.2d 472 (1979); Jones v. State, 129 Ga. App. 623, 625, 200 S.E.2d 487 (1973). See also Annot., "Consideration of Accused's Juvenile Court Record in Sentencing for Offense Committed as Adult," 64 A.L.R.3d 1291 (1975).

[24]State v. Tew, 54 Wis.2d 361, 195 N.W.2d 615 (1972).

[25]State v. Tew, 54 Wis.2d 361, 195 N.W.2d 615 (1972).

defendant's past criminal record;[26] (3) the defendant's past criminal behavior;[27] (4) the defendant's personality, character, and social traits;[28] (5) the results of any pre-sentence investigation;[29] (6) the vicious or aggravated nature of the crime;[30] (7) the degree of the defendant's actual participation and moral culpability in the crime;[31] (8) the defendant's demeanor at trial;[32] (9) the defendant's age, educational background, and employment record;[33] (10) the defendant's remorse, repentance, and cooperativeness;[34] (11) the defendant's need for rehabilitation, supervision, or control;[35] and (12) the rights and interests of society.[36]

Rule 33.6 of the Uniform Rules for the Superior Courts contains the following criteria to be considered in sentencing:

"(A) It is proper for the judge to grant charge and sentence leniency to defendants who enter pleas of guilty or *nolo contendere* where the interests of the public in the effective administration of criminal justice are thereby served. Among the considerations which are appropriate in determining this question are:

"(1) that the defendant by entering a plea has aided in ensuring the prompt and certain application of correctional measures;

"(2) that the defendant has acknowledged guilt and shown a willingness to assume responsibility for conduct;

"(3) that the leniency will make possible alternative correctional measures which are better adapted to achieving rehabilitative, protective, deterrent or other purposes of correctional treatment, or will prevent undue harm to the defendant from the form of

---

[26]Brown v. State, 52 Wis.2d 496, 190 N.W.2d 497 (1971). In United States v. Doyle, 348 F.2d 715 (2d Cir. 1965), the court held that unproven criminal activity of the defendant could be considered by the sentencing judge, if such activity was closely related to the crime at hand. The court saw no confrontation clause problem, as the unproven criminal conduct was admitted into the record only after the trial on the merits had ended and the resulting sentence was well within the statutory limits.

[27]Triplett v. State, 51 Wis.2d 549, 187 N.W.2d 318 (1971).

[28]State v. Morales, 51 Wis.2d 650, 187 N.W.2d 841 (1971).

[29]State v. Burgher, 53 Wis.2d 452, 192 N.W.2d 869 (1972).

[30]State v. Wells, 51 Wis.2d 477, 187 N.W.2d 328 (1971).

[31]State v. Schilz, 50 Wis.2d 395, 184 N.W.2d 134 (1971).

[32]State v. Schilz, 50 Wis.2d 395, 184 N.W.2d 134 (1971); Rogers v. State, 191 Ga. App. 855, 856 (2), 383 S.E.2d 331 (1989) (conduct and attitude at trial).

[33]State v. Cole, 50 Wis.2d 449, 184 N.W.2d 75 (1971).

[34]McCleary v. State, 49 Wis.2d 263, 182 N.W.2d 512 (1971). See Cottingham v. State, 213 Ga. App. 637 (1), 445 S.E.2d 384 (1994), and Dupont v. State, 204 Ga. App. 262, 265 (5), 418 S.E.2d 803 (1992), on lack of remorse. Cf. Jenkins v. State, 269 Ga. 282, 288 (c), 498 S.E.2d 502 (1998).

[35]McCleary v. State, 49 Wis.2d 263, 182 N.W.2d 512 (1971).

[36]Embry v. State, 46 Wis.2d 151, 174 N.W.2d 521 (1970).

conviction;

"(4) that the defendant has made public trial unnecessary when there are good reasons for not having the case dealt with in a public trial;

"(5) that the defendant has given or offered cooperation when such cooperation has resulted or may result in the successful prosecution of other offenders engaged in equally serious or more serious criminal conduct;

"(6) that the defendant by entering a plea has aided in avoiding delay (including delay due to crowded dockets) in the disposition of other cases and thereby has increased the probability of prompt and certain application of correctional measures to other offenders.

"(B) The judge should not impose upon a defendant any sentence in excess of that which would be justified by any of the rehabilitative, protective, deterrent or other purposes of the criminal law merely because the defendant has chosen to require the prosecution to prove the defendant's guilt at trial rather than to enter a plea of guilty or *nolo contendere*."

In *Ansley v. State*,[37] the Georgia Court of Appeals said that in making a determination as to a sentence, the following should be considered: "all aspects of the crime, the past criminal record or lack thereof, and the defendant's general moral character . . . the motive of the defendant, . . . [and] the defendant's predisposition to commit other crimes." In *McClain v. State*,[38] the court held that the sentencing courts are authorized to consider in aggravation "[a]ny lawful evidence which tends to show the motive of the defendant, his lack of remorse, his general moral character, and his predisposition to commit other crimes. . . ." However, it is reversible error for a court to refuse first offender status on the basis of hearsay evidence of other crimes or bad conduct by the defendant or to consider such evidence in aggravation of the sentence to be imposed.[39]

In *United States v. Grayson*,[40] the court held that generally there is no violation of due process when the sentencing judge

---

[37]Ansley v. State, 197 Ga. App. 765, 399 S.E.2d 558 (1990).

[38]McClain v. State, 220 Ga. App. 474, 476 (3), 469 S.E.2d 756 (1996) (citing Clark v. State, 186 Ga. App. 106, 108-109 (4), 366 S.E.2d 361 (1988)).

[39]See e.g., Humphrey v. State, 257 Ga. App. 312, 571 S.E.2d 187 (2002); Welborn v. State, 166 Ga. App. 214, 215, 303 S.E.2d 755 (1983).

[40]United States v. Grayson, 438 U.S. 41, 98 S.Ct. 2610, 57 L.Ed.2d 582 (1978); United States v. Gamboa, 543 F.2d 545 (5th Cir. 1976); United States v. Hendrix, 505 F.2d 1233 (2d Cir. 1974); United States v. Sneath, 557 F.2d 149 (8th Cir. 1977); United States v. Sanders, 435 F.2d 165 (9th Cir. 1970). But in Scott v. United States, 419 F.2d 264 (D.C.Cir. 1969), the court held that the trial judge is constitutionally prevented from relying on his

considers whether or not the defendant perjured himself at trial. However, in *Mitchell v. State*,[41] in a five to four decision of the United States Supreme Court, the Court held that the defendant's Fifth Amendment rights were violated where the sentencing judge drew adverse inferences from the refusal of the defendant to testify at trial.

In *Roberts v. United States*,[42] the United States Supreme Court said that a defendant, like any other citizen, is obliged to assist the authorities, and his refusal to cooperate with the police, when not justified on Fifth Amendment grounds, may be considered by the sentencing judge. However, the sentencing judge must also consider whether the defendant's refusal to cooperate was based on fear.

Although in a case that was later overruled, it has been held that the trial judge may consider the possibility that the defendant was insane or of diminished capacity at the time of the offense, even where the defendant specifically refuses to assert insanity as a defense.[43]

In Georgia, the failure of the trial judge to consider probating all or part of a sentence may constitute reversible error.[44] For instance, in the 2004 case of *Costin v. State*,[45] the court considered O.C.G.A. § 40-6-391(c)(1), which expressly limits a trial court's discretion in probating, suspending, or staying the prison sentence of a person convicted of driving under the influence to those cases in which the offender's blood-alcohol content was 0.08 grams or more. The court found the trial court's refusal to consider any sentencing option requiring the defendant to spend less than twenty-four (24) hours in jail was not mandated by the statute and thus failed to properly exercise its discretion.

The importance of the right to a fair and impartial trial, when accused of a violation of the law, has been emphasized and no practice is more to be abhorred than the coercion of guilty pleas.[46] Hence, it has been said that an accused "cannot be punished by a

---

belief that the defendant lied. See Case Note, "Judge's Disbelief of Defendant's Testimony May Justify an Increased Sentence," 30 Mercer L. R. 757 (1979). See also Annot., "Propriety of Sentencing Judge's Consideration of Defendant's Perjury or Lying in Pleas or Testimony in Present Trial," 34 A.L.R.4th 888 (1984).

[41]Mitchell v. United States, 526 U.S. 314, 119 S.Ct. 1307, 143 L.Ed.2d 424 (1999).

[42]Roberts v. United States, 445 U.S. 552, 100 S.Ct. 1358, 63 L.Ed.2d 622 (1980).

[43]Cross v. United States, 354 F.2d 512 (C.A.D.C. 1965), overruled by U.S. v. Marble, 940 F.2d 1543 (C.A.D.C. 1991).

[44]Knight v. State, 243 Ga. 770, 775 (2), 257 S.E.2d 182 (1979); Decker v. State, 139 Ga. App. 707, 711 (9), 229 S.E.2d 520 (1976).

[45]Costin v. State, 269 Ga. App. 632, 605 S.E.2d 73 (2004).

[46]Meeks v. State, 142 Ga. App. 452, 454, 236 S.E.2d 119 (1977). See Baldwin v. State, 217 Ga. App. 866,

more severe punishment because he unsuccessfully exercised his constitutional right to stand trial rather than plead guilty."[47] Likewise, "a sentencing judge may not penalize the exercise of a defendant's privilege against self-incrimination by enhancing his sentence based upon the defendant's failure to cooperate by implicating other persons or otherwise admitting guilt to crimes with which he is not charged."[48]

It has been held to be error for the sentencing judge to consider the following factors in reaching a sentencing decision: (1) that the defendant chose to go to trial instead of accepting a plea bargain;[49] (2) that the defendant continues to deny any guilt whatsoever;[50] or (3) that the defendant intends to appeal or gain a retrial.[51] Although in a case that was later overruled, it has been recognized that, in imposing sentence, a judge has no right to consider a case which has not been tried.[52]

However, the validity of much of the foregoing may be open to question in Georgia in view of Rule 33.6 of the Uniform Rules for the Superior Courts, which is set out above. In *Johnson v. State*,[53] the court held that this Rule "does not require a trial court to sentence a defendant [who exercises his right to trial] to the same sentence that would have been appropriate had a defendant entered a guilty plea."

---

460 S.E.2d 80 (1995) (not error for trial court to impose a greater sentence than pre-trial recommendation by the state after hearing evidence in that case).

[47]United States v. Rogers, 504 F.2d 1079 (5th Cir. 1974). However, thus far the Georgia appellate courts have refused to intervene where the trial judge imposes a greater sentence after an unsuccessful trial than after a guilty plea to the same offense. For example, in Thompson v. State, 154 Ga. App. 704, 708 (5), 269 S.E.2d 474 (1980), the defendant originally pled guilty and was sentenced to serve 3 years plus 3 years on probation. He withdrew his plea, was tried and sentenced to 6 years without probation. At the time of the second sentencing the judge said he accepted the original plea and sentenced the defendant the first time as he did because of the defendant's significant step toward rehabilitation and for that reason probated a part of the sentence. On appeal the defendant contended that there was a due process violation in the imposition of the second sentence. On appeal the case was affirmed as the court said the reason for the change was sufficiently set out and there was no showing of vindictiveness.

[48]U.S. v. Safirstein, 827 F.2d 1380, 1388(II)(D) (9th Cir. 1987).

[49]Scott v. United States, 419 F.2d 264 (C.A.D.C. 1969). See U.S. v. Jones, 997 F.2d 1475 (D.C. Cir. 1993). Compare Frank v. Blackburn, 646 F.2d 873 (5th Cir. 1980), opinion modified, 646 F.2d 902 (5th Cir. 1981).

[50]Thomas v. United States, 368 F.2d 941 (5th Cir. 1966); Scott v. United States, 419 F.2d 264 (C.A.D.C. 1969).

[51]Alabama v. Smith, 490 U.S. 794, 109 S. Ct. 2201, 104 L. Ed. 2d 865 (1989).

[52]Minis v. State, 150 Ga. App. 671, 675, 258 S.E.2d 308 (1979), overruled by Boney v. Tims, 254 Ga. 664, 333 S.E.2d 592 (1985).

[53]Johnson v. State, 224 Ga. App. 568, 570 (2), 481 S.E.2d 268 (1997).

Thus, it is generally not considered error for the trial judge to impose a greater sentence on a defendant after a trial than he might have imposed after a guilty plea.[54] However, it should be noted that the Court of Appeals has also found no error where the trial court refuses to recognize a notice of intent to seek a life sentence where such notice constitutes an apparent attempt by the state to punish a defendant who exercises his right to trial. In *Webb v. State*,[55] the state, following the defendant's rejection of a plea bargain offer on the eve of trial, informed the court that it would be required to sentence the defendant to life without parole if the defendant were convicted on the child molestation count as a recidivist. The Court of Appeals upheld the trial court's decision to disregard the state's recommendation, finding that the state's pre-trial negotiations with the defendant constituted an attempt to punish the defendant for exercising his right to go to trial.

In *North Carolina v. Pearce*,[56] the United States Supreme Court held that vindictiveness can play no role whatsoever in the sentencing decision. *Pearce* was subsequently overruled in *Alabama v. Smith*.[57] *Smith* restricted the presumption of vindictiveness created in *Pearce* to those cases where the evidence shows a "reasonable likelihood" that the increased sentence was "the product of actual vindictiveness on the part of the sentencing authority." Many jurisdictions hold that it is error merely for the sentencing judge to ask whether the defendant intends to appeal before imposing sentence.[58] In the 1983 decision of *Brock v. State*,[59] the Georgia Court of Appeals held that where the trial judge, in part, based his sentence on the fact that the defendant was appealing the case, the sentence had to be vacated.

In *United States v. Watts*,[60] the United States Supreme Court held that there was no double jeopardy violation when the trial

---

[54]Arnold v. State, 163 Ga. App. 94, 96, 292 S.E.2d 891 (1982); Arnold v. State, 228 Ga. App. 470, 473(2), 491 S.E.2d 819 (1997). Note, however, that a judge should not consider a separate case in which the defendant has been tried but in which the jury has not at that time returned a verdict. Newby v. State, 161 Ga. App. 805, 810 (5), 288 S.E.2d 889 (1982).

[55]Webb v. State, 270 Ga. App. 817, 608 S.E.2d 241 (2004).

[56]North Carolina v. Pearce, 395 U.S. 711, 89 S.Ct. 2072, 23 L.Ed.2d 656 (1969).

[57]Alabama v. Smith, 490 U.S. 794,

109 S. Ct. 2201, 104 L. Ed. 2d 865 (1989).

[58]See Annot., "Court's Pre-Sentence Inquiry as to, or Consideration of, Accused's Intention to Appeal as Error," 64 A.L.R.3d 1226 (1975).

[59]Brock v. State, 166 Ga. App. 649, 305 S.E.2d 180 (1983). See also Cook v. State, 256 Ga. App. 353, 568 S.E.2d 482 (2002) where it was held error for trial court to refuse to consider first offender sentence because the defendant insisted on trial.

[60]United States v. Watts, 519 U.S. 148, 117 S.Ct. 633, 136 L.Ed.2d 554 (1997).

judge considered in sentencing that the defendant had been found not guilty of an earlier crime but the trial court found by a preponderance of the evidence that the defendant was guilty.

The equal protection clause of the Fourteenth Amendment prohibits the sentencing judge from using race, religion, or other suspect classification as sentencing criteria.[61]

It should be kept in mind that O.C.G.A. § 17-10-5 provides: "When a defendant is found guilty of a felony punishable by imprisonment for a maximum term of ten years or less, the judge may, in his discretion, impose punishment as for a misdemeanor." However, since the trial judge sets the punishment and determines the sentence, it is not necessary for the judge to charge the jury that it could recommend misdemeanor punishment for the defendant.[62] O.C.G.A. § 16-11-106(d) prohibits reduction to misdemeanor punishment for the offense of possession of a firearm or knife during the commission of certain crimes.

In certain crimes where mandatory minimum sentences are generally required, the legislature provided the trial court with the discretion to depart from such sentences under certain conditions. Thus, pursuant to O.C.G.A. §§ 16-13-31 and 16-13-31.1, a trial judge may now depart from the mandatory sentencing requirements in drug and methamphetamine trafficking cases if the court concludes that the defendant was not a leader of the criminal conduct, the defendant did not use or possess a weapon during the crime, the crime did not result in the death or serious bodily injury of a person who was not a party to the crime, the defendant has no prior felony convictions and the interests of justice would not otherwise be served by the imposition of the mandatory sentences.[63] However, first offender sentences imposed under § 16-13-2 for drug trafficking and whose mandatory minimum sentences receive judicial discretionary downward departure pursuant to either § 16-13-31(g) or § 16-13-31.1(b) cannot be reduced by "any earned time, early release, work release, leave, or other sentence-reducing measures under programs administered by the Department of Corrections."

Under the provisions of O.C.G.A. § 17-10-1(b), if the trial judge is preparing to sentence a first offender, he may determine

---

[61]Pace v. Alabama, 106 U.S. 583, 1 S.Ct. 637, 27 L.Ed. 207 (1883); McLaughlin v. Florida, 379 U.S. 184, 85 S.Ct. 283, 13 L.Ed.2d 222 (1964); Moore v. Missouri, 159 U.S. 673, 16 S.Ct. 179, 40 L.Ed. 301 (1895). See § 26:4, supra, on equal protection.

[62]Wallace v. State, 188 Ga. App. 77, 78 (2), 371 S.E.2d 914 (1988).

[63]See O.C.G.A. § 17-10-6.1 and § 17-10-6.2 (court may depart from mandatory minimum sentences in case of person convicted of "serious violent felony" and sexual offenses where state and defense consent). See § 26:28, supra, on recidivism punishment.

whether the defendant should be considered for parole prior to the completion of any minimum time specified before parole eligibility. If the judge wishes to impose sentence under this provision, "he may specify in the sentence that the person is sentenced under this subsection and may provide that the State Board of Pardons and Paroles, acting in its sole discretion, may consider and may parole any person so sentenced at any time prior to the completion of any minimum requirement otherwise imposed. . . ."

Generally, under state law a bondsman on an appearance bond is automatically released from all liability as soon as sentence is imposed.[64]

In the case of federal law the United States Supreme Court has said "the judge has no enforceable expectations with respect to the actual release of a sentenced defendant. . . . [T]he actual decision is not his to make, either at the time of sentencing or later if his expectations are not met."[65]

O.C.G.A. § 17-10-15 provides that upon a verdict of guilty, a plea of guilty, or a plea of nolo contendere to any AIDS transmitting crime, the trial judge "shall" require the defendant to submit to an HIV test within 45 days of such verdict or plea. The statute also provides for the follow-up on such order. In *Adams v. State*,[66] O.C.G.A. § 17-10-15(b) was held constitutional in fact of a number of attacks. In *United States v. Ward*,[67] the Third Circuit held that there was no Fourth Amendment violation by a trial judge in ordering the defendant, who was convicted of a sexual assault, to undergo a HIV test.

See sections 25:2 and 25:3, supra, on merger of offenses. See § 26:31, supra, on merger of offenses of which a defendant has been convicted. See § 26:26, supra, on sexual offenders. See also § 14:54, supra, generally.

§ 26:44　The sentencing itself

The defendant has a right to be present at the time he is sentenced,[1] unless he has escaped during the trial, and he has

---

[64]City of Macon v. Davis, 251 Ga. 332, 305 S.E.2d 116 (1983). However, in the Davis 4 to 3 decision the court held valid a municipal ordinance extending the responsibility of the bondsman until the fine is collected.

[65]United States v. Addonizio, 442 U.S. 178, 99 S.Ct. 2235, 60 L.Ed.2d 805 (1979).

[66]Adams v. State, 269 Ga. 405, 498 S.E.2d 268 (1998).

[67]United States v. Ward, 131 F.3d 335 (3d Cir. 1997).

[Section 26:44]

[1]Ball v. United States, 140 U.S. 118, 11 S.Ct. 761, 35 L.Ed. 377 (1891). But see Smith v. Henderson, 190 Ga.

the right to be represented by counsel unless this right is waived.[2]

Defense counsel has the right to address the trial judge and to call the court's attention to any factor he believes will be helpful to his client.[3] There are a number of Georgia cases which hold that it is not reversible error for the trial judge to fail to ask the defendant if he has anything to say to show why sentence should not be imposed.[4] However, the court, in *Green v. United States*,[5] said that the defendant has the right of common-law allocution before he is sentenced, at least if this right is not waived. Before a defendant is sentenced, he has a right (1) to personally address the judge in his own behalf and (2) to present any information in mitigation of punishment.[6] O.C.G.A. § 17-10-2(a)(2) provides in part that the trial "judge shall also hear argument by the defendant or the defendant's counsel" at sentencing.

In addition to the right of the defendant and his counsel to address the court, the judge may be willing to hear from other interested persons on matters relating to the sentence to be imposed, particularly if there has not just been a pre-sentence hearing. If there is any doubt about whether a particular judge will hear from other witnesses at the sentencing, defense counsel should be doubly sure to have such persons present for the pre-sentence hearing.

At the time of sentencing, defense counsel may summarize the favorable comments which have been made about the defendant and urge the judge to consider some rehabilitative program or

---

886 (2), 10 S.E.2d 921 (1940). However, the voluntary absence of the accused amounts to a waiver of his right to be present. Byrd v. Ricketts, 233 Ga. 779, 780, 213 S.E.2d 610 (1975). Under Georgia law, a defendant does not have a right to be present when he is re-sentenced if the new sentence cannot be greater than the former sentence. See § 26:41, supra.

[2]See Welch v. State, 63 Ga. App. 277 (2), 11 S.E.2d 42 (1940).

[3]See Townsend v. Burke, 334 U.S. 736, 68 S.Ct. 1252, 92 L.Ed. 1690 (1948).

[4]See Guyton v. State, 281 Ga. 789, 642 S.E.2d 67 (2007); Seagraves v. State, 339 Ga. App. 258, 793 S.E.2d 164 (2016).

[5]Green v. United States, 365 U.S. 301, 81 S.Ct. 653, 5 L.Ed.2d 670 (1961).

In Murray v. State, 269 Ga. 871, 872 (1), 505 S.E.2d 746 (1998), the court failed to reach the question of whether there is a right of allocution under the Georgia Constitution.

[6]Green v. United States, 365 U.S. 301, 304, 81 S.Ct. 653, 5 L.Ed.2d 670 (1961). See 4 Torcia, Wharton's Criminal Procedure, 208, § 609 (12th Ed. 1976); Rule 32(a)(1) of the Federal Rules of Criminal Procedure; and Annot., "Necessity and Sufficiency of Question to Defendant as to Whether He Has Anything to Say Why Sentencing Should Not Be Pronounced Against Him," 96 A.L.R.2d 1292 (1964). Cf. Nash v. State, 225 Ga. App. 10, 11 (4), 482 S.E.2d 520 (1997).

Generally, see 21 Am. Jur. 2d 512, Criminal Law § 530 (1965). However, it is error for the trial judge in his charge to the jury to refer to the right of allocution. United States v. Haywood, 411 F.2d 555 (5th Cir. 1969).

other alternative to confinement.

Prior to 2005, the state did not have to provide the defense with evidence which it intended to introduce at sentencing in aggravation of punishment until the start of trial. That deadline was deleted by the legislature and a new one provided by O.C.G.A. § 17-16-4(a)(5). The state is now required to provide the defendant with notice of any evidence in aggravation of punishment which it intends to introduce at sentencing at least ten days prior to trial or at such time as the court directs, but in no event later than the start of trial. In addition, "sentencing Courts are authorized to consider in aggravation any *lawful evidence* which tends to show the motive of the Defendant, his lack of remorse, his general moral character, and his predisposition to commit other crimes."[7] This may even include conduct of the Defendant which occurred before or after trial, but prior to sentencing.[8]

Normally a trial judge in the exercise of sound discretion may sentence a defendant to any specific number of years within the limits set by the legislature.[9] "In the absence of any affirmative showing to the contrary, the trial court is presumed to have exercised its discretion in imposing . . . [a] sentence."[10] However, if there has been a change in punishment, the legislative act applicable at the time of the commission of the crime rather than that in effect at the time of sentencing controls.[11] As set out above, he may be authorized to probate a part or all of the sentence or

---

[7]Phillips v. State, 241 Ga. App. 689, 690, 527 S.E.2d 283 (1999).

[8]Demetrios v. State, 246 Ga. App. 506, 510(4), 541 S.E.2d 83 (2000); see, Pearce v. State, 256 Ga. App. 889, 570 S.E.2d 74 (2002), the state was not precluded by former O.C.G.A. § 17-10-2(a) from offering at sentencing evidence in aggravation about which it first became aware of on or about day of sentencing. Defendant's remedy is to ask for continuance, if necessary, in order to investigate new evidence. The same result should apply under O.C.G.A. § 17-16-4(a)(5) which replaced O.C.G.A. § 17-10-2(a) as the governing statute regarding notice of aggravation evidence at sentencing. Spencer v. State, 296 Ga. App. 82 (2), 676 S.E.2d 274 (2009).

[9]O.C.G.A. § 17-9-2, O.C.G.A.

§ 17-10-1, O.C.G.A. § 17-10-2(a); Baldwin v. State, 142 Ga. App. 758 (5), 237 S.E.2d 3 (1977). If there is an inconsistency between the name of the crime and the description of the crime in the indictment, the description of the crime determines the sentence which may be imposed. Hammock v. State, 146 Ga. App. 339, 340, 246 S.E.2d 392 (1978). In Hill v. Stynchcombe, 225 Ga. 122, 125 (6), 166 S.E.2d 729 (1969), the court said that any sentence within limits fixed by statute is not excessive.

But see § 26:2, supra, on cruel and unusual punishment.

[10]Hatcher v. State, 224 Ga. App. 747, 751 (2)(b), 482 S.E.2d 443 (1997).

[11]Searcy v. State, 162 Ga. App. 695, 698, 291 S.E.2d 557 (1982).

impose some special sentence.[12] However, where a sentence is given with a specified portion to be served and the balance served on probation, the judge may not provide that if the defendant is released from incarceration before the expiration of the time specified to be served, he will report to the probation department of the county. Such a sentence is regarded as a violation of the executive powers of the state.[13] Defendants that pled nolo contendere or guilty, or are convicted of offenses other than capital felonies, may, at the discretion of the sentencing judge, be released on bond or on the defendant's personal recognizance pending the defendant's surrender to a correctional institution or jail.[14]

In *Hirjee v. State*,[15] the defendant was found guilty of all counts, but the court failed to impose a sentence for one count. The court held that the trial judge retained authority to correct the sentence and impose sentence on the remaining count.

It has been held that the fact that the judge in sentencing the defendant expresses his belief in the defendant's guilt does not authorize an inference that the accused did not have a fair trial. However, such remarks may raise a question as to the ability of the judge to fairly try other such cases.[16]

In *Eubanks v. State*,[17] the court pointed out that under O.C.G.A. § 42-5-51, when a person is convicted of a felony and sentenced to serve time in any penal institution in Georgia, "he shall be committed to the custody of the 'commissioner [of corrections].' "The clerk is then to notify the commissioner, who shall designate the place of confinement.

After the trial judge has orally informed the defendant of his sentence, he normally should advise him of the following: (1) his right to appeal; (2) his right to appeal without cost if he is unable to pay the cost of appeal; (3) his right to appointment of counsel for the appeal if he is unable to employ counsel;[18] (4) his right to have the sentence reviewed by a panel of superior court judges if the sentence is for twelve years or more;[19] (5) the length of time within which an appeal must be filed; and (6) the length of time

---

[12]See § 26:18 et seq., supra, on suspended sentences.

[13]Johns v. State, 160 Ga. App. 535, 287 S.E.2d 617 (1981).

[14]O.C.G.A. § 17-10-9.1.

[15]Hirjee v. State, 226 Ga. App. 573 (2), 487 S.E.2d 40 (1997).

[16]Cf. Thomas v. State, 159 Ga. App. 249, 251 (4), 283 S.E.2d 37 (1981); Harkey v. State, 159 Ga. App. 112, 113 (3), 282 S.E.2d 648 (1981).

[17]Eubanks v. State, 229 Ga. App. 667, 494 S.E.2d 564 (1997).

[18]See § 28:6, infra, on indigent defendants' right to counsel.

[19]In Greenway v. State, 144 Ga. App. 558, 241 S.E.2d 453 (1978), the court stated that it was better procedure for the trial judge at the time of sentencing to advise defendant of the right to have his sentence reviewed. This right will expire to all cases where sentence was imposed prior to

in which he may petition to have his sentence reviewed by a panel of superior court judges.

Generally, until an oral sentence is reduced to writing, signed by the judge and filed by the clerk it is neither final nor appealable. Accordingly, a sentence which is merely pronounced may be modified by the court, either up or down, until such time as it is written, signed and filed.[20] One exception to this rule is the case where the defendant has already begun service of the sentence as announced. Thus, in *Stulb v. State*,[21] the trial court could not change a probated sentence to one which included incarceration after the defendant had reported to probation. See Studdard, *Daniel's Georgia Handbook on Criminal Evidence* (2018 ed.), § 4:59.

§ 26:45 Sentencing a defendant to life without parole

Previously in Georgia, the sentencing option of life without the possibility of parole in a capital case could only be imposed as an alternative where the state was seeking the death penalty and then only when the jury found that the state had proved one of the statutory aggravating circumstances.[1] In 2009, O.C.G.A. § 16-5-1 was amended to provide that, in the case of murder, the state can seek death or life in prison without the possibility of parole or life with the possibility of parole. In addition, proof of the statutory aggravating circumstances is now required only where the state is seeking the death penalty.[2] Life without the possibility of parole may also be imposed in the case of a recidivist violent offender pursuant to O.C.G.A. § 17-10-7. In addition, Code section 17-10-16.1 provides that a person may be sentenced to life without parole regardless of whether the state is seeking the death penalty.

July 2. 2007. O.C.G.A. § 17-10-6.3.

[20]Titelman v. Stedman, 277 Ga. 460, 591 S.E.2d 774 (2003). See Bell v. State, 294 Ga. 5, 8-9, 749 S.E.2d 672 (2013) ("It is the sentence signed by the judge, not his oral declaration, that is the sentence of the court.").

[21]Stulb v. State, 279 Ga. App. 547 (2), 631 S.E.2d 765 (2006). Compare Curry v. State, 248 Ga. 183 (4), 281 S.E.2d 604 (1981).

[Section 26:45]

[1]State v. Ingram, 266 Ga. 324, 467 S.E.2d 523 (1996).

[2]Laws 2009, Act. 6, § 8, provides that § 16-5-1 as amended applies only to offenses committed after July 1,

2009, provided however, that with the written consent of the state it may be applied to cases involving offenses committed earlier than that date if jeopardy has not attached or if the sentence or conviction in a case has been reversed on appeal and the state is not barred as a result from seeking the death penalty. O.C.G.A. § 16-5-1(e). See Blake v. State, 292 Ga. 516, 739 S.E.2d 319 (2013). See also Williams v. State, 291 Ga. 19, 727 S.E.2d 95 (2012) (other than the death penalty, there is no constitutional requirement that a court consider mitigating factors before imposing sentence of life without possibility of parole).

§ 26:46 Motion for reduction or correction of sentence— Felony cases

Prior to 2001, a trial judge only had authority to reduce a sentence if the defendant filed a motion for reduction at the same term of court as that at which the defendant was sentenced.[1] Since that time, the relevant Code section has been amended to provide the trial judge with authority to reduce a sentence "[w]ithin one year of the date upon which the sentence is imposed, or within 120 days after receipt by the sentencing court of the remittitur upon affirmance of the judgment after direct appeal, whichever is later[.]"[2] A pre-2001 Court of Appeals decision indicates that, except where a sentence is void, a motion to vacate a sentence would not be an appropriate remedy after the passage of the aforementioned time limit.[3] However, there is nothing to prevent a defendant from both appealing and making a motion to modify the sentence.[4] The argument and hearing on the motion to modify may be delayed until after the conviction has been affirmed.[5]

In *State v. Bradbury*,[6] the court held that even when a motion for reduction of sentence is not filed but a motion for new trial is filed, the trial judge at the term at which he denies the motion for new trial has authority then to reduce the sentence.

As a general proposition, a sentence is considered void if the punishment imposed exceeds that allowed by law.[7] However, a defendant

> cannot assert a claim that his conviction was unlawful in an untimely motion to vacate his sentence simply by dressing it up as a claim that his sentence was void. . . . Instead, a claim that a conviction was unlawful must be asserted by a motion for new trial, direct appeal from the judgment of conviction, extraordinary motion for new trial, motion in arrest of judgment, or petition for the writ of habeas corpus. Motions to vacate a void sentence generally are

---

[Section 26:46]

[1]Latham v. State, 225 Ga. App. 147, 148, 483 S.E.2d 322 (1997); Thomas v. State, 226 Ga. App. 409, 486 S.E.2d 673 (1997).

[2]O.C.G.A. § 17-10-1(f). See Grady v. State, 311 Ga. App. 620, 716 S.E.2d 747 (2011) (motion may not be used as vehicle to challenge underlying plea or conviction).

[3]Battle v. State, 235 Ga. App. 101, 102, 508 S.E.2d 467 (1998).

[4]Porterfield v. State, 139 Ga. App. 553, 228 S.E.2d 722 (1976). In State v. Hinson, 164 Ga. App. 66, 296 S.E.2d 386 (1982), the trial judge tried to avoid the time limitation on a motion for a reduction of sentence by granting an extraordinary motion for a new trial and re-sentencing the defendant. The Court of Appeals reversed.

[5]Burns v. State, 153 Ga. App. 529, 531, 265 S.E.2d 859 (1980).

[6]State v. Bradbury, 167 Ga. App. 390, 392 (4), 306 S.E.2d 346 (1983).

[7]See Franks v. State, 323 Ga. App. 813, 748 S.E.2d 291 (2013).

limited to claims that—even assuming the existence and validity of the conviction for which the sentence was imposed—the law does not authorize that sentence, most typically because it exceeds the most severe punishment for which the applicable penal statute provides.

Recidivist sentencing is no different. The existence and validity of three prior felony convictions are necessary predicates to the imposition of a recidivist sentence under OCGA § 17-10-7(c), see *Davis v. State*, 319 Ga.App. 501, 504(2), 736 S.E.2d 160 (2012), as is timely notice that the State intends to assert such convictions in aggravation of sentence.[8]

However, a plea of guilty can result in the waiver of claims that the predicate convictions to a recidivist sentence were unlawful and, hence, that the sentence was void.

In *McCrosky v. State*,[9] the defendant was convicted of criminal trespass. She asserted that the trial judge erred in not reducing her sentence and in not holding a hearing on her motion. The appellate court affirmed and held that under "Uniform Superior Court Rule 6.3 which is applicable to state court proceedings, the trial court is not required to hold a hearing on a motion to modify sentence."

On the other hand, in the case of a felony sentence where the sentence is to be served on probation, and as to the probated portion of a split felony sentence, the "sentencing judge shall not lose jurisdiction over any person placed on probation."[10] During the term of the person's probated sentence the judge "is empowered to revoke any or all of the probated sentence, rescind any or all of the sentence, or, in any manner deemed advisable by the judge, [to] modify or change the probated sentence, including ordering the probationer into the sentencing options system, as provided in [O.C.G.A. § 42-3-110], at any time during the period of time prescribed for the probated sentence to run." The judge retains this power regardless of whether or not there has been a violation of the existing conditions of probation.[11] The sentence, however, may not be increased after the defendant begins to serve the sentence.[12] While the statutes referred to in this section refer to the authority of the court to "modify" not "reduce" a sentence, the fact is that once a defendant begins to serve his sentence, the sentence may not be increased.[13]

---

[8]von Thomas v. State, 293 Ga. 569, 748 S.E.2d 446 (2013).

[9]McCrosky v. State, 234 Ga. App. 321, 322 (3), 506 S.E.2d 400 (1998).

[10]O.C.G.A. § 42-8-34(g).

[11]Edwards v. State, 216 Ga. App.

740, 456 S.E.2d 213 (1995).

[12]England v. Newton, 238 Ga. 534, 233 S.E.2d 787 (1977). Accord, Harp v. State, 228 Ga. App. 473, 474, 491 S.E.2d 923 (1997).

[13]England v. Newton, 238 Ga.

In *Penney v. State*,[14] the defendant was originally sentenced to ten years to serve. Four years later, a habeas corpus petition was granted and the case remanded. The defendant again pled guilty and "agreed to accept a sentence of five years on intensive probation *with no credit for* time served instead of pleading to the original ten years. The trial court accepted the plea. . . ." About two years later, defendant violated his probation and was sentenced to serve the balance of the five year sentence. In affirming, the appellate court held that the sentence was not void in providing that he was not to receive credit for the time served on the original sentence since it was clear that he "knowingly and voluntarily exchanged the time he served on his previous ten year sentence for a five year probated sentence. Credit for time served is a personal benefit Penney was authorized to waive by his decision to enter a plea and accept a negotiated sentence."

In *Beasley v. State*,[15] the Court of Appeals dismissed an appeal from an order denying a motion to modify a sentence in which the defendant complained that the Department of Corrections had failed to give him credit for time served between arrest and sentencing. The court ruled that because the defendant did not contest the validity of his guilty plea but only the computation of his sentence, his only available remedies were those of mandamus, injunction or perhaps habeas corpus depending on the timing of the action in relation to the point in time the defendant was in the service of his sentence.

On correction of clerical errors and increasing sentences, see § 26:1, supra. Also see the same section on modification of payments in an abandonment case.

§ 26:47 Motion for reduction or correction of sentence— Misdemeanor cases

A different rule applies in the case of modification of some misdemeanor cases. O.C.G.A. § 17-10-3 provides that a defendant may be sentenced (1) to pay a fine and/or to be confined in a county correctional institution or (2) confined under the jurisdiction of the Board of Corrections. If the defendant is sentenced under the first provision, the sentencing court retains "jurisdiction to amend, modify, alter, suspend, or probate" the sentence apparently at any time during the time the sentence is being

---

534, 536, 233 S.E.2d 787 (1977).

[14]Penney v. State, 236 Ga. App. 442, 443, 511 S.E.2d 275 (1999) (em-

phasis in original).

[15]Beasley v. State, 255 Ga. App. 522, 523, 566 S.E.2d 333 (2002).

served.[1] On the other hand if the defendant has been sentenced to the Board of Corrections, the sentence may only be modified as a felony sentence.[2] However, in a misdemeanor case if the defendant has been sentenced to probation under O.C.G.A. § 42-8-34(g), during the period of probation the trial judge may revoke or rescind the sentence at any time, but if a sentence is "divided between straight time and probation, a trial court may modify the probation portion of the sentence only."[3]

In 1996, Georgia amended O.C.G.A. § 17-10-1(a)(6) to provide that a judge shall not modify an imposed sentence to reduce a period of incarceration or probation and impose a financial payment which is in excess of the maximum fine or which is made to an entity not authorized to receive fines even if the defendant consents to such modification.

Nevertheless, the discretion of the trial court to amend or modify, alter, suspend or probate a misdemeanor sentence does not extend to a sentence for driving under the influence.[4]

§ 26:48   Illegal sentences

If a sentence is imposed which the law does not allow, the trial court has authority to vacate or modify after the term in which the sentence was imposed.[1]

If an illegal sentence is imposed, the remedy is for the trial court to re-sentence the defendant,[2] not withdrawal of the guilty plea. However, "[a] person may 'validly [waive his or her constitutional] rights through the plea bargaining process.' . . . Likewise, when a person 'knowingly and voluntarily enter[s] into [a] negotiated plea agreement and accept[s] [the conditions] of his [or her] probation in open court, he [or she waives] the right to challenge [the] issue on appeal.' "[3]"When a plea rests in any significant degree on a promise or agreement of the prosecutor, so that it can be said to be a part of the inducement or consideration,

---

[Section 26:47]

[1]Mauldin v. State, 139 Ga. App. 13, 227 S.E.2d 862 (1976) (dicta); Ga. Atty. Gen. 80-43.

[2]Mauldin v. State, 139 Ga. App. 13, 227 S.E.2d 862 (1976).

[3]State v. James, 211 Ga. App. 149, 150 (2), 438 S.E.2d 399 (1993).

[4]Patel v. State, 247 Ga. App. 815 (1), 545 S.E.2d 383 (2001).

[Section 26:48]

[1]Eddleman v. State, 247 Ga. App. 753 (2), 545 S.E.2d 122 (2001). See Humphrey v. State, 297 Ga. 349, 773 S.E.2d 760 (2015) (sentence is void to the extent it purports to limit parole eligibility in a way not authorized by law).

[2]Williams v. State, 221 Ga. App. 291, 292 (2), 470 S.E.2d 922 (1996).

[3]Phillips v. State, 236 Ga. App. 744, 746 (1), 512 S.E.2d 32 (1999) (quoting Allen v. State, 258 Ga. 424, 369 S.E.2d 909 (1988), and Darby v. State, 230 Ga. App. 32, 495 S.E.2d 146 (1997)).

such promise must be fulfilled."[4]

In *Withers v. State*,[5] the sentencing court imposed conditions upon the defendant during the period of any future parole. On appeal, the sentence was vacated with the direction that the defendant be resentenced. The Court of Appeals found that the sentence insofar as it attempted to direct the defendant's parole was an invalid effort to exercise control over the Executive branch of government.

In *O'Neal v. State*,[6] the defendant was sentenced to 20 years when the minimum sentence prescribed was 30 years. The appellate court affirmed the trial court in refusing the defendant's motion to correct the sentence since the mistake was a benefit to defendant.

In *Broadwell v. State*,[7] the court pointed out that a void sentence or a clerical error may be corrected after the expiration of the term in which it was imposed.

See §§ 16:14 and 16:15, supra, on withdrawal of a guilty plea.

§ 26:49 Felony sentences

When a defendant is sentenced for a felony, the trial judge has no authority to designate that he is sentenced to a specific institution. However, such a designation is treated as surplusage and does not void the sentence. "[W]hen a person is convicted of a felony and sentenced to serve time in any penal institution . . . 'he shall be committed to the custody of the commissioner [of corrections].' It is the duty of the clerk . . . to notify the commissioner . . . within 30 working days. . . . Thereafter, the commissioner . . . 'shall designate the place of confinement. . . .' "[1]

---

[4]Phillips v. State, 236 Ga. App. 744, 746 (2), 512 S.E.2d 32 (1999) (quoting Thompson v. Greene, 265 Ga. 782, 462 S.E.2d 747 (1995)).

[5]Withers v. State, 254 Ga. App. 833, 835 (3), 563 S.E.2d 912 (2002).

[6]O'Neal v. State, 238 Ga. App. 446 (2), 519 S.E.2d 244 (1999).

[7]Broadwell v. State, 224 Ga. App. 193, 194 (2), 480 S.E.2d 215 (1996).

[Section 26:49]

[1]Eubanks v. State, 229 Ga. App. 667, 494 S.E.2d 564 (1997) (quoting O.C.G.A. 42-5-51). Accord, Grimes v. State, 237 Ga. App. 654, 655, 516 S.E.2d 378 (1999).

Chapter 27

Contempt

KeyCite®: Cases and other legal materials listed in KeyCite Scope can be researched through the KeyCite service on Westlaw®. Use KeyCite to check citations for form, parallel references, prior and later history, and comprehensive citator information, including citations to other decisions and secondary materials.

---

§ 27:1 General

"Contempt" is a willful disregard or disobedience of public authority.[1] There are two kinds of contempt of court: (1) civil contempt and (2) criminal contempt.[2] Whether a contempt is civil or criminal depends on the purpose for which the power is exercised without regard to the kind of case in which it arose. The character and purpose of the penalty is said to distinguish civil from criminal contempt.[3] The United States Supreme Court in *Hicks v. Feiock*[4] held that the determination, from a federal constitutional standpoint, of whether a contempt proceeding is civil or criminal turns upon whether relief imposed or to be imposed upon the respondent is criminal or civil. "An unconditional penalty is criminal in nature because it is 'solely and exclusively punitive in character.' . . . A conditional penalty, by contrast, is civil because it is specifically designed to compel the doing of some act. 'One who is fined, unless by a day certain he [does the act ordered], has it in his power to avoid any penalty.

[Section 27:1]

[1]17 C.J.S. 3, 5 (1963).

[2]See Davis v. Davis, 138 Ga. 8 (1), 74 S.E. 830 (1912).

[3]In re Grand Jury Investigation, 610 F.2d 202 (5th Cir. 1980).

[4]Hicks v. Feiock, 485 U.S. 624, 108 S.Ct. 1423, 99 L.Ed.2d 721 (1988).

[And] those who are imprisoned until they obey the order, "carry the keys of their prison in their own pockets." '. . . Any sentence 'must be viewed as remedial' and hence civil in nature, 'if the court conditions release upon the contemnor's willingness to [comply with the order].' . . . On the contrary, a criminal contempt proceeding would be characterized by the imposition of an unconditional sentence for punishment or deterrence." In Georgia, it has generally been said that criminal contempt is the commission of a disrespectful act directed at the court itself which tends to obstruct justice, while civil contempt is the disobedience of a court order directing an act for the benefit or advantage of the opposing party to the litigation.[5] Likewise in Georgia, a proceeding to punish an offender for disrespect to or contumacious conduct towards the court constitutes criminal contempt,[6] while a contempt action brought because of a violation of a court order or decree is generally regarded as being a civil contempt proceeding.[7]

The court in *In re Earle*[8] pointed out that "[w]hen the trial court orders incarceration for an indefinite period until the performance of a specified act, the contempt is civil. . . . A trial court, however, may not continue incarceration for civil contempt when the respondent lacks the ability to purge himself. Imprisonment under civil sanctions is always conditional and a party found in contempt may apply for release at any time upon a showing of inability to comply with the terms for release."

In *Smith v. Orkin Exterminating Co., Inc.,*[9] the defendant was found guilty of contempt, ordered jailed for 20 days and fined $500 with a provision that he could purge himself by paying the $500. The court said the punishment was "unconditional in nature, which means that the court found appellant . . . guilty of criminal contempt."

In a very fine opinion by Judge Johnson in *Grantham v. Universal Tax Systems,*[10] the court points out that "the action the court takes to deal with the contempt determines whether the contempt is deemed 'criminal' contempt or 'civil' contempt. . . . The distinction between the two is that criminal contempt imposes unconditional punishment for prior acts of contumacy,

---

[5]United States v. Hilburn, 625 F.2d 1177 (5th Cir. 1980); In re Dinnan, 625 F.2d 1146 (5th Cir. 1980).

[6]Wagner v. Commercial Printers, 203 Ga. 1, 7, 45 S.E.2d 205 (1947).

[7]Davis v. Davis, 138 Ga. 8 (1), 74 S.E. 830 (1912); but see Alred v. Celanese Corp. of America, 205 Ga. 371, 388 (2), 54 S.E.2d 240 (1949).

[8]In re Earle, 248 Ga. App. 355, 358 (1), 545 S.E.2d 405 (2001).

[9]Smith v. Orkin Exterminating Co., Inc., 258 Ga. 705, 373 S.E.2d 740 (1988).

[10]Grantham v. Universal Tax Systems, 217 Ga. App. 676, 677 (2), 458 S.E.2d 870 (1995).

whereas civil contempt imposes conditional punishment as a means of coercing future compliance with a prior court order."

Despite the logic and clarity of *Grantham,* the distinction between civil and criminal contempt proceedings has not always been clear.[11] However, since contempt matters in criminal cases rarely arise out of the failure to abide by an order primarily issued for the benefit of a party, the contempt proceedings which are discussed in the remainder of this chapter emphasize criminal contempt proceedings which may sometimes arise out of the trial of a criminal case.

O.C.G.A. § 15-1-4 provides in part as follows:

"The powers of the several courts to issue attachments and inflict summary punishment for contempt of court shall extend only to cases of:

"(1) Misbehavior of any person or persons in the presence of such courts or so near thereto as to obstruct the administration of justice;

"(2) Misbehavior of any of the officers of the courts in their official transactions;

"(3) Disobedience or resistance by any officer of the courts, party, juror, witness, or other person or persons to any lawful writ, process, order, rule, decree, or command of the courts;

"(4) Violation of subsection (a) of O.C.G.A. § 34-1-3, relating to prohibited conduct of employers with respect to employees who are required to attend judicial proceedings; and

"(5) Violation of a court order relating to the televising, videotaping, or motion picture filming of judicial proceedings."

Superior courts have authority to punish *criminal*[12] contempt by fines not exceeding $1,000 and imprisonment not exceeding 20 days or both.[13] Thus, a judge has no authority to suspend counsel

---

[11]In Alred v. Celanese Corp. of America, 205 Ga. 371, 382, 54 S.E.2d 240 (1949), the court said that generally the classification of "civil" or "criminal" contempt depends on the facts of each case. A particular act may have characteristics of both classes. In Ensley v. Ensley, 239 Ga. 860, 238 S.E.2d 920 (1977), a contempt case for failure to pay child support, the court noted that the contempt could be either civil or criminal. If there is an unconditional order that the defendant be imprisoned it seems that the court has found the defendant in criminal contempt, but if he is ordered confined if he does not pay or until he does pay, it seems that the defendant has been found in civil contempt.

[12]The court held in In re Harvey, 219 Ga. App. 76, 80, 464 S.E.2d 34 (1995), that the limitations imposed by O.C.G.A. § 15-6-8(5) are not applicable to sanctions imposed for civil contempt.

[13]O.C.G.A. § 15-6-8(5); Aiken v. Richardson, 210 Ga. 728, 731 (2), 82 S.E.2d 646 (1954).

from the practice of law where he is found in contempt of court[14] or to bar an attorney, found in contempt, from practicing before a certain division of the court.[15] In the case of civil contempt where the real purpose of the proceeding is to force the respondent to do what he is obligated to do under a court order or decree, the respondent may, in the discretion of the trial judge, be confined to jail until he complies with the order or decree.[16] However, constitutional courts have inherent power to define and punish contempts, and this authority is not limited by the Code section referred to above.[17]

Sometimes criminal contempt is divided into two classes: (1) direct contempt and (2) indirect or constructive contempt.[18] "A direct criminal contempt relates to contumacious conduct, whether by word or deed, committed in the actual presence of the court. An indirect, or constructive contempt, consists of contumacious conduct outside the presence of the court which amounts to an obstruction of the administration of justice."[19] When a contempt is direct, it may be adjudged and punished summarily upon the court's own knowledge of the facts, without a hearing.[20] However, under the Federal Rules of Criminal Procedure, the judge must recite the specific facts upon which the contempt conviction rests.[21] When a contempt is indirect, or when it is not clear from the record whether the judge was personally aware of the contemptuous conduct at issue, the defendant is entitled to a fair hearing to show that the version of the event as understood by the judge is inaccurate, misleading, or incomplete.[22]

---

[14]In re Pruitt, 249 Ga. 190, 288 S.E.2d 208 (1982), s.c., 250 Ga. 836, 301 S.E.2d 481 (1983).

[15]In re August F. Siemon, 264 Ga. 641, 642(4), 449 S.E.2d 832 (1994).

[16]Gray v. Gray, 127 Ga. 345 (4), 56 S.E. 438 (1907).

[17]Cobb v. State, 187 Ga. 448, 200 S.E. 796 (1939).

[18]Ramirez v. State, 279 Ga. 13, 608 S.E.2d 645 (2005), provides an excellent discussion on the two varieties of criminal contempt. Clark v. State, 90 Ga. App. 330, 83 S.E.2d 45 (1954).

[19]Clark v. State, 90 Ga. App. 330, 331(2), 83 S.E.2d 45 (1954).

[20]Cooke v. United States, 267 U.S. 517, 534, 45 S.Ct. 390, 69 L.Ed. 767 (1925).

[21]See Rule 42(a) of the Federal Rules of Criminal Procedure; Johnson v. Mississippi, 403 U.S. 212, 91 S.Ct. 1778, 29 L.Ed.2d 423 (1971).

[22]Johnson v. Mississippi, 403 U.S. 212, 91 S.Ct. 1778, 29 L.Ed.2d 423 (1971). In Hopkins v. Hopkins, 244 Ga. 66, 67 (1), 257 S.E.2d 900 (1979), the father was jailed for two successive weekends for failure to pay child support promptly even though at the time of the hearing the father was current in his payments. The court pointed out that criminal contempt could be used to preserve the authority of the court to punish the father for disobedience of its orders. For a discussion of the notice and procedure to be followed in cases of indirect or constructive contempt, see In re: Harris, 289 Ga. App. 334, 657 S.E.2d 259 (2008).

In *Todd v. Casciano*,[23] the court observed: '[b]efore a person may be held in contempt for violating a court order, the order should inform him in definite terms as to the duties thereby imposed upon him, and the command must therefore be express rather than implied. . . . Indefiniteness and uncertainty in a judgement, decree or order may constitute a good defense in proceedings for contempt based on the violation of such judgement, decree, or order." For example, a trial judge's order to counsel to "reorganize" a cross-examination approach to a witness was considcred too vague a direction to warrant contempt sanctions despite the judge's finding that counsel was deliberately ignoring her instruction.[24]

In *Thomas v. Dept. of Human Resources*,[25] the court held that before the sanction of criminal contempt for violation of a court order can be imposed, "there must be proof beyond a reasonable doubt not only that the alleged contemnor violated a court order, but also that he did so willfully. And to show willfulness, there must be proof beyond a reasonable doubt that the alleged contemnor had the ability to comply with the court order: It is essential to constitute a contempt that the thing ordered be done be within the power of the person against whom the order is directed."

It has been held that an attempt to coerce a subpoenaed witness out of the presence of the court amounts to an indirect contempt,[26] while when a witness is harassed, browbeaten, and insulted as he attempts to leave the courthouse, the contempt is direct, as the witness is regarded as being present in the court if the court is still in session.[27] During a criminal contempt hearing, the offender has a constitutional right to counsel. In *Merritt v. State*,[28] the defendant represented himself in a criminal contempt hearing and was sentenced to a weekend in prison. The finding of contempt was reversed because the trial judge did not warn the defendant of the risks of self-representation nor did the judge obtain an express waiver of the defendant's right to counsel. See §27:4, infra, on procedure in contempt cases.

---

[23]Todd v. Casciano. 256 Ga. App. 631, 638 (3), 569 S.E.2d 566 (2002).

[24]In re: Butterfield, 265 Ga. App. 745, 595 S.E.2d 588 (2004).

[25]Thomas v. Department of Human Resources, 228 Ga. App. 518, 519–520, 492 S.E.2d 288 (1997). See In re Bowens, 308 Ga. App. 241 (1), 706 S.E.2d 694 (2011).

[26]Cf. Herring v. State, 165 Ga. 254, 140 S.E. 491 (1927).

[27]See Morgan v. State, 26 Ga. App. 83 (2), 85, 105 S.E. 449 (1920) (citing with approval In re Savin, 131 U.S. 267, 9 S.Ct. 699, 33 L.Ed. 150 (1889)).

[28]Merritt v. State, 261 Ga. App. 597, 583 S.E.2d 283 (2003).

§ 27:2   What constitutes contempt?

In order to determine the particular actions that constitute contempt, it is helpful to examine the various situations encountered by the Georgia courts. It should be kept in mind that the more recent cases, particularly those of the United States Supreme Court, have been less inclined to find persons in contempt than was formerly the case.

In the following situations, the appellate court held that either the conduct referred to amounted to contempt or there was sufficient evidence to support a finding of contempt: (1) Where an attorney in open court said, "I think your Honor has such antagonism toward me personally that I just can't, your Honor, seem to try a case before you without you jumping on me unnecessarily";[1] (2) Where a father called a judge in his private office and insisted on coming to see him to discuss the disposition of his son's case;[2] (3) Where an attorney failed to yield after three rulings of the trial judge adverse to him on the question of recalling a witness for further cross-examination, and insisted for the third time on recalling such witness;[3] (4) Where a defendant petitioned the judge to disqualify himself from passing on questions presented and averred that "with regret and humiliation, she is compelled to assert to this court that she cannot get a fair, impartial, and legal hearing";[4] (5) Where a sign was placed in a window of a theater which stated: "Due to selfish contemptible interests, we are temporarily restrained from showing 'Ecstasy.' We will bring this picture to you pending court decision."[5] (6) Where an attorney, during the selection of a jury, asked some 15 or more jurors the following questions: 1. "Do you believe in the principle of law that the presiding judge should be impartial as between the state and the accused?" 2. "Do you believe that the refusal of the court to accept the pleas of guilty or try the codefendant witnesses in this case concurred in by the solicitor's office until those witnesses have testified against the defendant in this case could have a bearing on the credibility of those codefendant witnesses?" He was found guilty of contempt where the court had never refused to accept guilty pleas nor to try codefendant witnesses;[6] (7) Where a threat to kill a subpoenaed witness to prevent him from testify-

---

[Section 27:2]

[1]White v. State, 71 Ga. App. 512, 31 S.E.2d 78 (1944).

[2]City of Macon v. Massey, 214 Ga. 589, 591, 106 S.E.2d 23 (1958).

[3]Crudup v. State, 106 Ga. App. 833, 129 S.E.2d 183 (1962).

[4]Jones v. State, 39 Ga. App. 1 (2), 145 S.E. 914 (1928).

[5]Carter v. State, 61 Ga. App. 430, 6 S.E.2d 175 (1939).

[6]Salem v. State, 101 Ga. App. 905, 906, 115 S.E.2d 447 (1960).

ing was made;[7] (8) Where one of two defendants delivered a carton of cigarettes to the bailiff in sight of some of the jurors to be given to the jury, and the other defendant gave liquor to the bailiff to be delivered to the jury;[8] (9) Where a party or a representative of a party attempts to influence a juror by communicating with the juror away from the court;[9] (10) Where a defendant attempted to induce a person on probation for a violation of the prohibition law to drink whiskey by saying to him, "Damn the court, take a drink";[10] (11) Where a defendant in a divorce action attempted to molest the other party, threatened to "get the judge," and stated that he could not get a fair trial and that he would not obey a court order regarding the custody of his children;[11] (12) Where a person attempts to get a witness to change his testimony by coercion;[12] (13) Where a witness who has been granted immunity refuses to testify because of the Fifth Amendment privilege;[13] (14) Where an attorney, in violation of a court's gag order, spoke about the case on a radio program.[14]

§ 27:3 What constitutes contempt? examples of noncontemptuous conduct

In the following situations, the appellate court held that either the conduct referred to was not contempt or there was not sufficient evidence to support a finding of contempt: (1) Where the defendant called the district attorney a "g-d-lying s.o.b." while the district attorney was in the presence of the grand jury in the grand jury room. The court said this statement was not so near the court as to obstruct the administration of justice;[1] (2) Where the comments of an attorney appeared in a newspaper, saying that the judge had adjourned court and gone to his home in another county to vote and criticizing the judge for leaving with undisposed of cases which were ready for trial, wasting the time of attorneys, and not acting in the best interest of the people.

---

[7]Burge v. State, 38 Ga. App. 690, 145 S.E. 463 (1928).

[8]Mays v. Willingham, 37 Ga. App. 478, 140 S.E. 789 (1927).

[9]Summers v. State ex rel. Boykin, 66 Ga. App. 648, 19 S.E.2d 28 (1942).

[10]Smith v. State, 36 Ga. App. 37, 38, 135 S.E. 102 (1926).

[11]Hodges v. Thibadeau, 122 Ga. App. 334, 177 S.E.2d 127 (1970).

[12]Herring v. State, 37 Ga. App. 594, 141 S.E. 89 (1928).

[13]United States v. Wilson, 421 U.S. 309, 95 S.Ct. 1802, 44 L.Ed.2d 186 (1975).

[14]Ramirez v. State, 279 Ga. 13, 608 S.E.2d 645 (2005). The trial court's determination that the attorney was in contempt was reversed because it incorrectly characterized the attorney's conduct as a direct contempt of the court's order when it should have been classified as indirect. The case provides an excellent discussion of the two varieties of criminal contempt.

[Section 27:3]

[1]Adams v. State, 89 Ga. App. 882, 81 S.E.2d 507 (1954).

This did not amount to contempt since it was done out of the presence of the court and did not obstruct the administration of justice;[2] (3) Where the court overruled a motion for continuance and, in summation, a defendant who was representing himself stated that the judge was biased and had prejudged the case and that the petitioner was a political prisoner. In the absence of any indication that the petitioner's statements were made in a boisterous tone or in any wise disruptive of the court proceedings, the statements did not constitute criminal contempt;[3] (4) Where an attorney, seeking to pursue a line of questioning which had been barred by the court, stated that he was going to continue the line of questioning unless the bailiff stopped him, it was held that this was not an obstruction of justice which justified summarily holding him in contempt;[4] (5) Where a lawyer gives good-faith advice to his client to refuse, in a civil case, to obey a judicial order for production of evidence;[5] (6) Where a defendant, during cross-examination, referred to his alleged assailant as "chicken shit," this single use of street language did not constitutionally support a conviction of criminal contempt, since it was not directed to the court;[6] (7) Where a subpoenaed witness who failed to appear in court was picked up and brought into by the sheriff's office, she could not be found in contempt for being intoxicated in court since she did not voluntarily come;[7] (8) Where a person interested in the outcome of a case spoke to a juror in the hall after a verdict had been returned and shook hands with the juror and said in an angry sarcastic voice, "I hope you are satisfied, you have something to live with all your life";[8] (9) Where counsel simply objects to the trial judge's instruction to the jury;[9] (10) Where counsel referred to the court's inquiry as a "sham proceeding" and "inquisition" from which the trial court would personally derive "political hay" the Georgia Supreme Court held that the remarks were not contemptuous where they were made outside the courtroom about a judge who had earlier recused himself. The court reasoned that the statements did not create a clear

---

[2]Townsend v. State, 54 Ga. App. 627, 188 S.E. 560 (1936).

[3]In re Little, 404 U.S. 553, 92 S.Ct. 659, 30 L.Ed.2d 708 (1972).

[4]In re McConnell, 370 U.S. 230, 82 S.Ct. 1288, 8 L.Ed.2d 434 (1962).

[5]Maness v. Meyers, 419 U.S. 449, 95 S.Ct. 584, 42 L.Ed.2d 574 (1975).

[6]Eaton v. City of Tulsa, 415 U.S. 697, 94 S.Ct. 1228, 39 L.Ed.2d 693 (1974).

[7]Moody v. State, 131 Ga. App. 355, 357 (1), 206 S.E.2d 79 (1974).

[8]Castellio v. State, 143 Ga. App. 386, 238 S.E.2d 746 (1977). Here the court pointed out that the trial had ended and the defendant's conduct could not have impaired the administration of justice.

[9]Spruell v. Jarvis, 654 F.2d 1090, 1094 (5th Cir. 1981).

and present danger to the administration of justice.[10]

§ 27:4 Procedure—General

The procedure to be used in a contempt case may depend upon whether the contempt is (1) a direct contempt, one committed in the presence of the court, or (2) an indirect or constructive contempt, one committed away from the judge. The idea is that there is more justification for summary action in a direct contempt situation, but even in this case some notice should be given by the court to the person whom he is considering finding in contempt.[1] The imposition of summary contempt and punishment should not be done in the presence of the jury.[2] If a direct contempt is not promptly punished, it appears that the same procedure must be used as in an indirect or constructive contempt.[3]

Except in the case of direct contempt, which must summarily

---

[10]Garland v. State, 253 Ga. 789, 325 S.E.2d 131 (1985).

[Section 27:4]

[1]In Hedquist v. Hedquist, 275 Ga. 188, 189, 563 S.E.2d 854 (2002), the Georgia Supreme Court explained: "The constitutional right to due process applies in criminal contempt proceedings because a conviction can result in the loss of liberty and the levy of a penal fine. Both the United States and Georgia Constitutions require that an accused be given notice and an opportunity to be heard before being convicted, except in rare instances. The notice must be reasonably calculated to inform persons of the charges against them and their opportunity for a hearing at a specific time and place to present their objections." Compare Knapp v. Cross, 279 Ga. App. 632, 632 S.E.2d 157 (2006). See Mayberry v. Pennsylvania, 400 U.S. 455, 91 S.Ct. 499, 27 L.Ed.2d 532 (1971). A.B.A. Standards, Special Functions of the Trial Judge, Vol. I, Standard 6-4.4 provides as follows:

Standard 6-4.4. Notice of charges and opportunity to be heard

(a) The trial judge should, as soon as practicable after he or she is satisfied that courtroom misconduct requires contempt proceedings, inform the alleged offender of the judge's intention to institute such proceedings.

(b) The trial judge should consider deferring adjudication of contempt for courtroom misconduct of a defendant, an attorney, or a witness until after the trial, and should defer such a proceeding unless prompt punishment is imperative.

[2]Davenport v. State, 216 Ga. App. 259, 260 (2), 454 S.E.2d 536 (1995).

[3]A.B.A. Standards, Special Functions of the Trial Judge, Vol. I, Standards 6-4.2 and 6-4.3 provide as follows:

"Standard 6-4.2. Admonition and warning

"No sanction other than censure should be imposed by the trial judge unless:

"(i) it is clear from the identity of the offender and the character of his or her acts that the disruptive conduct was willfully contemptuous, or

"(ii) the conduct warranting the sanction was preceded by a clear warning that such conduct was impermissible and that specified sanctions might be imposed for its repetition.

"Standard 6-4.3. Notice of intent to use contempt power; postponement of adjudication

"(a) The trial judge should, as soon as practicable after he or she is satisfied that courtroom misconduct requires contempt proceedings, inform

be dealt with, a contempt matter should be referred to another judge and handled by him.[4] Likewise, "[w]here the announcement of punishment is delayed, *and* where the contumacious conduct was directed toward the judge or where the judge reacted to the . . . conduct . . . as to become involved in the controversy, [the matter] *must* be conducted by another judge." (Emphasis added.)[5]

There is no federal constitutional right to a jury trial in a criminal contempt proceeding when the penalty actually imposed does not exceed six months.[6] O.C.G.A. § 15-1-4(b)(3) states that the judge in a contempt proceeding "shall cause questions to be propounded in writing to the jury and every question propounded shall be answered by the jury in its verdict."[7] Yet, apparently, this is not interpreted, even in a criminal contempt, to entitle the person charged to a trial by jury.[8]

An indirect or constructive criminal contempt proceeding may be initiated by an individual plaintiff,[9] but should more properly be brought by the district attorney in the name of the state. "The alleged contemnor, however, must have notice of the proceeding, and be given an opportunity to be heard. This is effected when the court grants a nisi order on the petition . . . , requiring the alleged contemnor to show cause at a certain time and place why he should not be adjudged in contempt, and provides for the ser-

---

the alleged offender of the judge's intention to institute such proceedings.

"(b) The trial judge should consider the advisability of deferring adjudication of contempt for courtroom misconduct of a defendant, an attorney or a witness until after the trial, and should defer such a proceeding unless prompt punishment is imperative."

[4]Offutt v. United States, 348 U.S. 11, 75 S.Ct. 11, 99 L.Ed. 11 (1954); Johnson v. Mississippi, 403 U.S. 212, 91 S.Ct. 1778, 29 L.Ed.2d 423 (1971); Cooke v. United States, 267 U.S. 517, 539, 45 S.Ct. 390, 69 L.Ed. 767 (1925); Mayberry v. Pennsylvania, 400 U.S. 455, 466, 91 S.Ct. 499, 27 L.Ed.2d 532, 540 (1971). A.B.A. Standards, Special Functions of the Trial Judge, Vol. I, Standard 6-4.5 provides as follows:

"Standard 6-4.5. Referral to another judge

"The Judge before whom courtroom misconduct occurs may impose

appropriate sanctions, including punishment for contempt, but should refer the matter to another judge if the original judge's conduct was so integrated with the contempt so as to have contributed to it or was otherwise involved, or the original judge's objectivity can reasonably be questioned."

Also see O.C.G.A. § 24-13-26.

[5]In re Adams, 215 Ga. App. 372, 375, 450 S.E.2d 851 (1994).

[6]Taylor v. Hayes, 418 U.S. 488, 495, 94 S.Ct. 2697, 41 L.Ed.2d 897, 905 (1974).

[7]O.C.G.A. § 15-1-4(b)(3).

[8]See In re Fite, 11 Ga. App. 665, 76 S.E. 397 (1912). It is clear that there is no right to a jury trial in a civil contempt proceeding. Branch v. Branch, 219 Ga. 601 (1), 135 S.E.2d 269 (1964).

[9]Welborn v. Mize, 107 Ga. App. 427, 428, 130 S.E.2d 623 (1963).

vice of the order. . . ."[10]

The evidence introduced at a rule nisi hearing is normally by affidavit.[11] In 1985, the Georgia Supreme Court concluded that "the evidence in any criminal contempt case must show that the defendant is guilty beyond a reasonable doubt."[12] Likewise, the United States Supreme Court has stated that the defendant must be proved guilty beyond a reasonable doubt in a criminal contempt case.[13] However, in *In re Harvey*,[14] the court held that "[t]he appropriate standard of proof in a civil contempt case is [the] preponderance of the evidence."

Formerly, where a defendant was found to be in contempt, it was necessary to set out findings of fact and conclusions of law upon which the order was based.[15] However, in 1989 the Georgia Supreme Court held in a criminal contempt case that findings of fact and conclusions of law are not necessary.[16]

There is no specific statute of limitations setting out the time within which a proceeding for contempt of court must be commenced. The Court of Appeals in the case of *In re Friedman*[17] specifically rejected the position that the two year statute for the prosecution of misdemeanors should apply.

§ 27:5 Procedure—Direct contempt

In the case of a contempt committed in the presence of the court during a trial, the offender is not entitled as a matter of right to a hearing before the court. The court may, in a summary

---

[10]Carson v. Ennis, 146 Ga. 726, 728 (3), 92 S.E. 221 (1917). In Martin v. Waters, 151 Ga. App. 149, 151, 259 S.E.2d 153 (1979), the court said that where a witness or litigant is ordered to appear and he does not, or where he is late, there is a question of whether or not the non-appearance on time was a result of willful conduct. The normal procedure is to issue a bench warrant and then inquire into the cause of the non-appearance. It is not proper to summarily sentence him without a hearing and in his absence.

[11]Clark v. State, 90 Ga. App. 330, 83 S.E.2d 45 (1954).

[12]Garland v. State, 253 Ga. 789, 790, 325 S.E.2d 131 (1985).

[13]Gompers v. Buck's Stove & Range Co., 221 U.S. 418, 444, 31 S.Ct.

492, 55 L.Ed. 797, 807 (1911).

[14]In re Harvey, 219 Ga. App. 76, 79, 464 S.E.2d 34 (1995).

[15]Brown v. Hames, 131 Ga. App. 148, 205 S.E.2d 716 (1974); Carter v. State, 129 Ga. App. 536, 537 (3), 199 S.E.2d 925 (1973).

[16]PBJ Development v. Holben, 259 Ga. 594 (1), 385 S.E.2d 658 (1989); In re Jones, 198 Ga. App. 228, 231 (7), 401 S.E.2d 278 (1990).

[17]In re Friedman, 257 Ga. App. 688(2), 572 S.E.2d 48 (2002). See Bales v. Bales, 156 Ga. 679, 681(3), 119 S.E. 635 (1923), where the court refused to bar an action for contempt when the lapse between the entry of a divorce decree and the filing of the contempt charge for failure to pay alimony was some seven years.

fashion, punish the offender for such contempt.[1]

In *White v. George*,[2] the court said that since the trial court may act on its own knowledge, it has been held that the offender can, in the discretion of the judge, be instantly punished without depriving the defendant of his due process right. However, the order of the court must "set forth fully and clearly the facts found and the conclusions of law upon which the order is based."[3] In *Salem v. State*,[4] the court said that "[i]n a direct summary criminal contempt proceeding there is no petition, rule nisi, or evidence" but any order holding the defendant in contempt must contain the facts specifying the misconduct of the defendant. In *In re Shafer*,[5] the court stated that "[i]n a summary contempt proceeding, objectively observable and describable behavior that causes an articulable interference with the administration of justice must be demonstrably present. Both the bad conduct and its adverse impact must be set forth with specificity in the ruling by the court that finds as a matter of fact that no justification exists for the alleged contemnor's behavior. If these procedural steps are taken verbally, as is usually the case with a court trying to restore some immediate order in its proceedings, the judge must *as soon as possible* create a written record that preserves the following: (1) the notice to the perpetrator of the offensive conduct subject to being viewed as contemptuous due to its actual or imminent adverse impact; (2) a detailed description of the bad acts committed or omitted by the perpetrator despite a contemporaneous warning by the court to refrain; (3) an explanation of the deleterious impact on the court's operations or its integrity; (4) a recitation of the perpetrator's reasons given as justification for the questionable conduct; (5) a finding of fact by the judge of direct conduct interfering with the court's administration of justice, or imminently threatening such consequences; and (6) an order declaring the respondent in contempt of court and imposing a statutorily authorized sanction."

[Section 27:5]

[1]Garland v. State, 99 Ga. App. 826, 830 (1), 110 S.E.2d 143 (1959).

[2]White v. George, 195 Ga. 465, 469, 24 S.E.2d 787 (1943).

[3]Spruell v. State, 145 Ga. App. 720, 244 S.E.2d 636 (1978). This case also holds that merely attaching pages of a colloquy between court and counsel in another case is not sufficient where the colloquy is only referred to in the order and it does not state the facts found or the conclusions drawn therefrom.

See Jordan v. Hodges, 162 Ga. App. 473 (2), 291 S.E.2d 778 (1982).

[4]Salem v. State, 101 Ga. App. 905 (3), 115 S.E.2d 447 (1960). Generally, see Annot., "Grand Jury Witness' Right to Hearing Before Summary Commitment for Contempt Under Recalcitrant Witness Statute (28 U. S. C. S. § 1826 (a))," 37 A. L. R. Fed. 875 (1978).

[5]In re Shafer, 216 Ga. App. 725, 726, 455 S.E.2d 421 (1995) (emphasis by the court).

Some United States Supreme Court cases may have altered many of the principles of Georgia law referred to above. For example, in *Mayberry v. Pennsylvania*,[6] the court pointed out that "[i]nstant treatment of contempt where lawyers are involved may greatly prejudice their clients but it may be the only wise course." A later case stated that "summary punishment always, and rightly, is regarded with disfavor."[7] In *Dowdy v. Palmour*,[8] the Georgia Supreme Court said, "During trial, a trial judge has power when necessary to maintain order in the courtroom, to declare conduct committed in his presence and observed by him to be contemptuous, and, after affording the contemnor an opportunity to speak in his or her own behalf, to announce punishment summarily and without further notice or hearing. The carrying out of the punishment announced during the trial may be postponed until after trial."

In *Taylor v. Hayes*,[9] the United States Supreme Court said that "where conviction and punishment are delayed, 'it is much more difficult to argue that action without notice or hearing of any kind is necessary to preserve order and enable [the court] to proceed with its business, . . . before an attorney is finally adjudicated in contempt and sentenced after trial for conduct during trial, he should have reasonable notice of the specific charges and opportunity to be heard in his own behalf." In *Dowdy v. Palmour*,[10] the Georgia Supreme Court explained the rule of the *Taylor* case as follows:

"Where the announcement of punishment is delayed, and where the contumacious conduct was not directed toward the judge and where the judge did not react to the contumacious conduct in such manner as to become involved in the controversy, the judge has the power to hold a contempt hearing at the conclusion of the trial and, after giving the attorney reasonable notice of the specific charges and opportunity to be heard, to impose punishment. . . . Where the announcement of punishment is delayed, and where the contumacious conduct was directed toward the judge or where the judge reacted to the contumacious

---

[6]Mayberry v. Pennsylvania, 400 U.S. 455, 91 S.Ct. 499, 539, 27 L.Ed.2d 532 (1971).

[7]In Crudup v. State, 106 Ga. App. 833, 839, 129 S.E.2d 183 (1962), the court said that "delay was 'a wise exercise of discretion . . . to allow the contemnor an opportunity to mitigate his offense by showing no contempt was intended'. . . ."

[8]Dowdy v. Palmour, 251 Ga. 135, 304 S.E.2d 52 (1983), rev'g 164 Ga. App. 804, 298 S.E.2d 521 (1982); Calhoun v. Findley, 168 Ga. App. 634, 637, 309 S.E.2d 907 (1983).

[9]Taylor v. Hayes, 418 U.S. 488, 498, 94 S.Ct. 2697, 41 L.Ed.2d 897, 907 (1974).

[10]Dowdy v. Palmour, 251 Ga. 135, 304 S.E.2d 52 (1983), rev'g 164 Ga. App. 804, 298 S.E.2d 521 (1982).

conduct in such manner as to become involved in the controversy, the judge may give the attorney notice of specific charges, but the hearing, including the attorney's opportunity to be heard, must be conducted by another judge." Furthermore, where there is no immediate punishment for contempt, the United States Supreme Court has held that because of the due process clause of the Fourteenth Amendment, a "defendant in criminal contempt proceedings should be given a public trial before a judge other than the one reviled by the contemnor."[11]

Specifically, in the case of attorneys, the Georgia Supreme Court has provided the following guidance in the case of *In re: Jefferson*:[12]

> Thus, to summarize, we hold that an attorney may be held in contempt for statements made during courtroom proceedings only after the court has found (1) that the attorney's statements and attendant conduct either actually interfered with or posed an imminent threat of interfering with the administration of justice and (2) that the attorney knew or should have known that the statements and attendant conduct exceeded the outermost bounds of permissible advocacy. Because contempt is a crime, the evidence must, of course, support these findings beyond a reasonable doubt.

> To assist in its analysis, it may be helpful for the court to consider the following non-exhaustive list of factors: (1) the extent to which the attorney was put on notice prior to the contempt citation that a continuation of the offending statements would constitute contempt; (2) the likely impact of the offending statements on the deliberations of the fact-finder, which calculus incorporates both the nature and timing of the offending conduct and whether the fact-finder is a judge or jury; (3) whether the offending statements occurred as an isolated incident or constituted a pattern of behavior; (4) the significance of the particular issue in question to the case as a whole and the relative gravity of the case; and (5) the extent, if any, to which the trial court provoked the offending statements with its own improper statements.

> Finally, in light of the important constitutional rights involved, we are of the opinion that, in adjudicating a case of possible contempt, doubts should be resolved in favor of vigorous advocacy. Indeed, where advocative expression is at issue, the need for such expression cannot merely be balanced *against* the court's interest in maintaining the integrity and continuity of a trial; advocacy is itself essential to the court's achieving that interest. Therefore, any balancing test for determining whether advocacy interferes suf-

---

[11]Mayberry v. Pennsylvania, 400 U.S. 455, 466, 91 S.Ct. 499, 27 L.Ed.2d 532, 540 (1971); In re Schoolcraft, 274 Ga. App. 271, 617 S.E.2d 241 (2005). But cf. Farmer v. Holton, 146 Ga. App. 102, 245 S.E.2d 457 (1978); Sussman v. Commonwealth, 374 Mass. 692, 374 N.E.2d 1195 (1978).

[12]In re Jefferson, 283 Ga. 216, 657 S.E.2d 830 (2008) citations and punctuation omitted. For an excellent review of contempt, see Newton v. Golden Grove Pecan Farm, 309 Ga. App. 764, 711 S.E.2d 351 (2011).

ficiently with justice to make it punishable must also consider the positive value of the advocacy to the very interest sought to be protected by the contempt power.

§ 27:6 Procedure—Indirect or constructive contempt

In the case of an alleged indirect contempt, the court has no right to a summary procedure such as that referred to in § 27:4, supra. The proceeding is by petition, order and hearing as set out heretofore.[1]

If a properly subpoenaed witness fails to come to court and he is subsequently found to be in contempt, there must be a citation, notice, and hearing at which he is entitled to representation by counsel.[2] The maximum punishment for failure to obey a subpoena is a fine of $300 and imprisonment of not more than 20 days.[3]

§ 27:7 Appeals

Where a defendant in a contempt action wishes to appeal, he must be sure the judge files a written, signed order before a notice of appeal is filed. The filing may not be accomplished by a nunc pro tunc order making it date back to the oral pronouncement.[1] As soon as the notice of appeal has been filed, a supersedeas should be sought from the trial judge. O.C.G.A. § 5-6-13 provides:

"(a) A judge of any trial court or tribunal having the power to adjudge and punish for contempt shall grant to any person convicted of or adjudged to be in contempt of court a supersedeas upon application and compliance with the provisions of law as to appeal and certiorari, where the person also submits, within the time prescribed by law, written notice that he intends to seek review of the conviction or adjudication of contempt. It shall not be in the discretion of any trial court judge to grant or refuse a supersedeas in cases of contempt.

"(b) This Code section shall not apply to contempt in the presence of the court during the progress of a proceeding."

In short, a defendant appealing a contempt conviction has an automatic right to a supersedeas except where the contempt was

---

[Section 27:6]

[1]See § 27:4, supra. For a discussion of the notice and procedure to follow in cases of constructive contempt, see In re Harris, 289 Ga. App. 334, 657 S.E.2d 259 (2008).

[2]Moody v. State, 131 Ga. App. 355, 360, 206 S.E.2d 79 (1974). See Apoian v. State, 313 Ga. App. 800, 723 S.E.2d 35 (2012).

[3]O.C.G.A. § 24-13-26.

[Section 27:7]

[1]In re Thomas, 134 Ga. App. 728, 215 S.E.2d 735 (1975).

"in the presence of the court during the progress of a proceeding." If the conviction was for a direct contempt, rather than an indirect contempt, the judge still has authority to issue a supersedeas.[2] If a supersedeas cannot be obtained in the trial court, it should be sought from the Court of Appeals[3] or the Georgia Supreme Court,[4] if that becomes necessary. The rules of both of our appellate courts provide that those courts, in emergency situations, may issue supersedeas to preserve the jurisdiction of an appeal and to prevent the issue from becoming moot.[5] "[O]n appeal of a criminal contempt conviction the appropriate standard of appellate review is 'whether, after viewing the evidence in the light most favorable to the prosecution, *any* rational trier of fact could have found the essential elements of the crime beyond a reasonable doubt.' "[6]

In addition to an appeal, it is possible to obtain some limited review of a conviction for contempt in a habeas corpus action. However, Georgia provides by statute that a person is not entitled to be discharged in a habeas corpus action "[w]hen the person is in custody for a contempt of court and the court has not exceeded its jurisdiction in the length of the imprisonment imposed . . . ."[7] If this statute were applied literally, habeas corpus proceedings in connection with a conviction for contempt would hardly be worth mentioning. While habeas corpus may not be used as a substitute for an appeal, the Georgia Supreme Court has indicated that habeas corpus relief may properly be sought where the contempt order is absolutely void or where some constitutional right of the defendant is violated in the contempt proceeding.[8]

If a defendant is confined because of an oral order finding him in contempt of court, it appears that a habeas corpus proceeding could be used at least to urge the trial judge into signing an order finding the defendant in contempt. An appeal could be filed once the signed order is filed in the trial court.

In the case of a criminal contempt action, if the trial judge determines that the defendant was not in contempt, the state has

---

[2]See Rule 40(a) of the Rules of the Court of Appeals; O.C.G.A. § 5-5-47, O.C.G.A. § 5-6-46, O.C.G.A. § 5-6-47.

[3]Rule 40(b) of the Rules of the Court of Appeals.

[4]Rule 9 of the Rules of the Supreme Court.

[5]Rule 9 of the Rules of the Supreme Court; Rule 40(b) of the Rules of the Court of Appeals.

[6]In re Henritze, 181 Ga. App. 560, 561, 353 S.E.2d 58 (1987) (quoting Jackson v. Virginia, 443 U.S. 307, 99 S.Ct. 2781, 61 L.Ed.2d 560 (1979)).

[7]O.C.G.A. § 9-14-16(6).

[8]White v. George, 195 Ga. 465 (1), 24 S.E.2d 787 (1943). But see Friedman v. Harbold, 150 Ga. App. 482, 483 (1), 258 S.E.2d 154 (1979).

a right to appeal the case.[9]

If the defendant has already served his sentence for contempt, an appeal will be dismissed because the validity of the contempt order has become a moot issue.[10] The rule is the same where the litigant satisfies the order of contempt by the payment of a fine.[11] Nonetheless, even in those cases where the alleged contemnor has been released from jail or paid a fine, appellate review may still be available if there is the potential for collateral adverse consequences, such as disciplinary action by a bar association in the case of an attorney, parole consequences, or even damage to reputation.[12]

---

[9]Welborn v. Mize, 107 Ga. App. 427, 130 S.E.2d 623 (1963).

[10]Endicott v. Glynn County, 235 Ga. 667, 221 S.E.2d 431 (1975); Cagle v. PMC Development Co., 227 Ga. 309, 180 S.E.2d 545 (1971); Cagle v. PMC Development Co. of GA, 227 Ga. 309, 180 S.E.2d 545 (1971).

[11]Herring v. Herring, 236 Ga. 43(1), 222 S.E.2d 331 (1976), compare Hamilton Capital Group, Inc. v. Equifax Credit Information Services., 266 Ga. App. 1 (1), 596 S.E.2d 656 (2004).

[12]In re Hatfield, 290 Ga. App. 134, 658 S.E.2d 871 (2008).

Part V

POST-TRIAL REMEDIES AND PROBATION REVOCATION

Chapter 28

Judicial Review

> **KeyCite®:** Cases and other legal materials listed in KeyCite Scope can be researched through the KeyCite service on Westlaw®. Use KeyCite to check citations for form, parallel references, prior and later history, and comprehensive citator information, including citations to other decisions and secondary materials.

§ 28:1 Scope

This work is intended to serve as a guide to criminal procedure in the trial courts of Georgia and not as a detailed treatment on post-conviction remedies. The sections which follow in this chapter are intended more to call the reader's attention to possible avenues of obtaining judicial review than to discuss these procedures in detail.

§ 28:2 Right to appeal—Defendant

The United States Supreme Court has never held that a defendant has a federal constitutional right to have his conviction reviewed under a system of appellate practice.[1] In fact, the courts have long recognized that there is a broad distinction between the right to be heard in a court of law on the one hand, and the right to have the court's decisions reviewed for error on the other.[2] For these reasons, and because an absolute right to appellate review was unknown at common law,[3] the right to appeal exists only where it is provided for by statutory or state constitutional authority.[4] Since the right of review is statutory, statutes limiting the scope of appellate review will usually pass constitutional muster.[5]

In Georgia, the right of a defendant to appeal his conviction exists by virtue of the Appellate Practice Act of 1965.[6] O.C.G.A. § 5-6-33 provides that "the defendant in any criminal proceeding in the superior, state, or city courts, may appeal from any sentence, judgment, decision, or decree of the court, or of the judge thereof. . . ." However, since the court below is presumed to have decided the case correctly,[7] the burden is on the defendant to show af-

---

[Section 28:2]

[1]McKane v. Durston, 153 U.S. 684, 14 S.Ct. 913, 38 L.Ed. 867 (1894).

[2]Ex parte Abdu, 247 U.S. 27, 38 S.Ct. 447, 62 L.Ed. 966 (1918).

[3]Alexander v. Blackmon, 129 Ga. App. 214, 216 (2), 199 S.E.2d 376 (1973).

[4]Alexander v. Blackmon, 129 Ga. App. 214, 216 (2), 199 S.E.2d 376 (1973); Bradford v. Southern R. R. Co., 195 U.S. 243, 25 S.Ct. 55, 49 L.Ed. 178 (1904).

[5]Fife v. Johnston, 225 Ga. 447, 169 S.E.2d 167 (1969).

[6]O.C.G.A. §§ 5-6-34 et seq.

[7]Saliba v. Saliba, 201 Ga. 681, 688, 40 S.E.2d 732 (1946).

firmatively that the judgment complained of was erroneous.[8] For this reason vague, indefinite, and uncertain assignments of error in the trial court present no questions for determination by the appellate court,[9] and lower court judgments will not be reversed if it is possible to sustain them on any ground apparent from the record.[10] In Georgia it has been held that each alleged error "must stand or fall upon its own merits and is not aggravated by the accumulative effect of other claims of error." Thus, the cumulative error rule does not apply.[11]

"The interpretation of a statute is a question of law, which is reviewed de novo on appeal."[12] A criminal statute "must be construed strictly against criminal liability and, if it is susceptible to more than one reasonable interpretation, the interpretation most favorable to the party facing criminal liability must be adopted."[13] Indeed, O.C.G.A. § 1-3-1(a) mandates that in "all interpretations of statutes, the courts shall look diligently for the intention of the General Assembly, keeping in view at all times the old law, the evil, and the remedy."

It has been held that the provisions of the Appellate Practice Act are mandatory and that non-compliance with those provisions should result in the dismissal of the appeal.[14] However, O.C.G.A. § 5-6-30 requires that the Act be liberally construed "so as to bring about a decision on the merits of every case appealed and to avoid dismissal of any case or refusal to consider any points raised therein. . . ."

In addition, a defendant may appeal from an adverse ruling in a criminal case on issues which are effectively final in that they "finally determine claims of right separable from, and collateral to, rights asserted in the action, too important to be denied review and too independent of the cause itself to require that appellate consideration be deferred until the whole case is adjudicated."[15] This is known as the "collateral order doctrine" and applies to an

---

[8]Saliba v. Saliba, 201 Ga. 681, 688, 40 S.E.2d 732 (1946); Dill v. State, 222 Ga. 793, 794, 152 S.E.2d 741 (1966).

[9]Dorsey v. Dorsey, 189 Ga. 662, 670, 7 S.E.2d 273 (1940); Dye v. Dotson, 201 Ga. 1, 9, 39 S.E.2d 8 (1946).

[10]Nobles v. Webb, 197 Ga. 242, 246, 29 S.E.2d 158 (1944).

[11]Butler v. State, 163 Ga. App. 475, 476 (4), 294 S.E.2d 700 (1982); Haas v. State, 146 Ga. App. 729, 734, 247 S.E.2d 507 (1978); Lee v. State, 177 Ga. App. 698, 701 (4), 340 S.E.2d 658 (1986).

[12]Joe Ray Bonding Co., Inc. v. State, 284 Ga. App. 687, 688, 644 S.E.2d 501 (2007).

[13]Fleet Finance, Inc. of Georgia v. Jones, 263 Ga. 228 (3), 430 S.E.2d 352 (1993).

[14]Baxter v. Long, 122 Ga. App. 500, 177 S.E.2d 712 (1970).

[15]Cohen v. Beneficial Indus. Loan Corp., 337 U.S. 541, 546, 69 S.Ct. 1221, 93 L.Ed. 1528 (1949). Compare U.S. v. MacDonald, 435 U.S. 850, 98 S.Ct. 1547, 56 L.Ed.2d 18 (1978) (no right to seek pretrial review of order

order which is effectively final and appealable because it comes within the terms of a relevant statutory right to appeal final judgments. The Appellate Practices Act authorizes a criminal defendant and the parties in a civil case to seek review from "all final judgments."[16] The state has no such right. O.C.G.A. § 5-7-1 sets out the sort of rulings that the state may appeal and the general right to appeal from a final judgment is not among them. Thus, a criminal defendant may appeal an order denying a motion to dismiss on double jeopardy grounds.[17]

In *Graham v. State*,[18] the court pointed out that a defendant may be deprived of due process "where there is an inordinate delay in the appellate process, including an excessive delay in the furnishing of a trial transcript." The four criteria of *Barker v. Wingo*[19] are to be used in determining whether or not a delay amounts to a due process violation. See § 14:70, supra. The *Graham* court also pointed out that "post-conviction incarceration, in and of itself, is [not] a violation of due process of law." Nonetheless, in 2012, the court noted in *Shank v. State*,[20] that extraordinary post-conviction, pre-appeal delays are occurring with "greater frequency" and admonished all of the participants in the criminal justice system to perform their respective duties "without unnecessary delay." Dissatisfied after several years with the post-*Shank* effort of defense attorneys, prosecutors, and trial courts, in *Owens v. State*,[21] the court directed the Council of Superior Court Judges in consultation with the State Bar and the Georgia Association of Criminal Defense Lawyers, the Prosecuting Attorneys' Council, and the Council of Superior Court Clerks, to craft a Uniform Rule of Superior Court to address the issue and to submit it to the court no later than September 17, 2018.

In cases where a transcript cannot be produced or those in which a party contends that the record does not accurately disclose what occurred at trial, O.C.G.A. § 5-6-41 establishes a procedure whereby a party may seek to have the record properly

---

denying motion to dismiss based upon constitutional right to speedy trial because such order is not considered "final").

[16]O.C.G.A. § 5-6-34(a)(1). See Sesniah v. State, 292 Ga. 35, 734 S.E.2d 362 (2012).

[17]Abney v. U.S., 431 U.S. 651, 97 S.Ct. 2034, 52 L.Ed.2d 651 (1977).

[18]Graham v. State, 171 Ga. App. 242, 250 (7), 319 S.E.2d 484 (1984). See Spradlin v. State, 262 Ga. App. 897, 899 (3), 587 S.E.2d 155 (2003).

Cf. Gaines v. Manson, 194 Conn. 510, 481 A.2d 1084 (1984); Chancey v. State, 256 Ga. 415, 436 (11), 349 S.E.2d 717 (1986).

[19]Barker v. Wingo, 407 U.S. 514, 92 S.Ct. 2182, 33 L.Ed.2d 101 (1972); St. John v. State, 182 Ga. App. 861, 863 (4), 357 S.E.2d 311 (1987).

[20]Shank v. State, 290 Ga. 844, 849, 725 S.E.2d 246 (2012).

[21]Owens v. State, 303 Ga. 254, 811 S.E.2d 420 (2018).

supplemented. The parties may stipulate as to what occurred at trial or the record may be completed based upon the recollection of the judge. The parties may recreate the transcript from memory and when they are unable to agree, the trial court may do so. "[W]hen the parties are unable to agree as to the correctness of such a supplemental transcript, the issue is to be decided by the trial judge, and such decision is final and not subject to review."[22]

In *Penrod v. State*,[23] the court pointed out that "neither the sixth amendment nor the fourteenth . . . requires . . . that the record reflect that the defendant made a knowing and intelligent decision not to appeal. . . ."

In *Smith v. Gwinnett County*,[24] the court held that a defendant may not file a petition for certiorari in the State Court of Gwinnett County from a conviction in the Recorder's Court.

See § 14:99, supra, on interlocutory appeals.

§ 28:3 Right to appeal—Defendant—Forfeiture and waiver of right to appeal

In *State v. Denson*,[1] the Georgia Supreme Court held that, notwithstanding the right of appeal provided for by the Appellate Practice Act,[2] a convicted party can, by his own conduct or by his own conduct in concert with that of his attorney, forfeit his appeal.[3] Absent a finding of ineffective counsel,[4] where the defendant and his attorney purposefully abuse or delay the appellate process, the appeal may be forfeited.[5] It has also been held that one cannot sit idly by and permit judgment to be taken against him and file no proper appeal; under such circumstances, the law will not provide relief.[6]

In addition, "Georgia law is clear . . . that where a defendant becomes a fugitive before filing any post-conviction motions and then remains a fugitive during the time in which he could assert

[22]Mosley v. State, 300 Ga. 521, 796 S.E.2d 684 (2017).

[23]Penrod v. State, 233 Ga. App. 532, 533, 504 S.E.2d 757 (1998) (quoting Murphy v. Balkcom, 245 Ga. 13, 262 S.E.2d 784 (1980)).

[24]Smith v. Gwinnett County, 246 Ga. App. 865, 867 (1), 542 S.E.2d 616 (2000).

[Section 28:3]

[1]State v. Denson, 236 Ga. 239, 223 S.E.2d 640 (1976).

[2]O.C.G.A. §§ 5-6-34 et seq.

[3]Cf. Thornton v. State, 216 Ga. App. 202, 203, 453 S.E.2d 802 (1995).

[4]The failure of counsel to inform a defendant of his right to appeal constitutes ineffective assistance of counsel, regardless of whether the attorney was appointed or retained. Kreps v. Gray, 234 Ga. 745, 747, 218 S.E.2d 1 (1975).

[5]State v. Denson, 236 Ga. 239, 240, 223 S.E.2d 640 (1976).

[6]Nix v. Nix, 138 Ga. App. 754, 756 (4), 227 S.E.2d 481 (1976).

such a motion, he waives his right to seek post-conviction relief."[7] Indeed, a fugitive defendant also waives the right to appear by counsel until he has returned to custody.[8]

It has been held that the right of appeal belongs to the defendant, who cannot be deprived of it because his counsel decides it is without merit and refuses to pursue it.[9] Similarly, an indigent defendant, not his counsel, has the prerogative of deciding whether or not to appeal.[10] However, where the Georgia Court of Appeals chose to believe defense counsel's assertion that he informed his client of his right to appeal, rather than the client's assertion that he was not so informed, such a holding will not be disturbed on appeal to the Georgia Supreme Court.[11]

In *Hudson v. State,*[12] the court pointed out "that criminal defense attorneys are often required to file appeals where there is no reasonable expectation of reversal, [but] this provides no excuse for disregard of appellate rules. . . ."

Where a defendant escapes while his appeal is pending, the appeal becomes moot and may be dismissed.[13] However, an escape does not prevent a defendant, after recapture, from raising in a habeas corpus petition issues which he could have raised in an appeal.[14] Also, if a defendant escapes before an appeal is filed and remains a fugitive during the time an appeal may be filed, he is said to have forfeited his right to appeal.[15] Likewise, a defendant who is an indigent and escapes forfeits his right to a trial transcript at state expense.[16] However, if a defendant is sentenced to death and he escapes, his appeal will not be dismissed because of the mandatory language requiring the Georgia Supreme Court

---

[7]Harper v. State, 300 Ga. App. 25, 28, 684 S.E.2d 96 (2009) (citations and punctuation omitted).

[8]Allen v. State of Ga., 166 U.S. 138, 17 S. Ct. 525, 41 L. Ed. 949 (1897); Worthen v. State, 342 Ga. App. 612, 804 S.E.2d 139 (2017). See also F.D.I.C. v. Pharaon, 178 F.3d 1159, 1161 (II) (11th Cir. 1999) (also known as the "fugitive disentitlement doctrine" because of the limits it places on access to the courts for fugitives).

[9]Lee v. State, 139 Ga. App. 65, 66, 227 S.E.2d 878 (1976).

[10]Barnes v. State, 135 Ga. App. 190, 217 S.E.2d 443 (1975).

[11]Murphy v. Balkcom, 245 Ga. 13, 262 S.E.2d 784 (1980).

[12]Hudson v. State, 246 Ga. App. 335, 337 (4), 539 S.E.2d 860 (2000).

[13]Gravitt v. State, 221 Ga. 812, 147 S.E.2d 447 (1966). However, in State Board of Corrections v. Smith, 238 Ga. 565, 567, 233 S.E.2d 797 (1977), the court held that where a defendant escapes during the pendency of an appeal and the appeal is dismissed, he may still file a state habeas corpus petition alleging ineffective assistance of counsel at his original trial.

[14]State Board of Corrections v. Smith, 238 Ga. 565, 566 (1), 233 S.E.2d 797 (1977).

[15]Saleem v. State, 152 Ga. App. 552, 263 S.E.2d 490 (1979).

[16]Seay v. Hubbard, 240 Ga. 464, 241 S.E.2d 220 (1978).

to review cases in which a death sentence has been imposed.[17] Even in a non-capital case if a defendant is captured or surrenders before his appeal is dismissed, the appeal at least cannot be dismissed summarily.[18]

If a defendant, who is convicted of a charge and sentenced to pay a fine or serve time, pays the fine and then files an appeal, the case is moot,[19] unless perhaps the defendant can show that there are adverse collateral consequences resulting from the conviction.[20] Thus, if a defendant wishes to appeal, he should obtain a supersedeas or post a bond so that he will not be held to have complied with his sentence which would otherwise render his appeal moot. However, the trial court in its discretion may consider a motion for new trial after the sentence has been served, but it is not obligated to do so.[21]

A defendant may voluntarily waive the right to appeal. "The fact that a waiver of the right to appeal is voluntary, knowing, and intelligent may be shown in two ways. First, a signed waiver may indicate that the defendant understands the right he is waiving. Second, and more important, detailed questioning of the defendant by the trial court that reveals that he was informed of his right to appeal and that he voluntarily waived that right is sufficient to show the existence of a valid, enforceable waiver."[22]

Pleas induced by an illusory promise of the state are not

---

[17]Sprouse v. State, 242 Ga. 831 (1), 252 S.E.2d 173 (1979).

[18]Yates v. Brown, 235 Ga. 391, 392 (1), 219 S.E.2d 729 (1975). In Golden v. State, 145 Ga. App. 36, 243 S.E.2d 303 (1978), the court said that unless a defendant is in custody in this state, after an escape his appeal may be dismissed summarily.

[19]Roberts v. State, 137 Ga. App. 801, 225 S.E.2d 90 (1976); Chaplin v. State, 141 Ga. App. 788, 234 S.E.2d 330 (1977).

[20]Gamble v. State, 181 Ga. App. 871, 354 S.E.2d 174 (1987); Ritchie v. State, 257 Ga. App. 149, 570 S.E.2d 435 (2002), adverse collateral consequences might include: potential enhancement of subsequent criminal punishment; the inability to vote or perform jury duty; and the disqualification from certain businesses or professions.

In Padilla v. Kentucky, 130 S. Ct. 1473, 176 L. Ed. 2d 284 (2010), the Supreme Court held that because the consequences of deportation are so drastic, the failure of counsel to advise the client that a plea could result in deportation is ineffective assistance. See Smith v. State, 304 Ga. App. 846, 698 S.E.2d 355 (2010) (Georgia Supreme Court follows *Padilla* holding that failure to advise non-citizen that guilty plea may result in deportation is ineffective assistance and satisfies first prong of *Strickland*). See also Taylor v. State, 304 Ga. App. 878, 698 S.E.2d 384 (2010) (failure to advise defendant of sex offender registry requirements mandated by plea was deficient representation).

[21]Baker v. State, 240 Ga. 431, 241 S.E.2d 187 (1978).

[22]Rush v. State, 276 Ga. 541, 542, 579 S.E.2d 726 (2003).

informed and voluntary and may be set aside. In *Hooks v. State*,[23] the defendant entered a plea of guilty and waived his right to appellate review in exchange for the most extreme punishment possible in his case. Although the sentence was not improper, the defendant's agreement to enter the plea was not made with an understanding that he receive no consideration for his plea. This, the court said, should have been made clear by the trial court at the time the plea was tendered. In *Nazario v. State*,[24] the court noted that a defendant does not "bargain away" or waive the right to challenge an illegal and void sentence simply because he knowingly enters into a plea agreement and accepts the benefit of the plea bargain.

In *Thomas v. State*[25] the court held that a criminal defendant could waive his statutory right to appeal a conviction in return for the state's waiver of the right to seek the death penalty.

Special problems exist where a person who is mentally incompetent refuses to assert a right of judicial review.[26]

"When notice of the entry of an appealable order is not given, the losing party should file a motion to set aside, and the trial court should grant the motion and re-enter the judgment, whereupon the 30-day appeal period would begin to run again."[27]

§ 28:4 Right to appeal—State

O.C.G.A. § 5-7-1 provides as follows:

(a) An appeal may be taken by and on behalf of the State of Georgia from the superior courts, state courts, and juvenile courts and such other courts from which a direct appeal is authorized to the Court of Appeals and the Supreme Court in criminal cases and adjudication of delinquency cases in the following instances:

(1) From an order, decision, or judgment setting aside or dismissing any indictment, accusation, or a petition alleging that a child has committed a delinquent act, or any count thereof;

(2) From an order, decision, or judgment arresting judgment of conviction or adjudication of delinquency upon legal grounds;

---

[23]Hooks v. State, 284 Ga. 531 (2), 668 S.E.2d 718 (2008), reversed on other grounds, Williams v. State, 287 Ga. 192, 695 S.E.2d 244 (2010) (challenge to a conviction as opposed to the sentence cannot be raised by O.C.G.A. § 16-1-7(a), motion to correct illegal sentence).

[24]Nazario v. State, 293 Ga. 480, 746 S.E.2d 109 (2013).

[25]Thomas v. State, 260 Ga. 262, 392 S.E.2d 520 (1990).

[26]E.g., Larkin, "The Eighth Amendment and the Execution of the Presently Incompetent," 32 Stanford L. R. 765 (1980). Roberta M. Harding, " 'Endgame': Competency and the Execution of Condemned Inmates-A Proposal to Satisfy the Eighth Amendment's Prohibition Against the Infliction of Cruel and Unusual Punishment, 14 St. Louis U. Pub. L. Rev. 105 (1994)."

[27]Veasley v. State, 272 Ga. 837, 838, 537 S.E.2d 42 (2000).

(3) From an order, decision, or judgment sustaining a plea or motion in bar, when the defendant has not been put in jeopardy;

(4) From an order, decision, or judgment suppressing or excluding evidence illegally seized or excluding the results of any test for alcohol or drugs in the case of motions made and ruled upon prior to the impaneling of a jury or the defendant being put in jeopardy, whichever occurs first;

(5) From an order, decision, or judgment excluding any other evidence to be used by the state at trial on any motion filed by the state or defendant at least 30 days prior to trial and ruled on prior to the impaneling of a jury or the defendant being put in jeopardy, whichever occurs first, if:

(A) Notwithstanding the provisions of Code Section 5-6-38, the notice of appeal filed pursuant to this paragraph is filed within two days of such order, decision, or judgment; and

(B) The prosecuting attorney certifies to the trial court that such appeal is not taken for purpose of delay and that the evidence is a substantial proof of a material fact in the proceeding;

(6) From an order, decision, or judgment of a court where the court does not have jurisdiction or the order is otherwise void under the Constitution or laws of this state;

(7) From an order, decision, or judgment of a superior court transferring a case to the juvenile court pursuant to subparagraph (b)(2)(B) of Code Section 15-11-28 or subsection (b) of Code Section 17-7-50.1;

(8) From an order, decision, or judgment of a court granting a motion for new trial or an extraordinary motion for new trial;

(9) From an order, decision, or judgment denying a motion by the state to recuse or disqualify a judge made and ruled upon prior to the defendant being put in jeopardy;" or

(10) From an order, decision or judgment issued pursuant to subsection (c) of Code Section 17-10-6.2."

(b) In any instance in which any appeal is taken by and on behalf of the State of Georgia in a criminal case, the defendant shall have the right to cross appeal. Such cross appeal shall be subject to the same rules of practice and procedure as provided for in civil cases under Code Section § 5-6-38.

(c) In any instance in which the defendant in a criminal case applies for and is granted an interlocutory appeal as provided by Code Section 5-6-34 or an appeal is taken pursuant to Code Section 17-10-35.1, the state shall have the right to cross appeal on any matter ruled on prior to the impaneling of a jury or the defendant being put in jeopardy. Such cross appeal shall be subject to the same rules of practice and procedure as provided for in civil cases under Code Section 5-6-38. The state shall not be required to obtain a certificate of immediate review for such cross appeal.[1]

[Section 28:4]

[1]See State v. Johnson, 292 Ga. 409, 738 S.E.2d 86 (2013) (state has no right to appeal an order transferring a case from superior court to juvenile court since it is not an order

Thus, the state has the right to appeal rulings related to certain evidentiary issues prior to trial, including orders suppressing evidence illegally seized or drug and alcohol test results. In addition, the state may also appeal orders which exclude evidence which the state seeks to use at trial. This direct appeal right, first provided to the state in 2013, is limited to orders entered thirty days prior to trial. Appeals taken pursuant to O.C.G.A. § 5-7-1 must be filed within two days of the entry of the subject order and the prosecuting attorney must certify that the appeal is not taken for purposes of delay. In addition, in any case in which the defendant is allowed an interlocutory appeal pursuant to O.C.G.A. § 5-6-34, or an appeal pursuant to O.C.G.A. § 17-10-35.1, the state has the right to file a cross-appeal on any matter ruled upon prior to the impaneling of a jury or the defendant otherwise being placed in jeopardy.

In *State v. Evans*,[2] the Georgia Supreme Court held that the state has no right to appeal an acquittal following a bench trial conducted over the objection of the state.

In addition to the more general rights of the state to appeal, O.C.G.A. § 17-10-6.1(b) provides that the state may "appeal any sentence which is imposed by the superior court which does not conform to the provisions of this subsection . . . ."

Pursuant to O.C.G.A. § 5-7-2, the state is not required to seek a certificate of immediate review and may file a direct appeal from a pre-trial order suppressing or excluding evidence as described in § 5-7-1(a)(4) and (5) and an order dismissing an indictment or delinquency petition as described in § 5-7-1(a)(1) and an order transferring a case to juvenile court as described in § 5-7-1(a)(7).

In *State v. Outen*,[3] the Georgia Supreme Court held that the Court of Appeals did not have jurisdiction over the state's appeal of the trial court's judgment, because the trial court judge did not issue a certificate of immediate review as required by O.C.G.A. § 5-7-2. The Court stated that even though "no question of the jurisdiction of the Court of Appeals was raised in that Court, it is incumbent upon the appellant courts of this State to inquire into their own jurisdiction, regardless of whether an issue of jurisdic-

---

"setting aside or dismissing an indictment").

[2]State v. Evans, 282 Ga. 63, 646 S.E.2d 77 (2007).

[3]State v. Outen, 289 Ga. 579, 714 S.E.2d 581 (2011). See State v. Osborne, 330 Ga. App. 688, 769 S.E.2d 115 (2015) (review of a trial court order denying state's motion to recuse is not subject to direct appeal and review can be had only by certificate of immediate review); State v. Green, 331 Ga. App. 107, 769 S.E.2d 804 (2015) (order dismissing some but not all charges in indictment is not "final" for purposes of O.C.G.A. § 5-7-1 and review was available only by way of certificate for immediate review, O.C.G.A. § 5-7-2).

tion is raised by the parties."

In *State v. King*,[4] the state claimed that the court imposed a void sentence after it accepted the defendant's plea but imposed a shorter term of imprisonment than that recommended in the plea agreement. According to the state, the court should have allowed it to withdraw from the plea agreement if it did not intend to impose the negotiated sentence. On appeal, the court noted that O.C.G.A. § 5-7-1(a) provides the state with a *limited* right of appeal in criminal cases and should the state attempt an appeal other than as provided therein "the appellate courts do not have jurisdiction to entertain it." The court rejected the state's position, holding that the sentence imposed was within the statutory guidelines and, thus, not void. As a result, the court found that it had no jurisdiction and dismissed the appeal.

For a further discussion of the State's right to appeal in a criminal case, see "Government Appeals in Criminal Cases in Georgia," Donald E. Wilkes, Jr., *The Georgia Defender*, Vol. 21 (3rd ed., 2002).

§ 28:5 Right of defendant to be released on bond pending appeal

A defendant who appeals a misdemeanor conviction in accordance with the provisions of the Appellate Practice Act[1] has a right to be released on a reasonable bond pending the appeal.[2] However, reasonable conditions to the granting of a bond may also be imposed.[3] Where the state appeals, the defendant has a right to be released on a reasonable bond in an amount fixed by the trial judge, unless the death penalty has been imposed.[4]

In *Wade v. State*[5] the court concluded that "[t]here is considerable doubt whether a direct appeal will lie from the interlocutory order denying bond during the pendency of a motion for new trial or an appeal." However, the court pointed out "the present practice is that a direct appeal from an order denying appeal bond should be considered on the merits." In *Johnson v. State*,[6] the court held that the entry of an order granting a new trial is a

---

[4]State v. King, 325 Ga. App. 445, 750 S.E.2d 756 (2013).

[Section 28:5]

[1]O.C.G.A. §§ 5-6-34 et seq.

[2]O.C.G.A. § 17-6-1; Boatner v. State, 122 Ga. App. 736, 737, 178 S.E.2d 699 (1970).

[3]Dudley v. State, 230 Ga. App. 339, 341, 496 S.E.2d 341 (1998).

[4]O.C.G.A. § 5-7-5. In the excep-

tional case where the court has orally ordered the suppression of evidence, the state may appeal the order provided it appears as a matter of record that the state requested the order be reduced to writing and the trial court declined. State v. Morrell, 281 Ga. 152, 635 S.E.2d 716 (2006).

[5]Wade v. State, 218 Ga. App. 377(1), 461 S.E.2d 314 (1995).

[6]Johnson v. State, 818 S.E.2d 601

final judgment thereby subjecting an order denying an appeal bond to direct appeal.

O.C.G.A. § 17-6-1(g) provides as follows:

"(g) No appeal bond shall be granted to any person who has been convicted of murder, rape, aggravated sodomy, armed robbery, aggravated child molestation, kidnapping, trafficking in cocaine or marijuana, aggravated stalking, or aircraft hijacking and who has been sentenced to serve a period of incarceration of seven years or more. The granting of an appeal bond to a person who has been convicted of any other felony offense or of any misdemeanor offense involving an act of family violence as defined in O.C.G.A. § 19-13-1, or of any offense delineated as a high and aggravated misdemeanor or of any offense set forth in O.C.G.A. § 40-6-391, shall be in the discretion of the convicting court. Appeal bonds shall terminate when the right of appeal terminates, and such bonds shall not be effective as to any petition or application for writ of certiorari unless the court in which the petition or application is filed so specifies."[7]

The case of *Birge v. State*[8] was decided before the enactment of the above statute. However, in that case the Georgia Supreme Court held that "[r]elease should not be granted unless the court finds that there is no substantial risk the . . . [defendant] will not appear to answer the judgment following conclusion of the appellate proceedings and that the . . . [defendant] is not likely to commit a serious crime, intimidate witnesses or otherwise interfere with the administration of justice, and that the appeal is not frivolous or taken for delay."

In *Jarrett v. State*,[9] the court held that "[t]he burden of seeking a stay of execution and a release on bond is upon the applicant."

(Ga. 2018).

[7]In Moran v. State, 268 Ga. 816, 819(4), 493 S.E.2d 126 (1997), the court found O.C.G.A. § 17-6-1 constitutional. See also Getkate v. State, 278 Ga. 585, 604 S.E.2d 838 (2004).

In those cases where the defendant is either denied an appeal bond or is not entitled to one because of the charges for which the defendant was convicted, the defendant does have a limited right to remain in the county jail pending the disposition of all appeals on the case. Defense counsel must make the request in writing setting out that the continued presence of the defendant in the county of conviction is necessary in order to prepare

and prosecute the appeal. O.C.G.A. § 42-5-50(c); see Helmeci v. State, 230 Ga. App. 866, 870-871(5), 498 S.E.2d 326 (1998). Note, however, that the trial court is empowered to deny such a motion " 'where an issue is properly raised before the trial court regarding jail security or other matters involving administration of the jail.' " Dorsey v. State, 279 Ga. 534, 615 S.E.2d 512 (2005) quoting In re Irvin, 254 Ga. 251, 252, 328 S.E.2d 215 (1985).

[8]Birge v. State, 238 Ga. 88, 230 S.E.2d 895 (1976); Prayor v. State, 214 Ga. App. 132, 447 S.E.2d 155 (1994).

[9]Jarrett v. State, 222 Ga. App. 521, 522, 474 S.E.2d 702 (1996).

The case of *Moore v. State*[10] set out a procedure, which the trial judge must follow, in such cases. " '[A]fter a sentence of imprisonment has been imposed, the question of the appellant's custody pending final decision on appeal should be reviewed and a *fresh determination* made by the trial court.' [Emphasis supplied.] . . . In doing so, the court must give applicant notice of the hearing and a chance to appear and be heard. At such hearing the burden of seeking a stay of execution and a release on bond is upon the applicant. Also, 'the trial judge may consider all the evidence adduced at the trial that is pertinent to this determination in addition to such other oral and documentary evidence that he may consider appropriate.' . . . After the appeal bond hearing conducted in accordance with the above guidelines, the court *must* make its decision as to the granting or denying of the appeal bond by answering the question[s] set out in the above paragraph. The answer of 'yes' to any one of the above questions will support the denial of an appeal bond, absent an abuse of discretion. If an affirmative finding is reached as to any one of the four *Birge* criteria, for this court to consider the appeal the record must include a transcript or meet the requirements of [O.C.G.A. § 5-6-41]. In the absence of a transcript we must assume as a matter of law that the evidence adduced at the hearing supported the findings of the court." In *Knapp v. State,*[11] the court held that while the trial judge "is free to exercise its discretion consistent with *Birge* . . . . it is not free to refuse to exercise its discretion or to provide defendant the opportunity to be heard on this issue at an evidentiary hearing."

In *Williford v. State,*[12] the court held that it is not error for a trial judge to make findings of fact and conclusions of law where the judge denies a bond pending an appeal of a criminal conviction and sentence.

In *Lipsey v. State,*[13] the Court of Appeals reversed the refusal of the trial judge to set an appeal bond. The court pointed out (1) "that in a non-capital case the length of the sentence alone . . . [is not] a sufficient basis for the denial of an appeal bond" and (2) evidence that the defendant's wife "sought prior to trial to influence the victim to change her testimony" is not to be attributed to the defendant solely because of the husband-wife relationship.

A direct appeal may be taken from the denial of an appeal

---

[10]Moore v. State, 151 Ga. App. 413, 415, 260 S.E.2d 350 (1979). See Glass v. State, 289 Ga. 542, 712 S.E.2d 851 (2011) (testimony at hearing on motion for new trial about what occurred at hearing on bond motion was not sufficient substitute for transcript of hearing or "reasonable substitute"

thereof pursuant to O.C.G.A. § 5-6-41).

[11]Knapp v. State, 223 Ga. App. 267, 268, 477 S.E.2d 621 (1996).

[12]Williford v. State, 218 Ga. App. 522, 462 S.E.2d 632 (1995).

[13]Lipsey v. State, 170 Ga. App. 212, 214, 316 S.E.2d 774 (1984).

bond.[14] Where there has been a denial of an appeal bond and the defendant is released on parole before an appellate court rules on the denial of the appeal bond, the issue is regarded as being moot.[15]

If the normal methods of obtaining an appeal bond as discussed fail or the bond fixed is excessive, consideration may be given to review by habeas corpus in federal court.[16]

Where a defendant is sentenced to death, a filing of a notice of appeal serves as a supersedeas.[17]

The filing of an appeal does not deprive the trial judge of his authority to revoke a bail bond pending appeal.[18]

See § 8:4, supra, on criteria for release on bond pending trial.

For a motion for bond pending appeal, see Studdard, *Daniel's Georgia Criminal Trial Practice Forms* (2018–2019 ed.), §§ 34:12 et seq.

§ 28:6 Indigent appellants—Right to counsel

An indigent defendant is entitled to have counsel appointed for him to handle an appeal,[1] but this right does not extend to having counsel in seeking certiorari from the United States Supreme Court.[2] The United States Supreme Court has held that the federal Constitution requires that an indigent defendant is entitled to the assistance of appointed counsel only on the first level of appellate review.[3] A specific request for the appointment of appellate counsel is unnecessary once a responsible state

---

[14]Johnson v. State, 818 S.E.2d 601 (Ga. Ct. App. 2018).

[15]Hazelrig v. State, 171 Ga. App. 97, 319 S.E.2d 32 (1984).

[16]See § 8:4, supra.

[17]O.C.G.A. § 5-6-45.

[18]Waters v. State, 174 Ga. App. 438, 330 S.E.2d 177 (1985).

[Section 28:6]

[1]Douglas v. California, 372 U.S. 353, 83 S.Ct. 814, 9 L.Ed.2d 811 (1963). See Note, "The Right of Appeal: Appointed Counsel's Advice to Indigent Client," 30 Mercer L. R. 1059 (1979).

[2]Strozier v. Hopper, 234 Ga. 597, 601, 216 S.E.2d 847 (1975). In Wooten v. State, 245 Ga. 724, 266 S.E.2d 927 (1980), the court held that an indigent defendant is not entitled to appointment of counsel to apply for writ of cer-

tiorari from the Georgia Supreme Court. In State v. Davis, 246 Ga. 200, 269 S.E.2d 461 (1980), the court at least implies that a trial judge has no authority to appoint counsel (who is to receive any payment) for a petitioner in a habeas corpus proceeding. See Murrell v. Young, 285 Ga. 182, 674 S.E.2d 890 (2009), no right to counsel on motion for extraordinary appeal.

[3]Ross v. Moffitt, 417 U.S. 600, 94 S.Ct. 2437, 41 L.Ed.2d 341 (1974). In Ross, counsel had been appointed to represent the defendant in an appeal to the North Carolina Court of Appeals. The United States Supreme Court held that it was not necessary for the state to also appoint counsel to represent the defendant in a discretionary appeal to the North Carolina Supreme Court. Accord, Evitts v. Lucey, 469 U.S. 387, 105 S.Ct. 830, 83 L.Ed.2d 821 (1985). Likewise, an indigent misdemeanant is entitled to court

agency knows that the defendant desires to appeal and that he or she is indigent.[4] In cases where an indigent defendant is improperly denied counsel for his first appeal, he is entitled to relief in the form of having counsel appointed to determine if there is any justifiable ground for an appeal, and if so, to the appointment of counsel to prosecute the appeal.[5] Although an indigent defendant is entitled to appointed counsel in connection with a timely motion to withdraw a plea, there is no right to appointed counsel for purposes of a motion to file an out-of-time appeal.[6] In addition, "[t]here is no constitutional right to counsel . . . in filing or litigating a post-conviction extraordinary motion for new trial or a discretionary application to appeal the ruling on such a motion."[7] The Georgia Supreme Court has held that in all cases where an indigent defendant wishes to raise the issue of ineffective assistance on appeal, trial counsel is conflicted from acting as counsel on appeal.[8]

Not only is an indigent defendant entitled to have counsel appointed to represent him on appeal, the record must show that he was made aware of his right to counsel on appeal and the dangers of proceeding without counsel.[9] If such a showing is made, a defendant may waive his right to counsel in post-conviction proceedings.[10]

From a federal constitutional standpoint, once a defendant has counsel appointed to represent him in an appeal, if the attorney wishes to withdraw he may do so only upon compliance with the rules set out in *Anders v. California*.[11] *Anders* requires that the appointed counsel accomplish the following: (1) submit to the court a request for permission to withdraw based upon counsel's

---

appointed counsel for the first level of appeal. Halbert v. Michigan, 545 U.S. 605, 125 S. Ct. 2582, 162 L. Ed. 2d 552 (2005).

[4]Swenson v. Butler, 386 U.S. 258, 87 S.Ct. 996, 18 L.Ed.2d 33 (1967). See Trauth v. State, 295 Ga. 874, 763 S.E.2d 854 (2014).

[5]Davis v. Frazier, 285 Ga. 16, 673 S.E.2d 215 (2009). See Milliken v. Stewart, 276 Ga. 712, 583 S.E.2d 30 (2003) (where the complaint is that counsel for first appeal was ineffective the remedy is a new trial).

[6]See Pierce v. State, 289 Ga. 893, 717 S.E.2d 202 (2011) (motion for out of time appeal cannot be construed as defendant's first appeal of right).

[7]Gable v. State, 290 Ga. 81, 720

S.E.2d 170 (2011). See Murrell v. Young, 285 Ga. 182, 674 S.E.2d 890 (2009).

[8]Garland v. State, 283 Ga. 201, 657 S.E.2d 842 (2008), this would include other attorneys in the office of appointed trial counsel or the office of the public or conflict defender who tried the case.

[9]Cochran v. State, 253 Ga. 10, 11, 315 S.E.2d 653 (1984).

[10]Weber v. State, 203 Ga. App. 356, 357, 416 S.E.2d 868 (1992). See Merriweather v. Chatman, 285 Ga. 765, 684 S.E.2d 237 (2009).

[11]Anders v. California, 386 U.S. 738, 87 S.Ct. 1396, 18 L.Ed.2d 493 (1967); Odum v. State, 145 Ga. App. 701, 244 S.E.2d 631 (1978).

opinion that, after conscientious examination of the transcript and record, the appeal would be "wholly frivolous"; (2) accompany the request with a brief setting forth anything of record which "might arguably support the appeal"; and (3) furnish the indigent client a copy of the brief in order to allow the defendant to raise any points he chooses to raise.

However, in the 2000 case of *Smith v. Robbins*,[12] the United States Supreme Court held that the Anders procedure was not the only way an appointed counsel could withdraw from an appeal. The court then approved the procedure followed in *People v. Wende*.[13] Under this procedure,

> counsel, upon concluding that an appeal would be frivolous, files a brief with the appellate court that summarizes the procedural and factual history of the case, with citations of the record. He also attests that he has reviewed the record, explained his evaluation of the case to his client, provided the client with a copy of the brief, and informed the client of his right to file a pro se supplemental brief. He further requests that the court independently examine the record for arguable issues. Unlike under the Anders procedure, counsel following Wende neither explicitly states that his review has led him to conclude that an appeal would be frivolous (although that is considered implicit . . . .) nor requests leave to withdraw. Instead, he is silent on the merits of the case and expresses his availability to brief any issues on which the court might desire briefing. . . . The appellate court, upon receiving a 'Wende brief,' must 'conduct a review of the entire record,' regardless of whether the defendant has filed a pro se brief. . . . The California Supreme Court in Wende required . . . a thorough review. . . . If the appellate court, after its review of the record pursuant to Wende, also finds the appeal to be frivolous, it may affirm. . . . If, however, it finds an arguable (i.e., nonfrivolous) issue, it orders briefing on that issue.

In *Penson v. Ohio*,[14] the United States Supreme Court considered a case in which appointed counsel for an appeal simply filed a two paragraphs petition in which he stated he had found nothing requiring reversal and requested to be permitted to withdraw. The court held that the withdrawal of counsel was presumptively prejudicial where counsel failed to follow the procedure set out in *Anders*. Here the error was in failing to call the appellate court's attention to anything in the record which might support the appeal. In *Bell v. State*,[15] the court held that an Anders motion should not be granted unless it is brought to the attention of the

[12]Smith v. Robbins, 528 U.S. 259, 120 S.Ct. 746, 145 L.Ed.2d 756 (2000).

[13]People v. Wende, 25 Cal.3d 436, 441-42, 158 Cal.Rptr. 839, 600 P.2d 1071, 1074-75 (1979).

[14]Penson v. Ohio, 488 U.S. 75, 109 S.Ct. 346, 102 L.Ed.2d 300 (1988).

[15]Bell v. State, 168 Ga. App. 336 (1), 308 S.E.2d 853 (1983).

court sufficiently before the scheduled hearing "for the court to consider the motion and give to the appellant the right to assert additional matters in event of a grant of the motion to withdraw."

From a federal constitutional standpoint, when the above requirements are satisfied by counsel, *Anders* requires the appellate court to examine fully the record and transcript and determine whether the appeal is, in fact, wholly frivolous. If not found to be so, the appellant must be furnished further assistance of counsel to continue the appeal. If found to be frivolous, counsel's request to withdraw may be granted, and the appeal will be dismissed.[16]

From a federal constitutional standpoint, if appellate counsel is permitted to withdraw pursuant to an Anders motion, the defendant is not entitled as a matter of right to have another counsel appointed to represent him in the appeal.[17]

However, the Georgia Supreme Court in *Huguley v. State*[18] concluded that an "Anders Motion is unduly burdensome in that it tends to force the court to assume the role of counsel for the appellant. . . . We therefore find and now announce to the bar that the Anders motion will no longer be entertained in this court." However, the rule of *Huguley* has not been applied to cases docketed before *Huguley*.[19] In December of 1988, in *Fields v. State*,[20] the Georgia Court of Appeals followed the *Huguley* case and stated that it will no longer entertain an Anders motion.

A defendant may waive the right to counsel during postconviction proceedings but "the record should reflect a finding on the part of the trial court that the defendant has validly chosen to continue pro se. The record should also show that this choice was made after the defendant was made aware of his right to counsel and the dangers of proceeding without counsel."[21] See § 7:3, supra, on waiver of counsel.

In *Jones v. Barnes*,[22] the United States Supreme Court held that appointed counsel, on appeal, has no "constitutional duty to raise every nonfrivolous issue requested by the defendant." The court "emphasized the importance of winnowing out weaker argu-

---

[16]Bethay v. State, 237 Ga. 625, 626, 229 S.E.2d 406 (1976); Fegan v. State, 154 Ga. App. 791, 270 S.E.2d 211 (1980).

[17]Garrett v. State, 159 Ga. App. 27, 282 S.E.2d 683 (1981).

[18]Huguley v. State, 253 Ga. 709, 710, 324 S.E.2d 729 (1985).

[19]O'Neal v. State, 254 Ga. 1, 3, 325 S.E.2d 759 (n. 2) (1985).

[20]Fields v. State, 189 Ga. App. 532, 533, 376 S.E.2d 912 (1988); Mapp v. State, 191 Ga. App. 622 (1), 382 S.E.2d 618 (1989).

[21]Weber v. State, 203 Ga. App. 356, 357, 416 S.E.2d 868 (1992). See Calmes v. State, 312 Ga. App. 769, 719 S.E.2d 516 (2011).

[22]Jones v. Barnes, 463 U.S. 745, 103 S.Ct. 3308, 77 L.Ed.2d 987 (1983).

ments on appeal and focusing on one central issue if possible or at most a few key issues. . . . A brief that raises every colorable issue runs the risk of burying good arguments. . . . For judges to second-guess reasonable professional judgments and impose on appointed counsel a duty to raise every 'colorable' claim suggested by a client would disserve the very goal of vigorous and effective advocacy that underlies *Anders.*"

In *Wainwright v. Torna,*[23] the United States Supreme Court considered a federal habeas corpus petition contending that Torna had been denied effective assistance of counsel by his retained attorney in that counsel failed to timely file an application for certiorari to the Florida Supreme Court. The United States Supreme Court said since Torna "had no constitutional right to counsel he could not be deprived of the effective assistance of counsel by the failure to timely file the application."

See § 30:6, infra, on the right of indigent defendants to have appointed counsel at a probation revocation hearing.

§ 28:7   Indigent appellants—Right to transcripts

An indigent defendant is entitled to obtain, free of charge, a transcript of his trial for purposes of a direct appeal of his conviction,[1] but the Georgia courts have taken the position that an indigent defendant is not entitled to a free transcript in collateral post-conviction proceedings.[2] It is error to require a defendant, who has filed a pauper's affidavit, to pay for the cost of an original transcript without a hearing simply because the defendant

---

[23]Wainwright v. Torna, 455 U.S. 586, 102 S.Ct. 1300, 71 L.Ed.2d 475 (1982).

[Section 28:7]

[1]Mitchell v. State, 280 Ga. 802(1), 633 S.E.2d 539 (2006). See Clay v. State, 122 Ga. App. 677, 679 (4), 178 S.E.2d 331 (1970). This is also true in a misdemeanor case unless the state can show that less than a full transcript is sufficient for an appeal. Mayer v. City of Chicago, 404 U.S. 189, 92 S.Ct. 410, 30 L.Ed.2d 372 (1971). It has also been held that an indigent defendant is entitled to a free transcript of a preliminary hearing. Roberts v. LaVallee, 389 U.S. 40, 88 S.Ct. 194, 19 L.Ed.2d 41 (1967).

The same rule applies to the appeal of a state habeas corpus. Gardner v. California, 393 U.S. 367, 89 S.Ct.

580, 21 L.Ed.2d 601 (1969). However, the Fourteenth Amendment does not require a state to furnish an indigent defendant in a murder case with a transcript of the first trial where the same counsel represents him in the second trial. Britt v. North Carolina, 404 U.S. 226, 92 S.Ct. 431, 30 L.Ed.2d 400 (1971).

[2]Holmes v. Kenyon, 238 Ga. 583, 584, 234 S.E.2d 502 (1977). Contra, Gardner v. California, 393 U.S. 367, 89 S.Ct. 580, 21 L.Ed.2d 601 (1969).

See Bell v. State, 337 Ga. App. 730, 788 S.E.2d 808 (2016) (petitioner must state particularized need for transcript and if court denies the request, it must make a factual determination that petitioner has failed to justify need for transcript).

was out on bond,[3] but it has been held that an indigent defendant is not entitled to a daily transcript of the trial at state expense.[4] Where evidence is introduced in support of a ground of a motion for new trial, an indigent defendant is entitled to a transcript of such evidence for his use in an appeal.[5] O.C.G.A. § 17-12-24(a) authorizes the public defender's office to determine indigence for purposes of appointed counsel but the authority to determine indigence for the purpose of requiring the county to pay for a trial transcript rests exclusively with the trial court pursuant to O.C.G.A. § 9-15-2(a)(2), the "costs statute," and that court's decision is not subject to review.[6]

In *Miller v. State,*[7] the defendant filed an affidavit for indigency and counsel was appointed. However, prior to trial, the defendant retained his own attorney, who tried the case. After conviction, the defendant's trial counsel filed a notice of appeal and requested inclusion of the trial transcript, but failed to let the court reporter know in a timely manner whether to provide the transcript. The court dismissed the appeal for unreasonable delay in filing of the transcript. The defendant challenged the dismissal "based on indigency." In affirming the dismissal, the Court of Appeals held that the defendant was at least obligated to make the trial judge aware that he was indigent and request a transcript at the state's expense. Since the defendant had paid for his trial counsel, it was reasonable for the judge to assume he could pay for the transcript.

"Unless it clearly appears that the delay in filing a transcript prevented the presentation of an adequate appeal or impaired a defense which would otherwise be available to an appellant where a new trial is ordered due to trial error, an appellant has not suffered the prejudice which turns a transcript delay into a violation of due process of law." Continued incarceration alone is not a basis for a new trial.[8] However, where a defendant is diligent and despite his/her efforts, a trial transcript cannot be found or substantial portions thereof are missing, a new trial is warranted should a court be unable to reach the merits of the petitioner's habeas case.[9]

---

[3]Clay v. State, 122 Ga. App. 677, 679 (4), 178 S.E.2d 331 (1970).

[4]Chenault v. State, 234 Ga. 216, 221, 215 S.E.2d 223 (1975).

[5]Hall v. State, 162 Ga. App. 713, 716 (4), 293 S.E.2d 862 (1982).

[6]Roberson v. State, 300 Ga. 632, 797 S.E.2d 104 (2017).

[7]Miller v. State, 222 Ga. App. 641, 475 S.E.2d 690 (1996).

[8]Proffitt v. State, 181 Ga. App. 564, 566 (3), 353 S.E.2d 61 (1987).

[9]See Sheard v. State, 300 Ga. 117, 793 S.E.2d 386 (2016). See also § 17:9, supra, on necessity of trial transcript.

In *Henderson v. State*,[10] the Supreme Court of Georgia held that O.C.G.A. § 15-3-3.1 excluded the Court of Appeals from jurisdiction over proceedings in which a sentence of death was or could have been imposed, and that the review of an order denying a post-trial motion for a record or transcript in such a case lay exclusively with the Supreme Court.

In *Miller v. State*,[11] the Court of Appeals held that an indigent defendant is not entitled to a state-provided copy of his probation revocation hearing transcript.

Generally, on the contents and existence of a transcript, see § 17:9, supra.

§ 28:8   Appellate review—Sufficiency of the evidence

The United States Supreme Court has held the "any evidence rule" unconstitutional in determining the question of the sufficiency of the evidence to support a conviction. The defendant is entitled to a reversal "if it is found . . . upon the record evidence . . . [that] no rational trier of fact could have found proof of guilt beyond a reasonable doubt."[1]

When reviewing the *legal* sufficiency of the evidence under *Jackson v. Virginia*,[2] rather than pursuant to O.C.G.A. § 5-5-21, the trial court does not act as a "thirteenth juror" and does not weigh the evidence or otherwise exercise its discretion.[3] In *Adams v. State*,[4] the court held that on an "appeal of a criminal conviction, the evidence is to be viewed 'in the light most favorable to the prosecution' (i.e., in the light most favorable to the jury's determination that the defendant is guilty), not in the light most favorable to the defendant."

In *Priest v. State*,[5] the court held that if the trial judge or the appellate court concludes that there is insufficient evidence to justify a conviction, double jeopardy prevents the state from

---

[10]Henderson v. State, 303 Ga. 241, 811 S.E.2d 388 (2018), overruling Coles v. State, 223 Ga. App. 491, 477 S.E.2d 897 (1996).

[11]Miller v. State, 301 Ga. App. 706, 689 S.E.2d 46 (2009), opinion vacated as moot, 288 Ga. 153, 702 S.E.2d 137 (2010).

[Section 28:8]

[1]Jackson v. Virginia, 443 U.S. 307, 99 S.Ct. 2781, 61 L.Ed.2d 560 (1979) (a federal habeas corpus action); Brown v. State, 250 Ga. 862, 864 (1), 302 S.E.2d 347 (1983). In Holloway v. McElroy, 632 F.2d 605 (5th Cir.

1980), the court held that *Jackson v. Virginia* was to be applied retroactively.

[2]Jackson v. Virginia, 443 U.S. 307, 99 S. Ct. 2781, 61 L. Ed. 2d 560 (1979).

[3]State v. Jackson, 294 Ga. 9, 748 S.E.2d 902 (2013).

[4]Adams v. State, 255 Ga. 356, 357, 338 S.E.2d 860 (1986) (quoting in part Jackson v. Virginia, 443 U.S. 307, 99 S. Ct. 2781, 61 L. Ed. 2d 560 (1979)).

[5]Priest v. State, 265 Ga. 399, 400 (1), 456 S.E.2d 503 (1995).

pursuing a retrial. See § 14:61, supra.

However, the Georgia Supreme Court in *State v. Clay*[6] recognized an exception to the foregoing where the jury, pursuant to request, is charged on a lesser included offense and the defendant is found guilty of the lesser offense. In this situation, if there is sufficient evidence to support a conviction for the greater offense, the defendant may not successfully contend that the evidence does not support the conviction for the lesser offense.

If a case is based entirely on circumstantial evidence, then a verdict of guilty will not be overturned unless it is "unsupportable as a matter of law."[7]

See § 14:99, supra, on interlocutory appeals.

§ 28:9 Motion for judgment notwithstanding mistrial or verdict

In the 1993 Court of Appeals decision in *Rhyne v. State,*[1] the court held that after a defendant has been convicted, such a defendant may no longer possess the post-conviction remedy of filing "a motion for judgment of acquittal notwithstanding the verdict nor a motion for judgment of acquittal notwithstanding mistrial."

In *Rhyne* the defendant moved for a directed verdict of acquittal at the conclusion of the state's evidence. The defendant moved for a directed verdict for a second time as the court considered the state's motion for a mistrial. In its assessment of whether the defendant's motion was valid under Georgia law, the court noted that the issue of such a motion's validity had not yet been addressed by the court. In fact, the only cases that had been before the court involving the trial court's denial of a motion for judgment of acquittal were either resolved on some other issue,[2] or were dismissed because of "the defendant's failure to follow the procedure for interlocutory appeal."[3]

Regardless, the Court of Appeals held that a motion for judgment of acquittal notwithstanding the verdict or mistrial is not valid pursuant to Georgia law. Further, the court noted that "the trial court should have dismissed rather than denied defendant's motion."[4]

---

[6]State v. Clay, 249 Ga. 250, 290 S.E.2d 84 (1982).

[7]Baugh v. State, 276 Ga. 736, 737, 585 S.E.2d 616 (2003).

[Section 28:9]

[1]Rhyne v. State, 209 Ga. App.

548, 551, 434 S.E.2d 76 (1993).

[2]Parham v. State, 137 Ga. App. 498, 224 S.E.2d 485 (1976).

[3]Phillips v. State, 153 Ga. App. 410, 265 S.E.2d 293 (1980).

[4]Rhyne v. State, 209 Ga. App.

In *Brown v. State*,[5] the court pointed out that "[a motion for acquittal notwithstanding the verdict] is treated simply as a motion for new trial." Although O.C.G.A. § 17-9-1 provides for a directed verdict of acquittal during trial, "that statute does not apply after the entry of a verdict."[6] A trial court may reserve ruling on a motion for directed verdict until after the verdict is returned, but the court loses the authority to grant the motion after the judgment is entered.[7]

§ 28:10 Motion for new trial

A convicted defendant may file a motion for a new trial and have the trial judge pass upon the points which the defense deems to be error.[1] Thus, having the trial judge pass on the motion means that an additional person will consider the case in the review process and of course a favorable ruling here eliminates an appeal unless the state has a right to appeal. See § 28:4, supra, on the state's right to appeal. Of course, if a defendant's motion for a new trial is not granted he still has the same right to appeal as he had initially. Also, the statute providing for a notice of appeal severely limits the time in which the appellant may file a transcript of the trial. This frequently means a number of extensions of time to file the transcript may have to be obtained. On the other hand, the trial judge has more discretion in setting a hearing on a motion for a new trial and he may set the hearing date when he realistically believes the transcript will be ready.[2] But the defense counsel is not relieved of his responsibility to appear on the date set in the rule nisi order, if such an order is signed as it normally is. Also, if any constitutional point is to be raised and the point has not previously been made, it seems to be better practice to raise it in a motion for a new trial, since appellate courts are very reluctant to consider a constitutional question unless it has been passed upon by the trial judge. A motion for a new trial, other than an extraordinary motion for a new trial, must be filed within 30 days of the entry of judgment.[3] Thus, it has been held that there is no such thing as an out-of-

---

548, 551, 434 S.E.2d 76 (1993).

[5]Brown v. State, 229 Ga. App. 87, 90 (4), 493 S.E.2d 230 (1997) (quoting State v. Bilal, 192 Ga. App. 185, 384 S.E.2d 253 (1989)).

[6]State v. Canup, 300 Ga. App. 678, 686 S.E.2d 275 (2009). See State v. Bilal, 192 Ga. App. 185, 384 S.E.2d 253 (1989).

[7]State v. Seignious, 197 Ga. App. 766, 399 S.E.2d 559 (1990); Ballentine

v. State, 194 Ga. App. 560, 390 S.E.2d 887 (1990).

[Section 28:10]

[1]See O.C.G.A. § 5-5-42 (forms for motion for new trial in civil and criminal cases).

[2]See O.C.G.A. § 5-6-39.

[3]See O.C.G.A. § 5-5-40.

time motion for a new trial,[4] unless this term is used to refer to an extraordinary motion for a new trial, which is discussed in § 28:12, infra.

Ordinarily a motion for new trial is filed on general grounds. The original motion is then usually amended after counsel has an opportunity to study the transcript. "A motion for a new trial may be amended at any time before the trial court's ruling thereon."[5] However, the trial judge may in his discretion pass on a motion for a new trial before the transcript of the trial has been prepared.[6] Thus, a hearing on the motion for a new trial may be conducted as soon as the motion is filed.[7]

In *State v. Reid*,[8] the court noted:

> Georgia law authorizes the trial court to independently assess a witness's credibility and grant a new trial if the court determines that the verdict of the jury "is . . . contrary to evidence and the principles of justice and equity," OCGA § 5-5-20, or if it is "decidedly and strongly against the weight of the evidence." OCGA § 5-5-21. "When properly raised in a timely motion, these grounds for a new trial—commonly known as the general grounds—require the trial judge to exercise a broad discretion to sit as a thirteenth juror." (Citation and punctuation omitted.) *White v. State*, 293 Ga. 523, 524(2), 753 S.E.2d 115 (2013). . . . In so doing, the trial court has an "affirmative duty" not only to assess witness credibility, but also to consider conflicts in the evidence and to weigh the evidence as a whole in order to determine whether the verdict is so decidedly against the weight of the evidence and/or the principles of justice and equity so as to warrant the Court setting it aside. . . . The court's discretion "should be exercised with caution, and the power to grant a new trial on this ground should be invoked only in exceptional cases in which the evidence preponderates heavily against the verdict." (Citation and punctuation omitted.) *Alvelo v. State*, 288 Ga. 437, 438(1), 704 S.E.2d 787 (2011).

Where the new trial is based on special grounds involving a

---

[4]Gibbs v. State, 213 Ga. App. 117, 443 S.E.2d 708 (1994).

[5]Horne v. State, 231 Ga. App. 864, 866 (2), 501 S.E.2d 47 (1998).

[6]Holmes v. State, 180 Ga. App. 787, 789 (4), 350 S.E.2d 497 (1986).

[7]McClure v. State, 163 Ga. App. 236, 237 (2), 293 S.E.2d 496 (1982); Thompson v. State, 175 Ga. App. 645, 650 (6), 334 S.E.2d 312 (1985). Where the motion for new trial is prepared by trial counsel, the first opportunity to raise the ineffectiveness of trial counsel after the motion is denied will likely be on appeal and then only after

different counsel is appointed or retained to prosecute the appeal. In that case the issue will be remanded to the trial court for an evidentiary hearing. Glover v. State, 266 Ga. 1832), 465 S.E.2d 659 (1996).

[8]State v. Reid, 331 Ga. App. 275, 277-78, 770 S.E.2d 665 (2015). See State v. Byrd, 341 Ga. App. 421, 801 S.E.2d 99 (2017) (fact that evidence may support verdict is not a bar to new trial on general grounds after judge weighs the credibility of witnesses).

question of law, the matter is subject to de novo review on appeal.[9] When reviewing the *legal* sufficiency of the evidence under *Jackson v. Virginia*,[10] and *not* pursuant to O.C.G.A. § 5-5-21, the trial court does not act as a "thirteenth juror" and does not weigh the evidence or otherwise exercise its discretion.[11] Pursuant to O.C.G.A. § 5-5-40(h), if a trial court grants a new trial on its own motion, it must do so within 30 days from the entry of the underlying judgment. After that time has passed, a trial court considering a timely filed motion for new trial is restricted to the grounds raised therein.[12] See § 28:8, supra, on Appellate reviews—sufficiency of the evidence.

Defects in an indictment may not be taken advantage of by a motion for a new trial.[13] "[U]nless the defects appearing in the indictment or accusation are so great that the indictment or accusation is absolutely void, [the] right to a perfect indictment or accusation may be waived, and is waived by going to trial under a defective indictment or accusation without complaint."[14] Further, if the accusation was void in any way the defendant needs to raise this complaint by demurrer before pleading to the merits, "or by motion in arrest of judgment after conviction."[15] Similarly, overruling of a motion in arrest of judgment does not furnish a valid ground for a motion for a new trial.[16] Also, it has been held that a motion for a new trial does not lie where a defendant has entered a guilty plea.[17] However, in *Smith v. State*,[18] a 1984 case, the Georgia Supreme Court stated, "We disapprove the statement that there is no appeal from a judgment entered on a guilty plea. Where the question on appeal is one which may be resolved by facts appearing in the record . . . a direct appeal will lie." See § 16:14, supra, on plea withdrawal.

---

[9]O'Neal v. State, 285 Ga. 361, 677 S.E.2d 90 (2009).

[10]Jackson v. Virginia, 443 U.S. 307, 99 S. Ct. 2781, 61 L. Ed. 2d 560 (1979).

[11]State v. Jackson, 294 Ga. 9, 748 S.E.2d 902 (2013).

[12]State v. Jones, 284 Ga. 302, 303(1), 667 S.E.2d 76 (2008).

[13]Abreu v. State, 206 Ga. App. 361, 363 (2), 425 S.E.2d 331 (1992); Scandrett v. State, 124 Ga. 141 (2), 52 S.E. 160 (1905). Likewise, a plea in abatement or a challenge to the array or other preliminary and collateral issues cannot be properly raised as a ground for a motion for a new trial. Herndon v. State, 178 Ga. 832 (1), 174 S.E. 597 (1934).

[14]Epps v. State, 262 Ga. App. 113, 584 S.E.2d 701 (2003) (citing Moore v. State, 94 Ga. App. 210, 94 S.E.2d 80 (1956)).

[15]Epps v. State, 262 Ga. App. 113, 584 S.E.2d 701 (2003) (citing Abreu v. State, 206 Ga. App. 361, 425 S.E.2d 331 (1992)).

[16]Watson v. State, 64 Ga. 61 (1) (1879).

[17]Romano v. State, 220 Ga. App. 322, 323 (1), 469 S.E.2d 726 (1996); Crosby v. State, 148 Ga. App. 215 (1), 251 S.E.2d 81 (1978); Amos v. State, 161 Ga. App. 281, 283 (2), 287 S.E.2d 743 (1982); Stevens v. State, 169 Ga. App. 646 (2), 314 S.E.2d 481 (1984).

[18]Smith v. State, 253 Ga. 169, 316 S.E.2d 757 (1984).

Generally, such questions as the adequacy and admissibility of evidence and correctness of the charge of the court are raised in a motion for a new trial.[19]

In *Cato v. State*,[20] the court held "that a post-trial declaration by a State's witness that his former testimony was false is not a ground for a new trial." Likewise, a new trial will not be granted on the basis of newly discovered evidence if its only effect is to impeach the testimony of the state's witness.[21]

If a new trial is sought on the grounds of newly discovered evidence, it appears that all of the essentials of an extraordinary motion for a new trial based on newly discovered evidence must be shown.[22] These requirements are discussed in § 28:12, infra.

It has been held that if a motion for a new trial is filed, both the statute and procedural due process require a hearing on the motion before a ruling is rendered.[23] If a party desires a hearing, he must affirmatively request one. He is entitled to a hearing, but in the absence of such request, a hearing on the motion is not necessary.[24] However, in *Mullins v. State*,[25] the court held that it was not error for a trial judge to deny the defendant's motion for a new trial where there was no rule nisi order or other request for a hearing. Without such a request, the trial judge has no duty to initiate a hearing. The defendant has no right to be present at such a hearing, which only involves a question of law.[26] However, in *Moore v. State*,[27] the Georgia Supreme Court held that a "defendant who is not laboring under the penalty of death has no right to be present during the hearing held upon his motion for a new trial." "Rather, due process affords him the right to be present at such a hearing only if his presence would contribute to the fairness of the proceeding."[28]

If a motion for a new trial is overruled, the defendant may

---

[19]O.C.G.A. § 5-5-20, O.C.G.A. § 5-5-22, O.C.G.A. § 5-5-24; Gale v. State, 138 Ga. App. 261, 226 S.E.2d 264 (1976); White v. Hammond, 129 Ga. App. 408, 199 S.E.2d 809 (1973).

[20]Cato v. State, 195 Ga. App. 619, 620 (2), 394 S.E.2d 413 (1990) (quoting Drake v. State, 248 Ga. 891, 287 S.E.2d 180 (1982)).

[21]Dowd v. State, 261 Ga. App. 306 (2), 582 S.E.2d 235 (2003).

[22]See Coalley v. State, 146 Ga. App. 526 (1), 246 S.E.2d 512 (1978). But in Holder v. Farmers' Exchange Bank of Stillmore, 30 Ga. App. 400 (3), 118 S.E. 467 (1923), the court said that the rule is stricter in the case of an

extraordinary motion for a new trial.

[23]Gantt v. Sweatman, 162 Ga. App. 738, 739, 293 S.E.2d 359 (1982).

[24]Cooper v. State, 249 Ga. App. 881, 549 S.E.2d 829 (2001).

[25]Mullins v. State, 224 Ga. App. 218 (1), 480 S.E.2d 264 (1997).

[26]Dobbs v. State, 245 Ga. 208, 209 (2), 264 S.E.2d 18 (1980).

[27]Moore v. State, 254 Ga. 525, 531 (4)(c), 330 S.E.2d 717 (1985); Backey v. State, 234 Ga. App. 265, 267 (4), 506 S.E.2d 435 (1998).

[28]Mantooth v. State, 303 Ga. App. 330, 336(2), 693 S.E.2d 587 (2010) (citation, punctuation and footnote

then take the case to the Court of Appeals or to the Georgia Supreme Court as discussed in § 28:11, infra. However, where a trial judge has granted or refused to grant a motion for a new trial, the judge, at the term at which the clerk entered the judgment, may amend or modify the earlier judgment.[29]

It has been held that if a motion for a new trial is filed after the case is on appeal to the Georgia Court of Appeals or Supreme Court, any attempted action by the trial judge is a nullity.[30] But see § 28:11, infra, on notice of appeal.

Counsel should take note that, pursuant to rule amendments effective January 1, 2019, Uniform Superior Court Rules 39.3.1 and 41 require that motions for new trial be "heard and decided upon as promptly as possible." To effectuate that purpose, Rule 39.3.1 requires that superior court clerks and judges monitor pending felony cases in which a motion for new trial is pending and prepare a schedule of such cases setting forth the date the sentence was imposed, the date the motion was filed, the date the trial transcript was submitted, the date the motion was ruled upon, the date a notice of appeal was filed, and whether the record is ready for transmittal. Rule 41 addresses scheduling issues relating to the hearing on the motion, transcript costs, and transmittal of the record for the appellate court.

For motions for new trial, order to show cause and supersedeas, see Studdard, *Daniel's Georgia Criminal Trial Practice Forms* (2018–2019 ed.), §§ 34:3 et seq.

§ 28:11 Notice of appeal

The most common method of taking a case to the Georgia Supreme Court or Court of Appeals is by a notice of appeal.[1] The notice of appeal must be filed within 30 days after the entry of the decision or judgment.[2] "[A] criminal case is not final but is pending in the trial court until a *written* judgment of conviction

---

omitted).

[29]Bowen v. State, 239 Ga. 517, 518 (2), 238 S.E.2d 62 (1977).

[30]Cf. Jinks v. State, 163 Ga. App. 841, 296 S.E.2d 624 (1982).

[Section 28:11]

[1]See O.C.G.A. § 5-6-37, O.C.G.A. § 5-6-51. In Raymond v. State, 162 Ga. App. 493, 292 S.E.2d 196 (1982), the court said that the filing of a notice of appeal within 30 days is essential in order to confer jurisdiction upon an appellate court. See Holman v. State, 329

Ga. App. 393, 765 S.E.2d 614 (2014) (notice must affirmatively request that a transcript of the evidence and proceedings be transmitted to the appellate court; statement that the clerk omit "nothing" from the record is not sufficient).

[2]O.C.G.A. § 5-6-38; Canup v. State, 150 Ga. App. 794, 258 S.E.2d 907 (1979); Grant v. State, 157 Ga. App. 390, 278 S.E.2d 53 (1981); Washington v. State, 158 Ga. App. 829, 282 S.E.2d 776 (1981).

and *sentence* is entered in the trial court."[3] In *Keller v. State*,[4] the Supreme Court applied this rule in a case involving several counts wherein sentence had been entered as to all but one count and determined that until the last count was finally resolved the case was not ripe for appeal. The trial court does have some discretion pursuant to O.C.G.A. § 5-6-39 to extend the time within which to file a notice of appeal.[5] Georgia courts may excuse non-compliance with a statutory requirement for appeal only where necessary to avoid or remedy a constitutional violation concerning the appeal.[6] Where a notice of appeal is filed before the entry of a written order denying a motion for a new trial, the appeal is valid.[7] The time within which a notice of appeal must be filed does not begin to run until the judgment signed by the judge is filed with the clerk. A judgment entered *nunc pro tunc* to an earlier date is "entered" for purposes of appeal on the date it is filed and does not relate back to the earlier date.[8]

In *Cain v. State*[9] the Georgia Supreme Court adopted the "functional equivalent" test with respect to the sufficiency of a notice of appeal. The defendant in the case filed a document labeled as a "motion to allow an out of time appeal." In fact, the paper was filed within thirty days of the date the order denying the defendant's motion for new trial was filed. Because the defendant expressed in the motion a desire to appeal his conviction and provided the State with sufficient notice thereof, the Court found that it was the "functional equivalent" of a timely notice of appeal and was consistent with a long standing principle in Georgia law which favors the construction of pleadings in such a way so as to promote a decision on the merits and avoid the dismissal of cases on technical or procedural grounds. The "functional equivalent" test has long been the rule in the Eleventh Circuit.[10]

In *Robinson v. State*,[11] the trial court granted the defendant the right to file an out-of-time appeal but would not allow him to file a motion for new trial. Reversing, the Supreme Court held that once an out-of-time appeal is allowed, the right to file a motion for a new trial is automatically included even if one had been

---

[3]Keller v. State, 275 Ga. 680, 571 S.E.2d 806 (2002).

[4]Keller v. State, 275 Ga. 680, 571 S.E.2d 806 (2002).

[5]See Campbell v. State, 192 Ga. App. 316, 385 S.E.2d 14 (1989) ("motion for reconsideration of the court's sentence" does not extend the time to file a notice of appeal).

[6]Gable v. State, 290 Ga. 81, 720 S.E.2d 170, 173 (2011).

[7]Livingston v. State, 221 Ga. App. 563 (1), 472 S.E.2d 317 (1996).

[8]Rocha v. State, 287 Ga. App. 446(1), 651 S.E.2d 781 (2007).

[9]Cain v. State, 275 Ga. 784, 573 S.E.2d 46 (2002).

[10]Harris v. Ballard, 158 F.3d 1164, 1166, n. 1 (11th Cir. 1998).

[11]Robinson v. State, 275 Ga. 143, 561 S.E.2d 823 (2002).

filed previously.

In *Burroughs v. State*,[12] the court held that an out-of-time appeal should be granted if the defendant was denied his right of appeal through counsel's negligence or ignorance or if the defendant was not adequately informed of his appeal rights.

In *Evitts v. Lucey*,[13] the United States Supreme Court held that an indigent defendant is entitled to the effective assistance of counsel on his first appeal. Hence, federal habeas corpus is properly granted where counsel for an indigent defendant fails to file an appeal in a timely manner. Also the Georgia Supreme Court has held that where trial counsel tells a defendant that an appeal will be filed and it is not timely filed, this is a basis for the granting of a petition for habeas corpus and granting a defendant an out-of-time appeal.[14]

In *Hasty v. State*,[15] the court pointed out that Georgia permits "out of time appeals if the appellant was denied his right of appeal through counsel's negligence or ignorance, or if the appellant was not adequately informed of his appeal rights. . . . An out of time appeal, however, is not authorized if the delay was attributable to the appellant's conduct, either alone or in concert with counsel." The denial of a motion for an out of time appeal is directly appealable when the criminal conviction at issue has not been the subject of a direct appeal.[16]

In *Smith v. State*,[17] the Georgia Supreme Court affirmed the denial of an out-of-time appeal for ineffective assistance of counsel filed after a guilty plea when the defendant failed to show a "good and sufficient" reason for the appeal. Thus, the defendant must make a showing that the questions he would raise could be resolved by the facts appearing in the record. See § 7:4, supra. If the defendant cannot demonstrate from the record ineffective assistance of counsel by failing to inform him of his right to appeal, his remedy is not a delayed appeal but a petition for a writ of habeas corpus.[18] The rule also applies where there is a question of

---

[12]Burroughs v. State, 239 Ga. App. 600, 521 S.E.2d 652 (1999). See Smith v. State, 252 Ga. App. 472, 556 S.E.2d 527 (2001), request for out of time appeal will require a hearing to determine as a matter of fact whether failure to timely file notice of appeal was due to negligence of counsel.

[13]Evitts v. Lucey, 469 U.S. 387, 105 S.Ct. 830, 83 L.Ed.2d 821 (1985). But see Cannon v. State, 175 Ga. App. 741, 334 S.E.2d 342 (1985).

[14]Webb v. State, 254 Ga. 130, 327 S.E.2d 224 (1985).

[15]Hasty v. State, 213 Ga. App. 731, 445 S.E.2d 836 (1994).

[16]Kemp v. State, 292 Ga. 795, 741 S.E.2d 652 (2013).

[17]Smith v. State, 266 Ga. 687, 470 S.E.2d 436 (1996).

[18]Smith v. State, 269 Ga. 21, 494 S.E.2d 668 (1998).

the voluntariness of the plea.[19]

"An out-of-time appeal is not authorized in every criminal case which involves a failure by counsel to comply with the applicable procedures necessary to invoke . . . [an appellate] court's jurisdiction. Such an appeal 'is not authorized if the loss of the right to appeal is not attributable to ineffective assistance of counsel but to the fact that the defendant himself slept on his rights.' "An appellate court cannot grant an out-of-time appeal unless a hearing has determined that the untimeliness of the motion for a new trial was not attributable to the defendant. Such a hearing must be held in the trial court.[20] "However, where the undisputed facts in the record show that the defendant waived or slept on her appellate rights, no hearing is required. [cits.]"[21]

An out-of-time appeal from a guilty plea will only be available if the issue is one which can be resolved by facts appearing on the record. Thus, for example, a request to file an out-of-time appeal based upon the claim of ineffective assistance of counsel would fail since the appellant would have to resort to extra record materials and testimony to establish the basis for the request.[22]

In *Ponder v. State*,[23] the court held that if a timely notice of appeal is filed and then a motion for a new trial is filed (presumably within 30 days from sentence), this has the effect of voiding the earlier notice of appeal. In *State v. Rimes*,[24] the court held that a notice of appeal is not valid if filed while a motion for a new trial is pending. However, *Rimes* was abrogated by *State v. Chambers*,[25] which held that in the absence of prejudice to an appellee, the fact that an appeal is prematurely filed will no longer serve as a basis for dismissal.

A notice of appeal may be filed without first filing a motion for new trial. This method of appeal bypasses the trial judge and usually results in an appellate court deciding the case more quickly than if a motion for a new trial is filed before the case is appealed. Yet, there are two factors which may be drawbacks to this particular method: First, the very fact that the trial judge

---

[19]Stewart v. State, 268 Ga. 886, 494 S.E.2d 665 (1998).

[20]Porter v. State, 271 Ga. 498, 499, 521 S.E.2d 566 (1999). See Bryant v. State, 257 Ga. App. 141, 570 S.E.2d 422 (2002); Dykes v. State, 266 Ga. App. 635, 597 S.E.2d 468 (2004) (no hearing necessary where undisputed facts in the record show that defendant waived or slept on his rights).

[21]Smith v. State, 263 Ga. App. 414, 416(1), 587 S.E.2d 787 (2003); Ray v. State, 287 Ga. App. 492, 652 S.E.2d 165 (2007).

[22]Johnson v. State, 275 Ga. 390, 565 S.E.2d 805 (2002).

[23]Ponder v. State, 164 Ga. App. 574, 298 S.E.2d 561 (1982).

[24]State v. Rimes, 177 Ga. App. 872, 341 S.E.2d 710 (1986).

[25]State v. Chambers, 194 Ga. App. 609, 391 S.E.2d 657 (1990).

does not get to reconsider the points raised eliminates the consideration of one person who could grant a new trial. Second, if there is a delay in obtaining the transcript, defense counsel must be careful to continue to obtain extensions of time in which to file the transcript before the time allowed expires.[26]

Although there is no federal constitutional right to a speedy appeal, there are circumstances where undue delay in the criminal appellate process can implicate the Due Process and Equal Protection Clauses of the Constitution. As the Georgia Court of Appeals observed in *Butler v. State*,[27] "[T]he balancing test adopted for speedy trial violations in *Barker v. Wingo*,[28] should be applied to situations in which a defendant claims that a delay in the appellate process is violative of due process of law. The four factors enunciated in *Barker* . . . are the length of delay, the reason for the delay and the defendant's assertion of his right, and prejudice to the defendant." Whether a defendant has been prejudiced by a delay in post conviction proceedings is tested by whether "there is a reasonable probability that, but for the delay, the result of the [proceedings] would have been different. A reasonable probability is a probability sufficient to undermine confidence in the outcome."[29]

If a motion for a new trial is filed and overruled, the defendant may have this decision, along with other alleged errors, reviewed by the filing of a notice of appeal.[30] A prematurely filed motion for new trial that sufficiently identifies the judgment involved becomes fully effective upon the entry of that judgment enabling the trial court, and ultimately the appellate court, pursuant to a properly filed notice of appeal, to review all the issues raised in the motion on their merits.[31] If a court fails to provide notice of one of its orders, the same should either be set aside and a new one entered from which the defendant may appeal or an out-of-time appeal should be allowed.[32] When the issue of notice becomes an issue in connection with a defendant's motion for an out of

[26]O.C.G.A. § 5-6-39, O.C.G.A. § 5-6-42.

[27]Butler v. State, 277 Ga. App. 57, 63-64 (5), 625 S.E.2d 458 (2005); Cail v. State, 287 Ga. App. 547(5), 652 S.E.2d 190 (2007).

[28]Barker v. Wingo, 407 U.S. 514, 92 S. Ct. 2182, 33 L. Ed. 2d 101 (1972).

[29]Chatman v. Mancill, 280 Ga. 253, 260-261(2)(e), 626 S.E.2d 102 (2006). See Chernowski v. State, 330 Ga. App. 702, 769 S.E.2d 126 (2015) ("speedy" appeal issue can arise in context of delay by clerk in assembling record).

[30]Cincinnati, N. O. & T. P. Ry. Co. v. Hilley, 121 Ga. App. 196, 197 (3), 173 S.E.2d 242 (1970).

[31]Southall v. State, 300 Ga. 462, 796 S.E.2d 261 (2017).

[32]See O.C.G.A. § 15-6-21(c) (court's duty to notify counsel of its decision); Williams v. State, 339 Ga. App. 158, 793 S.E.2d 485 (2016). See also Whitfield v. State, 313 Ga. App. 297, 721 S.E.2d 211 (2011). Compare Wright v. Young, 297 Ga. 683, 777 S.E.2d 475 (2015) (O.C.G.A. § 15-6-21(c) does not

time appeal, the court should make findings on the record as to whether notice was sent to the losing party.[33] However, a notice of appeal filed after a motion for a new trial is withdrawn without an order having been entered will not be timely if filed more than thirty days after sentence is imposed.[34]

In *Campbell v. State*,[35] the court held that where a defendant is sentenced in open court and thereafter files a notice of appeal, the notice of appeal is valid even though it is filed before the sentence is entered.

Because a guilty plea waives all defenses and objections, known or unknown, the general rule is that errors are not preserved for appeal.[36] However, in *Mims v. State*,[37] the Georgia Court of Appeals recognized the validity of an appeal from a conditional guilty plea. A conditional guilty plea permits a defendant to plead guilty to a charge and yet expressly reserve the right to appeal a specific adverse ruling. This reservation of the right to appeal is, however, at the discretion of the trial judge and must be agreed to by the state. Hence, "courts should precisely express on the record an approval of the reservation of appellate issues when exercising the discretion to accept the plea."[38] But, only three years later in *Hooten v. State*,[39] the same court held that it would no longer consider errors "preserved" by a conditional guilty plea, and that the rule prohibiting the acceptance of such conditional pleas (as was allowed in *Mims*) became effective as of July 9, 1994. See sections 16:14 and 16:15, supra.

In *Barber v. State*,[40] both the court and the defendant were unaware that the *Mims* plea was no longer available, but the court concluded that the defendant was entitled to withdraw such a plea, since the plea was not freely and voluntarily entered.

All murder convictions which are appealed are to go to the Georgia Supreme Court regardless of whether the defendant has

require court to set aside an order where court sent party notice which party claims it never received).

[33]Wright v. Young, 297 Ga. 683, 684 n. 3, 777 S.E.2d 475 (2015) (O.C.G.A. § 15-6-21(c) requires only that the court *send* the notice: it is not concerned with its receipt, disapproving cases holding that notice must be sent and received, e.g., Cambron v. Canal Ins. Co., 246 Ga. 147 (1), 269 S.E.2d 426 (1980)).

[34]Heard v. State, 274 Ga. 196, 197 (1), 552 S.E.2d 818 (2001).

[35]Campbell v. State, 178 Ga. App. 814 (1), 344 S.E.2d 745 (1986).

[36]Thomason v. Caldwell, 229 Ga. 637, 644, 194 S.E.2d 112 (1972); Polk v. Holland, 229 Ga. 169, 170 (2), 190 S.E.2d 35 (1972).

[37]Mims v. State, 201 Ga. App. 277, 278 (1), 410 S.E.2d 824 (1991). Cf. Chambers v. State, 210 Ga. App. 71, 435 S.E.2d 291 (1993).

[38]Springsteen v. State, 206 Ga. App. 150, 151, 424 S.E.2d 832 (1992).

[39]Hooten v. State, 212 Ga. App. 770, 775 (1), 442 S.E.2d 836 (1994).

[40]Barber v. State, 231 Ga. App. 176, 177 (2), 498 S.E.2d 758 (1998).

been sentenced to death or life imprisonment.[41]

In *Chambers v. State*,[42] the court held that a trial court has no jurisdiction to try and sentence a defendant before the remittitur from the appellate court is received and filed in the trial court, even where the appellate court has already ruled against the defendant on an interlocutory appeal. The court pointed out that this want of jurisdiction cannot be waived. In *Strickland v. State*,[43] the court held that the pending of an appeal merely deprives the trial court of its "power to execute the sentence," but does not *prevent* the court from entertaining the state's nolle prosequi petition or from amending its order denying a plea of former jeopardy, nunc pro tunc, to find the plea dilatory and frivolous.

In *Brooks v. State*,[44] the court held that the state has no right to cross appeal any issue other than those set out in § 28:4, supra.

See § 28:2, supra, on delay of an appeal as amounting to a due process violation. See § 28:10, supra, on matters which may be considered in a motion for a new trial.

§ 28:12 Extraordinary motion for new trial

An extraordinary motion for a new trial is one which is filed after the time fixed for the *filing of a regular motion* for a new trial.[1] Some good reason must be shown explaining the failure to file the motion within the usual time. These motions are not favored and are said to be addressed to the *sole* discretion of the trial judge.[2] The " 'trial court's authority to vacate or modify a judgment ends with the expiration of the term.' . . . This is so because courts must 'give stability to their decisions by maintaining the finality of the judgments.' . . . [C]ourts cannot at their pleasure reopen questions which have been concluded by solemn adjudication."[3]

The Georgia statute provides that only one extraordinary motion may be filed in a case. The defendant must give the opposite party 20 days notice of the motion.[4] The practical burden on the defendant is high.[5]

The usual ground stated for the filing of an extraordinary mo-

---

[41]Neal v. State, 290 Ga. 563, 722 S.E.2d 765 (2012).

[42]Chambers v. State, 262 Ga. 200, 415 S.E.2d 643 (1992).

[43]Strickland v. State, 258 Ga. 764, 765 (1), 373 S.E.2d 736 (1988). Cf. Isaac v. State, 237 Ga. App. 723, 726 (3), 516 S.E.2d 575 (1999).

[44]Brooks v. State, 206 Ga. App. 485, 489 (3), 425 S.E.2d 911 (1992).

[Section 28:12]
[1]See O.C.G.A. § 5-5-40, O.C.G.A. § 5-5-41.

[2]Van Scoik v. State, 142 Ga. App. 341, 235 S.E.2d 765 (1977).

[3]State v. Jones, 249 Ga. App. 199, 548 S.E.2d 29 (2001).

[4]O.C.G.A. § 5-5-41.

[5]See e.g. Davis v. State, 283 Ga. 438, 660 S.E.2d 354 (2008). Justice

tion for a new trial is the discovery of newly found evidence. The Georgia courts have held that in order to have an extraordinary motion for a new trial granted, "[i]t is incumbent on a party who asks for a new trial on the ground of newly discovered evidence to satisfy the court: (1) that the evidence has come to his knowledge since the trial;"[6] "(2) that it was not owing to the want of due diligence that he did not acquire it sooner;[7] (3) that it is so material that it would probably produce a different verdict;"[8] "(4) that it is not cumulative only;"[9] "(5) that the affidavit of the witness himself should be procured or its absence accounted for;" and "(6) that a new trial will not be granted if the only effect of the evidence will be to impeach the credit of a witness."[10] All six requirements must be complied with in order to secure a new trial. Hence, the failure to comply with one requirement is sufficient to justify the denial of a motion for a new trial. The burden is on the defendant to show that he has complied with each of the six requirements.[11] In addition to showing a compliance with these six requirements, if the motion is based on newly discovered evidence the defendant must "act without delay in bringing such a motion."[12] If the pleadings in an extraordinary motion for new trial fail to contain "a statement of *facts* sufficient to authorize

---

Sears was critical of the majority's failure to give serious consideration to newly discovered evidence and witness recantations.

[6]Timberlake v. State, 246 Ga. 488, 491, 271 S.E.2d 792 (1980). In Bradley v. State, 143 Ga. App. 767, 240 S.E.2d 124 (1977), the court said that if counsel for defendant was aware of a point when filing a motion for a new trial, which was not included in an ordinary motion for a new trial, he cannot later raise this point in an extraordinary motion.

[7]See Bharadia v. State, 297 Ga. 567, 774 S.E.2d 90 (2015).

[8]Timberlake v. State, 246 Ga. 488, 491, 271 S.E.2d 792 (1980); Garnto v. State, 247 Ga. 22, 273 S.E.2d 608 (1981).

[9]Timberlake v. State, 246 Ga. 488, 491, 271 S.E.2d 792 (1980). In Lee v. State, 146 Ga. App. 189, 193, 245 S.E.2d 878 (1978), the court said that testimony is not merely cumulative, even if it is very similar to other evidence, if it is of a higher and different grade from prior testimony. Thus,

where a witness was discovered who described a shooting much as the defendant had described it and none of the witnesses at the trial had corroborated the defendant's version of the incident, it was found to be error to refuse to grant an extraordinary motion for a new trial.

[10]Timberlake v. State, 246 Ga. 488, 491, 271 S.E.2d 792 (1980). See Sutton v. State, 295 Ga. 350, 759 S.E.2d 846 (2014) (GBI expert who testified at trial was later the subject of an investigation which concluded she had intentionally fabricated evidence in another case).

[11]Timberlake v. State, 246 Ga. 488, 491, 271 S.E.2d 792 (1980). See State v. Simmons, 321 Ga. App. 688, 742 S.E.2d 505 (2013); Burman & Fastman, "Newly Discovered Evidence—A Defendant's Chance for a New Trial," 28 N.Y. L. Sch. L. Rev. 31 (1983).

[12]Llewellyn v. State, 252 Ga. 426, 428 (2), 314 S.E.2d 227 (1984) (reason for requiring defendant to show that he acted with due diligence "is that litigation must come to an end").

that the motion be granted if the facts developed at the hearing warrant such relief, it is not error for the trial court to refuse to conduct a hearing on the extraordinary motion."[13]

O.C.G.A. § 5-5-41 allows for an extraordinary motion for new trial, based upon DNA evidence. In order to bring such a motion the petitioner must prove that the evidence was not tested at the time of trial, either "because the existence of evidence was un-known to the petitioner or to the petitioner's attorney prior to trial or because the technology for the testing was not available at the time of trial," and that identity of the convicted party was an important part of the trial.[14] A motion may also be granted even if testing has taken place if the proposed testing "would provide results that are reasonably more discriminating or proba-tive of the identity of the perpetrator than the prior test results." A hearing on a motion requesting DNA testing is unnecessary "if the DNA results hypothesized in a petitioner's motion, even when assumed valid, would not in reasonable probability have led to the petitioner's acquittal if those results had been available at trial . . . ."[15] However, pursuant to O.C.G.A. § 5-5-41(c)(12), fail-ure to set forth the rationale for the denial of such a motion or the denial of a request for a hearing on the motion is error.[16] An appeal taken from the denial of a motion requesting DNA testing should be by way of application for discretionary appeal.[17]

In *Riggins v. State*,[18] the trial judge was affirmed in denying an extraordinary motion where the newly discovered evidence came to the knowledge of the defendant during jury deliberations. The court pointed out that the defendant's "remedy was immediately to make a proffer of the evidence to the trial court and the cir-cumstances surrounding its belated discovery, and to move for the reopening of the evidence."

In *Hester v. State*,[19] the defendant made an extraordinary mo-tion for a new trial on the ground that he then had evidence which had not been available to him. That is, the defendant now had testimony of a co-defendant who invoked his Fifth Amend-ment right not to testify at the defendant's trial, but had since pled guilty. However, the court pointed out that there is a vast

---

[13]Dick v. State, 248 Ga. 898, 899 (2), 287 S.E.2d 11 (1982). See Davis v. State, 283 Ga. 438, 660 S.E.2d 354 (2008).

[14]See White v. State, 346 Ga. App. 448, 814 S.E.2d 447 (2018) (question is whether evidence is in a condition that would allow for testing; court need not consider the likelihood of whether DNA had deteriorated to point that testing would be fruitless).

[15]Crawford v. State, 278 Ga. 95, 97(2)(a), 597 S.E.2d 403 (2004).

[16]Johnson v. State, 272 Ga. App. 294, 612 S.E.2d 29 (2005).

[17]Crawford v. State, 278 Ga. 95(1), 597 S.E.2d 403 (2004).

[18]Riggins v. State, 230 Ga. App. 757, 759(2), 498 S.E.2d 117 (1998).

[19]Hester v. State, 219 Ga. App. 256(1), 465 S.E.2d 288 (1995).

difference between newly *discovered* evidence and newly *available* evidence: *First,* the testimony is not in fact new evidence since it was always known by the defendant. *Second,* "the once-unavailable defendant who now seeks to exculpate his co-defendant lacks credibility, since he has nothing to lose by testifying untruthfully regarding the alleged innocence of the defendant seeking a retrial." The court pointed out that "a defendant cannot postpone his trial until his co-defendant becomes 'available' after entering a plea or being convicted. . . ."

In addition to these hurdles, it has been held that newly discovered evidence must be admissible.[20] It should also be noted that a post-trial statement of a witness for the state that his trial testimony was false is not alone a ground for a new trial.[21] This rule seems to apply even if the state's key witness recants.[22] However, if the testimony of a material witness is a pure fabrication, the testimony is not regarded as merely impeaching; such testimony may entitle a defendant to a new trial.[23] In *Bennett v. State,*[24] the Georgia Supreme Court held that generally a void judgment was subject to attack at any time. However, because the courts have an interest in finality of judgments and where a period of years have elapsed, and where the state's conduct aided in causing the trial court to grant a new trial, the state will not be heard "to complain of or question on appeal a judgment which she invokes."

---

[20]Emmett v. State, 232 Ga. 110, 119, 205 S.E.2d 231 (1974). Here the Supreme Court affirmed the trial court's refusal to grant an extraordinary motion based on evidence that another person admitted committing the crime because the evidence was said to be inadmissible. In Scott v. State, 146 Ga. App. 25, 245 S.E.2d 360 (1978), the defendant made an extraordinary motion for a new trial based on the fact that she had taken and passed a polygraph examination since her conviction. In obiter dictum the court said that this could not be considered newly discovered evidence since it was not "valid evidence." However, in a similar case, the court did not mention inadmissibility of the evidence. Van Scoik v. State, 142 Ga. App. 341, 235 S.E.2d 765 (1977). Also see Dick v. State, 248 Ga. 898, 900, 287 S.E.2d 11 (1982).

[21]Richey v. State, 132 Ga. App. 188, 207 S.E.2d 672 (1974). See Cooper v. State, 287 Ga. 861, 862 (3), 700 S.E.2d 593 (2010) ("A post-trial statement purporting to state that trial testimony was false is merely impeaching of the trial testimony and insufficient to require a new trial in the absence of evidence that the trial testimony was the purest fabrication.").

[22]Drake v. State, 248 Ga. 891, 287 S.E.2d 180 (1982); Colquitt v. State, 213 Ga. App. 789, 790 (2), 446 S.E.2d 247 (1994).

[23]Fugitt v. State, 251 Ga. 451, 453, 307 S.E.2d 471 (1983); Anderson v. State, 276 Ga. App. 216, 622 S.E.2d 898 (2005).

[24]Bennett v. State, 268 Ga. 849, 494 S.E.2d 330 (1998).

In *Logan v. State*,[25] the court pointed out that provision "is made for setting aside verdicts resting on perjury, but there must first be a conviction" for perjury.

Finally, in *Pitts v. State*,[26] the court held that where there is an appeal from the denial of an extraordinary motion for a new trial, the appellant must file an application to appeal pursuant to O.C.G.A. § 5-6-35.

§ 28:13 Motion in arrest of judgment

It has been held that a motion in arrest of judgment must be filed at the term of court during which the judgment complained of was entered.[1] The motion need not be resolved or even heard during the term. Timely filing, however, is required.[2]

A motion in arrest of judgment will lie when there is a defect on the face of the record.[3] In criminal cases, the "face of the record" is composed of the (1) indictment, (2) plea, (3) verdict, and (4) judgment,[4] and only these four items are to be considered.[5] A motion in arrest of judgment lies only for some matter "affecting the real merits of the offense charged"[6] as the same is reflected on the face of the record, with the evidence in the case not being considered.[7]

It has been said that a motion in arrest of judgment must be predicated on some non-amendable defect appearing on the face

---

[25]Logan v. State, 212 Ga. App. 734, 738 (2), 442 S.E.2d 883 (1994).

[26]Pitts v. State, 254 Ga. 298, 328 S.E.2d 732 (1985); McDonald v. State, 180 Ga. App. 713, 350 S.E.2d 581 (1986).

[Section 28:13]

[1]O.C.G.A. § 17-9-61. See Spence v. State, 7 Ga. App. 825, 68 S.E. 443 (1910); Lacey v. State, 253 Ga. 711, 324 S.E.2d 471 (1985).

See Bonner v. State, 268 Ga. App. 170, 171 (1), 601 S.E.2d 478 (2004): "The authority for withdrawal in the same term of a plea of guilty after judgment is judicial in origin, and generally refers to an attack on a plea for defects dehors the record, as where the plea was rendered through mistake or undue influence. The statutory authority for modifications of criminal judgment is O.C.G.A. §§ 17-9-60 et seq., which authorizes a motion in arrest of judgment. A motion for arrest

of judgment, like a motion for withdrawal of a plea, must be made at the same term the judgment was obtained . . . and addresses only a non-amendable defect on the face of the record."

[2]State v. Fredericks, 256 Ga. App. 401, 568 S.E.2d 489 (2002)

[3]Hall v. State, 202 Ga. 42, 46, 42 S.E.2d 130 (1947); Darsey v. State, 17 Ga. App. 280, 86 S.E. 781 (1915).

[4]Gunn v. State, 227 Ga. 786, 787 (3), 183 S.E.2d 389 (1971).

[5]McClendon v. State, 81 Ga. App. 218, 219 (3), 58 S.E.2d 462 (1950); Pippin v. State, 172 Ga. 224 (1), 157 S.E. 185 (1931).

[6]O.C.G.A. § 17-9-63.

[7]Sessions v. State, 3 Ga. App. 13, 14 (1)(a), 59 S.E. 196 (1907). A motion for a new trial considers the evidence which was introduced.

of the record.[8] However, this statement may not be completely accurate, since an accusation is generally regarded as being, to some extent, amendable prior to verdict,[9] and a motion in arrest of judgment will lie in a case where there is a fatal defect in the accusation.[10] Perhaps the situation may be explained by saying that a motion for arrest of judgment will lie if the defect cannot be corrected by amendment at the time of the filing of the motion in arrest of judgment, or by saying that an accusation which is fatally defective may not be amended[11] and hence, a motion in arrest of judgment will lie.

After verdict, the indictment as well as the other documents which make up the face of the record are construed in favor of the state, and every presumption and inference is in favor of the verdict.[12] A motion in arrest of judgment because of a defect in an indictment may be filed even though the defendant did not file a demurrer to test the legal sufficiency of the indictment.[13] Yet, even if a demurrer to the indictment would have been good, it does not necessarily mean that the motion in arrest is valid.[14] Such a motion does not lie "for any matter not affecting the real merits of the offense charged."[15] However, the Georgia Supreme Court has said that a motion for arrested judgment is good if a general demurrer would have been valid.[16]

In the following situations it has been held that a motion in arrest of judgment was good: (1) Where a bigamy indictment failed to allege that the defendant had knowledge that his spouse was alive;[17] (2) Where an indictment for attempted burglary failed to allege any overt act;[18] (3) Where a defendant was charged with

---

[8]Smith v. State, 17 Ga. App. 612 (1), 87 S.E. 846 (1916).

[9]See § 13:23, supra.

[10]See Gilbert v. State, 17 Ga. App. 143 (4), (5), 86 S.E. 415 (1915).

[11]See §§ 13:20 and 13:23, supra.

[12]Lewis v. State, 55 Ga. App. 743, 744 (4), 191 S.E. 278 (1937).

[13]Register v. State, 65 Ga. App. 64 (2), 15 S.E.2d 251 (1941).

[14]Martin v. State, 95 Ga. 478 (1), 20 S.E. 271 (1894). As a matter of fact, if a motion in arrest of judgment successfully attacks an indictment, the indictment could have been attacked earlier by a valid demurrer. McClendon v. State, 81 Ga. App. 218 (2), 58 S.E.2d 462 (1950).

[15]Lampkin v. State, 87 Ga. 516, 523, 13 S.E. 523 (1891).

[16]Bramblett v. State, 239 Ga. 336, 338, 236 S.E.2d 580 (1977). Questioning of the constitutionality of a statute upon which the indictment is based must be timely and cannot be raised after the jury returns a guilty verdict. Hardeman v. State, 272 Ga. 361, 362, 529 S.E.2d 368 (2000). However, a constitutional challenge to the sentence to be imposed following conviction is timely if made after verdict but prior to sentencing. Woods v. State, 279 Ga. 28 (1), 608 S.E.2d 631 (2005).

[17]Herrin v. State, 27 Ga. App. 189, 107 S.E. 779 (1921).

[18]Ligon v. State, 25 Ga. App. 306 (2), 103 S.E. 189 (1920).

rape and was convicted of fornication;[19] (4) Where an indictment showed that the offense was barred by the statute of limitations, and no exception to the statute of limitations was alleged;[20] (5) Where the defendant was charged with a felony and the jury returned a "verdict" finding him guilty of a misdemeanor;[21] and (6) Where the defendant is tried in superior court on a uniform traffic ticket rather than on indictment or accusation.[22]

A motion in arrest of judgment has been held invalid in the following situations: (1) Where the record did not show that the defendant was present when sentence was pronounced;[23] (2) Where the indictment, because of a clerical error, used the word "accused" for the word "prosecutor";[24] (3) Where an indictment charging murder was returned as "true bill for voluntary manslaughter";[25] (4) Where an indictment alleged an impossible date or a date after the day the indictment was returned;[26] and (5) Where the defendant was charged with the misdemeanor of assault without specifying any act or acts constituting an assault.[27]

A motion in arrest of judgment which has been granted because of a defect in the indictment will not prevent the defendant from being re-indicted and re-tried.[28]

§ 28:14 Motion to set judgment aside

The only remedies for challenging a conviction after it has been affirmed on direct appeal are by way of: an extraordinary motion for new trial, O.C.G.A. § 5-5-41; a motion in arrest of judgment, O.C.G.A. § 17-9-61; or a petition for habeas corpus, O.C.G.A. § 9-14-40. *Chester v. State*,[1] which had recognized a motion to vacate judgment as a remedy to correct a void sentence, was overruled

---

[19]Holland v. State, 161 Ga. 492, 131 S.E. 503 (1926). The same rule applies when a defendant is convicted of any crime not charged in the indictment which is not a lesser included offense of the one charged. See Waller v. State, 107 Ga. App. 609, 131 S.E.2d 111 (1963).

[20]McLane v. State, 4 Ga. 335 (2) (1848); and see Hollingsworth v. State, 7 Ga. App. 16 (3), 65 S.E. 1077 (1909).

[21]Wells v. State, 116 Ga. 87, 89, 42 S.E. 390 (1902).

[22]Stone v. State, 151 Ga. App. 531, 260 S.E.2d 405 (1979).

[23]Rawlins v. Mitchell, 127 Ga. 24 (2), 55 S.E. 958 (1906).

[24]Lewis v. State, 55 Ga. App. 743 (3), 191 S.E. 278 (1937).

[25]Williams v. State, 13 Ga. App. 83, 78 S.E. 854 (1913).

[26]Dicta, Harris v. State, 58 Ga. 332 (2) (1877).

[27]Scott v. State, 35 Ga. App. 591, 134 S.E. 335 (1926).

[28]Hill v. Nelms, 122 Ga. 572, 50 S.E. 344 (1905). The same rule, of course, applies to a void accusation. Renfroe v. State, 10 Ga. App. 38 (1), 72 S.E. 520 (1911).

[Section 28:14]

[1]Chester v. State, 284 Ga. 162, 664 S.E.2d 220 (2008).

in *Harper v. State*.[2]

§ 28:15 Coram nobis

This method of review is included in this material principally to point out another possible means of obtaining judicial review.[1]

There have been a number of Georgia cases which have said that a party has a right to seek judicial review by a writ of error coram nobis.[2] However, it has been held that this common law writ, which is a part of Georgia law, will not lie where the party has an adequate statutory remedy.[3]

The Georgia Supreme Court has stated that the writ of coram nobis, in the states which have granted it, lies to correct "an error of fact not apparent on the record, not attributable to the accused's negligence and which, if before the court, would have prevented rendition of the judgment."[4] The court also pointed out that insofar as it has been able to ascertain, the writ has never actually been granted in Georgia.[5] The court concluded that the particular case under consideration did not involve an error in the facts of the case but a change in criminal procedure, thus making the writ of coram nobis inapplicable.

In *Waye v. State*,[6] the court indicated that this writ does not lie unless an extraordinary motion for a new trial based on newly discovered evidence would be appropriate, and hinted that this writ is inappropriate and obsolete, and should not be used in the future.

---

[2]Harper v. State, 286 Ga. 216, 686 S.E.2d 786 (2009). See Williams v. State, 287 Ga. 192, 695 S.E.2d 244 (2010) (*Harper* also applies to challenges to an illegal sentence).

[Section 28:15]

[1]For an interesting 60-page annotation, see "Availability Under 28 USCS § 1651 of Writ of Error Coram Nobis to Vacate Federal Conviction Where Sentence Has Been Served," 38 A.L.R.Fed. 617 (1978).

[2]E.g., Miraglia v. Bryson, 152 Ga. 828 (3)(b), 111 S.E. 655 (1922); South v. State, 72 Ga. App. 79 (1), 33 S.E.2d 23 (1945).

[3]Randall v. Whitman, 88 Ga. App. 803 (1), 78 S.E.2d 78 (1953); and cf. Riley v. State, 107 Ga. App. 639, 131 S.E.2d 124 (1963).

[4]Harris v. State, 225 Ga. 458, 461 (1), 169 S.E.2d 331 (1969).

[5]Harris v. State, 225 Ga. 458, 461 (1), 169 S.E.2d 331 (1969). However, since the Harris case, the writ was granted in the trial court in State v. Asinoff, 173 Ga. App. 573, 327 S.E.2d 237 (1985).

[6]Waye v. State, 239 Ga. 871, 873, 238 S.E.2d 923 (1977). In Grant v. State, 159 Ga. App. 2, 4, 282 S.E.2d 668 (1981), the court said that "a writ of error coram nobis . . . [is] an ancestor of the current extraordinary motion for a new trial." See Clemmons v. State, 340 Ga. App. 57, 796 S.E.2d 297 (2017) (this obsolete writ is "the ancestor of an extraordinary motion for new trial based on newly-discovered evidence").

§ 28:16 Petition to release insolvent

As previously noted, the imposition of a fine on indigents may amount to cruel and unusual punishment.[1] Georgia enacted a statute which addressed itself to the same situation long before the equal protection and cruel and unusual punishment provisions of the law were applied to the area of state fines.[2] Former GCA section 27-2804 provided as follows:

"If any prisoner in the common jail, after the time of his imprisonment expires, or otherwise, is detained merely until his costs, or his fine and costs, are paid, and the probate judge is satisfied that he is unable to pay the costs and fine, or either of them, said probate judge may discharge him from further confinement."

According to the Georgia Code Annotated, only one case[3] ever cited former GCA section 27-2804, and no decisions have been handed down by our appellate courts which have discussed or turned on the statute.

§ 28:17 State habeas corpus[1]

O.C.G.A. § 9-14-1 was enacted in 1967 to provide for state habeas corpus relief and states the following:

"(a) Any person restrained of his liberty under any pretext whatsoever, except under sentence of a state court of record, may seek a writ of habeas corpus to inquire into the legality of the restraint.

"(b) Any person alleging that another person in whom for any cause he is interested is kept illegally from the custody of the applicant may seek a writ of habeas corpus to inquire into the legality of the restraint.

"(c) Any person restrained of his liberty as a result of a sentence imposed by any state court of record may seek a writ of habeas corpus to inquire into the legality of the restraint."

As a general proposition, an individual must bring a writ for habeas relief within one year in the case of a misdemeanor, and

---

[Section 28:16]

[1]See §§ 26:4 and 26:15, supra.

[2]GCA § 27-2804 was enacted in 1861 and was not carried forward into the O.C.G.A.

[3]Lumpkin County v. Davis, 185 Ga. 393, 395 (4), 195 S.E. 169 (1938).

[Section 28:17]

[1]Generally, on Georgia habeas corpus, see the material of Thomas K. McWhorter, 14 E. G. L. Habeas Corpus (1999 Rev.).

Wilkes, "Postconviction Habeas Corpus Relief in Georgia: A Decade After the Habeas Corpus Act," 12 Ga. L. Rev. 249 (1978); Wilkes, "A New Role for an Ancient Writ: Postconviction Habeas Corpus Relief in Georgia (Part I)," 8 Ga. L. R. 313 (1974); (Part II), 9 Ga. L. R. 13 (1974).

four years in the case of a felony, from when their conviction becomes "final by the conclusion of direct review or the expiration of time for seeking such review. . . ."[2] There are several additional events beyond the conclusion of direct review that may also mark the start of this statute of limitations pursuant to O.C.G.A. § 9-14-42(c).[3]

In cases involving persons under sentence of a state court of record the petition must be brought in the county in which the petitioner is detained.[4] The petition should be verified, identify the proceeding in which the petitioner was convicted and clearly set forth "the respects in which the petitioner's rights were violated. . . . The petition shall identify any previous proceedings that the petitioner may have taken to secure relief from his or her conviction."[5] In cases involving a challenge to a Georgia conviction by a petitioner who is not incarcerated by the Georgia Department of Corrections, the petition should be filed against the State of Georgia.

In cases where the petitioner is not in custody or "is being detained under the authority of the United States, any of the several states other than Georgia, or any foreign state, the petition must be filed in the superior court of the county in which the conviction and sentence which is being challenged was imposed."[6] In cases where a custodial petitioner is transferred for detention in another county for legitimate or routine reasons, the case will be transferred to the new county since venue generally lies where the actual detention exists.[7]

In *Derrer v. Anthony*,[8] the court held that a habeas petition is not subject to dismissal on the ground that a constitutional viola-

---

[2]O.C.G.A. § 9-14-42(c). The court is also required to inform a defendant at sentencing of the periods of limitation applicable to a habeas petition.

[3]O.C.G.A. § 9-14-42(c) provides, inter alia, that the period of limitations for bringing a petition will also begin to run from the date on which the right asserted was first recognized by the Supreme Court of Georgia or the Supreme Court of the United States; and, from the date on which the facts supporting the petition could have been discovered. See Abrams v. Laughlin, 304 Ga. 34, 816 S.E.2d 26 (2018).

[4]O.C.G.A. § 9-14-43.

[5]O.C.G.A. § 9-14-44. In the event relief is granted, the filing of a notice of appeal shall operate as supersedeas.

Bond pending appeal can be obtained only in the court which rendered the judgment of conviction. O.C.G.A. § 9-14-52(c); O'Donnell v. Durham, 275 Ga. 860, 573 S.E.2d 23 (2002).

[6]O.C.G.A. § 9-14-43. See Hughes v. State, 259 Ga. 227, 378 S.E.2d 853 (1989).

[7]Preer v. Johnson, 279 Ga. 90, 610 S.E.2d 46 (2005). See Wilkes v. Terry, 290 Ga. 54, 717 S.E.2d 644 (2011) (decision to transfer venue is within trial court's discretion and transfer is not required solely on ground that petitioner's place of confinement is moved out of county after the petition is filed).

[8]Derrer v. Anthony, 265 Ga. 892, 894, 463 S.E.2d 690 (1995).

tion is not charged.

In *McDuffie v. Jones*,[9] the Georgia Supreme Court, in discussing the scope of the Georgia Habeas Corpus Act, stated that habeas corpus is appropriate where the defendant's conviction resulted from a substantial denial[10] of his rights under (1) the United States Constitution, or (2) the Constitution of the State of Georgia.[11] In the same decision the court outlined the steps to be followed in determining whether or not a petition should be granted: "[T]he threshold inquiry should be to ascertain whether the right asserted arises under the federal constitution, the state constitution, or state law. The next step in habeas corpus would be to see if waiver, under the corresponding standard, has occurred. In the absence of waiver the third step would be to determine if the habeas petitioner's rights were violated. If so, the final step would be to determine whether the error was harmless under the appropriate standard. We will examine each of petitioner's claims using this four step analysis."

A habeas corpus proceeding is not regarded as a criminal action.[12] The burden of proof is on the defendant to establish his claim by a preponderance of the evidence.[13] Although there is a mandatory hearing requirement provided by O.C.G.A. § 9-14-47, the State is under no obligation to produce the petitioner in court unless the petitioner is in the custody of the State or some other authority subject to the jurisdiction of the habeas court. The failure of a habeas petitioner to be present at the hearing may subject the petitioner to the same sanctions as any other civil litigant under O.C.G.A. § 9-11-41(b). Nonetheless, it is not absolutely necessary that the petitioner attend the hearing. Evidence may be presented through deposition, sworn affidavits, oral testimony or in any other proper form.[14] O.C.G.A. § 9-14-50 mandates that habeas corpus trials be transcribed and, if the petitioner is indigent, at state expense.[15] Ordinarily a petitioner for a writ of habeas corpus is not entitled to have counsel ap-

---

[9]McDuffie v. Jones, 248 Ga. 544, 283 S.E.2d 601 (1981), overruled on other grounds by West v. Waters, 272 Ga. 591, 533 S.E.2d 88 (2000).

[10]O.C.G.A. § 9-14-42.

[11]Parker v. Abernathy, 253 Ga. 673, 674, 324 S.E.2d 191 (1985).

[12]Hatton v. Smith, 228 Ga. 378, 185 S.E.2d 388 (1971).

[13]Stynchcombe v. Rhodes, 238 Ga. 74, 231 S.E.2d 63 (1976).

[14]Rickett v. State, 276 Ga. 609, 581 S.E.2d 32 (2003). See House v. Stynchcombe, 239 Ga. 222(1), 236 S.E.2d 353 (1977). But see Dickens v. State, 280 Ga. 320, 627 S.E.2d 587 (2006), where several justices were highly critical of an ineffective claim presented only through the proffer of the habeas attorney of what witnesses would have said and without any evidence either by way of live witnesses or in affidavit form.

[15]Flint v. State, 745 S.E.2d 277 (Ga. 2010) (O.C.G.A. § 9-14-50 is *mandatory* and not directory).

pointed to represent him.[16] See § 28:20, infra, on right of counsel in habeas corpus proceeding. When counsel is appointed for such a petitioner a trial judge has no authority to award attorney's fees to be paid out of state or county funds.[17] Likewise, it has been held that a petitioner for "habeas corpus is not constitutionally entitled to funds for investigation or litigation relating to his petition."[18]

A habeas corpus action is not to be thought of as a substitute for an appeal.[19] Indeed, a habeas court has no jurisdiction to authorize an out of time appeal.[20] An appeal seeks appellate review of the record in the trial court. When the claims can not be resolved without an expansion of the existing record, the remedy is a habeas corpus petition.[21]

It has been held that the failure of a petitioner "to pursue an appeal did not, ipso facto, render habeas corpus an '[in]appropriate remedy.' "[22] It will lie (1) where the court does not have jurisdiction to try the offense, (2) where the sentence was not authorized,[23] or (3) where the defendant was denied a fundamental constitutional right.[24] For example, a petitioner may allege that (a) he was deprived of the effective assistance of counsel;[25] (b) his guilty plea was not intelligently and voluntarily entered;[26] (c) he was not advised of his right to confront adverse witnesses or his

---

[16]O'Neal v. Caldwell, 231 Ga. 608, 203 S.E.2d 191 (1974); Jones v. Caldwell, 230 Ga. 775, 776 (3), 199 S.E.2d 248 (1973). In Johnson v. Avery, 393 U.S. 483, 488, 89 S.Ct. 747, 21 L.Ed.2d 718, 722 (1969), the Court said, "It has not been held that there is any general obligation of the courts, state or federal, to appoint counsel for prisoners who indicate, without more, that they wish to seek post-conviction relief." However, under the Federal Criminal Justice Act of 1970, counsel may be appointed in collateral proceedings. 18 U.S.C.A. § 3006A.

[17]Willis v. Price, 256 Ga. 767, 353 S.E.2d 488 (1987).

[18]Johnson v. Zant, 249 Ga. 812, 819 (11), 295 S.E.2d 63 (1982).

[19]Green v. Green, 231 Ga. 311, 312, 201 S.E.2d 440 (1973); Moye v. Hopper, 234 Ga. 230, 231, 214 S.E.2d 920 (1975).

[20]Milliken v. State, 259 Ga. App. 144, 575 S.E.2d 910 (2003).

[21]Rutledge v. State, 340 Ga. App.

765, 798 S.E.2d 355 (2017).

[22]Lewis v. Ford, 248 Ga. 820, 821, 286 S.E.2d 714 (1982).

[23]See Grimes v. Harvey, 219 Ga. 675, 676, 135 S.E.2d 281 (1964).

[24]14 E. G. L. Habeas Corpus (1999 Rev.), § 8.

[25]Graddy v. Hopper, 233 Ga. 65, 66 (2), 209 S.E.2d 636 (1974). In Williams v. Hopper, 243 Ga. 475, 254 S.E.2d 854 (1979), the petitioner had been convicted of robbery and was serving a 20-year sentence. He requested his retained counsel to appeal the case but no appeal was filed because his attorney was not paid. However, counsel failed to notify petitioner that he was withdrawing until long after the time for an appeal had expired. The court held that the facts demanded a finding that petitioner had been denied his right to counsel, reversed the habeas court and granted petitioner an out of time appeal.

[26]Dix v. Zant, 249 Ga. 810, 811, 294 S.E.2d 527 (1982); Capps v. Ault,

privilege against self-incrimination should he elect to proceed to trial;[27] or (d) the city ordinance under which he was sentenced was void.[28] Relief may also be sought by habeas corpus (4) where the defendant alleges that he was convicted of violating an unconstitutional statute, even if this issue has not been raised in a trial court before;[29] (5) where there is a *substantive* defect in the indictment on which the defendant was tried such that it failed to allege conduct which constituted a crime;[30] (6) where a prisoner is confined under a sentence longer than permitted by state statute;[31] and (7) where a prisoner is unlawfully confined beyond the term of his sentence.[32]

Habeas corpus relief will also be available in those cases where, after conviction and appeal, a defendant can establish that the law under which he was sentenced has been the subject of a new rule of substantive criminal law. For example, in *Brewer v. State*,[33] the Supreme Court ruled that the State could no longer prove the essential element of force simply by establishing the victim was a minor in an aggravated sodomy case. Instead, the Court ruled that proof of actual force was required even in cases involving victims under the age of consent.

In *Luke v. Battle*,[34] the habeas petitioner claimed that *Brewer* constituted a substantial change in the law that should be applied retroactively to reach his case. Agreeing, the court ruled that *Brewer* had effected a substantive change in the law and not merely in procedure. Had the court ruled otherwise and determined that *Brewer* was only of procedural consequence, Luke's habeas petition would have been denied under the "pipeline rule" which provides relief only to those cases on direct review or which are not yet final and would not apply to cases on collateral review, such as those in which habeas relief is sought.[35]

However, a habeas corpus action will not lie (1) to modify a

---

229 Ga. 873, 874, 195 S.E.2d 22 (1972).

[27]E.g., Bowers v. Moore, 266 Ga. 893, 471 S.E.2d 869 (1996) (overruled on other grounds by, Lejeune v. McLaughlin, 296 Ga. 291, 766 S.E.2d 803 (2014)).

[28]Giles v. Gibson, 208 Ga. 850, 69 S.E.2d 774 (1952).

[29]Hammock v. Zant, 243 Ga. 259, 253 S.E.2d 727 (1979). See Class v. U.S., 138 S. Ct. 798, 200 L. Ed. 2d 37 (2018) (negotiated guilty plea does not bar defendant from challenging the constitutionality of the statute of conviction).

[30]Hopper v. Hampton, 244 Ga.

361, 260 S.E.2d 73 (1979) (dicta).

[31]Manville v. Hampton, 266 Ga. 857, 858 (1), 471 S.E.2d 872 (1996).

[32]Lillard v. Head, 267 Ga. 291, 476 S.E.2d 736 (1996).

[33]Brewer v. State, 271 Ga. 605, 607, 523 S.E.2d 18 (1999).

[34]Luke v. Battle, 275 Ga. 370, 565 S.E.2d 816 (2002).

[35]See Luke v. Battle, 275 Ga. 370, 565 S.E.2d 816 (2002) for a thorough discussion of the difference between a "substantive" and "procedural" change in the law and the consequences thereof. See also Taylor v. State, 262 Ga. 584, 422 S.E.2d 430 (1992) (to

condition of probation believed to be illegal;[36] (2) to petition for "good time allowance" not received;[37] (3) to review the sufficiency of evidence supporting a probation revocation;[38] (4) to attack the treatment, discipline or conditions of confinement; or (5) to assert a pre-trial claim of ineffective assistance of counsel.[39] In *Littles v. Balkcom*,[40] the court held that the question of the sufficiency of the evidence to convict could not be raised in a state habeas corpus action. This decision does not appear to be sound.[41] It should also be kept in mind that regardless of whether or not the Georgia Supreme Court will grant relief in a state habeas corpus action in such a situation, the sufficiency of the evidence may be reviewed in a federal habeas corpus action if the point has been properly raised in a state proceeding.[42]

Jury instructions are generally not reviewable on habeas corpus.[43] However, in 1977 the Georgia Supreme Court held that charges which are fundamentally unfair may be reviewed even though not objected to at trial.[44] Also, in a death case the sentencing charge is regarded as so critical to the outcome of the trial that the court will consider jury instructions even though not objected to at the trial.[45]

---

qualify for the "pipeline rule," the claim must have been preserved for appellate review at trial). See § 14:64, supra, on retroactive application of new rules of criminal law.

[36]Dean v. Whalen, 234 Ga. 182, 183, 215 S.E.2d 7 (1975).

[37]Forbes v. Ricketts, 234 Ga. 316, 216 S.E.2d 82 (1975).

[38]Kreps v. Gray, 234 Ga. 745, 746, 218 S.E.2d 1 (1975).

[39]Myers v. St. Lawrence, 289 Ga. 240, 710 S.E.2d 557 (2011).

[40]Littles v. Balkcom, 245 Ga. 285, 264 S.E.2d 219 (1980). See also Stephens v. Balkcom, 245 Ga. 492 (1), 265 S.E.2d 596 (1980).

In DeFrancis v. Manning, 246 Ga. 307, 271 S.E.2d 209 (1980), the court held that the trial judge properly released the defendant pursuant to a habeas corpus action where he was charged with burglary of a truck and there was no evidence showing that anyone used the truck as a dwelling. The court said the release was mandatory under the due process clause of the Fourteenth Amendment.

[41]See Justice Hill's dissent in Littles v. Balkcom, 245 Ga. 285, 288, 264 S.E.2d 219 (1980). In Littles v. DeFrancis, 517 F.Supp. 1137 (M.D.Ga. 1981), the court quoted at length from Justice Hill's dissent in Littles v. Balkcom, 245 Ga. 285, 288, 264 S.E.2d 219 (1980), and granted Little's petition for federal habeas corpus.

[42]However, in Jackson v. Virginia, 443 U.S. 307, 99 S.Ct. 2781, 61 L.Ed.2d 560 (1979), reh. denied, 444 U.S. 890, 100 S.Ct. 195, 62 L.Ed.2d 126 (1979), the court held that in a federal habeas corpus the court may determine the sufficiency of the evidence. See Comment, Federal Review of the Evidence supporting State Convictions: Jackson v. Virginia, 79 Columbia L. Rev. 1577 (1979).

[43]See Byrd v. Hopper, 234 Ga. 248, 215 S.E.2d 251 (1975).

[44]Parrish v. Hopper, 238 Ga. 468 (1), 233 S.E.2d 161 (1977).

[45]Stephens v. Hopper, 241 Ga. 596, 602 (3), 247 S.E.2d 92 (1978).

In *Black v. Hardin*,[46] the Georgia Supreme Court said that the present rule is as follows: "A failure to make timely objection to *any* alleged error or deficiency or to pursue the same on appeal ordinarily will preclude review by writ of habeas corpus. However, an otherwise valid procedural bar will not preclude a habeas corpus court from considering alleged constitutional errors or deficiencies if there shall be a showing of adequate cause for failure to object or to pursue on appeal *and* a showing of actual prejudice to the accused. Even absent such a showing of cause and prejudice, the relief of the writ will remain available to avoid a miscarriage of justice where there has been a substantial denial of constitutional rights."

Generally, a petition for habeas corpus may not be filed until the conviction is final.[47] Thus, it has been held that such a petition is not valid if it is filed while petition for writ of certiorari is pending in the United States Supreme Court.[48] The Georgia Supreme Court "has not applied the doctrine of laches to habeas corpus cases."[49]

A habeas corpus proceeding may be brought to attack the validity of a sentence, which has already been served, if the petitioner can show that he is suffering from collateral consequence because of the conviction, e.g., where it is used to enhance the petitioner's sentence in a subsequent case.[50] If a defendant is convicted of several charges and incorrectly sentenced to consecutive sentences, he may raise this issue on habeas corpus.[51] Likewise, a defendant serving two concurrent sentences may attack one of them by habeas corpus since both convictions would delay his consideration for parole.[52] A habeas corpus petitioner may attack a future consecutive sentence even before he begins serving it.[53] A petition for habeas corpus will lie even where a

---

[46]Black v. Hardin, 255 Ga. 239, 240 (5), 336 S.E.2d 754 (1985); Schofield v. Meders, 280 Ga. 865, 632 S.E.2d 369 (2006).

[47]Kearse v. Paulk, 264 Ga. 509, 448 S.E.2d 369 (1994).

[48]Horton v. Wilkes, 250 Ga. 902, 302 S.E.2d 94 (1983).

[49]Zant v. Cook, 259 Ga. 299, 300 (1), 379 S.E.2d 780 (1989).

[50]Parris v. State, 232 Ga. 687, 688, 208 S.E.2d 493 (1974). See Ritchie v. State, 257 Ga. App. 149, 150, 570 S.E.2d 435 (2002) (a party proves adverse collateral consequences by showing "a substantial stake in the judgment of conviction which survives the satisfaction of the sentence").

[51]Johnson v. Caldwell, 232 Ga. 200, 201 (5), 205 S.E.2d 857 (1974); and see Middlebrook v. Allen, 234 Ga. 481, 216 S.E.2d 331 (1975).

[52]Jones v. Hopper, 233 Ga. 531, 532, 212 S.E.2d 367 (1975) (here there were two life sentences); Atkins v. Hopper, 234 Ga. 330, 331 (2), 216 S.E.2d 89 (1975) (here there was one life sentence and a 10-year sentence).

[53]Middlebrook v. Allen, 234 Ga. 481, 216 S.E.2d 331 (1975). See Hollis v. Allen, 235 Ga. 211, 212, 219 S.E.2d 108 (1975).

defendant has already completed a felony sentence.[54] In *Hicks v. Scott*,[55] the court held that a superior court has jurisdiction to hear a petition for habeas corpus where the petitioner is a federal prisoner in Georgia and the defendant's sentence in state court was used in the later federal case to enhance his federal sentence because the state conviction allegedly resulted from ineffective assistance of counsel.

If a sentence entered on a plea or a conviction is found to be null and void, the effect of this finding may not be limited by the court.[56]

In 1973, the Georgia legislature enacted a provision which is now O.C.G.A. § 9-14-51, providing that:

> All grounds for relief claimed by a petitioner for a writ of habeas corpus shall be raised by a petitioner in his original or amended petition. Any grounds not so raised are waived unless the Constitution of the United States or of this state otherwise requires or unless any judge to whom the petition is assigned, on considering a subsequent petition, finds grounds for relief asserted therein which could not reasonably have been raised in the original or amended petition.[57]

However, in 1982, this statute was changed so as to add a provision stating that habeas relief shall not be granted if no timely motion or objection was made at trial unless a showing of cause for such non-compliance is made. See O.C.G.A. § 9-14-48.

In 1995, the governor signed into law Georgia's Death Penalty Reform Act of 1995.[58] This Act amends O.C.G.A. § 9-14-44 and changes the required contents of certain state habeas corpus petitions.[59] The Act also "provides for comprehensive procedures with respect to challenging for the first time state court proceedings resulting in a death sentence[60] and requires the establishment of uniform court rules of certain time periods and schedules

---

[54]See Nix v. State, 233 Ga. 73, 75, 209 S.E.2d 597 (1974).

[55]Hicks v. Scott, 273 Ga. 358, 541 S.E.2d 27 (2001) (overruled on other grounds by, Crosson v. Conway, 291 Ga. 220, 728 S.E.2d 617 (2012)).

[56]Cooper v. State, 245 Ga. 60, 262 S.E.2d 816 (1980).

[57]Stevens v. Kemp, 254 Ga. 228, 230 (1), 327 S.E.2d 185 (1985). The United States Supreme Court has held that a state may properly require that a prisoner seeking post-conviction relief assert all known constitutional claims in a single case. Murch v. Mottram, 409 U.S. 41, 93 S.Ct. 71, 34 L.Ed.2d 194 (1972).

However, in Coker v. Hopper, 241 Ga. 288, 244 S.E.2d 873 (1978), the court said that if a habeas corpus petition is filed but is not considered on its merits, a later petition on the same grounds is not a successive petition and petitioner is entitled to a hearing on it.

[58]Ga. Laws 1995, p. 381, § 1 of the Act, which gives the statute its name, is uncodified.

[59]Ga. Laws 1995, pp. 381, 382, amending O.C.G.A. § 9-14-44.

[60]Ga. Laws 1995, pp. 381, 383, adding O.C.G.A. § 9-14-47.1(b).

applicable thereto."[61] Additionally, the Act "prohibits certain discovery except under certain circumstances; changes the time period for certain notice; changes certain requirements with respect to certain affidavits and changes certain provisions relating to review and granting of habeas corpus relief."[62] Also amended by the Act is O.C.G.A. § 15-1-9.1, which "changes certain requirements with respect to requesting judicial assistance from other courts."[63]

See the excellent summary of the Georgia 1995 Death Penalty Reform Act by Professor Donald Wilkes, Jr., in the November, 1995 issue of "Georgia Defender," published by The Georgia Association of Criminal Defense Lawyers.

In *Giles v. Ford*,[64] the court held that O.C.G.A. § 9-15-2(d) does not apply to a petition for habeas corpus. O.C.G.A. § 9-15-2(d) provides that a judge shall review a complaint to determine if "the pleading shows on its face such a complete absence of any justiciable issue" when presented with an affidavit of indigency and deny the filing of the complaint if it is so found.

In *Gaither v. Gibby*,[65] the court held that a petitioner who seeks release by writ of habeas corpus has the burden of proving by a preponderance of the evidence that the judgment attacked is invalid because the prisoner's constitutionally protected rights were violated in obtaining the judgment. Also "habeas proceeding[s] begin . . . with the presumption [that] the petitioner's judgment of conviction . . . [was] valid."

"[T]he failure of a respondent to reply to a writ requiring him to answer within a stated time may subject respondent to punishment for contempt, but it does not require that the prisoner be released."[66]

The Civil Practice Act "governs the sufficiency of pleadings, admissibility of evidence under the petition as drawn and amendments to the petition."[67] Hence, habeas corpus petitions are not limited to the grounds set out in the petition.[68] However, when the habeas court does not "rule on the grounds asserted in [the] petition," but bases his ruling on grounds not asserted in the petition, the parties should be given sufficient time to prepare to

---

[61]Ga. Laws 1995, pp. 381, 383, adding O.C.G.A. § 9-14-47.1(c).

[62]Ga. Laws 1995, pp. 381, 384, amending O.C.G.A. §§ 9-14-48(a), (b), (c), (d).

[63]Ga. Laws 1995, pp. 381, 384, amending O.C.G.A. § 15-1-9.1.

[64]Giles v. Ford, 258 Ga. 245 (1), 368 S.E.2d 318 (1988).

[65]Gaither v. Gibby, 267 Ga. 96, 97 (1), 475 S.E.2d 603 (1996).

[66]McLeod v. Barrett, 271 Ga. 569, 571 (2), 522 S.E.2d 219 (1999).

[67]Nelson v. Zant, 261 Ga. 358, 359 (1), 405 S.E.2d 250 (1991); Giles v. Ford, 258 Ga. 245 (1), 368 S.E.2d 318 (1988).

[68]Johnson v. Caldwell, 229 Ga. 548, 552, 192 S.E.2d 900 (1972).

address the issue before the court and "should have an opportunity to amend [the] petition to conform to the issues before the habeas court."[69] Also, a petition should not be dismissed for failure to comply with the technical requirements of O.C.G.A. §§ 9-14-41 et seq.[70] This interpretation gives added support to the provisions of O.C.G.A. § 9-14-51.[71] Once the Georgia Supreme Court[72] or the Georgia Court of Appeals[73] has passed on a legal issue, it will not be considered in a later petition for habeas corpus[74] "unless new facts have appeared or there has been a change in the relevant law"[75] or the petitioner can show that the writ is necessary to avoid a miscarriage of justice.[76] However, in a situation where a defendant is convicted of one crime and a short time later he is convicted of another, a habeas corpus petition involving the conviction of one of the crimes will not prevent a later habeas corpus petition relating to the other.[77]

In *Board of Pardons and Paroles v. Bridges,*[78] the court pointed out that although a motion of double jeopardy does not apply to a petition for habeas corpus, the doctrine of res judicata may be applicable.

In *Stone v. Powell,*[79] the United States Supreme Court held that "a federal court need not apply the exclusionary rule on habeas corpus review of a Fourth Amendment claim absent a showing that the state prisoner was denied an opportunity for a full and fair litigation of that claim at trial and on direct review."[80]

In *Jacobs v. Hopper,*[81] the Georgia Supreme Court stated that it would follow the same Stone rule in state habeas corpus review.

---

[69]King v. Hawkins, 265 Ga. 93, 454 S.E.2d 135 (1995).

[70]Mitchell v. Forrester, 247 Ga. 622, 623, 278 S.E.2d 368 (1981).

[71]See Fuller v. Ricketts, 234 Ga. 104, 214 S.E.2d 541 (1975).

[72]Strozier v. Hopper, 234 Ga. 597, 598 (1), 216 S.E.2d 847 (1975).

[73]Herring v. Ault, 230 Ga. 398 (1), 197 S.E.2d 354 (1973).

[74]Turpin v. Lipham, 270 Ga. 208 (1), 510 S.E.2d 32 (1998); Roulain v. Martin, 266 Ga. 353 (1), 466 S.E.2d 837 (1996); Treadwell v. Hopper, 235 Ga. 241, 242, 219 S.E.2d 155 (1975); Corn v. Hopper, 244 Ga. 28, 29 (3), 257 S.E.2d 533 (1979).

[75]Johnson v. Zant, 249 Ga. 812, 818, 295 S.E.2d 63 (1982).

[76]Walker v. Penn, 271 Ga. 609, 611 (2), 523 S.E.2d 325 (1999). The term "miscarriage of justice" is an extremely high standard to meet and demands a much greater showing than the defendant is not guilty. "[T]o establish a miscarriage of justice exception, petitioner is required to support allegations of constitutional error with new reliable evidence that was not presented at trial."

[77]Hunter v. Brown, 236 Ga. 168, 223 S.E.2d 145 (1976).

[78]Board of Pardons and Paroles v. Bridges, 268 Ga. 404, 489 S.E.2d 846 (1997).

[79]Stone v. Powell, 428 U.S. 465, 96 S.Ct. 3037, 49 L.Ed.2d 1067 (1976).

[80]Stone v. Powell, 428 U.S. 465, 494, 96 S.Ct. 3037, 49 L.Ed.2d 1067 (1976).

[81]Jacobs v. Hopper, 238 Ga. 461, 462, 233 S.E.2d 169 (1977).

In *Jacobs,* the court considered the issue of abandonment by the defendant of his right to habeas corpus relief. A motion to suppress had been filed under O.C.G.A. § 17-5-30, but the defendant failed to appear for the hearing. The motion was dismissed as having been abandoned. The court stated that the search and seizure issue would not be considered by it on appeal of the habeas corpus proceeding since the petitioner had a "full and fair opportunity to litigate his contention earlier and had not done so."

In *Farris v. Slaton,*[82] the court held that the failure of the state to respond in a timely manner to the petition for habeas corpus does not entitle the petitioner to a default judgment. The defendant in a habeas corpus action is entitled to a hearing in which to present evidence in opposition to the petition.[83] However, a habeas court may dismiss a petition without a hearing if it appears from the face of the pleading that it has not merit.[84]

In *State v. Hernandez-Cuevas,*[85] the court held that a state habeas court has no authority to direct that a defendant be tried or re-tried within a certain period of time.

According to "O.C.G.A. § 42-12-8, the statute which sets forth appellate procedural requirements under the Prison Litigation Reform Act, O.C.G.A. §§ 42-12-1 et seq. (PLRA), with some exceptions, a prisoner seeking to appeal an adverse judgment in a civil proceeding is restricted to discretionary rather than direct review.[86] One such exception is a petition for a writ of habeas corpus which is expressly exempted from the P.L.R.A. pursuant to O.C.G.A. § 42-12-3(1). The general rule for review of a denial of a post-trial habeas petition set forth in O.C.G.A. § 9-14-52 also requires a discretionary as opposed to a direct review. As the court explained in *Redmon v. Johnson,*[87]

> A habeas petitioner seeking to appeal a final superior court order denying his petition must file not only a timely application in this Court for a certificate of probable cause to appeal, but also a timely notice of appeal in the habeas court. See O.C.G.A. § 9-14-52(b); *Fullwood v. Sivley,* 271 Ga. 248, 250, 517 S.E.2d 511 (1999). The latter requirement leads to the record being forwarded to this Court so that it may be considered along with the application . . .. Under this Court's Rule 36, if a majority of the justices determine that the

---

[82]Farris v. Slaton, 262 Ga. 713 (2), 425 S.E.2d 291 (1993).

[83]Gearinger v. Taylor, 268 Ga. 73, 487 S.E.2d 600 (1997).

[84]Lucas v. Walker, 287 Ga. 864 (2), 700 S.E.2d 596 (2010). See Mitchell v. Forrester, 247 Ga. 622, 278 S.E.2d 368 (1981).

[85]State v. Hernandez-Cuevas, 202 Ga. App. 861, 862, 415 S.E.2d 713 (1992).

[86]Smith v. Nichols, 270 Ga. 550, 551 (1), 512 S.E.2d 279 (1999).

[87]Redmon v. Johnson, 302 Ga. 763, 764, 809 S.E.2d 468 (2018).

application shows that the case has "arguable merit", the application will be granted . . .. [A]rguable merit in this context . . . means that the petitioner has a fair probability of ultimately prevailing in his case by obtaining habeas relief.

In *Brown v. Crawford*,[88] the court held that pursuant to the Prison Reform Act, O.C.G.A. § 42-12-3(1), the only review mechanism available upon the denial of a petition for habeas relief, is that of an application for discretionary appeal as set forth in O.C.G.A. § 5-6-35 and overruled all authority to the contrary. In *Crosson v. Conway*,[89] the Supreme Court held that it was no longer necessary for a trial court to advise an unsuccessful habeas petitioner of the basic requirements of O.C.G.A. § 9-14-52(b) for filing a timely appeal.

Some special rules which apply to the appeal of a habeas corpus case are set out in O.C.G.A. § 9-14-52.[90] These provisions should be carefully considered before an appeal is instituted. In a habeas corpus action brought because of a restraint following a traffic conviction or plea, petitioner must apply for a certificate of probable cause to appeal.[91]

In the extreme case of *Howard v. Sharpe*,[92] the court held that where a petitioner shows a pattern of filing collateral grievances related to the prison and court systems, but unrelated to his criminal convictions or a violation of his constitutional rights, it is not error for the habeas court to fashion "an order, narrowly drawn with reasonable restrictions to prevent [the petitioner] from flooding the court with repeated, frivolous filings, while safeguarding [his] meaningful access to the courts."

Cases involving convictions rendered prior to July 1, 2004 are subject to dismissal because of laches. O.C.G.A. § 9-14-48(e) provides: "[A] petition, other than one challenging a conviction for which a death sentence has been imposed or challenging a sentence of death, may be dismissed if there is a particularized showing that the respondent has been prejudiced in its ability to respond to the petition by delay in its filing unless the petitioner

---

[88]Brown v. Crawford, 289 Ga. 722, 715 S.E.2d 132, 85 A.L.R.6th 699 (2011).

[89]Crosson v. Conway, 291 Ga. 220, 728 S.E.2d 617 (2012) (overruling Hicks v. Scott, 273 Ga. 358, 541 S.E.2d 27 (2001), and its progeny).

[90]See Massaline v. Williams, 274 Ga. 552, 554 S.E.2d 720 (2001) (adopts a "mailbox rule" for incarcerated, pro se habeas litigants that treats notices of appeal and applications for certificate of probable cause as "filed with the clerk" as of the date they are delivered to prison officials for forwarding to the appropriate court). See also Riley v. State, 280 Ga. 267, 626 S.E.2d 116 (2006) (*Massaline* is restricted to habeas corpus appeals and has no application otherwise).

[91]Patterson v. Earp, 257 Ga. 729, 730, 363 S.E.2d 248 (1988).

[92]Howard v. Sharpe, 266 Ga. 771, 773, 470 S.E.2d 678 (1996).

shows by a preponderance of the evidence that it is based on grounds of which he or she could not have had knowledge by the exercise of reasonable diligence before the circumstances prejudicial to the respondent occurred. This subsection shall apply only to convictions had before July 1, 2004."

In *Flint v. State*,[93] the Georgia Supreme Court remanded a habeas case because the trial court failed to have the hearing transcribed. Without a transcript, the court was not satisfied that it had a sufficient record to review holding that O.C.G.A. § 9-14-50 requires that the habeas hearing be transcribed.

In *Collier v. State*,[94] the Supreme Court held that a trial court may deny a habeas petition on the merits after a hearing or dismiss it without prejudice should petitioner fail to appear for a hearing. It may not dismiss a habeas claim on the merits because of petitioner's failure to prosecute.

See § 28:7, supra, on right of an indigent to a copy of the transcript of his trial. See § 16:14, supra, on the time limitation for challenges of traffic convictions. See § 28:23, infra, on forms to be used. See § 17:9, supra, on necessity of a transcript.

§ 28:18   State habeas corpus proceedings in death sentence cases

The Uniform Rules for the Superior Courts contain the following provisions which apply when the defendant receives a death sentence.

Rule 44. Habeas Corpus Proceedings in Death Sentence Cases

"44.1 Application.

This rule shall apply to all petitions seeking, for the first time, a writ of habeas corpus in state court proceedings for those cases in which the petitioner has received a sentence of death. O.C.G.A. § 9-14-47.1.

"44.2 Request for Judicial Assignment.

Within ten days of the filing of such a petition, the superior court clerk of the county where the petition is filed shall serve a copy of the petition upon the Executive Director of the Council of Superior Court Judges of Georgia. This service may be effected by mail and will constitute a request for judicial assistance under O.C.G.A. § 15-1-9.1(b)(3).

---

[93]Flint v. State, 745 S.E.2d 277 (Ga. 2010). See Lucas v. Walker, 287 Ga. 864, 700 S.E.2d 596 (2010) (petitioner's *inability* to attend hearing does not excuse trial court from con-ducting one where petition has merit and evidence can be presented by way of affidavit, deposition or other means).

[94]Collier v. State, 290 Ga. 456, 721 S.E.2d 903 (2012).

"44.3 Respondent's Answer or Motion to Dismiss.

The respondent shall answer or move to dismiss the petition within 20 days after the filing of the petition or within such further time as the court may set for good cause shown.

"44.4 Assignment of Judge for Habeas Corpus Proceedings.

"(A) The Executive Committee of the Counsel of Superior Court Judges shall promulgate guidelines for the assignment of such cases to the various superior court judges throughout Georgia, and shall provide that the case will not be assigned to a judge within the circuit in which the sentence was imposed. Within 30 days after the Executive Director receives the petition, the president of the council shall assign the case to a judge in accordance with the guidelines.

"(B) Pending assignment of a judge, or during a later vacancy of an assigned judge, a presiding judge of the court in which the petition is filed shall be authorized to act on emergency matters unless otherwise disqualified by Uniform Superior Court Rule 25.

"44.5 Preliminary Conference and Scheduling.

The assigned judge may wish to consider scheduling a preliminary conference with counsel for the petitioner and respondent as soon as practical. This conference may be conducted by telephone. The court may also wish to enter a scheduling order establishing specific dates in accordance with the guidelines set forth in this rule. The court may on its own or on motion of either party shorten any time period set forth hereinafter, and may extend such time period for good cause.

"44.6 Motions.

Within 60 days after the filing of the petition, the petitioner may file pre-trial motions. Within 90 days after the filing of the petition, the respondent may file any motions. Responses to motions shall be governed by Rule 6.2.

"44.7 Amendments to the Petition; Discovery.

No later than 120 days after the filing of the petition, the petitioner may amend the petition, and if discovery is allowed pursuant to O.C.G.A. § 9-14-48 it shall be completed.

"44.8 Pretrial Conference.

The court may wish to schedule a pretrial conference with counsel for the petitioner and the respondent and enter an appropriate pretrial order for proceedings in the case. This conference may be conducted with counsel only and by telephone if appropriate.

"44.9 Evidentiary Hearing.

Within 180 days after the filing of the petition, the court shall conduct an evidentiary hearing as provided by O.C.G.A. § 9-14-47 and O.C.G.A. § 9-14-48.

"44.10 Preparation of Transcript.

The evidentiary hearing shall be transcribed by a court reporter designated by the court hearing the case as set forth in O.C.G.A. § 9-14-50. Within 30 days after the evidentiary hearing, the transcript of the evidentiary hearing shall be made available to the parties and the court.

"44.11 Briefing.

Within 60 days after the evidentiary hearing, the petitioner may file any brief and if so directed by the court shall file proposed findings of fact and conclusions of law and a proposed order. Within 90 days after the evidentiary hearing, the respondent may file any responsive brief and if so directed by the court shall file proposed findings of fact and conclusions of law and a proposed order. Within 100 days after the evidentiary hearing, the petitioner may file any additional responsive brief.

"44.12 Ruling on Petition.

Within 90 days of the filing of the respondent's brief, or the petitioner's reply brief if one is filed, the court shall issue its ruling on the petition and its written findings of fact and conclusions of law as required by O.C.G.A. § 9-14-49.

"44.13 Effect of Rule.

Upon application of any party, the Supreme Court may order such relief as it finds necessary to assure compliance with this Rule. This Rule provides procedural guidelines and no substantive rights are hereby conferred upon any person. No violation of this Rule shall be the basis of any grant of habeas corpus relief."

See § 28:23, infra, on civil suits by prisoners.

§ 28:19   Federal habeas corpus

Reference has been previously made to the use of federal habeas corpus in connection with reducing or setting bail.[1] The basic federal statute on federal habeas corpus for persons convicted in a state court provides in part as follows:

"State custody—Remedies in Federal courts.

"(a) The Supreme Court, a Justice thereof, a circuit judge, or a district court shall entertain an application for a writ of habeas corpus in behalf of a person in custody pursuant to the judgment of a State court only on the ground that he is in custody in violation of the Constitution or laws or treaties of the United States.

[Section 28:19]
    [1]See § 8:4, supra.

"(b)(1) An application for a writ of habeas corpus on behalf of a person in custody pursuant to the judgment of a State court shall not be granted unless it appears that—

"(A) the applicant has exhausted the remedies available in the courts of the State; or

"(B)(i) there is an absence of available State corrective process; or

"(ii) circumstances exist that render such process ineffective to protect the rights of the applicant.[²]

"(2) An application for a writ of habeas corpus may be denied on the merits, notwithstanding the failure of the applicant to exhaust the remedies available in the courts of the State.

"(3) A State shall not be deemed to have waived the exhaustion requirement or be estopped from reliance upon the requirement unless the State, through counsel, expressly waives the requirement.

"(c) An applicant shall not be deemed to have exhausted the remedies available in the courts of the State, within the meaning of this section, if he has the right under the law of the State to raise, by any available procedure, the question presented.

"(d) An application for a writ of habeas corpus on behalf of a person in custody pursuant to the judgment of a state court shall not be granted with respect to any claim that was adjudicated on the merits in State court proceedings unless the adjudication of that claim—

(1) resulted in a decision that was contrary to, or involved an unreasonable application of, clearly established Federal law, as determined by the Supreme Court of the United States; or

(2) resulted in a decision that was based on an unreasonable determination of the facts in light of the evidence presented in the State court proceeding."[³]

The statute sets out a number of requirements and limitations. First, it should be noted that federal habeas corpus review is limited to a violation of the Constitution of the United States or its laws and treaties. Furthermore, there must be an exhaustion of state remedies before federal habeas corpus will be available.

[²]In Galtieri v. Wainwright, 582 F.2d 348 (5th Cir. 1978) (en banc) (an eight to six opinion), the majority concluded that a United States district court must dismiss a federal habeas corpus petition unless the petitioner had previously exhausted his state remedies as to each and all of the claims he presents.

[³]28 U.S.C.A. § 2254. Pub. L. No. 104-132, 110 Stat. 1221 et seq. added Chapter 153 to the Antiterrorism and Effective Death Penalty Act of 1996, entitled "Special Habeas Corpus Procedures in Capital Cases." See 28 U.S.C.A. §§ 2261 et seq. See also, Wiggins v. Smith, 539 U. S. 510, 123 S.Ct. 2527, 156 L.Ed.2d 471 (2003).

The prisoner must also be in custody. Also there is a presumption that the state trial court and appellate court factual findings are correct unless not supported by the record. Hence, a federal court granting habeas corpus relief must make a written explanation for not accepting the state's findings. The state's findings may not be overturned just on the basis of the preponderance of the evidence.[4] In *Price v. Vincent*,[5] the United States Supreme Court held that a federal court can grant habeas relief on the basis of a *de novo* review of the claims adjudicated in state court only if such claims qualify for the writ under the provisions of 28 U.S.C.A. § 2254(d).

In commenting upon the difficulty of meeting the standard for relief set by a § 2254 habeas petition, the United States Supreme Court noted:

"[C]learly established Federal law" for purposes of § 2254(d)(1) includes only " 'the holdings, as opposed to the dicta, of this Court's decisions.' " *Howes v. Fields,* 565 U.S. __, __, 132 S.Ct. 1181, 1187, 182 L.Ed.2d 17 (2012) (quoting *Williams v. Taylor,* 529 U.S. 362, 412, 120 S.Ct. 1495, 146 L.Ed.2d 389 (2000)). And an "unreasonable application of" those holdings must be " 'objectively unreasonable,' " not merely wrong; even "clear error" will not suffice. *Lockyer v. Andrade,* 538 U.S. 63, 75-76, 123 S.Ct. 1166, 155 L.Ed.2d 144 (2003). Rather, "[a]s a condition for obtaining habeas corpus from a federal court, a state prisoner must show that the state court's ruling on the claim being presented in federal court was so lacking in justification that there was an error well understood and comprehended in existing law beyond any possibility for fairminded disagreement." *Harrington v. Richter,* 562 U.S. __, __, 131 S.Ct. 770, 786-787, 178 L.Ed.2d 624 (2011).[6]

In *Terrell v. Bryson*,[7] the 11th Circuit noted: "[a]court may grant a stay of execution only if the moving party establishes that: '(1) he has a substantial likelihood of success on the merits; (2) he will suffer irreparable injury unless the injunction issues; (3) the stay would not substantially harm the other litigant; and (4) if issued, the injunction would not be adverse to the public

---

[4]Sumner v. Mata, 449 U.S. 539, 101 S.Ct. 764, 66 L.Ed.2d 722 (1981). See Cullen v. Pinholster, 131 S. Ct. 1388, 179 L. Ed. 2d 557 (2011) (where the issue is one which was resolved on the merits in state court proceedings, federal courts must use a "doubly deferential" standard of review that gives both the state court and the defense attorney the benefit of the doubt).

[5]Price v. Vincent, 538 U.S. 634, 123 S.Ct. 1848, 155 L.Ed.2d 877

(2003).

[6]White v. Woodall, 134 S. Ct. 1697, 1701, 188 L. Ed. 2d 698 (2014) (trial court's failure to give a blanket "no adverse inference" instruction following defendant's failure to testify during penalty phase did not violate Fifth Amendment privilege and was not unreasonable in the absence of settled precedent).

[7]Terrell v. Bryson, 807 F.3d 1276, 1278 (11th Cir. 2015) (citations and punctuation omitted).

interest.' And we review the denial of a stay of execution only for abuse of discretion."

The Supreme Court has held that where the petition is premised upon an Eighth Amendment challenge to a lethal injection protocol:

[P]risoners cannot successfully challenge a method of execution unless they establish that the method presents a risk that is sure or very likely to cause serious illness and needless suffering, and give rise to sufficiently imminent dangers. . . . To prevail on such a claim, there must be a substantial risk of serious harm, an objectively intolerable risk of harm that prevents prison officials from pleading that they were subjectively blameless for purposes of the Eighth Amendment. . . . [P]risoners cannot successfully challenge a State's method of execution merely by showing slightly or marginally safer alternative Instead, p[risoners must identify an alternative that is feasible, readily implemented, and in fact, significantly reduce[s] a substantial risk of severe pain.[8]

In *Rose v. Lundy*,[9] the Supreme Court considered whether or not there must be a "total exhaustion" of state remedies as a prerequisite to federal habeas corpus. The court concluded that a federal district court must dismiss a habeas corpus petition which contains both unexhausted and exhausted claims. The federal petitioner has the choice of exhausting all state claims before filing the habeas petition, or deleting those unexhausted claims from the petition at the risk of dismissal of subsequent federal petitions based upon those claims.

If a petitioner deliberately bypasses available state court procedures by escaping during the pendency of his appeal, this bars federal habeas corpus review.[10]

In *United States v. Frady*,[11] the Supreme Court stated that "to obtain collateral relief based on trial errors to which no contemporaneous objection was made, a convicted defendant must show both a [1] 'cause' excusing his double procedural default, and [2] 'actual prejudice' resulting from the errors of which he complains." In *Martinez v. Ryan*,[12] the U.S. Supreme Court held that "[A] procedural default will not bar a federal habeas court from hear-

---

[8]Glossip v. Gross, 135 S. Ct. 2726, 192 L. Ed. 2d 761 (2015) (internal quotes omitted), citing Baze v. Rees, 553 U.S. 35, 128 S. Ct. 1520, 170 L. Ed. 2d 420 (2008).

[9]Rose v. Lundy, 455 U.S. 509, 102 S.Ct. 1198, 71 L.Ed.2d 379 (1982).

[10]Glossip v. Gross, 135 S. Ct. 2726, 2737, 192 L. Ed. 2d 761 (2015) (citations and emphasis omitted); Potter v. Davis, 519 F.Supp. 621, 622 (E.D.Tenn.

1981); Strickland v. Hopper, 571 F.2d 275 (5th Cir. 1978).

[11]United States v. Frady, 456 U.S. 152, 102 S.Ct. 1584, 71 L.Ed.2d 816 (1982). Cf. Engle v. Isaac, 456 U.S. 107, 102 S.Ct. 1558, 71 L.Ed.2d 783 (1982).

[12]Martinez v. Ryan, 566 U.S. 1, 132 S. Ct. 1309, 1320, 182 L. Ed. 2d 272 (2012). See Trevino v. Thaler, 133 S. Ct. 1911, 185 L. Ed. 2d 1044 (2013)

ing a substantial claim of ineffective assistance at trial if, in the [state's] initial review collateral proceeding, there was no counsel or counsel in that proceeding was ineffective."

In *Daniels v. United States*,[13] and *Lackawanna County v. Coss*,[14] the United States Supreme Court held that post-conviction relief is unavailable on a motion under 28 U.S.C.A. § 2255 or a petition for federal habeas corpus relief under 28 U.S.C.A. § 2254 on the ground that a prior state conviction was used to enhance the sentence in the federal court. A petitioner who has bypassed state and federal opportunities to attack should not later be allowed federal habeas corpus relief because of the presumption of validity that attaches to the prior conviction. In *Coss*, the majority pointed out that "once a state conviction is no longer open to direct or collateral attack . . . because the defendant failed to pursue those remedies while they were available . . . the conviction may be regarded as conclusively valid." However, under *Custis v. United States*,[15] the United States Supreme Court held that section 2255 may be used to challenge a prior conviction on the ground that it was obtained in violation of the right to appointed counsel or possibly ineffective assistance of counsel.

In *Walker v. Zant*,[16] the Eleventh Circuit held that the "exhaustion requirement . . . does not require the prisoner to seek collateral review from the state judiciary of the same issues also raised on direct appeal."

In *McCleskey v. Zant*,[17] the United States Supreme Court attempted to clarify how federal courts should determine whether a petitioner for habeas corpus has "abused the writ" where a petitioner filed a second or subsequent petitions for habeas relief. The court began by pointing out that "the government bears the burden of pleading abuse of the writ" and that once the government makes a proper submission, the petitioner must show that he has not abused the writ in seeking habeas relief. "To excuse his failure to raise the claim earlier, he must show cause for failing to raise it and prejudice therefrom. . . . If petitioner cannot show cause, the failure to raise the claim in an earlier petition may nonetheless be excused if he or she can show that a

---

(*Martinez* could be applied to case where petition alleged that although he was represented at his first state collateral proceeding, counsel was ineffective for failing to raise a claim of ineffective assistance at trial).

[13]Daniels v. United States, 532 U.S. 374, 121 S.Ct. 1578, 149 L.Ed.2d 590 (2001).

[14]Lackawanna County v. Coss, 532 U.S. 394, 121 S.Ct. 1567, 149

L.Ed.2d 608 (2001).

[15]Custis v. United States, 511 U.S. 485, 114 S.Ct. 1732, 128 L.Ed.2d 517 (1994).

[16]Walker v. Zant, 693 F.2d 1087 (11th Cir. 1982).

[17]McCleskey v. Zant, 499 U.S. 467, 111 S.Ct. 1454, 113 L.Ed.2d 517 (1991).

fundamental miscarriage of justice would result from a failure to entertain the claim."

In 1993, the United States Supreme Court, in *Brecht v. Abrahamson*,[18] held that in determining whether there had been a federal constitutional error in a state criminal trial, the question in determining whether the error was harmless was "whether the . . . error 'had substantial and injurious effect or influence in determining the jury's verdict.' "However, in the 1995 case of *O'Neal v. McAninch*,[19] the same court held that "in cases of grave doubt as to harmlessness," the petitioner is entitled to the issuance of the writ.

In *Teague v. Lane*,[20] the United States Supreme Court ruled that "unless they fall within an exception to the general rule, new constitutional rules of criminal procedure will not be applicable to those cases which have become final before the new rules are announced." In *Horn v. Banks*,[21] the Supreme Court held that when the State raises retroactivity as a bar to habeas relief, the court must conduct a *Teague* analysis before considering the merits of the claim, i.e., determine whether the habeas petitioner's case became final before the new rule had been announced.

28 U.S.C.A. § 2254(d) requires that federal courts give deference to a state court's review of an ineffective assistance habeas claim. If the state court's decision is reasonably justified by the facts in the case, its decision is not subject to de novo review in a federal habeas action.[22]

In *Ryan v. Gonzalez*,[23] the United States Supreme Court held that based upon the "backward-looking" record-based nature of federal habeas proceedings, courts were not required to stay a habeas case based upon the petitioner's incompetency.

See Wilkes, *Federal Postconviction Remedies and Relief* (West 2003) and Wilkes, *State Postconviction Remedies and Relief* (West 2006).

---

[18]Brecht v. Abrahamson, 507 U.S. 619, 113 S.Ct. 1710, 123 L.Ed.2d 353 (1993), reh'g denied. See Chapman v. California, 386 U.S. 18, 24, 87 S. Ct. 824, 17 L. Ed. 2d 705, 24 A.L.R.3d 1065 (1967) ("before a federal constitutional error can be held harmless, the court must be able to declare a belief that it was harmless beyond a reasonable doubt").

[19]O'Neal v. McAninch, 513 U.S. 432, 115 S.Ct. 992, 130 L.Ed.2d 947 (1995).

[20]Teague v. Lane, 489 U.S. 288, 310, 109 S.Ct. 1060, 103 L.Ed.2d 334 (1989).

[21]Horn v. Banks, 536 U.S. 266, 122 S.Ct. 2147, 153 L.Ed.2d 301 (2002).

[22]Harrington v. Richter, 131 S. Ct. 770, 178 L. Ed. 2d 624 (2011) (in reviewing state court decision on effectiveness of counsel, federal habeas court is restricted to state court record).

[23]Ryan v. Gonzales, 133 S. Ct. 696, 184 L. Ed. 2d 528 (2013).

§ 28:20 Habeas corpus—Right to counsel for indigent petitioners

The United States Supreme Court has held that no court, state or federal, is required by the federal Constitution to provide counsel to indigent prisoners who, without more, merely indicate their wish to seek post-conviction relief.[1] The court has also held that the Sixth Amendment right to counsel is inapplicable to habeas corpus proceedings, which are civil rather than criminal, in nature.[2]

However, since a proceeding which may result in vacating a criminal conviction is not purely a civil matter,[3] federal courts at one time increasingly recognized a discretionary power to appoint counsel where "special circumstances" exist.[4] In 2008, Congress enacted 18 U.S.C.A. § 3599, which makes an important exception to this general rule in the case of persons seeking to set aside a death sentence pursuant to 28 U.S.C.A. §§ 2254 or 2255 and who are financially unable to employ counsel. It provides a statutory right to the appointment of counsel and the furnishing of other necessary assistance such as expert help in such cases.

In *Pennsylvania v. Finley*,[5] the United States Supreme Court held that "a defendant has no federal constitutional right to

---

[Section 28:20]

[1]Johnson v. Avery, 393 U.S. 483, 488, 89 S.Ct. 747, 21 L.Ed.2d 718 (1969).

[2]Ex parte Tom Tong, 108 U.S. 556, 2 S.Ct. 871, 27 L.Ed. 826 (1883).

[3]Dillon v. United States, 307 F.2d 445 (9th Cir. 1962).

[4]Pike v. United States, 330 F.2d 53 (5th Cir. 1964); Putt v. United States, 363 F.2d 369 (5th Cir. 1966); Ford v. United States, 363 F.2d 437 (5th Cir. 1966); Fleming v. United States, 367 F.2d 555 (5th Cir. 1966); Hollinger v. United States, 391 F.2d 929 (5th Cir. 1968).

Cf. Comment, "Discretionary Appointment of Counsel at Post-Conviction Proceedings: An Unconstitutional Barrier to Effective Post-Conviction Relief," 8 Pa. L. Rev. 434 (1974). In Dillon v. United States, 307 F.2d 445 (9th Cir. 1962), the court said that assistance of counsel may be constitutionally required by the equal protection clause in certain circumstances, notwithstanding the inap-plicability of the Sixth Amendment. The appointment of counsel becomes mandatory, according to Dillon court, when the circumstances of the defendant or the complexities of the matter are such that a fair and meaningful hearing would be impossible without the assistance of counsel. The Seventh Circuit has held that counsel should be appointed except where the motion is completely or utterly and hopelessly frivolous and devoid of merit. United States v. Farrar, 346 F.2d 375 (7th Cir. 1965).

In Douglas v. People of State of Cal., 372 U.S. 353, 83 S. Ct. 814, 9 L. Ed. 2d 811 (1963), the United States Supreme Court held, on equal protection grounds, that a right to appointed counsel for first appeals is required (see § 28:6, supra). Arguably, the Douglas rationale can be extended to habeas corpus proceedings, a position taken by the Fifth Circuit in Pike v. United States, 330 F.2d 53 (5th Cir. 1964).

[5]Pennsylvania v. Finley, 481 U.S. 551, 107 S.Ct. 1990, 95 L.Ed.2d 539

counsel . . . when attacking a conviction that has . . . become final. . . ." If counsel is appointed for an indigent person in a post-conviction proceeding and counsel determines that there is no arguable basis for collateral relief, he may advise the trial court and request permission to withdraw without following the procedure set out in *Anders v. California*.[6] See § 28:6, supra.

Even though an indigent prisoner has no absolute right to counsel to assist him with his habeas corpus petition,[7] his right to obtain legal assistance from other prisoners (the so-called "jailhouse lawyers") cannot be abrogated by statute in the interest of prison discipline, unless the state provides an alternative system of legal assistance to its indigent prisoners.[8]

In *Bounds v. Smith*,[9] the United States Supreme Court held "that the fundamental constitutional right of access to the courts requires prison authorities to assist inmates in the preparation and filing of meaningful legal papers by providing prisoners with adequate law libraries or adequate assistance from persons trained in the law." In *Portis v. Evans*,[10] the Georgia Supreme Court considered an action for mandamus filed by Portis, seeking to compel the Commissioner of the Department of Offender Rehabilitation (now Department of Corrections) to provide him with meaningful access to the courts. He alleged that he needed a law library to prepare a habeas corpus petition. He further alleged that the issues involved were beyond the scope of the experience of the attorney from the Prisoner Legal Counseling Project. The court held that it was error to grant a motion to dismiss for failure to state a claim.

In *Portis v. Evans*,[11] the court stated that "adequate law libraries or adequate assistance from persons trained in the law must be provided to prison inmates in their preparation and filing of meaningful legal papers in order to grant them meaningful access to the courts."

§ 28:21 Unified appeal in capital cases—Statutory basis

The name "Unified Appeal" is somewhat misleading in that the

(1987).

[6]Anders v. California, 386 U.S. 738, 87 S.Ct. 1396, 18 L.Ed.2d 493 (1967).

[7]Johnson v. Avery, 393 U.S. 483, 89 S.Ct. 747, 21 L.Ed.2d 718 (1969).

[8]Johnson v. Avery, 393 U.S. 483, 89 S.Ct. 747, 21 L.Ed.2d 718 (1969).

[9]Bounds v. Smith, 430 U.S. 817, 828, 97 S.Ct. 1491, 52 L.Ed.2d 72 (1977). Cf. Murray v. Giarratano, 492 U.S. 1, 109 S.Ct. 2765, 106 L.Ed.2d 1 (1989).

[10]Portis v. Evans, 249 Ga. 396, 291 S.E.2d 511 (1982). See Daker v. Humphrey, 294 Ga. 504, 755 S.E.2d 201 (2014) (holding that a petition for a writ of mandamus to compel a warden to allow a prisoner access to a law library or legal materials was not frivolous on its face).

[11]Portis v. Evans, 250 Ga. 239, 297 S.E.2d 248 (1982).

Unified Appeal Procedure does not just apply to appeals. It applies to various steps before, during and after a trial if the district attorney is seeking the death penalty. The various successive sections of this material on Unified Appeals should be consulted in death cases at each stage of the case.

In 1980, the Georgia General Assembly enacted O.C.G.A. § 17-10-36, which required the Supreme Court of Georgia to establish by rules a uniform review procedure of the "challenges to the trial, conviction, sentence, and detention of defendants" upon whom the death sentence has been sought.[1] These procedures apply "only in cases in which the death penalty is sought."[2]

The Georgia Unified Appeal Procedure includes an "outline of proceedings" and a "checklist." The checklist is to be utilized by the trial court, the prosecution, and the defense throughout the proceedings. The checklist delineates the categories of possible errors upon which the defendant may base a challenge. The checklist is excellent and may be helpful to defense counsel in other cases.

The purpose of these rules established by the Supreme Court of Georgia is to require "the trial court, the prosecuting attorney, and defense counsel, prior to, during, and after the trial of cases in which the death penalty is sought to make certain that all possible matters which could be raised in defense have been considered by the defendant and defense counsel and either asserted in a timely and correct manner or waived in accordance with applicable legal requirements. . . ."[3]

Thus, if the defendant is convicted and sentenced to the death penalty, the objective is to assure that the record and transcripts of the proceedings are complete for unified review by the sentencing court and by the Supreme Court and covers all possible challenges to the trial, judgment of conviction, sentence of death, and detention of the defendant.[4]

The rules are not to be interpreted so as to limit the defendant's grounds of review or "suspend the rights or remedies available through the procedures governing the writ of habeas corpus." The

---

[Section 28:21]

[1]O.C.G.A. § 17-10-36(a). The rules of the Supreme Court ("The Georgia Unified Appeal Procedure") were approved by the General Assembly April 14, 1981, and revised effective January 27, 2000. See § 28:22, infra. Georgia's Unified Appeal Procedure was held to be constitutional in Sliger v. State, 248 Ga. 316, 282 S.E.2d 291 (1981); Smith v. State, 249 Ga. 228, 230 (4), 290 S.E.2d 43 (1982).

[2]Unified Appeal Procedure, Outline of Proceedings.

[3]O.C.G.A. § 17-10-36(b).

[4]O.C.G.A. § 17-10-36(b); Unified Appeal Procedure, I.A.3. See O.C.G.A. § 17-10-2, which allots 45 days for the Supreme Court to either grant or deny review of pretrial proceedings in death penalty cases.

defendant may, through a writ of habeas corpus, pursue rights and remedies "if the procedures established in the rules . . . are inadequate or ineffective in any constitutional sense."[5]

However, in *Thomason v. State*,[6] the Georgia Supreme Court held that a conviction did not have to be reversed because of the failure to follow several procedures delineated in the Unified Appeal Procedure where the defendant suffered no harm as a result of the trial court's actions.

§ 28:22 Unified appeal in capital cases—Overview

Pursuant to O.C.G.A. § 17-10-36, the Georgia Supreme Court promulgated the Georgia Unified Appeal Procedure.[1] This procedure is applicable only in cases in which the death penalty is sought.

The Unified Appeal requires that *all* proceedings in the Superior Court be recorded and transcribed, and that the defendant be present during all proceedings in the Superior Court.[2]

The purposes of the Unified Appeal, in addition to those already mentioned in connection with the legislative intent behind O.C.G.A. § 17-10-36, are as follows:[3]

"1. [To ensure] that all legal issues which ought to be raised on behalf of the defendant have been considered by the defendant and defense counsel and asserted in a timely and correct manner.

"2. [To minimize] the occurrence of error and [correct] as promptly as possible any error that nonetheless may occur.

"3. [To make] certain that the record and transcripts of the proceedings are complete for unified review by the sentencing court and by the Supreme Court."

The Unified Appeal is divided into sections, based upon the various stages of the prosecution of a capital criminal case, as

---

[5]O.C.G.A. §§ 17-10-36(c), (d).

[6]Thomason v. State, 268 Ga. 298, 305 (4), 486 S.E.2d 861 (1997).

[Section 28:22]

[1]See Unified Appeal Procedure (Georgia Court and Bar Rules Manual). These rules were approved by Resolution (Ga. Laws 1981, p. 1532) and revised effective January 27, 2000. "The revised Unified Appeal should be followed in all cases for which the notice that the state intends to seek the death penalty is given after the effective date."

In Brown v. State, 250 Ga. 66, 72, 295 S.E.2d 727 (1982), the court held that the trial judge in his discretion may use the Unified Appeal Procedure in cases where the indictment was returned on or before August 25, 1980.

[2]See Unified Appeal Procedure, Note (emphasis in original).

[3]See Unified Appeal Procedure, I.A.

follows:[4] (1) pre-trial proceedings; (2) trial proceedings; (3) review proceedings. These sections are themselves subdivided into more specific areas of possible error.

§ 28:23　Inmates' actions against state and local governments and government agencies and officers

In *King v. State of Georgia*,[1] the court pointed out that Georgia has enacted O.C.G.A. § 9-10-14. This Code section provides that the Administrative Office of the Courts shall promulgate forms to be used by "inmates of state and local penal and correctional institutions in actions against the state and local governments and government agencies and officers." *King* holds that the dismissal of such an action is proper where the plaintiff does not use such forms.

See § 28:17, supra, regarding procedure for review of habeas corpus rulings.

---

[4]See Unified Appeal Procedure, Table of Contents.

[Section 28:23]

[1]King v. State of Georgia, 268 Ga. 384 (1), 493 S.E.2d 189 (1997).

Chapter 29

Administrative Review

§ 29:1 Sentence review
§ 29:2 Credit for pre-trial custody
§ 29:3 Earned time allowances
§ 29:4 Review by board of pardons and paroles
§ 29:5 Conditions of parole; revocation of parole or release

> **KeyCite®:** Cases and other legal materials listed in KeyCite Scope can be researched through the KeyCite service on Westlaw®. Use KeyCite to check citations for form, parallel references, prior and later history, and comprehensive citator information, including citations to other decisions and secondary materials.

---

§ 29:1 Sentence review

Pursuant to O.C.G.A. § 17-10-6.3, the Sentence Review Panel was to sunset on January 1, 2009. However, in *Sentence Review Panel v. Moseley*,[1] the Georgia Supreme Court declared O.C.G.A. § 17-10-6 to be unconstitutional holding that the Panel was a "separate judicial forum" not authorized by the constitution.

§ 29:2 Credit for pre-trial custody

When a defendant spends time in custody before he is tried, each day so spent in custody is credited on his sentence when he is sentenced.[1] This provision is "automatic" and the defendant cannot be deprived of it by sentence of the court.[2] This jail-time provision applies "only to time when a defendant is confined as a result of the charges leading to the sentence against which the credit is sought."[3] The custodian of the defendant during his pretrial incarceration is under a duty to make an affidavit specifying the number of days the defendant spent in custody and, within five days of sentencing, transmit it to the court, where the clerk

---

[Section 29:1]

[1]Sentence Review Panel v. Moseley, 284 Ga. 128, 663 S.E.2d 679 (2008).

[Section 29:2]

[1]Turner v. State, 151 Ga. App.

631, 634, 260 S.E.2d 756 (1979).

[2]Johnson v. State, 248 Ga. App. 454, 455 (3), 546 S.E.2d 562 (2001).

[3]Spann v. Whitworth, 262 Ga. 21, 24 (3), 413 S.E.2d 713 (1992). Accord, Johnson v. State, 241 Ga. App. 369, 526 S.E.2d 882 (1999).

sends it, together with the sentence, to the Department of Corrections.[4] However, in *Warren v. State,*[5] the court held that "the trial court did not err in refusing to modify its sentence as requested [since] the responsibility for computing credit for time served awaiting trial . . . [is] not . . . upon the trial court." A defendant is not entitled to credit for jail time for the time which he spends in jail waiting on a probation revocation hearing[6] nor where the defendant spent time in custody for an unrelated offense.[7] The remedy for a criminal defendant who believes that he or she has not received the proper amount of credit for time served would be by way of injunctive action or mandamus against the Department of Corrections.[8]

In the Washington case of *State v. Anderson,*[9] the court held that the defendant was entitled to credit for time served on electronic home detention before conviction.

See O.C.G.A. § 42-5-100 on allowance for earned time.[10]

The sentencing court has no authority to withhold good-time credit until a fine has been paid.[11]

However, a defendant is not entitled to earned time on a state sentence for time spent in the federal system.[12]

§ 29:3 Earned time allowances

O.C.G.A. § 42-4-7(b)(1) provides that an inmate being held in a county jail for a probation violation of a felony offense and an inmate serving time for a misdemeanor offense in a county jail may be entitled to an earned time allowance up to and including one-half of the period of confinement imposed based on the inmate's institutional behavior.

---

[4]O.C.G.A. § 17-10-12; Casario v. State, 169 Ga. App. 515, 313 S.E.2d 772 (1984).

[5]Warren v. State, 246 Ga. App. 894, 543 S.E.2d 38 (2000).

[6]Dickey v. State, 157 Ga. App. 13, 14 (2), 276 S.E.2d 75 (1981). *Dickey* points out, however, that a defendant gets credit on his original sentence as time served on probation that time spent in jail while awaiting a hearing on probation revocation.

[7]Wilson v. State, 273 Ga. 97, 538 S.E.2d 429 (2000).

[8]Anderson v. State, 290 Ga. App. 890, 660 S.E.2d 876 (2008). See Cutter v. State, 275 Ga. App. 888 (2), 622 S.E.2d 96 (2005).

[9]State v. Anderson, 132 Wash.2d 203, 937 P.2d 581 (1997).

[10]In Weaver v. Graham, 450 U.S. 24, 101 S.Ct. 960, 67 L.Ed.2d 17 (1981), the court held that a Florida statute reducing a prisoner's amount of good time credits violated the ex post facto clause. Cf. Lynce v. Mathis, 519 U.S. 433, 117 S.Ct. 891, 137 L.Ed.2d 63 (1997).

[11]Davis v. State, 181 Ga. App. 498, 353 S.E.2d 7 (1987).

[12]Wellons v. State, 164 Ga. App. 100, 296 S.E.2d 397 (1982).

§ 29:4 Review by board of pardons and paroles

The 1983 Georgia Constitution, Article IV, Sec. II, Par. II, provides that with certain exceptions "the State Board of Pardons and Paroles shall be vested with the power of executive clemency, including the powers to grant reprieves, pardons, and paroles; to commute penalties; to remove disabilities imposed by law; and to remit any part of a sentence for any offense against the state after conviction."[1]

The decision of the Board to grant or deny parole is not subject to judicial review. In addition, any attempt by a court "to impose as a part of a criminal sentence conditions operating as a prerequisite of or becoming automatically effective in the event of a subsequent parole . . . would be a nullity."[2]

Regardless of any other provision of the paragraph the Board has "authority to pardon any person convicted of a crime who is subsequently determined to be innocent of said crime."

Except where further limited by statute, the Board "shall not have the authority to grant a pardon to [a person whose death sentence has been commuted to life imprisonment] until such person has served at least 25 years in the penitentiary; and such person shall not become eligible for parole at any time prior to serving at least 25 years in the penitentiary. When a person is convicted of armed robbery, the board shall not have the authority to consider such person for pardon or parole until such person has served at least five years in the penitentiary."

The General Assembly by statute[3] may prohibit the Board "from granting and may prescribe the terms and conditions for the board's granting a pardon or parole to: (1) Any person incarcerated for a second or subsequent time for any offense for which such person could have been sentenced to life imprisonment; and (2) Any person who has received consecutive life sentences as the result of offenses occurring during the same series of acts."

"The chairman of the board, or any other member designated

[Section 29:4]

[1]In Greenholtz v. Inmates of the Nebraska Penal and Correctional Complex, 442 U.S. 1, 99 S.Ct. 2100, 60 L.Ed.2d 668 (1979), the court said that the mere possibility of a release on parole is not protected by due process. In Terry v. Hamrick, 284 Ga. 24 (2), 663 S.E.2d 256 (2008), the Georgia Supreme Court held that a trial court's sentence which included a special condition of parole violated the state's constitutional provision regarding separation of powers. See Pate v. State, 318 Ga. App. 526, 531 (3), 734 S.E.2d 255 (2012). See State v. Davis, 303 Ga. 684, 814 S.E.2d 701 (2018) (unconditional pardon obviates duty of a convicted sex offender to register as a sex offender).

[2]Pate v. State, 318 Ga. App. 526, 531 (3), 734 S.E.2d 255 (2012).

[3]O.C.G.A. § 42-9-39. See Ga. Const. 1983, Art. IV, § II, ¶ II.

by the board, may suspend the execution of a sentence of death until the full board shall have an opportunity to hear the application of the convicted person for any relief within the power of the board."[4] The Board's statutorily mandated guidelines provide that any offender who is convicted of a violent offense or residential burglary on or after January 1, 1998, will be required to serve a minimum of 90% of the court imposed term of incarceration in prison.

Pursuant to O.C.G.A. § 42-9-40, the Board is required to adopt a parole guidelines system for use in determining its parole decisions for all inmates eligible for parole. Accordingly, the Board adopted the Parole Decision Guideline System (PDG) which takes into account "the severity of the crime and the inmate's risk to re-offend" to produce a tentative parole month.[5] "The tentative parole month serves as a recommendation to the Board which may use its discretion in setting the month that the inmate will be considered for release or deny parole altogether. Once notified of their tentative parole month, inmates are permitted to contest the crime severity or likelihood of success factors that were used by the PDG, but the ultimate decision is left to the discretion of the Board."[6]

Pursuant to O.C.G.A. § 42-9-43, the Parole Board is required to consider all "pertinent information on the person in question" including, but not limited to, the general record of the person acquired while in custody in such areas as: education; physical and mental status; the observations of staff regarding the person's conduct and demeanor; and other information supplied by the victim, the victim's family or other witnesses having knowledge of the victim. The Board may also consider written statements or oral testimony and any recommendation offered by the district attorney. The Board also has the authority to consider a medical release for a person suffering from terminal illness.

The State Board has adopted Rule 475-3-.05(2), which provides in part, "The Board will inform inmates denied parole of the reasons for such denial without disclosing confidential sources of information or possibly discouraging diagnostic opinions."

O.C.G.A. § 42-9-43.1 specifically authorizes the Board of Pardons and Parole to consider whether the general purposes of a parole would be frustrated if the person to be paroled is not legally present in the United States and thus subject to deportation. The statute authorizes the Board to decline to grant parole to a prisoner in such a case "in furtherance of the state

---

[4]Ga. Const. 1983, Art. IV, § II, ¶ II(d).

[5]Ga. Comp. R & Regs. 475-3-. 05(5).

[6]Ray v. Carthen, 275 Ga. 459, 460, 569 S.E.2d 542 (2002).

interest in certain and complete execution of sentences." O.C.G.A. § 17-10-1.3 is a parallel statute for similar cases being considered for a suspended sentence or probation by a trial court.

In *Georgia State Board of Pardons and Paroles v. Turner,*[7] the court held that a mandamus does not lie to require the Board to give an inmate "a written explanation of its previous decision denying him parole including 'those specific reasons why parole was denied so as to duly inform . . . [inmate] of the basis for the Board's action upon . . . [his] application for parole.' "Due process also does not require this.

In *Sultenfuss v. Snow,*[8] the Eleventh Circuit held that the Georgia parole system does not create a liberty interest protected by the due process clause.

In the case of *Garner v. Jones,*[9] the United States Supreme Court pointed out that "[r]etroactive changes in laws governing parole . . ., in some instances, may be violative [of the ex post facto clause]. . . . The controlling inquiry . . . [is] whether retroactive application of the change . . . created 'a sufficient risk of increasing the measure of punishment attached to the covered crimes.' "The court then applied this question to the Georgia issue of lengthening the interval to reconsider parole after its initial denial from three years to at least every eight years. The court emphasized that "[s]tates must have due flexibility in formulating parole procedures and addressing problems associated with confinement and release." The court then stated that "[o]n the record . . ., [it could] not conclude the change in Georgia law lengthened the . . . [inmate's] time of actual imprisonment," and reversed the Eleventh Circuit's opinion which had found a violation of the ex post facto clause.

§ 29:5 Conditions of parole; revocation of parole or release

O.C.G.A. § 42-9-42(d)(1) provides the State Board of Pardons and Paroles with the authority to condition the granting of parole to inmates "on such terms and conditions as the board shall prescribe, and if he or she is serving a split sentence, the board's conditions shall include all the terms of probation imposed by the sentencing court."

Georgia has a statutory procedure, enacted in 1975, relating to

---

[7]Georgia State Board of Pardons and Paroles v. Turner, 248 Ga. 767, 285 S.E.2d 731 (1982).

[8]Sultenfuss v. Snow, 35 F.3d 1494 (11th Cir. 1994).

[9]Garner v. Jones, 529 U.S. 244, 120 S.Ct. 1362, 146 L.Ed.2d 236 (2000), followed in Ray v. Jacobs, 272 Ga. 760, 534 S.E.2d 418 (2000).

the revocation of parole or conditional release.[1] This statute provides for the arrest of an offender,[2] a preliminary hearing,[3] and a final hearing.[4] In *Morrissey v. Brewer,*[5] the United States Supreme Court set out certain minimum due process requirements for parole revocations.[6] These requirements are discussed in more detail in sections 30:4 and 30:5, infra, on "Probation Revocation." At least on the surface, the Georgia statute on parole revocation may fail to comply with these minimum due process requirements in one respect in that it fails to provide that the hearing officer be "neutral and detached."[7] Also, it should be pointed out that since 1981 a preliminary parole revocation hearing is not required by statute if the alleged violator (1) is not under arrest on a Board warrant, (2) has absconded from supervision, (3) has admitted any alleged violation to a Board representative in the presence of a third party (who is not a Board representative), (4) has been convicted of a crime in federal court or a court of any state, or (5) has waived the hearing.[8]

The United States Supreme Court has held that there is no federal constitutional right to a prompt parole revocation hearing where a parolee is convicted of a crime which clearly violated his parole. The court said that the whole revocation hearing may be held after he has served his sentence for the intervening conviction.[9] Also, from a constitutional standpoint, it should be pointed out that it has been held that a parolee has no due process right to confront the witnesses against him and investigators can testify after the parolee has testified and after he is no longer present.[10]

[Section 29:5]

[1]O.C.G.A. §§ 42-9-48 et seq.

[2]O.C.G.A. § 42-9-48. In Standlee v. Rhay, 557 F.2d 1303 (9th Cir. 1977), the court held that defendant's parole could be revoked even if he was acquitted of the offense which was the basis of revocation.

[3]O.C.G.A. § 42-9-50. Cf. Brannum v. United States Board of Parole, 361 F.Supp. 394 (N.D.Ga.1973); O'Brien v. Henderson, 353 F.Supp. 1378 (N.D.Ga. 1973). But see Cook v. United States Attorney General, 488 F.2d 667 (5th Cir. 1974).

[4]O.C.G.A. § 42-9-51.

[5]Morrissey v. Brewer, 408 U.S. 471, 92 S.Ct. 2593, 33 L.Ed.2d 484 (1972).

[6]Generally, see Ware v. State, 137 Ga. App. 673, 224 S.E.2d 873 (1976). See Note, "Due Process and Parole Revocation," 77 Mich. L. R. 120 (1978).

[7]However, the Georgia statute does say that the officer is not to be "directly involved in the case." O.C.G.A. § 42-9-50(c). See Rosenthal, "Due Process for Prisoners Facing Parole Boards," 21 ATLA L. Rep. 213 (1978).

[8]O.C.G.A. § 42-9-50(a).

[9]Moody v. Daggett, 429 U.S. 78, 97 S.Ct. 274, 50 L.Ed.2d 236 (1976).

[10]Christopher v. U. S. Board of Parole, 589 F.2d 924 (7th Cir. 1978).

In the 1982 Arizona case of *Meredith v. Raines*,[11] the court emphasized the broad discretion which a parole board has and concluded that parole can be revoked if a parolee fails to abide by an oral condition of his probation.

In *Welsh v. Mizell*,[12] the Seventh Circuit held that parole eligibility must be determined by the standard in effect at the time of the commission of the offense. The court pointed out that the use of the then current standards for release was, in effect, an ex post facto violation. However, in *In re Duarte*,[13] the Court of Appeals for California held that while an inmate's eligibility for parole date should be calculated based on the law in effect at the time of his conviction, the standards used to evaluate an inmate's suitability for parole when that eligibility date occurs should be those in effect at that time.

In *Hamm v. Ray*,[14] the Georgia Supreme Court held that "it is not sufficient for a probation officer to inform a defendant after sentencing of certain additional conditions of his *probation*. . . . Likewise, certain conditions of *parole* are particularly inappropriate subjects for the exercise of discretion by individual parole officers, and are better left for the Board to specify. . . . Conditions which are tailored to sex offenders and denominated accordingly are prime examples of conditions which individual parole officers should not be allowed to impose. . . . [T]he parole officer ha[s] no discretion or authority to condition continuation of [a defendant's] parole on compliance with so-called sex offender instructions." (Emphasis in original).

See § 26:2, supra, on a sentence of life without parole.

---

[11]Meredith v. Raines, 131 Ariz. 244, 640 P.2d 175 (1982).

[12]Welsh v. Mizell, 668 F.2d 328 (7th Cir. 1982).

[13]In re Duarte, 143 Cal. App. 3d 943, 193 Cal. Rptr. 176 (3d Dist. 1983).

[14]Hamm v. Ray, 272 Ga. 659, 660, 531 S.E.2d 91 (2000).

Chapter 30

Probation Revocation

> **KeyCite®:** Cases and other legal materials listed in KeyCite Scope can be researched through the KeyCite service on Westlaw®. Use KeyCite to check citations for form, parallel references, prior and later history, and comprehensive citator information, including citations to other decisions and secondary materials.

§ 30:1   Introduction—General

In Georgia, revocation of probation is governed generally by statute.[1] Once a condition of probation has been violated, the Georgia Code authorizes the arrest of the probationer.[2] Notably, pursuant to O.C.G.A. § 17-10-1(a)(4), a court lacks the authority to revoke the probation of a defendant "in the legal custody of the State Board of Pardons and Parole." This includes persons who are on parole.[3]

If the charges are not dismissed at the preliminary hearing, the statute provides that a final hearing be held at the earliest possible date.[4] Upon a determination that the probation terms have been violated, the court may revoke, modify or continue the probation.

A probationer is not entitled to a jury trial on the question of revocation,[5] but he is entitled to due process in the proceeding.[6] A

[Section 30:1]

[1]O.C.G.A. § 42-8-38.

[2]O.C.G.A. § 42-8-38.

[3]Hayward v. Danforth, 299 Ga. 261, 787 S.E.2d 709 (2016).

[4]O.C.G.A. § 42-8-38.

[5]Johnson v. State, 214 Ga. 818, 108 S.E.2d 313 (1959).

[6]Porter v. State, 142 Ga. App. 481, 482, 236 S.E.2d 172 (1977),

defendant has no right of discovery pursuant to a Brady motion.[7] In *Perry v. State,*[8] the court held that "there is no double jeopardy protection against revocation of probation . . . , [and a defendant may] be prosecuted in successive actions for probation revocation based on violations which were part of the same conduct."

A revocation proceeding may be held before the disposition of the criminal case which precipitated the revocation proceeding.[9] A judge may revoke a probated sentence which is to begin in the future,[10] but the court may not revoke a probated sentence which has expired at the time of the revocation hearing.[11] Probation may be revoked even though the defendant is found not guilty of the crime which is the basis of the revocation[12] and even though the probationer is not indicted or formally charged with the of-

---

overruled on other grounds, State v. Thackston, 289 Ga. 412, 716 S.E.2d 517 (2011).

[7]Baltimore v. State, 165 Ga. App. 741, 742 (1), 302 S.E.2d 427 (1983).

[8]Perry v. State, 213 Ga. App. 220, 221, 444 S.E.2d 150 (1994).

[9]Jackson v. State, 140 Ga. App. 659, 231 S.E.2d 554 (1976); King v. State, 154 Ga. App. 549, 269 S.E.2d 55 (1980).

In Evans v. State, 153 Ga. App. 764, 266 S.E.2d 545 (1980), the court said that there was no violation of due process or fundamental fairness in refusing to postpone a revocation hearing until after the trial of the charge which is the basis of the proposed revocation. However, in People v. Rocha, 86 Mich.App. 497, 272 N.W.2d 699 (1978), the court held on public policy grounds that a defendant's probation hearing could not be used at his later trial. In People v. Coleman, 13 Cal.3d 867, 120 Cal.Rptr. 384, 533 P.2d 1024 (1975), the court held "that the prosecutor must either grant use and derivative use immunity for the defendant's . . . revocation hearing testimony, or hold the violation hearing after the trial on the underlying charge." Accord, State v. DeLomba, 117 R.I. 673, 370 A.2d 1273 (1977); McCracken v. Corey, 612 P.2d 990 (Alaska 1980) (parole revocation). Contra, Flint v. Mullen, 499 F.2d 100

(1st Cir. 1974). In Melson v. Sard, 402 F.2d 653 (D.C.Cir. 1968), the court held that any incriminatory "statements made in a parole revocation hearing shall not be used affirmatively against the parolee in any subsequent criminal proceeding."

In Puckett v. State, 163 Ga. App. 156 (1), 293 S.E.2d 544 (1982), the court disapproved but declined to reverse the conducting of a combination probation revocation hearing and a commitment hearing.

[10]O.C.G.A. § 17-10-1(a)(1).

[11]Todd v. State, 108 Ga. App. 615, 616, 134 S.E.2d 56 (1963), disapproved on other grounds in Parrish v. Ault, 237 Ga. 401, 402, 228 S.E.2d 808 (1976).

[12]Johnson v. State, 142 Ga. App. 124, 235 S.E.2d 550 (1977). This opinion by Judge Shulman on revocation of probation is an excellent discussion of the whole subject, and the Johnson case was affirmed at 240 Ga. 526, 242 S.E.2d 53 (1978). See also Jones v. State, 142 Ga. App. 274, 235 S.E.2d 681 (1977); State v. Dupard, 93 Wash.2d 268, 609 P.2d 961 (1980).

In Mingo v. State, 155 Ga. App. 284, 287 (3), 270 S.E.2d 700 (1980), the court held that a defendant's probation could be revoked for committing an offense even though a grand jury returned a no bill if there is slight evidence of his guilt.

fense which is the basis of the revocation.[13] The state may delay a revocation proceeding when a probationer commits a later violation of a criminal statute, and it may consider both a conviction and a later escape in revoking the probation.[14] However, if the revocation proceeding is based on a conviction of another crime and the other conviction is reversed, this in effect reverses the probation revocation.[15] A defendant's probation may be revoked solely on a certified copy of his criminal conviction even if the case is being appealed.[16]

A general discharge of probation order which terminates probation early will operate as a bar to revocation initiated after the date of the order. Thus, in *White v. State*,[17] the Court of Appeals ruled that an early termination order by the Board of Pardons and Paroles which removes all disabilities resulting from the probationer's prior sentence leaves no sentence to revoke.

While there is no Georgia statute prescribing just what pleadings are to be used in a revocation proceeding, it is normally done with a petition.[18] A rule nisi order, directed to the probationer, is attached. In *Wolcott v. State*,[19] the Georgia Supreme Court found that O.C.G.A. § 42-8-29, allowing probation officers to file revocation petitions, does not violate the constitutional principle of separation of powers.

Where a defendant is placed on probation and as a condition thereof is ordered to pay a fine and make restitution and the payments are not made, the defendant must be given an opportunity to establish his inability to pay. "[T]he circumstances of the individual must be taken into consideration in determining whether revocation is warranted."[20]

In *Bearden v. Georgia*,[21] the United States Supreme Court held that "the trial court erred in automatically revoking probation

[13]DeFreese v. State, 148 Ga. App. 81, 251 S.E.2d 47 (1978).

[14]Aldridge v. State, 155 Ga. App. 916, 273 S.E.2d 656 (1980).

[15]Tift v. State, 133 Ga. App. 466, 211 S.E.2d 411 (1974).

[16]Crawford v. State, 166 Ga. App. 272 (1), 304 S.E.2d 443 (1983).

[17]White v. State, 274 Ga. App. 805, 619 S.E.2d 333 (2005). The court noted that the Board's power in this regard is provided by the Georgia Constitution. See, Ga.Const. 1983, Art. IV, Sec. II, Pr. II(a).

[18]E.g., Brogdon v. State, 136 Ga. App. 121, 220 S.E.2d 471 (1975).

In In re B. C., 169 Ga. App. 200, 311 S.E.2d 857 (1983), the court pointed out that revocation of probation of an adult was not analogous to a revocation of juvenile probation. Due process must be afforded in both. Due process requires timely notice and a hearing before revocation.

[19]Wolcott v. State, 278 Ga. 664, 604 S.E.2d 478 (2004).

[20]Malcom v. State, 162 Ga. App. 587, 291 S.E.2d 756 (1982).

[21]Bearden v. Georgia, 461 U.S. 660, 103 S.Ct. 2064, 76 L.Ed.2d 221 (1983), rev'g 161 Ga. App. 640, 288 S.E.2d 662 (1982) and remanding the case. See Johnson v. State, 307 Ga.

because petitioner could not pay his fine, without determining that petitioner had not made sufficient bona fide efforts to pay or that adequate alternative forms of punishment did not exist." The rule is different in cases where the defendant agrees to pay a specific amount of restitution by a date certain in order to avoid confinement. In such cases, a court need not concern itself with the defendant's ability to pay. The only issue is whether defendant satisfied his plea bargain.[22]

In 2009, the legislature amended Chapter 8 of Title 42 relating to probation by adding a new Article 9, known as the "Probation Management Act." The bill was summarized as follows in the 2009 Final Legislature Update from the Council of Superior Court Judges: "The trial judge may require that defendants who are sentenced to probation be ordered to the sentencing options system. Where a defendant has been ordered to the sentencing options system, the court shall retain jurisdiction throughout the period of the probated sentence and may modify or revoke any part of a probated sentence."

The Department of Corrections is authorized to establish a system of administrative sanctions as an alternative to judicial modifications or revocations for probationers who violate the terms and conditions of the sentencing options system. However, the department may not sanction probationers for violations of special conditions of probation or general conditions of probation for which the sentencing judge has expressed an intention that the violations be heard by the court. The department shall only impose restrictions which are equal to or less restrictive than the sanction cap set by the sentencing judge.

If an options system probationer files an appeal to a final decision, it must be filed within 30 days of the issuance of the decision by the senior hearing officer. It has to be reviewed first by the judge upon the record. At the judge's discretion, a de novo hearing may be held on the decision. The filing of the appeal shall not stay the department's decision. If the sentencing judge does not act on the appeal within 30 days of the date of the filing of the appeal, the department's decision shall be affirmed by operation of law. Code Section 42-8-157 provides: "Nothing

---

App. 570, 707 S.E.2d 373 (2011) (trial court required to make findings as to reasons for defendant's inability to pay fine or restitution as to defendant's ability to pay when revoking for that reason). Compare Dickey v. State, 257 Ga. App. 190, 570 S.E.2d 634 (2002) (revocation of probation was proper where defendant breached a negoti-

ated plea that required defendant to pay a specific amount of restitution by a date certain). See § 24:4, supra, on equal protection and § 30:8, infra, on violation of condition of probation.

[22]Dickey v. State, 257 Ga. App. 190, 570 S.E.2d 634 (2002). See Polly v. State, 323 Ga. App. 893, 748 S.E.2d 696 (2013).

contained in this article shall be construed as repealing any power given to any court of this state to place offenders on probation or to supervise offenders."

See §§ 26:18 et seq., supra, on terms of probation.

§ 30:2   Violation of conditions

It is provided by statute that if a probationer violates his probation "in a material respect," he may be arrested.[1] Thus, to put it another way, there seems to be no right to start a revocation proceeding unless the probationer violates one or more terms or conditions of his probation even if, as a matter of fact, he violates some law.[2] Where a probation order contains a general provision prohibiting the defendant from violating a state or federal law, his probation may not be terminated for violation of a city ordinance.[3] See §§ 26:18 and 26:19, supra, on terms of probation.

Thus, probation revocation for any reason other than a violation of a term or condition of probation is a due process violation.[4] However, in *Harp v. State*,[5] the defendant's probation was conditioned on his complying with the rules of a diversion center. The rules were not set out in the order but the defendant was fully informed of these rules. The court affirmed the revocation of his probation for possession of alcoholic beverages inside the center, which was contrary to its rules.

In *Thompson v. State*,[6] the Georgia Supreme Court determined that a Georgia statute which made it a felony offense for a registered sex offender to reside within 1,000 feet of a child day care facility or a school is not an unconstitutional ex post facto law when applied to an offender who was convicted before the

---

[Section 30:2]

[1]O.C.G.A. § 42-8-38. However, in Collins v. State, 151 Ga. App. 116, 117 (2), 258 S.E.2d 769 (1979), the court said that the charge against the defendant may not simply be that he violated "the rules of the Athens Diversion Center." The specific rule or rules violated must be set out so that he can adequately prepare his defense. See Legere v. State, 299 Ga. App. 640, 683 S.E.2d 155 (2009). Compare Wolcott v. State, 278 Ga. 664, 604 S.E.2d 478 (2004).

In Watson v. State, 155 Ga. App. 948, 274 S.E.2d 61 (1980), the court said the trial judge erred in failing to make a written statement of the evidence relied upon and the reason for revoking the probation.

[2]See Radcliff v. State, 134 Ga. App. 244, 214 S.E.2d 179 (1975); Kendrick v. State, 125 Ga. App. 326, 187 S.E.2d 580 (1972). Both of these cases actually hold that probation may not be revoked on any ground other than that set out in the petition for revocation.

[3]Nasworthy v. State, 169 Ga. App. 603 (1), 314 S.E.2d 446 (1984).

[4]Hinton v. State, 127 Ga. App. 853 (2), 195 S.E.2d 472 (1973).

[5]Harp v. State, 169 Ga. App. 670 (1), 314 S.E.2d 686 (1984).

[6]Thompson v. State, 278 Ga. 394, 603 S.E.2d 233 (2004); Denson v. State, 267 Ga. App. 528, 600 S.E.2d 645 (2004).

date the law was enacted. Likewise, in *Miller v. State*,[7] a sex offender registration requirement imposed as a condition of the defendant's probation was deemed not to be an ex post facto law because the defendant's failure to abide by the statute requiring that he register as a sex offender[8] would result in a new crime, even though the new crime would be based on his status as a sex offender.

However, in *Mann v. Georgia Dep't of Corrections*,[9] the Georgia Supreme Court held that a Georgia statute which made it a felony for a registered sex offender to reside or work within 1,000 feet of any child care facility, church, school, or area where minors congregate[10] was unconstitutional as a regulatory taking in that it required a sex offender to quit a residence that he acquired prior to a child care facility locating itself within 1,000 feet of the premises. The provision of the statute that prohibited sex offenders from working within 1,000 feet of a child care facility, school, or church was not held unconstitutional.

In 2008, the Georgia legislature amended the sex offender statute, attempting to bring it within constitutional bounds.[11] The amended version of the statute retains the provision making it unlawful for a registered sex offender to reside or work within 1,000 feet of any child care facility, school, church, or area where minors congregate. However, it provides for an exception where a sex offender owns and resides on real property and a child care facility, school, church, or area where minors congregate locates itself within 1,000 feet of that property. There is also an exception where a sex offender has established employment and a child care facility, school, church, or area where minors congregate locates itself within 1,000 feet of that employment, as well as an exception for individuals who established ownership of real property or employment within 1,000 feet of a prohibited location prior to July 1, 2006.

---

[7]Miller v. State, 291 Ga. App. 478, 662 S.E.2d 261 (2008); see also Watson v. State, 283 Ga. App. 635 (2), 642 S.E.2d 328 (2007).

[8]O.C.G.A. § 42-1-12. See Santos v. State, 284 Ga. 514, 668 S.E.2d 676 (2008) (O.C.G.A. § 42-1-12 is unconstitutionally vague in the case of the homeless because it fails to give fair notice of how to comply the statute's registration guidelines). Amended in 2010, O.C.G.A. § 42-1-12 no longer requires a sexual offender to register with an address of permanent or temporary residence. If the sexual offender is homeless, he or she must register in person with the sheriff of the county in which he or she sleeps within 72 hours of release and provide the sheriff the location of where he or she sleeps.

[9]Mann v. Georgia Dep't of Corrections, 282 Ga. 754, 653 S.E.2d 740 (2007).

[10]Former O.C.G.A. § 42-1-15.

[11]O.C.G.A. § 42-1-15.

In *Germany v. State*,[12] the court found that a special condition of probation which required a sex offender to submit to lie detector examinations did not violate the probationer's Fifth Amendment rights in the absence of a properly asserted right to the privilege against self-incrimination.

As previously mentioned, generally probation may not be revoked for any reason not set out in the petition,[13] but if a defendant admits in the hearing that he committed a crime not charged in the petition, his probation may be revoked because of this violation.[14] In *Oliver v. State*,[15] the court held that where the defendant was charged with being arrested for a named offense and the evidence showed that as a matter of fact he was guilty of that offense, the trial judge may revoke probation.

In *Shaw v. State*,[16] the defendant was found to have concealed marijuana when he checked into a diversion center after sentencing. His probation order had not been prepared or signed at the time. A petition for revocation was filed and his probation was revoked based on the possession of marijuana. In affirming the revocation, the court pointed out that in an earlier probation he had been advised that he had to obey all laws and not possess marijuana.

Where a defendant is sentenced as a first offender and his status is terminated because of a probation violation and he is then sentenced to serve for a specified period followed by the remainder of his sentence on probation, the terms of the earlier probation do not apply to the second probationary period.[17]

In 2001 the Legislature amended O.C.G.A. § 17-10-1(a) so as to provide that the trial court now has the "power and authority to suspend or probate all or any part of the entire sentence under such rules and regulations as the judge deems proper, including

---

[12]Germany v. State, 315 Ga. App. 717, 727 S.E.2d 240 (2012) (court based its decision on Minnesota v. Murphy, 465 U.S. 420, 104 S. Ct. 1136, 79 L. Ed. 2d 409 (1984)).

[13]Radcliff v. State, 134 Ga. App. 244, 214 S.E.2d 179 (1975). In Sosbee v. State, 155 Ga. App. 196, 270 S.E.2d 367 (1980), probation revocation was sought on the basis that defendant committed theft by taking. The trial judge erred in revoking probation where the evidence showed theft by receiving. Johnson v. State, 161 Ga. App. 506, 507 (1), 288 S.E.2d 366 (1982).

In Moore v. State, 165 Ga. App. 59, 299 S.E.2d 138 (1983), a petition for revocation of probation was filed on the ground that the defendant had committed a burglary. The evidence disclosed an indictment for burglary but a conviction of theft by receiving stolen property. The court pointed out that theft by receiving was not a lesser included offense of burglary and reversed the revocation.

[14]Frederick v. Davis, 231 Ga. 109, 200 S.E.2d 266 (1973).

[15]Oliver v. State, 169 Ga. App. 716, 717 (3), 314 S.E.2d 722 (1984).

[16]Shaw v. State, 164 Ga. App. 208, 296 S.E.2d 765 (1982).

[17]Helton v. State, 166 Ga. App. 565, 305 S.E.2d 27 (1983).

service of a probated sentence in the sentencing options system, as provided by Article 9 of Chapter 8 of Title 42, and including the authority to revoke the suspension or probation when the defendant has violated any of the rules and regulations prescribed by the court, even before the probationary period has begun. . .."[18] Thus, in *State v. Huckeba*,[19] the Court of Appeals determined that the trial court had the authority to revoke all or any part of the balance of the sentence to be served by the defendant because he violated a condition of probation while on parole but before the time the probated part of his sentence was to have begun.

In addition, O.C.G.A. § 17-10-1(a) as amended does not offend the constitutional prohibition against ex post facto laws and is applicable to persons sentenced prior to the effective date of the amendment.[20]

§ 30:3 Arrest or detention

The Georgia statute provides that a probation officer may arrest a probationer if he "believes" that such probationer under his supervision materially violated the terms of his probation.[1] Likewise, a law enforcement officer with general arrest powers may arrest a probationer without a warrant if the officer "has trustworthy information as to the probation violation."[2] After a probationer is arrested without a warrant, the probation officer may return him to the court granting probation, or if he is under the supervision of another county or circuit, he may be delivered to a court of equivalent jurisdiction in the county in which the probationer lives.[3] Also, any officer authorized to issue a warrant may issue an arrest warrant for the probationer "upon the affidavit of one having knowledge of the alleged violation, returnable forthwith before the court in which revocation proceedings are being brought."[4]

Pursuant to O.C.G.A. § 42-8-36(a)(1), a person on probation has a duty to keep his or her officer informed as to his or her residence. The court may also order that the probationer keep the officer informed as to his or her whereabouts. Pursuant to

---

[18]Ga. L. 2001, p. 94 § 5.

[19]State v. Huckeba, 258 Ga. App. 627, 629(1), 574 S.E.2d 856 (2002).

[20]Postell v. Humphrey, 278 Ga. 651, 604 S.E.2d 517 (2004).

[Section 30:3]

[1]In United States v. Basso, 632 F.2d 1007 (2d Cir. 1980), the court held that a "somewhat looser" standard is constitutionally permissible for arrest warrants for probation violations than

in the case of an ordinary arrest warrant.

[2]Battle v. State, 254 Ga. 666, 671, 333 S.E.2d 599 (1985).

[3]See Biddy v. State, 132 Ga. App. 264, 208 S.E.2d 22 (1974).

[4]Downs v. State, 163 Ga. App. 485, 295 S.E.2d 152 (1982); O.C.G.A. § 42-8-38. See Thompson v. State, 313 Ga. App. 294, 721 S.E.2d 106 (2011) (unsworn statement will not suffice).

O.C.G.A. § 42-8-36(a)(2), the running of a probated sentence is tolled upon the failure of a probationer to report as directed to his or her officer or by the failure of the probationer to appear at a revocation hearing. Either of these events may be proved by the affidavit of the officer. A probated sentence may also be tolled upon the filing of a non est inventus or other return of a probation revocation warrant for the violation of a condition of probation that the probationer cannot be found within the county of his or her residence. Pursuant to O.C.G.A. § 42-8-36(a)(3), the effective date of the tolling of the sentence shall be the date upon which the court enters a tolling order and continues until the probationer reports or is taken into custody.[5] The clerk of court must provide the Georgia Crime Information Center with a copy of the tolling order within 30 days of filing.

§ 30:4 Preliminary hearing

The Georgia statute provides that the probationer shall be brought before the court forthwith and also states that "[t]he court, upon the probationer being brought before it, may commit him or release him with or without bail to await further hearing or it may dismiss the charge. If the charge is not dismissed at this time, the court shall give the probationer an opportunity to be heard fully at the earliest possible date. . . ."[1] The statute also states "that, if the revocation proceeding is in a court other than the court of the original criminal conviction, the sentencing court shall be given ten days' written notice prior to a hearing on the merits."[2] O.C.G.A. § 42-8-34(g) mandates that the "sentencing judge" is to determine the question of revocation of probation. However, in *Smith v. State*,[3] the court held that a designated magistrate did not lack authority to hear the appellant's probation revocation because he was not the original sentencing judge. The court ruled that the state's reference to "sentencing judge" refers to the office and not a person, and the designated magistrate was acting under the authority of the superior court judge under whose authority the original sentence was entered.

The statutory procedure for probation revocation in Georgia does not seem to meet the minimum due process requirements as laid down by the United States Supreme Court in *Morrissey v.*

---

[5]See Anderson v. Sentinel Offender Services, LLC, 298 Ga. 854, 784 S.E.2d 791 (2016) (tolling applies to privately supervised misdemeanor sentences).

[Section 30:4]

[1]O.C.G.A. § 42-8-38.

[2]O.C.G.A. § 42-8-38.

[3]Smith v. State, 250 Ga. App. 128, 129 (1), 550 S.E.2d 683 (2001).

Brewer[4] and *Gagnon v. Scarpelli.*[5] In *Morrissey*, the court considered due process requirements of parole revocation. In *Gagnon*, the court concluded that the same requirements of due process applied to the revocation of probation which applied to parole revocation[6] and emphasized that a probationer was entitled to a preliminary and a final revocation hearing under the conditions set out in *Morrissey*. The following six due process requirements are taken from *Morrissey*:

First, there must be a prompt inquiry or preliminary hearing conducted at or near the place of the alleged parole violation or arrest while information is fresh and sources are available.[7] However, in *Wilson v. State*,[8] the Georgia Court of Appeals held that all due process requirements can be satisfied in a single court trial, and where they are so met the defendant is not entitled to a preliminary hearing.[9]

Second, this determination of whether or not reasonable

---

[4]Morrissey v. Brewer, 408 U.S. 471, 92 S.Ct. 2593, 33 L.Ed.2d 484 (1972).

[5]Gagnon v. Scarpelli, 411 U.S. 778, 93 S.Ct. 1756, 36 L.Ed.2d 656 (1973).

[6]Gagnon v. Scarpelli, 411 U.S. 778, 93 S.Ct. 1756, 36 L.Ed.2d 656 (1973).

[7]Morrissey v. Brewer, 408 U.S. 471, 485, 92 S.Ct. 2593, 33 L.Ed.2d 484, 496 (1972).

[8]Wilson v. State, 152 Ga. App. 695, 696 (1), 263 S.E.2d 691 (1979). Accord, McElroy v. State, 247 Ga. 355, 276 S.E.2d 38 (1981).

In Ware v. State, 137 Ga. App. 673, 675, 224 S.E.2d 873 (1976), the court said the requirements of the United States Supreme Court are "met and a probationer's constitutional rights are fully protected through a single dispositional hearing where, as here, the procedure included these successive steps: (1) a petition filed by the probation supervisor in the court where the original probation sentence has been entered; (2) such petition reciting (a) details of the original trial including nature of the offense, defendant's plea, the court's sentence and date thereof with a copy of the terms and conditions of the probation sentence; (b) specificity as to alleged viola-

tions of the probation conditions; (c) prayer for citation, petition for revocation and for a rule to show cause; (3) consideration of the petition by trial judge and his entry of an order requiring service of a copy of the petition and a show cause ruling for a specified date, time and place in open court; (4) service of the petition and court order; (5) a full fledged hearing in accordance with Code Ann. § 27-2713 [O.C.G.A. § 42-8-38]; and (6) a judicial determination in writing by the court stating the particulars in which the terms of the probation had been violated and a recital as to the specific term that remains to be served."

In Peters v. State, 150 Ga. App. 315, 257 S.E.2d 382 (1979), the court held that a probationer who is serving a sentence in Florida is not entitled to an immediate hearing. In United States v. Tucker, 524 F.2d 77 (5th Cir. 1975), the court said that where a probationer or parolee is incarcerated pursuant to a final conviction at the time of attempted revocation, he is not entitled to an immediate probable cause hearing.

Georgia provides by statute for a preliminary hearing in a parole violation case. O.C.G.A. § 42-8-38, O.C.G.A. § 42-9-50.

[9]For discussion suggesting that a bond and preliminary hearing are

grounds exist for revocation "should be made by someone not directly involved in the case."[10] "This independent person need not be a judicial officer."[11]

Third, the probationer "should be given notice that the hearing will take place and that its purpose is to determine whether there is probable cause to believe he has committed a . . . violation."[12]

Fourth, the probationer is entitled to be present and speak in his behalf. He "may bring letters, documents or individuals who can give relevant information to the hearing officer." If he requests it, he is entitled to the names of the persons who have given adverse information on which revocation is based unless an informer is involved whom the hearing officer determines would be subjected to the risk of harm.[13]

Fifth, the hearing officer has the duty of making a summary of what occurs at the hearing in terms of the responses of the probationer and the substance of evidence given.

Sixth, the officer should determine whether there is probable cause to hold the probationer for the revocation hearing. The officer should state the reasons for his determination and the evidence relied upon, but a formal finding of fact and conclusions of law are not required. The determination would be sufficient to warrant the probationer's continued detention pending the final revocation hearing.[14]

§ 30:5 Final revocation hearing—General

In *Smith v. Nichols,*[1] the Georgia Supreme Court pointed out "that due process in probation revocation proceedings does not require both a preliminary and a final hearing 'where all requirements of due process can be afforded in a single hearing procedure.'" However, a defendant's probation cannot be revoked on a ground which is not set forth in the petition to revoke.[2]

The Georgia statute provides only that if the probationer is not

---

required in probation revocation proceedings, see Volume XXIX, May 2003, *What's the Decision,* Gardner, Bond Hearings on Probation Warrants.

[10]Morrissey v. Brewer, 408 U.S. 471, 485, 92 S.Ct. 2593, 33 L.Ed.2d 484 (1972).

[11]Morrissey v. Brewer, 408 U.S. 471, 486, 92 S.Ct. 2593, 33 L.Ed.2d 484 (1972).

[12]Morrissey v. Brewer, 408 U.S. 471, 486, 487, 92 S.Ct. 2593, 33 L.Ed.2d 484 (1972); Hughes v. Hinks, 249 Ga. 416, 291 S.E.2d 545 (1982).

[13]Morrissey v. Brewer, 408 U.S. 471, 487, 92 S.Ct. 2593, 33 L.Ed.2d 484 (1972).

[14]Morrissey v. Brewer, 408 U.S. 471, 487, 92 S.Ct. 2593, 33 L.Ed.2d 484 (1972).

[Section 30:5]

[1]Smith v. Nichols, 270 Ga. 550, 554-55 (2)(b), 512 S.E.2d 279 (1999) (quoting McElroy v. State, 247 Ga. 355, 276 S.E.2d 38 (1981)).

[2]Jones v. State, 314 Ga. App. 442, 724 S.E.2d 454 (2012).

released when he is brought before the court the first time, he shall be given "an opportunity to be heard fully at the earliest possible date on his own behalf, in person or by counsel . . . ."[3] The Georgia Court of Appeals has interpreted the statute to mean that in the absence of "special circumstances . . . 30 days is an entirely reasonable time period between petition and hearing . . . ."[4]

Morrissey v. Brewer[5] and *Gagnon v. Scarpelli,*[6] as discussed in the last section, provide a minimum of due process requirements in proceedings of this kind. These minimum requirements in the final revocation hearing as set out in *Gagnon*[7] are as follows:

"(a) written notice of the claimed violations of probation . . . ;[8]

"(b) disclosure to the probationer . . . of evidence against him;

"(c) opportunity to be heard in person and to present witnesses and documentary evidence;

"(d) the right to confront and cross-examine adverse witnesses (unless the hearing officer specifically finds good cause for not allowing confrontation);

"(e) a 'neutral and detached' hearing body[9] . . . ; and

"(f) a written statement by the factfinders as to the evidence relied on and reasons for revoking probation. . . ."[10] However, in

---

[3]O.C.G.A. § 42-8-38. In the case of Baldwin v. Benson, 584 F.2d 953 (10th Cir. 1978), the court held that an indigent has a statutory right to court appointed counsel at his federal parole revocation hearing.

[4]Anderson v. State, 166 Ga. App. 521, 304 S.E.2d 747 (1983).

[5]Morrissey v. Brewer, 408 U.S. 471, 92 S.Ct. 2593, 33 L.Ed.2d 484 (1972).

[6]Gagnon v. Scarpelli, 411 U.S. 778, 786, 93 S.Ct. 1756, 36 L.Ed.2d 656 (1973).

[7]Gagnon v. Scarpelli, 411 U.S. 778, 93 S.Ct. 1756, 36 L.Ed.2d 656 (1973).

[8]In Harrell v. State, 162 Ga. App. 111, 290 S.E.2d 213 (1982), the court concluded that a revocation petition which only charged the defendant with violating the rules of the diversion center was not sufficient notice to the defendant to enable him to prepare an adequate defense.

In Kitchens v. State, 234 Ga. App. 785, 787 (2), 508 S.E.2d 176 (1998), the court emphasized that due process requires written notice of the claimed violation. Thus, where the probationer is charged with only a misdemeanor violation, this does not constitute sufficient notice to permit the trial court to revoke his probation on the ground of attempted rape even though the attempted rape was an alleged part of the charge of battery.

[9]The court said the reviewing board need not be judicial officers or lawyers.

[10]In Hillman v. State, 162 Ga. App. 121, 290 S.E.2d 219 (1982), the court concluded that a written statement of the evidence relied upon by the trial judge in revoking probation is not necessary when the basis of revocation can be determined from the record. Accord, Graves v. State, 168 Ga. App. 370 (2), 309 S.E.2d 390 (1983).

Johnson v. Boyington,[11] the Georgia Supreme Court held that "when the defendant and the appellate courts can ascertain the basis for revocation," it is not necessary for the trial court to submit its "findings on a separate piece of paper."

In *Kitchens v. State,*[12] the court emphasized that "[s]ince a probationer has no inflexible right to appointed counsel under the due process clause . . . , there is no absolute requirement that he be informed of that right. A probationer is entitled only to be informed of his right to *request* counsel. . . . *In every case in which a request for counsel at a preliminary or final hearing is refused, the grounds for refusal should be stated succinctly in the record.*" (Emphasis in original.) However, the "trial court's failure to inform an accused of his right to request counsel is not necessarily fatal to [the] case. 'Unless [the] revocation proceeding was one wherein the actual appointment of counsel was necessary to satisfy applicable due process requirements of fundamental fairness, then he would not have been entitled to have his request for counsel honored and the mere failure to have informed him of the right to make such a request could not have harmed him.' . . . However, the trial court must make the initial determination as to whether a probationer is entitled to counsel based upon the guidelines set forth in *Gagnon.*"

The final revocation hearing is not to be equated with "a criminal prosecution in any sense. It is a narrow inquiry; the process should be flexible enough to consider evidence including letters, affidavits and other material that would not be admissible in an adversary criminal trial."[13] However, the probationer must be given an opportunity to show that he did not violate the conditions and to show any factors of mitigation demonstrating that the violation does not warrant revocation.[14] The final hearing must be available to probationer within a reasonable time if he is in custody.[15]

In *Adams v. State,*[16] the court pointed out that counsel should be appointed for an indigent probationer "where, after being informed of his right to request counsel, . . . [he] makes such a request . . . based on a timely and colorable claim (i) that he has not committed the alleged violation of the conditions . . . ; or (ii)

---

[11]Johnson v. Boyington, 273 Ga. 420, 422, 541 S.E.2d 355 (2001).

[12]Kitchens v. State, 234 Ga. App. 785 (1), 508 S.E.2d 176 (1998) (quoting Vaughn v. Rutledge, 265 Ga. 773, 462 S.E.2d 132 (1995), and Elkins v. State, 147 Ga. App. 837, 250 S.E.2d 535 (1978)).

[13]Morrissey v. Brewer, 408 U.S. 471, 489, 92 S.Ct. 2593, 33 L.Ed.2d 484 (1972).

[14]See § 30:1, supra.

[15]Morrissey v. Brewer, 408 U.S. 471, 488, 92 S.Ct. 2593, 33 L.Ed.2d 484 (1972).

[16]Adams v. State, 207 Ga. App. 508 (1), 428 S.E.2d 613 (1993).

that, even if the violation . . . is uncontested, there are substantial reasons which justified or mitigated the violation and make revocation inappropriate, and that the reasons are complex or otherwise difficult to develop or present."

In *Vaughn v. Rutledge*,[17] the court held that it is only necessary to appoint counsel needed "to satisfy applicable due process requirements of fundamental fairness."

In *Kirby v. State*,[18] the Court of Appeals pointed out that, where the defendant at a revocation hearing contends that his plea was not freely and voluntarily entered, the state, before reaching the merits of the petition for revocation, must first establish that the plea *was* freely and voluntarily entered with an understanding of the nature of the charges and of the consequences of the plea. Likewise, a revocation of probation, which follows from a probationer's waiver of a hearing and admission of the violation alleged, will be set aside if the probationer can establish by independent evidence that "his or her admission of probation violation was not knowing and voluntary . . . ."[19]

If the "sole basis for probation revocation is failure to pay fines, statutory surcharges, or probation supervision fees," the sentencing judge must schedule the probationer to "appear on the court's next available court calendar for a hearing on such issue," but shall not issue a prehearing arrest warrant.[20] If the sole basis for revocation is failure to report as directed by a probation officer, the court may issue an arrest warrant if the probation officer submits an affidavit averring that:

(1) The probationer failed to report as directed at least twice;

(2) The officer attempted to contact the probation officer at least twice at their last known telephone number or email address, and list both;

(3) The officer has checked the local jail rosters and not seen the probationer on them;

(4) The officer sent a letter to the probationer's last known address advising the probationer that the officer will seek revocation if the probationer does not report within ten days of the mailing date of the letter; and

(5) The probationer failed to comply with the instructions in the letter and ten days passed since mailing the letter.

If the probationer reports to the officer as directed in the letter, "the probationer may be scheduled to appear on the next avail-

---

[17]Vaughn v. Rutledge, 265 Ga. 773, 774, 462 S.E.2d 132 (1995).

[18]Kirby v. State, 170 Ga. App. 11, 12, 316 S.E.2d 23 (1984).

[19]Meadows v. Settles, 274 Ga. 858, 862 (3), 561 S.E.2d 105 (2002).

[20]O.C.G.A. § 42-8-102(f)(2)(A).

able court calendar for a hearing to consider whether the probation sentence should be revoked in whole or in part."[21]

§ 30:6 Final revocation hearing—Right to counsel

Prior to 2005, an indigent probationer was not entitled to counsel as a matter of right in a probation revocation proceeding.[1] In 2005, the legislature enacted O.C.G.A. § 17-12-23, which provided, inter alia, that the circuit public defender provide representation to indigents at probation revocation proceedings in superior court and all direct appeals therefrom. Jurisdictions which do not have a circuit public defender are required by O.C.G.A. § 17-12-23(d) to appoint representation for indigents at such proceedings.[2]

§ 30:7 Final revocation hearing—Evidence

A number of Georgia cases have held that only slight evidence is necessary in order to justify the revocation of probation,[1] and the rules of evidence as applied in a civil or criminal trial are not

---

[21]O.C.G.A. § 42-8-102(f)(3).

[Section 30:6]

[1]See, e.g., Banks v. State, 275 Ga. App. 326, 620 S.E.2d 581 (2005).

[2]See Miller v. State, 301 Ga. App. 706, 689 S.E.2d 46 (2009), opinion vacated, 288 Ga. 153, 702 S.E.2d 137 (2010) (Appeals decision that indigent is not entitled to transcript of revocation hearing vacated as moot).

[Section 30:7]

[1]E.g., Harper v. State, 130 Ga. App. 545, 203 S.E.2d 866 (1974); Bishop v. State, 138 Ga. App. 382, 226 S.E.2d 476 (1976).

In Robinson v. State, 154 Ga. App. 591, 593, 269 S.E.2d 86 (1980), the court said that in a probation revocation proceeding it is not necessary that the evidence show a violation beyond a reasonable doubt or even by a preponderance of the evidence.

In Hicks v. State, 157 Ga. App. 79, 80(2), 276 S.E.2d 129 (1981), an experienced officer without expertise in the drug field was permitted to testify that the substance was hashish without describing what the substance looked like. This was found to be sufficient evidence to support a revocation of probation.

In Hayes v. State, 157 Ga. App. 659, 660(2), 278 S.E.2d 424 (1981), the court held that a GBI agent's testimony (based on training and experience) that the substance purchased from defendant was marijuana was sufficient to revoke defendant's probation.

In Hogan v. State, 158 Ga. App. 495(1), 280 S.E.2d 891 (1981), the court held that the testimony of both a probation officer and the defendant's mother that he had been convicted in another county is sufficient to revoke his probation. Accord, Mason v. State, 631 P.2d 1051 (Wyo.1981).

In United States v. O'Quinn, 689 F.2d 1359, 1361 (11th Cir. 1982), the court, quoting United States v. Rice, 671 F.2d 455, 458 (11th Cir. 1982), said that "all that is required is that the evidence reasonably satisfy the judge that the conduct of the probationer has not been as good as required by the conditions of probation." Cf. Smith v. State, 164 Ga. App. 384, 385(1), 297 S.E.2d 738 (1982).

In Humphrey v. State, 167 Ga. App. 30, 31(1), 306 S.E.2d 36 (1983), the court held that the slight evidence rule is not a violation of a defendant's

controlling.[2] In *State v. Thackston*,[3] the Georgia Supreme Court held that the exclusionary rule was not applicable in probation revocation proceedings and overruled all authority to the contrary. However, in 1988, the law was changed so as to permit a revocation only where the violation is established by a preponderance of the evidence unless the defendant admits the violation.[4] A plea of nolo contendere to a criminal charge will not suffice as an admission of a violation of a condition of probation for purposes of a revocation proceeding.[5]

In *Pennsylvania Board of Probation and Parole v. Scott*,[6] the United States Supreme Court held that the exclusionary rule of the Fourth Amendment does not apply at a state parole hearing.

In 1983, it was held that since only slight evidence is required to revoke probation, testimony of an officer experienced in narcotics that the substance which the defendant sold him was marijuana is sufficient to justify revocation.[7] The implication is that this is no longer true, since the defendant's violation must now be established by a preponderance of the evidence.

Previously in Georgia, hearsay testimony was deemed inadmissible and without probative value.[8] O.C.G.A. § 24-8-802 now allows consideration of hearsay as evidence in the absence of a timely objection. Defense counsel should be sensitive to the issue and ready with a timely objection if the state offers hearsay to

---

right to due process.

[2]Sellers v. State, 107 Ga. App. 516, 130 S.E.2d 790 (1963). In Smith v. State, 144 Ga. App. 631(2), 241 S.E.2d 499 (1978), the court held that the testimony of an officer that a substance sold him by defendant was marijuana was sufficient to authorize revocation of probation.

But in Commonwealth v. Maye, 270 Pa.Super. 406, 411 A.2d 783 (1979), the court concluded that reliance on hearsay testimony amounted to a denial of the right of cross-examination.

See Annot., "Sufficiency of Hearsay Evidence in Probation Revocation Hearings," 2004 A.L.R. 5th 1, § 1a (2004); and see "Admissibility of Hearsay Evidence in Probation Revocation Hearings," 11 A.L.R.4th 999 (1982).

[3]State v. Thackston, 289 Ga. 412, 716 S.E.2d 517, 92 A.L.R.6th 645 (2011).

[4]Former O.C.G.A. § 42-8-34.1(a)

(now O.C.G.A. § 42-8-34.1(b)). Preponderance of the evidence is also the burden of proof in probation revocation proceedings involving first offenders, Young v. State, 265 Ga. App. 425, 594 S.E.2d 667 (2004) and in proceedings to terminate a drug court contract, Wilkinson v. State, 283 Ga. App. 213(1), 641 S.E.2d 189 (2006).

[5]Bolden v. State, 275 Ga. 180, 563 S.E.2d 858 (2002).

[6]Pennsylvania Board of Probation and Parole v. Scott, 524 U.S. 357, 118 S.Ct. 2014, 141 L.Ed.2d 344 (1998).

[7]Chambers v. State, 165 Ga. App. 422, 301 S.E.2d 657 (1983); Oliver v. State, 169 Ga. App. 716 (1), 314 S.E.2d 722 (1984).

[8]Barnett v. State, 194 Ga. App. 892, 893, 392 S.E.2d 322 (1990). See Studdard, *Daniel's Georgia Handbook on Criminal Evidence* (2018 ed.), § 8:35; Smith v. State, 283 Ga. App. 317, 641 S.E.2d 296 (2007).

support a probation revocation petition.

§ 30:8 Result of violation of a condition of probation

Historically, if it is determined that a probationer has violated the terms of his probation, the court may decide to let him continue on probation under the original terms of his probation, or modify the terms, or revoke a part or all of the probation.[1] "At any revocation hearing, upon proof that the defendant has violated any general provision of probation or suspension other than by commission of a new felony offense, the court shall consider the use of alternatives to include community service, intensive probation, diversion centers, probation detention centers, special alternative incarceration, or any other alternative to confinement deemed appropriate by the court or as provided by the state or county. In the event the court determines that the defendant does not meet the criteria for said alternatives, the court may revoke the balance of probation or not more than two years in confinement, whichever is less[2] . . . . If the violation of probation or suspension alleged and proven by a preponderance of the evidence or the defendant's admission is the commission of a felony offense, the court may revoke no more than the lesser of the balance of probation or the maximum time of the sentence authorized to be imposed for the crime constituting the violation of probation."[3] Effective July 1, 2001, the statute was amended to provide that if the violation is one regarding a special condition of probation or suspension of the sentence, the court may revoke the probation or suspension and "require the defendant to serve the balance or portion of the balance of the original sentence in confinement."[4] In *Gardner v. State*,[5] the Court of Appeals clarified the amended statute's definition of a "special

---

[Section 30:8]

[1]Wood v. State, 142 Ga. App. 203, 235 S.E.2d 648 (1977). In Douglas v. Buder, 412 U.S. 430, 93 S.Ct. 2199, 37 L.Ed.2d 52 (1973), the court said that where a probationer received a traffic citation which was not reported to his probation officer for 11 days, this did not amount to a failure to report "all arrests" and was not a valid basis for revocation of probation.

[2]O.C.G.A. § 42-8-34.1(c).

[3]O.C.G.A. § 42-8-34.1(d).

[4]O.C.G.A. § 42-8-34.1(d); ("For purposes of this Code section, the term 'felony offense' means (1) A felony offense; (2) A misdemeanor offense committed in another state on or after July 1, 2010, the elements of which are proven by a preponderance of evidence showing that such offense would constitute a felony if the act had been committed in this state; or (3) A misdemeanor offense committed in another state on or after July 1, 2010, that is admitted to by the defendant who also admits that such offense would be a felony if the act had been committed in this state."); Gearinger v. Lee, 266 Ga. 167, 168 (1), 465 S.E.2d 440 (1996). See Chester v. State, 287 Ga. App. 70, 651 S.E.2d 360 (2007), reversible error to fail to consider alternatives to incarceration where defendant violated general, not special, conditions of probation.

condition" as having two specific requirements: "(1) a special condition must *expressly* be made a part of the sentence—in addition to general conditions, fines, and fees—as reflected in the sentencing sheet, *and also* (2) the sentencing sheet must state *in writing* that a violation of the special condition of probation will result in revocation and service of the balance of the probated sentence." (emphasis in original). Because the sentencing court in *Gardner* failed to set out in writing that a condition of probation was "special" and the consequences of a violation thereof, the court could not revoke more than two years of the defendant's probated sentence. In *Manville v. Hampton*,[6] the court held that where a defendant's probation is revoked *both* because he violated a special condition *and* committed a felony, the trial judge may revoke the balance of the probated sentence. However, where the only offenses supported by the record of the revocation proceedings are misdemeanors, no more than two years of probation may be revoked.[7]

If the defendant was sentenced to special alternatives to incarceration (shock incarceration) (§ 26:20, supra), the court may revoke the balance of probation or two years in confinement, whichever is less.[8]

In *Cockrell v. State*,[9] the court held that the trial judge could not revoke the defendant's probation for seven violations (none of which was a felony) and cause the defendant to serve three and one-half years. In fact, the period of confinement for a defendant who violates his probation by committing a misdemeanor shall not exceed two years.[10]

However, in considering revocation of probation for failure to pay a fine in *Bearden v. Georgia*,[11] the United States Supreme Court said a trial judge "could extend the time for making payments, or reduce the fine, or direct that the probationer perform some form of labor or public service in lieu of the fine . . . . *Only if the sentencing court determines that alternatives to imprisonment are not adequate in a particular situation to meet the State's interest in punishment and deterrence may the State imprison a probationer who has made sufficient bona fide efforts to pay.*" (Emphasis added.)

---

[5]Gardner v. State, 259 Ga. App. 375, 378, 577 S.E.2d 69 (2003).

[6]Manville v. Hampton, 266 Ga. 857, 858(2), 471 S.E.2d 872 (1996).

[7]Henley v. State, 317 Ga. App. 776, 732 S.E.2d 836 (2012).

[8]O.C.G.A. § 42-8-34.1.

[9]Cockrell v. Brown, 263 Ga. 345, 346, 433 S.E.2d 585 (1993).

[10]Gordon v. State, 217 Ga. App. 271, 456 S.E.2d 761 (1995).

[11]Bearden v. Georgia, 461 U.S. 660, 103 S.Ct. 2064, 2072, 76 L.Ed.2d 221 (1983); Massey v. Meadows, 253 Ga. 389, 321 S.E.2d 703 (1984); Gaither v. Inman, 253 Ga. 484, 322 S.E.2d 242 (1984).

The rule is different in those cases where the amount of restitution is negotiated at the time of the plea. Treating a negotiated plea as a contract, the Court of Appeals in *Dickey v. State*[12] was not willing to review the defendant's ability to pay a substantial amount of restitution in connection with a probation revocation where the amount had been negotiated at the time of sentencing.

Nevertheless, the United States Supreme Court in *Black v. Romano*[13] held that there was no violation of the due process clause of the Fourteenth Amendment where "the state judge did not explain on the record his consideration and rejection of alternatives to incarceration."

If the remainder of a probated sentence is revoked, the defendant is relieved from paying the outstanding balance of any fine or any other financial obligation imposed as condition of probation. O.C.G.A. § 42-8-36(b) provides "[a]ny unpaid fines, restitution, or any other monies owed as a condition of probation shall be due when the probationer is arrested; but, if the entire balance of his probation is revoked, all the conditions of probation, including monies owed shall be negated by his imprisonment . . . ."[14]

Generally, if the defendant is ordered to serve the remainder of his original sentence, he is entitled to credit for the time he has served under probation.[15] Except in the case of a First Offender Sentence, in revoking probation, the trial judge may not increase the term provided in the original sentence,[16] and sentences which were to run concurrently may not be changed so as to provide that they are to run consecutively.[17] Likewise, the court revoking probation may not provide that the revoked sentence is to run consecutively with a sentence which has been imposed since the

[12]Dickey v. State, 257 Ga. App. 190, 194(1), 570 S.E.2d 634 (2002).

[13]Black v. Romano, 471 U.S. 606, 105 S.Ct. 2254, 85 L.Ed.2d 636, 645 (1985).

[14]Compare, Rouse v. State, 256 Ga. App. 579, 569 S.E.2d 261 (2002). If the fine is a mandatory element of a sentence, e.g. the fine imposed as part of a DUI conviction under O.C.G.A. § 40-6-391, the defendant is not relieved of the obligation to pay following probation revocation.

[15]O.C.G.A. § 42-8-38(c). But in abandonment and bastardy cases a different rule applies. Turnipseed v. State, 147 Ga. App. 735, 736, 250 S.E.2d 186 (1978). "In abandonment and bastardy cases . . . the service of the sentence may be postponed ("suspended"), but remain viable in the first instance until the child is 18. . . . But once the suspension feature is eliminated, and the sentence modified to embrace confinement and/or probation as the case may be, the defendant does in fact enter upon the service of the sentence, and its probated feature, if any, cannot exceed the length of time applicable if incarceration instead of probation had been mandated."

[16]Inman v. State, 124 Ga. App. 190, 192, 183 S.E.2d 413 (1971).

[17]England v. Newton, 238 Ga. 534, 536, 233 S.E.2d 787 (1977).

original probated sentence.[18]

O.C.G.A. § 42-8-34.1 specifically allows for the revocation of the balance of a probated sentence upon the violation of a special condition imposed by the sentencing court.[19] A special condition of probation under subsection (a) of that Code section is defined as one "which: (1) is expressly imposed as part of the sentence in addition to general conditions of probation and court ordered fines and fees; and (2) is identified in writing in the sentence as a condition the violation of which authorizes the court to revoke the probation or suspension and require the defendant to serve up the balance of the sentence in confinement."

In *Harvey v. Meadows*,[20] the Supreme Court concluded that an oral designation by the trial court of a condition of probation as one which, if violated, could result in the revocation of the balance of the defendant's sentence was insufficient for purposes of O.C.G.A. § 42-8-34.1. The court ruled that an oral warning by the court of the consequences of a violation of a special condition of probation did not amount to "substantial compliance" with the statute's requirement that the designation of special conditions of probation be in writing and in the sentence of the court.

In *Hill v. State*,[21] the court concluded that it was not improper for a sentencing court to label all conditions of probation as "special" and thus allow for the revocation of more than two years of probation for failure to report or what would normally be the violation of a general condition of probation.

In *Syms v. State*,[22] the trial court's order revoking or modifying the defendant's probation to require that he serve five years in a probation detention center was affirmed where the defendant, a habitual violator, committed the offense of D.U.I. while on probation in violation of special conditions prohibiting the consumption of alcohol and the operation of a motor vehicle. The court ruled that the probation detention center was, under the statute, an "alternative to incarceration" and therefore not inconsistent with the two year maximum for confinement on a revoked probated sentence as provided by O.C.G.A. § 42-8-34.1(c).

In a felony case, if a fine was imposed as a condition of probation and such probation is later revoked, the defendant is not

---

[18]Mauldin v. State, 139 Ga. App. 13, 227 S.E.2d 862 (1976); Perdue v. State, 155 Ga. App. 802, 272 S.E.2d 766 (1980).

[19]See O.C.G.A. § 42-8-34.1(a) and (c).

[20]Harvey v. Meadows, 280 Ga. 166(2), 626 S.E.2d 92 (2006).

[21]Hill v. State, 270 Ga. App. 114(1), 605 S.E.2d 831 (2004).

[22]Syms v. State, 257 Ga. App. 521, 571 S.E.2d 514 (2002).

entitled to a rebate of any part of the fine which has been paid.[23]

While O.C.G.A. § 42-8-34(g) refers to the power to "revoke any or all of the probated sentence, rescind any or all of the sentence, or, in any manner deemed advisable by the judge, to modify or change the probated sentence," the fact is that a sentence may not be increased after the defendant has started serving the sentence unless the defendant was sentenced under the First Offender Act.[24]

In *Hulen v. State*,[25] the court held that when a trial judge revokes the remainder of a probated sentence, the judge lacks jurisdiction to revoke the probation again upon the defendant's release. Here the sentence unambiguously revoked the defendant's probation, required him to serve time in jail, and ordered his release. There was no indication in the sentence that the defendant's probation was to be reinstated, and thus the jail time served fully satisfied his sentence. Likewise, a court may not properly order in conjunction with a probation revocation that the custodian of the criminal defendant is to deny the defendant "good time", "earned time", or an "early release". The court has no jurisdiction over the executive branch of government in connection with such matters.[26]

If a defendant's probation is revoked, he must be informed of his right of appeal. If a probationer was not informed of this right by his counsel and did not know of the right, he is entitled to relief regardless of whether he had retained or appointed counsel.[27] There is no right to a bond pending an appeal from a revocation of probation even if the original offense was a misdemeanor.[28]

If a defendant wishes to appeal from an order revoking probation, he must first make an application to be permitted appeal as required by O.C.G.A. § 5-6-35(a)(5).[29] Any such application must be filed with the clerk of the Georgia Supreme Court or Court of Appeals (whichever court is appropriate) within 30 days of the entry of the revocation order.[30]

The State has a limited opportunity to appeal the denial of a petition to revoke probation under the discretionary appeals pro-

[23]O.C.G.A. § 17-10-8.

[24]See §§ 26:24 and 26:44, supra.

[25]Hulen v. State, 207 Ga. App. 465(1), 428 S.E.2d 405 (1993).

[26]Sanford v. State, 251 Ga. App. 190, 191, 553 S.E.2d 854 (2001).

[27]Kreps v. Gray, 234 Ga. 745, 747, 218 S.E.2d 1 (1975).

[28]Morrison v. State, 126 Ga. App. 565, 191 S.E.2d 449 (1972).

[29]Wells v. State, 236 Ga. App. 607, 608, 512 S.E.2d 711 (1999); Smith v. State, 202 Ga. App. 32, 413 S.E.2d 229 (1991); State v. Wilbanks, 215 Ga. App. 223, 450 S.E.2d 293 (1994).

[30]Hill v. State, 204 Ga. App. 582, 420 S.E.2d 393 (1992); Merciers v. State, 212 Ga. App. 424, 444 S.E.2d 416 (1994).

cedure pursuant to O.C.G.A. § 5-6-33 and O.C.G.A. § 5-6-35(a)(5) applicable to orders revoking probation. Jurisdiction may only be invoked by way of application.[31]

See § 30:1, supra, on Probation Management Act.

---

[31]See State v. Huckeba, 258 Ga.   App. 627(2), 574 S.E.2d 856 (2002).

Chapter 31

Crime Victim's Bill of Rights

> **KeyCite®:** Cases and other legal materials listed in KeyCite Scope can be researched through the KeyCite service on Westlaw®. Use KeyCite to check citations for form, parallel references, prior and later history, and comprehensive citator information, including citations to other decisions and secondary materials.

§ 31:1 General

In 1995, Georgia enacted a "Crime Victim's Bill of Rights." This material is codified in O.C.G.A. §§ 17-17-1 et seq. This chapter of the Code as amended contains some sixteen sections and is about nine or ten pages long. Because of limitations on space, no effort is being made to summarize the material, but it is cited for the reader's reference purposes.

APPENDICES

APPENDIX A*

Lesser Included Offenses

The following chart contains a sample of some of the lesser included offenses that have been approved by the appellate courts. In Georgia, a crime may be a lesser included offense of a charged offense either as a matter of law, or as a matter of fact. A crime is a lesser included crime as a matter of law if the lesser offense contains the same, but fewer elements as the greater offense, or if the same conduct occurs with a less culpable state of mind. A crime may be a lesser included offense as a matter of fact if the facts shown at trial establish that some lesser offense may have been all that was committed, regardless of whether the lesser offense contains certain elements that are not essential to the greater offense. O.C.G.A. § 16-1-6.

For example, voluntary manslaughter, as a matter of law, is a lesser included offense of murder; robbery is a lesser included offense, as a matter of law, of armed robbery; misdemeanor obstruction of an officer is a lesser included offense, as a matter of law, of felony obstruction of justice.

As a matter of fact, child molestation may be a lesser included offense of rape; reckless conduct may be a lesser included offense of murder; theft by taking may be a lesser included offense of armed robbery.

There are three ways in which the issue of lesser included offenses may arise: (1) the defendant may request a lesser included offense in order to provide the jury an option to avoid conviction on the greater offense; (2) the prosecutor may request a lesser included offense in order to provide the jury with a compromise verdict to avoid acquittal on the greater offense; (3) convictions on both the greater offense and a lesser included offense are barred by the double jeopardy clause.

With regard to lesser included offenses as a matter of law, either party may request such a charge to the jury if the facts would support a jury verdict finding the defendant guilty of the lesser offense. With regard to lesser included offenses as a matter of fact, the prosecutor may only request a lesser included verdict option if the indictment sets forth all the facts necessary to

---

*The materials were prepared by attorney Donald F. Samuel and were first published in *The Georgia Defender*, Vo. XXII, No. 1 (2003). Lesser Included Offenses.

sustain a verdict on the lesser offense. The defendant, however, may request a charge on a lesser included offense regardless of whether the indictment alleges all the essential elements, assuming, again, that the evidence would support a verdict on that offense. *Heggs v. State,* 246 Ga.App. 354, 540 S.E.2d 643 (2000).

Finally, the proper way to instruct the jury on the lesser included offense option invokes considerations of the *Edge v. State,* 261 Ga. 865, 414 S.E.2d 463 (1992) line of cases involving a sequential charge; and the cases that hold that the jury need not unanimously acquit the defendant of the greater charge before turning their attention to the lesser charge. *Cantrell v. State,* 266 Ga. 700, 469 S.E.2d 660 (1996); *Kunselman v. State,* 232 Ga.App. 323, 501 S.E.2d 834 (1998).

LESSER INCLUDED OFFENSES IN GEORGIA		
CRIME	LESSER IN-CLUDED OF-FENSE	AUTHORITY
ARSON	a. Criminal Damage to Property	a. Bryant v. State, 188 Ga.App. 505, 373 S.E.2d 289 (1988); Gunder v. State, 183 Ga.App. 122, 358 S.E.2d 284 (1987)

LESSER INCLUDED OFFENSES IN GEORGIA		
CRIME	LESSER IN-CLUDED OF-FENSE	AUTHORITY
AGGRAVATED AS-SAULT	a. Cruelty to children b. Reckless conduct c. Simple battery d. Terroristic threats e. Involuntary Manslaughter f. Simple Assault g. Obstruction of an officer h. Pointing weapon at another	a. Williams v. State, 144 Ga.App. 130, 240 S.E.2d 890 (1977). b. Shaw v. State, 238 Ga.App. 757, 519 S.E.2d 486 (1999); Brewton v. State, 216 Ga.App. 346,454 S.E.2d 558 (1998); Bowers v. State, 177 Ga.App. 36, 338 S.E.2d 457 (1985). c. Guevara v. State, 151 Ga.App. 444, 260 S.E.2d 491 (1979); Fulton v. State, 232 Ga.App. 898, 503 S.E.2d 54 (1998). d. Messick v. State, 209 Ga.App. 459, 433 S.E.2d 595 (1993). e. Givens v. State, 184 Ga.App. 498, 361 S.E.2d 830 (1987). f. Cordis v. State, 236 Ga.App. 629, 513 S.E.2d 45 (1999). g. Holeman v. State, 226 Ga.App. 879, 487 S.E.2d 700 (1997). h. Head v. State, 233 Ga.App. 655, 504 S.E.2d 499 (1998).

LESSER INCLUDED OFFENSES IN GEORGIA		
CRIME	LESSER IN-CLUDED OF-FENSE	AUTHORITY
BATTERY	a. Simple Battery	a. Hussey v. State, 206 Ga.App. 122, 424 S.E.2d 374 (1992).
BRIBERY	a. Violation of Oath of Office	a. Nave v. State, 171 Ga.App. 165, 318 S.E.2d 753 (1988).
BURGLARY	a. Criminal Trespass b. Theft by Taking	a. Hiley v. State, 245 Ga.App. 900, 539 S.E.2d 530 (2000); Huffman v. State, 153 Ga.App. 203, 265 S.E.2d 603 (1980); Echols v. State, 222 Ga.App. 598, 474 S.E.2d 766 (1996); Sellers v. State, 164 Ga.App. 637, 298 S.E.2d 623 (1982). b. Darden v. State, 165 Ga.App. 739, 202 S.E.2d 425 (1983).

LESSER INCLUDED OFFENSES IN GEORGIA		
CRIME	LESSER IN-CLUDED OF-FENSE	AUTHORITY
CHILD MOLESTA-TION	a. Sexual Battery b. Sodomy c. Statutory Rape	a. Watson v. State, 297 Ga. 718, 777 S.E.2d 677 (2015) (offense requires proof of lack of consent regardless of victim's age; state may not rely on Georgia law which holds that a person under age of 16 lacks capacity to consent to sexual intercourse to satisfy this burden). b. Horne v. State, 192 Ga.App. 528, 385 S.E.2d 704 (1989). c. Andrews v. State, 200 Ga.App. 47, 406 S.E.2d 801 (1991).
CRUELTY TO CHILDREN	a. Fighting words	a. Shuler v. State, 195 Ga.App. 849, 395 S.E.2d 26 (1990).
DRUGS - POSSES-SION WITH INTENT	a. Possession	a. Talley v. State, 200 Ga.App. 442, 408 S.E.2d 463 (1991); Stephens v. State, 219 Ga.App. 881,467 S.E.2d 201 (1996).

LESSER INCLUDED OFFENSES IN GEORGIA		
CRIME	LESSER IN-CLUDED OF-FENSE	AUTHORITY
DRUGS - TRAF-FICKING	a. Possession with intent and simple possession	a. Lumpkin v. State, 245 Ga.App. 627, 538 S.E.2d 514 (2000); Hancock v. State, 210 Ga. App. 528, 437 S.E.2d 610 (1993); Dalton v. State, 162 Ga.App. 7,289 S.E.2d 801 (1982); Howard v. State, 220 Ga.App. 579, 469 S.E.2d 746 (1996).
DRUGS - SALE	a. Possession	a. Harmon v. State, 235 Ga. 329, 219 S.E.2d 441 (1975).
FORGERY	a. Negotiating a fictitious check	a. Adams v. State, 217 Ga.App. 759, 458 S.E.2d 918 (1995).
MURDER	a. Aggravated Assault b. Armed Robbery c. Reckless conduct d. Involuntary manslaughter e. Voluntary man-slaughter	a. Fetty v. State, 268 Ga. 365, 489 S.E.2d 813 (1997). b. Burke v. State, 234 Ga. 512, 216 S.E.2d 812 (1975). c. Reinhardt v. State, 263 Ga. 113, 428 S.E.2d 333 (1993). d. Brooks v. State, 262 Ga. 902, 426 S.E.2d 374 (1993); Chambers v. State, 205 Ga.App. 16,421 S.E.2d 88 (1992). e. Swanson v. State, 216 Ga. App. 1, 453 S.E.2d 78 (1994).

LESSER INCLUDED OFFENSES IN GEORGIA		
CRIME	LESSER IN-CLUDED OF-FENSE	AUTHORITY
FELONY MUR-DER	a. The underlying felony b. Voluntary Man-slaughter	a. Jowers v. State, 259 Ga. 401, 382 S.E.2d 595 (1989). b. Young v. State, 141 Ga.App. 261, 233 S.E.2d 221 (1977); Woody v. State, 262 Ga. 327, 418 S.E.2d 35 (1992).
KIDNAPPING	a. Aggravated Assault b. Battery c. False Imprison-ment	a. Brown v. State, 247 Ga. 298, 275 S.E.2d 52 (1981). b. Holmes v. State, 229 Ga.App. 671, 494 S.E.2d 560 (1998). c. Sallie v. State, 216 Ga.App. 502, 455 S.E.2d 315 (1995); Ellis v. State, 181 Ga.App. 630, 353 S.E.2d 822 (1987).
OBSTRUCTION OF AN OFFICER (FELONY)	a. Obstruction (misdemeanor)	a. OCGA § 16-10-24 (a)
RICO	a. Predicate offen-ses	a. Martin v. State, 189 Ga.App. 483, 376 S.E.2d 888 (1988).

LESSER INCLUDED OFFENSES IN GEORGIA		
CRIME	LESSER IN-CLUDED OF-FENSE	AUTHORITY
RAPE	a. Assault with in-tent to rape b. Simple Battery c. Child molesta-tion	a. Padgett v. State, 205 Ga.App. 576, 423 S.E.2d 411 (1992). b. Johnson v. State, 195 Ga.App. 723, 394 S.E.2d 586 (1990). c. Pruitt v. State, 258 Ga. 583, 373 S.E.2d 192 (1988).
STATUTORY RAPE	a. Child Molesta-tion	a. Burgess v. State, 189 Ga.App. 790, 377 S.E.2d 543 (1989).
ROBBERY	a. Theft	a. Smith v. State, 244 GA.App. 667, 536 S.E.2d 561 (2000); Painter v. State, 237 Ga. 30, 226 S.E.2d 578 (1976); King v. State, 214 Ga.App. 311,447 S.E.2d 645 (1994).
ARMED ROB-BERY	a. Aggravated Assault b. Theft by taking c. Robbery by intimidation	a. Young v. State, 177 Ga.App. 756, 341 S.E.2d 286 (1986). b. Pearson v. State, 216 Ga.App. 333, 454 S.E.2d 205 (1995); Tisdol v. State, 158 Ga.App. 852, 282 S.E.2d 411 (1981). c. Studdard v. State, 185 Ga.App. 319, 363 S.E.2d 837 (1987).

LESSER INCLUDED OFFENSES IN GEORGIA		
CRIME	LESSER IN-CLUDED OF-FENSE	AUTHORITY
SODOMY, AGGRA-VATED	a. Sodomy	a. Gagnon v. State, 240 Ga.App. 754, 525 S.E.2d 127 (2000); Stover v. State, 256 Ga. 515, 350 S.E.2d 577 (1986).
THEFT BY TAK-ING	a. Criminal Trespass	a. Dix v. State, 206 Ga.App. 429, 425 S.E.2d 419 (1992).
THEFT BY RECEIVING	a. Theft by taking	a. Callahan v. State, 148 Ga.App. 555,251 S.E.2d 790 (1978).
VEHICULAR HO-MICIDE	a. DUI b. Vehicular homi-cide (second degree)	a. Duncan v. State, 183 Ga.App. 368, 358 S.E.2d 910 (1987); Chase v. State, 148 Ga.App. 690,252 S.E.2d 194 (1979). b. Lefler v. State, 210 Ga.App. 609, 436 S.E.2d 777 (1993).

APPENDIX B*

Recidivist Punishment under O.C.G.A. § 17-10-7

SUBSECTION (a)

1) If Defendant has ANY[1] prior felony conviction, O.C.G.A. § 17-10-7 (a) applies

ANY prior felony conviction invokes the application of O.C.G.A. § 17-10-7 (a), no matter how the defendant was sentenced (probation, jail time or a combination of both)

Webb v. State, 251 Ga.App. 414, 554 S.E.2d 563 (2001)

State v. Temple, 189 Ga.App. 284, 375 S.E.2d 300 (1988)

Hernandez v. State, 182 Ga.App. 797, 357 S.E.2d 131 (1987)

Bennet v. State, 132 Ga.App. 397, 208 S.E.2d 181 (1974)

A) MAXIMUM SENTENCE REQUIRED

Applying O.C.G.A. § 17-10-7 (a), the judge MUST sentence the defendant to the maximum

B) PROBATION, SUSPENSION OR STAY POSSIBLE

Though the judge must give the maximum under (a), she has the discretion to probate, suspend or stay some (or all) of the sentence IF THE SENTENCING PROVISIONS FOR THAT OFFENSE ALLOW IT.[2]

C) LIFE SENTENCE-PROBATION

The caveat here is that, if the maximum sentence is life, then the court cannot "probate, suspend or stay" any of the sentence. See O.C.G.A. § 17-10-1.

D) PAROLE ELIGIBLE FOR ANY OFFENSE

Any sentence under (a) is parole eligible.

SUBSECTION (c) and (a)

2) If Defendant has THREE OR MORE prior felony convictions, O.C.G.A. § 17-10-7 (a) and (c) apply

THREE OR MORE prior felony convictions invoke the applica-

---

*These materials were prepared by Marc A. Mallon, Assistant District Attorney, Fulton County, Georgia. Recidivist Punishment Under O.C.G.A. § 17-10-7.

tion of O.C.G.A. § 17-10-8 (a) and (c), which must be "read together".

State v. Jones, 253 Ga.App. 630, 560 S.E.2d 112 (2002).

Banks v. State, 225 Ga.App. 754, 484 S.E.2d 786 (1997).

State v. Carter, 175 Ga.App. 38, 332 S.E.2d 349 (1985).

Wallace v. State, 175 Ga.App. 685, 333 S.E.2d 874 (1985).

A) **MAXIMUM SENTENCE REQUIRED**

Applying O.C.G.A. § 17-10-7 (a) and (c), the judge MUST sentence the defendant to the maximum.

B) **PROBATION, SUSPENSION OR STAY POSSIBLE**

Though the judge must give the maximum under (a) and (c), he has the direction to probate, suspend or stay some (or all) of the sentence IF THE SENTENCING PROVISIONS FOR THAT OFFENSE ALLOW IT.

C) **LIFE SENTENCE-NO PROBATION**

The caveat here is that, if the maximum sentence is life, then the court cannot "probate, suspend or stay" any of the sentence. O.C.G.A. § 17-10-1.

D) **PAROLE *INELIGIBLE***

Any sentence of incarceration under (a) AND (c) is NOT parole eligible. Any jail sentence, *except MURDER,[3] MUST be served in its ENTIRETY.*

THE BOTTOM LINE

Instant Offense	Sentence length	Probation (?)	Parole (?)
2nd Felony	Maximum (even if life)	Yes (except life)	Yes
3rd Felony	Maximum (even if life)	Yes (except life)	Yes
4th-40th Felony	Maximum (even if life)	Yes (except life)	NO

EXAMPLES:

Priors/New Charges	Sentence	Legal or illegal?
Defendant has one prior non-7 deadly felony, now charged with Aggravated Assault	10P	ILLEGAL; not the max (20) under OCGA § 16-5-21
Same	20, serve 2, bal probated	LEGAL, sentence is the max (20)
Same	20P	LEGAL, no mandatory jail time under OCGA § 16-5-21
Defendant has one prior non-7 deadly felony, now convicted of rape, or armed robbery or kidnapping	20Y	ILLEGAL; not the max (life)

Priors/New Charges	Sentence	Legal or illegal?
Same	Life, probated	ILLEGAL; cannot probate a life sentence under OCGA § 17-10-1(a)(1)
Same	Life w/possibility	LEGAL
Same	Life without parole	ILLEGAL, parole eligible under OCGA § 17-10-7(a)
Defendant has three prior non-7 deadly felonies, now charged with Aggravated Assault	20P	LEGAL; sentence is the max
Same	20, serve 3 w/eligibility for parole, balance probated	ILLEGAL: while sentence is the max and probation is w/in judge's discretion, every day of three years must be served because parole ineligible under OCGA § 17-10-7 (c)
Defendant has three prior non-deadly felonies, now faces rape/armed robbery or kidnapping	Life w/possibility	ILLEGAL, parole ineligible under OCGA § 17-10-7 (c)
Same	Life WITHOUT	LEGAL under OCGA § 17-10-7 (c)
Defendant has three prior non-7 deadly felonies, now convicted of MURDER	Life WITHOUT parole possibility	ILLEGAL: While sentence is the max, OCGA § 17-10-7 (c) is INAPPLICABLE to a murder sentence because murder is a capital felony[4]
Defendant has one prior non-7 deadly felony, now convicted of car-jacking	20, serve 10, balance probated	ILLEGAL[5]: not the maximum
Same	Life, parole eligible	LEGAL
Defendant has two prior burglaries, now convicted of third burglary (no other record)	20, serve 2, balance probated	ILLEGAL[6]: while 20 is the maximum and though probation is OK, OCGA § 17-10-7 doesn't trump underlying Title 16 sentencing provisions unique to offense; 3rd burglary must include 5Y under OCGA § 16-7-1 (b)
Same	20, serve 5, balance probated	LEGAL

SUBSECTION (b)

3) **If Defendant has AT LEAST ONE prior "7 deadly sin"[7] (serious violent felony) conviction, and commits AN-OTHER 7 deadly sin offense, O.C.G.A. § 17-10-7 (b) applies**

   A) **LIFE SENTENCE IS REQUIRED** (unless the death

penalty is imposed)

Applying O.C.G.A. § 17-10-7 (b), the judge MUST sentence the defendant to LIFE WITHOUT PAROLE.

B) **PROBATION, SUSPENSION OR STAY IMPOSSIBLE**

Applying O.C.G.A. § 17-10-7 (b), the judge MUST sentence the defendant to LIFE WITHOUT PAROLE and the sentence can NEVER be suspended, probated, deferred or withheld.

C) **PAROLE *IN*ELIGIBLE**

Applying O.C.G.A. § 17-10-7 (b), the judge MUST sentence the defendant to LIFE WITHOUT PAROLE.

THE BOTTOM LINE

Instant Offense	Sentence length	Probation (?)	Parole (?)
2nd or subsequent 7 deadly sin	Life	No!	No!

EXAMPLES:

Priors/New Charges	Sentence	Legal or illegal?
Defendant has one prior 7 deadly felony, now convicted of rape, armed robbery or kidnapping, etc.	Life	ILLEGAL: must be life WITHOUT PAROLE
Same	Life without parole	LEGAL
Defendant has one prior 7 deadly felony, now convicted of MURDER	Life with parole	ILLEGAL: not eligible for parole
Same	Life WITHOUT parole	LEGAL
Defendant has three prior non-7 deadly felonies, now convicted of rape, armed robbery or kidnapping, etc.	Life with possibility	ILLEGAL: OCGA § 17-10-7 (b) doesn't apply because prior are not 7-deadly. And § 17-10-7 (c) DOES apply, so the sentence must be the max AND there can be no parole
Same	Life WITHOUT parole	LEGAL: no parole
Defendant has one prior non-7 deadly felony, now convicted of rape, armed robbery or kidnapping, etc.	Life WITHOUT parole	ILLEGAL: OCGA § 17-10-7(b) doesn't apply because prior is not a 7-deadly. Though OCGA § 17-10-7(a) DOES apply, the sentence is parole eligible
Same	Life with possibility	LEGAL

---

1.   Federal felony convictions and felony convictions from other states are acceptable.

2. Be particularly careful with sentencing of repeat drug offenders under O.C.G.A. § 16-13-30, § 16-13-32.5, etc.

3. O.C.G.A. § 17-10-7 (c) is inapplicable to "capital felonies," i.e., murder [Funderburk v. State, 276 Ga. 554, 580 S. E. 2d 234, 2003)], but the definition of a "capital felony" does NOT include armed robbery, rape, etc., see Cook v. State, 255 Ga. App. 405, 565 S. E. 2d 487 (2002) (**armed robbery** is not a "capital felony" for recidivist sentencing purposes); Collins v. State, 239 Ga. 400, 402, 236 S. E. 2d 759 (1977) (if death is not a possible sentence, insofar as punishment is concerned, the offense cannot be capital); Scott v. State, 172 Ga. App. 725 (1), 324 S. E. 2d 565, 1984 (same, **voluntary manslaughter** is not a "capital felony" for recidivist purposes); Davis v. State, 159 Ga. App. 356, 283 S. E. 2d 286 (1981) (same, **armed robbery** not "capital felony" for recidivist purposes); Getty v. State, 207 Ga. App. 736, 429 S. E. 2d 100 (1993) (same, **armed robbery**).

4. Funderburk v. State, 276 Ga. 554, 580 S. E. 2d 234 (2003) ("since murder is a 'capital felony' and O.C.G.A. § 17-10-7 (c) expressly excepts from its purview capital felonies, it follows that a sentence under [subsection (c)] is a punishment which the law does not allow").

5. Stephens v. State, 245 Ga. App. 823 (7), 558 S. E. 2d 882 (2000).

6. Norwood v. State, 249 Ga. App. 507, 548 S. E. 2d 478 (2001).

7. Under O.C.G.A. § 17-10-6.1 these offenses include murder or felony murder, armed robbery, kidnapping, rape, aggravated child molestation, aggravated sodomy and aggravated sexual battery (or a similar federal or other state offense).

APPENDIX C

Plea Litany Checklist*

PLEA LITANY CHECKLIST
SWEAR IN THE DEFENDANT

(1) State your true, correct and legal name?

[IF DEFENDANT IS INDICTED UNDER ALIAS OR KNOWN BY OTHER NAMES, INQUIRE: Are you also known as _____, _____, _____?]

(2) Do you waive any defect in the indictment with respect to your name? (If applicable)

(3) Are you at this time under the influence of any alcohol, drugs or medicine?

(a) If yes, name the medication and state whether it affects your ability to understand this proceeding. (Is it prescribed? Dosage? Purpose?)

(b) If no, is there a medication that you should be taking that you have not been given today?

(If yes to (b)): Does not having it affect your ability to understand this proceeding?

(4) How old are you and how far have you gone in school?

(5) Are you able to read, write, and understand the English language?

(If English is not native language, advise the following:

Do you understand that an interpreter may be provided to assist you if you do not understand what I am explaining to you?)

(6) Do you understand that you are charged with the following offense(s)?

(List offenses)_____, _____, _____

(7) Do you understand that you have the right to plead either "guilty" or "not guilty" to these charges and if you plead "not guilty" or remain silent, you may obtain a jury trial?

(8) Have you reviewed the Waiver of Rights Form which you have signed?

(Enter Waiver of Rights Form into record.)

---

*This form is used by the Office of the Fulton County District Attorney.

(9) Have you had sufficient time to speak with your lawyer, _____(attorney's name)_____, about all of the facts and circumstances known to you regarding the charges in this Indictment/Accusation, including any potential defenses?

(10) Do you need more time to discuss the case with your attorney?

(11) Are you satisfied with his or her services?

(12) Do you waive formal reading of the indictment?

(13) Do you waive any defect in the indictment with respect to your name? (If applicable)

(14) Has your attorney advised you of the minimum and maximum sentence for each charge?

STATE THE MINIMUM AND MAXIMUM SENTENCE FOR EACH CHARGE

[IF PRO SE DEFENDANT, ask: *Do you understand that upon reviewing your case, an attorney might discover facts which might be helpful to you. An attorney might find that you have a defense to the charges (s) or that there are mitigating circumstances which might be helpful to you. You should take these matters into consideration in deciding whether or not you want a lawyer. Knowing this, do you wish to continue to represent yourself?*]

(15) Do you understand that if you enter a plea of guilty, the State has promised to recommend a sentence of _____, but that the Court does not have to accept that recommendation, and can sentence you to the maximum on each charge, and can have you serve those sentences consecutively?

(16) Do you understand that this plea may be used to enhance sentencing pertaining to other convictions in this jurisdiction as well as other jurisdictions including those in the federal courts?

(17) Do you understand that you waive any and all defenses by entering a plea of guilty?

(18) Do you understand that if you went to trial, you have the right to trial by jury, the right to see, hear, and confront witnesses called to testify against you, and the right to remain silent and not incriminate yourself?

(19) Do you understand that by pleading guilty you are giving up the following rights:

(a) the right to trial by jury;

(b) the right to remain silent and not incriminate yourself;

(c) the right to confront witnesses against you;

(d) the right to assistance of counsel hired by you, or to court appointed if you cannot afford an attorney.;

(e) the right to the presumption of innocence;

(f) the right to testify on your own behalf and to present other evidence;

(g) the right to subpoena witnesses and compel the production of evidence;

(h) the right to have the charges against you proved beyond a reasonable doubt;

(i) the right to appeal should you be convicted of these charges;

(20) Has anyone forced, threatened, or promised you anything to get you to enter a guilty plea?

(21) Do you know that if you are not a United States citizen, a guilty plea may affect your immigration status, regardless of any contrary advice or representations by counsel or any other person?

(22) Is it your decision to waive **these** rights and enter a guilty plea because you are in fact guilty?

If the answer in (18) above is "NO," this is a guilty plea pursuant to *North Carolina v. Alford*

(23) Are you pleading guilty because you have decided that it is in your best interest to do so?

(24) Are you aware that even if you do not admit guilt, this is a plea of guilty and places you in the same position as if you were convicted by a jury at a trial?

(25) How do you plead to the charges of _____ in Indictment number _____?

(26) Is this guilty plea freely and voluntarily given with full knowledge of the charge(s) against you?

(27) Do you understand that you have a very limited right to appeal this guilty plea conviction?

(28) Do you understand that you have only 4 years from today for a felony charge, and 12 months from today for a misdemeanor charge, to file a *habeas petition* with respect to this guilty plea?

SUMMARIZE FACTUAL BASIS FOR THE PLEA

USE THIS SECTION IF NON-NEGOTIATED OR BLIND PLEA

(1) Do you understand that if your guilty plea is a blind plea, also called a non-negotiated plea, the court can impose any sentence authorized by law up to the maximum sentence on each charge?

(2) Do you understand that if you enter a non-negotiated plea, you will not be allowed to withdraw your plea once the sentence

has been announced?

(3)   Do you understand that this is a guilty plea which is permanently recorded on your criminal history?

USE IF DEFENDANT IS ON PROBATION

(4)   Do you understand that if you are currently on probation, that your probation may be revoked by entering a guilty plea today?

(5)   Do you understand that if you are placed on probation of any kind, you cannot violate any criminal laws of any **governmental** unit or any special conditions of probation without being subject to revocation for the balance of the sentence?

USE IF FIRST OFFENDER SENTENCE

(6)   Are you asking to be treated as a first offender under the provisions of the First Offender Act?

(7)   Have you ever pleaded guilty or *nolo contendere* to, or ever been convicted of a felony in the State of Georgia or any other jurisdiction?

(8)   Have you ever been sentenced for any crime, felony or misdemeanor under the First Offender Act to you?

(9)   Has your lawyer explained the First Offender Act to you?

(10)   Do you understand that if you violate the terms of your first offender probation or are convicted of a new offense while on first offender probation, that your 1st offender status could be revoked, you would be adjudicated guilty and that you can be resentenced up to the maximum sentence for each charge in this indictment?

Table of Laws and Rules

UNITED STATES CONSTITUTION

INTERNAL REVENUE CODE

UNITED STATES CODE ANNOTATED

UNITED STATES CODE ANNOTATED—Continued

UNITED STATES PUBLIC LAWS

CODE OF FEDERAL REGULATIONS

FEDERAL RULES OF CRIMINAL PROCEDURE

FEDERAL RULES OF EVIDENCE

GEORGIA CONSTITUTION

GEORGIA CODE

GEORGIA CODE—Continued

GEORGIA CODE—Continued

GEORGIA CODE—Continued

GEORGIA CODE—Continued

GEORGIA CODE—Continued

GEORGIA CODE—Continued

GEORGIA CODE—Continued

GEORGIA CODE—Continued

GEORGIA CODE—Continued

GEORGIA CODE—Continued

GEORGIA CODE—Continued

GEORGIA CODE—Continued

GEORGIA CODE—Continued

OFFICIAL COMPILATION RULES AND REGULATIONS OF THE STATE OF GEORGIA

GEORGIA RULES OF PROFESSIONAL CONDUCT

GEORGIA SUPERIOR COURT RULES

GEORGIA SUPERIOR COURT RULES—Continued

GEORGIA ATTORNEY GENERAL OPINIONS

Table of Cases

A

Ali v. State, 328 Ga. App. 203, 761 S.E.2d 601 (2014)—§ 10:2 n.27

Allaben v. State, 294 Ga. 315, 751 S.E.2d 802 (2013)—§ 25:6 n.18

Allanson v. State, 144 Ga. App. 450, 241 S.E.2d 314 (1978)—§ 20:7 n.2

Allen v. Estelle, 568 F.2d 1108 (5th Cir. 1978)—§ 6:9 n.2

Allen v. State of Ga., 166 U.S. 138, 17 S. Ct. 525, 41 L. Ed. 949 (1897)—§ 28:3 n.8

Allen v. People, 660 P.2d 896 (Colo. 1983)—§ 24:26 n.27

Allen v. Rhay, 431 F.2d 1160 (9th Cir. 1970)—§ 6:9 n.8

Allen v. Ricketts, 236 Ga. 294, 223 S.E.2d 633 (1976)—§ 26:23 n.4

Allen v. State, 296 Ga. 785, 770 S.E.2d 824 (2015)—§ 21:24 n.3

Allen v. State, 325 Ga. App. 156, 751 S.E.2d 915 (2013)—§ 3:7 n.22

Allen v. State, 286 Ga. 392, 687 S.E.2d 799 (2010)—§ 18:38 n.20

Allen v. State, 273 Ga. App. 227, 614 S.E.2d 857 (2005)—§ 7:3 n.34

Allen v. State, 248 Ga. App. 79, 545 S.E.2d 629 (2001)—§ 17:7 n.10

Allen v. State, 239 Ga. App. 899, 522 S.E.2d 502 (1999)—§ 18:24 n.12

Allen v. State, 237 Ga. App. 744, 516 S.E.2d 788 (1999)—§ 21:7 n.14

Allen v. State, 262 Ga. 240, 416 S.E.2d 290 (1992)—§ 14:48 n.38

Allen v. State, 259 Ga. 63, 377 S.E.2d 150 (1989)—§ 5:20 n.49

Allen v. State, 193 Ga. App. 670, 388 S.E.2d 889 (1989)—§ 15:3 n.10

Allen v. State, 258 Ga. 424, 369 S.E.2d 909 (1988)—§§ 26:19 n.39; 26:48 n.3

Allen v. State, 255 Ga. 513, 340 S.E.2d 187 (1986)—§ 14:72 n.44

Allen v. State, 172 Ga. App. 663, 324 S.E.2d 521 (1984)—§ 3:4 n.10

Allen v. State, 240 Ga. 567, 242 S.E.2d 61 (1978)—§ 4:6 n.8

Allen v. State, 144 Ga. App. 233, 240 S.E.2d 754 (1977)—§ 14:72 n.4, 5

Allen v. State, 235 Ga. 709, 221 S.E.2d 405 (1975)—§§ 17:7 n.22; 17:8 n.6

Allen v. State, 233 Ga. 200, 210 S.E.2d 680 (1974)—§ 26:33 n.15

Allen v. State, 128 Ga. App. 361, 196 S.E.2d 660 (1973)—§§ 14:4 n.27; 17:6 n.12

Allen v. State, 228 Ga. 859, 188 S.E.2d 793 (1972)—§ 21:1 n.4

Allen v. State, 120 Ga. App. 533, 171 S.E.2d 380 (1969)—§ 13:4 n.4

Allen v. State, 110 Ga. App. 56, 137 S.E.2d 711 (1964)—§§ 14:39 n.3; 14:42 n.6

Allen v. State, 123 Ga. 499, 51 S.E. 506 (1905)—§ 13:20 n.8

Allen v. Thomas, 265 Ga. 518, 458 S.E.2d 107 (1995)—§ 15:2 n.12, 13

Allen v. U.S., 164 U.S. 492, 17 S. Ct. 154, 41 L. Ed. 528 (1896)—§§ 20:3 n.4; 24:26 n.1, 2

Allenbrand v. State, 217 Ga. App. 609, 458 S.E.2d 382 (1995)—§ 3:2 n.55

Alleyne v. United States, 570 U.S. 99, 133 S. Ct. 2151, 186 L. Ed. 2d 314 (2013)—§§ 26:33 n.27; 26:43 n.9

Allison v. State, 288 Ga. App. 482, 654 S.E.2d 628 (2007)—§ 17:14 n.22

Allison v. State, 213 Ga. App. 195, 444 S.E.2d 347 (1994)—§ 6:6 n.5

Allison v. State, 129 Ga. App. 364, 199 S.E.2d 587 (1973)—§ 4:5 n.10

Allison v. State, 110 Ga. App. 266, 138 S.E.2d 335 (1964)—§ 25:2 n.3

Alliston v. State, 183 Ga. App. 462, 359 S.E.2d 220 (1987)—§ 26:14 n.1

Almeida-Sanchez v. U.S., 413 U.S. 266, 93 S. Ct. 2535, 37 L. Ed. 2d 596 (1973)—§ 4:45 n.2

Almon v. State, 151 Ga. App. 863, 261 S.E.2d 772 (1979)—§ 26:14 n.23

Anderson v. State, 142 Ga. App. 85, 235 S.E.2d 604 (1977)—§ 18:1 n.7

Anderson v. State, 141 Ga. App. 249, 233 S.E.2d 240 (1977)—§ 14:22 n.21

Anderson v. State, 133 Ga. App. 45, 209 S.E.2d 665 (1974)—§§ 4:43 n.2, 10, 22; 14:82 n.6

Anderson v. State, 196 Ga. 468, 26 S.E.2d 755 (1943)—§ 20:1 n.3

Anderson v. State, 63 Ga. 675, 1879 WL 2626 (1879)—§ 18:21 n.7

Anderson v. Warden, Maryland Penitentiary, 696 F.2d 296 (4th Cir. 1982)—§ 17:5 n.15, 23

Anderson v. Winfree, 85 Ky. 597, 4 S.W. 351 (1887)—§ 13:11 n.22

Andresen v. Maryland, 427 U.S. 463, 96 S. Ct. 2737, 49 L. Ed. 2d 627 (1976)—§ 5:22 n.14

Andreu v. State, 124 Ga. App. 793, 186 S.E.2d 137 (1971)—§ 4:35 n.18, 19

Andrews v. Hardwick, 29 Ga. App. 251, 114 S.E. 644 (1922)—§ 8:1 n.19, 22

Andrews v. State, 331 Ga. App. 353, 771 S.E.2d 59 (2015)—§ 4:33 n.26

Andrews v. State, 222 Ga. App. 129, 473 S.E.2d 247 (1996)—§§ 22:7 n.21; 23:9 n.14

Andrews v. State, 221 Ga. App. 492, 471 S.E.2d 567 (1996)—§ 3:10 n.14

Andrews v. State, 219 Ga. App. 808, 466 S.E.2d 909 (1996)—§ 4:12 n.18

Andrews v. State, 196 Ga. 84, 26 S.E.2d 263 (1943)—§ 13:9 n.10

Angevine v. State, 171 Ga. App. 658, 320 S.E.2d 578 (1984)—§ 7:11 n.11

Anglin v. Green, 254 Ga. 87, 326 S.E.2d 740 (1985)—§ 4:46 n.14

Anglin v. State, 302 Ga. 333, 806 S.E.2d 573 (2017)—§ 5:22 n.8

Anguiano v. State, 313 Ga. App. 449, 721 S.E.2d 652 (2011)—§ 5:12 n.4

Ansley v. State, 197 Ga. App. 765, 399 S.E.2d 558 (1990)—§ 26:43 n.37

Anthony v. Hopper, 235 Ga. 336, 219 S.E.2d 413 (1975)—§ 26:41 n.2, 6, 14

Anthony v. State, 303 Ga. 399, 811 S.E.2d 399 (2018)—§ 18:31 n.14

Anthony v. State, 213 Ga. App. 303, 444 S.E.2d 393 (1994)—§ 18:11 n.9

Anthony v. State, 160 Ga. App. 842, 287 S.E.2d 686 (1982)—§ 6:5 n.11

Apoian v. State, 313 Ga. App. 800, 723 S.E.2d 35 (2012)—§ 27:6 n.2

Appling v. State, 256 Ga. 36, 343 S.E.2d 684 (1986)—§ 17:24 n.11

Apprendi v. New Jersey, 530 U.S. 466, 120 S. Ct. 2348, 147 L. Ed. 2d 435 (2000)—§§ 26:11 n.24; 26:33 n.28; 26:43 n.7, 10

Aranza v. State, 213 Ga. App. 192, 444 S.E.2d 349 (1994)—§ 14:67 n.68

Arbegast v. State, 301 Ga. App. 462, 688 S.E.2d 1 (2009)—§ 14:70 n.34

Archer v. State, 217 Ga. App. 395, 457 S.E.2d 679 (1995)—§ 3:7 n.14

Archer v. State, 217 Ga. App. 257, 456 S.E.2d 754 (1995)—§ 3:7 n.10

Argersinger v. Hamlin, 407 U.S. 25, 92 S. Ct. 2006, 32 L. Ed. 2d 530 (1972)—§§ 7:2 n.11; 17:1 n.5; 26:8 n.51

Argot v. State, 261 Ga. App. 569, 583 S.E.2d 246 (2003)—§ 16:11 n.7

Arizona v. Evans, 514 U.S. 1, 115 S. Ct. 1185, 131 L. Ed. 2d 34 (1995)—§ 2:26 n.4

Arizona v. Fulminante, 499 U.S. 279, 111 S. Ct. 1246, 113 L. Ed. 2d 302 (1991)—§ 5:4 n.34

Arizona v. Gant, 556 U.S. 332, 129 S. Ct. 1710, 173 L. Ed. 2d 485, 47 A.L.R. Fed. 2d 657 (2009)—§§ 2:26 n.7; 4:28 n.14; 4:49 n.13

Arp v. State, 327 Ga. App. 340, 759 S.E.2d 57 (2014)—§ 2:5 n.14

Arp v. State, 249 Ga. 403, 291 S.E.2d 495 (1982)—§ 14:96 n.12

Arrington v. State, 286 Ga. 335, 687 S.E.2d 438 (2009)—§ 17:5 n.51

Arrington v. U. S., 382 A.2d 14 (D.C. 1978)—§ 4:49 n.23

Asbell v. State, 163 Ga. App. 514, 295 S.E.2d 182 (1982)—§ 14:30 n.39

Asberry v. State, 221 Ga. App. 809, 472 S.E.2d 562 (1996)—§ 14:54 n.15

Ashburn v. State, 15 Ga. 246, 1854 WL 1572 (1854)—§ 12:13 n.8

Ashcraft v. State of Tenn., 322 U.S. 143, 64 S. Ct. 921, 88 L. Ed. 1192 (1944)—§ 5:4 n.14

Ashe v. Swenson, 397 U.S. 436, 90 S. Ct. 1189, 25 L. Ed. 2d 469 (1970)—§ 14:57 n.3

Ashley v. State, 240 Ga. App. 502, 523 S.E.2d 901 (1999)—§ 21:8 n.6

Ashley v. State, 263 Ga. 820, 439 S.E.2d 914 (1994)—§ 17:5 n.12

Ashley v. State, 261 Ga. 488, 405 S.E.2d 657 (1991)—§ 5:20 n.24

Askea v. State, 153 Ga. App. 849, 267 S.E.2d 279 (1980)—§§ 5:5 n.13, 23; 5:26 n.6; 13:7 n.5

Askew v. State, 254 Ga. App. 137, 564 S.E.2d 720 (2002)—§ 19:2 n.4

Askew v. State, 145 Ga. App. 164, 243 S.E.2d 334 (1978)—§ 4:49 n.3

Askins v. State, 210 Ga. 532, 81 S.E.2d 471 (1954)—§ 23:8 n.10

Ates v. State, 155 Ga. App. 97, 270 S.E.2d 455 (1980)—§§ 3:7 n.1; 18:13 n.2; 18:34 n.2

Atkins v. Hopper, 234 Ga. 330, 216 S.E.2d 89 (1975)—§§ 14:73 n.23; 26:33 n.19; 28:17 n.52

Atkins v. Martin, 229 Ga. 815, 194 S.E.2d 463 (1972)—§ 14:48 n.1

Atkins v. State, 254 Ga. 641, 331 S.E.2d 597 (1985)—§§ 4:32 n.12; 4:34 n.6; 14:88 n.3

Atkins v. State, 173 Ga. App. 9, 325 S.E.2d 388 (1984)—§§ 4:32 n.12; 4:34 n.6

Atkins v. State, 228 Ga. 578, 187 S.E.2d 132 (1972)—§ 14:76 n.13

Atkins v. Virginia, 534 U.S. 1122, 122 S. Ct. 982, 151 L. Ed. 2d 963 (2002)—§ 26:6 n.33

Atkinson v. State, 219 Ga. App. 366, 466 S.E.2d 32 (1995)—§ 16:14 n.9

Atlanta Journal-Constitution v. State, 266 Ga. App. 168, 596 S.E.2d 694 (2004)—§ 17:4 n.2

Atlanta Newspapers, Inc. v. State by Webb, 216 Ga. 399, 116 S.E.2d 580 (1960)—§ 18:37 n.13

Attaway v. State, 244 Ga. App. 5, 534 S.E.2d 580 (2000)—§ 5:8 n.10

Attaway v. State, 236 Ga. App. 307, 511 S.E.2d 635 (1999)—§ 3:8 n.3

Atwater v. City of Lago Vista, 532 U.S. 318, 121 S. Ct. 1536, 149 L. Ed. 2d 549 (2001)—§ 2:6 n.27

Atwater v. State, 233 Ga. App. 339, 503 S.E.2d 919 (1998)—§ 14:80 n.3

Austin v. Carter, 248 Ga. 775, 285 S.E.2d 542 (1982)—§ 7:4 n.66

Austin v. State, 343 Ga. App. 118, 807 S.E.2d 1 (2017)—§ 26:24 n.24

Austin v. State, 275 Ga. App. 560, 621 S.E.2d 546 (2005)—§ 14:7 n.2

Austin v. State, 218 Ga. App. 90, 460 S.E.2d 310 (1995)—§ 21:17 n.20

Austin v. State, 261 Ga. 550, 408 S.E.2d 105 (1991)—§ 24:9 n.10

Austin v. State, 162 Ga. App. 709, 293 S.E.2d 10 (1982)—§ 26:24 n.38

Austin v. U.S., 509 U.S. 602, 113 S. Ct. 2801, 125 L. Ed. 2d 488 (1993)—§ 10:2 n.10

Bair v. State, 250 Ga. App. 226, 551 S.E.2d 84 (2001)—§ 25:3 n.2

Baird v. State, 263 Ga. 868, 440 S.E.2d 190 (1994)—§ 5:20 n.42

Baisden v. State, 279 Ga. 702, 620 S.E.2d 369 (2005)—§ 16:4 n.9

Baker v. McCollan, 443 U.S. 137, 99 S. Ct. 2689, 61 L. Ed. 2d 433 (1979)—§§ 2:12 n.9; 5:4 n.33

Baker v. State, 306 Ga. App. 99, 701 S.E.2d 572 (2010)—§ 26:28 n.9

Baker v. State, 270 Ga. App. 762, 608 S.E.2d 38 (2004)—§ 14:67 n.6

Baker v. State, 263 Ga. App. 462, 588 S.E.2d 288 (2003)—§ 14:53 n.6

Baker v. State, 252 Ga. App. 695, 556 S.E.2d 892 (2001)—§ 3:9 n.6, 7, 8, 10, 14

Baker v. State, 238 Ga. App. 285, 518 S.E.2d 455 (1999)—§§ 14:15 n.1; 14:20 n.6

Baker v. State, 230 Ga. App. 813, 498 S.E.2d 290 (1998)—§ 18:24 n.39

Baker v. State, 212 Ga. App. 731, 442 S.E.2d 815 (1994)—§ 14:67 n.69

Baker v. State, 202 Ga. App. 892, 416 S.E.2d 295 (1992)—§ 16:1 n.29

Baker v. State, 202 Ga. App. 73, 413 S.E.2d 251 (1991)—§ 4:26 n.23

Baker v. State, 190 Ga. App. 219, 378 S.E.2d 525 (1989)—§ 17:17 n.50

Baker v. State, 257 Ga. 567, 361 S.E.2d 808 (1987)—§§ 14:54 n.5; 14:55 n.12

Baker v. State, 449 N.E.2d 1085 (Ind. 1983)—§ 6:9 n.5

Baker v. State, 250 Ga. 187, 297 S.E.2d 9 (1982)—§§ 14:5 n.8; 14:93 n.1, 23; 14:94 n.2

Baker v. State, 243 Ga. 710, 257 S.E.2d 192 (1979)—§ 26:11 n.10

Baker v. State, 240 Ga. 431, 241 S.E.2d 187 (1978)—§ 28:3 n.21

Baker v. State, 39 Md. App. 133, 383 A.2d 698 (1978)—§ 6:9 n.7

Baker v. State, 238 Ga. 389, 233 S.E.2d 347 (1977)—§ 14:72 n.15

Baker v. State, 143 Ga. App. 302, 238 S.E.2d 241 (1977)—§ 14:22 n.37

Baker v. State, 131 Ga. App. 48, 205 S.E.2d 79 (1974)—§ 19:2 n.22, 33

Baker v. State, 230 Ga. 741, 199 S.E.2d 252 (1973)—§ 14:78 n.4

Baker v. State, 202 So. 2d 563 (Fla. 1967)—§ 7:11 n.2

Baker v. Wainwright, 422 F.2d 145 (5th Cir. 1970)—§ 7:11 n.20

Balbosa v. State, 275 Ga. 574, 571 S.E.2d 368 (2002)—§ 17:14 n.8, 19, 20

Baldasar v. Illinois, 446 U.S. 222, 100 S. Ct. 1585, 64 L. Ed. 2d 169 (1980)—§§ 26:14 n.3; 26:28 n.40

Baldivia v. State, 267 Ga. App. 266, 599 S.E.2d 188 (2004)—§ 11:4 n.6

Baldwin v. Benson, 584 F.2d 953 (10th Cir. 1978)—§ 30:5 n.3

Baldwin v. New York, 399 U.S. 66, 90 S. Ct. 1886, 26 L. Ed. 2d 437 (1970)—§ 18:1 n.2

Baldwin v. Sapp, 238 Ga. 597, 234 S.E.2d 513 (1977)—§ 11:2 n.5, 6

Baldwin v. State, 232 Ga. App. 335, 501 S.E.2d 548 (1998)—§ 14:21 n.2

Baldwin v. State, 217 Ga. App. 866, 460 S.E.2d 80 (1995)—§§ 7:6 n.21; 26:43 n.46

Baldwin v. State, 253 Ga. 721, 325 S.E.2d 128 (1985)—§ 5:21 n.18

Baldwin v. State, 51 Md. App. 538, 444 A.2d 1058 (1982)—§ 7:2 n.7

Baldwin v. State, 142 Ga. App. 758, 237 S.E.2d 3 (1977)—§ 26:44 n.9

Baldwin v. State, 120 Ga. 188, 47 S.E. 558 (1904)—§ 18:23 n.3

Bales v. Bales, 156 Ga. 679, 119 S.E. 635 (1923)—§ 27:4 n.17

Bales v. State, 227 Ga. App. 20, 488 S.E.2d 95 (1997)—§ 17:14 n.12

Barber v. State, 146 Ga. App. 523, 246 S.E.2d 510 (1978)—§ 14:60 n.8

Barclay v. State, 142 Ga. App. 657, 236 S.E.2d 901 (1977)—§§ 2:5 n.2; 2:6 n.13; 4:16 n.7, 8

Barfield v. Dampier, 241 Ga. 168, 243 S.E.2d 876 (1978)—§ 21:8 n.10

Barker v. State, 191 Ga. App. 451, 382 S.E.2d 115 (1989)—§ 17:5 n.13

Barker v. State, 144 Ga. App. 339, 241 S.E.2d 11 (1977)—§ 14:8 n.7

Barker v. State, 188 Ga. 332, 4 S.E.2d 31 (1939)—§ 21:10 n.5

Barker v. Wingo, 407 U.S. 514, 92 S. Ct. 2182, 33 L. Ed. 2d 101 (1972)—§§ 2:4 n.9; 10:1 n.9; 14:67 n.10; 14:70 n.6; 28:2 n.19; 28:11 n.28

Barlow v. Barlow, 272 Ga. 102, 526 S.E.2d 857 (2000)—§ 4:59 n.40

Barlow v. State, 148 Ga. App. 717, 252 S.E.2d 214 (1979)—§ 4:52 n.5

Barlow v. State, 280 A.2d 703 (Del. 1971)—§ 4:33 n.10

Barlow v. State, 127 Ga. 58, 56 S.E. 131 (1906)—§§ 12:17 n.14, 30, 32; 13:2 n.1

Barnard v. Henderson, 514 F.2d 744 (5th Cir. 1975)—§ 14:5 n.2

Barner v. State, 263 Ga. 365, 434 S.E.2d 484 (1993)—§ 22:7 n.10

Barnes v. Secretary, Department of Corrections, 888 F.3d 1148 (11th Cir. 2018)—§ 7:3 n.15

Barnes v. State, 287 Ga. 423, 696 S.E.2d 629 (2010)—§ 5:15 n.5

Barnes v. State, 275 Ga. 499, 570 S.E.2d 277 (2002)—§§ 7:2 n.13; 7:3 n.31

Barnes v. State, 239 Ga. App. 495, 521 S.E.2d 425 (1999)—§ 26:21 n.50

Barnes v. State, 269 Ga. 345, 496 S.E.2d 674 (1998)—§§ 18:31 n.52; 23:5 n.23, 24

Barnes v. State, 184 Ga. App. 513, 361 S.E.2d 876 (1987)—§ 11:2 n.14

Barnes v. State, 178 Ga. App. 205, 342 S.E.2d 388 (1986)—§§ 5:8 n.7; 21:24 n.2

Barnes v. State, 163 Ga. App. 61, 293 S.E.2d 717 (1982)—§ 5:13 n.1

Barnes v. State, 157 Ga. App. 582, 277 S.E.2d 916 (1981)—§ 14:36 n.13

Barnes v. State, 135 Ga. App. 190, 217 S.E.2d 443 (1975)—§§ 14:1 n.6; 28:3 n.10

Barnes v. State, 24 Ga. App. 372, 100 S.E. 788 (1919)—§ 22:3 n.1

Barnett v. Hopper, 548 F.2d 550 (5th Cir. 1977)—§ 26:4 n.9

Barnett v. Hopper, 234 Ga. 694, 217 S.E.2d 280 (1975)—§ 26:19 n.73

Barnett v. State, 300 Ga. 551, 796 S.E.2d 653 (2017)—§ 14:77 n.17

Barnett v. State, 270 Ga. 472, 510 S.E.2d 527 (1999)—§ 26:4 n.5

Barnett v. State, 204 Ga. App. 588, 420 S.E.2d 96 (1992)—§ 24:20 n.2

Barnett v. State, 194 Ga. App. 892, 392 S.E.2d 322 (1990)—§ 30:7 n.8

Barney v. State, 20 Miss. 68, 12 S. & M. 68, 1849 WL 2232 (1849)—§ 12:17 n.6

Barraza v. State, 149 Ga. App. 738, 256 S.E.2d 48 (1979)—§§ 24:19 n.12; 24:22 n.18

Barrett v. Kunzig, 331 F. Supp. 266 (M.D. Tenn. 1971)—§ 4:36 n.2

Barrett v. State, 212 Ga. App. 745, 443 S.E.2d 285 (1994)—§ 3:10 n.8

Barrett v. State, 157 Ga. App. 174, 276 S.E.2d 857 (1981)—§ 25:7 n.22

Barrett v. State, 146 Ga. App. 207, 245 S.E.2d 890 (1978)—§§ 14:85 n.27; 20:6 n.11; 24:9 n.4

Barrett v. State, 129 Ga. App. 72, 199 S.E.2d 116 (1973)—§ 21:16 n.6, 10

Barron v. State, 264 Ga. 865, 452 S.E.2d 504 (1995)—§ 21:3 n.5

Barrow v. State, 239 Ga. 162, 236 S.E.2d 257 (1977)—§ 12:9 n.18, 23

Baxter v. State, 134 Ga. App. 286, 214 S.E.2d 578 (1975)—§ 4:9 n.8

Baze v. Rees, 553 U.S. 35, 128 S. Ct. 1520, 170 L. Ed. 2d 420 (2008)—
§§ 26:6 n.52; 28:19 n.8

Bazemore v. State, 273 Ga. 160, 535 S.E.2d 760 (2000)—§ 16:4 n.8

Bazemore v. State, 233 Ga. App. 892, 506 S.E.2d 177 (1998)—§ 17:11 n.1

Bazemore v. State, 28 Ga. App. 556, 112 S.E. 160 (1922)—§ 12:5 n.8

B.C., In re, 333 Ga. App. 763, 777 S.E.2d 52 (2015)—§ 16:11 n.9

B.C., In re, 169 Ga. App. 200, 311 S.E.2d 857 (1983)—§ 30:1 n.18

Beal v. State, 175 Ga. App. 234, 333 S.E.2d 103 (1985)—§ 4:6 n.15

Beam v. State, 260 Ga. 784, 400 S.E.2d 327 (1991)—§ 18:21 n.9

Beaman v. City Of Peachtree City, 256 Ga. App. 62, 567 S.E.2d 715
(2002)—§ 13:23 n.4

Bean v. State, 81 Nev. 25, 398 P.2d 251 (1965)—§ 21:12 n.24

Bearden v. Georgia, 461 U.S. 660, 103 S. Ct. 2064, 76 L. Ed. 2d 221
(1983)—§§ 30:1 n.21; 30:8 n.11

Beardsley v. State, 149 Ga. App. 531, 254 S.E.2d 715 (1979)—§ 14:92 n.9

Beasley v. State, 345 Ga. App. 247, 812 S.E.2d 561 (2018)—§§ 16:13 n.9;
26:28 n.29

Beasley v. State, 255 Ga. App. 522, 566 S.E.2d 333 (2002)—§ 26:46 n.15

Beasley v. State, 244 Ga. App. 836, 536 S.E.2d 825 (2000)—§ 14:66 n.25

Beasley v. State, 269 Ga. 620, 502 S.E.2d 235 (1998)—§ 18:31 n.29

Beasley v. State, 204 Ga. App. 214, 419 S.E.2d 92 (1992)—§ 4:33 n.26

Beasley v. State, 168 Ga. App. 255, 308 S.E.2d 560 (1983)—§ 24:21 n.1

Beasley v. State, 165 Ga. App. 160, 299 S.E.2d 886 (1983)—§ 26:24 n.34

Beasley v. State, 161 Ga. App. 737, 288 S.E.2d 759 (1982)—§ 14:76 n.22

Beasley v. State, 115 Ga. App. 827, 156 S.E.2d 128 (1967)—§ 17:17 n.17

Beavers v. Henkel, 194 U.S. 73, 24 S. Ct. 605, 48 L. Ed. 882 (1904)—
§ 12:17 n.10

Beck v. Alabama, 447 U.S. 625, 100 S. Ct. 2382, 65 L. Ed. 2d 392
(1980)—§ 24:5 n.9

Beck v. State of Ohio, 379 U.S. 89, 85 S. Ct. 223, 13 L. Ed. 2d 142
(1964)—§§ 2:10 n.3; 2:11 n.3, 6, 7, 14; 2:12 n.2; 2:13 n.7

Beck v. State, 250 Ga. App. 654, 551 S.E.2d 68 (2001)—§ 14:15 n.6

Beck v. State, 235 Ga. App. 707, 510 S.E.2d 368 (1998)—§ 5:20 n.52

Beck v. State, 222 Ga. App. 168, 473 S.E.2d 263 (1996)—§ 16:8 n.13

Beck v. State, 216 Ga. App. 532, 455 S.E.2d 110 (1995)—§ 3:2 n.25

Beck v. State, 211 Ga. App. 125, 438 S.E.2d 391 (1993)—§ 24:2 n.16

Beck v. State, 261 Ga. 826, 412 S.E.2d 530 (1992)—§ 14:58 n.11

Beck v. State, 255 Ga. 483, 340 S.E.2d 9 (1986)—§ 18:26 n.35

Beck v. State, 76 Ga. 452, 1886 WL 1323 (1886)—§ 21:16 n.4, 10

Beckworth v. State, 281 Ga. 41, 635 S.E.2d 769 (2006)—§ 16:8 n.3, 4

Bedgood v. State, 100 Ga. App. 736, 112 S.E.2d 430 (1959)—§ 24:2 n.6

Beecham v. U.S., 511 U.S. 368, 114 S. Ct. 1669, 128 L. Ed. 2d 383
(1994)—§ 10:8 n.18

Beecher v. Alabama, 408 U.S. 234, 92 S. Ct. 2282, 33 L. Ed. 2d 317
(1972)—§ 5:4 n.21

Beecher v. State, 240 Ga. App. 457, 523 S.E.2d 54 (1999)—§ 26:13 n.14

Beecher v. State, 164 Ga. App. 54, 296 S.E.2d 374 (1982)—§ 26:33 n.8, 9

Blige v. State, 263 Ga. 244, 430 S.E.2d 761 (1993)—§§ 23:7 n.27; 23:8 n.11

Bliss v. State, 244 Ga. App. 160, 535 S.E.2d 251 (2000)—§ 26:24 n.36

Blitch v. State, 323 Ga. App. 677, 747 S.E.2d 863 (2013)—§ 4:33 n.11

Blitch v. State, 281 Ga. 125, 636 S.E.2d 545 (2006)—§ 3:11 n.33

Blitch v. State, 145 Ga. 882, 90 S.E. 42 (1916)—§ 12:13 n.12

Block v. Rutherford, 468 U.S. 576, 104 S. Ct. 3227, 82 L. Ed. 2d 438 (1984)—§ 4:44 n.18

Blockburger v. U.S., 284 U.S. 299, 52 S. Ct. 180, 76 L. Ed. 306 (1932)—§§ 14:52 n.3; 14:53 n.6; 26:32 n.8

Blocker v. State, 12 Ga. App. 81, 76 S.E. 784 (1912)—§ 13:13 n.3

Bloodworth v. Hopper, 539 F.2d 1382 (5th Cir. 1976)—§ 6:8 n.17

Bloodworth v. State, 233 Ga. 589, 212 S.E.2d 774 (1975)—§ 4:38 n.4, 20

Bloodworth v. State, 128 Ga. App. 657, 197 S.E.2d 423 (1973)—§ 13:6 n.14

Bloodworth v. State, 216 Ga. 572, 118 S.E.2d 374 (1961)—§ 5:1 n.3, 9

Bloodworth v. State, 161 Ga. 332, 131 S.E. 80 (1925)—§§ 17:1 n.16; 23:3 n.5

Blount v. State, 169 Ga. App. 215, 312 S.E.2d 197 (1983)—§§ 14:58 n.53; 18:1 n.11

Blount v. State, 214 Ga. 433, 105 S.E.2d 304 (1958)—§ 18:33 n.1

Blue v. State, 170 Ga. App. 304, 316 S.E.2d 862 (1984)—§ 6:6 n.41

Blue v. State, 168 Ga. App. 868, 310 S.E.2d 748 (1983)—§ 14:72 n.33

Blueford v. Arkansas, 566 U.S. 599, 132 S. Ct. 2044, 182 L. Ed. 2d 937, 77 A.L.R. Fed. 2d 737 (2012)—§§ 14:58 n.35; 24:27 n.11

B.N.D., In Interest of, 185 Ga. App. 906, 366 S.E.2d 187 (1988)—§ 14:48 n.23

Board of Education of Independent School District No. 92 of Pottawatomie County v. Earls, 536 U.S. 822, 122 S. Ct. 2559, 153 L. Ed. 2d 735, 166 Ed. Law Rep. 79 (2002)—§ 5:24 n.7

Board of Pardons and Paroles v. Bridges, 268 Ga. 404, 489 S.E.2d 846 (1997)—§ 28:17 n.78

Boatner v. State, 122 Ga. App. 736, 178 S.E.2d 699 (1970)—§ 28:5 n.2

Boatright v. State, 225 Ga. App. 181, 483 S.E.2d 659 (1997)—§ 3:10 n.12

Boatright v. State, 260 Ga. 534, 397 S.E.2d 689 (1990)—§§ 14:38 n.29; 21:25 n.2

Boatwright v. State, 26 Ga. App. 67, 105 S.E. 381 (1920)—§ 14:41 n.8

Bobo v. State, 254 Ga. 146, 327 S.E.2d 208 (1985)—§ 24:23 n.1

Bobo v. State, 153 Ga. App. 679, 266 S.E.2d 247 (1980)—§§ 3:8 n.2; 14:78 n.1

Bodiford v. State, 328 Ga. App. 258, 761 S.E.2d 818 (2014)—§ 3:11 n.20

Bodiford v. State, 169 Ga. App. 760, 315 S.E.2d 274 (1984)—§§ 2:13 n.11; 2:15 n.8

Bogan v. State, 165 Ga. App. 851, 303 S.E.2d 48 (1983)—§ 4:30 n.21

Boggs v. State, 261 Ga. App. 104, 581 S.E.2d 722 (2003)—§ 21:20 n.2

Boggs v. State, 194 Ga. App. 264, 390 S.E.2d 423 (1990)—§ 4:50 n.15

Boggs v. State, 268 Ala. 358, 106 So. 2d 263 (1958)—§ 20:7 n.30

Boggus v. State, 136 Ga. App. 917, 222 S.E.2d 686 (1975)—§§ 21:1 n.4; 22:5 n.3

Bohannon v. State, 230 Ga. App. 829, 498 S.E.2d 316 (1998)—§ 14:21 n.2

Brooks v. State, 311 Ga. App. 857, 717 S.E.2d 490 (2011)—§ 25:8 n.3

Brooks v. State, 285 Ga. 424, 677 S.E.2d 68 (2009)—§ 26:19 n.39

Brooks v. State, 292 Ga. App. 445, 664 S.E.2d 827 (2008)—§ 26:19 n.37

Brooks v. State, 267 Ga. App. 663, 600 S.E.2d 737 (2004)—§ 14:26 n.2

Brooks v. State, 243 Ga. App. 246, 532 S.E.2d 763 (2000)—§ 7:3 n.28

Brooks v. State, 271 Ga. 456, 519 S.E.2d 907 (1999)—§ 17:8 n.16

Brooks v. State, 237 Ga. App. 546, 515 S.E.2d 851 (1999)—§ 2:22 n.4

Brooks v. State, 224 Ga. App. 829, 482 S.E.2d 725 (1997)—§ 21:25 n.4, 18

Brooks v. State, 206 Ga. App. 485, 425 S.E.2d 911 (1992)—§ 28:11 n.44

Brooks v. State, 259 Ga. 562, 385 S.E.2d 81 (1989)—§§ 14:5 n.16; 21:10 n.29

Brooks v. State, 182 Ga. App. 144, 355 S.E.2d 435 (1987)—§ 14:34 n.8

Brooks v. State, 165 Ga. App. 115, 299 S.E.2d 167 (1983)—§ 26:28 n.57

Brooks v. State, 162 Ga. App. 485, 292 S.E.2d 89 (1982)—§ 14:48 n.26

Brooks v. State, 157 Ga. App. 650, 278 S.E.2d 463 (1981)—§ 21:11 n.4

Brooks v. State, 244 Ga. 574, 261 S.E.2d 379 (1979)—§§ 14:76 n.20, 23, 31; 20:6 n.36; 26:8 n.27

Brooks v. State, 238 Ga. 435, 233 S.E.2d 208 (1977)—§ 12:15 n.3, 4

Brooks v. State, 144 Ga. App. 97, 240 S.E.2d 593 (1977)—§§ 2:7 n.1; 3:6 n.2

Brooks v. State, 143 Ga. App. 523, 239 S.E.2d 207 (1977)—§ 24:5 n.2

Brooks v. State, 141 Ga. App. 725, 234 S.E.2d 541 (1977)—§§ 14:4 n.26; 14:8 n.18; 17:5 n.19

Brooks v. State, 140 Ga. App. 371, 231 S.E.2d 138 (1976)—§ 4:13 n.9

Brooks v. State, 129 Ga. App. 109, 198 S.E.2d 892 (1973)—§§ 2:25 n.6; 3:1 n.9; 3:2 n.43; 3:3 n.7

Brooks v. State, 229 Ga. 593, 194 S.E.2d 256 (1972)—§ 14:75 n.5

Brooks v. State, 125 Ga. App. 867, 189 S.E.2d 448 (1972)—§§ 21:25 n.17; 21:26 n.2, 6

Brooks v. State, 47 Ga. App. 226, 170 S.E. 406 (1933)—§ 13:20 n.2

Brooks v. Tennessee, 406 U.S. 605, 92 S. Ct. 1891, 32 L. Ed. 2d 358 (1972)—§ 19:2 n.17

Brooks v. U.S., 416 F.2d 1044 (5th Cir. 1969)—§ 5:19 n.32

Broom v. State, 209 Ga. App. 42, 432 S.E.2d 823 (1993)—§ 14:34 n.2

Broomfield v. State, 264 Ga. 145, 442 S.E.2d 242 (1994)—§ 17:19 n.20

Broughton v. Griffin, 244 Ga. 365, 260 S.E.2d 75 (1979)—§ 2:23 n.40

Brower v. County of Inyo, 489 U.S. 593, 109 S. Ct. 1378, 103 L. Ed. 2d 628 (1989)—§ 3:9 n.2

Brown v. Crawford, 289 Ga. 722, 715 S.E.2d 132, 85 A.L.R.6th 699 (2011)—§ 28:17 n.88

Brown v. Earp, 261 Ga. 522, 407 S.E.2d 737 (1991)—§ 16:14 n.28

Brown v. Hames, 131 Ga. App. 148, 205 S.E.2d 716 (1974)—§ 27:4 n.15

Brown v. Harris, 666 F.2d 782, 9 Fed. R. Evid. Serv. 1124 (2d Cir. 1981)—§ 6:12 n.1

Brown v. Illinois, 422 U.S. 590, 95 S. Ct. 2254, 45 L. Ed. 2d 416 (1975)—§§ 2:25 n.6, 11, 23; 2:29 n.5, 6; 2:31 n.2, 7

Brown v. Incarcerated Public Defender Clients Div. 3, 288 Ga. App. 859, 655 S.E.2d 704 (2007)—§ 7:1 n.13

Brown v. Kearney, 355 F.2d 199 (5th Cir. 1966)—§ 4:44 n.1

Burns v. State, 191 Ga. 60, 11 S.E.2d 350 (1940)—§ 14:42 n.12

Burns v. State, 89 Ga. 527, 15 S.E. 748 (1892)—§ 18:23 n.8

Burns v. State, 61 Ga. 192, 1878 WL 2826 (1878)—§ 5:6 n.3

Burrell v. State, 140 Ga. App. 900, 232 S.E.2d 172 (1977)—§ 14:22 n.31

Burroughs v. State, 239 Ga. App. 600, 521 S.E.2d 652 (1999)—§§ 16:12 n.2; 28:11 n.12

Burroughs v. U.S., 365 F.2d 431 (10th Cir. 1966)—§ 24:26 n.27

Burruss v. State, 242 Ga. App. 241, 529 S.E.2d 375 (2000)—§ 16:8 n.7

Burse v. State, 209 Ga. App. 276, 433 S.E.2d 386 (1993)—§ 3:7 n.13

Burt v. Panjaud, 99 U.S. 180, 25 L. Ed. 451, 1878 WL 18299 (1878)— § 18:24 n.24

Burton v. State, 212 Ga. App. 100, 441 S.E.2d 470 (1994)—§ 5:5 n.9

Burtts v. State, 269 Ga. 402, 499 S.E.2d 326 (1998)—§ 24:19 n.13

Busch v. State, 271 Ga. 591, 523 S.E.2d 21 (1999)—§§ 26:29 n.3; 26:35 n.8; 26:39 n.1

Bush v. State, 317 Ga. App. 439, 731 S.E.2d 121 (2012)—§ 21:24 n.1

Bush v. State, 268 Ga. App. 200, 601 S.E.2d 511 (2004)—§ 7:3 n.33

Bush v. State, 273 Ga. 861, 548 S.E.2d 302 (2001)—§ 13:23 n.12

Bush v. State, 149 Ga. App. 448, 254 S.E.2d 453 (1979)—§ 6:8 n.6

Bush v. State, 129 Ga. App. 160, 199 S.E.2d 121 (1973)—§ 19:2 n.9

Bussey v. State, 144 Ga. App. 875, 243 S.E.2d 99 (1978)—§ 5:8 n.3

Butler v. McKellar, 494 U.S. 407, 110 S. Ct. 1212, 108 L. Ed. 2d 347 (1990)—§§ 5:20 n.53; 14:64 n.8

Butler v. State, 290 Ga. 412, 721 S.E.2d 876 (2012)—§ 6:5 n.1

Butler v. State, 309 Ga. App. 86, 709 S.E.2d 293 (2011)—§ 14:70 n.39

Butler v. State, 277 Ga. App. 57, 625 S.E.2d 458 (2005)—§§ 5:25 n.14; 28:11 n.27

Butler v. State, 273 Ga. 380, 541 S.E.2d 653 (2001)—§ 23:1 n.7

Butler v. State, 225 Ga. App. 288, 483 S.E.2d 385 (1997)—§ 21:13 n.5, 12, 22

Butler v. State, 172 Ga. App. 405, 323 S.E.2d 628 (1984)—§ 14:22 n.42

Butler v. State, 163 Ga. App. 475, 294 S.E.2d 700 (1982)—§§ 22:3 n.5; 28:2 n.11

Butler v. State, 161 Ga. App. 251, 288 S.E.2d 306 (1982)—§ 21:16 n.13

Butler v. State, 159 Ga. App. 895, 285 S.E.2d 610 (1981)—§ 2:6 n.14

Butler v. State, 139 Ga. App. 92, 227 S.E.2d 889 (1976)—§ 14:22 n.11

Butler v. State, 134 Ga. App. 131, 213 S.E.2d 490 (1975)—§ 14:5 n.1

Butler v. State, 231 Ga. 276, 201 S.E.2d 448 (1973)—§ 18:20 n.22, 23

Butler v. State, 126 Ga. App. 22, 189 S.E.2d 870 (1972)—§ 14:67 n.87

Butterfield, In re, 265 Ga. App. 745, 595 S.E.2d 588 (2004)—§ 27:1 n.24

Butterworth v. Caggiano, 605 So. 2d 56, 16 A.L.R.5th 1118 (Fla. 1992)—§§ 10:2 n.29; 10:6 n.10

Butterworth v. Smith, 494 U.S. 624, 110 S. Ct. 1376, 108 L. Ed. 2d 572 (1990)—§ 12:10 n.9

Buttrum v. State, 249 Ga. 652, 293 S.E.2d 334 (1982)—§§ 4:38 n.15; 14:94 n.1

Butts v. State, 297 Ga. 766, 778 S.E.2d 205 (2015)—§ 13:28 n.8

Butts v. State, 273 Ga. 760, 546 S.E.2d 472 (2001)—§ 14:1 n.10

Butts v. State, 149 Ga. App. 492, 254 S.E.2d 719 (1979)—§ 3:7 n.26

C

Caito v. State, 130 Ga. App. 831, 204 S.E.2d 765 (1974)—§ 4:41 n.12

Caldwell v. Mississippi, 472 U.S. 320, 105 S. Ct. 2633, 86 L. Ed. 2d 231 (1985)—§§ 14:64 n.8; 23:8 n.15; 26:8 n.24

Caldwell v. State, 249 Ga. App. 885, 549 S.E.2d 449 (2001)—§§ 14:85 n.8; 18:22 n.3

Caldwell v. State, 245 Ga. App. 630, 538 S.E.2d 531 (2000)—§ 24:22 n.14

Caldwell v. State, 213 Ga. App. 531, 445 S.E.2d 560 (1994)—§ 16:6 n.1

Caldwell v. State, 171 Ga. App. 680, 320 S.E.2d 888 (1984)—§ 14:48 n.36

Caldwell v. State, 167 Ga. App. 692, 307 S.E.2d 511 (1983)—§§ 24:1 n.1; 24:13 n.4; 24:26 n.10

Caldwell v. State, 139 Ga. App. 279, 228 S.E.2d 219 (1976)—§§ 17:17 n.12; 21:8 n.15

Caldwell v. U.S., 651 F.2d 429 (6th Cir. 1981)—§ 7:4 n.64

Calhoun v. Couch, 232 Ga. 467, 207 S.E.2d 455 (1974)—§ 26:19 n.73

Calhoun v. Findley, 168 Ga. App. 634, 309 S.E.2d 907 (1983)—§ 27:5 n.8

Calhoun v. State, 144 Ga. 679, 87 S.E. 893 (1916)—§ 5:23 n.4

California v. Acevedo, 500 U.S. 565, 111 S. Ct. 1982, 114 L. Ed. 2d 619 (1991)—§§ 4:50 n.16; 4:53 n.3

California v. Beheler, 463 U.S. 1121, 103 S. Ct. 3517, 77 L. Ed. 2d 1275 (1983)—§ 5:12 n.3

California v. Brown, 479 U.S. 538, 107 S. Ct. 837, 93 L. Ed. 2d 934 (1987)—§ 26:10 n.19

California v. Byers, 402 U.S. 424, 91 S. Ct. 1535, 29 L. Ed. 2d 9 (1971)—§ 5:24 n.4, 5

California v. Carney, 471 U.S. 386, 105 S. Ct. 2066, 85 L. Ed. 2d 406 (1985)—§§ 4:48 n.3; 4:50 n.8

California v. Ciraolo, 476 U.S. 207, 106 S. Ct. 1809, 90 L. Ed. 2d 210 (1986)—§ 4:43 n.18

California v. Green, 399 U.S. 149, 90 S. Ct. 1930, 26 L. Ed. 2d 489 (1970)—§ 11:2 n.8

California v. Greenwood, 486 U.S. 35, 108 S. Ct. 1625, 100 L. Ed. 2d 30 (1988)—§ 14:83 n.36

California v. Hodari D., 499 U.S. 621, 111 S. Ct. 1547, 113 L. Ed. 2d 690 (1991)—§ 3:2 n.15

California v. Trombetta, 467 U.S. 479, 104 S. Ct. 2528, 81 L. Ed. 2d 413 (1984)—§ 14:6 n.1

Callaham v. State, 317 Ga. App. 513, 732 S.E.2d 88 (2012)—§ 24:26 n.13

Callaham v. State, 305 Ga. App. 626, 700 S.E.2d 624 (2010)—§ 17:5 n.47

Callahan v. State, 179 Ga. App. 556, 347 S.E.2d 269 (1986)—§ 4:7 n.39

Callahan v. State, 148 Ga. App. 555, 251 S.E.2d 790 (1978)—§§ 13:6 n.2; 16:1 n.26

Callahan v. State, 147 Ga. App. 301, 248 S.E.2d 561 (1978)—§ 21:8 n.3

Callahan v. State, 229 Ga. 737, 194 S.E.2d 431 (1972)—§ 18:30 n.6

Callaway v. State, 275 Ga. 332, 567 S.E.2d 13 (2002)—§§ 14:67 n.90; 14:70 n.40

Callaway v. State, 208 Ga. App. 508, 431 S.E.2d 143 (1993)—§§ 14:93 n.1; 24:27 n.2, 3

Callaway v. State, 197 Ga. App. 606, 398 S.E.2d 856 (1990)—§ 7:3 n.30

Calloway v. State, 303 Ga. 48, 810 S.E.2d 105 (2018)—§ 14:59 n.2

Carter v. State, 155 Ga. App. 49, 270 S.E.2d 233 (1980)—§ 12:17 n.25

Carter v. State, 150 Ga. App. 119, 257 S.E.2d 11 (1979)—§§ 14:8 n.8; 21:20 n.17

Carter v. State, 146 Ga. App. 681, 247 S.E.2d 191 (1978)—§ 20:4 n.4

Carter v. State, 142 Ga. App. 351, 235 S.E.2d 750 (1977)—§§ 14:35 n.21; 24:22 n.3

Carter v. State, 137 Ga. App. 824, 225 S.E.2d 73 (1976)—§§ 24:4 n.4; 25:2 n.1

Carter v. State, 129 Ga. App. 536, 199 S.E.2d 925 (1973)—§ 27:4 n.15

Carter v. State, 227 Ga. 788, 183 S.E.2d 392 (1971)—§ 21:1 n.4

Carter v. State, 61 Ga. App. 430, 6 S.E.2d 175 (1939)—§ 27:2 n.5

Carthern v. State, 238 Ga. App. 670, 519 S.E.2d 490 (1999)—§ 4:30 n.16

Carver v. State, 331 Ga. App. 120, 769 S.E.2d 722 (2015)—§ 18:26 n.62

Carver v. State, 185 Ga. App. 436, 364 S.E.2d 877 (1987)—§ 21:28 n.4

Carver v. State, 175 Ga. App. 599, 333 S.E.2d 697 (1985)—§ 14:38 n.9

Casario v. State, 169 Ga. App. 515, 313 S.E.2d 772 (1984)—§ 29:2 n.4

Casey v. State, 246 Ga. App. 786, 542 S.E.2d 531 (2000)—§ 4:2 n.27

Cash v. State, 231 Ga. 285, 201 S.E.2d 625 (1973)—§ 24:10 n.2

Cash v. State, 224 Ga. 798, 164 S.E.2d 558 (1968)—§ 5:13 n.8

Cason v. State, 134 Ga. 786, 68 S.E. 554 (1910)—§ 18:21 n.5

Caspari v. Bohlen, 510 U.S. 383, 114 S. Ct. 948, 127 L. Ed. 2d 236 (1994)—§ 14:64 n.8

Casper v. State, 244 Ga. 689, 261 S.E.2d 629 (1979)—§ 14:72 n.44

Castaneda v. Partida, 430 U.S. 482, 97 S. Ct. 1272, 51 L. Ed. 2d 498 (1977)—§ 12:9 n.5

Castell v. State, 250 Ga. 776, 301 S.E.2d 234 (1983)—§§ 14:34 n.7; 14:35 n.15

Castellio v. State, 143 Ga. App. 386, 238 S.E.2d 746 (1977)—§ 27:3 n.8

Caster v. State, 210 Ga. App. 809, 437 S.E.2d 608 (1993)—§ 4:32 n.7

Castillo v. State, 178 Ga. App. 312, 342 S.E.2d 782 (1986)—§ 26:1 n.14

Castillo v. State, 166 Ga. App. 817, 305 S.E.2d 629 (1983)—§ 4:12 n.36

Castro v. State, 295 Ga. 105, 757 S.E.2d 853 (2014)—§ 21:32 n.6

Castro v. State, 186 Ga. App. 248, 367 S.E.2d 42 (1988)—§ 18:38 n.11

Caswell v. State, 219 Ga. App. 787, 466 S.E.2d 907 (1996)—§ 4:10 n.21

Catchings v. State, 256 Ga. 241, 347 S.E.2d 572 (1986)—§ 18:17 n.25

Cates v. State, 232 Ga. App. 262, 501 S.E.2d 262 (1998)—§ 4:39 n.2

Cates v. State, 226 Ga. App. 519, 486 S.E.2d 654 (1997)—§ 14:67 n.75

Cato v. State, 195 Ga. App. 619, 394 S.E.2d 413 (1990)—§ 28:10 n.20

Caudell v. State, 262 Ga. App. 44, 584 S.E.2d 649 (2003)—§ 7:4 n.93, 94

Caudell v. State, 129 Ga. App. 229, 199 S.E.2d 550 (1973)—§ 4:9 n.2

Cauley v. State, 203 Ga. App. 299, 416 S.E.2d 575 (1992)—§ 7:4 n.10

Cauley v. State, 130 Ga. App. 278, 203 S.E.2d 239 (1973)—§§ 14:78 n.13; 18:7 n.1

Causey v. State, 334 Ga. App. 170, 778 S.E.2d 800 (2015)—§ 4:28 n.10

Causey v. State, 319 Ga. App. 841, 738 S.E.2d 672 (2013)—§ 18:38 n.8

Causey v. State, 215 Ga. App. 723, 452 S.E.2d 564 (1994)—§§ 14:29 n.40; 14:30 n.15

Cave v. State, 171 Ga. App. 22, 318 S.E.2d 689 (1984)—§ 23:7 n.49

Chandler v. State, 213 Ga. App. 46, 443 S.E.2d 679 (1994)—§ 14:72 n.13

Chandler v. State, 143 Ga. App. 608, 239 S.E.2d 158 (1977)—§§ 17:17 n.16; 24:18 n.6

Chaney v. State, 224 Ga. App. 663, 482 S.E.2d 398 (1997)—§ 14:33 n.11

Chaney v. State, 153 Ga. App. 882, 267 S.E.2d 300 (1980)—§ 14:94 n.5

Chaplin v. State, 141 Ga. App. 788, 234 S.E.2d 330 (1977)—§ 28:3 n.19

Chapman v. California, 386 U.S. 18, 87 S. Ct. 824, 17 L. Ed. 2d 705, 24 A.L.R.3d 1065 (1967)—§§ 23:8 n.1; 28:19 n.18

Chapman v. State, 275 Ga. 314, 565 S.E.2d 442 (2002)—§ 20:4 n.18

Chapman v. State, 273 Ga. 865, 548 S.E.2d 278 (2001)—§ 23:3 n.2

Chapman v. State, 266 Ga. 356, 467 S.E.2d 497 (1996)—§ 24:6 n.7

Chapman v. State, 259 Ga. 592, 385 S.E.2d 661 (1989)—§ 13:27 n.6

Chapman v. State, 90 Ga. App. 564, 83 S.E.2d 572 (1954)—§ 19:6 n.6

Chapman v. State, 148 Ga. 531, 97 S.E. 546 (1918)—§ 12:13 n.34

Chapman v. State, 18 Ga. 736, 1855 WL 1770 (1855)—§ 14:45 n.8

Chapman v. U.S., 365 U.S. 610, 81 S. Ct. 776, 5 L. Ed. 2d 828 (1961)—§§ 4:2 n.2; 4:30 n.11; 4:34 n.25

Chappell v. Stapleton, 58 Ga. App. 138, 198 S.E. 109 (1938)—§ 10:2 n.16

Chappell v. State, 164 Ga. App. 77, 296 S.E.2d 629 (1982)—§§ 13:18 n.12; 26:2 n.17

Character v. State, 285 Ga. 112, 674 S.E.2d 280 (2009)—§ 14:72 n.29

Charles v. U.S., 278 F.2d 386 (9th Cir. 1960)—§ 4:26 n.33

Charleston v. State, 292 Ga. 678, 743 S.E.2d 1 (2013)—§ 7:4 n.49

Chase v. State, 179 Ga. App. 71, 345 S.E.2d 149 (1986)—§ 14:29 n.8

Chase v. State, 148 Ga. App. 690, 252 S.E.2d 194 (1979)—§ 22:7 n.7

Chastain v. State, 255 Ga. 723, 342 S.E.2d 678 (1986)—§ 18:26 n.9

Chastain v. State, 177 Ga. App. 236, 339 S.E.2d 298 (1985)—§ 25:10 n.1

Chastain v. State, 158 Ga. App. 654, 281 S.E.2d 627 (1981)—§§ 14:85 n.32; 14:88 n.16

Chatham v. State, 247 Ga. 95, 274 S.E.2d 473 (1981)—§ 14:58 n.47

Chatman v. Mancill, 280 Ga. 253, 626 S.E.2d 102 (2006)—§ 28:11 n.29

Chattahoochee Brick Co. v. Sullivan, 86 Ga. 50, 12 S.E. 216 (1890)—§ 24:2 n.40

Chauncey v. State, 129 Ga. App. 207, 199 S.E.2d 391 (1973)—§ 13:23 n.15

Chavarria v. State, 248 Ga. App. 398, 546 S.E.2d 811 (2001)—§§ 18:20 n.16; 18:31 n.158

Chavis v. State of N.C., 637 F.2d 213, 7 Fed. R. Evid. Serv. 1243 (4th Cir. 1980)—§ 14:33 n.1

Cheddersingh v. State, 290 Ga. 680, 724 S.E.2d 366 (2012)—§ 24:16 n.14

Cheeks v. State, 218 Ga. App. 212, 460 S.E.2d 860 (1995)—§ 26:21 n.28

Cheeves v. State, 157 Ga. App. 566, 278 S.E.2d 148 (1981)—§ 6:6 n.19

Chenault v. State, 234 Ga. 216, 215 S.E.2d 223 (1975)—§§ 11:4 n.17; 14:93 n.12; 23:7 n.5; 28:7 n.4

Cheney v. U.S. Dist. Court for Dist. of Columbia, 541 U.S. 913, 124 S. Ct. 1391, 158 L. Ed. 2d 225 (2004)—§ 14:77 n.18

Chenoweth v. State, 281 Ga. 7, 635 S.E.2d 730 (2006)—§ 5:20 n.21

Chergi v. State, 234 Ga. App. 548, 507 S.E.2d 795 (1998)—§ 6:6 n.49

Chernowski v. State, 330 Ga. App. 702, 769 S.E.2d 126 (2015)—§ 28:11 n.29

Cobb v. State, 187 Ga. 448, 200 S.E. 796, 121 A.L.R. 210 (1939)—§ 27:1 n.17

Cochran v. State, 315 Ga. App. 488, 727 S.E.2d 125 (2012)—§ 26:17 n.19

Cochran v. State, 262 Ga. 106, 414 S.E.2d 211 (1992)—§ 7:4 n.48

Cochran v. State, 253 Ga. 10, 315 S.E.2d 653 (1984)—§ 28:6 n.9

Cochran v. State, 155 Ga. App. 418, 271 S.E.2d 864 (1980)—§ 12:9 n.40

Cochran v. State, 151 Ga. App. 478, 260 S.E.2d 391 (1979)—§§ 12:9 n.40; 19:2 n.36

Cochran v. State, 136 Ga. App. 125, 220 S.E.2d 477 (1975)—§ 21:16 n.6, 13

Cochran v. State, 9 Ga. App. 824, 72 S.E. 281 (1911)—§ 21:20 n.16

Cochran v. State, 62 Ga. 731, 1879 WL 2903 (1879)—§ 18:8 n.1, 4, 6

Cockrell v. Brown, 263 Ga. 345, 433 S.E.2d 585 (1993)—§ 30:8 n.9

Code v. Montgomery, 725 F.2d 1316 (11th Cir. 1984)—§§ 6:4 n.9; 6:8 n.29

Code v. State, 234 Ga. 90, 214 S.E.2d 873 (1975)—§ 4:33 n.10

Cody v. State, 278 Ga. 779, 609 S.E.2d 320 (2004)—§ 20:7 n.25

Coffey v. State, 339 Ga. App. 367, 793 S.E.2d 557 (2016)—§ 10:3 n.33

Coffin v. U.S., 156 U.S. 432, 15 S. Ct. 394, 39 L. Ed. 481 (1895)—§ 20:1 n.4

Cofield v. State, 247 Ga. 98, 274 S.E.2d 530 (1981)—§§ 2:19 n.20; 24:27 n.7; 26:8 n.30

Coggeshall v. Park, 162 Ga. 78, 132 S.E. 632 (1926)—§ 25:7 n.24

Cohen v. Beneficial Indus. Loan Corp., 337 U.S. 541, 69 S. Ct. 1221, 93 L. Ed. 1528 (1949)—§ 28:2 n.15

Cohen v. State, 7 Ga. App. 5, 65 S.E. 1096 (1909)—§ 14:39 n.8

Cohran v. State, 141 Ga. App. 4, 232 S.E.2d 355 (1977)—§ 22:7 n.9

Coker v. Georgia, 433 U.S. 584, 97 S. Ct. 2861, 53 L. Ed. 2d 982 (1977)—§ 26:6 n.1

Coker v. Hopper, 241 Ga. 288, 244 S.E.2d 873 (1978)—§ 28:17 n.57

Coker v. State, 181 Ga. App. 559, 353 S.E.2d 56 (1987)—§ 17:19 n.13

Colbert v. State, 178 Ga. App. 657, 344 S.E.2d 479 (1986)—§ 18:34 n.9

Colbert v. State, 124 Ga. App. 283, 183 S.E.2d 476 (1971)—§§ 5:19 n.1; 5:26 n.1, 4

Cole v. State, 334 Ga. App. 752, 780 S.E.2d 406 (2015)—§§ 13:6 n.4, 11; 13:10 n.4; 14:41 n.1

Cole v. State, 254 Ga. App. 424, 562 S.E.2d 720 (2002)—§ 4:33 n.28, 29

Cole v. State, 68 Ga. App. 179, 22 S.E.2d 529 (1942)—§§ 13:8 n.7; 14:41 n.17

Cole v. State, 6 Ga. App. 798, 65 S.E. 839 (1909)—§ 17:5 n.20

Coleman v. Alabama, 399 U.S. 1, 90 S. Ct. 1999, 26 L. Ed. 2d 387 (1970)—§§ 6:8 n.7; 7:2 n.22; 11:5 n.1, 4

Coleman v. Kemp, 778 F.2d 1487 (11th Cir. 1985)—§ 14:74 n.13

Coleman v. State, 301 Ga. 753, 804 S.E.2d 89 (2017)—§ 20:4 n.10

Coleman v. State, 337 Ga. App. 304, 787 S.E.2d 274 (2016)—§ 4:10 n.14

Coleman v. State, 286 Ga. 291, 687 S.E.2d 427 (2009)—§ 21:19 n.6

Coleman v. State, 256 Ga. 306, 348 S.E.2d 632 (1986)—§ 25:4 n.4

Coleman v. State, 163 Ga. App. 173, 293 S.E.2d 395 (1982)—§§ 14:54 n.3; 26:35 n.6

Coleman v. State, 160 Ga. App. 158, 286 S.E.2d 494 (1981)—§ 6:7 n.1

Colton v. State, 296 Ga. 172, 766 S.E.2d 38 (2014)—§§ 5:4 n.23; 5:19 n.21

Colton v. State, 292 Ga. 509, 739 S.E.2d 380 (2013)—§ 14:72 n.39

Columbus, Ga. v. Granco, Inc., 240 Ga. 850, 242 S.E.2d 607 (1978)—§ 9:2 n.9

Com. v. Almeida, 373 Mass. 266, 366 N.E.2d 756 (1977)—§ 3:8 n.1

Com. v. Bacon, 381 Mass. 642, 411 N.E.2d 772 (1980)—§ 3:6 n.2

Com. v. Barky, 476 Pa. 602, 383 A.2d 526 (1978)—§ 14:92 n.4

Com. v. Baseler, 419 Mass. 500, 645 N.E.2d 1179 (1995)—§ 24:2 n.44

Com. v. Carita, 356 Mass. 132, 249 N.E.2d 5 (1969)—§ 12:11 n.9

Com. v. Cherry, 474 Pa. 295, 378 A.2d 800 (1977)—§ 23:8 n.22

Com. v. Collini, 264 Pa. Super. 36, 398 A.2d 1044 (1979)—§ 2:12 n.10

Com. v. Davis, 264 Pa. Super. 574, 400 A.2d 1320 (1979)—§ 18:27 n.3

Com. v. DiSanto, 8 Mass. App. Ct. 694, 397 N.E.2d 672 (1979)—§ 4:31 n.3

Com. v. Ellis, 233 Pa. Super. 169, 335 A.2d 512 (1975)—§ 3:10 n.2

Com. v. Gable, 323 Pa. 449, 187 A. 393 (1936)—§ 21:12 n.24

Com. v. Johnson, 429 Pa. Super. 158, 631 A.2d 1335 (1993)—§ 3:10 n.13

Com. v. Jordan, 207 Mass. 259, 93 N.E. 809 (1911)—§ 12:11 n.7

Com. v. Levinson, 480 Pa. 273, 389 A.2d 1062, 2 A.L.R.4th 964 (1978)—§ 12:5 n.1

Com. v. Lombardi, 378 Mass. 612, 393 N.E.2d 346 (1979)—§ 14:92 n.4

Com. v. Louraine, 390 Mass. 28, 453 N.E.2d 437 (1983)—§ 14:93 n.6

Com. v. Maye, 270 Pa. Super. 406, 411 A.2d 783 (1979)—§ 30:7 n.2

Com. v. Meehan, 377 Mass. 552, 387 N.E.2d 527 (1979)—§ 2:34 n.3

Com. v. Podgurski, 386 Mass. 385, 436 N.E.2d 150 (1982)—§ 4:41 n.10

Com. v. Reid, 432 Pa. 319, 247 A.2d 783 (1968)—§ 21:16 n.16

Com. v. Riccardi, 220 Pa. Super. 72, 283 A.2d 719 (1971)—§ 4:16 n.8

Com. v. Richardson, 476 Pa. 571, 383 A.2d 510 (1978)—§ 4:38 n.1

Com. v. Rondeau, 378 Mass. 408, 392 N.E.2d 1001 (1979)—§ 14:4 n.8

Com. v. Sero, 478 Pa. 440, 387 A.2d 63 (1978)—§ 4:55 n.5

Com. v. Sexton, 485 Pa. 17, 400 A.2d 1289 (1979)—§ 6:9 n.8

Com. v. Silo, 480 Pa. 15, 389 A.2d 62 (1978)—§ 4:34 n.26

Com. v. Stetson, 384 Mass. 545, 427 N.E.2d 926 (1981)—§ 17:1 n.11

Com. v. Taylor, 10 Mass. App. Ct. 452, 409 N.E.2d 212 (1980)—§ 4:15 n.5

Com. v. White, 374 Mass. 132, 371 N.E.2d 777 (1977)—§§ 2:34 n.3, 4; 5:4 n.20

Comer v. State, 247 Ga. 167, 275 S.E.2d 309 (1981)—§ 24:5 n.2

Comley v. State, 218 Ga. App. 520, 462 S.E.2d 432 (1995)—§ 5:20 n.41

Commonwealth v. Meunley, 263 A. 2d 905 (Pa. 1970)—§ 4:41 n.5

Compton v. Porterfield, 155 Ga. 480, 117 S.E. 464 (1923)—§ 21:11 n.18

Compton v. State, 179 Ga. 560, 176 S.E. 764 (1934)—§ 18:20 n.21

Coney v. State, 290 Ga. App. 364, 659 S.E.2d 768 (2008)—§ 14:83 n.7

Congdon v. State, 262 Ga. 683, 424 S.E.2d 630 (1993)—§ 18:31 n.53, 104, 133

Congdon v. State, 261 Ga. 398, 405 S.E.2d 677 (1991)—§ 18:31 n.8

Conklin v. State, 254 Ga. 558, 331 S.E.2d 532 (1985)—§§ 14:30 n.7; 23:4 n.1; 23:8 n.19

Conley v. State, 21 Ga. App. 134, 94 S.E. 261 (1917)—§ 22:7 n.20

Crass v. State, 150 Ga. App. 374, 257 S.E.2d 909 (1979)—§ 20:3 n.3

Craver v. State, 246 Ga. 467, 271 S.E.2d 862 (1980)—§ 20:6 n.8

Crawford v. Crow, 114 Ga. 282, 40 S.E. 286 (1901)—§ 12:5 n.9

Crawford v. State, 288 Ga. 425, 704 S.E.2d 772 (2011)—§ 5:17 n.8

Crawford v. State, 278 Ga. 95, 597 S.E.2d 403 (2004)—§ 28:12 n.15, 17

Crawford v. State, 233 Ga. App. 323, 504 S.E.2d 19 (1998)—§ 13:6 n.12

Crawford v. State, 267 Ga. 881, 485 S.E.2d 461 (1997)—§ 14:5 n.16

Crawford v. State, 267 Ga. 543, 480 S.E.2d 573 (1997)—§§ 21:7 n.13;
    21:20 n.18

Crawford v. State, 220 Ga. App. 786, 470 S.E.2d 323 (1996)—§ 18:31
    n.118

Crawford v. State, 202 Ga. App. 653, 415 S.E.2d 300 (1992)—§ 21:13
    n.13

Crawford v. State, 257 Ga. 681, 362 S.E.2d 201 (1987)—§ 14:76 n.18

Crawford v. State, 166 Ga. App. 272, 304 S.E.2d 443 (1983)—§§ 26:24
    n.38; 30:1 n.16

Crawford v. State, 148 Ga. App. 523, 251 S.E.2d 602 (1978)—§ 14:72
    n.15

Crawford v. State, 240 Ga. 321, 240 S.E.2d 824 (1977)—§§ 5:8 n.1; 14:94
    n.7

Crawford v. State, 236 Ga. 491, 224 S.E.2d 365 (1976)—§ 26:2 n.15

Crawford v. Washington, 541 U.S. 36, 124 S. Ct. 1354, 158 L. Ed. 2d
    177, 63 Fed. R. Evid. Serv. 1077 (2004)—§§ 14:72 n.40; 20:7 n.31

Crawley v. State, 240 Ga. App. 891, 525 S.E.2d 739 (1999)—§ 14:20 n.4

Crawley v. State, 151 Ga. 818, 108 S.E. 238, 18 A.L.R. 368 (1921)—
    § 18:23 n.1

Crayton v. State, 298 Ga. 792, 784 S.E.2d 343 (2016)—§§ 23:5 n.27; 24:6
    n.6; 26:35 n.15

Crayton v. State, 145 Ga. App. 365, 243 S.E.2d 738 (1978)—§ 19:6 n.1

Creamer v. State, 168 Ga. App. 790, 310 S.E.2d 560 (1983)—§ 18:24 n.42

Creamer v. State, 229 Ga. 511, 192 S.E.2d 350 (1972)—§§ 5:22 n.12; 5:23
    n.1, 3; 5:25 n.6

Creecy v. State, 235 Ga. 542, 221 S.E.2d 17 (1975)—§ 26:36 n.7

Crenshaw v. State, 237 Ga. App. 511, 515 S.E.2d 642 (1999)—§ 24:16 n.3

Crews v. Flanders, 101 Ga. App. 914, 115 S.E.2d 628 (1960)—§ 18:19 n.4

Crews v. State, 226 Ga. App. 232, 486 S.E.2d 61 (1997)—§ 14:12 n.6

Crider v. State, 114 Ga. App. 523, 151 S.E.2d 792 (1966)—§ 4:33 n.8

Cridiso v. State, 200 Ga. App. 342, 408 S.E.2d 153 (1991)—§ 6:6 n.36

Crimley v. State, 330 Ga. App. 639, 768 S.E.2d 813 (2015)—§ 10:3 n.33

Crisp v. State, 195 Ga. App. 786, 395 S.E.2d 47 (1990)—§ 14:83 n.30

Crist v. Bretz, 437 U.S. 28, 98 S. Ct. 2156, 57 L. Ed. 2d 24 (1978)—
    § 14:51 n.1

Croker v. Smith, 225 Ga. 529, 169 S.E.2d 787 (1969)—§§ 13:18 n.10;
    26:14 n.30

Croker v. State, 114 Ga. App. 492, 151 S.E.2d 846 (1966)—§§ 2:6 n.1, 6,
    8, 9; 2:18 n.2

Cromwell v. State, 218 Ga. App. 481, 462 S.E.2d 388 (1995)—§ 5:21 n.8

Cronch v. State, 141 Ga. App. 851, 235 S.E.2d 40 (1977)—§ 14:93 n.21

Cronkite v. State, 293 Ga. 476, 745 S.E.2d 591 (2013)—§ 14:96 n.10

D

Darden v. State, 271 Ga. 449, 519 S.E.2d 921 (1999)—§ 25:6 n.14

Darden v. State, 212 Ga. App. 345, 441 S.E.2d 816 (1994)—§§ 18:35 n.4; 24:24 n.2, 3

Darling v. State, 248 Ga. 485, 284 S.E.2d 260 (1981)—§ 17:7 n.21

Darr, In re, 143 Cal. App. 3d 500, 191 Cal. Rptr. 882 (5th Dist. 1983)— § 7:12 n.2

Darracott v. State, 191 Ga. App. 675, 382 S.E.2d 664 (1989)—§ 3:6 n.3

Darsey v. State, 17 Ga. App. 280, 86 S.E. 781 (1915)—§ 28:13 n.3

Darst v. State, 323 Ga. App. 614, 746 S.E.2d 865 (2013)—§ 7:4 n.19

Darty v. State, 232 Ga. App. 814, 503 S.E.2d 76 (1998)—§ 21:7 n.12

D. A. S., Matter of, 391 A.2d 255 (D.C. 1978)—§ 5:7 n.13

Dasher v. State, 157 Ga. App. 664, 278 S.E.2d 465 (1981)—§ 17:17 n.36

Dasher v. Stripling, 685 F.2d 385 (11th Cir. 1982)—§ 17:17 n.37, 38

Datz v. State, 210 Ga. App. 517, 436 S.E.2d 506 (1993)—§ 7:4 n.47

Daugherty v. State, 248 Ga. App. 181, 546 S.E.2d 310 (2001)—§ 14:29 n.20

Daugherty v. State, 171 Ga. App. 95, 318 S.E.2d 803 (1984)—§ 4:21 n.24

Davenport v. State, 289 Ga. 399, 711 S.E.2d 699 (2011)—§§ 14:96 n.9, 10; 17:10 n.16

Davenport v. State, 283 Ga. 29, 656 S.E.2d 514 (2008)—§ 7:12 n.7

Davenport v. State, 277 Ga. App. 758, 627 S.E.2d 133 (2006)—§ 5:26 n.8

Davenport v. State, 216 Ga. App. 259, 454 S.E.2d 536 (1995)—§ 27:4 n.2

Davenport v. State, 172 Ga. App. 848, 325 S.E.2d 173 (1984)—§ 7:4 n.12

Davenport v. State, 172 Ga. App. 606, 324 S.E.2d 201 (1984)—§ 14:85 n.5

Davenport v. State, 170 Ga. App. 667, 317 S.E.2d 895 (1984)—§ 14:94 n.1, 5

Davenport v. State, 157 Ga. App. 704, 278 S.E.2d 440 (1981)—§ 17:6 n.17

Davenport v. State, 136 Ga. App. 913, 222 S.E.2d 644 (1975)—§§ 16:9 n.13; 16:14 n.21

Davey v. City of Atlanta, 130 Ga. App. 687, 204 S.E.2d 322, 67 A.L.R.3d 1010 (1974)—§ 17:9 n.20

David v. State, 279 Ga. App. 582, 631 S.E.2d 714 (2006)—§§ 16:4 n.2, 3; 16:10 n.4

Davidson v. State, 257 Ga. App. 260, 570 S.E.2d 698 (2002)—§ 3:2 n.11

Davidson v. State, 156 Ga. App. 457, 274 S.E.2d 807 (1980)—§ 14:38 n.12

Davidson v. State, 125 Ga. App. 502, 188 S.E.2d 124 (1972)—§ 4:51 n.1

Davis v. Davis, 646 F.2d 123 (4th Cir. 1981)—§ 26:2 n.23

Davis v. Davis, 138 Ga. 8, 74 S.E. 830 (1912)—§ 27:1 n.2, 7

Davis v. City of Fitzgerald, 6 Ga. App. 532, 65 S.E. 319 (1909)—§ 14:43 n.5

Davis v. Frazier, 285 Ga. 16, 673 S.E.2d 215 (2009)—§ 28:6 n.5

Davis v. Georgia, 429 U.S. 122, 97 S. Ct. 399, 50 L. Ed. 2d 339 (1976)— §§ 18:16 n.6; 18:17 n.14, 16

Davis v. Minnesota, 511 U.S. 1115, 114 S. Ct. 2120, 128 L. Ed. 2d 679 (1994)—§ 18:31 n.13

Davis v. Mississippi, 394 U.S. 721, 89 S. Ct. 1394, 22 L. Ed. 2d 676 (1969)—§ 2:25 n.6

Dempsey v. State, 156 Ga. App. 806, 275 S.E.2d 671 (1980)—§ 14:67 n.19

Dempsey v. State, 151 Ga. App. 784, 261 S.E.2d 733 (1979)—§ 17:17 n.47

Dempsey v. State, 225 Ga. 208, 166 S.E.2d 884 (1969)—§ 5:14 n.29

Dempsey v. State, 52 Ga. App. 35, 182 S.E. 56 (1935)—§ 20:4 n.6

DeNamur v. State, 156 Ga. App. 270, 274 S.E.2d 673 (1980)—§ 23:8 n.23

Denham v. State, 218 Ga. App. 191, 460 S.E.2d 869 (1995)—§ 18:33 n.4

Denham v. State, 144 Ga. App. 373, 241 S.E.2d 295 (1977)—§ 20:3 n.3

Denison v. State, 258 Ga. 690, 373 S.E.2d 503 (1988)—§ 18:20 n.14

Dennard v. State, 243 Ga. App. 868, 534 S.E.2d 182 (2000)—§§ 13:6 n.18; 13:10 n.1

Dennard v. State, 263 Ga. 453, 435 S.E.2d 26 (1993)—§§ 14:72 n.23; 26:37 n.14

Dennard v. State, 154 Ga. App. 283, 267 S.E.2d 886 (1980)—§§ 14:42 n.16; 14:66 n.4, 13

Dennis v. Grimes, 216 Ga. 671, 118 S.E.2d 923 (1961)—§ 14:68 n.3

Dennis v. State, 300 Ga. 457, 796 S.E.2d 275 (2017)—§ 26:2 n.30

Dennis v. State, 238 Ga. App. 343, 518 S.E.2d 745 (1999)—§ 18:31 n.72

Dennis v. State, 220 Ga. App. 420, 469 S.E.2d 494 (1996)—§§ 2:8 n.5; 24:26 n.15

Dennis v. State, 170 Ga. App. 630, 317 S.E.2d 874 (1984)—§§ 17:7 n.13; 21:10 n.1; 21:11 n.28

Dennis v. State, 226 Ga. 341, 175 S.E.2d 17 (1970)—§ 5:24 n.8

Dennis v. U.S., 384 U.S. 855, 86 S. Ct. 1840, 16 L. Ed. 2d 973 (1966)— § 12:11 n.8

Denny v. State, 226 Ga. App. 432, 486 S.E.2d 417 (1997)—§§ 14:92 n.19; 26:21 n.52

Denson v. State, 267 Ga. App. 528, 600 S.E.2d 645 (2004)—§ 30:2 n.6

Denson v. State, 149 Ga. App. 453, 254 S.E.2d 455 (1979)—§ 18:38 n.18

Denson v. State, 128 Ga. App. 456, 197 S.E.2d 156 (1973)—§ 4:56 n.22

Dent v. State, 243 Ga. 854, 257 S.E.2d 241 (1979)—§ 20:6 n.8

Department of Human Resources v. Long, 217 Ga. App. 763, 458 S.E.2d 914 (1995)—§ 14:95 n.1, 6

Department of Revenue of Montana v. Kurth Ranch, 511 U.S. 767, 114 S. Ct. 1937, 128 L. Ed. 2d 767 (1994)—§ 14:48 n.44

Depree v. State, 246 Ga. 240, 271 S.E.2d 155 (1980)—§ 14:72 n.33

Deren v. State, 237 Ga. App. 387, 515 S.E.2d 191 (1999)—§ 7:3 n.31

Derrer v. Anthony, 265 Ga. 892, 463 S.E.2d 690 (1995)—§§ 26:3 n.3; 28:17 n.8

DeSouza v. State, 285 Ga. App. 201, 645 S.E.2d 684 (2007)—§ 14:99 n.6

Detroit Free Press, Inc. v. Recorder's Court Judge, 409 Mich. 364, 294 N.W.2d 827 (1980)—§ 17:2 n.1

Devega v. State, 286 Ga. 448, 689 S.E.2d 293 (2010)—§ 4:2 n.54

Devenpeck v. Alford, 543 U.S. 146, 125 S. Ct. 588, 160 L. Ed. 2d 537 (2004)—§§ 3:2 n.54; 4:26 n.29

Devier v. State, 253 Ga. 604, 323 S.E.2d 150 (1984)—§§ 2:19 n.12; 2:29 n.5; 26:8 n.7

Devier v. State, 250 Ga. 652, 300 S.E.2d 490 (1983)—§ 12:9 n.27

Devier v. State, 247 Ga. 635, 277 S.E.2d 729 (1981)—§ 4:8 n.4

Devoney v. State, 717 So. 2d 501 (Fla. 1998)—§ 25:7 n.10

Dixon v. State, 12 Ga. App. 17, 76 S.E. 794 (1912)—§ 14:72 n.66

Dixon v. State, 113 Ga. 1039, 39 S.E. 846 (1901)—§ 5:6 n.4

D.L., Interest of, 228 Ga. App. 503, 492 S.E.2d 273 (1997)—§ 13:27 n.8

Dobbins v. State, 262 Ga. 161, 415 S.E.2d 168 (1992)—§ 4:14 n.14

Dobbs v. State, 245 Ga. 208, 264 S.E.2d 18 (1980)—§§ 17:8 n.29; 28:10 n.26

Dodd v. State, 324 Ga. App. 827, 752 S.E.2d 29 (2013)—§ 24:13 n.6

Dodd v. State, 240 Ga. App. 48, 522 S.E.2d 538 (1999)—§ 14:54 n.7

Dodd v. State, 236 Ga. 572, 224 S.E.2d 408 (1976)—§§ 6:6 n.29, 33, 34; 6:8 n.25; 17:10 n.10; 17:12 n.2

Dodson v. Grimes, 220 Ga. 269, 138 S.E.2d 311 (1964)—§§ 2:22 n.21; 11:4 n.5

Dodson v. State, 237 Ga. 607, 229 S.E.2d 364 (1976)—§ 6:11 n.1, 4

Dodys v. State, 73 Ga. App. 483, 37 S.E.2d 173 (1946)—§ 10:9 n.1

Doe v. U.S., 487 U.S. 201, 108 S. Ct. 2341, 101 L. Ed. 2d 184, 25 Fed. R. Evid. Serv. 632 (1988)—§ 5:22 n.15

Doe ex dem. Rowe v. Goetchius, 180 Ala. 381, 61 So. 330 (1913)—§ 25:1 n.1

Doehling v. State, 238 Ga. App. 293, 518 S.E.2d 137 (1999)—§ 14:67 n.78

Doggett v. U.S., 505 U.S. 647, 112 S. Ct. 2686, 120 L. Ed. 2d 520 (1992)—§ 14:70 n.28, 29

Dollar v. State, 168 Ga. App. 726, 310 S.E.2d 236 (1983)—§ 21:11 n.29

Dollar v. State, 161 Ga. App. 428, 288 S.E.2d 689 (1982)—§ 2:22 n.19

Dominguez v. State, 310 Ga. App. 370, 714 S.E.2d 25 (2011)—§ 3:11 n.20

Donaldson v. State, 244 Ga. App. 89, 534 S.E.2d 839 (2000)—§ 26:14 n.9

Donaldson v. State, 180 Ga. App. 879, 350 S.E.2d 849 (1986)—§ 7:4 n.29

Donaldson v. State, 249 Ga. 186, 289 S.E.2d 242 (1982)—§§ 5:19 n.23; 14:34 n.8

Donovan v. Dewey, 452 U.S. 594, 101 S. Ct. 2534, 69 L. Ed. 2d 262 (1981)—§ 4:46 n.11, 21

Doran v. Salem Inn, Inc., 422 U.S. 922, 95 S. Ct. 2561, 45 L. Ed. 2d 648 (1975)—§ 9:3 n.5, 15

Dorillas v. State, 224 Ga. App. 336, 480 S.E.2d 351 (1997)—§§ 18:20 n.24; 18:29 n.2

Dorsey v. Dorsey, 189 Ga. 662, 7 S.E.2d 273 (1940)—§ 28:2 n.9

Dorsey v. State, 279 Ga. 534, 615 S.E.2d 512 (2005)—§ 28:5 n.7

Dorsey v. State, 259 Ga. App. 254, 576 S.E.2d 637 (2003)—§ 16:2 n.1

Dorsey v. State, 206 Ga. App. 709, 426 S.E.2d 224 (1992)—§ 26:21 n.30

Dorsey v. State, 237 Ga. 876, 230 S.E.2d 307 (1976)—§ 14:59 n.1

Dorsey v. Willis, 242 Ga. 316, 249 S.E.2d 28 (1978)—§§ 17:23 n.7; 26:13 n.17; 26:14 n.23

Dorszynski v. U. S., 418 U.S. 424, 94 S. Ct. 3042, 41 L. Ed. 2d 855 (1974)—§ 26:43 n.15, 17

Doss v. State, 264 Ga. App. 205, 590 S.E.2d 208 (2003)—§ 18:25 n.9

Dossett v. State, 261 Ga. 362, 404 S.E.2d 548 (1991)—§ 18:1 n.16

Dotson v. State, 213 Ga. App. 7, 443 S.E.2d 650 (1994)—§§ 14:49 n.4; 14:58 n.55

Douglas v. State of Ala., 380 U.S. 415, 85 S. Ct. 1074, 13 L. Ed. 2d 934 (1965)—§ 20:7 n.29

Dye v. Dotson, 201 Ga. 1, 39 S.E.2d 8 (1946)—§ 28:2 n.9

Dye v. State, 114 Ga. App. 299, 151 S.E.2d 164 (1966)—§ 4:5 n.3

Dyer v. State, 167 Ga. App. 310, 306 S.E.2d 313 (1983)—§ 24:22 n.12

Dyer v. State, 162 Ga. App. 773, 293 S.E.2d 42 (1982)—§ 14:38 n.12

Dyke v. State, 232 Ga. 817, 209 S.E.2d 166 (1974)—§ 17:5 n.4

Dykes v. State, 266 Ga. App. 635, 597 S.E.2d 468 (2004)—§ 28:11 n.20

Dyson v. State, 155 Ga. App. 297, 270 S.E.2d 711 (1980)—§ 24:22 n.11

E

Eady v. State, 129 Ga. App. 656, 200 S.E.2d 767 (1973)—§ 17:10 n.7

Eafford v. State, 155 Ga. App. 865, 274 S.E.2d 37 (1980)—§ 18:26 n.46

Eagle v. State, 264 Ga. 1, 440 S.E.2d 2 (1994)—§§ 7:3 n.8; 20:6 n.35

Eaker v. State, 4 Ga. App. 649, 62 S.E. 99 (1908)—§ 2:15 n.4

Ealey v. State, 310 Ga. App. 893, 714 S.E.2d 424 (2011)—§ 17:14 n.27

Ealey v. State, 141 Ga. App. 94, 232 S.E.2d 620 (1977)—§ 20:1 n.5

Ealey v. State, 136 Ga. App. 292, 221 S.E.2d 50 (1975)—§ 13:5 n.8

Earle, In re, 248 Ga. App. 355, 545 S.E.2d 405 (2001)—§ 27:1 n.8

Early v. State, 218 Ga. App. 869, 463 S.E.2d 706 (1995)—§ 14:66 n.44

Earlywine v. Strickland, 145 Ga. App. 626, 244 S.E.2d 118 (1978)—§ 17:19 n.8

Eason v. State, 215 Ga. App. 614, 451 S.E.2d 820 (1994)—§§ 17:23 n.8; 26:13 n.18; 26:15 n.7

Eason v. State, 260 Ga. 445, 396 S.E.2d 492 (1990)—§ 17:11 n.11

East v. State, 135 Ga. App. 291, 217 S.E.2d 490 (1975)—§ 21:25 n.23

Eaton v. Grindle, 236 Ga. 324, 223 S.E.2d 670 (1976)—§ 18:23 n.4

Eaton v. State, 210 Ga. App. 273, 435 S.E.2d 756 (1993)—§ 4:8 n.7

Eaton v. State, 83 Ga. App. 82, 62 S.E.2d 677 (1950)—§ 2:6 n.18

Eaton v. City of Tulsa, 415 U.S. 697, 94 S. Ct. 1228, 39 L. Ed. 2d 693 (1974)—§ 27:3 n.6

Eaves v. State, 113 Ga. 749, 39 S.E. 318 (1901)—§§ 13:9 n.3; 13:10 n.3; 14:45 n.17

Eaves v. State, 236 Ga. App. 279, 511 S.E.2d 621 (1999)—§ 4:32 n.2

Echols v. State, 167 Ga. App. 307, 306 S.E.2d 324 (1983)—§ 16:11 n.4

Echols v. State, 149 Ga. App. 620, 255 S.E.2d 92 (1979)—§ 14:92 n.1

Eckles v. Atlanta Technology Group, Inc., 267 Ga. 801, 485 S.E.2d 22 (1997)—§ 14:47 n.14

Eckman v. State, 274 Ga. 63, 548 S.E.2d 310 (2001)—§ 14:76 n.23

Eddings v. Oklahoma, 455 U.S. 104, 102 S. Ct. 869, 71 L. Ed. 2d 1 (1982)—§§ 26:8 n.31; 26:10 n.11

Eddleman v. State, 247 Ga. App. 753, 545 S.E.2d 122 (2001)—§ 26:48 n.1

Eddy v. State, 255 Ga. 321, 338 S.E.2d 262 (1986)—§ 21:10 n.28

Edelman v. People of State of Cal., 344 U.S. 357, 73 S. Ct. 293, 97 L. Ed. 387 (1953)—§ 3:1 n.4

Edenfield v. State, 293 Ga. 370, 744 S.E.2d 738 (2013)—§ 18:19 n.19

Edge v. State, 345 Ga. App. 794, 815 S.E.2d 146 (2018)—§§ 18:38 n.3; 24:23 n.18

Edge v. State, 261 Ga. 865, 414 S.E.2d 463 (1992)—§§ 14:61 n.6; 24:5 n.27; 24:11 n.1; 26:37 n.11, 12, 13

Edge v. State, 194 Ga. App. 466, 391 S.E.2d 18 (1990)—§ 26:1 n.11

Ellington v. State, 292 Ga. 109, 735 S.E.2d 736 (2012)—§§ 18:19 n.19; 18:24 n.23; 23:5 n.20; 26:11 n.1

Ellis v. Grimes, 198 Ga. 51, 30 S.E.2d 921 (1944)—§ 2:23 n.9, 19

Ellis v. Reed, 596 F.2d 1195 (4th Cir. 1979)—§ 24:19 n.21

Ellis v. State, 292 Ga. 276, 736 S.E.2d 412 (2013)—§§ 18:19 n.17; 18:20 n.27

Ellis v. State, 285 Ga. 756, 684 S.E.2d 263 (2009)—§ 14:55 n.10

Ellis v. State, 279 Ga. App. 902, 633 S.E.2d 64 (2006)—§ 23:9 n.3

Ellis v. State, 245 Ga. App. 807, 539 S.E.2d 184 (2000)—§ 21:18 n.1

Ellis v. State, 235 Ga. App. 837, 510 S.E.2d 127 (1998)—§ 7:4 n.30

Ellis v. State, 221 Ga. App. 103, 470 S.E.2d 495 (1996)—§ 26:19 n.10, 30, 33

Ellis v. State, 216 Ga. App. 232, 453 S.E.2d 810 (1995)—§ 14:85 n.7

Ellis v. State, 256 Ga. 751, 353 S.E.2d 19 (1987)—§§ 4:2 n.73; 14:79 n.8

Ellis v. State, 164 Ga. App. 366, 296 S.E.2d 726 (1982)—§§ 14:5 n.13; 21:25 n.10

Ellis v. State, 248 Ga. 414, 283 S.E.2d 870 (1981)—§ 14:4 n.5

Ellis v. State, 137 Ga. App. 834, 224 S.E.2d 799 (1976)—§ 23:1 n.6

Ellison v. State, 299 Ga. 779, 792 S.E.2d 387 (2016)—§ 15:2 n.16

Ellison v. State, 242 Ga. App. 636, 530 S.E.2d 524 (2000)—§ 11:1 n.2

Ellison v. State, 158 Ga. App. 419, 280 S.E.2d 371 (1981)—§ 14:29 n.48

Ellison v. State, 82 Ga. App. 760, 62 S.E.2d 407 (1950)—§§ 12:17 n.34; 13:3 n.6

Ellzey v. State, 272 Ga. App. 253, 612 S.E.2d 77 (2005)—§§ 21:25 n.21; 24:12 n.3

Elom v. State, 248 Ga. App. 273, 546 S.E.2d 50 (2001)—§ 4:10 n.25

Elsasser v. State, 313 Ga. App. 661, 722 S.E.2d 327 (2011)—§ 26:21 n.42

Ely v. State, 172 Ga. App. 737, 324 S.E.2d 569 (1984)—§ 6:4 n.28

Elzey v. State, 239 Ga. App. 47, 519 S.E.2d 751 (1999)—§ 3:5 n.8

Embry v. State, 46 Wis. 2d 151, 174 N.W.2d 521 (1970)—§ 26:43 n.36

Emilio v. State, 263 Ga. App. 604, 588 S.E.2d 797 (2003)—§ 7:4 n.77

Emmett v. Ricketts, 397 F. Supp. 1025 (N.D. Ga. 1975)—§ 14:37 n.2

Emmett v. State, 232 Ga. 110, 205 S.E.2d 231 (1974)—§ 28:12 n.20

Encarnacion v. State, 295 Ga. 660, 763 S.E.2d 463 (2014)—§ 7:4 n.82

Endicott v. Glynn County, 235 Ga. 667, 221 S.E.2d 431 (1975)—§ 27:7 n.10

England v. Newton, 238 Ga. 534, 233 S.E.2d 787 (1977)—§§ 26:46 n.12, 13; 30:8 n.17

Engle v. Isaac, 456 U.S. 107, 102 S. Ct. 1558, 71 L. Ed. 2d 783 (1982)—§ 28:19 n.11

English v. State, 301 Ga. App. 842, 689 S.E.2d 130 (2010)—§ 21:4 n.2

English v. State, 202 Ga. App. 751, 415 S.E.2d 659 (1992)—§ 13:31 n.13

Enmund v. Florida, 458 U.S. 782, 102 S. Ct. 3368, 73 L. Ed. 2d 1140 (1982)—§ 26:6 n.13

Ensley v. Ensley, 239 Ga. 860, 238 S.E.2d 920 (1977)—§ 27:1 n.11

Ensley v. State, 330 Ga. App. 258, 765 S.E.2d 374 (2014)—§§ 14:79 n.10; 14:83 n.2

Ensley v. State, 294 Ga. 200, 751 S.E.2d 396 (2013)—§ 26:39 n.5

Eppinger v. State, 231 Ga. App. 614, 500 S.E.2d 383 (1998)—§ 18:31 n.169, 171

Evans v. State, 252 Ga. 312, 314 S.E.2d 421 (1984)—§§ 4:59 n.22; 13:19 n.1

Evans v. State, 161 Ga. App. 504, 288 S.E.2d 629 (1982)—§ 14:22 n.43

Evans v. State, 161 Ga. App. 468, 288 S.E.2d 726 (1982)—§§ 4:7 n.51; 26:40 n.4, 5

Evans v. State, 153 Ga. App. 764, 266 S.E.2d 545 (1980)—§ 30:1 n.9

Evans v. State, 148 Ga. App. 422, 251 S.E.2d 325 (1978)—§ 16:2 n.4

Evans v. State, 146 Ga. App. 480, 246 S.E.2d 482 (1978)—§ 23:1 n.3

Evans v. State, 138 Ga. App. 620, 227 S.E.2d 448 (1976)—§ 14:57 n.13

Evans v. State, 222 Ga. 392, 150 S.E.2d 240 (1966)—§ 18:26 n.5

Evans v. State, 17 Ga. App. 120, 86 S.E. 286 (1915)—§§ 12:5 n.5; 12:13 n.39; 12:17 n.5

Evans v. State, 106 Ga. 519, 32 S.E. 659 (1899)—§ 5:23 n.7

Evans v. Superior Court, 11 Cal. 3d 617, 114 Cal. Rptr. 121, 522 P.2d 681 (1974)—§ 6:9 n.8

Evans v. U.S., 408 F.2d 369 (7th Cir. 1969)—§ 17:6 n.13

Everett v. Clegg, 94 Ga. App. 725, 96 S.E.2d 382 (1956)—§ 18:23 n.28

Everritt v. State, 277 Ga. 457, 588 S.E.2d 691 (2003)—§ 13:31 n.9, 10, 11

Evitts v. Lucey, 469 U.S. 387, 105 S. Ct. 830, 83 L. Ed. 2d 821 (1985)—§§ 28:6 n.3; 28:11 n.13

E.W., In re, 290 Ga. App. 95, 658 S.E.2d 854 (2008)—§ 26:21 n.3

Ewing v. California, 538 U.S. 11, 123 S. Ct. 1179, 155 L. Ed. 2d 108 (2003)—§ 26:2 n.21, 22

Ewing v. Elliott, 51 Ga. App. 565, 181 S.E. 123 (1935)—§ 17:10 n.22

Ewish v. State, 110 Nev. 221, 871 P.2d 306 (1994)—§ 14:72 n.56

Ewumi v. State, 315 Ga. App. 656, 727 S.E.2d 257 (2012)—§ 3:6 n.29

Express-News Corp., In re, 695 F.2d 807, 12 Fed. R. Evid. Serv. 562 (5th Cir. 1982)—§ 25:9 n.1, 5

Eze v. State, 195 Ga. App. 503, 393 S.E.2d 758 (1990)—§ 17:17 n.45

Ezzard v. State, 230 Ga. App. 147, 495 S.E.2d 620 (1998)—§ 14:38 n.23

Ezzard v. State, 229 Ga. 465, 192 S.E.2d 374 (1972)—§ 16:7 n.5

F

Fagan v. Massey, 253 Ga. 483, 322 S.E.2d 59 (1984)—§ 2:23 n.23

Fain v. State, 259 Ga. 708, 386 S.E.2d 144 (1989)—§ 10:8 n.16

Fair v. State, 288 Ga. 244, 702 S.E.2d 420 (2010)—§§ 21:19 n.3; 26:4 n.7

Fair v. State, 284 Ga. 165, 664 S.E.2d 227 (2008)—§§ 4:10 n.10; 4:22 n.21; 21:17 n.11; 21:20 n.2

Fair v. State, 245 Ga. 868, 268 S.E.2d 316 (1980)—§§ 16:9 n.11; 26:11 n.5

Fair v. State, 129 Ga. App. 565, 200 S.E.2d 296 (1973)—§ 14:73 n.6

Fairfield v. State, 155 Ga. 660, 118 S.E. 395 (1923)—§ 5:1 n.16

Fajardo v. State, 191 Ga. App. 295, 381 S.E.2d 560 (1989)—§ 2:8 n.6

Falconer v. Lane, 905 F.2d 1129 (7th Cir. 1990)—§ 14:64 n.8

Falkenhainer v. State, 122 Ga. App. 478, 177 S.E.2d 380 (1970)—§§ 26:18 n.10; 26:19 n.23

Fallen v. State, 191 Ga. App. 233, 381 S.E.2d 410 (1989)—§ 5:15 n.11

Fambro v. State, 164 Ga. App. 359, 297 S.E.2d 111 (1982)—§ 25:2 n.5

Fantasia v. State, 268 Ga. 512, 491 S.E.2d 318 (1997)—§ 14:30 n.10

Fare v. Michael C., 442 U.S. 707, 99 S. Ct. 2560, 61 L. Ed. 2d 197 (1979)—§ 5:17 n.5

Ferguson v. Boyd, 566 F.2d 873 (4th Cir. 1977)—§ 5:5 n.5

Ferguson v. City of Charleston, 532 U.S. 67, 121 S. Ct. 1281, 149 L. Ed. 2d 205 (2001)—§ 4:2 n.43

Ferguson v. State of Ga., 365 U.S. 570, 81 S. Ct. 756, 5 L. Ed. 2d 783 (1961)—§ 14:1 n.1

Ferguson v. State, 226 Ga. App. 681, 487 S.E.2d 467 (1997)—§§ 14:35 n.1; 14:37 n.6

Ferguson v. State, 211 Ga. App. 218, 438 S.E.2d 682 (1993)—§ 6:4 n.3

Ferguson v. State, 606 P.2d 382 (Alaska 1980)—§ 26:43 n.15

Ferguson v. State, 219 Ga. 33, 131 S.E.2d 538 (1963)—§§ 14:51 n.1; 18:24 n.37; 18:33 n.9

Ferguson v. State, 215 Ga. 117, 109 S.E.2d 44 (1959)—§ 18:23 n.14

Fernandez v. California, 571 U.S. 292, 134 S. Ct. 1126, 188 L. Ed. 2d 25 (2014)—§ 4:34 n.35

Fernandez v. State, 171 Ga. App. 290, 319 S.E.2d 503 (1984)—§ 7:3 n.24

Ferrell v. Estelle, 568 F.2d 1128 (5th Cir. 1978)—§ 17:8 n.19

Ferrell v. State, 261 Ga. 115, 401 S.E.2d 741 (1991)—§§ 7:4 n.55; 17:8 n.25

Ferrell v. State, 198 Ga. App. 270, 401 S.E.2d 301 (1991)—§ 14:87 n.18

Ferrell v. State, 149 Ga. App. 405, 254 S.E.2d 404 (1979)—§§ 14:67 n.35; 14:78 n.31; 17:12 n.10; 23:5 n.6

Ferri v. Ackerman, 444 U.S. 193, 100 S. Ct. 402, 62 L. Ed. 2d 355 (1979)—§ 7:6 n.3

Ferron v. State, 216 Ga. App. 456, 454 S.E.2d 637 (1995)—§ 14:83 n.27

Ferry v. State, 161 Ga. App. 795, 287 S.E.2d 732, 26 A.L.R.4th 1 (1982)—§ 23:8 n.10

Ferry v. State, 245 Ga. 698, 267 S.E.2d 1 (1980)—§ 14:77 n.19

Ferry v. State, 151 Ga. App. 436, 260 S.E.2d 351 (1979)—§ 14:77 n.20

Fetty v. State, 268 Ga. 365, 489 S.E.2d 813 (1997)—§ 14:72 n.38, 68

Fex v. Michigan, 507 U.S. 43, 113 S. Ct. 1085, 122 L. Ed. 2d 406 (1993)—§ 14:71 n.22

Fiallo v. State, 240 Ga. App. 278, 523 S.E.2d 355 (1999)—§ 4:10 n.24

Fictum v. State, 188 Ga. App. 348, 373 S.E.2d 54 (1988)—§ 17:8 n.27

Fielding v. State, 266 Ga. 26, 463 S.E.2d 489 (1995)—§ 14:30 n.60

Fielding v. State, 30 Ga. App. 664, 118 S.E. 601 (1923)—§ 14:45 n.6

Fields v. Metropolitan Life Ins. Co., 147 Tenn. 464, 249 S.W. 798, 36 A.L.R. 1250 (1923)—§ 10:4 n.1

Fields v. State, 266 Ga. 241, 466 S.E.2d 202 (1996)—§§ 5:13 n.17; 5:19 n.6, 7; 5:20 n.12, 13, 14

Fields v. State, 260 Ga. 331, 393 S.E.2d 252 (1990)—§ 14:34 n.36

Fields v. State, 189 Ga. App. 532, 376 S.E.2d 912 (1988)—§ 28:6 n.20

Fields v. State, 232 Ga. 723, 208 S.E.2d 822 (1974)—§§ 5:3 n.5; 5:4 n.15

Fields v. State, 221 Ga. 307, 144 S.E.2d 339 (1965)—§§ 14:94 n.3; 21:10 n.11

Fields v. State, 190 Ga. 642, 10 S.E.2d 33 (1940)—§ 18:4 n.6

Fields v. State, 121 Ala. 16, 25 So. 726 (1899)—§ 12:17 n.24

Fife v. Johnston, 225 Ga. 447, 169 S.E.2d 167 (1969)—§ 28:2 n.5

Fife v. State, 306 Ga. App. 425, 702 S.E.2d 454 (2010)—§ 5:19 n.21

Fikes v. State of Ala., 352 U.S. 191, 77 S. Ct. 281, 1 L. Ed. 2d 246 (1957)—§ 5:4 n.4

Fletcher v. State, 157 Ga. App. 707, 278 S.E.2d 444 (1981)—§§ 13:4 n.10; 14:8 n.14

Fletcher v. Wainwright, 399 F.2d 62 (5th Cir. 1968)—§ 4:38 n.12

Fletcher v. Weir, 455 U.S. 603, 102 S. Ct. 1309, 71 L. Ed. 2d 490 (1982)—§§ 5:15 n.7; 5:21 n.8

Flint v. Mullen, 499 F.2d 100 (1st Cir. 1974)—§ 30:1 n.9

Flint v. State, 745 S.E.2d 277 (Ga. 2010)—§ 28:17 n.15, 93

Flint v. State, 12 Ga. App. 169, 76 S.E. 1032 (1913)—§§ 13:23 n.2; 14:66 n.36

Flippo v. West Virginia, 528 U.S. 11, 120 S. Ct. 7, 145 L. Ed. 2d 16 (1999)—§ 4:25 n.9

Florence v. Board of Chosen Freeholders of County of Burlington, 566 U.S. 318, 132 S. Ct. 1510, 182 L. Ed. 2d 566 (2012)—§§ 4:44 n.13; 4:57 n.24

Flores v. State, 818 S.E.2d 90 (Ga. Ct. App. 2018)—§ 3:11 n.10

Flores v. State, 308 Ga. App. 368, 707 S.E.2d 578 (2011)—§ 16:1 n.23

Flores v. State, 277 Ga. 780, 596 S.E.2d 114 (2004)—§ 25:6 n.18

Flores v. State, 159 Ga. App. 336, 283 S.E.2d 372 (1981)—§ 7:12 n.6

Florida v. Bostick, 501 U.S. 429, 111 S. Ct. 2382, 115 L. Ed. 2d 389 (1991)—§§ 2:2 n.14; 3:1 n.37, 40, 43; 3:2 n.13

Florida v. Harris, 568 U.S. 237, 133 S. Ct. 1050, 185 L. Ed. 2d 61 (2013)—§ 3:13 n.10

Florida v. Jardines, 569 U.S. 1, 133 S. Ct. 1409, 185 L. Ed. 2d 495 (2013)—§§ 4:1 n.4; 4:41 n.7

Florida v. Jimeno, 500 U.S. 248, 111 S. Ct. 1801, 114 L. Ed. 2d 297 (1991)—§§ 4:32 n.34; 4:53 n.5

Florida v. J.L., 529 U.S. 266, 120 S. Ct. 1375, 146 L. Ed. 2d 254 (2000)—§ 3:7 n.8

Florida v. Meyers, 466 U.S. 380, 104 S. Ct. 1852, 80 L. Ed. 2d 381 (1984)—§§ 4:50 n.14; 4:58 n.5

Florida v. Nixon, 543 U.S. 175, 125 S. Ct. 551, 160 L. Ed. 2d 565 (2004)—§ 7:4 n.62

Florida v. Powell, 559 U.S. 50, 130 S. Ct. 1195, 175 L. Ed. 2d 1009 (2010)—§§ 5:14 n.2; 5:18 n.1

Florida v. Riley, 488 U.S. 445, 109 S. Ct. 693, 102 L. Ed. 2d 835 (1989)—§ 4:43 n.19

Florida v. Rodriguez, 469 U.S. 1, 105 S. Ct. 308, 83 L. Ed. 2d 165 (1984)—§ 3:4 n.28

Florida v. Wells, 495 U.S. 1, 110 S. Ct. 1632, 109 L. Ed. 2d 1 (1990)— § 4:56 n.5

Florida v. White, 526 U.S. 559, 119 S. Ct. 1555, 143 L. Ed. 2d 748 (1999)—§ 4:56 n.35

Florida Pub. Co. v. Morgan, 253 Ga. 467, 322 S.E.2d 233 (1984)—§ 17:2

Flowers v. State, 252 Ga. 476, 314 S.E.2d 206 (1984)—§ 5:3 n.1

Flowers v. State, 166 Ga. App. 740, 306 S.E.2d 16 (1983)—§ 14:48 n.4

Floyd v. Anders, 440 F. Supp. 535 (D.S.C. 1977)—§ 9:3 n.8

Floyd v. State, 293 Ga. App. 235, 666 S.E.2d 611 (2008)—§ 7:4 n.77

Floyd v. State, 272 Ga. 65, 525 S.E.2d 683 (2000)—§ 18:20 n.19

Floyd v. State, 237 Ga. App. 586, 516 S.E.2d 96 (1999)—§ 14:83 n.28

Fortson v. State, 247 Ga. App. 533, 544 S.E.2d 719 (2001)—§ 2:18 n.4

Fortson v. State, 272 Ga. 457, 532 S.E.2d 102 (2000)—§§ 14:64 n.9; 16:14 n.31; 16:15 n.7

Fortson v. State, 240 Ga. 5, 239 S.E.2d 335 (1977)—§ 7:8 n.2

Foskey v. Battle, 277 Ga. 480, 591 S.E.2d 802 (2004)—§§ 16:4 n.4; 16:8 n.5, 6

Foskey v. Sapp, 237 Ga. 788, 229 S.E.2d 635 (1976)—§ 26:19 n.72

Foskey v. State, 232 Ga. App. 303, 501 S.E.2d 856 (1998)—§ 16:14 n.16

Foster v. California, 394 U.S. 440, 89 S. Ct. 1127, 22 L. Ed. 2d 402 (1969)—§§ 6:2 n.18; 6:3 n.16

Foster v. Chatman, 136 S. Ct. 1737, 195 L. Ed. 2d 1 (2016)—§ 18:31 n.165

Foster v. State, 294 Ga. 383, 754 S.E.2d 33 (2014)—§ 26:6 n.25

Foster v. State, 283 Ga. 484, 660 S.E.2d 521 (2008)—§§ 5:5 n.4; 5:6 n.5

Foster v. State, 283 Ga. 47, 656 S.E.2d 838 (2008)—§ 21:12 n.8

Foster v. State, 208 Ga. App. 699, 431 S.E.2d 400 (1993)—§ 3:2 n.18

Foster v. State, 258 Ga. 736, 374 S.E.2d 188 (1988)—§§ 5:14 n.20; 18:31 n.77, 106, 107, 114; 21:16 n.7

Foster v. State, 255 Ga. 425, 339 S.E.2d 256 (1986)—§ 18:38 n.23

Foster v. State, 170 Ga. App. 222, 316 S.E.2d 828 (1984)—§ 14:4 n.13

Foster v. State, 165 Ga. App. 137, 299 S.E.2d 420 (1983)—§§ 8:1 n.11; 8:4 n.4

Foster v. State, 160 Ga. App. 326, 287 S.E.2d 323 (1981)—§ 6:7 n.10

Foster v. State, 156 Ga. App. 672, 275 S.E.2d 745 (1980)—§§ 6:4 n.19, 25; 6:10 n.5; 6:11 n.1

Foster v. State, 240 Ga. 858, 242 S.E.2d 600 (1978)—§§ 18:12 n.9; 18:19 n.27; 24:8 n.1

Foster v. State, 213 Ga. 601, 100 S.E.2d 426 (1957)—§ 6:2 n.1

Foucha v. Louisiana, 504 U.S. 71, 112 S. Ct. 1780, 118 L. Ed. 2d 437 (1992)—§ 21:14 n.14

444 U.S. 890, 100 S.Ct. 195, 62 L.Ed.2d 126 (1979)—§ 28:17 n.42

Foushi v. State, 144 Ga. App. 608, 244 S.E.2d 14 (1978)—§ 24:10 n.7

Fouts v. State, 374 So. 2d 22 (Fla. 2d DCA 1979)—§ 21:16 n.13

Fouts v. State, 240 Ga. 39, 239 S.E.2d 366 (1977)—§ 12:9 n.36

Fowler v. State, 195 Ga. App. 744, 395 S.E.2d 254 (1990)—§ 3:12 n.4

Fowler v. State, 184 Ga. App. 177, 360 S.E.2d 918 (1987)—§ 26:21 n.53

Fowler v. State, 179 Ga. App. 492, 347 S.E.2d 322 (1986)—§ 19:2 n.5

Fowler v. State, 235 Ga. 535, 221 S.E.2d 9 (1975)—§ 26:28 n.21

Fowler v. State, 128 Ga. App. 501, 197 S.E.2d 502 (1973)—§ 4:12 n.34

Fowler v. State, 121 Ga. App. 22, 172 S.E.2d 447 (1970)—§§ 4:11 n.1, 6, 14; 4:16 n.2

Fox v. State, 272 Ga. 163, 527 S.E.2d 847 (2000)—§§ 4:44 n.6, 7; 26:18 n.6

Foy v. State, 40 Ga. App. 617, 150 S.E. 917 (1929)—§ 14:41 n.3

Frady v. State, 212 Ga. 84, 90 S.E.2d 664 (1955)—§ 13:9 n.10

Frain v. State, 40 Ga. 529, 1869 WL 1857 (1869)—§ 17:17 n.34

Francis v. Henderson, 425 U.S. 536, 96 S. Ct. 1708, 48 L. Ed. 2d 149 (1976)—§ 12:8 n.5

Francis v. Spraggins, 720 F.2d 1190 (11th Cir. 1983)—§ 7:4 n.96

Frank v. Blackburn, 646 F.2d 873 (5th Cir. 1980)—§ 26:43 n.49

Fugate v. New Mexico, 470 U.S. 904, 105 S. Ct. 1858, 84 L. Ed. 2d 777 (1985)—§ 14:60 n.1

Fugitt v. State, 254 Ga. 521, 330 S.E.2d 714 (1985)—§ 14:22 n.42

Fugitt v. State, 251 Ga. 451, 307 S.E.2d 471 (1983)—§ 28:12 n.23

Fulghum v. State, 246 Ga. 184, 269 S.E.2d 455 (1980)—§ 21:11 n.10

Fuller v. Oregon, 417 U.S. 40, 94 S. Ct. 2116, 40 L. Ed. 2d 642 (1974)—§ 26:19 n.9

Fuller v. Ricketts, 234 Ga. 104, 214 S.E.2d 541 (1975)—§ 28:17 n.71

Fuller v. State, 313 Ga. App. 759, 722 S.E.2d 453 (2012)—§ 24:23 n.17

Fuller v. State, 277 Ga. 505, 591 S.E.2d 782 (2004)—§ 24:19 n.7

Fuller v. State, 169 Ga. App. 468, 313 S.E.2d 745 (1984)—§ 14:60 n.10

Fuller v. State, 57 Ga. App. 809, 197 S.E. 58 (1938)—§ 13:11 n.26

Fullwood v. Sivley, 271 Ga. 248, 517 S.E.2d 511 (1999)—§ 21:13 n.19

Fullwood v. State, 290 Ga. 335, 720 S.E.2d 642 (2012)—§ 16:3 n.2

Fulton v. State, 278 Ga. 58, 597 S.E.2d 396 (2004)—§ 23:7 n.48

Fulton County v. State, 282 Ga. 570, 651 S.E.2d 679 (2007)—§ 14:99 n.14

Fuqua v. State, 183 Ga. App. 414, 359 S.E.2d 165 (1987)—§ 14:35 n.16

Furfano v. State, 212 Ga. App. 472, 442 S.E.2d 305 (1994)—§ 4:22 n.23

Furlow v. State, 172 Ga. App. 185, 322 S.E.2d 317 (1984)—§ 14:29 n.28

Furman v. Georgia, 408 U.S. 238, 92 S. Ct. 2726, 33 L. Ed. 2d 346 (1972)—§ 26:6 n.12

Fuss v. State, 31 Ga. App. 147, 120 S.E. 37 (1923)—§ 12:17 n.16

Futch v. State, 192 Ga. App. 345, 385 S.E.2d 18 (1989)—§ 6:6 n.45

Futch v. State, 151 Ga. App. 519, 260 S.E.2d 520 (1979)—§§ 17:5 n.19; 19:6 n.2

Futch v. State, 37 Ga. App. 151, 139 S.E. 110 (1927)—§§ 14:42 n.12; 14:46 n.2

G

Ga., State of v. Rachel, 384 U.S. 780, 86 S. Ct. 1783, 16 L. Ed. 2d 925 (1966)—§ 14:91 n.1

Gable v. State, 290 Ga. 81, 720 S.E.2d 170 (2011)—§§ 28:6 n.7; 28:11 n.6

Gabler v. State, 177 Ga. App. 3, 338 S.E.2d 469 (1985)—§ 7:4 n.12

Gaddis v. State, 1972 OK CR 145, 497 P.2d 1087 (Okla. Crim. App. 1972)—§ 4:26 n.39

Gadson v. State, 223 Ga. App. 342, 477 S.E.2d 598 (1996)—§ 4:33 n.27

Gadson v. State, 264 Ga. 280, 444 S.E.2d 305 (1994)—§ 24:5 n.10

Gagnon v. Scarpelli, 411 U.S. 778, 93 S. Ct. 1756, 36 L. Ed. 2d 656 (1973)—§§ 26:19 n.72; 30:4 n.5, 6; 30:5 n.6, 7

Gagnon v. State, 240 Ga. App. 754, 525 S.E.2d 127 (1999)—§ 24:5 n.8

Gainer v. State, 267 Ga. App. 408, 599 S.E.2d 359 (2004)—§§ 16:4 n.3; 16:10 n.4

Gainer v. State, 144 Ga. App. 703, 242 S.E.2d 286 (1978)—§§ 5:13 n.2; 5:14 n.8, 22

Gainer v. State, 142 Ga. App. 871, 237 S.E.2d 235 (1977)—§ 25:4 n.7

Gaines v. Manson, 194 Conn. 510, 481 A.2d 1084 (1984)—§ 28:2 n.18

Gaines v. State, 274 Ga. App. 575, 618 S.E.2d 197 (2005)—§ 24:23 n.1

Gaines v. State, 258 Ga. App. 902, 575 S.E.2d 704 (2002)—§ 18:31 n.174

Georgia R. & Banking Co. v. City of Atlanta, 118 Ga. 486, 45 S.E. 256 (1903)—§ 9:2 n.7

Georgia State Bd. of Pardons and Paroles v. Turner, 248 Ga. 767, 285 S.E.2d 731 (1982)—§ 29:4 n.7

Georgia Television Co. v. State, 257 Ga. 764, 363 S.E.2d 528 (1988)—§ 17:2 n.10

Gerisch v. Meadows, 278 Ga. 641, 604 S.E.2d 462 (2004)—§ 14:53 n.11

German v. State, 159 Ga. App. 638, 284 S.E.2d 654 (1981)—§ 14:62 n.1

Germany v. State, 315 Ga. App. 717, 727 S.E.2d 240 (2012)—§§ 26:19 n.49; 30:2 n.12

Gerstein v. Pugh, 420 U.S. 103, 95 S. Ct. 854, 43 L. Ed. 2d 54, 19 Fed. R. Serv. 2d 1499 (1975)—§§ 2:13 n.7; 11:2 n.1; 11:5 n.2, 4

Geter v. State, 129 Ga. App. 108, 199 S.E.2d 272 (1973)—§ 2:4 n.17

Getkate v. State, 278 Ga. 585, 604 S.E.2d 838 (2004)—§ 28:5 n.7

Geyer v. State, 289 Ga. App. 492, 657 S.E.2d 878 (2008)—§ 26:14 n.23

Gholston v. Gholston, 31 Ga. 625, 1860 WL 2426 (1860)—§ 24:2 n.40

Gibbs v. Bright, 330 Ga. App. 851, 769 S.E.2d 590 (2015)—§ 17:21 n.12, 14

Gibbs v. State, 217 Ga. App. 614, 458 S.E.2d 407 (1995)—§ 5:21 n.16, 17

Gibbs v. State, 213 Ga. App. 117, 443 S.E.2d 708 (1994)—§§ 7:6 n.14; 28:10 n.4

Gibson v. State, 335 Ga. App. 569, 782 S.E.2d 472 (2016)—§ 21:13 n.20

Gibson v. State, 319 Ga. App. 627, 737 S.E.2d 728 (2013)—§ 26:21 n.13

Gibson v. State, 288 Ga. 617, 706 S.E.2d 412 (2011)—§§ 17:5 n.31; 24:10 n.1

Gibson v. State, 281 Ga. App. 607, 636 S.E.2d 767 (2006)—§ 15:1 n.6

Gibson v. State, 272 Ga. 801, 537 S.E.2d 72 (2000)—§§ 24:19 n.19; 24:26 n.16, 17

Gibson v. State, 236 Ga. 874, 226 S.E.2d 63 (1976)—§ 26:11 n.2

Gibson v. State, 162 Ga. 504, 134 S.E. 326 (1926)—§ 12:17 n.24

Gidden v. State, 205 Ga. App. 245, 422 S.E.2d 30 (1992)—§ 24:2 n.42

Giddens v. State, 299 Ga. 109, 786 S.E.2d 659 (2016)—§ 14:57 n.3, 10, 11

Giddens v. State, 156 Ga. App. 258, 274 S.E.2d 595 (1980)—§§ 4:43 n.8; 23:5 n.11; 26:15 n.14; 26:16 n.9; 26:19 n.41

Giddens v. State, 154 Ga. 54, 113 S.E. 386 (1922)—§ 2:6 n.2

Giddens v. State, 152 Ga. 195, 108 S.E. 788 (1921)—§ 12:5 n.1

Gideon v. Wainwright, 372 U.S. 335, 83 S. Ct. 792, 9 L. Ed. 2d 799, 93 A.L.R.2d 733 (1963)—§§ 7:2 n.9, 10, 19; 14:64 n.7

Gifford v. State, 301 Ga. App. 50, 686 S.E.2d 831 (2009)—§ 14:67 n.59

Giglio v. U.S., 405 U.S. 150, 92 S. Ct. 763, 31 L. Ed. 2d 104 (1972)—§§ 14:4 n.27; 14:33 n.4; 14:34 n.5; 17:6 n.12

Gil v. Beto, 440 F.2d 666 (5th Cir. 1971)—§ 4:41 n.1

Gilbert v. California, 388 U.S. 263, 87 S. Ct. 1951, 18 L. Ed. 2d 1178 (1967)—§§ 2:24 n.16; 2:34 n.11; 5:25 n.7; 6:2 n.21; 6:3 n.12; 6:8 n.1; 6:10 n.3

Gilbert v. State, 306 Ga. App. 776, 703 S.E.2d 374 (2010)—§ 12:15 n.16

Gilbert v. State, 245 Ga. App. 809, 539 S.E.2d 506 (2000)—§ 14:83 n.16

Gilbert v. State, 226 Ga. App. 230, 486 S.E.2d 48 (1997)—§ 18:31 n.7, 94

Gilbert v. State, 163 Ga. App. 688, 295 S.E.2d 173 (1982)—§ 14:73 n.11

Glass v. State, 250 Ga. 736, 300 S.E.2d 812 (1983)—§ 25:1 n.6

Glass v. State, 26 Ga. App. 157, 106 S.E. 13 (1921)—§ 13:11 n.27

Glasser v. U.S., 315 U.S. 60, 62 S. Ct. 457, 86 L. Ed. 680 (1942)—§§ 7:11 n.1; 18:17 n.6

Glaze v. State, 2 Ga. App. 704, 58 S.E. 1126 (1907)—§ 24:2 n.9

Glazner v. State, 170 Ga. App. 810, 318 S.E.2d 233 (1984)—§ 2:21 n.13

Glean v. State, 268 Ga. 260, 486 S.E.2d 172 (1997)—§ 14:74 n.11

Glean v. State, 197 Ga. App. 34, 397 S.E.2d 459 (1990)—§ 5:13 n.14

Glenn v. State, 285 Ga. App. 872, 648 S.E.2d 177 (2007)—§ 4:50 n.19

Glenn v. State, 271 Ga. 604, 523 S.E.2d 13 (1999)—§ 14:38 n.30

Glenn v. State, 144 Ga. App. 557, 241 S.E.2d 447 (1978)—§ 2:4 n.6

Glenn v. State, 205 Ga. 32, 52 S.E.2d 319 (1949)—§ 17:1 n.1

Glidewell v. State, 279 Ga. App. 114, 630 S.E.2d 621 (2006)—§ 14:66 n.1

Glidewell v. State, 169 Ga. App. 858, 314 S.E.2d 924 (1984)—§ 14:70 n.6

Globe Newspaper Co. v. Superior Court for Norfolk County, 457 U.S. 596, 102 S. Ct. 2613, 73 L. Ed. 2d 248 (1982)—§§ 17:1 n.5; 17:2 n.3

Glossip v. Gross, 135 S. Ct. 2726, 192 L. Ed. 2d 761 (2015)—§ 28:19 n.8, 10

Glover v. State, 274 Ga. 213, 552 S.E.2d 804 (2001)—§ 25:7 n.19

Glover v. State, 266 Ga. 183, 465 S.E.2d 659 (1996)—§ 7:6 n.7, 8, 9, 10

Glover v. State, 203 Ga. App. 853, 418 S.E.2d 127 (1992)—§ 14:38 n.1

Glover v. State, 149 Ga. App. 369, 254 S.E.2d 492 (1979)—§ 14:22 n.36

Glover v. State, 139 Ga. App. 162, 227 S.E.2d 921 (1976)—§§ 4:28 n.3, 5; 4:49 n.1, 24

Glover v. State, 266 Ga. 1832—§ 28:10 n.7

G. M. Leasing Corp. v. U. S., 429 U.S. 338, 97 S. Ct. 619, 50 L. Ed. 2d 530 (1977)—§§ 4:25 n.3; 4:46 n.16

Go-Bart Importing Co. v. U.S., 282 U.S. 344, 51 S. Ct. 153, 75 L. Ed. 374 (1931)—§ 4:2 n.10

Gober v. State, 249 Ga. App. 168, 547 S.E.2d 656 (2001)—§ 21:34 n.1

Gober v. State, 264 Ga. 226, 443 S.E.2d 616 (1994)—§ 2:12 n.25

Gober v. State, 247 Ga. 652, 278 S.E.2d 386 (1981)—§ 18:13 n.3, 4

Goddard v. State, 310 Ga. App. 2, 712 S.E.2d 528 (2011)—§ 14:70 n.38

Goddard v. State, 27 Ga. App. 226, 107 S.E. 888 (1921)—§ 14:39 n.10

Godfrey v. Francis, 251 Ga. 652, 308 S.E.2d 806 (1983)—§§ 14:93 n.15; 26:8 n.34

Godfrey v. State, 248 Ga. 616, 284 S.E.2d 422 (1981)—§ 26:11 n.6, 7, 15

Godfrey v. State, 243 Ga. 302, 253 S.E.2d 710 (1979)—§ 12:8 n.9

Godinez v. Moran, 509 U.S. 389, 113 S. Ct. 2680, 125 L. Ed. 2d 321 (1993)—§§ 7:3 n.42; 16:5 n.1

Godwin v. Crowell, 56 Ga. 566, 1876 WL 3285 (1876)—§ 17:20 n.6

Goeke v. Branch, 514 U.S. 115, 115 S. Ct. 1275, 131 L. Ed. 2d 152 (1995)—§ 14:64 n.8

Goforth v. Wigley, 178 Ga. App. 558, 343 S.E.2d 788 (1986)—§ 23:2 n.7

Goggins v. State, 161 Ga. App. 571, 289 S.E.2d 771 (1982)—§ 4:19 n.6

Goins v. State, 177 Ga. App. 536, 339 S.E.2d 790 (1986)—§ 24:16 n.16

Goldberg v. State, 282 Ga. 542, 651 S.E.2d 667 (2007)—§ 26:28 n.66

Goldberg v. State, 22 Ga. App. 122, 95 S.E. 541 (1918)—§ 13:6 n.1

Gray v. Netherland, 518 U.S. 152, 116 S. Ct. 2074, 135 L. Ed. 2d 457 (1996)—§ 14:64 n.8

Gray v. State, 260 Ga. App. 197, 581 S.E.2d 279 (2003)—§ 14:80 n.3

Gray v. State, 222 Ga. App. 626, 476 S.E.2d 12 (1996)—§ 19:2 n.14

Gray v. State, 213 Ga. App. 507, 445 S.E.2d 328 (1994)—§ 14:34 n.17

Gray v. State, 204 Ga. App. 33, 418 S.E.2d 412 (1992)—§ 14:38 n.20

Gray v. State, 158 Ga. App. 582, 281 S.E.2d 328 (1981)—§ 21:7 n.2

Gray v. State, 43 Md. App. 238, 403 A.2d 853 (1979)—§ 14:85 n.26

Gray v. State, 145 Ga. App. 293, 243 S.E.2d 687 (1978)—§ 14:85 n.1

Gray v. State, 6 Ga. App. 428, 65 S.E. 191 (1909)—§§ 13:5 n.1; 13:10 n.7; 14:48 n.18

Grayer v. State, 181 Ga. App. 845, 354 S.E.2d 191 (1987)—§ 17:5 n.11

Grayson v. State, 39 Ga. App. 673, 148 S.E. 309 (1929)—§ 13:6 n.9

Greathouse v. State, 156 Ga. App. 491, 274 S.E.2d 835 (1980)—§ 14:71 n.20

Green v. Green, 231 Ga. 311, 201 S.E.2d 440 (1973)—§ 28:17 n.19

Green v. Loggins, 614 F.2d 219 (9th Cir. 1980)—§ 6:10 n.5

Green v. Russell, 176 Ga. 354, 168 S.E. 65 (1933)—§ 13:20 n.10

Green v. State, 299 Ga. 337, 788 S.E.2d 380 (2016)—§ 17:5 n.22

Green v. State, 331 Ga. App. 801, 771 S.E.2d 518 (2015)—§ 4:2 n.59

Green v. State, 295 Ga. 108, 757 S.E.2d 856 (2014)—§ 18:24 n.30

Green v. State, 324 Ga. App. 133, 749 S.E.2d 419 (2013)—§ 16:10 n.5

Green v. State, 303 Ga. App. 210, 692 S.E.2d 784 (2010)—§ 14:64 n.5

Green v. State, 282 Ga. 672, 653 S.E.2d 23 (2007)—§ 5:8 n.8

Green v. State, 279 Ga. 687, 620 S.E.2d 788 (2005)—§ 16:4 n.9

Green v. State, 275 Ga. 569, 570 S.E.2d 207 (2002)—§§ 4:15 n.10; 4:58 n.1

Green v. State, 274 Ga. 686, 558 S.E.2d 707 (2002)—§ 14:72 n.65

Green v. State, 250 Ga. App. 440, 550 S.E.2d 736 (2001)—§ 10:3 n.19

Green v. State, 240 Ga. App. 774, 525 S.E.2d 154 (1999)—§ 2:7 n.8

Green v. State, 266 Ga. 758, 470 S.E.2d 884 (1996)—§ 24:5 n.27, 28

Green v. State, 221 Ga. App. 694, 472 S.E.2d 457 (1996)—§ 7:11 n.38

Green v. State, 265 Ga. 263, 454 S.E.2d 466 (1995)—§§ 16:2 n.14; 16:7 n.4

Green v. State, 219 Ga. App. 24, 464 S.E.2d 21 (1995)—§ 18:31 n.68, 100

Green v. State, 260 Ga. 625, 398 S.E.2d 360 (1990)—§ 26:19 n.38

Green v. State, 170 Ga. App. 806, 318 S.E.2d 513 (1984)—§ 26:33 n.16

Green v. State, 165 Ga. App. 702, 302 S.E.2d 604 (1983)—§ 20:7 n.15

Green v. State, 159 Ga. App. 28, 283 S.E.2d 19 (1981)—§ 2:5 n.2

Green v. State, 615 S.W.2d 700 (Tex. Crim. App. 1980)—§§ 2:19 n.18; 2:31 n.12

Green v. State, 246 Ga. 598, 272 S.E.2d 475 (1980)—§§ 18:11 n.3; 24:15 n.3; 25:4 n.8, 14; 26:11 n.11

Green v. State, 154 Ga. App. 295, 267 S.E.2d 898 (1980)—§§ 5:26 n.5; 26:28 n.62

Green v. State, 127 Ga. App. 713, 194 S.E.2d 678 (1972)—§ 4:38 n.10

Green v. State, 124 Ga. App. 469, 184 S.E.2d 194 (1971)—§ 21:26 n.6

Green v. State, 223 Ga. 611, 157 S.E.2d 257 (1967)—§ 14:22 n.37

Green v. State, 115 Ga. App. 685, 155 S.E.2d 655 (1967)—§ 5:11 n.16

Green v. State, 112 Ga. App. 329, 145 S.E.2d 80 (1965)—§ 20:7 n.2

Griffin v. State, 230 Ga. App. 318, 496 S.E.2d 480 (1998)—§ 5:26 n.8

Griffin v. State, 267 Ga. 586, 481 S.E.2d 223 (1997)—§§ 21:21 n.1; 21:29 n.5; 24:2 n.20

Griffin v. State, 266 Ga. 115, 464 S.E.2d 371 (1995)—§§ 20:4 n.26; 26:35 n.9

Griffin v. State, 264 Ga. 232, 443 S.E.2d 612 (1994)—§ 14:58 n.53

Griffin v. State, 214 Ga. App. 813, 449 S.E.2d 341 (1994)—§ 24:4 n.7

Griffin v. State, 204 Ga. App. 270, 419 S.E.2d 115 (1992)—§ 21:16 n.13

Griffin v. State, 183 Ga. App. 386, 358 S.E.2d 917 (1987)—§ 14:30 n.17

Griffin v. State, 168 Ga. App. 696, 310 S.E.2d 278 (1983)—§ 26:37 n.17

Griffin v. State, 245 Ga. 345, 265 S.E.2d 20 (1980)—§ 12:8 n.11

Griffin v. State, 154 Ga. App. 261, 267 S.E.2d 867 (1980)—§ 21:25 n.26

Griffin v. State, 148 Ga. App. 311, 251 S.E.2d 161 (1978)—§ 14:5 n.7

Griffin v. State, 142 Ga. App. 362, 235 S.E.2d 724 (1977)—§ 17:5 n.21

Griffin v. State, 133 Ga. App. 508, 211 S.E.2d 382 (1974)—§ 14:22 n.33, 36

Griffin v. State, 229 Ga. 165, 190 S.E.2d 61 (1972)—§ 6:8 n.23

Griffin v. State, 12 Ga. App. 615, 77 S.E. 1080 (1913)—§ 17:20 n.1

Griffin v. Terry, 291 Ga. 326, 729 S.E.2d 334 (2012)—§ 7:4 n.98

Griffin v. Wisconsin, 483 U.S. 868, 107 S. Ct. 3164, 97 L. Ed. 2d 709 (1987)—§§ 4:44 n.5; 26:19 n.39

Griffith v. State, 264 Ga. 326, 444 S.E.2d 794 (1994)—§§ 17:24 n.14; 24:2 n.8

Griffith v. State, 188 Ga. App. 789, 374 S.E.2d 359 (1988)—§ 24:5 n.26

Griffith v. State, 172 Ga. App. 255, 322 S.E.2d 921 (1984)—§§ 2:31 n.4; 4:30 n.13

Griffith v. State, 223 Ga. 543, 156 S.E.2d 903 (1967)—§ 5:18 n.3

Griggs v. State, 262 Ga. 766, 425 S.E.2d 644 (1993)—§ 7:11 n.22

Griggs v. State, 241 Ga. 317, 245 S.E.2d 269 (1978)—§§ 14:92 n.9; 18:17 n.11; 21:10 n.11

Griggs v. State, 146 Ga. App. 694, 247 S.E.2d 219 (1978)—§ 5:2 n.7

Grimes v. Greer, 223 Ga. 628, 157 S.E.2d 260 (1967)—§ 26:29 n.7

Grimes v. Harvey, 219 Ga. 675, 135 S.E.2d 281 (1964)—§ 28:17 n.23

Grimes v. State, 293 Ga. 559, 748 S.E.2d 441 (2013)—§ 24:11 n.7

Grimes v. State, 303 Ga. App. 808, 695 S.E.2d 294 (2010)—§§ 4:28 n.14; 4:56 n.19

Grimes v. State, 237 Ga. App. 654, 516 S.E.2d 378 (1999)—§ 26:49 n.1

Grimes v. State, 168 Ga. App. 372, 308 S.E.2d 863 (1983)—§ 14:38 n.14

Grimsley v. Dodson, 696 F.2d 303 (4th Cir. 1982)—§ 2:34 n.8

Grimsley v. State, 251 So. 2d 671 (Fla. 2d DCA 1971)—§ 5:19 n.32

Grizzard v. State, 301 Ga. App. 613, 688 S.E.2d 402 (2009)—§ 14:70 n.33

Groban, Petition of, 352 U.S. 330, 77 S. Ct. 510, 1 L. Ed. 2d 376, 76 Ohio L. Abs. 368 (1957)—§ 12:18 n.7

Grogins v. State, 154 Ga. App. 606, 269 S.E.2d 98 (1980)—§ 5:11 n.8

Groh v. Ramirez, 540 U.S. 551, 124 S. Ct. 1284, 157 L. Ed. 2d 1068 (2004)—§ 4:22 n.4

Groom v. State, 212 Ga. App. 133, 441 S.E.2d 259 (1994)—§ 14:67 n.24, 40

Groppi v. Wisconsin, 400 U.S. 505, 91 S. Ct. 490, 27 L. Ed. 2d 571 (1971)—§ 14:74 n.4

H

Hair v. State, 262 Ga. 284, 417 S.E.2d 657 (1992)—§ 14:30 n.45

Haisman v. State, 242 Ga. 896, 252 S.E.2d 397 (1979)—§§ 2:4 n.10; 14:73 n.8

Halbert v. Michigan, 545 U.S. 605, 125 S. Ct. 2582, 162 L. Ed. 2d 552 (2005)—§ 28:6 n.3

Haley v. State, 124 Ga. 216, 52 S.E. 159 (1905)—§§ 13:15 n.1; 14:41 n.23

Hall v. Florida, 572 U.S. 701, 134 S. Ct. 1986, 188 L. Ed. 2d 1007 (2014)—§ 26:6 n.33

Hall v. Hopper, 234 Ga. 625, 216 S.E.2d 839 (1975)—§ 14:66 n.37

Hall v. State, 230 Ga. App. 378, 496 S.E.2d 475 (1998)—§ 14:72 n.44

Hall v. State, 223 Ga. App. 211, 477 S.E.2d 364 (1996)—§ 14:83 n.18

Hall v. State, 210 Ga. App. 792, 437 S.E.2d 634 (1993)—§ 7:4 n.74

Hall v. State, 261 Ga. 778, 415 S.E.2d 158 (1991)—§§ 14:4 n.18; 18:26 n.34; 18:31 n.45

Hall v. State, 180 Ga. App. 881, 350 S.E.2d 801 (1986)—§ 23:1 n.8

Hall v. State, 255 Ga. 267, 336 S.E.2d 812 (1985)—§ 5:20 n.35, 43

Hall v. State, 176 Ga. App. 498, 336 S.E.2d 604 (1985)—§ 20:6 n.18

Hall v. State, 163 Ga. App. 515, 295 S.E.2d 194 (1982)—§ 23:7 n.23

Hall v. State, 162 Ga. App. 713, 293 S.E.2d 862 (1982)—§ 28:7 n.5

Hall v. State, 161 Ga. App. 521, 289 S.E.2d 313 (1982)—§ 14:72 n.31

Hall v. State, 160 Ga. App. 508, 287 S.E.2d 223 (1981)—§ 26:14 n.3

Hall v. State, 155 Ga. App. 724, 272 S.E.2d 578 (1980)—§ 26:36 n.11

Hall v. State, 244 Ga. 86, 259 S.E.2d 41 (1979)—§ 14:58 n.36

Hall v. State, 241 Ga. 252, 244 S.E.2d 833 (1978)—§ 26:11 n.11

Hall v. State, 239 Ga. 832, 238 S.E.2d 912 (1977)—§ 4:32 n.2

Hall v. State, 143 Ga. App. 706, 240 S.E.2d 125 (1977)—§ 4:24 n.3

Hall v. State, 138 Ga. App. 20, 225 S.E.2d 705 (1976)—§ 19:5 n.3

Hall v. State, 136 Ga. App. 622, 222 S.E.2d 140 (1975)—§ 21:25 n.5

Hall v. State, 135 Ga. App. 690, 218 S.E.2d 687 (1975)—§§ 4:31 n.5; 18:26 n.22

Hall v. State, 131 Ga. App. 786, 206 S.E.2d 644 (1974)—§ 14:70 n.18

Hall v. State, 113 Ga. App. 587, 149 S.E.2d 175 (1966)—§ 4:5 n.4

Hall v. State, 202 Ga. 42, 42 S.E.2d 130 (1947)—§ 28:13 n.3

Hall v. State, 64 Ga. App. 644, 13 S.E.2d 868 (1941)—§ 18:19 n.8

Hall v. State, 8 Ga. App. 747, 70 S.E. 211 (1911)—§ 13:19 n.3

Hall v. State, 7 Ga. App. 115, 66 S.E. 390 (1909)—§ 12:7 n.4

Hall v. State, 120 Ga. 142, 47 S.E. 519 (1904)—§ 13:7 n.2

Hall v. U.S., 419 F.2d 582 (5th Cir. 1969)—§ 23:8 n.17

Hall v. Vargas, 278 Ga. 868, 608 S.E.2d 200 (2005)—§ 14:63 n.3

Hallman v. State, 141 Ga. App. 527, 233 S.E.2d 839 (1977)—§ 10:3 n.22

Halthon-Howard v. State, 234 Ga. App. 229, 506 S.E.2d 415 (1998)—§ 17:17 n.16

Ham v. South Carolina, 409 U.S. 524, 93 S. Ct. 848, 35 L. Ed. 2d 46 (1973)—§ 18:27 n.1

Hambrick v. State, 256 Ga. 148, 344 S.E.2d 639 (1986)—§ 26:33 n.16

Hambrick v. State, 174 Ga. App. 444, 330 S.E.2d 383, 58 A.L.R.4th 327 (1985)—§ 24:5 n.18

Hameen v. State, 246 Ga. App. 599, 541 S.E.2d 668 (2000)—§ 4:50 n.12

Hanifa v. State, 269 Ga. 797, 505 S.E.2d 731 (1998)—§§ 14:72 n.43, 44, 45; 24:19 n.6

Hankinson v. State, 129 Ga. App. 568, 200 S.E.2d 315 (1973)—§ 21:12 n.6

Hannah v. State, 125 Ga. App. 596, 188 S.E.2d 401 (1972)—§ 13:28 n.1

Hannah v. Stone, 236 Ga. 65, 222 S.E.2d 362 (1976)—§ 11:5 n.10

Hansen v. State, 222 Ga. App. 537, 474 S.E.2d 735 (1996)—§ 17:14 n.26

Hansford v. State, 54 Ga. 55, 1875 WL 2959 (1875)—§ 14:66 n.11

Hanson v. Kent, 263 Ga. 124, 428 S.E.2d 785 (1993)—§ 7:4 n.99

Hanvey v. State, 68 Ga. 612, 1882 WL 3201 (1882)—§ 21:16 n.12, 13

Happoldt v. State, 267 Ga. 126, 475 S.E.2d 627 (1996)—§ 14:74 n.10

Haralson v. State, 223 Ga. App. 787, 479 S.E.2d 115 (1996)—§ 21:25 n.26

Haralson v. State, 234 Ga. 406, 216 S.E.2d 304 (1975)—§§ 6:2 n.27; 6:6 n.8

Harbin v. State, 193 Ga. App. 248, 387 S.E.2d 367 (1989)—§ 14:78 n.32

Hardeman v. State, 272 Ga. 361, 529 S.E.2d 368 (2000)—§§ 14:2 n.2; 28:13 n.16

Hardeman v. State, 252 Ga. 286, 313 S.E.2d 95 (1984)—§ 5:12 n.5

Harden v. State, 184 Ga. App. 371, 361 S.E.2d 696 (1987)—§ 13:28 n.13

Harden v. State, 177 Ga. App. 531, 339 S.E.2d 793 (1986)—§ 16:14 n.14

Harden v. State, 160 Ga. App. 514, 287 S.E.2d 329 (1981)—§ 21:1 n.12, 13

Hardin v. Brookins, 275 Ga. 477, 569 S.E.2d 511 (2002)—§ 16:13 n.5

Hardin v. State, 344 Ga. App. 378, 810 S.E.2d 602 (2018)—§ 26:26 n.2

Hardin v. State, 277 Ga. 242, 587 S.E.2d 634 (2003)—§§ 3:9 n.18; 4:49 n.31

Hardin v. State, 269 Ga. 1, 494 S.E.2d 647 (1998)—§ 5:12 n.8, 11

Hardin v. State, 142 Ga. App. 795, 237 S.E.2d 202 (1977)—§ 14:22 n.32

Hardin v. State, 141 Ga. App. 115, 232 S.E.2d 631 (1977)—§ 26:36 n.11

Hardison v. Martin, 254 Ga. 719, 334 S.E.2d 161 (1985)—§ 16:14 n.27

Hardman v. Hardman, 185 Ga. App. 519, 364 S.E.2d 645 (1988)—§§ 26:19 n.28, 36; 26:24 n.8

Hardwick v. State, 264 Ga. 161, 442 S.E.2d 236 (1994)—§ 14:76 n.2

Hardwick v. State, 210 Ga. App. 468, 436 S.E.2d 676 (1993)—§§ 5:11 n.19; 24:23 n.12

Hardwick v. State, 231 Ga. 181, 200 S.E.2d 728 (1973)—§§ 12:9 n.34; 14:94 n.15; 16:1 n.12, 18

Hardy v. State, 223 Ga. App. 597, 478 S.E.2d 423 (1996)—§ 14:72 n.30

Hardy v. State, 192 Ga. App. 860, 386 S.E.2d 731 (1989)—§ 8:6 n.2

Hardy v. State, 162 Ga. App. 797, 292 S.E.2d 902 (1982)—§§ 4:9 n.9; 4:10 n.8

Hargett v. State, 151 Ga. App. 532, 260 S.E.2d 406 (1979)—§ 25:4 n.5

Harkey v. State, 159 Ga. App. 112, 282 S.E.2d 648 (1981)—§§ 17:5 n.32; 26:44 n.16

Harley-Davidson Motor Co., Inc. v. Daniel, 244 Ga. 284, 260 S.E.2d 20 (1979)—§ 14:78 n.15

Harley-Davidson Motor Co., Inc. v. Daniel, 149 Ga. App. 120, 253 S.E.2d 783 (1979)—§ 14:78 n.14

Harley v. State, 263 Ga. 875, 440 S.E.2d 178 (1994)—§ 14:30 n.47

Harris v. State, 344 Ga. App. 572, 810 S.E.2d 660 (2018)—§ 3:2 n.30

Harris v. State, 341 Ga. App. 831, 802 S.E.2d 708 (2017)—§ 3:13 n.10

Harris v. State, 331 Ga. App. 32, 769 S.E.2d 749 (2015)—§ 6:10 n.18

Harris v. State, 294 Ga. App. 668, 669 S.E.2d 706 (2008)—§ 24:8 n.9

Harris v. State, 284 Ga. 455, 667 S.E.2d 361 (2008)—§ 14:70 n.31

Harris v. State, 278 Ga. 596, 604 S.E.2d 788 (2004)—§ 18:35 n.6

Harris v. State, 258 Ga. App. 669, 574 S.E.2d 871 (2002)—§ 14:40 n.12

Harris v. State, 239 Ga. App. 537, 521 S.E.2d 462 (1999)—§ 3:10 n.12

Harris v. State, 218 Ga. App. 472, 462 S.E.2d 425 (1995)—§ 14:72 n.46

Harris v. State, 263 Ga. 526, 435 S.E.2d 669 (1993)—§ 24:26 n.23, 25

Harris v. State, 261 Ga. 859, 413 S.E.2d 439 (1992)—§ 26:21 n.60

Harris v. State, 205 Ga. App. 813, 423 S.E.2d 723 (1992)—§ 3:6 n.9

Harris v. State, 260 Ga. 860, 401 S.E.2d 263 (1991)—§§ 4:20 n.7; 14:30
n.18; 17:2 n.13

Harris v. State, 199 Ga. App. 457, 405 S.E.2d 501 (1991)—§ 13:23 n.28

Harris v. State, 197 Ga. App. 695, 399 S.E.2d 284 (1990)—§ 5:20 n.10

Harris v. State, 186 Ga. App. 756, 368 S.E.2d 527 (1988)—§ 21:30 n.1

Harris v. State, 255 Ga. 464, 339 S.E.2d 712 (1986)—§§ 18:19 n.28; 18:21
n.8; 18:26 n.5

Harris v. State, 181 Ga. App. 358, 352 S.E.2d 226 (1986)—§§ 21:10 n.30;
21:11 n.17

Harris v. State, 178 Ga. App. 735, 344 S.E.2d 528 (1986)—§§ 18:16 n.13;
18:19 n.24

Harris v. State, 170 Ga. App. 726, 318 S.E.2d 315 (1984)—§ 7:2 n.5

Harris v. State, 250 Ga. 889, 302 S.E.2d 104 (1983)—§ 21:16 n.15

Harris v. State, 167 Ga. App. 153, 306 S.E.2d 79 (1983)—§ 15:1 n.8

Harris v. State, 165 Ga. App. 249, 299 S.E.2d 924 (1983)—§ 26:36 n.5, 11

Harris v. State, 160 Ga. App. 47, 285 S.E.2d 781 (1981)—§ 26:28 n.40

Harris v. State, 145 Ga. App. 675, 244 S.E.2d 620 (1978)—§ 24:2 n.26

Harris v. State, 142 Ga. App. 37, 234 S.E.2d 798 (1977)—§§ 14:22 n.16;
17:17 n.2

Harris v. State, 237 Ga. 718, 230 S.E.2d 1 (1976)—§§ 5:1 n.12; 17:9 n.11

Harris v. State, 236 Ga. 242, 223 S.E.2d 643 (1976)—§ 13:31 n.1

Harris v. State, 225 Ga. 458, 169 S.E.2d 331 (1969)—§ 28:15 n.4, 5

Harris v. State, 120 Ga. App. 359, 170 S.E.2d 743 (1969)—§ 18:27 n.10

Harris v. State, 193 Ga. 109, 17 S.E.2d 573, 147 A.L.R. 980 (1941)—
§§ 14:42 n.14, 18; 14:57 n.3, 7

Harris v. State, 191 Ga. 243, 12 S.E.2d 64 (1940)—§ 20:4 n.1

Harris v. State, 188 Ga. 745, 4 S.E.2d 651 (1939)—§ 18:23 n.26

Harris v. State, 43 Ga. App. 485, 159 S.E. 603 (1931)—§ 14:42 n.17

Harris v. State, 37 Ga. App. 113, 138 S.E. 922 (1927)—§ 13:4 n.20, 32, 34

Harris v. State, 11 Ga. App. 137, 74 S.E. 895 (1912)—§ 16:1 n.2

Harris v. State, 3 Ga. App. 457, 60 S.E. 127 (1908)—§ 21:4 n.8

Harris v. State, 58 Ga. 332, 1877 WL 3017 (1877)—§ 28:13 n.26

Harris v. Superior Court, 19 Cal. 3d 786, 140 Cal. Rptr. 318, 567 P.2d
750 (1977)—§ 7:2 n.35

Harris v. Texas, 403 U.S. 947, 91 S. Ct. 2291, 29 L. Ed. 2d 859 (1971)—
§§ 18:16 n.6; 18:17 n.16

Harris v. Upton, 292 Ga. 491, 739 S.E.2d 300 (2013)—§§ 7:4 n.85; 16:10
n.15

Hatton v. Smith, 228 Ga. 378, 185 S.E.2d 388 (1971)—§ 28:17 n.12

Haugebrooks v. State, 196 Ga. App. 5, 395 S.E.2d 348 (1990)—§ 21:13 n.13

Haugh v. Jones & Laughlin Steel Corp., 949 F.2d 914, 34 Fed. R. Evid. Serv. 841 (7th Cir. 1991)—§ 25:7 n.7

Hawes v. State, 281 Ga. 822, 642 S.E.2d 92 (2007)—§ 16:8 n.3, 4

Hawes v. State, 266 Ga. 731, 470 S.E.2d 664 (1996)—§ 13:9 n.12

Hawes v. State, 240 Ga. 327, 240 S.E.2d 833 (1977)—§§ 7:4 n.9, 34; 23:8 n.15; 26:10 n.8

Hawes v. State, 239 Ga. 630, 238 S.E.2d 418 (1977)—§ 26:37 n.3

Hawkins v. Comparet-Cassani, 33 F. Supp. 2d 1244 (C.D. Cal. 1999)— § 17:7 n.23

Hawkins v. State, 290 Ga. 785, 723 S.E.2d 924 (2012)—§§ 4:2 n.89; 4:7 n.32; 4:26 n.17; 14:79 n.11

Hawkins v. State, 242 Ga. App. 603, 528 S.E.2d 853 (2000)—§ 24:5 n.22

Hawkins v. State, 267 Ga. 124, 475 S.E.2d 625 (1996)—§ 24:5 n.2

Hawkins v. State, 260 Ga. 138, 390 S.E.2d 836 (1990)—§ 13:8 n.3

Hawkins v. State, 165 Ga. App. 278, 300 S.E.2d 224 (1983)—§ 4:21 n.23

Hawkins v. State, 146 Ga. App. 312, 246 S.E.2d 343 (1978)—§ 4:38 n.2

Hawkins v. State, 130 Ga. App. 426, 203 S.E.2d 622 (1973)—§§ 4:5 n.12; 4:6 n.2

Hawkins v. State, 117 Ga. App. 70, 159 S.E.2d 440 (1967)—§§ 14:78 n.13; 14:84 n.1

Hawkins v. State, 86 Ga. App. 872, 72 S.E.2d 778 (1952)—§ 12:7 n.3, 7

Hayek v. State, 269 Ga. 728, 506 S.E.2d 372 (1998)—§ 14:67 n.27

Hayes v. Cady, 500 F.2d 1212 (7th Cir. 1974)—§ 4:33 n.8

Hayes v. Florida, 470 U.S. 811, 105 S. Ct. 1643, 84 L. Ed. 2d 705 (1985)—§ 3:12 n.8, 9

Hayes v. State, 292 Ga. App. 724, 665 S.E.2d 422 (2008)—§ 3:11 n.16

Hayes v. State, 249 Ga. App. 857, 549 S.E.2d 813 (2001)—§ 14:19 n.5

Hayes v. State, 236 Ga. App. 617, 512 S.E.2d 294 (1999)—§ 23:5 n.28

Hayes v. State, 268 Ga. 809, 493 S.E.2d 169 (1997)—§§ 23:2 n.10, 11; 23:3 n.1

Hayes v. State, 207 Ga. App. 520, 428 S.E.2d 425 (1993)—§ 14:99 n.4

Hayes v. State, 182 Ga. App. 319, 355 S.E.2d 700 (1987)—§ 4:7 n.26

Hayes v. State, 168 Ga. App. 94, 308 S.E.2d 227 (1983)—§ 14:34 n.32

Hayes v. State, 157 Ga. App. 659, 278 S.E.2d 424 (1981)—§ 30:7 n.1

Hayes v. State, 152 Ga. App. 858, 264 S.E.2d 307 (1980)—§ 20:6 n.63

Hayes v. State, 141 Ga. App. 706, 234 S.E.2d 360 (1977)—§ 4:21 n.11, 21, 22, 24

Hayes v. State, 138 Ga. App. 666, 226 S.E.2d 819 (1976)—§ 12:8 n.4

Hayes v. State, 138 Ga. App. 223, 225 S.E.2d 749 (1976)—§§ 19:6 n.4; 23:9 n.1

Hayes v. State, 136 Ga. App. 746, 222 S.E.2d 193 (1975)—§ 18:38 n.2

Hayes v. State, 57 Ga. App. 801, 196 S.E. 926 (1938)—§ 21:16 n.13

Hayes v. State, 58 Ga. 35, 1877 WL 2924 (1877)—§ 17:5 n.5

Haygood v. State, 225 Ga. App. 81, 483 S.E.2d 302 (1997)—§ 26:2 n.26

Hayles v. State, 188 Ga. App. 281, 372 S.E.2d 668 (1988)—§ 14:54 n.9

Hayles v. State, 180 Ga. App. 860, 350 S.E.2d 793 (1986)—§ 18:19 n.28

Hedquist v. Hedquist, 275 Ga. 188, 563 S.E.2d 854 (2002)—§ 27:4 n.1

Heidler v. State, 273 Ga. 54, 537 S.E.2d 44 (2000)—§ 18:17 n.22

Heidt v. State, 292 Ga. 343, 736 S.E.2d 384 (2013)—§ 7:12 n.5

Heien v. North Carolina, 135 S. Ct. 530, 190 L. Ed. 2d 475 (2014)—§§ 3:2 n.28; 4:26 n.7

Height v. State, 278 Ga. 592, 604 S.E.2d 796 (2004)—§ 26:8 n.47

Height v. State, 221 Ga. App. 647, 472 S.E.2d 485 (1996)—§ 18:31 n.75, 84

Height v. State, 214 Ga. App. 570, 448 S.E.2d 726 (1994)—§ 21:16 n.8

Heimlich v. State, 231 Ga. App. 662, 500 S.E.2d 388 (1998)—§ 3:9 n.8, 21

Heller v. New York, 413 U.S. 483, 93 S.Ct. 2789, 37 L.Ed.2d 745 (1973)—§ 4:23 n.6

Heller v. State, 275 Ga. App. 637, 621 S.E.2d 591 (2005)—§ 14:83 n.5

Helling v. McKinney, 509 U.S. 25, 113 S. Ct. 2475, 125 L. Ed. 2d 22 (1993)—§ 26:2 n.11

Helmeci v. State, 230 Ga. App. 866, 498 S.E.2d 326 (1998)—§ 28:5 n.7

Helmer v. State, 256 Ga. App. 717, 569 S.E.2d 606 (2002)—§ 7:3 n.27

Helton v. State, 206 Ga. App. 600, 426 S.E.2d 172 (1992)—§ 20:6 n.15

Helton v. State, 166 Ga. App. 565, 305 S.E.2d 27 (1983)—§ 30:2 n.17

Hemidi v. State, 245 Ga. App. 417, 537 S.E.2d 804 (2000)—§ 24:22 n.13

Henderson v. Commonwealth, 185 Ky. 232, 215 S.W. 53 (1919)—§ 14:4 n.17

Henderson v. Kibbe, 431 U.S. 145, 97 S. Ct. 1730, 52 L. Ed. 2d 203 (1977)—§ 24:8 n.12

Henderson v. Morgan, 426 U.S. 637, 96 S. Ct. 2253, 49 L. Ed. 2d 108 (1976)—§ 16:7 n.2

Henderson v. State, 303 Ga. 241, 811 S.E.2d 388 (2018)—§ 28:7 n.10

Henderson v. State, 295 Ga. 333, 759 S.E.2d 827 (2014)—§ 14:77 n.4

Henderson v. State, 250 Ga. App. 278, 551 S.E.2d 400 (2001)—§ 3:11 n.10

Henderson v. State, 236 Ga. App. 72, 510 S.E.2d 879 (1999)—§ 14:51 n.3

Henderson v. State, 206 Ga. App. 642, 426 S.E.2d 264 (1992)—§ 14:53 n.10

Henderson v. State, 204 Ga. App. 884, 420 S.E.2d 813 (1992)—§ 20:6 n.16

Henderson v. State, 182 Ga. App. 513, 356 S.E.2d 241 (1987)—§ 14:34 n.26

Henderson v. State, 255 Ga. 687, 341 S.E.2d 439 (1986)—§ 17:12 n.15

Henderson v. State, 173 Ga. App. 302, 326 S.E.2d 246 (1985)—§ 18:26 n.21

Henderson v. State, 251 Ga. 398, 306 S.E.2d 645 (1983)—§§ 18:24 n.19; 18:27 n.8; 18:30 n.9

Henderson v. State, 162 Ga. App. 320, 292 S.E.2d 77, 33 A.L.R.4th 289 (1982)—§§ 14:29 n.25, 43, 44; 14:30 n.38, 52; 14:38 n.12; 26:1 n.24

Henderson v. State, 234 Ga. 827, 218 S.E.2d 612 (1975)—§ 24:5 n.12

Henderson v. State, 227 Ga. 68, 179 S.E.2d 76 (1970)—§ 14:73 n.25

Henderson v. State, 5 Ga. App. 495, 63 S.E. 535 (1909)—§ 21:24 n.5

Henderson v. State, 113 Ga. 1148, 39 S.E. 446 (1901)—§ 13:15 n.3, 5

Henderson v. U.S., 405 F.2d 874 (5th Cir. 1968)—§ 4:26 n.12

Herring v. State, 334 Ga. App. 50, 778 S.E.2d 57 (2015)—§ 13:6 n.11

Herring v. State, 279 Ga. App. 162, 630 S.E.2d 776 (2006)—§ 4:30 n.9

Herring v. State, 224 Ga. App. 809, 481 S.E.2d 842 (1997)—§ 24:1 n.1

Herring v. State, 238 Ga. 288, 232 S.E.2d 826 (1977)—§§ 17:23 n.6; 26:13 n.16

Herring v. State, 37 Ga. App. 594, 141 S.E. 89 (1928)—§ 27:2 n.12

Herring v. State, 165 Ga. 254, 140 S.E. 491 (1927)—§ 27:1 n.26

Herring v. U.S., 555 U.S. 135, 129 S. Ct. 695, 172 L. Ed. 2d 496 (2009)—§ 2:26 n.5

Herrington v. State, 315 Ga. App. 101, 726 S.E.2d 625 (2012)—§ 14:58 n.17

Herrington v. State, 221 Ga. App. 354, 471 S.E.2d 289 (1996)—§ 3:2 n.21

Herrmann v. State, 235 Ga. 400, 220 S.E.2d 2 (1975)—§ 5:1 n.12

Herron v. State, 155 Ga. App. 791, 272 S.E.2d 756 (1980)—§§ 6:5 n.15; 6:10 n.5

Hersi v. State, 257 Ga. App. 63, 570 S.E.2d 365 (2002)—§ 17:8 n.21

Hess v. State, 296 Ga. App. 300, 674 S.E.2d 362 (2009)—§ 4:44 n.4

Hess v. State, 309 So. 2d 606 (Fla. 2d DCA 1975)—§ 4:57 n.8

Hester v. State, 268 Ga. App. 94, 601 S.E.2d 456 (2004)—§ 14:70 n.18

Hester v. State, 219 Ga. App. 256, 465 S.E.2d 288 (1995)—§ 28:12 n.19

Hester v. U.S., 265 U.S. 57, 44 S. Ct. 445, 68 L. Ed. 898 (1924)—§§ 4:2 n.31; 4:38 n.1, 2; 4:43 n.1, 2

Hewell v. State, 238 Ga. 578, 234 S.E.2d 497 (1977)—§ 26:41 n.4

Hewell v. State, 136 Ga. App. 420, 221 S.E.2d 219 (1975)—§ 20:6 n.26

Hewett v. State, 244 Ga. App. 112, 534 S.E.2d 867 (2000)—§ 26:32 n.2

Heyward v. State, 236 Ga. 526, 224 S.E.2d 383 (1976)—§ 6:8 n.10

Hiatt v. State, 144 Ga. App. 298, 240 S.E.2d 894 (1977)—§ 17:7 n.26

Hiatt v. State, 132 Ga. App. 289, 208 S.E.2d 163 (1974)—§ 18:20 n.5

Hibbert v. State, 195 Ga. App. 235, 393 S.E.2d 96 (1990)—§ 5:20 n.48

Hibbs v. State, 133 Ga. App. 407, 211 S.E.2d 24 (1974)—§ 14:22 n.20

Hickman v. State, 279 Ga. App. 558, 631 S.E.2d 778 (2006)—§§ 3:2 n.47; 3:12 n.16

Hickory v. U.S., 160 U.S. 408, 16 S. Ct. 327, 40 L. Ed. 474 (1896)— § 20:3 n.5

Hicks v. Oklahoma, 447 U.S. 343, 100 S. Ct. 2227, 65 L. Ed. 2d 175 (1980)—§ 14:1 n.9

Hicks v. Scott, 273 Ga. 358, 541 S.E.2d 27 (2001)—§ 28:17 n.55, 89

Hicks v. State, 315 Ga. App. 779, 728 S.E.2d 294 (2012)—§ 17:19 n.12

Hicks v. State, 221 Ga. App. 735, 472 S.E.2d 474 (1996)—§ 17:17 n.41

Hicks v. State, 262 Ga. 756, 425 S.E.2d 877 (1993)—§ 14:72 n.52

Hicks v. State, 200 Ga. App. 602, 409 S.E.2d 82 (1991)—§ 17:7 n.18

Hicks v. State, 256 Ga. 715, 352 S.E.2d 762 (1987)—§§ 12:9 n.15; 17:7 n.14; 19:2 n.30; 23:5 n.3; 23:7 n.31; 23:8 n.20; 24:2 n.37; 26:8 n.7, 37

Hicks v. State, 169 Ga. App. 542, 314 S.E.2d 113 (1984)—§ 7:4 n.11

Hicks v. State, 157 Ga. App. 79, 276 S.E.2d 129 (1981)—§ 30:7 n.1

Hicks v. State, 147 Ga. App. 814, 250 S.E.2d 558 (1978)—§ 16:1 n.22

Hicks v. State, 145 Ga. App. 669, 244 S.E.2d 597 (1978)—§ 16:1 n.20

Hicks v. State, 232 Ga. 393, 207 S.E.2d 30 (1974)—§§ 14:22 n.24; 14:34 n.33

Holiday v. State, 128 Ga. App. 817, 198 S.E.2d 364 (1973)—§ 21:26 n.7

Holland v. State, 221 Ga. App. 821, 472 S.E.2d 711 (1996)—§ 14:29 n.39, 40

Holland v. State, 218 Ga. App. 744, 463 S.E.2d 169 (1995)—§ 16:2 n.14

Holland v. State, 209 Ga. App. 821, 434 S.E.2d 808 (1993)—§ 16:6 n.5

Holland v. State, 204 Ga. App. 22, 418 S.E.2d 400 (1992)—§ 10:4 n.1

Holland v. State, 190 Ga. App. 169, 378 S.E.2d 513 (1989)—§ 14:29 n.28

Holland v. State, 161 Ga. 492, 131 S.E. 503 (1926)—§ 28:13 n.19

Holland v. State, 3 Ga. App. 465, 60 S.E. 205 (1908)—§ 24:2 n.15

Holley v. State, 157 Ga. App. 863, 278 S.E.2d 738 (1981)—§ 26:15 n.13

Hollinger v. U.S., 391 F.2d 929 (5th Cir. 1968)—§ 28:20 n.4

Hollingsworth v. State, 155 Ga. App. 878, 273 S.E.2d 639 (1980)—§ 4:38 n.22

Hollingsworth v. State, 7 Ga. App. 16, 65 S.E. 1077 (1909)—§§ 14:39 n.6; 14:66 n.14, 34; 28:13 n.20

Hollins v. State, 133 Ga. App. 183, 210 S.E.2d 354 (1974)—§ 22:6 n.8

Hollis v. Allen, 235 Ga. 211, 219 S.E.2d 108 (1975)—§ 28:17 n.53

Hollis v. State, 215 Ga. App. 35, 450 S.E.2d 247 (1994)—§ 25:8 n.4

Hollis v. State, 174 Ga. App. 627, 330 S.E.2d 817 (1985)—§ 5:21 n.8

Hollis v. State, 77 Ga. 74, 1886 WL 1447 (1886)—§ 11:2 n.12

Holloman v. State, 133 Ga. App. 275, 211 S.E.2d 312 (1974)—§ 14:66 n.21, 30

Holloway v. Arkansas, 435 U.S. 475, 98 S. Ct. 1173, 55 L. Ed. 2d 426 (1978)—§ 7:11 n.6

Holloway v. McElroy, 632 F.2d 605 (5th Cir. 1980)—§ 28:8 n.1

Holloway v. State, 257 Ga. 620, 361 S.E.2d 794 (1987)—§ 14:93 n.3

Holloway v. State, 178 Ga. App. 141, 342 S.E.2d 363 (1986)—§ 26:16 n.3

Holloway v. State, 168 Ga. App. 294, 308 S.E.2d 641 (1983)—§ 14:72 n.30

Holloway v. State, 137 Ga. App. 124, 222 S.E.2d 898 (1975)—§ 18:12 n.7

Holloway v. State, 134 Ga. App. 498, 215 S.E.2d 262 (1975)—§ 4:12 n.32

Holloway v. State, 90 Ga. App. 86, 82 S.E.2d 235 (1954)—§ 13:13 n.1, 6

Holman v. State, 329 Ga. App. 393, 765 S.E.2d 614 (2014)—§ 28:11 n.1

Holman v. State, 236 Ga. App. 111, 511 S.E.2d 240 (1999)—§ 16:9 n.3

Holmes v. Kenyon, 238 Ga. 583, 234 S.E.2d 502 (1977)—§ 28:7 n.2

Holmes v. King, 216 Ala. 412, 113 So. 274 (1927)—§ 10:1 n.4, 5

Holmes v. State, 270 Ga. App. 882, 608 S.E.2d 325 (2004)—§ 10:3 n.33

Holmes v. State, 273 Ga. 644, 543 S.E.2d 688 (2001)—§§ 18:3 n.1; 18:31 n.173

Holmes v. State, 269 Ga. 124, 498 S.E.2d 732 (1998)—§ 18:20 n.24

Holmes v. State, 233 Ga. App. 872, 506 S.E.2d 157 (1998)—§ 10:3 n.22

Holmes v. State, 187 Ga. App. 214, 369 S.E.2d 533 (1988)—§ 14:36 n.3

Holmes v. State, 180 Ga. App. 787, 350 S.E.2d 497 (1986)—§ 28:10 n.6

Holmes v. State, 5 Ga. App. 166, 62 S.E. 716 (1908)—§ 2:6 n.19

Holmes v. U.S., 876 F.2d 1545 (11th Cir. 1989)—§ 7:4 n.78

Holsey v. State, 306 Ga. App. 75, 701 S.E.2d 538 (2010)—§ 4:28 n.16

Holsey v. State, 291 Ga. App. 216, 661 S.E.2d 621 (2008)—§ 7:3 n.21

Holsey v. State, 271 Ga. 856, 524 S.E.2d 473 (1999)—§ 3:11 n.27

Huff v. State, 239 Ga. App. 83, 519 S.E.2d 263 (1999)—§ 18:38 n.8

Huff v. State, 197 Ga. App. 233, 398 S.E.2d 258 (1990)—§ 16:1 n.21

Huff v. State, 141 Ga. App. 66, 232 S.E.2d 403 (1977)—§ 14:22 n.18

Huff v. State, 113 Ga. App. 257, 147 S.E.2d 840 (1966)—§ 21:19 n.4

Huff v. Walker, 125 Ga. App. 251, 187 S.E.2d 343 (1972)—§ 4:7 n.1

Huffaker v. State, 119 Ga. App. 742, 168 S.E.2d 895 (1969)—§ 14:22 n.34

Huffman v. State, 257 Ga. 390, 359 S.E.2d 910 (1987)—§ 13:31 n.10

Hug v. State, 205 Ga. App. 746, 423 S.E.2d 700 (1992)—§ 26:34 n.4, 5

Huggins v. State, 173 Ga. App. 457, 326 S.E.2d 821 (1985)—§ 6:6 n.7

Hughes v. Hinks, 249 Ga. 416, 291 S.E.2d 545 (1982)—§ 30:4 n.12

Hughes v. Hopper, 629 F.2d 1036 (5th Cir. 1980)—§ 14:34 n.3

Hughes v. Montgomery Contracting Co., Inc., 189 Ga. App. 814, 377 S.E.2d 723 (1989)—§ 10:7 n.19

Hughes v. State, 296 Ga. 744, 770 S.E.2d 636 (2015)—§ 2:11 n.8

Hughes v. State, 309 Ga. App. 150, 709 S.E.2d 900 (2011)—§ 7:4 n.60

Hughes v. State, 269 Ga. 258, 497 S.E.2d 790 (1998)—§§ 3:6 n.13; 3:8 n.17

Hughes v. State, 259 Ga. 227, 378 S.E.2d 853 (1989)—§§ 3:12 n.3; 14:29 n.18; 28:17 n.6

Hughes v. State, 168 Ga. App. 413, 309 S.E.2d 409 (1983)—§ 17:17 n.28

Hughes v. State, 161 Ga. App. 824, 288 S.E.2d 916 (1982)—§§ 14:45 n.19; 18:20 n.25

Hughes v. State, 152 Ga. App. 80, 262 S.E.2d 245 (1979)—§ 21:25 n.27

Hughes v. State, 128 Ga. 19, 57 S.E. 236 (1907)—§ 19:2 n.37

Hughey v. State, 180 Ga. App. 375, 348 S.E.2d 901 (1986)—§ 18:24 n.34

Huguley v. State, 253 Ga. 709, 324 S.E.2d 729 (1985)—§ 28:6 n.18

Hulen v. State, 207 Ga. App. 465, 428 S.E.2d 405 (1993)—§ 30:8 n.25

Hulett v. State, 296 Ga. 49, 766 S.E.2d 1 (2014)—§§ 7:2 n.35; 7:4 n.76; 26:2 n.33; 26:37 n.1

Hulgan v. Thornton, 205 Ga. 753, 55 S.E.2d 115 (1949)—§ 10:8 n.12

Hull v. State, 613 S.W.2d 735 (Tex. Crim. App. 1981)—§ 3:8 n.16

Hullander v. State, 271 Ga. 580, 522 S.E.2d 658 (1999)—§ 14:30 n.9

Humkey v. State, 129 Ga. App. 750, 201 S.E.2d 190 (1973)—§ 4:51 n.3

Humphrey v. State, 297 Ga. 349, 773 S.E.2d 760 (2015)—§ 26:48 n.1

Humphrey v. State, 281 Ga. 596, 642 S.E.2d 23 (2007)—§ 6:10 n.8

Humphrey v. State, 257 Ga. App. 312, 571 S.E.2d 187 (2002)—§ 26:43 n.39

Humphrey v. State, 167 Ga. App. 30, 306 S.E.2d 36 (1983)—§ 30:7 n.1

Humphrey v. Walker, 294 Ga. 855, 757 S.E.2d 68 (2014)—§§ 21:10 n.19; 26:8 n.45

Humphrey v. Williams, 295 Ga. 536, 761 S.E.2d 297 (2014)—§ 7:4 n.77

Humphrey v. Wilson, 282 Ga. 520, 652 S.E.2d 501 (2007)—§ 26:2 n.6, 8

Humphreys v. State, 304 Ga. App. 365, 696 S.E.2d 400 (2010)—§ 18:19 n.30

Humphreys v. State, 287 Ga. 63, 694 S.E.2d 316 (2010)—§§ 5:19 n.11; 18:21 n.1; 18:22 n.4

Hunley v. State, 227 Ga. App. 234, 488 S.E.2d 716 (1997)—§ 24:4 n.6

Hunnicutt v. Hunnicutt, 248 Ga. 516, 283 S.E.2d 891 (1981)—§ 14:77 n.23

I

Illinois v. Allen, 397 U.S. 337, 90 S. Ct. 1057, 25 L. Ed. 2d 353 (1970)—
§ 17:8 n.11, 34, 35

Illinois v. Andreas, 463 U.S. 765, 103 S. Ct. 3319, 77 L. Ed. 2d 1003
(1983)—§ 4:58 n.7

Illinois v. Bean, 463 U.S. 1202, 103 S. Ct. 3530, 77 L. Ed. 2d 1383
(1983)—§ 2:22 n.15

Illinois v. Caballes, 543 U.S. 405, 125 S. Ct. 834, 160 L. Ed. 2d 842
(2005)—§§ 3:9 n.29; 4:2 n.29; 4:48 n.13; 4:57 n.14

Illinois v. Gates, 462 U.S. 213, 103 S. Ct. 2317, 76 L. Ed. 2d 527
(1983)—§§ 3:13 n.11; 4:7 n.5, 40; 4:10 n.14, 15

Illinois v. Krull, 480 U.S. 340, 107 S. Ct. 1160, 94 L. Ed. 2d 364
(1987)—§§ 4:2 n.83; 4:46 n.7

Illinois v. Lafayette, 462 U.S. 640, 103 S. Ct. 2605, 77 L. Ed. 2d 65
(1983)—§ 2:22 n.14

Illinois v. Lidster, 540 U.S. 419, 124 S. Ct. 885, 157 L. Ed. 2d 843
(2004)—§ 3:9 n.13

Illinois v. McArthur, 531 U.S. 326, 121 S. Ct. 946, 148 L. Ed. 2d 838
(2001)—§ 4:21 n.19

Illinois v. Perkins, 496 U.S. 292, 110 S. Ct. 2394, 110 L. Ed. 2d 243
(1990)—§§ 5:10 n.9; 5:13 n.20

Illinois v. Rodriguez, 497 U.S. 177, 110 S. Ct. 2793, 111 L. Ed. 2d 148
(1990)—§ 4:34 n.1, 4, 33

Illinois v. Somerville, 410 U.S. 458, 93 S. Ct. 1066, 35 L. Ed. 2d 425
(1973)—§§ 14:48 n.18; 14:51 n.16

Illinois v. Vitale, 447 U.S. 410, 100 S. Ct. 2260, 65 L. Ed. 2d 228
(1980)—§§ 14:55 n.20; 14:60 n.5

Illinois v. Wardlow, 528 U.S. 119, 120 S. Ct. 673, 145 L. Ed. 2d 570
(2000)—§ 3:8 n.14

Indiana v. Edwards, 554 U.S. 164, 128 S. Ct. 2379, 171 L. Ed. 2d 345
(2008)—§ 7:3 n.14

Indianapolis, City of v. Edmond, 531 U.S. 32, 121 S. Ct. 447, 148 L. Ed.
2d 333 (2000)—§ 3:9 n.4, 14

Inglett v. State, 239 Ga. App. 524, 521 S.E.2d 241 (1999)—§ 4:28 n.11

Ingram v. Prescott, 111 Fla. 320, 149 So. 369 (1933)—§ 12:14 n.7

Ingram v. State, 338 Ga. App. 552, 790 S.E.2d 641 (2016)—§ 7:4 n.86

Ingram v. State, 290 Ga. 500, 722 S.E.2d 714 (2012)—§ 25:2 n.14

Ingram v. State, 268 Ga. App. 149, 601 S.E.2d 736 (2004)—§ 25:6 n.12

Ingram v. State, 233 Ga. App. 356, 504 S.E.2d 254 (1998)—§ 6:2 n.23

Ingram v. State, 211 Ga. App. 252, 438 S.E.2d 708 (1993)—§ 13:20 n.1

Ingram v. State, 253 Ga. 622, 323 S.E.2d 801 (1984)—§§ 5:22 n.8; 12:6
n.1; 26:8 n.32

Ingram v. State, 237 Ga. 613, 229 S.E.2d 416 (1976)—§ 17:7 n.7

Ingram v. State, 137 Ga. App. 412, 224 S.E.2d 527 (1976)—§§ 14:72 n.10;
20:6 n.45

Inman v. State, 187 Ga. App. 652, 371 S.E.2d 230 (1988)—§ 12:12 n.1

Inman v. State, 124 Ga. App. 190, 183 S.E.2d 413 (1971)—§§ 26:19 n.13,
56, 74; 30:8 n.16

Inman v. State, 72 Ga. 269, 1884 WL 2157 (1884)—§ 18:8 n.3

I.N.S. v. Delgado, 466 U.S. 210, 104 S. Ct. 1758, 80 L. Ed. 2d 247
(1984)—§ 3:1 n.36

J

Jackson v. State, 280 Ga. App. 716, 634 S.E.2d 846 (2006)—§ 4:18 n.14

Jackson v. State, 276 Ga. 408, 577 S.E.2d 570 (2003)—§ 25:6 n.18

Jackson v. State, 253 Ga. App. 559, 560 S.E.2d 62 (2002)—§ 17:14 n.19

Jackson v. State, 250 Ga. App. 617, 552 S.E.2d 546 (2001)—§ 26:21 n.38

Jackson v. State, 272 Ga. 782, 534 S.E.2d 796 (2000)—§ 14:67 n.10

Jackson v. State, 272 Ga. 191, 528 S.E.2d 232 (2000)—§ 5:13 n.11

Jackson v. State, 246 Ga. App. 673, 541 S.E.2d 672 (2000)—§§ 14:48 n.48; 14:50 n.4

Jackson v. State, 244 Ga. App. 477, 535 S.E.2d 818 (2000)—§ 26:43 n.19

Jackson v. State, 270 Ga. 494, 512 S.E.2d 241 (1999)—§ 12:13 n.36

Jackson v. State, 237 Ga. App. 746, 516 S.E.2d 792 (1999)—§ 21:18 n.1

Jackson v. State, 236 Ga. App. 492, 512 S.E.2d 24 (1999)—§ 3:11 n.29

Jackson v. State, 231 Ga. App. 187, 498 S.E.2d 780 (1998)—§ 14:67 n.67

Jackson v. State, 267 Ga. 130, 475 S.E.2d 637 (1996)—§ 14:92 n.13

Jackson v. State, 223 Ga. App. 471, 477 S.E.2d 893 (1996)—§ 26:17 n.16

Jackson v. State, 222 Ga. App. 843, 476 S.E.2d 615 (1996)—§ 5:20 n.41

Jackson v. State, 220 Ga. App. 98, 469 S.E.2d 264 (1996)—§ 18:31 n.121

Jackson v. State, 265 Ga. 897, 463 S.E.2d 699 (1995)—§ 18:31 n.7, 42, 109

Jackson v. State, 218 Ga. App. 677, 462 S.E.2d 802 (1995)—§ 14:48 n.5

Jackson v. State, 214 Ga. App. 726, 448 S.E.2d 761 (1994)—§ 3:5 n.8

Jackson v. State, 213 Ga. App. 170, 444 S.E.2d 126 (1994)—§ 24:5 n.3

Jackson v. State, 209 Ga. App. 53, 432 S.E.2d 649 (1993)—§ 6:6 n.24

Jackson v. State, 208 Ga. App. 391, 430 S.E.2d 781 (1993)—§ 4:2 n.42

Jackson v. State, 207 Ga. App. 190, 427 S.E.2d 566 (1993)—§ 14:29 n.10

Jackson v. State, 261 Ga. 734, 410 S.E.2d 115 (1991)—§ 6:6 n.7

Jackson v. State, 258 Ga. 322, 368 S.E.2d 760 (1988)—§ 5:15 n.9

Jackson v. State, 183 Ga. App. 594, 359 S.E.2d 457 (1987)—§ 21:30 n.1

Jackson v. State, 180 Ga. App. 363, 349 S.E.2d 252 (1986)—§ 20:7 n.24

Jackson v. State, 172 Ga. App. 874, 324 S.E.2d 816 (1984)—§ 16:9 n.1

Jackson v. State, 172 Ga. App. 359, 323 S.E.2d 198 (1984)—§§ 14:67 n.53; 18:26 n.17

Jackson v. State, 154 Ga. App. 867, 270 S.E.2d 76 (1980)—§ 24:8 n.8

Jackson v. State, 154 Ga. App. 367, 268 S.E.2d 418 (1980)—§ 14:47 n.3

Jackson v. State, 150 Ga. App. 67, 256 S.E.2d 670 (1979)—§ 4:5 n.4

Jackson v. State, 149 Ga. App. 496, 254 S.E.2d 739 (1979)—§§ 7:3 n.4; 17:1 n.18; 17:7 n.26

Jackson v. State, 149 Ga. App. 253, 253 S.E.2d 874 (1979)—§ 14:92 n.4

Jackson v. State, 146 Ga. App. 736, 247 S.E.2d 512 (1978)—§ 14:88 n.8

Jackson v. State, 146 Ga. App. 375, 246 S.E.2d 407 (1978)—§ 5:8 n.4

Jackson v. State, 239 Ga. 40, 235 S.E.2d 477 (1977)—§ 24:5 n.16

Jackson v. State, 143 Ga. App. 406, 238 S.E.2d 752 (1977)—§ 26:35 n.5

Jackson v. State, 140 Ga. App. 659, 231 S.E.2d 554 (1976)—§ 30:1 n.9

Jackson v. State, 130 Ga. App. 6, 202 S.E.2d 206 (1973)—§§ 2:10 n.8; 4:11 n.2

Jackson v. State, 129 Ga. App. 901, 201 S.E.2d 816 (1973)—§§ 4:12 n.4, 15, 17; 4:18 n.8

Jackson v. State, 124 Ga. App. 488, 184 S.E.2d 185 (1971)—§ 20:6 n.18, 40

Jefferson v. State, 217 Ga. App. 747, 459 S.E.2d 173 (1995)—§§ 2:29 n.7; 2:31 n.3

Jefferson v. State, 216 Ga. App. 442, 454 S.E.2d 632 (1995)—§ 16:14 n.23

Jefferson v. State, 209 Ga. App. 859, 434 S.E.2d 814 (1993)—§§ 7:2 n.34; 7:4 n.64; 26:43 n.19

Jefferson v. State, 206 Ga. App. 544, 425 S.E.2d 915 (1992)—§ 6:12 n.13

Jefferson v. State, 256 Ga. 821, 353 S.E.2d 468 (1987)—§ 18:24 n.15

Jefferson v. State, 136 Ga. App. 63, 220 S.E.2d 71 (1975)—§ 13:6 n.10

Jefferson v. Zant, 263 Ga. 316, 431 S.E.2d 110 (1993)—§ 7:4 n.70

Jefferson, In re, 283 Ga. 216, 657 S.E.2d 830 (2008)—§ 27:5 n.12

Jeffrey v. State, 296 Ga. 713, 770 S.E.2d 585 (2015)—§§ 26:28 n.29; 26:33 n.29; 26:43 n.11

Jencks v. U.S., 353 U.S. 657, 77 S. Ct. 1007, 1 L. Ed. 2d 1103, 75 Ohio L. Abs. 465 (1957)—§ 14:4 n.29

Jenkins v. Anderson, 447 U.S. 231, 100 S. Ct. 2124, 65 L. Ed. 2d 86 (1980)—§ 5:21 n.7, 12

Jenkins v. Garrison, 265 Ga. 42, 453 S.E.2d 698 (1995)—§ 2:23 n.13

Jenkins v. Montgomery, 248 Ga. 696, 285 S.E.2d 706 (1982)—§ 26:1 n.8

Jenkins v. State, 278 Ga. 598, 604 S.E.2d 789 (2004)—§§ 14:46 n.10; 14:66 n.14, 22, 24

Jenkins v. State, 259 Ga. App. 47, 576 S.E.2d 300 (2002)—§ 17:14 n.19

Jenkins v. State, 269 Ga. 282, 498 S.E.2d 502 (1998)—§§ 17:6 n.22; 18:17 n.7; 18:22 n.17; 21:12 n.30; 26:43 n.34

Jenkins v. State, 268 Ga. 468, 491 S.E.2d 54 (1997)—§ 14:76 n.26

Jenkins v. State, 229 Ga. App. 556, 494 S.E.2d 311 (1997)—§§ 14:36 n.15; 14:45 n.19

Jenkins v. State, 223 Ga. App. 486, 477 S.E.2d 910 (1996)—§ 4:43 n.14

Jenkins v. State, 265 Ga. 539, 458 S.E.2d 477 (1995)—§ 26:8 n.43

Jenkins v. State, 172 Ga. App. 715, 324 S.E.2d 491 (1984)—§ 13:28 n.11

Jenkins v. State, 167 Ga. App. 840, 308 S.E.2d 14 (1983)—§§ 5:23 n.17; 6:4 n.7; 6:12 n.4; 14:29 n.47

Jenkins v. State, 159 Ga. App. 183, 283 S.E.2d 49 (1981)—§ 13:31 n.6

Jenkins v. State, 146 Ga. App. 458, 246 S.E.2d 466 (1978)—§§ 18:16 n.4; 18:20 n.29

Jenkins v. State, 121 Ga. App. 103, 172 S.E.2d 845 (1970)—§ 14:40 n.1, 4

Jenkins v. State, 65 Ga. App. 16, 14 S.E.2d 594 (1941)—§ 12:13 n.15

Jenkins v. State, 14 Ga. App. 276, 80 S.E. 688 (1914)—§ 14:50 n.1

Jenkins v. Thomas, 124 Ga. App. 286, 183 S.E.2d 489 (1971)—§ 9:2 n.11

Jennings v. State, 282 Ga. 679, 653 S.E.2d 17 (2007)—§ 23:7 n.6

Jennings v. State, 230 Ga. App. 661, 497 S.E.2d 13 (1998)—§ 14:48 n.14

Jensen v. City of Pontiac, 113 Mich. App. 341, 317 N.W.2d 619, 28 A.L.R.4th 1240 (1982)—§ 4:37 n.1

Jernigan v. State, 239 Ga. App. 65, 517 S.E.2d 370 (1999)—§ 14:70 n.21

Jesse v. State, 20 Ga. 156, 1856 WL 1894 (1856)—§ 18:19 n.4

Jester v. State, 193 Ga. 202, 17 S.E.2d 736 (1941)—§ 6:2 n.11

J.E.W. v. State, 256 Ga. 464, 349 S.E.2d 713 (1986)—§ 5:8 n.9

Jewell v. Franklin Life Ins. Co., 138 Ga. 576, 75 S.E. 592 (1912)—§ 17:12 n.9

Jewell v. State, 261 Ga. 861, 413 S.E.2d 201 (1992)—§ 18:11 n.12

Johnson v. State, 293 Ga. 641, 748 S.E.2d 896 (2013)—§ 18:2 n.12
Johnson v. State, 292 Ga. 22, 733 S.E.2d 736 (2012)—§ 14:57 n.2
Johnson v. State, 307 Ga. App. 570, 707 S.E.2d 373 (2011)—§ 30:1 n.21
Johnson v. State, 289 Ga. 532, 712 S.E.2d 811 (2011)—§§ 7:4 n.91; 15:1 n.10; 15:4 n.4
Johnson v. State, 305 Ga. App. 635, 700 S.E.2d 612 (2010)—§ 4:55 n.1
Johnson v. State, 298 Ga. App. 639, 680 S.E.2d 675 (2009)—§ 26:27 n.2
Johnson v. State, 297 Ga. App. 847, 678 S.E.2d 539 (2009)—§§ 3:10 n.18; 4:32 n.11; 4:33 n.19
Johnson v. State, 297 Ga. App. 254, 676 S.E.2d 884 (2009)—§ 2:12 n.26
Johnson v. State, 281 Ga. App. 455, 636 S.E.2d 178 (2006)—§ 14:12 n.5
Johnson v. State, 272 Ga. App. 294, 612 S.E.2d 29 (2005)—§ 28:12 n.16
Johnson v. State, 278 Ga. 344, 602 S.E.2d 623 (2004)—§ 17:5 n.36
Johnson v. State, 266 Ga. App. 171, 596 S.E.2d 693 (2004)—§ 10:3 n.19
Johnson v. State, 260 Ga. App. 897, 581 S.E.2d 407 (2003)—§ 16:9 n.13
Johnson v. State, 276 Ga. 57, 573 S.E.2d 362 (2002)—§ 26:2 n.8
Johnson v. State, 275 Ga. 390, 565 S.E.2d 805 (2002)—§ 28:11 n.22
Johnson v. State, 258 Ga. App. 33, 572 S.E.2d 669 (2002)—§ 14:58 n.57
Johnson v. State, 256 Ga. App. 730, 569 S.E.2d 625 (2002)—§ 14:58 n.57
Johnson v. State, 248 Ga. App. 454, 546 S.E.2d 562 (2001)—§§ 4:44 n.8; 29:2 n.2
Johnson v. State, 272 Ga. 468, 532 S.E.2d 377 (2000)—§ 14:19 n.1
Johnson v. State, 272 Ga. 254, 526 S.E.2d 549 (2000)—§§ 6:2 n.29, 30; 6:10 n.23, 24
Johnson v. State, 247 Ga. App. 157, 543 S.E.2d 439 (2000)—§ 26:39 n.2
Johnson v. State, 244 Ga. App. 128, 534 S.E.2d 480 (2000)—§ 14:35 n.23
Johnson v. State, 243 Ga. App. 891, 534 S.E.2d 563 (2000)—§ 17:7 n.1
Johnson v. State, 271 Ga. 375, 519 S.E.2d 221 (1999)—§§ 14:36 n.16; 23:7 n.26
Johnson v. State, 241 Ga. App. 369, 526 S.E.2d 882 (1999)—§ 29:2 n.3
Johnson v. State, 234 Ga. App. 116, 506 S.E.2d 234 (1998)—§ 5:12 n.13
Johnson v. State, 233 Ga. App. 450, 504 S.E.2d 290 (1998)—§ 14:40 n.2
Johnson v. State, 230 Ga. App. 535, 496 S.E.2d 785 (1998)—§ 4:9 n.10
Johnson v. State, 268 Ga. 416, 490 S.E.2d 91 (1997)—§ 14:70 n.11
Johnson v. State, 229 Ga. App. 400, 493 S.E.2d 926 (1997)—§ 26:28 n.21
Johnson v. State, 227 Ga. App. 390, 489 S.E.2d 138 (1997)—§ 16:2 n.7
Johnson v. State, 226 Ga. App. 503, 487 S.E.2d 90 (1997)—§ 26:17 n.20
Johnson v. State, 224 Ga. App. 568, 481 S.E.2d 268 (1997)—§ 26:43 n.53
Johnson v. State, 267 Ga. 77, 475 S.E.2d 595 (1996)—§ 26:20 n.1
Johnson v. State, 266 Ga. 775, 470 S.E.2d 637 (1996)—§ 5:13 n.25
Johnson v. State, 266 Ga. 624, 469 S.E.2d 152 (1996)—§ 21:22 n.4
Johnson v. State, 265 Ga. 833, 463 S.E.2d 123 (1995)—§ 14:30 n.60
Johnson v. State, 219 Ga. App. 547, 466 S.E.2d 63 (1995)—§ 18:16 n.7
Johnson v. State, 262 Ga. 652, 424 S.E.2d 271 (1993)—§ 18:25 n.1
Johnson v. State, 209 Ga. App. 632, 434 S.E.2d 169 (1993)—§ 26:35 n.5
Johnson v. State, 262 Ga. 527, 422 S.E.2d 648 (1992)—§ 14:92 n.16
Johnson v. State, 261 Ga. 236, 404 S.E.2d 108 (1991)—§ 24:4 n.12
Johnson v. State, 258 Ga. 506, 371 S.E.2d 396 (1988)—§ 17:6 n.4

Jones v. State, 129 Ga. App. 623, 200 S.E.2d 487 (1973)—§§ 26:14 n.17; 26:43 n.23

Jones v. State, 127 Ga. App. 137, 193 S.E.2d 38 (1972)—§§ 4:16 n.9; 4:18 n.6

Jones v. State, 126 Ga. App. 841, 192 S.E.2d 171 (1972)—§§ 3:10 n.5, 7, 8; 4:12 n.16; 4:21 n.12

Jones v. State, 223 Ga. 157, 154 S.E.2d 228 (1967)—§ 12:9 n.1

Jones v. State, 219 Ga. 848, 136 S.E.2d 358 (1964)—§ 14:43 n.1

Jones v. State, 101 Ga. App. 851, 115 S.E.2d 576 (1960)—§§ 14:76 n.16; 21:25 n.5

Jones v. State, 75 Ga. App. 610, 44 S.E.2d 174 (1947)—§ 13:15 n.6

Jones v. State, 68 Ga. App. 210, 22 S.E.2d 671 (1942)—§ 18:23 n.18

Jones v. State, 39 Ga. App. 1, 145 S.E. 914 (1928)—§ 27:2 n.4

Jones v. State, 27 Ga. App. 631, 110 S.E. 33 (1921)—§ 26:19 n.22

Jones v. State, 117 Ga. 710, 44 S.E. 877 (1903)—§ 24:19 n.20

Jones v. State, 115 Ga. 814, 42 S.E. 271 (1902)—§§ 14:41 n.11; 17:19 n.8

Jones v. State, 114 Ga. 73, 39 S.E. 861 (1901)—§ 2:6 n.21, 24

Jones v. State, 65 Ga. 506, 1880 WL 3686 (1880)—§ 23:9 n.8

Jones v. State, 55 Ga. 625, 1876 WL 2889 (1876)—§ 17:19 n.15

Jones v. Terry, 279 Ga. 623, 619 S.E.2d 601 (2005)—§ 16:3 n.2

Jones v. Thomas, 491 U.S. 376, 109 S. Ct. 2522, 105 L. Ed. 2d 322 (1989)—§ 26:29 n.13

Jones v. U.S., 526 U.S. 227, 119 S. Ct. 1215, 143 L. Ed. 2d 311 (1999)—§ 26:11 n.24

Jones v. U.S., 463 U.S. 354, 103 S. Ct. 3043, 77 L. Ed. 2d 694 (1983)—§§ 21:13 n.9; 21:14 n.10

Jones v. U. S., 391 A.2d 1188 (D.C. 1978)—§ 3:8 n.11

Jones v. U.S., 362 U.S. 257, 80 S. Ct. 725, 4 L. Ed. 2d 697, 78 A.L.R.2d 233 (1960)—§§ 14:79 n.5; 14:81 n.1, 2, 9; 14:84 n.3

Jones v. U.S., 357 U.S. 493, 78 S. Ct. 1253, 2 L. Ed. 2d 1514 (1958)—§§ 4:28 n.6; 4:30 n.14

Jones v. Walker, 540 F.3d 1277 (11th Cir. 2008)—§ 7:3 n.34

Jones v. Wharton, 253 Ga. 82, 316 S.E.2d 749 (1984)—§§ 7:3 n.39; 18:1 n.5

Jones, In re, 198 Ga. App. 228, 401 S.E.2d 278 (1990)—§ 27:4 n.16

Jordan v. Hodges, 162 Ga. App. 473, 291 S.E.2d 778 (1982)—§ 27:5 n.3

Jordan v. Com. of Massachusetts, 225 U.S. 167, 32 S. Ct. 651, 56 L. Ed. 1038 (1912)—§§ 18:21 n.4; 18:22 n.3

Jordan v. State, 281 Ga. App. 419, 636 S.E.2d 151 (2006)—§ 13:28 n.4

Jordan v. State, 259 Ga. App. 551, 578 S.E.2d 217 (2003)—§ 17:5 n.38

Jordan v. State, 272 Ga. 395, 530 S.E.2d 192 (2000)—§ 13:28 n.6

Jordan v. State, 242 Ga. App. 408, 530 S.E.2d 42 (2000)—§ 26:36 n.3

Jordan v. State, 267 Ga. 442, 480 S.E.2d 18 (1997)—§§ 5:17 n.12; 5:20 n.39

Jordan v. State, 217 Ga. App. 420, 457 S.E.2d 692 (1995)—§ 14:35 n.23

Jordan v. State, 211 Ga. App. 86, 438 S.E.2d 371 (1993)—§ 4:59 n.33, 39

Jordan v. State, 210 Ga. App. 30, 435 S.E.2d 256 (1993)—§ 14:72 n.20

Jordan v. State, 207 Ga. App. 710, 429 S.E.2d 97 (1993)—§ 20:6 n.38

Jordan v. State, 172 Ga. App. 496, 323 S.E.2d 657 (1984)—§§ 14:73 n.17; 23:5 n.8

K

Kastigar v. U.S., 406 U.S. 441, 92 S. Ct. 1653, 32 L. Ed. 2d 212 (1972)—§ 12:14 n.3, 6

Katz v. U.S., 389 U.S. 347, 88 S. Ct. 507, 19 L. Ed. 2d 576 (1967)—§§ 4:1 n.3, 12, 13; 4:2 n.9, 18; 4:27 n.1, 3; 4:43 n.20; 4:48 n.12; 4:59 n.3, 5, 6; 14:78 n.13; 14:81 n.3; 14:82 n.2

Katzensky v. State, 228 Ga. 6, 183 S.E.2d 749 (1971)—§ 5:17 n.3

Kaysen v. State, 191 Ga. App. 734, 382 S.E.2d 737 (1989)—§ 14:67 n.44, 45

Kazakos v. Baranan, 122 Ga. App. 594, 178 S.E.2d 222 (1970)—§ 20:7 n.10

Kearse v. Paulk, 264 Ga. 509, 448 S.E.2d 369 (1994)—§ 28:17 n.47

Keating v. State, 141 Ga. App. 377, 233 S.E.2d 456 (1977)—§ 3:3 n.2

Keaton v. State, 253 Ga. 70, 316 S.E.2d 452 (1984)—§ 21:25 n.4, 14

Keen v. State, 164 Ga. App. 81, 296 S.E.2d 91 (1982)—§§ 7:6 n.1; 17:8 n.14

Keenan v. State, 263 Ga. 569, 436 S.E.2d 475 (1993)—§ 5:24 n.10

Keener v. MacDougall, 232 Ga. 273, 206 S.E.2d 519 (1974)—§ 13:22 n.3

Keener v. State, 215 Ga. App. 117, 449 S.E.2d 669 (1994)—§ 14:72 n.64

Keener v. State, 254 Ga. 699, 334 S.E.2d 175 (1985)—§ 21:11 n.16

Keener v. State, 238 Ga. 7, 230 S.E.2d 846 (1976)—§§ 14:47 n.7, 10; 14:54 n.3, 14; 14:55 n.22, 23; 14:58 n.65; 14:61 n.5

Keener v. State, 97 Ga. 388, 24 S.E. 28 (1895)—§ 14:94 n.1

Keishian v. State, 202 Ga. App. 718, 415 S.E.2d 324 (1992)—§§ 14:80 n.4; 14:83 n.15

Keith v. State, 238 Ga. 157, 231 S.E.2d 727 (1977)—§§ 4:8 n.5; 14:86 n.1

Kelleher v. State, 185 Ga. App. 774, 365 S.E.2d 889 (1988)—§ 2:34 n.2

Keller v. State, 261 Ga. App. 769, 583 S.E.2d 591 (2003)—§ 18:34 n.5

Keller v. State, 275 Ga. 680, 571 S.E.2d 806 (2002)—§ 28:11 n.3, 4

Keller v. State, 208 Ga. App. 589, 431 S.E.2d 411 (1993)—§ 14:29 n.31

Keller v. State, 183 Ga. App. 717, 359 S.E.2d 714 (1987)—§ 14:67 n.26

Keller v. State, 245 Ga. 522, 265 S.E.2d 813 (1980)—§ 24:4 n.2

Kelley v. State, 235 Ga. App. 177, 509 S.E.2d 110 (1998)—§§ 21:10 n.3; 21:12 n.1; 21:17 n.12

Kelley v. State, 146 Ga. App. 179, 245 S.E.2d 872 (1978)—§§ 4:2 n.13; 4:30 n.14; 4:39 n.7

Kelley, Matter of, 433 A.2d 704 (D.C. 1981)—§ 6:9 n.6

Kellibrew v. State, 239 Ga. App. 783, 521 S.E.2d 921 (1999)—§ 26:34 n.3

Kellogg v. State, 288 Ga. App. 265, 653 S.E.2d 841 (2007)—§ 3:9 n.13

Kellum v. State, 258 Ga. 536, 371 S.E.2d 405 (1988)—§ 17:24 n.8, 12

Kelly v. Mangum, 145 Ga. 57, 88 S.E. 556 (1916)—§ 2:23 n.1

Kelly v. Robinson, 479 U.S. 36, 107 S. Ct. 353, 93 L. Ed. 2d 216 (1986)—§ 26:15 n.16

Kelly v. South Carolina, 534 U.S. 246, 122 S. Ct. 726, 151 L. Ed. 2d 670 (2002)—§ 26:6 n.45

Kelly v. State, 255 Ga. App. 813, 567 S.E.2d 36 (2002)—§ 18:34 n.13

Kelly v. State, 197 Ga. App. 811, 399 S.E.2d 568 (1990)—§ 14:4 n.13

Kelly v. State, 182 Ga. App. 7, 354 S.E.2d 647 (1987)—§ 5:3 n.4

Kelly v. State, 241 Ga. 190, 243 S.E.2d 857 (1978)—§ 22:7 n.9

Kelly v. State, 145 Ga. App. 780, 245 S.E.2d 20 (1978)—§ 14:58 n.48

Koritta v. State, 206 Ga. App. 228, 424 S.E.2d 799 (1992)—§ 24:12 n.5

Kornegay v. State, 174 Ga. App. 279, 329 S.E.2d 601 (1985)—§ 23:9 n.11

Kosal v. State, 204 Ga. App. 708, 420 S.E.2d 621 (1992)—§ 14:30 n.5

Koza v. State, 158 Ga. App. 709, 282 S.E.2d 131 (1981)—§ 17:5 n.5

Kremen v. U.S., 353 U.S. 346, 77 S. Ct. 828, 1 L. Ed. 2d 876 (1957)—§ 4:57 n.17

Kreps v. Gray, 234 Ga. 745, 218 S.E.2d 1 (1975)—§§ 28:3 n.4; 28:17 n.38; 30:8 n.27

Krier v. State, 249 Ga. 80, 287 S.E.2d 531 (1982)—§ 5:20 n.55

Krist v. Caldwell, 230 Ga. 536, 198 S.E.2d 161 (1973)—§ 14:76 n.20

K.S., In Interest of, 303 Ga. 542, 814 S.E.2d 324 (2018)—§ 13:27 n.1

Kugler v. Helfant, 421 U.S. 117, 95 S. Ct. 1524, 44 L. Ed. 2d 15 (1975)—§ 9:3 n.11

Kuhlmann v. Wilson, 477 U.S. 436, 106 S. Ct. 2616, 91 L. Ed. 2d 364 (1986)—§ 5:10 n.8

Kunselman v. State, 232 Ga. App. 323, 501 S.E.2d 834 (1998)—§ 25:2 n.13

Kuptz v. State, 179 Ga. App. 150, 345 S.E.2d 670 (1986)—§ 14:6 n.1

Kyler v. State, 270 Ga. 81, 508 S.E.2d 152 (1998)—§ 23:5 n.21

Kyles v. State, 254 Ga. 49, 326 S.E.2d 216 (1985)—§ 17:19 n.10

Kyles v. State, 243 Ga. 490, 255 S.E.2d 10 (1979)—§ 18:26 n.27

Kyles v. Whitley, 514 U.S. 419, 115 S. Ct. 1555, 131 L. Ed. 2d 490 (1995)—§§ 14:33 n.11, 16; 14:37 n.5

Kyllo v. U.S., 533 U.S. 27, 121 S. Ct. 2038, 150 L. Ed. 2d 94 (2001)—§§ 4:41 n.7; 4:48 n.14

L

Lacey v. State, 253 Ga. 711, 324 S.E.2d 471 (1985)—§ 28:13 n.1

Lackawanna County Dist. Attorney v. Coss, 532 U.S. 394, 121 S. Ct. 1567, 149 L. Ed. 2d 608, 176 A.L.R. Fed. 711 (2001)—§ 28:19 n.14

Lackey v. State, 246 Ga. 331, 271 S.E.2d 478 (1980)—§§ 2:25 n.1; 19:2 n.3

LaCount v. State, 237 Ga. 181, 227 S.E.2d 31 (1976)—§ 11:2 n.10

Ladd v. State, 228 Ga. 113, 184 S.E.2d 158 (1971)—§ 18:33 n.1

Lafler v. Cooper, 566 U.S. 156, 132 S. Ct. 1376, 182 L. Ed. 2d 398 (2012)—§ 7:4 n.86

LaFontaine v. State, 269 Ga. 251, 497 S.E.2d 367 (1998)—§§ 3:9 n.5, 21; 14:40 n.13

Lagyak v. State, 245 Ga. App. 546, 538 S.E.2d 467 (2000)—§ 14:67 n.25

Lahr v. State, 239 Ga. 813, 238 S.E.2d 878 (1977)—§ 18:9 n.3

Lajara v. State, 263 Ga. 438, 435 S.E.2d 600 (1993)—§§ 7:4 n.26; 24:5 n.28

Lam v. State, 208 Ga. App. 324, 430 S.E.2d 775 (1993)—§ 21:1 n.8

Lamar v. State, 278 Ga. 150, 598 S.E.2d 488 (2004)—§§ 7:3 n.11, 12, 13; 26:10 n.7

Lamb v. Dillard, 94 Ga. 206, 21 S.E. 463 (1894)—§ 2:8 n.7

Lamb v. State, 278 Ga. App. 97, 628 S.E.2d 165 (2006)—§ 16:10 n.22

Lamb v. State, 267 Ga. 41, 472 S.E.2d 683 (1996)—§ 7:11 n.10

Lamb v. State, 241 Ga. 10, 243 S.E.2d 59 (1978)—§§ 18:24 n.20; 18:28 n.1

Lamberson v. State, 265 Ga. 764, 462 S.E.2d 706 (1995)—§ 13:23 n.5, 34

Laster v. State, 268 Ga. 172, 486 S.E.2d 153 (1997)—§ 14:58 n.50

Laster v. State, 163 Ga. App. 294, 293 S.E.2d 75 (1982)—§ 20:6 n.64, 65

Latham v. State, 225 Ga. App. 147, 483 S.E.2d 322 (1997)—§ 26:46 n.1

Latimer v. State, 134 Ga. App. 372, 214 S.E.2d 390 (1975)—§§ 4:7 n.17; 13:4 n.30

Latta v. Fitzharris, 521 F.2d 246, 32 A.L.R. Fed. 135 (9th Cir. 1975)—§ 4:44 n.2

Lattimore v. State, 265 Ga. 154, 454 S.E.2d 496 (1995)—§ 5:21 n.15

Lattimore v. State, 265 Ga. 102, 454 S.E.2d 474 (1995)—§ 5:8 n.6

Lavelle v. State, 250 Ga. 224, 297 S.E.2d 234 (1982)—§ 14:84 n.11

Law v. State, 251 Ga. 525, 307 S.E.2d 904 (1983)—§ 14:30 n.4, 45, 53

Lawrence v. State, 267 Ga. App. 515, 600 S.E.2d 444 (2004)—§ 18:24 n.10

Lawrence v. State, 234 Ga. App. 603, 507 S.E.2d 490 (1998)—§ 16:9 n.1

Lawrence v. State, 265 Ga. 310, 454 S.E.2d 446 (1995)—§ 14:93 n.8

Lawrence v. State, 257 Ga. 423, 360 S.E.2d 716 (1987)—§ 12:15 n.10

Lawrence v. State, 259 Ind. 306, 286 N.E.2d 830 (1972)—§ 26:28 n.53

Lawson v. State, 280 Ga. 881, 635 S.E.2d 134 (2006)—§ 26:35 n.15

Lawson v. State, 224 Ga. App. 645, 481 S.E.2d 856 (1997)—§§ 14:12 n.3; 14:15 n.4; 14:21 n.1

Lawson v. State, 143 Ga. App. 776, 240 S.E.2d 188 (1977)—§ 4:6 n.5

Lay v. State, 242 Ga. 225, 248 S.E.2d 611 (1978)—§ 21:3 n.3

Layman v. State, 280 Ga. 794, 631 S.E.2d 107 (2006)—§ 17:19 n.2

Lazenby v. State, 221 Ga. App. 148, 470 S.E.2d 526 (1996)—§ 26:23 n.3

L.B.B. III v. State, 129 Ga. App. 163, 198 S.E.2d 895 (1973)—§§ 3:10 n.2; 4:51 n.2

L.C., In re, 273 Ga. 886, 548 S.E.2d 335 (2001)—§ 14:40 n.7

Leach v. State, 143 Ga. App. 598, 239 S.E.2d 177 (1977)—§ 22:6 n.1

Leadingham v. Commonwealth, 182 Ky. 291, 206 S.W. 483 (1918)—§ 18:23 n.11

Leath v. Rosser, 52 Ga. App. 587, 183 S.E. 839 (1936)—§ 10:5 n.3

Leatherwood v. State, 212 Ga. App. 342, 441 S.E.2d 813 (1994)—§§ 14:48 n.16; 22:3 n.6

Lebrun v. State, 255 Ga. 406, 339 S.E.2d 227 (1986)—§ 7:1 n.10

Ledbetter v. Benham, 463 U.S. 1222, 103 S. Ct. 3565, 77 L. Ed. 2d 1406 (1983)—§ 21:14 n.9, 11

Ledbetter v. Cannon, 192 Ga. App. 392, 384 S.E.2d 875 (1989)—§ 21:13 n.18

Ledbetter v. State, 234 Ga. App. 380, 506 S.E.2d 699 (1998)—§ 25:1 n.8

Ledbetter v. State, 190 Ga. App. 843, 380 S.E.2d 313 (1989)—§ 14:87 n.4

Ledesma v. State, 251 Ga. 885, 311 S.E.2d 427 (1984)—§§ 4:2 n.49; 4:14 n.2; 14:88 n.11

Ledesma v. State, 251 Ga. 487, 306 S.E.2d 629 (1983)—§§ 2:12 n.12; 14:29 n.37

Ledford v. State, 289 Ga. 70, 709 S.E.2d 239 (2011)—§ 17:5 n.40

Ledford v. State, 221 Ga. App. 238, 470 S.E.2d 796 (1996)—§ 3:9 n.23

Ledford v. State, 220 Ga. App. 272, 469 S.E.2d 401 (1996)—§ 3:7 n.14

Ledford v. State, 207 Ga. App. 705, 429 S.E.2d 124 (1993)—§ 18:31 n.98, 178

Lennard v. State, 104 Ga. 546, 30 S.E. 780 (1898)—§§ 12:13 n.9; 14:43 n.3

Lentile v. State, 136 Ga. App. 611, 222 S.E.2d 86 (1975)—§§ 2:10 n.9; 4:30 n.30; 4:41 n.9

Leonard v. State, 228 Ga. App. 792, 492 S.E.2d 747 (1997)—§ 14:38 n.11

Leonard v. State, 218 Ga. App. 369, 461 S.E.2d 309 (1995)—§ 26:36 n.7

Leonard v. State, 157 Ga. App. 37, 276 S.E.2d 94 (1981)—§ 14:94 n.10

Leonard v. State, 133 Ga. 435, 66 S.E. 251 (1909)—§ 24:2 n.12

Lepinsky v. State, 7 Ga. App. 285, 66 S.E. 965 (1910)—§ 13:23 n.23

Leslie v. State, 211 Ga. App. 871, 440 S.E.2d 757 (1994)—§§ 16:2 n.1; 24:5 n.30

Lester v. State, 278 Ga. App. 247, 628 S.E.2d 674 (2006)—§ 4:14 n.18

Lester v. State, 163 Ga. App. 604, 295 S.E.2d 566 (1982)—§ 14:83 n.27

Lester, In re, 77 Ga. 143, 1886 WL 1476 (1886)—§§ 12:13 n.11, 28; 12:17 n.2; 12:18 n.11

Letbedder v. State, 129 Ga. App. 196, 199 S.E.2d 270 (1973)—§ 14:67 n.53

Lett v. State, 164 Ga. App. 584, 298 S.E.2d 541 (1982)—§ 14:70 n.10

Lett v. State, 160 Ga. App. 476, 287 S.E.2d 384 (1981)—§§ 18:9 n.2; 21:17 n.17

Leverenz v. State, 140 Ga. App. 632, 231 S.E.2d 513 (1976)—§ 18:16 n.2

Leverette v. State, 291 Ga. 834, 732 S.E.2d 255 (2012)—§ 14:77 n.16

Levester v. State, 270 Ga. 485, 512 S.E.2d 258 (1999)—§ 14:68 n.3

Levin v. Morales, 295 Ga. 781, 764 S.E.2d 145 (2014)—§ 14:58 n.3

Levitt v. State, 170 Ga. App. 32, 316 S.E.2d 6 (1984)—§ 14:92 n.3

Lewis v. Ford, 248 Ga. 820, 286 S.E.2d 714 (1982)—§ 28:17 n.22

Lewis v. McDougal, 276 Ga. 861, 583 S.E.2d 859 (2003)—§ 17:5 n.61

Lewis v. State, 330 Ga. App. 412, 767 S.E.2d 771 (2014)—§ 15:1 n.12

Lewis v. State, 323 Ga. App. 709, 747 S.E.2d 867 (2013)—§ 3:6 n.20

Lewis v. State, 293 Ga. 110, 744 S.E.2d 21 (2013)—§ 14:21 n.2

Lewis v. State, 283 Ga. 191, 657 S.E.2d 854 (2008)—§§ 13:19 n.5; 23:2 n.13

Lewis v. State, 279 Ga. 756, 620 S.E.2d 778 (2005)—§§ 21:15 n.4; 26:6 n.51

Lewis v. State, 275 Ga. 194, 565 S.E.2d 437 (2002)—§ 14:77 n.10

Lewis v. State, 270 Ga. 891, 515 S.E.2d 382 (1999)—§ 21:20 n.12

Lewis v. State, 234 Ga. App. 873, 508 S.E.2d 218 (1998)—§ 4:10 n.14

Lewis v. State, 215 Ga. App. 486, 451 S.E.2d 116 (1994)—§ 14:30 n.26

Lewis v. State, 262 Ga. 679, 424 S.E.2d 626 (1993)—§ 18:31 n.51, 53, 171

Lewis v. State, 255 Ga. 101, 335 S.E.2d 560 (1985)—§ 2:11 n.4

Lewis v. State, 164 Ga. App. 549, 297 S.E.2d 303 (1982)—§ 17:8 n.42

Lewis v. State, 248 Ga. 566, 285 S.E.2d 179 (1981)—§ 14:58 n.25

Lewis v. State, 159 Ga. App. 135, 282 S.E.2d 750 (1981)—§ 14:22 n.23

Lewis v. State, 158 Ga. App. 575, 281 S.E.2d 318 (1981)—§ 24:10 n.3

Lewis v. State, 246 Ga. 101, 268 S.E.2d 915 (1980)—§ 18:17 n.11

Lewis v. State, 147 Ga. App. 794, 250 S.E.2d 522 (1978)—§ 17:9 n.11

Lewis v. State, 239 Ga. 732, 238 S.E.2d 892 (1977)—§ 21:12 n.20

Lewis v. State, 126 Ga. App. 123, 190 S.E.2d 123 (1972)—§§ 4:1 n.1, 5; 4:24 n.2; 4:39 n.7

Lewis v. State, 55 Ga. App. 743, 191 S.E. 278 (1937)—§ 28:13 n.12, 24

Liteky v. U.S., 510 U.S. 540, 114 S. Ct. 1147, 127 L. Ed. 2d 474 (1994)—§ 14:77 n.9

Little v. State, 280 Ga. App. 60, 633 S.E.2d 403 (2006)—§ 14:38 n.7

Little v. State, 279 Ga. App. 329, 630 S.E.2d 903 (2006)—§ 10:3 n.61

Little v. State, 230 Ga. App. 803, 498 S.E.2d 284 (1998)—§§ 14:38 n.26; 18:36 n.8

Little v. State, 188 Ga. App. 410, 373 S.E.2d 260 (1988)—§ 14:67 n.33

Little v. State, 300 Md. 485, 479 A.2d 903 (1984)—§ 3:9 n.22

Little v. State, 165 Ga. App. 441, 301 S.E.2d 660 (1983)—§ 26:21 n.46

Little v. State, 165 Ga. App. 389, 300 S.E.2d 540 (1983)—§§ 14:38 n.10, 12; 14:73 n.37

Little v. State, 157 Ga. App. 462, 278 S.E.2d 17 (1981)—§§ 23:1 n.2; 23:2 n.5

Little v. State, 153 Ga. App. 574, 266 S.E.2d 265 (1980)—§ 2:12 n.14

Little, In re, 404 U.S. 553, 92 S. Ct. 659, 30 L. Ed. 2d 708 (1972)— § 27:3 n.3

Littles v. Balkcom, 245 Ga. 285, 264 S.E.2d 219 (1980)—§ 28:17 n.40, 41

Littles v. DeFrancis, 517 F. Supp. 1137 (M.D. Ga. 1981)—§ 28:17 n.41

Lively v. Fulcher, 244 Ga. 771, 262 S.E.2d 93 (1979)—§ 2:23 n.10

Lively v. State, 262 Ga. 510, 421 S.E.2d 528 (1992)—§ 18:19 n.22

Lively v. State, 30 Ga. App. 633, 118 S.E. 476 (1923)—§ 14:45 n.18

Livingston v. State, 271 Ga. 714, 524 S.E.2d 222 (1999)—§ 18:31 n.28

Livingston v. State, 222 Ga. App. 298, 474 S.E.2d 1 (1996)—§ 14:29 n.14

Livingston v. State, 221 Ga. App. 563, 472 S.E.2d 317 (1996)—§ 28:11 n.7

Livingston v. State, 264 Ga. 402, 444 S.E.2d 748 (1994)—§ 26:5 n.2

Livingston v. Wynne, 147 Ga. 307, 93 S.E. 877 (1917)—§ 25:7 n.14

L.J.P., In re, 277 Ga. 135, 587 S.E.2d 15 (2003)—§ 6:2 n.27

L. L., In Interest of, 340 Ga. App. 445, 798 S.E.2d 1 (2017)—§ 14:92 n.7

Llewellyn v. State, 252 Ga. 426, 314 S.E.2d 227 (1984)—§ 28:12 n.12

Llewellyn v. State, 241 Ga. 192, 243 S.E.2d 853 (1978)—§ 24:2 n.41

Lloyd v. State, 339 Ga. App. 1, 792 S.E.2d 445 (2016)—§ 18:38 n.4

Lloyd v. State, 226 Ga. App. 401, 487 S.E.2d 44 (1997)—§§ 14:76 n.33; 26:17 n.4

Lloyd v. State, 258 Ga. 645, 373 S.E.2d 1 (1988)—§§ 7:4 n.74, 85; 15:1 n.3; 15:4 n.4; 16:10 n.15

Lloyd v. State, 139 Ga. App. 625, 229 S.E.2d 106 (1976)—§ 26:28 n.59

Lo-Ji Sales, Inc. v. New York, 442 U.S. 319, 99 S. Ct. 2319, 60 L. Ed. 2d 920 (1979)—§§ 4:14 n.13; 4:32 n.27; 4:41 n.15

Lock v. State, 122 Ga. 730, 50 S.E. 932 (1905)—§ 14:50 n.2

Locke v. State, 3 Ga. 534, 1847 WL 1366 (1847)—§ 13:4 n.13, 16

Lockett v. Ohio, 438 U.S. 586, 98 S. Ct. 2954, 57 L. Ed. 2d 973 (1978)— §§ 26:6 n.12; 26:8 n.17, 30; 26:10 n.8; 26:11 n.11

Lockett v. Ohio, 434 U.S. 889, 98 S. Ct. 261, 54 L. Ed. 2d 173 (1977)— § 23:8 n.1

Lockett v. State, 257 Ga. App. 412, 571 S.E.2d 192 (2002)—§ 13:23 n.10

Lockhart v. Fretwell, 506 U.S. 364, 113 S. Ct. 838, 122 L. Ed. 2d 180 (1993)—§ 7:4 n.24

Lockhart v. McCree, 476 U.S. 162, 106 S. Ct. 1758, 90 L. Ed. 2d 137 (1986)—§ 18:17 n.25

Love v. State, 144 Ga. App. 728, 242 S.E.2d 278 (1978)—§ 4:32 n.4

Loveless v. Carten, 64 Ga. App. 54, 12 S.E.2d 175 (1940)—§ 14:46 n.2

Loveless v. State, 344 Ga. App. 716, 812 S.E.2d 42 (2018)—§ 26:28 n.12

Loveless v. State, 337 Ga. App. 250, 786 S.E.2d 899 (2016)—§ 10:3 n.48

Lovell v. State, 235 Ga. App. 140, 508 S.E.2d 771 (1998)—§ 26:33 n.18

Lovell v. State, 189 Ga. App. 311, 375 S.E.2d 658 (1988)—§ 24:2 n.16

Lovett v. State, 80 Ga. 255, 4 S.E. 912 (1888)—§§ 14:58 n.5; 24:27 n.1

Lowe v. State, 245 Ga. App. 659, 538 S.E.2d 552 (2000)—§ 23:7 n.18

Lowe v. State, 267 Ga. 410, 478 S.E.2d 762 (1996)—§ 26:34 n.1

Lowe v. State, 185 Ga. App. 606, 365 S.E.2d 479 (1988)—§§ 5:23 n.13; 6:12 n.4

Lowe v. State, 253 Ga. 308, 319 S.E.2d 834 (1984)—§ 23:7 n.18

Lowe v. State, 141 Ga. App. 433, 233 S.E.2d 807 (1977)—§§ 6:6 n.29, 33, 34; 17:1 n.10, 14

Lowe v. State, 225 Ga. 56, 165 S.E.2d 861 (1969)—§ 5:3 n.5

Lowe v. Turner, 115 Ga. App. 503, 154 S.E.2d 792 (1967)—§ 2:19 n.10

Lowenfield v. Phelps, 484 U.S. 231, 108 S. Ct. 546, 98 L. Ed. 2d 568 (1988)—§ 24:19 n.23

Lowery v. State, 282 Ga. 68, 646 S.E.2d 67 (2007)—§ 24:19 n.26

Lowery v. State, 264 Ga. App. 655, 592 S.E.2d 102 (2003)—§ 18:13 n.4

Lowman v. State, 204 Ga. App. 655, 420 S.E.2d 94 (1992)—§ 14:66 n.27, 28

Lowman v. State, 197 Ga. App. 556, 398 S.E.2d 832 (1990)—§ 18:23 n.21

Lowrance v. State, 183 Ga. App. 421, 359 S.E.2d 196 (1987)—§ 7:1 n.14

Lowry v. Thompson, 53 Ga. App. 71, 184 S.E. 891 (1936)—§ 12:17 n.28

Loya v. State, 321 Ga. App. 430, 740 S.E.2d 382 (2013)—§ 26:19 n.50

Loyd v. State, 45 Ga. 57, 1872 WL 2506 (1872)—§ 18:20 n.7

Loyless v. State, 210 Ga. App. 693, 436 S.E.2d 814 (1993)—§ 14:73 n.9

Luallen v. State, 266 Ga. 174, 465 S.E.2d 672 (1996)—§ 5:17 n.12

Luangkhot v. State, 292 Ga. 423, 736 S.E.2d 397 (2013)—§ 4:59 n.22, 23

Lucas v. State, 273 Ga. 88, 538 S.E.2d 44 (2000)—§ 5:20 n.37, 46

Lucas v. State, 264 Ga. 840, 452 S.E.2d 110 (1995)—§ 25:6 n.8

Lucas v. State, 165 Ga. App. 468, 302 S.E.2d 121 (1983)—§ 21:26 n.6

Lucas v. State, 38 Ga. App. 449, 144 S.E. 138 (1928)—§ 14:41 n.15

Lucas v. Walker, 287 Ga. 864, 700 S.E.2d 596 (2010)—§ 28:17 n.84, 93

Luce v. U.S., 469 U.S. 38, 105 S. Ct. 460, 83 L. Ed. 2d 443, 16 Fed. R. Evid. Serv. 833 (1984)—§ 14:78 n.9

Luck v. State, 163 Ga. App. 657, 295 S.E.2d 584 (1982)—§ 14:30 n.42

Ludy v. State, 177 Ga. App. 767, 341 S.E.2d 224 (1986)—§ 14:29 n.34

Luke v. Battle, 275 Ga. 370, 565 S.E.2d 816 (2002)—§§ 14:64 n.4; 28:17 n.34, 35

Luke v. State, 324 Ga. App. 531, 751 S.E.2d 180 (2013)—§ 23:7 n.17

Luke v. State, 236 Ga. App. 543, 512 S.E.2d 39 (1999)—§ 23:5 n.14

Luke v. State, 180 Ga. App. 378, 349 S.E.2d 391 (1986)—§ 14:67 n.91

Luke v. State, 178 Ga. App. 614, 344 S.E.2d 452 (1986)—§ 26:19 n.37

Luke v. State, 171 Ga. App. 201, 318 S.E.2d 833 (1984)—§§ 26:33 n.16; 26:35 n.1

Lummus v. State, 17 Ga. App. 414, 87 S.E. 147 (1915)—§ 13:5 n.2

M

Mack v. State, 219 Ga. 829, 136 S.E.2d 320 (1964)—§ 14:40 n.8

Mackay v. State, 291 Ga. App. 733, 662 S.E.2d 814 (2008)—§ 4:30 n.37

MacKenna v. Ellis, 280 F.2d 592 (5th Cir. 1960)—§ 7:4 n.8, 9

Mackler v. State, 164 Ga. App. 874, 298 S.E.2d 589 (1982)—§ 14:30 n.49

Macon, City of v. Davis, 251 Ga. 332, 305 S.E.2d 116 (1983)—§ 26:43 n.64

Macon, City of v. Massey, 214 Ga. 589, 106 S.E.2d 23 (1958)—§ 27:2 n.2

Maddox v. Hall County, 162 Ga. App. 371, 291 S.E.2d 442 (1982)—§ 10:7 n.18

Maddox v. State, 322 Ga. App. 811, 746 S.E.2d 280 (2013)—§ 14:83 n.11, 12

Maddox v. State, 272 Ga. App. 440, 612 S.E.2d 484 (2005)—§ 14:76 n.23

Maddox v. State, 218 Ga. App. 320, 461 S.E.2d 286 (1995)—§ 14:67 n.8

Maddox v. State, 188 Ga. App. 883, 374 S.E.2d 810 (1988)—§ 4:49 n.8

Maddox v. State, 145 Ga. App. 363, 243 S.E.2d 740 (1978)—§ 20:4 n.8

Maddox v. State, 233 Ga. 874, 213 S.E.2d 654 (1975)—§§ 25:2 n.1; 25:4 n.4

Madigan v. State, 160 Ga. App. 656, 288 S.E.2d 34 (1981)—§ 14:30 n.35

Madison v. State, 281 Ga. 640, 641 S.E.2d 789 (2007)—§ 18:30 n.4

Madiwale v. Savaiko, 117 F.3d 1321 (11th Cir. 1997)—§ 2:10 n.2

Mafnas v. State, 149 Ga. App. 286, 254 S.E.2d 409 (1979)—§§ 14:96 n.2; 17:10 n.1

Mager v. State, 21 Ga. App. 139, 94 S.E. 82 (1917)—§ 14:67 n.73

Magher v. State, 199 Ga. App. 508, 405 S.E.2d 327 (1991)—§ 14:29 n.18

Magouirk v. State, 158 Ga. App. 517, 281 S.E.2d 283 (1981)—§ 14:72 n.16

Maguire, Appeal of, 571 F.2d 675 (1st Cir. 1978)—§ 6:9 n.6

Mahar v. State, 137 Ga. App. 116, 223 S.E.2d 204 (1975)—§ 4:13 n.5

Mahomet v. State, 151 Ga. App. 462, 260 S.E.2d 363 (1979)—§ 24:4 n.11

Maine v. Moulton, 474 U.S. 159, 106 S. Ct. 477, 88 L. Ed. 2d 481 (1985)—§ 5:10 n.11

Maines v. State, 330 Ga. App. 247, 765 S.E.2d 382 (2014)—§ 7:4 n.86

Majia v. State, 174 Ga. App. 432, 330 S.E.2d 171 (1985)—§ 14:67 n.26

Majmundar v. Veline, 256 Ga. 8, 342 S.E.2d 682 (1986)—§ 9:2 n.10

Major v. State, 306 Ga. App. 342, 702 S.E.2d 684 (2010)—§ 14:28 n.11

M.A.K. v. State of Georgia, 171 Ga. App. 151, 318 S.E.2d 828 (1984)— § 6:5 n.9

Malaguti v. State, 273 Ga. 398, 543 S.E.2d 1 (2001)—§ 14:19 n.2

Malcolm v. State, 263 Ga. 369, 434 S.E.2d 479 (1993)—§§ 20:4 n.30; 26:37 n.1

Malcom v. State, 162 Ga. App. 587, 291 S.E.2d 756 (1982)—§ 30:1 n.20

Mallarino v. State, 194 Ga. App. 212, 390 S.E.2d 114 (1990)—§ 26:41 n.11

Mallory v. State, 335 Ga. App. 852, 783 S.E.2d 370 (2016)—§ 26:19 n.51

Mallory v. State, 225 Ga. App. 418, 483 S.E.2d 907 (1997)—§ 7:3 n.22

Mallory v. State, 261 Ga. 625, 409 S.E.2d 839 (1991)—§§ 5:21 n.1, 2; 18:31 n.154

Mallory v. State, 230 Ga. 657, 198 S.E.2d 677 (1973)—§ 5:26 n.2

Malone v. State, 240 Ga. App. 732, 524 S.E.2d 770 (1999)—§ 18:20 n.29

Mason v. Banks, 242 Ga. 292, 248 S.E.2d 664 (1978)—§ 14:67 n.84

Mason v. Carter, 223 Ga. 2, 153 S.E.2d 162 (1967)—§ 13:6

Mason v. State, 274 Ga. 79, 548 S.E.2d 298 (2001)—§ 23:7 n.48

Mason v. State, 244 Ga. App. 247, 535 S.E.2d 497 (2000)—§ 24:24 n.3, 18

Mason v. State, 267 Ga. 314, 477 S.E.2d 568 (1996)—§ 26:33 n.19

Mason v. State, 197 Ga. App. 534, 398 S.E.2d 822 (1990)—§ 19:1 n.2

Mason v. State, 177 Ga. App. 184, 338 S.E.2d 706 (1985)—§ 5:12 n.4

Mason v. State, 162 Ga. App. 167, 290 S.E.2d 499 (1982)—§ 14:35 n.9

Mason v. State, 631 P.2d 1051 (Wyo. 1981)—§ 30:7 n.1

Mason v. State, 146 Ga. App. 557, 247 S.E.2d 118 (1978)—§ 4:2 n.16

Mason v. State, 239 Ga. 538, 238 S.E.2d 79 (1977)—§§ 18:37 n.6; 18:38 n.17

Mason v. U.S., 414 F.2d 1176 (D.C. Cir. 1969)—§§ 6:7 n.15; 6:9 n.8

Massachusetts v. Sheppard, 468 U.S. 981, 104 S. Ct. 3424, 82 L. Ed. 2d 737 (1984)—§ 4:20 n.2

Massachusetts v. Upton, 466 U.S. 727, 104 S. Ct. 2085, 80 L. Ed. 2d 721 (1984)—§ 4:25 n.4

Massachusetts v. White, 439 U.S. 280, 99 S. Ct. 712, 58 L. Ed. 2d 519 (1978)—§ 2:34 n.4

Massaline v. Williams, 274 Ga. 552, 554 S.E.2d 720 (2001)—§ 28:17 n.90

Massengale v. State, 189 Ga. App. 877, 377 S.E.2d 882 (1989)—§ 14:37 n.4

Massengale v. State, 164 Ga. App. 57, 296 S.E.2d 371 (1982)—§ 14:41 n.25

Massey v. Meadows, 253 Ga. 389, 321 S.E.2d 703 (1984)—§§ 21:28 n.2; 30:8 n.11

Massey v. State, 331 Ga. App. 430, 771 S.E.2d 122 (2015)—§ 14:30 n.11

Massey v. State, 270 Ga. 76, 508 S.E.2d 149 (1998)—§§ 18:36 n.7; 23:3 n.1

Massey v. State, 263 Ga. 379, 434 S.E.2d 467 (1993)—§ 14:22 n.5

Massey v. State, 251 Ga. 515, 307 S.E.2d 489 (1983)—§ 14:30 n.3

Massey v. State, 243 Ga. 228, 253 S.E.2d 196 (1979)—§ 5:8 n.5

Massey v. State, 127 Ga. App. 638, 194 S.E.2d 582 (1972)—§§ 17:9 n.14, 17; 17:17 n.10

Massiah v. U.S., 377 U.S. 201, 84 S. Ct. 1199, 12 L. Ed. 2d 246 (1964)—§§ 2:34 n.10; 5:4 n.6; 5:9 n.1, 3

Masters v. State, 186 Ga. App. 795, 368 S.E.2d 557 (1988)—§ 14:35 n.24

Mastrian v. Hedman, 326 F.2d 708 (8th Cir. 1964)—§ 8:6 n.5

Mata v. Sumner, 696 F.2d 1244 (9th Cir. 1983)—§ 6:6 n.44

Matchett v. State, 257 Ga. 785, 364 S.E.2d 565 (1988)—§ 18:38 n.19

Mathews v. U.S., 485 U.S. 58, 108 S. Ct. 883, 99 L. Ed. 2d 54 (1988)—§ 21:25 n.22

Mathis v. State, 336 Ga. App. 257, 784 S.E.2d 98 (2016)—§ 26:28 n.56

Mathis v. State, 273 Ga. 508, 543 S.E.2d 712 (2001)—§§ 14:48 n.50; 26:35 n.7

Mathis v. State, 249 Ga. 454, 291 S.E.2d 489 (1982)—§ 26:14 n.10

Mathis v. State, 153 Ga. App. 587, 266 S.E.2d 275 (1980)—§ 24:4 n.5

Mathis v. State, 242 Ga. 761, 251 S.E.2d 305 (1978)—§ 2:22 n.22

Mathis v. State, 145 Ga. App. 754, 245 S.E.2d 41 (1978)—§ 16:14 n.26

McDougal v. State, 277 Ga. 493, 591 S.E.2d 788 (2004)—§ 5:20 n.24

McDowell v. State, 290 Ga. App. 538, 660 S.E.2d 24 (2008)—§ 10:3 n.36, 38

McDowell v. State, 172 Ga. App. 643, 324 S.E.2d 211 (1984)—§ 4:49 n.8

McDowell v. U.S., 383 F.2d 599 (8th Cir. 1967)—§ 4:43 n.9

McDuffie v. Jones, 248 Ga. 544, 283 S.E.2d 601 (1981)—§§ 26:14 n.17, 24; 28:17 n.9

McElhannon v. State, 99 Ga. 672, 26 S.E. 501 (1896)—§ 18:23 n.20

McElmurray v. State, 76 Ga. App. 604, 47 S.E.2d 139 (1948)—§ 14:41 n.9

McElreath v. State, 163 Ga. App. 826, 296 S.E.2d 622 (1982)—§ 16:2 n.3

McElroy v. State, 247 Ga. 355, 276 S.E.2d 38 (1981)—§§ 30:4 n.8; 30:5 n.1

McElwee v. State, 147 Ga. App. 84, 248 S.E.2d 162 (1978)—§ 17:9 n.4

McFarland v. State, 137 Ga. App. 354, 223 S.E.2d 739 (1976)—§ 22:6 n.3

McFarley v. State, 268 Ga. App. 621, 602 S.E.2d 341 (2004)—§ 10:3 n.22

McFarlin v. State, 121 Ga. 329, 49 S.E. 267 (1904)—§ 12:7 n.7

McGee v. State, 287 Ga. App. 839, 652 S.E.2d 822 (2007)—§ 14:58 n.57

McGee v. State, 272 Ga. 363, 529 S.E.2d 366 (2000)—§§ 14:21 n.5; 14:34 n.26

McGee v. State, 133 Ga. App. 184, 210 S.E.2d 355 (1974)—§ 4:43 n.11

McGhee v. State, 253 Ga. 278, 319 S.E.2d 836 (1984)—§ 3:7 n.24

McGill v. State, 263 Ga. 81, 428 S.E.2d 341 (1993)—§ 7:4 n.9

McGinnis v. State, 208 Ga. App. 354, 430 S.E.2d 618 (1993)—§ 14:85 n.6

McGinnis v. State, 258 Ga. 673, 372 S.E.2d 804 (1988)—§ 18:26 n.28

McGlohon v. State, 228 Ga. App. 726, 492 S.E.2d 715 (1997)—§ 18:31 n.148

McGouirk v. State, 303 Ga. 881, 815 S.E.2d 825 (2018)—§ 14:95 n.3

McGowan v. State, 173 Ga. App. 438, 326 S.E.2d 805 (1985)—§ 5:3 n.6

McGraw v. State, 199 Ga. App. 389, 405 S.E.2d 53 (1991)—§ 18:24 n.13

McGriff v. State, 232 Ga. App. 546, 502 S.E.2d 482 (1998)—§ 18:19 n.28

McGuffie v. State, 17 Ga. 497, 1855 WL 1863 (1855)—§ 12:17 n.33

McGugan v. State, 215 Ga. App. 535, 451 S.E.2d 460 (1994)—§§ 3:10 n.20; 4:21 n.13

McGuire v. State, 200 Ga. App. 509, 408 S.E.2d 506 (1991)—§ 24:24 n.12

McGuire v. State, 288 Ark. 388, 706 S.W.2d 360 (1986)—§ 14:7 n.8

McGuyton v. State, 298 Ga. 351, 782 S.E.2d 21 (2016)—§ 16:11 n.1

McInturf v. State, 544 S.W.2d 417 (Tex. Crim. App. 1976)—§ 6:12 n.10

McIver v. State, 212 Ga. App. 670, 442 S.E.2d 855 (1994)—§ 14:67 n.13

McIver v. State, 205 Ga. App. 648, 423 S.E.2d 27 (1992)—§ 14:67 n.77

McKane v. Durston, 153 U.S. 684, 14 S. Ct. 913, 38 L. Ed. 867 (1894)—§ 28:2 n.1

McKaskle v. Wiggins, 465 U.S. 168, 104 S. Ct. 944, 79 L. Ed. 2d 122 (1984)—§ 7:3 n.7, 15

McKee v. Harris, 649 F.2d 927 (2d Cir. 1981)—§ 7:2 n.33

McKee v. State, 275 Ga. App. 646, 621 S.E.2d 611 (2005)—§ 26:33 n.9

McKee v. State, 168 Ga. App. 214, 308 S.E.2d 574 (1983)—§ 18:23 n.13

McKeiver v. Pennsylvania, 403 U.S. 528, 91 S. Ct. 1976, 29 L. Ed. 2d 647 (1971)—§ 18:1 n.15

McKenzey v. State, 138 Ga. App. 88, 225 S.E.2d 512 (1976)—§§ 17:7 n.11, 20, 22; 18:7 n.1; 18:11 n.8

Mills v. Rogers, 457 U.S. 291, 102 S. Ct. 2442, 73 L. Ed. 2d 16 (1982)—
§ 4:2 n.50

Mills v. State, 287 Ga. 828, 700 S.E.2d 544 (2010)—§ 21:29 n.1

Mills v. State, 160 Ga. App. 49, 286 S.E.2d 55 (1981)—§ 25:4 n.25

Mills v. State, 244 Ga. 186, 259 S.E.2d 445 (1979)—§ 26:14 n.17

Mills v. State, 137 Ga. App. 305, 223 S.E.2d 498 (1976)—§ 18:24 n.41

Millwood v. State, 191 Ga. App. 659, 382 S.E.2d 430 (1989)—§ 23:8 n.7

Milner v. State, 258 Ga. App. 425, 574 S.E.2d 457 (2002)—§ 6:2 n.17

Milner v. State, 180 Ga. App. 97, 348 S.E.2d 509 (1986)—§ 2:27 n.1

Milner v. U.S., 293 F. 590 (C.C.A. 5th Cir. 1923)—§ 25:6 n.22

Milton v. State, 232 Ga. App. 672, 503 S.E.2d 566 (1998)—§ 14:6 n.5

Mims v. State, 201 Ga. App. 277, 410 S.E.2d 824 (1991)—§§ 3:9 n.8;
28:11 n.37

Mincey v. Arizona, 437 U.S. 385, 98 S. Ct. 2408, 57 L. Ed. 2d 290
(1978)—§§ 2:32 n.4; 4:25 n.8; 4:30 n.32, 33; 4:57 n.16; 5:4 n.10; 5:15 n.16;
5:26 n.5

Mincey v. State, 186 Ga. App. 839, 368 S.E.2d 796 (1988)—§ 26:28 n.50

Mincey v. State, 180 Ga. App. 898, 350 S.E.2d 852 (1986)—§ 4:10 n.16

Mincey v. State, 180 Ga. App. 263, 349 S.E.2d 1 (1986)—§ 18:11 n.10

Mincey v. State, 251 Ga. 255, 304 S.E.2d 882 (1983)—§§ 2:13 n.10; 14:4
n.15; 18:17 n.24; 26:2 n.16

Minchey v. State, 155 Ga. App. 632, 271 S.E.2d 885 (1980)—§ 16:11 n.2,
3

Minder v. State of Ga., 183 U.S. 559, 22 S. Ct. 224, 46 L. Ed. 328
(1902)—§ 14:96 n.2

Minder v. State, 113 Ga. 772, 39 S.E. 284 (1901)—§ 14:96 n.2

Miner v. State, 268 Ga. 67, 485 S.E.2d 456 (1997)—§§ 24:2 n.42; 24:11 n.2

Miners v. State, 250 Ga. App. 443, 550 S.E.2d 725 (2001)—§ 17:15 n.2

Mingo v. State, 155 Ga. App. 284, 270 S.E.2d 700 (1980)—§ 30:1 n.12

Mingo v. State, 133 Ga. App. 385, 210 S.E.2d 835 (1974)—§ 17:1 n.4

Minhinnett v. State, 106 Ga. 141, 32 S.E. 19 (1898)—§ 13:6 n.7

Minis v. State, 150 Ga. App. 671, 258 S.E.2d 308 (1979)—§ 26:43 n.52

Minnesota v. Carter, 525 U.S. 83, 119 S. Ct. 469, 142 L. Ed. 2d 373
(1998)—§ 14:81 n.22

Minnesota v. Dickerson, 508 U.S. 366, 113 S. Ct. 2130, 124 L. Ed. 2d
334 (1993)—§ 3:10 n.12

Minnesota v. Murphy, 465 U.S. 420, 104 S. Ct. 1136, 79 L. Ed. 2d 409
(1984)—§§ 5:12 n.23; 26:19 n.49; 30:2 n.12

Minnesota v. Olson, 495 U.S. 91, 110 S. Ct. 1684, 109 L. Ed. 2d 85
(1990)—§§ 4:31 n.1; 14:81 n.21; 14:83 n.30

Minnick v. Mississippi, 498 U.S. 146, 111 S. Ct. 486, 112 L. Ed. 2d 489
(1990)—§ 5:20 n.27

Minor v. State, 328 Ga. App. 128, 761 S.E.2d 538 (2014)—§ 18:31 n.34,
144

Minor v. State, 298 Ga. App. 391, 680 S.E.2d 459 (2009)—§ 2:5 n.5

Minor v. State, 264 Ga. 195, 442 S.E.2d 754 (1994)—§ 18:31 n.113

Minor v. State, 63 Ga. 318, 1879 WL 2517 (1879)—§ 13:8 n.5

Minton v. State, 99 Ga. 254, 25 S.E. 626 (1896)—§ 5:5 n.15

Miracle v. Estelle, 592 F.2d 1269 (5th Cir. 1979)—§ 14:61 n.1

Mitchell v. U.S., 526 U.S. 314, 119 S. Ct. 1307, 143 L. Ed. 2d 424 (1999)—§ 26:43 n.41

Mitchum v. Foster, 407 U.S. 225, 92 S. Ct. 2151, 32 L. Ed. 2d 705 (1972)—§ 9:3 n.10, 12

Mitchum v. State, 11 Ga. 615, 1852 WL 1365 (1852)—§ 23:5 n.5

Mixon v. State, 184 Ga. App. 623, 362 S.E.2d 111 (1987)—§ 4:32 n.10

Mize v. State, 269 Ga. 646, 501 S.E.2d 219 (1998)—§§ 23:5 n.30; 26:7 n.13

Mize v. State, 190 Ga. App. 166, 378 S.E.2d 392 (1989)—§ 18:28 n.3

Mize v. State, 135 Ga. 291, 69 S.E. 173 (1910)—§§ 12:7 n.3, 6; 12:8 n.12

M.J.H., In re, 239 Ga. App. 894, 522 S.E.2d 491 (1999)—§ 3:2 n.9

Moak v. State, 222 Ga. App. 36, 473 S.E.2d 576 (1996)—§§ 18:26 n.6; 18:31 n.117

Mobley v. State, 346 Ga. App. 641, 816 S.E.2d 769 (2018)—§ 4:2 n.90

Mobley v. State, 345 Ga. App. 393, 812 S.E.2d 796 (2018)—§ 26:36 n.16

Mobley v. State, 277 Ga. App. 267, 626 S.E.2d 248 (2006)—§ 6:4 n.15

Mobley v. State, 269 Ga. 738, 505 S.E.2d 722 (1998)—§§ 5:25 n.17; 21:22 n.5

Mobley v. State, 219 Ga. App. 789, 466 S.E.2d 669 (1996)—§§ 14:36 n.8; 14:37 n.3

Mobley v. State, 218 Ga. App. 739, 463 S.E.2d 166 (1995)—§ 24:22 n.20

Mobley v. State, 164 Ga. App. 154, 296 S.E.2d 617 (1982)—§§ 13:7 n.4; 14:41 n.26

Moceri v. State, 338 Ga. App. 329, 788 S.E.2d 899 (2016)—§ 14:20 n.9

Mock v. State, 163 Ga. App. 320, 293 S.E.2d 525 (1982)—§ 7:2 n.26

Mock v. State, 163 Ga. App. 319, 294 S.E.2d 361 (1982)—§ 14:72 n.36

Mock v. State, 156 Ga. App. 763, 275 S.E.2d 393 (1980)—§ 26:19 n.33

Mohammed v. State, 226 Ga. App. 387, 486 S.E.2d 652 (1997)—§ 26:24 n.35, 36, 37

Mojica v. State, 210 Ga. App. 826, 437 S.E.2d 806 (1993)—§ 17:14 n.25

Molaro v. State, 236 Ga. App. 35, 510 S.E.2d 886 (1999)—§ 3:1 n.30

Molina v. State, 304 Ga. App. 93, 695 S.E.2d 656 (2010)—§§ 3:1 n.25; 4:54 n.7

Monday v. State, 32 Ga. 672, 1861 WL 1437 (1861)—§ 17:17 n.8

Mondy v. State, 229 Ga. App. 311, 494 S.E.2d 176 (1997)—§ 14:9 n.2

Monge v. California, 524 U.S. 721, 118 S. Ct. 2246, 141 L. Ed. 2d 615 (1998)—§ 14:47 n.5

Monroe v. Blackburn, 607 F.2d 148 (5th Cir. 1979)—§ 14:34 n.3

Monroe v. State, 272 Ga. 201, 528 S.E.2d 504 (2000)—§ 23:3 n.1, 3

Monroe v. State, 5 Ga. 85, 1848 WL 1538 (1848)—§ 24:10 n.1

Montana v. Egelhoff, 518 U.S. 37, 116 S. Ct. 2013, 135 L. Ed. 2d 361 (1996)—§ 21:16 n.3

Monteagudo v. State, 247 Ga. App. 801, 545 S.E.2d 351 (2001)—§ 13:28 n.10

Montejo v. Louisiana, 556 U.S. 778, 129 S. Ct. 2079, 173 L. Ed. 2d 955 (2009)—§ 5:20 n.18

Montero v. State, 245 Ga. App. 181, 537 S.E.2d 429 (2000)—§ 3:2 n.47

Montford v. State, 164 Ga. App. 627, 298 S.E.2d 319 (1982)—§ 17:9 n.4

Montgomery v. Louisiana, 136 S. Ct. 718, 193 L. Ed. 2d 599 (2016)—§§ 26:2 n.30, 31; 26:6 n.24

Morrow v. City of Atlanta, 162 Ga. 228, 133 S.E. 345 (1926)—§ 9:2 n.2

Morrow v. State, 257 Ga. App. 707, 572 S.E.2d 58 (2002)—§ 3:2 n.26

Morrow v. State, 272 Ga. 691, 532 S.E.2d 78 (2000)—§ 12:9 n.41, 47

Morrow v. State, 226 Ga. App. 833, 487 S.E.2d 669 (1997)—§ 14:73 n.38

Morrow v. State, 186 Ga. App. 615, 367 S.E.2d 854 (1988)—§ 10:2 n.17

Morrow v. State, 162 Ga. App. 183, 290 S.E.2d 137 (1982)—§ 14:93 n.2

Morrow v. State, 147 Ga. App. 395, 249 S.E.2d 110 (1978)—§ 14:68 n.2

Morse v. State, 288 Ga. App. 725, 655 S.E.2d 217 (2007)—§ 4:43 n.5

Mortimer v. State, 177 Ga. App. 679, 340 S.E.2d 649 (1986)—§ 2:25 n.2

Morton v. State, 181 Ga. App. 781, 353 S.E.2d 852 (1987)—§ 14:72 n.37

Morton v. State, 166 Ga. App. 170, 303 S.E.2d 509 (1983)—§§ 8:1 n.10, 12; 10:8 n.9

Moseley v. State, 165 Ga. 290, 140 S.E. 754 (1927)—§ 21:8 n.3

Mosely v. State, 269 Ga. 17, 495 S.E.2d 9 (1998)—§ 18:19 n.15

Moser v. Richmond County Bd. of Com'rs, 263 Ga. 63, 428 S.E.2d 71 (1993)—§ 14:48 n.39

Moses v. State, 264 Ga. 313, 444 S.E.2d 767 (1994)—§ 5:12 n.2

Moses v. State, 167 Ga. App. 556, 307 S.E.2d 35 (1983)—§ 21:13 n.10

Moses v. State, 245 Ga. 180, 263 S.E.2d 916 (1980)—§ 21:11 n.29

Mosher v. State, 268 Ga. 555, 491 S.E.2d 348 (1997)—§§ 18:20 n.15; 26:6 n.27

Mosier v. State, 160 Ga. App. 415, 287 S.E.2d 357 (1981)—§ 4:12 n.25

Mosley v. State, 300 Ga. 521, 796 S.E.2d 684 (2017)—§ 28:2 n.22

Mosley v. State, 230 Ga. App. 890, 497 S.E.2d 608 (1998)—§ 14:58 n.25

Mosley v. State, 257 Ga. 382, 359 S.E.2d 653 (1987)—§§ 18:24 n.31; 24:5 n.10

Mosley v. State, 145 Ga. App. 651, 244 S.E.2d 610 (1978)—§ 24:19 n.16

Moss v. State, 220 Ga. App. 150, 469 S.E.2d 325 (1996)—§ 14:66 n.12, 35

Moss v. State, 206 Ga. App. 310, 425 S.E.2d 386 (1992)—§ 13:18 n.3

Moss v. State, 196 Ga. App. 81, 395 S.E.2d 363 (1990)—§ 7:4 n.30

Moss v. State, 250 Ga. 368, 297 S.E.2d 459 (1982)—§§ 14:93 n.18; 18:19 n.21

Mote v. State, 212 Ga. App. 551, 442 S.E.2d 799 (1994)—§ 21:32 n.4

Motes v. State, 256 Ga. 831, 353 S.E.2d 348 (1987)—§ 14:92 n.21

Motley v. State, 273 Ga. 732, 546 S.E.2d 468 (2001)—§ 16:4 n.10

Moultrie Milk Shed v. City of Cairo, 206 Ga. 348, 57 S.E.2d 199 (1950)—§ 9:2 n.10

Mowery v. State, 234 Ga. App. 801, 507 S.E.2d 821 (1998)—§ 14:28 n.4

Mowoe v. State, 328 Ga. App. 536, 759 S.E.2d 663 (2014)—§ 23:7 n.17

Mowrer v. State, 447 N.E.2d 1129 (Ind. Ct. App. 1983)—§ 2:5 n.15

Moye v. Hopper, 234 Ga. 230, 214 S.E.2d 920 (1975)—§ 28:17 n.19

Moye v. State, 129 Ga. App. 52, 198 S.E.2d 514 (1973)—§ 14:22 n.17

Moye v. State, 122 Ga. App. 14, 176 S.E.2d 180 (1970)—§ 6:8 n.18

Moyer v. State, 164 Ga. App. 629, 298 S.E.2d 308 (1982)—§ 25:2 n.19

Mozier v. State, 207 Ga. App. 264, 427 S.E.2d 551 (1993)—§ 4:42 n.12

Muckle v. State, 233 Ga. 337, 211 S.E.2d 361 (1974)—§§ 26:8 n.35; 26:14 n.19

Muehler v. Mena, 544 U.S. 93, 125 S. Ct. 1465, 161 L. Ed. 2d 299 (2005)—§§ 2:2 n.14; 3:11 n.13

Murray v. State, 253 Ga. 90, 317 S.E.2d 193 (1984)—§ 21:11 n.17

Murray v. State, 155 Ga. App. 816, 273 S.E.2d 219 (1980)—§ 5:13 n.19

Murray v. State, 151 Ga. App. 122, 258 S.E.2d 919 (1979)—§ 20:6 n.59

Murray v. State, 135 Ga. App. 344, 217 S.E.2d 448 (1975)—§ 26:19 n.26

Murray v. U.S., 487 U.S. 533, 108 S. Ct. 2529, 101 L. Ed. 2d 472 (1988)—§§ 2:25 n.13; 2:27 n.8

Murrell v. Young, 285 Ga. 182, 674 S.E.2d 890 (2009)—§ 28:6 n.2, 7

Mydell v. State, 238 Ga. 450, 233 S.E.2d 199 (1977)—§ 26:2 n.14

Myers v. State, 143 Ga. App. 195, 237 S.E.2d 662 (1977)—§ 21:12 n.14

Myers v. State, 140 Ga. App. 641, 231 S.E.2d 496 (1976)—§ 21:25 n.19

Myers v. State, 97 Ga. 76, 25 S.E. 252 (1895)—§ 17:1 n.11

Myers v. St. Lawrence, 289 Ga. 240, 710 S.E.2d 557 (2011)—§ 28:17 n.39

Myrick v. State, 168 Ga. App. 223, 308 S.E.2d 563 (1983)—§ 14:88 n.9

Myrick v. State, 155 Ga. App. 496, 271 S.E.2d 637 (1980)—§ 14:72 n.14

N

Nagel v. State, 264 Ga. 150, 442 S.E.2d 446 (1994)—§ 21:13 n.21

Nagel v. State, 262 Ga. 888, 427 S.E.2d 490 (1993)—§ 21:13 n.20

Nalley v. Howell, 268 Ga. 63, 487 S.E.2d 600 (1997)—§ 9:2 n.17

Nalls v. State, 304 Ga. 168, 815 S.E.2d 38 (2018)—§ 13:28 n.6

Nance v. State, 280 Ga. 125, 623 S.E.2d 470 (2005)—§ 17:7 n.16

Nance v. State, 274 Ga. 311, 553 S.E.2d 794 (2001)—§ 14:58 n.8

Nance v. State, 272 Ga. 217, 526 S.E.2d 560 (2000)—§ 21:10 n.18

Nance v. State, 266 Ga. 816, 471 S.E.2d 216 (1996)—§ 14:48 n.20

Nance v. State, 123 Ga. App. 410, 181 S.E.2d 295 (1971)—§ 14:22 n.42

N & N, Inc. v. Veline, 253 Ga. 51, 315 S.E.2d 908 (1984)—§ 4:23 n.5

Napier v. State, 276 Ga. 769, 583 S.E.2d 825 (2003)—§ 20:4 n.10

Napue v. People of State of Ill., 360 U.S. 264, 79 S. Ct. 1173, 3 L. Ed. 2d 1217 (1959)—§ 14:33 n.2, 3

Nardone v. U.S., 308 U.S. 338, 60 S. Ct. 266, 84 L. Ed. 307 (1939)— § 2:25 n.14, 15

Nash v. Hess Oil & Chemical Corp., 123 Ga. App. 132, 179 S.E.2d 778 (1970)—§ 14:78 n.27

Nash v. State, 271 Ga. 281, 519 S.E.2d 893 (1999)—§§ 14:77 n.11; 16:14 n.25; 17:23 n.6; 18:2 n.4; 18:17 n.21; 26:14 n.11, 12; 26:28 n.35

Nash v. State, 233 Ga. App. 75, 503 S.E.2d 23 (1998)—§ 26:28 n.45

Nash v. State, 225 Ga. App. 10, 482 S.E.2d 520 (1997)—§ 26:44 n.6

Nasir v. Gwinnett County State Court, 341 Ga. App. 63, 798 S.E.2d 695 (2017)—§ 17:21 n.11

Nasworthy v. State, 169 Ga. App. 603, 314 S.E.2d 446 (1984)—§ 30:2 n.3

Nation v. State of Ga., 645 F. Supp. 179 (N.D. Ga. 1986)—§ 26:43 n.20

National Treasury Employees Union v. Von Raab, 489 U.S. 656, 109 S. Ct. 1384, 103 L. Ed. 2d 685 (1989)—§ 4:2 n.40

National Viatical, Inc. v. State, 258 Ga. App. 408, 574 S.E.2d 337 (2002)—§ 4:60 n.5

Natson v. State, 242 Ga. 618, 250 S.E.2d 420 (1978)—§ 14:8 n.8

Navarette v. California, 572 U.S. 393, 134 S. Ct. 1683, 188 L. Ed. 2d 680 (2014)—§ 3:7 n.7

Oregon v. Ice, 555 U.S. 160, 129 S. Ct. 711, 172 L. Ed. 2d 517 (2009)—
§ 26:43 n.10

Oregon v. Kennedy, 456 U.S. 667, 102 S. Ct. 2083, 72 L. Ed. 2d 416
(1982)—§ 14:58 n.9, 11, 49

Oregon v. Mathiason, 429 U.S. 492, 97 S. Ct. 711, 50 L. Ed. 2d 714
(1977)—§ 5:12 n.3

Organization for a Better Austin v. Keefe, 402 U.S. 415, 91 S. Ct. 1575,
29 L. Ed. 2d 1 (1971)—§ 17:2 n.19

Orkin v. State, 236 Ga. 176, 223 S.E.2d 61, 82 A.L.R.3d 344 (1976)—
§§ 4:59 n.14; 21:25 n.16

Orozco v. Texas, 394 U.S. 324, 89 S. Ct. 1095, 22 L. Ed. 2d 311 (1969)—
§ 5:12 n.3

Orr v. State, 209 Ga. App. 832, 434 S.E.2d 723 (1993)—§ 14:29 n.26, 38

Orvis v. State, 237 Ga. 6, 226 S.E.2d 570 (1976)—§ 14:58 n.16

Osborn v. State, 161 Ga. App. 132, 291 S.E.2d 22 (1982)—§§ 13:28 n.9,
16; 13:32 n.4, 11, 12; 14:36 n.2

Osborn v. United States, 385 U.S. 323, 87 S.Ct. 429, 17 L.Ed.2d 394
(1966)—§ 4:59 n.1

Osborne v. State, 263 Ga. 214, 430 S.E.2d 576 (1993)—§ 18:31 n.137

Osborne v. State, 193 Ga. App. 276, 387 S.E.2d 383 (1989)—§ 5:15 n.10

Osborne v. State, 166 Ga. App. 439, 304 S.E.2d 416 (1983)—§§ 14:29
n.44; 14:30 n.52

Oswell v. State, 181 Ga. App. 35, 351 S.E.2d 221 (1986)—§ 4:56 n.36

Otis v. State, 298 Ga. 544, 782 S.E.2d 654 (2016)—§§ 14:58 n.47; 14:92
n.15; 22:1 n.5

Ottis v. State, 269 Ga. 151, 496 S.E.2d 264 (1998)—§ 5:20 n.45

Otuwa v. State, 303 Ga. App. 410, 693 S.E.2d 610 (2010)—§ 26:24 n.38

Outdoor Am. Corp. v. City of Philadelphia, 333 F.2d 963 (3d Cir.
1964)—§ 9:3 n.3, 6

Overand v. State, 240 Ga. App. 682, 523 S.E.2d 610 (1999)—§ 3:7 n.23

Overby v. State, 315 Ga. App. 735, 728 S.E.2d 278 (2012)—§ 26:21 n.36

Overman v. State, 250 Ga. 494, 299 S.E.2d 542 (1983)—§ 4:30 n.40

Overstreet v. State, 250 Ga. App. 336, 551 S.E.2d 748 (2001)—§ 24:7 n.1

Owen v. State, 266 Ga. 312, 467 S.E.2d 325 (1996)—§ 14:72 n.16, 18, 29,
51

Owens v. McLaughlin, 733 F.3d 320 (11th Cir. 2013)—§ 20:4 n.13

Owens v. State, 303 Ga. 254, 811 S.E.2d 420 (2018)—§ 28:2 n.21

Owens v. State, 298 Ga. 813, 783 S.E.2d 611 (2016)—§ 7:3 n.23

Owens v. State, 236 Ga. App. 534, 512 S.E.2d 394 (1999)—§ 4:30 n.18

Owens v. State, 204 Ga. App. 5, 418 S.E.2d 631 (1992)—§ 14:30 n.56

Owens v. State, 193 Ga. App. 661, 388 S.E.2d 712 (1989)—§ 14:72 n.51

Owens v. State, 173 Ga. App. 309, 326 S.E.2d 509 (1985)—§§ 24:4 n.7;
24:12 n.4

Owens v. State, 251 Ga. 313, 305 S.E.2d 102 (1983)—§ 24:19 n.2

Owens v. State, 161 Ga. App. 184, 288 S.E.2d 262 (1982)—§ 20:6 n.24

Owens v. State, 427 N.E.2d 880 (Ind. 1981)—§ 17:10 n.24

Owens v. State, 248 Ga. 629, 284 S.E.2d 408 (1981)—§ 20:6 n.66

Owens v. State, 233 Ga. 905, 213 S.E.2d 860 (1975)—§ 14:73 n.20

Owens v. State, 233 Ga. 869, 214 S.E.2d 173 (1975)—§§ 17:9 n.8; 18:6 n.1

Parham v. State, 342 Ga. App. 754, 805 S.E.2d 264 (2017)—§ 26:28 n.67

Parham v. State, 137 Ga. App. 498, 224 S.E.2d 485 (1976)—§§ 14:58 n.22; 28:9 n.2

Parham v. State, 135 Ga. App. 315, 217 S.E.2d 493 (1975)—§§ 14:22 n.29; 18:33 n.8; 19:2 n.12, 15

Parham v. State, 28 Ga. App. 569, 112 S.E. 289 (1922)—§ 25:2 n.29

Parish v. Weed Sewing-Machine Co., 79 Ga. 682, 7 S.E. 138 (1887)— § 17:12 n.10

Park v. State, 260 Ga. App. 879, 581 S.E.2d 393 (2003)—§ 18:25 n.4

Park v. State, 230 Ga. App. 274, 495 S.E.2d 886 (1998)—§§ 5:23 n.20; 14:29 n.1

Park v. State, 154 Ga. App. 348, 268 S.E.2d 401 (1980)—§§ 4:34 n.7; 17:12 n.3

Park v. State, 126 Ga. 575, 55 S.E. 489 (1906)—§ 24:18 n.2

Parke v. Raley, 506 U.S. 20, 113 S. Ct. 517, 121 L. Ed. 2d 391 (1992)— § 26:28 n.37, 44

Parker v. Abernathy, 253 Ga. 673, 324 S.E.2d 191 (1985)—§ 28:17 n.11

Parker v. Gladden, 385 U.S. 363, 87 S. Ct. 468, 17 L. Ed. 2d 420 (1966)—§§ 24:19 n.10; 25:7 n.2, 15

Parker v. Randolph, 442 U.S. 62, 99 S. Ct. 2132, 60 L. Ed. 2d 713 (1979)—§ 14:72 n.41

Parker v. State, 296 Ga. 586, 769 S.E.2d 329 (2015)—§ 14:96 n.10

Parker v. State, 320 Ga. App. 319, 741 S.E.2d 159 (2013)—§ 26:21 n.45

Parker v. State, 277 Ga. 439, 588 S.E.2d 683 (2003)—§ 19:5 n.6

Parker v. State, 249 Ga. App. 509, 548 S.E.2d 475 (2001)—§ 18:38 n.25

Parker v. State, 229 Ga. App. 217, 493 S.E.2d 558 (1997)—§ 4:41 n.12

Parker v. State, 226 Ga. App. 462, 486 S.E.2d 687 (1997)—§ 25:2 n.12

Parker v. State, 220 Ga. App. 303, 469 S.E.2d 410 (1996)—§ 7:2 n.11

Parker v. State, 219 Ga. App. 361, 464 S.E.2d 910 (1995)—§ 18:31 n.80, 123, 127

Parker v. State, 255 Ga. 167, 336 S.E.2d 242 (1985)—§ 20:6 n.19

Parker v. State, 172 Ga. App. 540, 323 S.E.2d 826 (1984)—§ 18:26 n.27

Parker v. State, 170 Ga. App. 333, 317 S.E.2d 209 (1984)—§ 14:60 n.10

Parker v. State, 161 Ga. App. 478, 288 S.E.2d 297 (1982)—§ 5:19 n.24

Parker v. State, 161 Ga. App. 37, 288 S.E.2d 852 (1982)—§§ 4:32 n.4; 4:50 n.20, 25

Parker v. State, 155 Ga. App. 617, 271 S.E.2d 871 (1980)—§ 21:25 n.17

Parker v. State, 154 Ga. App. 668, 269 S.E.2d 518 (1980)—§ 17:9 n.18

Parker v. State, 81 Ga. 332, 6 S.E. 600 (1888)—§ 25:4 n.19

Parker v. State, 34 Ga. 262, 1866 WL 1120 (1866)—§§ 18:16 n.4; 18:20 n.29

Parkerson v. State, 156 Ga. App. 440, 274 S.E.2d 799 (1980)—§ 26:19 n.27

Parks v. State, 281 Ga. App. 679, 637 S.E.2d 46 (2006)—§ 5:21 n.10

Parks v. State, 275 Ga. 320, 565 S.E.2d 447 (2002)—§ 17:8 n.3

Parks v. State, 241 Ga. App. 381, 526 S.E.2d 893 (1999)—§ 24:11 n.9

Parks v. State, 223 Ga. App. 694, 479 S.E.2d 3 (1996)—§ 16:4 n.1

Parks v. State, 180 Ga. App. 31, 348 S.E.2d 481 (1986)—§ 14:22 n.14

Parks v. State, 254 Ga. 403, 330 S.E.2d 686, 62 A.L.R.4th 833 (1985)— §§ 12:9 n.14, 21; 14:35 n.17

Patterson v. State, 154 Ga. App. 877, 270 S.E.2d 86 (1980)—§§ 14:8 n.17; 17:12 n.10, 11; 18:26 n.46

Patterson v. State, 239 Ga. 409, 238 S.E.2d 2 (1977)—§ 18:20 n.2

Patterson v. State, 238 Ga. 204, 232 S.E.2d 233 (1977)—§ 14:5 n.4

Patterson v. State, 138 Ga. App. 290, 226 S.E.2d 115 (1976)—§ 21:27 n.4

Patterson v. State, 233 Ga. 724, 213 S.E.2d 612 (1975)—§ 21:8 n.11, 12

Patterson v. State, 133 Ga. App. 742, 212 S.E.2d 858 (1975)—§ 4:41 n.6

Patterson v. State, 124 Ga. 408, 52 S.E. 534 (1905)—§ 23:5 n.1

Patterson v. State, 122 Ga. 587, 50 S.E. 489 (1905)—§ 13:11 n.25

Pattman v. State, 236 Ga. App. 786, 513 S.E.2d 761 (1999)—§ 14:12 n.8

Patton v. State, 148 Ga. App. 793, 252 S.E.2d 678 (1979)—§ 4:21 n.14

Patton v. U.S., 281 U.S. 276, 50 S. Ct. 253, 74 L. Ed. 854, 70 A.L.R. 263 (1930)—§ 17:14 n.13, 17

Patton v. Yount, 467 U.S. 1025, 104 S. Ct. 2885, 81 L. Ed. 2d 847 (1984)—§ 14:76 n.18

Paul v. State, 274 Ga. 601, 555 S.E.2d 716 (2001)—§ 21:20 n.6

Paul v. State, 272 Ga. 845, 537 S.E.2d 58 (2000)—§ 17:5 n.15

Paul v. State, 170 Ga. App. 746, 318 S.E.2d 200 (1984)—§ 26:1 n.16

Paul, In re, 270 Ga. 680, 513 S.E.2d 219 (1999)—§ 14:99 n.15

Paulhill v. State, 229 Ga. 415, 191 S.E.2d 842 (1972)—§ 18:36 n.1

Paulk v. State, 5 Ga. App. 567, 63 S.E. 659 (1909)—§ 17:17 n.20

Paxton v. State, 160 Ga. App. 19, 285 S.E.2d 741 (1981)—§§ 2:11 n.17; 6:10 n.6

Paxton v. State, 159 Ga. App. 175, 282 S.E.2d 912 (1981)—§ 5:8 n.7, 8

Payne v. State of Ark., 356 U.S. 560, 78 S. Ct. 844, 2 L. Ed. 2d 975 (1958)—§ 5:4 n.5

Payne v. State, 269 Ga. App. 662, 605 S.E.2d 75 (2004)—§ 14:58 n.53

Payne v. State, 248 Ga. App. 158, 545 S.E.2d 336 (2001)—§§ 22:7 n.9; 24:2 n.39

Payne v. State, 232 Ga. App. 591, 502 S.E.2d 526 (1998)—§ 3:9 n.8

Payne v. State, 219 Ga. App. 318, 464 S.E.2d 884 (1995)—§ 26:8 n.6

Payne v. State, 217 Ga. App. 386, 460 S.E.2d 297 (1995)—§ 17:14 n.10

Payne v. State, 195 Ga. App. 523, 394 S.E.2d 781 (1990)—§ 18:35 n.5

Payne v. State, 168 Ga. App. 485, 309 S.E.2d 667 (1983)—§ 22:6 n.10

Payne v. State, 161 Ga. App. 233, 291 S.E.2d 236 (1982)—§ 7:4 n.41

Payne v. State, 233 Ga. 294, 210 S.E.2d 775 (1974)—§ 6:8 n.18

Payne v. Tennessee, 501 U.S. 808, 111 S. Ct. 2597, 115 L. Ed. 2d 720 (1991)—§ 26:5 n.2, 3

Payton v. New York, 445 U.S. 573, 100 S. Ct. 1371, 63 L. Ed. 2d 639 (1980)—§§ 2:5 n.3, 5, 16; 2:6 n.12; 2:31 n.17; 3:1 n.29; 4:28 n.6

Payton v. State, 177 Ga. App. 104, 338 S.E.2d 462 (1985)—§ 4:19 n.9

PBJ Development Co. v. Holben, 259 Ga. 594, 385 S.E.2d 658 (1989)—§ 27:4 n.16

Peachtree City, City of v. Shaver, 276 Ga. 298, 578 S.E.2d 409 (2003)—§ 13:23 n.12

Peacock v. State, 170 Ga. App. 309, 316 S.E.2d 864 (1984)—§ 4:10 n.18

Pealor v. State, 165 Ga. App. 387, 299 S.E.2d 904 (1983)—§ 14:29 n.15, 21

Pearce v. State, 256 Ga. App. 889, 570 S.E.2d 74 (2002)—§ 26:44 n.8

People v. Williams, 25 Cal. 4th 441, 106 Cal. Rptr. 2d 295, 21 P.3d 1209 (2001)—§ 24:24 n.16

People v. Williams, 51 Cal. App. 3d 346, 124 Cal. Rptr. 253 (4th Dist. 1975)—§ 4:57 n.14

People v. Wilson, 24 Ill. 2d 425, 182 N.E.2d 203 (1962)—§ 14:4 n.16

People v. Yopp, 25 Mich. App. 69, 180 N.W.2d 897 (1970)—§ 6:7 n.6

Perault v. State, 162 Ga. App. 294, 291 S.E.2d 122 (1982)—§ 18:37 n.7

Perdue v. State, 256 Ga. App. 765, 578 S.E.2d 456 (2002)—§ 3:9 n.9

Perdue v. State, 155 Ga. App. 802, 272 S.E.2d 766 (1980)—§ 30:8 n.18

Perdue v. State, 147 Ga. App. 648, 249 S.E.2d 657 (1978)—§ 17:5 n.16, 25

Perez v. Ledesma, 401 U.S. 82, 91 S. Ct. 674, 27 L. Ed. 2d 701 (1971)—§ 9:3 n.8

Perez v. State, 283 Ga. 196, 657 S.E.2d 846 (2008)—§§ 5:15 n.4; 5:17 n.12; 5:20 n.40

Perez v. State, 263 Ga. App. 411, 588 S.E.2d 269 (2003)—§ 14:99 n.13

Perez, In re, 682 F.3d 930 (11th Cir. 2012)—§ 7:4 n.87

Perkins v. State, 279 Ga. 506, 614 S.E.2d 92 (2005)—§ 14:51 n.13

Perkins v. State, 269 Ga. 791, 505 S.E.2d 16 (1998)—§ 21:33 n.1

Perkins v. State, 220 Ga. App. 524, 469 S.E.2d 796 (1996)—§ 4:10 n.26, 29

Perkins v. State, 197 Ga. App. 577, 398 S.E.2d 702 (1990)—§ 14:83 n.36

Perkins v. State, 151 Ga. App. 199, 259 S.E.2d 193 (1979)—§ 5:13 n.8

Perkins v. State, 143 Ga. App. 124, 237 S.E.2d 658 (1977)—§ 14:60 n.14

Perkinson v. State, 279 Ga. 232, 610 S.E.2d 533 (2005)—§ 14:76 n.28, 29

Perkinson v. State, 273 Ga. 491, 542 S.E.2d 92 (2001)—§ 20:4 n.29

Perry v. Leeke, 488 U.S. 272, 109 S. Ct. 594, 102 L. Ed. 2d 624 (1989)—§ 7:1 n.2, 12

Perry v. Mitchell, 253 Ga. 593, 322 S.E.2d 273 (1984)—§ 14:70 n.18

Perry v. New Hampshire, 565 U.S. 228, 132 S. Ct. 716, 181 L. Ed. 2d 694 (2012)—§ 6:3 n.25

Perry v. State, 232 Ga. App. 484, 500 S.E.2d 923 (1998)—§ 23:7 n.13

Perry v. State, 216 Ga. App. 661, 455 S.E.2d 607 (1995)—§ 18:27 n.5

Perry v. State, 213 Ga. App. 220, 444 S.E.2d 150 (1994)—§ 30:1 n.8

Perry v. State, 255 Ga. 490, 339 S.E.2d 922 (1986)—§§ 14:30 n.53; 18:35 n.3; 24:15 n.4

Perry v. State, 154 Ga. App. 559, 269 S.E.2d 63 (1980)—§ 20:4 n.35

Perry v. State, 143 Ga. App. 227, 237 S.E.2d 705 (1977)—§ 21:25 n.27

Perry v. State, 62 Ga. App. 115, 8 S.E.2d 425 (1940)—§ 13:19 n.6

Perry v. State, 102 Ga. 365, 30 S.E. 903 (1897)—§ 19:6 n.3

Perryman v. State, 149 Ga. App. 54, 253 S.E.2d 444 (1979)—§ 14:84 n.6

Perryman v. State, 63 Ga. App. 819, 12 S.E.2d 388 (1940)—§ 21:24 n.2

Peruzzi v. State, 275 Ga. 333, 567 S.E.2d 15 (2002)—§ 3:5 n.9

Pervis v. State, 181 Ga. App. 613, 353 S.E.2d 200 (1987)—§ 4:46 n.15

Pestana v. State, 328 Ga. App. 454, 762 S.E.2d 178 (2014)—§ 14:98 n.2

Peterkin v. State, 147 Ga. App. 437, 249 S.E.2d 152 (1978)—§ 2:23 n.32

Peters v. Kiff, 407 U.S. 493, 92 S. Ct. 2163, 33 L. Ed. 2d 83 (1972)—§§ 12:4 n.5, 7; 12:9 n.19, 20

Peters v. State, 242 Ga. App. 816, 531 S.E.2d 386 (2000)—§ 3:10 n.1

Pope v. State, 256 Ga. 195, 345 S.E.2d 831 (1986)—§§ 14:77 n.11; 18:2 n.4; 18:17 n.21

Pope v. State, 172 Ga. App. 396, 323 S.E.2d 268 (1984)—§ 21:14 n.3

Pope v. State, 170 Ga. App. 799, 318 S.E.2d 223 (1984)—§ 18:19 n.13

Pope v. State, 169 Ga. App. 969, 315 S.E.2d 685 (1984)—§ 26:14 n.13

Pope v. State, 167 Ga. App. 328, 306 S.E.2d 326 (1983)—§ 21:17 n.17

Pope v. State, 157 Ga. App. 154, 276 S.E.2d 666 (1981)—§ 24:18 n.8

Pope v. State, 52 Ga. App. 411, 183 S.E. 630 (1936)—§ 24:2 n.1

Pope v. State, 42 Ga. App. 680, 157 S.E. 211 (1931)—§ 17:17 n.40

Pope v. U.S., 372 F.2d 710 (8th Cir. 1967)—§ 14:93 n.17

Pope v. U.S., 298 F.2d 507 (5th Cir. 1962)—§ 21:12 n.24

Porter v. State, 272 Ga. 533, 531 S.E.2d 97 (2000)—§ 21:20 n.5

Porter v. State, 243 Ga. App. 498, 532 S.E.2d 407 (2000)—§§ 14:93 n.19; 21:11 n.1

Porter v. State, 271 Ga. 498, 521 S.E.2d 566 (1999)—§ 28:11 n.20

Porter v. State, 209 Ga. App. 27, 432 S.E.2d 629 (1993)—§ 4:59 n.16

Porter v. State, 258 Ga. 94, 365 S.E.2d 438 (1988)—§ 7:6 n.18

Porter v. State, 143 Ga. App. 640, 239 S.E.2d 694 (1977)—§§ 5:5 n.2; 20:6 n.33

Porter v. State, 142 Ga. App. 481, 236 S.E.2d 172 (1977)—§ 30:1 n.6

Porter v. State, 141 Ga. App. 602, 234 S.E.2d 100 (1977)—§ 24:9 n.3

Porter v. State, 237 Ga. 580, 229 S.E.2d 384 (1976)—§ 18:11 n.14

Porter v. State, 200 Ga. 246, 36 S.E.2d 794 (1946)—§ 13:28 n.17

Porter v. State, 124 Ga. 297, 52 S.E. 283 (1905)—§§ 2:6 n.3, 4, 5, 6; 2:13 n.3, 4, 5

Porterfield v. State, 139 Ga. App. 553, 228 S.E.2d 722 (1976)—§ 26:46 n.4

Portis v. Evans, 250 Ga. 239, 297 S.E.2d 248 (1982)—§ 28:20 n.11

Portis v. Evans, 249 Ga. 396, 291 S.E.2d 511 (1982)—§ 28:20 n.10

Portuondo v. Agard, 529 U.S. 61, 120 S. Ct. 1119, 146 L. Ed. 2d 47, 53 Fed. R. Evid. Serv. 337 (2000)—§ 23:8 n.6

Posey v. State, 222 Ga. App. 405, 474 S.E.2d 206 (1996)—§ 14:22 n.28

Posey v. U.S., 416 F.2d 545 (5th Cir. 1969)—§ 24:26 n.19

Poss v. State, 167 Ga. App. 86, 305 S.E.2d 884 (1983)—§ 2:21 n.12

Poss v. State, 114 Ga. App. 609, 152 S.E.2d 695 (1966)—§ 26:19 n.17

Post v. State, 298 Ga. 241, 779 S.E.2d 624 (2015)—§ 14:77 n.5

Postell v. Humphrey, 278 Ga. 651, 604 S.E.2d 517 (2004)—§ 30:2 n.20

Postell v. State, 226 Ga. App. 843, 487 S.E.2d 422 (1997)—§ 5:1 n.16

Postell v. State, 264 Ga. 249, 443 S.E.2d 628 (1994)—§ 3:6 n.19

Potter v. Davis, 519 F. Supp. 621 (E.D. Tenn. 1981)—§ 28:19 n.10

Potter v. State, 283 Ga. 576, 662 S.E.2d 128 (2008)—§ 5:10 n.18

Potter v. State, 273 Ga. 325, 540 S.E.2d 184 (2001)—§ 7:4 n.36

Potts v. State, 207 Ga. App. 863, 429 S.E.2d 526 (1993)—§ 14:35 n.8

Potts v. State, 261 Ga. 716, 410 S.E.2d 89 (1991)—§§ 14:53 n.11, 14; 14:55 n.19; 23:7 n.32; 24:22 n.16

Potts v. State, 259 Ga. 812, 388 S.E.2d 678 (1990)—§§ 7:4 n.39; 12:9 n.16

Potts v. State, 257 Ga. 402, 359 S.E.2d 916 (1987)—§ 14:58 n.10

Potts v. State, 241 Ga. 67, 243 S.E.2d 510 (1978)—§ 21:11 n.15

Presnell v. State, 241 Ga. 49, 243 S.E.2d 496 (1978)—§§ 14:93 n.14; 21:10 n.21; 26:9 n.8; 26:11 n.4

Press-Enterprise Co. v. Superior Court of California for Riverside County, 478 U.S. 1, 106 S. Ct. 2735, 92 L. Ed. 2d 1 (1986)—§ 17:2 n.4

Press-Enterprise Co. v. Superior Court of California, Riverside County, 464 U.S. 501, 104 S. Ct. 819, 78 L. Ed. 2d 629 (1984)—§ 18:15 n.1

Pressel v. State, 163 Ga. App. 188, 292 S.E.2d 553 (1982)—§§ 4:6 n.3; 14:5 n.5

Pressley v. State, 158 Ga. App. 638, 281 S.E.2d 364 (1981)—§ 26:41 n.5

Preston v. State, 296 Ga. App. 655, 675 S.E.2d 553 (2009)—§ 4:34 n.32, 36

Preston v. State, 282 Ga. 210, 647 S.E.2d 260 (2007)—§ 21:20 n.5

Preston v. U.S., 376 U.S. 364, 84 S. Ct. 881, 11 L. Ed. 2d 777 (1964)— §§ 4:26 n.3; 4:49 n.3

Price v. Cobb, 60 Ga. App. 59, 3 S.E.2d 131 (1939)—§ 17:19 n.2

Price v. Georgia, 398 U.S. 323, 90 S. Ct. 1757, 26 L. Ed. 2d 300 (1970)—§§ 14:55 n.14, 15, 16; 14:61 n.1

Price v. State, 310 Ga. App. 132, 712 S.E.2d 135 (2011)—§ 17:5 n.22

Price v. State, 289 Ga. 459, 712 S.E.2d 828 (2011)—§ 21:7 n.2

Price v. State, 269 Ga. 222, 498 S.E.2d 262 (1998)—§ 14:30 n.11

Price v. State, 223 Ga. App. 185, 477 S.E.2d 353 (1996)—§§ 14:22 n.12; 16:2 n.15

Price v. State, 194 Ga. App. 453, 390 S.E.2d 663 (1990)—§§ 5:23 n.10; 6:8 n.24

Price v. State, 179 Ga. App. 598, 347 S.E.2d 608 (1986)—§ 21:12 n.5

Price v. State, 175 Ga. App. 780, 334 S.E.2d 711 (1985)—§ 23:8 n.10

Price v. State, 247 Ga. 58, 273 S.E.2d 854 (1981)—§ 26:40 n.1, 2

Price v. State, 160 Ga. App. 245, 286 S.E.2d 744 (1981)—§ 2:22 n.7

Price v. State, 159 Ga. App. 662, 284 S.E.2d 676 (1981)—§ 6:10 n.4, 22

Price v. State, 155 Ga. App. 844, 273 S.E.2d 225 (1980)—§ 14:72 n.16

Price v. State, 155 Ga. App. 206, 270 S.E.2d 203 (1980)—§ 14:73 n.13

Price v. State, 149 Ga. App. 397, 254 S.E.2d 512 (1979)—§ 17:1 n.1

Price v. Vincent, 538 U.S. 634, 123 S. Ct. 1848, 155 L. Ed. 2d 877 (2003)—§ 28:19 n.5

Pride v. Kemp, 289 Ga. 353, 711 S.E.2d 653 (2011)—§ 15:4 n.5

Priest v. State, 265 Ga. 399, 456 S.E.2d 503 (1995)—§§ 14:58 n.23; 28:8 n.5

Priester v. State, 249 Ga. App. 594, 549 S.E.2d 429 (2001)—§ 24:2 n.27

Prince v. State, 277 Ga. 230, 587 S.E.2d 637 (2003)—§ 18:21 n.13

Prince v. State, 142 Ga. App. 734, 236 S.E.2d 918 (1977)—§ 24:5 n.3

Prindle v. State, 240 Ga. App. 461, 523 S.E.2d 44 (1999)—§§ 13:23 n.26, 31; 14:30 n.28

Printup v. State, 142 Ga. App. 42, 234 S.E.2d 840 (1977)—§ 21:12 n.23

Pritchard v. State, 300 Ga. App. 14, 684 S.E.2d 88 (2009)—§ 4:21 n.20

Pritchard v. State, 224 Ga. 776, 164 S.E.2d 808 (1968)—§ 21:1 n.4

Pritchett v. State, 92 Ga. 65, 18 S.E. 536 (1893)—§ 17:5 n.5

Prock v. State, 246 Ga. App. 703, 541 S.E.2d 685 (2000)—§ 14:48 n.10

Proctor v. State, 235 Ga. 720, 221 S.E.2d 556 (1975)—§ 20:6 n.64, 65

Raymond v. State, 162 Ga. App. 493, 292 S.E.2d 196 (1982)—§ 28:11 n.1
Raymond v. State, 129 Ga. App. 17, 198 S.E.2d 430 (1973)—§ 4:52 n.6
R.D.F., In Interest of, 266 Ga. 294, 466 S.E.2d 572 (1996)—§ 5:8 n.4
Reaves v. State, 292 Ga. 582, 740 S.E.2d 141 (2013)—§ 5:20 n.40
Reaves v. State, 284 Ga. 181, 664 S.E.2d 211 (2008)—§§ 4:22 n.3; 5:4 n.9; 14:5 n.12
Reaves v. State, 242 Ga. 542, 250 S.E.2d 376 (1978)—§§ 12:13 n.35; 14:67 n.89; 14:71 n.5; 14:76 n.31; 18:37 n.16
Reaves v. State, 284 Ga. App. 181—§ 5:26 n.13
Rebeiro v. State, 186 Ga. App. 518, 367 S.E.2d 857 (1988)—§ 3:4 n.24
Recoba v. State, 179 Ga. App. 31, 345 S.E.2d 81 (1986)—§ 24:19 n.2
Recoba v. State, 167 Ga. App. 447, 306 S.E.2d 713 (1983)—§ 14:90 n.2
Rector v. State, 213 Ga. App. 450, 444 S.E.2d 862 (1994)—§ 18:31 n.79, 135, 161
Redd v. State, 229 Ga. App. 364, 494 S.E.2d 31 (1997)—§ 3:10 n.21
Redd v. State, 242 Ga. 876, 252 S.E.2d 383 (1979)—§§ 14:62 n.9; 18:17 n.10
Redd v. State, 240 Ga. 753, 243 S.E.2d 16 (1978)—§ 26:10 n.5
Reddick v. State, 264 Ga. App. 487, 591 S.E.2d 392 (2003)—§ 25:6 n.18
Reddick v. State, 249 Ga. App. 678, 549 S.E.2d 151 (2001)—§ 26:33 n.23
Redding v. State, 296 Ga. 471, 769 S.E.2d 67 (2015)—§ 24:22 n.6
Redding v. State, 205 Ga. App. 613, 423 S.E.2d 10 (1992)—§ 14:65 n.1
Redding v. State, 192 Ga. App. 87, 383 S.E.2d 640 (1989)—§§ 4:7 n.25; 4:10 n.28; 14:87 n.9
Redding v. State, 151 Ga. App. 140, 259 S.E.2d 146 (1979)—§ 23:8 n.3
Redding v. State, 214 Ga. 524, 106 S.E.2d 5 (1958)—§ 22:7 n.12
Reddish v. State, 161 Ga. App. 170, 288 S.E.2d 266 (1982)—§ 4:11 n.6
Reddish v. State, 238 Ga. 136, 231 S.E.2d 737 (1977)—§ 14:72 n.33
Reddish v. State, 101 Ga. App. 759, 115 S.E.2d 736 (1960)—§ 13:7 n.2
Redeford v. State, 93 Nev. 649, 572 P.2d 219 (1977)—§ 24:26 n.19
Redfearn v. Thompson, 10 Ga. App. 550, 73 S.E. 949 (1912)—§ 25:7 n.17
Redmon v. Johnson, 302 Ga. 763, 809 S.E.2d 468 (2018)—§ 28:17 n.87
Redmond v. State, 252 Ga. 142, 312 S.E.2d 315 (1984)—§ 14:22 n.22
Reece v. State of Ga., 350 U.S. 85, 76 S. Ct. 167, 100 L. Ed. 77 (1955)—§ 12:8 n.8
Reece v. State, 257 Ga. App. 137, 570 S.E.2d 424 (2002)—§ 4:44 n.4
Reece v. State, 152 Ga. App. 760, 264 S.E.2d 258 (1979)—§ 4:43 n.2
Reed v. Farley, 512 U.S. 339, 114 S. Ct. 2291, 129 L. Ed. 2d 277 (1994)—§ 14:71 n.20
Reed v. State, 318 Ga. App. 412, 734 S.E.2d 113 (2012)—§ 24:15 n.9
Reed v. State, 267 Ga. 482, 480 S.E.2d 27 (1997)—§ 18:38 n.12
Reed v. State, 222 Ga. App. 376, 474 S.E.2d 264 (1996)—§§ 14:58 n.11; 21:28 n.5
Reed v. State, 205 Ga. App. 209, 422 S.E.2d 15 (1992)—§§ 13:20 n.12; 14:99 n.6
Reed v. State, 195 Ga. App. 821, 395 S.E.2d 294 (1990)—§ 4:56 n.28
Reed v. State, 163 Ga. App. 364, 295 S.E.2d 108 (1982)—§ 14:29 n.24, 46
Reed v. State, 126 Ga. App. 323, 190 S.E.2d 587 (1972)—§§ 4:12 n.28; 14:78 n.13; 14:88 n.12

Riley v. State, 242 Ga. App. 720, 531 S.E.2d 138 (2000)—§ 14:34 n.15

Riley v. State, 212 Ga. App. 519, 442 S.E.2d 7 (1994)—§ 14:67 n.76

Riley v. State, 257 Ga. 91, 355 S.E.2d 66 (1987)—§ 5:3 n.6

Riley v. State, 180 Ga. App. 409, 349 S.E.2d 274 (1986)—§§ 14:69 n.1, 2; 17:8 n.8

Riley v. State, 174 Ga. App. 607, 330 S.E.2d 808 (1985)—§ 17:17 n.49

Riley v. State, 237 Ga. 124, 226 S.E.2d 922 (1976)—§ 20:6 n.49

Riley v. State, 107 Ga. App. 639, 131 S.E.2d 124 (1963)—§ 28:15 n.3

Rimmer v. State, 197 Ga. App. 294, 398 S.E.2d 282 (1990)—§ 14:87 n.17

Rinaldi v. U. S., 434 U.S. 22, 98 S. Ct. 81, 54 L. Ed. 2d 207 (1977)—§ 14:59 n.3, 5

Ring v. Arizona, 536 U.S. 584, 122 S. Ct. 2428, 153 L. Ed. 2d 556 (2002)—§§ 26:11 n.24; 26:43 n.8

Rini v. State, 236 Ga. 715, 225 S.E.2d 234 (1976)—§ 14:34 n.33

Rini v. State, 235 Ga. 60, 218 S.E.2d 811 (1975)—§ 14:34 n.35

Rinker v. State, 228 Ga. App. 767, 492 S.E.2d 746 (1997)—§ 25:4 n.7

Rios v. U.S., 364 U.S. 253, 80 S. Ct. 1431, 4 L. Ed. 2d 1688 (1960)—§ 4:38 n.3

Ristaino v. Ross, 424 U.S. 589, 96 S. Ct. 1017, 47 L. Ed. 2d 258 (1976)—§ 18:27 n.1

Ritchie v. State, 257 Ga. App. 149, 570 S.E.2d 435 (2002)—§§ 28:3 n.20; 28:17 n.50

Rivas v. U.S., 368 F.2d 703 (9th Cir. 1966)—§ 4:45 n.8

Rivera v. Illinois, 556 U.S. 148, 129 S. Ct. 1446, 173 L. Ed. 2d 320 (2009)—§ 18:31 n.168

Rivers v. State, 225 Ga. App. 558, 484 S.E.2d 519 (1997)—§ 14:73 n.15

Rivers v. State, 265 Ga. 694, 461 S.E.2d 205 (1995)—§ 2:22 n.6

Rivers v. State, 250 Ga. 303, 298 S.E.2d 1 (1982)—§§ 7:2 n.28; 7:4 n.64

Rivers v. State, 250 Ga. 288, 298 S.E.2d 10 (1982)—§§ 4:16 n.3; 4:24 n.6; 21:8 n.6; 26:11 n.14

Riverside, County of v. McLaughlin, 500 U.S. 44, 111 S. Ct. 1661, 114 L. Ed. 2d 49 (1991)—§§ 5:4 n.32; 11:1 n.3

Rizzo v. Goode, 423 U.S. 362, 96 S. Ct. 598, 46 L. Ed. 2d 561 (1976)—§ 9:3 n.13

Robbins v. State, 290 Ga. App. 323, 659 S.E.2d 628 (2008)—§ 4:60 n.20

Roberson v. State, 300 Ga. 632, 797 S.E.2d 104 (2017)—§ 28:7 n.6

Roberson v. State, 246 Ga. App. 534, 540 S.E.2d 688 (2000)—§§ 4:7 n.11; 4:10 n.3

Roberson v. State, 265 Ga. 658, 461 S.E.2d 212 (1995)—§ 5:20 n.56

Robert Hawthorne, Inc. v. Director of Internal Revenue, 406 F. Supp. 1098 (E.D. Pa. 1975)—§ 12:2 n.4

Roberts v. Gordon, 86 Ga. 386, 12 S.E. 648 (1890)—§ 8:1 n.23

Roberts v. Greenway, 233 Ga. 473, 211 S.E.2d 764 (1975)—§§ 16:2 n.9; 16:15 n.3

Roberts v. LaVallee, 389 U.S. 40, 88 S. Ct. 194, 19 L. Ed. 2d 41 (1967)—§§ 11:4 n.17; 28:7 n.1

Roberts v. Reilly, 116 U.S. 80, 6 S. Ct. 291, 29 L. Ed. 544 (1885)—§ 2:23 n.1

Roberts v. State, 278 Ga. 610, 604 S.E.2d 781 (2004)—§ 14:2 n.7

Robinson v. State, 179 Ga. App. 616, 347 S.E.2d 667 (1986)—§ 6:6 n.39

Robinson v. State, 173 Ga. App. 285, 326 S.E.2d 245 (1985)—§ 16:13 n.8

Robinson v. State, 166 Ga. App. 741, 305 S.E.2d 381 (1983)—§ 2:31 n.6

Robinson v. State, 164 Ga. App. 379, 296 S.E.2d 225 (1982)—§§ 6:4 n.27; 17:5 n.6

Robinson v. State, 248 Ga. 627, 284 S.E.2d 400 (1981)—§ 24:5 n.12

Robinson v. State, 154 Ga. App. 591, 269 S.E.2d 86 (1980)—§ 30:7 n.1

Robinson v. State, 146 Ga. App. 318, 246 S.E.2d 518 (1978)—§ 18:1 n.9

Robinson v. State, 145 Ga. App. 17, 243 S.E.2d 257 (1978)—§ 21:25 n.27

Robinson v. State, 238 Ga. 291, 232 S.E.2d 561 (1977)—§ 18:16 n.2

Robinson v. State, 232 Ga. 123, 205 S.E.2d 210 (1974)—§§ 5:1 n.7, 8; 5:2 n.1

Robinson v. State, 229 Ga. 14, 189 S.E.2d 53 (1972)—§ 5:5 n.11

Robinson v. State, 93 Ga. App. 203, 91 S.E.2d 52 (1956)—§ 13:20 n.1, 3

Robinson v. State, 209 Ga. 650, 75 S.E.2d 9 (1953)—§ 25:2 n.26

Robinson v. State, 86 Ga. App. 375, 71 S.E.2d 677 (1952)—§ 14:76 n.5

Robinson v. State, 109 Ga. 506, 34 S.E. 1017 (1900)—§ 25:4 n.8

Robinson v. State, 93 Ga. 77, 18 S.E. 1018 (1893)—§ 2:6 n.22

Robles v. State, 277 Ga. 415, 589 S.E.2d 566 (2003)—§ 14:2 n.2

Rocco v. State, 267 Ga. App. 900, 601 S.E.2d 189 (2004)—§ 8:3 n.16, 19

Rocha v. State, 287 Ga. App. 446, 651 S.E.2d 781 (2007)—§ 28:11 n.8

Rochin v. California, 342 U.S. 165, 72 S. Ct. 205, 96 L. Ed. 183, 25 A.L.R.2d 1396 (1952)—§ 4:57 n.21

Rockdale Citizen Pub. Co. v. State, 266 Ga. 92, 463 S.E.2d 864 (1995)— § 17:2 n.14

Rockdale Citizen Pub. Co., Inc. v. State, 266 Ga. 579, 468 S.E.2d 764 (1996)—§ 17:2 n.7

Rockholt v. State, 129 Ga. App. 99, 198 S.E.2d 885 (1973)—§§ 2:14 n.5; 26:8 n.11

Roden v. State, 181 Ga. App. 287, 351 S.E.2d 713 (1986)—§§ 14:38 n.14; 21:25 n.12; 21:26 n.5

Rodriguez v. State, 295 Ga. 362, 761 S.E.2d 19 (2014)—§ 3:2 n.39

Rodriguez v. State, 191 Ga. App. 241, 381 S.E.2d 529 (1989)—§ 4:25 n.6

Rodriguez v. State, 378 So. 2d 7 (Fla. 2d DCA 1979)—§ 26:19 n.13

Rodriguez v. U.S., 135 S. Ct. 1609, 191 L. Ed. 2d 492 (2015)—§§ 3:9 n.29; 4:48 n.15; 4:57 n.13

Rodriguez v. U.S., 227 F.2d 912 (5th Cir. 1955)—§ 21:25 n.19

Roe v. Flores-Ortega, 528 U.S. 470, 120 S. Ct. 1029, 145 L. Ed. 2d 985 (2000)—§ 7:5 n.3

Roe v. Wade, 410 U.S. 113, 93 S. Ct. 705, 35 L. Ed. 2d 147 (1973)—§ 9:3 n.9

Roebuck v. State, 261 Ga. App. 679, 583 S.E.2d 523 (2003)—§ 18:24 n.43

Roebuck v. State, 57 Ga. 154, 1876 WL 3117 (1876)—§ 14:67 n.13

Roesser v. State, 294 Ga. 295, 751 S.E.2d 297 (2013)—§ 14:57 n.9

Rogers v. Hall, 567 Fed. Appx. 873 (11th Cir. 2014)—§ 17:8 n.11

Rogers v. McMackin, 884 F.2d 252 (6th Cir. 1989)—§ 14:72 n.57

Rogers v. Richmond, 365 U.S. 534, 81 S. Ct. 735, 5 L. Ed. 2d 760 (1961)—§§ 4:32 n.31; 5:7 n.2

Rogers v. Rogers, 138 Ga. 803, 76 S.E. 48 (1912)—§ 17:10 n.22

S

Sachtjen v. State, 340 Ga. App. 612, 798 S.E.2d 114 (2017)—§ 14:6 n.9

Saffle v. Parks, 494 U.S. 484, 110 S. Ct. 1257, 108 L. Ed. 2d 415 (1990)—§ 14:64 n.8

Safford v. State, 240 Ga. App. 80, 522 S.E.2d 565 (1999)—§ 4:45 n.12

Safford Unified School Dist. No. 1 v. Redding, 557 U.S. 364, 129 S. Ct. 2633, 174 L. Ed. 2d 354, 245 Ed. Law Rep. 626 (2009)—§ 4:60 n.25

Saine v. State, 170 Ga. App. 610, 317 S.E.2d 650 (1984)—§ 26:14 n.17

Sakobie v. State, 115 Ga. App. 460, 154 S.E.2d 830 (1967)—§ 18:33 n.3

Salazar-Balderas v. State, 343 Ga. App. 201, 806 S.E.2d 644 (2017)— § 21:19 n.1

Sale v. Leachman, 218 Ga. 834, 131 S.E.2d 185 (1963)—§ 10:2 n.15

Saleem v. State, 152 Ga. App. 552, 263 S.E.2d 490 (1979)—§ 28:3 n.15

Salem v. State, 228 Ga. 186, 184 S.E.2d 650 (1971)—§ 24:18 n.1, 7

Salem v. State, 101 Ga. App. 905, 115 S.E.2d 447 (1960)—§§ 27:2 n.6; 27:5 n.4

Saliba v. Saliba, 201 Ga. 681, 40 S.E.2d 732 (1946)—§ 28:2 n.7, 8

Salinas v. Texas, 570 U.S. 178, 133 S. Ct. 2174, 186 L. Ed. 2d 376 (2013)—§ 5:21 n.13

Salisbury v. State, 223 Ga. 414, 156 S.E.2d 48 (1967)—§ 6:2 n.7

Salisbury v. State, 221 Ga. 718, 146 S.E.2d 776 (1966)—§ 23:8 n.2

Sallie v. State, 276 Ga. 506, 578 S.E.2d 444 (2003)—§ 14:66 n.16

Sallie v. State, 269 Ga. 446, 499 S.E.2d 897 (1998)—§ 7:11 n.39

Sallie v. State, 216 Ga. App. 502, 455 S.E.2d 315 (1995)—§§ 14:53 n.13; 20:4 n.29

Salmeron v. State, 280 Ga. 735, 632 S.E.2d 645 (2006)—§§ 3:2 n.31; 3:11 n.14; 4:32 n.39

Salmon v. State, 206 Ga. App. 469, 426 S.E.2d 160 (1992)—§ 4:59 n.27

Salter v. Greene, 226 Ga. App. 384, 486 S.E.2d 650 (1997)—§ 8:3 n.13

Salter v. State, 257 Ga. 88, 356 S.E.2d 196 (1987)—§ 21:11 n.11

Salyer, In Interest of, 44 Ill. App. 3d 854, 3 Ill. Dec. 648, 358 N.E.2d 1333 (3d Dist. 1977)—§ 4:34 n.43

Sammons v. State, 279 Ga. 386, 612 S.E.2d 785 (2005)—§§ 17:8 n.1; 24:19 n.7

Sammons v. State, 53 Ga. App. 369, 185 S.E. 923 (1936)—§ 17:14 n.3

Samples v. State, 217 Ga. App. 509, 460 S.E.2d 795 (1995)—§ 18:26 n.38

Sampson v. State, 165 Ga. App. 833, 303 S.E.2d 77 (1983)—§§ 4:5 n.13; 21:29 n.2

Sampson v. State, 124 Ga. 776, 53 S.E. 332 (1906)—§ 12:17 n.37

Samson v. California, 547 U.S. 843, 126 S. Ct. 2193, 165 L. Ed. 2d 250 (2006)—§ 4:44 n.10

Samuels v. Mackell, 401 U.S. 66, 91 S. Ct. 764, 27 L. Ed. 2d 688 (1971)—§ 9:3 n.14

Sanabria v. U. S., 437 U.S. 54, 98 S. Ct. 2170, 57 L. Ed. 2d 43 (1978)— § 14:58 n.26

San Antonio Independent School Dist. v. Rodriguez, 411 U.S. 1, 93 S. Ct. 1278, 36 L. Ed. 2d 16 (1973)—§ 26:4 n.8

Sanborn v. State, 251 Ga. 169, 304 S.E.2d 377 (1983)—§ 14:83 n.14

Sanchez-Villa v. State, 341 Ga. App. 264, 799 S.E.2d 364 (2017)—§ 14:83 n.9

Seaman v. State, 196 Ga. App. 634, 396 S.E.2d 525 (1990)—§ 10:2 n.7

Searcy v. State, 168 Ga. App. 233, 308 S.E.2d 621 (1983)—§ 24:4 n.6

Searcy v. State, 162 Ga. App. 695, 291 S.E.2d 557 (1982)—§ 26:44 n.11

Sears v. Humphrey, 294 Ga. 117, 751 S.E.2d 365 (2013)—§ 26:8 n.20

Sears v. State, 270 Ga. 834, 514 S.E.2d 426 (1999)—§§ 18:24 n.30; 24:14 n.4; 24:27 n.1

Sears v. State, 268 Ga. 759, 493 S.E.2d 180 (1997)—§§ 23:5 n.23, 24; 25:9 n.8

Sears v. State, 262 Ga. 805, 426 S.E.2d 553 (1993)—§§ 4:3 n.2; 12:9 n.37; 14:77 n.17; 18:3 n.1

Sears v. State, 182 Ga. App. 480, 356 S.E.2d 72 (1987)—§ 14:66 n.26

Sears v. State, 161 Ga. App. 515, 288 S.E.2d 757 (1982)—§ 14:30 n.54

Sears v. U.S., 343 F.2d 139 (5th Cir. 1965)—§ 21:25 n.20

Seay v. Hubbard, 240 Ga. 464, 241 S.E.2d 220 (1978)—§ 28:3 n.16

Seay v. State, 276 Ga. 139, 576 S.E.2d 839 (2003)—§ 24:13 n.12

Seckinger v. State, 267 Ga. 260, 477 S.E.2d 129 (1996)—§ 24:12 n.7

Segura v. U.S., 468 U.S. 796, 104 S. Ct. 3380, 82 L. Ed. 2d 599 (1984)—§§ 2:27 n.1; 4:28 n.21

Seitman v. State, 320 Ga. App. 646, 740 S.E.2d 368 (2013)—§ 17:14 n.9

Self v. State, 232 Ga. App. 735, 503 S.E.2d 625 (1998)—§ 14:30 n.25

Selfe v. State, 290 Ga. App. 857, 660 S.E.2d 727 (2008)—§ 20:4 n.15

Sell v. U.S., 539 U.S. 166, 123 S. Ct. 2174, 156 L. Ed. 2d 197, 188 A.L.R. Fed. 679 (2003)—§ 14:95 n.4

Sellers v. Smith, 412 F.2d 1002 (5th Cir. 1969)—§ 5:13 n.4

Sellers v. State, 263 Ga. App. 144, 587 S.E.2d 276 (2003)—§ 13:10 n.4

Sellers v. State, 107 Ga. App. 516, 130 S.E.2d 790 (1963)—§ 30:7 n.2

Semega v. State, 302 Ga. App. 879, 691 S.E.2d 923 (2010)—§ 24:24 n.18

Semple v. State, 271 Ga. 416, 519 S.E.2d 912, 86 A.L.R.5th 767 (1999)—§ 6:8 n.20

Senior v. State, 186 Ga. App. 861, 369 S.E.2d 49 (1988)—§ 21:15 n.3

Sentence Review Panel v. Moseley, 284 Ga. 128, 663 S.E.2d 679 (2008)—§ 29:1 n.1

Septum, Inc. v. Keller, 614 F.2d 456 (5th Cir. 1980)—§ 9:3 n.5

Serdula v. State, 344 Ga. App. 587, 812 S.E.2d 6 (2018)—§ 14:77 n.12

Seritt v. State of Ala., 731 F.2d 728 (11th Cir. 1984)—§ 26:2 n.29

Sermons v. State, 262 Ga. 286, 417 S.E.2d 144 (1992)—§§ 26:5 n.9; 26:14 n.20

Serrano v. State, 146 Ga. App. 781, 247 S.E.2d 593 (1978)—§ 20:6 n.62

Sessions v. State, 3 Ga. App. 13, 59 S.E. 196 (1907)—§ 28:13 n.7

Setser v. State, 209 Ga. App. 57, 432 S.E.2d 652 (1993)—§ 4:33 n.13

Sevilla-Carcamo v. State, 335 Ga. App. 788, 783 S.E.2d 150 (2016)—§ 4:34 n.38

Sevostiyanova v. State, 313 Ga. App. 729, 722 S.E.2d 333 (2012)—§ 21:21 n.2

Sewell v. State, 283 Ga. 558, 662 S.E.2d 537 (2008)—§ 5:12 n.6

Sewell v. State, 229 Ga. App. 685, 494 S.E.2d 512 (1997)—§§ 13:20 n.11; 14:1 n.7; 14:48 n.30

Seymour v. State, 312 Ga. App. 462, 718 S.E.2d 354 (2011)—§ 7:3 n.35

Shabazz v. State, 259 Ga. App. 339, 577 S.E.2d 45 (2003)—§ 16:10 n.21

Sherman v. United States, 356 U.S. 369, 78 S. Ct. 819, 2 L. Ed. 2d 848 (1958)—§ 21:25 n.5

Shields v. State, 264 Ga. App. 232, 590 S.E.2d 217 (2003)—§ 26:28 n.3

Shields v. State, 202 Ga. App. 659, 415 S.E.2d 478 (1992)—§§ 18:24 n.21; 18:26 n.12

Shields v. State, 162 Ga. App. 388, 291 S.E.2d 448 (1982)—§ 18:23 n.28

Shields v. State, 147 Ga. App. 131, 248 S.E.2d 205 (1978)—§ 20:7 n.20

Shields v. United States, 273 U.S. 583, 47 S. Ct. 478, 71 L. Ed. 787 (1927)—§ 24:19 n.11

Shifflett v. Com., 221 Va. 760, 274 S.E.2d 305, 17 A.L.R.4th 1260 (1981)—§ 21:10 n.16

Shinholster v. State, 150 Ga. App. 221, 257 S.E.2d 342 (1979)—§ 14:76 n.20

Shire v. State, 225 Ga. App. 306, 483 S.E.2d 694 (1997)—§ 14:67 n.27

Shirley v. State, 297 Ga. 722, 777 S.E.2d 444 (2015)—§ 4:9 n.15

Shirley v. State, 330 Ga. App. 424, 765 S.E.2d 491 (2014)—§ 4:9 n.14

Shirley v. State, 166 Ga. App. 456, 304 S.E.2d 468 (1983)—§§ 7:11 n.20; 14:85 n.12; 14:88 n.1

Shivers v. State, 286 Ga. 422, 688 S.E.2d 622 (2010)—§ 24:6 n.5

Shivers v. State, 188 Ga. App. 21, 372 S.E.2d 2 (1988)—§ 16:1 n.26

Shoemake v. State, 213 Ga. App. 528, 445 S.E.2d 558 (1994)—§ 16:14 n.1

Short v. State, 140 Ga. 780, 80 S.E. 8 (1913)—§ 21:20 n.15

Shorter v. State, 239 Ga. App. 625, 521 S.E.2d 684 (1999)—§ 3:7 n.21

Shorter v. Waters, 278 Ga. 558, 604 S.E.2d 472 (2004)—§ 7:4 n.97

Shorter v. Waters, 275 Ga. 581, 571 S.E.2d 373 (2002)—§ 7:4 n.97

Shuler v. State, 125 Ga. 778, 54 S.E. 689 (1906)—§ 13:23 n.21

Shumake v. State, 257 Ga. App. 209, 570 S.E.2d 648 (2002)—§ 16:12 n.2

Shuman v. State, 146 Ga. App. 822, 247 S.E.2d 561 (1978)—§ 25:1 n.10

Shy v. State, 234 Ga. 816, 218 S.E.2d 599 (1975)—§§ 5:12 n.6; 5:13 n.2, 3; 5:14 n.15

Sibert v. State, 259 Ga. 323, 380 S.E.2d 698 (1989)—§ 14:22 n.3

Sibron v. New York, 392 U.S. 40, 88 S.Ct. 1889, 20 L.Ed.2d 917 (1968)—§ 3:1 n.19

Siemon, In re, 264 Ga. 641, 449 S.E.2d 832 (1994)—§ 27:1 n.15

Sikes v. State, 268 Ga. 19, 485 S.E.2d 206 (1997)—§ 21:13 n.16

Sikes v. State, 105 Ga. 592, 31 S.E. 567 (1898)—§ 18:23 n.23

Silverthorne Lumber Co. v. U.S., 251 U.S. 385, 40 S. Ct. 182, 64 L. Ed. 319, 24 A.L.R. 1426 (1920)—§§ 2:24 n.10; 2:25 n.12, 13

Simile v. State, 259 Ga. App. 106, 576 S.E.2d 83 (2003)—§ 14:48 n.43

Simmons v. South Carolina, 512 U.S. 154, 114 S. Ct. 2187, 129 L. Ed. 2d 133 (1994)—§§ 14:64 n.8; 26:6 n.43; 26:8 n.26

Simmons v. State, 292 Ga. 265, 736 S.E.2d 402 (2013)—§ 15:2 n.9

Simmons v. State, 282 Ga. 183, 646 S.E.2d 55 (2007)—§ 18:26 n.6

Simmons v. State, 276 Ga. 525, 579 S.E.2d 735 (2003)—§ 7:5 n.2

Simmons v. State, 223 Ga. App. 781, 479 S.E.2d 123 (1996)—§ 3:11 n.19

Simmons v. State, 174 Ga. App. 906, 331 S.E.2d 923 (1985)—§ 26:36 n.5

Simmons v. State, 172 Ga. App. 695, 324 S.E.2d 546 (1984)—§ 22:7 n.3

Simmons v. State, 249 Ga. 860, 295 S.E.2d 84 (1982)—§ 17:14 n.2

Smith v. Williams, 277 Ga. 778, 596 S.E.2d 112 (2004)—§§ 7:4 n.79; 16:15 n.4

Smithwick v. Olson, 229 Ga. 494, 192 S.E.2d 337 (1972)—§ 2:23 n.24

Smithwick v. State, 199 Ga. 292, 34 S.E.2d 28 (1945)—§ 20:6 n.64

Snellings v. State, 194 Ga. App. 552, 391 S.E.2d 36 (1990)—§ 17:14 n.22

Snider v. State, 292 Ga. App. 180, 663 S.E.2d 805 (2008)—§ 14:83 n.30

Snow v. State, 229 Ga. App. 532, 494 S.E.2d 309 (1997)—§ 14:70 n.32

Snyder v. Louisiana, 552 U.S. 472, 128 S. Ct. 1203, 170 L. Ed. 2d 175 (2008)—§ 18:31 n.131

Snyder v. Com. of Mass., 291 U.S. 97, 54 S. Ct. 330, 78 L. Ed. 674, 90 A.L.R. 575 (1934)—§ 17:8 n.8, 22

Snyder v. State, 585 P.2d 229 (Alaska 1978)—§ 4:35 n.19

Solano-Rodriguez v. State, 295 Ga. App. 896, 673 S.E.2d 351 (2009)—§ 3:1 n.42

Solem v. Helm, 463 U.S. 277, 103 S. Ct. 3001, 77 L. Ed. 2d 637 (1983)—§ 26:2 n.25

Soles v. City of Vidalia, 92 Ga. App. 839, 90 S.E.2d 249 (1955)—§ 3:1 n.4

Solina v. U.S., 709 F.2d 160 (2d Cir. 1983)—§ 7:4 n.1

Soloman v. State, 143 Ga. App. 449, 238 S.E.2d 573 (1977)—§ 4:34 n.10

Solomon v. State, 232 Ga. 306, 206 S.E.2d 436 (1974)—§ 9:2 n.13

Somchith v. State, 272 Ga. 261, 527 S.E.2d 546 (2000)—§ 18:19 n.10, 24

Sorrells v. State, 218 Ga. App. 413, 461 S.E.2d 904 (1995)—§ 18:31 n.117

Sorrells v. U.S., 287 U.S. 435, 53 S. Ct. 210, 77 L. Ed. 413, 86 A.L.R. 249 (1932)—§ 21:25 n.5

Sosbee v. State, 155 Ga. App. 196, 270 S.E.2d 367 (1980)—§ 30:2 n.13

Sosebee v. State, 190 Ga. App. 746, 380 S.E.2d 464 (1989)—§§ 14:4 n.14; 17:17 n.41

Sosebee v. State, 169 Ga. App. 370, 312 S.E.2d 853 (1983)—§ 2:7 n.2

Sosniak v. State, 292 Ga. 35, 734 S.E.2d 362 (2012)—§§ 14:67 n.90; 14:70 n.40; 28:2 n.16

Souder v. State, 170 Ga. App. 413, 317 S.E.2d 251 (1984)—§ 5:20 n.34

South v. State, 268 Ga. App. 110, 601 S.E.2d 378 (2004)—§ 13:6 n.18

South v. State, 72 Ga. App. 79, 33 S.E.2d 23 (1945)—§ 28:15 n.2

Southall v. State, 300 Ga. 462, 796 S.E.2d 261 (2017)—§ 28:11 n.31

South Carolina v. Gathers, 490 U.S. 805, 109 S. Ct. 2207, 104 L. Ed. 2d 876 (1989)—§ 26:5 n.4

South Dakota v. Neville, 459 U.S. 553, 103 S. Ct. 916, 74 L. Ed. 2d 748 (1983)—§ 5:22 n.7

South Dakota v. Opperman, 428 U.S. 364, 96 S. Ct. 3092, 49 L. Ed. 2d 1000 (1976)—§§ 4:2 n.19; 4:48 n.5; 4:56 n.2; 4:57 n.19

Southern Exp. Co. v. State, 1 Ga. App. 700, 58 S.E. 67 (1907)—§ 13:15 n.6

Sovereign News Co. v. U.S., 690 F.2d 569 (6th Cir. 1982)—§ 4:14 n.16

Sowers v. State, 146 Ga. App. 701, 247 S.E.2d 225 (1978)—§§ 3:1 n.11; 3:9 n.22

Spain v. State, 243 Ga. 15, 252 S.E.2d 436 (1979)—§ 5:19 n.11

Spann v. State, 126 Ga. App. 370, 190 S.E.2d 924 (1972)—§ 23:8 n.2, 3

Spann v. Whitworth, 262 Ga. 21, 413 S.E.2d 713 (1992)—§ 29:2 n.3

Sparks v. State, 232 Ga. App. 179, 501 S.E.2d 562 (1998)—§ 15:2 n.5

Stack v. State, 234 Ga. 19, 214 S.E.2d 514, 88 A.L.R.3d 216 (1975)—
§ 18:26 n.8

Stafford v. State, 251 Ga. App. 203, 554 S.E.2d 219 (2001)—§ 26:24 n.10

Staggers v. State, 225 Ga. 581, 170 S.E.2d 430 (1969)—§ 14:58 n.2

Staley v. State, 224 Ga. App. 806, 482 S.E.2d 459 (1997)—§ 4:56 n.14

Stancil v. State, 155 Ga. App. 731, 272 S.E.2d 511 (1980)—§ 26:36 n.12

Standefer v. U.S., 447 U.S. 10, 100 S. Ct. 1999, 64 L. Ed. 2d 689
(1980)—§ 25:6 n.21

Standlee v. Rhay, 557 F.2d 1303 (9th Cir. 1977)—§ 29:5 n.2

Stanford v. Kentucky, 492 U.S. 361, 109 S. Ct. 2969, 106 L. Ed. 2d 306
(1989)—§ 26:6 n.23

Stanford v. State, 251 Ga. App. 87, 553 S.E.2d 622 (2001)—§ 3:2 n.41

Stanford v. State, 272 Ga. 267, 528 S.E.2d 246 (2000)—§§ 4:10 n.2; 17:7
n.23

Stanford v. State of Tex., 379 U.S. 476, 85 S. Ct. 506, 13 L. Ed. 2d 431
(1965)—§§ 4:12 n.3; 4:14 n.4

Stanley v. Georgia, 394 U.S. 557, 89 S. Ct. 1243, 22 L. Ed. 2d 542
(1969)—§ 4:23 n.1

Stanley v. State, 267 Ga. App. 656, 601 S.E.2d 141 (2004)—§ 17:14 n.11

Stanley v. State, 267 Ga. App. 379, 599 S.E.2d 331 (2004)—§ 17:14 n.19

Stanley v. State, 213 Ga. App. 95, 443 S.E.2d 633 (1994)—§ 3:7 n.6

Stanley v. State, 206 Ga. App. 125, 424 S.E.2d 90 (1992)—§ 14:84 n.10

Stanley v. State, 191 Ga. App. 603, 382 S.E.2d 686 (1989)—§ 3:6 n.4

Stanley v. State, 153 Ga. App. 42, 264 S.E.2d 533 (1980)—§ 24:2 n.28

Stanley v. State, 240 Ga. 341, 241 S.E.2d 173 (1977)—§ 26:11 n.3

Stanley v. State, 129 Ga. App. 759, 201 S.E.2d 182 (1973)—§ 2:14 n.6

Stanley v. State, 94 Ga. App. 737, 96 S.E.2d 195 (1956)—§ 20:7 n.28

Stansbury v. California, 511 U.S. 318, 114 S. Ct. 1526, 128 L. Ed. 2d 293
(1994)—§ 5:12 n.8

Stansell v. State, 270 Ga. 147, 510 S.E.2d 292 (1998)—§ 7:4 n.70

Staples v. State, 209 Ga. App. 802, 434 S.E.2d 757 (1993)—§ 18:31 n.24

Stapleton v. State, 235 Ga. 513, 220 S.E.2d 269 (1975)—§ 5:16 n.3

Stapleton v. Superior Court of Los Angeles County, 70 Cal. 2d 97, 73
Cal. Rptr. 575, 447 P.2d 967 (1968)—§ 4:60 n.13

Stapp v. State, 249 Ga. 289, 290 S.E.2d 439 (1982)—§ 16:9 n.1

Starks v. State, 262 Ga. 244, 416 S.E.2d 520 (1992)—§ 5:10 n.19

Starks v. State, 157 Ga. App. 579, 278 S.E.2d 156 (1981)—§ 24:18 n.4

Starling v. State, 242 Ga. App. 685, 530 S.E.2d 757 (2000)—§ 20:4 n.18

Starr v. State, 269 Ga. App. 466, 604 S.E.2d 297 (2004)—§§ 5:5 n.7; 17:5
n.48

State v. Abbott, 303 Ga. 297, 812 S.E.2d 225 (2018)—§ 2:29 n.11

State v. Abdi, 162 Ga. App. 20, 288 S.E.2d 772 (1982)—§ 14:58 n.42

State v. Abernathy, 289 Ga. 603, 715 S.E.2d 48 (2011)—§§ 7:11 n.18;
14:93 n.28; 17:1 n.13; 21:15 n.2

State v. Achter, 512 S.W.2d 894 (Mo. Ct. App. 1974)—§ 4:55 n.2, 3

State v. Addaquay, 302 Ga. 412, 807 S.E.2d 413 (2017)—§§ 7:4 n.84;
14:64 n.2

State v. Aduka, 303 Ga. 309, 812 S.E.2d 266 (2018)—§ 7:4 n.90

State v. Aguillard, 357 So. 2d 535 (La. 1978)—§ 4:26 n.12

State v. Philpot, 299 Ga. 206, 787 S.E.2d 181 (2016)—§ 5:20 n.45

State v. Pickens, 330 Ga. App. 862, 769 S.E.2d 594, 315 Ed. Law Rep. 1099 (2015)—§ 21:17 n.9

State v. Pickett, 288 Ga. 674, 706 S.E.2d 561 (2011)—§ 14:70 n.11

State v. Picot, 255 Ga. App. 513, 565 S.E.2d 865 (2002)—§ 2:21 n.12

State v. Pinkerton, 262 Ga. App. 858, 586 S.E.2d 743 (2003)—§ 7:3 n.26

State v. Pless, 282 Ga. 58, 646 S.E.2d 202 (2007)—§ 26:21 n.54

State v. Porter, 288 Ga. 524, 705 S.E.2d 636 (2011)—§ 14:70 n.19, 38

State v. Porter, 167 Ga. App. 293, 306 S.E.2d 377 (1983)—§ 4:13 n.6

State v. Preston, 411 A.2d 402 (Me. 1980)—§ 2:34 n.3

State v. Pruiett, 324 Ga. App. 789, 751 S.E.2d 579 (2013)—§ 14:55 n.6

State v. Purdy, 147 Ga. App. 340, 248 S.E.2d 683 (1978)—§ 3:6 n.1

State v. Ramos, 145 Ga. App. 301, 243 S.E.2d 693 (1978)—§ 13:7 n.1

State v. Ramsey, 147 Ga. App. 150, 248 S.E.2d 289 (1978)—§ 14:67 n.2

State v. Ramsey, 143 Ga. App. 191, 237 S.E.2d 666 (1977)—§ 14:60 n.15

State v. Randle, 298 Ga. 375, 781 S.E.2d 781 (2016)—§ 26:19 n.52

State v. Ray, 272 Ga. 450, 531 S.E.2d 705 (2000)—§ 5:5 n.13

State v. Redd, 248 Ga. App. 312, 546 S.E.2d 68 (2001)—§ 7:12 n.14

State v. Redding, 274 Ga. 831, 561 S.E.2d 79 (2002)—§ 17:18 n.7

State v. Reid, 331 Ga. App. 275, 770 S.E.2d 665 (2015)—§ 28:10 n.8

State v. Reid, 167 Ga. App. 81, 306 S.E.2d 61 (1983)—§ 4:33 n.21

State v. Reid, 247 Ga. 445, 276 S.E.2d 617 (1981)—§ 3:4 n.9

State v. Reid, 156 Ga. App. 78, 274 S.E.2d 164 (1980)—§ 3:4 n.8

State v. Reid, 149 Ga. App. 685, 255 S.E.2d 71 (1979)—§ 3:4 n.7

State v. Rezvani, 181 Ga. App. 328, 352 S.E.2d 197 (1986)—§ 4:32 n.32

State v. Rimes, 177 Ga. App. 872, 341 S.E.2d 710 (1986)—§ 28:11 n.24

State v. Rish, 222 Ga. App. 729, 476 S.E.2d 50 (1996)—§§ 13:23 n.33; 17:6 n.6

State v. Ritter, 268 Ga. 108, 485 S.E.2d 492 (1997)—§ 5:7 n.5, 6, 8

State v. Roadenbaugh, 234 Kan. 474, 673 P.2d 1166 (1983)—§ 5:14 n.21

State v. Roberts, 247 Ga. 456, 277 S.E.2d 644 (1981)—§ 22:6 n.7, 11

State v. Robins, 296 Ga. App. 437, 674 S.E.2d 615 (2009)—§ 14:66 n.16

State v. Robinson, 326 Ga. App. 63, 755 S.E.2d 869 (2014)—§ 5:5 n.13

State v. Robinson, 142 Ga. App. 705, 237 S.E.2d 1 (1977)—§ 4:6 n.6, 8

State v. Roca, 203 Ga. App. 267, 416 S.E.2d 836 (1992)—§§ 12:17 n.27; 14:48 n.29

State v. Rocco, 255 Ga. App. 565, 566 S.E.2d 365 (2002)—§ 4:16 n.6

State v. Rocco, 259 Ga. 463, 384 S.E.2d 183 (1989)—§ 16:13 n.11

State v. Roddy, 231 Ga. App. 91, 497 S.E.2d 653 (1998)—§§ 14:78 n.25; 14:84 n.14, 19

State v. Rodriguez, 274 Ga. 728, 559 S.E.2d 435 (2002)—§ 5:8 n.11

State v. Rogers, 173 Ga. App. 653, 327 S.E.2d 782 (1985)—§ 5:10 n.6

State v. Rosof, 180 Ga. App. 637, 350 S.E.2d 36 (1986)—§ 4:35 n.11

State v. Ross, 155 Ga. App. 659, 272 S.E.2d 524 (1980)—§ 14:85 n.1

State v. Rowe, 138 Ga. App. 904, 228 S.E.2d 3 (1976)—§§ 14:46 n.3; 14:67 n.81

State v. Royal, 247 Ga. 309, 275 S.E.2d 646 (1981)—§§ 14:38 n.10; 21:25 n.28

State v. Springer, 297 Ga. 376, 774 S.E.2d 106 (2015)—§ 25:6 n.17

State v. Stafford, 277 Ga. App. 852, 627 S.E.2d 802 (2006)—§ 4:16 n.4

State v. Staley, 249 Ga. App. 207, 548 S.E.2d 26 (2001)—§ 4:13 n.2

State v. Stamey, 211 Ga. App. 837, 440 S.E.2d 725 (1994)—§§ 13:6 n.17; 13:11 n.16

State v. Starke, 81 Wis. 2d 399, 260 N.W.2d 739 (1978)—§ 4:22 n.17

State v. Stasio, 78 N.J. 467, 396 A.2d 1129 (1979)—§ 21:16 n.13

State v. Stearns, 240 Ga. App. 806, 524 S.E.2d 554 (1999)—§ 3:9 n.24

State v. Steien, 214 Ga. App. 345, 447 S.E.2d 701 (1994)—§ 14:55 n.5

State v. Stephens, 252 Ga. 181, 311 S.E.2d 823 (1984)—§§ 4:7 n.5; 4:10 n.16

State v. Stephens, 300 N.C. 321, 266 S.E.2d 588 (1980)—§ 5:19 n.1

State v. Stevens, 181 Wis. 2d 410, 511 N.W.2d 591 (1994)—§ 4:16 n.9

State v. Stevens, 120 Wis. 2d 334, 354 N.W.2d 762 (Ct. App. 1984)—§ 4:38 n.17

State v. Stewart, 317 Ga. App. 82, 729 S.E.2d 478 (2012)—§ 14:53 n.15

State v. Stewart, 191 Ga. App. 35, 381 S.E.2d 50 (1989)—§ 14:67 n.56, 61

State v. Stilley, 261 Ga. App. 868, 584 S.E.2d 9 (2003)—§ 4:50 n.12

State v. Stinson, 278 Ga. 377, 602 S.E.2d 654 (2004)—§ 16:14 n.21, 22

State v. Stinson, 244 Ga. App. 622, 536 S.E.2d 293 (2000)—§ 5:6 n.9, 11

State v. Stokes, 185 Ga. App. 718, 365 S.E.2d 477 (1988)—§ 20:7 n.17

State v. Stonaker, 236 Ga. 1, 222 S.E.2d 354 (1976)—§ 24:5 n.4

State v. Stone, 304 Ga. App. 695, 697 S.E.2d 852 (2010)—§ 14:99 n.13

State v. Stone, 165 W. Va. 266, 268 S.E.2d 50 (1980)—§§ 2:34 n.2; 4:7 n.47

State v. Stowe, 167 Ga. App. 65, 306 S.E.2d 663 (1983)—§ 14:54 n.12

State v. Stringer, 258 Ga. 605, 372 S.E.2d 426 (1988)—§§ 2:19 n.26; 2:26 n.10

State v. Sutton, 258 Ga. 382, 369 S.E.2d 249 (1988)—§ 4:32 n.13

State v. Swift, 290 N.C. 383, 226 S.E.2d 652 (1976)—§ 13:9 n.11

State v. Swift, 232 Ga. 535, 207 S.E.2d 459 (1974)—§§ 3:9 n.22; 4:49 n.31; 14:88 n.10

State v. Sykes, 137 Ga. App. 297, 223 S.E.2d 491 (1976)—§ 22:5 n.10

State v. Tansimore, 3 N.J. 516, 71 A.2d 169 (1950)—§ 21:16 n.16

State v. Tedford, 195 Ga. App. 372, 393 S.E.2d 502 (1990)—§ 4:21 n.25

State v. Telenko, 225 Ga. App. 724, 484 S.E.2d 725 (1997)—§ 24:27 n.12

State v. Templeman, 229 Ga. App. 6, 492 S.E.2d 902 (1997)—§ 3:6 n.25

State v. Terrebonne, 256 La. 385, 236 So. 2d 773 (1970)—§ 12:10 n.11

State v. Terry, 257 Ga. 473, 360 S.E.2d 588 (1987)—§ 16:1 n.11

State v. Tew, 54 Wis. 2d 361, 195 N.W.2d 615 (1972)—§ 26:43 n.24, 25

State v. Thackston, 289 Ga. 412, 716 S.E.2d 517, 92 A.L.R.6th 645 (2011)—§§ 2:34 n.9; 30:7 n.3

State v. Thomas, 331 Ga. App. 220, 770 S.E.2d 301 (2015)—§ 14:41 n.5

State v. Thomas, 150 Ga. App. 170, 257 S.E.2d 28 (1979)—§ 14:84 n.13

State v. Thompson, 284 Ga. App. 744, 644 S.E.2d 889 (2007)—§ 14:71 n.37

State v. Thompson, 261 Ga. App. 828, 584 S.E.2d 7 (2003)—§ 14:66 n.37

State v. Thompson, 256 Ga. App. 188, 569 S.E.2d 254 (2002)—§§ 3:6 n.20; 4:51 n.2

State v. Westmoreland, 204 Ga. App. 312, 418 S.E.2d 822 (1992)—§ 4:32 n.25

State v. Whetstone, 264 Ga. 135, 441 S.E.2d 842 (1994)—§ 21:9 n.9

State v. White, 660 So. 2d 664 (Fla. 1995)—§ 2:26 n.9

State v. White, 196 Ga. App. 685, 396 S.E.2d 601 (1990)—§ 4:9 n.11

State v. Whitehead, 184 Ga. App. 162, 361 S.E.2d 41 (1987)—§ 14:58 n.11

State v. Wilbanks, 215 Ga. App. 223, 450 S.E.2d 293 (1994)—§ 30:8 n.29

State v. Wilkins, 302 Ga. 156, 805 S.E.2d 868 (2017)—§ 13:31 n.8

State v. Williams, 818 S.E.2d 256 (Ga. Ct. App. 2018)—§§ 13:5 n.11; 26:33 n.12

State v. Williams, 336 Ga. App. 97, 783 S.E.2d 700 (2016)—§ 3:7 n.10

State v. Williams, 275 Ga. App. 612, 621 S.E.2d 581 (2005)—§ 4:18 n.2

State v. Williams, 264 Ga. App. 199, 590 S.E.2d 151 (2003)—§ 3:10 n.3

State v. Williams, 242 Ga. App. 34, 528 S.E.2d 554 (2000)—§ 2:12 n.18

State v. Williams, 226 Ga. App. 346, 486 S.E.2d 637 (1997)—§ 3:3 n.4

State v. Williams, 225 Ga. App. 736, 484 S.E.2d 775 (1997)—§ 3:7 n.5

State v. Williams, 220 Ga. App. 100, 469 S.E.2d 261 (1996)—§ 3:10 n.17

State v. Williams, 212 Ga. App. 164, 441 S.E.2d 501 (1994)—§ 4:33 n.2

State v. Williams, 181 Ga. App. 204, 351 S.E.2d 727 (1986)—§§ 12:12 n.1; 12:13 n.3, 28

State v. Williams, 172 Ga. App. 708, 324 S.E.2d 557 (1984)—§ 14:66 n.38

State v. Williams, 247 Ga. 200, 275 S.E.2d 62 (1981)—§§ 13:6 n.8; 13:19 n.1, 8

State v. Williams, 297 So. 2d 52 (Fla. 2d DCA 1974)—§ 4:37 n.1

State v. Williams, 279 N.C. 663, 185 S.E.2d 174 (1971)—§ 6:7 n.4

State v. Willis, 218 Ga. App. 402, 461 S.E.2d 576 (1995)—§ 6:6 n.37

State v. Willis, 207 Ga. App. 76, 427 S.E.2d 306 (1993)—§§ 2:11 n.12; 3:2 n.14

State v. Willis, 149 Ga. App. 509, 254 S.E.2d 743 (1979)—§ 14:54 n.16

State v. Wilson, 220 Ga. App. 538, 469 S.E.2d 804 (1996)—§ 20:4 n.32

State v. Wilson, 112 N.C. App. 777, 437 S.E.2d 387 (1993)—§ 3:10 n.13

State v. Wilson, 179 Ga. App. 334, 346 S.E.2d 111 (1986)—§ 2:13 n.10

State v. Winnie, 242 Ga. App. 228, 529 S.E.2d 215 (2000)—§ 3:8 n.5

State v. Wintker, 223 Ga. App. 65, 476 S.E.2d 835 (1996)—§ 5:12 n.8

State v. Wood, 53 N.H. 484, 1873 WL 4197 (1873)—§ 12:10 n.11

State v. Woods, 280 Ga. 758, 632 S.E.2d 654 (2006)—§§ 2:33 n.2; 5:7 n.5; 5:10 n.3; 5:20 n.23; 5:26 n.11

State v. Wooten, 273 Ga. 529, 543 S.E.2d 721 (2001)—§ 17:15 n.2

State v. Wright, 221 Ga. App. 584, 472 S.E.2d 144 (1996)—§ 14:67 n.71

State v. Wright, 316 So. 2d 380 (La. 1975)—§ 6:9 n.9

State v. Wyatt, 295 Ga. 257, 759 S.E.2d 500 (2014)—§§ 14:40 n.3; 14:41 n.6

State v. Yapo, 296 Ga. App. 158, 674 S.E.2d 44 (2009)—§ 21:17 n.24

State v. Yates, 223 Ga. App. 403, 477 S.E.2d 670 (1996)—§ 14:70 n.16

State v. Young, 135 Ariz. 437, 661 P.2d 1138 (Ct. App. Div. 1 1982)—§ 4:57 n.4

State v. Young, 15 Wash. App. 581, 550 P.2d 689 (Div. 1 1976)—§ 4:57 n.22

Thomason v. Caldwell, 229 Ga. 637, 194 S.E.2d 112 (1972)—§ 28:11 n.36

Thomason v. State, 268 Ga. 298, 486 S.E.2d 861 (1997)—§§ 14:4 n.19; 14:5 n.16; 17:9 n.13; 28:21 n.6

Thomason v. State, 148 Ga. App. 513, 251 S.E.2d 598 (1978)—§ 4:6 n.3

Thompkins v. State, 181 Ga. App. 158, 351 S.E.2d 475 (1986)—§ 18:33 n.3

Thompkins v. State, 180 Ga. App. 473, 349 S.E.2d 768 (1986)—§ 24:5 n.25

Thompson v. Eubanks, 557 Fed. Appx. 855 (11th Cir. 2014)—§ 26:19 n.27

Thompson v. Greene, 265 Ga. 782, 462 S.E.2d 747 (1995)—§§ 16:8 n.8; 26:48 n.4

Thompson v. Keohane, 516 U.S. 99, 116 S. Ct. 457, 133 L. Ed. 2d 383 (1995)—§ 5:12 n.10

Thompson v. Louisiana, 469 U.S. 17, 105 S. Ct. 409, 83 L. Ed. 2d 246 (1984)—§ 4:30 n.39

Thompson v. McNeil, 556 U.S. 1114, 129 S. Ct. 1299, 173 L. Ed. 2d 693 (2009)—§ 26:2 n.33

Thompson v. Oklahoma, 487 U.S. 815, 108 S. Ct. 2687, 101 L. Ed. 2d 702 (1988)—§ 26:6 n.21

Thompson v. Secretary for Dept. of Corrections, 517 F.3d 1279 (11th Cir. 2008)—§ 26:2 n.33

Thompson v. State, 332 Ga. App. 204, 770 S.E.2d 364 (2015)—§ 26:28 n.9

Thompson v. State, 295 Ga. 96, 757 S.E.2d 846 (2014)—§ 14:93 n.28

Thompson v. State, 294 Ga. 693, 755 S.E.2d 713 (2014)—§ 18:19 n.11

Thompson v. State, 313 Ga. App. 844, 723 S.E.2d 85 (2012)—§ 5:12 n.24

Thompson v. State, 313 Ga. App. 294, 721 S.E.2d 106 (2011)—§ 30:3 n.4

Thompson v. State, 294 Ga. App. 363, 670 S.E.2d 152 (2008)—§ 4:2 n.69

Thompson v. State, 289 Ga. App. 661, 658 S.E.2d 122 (2007)—§ 3:2 n.52

Thompson v. State, 278 Ga. 394, 603 S.E.2d 233 (2004)—§§ 14:63 n.2, 5; 30:2 n.6

Thompson v. State, 277 Ga. 102, 586 S.E.2d 231 (2003)—§ 20:4 n.17

Thompson v. State, 260 Ga. App. 253, 581 S.E.2d 596 (2003)—§ 18:38 n.24

Thompson v. State, 271 Ga. 105, 519 S.E.2d 434 (1999)—§ 25:6 n.24

Thompson v. State, 240 Ga. App. 539, 524 S.E.2d 239 (1999)—§ 16:10 n.3

Thompson v. State, 240 Ga. App. 26, 521 S.E.2d 876 (1999)—§ 14:21 n.2

Thompson v. State, 237 Ga. App. 91, 514 S.E.2d 870 (1999)—§ 22:3 n.9

Thompson v. State, 234 Ga. App. 74, 506 S.E.2d 201 (1998)—§ 14:83 n.5

Thompson v. State, 229 Ga. App. 526, 494 S.E.2d 306 (1997)—§ 14:48 n.7

Thompson v. State, 212 Ga. App. 175, 442 S.E.2d 771 (1994)—§ 18:20 n.15

Thompson v. State, 263 Ga. 23, 426 S.E.2d 895 (1993)—§§ 18:16 n.6; 26:8 n.27; 26:37 n.3

Thompson v. State, 186 Ga. App. 379, 367 S.E.2d 247 (1988)—§ 14:71 n.21

Thompson v. State, 257 Ga. 386, 359 S.E.2d 664 (1987)—§ 7:6 n.18

Thompson v. State, 181 Ga. App. 163, 351 S.E.2d 483 (1986)—§ 14:73 n.8

Tibbs v. State, 211 Ga. App. 250, 438 S.E.2d 706 (1993)—§ 21:1 n.10

Tidwell v. Paxton, 282 Ga. 641, 651 S.E.2d 714 (2007)—§ 11:4 n.5

Tidwell v. State, 285 Ga. 103, 674 S.E.2d 272 (2009)—§ 4:34 n.3, 28

Tidwell v. State, 216 Ga. App. 8, 453 S.E.2d 64 (1994)—§ 13:4 n.1

Tierney, In re, 465 F.2d 806 (5th Cir. 1972)—§ 12:18 n.8

Tieu v. State, 257 Ga. 281, 358 S.E.2d 247 (1987)—§ 14:51 n.4

Tifford v. Wainwright, 588 F.2d 954 (5th Cir. 1979)—§ 14:72 n.34

Tift v. Bush, 209 Ga. 769, 75 S.E.2d 805 (1953)—§ 20:7 n.8

Tift v. State, 133 Ga. App. 466, 211 S.E.2d 411 (1974)—§ 30:1 n.15

Tigner v. State, 119 Ga. 114, 45 S.E. 1001 (1903)—§ 13:13 n.2

Tiller v. State, 261 Ga. App. 363, 582 S.E.2d 536 (2003)—§§ 3:11 n.10; 14:81 n.24

Tiller v. State, 267 Ga. 888, 485 S.E.2d 720 (1997)—§§ 19:2 n.26; 25:3 n.7

Tiller v. State, 222 Ga. App. 840, 476 S.E.2d 591 (1996)—§ 6:10 n.8

Tiller v. State, 118 Ga. App. 590, 164 S.E.2d 915 (1968)—§ 21:8 n.4

Tilley v. Page, 181 Ga. App. 98, 351 S.E.2d 464 (1986)—§ 16:13 n.10

Tilley v. State, 201 Ga. App. 360, 411 S.E.2d 100 (1991)—§ 17:8 n.42

Tillman v. State, 249 Ga. 792, 294 S.E.2d 516 (1982)—§ 26:1 n.17

Tillman v. U.S., 406 F.2d 930 (5th Cir. 1969)—§ 14:72 n.19

Tilton v. State, 5 Ga. App. 59, 62 S.E. 651 (1908)—§ 17:1 n.13

Timberlake v. State, 246 Ga. 488, 271 S.E.2d 792 (1980)—§ 28:12 n.6, 8, 9, 10, 11

Timberlake v. State, 100 Ga. 66, 27 S.E. 158 (1896)—§ 13:9 n.8

Timmons v. State, 13 Ga. App. 376, 79 S.E. 216 (1913)—§ 22:4 n.1

Tinetti v. Wittke, 620 F.2d 160 (7th Cir. 1980)—§ 4:57 n.3

Tipton v. State, 321 Ga. App. 870, 743 S.E.2d 532 (2013)—§ 10:2 n.13

Tipton v. State, 119 Ga. 304, 46 S.E. 436 (1904)—§ 13:6 n.2

Tison v. Arizona, 481 U.S. 137, 107 S. Ct. 1676, 95 L. Ed. 2d 127 (1987)—§ 26:6 n.14

Titelman v. Stedman, 277 Ga. 460, 591 S.E.2d 774 (2003)—§ 26:44 n.20

Todd v. Casciano, 256 Ga. App. 631, 569 S.E.2d 566 (2002)—§ 27:1 n.23

Todd v. State, 172 Ga. App. 231, 323 S.E.2d 6 (1984)—§ 26:24 n.8, 20

Todd v. State, 163 Ga. App. 814, 294 S.E.2d 714 (1982)—§ 26:28 n.47

Todd v. State, 243 Ga. 539, 255 S.E.2d 5 (1979)—§ 18:26 n.45

Todd v. State, 108 Ga. App. 615, 134 S.E.2d 56 (1963)—§ 30:1 n.11

Tokars v. Superior Court of Cobb County, 264 Ga. 180, 442 S.E.2d 454 (1994)—§ 17:5 n.1

Toland v. State, 115 Ga. App. 786, 156 S.E.2d 215 (1967)—§ 20:4 n.4

Tolbert v. State, 260 Ga. 527, 397 S.E.2d 439 (1990)—§ 14:92 n.21

Tolbert v. State, 224 Ga. 291, 161 S.E.2d 279 (1968)—§ 4:34 n.10

Tollett v. Henderson, 411 U.S. 258, 93 S. Ct. 1602, 36 L. Ed. 2d 235 (1973)—§ 16:2 n.12

Tollette v. State, 280 Ga. 100, 621 S.E.2d 742 (2005)—§§ 18:17 n.13; 23:8 n.12

Tolliver v. State, 276 Ga. App. 755, 625 S.E.2d 403 (2005)—§ 10:3 n.22

Tolliver v. State, 243 Ga. App. 180, 531 S.E.2d 383 (2000)—§ 26:24 n.8

Tomlinson v. State, 242 Ga. App. 117, 527 S.E.2d 626 (2000)—§ 4:9 n.6

Tommie v. State, 158 Ga. App. 216, 279 S.E.2d 510 (1981)—§ 26:43 n.15

Trulock v. Freeh, 275 F.3d 391 (4th Cir. 2001)—§§ 4:27 n.5; 4:34 n.41

Trussell v. State, 67 Md. App. 23, 506 A.2d 255 (1986)—§ 14:85 n.11

Tubbs v. State, 276 Ga. 751, 583 S.E.2d 853 (2003)—§ 14:19 n.3, 7

Tucci v. State, 255 Ga. App. 474, 565 S.E.2d 831 (2002)—§ 7:3 n.28

Tucker v. Francis, 723 F.2d 1504 (11th Cir. 1984)—§ 23:7 n.29

Tucker v. State, 238 Ga. App. 645, 519 S.E.2d 745 (1999)—§ 24:5 n.7

Tucker v. State, 231 Ga. App. 210, 498 S.E.2d 774 (1998)—§ 14:98 n.1

Tucker v. State, 228 Ga. App. 321, 491 S.E.2d 420 (1997)—§ 5:20 n.39

Tucker v. State, 222 Ga. App. 517, 474 S.E.2d 696 (1996)—§§ 4:2 n.86; 14:14 n.2

Tucker v. State, 182 Ga. App. 625, 356 S.E.2d 559 (1987)—§ 21:4 n.3

Tucker v. State, 172 Ga. App. 86, 321 S.E.2d 817 (1984)—§ 7:4 n.42

Tucker v. State, 170 Ga. App. 782, 318 S.E.2d 147 (1984)—§ 5:20 n.35

Tucker v. State, 249 Ga. 323, 290 S.E.2d 97 (1982)—§ 18:24 n.8

Tucker v. State, 245 Ga. 68, 263 S.E.2d 109 (1980)—§ 23:8 n.12

Tucker v. State, 244 Ga. 721, 261 S.E.2d 635 (1979)—§ 26:10 n.3

Tucker v. State, 237 Ga. 777, 229 S.E.2d 617 (1976)—§ 5:13 n.2

Tucker v. State, 136 Ga. App. 456, 221 S.E.2d 664 (1975)—§ 17:17 n.27

Tucker v. State, 112 Ga. App. 622, 145 S.E.2d 751 (1965)—§ 13:11 n.10, 13

Tucker v. State, 180 Ga. 87, 178 S.E. 152 (1935)—§ 21:24 n.5

Tuff v. State, 278 Ga. 91, 597 S.E.2d 328 (2004)—§ 24:14 n.6

Tuff v. State, 202 Ga. App. 772, 415 S.E.2d 702 (1992)—§ 14:38 n.15

Tuggle v. State, 165 Ga. App. 53, 299 S.E.2d 121 (1983)—§ 24:13 n.3

Tuggle v. State, 145 Ga. App. 603, 244 S.E.2d 131 (1978)—§ 13:4 n.25

Turk v. U.S., 429 F.2d 1327 (8th Cir. 1970)—§ 4:7 n.33

Turman v. State, 272 Ga. App. 570, 613 S.E.2d 126 (2005)—§§ 7:1 n.4; 17:17 n.29

Turner v. Evans, 251 Ga. 486, 306 S.E.2d 921 (1983)—§ 10:7 n.18

Turner v. State of La., 379 U.S. 466, 85 S. Ct. 546, 13 L. Ed. 2d 424 (1965)—§§ 18:5 n.6; 18:17 n.6; 18:37 n.18

Turner v. Murray, 476 U.S. 28, 106 S. Ct. 1683, 90 L. Ed. 2d 27 (1986)—§ 18:27 n.2

Turner v. State, 259 Ga. App. 902, 578 S.E.2d 570 (2003)—§§ 17:23 n.8; 26:13 n.18, 19; 26:15 n.7; 26:42 n.2

Turner v. State, 246 Ga. App. 49, 539 S.E.2d 553 (2000)—§§ 4:34 n.5; 5:11 n.8

Turner v. State, 245 Ga. App. 294, 536 S.E.2d 814 (2000)—§ 5:20 n.35

Turner v. State, 238 Ga. App. 438, 518 S.E.2d 923 (1999)—§ 14:54 n.5

Turner v. State, 268 Ga. 213, 486 S.E.2d 839, 79 A.L.R.5th 723 (1997)— § 26:5 n.7

Turner v. State, 210 Ga. App. 303, 436 S.E.2d 229 (1993)—§ 21:7 n.5, 14

Turner v. State, 262 Ga. 359, 418 S.E.2d 52 (1992)—§§ 21:29 n.4; 24:12 n.6

Turner v. State, 188 Ga. App. 267, 372 S.E.2d 826 (1988)—§ 14:67 n.50

Turner v. State, 152 Ga. App. 354, 262 S.E.2d 618 (1979)—§ 13:25 n.1

Turner v. State, 151 Ga. App. 631, 260 S.E.2d 756 (1979)—§§ 26:41 n.5; 29:2 n.1

Turner v. State, 78 Ga. 174, 1886 WL 1691 (1886)—§ 12:7 n.11

U

U.S. v. Hernandez, 739 F.2d 484 (9th Cir. 1984)—§ 4:45 n.11

U.S. v. Hernandez, 574 F.2d 1362 (5th Cir. 1978)—§ 5:19 n.16

U.S. v. Hernandez, 572 F.2d 218 (9th Cir. 1978)—§ 14:57 n.12

U.S. v. Herrera, 711 F.2d 1546 (11th Cir. 1983)—§ 3:5 n.4

U.S. v. Herring, 568 F.2d 1099 (5th Cir. 1978)—§ 18:38 n.15

U.S. v. Herzbrun, 723 F.2d 773 (11th Cir. 1984)—§ 4:35 n.4

U.S. v. Hickman, 592 F.2d 931 (6th Cir. 1979)—§ 17:5 n.33

U.S. v. Hidalgo-Gato, 703 F.2d 1267 (11th Cir. 1983)—§ 3:5 n.4

U.S. v. Highfill, 334 F. Supp. 700 (E.D. Ark. 1971)—§§ 4:20 n.4; 4:57 n.6

U.S. v. Hilburn, 625 F.2d 1177 (5th Cir. 1980)—§ 27:1 n.5

U.S. v. Hill, 655 F.2d 512, 8 Fed. R. Evid. Serv. 1021 (3d Cir. 1981)—
§ 21:25 n.9

U.S. v. Hill, 626 F.2d 429 (5th Cir. 1980)—§ 3:4 n.7

U.S. v. Hill, 508 F.2d 345 (5th Cir. 1975)—§ 4:32 n.28

U.S. v. Hill, 500 F.2d 315 (5th Cir. 1974)—§ 4:7 n.9

U.S. v. Hill, 473 F.2d 759 (9th Cir. 1972)—§ 14:49 n.1

U.S. v. Hittle, 575 F.2d 799 (10th Cir. 1978)—§ 4:7 n.7

U.S. v. Hobson, 672 F.2d 825 (11th Cir. 1982)—§ 7:12 n.3, 4

U.S. v. Hodge, 496 F.2d 87 (5th Cir. 1974)—§ 12:13 n.37

U.S. v. Hoffman, 733 F.2d 596 (9th Cir. 1984)—§ 7:4 n.5

U.S. v. Hoker, 483 F.2d 359 (5th Cir. 1973)—§ 17:5 n.33

U.S. v. Holland, 755 F.2d 253 (2d Cir. 1985)—§ 2:5 n.6

U.S. v. Holloway, 290 F.3d 1331 (11th Cir. 2002)—§ 4:30 n.41

U.S. v. Holt, 264 F.3d 1215 (10th Cir. 2001)—§ 3:11 n.28

U.S. v. Hopkins, 464 F.2d 816 (D.C. Cir. 1972)—§ 6:6 n.31

U.S. v. Hoyland, 264 F.2d 346 (7th Cir. 1959)—§ 14:49 n.1

U.S. v. Hubbell, 530 U.S. 27, 120 S. Ct. 2037, 147 L. Ed. 2d 24 (2000)—
§ 5:25 n.2

U.S. v. Humphrey, 104 F.3d 65, 46 Fed. R. Evid. Serv. 286 (5th Cir.
1997)—§ 4:22 n.2

U.S. v. Hunley, 567 F.2d 822 (8th Cir. 1977)—§ 4:8 n.4

U.S. v. Hyde, 520 U.S. 670, 117 S. Ct. 1630, 137 L. Ed. 2d 935 (1997)—
§ 15:2 n.4

U.S. v. Inmon, 568 F.2d 326 (3d Cir. 1977)—§ 14:55 n.13

U.S. v. Irizarry, 673 F.2d 554 (1st Cir. 1982)—§ 4:57 n.4

U.S. v. Isenberg, 343 F. Supp. 25 (W.D. Pa. 1972)—§§ 6:5 n.14; 6:7 n.7

U.S. v. Italiano, 894 F.2d 1280 (11th Cir. 1990)—§ 14:66 n.40, 42

U.S. v. Jacobs, 97 F.3d 275, 45 Fed. R. Evid. Serv. 1013 (8th Cir.
1996)—§ 14:7 n.4

U.S. v. Jacobsen, 466 U.S. 109, 104 S. Ct. 1652, 80 L. Ed. 2d 85
(1984)—§§ 4:1 n.3; 4:42 n.13; 4:58 n.10

U.S. v. James Daniel Good Real Property, 510 U.S. 43, 114 S. Ct. 492,
126 L. Ed. 2d 490 (1993)—§ 10:6 n.9

U.S. v. Janis, 428 U.S. 433, 96 S. Ct. 3021, 49 L. Ed. 2d 1046 (1976)—
§§ 2:35 n.2; 4:60 n.8

U.S. v. Jaras, 86 F.3d 383 (5th Cir. 1996)—§ 4:53 n.6

U.S. v. Jeffers, 520 F.2d 1256 (7th Cir. 1975)—§ 7:11 n.33

U.S. v. Jeffers, 342 U.S. 48, 72 S. Ct. 93, 96 L. Ed. 59 (1951)—§§ 4:2 n.8;
14:82 n.4

U.S. v. Koblitz, 803 F.2d 1523 (11th Cir. 1986)—§ 7:1 n.5, 6

U.S. v. Kordel, 397 U.S. 1, 90 S. Ct. 763, 25 L. Ed. 2d 1, 13 Fed. R. Serv. 2d 868 (1970)—§ 14:4 n.20

U.S. v. Kramer, 711 F.2d 789, 13 Fed. R. Evid. Serv. 904 (7th Cir. 1983)—§ 4:38 n.17

U.S. v. Kreimes, 649 F.2d 1185 (5th Cir. 1981)—§ 4:31 n.8

U.S. v. Kubiak, 704 F.2d 1545, 13 Fed. R. Evid. Serv. 129 (11th Cir. 1983)—§ 3:5 n.3

U.S. v. Ladd, 704 F.2d 134 (4th Cir. 1983)—§ 4:22 n.21

U.S. v. Laist, 702 F.3d 608 (11th Cir. 2012)—§ 4:21 n.19

U.S. v. Lakhani, 480 F.3d 171, 72 Fed. R. Evid. Serv. 881 (3d Cir. 2007)—§ 25:7 n.8

U.S. v. Lall, 607 F.3d 1277 (11th Cir. 2010)—§ 5:13 n.29

U.S. v. Lamerson, 457 F.2d 371 (5th Cir. 1972)—§ 23:5 n.16

U.S. v. Lang, 644 F.2d 1232 (7th Cir. 1981)—§ 12:17 n.6

U.S. v. Lara, 517 F.2d 209 (5th Cir. 1975)—§ 4:41 n.12

U.S. v. La Vecchia, 513 F.2d 1210 (2d Cir. 1975)—§ 4:56 n.34

U. S. v. Lawrance, 480 F.2d 688 (5th Cir. 1973)—§ 21:11 n.2

U.S. v. Lee, 274 U.S. 559, 47 S. Ct. 746, 71 L. Ed. 1202 (1927)—§§ 4:39 n.5; 4:41 n.11

U.S. v. Lefkowitz, 285 U.S. 452, 52 S. Ct. 420, 76 L. Ed. 877, 82 A.L.R. 775 (1932)—§§ 4:2 n.11; 4:41 n.8

U.S. v. Leon, 468 U.S. 897, 104 S.Ct. 3405, 82 L.Ed.2d 677 (1984)—§§ 2:26 n.1; 2:29 n.1

U.S. v. LeQuire, 424 F.2d 341 (5th Cir. 1970)—§ 5:14 n.15

U.S. v. Lichenstein, 610 F.2d 1272 (5th Cir. 1980)—§ 25:6 n.5

U.S. v. Lifshitz, 369 F.3d 173, 4 A.L.R.6th 697 (2d Cir. 2004)—§ 4:27 n.4

U.S. v. Lindsey, 451 F.2d 701 (3d Cir. 1971)—§ 4:35 n.14

U.S. v. Lisenby, 716 F.2d 1355 (11th Cir. 1983)—§ 5:10 n.7

U.S. v. Liu, 731 F.3d 982 (9th Cir. 2013)—§ 14:66 n.41

U.S. v. Logan, 210 F.3d 820 (8th Cir. 2000)—§ 14:72 n.43

U.S. v. Lomas, 706 F.2d 886 (9th Cir. 1983)—§ 4:1 n.11

U.S. v. Lopez, 328 F. Supp. 1077, 14 A.L.R. Fed. 252 (E.D. N.Y. 1971)—§ 4:35 n.9

U.S. v. Lot 5, Fox Grove, Alachua County, Fla., 23 F.3d 359 (11th Cir. 1994)—§§ 10:2 n.30; 10:6 n.11

U.S. v. Loud Hawk, 474 U.S. 302, 106 S. Ct. 648, 88 L. Ed. 2d 640 (1986)—§ 14:70 n.22

U. S. v. Lovasco, 431 U.S. 783, 97 S. Ct. 2044, 52 L. Ed. 2d 752 (1977)—§§ 2:4 n.4, 5, 6, 8; 14:70 n.25

U.S. v. Lovvorn, 524 Fed. Appx. 485 (11th Cir. 2013)—§ 4:11 n.5

U.S. v. Lumpkin, 159 F.3d 983, 1998 FED App. 0330P (6th Cir. 1998)—§ 4:56 n.12

U.S. v. MacDonald, 456 U.S. 1, 102 S. Ct. 1497, 71 L. Ed. 2d 696 (1982)—§ 14:70 n.27

U. S. v. MacDonald, 435 U.S. 850, 98 S. Ct. 1547, 56 L. Ed. 2d 18 (1978)—§§ 14:99 n.1; 28:2 n.15

U.S. v. Magda, 547 F.2d 756 (2d Cir. 1976)—§ 3:8 n.11

U.S. v. Malatesta, 583 F.2d 748 (5th Cir. 1978)—§ 23:7 n.7

U. S. v. Procter & Gamble Co., 356 U.S. 677, 78 S. Ct. 983, 2 L. Ed. 2d 1077 (1958)—§ 12:10 n.2

U.S. v. Provenzano, 423 F. Supp. 662 (S.D. N.Y. 1976)—§ 12:13 n.33

U.S. v. Purcell, 236 F.3d 1274 (11th Cir. 2001)—§§ 3:2 n.32; 3:11 n.8

U.S. v. Quesada-Rosadal, 685 F.2d 1281, 11 Fed. R. Evid. Serv. 778 (11th Cir. 1982)—§ 14:85 n.26

U.S. v. Quinn, 728 F.3d 243 (3d Cir. 2013)—§ 12:15 n.15

U.S. v. Rabinowitz, 339 U.S. 56, 70 S. Ct. 430, 94 L. Ed. 653 (1950)—§ 2:9 n.2

U.S. v. Rada-Solano, 625 F.2d 577 (5th Cir. 1980)—§ 5:26 n.4

U.S. v. Ramapuram, 632 F.2d 1149 (4th Cir. 1980)—§ 4:50 n.13

U.S. v. Ramirez, 523 U.S. 65, 118 S. Ct. 992, 140 L. Ed. 2d 191 (1998)—§ 4:18 n.5

U.S. v. Ramsey, 431 U.S. 606, 97 S. Ct. 1972, 52 L. Ed. 2d 617 (1977)—§§ 4:45 n.1; 4:46 n.17

U.S. v. Rangel-Portillo, 586 F.3d 376 (5th Cir. 2009)—§ 3:4 n.30

U.S. v. Ravich, 421 F.2d 1196 (2d Cir. 1970)—§ 6:9 n.8

U.S. v. Reed, 639 F.2d 896, 7 Fed. R. Evid. Serv. 918, 64 A.L.R. Fed. 276 (2d Cir. 1981)—§ 2:25 n.4

U.S. v. Reed, 572 F.2d 412, 3 Fed. R. Evid. Serv. 155 (2d Cir. 1978)—§§ 2:5 n.19; 4:28 n.6; 4:30 n.21

U.S. v. Reese, 463 F.2d 830 (D.C. Cir. 1972)—§ 8:1 n.1

U.S. v. Reinholz, 245 F.3d 765 (8th Cir. 2001)—§ 14:87 n.21

U.S. v. Reyna, 563 F.2d 1169 (5th Cir. 1977)—§ 5:19 n.28

U.S. v. Reynoso, 6 F. Supp. 2d 269 (S.D. N.Y. 1998)—§ 7:11 n.34

U.S. v. Rice, 671 F.2d 455 (11th Cir. 1982)—§ 30:7 n.1

U.S. v. Richards, 638 F.2d 765 (5th Cir. 1981)—§ 4:45 n.18

U.S. v. Richardson, 651 F.2d 1251 (8th Cir. 1981)—§ 6:10 n.11

U.S. v. Robertson, 582 F.2d 1356, 3 Fed. R. Evid. Serv. 1499 (5th Cir. 1978)—§ 5:5 n.5

U.S. v. Robinson, 485 U.S. 25, 108 S. Ct. 864, 99 L. Ed. 2d 23 (1988)—§ 23:7 n.20

U.S. v. Robinson, 690 F.2d 869 (11th Cir. 1982)—§ 3:4 n.19

U.S. v. Robinson, 625 F.2d 1211 (5th Cir. 1980)—§ 3:4 n.7

U.S. v. Robinson, 414 U.S. 218, 94 S.Ct. 467, 38 L.Ed.2d 427 (1973)—§ 4:26 n.21

U.S. v. Rochan, 563 F.2d 1246 (5th Cir. 1977)—§ 23:7 n.22

U.S. v. Rodriguez-Franco, 749 F.2d 1555 (11th Cir. 1985)—§ 3:1 n.35

U.S. v. Rogers, 504 F.2d 1079 (5th Cir. 1974)—§ 26:43 n.47

U.S. v. Rojas-Colombo, 462 F.2d 1091 (5th Cir. 1972)—§ 26:2 n.9, 10

U.S. v. Romano, 482 F.2d 1183 (5th Cir. 1973)—§ 17:10 n.8

U.S. v. Ronder, 639 F.2d 931 (2d Cir. 1981)—§ 24:19 n.14

U.S. v. Roper, 702 F.2d 984 (11th Cir. 1983)—§§ 2:12 n.16; 3:2 n.49; 3:12 n.1

U.S. v. Ross, 33 F.3d 1507, 41 Fed. R. Evid. Serv. 303 (11th Cir. 1994)—§ 7:11 n.33

U.S. v. Ross, 456 U.S. 798, 102 S. Ct. 2157, 72 L. Ed. 2d 572 (1982)—§§ 4:25 n.11; 4:26 n.43; 4:50 n.2, 10, 11; 4:53 n.1

U.S. v. Rubin, 474 F.2d 262 (3d Cir. 1973)—§ 4:30 n.7, 8

Vansant v. State, 264 Ga. 319, 443 S.E.2d 474 (1994)—§§ 3:7 n.16; 14:88 n.15

Van Scoik v. State, 142 Ga. App. 341, 235 S.E.2d 765 (1977)—§ 28:12 n.2, 20

Vanvelsor v. State, 162 Ga. App. 467, 291 S.E.2d 772 (1982)—§ 16:9 n.1

Van Voltenburg v. State, 138 Ga. App. 628, 227 S.E.2d 451 (1976)—§ 26:8 n.51

VanVoorhis v. State, 234 Ga. App. 749, 507 S.E.2d 555 (1998)—§ 21:10 n.6

Varnadoe v. State, 227 Ga. App. 663, 490 S.E.2d 517 (1997)—§ 17:6 n.14

Varriano v. State, 312 Ga. App. 266, 718 S.E.2d 14 (2011)—§ 4:34 n.12

Vasquez v. Hillery, 474 U.S. 254, 106 S. Ct. 617, 88 L. Ed. 2d 598 (1986)—§ 12:8 n.2

Vasser v. State, 272 Ga. App. 327, 612 S.E.2d 543 (2005)—§ 5:20 n.9, 38

Vaughan v. State, 210 Ga. App. 381, 436 S.E.2d 19 (1993)—§ 5:19 n.9

Vaughan v. State, 161 Ga. App. 265, 287 S.E.2d 728 (1982)—§ 16:14 n.24

Vaughn v. Rutledge, 265 Ga. 773, 462 S.E.2d 132 (1995)—§ 30:5 n.12, 17

Vaughn v. State, 324 Ga. App. 289, 750 S.E.2d 375 (2013)—§ 26:21 n.33

Vaughn v. State, 281 Ga. App. 475, 636 S.E.2d 163 (2006)—§ 24:19 n.6

Vaughn v. State, 259 Ga. 325, 381 S.E.2d 30 (1989)—§ 12:13 n.27

Vaughn v. State, 248 Ga. 127, 281 S.E.2d 594, 18 A.L.R.4th 735 (1981)—§§ 5:4 n.31; 5:20 n.22

Vaughn v. State, 247 Ga. 136, 274 S.E.2d 479 (1981)—§§ 2:11 n.7; 2:13 n.9; 2:15 n.7

Vaughn v. State, 141 Ga. App. 453, 233 S.E.2d 848 (1977)—§ 4:12 n.24

Vaughn v. State, 88 Ga. 731, 16 S.E. 64 (1892)—§ 18:8 n.2

Vauss v. U.S., 370 F.2d 250 (D.C. Cir. 1966)—§ 4:30 n.18

Veal v. State, 303 Ga. 18, 810 S.E.2d 127 (2018)—§ 26:2 n.32

Veal v. State, 298 Ga. 691, 784 S.E.2d 403 (2016)—§ 26:2 n.31

Veal v. State, 116 Ga. 589, 42 S.E. 705 (1902)—§ 13:9 n.7

Veasey v. State, 234 Ga. App. 795, 507 S.E.2d 799 (1998)—§ 21:7 n.7

Veasley v. State, 272 Ga. 837, 537 S.E.2d 42 (2000)—§ 28:3 n.27

Vedder v. State, 241 Ga. App. 578, 527 S.E.2d 249 (1999)—§ 14:67 n.29

Velazquez v. State, 282 Ga. 871, 655 S.E.2d 806 (2008)—§ 14:94 n.9

Velez v. Schmer, 724 F.2d 249 (1st Cir. 1984)—§ 6:10 n.3

Venner v. State, 30 Md. App. 599, 354 A.2d 483 (1976)—§ 4:38 n.18

Verdugo v. U.S., 402 F.2d 599 (9th Cir. 1968)—§ 26:2 n.7

Vergara v. State, 287 Ga. 194, 695 S.E.2d 215 (2010)—§ 13:28 n.2

Vergara v. State, 283 Ga. 175, 657 S.E.2d 863 (2008)—§§ 2:29 n.6; 2:33 n.4; 5:6 n.1; 5:8 n.10; 5:26 n.14

Vermont v. Brillon, 556 U.S. 81, 129 S. Ct. 1283, 173 L. Ed. 2d 231 (2009)—§ 14:70 n.8

Vernon v. State, 12 Md. App. 430, 278 A.2d 609 (1971)—§ 6:7 n.14

Vernonia School Dist. 47J v. Acton, 515 U.S. 646, 115 S. Ct. 2386, 132 L. Ed. 2d 564, 101 Ed. Law Rep. 37 (1995)—§ 5:24 n.7

Verscharen v. State, 188 Ga. App. 746, 374 S.E.2d 349 (1988)—§ 14:67 n.70

Vescuso v. Com., 5 Va. App. 59, 360 S.E.2d 547, 70 A.L.R.4th 619 (1987)—§ 17:1 n.6

W

Warbington v. State, 316 Ga. App. 614, 730 S.E.2d 90 (2012)—§ 14:78 n.9

Ward v. Jarvis, 240 Ga. 668, 242 S.E.2d 134 (1978)—§ 2:23 n.40

Ward v. Village of Monroeville, Ohio, 409 U.S. 57, 93 S. Ct. 80, 34 L. Ed. 2d 267 (1972)—§ 17:5 n.3

Ward v. State, 288 Ga. 641, 706 S.E.2d 430 (2011)—§§ 17:8 n.12, 33; 18:35 n.10

Ward v. State, 277 Ga. App. 790, 627 S.E.2d 862 (2006)—§ 3:2 n.42

Ward v. State, 262 Ga. 293, 417 S.E.2d 130 (1992)—§ 23:7 n.42

Ward v. State, 205 Ga. App. 485, 423 S.E.2d 22 (1992)—§ 12:19 n.1

Ward v. State, 195 Ga. App. 166, 393 S.E.2d 21 (1990)—§ 26:15 n.15

Ward v. State, 165 Ga. App. 163, 300 S.E.2d 528 (1983)—§ 7:4 n.42

Ward v. State, 248 Ga. 60, 281 S.E.2d 503 (1981)—§§ 16:3 n.1; 26:19 n.58

Ward v. State, 239 Ga. 205, 236 S.E.2d 365 (1977)—§§ 14:62 n.6; 20:6 n.42; 26:9 n.11; 26:41 n.16

Warden, Md. Penitentiary v. Hayden, 387 U.S. 294, 87 S. Ct. 1642, 18 L. Ed. 2d 782 (1967)—§§ 4:3 n.7; 4:14 n.1; 4:22 n.15; 4:31 n.1, 3; 14:78 n.2; 14:81 n.21

Ware v. State, 298 Ga. App. 232, 679 S.E.2d 797 (2009)—§§ 14:19 n.4; 14:20 n.2

Ware v. State, 267 Ga. 510, 480 S.E.2d 599 (1997)—§ 14:67 n.9

Ware v. State, 191 Ga. App. 896, 383 S.E.2d 368 (1989)—§ 18:31 n.99

Ware v. State, 137 Ga. App. 673, 224 S.E.2d 873 (1976)—§§ 17:17 n.27; 29:5 n.6; 30:4 n.8

Warner v. State, 299 Ga. App. 56, 681 S.E.2d 624 (2009)—§ 4:34 n.25

Warner v. State, 281 Ga. 763, 642 S.E.2d 821 (2007)—§ 19:2 n.13

Warner v. State, 214 Ga. App. 343, 447 S.E.2d 692 (1994)—§ 16:6 n.8

Warren v. Hiers, 105 Ga. App. 202, 124 S.E.2d 445 (1962)—§ 17:10 n.22

Warren v. State, 297 Ga. 810, 778 S.E.2d 749 (2015)—§ 14:90 n.4

Warren v. State, 314 Ga. App. 477, 724 S.E.2d 404 (2012)—§ 24:27 n.5

Warren v. State, 281 Ga. App. 490, 636 S.E.2d 671 (2006)—§ 23:2 n.13

Warren v. State, 246 Ga. App. 894, 543 S.E.2d 38 (2000)—§ 29:2 n.5

Warren v. State, 239 Ga. App. 468, 521 S.E.2d 424 (1999)—§ 17:21 n.15

Warren v. State, 32 Ga. App. 359, 123 S.E. 182 (1924)—§ 13:19 n.2

Washburn v. Foster, 87 Ga. App. 132, 73 S.E.2d 240 (1952)—§ 8:1 n.16

Washington v. City of Atlanta, 201 Ga. App. 876, 412 S.E.2d 624 (1991)—§ 16:10 n.20

Washington v. Chrisman, 455 U.S. 1, 102 S. Ct. 812, 70 L. Ed. 2d 778, 1 Ed. Law Rep. 1087 (1982)—§§ 4:26 n.2; 4:28 n.7

Washington v. State, 333 Ga. App. 236, 775 S.E.2d 719 (2015)—§ 25:2 n.15

Washington v. State, 276 Ga. 655, 581 S.E.2d 518 (2003)—§§ 7:4 n.99; 26:35 n.9, 11

Washington v. State, 238 Ga. App. 561, 519 S.E.2d 234 (1999)—§§ 17:23 n.3; 26:13 n.12

Washington v. State, 216 Ga. App. 352, 454 S.E.2d 214 (1995)—§ 7:4 n.42

Washington v. State, 192 Ga. App. 678, 385 S.E.2d 767 (1989)—§ 5:13 n.22

Watt v. State, 204 Ga. App. 839, 420 S.E.2d 769 (1992)—§ 16:6 n.7

Watters v. State, 241 Ga. 307, 245 S.E.2d 281 (1978)—§ 5:14 n.7

Watts v. Cannon, 224 Ga. 797, 164 S.E.2d 780 (1968)—§§ 2:6 n.9; 2:19 n.24

Watts v. Pitts, 253 Ga. 501, 322 S.E.2d 252 (1984)—§ 8:2 n.1

Watts v. State, 334 Ga. App. 770, 780 S.E.2d 431 (2015)—§ 4:48 n.15

Watts v. State, 261 Ga. App. 230, 582 S.E.2d 186 (2003)—§ 14:84 n.8

Watts v. State, 253 Ga. App. 227, 558 S.E.2d 791 (2002)—§ 4:7 n.45

Watts v. State, 274 Ga. 373, 552 S.E.2d 823 (2001)—§§ 4:7 n.45; 14:85 n.14, 15; 14:87 n.6, 10, 18, 19, 20

Watts v. State, 170 Ga. App. 614, 317 S.E.2d 654 (1984)—§ 14:36 n.3

Watts v. State, 142 Ga. App. 857, 237 S.E.2d 231 (1977)—§§ 17:17 n.17; 25:4 n.15

Watts v. State, 141 Ga. App. 127, 232 S.E.2d 590 (1977)—§§ 14:34 n.33; 18:6 n.3; 26:14 n.17

Waxelbaum Co. v. Atlantic Coast Line R. Co., 3 Ga. App. 394, 59 S.E. 1129 (1908)—§ 17:17 n.6

Way v. State, 239 Ga. 316, 236 S.E.2d 655 (1977)—§ 14:72 n.10

Waye v. State, 219 Ga. App. 22, 464 S.E.2d 19 (1995)—§ 14:47 n.12

Waye v. State, 239 Ga. 871, 238 S.E.2d 923 (1977)—§ 28:15 n.6

Wayne v. State, 269 Ga. 36, 495 S.E.2d 34 (1998)—§ 7:3 n.34

Wayne v. State, 184 Ga. App. 160, 361 S.E.2d 39 (1987)—§ 21:16 n.7

Wayne v. U.S., 318 F.2d 205 (D.C. Cir. 1963)—§§ 2:28 n.6; 4:30 n.15, 33

Wayte v. U.S., 470 U.S. 598, 105 S. Ct. 1524, 84 L. Ed. 2d 547 (1985)— § 21:28 n.7

Wearry v. Cain, 136 S. Ct. 1002, 194 L. Ed. 2d 78 (2016)—§ 14:34 n.5

Weatherbed v. State, 271 Ga. 736, 524 S.E.2d 452 (1999)—§§ 13:24 n.1; 14:51 n.13

Weatherford v. Bursey, 429 U.S. 545, 97 S. Ct. 837, 51 L. Ed. 2d 30 (1977)—§ 14:4 n.4

Weatherly v. Beavers, 139 Ga. 122, 76 S.E. 853 (1912)—§ 8:1 n.20

Weaver v. Graham, 450 U.S. 24, 101 S. Ct. 960, 67 L. Ed. 2d 17 (1981)—§ 29:2 n.10

Weaver v. Massachusetts, 137 S. Ct. 1899, 198 L. Ed. 2d 420 (2017)— § 7:4 n.57

Weaver v. State, 288 Ga. 540, 705 S.E.2d 627 (2011)—§ 17:8 n.36

Weaver v. State, 224 Ga. App. 243, 480 S.E.2d 286 (1997)—§ 14:51 n.5

Weaver v. State, 206 Ga. App. 560, 426 S.E.2d 41 (1992)—§ 14:73 n.38

Weaver v. State, 179 Ga. App. 641, 347 S.E.2d 295 (1986)—§ 13:23 n.25

Weaver v. State, 170 Ga. App. 731, 318 S.E.2d 196 (1984)—§ 24:15 n.7

Weaver v. State, 169 Ga. App. 890, 315 S.E.2d 467 (1984)—§ 14:73 n.16

Weaver v. State, 145 Ga. App. 194, 243 S.E.2d 560 (1978)—§ 23:7 n.16

Webb v. Hutto, 720 F.2d 375 (4th Cir. 1983)—§ 14:58 n.56

Webb v. State, 284 Ga. 122, 663 S.E.2d 690 (2008)—§ 21:20 n.7

Webb v. State, 270 Ga. App. 817, 608 S.E.2d 241 (2004)—§§ 26:28 n.4, 6; 26:43 n.55

Webb v. State, 270 Ga. 556, 512 S.E.2d 633 (1999)—§ 21:10 n.6

Webb v. State, 254 Ga. 130, 327 S.E.2d 224 (1985)—§ 28:11 n.14

Webb v. State, 176 Ga. App. 576, 336 S.E.2d 838 (1985)—§ 14:54 n.7

White v. Woodall, 572 U.S. 415, 134 S. Ct. 1697, 188 L. Ed. 2d 698 (2014)—§ 28:19 n.6

Whitehead v. State, 211 Ga. App. 121, 438 S.E.2d 128 (1993)—§ 15:1 n.9

Whitehead v. State, 207 Ga. App. 891, 429 S.E.2d 536 (1993)—§ 26:19 n.27

Whitehead v. State, 126 Ga. App. 570, 191 S.E.2d 336 (1972)—§ 14:43 n.7

Whitehead v. State, 107 Ga. App. 15, 128 S.E.2d 552 (1962)—§ 24:2 n.15

Whiteley v. Warden, Wyo. State Penitentiary, 401 U.S. 560, 91 S. Ct. 1031, 28 L. Ed. 2d 306 (1971)—§§ 2:11 n.5, 18; 2:19 n.17, 18, 25; 2:25 n.6

Whitener v. State, 272 Ga. App. 28, 611 S.E.2d 707 (2005)—§ 2:7 n.1

Whitfield v. State, 313 Ga. App. 297, 721 S.E.2d 211 (2011)—§ 28:11 n.32

Whitfield v. State, 217 Ga. App. 402, 457 S.E.2d 682 (1995)—§ 14:73 n.5

Whitfield v. State, 143 Ga. App. 779, 240 S.E.2d 189 (1977)—§ 19:2 n.15

Whitley v. State, 137 Ga. App. 245, 223 S.E.2d 279 (1976)—§ 26:13 n.2, 4

Whitlock v. State, 148 Ga. App. 203, 251 S.E.2d 59 (1978)—§ 14:72 n.13

Whitlock v. State, 230 Ga. 700, 198 S.E.2d 865 (1973)—§ 24:19 n.3

Whitlock v. State, 124 Ga. App. 599, 185 S.E.2d 90 (1971)—§§ 4:38 n.6; 4:52 n.6; 4:55 n.7

Whitsell v. State, 179 Ga. App. 358, 346 S.E.2d 130 (1986)—§ 23:4 n.1

Whitt v. State, 215 Ga. App. 704, 452 S.E.2d 125 (1994)—§ 18:11 n.5

Whittington v. State, 252 Ga. 168, 313 S.E.2d 73 (1984)—§ 18:16 n.11

Whittington v. State, 165 Ga. App. 763, 302 S.E.2d 617 (1983)—§§ 4:40 n.5; 4:42 n.11

Whittington v. State, 155 Ga. App. 667, 272 S.E.2d 532 (1980)—§ 17:7 n.2

Whitus v. State of Ga., 385 U.S. 545, 87 S. Ct. 643, 17 L. Ed. 2d 599 (1967)—§ 12:9 n.5

Whren v. U.S., 517 U.S. 806, 116 S. Ct. 1769, 135 L. Ed. 2d 89 (1996)—§§ 3:2 n.54; 3:3 n.15; 4:26 n.29

Widdowson v. State, 171 Ga. App. 134, 318 S.E.2d 820 (1984)—§ 5:20 n.23

Wiggins v. Estelle, 681 F.2d 266 (5th Cir. 1982)—§ 7:3 n.15

Wiggins v. Henson, 68 Ga. 819, 1882 WL 3270 (1882)—§ 6:2 n.6

Wiggins v. Lemley, 256 Ga. 152, 345 S.E.2d 584 (1986)—§ 17:6 n.26

Wiggins v. Smith, 539 U.S. 510, 123 S. Ct. 2527, 156 L. Ed. 2d 471 (2003)—§§ 7:4 n.61; 28:19 n.3

Wiggins v. State, 298 Ga. 366, 782 S.E.2d 31 (2016)—§ 7:3 n.2

Wiggins v. State, 331 Ga. App. 447, 771 S.E.2d 135 (2015)—§ 4:10 n.1

Wiggins v. State, 280 Ga. 268, 626 S.E.2d 118 (2006)—§ 12:16 n.5

Wiggins v. State, 272 Ga. App. 414, 612 S.E.2d 598 (2005)—§ 26:21 n.29

Wiggins v. State, 245 Ga. App. 527, 538 S.E.2d 180 (2000)—§ 16:10 n.3

Wiggins v. State, 252 Ga. 467, 314 S.E.2d 212 (1984)—§ 18:26 n.16

Wiggins v. State, 172 Ga. App. 433, 323 S.E.2d 290 (1984)—§ 18:16 n.2

Wiggins v. State, 171 Ga. App. 358, 319 S.E.2d 528 (1984)—§ 14:48 n.35

Wiggins v. State, 249 Ga. 302, 290 S.E.2d 427 (1982)—§§ 14:40 n.6; 14:78 n.21

Wiggins v. State, 221 Ga. 609, 146 S.E.2d 294 (1965)—§ 21:16 n.15

Y

Z

Index

RESULTS—Cont'd
Illegally obtained evidence, confessions and admissions, **5:26**
Probation revocation, violation of condition of probation, **30:8**

RETARDATION
Defenses, release of defendant found guilty but mentally retarded, **21:15**

RETENTION BRIEFLY OF INANIMATE OBJECTS WITHOUT PROBABLE CAUSE
Stop-and-frisk, **3:13**

RETRIAL
Double jeopardy, **14:61**

RETROACTIVE APPLICATION OF LAWS AND RULES
Criminal law rules, **14:64**
Penal statutes, **14:63**
    Statutes, **14:63**

RETURN OF PROPERTY IN CUSTODY OF LAW ENFORCEMENT
Condemnations and forfeitures, **10:2**

RETURN OF SEARCH WARRANT BY OFFICER
Generally, **4:24**

REVERSAL
Charge to jury, errors, **24:13**

REVERSE STING OPERATIONS
Defenses, **21:34**

REVIEW
Appeal and Review, this index

REVOCATION
Bond, **8:7**
Parole, administrative review of sentences, **29:5**
Probation, **30:1 to 30:8**
Release, administrative review of sentences, **29:5**

RIGHTS
Appeal and Review, this index
Arrest that is illegal, right to resist, **2:7**
Condemnations and forfeitures, restoration of civil rights, **10:8**
Confessions and Admissions, this index
Counsel, this index
Jury and jury trial, right of counsel to further argument, **24:17**
Opening statements, right of victim and defendant to be present, **19:3**
Search without warrant based on plain view, right of officer to be where he was
    at time of discovery, **4:41**
Speedy trial, **14:70**
Venue, right of trial judge to change because of danger, **14:75**